ENCYCLOPEDIA
OF AMERICAN
INDUSTRIES

2ND EDITION

VOLUME 1:
MANUFACTURING INDUSTRIES

ENCYCLOPEDIA OF AMERICAN INDUSTRIES

2ND EDITION

VOLUME 1:
MANUFACTURING INDUSTRIES

SCOTT HEIL AND
TERRANCE W. PECK,
EDITORS

GALE

DETROIT • NEW YORK • TORONTO • LONDON

ENCYCLOPEDIA OF AMERICAN INDUSTRIES

2ND EDITION

Scott Heil and Terrance W. Peck, *Editors*

Sheila Dow, *Coordinating Editor for Research*

Rebecca Marlow-Ferguson, *Coordinating Editor for Data Entry*

Nick Sternberg, *Coordinating Editor for Graphics*

Mike Weaver, *Coordinating Editor for Indexing*

Deborah Burek, Donna Craft, Eva M. Davis, Melissa Fernandez, Laurie Fundukian, Kelly Hill, Sonya Hill, Monica Hubbard, Kim Hunt, Karin Koek, Jesse Levine, Jane Malonis, Wendy Mason, Jacqueline Mueckenheim, Annette Novallo, Amy Park, Tyra Phillips, Camille Pippen, Holly Selden, Angela Shupe, Margaret Strickland, *Contributing Editors*

Jennifer L. Carman, Susan J. Cindric, Mark J. Elliot, *Assistant Editors*

Diane Maniaci, *Managing Editor*

Mary Beth Trimper, *Production Director*
Deborah Milliken, *Production Assistant*
Cynthia Baldwin, *Production Design Manager*

Pamela Galbreath, *Art Director*

Kenneth Benson, *Data Entry Coordinator*
Eleanor M. Allison, *Data Entry Services Manager*
Nikkita Bankston, Lysandra Davis-Hill, Maleka Imrana, Beverly Jendrowski, Frances Monroe, Cynthia Morgan, Elizabeth Pilette, Nancy Sheridan, *Data Entry Associates*

Jeffrey Muhr, *Technical Support Services*

Library of Congress Cataloging-in-Publication Data

Encyclopedia of American Industries / Scott Heil, Terrance W. Peck, editors. -- 2nd ed.
   p.   cm.
   Includes bibliographical references and index.
   ISBN 0-7876-2732-1 (set). -- ISBN 0-7876-0146-2 (v. 1). -- ISBN 0-7876-0147-0 (v. 2)
    1. Industries--United States--Encyclopedias. 2. Industries--United States--Classification. I. Heil, Scott. II. Peck, Terrance W.
   HC102.E53   1997
   338.0973'03--dc21
                               97-36045
                                       CIP

™ This book is printed on acid-free paper that meets the minimum requirements of the American National Standard for Information Sciences— Permanence Paper for Printed Library Materials, ANSI Z39.48-1984.

Copyright © 1998 by Gale Research
835 Penobscot Bldg.
Detroit, MI 48226-4094

ISBN 0-7876-2732-1 (set)
ISBN 0-7876-0146-2 (volume one)
ISBN 0-7876-0147-0 (volume two)

OVERVIEW OF CONTENTS

VOLUME ONE: MANUFACTURING INDUSTRIES

VOLUME TWO: SERVICE & NON-MANUFACTURING INDUSTRIES

INTRODUCTION

The *Encyclopedia of American Industries (EAI)* is a major business reference tool that provides detailed, comprehensive information on a wide range of industries in every realm of American business. Volume one provides separate coverage of 461 manufacturing industries. Volume two presents 544 essays covering the vast array of service and other non-manufacturing industries in the United States. Combined, these two volumes provide individual essays on every industry recognized by the U.S. Standard Industrial Classification (SIC) system. Both volumes of the *Encyclopedia* are arranged numerically by SIC code for easy use.

CONTENT AND ARRANGEMENT

Industry Essays. The *Encyclopedia*'s business coverage includes information on historical events of consequence as well as relevant trends and statistics entering the twenty-first century. Sections of coverage in an article may include the following:

- **Industry Snapshot.** Provides an overview of the industry and identifies key trends, issues, and statistics.

- **Organization and Structure.** Discusses the configuration and functional aspects of the industry, including government regulation, subindustry divisions, and interaction with other industries.

- **Background and Development.** Relates the industry's genesis and historical development, including major technological advances, scandals, pioneering companies, major products, important legislation, and other factors that shaped the industry.

- **Current Conditions.** Provides information on the status of the industry in the mid- to late 1990s, with an eye to industry challenges on the horizon.

- **Industry Leaders.** Profiles major companies within the industry and includes discussion of financial performance.

- **Work Force.** Contains information on the size, diversity, and characteristics of the industry's work force.

- **America and the World.** Discusses the global marketplace for the U.S. industry, as well as international participation in U.S. markets.

- **Research and Technology.** Furnishes information on major technological advances, areas of research, and their potential impact on the industry.

- **Further Reading.** Provides users with suggested further reading on the industry. These sources, many of which were also used to compile the essays, are publicly accessible materials such as magazines, general and academic periodicals, books, annual reports, and government sources, as well as material supplied by industry associations. This edition also includes references to numerous Internet sources. When available, the URL address of these resources is included.

Graphs. The *Encyclopedia of American Industries* includes hundreds of informative, easy-to-read graphs that detail a wide range of key economic and business information. Graphs without source information have been compiled from the research material used to write the essay or from original research.

Conversion Tables. Two industry classification tables allow cross-referencing of SIC categories with the North American Industry Classification System (NAICS) industry codes. (Please see below for additional information.)

Index. Contains alphabetic references from both volumes to companies, trade associations, significant business trends, government agencies, historical figures, court cases, and key legislation. Includes cross-references for acronyms and variant names.

ABOUT INDUSTRY CLASSIFICATION

Encyclopedia of American Industries offers tools to analyze industries using two industry classification systems. The primary system, the Standard Industrial Classification, was established by the U.S. government to provide a uniform means for collecting, presenting, and analyzing economic data. SIC codes are widely used by federal, state, and local government agencies; trade associations; private research organizations; and business professionals to promote comparability in the presentation of statistical data. In addition, *EAI* includes reference tables for the 1997 North American Industry Classification System, which has been adopted by the U.S. government as its new standard for economic data.

1987 Standard Industrial Classification (SIC). Each SIC code classifies business and nonprofit establishments by the types of activities in which they are engaged. An establishment is an economic unit where a service is performed or a product is manufactured or sold (generally at a single physical location). To be recognized as a separate industry within the SIC system, a set of establishments must be statistically significant according to criteria such as the number of persons employed and the volume of business conducted. Each establishment is placed in an SIC according to its primary activity, which is determined by the industry category from which it derives the most revenue. Many large companies, however, operate multiple establishments and may participate in several industries, thus it is possible for a company to be a leading force in SIC categories outside of its primary industry.

The SIC system comprises four levels of classification, as described below:

- **Divisions.** The broadest SIC categories are divisions that define an activity in very general terms: Agriculture, Forestry, and Fishing; Mining; Construction; Manufacturing; Transportation, Communications, Electric, Gas, and Sanitary Services; Wholesale Trade; Retail Trade; Finance, Insurance, and Real Estate; Services; and Public Administration.

- **Major Groups.** Within these broad categories are major groups. Each begins with a unique two-digit code that makes up the first two numbers of the complete four-digit SIC code. In the case of Manufacturing, the major group codes range between 20 and 39. Examples of two-digit groups in Manufacturing are: Food & Kindred Products (20); Tobacco Products (21); Furniture & Fixtures (25); Printing, Publishing, & Allied Industries (27); and Industrial & Commercial Machinery & Computer Equipment (35).

- **Industry Groups.** Major groups are further subdivided into three-digit industry groups. Each is assigned a three-digit code based on the two-digit code for its major group. For example, Printing, Publishing & Allied Industries is broken down into: 271 for Newspapers, 272 for Periodicals, and 273 for Books.

- **Industries.** Industry Groups are divided still further into specific Industry classifications which are assigned complete, four-digit codes based on the Industry Group. These four-digit classifications are the basis for industries detailed in *EAI.*

1997 North American Industry Classification System (NAICS). While industry information is still maintained in SIC categories for this edition, *Encyclopedia of American Industries* provides conversion tables to compare SIC data with the new North American Industry Classification System, which the governments of Canada, Mexico, and the United States jointly adopted. The NAICS is similar in principle to the SIC system but differs in industry specificity and grouping. It includes broad classifications that are common among the three nations as well as unique national-level classifications. Industries are specified in the NAICS by up to six digits, however in some cases the most specific category is only five digits. The conversion tables provided in this book reflect the U.S. version of the NAICS.

The new system will be implemented over several years by the respective governments, and preliminary U.S. economic data in NAICS categories was scheduled for release in 1998.

ACKNOWLEDGEMENTS

The editors would like to thank the members of the advisory board for their invaluable help:

- **Wendy Diamond,** Business Librarian, Meriam Library, California State University, Chico, California.

- **Mark Leggett,** Librarian, Indianapolis-Marion County Public Library, Indianapolis, Indiana.

- **Judith M. Nixon,** Librarian, Consumer & Family Sciences Library, Purdue University, West Lafayette, Indiana.

- **James R. Rettig,** Assistant University Librarian for Reference and Information Services, Swem Library, College of William and Mary, Williamsburg, Virginia.

- **Beth Stanton,** Librarian, Comerica Inc. Library, Detroit, Michigan.

COMMENTS AND SUGGESTIONS

Questions, comments, and suggestions regarding the *Encyclopedia of American Industries* are welcomed. Please contact:

The Editors
Encyclopedia of American Industries
Gale Research
835 Penobscot Bldg.
Detroit, MI 48226-4094
Telephone: (313) 961-2242
Toll-Free: 800-347-GALE
Fax: (313) 961-6815
http://www.gale.com

Industry in the Postindustrial Economy

The State of U.S. Industry Today and in the Twenty-First Century

Originating at least as early as the 1960s and flourishing in the 1980s and 1990s, new patterns have begun to reshape the U.S. economy. The result has been variously described as the "new era" or "postindustrial" economy. Common threads include the rise of service and idea-based industries, a domestic manufacturing base being supplanted by imports, the realignment of labor to better match growing industries and emerging technologies, and a changing market infrastructure underpinning the new economy. While uncertainties accompany some of these transitions, they do not necessarily lead to a weakened economy. In fact, another tenet of the new era theory is that the new economy is capable of sustaining longer, higher-volume periods of growth with fewer and smaller downturns. The extent to which the theory is accurate remains to be seen, but there can be no doubt that U.S. industries made solid advances in the 1990s.

Economic Status of the 1990s

Emerging from recession in the early 1990s, the U.S. economy was by late decade enjoying healthy growth. Low inflation and high consumption have sustained the economy with low interest rates, low unemployment rates, and moderate sales growth. Within the overlying picture, the U.S. economic terrain varies by sector: some industries are fundamentally healthy and expanding while others are unstable or declining. The industry-specific chapters in the second edition of *Encyclopedia of American Industries* detail the strengths and liabilities that converge to form the broad trends summarized here.

According to U.S. Census Bureau figures, in the mid-1990s approximately 4.8 million for-profit enterprises operated more than 6 million business

locations, or establishments, in the United States (excluding single-person or other nonemployer businesses). An additional few hundred thousand nonprofit organizations also participated in the U.S. economy. Combined, these employed a work force of more than 100 million Americans.

The net value of these establishments' output, minus the value of imports, comprises the nation's gross domestic product (GDP), which in 1996 totaled $7.3 trillion. Annual GDP growth, however, has been slower in the 1990s than in previous decades. Controlling for inflation, annual growth averaged just 1.9 percent from 1990 to 1996, which included one year (1991) of decline. By contrast, GDP growth averaged 2.8 percent annually in the 1980s, 3.2 percent in the 1970s, and 4.4 percent in the 1960s. Declining annual growth reflects in part the gradual maturation of domestic markets for many industries' goods and the greater consumption of imports in recent years.

While growth in the 1990s has been slower at the aggregate level, it has also been less volatile. The 1980s saw annual peaks as high as 7 percent and setbacks as low as 2.1 percent; in the 1990s the respective figures were 3.5 percent and 0.9 percent. Still, the 1990s have seen several GDP milestones surpassed. In current dollar terms, the U.S. GDP first topped the $6 trillion mark in 1992, exceeded $7 trillion by 1995, and was expected to reach $8 trillion in 1998. Continuing at this pace, the U.S. economy will have doubled in size for the 20 years ending in 2000, as it had over the previous 20 years.

The economy was robust by other measures as well. Stock markets posted unprecedented gains in the mid-1990s. In less than eight years the Dow Jones Industrial Average nearly tripled from 2,800

REAL U.S. GROSS DOMESTIC PRODUCT
Figures in constant (1992) dollars

1960	$2.26 trillion
1970	$3.40 trillion
1980	$4.62 trillion
1990	$6.14 trillion
1995	$6.74 trillion
1996	$6.91 trillion
1997	$7.11 trillion*
1998	$7.25 trillion*

*estimate

Source: U.S. Bureau of Economic Analysis

in 1990 to more than 8,200 by 1997, escalating particularly from 1995 to 1997. In contrast, the index of 30 stocks took from 1972 to 1987 to double from 1,000 to 2,000. Similar, though less dramatic, growth was also recorded in the composite indexes of the New York Stock Exchange and the Nasdaq. Contributing to these rises were low interest rates and increasing consumer comfort with stock-derived investments such as mutual funds, which helped channel more dollars into stocks.

Corporate performance in the 1990s has accordingly been strong. While several notable corporate giants floundered at least temporarily, many have reaped substantial profits. Central to most companies' growth strategies have been various reengineering or restructuring programs intended to configure a more profitable organization. In some cases, such as with AT&T Corporation in 1994 and 1995, this involved mass layoffs and the break-up and sale of discrete business units. It became almost cliché for corporations to announce they were focusing on core businesses and selling off or cutting back resources from noncore product lines.

Perhaps just as often, however, companies have pursued mergers, acquisitions, alliances, and international expansion for market share growth or vertical integration. Sizable mergers in the mid-1990s were widespread in banking, network and cable television, telecommunications, paper mills, aerospace, and retailing. Likewise, significant growth was realized in international markets even while companies' U.S. sales lagged.

According to an annual *Industry Week* ranking, the five leading multibillion-dollar U.S. companies by 1996 profit margin were chemical giant W.R. Grace & Co., with an 82 percent margin; drug maker Amgen Inc., with 30 percent; software behemoth Mi-

crosoft Corporation, with 25 percent; microprocessor chip leader Intel Corporation, with 25 percent; and computer network hardware manufacturer Cisco Systems Inc., with 22 percent. The report also noted that certain nondurable goods, particularly petroleum, pharmaceuticals, and other chemicals, were some of the most profitable sectors in manufacturing.

Modest productivity gains have played a noteworthy supporting role. According to U.S. Department of Labor figures, productivity—as measured in real hourly output per person—advanced by more than 6 percent in nonfarm businesses between 1990 and 1997. Some economists believe this figure underestimates actual gains in efficiency. Increases in productivity had averaged roughly 1 percent through the 1970s but have tended to be lower since then. After sluggish advances in the early 1990s, productivity climbed by 0.7 percent in 1996 and was expected to reach a similar growth figure for 1997. Coupled with slow wage growth, higher productivity has contributed to corporate profitability, arguably at the expense of better compensation for workers, and has helped suppress inflation.

THE EMPLOYMENT LANDSCAPE

The U.S. economic transition has effected a profound restructuring of the work force in the past few decades. While there has been net job growth, a substantial turnover and reconfiguration has occurred since the 1980s. According to *The New York Times* and government figures, nearly 70 million jobs were created between 1979 and 1996. Job losses, however, amounted to more than 40 million, bringing the net gain to just under 30 million new jobs for the period. New jobs were increasingly in retail and service industries and on average paid less than jobs that were cut. Since the mid-1980s most manufacturing industries have decreased net employment—a 4 percent reduction in total manufacturing employment between 1987 and 1992 alone—even while production and revenues continued to rise.

The shift was largely driven by competition from lower-cost foreign producers and was achieved through improved efficiency and through sourcing cheaper labor from outside the United States. In the early and mid-1990s, layoffs figured prominently in numerous reengineering programs. Many of these cuts were noteworthy in that the employers were turning profits but were simply not as profitable as shareholders and management wished.

A portion of the trend was cyclical. The recession of the late 1980s and early 1990s pushed U.S. civilian unemployment upward to peak at a seasonally adjusted 7.8 percent in mid-1992. By late

1994, however, unemployment was down to its pre-recession level of 5.4 percent. After edging up again in 1995, the national unemployment rate dropped further by 1997 to reach 4.8 percent, its lowest rate in a quarter century. In 1997 the tighter labor market began to drive up wages slightly and was expected to continue upward pressure on wages for the short term. Some economic observers warned, however, that wage inflation could trigger broader inflation as employers passed higher labor costs on to consumers. Continued productivity growth should cushion price inflation somewhat.

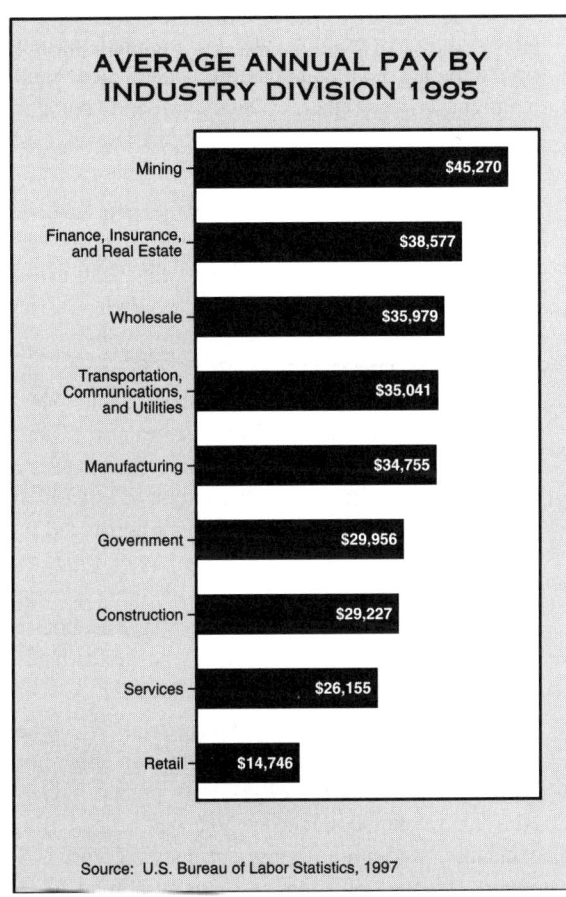

AVERAGE ANNUAL PAY BY
INDUSTRY DIVISION 1995

Industry	Pay
Mining	$45,270
Finance, Insurance, and Real Estate	$38,577
Wholesale	$35,979
Transportation, Communications, and Utilities	$35,041
Manufacturing	$34,755
Government	$29,956
Construction	$29,227
Services	$26,155
Retail	$14,746

Source: U.S. Bureau of Labor Statistics, 1997

Wages, however, have stagnated for most of the 1990s and increases have simply kept pace with inflation. Based on Labor Department statistics, real hourly compensation across all industries grew by less than 2 percent between 1987 and 1996. And while the economy continues to add high-skill jobs, increasingly new jobs in the United States are concentrated in lower-paying occupations. In 1997, the average hourly wage in the United States was slightly over $12 per hour.

The Labor Department forecasts the United States to generate 17.7 million new jobs between 1994 and 2005. Importantly, almost all of this growth—more than 91 percent—is expected to come from non-manufacturing industries, with service industries accounting for up to 70 percent and retail industries producing 26 percent. While there will still be thousands of job openings in manufacturing, most new jobs will be offset by cutbacks elsewhere. A net loss of more than a million manufacturing jobs by 2005 is forecast. In 1997, non-manufacturing industries employed more than three-quarters of the U.S. work force, a proportion that has edged up by about 7 percent in ten years.

A related facet of the new labor structure is a shift away from the one-job career: job security is waning. In a given period the majority of workers will not face layoffs or work shortage, and there will be sizable numerical gains in specialty and technical professions among others. But as certain jobs become obsolete or radically altered, the typical U.S. worker can expect to have more jobs of shorter duration than in the past—and potentially fewer well-paying ones. More so now than in the past, as well, ongoing training and education are key to effective job transition.

GLOBAL INTEGRATION

Still larger than that of any other national economy, U.S. GDP entering the late 1990s was nearly 60 percent greater than that of the next-largest market economy, Japan. Until the European Union's (EU) 1995 expansion to 15 members, the United States' GDP had been roughly equivalent to that of the 12 EU economies combined. According to figures compiled by the Organization for Economic Cooperation and Development (OECD), an organization of industrialized market-economy nations, in 1996 U.S. GDP was nearly $7.3 trillion in current dollars. Between 1990 and 1996, U.S. real GDP increased by roughly 14.7 percent. By comparison, real GDP in Japan grew by 10.5 percent and the 15 EU member nations grew by 8.6 percent in the same period.

Some estimates place China at number two in terms of purchasing power parity, that is, compared to the relative cost of goods and services. In 1996, China had an estimated GDP of more than $4 trillion by purchasing parity, but it fell only in the $700 billion range on a current value basis. Among the market economies, Japan produced the second-largest GDP in 1996, at nearly $4.6 trillion in current dollars. It was followed by Germany, with $2.4 trillion; France, with $1.5 trillion; Italy, with $1.2 trillion; and the United Kingdom, with $1.1 trillion. Together with the United States, these five economies made up the only multitrillion dollar GDPs in the world. Canada, although eighth-largest in terms of GDP after Spain's $586 billion, made up the seventh member of the Group of Seven (G-7) leading industrial states, with $578 billion.

On a per capita basis, the U.S. GDP also ranked among the highest. Second only to Luxembourg among OECD countries, U.S. GDP per capita in the mid-1990s totaled more than $26,000. Japan followed at $21,800 and the remainder of the G-7 economies fell between that level and the United Kingdom's low of $17,800 per capita. Two smaller but powerful Asian economies, Hong Kong and Singapore, ranked higher than most of the G-7, at $23,000 and $22,800 per capita, respectively. These figures can be deceiving, however, because they do not reflect the respective income distributions or even the proportion of GDP earmarked under personal consumption, which is a more reliable indicator of standard of living.

U.S. public debt still proportionately exceeded that of most other leading economies. As a percentage of GDP, U.S. national debt tallied sixth-largest among OECD countries. Within the G-7, the United States trailed Italy and Canada with the largest debt shares; for 1997 the U.S. debt equaled roughly 50 percent of GDP. This figure has remained relatively steady in the 1990s, though, because of tighter U.S. fiscal policy.

With total trade volume approaching $2 trillion, the United States is the world's largest merchandise exporter, at $600 billion or nearly 12 percent of world exports in 1996. As a U.S. trade deficit in goods persists, imports accounted for an even larger segment, reaching approximately $780 billion. In services, however, the United States has regularly enjoyed a trade surplus. Service exports in the mid-1990s reached $210 billion versus imports of $140 billion. While trade deficits have fueled protectionist urges in U.S. politics, little long-term headway has been made to avert future deficits and economically the benefits of doing so are questionable.

Electronics and transportation equipment trade volume surpasses all other categories both in imports and exports. In exports, these are joined by chemicals, agricultural commodities, and machinery to make up more than three-quarters of U.S. goods exported. In imports, minerals, fuels, and machinery combine with electronics and transportation equipment to comprise two-thirds of merchandise imports. In the mid-1990s imports typically exceeded exports in all merchandise categories except agricultural products, which averaged a $20 billion to $30 billion surplus, and chemicals, which averaged a $12 billion to $16 billion surplus. Some of the highest-growth products within the top export industries include data processing equipment, elec-

tronic parts and semiconductor component technology, cereals, wood pulp, and semiconductor and similar high-precision manufacturing equipment. Significant export declines occurred in aircraft, nuclear materials, cigarettes, and some food and agricultural products. Among imports, electronic parts, data processing equipment, automobiles, crude petroleum, and high-precision manufacturing equipment purchases grew the most in dollar value, compared to sizable import drops in refined petroleum, steel, lumber, and aircraft components.

In services trade, leading exports include travel and tourism, freight transportation, intellectual property (including patents, license royalties, and films), passenger transportation, and professional services (including accounting, consulting, health care, legal, maintenance and repair, architectural, and engineering services), which together totaled more than 85 percent of U.S. service exports. The major service imports were virtually the same: travel and tourism, freight transportation, passenger transportation, telecommunications, and intellectual property, which amounted to nearly 90 percent of the total.

By combined import and export volume, the United States' largest trading partners entering the late 1990s were, in descending order, Canada, Japan, Mexico, the United Kingdom, China, Germany, Korea, Taiwan, Singapore, and France. Mexico was expected to eclipse Japan for the number two spot as early as year end 1997. Together, these nations accounted for roughly two-thirds of all U.S. trade. As of 1997, the United States held its greatest trade deficits with China, Japan, Canada, Germany, and Mexico; its largest trade surpluses were with the Netherlands, Australia, Hong Kong, Korea, and Brazil.

Changes in currency exchange rates over time, as opposed to short-term fluctuations, can either bolster or diminish U.S. industries' trade positions. Generally, a weaker dollar—one that has a decreasing exchange rate with a foreign currency—favors U.S. exports by making them less costly abroad while raising the relative cost of imports. A strong dollar has the reverse effect on trade but also reflects broader economic health. In practice, prices of goods and services tend to fluctuate much less than exchange rates, and the difference in currency values, particularly in the short run, may simply be absorbed by companies in the form of increased or decreased revenues without changing the selling price.

Since the late 1980s, the U.S. dollar has chartered a fairly stable course, depreciating slightly through the mid-1990s. In late 1996 and much of 1997, though, the dollar climbed considerably relative to the currencies of some of its largest trading partners. Comparatively low U.S. unemployment, minimal inflation, and strong corporate performance contributed to the dollar's rise.

As the U.S. government continues to pursue its predominantly free-trade economic policy, better trade opportunities will arise in well-established markets, such as Japan, as well as in formative markets such as South America and sub-Saharan Africa. At the same time some U.S. industries will continue to lose domestic market share and the move toward relocating manufacturing facilities in cheaper labor markets abroad will likely accelerate.

INDUSTRY TRENDS

As noted, economic performance has not been uniform across industries. The following is a short description of the size and major trends in the nine private-sector Standard Industrial Classification (SIC) divisions:

Agriculture, Forestry, and Fishing. The smallest sector of the economy, agriculture and related industries employed in the mid-1990s roughly 590,000 workers at 100,000 separate establishments. Total output in this category was valued at more than $30 billion annually. While sweeping legislative reform in 1996 promised to reconfigure these industries by eliminating U.S. government price supports, in the long term the United States is expected to produce a declining share of its own and the world's food. Employment, nonetheless, is expected to rise slightly in this sector.

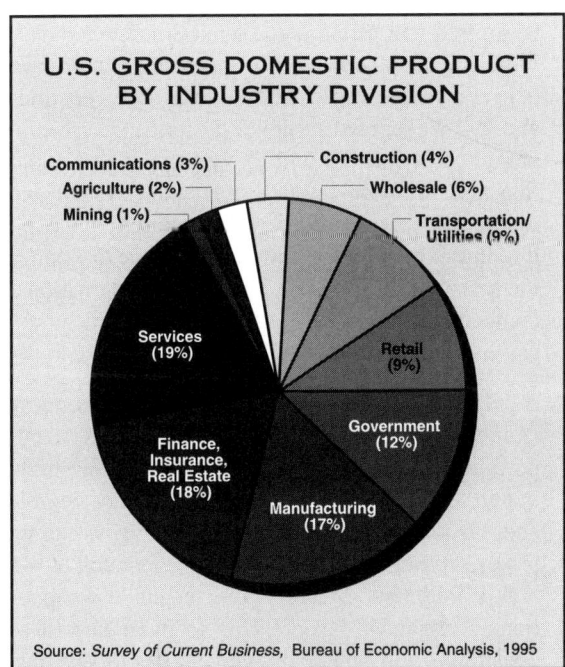

U.S. GROSS DOMESTIC PRODUCT BY INDUSTRY DIVISION

Communications (3%)
Agriculture (2%)
Mining (1%)
Construction (4%)
Wholesale (6%)
Transportation/ Utilities (9%)
Services (19%)
Retail (9%)
Finance, Insurance, Real Estate (18%)
Government (12%)
Manufacturing (17%)

Source: *Survey of Current Business,* Bureau of Economic Analysis, 1995

Mining. Valued at roughly $160 billion in annual revenues, U.S. mining operations employed a mid-1990s work force of 560,000 at 28,000 establishments. On a relatively lean work force, mining as a whole posts regular double-digit pretax profit margins, in the range of 12 percent to 16 percent, according to the Census Bureau's *Quarterly Financial Reports.* While mine production in some categories continues to reach new highs, in many areas industry employment has fallen precipitously. Those who remain in mining enjoy on average a higher annual salary than for any other broad sector, however production workers still must contend with some of the most hazardous and demanding work anywhere. The Labor Department forecasts further employment declines heading into the new century.

Construction. In the mid-1990s construction industries employed nearly 5 million workers at 600,000 establishments. Together, these firms generated yearly sales of more than $570 billion. Traditionally a cyclical sector, construction suffered heavily in the early 1990s from a dearth of new projects because of excess supply created in the 1980s and from lean capital spending during the recession. When the economy picked back up, housing starts improved considerably, as did to a lesser extent commercial and industrial construction, and some ground was regained. Entering the late 1990s, however, the market was still considered soft and signs of another slowdown loomed; as an employment sector, construction is forecast to grow.

Manufacturing. U.S. manufacturers employed about 18 million at mid-decade in roughly 370,000 business locations. The total value of U.S. manufacturing exceeded $3.5 trillion in revenues. In terms of employment, leading industries include industrial machinery, transportation equipment, printing and publishing, and food manufacturing. Some of the most profitable categories include nondurable goods such as pharmaceuticals and chemicals (and often petroleum, although it is highly volatile). Manufacturing as a whole posted mid-1990s profit margins between 6 percent and 8 percent.

Employment and sales declines in some domestic manufacturing industries will continue as foreign producers gain market share through lower prices. Competition at home and abroad will increasingly create commodity-like markets for manufactured goods, and employment numbers will continue to slide overall. Growth opportunities will still abound in numerous categories, including biotechnology, specialty machinery, computer-related goods, and other electronics.

Transportation, Communications, and Utilities. Collectively valued at roughly $1 trillion in revenues, these three sectors largely function independently despite their linkage in the SIC system. Transportation services, which do not include vehicle and equipment production, employed nearly 4 million (not including the U.S. Postal Service); communications services employed more than 1.3 million; and utilities employed approximately 900,000. Automation in telecommunications has decimated some job categories, but the overall trend is toward employment growth in communications industries.

Already the second-largest service trade category, transportation industries will continue to benefit from increased cross-border trade. U.S. deregulation in telecommunications and utilities will result in growing competition and downward pressure on prices throughout these industries. Although the technology and new delivery media continue to re-shape the communications industries, communications firms will likely enjoy the greatest growth in this category by bundling services—such as telephone service, cable television, cellular service, and Internet access—and crossing into new markets. The television segment will likewise invest heavily in digital broadcasting technology to comply with new high-definition television (HDTV) standards, which will supplant analog transmissions by 2006. Deregulation abroad will provide additional growth opportunities for telecommunications firms.

Wholesale Trade. U.S. wholesalers employed more than 6.4 million at mid-decade for gross revenues of more than $3.5 trillion. Over 500,000 establishments conducted wholesale trade. While wholesale is a lucrative and growing sector, its aggregate numbers can be deceiving because the industry incurs a relatively higher cost of sales than other industries. Traditionally the go-between for manufacturers and retailers, some wholesalers are losing sales as larger retailers focus on direct relations with manufacturers. Internet and other improved communications technology could potentially threaten some wholesalers as well by offering new or non-wholesale channels for buyers to locate goods rather than relying on local suppliers. Wholesale profits tend to be slim on the aggregate level, based on Census Bureau data, often ranging at just 2 percent to 3 percent of sales.

Retail Trade. The retail sector generated some $2 trillion in mid-1990s sales through 1.6 million business locations. The second-largest employer after services, retail industries provided more than 20 million U.S. jobs. Average wages, however, are considerably lower than in all other sectors. Coupled with services, retail operations have picked up some of the slack from the downsizing of U.S. manufacturing. With the exception of some highly profitable niches, large retailers achieve profits primarily through a high sales volume of low-margin goods. Entering the late 1990s, aggregate profits in the retail sector hovered around 5 percent of sales.

Finance, Insurance, and Real Estate. In the mid-1990s finance and related industries garnered $2 trillion in receipts and employed 6.9 million at more than 600,000 establishments. With steady performance overall, the finance industry, particularly commercial banking, witnessed a surge in mergers and acquisitions in the mid-1990s. More cyclical than finance and insurance, real estate sales have improved greatly from a slump early in the decade as the glut of available properties diminished. Employment growth has been somewhat sluggish in the finance industries versus real estate and insurance, which are expected to continue to outpace finance in creating new jobs.

Services. Service industries employ more workers than any other sector in the United States, with more than 33 million workers. Combined, these industries have revenues of more than $2 trillion from more than 2.3 million business locations. Along with retail, services are expected to account for 16.2 million new jobs by 2005, according to the Labor Department. Health care is expected to be among the largest growth areas.

FUTURE PROSPECTS

As this survey suggests, the U.S. economy is on track for modest growth in the coming years, but its growth will be tempered by new economic realities. The labor force will be increasingly polarized between well-compensated, high-skill occupations and low-wage, high-turnover positions. These economic consequences will likely place added attention and strain on the U.S. education system and will propel reform efforts and alternative modes of training. Foreign trade, too, will continue to reshape the sensibilities of U.S. industry as international competitors quickly ascend to fill voids left by decay in domestic businesses.

U.S. industries in the postindustrial economy simultaneously face new constraints and new opportunities. The constraints include increasingly mature domestic markets, the need to stay flexible and respond quickly to market changes, falling prices, continuing high costs of technology, and highly fragmented markets due to global competition. Companies that are able to overcome these constraints will potentially gain access to vast new markets abroad, will vie for market share growth or even dominance, and will likely enjoy higher than average revenue and profit growth.

But whether a company is able to attain future success will also be influenced by the nature of the goods or services it offers. For some it could be a mortal struggle if they participate in receding industries; others in high-growth and emerging industries may find success hard to elude.

CONTENTS

VOLUME ONE: MANUFACTURING INDUSTRIES

FURNITURE & FIXTURES

PAPER & ALLIED PRODUCTS

PRINTING, PUBLISHING, & ALLIED INDUSTRIES

CHEMICALS & ALLIED PRODUCTS

PETROLEUM REFINING & RELATED INDUSTRIES

RUBBER & MISCELLANEOUS PLASTICS PRODUCTS

LEATHER & LEATHER PRODUCTS

STONE, CLAY, GLASS, & CONCRETE PRODUCTS

PRIMARY METAL INDUSTRIES

FABRICATED METAL PRODUCTS, EXCEPT MACHINERY AND TRANSPORTATION EQUIPMENT

TRANSPORTATION EQUIPMENT

MEASURING, ANALYZING, & CONTROLLING INSTRUMENTS

MISCELLANEOUS MANUFACTURING INDUSTRIES

ENCYCLOPEDIA
OF AMERICAN
INDUSTRIES

2ND EDITION

VOLUME 1:
MANUFACTURING INDUSTRIES

BIOTECHNOLOGY

BIOTECHNOLOGY

Biotechnology includes firms engaged in manipulating living organisms or biological components at the molecular, submolecular, or cellular levels to create marketable products. Such products include bacterial and viral vaccines, toxoids, serums, plasmas, and various microbiological substances. In vitro and in vivo diagnostic substances are covered in **SIC 2835: In Vitro and In Vivo Diagnostic Substances.**

INDUSTRY SNAPSHOT

On February 22, 1997, a Scottish embryologist named Ian Wilmut announced to the world that he and colleagues at the Roslin Institute near Edinburgh had cloned an adult Dorset sheep. "Dolly," a precise genetic copy of a sheep, became literally an overnight sensation. Concocted from the DNA of a sheep's mammary gland, she represented endless technological possibilities and fears, the most obvious of which was: Could humans also be cloned eventually or even someday soon? Within forty-eight hours of Wilmut's announcement, President Clinton suggested a national commission should review the "troubling" ramifications of cloning.

As extraordinary as Wilmut's achievement was, it was only one feat in an industry whose 1996 national sales and revenues, according to an annual industry report by Ernst & Young LLP, reached $12.7 billion. This figure, as compared to 1995's $11.3 billion total, represented something of an industry turnaround, especially in light of the American Stock Exchange biotech index plummeting 25 percent in the summer of

1996. According to the Biotechnology Industry Organization, as of 1996 there were nearly 1,300 biotechnology companies employing more than 100,000 people. A 1996 CorpTech survey reported that biotech firms were expanding at an average yearly employment and revenue rate of roughly 25 percent. Roughly 33 percent of the biotech industry's capitalization, according to a *Forbes* article, is found in just a few established industry leaders, including Amgen, Biogen, Chiron and Genentech. Of the approximately 350 publicly held companies, only a small number have actually had the success of bringing an FDA-approved product to the market. Hence, much trading rested on innuendo and future prospects. With the rate of new company creation slowing down, industry consolidation has escalated in an atmosphere of acquisitions, mergers, and alliances.

Until recently, the U.S. government mostly restricted its biotechnology investment to the health care realm. While this focus has had and continues to show enormous consequences for the diagnosis, prevention, and treatment of disease, federal researchers in the 1990s rapidly explored other biotechnology applications. In a recent report, the Biotechnology Research Subcommittee (BRS) of the Committee on Fundamental Science of the National Science and Technology Council (NSTC) delineated four investment areas. They included, as of 1996: agricultural biotechnology; environmental biotechnology, with a focus on bioremediation; manufacturing/bioprocessing, including energy; and marine biotechnology and aquaculture.

One biotechnology trend is toward more globalization, with many more foreign companies financing new American businesses. Conversely, numerous American industry leaders have invested in operations abroad. Like many other industries, biotechnology has made the transition from the 1980s lavish-spending, heavy-investment mood to the downsizing theme of the 1990s. In keeping with this new atmosphere, many biotechnology firms have formed partnerships with pharmaceutical businesses as a means to secure capital.

ORGANIZATION AND STRUCTURE

Robert F. Curl, the 1996 Nobel prize-winning chemist, said in a 1997 *Newsweek* article, "This was the century of physics and chemistry. But the next century will be the century of biology." Biotechnology overlaps many areas of science and technology, including agriculture, genetic engineering, and health and medicine. In the United States, the federal government, the private sector, and academic institutions are all significant players in the biotechnological realm. In the broadest sense, the federal government's chief goal is to sponsor research to enhance fresh knowledge and to assure that technological progress is in keeping with the public good and national welfare. In 1997, the 13 federal departments and agencies supporting biotechnology research were: Agency for International Development; Department of Agriculture; Department of Commerce; Department of Defense; Department of Energy; Department of Health and Human Services; Department of Interior; Department of Justice; Department of State; Department of Veteran Affairs; Environmental Protection Agency; National Aeronautics and Space Administration; and National Science Foundation.

In terms of overseeing the area of agricultural biotechnology, the Food and Drug Administration (FDA) has general authority to regulate the introduction of all new food crops. Every company or individual that manufactures whole foods or any other food products must ensure the safety and quality of any product they introduce into the food supply. As of 1997, the FDA required that genetic modifications that vary the nutritional value of the host food, use genetic material not within the traditional food supply, or use recognizable allergens be subjected to strict premarketing testing and scrutiny. The USDA and the EPA impose safety requirements and performance standards on the development of pesticides, herbicides, and genetically modified test crops.

The burgeoning globalization of the biotech market through direct investment in American companies, in particular pharmaceuticals, spurred on greater competition and an increasingly fuzzy national identity of products in the 1990s. All indications say this trend

will persist. A scarcity of operating capital permeated the modern biotechnology field since the beginning, an albatross unlikely to disappear. Some blame the FDA for excessive regulation, and according to Oregon Business Media, the vast majority of biotechnology companies incur net losses virtually every year, subsidizing their businesses through the selling of stock or through alliances with pharmaceutical giants. Oregon Business Media also claims the roughly 50 percent of the biotechnology companies have no more than two years cash reserves to sustain them.

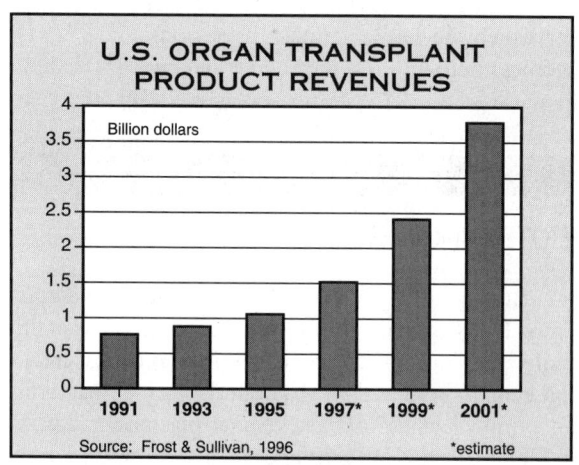

U.S. ORGAN TRANSPLANT PRODUCT REVENUES

Source: Frost & Sullivan, 1996 *estimate

Up until 1996, patent law did not apply directly to biotechnology. Under normal circumstances, patents shielded companies that have devised an innovative product or employed a novel procedure to manufacture it. According to an article in *Science,* however, the majority of the biotechnology operations often use standard genetic engineering methods to make naturally occurring proteins. In November 1995, President Clinton signed a law that amended a section of the U.S. Code on patents by saying that a familiar biotechnological process may be considered novel in the circumstances that it uses or produces a novel material. Formerly, businesses could patent genes or cell lines, but could not necessarily patent the whole process of employing a specific gene in a specific cell line to manufacture a product. The new law contradicts *In Re Durden,* a 1985 ruling by the U.S. Court of Appeals for the Federal Circuit in Washington, D.C. *In Re Durden* concerned the utilization of a chemical procedure to produce compounds named oximes; the court decided that although a certain process may result in a novel substance, it cannot be patented if the result is evident. Under the new law, biotechnology companies will have at least some of the process protection denied to them previously.

BACKGROUND AND DEVELOPMENT

Although the possibilities for biotechnology are expanding at an unprecedented rate, in some sense this science existed even in the prehistoric period. From time immemorial, humans have manipulated live organisms to sustain their survival or to make their lives more pleasant. Roughly 10,000 years ago, beer, wine, and bread were made through a process known as fermentation, a biochemical process that transforms substances through enzyme activity. In discovering and applying fermentation, our ancestors made food by permitting living organisms to interact with other ingredients. By experimenting with the conditions under which the fermentation process took place, early peoples could improve the quality and quantity of their foods.

Plant science is a more modern application of biotechnology, although ancient farmers practiced a form of it with crop rotation and seed selection. By the middle of the nineteenth century, Austrian botanist Gregor Mendel had explored the possibilities of hereditary features of peas. Through his and other scientists' vision and efforts, the concept of cross-breeding evolved. That different plants with a wide variety of benefits could be eventually combined became the basis for hybridization.

The principles of biotechnology have been employed on countless occasions worldwide in the twentieth century. Among the most important medical breakthroughs was Alexander Fleming's discovery of penicillin in 1928. However, this antibiotic, which comes from the mold *penicillium,* was not available on a widespread basis until the mid-1940s. Gradually, the biotechnology realm branched out in many directions, including pharmaceuticals, biological and chemical warfare, pesticides, and herbicides. More recently, with the innovations of gene splicing and recombinant DNA technology, scientists merged the genetic components of two or more living cells. While biotechnology extends to many scientific areas, it can, for purposes of simplification, be divided into three general sub-categories: genetic engineering, diagnostic applications, and cell/tissue applications.

The distinction between a biotechnological company and a pharmaceutical company is often not always easy to make, particularly since the two industries overlap in many ways. As indicated in *Standard & Poor's Industry Survey,* pharmaceutical companies usually use inorganic chemicals to develop new drug compounds. In contrast, biotechnology firms rely on natural elements from the human body, in addition to organic substances from animals and vegetation, to create other substances to combat disease.

According to *Standard & Poor's Industry Survey,* in the early 1980s, the biotech industry offered virtually no products; by 1994, the sector had manufactured about 25 thriving drugs, which collectively totaled almost $8 billion in product sales, according to the Biotechnology Industry Organization. According to *Chemical & Engineering News,* with the biotech industry having more new products from more new companies than ever before, the industry was more secure in the mid-1990s than earlier in the decade.

CURRENT CONDITIONS

As the biotechnology industry entered the 1990s, the Human Genome Project (HGP) had already commenced. A collaboration of the DOE Human Genome Program and the NIH National Center for Human Genome Research (NCHGR), the HGP was conceived to account for the 50,000 to 100,000 human genes, as well as ascertain the entire sequence of the 3 billion DNA sub-units. Formally begun on October 1, 1990, HGP has been scheduled to continue at least until 2005. DOE and NIH funding for human genome research extends to many colleges, universities, and laboratories.

As of October 1996, approximately 16 other countries—including Australia, Brazil, Canada, China, Denmark, France, Germany, Israel, Italy, Japan, Mexico, Netherlands, Russia, Sweden, and United Kingdom—had organized human genome research programs. As of the mid-1990s, roughly 1,000 persons from about 50 nations were members of HUGO, an organization that serves to promote international collaboration in the genome project.

The development of a new drug is typically an expensive and slow procedure. Most drugs fail to withstand the pressure of clinical trials; of the minority that do, less than 10 percent have ever been approved for sale. The arduous approval process and the newness of the contemporary biotechnology industry explained why most biotech firms have no immediate plans for releasing a commercial product on the market. Simply staying in business has always been a great struggle for most biotech firms; in the mid-1990s, almost 90 percent of the firms in the industry had under 200 employees and no significant product revenues. Also, even though the industry's overall revenues improved in the mid-1990s, research and development expenses have escalated. Even in the aftermath of a successful product's release, most biotech operations struggle economically for years, even decades.

Oregon Business Media anticipated that sales for biotechnology merchandise would increase somewhere between 15 to 20 percent by the year 2000.

However, the organization also said there were only 125 biotech-derived drugs on the market and over 700 diagnostic kits for disease screening. While at least 100 new biotech companies emerged worldwide since 1994, a scarcity of operating capital has been at least partly to blame for the decreasing rate of new business starts.

The market for artificial organs and replacement skin, although still in its infancy, has already shown an enormous capacity for growth. A 1995 Frost & Sullivan study anticipated that U.S. markets for artificial parts and organ transplantation products will boom from $963 million in 1994 to $3.8 billion by 2001. With the scarcity of natural human organs obtainable for transplantation, the artificial organ technology may also extend to partial organs, as well as complete ones. By the mid-1990s, some companies had developed artificial heart valves designed to withstand the ravages of human heart disease. Frost and Sullivan also predicted that with the replacement parts industry skyrocketing from less than 1 percent of the total combined organ product revenues in 1996 to 28 percent in 2001, the market for immunosuppressive drugs will plummet from 85 percent to 44 percent for the same period.

According to *Cancer Researcher Weekly,* biotech research for cancer drugs and therapies receded by the mid-1990s because of an investment shortage. In a 1994 Biotechnology Industry Organization (BIO) survey, 44 percent of companies answered that their cancer research had been cut back or postponed. Of this group, slightly more than 40 percent believed the rationale for less emphasis on research was uncertainty in regard to the Clinton administration's suggestions for de facto price controls on new breakthrough drugs. A total of 62 percent anticipated that their own cancer research efforts would diminish if the Clinton administration's recommendations passed into law.

However, in 1996 sales and earnings performance for many companies in the U.S. biopharmaceutical sector was consistently strong. The total sales for the top ten U.S. drug producers in the second quarter of 1996 rose 10 percent from the same period in 1995 to $29.1 billion. For the first half of 1996, sales increased 11 percent from first half 1995 to a combined $58 billion.

INDUSTRY LEADERS

By the mid-1990s, Genentech, Amgen, Biogen, and Chiron represented some of the most established and successful biotech companies in the world. Genentech, Inc., having achieved almost $1 billion in annual sales by 1996, has been possibly more involved in genetic engineering than any other company in the world. The San Francisco-based business that went public in 1980 and employed almost 3,000 by 1996 has developed several new significant biotech products, including genetically produced human insulin for diabetes; a hepatitis-B vaccine; and Pulmozme, a drug to treat cystic fibrosis; and a hairy cell leukemia treatment. With 10 products on the market by 1996, Genentech's sales grew by 5.5 percent during that year.

Amgen Inc., another industry leader, manufactured anti-anemia drugs and has developed hepatitis C and neutropenia therapeutics. The company received much publicity for its discovery of a "fat gene" in the summer of 1995. In a collaboration with the Howard Hughes Medical Institute, Amgen located a gene in mice which controls fat storage. Hence, scientists proceeded to decrease the size and weight of these oversized mice. Subsequently, they found a similar human gene, although Amgen also anticipated that not until the year 2000 would a commercial therapy emerge from its efforts. It is worth noting that Amgen outbid more than ten companies for products to be eventually developed from the "fat gene." In the short term, Amgen's stock skyrocketed and its 1996 sales grew by more than 15 percent to $2.2 billion. Amgen made the news on other occasions in the mid-1990s. On August 12, 1996, the company began the first human clinical trial of moderate to severe Parkinson's disease. On August 21, 1996, it received a U.S. patent for an anemia drug for people with kidney failure.

Biogen, Inc. is another significant player in the industry. This company's main business in the 1990s was the development of drugs for multiple sclerosis, respiratory, and autoimmune ailments. In August 1996, Biogen signed two exclusive European distribution agreements for Interferon beta-1a (AVONEX), a drug for treating relapses of multiple sclerosis. Under one agreement, the company of Astra AB (A), when the drug is approved, will have the rights to distribute, market and sell it in Denmark, Finland, Iceland, Norway, and Sweden. In the other agreement, Schering-Plough will acquire the rights to distribute interferon beta-1a in Spain when the drug is approved. For 1996 Biogen had revenues of $259 million, a 92 percent increase over the previous year. However, Biogen did not fare so well in November 1996 when the House of Lords in England turned down the company's patent claim for a recombinant DNA coding for a polypeptide showing Hepatitis B virus antigen specificity. This decision represented the first time that the House of Lords had even pondered a patent claim based on products that evolved out of genetic engineering.

Famous for its discovery of the hepatitis C virus (HCV) and its development of an HCV antibody test, Chiron Corporation also developed a genetically engineered vaccine for the hepatitis B virus (HBV). The company has four markets in health care: diagnostics; pediatric and adult vaccines; therapeutics, with an emphasis on oncology; and ophthalmics. In January 1995, Ciba Geigy Limited bought out 49.9 percent ownership of Chiron's outstanding common stock. In their agreement, Ciba has contracted to provide $1.2 billion to Chiron in research funding, debt guarantees and equity purchases for a five-year term. For its fiscal year 1996, Chiron had revenues of $1.3 billion, a 19 percent increase from 1995.

In the middle 1990s, drug-delivery companies also demonstrated a solid niche in the biotech market. According to *Fortune,* trendsetters such as Elan, Dura Pharmaceuticals, Alza, and TheraTech offer a host of products that help the human body to better absorb certain medications. Time-release capsules and sweet-tasting sedative painkillers are just two examples. In this corner of the biotechnological realm, Alza and Elan are particularly prominent, both having tackled such innovations as nitroglycerin patches, and wristwatch types of products that electrically maneuver drugs into the human skin. According to *Fortune* Alza had 1995 sales of $350 million and profits of $72 million; Elan had $223 million in sales and $89 million in profits for a similar period.

By the mid-1990s, some new biotechnology companies had entered in the field of genomics, a science dominated by the desire to manipulate the human genome to understand disease. Consultant Cynthia Robbins-Roth said in a *Business Week* article that the six biggest genomics operations have invested possibly as much as $1 billion with powerful pharmaceutical companies. With so many gene discoveries in such diseases as Alzheimer's, cancer, and mental illness, the stakes are indeed high. Ultimately, of course, the goal is not simply to understand the high-profile diseases that have plagued mankind for so long, but to cure and finally prevent them. Among the up-and-coming, genomics/genetics firms included in the mid-1990s: Affymetrix, Cadus, Exelixis, Human Genome Sciences, Incyte, and Millennium.

AMERICA AND THE WORLD

With the biotech industry more of a global enterprise than ever before, the concept of a strictly American biotech business—or any biotech business rigidly representing just one nationality—has become somewhat outdated. According to Oregon Business Media, although the United States leads the world in research and development investment, six of the world's leading pharmaceutical companies are in Europe, all of which have committed some degree of interest in biotechnology. The Organization for Economic Cooperation and Development (OECD), which includes 24 countries, predicts that "the [biotechnology] market could reach $50 billion in Europe alone by the year 2000." While Europe is generally America's strongest competitor, Asia in the 1990s showed some interest in entering the biotech market. According to Oregon Business Media, U.S. biotechnology businesses totaled global sales of about $7 billion, and research and development expenditures averaged nearly four-fifths of sales.

To date, most of the domestic and international interest in biotechnology revolved around health care. However, endless other opportunities abound, including genetic engineering, forensics, environmental science, agriculture, and even as a means to combat crime. Among the trends most likely to continue is the increasing interdependence between pharmaceutical firms and biotech companies; in fact, according to Oregon Business Media, more than 150 alliances between the two overlapping industries were formed in 1994 alone.

RESEARCH AND TECHNOLOGY

While the future of the biotechnology industry seemed extremely uncertain in the 1990s, particularly in terms of which companies would thrive and which ones would not survive, no one could deny the impact of certain innovations. The 1997 cloning of an adult Dorset sheep had ramifications for every biotech-related industry, as well as for many non-biotech related businesses. As reported in *Standard & Poor's Industry Survey,* another 1990s milestone occurred when Calgene Inc. released the *MacGregor FlavrSavr*—a genetically engineered tomato—in parts of California and Illinois. With an additional gene that helps it ripen on the vine, the *MacGregor FlavrSavr* demonstrated that its freshness lasts for about two weeks after the fruit has been picked. Another significant agricultural/biotech development that occurred in the 1990s: the FDA approved a bovine hormone that swells milk turnout.

Generally, gene therapy, a process in which a person is injected with genetically-transformed cells, focused on cancer treatment more than any other disease in the 1990s. According to *Standard & Poor's,* many scientists' original intention of gene therapy—to treat heredity diseases or to repair defective genes—did not develop significantly in the 1990s, although the promise still looms large. Such companies as Genetic

Therapy, Somatix and Cell Genesys were particularly active in gene therapy. Vector, a method of gene transfer, offered exciting possibilities although by 1997 it existed mostly only in laboratories.

Antibodies, products of the immune system in combating infection and sickness, have figured prominently into biotechnology. According to *Standard & Poor's,* specific approaches utilizing monoclonal antibodies were effective in diagnostics, but they generally did less well in the biotech market. For example, Xoma, Chiron, and Centocor all used monoclonal antibodies in attempts to target septic shock, but none had really succeeded by 1997. On the other hand, Centocor showed some promise with *ReoPro,* a recent drug that employs antibodies to combat clotting in angioplasty operations. Cytogen, Icos, and NeoRx all represent businesses that have invested much in antibody-based therapy.

Given the enormous monetary investment, patience, and vision required by all biotech firms, regardless of their size and the nature of their specific business, this is a particularly precarious industry. Of course, the relative newness of the modern biotech realm only enhances that aura of uncertainty.

FURTHER READING

"All The Genes There Are." *Economist,* 25 February 1995.

"Artificial Organs, Replacement Skin Markets to Explode Late-Decade, Top $2 Billion by 2001." *Business Wire,* 30 April 1995.

"Biohazard." *Forbes,* 18 November 1996.

"Biodiversity and Human Health." *Lancet,* 22 April 1995.

Biotechnology at Work. Biotechnology Industry Organization, 1989-1990.

Biotechnology for the 21st Century: New Horizons. Biotechnology Information Center, National Agricultural Library, July 1995.

"Biotechnology: Global State of the Industry." *Oregon Business Media,* 1996.

Biotechnology in Perspective, Biotechnology Industry Organization, 1989-1990.

Brahms, Diane, "Biogen Loses Its Landmark Status." *Lancet,* November 16, 1996

"Environmental Biotechnologies." *EUREKA News,* January, 1996.

LaFemina, Lorraine. "Biotech Companies' Comeback." *Long Island Business News,* 06-10-1996.

Murphy, Ann, and Perrella, Judy. *A Further Look At Biotechnology.* Woodrow Wilson National Fellowship Foundation, 1993.

"New Biotech Law Shores Up U.S. Firms." *Science,* 3 November 1995.

Peters, Pamela. *Biotechnology: A Guide to Genetic Engineering.* Wm. C. Brown Publishers, Inc., 1993.

"Research Suffers from Investment Crunch." *Cancer Researcher Weekly,* 9 May 1994.

"Special Report: The Biotech Century." *Business Week,* 10 March 1997.

Thayer, Ann. "Biotech Industry Still Breeding Growth." *Chemical & Engineering News,* 6 January 1997.

———. "Drug, Biopharmaceutical Company Sales Rise in Second Quarter and First Half." *Chemical & Engineering News,* 19 August 1996.

Unger, Michael. "Separated at Birth." *Newsday,* 23 September 1996.

Welles, Edward O. "The Awakening." *Inc. Online,* January 1995.

"Yum! The New Treat in Biotech." *Fortune,* 14 October 1996.

—David Levine

Food & Kindred Products

MEAT PACKING PLANTS

This industry includes establishments primarily engaged in the slaughtering (for their own account or on a contract basis for the trade) of cattle, hogs, sheep, lambs, and calves for meat to be sold or to be used on the same premises in canning, cooking, curing, and freezing, and in making sausage, lard, and other products. The industry also includes establishments primarily engaged in slaughtering horses for human consumption. Businesses primarily engaged in slaughtering, dressing, and packing poultry, rabbits, and other small game are classified in **SIC 2015: Poultry Slaughtering and Processing.** Those primarily engaged in slaughtering and processing animals not for human consumption are classified in **SIC 2048: Prepared Feeds and Feed Ingredients for Animals and Fowls, Except Dogs and Cats.** Businesses primarily involved in manufacturing sausages and meat specialties from purchased meats are classified in **SIC 2013: Sausages and Other Prepared Meat Products.**

INDUSTRY SNAPSHOT

With annual sales in the $90 billion range, meat packing is one of the largest agriculture-based industries in the United States in the 1990s. In recent years, however, changing consumer eating habits have impacted the beef and pork industries, by far the largest sectors in this industry category. As Americans ate less beef, the beef industry retrenched, eliminating smaller and inefficient plants and expanding their operations to incorporate poultry products. At the same time, the pork industry was striving to reposition pork as "the meat of choice." Although technically a "red" meat,

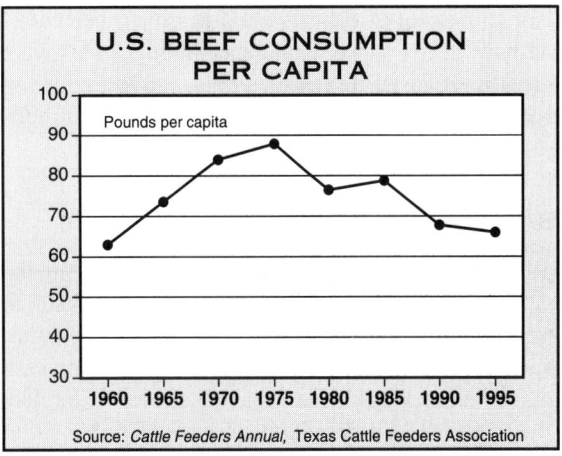

U.S. BEEF CONSUMPTION PER CAPITA

Source: *Cattle Feeders Annual,* Texas Cattle Feeders Association

it was gaining acceptance as an alternative to the other white meat, chicken.

In the mid-1990s there were 1,312 establishments in the industry, a 1 percent increase since 1990. In 1995, the industry shipped $46.7 worth of products, an 8 percent decrease since 1990.

ORGANIZATION AND STRUCTURE

The American Meat Institute (AMI) reported that there were more than 1.25 million livestock operations, raising beef cattle, hogs, and sheep destined for human consumption in the United States in the early 1990s. According to USDA statistics for 1994, gross income from livestock totaled $36.4 billion, $506 million for sheep and lambs, and $9.86 billion for hogs. Cattle numbers were expected to peak in 1997, when approximately 107 to 108 million head will be slated for consumption.

The meat packing plants that processed these animals into food and nonfood products ranged in size from those handling small numbers of livestock to operations processing millions of animals a year. According to the AMI, federally inspected slaughter and processing plants numbered 6,200 in 1997. The dominance of a few major companies is demonstrated by the fact that four packers processed approximately 82 percent of the beef, and three packers processed close to 35 percent of the pork. The USDA reports that in 1996, nearly 36.6 million commercial cattle were slaughtered, representing a three percent increase from 1995. Also in 1996, 92.4 million commercial hogs and 4.18 million sheep and lambs were slaughtered.

According to the AMI, the U.S. meat and poultry industry is spread among 44 states. Industry sources indicate that the Midwestern states raised about 46 percent of the cattle and over 15 percent of the hogs in the early 1990s, while South Central states raised more than 15 percent of the cattle and nearly 70 percent of the hogs. The top five cattle slaughtering states were Kansas, Nebraska, Texas, Colorado, and Iowa; the top five states in the slaughter of hogs were Iowa, Illinois, Minnesota, North Carolina, and South Dakota.

BACKGROUND AND DEVELOPMENT

Salt was used by the first meat packers in the United States, the colonial farmers of New England, to preserve meat. As the nation grew and moved westward, slaughterhouses were built near population centers so that meat could reach the table before it spoiled. The livestock herds were driven overland or barged to these early packing plants. So many hogs were slaughtered in Cincinnati, Ohio, that the city was called "Porkopolis."

For sanitary reasons, meat packing operations could only be carried out during the cold winter months, with ice used for refrigeration. The development of mechanical refrigeration and refrigerated railroad cars in the second half of the nineteenth century changed this. From late 1865 until the 1920s, Chicago, a hub city for the railroads, became renowned for its array of stockyards that collected and slaughtered livestock, often under harrowing working conditions.

With the turn of the century came mechanized disassembly and conveyor procedures in the plants, and the 1950s saw major improvements in plant sanitation and packaging. By the 1980s, the meat packing industry had again dispersed. Slaughterhouses moved closer to the feedlots where the animals were raised. Not having to ship them long distances reduced the stress, weight loss, and injury to the animals that was the inevitable effect of long journeys in crowded cattle cars and trucks.

Regulations. Under the 1906 Meat Inspection Act, U.S. pre- and post-mortem inspection of meat entering interstate and foreign commerce became mandatory. Meat to be used entirely within a single state may be inspected by that state's agriculture department. The Federal program was conducted by the Food Safety and Inspection Service (FSIS) of the U.S. Department of Agriculture (USDA). During the late 1980s and early 1990s, unfavorable media criticism of the inspection system spurred an overhaul of FSIS procedures.

In 1993, after four people died and hundreds more fell ill from ingestion of E. coli bacteria in undercooked hamburgers, food safety returned as a major industry issue. The USDA proposed a new labeling policy for red meat that was not ready for consumption. Under the new policy, labels with safe-handling instructions would be attached to meat and meat products. In issuing the new labeling recommendations, the USDA cited consumer surveys of 1985 and 1990 that revealed consumer ignorance of basic food-safety procedures.

Slaughter. The desirability of stunning animals prior to slaughter was recognized in both Europe and the United States before the end of the nineteenth century. It wasn't until 1960—with the passage of the Humane Slaughter Act—that the practice became mandatory in the United States. The Act required that, before being slaughtered, animals must be rendered unconscious by mechanical, electrical, or chemical (carbon dioxide gas) means that cause the animal the minimum of excitement or discomfort. Captive-bolt pistols or pneumatic guns may be used on cattle; with sheep and pigs, pistols, electric shock, or anesthetization in a carbon dioxide chamber is allowed. Compressed-air stunners and gas chambers for smaller animals came into use for cattle after World War II. Exceptions to federal requirements are made for ritual slaughters that satisfy the requirements of a particular faith. In kosher inspection, for example, a member of the Jewish faith cuts the throat and bleeds the animal without first stunning it, and then examines it for abnormalities before approving it for food use.

After stunning, cattle are suspended by one or both hindlegs while the carotid arteries and jugular veins are cut. Hides are then removed by an automated process. A straight cut opens the center of the belly to remove the viscera. Next, the carcasses are split down the center of the backbone. Beef carcasses might then be shrouded, a procedure in which the carcasses are cooled for 24 hours after being tightly wrapped in muslin that has been soaked in warm water. The carcass fat is smooth and trim when the shroud is removed. Specialty meat items like the brains, kidneys, tail, tongue, and sweetbreads do not accompany the carcass but are an important income source for packers. The procedures for veal carcasses are similar except that the hides are left on during chilling. Veal carcasses have very little fat and would shrink during chilling if the hides were removed.

In hog slaughter, the animals are bled after stunning by severing a large vein. The carcasses are then submerged in hot water to loosen the hair. After the removal of the hair, the carcass is eviscerated, split, and chilled.

Grading. While meat inspection is mandatory, grading is a voluntary program. Funded by fees paid by the packers, the service is offered by the USDA's Agricultural and Marketing Service. Grading establishes uniform trading standards and helps to determine the value of various meat cuts. Meat carcasses are graded by both quality and yield.

The quality grades for beef are prime, choice, good, standard, commercial, utility, cutter, and canner. Carcass characteristics that determine the grade include marbling (the streaks of fat in the lean portions), the color and texture of the lean, and maturity. Consumers tend to interpret grading as an indication of taste and tenderness, although it was not designed for this purpose. Growing consumer perceptions that lean meat is healthier have increased the demand for lower-fat grades. The ratio of usable meat to bone and fat determines a carcass's yield grade. Combined with the quality grade it is used to establish the monetary value of a carcass.

Working Conditions. The slaughterhouses of the United States in the early twentieth century were grim and dangerous places to work. Low wages coupled with unsafe conditions made the stockyards of Chicago and other cities hazardous work sites. But it was not until reports on conditions there grew widespread—thanks in part to Upton Sinclair's novel *The Jungle,* which depicted in chilling detail the deplorable environment of the stockyards of Chicago—that the government turned its attention to the industry. Slaughterhouse conditions furthered the cause of fledgling unions, who grew in strength over the ensuing years.

At the end of the twentieth century, automation had not replaced manual labor and the extensive use of sharp knives and other hand tools, workers were still lifting and lugging heavy carcasses, abattoir floors were slippery, and workers suffered from exposure due to the need for continuous refrigeration systems. Despite AMI and the OSHA guidelines, 36 percent of meatpacking employees are injured on the job each year. The meatpacking industry still has the highest injury rate of any U.S. industry. So long as there is no economical and reliable cutting machinery that could accommodate the physical variety of animal carcasses, processing would continue to be a manual operation.

In the early 1990s, the industry's rate of cumulative trauma disorders (CTDs) was higher than all other manufacturing industries. The illness usually took the form of carpal tunnel syndrome, in which repeated, rapid, and forceful motions pinch and compress the nerve that runs through the wrist to the hand. Lower back and various tendon disorders were also reported. However, it appears that the rate of on-the-job illness and injury may have declined since 1991, following OSHA's establishment of the Ergonomics Guidelines for the Meat Packing Industry. Under-reporting of injury and illness still remains a chronic problem, as the majority of the meatpacking workforce is comprised of illegal aliens.

Two of the nation's largest meat packers, IBP, Inc. and John Morrell, were cited by the Occupational Safety and Health Administration (OSHA) for under-reporting or failing to record injuries and illnesses. Both companies contested the OSHA fines, which were greatly reduced. More important, OSHA recognized that the CTDs plaguing meat industry workers needed new solutions. In 1990 OSHA issued ergonomic (fitting the job to the employee rather than the other way round) guidelines after consultation with AMI and labor groups. The guidelines emphasized worker training in proper techniques, strengthened by refresher courses, and the importance of workers to report CTD symptoms early to prevent permanent injury. Medical management by trained health care providers was another program component.

OSHA offered special incentives to meat packers who entered into voluntary agreements with the agency to lessen their ergonomic hazards. While they would still be subject to OSHA inspections, they would not be cited or penalized on ergonomic grounds. Opinions on OSHA's voluntary guidelines were mixed. Jim Marsden, AMI vice-president for scientific and technical affairs, said in *Occupational Hazards,* that they were "especially effective because they're geared toward hazard prevention." Industry critics did not always agree. Phillip L. Immesote, president of the United Food and Commercial Workers Union, testified at a hearing of the House Employment and Housing Subcommittee that OSHA was about to repeat earlier disastrous experiences with "a new program of exemptions and voluntary compliance in the nation's packing houses."

CURRENT CONDITIONS

Per capita meat consumption has increased from 116.1 pounds in 1992 to 143 pounds in 1996. Industry observers expect red meat consumption to remain stable, and for the next several years, the USDA forecasts larger meat supplies at lower wholesale prices, with resulting competition for consumer dollars at the retail level.

Beef. With demand for red meat declining, the number of companies producing it decreased by 22 percent from 1982-1992, according to the *1992 Census of Manufactures.* The USDA expects per capita consumption of beef to decrease in 1997, due in part to a decrease in cattle, increased exports, fewer imports, and a growing population. As such, meat processors have sought to improve their business outlook by expanding into the fast-growing poultry market. The number of major meat producers who also engaged in production of poultry products has risen dramatically in the last ten years.

There were reasons other than health concerns for the decline in beef consumption, according to Robert Adams, vice-president of Continental Grain Company's cattle feeding division. A 1994 article in *Feedstuffs* noted Adams' belief that the beef industry is disorganized, divided among a great many operations that vary enormously in their size and handling of as many as 80 different breeds of cattle. Supermarket meat cases were overwhelming, too, said Adams, with a profusion of cuts creating confusion instead of convenience.

Enhanced genetics, the introduction of new feed additives and growth stimulants, and nutritional advances all played a part in the improvements in cattle growth rate during the last quarter of the twentieth century. Consumer demand for lean beef, as well as environmental concerns, are expected to continue to have an impact on the beef industry.

Pork. Nationwide, the number of hog enterprises has dwindled in recent years. In 1993 the number of hog farms was half of what it had been in 1980. Many of the smaller operations dropped out, while the larger outfits expanded. For pig-slaughtering operations, however, this consolidation of sources didn't adversely impact their production.

According to the *Statistical Abstract of the United States: 1996,* Iowa had the largest number of hogs and pigs on farms, with 15,000. Illinois and North Carolina were the next two largest, with 5,450 and 5,400 hogs and pigs respectively.

In the mid-1990s, the National Pork Producers Council announced a comprehensive plan to promote pork as the meat of choice both domestically and worldwide. The plan was the joint output of the National Pork Board (NPPC), the National Live Stock and Meat Board's pork section, and hundreds of producers. Goals included building demand for pork by creating new products and expanding current uses; ensuring that pork met or surpassed consumer expectations of safety, quality, value; and positioning the industry as socially responsible.

Whether the potential for larger herds and increased production could be parlayed into industry growth was dependent on other factors, such as cost competitiveness, exports, and the continued popularity of pork products. In the early to mid-1990s that popularity remained stable. The United States reported an increase in per capita pork consumption since 1991, with Americans' per capita consumption at 68 pounds in 1995. This continuing viability was due in part to new breeding techniques that produce pork lower in calories and cholesterol and with one-third less fat than ten years earlier.

INDUSTRY LEADERS

Industry sources report that IBP, Inc., ConAgra, Inc., and Cargill Incorporated are the top three beef slaughterers, while IBP, ConAgra, and John Morrell operated the country's top three pork slaughter operations.

IBP, Inc. Competition for the number one spot in the meat packing industry was strong, but Nebraska-based IBP, Inc., a subsidiary of Occidental Petroleum Corp., held on with sales of $13 billion in 1996. These posted earnings continued the company's growth pattern. IBP, Inc. touts itself as the world's largest producer of fresh beef and pork, and operates 24 plants in North America. With the acquisition of Foodbrands America, Inc. in early 1997, IBP enjoyed an increased work force. Foreign exports accounted for a small percentage of sales, most of them to the Far East (Japan, Korea, Taiwan). Mexico was a strong beef market for IBP, and the company's sales of pork in Europe increased sevenfold in 1992. IBP continued to concentrate on beef and pork slaughter and processing, leaving the diversification into poultry products to competitors like ConAgra, Inc., and Cargill Meat Sector in Minneapolis.

By relocating its slaughterhouses in 1961 to where the beef was, near Nebraska's and Iowa's cattle farms, IBP changed the meat-packing industry. At the company's plant in Dakota City, Nebraska, animal carcasses were carried over 20 miles of conveyor systems. Within 48 hours, a 650-pound carcass could be broken, cut, and packed into 65- to 80-pound boxes for shipment to supermarkets. Pork became an important part of IBP's success starting in 1976, and by the late 1980s the company planned six plants in Iowa and Nebraska, all within a 100-mile radius of the nation's largest hog-producing area.

ConAgra, Inc. Originally known as Nebraska Consolidated Mills, ConAgra's expansion to its present status as a leading food producer began in earnest with its development of Duncan Hines cake mix in the 1950s. The company became a multifaceted food provider in the 1960s and 1970s, establishing a number of poultry processing plants to complement their growing flour mill business. In 1971 the company changed its name to ConAgra and continued its expansion into a variety of manufacturing industries. The company's purchases in recent years have included United Agri Products (1978), Banquet Frozen Foods (1980), Armour Food Company (1983), and Beatrice (1990), as well as a number of other businesses. In 1996, ConAgra announced plans to close 29 of its facilities in effort to weed out its lowest profit producers. ConAgra offers over 50 brands, including Hunt's, Wesson, Armour, and Butterball, and operates more than 200 retail outlets.

Cargill. Founded in 1865, Cargill built its reputation in commodity trading, but by 1993 was one of the country's largest suppliers of raw foods and ingredients, with sales reaching $11 to $13 billion from diversified activities ranging from corn and flour milling to oilseed processing.

In 1993, although Cargill still regarded itself primarily as an ingredient supplier, it had become the nation's third largest meat packer. Cargill had acquired Excel Corp., a leading name in boxed beef and pork, in 1979. When Cargill formed its Meat Sector in the early 1990s, it included the Excel Corp. and Cargill Meat Products (which further processed beef and pork). In 1993, Cargill announced that it would sell its meat processing business in Japan, although it continues to export beef to Japan. Excel distributed most of its products under private label. Estimated annual sales in the 1990s of $8 billion were split almost equally between retail and industrial/foodservice customers.

WORK FORCE

The number of employees in the meat packing and processing industry began registering modest increases in the early 1990s, up to 467,800 in 1995, according to the AMI. In the food industry as a whole, meat packing and processing is the largest employer. According to U.S. Department of Labor statistics, meat packing and processing workers' weekly earnings averaged $409.26, or $9.43 an hour in 1995,

MEAT PACKING INDUSTRY EMPLOYMENT

Employment in thousands

Source: Department of Labor

lagging behind reported wages in meat processing ($431.15). Meat packing is also a highly labor-intensive industry, and a higher proportion of total employees (84 percent) was production workers, compared to 72 percent in all food preparation sectors and 67 percent in all manufacturing industries.

Because of the low wages of the industry, employee turnover has increased. In 1977, the average pay in the meat packing industry was 17 percent higher than that for all manufacturing. By 1986, when the pay advantage had dropped to 15 percent below the factory average, growing numbers of workers quit the industry. Meat packing had traditionally recorded high lay-off and recall rates, but until the sharp drop in pay scale, the number of workers who quit had been lower than in manufacturing as a whole. Labor agreements with some of the large packers in the early 1990s seemed to be attempting to address the wage discrepancy, both to attract and hold workers. However, according to a report in *Dollars and Sense,* it is not unusual for a turnover of the entire labor force in the course of a year.

AMERICA AND THE WORLD

The marketing of meat to American consumers in the supermarket lagged behind changes taking place elsewhere in the world, according to *Progressive Grocer* magazine. Centralized meat cutting that did away with the need for cutting operations in the supermarket was common in France, while retailers in the United Kingdom used new packaging technologies to extend product quality and shelf life. Across the Pacific, meat was often displayed in Japanese and Australian markets by its method of preparation rather than by animal, a system that exposed consumers to more varieties of meat.

International Trade. The United States enjoyed a favorable trade balance in red meat products, with exports valued at about $2.4 billion. In 1996, the United States became the second-largest pork exporter in the world, representing an increase of 19.7 percent from 1994. The major destination for beef exports was Japan, which imports over 62 percent of U.S. beef, accounting for $1.5 billion in sales. Sales of beef to Mexico have also increased in the mid-1990s to $500 million. South Korea became the fourth-largest importer of U.S beef. Japan made up an estimated 48 percent of the export market for pork in 1996. This amount, a sudden increase over figures posted in previous years, was attributed to a scandal involving Taiwan's falsification of documents to avoid Japanese taxes. Even though high-end U.S. pork products were likely to remain competitively priced in Japan, Taiwan was expected to regain its market dominance. However, a recent outbreak of foot and mouth disease has affected the Taiwanese pork supply, boding well for continued growth in U.S. pork exports to Japan.

For the late 1990s, the USDA predicted a small improvement in meat trade, as Japan's economy remained slow, and the recent E. Coli scare has made Japanese meat consumers wary. Both Canada and Mexico were expected to increase their exports. In 1994, U.S. export sales of meat and related products totaled nearly $10 billion.

Five countries accounted for 86 percent of all red meat imports in 1992: Australia (32 percent), Canada (24 percent), New Zealand (21 percent), Denmark (7 percent), and Argentina (2 percent). Pork imports came primarily from Canada and Denmark (60 percent). Strong pork prices in the European Economic Community compared to weaker pricing in the United States, combined with political upheavals in Eastern Europe and the former Yugoslavia, led to lower imports from these areas.

FURTHER READING

1993 Meat & Poultry Facts. Washington: American Meat Institute, 1993.

Bain, Herbert B. "The First 75 Years of the American Meat Institute." *American Meat Institute 75th Anniversary Commemorative Magazine.* Arlington, VA, 1980.

Baldo, Anthony. "Boxed In: For Two Decades, Iowa Beef Packing Prospered in the Rough-and-Tumble Meat-Cutting Business Without Much Fear of Competition." *Financial World,* 21 March 1989.

Brown, Robert H. "AMI Testifies Against FDA Meat Inspection." *Feedstuffs,* 22 November 1993.

"Cargill to Quit Meat Packing Line in Japan." *Wall Street Journal,* 26 November 1993.

Carlson, Gordon S. "Larger Meat Supplies, Lower Prices on Tap." *Feedstuffs,* 13 December 1993.

Cross, H. Russell. "HACCP: Pivotal Change for the Meat Industry." *Food Technology,* August 1996.

Frazier, Frank. "Poultry Inspection History Shows New Tactics Tried Before." *Feedstuffs,* 14 February 1994.

Hawkins, Dana. "The Most Dangerous Jobs." *U.S. News and World Report,* 23 September 1996.

Just the Facts: Fact Sheet: Meat Consumption in the U.S. Washington: American Meat Institute, 1996. Available from http:www.meatami.org/FactBK02.HTM.

Just the Facts: The Role of the Meat Industry in the U.S. Economy. Washington: American Meat Institute, 1996. Available from http:www.meatami.org/FactBK01.HTM.

Kushner, Gary Jay. "1994 Food Industry Legislative and Regulatory Outlook." *Food Processing,* January 1994.

LaBell, Fran. "Vegetarianism on the Rise." *Prepared Foods,* February 1994.

Marberry, Steve. "Pork Production 2000: Fewer Farms Doing More." *Feedstuffs,* 28 February 1994.

"Meat Plant Escapes Cuts: ConAgra Says Facility in Nampa is Doing Well." *Idaho Statesman,* 31 May 1996.

"Meatpacking Industry Cuts Comp. Claims." *Occupational Hazards,* May 1996.

Pehanich, Mike. "The Quiet Giant Climbs the Value Chain." *Prepared Foods,* October 1993.

Personick, Martin E., and Katherine Taylor-Shirley. "Profiles in Safety and Health." *Monthly Labor Review,* January 1989.

"Product Handbook: Pork." *ID,* 15 September 1993.

"Product Handbook: Processed Meats." *ID,* 15 September 1993.

"Record U.S. Meat Production Expected in 1993." *AgraEurope,* December 1992.

"Red Meat Will Get Largest Cut of USDA Export Promotion Funds." *Journal of Commerce and Commercial,* June 1995.

Rhoads, Alexander. "Grinding Workers Down." *Dollars & Sense,* March 1992.

Scheid, Jon F. "Beef Industry Striving to Be More Direct." *Feedstuffs,* 21 February 1994.

———. "Food Poisoning Cases Inspire New Policy." *Feedstuffs,* 22 November 1993.

Sheridan, Peter J. "Meatpackers Move to Cut Injury Rates." *Occupational Hazards,* May 1991.

Smith, Rod. "Pork Industry's Long-range Plan Ready to Go to Producers." *Feedstuffs,* 24 January 1994.

Spears, Jerry W. "Environment, Consumers, to Influence Beef Production." *Feedstuffs,* 21 February 1994.

U.S. Department of Agriculture. *Cattle and Beef Industry Statistics.* Available from http://www.cowtown.org./library/stats/cbis0497.html.

———. *Livestock, Dairy, and Poultry Monthly.* Available from http://usda.mannlib.cornell.edu/reportsà97/livestock_dairy_and_poultry_04.16.97.

———. *Livestock Slaughter - 1996 Summary.* http://usda.mannlib.cornell.edu/reportsàstock_slaughter_annual_summary_03.14.97.

———. *U.S. Beef Industry: May 1996 Situation.* Available from http://www.ncanet.org/market_watch/sit_596.html.

———. *U.S. Cattle on Feed up 6 Percent.* Available from http://www.usda.gov/nass/PUBS/TODAYRPT/SR889.COF0497.DATA.

"U.S. Now World's Second Biggest Pork Exporter." National Pork Board, 1996. Available from http://www..nppc.org/NEWS/npbtrade.html.

Zbytniewski, Jo-Ann. "Marketing Methods: Meat products: Merchandising." *Progressive Grocer,* December 1992.

—Mary Ratcliffe, updated by Kris Barnett

SIC 2013

SAUSAGES AND OTHER PREPARED MEAT PRODUCTS

Establishments in this category are primarily engaged in manufacturing sausages, cured meats, smoked meats, canned meats, frozen meats and other prepared meats and meat specialties, from purchased carcasses and other materials. Products include bologna, bacon, corned beef, frankfurters (except poultry), headcheese, luncheon meat, pigs' feet, sandwich spreads, stew, pastrami, and hams (except poultry). Prepared meat plants operated by packing houses as separate establishments are also included in this industry.

Establishments primarily engaged in canning or otherwise processing poultry, rabbits, and other small game are classified in **SIC 2015: Poultry Slaughtering and Processing.** Establishments primarily engaged in canning meat for baby food are classified in **SIC 2032: Canned Specialties.** Establishments primarily engaged in the cutting up and resale of purchased fresh carcasses, for the trade, are classified in **SIC 5147: Meats and Meat Products,** a wholesale trade industry.

INDUSTRY SNAPSHOT

There were 1,200 establishments in the industry in the mid-1990s, up 2 percent since 1990. In 1995 U.S. companies in this industry shipped products worth $20.685 billion; the value of shipments for all meat products was $100.2 billion. Imports of red meat in the mid-1990s were valued at $3 billion, while red meat exports were worth an estimated $5.2 billion. Prepared meats also found a niche among the salty snack category, evinced by recent sales increases in this market.

In 1995, the red meat industry, which included meat-packing plants and establishments that produced processed pork and beef products, accounted for only 71 percent of the entire meat industry, which included poultry and poultry products, compared to 80 percent in 1988. The consensus among analysts is that this shifting market share is due to increasing consumer demand for healthier foods. The shift does not appear to be away from meat according to USDA data, as red meat production hit an all time high of 42.6 million pounds in 1995.

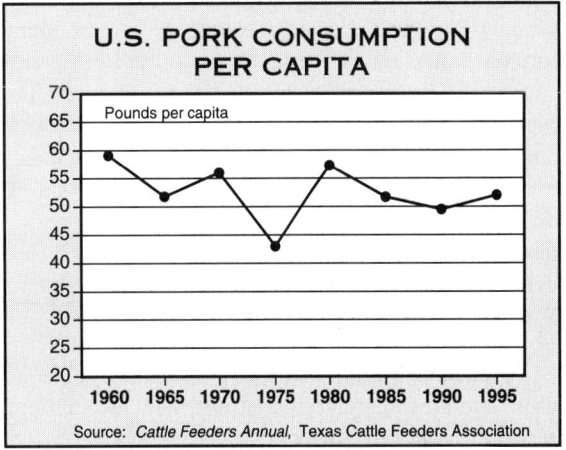

U.S. PORK CONSUMPTION PER CAPITA

Source: *Cattle Feeders Annual,* Texas Cattle Feeders Association

Per capita consumption of red meat continued to increase throughout 1996, and studies done by both the USDA and the American Meat Institute (AMI) show that 99 percent of Americans eat meat and 94 percent eat red meat. Total meat, poultry, and fish consumption has risen by 16 pounds per person over the past decade. The USDA estimates that the average American ate 125.5 pounds of red meat, 95 pounds of poultry, and 15 pounds of fish in 1996; of that amount, 34.2 pounds were processed meat. The average amount spent by an individual on processed meat products per week is $1.88.

ORGANIZATION AND STRUCTURE

Prepared meat products are marketed to supermarkets and wholesale clubs, and often times the "store brand" purchased was produced by a large company and labeled locally. The pizza industry (for toppings), food services, and in-store delicatessens make up the rest of the market share. Companies in this category also manufacture private label meats for restaurants.

Meat processors often work closely with vendors from other industries to develop innovative new packaging ideas, mindful of the importance of packaging from a marketing and a practical point of view. Because meat is a highly perishable item, packaging must ensure that the food inside will not spoil and that it will retain its flavor for long periods of time. The packaging must also be convenient and attractive to the consumer. The concept of meeting consumer demands through marketing is reflected in packaging, which presents each product's traits, i.e. low-fat, low-sodium, etc.

In addition to the large national brands, many regional brands of hams, sausages, hot dogs, lunch meats and other prepared meats are available for family-run companies. A proliferation of processed meat products has put shelf and cooler space at a premium, forcing producers to create niches in major markets and design more convenient and tasty products. The prepared meat industry's practice of creating products and the demand for them that had not previously existed among consumers is part of a larger food industry trend called differentiation. With differentiation, similar foods are altered enough to appear different either in preparation, flavor, or packaging, and are then marketed as new products.

Prepared meat businesses owe much of their growth to the creation of variations, such as premium, economy, flavored, low-salt, low-fat, high-protein, or more convenient versions of a basic meat product. The industry devised creations such as microwave bacon and sausages, shelf-stable stews and dinners, low-fat deli meats, frozen microwaveable hamburgers, or cheese-filled hot dogs. Reduced fat products are among the fastest growing markets of all processed meats. Changes in the production of such "healthier" versions to improve their taste and texture have appealed to consumers and have spawned a devoted following.

Costs and prices in this industry are greatly affected by the hog commodities market. Some companies not only operate their own packinghouses, but they also raise hogs in order to avoid the price swings that often occur in the commodities market. When hog supplies increase, manufacturers' profit margins generally expand because only a small part of that savings is passed on to the consumer. When hog supplies decrease, forcing prices up, the manufacturers' profit margin narrows. Another factor affecting price is the strict guidelines aimed at safer meat processing. Techniques required to prevent bacteria and disease have increased the cost of production.

Package labeling. Nutrition labeling laws designed to enforce the 1990 Nutrition Labeling and Education Act were announced in 1992. The regulations required food processors to provide consumers with additional nutrition information on labels. The rules went into effect in 1995, but most companies voluntarily switched their labels before the deadline.

The new labels require the manufacturer to list the total fat content, amount of saturated fat, number of calories derived from fat, and cholesterol, sodium, carbohydrates and protein content in its products. According to the regulations, meat processors may use the term "light in sodium" if the meat product's sodium levels have been reduced 50 percent. In addition, the rules defined terms such as "lite or light," "low fat," "fat-free," "reduced calories," "low in saturated fat," "high fiber," and other terms that manufacturers have been using to tout the "healthiness" of products. In order to use any of those terms on the label, food must meet the requirements of the definition. For example, a "low-fat" product must have only three grams of fat or less in a serving. The government also established standard serving sizes for many foods so that food manufacturers could no longer decrease serving sizes in order to meet claims that products were low-calorie or low-sodium.

The regulations were designed to eliminate much of the hype routinely utilized by food manufacturers. Companies that bring in less than $500,000 in annual sales were exempt from the laws. However, it was expected that the entire food industry, including prepared meat businesses, would spend about $2.8 billion on new labels and other related expenses.

Environmental concerns. Many highly processed or packaged meat products provided convenience to consumers, but at a price to the environment. Disposable microwaveable packages, such as microwave bacon, free up consumers from dirty dishes, but create more waste. Because of increasing public concern about the problem of garbage disposal, products packaged in disposable containers face growing criticism. Laws that require recyclable packaging could have an impact on the companies that produce some processed meat products. Environmentalists and relief workers also continue to voice their criticism of the meat industry and its use of immense amounts of grain crops, water, energy, grazing areas, and other natural resources in the development of its product.

BACKGROUND AND DEVELOPMENT

Many of the companies in this industry began as meat-packing companies and sold nonbranded meat to stores, food services, and meat product manufacturers.

They diversified, however, as it became clear that the food processing business was more profitable and less susceptible to swings in commodity prices and the cyclical nature of the fresh pork business. A company that processed pork earned ten times as much on every dollar of sales as a company that derived most of its income from slaughtering.

Many of the establishments that produce prepared meat products also own and run the packinghouses that supply them with meat. Hormel, once a large meatpacking concern, severely limited its packing operations and concentrated most of its resources on processing hot dogs, cold cuts, sausages and other prepared meats. In some cases, meat manufacturing establishments have leased packing services or have exclusive contracts from meatpackers to supply only that manufacturer. Hormel leased one of its slaughter plants to a pork processing company to operate, but it provided the hogs and purchased all of the plant's prime cuts and processed product output.

Establishments that pack or process red meat suffered in the late 1980s and early 1990s, as a result of increased consumer demand for poultry products. Between 1982 and 1987, the total number of companies in the red meat business fell 10 percent, leaving 2,562 companies, according to the *1987 Census of Manufacturers*. Between 1982 and 1992, the number of red meat processors also producing poultry products nearly tripled, from 11 companies to 32.

In addition, companies closed inefficient plants and introduced innovative new products. Companies processing red meat expanded into other product areas, especially poultry, through acquisitions or mergers. Meat packers diversified, shifting attention from meat packing to processing of low-fat cold cuts and other meat products. In 1980, half of all beef shipped in this country was shipped as noncarcass, or processed, beef; in 1992, almost seven-eighths was noncarcass beef.

CURRENT CONDITIONS

As a result of consumer demands for healthier prepared-meats, meat processing companies introduced many "light" or "low-fat" versions of popular products. Chicken or turkey cold cuts and hot dogs stole market share from beef and pork products. According to Marketing Intelligence Service, Ltd. and reported by AMI, "more than 50 percent of the product lines in the lunch meat and hot dog categories contain a reduced fat or nutritional claim. The extra low-fat (97 percent fat free) hot dog and bologna market has grown by more than 21 percent."

It is likely that processors will continue to diversify their product offerings. According to some estimates, by 1997 at least 70 percent of the top 25 poultry and meat producers will market both poultry and red meat products, compared to only 40 percent in 1992. Companies are also looking to fish and seafood products to further bolster their sales.

Sales of bacon have declined, in all probability because of bacon's fat and cholesterol content; sales of bacon in restaurants remained steady, however, suggesting that consumers allow themselves some leeway in their quest for a healthier diet. The introduction of "lower salt", "reduced fat", and "fat free" bacon should help compensate for this trend.

In any event, the increased emphasis on healthy nutrition has revolutionized the prepared meat product industry. Philip Morris' Oscar Mayer Foods Corp. cut nearly 300 slow-selling products, dropped prices on bacon, hot dogs, and bologna and added light bologna and turkey bacon as part of an ambitious low-fat lunch meat line. In 1992 ConAgra's Armour Swift-Eckrich Inc. subsidiary introduced a full line of Healthy Choice brand lunch meats and hot dogs to compete against Oscar Mayer's Healthy Favorites and a Weight Watchers lunch meat line, produced by Hillshire Farms which is owned by Sara Lee Corporation.

Oscar Mayer led the cold cuts or lunch meat market with a 33 percent share in 1991-92. While prepared luncheon meat products were the cornerstone of the company's stature, Oscar Mayer's Lunchables, a packaged meal of cheese, cold cuts, and crackers, was also a part of this success. This lunchtime fare was introduced in 1989, and by 1992 had reached sales of more than $130 million a year, with about 40 percent consumed by children and the rest evenly split between men and women.

ConAgra's Healthy Choice line of products has grown steadily since its introduction in 1988. As of 1996 there were 300 products in the line, with sales of $1.4 billion. The Healthy Choice products include beef, pork, and poultry-based meats. It is sold in prepackaged form as well as at supermarket deli counters; the company also plans to market it to food services. Company officials from Armour Swift-Eckrich predicted that its new line of 97-percent fat-free lunch meats would expand the existing market by turning light users of lunch meats into medium and heavy users, possibly reversing a trend away from lunchmeat sandwiches that confronted the industry and sent processors looking for convenient substitutes to entice "brown baggers."

Lunch preferences. According to the *Wall Street Journal,* the number of people who brought their lunch to work every day had risen throughout the 1980s. That number rose to 11 percent of all Americans in 1992, a very lucrative market. While the nation's work force was bringing its lunch to work in record numbers, demand for sandwiches and sandwich meats was falling. The article said that the average American carried 42 meals from home in 1984; 71 percent of those lunches included a sandwich. In 1991-92, the average working American brought 53 meals from home, but only 58 percent included a sandwich. During that same year, cold cut sales fell almost two percent to $2.4 billion. Sales of low-fat sandwich meats, however, rose 14 percent.

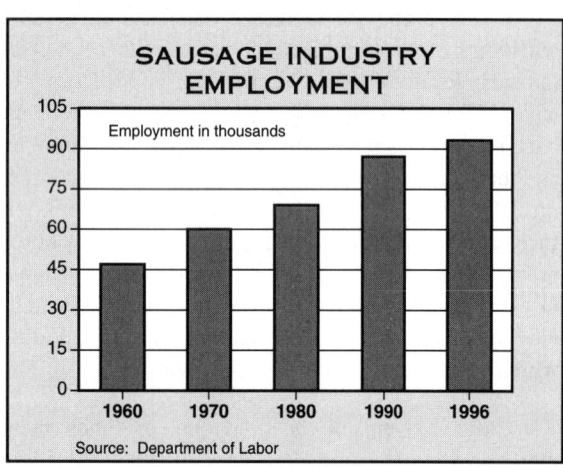

SAUSAGE INDUSTRY EMPLOYMENT

Employment in thousands

Source: Department of Labor

INDUSTRY LEADERS

A majority of widely recognized processed meat brands are now owned by large conglomerates, and many of them started out as small, regional, independent meatpacking and meat processing companies. Three national industry leaders are Sara Lee Corporation, Hormel Foods Corporation, and Oscar Mayer Foods Corporation, a subsidiary of Philip Morris Companies, Inc. There are still many localized companies, however, but their sales only account for a small percentage of total industry sales.

Sara Lee Corporation (known as Consolidated Foods until 1985) was one of the largest meat processing establishments in the United States. Sara Lee held the number one position in sales in three of the major categories of packaged and processed meats. The company's Hillshire Farm smoked sausage product commanded a 38 percent share of the $1 billion retail market. Its Jimmy Dean breakfast sausage and Ball Park hot dog brands each owned a 22 percent share of their respective billion-dollar markets. Sara Lee also boasts a number of very strong regional brands, such as Bryan, Kahn, and others. Sara Lee had total sales of $18.624 billion in 1996.

With the purchase of Kraft General Foods in 1988 for $12.9 billion, Philip Morris acquired Oscar Mayer and Louis Rich meat products. In 1991 the Oscar Mayer division of Philip Morris had revenues of $2.3 billion. One of Oscar Mayer's products, Lunchables, a pre-packaged lunch in a box, was marketed towards parents. Containing lunch meat, crackers, cheese, etc., it was to be the ideal "take along" lunch for school children. In 1996 and 1997 various consumer advocate groups claimed that Lunchables were too high in fat to be considered a nutritious lunch.

Conglomerate agribusiness ConAgra had total annual sales of more than $24 billion in 1996, and employed more than 90,000 people in 27 countries. ConAgra acquired Armour from Greyhound in 1983, and Swift-Eckrich from the Beatrice Co. in 1990. Armour and Swift-Eckrich became a single subsidiary of ConAgra, which manufactures Sizzlean, Swift Premium Brown 'N Serve Sausage and Eckrich sausages, and other Armour and Swift products. Before the acquisition, Swift had been the third-largest manufacturer of processed meat after Oscar Mayer and Sara Lee. ConAgra also owns meatpacking companies Swift Independent Packing and Monfort.

George A. Hormel & Company was founded in Austin, Minnesota, in 1891 as a slaughterhouse and retail meat products shop. Its earnings for the first year were $220,000. About 100 years later, the company name was changed to Hormel Foods Corporation, reflecting its change in focus from a packing and meat company to a food processing company offering meat products, frozen foods, and microwave products, as well as branded fresh pork and beef. One of the most widely recognized products from the line is SPAM, a pork based luncheon meat in a can. Hormel was one of the few older meat companies that remained independent after a wave of takeovers in the 1980s. It had sales of $3.1 billion in 1996.

Hormel became known as the industry's innovator in the late 1980s. It was one of the largest meatpackers in the country, but its president, Richard Knowlton, closed many of its slaughtering facilities in the 1980s and began focusing on producing processed and branded meat products. Since the early 1980s, Hormel's hog slaughter capacity has been cut 75 percent. The portion of its revenues generated by prepared meat and other food products rose to between 65 and 75 percent.

In the first half of the 1980s, Hormel introduced two or three new products annually. In one 18-month period during the second half of the decade, however, it introduced 134 new products, including those made from chicken, turkey, and fish. After a large investment and the acquisition of the necsessary research equipment, the company achieved an industry breakthrough in 1987 with the debut of Top Shelf, a line of microwaveable dinner entrees that remained fresh unrefrigerated for 18 months. Despite initial success, Top Shelf sales declined throughout the 1990's and the product is non-existent in most markets.

Like Hormel, Smithfield Foods was an independent company, but on a smaller scale. It initially produced only pork products, and it spent a fraction of the more than $70 million on advertising that Hormel spent. In 1992 the company had sales of more than $1 billion, which more than doubled by 1996 to $2.3 billion.

The name recognition of Smithfield canned hams enabled it to diversify into production of hot dogs, bacon, sausages and lunch meats from its main pork-packing operations. About half of its sales in 1988 were in nonbranded items—spareribs, pork chops, or hot dogs packaged for other companies' private labels. Smithfield Foods distributes on both a national and international level.

Thorn Apple Valley, Inc., is one of the largest producers of customer-owned private label meat products, as well as one of the largest regional producers of bacon, hot dogs, lunch meats, and smoked sausages. Its private label meats account for approximately 60 percent of its processed meat sales. It traditionally aimed its other products at the economy shopper; however, the company has begun to stress premium brands, including its own and strong regional ones. In response to the healthy-eating trend among consumers, Thorn Apple also increased its sales of poultry-based products. Thorn Apple Valley is one of the largest hog slaughtering companies in the United States. In 1996 sales totaled $983 million, 50 percent of which were processed meat products.

AMERICA AND THE WORLD

For many foreign companies, the new label laws created by the 1990 Nutrition Labeling and Education Act were difficult to comply with because businesses were not accustomed to providing such complete product content analyses. Although the labels could be considered a barrier to trade and, therefore, incompatible with the General Agreement on Tariffs and Trade (GATT), it was unlikely that any challenge would hold up as both foreign and domestic companies had to observe the same regulations.

In 1993 Oscar Mayer prepared to compete in the Mexican market by signing an agreement insuring that Sigma Alimentos, Mexico's largest processed meat company, would be Oscar Mayer's sole distributor in Mexico. Like Oscar Mayer, Sigma Alimentos was a subsidiary of one of its country's largest corporations. Its share of the processed meat market in Mexico was 32 percent, reflecting a standing in the Mexican marketplace similar to that enjoyed by Oscar Mayer in the American market. Sigma Alimentos agreed to distribute Oscar Mayer meats, as well as Louis Rich turkey products and Claussen pickles. This was the first national distribution of Oscar Mayer products in Mexico. The company also exports products to the Caribbean, Asia, and the Middle East.

FURTHER READING

American Meat Institute. ''Just The Facts, 1997.'' Washington, 1996. Available from http://www.meatami.org.

Barrows, John. ''Nabisco Introduces Health Choice Cookies and Snacks.'' Nabisco, 1997. Available from http://www.nabisco.com.

Berss, Marcia. ''This Isn't Ross Perot and GM.'' *Forbes,* 8 June 1992, 103-4.

Coletti, Richard. ''Living Higher on the Hog.'' *Financial World,* 27 November 1990, 29.

Deveny, Kathleen. ''Firms See a Fat Opportunity in Catering to Americans' Quest for 'Easy' Lunches.'' *Wall Street Journal,* 3 November 1992, B1.

Erickson, Julie Liesse. ''Meatpacker's Makeover.'' *Advertising Age,* 21 November 1988, 53.

Gutfield, Rose. ''Food Label 'Babel' to Fall as Uniform System Is Cleared.'' *Wall Street Journal,* 3 December 1992, B1.

Ingersoll, Bruce. ''Food Concerns, Public in Limbo over Labeling.'' *Wall Street Journal.* 9 November 1992, B1.

Koselka, Rita. ''$Oink $Oink.'' *Forbes,* 3 February 1992, 54-56.

Reier, Sharon. ''High on the Hog.'' *Financial World,* 28 June 1988, 29-31.

U.S. Department of Agriculture. ''The Status of U.S. Meat Product Exports in 1996.'' Washington, 1996. Available from http://www.ffas.usda.gov.

—Wendy Stein, updated by Jennifer Stong

POULTRY SLAUGHTERING AND PROCESSING

This industry includes establishments primarily engaged in slaughtering, dressing, packing, freezing, and canning poultry, rabbits, and other small game, or in manufacturing products from such meats, for their own account or on a contract basis for the trade. This industry also includes the drying, freezing, and breaking of eggs.

INDUSTRY SNAPSHOT

Beginning in the early 1930s, the poultry industry was dominated by many small growers and processors. The U.S. poultry business evolved into a vertically integrated industry in the mid-1930s, in which a few top companies accounted for most of the country's broiler (chicken) and turkey production. Vertical integration combined the previously independent and fragmented operations of feedmills, hatcheries, farms, slaughterers, and processors into giant conglomerates that managed all stages of production.

Broilers, which are chickens raised specifically for table consumption, represented by far the largest component of the industry, with the value of production exceeding $11.8 billion in 1995, compared to $3 billion for turkey. Other poultry, such as ducks and geese, accounted for only about $300 million in industry sales. Broiler production was concentrated in 17 southeastern states on the eastern seaboard and Gulf of Mexico. This so-called ''broiler belt'' was the source of 90 percent of production. No such regional concentration existed in the turkey sector. The top four turkey producing states were North Carolina, Minnesota, California, and Arkansas. Broilers averaged $0.86 per pound in price in 1995. There were 7.33 billion broilers produced in 1995 alone, the equivalent of 25.2 billion pounds of broiler meat. It is anticipated that the amount of broilers produced per year will continue to rise.

ORGANIZATION AND STRUCTURE

According to the U.S. Department of Agriculture (USDA), there were 508 federally inspected poultry slaughtering and processing plants in 1990, and 3,180 plants that slaughtered and/or processed both meat and poultry. Poultry processing firms totaled about 100 that year, with 54 of them being integrated broiler processors. The remainder were 32 turkey processors and 14 processors of ducks, geese, and guineas.

Most broilers (99 percent) in the 1990s were produced under contractual arrangements in which the broiler company provided a grower with day-old chicks, and the grower then raised the birds in the carefully controlled environment of the grow-out house. Protected from disease and predators in an enclosed system, the birds would be fed mostly a diet of vitamin- and mineral-fortified corn and soybean meal during the six-and-a-half week period it took to bring them to market weight of about four pounds. Prior to being sent to the processing plant, the birds might be tested for traces of pesticides, toxins, or antibiotics in the ongoing USDA residue monitoring program. In 1935 it took approximately 16 weeks for a 3.5 to 4.5 pound broiler to be fully produced. In the 1990s, with advanced technology, that time has been reduced to 6-7 weeks.

The five primary product categories handled within the poultry processing industry were: chicken, turkeys, ducks, geese, and egg products. Available chicken types included young broilers/fryers weighing an average of 3 pounds; specially grown, 6- to 8-pound young roasters; capons, surgically desexed male birds weighing more than 9 pounds; heavy hens (often called stewing hens), over a year old and weighing 4 to 6 pounds; and Rock Cornish or Cornish game hens, young chickens weighing about 1 to 2 pounds. About 18 percent of ready-to-cook chickens were sold as whole birds; the rest were sold as broiler parts or as boneless chicken breasts or thighs.

Annual per capita consumption of turkey stabilized in 1994 to about 18.1 pounds. Total annual turkey production for 1995 was 2.77 billion turkeys. The methods used in breeding, raising, slaughtering, and processing turkeys were almost identical with those used for chicken. Turkey hens reached maturity at about 16 weeks, with a market weight of 16 to 18 pounds. Toms took 19 weeks to reach market weight of 28 to 30 pounds. Most turkeys were sold whole, either fresh or frozen. The USDA ranks North Carolina as the number one state for turkey production in 1995.

The White Pekin was the most popular duck breed for mass production in the 1990s. Annual production was about 21 million ducks, which were generally packaged and sold whole and frozen. Duck feathers and down used by bedding manufacturers were valuable by-products. The total population of geese in the United States rarely exceeded 5 million; most were raised in Minnesota and Iowa.

Value-added egg products—including liquid, frozen, and dried—fell into two categories, commodities and branded products (such as Egg Beaters, Healthy Choice, and Simply Eggs). From 1980 to 1992, sales of value-added egg products rose from 24.1 to 41.4 million cases. Food manufacturers accounted for 24.6 million cases; 11.4 went for institutional use; 2.4 were sold at the retail level; and 3.0 million cases were exported.

BACKGROUND AND DEVELOPMENT

History. Poultry processing was one of the nation's first agribusinesses, characterized by many small farms. In the early days, raising meat and poultry was secondary to egg production. One of the first stages in the mechanization of poultry processing was the accelerated development in the 1920s of incubators that could hold thousands of eggs. Farmers could start with 500 chicks and no longer depended on hens to hatch them.

Prior to World War II, home cooks were likely to buy chickens live. After the war, more and more consumers purchased either ''New York dressed'' chickens—with only the blood and feathers removed—or in some areas, ''dressed and drawn'' birds—with head, feet, and intestines removed. The change had far-reaching effects, transferring the preparation of poultry to the processing plant, which consumers trusted to be as clean as their own kitchens.

Starting in the 1940s, the poultry industry went through three major changes: an increasing rate of vertical integration, which was largely completed by the mid-1950s; the phasing out of small operations and the concentration of production among a few large firms; and the movement of processing operations to the southeastern states to be closer to the broiler supply.

Regulations. Since mandatory federal inspection began in 1957, all commercially produced chickens were inspected by USDA for wholesomeness before going to market. Traditionally, inspection took place in the processing plant, conducted by a USDA inspector who relied on sight, touch, and smell to determine the wholesomeness of each bird as it passed by on a swiftly moving conveyer line. In 1978, USDA introduced a faster, modified system in which three inspectors divided the task. One inspected the bird's exterior, another its viscera, and a third made a final inspection of the bird. A more scientific system, Hazard Analysis and Critical Control Points (HACCP), was proposed in the early 1990s. Under this program, inspectors would identify hazards, determine the points at which they could be controlled, and recommend corrective action. In December 1996 the USDA's Food Safety & Inspection Service (FSIS) completed their ruling on the validity of labeling poultry as ''fresh.'' Starting in December 1997, poultry may only carry the fresh label if the chicken has not been chilled below 26 degrees Fahrenheit. These rulings are part of the truth in labeling issues that have changed food labeling throughout all industries.

In terms of processing, USDA regulations required that washed and eviscerated chickens be submerged in a water-filled chill tank that quickly reduced the birds' body temperatures to 40 degrees or less to prevent multiplication of salmonella and other microorganisms commonly found on chicken skin. The regulations further required that the water in continuous chill systems be replaced at a rate of one-half gallon per chicken as birds were added to the system.

Food safety continued to be an issue for poultry processors in the 1990s. Following an outbreak of foodborne illnesses, USDA proposed a new labeling policy under which safe-handling instructions would explain the need to refrigerate poultry until it was cooked, cook it thoroughly, refrigerate or discard leftovers immediately, and keep work areas clean. In issuing the new labeling recommendations, USDA cited surveys of 1985 and 1990 that revealed consumer ignorance of such basic food safety procedures. The government also cited data from the Centers for Disease Control (CDC) in Atlanta, Georgia, which showed that one-third of at-home food poisoning incidents were caused by undercooking, and another 12 percent resulted from holding precooked food at unsafe temperatures. Safe-handling instructions were publicized by the leading industry associations, the National Broiler Council and the National Turkey Federation.

In 1992, USDA ruled that fresh or frozen uncooked whole carcasses or parts could be treated by irradiation. In 1993 irradiated, packaged poultry became commercially available, albeit in only four independently owned retail stores. Irradiation eliminated up to 99.9 percent of salmonella and 100 percent of campylobacter organisms, and probably any listeria bacteria as well. Given public concern over foodborne illnesses, the technology showed promise, but whether it would gain widespread consumer acceptance remained to be seen. The treatment was still controversial and even banned in some regions.

CURRENT CONDITIONS

A 1993 survey of the country's largest broiler companies, whose output of ready-to-cook product totaled 99 percent of U.S. production, showed a 6 percent production increase, slightly higher than in 1992 (5.3 percent) and 1991 (5.8 percent). Average weekly production for all companies was 475.81 million pounds.

In 1995, America's annual per capita consumption (PCC) of chicken increased to 47.4 pounds and turkey consumption was 14.2 pounds per person. In the same period, red meat PCC, which included beef, pork, veal, and lamb, dropped 14 percent to 122 pounds. Starting in 1992, chicken consumption for the first time surpassed that of beef, America's former top meat choice.

Forecasting the continuation of 4 percent annual growth in the industry, the nation's largest poultry processor, Tyson Foods, announced plans for a major expansion of its poultry production and processing capability with the addition of four new operating complexes. Each would include a feedmill, hatchery, and processing plant. Chairman Don Tyson also cited passage of the North American Free Trade Agreement and likely approval of the General Agreement on Tariffs and Trade as increasing demand for poultry.

Donald E. Wray, chief operating officer of Tyson Foods, Inc., predicted in *Consumer News* that demand for unadulterated (no filler) chicken products of high quality would increase, and that further-processed chicken would be even more important as sales of whole birds and cut-up parts continued to decline. Protein, including chicken, Wray claimed, "will be used more as an ingredient in foods, rather than as a center-of-the-plate feature." Product innovation would be the key to continued growth, especially the development of ethnic and regional foods offering new flavor combinations. By 2001, one-third of the U.S. population would be immigrants, and two-thirds would be in the 45-65 age bracket. These changing demographics would impact on the consumer-driven poultry industry.

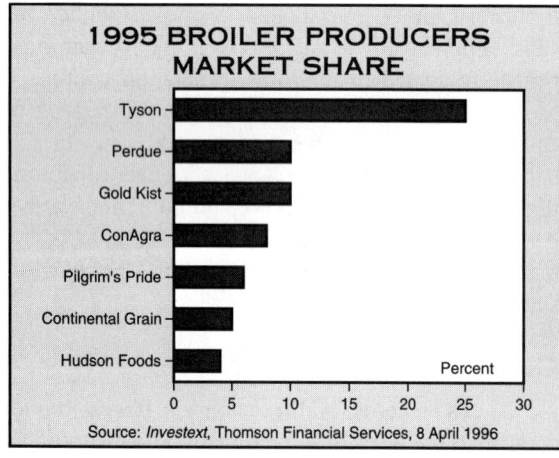

1995 BROILER PRODUCERS MARKET SHARE

Source: *Investext*, Thomson Financial Services, 8 April 1996

INDUSTRY LEADERS

The nation's leading producer, processor, and marketer of poultry and poultry products throughout the 1990s has been Arkansas-based Tyson Foods, Inc. Sales in fiscal 1996 reached $6.45 billion, up from $4.2 billion in fiscal 1992. Predictions estimate that by the year 2005, annual sales for Tyson will reach $10 billion. Weekly production of ready-to-eat broiler meat reached 84.15 million pounds in 1993, making Tyson not only America's largest poultry producer, but also the third-largest in the world, after Brazil and China. Only 8 percent of Tyson's consumer poultry product sales were basic poultry; value-added products accounted for 73 percent. Tyson owns 50 percent of the Rock Cornish Hen market alone. The company's 1989 purchase of Holly Farms resulted in an increase of 31.9 million ready-to-cook poultry pounds per week. Tyson produced 1.59 billion chickens in 1995, which is the equivalent of 35 million chickens per week. By 1995 Tyson employed 64,000 employees.

In 1995, Tyson operated 76 processing and further-processing plants and one fowl slaughter plant. The company derived only 19 percent of sales from its non-poultry operations, which included beef, pork, prepared foods, live swine operations, and other activities. The purchase in 1992 of the North Atlantic's largest catching and at-sea processing fleet, Arctic Alaska Fisheries Corporation, moved Tyson into yet another protein sector. Europe and Japan were the company's biggest foreign markets in the early 1990s, but John Tyson foresaw further growth potential in Southeast Asia. Tyson exports to over 43 countries and is the United States' number one poultry exporter.

Started in 1933 as a cotton cooperative, Georgia-based Gold Kist Inc. was the second-ranked poultry processor with 14 million broilers processed per week in 1995. Sales in 1995 reached $2 billion. The cooperative operated 11 processing plants in Georgia, Alabama, Florida, and the Carolinas. Gold Kist employed over 17,500 employees in 1995. Yet another leading broiler company in the United States was Perdue Farms Incorporated, with average weekly ready-to-cook production of 28 million pounds.

Another Arkansas-based company, ConAgra, ranked third in broiler production in 1993, with weekly production of 40.53 million ready-to-cook pounds, based on slaughtering 11.25 million broilers a week weighing an average of 4.75 pounds. From 1988 to 1993, broiler production at ConAgra grew by 29 percent. The company's principal broiler operation was the ConAgra Broiler Company, with 14 processing plants and fiscal 1993 sales of more than $1.5 billion. Products included Country Pride Roasted Chicken and a line of 20 premium boneless and bone-in Butterball products. The ConAgra Frozen Foods Co. added 5.7 million pounds per week in six processing plants.

Hudson Foods, Inc., was the nations seventh largest poultry processor. Founded in 1972, the company has grown into a $1.38 billion a year business. With the purchase of Armour Foods in 1982, Hudson has been growing at a steady pace. The company owned seven chicken processing plants, seven feed mills, nine broiler hatcheries and five protein facilities in 1995.

The largest turkey producers in 1993 were Butterball Turkey Corp., with four plants producing 700 million pounds of product; Jennie-O Foods Inc., with five plants producing 494 million pounds; and Rocco Turkeys, Inc., which operated three plants and produced 482 million pounds.

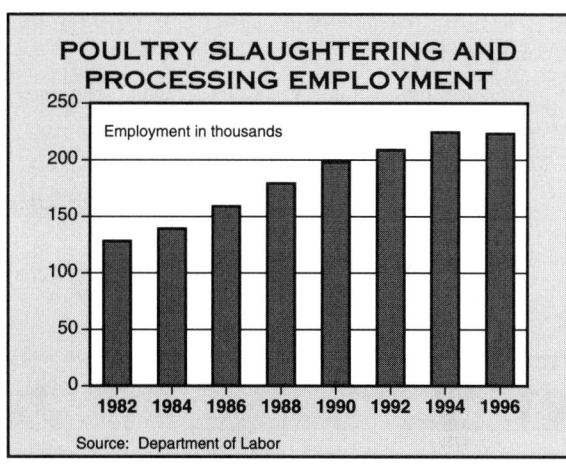

POULTRY SLAUGHTERING AND PROCESSING EMPLOYMENT

Employment in thousands

Source: Department of Labor

WORK FORCE

Between 1963 and 1985, the average annual rate of increase in employee output per hour at poultry processing plants was 2.9 percent, slightly greater than industry as a whole. Productivity gains were higher in the 1970s, when automated eviscerating and cutting machines were widely introduced. In the first half of the 1980s, productivity rose again to meet growing consumer demand for value-added poultry products and the requirements of an expanding number of fast food outlets.

Low wages were characteristic of the poultry industry; despite increases of 17 percent from 1986 to 1990, pay was usually lower than in any other sector of the food industry. While the industry employed a high proportion of low-wage production workers, it also required highly skilled personnel in research and development and to manage and maintain the increasingly efficient and technologically advanced processing operations.

AMERICA AND THE WORLD

In 1990, the United States controlled about 30 percent of the world's poultry production. The country ranked as the world's largest producer and consumer of poultry products, as well as its second-leading exporter. Poultry exports in 1996 increased to $2.5 billion. About 69 percent of U.S. exports went to four markets: Japan (23 percent), Mexico (17 percent), Canada (15 percent), and Hong Kong (14 percent). Chicken parts accounted for most poultry exports, but turkey exports rose 15 percent in 1992. Mexico and South Korea were the major markets for turkey products. U.S. poultry production supplied virtually all domestic consumption. Imports declined an estimated 8 percent in 1992; nearly half came from Canada and New Zealand.

RESEARCH AND TECHNOLOGY

New processing and packaging technologies facilitated the poultry industry's rapid growth in the last half of the twentieth century. Over the years, numerous automated processes took the place of manual labor at various stages of production. For example, mechanized killing machines capable of killing five birds per second—five times more than a skilled worker could accomplish with a sharp knife—were introduced in the 1960s. Defeathering operations were also automated.

Mechanical eviscerating machines came into use in the 1970s. At about the same time, mechanized cutting of the birds into parts was increasingly performed in processing plants rather than by meatcutters in retail outlets. The late 1970s also saw the introduction of automatic deboning machines capable of processing up to 800 pieces of chicken a minute and separating edible meat from bonier parts. The machines also collected meat scraps from partially defleshed carcasses; the scraps were used in the further processing of patties, soups, luncheon meats, and other products.

By the 1990s, as consumers began to expect the ready-to-cook convenience of portioned chicken, ultra-thin, high-pressure waterjet cutting and shaping delivered it. Video cameras sensed the changing pattern from a light projected on a partially prepared carcass. A computer received the information, calculated the best cutting patterns, and sent directions to waterjet nozzles, which then made precise cuts, trimming and portioning the chicken at the same time. Another machine used pistons to force chopped chicken through molds that created three-dimensional formed products. The possibilities included geometric shapes, concave patties, and pieces that looked like boneless breasts.

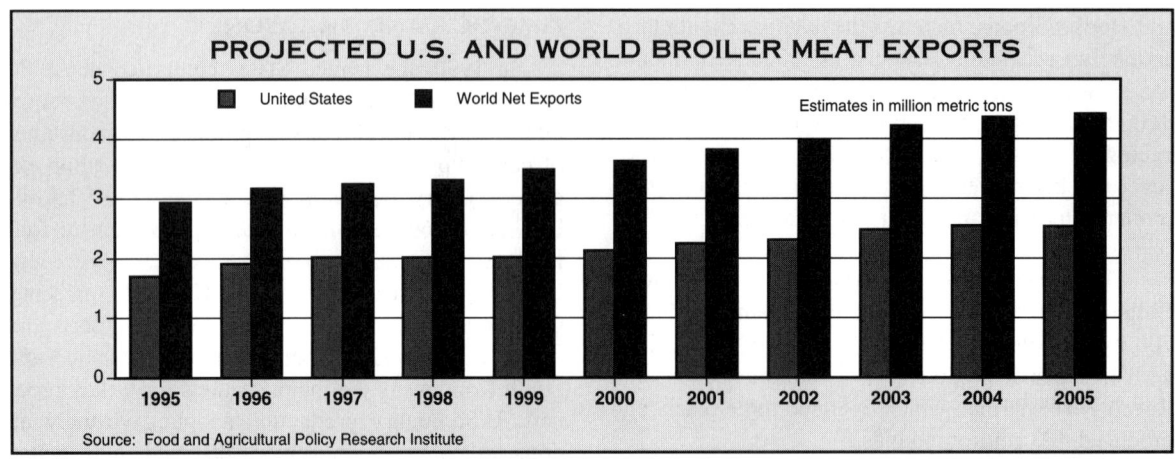

PROJECTED U.S. AND WORLD BROILER MEAT EXPORTS

Source: Food and Agricultural Policy Research Institute

Since sanitation was always a concern, the poultry processing industry continued research into chemical cleansers and new dispensing techniques in the 1990s. For example, some firms experimented with low-cost robots that could transfer a variety of poultry products from conveyer belts to other processing areas.

FURTHER READING

Ahmed, Ziaul Z., and Mark Sieling. ''Two Decades of Productivity Growth in Poultry Dressing and Processing.'' *Monthly Labor Review,* April 1987.

Berne, Steve. ''Poultry Takes the Lead.'' *Prepared Foods,* January 1994.

Broiler Industry Reference Guide. Washington: National Broiler Council, 1990.

Brown Robert H. ''Tyson to Expand Poultry Output, Processing.'' *Feedstuffs,* 10 January 1994.

Frazier, Frank. ''Poultry Inspection History Shows New Tactics Tried Before.'' *Feedstuffs,* 14 February 1994.

Industry and Trade Summary: Poultry. Washington: U.S. International Trade Commission, June 1992.

Looper, Ken. ''The Potential for Value-Added Egg Products.'' *Poultry Yearbook,* 1993.

Raising Turkeys. Reston, Virginia: National Turkey Federation, 1993.

Turkey Statistics 1993. Reston, Virginia: National Turkey Federation, 1993.

Pszczola, Donald. ''Irradiated Poultry Makes U.S. Debut in Midwest and Florida Markets.'' *Food Technology,* November 1993.

''Salmonella Treatment Minimizes Liabilities.'' *Prepared Foods,* February 1993.

Thornton, Gary. ''Nation's Broiler Industry.'' *Broiler Industry,* December 1993.

———. ''Profiles of the Nation's Top 10 Broiler Companies.'' *Broiler Industry,* December 1993.

U.S. Industrial Outlook. Washington: U.S. Department of Commerce, 1993.

Wray, Donald E., ''Poultry Market Trends.'' *Consumer News,* Winter 1994.

USDA Online. 1997. Available at http://www.usda.gov.

Tyson Foods Factbook. 1997. Available at http://www.tyson.com.

—Wendy Stein, updated by Jennifer L. Stong

SIC 2021

CREAMERY BUTTER

This industry consists of establishments primarily engaged in manufacturing creamery butter.

Despite modern sanitary production methods, entering the twenty-first century butter is not much different from that enjoyed centuries ago by people who churned milk in animal skins slung from the backs of camels and horses. Butter manufacturing and marketing, a sector of the dairy industry, is extremely regionalized and competitive. The industry's quality standards and farm pricing are highly regulated by the U.S. government.

Commercial production of butter is a relatively recent development. In 1870 nearly all of the 514 million pounds of U.S. butter was produced on farms. The spreading effects of the Industrial Era and the invention of machinery changed all that. In 1864, a Bavarian brewmaster applied the process of centrifugation to butter making. A cream batching machine was introduced in 1877, followed two years later by the continuous cream separator.

Other innovations helped to advance the industry. The Babcock test, perfected in 1890, accurately measured the percentage of fat in milk and cream. Pasteurization insured a high quality of milk and cream. The use of pure cultures of lactic acid bacteria and the invention of refrigeration also aided the preservation of quality.

The first U.S. butter manufacturing creamery was built in Manchester, Iowa, in 1871. By 1991, commercial production exceeded 1.3 billion pounds. Wisconsin and California were the leading butter producers in 1991, accounting for 654 million pounds. Approximately one-quarter of milk produced on dairy farms is used to make butter.

Under federal regulations, butter sold in the United States is made exclusively from milk or cream, or both, and must contain at least 80 percent milkfat by weight. Coloring or salt may be added. Butter is labeled by the U.S. Department of Agriculture (USDA) as Grade AA, A, or B, according to flavor intensity, texture, color, and salt taste.

In the 1990s butter producers sold their butter products through supermarkets, club stores, and other retail outlets. In addition to individual consumers, butter producers served the foodservice industry (restaurants, fastfood operations), institutions (hospitals, schools), and industrial customers. At the retail level, Grade A butter was typically packaged in quarter pound sticks packed four to a cardboard carton, and whipped butter, developed for easier spreadability, was packaged in tubs. Industrial and foodservice packaging ranged from 68 pound blocks to individually wrapped, single-serve pats. Butteroil, the anhydrous form of butter developed to use up surpluses during a period of lowered public consumption, has been used by the confectionery and baking industries and as a cooking oil.

During the 1980s butter consumption slowed as health and calorie-conscious consumers switched to margarine and other spreads. From 1981 to 1991, annual per capita butter consumption increased only slightly from 3.7 to 3.9 pounds. In 1995 supermarket sales of butter were $689 million, down from the 1991 figure of $917.5 million. Total U.S. butter sales in 1995 were $1.3 billion, virtually unchanged from 1991.

To offset the decrease in butter consumption, the industry researched alternate ways to market its product. One was the use of butteroil as a substitute for other oils in cooking and baking. Butteroil is produced by heating butter until its emulsion breaks down. The milk serum is then removed through centrifugation. According to the *Prepared Foods* 1996 New Product

Survey, butter producers will also be introducing flavored butters.

The largest butter producers in the United States were also among the largest of the midwest dairy cooperatives, Land O'Lakes and MidAmerica Dairymen, Inc. These co-ops, which had originated to represent farmers in obtaining the best milk prices, grew to become manufacturers and marketers of butter and other dairy products. The Land O'Lakes cooperative, established in 1921, led the retail butter industry in the 1990s with a 35 percent market share. MidAmerica Dairymen, Inc. sold its butter products to retailers under its Mid-Am name and to private label customers. Kraft sold butter made by MidAm under its Breakstone brand. Associated Milk Producers, Inc. and Darigold, Inc. were other major cooperatives with strong butter manufacturing operations. By the late 1990s, however, the West Coast was replacing the Midwest as the leading producer of dairy products. Many distributors blamed Midwest farmers' reluctance to modernize.

At the close of the century, the use of recombinant bovine growth hormone (RBGH) to stimulate cows' milk production was the dominant issue in the dairy industry. Manufactured by Monsanto and approved for use by the U.S. Food and Drug Administration in 1995, RBGH was criticized for its tendency to create udder infections in cows. Antibiotics administered to the cows passed into their milk and subsequently into consumers. Critics charged that humans were in danger of developing a resistance to antibiotics, which could prove fatal when needed for disease control. There was also concern that RBGH could cause cancer. Land O' Lakes, a vocal supporter of RBGH, was often targeted by protestors. In early 1997, a Vermont campaign to require labeling of all dairy products containing RBGH milk was struck down by the courts.

FURTHER READING

"BGH Label Law Struck Down." *Vegetarian Times,* January 1997.

Butter. Springfield, MO: MidAmerica Dairymen, Inc.

Butter Facts. California Manufacturing Milk Advisory Board, 1991.

"Consumer Expenditures Study." *Supermarket News,* September 1996.

"Europe Bans RBGH," *Health News & Review,* Spring 1995.

Garrison, Bob. "Dynamic Duo." *Refrigerated & Frozen Foods,* May 1993.

"How Now Drugged Cow." *Harper's,* October 1994.

"Land O' Low Returns." *Forbes,* 15 August 1994.

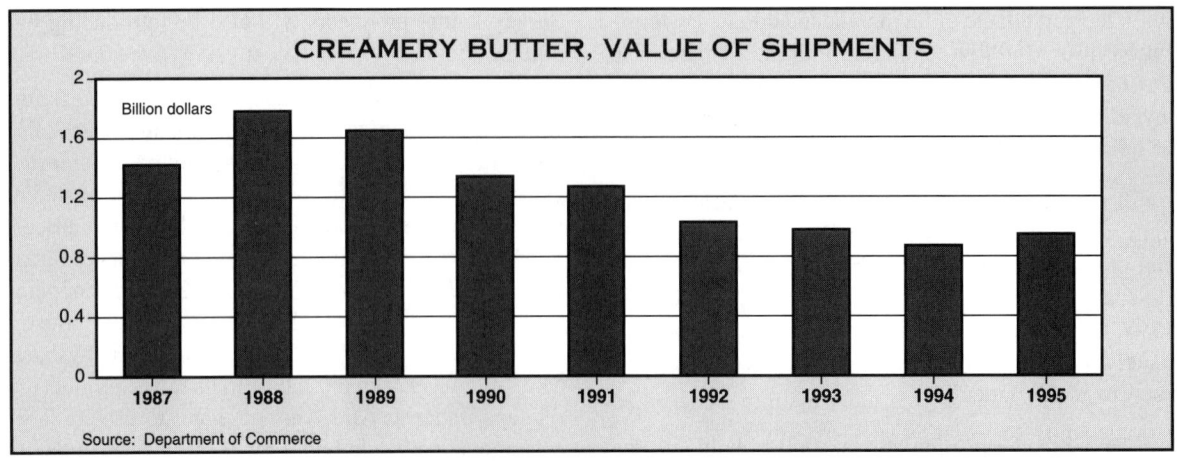

CREAMERY BUTTER, VALUE OF SHIPMENTS

Source: Department of Commerce

"Market Stats and Data." *Dairy Field.* December 1992.

Milk Facts. Washington: Milk Industry Foundation, 1992.

"Rediscover the Values of Butter." Wisconsin Milk Marketing Board, 1993.

Reeves, James L. *The First 20 Years: The Story of MidAmerica Dairymen.* Republic, MO: Western Printing Company, 1989.

"Robocow." *Village Voice,* 14 March 1995.

"U.S. Food Consumption." *Food Review,* May 1996.

—Mary Ratcliff, updated by Mary McNulty

SIC 2022

NATURAL, PROCESSED AND IMITATION CHEESE

This industry encompasses establishments primarily engaged in manufacturing natural cheese (except cottage cheese), cheese foods, cheese spreads, and cheese analogues (imitations and substitutes). These establishments also produce byproducts, such as raw liquid whey.

INDUSTRY SNAPSHOT

Cheese is one of the principal product groups in the dairy industry and has become increasingly important to the growth of the entire dairy industry in the United States. Wisconsin has been the leading cheese producer of the 21 major cheese-producing states in the nation. California was the number-two cheese producer in 1996, following an aggressive promotional campaign. Annual per capita consumption of cheese increased yearly during the 1990s, with projections at more than 35 pounds per person by 2005. The total value of industry shipments increased from $11 billion in the mid-1980s to approximately $18 billion by the mid-1990s.

The United States has developed very few cheeses of its own. Processors have instead replicated European cheeses and used their European names, except for Roquefort, which is a protected name. Some of the cheeses created in this country are monterey jack, brick, colby, and herkimer; all of these cheeses are firm, ripened cheddar-type cheeses.

ORGANIZATION AND STRUCTURE

Kraft, the leading cheese producer, is part of a diversified conglomerate. In 1988, Kraft was purchased by the tobacco producer, Philip Morris Companies Inc., for $12.9 billion. Philip Morris combined Kraft with an 1985 acquisition to form Kraft General Foods, the largest coffee and cheese producer in the United States. Its strongest competition in the cheese area of its operations came from large dairy companies and dairy cooperatives like Beatrice, Sargento, Inc., and Tillamook.

As Americans' cheese palate became more adventurous in the early 1990s, there were growing numbers of small, regional cheese makers sending their specialty products to market. U.S. cheese producers obtain the raw milk from which their products are made from thousands of commercial dairy farms. The number of farms has been dwindling steadily for decades, but they have grown larger in size, and milk production efficiency has been vastly improved. Many of the farmers are members of one of the several hundred regional dairy co-ops. These co-ops, formed to represent milk producers in price setting, are beginning to take over other dairy operations, including the manufacture and marketing of a broad range of cheese products and ingredients. Large food processors either own their own farms or purchase raw milk from the co-ops and independent farmers. Approximately one-third of the 157,483 million pounds of raw milk produced by the country's 9.4 million dairy cows in 1996 was used to make cheese.

The dairy industry has been heavily regulated by the government. Cheese manufactured in the United States must meet Standards of Identity, which define such product characteristics as content levels of milkfat and manufacturing methods. Either Class I milk or milk of manufacturing grade may be used to make cheese. Class I fluid milk meets stricter standards, which include regular inspections of the herd, herd housing facilities, and dairy equipment and milk storage units to ensure that they satisfy health and sanitation requirements. It is used for human consumption as a beverage or in manufactured products such as cheese. Milk of manufacturing grade meets less stringent standards and may only be used for manufactured products.

The government has regulated milk pricing through the Federal Milk Marketing Orders authorized by the Agricultural Marketing Act of 1937, or the Agricultural Act of 1949, which established the ongoing dairy price support program. The complex pricing system affected all segments of the dairy industry.

BACKGROUND AND DEVELOPMENT

Although there is no record of when cheese was first used as a food, its origins have been estimated to date back to 6000-7000 B.C. Its lasting quality made it a source of nourishment both at home and on journeys, and armies often carried cheese among their provisions. The first U.S. cheese plant was built in 1851 in Rome, New York, and the area remained the center of American cheesemaking for the next 50 years. The U.S. cheesemaking industry began shifting westward toward Wisconsin in the early 1900s.

There are hundreds of varieties of cheese worldwide and numerous ways of classifying them, usually according to the coagulating agent (rennet, acid, etc.) or texture (very hard, hard, semisoft, soft, or acid). Natural cheeses are made directly from milk (or sometimes whey) by pressing the curd that forms when milk has been coagulated (or curdled), then heated and stirred, and finally by draining off the whey (the remaining liquid part of the milk). Processed cheeses are made from a combination of one or more batches of natural cheeses, heated to pasteurization temperatures. They were developed in the 1920s to extend shelf life, ensure product uniformity, and make slicing easier, while simulating natural cheese. The first U.S. patent for processed cheese was issued to J.L. Kraft in 1916; it described a method of emulsifying the heated cheese mixture using alkaline salts.

Cheese analogues are made without butterfat and are designed to resemble natural or processed cheese in appearance, taste, texture, and nutrition. The cost savings of using less expensive fats, such as vegetable oils instead of butterfat, provided the incentive to produce cheese analogues. Early examples were produced in the early 1900s by skimming butterfat from whole milk, replacing it with another fat, and then following regular cheesemaking procedures. Technology using dried milk protein, hydrogenated vegetable oil, emulsifiers, and other ingredients was developed in the early 1970s to simulate processed american and mozzarella cheeses.

Some of the principal cheese products are: cheddar, swiss (hard); parmesan, romano (very hard); mozzarella, brick, havarti, blue (semisoft); brie, bel paese, camembert (soft); powders and blends; and reduced-fat.

The economic health of the cheese industry was varied at the start of the 1990s. Both sales and production of cheese hit record highs in the early 1990s as

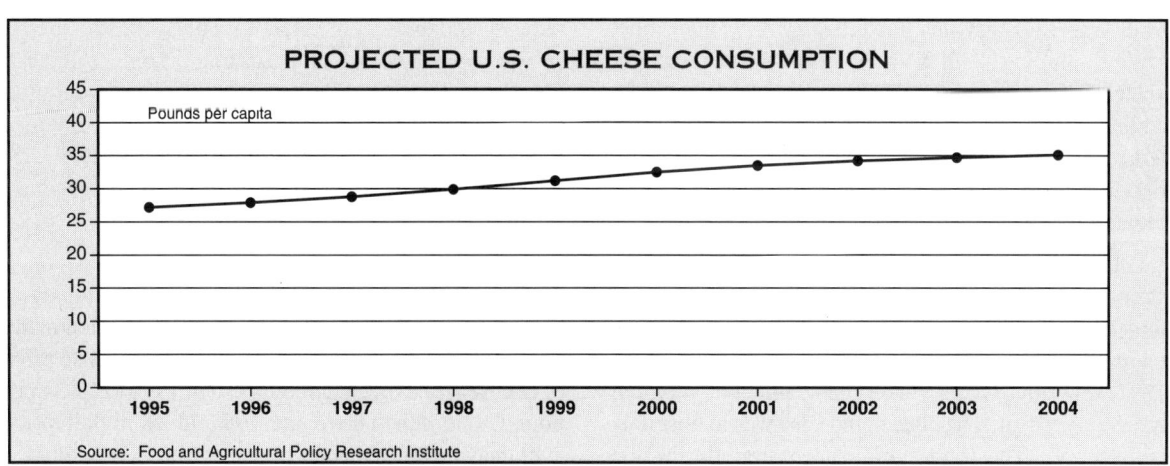

PROJECTED U.S. CHEESE CONSUMPTION

Pounds per capita

Source: Food and Agricultural Policy Research Institute

indicated by the following statistics: $18 billion in sales; 6.1 billion pounds of natural cheese; and 2.2 billion pounds of processed cheese. Overall industry growth, however, was flat, and in 1992, supermarket sales of $5.36 billion had dipped 3.06 percent from 1991. Sales were fairly evenly divided among three major markets: retail, foodservice (restaurants, fast-food outlets, institutions), and industrial (ingredients used by other food processors).

The biggest supermarket sellers were unshredded american and other natural cheeses. The biggest gains, however, were registered in natural (11.28 percent) and processed (72.6 percent) shredded cheeses. Sales of Italian cheeses in particular were projected to continue their upward curve in all areas. Although per capita consumption of cheese had hovered at a fairly steady amount of 11-12 pounds since the mid-1980s, annual Italian cheese consumption had surged by 50 percent, from 6.5 to 9.4 pounds per person in that period. Most of this increase was in mozzarella, with consumption exceeding 7 pounds per capita in 1991.

Pre-sliced, packaged process cheeses represented a healthy chunk of cheese sales, and processors followed up with packaged shredded cheese in such flavored varieties as ''taco'' and ''pizza.'' Retailers also found that pre-sliced cheeses were popular among consumers at the deli counter as well. Vacuum-packed, pre-sliced cheese allowed deli counter staff to deal with other tasks instead of slicing cheese to order and reduced the time that customers spent waiting in line.

Industrial sales of cheese ingredients continued to grow. They accounted for about 28 percent of the industry's $18 billion sales figure for the early 1990s. Here, too, much of the growth was in Italian-style cheeses, but processed cheeses, powders, and other natural cheeses were also big sellers. Industrial uses of cheese expanded as the country's changing demographics resulted in increased popularity of prepared and frozen foods. According to Jim Lauderdale of Mid-America Dairymen Inc. in *Dairy Field* magazine, ''We're finding with both parents working, people want bigger variety . . . Cheese plays a large part in adding variety and making a nutritious meal.'' Mid-Am offered mozzarella, provolone, parmesan, romano, ricotta, and such american-style cheeses as colby and monterey jack, as well as cottage cheese.

Pizza's continuing popularity contributed to the strength of the foodservice market, which is the third largest market for cheese makers. Italian cheese sales increased approximately 10 percent from 1987 to 1991, a period during which the segment as a whole grew 6.6 percent. The biggest increase was in hospitals and schools. The most significant change during the period was the waning popularity of cheddar compared to processed cheese.

Portions of the cheese industry were suffering in the early 1990s. Declining cheese production in Minnesota was costing the state economy nearly $831 million annually and more than 12,000 jobs, according to a University of Minnesota study. Milk product sales of cheese (and ice cream) were down 10 percent from 1985. As production and sales dropped, so did dairy farm purchases from related industries. The milk production declines were triggered in part by sell-outs due to lower milk pricing and a relatively low per-cow production.

In a move that the industry hoped would alleviate erratic pricing, the New York Coffee, Sugar & Cocoa Exchange (CSCE) began trading in futures contracts for cheddar cheese in June, 1993. Each contract was for 40,000 pounds of cheddar in 40-pound blocks, with FOB delivery in the continental United States. In futures contracts, buyers and sellers agree to the price for a commodity on a fixed date. The contracts allowed cheese producers and processors a degree of control over the volatile pricing that had afflicted the industry in the 1980s, when the federal government reduced price supports and cheese became more subject to market forces. The first day of trading slightly exceeded the CSCE's pre-opening day estimate of 100 contracts, but whether the experiment would succeed over the long run was uncertain. Kraft General Foods supported the trading as did some dairy co-ops like Land O'Lakes, which had experienced some very wide swings in earnings for several years. Other producers, like Darigold, Inc., a Seattle co-op, planned to study the trading carefully before plunging into the unfamiliar CSCE market.

Legislation. The Nutritional Labeling Education Act (NLEA) mandated sweeping changes in labeling, emphasizing the relationship between nutrition and chronic disease over the vitamin/mineral content. The redesigned labels were meant to reduce consumer confusion by standardizing serving sizes (reference amounts), establishing rules for health claims, defining comparative nutritional claims, and relating them to U.S. Recommended Daily Intakes (RDIs) and U.S. Recommended Daily Allowances (RDAs) for vitamin/mineral percentages.

CURRENT CONDITIONS

The size of the cheese market was $4 billion in the fiscal year ended September 1996. The wholesale price of cheese was expected to increase in 1996 to $1.34 per pound, one cent above the 1994 level. Retail price averaged $3.09 per pound.

Of the 7.9 billion pounds of cheese produced in 1996, 123 million pounds were sent abroad, while domestic use accounted for 7.5 billion pounds. Per capita consumption in the United States was 27.9 pounds.

Lowfat. Of the 7.5 billion pounds of cheese sold in the United States in 1996, some 15.3 percent consisted of low-fat products, but their flavor and texture could not match that of full-fat standard cheeses. A prime research effort of the cheese industry in the 1990s was to develop ways to improve the flavor of low-fat and fat-free products. Some success was achieved by using new adjunct cultures to enhance flavor. The development of new starter cultures created especially for low-fat cheeses also allowed for greater flavor with lower acidity.

By mid-decade, one of every four dollars consumers spent on cheese went toward the purchase of reduced-fat or no-fat cheeses. Improved technology continued to enhance taste and texture of these products. The Wisconsin Center for Dairy Research patented a manufacturing protocol that used a firmer milk coagulum to increase flavor and moisture of reduced- and no-fat products. It was projected that sales of reduced- and no-fat cheese would represent 50 percent of all cheese purchases after 2000.

INDUSTRY LEADERS

Kraft, long the country's top cheese producer, held 26.8 percent of the $1.6 billion natural cheese market and 61.3 percent of the processed cheese market in 1995. The cheese giant suffered from the recession of the early 1990s, and consolidated two cheese plants into one in Illinois and closed another in Michigan.

Kraft's Specialty Products Division planned strong promotional activity for its Italian and specialty cheeses in foodservice, in-store deli, and institutional markets. In the industrial market, Kraft Food Ingredients (KFI) sold a wide range of natural and processed cheeses and cheese substitutes to other food processors for use as food ingredients. The company that built its reputation on the pasteurized processed cheese it patented in 1916 continued to add to its consumer product line. "Marketers like Kraft are facing more competition than they ever have before," according to Robert Eckert, of Kraft USA's Retail Division, in *Dairy Field* magazine. In the fall of 1992, the company launched Kraft Healthy Favorites, a 23-item line of 50 percent reduced-fat cheese products.

Some of Kraft's competition was coming from Sargento Cheese Company Inc., which knocked the giant from its number-one-in-the-market perch in the shredded cheese area. With its $320 million in sales versus Kraft's $2 billion, Wisconsin-based Sargento Cheese Co. wouldn't displace Kraft, but its 20 percent increase over 1991 sales made it a company to watch. Kraft sales had also dropped in the $1.5 billion processed cheese slices section of the dairy case as consumers opted for regional brand names or lower-priced private label brands. ConAgra's Beatrice Cheese unit also planned to do battle with Kraft's longstanding dominance with a line of 30 new fat-free cheeses under its Healthy Choice label. Kraft fought back and by 1995, had regained the number one spot in the $1.1 billion shredded cheese market by a slim margin— 25.1 percent to Sargento's 22.6 percent.

Co-ops that processed the raw milk from their dairy farm membership were strong contenders in the competitive cheese industry. Mid-America Dairymen, Inc. (Mid-Am), the country's second-largest dairy co-op in the early 1990s, produced cheese from the milk of its member farms. Mid-Am used both milk of manufacturing grade and Class I (Grade A) milk that was not bottled for beverage use. It was one of the largest manufacturers of natural cheese in the country and also produced a range of specialty cheeses. Its output of mozzarella alone, largely destined for its fresh pizza customers, came to 180 million pounds a year. Under its Mid-America Farms label, it sold its cheese products to consumers, institutional and foodservice markets, and to food manufacturers for use as food ingredients.

WORK FORCE

The 1992 U.S. Census of Manufactures reported that 34,500 people were employed in the cheese industry. Of these employees, approximately 26,900 were production workers, earning an average hourly wage of $10.64. By 1996, total industry employment had increased to an estimated 36,600, 29,600 of which were production workers.

AMERICA AND THE WORLD

U.S. cheese exports reached 77 million pounds in 1996. Japan was the leading importer of the world's cheese, receiving 156,000 metric tons of cheese in 1996. The U.S. imported 115,000 metric tons of cheese in 1996.

RESEARCH AND TECHNOLOGY

New technologies in the industry focused on product safety, automation, and quality controls. An increasing number of large cheddar cheese plants operate non-stop, seven days a week, using sophisticated

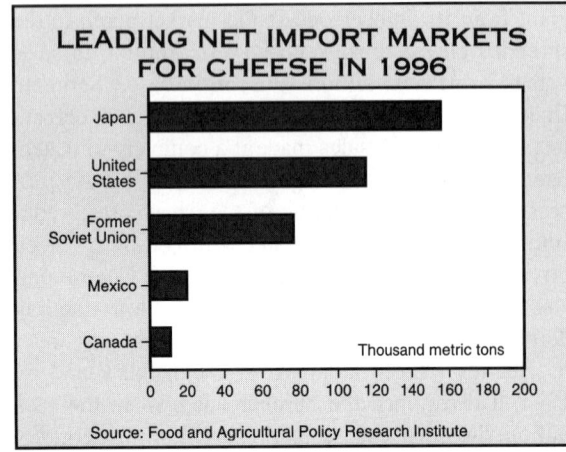

LEADING NET IMPORT MARKETS FOR CHEESE IN 1996

Source: Food and Agricultural Policy Research Institute

computer control systems that are able to pump 50,000 pounds of milk per hour. Many of these systems allow a single operator to oversee the following processes: pasteurizing the milk, adding the starter culture, making the cheese, draining the whey, cheddaring, and milling and salting. In 1991, there were less than one-tenth the number of U.S. cheese plants than there had been in 1940, but they were producing four times as much cheese.

FURTHER READING

Campbell, Alta, Gary Hoover, and Patrick J. Spain, eds. *Hoover's Handbook of American Business 1993*. Austin, TX: The Reference Press, Inc., 1996.

"Cheese." *Institutional Distribution,* 15 May 1991.

"Cheese Sales Climb as Processors Diversify." *Dairy Field,* December 1992.

Considine, Douglas M., P.E., ed. *Foods and Food Production Encyclopedia*. New York: Van Nostrand Reinhold Company, 1982.

Dexheimer, Ellen et al. "Navigators of the '90s." *Dairy Foods,* April 1993.

Doeff, Gail Rosenbaum. "Ready, Set, Hedge!" *Dairy Foods,* July 1993.

Dryer, Jerry. "Convenience: More Than Just a Fact of Life." *Dairy Field,* July 1992.

Fabricant, Florence. "Looking for Flavor? Say 'Cheese'." *The New York Times*, 28 July 1993.

Food and Agricultural Policy Research Institute 1996 Outlook. Available from http://ssu.agri.missouri.edu/ssu/fapristaffp/fap196/text/.

Friend, Janin. "Reduced-Fat Cheese Sales Expected to Gain." *Supermarket News*, 46:42, 14 October, 1996, 47.

Garrison, Bob. "Dynamic Duo." *Refrigerated and Frozen Foods,* May 1993.

Getler, Warren, and Scott Kilman. "Cheddar Lovers May Take a Slice of These Futures." *Wall Street Journal*, 14 January 1993.

Godfrey, Patricia, R.D., and Dan Best. "NLEA in a Nutshell." *Prepared Foods*, December 1992.

Honer, Clem. "Technology Update." *Dairy Field,* February 1993.

———. "Serious About Mozzarella." *Dairy Field,* August 1992.

"Infoscan Report, Full Year 1992 Figures." *Food & Beverage Marketing*, March 1993.

Kimbrell, Wendy. "Cheese Rap." *Dairy Field,* November 1992.

LaBell, Fran. "Cultures Improve Low-fat Cheese." *Food Processing*, September 1992.

———, et al. "Current Dairy Research Highlights Lowfat Cheese." *Food Processing,* September 1992.

Lazich, Robert S. *Market Share Reporter 1997*. Detroit: Gale Research, 1997.

Lenius, Pat Natschke. "Presliced Adds Up." *Supermarket News,* 7 June 1993.

Levitt, Alan. "Versatility Is Its Virtue." *Dairy Foods,* August 1993.

Liesse, Julie. "Brand Scorecard: Foes Poke Holes in Kraft Cheese Stranglehold." *Advertising Age,* 7 December 1992.

———. "ConAgra, Kraft Start Cheese War." *Advertising Age,* 6 July 1992.

Milk Facts. Washington: Milk Industry Foundation, 1992.

"Milk Production Declines Expensive for Minnesota." *Feedstuffs,* 14 June 1993.

"More Than Just a Milk Check . . . " Mid-America Dairymen, Inc., 1991.

Ruland, Susan. "Bright Spot." *Dairy Field,* February 1993.

———. "Ready for Change." *Dairy Field,* August 1992.

U.S. Census of Manufactures. U.S. Bureau of the Census. 1992. Available from http://www.census.gov/epcd/www/mc92ht20.html/.

Williams, Mina. "Cheese Campaign Expands in Second Year," *Supermarket News*, 46:31, 29 July 1996, 23.

—Mary Ratcliffe, updated by Marinell Jochnowitz

SIC 2023

DRY, CONDENSED, AND EVAPORATED DAIRY PRODUCTS

This classification covers establishments primarily engaged in manufacturing dry, condensed, and evaporated dairy products. Included in this industry are establishments primarily engaged in manufacturing mixes for the preparation of frozen ice cream and ice milk and dairy and nondairy base cream substitutes and dietary supplements.

INDUSTRY SNAPSHOT

The dry, condensed, and evaporated dairy products sector of the highly regionalized dairy industry embraces both small family operations and multinational giants, reporting sales in the billions of dollars. The spectrum of products produced by this industry is just as broad, ranging from retail staples like canned, evaporated milks, which have been familiar on market shelves for more than a century, to sophisticated milk protein ingredients which are constantly being refined in research laboratories for new food uses. With products as comforting as mother's milk and as baffling to consumers as the sodium caseinates that appear on the labels of the latest sports drinks, it was a $9.36 billion industry by the 1990s.

ORGANIZATION AND STRUCTURE

From World War II, a dwindling number of dairy farms has supplied the raw milk from which dry, condensed, and evaporated milk products are processed, but the farms have become much larger. Huge dairy farm cooperatives combined with operations that processed the raw milk to produce branded consumer products and milk ingredients marketed to food and animal feed processors. Darigold Inc. was the largest Pacific Northwest cooperative in 1992. With 1,400 dairy farmer members and its own processing plants and distribution centers, it was a top producer of powdered milk, with 1963 sales of $930 million.

The small companies that had pioneered condensed and evaporated milk technology and production in the nineteenth century were still in business more than 100 years later, producing the same products with which they had started out—and many, many others. Borden, Inc., and Pet, Inc., had grown into diversified giants ranked in the top 50 food companies nationwide. Pharmaceutical companies also reached into this dairy food category with their infant formulas. There was always room, though, for smaller companies, often specializing in milk ingredients like whey proteins and ice cream/yogurt/milkshake mixes.

BACKGROUND AND DEVELOPMENT

Removal of all or part of the water from milk not only reduces transportation costs and makes handling easier, but also it allows unrefrigerated storage of sterilized or dried products for prolonged periods.

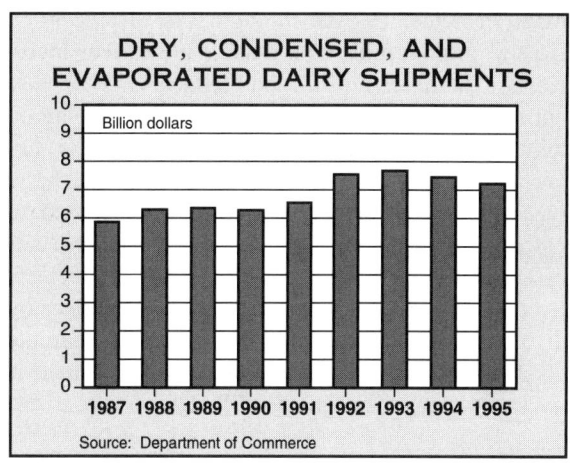

DRY, CONDENSED, AND EVAPORATED DAIRY SHIPMENTS

Billion dollars

Source: Department of Commerce

Such products may be intended for consumer use or as ingredients in diverse processed foods.

The Federal Drug & Cosmetic Act has established Standards of Identity (SID) for milk products which define what can be packaged under a given product name. The Food and Drug Administration (FDA) designates food ingredients to be generally recognized as safe (GRAS) when extensive past use has not shown any harmful effects.

Dry Milk. Marco Polo, it is said, encountered sundried milk in his travels through Mongolia in the thirteenth century. It remained for later scientists to develop commercial production processes. An early patent for a commercial process to manufacture dried milk was granted in 1855. Technological advances since then have enabled a wide variety of manufactured milk products with applications in frozen dairy desserts, ice cream, frozen soft and hard yogurt, bakery goods, confectionery products, dry mixes, soups, animal feeds, and countless other nutritional and functional uses.

Nonfat dry milk (NDM) results when both fat and water are removed from milk. Lactose (milk sugar), milk proteins, and milk minerals are present in the same relative proportions as in fresh milk. Moisture is not more than 5 percent by weight, and fat content is not more than 1.5 percent by weight unless otherwise indicated. In the 1990s, nearly a billion pounds of NDM were being produced every year.

Dry whole milk results from the removal of water from milk. It contains not less than 26 percent milk fat and not more than 4 percent moisture. Dry buttermilk is made by removing the water from buttermilk derived from butter manufacture. It has not less than 4.5 percent milk fat content and not more than 5 percent moisture.

Milk Proteins. Derived through various processing steps from skim milk, milk proteins are used as ingredients in a wide range of food products both for their nutritional value and for their functionality. Casein, milk's principal protein, has been commercially isolated from skim milk since 1900. There are two basic types, depending on the coagulating agent used to precipitate the casein from the milk: lactic (acid) casein and rennet casein. Most acid caseins intended for food applications were converted to caseinates by dissolving the acid casein curd with water and dilute alkali and then drying the solution. Sodium caseinate is generally recognized as safe (GRAS).

Casein has a higher Protein Efficiency Ratio (PER) than vegetable proteins. Under the *Code of Federal Regulations,* "if the protein efficiency ratio of protein is equal to or better than that of casein, the U.S. Recommended Daily Allowance (RDA) is 45 grams." However, if the PER is lower than that of casein (2.5), then 65 grams of protein are required to meet the USRDA. Because of its high protein quality and content, low lactose, and bland flavor, casein is used in nutritional supplements. Nutritional foods commonly formulated with casein include high-protein beverage powders, fortified cereals, infant formulas, and nutrition bars. Products incorporating casein for its functional properties of imparting texture, viscosity, emulsification, and opacity included coffee creamers, soups, sauces, ice cream, whipped toppings, yogurt, and salad dressings.

Whey seemed to have been the "forgotten" milk protein until April 1971, when representatives of 56 firms gathered to consider the potential of these milk solids that remain after cheese manufacture. Warren S. Clark, Jr., executive director of the American Dairy Products Institute, wrote in the *Encyclopedia of Food Science and Technology,* "In no area of the modern dairy industry have changes of a technical nature been as innovative and rapid as in the whey products segment." The Food and Drug Administration affirmed the safety of whey products and their manufacture in 1984 with a declaration of common and usual names for diverse whey products ("Whey," "Reduced Minerals Whey," and "Whey Protein Concentrate") and by granting them GRAS status.

Evaporated Milk. When Gail Borden returned to the United States from England in 1851, it was on a ship that had to carry cows to provide milk for the immigrant children on board. There was no way to carry fresh milk on a long sea voyage without it spoiling. Five years later, in 1856, Borden was granted patents in the United States and England for the preservation

of milk after it had been evaporated in a vacuum. The method used no added sugar, but sweetened condensed milk was to be Borden's first commercial product in 1861.

Thirty years later, the Helvetia Milk Condensing Company began production of the world's first unsweetened evaporated milk in 1885, calling it Highland Evaporated Cream after the plant's home in Highland, Illinois. The company was later to change its name to Pet, Inc.

Evaporated milk is a canned whole milk concentrate with a specified quantity of added vitamin D. Vitamin A may also be added. Related products are evaporated skimmed milk, evaporated low fat milk, evaporated filled milk, and evaporated goat milk.

Dairy and Non-Dairy Creamers. Health-conscious consumers in the 1990s regarded non-dairy creamers as cholesterol free and, therefore, better for you than milk-based products. Nestlé's Carnation, which introduced Coffee-Mate in 1961, added Coffee-Mate Lite in 1989, and again extended this top-selling non-dairy creamer line in 1992 with Hazelnut, Irish Creme, and Amaretto flavored powders. Pet, Inc. also marketed a non-dairy creamer.

Infant Formulas. Infant formulas that approximate human milk are fed to infants all over the world, sometimes as their sole source of nutrients during the first months of life. Such products were unknown until the twentieth century, when they became a reliable alternative to breast-feeding. In the London of the early 1800s, only about 10 percent of infants not breast-fed lived past their first birthdays.

In the United States, the Infant Formula Act of 1980 and its 1986 amendments very specifically govern the manufacture of commercial infant formulas. The Act authorized the FDA to implement quality control regulations and recall procedures, labeling and nutrient requirements, and requirements for exempt infant formulas. Additionally, infant formulas must satisfy Federal Food, Drug and Cosmetic Act regulations dealing with foods for special dietary use, good manufacturing practices, and canned foods (for liquid infant formulas only).

The stringent regulations governing infant formulas have included setting maximum levels for 29 nutrients and minimum levels for 10. Labels were required to include a nutrient declaration; "use by" date information; a statement such as "use as directed by a physician"; a warning statement of the consequences of improper preparation; preparation and use directions that included pictograms if appropriate; and more. All of these requirements had long been standard practices of its member manufacturers, according to the Infant Formula Council.

Infant formulas were a $1.9 billion business in the 1990s, presenting their products as the best substitute for mother's milk. Yet, the industry was mired in federal and state price-fixing investigations. Antitrust inquiries were directed at contracts awarded to the three top producers under the Special Supplemental Food Program for Women, Infants and Children (WIC), designed for low-income families. Although federally funded, WIC was administered by the states, which were paying full retail prices for formula because there was no competitive bidding.

In the early 1990s, Abbott Laboratories, which marketed infant formulas through its Ross Laboratories unit, and Bristol-Myers Squibb, whose infant formulas were sold through its Mead Johnson Nutritional Group, shared 85 percent of the market. American Home Products accounted for about 9 percent of the market, selling through Wyeth-Ayerst Laboratories. The other major producers were Nestlé's Carnation unit and Gerber, which marketed a Bristol-Myers product.

In June 1992, after a two-year investigation into the three biggest producers, the Federal Trade Commission charged them with price-rigging, contending that they had rigged contracts awarded under the federally-funded Special Supplemental Food Program for Women, Infants and Children. This program accounts for approximately one of every three cans of formula sold. The cost to the government was estimated at $25 million. Mead-Johnson and American Home, while admitting no wrongdoing, agreed to settle. Abbott Laboratories initially planned to fight the charges in federal court. The *Wall Street Journal* quoted Duane Burnham, Abbott's chairman and chief executive officer: ''We have competed responsibly, aggressively, and completely within the law.'' In May 1993, however, Abbott Laboratories agreed to pay more than $140 million to settle a number of suits filed against the company nationwide and consolidated in Florida to simplify proceedings. The Federal Trade Commission's actions against Abbott remain in place.

Value of shipments in this industry was expected to increase to $8.1 billion in 1997, over 1996 shipments of an estimated $7.9 billion. Value of imports dropped from $345 million in 1989 to $247 million (forecast) in 1993, but increased to $383 million by 1995. Exports jumped from $519 million in 1994 to $583 million in 1995.

CURRENT CONDITIONS

In the mid-1990s the dairy industry was witnessing the highest raw milk and milkfat prices in history due to low grain yields, high feed costs, and high demand for dairy products. According to *Dairy Foods,* despite a subsequent increase in retail dairy prices, however, most dairy categories posted good growth for 1996 as consumers continued to eagerly patronize dairy products.

The baby foods segment in particular saw significant growth in the mid-1990s. The baby formula market grew 7.8 percent in 1995 compared with 1994 due to an increase in babies and an increase in formula prices. According to *Advertising Age* the leader in market share was Abbott Laboratories' Ross Products Similac with 36.6 percent of the market.

Dry whole milk production during March 1996 totaled 10.6 million pounds, down 39 percent from 1995. Production of nonfat dry milk during March 1996 was 110 million pounds, down 7 percent from March 1995. Canned milk production during March 1996 totaled 35 million pounds, down 27 percent from March 1995.

INDUSTRY LEADERS

The top three companies in the industry, Borden, Inc., Mid-America Dairymen Inc., and Pet, Inc., were all long-established producers of staple products for retail consumers.

Mid-America Dairymen Inc. was headquartered in Springfield, Missouri. With 5,000 employees and $3.68 billion in mid-1990s sales, it was one of the largest companies in this industry. The cooperative served approximately 18,000 farms in 30 states in 1996. According to *Prepared Foods,* Mid-America Dairymen Inc. adhered to strict quality control and hazard analysis and critical control point standards to ensure the quality of its dairy products.

Borden Inc., headquartered in Columbus, Ohio, brought in total sales of $5.77 billion in 1996 and employed approximately 20,000 people. The originator of sweetened condensed milk in the nineteenth century, Borden continued to market the product under its Eagle brand name, while KLIM dried milk, sold in 85 countries, recorded a record sales revenue of $2.04 billion. The KLIM line was extended with KLIM Lite-line low fat milk powder, while KLIM Superkid fortified milk powder was formulated for children from three to seven.

In addition to its dairy product line, Borden produces adhesives, wall coverings, industrial inks and resins, and vinyl films. As of early 1997, there were discussions of Borden selling its dairy division to Mid-America Dairymen Inc.

Pet, Inc., which introduced the first commercially produced evaporated milk in 1885, was the third largest company in the industry with $1.58 billion in mid-1990s sales and 5,739 employees. Its evaporated milk was still on market shelves nationwide, but the company had diversified to market many other food products.

Rich Products Corp. of Buffalo New York, with a sales revenue of $1.02 billion was another major industry player. With 5,100 employees, Rich Products was a billion dollar enterprise with a small business approach. According to *Prepared Foods,* Rich Product's research and development department pervaded every aspect of the frozen foods business, from plant start-up and commercialization to logistics, engineering, and marketing. Consumer trends were effectively gauged in this manner and executed accordingly, making the company successful and a national leader. Rich's market for its assorted baked goods, non-dairy toppings, creamers and icings, extended to all corners of the globe.

Other leaders in this industry, that figured in the top 10 in terms of sales revenues were: Ross Products of Columbus, Ohio, with sales of $1 billion; Dairyman's Cooperative Creamery Association, of Tulare, California, with sales of $560 million; Wisconsin Dairies Cooperative of Barabo, Wisconsin, with sales of $530 million; D.P.D. Div of Minneapolis, Minnesota, with sales of $412 million; International Dairy Queen of Minneapolis, Minnesota, with sales of $372 million; and Agrimark Inc. of Lawrence Massachusetts, with sales of $350 million.

WORK FORCE

Employment increased steadily from 1987 (8,700 employees) through the early 1990s (9,900 in 1992), but began to decline by the mid-1990s. Hourly earnings in 1987 were $11.47 compared to $12.75 (estimated) in 1992, and reached $14.00 by mid-decade.

AMERICA AND THE WORLD

According to a 1993 National Dairy Promotion and Research Board market plan, nonfat dry milk (NDM) production in the United States decreased between 1987 and 1992 by 4.3 percent, from $480 million to $385 million, while consumption increased slightly from 329 to 339 million tons. During that same period, the European Union (EU) and Australasia produced far more NDM than they consumed, with most overproduction available for export. Underproducing countries were Mexico and Japan. U.S. exports of dry whole and nonfat dry milk to Mexico alone increased almost 165 percent in the early 1990s, to $318 million.

Overall, early decade exports of all dairy products jumped 67 percent, marking the first trade surplus since 1972. Dry, evaporated, and condensed milk exports, which accounted for almost 69 percent of dairy exports, more than doubled. The U.S. Government, through the Dairy Export Incentive Program (DEIP), continued to subsidize exports. The dairy industry was expected to continue profiting from the historic North American Free Trade Agreement (NAFTA), which combined Mexico, the United States, and Canada as the world's largest single consumer market, with a population topping 360 million people and an economy close to $6.5 trillion. American processors could look forward to barrier-free trade with the Mexican market, traditionally a major dairy importer.

RESEARCH AND TECHNOLOGY

Evaporation and Drying. Water is removed from milk either by evaporation, in which heat is applied under a vacuum, or by drying. Spray drying has been the more widely used method for preparing dried milk products. In this process, the condensed fluid milk is pumped from the vacuum pan while it is still hot and atomized in the heated air of the spray dryer either by the centrifugal force of being discharged from a rapidly turning disk or by being forced through a narrow nozzle. Drying is almost instantaneous.

Roller drying has rarely been used to dry milk for human use. In this process, condensed milk is fed between a pair of heated rollers and adheres to them in a thin film. The dried milk is scraped off by a sharp blade and hammered into uniform, fine particles. In addition to roller and spray drying, these products could be made by foam or freeze drying. It was also possible to make them more readily soluble; such products were called "instantized."

Ultra-High Temperature Processing. Ultra-high temperature processing, which produced liquid soft-serve ice cream and yogurt mixes with a 90-day shelf life, six to nine times that of standard processing, enabled food service distributors in the 1990s to compete with local and regional dairies with a full line of dairy products. Until then, the dairies had a tight hold on this lucrative segment of the dairy industry, selling to giant fast food outlets like McDonald's as well as mom-and-pop stores.

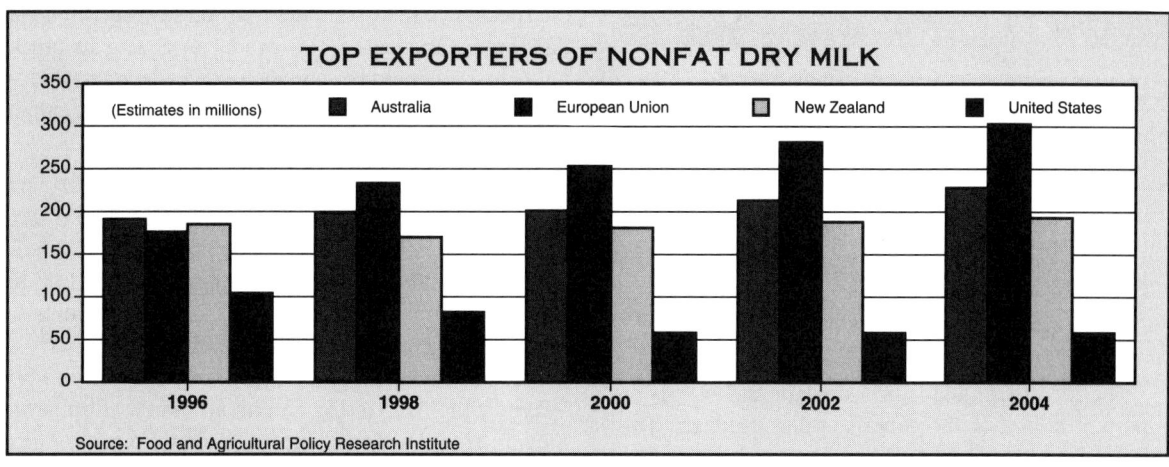

TOP EXPORTERS OF NONFAT DRY MILK

(Estimates in millions)   Australia   European Union   New Zealand   United States

Source: Food and Agricultural Policy Research Institute

FURTHER READING

"All Around the World, Borden Growth, Innovation Continue." *Borden Eagle,* April/May 1992.

Anderson, Sue Ann, Hermin I. Chinn, and Kenneth D. Fisher. "History and Current Status of Infant Formulas." *The American Journal of Clinical Nutrition,* February 1982.

Collins, James H. "The Story of Condensed Milk." Columbus, OH: The Borden Co., 1922.

"Creating a Masterpiece: The First 100 Years of Pet Incorporated." St. Louis: Pet Inc., 1985.

"Current Legislation and Regulations Regarding Infant Formulas." Atlanta: Infant Formula Council, 1992.

"Dairy Products." *Institutional Distribution,* 15 May 1993.

"Dairy Speaks': The Big Picture: Higher Prices, But Higher Demand," *Dairy Foods,* 15 October 1996.

"Dry Milk and Whey Products Production & Markets—1992." Chicago: American Dairy Products Institute, 1992.

Friedman, Marty. "Non-Dairy Creamers Build Their Case." *Dairy Foods,* April 1992.

General Business File. Universty of Michigan Kresge Library Online Database. February 1997.

Hui, Y. H., ed. *Encyclopedia of Food Science and Technology.* New York: John Wiley & Sons Inc., 1992. S.v. "Casein and Caseinates," by C. R. Southward and N. J. Walker.

Hui, Y. H., ed. *Encyclopedia of Food Science and Technology.* New York: John Wiley & Sons Inc., 1992. S.v. "Dry Milk," by Warren S. Clark, Jr.

Hui, Y. H., ed. *Encyclopedia of Food Science and Technology.* New York: John Wiley & Sons Inc., 1992. S.v. "Evaporated Milk," by Warren S. Clark, Jr. and J. C. Flake.

Hui, Y. H., ed. *Encyclopedia of Food Science and Technology.* New York: John Wiley & Sons Inc., 1992. S.v. "Whey Processing: History and Development," by Warren S. Clark, Jr.

Landa, Marinell. "A Look at America's Most Popular Non-Dairy Creamer." San Francisco, CA: Nestlé Beverage Products, 1992.

"Market Development Plan for the Pacific Rim and Latin America." Arlington, VA: National Dairy Promotion and Research Board, July 1992.

McGraw-Hill Encyclopedia of Science & Technology. Vol. 11. McGraw-Hill, Inc., 1992. S.v. "Milk," by Robert L. Bradley, Jr.

Meier, Barry. "Abbott Labs Settles in Florida Suits." *New York Times,* 25 May 1993.

———. "What Prompted Investigations Into Pricing of Baby Formula?" *The New York Times,* 19 January 1991.

"NAFTA Negotiations Conclude." *Dairy Field,* October 1992.

Noble, Barbara Presley. "Price-Fixing and Other Charges Roil a Once Placid Market." *The New York Times,* 28 July 1991.

O'Donnell, Claudia, D. "The Right Mix: At Rich Products, R&D Is Incorporated Into Every Phase of the Business," *Prepared Foods,* March 1996.

Rickard, Leah. "Price Hikes, Baby Boom Nurture Formula Sales." *Advertising Age,* 10 April 1995.

Rice, Judy. "Conquering a Critical Control Point." *Prepared Foods,* October 1996.

Ruland, Susan. "Milk Shaker." *Dairy Field,* May 1992.

Salwen, Kevin G. "Firms Rigged Bids, U.S. Says." *Wall Street Journal,* 12 June 1992.

U.S. Industrial Outlook. Washington: U.S. Department of Commerce, 1993.

Van Wagner, Lisa R. "Government Agencies." *Food Processing,* August 1992.

—Mary Ratcliffe, updated by Visi Tilak

SIC 2024

ICE CREAM AND FROZEN DESSERTS

This industry classification encompasses establishments primarily engaged in manufacturing ice cream and other frozen desserts: frozen yogurt, ice milk, ices and sherbets, frozen custard, mellorine, frozen tofu, and pops (frozen desserts on sticks).

INDUSTRY SNAPSHOT

The ice cream and frozen desserts industry is an important sector of the American dairy industry. Increasing consumption of frozen desserts has been attributed to the introduction of products containing less milkfat, which were developed to address consumers' interest in healthier diets. Frozen yogurt, for example, was a $585 million market in 1995, while sherbet and sorbet sales combined hit $161 million that year. Although domestic sales of ice cream were down 1.5 percent in 1996, sales of super premium brands rose 3.2 percent. The value of ice cream and frozen dessert shipments has steadily increased throughout the 1990s, reaching nearly $6 billion in 1996. Industry employment also increased, from 20,700 in 1990 to an estimated 21,500 by 1996.

ORGANIZATION AND STRUCTURE

The production of ice cream begins with the milk produced by America's dairy farmers, many of whom belong to large dairy cooperatives that market their milk to processors or, in some cases, operate their own processing facilities for the manufacture of ice cream and other dairy products. In the early 1990s, America's 10 million dairy cows produced 148,526 million pounds of milk; approximately 8.6 percent of it, or 12.8 million pounds, was used to make frozen dairy products.

Manufacturers of ice cream and other frozen desserts range in size from small operations with sales under $1 million a year to subsidiaries or divisions of giant, diversified companies with annual sales in the billions of dollars and for which frozen desserts are only a portion of their total product lines. In the early 1990s, there were approximately 675 establishments making ice cream, 305 making ice milk, and 175 making water ice. Most of these plants made more than one type of frozen dessert product.

In the highly regionalized and extremely competitive dairy industry, many top producers' brand names are known only in the geographic areas in which they are distributed. Distribution to sales outlets is vital to the success of the frozen desserts, and competition for distributors is keen. Small producers trying to break into a market could be "frozen out" by leading producers who demand absolute loyalty from their regional distributors.

Licensing agreements sometimes make partners of competitors. For example, in the San Francisco Bay area, Dreyer's/Edy's Grand Ice Cream was a co-packer and distributor for Vermont-based Ben & Jerry's, and according to a filing with the Securities & Exchange Commission, 42 percent of Ben & Jerry's ice cream was being made by a Dreyer's plant in Fort Wayne, Indiana, using Vermont milk. Similarly, Steve's Homemade produced Yoplait frozen yogurts under an agreement with Yoplait's parent company, General Mills.

BACKGROUND AND DEVELOPMENT

Whether ice cream originated in China or Rome is a matter of debate, but there was little debate in the early 1990s that ice cream and its frozen dessert relatives had regained their position as one of Americans' favorite treats. Ice cream as we know it—smooth and creamy—was introduced in the United States early in the twentieth century as a result of two technological advances: homogenization, which reduced the fat particle size in milk; and a continuous freezing process that enabled a consistent ice crystal structure. Production and manufacturing advancements that have since been realized have centered primarily on formulation refinements and stabilizer and process systems.

Ice cream is a frozen, pasteurized mixture of milk, cream, nonfat milk solids, sugars, and stabilizers. Its contents and manufacture are regulated by the government and must meet Standards of Identity. To be called ice cream, a product must contain a minimum of 10 percent butterfat, which is dispersed throughout the mix to impart smooth texture. Fresh sweet cream is the best source of butterfat; unsalted butter, which is about 82.5 percent fat, can replace 50 to 75 percent of sweet cream fat. Other fat sources that can be used include anhydrous butter oil, concentrated sweet cream, and dried cream. French ice cream, or frozen custard, also contains more than 1.4 percent egg yolk solid. Consumer concerns about the negative health effects of fat in the diet, however, led to the popularity of lower-fat products such as ice milk, which contained between 2 percent and 7 percent butterfat. "Ice milk" as a product name, however, was headed for extinction with passage of the Nutrition Labeling and Education Act.

Other standard ice cream ingredients include sugars and sweeteners, milk proteins, stabilizers, and emulsifiers. Sweetening agents can be natural (using corn sweeteners, sucrose processed from cane and beet sugars, or fructose) or artificial (using aspartame). The milk proteins used are whey proteins and casein. Milk and milk products themselves have some natural stabilizing and emulsifying properties that often eliminate the need for additional stabilizers and emulsifiers. Stabilizers help to prevent texture deterioration caused by inevitable temperature fluctuations that occur during distribution, which cause ice crystals to melt and then reform into larger crystals. Emulsifiers enhance the whipping qualities of the ice cream mix by creating a smoother texture and body.

Flavorings may be added before or after pasteurization, and may be pure flavor extracts, pure extracts with some synthetic or artificial components, or artificial flavors. As a general rule, premium ice creams use pure extracts, and fruits, nuts, candies, and syrups to add flavor. In the 1990s, mix-in flavors like Chocolate Chip Cookie Mix, Carrot Cake Passion, and Cappuccino Commotion were very popular.

The luxury, or super premium, ice creams that were regaining popularity in the 1990s were pioneered by Reuben Mattus in the early 1960s. Using all top-quality, natural ingredients, and no artificial stabilizers or other additives, Mattus created Häagen-Dazs, a highly successful product that set the pattern for rich, clean-tasting ice creams. In the 1980s, such ice cream novelties as ice pops, fudgesicles, and ice cream sandwiches, which had been originally marketed at children, were becoming popular with adults. Häagen-Dazs entered this market with such products as Dove bars and Häagen-Dazs frozen yogurt bars.

Sherbets were defined by the Federal Code of Regulations to contain between 1 and 2 percent butterfat and between 2 and 5 percent total milk-derived solids. Ices contain no milk-derived ingredients or egg ingredients other than egg white; they can be made with non-pasteurized mixes because of their typically high acidity formulation. Mellorine products, although similar to ice cream, contain a combination of vegetable and animal fat in place of butterfat. Federal Standards of Identity require mellorine products to contain at least 6 percent fat and no less than 3.5 percent protein.

Frozen yogurts are made using the bacteria cultures *streptococcus thermophilus* and/or *lactobacillus bulgaricus*. As most refrigerated yogurts were lowfat and had a healthy image with consumers, frozen yogurt was assumed to have the same health benefits as the refrigerated product. The Code of Federal Regulations, however, which required specific starting cultures and acidity levels for refrigerated yogurt, set no such product characteristic requirements for frozen yogurt. The National Yogurt Association (NYA) endorsed a 1991 International Ice Cream Association petition to the government that would standardize manufacturing procedures and require frozen yogurt to be made with specific characterizing yogurt cultures.

Nutrition Labeling and Education Act. By defining terms that had been unclear, the U.S. Food and Drug Administration's (FDA) Nutrition Labeling and Education Act (NLEA), with its May 1994 compliance deadline, enabled many frozen food processors to call their products "lowfat ice cream." The act also separated the link between calories and fat, so that desserts getting more than half their calories from fat could be labeled "light" if its fat content had been reduced 50 percent from its reference product. The "light" label was also permitted on products getting less than half their calories from fat if the products had either a 50 percent fat reduction or a one-third reduction in calories.

A significant change in the new labeling did away with the term "ice milk." Lower-fat ice creams, which previously had to be called "ice milk," are now labeled as "reduced fat," "light," "lowfat," "nonfat," or "fat-free," depending on the product's fat content.

Although the definitions of the terms were clear, the actual fat content percentages were not, because they were tied to an indefinite term, "reference food." Thus, a "reduced fat" claim meant that a product had 25 percent less fat than its "reference food." "Light" referred to a product that had a 50 percent fat reduction from "the reference food," and a "lowfat" product was defined as having not more than 3 grams of total fat in a half-cup serving. "Nonfat" and "fat-free" were defined as products having less than 0.5 grams total fat per reference amount. The reference amount was a half-cup for ice cream and frozen yogurt products and 85 grams for flavored ices and juice bars.

To determine the "reference food," processors first had to find the marketplace average fat or calorie content by looking at the leading brands in the area where the product was to be sold. For example, a processor would have to compare its "light" Fudge Ripple with leading brands of Fudge Ripple to calculate how much of a reduction in fat or calories would satisfy the "50 percent less" requirement. If, on average, the leading brands contained 16 grams of fat, then a product containing 8 grams of fat could be labeled "light."

In 1991, ice cream and frozen dessert sales ranked third behind the fluid milk and cheese sectors of the dairy industry, exceeding $9 billion and representing over 15 percent of the dairy industry's overall sales of

$62.8 billion. Measured by consumption, frozen desserts led the entire dairy industry segment in 1992. Consumption of frozen yogurt, a lowfat alternative to ice cream, rose by 17 percent, and ice cream's 7.3 percent gain was attributed largely to reduced-fat products.

With sales of $3.2 billion in 1991, ice cream was making a comeback as America's favorite dessert. Sales of other frozen desserts (ice milk, frozen yogurt nonfat/lowfat products, novelties, sherbets and sorbets, tofu-based products, mellorine and miscellaneous products) brought the industry total to $9.5 billion for the year. Overall, production increased 4 percent from 1990, with full-fat ice creams still leading the market at 61 percent. Frozen yogurt production, however, increased by 25 percent. The number of reduced-fat ice creams, which represented 54 percent of all reduced-fat product introductions in 1990, declined from 311 to only 94, or 23 percent of the market segment, in 1992.

Dannon, a subsidiary of BSN Groupe, a French company that in 1991 laid claim to being the world's largest dairy processor, introduced its first frozen yogurts in 1992. A leader in the U.S. refrigerated yogurt category, Dannon sent both sugar-free, nonfat products, and premium, full-fat, frozen yogurts to America's retail dairy cases. Frank Palantoni, Dannon's vice president for marketing, said in *Dairy Field* magazine, "In 1991, growth of frozen desserts was driven by frozen yogurt. [It was] up 26 percent." He added that, consistent with NYA guidelines, Dannon's frozen products would be "full of live active cultures . . . a true yogurt product."

Americans spent $5 billion on frozen desserts to eat at home, and another $4.5 billion was spent on away-from-home purchases. Whether indulging in full-fat super premium brands or following the trend to purchase healthier lowfat foods, Americans of all ages were purchasing more frozen desserts at supermarkets, restaurants, and ice cream shops.

The United States was the world's second largest ice cream exporter, sending 21,800 tons out of the country in 1991. This was a 76 percent increase over the previous year and three-and-a-half times the tonnage exported in 1988. Some of this share was taken from the European Community (EC). EC exports fell from 51 percent to 41 percent of the world total, and the U.S. share jumped from 13 percent to 27 percent. The value increase in that same period was over 700 percent, from $6.5 million to $46.3 million, indicating the volume increase was higher in premium or super premium products.

In terms of value, Japan led with imports of $13 million, followed by Mexico, then France and the United Kingdom (UK). The UK, France, and other European Community nations, however, were unlikely to continue importing premium ice cream at the same rate when the new Häagen-Dazs plant in France started production in 1992.

Worldwide production and consumption data for frozen dairy desserts were not very reliable, but based on available figures, the National Dairy Board estimated that the United States was by far the largest producer. Japan was the second largest producer, but its production was far less than that of the United States. The United States also led in per capita consumption, with Finland, New Zealand, and Australia close runners-up.

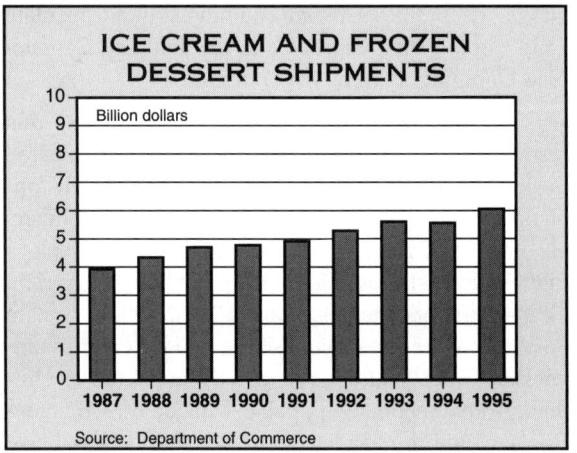

ICE CREAM AND FROZEN DESSERT SHIPMENTS

Billion dollars

Source: Department of Commerce

CURRENT CONDITIONS

Ice cream was a $3.3 billion market in 1995, while frozen yogurt represented a $585 million market. Leading ice cream brands included Unilever, Dreyer's, Häagen-Dazs, and Ben & Jerry's. Top frozen yogurt brands were Dreyer's/Edy's, Kemps, and Ben & Jerry's.

Fat content continued to be of concern to many consumers, as reflected in the marked growth of the sherbet and sorbet market to $161 million in 1995. Top brands in this market niche included Häagen-Dazs, Dreyer's/Edy's, and Real Fruit. One survey found that nearly two-thirds of respondents regularly chose lowfat dairy foods. Older people and couples were more apt than single people to opt for lowfat regularly.

INDUSTRY LEADERS

Häagen-Dazs Co., whose parent company, Pillsbury, was in turn owned by the United Kingdom giant

Grand Metropolitan PLC, set a course in the 1990s aimed at leaving the competition trailing. The company offered something for everyone in the frozen dessert segment: premium ice creams, frozen yogurt novelties on a stick, 98 percent fat-free frozen yogurts, and a new super premium line of mix-in flavored frozen yogurts and ice creams that Häagen-Dazs dubbed Exträas. The new products were designed to meet increasingly stiff competition in the marketplace and to regain market share from Ben & Jerry's. Sales volume jumped 10 percent after the introduction of Exträas, and the company's market share jumped from 5.9 percent to 8.3 percent in just 12 weeks. Kate Boyle, marketing director of frozen novelties, said in *Dairy Foods* magazine that frozen yogurt stick bars were "somewhat of an afterthought." The afterthought had rewarding results. Overall, market sales of frozen yogurt novelties tripled after their introduction early in 1992, and Häagen-Dazs claimed 52 percent of that market niche.

Häagen-Dazs took its cue for mix-in flavored super premium frozen yogurts from Ben & Jerry's Homemade, Inc., the successful Vermont ice cream maker.

In response to consumer demand for up-scale, low-fat ice cream, Häagen-Dazs announced in early 1997 that it would introduce a new line of ice creams with only 3 grams of fat. The new low-fat flavors were formulated with a concentration of proteins from lactose-reduced skim milk.

At Ben & Jerry's Homemade, which built its success on full-fat, super premium ice cream, efforts to develop a satisfactory lowfat ice cream yielded a 7 percent fat product. "This was lowfat according to Ben & Jerry's interpretation," said Peter Lind, the company's "primal ice cream therapist" (other companies called this research and development). The company did, however, develop a true lowfat frozen yogurt. The technical challenge for this was great, given B&J's requirement that the ingredients had to be easy to pronounce and not include "chemical sounding" words.

Ben & Jerry's is known for its social action programs as well as its unusual ice cream flavors. The company's strategy of supporting charitable and political programs and introducing unique mix-in flavors paid off in 1992 with $6.7 million in profits, a 78 percent rise from the previous year, and nearly $132 million in sales, a 36 percent increase. In 1993, Ben & Jerry's followed its very successful vanilla-based Chocolate Chip Cookie Dough flavor with Peanut Butter Cookie dough and had ice cream lovers begging for more.

On the social action front, the company waived its usual $30,000 franchise free for a scoop shop in New York City's Harlem; 75 percent of the profits went to HARKhomes, an organization for homeless men, and the shop employed the homeless as well. Through the Children's Defense Fund, Ben & Jerry's also fought to give children's issues higher priority in the national agenda. By 1995, B&J's had $149 million in sales and ranked seventh in the ice cream market.

Dreyer's Grand Ice Cream of Oakland, California, with 1996 sales of $681 million, continued to expand its markets and its product line. Its acquisition of a New York dairy's premium ice cream brand and distribution brought it into the New York tri-state market, which includes New Jersey and Connecticut. The company also became the exclusive New York supermarket distributor for Dolly Madison ice creams and struck distribution agreements with Steve's Homemade Ice Cream, Inc. New products for the 1990s included low fat, sugar-free, and fat-free ice cream, Grand Delights frozen novelties, and a line of ice cream pies and mid-priced ice cream for food service companies. Additionally, Dreyer's and Ben & Jerry's were the only two companies that had mastered the art of making an ice cream stick bar with added-in chunks.

Gold Bond-Good Humor Ice Cream, a division of T.J. Lipton Co., specialized in high-sale frozen novelties. The company made up for the loss of its licensing rights to Walt Disney characters by acquiring the rights to Peanuts cartoon characters and launching a Snoopy ice cream bar. Gold Bond's plans included a full line of novelties, including a water ice Dinosaur Bar with a bubble gum ball in the center. The company's 1995 sales were $320 million.

WORK FORCE

Employment in the ice cream/frozen dessert industry was 20,900 in 1992. Production workers earned an average of $11.10 an hour in 1991, up 4.1 percent over the previous year. Although management salaries for the industry were undocumented, *Food Engineering* magazine's annual salary survey reported average 1992 increases of 4.7 percent. Over the course of the decade, employment continued to decline. By 1995, there were 15,900 workers in the industry.

FURTHER READING

Dexheimer, Ellen, et al. "Navigators of the '90s." *Dairy Foods,* April 1993.

Dillon, Patricia M. "Salary Survey: The High Price of an Average Raise." *Food Engineering,* December 1992.

Doeff, Gail Rosenbaum. "Competition for Ice Cream Distribution Heats Up." *Dairy Foods,* July 1993.

Dryer, Jerry. "Taking Lowfat Dairy Products Seriously." *Dairy Foods,* July 1993.

Fiscal Year 93 Market Development Plan. National Dairy Board, 1993.

Food and Agricultural Policy Research Institute 1996 Outlook. Available from http://ssu.missouri.edu/ssu/fapri/.

Friday, Carolyn. "Cookies, Cream 'n' Controversy." *Newsweek,* 5 July 1993.

"Frozen Desserts Go Back to Basics with a Gusto." *Dairy Field,* December 1992.

Gerson, Vicki. "Fast and Furious." *Dairy Field,* March 1993.

Gibson, Richard. "Häagen-Dazs' New Ice Creams Have Less Fat." *Wall Street Journal,* 10 January 1997, B14.

Goerne, Carrie. "Häagen-Dazs Adds Flavors to Ice Its Super premium Competitors." *Marketing News,* 31 August 1992.

Hui, Y. H., ed. "Ice Cream and Frozen Dessert." *Encyclopedia of Food Science and Technology.* New York: John Wiley & Sons, Inc., 1992.

Kimbrell, Wendy. "Healthy Culture." *Dairy Field,* April 1992.

Lazich, Robert S., ed. *Market Share Reporter.* Detroit: Gale Research, 1997.

"Market Stats and Data." *Dairy Field,* December 1992.

Milk Facts. Washington: Milk Industry Foundation, 1992.

O'Donnell, Claudia Dziuk. "Cutting the Fat." *Dairy Foods,* July 1993.

———. "Benefiting from a Healthy Image." *Dairy Foods,* April 1993.

Ruland, Susan. "Exträa Energy." *Dairy Field,* September 1992.

U.S. Bureau of the Census. *1992 Census of Manufactures.* Available at http://www.census.gov/ftp/pub/mcd/mancen/download/mc92f202.sum/.

—Mary Ratcliffe, updated by Marinell Jochnowitz

SIC 2026

FLUID MILK

This industry encompasses establishments primarily engaged in processing fluid milk, cream, and related products that included cottage cheese, yogurt (except frozen), and other cultured milk products.

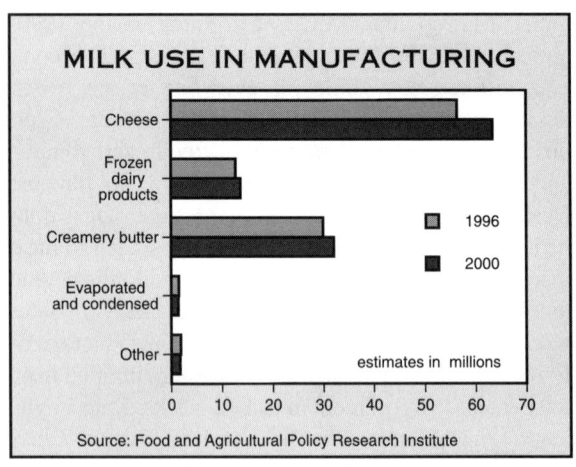

MILK USE IN MANUFACTURING

Cheese
Frozen dairy products
Creamery butter
Evaporated and condensed
Other

1996
2000

estimates in millions

0 10 20 30 40 50 60 70

Source: Food and Agricultural Policy Research Institute

INDUSTRY SNAPSHOT

The fluid milk industry is an important subsector of the nation's dairy business. Fluid milk producers are often huge, sophisticated, diversified operations with product lines crossing industry boundaries. They manufacture and market a mix of fluid milk products, cheeses, ice creams, butter, dairy ingredients, and sometimes extensive lines of non-dairy products as well.

The 1990s brought a variety of changes and challenges for the industry. The pace of consolidation quickened. The number of dairy farms and dairy farm cooperatives was shrinking, and the federal government passed the FAIR Act, which started the phasing out of dairy price supports starting in 1996. In addition, although production was increasing, controversy concerning the introduction of scientific methodologies responsible for these increases, such as the use of Bovine Growth Hormone (rBST), was considerable. Consequently, the fragmented industry began an effort to pull together in order to address the changes on the horizon.

ORGANIZATION AND STRUCTURE

The highly regionalized fluid milk industry started on the dairy farm—where the raw milk was produced—and extended out to processors and manufacturing plants owned by dairy farm cooperatives, general food processors, and even by supermarket chains marketing their own private label product lines. These processing plants made a variety of milk products destined for retail outlets, food service and institutional markets, and, to a lesser degree, other countries.

Milk is an extremely perishable commodity, and supply and demand can fluctuate unpredictably, depending on such variables as the output of individual cows, weather conditions, and even road conditions

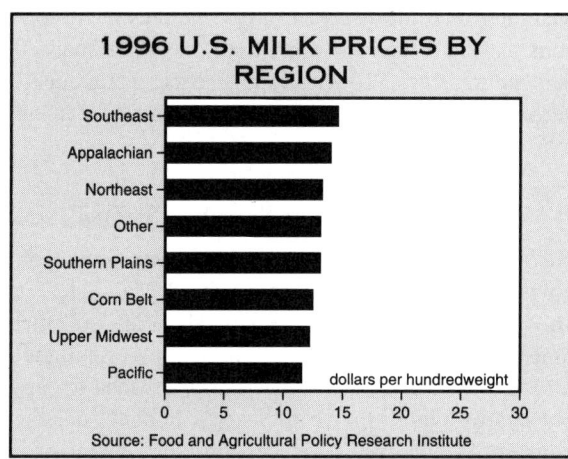

1996 U.S. MILK PRICES BY REGION

dollars per hundredweight

Southeast, Appalachian, Northeast, Other, Southern Plains, Corn Belt, Upper Midwest, Pacific

0 5 10 15 20 25 30

Source: Food and Agricultural Policy Research Institute

met by tank trucks. But, as pointed out in *Dairy Field* magazine by Don Blayney of the U.S. Department of Agriculture's (USDA) Agricultural Research Service, "Milk is produced every day. You can't store it on the farm. It has to move to someone who can do something with it."

In the 1990s, changes in the dairy industry were transforming the complex relationships between cooperatives and processors. Dairy cooperatives traditionally helped to reduce the impact of such fluctuations on milk handlers by more efficiently coordinating supply arrangements and routing raw milk supplies not needed for fluid milk. Dairy cooperatives assisting the producers in price setting, have in many cases taken over all stages of dairy operations, including: herd management and milking; management of fluid milk supplies and surpluses; development of competitive new products; fluid milk processing; and the manufacture and marketing of a broad range of dairy products and ingredients.

Government pricing regulations were another means of insuring market stability. The government regulated milk pricing to farmers through Federal Milk Marketing Orders authorized by the Agricultural Marketing Act of 1937 or the Agricultural Act of 1949, which established the ongoing dairy price support program for areas where producers had agreed to abide by it. The pricing system was described in *The Wall Street Journal* as "so antiquated and complex that [it filled] three volumes of the Code of Federal Regulations." Supervised regionally by the USDA, prices were established geographically and according to the milk supply, fat content, weight, and the end use of the milk. From its inception, the support price fluctuated according to market conditions. In addition to the federal pricing structure, almost one-third of milk producing states also regulated milk pricing to farmers.

Milk Processing. Cow milk is the principal source of America's fluid milk supply. It contains about 87 percent water and 13 percent solids, which are composed of solids-not-fat (SNF) and milk fat. Components of SNF are mostly protein (caseins and whey), lactose, and minerals important to human nutrition. An excellent source of calcium, phosphorous, and vitamins A and B-2, and a good source of vitamins A, B-1 and B-12, milk's nutritional components earned it the label of "most perfect food." It is, however, a poor source for iron, copper, manganese, nicotinic acid, and vitamins C and D. Since the 1920s, most milk sold in the United States has been fortified with vitamin D.

Class I fluid milk meets strict standards, which include regular inspections of the herd and herd housing facilities, dairy equipment, and milk storage units to insure that they satisfy health and sanitation requirements. Class I milk is used for human consumption or in manufactured milk products. Milk of manufacturing grade does not meet such strict standards and is priced lower.

In most dairy operations, raw milk is piped from a milking machine to a refrigerated bulk storage tank before it is transferred to a tank truck for delivery to a plant. There it undergoes the following processing operations:

- Separation: The milk is split into cream (fat) and skim milk. The cream is then added back to the milk stream to achieve the desired fat content.

- Pasteurization: The milk is heated to destroy pathogenic bacteria and other undesirable organisms that might lead to spoilage. In continuous high-temperature-short-time pasteurization (HTST), milk is heated to 161°F (72°C) for a minimum of 15 seconds. Since about 1970, ultrahigh temperature pasteurization (UHT), through which milk is heated at temperatures as high as 265°F (130°C) for three seconds, has been used with products such as heavy and light cream, and half-and-half. This process has extended their shelf life for several months.

- Homogenization: This process breaks up the fat globules in milk, forming a stable emulsion that does not separate. Most fluid milk is homogenized.

Fresh Milk. The following products are included in the fresh milk category: whole milk, lowfat milk, skim or nonfat milk, cream, half-and-half, and buttermilk.

Whole milk contains not less than 3.25 percent milkfat and 8.25 percent SNF. Vitamins A and D may be added at levels of at least 2,000 International Units

(IU) per quart for vitamin A and 400 IU for vitamin D. Flavoring ingredients may also be added.

Lowfat milk contains milkfat at levels of 0.5, 1.5, or 2 percent, not less than 8.25 percent SNF, and at least 2,000 IU of vitamin A per quart. If vitamin D is added, it must be present at a level of 400 IU per quart. Flavoring ingredients are also permitted.

Skim or nonfat milk contains less than 0.5 percent milkfat and not less than 8.25 percent SNF. It must contain 2,000 IU of vitamin A per quart. If vitamin D is added, it must be present at a level of 400 IU per quart. Flavoring ingredients are permitted.

Cream is made by separating out most of the skim milk and is rich in milkfat. Light (coffee) cream contains at least 18 percent and no more than 30 percent milk fat. Heavy (whipping) cream contains at least 36 percent milkfat. Half-and-half, a mixture of milk and cream, contains between 10.5 percent and 18 percent milkfat. It was often preferred over coffee cream for its lower fat and calorie content and lower cost.

Buttermilk is a byproduct of churning cream into butter. Similar in composition to skim milk, it is condensed and dried for commercial use in baking and packaged cake mixes; it is not sold for consumption.

Cultured Milk Products. For centuries, people have known how to preserve the nutritional values of fresh milk for weeks or months by using bacterial cultures. Lactic-acid producing bacteria and certain characterizing ingredients may be added to fresh milk products and, depending on the level of milkfat, they may be labeled "cultured buttermilk," "cultured lowfat buttermilk," or "cultured skim milk (or nonfat) buttermilk." Yogurt, sour cream, dry curd cottage cheese, and cottage cheese are included in the cultured milk products category.

Yogurt is made by culturing a mixture of milk and cream with lactic acid-producing bacteria, *Lactobacillus bulgaricus* and *Streptococcus thermophilus,* and contains not less than 3.25 percent milkfat and 8.25 percent SNF. Often sweeteners, flavorings, and other ingredients are added. Lowfat yogurt contains no more than 2 percent milkfat, and nonfat yogurt contains less than 0.5 percent milkfat. Sour cream results from the addition of lactic acid-producing bacteria to pasteurized cream containing not less than 18 percent milkfat.

Dry curd cottage cheese is made by adding either lactic-acid producing bacteria or acidifiers to skim milk and/or reconstituted nonfat dry milk. Rennet and/or other enzymes may also be added to help curd formation. The soft, unripened cheese contains less than 0.5 percent milkfat and no more than 80 percent moisture. Cottage cheese is made by the addition of a creaming mixture to dry curd cottage cheese. It contains at least 4 percent milkfat and no more than 80 percent moisture. Lowfat cottage cheese contains 2 percent or less milkfat and no more than 82.5 percent moisture.

BACKGROUND AND DEVELOPMENT

History. The first cows landed at the Jamestown Colony in North America in 1611, and 13 years later, in 1624, cows were brought to Plymouth Colony. At that time, dairying was a family affair, and it was not until urbanization that dairy farms were established to supply nearby cities. In the industry's infancy, a large number of small, local producers provided the milk for their immediate areas. With the introduction of milk preservation and sanitation methods, it became possible for large dairy processors, often far removed from their raw milk sources, to supply ever more distant markets.

A creamery built in Goshen, Connecticut, in 1810, was one of the first formal business units established as a cooperative venture. Cooperative cheese rings and dairy cooperatives in eastern states soon followed, and the movement spread to Wisconsin and other midwestern states. It did not gain momentum, however, until after the Civil War, when the Grange and other farm organizations sponsored a number of experimental cooperatives. By 1900 there were approximately 1,000 farmer cooperatives. A period of dynamic growth occurred from 1915 to 1930 when cooperatives were placed under statute laws rather than common law. Passage of the Capper-Volstead Act in 1992 established the right of agricultural producers to band together in voluntary associations for their mutual benefit in collective processing, handling, and marketing of agricultural products in interstate and foreign commerce.

Some milestones along the way: Louis Pasteur's experiments using heat to kill microorganisms in milk (1856); Gail Borden's first successful milk condensery in Burrville, Connecticut (1857); development of the milk bottle by Dr. Hervey D. Thatcher, Potsdam, New York (1884); introduction of tuberculin testing for dairy herds and Dr. S. M. Babcock's perfection of a fat content test for milk and cream (1890); introduction of commercial pasteurizing machinery (1895); perfection of the automatic bottle filler and capper (1911); the first use of tank trucks for milk transport (1914); successful sale of homogenized milk in Torrington, Connecticut (1919); introduction of vitamin D-fortified milk (1932); perfection of a vacuum pasteurization process (1946); introduction of ultra-high temperature (UHT) pasteurization (1948); the start of nutrition labeling for fluid milk products (1974); widespread acceptance of UHT milks (1981); increased popularity of low fat and skim milk, with sales surpassing whole milk for the first time (1988); mandatory nutrition labeling under the Nutrition Labeling and Education Act (1991).

In 1991 nearly 10 million dairy cows were on cooperative farms or—on the increasingly rare—small and independent dairy farms in the United States. They yielded an annual average of 14,867 pounds of milk per cow, for a total of 148,526 million pounds. *Holstein Association News* reported in 1993 that a 5-year-old cow, prophetically christened Royalty Maxima, had set a new world record by producing 58,952 pounds of milk, surpassing the previous record set in 1975. Breeding efficiency, the ability to improve the herds rapidly using artificial insemination techniques introduced in the 1940s, and the selection of superior sires brought milk production a long way from the mid-1800s, when cows produced an average of only 322 gallons annually.

Also by 1991, fluid milk accounted for 39.3 percent of all dairy industry sales: $24.7 billion out of a total of $62.8 billion for the entire dairy industry. By the mid-1990s, however, per-capita milk sales had experienced a decline of 15 percent since 1975.

Record-breaking floods and drenching rains left tens of thousands of acres in the Mississippi River valley under water in the summer of 1993. Despite damage measured in tens of billions of dollars, it looked as if dairy farmers would be spared the worst of it. Minnesota farmers, for example, were unable to plant vast portions of acreage, but the cows responded to cooler-than-usual temperatures by giving more milk. A Land O'Lakes spokesman expected this to offset higher feed cost and increased risk of udder infections from the sloppy conditions.

Scandal in the Dairy Industry. Computerized bid-analysis techniques uncovered conspiracies in Florida in the mid-1980s, where the court said that illegal bid-rigging had raised the price of milk by as much as 14 percent. The U.S. Department of Justice and some other states began their own investigations, and by mid-1987, signs of illegal bid-rigging extended into Georgia, Alabama, and Mississippi. Said Gina Talomona of the Justice Department in *The American School Board Journal,* these federal and state bid-rigging probes constituted the country's "biggest antitrust case in at least the last 10 years." The dollars involved were considerable. According to the Milk Industry Foundation, from 1981 to 1991 a steady 7 percent of fluid milk sales had been to schools. Fines

and settlements had come to more than $100 million by 1993.

Even as investigations and prosecutions proceeded, a report from the General Accounting Office (GAO) criticized the government for its share of responsibility for the schemes. Once bid-rigging had been discovered, said the GAO, the USDA had the authority to halt federal funding to companies found guilty of bid-rigging and to bar their future participation in the federally financed programs. Under federal marketing and price-support programs, moreover, dairies were aware of competitors' minimum prices, creating a situation that provided opportunities for collusion.

The USDA countered that debarment of private companies was inappropriate if the companies paid the penalties imposed and satisfied the federal agency's requirements.

Controversy. Monopolistic practices and political contributions have been the main controversies attached to dairy co-ops. Consumer advocate Ralph Nader accused the three largest dairy co-ops, Associated Milk Producers, Inc. (AMPI), Dairymen, Inc., and Mid-America Dairymen, Inc. (Mid-Am) of illegal contributions totaling $422,000 to President Richard Nixon's re-election campaign in order to influence the administration to enact higher price supports (enacted in 1971) and to drop antitrust suits against the three co-ops.

Eventually, AMPI pleaded guilty to having made illegal contributions in 1968, 1970, and 1971. This, however, was not the end of AMPI's legal battles; in 1989 the U.S. Supreme Court upheld an appeals court ruling, filed in 1971 by the National Farmers' Organization (NFO), which determined that AMPI had conspired to eliminate competitive milk producers.

Meanwhile, after decades of backing the industry through price support programs and the purchase of surpluses, the federal government was gradually reducing its role, although no one was predicting the elimination of supports in the near future. As with many issues in the dairy industry, opinions were divided as to whether supports protected the dairy farmers or whether a free market would serve them better.

In the early 1990s, industry analysts forecasted that fluid milk sales were likely to drop between 1 and 1.5 percent annually. According to a 1992 *Supermarket Business* magazine Consumer Expenditures Study, sales declined in every major milk product except yogurt, which posted a 5.8 percent gain. The figures illustrated the trend reported by the Milk Industry

Foundation (MIF), which said that from 1974 to 1991, total fluid milk product sales (plain whole milk, lowfat milk, skim milk, flavored milk and drinks, and buttermilk) had risen a scant 0.05 percent, from 52,476 million pounds to 55,227 pounds. Sales of whole milk had plummeted 43.7 percent in that period, from 36,765 million pounds to 20,680 pounds, while lowfat milk sales had jumped from 9,763 to 25,221 million pounds.

Consumers' health concerns about fat in their diets presented opportunities for the introduction of flavorful low-fat and skim milk products, and dairy companies were working to improve the taste of these products in order to compete with non-dairy beverages like soft drinks, bottled waters, beer, juices, and sports drinks.

Per capita sales from 1974 to 1991 dropped 10.6 percent, from 245.9 pounds to 219.0 for all milk products, and from 172.3 to 82.0 for whole milk. During the same period, lowfat milk sales more than doubled, from 45.8 to 100.0 pounds per capita.

Dairy Field magazine quoted a report by Bozell Worldwide consultants with even worse statistics for the industry. The report detailed a 23 percent drop in per capita milk consumption reported for the 35 years from 1955 to 1990, and it noted a dramatic drop in milk drinking after age 17; at the time, 64 percent of the U.S. population was 25 or older. Still, nearly 95 percent of American households purchased milk, usually from supermarkets, where milk posted 1991 sales of nearly $6.8 billion and accounted for 31.06 percent of dairy case sales. It was the most frequently purchased supermarket item for the year ending March 1992, just ahead of bread.

Nevertheless, milk's image as the most perfect and nutritionally complete food was slipping. Studies linked it to diabetes and certain infant allergies. Consumers also expressed concern about the fat in milk, although a 1990 Pennsylvania State University study found that more than half of the survey's respondents didn't know the fat content of whole and skim milks, and 40 percent didn't know the fat content of lowfat milk. Even those who thought they knew milk's fat content tended to overstate it. A National Dairy Board study found that many Americans believed, erroneously, that reducing fat content also depleted milk's nutrients.

Facing slow sales growth and virtually no increase in consumption, fluid milk producers began to take aggressive steps to improve the industry's outlook. A combination of consumer education, advertising and promotion, and consumer-responsive new products was seen as imperative to restoring consumer demand for and confidence in fluid milk and fluid milk products.

In 1993, the Milk Industry Foundation (MIF) took steps to set up a fund for a $55-million national consumer education program, the only strategy on which the fragmented industry was likely to unite. The money was to come from an assessment on Class I fluid milk sales. Said Bill Tinklepaugh, MIF vice president, in *Dairy Field* magazine, "Although the 1990 Farm Bill authorized a national advertising program, here we are in 1992 still trying to build a coalition of support for any program. That's because milk processors have so many divergent points of view." Howard Dean, chairman and chief executive officer of Dean Foods Co. and 1991-92 MIF chairman, said in the same article, " . . . we've never been able to get our act together and coordinate the industry."

As sales of fluid milk flattened out and cottage cheese sales plunged in the 1980s, sales of cultured milk products increased.

Yogurt sales soared by 88 percent—from 583 to 1,098 million pounds—from 1980 to 1991, and sour cream and dips jumped 61 percent, from 408 to 657 million pounds. Growing popularity of ethnic foods, especially Mexican, in the late 1980s and early 1990s, spurred growth in the $750 million sour cream and dip market. Combined sales of cultured products reached $4 billion in 1991.

In 1992 the International Dairy Foods Association predicted that the number of fluid processing plants would decrease by as much as one-third, to under 400, by the year 2000. They foresaw 90,000 dairy farms (in 1954, there had been 1,475,000) and 8.5 million cows, each producing an annual average of 18,000 pounds of milk for a total of 157 million pounds. Top dairy co-op executives expected that the number of national cooperatives would drop to four or five.

On the heels of depressed profitability in 1990, Dun & Bradstreet reported median ratios on industry profitability in 1991 that showed a strong comeback: returns on sales were 1.6 percent in 1991, following a drop from 1 percent in 1989 to 0.8 percent in 1990; returns on assets were 5.3 percent, up from 1990's 2.9 percent; returns on net worth were 12.5 percent, up from 7.4 percent in 1990. A return on net worth of 10 percent is generally considered desirable to provide for both dividends and future growth.

CURRENT CONDITIONS

In the last decade of the twentieth century, the industry appeared poised to tackle changes in the fluid milk market in united fashion and form a probable position of financial strength. A major development was the passage of the Federal Agricultural Improvement and Reform Act of 1996 (FAIR), which called for a phased elimination of government supports for dairy products. In 1996, the support price was $10.35 per cwt level. This was expected to move to $9.90 by 1999. Price supports were to be eliminated altogether by 2000.

In 1996, rBST was in its second year, and the industry saw increasing rates of adoption. It was estimated that one-third of dairy cows received rBST in 1996. Usage of hormonal injections was expected to increase steadily each year through the end of the decade, leveling off at 50 percent by 2002.

Milk prices were unusually high by mid-decade, due to rising production costs and weather-related feed grain shortages that drove up farmers' costs of feeding dairy cows. With the higher costs, milk production was down 1.16 billion pounds in 1996. The number of dairy cows was projected to drop to less than 9 million head by January 2000.

In an effort to counteract these trends by boosting consumption of milk, the industry introduced national advertising campaigns, such as the "milk mustache" series of ads that featured well-known athletes and celebrities. The industry also petitioned the Food & Drug Administration to eliminate strict labeling standards for milk and other products. In late 1996, the FDA announced a new policy that would make labeling of dairy products consistent with that of other low-fat and nonfat foods. For example, under the new policy, 2 percent milk was to be renamed "reduced-fat," 1 percent relabeled as "low-fat," and skim milk as "fat-free" or "nonfat." The new rules were applauded by the International Dairy Foods Association as opening the way for the industry to formulate more lower-fat products.

INDUSTRY LEADERS

The two major producers in the fluid milk industry were representative of the food industry as a whole in that their manufacturing activities were not limited to a single SIC category. Borden, Inc., which in the 1990s was the leading maker of fluid milk products, was also a leading manufacturer of pastas and chemical adhesives. Dean Foods, second only to Borden, also made vegetable products.

Borden, Inc. Incorporated in 1899, this venerable U.S. company was founded by Gail Borden in the mid-nineteenth century when it introduced condensed milk.

By 1875 the company was producing fresh milk, which it sold door-to-door in New York City. Despite steady expansion into other food and chemical product lines, management focus remained on the dairy business until 1956. Over the years, the company grew and prospered through a policy of aggressive acquisition.

In the late 1980s and early 1990s, the industry giant embarked on a major restructuring and consolidation of its business, including its dairy operations. Between 1988 and 1991, the company closed 15 dairy plants and sold off five more while folding its Dairy Division into its Grocery Products Division. Withdrawal from the fluid milk and cultured products markets in the East and Southeast was announced in 1989, due to market overcrowding and low profits. Borden continued to market its milk in southern, western and midwest states. The company also announced record capital expenditures for what it called "hyperplants." Three of the 11 planned state-of-the-art, high efficiency, mostly large-scale manufacturing facilities were slated to make dairy products.

Throughout this restructuring process, Borden continued to hold the number one position in the dairy industry, even as its dairy business shrank. The company reported a $21.4 million operating loss in its dairy operations for 1992, compared to operating income of $85 million in 1991. The difference was attributed to the high cost of raw milk and the $47.3 million reorganization costs. At the same time, the company posted $1.5 billion in total dairy sales, a 1.5 percent increase and 25 percent of the company's 1992 income. "We probably don't have as much of a battle overcoming the commodity image of milk as many of our competitors do," said company spokesman John Rutan in *Dairy Field* magazine. "We have very strong regional brand equities . . . We're the #1 or #2 brand in all the markets we participate in." In 1992 Borden planned to reinforce its brand name with their Elsie the Cow trademark as advertising "spokescow." Elsie was also scheduled to make a strong reappearance on product packaging. Although she had been out of the limelight for nearly 20 years, Borden said more than half of all American adults still recognized Elsie.

By mid-decade, Borden was still the industry leader, with 27,500 employees and sales of $5.9 billion in 1995.

Dean Foods. With 6 percent of the total market and sales of $2.6 billion in 1996, Dean Foods was catching up to Borden. The company appeared to be recovering from a slump that came after 40 years of uninterrupted earnings growth. Dean's 21 milk processing plants bought raw milk directly from farmers and processed it into skim milk, half-and-half, whipping cream, yogurt, sour cream, buttermilk, and cottage cheese. Typically, some 75 percent of plant output was marketed to supermarkets and other retail food outlets within a 250-mile radius of the plant. The rest was supplied to restaurants, hotels, schools, hospitals, military installations, and fast food chains. Industrial sales accounted for a relatively small portion of Dean's business.

For decades the company's strategy had been growth through acquisition, a policy Dean planned to continue through the 1990s as milk consumption flattened. Typically, Dean sought to purchase larger dairies with sales in the $25 million to $80 million dollar range, often retaining their strong regional brand names. In 1993 the company entered into negotiations to purchase the Flav-O-Rich, Inc. fluid milk and ice cream business. Flav-O-Rich, which operated nine fluid milk plants in the southeastern United States and had 1992 sales of approximately $400 million, was the milk-processing subsidiary of Dairymen, Inc., one of the country's largest dairy cooperatives. Dean was also looking to Mexico for growth. With half of the country's population under 18, the prime age group for milk drinking, and a chronic shortage of fresh milk, Mexico was an attractive new market for expansion.

Despite its emphasis on acquisitions, 50 percent of the company's growth over 20 years could be attributed to expanding markets and new product introductions.

Cooperatives. The largest cooperative in the United States, the San Antonio-based Associated Milk Producers, Inc. (AMPI), was planning a reorganization of its management structure to allow quicker reactions to the changes in consumer demands, milk supplies, and market opportunities. The co-op had registered 16,321 member farms in 20 states in 1991.

Other cooperatives were developing new strategies to deal with changing market conditions. Mid-America Dairymen, Inc. (Mid-Am), one of the largest of the dairy co-ops, with $1.85 billion in 1992 sales, reported that approximately 50 percent of its milk production was sold as fluid milk. Mid-Am entered into joint ventures with other co-ops and processors and also bought into an independent dairy company, which did not handle Mid-Am milk at all. The co-op's fluid milk operations were turned over to Prairie Farms, an Illinois cooperative, which managed Mid-Am plants profitably, something which had eluded Mid-Am, without sharing ownership in them.

Dairymen's sale of its Flav-O-Rich subsidiary, if successful, would take it out of the milk-processing

business; it would revert to a raw-milk cooperative supplying other processors, including Dean. The sale would also catapult Dean Foods into the leading position in the dairy industry, over Borden.

Leaders in the burgeoning refrigerated yogurt category were Dannon—with close to a 33 percent market share and 1992 sales of $388.3 million, up 13.8 percent over 1991—and the General Mills subsidiary Yoplait, with its 17.8 percent market share and 1992 sales of $210.5 million. Private label brands ranked third in 1992, with sales of $153.3 million and a 13.3 percent market share.

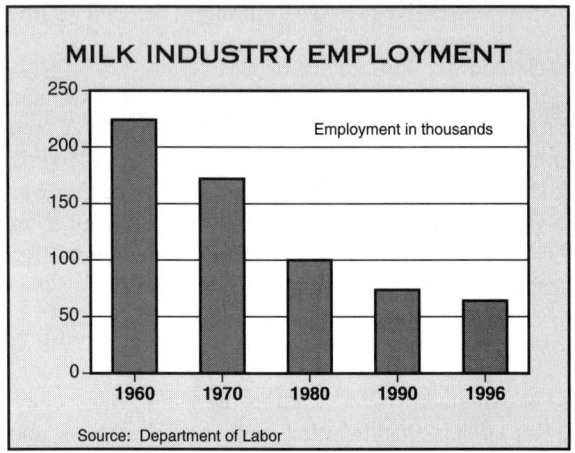

MILK INDUSTRY EMPLOYMENT

Employment in thousands

Source: Department of Labor

WORK FORCE

From 1982 to 1991, employment in the fluid milk industry declined 18 percent, from 84,000 to 69,000 jobs, according to the U.S. Bureau of the Census and MIF estimates. The number of production workers in the industry dropped from 37,900 to 33,400, while their wages rose from $693 million to $892 million. The average annual compensation for a production worker rose from $18,285 in 1982 to $26,707 in 1991.

Many food industry companies were restructuring and reducing personnel in the early 1990s in response to the overall economic recession. Most of the job losses between 1991 and 1992 were in the supervisory (28.8 percent) and middle management (26.6 percent) areas; only 8.1 percent of professional/technical positions were lost.

Jobs in the dairy industry requiring a college degree included farm and processing plant management, quality control, and research. Training for herd management, milk production, processing, distribution, and sales could be obtained from secondary and vocational schools.

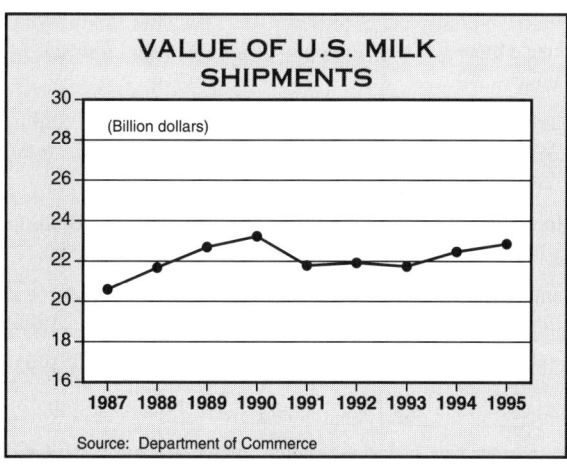

VALUE OF U.S. MILK SHIPMENTS

(Billion dollars)

Source: Department of Commerce

AMERICA AND THE WORLD

NAFTA. The North American Free Trade Agreement (NAFTA) will do away with existing tariffs and other trade barriers among the United States, Canada, and Mexico for the next fifteen years, creating the world's largest consumer market with a combined economy of nearly $6.5 trillion. Negotiations for the agreement concluded in 1992, and the legislation was passed by the U.S. Congress late in 1993.

The International Dairy Foods Association predicted that the treaty would be an overall benefit to the U.S. dairy industry, including the fluid milk sector. With or without NAFTA, Mexico was seen as a potential growth area by the dairy industry. Mexico, which had been a major importer of dry milk and cheese products, had also increased its imports of such fresh dairy products as fluid milk and yogurt. The impact of the treaty on dairymen was likely to be less in Canadian trade.

The opportunities NAFTA would create for fluid milk products in Mexico in the 1990s also presented many challenges for U.S. companies. Only about one-half of Mexico's households had refrigerators. Moreover, Mexican consumers often bought their food at small neighborhood stores, also with little refrigeration. Even some of the better equipped supermarkets turned off their electricity overnight. Quality controls for dairy products in Mexico were also much less stringent than those in the United States. As much as 40 percent of Mexican-produced milk went straight from the cow to the consumer, without being pasteurized.

Europe. The introduction of milk quotas in 1984 to curtail surplus milk production under the European Commission's Common Agriculture Policy (CAP), had apparently backfired by the 1990s. Production efficiency was suffering and competition was down.

The industry was becoming polarized, as large producers were growing in size and smaller companies found it increasingly difficult to survive. Restrictive quotas also had an impact on available milk volumes in the domestic market. Processors, if strong enough, could purchase dairies in new markets to assure raw milk supply. Those unable to do this were threatened with takeover. Buying power, too, was becoming concentrated in a small number of powerful and aggressive retailing groups. The large, well-established international dairy suppliers were able to stand up to their demands, but smaller, national producers were at risk.

World Milk Production. There was very little international trade of fluid milk in the early 1990s. According to a National Dairy Board (NDB) market development plan for 1993, there was no change in the average rate of worldwide milk production from 1987 to 1991, but there was a significant drop in production in the USSR and Eastern Europe after the disintegration of communist rule. Much of the NDB data was drawn from the Foreign Agricultural Service (FAS) Dairy Livestock, Dairy and Poultry Division (DLP), so it does not include data from non-reporting countries.

The world's largest milk producer was the European Community, with an estimated production of 112.9 million tons in 1992. The former USSR followed, with an estimated production of 95 million tons, and the United States ranked third, with an estimated 1992 production of 68.2 million tons. Worldwide, a production decline of 1 percent from 1991 to 1992 was predicted. Long range trends indicated that large, populous developing nations like Mexico, India, and China would increase their production capabilities.

RESEARCH AND TECHNOLOGY

Bovine Growth Hormone (BST). There was consternation and divided opinion among dairy farmers and processors in the late 1980s and early 1990s on how, and whether, they would make use of bovine somatotropin (BST), even though it had been found safe for human consumption by the National Institutes of Health. This genetically engineered version of a hormone that occurs naturally in cows increases milk production by as much as 15 percent. Marketed by its producer, Monsanto, under the trade name Posilac, proponents argue that milk from BST-treated cows is indistinguishable from those produced by ordinary cows. Critics, however, note that cows that have been treated with BST (or BGH-bovine growth hormone, as its also known) are more likely to contract mastitis, an udder infection.

Approved by the U.S. Food and Drug Administration (FDA), the hormone was the subject of labeling debate as well. If milk products produced from BST-treated cows were required to be labeled as such, it would open the door to similar requirements for other undisclosed substances in foods, such as pesticides and antibiotic residues.

FURTHER READING

Baker, Stephen, and Lois Therrien. "Market Share Con Leche?" *Business Week/Reinventing America,* 1992.

Blamey, Pamela. "Rising Production Costs Continue to Milk High Dairy Prices." *Supermarket News,* 14 October 1996, p.47.

Borden, Inc. "A History of Borden, Inc." *Borden, Inc.,* June 1992.

Bradley, Jr., Robert L. "Milk." *The Encyclopedia Americana International Edition,* Danbury, CT: Grolier Incorporated, 1991.

Burros, Marion. "Eating Well." *The New York Times,* 12 May 1993.

Calbert, Harold E. "Dairy Industry." *The Encyclopedia Americana International Edition,* Danbury, CT: Grolier Incorporated, 1991.

Campbell, Alta, Gary Hoover, and Patrick J. Spain, eds. *Hoover's Handbook of American Business 1993.* TX: The Reference Press, Inc., 1992.

Considine, Douglas M., P.E., ed. *Foods and Food Production Encyclopedia,* New York: Van Nostrand Reinhold Company, 1982.

Corbett, David. "Milk Quotas - Benefit or Constraint?: Why a Common Agricultural Polich?" *British Food Journal,* 1992.

Doeff, Gail Rosenbaum. "Cultured Comeback." *Dairy Foods,* April 1993.

Dexheimer, Ellen. "Dean Dynasty." *Dairy Foods,* November 1991.

Dillon, Patricia M., Christopher Glenn, Leticia Mancini, and Charles E. Morris. "State of the Food Industry." *Food Engineering,* May, 1993.

Elmer-Dewitt, Philip. "Brave New World of Milk," *Time,* 14 February 1994, 31.

FAPRI 1996 U.S. Agricultural Outlook — U.S. Dairy Products. Available from http://ssu.agri.missouri.edu/ssu/fapri.

Feder, Barnaby J. "Beyond the Flood, Farmers Worry about Drought and an Early Frost." *The New York Times,* 31 July 1993.

Gatty, Bob. "The Regulatory Web." *Dairy Field,* April 1993.

Gerson, Vicki and Susan Ruland. "Pouring It On." *Dairy Field,* November 1992.

Getler, Warren, and Scott Kilmant. "Cheddar Lovers May Take a Slice of These Futures." *The Wall Street Journal,* 14 January 1993.

Harbrecht, Douglas, William C. Symonds, and Geri Smith. "Why NAFTA Just Might Squeak Through." *Business Week,* 30 August 1993.

Henriques, Diana B. "Evidence Mounts of Rigged Bidding in Milk Industry." *The New York Times,* 23 May 1993.

Janis, William V. "Dairy Products." *U.S. Industrial Outlook,* Washington: U.S. Department of Commerce, 1992.

Kimbrell, Wendy. "Fresh Focus." *Dairy Foods,* July 1992.

"Market Stats and Data." *Dairy Field,* December 1992.

Mid-American Dairymen, Inc. "News Update." *Mid-Am Reporter,* April 1993.

———. "Mid-Am Resolutions." *Mid-Am Reporter,* April 1993.

Milk Industry Foundation. *Milk Facts,* Washington: Milk Industry Foundation, 1992.

"Milk Sales Inch On in the Face of Misconceptions." *Dairy Field,* December 1992.

"NAFTA Negotiations Conclude; Dairy Industry Should Profit." *Dairy Field,* October 1992.

National Dairy Board. *NDB FY 93 Market Development Plan.*

Otolski, Greg. "Dairymen Hopes to Sell Flav-O-Rich to Dean Co." *The Courier Journal,* 10 June 1993.

"New Labeling Rules for Dairy Products are Planned by FDA." *The Wall Street Journal,* 20 November 1996, B11D.

Palmer, Jay. "Growing Again." *Barron's,* 6 July 1992.

Pehanich, Mike. "Quality to the Core." *Dairy Foods,* November 1991.

Rist, Marilee C. "Cheating the Children." *The American School Board Journal,* May 1993.

Rogers, Paul. "To BST or not to BST. . . ." *Dairy Foods,* July 1993.

Salvage, Bryan. "Private Label Renaissance." *Dairy Field,* August 1992.

Schmidt, Peter. "G.A.O. Says U.S. May Have Aided Milk Bid-rigging Schemes." *Education Week,* 2 December 1992.

Sole, Catherine. "The Changing Structure of Retailing: Consequent Impact on Players in the Dairy Industry." *British Food Journal,* 1992.

"Some Cultured Products Experienced New Vitality." *Dairy Field,* December 1992.

"The 1992 Supermarket Sales Manual." *Progressive Grocer,* July 1992.

U.S. Census Bureau. "1992 Census of Manufactures: Food and Kindred Products." Available from http://www.census.gov/epcd/www/mc92ht20.html.

Wagner, Jim. "Borden: One Company, One R&D." *Dairy Field,* July 1992.

—Mary Ratcliffe, updated by Marinell Jochnowitz

SIC 2032

CANNED SPECIALTIES

This category covers establishments primarily engaged in canning specialty products, such as baby foods, nationality specialty foods, and soups, except seafood.

INDUSTRY SNAPSHOT

Canned foods suffered a decline at the beginning of the 1990s as consumers turned to fresh and frozen products in a search of healthier foods. However, thanks to new nutritional labeling and canned products that featured lower salt and lighter syrups, that trend showed signs of reversing in the latter part of the decade. In 1995, 37 companies listed the manufacture of canned specialties as their primary business, generating $9.2 billion in sales. Soup led the category in sales, with condensed soup as the best-selling canned food item on the shelf. Ethnic foods were the fastest growing aspect of the industry.

BACKGROUND AND DEVELOPMENT

Cans have unquestioned advantages as food containers. Hermetically sealed, they protect their contents from contamination as well as prevent undesirable fluctuations in moisture content, the absorption of oxygen, gases, undesirable odors, and exposure to light. In addition, they allow for high-speed filling, sealing, and casing, and retailers can display them easily and attractively.

Compared to other methods of food preservation, canning is a recent development. Freezing goes back to the ice ages, and even smoking and drying were used before recorded history. Canning did not come along until the first quarter of the nineteenth century.

Nicholas Appert, a French confectioner and chef, theorized in 1795 that if food is heated in a container with no air in it, the food will keep. He worked on his theorem for 14 years, cooking foods in cork-stoppered bottles in boiling water. Sent around the world on sailing ships, Appert's preserved fruits and vegetables remained wholesome. Eventually an English merchant, Peter Durand, would develop the use of tin canisters in 1810.

The first U.S. patent for tin containers was granted in 1825. At first, cans were made by hand; even an expert in the process could turn out only five or six an hour. The term canning came to mean sterilizing food by heat and sealing it in airtight containers, either metal or glass, at an individual's home or in a processing plant.

The Civil War accelerated the need for canned foods, and by the war's end production of canned foods had increased six times, and Americans had learned to trust them. The importance of canned foods to the military was underscored again during World War II, when two-thirds of the food supplies for the U.S. and Allied forces came in cans. When the Japanese capture of Malaya cut off important sources of tin, conservation of the metal in the United States became critical. At the same time, glass containers, which had always been used for some foods, were used to replace tin cans.

Technological advances in the canning industry accelerated after the Civil War. The invention of the retort, or pressure cooker, in 1874 made it possible to control cooking temperatures for the sealed cans. The invention of the so-called sanitary can in 1900 was a cylindrical can that had an open top, enabling canners to deposit larger food pieces without the damage that occurred when filling the old hole-and-cap can. The lid for the new can could be attached mechanically, without the solder seal coming into contact with the food.

Near the end of the twentieth century, when consumers were concerned about lead in food, tin replaced lead in soldering. Other packaging developments included the flexible pouch for low-acid foods and cans made of aluminum and of steel.

CURRENT CONDITIONS

Canned Soups. Sales of canned soup totalled $2.6 billion in 1995, with condensed versions accounting for more than $1.8 billion. Sales of single-serving cans were just over $800 million. The canned soup market was huge, with sales coming from commercial outlets, such as restaurants, cafeterias, fast-food chains, and non-commercial institutions, such as schools, hospitals, and the military.

"Healthy" was the hot word in canned soups in the 1990s. Campbell Soup Company, long the industry leader, started the decade by launching 11 new soups under its Healthy Request label. By 1996, Campbell was introducing a new line with natural pharmacological qualities.

ConAgra, Inc. entered the arena with its Healthy Choice line of soups. Even with no experience in soups, ConAgra, the second-largest food company in the country, was optimistic about its low-sodium, low-fat, low-cholesterol product.

Pet, Inc., maker of Progresso soups, lowered salt in its Sodium Watch Soups, while Pritikin Systems, a division of Quaker Oats, put out a line of Healthy Soups. Pet's Progresso brand continued to capitalize on eating trends in the 1990s with six new ready-to-serve canned soups, containing pasta combined with a flavorful broth and plenty of vegetables.

Campbell Soup Company added Dinosaur Vegetable and Souper Stars soups targeted to children. In the latter part of the 1990s, Campbell's introduced ready-to-serve soup in glass jars and embarked on a $15 million advertising campaign to promote the new line. Soups with an emphasis on of fresh appearance and flavor, and healthier formulations (i.e., low-sodium, low-fat, no-MSG) were put on the market; they were more appealing than ever. Vegetable broths increased in popularity as a result of consumers' focus on healthy eating.

Baby Foods. By 1995 the baby food sales in the United States reached $1 billion. The major manufacturers spent much of the 1990s cutting prices to win back customers who had switched over to value-price store brands. Additional customers were lost when the Center for Science in the Public Interest admonished several top brands for having excessive water and fillers in their baby foods.

In response to the criticism, Gerber Products Company, the leader in the category, introduced new versions of its core foods without added starch or sugar. The company also produced a line of Tropical Baby Foods targeting the Hispanic market. Beech-Nut, a division of St. Louis, Missouri-based Ralston-Purina, introduced its chemical and pesticide-free Special Harvest line of fruits, vegetables, cereals, dinners, and juices from organic sources in 1991, but poor sales caused the company to abandon the line two years later.

Several independent companies marketing organic baby foods appeared in the 1990s—notably Earth's Best and Growing Healthy, Inc. In spite of the popularity of so-called health foods among the general public, the market for infant health foods was slow to catch on. One reason was fierce brand loyalty among consumers for Gerber and Heinz. That outlook could change, however; in March of 1996, H.J. Heinz Company acquired Earth's Best, and Gerber introduced four new vegetarian products with pasta and increased protein.

Ethnic Foods. The market for ethnic foods grew an average of 9.4 percent annually in the 1990s. As discounted and private label products, as well as new products geared toward niche markets, crowded supermarket shelves in the 1990s, many famous old brands began to disappear. La Choy and Chun King were typical of threatened brands, with competition coming from the increasing availability of fresh Chinese food.

Mexican specialties and southern soul food were the top sellers in the 1990s. Their growth spurred the growth of minority-owned businesses such as Goya Foods, Glory Foods and Garcia Canning Co. The latter, established in Columbus, Ohio, markets collared greens, kale, pinto beans, sweet potatoes, and field peas. In 1995, Glory Foods posted sales figures of $4 million. Goya's products included olives, olive oil, and a variety of Mexican products. Garcia Canning Co. of Tampa, Florida, specialized in kosher and vegetarian products such as black beans, lentils, and chili made without MSG, lard, or saturated fats.

Canned pasta faced tough competition from the dried and fresh pasta industries. The Chef Boyardee brand of canned spaghetti was the industry leader with a 59 percent share of the market by mid-decade. Acquired by International Home Foods in 1996 from long-time parent American Home Food Products, Chef Boyardee launched its ABCs and 123s pasta shapes with an aggressive media campaign. Campbell Soup's Franco-American brand was second with a 36 percent share. In the late 1990s, Franco-American promoted its Superiore variety in an effort to attract more adult consumers.

Canned Gravy. In the early 1990s, Campbell's launched a line of bottled gravies in seasoned turkey, hearty beef, mushroom and wine, and golden chicken varieties under its Pepperidge Farm label. After considering its Campbell's and Franco-American brands, the company chose Pepperidge Farm, explained Campbell Soup manager of communications Judy Dagnoli in *Supermarket News,* "because it communicates authenticity, taste and high quality. Although it's 98 percent fat free, we also wanted to communicate the fact that it tastes really, really good." Campbell Soup Company was so confident that it did not even test market the product before rolling it out nationally. Pepperidge Farm, a brand usually reserved for baked goods, also offered a line of exotic canned soups in such flavors as bacon, lettuce, and tomato.

Early in 1993, Heinz introduced a peppery, milk- and cream-based HomeStyle Gravy. The company promoted it with regional events and endorsements from local radio personalities in 37 markets, a strategy designed to "really get down to the personal level with consumers," noted Tom Becker, the associate product manager for the gravy in *Food Business.*

INDUSTRY LEADERS

Campbell Soup Company. The undisputed leader of the industry in the 1990s and indeed throughout its long history, Campbell Soup Company was selling 5 billion cans of soup a year, or close to half of all soup sales in the $2 billion market. Founded in 1869 by Joseph Campbell, a fruit merchant, and Abram Anderson, an ice box manufacturer, the company ranked tenth among U.S. and Canadian public food and beverage manufacturers in 1995, with sales of $7.2 billion.

Perhaps no event in the Campbell Soup Company's long history was more momentous than the arrival in 1897 of a 24 year-old chemist, Dr. John T. Dorrance, who signed on at a salary of $7.50. When he died 33 years later, he was sole owner of the Campbell Soup Company and amassed a personal fortune of $115 million, an amount equal to $850 million in the 1990s.

Young Dorrance was a man with an idea: condensed soup. When he joined Campbell Soup Company, soup was sold in 32-ounce cans for about 30 cents. Since soup was made mostly of water, Dorrance reasoned, the removal of water would save on shipping, cans, and weight. Dorrance introduced condensed soups in ten and a half ounce cans selling for 10 cents. To win over consumers who tended not to trust the quality of such a low-cost product, he spent heavily on advertising and promotion. In 1990 Campbell produced its 20 billionth can of condensed tomato soup.

Campbell Soup Company's marketing high points include the 1904 introduction of the enduring image of the Campbell kids, created by Philadelphia artist Grace Gebbie Drayton. In the 1930s, the slogan "M'm! M'm! Good!" entered the nation's consciousness when Campbell sponsored the "Amos 'n' Andy" and the George Burns and Gracie Allen radio shows.

Gerber Products Company. A symbol of quality and trust, the Gerber baby was adopted as an official trademark in 1931, three years after Fremont Canning Company of Fremont, Michigan, began pureeing foods for babies. Commercial artist Dorothy Hope Smith created the unfinished charcoal sketch of a neighbor's child, who was the first Gerber baby.

Sales figures in the 1990s continued to support Gerber Products' dominance in baby food; it held a 70 percent share of the market. Gerber was also second in the canned specialties industry overall with $1.1 billion in sales in 1995. Being almost synonymous with baby food in the minds of American consumers, however, had occasional drawbacks. When it was revealed that competitor Beech-Nut was marketing an apple juice product without real juice, Gerber too lost sales.

In 1995, American Home Products was the third largest manufacturer of canned specialties with $866 million. However, that changed radically the following year when American Home Products sold off its food divisions.

AMERICA AND THE WORLD

NAFTA. The controversial North American Free Trade Agreement (NAFTA), ratified in 1993, did away with tariffs and other barriers to trade between the United States, Canada, and Mexico, creating the world's largest consumer market, with a population of more than 360 million and a combined economy close to $6.5 trillion. Even before a heated debate led to U.S. ratification of NAFTA in November of 1993, the country's food companies were becoming active in Mexico and Canada. Campbell Soup Company went so far as to reorganize the company, combining its North and South American units into one division.

With its $25 million acquisition in 1991 of Alima S.A., a Polish infant food and juice company, Gerber ventured into the untapped Eastern European market. The venture presented hurdles, not all of them anticipated. Polish mothers were accustomed to making their own baby food, and distribution to small stores via treacherous roads was not as smooth as delivering to U.S. supermarkets. Production workers had to be trained in U.S. quality control standards.

When David Johnson became president and chief executive officer of Campbell Soup, his first moves were to refocus the company on the home front. By 1993 the company was ready to expand on a grander scale into the global marketplace. The purchase of Australian manufacturer Arnotts had given Campbell a Pacific base from which to penetrate China and the rest of the burgeoning Far East market. Campbell was already selling soup in China, South America, and Poland. Nevertheless, exports accounted for only 5 percent of the company's soup sales. Management proposed to capitalize on the lucrative potential in Poland, where per capita consumption of soup was 2.5 times more than in the United States.

After more than a century of doing business in the United Kingdom, Heinz was hit hard by the recession in the early 1990s. Its best known product was baked beans, followed by baby food. "In Third World countries," commented Barry Tilley, general manager of the company's Western Hemisphere Trading Division, in *Prepared Foods* magazine, "baby food would top the list.'' Heinz still held 58 percent of the British canned soup market, but that category was gradually shrinking. Only premium soups were experiencing growth, and Heinz sought to protect and revitalize its position with the introduction of a new, ''almost'' premium soup line, HJ Heinz.

Like many other companies in the years just after the breakdown of the Cold War, Heinz was looking to China and Russia to expand its global marketing activities, especially its baby food line. Tilley remarked, ''Heinz is building a platform at an early stage with baby food. Mothers today feed their babies Heinz baby food and then move onto other Heinz products. It's a natural progression.''

RESEARCH AND TECHNOLOGY

Product Development. At Campbell Soup, research and development concentrated on products. ''Fat is our No. 1 area of concern,'' noted Herb Baum, then president of Campbell North and South America, in *Prepared Foods* magazine. Also, low sodium technology that was highly proprietary to Campbell Soup Company led to more flavorful low-sodium products.

FURTHER READING

Amin, Melanie. ''Health Craze Settles on Soup.'' *Prepared Foods,* Mid-April, 1992.

''Baby Foods.'' *Supermarket Business,* September 1996.

Bivens, Terry, Carol Horner, and Jennifer Lin. ''The Dorrance Legacy of Control.'' *Philadelphia Inquirer,* 18 March 1981.

Bowens, Greg. ''Wiping the Mess Off Gerber's Chin.'' *Business Week,* 1 February 1993.

Brandweek, 27 January 1997.

''A Brief History of Canning.'' *Guidelines for Evaluation and Disposition of Damaged Canned Food Containers.* Washington: National Food Processors Association, December 1990.

''Campbell Hopes to Find Polish Market M-M-M Good.'' *Journal of Commerce,* 3 November 1992.

Campbell Soup Company Chronology. Campbell Soup Company.

''Canned Foods Get Some Soul.'' *Black Enterprise,* October 1993.

Corrections Today, July 1994.

Davis, Sue. ''You've Come a Long Way, Baby.'' *Prepared Foods,* Mid-April 1992.

''Emerging Entrepreneurs.'' *Black Enterprise,* November 1995, 100.

''The Ghost Brigade of the Future?'' *New York Times,* 7 November 1993.

''Healthy Soups Heat Up the Category.'' *Food Business,* 23 November 1992.

Heid, J. L., and Maynard A. Joslyn. *Fundamentals of Food Processing Operations: Ingredients, Methods and Packaging.* Westport, CT: The AVI Publishing Co., 1967.

''Importance of Canned Foods.'' *Guidelines for Evaluation and Disposition of Damaged Canned Food Containers.* Washington: National Food Processors Association, December 1990.

''Infoscan Report: Full Year 1992 Figures.'' *Food and Beverage Marketing,* March 1993.

Kanner, Bernice. ''Soupy Sales.'' *New York,* 1 November 1993.

Koranteng, Juliana. ''Heinz Finds New Niche.'' *Marketing,* 3 December 1992.

Kuhn, Mary Ellen. ''Heinz Goes Country for Promotion.'' *Food Business,* 6 September 1993.

''Landing the Big One.'' *Food Processing,* September 1992.

Littman, Margaret. ''Yes Sir, That's My Baby (Food).'' *Prepared Foods,* September 1992.

Meyer, Ann. ''Food Companies Make Post-NAFTA Plans.'' *Food Business,* 1 November 1993.

Pawlosky, Mark. ''Health Food for Babies is Slow to Grow.'' *The Wall Street Journal,* 14 June 1995.

Pehanich, Mike. ''Brand Power.'' *Prepared Foods,* Mid-April 1993.

Perlez, Jane. ''In Poland, Gerber Learns Lessons of Tradition.'' *New York Times,* 8 November 1993.

Pollack, Judann. ''Franco-American Ads Go Comparative.'' *Advertising Age,* 21 October 1996.

Prepared Foods, July 1996.

''Private Label's Tally.'' *Food & Beverage Marketing,* July 1993.

''Product Handbook: Soup.'' *ID* 15 September 1993.

Turcsik, Richard. ''Campbell Soup Adding Pepperidge Farm Gravy.'' *Supermarket News,* 31 August 1992.

U.S. Department of Commerce. International Trade Administration. *U.S. Industrial Outlook 1994.* Washington: GPO, 1994.

U.S. Department of Commerce. ''Preserved Fruits and Vegetables.'' *1987 Census of Manufactures.* Washington: GPO, 1990.

Wagner, Jim. ''Campbell Soup Reshuffles, Strengthens Global Commitment.'' *Food Business,* 26 July 1993.

Wellman, David. ''New Products: Pass da Soup.'' *Food & Beverage Marketing,* September 1993.

—Mary Ratcliffe, updated by Mary McNulty

CANNED FRUITS, VEGETABLES, PRESERVES, JAMS, AND JELLIES

This industry includes establishments primarily engaged in canning fruits, vegetables, and fruit and vegetable juices; and in manufacturing ketchup and similar tomato sauces, or natural and imitation preserves, jams, and jellies. Establishments primarily engaged in canning seafoods are classified in **SIC 2091: Canned and Cured Fish and Seafoods;** and those manufacturing canned specialties, such as baby foods and soups, except seafood, are classified in **SIC 2032: Canned Specialties.**

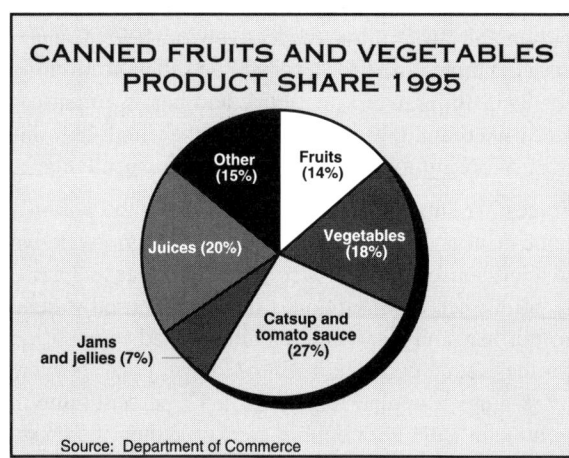

CANNED FRUITS AND VEGETABLES PRODUCT SHARE 1995

Other (15%)
Fruits (14%)
Juices (20%)
Vegetables (18%)
Jams and jellies (7%)
Catsup and tomato sauce (27%)

Source: Department of Commerce

INDUSTRY SNAPSHOT

The canned foods industry generated more than $14.5 billion in sales in 1995. Canned food processors were the primary market for many of the nation's farmers. By contracting and paying in advance for a large part of the harvest, the industry guaranteed farmers and growers a cash income, helping to absorb the risks of marketing produce on the fresh market.

More than 80 percent of all tomatoes are processed into canned products, while almost 100 percent of table beets, 40 percent of sweet corn, 40 percent of Appalachian area apples, 60 percent of pears, and over 40 percent of peaches are canned.

Payments to farmers for fruits and vegetables accounted for 30 percent of the production cost of canned goods; 25 percent went for containers and labels. Labor took another 17 percent, while approximately 3 percent of production costs were attributable to fuel and energy. Miscellaneous costs such as machinery, overheads, rental and leasing payments, and insurance came to about 20 percent.

BACKGROUND AND DEVELOPMENT

Napoleon has been credited with saying, "An army marches on its stomach." Whether he did or not, he knew the importance to a successful military campaign of adequate, wholesome food for his troops. When the governing French Directorate offered a prize in 1795 to the citizen who found a way to keep food fresh during campaigns, Napoleon supported the project. Fourteen years later, in 1810, Emperor Napoleon would award the prize to Nicholas Appert, an obscure French confectioner and chef, whose accomplishment secured his place in history.

Appert theorized that if food is heated in a container with no air in it, the food will keep. He cooked foods in cork-stoppered bottles in boiling water, perfecting his methods. Proof of his success came when Appert's preserved fruits and vegetables were sent around the world on sailing ships and remained edible. Two months after Appert published his procedures, an English merchant, Peter Durand, applied to King George III for a patent for a "Method of Preserving Animal Food, Vegetable Food, or Other Perishable Articles a Long Time from Perishing or Becoming Useless." Durand's use of tin canisters in his process revolutionized food packaging and launched the canning industry as we know it. population. Captain Edward Perry took tinned foods on his Arctic expeditions in the first quarter of the nineteenth century. Tinned pea soup and beef left behind by his party were recovered and eaten in 1911, and tins of veal and carrots from Perry's 1824 expedition were found to have been safely preserved when they were opened more than 100 years later, in 1939.

Around 1822 tinned foods came to the United States; the first American patent for tin containers was granted in 1825. By the mid-1800s, vegetable processing in steel canisters coated with tin to protect against rust and erosion was becoming widespread, and the words "tin can" and "canning" entered the language. Canning came to mean sterilizing food by heat and sealing it in airtight containers, either metal or glass. Canning activities were undertaken both in food processing plants and in households across the country.

In 1861 canners began adding calcium chloride to the water in which they cooked their closed cans. This enabled canners to use higher temperatures; production time was thus shortened and production volume increased. The improved technology came just in time for the Civil War, which spurred a demand for canned products. By the time the war was over, production of canned foods had grown six times over, and Americans had learned to trust the quality of the products contained therein.

The importance of canned foods to the military was underlined during World War II, when fully two-thirds of the food supplies for the U.S. and allied forces came in cans. When the Japanese capture of Malaya cut off important sources of tin, conservation of the metal on the home front became critical. At the same time glass containers, which had previously used for some foods, were often used in place of tin cans.

The advent of a wide variety of food package choices in the 1980s led to a decline in the sales of canned food in metal cans. Microwave-safe plastic containers, high-barrier film pouches, and form-fill and seal cups were some of the choices offered to consumers. Furthermore, some advertising claimed superior freshness for foods packed in glass jars. In 1986 the Can Manufacturers Institute, the National Food Processors Association, and the American Steel Institute formed the Canned Food Information Council (CFIC) to restore canned foods' former level of acceptance and popularity and disseminate positive information about the nutritional quality and appetizing nature of foods in metal cans.

Regulations. The U.S. Department of Agriculture (USDA) grades canned vegetables on a point system, rating them on such characteristics as texture, size, variety, maturity, taste, odor, and absence of defects. Three more standards were applied to canned foods by the Food and Drug Administration (FDA). Standard of Quality referred to the permitted number of defects or foreign materials; Standard of Fill specified the minimum content for a particular size can or jar; Standard of Identity regulated what was in the container.

Nutritional Quality of Canned Foods. Because canned foods are heat sterilized in a sealed steel can, there is no need at all for preservatives. As consumer tastes changed, the levels of salt and sugar, which had been commonly added for flavor, were reduced to satisfy consumer demand for low-salt and low-sugar products. As for their nutrition, the CFIC reported a National Food Processors Association study conducted for the USDA. Because canned foods are already cooked, the comparison was made with home-cooked fresh lima beans, peas, spinach, sweet potatoes, carrots, and squash, and with frozen vegetables that were boiled or microwaved according to package directions. Vitamin, mineral, and fiber content were found to be similar and, in some cases, the canned product exceeded even the fresh in vitamin content. Studies comparing canned fruits to fresh and frozen counterparts achieved similar results. Canning actually protects foods from oxygen that can destroy vitamins A, B, C, D, and carotene. The process can also eliminate up to 99 percent of pesticide residues and destroy the bacteria that leads to spoilage.

Vegetables and Fruits. Most produce destined for canning goes directly from the growing fields to a nearby processing plant. Production methods allow vegetables to be canned within hours of harvest. It is in the plant that vegetables and fruit are chopped, sliced, peeled, or otherwise prepared for packing in cans. Blanching helps to preserve texture and flavor. Once they are in vacuum-packed cans and sealed, they are sent into the retort, or cooker, to be heat-processed. Cooling is the final step before the cans are labeled and prepared for distribution.

Sales of canned vegetables and fruits were $3.6 billion and $1.9 billion, respectively, in 1995. Canned corn continued to be the number one seller, accounting for $635 million in sales. Pork and beans, tomatoes, and waxed and green beans were next with $484 million, $466 million, and $452 million, respectively.

Juices. Traditionally children have been the nation's juice drinkers. The 1990s, however, brought a decline in adult consumption of alcoholic beverages and a rise in adult juice consumption. Makers of bottled waters, soft drinks, and juices entered into spirited competition for these adult consumers. Blended fruit juices became increasingly popular, registering a 9.7 percent jump in volume in 1991 after double-digit growth in the previous two years. By 1995, sales of canned and bottled juices totaled $2.7 billion. An additional $2 billion was spent on blended fruit drinks.

Apple cider and juice accounted for $1.1 billion of fruit juice sales, followed by cranberry juice at $438 million, and grape juice at $253 million. Although orange juice remained the number one choice of restaurant patrons, it ranked sixth in total retail sales at $82 million.

Some juice manufacturers came under fire in the late 1980s and early 1990s for misleading product labeling. A $2 million fine was levied by the federal government in 1987 on Beech-Nut Nutrition Corporation for selling a mix of sweetened water and chemicals as ''apple juice.'' Investigators estimated that as much as 10 percent of juice sold, most of it orange juice, was adulterated, usually with sugar or watery orange byproducts. Manufacturers cited in cases from 1987-1993 were mostly major wholesalers to important producers and grocery chains, not companies familiar to the public.

Adulteration cases were pursued haphazardly, in part because labeling claims were misleading, they posed no threat to public safety. Furthermore, the FDA was hindered by its lack of the statutory powers to pursue the cases more aggressively. In 1993 the *New York Times* reported that some manufacturers were using preservatives not approved as safe for use in juice. The former general counsel for the Florida Department of Citrus, said in the *Times* that diluted juice had been around for a long time. Common dilutants were cheap but generally harmless ingredients such as beet sugar and the pulp wash from re-squeezing oranges that had been soaked in water. Such juice spoiled more readily, and the industry looked for less detectable preservatives, some of which had been banned by the Food and Drug Administration in the belief that they were potentially hazardous.

Jams, Jellies, and Preserves. This category is comprised of several distinct products. Jellies, a mixture of fruit juice, sugar, and pectin, are clear and bright with a tender but firm texture. Jams and preserves are thicker, made by cooking fruit, pectin, and sugar until the texture is almost a puree. In preserves, the fruit chunks are larger. Conserves, similar to jam, mix more than one kind of fruit and perhaps nuts. Marmalade contains citrus fruit rind, most often Seville oranges. Fruit butter is made by stewing fruit, sugar, and spices to a thick, smooth, spreadable consistency. Under federal guidelines, in order for a product to be called a jam or jelly it had to contain 55 percent sugar and be so labeled. Reduced-sugar products that catered to a health-conscious consumer were sweetened with fruit juice and had to be called something other than ''jam'' or ''jelly.''

Despite a more weight-conscious population in the late 1980s and 1990s, the category experienced some growth during the period, albeit slow. Sales reached $1.2 billion in 1995, a decrease of 2 percent from 1994. Citrus marmalades registered the largest percent increase. outlets, with about 13 percent sold for industrial use and 9 percent to the foodservice market. Industrial uses included baked goods, where the products were used as fillings for coffee cakes and donuts, and as flavor components for yogurt.

According to *Prepared Foods,* Ohio-based jam and jelly maker J.M. Smucker was third in the magazine's list of top sales gainers from 1994 to 1995 with a 29 percent gain. Sales for that year were $628 million.

Spaghetti Sauces. Americans spent more than $2 billion on pasta products in 1995, and sales of spaghetti sauces kept pace at $2 billion as well. Leaders in the field were Van den Bergh Food Co.'s Ragu, Campbell Soup Co.'s Prego, and ConAgra's Hunt's label. These ranged from traditional, meat- and mushroom-flavored sauces to a no-fat, no-cholesterol line of ''light''

sauces. In the latter part of the 1990s, Van Den Bergh and Campbell's were embroiled in a three-year legal battle over Campbell's advertisement that claimed its Prego sauce was thicker than Van Den Bergh's Prego Old World Style. In the fall of 1996, a judge ruled in Campbell's favor. At the decade's end, Van Den Bergh, now merged with the Thomas J. Lipton Company to become the Lipton Company (a wholly owned subsidiary of Unilever) planned new packaging, new flavors and a new aggressive advertising campaign.

Salsa. Salsa includes an array of sauces that includes picante, enchilada, taco, and other chili-based sauces. In 1991, when it outsold ketchup in retail stores by $40 million, David A. Weiss, President of the market research company Packaged Facts Inc., commented in *Supermarket Business* that the taste for salsa has become as mainstream as apple pie. The first seven months of that year saw the introduction of 147 new salsa products. Retail sales in 1995 for salsa and other Mexican sauces were $943 million, outselling ketchup by $300 million.

San Antonio-based Pace Foods, which introduced American consumers to salsa in 1947, was acquired by the Campbell Soup Co. in 1995. Hormel, Nabisco, Frito-Lay, and PET Inc. all introduced Mexican-style products. H.J. Heinz Co., long dominant in the ketchup category, was so confident of its salsa style ketchup that it introduced the product nationally in 1993 without any test marketing. At Campbell Soup Co., salsa first appeared as V8 Picanta Vegetable Juice, a line extension of its V8 vegetable juice.

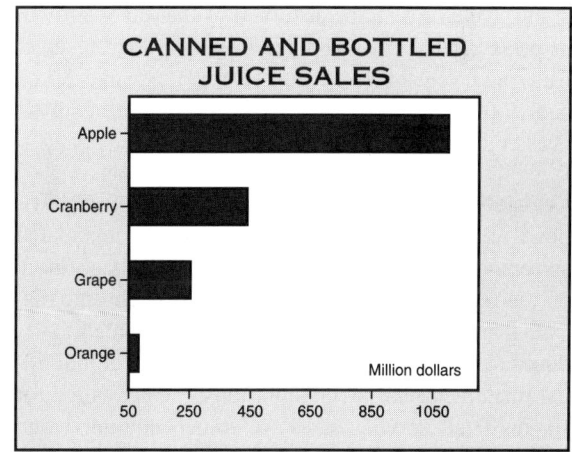

CANNED AND BOTTLED JUICE SALES

CURRENT CONDITIONS

Cost-conscious consumers and strong competition took a toll in the food industry overall in the 1990s. The canning industry faced continued competition from the fresh and frozen food industries. Some canners focused on the so-called value-added segment, such as asparagus, specialty corn, glass jar mushrooms, and tomatoes, to boost sales. Recognizing and serving regional preferences, as well as larger-sized packaging were two other marketing tactics used by the canning industry.

Widespread flooding in the prime midwest growing region in the early 1990s, coupled with crop damage from cool, wet weather, and planned-for reductions in planted acreage reduced the harvest by as much as 20 percent compared to 1992. Prices of canned tomato paste, typically an industry indicator, jumped 33 percent from $.33 per pound to $.40 per pound. By mid-decade, however, tomato crops were once again abundant.

Other industry concerns include the proliferation of warehouse club stores, which have induced retailers to look for ways to compete by forcing stronger competition among top brands; premiums on shelf space in retail outlets, combined with a stronger emphasis among retailers on their own private label products; nervous investors; and new, costly labeling laws.

Co-branding was a popular marketing venture in the late 1990s. H.J. Heinz teamed with Louisiana-based McIlhenny Company's Tabasco sauce to produce a spicy ketchup. Campbell's Pace salsa joined with Kraft Foods for a ready-to-eat salsa and cheese dip.

Private Labels. Leading manufacturers of name brands have cause to be disturbed by the steady growth in private label (store brand) products. Private label fruits and vegetables accounted for a sizeable 30.83 and 27.02 percent dollar share, respectively, of supermarket sales in the canned food category.

Legislation. In the first half of the 1990s, the Nutritional Labeling Education Act (NLEA) mandated sweeping changes in labeling, with the emphasis more on the relationship between nutrition and chronic disease than on vitamin/mineral content. Intended to reduce consumer confusion and end the chaos of individual manufacturers' label definitions, the act called for standardized serving sizes (reference amounts) and established rules for health claims and relating them to U.S. Recommended Daily Intakes (RDIs) and U.S. Recommended Daily Allowances (RDAs) for vitamin/mineral percentages. Because this legislation called for dramatic changes in the packaging for canned foods, some manufacturers contend that meeting the requirements of the NLEA legislation will substantially increase their production costs.

INDUSTRY LEADERS

Among the leading fruit and vegetable canners are H.J. Heinz Co., Del Monte Corporation, and Ocean Spray Cranberries, Inc.

At the $8 billion H.J. Heinz Company, brand equity was a 1990s priority. Heinz ketchup managed to hold onto its 54-percent market share despite stiff competition from salsa. A new ketchup label was introduced in 1996, replacing the previous design, which had graced bottles for 56 years. The new label, projecting a more whimsical image, was targeted to appeal to children, ketchup's primary market.

Following the Kohlberg Kravis Roberts & Co. purchase of Del Monte in a leveraged buyout from RJR Nabisco, the company increased its leading share of the canned fruit and vegetable market. Del Monte's 1995 food and beverage sales were reported at $1.5 billion. That same year, Del Monte introduced the D'Italia pasta sauce line. In early 1997, the Texas Pacific Group announced plans to acquire Del Monte.

Massachusetts-based Ocean Spray Cranberries Inc. remained the leading producer of canned and bottled juices in North America. A cooperative of 900 cranberry and citrus growers in the United States and Canada, Ocean Spray posted sales of $1.3 billion in 1995.

AMERICA AND THE WORLD

The 1993 North American Free Trade Agreement (NAFTA) did away with trade barriers between the United States, Canada, and Mexico for 15 years and created the world's largest consumer market, with a population of more than 360 million people and a combined economy close to $6.5 trillion in size. Even before NAFTA's passage, canned food companies were expanding operations into Canada and Mexico.

The United States exported $25 billion worth of processed food in 1994. Canned fruits and vegetables were among the top five industries in foreign trade. Canada and Japan continued to be the top export markets, followed by Mexico, the United Kingdom, and Germany.

According to *Forbes'* 1997 Annual Report on American Industry, food processors must increase their focus on foreign markets if they are to continue to succeed. Developing nations, with their growing middle classes, are a prime market for packaged foods.

RESEARCH AND TECHNOLOGY

The 1990s saw the installation of new retort systems at a number of plants. Some automated systems were flexible enough to process food in glass jars, flexible pouches, plastic tubs, or irregular shapes. In batch retorting, a single operator can handle a system that automatically stacks cans in trays, conveys them into the retort, removes them after sterilization and cooling, and carries them back to a destacker.

Packaging Advances. The 1990s saw the development of new, upscale cans to rival glass containers in style and sophistication. Not unlike the innovative changes in plastic packaging that had marked the 1980s, the new cans were designed to increase the containers' appeal and convenience to consumers.

Campbell launched Cianto pasta sauce in the United Kingdom in a Quantum can. Produced by the Foodcan Group of CarnaudMetalbox (CMB), the distinctive, vertically fluted can with labeling graphics lithographed directly onto the metal won a 1992 Worldstar Award from the World Packaging Organization. CMB has also licensed the technology for its Ferrolite can to North American can makers. The Ferruled can, a plastic-laminated, microwaveable, recyclable, fully retortable steel can, was another Worldstar winner for CMB.

FURTHER READING

"49th Annual Consumer Expenditures Study." *Supermarket News,* September 1996.

"A Brief History of Canning." *Guidelines for Evaluation and Disposition of Damaged Canned Food Containers.* Washington: National Food Processors Association, December 1990.

Buss, Dale D. "Canners Set to Harvest Higher Profits." *Food Business,* 6 September 1993.

"Canned Goods." *Supermarket Business,* September 1996.

"Canned Vegetables." *Industrial Distribution* 15 May 1991.

"Del Monte Cooking up Pasta Sauce." *Advertising Age,* March 1996.

"Del Monte to Be Purchased by Texas Pacific Group." *The New York Times,* 1 March 1997.

Dyslin, John. "Globe Trotting." *Prepared Foods,* April 1993.

———. "The Leading 150." *Prepared Foods,* July 1993.

"Annual Report on American Industry" *Forbes,* 13 January 1997.

Friedman, Marty. "New Products Fuel Salsa's Fire." *Prepared Foods,* October 1993.

———. "New Sauces Heed Pastamania's Call." *Prepared Foods,* April 1993.

Furman, Phyllis. "Tin Tizzy: Public Image of Canned Food and Alternatives."

"Gourmet Products and New Packaging Are Hot Topics in Jams and Jellies." *Fancy Food,* June 1991.

Henriques, Diana B. "10% of Fruit Juice Sold in U.S. Is Not All Juice, Regulators Say." *New York Times,* 31 October 1993.

Larson, Melissa. "New Ideas Come in Cans." *Packaging,* April 1993.

Littman, Margaret. "And the Brand Played On." *Prepared Foods,* August 1992.

McDermott, Michael J. "Juicing Up Adults." *Food & Beverage Marketing,* November 1992.

Meyer, Ann. "Food Companies Make Post-NAFTA Plans." *Food Business,* 1 November 1993.

Miller, Cyndee. "Moves by P&G, Heinz Rekindle Fears That Brands Are in Danger." *Marketing News,* 8 June 1992.

Morris, Charles E. "Shelf-Stable Convenience." *Food Engineering,* April 1993.

"New Labels for Ketchup's Real Fans." *The New York Times,* 12 June 1996.

O'Neil, Molly. "New Mainstream: Hot Dogs, Apple Pie and Salsa." *Supermarket Business,* May 1992.

Pollack, Judann. "Prego Prevails in Battle over Comparative Ad." *Advertising Age,* 16 September 1996.

"Private Label's Tally." *Food & Beverage Marketing,* July 1993.

"Product Handbook: Canned Vegetables." *ID,* 15 September 1993.

Rice, Judy. "Retortable Plastic Packaging Evolving." *Food Processing,* January 1993.

Sellers, Patricia. "H. J. Heinz: Has Cost Cutting Gone Too Far?" *Fortune,* 2 November 1992.

Swientek, Robert J. "Retorting Heats Up!" *Food Processing,* January 1993.

"Talk Around Town." *San Antonio Business Journal,* 23 June 1995.

"Unilever's New Lipton Recasts, Repackages Ragu." *Brandweek,* 13 January 1997.

—Mary Ratcliff, updated by Mary McNulty

SIC 2034

DRIED AND DEHYDRATED FRUITS, VEGETABLES, AND SOUP MIXES

This category covers establishments primarily engaged in sun drying or artificially dehydrating fruits and vegetables, or in manufacturing packaged soup mixes from dehydrated ingredients. Establishments primarily engaged in the grading and marketing of farm dried fruits, such as prunes and raisins, are classified in **SIC 5149: Groceries and Related Products, Not Elsewhere Classified.**

Dried and dehydrated fruits, vegetables, and soups generated $3 billion in 1995. Some 160 establishments employing 13,000 workers made up this industry. California was the site of 90 percent of U.S. dried fruit production, although makers of dried potato products were mostly based in Idaho. Industry leaders included Sun-Diamond Growers of California, Basic American, Inc., and Dole Dried Fruit and Nut Co., with combined sales of $1.6 billion.

Sun drying, one of the oldest known methods of fruit preservation, originated thousands of years ago. Dehydration preserved foods by removing the moisture that microorganisms needed to thrive. Although the technique remained in use in the 1990s, mechanical drying methods increased beginning in the late nineteenth century. Besides preservation, reduction in bulk and weight were considerations in the drying of fruits and vegetables.

As consumer interest in healthy eating intensified continued to rise during the 1990s, processors of dates, raisins, dried apricots, apples, cherries, and other fruits promoted their products as nutritious, year-round snacks as well as ingredients for home baking and cooking. Processors used dried fruits in a wide variety of food products. Dates—popular with retail shoppers—lent texture, flavor, and sweetness to processed cereals, baked goods, snack bars and confections, and frozen desserts. Along with dates, raisins enjoyed a variety of uses in food processing. Products introduced in the 1990s included donuts with raisins, fat-free raisin cookies and fruit bars, and even raisin salami.

In exports, shipments of dried and tropical fruits increased during the 1990s—to 627 million by 1995—partly as a result of more favorable climate following the finalization of the General Agreement on Tariffs and Trade (GATT) among the international community. American-produced dried fruits found favorable markets in the United Kingdom, Germany, the Netherlands, and Japan.

The industry also witnessed the introduction of sophisticated processing technology, such as quality-monitoring computer programs and lasers. New dehydration processes, such as a three-stage vegetable dehydrator employed by Breedlove Dehydration Foods of Lubbock, Texas, were used to save surplus food for later distribution to a national network of food banks to feed the homeless.

In 1996 industry giant performer Sun-Diamond was rocked by scandal when it was revealed that a lobbyist for the company—actually an organization of cooperative growers—had given improper gifts to Secretary of Agriculture Mike Espy. Gilroy Foods, the company that held the fifth spot in the industry according to 1994 figures, was sold by its parent company, McCormick & Co., to ConAgra.

FURTHER READING

Darnay, Arsen J., ed. *Manufacturing USA.* 5th ed. Detroit: Gale Research, 1996.

U.S. Bureau of the Census. *1995 Annual Survey of Manufactures.* Washington: GPO, 1997.

—Mary Ratcliffe, updated by Carol Brennan

SIC 2035

PICKLED FRUITS AND VEGETABLES, VEGETABLE SAUCES AND SEASONINGS, AND SALAD DRESSINGS

This category covers establishments primarily engaged in pickling and brining fruits and vegetables, and in manufacturing salad dressings, vegetable relishes, sauces, and seasonings. Establishments primarily engaged in manufacturing catsup and similar tomato sauces are classified in **SIC 2033: Canned Fruits, Vegetables, Preserves, Jams, and Jellies,** and those packing purchased pickles and olives are classified in wholesale or retail trade. Establishments primarily engaged in manufacturing dry salad dressing and dry sauce mixes are classified in **SIC 2099: Food Preparations, Not Elsewhere Classified.**

Diversified multi billion dollar companies such as H.J. Heinz Company, Kraft General Foods, Inc., and Best Foods Division of CPC International, Inc. were the major producers of pickles, sauces and seasonings, and salad dressings in the 1980s and 1990s. However small, regional independents accounted for many familiar products.

The industry reflected the trends that were influencing other food processors; consumers were concerned with healthier eating and developed the taste for exotic flavors and ethnic cuisines. Retail sales of sauces and dressings exceeded $3 billion in 1995. Pourable salad dressings outstripped all other products in the category with $1.3 billion, closely followed by mayonnaise and other sandwich spreads, and gravy and sauce mixes. Pickles accounted for $1 billion of the $1.5 billion relish market at mid-decade. According to the Calorie Control Council, low-fat salad dressings, sauces, and mayonnaise were one of the top choices of adults who reported using so-called lite products. The proliferation of pre-made salad kits were also seen as a reason for the boost in salad dressing sales.

In 1950, the Food and Drug Administration established standards of identity for mayonnaise, salad dressing, and French dressing, which regulated their ingredients and manufacture. Other dressings, though not regulated, had predictable flavors and characteristics. Italian, ranch, thousand island, French, and bleu cheese were America's favorite salad dressings in the 1990s according to an Association for Dressings and Sauces (ADS) survey reported in *Institutional Distribution* magazine. Steady growth in the sector was in line with the findings of the same ADS survey that three out of four people ate a tossed salad every other day.

Low-fat, low-calorie dressings were introduced to meet consumers' dietary concerns, but achieving the flavor and texture to which people were accustomed was a challenge. "We were never able to reduce fat and keep the taste," said Jessie Ristic, spokesperson for Best Foods, maker of the top ranking Hellmann's mayonnaise line. But as suppliers "grew more sophisticated with fat replacers and low-fat flavor systems . . . we were finally able to come out with a reduced-fat mayonnaise that tasted good." Indeed, by the end of the twentieth century the food additives industry was growing faster than the food industry as consumers demanded improved flavor, texture, color, and nutritional benefits. Offered in a variety of flavors, these sauces were added to meat—notably chicken—to create quick, more enticing meals. Such sauces were part of the "fastest-growing category in supermarkets" during the third quarter of 1992, according to Michael J. McDermott in *Food & Beverage Marketing.*

Pickle Packers International, Inc., reported that consumption of pickles had more than doubled from the mid-1940s to the early 1990s to an estimated nine pounds per person annually. According to the May 1996 issue of *Food Review,* this figure decreased markedly by mid-decade to 4.7 pounds. The industry association reported 50 known processors in the United States, but this figure did not include the many regional family producers. Heinz, Clausson, and Vlasic were the only national brands.

FURTHER READING

Agricultural Research, October 1994.

Boehning, Julie C. "Dressing Up." *Supermarket News,* 3 June 1996.

"Food Producers Appeal to Fat-Free Crowd." *Marketing News,* 14 August 1995.

Hui, Y. H., ed. *Encyclopedia of Food Science and Technology,* 4 vols. New York: John Wiley & Sons Inc., 1992.

"Ingredients." *Food & Beverage Marketing,* March 1993.

Lingle, Rick. "Four Packages You Wish You Had Introduced." *Prepared Foods,* April 1992.

McDermott, Michael J. "Battle Simmering in Sauces." *Food & Beverage Marketing,* February 1993.

"Mustard." *Prepared Foods,* October 1986.

"The 1992 Supermarket Sales Manual." *Progressive Grocer,* July 1992.

Supermarket News, September 1996.

Tanyeri, Dana. "Salad Dressings." *Institutional Distribution,* December 1991.

"U.S. Food Consumption." *Food Review,* May 1996.

Ward's Business Directory of U.S. Private and Public Companies, Vol. 5, Detroit: Gale Research, 1996.

—Mary Ratcliffe, updated by Mary McNutty

SIC 2037

FROZEN FRUITS, FRUIT JUICES, VEGETABLES

This classification covers establishments primarily engaged in freezing fruits, fruit juices, and vegetables. These establishments also produce important by-products such as fresh or dried citrus pulp.

INDUSTRY SNAPSHOT

Frozen foods became available commercially beginning in 1930, making this category a comparative newcomer to the U.S. food industry. By 1995, the manufacture of frozen food constituted a $50 billion business. Frozen fruits, fruit juices, and vegetables accounted for $12 billion of that total.

Consumers receive frozen fruits, fruit juices, and vegetables through two main sales outlets: grocery stores and foodservice. Grocery stores, include supermarkets, other retail stores, and the emerging warehouse clubs; foodservice is a highly fragmented market comprised of restaurants, lodging and recreation outlets, separate eating and drinking establishments, health care institutions, colleges and universities, primary and secondary schools, airlines, business and industry, the military, and more. The division of sales between retail and foodservice had once weighed in favor of retail, but that changed in the 1990s. Variation among the product groups was too great for easy generalization, but *Quick Frozen Foods International* indicated the split was approximately 45 percent retail to 55 percent institutional. For frozen fruits and vegetables the difference was more pronounced: 38 percent retail and 62 percent institutional.

The frozen fruits, fruit juices, and vegetables industry has been greatly influenced by changes in the needs of the American consumer. Single parent families, two-income families, and growing numbers of women in the work force fueled the demand for convenience foods in convenient packaging. To compete in this changing marketplace, processors of commodity frozen vegetables extended their product lines with value-added items such as prepared meals, sauced vegetables, frozen entrees, pasta, and vegetable mixes; although changing demographics affected more than new product introductions. Single-serving frozen vegetables were an example of packaging that targeted changing demographic patterns, but they sold well only in stores with a high proportion of singles, or younger and elderly couples for customers.

ORGANIZATION AND STRUCTURE

The major producers of frozen fruits, fruit juices, and vegetables were subsidiaries or divisions of diversified, multinational, multibillion dollar conglomerates. Ore-Ida, a leading producer of frozen potato products in the 1990s, was, for most of the decade, a subsidiary of H. J. Heinz. Minute-Maid, the top frozen orange juice concentrate, was produced by a division of Coca-Cola. Birds Eye, named for Clarence Birdseye, the ''father'' of the frozen food industry in the United States, was a Kraft General Foods (KGF) brand; KGF belonged to the Philip Morris family of companies. Green Giant was a subsidiary of Pillsbury Co. J. R. Simplot and its Food Group division were the lone privately held companies among the major ones. Alongside these industry giants, smaller newcomers and regional processors carved out significant markets for themselves. McCain Foods USA, for example, laid claim to being the fastest growing frozen food company in the United States, increasing its business fivefold in six years and predicting sales of $1 billion by 1997. McCain made a significant step in that direction when it purchased Ore-Ida from Heinz in 1997.

David McDonald, president and chief executive officer of Curtice Burns Foods, said in *Refrigerated & Frozen Foods,* ''At $1 billion in sales, I rate [us] a small company. Our main competitors average anywhere from $10 to $15 billion.'' He continued, ''The frozen vegetable market is really in dramatic transition. In the last couple of years, the oversupply situation has been fueled by the overcapacity in the industry . . . It's harder to make money in this business.'' Nevertheless, Curtice Burns saw growth potential in foodservice and private label, and targeted its efforts there.

BACKGROUND AND DEVELOPMENT

History. Humans have been using cold to preserve food quality for as long as they have been eating. Over 100,000 years ago, food was stored in caves where the temperatures were naturally low. Ice and snow were used to preserve food when they were available. It was not until the twentieth century, however, that scientific research into freezing foods really began. The ability to deliver frozen food to consumers is generally dated from October 14, 1924, when Clarence Birdseye received a patent for his revolutionary new apparatus called a plate freezer. A few more years passed before M.A. Joslyn and W.V. Cruess reported the necessity of blanching vegetables prior to freezing.

The industry has advanced steadily ever since. In 1930, June peas and spinach were the first commercially available frozen vegetables, making their debut in Massachusetts supermarkets. A shortage of tin for cans during World War II spurred the growth of frozen foods. Mechanically refrigerated railroad cars came into use in 1949, and the early 1960s saw the development of individually quick frozen (IQF) foods.

All food preservation systems are designed to prevent deterioration and spoilage during storage. Lowering food temperature decreases or inhibits the speed of chemical and physical reactions that result in spoilage. Microorganisms are a factor in the deterioration of food quality, but microbiologic growth stops when food temperature is reduced to less than -10 C. Foods frozen at temperatures as low as -40 C were not unusual towards the end of the 20th century.

Manufacturing. Processors used several methods of freezing foods. High quality could be achieved with individual quick freezing. Its advantages were rapid freezing rates, and the fact that, because food pieces did not cohere into a solid block, individual portions could be stored in large containers. This made it particularly suitable for foodservice. In blast freezing, fans passed cold air over the food. Food could also be frozen between plates containing freezing coils, or by immersion into freezing liquid such as salt solutions, liquid nitrogen and liquid carbon dioxide.

After a period of steady growth since 1986, the frozen food market dropped in the recessionary 1990s. Even though poundage production was up slightly, production value was down for the first time since

1947, as a surplus of vegetables had lowered prices. Sales in the frozen fruit and juice concentrate sectors were also down.

CURRENT CONDITIONS

Increased supply tied to lower prices was particularly dramatic in concentrated juices. Retail sales of frozen juice concentrates fell to $1 billion in 1995, a 7.2 percent decrease from the year before. All varieties except grape juice suffered losses. These figures did not include sales in warehouse clubs, which processors were anticipating to give a boost to sales of bulk packaged frozen fruits and vegetables. Club stores, characterized by membership fees, low prices, cash-only policies and limited selection, were a popular new marketing channel in the 1990s. An alternative to traditional retail and foodservice distribution channels, club stores were becoming more open to carrying regional brands and control label and private label products.

Some analysts predicted improving sales opportunities based on government recommendations of fruit and vegetable consumption and the Nutritional Labeling Education Act (NLEA). The NLEA mandated sweeping changes in labeling, with the emphasis more on the relationship between nutrition and chronic disease than on vitamin/mineral content. The redesigned labels were meant to reduce consumer confusion and end the chaos of individual rules for health claims, defining comparative nutritional claims and relating them to U.S. Recommended Daily Intakes (RDIs) and U.S. Recommended Daily Allowances (RDAs) for vitamin/mineral percentages.

Vegetables. The most popular frozen vegetable in both supermarket and foodservice markets has long been the potato. The average American consumed more than 26 pounds of frozen potatoes annually by 1995. According to Gallup Organization data published in November 1991 and reported in *Institutional Distribution,* potatoes were the favorite side dish for 40 percent of Americans. French fries were second in popularity only to hamburgers as a restaurant choice. By the mid-1990s, the consumption of frozen french fries surpassed that of fresh potatoes, and 89 percent of those french fries were sold by food-service outlets.

Retail sales statistics compiled by *Supermarket News* for 1995 listed vegetable mixes, green peas, corn, green beans, broccoli, and spinach as the top frozen vegetable categories after potatoes. Since most frozen vegetables were individually quick frozen within hours of harvest, they offered home cooks and foodservice operations the advantages of labor-saving convenience plus nutrient value, no waste, speed and ease of preparation, and year-round availability. Frozen vegetables retail sales in 1995 were $2.6 billion. Vegetables made up the bulk of the $3.9 billion in sales of frozen vegetables and fruits to the foodservice industry.

Fruits. The U.S. Department of Agriculture (USDA) provides voluntary grade standards for fruits and vegetables to help processors achieve uniform product quality. The best quality fruit is usually either sold as fresh produce or individually quick frozen, which results in a product close to fresh fruit. In the latter process, no sugar is added, and the speed of freezing minimizes ice crystal damage. Factors affecting fruit quality are color, size, blemishes, flavor, firmness, and unwanted portions such as skin, pits, or leaves. In bulk freezing, the fruit is filled into containers and then frozen. Such fruit can be frozen alone or with sugar or syrups added; sometimes fruit is frozen in its own juice.

Retail frozen fruit sales in 1995 were $181 million, with strawberries the undisputed favorite, accounting for $63 million in retail sales alone. However, a 1996 outbreak of hepatitis A traced to frozen strawberries grown in Mexico and processed in California put a damper on sales that year. Raspberries and blueberries were second and third with 1995 retail sales of $25 million and $21 million, respectively.

Fruit Juices. Citrus juices are regulated at the federal level by the Federal Food, Drug and Cosmetic Act, which established Standards of Identity under a grading system that considered flavor, color, absence of defects, and Brix, a designation which refers to the percent of solids, mostly dissolved sugar, in fruit juices and other fruit products having a high moisture content. The Florida Department of Citrus also imposes quality standards. The primary standard was also the Brix; it guaranteed that the strength of the Florida concentrates would be consistent regardless of the packer and flavor variations. Frozen juice concentrate sales in 1995 were $2.2 billion; retail at $1.4 billion surpassed foodservice sales of $850 million.

INDUSTRY LEADERS

Simplot Food Group set its sights in the early 1990s on a 50 percent sales increase—to $1.5 billion by the decade's end—a goal the company reached by February of 1996. The company accomplished this goal by adding other vegetables, as well as meat and dairy products, to its potato line. Best known as a major supplier of French fries to the McDonald's restaurant chain, Simplot also processed 15 varieties of fruits and vegetables at plants in California, Washington, Iowa, and Mexico, with more than half of them destined for foodservice use. The company also offered preblended, preportioned vegetables as well as commodity bins of frozen vegetables to processors of prepared dinners and entrees. Simplot took the private label route into supermarkets, shipping frozen bulk product to facilities that would repack them for retail customers under their own brand names.

Industry leaders were not recession-proof in the 1990s. The Heinz subsidiary Ore-Ida, with a 54 percent share of retail frozen potato sales, experienced volume slippage and sought to come back with the introduction of Fast Fries, a shoestring fry designed to compete with fast-food fries in flavor and crisp texture. Ore-Ida executive Bob Ginkel told *Food Business,* ''We've seen for several years that the category has been, if not flat, then just barely growing.'' Adding that there were 3.5 billion pounds of fast food restaurant fries being sold, Ginkel continued, ''When you consider that Ore-Ida retail sales are about equal to that, I think you start to see the huge category-building potential [we can achieve]. . . .'' The Boise, Idaho, processor reported $900 million in sales in 1992, and dominated supermarket freezer cases with 35 potato items. But, by 1997, Heinz was throwing in the towel, selling Ore-Ida.

In the 1990s, Green Giant USA took first place in supermarket freezer units from longtime frozen vegetable leader, Birds Eye. Green Giant president Gary Klingl, quoted in *Food Business,* attributed the company's success to selling frozen vegetables in plastic bags, which accounted for 50 percent of the frozen vegetable market. Green Giant's sales of bagged vegetables were 7 million cases a year, up from 1 million cases ten years earlier.

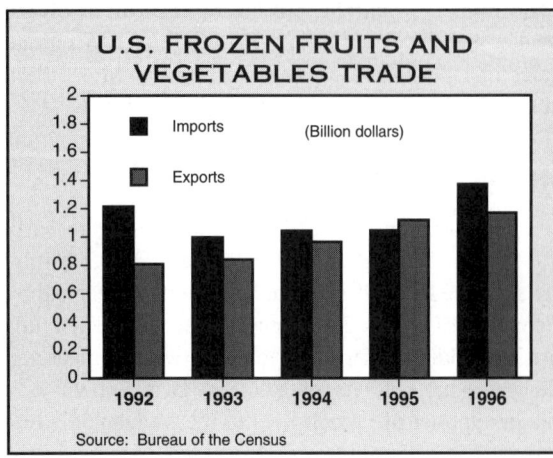

U.S. FROZEN FRUITS AND VEGETABLES TRADE

(Billion dollars)
■ Imports
■ Exports

Source: Bureau of the Census

AMERICA AND THE WORLD

In the 1990s, manufacturers of frozen fruits, fruit juices, and vegetables looked overseas for opportunities to expand. As the U.S. market for orange juice matured in the 1990s, the three leading producers, Minute Maid, Citrus Hill, and Tropicana, were looking to Europe and Japan for increased sales.

Stiff competition from European-based giants like Unilever and Nestle SA encouraged U.S. producers to explore the Americas for new markets and investment opportunities. Green Giant moved the broccoli and cauliflower growing and cutting operations from its Watsonville, California, plant to Irapuato, Mexico, where labor was cheaper. The Institute for Agriculture and Trade Policy, a Minneapolis-based labor-oriented research group, predicted that economic pressure would induce Green Giant to move more operations to Mexico. Simplot also looked to Irapuato, acquiring an equity interest in a leading Mexican processor which exported 100 percent of its frozen vegetables, most of them to the United States. In Canada, Simplot jointly owned a 210-million pound potato facility with Nestle Foodservice of Canada and predicted that it could import up to 150 million pounds of potatoes from Canada once the North American Free Trade Agreement (NAFTA) went into effect in 1997.

RESEARCH AND TECHNOLOGY

In 1989, the Chicago-based Institute of Food Technologists (IFT) named the ten most significant food science innovations to have taken place during its 50-year history. Third on their list was the development of frozen concentrated citrus juices at the U.S. Department of Agriculture research laboratories in the mid-1940s. The addition of approximately 7 percent fresh juice to the concentrate was the key to the product's success. Since that time, processors have further refined the process with the addition of essential oils and natural flavors to the concentrate before it is packaged and frozen. Also making IFT's top ten list was the development of new freezing methods that enabled the prediction of optimal freezing and storage conditions, an important advance because nutrient loss is negligible when foods are properly frozen and stored.

Another breakthrough in the twentieth century was the development of plastic packaging. Among plastic's advantages: it is heat sealable, microwavable, resistant to corrosion, and easily made. More than 80 percent of American households had microwave ovens by the early 1990s, and makers of frozen vegetables and fruits used dual-purpose plastics in packaging that enabled consumers to use either traditional top-of-the-stove cooking methods or the popular microwave ovens.

Agriculturalists in the field of plant breeding were focusing on improving the taste and nutritional value of vegetables used in frozen products, particularly onions, carrots, cucumbers, and garlic.

FURTHER READING

Agricultural Research, October 1994.

American Frozen Food Institute. Available from http://www.affi.com/facts/decafood.htm.

"Annual Consumer Expenditures Study." *Supermarket News,* September 1996.

Arble, Meade. "Big-3 Orange Juice Firms Eyeing Europe for Growth." *Supermarket News,* 1 June 1992.

Best, Daniel and Patricia Godfrey. "NLEA in a Nutshell." *Prepared Foods,* December 1992.

Blalock, Cecelia. "Sharp Focus." *Refrigerated & Frozen Foods,* February 1993.

"Business Linked to Berries Is Not New to Controversy." *The New York Times,* 3 April 1997.

"Frozen Food Timeline." *Frozen Food Report,* January-February 1992.

Garrison, Bob. "Market Maverick." *Refrigerated & Frozen Foods,* January 1993.

"Green Giant Squashing U.S. Labor?" *Food Business,* 12 August 1991.

"How Frozen Vegetables Have Grown." *Frozen Food Report,* January-February 1992.

Hui, Y. H., ed. *Encyclopedia of Food Science and Technology.* New York: John Wiley & Sons, 1992.

"Heinz Cutting 2500 Jobs in Revamping," *The New York Times,* 15 March 1997.

"J.R. Simplot," *Nation's Restaurant News,* 2 February 1996.

Kimbrell, Wendy. "Regional Edge." *Refrigerated & Frozen Foods,* July 1992.

Kuhn, Mary Ellen. "Take-out Fry Taste Comes Home." *Food Business,* 4 January 1993.

Kuntz, Lynn A. "Fruit Applications: From Down on the Farm to Up on the Shelf." *Food Product Design,* December 1992.

———. "Fruit Applications: After the Harvest." *Food Product Design,* December 1992.

Liesse, Julie. "Green Giant Heats Up in Freezer Case." *Advertising Age,* 11 November 1991.

Lingle, Rick. "How to Gain Clout with Warehouse Clubs." *Prepared Foods,* September 1992.

"Looking Up." *Refrigerated & Frozen Foods,* November 1992.

Neff, Jack. "McCain USA Hits the Big Time." *Food Business,* 20 July 1992.

"1992 Global Frozen Foods Almanac: Recession and Soft Commodity Prices Put Crimp on US Frozen Food Industry." *Quick Frozen Foods International,* October 1992.

"The 1992 Supermarket Sales Manual." *Progressive Grocer,* July 1992.

Pacyniak, Bernard. "Filling the Food Service Order." *Prepared Foods,* April 1992.

Sender, Isabelle. "Single Serve Caters to Single Shopper." *Supermarket News,* 23 September 1991.

Staff report. "Top 10 Food Science Innovations 1939-1989." *Food Technology,* September 1989.

"A Strawberry Profile." *Frozen Food Report,* January-February 1993

Tanyeri, Dana. "Any Way You Slice Them, Potatoes Mean Profit." *Institutional Distribution,* February 1993.

———. "Frozen Vegetables." *Institutional Distribution,* 1 November 1991.

"U.S. Food Consumption." *Food Review,* May 1996.

Van Wagner, Lisa R. "1993 Food Industry Economic Outlook." *Food Processing,* February 1993.

———. "Government Agencies." *Food Processing,* August 1992.

—Mary Ratcliffe, updated by Mary McNulty

SIC 2038

FROZEN SPECIALTIES NOT ELSEWHERE CLASSIFIED

Establishments primarily engaged in manufacturing frozen food specialties, not elsewhere classified, such as frozen dinners and frozen pizza. The manufacture of some important frozen foods and specialties is classified elsewhere. For example, establishments primarily engaged in manufacturing frozen dairy specialties are classified in **SIC 2024: Ice Cream and Frozen Desserts;** those manufacturing frozen bakery products are classified in **SIC 2051: Bread and Other Bakery Products** and **SIC 2053: Frozen Bakery Products, Except Bread;** those manufacturing frozen fruits and vegetables are classified in **SIC 2037: Frozen Fruits, Fruit Juices, and Vegetables;** and those manufacturing frozen fish and seafood specialties are classified in **SIC 2092: Prepared Fresh or Frozen Fish and Seafood.**

INDUSTRY SNAPSHOT

Companies in the industry shipped $8.6 billion worth of products in 1995, an increase of 12 percent since 1990. There were 333 establishments in the industry in the mid-1990s, an increase of 20 percent since 1990. In the mid-1990s, the industry employed 44,429, an increase of 10 percent since 1990.

BACKGROUND AND DEVELOPMENT

Clarence Birdseye is considered the father of the frozen food industry. He created the freezing process that preserved foods so they did not need to be cooked immediately. Birdseye formed Birds Eye Foods Ltd. in London in 1954; it later became a subsidiary of Unilever. According to *Quick Frozen Foods International,* Birds Eye "virtually held an umbrella over the industry during the squalls of its infancy."

The frozen food industry evolved during the early 1960s as the proliferation of supermarkets and self-service stores made mass marketing of frozen food products profitable. At the same time, refrigerator-freezers and stand-alone freezers gained in popularity. The first frozen food products were vegetables, poultry, fish, and fruit in boilable pouches. Items such as frozen juice concentrate, ice cream novelties, baked goods, variety dinners, seafood, breakfast items, and pizza gradually entered the industry from the mid-1960s through the 1990s.

Beginning in the 1980s, standard TV dinners gave way to a variety of meals and frozen specialty items that offered more choices and met specific dietary requirements. Frozen food manufacturers targeted their products at the needs of busy families who desired quick meal preparation and a large variety. They also developed new frozen entrees for children.

The rapid growth in the industry is also attributable to the introduction of the microwave oven. In fact, *Quick Frozen Foods International* called the combination of the microwave oven and frozen food a "marriage of convenience": "Frozen food performs better in a microwave oven." The magazine reported that microwave oven owners spent 34 percent more on pizza, 29 percent more on breakfast foods, 19 percent more on entrees, and 16 percent more on dinners than non-microwave owners. Improvements in taste over the past 40 years also made frozen food specialties increasingly attractive to busy families.

Leading frozen food manufacturers engaged in damaging price wars and expensive trade promotions in the early 1990s. As a result, many companies began shifting their focus toward generating profits from existing products instead of launching new brands and line extensions.

CURRENT CONDITIONS

The frozen food grew from a $250 million retail business in 1947 to more than $50 billion by the 1990s, according to the National Frozen Food Association. Frozen food specialties comprised $7.3 billion of the total sales in 1995. Frozen dinners and entrees generated sales of $4 billion and were available in over 500 products. Within that category, pizza was the number one seller, generating $1.5 billion retail sales in 1995. Frozen pizza accounted for 7.2 percent of the $24 billion pizza industry and had a U.S. household use of 65 percent by mid-decade. Another favorite entree, frozen pot pies, had 1995 sales of $279 million.

In the 1990s, dual-income households and the convenience of microwave ovens contributed to annual growth in the frozen food category. However, consumers also complained about the poor texture and inferior browning effect of microwaveable foods. In a 1995 report, The Food Channel predicted a bleak future for most frozen microwaveable items. Cognizant of this concern, technicians in the food additives field increased research into methods to improve the flavor, texture, color, shelf-life and nutritional benefits of frozen foods.

One of the fastest-growing new products were frozen appetizers. According to the 1995 Menu Census conducted by *Restaurants and Institutions,* half of the top selling appetizers in the foodservice industry were frozen items such as onion rings, chicken wings, mozzarella sticks, breaded calamari and breaded vegetables.

Convenience in preparation is the primary appeal of frozen foods. Americans used fewer and fewer ingredients to prepare their meals in the 1990s, and often substituted frozen foods for fresh produce. Concerns about health and nutrition also led consumers to reduce their intake of foods containing fat and sodium. The specialty frozen food industry responded by offering low-cholesterol and low-fat products. H. J. Heinz, for example, introduced a 98 percent fat-free frozen dinner for its Budget Gourmet brand.

Because of tough economic conditions, the frozen food industry had to refine its marketing techniques to communicate value and quality to wary consumers. *Supermarket News* claimed that frozen food manufacturers should target the 40- to 54-year-old demographic group, which was expected to grow by about 20 percent through the mid-1990s, as well as the over 55-year-old group, which was projected to increase by about 7 percent. These two groups made up about 60 percent of the American population. Frozen food items heavily purchased by those in the over 55 group included pizzas, pies, and entrees.

According to *Supermarket News,* "frozen Mexican and Tex-Mex foods have outgrown their purely regional appeal to gain acceptance in the diets of many Americans." Double-digit dollar gains for frozen ethnic foods are expected to continue into the twenty-first century. In 1996, Italian one-dish frozen entries generated $973 million in sales; Mexican one-dish items, $286.1 million. Oriental one-dish meals generated $259.5 million. Stouffer's, Healthy Choice, Swanson, Banquet and Weight Watchers all had success with new ethnic offerings. Weight Watchers' International Selections line, for example, realized retail sales of $47.4 million in 1996. Less well-known companies were also increasing sales of ethnic foods in the 1990s. The Tai Pan oriental brand of VIP Sales Co. of Tulsa, Oklahoma, had sales of $10 million in 1996. Sales of Yu Sing oriental foods by Luigino's Inc. of Duluth, Minnesota, reached $48 million the same year. The increasing popularity of frozen ethnic foods prompted some manufacturers to seek shelf placement in the mainstream food aisle. Others, particularly small companies with a large percentage of non-English speaking customers, preferred to remain in the ethnic foods aisle.

At the close of the 1990s, industry analysts are urging the frozen food industry to develop new prepared foods in order to avoid losing additional market share to ready-to-eat meals, including microwavable shelf-stable and refrigerated items. Sales of such products could erode the market share held by frozen foods from 66 percent in the mid-1990s to 34 percent by the year 2000.

Another challenge facing the industry is the strict product labeling guidelines imposed by the Nutrition Labeling and Education Act of 1990, which went into effect in 1994. The law requires accuracy in labeling information, nutritional content claims, and definitions of serving sizes. Upon enactment of the legislation, the industry was forced to discard products that were packed and labeled before the deadline.

INDUSTRY LEADERS

Among the leading manufacturers of frozen food specialties in 1996 were Sara Lee Corporation, with $17.7 billion in sales; Rich Products Corporation, with $940 million in sales; and Nestle Frozen Food Company, with $833 million. Popular frozen products are Campbell Soup's Swanson Frozen Foods, Weight Watchers, Stouffer's Lean Cuisine, and ConAgra's Healthy Choice lines.

FURTHER READING

American Frozen Food Institute home page. Available from http://www.affi.com/facts/decafood.htm.

Darnay, Arsen, ed. *Manufacturing USA.* 5th ed. Detroit: Gale Research, 1997.

"The Decline and Fall of the Microwave." *Futurist,* March/April 1995.

DeNitto, Emily. "Frozen Food Results Chill Top 100." *Advertising Age,* 29 September 1993.

Dowdell, Stephen. "Increasing the Volume." *Supermarket News.* 4 October 1993.

Friedman, Michael. "International Foods Growing." *Frozen Food Age,* Feburary 1997.

"In Praise of Mighty Microwave Oven, FF Leaders Call for Standardization." *Quick Frozen Foods International,* January 1988.

Karolefski, John. "Industry Urged to Jazz Up Meal Offerings." *Supermarket News,* 5 March 1990.

———. "New Technology Expected to Increase Market Share." *Supermarket News,* 5 March 1990.

Klepacki, Laura. "Demographics, Value Stressed as Key to Frozen Food Growth." *Supermarket News,* 9 November 1992.

———. "Mexican Style Fast Foods Securing Niche in Frozens," *Supermarket News,* April 19, 1993.

Predicasts Forecasts. Foster, California: Information Access Co., Fourth Quarter 1993.

Saxton, Lisa. "Meals on Deals." *Supermarket News,* 4 October 1993.

Sternman, Mike. "Would You Believe This Frozen Food Season." *Supermarket Business,* 3 January 1994.

———. "Sorting Out the Labels." *Supermarket News,* 4 October 1993.

"Thirty Years around the World with Frozen Foods: 1959-1989." *Quick Frozen Foods International,* October 1989.

Turcsik, Richard. "Realignment at Campbell Splits Frozens, Condiments." *Supermarket News,* 3 May 1993.

———. "A Period of Cool Change." *Supermarket News,* 28 December 1992.

Ward's Business Directory of U.S. Public Companies. volume 5. Detroit: Gale Research, 1996.

—Evelyn Dorman, updated by Mary McNulty

SIC 2041

FLOUR AND OTHER GRAIN MILL PRODUCTS

This industry is comprised of establishments primarily engaged in milling flour from wheat, rye, and other grains except rice. Rice millers are categorized in **SIC 2044: Rice Milling.** Establishments involved in corn milling by the wet process are categorized in **SIC 2046: Wet Corn Milling.**

Products of this industry include plain flour or mixes and doughs prepared from milled ingredients. Establishments who supply mixes and doughs prepared from purchased ingredients are categorized in **SIC 2045: Prepared Flour Mixes and Doughs.**

INDUSTRY SNAPSHOT

In 1995, sales from flour and grain mill products totaled an estimated $6.6 billion, a substantial drop from sales of $7 billion in 1994. Nonetheless, the industry's sales and production were larger than those of the 1980s and the early 1990s. According to a U.S. Census of Manufacturers estimate, the industry had 354 active mills in 1996. In addition, states with the largest number of active mills included Kansas, New York, Minnesota, Ohio, California, and Missouri in 1996.

Although any grain (rice, oats, barley, corn, millet, sorghum, and wheat) can be ground into flour, most of the world's flour was produced from wheat. Using standard milling procedures, 100 pounds of wheat yielded approximately 72 pounds of white flour. In addition to flour, the milling process produced millfeeds, which were made from pieces of bran and other portions of the wheat kernel. Millfeeds were used as ingredients in livestock food.

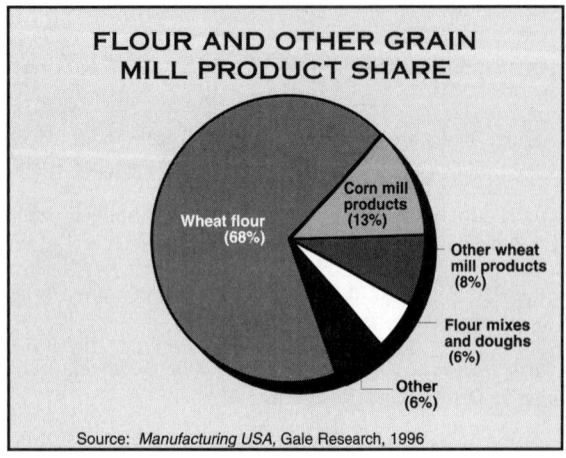

FLOUR AND OTHER GRAIN MILL PRODUCT SHARE

Wheat flour (68%)
Corn mill products (13%)
Other wheat mill products (8%)
Flour mixes and doughs (6%)
Other (6%)

Source: *Manufacturing USA*, Gale Research, 1996

Flour could be packaged for sale to the household or bakery markets or used as an ingredient in bakery mixes, breads or doughs, or pastas. Different bread varieties were made with varying recipes, but on average 100 pounds of flour could make about 150 one-pound loaves of bread. The bread and cake industry consumed approximately 70 percent of the flour milled in the United States. Other flour products included cookies, cereals, gravies, soups, whiskeys, and beers. Flour products were also used in nonfood applications such as the manufacture of plywood adhesives, industrial starches, fertilizers, paving mixes, polishes, and cosmetics. Approximately 85 percent of the flour used by industrial users was milled from hard and durum wheat varieties.

Furthermore, mills used a process called fractionation to separate the flour according to the fineness of its particles. Course fractions were reground. Intermediate fractions were used in applications requiring low amounts of protein, and fine fraction flour was blended with other flours or used alone in applications where high protein content was necessary. White flour was often bleached with agents such as potassium bromide, iodate, acetone peroxide, azodicarbonamide, ascorbic acid, and chlorine dioxide. In addition to providing consistent coloring, bleaching improved the condition of the flour gluten which improved its baking quality.

White flour is made only with the endosperm portion of the wheat kernel. Farina is also made from the endosperm, but it is ground to produce a granular product. The term ''wheat germ'' refers to the part of the wheat kernel from which a seed sprouts. It contains oil which is sometimes extracted for separate processing. Wheat germ is also used in breakfast cereals, breads, and other bakery products. Whole wheat flour, also called graham flour, is made from the endosperm, bran, and germ combined. It has a higher protein content than regular white flour. Pastas such as spaghetti, macaroni, and noodles are made from durum wheat. A popular pasta ingredient, ''semolina'' is a granular grind of durum endosperm, comparable to farina.

BACKGROUND AND DEVELOPMENT

Milled grains have been used as principal food staples for thousands of years. Corn has been the predominant grain used by people in Latin America and the sub-Saharan regions of Africa, while many Asian nations have depended on rice. Inhabitants of Europe and North America relied primarily on wheat products.

The origins of wheat farming and milling are obscure. Historians estimate that wheat cultivation began between 10,000 and 15,000 years ago, marking the beginning of civilization. Because they could be stored, stocked, and transported, grains led to the evolution of trading practices. Documents in the form of artistic depictions and early writings chronicled the development of wheat grinding technologies and baking methods in ancient Egypt, Assyria, Greece, and China.

One of the oldest types of wheat known is bulgur wheat, and the earliest means employed to separate the parts of the wheat kernel involved rubbing the grain between the hands. Another method used the action of hoofed animals walking over grains which had been spread on hard ground. Winnowing was a process in which grains were tossed in the air so that the chaff would blow away. Removing the individual grains from the rest of the plant was necessary before milling could take place.

Wheat kernels are made up of three components: "endosperm," "bran," and "germ." The endosperm represents about 83 percent of the kernel and contains the starchy portion used to make white flour. The bran accounts for about 14.5 percent of the wheat kernel and is used in whole wheat flour and animal feeds. The smallest portion of the kernel, the germ, represents only about 2.5 percent of the kernel. The most common uses of wheat germ are in human food products and in animal feeds. Historically, the germ was separated from the rest of the wheat kernel because it contained fat and did not keep well in long term storage.

Grain milling practices were developed to separate the kernel components and make flour. The first types of milling procedures involved the use of rubbing stones, mortar and pestles, or querns. Querns were devices made from two stacked, disk-shaped stones. Wheat grains were poured into the quern through a hole in the top stone. As the two stones turned against each other, the abrasive movement separated the parts of the wheat kernels and ground the endosperm into flour. The flour was then discharged between the stones.

More efficient methods of grinding grain progressed along with the development of alternative power supplies. Horses and oxen could turn millstones better than human power. Wind- and water-operated mills supplanted animal power. As the United States was settled, mills were constructed in almost every town. Typically the mill relied on water power and was, therefore, located near a source of running water.

The first continuous system for milling wheat into flour was developed during the last part of the eighteenth century by an American, Oliver Evans. Evans's mill design utilized steam technology and employed conveyors and bucket elevators to move the grain through a multi-phase milling process. Further advances in milling technology occurred during the nineteenth century. In 1865, Edmund La Croix developed a middlings purifier that separated the granular endosperm from the bran so that it could be reground to produce a better grade of flour. During the 1870s, the first roller mills in the United States were constructed. Roller mills possessed several advantages: they eliminated the need of dressing millstones; they were able to produce flour through a more gradual extraction process, which enabled millers to yield a larger percentage of better grade flour; and they lent themselves to greater efficiency, thereby making the construction of larger mills more feasible.

As U.S. citizens moved westward, milling centers moved with them. Mills became larger in size but fewer in number. In 1870, an estimated 22,000 mills served the nation's population of about 30 million. One hundred and ten years later in 1980, the nation's population of 220 million was served by an estimated 150 to 250 mills. In Michigan, the number of mills fell from 534 at the turn of the century to six in 1990. The consolidation of mills and the trend toward facilities with greater capacities led to the creation of giant corporations such as Pillsbury Co. and General Mills, Inc. Millers began offering a wider variety of products during the early 1900s. Self-rising flour, biscuit and cake mixes, and prepared doughs were introduced during the 1920s and 1930s but failed to gain widespread popularity until after World War II.

During the middle of the twentieth century, fundamental changes occurred in the primary location of mills. Prior to the 1950s, the cost of shipping wheat and the cost of shipping flour were approximately equal, and mills were frequently built close to wheat fields. During the early 1960s, the cost of shipping grain decreased following the introduction of hopper rail cars. At the same time, costs surrounding sanitation requirements increased the price of shipping flour. As a result, mills were constructed in close proximity to end markets rather than near the wheat fields.

Granular flour, a product made with particles of a uniform size with carefully controlled amounts of atomized moisture to reduce clumping, was introduced during the 1960s. Although granular flower was more expensive than regular flour, it offered several advantages. It had less dust, was easier to pour, did not require sifting, and it dispersed in cold liquids.

During the 1970s, sales of household flour declined as society moved away from home baking and homemakers demonstrated a preference for the convenience and consistency of prepared mixes. In addition, many mixes were less expensive than individual ingredients. Baking from ''scratch'' ceased to be an activity of necessity and was relegated to hobby status. Demographic information revealed that households with higher incomes were more likely to use flour than lower income households. Flour volume losses within the household sector were partially offset by increases of flour sales to commercial bakers.

CURRENT CONDITIONS

Although overall flour consumption declined somewhat during the early 1970s, annual per capita flour consumption increased by about 69 pounds between 1970 and 1994 to a total of 179.7 pounds. Industry analysts attributed gains to increased consumption of fiber, bran, and whole grain products along with growing consumption of such flour-based convenience foods as sandwiches and pizzas. Wheat flour consumption lead at 144.5 pounds per person, followed by milled corn at 23.7 pounds, milled oats at 9.2 pounds, and milled rye at .6 pounds.

The diverse end uses of flours required a wide variety of milled grain products produced from different types of wheat. During the latter part of the twentieth century, 14 different wheat species were grown. The three most frequently used varieties were common wheat (*Triticum aestivum*), club wheat (*Triticum compactum*), and durum wheat (*Triticum durum*). Together, these three accounted for 90 percent of the wheat grown in the United States.

Different wheats were classified as ''hard,'' ''soft,'' or ''durum.'' Hard wheats were used to make flours for breads and rolls. Soft wheats were used primarily in cakes, cookies, crackers, and prepared mixes. Durum wheat was almost exclusively used to make pasta products. Although a single modern flour mill might offer more than one product, it typically ground only one class of wheat. Approximately 70 percent of the U.S. milling capacity during the late 1980s was devoted to hard wheat. Soft wheat mills accounted for 20 percent, durum wheat accounted for 8 percent, and mills dedicated to whole wheat production represented 2 percent of the nation's milling capacity.

As the grain mill products industry entered the 1990s, the number of mills declined, but the capacity per mill continued to increase. Between 1973 and 1990, the average mill increased in size by 70 percent, but the total number of mills in the United States fell by 25 percent. However, the number of mills remained steadier throughout the mid-1990s with only mild declines in the number of operations, and analysts predicted that it would remain steady throughout the end of the 1990s.

In the 1990s, more than half of the nation's milling capacity was concentrated in mills with individual daily capacities exceeding a million pounds. The trend toward corporate mills was driven by the goals of reducing labor and transportation costs and thereby increasing profits. The average daily wheat milling capacity, for example, was about 14 million pounds in 1996, up about 1 million pounds from 1994's daily capacity of 13 million.

One of the biggest challenges facing the grain mill industry was the charge that flour performance was diminishing. Industry researchers speculated that one cause of deteriorating quality was a national grain breeding program that had emphasized increasing yield per acre without paying sufficient attention to the quality of the end products produced with the grain. Other possible causes included: a drop in the amount of protein; a declining protein quality; an ever-increasing number of wheat varieties; the impact of agricultural practices such as irrigation and fertilizers; and milling practices which improved efficiency but potentially produced inferior results.

INDUSTRY LEADERS

One of the leading companies within the flour and grain mill products classification was Pillsbury Co., a division of Grand Metropolitan PLC. Grand Metropolitan, a British firm, purchased Pillsbury in 1989 for $5.8 billion. In fiscal 1996, Grand Metropolitan reported that Pillsbury employed 15,000 workers worldwide, and its profits totaled $702.5 million from sales of $6.1 billion, accounting for a third of Grand Metropolitan's earnings. Pillsbury operated three major groups: Pillsbury and Hungry Jack; Pizza; and Green Giant. The Pillsbury and Hungry Jack group offered flour to both the home and institutional markets, as well as pastries, prepared dough, baked goods, baking mixes, and specialty potatoes. The company also pioneered microwave products in the 1970s. Pizza products were sold under two brands, Jenos and Totinos. Vegetable products were marketed under the Green Giant label.

Pillsbury, originally a flour milling company, was established in 1869 in Minneapolis, Minnesota. In 1929, the company developed and patented a vented package that allowed dough to rise. The innovation enabled the company to boost its position in dough product sales. In 1996, the refrigerated dough product line represented the company's largest segment, and Pillsbury held the top position in U.S. refrigerated dough sales. In early 1997, Pillsbury introduced its own line of bread.

Though Pillsbury held the top position in refrigerated doughs, it lagged behind Duncan Hines and General Mills, Inc. in overall bakery goods. In addition, the company relinquished its position as the nation's top flour miller in the late 1970s. Pillsbury's milling capacity grew by 39 percent between 1973 and 1987, but it was surpassed by three competitors: ConAgra, Inc., Archer Daniels Midland Milling, and Cargill Corp. Between 1987 and 1990 Pillsbury's milling capacity decreased by 9 percent, and in 1991 the company announced plans to sell four of its eight mills to Cargill.

Another one of the nation's largest grain miller, as measured by capacity, was ConAgra. ConAgra moved into the top spot following its acquisition of Pevney and International Multifoods. In 1990s ConAgra's milling capacity totaled about 27 million pounds per day.

ConAgra, a large, diverse food products organization, operated divisions in three areas: Prepared Foods, Trading and Processing, and Agri-Products. The company's total sales for fiscal 1996 totaled $24.5 billion. In addition to its wheat flour production mills, ConAgra operated oat, dry corn, and barley processing facilities. In the United States, the company's grain processing division operated 27 mills located in 14 states. An additional three U.S. mills were operated under joint venture agreements. ConAgra also operated mills in Canada and the United Kingdom.

Another industry leader was General Mills. In 1996, General Mills earned $5.4 billion in part for its milling and backed goods concerns. The company's household flours, sold under the Gold Medal and Robin Hood labels, held a 34 percent share of the market. The company's Bisquick mix held a 73 percent market share within the baking mix category, and its Betty Crocker mixes held a 48 percent share of the dessert market.

WORK FORCE

According to a Census of Manufacturers estimate, employment within the U.S. flour and grain mills products industry totaled 12,300 in 1996. This figure represents a drop of about 1,000 employees since 1993. As of 1994, employees within this industry earned about $12 per hour. Out of the 354 active mills, 168 maintained a staff of 20 or more workers. Establishments in this industry maintained an average of 49 employees and each laborer cost the industry about $102,970. Mills also produced 279,017 shipments per employee.

Safety issues within the industry included dust control, noise abatement, and controlling hazards that presented risks for fire and explosions. Concentrations of grain dust above certain limits were susceptible to burning rapidly if ignited. Dust control was also necessary to limit possible worker exposure to microorganisms, pesticide residues, toxins, insect parts, and animal hairs. Some studies suggested that workers with high levels of exposure to grain dust might be susceptible to respiratory diseases such as chronic bronchitis. Noise in mills was primarily attributed to pneumatic blowers and vehicles.

To control potential work place hazards, modern mills reduced dust generation by minimizing grain handling, reducing the velocity of grain movement, and installing enclosed conveyor systems. Protection from excessive noise was achieved by isolating work stations and limiting exposure.

FURTHER READING

Blackwood, Alan. *Spotlight on Grain.* Vero Beach, FL: Rourke Enterprises, 1987.

Bush, Paul. "Pillsbury's Predictable Quality." *Prepared Foods,* January 1991.

Darnay, Arsen J., ed. *Manufacturing USA.* 5th ed. Detroit: Gale Research, 1996.

Grand Metropolitan Annual Report 1996. London: Grand Metropolitan, 1996.

Harwood, Joy. "U.S. Flour Milling on the Rise." *Food Review,* April - June 1991.

Mutchler, John E. and Stephen W. Bell. "Grain Handling and Processing." *Industrial Hygiene Aspects of Plant Operations.* New York: Macmillan, 1985.

U.S. Census Bureau. "Current Industrial Reports. Washington: 2 April 1997. Available from: http://www.census.gov/ftp/pub/industry/m20a9702.txt.

Waldrop, Judith. "Scratch and Mix." *American Demographics,* October 1992.

Wheat Flour Institute. *From Wheat to Flour,* Washington: Wheat Flour Institute, 1981.

—Karen Bellenir, updated by Karl Heil

SIC 2043

CEREAL BREAKFAST FOODS

This industry is comprised of establishments that manufacture cereal breakfast foods. Establishments that primarily manufacture granola and other types of breakfast bars are categorized in **SIC 2064: Candy and Other Confectionary Products.**

INDUSTRY SNAPSHOT

In the mid-1990s breakfast cereal makers underwent major repositioning, rethinking their product development procedures. Burdened with high development costs and new product failure rates, manufacturers were scaling back product introductions. Even though co-branding products slowed the development process, co-branded products were being introduced by many national manufacturers.

Consumer awareness of health and nutrition played a major part in shaping the industry during the mid-to-late 1990s. Many national cereal manufacturers were also playing the acquisitions and mergers game to enter popular breakfast foods markets; for example, Kellogg Company purchased Lender's Bagels from Kraft Foods to enter the very popular and trendy bagel market. Bagels were the fastest growing segment of the cereal foods market in the mid to late 1990's.

BACKGROUND AND DEVELOPMENT

Ready-to-eat cereals first appeared during the late 1800s. According to one account, John Kellogg, a doctor who belonged to a vegetarian group, developed wheat and corn flakes to extend the group's dietary choices. John's brother, Will Kellogg, saw potential in the innovative grain products and initiated commercial production and marketing. Patients at a Battle Creek, Michigan, sanitarium were among Kellogg's first customers.

Another cereal producer with roots in the nineteenth century was the Quaker Oats Company. In 1873, the North Star Oatmeal Mill built an oatmeal plant in Cedar Rapids, Iowa. North Star reorganized with other enterprises and together they formed Quaker Oats in 1901.

The Washburn Crosby Company, a predecessor to General Mills, entered the market during the 1920s. The company's first ready-to-eat cereal, Wheaties, was introduced to the American public in 1924. According to General Mills, Wheaties was developed when a Minneapolis clinician spilled a mixture of gruel that he was making for his patients on a hot stove. The clinician approached the Washburn Crosby Company with his product and, following many tests and refinements, Wheaties was born. Other General Mills cereals followed in rapid succession. In 1937 Crispy Corn Kix was introduced. The company also launched the world's first ready-to-eat oat cereal in 1941. Originally

named Cheerioats, the product later became "Cheerios."

During the 1940s cereal makers benefited from improved methods of puffing cereal products. Puffing methods employed a principle somewhat analogous to popping corn. Cereal ingredients were cooked and formed into pellets with precisely monitored amounts of water. The product was heated in an enclosed container called a "gun." As the heat increased, the water within the pellets turned to steam. The steam expanded and built up pressure within the gun until the intensity of the pressure caused the end of the gun to open. When the gun opened, the force of the escaping steam propelled the pellets out of the gun into a receiving bin, and as the steam erupted from the pellets it left them permeated with thousands of air holes. These air holes caused the pellet to become larger and less dense. For example, one type of puffed product made with a pellet measuring 0.156 inches in diameter, measured 0.5 inches after puffing. During the first decade of the 1900s, before the development of modern puffing procedures, puffed products were actually shot from cannons.

Many kinds of cereal were manufactured with a device called a food extruder. The extruder mixed and cooked cereal ingredients in a process that also shaped and colored the mixture. Ingredients were added at one end of the extruder and conveyed through its inner mechanisms by spiraling screws. A die at the other end of the extruder squeezed out cereal shapes and a blade cut the pieces at a predetermined size.

These food extruders were similar in operation to meat grinders. The first extruders, used during the 1930s, had only a single screw and often had problems caused by dried pieces of food. The machines were improved by the development of twin screws. Twin screw extruders had two screws that intermeshed and cleaned each other as they propelled the cereal mixture.

The second half of the twentieth century brought rapid increases in brand offerings and growing national interest in ready-to-eat cereals. Many popular pre-sweetened cereals aimed at the children's market were introduced during the 1950s. Trix and Lucky Charms were launched in 1954. Cocoa Puffs made its first appearance in 1958. Adult cereals made an impact during the 1960s. Total, touted as a product containing 100 percent of the officially established U.S. RDA (recommended daily allowance) of vitamins and iron, was introduced in 1961. In 1970, the ready-to-eat cereal market was valued at $659 million, and it had reached $1.9 billion by 1979.

In the 1980s, U.S. consumers became increasingly interested in health issues and consequently in improving their diets. In response, Kellogg introduced Nutri-Grain, the first line of flaked, whole grain ready-to-eat cereals with no sugar or preservatives. Other Kellogg offerings aimed at the health-conscious market included Crispix in 1983 and Just Right in 1985.

In 1985, Kellogg held a 40 percent share of the total ready-to-eat cereal market, which had grown to $4.35 billion. General Mills held a 22 percent share, followed by Post (14 percent), Quaker Oats (8 percent) and Ralston Purina (6 percent). All other cereal manufacturers combined held the remaining 10 percent. According to a report published by *Prepared Foods,* 92.4 percent of U.S. households used ready-to-eat cereal. The average household had four packages and the country consumed more than 20 billion bowls annually.

According to figures published by the U.S. Department of Commerce, the cereal breakfast foods industry shipped $6.6 billion worth of products in 1987. The total included $5 billion of products considered primary to the industry and $1.3 billion of secondary products. Miscellaneous transactions accounted for $319 million. These figures yielded a specialization ratio of 79 percent, an increase from the 77 percent specialization ratio recorded in 1982.

The largest and most rapidly growing segment within the industry consisted of ready-to-eat (RTE) cereals. By the end of the 1980s, the RTE market was estimated at $4.8 billion. By 1992, industry analysts valued it at $7.3 billion, and industry forecasters expected it to reach $8 billion in 1993.

A much smaller segment, hot cereals, experienced virtually no growth between 1982 and 1987. In 1988, however, the hot cereal market garnered sales of $600 million, a 20 percent increase over figures for the previous year. The sudden surge was attributed to a national focus on the reported health benefits of oat bran.

Much of the growth within the ready-to-eat cereal segment during the later part of the 1980s was attributed to interest in oat bran. Products specifically labeled "oat bran" were valued at $34.9 million in 1987, at $105.2 million in 1988, and at $328.2 million in 1989. Oat bran's popularity, however, was short-lived. A study published in the *New England Journal of Medicine* debunked advertising claims that oat bran possessed the ability to lower cholesterol levels. The study led to consumer skepticism and a downturn in the success of new products based on key ingredients.

In 1990 ready-to-eat cereal sales increased only 0.2 percent.

Another ingredient to suffer from health controversies was psyllium. Psyllium, a grain grown mainly in India, was said to help reduce cholesterol and thereby reduce risks of heart disease. A study done by the University of Minnesota, reporting a 9 percent reduction in cholesterol levels among people who ate a cereal containing psyllium, was used to document the claims. Subsequently, General Mills incorporated it in "Benefit" and Kellogg used it in "Heartwise."

Psyllium had been previously approved by the Food and Drug Administration (FDA) for use as a laxative, but its use as a food had not been certified. The FDA expressed concern that it could result in damaging health consequences to the intestinal tract such as constipation, fecal impaction, depletion of necessary colon bacteria, and shifts in the body's ability to absorb nutrients. Allergic reaction posed another problem related to psyllium use. Consequently, General Mills discontinued Benefit in January 1990, and Kellogg encountered problems with regulatory challenges to its advertising. Six states—Iowa, California, Florida, Minnesota, Texas, and Wisconsin—brought suit against the company regarding the health benefit claims for Heartwise and other products including Special K, 40+, Bran Flakes, and Frosted Flakes. In addition, Texas banned Heartwise. The suits were settled in 1991 when Kellogg agreed to pay each of the six states $30,000 to use for consumer or nutritional education and changed the name from "Heartwise" to "Fiberwise."

The early 1990s were notable for shifts in traditionally held markets. Kellogg's Frosted Flakes had lost its top position to General Mills' Cheerios in 1989, and the cereal giant's previous 40 percent market share slipped to 37.5 percent in 1991. At the same time, General Mills market share increased to 25.1 percent. *Fortune* magazine estimated each percentage point was worth about $75 million dollars per year.

In addition, many of the country's major cereal manufacturers faced problems because of changing patterns regarding brand loyalty. Customers preferred purchasing a variety of cereals rather than one favorite. Another challenge was the growing percentage of market share being captured by private labels marketed by a supermarket or grocer. For a 12-week period that ended in January 1991, private labels accounted for 7 percent of the pound volume sales in the ready-to-eat cereal market and 4 percent based on dollar amount. The percentage varied by cereal type. For example, as measured in dollars, private labels captured 13 percent of the crisp rice segment and 11 percent of the frosted flakes segment. Many of these private label brands were manufactured by Ralston Purina.

Another change noted during the early 1990s was a shift away from products promoted solely on the basis of their health benefits. Although consumers continued to look at nutritional content, other factors such as taste, variety, convenience, and price were also important. The "all-family" cereal segment held almost half of the ready-to-eat market. All-family cereals were not as sweet as children's cereals but had more sugar than traditional adult cereals. Examples included General Mills' Wheaties Honey Gold and Kellogg's Frosted Bran.

The snack market, which was estimated to be more than three times larger than the ready-to-eat cereal market, represented an emerging growth area for cereal makers. Following the U.S. Department of Agriculture's release of its recommendation that Americans eat six to 11 servings of grain per day, cereal makers began promotions touting their products as tasty treats with positive health benefits. An estimated 7 percent of ready-to-eat cereals were consumed as snacks throughout the day. For example, Cheerios was promoted as a snack for toddlers, and an estimated one-third of all Chex cereal, made by Ralston Purina, was purchased for use as an ingredient in snack mixes rather than for breakfast consumption. Two new products aimed directly at the snack market were Kellogg's Rice Krispies Treats and General Mills' Fingos.

CURRENT CONDITIONS

Sales of cereals rose from 2.3 percent in 1988 to 3.1 percent in 1993. The primary reason for this according to *ID: The Voice of Foodservice Distribution* was the growing awareness of consumers on the nutritional aspects of foods they ate. One of the hottest growth segments in the early 1990s was the ready-to-eat cereals, which were available as rolled, puffed, and extruded in a variety of flavors.

Hot cereals, which included oat, corn, wheat, and rice, continued to dominate sales during the cooler seasons, while the sales of cold cereals remained consistent through the year. Cold weather increased sales of hot cereals with a total of 75 percent of hot cereal sales being made between October and February. Between September 1993 to September 1994 hot cereal sales was at $367.6 million an increase of 6.9 percent over hot cereal sales between September 1992 and September 1993, according to *Supermarket News*. The entire breakfast cereal industry generated $8.1 billion in 1994, up from $7.7 billion in 1993.

The breakfast cereal industry's product development activity in 1995 seemed to have been affected by criticisms from consumer advocates, politicians and food editors, according to *Prepared Foods*. Critics lambasted cereal producers over, alleged high cereal prices and profits which as a result inhibited product product introductions. According to *Prepared Foods*, only 128 new labels were launched in 1995 with very few of them coming from the Big Five cereal companies.

A price war erupted in the U.S. breakfast cereal market in 1996 following a long period of high cereal prices. According to *The Financial Times*, analysts said that producers had been greedy and continued to raise prices in the belief that their brands were so strong that consumers would pay inflated prices. The exorbitant prices of national brand name cereals forced consumers to seek lower price brand name cereals.

As a result, according to *Supermarket Business*, private cereal brand name products took 9 percent of the market away from the top national brand manufacturers during the period ending April 21, 1996. To compensate for the lost sales large brand manufacturers decided to reduce prices of cereals. According to *Supermarket Business*, analysts predicted that such a price reduction would hurt sales in the short-run but would eventually help improve the companies' long-term profits.

INDUSTRY LEADERS

Kellogg Company was the leader among national cereal makers with a 1996 sales revenue of $7.003 billion. Established in 1906, Kellogg Company was the world's market leader in ready-to-eat cereals throughout most of the twentieth century. In 1992, Kellogg operated manufacturing facilities in 17 nations, and the company's global distribution network reached 150 countries. Canada, the United Kingdom, and Australia represented Kellogg's three largest overseas markets.

A few well-known Kellogg products were Corn Flakes, Frosted Mini-wheats, Corn Pops, and Froot Loops. In addition to its ready-to-eat cereal division, Kellogg also operated Mrs. Smith's Frozen Foods. The Mrs. Smith's division manufactured Eggo waffles and frozen pies. Kellogg introduced the "Temptations" line of cereals in 1995. This product set itself apart from competitors by emphasizing its excellent taste and exceptional nutritional profile. In 1996 Kellogg purchased Lenders Bagels, which controlled 72.6 percent of the frozen bagels market, from Kraft Foods Inc.

Another leading cereal maker, ranked second with $5.954 billion in 1996 sales revenues, was the Quaker Oats Company. The company's first puffed product, "Puffed Rice," was introduced in 1905. In 1992, Quaker Oats held a 7.1 percent share of the ready-to-eat cereal market, and its principal product was Cap'n Crunch. Quaker Oats' market share within the ready-to-eat segment peaked in 1988 at 8 percent but slowly eroded in subsequent years. Within the smaller hot cereal segment, however, the company held approximately 60 percent of the market. In addition to cereal products, Quaker Oats produced Aunt Jemima Pancake mix and Gatorade sports drinks.

General Mills, with 1996 sales revenue of $5.416 billion, was the third largest cereal manufacturer in terms of ready-to-eat market share. Its consumer foods division included its line of Big G cereals, Gold Medal Flour, Betty Crocker mixes, and Hamburger Helper. Outside its consumer foods division, the company also owned the Red Lobster and Olive Garden Restaurants. The restaurants accounted for approximately one-third of General Mills' total revenues.

General Mills operated seven cereal manufacturing plants within the United States and an eighth in Toronto, Ontario and employed 121,000 people. Big G cereals included flaked products such as Total, Raisin Bran, and Country Corn Flakes; the company's puffed varieties included Kix, Trix, and Cocoa Puffs. Innovations undertaken during 1993 included the introduction of "Fingos," a dry, finger-food cereal aimed at the snack market, and the addition of X's to Cheerios. The Cherrios and X's were packaged with a detachable game board on the back of the box.

Philip Morris Companies Inc. located in New York, was another industry leader in the mid- to late 1990s with sales revenue of $66.071 billion and 151,000 employees. Founded in 1847, Phillip Morris is the parent company for such large brands as Kraft, Post, and Nabisco.

AMERICA AND THE WORLD

Kellogg was the first American company to enter the foreign market for ready-to-eat cereals. In 1914 the company began distribution in Ontario, Canada, and ten years later the company began operations in Australia. Kellogg opened its first plant in England in 1938 and began operations on the European continent in the 1950s. By the early 1990s Kellogg distributed its products to 150 nations and in some of these markets held a market share as large as 80 percent.

English-speaking nations represented the largest cereal markets. Consumption in non-English markets was estimated at only one-fourth the amount consumed by English speakers. For example, during the early 1990s per capita consumption of ready-to-eat cereal in England was 13.3 pounds per person, but in France it was only 1.8 pounds. On the European continent, consumption averaged 3.0 pounds per year. Shifting attention away from traditional breakfasts and focusing interest on low-cholesterol, convenient snack alternatives, cereal makers viewed low per capita consumption areas as potential growth fields. In Spain sales were growing at a rate of 20 percent per year; in Portugal they were growing at an annual rate of 50 percent. Some industry forecasters estimated that by the year 2000 the European cereal market would experience more than a four-fold increase and reach $6.5 billion.

In 1991, Kellogg announced a joint venture plan to build a cereal plant in Eastern Europe to supply the Baltic states and parts of the former Soviet Union. The plant, located in Riga, Latvia, was expected to be ready for production in 1994. Kellogg also announced plans to build plants in India and China. Ground-breaking for the production facility in Bombay, India, was accomplished in October 1992 and the plant was also expected to begin production in 1994. The company's Chinese facility, to be located in the Guangdong Province, was scheduled for completion in 1995.

General Mills was also active in expanding its overseas operations. In Europe, General Mills and Nestle formed a joint venture called Cereal Partners Worldwide (CPW). In 1992, CPW claimed a 15 percent share of the United Kingdom market and planned an aggressive expansion campaign on the European continent. CPW also planned to enter the Mexican market and expand into Malaysia, Thailand, Philippines, Singapore, Indonesia, and Brunei.

FURTHER READING

1993 Annual Report, Minneapolis, MN: General Mills, June 1993.

Austin, Beth. "Quaker in $45.6M Push." *Advertising Age,* 13 July 1987.

Biesada, Alexandra. "A Case of Heartburn." *Financial World,* 11 June 1991.

———. "Life After Oat Bran." *Financial World,* 11 June 1991).

Brumback, Nancy. "Cereal's Sweeter Family." *Supermarket News,* 31 May 1993.

Dworetzky, Tom. "The Churn of the Screw." *Discover,* May 1988.

Ferguson, Bob. "Cereal Science." *Brandweek,* 2 May 1994.

Friedman, Martin. "Breakfast Cereals-Asleep at the Table?" *Prepared Foods,* 15 April 1996.

General Mills, Inc. "Big 'G' Cereals." Minneapolis, MN: General Mills, (January 1993).

"Going With the Grain." *Progressive Grocer,* August 1989.

Hammel, Frank. "Cereal." *Supermarket Business,* September 1990.

Haran, Leah. "Promos Go Soggy as Co-marketing, Intro's Freshen Cereals." *Advertising Age,* 27 September 1995

Holleran, Joan. "Kelloggs Gets Back on Track." *Food Processing,* January 1995.

"How to Play With Cereal, But Without the Milk." *New York Times,* 23 June 1993.

Hunter, Beatrice Trum. "Foods or Drugs?" *Co nsumers' Research,* April 1990.

Kelley, B.G. "Breakfast Foods." *Supermarket Business,* September 1996.

"Kellogg Pays Six States." *New York Times,* 4 October 1991.

"Kellogg Will Buy Lenders Bagels from Kraft." *The New York Times,* 19 November 1996.

Knowlton, Christopher. "Europe Cooks Up a Cereal Brawl." *Fortune,* 3 June 1991.

Liesse, Julie. "Private-label Cereals Surge." *Advertising Age,* 4 March 1991

———. "Quaker's New Cereals Run Hot and Cold." *Advertising Age,* 20 July 1992.

Mans, Jack. "From Quaker's Tiny Oats, A Mighty Plant Grows." *Prepared Foods,* August 1988.

Messenger, Robert. "No More Blues in Battle Creek." *Prepared Foods,* February 1987.

Meyer, Ann. "Can't Catch Kellogg." *Prepared Foods,* February 1992.

Naude, Alice. "'Heartwise' Is Launched Amid Food Labeling Debate." *Chemical Marketing Reporter,* 4 September 1989.

"Not Just For Breakfast." *ID: The Voice of Foodservice Distribution,* 15 May 1995.

Saxton, Lisa. "Instant Replay? Buyers Say a Repeat of Last Year's Strong Hot Cereal Sales Will Depend Largely on Old Man Winter." *Supermarket News,* 23 January 1995.

Spethmann, Betsy. "Snack Time? Give Me My Cereal Bowl!" *Brandweek,* 3 May 1993.

Therrien, Lois, and Charlie Hoots. "Cafe Au Lait, A Croissant — and Trix." *Business Week,* 24 August 1992.

Thompson, Stephanie. "Kelloggs Lenders Buy: The Right Category?" *Brandweek,* 2 December 1996.

Tomkins, Richard. "Crunch Time for US Cereal Makers." *The Financial Times,* 27 June 1996.

U.S. Department of Commerce. *1987 Census of Manufactures.* Washington: Bureau of the Census, 1990.

—Karen Bellenir, updated by Visi Tilak

SIC 2044

RICE MILLING

This industry is comprised of establishments that clean, polish, or process rice. Principal products include rice flour, rice meal, white rice, brown rice, and rice bran. The growing of rice is discussed under **SIC 0112: Rice.**

One of the smaller segments of U.S. grain milling, rice milling was worth $1.723 billion in 1995, according to the U.S. Census Bureau, a 6 percent drop from the previous year. Industry sales were expected to recover slowly to the $1.8 billion level between 1996 and 1998. At 5.8 million metric tons, the United States produced just 1.7 percent of the world's milled rice in 1995, however its 2.9 million tons of exports commanded an 18 percent share of world exports for the same year. Because rice growing is concentrated heavily in the southern and western United States, most of the estimated 50 U.S. rice mills operate in these regions.

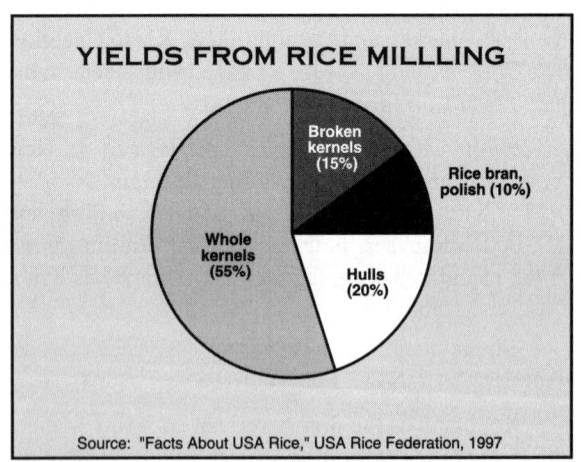

YIELDS FROM RICE MILLLING

Broken kernels (15%)

Rice bran, polish (10%)

Whole kernels (55%)

Hulls (20%)

Source: "Facts About USA Rice," USA Rice Federation, 1997

At an average of 25 pounds per person in 1995, U.S. per capita rice consumption has nearly tripled since 1970. The USA Rice Federation estimated that more than 90 percent of this consumption was domestic rice. Increases reflect the product's nutritional merits, low cost, and consumer appeal. Marketed as a healthy food, rice contains only trace amounts of fat and naturally provides protein, thiamin, riboflavin, niacin, phosphorous, iron, and potassium. It is also cholesterol free, gluten free, and low in sodium.

When rice is harvested, it is first dried for stable storage and then sold to a rice mill. At this stage, the rice is referred to as "paddy" or "rough" rice. Using high-tech machinery, millers shell the rice by removing the inedible hull surrounding each individual grain. Beneath the hull, rice grains still possess seven natural bran layers. In this state, the rice is sold as brown rice, or "polished" to remove the bran and produce white rice kernels. Discarded bran may be used to extract oils or as a food ingredient.

Because polishing rice removes some of the grain's natural ingredients, some millers employ a procedure called "parboiling" to ameliorate nutrient losses. Parboiled rice is soaked in pressurized water, steamed, and dried before milling. In addition to helping grains preserve their nutrients, parboiling helps produce grains that fluff better and are less sticky when cooked. Parboiled grains, however, take longer to cook.

Other rice mill products include brewers rice, enriched rice, and precooked rice. Brewers rice is made of small, broken rice fragments leftover after shelling and polishing and is primarily used by pet food manufacturers and brewers. Enriched rice contains artificially replaced nutrients. Precooked rice is cooked and dehydrated after it is milled.

The industry is dominated by Riceland Foods, Inc., an Arkansas-based cooperative that is the largest rice milling operation in the world. In the mid-1990s, Riceland reported milling and marketing 20 percent of the roughly 390 million bushels of domestic rice produced annually. Also engaged in grain storage and related processing activities, the privately held firm generated revenues of $806 million in the mid-1990s and employed approximately 2,000 workers. Riceland was also a major exporter of U.S. rice products.

Employment in rice milling has generally declined since its 1989 peak of 4,700 workers. By 1996 this number was down to an estimated 3,500 workers and was expected to drop by an average of 100 employees per year in 1997 and 1998. The average wage in the industry was $10.15 per hour in the mid-1990s. Approximately 84 percent of the industry's employment was concentrated in the four states of Arkansas, Texas, California, and Louisiana.

FURTHER READING

Riceland Foods, Inc. "About Riceland." Stuttgart, AR, 1996.

USA Rice Federation. *About USA Rice.* Washington, 1996. Available from http://www.usarice.com/rice.html.

U.S. Bureau of the Census. *1995 Annual Survey of Manufactures.* Washington: GPO, 1997.

SIC 2045

PREPARED FLOUR MIXES AND DOUGHS

This industry classification is comprised of establishments primarily involved in manufacturing prepared mixes and doughs from purchased flours. Establishments primarily involved in milling flour from grain and manufacturing grain mill products, including prepared mixes and doughs, are classified in **SIC 2041: Flour and Other Grain Mill Products.**

In 1995 establishments classified in **SIC 2045: Prepared Flour Mixes and Doughs** shipped products totaling $4.8 billion. This represented a 17 percent increase over the $4.1 billion total for 1994, and a 23 percent increase over 1992 figures. Total costs of material for the industry amounted to $2.0 billion in 1992, but by 1994, this had risen to $2.2 billion, an increase of 8 percent, and in 1995 the costs were at $2.4 billion, an increase of 20 percent over the 1992 figure.

The concept of commercial mixes first developed when millers began adding a leavening agent and salt to flour products to make "self-rising" formulations. Self-rising flours became popular in the southeastern portion of the United States because traditional leavening agents, such as baking powder, had limited shelf life in hot, humid climates.

The development of a stable shortening led to the introduction of the nation's first biscuit mix in the 1920s. Cake mixes tentatively appeared during the 1930s after the industry learned how to dehydrate eggs. Because mixes were convenience products rather than necessities, further commercial development was hampered by the economic hardships and product shortages associated with the Depression and World War II. Following World War II, however, the country embraced convenience. Cake mixes reappeared and began to find increasing popularity not only with homemakers but also among restaurants and institutional users.

During the early 1990s, mixes continued to enjoy widespread popularity. Many bakers preferred mixes to traditional "from scratch" recipes because in addition to offering convenience, they provided consistently favorable results, even for inexperienced cooks.

Prepared mixes were available for a wide variety of products including breads, rolls, cakes, cookies, and pancakes. Mixes were generally one of two kinds. One type required only the addition of a specified amount of liquid. Another type required the addition of other ingredients such as eggs and shortening.

According to a report published by *Institutional Distribution* in 1990, the best selling cake mixes to food service establishments were chocolate, white, devil's food, spice, and pound cakes. In addition, carrot, crumb, gingerbread, lemon, sponge, angel food, applesauce, banana, and brownie mixes were also popular.

Three of the leading companies in this industry in the mid-1990s included Dawn Food Products Inc. of Jackson, Michigan, with $350 million in sales and 1,200 employees; Cereal Food Processors Inc. of Mission Woods, Kansas, with $240 million in sales and 400 employees; and Continental Mills Inc. of Seattle, Washington, with about $110 million in sales and 600 employees.

According to government statistics, this industry employed 15,100 workers in 1995, a 25 percent increase over 1987 figures. The leading states in employment in 1987 were Illinois, Tennessee, Indiana, and Missouri, but by the mid-1990s, California displaced Indiana. Small, single-establishment companies with less than 10 employees accounted for only 7 percent of the industry's total shipments.

FURTHER READING

"Cake Mixes." *Institutional Distribution,* 15 May 1991.

From Wheat to Flour. Washington: Wheat Flour Institute, 1981.

Koselka, Rita. "A Family Affair." *Forbes,* 11 June 1990.

Tanyeri, Dana. "Mixes Offer Fresh Benefits and Low Food Cost." *Institutional Distribution,* July 1990.

U.S. Bureau of the Census. *1992 Census of Manufactures.* Washington: GPO, 1992.

U.S. Bureau of the Census. *1995 Annual Survey of Manufactures.* Washington: GPO, 1997.

—Karen Bellenir, updated by Kenneth R. Shepherd

SIC 2046

WET CORN MILLING

Establishments primarily engaged in milling corn or sorghum grain (milo) by the wet process, and producing starch, syrup, oil, sugar, and by-products, such as gluten feed and meal. Also included in this industry are establishments primarily engaged in manufacturing starch from other vegetable sources (e.g., potatoes, wheat). Establishments primarily engaged in manufacturing table syrups from corn syrup and other ingredients, and those manufacturing starch base dessert powders, are classified in **SIC 2099: Food Preparations, Not Elsewhere Classified.**

Also known as corn refining, wet corn milling in the United States grew by more than 50 percent from 1987 to 1995, expanding shipments from $4.8 billion in 1987 to $7.53 billion in 1995. Performance in 1995 showed a 17 percent increase in value over shipments in 1992, when the industry totaled $6.415 billion in shipments. Growth in the 1990s was not steady, however, with 1993 actually showing a decrease of 3.8 percent in the value of wet corn milling shipments from 1992. Shipments were expected to continue to rise in the late 1990s. The industry processed an estimated 1.5 billion bushels of corn in 1996, or roughly 20 percent of the U.S. corn crop in that year. Processed corn exports generated approximately $1.4 billion in sales in 1995.

Use of the corn kernel differs by product. Corn starch is used in a variety of industries, including food products, paper, adhesives, textiles, and pharmaceuticals. Starch can also be converted to ethanol. Wet corn millers advocated using ethanol as part of an overall national energy policy. Between 1981 and 1991 drivers around the world traveled almost one trillion miles on fuels made with ethanol blends. Also produced from starch, corn sweeteners—corn syrup, dextrose, and high fructose corn syrup (HFCS)—accounted for more than 55 percent of U.S. sweetener consumption in the mid-1990s, according to the Corn Refiners Association. An estimated 400 million bushels of corn were used annually to make HFCS, which since 1980 has been the sweetener of choice for the major U.S. soft drink manufacturers.

Germ is the portion of the kernel from which a seed would sprout. The germ contains oils used to make margarine, mayonnaise, salad dressings, and shortening. Other portions of the corn kernel are made up of protein and are used to produce corn gluten feed and corn gluten meal for animals and poultry.

According to the U.S. Census Bureau, the industry's product share in 1995 was divided among corn sweeteners, which accounted for 48.7 percent of industry shipments by value, followed by wet process corn by-products at 19.9 percent, manufactured starch at 18.6 percent, corn oil at 12.5 percent, and miscellaneous products at 0.3 percent.

Approximately 28 companies operating some 50 plants comprised the industry in the mid-1990s. Such multibillion dollar agribusiness concerns as Archer Daniels Midland Company (ADM) of Decatur, Illinois, Cargill, Incorporated of Minneapolis, Minnesota, and CPC International Inc. of Englewood Cliffs, New Jersey were among the leading producers. ADM, which operated four wet corn milling facilities, employed 14,811 workers and generated sales of $13.31 billion in 1996. Corn product sales made up about 19 percent of ADM's 1996 sales, and increased by 3 percent over 1995. Cargill, Inc., the largest privately owned company in the United States, employed more than 76,000 people worldwide and topped $56 billion in sales for fiscal 1996. Marketer of well-known consumer brands like Mazola corn oil and Hellmann's mayonnaise, CPC International posted sales of $9.84 billion in 1996, approximately 15 percent of which was attributed to its corn refining business.

The industry work force averaged 9,000 people in the mid-1990s, with Iowa, Illinois, and Indiana providing more than 70 percent of the industry's labor. Employment fluctuated considerably during the 1980s and 1990s, varying from a low of 8,300 in 1989 to a high of 9,700 in 1991.

FURTHER READING

Archer Daniels Midland Company. *Annual Report.* Decatur, IL, 1996.

Cargill Inc. *Cargill.* Minneapolis, 1997. Available from http://www.cargill.com.

Corn Refiners Association. *Welcome to the Corn Refiners Association, Inc. Home Page.* Washington, 1997. Available from http://www.corn.org.

CPC International Inc. *Annual Report.* Englewood Cliffs, NJ, 1996.

Darnay, Arsen J., ed. *Manufacturing USA.* 5th ed. Detroit: Gale Research, 1996.

U.S. Bureau of the Census. *1987 Census of Manufactures.* Washington, 1990.

U.S. Bureau of the Census. *1992 Census of Manufactures.* Washington, 1995.

U.S. Bureau of the Census. *1995 Annual Survey of Manufactures.* Washington: GPO, 1997.

SIC 2047

DOG AND CAT FOOD

This industry consists of establishments primarily engaged in manufacturing dog and cat food from cereal, meat, and other ingredients. These preparations may be canned, frozen, or dry. Establishments manufacturing feed for animals other than dogs and cats are classified in **SIC 2048: Prepared Feeds and Feed Ingredients for Animals and Fowls, Except Dogs and Cats.**

INDUSTRY SNAPSHOT

Retail sales of dog and cat food totaled $8.2 billion in 1997. The industry's growth rate in the 1980s was relatively flat, with an average growth of 1 or 2 percent annually. As a vice-president for Quaker Oats told the *New York Times* in 1993, "This is a very competitive market. Unlike beverages where there is no limit to how much people will drink, dog food is driven by the change in dog population and we have only seen 1 to 2 percent (growth) a year." However, in the mid-to-late 1990s, the growth of the market expanded approximately 4 percent.

The flat growth of the 1980s led to price wars in the early 1990s as the various manufacturers vied to take a larger share of a stagnant market. Flat growth in U.S. sales also led the U.S. pet industry to look to exports as a means of expanding the market. At the same time, the Pet Food Institute—the association to which 95 percent of all U.S. pet food manufacturers belong—tried to expand the number of U.S. pet owners by targeting groups not usually associated with pet ownership, such as singles. Their success in increasing ownership was primarily through promoting cat ownership since cats need less attention and are more adaptable to the lifestyle of the single person.

Another 1990s effort to overcome flat sales was the development of "upscale" healthy and gourmet pet food products. This paralleled a similar trend in the larger food industry. Established specialists in this area of the pet food market benefitted greatly. According to *Advertising Age,* pet food advertisers were generally among the top ten annual spenders in advertising during the 1980s, although this trend has diminished somewhat over the last few years. *Advertising Age* reported in 1993, for instance, that one of the effects of the price wars was a cut-back on the advertising budgets of most pet food firms in order to sustain a profit. Downsizing product packages to sell more product units was another tactic adopted by many of the manufacturers in the early 1990s to increase profits in a time of slow growth.

Beginning in the mid-1990s, pet owners began following the general food trend toward healthy diets, leaving behind traditional pet foods for those with more protein and fewer chemical additives and preservatives. According to *Advertising Age,* nearly 20 percent of the 1994 pet food market—or about $1.7 billion—was made up of superpremium brands, up from 15 percent and $1.2 billion in 1992. In April 1996, *Barron's* reported that premium pet foods totaled $2.5 billion a year, or 25 percent of the market.

ORGANIZATION AND STRUCTURE

The dog and cat food segment of the pet food industry is comprised primarily of two types of firms. One is the large, general manufacturer producing a variety of dog and cat foods along with other types of feed and/or food for humans in other divisions or subsidiaries. These manufacturers sell their products primarily through grocery stores. The other type is the specialty firm that exclusively produces pet food— usually a health-related or other specialized type. Traditionally, the general firms usually sell their product in grocery stores while the specialty firms sell their products through veterinary offices.

The pet food industry is subject to regulation at the federal and state levels. In 1958 the manufacturers of pet food formed The Pet Food Institute (PFI), a national trade association. PFI acts as a spokesman for the industry before the various regulatory agencies and bodies, sponsors research, represents the U.S. industry in international meetings, and works on uniform standards for pet food. PFI worked with the American Association of Feed Control Officials (AAFCO) to develop a uniform law on pet food standards that states may use as a model whenever they consider changes to their laws and regulations on the topic. Each state has its own set of laws and regulations which apply to pet food.

Regulation of the Pet Food Industry. At the federal level, pet food labeling and advertising claims are regulated by the Food and Drug Administration (FDA), the Federal Trade Commission (FTC), and the Department of Agriculture. All pet food plants are subject to FDA inspection, and many of the FDA's canned food regulations apply to pet foods. Many manufacturers produce and/or sell products in more than one state, which means their product and its labels much also meet each state's regulations. In August 1996, the AAFCO passed new regulations, that must be complied with by January 1998. These regulations govern the use of the terms "lite" and "less fat" on the U.S. petfoods labels.

Sales Outlets/Product Distribution. Dog and cat food has traditionally been sold in grocery stores, pet stores, and by veterinarians. Veterinarian sales are especially prevalent for those brands that are marketed as a health specialty. Health consciousness for pets paralleled the general trend toward health conscious-

ness for humans in recent years. This movement led to increased attention to labeling and awareness of obesity in pets and the development of more specialized pet foods, with greater emphasis on health in the marketing of the product. Grocery stores, however, still remained the largest outlet for sales of pet food.

In the 1980s and early 1990s, the advent of the discount retailer as a major economic force in America began to change that trend. The biggest loser was the grocery store. The interest in health foods allowed those brands traditionally marketed through veterinarians and breeders to retain market share while the share of the grocery store fell to the discount chain. According to a 1996 article in *Barron's,* supermarket chains saw their share of the total pet food market fall from 85 percent to 60 percent since 1986, with projections of the market share falling further to 50 percent. Efforts to stem the flow with cheaper, in-house brands had only moderate success since people continued to prefer national brands, but they wanted them at a lower price.

The downward trend in supermarket sales was also due to the proliferation of pet megastores—such as PetSmart and Petco—which sell premium brands at discount prices, undercutting supermarkets by 10 to 30 percent.

BACKGROUND AND DEVELOPMENT

The first commercially prepared dog food was a biscuit product introduced in England in about 1860, according to the Pet Food Institute. Dry dog foods were subsequently developed with formulas based on the nutritional knowledge of the day. After World War I, canned horse meat for dog food was introduced into the United States. In the late 1920s, the first commercial pet food diet was developed by the Ralston Purina Company. In the 1930s canned cat food and dry meat meal dog foods came into use. These were succeeded by dry expanded type pet foods, which came onto the market during the 1950s. The 1960s, notes the Institute, "were marked with great diversification in the types of food available to the pet owner—dry cat food, many more varieties of canned products, and new soft-moist products. With the growth of the industry has come a greatly expanded use of by-products from the meat, poultry, and seafood processing industry. Approximately 1.1 million tons of these by-products are . . . now used annually in pet foods."

According to *Prepared Foods*, there were 174 new pet foods introduced in 1995, including such gourmet items as Kal Kan's Whiskas Crunch, a lowfat snack to stimulate a cat's appetite; Novapet's Cow Ear Chews, an alternative to pig's ears; and Nature Animal

Biscuits, baked fresh daily for sale in health food stores.

CURRENT CONDITIONS

As of 1997, the pet market was one of the fastest growing industries in the United States, with Americans spending $20 billion annually on their pets. The number of dogs in the United States in 1997 was 54.9 million, and cats numbered 65.8 million. The industry saw an increase of 22 percent from 1995 to 1997 in the purchase of nutritional supplements and a 7.5 percent increase in the purchase of treats.

INDUSTRY LEADERS

Leading companies involved in the manufacture of dog and cat food in the United States include the Ralston Purina Company of St. Louis, with mid-1990s sales of $2.2 billion; Hartz Mountain Corp. of Harrison, New Jersey, with sales of $850 million; Quaker Oats Pet Food Co. of Chicago, with sales of $538 million; Alpo Petfoods Inc. of Lehigh Valley, Pennsylvania, with sales of $240 million; and Kal Kan Foods Inc. of Vernon, California, with sales of $220 million.

According to *Petfood Industry,* in 1994 canned cat food sales were led by Carnation's Friskies Buffet product line, with $294.2 million in sales, while the leading brand of canned dog food was Kal Kan's Pedigree brand, with 1994 sales of $230.1 million. The leading semi-moist dog food that year was Ralston Purina's Moist & Meaty brand, with $30.2 million in sales, while the leading semi-moist cat food in 1994 was Ralston Purina's Tender Vittles brand, with $55.2 million in sales. Kibbles 'N Bits 'N Bits 'N Bits led in the dry dog food category with $134.5 million in sales, and Cat Chow led the dry cat food category with $138.9 million in sales.

AMERICA AND THE WORLD

According to *Petfood Industry Magazine,* the United States has managed to maintain a favorable trade balance in the petfood industry. Exports amounted to $433 million in 1995, and increased almost nine times between 1986 and 1995 according to the U.S. Department of Commerce.

During the 1980s pet food exports were around $50-60 million annually, but the size of the export market began to expand in the middle of that decade and has continued to grow since that time. Canada, Japan, and the European Community are the three biggest markets for U.S. dog and cat food product exports. Products from Thailand are the biggest competitors with U.S. products on the world market, especially in the Common Market countries. Australia, meanwhile, provides the keenest competition for the Japanese market.

FURTHER READING

Blaesing, Dana. "Special (Pet) Treatment." *Prepared Foods,* April 1996.

Dzanis, Dr. David A. "The 'Lite' Stuff." *Petfood Industry,* March/April 1997.

Gibson, Rachel. "Pet-Food Shoppers Watch Their Pennies." *Wall Street Journal,* 22 October 1992.

"The Iams Company." Lewisburg, OH: Iams, 1992.

Immudyne Pet Health. "Markets for Companion Animal Health and Nutrition." Available from http://www.immudyne.com/mkvet.htm.

Keating, James and Kevin Fleming. "Petfood 2000: Growing Your Petfood Business Over the Next Four Years." *Petfood Industry,* March/April 1997.

Liesse, Julie. "Price War Bites at Pet Food Ad $." *Advertising Age,* 5 April 1993.

Palmer, Jay. "Well, Aren't You the Cat's Meow." *Barron's,* 1 April 1996.

Pet Food Institute Materials. Washington: Pet Food Institute, 1993.

"Pet Foods—1992 Supermarket Sales Manual." *Progressive Grocer,* July 1992.

PFI Monitor. March 1993.

Ralston, Julie. "Deluxe Brands, Pet Supers Wag the Market." *Advertising Age,* 17 September 1995.

"Ralston Purina Company History." Available from http://www.ralston.com/rph.html.

"Ten Insights." *Petfood Industry Magazine.* November/December 1992.

"Who's Who in Pet Food." *Petfood Industry Magazine,* January 1991.

—Joan Leotta, updated by Sharon Kolberg

SIC 2048

PREPARED FEEDS AND FEED INGREDIENTS FOR ANIMALS AND FOWLS, EXCEPT DOGS AND CATS

This classification covers establishments primarily engaged in manufacturing prepared feeds and feed ingredients and adjuncts for animals and fowls, except dogs and cats. Included in this industry are poultry and livestock feed and feed ingredients such as alfalfa meal, feed supplements, and feed concentrates and pre-mixes. Also included are establishments primarily engaged in slaughtering animals for animal feed. Establishments primarily engaged in slaughtering animals for human consumption are classified in **SIC 2011: Meat Packing Plants, SIC 2013: Sausages and Other Prepared meat Products,** and **SIC 2015: Poultry Slaughtering and Processing.** Establishments primarily engaged in manufacturing cat and dog foods are classified in **SIC 2047: Dog and Cat Food.**

INDUSTRY SNAPSHOT

Feed is by far the largest input cost of producing food and fiber of animal origin, exceeding even the initial cost of the animals themselves. The cost of feed represents 50 to 70 percent of the cost of producing meat, milk, and eggs at the farm level. For instance, the United States Department of Agriculture calculates that it requires 88 pounds of feed of feed to produce 100 pounds of milk; 9,523 pounds of feed to produce a steer; 1,273 pounds to produce a lamb; 50 pounds of feed for 100 eggs; 261 pounds of feed to produce 100 pounds of poultry; and 629 pounds of feed for 100 pounds of pork. In the case of grass-eating livestock such as cattle and sheep, a great deal of their nutrition may come from foraging pasture land, although the latter stages of their lives often include significant portions of prepared feeds. With poultry and hogs, however, nourishment is supplied primarily through prepared feed mixes.

According to the American Feed Industry Association, as much as $18 billion worth of feed ingredients are purchased each year. These products range from grain mixes to orange rinds to beet pulps. The feed is prepared in 3,000 primary feed manufacturing plants and 5,500 secondary or custom mix plants. Animal feed is manufactured in every state in the nation and is sold by 17,500 feed dealers; the feed industry as a whole employs 175,000 workers nationwide, with approximately 42,000 of those workers operating in the manufacturing sector.

The four largest feed dealers in the country produce less than 25 percent of the total animal feed consumed. Tens of thousands of farmers with feed mills on their own farms are able to compete with huge conglomerates with national distribution. The feed industry is one of the most competitive businesses in the agricultural sector, and is by far the largest purchaser of U.S. corn, feed grains, and soybean meal.

ORGANIZATION AND STRUCTURE

Owning a feed mill is a capital intensive operation. Many modern feed mills increasingly rely on computer technology; human hands rarely touch the feed ingredients. Not only can the feed mill itself be a multi-million dollar investment—with attendant costs associated with maintaining a competitive position regarding machinery—but the feed manufacturer must also have an expensive commodity inventory on hand at all times. Mill managers attempt to purchase their ingredients up front, often contracting for goods months in advance. To hedge the risks associated with fluctuating grain and commodity prices, many feed manufacturers utilize the option of futures trading. Most feed manufacturers also have a sizable investment in a truck fleet used to deliver bulk feed to dairies, poultry, and swine operations. Virtually all cattle feedlots in the United States, however, prepare all their feed on the premises in bulk form. Many poultry processing companies own their own feed mills and sell the feed to contracting poultry producers who in turn sell their broilers back to the processor.

Retail outlets often will carry only one brand of feed. In return, the feed companies do extensive advertising in the rural press, usually on a regional basis. Another important aspect of the feed industry is the production of sacked feed which is sold through farm supply stores and feed dealers. This feed is often used for 4-H and Future Farmers of America projects, backyard poultry projects, and for feeding of horses and small animals such as rabbits and guinea pigs. The sacked feed sold in farm supply stores is prepared in the same manner as the feed delivered in bulk form, but it is more expensive because of the extra packaging.

Nutritional experts. More than 150 micro- and macro-ingredients are covered in a guide prepared by the Nutrition Council that has become the authoritative source for the feed industry. Nutritionists are commonly employed in the feed manufacturing industry to determine the needs of domestic livestock. Animal nutritionists rely heavily on university research and industry publications for information on the chemical properties of various feed ingredients and their use and availability.

The role of the nutritionist is to calculate a ration that fits the nutritional requirements for the least cost. This is known as a ''least cost ration'' and is the ultimate goal of all rations. There are thousands of professional nutritionists working for livestock feed suppliers, poultry feed manufacturers, feedlots, and poultry raising operations who spend a great deal of their time determining the needs of each animal for different phases of its productive life cycle. Nutritionists use the most sophisticated computer hardware and software to make these calculations on a daily basis. Nutritionists either are employed "in house" or work on a consulting basis.

The role of the feed manufacturer is to buy the commodities and blend them in the feed mill according to the specifications outlined by the nutritionist. There is little room for error because if the ration is not apportioned correctly, it can manifest itself in lowered animal production and diminished outward appearance.

CURRENT CONDITIONS

According to the USDA, in 1991 animals consumed 25 million tons of oil seeds, cakes, and meals; 3.3 million tons of animal proteins such as fish meal, meat, and bone meal; and 46.8 million tons of other by-products. This does not include liquid feeds, which are usually molasses-based supplements used on the range to supplement the grass diet of grazing cows and sheep. The main ingredients used in commercially prepared feed are the feed grains. In 1991, 137.2 million tons of corn, 23 million tons of soybeans, 9.7 million tons of sorghum, and 8.4 million tons of oats and barley were used in the preparation of commercial feeds.

In the mid-1990s, the shipment value was increasing—from about $1.6 billion in 1995 to about 1.7 billion in 1997. According to the delivered cost, field corn and soybean cake and meat were by far the most profitable ingredients of prepared feeds at $4.25 million.

In the mid-1990s, the shipment value was increasing—from about $1.6 billion in 1995 to about $1.7 billion in 1997. According to the delivered cost, field corn and soybean cake and meal were by far the most profitable ingredients of prepared feeds—$4.25 million, combined.

The sale and manufacture of pre-mixes is an industry within an industry. Pre-mixes are micro-ingredients such as vitamins, minerals, chemical preservatives, antibiotics, fermentation products, and other essential ingredients that are purchased from pre mix companies, usually in sacked form, for blending into commercial rations. Because of the availability of these products, a farmer who uses his own grain can formulate his own rations and be assured that his animals are getting the recommended levels of minerals and vitamins.

INDUSTRY LEADERS

Leading companies involved in prepared feeds production include ConAgra Inc., an Omaha, Nebraska based firm; and Ralston Purina, based in St. Louis, Missouri. Other significant industry players include SmithKline Beecham, Moorman Manufacturing Company, Hubbard Milling Company, Central Soya Company, Farmland Industries, and Baywood International Incorporated.

The 1992 merger between the National Feed Ingredients Association (NFIA) and the American Feed Industry Association (AFIA) under the AFIA name brought the entire feed industry under representation by a single organization for the first time since 1909. The membership of the American Feed Industry Association includes companies that manufacture feed to sell, firms that manufacture feed for their own animals, and those who provide equipment, ingredients, services and supplies to feed manufacturers. AFIA headquarters are located in Arlington, Virginia.

One of the primary goals of the AFIA is to represent the interests of the feed industry on federal legislation and regulation. The AFIA meets often with Food and Drug Administration officials to coordinate such things as mill inspections, manufacturing practices, labeling requirements, feed additives, and the administration of laws and regulations. The AFAI played a leading role in the development of the Uniform State Feed Law and other regulations mandating uniform feed labels.

WORK FORCE

This industry, according to the United States Bureau of Labor Statistics, employed approximately 42,000 workers in 1992, the last year that figures were made available. This marks a significant drop from 1982, when the industry supported 53,600 employees. By 1996 the employment rate fell to about 35,000. Of those employed in prepared feeds manufacturing, the bulk of them are engaged as production workers—nearly 19,600 in 1996. Average hourly earnings in the industry for production workers reached $9.83 in 1992, up from $9.07 in 1990 and $8.52 in 1988. By 1998 hourly wages were expected to increase to $11.30.

FURTHER READING

Agricultural Statistics. U.S. Department of Agriculture, 1991.

Agricultural Statistics Board. *Cattle and Livestock Report.* Washington: NASS/USDA, 1992.

American Feed Industry Association materials. Arlington, VA: AFIA, 1993.

Cattle and Beef Handbook. Englewood, CO: National Cattlemen's Association, 1992.

Factbook On U.S. Agriculture. USDA Office of Government and Public Affairs, 1991.

U.S. Department of Commerce. International Trade Administration. *U.S. Industrial Outlook 1994.* Washington: GPO, 1994.

—Lee Pitts, updated by Jennifer L. Stong

SIC 2051

BREAD, CAKE, AND RELATED PRODUCTS

This industry is comprised of establishments that make fresh or frozen breads or rolls and perishable bakery products such as cakes, pies, and pastries. Manufacturers of dry bakery products such as cookies and crackers are classified in **SIC 2052: Cookies and Crackers.** Establishments involved in manufacturing frozen bakery products other than bread are classified in **SIC 2053: Frozen Bakery Products, Except Bread.** On-premises, retail bakeries are classified in **SIC 5461: Retail Bakeries.**

INDUSTRY SNAPSHOT

In the United States, 2,535 bread and cake plants operated during 1992, according to the U.S. Census Bureau Survey of Manufactures. Total shipments for the bread, cake, and related products industry approximated $18.1 billion that year. Primary products represented $14.1 billion. Secondary products were valued at $680.5 million, and miscellaneous transactions represented $3.3 billion of the industry's total shipments.

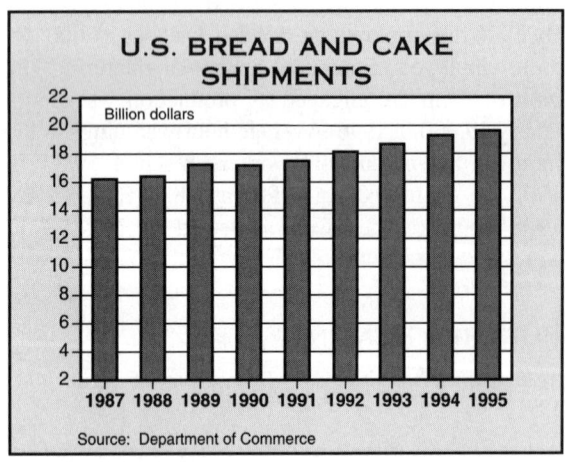

U.S. BREAD AND CAKE SHIPMENTS

Billion dollars

Source: Department of Commerce

ORGANIZATION AND STRUCTURE

Historically, the baking industry established itself close to population centers. Because bread and cake products were perishable, proximity to a customer base was a primary concern. One way growing bakeries overcame this geographic constraint was through the purchase of companies in other areas. Many acquisitions and mergers within the industry during the last decades of the twentieth century transformed baking establishments with regional shipping systems into large conglomerates with national distribution networks. In addition, large baking establishments often attracted the attention of other investors. According to a report published in *Food Review,* since 1960 many of the nation's top wholesale bakeries were purchased by food processing companies. Joy Harwood, an agricultural economist writing for *Food Review,* stated that "control of every major wholesaler, except Flowers Industries, has changed."

The practice of buying or merging with existing firms had benefits in addition to overcoming problems related to delivering fresh products to the marketplace. Buying and refurbishing existing facilities was often less expensive than building new plants. Buying also helped avoid problems associated with creating excess capacity in specific geographic areas. Despite the trend toward building large corporations, many independent family-owned bakeries remained successful. In 1987 an estimated 56.3 percent of all wholesale bread and cake plants operated with less than 20 employees. These small establishments, however, captured only 2.3 percent of the industry's total sales.

The baking industry was monitored and regulated by several governmental agencies. For example, the U.S. Department of Health, Education and Welfare set the definitions and standards used to identify wheat and related products. The Food and Drug Administration (FDA) regulated product quality and mandated procedures by which food additives were to be approved prior to use. And, the National Research Council's Food and Nutritional Board (along with the American Medical Association's Council on Foods and Nutrition) published guidelines for enriching bread products with nutrients.

BACKGROUND AND DEVELOPMENT

The oldest existing written record of a baked grain product dates back to about 2600 B.C. The earliest known breads were flat and were baked them on smooth stones or clay plates. According to a theory held by some historians, the ancient Egyptians created the world's first leavened breads. Leavened bread was made with ingredients possessing the chemical properties necessary to make dough rise. By contrast, unleavened breads were made from doughs that did not rise.

The ability to bake leavened breads may have been developed along with the ability to brew beer, as both processes relied on fermentation. Fermentation refers to a complex chemical process in which organic compounds are broken down into simpler substances. In alcoholic fermentation, the yeast converts a mixture's sugar or starch into carbon dioxide and alcohol. Recipes with sufficient liquid produced beer-like beverages. In mixtures with less liquid, the carbon dioxide produced by the fermentation process made the dough rise.

Fermentation of wheat and water mixtures was accomplished through the incorporation of yeast. Yeast is a member of the fungus family. Although an individual ''yeast'' is a single-celled organism, it lives and grows by multiplying into cultures consisting of thousands of cells. In order to grow, the cells eat the sugar and starch in dough mixtures. Early yeasts were incorporated into recipes by letting doughs sit out for a period of time to ''sour.'' These wild yeast cultures, once established in a dough mixture, were carefully maintained through a process whereby some dough from each batch was saved to incorporate into the next batch. Before the development of commercial yeast, all leavened bread was made from sourdoughs. Sourdough breads are still made from flour, water, yeast, and bacteria.

Although many grains and other products could be fermented, wheat flours were the only ones to exhibit leavening. Wheat possessed a type of gluten (plant protein) unlike the gluten of other grains. Wheat gluten, when kneaded, formed an elastic structure that had the unique ability to trap the carbon dioxide given off by the yeast and to stretch and expand as more gas was created. When leavened doughs were baked, the heat killed the yeast but the dough's expanded structure remained. As a result, leavened breads were lighter and more airy than their unleavened counterparts.

The ancient Egyptians are also sometimes credited with inventing ovens. According to one theory, the first ''ovens'' were earthen pots. Early bakers discovered that when dough was placed inside preheated pots, it cooked more evenly than it did when placed on top of a heat source. The construction of permanent oven structures soon followed. Along with the development of ovens came the development of bread varieties as bakers experimented with different shapes and different ingredients. Sweet cakes first appeared in the twelfth century B.C. During the classical era, the Greeks modified oven designs and introduced the use of more innovative ingredients including milk, oil, wine, cheese, and honey.

Commercial bakeries first appeared in the Roman Empire. Under early Roman rule, baking progressed to an art form. As the Empire began to crumble, however, bakeries were taken over by the government and commercial baking became virtually nonexistent. White flour was a luxury available only to royalty. During the Middle Ages, only monasteries and manor houses baked large quantities of leavened products. Monasteries were also credited with the development of pie crusts, an early pastry product. Although pie crusts were originally used only with meat dishes, they gained popularity for dessert items when sweetening ingredients were used. Early sweeteners in baked goods consisted of honey, raisins, and other types of fried fruits. The use of sugar was introduced during the 1500s. Innovative bakers using sugared batters and doughs developed cakes and pastries.

Commercial baking as a trade began to rise again during the urbanization that accompanied the early Industrial Revolution. Innovations of the late nineteenth and early twentieth century enabled the mass-production of baked goods. As a result, large baking facilities began to supplant small local establishments. One of the most important innovations was the development of ''tame'' yeast, because these yeast cultures produced uniform, predictable results. Wild yeast cultures were too time consuming and too unpredictable to make automatic production feasible. The first yeasts used by commercial bakers were obtained from brewers, and in 1868 Charles Fleischmann made a compressed, distiller's yeast. The selective breeding of pure yeast cultures began in 1883, and by the early 1900s fast acting yeasts were well established.

Another innovation that helped shorten the time required to make bread was the mechanization of dough kneading. Kneading was necessary to develop gluten elasticity. The introduction of harder wheat hybrids that produced stronger flours enabled bakers to formulate doughs capable of withstanding the stress of mechanical kneading. The practice was introduced in the 1920s and had gained widespread acceptance by the 1950s.

The automation of milling and baking practices, however, did not produce uniformly beneficial results. In the 1930s, the U.S. Department of Agriculture (USDA) conducted nutritional surveys and found extensive thiamine and riboflavin deficiencies in some segments of the population. The deficiencies were attributed to milling methods that yielded finer white flours with diminished nutritional value. For example, stone-ground white flour contained 60 percent of the grain's original thiamine content, and roller-milled white flour contained only 12-20 percent of the wheat's original thiamine content. Concomitant with the surveys that identified these nutritional deficiencies, researchers developed the ability to synthesize vitamins.

During the 1940s efforts were made to restore the vitamins lost by milling practices. In 1941, the National Research Council recommended enriching white flour and white bread. Within a year, an estimated 75-80 percent of the nation's white bread was enriched on a voluntary basis. During World War II bread enrichment was mandated by the federal government, and to ensure continuation after the war, 27 individual states passed enrichment regulations. The Food, Drug, and Cosmetic Act, which became law in 1952, defined minimum and maximum levels for thiamine, riboflavin, and niacin enrichment.

Congress gave the Food and Drug Administration (FDA) the responsibility of establishing guidelines concerning the practice of adding nutrients to food products. According to recognized standards, the word "enriched" meant adding B-vitamins, iron, and optionally calcium to flour or cereal grain products. "Restored" referred to the practice of replacing natural nutrients that were lost during processing. "Fortification" involved the addition of nutrients not naturally present in a food. A few well known examples were the addition of vitamin D to milk or iodine to salt. During the early 1980s, an estimated 90 percent of all standard commercial white bread was enriched.

Three bread-making techniques produced most of the commercial bread in the United States. These were called the straight dough process, the sponge method, and continuous production. In the straight dough process, all ingredients, including the yeast, were combined. The resulting dough rested during the fermentation process. Following fermentation, mechanical means were used to form loaves and the loaves were permitted to rise again before baking.

The sponge method was based on traditional bread making techniques but employed highly mechanized procedures. Recipes were based on ingredient weight rather than volume measurements. Flour was mixed with yeast and water to make a dough or "sponge," which was then permitted to ferment for several hours. After fermentation, other ingredients and additional flour were added and the dough was remixed. Following a time of rest, the dough was cut into pieces and placed in pans. After placement in pans, the dough was allowed to rise and was then moved to an oven for baking. Typical fermentation resulted in a five-fold volume increase. Resting times averaged 20-30 minutes, and rising times were approximately one hour.

The continuous production method was also highly automated. Flour and other ingredients were fed into a production line under carefully monitored conditions. The resulting dough was extruded through dies, pressed, or cut and placed in pans. The pans moved by conveyor through a large oven. Slicing machines cut finished loaves and packaging machines blew wrappers open with a puff of air to receive the finished product.

The commercial baking industry produced two basic types of breads—yeast breads and quick breads. Yeast breads were leavened with yeast. Quick breads used other leavening agents such as baking powder. Baking powder, which also worked by producing carbon dioxide, produced results more quickly than yeast. Quick breads included such products as muffins, loaves, and biscuits.

According to Ed Wood, a researcher of the history of bread making, 75 percent of the bread consumed in industrialized nations is produced by large commercial bakeries. The Wheat Flour Institute calculated that during the early 1980s, U.S. bakers produced approximately 250 million pounds of bread every week. Bread products were available in many varieties and some individual bakers' lines exceeded 200 different products.

The most popular kind of bread is white bread made from white flour. French breads are made without milk, sugar, and shortening. Their characteristic texture is created by injecting steam into the oven during baking, and the flavor comes from the wheat itself. "Whole wheat breads" are made from whole wheat flour, and "wheat bread" is made from a blend of white flour and whole wheat flour. Cracked wheat breads are made from white flour and crushed wheat meal. Other bread varieties are made with white flours of varying coarseness. Rye breads are made with a mixture of rye flour and wheat flour because rye flour by itself does not possess the chemical properties necessary to produce a leavened product. Two types of rye flours are used to produce different rye breads. Light rye is made from the grain's endosperm; dark rye is made from the entire kernel.

In addition to its bread products, the baking industry also produces cakes. Cakes are typically made from pourable batters. The basic ingredients are flour, liquid, eggs, and leavening agents plus flavorings and sometimes fat. The rising action of a baking cake is similar to the leavening action of bread. When a cake bakes, steam and gases cause the batter to expand. Different types of cakes are classified according to how they are leavened and whether they contain fat.

Two broad cake classifications are foam cakes and butter cakes. Foam cakes, typically airy and mild, are primarily leavened with air. One way in which this is accomplished is by beating egg whites and folding them into the mixture. Examples of foam cakes include angel food cake and sponge cake. Butter cakes rely on leavening agents such as baking powder, baking soda, or yeast. Butter cakes are typically more tender and possess a smoother texture than foam cakes. Examples include layer cakes and pound cakes. Other types of cakes do not easily fit these traditional distinctions. Chiffon cakes use egg whites and baking powder for leavening. Tortes are similar to sponge cakes but rely on ground nuts or crumbs to replace some or all of their flour.

According to figures for 1990, annual per capita consumption of bread products was increasing slightly. The average U.S. citizen consumed 28 pounds of white bread, 23 pounds of variety breads, 23 pounds of rolls, 15 pounds of cake, and four pounds of doughnuts and other sweet yeast products. Between 1991 and 1992 the value of the industry's shipments increased by 3.1 percent to $18.4 billion. Projections for 1993 anticipated that production would reach $19.2 billion. Forecasters predicted that annual per capita bread consumption would reach 60 pounds by the end of the century. One factor expected to drive the increase was the release of the Department of Agriculture's new four-tiered Food Guide Pyramid. The updated Food Guide Pyramid recommended 6-11 daily servings from the bread and grain food group.

Consumption increases varied by product, however, and overall industry growth was expected to be less than 1 percent in 1993, and only about 1.5 percent annually between 1993 and 1997. Industry watchers expected white bread to capture 58 percent of the total bread market. Demand for snack cakes was expected to increase 2-2.5 percent annually as manufacturers improved quality and offered new packaging options such as individually wrapped, single-servings within larger boxes. Sales of sweet yeast doughnuts were expected to increase 2.5 percent per year. With the continuing emphasis on healthy, low-fat foods, the consumption of fresh bagels exceeded $500 million in 1992, with sales growing at more than 30 percent annually.

A number of products, however, experienced declining consumption. Dinner roll consumption tapered off when pasta products gained popularity as bread substitutes. Sales of large pies, snack pies, full-size cakes, and cake-type doughnuts slackened as part of a national trend toward health consciousness. Some analysts noted that the increased consumption of sweet yeast doughnuts and snack cakes was contrary to the general trend toward more healthy products. They attributed the continuing popularity of these items to convenience.

Recessionary conditions prevalent in the United States during the early 1990s also impacted the bread and cake products industry. Lower priced products, particularly white breads, attracted renewed interest. In 1992, white bread averaged $0.75 per pound. Whole wheat bread sold for $1.02 per pound, and French breads averaged $1.26 per pound.

As the bread and cake industry entered the 1990s, its products were available virtually everywhere within the United States. Most of the products produced by commercial bakers were sold through grocery stores where breads and rolls represented the fifth largest selling category of grocery items. Additionally, the baking industry was the nation's largest consumer of nonfat dried milk. One industry analyst stated that 9 million tons of bread, rolls, and buns were sold annually. Another report pointed out that U.S. commercial bakeries consumed 73 percent of the nation's milled flour in 1980.

Despite its ubiquitous presence, however, the bread and cake industry faced several challenges in the early 1990s. One challenge was increased competition from in-store bakeries. Supermarkets with large numbers of in-store bakeries in 1990 included Winn-Dixie (with 1,117), Kroger (946), and A&P (716). Although goods baked on the premises were often priced higher than prepackaged goods, they held several advantages. Customers perceived them as fresher, and on-premises bakeries could offer specialty cakes and breads that were not available from mass producers. In-store bakeries often promoted products as impulse items, placing them near the front of the store to take advantage of baking aromas.

To meet the competition from in-store bakeries, commercial wholesalers began offering more variety in single-serving packages and increasing the assortment of specialty products. Industry analysts disagreed about the long-term effect in-store bakeries would have on traditional distribution networks. Although sales from in-store bakeries increased from $4.9 billion in 1986 to $8 billion in 1990, the rate at which they were being developed slowed during the early 1990s.

In addition to competition from in-store bakeries, wholesalers faced increased competition from prepared mixes. Prepared mixes were marketed to customers who wanted the convenience of purchased items and the freshness of newly baked goods. Competition from prepared mixes came not only within the household market, but also in the institutional market as users such as restaurants turned increasingly toward mixes.

Private label manufacturers also captured a growing portion of the bread and cake market. As the nation endured recessionary times during the early 1990s, consumers paid more attention to food prices. In order to retain market share, major manufacturers increased use of couponing and discounting.

Another challenge facing the industry during the early 1990s was increased concern about the environment. During the leavening process ethyl alcohol was released into the atmosphere. As a result, Southern California's South Coast Air Quality Management District Board ordered smog controls on the ovens of 24 large commercial bakeries. In addition, some environmental groups criticized the industry for its use of excess packaging. Officials countered the charges with claims that the packaging was necessary to prevent spoilage. To ameliorate the criticism, bakery wrapper recycling programs were instituted in some areas.

The bread and cake industry also faced the challenge of producing products for a nation caught up in a conflict between health consciousness and a desire for taste gratification. In 1989, many items were reformulated to eliminate ingredients viewed as unhealthy. These included such ingredients as tropical oils and other fat, sugar, and salt. The elimination of fat from many classes of bakery items was a difficult accomplishment because the fat incorporated in batters and doughs served many technical and aesthetic functions. Technically, it assisted the leavening process by incorporating air into mixtures, enabling the even transfer of heat during baking, and giving moisture to the final product. Aesthetically, the fat produced a favorable texture and added flavor.

To reformulate recipes without fat, different types of fat replacers were studied. Entenmann's Bakery, a subsidiary of CPC Baking, Inc., was the first national company to offer a line of fat-free products. It began test marketing them in 1989 and reported sales of $200 million during the first full year of production. To honor Entenmann's achievement, the American Marketing Association awarded the company with the 1990 Edison Award for New Product Marketer of the Year. Entenmann's also received the grand prize from the Gorman's New Product Contest. The introduction of fat-free items helped increase consumption among consumers who traditionally skipped dessert items.

Following the launch of fat-free products during the early 1990s, many consumers reported that choles-

terol and overall fat content were important in purchasing decisions. As the trend expanded and many companies began bringing fat-free products to the marketplace, Campbell Taggart introduced an enriched bread with the name IronKids in 1989. The bread was made with the same fiber content as the company's whole wheat bread, and the FDA therefore challenged the product's name and marketing methods. Campbell Taggart and the FDA reached a compromise in 1992. Under the terms of the compromise, Campbell Taggart printed a disclaimer under the IronKids logo stating that the name ''refers only to a children's fitness program, and has no reference to either extra iron in this bread or to the bread resulting in superior strength or performance.''

Interest in healthy products, however, appeared to be waning in 1992. *Prepared Foods* published the results of a study conducted by the NPD Group of Port Washington, New York, which documented a shift toward snacking and diminished concern about calorie content. Consumers were also less likely to read labels. More emphasis was placed on upscale, indulgent products than on products aimed at health-conscious consumers. A similar trend was revealed by the results of a Gallup Poll published in *Progressive Grocer,* in which consumer statements about health concerns contradicted consumer spending habits. Industry analysts theorized that low-fat sweet goods were of an inferior quality and priced higher than traditional formulas. One exception was noted within the bread category where multigrain items with high-fiber and low-fat contents were doing well.

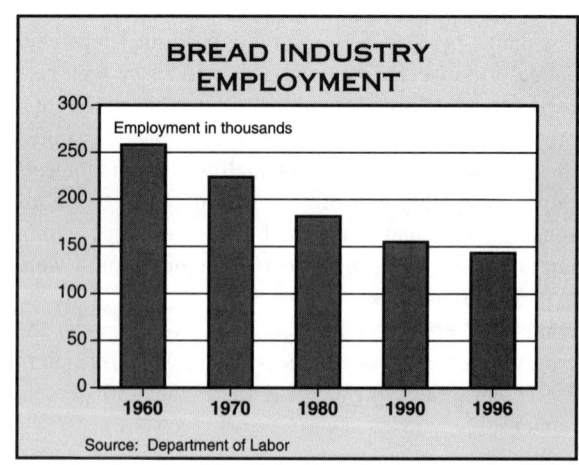

BREAD INDUSTRY EMPLOYMENT

Employment in thousands

Source: Department of Labor

CURRENT CONDITIONS

In the mid-1990s, increased costs of raw materials cut into the profit margins of large and small players in the industry. In 1996, bread and cake products constituted an $18.4 billion industry that employed 183,000 workers. Shipments by mid-decade were valued at $16.1 billion, with bread accounting for almost one-third of that total.

INDUSTRY LEADERS

Interstate Bakeries Corporation was the nation's largest baker and distributor of fresh bread and cake products by mid-decade. In 1996, Interstate reported net sales of $753 million. That year, the company operated 63 bread and cake bakeries throughout the U.S.

Interstate was formed in 1937 following the consolidation of two baking companies in Kansas City. Interstate operated two major divisions, the Bread Division and the Cake Division. Its major brands included Dolly Madison, Butternut, and Holsum. Interstate distributed products through more than 100,000 food outlets located along 4,200 routes. The distribution network covered all regions of the United States except the northeast. Interstate's thrift store network, which had 780 operating stores, was the industry's most extensive.

In 1996, Flowers Industries was another major player in the industry through co-ownership of the second-largest cookie and cracker business in the U.S.: the newly combined Keebler & Sunshine Biscuit Co. Flowers, which was founded in 1919, operated in 16 states by 1996. The company's products included white and variety breads, buns, rolls, snack cakes, pastries, pies, doughnuts, and brownies. Its major brands were Nature's Own, Cobblestone Mill, Bluebird, Holsum, and Country Hearth, and Mrs. Smith's Frozen Pies, which had been acquired in a merger with Shipley Baking Co. of Fort Smith, Arkansas. In addition, the company manufactured products under regional brands and private labels. Flowers reported revenues of $1.2 billion in 1996. The company operated 48 production and distribution companies and employed more than 7,000 people.

Many other major bread and cake establishments were owned by other corporations. For example Campbell Taggart was owned by Anheuser-Busch; and, Pepperidge Farm, with revenues of $520 million in 1996, was owned by Campbell Soup Company. In 1995, food conglomerate CPC International Inc. purchased Entenmann's from Kraft Foods, Inc., which itself was a subsidiary of Philip Morris Companies Inc.

Entenmann's was established in 1898 by William Entenmann. The company made its deliveries with a horse and buggy, but in 1957 a decision was made to switch from delivery routes to wholesale distribution

through supermarkets. In 1978 the company was purchased by Warner-Lambert Company and was then sold, in 1982, to General Foods Corporation. After General Foods was acquired by Philip Morris and its operations merged with Philip Morris' Kraft subsidiary, the bakery line was considered outside of the company's core business and was sold in 1995 to Kraft competitor CPC International Inc. The Entenmann's line included more than 200 different products in eight categories: danish, sweet cakes, pastry, cakes, cupcakes, pies, cookies, and doughnuts.

RESEARCH AND TECHNOLOGY

One of the most extensive areas of ongoing research within the industry involved investigating methods of extending shelf life and preserving product freshness. One method, modified atmosphere packaging (MAP), involved introducing a predetermined atmosphere inside special barrier packaging materials at the time products were sealed for shipping. Nitrogen and carbon dioxide were the most frequently used gases in MAP. The technique was used to replace oxygen, a primary contributor to product staleness. According to published reports, MAP extended shelf life up to 30 days and increased freezer life up to six months.

Another, more advanced method of controlling the atmosphere within a product package was called controlled atmosphere packaging (CAP). CAP relied on active means of manipulating the gas in a package's "headspace." Products were packed with chemical inserts to actively manipulate the environment within the package. For example, oxygen scavengers, frequently composed of iron compounds, would absorb any oxygen remaining after a package was sealed. Eliminating oxygen from packaging was important because it inhibited mold growth. Studies indicated that CAP extended the time period in which a product would remain mold-free by 300 percent.

MAP and CAP technologies presented many benefits. They eliminated the need for preservatives, and reduced distribution costs by eliminating the need for freezing and chilling during transportation. They also increased customer convenience because products did not require freezing following purchase. They also helped maintain appropriate moisture levels so products did not dry out. Two of the biggest problems surrounding MAP and CAP usage were customer perception and price. Customers did not view bakery products with extended shelf life as fresh, and products packaged with MAP and CAP were more expensive than those packaged with traditional methods. One industry analyst suggested that CAP and MAP technologies were best suited for wholesalers with large geographic distribution networks, rather than local baking operations.

FURTHER READING

Amin, Melanie. "Baking Ingredients Offer the Right Mix." *Prepared Foods* 15 April 1992.

Berger, Melvin. "Baking and Grain Processing." *Food Processing: Industry at Work.* New York: Franklin Watts, 1977.

Best, Daniel, Claudia Dziuk-O'Donnell, and Lisa Nelson. "Fat-busters for Bakery Foods." *Prepared Foods,* July 1992.

Dornblaser, Lynn. "Have Your Cake and Eat It, Too." *Prepared Foods,* 15 April 1992.

Dornblaser, Lynn, and Marty Friedman. "New Product Numbers Down: Slow Down or Postponement?" *Prepared Foods,* February 1993.

Entenmann, Jackie. "Entenmann's." Bay Shore, NY: Entenmanns, nd.

"Flowers Industries Announces Record Sales for Fiscal 1996." Available from http://www.prnewswire.com/cgi-bin/
.

"Frozen Cake and Pastry." *Institutional Distribution,* 15 May 1991.

Harwood, Joy. "U.S. Baking Industry Responds to Customers." *Food Review,* April-June 1991.

———. "U.S. Flour Milling on the Rise." *Food Review,* April-June 1991.

Horovitz, Bruce. "Bagels Hit the Big Time." *Los Angeles Times,* 21 December 1993, D1.

"IBC: A Short Biographical Sketch." Kansas City, MO: Interstate Bakeries, nd.

"IBC Quick Facts." Kansas City, MO: Interstate Bakeries, nd.

Lazich, Robert S., ed. *Market Share Reporter 1997.* Detroit: Gale Research, 1997.

Lingle, Rick. "CAP for U.S. Bakery Products: To Be, or Not To Be?" *Prepared Foods,* March 1988.

Pyler, Ernst John. *Our Daily Bread.* Chicago: Siebel Publishing, 1958.

"Shipley Baking Company Joins Flowers Industries, Inc." Available from http://www2.flowersindustries.com/flowers/archive/news6.html/.

Tanyeri, Dana. "Mixes Offer Fresh Benefits and Low Food Cost." *Institutional Distribution,* July 1990.

Turner, Dorothy. *Bread.* Minneapolis, MN: Carolrhoda Books, 1989.

U.S. Bureau of the Census. *1995 Annual Survey of Manufactures.* Washington: GPO, 1997.

U.S. Department of Commerce. *1987 Census of Manufactures.* Washington, DC: Bureau of the Census, 1990.

U.S. Department of Commerce. *U.S. Industrial Outlook 1993.* Washington: U.S. Department of Commerce, 1993.

Wheat Flour Institute. *From Wheat to Flour.* rev. ed. Washington: Wheat Flour Institute, 1981.

Wood, Ed. *World Sourdoughs from Antiquity.* Cascade, ID: Sinclair Publishing, 1989.

—Karen Bellenir, updated by Marinell Jochnowitz

SIC 2052

COOKIES AND CRACKERS

This category includes establishments primarily engaged in manufacturing fresh cookies, crackers, pretzels, and similar "dry" bakery products. Secondary products that are part of this industry include biscuits, graham crackers, saltines, cracker meal and crumbs, cracker sandwiches made from crackers, wafers, and ice cream cones and cups.

INDUSTRY SNAPSHOT

Although mom is still America's favorite cookie maker, the bakeries that attempt to make cookies and crackers as good as mom's have become a huge industry. Total sales of cookies and crackers was estimated to be approximately $11.5 billion in 1996.

Adult consumers have proven to be attracted to relatively new brands of items such as low-fat parmesan and romano cheese crackers now on the shelves. While sales of expensive national brand cookies have declined somewhat, sales of lower-priced private labels rose. It is reasonable to assume that price, convenience, and health concerns will continue to influence the consumption of cookie and cracker goods in the near future.

ORGANIZATION AND STRUCTURE

According to *Ward's Business Directory of U.S. Private and Public Companies,* there are 72 cookie and cracker manufacturing companies listed under SIC 2052. In the major bakery companies, the cookies and crackers segment of business often operates as a separate division of the bakery division of the company. Many bakery companies today are often divisions of holding companies that are also involved with the diversification of products that include food, beverages, and, as is the case with RJR Nabisco, Inc., tobacco.

Other manufacturers of cookies and crackers operate strictly under the bakery goods heading.

Companies such as Mrs. Field's Cookies and Famous Amos at one time operated exclusively out of their own retail outlets. They later expanded to supermarkets and specialty stores. A number of these private label companies work through distributors, who can handle a number of varied products. Many of the larger companies handle their own distribution, working directly with supermarkets and retailers.

BACKGROUND AND DEVELOPMENT

The U.S. Department of Agriculture estimated that the makers of bakery products constitute a $29.1 billion industry. The cookie and cracker segment of that industry is a significant one, as more than 3 billion pounds of cookies and 2.1 billion pounds of crackers were consumed in 1992, according to government estimations. According to the U.S. Bureau of the Census, the cost of materials, services, fuels, and electric energy used by the cookies and crackers industry amounted to about $2.2 billion. The total value of shipments for establishments classified in this industry is estimated to be about $6.5 billion.

The U.S. Chamber of Commerce notes that cookie and cracker manufacturing is the fastest growing segment of the bakery industry. Shipments of all bakery products rose on the average of 1.3 percent per year from the years 1987 to 1992. Sales of cookies and crackers for the same years, however, increased by rates of 2.3 percent. The primary reason given for the projected increase in sales is the recent introduction of low-fat, low-calorie, low-cholesterol cookies and crackers.

Well into the late 1980s, bakery goods showed a consistent increase in sales. But consumption of sweet baked goods began to decline around 1992. Consumers were changing their buying habits and sought out bakery products that were lower in calories. Cookie and cracker sales also slowed by 1992, but showed signs of growth due to the availability of the new low-fat varieties. Sales of high-priced national brand cookies also declined, as consumers turned to lower-priced private labels.

Health Valley Natural Foods Inc. and R.W. Frookies were also making a bid for the fat-free cookie market. Health Valley claims its cookie is the number one fat-free cookie. Frookies now has four flavors of fat-free cookies on the shelf. Frookies founder Richard Worth claims that Frookies shares equal shelf space with Nabisco in many supermarkets. He is convinced that Frookies is more of a health food than Nabisco's. Moreover, Campbell Soup Company's Pepperidge Farm division launched a low-fat cookie line called, Wholesome Choice. It claims it has no preservatives and no artificial flavors. Pepperidge Farm holds about six percent of the cookie market, according to Michael Wilke of *Advertising Age.*

The industry has also seen the merger and/or purchase of some major producers. *Business Week* reported the 1992 purchase of the Famous Amos brand of chocolate chip cookies by President Enterprises Corp., the Taiwanese food giant, for an estimated $60.6 million. George K. Liu, chief executive of President's U.S. division, implied that it was the first of many acquisitions. President's corporate CEO, C.Y. Kao, promised that "in 25 years, we will be one of the biggest food companies in the world". At the same time, Campbell Soup Company made an unsolicited bid for Arnotts Ltd., an Australian maker of cookies and crackers.

Nabisco made efforts to reverse its losses in the cookie business. The *Wall Street Journal* noted that Nabisco sales have been slipping in part because baby boomers are giving up their old favorite high-fat, high-cholesterol cookies and discouraging their children from buying them. Another important reason for declines in Nabisco's cookie and cracker business is that, during the good years in the 1980s, Nabisco aggressively increased its prices until the consumers started to fight back by not buying. Commenting on this strategy, Robert Urbain, a vice president with Pepperidge Farm, said, "Prices have gone beyond the levels that are justified." Nabisco still holds the lion's share of the business—28.2 percent, compared to total private labels of 13.7 percent, and Keebler's 12.4 percent. Private labels, however, have begun to cut heavily into Nabisco's market share. Nabisco is said to be working overtime to undercut its private label competition. In an effort to bolster its market, Nabisco is making an effort to gain market space in discount outlets and convenience stores. But private labels are slowly making inroads in all the major cookie and cracker markets.

Because it is the leader in the cookie and cracker industry, the private labels appear to be pointing their big guns at Nabisco. There are a number of upscale private lines available, including Sam's Choice, a line being sold at Wal-Mart stores, and Master Choice, sold at A & P stores. One of the front-runners, and a leader of the upscale private label pack, is President's Choice. Produced by Canada's Loblaw Companies, the chocolate chip entry is beginning to chip away at Nabisco's Chips Ahoy! brand.

CURRENT CONDITIONS

The consumer segment most responsible for boosting the sales of baked goods is the 35- to 54-year-

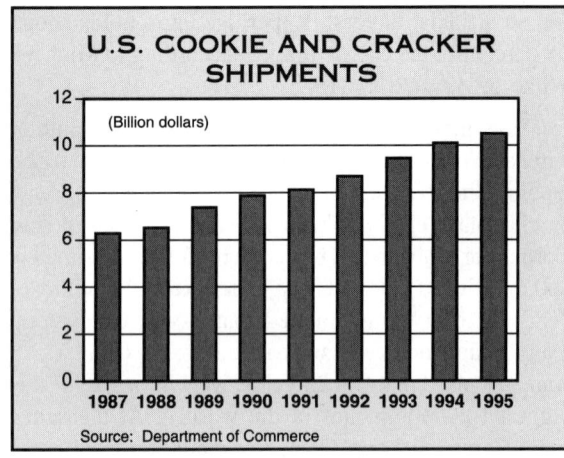

U.S. COOKIE AND CRACKER SHIPMENTS

(Billion dollars)

Source: Department of Commerce

old age group, according to a survey compiled by the U.S. Bureau of Labor Statistics. The survey showed that people in this age group regularly spend more for bakery products. Happily for cookie and cracker manufacturers, this consumer segment was growing at a rate of 2.7 percent yearly, and by 1997, it was expected to represent 29.3 percent of the total U.S. population. One explanation for heightened consumption was that this group was at the peak of their earning potential, and therefore they had more disposable income. The consumption of cookies and crackers also went up due in part to manufacturers reacting to the health consciousness of the consumer. Many manufacturers replaced tropical oils and white flour with healthier canola oil and whole wheat flour. Price and health concerns are expected to continue to be the prime influence in consumption changes.

In today's market, consumers have been purchasing healthy cookies and crackers, and manufacturers are responding. Diana Morgan, writing in *In Health* magazine, accused the bakery industry of "the poisoning of America." Morgan lambasted Fruit and Fibre cereal, Triscuits crackers, Hydrox cookies, and Cracklin' Oat Bran as being laced with coconut palm or palm kernel oils that can clog arteries as badly as fatty pork chops and London broil. The food companies promptly promised to change their ways, but many of them are finding it difficult to make cookies with unsaturated oils unless they are resaturated. Dumping the high cholesterol tropical oils that do so much to enhance the product's flavor has not been easy. Unsaturated oils cause the product to lose the crunch that consumers favor, and usually result in premature staleness. While partially resaturated unsaturated products like "Partially hydrogenated vegetable oil" help manufacturers solve the problem, the fact is that products are probably no healthier than they were before. According to Morgan, "partially hydrogenated oils

can act even more saturated than they really are." The experts are working at it, however, and they still hope to come up with the answer.

A number of companies have introduced products to suit this changing market. Nabisco introduced a new line of fat-free cookies and crackers called SnackWells. As reported in *Advertising Age,* Nabisco management insists that "The company is placing substantial corporate emphasis behind product categories that health-wise consumers are increasingly demanding." The company added that SnackWell cookies have one gram of fat compared with three grams in traditional cookies on the market.

By 1997, SnackWells was the top-selling brand of cookie and cracker in the country. The brand's popularity reflected the fact that 173 million Americans were eating reduced-fat and fat-free foods—an 81 percent increase from 1993.

Food and Drug Administration (FDA) approval in 1996 of a new fat substitute, Olestra, promised to change the low-fat cookie and cracker market even further. Olestra, which was developed by Procter & Gamble, added no fat or calories to foods and was expected to appear in new formulations of crackers, tortilla chips and other snacks.

Concern for the environment has affected the operations of bakery companies. Most are now spending more of their dollars on environmental protection. Many companies are introducing pollution abatement equipment, especially for their ovens, and will be introducing other pollution control measures. Many are converting their delivery vans so they can operate on cleaner-burning propane instead of gasoline. It is expected that environmental control efforts will eventually increase operating costs by as much as 10 percent.

Bakery companies are also generally making changes in the ingredients they have been using for years. They are making efforts to minimize the use of chemical agents. Companies are beginning to phase out potassium bromate, which has always been a integral part of their recipes. Health conscious, label-reading consumers are turning from products with potassium bromate to products that contain acceptable alternatives, such as barley malt. The *U.S. Industrial Outlook* reported that the per capita consumption of crackers edged up mainly due to bakery companies changing ingredients to satisfy consumer demands and tastes. The increase, it was believed, was due to cracker manufacturers eliminating questionable ingredients like tropical oils and white flour, and using canola oil and whole wheat flour in their place. This combination is preferred by health-conscious adults who purchase crackers and examine ingredient labels.

Some manufacturers are employing extrusion used in other food industries. This engineering process permits continuous blending of ingredients. It results in a greater variety of products being made available to the consumer, and it results in less waste during production time, and also consumes less energy. Changes in ingredients and procedures are monitored carefully by the Food and Drug Administration.

Manufacturers of cookies and crackers are working harder at expanding their sources of sales. They are exploring non-traditional outlets such as toy retailers, drug stores, and children's stores to sell their products. They are incorporating the use of licensed characters for their cookies, hoping to increase consumption of cookies among children aged 5 to 14.

The inflation-adjusted prices of agricultural commodities are not expected to represent a factor in the cookies and crackers manufacturing industry. Although there have been periodic price increases, the average index of real prices of ingredients has actually shown a decline. This pattern should continue. Also, with the use of computers and better telecommunications, bakery companies today are more sophisticated and more easily able to protect themselves against sudden price increases of agricultural commodities.

INDUSTRY LEADERS

Nabisco has consistently been the leader in the industry. The Nabisco Company produces, distributes, and markets a broad range of cookies, crackers, and snacks. Nabisco Biscuit Company sells 9 of the top 10 cookies and crackers worldwide, including Chips Ahoy! and Oreo Chocolate sandwich cookies, the world's largest-selling cookie brands; Ritz crackers; and SnackWell's cookies and crackers. Nabisco Biscuit held 35 percent of the cookie market and 46.2 percent of the cracker market in 1995. It is the operating company of Nabisco, Inc., a $8.3 billion company.

Nabisco markets its products through a direct store delivery system. To boost its share of the cookie market, Nabisco signed a licensing agreement with ConAgra in 1997 to market cookies and bread crisps under the Healthy Choice brand name.

The second largest cookie manufacturer in terms of market share is Keebler, a subsidiary of United Biscuit Holding Corporation, based in Britain. Keebler held 11 percent of the cookie market and 16.3 percent of the cracker market in 1995. Like Nabisco's, Keebler's products are represented in major supermarkets throughout the country. Keebler also produces and distributes a wide range of crackers and snacks.

WORK FORCE

In 1995 the cookies and cracker industry employed approximately 49,200 people, 38,700 of whom fall into the category of production workers. The average hourly wages for those workers came to about $12.57 per hour. The states with the most employees in the cookies and crackers industry are North Carolina, Illinois, Pennsylvania, and Georgia.

AMERICA AND THE WORLD

The export trade of bakery goods has amounted to a small portion of the total bakery production in the United States, because of the problem of perishability and consumer preference in other countries. Nevertheless, bakery exports are growing. Exports consist mainly of cookies, crackers, and specialty cakes that have adequate shelf life, attractive packaging, and competitive prices.

The real value of U.S. export shipments for all bakery items was not likely to grow more than 1.5-2.0 percent annually from 1993 to 1997. The fastest growth was expected to be from cookies and crackers exports which is expected to grow about 2 percent yearly. International competitiveness of bakery products is still a long way off.

It is conceivable, however, that in the coming years exports and imports of bakery products, with cookies and crackers leading the way, will become more of a viable international fixture. According to *U.S. Industrial Outlook,* international trade in bakery products will continue to increase.

FURTHER READING

"Campbell Soup Acquires Majority Stake in Arnotts." *Wall Street Journal,* 5 February 1993.

"FDA Approves Fat Substitute, Olestra." Available from http://vm.cfsan.fda.gov/.

Hwang, Suein L. "Campbell Makes $590 Bid for Cookie Firm; Offer for Australia's Arnotts Is Aimed at Establishing Base for Asian Market." *Wall Street Journal,* 13 October 1992.

Hwang, Suein L. "Healthy Eating, Premium Private Labels Take a Bite Out of Nabisco's Cookie Sales." *Wall Street Journal,* 13 July 1992.

Konrad, Walecia. "Famous Amos Gets a Chinese Accent." *Business Week,* 28 September 1992.

Lazich, Robert S., ed. *Market Share Reporter, 1997.* Detroit: Gale Research, 1997.

Morgan, Diana. "Mixed-Up Munchies." *In Health,* April 1990.

"Nabisco Introduces Snack Products with Less Fat." *New York Times,* 15 July 1992.

Rice, Faye. "Eco-correct Crackers." *Fortune,* 9 September 1991.

U.S. Industrial Outlook 1993. Washington: U.S. Department of Commerce, January 1993.

Ward's Business Directory of U.S. Private and Public Companies. Detroit: Gale Research, 1997.

Wilke, Michael. "New Nabisco Line Joins Healthy Cookie Parade." *Advertising Age,* 13 July 1992.

—Ron Schultz, updated by Marinell Jochnowitz

SIC 2053

FROZEN BAKERY PRODUCTS, EXCEPT BREAD

This industry is comprised of establishments primarily involved in manufacturing frozen bakery products other than bread and bread-type rolls. Products include frozen cakes, croissants, doughnuts, pies, and sweet yeast goods. Manufacturers of frozen bread and bread-type rolls are classified in **SIC 2051: Bread, and Other Bakery Products. Except Cookies and Crackers.**

INDUSTRY SNAPSHOT

Twenty-four companies were primarily involved in the manufacture of frozen bakery products with total sales of $848 million in 1995, down from $1 billion in 1987. Industry employment was also down in 1995 to 6,100, from 9,900 in 1987.

Retail prices dipped slightly in 1995, with baked goods ringing in at $1.6 billion, cakes and pastries at $374 million, and pies at $385 million. The reduction was partly attributed to consumer preferences for products that required no thawing or baking time. Additionally, according to a report published by *The Food Channel,* the forecast was bleak for most frozen microwaveable products. The cable station blamed the industry for failing to adequately address consumers issues of poor texture and poor browning effects. However, the report did forecast

BACKGROUND AND DEVELOPMENT

One of the first companies to offer frozen bakery products to the American marketplace was Sara Lee. Sara Lee Bakery was founded in 1949 by Charles

Lubin. Originally the company offered a line of premium, fresh-baked products and made shipments within a 200-mile radius of its Chicago location. In 1953, in order to accommodate the needs of long-distance clients, the company pioneered freezing methods and nine years later made the decision to switch its production exclusively to frozen products.

CURRENT CONDITIONS

According to the January 27, 1997 issue of *Brandweek,* 82 percent of American consumers were eating breakfast at home, creating a $16 billion market. Manufacturers targeted those consumers who were looking for convenience, as well as attempting to woo those who were purchasing breakfast at fast-food restaurants and convenience stores.

The late 1990s saw the beginnings of a breakfast foods war among manufacturers of frozen and fresh products. Kellogg's added Eggo Banana Bread waffle to its nine other flavors. Pillsbury introduced Toaster Scrambles in three varieties: cheese and egg; cheese, egg, and bacon; and cheese, egg, and ham. Sara Lee planned to redirect its marketing efforts to its new fresh division in an attempt to tap into the $300 million supermarket bagel business.

INDUSTRY LEADERS

Chicago-based Sara Lee is not only the leader among manufacturers of frozen baked goods, but one of the top-ten public food and beverage companies in the United States and Canada. Initially, Sara Lee's more than 200 different items were sold in supermarkets and in 40 nations around the globe. Sales figures for 1995 topped $8 billion.

Another industry leader was Mrs. Smith's. Mrs. Smith's, a subsidiary of Kellogg, offered two product lines, Eggo frozen waffles and Mrs. Smith's frozen pies. Both were market leaders within their categories and sold predominantly to convenience-conscious customers. For example, Mrs. Smith's Pie in Minutes, a microwaveable product introduced in 1985, was ready to serve in less than half the time normally required to bake a pie.

In addition to being promoted for their convenience, Eggo Waffles were also marketed at the health market. Nutri-Grain Waffles were introduced in 1984 and Nutri-Grain Bran and Raisins appeared in 1985. By the mid-1990s, there were nine flavors of Eggo waffles on the market. Mrs. Smith's expanded its market territory at the beginning of the 1990s by offering products in Canada.

FURTHER READING

Friedman, Marty. "New Products Dawn on Breakfast Market." *Prepared Foods,* September 1987.

"Frozen Baked Goods: Nobody Does It Like Sara Lee." *Frozen Food Digest,* April/May 1993.

Kellogg 1992 Annual Report. Battle Creek, MI: Kellogg, 1993.

Messenger, Robert. "No More Blues In Battle Creek." *Prepared Foods,* February 1987.

U.S. Department of Commerce. *1987 Census of Manufactures.* Washington: U.S. Department of Commerce, 1987.

—Karen Bellenir, updated by Mary McNulty

SIC 2061

CANE SUGAR, EXCEPT REFINING

This classification includes establishments primarily engaged in manufacturing raw sugar, syrup, or finished (granulated or clarified) sugar from sugar cane. Establishments primarily engaged in refining sugar from purchased raw sugar or sugar syrup are classified in **SIC 2062: Cane Sugar Refining.**

INDUSTRY SNAPSHOT

The sugar cane industry is confined by the crop's growing conditions and the logistics of transporting sugar cane. United States production is limited to Florida, Hawaii, Louisiana, Texas and Puerto Rico. Mills that process the sugar cane into raw sugar must be located near cane plantations since cut sugar cane is too bulky and heavy to ship. Mills in this category process cane into crystals of raw sugar that can be transported in bulk, like grain, aboard ships or by land.

Sugar cane milling profitability in the United States depends on federal government subsidies and import controls. Since the late 1700s, producing raw sugar has been a lucrative business for growers and millers. Domestic sugar prices have been government-controlled and foreign imports severely limited. Some members of Congress, as well as numerous American agricultural policy critics, have been advocating less government involvement. They have been pushing for decreased price supports for domestic sugar cane as well as lifting or easing foreign sugar quotas. Critics claim import controls hurt small sugar-producing Caribbean nations, as well as the Philippines.

ORGANIZATION AND STRUCTURE

Sugar mills are located near the plantations on which sugarcane is grown and harvested. In many cases, these are operated by the plantations or as cooperatives by the owners of several sugarcane plantations. United States Sugar Corporation in Clewiston, Florida, for example, is both a grower and manufacturer of raw cane sugar. (Plantations primarily involved in production of sugarcane and sugar beets are classified under **SIC 0133: Sugarcane and Sugar Beets.**)

Mills run continuously, day and night, from fall until spring, when the last cane is harvested. To facilitate the constant milling, growers cultivate a variety of sugar cane that they can harvest throughout the season. The variety of cane available, however, depends on the soil and climate on a particular plantation.

Government Supports. The U.S. government has supported sugar prices for more than 200 years. In 1789, the federal government imposed an import tariff to raise revenue, and for the next 100 years, this sugar tariff yielded almost 20 percent of all import duties, the main source of government money before the Civil War. The Sugar Act of 1934 regulated domestic sugar production, imports, and prices. Import quotas were assigned to foreign sugar-growing countries.

Price supports were applied sporadically during the 1970s, depending upon the price of sugar on the world market. Temporary suspensions of price controls in 1974 and 1980 resulted in increased sugar prices. Shortages soon followed and with that, sugar prices plummeted.

As a result, in the Agriculture and Food Act of 1981 the government agreed to purchase raw cane sugar and refined beet sugar for a specific price per pound if commercial prices were not high enough. In order to avoid payments, the government imposed tariffs to discourage imports, limit the supply of sugar, and therefore keep sugar prices level at or above the government's minimum price. Farmers claim to get no benefit from the subsidies. Industry claims are that United States consumers pay 28 percent less for sugar than consumers anywhere else worldwide, however, the United States price for sugar in 1995 was more than double the world price. Subsequent agricultural acts continued to provide price supports for sugar, keeping quotas low and prices high in the domestic market.

In recent decades, the United States has imposed strict quotas on import of foreign sugar, cutting imports 80 percent since 1975. The tariff on sugar imports in excess of the quota was also high enough to discourage imports. This quota has created great controversy regarding U.S. trade with developing nations. More than 110 countries grow sugar cane or sugar beets, and many of the developing nations have become dependent on sugar as a source of employment and income. In the early 1990s, the United States imported less than 1.5 million tons of sugar to make up the difference between the sugar cane produced domestically and the approximately 9 million tons used.

Some critics of U.S. foreign trade policy have blamed the federal sugar support program for the rise in cocaine traffic into the United States. These critics claimed that, not only did the sugar program hurt other countries financially, but also the loss of sugar trade with the United States contributed to increased coca (from which cocaine is derived) production in Bolivia and Peru. U.S. sugar producers disputed this claim, maintaining a primary factor in the decline was nationalization of Peru's sugar industry, not cuts in U.S. sugar imports.

Price supports for sugar in the United States are provided in the form of nonrecourse loans, so that sugar growers can borrow money with the crop as collateral. The government sets the value of the crop-collateral at a minimum price per pound, guaranteeing that the sugar producer will receive at least that price, even if the commodity price drops. Loans are made to the processor because the raw sugarcane must be milled before being sold or stored. When the raw sugar is sold, the growers reportedly receive payment as well. In many cases the processor and the grower are the same concern. In 1996, to protest the United States policies surrounding subsidies, the Sugar Cane Growers Cooperative of Florida said it would decline $28,000 in government payments.

Processing. The harvesting of sugar cane poses many challenges to producers. Harvesting is either carried out by hand-cutting or machine-cutting. While harvesting by machine costs half as much as harvesting by hand, mills complain that machine harvest includes too much debris, such as roots, dirt, leaves, and dead animals, according to Alec Wilkinson in his book *Big Sugar, Seasons in the Cane Fields of Florida*. He notes that mill owners estimate machine-harvested sugar cane includes 7 to 10 percent trash, while hand-cut cane includes only about 2 percent. Mill owners complain that trash costs them money because it clogs the machines and absorbs juice during milling. According to Wilkinson, mill owners claim machines leave too much cane in the field. Machines cannot cut as close to the ground as the hand cutters and owners claim every half inch of cane stubble left on an acre would have made another half ton of cane to be milled.

Sugar cane stalks are transported to nearby mills in trucks or railroad cars to be washed and shredded, then placed in crushing machines or vats of hot water to dissolve the sugar. Crushing machines break open the cane and squeeze out the sugary juice. Water dissolves more of the sugar in the stalk, creating a sugary mixture called cane juice. The cane juice is heated, and lime is added to settle impurities; then carbon dioxide is used to remove the lime. The clear juice moves on to giant evaporator tanks. After removing most of the water, the thickened mixture is transferred to a vacuum pan where the mixture is heated to remove still more water. When crystals form in the syrup, the mixture is transferred to a centrifuge. The mixture in spun at high speeds to separate large sugar crystals from the thick syrup. The crystals, 97 to 99 percent sucrose, are called raw sugar. Producers may package the raw sugar, as turbinado, for consumer use or sell it to cane sugar refiners classified under **SIC 2062: Cane Sugar Refining** for the manufacture of granulated or powdered sugar. Any foreign sugar shipped to the United States is also transported in raw form.

CURRENT CONDITIONS

Sugar and other agricultural supports continue to be criticized by members of Congress and other government officials. Although cuts in price supports are likely, the government is unlikely to remove all supports. Sugar producers claimed that the federal sugar program protected U.S. consumers from wild swings in world prices. Critics say U.S. consumers spend an extra $1.4 billion annually because of the government program. The industry contends that figure should be about $200 million.

U.S. companies including Coca-Cola, Mars, Inc. and Kraft, are among the critics of sugar tariffs. In 1991, E. J. Brach's, a candy manufacturer, asked that a part of Chicago be declared a free trade zone so the company could import sugar at the world price. Brach's officials said that if the company had to continue to pay inflated U.S. sugar prices, it would be forced to move its operations out of the country. The sugar industry successfully blocked the company's application for free trade status.

The U.S. sugar industry and its very powerful lobby claimed that 80 percent of the sugar in the United States is consumed by food processors, who did not pass drops in sugar prices on to consumers. They cited government reports that said, from 1982 to 1992, the average cost of sweeteners (cane sugar, beet sugar, and high fructose corn syrup) rose only about 9 percent, less than the rate of inflation, however prices for products containing sugar rose 54 percent. The chair-

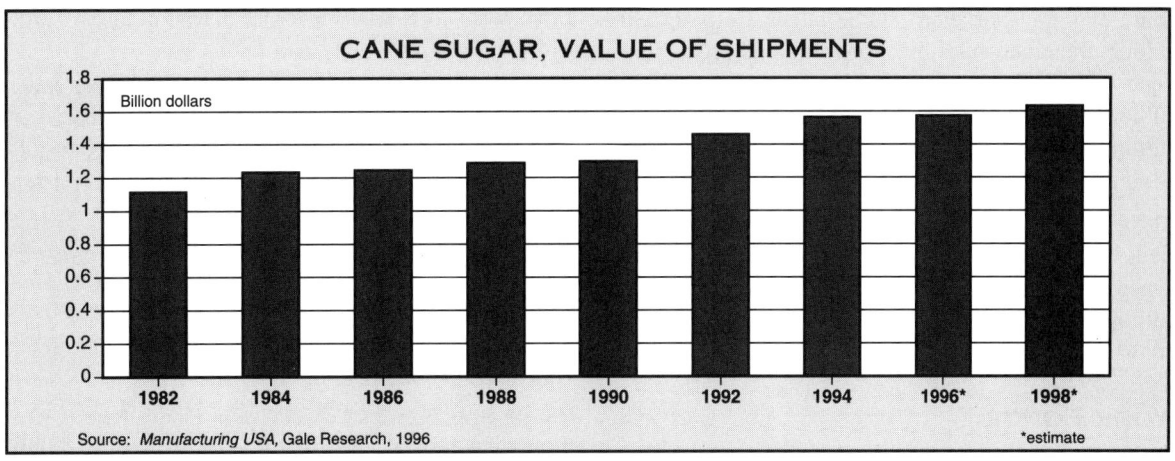

CANE SUGAR, VALUE OF SHIPMENTS

Billion dollars

Source: *Manufacturing USA*, Gale Research, 1996   *estimate

man of the American Sugar Alliance also claimed that U.S. consumers pay 25 percent less for sugar than consumers in other developed nations and that the U.S. price for sugar was 10 percent less than the world average retail price. The American Sugar Alliance asserted that since the United States was not self-sufficient in sugar production, it imported 27 percent of its sugar in 1991 and that exporters of sugar to the United States received the same level of price supports as U.S. sugar cane producers.

The North American Free Trade Agreement promised to open up the sugar market to Mexico; however, rather than increasing overall import of sugar, it would probably reduce U.S. purchases from the Philippines or Caribbean nations. According to a 1988 *Monthly Review* article, "the industry is confronted with virtual extinction over the next decade," attributing the move to "policy decisions adopted in the boardrooms of a minuscule number of beverage companies with no consideration whatsoever for the millions of sugar workers and their families around the world." In other words, a shift to corn sweeteners and other sugar substitutes was to blame.

The shift to high fructose corn syrup use by the U.S. beverage industry began in the 1980s. Its price in 1985 was approximately seven U.S. cents per pound less than sugar, and the savings to the industry megaliths the previous year had been $90 million. This move by the beverage industry was assisted, contended *Monthly Review*, by the push of conglomerates such as Archer-Daniels-Midland Company and Cargill. That same year the U.S. sugar market declined by about 8 percent.

United States sugar production in 1994-95 reached a record high, but was soon beset by problems. Freezing temperatures in Louisiana, droughts and lack of irrigation in Texas, storms in Florida and continuing plant closures in Hawaii all decreased sugar produc-

tion. Projections past the 1996-97 harvest by the U.S. Department of Agriculture continued to show lower production.

Pollution in the Everglades. According to environmentalists, agricultural run-off from sugar plantations and milling processes in southern Florida have been responsible for damage to the Everglades. In 1991, United States Sugar Corporation was fined $3.75 million for improper disposal of hazardous materials from one of its Clewiston mills in the Everglades. The company pleaded guilty to knowingly allowing hazardous wastes into local landfills during three harvest years. Environmentalists continue to raise concerns about the impact of the sugar industry on the fragile ecosystem of the Everglades.

INDUSTRY LEADERS

According to the *Wall Street Journal* and *US News & World Report,* one family supplies the United States with more than 15 percent of its cane sugar: the Fanjuls, through Flo-Sun, Inc., own 180,000 acres of cane fields and milling facilities in southern Florida. In 1959, after Fidel Castro took over Cuba, fifth-generation members of one of Cuba's largest sugar-growing families, the Fanjuls, bought a 25 percent share in a new sugar company. That company moved a Louisiana sugar mill to Florida, and the mill and sugar cane fields were established on 4,000 acres of land newly drained by the U.S. Army Corps of Engineers. In 1985, the Fanjuls purchased Gulf & Western's sugar operations in Florida and the Dominican Republic; although the price was not disclosed, experts estimated the acquisition cost between $200 million and $240 million. The family reportedly profits heavily from government subsidies, receiving more than $60 million each year.

Other large Florida sugar cane concerns include: St. Joe Paper Co. (its $685.7 million in sales includes diverse businesses in paperboard mills, communications, and transportation); U.S. Sugar Corp. ($430 million combined sales from growing and processing sugar cane and sugar beets); Okleelanta Corp. ($200 million in sales); Osceola Farms Company Inc. ($130 million); and Atlantic Sugar Association ($65 million).

Large sugar cane concerns in Hawaii include: Alexander and Baldwin (its $1.02 billion in sales includes diverse businesses in agriculture, real estate and transportation); Hamakua Sugar Company, Inc. ($25 million); and Oahu Sugar Company, Ltd. ($36 million).

WORK FORCE

Although cutters are employed by the sugar growers, they are discussed here because many southern Florida plantations are owned by the large sugar mills and are therefore part of this industry in the country's leading sugar-producing state. Sugar harvesters, called cane cutters, face one of the most grueling jobs imaginable. For decades, the Florida sugar cane industry came under fire for the severe, even slave-like conditions in which the cutters lived and for illegal practices concerning wages. Most Florida cane cutters were seasonal workers migrating from the Caribbean for the harvest.

A 1991 congressional report accused the sugar cane industry of violating labor laws. In 1992, U.S. Sugar Corp., one of the largest sugar concerns in Florida, agreed to a wage increase and other improvements. Farm-worker advocacy groups were hoping to win reforms for cane cutters working at other sugar companies. However, southern Florida producers were increasingly turning to machine cutting because of the historical controversy about the treatment of immigrant labor by the industry.

Employment in the fields and in the mills is seasonal, peaking between fall and spring. According to the Bureau of Labor Statistics, in 1990, total employment of production workers in the industry was 3,500 in July and 6,400 in November. One cooperative based in a single county in Florida reported employing about 900 people in 1996 on a payroll exceeding $26 million.

FURTHER READING

Bacon, Kenneth H. "U.S., Mexico Have Tentative Pact on Sugar Trade." *Wall Street Journal,* 29 July 1992, A2.

Barry, Robert D. "The U.S. Sugar Program in the 1980s." *National Food Review,* January-March 1990, 55-61.

Cheney, Carolyn. "Letter to the editor: Sugar Study's Sticky Trap." *Wall Street Journal,* 21 August 1991, A13.

Clairmonte, Frederick, and John Cavanagh. "Destruction of the Sugar Industry." *Monthly Review,* May 1988, 38-45.

Egan, Jack. "A New Battle for the Sultans of Sugar." *U.S. News & World Report,* 17 July 1995.

Ingersoll, Bruce. "Sugar Subsidies Assailed for Drug, Environment Links." *Wall Street Journal,* 24 July 1990, 2A.

James, Canute. "Caribbean Nations Lose as U.S. Farms Automate." *Journal of Commerce and Commercial,* 31 August 1992, 4A.

Lawrence, Richard. "Bitter Aftertaste for 'Big Sugar.'" *Journal of Commerce and Commercial,* 5 Oct, 1995, 6A.

Mayer, Jane, and Jose de Cordoba. "Sweet Life: First Family of Sugar Is Tough on Workers, Generous to Politicians." *Wall Street Journal,* 29 July 1991, A1.

"Sugar Cane Growers Cooperative of Florida Rejects Payment from Federal Government," PR Newswire, 3 July 1996.

U.S. Department of Agriculture. "Sugar and Sweeteners— Summary." M2 Presswire, 20 December 1996.

"U.S. Sugar Program Is Getting Shaft." *Food & Drink Daily,* 27 June 1995.

Wilkinson, Alec. *Big Sugar, Seasons in the Cane Fields of Florida.* New York: Alfred A. Knopf, 1989.

—Wendy Stein, updated by Linda Paulson

SIC 2062

CANE SUGAR REFINING

This entry includes establishments primarily engaged in refining purchased raw cane sugar and sugar syrup. Sugar cane is cut and milled into raw cane sugar, then shipped in that form to refiners to be processed into syrup, granulated sugar, powdered sugar, or brown sugar. Establishments that manufacture the raw cane sugar from sugar cane are included under **SIC 2061: Cane Sugar, Except Refining.**

The U.S. cane sugar refining industry has been facing heavy competition and increased economic challenges that make their viability into the year 2000 questionable. Manufacturers of beet sugar, high fructose corn syrup (HFCS) and artificial sweeteners have all taken a large share of the market away from cane sugar refiners. Ten out of 21 refineries closed between 1981 and 1990, according to *National Food Review.* *Journal of Commerce and Commercial* states an estimated 3,000 people were left jobless as a result.

Soft drink manufacturers switched to HFCS from liquid cane sugar in the 1980s, striking a severe blow to the sugar industry. To compensate for the losses, cane sugar refiners diversified, adding sugar beet processing operations and/or wet-milling operations to produce HFCS and other corn sweeteners. Beet sugar's share of the sugar market increased from 30 percent in the 1970s to 40 percent in the 1980s, and its market share continued to rise into the 1990s.

In addition to the rise in HFCS, there were other problems for cane sugar refiners. Domestic production of sugar cane dropped, and a strict quota on imported raw cane sugar was imposed by the federal government. The drop in availability of imported raw sugar was especially serious to the industry since sugar refineries in the United States processed more imported raw sugar than domestically-milled raw sugar.

Price, in addition to new product competition, plagued the cane sugar refining industry in the 1990s. Federal programs kept the price of domestic sugar higher than world market prices. In 1992, for example, when the world price of sugar was 10 cents a pound, the price in the United States was 21 cents a pound. The government also imposed a quota to prevent cheaper imported sugar from flooding the U.S. market. The United States continued to import some raw sugar, because it did not grow enough to meet U.S. demand. Additional problems with crops—drought years in Texas, storms in Florida, and freezing temperatures in Louisiana—in the mid-1990s further depressed yields.

High fructose corn syrup producers have been able to undercut the sugar market—both beet sugar and cane sugar—and make HFCS a cheaper alternative sweetening agent for processed foods. Americans consumed more corn syrup than refined sugar in the early 1990s, particularly in soft drinks. The beverage industry is said to be a primary force behind the demise of cane sugar production. Coca-Cola was the largest sugar buyer in the United States in the 1980s, accounting for 10 percent of the market.

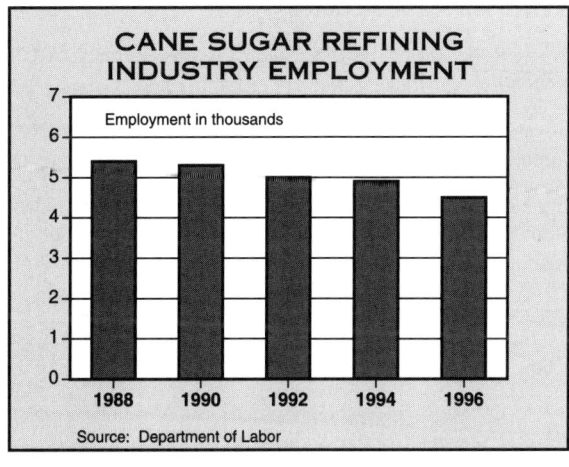

CANE SUGAR REFINING INDUSTRY EMPLOYMENT

Source: Department of Labor

At least one market continued to prefer cane sugar to its competitors. Candy and pastry makers were not impressed with substitutes for refined cane sugar. They insisted that beet sugar was not suitable for their purposes and that they achieved better results with pure cane sugar. According to the U.S. government, cane sugar and beet sugar have the same chemical formula so refiners cannot claim any difference between them.

To produce refined sugar from raw sugar, the raw sugar crystals are transported, aboard ships or trains to refineries where first the yellow-brown film is rinsed off. The sugar crystals are dissolved in water and poured through a series of filters until the liquid is clear. The syrup is heated so the liquid evaporates leaving crystals again. The crystals are spun in a centrifuge, and then the white sugar is separated into a drying drum where any remaining moisture is eliminated. Syrup that does not form crystals is used to make brown sugar. Molasses is another by-product of the refining process.

Leading American sugar refiners include: Tate and Lyle, Inc., which also processes beet sugar; Savannah Foods and Industries; Domino Sugar Corp.; and Imperial Holly Corp., which also processes beet sugar.

FURTHER READING

Bacon, Kenneth. "Politics & Policy: U.S., Mexico Have Tentative Pact on Sugar Trade." *Wall Street Journal,* 29 July 1992, A2.

Carlsen, Clifford. "Business is Sweet at C&H Sugar Co." *San Francisco Business Times,* 6 September 1991, 1.

Clairmonte, Frederick, and John Cavanagh. "Destruction of the Sugar Industry." *Monthly Review,* May 1988.

Ingersoll, Bruce. "Range War: Small Minnesota Town is Divided by Rancor over Sugar Policies." *Wall Street Journal,* 26 June 1990, 1A.

Kochilas, Diane. "Sweet Sense." *Restaurant Business,* 10 December 1990, 155.

Lawrence, Richard. "Bitter Aftertaste for 'Big Sugar.'" *Journal of Commerce and Commercial,* 5 October 1995.

Schontak, Judith. "Savannah Foods: Sweet on Profits." *Business Atlanta,* October 1988, 42.

—Wendy Stein, updated by Linda Paulson

SIC 2063

BEET SUGAR

This entry includes establishments primarily engaged in manufacturing sugar from sugar beets.

Sugar beets are one of the world's main sugar sources and an important source of sugar for the United States. Reduced raw cane sugar imports hurt U.S. refiners in the 1980s, and the sugar industry turned to sugar beets to make up the difference. The United States processes more sugar from domestically-grown sugar beets than from domestically-grown sugar cane. Many cane refiners also invested in sugar beet processing firms in the 1980s as the sugar beet market share (including imports) climbed from 30 percent in the 1970s to 40 percent in 1988.

The beet sugar industry traces its origins to ancient Babylonia, Egypt, and Greece, where sugar beets were grown. In 1744, a German chemist discovered that sugar from sugar beets was the same as sugar from sugar cane. About 50 years later, another German chemist developed a method for extracting sugar from the beets. Sugar mills were soon built in Europe and Russia. In 1838, sugar beets were being processed in the United States as well. The first successful commercial beet sugar mill was built in Alvarado, California, by American businessman E.H. Dyer.

Unlike sugarcane, which is processed into raw sugar (see **SIC 2061: Cane Sugar, except Refining**) to be marketed to cane refiners (see **SIC 2062: Cane Sugar Refining**), beets are processed directly into refined sugar. Beet sugar is produced from the root of the sugar beet plant, which is shipped to factories to be washed and cut into thin slices called cossettes. These cossettes are soaked in diffusers to remove the sugar. Resulting pulp is dried and mixed with molasses to make cattle feed. The sugar-water mixture goes through a series of purification processes in which lime, carbon dioxide, and filtration are used to remove impurities. Finally, the liquid is reheated until evaporation leaves a crystallized sugar product. Sugar products manufactured from sugar beets include dried beet pulp, beet sugar, molasses, granulated sugar, liquid sugar, invert sugar, powdered sugar, and syrup.

Traditional sugar beet producing states are California, Idaho, Michigan, North Dakota and Wyoming. Leading beet sugar producers include Contran Corp. and Valhi, Inc., both with headquarters in Dallas; Imperial Holly Corp. of Sugar Land, Texas; Tate & Lyle, which also produces cane sugar; and Holly Sugar Corp. of Colorado Springs.

The federal government has provided price supports to the U.S. sugar industry for almost 200 years. Nonrecourse loans to processors guarantee a minimum price for beet sugar. (This subject is fully explained in **SIC 2061: Raw Cane Sugar**). Many consumer groups and commentators are critical of the U.S. program that protects the sugar industry. In 1990, James Bovard, a policy analyst, wrote in *USA Today* that the sugar program results in American sugar prices that are double or triple world prices, keeps out foreign sugar to create "artificial shortages," and costs sugar-cane-producing allies such as the Philippines hundreds of millions of dollars in lost trade. When market conditions became bad in 1993 and 1994—reportedly the second time in history— industry leaders asked the U.S. Department of Agriculture to help stimulate prices by imposing an allotment system, to balance beet sugar supply and demand.

California's sugar beet industry best exemplifies the results of these problems of the mid 1990s. Plagued by drought, disease and other problems, the state's once vibrant sugar beet industry, for the most part, never recovered. Crop yields in 1993 were down significantly. Between 1990 and 1996, the land devoted to sugar beet cultivation was cut by about 50 percent to about 90,000 acres. Two of California's eight sugar beet processing plants closed between the 1993 and 1994 harvests.

In the 1994 season, growers for Spreckels Sugar Co.—founded in 1898, once California's leading beet refiner—began reporting yields more than 20 percent lower than the previous year. Coupled with rock bottom prices and an over-abundance of beets in other states for the second year running, it was a disaster. Spreckels didn't survive. Its assets and debts were purchased in 1996 by Imperial Holly, now the lone beet refiner in the state.

FURTHER READING

Barry, Robert D. "The U.S. Sugar Program in the 1980s." *National Food Review,* January- March 1990.

Bovard, James. "Farm Subsidy Follies." *USA Today,* November 1990.

Graebner, Lynn. "Spreckels Scrapes Bowl After Another Sour Year." *The Business Journal Serving Greater Sacramento,* 27 June 1994.

———. "Sugar Beet Industry Falls on Tough Times." *The Business Journal Serving Greater Sacramento,* 26 August 1996.

———. "Sugar Industry Has Gone Sour." *The Business Journal Serving Greater Sacramento,* 25 January 1993.

"Holly Sugar Corp. to Acquire Spreckels Sugar Operation." *Milling & Baking News,* 16 January 1996.

—Wendy Stein, updated by Linda Paulson

CANDY AND OTHER CONFECTIONERY PRODUCTS

This category includes establishments primarily engaged in manufacturing candy, including chocolate candy, other confections, and related products, including: chocolate-covered candy bars; breakfast bars; candy, except solid chocolate; chocolate bars made from purchased chocolate; chocolate candy, except solid chocolate; confectionery cake ornaments; fudge; granola bars; marshmallows; candy-covered nuts; candied, glazed or crystallized fruits; and popcorn balls and candy-covered popcorn products. Establishments engaged primarily in manufacturing solid chocolate bars from cacao beans are classified under **SIC 2066: Chocolate and Cocoa Products.** Establishments manufacturing chewing gum are included under **SIC 2067: Chewing Gum**, while those primarily engaged in roasting and salting nuts are classified in **SIC 2068: Salted and Roasted Nuts and Seeds.** Establishments primarily engaged in manufacturing confectionery for direct sale on the premises to household consumers are classified in **SIC 5441: Candy, Nut, and Confectionery Stores.**

INDUSTRY SNAPSHOT

America and the rest of the world have an appetite for candy. The candy industry is very competitive and features a long rivalry between leading manufacturers such as Mars, Inc., Hershey Foods Corporation, Nestle Foods USA, and Nabisco.

Market growth was exceptional through the late 1990s. In keeping with the health conscious consumers, low-fat/low-calorie candies gained prominence in the industry. However, the level of new product introductions in the industry was low during the mid-1990s.

Many members of this industry continued to be family owned, especially the gourmet candy and confectionery manufacturers—even leading candy maker Mars, Inc. is privately held by the Mars family.

BACKGROUND AND DEVELOPMENT

Many of the most popular candy bars sold today were developed between the 1890s and 1920 by various candy makers around the country. Rights to many of these candies have been bought and sold many times since they were developed and now are owned by large corporations such as Mars, Hershey Foods, Warner-Lambert, and RJR Nabisco.

Milton S. Hershey manufactured the first chocolate bar in the United States in 1894. Hershey Kisses were introduced in 1907. The Bunte Brothers are credited with manufacturing the first chocolate-covered candy bars in 1911. During World War I, Hershey and other candy makers shipped large blocks of chocolate to army training camps, where the blocks were cut into smaller chunks for distribution. This task became too time-consuming for military personnel, and the manufacturers started wrapping individual chocolate bars before shipping them. After the war, the candy makers continued to sell candy commercially in this form, and this method of selling candy became popular and convenient.

Many lines of candy bars were first sold for a dime, but sales did not catch on since consumers could buy a pound of loose candy for that same dime. Immediately after World War I, however, sugar and chocolate prices dropped and the price of most candy bars was dropped to a nickel. The price remained fairly constant until the late 1960s, when the price went back to a dime because of rising costs. Since then, prices have steadily climbed.

The forerunners of NECCO wafers and Canada Mints were first produced in 1847 by Chase and Company, with Canada Mints themselves introduced in Canada in the late 1880s and brought to the United States in 1908. NECCO wafers were introduced in 1912 by New England Confectionery Company, a company formed by Chase and two other candy companies; the NECCO brand name is derived from the company's initials. Cracker Jack entered the confectionery market in 1893 at Chicago's World's Fair but was not named until 1896.

LifeSavers first rolled into production in 1912 in a small factory in Cleveland, Ohio, when Cornelius Crane, a chocolate maker, developed mint tablets as a summertime product to compensate for the drop-off in sales of chocolate during the hot summer months. Crane went to a pill manufacturer to produce the mints and a malfunctioning machine produced mints with a hole in the center, thus creating the first LifeSavers product.

The first part of the twentieth century marked an explosive period of growth for the industry. Dozens of new candy products were introduced during this period, and many have endured. Ferrara Pan, a candy company formed in 1919 in Illinois, produced Jaw Breakers, Atomic Fireballs, and Boston Baked Beans. In 1919 the Oh Henry! bar was first manufactured by the Williamson Candy Company of Chicago. Charleston Chews! were first sold in 1922 by the Fox-Cross Candy Company near San Francisco. Goobers were first made by the Blumenthal Chocolate Company in 1925. Holloway Milk Duds were introduced in 1926 by the Holloway Company. During the 1920s and 1930s, the James O. Welch Company introduced several favorites that are still around today, including Sugar Daddy, Sugar Babies, Pom Poms, and Junior Mints. Heath Bars, manufactured by the L.S. Heath Company, went on the market in 1932. Chunky was developed in the mid-1930s by Philip Silverstein, a New York candy maker.

In 1930 the most popular candy bar in America was created—Snickers. Snickers is one of the few candy bars still produced by its originator—Mars, Inc., which today is one of the largest private companies in the United States. Mars introduced the Milky Way bar in 1923, 3 Musketeers and the Mars Bar in the 1930s, and M&M's in 1941.

Peter Paul Candies was formed in 1919 and introduced its first candy bar, the Konabar. Three years later, the company introduced the dark chocolate-covered coconut bar that served as the cornerstone of the company's product line—Mounds. The first Mounds was a single bar for a nickel, but during the Depression, Peter Paul doubled the size of the package by adding a second bar without increasing the price. This two-for-one tactic increased sales, despite the hard times. Peter Paul replaced hand-wrapping with machine-wrapping by converting a machine designed to wrap soap bars. The company also became one of the first to venture into broadcast advertising. In 1948 the company combined almonds with coconut to launch Almond Joy. Peter Paul acquired York Peppermint Patty in 1972. Several years later, the company was acquired by Cadbury Schweppes PLC for $58 million.

The candy industry has gone through a period of consolidation during the past 20 to 30 years. In the 1960s Hershey acquired Reese's, maker of Reese's Peanut Butter Cups since 1923; in 1977 Hershey acquired Y&S Candies, which had marketed licorice Twizzlers and Nibs since the 1920s. Hershey's acquisition of Cadbury Schweppes' U.S. division in 1988 propelled Hershey past Mars to become the leading U.S. candy maker. The purchase gave Hershey the rights to Peter Paul Almond Joys and Mounds, as well as Cadbury and Caramello products, to buttress its already impressive product line.

Despite the presence of such corporate giants as Mars, Inc. and Hershey Foods Corporation, several independent companies have maintained a significant presence in the industry. Tootsie Roll Industries has remained an independent company since its founding in 1896. It markets a line of Tootsie Roll products, as well as several products, including Mason Dots and Bonomo Turkish Taffy, it acquired through the purchase of smaller companies.

Another company that remained independent since its beginnings is PEZ Candy Inc., with its flavored rectangular sugar tablets and vast array of plastic, flip-top dispensers. PEZ was founded in 1952 and is based in Orange, Connecticut. The first PEZ tablets were invented in 1927 as a peppermint tablet and cigarette substitute. PEZ was an abbreviation for *pfefferminz,* the German word for peppermint.

Sales for candy rose in 1992, after steep declines in 1990 and 1991. Manufacturers launched aggressive new product campaigns in 1992 and maintained the recent trend towards products with reduced fat and sugar content.

Candy exports were strong, especially with Mexico and Canada, and were expected to improve further with the passage of the North American Free Trade Agreement. Candy makers, though, are also concerned about the ramifications of new environmental regulations that might require them to provide recyclable packaging.

The industry has grown steadily in the 1990s. By 1992, shipments were valued at $8.9 billion. Adjusted for inflation, the value of candy and confectionery shipments rose an estimated 3.2 percent in that year. Between 1987 and 1991, the inflation-adjusted value of industry shipments rose 2.2 percent annually.

Although sales of regular candy have been substantial, the candy makers have increasingly taken notice of the relatively recent nutritional health emphasis and used it as a source of growth. In 1992 sugar-free and other ''healthier'' candies accounted for only one percent of the confectionery market, but industry members anticipate the market will grow, especially as new low-fat or low-calorie ingredients improve the taste of the so-called ''healthier'' chocolate candies.

Caprenin, developed by The Procter & Gamble Company, combined the taste and consistency of ordinary fat, but contained half the calories. Mars used it in its reduced-fat, reduced-calorie Milky Way II, which contained half the calories of the original Milky Way and eight grams of fat. Smaller companies were also trying to capitalize on the health market. In 1992, 92 percent of supermarkets and other stores sold some kind of sugar-free candy. Although most retail outlets said that sugar-free candy sales represented a very small market share, 87 percent of the store buyers surveyed expected demand for sugar-free items to continue to increase well into the 1990s. At the beginning of 1993, all ten candy bars on the top-selling candy list in the United States were manufactured by Mars,

Hershey, or Nestle. Snickers remained the number one candy bar with sales of more than $61 million annually; Hershey products were second and third on the list, with Reese's Peanut Butter Cups (sales of $41 million) and Kit Kat ($36 million). The rest of the list included M&M's Plain (Mars, almost $32 million); Butterfinger (Nestle, almost $32 million); M&M's Peanut (Mars, almost $30 billion); Crunch (Nestle, $26 million); Hershey Milk Chocolate ($24 million); Hershey Almond (24 million); and 3 Musketeers (Mars, $20 million).

CURRENT CONDITIONS

The mid-1990s was an exceptional growth period for this industry. The National Confectioners Association and the Chocolate Manufacturers Association showed a 4.8 percent sales growth in 1995 while shipments increased by 2.9 percent. Confectionery sales in grocery stores, drug stores, and mass merchandise stores also increased by 6.3 percent to reach $2.892 billion. Candy sales to vending machine operators grew by 3.8 percent.

The non-chocolate candy segment showed admirable growth with a 9.2 percent increase in dollars to $2.4 billion and 7.9 percent in volume to 1.54 billion pounds in 1995 as compared to respective growth percentages of only 2.2 percent and 2.5 percent the previous year. Bulk Candy sales in stores accounted for about 8 percent to 14 percent of total candy sales with average weekly sales exceeding $275. Even though the level of new product introductions was low in the industry, candy consumption continued to increase steadily.

Candy makers are also cashing in on the holiday markets. The seasonal candy market posted overall respective dollar and unit volume gains of 10.4 percent and 9.7 percent in 1995, according to the *Candy Industry* overview of this industry.

Mars, Hershey, and Nestle had traditionally stayed away from the holiday candy market, but when candy consumption and sales remained flat, the candy giants saw great opportunity to capture a major share of the holiday sales. The three companies repackaged many of their most famous goodies in pastel colors for Easter. Their entry into the holiday market shoved aside many of the usual holiday candy manufacturers.

Many other confectioners are looking to the kids' market for growth. Industry experts and retailers note that over half the children in the United States between the ages of four and twelve possess an average of $4 a week to spend. Many candy makers were thus pitching their products directly to this market segment.

The adult health conscious market was seen as a major growth market for this industry. Nabisco's Snackwell's brand of products pioneered a new era in this industry. The resounding success of Snackwell's motivated many manufacturers to join this era of new comparable products designed to placate consumers worried about the fat and calorie content in existing products. Hershey and Mars offered their new alternatives with the launch of Sweet Escapes and Milky Way Lite respectively. Other smaller companies were quick to join the growing fray as well. The market for sugar-free candies was valued at more than $50 million in the mid-1990s.

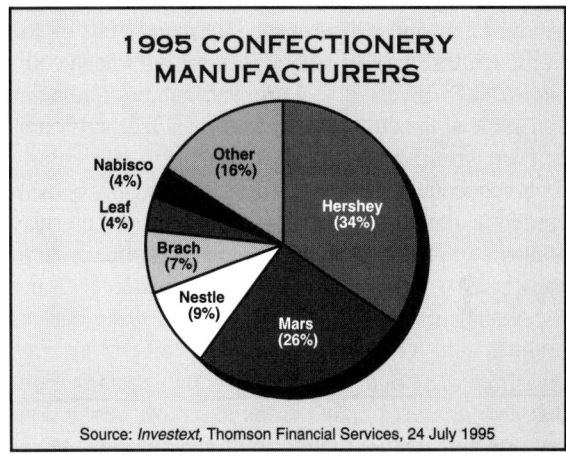

1995 CONFECTIONERY MANUFACTURERS

Nabisco (4%)
Leaf (4%)
Brach (7%)
Nestle (9%)
Mars (26%)
Other (16%)
Hershey (34%)

Source: *Investext*, Thomson Financial Services, 24 July 1995

INDUSTRY LEADERS

Mars, Inc. of McLean, Virginia was the largest company primarily in the candy business, employing 28,000 and generating a sales revenue of approximately $13 billion in 1996. Mars' Snickers was the top-selling candy bar in the United States in the mid-1990s. However, Hershey Foods Corporation, of Hershey, Pennsylvania, generated the largest sales volume specific to the industry. In 1996, Hershey had $4 billion in revenues and 15,300 employees. RJR Nabisco Holdings Corp. of New York, a highly diversified company, also had sizable presence in this industry primarily through its Nabisco, Inc. subsidiary. RJR Nabisco had $17 billion in 1996 sales and more than 79,000 employees. The astounding sales of Snackwell's was one key reason for Nabisco's success in this category.

Other leading U.S. candy makers include Leaf Inc. ($700 million in sales), Lance Inc. ($474 million in sales), Russell Stover Candies Inc. ($420 million in sales), E.J. Brach Corp. ($400 million in sales), Sathers Inc. ($360 million in sales), Archibald Candy Corp. ($350 million in sales), Farley Foods U.S.A. ($330 million in sales), and Tootsie Roll Industries Inc. ($312.7 million in sales).

AMERICA AND THE WORLD

The value of U.S. candy and confectionery exports in 1995 was about $527 million, a decrease of more than 3 percent from the previous year. Exports to Canada and Mexico accounted for about 64 percent of all U.S. candy exports, while exports to South Korea and Japan accounted for another 13 percent of export value.

Although Europeans consume a great amount of candy, Europe continued to be a poor market for U.S. candy. High duties have kept U.S. candy out of the European Union (EU), although some American companies have invested in European candy companies and avoided the duties. U.S. companies face stiff competition from European confectioners, particularly Swiss chocolate producers, which are typically considered to market finer quality confections than American companies. Hershey purchased its first European company in 1991 with the $31 million acquisition of Gubor Schokoladen, a chocolate company that manufactures pralines and chocolates. Warner-Lambert, a large pharmaceutical and consumer products manufacturer that also produces cough drops and other confectionery products, entered into a joint venture with Alivar S.p.A to sell cough drops and candies in Italy, a large confectionery market.

The value of U.S. candy imports in 1995 exceeded $1 billion. The EU provides most U.S. candy imports. In the early 1990s Germany, the United Kingdom, Italy, the Netherlands, France, and Spain accounted for more than 40 percent of U.S. candy imports. Canada was the single most important source of candy imports, though, providing 24 percent. Mexico provided 4 percent of import value.

FURTHER READING

"Annual Update Unveils Industry's Fortune." *Candy Industry,* January 1995.

"Champions a Gold Medal Year." *Candy Industry* July 1996.

Deveny, Kathleen. "Pushing Chocolate Chicks and Bunnies." *Wall Street Journal.* 3 April 1993, B1.

Dornblaser, Lynn. "Candy Is More than Dandy." *Prepared Foods,* 15 April 1996.

"The Expanding Market for Bulk Candy." *Candy Industry,* July 1996.

Henry, Jim. "Keeping it in the Family: and Industry Discussion." *Candy Industry,* January 1996.

Rutherford, Andrea C. "Candy Firms Roll Out 'Healthy' Sweets." *Wall Street Journal,* 10 August 1992, B1.

Yoshihashi, Pauline. "New Candies for Kids May Seem Tasteless to Adults." *Wall Street Journal,* 8 April 1993, B1.

—Visi Tilak

SIC 2066

CHOCOLATE AND COCOA PRODUCTS

Included in this industry classification are establishments primarily engaged in shelling, roasting, and grinding cocoa beans for the purpose of making chocolate liquor—from which cocoa powder and cocoa butter are derived—and in the further manufacture of solid chocolate bars, chocolate coatings, and other chocolate and cocoa products. Also included is the manufacture of similar products, except candy, from purchased chocolate or cocoa. Establishments primarily engaged in manufacturing candy from purchased cocoa products are classified in **SIC 2064: Candy and Other Confectionery Products.**

INDUSTRY SNAPSHOT

The chocolate and cocoa products industry has traditionally been subject to significant fluctuations in demand. Chocolate products tend to be seasonal in nature, with demand increasing sharply during the holidays. In addition, several consumer trends have had an impact on demand. These include rising sales of premium-priced chocolates and the growing concern about the health risks associated with the consumption of such high-fat foods like chocolate.

In 1995, the chocolate and cocoa products industry shipped $3.2 billion worth of products, a slight increase over 1990 figures, when products shipped totaled $3.0 billion. The number of establishments in the industry has decreased from 186 in 1990 to 157 in the mid-1990s. The balance of trade for U.S. cocoa and chocolate has usually run at a deficit. In 1995, cocoa imports totaled $722 million, while exports totaled $39 million.

ORGANIZATION AND STRUCTURE

All cocoa beans processed by U.S. manufacturers must be imported, by direct purchase or through the services of a broker, as cocoa trees require a tropical climate to flourish. Growers are paid for the beans at market price, which is determined primarily by the quality and availability of the crop worldwide. A testament to cocoa's importance as a commodity is the existence of cocoa exchanges, similar to standard stock exchanges, in New York City, London, Hamburg, and Amsterdam. The beans are then processed to make chocolate liquor, which is in turn used to further manufacture such products as cocoa, chocolate syrup, and solid chocolate chips and baking bars. The chocolate liquor is also often sold to other manufacturers that combine it with additional ingredients to produce confections, bakery items, and dairy products.

Manufacturers roast, shell, and grind the beans to produce unsweetened chocolate, the chocolate liquor that is the basic ingredient of all chocolate products. Further processing of chocolate liquor falls into two categories: cocoa manufacture and chocolate manufacture.

In cocoa production the fat is pressed from chocolate liquor, leaving cocoa cake that is crushed to form cocoa powder. The powder may be sweetened and sold as a cocoa beverage or left unsweetened for use in bakery and dairy products and for home cooking use. Cocoa butter, the fat removed from the chocolate liquor, is used mainly in sweetened chocolate, but is also used as a moisturizer in soaps, creams, and medications.

The production of chocolate requires the addition of sugar or other sweeteners and cocoa butter to chocolate liquor. Milk solids are also added in the manufacture of milk chocolate. Bulk quantities of sweetened chocolate (blocks of at least 4.5 kilograms) are considered chocolate coating and are used for candy coverings and baked goods. Chocolate coating is generally more expensive than the confectioners' coatings, which are made from cocoa powder.

Chocolate manufacturers sell these semiprocessed cocoa products to other firms that use the items in the production of confectionery, baked goods, and dairy products such as chocolate milk. In addition, some producers also manufacture their own confectionery. Exports of chocolate products consist mainly of confectionery items rather than semiprocessed chocolate.

BACKGROUND AND DEVELOPMENT

The history of the chocolate and cocoa products industry in the United States dates from 1765. In that year, supplied by cocoa beans from the West Indies, the first chocolate factory was established in New England. Physician James Baker funded the venture, whose brands (Baker's) continue to be produced today by Kraft General Foods, Incorporated.

During World War I, the U.S. government recognized chocolate's worth as both nourishment and a morale booster to those in the armed forces. Space was made on cargo planes coming into the country so a sufficient supply of cocoa beans would be available to manufacture chocolate products. The U.S. Army D-rations still include 4-ounce chocolate bars, and cocoa bean products are part of the rarified rations of NASA space travelers.

The chocolate industry did not escape the effects of the recession of early 1990s. Few cocoa-based companies in North America have not experienced layoffs, mergers and consolidations, plant closings, shift cutbacks, advertising budget slashes, and operational streamlining, reflected in poor sales figures and fiscal restraint. Between 1989 and 1991, the industry experienced 50 acquisitions, mergers, licensing agreements, or joint ventures, and companies have been intent on expanding and diversifying their product base.

CURRENT CONDITIONS

Demand for cocoa continues to increase worldwide. The decline in world output of cocoa and the increase in demand for chocolates in new markets such as China, Russia, and other emerging economies indicate the arrival of a long-awaited bull market in cocoa. Another area in which the demand for cocoa increased was the beverage industry. Of the 2,894 new product introductions in 1995, approximately one-half of the beverage products consisted of either cocoa, coffee, or tea.

In the mid-1990s, more producers began catering to health conscious consumers. Popularity of lite (low-fat) candy and lite desserts increased dramatically. Bakers also began offering reduced fat and fat-free chocolate items.

INDUSTRY LEADERS

Industry leaders in the mid-1990s included Hershey Foods Corporation, Farley Candy Company, World's Finest Chocolate, Inc., Merckens Chocolate Company, and Ghirardelli Chocolate Company. Sales figures and employee counts for these companies for 1996 was as follows: Hershey Foods Corporation: $3.7 billion, 15,300; Farley Candy Company: $275 million, 2,300; World's Finest Chocolate, Inc.: $120 million, 600; Merckens Chocolate Company: between $50 and $100 million, 200; and Ghirardelli Chocolate Company: $30 million, 100.

RESEARCH AND TECHNOLOGY

In an effort to compensate for lagging sales, a number of chocolate and cocoa-based companies have adopted technological solutions to increase efficiency and lower production costs. Grace Cocoa's new Choc-

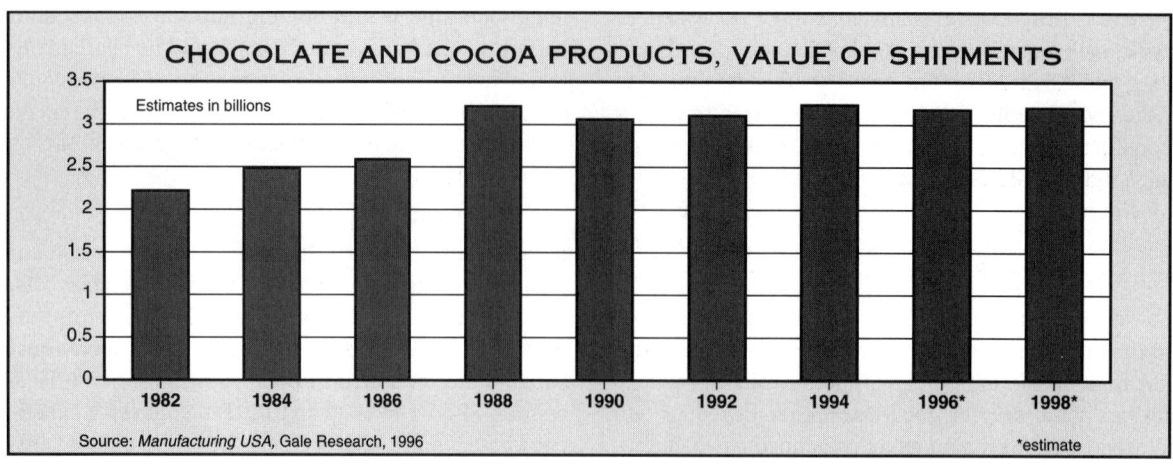

CHOCOLATE AND COCOA PRODUCTS, VALUE OF SHIPMENTS

Estimates in billions

Source: *Manufacturing USA*, Gale Research, 1996   *estimate

olate Americas Division headquarters, for example, built a $95 million plant with 335,000 square feet of computer-integrated manufacturing constructed on a barren site in a Milwaukee, Wisconsin, industrial park. According to a *Candy Industry* interview with Dave Pollock, director of manufacturing at the new factory, "This really is the future."

Part of the new technology in the plant includes the computerization of a number of production processes. While this has helped facilitate more efficient productivity, it also engendered a number of challenges. One of these was retraining employees who were familiar with only rudimentary chocolate making procedures. The state of Wisconsin helped offset some of the retraining costs by contributing half the cost of employees' tuition at local technical colleges.

Cocoa has become such an intrinsic and valuable part of the U.S. economy that efforts by industry and science are underway to better understand the bean itself. The American Cocoa Research Institute contributed $1.5 million to Penn State University's Molecular Biology of Cocoa program. The main objective of the program is to increase understanding of the biology, botany, and genetics of the cocoa plant. The objectives of the study include the study of disease resistance, quality, plant delivery, and tools.

FURTHER READING

Dornblaser, Lynn. "Adult Drinks Lead the Beverage Pack." *Prepared Foods,* 15 April 1996.

Hoover's Handbook of American Business, 1993. Austin, TX: The Reference Press, Inc., 1992.

Ingram, Molly. "Glaze, Drizzle, Dip and Chip—Chocolate Does It All." *Bakery Production and Marketing,* 15 February 1996.

Lemonick, Michael D. "No Wonder You Can't Resist: Chocolate and Marijuana Share the Same Chemistry." *Time,* 2 September 1996.

Miller, Hilary S. "Yoo-Hoo Chocolate Lovers: Beverage Makers Are Flocking to the Chocolate Drink Category." *Beverage Industry,* May 1994.

Mitchell, Dennis P. "An Industry in Turmoil." *Snack Food,* June 1992.

Sanik, Sholom. "How 'Bout a Nice Hot Cocoa Contract." *Futures,* December 1996.

Tiffany, Susan. "Grace Cocoa Unveils Engineering Marvel." *Candy Industry,* April 1993.

U.S. International Trade Commission Office of Industries. *Industry & Trade Summary: Cocoa, Chocolate, and Confectionery.* Washington: GPO, 1993.

Ward's Business Directory of U.S. Private and Public Companies 1997, Detroit: Gale Research, 1996.

—Visi Tilak

SIC 2067

CHEWING GUM

This industry consists of establishments primarily engaged in manufacturing chewing gum or chewing gum base.

INDUSTRY SNAPSHOT

The American chewing gum industry has been marked by strong periods of growth and decline throughout the twentieth century. Since the 1970s this industry has been growing at a faster pace overseas than within the United States. The industry's overall success has been the result of low manufacturing costs and aggressive marketing campaigns. In 1996, there were 19 U.S. manufacturers in this industry.

As one of the best performers in the candy industry, chewing gum continues to be a favorite among American consumers. Sales of sugar and sugar-free gum continued to rise steadily since 1990. Consumers, adults, seniors, and children alike continue chewing various types of gum for a variety of reasons, thereby adding to the market demand in this industry.

ORGANIZATION AND STRUCTURE

Chewing gum companies use two main channels of distribution: one channel is through wholesalers, who supply retail stores in the areas they serve; the other channel is the delivery of boxes of chewing gum directly to large retail outlets from the manufacturers' warehouses and factories. The retail distribution chain includes food, drug, variety, and convenience stores, gas stations, newsstands, and restaurants. Another important channel for these manufacturers has been distributors who stock vending machines.

BACKGROUND AND DEVELOPMENT

History. Though chewing gum bases are primarily synthetic today, gum was originally derived from natural sources such as tree resins and saps. The use of chewing gum made from tree resin dates back to ancient Greek and Mayan civilizations. In North America, Wampanoag Indians introduced chewing gum to European settlers. The gum was made from the resin of spruce trees.

Americans began manufacturing gum in the mid-1800s, adding paraffin wax, which was used to make the gum softer and last longer. At about this time flavors such as mint were added to the gum, helping to increase the product's popularity. In 1848, John Curtis of Maine started producing the first commercial spruce gum.

American settlers traveling west learned about chewing chicle, the hardened sap of sapodilla trees, from the Osage Indians. The sapodilla tree is found mainly in the tropical rain forests of the Yucatan Peninsula of Mexico and Guatemala. By 1869, the first commercial chicle was manufactured, and in 1906 paraffin was added to chicle.

During the late 1800s, companies that would become the industry leaders entered this business, making valuable contributions to the industry as a whole. William Wrigley, Jr., was a baking soda salesman who started offering two packages of chewing gum with each can of baking soda. When this promotion proved successful, Mr. Wrigley decided to enter the relatively undeveloped chewing gum business. His first two brands were Lotta and Vassar; later in 1893 he introduced Juicy Fruit and Wrigley's Spearmint. In the early days, Wrigley used premiums to encourage merchants to stock his chewing gum. The success of this method of marketing led to a published catalog of premiums for retailers. Wrigley was also one of the pioneers in the use of advertising to promote brand name merchandise. Advertisements for Wrigley's gum ran in newspapers, magazines, and on outdoor posters. Even during industry slumps, Wrigley continued advertising.

By 1910, Wrigley's Spearmint gum was the largest selling chewing gum in the United States. Later that year, the company expanded by opening a factory in Canada. By 1927, Wrigley plants were being built in Great Britain and Australia. The different preferences in international markets led to new types of products and flavors. Perhaps the most successful product for the company outside the United States was the pellet-shaped chewing gum sold under the PK brand.

Another industry leader, Franklin Channing, invented the first dental gum, Dentyne, in 1899. About the same time, Henry Fleer created Chiclets, the first candy-coated chewing gum.

Bubble gum was first developed in 1906, but early batches were too sticky to sell and it was not until 1928 that bubble gum was first marketed. Another important development in this industry was the first sugarless gum, which was created in the late 1940s (but not marketed until the 1950s). LifeSavers' CareFree and American Chicle's Trident appeared in the mid-1960s and dominated the sugarless gum market early on. In the 1980s, Wrigley's Extra gum was launched, and by 1990 it controlled 40 percent of the $480 million sugar-free gum market.

Sugar-free gums began using xylitol, an artificial sweetener, in the late 1970s. However, in 1978, the U.S. Food and Drug Administration began investigating possible links between xylitol and cancer; though no link was ever established, products made with xylitol were reformulated using other artificial sweeteners. In the early 1990s, xylitol was reintroduced by Leaf Specialty Products, who manufactured XyliFresh, a chewing gum intended for fighting plaque.

Chewing gum manufacturers have also enjoyed heightened success during war times. The Wm. Wrigley Jr. Company recorded an increase in chewing gum demand during World War I and II and during the 1990-91 conflict in the Persian Gulf. In fact, during World War II, when top-grade ingredients were scarce, production was limited to the armed forces, and civilians were sold a lesser quality gum under the brand name Orbit.

Marketing and Product Trends. The chewing gum industry spends roughly 10 percent of its revenues on marketing, primarily on television advertising. According to *Adweek's Marketing Week,* Amurol Products had brought roughly 12 new products to the market each year, eight of which last two years and only four of which last longer. Because of the short life span, companies have incentive to continue creating new products.

Since it was first sold in America, gum has been packaged with novelties, such as sports cards, toys, and comic strips. In the twentieth century, companies launched novelty bubble gums, which were packaged in a variety of shapes and unusual forms, such as school lockers and toothpaste tubes.

In the early 1990s, sour gum became popular with children. These chewing gums have an extremely sour taste that becomes sweet and eventually has a neutral or tangy taste. Children often used these gums to play jokes on friends or to prove their mettle. In 1992 sour gum brought in an estimated $70 million in retail sales. Moreover, as the demand for sour gum caught suppliers by surprise, a "black market" for the product emerged.

In the 1980s, chewing gum sales were boosted by campaigns that promoted chewing gum as an alternative to smoking. Other advertisements have endorsed sugar-free gums as being good for teeth. In addition to advertisements on television, radio, and in newspapers, companies in this industry use sales representatives to market their products. These representatives regularly visit retailers and assist them with display designs and layouts.

In 1993, LifeSavers made industry news with its innovative approach to selling bubble gum. Its Bubble Yum product was promoted through a traveling virtual reality arcade game, and LifeSavers was the first company to use the game as a marketing tool. The game, called Planet Bubble Yum, featured chunks of bubble gum flying around in three-dimensional animation. Bubble Yum charged proof of purchase seals for admission. The tour traveled to shopping malls in major U.S. cities, with an average attendance of 1,100 people per location.

After a slump during the 1970s and early 1980s, chewing gum manufacturers entered the 1990s on a slight upswing. A new interest in chewing gum emerged in the United States since gum was promoted as an alternative to smoking when more public places began to prohibit smoking. Domestic per capita consumption of chewing gum increased from 168 sticks in 1986 to 183 in 1992, resulting in a 1.3 percent average annual rise in gum sales.

In the 1990s there were an estimated 550 chewing gum companies around the world. Turkey had the most with 60 companies. Seven companies comprised the U.S. industry, which took in over $1.4 billion in sales in 1996. The two industry leaders, Wm. Wrigley Jr. Company and Warner-Lambert Company accounted for 75 percent of domestic chewing gum sales in 1992.

Companies that sell their gum through the sale of sports and entertainment cards have experienced sharp declines in their sales as a result of oversupply. In 1993 Topps Company reported a 13 percent drop in their bubble gum card sales.

Production. The cost of producing chewing gum has always been low. High demand for chewing gum, allowing for high volume production, and advances in automation have helped to reduce costs further. The price of ingredients, such as corn syrup and gum base, has also declined since the 1970s, thus reducing costs and increasing profit margins.

Modern methods and new materials have changed the character of chewing gum. Natural ingredients have become scarce due to changing climatic conditions, demand, and development in regions where the ingredients were harvested. Chicle and other products from trees are now used in conjunction with synthetic materials. Most chewing gums are made with five basic ingredients: chewing gum base, sugar, corn syrup, softeners (such as glycerin and other vegetable oils), and flavors (mostly extracted from mint plants). In sugar-free gums, sugar and corn syrup are usually replaced with aspartame, mannitol, and/or sorbitol.

Manufacturers typically employ food chemists to inspect and test all ingredients and materials. The Wm. Wrigley Jr. Company maintains a central quality assurance laboratory where samples from each factory are tested regularly so that flavor and texture are consistent in their products throughout the world.

Demographics Industry experts have foreseen several trends affecting the gum industry over the next few years. A continued increase in the older population (55 and older) was expected to make the market very strong for sugar free brands. This group was consumed 22 percent of the volume of Care Free sugarless chewing gum. Kids under the age of 12 favored strong fruit flavors; teens and adult women preferred chocolate; and older consumers preferred lemon, peppermint, and butterscotch hard candies, according to a LifeSavers spokesperson in *U.S. Distribution Journal.* Males represented 45 percent of gum buyers and were more likely than females to buy singles (5-or 7-packs).

CURRENT CONDITIONS

In spite of the consistent demand for products in this industry, the gum sector of the candy industry exhibited major weaknesses, with 1995 dollar sales down by 7.1 percent and pound volume off by 4.5 percent from 1994 levels. Chewing gum and bubble gum sales through drug stores fell by 9 percent in overall dollars, while unit volume was down by 11.4 percent.

Gum manufacturers continued to introduce new products, especially to cater to one of their biggest group of consumers—kids. It was found that kids make 270 visits to stores a year averaging 5.2 purchases a week. Therefore, gum manufacturers have spent a lot of money and time researching new products that would appeal to kids.

Packaging played an important role in gum purchases. Innovative products like gum squeezed out of a tube, Roller Racer Bubble Gum, Bubble Cube, a 3-D puzzle toy filled with bubble bits, and gum rolled up like ribbon several feet long were some of the hot gum products on the market.

The sugar-free chewing gums sector, primary consumers of which were adults, represented a $700 million category across the grocery, mass, and chain drug classes of trade. This segment grew at an annual clip of 4 percent across all channels.

Another type of gum that was gaining popularity in the gum industry was smoking cessation products. In 1996, however, supermarket sales of these products were lagging behind sales at alternative formats, especially drug stores. According to sales figures from Chicago-based Information Resources Inc. in *Supermarket News,* food stores held 12 percent of the smoking cessation market, mass merchandisers held 20 percent of the market, and drug stores held a whopping 68 percent of the market.

INDUSTRY LEADERS

The Nabisco Foods Group, located in East Hanover, New Jersey, was the industry leader with sales revenues of $8.3 billion in 1996. With 53,200 employees, the Nabisco Foods Group is a subsidiary of RJR Nabisco Inc. and was founded in 1898.

Warner-Lambert Company was the second-ranked industry leader, with more than $7.03 billion in overall sales revenues and 37,000 employees in 1996. Its American Chicle Company, maker of Chiclets, was founded in 1856. The company also manufactures breath mints and other confectioneries. Its main chewing gum product, Chiclets, accounted for 12 percent of the company's worldwide sales in the early 1990s.

Other large sellers for Warner-Lambert have been Clorets and Trident brand gum.

Wm. Wrigley Jr. Company was also an industry leader in 1996. The parent company posted nearly $1.75 billion in sales, followed by two of its subsidiaries: L.A. Dreyfus Company with $150 million and Amurol Products Company with $66 million. The Wm. Wrigley Jr. Company, formed in 1893, manufactures and sells wholesale chewing gum throughout the United States and overseas.

In 1996, Leaf Incorporated, with a sales revenue of $700 million was the fourth largest company in the industry.

In 1996, Topps had a sales revenue of $265 million and was the fifth largest company in the industry. Topps Company, has also been a leader in commercial printing (see **SIC 2759: Commercial Printing, Gravure**) for their bubble gum sports cards, carrying over 30 percent of the market in sports and entertainment cards. In 1993 Topps' sales were over $263 million. This company has been most noted in the gum industry for producing Bazooka Bubble Gum. Despite the risky nature of the card end of their business, which relies on entertainment fads, some lines of cards developed in the early 1990s omitted the bubble gum.

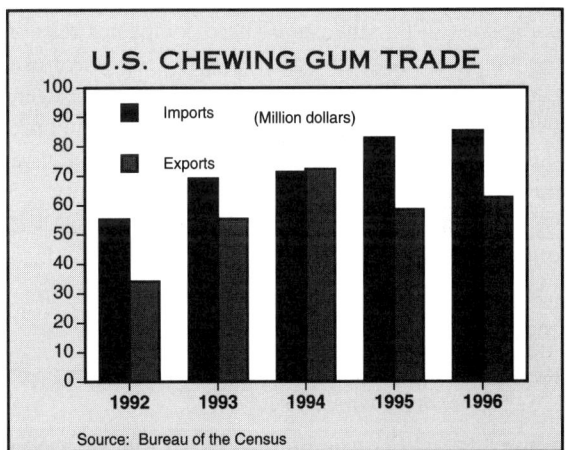

AMERICA AND THE WORLD

Much of American-produced chewing gum is sold overseas. Wrigley has operated in Europe since the 1910s and has had 80 percent of the chewing gum market in Britain and Germany. However, Wrigley did not position itself in Latin America, where many governments required joint ventures. In mid-1990s, Wrigley's business abroad was rising over 10 percent annually; during that time the company opened a factory in China, where people had already been introduced to chewing gum through shipments from Singapore. In addition, 42 percent of Wrigley's mid-1990s earnings came from sales overseas, where the company has dominated most of its 109 markets.

Warner-Lambert has also done well in overseas markets. In the mid-1990s about 50 percent of their sales were from overseas. Their markets have included Canada, Europe, Asia, the Middle East, and Latin America. In 1993, Warner-Lambert launched an aggressive advertising campaign in Latin America, which included materials to help their products stand out in crowded street kiosks. According to the company, it held 79 percent of the Colombian market and 41 percent of the Brazilian market in 1993 chewing gum sales.

RESEARCH AND TECHNOLOGY

Companies in this industry are continually seeking ingredients and processes that can improve product quality and packaging. In the 1980s, new synthetic gum bases were developed to overcome the limitations of previously used natural ingredients. These new materials are aimed at increasing gum flavor, improving texture, and reducing stickiness.

The environmental impact of the packaging used for chewing gum has been of considerable concern for companies in this industry. These companies rely on the wrappers and plastic packaging to keep gum fresh, yet these materials result in considerable waste. Scientists at gum companies have been evaluating and making changes to packaging and researching materials to meet future disposal and recycling requirements.

FURTHER READING

"Champions a Gold Medal Year." *Candy Industry,* July 1996.

Kaplan, Andrew. "Gum and Mints: Categories with Pop." *U.S. Distribution Journal,* 15 July 1995.

Warner, Fara. "Chewing Up Competitors with an Ancient Marketing Formula *Brandweek,* 4 July 1994.

"Topps in Bazooka Bursts Rollout." *ADWEEK,* 23 May 1994.

Malbin, Peter. "Butting Out: Retailers Are Caught in Swirl of Potential—and problems—in Merchandising High-Priced Smoking Cessation Products." *Supermarket News,* 4 November 1996.

Aho, Debra. "Bubble Yum Steps into Virtual Reality." *Advertising Age,* 4 October 1993.

Berry, Jon. "From Wrigley's, Gum in a Tube." *Adweek's Marketing Week,* 16 December 1991.

"Candy and Gum." *Progressive Grocer,* July 1993.

Davis, Ricardo. "Bubble Yum Kicks off Virtual Reality Game." *Advertising Age,* 22 March 1993.

Goldman, Kevin. "Rapid-Fire Topps TV Ads Ignore Nostalgia." *Wall Street Journal,* 10 December 1993.

Khalaf, Roula. "Card Glut." *Forbes,* 21 December 1992.

Klein, Carrie. "Wm. Wrigley: Chew on This." *Financial World,* 1 September, 1992.

Lesley, Elizabeth. "A Burst Bubble at Topps." *Business Week,* 23 August 1993.

Liesse, Julie. "Leaf Unwraps Gum with Xylitol." *Advertising Age,* 8 October 1990.

Malkin, Elizabeth. "Chiclets Tries New Language." *Advertising Age,* 19 April 1993.

Quintanilla, Carl. "If You Walk and Chew This Gum, You'll Stumble with a Smile." *Wall Street Journal,* 8 June 1993.

Rudnitsky, Howard. "Chicle Is Chic." *Forbes,* 8 November 1993.

Young, Robert. *The Chewing Gum Book.* Minnesota: Dillion Press, 1989.

Zinn, Laura, and Sandra D. Atchison. "Tastes Yucky, Sells Like Hotcakes." *Business Week,* 18 May 1992.

—Paola Trimarco, updated by Visi Tilak

SIC 2068

SALTED AND ROASTED NUTS AND SEEDS

This category includes establishments primarily engaged in manufacturing salted, roasted, dried, cooked, or canned nuts or in processing grains or seeds in a similar manner for snack purposes. Establishments primarily engaged in manufacturing confectionery-coated nuts are classified under **SIC 2064: Candy and Confectionery Products** and those manufacturing peanut butter are classified under **SIC 2099: Food Preparations, Not Elsewhere Classified.**

INDUSTRY SNAPSHOT

Salted or dried peanuts account for about 53 percent of the snack-nut market. The rest of the snack-nut market is split among mixed nuts, cashews, walnuts, almonds, pistachios, and macadamia nuts. Salted or roasted sunflower seeds, pumpkin seeds, and other seeds are also included in this category. Nuts and seeds are sold both packaged and as bulk food in grocery stores.

The industry shipped $2.8 billion worth of goods in 1995, up from $2.3 billion in 1990. Industry exports totaled 983 million tons in 1995. The number of establishments in the industry has increased 13 percent since 1990, from 87 to 98 in 1995.

ORGANIZATION AND STRUCTURE

The market for snack nuts has remained fairly level for a decade. Snack-food nuts have strong competition from potato chips, tortilla chips, pretzels, and microwave popcorn for the nation's snack dollars. The snack-nut and seed industry has handled its competition by introducing new flavors of seeds and nuts. Blue Diamond introduced lemon-chili and ranch-flavored almonds in some parts of the country, and Planters introduced hot and mild versions of spicy peanuts.

Manufacturers have also tried more creative packaging to expand their markets. Planters brought out a line of snacks in small, narrow bags and called them Munch-and-Go Tube Nuts. But merchandising efforts for nut and seed snacks are minimal compared to those for potato chips. Manufacturers have also been pushing for more shelf space and displays in grocery stores. While salted snack nuts and seeds showed flat sales, many producers and distributors were optimistic about sales of dried nuts because of their nutritional value.

Price has been another factor working against the industry. About 20 to 25 percent of domestic peanuts are used for snack nuts. With peanut prices kept high by government quotas, restrictions against imports, and support prices, peanut snack manufacturers are somewhat restricted in their supplies and prices. While almond processors and processors of other nuts can buy foreign nuts, peanut processors must buy domestically-grown peanuts. A drought in 1990 sent peanut prices soaring, resulting in deep profit losses for peanut processors.

Peanuts for snack nuts are usually purchased raw by a nut sheller. Processors, such as Planters, purchase the shelled nuts and send them on to blanchers to have the skins removed. Finally, the processing company receives them for roasting. Some snack nut companies, however, do the shelling and blanching themselves.

Many non-peanut nuts are sold through grower-owned co-operatives such as Blue Diamond Almonds and Diamond Walnuts. In 1992 Blue Diamond marketed 40 percent of the almonds grown in California, the only state in which almonds are grown commercially. Ten years earlier, Blue Diamond was handling 55 percent of the crop, but some growers dropped out to sell their almonds to other California and out-of-state processors.

CURRENT CONDITIONS

Sale of processed nuts rose from 36 million pounds in 1990 to 42 million pounds in 1994, an increase of only 4 percent. The 1996 nut market was marked by fluctuations. The estimated peanut yield for 1997 was at 1.7 million tons. Growth in specialty nuts was the most encouraging in the market due to the greater interest in ethnic food and various-flavored nuts among consumers. Middle-aged consumers were the largest purchasers of processed nuts.

The nut industry was no different from other food industries when it came to catering to health conscious consumers. Reduced-fat nuts appeared in the market in the mid-1990s and were expected to increase nut sales in supermarkets. Planters introduced low-fat honey roasted peanuts in 1995.

INDUSTRY LEADERS

The industry sales leader in 1996 was Nabisco Foods Group, with an overall sales revenue of $8.3 billion. Dole Food Company was second, with overall sales of $3.8 billion, and Nabisco Foods Group's, Planters Division, was third with overall sales revenue of $1.23 billion. Lance Inc., an independent company located in Charlotte, North Carolina was fourth largest, with overall sales of $477.5 million. Blue Diamond Growers was fifth, with sales revenue of $330 million.

Other industry sales leaders in 1996 were John B. Sanfilippo and Son Inc.($277.7 million revenue), Eagle Snacks Inc. ($240 million), Sunmark Inc. ($200 million), W.B. Rodenberry Company Inc. ($120 million), Magna Loa Macadamia Nut Corp. ($86 million), David and Sons Inc. ($48 million), Fisher Nut Co. ($48 million), Dahlgren and Co. Inc. ($40 million), and Georgia Nut Co. ($40 million).

FURTHER READING

Bovard, James. "Trade Nuttiness." *Wall Street Journal,* 13 December 1990, A14.

Dorn, Chad A. "Nut Market Going 'Nutty in 1996." *Candy Industry,* October 1996.

Graebner, Lynn. "Blue Diamond Has Competition for Hearts of Farmers." *Business Journal Serving Greater Sacramento,* 7 December 1992, 1.

Ingersoll, Bruce. "Shell Game: Peanut Quota System Comes Under Attack." *Wall Street Journal.* 1 May 1990, A1.

McClure, Barney H. "Cooperating on Dried Fruit and Nuts." *Supermarket Business Magazine,* November 1990, 21-22.

"Processed Nuts." *Retail Business: Market Surveys,* September 1995.

Saxton, Lisa. "Health Nuts: Buyers Are Hoping Reduced-fat Peanuts Will Whip the Category into Better Shape." *Supermarket News,* 25 September 1995.

Wold, Marjorie. "Nuts Can't Crack the Snack Market." *Progressive Grocer,* May 1992, 179-180.

—Wendy Stein, updated by Visi Tilak

SIC 2074

COTTONSEED OIL MILLS

This category covers establishments primarily engaged in manufacturing cottonseed oil, cake, meal, and linters, or in processing purchased cottonseed oil into forms other than edible cooking oils. Businesses primarily involved in refining cottonseed oil into edible cooking oils are covered in **SIC 2079: Shortening, Table Oils, Margarine, and Other Edible Fats and Oils, Not Elsewhere Classified.**

The first successful cottonseed oil mill began production in Natchez, Mississippi, in 1833. Up to that point, cottonseed left over from planting had been regarded as a health hazard and a source of pollution. The cottonseed industry grew swiftly after the Civil War, making the United States the largest consumer of cottonseed in the world. Total U.S. cottonseed production reached 7.6 million tons in 1996.

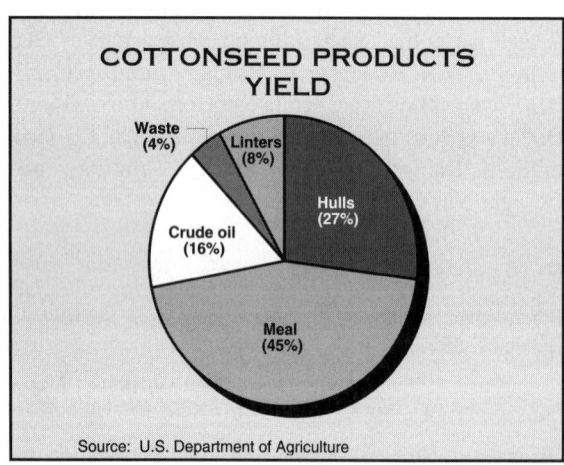

COTTONSEED PRODUCTS YIELD

Waste (4%)
Linters (8%)
Hulls (27%)
Crude oil (16%)
Meal (45%)

Source: U.S. Department of Agriculture

The milling of raw cottonseed yields three products: hulls, linters, and kernels. The hull is typically used as livestock feed, the linters for the manufacturing of various products, and the kernels are crushed for oil and meal production. Cottonseed meal typically represents 60-80 percent of total crushed production. Aside from its role in the production of salad dressings, margarine, and shortening, the chief use for the oil is in the manufacture of lubricants, paint, and soap. The principal use for cottonseed meal is as a high-protein feed supplement for cattle, swine, and poultry, and it is also used as a fertilizer. In 1996, U.S. meal production reached 1.73 million tons, and oil production reached 635,500 tons.

Linters. Before the crushing of cottonseeds, but after the removal of the longer fibers processed in the manufacture of fabrics, the linters—shorter cotton fibers—are removed by a range of methods suited to their various uses in the production of sterile absorbent cotton, felt, and padding; in the manufacture of paper, film, explosives, plastics, and rayon; and as a source of essentially pure cellulose for the chemical industry.

Mill-run processing of linters is a one-step procedure used for smaller quantities than are handled in alternative processing methods. Various production approaches yield both longer and shorter linters for use either in the chemical industry or for other purposes. A two-step processing method yields, at the first stage, the longer and softer first-cut linters well suited to the production of absorbent cotton, felt, and padding. At the second stage (the portion of the production process that generally represents the bulk of total linter production), the shorter and tougher second-cut linters usually reserved for use in the chemicals industry are garnered.

Genetics. Any part of cottonseed intended for consumption by humans or by nonruminant animals has to be processed in such a way as to extract the gossypol, a pigment toxic to all nonruminants. Because this pigment is located in the tiny glands of cottonseed, the development of a glandless strain of cottonseed was seen as holding potentially great promise for the future of the cottonseed industry. In the mid-1990s a new cottonseed variety with a "healthier" high-oleic acid profile was developed, which could increase market share for cotton in the cooking and salad oil industries then dominated by soybean oil.

The leading company in the industry was Southern Cotton Oil Co., Inc., located in Decatur, Illinois, with $450 million in sales. Plains Cooperative Oil Mill Inc. of Lubbock, Texas, ranked second with $128 million in sales. Other companies included Yazoo Valley Oil Mill Inc., a privately owned company in Greenwood, Missouri, Chickasha Cotton Oil Co., based in Chandler, Arizona, and Osceola Products Co. of Osceola, Arizona. The top ten companies had less than $1 billion in sales, and the majority of establishments had less than 100 employees.

FURTHER READING

"Feed Marketing and Distribution," *Feedstuffs,* 16 July 1992, 6-22.

Food and Agriculture Policy Research Institute. *FAPRI 1996 Agricultural Outlook.* Columbia, Missouri, 1996. Available from http://ssu.agri.missouri.edu/SSU/FAPRI/REPORTS/staffp/fap196/text/introd/title.html.

McCormick, Ian, and Bengt Hyberg "What's in the Future for Canola?" *Agricultural Outlook,* August 1992, 15-18.

U.S. Dept of Agriculture. National Agricultural Statistics Service. *1997 Agricultural Outlook.* Washington: Economic Research Service, 1997. Available from http://usda.mannlib.cornell.edu/reports/erssor/economics/ao-bb/complete/1997.

U.S. Department of Commerce. International Trade Administration. *U.S. Industrial Outlook 1994.* Washington: GPO, 1994.

SIC 2075

SOYBEAN OIL MILLS

This category covers establishments primarily engaged in manufacturing soybean oil, cake, and meal, and soybean protein isolates and concentrates, or in processing purchased soybean oil into forms other than edible cooking oils. Businesses primarily engaged in refining soybean oil into edible cooking oils are classified in **SIC 2079: Shortening, Table Oils, Margarine, and Other Edible Fats and Oils, Not Elsewhere Classified.**

Traditionally one of the largest U.S. crops, soybeans are especially valuable because the same automated presses yield two important products with closely linked markets—soybean oil, and (representing more than 80 percent of the total) soybean meal.

In the 1950s and 1960s, the largest food market for soybean meal was in meat processing, which used soy flour as a protein filler. This product eventually became outmoded as improved refining techniques yielded isolated soy proteins and concentrates having a wider range of applications and little or no independent flavor. These ingredients grew in popularity after legislation was passed that freed meat product manufacturers from regulations that insisted on prominent package labeling of the presence of such ingredients. In the 1970s and 1980s, increasing desirability of high-protein animal feeds, and soy's enhanced status as a healthy ingredient in food, led to increased demand for meal. Soybean meal and oil production volume increased proportionally.

A record U.S. soybean crop in 1994 resulted in lower prices, as the farm price dropped from $6.40 in 1994 to $5.35 per bushel in 1995. Domestic use of soybean oil increased in 1995, reaching almost 13 billion pounds, and is projected to increase through 2004, while slow growth is projected for many competing fats and oils. Total U.S. production of soybeans totaled 2.38 billion bushels in 1996, up 9 percent from 1995, ranking second behind the bumper crop of 1994. As a result of 1994 volume, soybean oil production in 1994 rose 8 percent from 1993, to 6.8 million metric tons. Production in 1996 was projected to recede 4 percent from 1995 figures, and then resume steady growth, reaching 7.1 million metric tons by the year 2000.

The *1996 USDA Agricultural Outlook* predicted that world grain and oilseed markets will face tight supplies and strong prices through the rest of the century, due primarily to stronger economic and population growth in developing countries, such as Asia and Latin America. U.S. exports of soybeans and soybean meal—dominant in the global meal market—were expected to account for the bulk of the growth in world soybean output, as the U.S was projected to increase its share of world output from 48 percent in 1995 to 50 percent by 2000, with Asia importing half of all U.S. grain shipments.

The trend in the United States appeared to be in favor of greater acceptance and more widespread use of soybean products, especially in the form of isolated soy proteins and concentrates. Isolated soy proteins—ISPs—have been shown to equal the protein quality of milk and egg protein, to make logical substitutes for dairy protein because of their lack of fiber and 90 percent protein content, and to have uses in coffee creamers, protein-fortified beverages, both weight-loss products and body-building supplements, certain medical foods, and milk-free infant formulas.

The leading company in the industry in 1996 was Ag Processing Inc., of Omaha, Nebraska, with 1.37 billion in sales and 3,000 employees. Central Soya Company Inc., of Fort Wayne, Indiana, was second with 1 billion in sales and 1,200 employees. Other industry leaders included Harvest States Cooperatives' Honeymead Products Co., Ralston Purina Co.'s Protein Technologies International Holdings Inc., and Riceland Foods.

In the mid-1990s, there were significant technological advances in the production of biodiesel, a biodegradable, nontoxic, lower-emitting alternative to pe-

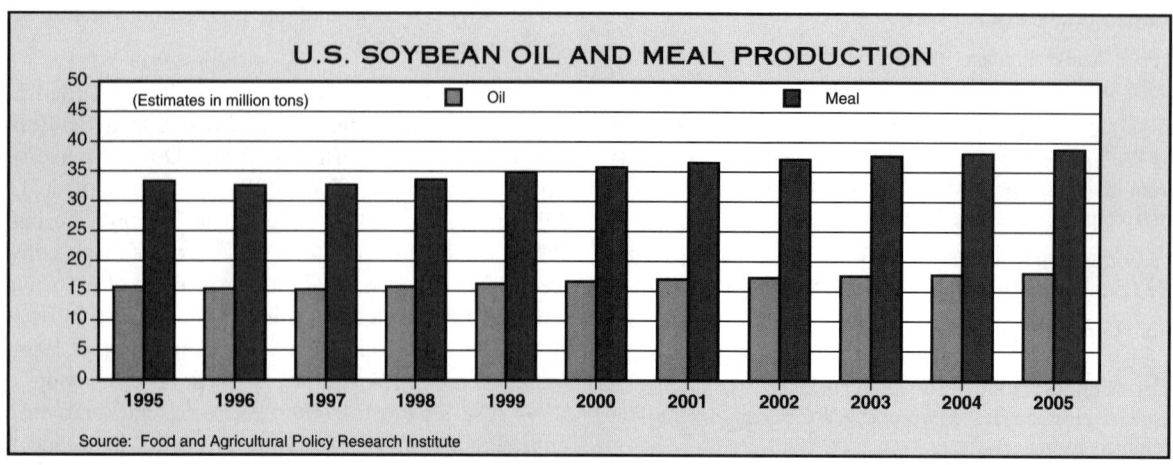

Source: Food and Agricultural Policy Research Institute

troleum diesel fuel. Biodiesel is fuel and edible oil blend for use in diesel engines, and was expected to boost demand for soybean oil. The Chicago Biodiesel Plant, operated by Columbus Foods Company, which began production in 1997, was the first plant in the United States to produce biodiesel from combinations of used vegetable oils and fresh soybean oil, and is expected to act as a model for future biodiesel production.

FURTHER READING

"Feed Marketing and Distribution." *Feedstuffs,* 16 July 1992, 6-22.

Food and Agriculture Policy Research Institute. *FAPRI 1996 Agricultural Outlook.* Columbia, Missouri, 1996. Available from http://ssu.agri.missouri.edu/SSU/FAPRI/REPORTS/staffp/fap196/text/introd/title.html.

Mancini, Leticia. "Giving Soy a Second Look." *Food Engineering,* August 1993, 94-95.

U.S. Dept of Agriculture. National Agricultural Statistics Service. *1997 Agricultural Outlook.* Washington: Economic Research Service, 1997. Available from http://usda.mannlib.cornell.edu/reports/erssor/economics/ao-bb/complete/1997.

SIC 2076

VEGETABLE OIL MILLS, EXCEPT CORN, COTTONSEED, AND SOYBEAN

This category covers establishments primarily engaged in manufacturing vegetable oils, cake, and meal, with the exception of corn, cottonseed, and soybean, or in processing such vegetable oils into forms other than edible cooking oils. Businesses primarily engaged in manufacturing corn oil and its byproducts are classified in **SIC 2046: Wet Corn Milling;** those refining

vegetable oils into edible cooking oils are covered in **SIC 2079: Shortening, Table Oils, Margarine, and Other Edible Fats and Oils, Not Elsewhere Classified;** and those primarily refining these oils for medicinal purposes are discussed in **SIC 2833: Medicinal Chemicals and Botanical Products.**

High vegetable oil prices in 1994-95 increased oil's contribution to the value of seeds. This stimulated production of high-oil-content seeds such as rapeseed and sunflowers in 1995-96. However, U.S. oilseed production was estimated at 70.2 million tons, down 9.5 million tons from 1994-95. In that same year, production of palm oil rose 6 percent, and rapeseed continued to increase its market share, with 12 percent of world protein meal consumption in 1996. Industry analysts paid particular attention to sunflowers (along with soy beans and corn, one of the biggest U.S. crops) and to rapeseed, due to a significant boost in production levels in the mid-1990s, up nearly 37 percent from 1993 to 1996.

Sunflower Seed Oil. Sunflowers can be processed using the same automated presses as corn and soy beans, but use less water and are drought resistant. These advantages, together with the Sunflowerseed Oil Assistance Program (SOAP), which helps to offset the competitiveness of highly subsidized European Community vegetable oils, helped overcome reduced levels of production and the loss of two major export markets in the early 1990s—Egypt and Russia—and boost U.S. sunflowerseed oil exports to 270,00 metric tons in 1992-93. However, 1995-96 exports fell 27 percent from 1994-95, to 209,000 metric tons. Total U.S. sunflowerseed production also declined, to 4.009 billion pounds, down 17 percent from the bumper crop of 1994.

Canola. Canola is the name for a group of rapeseed varieties, and accounts for the majority of rapeseed grown in the United States and Canada. As a relatively new contender in the United States, canola in the early 1990s faced an uncertain future, when the product was seen as one that might join the so-called specialty oils market—alongside such products as linseed oil, coconut oil, and walnut oil. However, in the mid-1990s canola is now sought after by increasingly health-conscious food and edible oil industries because of its low saturated fat content, which is the lowest among major vegetable oils. Most of the canola oil consumed in the United States is imported from Canada, and domestic use increased 10 percent in 1995-96, as U.S. rapeseed consumption reached 316 million pounds. Canola meal (originally known as rapeseed meal) has similar nutritional qualities to soybean meal, and is often used as a cattle feed supplement. Canola was also likely to see increased industrial use, as a genetically-engineered variety of canola called high-lauric acid canola was being produced in the mid-1990s. Lauric acid, previously only available from coconut or palm kernel oil, is a key ingredient in soaps, detergents, lubricants, cosmetics, and confections.

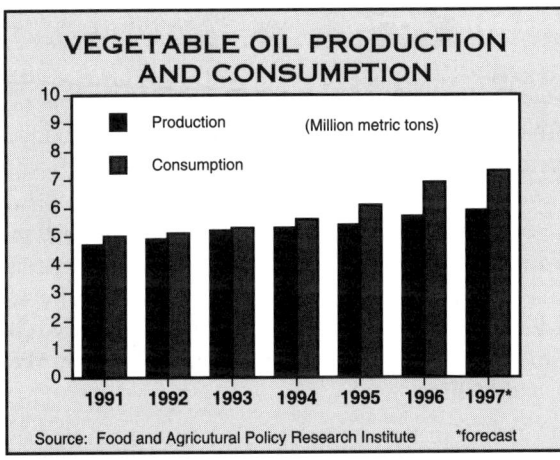

VEGETABLE OIL PRODUCTION AND CONSUMPTION

Source: Food and Agricultural Policy Research Institute   *forecast

The leader in the industry for 1996 was Cargill Peanut Products, of Dawson, Georgia, with $140 million in sales and about 300 employees. Parent company Cargill Inc. had $56 billion in sales. Other industry leaders included Colfax Inc., of Pawtucket, Rhode Island, CasChem, of Bayonne, New Jersey, and SVO Specialty Products, Inc. of Eastlake, Ohio.

The U.S. typically produces less than 10 percent of world sunflowerseeds. Among international producers in 1995-96, Argentina and the Former Soviet Union were the largest producers and exporters, producing 5.4 and 5.21 million metric tons respectively, while Argentine exports of sunflowerseed are expected to fall dramatically to 200,000 tons in 1997. Canada was the principal producer and exporter of canola, and palm oil was the most heavily traded oil in the world.

In the mid-1990s, there were significant technological advances in the production of biodiesel, a biodegradable, nontoxic, lower-emitting alternative to petroleum diesel fuel. Biodiesel is a diesel fuel and edible oil blend for use in diesel engines, and was expected to boost demand for compatible oils. The Chicago Biodiesel Plant, operated by Columbus Foods Company, which began production in 1997, was the first plant in the United States to produce biodiesel from combinations of used vegetable oils and fresh soybean oil, and is expected to act as a model for future biodiesel production.

FURTHER READING

American Soybean Association. *Soy Stats 1996.* St. Louis, 1996. Available from http://www.ag.uiuc.edu/%7Estratsoy/96soystats/pg2.html.

Best, Annie. "U.S. Oilseed Crusher Sees Expanding Markets." *Feedstuffs,* 7 December 1992, 25.

"Feed Marketing and Distribution." *Feedstuffs,* 16 July 1992, 6-22.

Food and Agriculture Policy Research Institute. *FAPRI 1996 Agricultural Outlook.* Columbia, Missouri, 1996. Available from http://ssu.agri.missouri.edu/SSU/FAPRI/REPORTS/staffp/fap196/text/introd/title.html.

Good, Darrel, and George Flaskerud. "Oilseeds Policy." College Station, Texas: Texas A&M University, 1996. Available from: http://ianrwww.unl.edu/farmbill/oilseed.htm.

McCormick, Ian, and Bengt Hyberg, "What's in the Future for Canola?" *Agricultural Outlook,* August 1992, 15-18.

U.S. Dept of Agriculture. National Agricultural Statistics Service. *1997 Agricultural Outlook.* Washington: Economic Research Service, 1997. Available from http://usda.mannlib.cornell.edu/reports/erssor/economics/ao-bb/complete/1997.

U.S. Census Bureau. *Current Industrial Report Series, Fats and Oils: Oilseed Crushing.* GPO: Washington, 1996. Available from http://www.census.gov/industry/m20j9605.txt.html.

SIC 2077

ANIMAL AND MARINE FATS AND OILS

This category covers establishments primarily engaged in manufacturing animal oils (including fish oil and other marine animal oils) and fish and animal meal, together with those rendering inedible stearin, grease, and tallow from animal fat, bones, and meat scraps. Establishments primarily engaged in manufacturing lard and edible tallow and stearin are classified in meat-producing industries; those which refine marine animal oils for medicinal purposes are classified in **SIC 2833: Medicinal Chemicals and Botanical Products;** and those manufacturing fatty acids are classified in **SIC 2899: Chemicals and Chemical Preparations, Not Elsewhere Classified.**

The majority of the industry in the mid-1990s was engaged in the manufacture of feed and fertilizer byproducts, which represented 52 percent of total shipments in 1995. Grease and inedible tallow accounted for 40 percent of industry shipments, and other animal and marine oil mill products made up the remaining 8 percent. The total value of shipments for this industry in 1995 was $3.13 billion.

Though the output quantities for meat meal and tankage were much larger than those for fish meal and oil in this industry in the 1990s, and though fish meal typically constituted a small portion of the feeds given to poultry, pigs, and cattle (among such other ingredients as feather meal, meat meal, bone meal, and soybean meal), fish meal could make up over half the content of feeds manufactured for pond-raised salmon and trout.

In addition, fish meal represented a uniquely valuable source of nutrition because of its especially rich crude protein content and prominence of essential amino acids, and because its consumption was linked to faster growth and reproduction in livestock and larger quantities of eggs and milk. Moreover, fish oil—a natural by-product of fish meal manufacturing, released when steam-cooked fish are passed through large screw presses—had significant value in the domestic food industry.

There were several companies of significant size engaged in this industry in the mid-1990s. Darling International Inc., based in Irving, Texas, had over $400 million in sales and employed around 1,600 workers. Other leading members of the industry included National By-Products Inc., of Des Moines, Iowa, with $175 million in sales and 1,000; employees, and American Proteins Inc., based in Roswell, Georgia, with $170 million in sales. Other leaders included Georgia Protein Co. of Cumming, Georgia, and Farmers Union Marketing and Processing Association of Redwood Falls, Minnesota. The outlook for employment in the industry was bleak in the mid-1990s. The total number of employees in 1995 was 8,600, down nearly 20 percent from 1988, and jobs for production workers were expected to decline steadily through 2000. Production workers made up about 66 percent of the work force in 1995, and the average annual salary per production worker was $26,000.

FURTHER READING

Bahner, Benedict. ''Fish Oil, Meal Markets Look toward US Recovery.'' *Chemical Marketing Reporter,* 19 April 1993, 10.

Darnay, Arsen J., ed. *Manufacturing USA.* 5th ed. Detroit: Gale Research, 1996.

''Feed Marketing and Distribution'' *Feedstuffs,* 16 July 1992, 6-22.

U.S. Dept of Agriculture. National Agricultural Statistics Service. *1997 Agricultural Outlook.* Washington: Economic Research Service, 1997. Available from http://usda.mannlib.cornell.edu/reports/erssor/economics/ao-bb/complete/1997.

U.S. Department of Commerce. Economics and Statistics Administration. Bureau of the Census. *1995 Annual Survey of Manufactures.* Washington: GPO, 1997. Available from http://www.census.gov/prod/www/titles.html#mm.

U.S. Industrial Outlook 1994 Washington, DC: U.S. Department of Commerce, 1994.

SIC 2079

SHORTENING, TABLE OILS, MARGARINE, AND OTHER EDIBLE FATS AND OILS, NOT ELSEWHERE CLASSIFIED

This category covers establishments primarily involved in manufacturing shortening, table oils, margarine, and other edible fats and oils that are not elsewhere classified. Companies primarily engaged in producing corn oil are discussed in **SIC 2046: Wet Corn Milling.**

Many of the goods classified in this industry are long-time staples of the American kitchen. Commonly utilized for cooking and baking purposes, products such as shortening, vegetable oil, and margarine have become established presences in the marketplace. The market in the mid-1990s was dominated by shortenings and cooking oils, which represented 77 percent of shipments, while margarine accounted for 22 percent. The industry shipped $5.748 billion in goods in 1995.

Margarine is a key product in this industry. Invented in France in 1869, margarine's introduction to the United States was initially impeded by low quality and the efforts of a powerful butter lobby, which led to discriminatory taxes. With technical improvements and altered legislation, margarine enjoyed increased acceptance. It came to be largely regarded as a healthier and cheaper alternative to butter. By the early 1990s, however, the $1.5 billion margarine industry began to falter while butter, which offered bargain prices, increased its market share. Now, many consumers who switched from butter to margarine for health reasons have become disillusioned after learning that vegetable shortenings may also raise the risk of cardiovascular disease. Margarine remains a major moneymaker for its producers, however. The leader in margarine industry sales was Nabisco Foods.

The fastest growing segment of the industry in the mid-1990s was the specialty oils market, which included blended oils such as canola/corn oil, corn/palm oil, olive/canola oil, and peanut/sesame oil, and flavored cooking oils that infuse herbs and other seasonings, like garlic. The specialty oils market averaged 50 percent annual gains in the mid-1990s, and was worth over $100 million in 1995. In addition, newer contenders like canola and olive oil grabbed the attention of increasingly health-conscious consumers in the mid-1990s. Physicians were impressed by reports that stated that the rate of heart disease in certain regions of the Mediterranean—where olive is the principal oil consumed—was relatively low, and that dietary monounsaturated fat was capable of lowering total cholesterol and LDL without lowering HDL. U.S. imports of olive oil during 1996 totaled 118,000 tons, an 18 percent increase from 1991 figures. Leading olive oil manufacturers include Bertolli, Filippo Berio, and Pompeian.

The industry employed 7,000 people in 1995, 70 percent of whom were production workers. The average annual salary for production workers was $29,700. Due to increased productivity and increased automation, gradual reductions in the work force were projected through 2000.

FURTHER READING

Darnay, Arsen J., ed. *Manufacturing USA*. 5th ed. Detroit: Gale Research, 1996.

Davis, Riccardo A. "New Spread Formation." *Advertising Age,* 2 August 1992.

DeNitto, Emily. "Olive Oil Sales Climb Out of the Pits." *Advertising Age,* 6 September 1993, 8.

Deveny, Kathleen. "Health Doubts Cut Into Margarine Sales." *Wall Street Journal,* 24 June 1993, B1, B10.

Mancini, Leticia. "Low Fat Comes of Age" *Food Engineering,* June 1993.

Spethmann, Betsy. "Flavors Fuel Run on Oils." *Brandweek,* 27 November, 1995, 24.

U.S. Department of Commerce. Economics and Statistics Administration. Bureau of the Census. *1995 Annual Survey of Manufactures.* Washington: GPO, 1997. Available from http://www.census.gov/prod/www/titles.html#mm.

SIC 2082

MALT BEVERAGES

This category includes establishments primarily engaged in the manufacturing of malt beverages, including ale, beer, malt liquor, nonalcoholic beer, porter, and stout.

INDUSTRY SNAPSHOT

Beer has been a part of the American lifestyle since the discovery of America and the creation of the United States. Records show that beer was brewed in colonial America and was made by American Indians. Through the years, beer has served cultural, spiritual, and even medicinal purposes. With nearly 80 million American beer drinkers, beer has become one of the most popular beverages, second only to water and tea.

Each year, the U.S. malt beverage industry produces and sells more than 2.5 billion cases of beer, or about 190.2 million barrels. A barrel of beer is equal to two kegs or 31 gallons, which is roughly 13.8 24-unit cases of 12-ounce cans or bottles. The wholesale value of malt beverage shipments averages approximately $15 billion annually. According to the Beer Institute, the trade association for the malt beverage industry, the United States is the world's largest producer of beer, brewing more than 20 percent of the world's volume.

Domestic sales for beer rose a small but significant 1 percent in 1996, breaking a ten-year stalemate in consumption rates. This growth can be attributed to the strength of microbrews, which continue to post double-digit growth, and imported beer, which saw record figures in 1995.

Three major companies hold nearly 78 percent of the market share in the United States. These breweries are Anheuser-Busch, located in St. Louis, Missouri; Miller Brewing Company in Milwaukee, Wisconsin; and Coors Brewing Company in Golden, Colorado.

The two top-selling brands, Budweiser and Bud Light, both belonged to Anheuser-Busch, along with 45 percent of the market share and 75 percent of the industry profits. In second place was Miller with the third-best selling product, Miller Light. Ranked third was Coors Brewing Company with the fourth most-popular beer, Coors Light.

Although light beer continues to dominate the market with a 37 percent share, consumption rate of micro brews or specialty beer also continued to grow in popularity. Since the industry-leader Boston Beer Company was founded in 1984, the microbrew business has grown into a $1 billion industry. And the market segment is projected to grow from now through 2000, capturing 6 percent of the total domestic beer market.

Another good sign for the U.S. beer industry is its strong showing overseas. Various markets are starting to become accessible, especially the most eagerly sought Asian market. Japan continues to be the largest market for U.S. beer, but export rates also have climbed in Hong Kong, Brazil, Taiwan, Canada, and Russia.

ORGANIZATION AND STRUCTURE

This industry includes only those companies that manufacture beer. The industry has consistently been dominated by three major U.S. breweries, yet, regardless of size, all breweries have to sell their products through wholesalers and retailers. This distribution channel is the result of accommodating the variety of federal, state, and local regulations regarding the sale of alcoholic beverages.

Federal and State Regulation. The Federal Alcohol Administration Act (FAA) was put into place at the end of Prohibition in 1933. Since that time, the Bureau of Alcohol, Tobacco and Firearms (ATF) has been responsible for administering and enforcing the FAA, including qualifying brewers, collecting brewer and wholesaler occupational taxes, and regulating trade practices, advertising, and labeling.

Beyond the uniformity of the FAA, regulations varied greatly among the 50 states, as the Beer Institute reported in their testimony to the U.S. Senate regarding the Malt Beverage Interbrand Competition Act. Probably the most dramatic example of regulatory diversity has been the way that states have allowed beer to be sold. States sell beer in one of two ways, either in a controlled environment or using an open, licensed method. ''Open'' states license retailers and wholesalers to handle the distribution and sale of alcoholic beverages. Thirty-two states and the District of Columbia are considered ''open'' states. The other 18 states operate under the control method, in which each state government buys and sells alcoholic beverages at the wholesale and retail levels.

In addition to federal regulations, some states have set up independent agencies that have been responsible for the administration, licensing, and enforcement of state laws and the collection of state revenues. Additionally, some state legislatures created their own Alcoholic Beverage Control (ABC) agencies with rule-making power, and 32 states have allowed citizens to vote for or against the sale of liquor in various cities or counties.

BACKGROUND AND DEVELOPMENT

The foundation of the U.S. beer industry can be traced to the ancient times of kings and pharaohs. Babylonian clay tablets more than 8,000 years old depicted beer being brewed and gave detailed recipes. Other writings indicated that beer was brewed by the Egyptians as early as 3000 B.C. and by the Chinese in the 23rd century B.C. One of the world's oldest breweries still in existence is Brauerei Beck in Germany, where Beck's beer was first brewed in 1533.

Beer was first brewed in America in 1587 at Sir Walter Raleigh's colony in Roanoke, Virginia, and Puritan settlers brewed beer in Boston as early as 1620. In 1791, Congress levied the first tax on alcohol. By 1870, Adolphus Busch had pioneered the use of refrigerated railroad cars to ship beer over long distances. Following the steady development of temperance groups, the Pure Food and Drug Act, more commonly known as the Volstead Act, went into effect on January 16, 1920. This act ushered in the era of Prohibition, which banned the sale of alcoholic beverages. Prohibition, which banned the sale of alcoholic beverages for 13 years, during which the production and distribution of millions of gallons of alcohol fell into the hands of gangsters called ''bootleggers.''

After Prohibition was repealed in 1933, federal and state governments tightened regulations under the Federal Alcohol Act (FAA) and various state regulations. Brewers also adopted policies of self-regulation, such as the Distilled Spirits Council of the United States (DISCUS) voluntary ''code of good practice.'' Following Prohibition, beer was produced in 750 locations throughout the country. It was distributed to wholesalers and retailers in limited geographic regions that seem extremely small when compared to current distribution areas. By the 1930s, the primary way to sell beer was in draft form and in refillable bottles.

In order for breweries to continue expanding, however, less costly containers were needed. The beer can, introduced in 1935, filled those needs perfectly. By the end of World War II, the beer can had become such a popular container that glass companies soon created the one-way bottle to keep up with the competition. Both of these less-expensive products allowed brewers to ship products and expand markets. By 1946, breweries served markets that were at one time only accessible to local and regional companies, and this expansion soon created the nationwide market of the major breweries.

Beyond the complexities of the regulations for producing and selling beer, brewing beer is a simple process. Beer is nothing more than a fermented alcoholic beverage made from malted barley and flavored with hops. Beer is produced by grinding barley, malt, and rice or corn and then mixing the combination with boiling water. The resulting "mash" is slowly cooked to convert the grain starches to fermentable sugars. The mash then is strained and the clear amber liquid that remains is called "wort." The strained wort is piped to a brew kettle where it is boiled. Hops are added to give the brew the aroma and flavor associated with beer. The wort then is chilled and pumped to fermenting cellars, where yeast is added. This begins the fermentation process, producing the alcohol and carbonation in the beer. Upon completion, the yeast is filtered out and the brew is piped to aging tanks. There, the beer will age 10-14 days prior to being packaged in bottles, cans, or kegs.

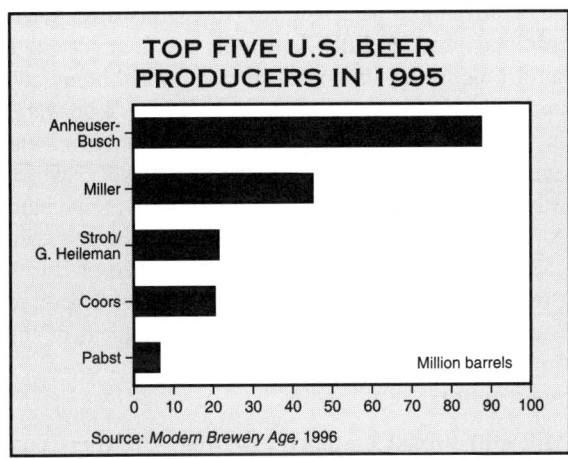

TOP FIVE U.S. BEER PRODUCERS IN 1995

Source: *Modern Brewery Age,* 1996

CURRENT CONDITIONS

Total sales volume for the domestic beer market rose 1 percent in 1996, a small but symbolic gesture breaking a decade-long stagnation in consumption rates. Although incremental, this industry growth can be attributed to the continued rise in microbrews, which has been posting double-digit growth since 1995, and to imported beers. Both segments are significant but small; microbrews make up only 2 percent of the market and imports are just 5 percent.

"I think that the issue that the major brewers have to deal with is that the combination of microbrews and imports are skimming the cream off the top," says Emanuel Goldman, a leading drink analyst for Paine Webber. "It's an industry that is basically not growing. The beer per cap is undergoing a very gradual decline, and so what you have is what has existed for

some time in the distilled spirits business, people drinking less but drinking better," said Goldman.

The three big leaders in the beer industry continue to be Anheuser-Busch, Miller, and Coors. With the two top-selling brands, Budweiser and Bud Light, A-B dominates the domestic beer market. In 1996, A-B increased its market share from 44 percent to 45.2 percent, according to a report published in *Beer Marketer's Insights.* A-B shipped more than twice as much beer than second-place Miller, who has 21.8 percent of the market and the third best-selling product, Miller Light. Coors Brewing Company, with its fourth-place Coors Light, dropped market share from 10.1 percent in 1995 to 9.9 percent in 1996.

A-B sells 45 percent of U.S. beer volume, but controls over 75 percent of the industry's profits. The rest of the industry battles for the remaining 25 percent of the profit pool. As a result, companies have begun to consolidate with others to save in operational expenditures. So, in 1995 fourth-place Stroh Brewery Company acquired G. Heileman, makers of Colt 45, Old Style, and Henry Weinhard, among other labels.

"Stroh and Heilman are partners now under a common umbrella. . . .because of the necessity of it. Coors will have to find a partner with which to consolidate to achieve long-term profitability. And although it's part of a very large and wealthy company, Miller's share of industry profits is declining even while its share of market has been relatively stable," said Martin Romm, a leading industry analyst for First Boston.

Causes for this stagnant market have and continue to be attributed to the effects of the federal excise tax hike in 1991, unfavorable demographics (not enough 21-year-olds), and continuing health concerns regarding alcohol consumption. A bit of good news for the beer industry is that the mini baby-boom generation is about to come of age, so the flat market of 21-year-olds should be growing soon.

Attempting to boost incremental sales and grow the beer market, companies have been continue to introducing new products—often creating entirely new segments such as light beer, nonalcoholic beer, ice beer, bottled draft beer, and clear malt liquor drinks such as Zima.

Light beer has maintained the largest share of beer consumption at 37.25 percent—more than 70 million barrels in 1996, according to figures from R.S. Weinberg & Associates. Nonalcoholic beer also has helped grow the beer business. Although small compared to total beer consumption, volume of nonalcoholic beer has more than doubled since its 1989 level and remained steady since 1991. O'Doul's by Anheuser-Busch accounts for half of the non-alcoholic category.

The one market segment that everyone has been turning to is the craft beer or microbrews. Sales in this segment have been growing at an average of 40 percent a year for the last ten years. According to the Institute for Brewing Studies, specialty brewing in the United States grew from a $600-million industry in 1992 to a $1-billion industry in 1994.

In an industry of mature brands, companies were looking at the future of microbrews. Even the big names were offering craft brews. In 1994, A-B, the largest brewer in the United States, bought a stake in Seattle's Redhook Ale Brewery, while Coors Brewing Company landed Killian's Irish Red.

The undisputed leader of the microbrew segment has been the Boston Beer Company (BBC) and its product Samuel Adams. The tenth largest beer producer in the country, BBC manufactured 700 barrels in 1994, only about three one-thousandths of the beer sold in the United States. However small, its volume still is greater than the total of the next six microbrewers combined.

When the BBC was founded in 1984, fewer than 40 micro-breweries existed. Since then, an estimated 500 small breweries and brew pubs have opened, with an additional 50 added each year from 1985 on.

''The microbrewery segment is expected to grow to a six percent domestic market share by 2000 from 2.5 percent now, but not every brewer in business today will be around then,'' says Mike Gerend, president of Wisconsin Brewing Co. So many companies have tried to cash in on the microbrewing craze that there may be too many. Gerend thinks a true microbrew will be most successful in its hometown market and will survive on consumer loyalty.

INDUSTRY LEADERS

Anheuser-Busch, Inc. Anheuser-Busch, Inc. is the world's largest brewer and the main subsidiary of the Anheuser-Busch Companies, based in St. Louis, Missouri. With 13 breweries, Anheuser-Busch produces 15 naturally brewed beers, one non-alcoholic beer, and imports three beers for distribution in the United States. By 1992, Anheuser-Busch sold an all-time industry record of 86.8 million barrels of beer in one year. Anheuser-Busch was the first brewer to use pasteurization to help keep beer fresh in transit, and most packaged beer is still pasteurized.

Anheuser-Busch brands are exported to more than 40 countries and brewed under the company's supervision in five countries. Anheuser-Busch employs over 44,000 people and works with approximately 900 independent wholesale distributors. Anheuser-Busch also operates 11 company-owned distributorships. Other beer-related Anheuser-Busch subsidiaries are Anheuser-Busch International, Inc.; Busch Agricultural Resources, Inc.; Metal Container Corporation; Anheuser-Busch Recycling Corporation; Busch Media Group, Inc.; Busch Creative Services Corporation; St. Louis Refrigerator Car Company; Manufacturers Railway Company; and the International Label Company. Anheuser-Busch brands are Budweiser, Bud Light, Bud Dry Draft, Michelob, Michelob Light, Michelob Classic Dark, Michelob Dry, Michelob Golden Draft, Michelob Golden Draft Light, Busch, Busch Light, Natural Light, Natural Pilsner, O'Doul's, King Cobra, Carlsberg, Carlsberg Light, and Elephant Malt Liquor.

Adolphus Busch, founder of the Anheuser-Busch Brewing Company, immigrated to the United States in 1857, arriving in St. Louis via New Orleans. In 1861, Adolphus married Lilly Anheuser, and after serving a short time in the Union Army, he returned home and joined the management of his father-in-law's brewery. In 1869, Adolphus purchased half ownership of another brewery, called the Bavarian Brewery, which was restructured with his father-in-law, Eberhard Anheuser, as president and Busch as secretary. In 1879, the company was renamed Anheuser-Busch Brewing Association. Upon the death of Eberhard Anheuser, Adolphus Busch became president of the brewery. He continued in this position for the next 33 years until his death in 1913.

Miller Brewing Company. The Miller Brewing Company is a wholly owned subsidiary of Phillip Morris Companies Inc., with corporate headquarters in Milwaukee, Wisconsin. With approximately 10,000 employees, the company operates seven breweries, five manufacturing plants, a glass-bottling plant, a hops processing plant, a malting factory, and a packaging/printing plant. The Miller Brewing Company produces over 40 million barrels of beer each year. The company's major brands are Miller High Life, Miller Lite, Lowenbrau, Miller Genuine Draft, Meister Brau, Milwaukee's Best, Magnum Malt Liquor, Leinenkugal, and Sharp's nonalcoholic beer. Miller products are distributed to retailers in the United States, Puerto Rico, and the Virgin Islands by a network of approximately 690 distributors. The company's products are also sold in approximately 50 foreign markets in Europe, Asia, and the Caribbean, including U.S. military bases.

The Miller Brewing Company was founded by German immigrant Frederick Miller, who settled in

Milwaukee after a brief stay in New York City. He bought the Plank Road Brewery in 1855, and soon after opened a 20-acre park or "sommer-garten." After Frederick's death, the Milwaukee Brewery was passed on to Miller's children. The W.R. Grace Co. purchased most of the children's stock in the Miller Brewing Company in 1966. Phillip Morris Inc. purchased the company in 1969 and the rest of the family's stock in 1970.

Coors Brewing Company. The Adolph Coors Company, founded in 1873, is America's third-largest brewer. Headquartered in Golden, Colorado, Coors sells approximately 17 million barrels of beer annually in 49 states and the District of Columbia. The Coors Brewing Company employs 7,100 people, works with 597 independent distributors, and has seven company-owned distributorships. The Adolph Coors Company has three autonomous business units that are operated by fourth-generation Coors family members. These are the Coors Brewing Company, the Coors Ceramics Company, and the Coors Technology Companies. The Coors Brewing Company produces beer from all natural ingredients including pure Rocky Mountain water, and it is the only brewery that does not pasteurize any of its beer. Instead, it uses a sterile filtration process that the company developed in the late 1950s. Coors is the only company with a complete line of draft or non-pasteurized beers.

The Coors Brewing Company operates three breweries, including the world's largest single-site brewery. Coors products are exported to 12 foreign markets and to U.S. military bases in 16 countries worldwide. The company also has licensing agreements to brew and distribute Coors products in Japan, Canada, Scotland, and Korea. Coors brands include original Coors, Coors Light, Coors Extra Gold, George Killian's Irish Red, Keystone and Keystone Light, Coors Winterfest (a seasonal beer), and Coors Cutter (a nonalcoholic beer).

German immigrant Adolph Coors founded the Coors Brewing Company. Upon his arrival in the United States in 1868, Adolph spent many years as a laborer and saved his money to fulfill his dream of owning a brewery. During one of his day's off from work, Adolph Coors found an abandoned tannery in the town of Golden at the base of Table Mountain. He and other investors remodeled the tannery and soon began brewing Coors beer. By 1880, Adolph was able to buy out his investors. The company was sustained during Prohibition by divesting into other industries, including a cement manufacturing facility and a porcelain plant. The Coors Ceramics Company has been one of the world's largest producers of industrial technical

ceramics, and the sole supplier of chemical porcelain used in the United States, Mexico, and Canada.

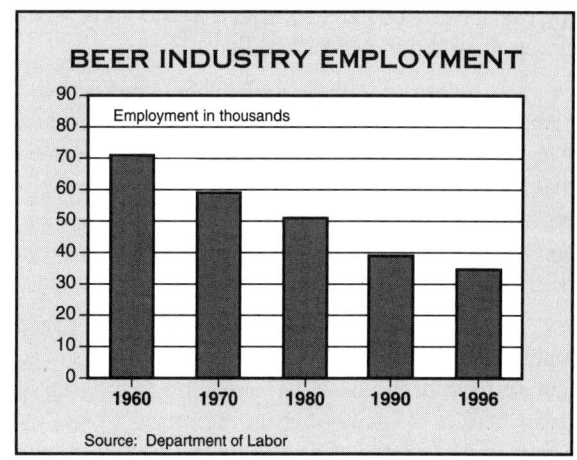

WORK FORCE

The U.S. beer industry consisted of 54 leading breweries that employ approximately 97,000 people in all areas of the industry (including non-manufacturing areas). According to the Beer Institute, "Brewery workers' wages are among the highest of more than 350 industries annually surveyed by the U.S. Department of Labor. These men and women take home approximately $2.2 billion a year in salaries and wages with additional millions paid in the form of fringe benefits and retirement programs." Bureau of Labor Statistics data indicate, however, that the number of employees directly involved in the industry has dropped over the past several decades, from more than 71,000 workers in 1960 to less than 40,000 in the late 1990s.

The top five states that were home to the largest number of brewery employees are New York, Wisconsin, Pennsylvania, California, and Washington. The largest numbers of employees worked as packaging and filling machine operators, driver-sales workers, salespeople, truck drivers, tractor operators, supervisors, and laborers. Estimates by the Bureau of Labor Statistics showed that virtually all occupations within the beer industry would decline in the percentage of total employed by the year 2000. Those jobs that include "hands-on" involvement, such as freight, stock and material movers, hand packers, and testers, were predicted to decline by at least 25 percent.

AMERICA AND THE WORLD

Exports. Faced with consumption rates at a stand still at home, U.S. companies turned to the international arena to grow their markets. A-B was considering opportunities from Latin America to Europe and the Far East. Competitors feared that the company would eventually work with French company Kronenbourg (part of the Danone group), which would give A-B a strong distribution network in Europe.

U.S. companies were looking for markets with financial strength and disposable income, such as Latin America and the Asian marketplace. In fact, it seemed that beer companies throughout the world were rushing into the exploding markets of Thailand, Vietnam, and most importantly China—which was believed to be the largest beer market by the end of the decade.

"The marketplace around the world has opened up in the very recent past. So, in part, our abilities to go abroad have been enable by the world freeing up in terms of access," said Michael Marranzino, chief international officer at Coors Brewing Company and reported in *Beverage Industry*.

According to the U.S. Department of Commerce, Japan was the largest market for U.S. beer in the mid-1990s, although sales were actually down 16.6 percent in the country in 1995. Sales came in 62 percent higher than in 1994 in Hong Kong, 214.5 percent higher in Brazil, 108.6 percent higher in Taiwan, 33.6 percent higher in Canada, and 78.9 percent higher in Russia.

Imports. The total U.S. imported beer market hit an all-time high in 1995, with volume topping out at an estimated 343.5 million gallons, as reported by *Beverage Marketing*. This growth represented a 5.5 percent jump in volume from 1994 and was almost a 40 percent improvement of U.S. imported beers as compared to ten years ago.

"Thirty years ago the imported beer market in the US basically did not exist," says Michael Bellas, president of *Beverage Marketing*. "In 1965, only 8.8 million cases [19.8 million gallons] of beer was imported into the United States. Since that time, the imported beer market has sustained compound annual volume growth of 10 percent. In 10 of the last 20 years, import growth rates have been in the double-digits."

The surge in imports to the United States was attributed to the American consumer's desire for high quality, full-bodied brews; lower total alcohol consumption; and becoming accustomed to higher prices for both domestic craft brews and imported brands. Among the world's best-selling beers, only Heineken, the Danish Carlsberg, and Guinness may be regarded as truly international. The Dutch sell 90 percent of the their beer outside the Netherlands.

North America and the Caribbean countries (Mexico, Canada, Jamaica) led exports in 1995, with 165.8 million gallons of beer shipped to the United States, up from 160 million gallons in 1994. The Europeans exported a record 161.8 million gallons of beer to the United States, up almost 8 percent from 1994. The Asian/Pacific region exported 7.4 million gallons to the United States—virtually the same figure as in 1994.

FURTHER READING

"Adolph Coors 1992 Annual Report." Golden, CO: Coors Brewing Company, 1992.

"Anheuser-Busch Reports Record Year." *Supermarket News,* 10 March 1997.

"Anheuser-Busch 1992 Fact Book." St. Louis, MO: Anheuser-Busch, 1992.

Brandes, Richard. "Beverage Trends: The Shape of Drinks to Come." *Beverage Dynamics,* May 1993.

"Buzz about Beer. *Beverage World,* 15 February 1997.

Causey, James. "Miller, Pabst Beverages Shipments Fall as Anheuser-Busch's Rise." *Knight-Ridder/Tribune Business News,* 15 January 1997.

Causey, James. "Only Icehouse, Lite Sell More for Miller in 1996." *Knight-Ridder/Tribune Business News,* 20 January 1997.

"Coors 1990 Facts & Figures." Golden, CO: Coors Brewing Company.

Dawson, Havis. "Something for Everyone." *Beverage World,* February 1996.

"Economic Impact of the Beer Industry." Washington: Beer Institute.

"Facts About Beer, the Brewing Industry and Miller Brewing Company." Milwaukee, WI: Miller Brewing Company, 1990-91.

Goodman, Ellis M. "Trends and Opportunities in Imported Beer." *Beverage Dynamics,* September 1992.

Henry, William L. "The Truth About Beer." *Beverage Dynamics,* September 1992.

"The History of Anheuser-Busch Companies: A Fact Sheet." St. Louis, MO: Anheuser-Busch.

Holleran, Joan. "Craft brews, a beer rabbit?" *Beverage Industry,* January 1997.

"It's a Small World for US Brewers." *Beverage Industry,* May 1996.

Kelley, Kristine Portnoy. "Liquor and Wine: slow but steady." *Beverage Industry,* August 1995.

"The Malt Beverage Interbrand Competition Act." Washington: United States Brewers Association, Inc., 21 June 1982.

Mamis, Robert A. "Market Maker." *Inc.,* December 1995.

"Miller History." Milwaukee, WI: Miller Brewing Company.

Morice, James L. "Anheuser-Busch Announces Record 1992 Beer Sales and Market Share Increase." Fleishman-Hillard, Inc. 19 January 1993.

Mullins, Robert. "Microbrewers See Slower Growth, Shakeout." *The Business Journal-Milwaukee,* 4 January 1997.

Prince, Greg W. "Shut Up and Drink. *Beverage World,* February 1996.

————. "This seat is taken." *Beverage World,* March 1996.

Sfiligoj, Eric. "The Europeans strike back." *Beverage World,* February 1996.

————. "Important Gains," *Beverage World,* February 1993.

Sherer, Michael. "Specialty Brews." *Beverage Dynamics,* November/December 1992.

Smit, Barbara. "Global Beer War Set to Explode." *The European,* 25 July 1996.

"Standing on Their Own." *Beverage Dynamics,* April 1993.

Student, John, and Brad Edmondson. "True Brew." *American Demographics,* May 1995.

—Catherine A. Quagliana

SIC 2083

MALT

This classification covers establishments primarily engaged in manufacturing malt or malt by-products from barley or other grains.

Malt is a barley kernel that has been allowed to sprout and is used primarily for brewing and distilling. It has long been a central element in beer production. Anywhere from 25 to 50 pounds of malt are used to make one barrel of beer.

In October 1996, the U.S. Department of Agriculture (USDA) estimated barley production to be 397 million bushels, up 10 percent from 1995. North Dakota is the largest producer of barley in the United States, producing 28 percent of the nation's barley in 1995. Montana, Idaho, and Minnesota are the next largest producers, respectively.

Malt is created by germinating moistened barley under controlled conditions for a short period of time, usually four days. The germination process activates the enzyme systems, specialized proteins that break down the barley's starch and protein. Once germinated, the "green malt" must be kilned, or dried with heat. Essentially, the malt is cooked to stop its growth, although the enzyme activity continues. Prior to kilning, the rootlets that appear during germination

are removed and discarded. What is left after kilning is considered to be malt.

Ninety percent of all malting barley grown is used by brewers, with the remainder used as feedstock. Brewers create a mash with the malt by mixing it with water and heating it under controlled conditions. During the mashing process, the enzymes break down the starch into sugars and proteins, creating a soluble mixture or extract. The soluble product is filtered and yeast is added. Other starches such as corn or rice are added at this time, along with hops for flavor.

All beer has some malt content. Budget beers usually are 50 percent malt and 50 percent corn or rice, while premium beer composition may be as high as 70 percent malt. Brewers generally specify to barley growers the variety of malt needed for particular brands.

A number of the major American beer producers maintain in-house malt operations. Examples include Busch Agricultural Resources, Inc., a subsidiary of Anheuser-Busch Inc., which operates three malt plants that together supply the company with approximately one-third of Anheuser-Busch's malt needs; and Miller Brewing Company's malt plant in Waterloo, Wisconsin.

Leading malt producers in America include the Great Western Malting Company, the largest producer of malt in the western United States with more than $100 million in annual sales. Great Western is a subsidiary of Canada Malting Co., Ltd., which was acquired by agribusiness and food service manufacturer ConAgra, Inc. in 1995 for $288.7 million. A year later, a 50 percent interest in ConAgra was acquired by South Africa-based Tiger Oats Ltd. Worldwide annual sales for ConAgra's malting business was $480 million. Other U.S. industry leaders include Froedtert Malt Corp. with $70 million in annual sales; Schreier Malting Co. with $34 million; Rahr Malting Co. with $14 million; and Minnesota Malting Co. with $20 million in annual sales in 1995.

Strong prices drove up barley production to higher levels in 1996, according to the National Barley Growers Association. However, Association President Craig Corbett has cautioned against over-optimism, saying "there are no indications that the long-term downward spiral which continues to plague the industry will bottom out anytime soon," as reported in *Feedstuffs.*

Both feed and malting barley reached more than $3 per bushel in the spring of 1996. Strong barley prices encouraged producers to plant 7.1 million acres in 1996, 435,000 more acres than planted in 1995.

Short stocks, domestic demand for feed grains, and feed grain exports also were factors.

But the big issue for malsters and brewers has been vomitoxin levels and growing scab-resistant barley. Growing malting-grade barley has been difficult over the past years due to a vomitoxin-producing scab that affects the malting of barley. Although it does not affect humans, barley affected with vomitoxin disturbs the malting process. An experimental barley line called MNS85 was introduced at the Small Grains Institute in March 1997. Depending on the success of MNS85 trials, a commercial scab-resistant variety was expected to become available in 1998.

The USDA Economic Research Service forecast U.S. barley imports for 1996-97 to fall 5 million bushels to 40 million. In 1995, Japan became the largest importer of U.S. barley, and China is slowly importing barley. The world market for barley continues to increase, especially in China where beer production increased 24.5 percent in 1995.

FURTHER READING

Bailey, Ann. "Agweek Magazine Malting Barley Outlook Column" *Knight-Ridder/Tribune Business News,* 24 September 1995. (Originated from *Agweek Magazine*).

"Barley Research." Milwaukee: American Malting Barley Association, 1993.

Campbell, Erin. "Red River Valley Awaits Experimental Scab-Resistant Barley" *Knight-Ridder/Tribune Business News,* 6 March 1997. (Originated from Grand Forks Herald, North Dakota).

Canada Malting Co. Limited Annual Reports. Toronto: Canada Malting Co., 1991, 1992. "ConAgra Bids on Malting Concern" *Nation's Restaurant News,* 2 October 1995.

Davis, Michael. "Malting Barley Quality Factors." American Malting Barley Association, 1993.

Flaskerud, George. "U.S. Barley Production Estimates Increase" *Knight-Ridder/Tribune Business News,* 28 October 1996. (Originated from *Grand Forks Herald,* North Dakota).

Menke, Jayson. "Barley Growers at North Dakota Conference Want Worldwide Identity, Farm Bill" *Knight-Ridder/Tribune Business News,* 10 January 1996. (Originated from *Grand Forks Herald,* North Dakota).

———. "Demand Drives Barley Acres Higher" *Knight-Ridder/Tribune Business News,* 30 December 1996. (Originated from *Agweek Magazine*).

"Proceedings, 29th Barley Improvement Conference." Milwaukee: American Malting Barley Association. January, 1993.

"Tiger Oats to Buy 50% of ConAgra's Malting Business" *Feedstuffs,* 6 May 1996.

—Catherine A. Quagliana

WINES, BRANDY, AND BRANDY SPIRITS

This category includes establishments primarily engaged in manufacturing wines, brandy, and brandy spirits. This industry also includes bonded wine cellars which are engaged in blending wines. Establishments which primarily bottle purchased wines, brandy, and brandy spirits but which do not manufacture wines and brandy are classified in **SIC 5182: Wine and Distilled Alcoholic Beverages.**

INDUSTRY SNAPSHOT

The first commercial wine venture in the United States was in Pennsylvania in 1793. However, the majority of modern American wineries have been located in California, with Washington and New York coming in a distant second and third, respectively. California has accounted for over 90 percent of all U.S. wine production and over 70 percent of all wine sold in the United States. According to the Wine Institute, "If viewed as a nation, California would rank sixth in worldwide wine production, following Spain but bigger than Germany." The dominate wine producer in California continues to be the Gallo family, controlling nearly 40 percent of the wine market.

According to a five-year study of wine consumption patterns in the United States, wine is drunk in moderation and usually with a meal. The report found that 49 percent of wine drinkers are between the ages of 45 and 64, and 82 percent of wine consumption takes place with a meal, typically dinner.

Table wine has been the most popular kind of wine sold in the United States. Varietals, table wines made predominately of one kind of grape, have continued to grow in popularity, following the trend that consumers are drinking less, but better wines.

Wine sales in the United States have been on the rise since 1994, while per capita consumption rates have remained steady at 1.8 gallons. Consumer tastes have progressed to upscale wines, which has boosted the sales of varietals. As consumer demand for wine strengthens, the availability of grapes has weakened, driving up the price of grapes to an all-time high in 1995.

Fueling this increase in wine consumption has been the improved U.S. economy and the publicity of reports touting the benefits of moderate wine consumption. In 1996, the U.S. government for the first time acknowledged moderate wine consumption to be a part of a heart-healthy diet. This statement of public policy should only further fuel the growth of wine sales in the United States in the years to come.

Imported wine also has seen tremendous growth in the United States, and many California wine companies have established relationships with producers in Chile and Argentina to sell their wine. For example, the Canandaigua Wine Company, the second-largest wine seller in the United States, has established a relationship with Vino Santa Carolina Chilean wines to become that company's sole agent and exclusive importer for the United States.

U.S. WINE, BRANDY, AND SPIRITS SHIPMENTS

(Billion dollars)

1987 1988 1989 1990 1991 1992 1993 1994 1995

Source: Department of Commerce

ORGANIZATION AND STRUCTURE

All winemakers have to sell their products through wholesalers and retailers to accommodate various federal, state, and local regulations regarding the sale of alcoholic beverages. The Federal Alcohol Administration Act (FAA) was established after the 13-year Prohibition Era ended in 1933. The Bureau of Alcohol, Tobacco and Firearms (ATF) is responsible for administering and enforcing the FAA, including qualifying wine makers, collecting producer and wholesaler occupational taxes, and regulating trade practices, advertising, and labeling. Beyond the uniformity of the FAA, regulations vary greatly among the 50 states.

States can sell wine in one of two ways, either in a controlled environment or using an open, licensed method. "Open" states have licensed retailers and wholesalers that handle the distribution and sale of alcoholic beverages. Thirty-two states and the District of Columbia are "open" states. The other 18 states operate under the control method, in which each state government buys and sells alcoholic beverages at the wholesale and retail levels. In addition to federal regulations, some states have set up their own independent agencies that are responsible for the administration,

licensing, and enforcement of state laws and the collection of state revenues. Some state legislatures even have created their own Alcoholic Beverage Control (ABC) agencies with rule-making power, and 32 states allow their citizens to vote for or against the sale of liquor on a city or county-wide basis.

BACKGROUND AND DEVELOPMENT

California wine growing began in 1769 when Father Junipero Serra planted vines at Mission San Diego. In September 1772, the grapes were harvested and pressed, creating California's first vintage. These early wines were produced for sacramental purposes and personal consumption at the missions.

The commercial era of wine production began in 1830 with the efforts of Frenchman Jean Louis Vignes from Bordeaux, France. His vineyard was located in what is now downtown Los Angeles, California. The wine industry boomed as an ancillary result of the discovery of gold in California in 1848. A surge of Europeans came to the state seeking their fortune. Immigrants from Italy, France, and Germany who had no luck finding gold turned to a trade they already knew—winemaking.

Between 1860 and 1880, the industry grew rapidly as numerous wineries were established. By 1890, several of the state's famous wine regions already had taken shape and the industry was producing 25 million gallons of wine per year. After suffering losses from a vine pest called phylloxera, the industry virtually disappeared with the passage of Prohibition in 1919. The repeal of Prohibition in 1933, however, prompted the industry to rebuild. Growth was steady between 1949 and 1960, with annual output increasing from 117 million gallons to 129 million gallons. By the 1970s, the demand for California table wines had doubled.

As the industry evolved, so did consumer preferences. From 1933 to 1967, dessert wine was the most popular kind of wine in the United States. During the 1970s, generic table wines, like California Chablis and California Burgundy, dominated sales. By the late 1980s, varietal wines, those labeled with the name of the grape, had taken over. These wines were expected to remain prominent throughout the 1990s.

Production. The making of wine begins with the grape harvest, which generally occurs from August through November, depending upon the grape variety and the weather. The grapes are placed in a crusher that separates the stems from the fruit and breaks up the berries. The stems are then discarded, leaving a combination of juice, seeds, pulp, and skins, called "must." Juice from red or white wine grapes is colorless.

To make white wine, the skins and seeds usually are removed from the must after a few hours. The remaining juice is called ''free-run.'' The discarded skins also are pressed to extract the ''press juice.'' Both juices then are filtered, placed in storage, and given yeast to facilitate the fermentation process. White wine fermentation can last anywhere from three days to three weeks. Upon completion, the wine is filtered for solids or remaining yeast. The wine then is aged for a period of one week to a year in stainless steel, oak, or redwood containers. It also can be aged in the bottle. After aging, the wine can be blended with other wines to create a desired style or is sent to be finished, a process that stabilizes and filters the wine before bottling.

Production of red wine is slightly different than the process of making white wine. Red wine is fermented at warmer temperatures than white wine. For red wine production, the skins are fermented with the crushed juice to give it color and flavor. The skins float to the top and are moistened regularly with juice to extract color and flavor. Red wine usually is fermented for five to ten days and then is filtered, clarified, and preserved with sulfites. Red wine commonly is aged in oak barrels for one to two years.

Types of Wines. Wines sold in the United States generally are divided into the following categories: champagne, aperitifs, dessert, table, and varietal wines. Also included in SIC 2084 are brandy and other fortified wines. Wines can be named one of four ways; by variety, which tells the predominant type of grape; by a generic name describing the color, such as blush; by the region that originally inspired the wine, such as Chablis; or by a proprietary name a label created by the winery.

Champagne and sparkling wines are names used interchangeably in the United States for wines with effervescence. These wines range from very dry (Natural), to dry (Brut), to slightly sweet (Extra Dry), to sweet (Sec and Demi-Sec). Aperitifs are appetizer wines usually served prior to a meal and can include champagnes and sherries. Dessert wines are officially classified as those with an alcohol content of 17 percent to 21 percent. They can be sweet or dry and include sherries and port.

Table wine is a term commonly used to describe all red, white, blush, and rose wines that contain 7 to 14 percent alcohol. These wines are still rather effervescent and are served mainly with meals. Table wines can be made from any grape or combination of grapes and in any style that the winemaker chooses. Varietal wines are table wines that are made from a minimum of 75 percent of a particular grape variety. They carry the name of the grape variety from which they are produced, such as Chardonnay or Merlot.

The red table wine category has been led by Cabernet Sauvignon, a full-bodied, rich, intense wine with noticeable tannins. A leading prestigious varietal, Cabernet Sauvignon has been one of the most widely available wines from California. Other red varietals include Merlot, Petite Sirah, and Zinfandel. Merlot is a medium- to full-bodied wine that originally was made for the sole purpose of blending with Cabernet Sauvignon. Petite Sirah is a wine with deep color, full body, and fresh-berry, spicy personality. Zinfandel, known as the classic California wine, is known for its versatility, range of style, and its raspberry-spicy aroma and flavor.

White table wines have been dominated by Chardonnay, the most widely planted variety in California, making up more than 56,000 acres. It is a dry wine, which has a balance of fruit, acidity, and texture. Depending upon what the winemaker uses for storage, Chardonnay can range from clean and crisp wines to rich, complex, oak-aged wines. A second wine popular in California has been Chenin Blanc. It is made in dry to off-dry or slightly sweet styles.

Other white varietals include French Columbard, Sauvignon Blanc, Johannisberg Reisling, Gewurztraminer, and Pinot Blanc. French Columbard is generally fresh and fruity, ranging from light to medium in body. Sauvignon Blanc has been one of the fastest growing varietals in California. Sometimes called Fume Blanc, it is best known for its grassy, herbal flavors and is often consumed with fish and shellfish. Johannisberg Riesling, from the German Riesling grape, is aromatic, delicate, and slightly sweet. Late Harvest Rieslings are good accompaniments for dessert. Gewurztraminer offers full floral, spicy aromas and flavors, and a slight wisp of residual sweetness. Often this wine goes well with Asian food. Pinot Blanc is a unique, dry white wine, with styles ranging from bold, oak-aged to crisp, and medium-bodied.

Brandy is ''burnt wine'' or fruit wine that is boiled and aged in wood. Virtually any type of fruit can be used to make brandy, although grapes have been the most common. Brandy has been produced primarily in Spain, Italy, and France and most recently in the United States. Cognac has been considered to be the best of all brandies. Cognac's discerning characteristic has been its blending. ''While other brandies . . . are sometimes unblended or vintage-dated, cognacs, from the most basic V.S. to the rarest X.O., are almost always the final product of tens of cognacs, which have been married to achieve the proper balance, flavor and style,'' according to the *New York Times Magazine*.

Fortified wines were the creation of the Spanish and Portuguese and included port, sherry, and madeira. Sherry is made by blending younger sherries with older sherries in oak casks. It varies in dryness levels, ranging from bone-dry to extremely sweet and in hues ranging from pale gold to chestnut. Harvey's Bristol Cream, imported by Hiram Walker & Sons, has been the top selling sherry in the United States, with a nearly 41-percent market share. The best seller is a blend of aged oloroso, a fortified full-bodied sherry, and Pedro Ximines grapes, which sweetens the mixture.

Port is red wine fortified with grape brandy. It was created unintentionally in the seventeenth century when Portugal tried to ship its table wine to England. In order to stabilize the wine during its voyage over the Atlantic, the wine needed the addition of grape brandy. England has remained the most popular market for port.

Madeira comes from a tropical island of the same name and is a raisiny, sweet wine. Madeira has been closely linked with the history of the United States, according to the *New York Times Magazine*. It was considered to be the wine of choice for American Revolutionary notables such as Thomas Jefferson, George Washington, and Ben Franklin. One reason this wine became so popular in the New World was because unlike other wines that soured during the long, hot voyage across the Atlantic, madeira was the only wine known to improve dramatically with the introduction of heat.

CURRENT CONDITIONS

Following a 6.5 percent loss in 1993, wine sales in the United States have been rising for the past three years, while per capita consumption remains steady at 1.8 gallons. According to the San Francisco-based Wine Institute, consumer demand for premium varietal wines spurred a 5 percent increase in California table wine sales in 1994—the strongest performance in more than a decade.

While most of the largest wine producers reported record sales, and consumer tastes moved upscale to more expensive wines, 1994 was noted as the best year for the wine industry since the late 1980s. ''The end of the drought, the waning of phylloxera root louse problems and increased consumer demand all have wine makers singing a new tune,'' reported Clifford Carlsen of *The San Francisco Business Times*.

Total U.S. production again rose in 1995, up 10.3 percent at 437 million gallons. According to wine industry analyst Jon Frederickson of Gomberg, Fredrickson and Associates of San Francisco, California wine sales increased 8 percent in 1995 to a record $4.4 billion. Increased consumer demand and a relatively strong supply of fruit contributed to the industry's continued strong growth.

Following record wine sales and all-time high prices for grapes in 1995, the industry experienced another banner year in 1996. In fact, many North Coast wineries, with sales increases of 30 to 40 percent, didn't have enough wine to meet the staggering demand.

''The only regret anyone has the moment is that there isn't enough wine to sell, which is a good position to be in given some of the times in the past,'' said Patrick Campbell, owner of the Laurel Glen Winery in Glen Ellen.

The improved economy and continuing news reports about the health benefits of moderate wine consumption has fueled the continued growth of the industry. Wine sales have been on the rise since the 1991 broadcast of a ''60 Minutes'' report linking moderate wine consumption with a reduced risk of heart attack. Called the French Paradox, two scientists found that despite similar fat intake, France's heart attack rate was one-third that of the United States. A key factor they attributed to this was the French custom of drinking wine with meals. Red wine sales have increased more than 75 percent since that 1991 report.

Wine sales should continue to increase as the federal government took an unprecedented step in advocating moderate consumption. When the U.S. government issued new dietary guidelines in 1996, it acknowledged for the first time the benefits of moderate wine consumption. Previously, the government had warned that even small amounts of alcohol had ''no net health benefit.''

''Writing that language into the dietary guidelines was an extraordinary statement of public policy change in the United States. It's a foundation we can build on into the next century,'' said John De Luca, president of the Wine Institute, the trade association for wine industry. He added that the revised guidelines culminated five years of work to redefine the image of wine, ''putting it back on the dining room table where it's been for 2,000 years.''

Leading the pack in wine sales have been the varietals, especially the fighting one. Relatively new to the industry, a ''fighting'' varietal has been defined as a value-priced, cork-finished 750 ml varietal wine. The leader in fighting varietals has been Glen Ellen, followed by Fetzer's Bel Arbors, Sebastiani's Country

Wines and Swan Cellar label, Beringer's Napa Valley, and Robert Mondavi's Woodbridge. Tim Wallace, a Glen Ellen executive, told *Beverage Dynamics* that "fighting varietals are the foundation for the American wine industry in the future." And in 1996, the fighting varietal category has remained the largest single segment among growth markets.

Additional growth has come from consumers trading up from generic table wines into the fighting varietal category, or those moving from fighting varietals into the premiums.

On the other hand, champagne sales continued to drop despite increases of specific brands. From a peak of 18.2 million 9-liter cases of sparkling wine and champagne in the United States in 1986, consumption fell to 12.3 million 9-liter cases in 1995. Causes for the decline are high prices for champagne, high taxes, high cost of shipping, and lack of consistent, high-profile marketing programs.

The good news is that quality of champagne, both domestic and imported has been rising. "Champagne producers have begun to make a lighter, more elegant non-vintage brut, one that better suits the American palate. Dramatic improvements in taste and technique all have been pioneered in California's best sparkling wine regions—Carneros, Mendocino County, and the central coast. In return, these domestic producers have seen consumers move to brands that offer high quality at affordable prices.

INDUSTRY LEADERS

As dominant as the state of California is in the wine industry, so too are the wineries of California winemakers Ernest & Julio Gallo. Controlling nearly 40 percent of the U.S. wine market, E. & J. Gallo Wineries lead every wine category in which they compete. According to the *Wine Spectator,* one out of every three bottles of wine made in America is a Gallo product. The world's largest wine maker, E. & J. Gallo Wineries had annual sales of over $1 billion.

In 1933, the original Ernest and Julio Gallo brothers winery was founded in Modesto, California. Unable to obtain bank financing, they bought crushing and fermenting equipment on 90-day terms and rented a warehouse to make their first commercial wine. Using pamphlets on winemaking from the local library and grapes bought on a promise to pay from sales proceeds, the two brothers made their first batch of wine. By 1993, Gallo owned five separate vineyards totaling more than 2,000 acres. The company has remained a private, family-owned business and is one of the largest organic farms in the United States.

The company's success has been due in part to the partnership of the Gallo brothers; Ernest marketed the wine that Julio made. Another part of Gallo's success has been its quest for improving the quality of the wine it produced. To this end, Gallo replanted its vineyard in Livingston in 1946 using grape varieties that had not been previously grown in the area. Various viticultural techniques were experimented, and in 1947 a formal research program was established to evaluate the results. Specific standards were developed for wine making and have been used ever since.

In 1965, Julio Gallo established the first Growers Relations Department and shared research findings with area growers. In 1967, Gallo offered long-term contracts to selected growers, giving economic security and incentive to replant vineyards with the better grapes varieties recommended by Gallo. During the 1970s, the winery shifted to producing premium varietal wines, and in 1991 introduced its first ultra-premium wine, 1991 Sonoma Estate Chardonnay. Leading brands for E. & J. Gallo Wineries have been Gallo, Andre, Bartles & James, and Carlo Rossi.

Recent newcomer, Canandaigua Wine Company, became the number two seller in the U.S. wine market in 1995 with the acquisition of the Almaden and Inglenook wine labels (in 1994) from Heublein for $130.5 million. And although the company name may not be well known, its products such as Almaden, Inglenook, Taylor California Wines, and Paul Masson Wines are household names.

The company is a father-and-son operation located in upstate New York, and was started in 1945 by Marvin Sands, who bought a sauerkraut factory turned winery for $60,000. For ten years, Canandaigua Industries sold fruit wines in bulk to local bottlers who would then sell them under their own brand names. In 1954, Sands turned away from bulk wines and created a brand for himself—Richards Wild Irish Rose, a blended red dessert wine. During the 1960s, Wild Irish Rose represented nearly all of the company's sales.

Working from that base, Sands slowly expanded, acquiring 11 small wineries through 1984. Then the company jumped on the wine cooler bandwagon with their Sun Country Wine Coolers. Although they suffered an operating loss of $20 million in 1987 and 1988 due to expensive advertising, the Sandses realized the power of their distribution network, and began looking for established brands.

In 1991, Canadaigua made its first major purchase with Cook's Champagne for $60 million. Then came additional purchases in 1993 and 1994. Today Canandaigua's brands total 21 percent of the domestic table wine market, making it runner-up to Gallo's 32 percent.

The Seagram Company, Ltd. has been one of the world's leading producers and marketers of distilled spirits and wines. Originally, Seagram divided its wine collection into two specialized divisions: The Seagram Classics Wine Company and Seagram Chateau & Estates Wine Company.

Based in San Mateo, California, the Classics Wine Company has produced, marketed and exported the wines of Sterling Vineyards, the Monterey Vineyard, and Mumm Napa Valley. The division also has imported and marketed Mumm Champagnes and Barton & Guestier Wines from France and has acted as sales agent for select California and overseas wines.

Based in New York, the Seagram Chateau & Estates Wine Company has imported many European wines, including 35 percent of all classified Bordeaux. The company also has imported Seagram-owned Perrier-Jouet Champagnes, the third best-selling champagne in the United States, Sandeman Ports and Sherries, and Janneau Armagnacs.

In an effort to improve customer service, Seagram merged these two U.S. based wine companies in 1996. Sam Bronfman II, president of The Seagram Classic Wine Company, was selected to head this new operation.

Kentucky-based Brown-Forman has been well known for its collection of distilled spirits, especially bourbon. During the 1960s and 1970s the company expanded into the wine industry with the acquisition of Korbel champagne and brandy in 1965, and Bolla and Cella wines in 1968. By the early 1990s, Brown-Forman established a separate division for its wine operations and embarked on an aggressive plan to expand its business through long-term marketing and distribution contracts. Its base of wine products by 1991 included Bolla, Fontana, Candida, Brolio, Korbel, and Noilly Prat.

Aiming to expand in the wine market, Brown-Forman acquired Californian Fetzer in 1995. The Fetzer line sells 2.2 million cases in the United States, and with the help of Brown-Forman, the brand was expected to make significant progress in export markets.

WORK FORCE

The *Ward's Business Directory of U.S. Private and Public Companies 1997* lists 144 companies that have produced wine and brandy in the United States. Most of these companies are privately held, with a handful of public companies such as Heublein, Hiram

Walker, and the Seagram Company. In total, the winemaking industry employed over 17,000 workers. The majority of wineries have been family-owned, located predominately in California, and have created a tremendous impact on that state's economy. Los Angeles-based Recon Research Corporation reported that the California wine industry has contributed nearly $1.5 billion annually to the Sonoma County economy, employing more than 3,600 people and creating secondary industrial employment of an additional 2,500 jobs.

U.S. WINE, BRANDY, AND SPIRITS IMPORTS

(Billion dollars)

Source: U.S. Bureau of the Census

AMERICA AND THE WORLD

The impending shortage of California wine combined with growing consumer demand should open the door for wines coming into the United States from Italy, France, Chile, Argentina, and other wine-producing countries. Overseas planting of premium varietals have been growing at a fast pace and will be a significant new source of wine for U.S. consumers. In fact, California wineries already were buying unprecedented amounts of overseas wine to meet consumer demand for low-priced everyday wine and to expand their existing line of products in the mid-1990s.

For example, in 1996 Robert Mondavi began importing a Chilean line of wines, the Caletara brand, priced in the $6 to $9 range. A second brand, Edwardo Chadwick was introduced in the $12 to $15 range, followed by a brand in an even higher price range. In 1995, the winery also launched a line of Italian varietals.

Said Bill Turrentine of Turrentine Wine Brokerage, "It would be naïve for us not to recognize the importance of this new premium wine. It is already an important factor in the marketplace and it's going to be an increasingly important factor. If you go to the store now and look around, you'll find some inexpensive

Merlots from Chile, Eastern Europe and elsewhere. The beachhead already has been established," as reported in *Wine Business Monthly.*

Wines from Chile continue to make inroads into the American market. According to *Beverage Dynamics,* wines from Chile have sold well in the United States since 1986. Chilean wines exports grew from $10.4 million in 1985 to $181.7 million in 1995. The United States alone imported about $40 million worth of Chilean wine in 1995. Again, U.S. companies were seizing the opportunity to push Chilean wines. The Brown-Forman Beverage Company began working with a line of Chilean wine with the brand name, Carmen, in 1993. In the mid-1990s, the nation's second-largest wine marketer, Canandaigua, became sole agent and exclusive importer for Vino Santa Carolina Chilean wines.

Another emerging wine growing country has been Australia. Demand for Australian wine skyrocketed as American consumers enjoy the Australian style of wine. Its worldwide trademark of generous flavors, soft tannins, and accessible fruit made this wine easier to like when young, a perfect style of wine for Americans. In 1990, the Australians shipped only 578,000 cases of wine to the United States. In comparison, case shipments to the United States by the end of 1996 were projected to reach 2 million. Moreover, the Australian Wine Bureau reports that more than 4 million cases of Australian wine would be shipped to the United States by 2001, and by 2026, shipments should total more than 10 million cases with an estimated value of $440 million.

FURTHER READING

Amerman, Don. "Deluges haven't dampened vinters' spirits (A Special Report: Wine & Spirits)." *Journal of Commerce and Commercial,* 29 July 1996.

Bellamy, Gail. "Wine update." *Restaurant Hospitality,* October 1995.

Berger, Dan. "Australian Wines." *Beverage & Food Dynamics,* January/February 1997.

Berger, Dan. "Making the Most of Port and Sherry." *Beverage Dynamics,* November/December 1992.

Berger, Dan. "Sparkling Sells." *Beverage Dynamics,* November 1996.

Boyd, Gerald. "In This Corner . . . " *Beverage Dynamics,* March 1992.

———. "Southern Exposure. Trapiche, Argentina's Largest Winery, Is Making a Mark in the U.S." *Beverage Dynamics,* June 1992.

———. "Brown-Forman Puts Weight Behind Fetzer." *Grocer,* 12 August 1995.

———. "The Wines of Chile." *Beverage Dynamics,* July/August 1993.

"Brown-Forman Cultivates Its Growing Wine Business." *Beverage Dynamics,* March 1992.

Carlsen, Clifford. "Full-bodied Sales Make 1994 Vintage Year for Wineries." *San Francisco Business Times,* 4 August 1995.

Carlsen, Clifford. "Robust Year of Sales Gives Wine Makers a Healthy Glow." *San Francisco Business Times,* 15 November 1996.

———. "Chile is Hot." *Beverage World,* September 1996.

"Distillations, Libations, and Celebrations: A Consumer Guide to Liqueurs, Cognac, Fortified Wines & Brandy." *New York Times Magazine,* 13 December 1992.

"E. & J. Gallo Winery History." Modesto, CA: E. & J. Gallo Wineries, 1993.

———. "Enjoying California Wine." San Francisco: Wine Institute, 1992.

———. "The Fine Wines of Ernest and Julio Gallo." Modesto, CA: E. & J. Gallo Wineries, 1993.

———. "Gallo Introduces First Sonoma Estate Wine." Modesto, CA: E. & J. Gallo Wineries, 1993.

Holmgren, Elizabeth. "60 Minutes Revisits the French Paradox with More Good News!" Wine Trader: Health and Social Issues Report, 1996. Available from http://www.Wines.com/winetrader/196his.html.

Hood, Donna Jean. "From Sweet to Sophisticated." *Beverage Dynamics,* June 1992.

———. *Jobson's Handbook Advance 1993.* New York: Jobson Beverage Group, 1993.

Kelley, Kristine Portnoy. "Liquor and wine: slow but steady: consumptions is still down but consumers are trading up; companies are surfing the Net for more business." *Beverage Industry,* August 1995.

Lane, Randall. "Who's afraid of big, bad Gallo?" *Forbes,* 13 February 1995.

"1991 Wine Industry Statistical Report." San Francisco: Wine Institute, October 1992.

———. "The Positive Power of the Press." *Beverage Dynamics,* March 1992.

———. "Quality Across the Board." *Beverage and Food Dynamics,* November 1996.

———. "A Scientific Look at Wine." San Francisco: Wine Institute, 1990.

The Seagram Company. *Seagram Company Annual Report.* New York: The Seagram Company Ltd., 1991-1992.

———. "Seagram Puts it all together." *Beverage World,* October 1996.

Sfiligoj, Eric. "Wine (The Beverage Market Index 1995)." *Beverage World,* May 1995.

Shore, Teri. "More Import Perspectives. Foreign Supplies Could Help California Wines." *Wine Business Monthly,* February 1996.

———. *Standard & Poor's Industry Surveys.* New York: Standard & Poor's, 1993.

———. "The Story of American Wines." San Francisco: Wine Institute, 1985.

Tesconi, Tim. "California Wine Business Sparkles." *Santa Rosa Press Democrat,* Outlook Online. Available from http://www.pressdemo.com/outlook/econ3.html. 1996.

U.S. Department of Commerce. *U.S. Industrial Outlook 1993.* Washington, DC: U.S. Department of Commerce, 1993.

Ward's Business Directory of U.S. Private and Public Companies. Detroit: Gale Research, 1997.

"Wine Drinker Profiled." *Beverage Dynamics,* March 1992.

—Catherine A. Quagliana

SIC 2085

DISTILLED AND BLENDED LIQUORS

This category includes establishments primarily engaged in manufacturing alcoholic liquors by distillation and in manufacturing cordials and alcoholic cocktails by blending, processing, or mixing liquors and other ingredients. Establishments primarily engaged in manufacturing industrial alcohol are classified in **SIC 2869: Industrial Organic Chemicals, Not Elsewhere Classified,** and those bottling purchased liquors are classified in **SIC 5182: Wine and Distilled Alcoholic Beverages.**

INDUSTRY SNAPSHOT

American consumption of distilled spirits rose slightly in 1996, breaking a dramatic 15-year decline. Nearly 135 million cases of liquor were sold in 1996, with Absolut's Vodka leading the way with 3.3 million cases. In second place was Jose Cuervo tequila with 2.5 million cases.

As American consumers continued to drink less frequently but better quality products, the premium category of distilled spirits grew. The resurgence of classic cocktails such as Martinis and Manhattans also helped the sale of premium dark spirits, although white spirits such as vodka and gin remained more popular.

Despite this small jump in sales, the liquor industry, which consisted of large, multinational corporations, was trying to counter the 23 percent decline in U.S. consumption rates since 1981. Citing the need to compete with marketers of beer and wine, the liquor industry made a controversial decision to lift a 48-year-old voluntary ban on television advertising.

Response to this decision was swift and came from a variety of sources, including President Clinton and various public interest organizations. Congress began to hold hearings regarding all advertising for alcoholic beverages on radio and television. The outcome of these hearings also would affect the ever-popular and growing presence of liquor companies on the World Wide Web.

On a brighter note, American liquor marketers continued to make inroads with product exportation. Claiming a banner year in 1995, U.S. exports of distilled spirits totaled 22 percent of industry sales. Volumes of whiskey, rum, and neutral grain spirits all increased in 1995.

All the major liquor companies had their eye on the international arena, especially the Asian market. Japan was already at the top of the U.S. export list, and has been a favorite home for American whiskey. Latin America also has been noted for its tremendous growth opportunity, especially for premium-priced products.

ORGANIZATION AND STRUCTURE

The distilled spirits industry has been dominated by a few large companies that offer a variety of alcoholic beverages. Most started with a flagship brand, such as Jim Beam Bourbon, and have diversified into a family of products that includes whiskey and non-whiskey items, such as gin, vodka, rum, tequila, cordials, mixed cocktails, and even fruit juices and other nonalcoholic or low-alcohol beverages.

This category includes only those companies that produce distilled spirits. All distillers have to sell their products through wholesalers and retailers, in order to accommodate various federal, state, and local regulations regarding the sale of alcoholic beverages. The Federal Alcohol Administration Act (FAA) was established at the end of the 13-year Prohibition Era in 1933. The FAA, which is enforced by the Bureau of Alcohol, Tobacco and Firearms (ATF), qualifies distillers, collects producer and wholesaler occupational taxes, and regulates trade practices, advertising, and labeling. Beyond the uniformity of the FAA, regulations vary greatly among the 50 states.

States can sell distilled spirits in one of two ways, either in a controlled environment or using an "open," licensed method. Open states have licensed retailers and wholesalers that handle the distribution and sale of alcoholic beverages. Thirty-two states and the District of Columbia are open states. The other 18 states operate under the control method, in which each state government buys and sells alcoholic beverages at the wholesale and retail levels.

In addition to federal regulations, some states have set up their own independent agencies that are responsible for the administration, licensing, and enforcement of state laws, and the collection of state revenues. Some state legislatures have created their own Alcoholic Beverage Control (ABC) agencies with rule-making power, and 32 states allow their citizens to vote for or against the sale of liquor on a city or county-wide basis.

BACKGROUND AND DEVELOPMENT

All forms of alcoholic beverages—beer, wine and liquor—are based on fermentation, the natural process of decomposition of organic materials containing carbohydrates. Liquor production involves the extra step of distillation, which reduces the original water content and greatly increases the alcoholic strength. While beer averages 2-8 percent alcohol content, and wine averages from 8 to 14 percent, distilled spirits range from 35 to 50 percent alcohol. Two types of raw materials are used to make a distilled spirit: sugar and carbohydrates. Sugary materials include grapes, sugarcane, agave, molasses, and sugar. Those materials with high levels of carbohydrates are corn, rye, rice, barley, wheat, and potatoes.

Civilizations in almost every part of the world have developed some type of alcoholic beverage. The Chinese distilled a beverage from rice beer before 800 BC. The Arabs developed a method used to produce a distilled beverage. A reference to distillation appears in the writings of the Greek philosopher Aristotle. And the Romans produced distilled beverages, although no written references can be found prior to 100 AD. Liquor production was reported in Britain before the Roman conquest. But producing distilled spirits in Western Europe was limited until the eighth century, after contact with the Arabs.

Distilled spirits can be classified into two categories: brown goods and white goods. Brown goods include all whiskies, bourbons, and scotches. White goods are vodka, gin, rum, and tequila. Other major segments in the distilled spirits market are the cordial or liquor category and the assortment of ready-to-drink cocktails.

Whiskey. Whiskey is an all-encompassing term for any distilled liquor made from a fermented mash of grain. However different in taste, all whiskey is distilled in a similar manner. The four primary steps to make whiskey are mashing, fermenting, distilling, and aging. The grains of corn, barley, rye, and/or wheat are ground into a fine meal, mixed with water, and cooked until the starches have been converted into sugars. This creates a ''mash'' that is mixed with yeast, converting the sugars into alcohol. The fermented mixture is then pumped into a still where steam condensation allows the alcohol to separate from the water and by-products. Fresh from the still, the whiskey is colorless, harsh, and in need of aging. It is the aging process that enhances the spirit and refines the whiskey, giving it an amber color.

Federal regulations specify that whiskey must be ''produced at less than 190 proof and bottled at not less than 80 proof.'' American-distilled whiskeys include Tennessee, rye, and blended. Tennessee whiskey, such as Jack Daniel's and George Dickel, is a distinct product due to filtering the whiskey through charcoal prior to aging. Rye whiskey is made from at least 51 percent rye and distilled at no more than 160 proof. The whiskey then is stored at no more than 125 proof in new oak barrels. Blended whiskey, such as Seagram's Seven Crown, comes from at least 20 percent straight whiskey mixed with other whiskey grain neutral spirits. Blended whiskey became popular during World War II when whiskey was in short supply and distillers stretched its availability by adding grain neutral spirits.

Bourbon. Part of the whiskey group, bourbon is a uniquely American product. The drink was created unintentionally in 1789 when a Bourbon County, Kentucky farmer sealed his whiskey in a charred barrel. This aging process picked up the mellow smoky flavor of the wood, giving bourbon its distinctive taste. In 1964, the U.S. Congress officially named bourbon America's ''Native Spirit,'' and has tightly regulated bourbon's production to ensure a consistent, quality product. Straight bourbon whiskey is required by law to contain at least 51 percent corn; to be distilled at no more than 160 proof; and to be aged a minimum of two years in new, charred oak containers. Jim Beam Kentucky Straight Bourbon Whiskey continues to be the best-selling bourbon in the United States.

Scotland, a world-class whisky-producing region, remains the international leader in high quality whiskey making. Blessed with natural resources and the ideal climate for making whisky, Scotland boasts a long and rich history of distillation and a devotion to creating distinctly individual malts. By law, all Scotch whisky must be aged at least three years, although few brands enter the United States without being aged at least four. Scotch can be bottled in the country of origin or it can be shipped in bulk to the United States and bottled here, which can be more cost efficient.

More than 95 percent of Scotch consumed worldwide is blended whisky. Blends are a result of mixing both single malts and grain whiskies and are created to "soften" the harsher characteristics of individual malt whiskies.

Although still a small percentage of overall Scotch consumption in the United States, single-malt whiskies have been made by Scottish distillers for more than 500 years. Single malts, the original Scotch whiskies, are derived from sprouted barley that has been dried in kilns fired by peat and coal, which imparts a distinctive smoky character to the spirit. Produced by more than 100 Scotch distilleries, each single malt has a style and flavor all its own.

Canadian whiskey is a blend of mostly rye with corn, wheat, and barley malt. By Canadian law, no more than 9.09 percent of a Canadian label may include whiskey from other countries; it must be blended from cereal grains; and it has to age at in wood at least three years. As a rule, Canadian whiskies are light-bodied, slightly pale with a reputation for having a mellow quality.

Irish whiskey is made from a fermented mash of malted and unmalted barley, corn, rye, and lesser amounts of other cereal grains. Unlike the Scots who dry malt over an open peat fire to give it a smoky flavor, the Irish dry malt in closed kilns. Irish whiskies are full-bodied and possess a smooth malty flavor. All Irish whiskies are tripled-distilled in copper pot stills and are aged three to nine years in reused sherry, brandy, bourbon, or rum oak casks. Irish Whiskey remains the smallest of all the distilled spirits categories in the United States, accounting for less than 1 percent of all distilled spirits consumption.

Vodka. Vodka continues to be the most popular liquor in America, accounting for more than one out of every five bottles of distilled spirits sold. According to U.S. federal regulations, vodka lacks aroma, taste, and color. It is distilled at a high proof, extracting all of the congeners, or the natural compounds in the distillate that give the product its taste and aroma. Because vodka is highly neutral, it is possible to make it from a mash of the cheapest and most readily available raw ingredients. Although potatoes traditionally were used, vodka now generally is produced by cereal grains, including rye, wheat, and barley, but mostly corn.

According to numerous sources, vodka originated in Russia during the fourteenth century and has remained commonplace in Russia, Poland, and the Baltic States. It became popular in the United States after World War II with the introduction of a drink called the Moscow Mule. In the land of its origin, vodka usually is consumed chilled, straight up in small glasses and accompanied by appetizers. In the United States, vodka is the base ingredient in a variety of popular cocktails.

Gin. Gin is the distilled product of juniper berries mixed with a clear grain-based spirit. First created in 1650 by a chemist in Holland, gin quickly became a popular drink in Britain and later in the United States. Government regulations require that gin be bottled at 80 proof or higher, have a juniper berry flavor, and be made either by distillation or compounding. Compound gin, a less costly method, is the combination of neutral spirits with the oil and extracts of the botanicals.

Aging is not a factor with gin. Instead, each gin achieves its distinct taste through the distiller's specific combination of gin botanicals, such as cassia, anise, coriander, angelica, and juniper. Gin is a flavored spirit. Without the flavoring, it would be vodka.

Rum. A favorite American spirit long before bourbon whiskey, rum is a sweet, distilled spirit made from sugar cane. Although the debate continues regarding where rum was first produced, by the late seventeenth century, the liquor was being distilled in the American colonies using molasses from the West Indies. In fact, the first distillery in what is now called the United States was built on Staten Island and was already producing rum when the English seized the Dutch colony in 1664.

By federal law, rum must be distilled from the fermented juice of sugar cane, sugar cane syrup, sugar cane molasses, or other sugar cane by-products at less than 190 proof. It can be made anywhere, although more than 80 percent of rum is produced in Puerto Rico. The two main types of rum are light-bodied rums, which have a dry, subtle flavor; and full-bodied rums, a more aromatic variety.

Tequila. Made from the heart of the agave plant, Tequila is produced in its namesake town located in the central Mexican state of Jalisco. The core of the plant, which resembles a large pineapple, is harvested, cut into chunks, and baked in steam ovens. The juice is extracted by steaming and compressing the core. After fermenting for several days, the juice is distilled at a low proof. The tequila then is double distilled to a powerful 110 proof and reduced to 80 proof with water before bottling.

Although tequila can be bottled as a clear product, the gold and "añejo" products are aged in wood. Gold tequila is kept in large oak vats for about nine months to a year, acquiring its pale gold color. By law, tequila designated anejo must be aged in a wood container for at least one year, although most anejo products are aged for three to seven years.

Cordial. The cordial or liquor category is the largest and most diverse in terms of the number of brands, flavors, and alcohol content. It also is one the largest as far as total case sales. Products in this category encompass all flavors, and are used as after-dinner drinks, aperitifs, components of classic cocktails or popular shooters, or as flavorful enhancements to foods.

Originating in Europe, cordials and liqueurs are alcoholic beverages that are prepared by mixing or compounding various spirits with flavorings. The cordial category includes schnapps, liqueurs, cremes, and brandies. Cordials must contain at least 2.5 percent sugar by weight, although most are considerably higher in their sugar content and may contain up to 35 percent of a sweetening agent.

Cordials are produced by one of the following methods: percolation, maceration, or distillation. The percolation process starts with pouring the spirits in the bottom of a large tank with a basket-like container filled with fruit and spices near the top. The sprits then are ''percolated'' up through the basket, extracting the flavors of the fruit. With maceration, the fruit and other ingredients are mixed with the spirit and allowed to steep until all the flavors have been extracted. In the distillation process, all the ingredients are placed in the still with grain neutral spirits and gently heated.

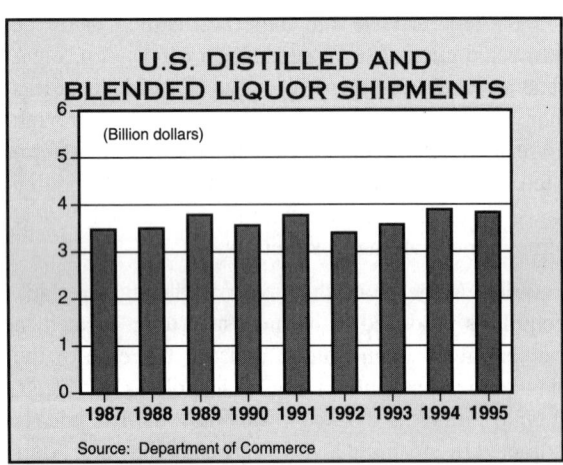

U.S. DISTILLED AND BLENDED LIQUOR SHIPMENTS

(Billion dollars)

1987 1988 1989 1990 1991 1992 1993 1994 1995

Source: Department of Commerce

CURRENT CONDITIONS

For the first time in 15 years, American consumption of distilled spirits increased in 1996—albeit only a 0.3 percent rise. This small but significant jump bolstered the hopes of liquor industry leaders who long anticipated consumption rates to turn around.

Approximately 135 million cases of liquor goods were consumed in 1996, according to *Impact,* an industry trade journal. The biggest sellers were Seagram's Absolut Vodka (3.3 million cases, up 5.2 percent from 1995) and Grand Met's Jose Cuervo tequila (2.5 million cases, up 6 percent).

As with previous years, the recovery appears to be gaining at a much faster pace with white goods rather than dark. Vodka topped US distilled liquor sales in 1994, with more than 31 million cases sold. Canadian whiskey led sales of dark spirits with slightly more than 16 million cases.

The sales breakdown of other distilled spirits in 1994 were rum, 10.6 million cases; gin, 11.6 million cases; tequila, 4.5 million cases; cordials, 14.9 million cases; bourbon(including blended and straight), 13 million cases; blended whiskey, 7.2 million cases; scotch, 8.9 million cases; and Irish whiskey, 242,000 cases.

With 25 percent of the distilled market, vodka continue to surpass all other types of distilled spirits. In the past, vodka was popular because American consumers wanted lighter, less flavorful beverages. But as classic cocktails were revived in the 1990s, many were resurrected with a vodka base. Moreover, premium vodkas such as Ketel One, Absolut, and Skyy, were growing in popularity, as well as infused vodkas such as Absolut Citron, Absolut Kurrant, Finlandia Cranberry, Finlandia Pineapple, and Tanqueray Sterling Citrus.

Following in the footsteps of infused vodka, rum flavored with spices or citrus was also gaining popularity with American consumers. Captain Morgan Original Spiced Rum from Seagram captured the number two spot in the rum category with sales of 1 million cases in 1995, and Bacardi Limon claimed sales of more than 300,000 cases in its first nine months on the market.

Gin also posted a slight gain, but due more to the resurgence of gin cocktails rather than the introduction of new products. Marck Schuermann, director of public issues for DISCUS, cites what he calls ''anecdotal evidence,'' with the return of classic cocktails and martini bars.

The popularity of classic cocktails such as Manhattans and Rob Roys may explain why dark spirits have shown increases, especially in the premium category. According to *Impact,* the top 25 premium and super-premium brands are expected to be up 4.9 percent to 28.8 million cases in 1996.

This good news for the liquor industry still can't match the 23 percent decline in distilled spirits consumption in the United States since 1981. Citing falling sales and the need to compete with wine and beer marketers, in November 1996 the board of the Distilled Spirits Council of the United States unanimously voted to lift a 48-year-old voluntary ban on television advertising.

Seagram Americas became the first spirits marketer to break the ban in June 1996 with its ad for Crown Royal Canadian whiskey on KRIS-TV in Corpus Christi, Texas. ABC, CBS, NBC, and Fox so far have refused to take liquor ads. But more than 1,000 television and cable providers may follow the lead of Black Entertainment Television and accept advertisements from distilled spirits marketers.

The issue of liquor advertising opened a floodgate of controversy, including admonishments from President Clinton, Mothers Against Drunk Drivers, and Reed Hundt, chairman of the Federal Trade Commission. All of these parties said the ban should remain to protect children. George Hacker of the advocacy group, Center for Science in the Public Interest, said the repeal of the broadcast ad ban "marks the beginning of an open liquor-marketing season on America's children and teens."

The Federal Communications Commission (FCC) began a formal inquiry into the placement and content of Seagram's ads, while the Federal Trade Commission (FTC) followed with its own investigation. Congress also had taken up this issue with the Senate Commerce Committee telecommunications subcommittee hearings in March 1997. Witnesses include the FTC Chairman Robert Pitofsky, FCC Chairman Reed Hundt, industry critics including former Senator George McGovern, the official spokesperson of the National Council on Alcoholism and Drug Dependence, and representatives of the beer, liquor, broadcast, and cable industries.

The outcome of these hearings would not only affect liquor advertising on broadcast and cable television, but also distilled spirits marketers presence on the Internet. All liquor companies—beer, wine and distilled spirits—turned to the Internet to disseminate product information. However, some organizations, such as the Center of Media Education, were claiming that beer and liquor companies were using the World Wide Web to attract underage drinkers. Some companies included a warning on their web sites that visitors must be at least 21 years old. These include Heublein Inc.'s web sites for Smirnoff vodka and Cuervo Gold tequila, and Joseph E. Seagram & Son's site for Captain Morgan's rum.

INDUSTRY LEADERS

International Distillers & Vinters (IDV) was the largest wine and spirits group in the world, and is the beverage division of Grand Metropolitan PLC, a London-based multinational company. IDV is known for its successful development of Smirnoff Vodka, J&B Whiskey, and Bailey's Irish Cream. IDV also is the parent company for Heublein, the marketer of Jose Cuervo Tequila.

Joseph Seagram & Sons is one of the world's leading producers and marketers of distilled spirits and wine with 1996 sales of over $4.6 billion. The business was organized on a global basis and conducted through subsidiaries and affiliates in 30 countries. Known as the Seagram Spirits and Wine Group, this division has been responsible for the production, brand management, business development, marketing, sales, and distribution of nearly all of Seagram's beverage alcohol business. The only exceptions have been Seagram's U.S. cooler business and the U.S.-based, specialized, premium wine operations. Focusing on premium and core brands, Seagram sold the trademark rights to seven distilled spirits brands in December 1991. A subsidiary of American Brands, Inc. purchased the trademark rights to Lord Calvert Canadian Whisky, Calvert Extra and Kessler Blended American Whiskeys, Calvert Gin, Wolfschmidt Vodka, Ronrico Rum, and the Leroux line of cordials.

In 1988, Seagram acquired Martell, the world's second largest cognac producer. Other well known Seagram brands include Chivas Regal, Mumm, Crown Royal, Seagram's Gin, and V.O. With this portfolio of premium products, Seagram's was successfully developing a worldwide market. As expected, the acquisition of Martell delivered enhanced growth for Seagram in the Asia-Pacific market, the fastest growing area in the world for beverage alcohol products. In this market, cognac has been the most prestigious drink, and Martell has been the pre-eminent cognac. This brand also has been popular in the markets of Singapore, Malaysia, and Hong Kong.

The largest U.S. distilled spirit company is Kentucky-based Brown-Forman Corporation ($1.6 billion in 1996 sales), which was created in 1870 when George C. Brown and John Forman opened their distillery in Louisville to producer Old Forester bourbon. In 1902, Forman sold his interest in the company to the Brown family, which has remained in control of the business ever since. The company's first acquisition was Early Times in 1923. Brown-Forman went public prior to the onset of Prohibition and was allowed to remain open to produce alcohol for medicinal purposes. During World War II, alcoholic beverage production was curtailed in order to produce alcohol for the war effort. In 1941, Brown-Forman began the process for a new batch of bourbon to be complete by 1945. As a result, Early Times dominated the bourbon market following the end of World War II.

In 1956, the company purchased Jack Daniel's sour mash whiskey produced in Lynchburg, Tennessee. Brown-Forman retained the Jack Daniel's label and promoted the image of a small distillery. This product has become so popular that it sells at least 4 million cases annually throughout the world.

Brown-Forman continued its expansion during the 1970s, adding lines of wine, champagne, brandy, scotch, gin, whiskey, and cordials. By the early 1990s, the company established a separate division for its wine operations and embarked on an aggressive expansion plan that included long-term marketing and distribution contracts.

Jim Beam Brands Company is the second largest distilled spirits company in the United States with $1.2 billion in 1996 sales, and producing and marketing more than 70 products, including six of the top 30 brands sold in the United States. Jim Beam Bourbon has been the company's flagship brand and the best selling bourbon in the United States and worldwide. The company started up in 1795 when Jacob Beam, a Kentucky farmer, developed his recipe for Kentucky bourbon whiskey. His son, David, joined the business, and with the assistance of new roads the distillery business grew as distribution broadened into the surrounding counties. In the following years, the distillery was moved twice, first to take advantage of an abundance of spring water and again to be closer to the railroad lines. The company's distillery is located on 430 acres in Clermont, 30 miles south of Louisville. Booker Noe, grandson of Jim Beam, is the Master Distiller at Clermont.

Beyond the company's portfolio of bourbons, its other main brands include Gibley's Gin, Canadian Supreme Whisky, Lord Calvert Canadian Blended Whisky, Kamchatka Vodka, and DeKuyper, the top selling cordial line in the United States. Jim Beam Brands Company operates its sales office and corporate headquarters in Deerfield, Illinois.

AMERICA AND THE WORLD

U.S. exports of distilled spirits reached a record high in 1995, according to DICUS. Since 1991, U.S. distilled spirits have doubled both in value and volume. In 1991, U.S. distilled spirits exports were less than 10 percent of total industry sales; in 1995, they totaled 22 percent of industry sales. Volume exports of

U.S. DISTILLED AND BLENDED LIQUOR IMPORTS

Billion dollars

Source: Bureau of the Census

U.S. whiskey, rum, and neutral grain spirits categories all increased in 1995, while U.S. whiskey, brandy, gin, cordials, and neutral grain spirits increased in value.

"International expansion represents a great opportunity for distillers. Leading spirit brands already enjoy worldwide cachet, especially within the whiskey and cognac categories," reported Jim Barrett in the *Value Line Investment Survey*. Export opportunities can be found in the fast-growing markets of the Asia Pacific region, Latin America, and the former Soviet Bloc. "Not only are these expanding markets, but the growth is generally occurring among higher-margin, deluxe brands. What's more, trade barriers have recently been lifted in a number of countries, such as India and Taiwan," added Barrett.

The Asia Pacific area has included some of the largest whiskey markets in world, with Japan at the top of the U.S. export list. The rapid ascent of a middle class in these countries bodes well for the future of beverage alcohol marketers. "Export is the hot spot," Barry M. Berish, president of Jim Beam Brands Co., noted in *Business Week*.

U.S. whiskey exports led the product categories with a 15.5 percent increase in value to $278 million and a 9.8 percent increase in volume. Japan, Germany, and Australia were significant growth markets for exporting U.S. whiskey in 1995. Japan accounts for 26 percent of the total value of U.S. exports with an 11 percent increase in sales over 1994. Germany accounts for 17.6 percent with an 18 percent increase compared to 1994. Australia accounts for 12.8 percent, with a 21 percent increase in 1995 sales.

Beverage alcohol marketers also were beginning to focus on growth in other countries. After successful penetration of the Japanese market, whiskey advertising could be found in Britain and other affluent markets. Latin America, for example, has become the second greatest growth opportunity, particularly for premium-priced scotch marketers like Seagram. Sales of scotch grew over 50 percent in 1991 in Venezuela, with much of the growth occurring among higher-priced brands, such as Chivas Regal Scotch. Scotch whisky has remained the most popular distilled spirit in the world and has been sold in 190 countries.

FURTHER READING

Brandes, Richard. "Beverage Trends: The Shape of Drinks to Come." *Beverage Dynamics,* May 1993.

———. "Discus Annouces Record Year for U.S. Distilled Spirits Exports (press release)." Washington, D.C.: Distilled Spirits Council of the US, 24 April 1996.

———. "The Dow Lifts Some Spirits." *Time,* 17 February 1997.

Fried, Eunice. "High-Powered Drinks: Cost Aside, Ultra Premium Vodka is Surging in Popularity." *Black Enterprise,* March 1996.

Hood, Donna Jean. "The Value of Vodka." *Beverage Dynamics,* March 1992.

———. Jim Beam Brands Co. publicity materials, Deerfield, IL: Jim Beam.

Kelley, Kristine Portnoy. "Liquor and Wine: Slow but Steady: Consumptions is Still Down, but Consumers are Trading Up." *Beverage Industry,* August 1995.

———. "Knowing and Understanding Distilled Spirits." BeverageNet Home Page, 1996. Available from http://www.aip.com.

Levin, Gary. "Liquor Sales Go Dry." *Advertising Age,* 10 February 1992.

———. "Liquor Ad Ban May Become Official." *Time,* 8 November 1996.

———. "Liquor Ads Hearing Postponed." *Advertising Age,* 30 January 1997.

Power, Christopher. "Sweet Sales for Sour Mash— Abroad." *Business Week,* 1 July 1991.

Prince, Greg W., and Eric Sfiligoj. "The Beverage Market Index for 1993." *Beverage World,* May 1993.

Riell, Howard. "Margarita Mania." *Beverage Dynamics,* April 1993.

———. "Spirits Not So Down, Consumption Continues to Sink, but Shows Signs of Leveling Off." *Beverage Industry,* August 1996.

———. "Spirits sales drought eases." *Advertising Age,* 12 December 1996.

———. "Ten Events That Made News (Spirits TV advertising)." *Advertising Age,* 23 December 1996.

———. "Thirst of the Lonely." *The Economist,* 10 April 1993.

———. "Top Selling Liquor Brands." *Advertising Age,* 15 February 1993.

Tougas, Jane Grant. "Scotch: Spirit of Tradition," *Beverage Dynamics,* May 1993.

U.S. Industrial Outlook 1994. Washington, DC: U.S. Department of Commerce, 1994.

Ursin, Cheryl. "Mixing It Up." *Beverage Dynamics,* July/August 1993.

Warner, Fara. "Beam's Hot Shots." *Brandweek,* 26 April 1993.

—Catherine A. Quagliana

SIC 2086

BOTTLED AND CANNED SOFT DRINKS AND CARBONATED WATERS

This category includes establishments primarily engaged in manufacturing soft drinks and carbonated waters. Establishments primarily engaged in manufacturing fruit and vegetable juices are classified in various canned, frozen, and preserved food classifications. Those manufacturing fruit syrups for flavoring are classified in **SIC 2087: Flavoring Extracts and Flavoring Syrups, Not Elsewhere Classified;** those manufacturing nonalcoholic cider are classified in **SIC 2099: Food Preparations, Not Elsewhere Classified.** Establishments primarily engaged in bottling natural water are classified in **SIC 5149: Groceries and Related Products, Not Elsewhere Classified.**

INDUSTRY SNAPSHOT

Soft drinks have become intrinsically tied to the "American way of life," and the leading soft drink, Coca-Cola, is a virtual icon of American culture. Close to 500 soft drinks manufacturers and bottling companies operate in the United States. According to the National Soft Drinks Association (NSDA), in 1995, the retail sale of soft drinks totaled more than $52 billion. In 1995, Americans consumed over 51 gallons of soft drinks per capita, a total of more than 13 billion gallons. Soft drinks accounted for more than 27 percent of Americans' beverage consumption. The U.S. market included nearly 450 different soft drinks.

Two companies, Coca-Cola and Pepsi-Cola, controlled nearly three-quarters of the U.S. soft drink market, with each company producing four of the top ten best-selling brands. Approximately 500 bottlers operate across the United States. Modern bottling plants produce more than 2,000 soft drinks per minute on each line of operation. The soft drink industry employed more than 136,000 people nationwide.

The Economic Impact of the Industry. There is more to America's soft drink industry than just the companies that provide consumers with their favorite refreshments, according to the NSDA. It's also a big part of the U.S. economy, buying products and services from many different industries, creating thousands of jobs and contributing to worthwhile causes in local communities. According to the NSDA, bottlers and canners spend more than $65 billion annually purchasing supplies from 116 separate industries, accounting for 744,000 jobs across the United States in addition to the 136,000 people directly employed by the soft drink industry.

Soft drink flavorings are the number one product purchased, followed by metal cans in second place, and plastics used for packaging in third place. The soft drink industry also is a big buyer of corn syrup, advertising services, glass containers, boxes for shipping bottle caps, warehousing, fruits and vegetables, motor freight, carbonated water, sugar, and many other products and services that contribute to the manufacture of soft drinks. NSDA states that, each year, the soft drink industry pays $4.3 billion in payroll dollars, pays more than $1 billion in state and local taxes, and contributes more than $95 million to charities.

ORGANIZATION AND STRUCTURE

Soft drink companies manufacture and sell beverage syrups and bases to bottling operations, which add sweeteners and/or carbonated water to produce the final product. Independent bottlers work under contract with various soft drink manufacturers and are allotted specific territories to serve. The manufacturers provide the bottlers with syrups and bases, but also with a variety of business services, including product quality control, marketing, advertising, engineering, and financial and personnel training. In turn, the bottlers supply the required capital investment for land, buildings, machinery, equipment, trucks, bottles, and cases.

During the past few years the number of independent bottlers declined as major soft drink manufacturers consolidated their bottling operations by acquiring independent companies and combining them into one large operation. Both Coke and Pepsi have such arrangements. Coca-Cola Enterprises (CCE) has become the world's largest soft drink bottler; their production accounted for 55 percent of all the bottled and canned Coke products sold in the United States. The company operates in 37 states, Washington, D.C. and the U.S. Virgin Islands. Meanwhile, Pepsi's company-owned bottling operations have been responsible for 52 percent of its bottling volume. Both companies promoted the purchase of franchised bottling operations as a way of preparing for long-term strategic growth, domestically and internationally. As the economies of various countries have become more sophisticated and complex, so must soft drink manufacturers in their ability to produce, distribute, and market their products.

The soft drink industry sells its product in two forms, packaged and fountain service. The packaged form of cans and bottles represented 75 percent of the total soft drink market, with 9.3 billion gallons sold in 1992. With fountain service, the soft drink product is dispensed and served in cups, typically in a restaurant or any location with a food service station. Fountain service volume increased 2.3 percent in 1992, reaching nearly 3.1 billion gallons or 25 percent of the market share.

BACKGROUND AND DEVELOPMENT

The soft drink industry began in the mid-1880s, with the creation of a syrup that was mixed with carbonated water and served at drug store lunch counters. During the early years, soft drinks were sold only in stores that could provide fountain service. Increasing distribution was tied to building additional syrup manufacturing plants.

With the advent of bottling machinery, soft drinks began to be distributed beyond the town drug store. The first merchant to bottle Coca-Cola was Joseph A. Biedenharn of Vicksburg, Mississippi, who installed a bottling machine in his candy store in 1894. The development of large-scale bottling assisted the proliferation of Coca-Cola and by 1895 the drink was sold in nearly every part of the United States. An infrastructure of independent bottlers working under contract with Coca-Cola, producing the drink to exact specifications, and distributing it within a specific region soon became the model distribution method for Coke and was emulated by others.

The 1960s and 1970s brought acquisitions and diversification for Coca-Cola and Pepsi-Cola. In 1960, Coke purchased Minute Maid and later acquired Duncan Foods. The Coca-Cola Company Foods Division was created in 1967, and later renamed Coca-Cola Foods. Meanwhile, Pepsi-Cola merged with Frito-Lay in 1965, changing its name to PepsiCo, but maintaining its beverage division under the name Pepsi-Cola. PepsiCo soon ventured into food service and snack foods with the acquisition of Pizza Hut, Taco Bell, and Kentucky Fried Chicken restaurants.

During the 1980s, as consumers became more interested in health and fitness, the soft drink industry faced stiff competition from the makers of bottled water. In response, soft drink manufacturers developed low-calorie and caffeine-free beverages, such as Diet Coke and Diet Pepsi. The start of the 1990s ushered in a new kind of competition focussed on "New Age" beverages like ready-to-drink teas, fruit juice beverages, and flavored waters. Gatorade, the perennial leader among sports drinks, saw new competitors in the 1990s.

From the simple beginnings of one cola, the soft drink industry exploded into a kaleidoscope of traditional sodas, natural sodas, fruit juice drinks, and various kinds of bottled water. Coca-Cola Classic was the best selling soft drink in the United States in 1992 and around the world, controlling nearly 20 percent of the domestic market and 46 percent of the worldwide market. Coke Classic controlled 19.3 percent of the soft drink market and posted a sales increase of 1.5 percent for the year. Pepsi-Cola was the second best-selling soft drink for the year, with 16.1 percent market share, down 0.8 percent over 1991. Diet Coke, Diet Pepsi, and Dr Pepper completed the list of the top five soft drink brands for 1992.

The average American consumes more soft drinks than water, quaffing 49 gallons, or 296 eight-ounce servings, each year. The soft drink industry (excluding bottled water and fruit juices and drinks) generated $48.9 billion dollars in retail sales in 1992 and dominated total beverage consumption in the United States with 51.3 percent. Beer came in second place with 24.0 percent, fruit juices and drinks at 12.5 percent, bottled water at 8.7 percent, wine with 2.0 percent, and spirits at 1.5 percent.

Some industry leaders contend that the U.S. soft drink market has begun a slow, steady decline, citing its failure to post double-digit growth since the end of the 1980s. Pointing to an aging U.S. population and changing consumer tastes, industry analysts predicted that per capita consumption and the total consumption rate will not increase significantly in the near future. To combat a weak U.S. market, soft drink manufacturers aggressively pursued overseas markets. Although no other country has a soft drink consumption rate as high as the United States, many areas have been targeted as potential for expansion, especially the underdeveloped and highly populated areas of China and India. The Coca-Cola Company has been the clear leader in overseas expansion with nearly 75 percent of its operating profits coming from areas outside the United States.

The traditional cola producers were caught off-guard by the rise of generic store brands during the early 1990s, as the recession drove consumers to experiment with these lower-priced drinks. These colas are not expected to create a significant amount of brand loyalty, however, and therefore have not appeared as a substantial threat to the major soft drink manufacturers.

Despite their market dominance, traditional cola products continued to lose market share. Total soft drink consumption grew roughly 5 percent annually between 1983 and 1989, but slowed to 3 percent in 1990, and only 1.6 percent by 1991. Even the diet cola market has faltered since 1990, losing ground to new drinks commonly called "New Age" beverages. In a category that enjoyed a 10-20 percent growth rate during the 1980s, sales growth for diet colas was cut to approximately 3 percent per year. Industry analysts suggest that new drinks, including sodas and bottled water, are the most formidable opponents to traditional colas. This market segment began with the rise of the bottled water industry in the United States and expanded into the creation of the "New Age" category.

Bottled Water. Strongest during the 1980s, bottled water remained a vibrant and growing segment of the beverage market into the 1990s. This industry can be divided into two segments, bulk water and refreshment beverages. Bulk water is nonsparkling water that is consumed instead of tap water, and represented about 80 percent of the market. Refreshment beverages ranged from still water such as Evian to flavored, vitamin-enriched sparkling mineral water from Crystal Geyser. While bulk water usually is bought through a delivery service in five-gallon containers or larger; refreshment beverages are premium, image-driven brands, prepared in smaller containers, and are sold for both on- and off-premise consumption. These products compete directly with sodas and mixers.

Since 1980, the U.S. bottled water market has grown to nearly three billion gallons in annual consumption. After a decade of double-digit growth, the market faltered in 1991, showing only a 0.5 percent gain in volume. Analysts blamed the recession and concern over safety, prompted by the Perrier recall in 1990, for the downturn. The industry began to rebound in 1992 with a 3.7 percent increase in volume and a 3.2 percent increase in sales. By 1993, more than 700 brands of bottled water were produced in the United States at 430 bottling facilities. Another 75 brands of water were imported.

The Perrier Group has been the largest bottled water company in the United States. Acquired in 1992 by Nestle, the Perrier Group includes a collection of strong regional domestic waters plus its flagship brand. The second largest bottled water company in the United States has been McKesson Water Products, with most of its business centered around home and office delivery. More than 80 percent of the company's sales have been in California with its Sparkletts brand. In a recent survey by Business Trends Analysts, consumers reported the most important reasons for drinking bottled water were health concerns and taste. "The more Americans learn about water the more they will drink it much the same way that Europeans do," Evian marketing director Ed Slade told *Beverage Dynamics.*

Beyond bottled water, an entirely new market segment appeared, answering Americans' call for flavored drinks that are lighter, less filling, less sweet, "healthier" and more sophisticated than traditional sodas. The "New Age" beverages have covered everything from flavored sparkling waters to natural sodas to fruit juice drinks to flavored teas and bottled coffee products. A beverage fits in the New Age category if it is "relatively new to the market, considered by the consumer as 'good for me' and containing natural and/or healthy ingredients without preservatives," industry analyst Michael Bellas told *Beverage World.*

The all-natural soda division has been the most active New Age segment. Although sales slumped in 1990, "all-natural sodas stormed back to reach $309.8 million in sales in 1991, up a whopping 51 percent," reported Eric Sfiligoj in *Beverage World.* Consumption of all-natural sodas reached 81.3 million gallons annually by 1991, second in the category only to flavored waters. The healthy growth of all-natural sodas has been in direct response to the success of Vancouver-based Clearly Canadian. Launched in 1987, Clearly Canadian is Canadian water pumped from deep artesian wells and mixed with fruit flavors. The product is sweetened with fructose and does contain preservatives.

Sales of New Age beverages have been projected to grow at 8 percent annually through 1995, with growth rates hitting 11 percent by 1996, according to *Beverage Dynamics.* With projections such as these, it was only a matter of time before the national cola brands added their own products to the plethora of New Age drinks. In early 1992, Pepsi introduced Crystal Pepsi, a clear, cola-flavored beverage that is 100 percent naturally flavored and contains no preservatives or caffeine. During its first year of national distribution in 1993, Crystal Pepsi captured more than 2 percent of the soft drink market or roughly $1 billion in sales.

Coca-Cola also launched its New Age soda, Nordic Mist, in 1992. The Coke product is a mixture of sparkling water, high fructose corn syrup, citric acid, potassium, and 1 of 5 natural fruit flavors. "New Age isn't our bread and butter," said Bob Bertini of Coca-Cola USA in *Beverage Dynamics,* "but it deserves a place at the table. We want to be fully represented in every category that makes sense for us. We're trying to respond to changes in the market, but our priority is still colas and traditional soft drinks."

In the face of rising competition from all fronts of the beverage market, both Coke and Pepsi turned to joint ventures with other beverage companies. Pepsi-Cola has been working with Ocean Spray to provide all of their ready-to-drink beverages, including Ocean Spray Splash, a five-flavor line of fruit sparklers, and Ocean Spray Lemonade. In this alliance, Pepsi has become the exclusive distributor of all new Ocean Spray single-serve products.

In a joint venture with Nestle, Coca-Cola created the Coca-Cola Nestle Refreshment Company (CCNR) in 1991 to market ready-to-drink coffee, tea, and chocolate beverages. Nestea Iced Tea, CCNR's first project, was introduced in the United States in March 1992. The bottled tea has no preservatives, artificial flavors or colors, and comes in regular and diet version.

Both cola manufacturers have also been test marketing sports drinks, such as All Sport by Pepsi and PowerAde by Coke. Sports drinks replenish fluids, minerals, and energy lost during exercise, and the market for these drinks has grown into a billion-dollar retail segment. Gatorade accounted for nearly 90 percent of nationwide sales, and will be the one brand for both Coke and Pepsi to beat. "Gatorade defines the category," says Jesse Meyers, publisher of *Beverage Digest,* in *Time.* "There is not a beverage category in any country in the world that is so dominated by one producer."

The movement of major players like Coke and Pepsi into nontraditional beverage markets has shown the affect of changing consumer preferences. Should the New Age category remain as a firmly established and viable drink alternative, these two manufacturers are likely to increase their domestic rivalry, possibly to the detriment of the smaller firms in the marketplace. Moreover, both Coca-Cola and Pepsi-Cola have set their sites on a much larger piece of the beverage market pie, overseas expansion. With improving distribution systems, these two giants have been preparing for what they do best, promoting worldwide consumption of their well-known and well-loved products.

CURRENT CONDITIONS

At the turn of the century, the soft drink industry, having played it's cards right, was doing well again, after its slump in the early to mid-1990s. One of the

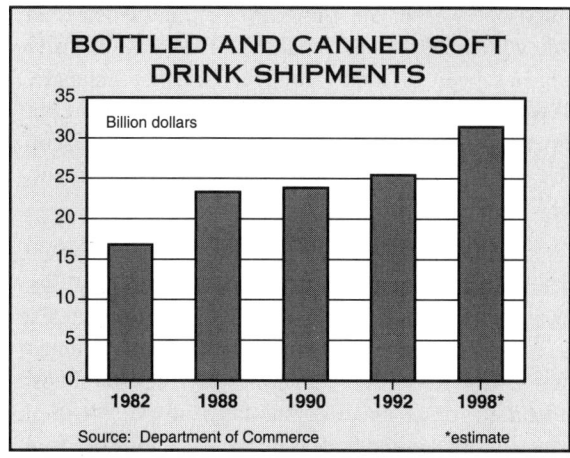

BOTTLED AND CANNED SOFT DRINK SHIPMENTS

Billion dollars

Source: Department of Commerce   *estimate

biggest reasons for this was the industry's expansion into fertile overseas markets. Innovative marketing strategies and timely new product introductions, caused U.S. consumption of soft drinks to improve. According to *Beverage World,* carbonated soft drink consumption increased to 13.3 billion gallons in 1994, an increase of 4.3 percent over 1993 consumption. Fruit beverages consumption was 3.3 billion gallons in 1994 an increase of 3.8 percent from 1993.

New age drinks were the best performers in the mid-1990s. Bottled water consumption reached 2.5 billion gallons in 1994, an increase of 10.4 percent over 1993. Sports drinks performed even better, with the consumption reaching 391.1 million gallons in 1994, an increase of 11.4 percent over consumption in 1993.

Bottled water was seen as the best performing star of the soft drinks industry in the mid- to late 1990s. It's success was attributed to many factors including, "A perception of a healthy, natural, good-for-you product," according to *Beverage World.* Given the concerns over municipal water, it was considered the only beverage category that was driven because it was a tap water replacement. The bottled water industry saw many "firsts" in the mid-1990's. It was the first time that this industry "topped 2.5 billion gallons, measured more than 10 gallons per capita, and totaled more than 3 billion in wholesale receipts," according to *Beverage World.* The sparkling water segment, however, was the only down spot in the industry, with dollar sales going down almost 10 percent according to *Beverage World.*

Bottled coffee was seen as the other rising trend of the 1990s. The well known coffee maker, Starbucks, teamed up with PepsiCo to produce Frappucino, which was expected to make it's debut in the middle of 1996. This was expected to be a challenging venture for the

company, since cold bottled coffee was seen as a tough sell according to *Business Week.* In spite of the failure of Maxwell House's Cappio, and Mazagran, a carbonated coffee drink, from the Starbucks-Pepsi partnership, Frappuccino was seen as a drink that would succeed because of two reasons—the Starbucks name brand and coffee by itself, which was the fastest growing beverage segment after carbonated drinks.

Packaging and Recycling. Since 1989, soft drink container recycling has risen from 48.7 percent to more than 60.0 percent—a 23 percent increase. Nearly 48 billion soft drink containers were recycled in 1995. Soft drink containers account for less than 1 percent of the U.S. solid waste stream. Although beverage containers account for less than 20 percent of materials collected in most curbside programs, they generate up to 73 percent of total scrap revenue. Packaging innovations lightened the weight of soft drink containers by an average of 30 percent since 1972. Nearly 78 percent of soft drinks are packaged, while the remaining 22 percent are dispensed from fountains. In 1995, 62.6 billion soft drinks were packaged in cans, 16.8 billion were packaged in PET bottles, and 3.6 billion were packaged in glass bottles.

INDUSTRY LEADERS

Following is a list of the largest companies in this industry: Coca-Cola Co. of Atlanta, Georgia, with a sales revenue of $18.02 billion and 32,000 employees; McKesson Corporation of San Francisco, California, with a sales revenue of $13.2 billion and 11,000 employees; Pepsi-Cola Co. of Somers, New York, with a sales revenue of $10.55 billion and 30,000 employees; Joseph E. Seagram and Sons Inc. of New York, New York, with a sales revenue of $4.65 billion and 16,000 employees; Whitman Corp. of Rolling Meadows, Illinois, with a sales revenue of $2.95 billion and 16,841 employees; Perrier Group of America Inc., located in Greenwich, Connecticut, with a sales revenue of $1.91 billion and 4400 employees; Gatorade of Oakland, California, with a sales revenue of $1.26 billion and 2600 employees; RC/Arby's Corp. of Fort Lauderdale, Florida, with a sales revenue of $610 million and 9000 employees; Snapple Beverage Corp. of East Meadow, New York, with a sales revenue of $513 million and 176 employees; Cadbury Beverages Inc. of Stamford, Connecticut, with a sales revenue of $513 million and 1100 employees.

Coca-Cola has been the world's most popular soft drink, holding as high as 46 percent global market share. Using a franchise system for distribution, the company and its subsidiaries sold the flagship brand

and other brands in the Sprite, Tab, and Diet Coke families in more than 195 countries and territories. Coca Cola had 1996 sales of $18.45 billion.

Coca-Cola originated in Atlanta, Georgia, on May 8, 1886, when pharmacist Dr. John Styth Pemberton created a caramel-colored syrup in his backyard. He took a jug of the syrup to Jacob's Pharmacy in Atlanta where the product debuted as a soda fountain drink for five cents a glass. Thinking that two C's would look good in advertising, Dr. Pemberton's partner and bookkeeper Frank M. Robinson suggested the name Coca-Cola and designed the now-famous script trademark. Dr. Pemberton, in poor health and in need of funds, soon sold portions of his company. Asa G. Candler, a druggist and Atlanta businessman, acquired complete control of the company for $2,300 in 1891.

In 1892, Candler, along with his brother John S. Candler and two other associates, formed ''The Coca-Cola Company.'' In 1894, the first syrup manufacturing plant outside of Atlanta was opened in Dallas, Texas. The following year, two more were opened in Chicago and Los Angeles. By 1895, Coca-Cola was available in every state in the United States. Large-scale bottling began in 1899, when Benjamin F. Thomas and Joseph B. Whitehead of Chattanooga, Tennessee, obtained the exclusive rights to bottle and sell Coca-Cola. With the financial assistance of John T. Lupton, these men developed a regional franchise bottling system, engaging over 1,000 bottlers in 20 years.

In 1919, The Coca-Cola Company was sold to Atlanta banker Ernest Woodruff for $25 million. Ernest's son Robert was elected president of The Coca-Cola Company in 1923, when the business was reincorporated in Delaware and 500,000 shares of common stock were sold publicly for $40 per share. The new president led the company for six decades.

Coca-Cola's diversification into the food industry began with the purchase of Minute Maid Corporation in 1960, and the Minute Maid and Hi-C trademarks joined Coke's family of beverages. The company acquired Duncan Foods and formed The Coca-Cola Company Foods Division in 1967, now known as Coca-Cola Foods. In 1986, the company consolidated its U.S. bottling operations, creating Coca-Cola Enterprises (CCE), 51 percent of which was sold to the public.

To sell its products throughout the world, The Coca-Cola Company divided its operations into two sectors, the North America Soft Drink Business Sector and the International Soft Drink Business Sector. The North American division covers Coca-Cola USA, which operates in the United States, and Coca-Cola, Ltd., which operates in Canada. The International division has been divided into five operating units: EC Group, Northeast Europe/Middle East Group, Latin America Group, Pacific Group, and the Africa Group. The Coca-Cola Company employs over 31,300 people.

Pepsi-Cola, the beverage division of PepsiCo, Inc., a worldwide consumer products company, was the second leader with sales of $10.55 billion. The Pepsi brand, in addition to Diet Pepsi, Slice, Mountain Dew, Mug Root Beer, and the new Crystal Pepsi, accounted for as much as one-third of the soft drink market in the United States. Pepsi, a leading soft drink with nearly $17 billion in worldwide retail sales, was first created in 1898. Caleb D. Bradham, a druggist in New Bern, North Carolina, invented the drink and named it Pepsi-Cola, claiming it cured dyspepsia or indigestion. Various owners operated the Pepsi-Cola Company from 1923 through 1963. Under the direction of Donald M. Kendall, who became company president in 1963, Pepsi acquired Frito-Lay, the largest snack chip company in the United States, and became PepsiCo, Inc. Additional acquisitions have included Pizza Hut (1977), Taco Bell (1978), and Kentucky Fried Chicken (1986).

Pepsi-Cola North America manufactures and sells soft drink concentrate to company-owned and independent franchised bottlers operating facilities throughout the United States and Canada. The company also provides fountain beverage syrups to restaurants, including the 18,000 kitchens at Taco Bell, KFC (formerly Kentucky Fried Chicken), and Pizza Hut. Pepsi-Cola International (PCI) controls the company's international soft drink operations. Through this division, Pepsi-Cola products are sold in 155 countries and territories throughout the world. PCI produces nearly 18 percent of all soft drinks sold internationally, including the business of Seven-Up International. World headquarters for PepsiCo, Inc. are located in Purchase, New York, and the company employs 370,000 people.

Dr Pepper/Seven-Up Companies, Inc. was the third largest soft drink manufacturer in the United States with an 11 percent market share in the early 1990's. Dr Pepper and Seven-Up manufacture and market syrup to more than 750 licensed bottlers, and its products have been served in more than 100,000 food service outlets in the United States. Dr Pepper remained the nation's fifth largest selling soft drink, behind the regular and diet versions of Coke and Pepsi. In addition to the family of Dr Pepper and Seven-Up brands, the company also sells IBC brand sodas and Welch's soft drinks.

The Dr Pepper Company was publicly traded on the NYSE from 1946 until February 1984, when it was taken private in a leveraged buy out. In November 1986, the company was sold to an owner equity group, which included members of the management team and other investors. Later that year, the company management arranged a separate owner equity group to buy the domestic operations of The Seven-Up Company, then owned by Philip Morris, Inc.

The Dr Pepper brand was first sold at Morrison's Old Corner Drug Store in Waco, Texas, in 1885. Created by pharmacist Charles Alderton and sold by store owner Wade Morrison, the new drink was named after one of Morrison's friends from Virginia. A bottler in Waco, Robert Lazenby, began producing the syrup and bottling the drink and soon formed a company with Morrison. In 1923, they moved the headquarters to Dallas, and in 1924 named their business the ''Dr Pepper Company.''

The Seven-Up Company began in 1929, when C. L. Grigg, owner of The Howdy Company in St. Louis, introduced his lemon-lime drink. In 1936, the company name was changed to The Seven-Up Company, in recognition of its popular drink. The company went public in 1967 and was bought by Philip Morris in 1978.

In August 1993, Cadbury Schweppes PLC, a British candy and soft drink maker, purchased 12.2 million Dr Pepper shares for $231.3 million, increasing its stake in the company to nearly 26 percent. Cadbury officials described the stock purchase as an excellent investment opportunity. However, industry analysts speculated that Cadbury's increased ownership could help Dr Pepper expand into international markets. Cadbury sells its candy and soft drink products in 170 countries and posted $5 billion in worldwide sales in 1992.

The Dr Pepper/Seven-Up Companies operates one of the industry's most modern manufacturing plants near St. Louis, Missouri, which produces all of the company's concentrates, extracts, and syrups. The plant also makes most of Cadbury's concentrate sold in North America. Dr Pepper/Seven-Up Companies' administrative headquarters are located in Dallas. Operating divisions are Dr Pepper USA, Seven-Up USA, Premier Beverages, Dr Pepper/Seven-Up Foodservice, and International. The company employs approximately 930 workers. President, chairman, and CEO is John R. Albert.

WORK FORCE

According to *Ward's Business Directory of U.S. Public and Private Companies,* 292 soft drink manufacturers and bottling companies operated in the United States in the early 1990s, employing approximately 207,300 workers. By the turn of the decade there were 500 bottling operations in the United States employing about 136,000 workers. According to the U.S. Department of Labor, overall employment in food processing (which includes beverages) has been projected to decline 6 percent by the year 2005. Like other manufacturing industries, food processing has become less labor intensive, and occupational projections reflected this predicted decline. According to *Manufacturing USA,* by the year 2000, employment for packaging and filling machine operations will drop 26.9 percent, industrial truck and tractor operators 23.4 percent, freight stock and materials movers (by hand) 23.8 percent, and hand packers and packagers 32.3 percent. Professional specialty occupations, such as engineers and computer scientists, have been expected to grow, which reflects the industry's continued emphasis on scientific research to improve food products and production processes. However, these jobs have comprised a very small proportion of industry employment.

AMERICA AND THE WORLD

Soft drinks have been produced or consumed in nearly every corner of the world. Growing consumption trends can be attributed to rising disposable incomes, falling trade barriers, universal product acceptance, and a rising demand for American consumer goods. Both Pepsi-Cola and Coca-Cola have company-owned franchised bottling plants in more than 120 countries that produce their respective brands within each country rather than exporting them from the United States.

Beverages that are exported from the United States include unsweetened bottled water, but these figures have remained relatively low as the worldwide market for bottled water has been dominated by a few well-established European producers. However, United States producers of sweetened water or New Age beverages have fared better in the export market. The international beverage market has seen the dominance and continued development of Coke and Pepsi in all parts of the world. These companies have taken their rivalry overseas and have been spending millions to develop new markets for their products. One market that Pepsi-Cola dominated has been Russia, controlling twice the market share of Coke. Establishing its presence in Russia during the Nixon administration,

Pepsi gained entry into the country through a barter deal involving the exportation of vodka. By 1993, Pepsi-Cola controlled 4 percent of the market compared to Coke's 2 percent. The obvious market growth potential has made this former Soviet state a prime target for an American invasion of the cola wars.

In April 1993, Coke announced the construction of a $15 million production plant and training facility near Moscow. These facilities will serve the kiosks that have been installed in various Russian communities. Coca-Cola owns these kiosks, which are shaped like giant Coke cans, and rents them to a wholesaler, who in turns employs local citizens to operate the small soda stands. The acceptance of Russian rubles instead of American dollars differentiates this enterprise from the other American operations in Russia. ''The idea,'' reported Laurie Hays in the *Wall Street Journal,* ''is that such transactions will help the economy firm up and ultimately put more money into the pockets of citizens—more money they can use to buy Coke.''

In August 1993, PepsiCo announced its plans to invest $500 million in Poland over the next five years, with $200 million expressly for the development of a Pepsi market among the country's 38 million consumers. This investment was the third such announcement made by Pepsi. The company previously revealed a $115 million, five-year investment plan for Hungary and a $750 million plan for Mexico.

With per-capita consumption second only to the United States, Mexico has been set up as another major battleground for the cola wars. The largest Pepsi bottler outside of the United States has been Grupo Embotellador de Mexico SA, or Gemex, located in Mexico City. Meanwhile, Fomento Economico Mexicano SA, or Femsa, owns the largest Coke franchise in the world and is located in Monterrey. Needless to say, Pepsi dominated Mexico City while Coke covered the southern Mexico market. With the assistance of market reforms enacted by Mexico's President Carlos Salinas de Gortari, both Coke and Pepsi have been working to compete in each other's established territories.

In the United States, imported unsweetened bottled waters, both still and carbonated, have continued to dominate their segment of the U.S. water and soft drink market. In 1991, France was responsible for 60 percent of unsweetened water imports and 34 percent of all water and soft drink imports. Canada had 24 percent of the unsweetened water imports, mainly with Clearly Canadian, and 42 percent of carbonated soft drinks. Due to the cost of shipping and distribution, imported products generally have been more expensive than domestically produced drinks and can be found at the luxury end of the U.S. market.

RESEARCH AND TECHNOLOGY

Advances in computer technology and automation improved all aspects of the soft drink manufacturing industry from inventory control to ''smart'' vending machines. Those companies with computerized operations have found both increased profitability and improved product quality. One example of a computerized system is a plant-wide automated measurement system used in some syrup manufacturing plants. Working with a personal computer, the automated system can measure nearly every important segment of beverage production, including syrup usage, Brix count (percent sugar) and beverage carbonation. Other system checks include monitoring the purification system for failures, and checking the warehouse temperature for the precise dew point. ''By keeping much closer control on all critical process variables, we (Abex Beverage Corporation) have been able over time to significantly improve yields, while also increasing the quality and consistency of our product,'' reported Randy Mostert, Abex production manager, in *Beverage World.*

Another technological advancement can be found on the user-end of the soft drink industry with the ''smart'' vending machines. These products use computerized components that keep track of stock supplies, sales patterns, breakdowns, and other conditions. ''Bottlers are looking for ways to increase revenues and reduce their costs,'' Bill Astin, senior VP/sales and marketing at the Vendo Co., told *Beverage Industry.* ''This improved technology allows them to do just that.''

General Programming Inc. introduced a wireless communications package called Vending Manager. This program allows vending machines to place orders as they are required, rather than have someone manually check the stock level. ''Loss of sales from a stock-out situation or out-of order situations will be eliminated, as machines will immediately notify the dispatcher of their status,'' said H.O. Bransom, president of General Programming Inc., in *Beverage Industry.*

Claiming that it could be the wave of the future, Coca-Cola USA already has begun to test market their own version of the smart vending machine called the Generation II, manufactured by Royal Vendors. ''With the GII, it [collecting data] is as simple as plugging a hand-held computer into the vendor controller, or keying the LED readout to deliver the information for the route person . . .,'' said Ray Steeley, president of Royal Vendors, in *Beverage Industry.*

The final outcome of computerized operations eventually will be the paperless warehouse, where computers, robotics, and electronic information transmission will control all operations. "Computer control gives instant information on the whereabouts of any material within the system," said Jim Larsen, VP of Eaton-Kenway, the company that installed a real-time management system (along with Operations Management Inc.) in Coca-Cola Enterprises Market Service Center in Cincinnati, Ohio, in 1991. "Those who use a real-time communications system in the warehouse also report better inventory control, faster truck check-in and check-out, better stock rotation in the distribution center and elimination of truck load errors," added Norand Corporation executive Tom Miller in *Beverage Industry.*

FURTHER READING

"Beverages—Pepsi (Fact Sheet)." Somers, NY: PepsiCo, Inc., 1993.

Browder, Seanna. "Starbucks Does Not Live By Coffee Alone." *Business Week,* 5 August 1996.

"The Coca-Cola Company Annual Report." Atlanta: The Coca-Cola Company, 1993.

"The Coca-Cola Company: A Brief Profile of a Worldwide Business." Atlanta: The Coca-Cola Company, 1993.

"Crystal Pepsi to Roll in North America." Somers, NY: Pepsi-Cola Company, 8 December 1992.

"Dr Pepper/Seven Up Companies, Inc. Annual Report." Dallas: Dr Pepper/Seven Up Companies, 1992.

"Dr Pepper/Seven-Up Companies, Inc. Goes Public." *Clockdial,* Spring 1993.

"The Economic Impact of the Industry." National Soft Drinks Association. Washington, D.C.

Flaherty, Francis. "Pepsi's $500 Million for Poland." *New York Times,* 15 August 1993.

"The 49th Annual Report on the American Industry." *Forbes,* 13 January, 1997

General Business File. University of Michigan Kresge Library Online Database. February 1997.

Guyette, James E. "Vending Smart, Bottlers Can Profit from High-Tech Breakthroughs," *Beverage Industry,* January 1993.

Hays, Laurie. "Building a Market: Amid Russian Turmoil, Coca-Cola Is Placing a Bet On the Future." *Wall Street Journal,* 6 April, 1993.

Jaroff, Leon. "A Thirst for Competition." *Time,* 1 June, 1992.

Moffett, Matt. "A Mexican War Heats Up for Cola Giants." *Wall Street Journal,* 20 April, 1993.

"More Fun Facts." National Soft Drinks Association. Washington, DC.

Mostert, Randy. "Not by the Manual." *Beverage World,* October 1992.

"Nestea Ice Tea Launched." *Beverage Dynamics,* March 1992.

Oman, Bruce. "From the Bottom Up." *Beverage World,* January 1993.

"PepsiCo, An Overview." Somer, NY: PepsiCo, Inc., 1993.

Prince, Greg W. "In Hot Water." *Beverage World,* March 1995.

Prince, Greg W., and Eric Sfiligoj. "The Beverage Market Index for 1993." *Beverage World,* May 1993.

———. "A League of Their Own." *Beverage World,* March 1993.

———. "Reality Drinks." *Beverage World,* September 1994.

Sanborn, Stephen. "Soft Drink Industry." *Value Line Investment Survey,* 20 August, 1993.

Sfiligoj, Eric. "Alive and Fizzing." *Beverage World,* August 1992.

———. "The Big Get Smaller." *Beverage World,* January 1996.

———. "Bottled Water." *Beverage World,* May 1995.

———. "Fruit Beverages." *Beverage World,* May 1995.

———. "Is Gatorade a Sleeping Giant?" *Beverage World,* August 1992.

———. "Soft Drinks." *Beverage World,* May 1995.

———. "Sports Drinks." *Beverage World,* May 1995.

———. "Time and Tide." *Beverage World,* October 1995.

"Soft Drink Facts." National Soft Drinks Association. Washington, DC.

Standard & Poor's Industry Surveys 1993. New York: Standard & Poor's, 1993.

Tougas, Jane Grant. "Coke and Pepsi Go New Age." *Beverage Dynamics,* July/August 1993.

———. "Go With The Flow." *Beverage Dynamics,* June 1993.

———. "New Age Beverages Go Mainstream." *Beverage Dynamics,* July/August 1993.

Ursin, Cheryl. "Water, Water, Everywhere." *Beverage Dynamics,* March 1992.

Walker, Tracey L. "Warehousing . . . A Paperless Trek Through Time and Space." *Beverage Industry,* July 1992.

Walsh, Matt. "Juice Wars." *Forbes,* 11 April 1994

Zimmerman, Martin. "Cadbury Raises Dr Pepper Stake." *Dallas Morning News,* 21 August 1993.

—Catherine A. Quagliana, updated by Visi Tilak

SIC 2087

FLAVORING EXTRACTS AND FLAVORING SYRUPS, NOT ELSEWHERE CLASSIFIED

This category includes establishments primarily engaged in manufacturing flavoring extracts, syrups, powders, and related products, not elsewhere classified. The products are generally used at soda fountains or during the manufacture of soft drinks, as well as for adding color to baked products and confectioneries. Establishments primarily engaged in manufacturing chocolate syrup are classified in **SIC 2066: Chocolate and Cocoa Products.**

INDUSTRY SNAPSHOT

While most foods have some flavor, certain agents can enhance the taste of these foods. These products encompass a wide range of materials that can be used alone or mixed into a blend. Substances used for flavoring "are those predominately purchased for flavoring contributions rather than functional characteristics," Kraft Food Ingredients marketing director Russ Williams told *Food Product Design.*

The $3-billion global flavors market is estimated to grow at 6 percent a year to 2001. The continued growth of the beverage industry—especially drinks such as Snapple and prepared iced teas—have helped grow the flavors industry. In fact, some 20,000 new flavors, colors, or varieties of new products were introduced in 1995.

Consumer trends continue to focus on natural ingredients and products that are perceived as "healthy." Medicinal ingredients such as ginseng and garlic have become more commonplace. Tropical flavors also have regained popularity, and have been most effective when mixed with a more-established fruit flavor, such as kiwi strawberry.

The flavors industry began to focus on Asia in the 1990s for both its ethnic tastes and expansion into the consumer market. As the middle class grows in Asia, so does the demand for western-style beverage such as prepared juices and teas.

Approximately 100 companies produce flavors in the United States. Of these, about 11 companies account for almost two-thirds of the flavor industry's sales to beverage and food processors. New York-based International Flavors & Fragrances remains the flavor industry leader in the United States and throughout the world.

Colorants continue to be one of the smallest segments of the food additives industry. With $245 million in 1991 sales, the segment was projected to reach $268 million annually by 1996. The natural colorants, mainly caramel color used in cola drinks, have dominated the industry with $155 million in sales annually. Synthetic colorants also have been used largely by the beverage industry, followed by usage in pet food, confections and gums, and dry mixes. Financial concerns led the colorant industry into major consolidations, leaving four major suppliers in the United States: Warner-Jenkinson, Colorcon, Hilton-Davis, and Compton & Knowles.

ORGANIZATION AND STRUCTURE

Flavoring manufacturers, sometimes called "flavor houses," create extracts, syrups, powders, and other forms of flavoring materials. These manufacturers work with natural base ingredients purchased from suppliers throughout the world. The manufacturers' dependence on natural sources leaves the flavor chemicals open to price fluctuation due to the availability and cost of the raw materials. Once processed, flavoring ingredients are sold to soft drink companies and other makers of processed foods.

Flavor manufacturers and food producers cooperated increasingly in research and development efforts to create new food products. Flavor producers also provide technical support on flavor issues, especially with the beverage industry. Flavor houses custom tailor flavors, relying heavily on work in application laboratories. "Each flavor is so application-specific that flavor companies and product developers must work closely together with flavor chemists to make it work," Marcia Sprague, vice-president of Merlin Development, told *Prepared Foods.*

Although the starting materials may be of natural origin, all flavoring materials are processed in some manner. The distillation process uses hot water or steam to extract the aromatic materials from the flavoring materials. The quality of the flavor depends on the raw materials and the process. The product derived from this process is called a volatile or essential oil.

Extraction is used to obtain characteristic flavoring attributes provided by non-volatiles. Organic solvents are used to dissolve volatile and nonvolatile compounds from the natural starting material. After removing the solvent, usually with a high vacuum process, the flavoring compounds remain. An extracted flavor often is fractionated into many parts and only certain ones are selected for the final flavor.

Extraction and distillation remain important methods for obtaining natural flavor components. Types of extracted/distilled flavor components are essential oils, aromatic fractions of the plant, oleoresins (which are extracts without volatiles), standardized oleoresins (added with extra essential oils), and concentrated oils (which are essential oils fractionated to a specific degree of concentration).

The flavoring industry worked closely with the Food and Drug Administration (FDA), primarily through the efforts of industry trade association Flavor Extract Manufacturers Association (FEMA). FEMA has been participating in the development of the Nutritional Labeling and Education Act of 1990. This legislation mandated that producers detail the ingredients used in processed food formulations. This act was implemented in May 1993.

BACKGROUND AND DEVELOPMENT

Development of the modern flavor industry occurred in the last 50 years. Some of the earliest flavors were manufactured by extraction during the 1940s, but by the 1950s and 1960s the industry moved toward the use of synthetic flavor compounds as flavoring agents. By the 1970s, "natural" began to be a selling point and methods were sought to develop pure, natural chemicals. One problem with these natural extracts was that the raw materials varied in taste and intensity. However, the modern flavor industry resolved this issue by compounding natural flavor chemicals rather than using the extracts as final flavors. This procedure provided food manufacturers with consistent flavors.

CURRENT CONDITIONS

The global flavor market, estimated at $3 billion, is expected to grow at the rate of 6 percent from 1996 to 2001. Growth of the flavor industry has been carried on the shoulders of the beverage sector—a segment that already represents $1 billion of the overall flavor market—and is expected to continue at a 6 to 8 percent clip, according to Michael Goodman, director of research publications at Decision Resources. This growth is based on continued consumer demand for alternative beverages, including still and carbonated flavored waters, ready-to-drink iced teas, and fruit beverages.

Flavor companies claimed that consumers wanted more choices and product diversity. In response, 20,076 new flavors, colors, or varieties of new products were introduced in 1995, according to New Product News (NPN), a Chicago-based new product tracking firm.

Consumers also had a growing interest in natural flavors and healthful drinks. In a survey of juice manufacturers, bottlers, and soft drink franchises, 74 percent said they planned to increase their use of natural flavors, according to Beverage Industry. Around 44 percent said they planned to increase the use of lemon. Use of orange and lime will rise from 43 and 38 percent of those surveyed, respectively. Medicinal ingredients such as ginseng, garlic, and calcium also became popular ingredients. Growth for this subsection of healthy, energy drinks was expected to at least match overall beverage growth.

Another major trend in flavorings was the return of tropical fruit flavorings. "But consumers are more educated and tropicals are no longer just pineapple, coconut and banana," said Diane Barrera, in Beverage Industry. "Consumers now know lychee, guanabana and such."

Flavor experts report that while passion fruit and guava once were among the trendiest tropicals, kiwi and mango topped the list in the mid-1990s. Mango, in particular, is a rising star, according to Dave Watkins. He points out that tropical flavors have the advantage of being perceived as both refreshing and healthful, as reported in Food Processing.

"Combining tropicals with more familiar fruit flavors has become an effective strategy for broadening their appeal," says Paulette Lanzoff in Food Processing. Popular combinations include tangerine, mango melon, and kiwi strawberry.

Asian cuisine seemed to also be gaining greater attention. At the Institute of Food Technology (IFT96), no fewer than ten flavor companies featured beverages at their booths with an Asian taste. These ranged from apple ginger cider tea from Systems Bio-Industries (SBI) to exotic fruit/flower combinations like strawberry chamomile and raspberry-hibiscus from Beck Flavors.

INDUSTRY LEADERS

The flavor producing companies have become larger and are based more multinationally, while using a smaller sales force and a leaner corporate staff. Specific information related to job descriptions or other work force information was closely guarded due to the competitive and rather secretive nature of the flavor industry. In the United States, International Flavors and Fragrances (IFF) was the leader, followed by Givaudan-Roure Corporation, Tastemaker and Universal Flavor.

International Flavors and Fragrances (IFF) is a leading creator and manufacturer of flavors and fragrances used by other companies to impart or improve the flavor or fragrance of various consumer products. The company has more than 80,000 recipes on file, with most of the flavors sold primarily to the makers of dairy, meats, and other processed foods, beverages, snacks, and savory foods.

As the makers of Halston and Calvin Klein's Eternity perfumes, IFF has been a well known leader within the fragrance market. By 2000, current sales split between flavors and fragrances is expected to shift toward the flavor segment. Industry analysts have projected that this shift will bring in $1 billion in flavor sales out of the company's total estimate of $1.7 billion in sales. This shift to flavors will be backed by stronger growth in traditional markets along with ventures into booming new regions.

Approximately 69 percent of IFF sales has been from overseas, providing a strong position for the company in a growing global economy. IFF reported strong sales in the early 1990s in Argentina, Brazil, China, and Indonesia. Overall, these countries accounted for total expansion level for flavors of 14 percent. For China, IFF reported $15 million worth of sales for its 51-percent-owned flavor joint venture, its 80-percent-owned aroma chemical operation and a wholly owned fragrance unit.

Universal Flavor manufactures beverage and food flavors in liquid and dry form, as well as fruit and specialty flavor ingredient systems for dairy and baking applications. In the North American flavor market, Universal Flavor gained an 18 percent market share, compared to IFF's 13 percent. In the rest of the world, IFF is the industry leader, with an estimated 13 percent of the market, while Universal Flavor has a 7 percent share, tying it for fifth place in the industry. Universal Flavor has manufacturing and processing centers in three states in the United States. It also operates 14 color and flavor plants in 11 countries and has investments in 16 companies that operate yeast and allied product facilities in 12 foreign countries.

Universal Flavor's Color Division accounted for 14 percent of sales and 18 percent of operating income in 1993. The division supplied synthetic and natural colors to food processors (80 percent of sales) and cosmetic and pharmaceutical manufacturers (20 percent). In the color field, Universal Flavor holds a leading market share in North America, with a 44 percent share of the market, as well as holding an estimated 16 percent share internationally.

Tastemaker was started by one of the most publicized mergers in the flavors industry, with the combination of IMCERA's Mallinckrodt Specialty Chemicals Company (Fries and Fries) and Hercules PFW Flavors and Citrus Specialty Business in a 50/50 joint venture. Becoming the fifth largest flavor house in the world, the new company adopted the name Tastemaker and is headquartered in Cincinnati, Ohio.

AMERICA AND THE WORLD

The strongest area of growth for the flavors industry was expected to occur in the Pacific Rim countries, largely due to consumer trends. Studies showed that consumption of flavored products is directly proportional to per-capita income. As the middle class grows in Asian countries, demand for Western-style beverages was likely to gain ground. Growth in Asia was projected to have the ability to drive flavor growth higher well into the next century. Expansion into Asia also would allow companies easier access to newer, more exotic flavors.

RESEARCH AND TECHNOLOGY

New technologies, particularly in extraction techniques and applications of biotechnology were being applied in the flavors industry, which was expected to post dramatic results in the coming years. Biotechnology is the most advanced of the new flavor technologies, and will be used to create "natural flavors of the future."

The flavors industry claims that commercially growing an entire plant for a single flavor molecule is unnecessary and wasteful. Plant cell culture technology allows scientists to grow only the part of the plant that contains the desired flavor molecule.

Cost advantages of this type of cell manufacture are numerous. According to Decision Resources, yields would be increased per unit mass of plant tissue; processing costs would be reduced since very little plant tissue needs to be removed; and the quality of the extracted oil would be higher. This technology should also save time because it should be possible to grow or generate exotic plants in a short time span compared with traditional plant growing methods.

FURTHER READING

"A 'Berry' Exciting Flavor Forecast." *Beverage World,* April 1990.

Best, Daniel. "Flavor Industry Survey Targets Customer Needs." *Prepared Foods,* April 1990.

"Colorful Growth." *Chemical Marketing Reporter,* 15 June 1992.

Cummins, R. J. "Universal Flavors Company Report." Wertheim Schroder & Co., 30 October 1992.

Fitzell, Phil. "Back To Nature." *Beverage World,* August 1990.

Floreno, Anthony. "Flavors Taste Brave New World: Expansion into Asia and Beverage are Driving Growth and New Product Development, While Biotechnology Holds Promise for the Future. (Food Additives '96). *Chemical Marketing Reporter,* 24 June 1996.

"Food Additives-Worldwide." *Speciality Chemicals, SRI International,* November 1988.

Gallagher, Matthew. "Tasting Success: Global Producers of Flavors and Fragrances Are Shifting Emphasis Towards the Flavor Side of their Operations. (Food Additives '94) (Industry Overview)." *Chemical Marketing Reporter,* 27 June 1994.

"International Flavors & Fragrances 1992 Annual Report." New York, NY: International Flavors & Fragrances, 1993.

Kuhn, Mary Ellen. "Flavoring Forecast: Anything Goes! (trends in the flavors and seasonings business). *Food Processing,* August 1995.

Kuntz, Lynn A. "Flavors in Use and Practice: Tapping the Genie in the Bottle." *Food Product Design,* August 1993.

La Bell, Fran. "Beyond Refreshment: Flavors Influence Moods." *Food Processing,* October 1991.

———"The Launching of McCormick and Wild." *Beverage World,* August 1990.

———"Past, Present and Future: 50 Years of Flavors & Spices." *Food Processing,* October 1990.

Roman, Monica. "Beef-Fat Flavor May Not Sound Glamorous, But . . . " *Business Week,* 11 March 1991.

Sfiligoj, Eric. "A World of Possibilities. (New flavors at the 1996 Institute of Food Technology Show)." *Beverage World,* August 1996.

———. "Fit to a Tea." *Beverage World,* December 1992.

"Shared Rule." *Beverage World,* April 1993.

"Title Wave of Trends: No Single Flavor Trend Dominates the Beverage Industry." *Beverage Industry,* November 1996.

Topfer, Kurt. "Adding Spice: Food Additives 92 Special Report." *Chemical Marketing Reporter,* 15 June 1992.

Wilkes, Ann Przybyla. "Flavor Development Combining Creativity with Modern Science." *Food Product Design,* September 1992.

Wittenburg, B. "Universal Flavors Corporation Company Report." Dain, Bosworth, Inc., 1992.

Wolf, A. E. "Colour My World." *Beverage World,* September 1991.

—Catherine A. Quaglina

CANNED AND CURED FISH AND SEAFOODS

This category covers establishments primarily engaged in cooking and canning seafood products such as fish, shrimp, oysters, clams, and crab or in curing seafood products by means such as smoking, salting or drying. It also includes manufacturers of seafood soups, chowders, stews, broths, and juices. Establishments primarily engaged in preparing fresh fish or shucking and packing fresh oysters in nonsealed containers are classified in **SIC 2092: Prepared Fresh or Frozen Fish and Seafoods.**

INDUSTRY SNAPSHOT

Retail sales of canned fish and seafood continued to decrease in the mid-1990s, with postings at $1.854 billion in 1995, down 3.2 percent from $1.916 billion in 1994. Although canned tuna continued to be the most popular form of canned seafood consumed in the United States, sales fell from $1.459 billion in 1994 to $1.419 billion in 1995. Sales of canned salmon, the industry's second most popular product, dropped 6.0 percent from $298 million in 1994 to $280 million in 1995.

Other products included six different species of clam in East Coast production centers located in Maine, Maryland, Massachusetts, and Florida; and on the West Coast areas in Oregon, Washington, and Alaska. East Coast canners principally packed hard and soft shell clams, while most West Coast production involved razor clams, which were most often sold as minced clam meat. Other types of mollusks (soft-bodied shellfish) canned in the United States included oysters, mussels, abalone, cockles, donax, snails, and squid.

Per capita consumption of fisheries products peaked in 1987 at 16.2 pounds, but fell to 15 pounds in the mid-1990s. Fresh and frozen products represented 9.7 pounds, canned products represented 4.9 pounds, and cured products only 0.3 pounds. Although industry observers noted a slight increase in per capita consumption of fresh and frozen products in 1992 (up to 9.9 pounds), consumption decreased in the mid-1990s. Continued declines within the canned category, which fell to 4.6 pounds in 1992, rebounded slightly in 1995 with a 0.2 pound increase. Per capita consumption of cured seafood products remained at 0.3 pounds per person, a level unchanged since 1980 but reduced from 0.4 pounds in the late 1970s and 0.5 pounds in 1974.

Although government projections anticipated stable catches for most commercial fisheries species through the mid-1990s, problems attributed to overfishing were threatening some individual stocks. Tuna catches declined, as did takes of some varieties of salmon. In 1992 Alaskan salmon fishermen reported reduced catches of pink salmon, but increased takes of sockeye salmon. The 1995 net of 50 million salmon by Alaskan fishereries far surpassed industry estimates and caused some to speculate that the rising number would drive prices down to the detriment of the individual fisherman.

BACKGROUND AND DEVELOPMENT

Fish curing is one of the oldest industries in North America. Even before permanent European settlements had been established, fishermen were harvesting cod and other species off the northeastern coastline of the American continent. Fish were preserved and prepared for marketing by salting. According to Roy E. Martin of the National Fisheries Institute, ''As early as 1580 more than three hundred ships from Europe were salting cod in this area.''

New England colonists depended on salted cod and smoked herring for food and as trade items. During the seventeenth and eighteenth centuries, cured fish products made major contributions to the economies of New England and eastern Canada. Disputes over fishing rights and restraints on trade contributed to the political climate leading up to the Revolutionary War. Martin, writing in *The Seafood Industry,* stated, ''The English Parliament in 1775 prohibited the New England colonies from trading directly with foreign countries and prevented New England vessels from fishing on the banks off Newfoundland, in the Gulf of St. Lawrence, and on the coasts of Labrador and Nova Scotia where they had been accustomed to fishing. This restriction meant ruin to the New England fish-curing industry, and the edict was one cause of the Revolutionary War.''

Another type of preservation, pickling, was also used commercially with fish and molluscan products through the 1800s. Pickled and cured fish products continued to be major industries until the processes were gradually supplanted by canning technology and by innovations enabling fresh and frozen seafood products to be delivered to inland markets.

During the early years of the nineteenth century, the first canned seafood products appeared in the United States. Initial offerings included salmon, lobsters, and oysters. Of these three, the most popular, and first to be canned on an industrial scale, was the Chesapeake Bay oyster. Canning technology enabled the sale of oysters to inland people who had previously been unable to purchase them. As canning technology improved, other products were added to the menu. Sardines, for example, were first successfully canned in Maine around the middle of the nineteenth century. As more products became available, consumer acceptance increased. The Civil War also helped the new industry gain favor by introducing many soldiers to canned products.

The 1860s saw the beginning and rapid expansion of canning operations for Pacific salmon. From a small beginning in California, salmon canners spread north into Washington and Canada. The first canneries opened in Alaska in 1878. The 1870s also brought the first menhaden cannery. It opened on Long Island in 1872. Canned fish cakes (cod and haddock products) were introduced in 1878. By 1880, other canned items included mackerel, clams, and crabs. U.S. production of canned products in 1880 was valued at $15 million. Finnan haddie (smoked haddock) was first offered commercially in 1890. ''Salad Fish,'' canned flaked meat from cod and haddock, was introduced in 1898. Other turn-of-the-century products included pickled sturgeon, carp, and shark meat.

During the early years of the twentieth century, the sardine canning industry moved from the East Coast to the West Coast. Canneries sprang up in the Monterey Bay area of California. As sardine canning operations expanded, demand for fish exceeded availability. To help increase catches, new fishing methods were developed using a special type of net, called a lampara net. Lampara nets encircled entire schools of fish and yielded large harvests. Canners also continued bringing new products to American consumers. Items added during the early years of the twentieth century included shad, alewives, and tuna. The first commercial offering of tuna was made in 1909 by the Southern California Fish Company. Only albacore tuna was used, and the first year's production equaled 2,000 cases.

In the following decade many major participants in the U.S. canned and cured seafood industry were founded. Ocean Beauty Seafoods was founded in 1910, Ward's Cove Packing Company in 1912, and in 1914 Peter Pan Seafoods and Van Camp Seafoods were established. By 1915, only six years after the first commercial offering of albacore, California processors packed 237,265 cases. In the Monterey Bay area, the sardine cannery industry was well established and continued growing. In 1918 nine sardine canning plants in Monterey packed a total of 1.4 million cases.

The 1920s saw expansion of Pacific mackerel canneries and increased activity in the Alaskan salmon industry. By the end of the decade, 159 canneries were operating in Alaska. Improvements in cold storage technology enabled canners to receive and process larger quantities of fish. Refined fishing techniques developed during the 1920s helped fishermen meet ever-growing demand. Purse seines, a type of large net closed by a drawstring-like apparatus, were capable of dropping to a depth of 100 feet and enclosing an area 100 feet across. Newer boats were built to operate hundreds of miles offshore and carry up to 150 tons of fish.

Catches of albacore, however, began decreasing during the 1920s and tuna canners consolidated. In 1926 albacore catches plummeted. As a substitute, Van Camp Seafood Company offered yellowfin tuna and marketed it as ''Fancy Light Meat Tuna.'' Sardine catches continued in large numbers and canneries prospered through the 1930s and early 1940s. Owners expanded operations by adding fish by-products such as poultry and livestock feed, fertilizer, and fish oil to their product lines.

During World War II the canning industry faced several challenges. Tuna boats were requisitioned by the Maritime Commission and by the U.S. Navy, primarily for use in delivering supplies. Fish harvests were reduced as fishermen enlisted or were drafted into armed service. Anti-submarine efforts along the Pacific coast restricted fleet movement. And inside the canneries, labor shortages persisted, intensified by a governmental policy of moving Japanese workers to internment camps. Despite the problems, however, the war years proved to be profitable ones for tuna and other fish packers because of the heavy demand spurred by government requisitions for canned products to feed troops.

During the second half of the 1940s, sardine catches began declining and forced canneries, one after another, to close. By 1952, Monterey's sardine era had ended. Industry analysts have attributed the declining sardine catches to various causes including pollution, climate and current changes, natural fish cycles, and fished-out stocks. Although the 1950s saw the demise of many sardine canners, other segments of the industry prospered. Larger fishing boats traveled greater distances from shore and some companies opened canneries in more distant locations. For example, in 1954, the Van Camp Seafood Company opened canning facilities in Pago Pago (Samoan Islands). The plant received fish from Japan, Korea, and Taiwan. It employed 600 people and averaged 145 tons of production daily. The modernization of fishing techniques continued to improve catches. By 1961, most commercial fishing vessels shifted from hook-and-line gear to

mechanized purse seining. By the 1980s, tuna fishermen were using seines measuring up to 4,800 feet by 702 feet that were capable of hauling 200 ton catches.

These large nets, however, drew criticism because the seines indiscriminately captured all fish swimming in a school. For reasons not completely understood, dolphins often schooled with yellowfin tuna and reports of dolphin mortality increased. To help alleviate problems associated with dolphin mortality, the Marine Mammal Protection Act of 1972 banned the importation of fish and fish products caught in ways that posed excessive risks to ocean mammals. Another piece of legislation, the Boxer-Biden Dolphin Protection Consumer Information Act of 1991 was passed to govern the conditions under which fishing operations could operate if their products carried a ''dolphin-safe'' label. In 1990 three major U.S. tuna canners, Star-Kist (owned by H. J. Heinz), Bumble Bee Seafoods, and Van Camp Seafood (''Chicken of the Sea'' brand) promised to provide dolphin-safe tuna.

At the close of the twentieth century, the U.S. government, backed by several mainstream environmental groups, was poised to rescind the embargo on tuna caught by boats not adhering to the Marine Mammal Protection Act.

CURRENT CONDITIONS

At the close of the 1990s, tuna fish continued to be the top-selling product in the canned and cured fish and seafood industry. According to a *U.S. News and World Report-CNN Poll,* of the 87 percent of Americans who reported eating tuna, 76 percent prefer the canned variety. On the other hand, canned salmon decreased in popularity significantly during the 1990s. The decrease prompted the Alaska Seafood Marketing Institute to ask the federal government to purchase canned salmon surpluses for use in public schools and prisons.

Per capita consumption of canned sardines was also declining. In 1972 it totaled 0.4 pounds. During much of the 1980s, it stood at 0.3 pounds and in 1991 and 1992 measured only 0.2 pounds. In 1992 United Food Processors (UFP), a California sardine canning operation, declared bankruptcy. Company owners hoped to enter into a joint venture or partnership with investors who could provide the capital necessary to modernize their facility and install an oval-tin sardine processing line.

Several reasons were cited for the decreased consumption of canned salmon and sardines. Primarily, seafood products faced stiff competition from other food items, particularly fast food. The declining number of advertising dollars spent by major producers was also seen as a contributor. In 1975, an average of $0.31 per case was spent on promotions. That figure decreased to $0.10 per case in the early 1990s. The switch to a smaller tuna can size, from 6.5 ounces to 6.0 ounces, also contributed to the decreased consumption statistics.

Technological advances in making fish products shelf stable enabled the development of new items such as smoked oysters and gourmet smoked salmon. Mackerel, offered as a smoked product, faced an uncertain future. California fish landings diminished during the early years of the 1990s. Fishermen and processors voiced concern about the possibility of reductions in quotas, which would limit availability.

INDUSTRY LEADERS

One of the largest companies involved in canning and curing fish and seafood products was Trident Seafoods Corp. Trident, a privately owned company headquartered in Seattle, Washington, was founded in 1973. Trident operated as a vertically integrated harvesting, processing, and marketing company.

In 1995 Trident's sales were estimated at $540 million. The company employed 600 permanent workers and 4,000 during its peak season. Trident operated floating processing vessels and processing plants in Alaska and Washington. A company spokesman estimated that the company's product mix in the 1990s was 80 percent frozen products and 20 percent canned. Trident's canned salmon was offered under several brands: Faust, Lily, Prelate, Rubinstein's, Sea-Alaska, Tulip, and Whitney's. The highest-volume species canned was pink salmon. According to information provided by Trident, most of the canned salmon produced in the United States was packed in 14.75 ounce cans. The second most popular size was 7.5 ounce cans. Other common sizes were 3.75 ounces and four pounds.

Another major participant in the seafood canning industry was Van Camp Seafoods Company with 1995 sales figures of $440 million and 2,700 employees. Van Camp was founded by a father-and-son team, Frank and Gilbert Van Camp. The company processed its first load of albacore tuna on June 6, 1914. Van Camp pioneered many of the technologies and practices that developed as the tuna industry evolved, including cold storage, advanced fishing methods, mechanized production, and "tendering," the practice of buying fish from boats at sea and ferrying them back to the cannery. Another Van Camp accomplishment was the establishment of Van Camp Laboratories to extract vitamins from fish scraps, organs, and oils. Van Camp adopted its "Chicken of the Sea" mermaid logo in

1953. During the 1960s the company was the largest canner of an advertised brand of tuna in the United States. In addition to its tuna line, the "Chicken of the Sea" brand includes canned salmon products. "Chicken of the Sea" was the first to offer skinless/boneless canned salmon.

Other industry leaders included Icicle Seafoods with $240 million in sales for 1995 and 2,500 employees; and Star-Kist with $200 million in sales and 1,500 employees.

WORK FORCE

According to figures released by the U.S. Department of Commerce, employment within the canned and cured fish and seafoods industry fell to 6,700 in 1987, a 52 percent drop from the 13,900 employed in 1982. However, in 1995, that number increased to 14,000. States with the highest employment were California, Maine, Alaska, and Washington.

FURTHER READING

"Around the Coasts." *National Fisherman,* October 1996.

"Alaska Canned Salmon." Juneau: Alaska Seafood Marketing Institute, 1988.

Chicken of the Sea Tuna and Salmon. St. Louis: Van Camp Seafood Company, Inc., 1988.

"Consumers Expenditures Survey." *Supermarket News,* September 1996.

Hutchinson, William. "Net Gains." *Supermarket News,* 20 September 1993.

Kronman, Mick. "Outlook: Wetfish Cannery Closure Bursts Sardine Bubble." *National Fisherman,* October 1992.

Lang, Linda. "Seafood Processors." *Puget Sound Business Journal,* 29 May 1992.

Litwak, David, and Nancy Maline. "Fifth Annual Seafood Operations Review." *Supermarket Business,* November 1992.

Martin, Roy E., and George J. Flick, eds. *The Seafood Industry.* New York: Van Nostrand Reinhold, 1990.

McDowell, Eric, and Jim Calvin. *Alaska Seafood Industry Study: A Summary.* Juneau, AK: The McDowell Group, March 1989.

McMath, Robert. "Fishy Snacks and Franks Swim Into Stores." *Adweek's Marketing Week,* 30 July 1990.

Salmon 2000: Yearbook 1993. Juneau, AK: Alaska Seafood Marketing Institute, 1993.

"Trident Seafoods Corporation." *From the Source to the Plate.* Seattle, WA: Trident.

"Tuna Without the Guilt." *Time.* 23 April 1990.

U.S. Bureau of the Census. *Statistical Abstract of the United States: 1992.* Washington: GPO, 1992.

U.S. Department of Commerce. International Trade Administration. *U.S. Industrial Outlook 1993.* Washington: GPO, 1994.

Warren, Brad. "Salmon Glut May Force Changes." *National Fisherman,* March 1996.

—Karen Bellenir, updated by Mary McNulty

SIC 2092

PREPARED FRESH OR FROZEN FISH AND SEAFOODS

This category covers establishments that prepare fish, seafoods, and other seafood preparations (such as shrimpcakes, crabcakes, fishcakes, chowders, stews, and stews), in fresh and raw or cooked frozen form. Prepared fresh fish are eviscerated or processed by removal of heads, fins, or scales. This industry also includes establishments primarily engaged in the shucking and packing of fresh oysters in nonsealed containers.

INDUSTRY SNAPSHOT

During the 1980s, health and diet concerns led American consumers to think about fish and seafoods in two ways. These years marked a significant trend towards higher levels of consumption of poultry, fish, and seafoods at the expense of red meat. But perennial worries about the quality of fish and seafoods, which swiftly lose their taste and freshness, were compounded by growing consumer knowledge about the potential harmful effects of pollution and the consequences of improper handling and storage. A *Consumer Reports* analysis in early 1992 found that much of the seafood consumed by Americans was often of poor quality. Reactions in the industry ranged from concern that the samples were not representative, to genuine uncertainty as to what the quality standards should be, and how best to achieve them. The lengthy chain of production separating harvested fish the consumer's plate made it difficult to determine which processes contributed to poor quality.

The fishing industry was also under attack from recreational fishers and environmental groups who charged that certain waters were being overfished. The Gulf Coast Conservation Association has been successful in pushing through legislation in Texas, Florida, Alabama, and Louisiana to prevent commercial fishers from destroying wetlands and endangering certain fish species. In noting the collapse of the Pacific anchovy fisheries and the 109 million tons of finfish

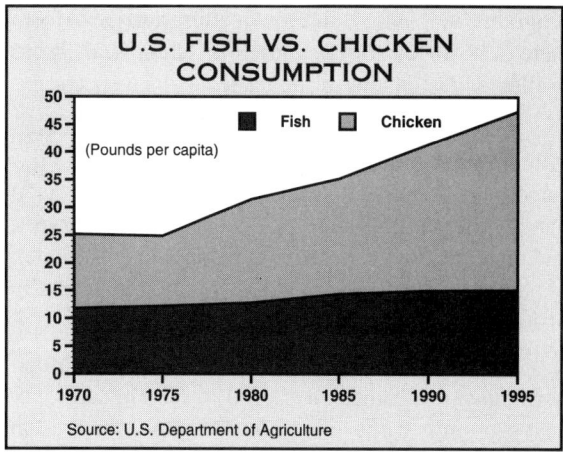

U.S. FISH VS. CHICKEN CONSUMPTION

Fish | Chicken

(Pounds per capita)

50
45
40
35
30
25
20
15
10
5
0

1970   1975   1980   1985   1990   1995

Source: U.S. Department of Agriculture

harvested in 1994, WorldWatch warned that continuing increases are dangerous. In *Science News,* Meryl Williams, director general of the International Center for Living Aquatic Resources Management, stated that 25 percent of the primary 200 fish stocks are overfished and another 38 percent are being fully exploited.

ORGANIZATION AND STRUCTURE

Small-scale processing plants were tied to local fleets that were in turn tied to specific stocks of fish that in many cases fluctuated dramatically, discouraging processors from expanding operations, developing new products, or adopting new technology. Those fleets not equipped for processing at sea were obliged to return to land at short intervals, rather than when full, so that their harvest could be processed while still fresh. The needs of processors and harvesters did not always agree: fleets were reluctant to harvest such bottomfish species as Alaska pollock, Pacific cod, flounder, and sablefish, although processors regarded them as a potentially lucrative source. In addition to an expansion of at-sea processing operations and a greater use of fish and shellfish raised by aquacultural means, vertical integration was seen as the key to a profitable restructuring of the American fish and seafoods processing industry. Some industry observers felt restructuring was necessary to bring about large-scale, sustained investment in underutilized species, greater speed to market, and the ability to respond to shortages and gluts.

A better program of inspection was regarded as a necessity for the future of the industry. While there was no mandatory inspection of fish and seafood by the federal government, processors, retailers, and wholesalers could pay for a U.S. Department of Commerce inspection. Approximately 10 percent of processors were participating in such voluntary inspection programs in 1992. But even in this restricted form there was no uniformity; three different seals were available, designating different levels of inspection.

Regulations at the state level differed from region to region but in general gave little protection to consumers. A majority of states required stores to keep records identifying the initial source, date of harvest, and the company responsible for shipping every batch of shellfish. But these records were often kept poorly or not at all.

By the mid-1990s, the rising incidence of seafood poisoning—an estimated 20,000 to 60,000 cases per year—prompted the Food and Drug Administration (FDA) to apply the Hazard Analysis and Critical Control Points (HACCP) program to the seafood industry. A final set of regulations was formulated in 1995 with compliance to begin in 1997.

Followed on a voluntary basis by other food industries since 1959, HACCP is a scientific and systematic method to monitor the microbiological, chemical, and physical safety of prepared foods. Under the plan, seafood distributors must identify any critical points at which their product's quality is endangered and then install safeguards. Although the regulations do not apply to fishing vessels or transporters, the processors are responsible for ensuring that the product reaches them in the purest form. For example, distributors are expected to only accept fish from government-approved waters.

Compliance with the HACCP program will be expensive for the industry: $70 to $160 million to institute and $40 to $80 million per year thereafter. However, the FDA says the cost will be offset by the reduced incidence of food poisoning, the nutritional benefits of more people eating seafood, and increased export income.

BACKGROUND AND DEVELOPMENT

Soon after World War II, American consumers began to rely increasingly on the convenience of fully or partially prepared fish and seafoods, often available in frozen form. These fish products were available with or without coatings of breading; batter coatings were introduced in the 1960s. Batter-fried fish and seafood reached the consumer only after an extensive preparation in which the product was dusted with flour, encased in batter, and then lightly fried to fix the batter and achieve specified standards of texture and quality.

Fish and seafood constituted about half of the frozen battered and breaded products consumed in the United States, the largest consumer of breaded fish and seafood in the world. The most frequently consumed type of coated seafood was precooked and raw portions of fish, followed by shrimp, fishcakes, and scallops. Among the breaded products most typically sold in frozen form were scallops, oysters, clam strips, clamcakes, and squid rings (calamari).

Freezing technology permitted great advances in an industry dependent on a product subject to rapid spoilage. However, not all species of fish and seafood responded well to freezing, often delicacies of texture and flavor could be lost. For instance, whereas crabmeat generally was found to freeze less well and have a briefer shelf life than many other types of fish and seafoods, king crab was discovered to lend itself rather well to freezing. Well-suited to shrimp, catfish, and halibut, the technique of rapid freezing proved especially effective because it minimized losses of texture and flavor by guaranteeing uniformity of freezing. The ''I.Q.F.'' marking, which referred to individually quick frozen products, thus became a selling point for the American consumer. The equipment used for this operation included automated loading and unloading units (mechanically or electronically controlled to adapt to the specific requirements of each type of product), and labor-intensive batch-freezing units.

The United States was for a long period the world leader in terms of its versatility in processing, handling, distributing, and marketing frozen fish and seafoods. It was also an early leader in deploying techniques for freezing catches aboard ship, yet lost its edge in the commercial application of this technology, which allowed fishing vessels to remain at sea for greater periods of time. Ships could remain at sea until their load was full instead of frequently returning to share to ensure the freshness of their catch.

CURRENT CONDITIONS

Already appealing by virtue of their convenience, prepared fish and seafoods gained popularity when dieticians began advising American consumers to eat less red meat and instead consume greater quantities of poultry and fish. Some analysts felt that the increasing consumption of fish and seafoods in the United States during the 1980s had reached a plateau of roughly 15 pounds per person annually. However, the U.S. Department of Commerce noted that the proportion of domestic landings used for human food in 1992 increased by 5 percent from 1991.

In fact, after rising to 17 pounds per capita in 1993, American consumption of seafood dropped back to 15 pounds in 1995. According to the National Marine Fisheries Service, a decrease in the consumption of fresh and frozen seafood accounted for this drop. On the other hand, consumption of canned seafood rose 0.2 pounds to 4.7 pounds per capita.

The continued demand for Alaskan salmon in the late 1990s raised speculation of a worldwide glut that would drive down prices. In 1995, 50 million salmon were caught by Alaskan commercial fishers.

A summary of a National Fisheries Institute report published in *Prepared Foods* noted that annual per capita consumption of fish and seafoods in America was forecast to reach 20 pounds in the year 2000, with consumption of shrimp alone increasing to one billion pounds (from 567 million pounds in 1989). It furthermore noted that demographic trends within the United States indicated growing numbers of Asian and Hispanic consumers whose diets have traditionally favored relatively high levels of fish and seafood. In addition, the National Restaurant Association predicted that by the year 2000 fish and seafood would constitute about 8 percent of total meat and group poultry consumption in America, compared to 7 percent in 1964.

INDUSTRY LEADERS

In the 1990s, 65 U.S. companies were involved in the processing of fish and seafoods. These companies ranged in size from tiny operations, employing a handful of workers and concentrating on a single species or type of preparation, to large businesses engaged in many other areas. Major companies in this industry include Gorton's, with 1,000 employees and $400 million in sales, King & Prince Seafood Corporation (800 employees, $120 million in sales), and Ore-Cal Corporation (100 employees, $90 million in sales).

WORK FORCE

According to the U.S. Department of Labor, little change in employment in the American fish and seafoods processing industry is expected through the year 2005, though there is likely to be a shift in the distribution of the work performed, with an increase of semiskilled workers for processing plants and a decrease in skilled workers for markets and other retail centers.

The skills most important to processors include good eye-hand coordination, manual dexterity, depth perception, and color discrimination, and these were usually acquired in apprenticeship programs or on the job, rather than in any formal educational settings. Work environments often require extended periods of standing for employees, as well as low temperatures needed to keep product fresh.

Aside from promotion to a supervisory position, employment in processing of fish and seafoods offers few career prospects. In this area, as in other areas of the fishing industry, wages are typically low, although there are some variances in salary scales based on geographic location.

AMERICA AND THE WORLD

In 1966 the United States was heavily dependent on imported frozen fish and seafoods, which made up about half of its supply. In the next few decades, however, the industry achieved a more equitable balance between imports and exports. Imports of processed fishery products reached $5.3 billion in 1992, while exports reached $3.2 billion. However, in 1995, fully 75 percent of the shrimp consumed by Americans was imported. In the eight-year period from 1987 to 1995, the number of Louisiana shrimping licenses dropped from 44,000 to 25,000.

RESEARCH AND TECHNOLOGY

According to *Frozen Food Digest,* between 1980 and 1990 the quantity of farm-raised processed catfish in the United States rose from 46 million pounds to 377 million pounds, and production of surimi also increased between 1987 and 1989 from 67 million pounds to 300 million pounds. Processing of both continued to rise during the 1990s. By 1995, catfish processing was up more than 22 percent. Surimi processing, while continuing to grow, showed signs of leveling off by mid-decade. The growth of catfish consumption partly reflected a substantial increase in aquaculture, which *Frozen Food Digest* noted was ''outpacing all other types of farming'' in the United States. The trend towards aquaculture was a significant one, not only because of the growing proportion of the U.S. supply of fish and seafood that it contributed, but also because it brought harvesting and processing into closer conjunction and thereby assured a higher and more consistent quality of product.

The Minaqua fish farm in Beckley, West Virginia has devised a method for raising trout and arctic char in abandoned coal mines. The pure mine water remains a steady 55 degrees Fahrenheit year-round, which the company claims is perfect for breeding. If the venture is successful, it could turn a landlocked state into fishing industry leader.

New processing and packaging technologies that extend the shelf life of fresh and prepared fish and seafoods are keys to growth in the processing industry. Other challenges facing this industry include developing seafood products that can be microwaved without any loss of crispness, and improving the overall quality of such products (which have been subject to unevenly distributed coatings and minor flaws in composition that substantially affect both cooking time and batter adhesion).

FURTHER READING

"Around the Coasts." *National Fisherman,* October 1996, 10.

Brown, Robert H. "Florida Has Its First Major Catfish Processor." *Feedstuffs,* 30 September 30 1991, 9.

Foodservice Industry Forecast. Washington: National Restaurant Association, 1990.

Garry, Michael. "Seafood Standoff." *Progressive Grocer,* March 1993, 85.

Hunter, Beatrice Trum. "Food for Thought." *Consumers' Research,* July 1996, 8.

Kummer, Corby. "Farmed Fish." *The Atlantic,* August 1992.

Martin, Roy E., and George J. Flick, eds. *The Seafood Industry.* New York: Osprey, 1990.

McGoodwin, James R. *Crisis in the World's Fisheries.* Stanford, CA: Stanford University Press, 1990.

"Struggling to Stay Afloat." *U.S. News and World Report,* 5 August 1996, 50.

Sullivan, Jeremiah J., and Per O. Heggelund. *Foreign Investment in the U.S. Fishing Industry.* Pacific Rim Research Series 3. Lexington, MA: D.C. Heath, 1979.

Warren, Brad. "Salmon Glut May Force Changes." *National Fisherman,* March 1996, 24.

Wold, Marjorie. "FMI Probes Food Safety." *Progressive Grocer,* March 1992, 7.

"Why Doesn't the U.S. Inspect More Fish?" *Consumer Reports,* February 1992, 113.

—Richard Hillyer, updated by Mary McNulty

SIC 2095

ROASTED COFFEE

This category covers establishments primarily engaged in roasting coffee and in manufacturing coffee concentrates and extracts in powdered, liquid, or frozen form, including freeze-dried. Coffee roasting by wholesale grocers is covered in **SIC 5149: Groceries and Related Products, Not Elsewhere Classified.**

INDUSTRY SNAPSHOT

In the early 1990s, coffee consumption continued to remain strong, with coffee shops maintaining their presence throughout the country. Roasters, small and large, continued to enjoy strong markets. Starbucks continues to expand with plans to add 2,000 stores by the year 2000. Other players moved to enter the specialty coffee market—Procter & Gamble acquired Millstone Coffee, a privately held firm that roasts and distributes gourmet, whole-bean coffee products to supermarkets in December 1995.

Coffee hasn't always enjoyed this popularity. Between 1970 and 1980, U.S. per capita consumption of coffee in gallons had dropped from 33.4 to 26.7, although it held steady at that approximate rate throughout the 1980s. At an estimated 1.75 cups, daily per capita consumption of coffee in 1991 was a far cry from that of the all-time high of 3.1 cups reached in 1962. The advent of specialty coffees seemed to signal a turnaround in the coffee industry. Having in past decades exported a taste for instant coffee, the United States began importing a demand for specialty coffees.

A nationwide rediscovery of coffee led to increased growth in this industry beginning in the late 1980s, with production growing from a level of $96 billion in 1986 to more than $110 billion in 1994. In early 1997 coffee futures soared due to heavy roaster buying—the biggest one-day gain since July 1994.

ORGANIZATION AND STRUCTURE

Due to a climate that cannot support coffee trees in areas other than Hawaii and Puerto Rico, U.S. production of coffee beans has been negligible. Instead the United States has become the largest importer of the beans, purchased from producing nations through traders. For this reason traders play an important role in the U.S. coffee industry, albeit one constrained by their obligation to serve the requirements of roasters. Thus the National Coffee Association, formed in the early 1970s, is dominated by the roasters.

Processing of coffee beans is performed by manufacturers that roast the beans for packaging. Also, roasters often further process the beans to be sold for brewing and instant coffee. At least until the mid-1980s, coffee produced in the United States was thought to be less superior than that of other countries. According to Michael Sivetz and Norman W. Desrosier in *Coffee Technology,* this was explained by the fact that many of the leading manufacturers were owned by multinational conglomerates: "Most of the bad features in handling coffee in the U.S.A. (and elsewhere too) are due to mass production and centralized marketing and sales. The indicated particular treatment of green, roast ground coffees and their brewing is in conflict with corporate mass production and selling policies. . . . Commercial aspects, that is profit-making, invariably override technical considerations and process technology."

BACKGROUND AND DEVELOPMENT

The U.S. coffee industry can be traced back to the seventeenth century, when coffeehouses, already quite popular in Europe, began to open in the colonies. Indeed, Revolutionary War strategy was often plotted in these establishments. At that point in time, only whole coffee beans were available, and these were sold from a barrel to be blended and ground in the home for boiling.

This method of preparing coffee proved its inconvenience during the Civil War, when transporting beans and grinders was quickly found to be unwieldy. As an alternative, coffee was made into a sort of concentrate by grinding it into a pulp that was fashioned into bricks and allowed to harden. This allowed soldiers to slice off an appropriate amount for boiling. In the meantime, however, entrepreneurs saw an opportunity. By roasting, blending, grinding, and packaging the coffee for sale, they offered consumers a welcome convenience.

Coffee beans are mainly categorized into two major varieties: arabica and robusta. Arabica beans are the most flavorful, and gourmet coffees are made with this type. Robusta beans are used in commercially packaged and instant coffees. Roasters store the purchased beans in silos until they are blended, which occurs immediately prior to roasting. Control of the blending process is usually done electronically, with preset percentages of the different varieties to go into the blend. In addition to the type of bean used in a blend, roasting plays an important role in the resulting coffee's taste. Roasting eliminates the moisture from the bean, releasing the flavor. The color of the roasted beans determines the flavor, and consistency of color throughout a bean produces a high-quality brew. The beans should be dark enough to give the maximum amount of flavor, though not so dark that the coffee tastes scorched.

Until the end of World War II, robusta beans commanded a significantly lower price than arabica, not only because they are less flavorful, but also because they can be harvested more easily. Thereafter, the price differential was reduced by two developments: demand for robusta was boosted by coffee-consuming nations' shift toward blends that combined both kinds of beans and, on an even larger scale, the introduction and great success of soluble coffee (or "instant" as it would later be known) derived largely, though not exclusively, from robusta.

According to Richard L. Lucier, author of *The International Political Economy of Coffee,* "Only 8 percent of world production was of robusta coffee in

the late 1940s, but robusta's share more than tripled by the early 1970s. Over the same time period, soluble coffee's share of world consumption grew from virtually zero (i.e. consumption was of regular coffee) to nearly 25 percent." Key points in the rapid development of the U.S. coffee industry during the decades after World War II included the pioneering of a soluble process by Hills Brothers in 1953, Nestlé's introduction in the same year of decaffeinated instant coffee, the emergence of freeze-dried coffee in 1965, and the creation of continuous freeze-drying systems in 1975.

The increasing demand for robusta had a sharp impact on the coffee-producing nations. Central and South America, where much of the world's arabica is grown, dominated coffee production before the 1950s. By the late 1980s, however, more than a third of world coffee production took place in the robusta-growing countries of Africa and Southeast Asia.

Latin America also suffered when the coffee boom, occurring from 1955 to 1962, was followed by a slump in prices triggered by over-production, a crisis that led in 1962 to the first of several International Coffee Agreements intended to stabilize prices. As M. Th. A. Pieterse and H. J. Silvis explained in *The World Coffee Market* and the International Coffee Agreement, "The instrument used is a system of export quotas, which—depending on price developments—limits producing members' exports to consuming members' markets. The role of consuming members is to police producing members' adherence to the quota provisions." According to Richard Lucier's analysis, the swift and concerted response by the U.S. coffee industry to the slump-induced crisis in Latin America reflected the political climate of the time (fear of Communist inroads into countries with deteriorating economies) as well as concern about the possible overall disruption of world coffee production and an attachment to neighbors and long-term trading partners.

CURRENT CONDITIONS

Despite numerous reports linking various health problems with coffee consumption, the results of such studies have been inconclusive and ambiguous, showing no clear reason to suppose that coffee drinkers are at risk for high cholesterol, heart disease, birth defects, cancer of the bladder or pancreas, and high blood pressure. Though the drop in coffee consumption through the 1960s and 1970s may have reflected anxiety induced by the sheer number of these reports, it may also have been prompted in part by dissatisfaction with the quality of the product.

The increasing demand for specialty coffees suggested that consumers were attracted to higher quality brews, especially when accompanied by lower levels of caffeine—arabica beans are not only less bitter than robusta but also contain about half as much caffeine, the component of coffee most frequently cited in connection with potentially harmful side-effects.

Coffee shops continued to enjoy prominence throughout American culture during the mid-1990s, with Starbucks the unchallenged leader. Numerous smaller roasters, however, had also entered the market, enjoying measured success on a less dominant basis.

The industry showed strong signs in early 1997, with coffee markets showing record levels as roasters took advantage of favorable prices and rising inventories. Speculation about the amount of coffee that Brazil, the world's leading producer, would harvest in late spring, 1997, indicated some uncertainty about whether these strong levels could be maintained.

INDUSTRY LEADERS

In a 1995 ranking in *Advertising Age,* year-to-date leaders in sales of ground coffee were Folgers with 27.4 percent of the market, followed by a 19.5 percent share for Kraft's Maxwell House. These two brands strongly dominate the market with private label brands showing the next highest share of market at only 7.6 percent.

According to an analysis by Bill Saporito that appeared in *Fortune,* Kraft General Foods became more aggressive in its promotion of Maxwell House when Philip Morris acquired the company in 1988, introducing a risk-taking mood. Saporito noted several reasons why such aggressiveness in the battle for market share in the ground and soluble coffee markets seemed ill-advised: with a profit of less than a penny per cup of coffee at stake, such coffee manufacturers had been competing against each other in expensive advertising campaigns, together with costly promotions aimed at supermarkets (in the form of incentives) and consumers (in the form of coupons), all the while neglecting opportunities to take advantage of a burgeoning taste for the more profitable specialty coffees, except by cautiously introducing upscale versions of already popular brands.

Because the giants in the U.S. coffee business imported in pre-roasted or even ready-soluble form so much of the coffee they used, much of the coffee processing actually done in this country was performed by smaller concerns, including those companies marketing the increasingly popular specialty coffees.

The Procter & Gamble Company entered this market in late 1995 with the acquisition of Millstone

Coffee, a privately held firm. Millstone roasts and distributes more than 70 varieties of whole-bean, gourmet coffee products. P&G sales for 1996 were $17.1 billion, up 6 percent from the prior year level of $16.2 billion. Its Food and Beverage segment achieved 7 percent unit volume growth in 1996, led by the coffee category. General Mills, maker of Maxwell House, achieved record results in 1996, with sales growing 8 percent to exceed $5.4 billion and earnings a record 28 percent.

Among coffee manufacturers Starbucks Corporation led the way. Starbucks is the leading retailer, roaster, and brand of specialty coffee in North America. The company opened its first store in Seattle in 1971 and just over two decades later operated more than 1,100 coffee shops throughout the United States in office buildings, shopping centers, airport terminals, cruise ships and supermarkets. Starbucks went public in 1992, with continued success well into the late 1990s as Americans continued their obsession with gourmet coffee and related products. Starbucks has also introduced coffee-flavored ice cream and beer. It has also launched a cold coffee drink called Frappuccino with Pepsico. The company expanded outside the U.S. in 1996 with its first international stores in Tokyo and Toronto. Sales in 1996 were $696.5 million. Demonstrating the level of increasing sales, Starbucks reported consolidated revenues of $109.9 million for the five-week fiscal month ending December 29, 1996, an increase of 39 percent from revenues of $79.1 million for the same period in fiscal 1995. The company planned to open more than 227 new stores in 1997 and enter at least two major new North American markets.

AMERICA AND THE WORLD

With the exception of several countries in Latin America and a few in Africa that both produce and consume coffee, the world is divided between developed coffee-consuming nations and developing coffee-producing nations. In terms of kilograms of coffee per person consumed in 1985, the United States at 4.7 ranked tenth, behind Sweden (11.6), Denmark (11.0), Finland (10.1), Holland (9.5), Germany (6.8), France (5.5), and Italy (4.9) among the coffee-consuming nations, and behind Costa Rice (6.5) and Brazil (5.5) among the coffee-producing nations. Overall, in the decade between 1975 and 1985 European Community levels of imported coffee rose significantly, those of Japan doubled, while those of the United States remained steady despite increased population—an indication of a drop in per capita consumption.

Unlike other coffee-consuming nations, the United States imposed no import duty on this particular commodity. Another unique feature of the U.S. market is the nation's close cultural, geographical, political, and economic ties to Latin America, and thus to such major coffee producers as Brazil, Colombia, and Mexico. Although Mexico has been by far the least important of these in terms of output, its close proximity to roasters in the southern United States and its consequent ability to transport coffee overland have been advantageous.

Drawing parallels between America and most of Europe (roughly equivalent markets in terms of the sheer volume of their coffee imports), C. F. Marshall noted several contrasts in his 1983 study *The World Coffee Trade.* The quality of the coffee shipped to the United States appeared generally lower than that intended for Europe, and much of it was already roasted and ground or turned into soluble form, with a lighter roast than was customary in Europe, where "the higher roast forces the roaster to pay more attention to the regularity of bean and to avoid a large proportion of broken or thin textured shells which can scorch and spoil the taste." Marshall attributed these compromises on quality to the "intense competition" among coffee manufacturers in the United States, concluding that "some miracle is needed to switch the competition from one of price to one of quality."

Within just a few years of Marshall's analysis, the miracle in question had begun, driven by American consumers' increasing preference for precisely the kind of high-quality specialty coffees favored in Europe. However, a decade later Ted. R. Lingle, executive director of the Specialty Coffee Association of America, noted in the *Vending Times* that "the continued surplus of lower grades of coffee" meant that consumers in the United States were still faced with coffee that was "merely acceptable because it 'contained' too high a proportion of low-grade coffees in the blend."

RESEARCH AND TECHNOLOGY

For several reasons, the leading manufacturers of coffee in the United States, despite their dependence on imported beans, managed to resist any competition from among the coffee-producing nations. One key advantage was that of patented technology, and consequently automated production on a huge (and therefore highly economical) scale. Eliminating much repetitive labor in loading and unloading, the introduction of the continuous roaster enabled a single person to operate two units continuously producing 5000 kilograms per hour, thereby doubling productivity to the level of 1600 bags per person-day. The developing coffee-producing nations could neither match this technological

advantage nor afford to compete with U.S. manufacturers in a field characterized by heavy promotional and advertising costs.

Another obstacle preventing coffee-producing nations from manufacturing coffee for the U.S. market was that the industry leaders had used their technological advantage to shape local tastes to specific blends manufactured with great consistency. A single coffee-producing nation could not possibly draw on a sufficient variety of coffees to match these exact blends.

With the shift in national taste towards specialty coffees, quality of beans became a paramount concern for new producers entering the developing gourmet market. In response, the established American manufacturers began experimenting with refined versions of popular lines and researching possible new products, such as iced coffee. Based on its success in Japan, and given its potential appeal to younger consumers, iced coffee was regarded by a number of analysts as a probable strong seller in the American market during the 1990s. Others, however, remained skeptical of this product's ability to reproduce the success achieved by iced teas, diet sodas, or health drinks.

FURTHER READING

"Comeback Time for Coffee." *Time,* 22 October 1990, 59.

De Graaff, J. "The Economics of Coffee." *Economics of Crops in Developing Countries 1.* Wageningen, The Netherlands: Center for Agricultural Publishing and Documentation, 1986.

"Gourmet Coffee Stirs Market." *Advertising Age,* 1 October 1990, 19.

Lucier, Richard L. *The International Political Economy of Coffee.* New York: Praeger, 1988.

Marshall, C. F. *The World Coffee Trade.* Cambridge, England: Woodhead-Faulkner, 1983.

"No Break for Coffee Prices." *Fortune,* 13 June 1994, 13.

Pieterse, M. Th. A., and H. J. Silvis. *The World Coffee Market and the International Coffee Agreement.* Wageningen, The Netherlands: Wageningen Agricultural University, 1988.

Rothman, Howard. "You Love the Java, But Does It Love You?" *Nation's Business,* February 1992, 55.

Rothman, Matt. "Into the Black." *Inc.,* January 1993, 59-60, 62, 64-65.

Saporito, Bill. "Can Anyone Win the Coffee War?" *Fortune,* 21 May 1990, 97, 100.

Sivetz, Michael, and Norman W. Desrosier. *Coffee Technology,* second ed. Westport, CT: AVI, 1979.

Tantillo, L. "Iced Coffee Market Heats Up." *Beverage World Periscope.* 30 June 1990, 10.

Willman, Michelle L. "Romancing the Bean." *Beverage Industry,* April 1993, 42-43.

—Richard Hillyer, updated by Lin Grensing-Popal

SIC 2096

POTATO CHIPS, CORN CHIPS, AND SIMILAR SNACKS

Establishments primarily engaged in manufacturing potato chips, corn chips, and similar snacks. Establishments primarily engaged in manufacturing pretzels and crackers are classified in **SIC 2052: Cookies and Crackers;** those manufacturing candy covered popcorn are classified in **SIC 2064: Candy and Other Confectionery Products;** those manufacturing salted, roasted, cooked, or canned nuts and seeds are classified in **SIC 2068: Salted and Roasted Nuts and Seeds;** and those manufacturing packaged unpopped popcorn are classified in **SIC 2099: Food Preparations, Not Elsewhere Classified.**

INDUSTRY SNAPSHOT

The so-called "salty snack" industry included potato chips, corn chips, tortilla chips, ready-to-eat popcorn (except candy-coated), pork rinds, potato sticks, and extruded snacks such as cheese puffs. The mid-1990s were lackluster for the salty snack industry, according to the Snack Food Association. Retail dollar sales for snacks overall for 1995 totaled $15.09 billion, an increase of .4 percent from 1994's dollar sales of $15.05 billion. Potato chips and tortilla chips controlled the snack foods market. Sales of potato chips for 1995 was $4.818 billion and that of tortilla chips was $3.195 billion, an increase of 2.5 and 5.3 percent, respectively, from 1994.

In the mid 1990s private label brands of salty snacks grew at unprecedented rates. According to *Brandweek* from statistics presented at the Private Label Manufacturers Association trade show, store brands reported a 15.4 percent increase compared to an 11 percent increase in sales of national brands.

Even though the salty snacks industry experienced an almost flat overall growth rate in the mid 1990s, the low fat and no fat salty snacks experienced tremendous growth. Low-fat and no-fat potato chip sales grew 48 percent in 1995 as compared to 1994 and low fat and no fat tortilla chips grew 67 percent in 1995 from 1994 sales. Pretzels were the biggest competitor to the salty snacks industry experiencing a 339 percent growth rate between 1994 and 1995.

According to *Food Processing,* marketing research on the snack food industry revealed that healthy snack foods were stealing a large portion of the market from traditional snack foods. The announcement of a major snack food manufacturer's $225 million investment in the production of low-fat and no-fat snacks in January of 1995 further substantiated the results. According to *Advertising Age,* sales of the ten fastest selling supermarket food categories for 1994 reflected the shift toward low fat and no fat eating. New labeling regulations were responsible for accentuating this trend.

ORGANIZATION AND STRUCTURE

The salty snack foods industry had a unique structure, since Frito-Lay controlled roughly half of the total market share with retail sales of about $5.6 billion in 1992. Its nearest competitor, Borden Snacks Group, had retail sales of just over $1 billion that same year. Eagle Snacks, a unit of Anheuser-Busch breweries, was the third-largest maker of salty snacks with $600 million of retail sales. Several other companies showed retail sales from one quarter to one half a billion dollars that same year. Although the industry had some elements of a monopoly, aggressive pricing and distribution policies among chip makers, along with the regional presence of many large and small manufacturers, kept it highly competitive.

Numerous companies of descending size made up the snack industry. Many competed only on a regional level, and some found it difficult to price their products competitively with the larger manufacturers. Others, however, created a market niche, sometimes with a specialty product such as kettle style potato chips or baked chips sold through health food stores. If their product met with success among customers, the smaller makers could often charge higher prices for their products than the biggest manufacturers. Larger manufacturers were generally full-service snack companies—those which offered a full range of products, including potato chips, tortilla chips, and other salty snacks. The smaller producers were more likely to specialize.

One such small manufacturer was Cape Cod Potato Chip Co., a Massachusetts-based firm that began frying chips over a kitchen stove before purchasing a storefront potato chip shop in 1980. The hand-operated frying kettles produced only 120 pounds of chips per hour, in contrast with the industry standard commercial cookers that produced 4,000 pounds. A decade after opening, Cape Cod employed 200 people—although the operation was purchased in 1985 by Eagle Snacks.

BACKGROUND AND DEVELOPMENT

The potato chip was born accidentally in 1853, when railroad magnate and naval commodore Cornelius Vanderbilt was vacationing in a popular East Coast inn. He ordered fried potatoes but disliked them and returned the fries to the kitchen, complaining that they were ''too thick.'' The cook, a Native American named George Crumm, reacted with indignation. He sliced a potato into slivers as thin as he could, fried them, and served them to Vanderbilt.

The newly invented snack gained popularity among other customers, but remained primarily a restaurant item for several decades. This style of potatoes became known as Saratoga chips, named after the town in which they were first consumed. In 1895, William Tappenden of Cleveland began manufacturing potato chips for home consumption. Snack food innovations included the introduction of ridged potato chips in 1966 and fabricated potato chips in the 1970s.

Popcorn is perhaps the oldest salty snack food still widely consumed. Indigenous peoples in what became Peru were known to toast corn kernels over flames until they burst. This tradition was recorded as early as the fifteenth century. North American natives also prepared popcorn, and it was believed to have been shared at the first Thanksgiving dinner in Plymouth, Massachusetts. The term popcorn became accepted around 1820. Early American settlers may have eaten it—sprinkled with sugar and doused in cream—as the first breakfast cereal. It was also used decoratively from the beginning of its history, having been strung and draped on Christmas trees during the 1800s.

The snack food received a boost from the invention of the first popping machine in 1885 by a Chicago inventor named Charles Cretors. His machine used oil to pop the corn and was used for about a century until the development of the hot-air popper. In the mid-1960s the snack began to be manufactured on a mass scale by Orville Redenbacher—who then promoted his brand as a gourmet hybrid popcorn. The next major innovation came in 1986, when Pillsbury introduced microwavable popcorn.

Industry analysts reported that the snack food industry fared well in the early 1990s, given the economic downturn. In fact, over time the industry developed a reputation for being recession proof. However, stiff competition required increasingly aggressive promotions to grab the consumer dollar, so some viewed salty snacks as a no-growth industry.

Dollar sales of savory snacks—in a broad category including pretzels and snack nuts—grew from $10.6 billion in 1987 to $13.8 billion in 1992, an increase of 30 percent. Per capita consumption jumped from 17.49 pounds in 1987 to 20.55 pounds in 1992. The field was dominated by Frito-Lay, a subsidiary of Pepsi Co., which claimed nearly half of the overall salty snack food market in 1992. But Americans' appetite for specialty and relatively ''healthy'' snacks kept the industry competitive. Over 400 new products were introduced in both 1991 and 1992, including several varieties of multigrain chips, flavored ready-to-eat popcorn, and diet cheese puffs.

The industry experienced steady sales growth, even during the recession of the early 1990s. But pound sales volume rose faster than dollar sales volume in both 1991 and 1992 due to the keen competition that characterized the industry. The decline in price per pound was also consistent with falling retail grocery prices nationwide. The issues described by snack food companies as posing the biggest challenges to profitability in the mid-1990s included: competitive pricing, government mandated nutritional labeling, changing distribution patterns, and rising supermarket shelf fees.

Profits for salty snack manufacturers were 7.5 percent in 1992, representing a slight drop from the previous year. These figures included additional snacks, such as pretzels and packaged nuts, which were made by ''full-service'' salty snack companies such as Frito-Lay and Borden. Pre-tax profit margins for this broad category of snacks slipped from 6.8 percent in 1991 to 4.2 percent in 1992. Domestic dollar sales in 1992 were $9.6 billion—up overall from 1991 sales. Consumers bought 3.56 billion pounds of salty snacks, or nearly 18 pounds per capita consumption.

Potato chips led the way in salty snack consumption in 1992, with a retail sales volume of $4.41 billion. This dollar amount represented the sale of over 1.66 billion pounds of potato chips, which claimed 32 percent of the market for all savory snacks, including popcorn, meat snacks, pretzels, and snack nuts. Tortilla chips were the second most consumed salty snack. Over $2.57 billion worth were sold in 1992—a volume of 1.06 billion pounds. This represented a 20.5 percent market share by pound volume, or 18.6 percent by dollar sales. Potato chips and tortilla chips combined accounted for about one-half of the savory snack market.

Over 40 percent of all purchases of salty snacks were made in supermarkets—food stores which reported annual sales of at least $2 million. Grocery stores—food stores with sales of under $2 million annually—accounted for between 10 percent and 20 percent of salty snack sales in 1992, depending on the product. The remaining salty snacks were sold in convenience stores, mass merchandisers—large general merchandise stores which also carried grocery items— warehouse club stores, drug stores, vending machines, and other retail outlets such as delicatessens, liquor stores, and sports stadiums.

Shifting Distribution Patterns. A market research study found that consumers paid an average price of $2.66 per pound of savory snacks in 1992, down 2.6 percent from $2.73 per pound the previous year. This was attributed to several factors—including the recession and the competitive nature of retail products—but another major factor was a shift in distribution patterns. Large warehouse club stores and mass merchandisers charged lower prices for snacks in order to attract customers from smaller supermarkets and grocery stores. While supermarkets accounted for nearly half of salty snack sales, sales by dollar volume rose only about 1 percent. By contrast, warehouse clubs saw an increase of over 50 percent in savory snack sales, and mass merchandisers also saw double digit growth. Since these larger outlets charged less per pound for snacks than supermarkets, the increased sales represented a decline in profitability.

Convenience stores charged the highest prices for both potato chips and corn chips. In 1992, average potato chip prices were $3.06 per pound—the only outlet where prices passed the $3 mark. By contrast, potato chips sold for $2.49 per pound in supermarkets and $2.44 at mass merchandisers. Corn chips in that same year sold for $2.74 per pound in convenience stores, compared with $2.44 in supermarkets and $2.00 in warehouse clubs.

Prices began a trend toward equalization in the early 1990s, however. Convenience store prices of tortilla chips, for instance, were $2.61 per pound in 1992—the highest of any outlet, though 10 percent lower than the previous year. Supermarkets, grocery stores, mass merchandisers, and drug stores saw only a modest shift in tortilla chip prices. However, the price at warehouse clubs jumped almost 30 percent to $2.27 per pound. This trend also reflected the fierce competition that kept profits low throughout the recession.

Moreover, savory snacks experienced intensely competitive pricing in supermarkets. Full-line snack companies reported spending 52 cents of each promotional dollar on price reductions. Another 25 percent of promotional expenses went toward advertising, and 16 percent was used for in-store promotions. On the whole, 72 percent of full-line manufacturers reported spending more money for advertising and other promotional endeavors in 1992 than in 1991. In addition, retail shelf space increased in price during the early 1990s. The average cost per section foot per store paid by salty snack manufacturers leaped from $283.33 in 1991 to $342.86 in 1992.

Health Implications. The salty snack industry adapted to shifting consumer demands and perceptions throughout the last several decades. During the late 1960s and 1970s, Americans learned from health experts that they were consuming salt in greater quantities than was necessary or healthy. The average individual needed about one-third teaspoon of salt per day. High consumption of salty snacks and other prepared or processed foods resulted in more than double the recommended intake.

In more recent years, university studies linked low fat diets to reduced rates of cancer and heart disease. Research showed that low fat diets, typical of those in the Far East, were associated with low or virtually nonexistent incidence of cancer. This was particularly true, for instance, in breast cancer for women, which was much more prevalent in the United States and other western nations than it was in China. Moreover, when women of Chinese descent lived in the United States and adopted the high fat diet typical of Americans, the incidence of breast cancer jumped to the rate found among westerners. Consumers were advised to reduce their fat intake, and many began to do so. Whereas in the 1960s, Americans typically consumed about one-half of their calories in the form of fat, a healthy diet was said to be one in which a maximum of 30 percent of calories ought to be consumed through fats.

Thus, manufacturers of salty, high fat foods battled public perception that their products were unhealthy. Salty snack makers responded to changing consumer tastes by creating potato chips, corn chips, and tortilla chips that were perceived as healthy—or at least not too harmful. No salt potato chips were developed in response to consumer demand, although in 1992 they accounted for less than 1 percent of potato chip sales. Following the unspectacular success of no-salt chips, low salt varieties were introduced and proved more successful, showing double digit market share growth in the early 1990s.

Low oil potato chips proved more successful, making up 3.7 percent of chip sales by volume. From 1991 to 1992 alone, this category of potato chip jumped by 24.3 percent. One low oil chip maker claimed its product to contain only 4 grams of fat per one-ounce serving, and just 140 calories. Other specialty chips were baked rather than fried, and another manufacturer sold chips that were cooked in the potato's own juices, resulting in a fat-free chip. Similar innovations were found in the tortilla chip industry in the early 1990s. Low salt and low oil tortilla chips combined to make up about 9 percent of overall volume.

Despite the responsiveness of manufacturers to consumer demand for healthier products, the desire to eat foods lower in fat nevertheless affected the salty snack industry. Among industry products, popcorn consumption virtually exploded in the late 1980s and early 1990s. Multigrain snacks also showed remarkable growth for the first few years after their introduction. Other foods that competed with the potato chip and similar snacks included pretzels and snack nuts, both of which gained market share much more rapidly than potato chips and tortilla chips in the early 1990s. Double digit growth was observed in both ready-to-eat popcorn and in pretzels from 1991 to 1992: 12 percent and 15.5 percent, respectively. This was due at least in part to consumer perception of pretzels and nuts as having more nutritive value than potato chips. Even low oil chips contained more fat than pretzels, for instance, which were baked rather than fried. Snack nuts contained relatively little salt and oil and featured nutrients such as protein and minerals not found in potato or tortilla chips.

Flavor Variety. The development of flavored chips and snacks throughout the 1980s and 1990s was generally successful in keeping snack consumption on the rise. Small manufacturers introduced kettle-style potato chips—cooked in kettles as done previously. Many larger manufacturers followed suit, either developing their own versions of kettle chips or buying smaller companies that developed them for regional markets. In 1992, kettle style chips made up 5.5 percent of pound volume consumed.

Regularly shaped chips made up 46.2 percent of pound volume, and ridged chips of all flavors accounted for 34.4 percent in 1992. Fabricated chips represented 13.9 percent of the market for potato chips in that same year. Flavored potato and corn chips also multiplied, accounting for much of the introduction of new products during the late 1980s and early 1990s. In addition to barbecue flavored potato chips, consumers purchased sour cream and onion, ranch, and other flavors.

Tortilla chips experienced the most success of any salty snack food with the introduction of flavor varieties. Regular flavored chips made up 61.4 percent of the tortilla chip market in 1992, while cheese flavored tortilla chips accounted for 26.3 percent of the market. The third most popular flavor that year was ranch, which represented just under 8 percent of the market. Other varieties included salsa, spicy hot, jalapeno, chili, and oat bran flavors. In addition, white corn

tortilla chips were introduced in the early 1990s and apparently found favor with consumers.

Ready-to-Eat Popcorn. The ready-to-eat (RTE) popcorn category of snack grew in popularity during the late 1980s and early 1990s. Dollar sales jumped from $248 million in 1987 (including caramel coated) to over half a billion dollars in 1992. This was in contrast to more sluggish growth in the microwavable popcorn category, in which sales remained flat from 1990 to 1992 after booming during the 1980s. Analysts attributed this slowdown to market maturation— almost 90 percent of consumers owned a microwave oven by 1990.

While caramel coated RTE popcorn made up the largest market share of any individual type—39.2 percent in 1992—non-coated popcorn accounted for 60.8 percent of total RTE consumption. Regular flavor had the largest share of sales after caramel, with nearly 20 percent of the market. White cheddar and cheese combined made up over 17 percent of the market, with butter flavor accounting for nearly 12 percent, and cinnamon and other flavors combining to total about 2 percent. Sales of all varieties grew in double digits from 1991 to 1992, except for white cheddar flavored popcorn, which dropped 13.2 percent in the latter year. Low salt RTE sold well, claiming 6.3 percent of pound volume in supermarkets.

Whereas total popcorn sales slid downward 4.2 percent to $1.358 billion in 1992, RTE popcorn sales (including caramel flavored) increased 12 percent to $510 billion that same year. Measured in pound volume, sales grew 15.4 percent between 1991 and 1992, with 154.2 million pounds consumed. Many RTE brands were air popped, making them virtually fat free. Moreover, RTE popcorn could be purchased and eaten immediately, making it even more convenient than its microwavable competitors. RTE varieties appeared to be causing the demise of a second competitor, unpopped popcorn, for which dollar sales slumped 11.3 percent to $117.4 million in 1992. This trend suggested that RTE popcorn would eventually split the market with microwavable brands, while unpopped popcorn would become a supermarket dinosaur.

Showing similar pricing and distribution patterns to potato and tortilla chips, RTE popcorn commanded the highest price in convenience stores in 1992—$3.46 per pound. The lowest price, $2.28 per pound, was found in the warehouse club stores, which nevertheless saw an 11.8 percent price increase over the previous year. As of the early 1990s, RTE popcorn was produced by only a few manufacturers, but as others took note of its popularity and profitability, new companies began marketing their own products.

Extruded Snacks. Extruded snacks was the industry term for cheese puffs, corn puffs, and onion rings. By far the largest segment of this snack category—about 96 percent—was controlled by cheese flavored products. Sales of extruded snacks remained flat relative to other salty snacks from 1987 to 1992. Dollar volume was $694.3 million in 1987, and $774.0 in 1992, having dropped from its peak of $813 million in 1991. Like other savory snacks, extruded snacks were characterized by the introduction, in the late 1980s and early 1990s, of many flavor varieties. A diet company even introduced individual serving-size low-calorie cheese curls. But the new varieties failed to bring as much growth as expected to the industry overall.

Extruded cheese snacks, although no higher in fat content than potato chips and corn chips, suffered from a consumer perception that they were highly processed and therefore not as healthful as related snack foods. Throughout the last decade, consumers showed a preference for more natural, less processed foods—including snack foods. Although consumers wanted convenience, there was nevertheless a trend toward the use of whole foods rather than refined foods, which might have implications for the extruded snack industry.

Pork Rinds. The pork rind segment of the salty snack industry grew steadily over the past five years, increasing in sales volume from $163.4 million in 1987 to $236 million in 1992. Double-digit sales growth in the late 1980s slowed to about 5 percent annually in the early 1990s. One reason for growth in this segment was that the industry leader, Frito-Lay, increased its focus on pork rinds in its promotions—particularly in the southern United States. The South represented over half of total pork rind consumption, with Pacific states totaling another 20 percent. The New England and mid-Atlantic states had virtually no market, with only 4 percent of national pork rind sales.

Supermarkets sold only 18 percent of pork rinds in 1992, while grocery stores—the smaller volume of the two types—saw 27 percent of the snack's sales. Convenience stores, which charged the highest price for pork rinds—$6.12 per pound—accounted for 18 percent of sales. Boosting this snack's popularity was the introduction of microwavable brands in 1992. The new product offered a 60 percent to 70 percent reduction in fat—undoubtedly a source of appeal to consumers. In addition, pork rinds, like other salty snacks, appeared in flavor varieties including Cajun, jalapeno, barbecue, and chili.

Multigrain Chips. Of all the salty snacks manufactured and sold in the early 1990s, the type that demonstrated the greatest growth was the multigrain chip.

Although only a $198 million industry in 1992, this sales volume represented a growth of 76.5 percent from the previous year. The first-year sales of Frito-Lay's multigrain product, Sunchips, totalled $115 million.

Introduced in 1990 by Frito-Lay, multigrain chips grew quickly enough that industry observers expected the product to become a substantial segment of the salty snack industry. Two competitors introduced their own versions of multigrain chips, but Frito-Lay still cornered the market in 1992 with $192 million in sales—nearly all of the product's volume. The success of multigrain chips was attributed to the perceived health value of the snack, which was made of grains and was relatively low in salt and oil.

By contrast, the decline in sales for four straight years signaled a maturing market for corn chips. In 1987, the corn chip industry saw $560 million in sales, but by 1992 that figure had grown to only $598 million. The introduction of flavor varieties did not boost sales—which peaked in 1989 at $668 million and slid each year thereafter. Efforts by Frito-Lay to bolster sales through redesigned packaging and new marketing campaigns met with consumer apathy. Nevertheless, corn chips represented 4.3 percent of the overall snack market.

Industry Challenges. In a 1993 survey of salty snack manufacturers, increased government regulations were cited most often as the biggest challenge facing the industry in the mid-1990s. This concern arose from the passage of the Nutrition Labeling and Education Act of 1990, which required that all food manufacturers list nutrients in greater detail beginning in May 1994. In addition, the NLEA required manufacturers to list nutritional components of foods by serving sizes determined at the discretion of the government. Previously, food makers determined portion size and listed vitamins, protein, minerals, fat, and calorie content accordingly.

The trend mentioned second most frequently in the survey was the increasing consolidation of the industry. Some snack makers expressed concern that the large, national companies steadily purchased successful smaller firms that cut into their profits. This trend was perceived as a possible threat to the healthy competitiveness of the industry provided by innovative regional and family-owned firms. Increasing consumer emphasis on the health value of foods was cited as the third most important trend in the mid-1990s. Other trends noted were increasing retail shelf space fees, continued intense pricing competition with other manufacturers, demographic changes, and rising environmental concerns.

CURRENT CONDITIONS

The 1995 per-capita consumption of snacks was 21.31 pounds, a decrease of 1.9 percent from 1994, however per-capita sales increased 1.4 percent to $57.90 in 1995. In the overall 1995 snacks market, potato chips held a 31.9 percent market share in terms of dollar sales, tortilla chips held 21.4 percent, corn chips held 3.6 percent, popcorn held 8.1 percent, pork rinds held 1.8 percent, multigrain chips held 1 percent and extruded snacks held 5.1 percent of the market share.

Potato Chips. Potato chips increased 2.5 percent in sales from 1994 to $4.817 billion in 1995, with pound volume decreasing 2.8 percent from 1994 to 1.689 billion pounds in 1995. The explosive growth of low fat and no fat potato chips drove sales in 1995. The most liked flavor was the regular variety, followed by barbecue and sour cream and onion. The top potato chips brands in the order of ranking were: Lay's with 26 percent of the supermarket dollar share; Ruffles with 19.1 percent of the supermarket dollar share; Pringles with 9.6 percent of the supermarket dollar share; and with the remaining share, Eagle brand, private label, Wise, Utz, Herr's, Keebler, Golden Flake and Jays. 48.5 percent of the potato chips sold in 1995 were through supermarkets.

Tortilla Chips. Retail dollar sales of tortilla chips was $3.195 billion in 1995, an increase of 5.4 percent from 1994, with the 1994 pound volume increasing 2.4 percent to 1.288 billion pounds in 1995. The most favored flavor was regular, followed by cheese and ranch. Supermarkets dispensed 47.4 percent of tortilla chips in 1995. The top brands were: Dorito's with 36.4 percent of the supermarket dollar share; Tostito's with 33.4 percent of the supermarket dollar share; Eagle brand with 5 percent of the supermarket dollar share; and Private Label, Santitas, Mission, Padrino's, Chachos, and Le Famous with the remaining share.

Corn Chips. Corn chips decreased 18.8 percent in sales from 1994 to $562.7 million in 1995, with pound volume decreasing 17.9 percent from 1994 to 218.6 million pounds in 1995. According to the Snack Foods Association, low fat was most popular in the market, and unfortunately, corn chips were not low in fat. The most liked flavors in the mid-90's were the regular variety, followed by barbecue and spicy cheese.

Popcorn. Retail dollar sales of popcorn were $1.234 billion in 1995, a decrease of 8.8 percent from 1994. The 1995 pound volume decreased 9.9 percent to 592.8 million pounds. The most favored salty flavored ready to eat popcorn in the mid 1990s was regular, followed by butter, cheese, and white cheddar cheese.

Extruded Snacks. According to the Snack Foods Association, extruded snacks were slowly catching on to the low fat and no fat trend. Extruded snacks sales decreased 3.4 percent from 1994 to $768.1 million in 1995, with pound volume decreasing 1.8 percent from 1994 to 285 million pounds in 1995. Cheese flavored extruded snacks were liked by 91.1 percent of the consumers.

Pork Rinds. The 1995 retail dollar sale of pork rinds was $269.6 million, an increase of 1.6 percent from 1994. The 1995 pound volume decreasing 4.4 percent to 44.6 million pounds. According to the Snack Foods Association, a shortage of pork skins restricted pork rind growth in the mid-1990s. The most favored flavor of pork rinds was regular, followed by hot and spicy and barbecue flavors.

Multigrain Chips. According to the Snack Foods Association, multigrain chips, which generated more than $100 million in retail sales in the segments first year of introduction, steadily lost sales—falling almost 14 percent in both dollar sales and pound volume. 1995 dollar sales were at $154.7 million, a decrease of 13.7 percent from 1994 and 1995 pound volume was at 46.6 million a decrease of 13.3 percent from 1994. Regular was the most favored flavor, followed by onion and cheese.

INDUSTRY LEADERS

According to *Knight Ridder/Tribune Business News,* the top ten salty snacks brands for 1994 was led by Private Labels with $638.2 million in sales, Doritos with $559 million in sales, Lay's with $555.7 million in sales, Ruffles with $405.3 million in sales, Tostito's with $379.7 million in sales, Planters with $377.3 million in sales, Eagle Brand with $376.7 million in sales, Orville Redenbacher with $268.9 million in sales, Pringles with $241.1 million in sales, Fritos with $235.2 million in sales, and Keebler with $129.1 million in sales. The leading company in the industry according to the Snack Food Association was The Frito-Lay Company, followed by Eagle Snacks, and the Keebler Company.

The Frito-Lay Company's snack sales increased 10 percent to $5.495 billion in the mid-1990s. The Frito-Lay Company was based in Plano, Texas and had 30,000 employees. Because of its 45 to 50 percent market share, Frito-Lay's activities and innovations reverberated throughout the salty snack food industry. Profits from the manufacturer accounted for 39 percent of the total of its parent company—Pepsi Co. A competitive battle for market share during the early 1990s prompted Frito-Lay to carry out a reorganization, which included repricing products and laying off 1,800 executives. In addition, 2,000 employees were shifted from administrative positions into sales jobs.

The rising success of its nearest competitors—Borden, which controlled 8 percent market share in 1992, and Anheuser-Busch's Eagle Snacks, which claimed 6 percent—provided the impetus for the restructuring. In the late 1980s, Frito-Lay increased prices faster than the rate of inflation and allowed quality control to lapse, resulting in a higher rate of broken chips. In addition, Frito-Lay did not respond to aggressive product promotions by its competitors in certain cities.

The result was that Eagle's potato chips began to win taste test competitions with Lay's and were priced as much as 20 percent lower. Even though Eagle was still unprofitable, its market share gains left the larger manufacturer vulnerable. Frito-Lay responded in 1991 with price reductions, a new advertising campaign, and the reorganization. About 60 percent of its management and administrative positions were eliminated, and decision making was dispersed throughout operations. Four out of 40 plants were closed or sold, and the product lineup was substantially streamlined. These changes brought about $100 million in cost savings in the first year, and Frito-Lay's operating profits rose 15 percent in the first six months of 1992. Frito-Lay gained one percentage point in market share, while Borden lost almost a percentage point.

The number two ranked Eagle Snacks, a subsidiary of Anheuser-Busch, admitted defeat in October 1995. After four months on the block and no buyer, Anheuser-Busch announced in February 1996 that it was closing down it's Eagle division and selling four plants to The Frito-Lay Company.

The number three ranked Keebler Company, based in Elmhurst, Illinois, was a $1.8 billion dollar company with 9000 employees. "In July 1995 Keebler announced it's intentions to sell it's savory snacks business in order to focus greater resources on strengthening and advancing the company's cookie and cracker business," according to the Snack Foods Association.

AMERICA AND THE WORLD

Two snack food industry leaders exported their product, producing overseas sales of about $4 billion. Pepsi Co. Foods International, the overseas counterpart to Frito-Lay, reported selling $2.18 billion in salty snacks in 1992. Its competitor, Borden, recorded nondomestic sales of $1.87 billion in that year. These figures encompassed the broad category of snacks, including pretzels and snack nuts. The international

snack food market was more than one-quarter the size of the domestic market in 1992. The passage in fall 1993 of the North American Free Trade Agreement (NAFTA) was expected to result in increased sales of these products in Mexico and Canada. In addition, the ramifications of NAFTA on trade with European nations could expand the market overseas throughout the 1990s.

In 1995, 26 percent of the snacks exported by the United States was potato chips. Corn chips and pretzels made up 8.9 percent of exports, and 13.5 percent of popcorn was exported. In 1995, $19.7 million worth of potato chips was exported to Canada, $49.4 million worth to Japan, and $50.5 million to the European Union.

RESEARCH AND TECHNOLOGY

The salty snack food industry witnessed an innovative use of computer technology in the late 1980s, when Frito-Lay issued hand-held computers to each of its 10,000-member sales force. Prior to this change, the route salespeople tallied the inventory of product on supermarket shelves on paper. These data were returned manually to regional offices, compiled, and eventually sent to the company's headquarters in Dallas. The resulting reports were clumsy and slow to produce.

Following the issuance of the small computers, however, the sales staff punched in inventory counts while still in the stores. The figures were instantly transmitted via satellite to Frito-Lay's mainframe computer. This instantaneous sending of data allowed analysts in Dallas to see sales figures much more quickly. As a result, Frito-Lay sales people gained discretion to lower prices on the spot if necessary to remain competitive with other products. Although this computer system, purchased from Fujitsu, cost $40 million in 1987, Frito-Lay maintained that the technology paid for itself several times over by eliminating stale product in stores. Following this innovation, Frito-Lay's major competitors introduced hand-held computers, and manufacturers in other packaged foods industries were expected to follow suit.

FURTHER READING

1993 SFA State-of-the-Industry Report. Alexandria, Virginia: Snack Food Association, 1993.

Fink, Ronald. "Data Processing: Pepsi Co." *Financial World,* 29 September 1992.

Freeman, Laurie. "Hot Categories Prove Americans Make the Healthy Choice when Possible." *Advertising Age,* 27 February 1995.

General Business File. University of Michigan Kresge Library Online Database. February 1997.

Gutner, Toddi. "Chip Mania." *Forbes,* 19 July 1993.

Kuhn, Mary Ellen. "The Skinny on Snacks: Healthy Is Hot." *Food Processing,* March 1995.

LeDuc Doug. "Snack Food Makers Foresee Less Price Pressure After Eagle Brands Demise." *Knight Ridder/Tribune Business News,* 19 March 1996.

Macnow, Glen. "A Taste of Old Cape Cod." *Nation's Business,* February 1990.

Main, Jeremy. "Frito-Lay Shorts Its Business Cycle." *Fortune,* 15 January 1990.

Sellers, Patricia. "If It Ain't Broke, Fix It Anyway." *Fortune,* 28 December 1992.

Snack Foods Association. "1996 State of the Industry Report" *Snack World,* June 1996.

Thompson, Stephanie. "Frito-Lay Brand Dominance Breeds P-L Snack Upstarts." *Brandweek,* 25 November 1996.

Zellner, Wendy. "Frito-Lay is Munching on the Competition." *Business Week,* 24 August 1992.

—Karen Withem, updated by Visi Tilak

SIC 2097

MANUFACTURED ICE

This category covers ice plants operated by public utilities and establishments manufacturing artificial ice for sale in the form of blocks or cubes; it excludes makers of dry ice, which are categorized in **SIC 2813: Industrial Gases.**

Technological advances freed consumers from their long dependence on the harvest of local, naturally occurring sources of ice by permitting first its export and then its manufacture. This production, whether by private companies or by public utilities, was based on developments that also heralded the era of domestic refrigeration, and the ice trays found in most American kitchens became the major rival of commercial ice manufacturers. In terms of volume, however, domestic refrigerators could not compete with ice plants, and manufactured ice has sold well in outlets where goods for parties, receptions, and other entertainments are routinely purchased.

In the 1990s, ice manufacturers' products ranged from pound bags of ice cubes in varying quantities, to blocks of ice in weights of 10 to 300 pounds. The larger blocks were particularly popular for ice carvings at outdoor festivals and banquet buffets.

Much of the industry's annual revenues depends on the weather. The warmer the temperature, the more ice consumers buy. Logically, sales of manufactured ice are highest during the summer months of June, July, and August. Due to the ever-increasing efficiency of ice-making machinery and delivery, the wholesale price of ice has increased only by five cents since the late 1970s, to between 45 cents and 50 cents per pound in the late 1990s.

Purity is a primary issue among ice suppliers. As Michael R. Enright explained in *Nation's Business,* many ice suppliers have learned to enhance the purity of their product by creating a hole in the center of each cube and then flushing it, rinsing away the sulphur, iron, and other impurities in water that had concentrated there during the formation of the cube.

Such purity concerned not only consumers but also businesses that required large quantities of ice to keep food cool and fresh. Despite the convenience and cheapness of ice produced in-house by such businesses, ice manufacturing specialists had the potential to create a product of greater purity.

Both the continuing quest for purity and a heightened consciousness about ecological issues on the part of consumers have made one promising development in the 1990s—the marketing of gourmet ice, as harvested from glaciers, springs, and other sources predating or little affected by human pollution—a return to the very origins of the ice industry, though with the probable addition of innovative packaging this time around.

Since the late 1980s, legislation at various levels of government led to tightened controls on sanitation and an improved standard of quality in the ice industry, with the result that mandating drug testing of truck drivers further regulated the industry.

Three of the five leading companies in the ice manufacturing business are located in California: Union Ice Co. of Los Angeles, with 100 employees and $16 million in sales; Glacier Ice Co. of Fremont, with 75 employees and $10 million in sales; and Riverside Ice Company of Riverside, with 20 employees and $3 million in sales. Other leaders include Pelican Ice and Cold Storage Inc. of New Orleans with 100 employees and $16 million in sales; and Crystal Ice and Cold Storage Inc. of Phoenix with 150 employees and $7 million in sales.

FURTHER READING

Bryan, Dave. "Ice Company Has Stood the Heat for 20 Years." *Triangle Business Journal,* 14 July 1995.

Cuneo, Alice Z. "California Warms Up to Spring-Water Ice." *Advertising Age,* 7 October 1989, 30MW.

Enright, Michael R. "Hot Ice." *Nation's Business,* July 1987, 57.

Morris, David. *Self-Reliant Cities,* San Francisco: Sierra Club, 1982.

NPN: National Petroleum News, Mid-June 1993, 142.

Ward's Business Directory of U.S. Private and Public Companies. Detroit: Gale Research, 1996.

—Richard Hillyer, updated by Mary McNulty

SIC 2098

MACARONI, SPAGHETTI, VERMICELLI, AND NOODLES

This category covers establishments primarily engaged in manufacturing dry macaroni, spaghetti, vermicelli, and noodles. Establishments primarily engaged in manufacturing canned macaroni and spaghetti are classified in **SIC 2032: Canned Specialties,** and those manufacturing fried noodles, such as Chinese noodles, are classified in **SIC 2099: Food Preparations, Not Elsewhere Classified.**

INDUSTRY SNAPSHOT

In the two decades from 1975 to 1995, Americans increased their pasta consumption by 90 percent. Pasta was manufactured almost exclusively in the United States from durum semolina wheat. A growing consumer preference for nutritious, low-fat foods boosted the health of the industry, nearly doubling mean annual per capita consumption in the last 20 years to 24 pounds. In 1995, the typical consumer ate pasta an average of 2.7 times a week. The increased consump-

tion was also due to a shift in consumer perceptions: it gained popularity among middle class and affluent adults and seniors, rather than being viewed as a meal for children or the working poor, as was the case during the 1960s.

Industry sales in 1995 totaled nearly $2.1 billion, up from $1.3 billion in 1991. Slightly more than 6,000 people were employed by the nation's approximately 180 pasta manufacturing establishments. The industry faced challenges entering the mid-1990s, however, as foreign producers flooded the market and the nation's durum wheat was attacked by Karnal Bunt disease. Additionally, tougher labeling requirements, made effective in 1994, affected pasta industry profit levels, as did environmental protection and laws designed to protect employees, such as mandatory health care provisions.

ORGANIZATION AND STRUCTURE

Fifty companies produce virtually all the pasta made in the United States through approximately 180 establishments. Half of those firms were divisions or subsidiaries of larger companies. The bulk of dried pasta and noodles was sold through retail outlets such as supermarkets, convenience stores, and gourmet shops, for personal consumption. A scant 5 percent was sold to the food service industry.

Pasta Manufacturing. Dried pasta was manufactured from coarsely ground durum wheat, or "semolina." Durum was a hard, winter wheat, known for its high level of gluten, which made a stiff dough appropriate for pasta. Farina, a softer wheat, was sometimes added, as were powdered flavorings such as tomato or spinach. Gluten was also sometimes added to the dough, and "enriched" pasta received nutritional supplements such as thiamin, niacin, riboflavin, and iron. Most pasta was made without eggs, but noodles were formed by adding eggs to the dough before processing.

Prior to the formation of pasta into its characteristic shape, the wheat was harvested and tested for moisture content, volume, color, insects, chaff, and bran. Once the wheat was determined to meet sufficient standards, the process of milling began. Wheat was first "tempered," or soaked in water, to separate the bran from the berry. Tempering also gave the berry enough moisture to prevent shattering when it was ground—the next part of the process. Once ground, the wheat was sifted numerous times to create semolina—coarsely ground flour, with particles about the size of sugar crystals. A byproduct of this repeated sifting was durum flour, which was sold for other uses. The semolina was added to water and any other ingredients, such as dyes, to create dough, which was then extruded through machines that formed the pasta into its ultimate shape. The pasta was then dried, packaged, and distributed.

BACKGROUND AND DEVELOPMENT

Although pasta was generally associated with Italy, and indeed many of the varied shapes originated from that country, the first pasta was actually Chinese. The development of an agricultural civilization led to pasta, possibly around 3000 B.C. ancient Greeks considered pasta ''marcus''—meaning ''divine food.'' An Etruscan tomb created around 400 B.C. depicted the making of the grain product. Horace, a poet who lived in the first century B.C., described lasagna as one course of a Roman banquet.

Pasta was also a part of the cuisine of the Middle East. The Jewish and Arabic cultures, as well as that of Persia, discussed pasta as well as noodles. Germans consumed it, and the Genoese ate it in the thirteenth century. All of this took place before Marco Polo's legendary expedition to China, which led to the widespread consumption by Italians, who added red tomatoes to the recipe.

Noodles were consumed in the New World, prepared in the manner popular among the British—accompanied with a cream sauce and cheese. Thomas Jefferson was the first prominent American to embrace pasta, when he purchased a ''macaroni'' machine in Italy and shipped it to the United States. An Italian restaurateur in Richmond, Virginia, served pasta to his influential clientele, which included Jefferson.

By 1848, French miller Antoine Zerega opened the first macaroni factory. He followed both Chinese and Italian traditions, drying strands of spaghetti on the rooftop of his Brooklyn factory. The subsequent immigration of large numbers of Italians to New York helped bring pasta into the mainstream of American cuisine.

A subtle wheat flavor was considered the ideal taste for pasta, since blandness prevented the pasta noodle from competing with the flavor of the sauce. The ideal texture of pasta was obtained when it was cooked ''al dente.'' This translated from Italian literally as ''to the tooth,'' but it described a noodle that was firm when chewed.

CURRENT CONDITIONS

Retail sales of dried pasta were $2.3 billion in 1995, a 50 percent increase from 1991. One reason for this dramatic trend was research about cancer and heart disease prevention combined with the nutritional qualities of pasta. Numerous public and private studies

during the 1970s and 1980s linked diets high in fat content with various types of cancers and heart disease. During this same time period, separate research of individuals in developing countries demonstrated the benefits of a diet high in fiber—a non-nutritional substance found in whole grains, vegetables, and fruits. In addition, studies revealed the importance of complex carbohydrates, which were also found in grains such as durum wheat. Consuming complex carbohydrates helped to provide a steady flow of energy because they took longer to digest than simple carbohydrates.

All of these findings rippled throughout the food industry, causing consumer preference to shift away from meals high in fat toward foods low in fat. Americans reduced their consumption of meat and dairy products as part of a healthier overall diet. Simultaneously, consumers embraced diets with a higher percentage of whole grain foods—including pasta. In fact, the popularity of pasta among athletes led to the term ''carbo-loading,'' which was frequently accomplished through the ingestion of pasta or other grains. The consumption of foods high in complex carbohydrates prior to a marathon or other athletic endurance event was widely believed to boost performance.

In addition to being high in carbohydrates, pasta products became widely recognized for their nutritional value and relatively low levels of fat. A 10-ounce serving of cooked pasta contained 420 calories, 14 grams of protein (although wheat protein was considered incomplete), and only 1 gram of fat. It also provided one-fifth of the iron, niacin, and riboflavin, and one-third of the thiamin, needed for one day.

The general perception of pasta also evolved over the last three decades. In the 1960s, consumers thought of meatballs and spaghetti as a child's meal, too unsophisticated for adults. With the introduction of pasta varieties—lasagna, fettucine, manicotti, linguine, ravioli, cannelloni, tortellini, and angel hair pasta—the age-old grain food gained acceptance among affluent adults, for both dining out and eating in. Moreover, the typical marinara, or tomato-based, sauce served with ground beef or meatballs gave way to a multitude of flavored toppings—ranging from basil and pine nuts to Alfredo or cream sauces. Another popular accompaniment to the noodle was a mixture of vegetables, often in a marinara sauce, known as ''pasta primavera.''

As the popularity of pasta grew, so did the market for value-added, or flavored, varieties. At the end of the 1990s, popular flavors included smoked salmon, porcini mushroom, tomato basil, lemon pepper, and chili pepper.

Other factors contributing to pasta's popularity included its convenience, durability, and economy. A box of dried pasta lasted up to seven years on the shelf. It was a relatively good food value, at a cost of about a quarter per 10-ounce serving. The nationwide availability of prepared sauces added to the ease with which a pasta meal could be prepared. Pasta could be cooked on the stove top in about 10 to 15 minutes. It could be reheated—along with the accompanying sauce—in a microwave oven in half of that time. These factors had significant appeal to the increasing numbers of dual-income and single-parent households in the United States.

Most pasta was served for dinner (approximately 75 percent in the mid-1990s), but the trend went toward more frequent pasta lunches, with a 20-percent increase in consumption at this meal. The most popular shapes were macaroni, which saw a 33-percent increase in consumption, and lasagna, which showed 31-percent growth. Pasta products also dominated the side dish market, with 669 varieties offered in 1995, far exceeding the amount of rice dishes (137), salads (41), potato products (17), and stuffing mixes (14).

Regulatory Challenges. Like much of the food industry, pasta manufacturers faced increased regulation under new federal laws. The Nutrition Labeling and Education Act (NLEA) of 1990, which took effect in May 1994, required that pasta packaging list nutrients in greater detail than in the past. In addition, the NLEA provided for the Food and Drug Administration to determine the serving size on which nutritional information was based—something that had previously been determined by the manufacturers themselves.

Another trend in regulation in the early 1990s was based on concern over the effects of fumigants on the ozone layer. Many pasta manufacturers employed methyl bromide to rid storage areas of weevils and other pests that consumed wheat. One bill considered in 1993 declared methyl bromide a class one ozone depleter and called for its production to be discontinued by the year 2000.

Competitive Challenges. The greatest challenge to the dry pasta and noodle industry was expected to come from competition with other types of pasta. For example, the sales volume of frozen pasta grew at an annual rate of 19.1 percent from 1980 to 1985 and 13.4 percent from 1986 to 1991. Although growth was expected to slow to about 6.7 percent per year in the latter part of the 1990s, the popularity of frozen pasta was expected to continue throughout the remainder of the decade, with consumption estimated at 62 billion pounds in 1995.

This growth was attributable to the convenience of frozen pasta, which came with a variety of sauces and required nothing more than heating in the microwave or the conventional oven. While cooking dry pasta was simple and required little time, preparation of the sauce could be more complex, and working individuals were increasingly reluctant to create meals from intricate or lengthy recipes.

Shelf-stable pasta was yet another product that eroded market share of dry pasta, and was expected to continue to do so. The shelf-stable category included dry packages like macaroni and cheese, pasta and noodle side dish mixes, add-meat dinner mixes, and soups or other meals that came in microwaveable containers. Shelf-stable pasta sales grew 6.7 percent annually in the early 1980s, but its popularity grew during the latter part of the decade by about 10 percent. Sales of this product were expected to grow at an annual rate of better than 10 percent through the remainder of the 1990s.

Fresh pasta, which showed an increase in sales volume of 60 percent annually from 1988 to 1991, experienced a decrease in the latter half of the 1990s. Initially, fresh pasta gained market share among the affluent at the expense of its dry counterpart, as it was perceived to be more flavorful and nutritious. It was sold in gourmet shops, as well as restaurants and supermarkets. The drawback of fresh pasta was its perishability, a result of its high moisture content. The greater ease of distribution enjoyed by dry pasta manufacturers was believed to be a primary reason that dry pasta held its own in market share.

Canned pasta posed no competitive threat to dry pasta and noodles. Despite attempts to upgrade its image to a premium food product, canned pasta was still perceived to be most appropriate for children or for lower income individuals. Canned food was also viewed as having depleted nutritional value, and the health value that drove much of the rise in pasta consumption was perceived to be lacking in canned dishes. Moreover, canned spaghetti with sauce was not believed by consumers to be as flavorful as that of either fresh, frozen, or dry pasta.

New Jersey-based Campbell Soup Company, a leader in the canned pasta market under the name Franco-American, continued to introduce new children's dishes—including teddy bear shaped pasta and sporty shapes, like bicycles, in sauces—and an upscale variety called Superiors targeted at adults. Despite such innovations, canned pasta market analysts did not anticipate that this product would pose a threat to dry pasta's market share. After sales volume of this product grew 3.3 percent annually from 1980 to 1985, and

5.3 percent per year from 1986 to 1991, it was projected to increase less than 1.0 percent annually through the mid- and late 1990s.

INDUSTRY LEADERS

Hershey Foods Corporation, a $3 billion company located in Hershey, Pennsylvania, was the largest pasta manufacturer. The company's Pasta Division produced approximately 600 pounds of pasta in 1995 through such brands as Ronzini, Skinner, American Beauty, and Delmonico. Minneapolis-based Borden Incorporated's Pasta Division, also manufactured 600 pounds of pasta in 1995, primarily through its Creamette and Prince lines. That same year, Borden Incorporated, which posted sales of $5.9 billion, became a privately owned company when it was purchased by partners of the investment firm Kohlberg, Kravis, Roberts, and Co. Independently owned A. Zerega Sons, Inc., of New Jersey, turned out 270 pounds of pasta in 1995 and reported sales of $100 million.

WORK FORCE

Due to technological advances in the pasta industry, including the use of computers in the manufacturing process, the number of workers declined from the early 1980s to the mid-1990s. About 8,400 people were employed in the manufacture of dry pasta in 1982; by 1995, that figure dropped to 6,300. Seventy-nine percent of those employees were involved in production activities.

AMERICA AND THE WORLD

Until the 1990s, the United States imported a negligible volume of manufactured pasta. That situation changed drastically as foreign producers moved to take advantage of the expanding U.S. pasta market. U.S. pasta distributors complained about the inferior quality of some pastas from Italy and Turkey, charging that those countries were purposely dumping inferior products on the U.S. market at lower-than-market prices. The outcry prompted the International Trade Commission and the Commerce Department to impose stiff tariffs on the imported products. The targeted importers were expected to appeal the tariffs.

The durum wheat from which pasta was made grew steadily as an export beginning with the 1959-60 growing season. Exports of this wheat variety were zero that year, but climbed to peak annual levels of 80 million bushels during the 1980s. By the 1990s, the United States was exporting 50 percent of its annual production. Algeria was the largest importer of U.S. durum wheat, with Tunisia second. Trade with those

countries was part of the Export Enhancement Program, an incentive program to facilitate U.S. exports to North African nations.

As domestic pasta consumption skyrocketed, durum farmers were hard-pressed to meet the demand. In 11 of the 15 years from 1981 to 1996, domestic use of durum for pasta production combined with export sales exceeded domestic production. The shortage of durum wheat drove prices up to $7.50 per bushel, a substantial increase from the $4.50 price of the late 1980s.

After the passage of the Canada/United States Free Trade Agreement (CUSTA), in 1988 U.S. farmers in Minnesota, North Dakota, and Montana voiced concern over the growing volume of Canadian wheat sold in the U.S. By the 1990s, Canadian wheat accounted for 14 percent of U.S. durum production. The situation was exacerbated when U.S. durum wheat fields were hit by Karnal Bunt disease, which reduced the wheat to a powdery soot. Canada banned imports of all U.S. durum and many U.S. producers refused to accept durum from states where infected wheat was reported.

The United States ranked fourth in the world in mean annual per capita pasta consumption. Italians consumed over 59 pounds per capita annually and Venezuelans nearly 28 pounds, while Americans ate 19 pounds apiece annually. With popularity of pasta on the increase due to its perceived convenience and nutritional value, however, per capita consumption in the United States was predicted to surpass that of every nation in the world except Italy by the year 2000.

FURTHER READING

"Annual Consumer Expenditures Survey." *Supermarket News,* September 1996.

"The Bunt Bonanza." *Alberta Report/Western Report,* 16 April 1996.

Business Trend Analysts, Inc. "The U.S. Pasta Market." *Pasta Journal,* November/December 1991.

Dornblaser, Lynn. "Pasta Garnishes More Meals." *Prepared Foods,* Mid-April 1996.

Fisher, Neal, "Growth in Durum Markets Benefits Producers and Industry," *Pasta Journal,* November/December 1990.

"International Pasta." *Pasta Journal,* November/December 1990.

Kardong, Don. "Yankee Noodles." *Runner's World,* October 1992.

"Making Tons of Pasta Helps to Form Northland's Economic Foundation." *Kansas City Business Journal,* 1 March 1996.

Darnay, Arsen, J., ed. *Manufacturing USA.* 5th ed. Detroit: Gale Research, 1996.

National Pasta Association. "And on the Ninth Day There Was Pasta." *Pastahh,* Winter 1989-90.

"Pasta Is Growing Strong." *Pasta Journal,* May/June 1993.

"Spaghetti." *Consumer Reports,* August 1988.

Tagliabue, John. "Pasta Makers of the World Unite." *The New York Times,* 28 October 1995.

Turcsik, Richard. "Stiff Tariffs Expected on Imports of Pasta." *Supermarket News,* 7 August 1995.

"The United States-Canada Durum Wheat War." *Choices: The Magazine of Food, Farm & Resource Issues,* 1995.

"U.S. Food Consumption." *Food Review,* May-August 1995.

—Karen Withem, updated by Mary McNulty

SIC 2099

FOOD PREPARATIONS, NOT ELSEWHERE CLASSIFIED

This classification includes establishments primarily engaged in manufacturing food preparations not classified under another category. It includes manufacturers of items such as syrups, leavening agents, dry mixes (for sauces and gravies), packaged mixes (made from pasta, rice, and potatoes), seasonings and spices, and ready-to-eat meals and salads. Also included are manufacturers of miscellaneous food specialties, such as fried Chinese noodles, sorghum, tortillas, honey, marshmallow creme, peanut butter, popcorn, tea, tofu, and vinegar.

Miscellaneous food preparations with separate classifications include: **SIC 2091: Canned and Cured Fish and Seafoods; SIC 2092: Fresh or Frozen Prepared Fish and Seafoods; SIC 2095: Roasted Coffee; SIC 2096: Potato Chips and Similar Snacks; SIC 2097: Manufactured Ice;** and **SIC 2098: Macaroni and Spaghetti.** Manufacturers of flour mixes are classified in Industry Group 204.

INDUSTRY SNAPSHOT

According to government statistics, the total value of goods shipped by establishments classified in SIC 2099 totaled $9.8 billion in 1987. In addition, some businesses with other classifications manufactured products considered primary to the industry. Combined, the value of all product shipments for items classified in the industry, irrespective of their source, in 1987 totaled $10.7 billion. This represented a 30 percent increase over the total $8.1 billion in 1982 shipments. By 1995, miscellaneous food preparations had grown to a $14 billion industry in current dollars.

The leading companies in this industry segment are diversified and manufacture a wide variety of food stuffs found on grocers' shelves. These include Kraft Foods, Inc., with sales exceeding $29 billion; SUPERVALU, Inc., RJR Nabisco Corp., American Home Products Corporation, and Abbott Laboratories each had sales greater than $10 billion. Kellogg Company, Borden, Inc., General Mills, Inc. are among the other leading companies in this industry segment whose brand names are immediately recognizable to American consumers.

In 1995, vinegar and cider shipments reached $219.6 million, down from a 1993 high of $235 million. Retail consumption of pasta dropped 2 percent in 1995 over the previous year's period. This 1996 survey, conducted for the National Pasta Association, tallied a wide range of products on grocers' shelves—from dried pasta to pasta included in prepackaged dinners—but did not take into account pasta sold to the so-called "warehouse clubs" or to foodservice establishments.

Despite these declines, many categories experienced substantial increases. Fast-growing classifications included: dry mix preparations (such as dips, salad dressings, gravy and sauces, seasonings, and frostings), which increased from $1.2 billion to $2.2 billion; nonfrozen, perishable prepared foods (such as salads, peeled vegetables, tortillas, and tofu), which increased from $769.1 million to more than $1.3 billion; tea packaged for consumers, which increased from $747.6 million to $936.3 million; and spices, which accounted for an estimated $2 billion in 1994.

BACKGROUND AND DEVELOPMENT

Vinegar. One of oldest products classified within SIC 2099 is vinegar. Records of vinegar use date back 5,000 years, and some historians estimate it was known as long ago as 10,000 years. During the Civil War, vinegar was used to prevent scurvy, a disease caused by vitamin C deficiency. Throughout vinegar's long history, it has had a wide variety of applications, including use as a preservative and as a cleaning agent.

Vinegar, derived from two French words meaning "sour wine," is a product of fermentation. When natural sugars ferment they produce alcohol, which after undergoing further acetic fermentation becomes vinegar. One of the best known types is wine vinegar, but throughout history many other types of vinegar have been produced. These include vinegars made from naturally sweet products like molasses, sorghum, honey, and syrup, and vinegars made from fruits, potatoes, and grains.

Four different methods have evolved to control the fermentation process by which vinegars are made. Under the most labor-intensive method, called the solera system, vinegar is aged in different types of wood, a process that can take decades. Another technique, termed the Orleans method, uses a starter culture in a manner similar to the process by which bakers ferment bread dough in sourdough preparation. The Orleans method is implemented to produce vinegar in wooden barrels and takes up to six months. A faster method, termed the ''quick process,'' involves the aeration of wine along with organic materials to produce vinegar in about a week. The quickest vinegar production, however, occurs in a process called continuous production, which requires holding wine in a pressurized tank under carefully controlled conditions. Air is forced through the liquid to aid the fermentation process. Wine is continually added and finished vinegar taken off the top of the tank. Converting wine into vinegar using this process takes approximately one day.

In the United States, the vinegar industry formed alongside the apple industry. As a result, it was concentrated in areas with large harvests of apples. Cider vinegar was made from apples or apple juice. As the U.S. vinegar industry developed, it offered a variety of products to perform different functions. White vinegar, also called distilled vinegar, is primarily used in home canning and for making pickles, salsa, and relishes. Wine vinegar is an integral ingredient in vinaigrettes. Malt vinegar, a mildly sweet product, complements salads and fish and chips. Rice vinegar, a particularly strong variety, is added to sushi rice. A rich, dark product, balsamic vinegar is used for vinaigrettes and as a condiment. Sherry vinegar, another variety with a strong flavor, is a cooking vinegar. In addition to the types of vinegar produced by using varying sources, infused vinegars are made by adding flavorings such as berries, garlic, or herbs.

Tofu. A product with a long history, tofu is a white, gelatinous substance made from soybean curd. It bears a slight resemblance to cream cheese but has a softer texture that has sometimes been described as ''squishy.'' Although tofu by itself is considered bland, when cooked in a recipe it picks up flavors from other ingredients. To make tofu, manufacturers begin by soaking soybeans for 12 to 18 hours. After soaking, the beans are mashed and strained. The retained juice solidifies, is cut into portions, and packaged for sale.

Originating in China approximately 1,000 years ago, tofu was a staple in Oriental cooking for centuries. Tofu began gaining popularity in the United States following World War II when returning servicemen, accustomed to eating it abroad, began eating tofu at home.

Tea. Another food product with historic ties to China is tea. Tea was originally made from the dried, processed leaves of an Asian shrub. One of the oldest companies in the U.S. tea industry was founded by Sir Thomas Lipton, a Scotsman, who began importing tea into the United States in 1890. The first instant tea was marketed by the Nestle Beverage Company in 1948.

Peanut butter. One product native to the Americas is peanut butter. While not indigenous to North America, peanuts were grown by South Americans at least 1,000 years ago. Although the circumstances of their introduction to North America is unknown, historians believe peanuts were grown by early European settlers, who used them as food for hogs. George Washington Carver is credited with developing more than 300 uses for peanuts and helping establish them as an important crop. Improvements made between the 1930s and the 1990s helped peanut farmers experience a fivefold increase in per acre yields. During the early 1990s, most U.S. peanut production came from Georgia. Other leading peanut cultivation states were Alabama, Texas, North Carolina, and Virginia.

Approximately half the peanuts eaten in the United States are consumed in the form of peanut butter. *Consumer Reports* calculated that on any given day peanut butter is consumed by one out of every six Americans. Although peanut butter is considered a good source of protein, dietary fiber, and B vitamins, it contains a high percentage of fat. To make peanut butter, manufacturers remove peanut skins and grind the nuts into a thick, pasty substance. Frequently, hydrogenated vegetable oil is added as a stabilizer, and salt and sugar are added to improve flavor. Chunky varieties, containing pieces of peanuts, were also developed.

One of the problems associated with peanut butter is the presence of aflatoxin. Aflatoxin is a carcinogenic poison produced by *aspergillus flavus,* a mold that grows on peanuts when they are not properly stored. Aflatoxin problems first appeared in the 1960s and led U.S. officials to establish limits on the amount of the substance allowable in peanut products. A 1990 *Consumer Reports* study noted that some peanut butter exceeded allowable levels of aflatoxin.

CURRENT CONDITIONS

During the early 1990s, the top U.S. peanut butter brands—Jif, Skippy, and Peter Pan—accounted for two-thirds of all peanut butter sales. Specialty and health food stores offered "natural" peanut butters that lacked sweeteners and stabilizers and some featured "grind your own" peanut butter options.

In 1993 industry watchers noted a decline in peanut butter sales. The drop was attributed to calorie-consciousness. Consumers also turned away from name brands in favor of private labels. According to a September 1993 report in the *Wall Street Journal*, peanut butter sales declined 12.2 percent during the 13-week period ending July 4, 1993. Chunky peanut butter sales fell the most, declining 15.7 percent, while creamy sales dropped 10.9 percent.

One of the fastest growing sectors within the industry during the early 1990s was prepackaged convenience foods, which were often sold as "kits" with premeasured ingredients that could be prepared quickly and easily by the consumer. These ranged from salads to stir fry.

Tofu was also experiencing rapid growth. Because it is a good protein source naturally low in saturated fat, with no cholesterol, its popularity was increasing particularly among vegetarians and health- conscious consumers. Tofu also benefited from a growing interest in ethnic cooking. The tofu expansion could be attributed in part to improvements in packaging technology, giving products a longer shelf life. Most tofu was sold in packages of water and had a short shelf life of only about 10 days. In 1990 one producer, Mori-Nu, reported the development of innovative packaging enabling its product to have a 10 month shelf life without refrigeration.

One of the nation's largest tofu producers, Azumaya, Inc., of San Francisco, began producing tofu in 1927. In 1991 the company reported daily production of 3.5 tons of tofu. Some industry analysts predicted that tofu would become as popular as yogurt.

Another rapidly growing product in the United States during the 1990s was tea. According to Information Resources Inc. of Chicago, the sales of loose teas and tea in bags grew 1 percent to $640 million; ready-to-drink teas sold in the United States increased 1.8 percent to $421 million in 1995. The market is no longer relegated to a simple hot drink served with lemon and honey; it has married tea—black, green, or herbal—to all sorts of flavor permutations.

Herbal teas in supermarkets passed the $100 million sales mark in 1991. The top three companies in herbal tea sales were Celestial Seasonings, Inc. with 49.1 percent of the market (and with a new line of herbal "remedy" teas in 1995), Lipton with 23.1 percent, and Bigelow with 14.6 percent. In 1992 enough herbal tea was sold in the United States to brew 58 million gallons. Sales represented a 5 percent increase over the previous year. According to a report in *Brandweek,* one of every eight cups of tea consumed in the United States is either decaffeinated or herbal, and approximately 80 percent is consumed as iced tea. In 1993 *Beverage World* estimated that iced tea sales would continue growing at an annual rate of 50 percent.

Product expansions in the tea category, according to *Prepared Foods* are attributable to introductions of green teas and chai. Green teas purportedly provide healing benefits, which is why numerous companies now provide green tea products, including John Wagner & Sons and AFC. Chai is a rich, milky tea-based drink often used as part of Indian ceremonial meals and tastes of vanilla, honey, and spices. Oregon Chai introduced its chai liquid concentrates to consumers in 1995.

Tea-juice hybrids increased in popularity through 1995, with a great number of product introductions that year—and not only from Snapple. Nestle added numerous products to its Nestea line in 1995, including an instant Lemonade Tea, and Suntea Style mix, and several fruit-flavored beverage mixes. Snapple Cider Tea—a combination of black tea and apple cider that may be served hot or cold—was introduced by The Quaker Oats Company. (Snapple was sold to Triarc Companies in 1997.)

According to the U.S. Department of Agriculture, the average U.S. spice consumption was an estimated 815 million pounds between 1990 and 1994, compared with 541 million for the period between 1980 and 1984 Per capita consumption rose a point from a period a decade ago. Domestic production increased to meet the demand.

Total sales of spices, domestic and imported, in the United States were about $2 billion in 1994, double that of a decade ago, and compared to sales of between $400 and 450 million in the mid-1970s. Dehydrated garlic and onions accounted for about two-thirds of national spice production in 1994, with cayenne or red peppers representing an estimated 30 percent, and then mustard seed and various herbs account for the balance.

Sales are anticipated to continue unabated. "If the current rate of per capita consumption continues and the U.S. population reaches the forecasted 274.8 million by the year 2000," predicted analysts Peter J.

Buzzanell and Kathryn L. Lipton, "total domestic use of spices would increase 8 percent from 1990-94 to an estimated 877 million pounds. But all indications are that the growth likely will be even higher. The trend toward less salt in foods will likely continue to stimulate more spice use to compensate for flavor loss."

An estimated 60 percent of spices sold in the United States are to add flavor to the food processing and foodservice industries. Population growth (particularly census figures noting increased Asian and Hispanic populations), increased popularity of ethnic foods and prepared meals, and increased consumption of food outside the home can be attributed to the continued growth in spice sales. Major spice users include fast-food outlets such as Kentucky Fried Chicken and McDonald's, which not only spice their foods, but provide prepackaged condiments to customers.

INDUSTRY LEADERS

A leader within the tea segment of SIC 2099 is the Thomas J. Lipton Company, a wholly owned subsidiary of Unilever PLC. Lipton, headquartered in Englewood Cliffs, New Jersey, reported sales of $3 billion in fiscal 1996. This represented a substantial increase over the $1.4 billion in sales posted in 1992, which was a 4.3 percent increase over 1991 sales. According to one report, Lipton controlled about half of the black tea market, estimated at $423 million in 1992.

Lipton, a pioneer in the development of naturally decaffeinated teas, was founded in 1915 by Sir Thomas Lipton, who had been selling his teas in the United States since 1890. In 1992 Lipton reported that its Suffolk, Virginia, production facility blended more than 36 million pounds of tea. Lipton's tea products include tea bags, instant iced tea, and ready-to-drink iced tea. In 1991 the company established the Pepsi Lipton Tea Partnership, a venture undertaken to bring together expertise from Lipton's tea producers and Pepsi's bottling and distribution system. In addition to tea products, Lipton also marketed Lipton Soup Mixes, Recipe Secrets, Lipton Side Dishes, and Cup-a-Soup. The company's Lawry's division offered spice and seasoning blends, sauces, and Mexican food products.

Another major participant in this market segment was Nestle USA, Inc., which had 15 food and beverage companies. Products of the Nestle Beverage Company include Nestea, Carnation hot cocoa, and Nestle Quick, while the Nestle Refrigerated Food Company produces Contadina refrigerated pizza kits and sauces. Other major Nestle divisions include Nestle Food Company, Nestle Frozen Food Company, and Nestle Brands Foodservice. In 1992 the Nestle organization

reported net sales of $7 billion and a staff of 43,000. Nestle USA Inc., which is the segment of the corporation that manufactures products including chocolate, frozen dinners under the Stouffer's brand, ice cream and chocolate milk, posted sales in excess of $3.5 billion in 1994.

At the helm of the spice segment within this industry classification is McCormick & Company, Inc., founded in 1889 and—according to company literature—the largest spice company in the world. Its product line, sold in the United States on the East Coast under the McCormick label and on the West Coast under the Schilling label, features a wide variety of spices from 18 areas around the world. The company's other primary business involves plastic bottle and tube manufacturing.

McCormick/Schilling had a 37 percent share in the U.S. retail spice market in 1994. In fiscal year 1995 the company posted sales of $1.9 billion and about 8,900 employees; in 1992 that figure McCormick reported sales of $1.5 billion and had a work force of 8,000. McCormick's industrial and food service divisions provide flavors, seasonings, and specialty food products to more than 80 of the top 100 food manufacturers in the United States as well as to many major restaurant chains. In addition to the United States, McCormick sold products globally; in 1993 the company announced intentions to develop markets in China and the Pacific Rim.

Universal Foods Corporation, a major producer in several of this industry's segments, is an international company involved in manufacturing and marketing a wide variety of food products, including flavors and colors, dehydrated vegetables, frozen french fried potatoes, and yeast products. The company posted sales of $806.4 million in 1996. The company's yeast products are marketed under the Red Star label.

Red Star yeast production began during the latter part of the 1800s. In the 1920s the company perfected an aeration process that enabled it to make an improved compressed yeast product. Further work led to the development of a less perishable yeast. In the early 1990s Universal Foods claimed it was the largest and most diversified manufacturer and distributor of yeast products within the United States. Red Star reported sales of $160.0 million in 1995.

In 1993 Universal Foods reported a 7 percent increase in yeast revenue, a significant portion of which was attributable to trends within the pizza industry toward producing extra large pizzas. Within the consumer baking market, a rise in yeast sales was attributed to the growing popularity of bread machines. According to company statistics, U.S. households owned an estimated three million bread machines in 1993.

WORK FORCE

According to the U.S. Department of Commerce, industry employment totaled 57,900 in 1987. The industry's combined payroll topped $1.1 billion. The leading states in employment were California, Illinois, New York, and Texas.

FURTHER READING

Applebaum, Cara. "Tetly Heats Up Iced Tea." *Adweek's Marketing Week* 6 April 1992.

"Background on Thomas J. Lipton Company." Englewood Cliffs, NJ: Thomas J. Lipton Co., 1996.

Bittman, Mark. "Vinegar." *Restaurant Business Magazine* 1 March 1992.

"Brand Scorecard." *Advertising Age,* 5 October 1992.

Buzzanell, Peter J.; Lipton, Kathryn L. "Whether a Pinch or a Dash, It Adds up to a Growing U.S. Spice Market. *Food Review,* September-December 1995.

Carlsen, Clifford. "Utilitarian Soybean Curd Goes Exotic." *San Francisco Business Journal* 28 June 1991.

Deveny, Kathleen. "Peanut Butter Makers Feel Crunch With Sales Decline in 2nd Quarter." *Wall Street Journal,* 16 September 1993.

Dornblaser, Lynn. "Adult Drinks Lead the Beverage Pack." *Prepared Foods,* 15 April 1996.

"Estimated Retail Pasta Consumption." National Pasta Association, 1996.

Friedman, Martin. "Food Kits Foster One-Stop Shopping." *Prepared Foods,* August 1992.

McMath, Robert. "Whether Regular or Herbal, It's Increasingly Time for Tea." *Brandweek,* 31 May 1993.

Meeting the Growing Demand for Diversified Yeast Products. Milwaukee: Universal Foods, 1996.

Miller, Cyndee. "Seeking an Image: Tofu Tired of Being 'Yucky,' Car Agency Has 'Smart' Idea." *Marketing News,* 29 October 1990.

Prince, Greg W. "Together Forever." *Beverage World,* April 1993.

—Karen Bellenir, updated by Linda Dailey Paulson

TOBACCO PRODUCTS

CIGARETTES

This category covers establishments primarily engaged in manufacturing cigarettes from tobacco or other materials.

INDUSTRY SNAPSHOT

The cigarette manufacturing industry in America is among the most powerful and controversial in the country's history. Spearheaded by highly diversified international conglomerates Philip Morris Companies Inc. and RJR Nabisco Holdings Corp., who continue to champion their cigarette interests along with their other myriad businesses, the cigarette industry is a formidable economic force. According to *Business Week,* the leading tobacco companies posted total sales in 1993 of more than $80 billion. Moreover, the long-time slide in American consumption of cigarettes appears to have halted in the mid-1990s; the percentage of smokers in the American population has remained stable since 1991 at about 26 percent. Finally, American cigarette companies are optimistic about opportunities in international markets, where demand for their product is high and rules and legislation regarding usage are largely absent.

Nonetheless, the cigarette industry is a beleaguered one in many ways, all ultimately traceable to the health risks associated with consumption of their product. As *Time* noted in April 1994, "in the past few months, a rash of new restrictions, legislation and government tough talk has elevated the antismoking campaign to new heights. Before, it was a matter of health warnings, moral persuasion and segregation of the warring parties. Now smoking [in the United States] is in danger of being legislated virtually out of existence."

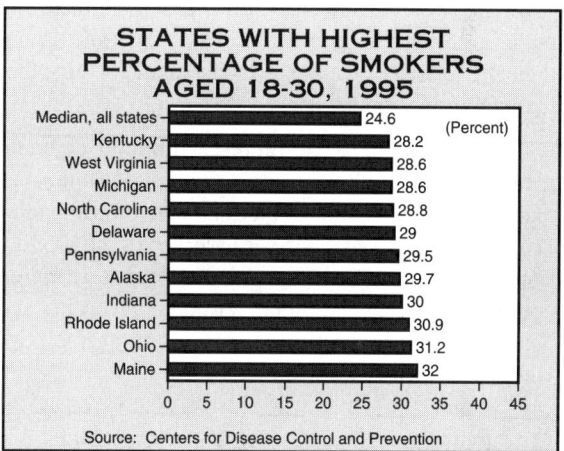

STATES WITH HIGHEST PERCENTAGE OF SMOKERS AGED 18-30, 1995

	(Percent)
Median, all states	24.6
Kentucky	28.2
West Virginia	28.6
Michigan	28.6
North Carolina	28.8
Delaware	29
Pennsylvania	29.5
Alaska	29.7
Indiana	30
Rhode Island	30.9
Ohio	31.2
Maine	32

Source: Centers for Disease Control and Prevention

ORGANIZATION AND STRUCTURE

The group of manufacturers leading the industry in the 1990s was a small, entrenched collection of competitors. From the industry's nascence in the mid-nineteenth century, when many cigarette manufacturers began as tobacco farmers, to the 1990s, the number of participants generally has been limited to slightly more than a handful. Early cigarette producers were located in proximity to the tobacco fields of the southern United States, typically operating in the same region as their competition. It was an industry in which everyone knew each other's names.

Nearly a century and a half later, the cigarette industry still consisted of a small, almost fraternal group of manufacturers, several of whom had been in competition with one another since the nineteenth century. In 1992 there were 15 cigarette manufacturers in the United States generating at least $3 million in revenue each. Roughly a quarter of these companies were subsidiary operations of the industry's two largest participants, Philip Morris Companies Inc. and RJR Nabisco Holdings Corp. Moreover, the disparity in revenue volumes among these manufacturers was vast, as great as the nearly $50 billion gulf separating Philip Morris, the tenth largest publicly held corporation in the United States, and Eagle Tobacco Corp., with annual sales of roughly three million dollars.

While the number of companies involved in the industry in the early 1990s was relatively small, its revenue volume was not; it totaled over $25.52 billion in 1990. This amount, particularly large considering the limited number of manufacturers in the industry, more than doubled during the 1980s, climbing from $12.12 billion in 1982. The enormous amount of capital required to operate in the industry limited new entrants from establishing manufacturing facilities. In 1989 the average amount paid for raw manufacturing materials was $352.5 million, nearly 80 times more than the average cost per establishment for all other manufacturing industries.

Geographically, the representation of cigarette manufacturing establishments in the United States is as narrow in scope as the limited number of companies involved in the industry. In the early 1990s the production of cigarettes was confined to the four-state region comprising North Carolina, Virginia, Georgia, and Kentucky. The bulk of these manufacturing facilities were located in North Carolina.

BACKGROUND AND DEVELOPMENT

The origins of tobacco in the United States date back to before the formation of the nation itself, and the growth and sale of this product represented one of the key agricultural crops that spurred the country's growth in the eighteenth and nineteenth centuries. The use of tobacco to produce cigarettes in any widespread fashion did not occur, however, until the dawn of the twentieth century. Other uses for tobacco precluded the popularity of cigarettes, as Americans in the early nineteenth century enjoyed plug and twist tobacco, then smoking tobacco, and finally cigars, all of which overshadowed cigarette production in terms of volume for most of the century. Even in the mid-1800s, the use of tobacco had its detractors, and cigarette smokers, many of whom were women, suffered from a somewhat ignoble image. As a social commentator in 1854 wrote in reference to New York: "Some of the *ladies* of this refined and fashion-forming metropolis are ap-

ing the silly ways of some pseudo-accomplished foreigners in smoking Tobacco through a weaker and more *feminine* article which has been most delicately denominated *cigarette.*"

A decade later, however, the production volume of cigarettes had increased enough to become the object of special federal taxation, which, according to the Internal Revenue Law promulgated in June of 1864, levied one dollar per one hundred packages not exceeding five dollars in aggregate value. The following year, 19.7 million cigarettes were produced, and manufacturers were buffeted by a series of tax hikes, first to two dollars per thousand and then to five dollars per thousand. This arrested the growth of the industry just as sales were beginning to elevate cigarette manufacturers' importance in the tobacco industry. In 1868 tax rates were cut back to $1.50 per thousand and growth resumed, marking the beginning of 20-year period that would witness the most rapid percentage growth rate in the production of cigarettes in the history of the industry.

Cigarette production reached 500 million in 1880 and eclipsed the one billion mark five years later. By the 1880s, there were five principal manufacturers of cigarettes: Washington Duke Sons & Co., Allen & Ginter, Kinney Tobacco Co., William S. Kimball & Co., and Goodwin & Co. Together these companies produced 2.18 billion cigarettes annually by the end of the decade, 91.7 percent of the national output of 2.41 billion. These companies, referred to as the "Tobacco Trust," essentially controlled the cigarette market, enjoying a virtually unassailable lead over other, smaller manufacturers. This monopolistic trait would characterize the industry throughout much of its existence.

The ability of these companies to secure such a wide advantage over their competition was partly due to significant technological innovations achieved during the 1880s that ended the time-consuming chore of rolling cigarettes by hand. On a good day, a skilled laborer could roll 3,000 cigarettes during a ten-hour workday—a production rate that threatened to place a ceiling on the industry's growth. But beginning in 1872, the age of mechanization in the cigarette industry was initiated. The first cigarette manufacturing machine, patented by Albert H. Hook, earned a modicum of success, but did not prove to be commercially viable. By 1881, however, significant improvements had been made in a design patented by James A. Bonsack. This machine could churn out 200 to 220 cigarettes per minute, accomplishing in 15 minutes what it took an experienced production worker ten hours to complete.

Bolstered by the ability to produce more cigarettes with lower labor costs, the five companies that occupied the industry's leading positions grew quickly by moving into untapped markets and securing their overwhelming lead in the U.S. market. In 1890 the composition of the industry's manufacturers became more homogeneous when the five leading companies, at the urging of James Duke of Washington Duke & Sons Co., merged to form the American Tobacco Co., which initially focused primarily on the production of cigarettes. Over the next 20 years, the American Tobacco Co. acquired an interest in roughly 250 companies. This cigarette giant developed into a tobacco giant, securing commanding leads in every product branch of the tobacco industry with the exception of cigars. In the manufacture of cigarettes, plug, smoking tobacco, fine cut tobacco, snuff, and little cigars, the conglomerate's production output in the first decade of the twentieth century represented no less than 76 percent of the country's total volume, giving smaller manufacturers little hope of wresting market share away from the industry's predominant leader.

If the five leading manufacturers in the 1880s justly earned the moniker "Tobacco Trust" when operating as separate companies, then their union certainly deserved the same label. The U.S. Supreme Court came to this realization in May of 1911, when it found the American Tobacco Co. in violation of the Sherman Act. Six months after the ruling, the court issued a decree stipulating that the enormously powerful tobacco company be divided into 16 independent corporations, none which could wield monopolistic control over any one product branch within the tobacco industry.

Although certainly a significant chapter in the history of the cigarette industry, the parceling of the American Tobacco Co.'s sundry divisions and subsidiaries did not affect the cigarette industry as greatly as the cigar industry, primarily because cigarettes still did not represent a major branch of the tobacco industry. The cigarette industry was burgeoning, however, and stood on the brink of catapulting past all other branches of the tobacco industry. The first step toward this end came six years after the restructuring of the industry, when the United States entered World War I and cigarettes were issued to soldiers in the U.S. Army and Navy.

Once the habit of smoking cigarettes had extended to women, thereby doubling the potential customer base of the industry, sales began to mushroom and the cigarette branch of the industry at last overtook all other branches. Over the ensuing 20 years, during which time many of the widely popular brands— Chesterfield, Lucky Strike, Old Gold, Camel, Raleigh, and Marlboro—emerged, the consumption of ciga-

rettes grew rapidly. Domestic tobacco leaf consumption increased 42.5 percent between 1910 and 1930, while the production of cigarettes increased from 8.64 billion to 125.2 billion, a 1,339 percent increase. In these first two decades following the dissolution decree, there were approximately 15 to 20 manufacturers deriving the bulk of their revenue from the production of cigarettes. Only four of these manufacturers, commonly referred to as the "Big Four," held any appreciable share of the market. Indeed, these manufacturers—the restructured American Tobacco Co., R.J. Reynolds Tobacco Co., P. Lorillard Co., and Liggett & Meyers Tobacco Co.—held as firm a grip on the U.S. cigarette market as American Tobacco had before the U.S. Supreme Court's ruling; they controlled more than 95 percent of the market.

Clearly, the dissolution of American Tobacco had not produced the U.S. Supreme Court's intended effects; a monarchy had merely been replaced with an oligarchy. Smaller, independent cigarette manufacturers were able to record enviable profits during this period, largely because of the bountiful market itself, but none could challenge the "Big Four" in magnitude. Accordingly, as the cigarette industry continued to grow, these powerful manufacturers became more formidable, further widening the gulf separating the industry's upper echelon and the rest of the competition.

The next two decades of business brought continued success to the industry's four largest manufacturers and witnessed the rise of an additional member to the industry's elite, Philip Morris & Company Ltd., Inc. Philip Morris introduced its mainstay Marlboro brand in 1925, which reached an annual production total of approximately 500 million cigarettes. But the industry's leading brands during these years, Camel and Lucky Strike, each sold 25 billion cigarettes a year, by far outpacing Philip Morris' production volume and providing little room for the future ascension of the smaller, formerly British-based manufacturer. Instead, Philip Morris was able to climb the industry's ranking list due to a strong relationship with cigarette jobbers throughout its distribution network and by virtue of prudent management. By the end of the 1940s, after Philip Morris had already unseated Lorillard to occupy the industry's fourth place position, the "Tobacco Trust" now included five members, generating an aggregate sales total of $357.3 million.

The 1950s heralded a new era for cigarette manufacturers, one in which it became necessary to defend growing criticism of the product being sold. Since the industry's emergence, anti-cigarette and anti-tobacco factions from both the federal and consumer sector had railed against the sale and use of tobacco. Manufacturers had fared fairly well, effectively beating back the rising tide of protest against their business. While industry manufacturers had suffered run-ins with the Federal Trade Commission concerning misleading advertising, the federal government had subsidized a large portion of the industry before World War II, which helped to allay the fears of manufacturers.

During the 1950s, however, medical reports linking health problems to smoking began to surface. In 1953 the Sloan-Kettering Cancer Institute's report showed a relationship between cancer and tobacco, and manufacturers consequently found themselves fighting against an entirely new and much more formidable foe—scientific fact.

In 1964 the U.S. Surgeon General issued a landmark report linking smoking with lung cancer and heart disease. A year later, the U.S. Congress promulgated the Cigarette Advertising and Labeling Act, which stipulated that health warnings be placed on each cigarette package. In 1971 cigarette advertisements on radio and television were banned. Although these announcements and restrictions did not cause the industry to collapse, the rate of smoking in the United States began to spiral downward.

Cigarette manufacturers had already begun creating different types of cigarettes—filter tips during the 1950s, then low-tar cigarettes during the 1960s and 1970s—and marketed these products not to create more customers, but to capture their competitor's customers. By the 1970s, however, Philip Morris and R.J. Reynolds had gained considerable ground on their competition, making the industry essentially a battle between these two behemoth corporations. Philip Morris won the battle, albeit temporarily, when the manufacturer's Marlboro brand passed R.J. Reynolds' Winston brand in 1976.

During the 1980s, lower-priced, discount cigarettes began to enter the market with increasing frequency. This enabled smaller cigarette manufacturers to thrive for a short time, until the industry's preeminent leaders dropped their own prices and set about capturing the low-end market. By this time, the reams of medical reports delineating the hazardous effects of smoking had firmly grabbed the attention of the American populace, transforming anti-tobacco factions into a powerful nationwide movement. Cigarette taxation doubled in 1983 and continued to rise, particularly during the late 1980s, increasing the popularity of lower-priced cigarettes. Consequently, cigarette manufacturers diversified their operations with unprecedented fervor, while casting an eye to international business opportunities.

CURRENT CONDITIONS

As the national economy began to recover from the recessive economic conditions of the early 1990s, manufacturers in the cigarette industry were saddled with problems much larger and more threatening than the vagaries of the economic climate. These difficulties had always confronted the industry, but the intensity of the groups fighting against the industry in the mid-1990s was increasingly vehement. In June 1992 the U.S. Supreme Court reversed an appeals court ruling concerning the product liability of cigarette manufacturers. Earlier, two lower courts in Minnesota and New Jersey had ruled that the family of a woman who had died of lung cancer in 1984 could not sue Philip Morris, Loews Corporation, and the Liggett Group on grounds that these cigarette manufacturers had withheld information concerning potential health dangers. The Court's reversal sent cigarette manufacturers' stock prices cascading downward, as industry participants braced themselves for a rash of lawsuits.

Perhaps a more disheartening development for cigarette manufacturers in the early 1990s was their diminishing influence over federal lawmakers. In the past, through the combined efforts of the tobacco lobby and elected representatives from tobacco-growing states in the Southeast, manufacturers had been able to slow the rate of federally imposed cigarette taxes and mitigate, to a certain extent, federal legislation aimed at curbing cigarette use. But in the early 1990s, cigarette makers were assailed on several fronts with renewed energy. As *Business Week* noted, "smokers are confronting an unprecedented rush to tax their cigs. Tobacco levies passed during the 1993 legislative sessions will provide 15 percent of new state tax revenue in fiscal 1994—even though cigarette taxes are less than two percent of state tax collections nationwide, according to the National Conference of State Legislatures. Several states, including Washington and New York, levy a tax above 50 cents a pack. Michigan voters recently approved raising the state's tax to 75 cents a pack to finance public education."

Additional restrictions on smoking in public areas are increasingly common as well, in part as a result of a 1993 Environmental Protection Agency (EPA) report that classified environmental tobacco smoke as a class-A carcinogen and charged that 3,000 nonsmokers die annually from second-hand smoke. *Time* reported in 1994 that "in May, Maryland will institute the tightest state-wide restrictions in the nation, banning smoking in virtually all work places, except in sealed, separately ventilated rooms." Many communities across the country are instituting strict rules regarding cigarette use, and even the U.S. Department of Defense issued restrictions that ban smoking in all military work spaces, including military bases. Businesses, too, (including fast-food giant McDonald's) are banning smoking in their establishments. The poor publicity associated with such legislation, coupled with scathing reports in the news media that charge cigarette manufacturers with duplicity and disregard for public health, have further damaged the industry's reputation. Controversy over the "Joe Camel" advertising campaign launched by R.J. Reynolds Tobacco Co. was also heated. Critics charged that the campaign snared a large number of under-age smokers, while the company insisted that such charges are baseless.

Another ominous threat to the cigarette industry, according to *Time,* was "the activist Food and Drug Administration, [which] is taking a look at whether to classify nicotine as a drug—a move that could effectively remove cigarettes from the over-the-counter market. FDA Commissioner David Kessler told Congress [in 1994] he believes that nicotine is a 'highly addictive agent' and that cigarette producers control the level of nicotine 'that creates and sustains this addiction.'" The FDA further charged in June 1994 that the Brown & Williamson Tobacco Corp. cultivated a strain of high-nicotine tobacco in Brazil expressly for use in producing its cigarettes, a charge the company denied.

By 1996, the cigarette industry seemed to be breathing a little easier. Philip Morris had successfuly sued the ABC television network for libel, forcing ABC to apologize for reporting that the company reconsituted tobacco to control nicotine levels. On the legislative front, President Clinton's ambitious health reform package, which had included major tax increases on cigarettes, had collapsed, the FDA's efforts to classify nicotine as a drug were being stymied by lawsuits launched both by tobacco companies and tobacco-growing states, and a new anti-tax Republican congress seemed likely to prevent any attempts on the part of the Clinton Administration to hike the tobacco tax.

In early 1997, however, the anti-tobacco forces continued to battle, successfully splitting the tobacco companies' united front by pressuring the Liggett Company to settle a class action lawsuit out of court. Liggett's move was not entirely unexpected—with only a 2 percent share of the U.S. market, the company lacked the resources to fight an extended court battle. But when the company turned against long-established industry policy and admitted that cigarettes do indeed cause cancer and that nicotine is addictive, the other companies were forced to move quickly to reduce the damage. Reports soon surfaced that Philip Morris and

the R.J. Reynolds Tobacco Co. were seeking to make an out-of-court deal.

The reports proved to be accurate. Riddled by lawsuits from private citizens and state governments alike, in mid-1997 the tobacco industry, seeking to minimize costs and negative publicity, proposed a settlement with the federal government. The $368.5 billion deal, reached after months of negotiations between representatives for the attorneys general, FDA, and the tobacco industry, would bring the plague of lawsuits against the industry to a final resolution. For its part, the tobacco industry agreed to reimburse states for health costs, fund anti-smoking campaigns, severely limit—if not virtually put an end to—cigarette advertising, and work toward reducing underage smoking. In return, however, the industry sought both immunity from future liability, and limits on the power of the FDA to regulate nicotine in cigarettes. In the midst of settlement negotiations R.J. Reynolds, perhaps as a show of good faith, gave in to private and governmental pressures, agreeing in July of 1997 to retire its most well known (and marketable) mascot, "Joe Camel." Despite this gesture, however, the Clinton Administration refused to approve the settlement, citing both the restrictions it would impose on the FDA and the terms it would outline for penalizing tobacco companies if they failed to fulfill their end of the settlement. The administration planned to write and send its own legislation to Congress—without further negotiations. In an ironic twist to the tobacco wars, the country home of the president of the R.J. Reynolds Tobacco Co. burned down in April 1997— apparently as the result of careless smoking.

Beyond these developments, the nature of the industry itself was transforming, creating further anxiety for cigarette manufacturers and particularly the industry's large, leading manufacturers. The popularity of discount cigarettes continued to climb, and by 1993, discount cigarettes had accounted for nearly one-third of the volume retail sales of cigarettes in the United States. Several of the larger manufacturers were slow to acknowledge this consumer trend. Philip Morris and R.J. Reynolds Tobacco Co., however, had aggressively entered into the production of discount cigarettes, realizing that cheaper cigarettes did not represent a fleeting consumer trend, but an economic choice driven by the 12 cent annual increases in cigarette prices for the previous five years. Controlling 60 percent of the discount market by 1993, Philip Morris and R.J. Reynolds regained the market share they had been ceding to smaller manufacturers. However, the production of discount cigarettes generated far less profit—as much as ten times less—than traditional, higher-priced brands, further clouding the industry's financial future. To counter this, both Philip Morris and R.J. Reynolds increased advertising and promotion of premium brands, a move that the two companies helped stall growth of the discount cigarette market. At the same time, the two companies worked to reduce the allure of discount brands by sharply raising the prices of discount cigarettes while cutting the prices of premium brands. By 1995, these moves had succeeded in reversing the trend towards discount cigarettes, with premium cigarettes capturing a 68 percent market share, compared with a 66.5 percent share in 1993. A beneficial side effect of this strategy was to curtail overall growth in the price of cigarettes, thus helping slow the decrease in the number of smokers. In fact, by 1996, a number of reports indicated that the number of smoking had actually increased somewhat—especially among the young.

Over the long term, however, downward pressure on cigarette sales in the United States is likely to continue. In addition to taxes and regulatory restrictions, the increasing number of restrictions on where people can smoke, heightened awareness of the dangers of smoking, and the growing social stigma attached to the habit, all are expected to gradually erode the market base for cigarettes.

Faced with these formidable challenges, cigarette manufacturers quickly sought to ameliorate their position, as they had frequently done in the past. With the hope of alleviating some of the pressure from the legislative sector, manufacturers compiled databases of ''confirmed'' smokers, registering names and addresses of consumers responding to direct mail advertising and promotional offers. The marshalling of forces to combat the growing movement against the tobacco industry represented, at best, a long-term solution to manufacturers' problems. For more immediate relief, the industry increasingly looked toward foreign markets to sell their traditional, higher-priced line of cigarettes. Toward this end, U.S. manufacturers were recording considerable success, tapping into a market in which sales tripled between 1985 and 1993.

INDUSTRY LEADERS

Ranked according to sales volume, the two largest cigarette manufacturers in the United States during the early 1990s were Philip Morris Companies Inc. and R.J. Reynolds Tobacco Co., both perennial leaders in the industry. Together, the two manufacturers controlled 71 percent of the U.S. cigarette market in 1993.

Philip Morris' ascension to the number one position in the cigarette industry began shortly after the 1911 decree intended to dilute the staggering power of the American Tobacco Co. Although Philip Morris' initial magnitude paled in comparison to the industry's ''Big Four''—the American Tobacco Co., R.J. Reynolds, Lorillard, and Liggett & Meyers— its rise stands as a remarkable achievement. Beginning as the U.S. operations of a British manufacturing company named Philip Morris Company, the manufacturing facilities were purchased by U.S. financier George J. Whelan, who acquired several of the small manufacturing concerns left for sale after the break up of American Tobacco. Formed as a U.S. company in 1919 and renamed Philip Morris & Company Ltd., Inc., the company introduced the brand of cigarette that would eventually catapult the fledgling manufacturing concern toward the top of its market in 1925. That brand, Marlboro, did not begin its meteoric rise until the ubiquitous Marlboro Man, the rough-hewn American cowboy, first appeared on cigarette packages in 1955. In the interim, Philip Morris slowly climbed the industry's ladder through effective marketing and a strong relationship with cigarette jobbers on the East Coast, ensuring that the company's products received preferential treatment during the all-important journey from manufacturing site to retail stores.

By 1936, Philip Morris maintained a firm grip on the industry's fourth position through its widely popular English Blend cigarettes introduced three years earlier. Following World War II, several poor management decisions, including an overestimation of the nation's consumption capacity and a belated entry into the filter segment of the industry sent the company's sales spiraling downward. By 1960, Philip Morris had fallen to sixth place in the U.S. cigarette market—last among the major U.S. manufacturers.

The introduction of the Marlboro Man in 1955, however, strengthened Philip Morris' domestic sales, while an early move into foreign markets underpinned the company's domestic resurgence. By 1973, Marlboro cigarettes were the second most popular brand in the United States, ranking only behind RJR's Winston brand. Three years later, Marlboro eclipsed Winston, and Philip Morris became the second-largest seller of tobacco in the world. As Marlboro became the nation's preferred cigarette, Philip Morris branched into the production of low-tar cigarettes with its Merit brand, then intensified its efforts toward overseas expansion. As a result of these two marketing strategies, plus the growing popularity of Marlboro cigarettes, Philip Morris surpassed RJR in 1983 to become the world's largest cigarette manufacturer. By 1995, the company held a commanding share of the U.S. market, accounting for 47 percent of domestic sales.

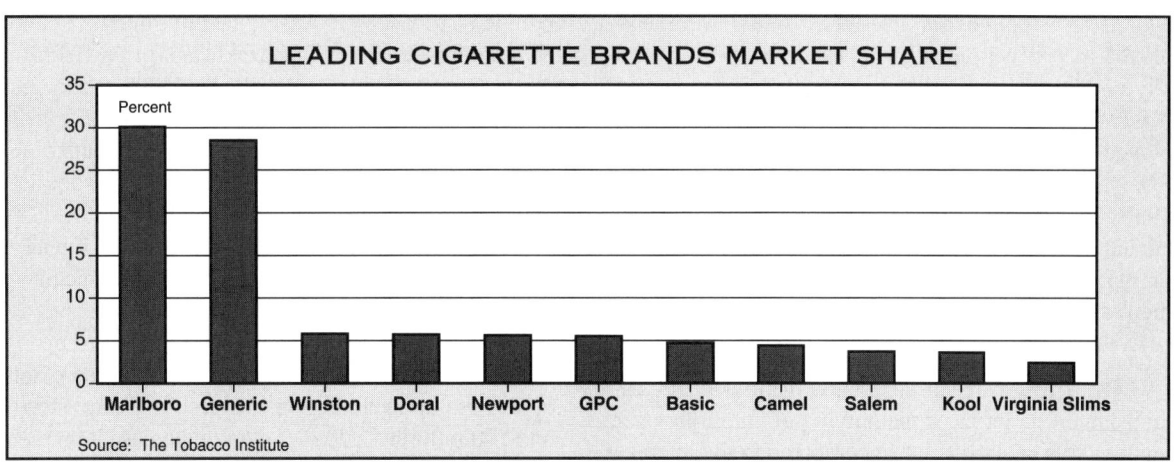

LEADING CIGARETTE BRANDS MARKET SHARE

Source: The Tobacco Institute

Incorporated in 1879 as R.J. Reynolds Tobacco Company, RJR Nabisco Holdings Corp. garnered initial success through the efforts of the company's founder, Richard Joshua Reynolds, and by virtue of its association with the American Tobacco Co. during the lucrative "trust years" in the tobacco industry. Operating as a subsidiary of American Tobacco from 1899 until the dissolution decree of 1911, Reynolds' company thrived, earning a majority of its profits through the sale of chewing and smoking tobacco under the respective Schnapps and Prince Albert brands. The company did not manufacture cigarettes until 1913—shortly after Reynolds had resumed control of the company following the U.S. Supreme Court's ruling—but once it did, the company's success came quickly with its widely popular Camel brand of cigarettes.

For the next 20 years, the company's success was primarily predicated on the popularity of Camel cigarettes, but by the late 1930s and throughout the 1940s, the company's exponential growth began to slow due to labor problems, antitrust suits, and one particular product flop, Cavalier cigarettes. By the 1950s, however, R.J. Reynolds began to effect a turnaround by selling its new filter tip brand of cigarettes, Winston, which first appeared in 1954. Two years later, the company introduced its Salem brand, the industry's first king-size filter-tipped menthol cigarette. This, combined with the continuing success of the Camel and Winston brands, elevated the company's standing in the market above all others.

When Philip Morris' Marlboro surpassed R.J. Reynolds' Winston in domestic sales in 1976, the company countered with the introduction of a "back-to-nature" brand of cigarettes called Real, but the effort failed miserably and the product was discontinued in 1980. In that same year, the company's management sought to ameliorate its position by expanding overseas, leading to an agreement with the People's

Republic of China to manufacture and sell cigarettes there, the first U.S. company to reach an accord with that country.

However, this historic move abroad was not enough to stop the company's slide to the industry's number two position three years later, when Philip Morris ascended to the industry's number one position. In 1985, to stave off further losses, R.J. Reynolds purchased Nabisco Brands, Inc. for $4.9 billion (the same year in which Philip Morris acquired General Foods Corporation). Three years after the Nabisco purchase, the biggest leveraged buyout in U.S. history occurred when Kohlberg Kravis Roberts & Co., an investment firm purchased RJR Nabisco for $24.88 billion. Once the company became privately held, several subsidiaries were sold to streamline the company's operations, then it once again went public in 1991 with a new issue of stock.

WORK FORCE

Moving in inverse proportion to the industry's sales during the 1980s, the number of people employed by cigarette manufacturers declined over the course of the decade. In 1980 the industry's total work force, including both hourly and salaried workers, amounted to 46,000. By the end of the decade, the industry's employment base had dropped by more than 10,000 workers, descending to 35,000 by 1990, then dropping again to 34,000 in 1992.

Throughout its history, the bulk of the industry's work force has been comprised of production workers, or those employees paid on an hourly basis to operate manufacturing machinery and perform manual tasks in the production of cigarettes. This preponderance of production workers, whose proportional representation in the cigarette industry's work force dropped by roughly four percent during the 1980s, continued to characterize the industry in the early 1990s. Of the

34,000 total employees in 1992, 26,000 were employed as production workers. These workers, generally employed on a full-time basis, but averaging 11 percent fewer hours than production workers employed by all other manufacturing industries, earned $20.68 per hour in 1992, up from $9.23 per hour in 1980. Salaried employees, or those workers paid an annual salary for performing administrative, technical, or managerial duties, composed the balance of the industry's work force, earning an average of $47,915 per year in 1991.

The average size of a cigarette manufacturing establishment, in terms of the number of employees per facility, was enormous when compared to the average size of manufacturing establishments in all other manufacturing industries. In 1989, the typical manufacturing establishment comprised 54 employees, 37 of whom were employed as production workers, while the cigarette industry averaged 2,277 employees per establishment, more than 42 times the size of all other manufacturing industries. Of these 2,277 employees per establishment in 1989, 1,700 were employed as production workers.

AMERICA AND THE WORLD

As legislation and taxation affecting the cigarette industry in the United States has become more commonplace, leading companies have increasingly turned to global opportunities. As *Newsweek* pointed out in 1994, "sixty percent of Philip Morris's sales already come from outside the United States; in the next decade it hopes to push its overseas profits closer to that 60 percent mark." By 1995, the company's overseas sales accounted for more than seventy percent of total sales, with overseas shipments accounting for 593 million units, compared to 222 million in the United States. This move to international markets is expected to be an expensive one, for although American cigarette exports are growing 6 to 8 percent annually, cigarette companies recognize that establishing facilities in targeted countries is a priority. Plant construction or acquisition is expected to impact industry players for the next several years as a result.

The cigarette industry, however, views the potential profitability in those regions as too lucrative to ignore. *Forbes* pointed out in 1994 that "the tobacco companies have been buying every major Russian and Eastern European tobacco plant in sight. During 1995, Philip Morris modernized and expanded a manufacturing plant in the Czech Republic, began construction of a new plant in Lithuania, and undertook plant renovations in Russia and the Ukraine. The company also announced plans to increase capacity in Holland,

upgrade its tobacco processing facility in Switzerland, and build a new factory in Kazakhstan. In 1996, Philip Morris acquired a 33 percent share of Poland's largest tobacco company, completed construction of a leaf-processing facility in Malaysia, and concluded an agreement under which a third party would contract-manufacture Marlboro cigarettes in China for the Chinese market. RJR has invested in plants in Hungary, Poland, Ukraine, and Russia, as well as manufacturing its brands through licensing agreements in about 20 other countries . . . In two to five years, company executives say, these new and recently acquired plants could gross up to $1 billion in sales for Philip Morris and $500 million for RJR. Both companies claim their Russian operations are already profitable." Smoking is on the rise in heavily-populated regions of the world such as Asia as well, and "American companies must sell cheaper, less profitable smokes in the Third World, but margins will improve as those economies develop and prices rise."

FURTHER READING

"Alcoholic Beverages and Tobacco." *Standard and Poor's Industry Surveys.* New York: McGraw Hill, January 1997.

Faison, Seth Jr. "Cigarette Ruling: Hour of Confusion." *New York Times,* 26 June 1992, D1.

Farley, Christopher John. "The Butt Stops Here." *Time,* 18 April 1994.

Farrell, Christopher. "This Sin Tax is Win-Win." *Business Week,* 11 April 1994.

Hass, Nancy. "Fighting and Switching." *Newsweek,* 21 March 1994.

Henslein, William. "Food, Drink, and Tobacco." *Forbes,* 1st January 1996.

Kent, Christine. "Tobacco Firm Pays for Failure to Warn." *American Medical News,* 26 August 1996.

Klebnikov, Paul. "Opiate of the Masses." *Forbes,* 11 April 1994.

Mallory, Maria. "Is the Smoking Lamp Going Out for Good?" *Business Week,* 11 April 1994.

———. "That's One Angry Camel." *Business Week,* 7 March 1994.

Reynolds, Patrick, and Tom Shachtman. *The Gilded Leaf: Triumph, Tragedy, and Tobacco.* Boston: Little, Brown and Company, 1989.

Shapiro, Eben. "Marlboro Smokers Defect to Discounters." *Wall Street Journal,* 13 January 1993, B1.

Simon, Howard. "US Tobacco Lights up Overseas," *Journal of Commerce,* 27 August 1996.

"Smoking Rate in U.S. Rises for First Time in 25 Years. *Wall Street Journal,* 2 April 1993, B6.

Smothers, Ronald. "Tobacco Country Is Quaking Over Cigarette Tax Proposal." *New York Times,* 22 March 1993 A1.

Statistical Abstract of the United States: 1993. Washington: U.S. Bureau of the Census, 1993.

"Still Smoking." *The Economist,* 11 March 1995, 61.

"Tobacco Sales Heat Up." *Triad Business News,* 1 September 1995.

Walmac, Amanda. "Empty the Ashtray: Time is Running Out on Tobacco Stocks." *Money,* November. 1996.

"When Smoke Got in their Eyes." *The Economist,* 10 April 1993, 65.

— Jeffrey L. Covell, updated by Chris Hunt

LEADING EXPORTERS OF CIGARS TO U.S.

Cuba (3%)
Nicaragua (2%)
Mexico (6%)
Jamaica (9%)
Dominican Republic (48%)
Honduras (32%)

Source: Cigar Association of America, 1996

SIC 2121

CIGARS

This industry consists of establishments that primarily are engaged in the manufacture of cigars. Manufacturers of other tobacco items are treated in **SIC 2111: Cigarettes**; **SIC 2131: Chewing and Smoking Tobacco and Snuff**; and **SIC 2141: Tobacco Stemming and Redrying.**

The cigar industry has experienced a boom in recent years thanks to increasing acceptance of cigar smoking among the "Generation X" population, a resurgence in "cigar evenings," and the popularity of the Internet where cigars are being sold in record numbers. The magazine *Cigar Aficiando,* introduced in 1992, is generally credited with the upturn in the cigar industry. No longer a passion for older men alone, changing demographics find "twentysomethings," men and women, participating in cigar evenings and joining the traditional 35-65 year old traditionalists in the purchase of premium cigars. Celebrities have also helped to add to the allure, adorning the cover of *Cigar Aficiando* and showing up frequently at soirees boasting "stogies."

Like other tobacco products, the sale of cigars had dropped off as Americans became increasingly concerned about the effects of tobacco smoking on health and fitness. In the mid-1970s, volume was more than 5.5 billion, and at the industry's peak in 1964, unit sales reached 9 billion cigars. The volume of cigar sales fell about five percent a year during a 15-year period, dropping to 2.2 billion units sold in 1991.

While the upswing in the cigar market is strong, consumption still doesn't match the record highs of the mid-1960s. Cigar smokers have traded quantity for quality. They smoke fewer cigars, but when they do

smoke, they often smoke cigars of a high quality. Declines in volume have been offset by increases in prices and a growing market for premium cigars. Sales in dollars have risen to about $700 million in the early 1990s. In 1995 imports of premium cigars rose to 176.3 million units, an increase from 1994's level of 132.4 million. In 1996 imports increased to 294 million.

Changes in distribution systems also helped the industry, as more discount stores and supermarkets began carrying a wider variety of cigars, especially the higher-priced cigars. The Internet has also played a role in cigar sales, with companies like J.R. Cigar finding it difficult to match demand. In late 1996, J.R. Cigar even began turning down orders from new customers as it struggled to fill orders. Mike's Cigars, Famous Smoke Shop, and J.R. Tobacco make up the "big three" of the discount cigar mail-order business. All are enjoying a renaissance in the mid-1990s. Manufacturers were sitting on back orders in the 5 to 6 million unit range in 1996.

Laws prohibiting smoking in public places, increased taxes on tobacco products, and medical findings that cigars cause mouth, throat, and pancreatic cancer have had an impact on the U.S. cigar industry. Cigar manufacturers have been combating these obstacles by increasing promotional activities with wholesalers and by introducing new products in various sizes.

The cigar industry also continues to deal with the sale of both authentic and counterfeit Cuban cigars in the United States. The Cigar Association of America has been trying to halt the sale of these illegal products, estimating that they cost U.S. cigar makers $28 million a year. Approximately 6 million Cuban cigars are smuggled into the United States every year. In August 1996, government officials found over $50,000 of contraband cigars on one boat in Florida. The sale of

Cuban cigars has been illegal in the U.S. since 1962, when President Kennedy signed the Cuban trade embargo.

The Cigar Association of America, established more than 50 years ago, consists of regular members (the cigar makers headquartered in the United States) and associate members (including foreign cigar manufacturers, importers, leaf dealers, and other suppliers.) The organization's principle activities involve maintaining cigar industry statistics, public relations efforts, and lobbying federal and state governments on issues of import to the industry, especially taxation of their products.

The number of cigar manufacturers in the U.S. has steadily shrunk during the last part of this century. The 1992 census reports only 27 establishments with total employment of 2600. However production has witnessed an upturn. The value of shipments in 1990 (the last year for which data is available) was at $120 million, up from $107 million in 1989 — the first upward trend since 1983.

Still, the industry has needed to respond to change. While cigars were once handmade products, technology has taken over in most companies. In Miami, however, Cuban and Central American immigrants in a half dozen small cigar factories have continued to make hand-rolled cigars. With a decline of qualified cigar rollers, cigar-rolling is becoming a lost craft.

The cigar industry is enjoying a rebirth of sorts in the late 1990s. The United States has about 1 million premium cigar smokers. However, the anti-smoking trend among consumers and the government will continue to impact cigar sales.

FURTHER READING

"Cigar Industry Campaigns Against Cuban Imports, Fakes." *U.S. Distribution Journal,* August 1989.

Edelman, Vladimir. "Blowing Smoke: The Cigar Renaissance." *Inc. Online,* 1 July 1996.

Flanagan, William G. "Cigar Madness." *Forbes,* 21 April 1997.

Fucini, Suzi. "Taking a New Look at an Old Mainstay." *U.S. Distribution Journal,* January 1990.

Maldonado, Patricia. "Keeping Tradition Alive." *South Florida Business Journal,* 13 March 1990.

"Puffery." *Forbes,* 22 June 1992.

"Split in Cigar Sales Continues." *U.S. Distribution Journal,* January 1991.

—Wendy Stein, updated by Lin Grensing-Pophal

CHEWING AND SMOKING TOBACCO AND SNUFF

This industry consists of establishments primarily engaged in manufacturing chewing and smoking tobacco and snuff. Other tobacco product industries are discussed in **SIC 2111: Cigarettes; SIC 2121: Cigars; and SIC 2141: Tobacco and Redrying.**

In 1997, the U.S. tobacco industry was clearly in the hands of three companies: R.J. Reynolds Tobacco Co., Brown and Williamson Tobacco Corp., and United States Tobacco Co. Of these top companies, the leader was R.J. Reynolds, with $7.7 billion in annual sales—almost five times number two Brown and Williamsons' sales of $1.7 million.

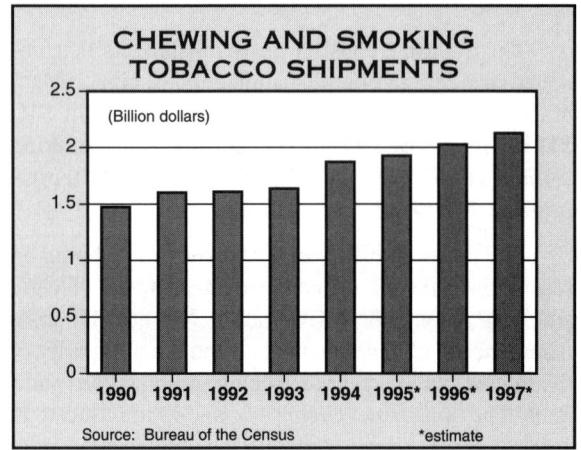

CHEWING AND SMOKING TOBACCO SHIPMENTS

(Billion dollars)

Source: Bureau of the Census   *estimate

In the early 1990s, as cigarette and cigar volume dropped, smokeless tobacco products grew 3-5 percent in sales volume annually. Among smokeless products, moist snuff was the leader, with total U.S. output rising 83 percent—from 30 million pounds in 1981 to almost 55 million pounds in 1993. The increase in use of moist snuff was due to a number of factors: increased smoking restrictions in many places; promotions and advertising; and the waning impact of tax hikes, negative publicity, and health warnings. Manufacturers of loose leaf, plug, and dry snuff experienced a slow slide in volume sales but maintained profits through price increases. In addition, use of smoking tobacco— including pipe tobacco and self-rolled cigarettes— showed a slight increase in the early 1990s. The mid- to late 1990s also saw a resurgence in the consumption of cigars.

U.S. Tobacco Co. has been the overwhelming market leader in moist snuff sales with its Copenhagen and Skoal brands. In the looseleaf category, Pinkerton Tobacco Co. has established itself as a consistent market leader with its Red Man and Granger brand lines.

Industry Issues in the Twentieth Century. The snuff business enjoyed an upsurge in use in the mid-1970s after nearly half a century of lackluster sales, due in large part to a health-related scare about smokeless tobacco at the beginning of the twentieth century; people were alerted to the danger of contracting tuberculosis from sputum, and spitting was considered the greatest hazard of tobacco. The hardcore market remained in the South among the older population. However in the mid-1970s, snuff began to regain some popularity, especially as young men turned to it because they thought it was a safe alternative to cigarettes. Labels warning of dangers and a ban on television and radio advertising of smokeless tobacco were not required until 1986, when the U.S. Surgeon General proclaimed it a cause of mouth cancer and other oral diseases.

The industry faced many challenges in the 1980s and 1990s as the public became more concerned about tobacco-related health issues. The mid-1990s saw a flurry of legal activity as states sued companies to compensate state healthcare providers for the cost of treating tobacco related illnesses. In addition to the suits for smoking tobacco, U.S. Tobacco and other smokeless tobacco producers were sued for injuries that plaintiffs claimed were caused by chewing tobacco. In 1996, President Clinton announced sweeping regulatory measures, which included the regulation of the nicotine in tobacco as a drug, more stringent control of advertising, and efforts to keep tobacco away from minors. In 1997, state attorney generals and tobacco companies were working toward out-of-court settlements of anti-tobacco lawsuits in exchange for longterm regulation at the state and federal levels.

With rising pressures on the $45 billion domestic tobacco industry, the strategy for maintaining profits included a heavy emphasis on foreign markets. Of Philip Morris's 1995 sales of $66.1 billion, $5.5 billion was profit. With close to half of its revenues coming from foreign sales, the company expected to have an earnings gain of about 17 percent in 1997. Likewise, RJR Nabisco, with more than 170 markets worldwide, was expecting a 15 percent increase in earnings.

FURTHER READING

American Cancer Society. *Cancer Facts & Figures — 1997.* Available from http://www.cancer.org/97tobacc.html.

Frank, Allan Dodds. "Tobacco Under Fire." *CNNfn Archives,* Cable News Network. 15 May 1996. Available from http://www.cnnfn.com/news/9605/15/tobacco_attack_pkg/index.htm.

Forbes Annual Report on American Industry, 13 January 1997. Available from http://www.forbes.com/forbes/97/0113/5901160a.htm.

Greising, David and Catherine Yang. "Peace Talks in the Tobacco Wars?" *Business Week,* 10 February 1997, 88.

"Moist Snuff Lifts Smokeless Market." *U.S. Distribution Journal,* May 1990.

"Smokeless Sales Show Effects of Recent Pressures." *U.S. Tobacco and Candy Journal,* 25 October 1987.

"Smokeless Tobacco Producers Come Under Fire." *CNN Archives,* Cable News Network. 28 December 1995.

"Taking Stock." *Beverage World,* July 1996.

"To Your Health." *PBS News Hour,* 23 August 1996. Available from http://www1.pbs.org/newshour/bb/health/august96/kwame_kessler_8-23.html.

"U.S. Volumes Decline Again." *Standard and Poor's Industry Survey,* 6 August 1992.

White, Larry C. *Merchants of Death: The American Tobacco Industry,* New York: William Morrow, 1988.

—Wendy Stein, updated by Brett Alan King

SIC 2141

TOBACCO STEMMING AND REDRYING

Establishments in this industry classification are primarily engaged in the stemming and redrying of tobacco or in manufacturing reconstituted tobacco. Establishments which sell leaf tobacco as merchants, wholesalers, agents, or brokers, and which may also be engaged in stemming tobacco, are classified in **SIC 5159: Farm Product Raw Materials, Not Elsewhere Classified.** Leaf tobacco warehouses that also may be engaged in stemming tobacco are classified in **SIC 4221: Farm Product Warehousing and Storage.**

INDUSTRY SNAPSHOT

In early 1997, tobacco processors, like the tobacco industry as a whole, faced an uncertain outlook in the United States. The long-term trend of domestic cigarette consumption was down, owing to higher prices, tougher restrictions on smoking in public places, greater awareness of the health risks of tobacco use, and declining social acceptance. Cigarette companies were roundly criticized for promoting smoking among teenagers, and in March 1997 tough rules went into effect to reduce teen smoking. Thousands of tobacco farmers, whose families had often been in the business for generations, were shifting out of the product and into other crops—cotton, in many cases.

Tobacco processing is truly an international business, however, and all of the major companies in the segment have extensive growing, processing, and sales operations overseas. Overseas markets presented a brighter picture. While U.S. usage was on a downward trend, consumption overseas (about 10 times the size of the domestic market) was expanding; overall cigarette consumption was growing 1 to 2 percent a year. Demand in some countries had grown enormously—cigarette consumption in China, for example, was more than five times greater than in 1965. U.S. cigarette exports tripled between 1985 and 1992, owing to the popularity of American tobacco products and reduced trade barriers in countries such as Japan. The trend continued into the mid-1990s: exports of domestically produced cigarettes in 1995 totaled 35.1 percent of production, up from 31.8 percent in 1994 and 30.9 percent in 1993.

ORGANIZATION AND STRUCTURE

The processing of tobacco in the United States is dominated by three major companies (Universal Corporation, DiMon, and Standard Commercial) that have large operations in the important tobacco-growing regions of the world. These companies will purchase the farmer's tobacco at auction (common in the United States) or contract to purchase tobacco directly from the farmer. In certain overseas markets where the firms have contracted to buy the farmer's entire crop, they will often provide financial and technical assistance as well to ensure the tobacco's quality. In the United States, most of the processors' tobacco purchases at auction are made to fill specific orders from the major domestic and overseas cigarette producers, with whom they often have relationships extending over many years.

After purchase, the tobacco is processed to meet the specific needs of the cigarette manufacturer, whose representatives are frequently at the processor's facilities to monitor the work on their particular orders. At the factory, the tobacco is reclassified according to grade; blended to meet customer requirements regarding color, body, and chemistry; and threshed to remove the stem from the leaf (although some tobacco is processed in whole leaf form). The processed tobacco is redried to remove excess moisture so it can be held in storage for long periods of time. The companies also perform most of the processing of tobacco that is not purchased at auction and thus enters the U.S. stabilization pool, under the auspices of the Department of Agriculture. The companies generally do not manufacture cigarettes or other consumer tobacco products.

In the United States, primarily two major types of tobacco are grown: flue-cured and burley. Flue-cured is one of the most widely grown tobaccos in the world. It is cured by the grower, usually with gas- or oil-generated heat, and it serves as the basic ingredient in light blended or "American type" cigarettes. In the United States, flue-cured tobacco is grown on the east coast, from Virginia to Florida, and especially in North Carolina. Burley tobacco, on the other hand, is air cured and is grown primarily in Kentucky and Tennessee. Mature tobacco is a perishable commodity that must be processed relatively quickly to prevent fermentation or deterioration. Tobacco processors thus locate their facilities near the principal sources of the crop.

CURRENT CONDITIONS

While the domestic consumption of tobacco products continued to trend downward in the 1990s, the major processors remained relatively unscathed. One reason was that to increase or maintain margins on cheaper cigarettes, the manufacturers imported more foreign tobacco, which was relatively inexpensive—but significantly more profitable for the processors to supply. Between 1989-92, U.S. tobacco imports—the bulk of which were from Brazil, Zimbabwe, Argentina, Thailand, and Malawi—had more than doubled, while domestic output had risen only 26 percent.

Moreover, primarily because of increased smoking in Asia, worldwide tobacco consumption had jumped 75 percent in the 1970s and 1980s and was continuing to trend upward at 1 to 2 percent a year. Demand for so-called American-blend cigarettes, which tasted milder compared with the stronger and harsher cigarettes smoked in most of the world, was increasing—even in countries where overall demand was flat or down. Overseas demand for milder cigarettes, coupled with reduced trade barriers in important markets like Japan, helped U.S. cigarette exports to surge to 260 billion cigarettes in 1995, versus 100 billion in 1987 and 59 billion in 1985. U.S. processors were well positioned to supply the flue-cured and burley tobaccos that are used to make the relatively low-tar, low-nicotine American-blend cigarette.

Of course, the industry wasn't immune to temporary downturns, and in 1993 and 1994 market conditions weakened. The enactment of legislation that required U.S.-produced cigarettes contain at least 75 percent domestically grown tobacco (the "75/25 Rule") induced U.S. manufacturers to reduce purchases of overseas tobacco. Moreover, lower-than-expected initial demand for imported tobacco products in Central and Eastern Europe and the former Soviet Union and an oversupply attributable to record foreign tobacco crops dampened prices. Together, reduced demand and lower prices hurt the financial performance of the leaf tobacco merchants.

In late 1994 and 1995, however, the demand and supply imbalance in world tobacco markets began to improve. Leaf tobacco production outside the U.S. was curtailed in response to the market overhang. The 75/25 Rule was repealed in September 1995, since it violated GATT; it was replaced by a string of less stringent import quotas. U.S. cigarette manufacturers began to buy more tobacco from outside the United States, and the overall tenor of the market brightened. U.S. imports of unmanufactured tobacco increased 20 percent between July 1994-June 1995 and July 1995-June 1996.

Tobacco output on a per-acre basis remained quite profitable in the United States, but farmers remained wary and uncertain. As Kentucky Farm Bureau President William Sprague told the *Lexington Herald Leader* in 1996, ''It's a paradox: we have an increasing world demand for something we can produce in this state very well. But all farmers are seeing and reading about is the ill effects of tobacco. It has our farmers gun shy.'' The long-term downward trend in domestic consumption had forced some growers to switch to alternative crops like cotton. The number of tobacco farms in North Carolina, which grows about two-thirds of the country's flue-cured tobacco, dropped from about 100,000 in the mid-1980s to 42,000 in 1991.

While their own segment remained profitable, the processors, like other industry participants, were concerned about the increasingly strong steps being taken to limit tobacco use. Dozens of localities around the country had passed measures that curtailed smoking in offices, restaurants, and other public places, and nationwide restrictions were being suggested by some in Congress. Studies that determined second hand cigarette smoke could cause lung cancer were gaining credence. States were suing the cigarette manufacturers to pick up their health-care costs and were gaining significant court victories. In March 1997, bipartisan legislation was unveiled that would hike Federal cigarette taxes 43 cents per pack to fund health insurance costs for children and reduce the deficit. The outlook for the domestic tobacco industry could only be described as bleak.

INDUSTRY LEADERS

Universal Corporation is the largest tobacco processor in the United States. In the fiscal year ending June 1996, net income almost tripled to $72 million, as sales rose about 9 percent to $3.6 billion. The profit improvements reflected better market conditions, larger leaf volumes, and the company's restructuring efforts. More than two-thirds of Universal's revenues came from the tobacco business, with the balance generated by lumber and agricultural products. Universal estimates that in fiscal 1996 it purchased or processed nearly 40 percent of the flue-cured and burley tobacco produced in aggregate in the United States, Brazil, Zimbabwe, and Malawi. It also is an important participant in dark tobacco (used in cigars and smokeless tobacco) markets, such as the United States, the Dominican Republic, and Indonesia. During 1993, Universal added to its international holdings with the acquisition of Britain's Casalee, the world's fifth-largest processor.

In April 1995, Dibrell and Monk-Austin, two giants of the tobacco processing industry, merged to form a new firm called DiMon. In 1996, it was the second-largest leaf tobacco processor, with about 30 percent of the world market. Approximately 80 percent of its revenues come from tobacco operations, with the balance derived from fresh-cut flowers. Sales for the year ending 30 June 1996 were $2.2 billion, up 12 percent, and net income was $41 million, against a $30 million loss in the prior year. Better market conditions and consolidation of overlapping functions in the merged company were responsible for the turnaround. During the year, approximately 57 percent of the dollar value of DiMon's tobacco purchases were made in the United States. Purchases in Brazil, Malawi, and Zimbabwe accounted for 17 percent, 9 percent, and 3 percent of all buys.

On 14 February 1997, DiMon announced an agreement to buy Intabex, the world's fourth-largest tobacco dealer, with annual sales of $700 million. Intabex was owned by Folium, Inc., an investment company, and Tabacalera, the Spanish cigarette company.

Standard Commercial has expanded since its founding in 1910 as a small marketer of oriental tobaccos to become one of the three largest tobacco processors. Sales in fiscal 1996 (ending March 31) rose 12 percent to $1.2 billion, and the company cut its annual loss in half to about $9 million. However, its tobacco operations, which account for about 70 percent of sales, did quite well. (The company derives the balance of its sales from wool operations.) Revenues rose 22 percent to $925.5 million and income from operations (before interest) increased 86 percent to $71 million.

WORK FORCE

In the United States, the tobacco processors purchase flue-cured tobacco during the five-month period from July-November; for burley tobacco, the season runs from late November until January or February. Processing takes place throughout the buying season and is usually finished within two to three months following purchase. During these periods, the industry's work force swells. Some of the processors' seasonal employees are covered by collective bargaining agreements with unions. Seasonal labor is also used extensively in overseas operations.

AMERICA AND THE WORLD

Both in terms of supply and demand, in the 1990s the U.S. tobacco processing industry was increasingly looking abroad. The elimination of trade barriers and the rising popularity of lighter, American-blend cigarettes were expanding overseas markets. Following the fall of the Berlin Wall in 1989, new markets for U.S. exports sprung up in the former Soviet republics and in Eastern Europe. And, as international suppliers of tobacco, the processors were also selling tobacco grown overseas for cigarette manufacture in non-U.S. factories.

In terms of supply, the large processors had major operations in Brazil, Zimbabwe, Malawi and other leading tobacco-growing countries. In several countries, the processor will contract directly with tobacco farmers, in some cases before harvest, and thus take the risk that the delivered product will meet the market's quality requirements. In some countries, the major processors also provide agronomy services and advances for fertilizers and supplies.

FURTHER READING

Bickers, Christopher. "Quotas Go Begging, But Imports Rise." *World Tobacco,* November 1996.

Bridges, Roger. "Record Exports Set to Continue." *World Tobacco,* September 1995.

"DIMON Announces Acquisition of Intabex." *PR Newswire,* 14 February 1997.

Greising, David. "A Cotton-Picking Land Rush." *Business Week,* 9 May 1994.

Lucke, James. "Kentucky Farmers Fear Tobacco Shortage May Harm State in World Markets." *Knight-Ridder/Tribune Business News,* 15 July 1996.

Sandlin, Nina. "The Anti-Smoking Movement Isn't Killing the Tobacco Industry, It's Dying a Natural Death." *American Medical News,* 14 November 1994.

"Zimbabwe." *World Tobacco,* November 1996.

—Bob Schneider

TEXTILE MILL PRODUCTS

BROADWOVEN FABRIC MILLS, COTTON

This category covers establishments primarily engaged in the production of woven fabrics more than 12 inches (30.48 centimeters) in width, wholly or chiefly by weight of cotton. Broadwoven fabrics primarily of cotton are utilized in three general end-product categories: apparel, homefurnishings, and industrial products. Most of the broadwoven cotton apparel fabrics serve the outerwear market—men's, ladies' and children's shirts, blouses, pants, and dresses. Some lightweight jackets and boxer shorts are also produced from broadwoven cotton fabric. The homefurnishings market includes terry towels; sheets, pillowcases, blankets, bedspreads, and other bedding accessories; table linens, dish towels and dish rags; draperies; and upholstery fabrics and wall coverings. Carpet and rug manufacturers are classified in **SIC 2273: Carpets and Rugs.** Establishments involved in tire cord and fabric production are classified in **SIC 2296: Tire Cords and Fabrics.** Those establishments engaged in finishing cotton broadwoven fabrics are classified in **SIC 2261: Finishers of Broadwoven Fabrics of Cotton.**

INDUSTRY SNAPSHOT

Manufacturing of cotton broadwovens—like most segments of textiles—is a mature industry. Since the mid-1980s, major U.S. firms in the industry have pursued growth largely through mergers, acquisitions, and foreign markets; they have maximized profits typically through cost cutting and sourcing low-cost labor from foreign countries. The industry faces formidable competition on price from imported textiles, particularly those from Asian nations and Mexico. Nonethe-

less, the value of U.S. industry shipments rose modestly throughout the first half of the 1990s and totaled more than $6.5 billion by 1995. Real growth after inflation, however, was only at about 7 percent for the six-year period.

ORGANIZATION AND STRUCTURE

Fabric weavers generally are vertically integrated companies that produce their own yarn. The primary reason for integrated weaving plants is that despite fashion changes that occur in the woven segment, yarn counts—the size of the yarn—as well as fabric constructions remain fairly stable. Fabric knitters, on the other hand, are faced with constant changes in yarn size and construction. Therefore, most knitters find it more economical to purchase yarn from sales yarn companies.

CURRENT CONDITIONS

Cotton remains a viable material for the textile market despite predictions in the 1960s and 1970s that manmade products would completely replace natural fiber. Cotton's inherent qualities, such as absorbency and breathability, and new fabric finishes have kept the fiber's market share strong. In 1995, U.S. manufacturers produced some 4.5 billion square yards of broadwoven cotton fabrics, according to the U.S. Department of Commerce. That same year, Cotton Incorporated reported that among the different fibers used in apparel and home fabrics, cotton use was larger than for any other single fiber. Cotton's competitiveness can be partially attributed to improvements such as the all-cotton, wrinkle resistant fabrics that are particularly popular for making men's pants, softer finishes, and flame-retardant treatments. Researchers are also developing antibacterial finishes and temperature responsive treatments for cottons.

The general state of the economy, coupled with the level of consumer confidence, has a great impact on operations engaged in the manufacture of broadwoven cotton fabrics for apparel products. This has obviously been the case over the last several years, with companies producing fabrics for apparel enjoying success or decline in direct relationship to the state of the economy.

New housing starts, which showed strength in the mid-1990s, are the chief factor outside of trade matters affecting manufacturers of broadwoven cotton fabrics for homefurnishings. Although a large market exists for replacement sheets, pillow cases, towels, etc., nothing spurs this segment of the industry as much as new housing starts.

Several factors affect the demand for broadwoven cotton fabrics for industrial use. These include the success of the automotive industry, the activity in new highways, bridges, etc., and the nature of the agriculture industry. A significant section of the agriculture industry—cotton farming—also has a tremendous influence on the annual success of producers of broadwoven cotton fabrics for any application. The price of raw materials are often affected by weather and other natural factors. Shortages in U.S. cotton production plagued the industry in 1995, when prices shot above $1.00 per pound—costs that have not been seen since the American Civil War. At the same time, foreign crops were reduced by the boll worm in China and by the leaf curl virus in Pakistan. In 1996-97 cotton acreage in the United States was expected to fall by 10 percent because of the higher returns then available in the soybean, corn, and wheat markets.

In 1993, the textile industry and the U.S. government signed the American Textile Partnership Agreement (AMTEX), which was expected be a major stimulus to the industry. AMTEX links eight Department of Energy laboratories with the textile and apparel industries and supporting research groups. The agreement's goal is to create programs and develop technologies for the U.S. textile and apparel industries.

AMERICA AND THE WORLD

A number of factors influence the success of companies engaged in the manufacturing of broadwoven cotton fabrics, but none has the impact to equal that of international trade. For a number of years, imports—particularly in the apparel fabrics sector—have steadily risen, severely affecting operation of U.S. manufacturers of broadwoven cotton fabrics. Manufacturers of broadwoven cotton fabrics are impacted by imported garments—which are usually cut and sewn from fabrics manufactured in the same country as the garments—as well as fabrics.

The summer of 1993 was a watershed in the history of textile and apparel imports. The months of June, July, August, and September represented the four largest importing months in history in this area for America. Each month set a new all-time record for that particular period. Total imports during the trimester were 5.85 billion square meters, more than was imported during the entire year of 1982. The trade deficit is of increasing concern to the textile industry, as companies look for growth in international sales. U.S. textile exports experienced steady growth during the 1980s and the first half of the 1990s. In 1995, however, the United States still imported twice the dollar amount of cotton broadwovens it exported.

The North American Free Trade Agreement (NAFTA) of 1993 was expected to benefit U.S. manufacturers of broadwoven cotton fabrics in the long run, according to the American Textile Manufacturers Institute (ATMI). The General Agreement on Tariffs and Trade (GATT), however, could be detrimental to the long-range success of U.S. broadwoven cotton manufacturers, according to ATMI.

NAFTA, which became official January 1, 1994, effectively eliminates trade barriers between Canada, Mexico, and the United States. Gradual elimination of tariffs on U.S. textile exports to Mexico is seen as a major motivator for sales. Some U.S. companies are, in fact, spending millions of dollars to increase capacity as a result of the passage of NAFTA. The agreement was to eliminate tariffs on 89 percent of U.S.-made fabric exports to Mexico over a five-year period beginning January 1, 1994. Mexico eliminated tariffs on U.S. products such as denim, twills, cotton terry towels, curtains, and drapes immediately in 1994.

By early 1997, U.S. Department of Commerce data indicated that increased trade with Mexico and Canada had begun to reduce the dominance of Asian countries in textile imports to the United States. Mexican textile/apparel imports had increased 40 percent in the first three quarters of 1995, while Canadian shipments to the United States increased by 18 percent. At the same time, Chinese imports dropped by 23 percent and shipments from Hong Kong, Korea, and Thailand fell by 10 to 12 percent. U.S. textile mills benefited from this scenario because U.S. yarns and fabrics are used in 80 percent of Mexican apparel, while China uses very little of these products. Caribbean nations, which have made a special trade pact with the United States, are also enjoying increased textile and apparel imports, and should further stimulate U.S. mill performance.

Growth of the Mexican apparel manufacturing industry is credited to the lower wages generally paid in that country. This advantage may also benefit U.S. textile companies who are interested in undertaking joint ventures with Mexican companies. One such U.S.-Mexican partnership to form following NAFTA implementation was between Cone Mills Corp. and Compania Industrial de Parras SA, Mexico's largest denim maker. Together they formed Parras Cone de Mexico and built a 650,000 square foot, state-of-the-art manufacturing facility in Parras, Coahuila. The plant's general manager, Marcus Bradsher, noted in *Textile World* that his new work group was "relatively young . . . About 25 percent are female, and 40 percent of them never had a job before this plant was built."

While the signing of NAFTA raised the hopes of manufacturers of broadwoven cotton fabrics, signing of GATT had just the opposite effect. Known as the Uruguay Round of GATT, the agreement was signed in 1993 by 117 nations following seven years of negotiations. This agreement phased out tariffs on textiles set by the MultiFiber Arrangement (MFA) by 2005. In January of 1995 the administration and enforcement of GATT was assumed by the newly formed World Trade Organization.

RESEARCH AND TECHNOLOGY

Manufacturers of broadwoven cotton fabrics are replacing shuttle looms with shuttleless weaving machines as rapidly as economically feasible. In 1993 approximately half of the approximate 100,000 weaving machines in the United States were shuttleless, which offer geometrically higher weaving speeds than those of shuttle systems. Use of electronics in the broadwoven manufacturing process has permitted even higher increases in speeds. Speeds on any filling insertion system vary depending on type and width of fabric being woven.

When first developed, each shuttleless filling insertion system was designed specifically for a somewhat narrow fabric application range. As systems have been improved, modified, and computerized, the application ranges have broadened considerably. Projectile, flexible rapier, and rigid rapier systems are more versatile and can handle heavier, more complicated styles such as plaid upholstery. However, modifications to air-jet systems have broadened the application range to include more than just simple, lightweight styles such as printcloth and sheeting. Burlington Industries and Swift Textiles now both produce heavyweight denim on air-jet machines, and a few companies have begun

experimenting with heavyweight upholstery fabrics on air jets as well.

Electronic technology has contributed greatly to the operation of shuttleless weaving machines in the broadwoven cotton sector. Systems have provided more control in the air bursts from the series of nozzles on air-jet machines, permitting greater manufacturing speeds and production of a broader range of fabric weights. Jacquard machines—which control multi-colored, extremely complicated patterns—have incorporated electronics that permit higher speeds in the production of fancy upholstery fabrics on flexible and rigid rapiers. Electronic advances also paved the way for the installation of automation features on shuttleless weaving machines such as automatic filling break repair, automatic cloth removal at specified lengths and automatic filling supply cone replenishment.

The biggest contribution made by electronic technology to broadwoven cotton manufacturing is in monitoring and control of the operation. Microprocessor-driven systems monitor and provide real-time data on efficiency, production, and quality. The data can be provided for any time period the manufacturer wishes to designate. This data can also be supplied for an individual machine or several machines grouped by style, job assignment, etc. Such information permits the evaluation of styles, fabrics, etc. and gives the broadwoven fabrics manufacturer the ability to select those materials most suited for the production machinery available.

As electronic systems become more advanced, they not only permit monitoring of the operation, but control of many of the functions as well. Modern systems can detect many mechanical and electrical problems. Depending on the sophistication of the system and the severity of the problem, the system can correct the problem, signal technicians as to the nature of the problem, or stop the machine until the problem is corrected. Totally automated systems (known as "lights out" operations) have been created for spinning machines, while complete automation of the weaving process is still far from being cost effective.

Computerization of the textile industry has been a critical part of the quick response (QR) programs that are being adopted by companies in an attempt to shorten the time between the placement of retail orders and the delivery of textile goods to their stores. The companies coordinating such programs communicate using bar codes and electronic data interchange. With the ability to pinpoint production times and quantities, mills can direct production according to individual orders. The mills, as well as apparel manufacturers and retailers, benefit from the resulting reduction in inventory costs. QR programs also reduce forced markdowns and stockouts on the retail level.

FURTHER READING

"ATME-I '93 Quickens Textiles' Time to Market." *Textile World,* June 1992.

"At 150 Years, Collins & Aikman is Dedicated to its Markets." *Textile World,* June 1993.

Cotton Incorporated. "Cotton Perspective." April 1996.

"Dundee Puts on the Ritz with Hot New Product Mix." *Textile World,* June 1988.

"GATT Disappoints U.S. Textile Leaders." *Textile World,* January 1994.

Isaacs III, McAllister. "Machinery Makers Are Responding to the Needs of Weaving Plants." *Textile World,* December 1993.

———. "Textile World's Weaving Machinery Chart for 1993," *Textile World,* December 1993.

Jablonski, Mary. "Multifactor Productivity: Cotton and Synthetic Broadwoven Fabrics." Monthly Labor Review, July 1995.

Lee, Jill. "Textile Advances Enhance Cotton Markets." *Agricultural Research,* May 1996.

Linton, George C. *The Modern Textile and Apparel Dictionary.* Plainfield, NJ: Textile Book Service, 1973.

McClenahen, John S. "A Yarn That's No Tall Tale." *Industry Week,* 1 July 1996.

Reichard, Robert S. "Positives . . . Nudge . . . Textiles . . . Toward . . . Recovery." *Textile World,* January 1996.

———. "Do positive signs point to prosperity?" *Textile World,* January 1997.

Rozelle, Walter N. "Parras Cone: A Product of A NAFTA Partnership." *Textile World,* February 1996.

———. "Business Outlook." *Textile World,* January 1997.

Standard & Poor's Industry Surveys. New York: Standard & Poor's Corporation, 1996.

"Stevens Breakup Realigns Industry." *Textile World,* June 1988.

U.S. Bureau of the Census. "Broadwoven Fabrics." *Current Industrial Reports,* 10 June 1996. Available from http://www.census.gov.

"Textiles Ready to Reap NAFTA Rewards." *Textile World,* December 1993.

"Weaving Speeds are not all in Machines." *Textile World,* June 1993.

"Who's the Real Winner in Burlington Match?" *Textile World,* June 1987.

—McAllister Isaacs III, updated by Paula Pyzik Scott

BROADWOVEN FABRIC MILLS, MANMADE FIBER AND SILK

This category covers establishments primarily engaged in the production of woven fabrics more than 12 inches (30.48 centimeters) in width, wholly or chiefly by weight of manmade fiber and/or silk. Broadwoven fabrics primarily of manmade fiber are utilized in three general end-product categories: apparel, home furnishings, and industrials. Broadwoven fabrics primarily of silk are for the most part utilized in apparel products. Occasionally, broadwoven silk fabrics serve the home furnishings market.

Production of broadwoven fabrics with content wholly or primarily by weight of cotton is included in **SIC 2211: Broadwoven Fabric Mills, Cotton.** Production of broadwoven fabrics with content wholly or chiefly by weight of wool, mohair, or other similar animal fiber is included in **SIC 2231: Broadwoven Fabric Mills, Wool (Including Dyeing and Finishing).** Production of narrow fabric, generally 12 inches or less in width, of cotton, wool, silk, and manmade fiber is included in **SIC 2241: Narrow Fabric and Other Smallwares Mills: Cotton, Wool, Silk, and Manmade Fiber.**

INDUSTRY SNAPSHOT

There are more than 300 companies, with some 436 establishments, engaged in the production of manmade fiber or silk broadwoven fabrics in the United States. In 1992 makers of such fabric employed 87,400 workers, of which some 79 percent were employed in South Carolina, North Carolina, Georgia, and Virginia. In 1995, these establishments produced 11.75 billion square yards, according to the U.S. Department of Commerce, Bureau of the Census. While manmade and silk broadwoven fabric production totaled more than twice that of broadwoven cotton fabrics—over 11.75 billion square yards vs. 4.48 billion square yards—no single manmade fiber or silk accounted for as much production as cotton by itself.

Principal fibers used in broadwoven manmade fiber fabrics for apparel are polyester, rayon, and nylon with occasional use of polypropylene or olefin fiber. These fabrics are generally used for men's, ladies', and children's outerwear including shirts, blouses, pants, and dresses; leisure and activewear; heavy and lightweight jackets and coats; suits; sleepwear and lingerie; etc.

The home furnishings market for manmade broadwoven fabrics includes sheets, pillowcases, blankets, bedspreads, and other bedding accessories; table linens or napery products; draperies; upholstery fabrics and wall coverings. The principal manmade fibers used in home furnishings are polyester, rayon, polypropylene, acrylic and occasionally nylon. Carpet and rug manufacturers are included in **SIC 2273: Carpets and Rugs.**

Industrial applications for broadwoven manmade fibers include materials used in the automotive, agricultural, geotextile, medical, recreational, and transportation industries. Broadwoven manmade fiber fabrics also find use in conveyor and other industrial belting products as well as in specialized applications such as soft-sided luggage and protective clothing. Tire cord and fabric production is included in **SIC 2296: Tire Cord and Fabrics.**

Broadwoven fabrics of manmade fiber for industrial applications are made from the widest variety of fiber types. Traditional manmade fibers such as nylon, polyester, acrylic, polypropylene or olefin, and rayon find numerous uses in the area of industrial fabrics. A number of industrial applications products, however, require the characteristics of some specialized manmade fibers. Some of these fibers include the aramid family with such fibers as Nomex and Kevlar, both manufactured by Du Pont. Nomex is highly flame resistant, and fabrics manufactured from this fiber are used in such products as protective clothing for firefighters, space suits, and race-car-driver clothing. Kevlar, with strength characteristics superior to steel, can be found in fabrics manufactured for bullet-proof vests and other protective devices.

Other manmade fibers with high-performance characteristics for use in specialized applications and their major producers include carbon fiber, BASF and Courtaulds; glass fiber, Owens-Corning Fiberglass Corp. and PPG Industries Inc.; polybenzimidazole, Hoechst Celanese; polyetheretherketone, Albany International and Shakespeare Monofilament; and sulfur, Albany International and Phillips Fibers Corp.

Of the numerous producers of traditional manmade fibers that are used in broadwoven fabrics, some of the principal U.S. producers are Eastman Chemical Products Inc. (Acetate); Mann Industries and Monsanto (Acrylic); Albany International, Allied Fibers, BASF Corp., and Hercules Inc. and Phillips Fibers Corp. (Olefin polypropylene; Courtaulds Fibers Inc. and North American Rayon Corp. (Rayon); and Globe Mfg. Co. (Spandex).

ORGANIZATION AND STRUCTURE

Producers of broadwoven fabrics of manmade fiber and silk, like the producers of other broadwoven fabrics, are for the most part vertically integrated textile manufacturing companies. That is, most broadwoven companies manufacture their own yarn requirements; many of them dye and finish their own fabrics.

Aside from the many different generic types of manmade fiber—i.e., polyester, nylon, rayon, etc.—and the different brands within each generic type—i.e., Du Pont's Dacron, Eastman's Kodel, Hoechst Celanese's Trevira, and other polyesters—fabrics may be woven from two forms of manmade fiber yarn: filament or staple. Filament yarn is a continuous strand of manmade fiber. Staple manmade fiber yarn consists of many individual fibers cut to a specific length. These fibers measure approximately one to one-and-a-half inches in length if they are to be spun into yarn on a cotton system spinning process. If they are to be spun on a woolen or worsted system spinning process, the fibers are cut up to six or eight inches in length. The form of manmade fiber yarn to be woven depends on the end-use application of the fabric. Staple fiber arrives at the textile plant in bales, just like cotton or wool. It is processed just like cotton or wool on the same machinery.

Of the more than 11.75 billion square yards of manmade fiber and silk broadwoven fabric woven in 1995, more than half was produced using 85 percent or more continuous filament yarn. The percentage of manmade fiber broadwoven fabrics produced from continuous filament yarn has trended upward since 1980 when this type represented 37 percent of the 10.7 billion square yards produced. In 1988, the amount of the manmade fiber broadwoven fabric produced from continuous filament yarn reached 50 percent for the first time. Consumption of filament fiber by broadwoven manmade fabric producers has remained at or above this level since that time.

BACKGROUND AND DEVELOPMENT

A discussion of weaving systems types and the emergence of shuttleless weaving as the most efficient, productive and quality producing system can be found in **SIC 2211: Broadwoven Fabric Mills, Cotton.** All of the shuttleless weaving systems—projectile, rigid and flexible rapier and air-jet—described in the broadwoven cotton fabrics section are in use in weaving broadwoven fabrics from manmade fiber and silk. Producers of many of the styles of broadwoven manmade fiber fabrics can also use the water-jet system of weaving as well. This requires the yarn to be hydrophobic—the fiber must not absorb moisture, the styles must be relatively simple in construction, and the material must be relatively light in weight so that a stream of water can carry the yarn across the weaving machine. Most manmade fibers are hydrophobic, rayon and its variants being the notable exceptions.

Water-jet weaving machines are manufactured by Nissan Motor Co. Ltd. and Tsudakoma Corp. of Japan and Zbrojovka-Vsetin of the Czech Republic. Water-jet weaving machines operate at a production rate of over 1,000 ppm, which is more than 500 percent faster than conventional shuttle weaving systems, approximately 200 percent faster than projectile and both rapier systems, and at least 25 percent faster than the average air-jet weaving machine.

CURRENT CONDITIONS

As a group—and aside from competition within the group—producers of broadwoven fabrics of manmade fiber and silk face two types of competition for market share, especially in the apparel sector and, to a lesser extent, in the homefurnishings market. Those two types of competition are (1) fabrics and garments imported from developing countries and (2) a trend toward increasing consumer preference for products made from natural fibers.

Increasing consumer preference for products made from natural fibers—cotton, wool, etc.—stems from several factors. The first of these is marketing and promotional campaigns conducted by Cotton Incorporated, an organization sponsored and paid for by the cotton growers of the United States. Formed in 1971 in an attempt to offset the huge gains in market share being made by polyester, the organization's purpose is to promote the use of cotton in fabrics. Since its formation, cotton has increased in market share in the United States at the expense of manmade fiber in production of broadwoven fabrics every year. With headquarters and marketing offices in New York and research facilities in Raleigh, North Carolina, Cotton Incorporated's principal means of promotion of cotton as a fiber of choice in broadwoven fabrics are (1) massive television commercials: "The Fabric of Our Lives;" and (2) use of the cotton bowl logo in products made of 100 percent cotton or the cotton-blend logo in products made of at least 60 percent cotton. In a recognition survey of 12 leading product logos among consumers in 1993, the cotton logo was deemed the second most recognizable logo, behind only the Shell Oil Co. logo. The survey found that the cotton logo was more recognizable than such logos as those of CBS, Chrysler, Dutch Boy, Merrill Lynch, Prudential, Maxwell House, Kodak, Travelers and Wrigley's.

The second factor playing a part in decreasing market share among manmade fiber broadwovens compared to natural fiber broadwovens has to do with increasing environmental concerns among consumers. Most manmade fibers are produced in chemical plants from a variety of chemicals with inherent potential for environmental problems. Few, if any, fiber producers violated any environmental regulations in 1993, but the perception of potential problems is a factor producers of manmade fiber fabrics must overcome.

The third factor playing a part in decreasing market share among manmade fiber broadwovens is the minimization, if not elimination, of what has historically been the major objection to broadwoven fabrics of cotton. With current capabilities that reduce wrinkles in cotton fabrics and that make the products more in the line of "easy care" or "wash-and-wear" polyester products, cotton fabric producers have taken a giant step toward attracting additional consumers. The makers of manmade fabrics have responded by improving existing fabrics and creating new products. Lycra has been adapted to include some cotton-like attributes—breathability and washability—while providing excellent stretchability. Lycra was especially important in the marketing of 1996 garments constructed of manmade fibers, when manufacturers promoted the "high-tech" look of stretch twills and suitings. The relatively new microdernier fabrics, although they were initially very expensive, are also expected to become popular for their easy care, breathability, and dense, soft characteristics. Specialty fabrics such as DuPont's CoolMax polyester and Cordura Plus nylon are being introduced into apparel manufacturing.

Three agreements enacted during 1993 could have a significant effect on producers of manmade fiber and silk broadwoven fabrics: North American Free Trade Agreement (NAFTA), General Agreement of Tariffs and Trade (GATT), and American Textile Partnership (AMTEX). The first two are agreements between the United States government and governments of other countries, while the third is an agreement between the United States government and the United States textile/apparel complex.

NAFTA went into effect January 1, 1994. It eliminates tariffs on most products traded among Canadian, U. S., and Mexican businesses over a five-year period. Some of those involving textile and apparel products were eliminated on the day the NAFTA took effect. Industry leaders from the American Textile Manufacturers Institute (ATMI) expect NAFTA to benefit the U.S. textile industry, including producers of manmade and silk broadwoven fabrics, from two standpoints.

First, it removes barriers and eliminate tariffs from the United States' trading partners, Mexico and Canada. Second, over the long run, many feel that due to NAFTA, the standard of living will rise in Mexico, creating a larger market for U.S. textile and apparel products.

The December 1993 issue of *Textile World* reported that several U.S. textile companies were increasing their capacities strictly because of the passage of NAFTA. Guilford Mills spent $280 million in 1993 on capital improvements to increase productivity for expected increased demand for apparel fabric. Swift Textiles expanded its denim capacity. John A. Boland III, Swift's president and CEO, said that the $20-million expansion was due to growing interest in denim in Mexico. ''There's a great appeal in Mexico for denim and that will continue to grow,'' he said.

The wisdom of such investments was proven when Mexico and Canada succeeded in reducing the dominance of imports from the Far East during the mid-1990s. Four of the top five exporters of textiles and apparel to the United States in 1993 had been China (2.1 billion sme), Taiwan (1.2 billion sme), Hong Kong (936 million sme) and South Korea (872 million sme). In January 1996, however, Mexico surpassed China in exports to the United States—as well as Canada, Taiwan, and Hong Kong—for the first time. The textile industry heralded this achievement as a victory for U.S. manufacturers because 80 percent of Mexican imports are made with U.S. fabric and yarn.

U.S. producers of broadwoven fabrics of manmade fiber and silk were not so enthusiastic about the completion of the Uruguay Round of the GATT. After a seven-year marathon of negotiations, this agreement was concluded on December 15, 1993, and signed on April 15, 1994. The pact, approved by 117 nations, phases out tariffs on textiles by 2005—thus ending the former MultiFiber Arrangement (MFA). In January of 1995 the administration and enforcement of GATT was adopted by the newly-formed World Trade Organization. Some analysts predict that the expected rise in textile and apparel imports will mean the elimination of one million textile and apparel jobs over that period of time.

Imports of textile and apparel products have been increasing steadily over the last several years. Following a record-breaking surge in 1992, imports of textiles and apparel jumped again in 1993, rising 9.1 percent and setting a new record of 15.8 billion square-meter equivalents (sme). Textiles bore the brunt of the increase, rising 11.5 percent to reach 8.3 billion sme. Manmade fiber broadwoven fabric imports grew 10 percent in 1993. Looking at import penetration over

nearly a ten-year span, the increase is just as dramatic: the U.S. textile and apparel market was made up of just 23.3 percent imported goods in 1975, as compared to 69.8 percent in 1993, according to *Standard and Poor's Industry Surveys* for 1996.

U.S. textile mill operators were therefore increasingly intent on growing exports and reducing a trade deficit that showed signs of peaking at the 1995 ratio of 4:1 (imports/exports). Such a turnaround would mark a significant change for the industry, which has not enjoyed a trade surplus since 1981. Among the keys to improved international competitiveness were greater efficiency, improved quality of fabrics, and specialization.

The third agreement—the AMTEX—is between the United States Department of Energy (DOE) and the U.S. textile/apparel complex to provide research and existing government technologies to boost U.S. competitiveness. In 1997, eight projects were in progress as joint industry-DOE efforts:

- Computer-Aided Fabric Evaluation (CAFE): Currently, this technology is used for computer vision target recognition systems that can tell the difference between military and civilian aircraft or vehicles. It is also used for high-speed inspection systems that detect pattern and color defects in U.S. currency and postage stamps. Through AMTEX, this technology will be used to detect and classify defects as hundreds of square yards of fabric per minute ''fly by'' an inspection system.

- Cotton Biotechnology: Researchers sought to improve cotton fiber performance and plant yield, with the result of developing longer, stronger, and more uniform plant fibers.

- Demand-Activated Manufacturing Architecture (DAMA): The government has invested extensively in advanced computing, in analysis of large and complex data sets, and in simulation of complex systems. AMTEX proposed an industry-wide computer system linking fiber producers, textile and apparel manufacturers and retailers in an electronic marketplace. U.S. companies will optimize business relationships and production practices to be more responsive to customer needs and reduce costs of shipping, handling, over-production and inventory time. DAMA was slated to be in place by 2000.

- Electronic Embedded Fingerprints: Tiny electronic microchips and radio transponders were developed by DOE to permanently identify or tag missiles or items that were to be controlled under international treaties. While current devices are about the size of a penny, AMTEX proposes to develop a smaller version about the size of a grain of rice. It will include a small radio transmitter and will be packaged for permanent encasement in apparel or other products counterfeited in foreign markets.

- On-Line Process Control (OPCon): AMTEX was working to identify and develop technologies that would allow for faster transitions between products, cost effective production of small lots, and eliminate off-quality productions and off-line testing.

- Rapid Cutting: The government invested in developing high-power lasers for the Strategic Defense Initiative program, isotope separation, and scientific investigations. The new use of these technologies will be to create a new generation of high-speed cutting machines ten to twenty times faster than current machines. This will allow both small and large companies to enter the era of demand-activated-manufacturing and custom apparel manufacturing.

- Sensors for Agile Manufacturing (SFAM): The AMTEX partnership was developing sensors and feedback control methods to increase the industry's productivity, flexibility, and sewing safety.

- Textile Resource Conservation (TReC): Methods were being developed for eliminating the discharge of waste into the environment. Manufacturing processes were being revised to use less energy and natural resources.

Technological advances were matched by corporate interest in improving productivity, which resulted in industry-wide investments in new machinery and equipment. The central thrust of these purchases was to allow mills, apparel manufacturers, and retailers to participate in quick response (QR) programs. Using computer technology—bar codes and electronic data transmission—these groups can cut the time between an initial order and delivery of the desired goods by several weeks. The resulting cost savings is shared by all three players, as each benefits from reduced inventory costs. The system should also share savings from a reduction in forced markdowns and product shortages at the retail level. At the same time, the new machines require fewer and fewer personnel to operate them, as the industry heads toward "lights out" or fully-automated operations. The cost of implementing such programs will likely limit their use for the near future, but related technological advances will undoubtedly reduce the number of jobs for mill employees.

FURTHER READING

American Textile Partnership. "AMTEX Project Descriptions." Available from http://cbmt1.energylan.sandia.gov/amtex/cafe.html.

"ATME-I '93 Quickens Textiles' Time to Market." *Textile World*, June 1992.

"Broadwoven Goods Production, 1993." Washington: Bureau of the Census, United States Department of Commerce.

"The Business Week 1000 Tables." *Business Week*, 1993 Bonus Issue.

"Cotton Incorporated Is 'Textiles' Partner'." *Textile World*, August 1993.

"GATT Disappoints U.S. Textile Leaders." Textile World News, *Textile World*, January 1994.

Isaacs III, McAllister. "Machinery Makers Are Responding to the Needs of Weaving Plants." *Textile World*, December 1993.

Isaacs III, McAllister. "Textile World's Weaving Machinery Chart for 1993." *Textile World*, December 1993.

Jablonski, Mary. "Multifactor Productivity: Cotton and Synthetic Broadwoven Fabrics." *Monthly Labor Review*, July 1995.

Luther, Michael. "Dupont's Fall 1996 Vision: Wardrobe of High-Tech Versatility." *Textile World*, January 1996.

McClenahen, John S. "A Yarn That's No Tall Tale." *Industry Week*, 1 July 1996.

"Microfibers: All Dressed Up and Everywhere to Go." *Textile World*, August 1992.

Reichard, Robert S. "Positives . . . Nudge . . . Textiles . . . Toward . . . Recovery." *Textile World*, January 1996.

———. "Do Positive Signs Point to Prosperity?" *Textile World*, January 1997.

"Springs Psyched for a Second Century of Success." *Textile World*, June 1987.

Standard & Poor's Industry Surveys. New York: Standard & Poor's Corporation, 1992, 1993, 1996.

Textile Highlights. Washington: American Textile Manufacturers Institute, December 1993 and March 1994.

"Textiles Ready to Reap NAFTA Rewards." Textile World News, *Textile World*, December 1993.

"Textile World 1992 Manmade Fiber Chart." *Textile World*, August 1992.

U.S. Bureau of the Census. "Broadwoven Fabrics." *Current Industrial Reports*. Washington: GPO. 1996.

———. "Description of Industries and Summary of Findings: Industry 2221, Broadwoven Fabric Mills, Manmade Fiber and Silk."

"Washington Outlook." *Textile World*, January 1996.

"Weaving Speeds Are Not All in Machines." *Textile World*, June 1993.

—McAllister Isaacs III, updated by Paula Pyzik Scott

BROADWOVEN FABRIC MILLS, WOOL (INCLUDING DYEING AND FINISHING)

This category covers establishments primarily engaged in the production of woven fabrics more than 12 inches (30.48 centimeters) in width, wholly or chiefly by weight of wool, mohair or similar animal fibers; dyeing and finishing of woven wool fabrics; and those shrinking and sponging wool goods for the trade. These fabrics are used primarily for production of apparel (especially outerwear), home furnishings (especially blankets), and specialty items, such as billiard table cloth.

Establishments primarily engaged in weaving or tufting wool carpets and rugs are classified in **SIC 2273: Carpets and Rugs.** Production of broadwoven fabrics with content wholly or primarily by weight of cotton is included in **SIC 2211: Broadwoven Fabric Mills, Cotton.** Production of broadwoven fabrics with content wholly or chiefly by weight of manmade fiber and silk is included in **SIC 2221: Broadwoven Fabric Mills, Manmade Fiber and Silk.** Production of narrow fabric, generally 12 inches or less in width, of cotton, wool, silk and manmade fiber is included in **SIC 2241: Narrow Fabric and Other Smallwares Mills: Cotton, Wool, Silk, and Manmade Fiber.**

INDUSTRY SNAPSHOT

There are some 106 companies that operate 118 establishments engaged in the production of broadwoven fabrics of wool, mohair or of similar animal fiber, according to the U.S. Department of Commerce, Bureau of the Census. By far, the greatest amount of production was from wool fiber. According to the Department of Commerce, the value of production shipments in 1991 for these fabrics totaled $1.5 billion. The preponderance of these fabrics, nearly $1.3 billion, were produced for the apparel industry, while blankets accounted for $27.9 million in shipments. World wool production proceeded to decrease during the first half of the 1990s. However, U.S. mill use was steady during the 1991-1996 period at 150 million pounds. U.S. mills produced some 162.2 million square yards of broadwoven gray (unfinished) chiefly-wool fabrics in 1995, a fraction of the quantities produced of cotton fabrics (4,488.4 million square yards) and manmade/silk fiber fabrics (11,754.1 million square yards).

The leading employers engaged in the production of wool and other animal fiber fabrics were located in Virginia, Georgia, Maine, and North Carolina. As of 1992, some 13,700 individuals were employed by the industry, a number that is falling regularly. Automation has been partially responsible for the decrease, as has international competition. At the same time, employee requirements are changing; while mill personnel had an average of 7th to 8th grade education during the mid-1990s, Neil Cahill of the Institute of Technology estimated in *Textile World* that new machine technology would soon require a 12th to 14th grade education.

The two largest producers of wool fabrics were Burlington Industries and Forstmann & Co., formerly the wool division of J.P. Stevens. In 1996 Burlington was posting profits after several years of losses; the company was restructured following a 1987 leveraged buyout and became a public corporation in 1992. Forstmann & Co. has suffered financial difficulties and filed a Chapter 11 bankruptcy petition in 1995.

ORGANIZATION AND STRUCTURE

Producers of woolen broadwoven fabrics are for the most part engaged in processes that are similar in principle to those that produce broadwoven fabrics in the cotton and manmade sectors. However, wool and other animal fibers must first be scoured before being processed into yarn. This is necessary to remove animal greases and other debris that naturally become entangled in the wool prior to shearing.

In the processes involved in the manufacture of yarns—opening, carding, drafting, roving and spinning—machines are larger and designed to process long-staple fibers. These fibers measure four to eight inches in length, as opposed to cotton, which measures from seven-eighths to one and three-eighths inches. Most manmade fiber is cut to process on the cotton system of yarn manufacturing and is thus approximately the same length as the cotton fibers. There are some manmade fibers that are designed to go into products that replace woolen fabrics—suitings, blankets, etc.—or that will be blended with wool fibers (i.e., polyester-wool blends, which are cut to process on woolen machinery).

Like the producers of broadwoven cotton and manmade fabrics, producers of woolen fabrics are generally fully integrated; they produce, weave, then dye the yarn, and finish the woven fabric. Some companies, such as Forstmann & Co., maintain yarn manufacturing and weaving operations in one manufacturing plant and dyeing and finishing in another. Frequently, however, producers of woolen yarn and fabrics buy wool that has already been scoured. The scoured wool purchased by producers of woolen fabrics is generally known as "woolen tops."

There are three categories of manufacturing machinery for production of wool yarns: woolen, worsted, and semiworsted. The category used is determined by the intended fabric's end use. The largest global manufacturer of woolen and worsted yarn manufacturing equipment was N. Schlumberger & Cie, of France. Other producers of this type of equipment included Savio, of Italy, and Octir and Ommi, of Germany. Those companies also produced semiworsted yarn manufacturing machines along with James Mackie & Sons Ltd. of Ireland, Walker Technical Inc. of the United States, and Bigagli of Italy. Mohair and other animal fibers were processed on standard woolen, worsted, and semiworsted yarn manufacturing machines with occasional modifications to adjust for variations in fiber length.

Most woolen and other animal fiber broadwoven fabrics are produced on projectile, rigid, and flexible rapier weaving machines. Air-jet weaving machines are not suitable for production of heavyweight woolen fabrics but are used occasionally if the woolen fabric is a very lightweight worsted product. Water jet weaving machines cannot be used to produce broadwoven fabrics of wool and similar animal fibers.

In the early 1990s, only Japan's Tsudakoma Corp. and Toyoda Automatic Loom Works Ltd. manufactured air-jet weaving machines for the production of worsted fabrics. Sulzer Ruti of Switzerland manufactured projectile machines that were widely used in the production of broadwoven fabrics of wool and similar animal fibers. There were a number of weaving machine manufacturers that produced flexible and rigid rapier looms that were used for weaving broadwoven fabrics from woolen and other animal fiber yarns. Flexible rapier weaving machines were available from a small number of Italian and Belgian companies. Rigid rapier weaving machines were available through several European woolen broadwoven fabric makers.

Dyeing and finishing of woolen fabrics was performed on machinery similar to that found in the processing of cotton and manmade fibers. However, chemicals designed specifically for woolen and other animal fibers were used. Frequently, and more often in woolen fabrics than in other types, dyeing was done prior to the manufacture of the fabric. This was done by dyeing the raw wool after scouring or by dyeing the wool yarn. Dyeing the wool before it was made into fabric was absolutely necessary if the finished product was going to contain a plaid, stripe, or any multicolored pattern (unless the fabric was going to be printed with the design). Since many of the wool fabrics that were woven would be printed with multicolored patterns, stripes, or plaids, predyeing of the raw material or yarn was more common in woolen operations than in those processing cotton and/or manmade fiber.

Most wool is raised in Australia, New Zealand, and the United Kingdom, increasing its cost to textile plants in the United States (where wool production is insignificant). The added cost of scouring plus the increased cost of wool processing machinery further increase the price of woolen products. The cost of mohair is even more expensive than that of wool. Subsequently, wool, mohair, and similar animal fibers used to produce broadwoven fabrics have been more expensive (as raw materials) than cotton and most manmade fibers. For this reason, apparel, blankets, and other common applications for wool and animal fibers are often considered by many to be luxury items. The most expensive fibers used in textile applications include certain manmade fibers and those with special applications for high strength or resistance to heat.

CURRENT CONDITIONS

Wool prices were exceptionally high in 1989-1990, which contributed to a dramatic market loss for wool. By 1996, however, a significant improvement in wool prospects was reported. The managing director of the U.S. Wool Bureau, Pete Peter, noted : "With wool prices low and competitive with other fibers, consumers don't have to pay a premium for [wool]." At the same time, wool yarns and fabrics for the apparel industry were being designed that incorporated manmade fibers and that were washable and dryable. An agreement with DuPont was to result in a new Lycra-wool blend. And, just as cotton apparel fabrics had benefited from easy-care adaptations such as wrinkle resistant 100 percent cotton, woolen mills anticipated increased consumer interest in "transeasonal," lightweight woven wools that can be machine washed.

Mohair is a product that has seemingly enjoyed more success in European countries than in the United States, where most users of this animal fiber blend it with other fibers such as wool. With the end of the U.S. government's mohair price support program set for 1996, many industry observers expected U.S. production of mohair raw material to decline by 50 percent throughout the mid-1990s. The incentive program, part of the National Wool Act of 1954, paid $58.2 million to producers based on 1992 production. Payments dropped to 75 percent of the incentive for 1993, then to 50 percent in 1995, and were phased out completely in 1996.

Mohair was produced in 33 states in the United States in the early 1990s, but 86 percent of total production came from about 4,000 ranchers in the Edwards Plateau region of southwestern Texas. Other states with significant production were New Mexico, Oklahoma, Missouri, and North Dakota. U.S. mohair production hit an all-time high in 1965 with 32.4 million pounds. In 1992, production was 15.7 million pounds and was expected to drop still further. Figures from the U.S. Department of Commerce for fibers consumed in woolen spinning during 1994 bear this out; of the 842 million pounds of fiber used that year, just 1.36 million pounds were comprised of mohair, alpaca, vicuna, and other non-sheep wools.

FURTHER READING

"ATME-I '93 Quickens Textiles' Time to Market." *Textile World,* June 1992.

"GATT Disappoints U.S. Textile Leaders." *Textile World,* January 1994.

Hoover's Handbook of American Business. Austin, TX: Hoover's Inc., 1996.

Isaacs III, McAllister. "Machinery Makers Are Responding to the Needs of Weaving Plants." *Textile World,* December 1993.

McCurry, John W. "Is Mohair in for More Woes?" *Textile World,* December 1993.

———. "Wool Changing Its Image." *Textile World,* May 1996.

Standard & Poor's Industry Surveys. New York: Standard & Poor's Corporation, 1996.

Textile Highlights. Washington, DC: American Textile Manufacturers Institute, March 1994.

U.S. Bureau of the Census. *Current Industrial Reports.* Washington, 1996. Available from http://www. census. gov.

—McAllister Isaacs III, updated by Paula Pyzik Scott

SIC 2241

NARROW FABRIC AND OTHER SMALLWARES MILLS: COTTON, WOOL, SILK AND MANMADE FIBER

This category covers establishments primarily engaged in weaving or braiding narrow fabrics of cotton, wool, silk, and man-made fibers, including glass fibers. These fabrics are generally 12 inches or less in width in their final form but may be made initially in wider widths that are specially constructed for cutting to narrower widths. Also included in this industry are establishments primarily engaged in producing fabric-covered elastic yarn or thread.

Weavers of broadwoven fabrics, those that are generally greater than 12 inches in width, are covered in **SIC 2211: Broadwoven Fabric Mills, Cotton**; **SIC 2221: Broadwoven Fabric Mills, Manmade Fiber and Silk**; and **SIC 2231: Broadwoven Fabric Mills, Wool (Including Dyeing and Finishing).**

Products that fall into the narrow fabrics category include webbing for military use, industrial belting, automotive seat belts, etc.; narrow apparel products such as waistbands, straps, etc.; tapes for venetian blinds, insulating, zippers, fasteners, etc.; ribbons, laces, fringe and other trimmings; and labels, strapping, and shoe laces.

INDUSTRY SNAPSHOT

In 1995, some 260 U.S. operations engaged in the production of narrow fabrics, according to the U.S. Census Bureau. These companies produced and shipped $1.54 billion worth of narrow fabric products and provided employment to more than 17,000 Americans in 1995. The industry exported $402 million worth of products in 1995, up almost 17 percent from the previous year. Imports, which increased by 10 percent in 1995, trailed exports at $302 million.

ORGANIZATION AND STRUCTURE

Narrow fabrics are usually divided into two categories: elastic and rigid (or nonelastic). Narrow fabrics that, when stretched, will then return to the original shape and size fall into the elastic group. Elastic narrow fabrics include waistbands, some straps, etc.

Narrow fabrics weaving machines differ from broadwovens weaving machines in more ways than the width of fabrics produced. Narrow fabrics weaving machines produce more than one fabric at a time. Generally speaking, the wider the fabric, the fewer multiples of fabric pieces are woven. Narrow fabrics weaving machine speed is measured in the same manner as broadwoven fabrics weaving machine speed, i.e., picks per minute (ppm).

Most narrow fabrics weaving machines operate by the needle-loom principle. There are rapier narrow fabrics weaving machines as well. Some narrow fabrics are produced on broadwoven weaving machines with the fabric being slit into the narrow widths following weaving. Fabrics requiring woven selvages (edges), however, must be produced on standard narrow fabrics weaving machines. For some end uses, such as ribbons, fabrics made of man-made fibers such as polyester and nylon may be slit with a hot slitting system. This action causes the selvages to fuse, thus preventing raveling of the fabric edges.

BACKGROUND AND DEVELOPMENT

Business remains fairly stable for the narrow fabrics producer. Many items do not reflect economic conditions—as do some other textile products. This is especially true for webbings for industrial and military use and tapes, bandages, gauze, etc., for the medical trade. Automotive seat belt fabrics and decorative trimmings are, however, affected by the general economic conditions, and safety issues that emerged in the mid-1990s about the possible dangers of automotive air bags once again renewed interest among consumer advocates about the seat-belt use.

CURRENT CONDITIONS

According to the Industrial Fabrics Association International, its member companies were looking to Asia as an expanding market in the late 1990s. Products made for cargo and transport, such as cargo lifting straps and automotive tow straps, remained a primary source of income. Sporting goods products—golf-bag straps, for instance—came in second, followed by seat belts. Sling devices (encompassing many products for use in medicine) and pet products such as leashes and collars rounded out the field.

Like other textile producers, narrow fabrics firms in the middle 1990s were controlling inventory at all-time low levels. When the garment manufacturers need a change in a hurry, the label supplier has to be able to respond quickly. This need for versatility places increased emphasis on electronics machinery and, in particular, computer-controlled design stations.

FURTHER READING

Isaacs, McAllister III. ''Textile World 1992 Guide To Narrow Fabrics Looms.'' *Textile World,* January 1992, 49-66.

Textile Highlights, Washington: American Textile Manufacturers Institute, March 1994.

U.S. Bureau of the Census. *1995 Annual Survey of Manufactures.* Washington: GPO, 1997.

—McAllister Isaacs III, updated by Carol Brennan

SIC 2251

WOMEN'S FULL-LENGTH AND KNEE-LENGTH HOSIERY, EXCEPT SOCKS

This industry category includes establishments primarily engaged in knitting, dyeing or finishing women's and misses' full-length and knee-length hosiery (except socks), both seamless and full-fashion, and panty hose. Those establishments primarily engaged in knitting, dyeing or finishing women's and misses' knee-length socks and anklets can be found in **SIC 2252: Hosiery, Not Elsewhere Classified.** Establishments primarily engaged in manufacturing elastic (orthopedic) hosiery are classified in **SIC 3842: Orthopedic, Prosthetic, and Surgical Appliances and Supplies.**

According to the National Association of Hosiery Manufacturers, there were 91 companies engaged in the production of women's full-length and knee-length hosiery in 1995, a decrease from the 109 companies operating 161 establishments in 1991, and the 206 establishments registered a decade earlier. Women's sheer hosiery production decreased 3 percent from 1995 to 1996: tights and opaques fell 14 percent while Spandex Leg rose 10 percent. In 1996, shipments of sheer hosiery also declined; shipments of tights/opaques decreased by 11 percent to approximately 8.5 million dozens of pairs. Over 24,000 people in 28 states were employed in the industry.

In 1995, 55 percent of all hosiery was produced in North Carolina, home to the three largest companies producing women's hosiery (except socks). The southern part of the U.S. housed most of the industry with major producing establishments in Alabama, Tennessee, Georgia, Kentucky, and South Carolina. The top producing establishments in the North were concentrated in Pennsylvania and New York, and in the Midwest, Wisconsin was the top producing state.

Most women's hosiery products are made of textured nylon and produced on small-diameter knitting machines. The processes involved in production of the goods covered by this category include: production of POY (partially oriented yarn) nylon filament by fiber producers; texturizing (or texturing) the nylon filament; knitting the filament nylon into the hosiery product; boarding the hosiery to obtain proper size and shape; and finishing the hosiery products and packaging them. Texturing of the nylon hosiery yarn is covered in **SIC 2282: Yarn Texturizing, Throwing, Twisting, and Winding Mills.**

The biggest single event in the evolution of hosiery manufacturing was Du Pont's invention of nylon, which was introduced to the public in 1938, replacing the baggier cotton or more expensive silk stockings. Finding a commercially palatable name for what was officially polyhexamethyleneadipamide took more than two years. "Delawear" was one suggestion submitted by Lammot du Pont, then president of the company. Others were "Duparooh," an unwieldy acronym for "Du Pont pulls a rabbit out of a hat," "Neosheen," "Duponese," and "klis" (silk spelled backwards). Nylon, the word, is in fact a derivative of nylon stockings' wide rumored "no-run" feature.

Sales growth in the women's hosiery industry slowed in 1993 and 1994 and remained sluggish in 1995. Women's sheer hosiery sales were $2.7 billion, up 2 percent from 1994, and tights and opaques sales dropped by almost 2 percent. In 1996, however, tights and opaques sales rose 16 percent to $681 million and Spandex Leg sales climbed 12 percent, while sheer hosiery sales dropped nearly 1 percent due in large part to the 19 percent drop in all-nylon-non-control-top hosiery sales. Sara Lee Corp. L'eggs Products Division, the largest U.S. producer of hosiery within this industry, announced a 10 percent drop in unit sales of sheer hosiery in the second quarter of 1996 citing "continued emphasis on sales of higher margin products and reductions on hosiery sold on promotion in both the U.S. and European markets." Sara Lee posted sales of $660 million in 1996 and employed 6,000.

Other industry leaders included Ithaca Industries Inc., of Wilkesboro, North Carolina; Hanes Hosiery Inc., of Winston-Salem, North Carolina; Hampshire Group Ltd., of Anderson, South Carolina; and Kentucky Derby Hosiery Company, Inc. of Hopkinsville, Kentucky. Ithaca Industries, the largest employer in this category, employed approximately 6,900 people in 1996 and posted sales of $380 million.

Trade negotiations during the 1990s opened up opportunities for a potential export market. In 1994, trade barriers were reduced in Japan, Canada, and Mexico as a result of the North American Free Trade Agreement (NAFTA). In the third quarter of 1996, U.S. total hosiery exports dropped 5 percent from 1995 figures, with most of the decrease attributed to the 77 percent decline in women's full and knee length hosiery. Pantyhose and tights exports grew 15 percent to 7.8 million dozens of pairs, with 1.8 million dozens of pairs exported to El Salvador and another 1.5 million dozens of pairs to Mexico. A new World Trade Organization (WTO) was established in 1995, and the Multifiber Arrangement (MFA) which allowed importing countries to limit the flow of imports from lower cost,

developing countries was replaced by the Agreement on Textiles and Clothing (ATC) which required the phasing out of MFA quotes over a ten-year period. According to Linda Shelton in an *Industry, Trade, and Technology Review* report, "The elimination of MFA quotas likely will have a significant impact on the U.S. textile and apparel sector given the level of protection that such restrictions have provided domestic producers over the past two decades." Since the U.S. has until 2005 to implement the ATC, the legislation's impact on the hosiery industry may not be realized for several years.

FURTHER READING

1996 Hosiery Sales Leap Ahead. Charlotte, NC: National Association of Hosiery Manufacturers, 1996. Available from http://www.nahm.com/601d.htm.

Annual Summary. Charlotte, NC: National Association of Hosiery Manufacturers, 1995. Available from http://www.nahm.com/601c.htm.

Brady, Jennifer L. "Sara Lee Reports 12.8% Profit Hike in Second Quarter." *Women's Wear Daily,* 26 January 1996. Available from http://207.51.71.250/samples/archive/1996/000/497.htm.

Imports of Tights from Mexico Increase. Charlotte, NC: National Association of Hosiery Manufacturers, 1995. Available from http://www.nahm.com/601f.htm.

Linton, George C. *The Modern Textile and Apparel Dictionary.* Plainfield, NJ: Textile Book Service, Div. of Bonn Industries Inc., 1973.

Shelton, Linda and Robert Wallace. "World Textile and Apparel Trade: A New Era." *Industry, Trade, and Technology Review,* October 1996.

Sock Production Soars in 1996. Charlotte, NC: National Association of Hosiery Manufacturers, 1995. Available from http://www.nahm.com/601e.htm.

Standard & Poor's Industry Surveys. New York: Standard & Poor's Corporation, 1993.

Textile Highlights. Washington: American Textile Manufacturers Institute, March 1994.

Thomas, Marita, and Richard G. Mansfield. "Happy Birthday, Nylon!" *Textile World,* March 1988.

—MacAllister Isaacs III,
updated by AnnaMarie L. Sheldon

SIC 2252

HOSIERY, NOT ELSEWHERE CLASSIFIED

This category covers establishments primarily engaged in knitting, dyeing, or finishing hosiery, not elsewhere classified. Establishments engaged in the knitting, dyeing, or finishing of anklets, boys' hosiery, children's hosiery, leg warmers, men's hosiery, socks, slipper socks, and men's and children's tights are included in this category. Establishments engaged in the production of women's full-length and knee-length hosiery and panty hose are classified in **SIC 2251: Women's Full-Length and Knee-Length Hosiery, Except Socks.** Establishments engaged in manufacturing elastic (orthopedic) hosiery are classified in **SIC 3842: Orthopedic, Prosthetic, and Surgical Appliances and Supplies.**

According to the National Association of Hosiery Manufacturers Annual Report 1996, there were 334 hosiery production companies operating 440 plants around the United States in 1996. Eighty-five of these plants were in the women's sheer hosiery business. The other 355 were in the sock industry.

North Carolina, Alabama, Kentucky, and South Carolina were the top producers in the manufacture of hosiery. In the north, Pennsylvania and New York were the top producers, and Wisconsin was top in the Midwest. Hosiery imports increased 25 percent in 1996. 29.7 percent of these imports were "9802" transactions (hosiery partially made in the United States and shipped out of the country for further work, then brought back into the United States to be sold). Imported socks made up 42 percent of the total hosiery imported in 1996. Tights/opaques were 13 percent and pantyhose imports were 41 percent. Women's full-length hosiery accounted for 4 percent.

Hosiery manufactured in this category was produced on small-diameter knitting machines. These establishments, unlike most companies engaged in the weaving process of fabric formation, do not usually have yarn manufacturing facilities on site, necessitating the purchase of all yarn requirements. The primary reason for this is that socks and other miscellaneous hosiery products can be made from many different yarn types, making it costly and ineffective for one establishment to produce all the different yarn types required by one knitting establishment.

Most companies classified in this category do, however, operate their own dyeing, finishing, and packaging processes. Thus, after buying the necessary yarn requirements, these establishments can produce finished products that are packaged and ready for sale at the retail level.

Products in this category are made from lightweight to heavyweight yarns, depending on the end-use requirements. They range from heavy woolen socks used by hunters to lightweight anklets worn by small children. Products in this category can be made from cotton, wool, nylon, polyester, polypropylene, rayon, mohair, and other fibers, as well as blends of two or more fibers to reach the desired properties.

Sales indicated growth in this category during the early 1990s. A turn toward more casual styles of dress and a strong movement toward active wear by most regions in the United States were indicators of continued prosperity in this industry. Men's finished seamless hosiery and anklets made of natural fibers made up slightly over 60 percent of sales within this category.

The leading hosiery producer was Kayser-Roth Corporation, of Greensboro, North Carolina, with sales estimated at $400 million in 1994 and approximately 7,000 employees. Other leaders in the industry were Sara Lee Corp., Adams-Millis Division, of High Point, North Carolina; Americal Corp., Renfro Corp., of Mount Airy, North Carolina; Jockey International, Acme/McCrory and Clayson Knitting Company Inc., of Star, North Carolina, Clausen Knitting, and Adams/Millica.

There was an average of 60,600 workers employed in this industry in 1996 in 28 states, representing an increase of almost 37,000 people from a decade earlier. Of these, 20,600 were in the women's sheer hosiery industry and 40,00 in the sock industry. Women represented more than 72 percent of the work force, reflecting little change from 1982, when it was 71 percent.

FURTHER READING

Gibson, Richard. "Sara Lee Plans To Take Charge of $495 Million." *The Wall Street Journal,* June 1994.

Linton, George C. *The Modern Textile and Apparel Dictionary.* Plainfield, NJ: Textile Book Service, Div. of Bonn Industries Inc., 1973.

Standard & Poor's Industry Surveys. New York: Standard & Poor's Corporation, 1996.

Textile Highlights. Washington: American Textile Manufacturers Institute, March 1994.

"The Business Week 1000 Tables." *Business Week,* 1993 Bonus Issue, 118-163.

The 1996 Annual Report of the National Association of Hosiery Manufacturers. Charlotte, NC, 1997.

—McAllister Isaacs III, updated by Kathleen Vyn

SIC 2253

KNIT OUTERWEAR MILLS

Manufacturers in this category are primarily engaged in knitting outerwear from yarn or in the production of outerwear from knit fabrics produced in the same establishment. Establishments that are primarily engaged in hand knitting outerwear for the trade are included in this industry. Establishments primarily engaged in knitting gloves and mittens are classified in **SIC 2259: Knitting Mills, Not Elsewhere Classified.** Those manufacturing outerwear from purchased knit fabrics are classified in the major group for apparel and other finished products made from fabrics and similar materials.

Products manufactured under this category include such diverse products as bathing suits, bathrobes, beachwear, blouses, body stockings, caps, collar and cuff sets, dresses, hats, headwear, housecoats, jackets, jerseys and sweaters, jogging suits, leotards, lounging robes, mufflers, neckties, pants, scarves, shawls, shirts, outerwear, shoulderettes, ski suits, skirts, slacks, suits, sweat bands, sweat pants, sweat shirts, sweaters and sweater coats, tee-shirts, tank tops, ties, trousers, warm-up suits, and wristlets.

INDUSTRY SNAPSHOT

This category contained more companies and establishments, 677, than any other category classified in Industry Group 225 (knitting mills). In 1995, according to the U.S. Economic Census, the value of shipments from this industry was $5.68 billion. There are a reported 48,800 employees working in the knit outerwear industry.

One of the largest companies in this sector was Sara Lee Corp., Sara Lee Knit Products Div. (SLKP), headquartered in Winston-Salem, North Carolina. The next two companies in order of size were Tultex Corporation headquartered in Martinsville, Virginia and Dyersburg Corporation of Dyersburg, Tennessee.

These companies capitalized on one of the fastest growing product areas in the textile industry and the fastest growing section of apparel textile products: leisure and active wear. Products common among the three companies included tee-shirts and golf shirts (knit shirts with collars) for men, women, and children. The tee-shirt business has been one of the fastest growing businesses in the textile industry, especially with the trend toward putting messages and company names on them.

ORGANIZATION AND STRUCTURE

Two broad categories of knitting machines produced the products in this classification: circular and flat. Circular machines are much more prominent in this category because flat machines generally are used in the production of sweaters. Major producers of circular knitting machines were Camber International, of Leicester, England; Fukuhara Ltd., of Osaka, Japan; Mayer & Cie, of Albstadt, Germany; Monarch Knitting Machine Corp., of St. Glendale, New York; Terrot Strickmaschen GmbH, of Stuttgart, Germany; Tritex International Ltd., of Leicester, England; and Vanguard-Supreme, of Monroe, North Carolina. Monarch and Mayer were among the major producers of flat knitting machines as well as Liba Maschinenfabrik GmbH, of Naila/Bavaria, Germany, and Karl Mayer, of Obertshauesen, Germany.

While it is a generally accepted practice that companies engaged in the weaving business are fully integrated, (i.e., produce their own yarn requirements), it is also a general rule that companies engaged in knitting are not fully integrated, that is they buy their yarn requirements. The reason for this is that most manufacturers of knit products require so many different types of yarn that it is not economically feasible for them to produce their own yarn requirements. The notable exceptions to this practice in the knitting sector were the largest companies in the industry, including SLKP. Larger companies are able to do this for several reasons: they have the ability to confine specific products to certain plants, invest in modern yarn manufacturing machinery and equipment, and although these companies produced a larger volume than most other knitting companies, they did not produce as many types of products.

One similarity about the operations of large companies such as SLKP to the other knitting companies that are not integrated is that knitting operations are not located in the same facilities as the yarn manufacturing operations. Dyeing and finishing of the knit fabrics is, however, usually located in the same plant building with the knitting operation.

SLKP's Mountain City Plant produced over one million pounds each week of 100 percent cotton yarn for the company's Hanes Beefy-T Tee-shirt products. The plant was not only modern from a machinery and equipment standpoint, but also contained state-of-the-art electronic information system technology and the latest in management techniques. At the fully automated plant, bales of cotton had to be manually unloaded from the delivery trucks, but no one touched any part of the product after that until palletized cartons of yarn were readied to be put back on the same trucks for shipment to SLKP knitting plants.

The SLKP Mountain City Plant was also a fully computer-integrated manufacturing facility. A computerized network system monitored each machine for quality, production, and efficiency. A series of alarms and shut-down capabilities alerted teams if problems occurred.

The unique management technique implemented at Mountain City broke industry norms. No supervisors were employed, with the exception of the plant manager. It operated 24 hours each day, seven days per week, with two pairs of 12-hour shifts. Each shift had two 20-person teams that were responsible for each half of the plant. These teams patrolled operations, monitored electronic information systems, and together controlled the manufacturing facility. Teams hired and fired team members and participated in extensive training in such subject areas as problem solving, consensus decision making, etc. All employees were salaried and had business cards. As a symbol of ownership, each employee had a tree planted on the plant's property with his or her name on a plaque by the tree. In addition, all employees were paid an incentive bonus based on plant production and quality evaluated at the knitting plant.

BACKGROUND AND DEVELOPMENT

While the basic principles of knitting have not changed over the years, the use of electronic technology in recent years has enhanced the process tremendously. The use of CAD/CAM (computer-aided design/computer-aided manufacturing) systems has been the most prominent infusion of electronics into knitting. The best known system was manufactured by Monarch Design Systems, which produced a system that increased creativity, productivity, and versatility. Products designed to be knitted on an electronic knitting machine were transferred onto a 3.5 inch disk, and then loaded on a Macintosh computer. The disk was then subsequently transferred to the knitting machine by a loading device on the knitting floor. This process, like new electronic processes in weaving, reduced to hours (in some cases minutes) processes that at one time took weeks.

Another form of electronics used in the knitting process was a program for monitoring performance of the process as well as production of the product. One such system was STARFISH (start as you intend to finish), developed by Cotton Technology International, of Manchester, England. STARFISH was a set of computer programs that related the properties and dimensions of a knitted cotton fabric to the knitting

parameters and the finishing route. By the use of such programs, manufacturers and buyers were able to quickly calculate the performance of the most popular fabric constructions after dyeing and finishing. Thus, major savings in development time and money were achieved and decision making enhanced.

The knitting industry has also taken advantage of the textile industry's advancements in using technology to control costs. The American Textile Partnership (AMTEX) has collaborated on many projects to increase efficiency in the industry, including fostering research and development between the integrated U.S. textile industry and National Laboratories. The Demand Activated Manufacturing Architecture (DAMA) project is developing a communications system for the total textile industry to the consumer. This rapid communication allows the industry to quickly respond to changes in the market place with appropriate manufacturing processes and inventories and therefore cut overall costs.

CURRENT CONDITIONS

With the increased use of leisure and active wear, business in this industry has continued to improve over the past several years. The passage of the North American Free Trade Agreement (NAFTA) also portends well for manufacturers of products in this classification. North American countries already make up the U.S. textile industry's most important export markets, and demand for U.S.-made and U.S.-style products in Mexico is expected to increase, especially for affordable tee-shirts, sweat suits, and jogging suits, making international markets for U.S. products a promising trend.

FURTHER READING

Brookstein, David. ''U.S. Textiles Has Global Opportunities.'' *Textile World,* February 1997, 79-81.

''DAMA Pilot Project Under Way.'' *Textile World,* October 1996, 25.

Dun & Bradstreet Million Dollar Directory: America's Leading Public & Private Companies 1996. New York: Dun & Bradstreet, 1996.

Gibson, Richard. ''Sara Lee Plans to Take Charge of $495 Million.'' *The Wall Street Journal,* 7 June 1994.

Isaacs III, McAllister. ''Mountain City's Whiz Bang Is On the Move.'' *Textile World,* October 1993, 61-66.

Malone, Dr. Thomas. ''The AMTEX Partnership After One Year.'' *Textile World,* May 1994, 34-35.

Morrissey, James A. ''Textile Firms Turn Trash to Treasure.'' *Textile World,* February 1997, 74-76.

"Mountain City: Oh What a Yarn Mill!" *Textile World,* June 1991, 38-40.

"NAFTA Boosts U.S. Textiles." *Textile World,* January 1997, 28.

Richard, Robert. "Market Outlook." *Textile World,* March 1996, 17.

Rozelle, Walter. "Business Outlook." *Textile World,* March 1996, 15.

Standard & Poor's Industry Surveys. New York: Standard & Poor's Corporation, 1996.

Textile Highlights. Washington: American Textile Manufacturers Institute, March 1994.

"Textile World 1993-94 Buyer's Guide For Machinery, Equipment & Supplies." *Textile World,* July 1993.

Ward's Business Directory of U.S. Private and Public Companies. Detroit: Gale Research, 1997.

—Isaacs McAllister III, updated by Tami L. Powell

SIC 2254

KNIT UNDERWEAR AND NIGHTWEAR MILLS

This category covers those establishments primarily engaged in knitting underwear and nightwear from yarn or in manufacturing underwear and nightwear from knit fabrics produced in the same establishment. Companies primarily engaged in manufacturing underwear and nightwear from purchased knit fabrics are classified in the Major Industry Group 23 (apparel and other finished products made from fabrics and similar materials). Those establishments that produce knitted robes are classified in **SIC 2253: Knit Outerwear Mills.**

Products manufactured by companies in this classification include underwear briefs and knitted underwear drawers, night gowns, negligees, knit pajamas, ladies' and girls' panties, undershirts, T-shirts used as undershirts (both V-neck and regular neck), slips, and union suits or long (winter) underwear.

There were 70 establishments engaged in the production of underwear and nightwear in the mid-1990s, according to the U.S. Department of Commerce, Bureau of the Census. In 1995, establishments in this segment shipped $1.48 billion worth of products, up from $1.14 billion in 1992. Total employees in 1995 numbered 11,400, a 40 percent drop from 18,900 in 1990. Average hourly wages rose from $7.29 in 1990 to $8.84 in 1995. According to the Census Bureau's 1995 Current Industrial Report on Apparel, underwear and nightwear accounted for the bulk of all women's and men's apparel production. There were 1.1 billion units of mens' underwear and nightwear produced and 1.3 billion units of women's. However, the value of the underwear is far below that of all other apparel.

The early 1990's saw a healthy growth in underwear and nightwear exports and in 1995, total underwear exports were valued at $618 million. The export trend is likely to continue in this industry, as well as most other industries, with the reduction of trade restrictions resulting from the 1994 passage of the North American Free Trade Agreement.

Almost all products in this category are made on circular knitting machines. Most men's and boys' underwear is made from 100 percent cotton or cotton-polyester blends. Until recently, most women's and girls' underwear was produced from nylon, with silk used as somewhat of a luxury item. Now the trend in women's underwear is to use cotton. During the late 1980s and early 1990s, companies such as Jockey and Fruit Of The Loom began modeling women's lines after men's cotton briefs. Such products were successful.

Jockey International Inc., of Kenosha, Wisconsin, showed strongest sales in the knit underwear industry, with 1996 revenues of approximately $440 million and approximately 4,500 employees. Fruit Of The Loom Inc., of Lexington, South Carolina, is one of the largest manufacturers of men's briefs. Their 1996 revenues totaled $2.4 billion, and they employed 22,000 people in the United States and 11,000 worldwide. Maidenform Worldwide, Inc., headquartered in New York, is one of the leading women's intimate apparel manufacturers with 1996 revenues of $410 million and total employment of 9,000. Other industry leaders include Spring City Knitting Company Inc., of Cartersville, Georgia; Martin Mills Inc., of Martinville, Louisiana; and Spring Ford Knitting Company Inc., of Spring City, Pennsylvania.

FURTHER READING

"Forbes 500 Largest Private Companies." Forbes Inc, 1997. Available from http://www.forbes.com.

"Fruit of the Loom Company." Fruit of the Loom, Inc. Available from http://www.fruit.com/company.

Linton, George C. *The Modern Textile and Apparel Dictionary.* Plainfield, NJ: Textile Book Service, Div. of Bonn Industries Inc., 1973.

Standard & Poor's Industry Surveys. New York: Standard & Poor's Corporation, 1993.

Textile Highlights. Washington: American Textile Manufacturers Institute, December 1993.

"Textiles Ready to Reap NAFTA Rewards." *Textile World,* December 1993, 23-24.

U.S. Bureau of the Census. *1995 Annual Survey of Manufactures.* Washington: GPO, 1997.

U.S. Department of Commerce. *Current Industrial Reports: Apparel 1995.* Washington: GPO, 1996.

—McAllister Isaacs III, updated by Paula Hartman Cohen

SIC 2257

WEFT KNIT FABRIC MILLS

Establishments in this classification are primarily engaged in knitting weft, or circular, fabrics or in the dyeing or finishing of weft, or circular, fabrics. These companies may sell their fabrics to manufacturers of outerwear, underwear, or other products in the apparel or home furnishings industries. Companies engaged in knitting weft outerwear fabrics and subsequently producing outerwear in the same establishment are discussed in **SIC 2253: Knit Outerwear Mills.** Also, establishments engaged in knitting circular underwear and nightwear products and that manufacture the end-product at the same site are discussed in **SIC 2254: Knit Underwear and Nightwear Mills.** Overall, those companies who buy knit fabrics for the production of outerwear and underwear are described in the major group for apparel and other finished products made from fabrics and similar materials.

As many as 716 establishments produced weft knit fabrics in 1995. These companies shipped $5.2 billion worth of fabric that year, up from $3.8 billion in 1991. This category employed approximately 37,400 workers in 1995 (31,600 of whom were production workers), with a total payroll estimated at $828 million. The average hourly wage for all textile mill workers at the end of 1996 was $9.90 per hour.

The handling of circular knit fabrics is a more delicate process than handling of woven goods, because the fabrics are not as stable in the finished state. Extreme care must be taken and special shipping containers must be used when shipping circular knit fabrics. Fabrics produced in this category are used across the spectrum of finished goods, from leisure and activewear, to more expensive evening wear.

Guilford Mills, Inc., Fashion Apparel Division, of Lumberton, North Carolina led this category in 1995 with sales of $415 million. The Fashion Apparel Division had 3,000 employees as of 1995. Some of the company's circular-knit fabrics consist of lycra-blended cotton or synthetic stretch knits made for dresses, swimwear, and lingerie, and were sold to Guilford Mills' client, Victoria's Secret. The company also produces a woven velour fabric, suitable for upholstery, for General Motors and Ford.

The second largest manufacturer in this category, Stevcoknit Fabrics Co. of Greer, South Carolina, posted 1995 sales of $100 million and employed approximately 1,500 people. Despite Stevecoknit's strong showing in this category, its parent company, Delta Woodside Industries overall stock price fell 66.9 percent from 1991-96, and the parent company showed no profit for 1996. Another leader within this category was Andrex Industries Corp., of New York, New York, a privately held company with approximately 200 employees and $50 million in sales for 1995.

One industry trend worth noting during 1997 was the rise of micro-denier fabrics. These densely woven fabrics mimic a soft silk because they are woven from fabrics containing less than one denier per filament. This creates a fabric that feels like silk and costs considerably less.

FURTHER READING

"Annual Report on American Industry." *Forbes Magazine,* 13 January 1997, 90-258.

"The Business Week 1000 Tables." *Business Week,* 1993 Bonus Issue, 118-163.

Guilford Mills corporate website. Available from http://www.guilfordmills.com.

Hoover's Company Capsules. Austin, TX: Hoover's, Inc., 1997. Available from http://www.hoovers.com.

Standard & Poor's Industry Surveys. New York: Standard & Poor's Corporation, 1993.

"Starfish Technology For Upgrading the Performance of Circular Knitted Cotton Fabrics." Manchester, England: Cotton Technology International.

Textile Highlights. Washington, DC: American Textile Manufacturers Institute, March 1994.

Textile Highlights. Washington, DC: American Textile Manufacturers Institute, March 1997.

U.S. Department of Commerce. *1995 Annual Survey of Manufactures.* Washington, DC: GPO, 1997.

—McAllister Isaacs III, updated by Dave Fagan

SIC 2258

LACE AND WARP KNIT FABRIC MILLS

Establishments in this category are those that are primarily engaged in knitting, dyeing, or finishing warp (flat) knit fabrics; or in manufacturing, dyeing, or finishing lace goods. Products produced under this category include lace bed sets; lace covers for chairs, dressers, pianos, and tables; curtains and lace curtain fabrics; lace edgings; knit netting; warp knit pile fabrics; and tricot fabrics.

There were an estimated 261 establishments engaged in the production of warp knit goods or lace products in 1996. Of these, 167 employed 20 or more people. Overall, employment slightly slipped from a high in 1982 of 21,100 employees working within this classification to 20,500 in 1988, a trend that continued into the 1990s, decreasing to an estimated 19,800 by 1996. New York had the most mills in this category, with 89 in 1992. Other states with high concentrations of companies in this industry included North Carolina, New Jersey, Pennsylvania, Rhode Island, Georgia, California, and South Carolina.

Employees worked as sewing machine operators, textile draw-out and winding machine workers, hand packers and packagers, inspectors, laborers, industrial machinery mechanics, textile bleaching and dyeing machine workers, hand workers, textile machine setters and set-up operators, blue collar worker supervisors, general managers, top executives, and freight and stock handlers.

Warp, or flat, knitting machines resemble weaving machines in appearance, but produce fabrics more nearly like those produced on circular knitting machines. Warp knit is a specialized fabric made by a machine knit process consisting of running nylon, acetate, and polyester yarns in a lengthwise direction in the fabric, forming interlocking loops. The cost, compared to circular knit techniques, is relatively low. Major U.S. producers of these types of machines include Chima Inc., of Reading, Pennsylvania and Mayer Textile Machine Corp., of Clifton, New Jersey.

During the 1980s, sales took a slight downturn in this industry. A slump in clothing sales and a growing flood of inexpensive imports slowed growth considerably. Throughout the early to mid-1990s, domestic manufacturers remained competitive by introducing new specialty fabrics, like microdeniers and spandex blends. Microdenier fabrics are stretchy and have a high-filament count that gives them a silky feel. Introduced by Guilford Mills, Inc. in 1991, this fabric quickly gained a niche market in the warp knit industry. By early 1997, the market for spandex blends had grown markedly. Spandex was being used in a wide range of warp knit fabrics: foundation garments, swimwear, activewear, lace, hosiery, and medical supplies/clothing. Worldwide demand for spandex is expected to grow to 220 million pounds annually by 1999, which should result in increased sales for warp knit manufacturers. Other markets that are expected to grow include woven fabrics with two-way stretch; sheer fabrics in the 15-, 20- and 30-den range; high-denier fabrics for foundation and control garments, blends with Tencel microdenier and acrylic, and performance fabrics with u-v resistance and thermal and antimicrobal properties.

In 1994, the North American Free Trade Agreement created a large new market for lace and warp knit fabrics by reducing trade barriers between Canada, Mexico, and the United States. However, in 1995, the General Agreement on Tariffs and Trade was passed, which will continue to increase foreign competition by reducing tariffs and quotas placed on imported textiles and apparel over the next ten years.

In 1996, the largest company in this category was Guilford Mills, Inc., of Greensboro, North Carolina, a public company with sales of $830.3 million and 6,715 employees. In 1994, Guilford represented the only U.S. automotive textile company with manufacturing facilities abroad, with production plants in the United Kingdom, and part-ownership in the largest warp knitting company in Mexico. Its clients include Ford, General Motors, and Victoria's Secret.

Other industry leaders are Liberty Fabrics Inc., of New York; FAB Industries Inc., of New York; Lida Inc., of Charlotte, North Carolina; Mohican Mills Inc., of Lincolnton, North Carolina; and Carisbrook Industries Inc. Native Textiles of New York.

FURTHER READING

Hoover's Company Capsules. Austin, TX: Hoover's Inc., 1997. Available from http://www.hoovers.com.

Moody's Industry Review. New York: Moody's Investors Service, Inc., 1996.

Rozelle, Walter N. ''Miracle Fiber Now Coming Into Its Own.'' *Textile World* Atlanta: Intertec Publishing, January 1997.

Standard & Poor's Industry Surveys. New York: Standard & Poor's Corporation, 1996. *Textile Highlights.* Washington: American Textile Manufacturers Institute. March 1994.

''The Business Week 1000 Tables.'' *Business Week,* 1993 Bonus Issue, 118-163.

—McAllister Isaacs III, updated by Kathy Seablom

SIC 2259

KNITTING MILLS, NOT ELSEWHERE CLASSIFIED

Companies in this classification are primarily engaged in knitting gloves and other articles, not elsewhere classified. Establishments primarily making woven or knit fabric gloves and mittens from purchased fabrics are classified in **SIC 2381: Yarn Spinning Mills.**

Products manufactured by companies in this category include bags and bagging, bedspreads, curtains, dishcloths, elastic girdle blanks, girdles and other foundation garments, gloves, shoe linings, mittens, stockinettes, towels, and washcloths.

Many companies in this category were small, family-owned businesses serving niche markets. In 1995, there were 90 establishments classified in this industry category, up from 77 establishments operating in 1988. These companies shipped $308.1 million worth of fabric in 1995, compared to $222.9 million in 1988. This category employed approximately 3,700 workers in 1995 (3,200 of these were production workers), with a total payroll estimated at $74.1 million.

Employees of this industry worked as sewing machine operators, textile draw-out and winding machine workers, hand packers and packagers, inspectors, industrial machinery mechanics, textile bleaching and dyeing machine workers, testers, hand workers, textile machine setters and set-up operators, blue collar worker supervisors, general managers, and material movers and handlers.

Like many companies in the knitting business, businesses in this category tend to buy their own yarn requirements. Companies in this category rarely have their own dyeing and finishing operations. When dyeing and finishing is required, the companies either have the work done on a commission basis or, in some cases, sell goods to dyers and finishers who in turn deliver the finished fabric. For some types of knit work gloves, dyeing and finishing is not necessary—the gloves are made from greige fabric and left the natural color.

Technological advances during the 1990s occurred in three areas within the entire textile industry: computer-aided design (CAD), production, and communications; new modular manufacturing systems; and ergonomics (work place instruments designed to improve the safety, health, and efficiency of workers). Only about 60 percent of textile businesses used any of the new technology offered. Smaller firms were often the least efficient. Miscellaneous knitting mills usually had only a few knitting machines, which were either circular or flat machines depending on the product made.

New technology also brought machines that were quieter, easier-to-operate, and designed to reduce workers' stress and injury. Particular emphasis was placed on reducing the repetitive motion injuries typical of apparel workers, which has led to more government regulations, higher workers' compensation costs, and rising health care costs. Between 1987 and 1995, the number of companies with 20 or more employees increased in this category. The total number of people employed rose also, despite a shift away from smaller, inefficient, and costly manufacturing sites to larger companies with greater automation. The U.S. Bureau of Labor predicts jobs in this industry may decline due to technological advances.

In 1995, the largest U.S. company within this classification was privately held H. Warshow and Sons, Inc., of New York, New York, with sales of $50 million and 600 employees. The number two firm in this category was Scott Mills, Inc. of Plymouth Meeting, Pennsylvania, with sales of $17 million and 200 employees. Scott Mills, Inc. knits cotton, polyester, cotton/polyester blend, and acrylic fabrics for the women's and children's apparel markets. Another industry leader, Kleinert's, Inc. of Alabama, purchased Scott Mills in 1996. Privately-held Arlington Hat Co., Inc. of Long Island City, New York, also competed in this category with annual sales of $6 million and a workforce of 100.

FURTHER READING

''Annual Report on American Industry.'' *Forbes Magazine,* 13 January 1997, 90-258.

''The Business Week 1000 Tables.'' *Business Week,* 1993 Bonus Issue, 118-163.

Hoover's Company Capsules. Austin, TX: Hoover's, Inc., 1997. Available from http://www.hoovers.com.

Linton, George C. *The Modern Textile and Apparel Dictionary.* Plainfield, NJ: Textile Book Service, Div. of Bonn Industries Inc., 1973.

Standard & Poor's Industry Surveys. New York: Standard & Poor's Corporation, 1993.

Textile Highlights. Washington, DC: American Textile Manufacturers Institute, March 1994.

U.S. Department of Commerce. *1995 Annual Survey of Manufactures: Statistics for Industry Groups and Industries.* Washington, DC: GPO, 1997.

—McAllister Isaacs III, updated by Dave Fagan

SIC 2261

FINISHERS OF BROADWOVEN FABRICS OF COTTON

This category covers establishments primarily engaged in finishing purchased broadwoven cotton fabrics or finishing such fabrics on a commission basis. These finishing operations include bleaching, dyeing, printing (roller, screen, flock, plisse), and other mechanical finishing, such as preshrinking, calendering, and napping. Also included in this industry are establishments primarily engaged in shrinking and sponging of cotton broadwoven fabrics for the trade and chemical finishing for water repellency, fire resistance, and mildew proofing. Establishments primarily engaged in finishing wool broadwoven fabrics are classified in **SIC 2231: Broadwoven Fabric Mills, Wool (Including Dyeing and Finishing)**; those finishing knit goods are classified in knitting mill industries; and those coating or impregnating fabrics are classified in **SIC 2295: Coated Fabrics, Not Rubberized.**

INDUSTRY SNAPSHOT

In 1995, there were approximately 300 establishments in the United States engaged in dyeing and/or finishing of broadwoven cotton fabrics with 18,300 employees. The vast majority of these are located in the southeastern United States, particularly in North and South Carolina. Some establishments, such as Burlington Industries Inc., Cone Mills Corp., and Thomaston Mills Inc. are engaged in both manufacturing and finishing of broadwoven cotton fabrics. Some companies, such as Cranston Print Works, are engaged only in the dyeing and finishing of broadwoven cotton fabrics.

More than 95 percent of manufactured broadwoven cotton fabrics receive some form of dyeing and/or finishing treatment. Even industrial products that require no coloration still require some type of finishing process to render the fabric useful in its intended application. In the early 1990s, environmentally conscious products began attracting consumer attention. Sheets and pillowcases that were produced without dyeing or chemical processing became popular in department stores. But even these products necessitate a finishing process, albeit one without chemicals, to become useful bedding products.

ORGANIZATION AND STRUCTURE

The finishing of broadwoven fabrics is subdivided into three general processing categories: fabric preparation, fabric coloration, and fabric finishing. Fabric preparation consists primarily of bleaching and preparing fabrics with chemical agents to aid in subsequent processing. Such processes, depending on the end result desired, may be performed in open-width fabric form or in fabric rope form.

Coloration of fabrics consists of a variety of dyeing methods executed via batch or continuous process procedures and printing. Printing of broadwovens may be performed by screen printing machines, roller printing machines, roller-screen printing machines, or by a process known as transfer printing.

Fabric finishing is accomplished either through surface (dry) finishing or wet finishing. Surface or dry finishing consists of such processes as sueding, sanding, and napping and imparts a certain texture or feel to the fabric. Wet finishing consists of preshrinking or sanforizing, mercerization, or heat-setting. Chemical finishes for water repellency, flame retardancy, mildew proofing, and wash-and-wear characteristics are applied during finishing processes. Fabric straightening (elimination of bow and bias) and width setting is also performed during finishing.

Virtually all establishments engaged in dyeing and finishing of broadwoven cotton fabrics have at least part of their operations involved in commission work—dyeing and finishing services performed on fabrics owned by other companies. Dyeing and finishing facilities generally utilize much more complicated production processes than do facilities designed for other textile processes. This is due both to the volume of water used in dyeing and finishing operations and the amount of chemicals used in each dyeing and finishing process. Dyeing and finishing machines and equipment are generally custom-designed to meet specific applications and needs. Piping requirements for water, steam, and chemicals will vary from one installation to another as well. Therefore, building facilities used for dyeing and finishing operations are usually custom-designed. While buildings for other textile processes, such as yarn manufacturing, knitting, and weaving, carry structural specifications due to the weight and vibration potential of the machines, dyeing and finishing building specifications must consider machine weight plus machine and piping design and configuration.

Establishments engaged in dyeing and finishing of broadwoven cotton fabrics generally serve three market categories: apparel, home furnishings, and industrials. In the United States, apparel and home furnishings account for 75 to 80 percent of the broadwoven cotton fabric production. Imports are eroding those markets, however, at a time when industrial fabrics are growing in end uses. Some industry observers expect industrial fabrics to account for approximately 35 percent of production by the end of the 1990s.

In the apparel area, companies dye and finish broadwoven cotton fabrics for men's and ladies' shirts and blouses, children's wear, men's trousers and ladies' pants, leisure and sports wear, and other clothing. Because of some advances developed by Cotton Incorporated, the research arm of the Cotton Growers' Association, companies can now produce water repellent broadwoven cotton rain wear. Cotton Incorporated has also developed some finishes that allow production of wash-and-wear (easy care, no-iron) cotton fabrics.

In home furnishings, dyers and finishers of broadwoven cotton fabrics supply bedding products—sheets, pillowcases and shams, light comforters and blankets, and dust ruffles; bath products—bath towels, hand towels, and wash cloths; and other household items such as draperies and curtains, napery products (napkins and tablecloths), kitchen towels, upholstery fabrics, and cushion covers. In the industrial area, broadwoven cotton fabrics are dyed and/or finished toward production of medical and hospital goods, abrasive fabrics such as sanding belt fabrics, conveyor belts, tents, awnings, luggage, and other products.

CURRENT CONDITIONS

Along with immense technology advancements, recent trade agreements have had a significant impact on finishers of cotton broadwoven fabrics. Trade agreements enacted in the early 1990s give the industry the opportunity to compete in the global marketplace through effective brand recognition and marketing together with capital investments in systems such as DAMA that increase efficiency.

The General Agreement on Tariffs and Trade (GATT), which reduces or eliminates tariffs among 117 nations throughout the 1990s, will not, according to American Textile Manufacturers Institute (ATMI) officials, have a positive impact on U.S. producers of dyed and finished broadwoven cotton fabrics. However, since global textile usage could grow dramatically in the future due to developing economies and increasing populations, how much of a negative impact this agreement will have on U.S. dyers and finishers remains to be seen.

The North American Free Trade Agreement (NAFTA), enacted in 1993, which essentially removes all trade restrictions among Canadian, American, and Mexican businesses, has already had a positive economic effect for U.S. dyers and finishers of broadwoven cotton fabrics. North American countries

were the U.S. textile industry's most important export markets throughout the 1990s, and Mexico is expected to continue to be a growing market.

INDUSTRY LEADERS

The largest company engaged only in finishing broadwoven cotton fabrics is Cranston Print Works headquartered in Cranston, Rhode Island. In 1996, Cranston Print Works had approximately 1,700 employees and $253 million in sales. The next two largest companies in this industry, both with an estimated $55 million in sales, are Santee Print Works headquartered in Sumter, South Carolina and Cecil Saydah Co. headquartered in Los Angeles, California.

RESEARCH AND TECHNOLOGY

As a part of industry-wide efforts to remain competitive in the international arena, cotton broadwoven fabric finishers have explored several new operating systems. One such system, called Quick Response, demonstrated throughout the 1990s that as a communications process it could boost production of U.S.-made broadwoven cotton products. The Quick Response system requires partnerships throughout the softgoods pipeline—fiber producers, textile manufacturers, apparel manufacturers and retail establishments—and makes use of electronic technology, especially bar coding and Electronic Data Interchange (EDI), to receive up-to-date information. This immediate market feedback enables every member of the pipeline to reduce inventories, shorten delivery times between each pipeline partner, and eliminate processing steps at some partner members' operations without adding them at others.

The system also permits orders from retail establishments that are smaller than season requirements and enables these retail establishments to reorder in mid-season after buying trends and patterns have been established. This process, when all elements are in place, reduces costs at all pipeline partner establishments and reduces the number of necessary markdowns at the end of the season in the retail establishments.

The American Textile Partnership (AMTEX) also aided U.S. producers of dyed and finished broadwoven cotton fabrics throughout the mid-1990s. AMTEX enacted a pact in 1993 in which national laboratories, in conjunction with the U.S. Department of Energy, work on selected projects with the U.S. textile industry and its research facilities to develop systems to make the industry more competitive.

The AMTEX project with the most immediate results is Demand Activated Manufacturing Architecture (DAMA), which expands on the Quick Response system. Under the DAMA system, electronics inform pipeline partners of each garment sold by making use of point-of-sale data generated during scanning of barcoded hang tags. The DAMA pilot project began in September of 1996, and results have shown that the creation of an electronic marketplace will improve operations and reduce costs through controlling warehouse costs and inventory size and reducing wastes, while improving customer responsiveness and product development. The years of preparation with the Quick Response system has allowed the industry to quickly realize the competitive advantages of capitalizing on the national information super highway.

FURTHER READING

Brassil, Robert D. "Practical Aspects of Fabric Preparation." *Theory and Practice of Fabric Preparation Conference.* Clemson, South Carolina: FMC Corp., 1982.

U.S. Bureau of the Census. "Broadwoven Goods Production, 1993." Washington: GPO, 1993.

Dun & Bradstreet Million Dollar Directory: America's Leading Public & Private Companies 1996. New York: Dun & Bradstreet, 1996.

"1993 Industry Outlook: What's Ahead for America's 24 Key Industries." *Business Week,* 11 January 1993.

"GATT Disappoints U.S. Textile Leaders." *Textile World,* January 1994, 23-24.

Goldstein, Herman B. "Basics of Textile Finishing: Chemical and Mechanical." Chester, South Carolina, 1987.

Malone, Dr. Thomas. "The AMTEX Partnership After One Year." *Textile World,* May 1994, 34-35.

Morrissey, James A. "Textile Firms Turn Trash to Treasure." *Textile World,* February 1997, 74-76.

"NAFTA Boosts U.S. Textiles." *Textile World,* January 1997, 28.

Richard, Robert. "Market Outlook." *Textile World,* March 1996, 17.

Rozelle, Walter. "Business Outlook." *Textile World,* March 1996, 15.

"Springs Psyched for a Second Century of Success." *Textile World,* June 1987, 44-85.

Standard & Poor's Industry Surveys. New York: Standard & Poor's Corporation, 1996.

Textile Highlights. Washington, DC: American Textile Manufacturers Institute, December 1993.

"Textiles Ready to Reap NAFTA Rewards." *Textile World,* December 1993, 23-24.

"Who's the Real Winner in Burlington Match?" *Textile World,* June 1987, 23.

Ward's Business Directory of U.S. Private and Public Companies. Detroit: Gale Research, 1997.

—McAllister Isaacs III, updated by Tami L. Powell

SIC 2262

FINISHERS OF BROADWOVEN FABRICS OF MANMADE FIBER AND SILK

Establishments in this category are primarily engaged in finishing purchased manmade fiber and silk broadwoven fabrics or finishing such fabrics on a commission basis. Those companies engaged in the dyeing and finishing of broadwoven cotton fabrics are discussed in **SIC 2261: Finishers of Broadwoven Fabrics of Cotton.** Establishments primarily engaged in finishing wool broadwoven fabrics are classified in **SIC 2231: Broadwoven Fabric Mills, Wool (Including Dyeing and Finishing)**; those finishing knit goods are classified in knitting mills industry group; and those coating or impregnating fabrics are classified in **SIC 2295: Coated Fabrics, Not Rubberized.** Finishing operations found in **SIC 2262: Finishing Plants, Manmade** include bleaching, dyeing, printing, preshrinking, calendering, and napping.

INDUSTRY SNAPSHOT

There are 195 establishments engaged in the finishing of broadwoven manmade and silk fabrics, according to the United States Bureau of the Census. By far, the great majority of those are engaged in finishing polyester fabrics. In 1995, these companies, and their 23,800 employees, finished and shipped $3.9 billion worth of fabrics.

ORGANIZATION AND STRUCTURE

Finishing of broadwoven fabrics is subdivided into three general processing categories: fabric preparation, fabric coloration, and fabric finishing. Fabric preparation consists primarily of bleaching and preparing fabrics with chemical agents to aid in subsequent processing. Such processes, depending on the end result desired, may be performed in open-width fabric form or in fabric-rope form. Severe bleaching of fabrics of manmade fibers isn't necessary to the extent broadwoven cotton fabric bleaching is required, because impurities from the cotton plant are found in broadwoven cotton fabrics. Machines most commonly used in the preparation process include kiers, J-boxes, roller steamers, conveyor steamers, semi J-box steamers, and high-temperature pressure steamers. The most common chemical agent used is hydrogen peroxide.

Coloration of fabrics consists of a variety of dyeing methods, either in batch or continuous process procedures and printing. The continuous process is by far the most popular in the United States as it is based on high-volume, low-cost-per-unit operations. However, as more and more companies begin participating in Quick Response or Demand Activated Manufacturing Architecture (DAMA) partnerships, it may become necessary to increase the number of batch operations, which are generally geared toward shorter-run, lower-volume products. Printing of broadwovens may be performed by screen printing machines, roller printing machines, roller-screen printing machines, or by a process known as transfer printing.

The subcategory of finishing divides again into surface or dry finishing and wet finishing. Surface or dry finishing consists of such processes as sueding, sanding, and napping and imparts a certain texture or feel to the fabric. Wet finishing consists of preshrinking or sanforizing, mercerization, or heat-setting. Chemical finishes for water repellency, flame retardancy, mildew proofing, and wash-and-wear characteristics, are applied during finishing processes.

The practice of treating fabrics with resins or other agents to impart shrinkage stabilization, creaseproofing, and shape retention has grown to tremendous importance. Collectively, these properties are now known as durable press. Compressive shrinking, generally known as sanforizing, takes place during finishing and prevents shrinking of finished garments. In finishing, widths are set, while fabrics are straightened and given particular feels or hands. It is the final process in textile manufacturing of broadwoven fabrics.

Establishments engaged in dyeing and finishing of broadwoven manmade fiber and silk fabrics generally serve three market categories: apparel, homefurnishings, and industrials. In the United States, apparel and homefurnishings account for 75 to 80 percent of broadwoven fabric production. Because imports are eroding those markets and industrial fabrics are growing in end uses, however, industrials are expected to account for approximately 35 percent of production by the year 2000.

CURRENT CONDITIONS

Two trade agreements enacted at the end of 1993 have had an effect on the future of this industry. The General Agreement on Tariffs and Trade (GATT), which reduces or eliminates tariffs among 117 nations over the next 10 years will not, according to American Textile Manufacturers Institute (ATMI) officials, have a positive impact on U.S. producers of dyed and finished broadwoven manmade fiber and silk fabrics. How much of a negative impact this agreement will have on U.S. dyers and finishers remains to be seen. In part, it will depend on the results of efforts put into cooperative systems such as the Quick Response and DAMA systems. The North American Free Trade Agreement (NAFTA), which essentially removes all trade restrictions among Canadian, U.S., and Mexican businesses, has shown short-term positive impacts on the U.S. textile industry since North American countries were the U.S. textile industry's most important export markets throughout the 1990s, and Mexico is expected to continue to be a growing market. The agreement should continue to have a long-range positive effect on U.S. dyers and finishers of broadwoven manmade fiber and silk fabrics, according to officials at the ATMI.

INDUSTRY LEADERS

Kenyon Industries Inc., headquartered in Kenyon, Rhode Island, and founded in 1989, had 400 employees and $25 million in sales in 1996. The second largest company in the industry, Amerbelle Corporation of Vernon, Connecticut, also had and estimated $25 million in sales, and the third largest company, J&J Flock Products Inc. of Easton, Pennsylvania, had $17 million in sales in 1996.

RESEARCH AND TECHNOLOGY

Research and technological developments have played a vital role in keeping the U.S. textile industry competitive, and as a part of this industry-wide effort to remain competitive in the international arena, cotton broadwoven fabric finishers have explored several new operating systems. One such system, called Quick Response, demonstrated throughout the 1990s that as a communications process it could boost production of U.S.-made broadwoven cotton products. The Quick Response system requires partnerships throughout the softgoods pipeline—fiber producers, textile manufacturers, apparel manufacturers, and retail establishments; and makes use of electronic technology, especially bar coding and Electronic Data Interchange (EDI), to receive up-to-date information. This process, when all elements are in place, reduces costs at all pipeline partner establishments and reduces the number of necessary markdowns at the end of the season in the retail establishments. The system also overcomes some of the advantages held by establishments exporting products from low-wage, developing countries into the United States.

The American Textile Partnership (AMTEX) enacted a pact in 1993 in which national laboratories, in conjunction with the United States Department of Energy, work on selected projects with the U.S. textile industry and its research facilities to develop systems to make the industry more competitive. The AMTEX project with the most immediate and far-reaching results is Demand Activated Manufacturing Architecture (DAMA), which expands on the Quick Response system. Under the DAMA system, electronics inform each pipeline partner of each garment sold by making use of point-of-sale data generated during scanning of bar-coded hang tags. The DAMA pilot project, begun in September of 1996, has shown that the creation of an electronic marketplace will improve operations and reduce costs through controlling warehouse costs and inventory size and reducing wastes, while improving customer responsiveness and product development. The seven years of perpetration with the Quick Response system has allowed the textile industry to quickly realize the competitive advantages of capitalizing on the national information super highway.

FURTHER READING

Brassil, Robert D. "Practical Aspects of Fabric Preparation." *Theory and Practice of Fabric Preparation Conference.* Clemson, South Carolina: FMC Corp., 1982.

"Broadwoven Goods Production, 1993." Washington: Bureau of the Census, United States Department of Commerce, 1993.

Brookstein, David. "U.S. Textiles Has Global Opportunities." *Textile World,* February 1997, 79-81.

"DAMA Pilot Project Under Way." *Textile World,* October 1996, 25.

Dun & Bradstreet Million Dollar Directory: America's Leading Public & Private Companies series 1996. New York: Dun & Bradstreet, 1996.

"GATT Disappoints U.S. Textile Leaders." *Textile World,* January 1994, 23-24.

Goldstein, Herman B. "Basics of Textile Finishing: Chemical and Mechanical," Consultant, Chester, South Carolina, 1987.

Malone, Dr. Thomas. "The AMTEX Partnership After One Year." *Textile World,* May 1994, 34-35.

Morrissey, James A. "Textile Firms Turn Trash to Treasure." *Textile World,* February 1997, 74-76.

"1993 Industry Outlook: What's Ahead for America's 24 Key Industries." *Business Week,* 11 January 1993.

"NAFTA Boosts U.S. Textiles." *Textile World,* January 1997, 28.

Richard, Robert. "Market Outlook." *Textile World,* March 1996, 17.

Rozelle, Walter. "Business Outlook." *Textile World,* March 1996, 15.

"Springs Psyched for a Second Century of Success." *Textile World,* June 1987, 44-85.

Standard & Poor's Industry Surveys. New York: Standard & Poor's Corporation, 1996.

Textile Highlights. Washington: American Textile Manufacturers Institute, December 1993.

"Textiles Ready to Reap NAFTA Rewards." *Textile World,* December 1993, 23-24.

"Who's the Real Winner in Burlington Match?" *Textile World,* June 1987, 23.

Ward's Business Directory of U.S. Private and Public Companies. Detroit: Gale Research, 1997.

—Isaacs McAllister III, updated by Tami L. Powell

SIC 2269

FINISHERS OF TEXTILES, NOT ELSEWHERE CLASSIFIED

Companies included in this category are those which dye and finish textiles, not elsewhere classified, such as bleaching, dyeing, printing, and finishing of raw stock, yarn, braided goods, and narrow fabrics, except wool and knit fabrics. These establishments perform finishing operations on purchased textiles or on a commission basis.

There were approximately 450 U.S. companies engaged in finishing textiles, not elsewhere classified. This represents a substantial increase from the 178 firms reported in 1991. In 1995, these businesses shipped $1.1 billion worth of goods, which was less than the $1.2 billion shipped in this category in 1991. Textile finishers employed 9,700 people in 1995, with a total annual payroll of $222.5 million.

Most companies in this category dye raw stock or yarn. (Any fiber may be dyed in the raw stock or yarn form.) The top dyeing and finishing companies in the United States in 1995 were: Meridian Industries Inc. of Milwaukee, Wisconsin ($190 million in revenues, 1,300 employees); Brittany Dyeing and Printing, Inc. of New Bedford, Massachusetts ($33 million in revenues, 300 employees); and India Ink Co. of Los Angeles, California ($33 million in revenues, 300 employees). Each industry leader was a privately held company.

Business grew steadily throughout the 1990s for companies engaged in raw stock or package dyeing. Analysts expect business to keep rising. This is because "fancy" fabrics, such as plaids, stripes, and various patterns, require that yarn be colored prior to weaving or knitting. This may be done in either the raw stock form or the yarn form. As of early 1997, the North American Free Trade Agreement brought increased exports from this and most other textile categories to Canada and Mexico.

FURTHER READING

"ATME-I '93 Quickens Textiles' Time to Market." *Textile World,* June 1992, 74-75.

"GATT Disappoints U.S. Textile Leaders." *Textile World,* January 1994, 23-24.

Linton, George C. *The Modern Textile and Apparel Dictionary.* Plainfield, NJ: Textile Book Service, Div. of Bonn Industries Inc., 1973.

"Microfibers: All Dressed Up and Everywhere to Go." *Textile World,* August 1992, 37-48.

Standard & Poor's Industry Surveys. New York: Standard & Poor's Corporation, 1993.

Textile Highlights. Washington: American Textile Manufacturers Institute, December 1993.

Textile Highlights. Washington: American Textile Manufacturers Institute, March 1994.

Textile Highlights. Washington: American Textile Manufacturers Institute, March 1997.

"Textiles Ready to Reap NAFTA Rewards." *Textile World,* December 1993, 23-24.

"Textile World 1992 Manmade Fiber Chart." *Textile World,* August 1992, 49-73.

"Textile World 1993-94 Buyer's Guide for Machinery, Equipment & Supplies." *Textile World,* July 1993.

"The Business Week 1000 Tables." *Business Week,* 1993 Bonus Issue, 118-163.

U.S. Department of Commerce. *1995 Annual Survey of Manufactures: Statistics for Industry Groups and Industries.* Washington: GPO, 1997.

—McAllister Isaacs III, updated by Dave Fagan

SIC 2273

CARPETS AND RUGS

This industry includes establishments primarily engaged in manufacturing woven, tufted, and other carpets and rugs such as art squares, floor mattings, needle punch carpeting, and doormats and mattings from textile materials or from twisted paper, grasses, reeds, coir, sisal, jute, or rags. Coverage includes aircraft and automobile floor coverings, except rubber or plastics; bathmats and sets, textile; dyeing and finishing of rugs and carpets, and wilton carpets.

INDUSTRY SNAPSHOT

After a ten-year span of steady sales in the 1980s, the carpet industry's primary residential and commercial clients were faced with decreased buying power and constrained budgets and thereby placed carpet buying as a low priority. Higher interest rates, slower starts in new home construction, and sluggish real estate further reduced residential interest in new carpet. Industrywide sales plunged from $8.5 billion in 1990 to less than $7 billion in 1991. Burgeoning consumer confidence and new home construction helped drive a recovery mid-decade, and gross carpet and rug sales increased to over $9.5 billion on volume of 1.6 billion square yards in 1995. The vast majority—over 90 percent—of those sales came from tufted carpet and rugs, while woven and other floorcoverings constituted the remainder.

Corporate consolidation was one of the industry's biggest issues in the late 1980s and early 1990s. Mergers and acquisitions reduced the number of participating companies from over 300 in 1980 to 100 by the mid-1990s, with vertically-integrated "megamills" emerging at the top of the heap. The top three players—one of them foreign-owned—commanded an estimated 50 percent of industry sales volume in 1995.

ORGANIZATION AND STRUCTURE

In the mid-1990s, 238 of America's 383 manufacturing plants were located in the state of Georgia. Carpet mills specialize in producing carpet backing as well as carpets and rugs. Intense competition in the 1980s led forward-looking companies to acquire both manufacturing and retailing operations in an effort to cut costs.

Tradition, profits, and consumer preferences, more than a specific management approach, have historically dictated the organization of the carpet industry. The product flows to residential and contract clients primarily via the following two methods: (1) directly from mill to client or (2) from mill to dealer or wholesale distributor, then to a retailer who sells to a client. If manufacturers in the industry continue to follow the lead of Shaw Industries, Inc., the contemporary industry leader, the industry's organizational mode may be revamped. According to analysts, Shaw's acquisition-based growth coincided with the company's novel management approach. First the company hired aggressive, no commission, straight salary sales representatives. Next, in another cost savings move, Shaw signed shorter, more flexible agreements with retailers and in the process eliminated distributors, a long standing entity in carpet promotion. Whether this strategy is adaptable industry wide remains to be seen; however, carpet manufacturers foresee several outcomes. For example, retailers are expected to begin buying most carpet directly from the mills. Secondly, total industry recovery will require the development of strategies to create more unified partnerships between manufacturers, retailers, and cleaners that would allow them to serve and sustain customer confidence.

BACKGROUND AND DEVELOPMENT

The first carpet mill opened in Philadelphia in the 1791. Until the mid-1800s, carpet manufacturing in the United States was a tedious process using hand operated machines. High quality, artful appeal, and high cost described the carpets of this period. However, during this period and continuing over the next century, several events changed the manufacturing and utility of rugs and carpets. Much of the impetus for industrialization of the carpet industry began when Erastus B. Bigelow, known as the "Father of the Modern Carpet Industry," obtained a patent for his invention of a power driven loom. As power looms became more refined and functional, carpet manufacturing became a profitable venture.

The next milestone in the carpet industry came with changes in the composition of carpet. Originally all carpets were made entirely of wool because it insulated against cold and repelled water. Because of these characteristics, wool was declared an essential commodity during World War II, and consequently carpet production was severely curtailed in favor of war goods production. This setback served as an incentive for researching wool substitutes, which in turn led to the development and upgrade of new natural and synthetic carpet fabrics. By the 1960s, E.I. DuPont de Nemours and Co.'s man-made continuous filament carpet nylon and Chemstrand's acrylic fibers were supplying most of the fibers for broadloom carpets in the industry. Today, nylon accounts for 67.8 percent of the fibers used in carpet manufacturing, followed by 22.2 percent polypropylene, and 9.4 percent polyester, with wool constituting a little over 0.6 percent of the total.

Weaving, needle-punch, and bonding and tufting are the principle carpet manufacturing processes, with the tufting method accounting for 95 percent of all

carpets currently produced and sold in the United States. Tufting differs from weaving and other processes in that yarn is pushed through a previously manufactured backing material, while weaving produces the carpet backing simultaneously as the carpet is being manufactured. As tufting became popularized as a faster and more economical alternative to the traditional weaving process, carpet manufacturers discovered several other cost and labor advantages. Utilization of the tufting process produced broadloom eight to ten times faster, required less fined-tuned weaving skills, and ultimately lowered prices sufficiently to attract lower and middle income groups. Nearly 63 percent of the industry's tufting mills were located in the South due the area's abundance of low-cost labor and excellent water supply.

The impact of these milestones solidified the "homing" of the carpet industry. Between 1950 and 1968, U.S. production of residential and commercial broadloom carpet and rugs rose from 85.7 to 435.0 million square yards, with tufted carpet shipments topping woven Axminster, Wilton, velvet, chenille, and knitted carpets by more than 81 percent in 1968. Price, aesthetics, and utility changed the image of carpet from a luxury item to an essential accessory for every home. By the 1980s, consumer carpet selections included an enormous variety of colors and patterns suitable as indoor/outdoor floor or wall coverings. Moisture repellents and stain resistant treatments increased the life spans of some carpets by as much as ten years and allowed manufacturers to extend carpet warranties. Residential or "home use" carpet, one of the industry's major markets, comprised 76 percent of all residential floor coverings, 55 percent of which was used for remodeling and replacement purposes, and 45 percent in new home construction in the early 1990s. Carpets for commercial or contract use formed the next primary market and represented the preferred floor covering for 73 percent of all commercial space in offices, schools, hotels, hospitals, airplanes, and other heavily trafficked public areas.

Ironically, just as the "homing phase" of the carpet appeal became entrenched in American living, both residential and commercial users began voicing concerns regarding health and environmental hazards attributed to carpet. In 1987, the Consumer Product Safety Commission received more than 130 complaints about carpeting, mostly focusing on eye and throat irritation beginning after installation of new carpet. One such incident occurred at the Environmental Protection Agency, where employees complained of flu-like symptoms within days after a new carpet was installed. Specific causes of the illnesses were never identified, but several areas were investigated. No toxic chemicals were found in the carpet, but questions remained regarding toxic ingredients in the carpet adhesives. Another theory postulated that noxious fumes resulted from carpet deterioration. Later tests, so named the Anderson tests after the testing company, Anderson Laboratories Inc., introduced the possibility that carpet emissions capable of killing mice could also produce adverse effects on human life.

Despite disclaiming some of the hazards, the carpet industry vowed to reassess its overall manufacturing process, including the type and quality of raw materials used, the use of pesticides, microbiological contamination, and carpet installation and maintenance processes. Consistent with the industry's objectives to improve consumer confidence, the Carpet and Rug Institute, the industry's trade association, launched a labeling program listing various characteristics of carpet. The Institute is also collaborating with Environmental Protection Agency in the development of indoor air quality guidelines for carpet.

Because consumers remained unconvinced of the carpet industry's intent to alleviate the health hazards of carpet, a consumer lawsuit was filed in 1993 against several carpet manufacturers. Consumers involved in the suit were seeking monetary compensation and other rewards from manufacturers accused of promoting misleading claims regarding carpet air emissions hazards and so-called environmentally friendly carpets.

In the early 1990s, many homeowners took advantage of falling interest rates and refinanced their mortgages. This allowed homeowners to spend more money on remodeling expenditures and new carpeting. A stabilized real estate market with increased new housing starts and greater turnover in home sales would also have a positive impact on carpet sales. As businesses recovered from the recession, contract carpet dealers sought increased business with hospital, health care, and retail facilities. Schools were also seen by many in the industry as a potential growth market.

CURRENT CONDITIONS

Carpet and rug sales totaled $9.5 billion in 1995 on volume of 1.6 billion square yards. As they had throughout the postwar era, tufted carpet and rugs continued to dominate, with 87 percent of volume and over 90 percent of revenues. Over 85 percent of tufted carpet yardage sold was in roll goods. Over two-thirds of all tufted floorcovering yardage was made with nylon face yarn, while about 20 percent were made from polypropylene and another six percent was constituted of polyester.

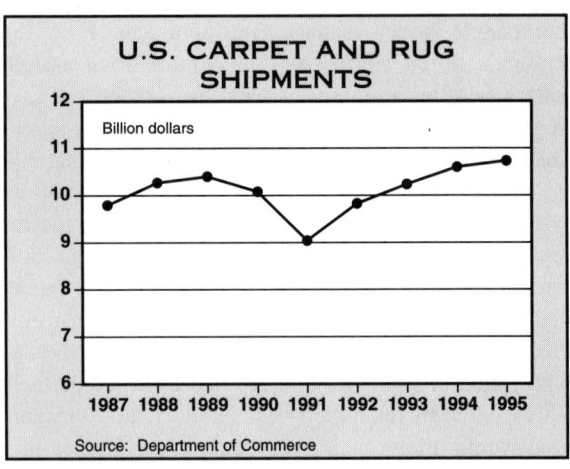

U.S. CARPET AND RUG SHIPMENTS

Billion dollars

Source: Department of Commerce

Over the last twenty years, one consistent indicator of this industry's condition has come from tracking real disposable income—as it rose or decreased, so did carpet and rug sales. The 1996 edition of *Manufacturing USA: Industry Analyses, Statistics, and Leading Companies* forecast total U.S. carpet and rug production to grow to $12.5 billion by 1998. Some observers expected the industry's consolidation to bring increased prosperity by eliminating overcapacity. Increases in residential construction and consumer confidence also seemed to bode well for the industry.

INDUSTRY LEADERS

Certainly bigger is not always better, yet it appeared to be very helpful for several manufacturers in the carpet industry. Companies undergoing a consolidation or merger found that infusion of capital frequently meant new equipment and expansion of research and development. Such organizational changes represented the norm for the carpet and rug industry in the early and mid-1990s. Acquisitions within the industry created a new crop of mega-mills with Shaw Industries, Inc. topping the list.

Founded in 1967 by brothers Robert Shaw and J.C. Shaw, Shaw Industries, Inc. has long utilized acquisitions to carve out a profitable niche in the carpet industry. In fact, it entered the market via the acquisition of a Georgia carpet mill. The 1987 purchase of West Point-Pepperell Inc. pushed Shaw's revenues over the $1 billion mark and made it the world's largest carpet manufacturer in 1987. Growth via acquisition merely accelerated from that point. By 1995, the company had garnered over one-fourth of wholesale carpet sales.

Having achieved its goal of establishing a worldwide niche in each important aspect of carpet manufacturing, it began to acquire carpet retail chains with hundreds of outlets, including Carpetland USA Inc.;

The Carpet Exchange; and New York Carpet World. Shaw's sales increased at an average annual rate of 15.3 percent during the early 1990s, from $1.6 billion in 1991 to $2.9 billion by 1995. But rising raw materials prices slashed the company's net from $127 million in 1994 to $52.3 million in 1995. At that time, the Dalton, Georgia-based company employed 25,000 workers.

Calhoun, Georgia's Mohawk Industries, Inc. placed a distant second to Shaw, with 11,450 employees and sales of $1.6 billion in 1995. Founded in 1878, Mohawk found itself scrambling to keep up with its much younger, but larger, competitor in the early 1990s. Following a public stock offering in 1992, the company made four acquisitions in two years, including Horizon Industries Inc., Karastan-Bigelow Inc. and American Rug Craftsmen Inc. In 1994, Mohawk merged with highly profitable Aladdin Mills Inc. The purchases catapulted Mohawk from eleventh in the industry to number two, increased its sales from $761 million in 1992 to $1.6 billion in 1995, and multiplied its market share from less than 4 percent to 17 percent. The company boasts three of the industry's most recognizable brands: Mohawk, Karastan, and Bigelow. Notwithstanding its impressive growth, Mohawk Industries struggled to cut costs and thereby raise its profitability. Net income shriveled from a high of $39.5 million in 1993 to a mere $6.4 million in 1995.

While high-level mergers raised eyebrows regarding anti-trust issues, many analysts noted the negative impact of these mergers on smaller companies. Smaller companies have more limited pricing options. Therefore, attempts by small manufacturers to duplicate the cost cutting strategies of the mega-mills generally threaten their profitability and ultimately their survival.

WORK FORCE

Having risen to 55,000 in the late 1980s, carpet and rug industry employment declined to less than 50,000 in the early 1990s before rebounding to 55,200 in 1994. Well over half of those workers were employed in Georgia, "The Carpet Capitol of the World." Production workers made up approximately 78 percent of the work force, according to the 1996 edition of *Manufacturing USA: Industry Analyses, Statistics, and Leading Companies,* which also projected a rise in employment, to 57,000 by 1998.

While machine operators constituted the industry's largest employment category, computerization of carpet manufacturing was changing job functions and requirements. Machines for tufting, shearing, and many other functions connected to computers were

expected to eliminate many low-skilled jobs. The industry was expected to require higher skilled laborers to operate the sophisticated machinery.

By and large, the majority of the industry's production employees had low literacy levels and were unable to interpret computer feedback. Without upgrading the literacy skills of their production workers, manufacturers stood to lose the potentially high returns from converting to a high-tech environment. With more than one-third of their 560 employees deficient in these literacy skills, Collins & Aikman Corp., a Georgia-based carpet mill, developed programs combining remedial education and computer training on company time.

AMERICA AND THE WORLD

In the early 1990s, the United States accounted for over half of the world's carpet consumption. According to the *U.S. Census of Manufactures,* imports to the United States constituted less than 6 percent of the quantity of carpeting purchased and less than 10 percent of the value in 1995. As Shaw Industries CEO Robert Shaw noted in a 1996 interview for *Textile World,* "We have no foreign competition for all practical purposes." China and Iran were historically the largest importers, but with an embargo against Iran since 1979 and China's Most Favored Nation status under question in the 1990s, carpet and rug importers turned to India, the Philippines and Vietnam (after the Clinton Administration lifted an embargo against that nation in 1994) for supplies. Exports from the U.S. made up just over 7 percent of the quantity and value that year. Several factors constrain international carpet and rug trade, among them quotas and duties, high shipping costs, and the influence of America's leading carpet makers, who are often able to price imports out of the market. Most of America's carpet exports go to Canada. While Americans attributed their spectacular performance in this neighboring market to Canada's lack of competitiveness, Canadians viewed the growth as unfair competition. American carpet companies were accused of "dumping" their goods in Canada at unfairly low prices. The resulting failure of scores of Canadian carpet businesses prompted the Canadian government to institute recovery measures by imposing a permanent duty averaging 12 percent on all American carpets. Although the "dumping" issue had strained relations between the Canada and the United States, Canada was expected to remain an important export market.

In the future, outcomes of other trade issues may well expand or reduce opportunities for U.S. manufacturers to create a global presence. Carpet mills downplayed the impact of the North American Free Trade Agreement (NAFTA) which merged Canada, Mexico, and the United States into one market. The European Community Agreement (EC), another international trade agreement affecting the textile industry, was also expected to enhance international opportunities in textile production.

In the early 1990s industry leaders were aggressively pursuing international trade, though not necessarily through export. Shaw Industries entered both the Australian and Mexican markets via joint ventures. If finding an international niche meant physically relocating to a lucrative market, more companies could be expected to follow the example of Belgium's Beaulieu Group, which established a facility in Georgia as part of its objective to diversify and penetrate the American market.

RESEARCH AND TECHNOLOGY

Research and technology for the carpet industry has focused on producing high quality and environmentally-friendly products, and responding to contemporary customer needs. To these ends, several innovations were in progress in the early 1990s. New backing materials were being developed to replace the environmentally-unfriendly latex. As a secondary backing bond to tufted and needle punched carpets, hot melt adhesive films produced no fumes inside or outside the mills, offered between 70 percent and 80 percent energy savings, and resulted in a 50 percent reduction in backing application time. Waste reduction and reclamation were also key issues under study. Some in the industry campaigned to reduce carpet trim waste, which not only cost U.S. carpet companies an estimated $25 million per year, but also generated tons of useless material destined for landfills. Other ideas being studied for waste reduction included reducing widths of backings and developing pure synthetic backings to match face fibers which would allow burning or recycling of the whole carpet. Many, including industry leader Shaw Industries, adopted the goal of "zero manufacturing waste."

Recycling programs focused on recycling or converting packaging materials like PET bottles and used carpet into everything from floor tiles to concrete reinforcement material and highway guard rails, to like-new carpet fiber. While these solutions required a concerted industry-wide effort, a few company initiatives showed some merit. DuPont maintained a joint program with Sonoco Products Co. which involved reclaiming cardboard drums used to deliver its fluorochemical products. Hoechst Celanese Corp.'s introduction of a new environmentally friendly carpet not only eliminated latex and the usual odor connected with indoor air quality problems, but also totally eliminated carpet waste because it was made of 100 percent recyclable polyester.

Another area of research addressed utilization of carpet to reduce physical stress, injuries, and fatigue in a variety of environments. While carpet's nonslip, pliant properties remain favorable, biomechanical studies could lift the carpet industry's sales by measuring how the human body reacts to subtle differences in floor surface properties. Research at the University of Pittsburgh's Medical and Engineering Schools is currently studying body reactions to different carpet and cushion combinations in different facilities, such as high and low-impact aerobic exercise settings.

FURTHER READING

"Allied Signal Fibers Offers 1993 Carpet Forecast." *Carpet & Rug Industry,* March 1993.

"Another Merger Creates New Member of Top 50." *Carpet & Rug Industry,* February 1993.

"BASF Takes Concepts '93 on the Road." *Carpet & Rug Industry,* March 1993.

"BASF Unveils New Carpet-recycling Program." *Hotel & Motel Management,* 2 November 1992.

"The Carpet Industry Answers Environmental Challenges." *Carpet & Rug Industry,* March 1993.

"The Carpet Manufacturing Process." *On Carpet,* September 1991.

"Carpet Sales Down 2.4 Percent for First Half of Year." *Carpet & Rug Industry,* December 1992.

"Changing Times." *Carpet & Rug Industry,* October 1992.

Cooper, Helene. "The New Educators: Carpet Firm Sets Up an In-house School to Stay Competitive. . . ." *The Wall Street Journal,* October 1992.

"CRI Responds to New Adverse Health Allegations Concerning Carpet Emissions." *Carpet & Rug Industry,* September 1992.

Darnay, Arsen J., ed. *Manufacturing USA: Industry Analyses, Statistics, and Leading Companies.* Detroit: Gale Research Inc., 1996.

Elliott, Michelle. "1993 Annual Backings Report." *Carpet & Rug Industry,* February 1993.

Farnsworth, Clyde H. "Called on the Carpet." *The New York Times,* 26 April 1992.

Feldman, Andy. "A Slippery Rug." *Forbes,* 22 May 1995, 68-69.

"1993 Forum & Forecast." *Carpet & Rug Industry,* January 1993.

Herlihy, Janet. "'92 Tufting." *Carpet & Rug Industry,* December 1992.

Herlihy, Janet, and Janice Kirby. "The World's Top Carpet & Rug Manufacturers." *Carpet & Rug Industry,* November 1992.

"Hoechst Celanese Plans Shift to Recyclable Carpets." *The Wall Street Journal,* 4 January 1993.

Kirk, Robert W. *The Carpet Industry: Present Status and Future Prospects.* Philadelphia: University of Pennsylvania, 1970.

Kolb, David L. "The Metamorphosis of Mohawk From LBO to Big Acquirer." *Mergers & Acquisitions,* November-December 1994, 47-50.

Kurtz, Josh. "After a Decade of Consolidation, Hard Times Await Carpet Makers." *The New York Times,* 27 May 1990.

Macdonald, Julie. "Carpet Magic." *Hotel & Motel Management,* 6 Feburary 1995, 15.

McCurry, John W. "Shaw Industries Near $3-Billion Sales Plateau." *Textile World,* May 1996, pp.40-41.

"Mohawk Industries Agrees to Purchase Horizon Industries." *The Wall Street Journal,* 28 July 1992.

Naughton, Julie. "State of the Union: Consolidation of U.S. Mills May Not Bode Well for Importers of Lower-End Machine-Mades." *HFD-The Weekly Home Furnishings Newspaper,* 13 June 1994, 14-15.

———"Capel: 'Inscrutable Chinese' No Longer." *HFN: The Weekly Newspaper for the Home Furnishing Network,* 9 January 1995, 25-26.

Schut, Jan H. "'Impossible' Carpet Compound Makes Good." *Plastics World,* February 1996, 16.

"Shaw Updates Global Strategy at Domotex." *Carpet & Rug Industry,* February 1993.

Smith, G. Wentworth. "Ergonomic Floor Covering Studies." *Carpet & Rug Industry,* January 1993.

"Space Dyeing." *On Carpet,* August 1991.

"The Top Fifty Carpet & Rug Manufacturers' Sales Totals—1991." *Carpet & Rug Industry,* June 1992.

Tucker, Katherine Hayes. "Carpet is Still King in Dalton After Shakeout." *Georgia Trend,* April 1994, 39-40.

U.S. Department of Commerce. *U.S. Census of Manufactures.* Washington: GPO, 1987.

Walton, Frank L. *Tomahawks to Textiles.* New York: Appleton-Century-Crofts, Inc., 1953.

Wilson, Frank C. "Carpet Trim Waste: Money Down the Drain." *Textile World,* September 1996, 32.

Wyman, Lissa. "The China Syndrome: Rug Import Options." *HFN: The Weekly Newspaper for the Home Furnishing Network,* 8 July 1996, 15-16.

———"Rug Makers Proudly Recycle." *HFN: The Weekly Newspaper for the Home Furnishing Network,* 9 October 1995, 18-19.

—Attrices Dean Griffin, updated by April Dougal Gasbarre.

SIC 2281

YARN SPINNING MILLS

This industry is made up of establishments primarily engaged in spinning yarn wholly or chiefly by weight of cotton, manmade fibers, silk, wool, mohair, or similar animal fibers. Products include acetate and acrylic yarn, made from purchased staple, spun; carded yarn, carpet yarn, combed yarn, cordage yarn (all of cotton); crochet yarn, cotton, silk, wood, and manmade staple.

There were approximately 400,000 establishments involved in the yarn spinning mills industry in 1994. This number was estimated to have increased to 410,000 by 1997. The value of industry shipments increased approximately 12.5 percent from 1994 ($8.01 billion) to 1997 ($9.42 billion).

An average two-piece suit currently includes about 67,000 yards of yarn composed of roughly 350 million manmade fibers, textured and colored to produce a natural look. These characteristics basically describe the product flow of yarn spinning mills— from fiber, to yarn, to apparel and home accessories. The actual yarn spinning process entails first cleaning of cotton, wool, silk, or other fibers and then a combing or carding process which turns tangled fibers into straight, even rolls that resemble loose ropes of soft cotton yarn. Depending on the specifications, machines are set to spin yarn of multiple lengths and textures.

Consumers with active lifestyles have called for more livable fabric combining fashion with rough-ready, easy care qualities, and stretchable wear. "Casual Fridays" in the United States, a move toward casual business dress, further enforces this trend that has been particularly good for cotton. The volume of cotton increased more than 30 percent since 1990, compared to 8 percent for all other fibers.

During the early establishment of the industry in the eighteenth century, most spinning mills operated as independent entities. Later, mergers and consolidations in the yarn spinning industry opened diversification opportunities, and many spinning mills became subsidiaries or integrated components of larger carpet or textile mills, or they combined with specialized dyeing facilities. In the 1990s, these mills increasingly use high technology in order to meet the demands of efficient production and improved fiber quality—at the same time protecting the environment and conserving resources.

One of the first objectives of the Occupational Safety and Health Administration (OSHA), formed in 1970, was to minimize illness and death resulting from cotton dust in textile mills. Referred to as "brown lung" disease, 1988 statistics estimated that 35,000 current and former textile employees had severe cases of "brown lung," and another 100,000 workers had symptoms that indicated early stages of the disease. As unions worked to improve hazardous mill conditions, textile manufacturers often opposed strict sanitation measures imposed by OSHA. In the early 1990s, questions remained as to the legality of some of the restrictions and how best to provide safer factory conditions.

Yarn spinning mills shared the textile industry's apprehension regarding the impact of the North American Free Trade Agreement (NAFTA). Some yarn spinners foresaw a negative impact based on claims that NAFTA would benefit Canada and Mexico more than the United States. Other spinners envisioned more positive results for the United States, particularly if NAFTA requires Canada and Mexico to use yarns produced in North America. The threat of mills closing or a possible mass exodus of plants to Mexico was not perceived as an immediate threat; however, the president of the American Yarn Spinners Association did envision possible long term drawbacks resulting from NAFTA. In his opinion, the more imminent threat on American yarn spinning mills was posed by GATT, another trade agreement, which in draft form, proposed to cut U.S. textile apparel import duties.

In contrast to other industries, the current growth in technological advances allows a clear vision of twenty-first century yarn spinning mills. Already industry literature refers to spinning systems rather than spinning mills. By the year 2000, *Textile World* predicts daytime operations of spinning departments will be staffed with maintenance technicians, monitoring personnel, and a single supervisor. Night operations are expected to be staffless and monitored by sophisticated computers.

Changes in yarn, speed, styles, and other functions will become increasingly programmable or electronic functions. One certain outcome of computerization will be severely reduced manpower needs. In preparing for the coming high tech environment, industry research and development focused on refining and developing new equipment in the mid-1990s. Air-jet spinning machines, long recognized for good evenness and less defects, will achieve increased acceptance because of their ability to spin cotton-polyester blend yarn. If slippage problems can be overcome, the friction spinning machine, considered excellent in producing evenness and less defects, will be introduced for

medium and fine yarn count range, especially for cotton.

Yarn spinners continue to develop new more colorful and functional yarns. In the 1990s, three variations on DuPont's Cordura nylon went on the market. Originally introduced as a tire cord fiber, Cordura has been introduced as a fabric for outdoor recreational apparel. In addition to its light weight qualities, the Cordura/acrylic blend offered twice the abrasion resistance of ballistic nylon, three times that of vinyl or standard nylon, and four times that of cotton. Previous applications included luggage, backpacks, boots, and rugged ski apparel.

FURTHER READING

Black, Jeff. "Yarn Spinning Get New Spin." *Daily News Record,* 11 August 1992.

"Candlewick: Yarns That Fit a Niche." *Carpet & Rug Industry,* March 1993.

Clune, Ray. "Yarn Spinners Optimistic for '93." *Daily News Record,* January 1993.

———. "Prices of Cotton Yarns Stable in Spotty Market." *Daily News Record,* 26 August 1992.

"Conner Plays Down NAFTA Effect." *Daily News Record,* January 1993.

Copeland, Melvin Thomas. *The Cotton Manufacturing Industry of the United States.* New York: Augustus M. Kelley Publishers, 1966.

"Dura-fleece, Spandura, New Blend Move Outdoors." *Textile World,* December 1992.

Isaacs, McAllister III. "Automation and Quality Key Spinning in the '90s." *Textile World,* January 1990.

"Late News Report." *Textile World,* February 1993.

"'Lights Out' for Yarn Making Is Here - Now." *Textile World,* December 1992.

"What's New in Cotton Research." *Cottong Incorporated,* July 1996.

Sawhney, A. P. S. "Air-jet Weaving Requires Special Attention to Yarn." *Textile World,* December 1992.

Stuart, Frank. "Yarn Fair Rolls a Natural." *Daily News Record,* 19 August 1992.

"U.S. Textiles Averts Bush's Tariff Cut." *Textile World,* February 1993.

Welch, Susan, John Gruhl, Michael Steinman, and John Comer. *American Government.* 2nd ed. St. Paul: West Publishing Company, 1988.

—Attrices Dean Griffin, updated by Gertrude Mandeville

SIC 2282

YARN TEXTURIZING, THROWING, TWISTING, AND WINDING MILLS

Establishments included in this classification are those that are primarily engaged in texturizing (or texturing), throwing (another name for texturizing), twisting, winding, or spooling purchased yarns or manmade fiber filaments wholly or chiefly by weight of cotton, manmade fibers, silk, or wool, mohair, or similar animal fibers, or in performing such activities on a commission basis. Establishments primarily engaged in dyeing or finishing purchased yarns or finishing yarns on a commission basis are classified in **SIC 2231: Broadwoven Fabric Mills, Wool (Including Dyeing and Finishing)** if the yarns are of wool and in **SIC 2269: Finishers of Textiles, Not Elsewhere Classified** if they are of other fibers. Establishments primarily engaged in producing and texturizing manmade fiber filaments and yarns in the same plant are classified in **SIC 2823: Cellulosic Manmade Fibers.**

INDUSTRY SNAPSHOT

According to the U.S. Bureau of the Census, there are 147 establishments in this classification. In 1995, these establishments and their 15,400 employees shipped $3.7 billion worth of products. While texturizing establishments are just a small part of the total number of companies and establishments in this classification, the texturizing plants accounted for the largest portion of sales, shipping $2.87 billion worth of products in 1995. Unifi Corporation of Greensboro, North Carolina, is the world's largest texturizing company and accounts for well over half of the total texturizing sales.

Texturizing is a process whereby partially oriented filament yarn (POY) is stabilized through heating and drawing, providing a crimped continuous filament yarn. Generally speaking, two types of manmade POY is texturized: nylon and polyester. Ladies' hosiery is the primary end-use application for texturized nylon, while texturized polyester is used in a wide variety of apparel and homefurnishings products and, to a lesser extent, in some industrial fabric applications. There are two different types of texturizing machines. The majority of POY products are texturized on false-twist texturizing machines, but some applications require the use of air-jet texturizing machines.

ORGANIZATION AND STRUCTURE

POY comes to the texturizing plant wound on tubes, which serve as the supply packages for the texturizing machines. These are purchased from manmade fiber producers such as Du Pont, Eastman Chemical Co., Hoechst Celanese, Tollaram Fibers, American Micrell, and Wellman. These packages contain anywhere from 10 to 100 pounds of POY. In order to receive the more economical larger packages, a texturizing plant must be equipped with automated package-handling equipment, which has been available since 1990. Some older plants, especially those involved in small niche markets, opted not to purchase the automated equipment and must order the smaller package size.

Most texturized yarn is produced by companies such as Unifi for sale to weaving and knitting establishments. Some weaving plants, such as Burlington Industries and Milliken & Co., produce yarn for their own consumption. Texturizing machines are not manufactured in the United States; instead, false-twist and air-jet texturizing machines are made by companies in Europe and Japan.

BACKGROUND AND DEVELOPMENT

Texturizing as an industry is relatively new compared to other segments of the textile industry, most of which have been around for centuries. The beginnings of texturizing go back to the invention of nylon just over 50 years ago when texturizing was used to process nylon yarn for hosiery. But it really blossomed in the 1970s as the system to produce polyester filament yarns for use during the doubleknit polyester craze. As rapidly as doubleknit polyester leisure suits grew in popularity, texturizing grew as a necessary process. And, unfortunately for the more than one hundred polyester texturizing plants that sprang up overnight, polyester texturizing died with doubleknit polyester leisure suits.

Despite its relatively young age, texturizing enjoyed more technological advances over the last two decades than any other textile process. The Textured Yarn Association of America (TYAA) formed in 1972 with the original purpose of establishing quality standards for what was then still considered a fledgling process. TYAA members learned at the association's twentieth anniversary meeting in July of 1992, that since the association's first meeting, texturizing speeds more than quadrupled to a one thousand meters per minute delivery speed of finished texturized yarn. Package sizes tripled during that time period. Electronics now controlled operations, temperatures, speeds, and twists and monitored quality, temperature, and efficiency. Nearly every machine maker offers at least one model loaded with automation: doffing, package handling, and creeling.

CURRENT CONDITIONS

At the first organizational meeting TYAA hosted over one hundred texturizing companies. Most of these were supplying yarn for the doubleknit polyester trade. At TYAA's 1993 annual meeting, there were ten texturizing companies represented. Membership in TYAA today, however, includes suppliers to the industry, end users of texturized yarn, and companies who actually perform the texturizing process. Annual poundage for texturizing at TYAA's beginning was in the neighborhood of 1.6 billion. Today the figure is something less than 1.0 billion. But the dollar value is way up, even with inflation. Those companies who divorced themselves from the doubleknit disaster are today producing products requiring high-tech specifications and much higher quality. And those companies are reportedly running flat out.

Yarn texturizing, along with the rest of the U.S. textile industry, is also benefiting from competing in a growing global market. A growing global population, developing world economies, the U.S. Industry's growing technical advantages of using systems such as Quick Response and DAMA, and new trade agreements are working together to positively effect this segment of the industry. The North American Free Trade Agreement (NAFTA), which essentially removes all trade restrictions among Canadian, U.S., and Mexican businesses, has already shown short-term positive impacts on the U.S. textile industry. With North American countries as the U.S. textile industry's most important export markets throughout the 1990s, the agreement should have a long-range positive effect on the industry.

INDUSTRY LEADERS

Unifi Corporation represents more than a microcosm of today's texturizing industry. The company, founded in 1971, has long been the industry leader in texturizing in the United Sates thanks in part to their continued quest for technology and willingness to pay for capital improvements. Unifi reached record growth with $1.35 billion in sales in 1996. In Kurt Salmon Associate's annual profile of publicly held textile companies for 1992, Unifi ranked sixth in total sales, behind such industry giants as Burlington Industries, Springs Industries, Shaw Industries, Dominion Textiles, and Fieldcrest Cannon. But, amazingly, its net income of $62 million led all publicly held textile companies.

Until 1991, Unifi's largest texturizing competitor was Macfield, a company also born during the doubleknit polyester craze. In that year, Unifi acquired Macfield, thus obtaining the capacity to produce over half of the texturized yarn in the United States. In 1996, the second and third largest companies in this sector of the textile industry was Jefferson Mills Inc. of Pulaski, Virginia, with $48 million in sales and Burke Mills Inc. of Valdese, North Carolina, with $34 million in sales.

One thing Unifi has always done that other textile companies are just now learning to do is export. Since the company was founded, it has had a commitment to export a minimum of 20 percent of its capacity. The company has done this even in years when, because of circumstances, it might have been more profitable to utilize its entire capacity for production of products ticketed for the domestic market. Such a philosophy and experience insofar as exporting products are concerned portends well for Unifi over the next several years following the passage of the North American Free Trade Agreement (NAFTA).

RESEARCH AND TECHNOLOGY

Research and technology played a vital role in keeping the U.S. textile industry competitive by exploring several new operating systems. One such system, called Quick Response, creates partnerships up and down the softgoods pipeline—fiber producers, textile manufacturers, apparel manufacturers, and retail establishments—and makes use of electronic technology, especially bar coding and Electronic Data Interchange (EDI), to receive up-to-date information. When all the elements are in place and the process works as it should, the system overcomes some of the advantages held by establishments exporting products from low-wage, developing countries into the United States.

The American Textile Partnership (AMTEX) enacted a pact in 1993 where national laboratories, in conjunction with the United States Department of Energy (DOE), work on selected projects with the U.S. textile industry and its research facilities to develop systems to make the industry more competitive. The AMTEX project with the most immediate results is Demand Activated Manufacturing Architecture (DAMA), which expands on the Quick Response system. Under the DAMA system, electronics inform pipeline partners of each garment sold by making use of point-of-sale data generated during scanning of barcoded hang tags. Results of the DAMA pilot project, begun in September of 1996, have shown that the creation of an electronic marketplace will improve operations and reduce costs by controlling warehouse costs and inventory size and reducing wastes, while improving customer responsiveness and product development.

FURTHER READING

"ATME-I '93 Quickens Textiles' Time to Market." *Textile World,* June 1992, 74-75.

Brookstein, David. "U.S. Textiles Has Global Opportunities." *Textile World,* February 1997, 79-81

"The Business Week 1000 Tables." *Business Week,* 1993 Bonus Issue, 118-163.

"DAMA Pilot Project Under Way." *Textile World,* October 1996, 25.

Dun & Bradstreet Million Dollar Directory: America's Leading Public & Private Company series 1996. New York: Dun & Bradstreet, 1996.

"GATT Disappoints U.S. Textile Leaders." Textile World News. *Textile World,* January 1994, 23-24.

Isaacs III, McAllister. "Aaair-Jet Texturing Machine Chart 1992." *Textile World,* May 1992, 64-66.

———. "False-Twist Texturing Machine Chart 1992." *Textile World,* May 1992, 56-62.

———. "Texturing Gets Automation as TYAA Turns 20." *Textile World,* May 1992, 54-55.

———. "Unifi Tops the Sales Yarn Market and Is Still Moving." *Textile World,* August 1993, 33-37.

Linton, George C. *The Modern Textile and Apparel Dictionary.* Plainfield, NJ: Textile Book Service, Division of Bonn Industries Inc., 1973.

Malone, Dr. Thomas. "The AMTEX Partnership After One Year." *Textile World,* May 1994, 34-35.

McCurry, John. "Technology Underscores Unifi's Success." *Textile World,* January 1997, 62-66.

"Microfibers: All Dressed Up and Everywhere to Go." *Textile World,* August 1992, 37-48.

Morrissey, James A. "Textile Firms Turn Trash to Treasure." *Textile World,* February 1997, 74-76.

"Nafta Boosts U.S. Textiles." *Textile World,* January 1997, 28.

Richard, Robert. "Market Outlook." *Textile World,* March 1996, 17.

Rozelle, Walter. "Business Outlook." *Textile World,* March 1996, 15.

Standard & Poor's Industry Surveys. New York: Standard & Poor's Corporation, 1996.

Textile Highlights. Washington: American Textile Manufacturers Institute, December 1993 and March 1994.

"Textile World 1992 Manmade Fiber Chart." *Textile World,* August 1992, 49-73.

"Textiles Ready to Reap NAFTA Rewards." Textile World News. *Textile World,* December 1993, 23-24.

—McAllister Isaacs III, updated by Tami L. Powell

SIC 2284

THREAD MILLS

Establishments in this classification are those that are primarily engaged in manufacturing thread from cotton, silk, manmade fibers, wool, or similar animal fibers. Important products in this category include sewing, crochet, darning, embroidery, tatting, hand-knitting, and other handicraft threads. Establishments primarily engaged in manufacturing thread from flax, hemp, and ramie are included in **SIC 2299: Textile Goods, Not Elsewhere Classified.**

The thread industry has enjoyed continued growth in sales throughout the 1990s, with an estimated $986.6 million worth of products shipped in 1997, up from $799.3 million in 1991. The largest component of this category is sewing thread, purchased mainly by the apparel industry. American & Efird, Inc., with annual sales of $265 million, and Coats Industrial North America, with annual sales of $160 million, are the largest manufacturers of thread.

While sales are up, total thread industry employment figures dropped from 6,200 in 1992 to an estimated 4,900 in 1997. Employment of machinery operators in the textile industry as a whole is expected to decline through the year 2005 due to changing trade regulations and labor saving machinery. Hourly production workers in thread mills earned less, on average, than many of their counterparts in other industries, with pay scales increasing slightly from $7.34 in 1992 to $8.19 in 1997. States with the most thread mills and the highest number of employees in this industry include North Carolina, Massachusetts, and Georgia.

The future for thread sales appears to be good, with natural fibers outselling manmade fibers due to strong demand by the carpet, apparel, and household furnishing markets.

FURTHER READING

Davison's Textile Blue Book. Atlanta, GA: Apparel Exchange, 1997. Available from http://apparelex.com/bluebok/thr_573.htm.

Manufacturing USA: Industry Analyses, Statistics, and Leading Companies. Detroit: Gale Research, 1996.

Occupational Outlook Handbook 1996-97,

U.S. Bureau of Labor Statistics. Available from http:// stats.bls.gov.

—McAllister Isaacs III, updated by Laurette Koserowski

SIC 2295

COATED FABRICS, NOT RUBBERIZED

This industry includes establishments primarily engaged in manufacturing coated, impregnated, or laminated textiles, and in the special finishing of textiles, such as varnishing and waxing. Establishments primarily engaged in rubberizing purchase fabrics are classified in **SIC 3069: Fabricated Rubber Products, Not Elsewhere Classified,** and those establishments engaged in dyeing and finishing textiles are classified in various textile industries or **SIC 2231: Broadwoven Fabric Mills, Wool (Including Dyeing and Finishing).**

The coated fabrics (not rubberized) manufacturing industry is regarded as a part of the larger miscellaneous textile goods business sector. While the textile goods industry as a whole has seen its employment figures gradually drop over the past decade, employment figures for the coated fabrics industry have not decreased significantly. In 1992, the total number of workers in the coated fabrics (not rubberized) industry was 9,200, with 1997 figures estimated at 9,100. The work force is composed primarily of hourly production workers earning an average of $14.90 per hour in 1997, up from $12 an hour in 1992.

During the nineties, the industry saw significant growth in the value of products shipped, with 1997 figures projected at approximately $1.8 billion up from $1.5 billion in 1992. A large percentage of companies engaged in coated fabrics manufacturing post annual sales in excess of 20 million. Industry leaders include Ludlow Corp. of Exeter, New Hampshire, with annual sales of about $130 million; Seaman Corp. of Wooster, Ohio, with annual sales of $50 million; Uniroyal Engineered Products of Troy, Michigan, with annual sales of $49 million; Health-Chem Corp. of New York, New York, with annual sales of $47 million; and Cooley Inc. of Pawtucket, Rhode Island, with annual sales of $35 million. Other significant companies in this industry include Athol Mfg. Corp., Great Lakes Paper Co., and JB Group Inc. High demand for non-rubberized coated fabrics is in the area of furniture and wall coverings. Non-rubberized coated fabrics are also used in the manufacture of children's toys, nonwoven shoes, soft luggage, awnings and canopies, tents,

sports equipment, industrial and marine supplies, protective clothing, etc. Strong specialty markets include vehicle air bags used by the automotive industry.

FURTHER READING

Manufacturing USA: Industry Analyses, Statistics, and Leading Companies. Detroit: Gale Research, 1996.

U.S. Department of Commerce. *U.S. Industrial Outlook 1994.* Washington: 1994.

—Laurette Koserowski

SIC 2296

TIRE CORD AND FABRICS

This category covers establishments which produce cord and fabric of manmade fibers, cotton, glass, steel, or other materials used for reinforcing rubber tires, industrial belting, fuel cells, and similar applications. Manufacturers of coated fabrics that are not rubberized are covered under **SIC 2295: Coated Fabrics, Not Rubberized.** For discussion of weaving systems, refer to **SIC 2211: Broadwoven Fabric Mills, Cotton.**

The U.S. Department of Commerce 1993 Census reported nine U.S. companies produced tire cord and fabrics for the rubber tire industry. In 1995, the largest of these was Goodyear Tire and Rubber Co., with principal plants in Decatur, Alabama, and Cartersville, Georgia. The next largest manufacturer of tire cord and tire cord fabrics was Firestone Fibers and Textiles Co. of Kings Mountain, North Carolina. This Bridgestone subsidiary posted 1995 sales of $80 million and employed 400 people. The third largest business in this industry was Page Belting Co. of Concord, New Hampshire. This private company employed 100 people and had sales of $2 million in 1995. Overall, this industry employed 5,000 workers in 1995 and shipped $1 billion worth of goods.

While some tire cord came from steel in the 1990s, most tire reinforcement came from such synthetic materials as nylon, polyester, and rayon fiber. Of the 744 million tons of manmade fiber used as tire reinforcement worldwide in 1993, 57 percent was nylon, nearly 24 percent was polyester, and approximately 19 percent was rayon. Worldwide projections called for 811 million tons of tire cord to be produced in 1998, of which 57 percent would be nylon, nearly 15 percent rayon, and nearly 27 percent polyester.

In North America, the 165 million tons of manmade fiber used in 1993 was 55 percent polyester, nearly 43 percent nylon, and nearly 2 percent rayon. For 1998, projections called for 161 million tons to be produced in North America: 64 percent polyester, nearly 36 percent nylon, and less than 1 percent rayon.

Specifications for tire cord were generally dictated by the type of tire made. The three most common types of tires manufactured in the early 1990s were radial, bias, and high performance. In the United States, radial tires were the most popular, holding about 90 percent of the market in the early 1990s. This, however, was expected to change as high-performance tires increased in popularity, potentially comprising between 20 and 25 percent of the market by the year 2000. Production demands for tire cord fabric were directly related to the number of new cars and trucks sold as well as the need for replacement tires on existing automobiles and trucks.

The manufacture of tire cord fabrics involved two general processing steps: twisting and weaving. In the twisting process, two or three ends of the tire cord material are twisted together to form a two- or three-ply yarn. The plied yarn then goes through a second round of twisting called cabling, in which two or three strands of the plied yarn are twisted together to form 2/2, 2/3, 3/2, or 3/3 cabled yarn. During weaving, the cabled tire cord serves as the warp or lengthwise yarn in the tire cord fabric. Tire cord makers use a light cotton thread to form the filling or crosswise yarn in the fabric. This lightweight yarn, which holds the cabled tire cord in place, dissolves during the rubberizing process, leaving only lengthwise strands of tire cord in the fabric.

Traditionally, all tire cord fabrics were produced on shuttle system weaving machines. By the end of the 1980s, however, two companies—Draper Corp. of Spartanburg, South Carolina, and Gunne GmbH of Moehnesse-Gunne, Germany—began making air-jet weaving machines for production of tire-cord fabrics. Air-jet weaving machines produced tire cord fabric about 3.5 times faster than shuttle system weaving machines, increasing tire cord fabric production tremendously. However, few companies produced the air-jet weaving machine for tire cord in the 1990s, as few companies were engaged in that business.

FURTHER READING

''1993 Industry Outlook: What's Ahead for America's 24 Key Industries.'' *Business Week,* 11 January 1993.

Isaacs, McAllister, III, ''Machinery Makers Are Responding to the Needs of Weaving Plants.'' *Textile World,* December 1993, 42-43.

Isaacs, McAllister, III. ''Textile World's Weaving Machinery Chart for 1993.'' *Textile World,* December 1993, 44-60.

Linton, George C. *The Modern Textile and Apparel Dictionary,* Plainfield, NJ: Bonn Industries Inc., 1973.

Textile Highlights. Washington: American Textile Manufacturers Institute, December 1993.

''Weaving Speeds Are Not All in Machines.'' *Textile World,* June 1993, 78-87.

U.S. Department of Commerce. *1995 Annual Survey of Manufactures.* Washington: GPO, 1997.

—McAllister Isaacs III, updated by Dave Fagan

SIC 2297

NONWOVEN FABRICS

Included in this category are establishments that are primarily engaged in manufacturing nonwoven fabrics by mechanical, chemical, thermal, or solvent means, or by combinations thereof. Establishments that are primarily engaged in producing woven felts are classified in **SIC 2231: Broadwoven Fabric Mills, Wool (Including Dyeing and Finishing).** Those producing other felts are classified in **SIC 2299: Textile Goods, Not Elsewhere Classified.**

A wide variety of products are made using the nonwoven process. They are generated by textile-, paper-, and/or extrusion-type processes. Nonwovens produced from textile-type processes include filtration fabrics, shoe furnishings, insulation padding, apparel components, wipes, medical dressing, medical apparel, coverstock, foodservice wipes, and automotive headliner. Nonwovens from paper-type processes include tea bags, surgical drape, apparel components, air filtration, premoistened towelettes, and wet wipes. Those nonwovens produced from extrusion-type processes include geotextiles (fabrics used as road beds and erosion prevention systems), protective clothing, reinforcement fabrics, coverstock, filtration fabrics, roofing, automobile carpet backing, laundry aids, homefurnishings, and regular carpet backing. Some nonwovens products are produced from a combination or hybrid of processes; these include surgical drape, wound dressing, sorbent media, medical apparel, and disposable components.

INDUSTRY SNAPSHOT

The nonwoven fabrics industry is probably the fastest growing sector of the textile business. New end uses, replacing those in the woven and knitted sector, are being developed every day. It is generally immune from import competition. Nonwovens as an operation is highly capital intensive and relatively low in labor intensity. It is therefore not an attractive process for developing countries where putting a lot of people into the workplace is one of the prime objectives.

Like **SIC 2295: Coated Fabrics, Not Rubberized,** this category requires sophisticated, electronically controlled machinery, and sophisticated, highly trained fabric engineers. In almost all cases where nonwoven fabrics can be substituted for woven and knitted fabrics, the result is a less expensive product. The U.S. Bureau of the Census reports that in 1994 there were 198 establishments engaged in primary production of nonwoven fabrics. In 1995, these establishments, with 11,100 employees, shipped $1.86 billion worth of products. Three of the largest companies involved solely in the nonwoven fabrics industry are Dexter Nonwovens of Windsor Locks, Connecticut with $300 million in sales; Reemay Inc. of Old Hickory, Tennessee, with $180 million in sales; and National Nonwovens of Easthampton, Massachusetts, with $32 million in sales.

ORGANIZATION AND STRUCTURE

Nonwoven is a generic term used to describe a fabric that is produced differently from a fabric made by weaving or, more broadly, a fabric that is different from traditional woven or knitted fabrics. Like all fabrics, nonwovens are planar structures that are relatively flat, flexible, and porous. Unlike traditional fabrics that are made by mechanically interlacing (weaving) or interlooping (knitting) yarns composed of fibers or filaments, nonwovens are fabrics that are made by (a) mechanically, chemically, or thermally interlocking layers or networks of fibers or filaments or yarns; (b) interlocking fibers or filaments concurrent with their extrusion; (c) perforating films; or (d) forming porous films concurrent with their extrusion.

Terminology used in the trade to describe nonwoven fabrics has been coined from the method used to form the web, the technology used to bond the web into a fabric, the forming/bonding combination, and the end-use application. Web formation jargon includes dry laid, carded, crosslapped, garnetted, air laid, wet laid, cylinder formed, extruded, meltblown, cast film, coformed, and flashspun. Terms associated with bonding include mechanically bonded, stitchbonded, needlefelted, needlepunched, spunlaced, jetlaced hydroentangled, apertured, chemically bonded, resin bonded, latex bonded, powder bonded, print bonded, saturated, spray bonded, foam bonded, frothed, thermal bonded, point bonded, and ultra-

sonically welded. Examples of forming/bonding terms for nonwovens are card/bond and spunbond. Examples of end-use application terminology are disposables, durables, semidurables, coverstock, geotextiles, filter fabric, sorbers, medical dressing, premoistened towellete, and wipe. Also, nonwovens are often described according to their fiber content such as polyester nonwoven, rayon nonwoven, polypropylene nonwoven, cotton/polyester nonwoven, pulp/polyester nonwoven or polypropylene/pulp nonwoven. Other nonwoven terms frequently encountered include film laminate, composite, SMS, and hybrid.

BACKGROUND AND DEVELOPMENT

The nonwoven fabrics industry is international in scope. The concept of making fabrics directly from fibers on needlepunch machinery achieved commercial viability in North America and Europe over 75 years ago. Facilities for producing commercial quantities of technical fabrics using wet-laid technology were established in the United States during the 1930s. Large-scale commercial production facilities for chemically bonded nonwovens were placed in operation in the United States during the early 1940s and in Europe and Japan following World War II.

The first extrusion operations dedicated to making fabrics directly from polymer melts were opened in the United States and Europe during the mid- to late 1960s. Currently, about half of the worldwide nonwoven fabric production capacity is located in North America, a third in Europe, and an eighth in Japan. Capacities in these areas are expanding at annual growth rates ranging 6 to 10 percent through both productivity improvements and the installation of new facilities. In addition, new nonwoven enterprises are currently starting up throughout Asia and South America. About two-thirds of all nonwovens are directly from fibers, and one-third are made directly from polymers.

An interesting history of technical, market, and product emphasis has occurred during the relatively short period of nonwoven industrialization. The early thrust in nonwoven usage emphasized replacing traditional woven and knitted fabrics. During this initial phase, proprietary technology was used not only to produce fabric structures that performed better than the items they were designed to replace, but it also was used when traditional fabrics could not be used. As a result, new applications and markets were established and the industry expanded.

As the industry matured and technology became publicly available, emphasis in the various sectors of the industry changed. Currently, some portions of the nonwovens industry are technology driven while others are market driven. A number of firms are proprietary technology-based while others are turn-key plant operations. Some are commodity roll-goods producers while others are more oriented to niche markets with high value-added products. Many nonwovens producers continue the quest for new markets and more opportunities to compete with traditional textiles, papers, and plastics.

CURRENT CONDITIONS

Production of nonwoven roll goods in the United States climbed over the 2.5 billion pound level for the first time in 1992. By nonwoven type, application distribution is as follows: The majority of card/ resinbond and card/thermalbond fabrics go into coverstock, while interlinings, wipes, and carrier sheets account for most of the remainder. Interlinings are one of the largest growing markets for nonwoven fabrics with 40 million pounds of fiber going to meet interlinings demand in 1995 according to Dlemson's School of Textiles, Giber & Polymer Science. To continue to expand in this growing market the nonwoven industry must increase the perception of nonwovens as a quality alternative to wovens and knits, and increase their exports by pursuing markets in other countries.

More than half of the highloft volume is used in furniture and sleeping applications. Filtration, apparel, insulation, healthcare, and geotextile products account for most of the remainder. Stitchbond fabrics are used in bedding, shoes, and a variety of coated products. Automotive trim and geotextiles account for 50 to 60 percent of all needlepunch fabrics. Other major applications are filtration, bedding, homefurnishings, and coating.

As much as two-thirds of all spunlace fabrics are used in medical products. Other applications are wipes, industrial apparel, interlinings, absorbent components, filtration, and coating. Medical product applications also account for about one-third of all wet laid nonwovens. Other applications include tea bags, meat casings, filter media, battery separators, and wipes.

Most bonded pulp fabrics are used as wipes or absorbent components. The largest yardage applications for spunbonds is coverstock. Other major uses are geotextiles, roofing, carpet backing, medical, filtration, furniture, and packaging. About one-half of all meltblown nonwoven roll goods are used in filtration and medical applications. Other applications include sorbents, wipes, and sanitary products. Porous film applications include coverstock, medical products, and laminating media. Nonwoven hybrids are used in absorbent products, wipes, filtration, and barrier applications.

The effect of the North American Free Trade Agreement (NAFTA) on the nonwovens sector is expected to be more long range than near term. Removing the trade barriers on textile products shouldn't have much of an impact immediately in this area because of the typical end-use applications for nonwoven products. However, as the standard of living in Mexico rises, and as such industries as automotives increase their presence in Mexico, and areas such as Mexico's highway systems undergo extensive improvements, NAFTA's effect on the nonwovens sector will be a positive one.

FURTHER READING

"ATME-I '93 Quickens Textiles' Time to Market." *Textile World,* June 1992, 74-75.

"The Business Week 1000 Tables." *Business Week,* 1993 Bonus Issue, 118-63.

"Cotton Incorporated Is 'Textiles' Partner'." *Textile World,* August 1993, 47-48.

Brookstein, David. "U.S. Textiles Has Global Opportunities." *Textile World,* February 1997, 79-81.

"DAMA Pilot Project Under Way." *Textile World,* October 1996, 25.

Dun & Bradstreet Million Dollar Directory: America's Leading Public & Private Company Series 1996. New York: Dun & Bradstreet, 1996.

"GATT Disappoints U.S. Textile Leaders," Textile World News. *Textile World,* January 1994, 23-24.

Linton, George C. *The Modern Textile and Apparel Dictionary.* Plainfield, NJ: Textile Book Service, Division of Bonn Industries Inc., 1973.

Malone, Dr. Thomas. "The AMTEX Partnership After One Year." *Textile World,* May 1994, 34-35.

"Microfibers: All Dressed Up and Everywhere to Go." *Textile World,* August 1992, 37-48.

Morrissey, James A. "Textile Firms Turn Trash to Treasure." *Textile World,* February 1997, 74-76.

"Nafta Boosts U.S. Textiles." *Textile World,* January 1997, 28.

Richard, Robert. "Market Outlook." *Textile World,* March 1996, 17.

Rozelle, Walter. "Business Outlook." *Textile World,* March 1996, 15.

———. "Nonwovens: Growth in New and Established Markets." *Textile World,* August 1996, 52, 77-78.

Standard & Poor's Industry Surveys. New York: Standard & Poor's Corporation, 1996.

Textile Highlights. Washington: American Textile Manufacturers Institute, December 1993 and March 1994.

Ward's Business Directory of U.S. Private and Public Companies. Detroit: Gale Research, 1997.

"Textiles Ready to Reap NAFTA Rewards." Textile World News. *Textile World,* December 1993, 23-24.

"Textile World 1992 Manmade Fiber Chart." *Textile World,* August 1992, 49-73.

Vaughn, E. A. *Nonwoven Fabric Primer and Reference Sampler.* Association of the Nonwovens Fabrics Industry, 1992.

—McAllister Isaacs III, updated by Tami L. Powell

SIC 2298

CORDAGE AND TWINE

This classification covers businesses that make rope, cable, cordage, twine and related products from abaca (Manila) sisal, henquen, hemp, cotton, paper, jute, flax, manmade fibers including glass, and other fibers. Products include binder and baler twine, blasting mats and rope, fiber cable, camouflage nets not made in weaving mills, cargo nets, braided cord, fish nets and seines, fishing lines, insulator pads, rope nets, rope, rope slings, and wire ropes.

In the early 1990s, 181 companies produced cordage and twine products according to the U.S. Department of Commerce, Bureau of the Census. In 1995, these businesses shipped $817.4 million worth of products, down from $880 million in 1991. As of 1995, the industry employed 7,500 people (5,900 were production workers), with a total estimated payroll of $165.8 million.

Most establishments in this industry are relatively small. More than 100 of the 187 establishments have fewer than 20 employees. Generally, cordage and twine plants are not as modern as other textile producers. Most serve niche markets with closely controlled product specifications.

The largest company engaged in this industry was Wire Rope Corporation of America, Inc. of St. Joseph, Missouri. This private company employed 950 people and had 1995 sales of approximately $95 million. Wire Rope Corporation makes such lifting products as wire rope, wire rope slings, high carbon wire, and structural strand especially for use in oil fields, mines, cranes, construction sites, and logging operations.

The second largest company in this category for 1995 was Tolaram Fibers, Inc. of Charlotte, North Carolina, with 200 employees and annual sales of $52 million. The British conglomerate, Cookson Group, plc bought out Tolaram in 1995, changing its name to Cookson Fibers. The company is now the largest contract manufacturer of dental floss, a nylon yarn product, in the world, producing 3.5 miles of yarn per minute.

Almost all cordage and twine makers buy their yarn requirements from sales yarn mills. This yarn is then twisted (plied) by taking two or more strands of yarn and twisting them a certain number of turns per inch. Depending on the end-use application, cabling follows the twisting process. Cabling is similar to twisting except that where twisting involves wrapping several single strands of yarn together, cabling twists several strands of plied yarns together. The cabling continues until the proper size twine, cord, or rope is developed.

As of the mid-1990s, some experts thought sales in this industry would remain stable throughout the decade. The marine industry constitutes one of the largest markets for this industry. Increased demand for certain products has been offset by the decline in boat sales following the institution of the luxury tax in this area. The North American Free Trade Agreement has had little, if any, effect on this industry segment.

FURTHER READING

"ATME-I '93 Quickens Textiles' Time to Market." *Textile World,* June 1992.

"Cotton Incorporated Is 'Textiles' Partner." *Textile World,* August 1993.

Cookson Group, plc corporate website. Available from http://www.cooksongroup.com/plastics/home.html.

"GATT Disappoints U.S. Textile Leaders." *Textile World,* January 1994.

Hoover's Company Capsules. Austin, TX: Hoover's, Inc., 1997. Available from http://www.hoovers.com.

Linton, George C. *The Modern Textile and Apparel Dictionary.* Plainfield, NJ: Textile Book Service, Div. of Bonn Industries Inc., 1973.

"Microfibers: All Dressed Up and Everywhere to Go." *Textile World,* August 1992.

Standard & Poor's Industry Surveys. New York: Standard & Poor's Corporation, 1993.

Textile Highlights. Washington, DC: American Textile Manufacturers Institute, 1993, 1994.

"Textiles Ready to Reap NAFTA Rewards." *Textile World,* December 1993.

"Textile World 1992 Manmade Fiber Chart." *Textile World,* August 1992.

"The Business Week 1000 Tables." *Business Week,* 1993.

U.S. Department of Commerce. *1995 Annual Survey of Manufactures.* Washington: GPO, 1997.

Wire Rope Corporation of America, Inc. company website. Available from http://www.wrca.com.

—McAllister Isaacs III, updated by Dave Fagan

SIC 2299

TEXTILE GOODS, NOT ELSEWHERE CLASSIFIED

This category covers companies making textile products not included in other industry classifications. These include linen, jute, and felt goods; padding and upholstery filling; and processed waste and recovered fibers and flock. Establishments that prepare textile fibers for spinning, such as wool scouring and carbonizing, and combing and converting tow to top, are also grouped here.

Companies that primarily weave wool felts and wool haircloth are classified in **SIC 2231: Broadwoven Fabric Mills, Wool (Including Dyeing and Finishing).** Those that primarily make needle punch carpeting are classified in **SIC 2273: Carpets and Rugs.** Companies that primarily make embroideries are classified in Industry Group 239. Businesses that primarily make lace goods are classified in **SIC 2258: Lace and Warp Knit Fabric Mills**, and those that primarily sort wiping rags or waste are classified in **SIC 5093: Wholesale Trade.**

Approximately 1,900 companies are grouped in this category, up from 591 listed in 1991. The U.S. Department of Commerce, Bureau of the Census reports that companies in this category shipped $2.36 billion worth of goods in 1995, up substantially from $1.61 billion in 1991. In 1995, this category employed 19,900 workers (15,500 in production), with a total estimated payroll of $450 million.

As of 1995, the industry leader for this category was Albany International Corp. of Albany, New York, a public company with 5,400 employees and $692 million in sales (1996). This company made paper machine clothing (i.e., engineered fabrics), such as felt, used inside paper manufacturing machinery. Another industry leader was Quaker Fabric Corp. of Fall River, Massachusetts, with 1,600 employees and $198 million in sales (1996). Quaker Fabric made jacquard-patterned fabrics for residential furniture upholstery. Third in this category was William Barnet and Son, Inc. of Arcadia, South Carolina, a private company with $100 million annual sales and approximately 600 employees.

In the mid-1990s, environmental concerns affected business in this category, especially those using textiles by-products. Taking by-products to the landfill used to be common practice among all textile plants. Now that this is neither economically feasible nor environmentally acceptable, plants must find other outlets for their by-products. This has opened up new opportunities for companies in this classification. By 1997, the North American Free Trade Agreement had little effect on this industry segment.

FURTHER READING

"ATME-I '93 Quickens Textiles' Time to Market." *Textile World,* June 1992.

"GATT Disappoints U.S. Textile Leaders." *Textile World,* January 1994.

Hoover's Company Capsules. Austin, TX: Hoover's, Inc., 1997. Available from http://www.hoovers.com.

Linton, George C. *The Modern Textile and Apparel Dictionary.* Plainfield, NJ: Textile Book Service, Div. of Bonn Industries Inc., 1973.

"Microfibers: All Dressed Up and Everywhere to Go." *Textile World,* August 1992.

Textile Highlights. Washington: American Textile Manufacturers Institute, December 1993; March 1994.

"Textiles Ready to Reap NAFTA Rewards." *Textile World,* December 1993.

"The Business Week 1000 Tables." *Business Week,* 1993.

U.S. Department of Commerce. *1995 Annual Survey of Manufactures.* Washington: GPO, 1997.

—McAllister Issacs III, updated by Dave Fagan

APPAREL & OTHER FINISHED FABRIC PRODUCTS MADE FROM FABRICS & SIMILAR MATERIALS

MEN'S AND BOY'S SUITS, COATS, AND OVERCOATS

This category covers establishments primarily engaged in manufacturing men's and boy's tailored suits, coats, and overcoats from purchased woven or knit fabrics. Establishments primarily engaged in manufacturing uniforms (except athletic and work uniforms) are also included in this industry. Establishments primarily engaged in manufacturing men's work uniforms and clothing are classified in **SIC 2326: Men's and Boys' Work Clothing,** and those manufacturing men's and boys' athletic uniforms are classified in **SIC 2329: Men's and Boys' Clothing, Not Elsewhere Classified.** Knitting mills primarily engaged in manufacturing suits and coats are classified in **SIC 2253: Knit Outerwear Mills.**

INDUSTRY SNAPSHOT

In the mid 1990s, output and employment in the men's and boys' suit and coat industry continued the long-term pattern of contraction that had begun over two decades earlier. In 1979, industry sources estimated that, of the 25 million suits sold in the U.S., approximately 80 percent were U.S.-made; in 1994, by contrast, according to Department of Commerce figures, U.S. manufacturers accounted for a much smaller share—55 percent—of the much smaller number of suits, just 13 million, sold in this country. The number of people employed making suits and coats had fallen from well over 100,000 in the late 1960s to just 34,000 by 1994. The outlook of this branch of production was being shaped by a number of processes—cyclical changes in the broader economy, a changing retail structure, the impact of imports produced with cheap labor—that were having similar effects across the entire apparel industry. One key factor, however, changing dress habits among American men, was having an especially acute impact on the suit and coat industry.

ORGANIZATION AND STRUCTURE

About 250 companies in the United States produced men's and boys' suits and coats in the early 1990s, down from over 400 a decade earlier. The great majority of these were small enterprises, with 200 or fewer employees. The industry consisted of three major types of companies: manufacturers, contractors, and jobbers. Manufacturers cut and sewed finished products entirely within their own facilities. Jobbers, on the other hand, specialized in cutting the fabric, which they then supplied to contractors for sewing. The major suppliers of these manufacturers were textile mills, which produced the broad-woven fabrics accounting for roughly three-quarters of the materials consumed by the industry. Manufacturers in this industry sold their goods primarily to three types of retailers; small specialty clothing stores, department stores, and large menswear discount chains. Over the course of the 1990s, manufacturers became more dependent on the large discounters—such as Men's Wearhouse, Today's Man, and S&K Famous Brands—which expanded their operations often at the expense of the small stores, some 4,000 of which closed in the first half of the decade.

BACKGROUND AND DEVELOPMENT

The clothing industry in the United States began to develop in the eighteenth century, but most clothing was still made in homes until the Civil War. Quality menswear was long the province of skilled tailors, while most ready-to-wear clothing was imported. In the nineteenth century, however, urban migration, the sewing machine, and a demand for uniforms during the Civil War changed the industry.

Urban Migration. Urban growth in the nineteenth century changed the way Americans dressed. As people began moving to cities, they also became more concerned with their clothing. As Claudia B. Kidwell and Margaret C. Christman pointed out in *Suiting Everyone: The Democratization of Clothing in America,* ''For the most part factory workers could not afford the services of a good tailor, but they still wanted clothing which looked in no way appreciably different from the mainstream fashion. Consequently, the demand was there—not for the inferior or specialized clothing that had previously distinguished 'ready-made,' but rather for 'equal clothing' for anyone, which anyone could afford to buy.''

Tailors began to develop ''scientific principles'' and ''proportional systems'' for making clothing that would fit almost anyone. In 1848, Oliver Hudson, a men's clothier in Boston, advertised that ''sizes are indicated by number and a printed tag is attached to each article, so that anyone after becoming familiar with the size will seldom find it necessary to try a second garment.'' Tailors also began hiring workers, usually women who worked in the home, for many of the less skilled tasks, such as sewing straight seams.

Brooks Brothers, the famous New York clothier, is believed to have introduced the first ready-to-wear men's suits in the United States in 1845, and would later introduce the ''sack suit'' around the turn of the century. The comfortable, boxy-looking sack suit was a stark departure from the tight-fitting suits with padded shoulders and pleated trousers that were then popular in Europe, and was considered the first genuinely American business attire. The sack suit evolved into the Ivy League look of the 1950s and the celebrated gray flannel suit of the 1960s.

Sewing Machine. Although many people contributed to the invention of the sewing machine, Elias Howe Jr., an American machinist, demonstrated a working model in 1845 and received a patent the following year. Isaac Merritt Singer, another American, made improvements to Howe's machine, and introduced ''The Perpetual Action Belay Stitch Machine'' in 1850. Singer's was considered the first practical sewing machine. Although the two inventors would squabble over patent rights for years, I.M. Singer & Co. was formed in 1851 and garment manufacturers began placing their orders.

By some estimates, sewing machines reduced the cost of manufacturing simple ready-to-wear clothes by as much as 80 percent. In the mid-1860s, Brooks Brothers noted that a top-quality overcoat that took six days to sew by hand could be made in three using a sewing machine. A foot treadle was added in 1871, which increased productivity even more, and the Singer Sewing Machine Co., renamed after Singer's death in 1875, introduced the first electric sewing machine in 1889.

Civil War. Although most clothing in the United States was made in homes before the Civil War, military uniforms were an exception. At first, the U.S. government hired outside contractors to produce uniforms that were somewhat consistent in color and style. In 1812, however, the United States Army Clothing Establishment—perhaps the first true clothing factory in the United States—was created in Philadelphia. Fabric was cut to a standard pattern and then packaged along with padding, facing cloth, thread, and buttons. The materials were then delivered to ''widows and other meritorious females'' who sewed them into uniforms working at home. As private clothing factories appeared, they copied the same structure.

The demand for uniforms during the Civil War had several consequences. Since the Army's Establishment could not supply enough uniforms by itself, the government awarded contracts to other clothiers, many of whom received their first exposure to mass production. Second, military demand stimulated improvements in technology, including the development of better cutting machines, pressers, and buttonholers. The Establishment also kept the first detailed records on measurements, which helped manufacturers develop regular ready-to-wear sizes after the war. In 1879, Albert S. Bolles wrote in the *Industrial History of the United States* that ''the home manufacture of men's garments has virtually ceased, and every one, from ploughman to railroad president, goes to the store for his goods, and can be suited, if he chooses, from the shelves of the store at once.''

Immigration. Many of the people who worked in the early clothing industry, both as inside cutters and contract seamstresses, were immigrants, primarily Irish in the 1840s and Germans in the 1850s. Many of the Jews who emigrated from Germany after 1860 also entered the clothing trade (although more often as retailers). The industry continued to provide thousands of low-paying jobs to later immigrants, including thousands of Italians and Russian Jews, who arrived between 1880 and 1910. Many of these immigrants worked long hours in overcrowded, poorly ventilated buildings that came to be known as sweatshops.

Immigrants not only provided labor for the menswear industry; they also fueled demands for its products. One of the first purchases a new arrival made was a new American-made suit, which, according to Kidwell and Christman could instantly transform him "from 'greenhorn' to 'someone who belonged.'" In the cities, men began wearing suits to work no matter what their occupations, even if they wore aprons or other work garments to keep them clean.

In 1869, garment workers in Philadelphia, led by Uriah Stephens, formed the Noble Order of the Knights of Labor, one of the first labor unions in the United States. Among its goals were an eight-hour workday and the abolition of child labor. The Knights of Labor remained a secretive, fraternal organization until 1879, when members elected Terence V. Powderly as Grand Master Workman. Powderly called for "one big union" and welcomed workers from other industries, including Catholics, who had been excluded under Stephens. Membership in the Knights of Labor rose from about 10,000 in 1879 to more than 100,000 in 1885. In 1885, the Knights of Labor led an unsuccessful strike against the Texas and Pacific Railroad, and its influence waned. Eventually, it was supplanted by the American Federation of Labor (AFL) as the most powerful union in the United States. In the early 1900s, the United States passed laws outlawing sweatshops and regulating child labor.

Hart, Schaffner & Marx. The first men's clothing manufacturer to eliminate outside contract labor was Hart, Schaffner & Marx in 1911. Originally known as Harry Hart & Brother, the company was started as a retail outlet in Chicago in 1871 by brothers Harry and Max Hart. In 1897, Hart, Schaffner & Marx became the first clothing manufacturer to advertise nationally, and within a few years, had become the leading men's clothing label in the United States. Hart, Schaffner & Marx also promoted standards for the clothing industry, such as insisting that an "all-wool" suit should be made of 100 percent wool (although the federal Wool Products Labeling Act was not passed until 1939). In 1906, Hart, Schaffner & Marx announced that its ready-to-wear men's clothing came in 14 basic body types so customers could get a more tailored look. The company boasted: "We design models especially for men who call themselves hard to fit. Stouts, slims, short stout men, big and little men, men who are built 'close to the ground,' long bodies and short legs, men with slightly stooping shoulders; all the odd sizes have their special models, made to fit."

Fashion. Men's fashions were never as volatile as women's fashions, except perhaps during the leisure-suit phenomenon of the 1970s. Leisure suits were an urban adaptation of the safari jacket, and accounted for more than half of all men's and boy's suits produced in the United States in 1975 when more than 12 million were sold. But sales of leisure suits were less than half that in 1976, and by 1983 the leisure suit had disappeared altogether. Similarly, knit fabrics were used in nearly 75 percent of the suits and coats made in the 1970s, but also virtually disappeared by the mid-1980s.

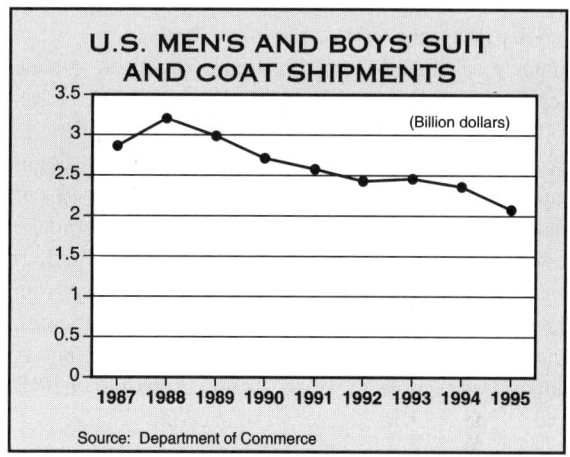

U.S. MEN'S AND BOYS' SUIT AND COAT SHIPMENTS

(Billion dollars)

Source: Department of Commerce

CURRENT CONDITIONS

The persistent downward trend in U.S. production of suits and coats, which began in the 1970s, continued in 1995. U.S. manufacturers produced 9.6 million suits in 1995, valued at $930 million, and 11.6 million tailored coats, valued at $737 million. For these two classes of products, which make up the vast majority of goods produced by this branch of the apparel industry, these figures represented a significant drop in quantity and value from 1994 (when 11.2 million suits and 13.5 million tailored coats were produced). Industry analysts explained the continued contraction of this industry, during a period of overall growth, as a result of two major factors: competition from inexpensive imported clothes, and an acceptance of more casual dress in settings where suits were once required. A central part of this trend were relaxed dress-codes at large corporations, most famously IBM, which instituted "dress down" days on which employees could show up for work in casual clothes. One Boston mortician reported that formal attire was no longer universal even on corpses. Simply put, American men were wearing, and therefore buying, suits much less often than before. Another trend that clothing manufacturers were watching carefully was the growing percentage of men's clothing that was actually purchased by men. In 1989, only about half of all men's clothing was purchased by men, but in 1993, men made nearly 70 percent of the purchase decisions.

INDUSTRY LEADERS

Oxford Industries Inc. and Hartmarx Corp. were the two largest manufacturers of men's and boys' and suits in the mid-1990s. Hartmarx's 1995 sales of men's tailored clothing represented 61 percent (about $363 million) of its total sales of $595 million. Oxford reported overall sales of $657 million, although it was not clear what share of these sales came from suits and coats.

By the mid-1990s, Hartmarx had undergone a major reorganization and financial comeback. At the beginning of the decade, with a debt of over $300 million and annual net losses reaching $220 million in fiscal 1992, the company was surrounded by bankruptcy rumors, and its stock price plunged to $3 per share, from $34.75 per share in 1987. The company responded by closing unprofitable retail stores, including selling the Kuppenheimer unit, downsizing from 35 to 22 factories, developing casual menswear lines, and establishing new ties with retailers. The newly downsized company was once again profitable in 1993 and 1994, and had succeeded in shedding a large portion of its debt.

WORK FORCE

The suit and coat industry employed 34,000 people in 1994, 28,700 of whom were production workers. At Hartmarx, the largest producer, most production workers were covered by contracts with the Union of Needletrades, Industrial and Textile Employees (UNITE). For the industry as a whole, production workers' wages averaged $7.97 per hour in 1992, among the highest for the apparel industry, but well below the $11.55 average for all manufacturing industries in that year. Sewing machine operators, mostly women, were the largest group in the work force. The assembly of suits and coats was organized largely according to the bundle system, in which each operator performed one task on a bundle of pieces, which was then taken to the next operator, until the piece was finished. Production of a typical men's suit was broken down, in this way, into as many as 100 different operations.

AMERICA AND THE WORLD

Imported goods met a substantial share of U.S. consumers' demand for suits and coats in the mid-1990s. In 1994, for example, 70 percent of tailored coats and 45 percent of suits bought by U.S. consumers were imports. The value of imported suits and coats rose rapidly in the first half of the 1990s: between 1991 and 1994, for example, imports of men's and boys' wool suits rose from $258 million to $354 million.

International trade treaties ratified in the mid-1990s were expected to substantially affect domestic apparel industries, including production of suits and coats. The Agreement on Textiles and Clothing (ATC), which took effect on January 1, 1995, called for the phase-out, over a ten-year period of the bilateral import quotas that the U.S. had negotiated with textile- and apparel-exporting countries under the Multifiber Agreement. The terms of the ATC, however, preserve import quotas on most apparel items, including suits and coats, until 2005, while accelerating the rise of quota limits up until that year.

RESEARCH AND TECHNOLOGY

Following World War II, improvements in the sewing machine eliminated the need to stitch button holes, pockets, belt loops, and lapels by hand. New technology introduced since the 1960s has also increased productivity, although some promising technologies were later abandoned. In the 1960s, some manufacturers replaced reciprocating blade cutting machinery with lasers. However, the lasers tended to fuse layers of synthetic fabrics. Computer-controlled spreading, marking, and cutting systems were introduced in the late 1970s and early 1980s. Sewing machines also became more sophisticated beginning in the late 1960s, eliminating much of the manual labor involved in handling and positioning garments as they moved from one sewing-machine operator to another. These advances led to significant increases in productivity, and employment has dropped significantly faster than the value of output since the early 1980s.

FURTHER READING

Adler, Jerry. "Have We Become a Nation of Slobs?" *Newsweek,* 20 February 1995.

Bailey, Thomas. "Organizational Innovation in the Apparel Industry." *Industrial Relations,* Winter, 1993.

Brown, Christie. "Dressing Down." *Forbes,* 5 December 1994.

Cleary, David Powers. *Great American Brands.* New York: Fairchild Publications, 1981.

Cocks, Jay. "Bonfire of the Business Suits." *Time,* 19 November 1990.

Darnton, Nina. "Good Taste for Tough Times." *Newsweek.* 28 May 1990.

Darnay, Arsen J., ed. *Manufacturing USA.* Detroit: Gale Research, 1996.

Gross, Michael. "Suit Wars." *New York.* 3 October 1988.

Kidwell, Claudia B., and Margaret C. Christman. *Suiting Everyone: The Democratization of Clothing in America.* Washington, D.C.: Smithsonian Institution Press, 1974.

Landler, Mark. "Suddenly, the Stylish Male Gets Discovered." *Business Week,* 1 October 1990.

1993 Focus: An Economic Profile of the Apparel Industry. Arlington VA: American Apparel Manufacturers Association, 1993.

Patterson, Gregory. "Hartmarx, Having Restyled Itself, Sees Robust Profits." *Wall Street Journal,* 31 May 1995.

Patterson, Gregory. "Nineties Men Want Cheap Suits and these Three Chains Oblige." *Wall Street Journal,* 19 October, 1994.

Shelton, Linda and Robert Wallace. "World Textile and Apparel Trade: A New Era." *Industry, Trade, and Technology Review,* October 1996. Available from http://www.usitc.gov/ittr.htm.

Sieling, Mark Scott, and Daniel Curtin. "Patterns of Productivity Change in Men's and Boys' Suits and Coats." *Monthly Labor Review,* November 1988.

U.S. Bureau of the Census. *Current Industrial Reports: Apparel,* MQ23A, 1995, tables 2B, 6. Available from http://www.census.gov/cir/www/mq23a.html.

U.S. International Trade Commission. *U.S. Imports of Textiles and Apparel Under the Multifiber Agreement: Annual Report for 1994.* Washington: 1995.

Zinn, Laura. "The Suit Market is Coming Apart at the Seams." *Business Week,* 12 August 1991.

Manufacturing USA. Detroit: Gale Research, 1996.

—Dean Boyer, updated by Jonathan Mogul

SIC 2321

MEN'S AND BOYS' SHIRTS

This category includes establishments primarily engaged in manufacturing men's and boys' shirts (including polo and sport shirts) from purchased woven or knit fabrics. Establishments primarily engaged in manufacturing work shirts are classified in **SIC 2326.** Knitting mills primarily engaged in manufacturing outerwear are classified in **SIC 2253.**

INDUSTRY SNAPSHOT

Slow and steady growth in production and declines in employment were characteristics of the men's and boys' shirt industry as it entered the second half of the 1990s. From 1982 to 1994, the value of shipments by firms in this industry climbed from roughly $3.5 to $5.1 billion dollars, at the same time as total employment dropped from 88.7 to 73.6 thousand people. However, if the aggregate figures indicated relatively incremental changes in output and employment, the two major branches of the industry—woven shirts and knit shirts—were experiencing much larger changes, in opposite directions. While production of woven shirts—including dress and sport shirts—declined in the 1990s, production of knit shirts, especially T-shirts increased rapidly.

Conditions in the men's and boys' shirt industry reflected the impact of a number of broader forces, including domestic market conditions, economic globalization, and new technological possibilities. Slow overall growth in this branch of the apparel industry, as in other branches as well, was partly attributable to the declining share of personal income which Americans were spending on clothing, which kept demand in check even during a period of prolonged economic growth since the early 1990s. Cost-conscious consumers increasingly turned to "non-traditional" retailers, such as discount menswear stores, factory outlets, or direct-mail catalogues. U.S. manufacturers had to compete for space on the shelves of all retailers with foreign-produced shirts, and this competition was expected to become more intense with the passage of new international trade treaties in the mid-1990s. U.S. firms attempted to stay competitive, in part, by taking advantage of opportunities to "source" work abroad, shipping cut cloth to contractors in the Caribbean Basin or Mexico, and then importing the sewn products at preferential duties. At the same time, new technologies, especially communications systems, provided domestic shirt manufacturers with a potential competitive advantage vis-à-vis foreign producers on the basis of flexibility, rather than cost alone.

The industry's larger firms were busy exploiting the competitive advantages offered by their size. In an effort to preserve or extend their dominance in the market, better-positioned firms used internally generated funds to invest in the latest apparel-related technology. At the same time, the future looked less than rosy for firms which found themselves either too late in implementing new investments or unable to arrange financial backing to undertake such improvements in plant and equipment. The forward momentum of both industry downsizing and shifting market-share concentration were expected to continue through the 1990s.

ORGANIZATION AND STRUCTURE

In 1992, there were 658 establishments, owned by 528 companies, producing men's and boys' shirts in the U.S. Shirt production was heavily concentrated in the southeastern states, especially North Carolina, Alabama, Kentucky, South Carolina and Georgia, which together accounted for about 55 percent of total shipments.

Manufacturers assembled shirts from cut pieces of fabric primarily according to the ''bundle system,'' characteristic of the apparel industry as a whole. Sewing a dress-shirt requires anywhere from 20 to 40 operations, each of which was the specialty of certain sewing-machine operators. In the bundle system, each operator performed his or her single task on a large bundle of cut pieces, retied the pieces in the bundle, and sent them along to the next operator in the sequence. At any one moment, there were thousands of garment-pieces lying in wait on the factory floor, a huge ''work-in-process'' inventory. The less than 20 minutes of actual labor required to assemble a shirt, in this system, was often extended over a production cycle as long as six weeks, from the time the separate pieces were cut to the time they were ready to be packaged for distribution. As early as the 1980s, industry analysts recognized the considerable disadvantages that the bundle system carried. This system, which maximized the productivity of an individual operator, at the same time resulted in a costly build-up of in-process inventory and hindered manufacturers' flexibility to respond to changing consumer demand.

The two most important supplies for men's and boys' shirt establishments were knit fabrics and broad-woven cloths, which accounted for, respectively, 61 percent and 21 percent of the $2.24 billion in materials consumed by the industry in 1992. The industry's largest firms reported that department stores and mass merchandisers were the largest consumers of their products. In addition, a number of firms were expanding sales of their products through their own retail divisions, especially factory stores at outlet malls.

BACKGROUND AND DEVELOPMENT

The historical development of the men's and boys' shirt industry can be divided into two basic periods: the eras before and after the 1918 introduction of the soft-collar-attached shirt. The current state of the men's and boys' shirt industry is the result of a range of influences: wars; political, industrial, and technological revolutions; government policies; apparel construction and design changes; introductions of new natural and synthetic fibers and/or improvements in their resiliency; and the fleeting nature of fashion preferences.

The event that gave birth to the U.S. apparel industry was the American Revolution of 1776. It created a climate in which the activities of urban-based industrialists, bankers, merchants, and various other professions and crafts could flourish. Progressing in step with this newly emergent and triumphant political/economic class of white males were styles of dress reflective of their own particular preferences. For the most part, these tastes were uniformly utilitarian in design and style. In the long-run, this uniformity of fashion tastes offered the possibility of mass-producing ready-made shirts.

The U.S. apparel industry, from its infancy at the end of the American Revolution to the outbreak of the Civil War, was nurtured by a highly protectionist trade policy. Between 1816 and 1829, the tariff on any type of imported clothing rose from 25 percent to 50 percent, where it remained until 1860. And, if imported clothing arrived in the United States on board a ship of foreign origin, additional penalties were imposed.

The decision to finally lift the tariff and compete in international markets was motivated by the introduction of sewing-machine technology in the 1850s. The increased productivity generated by the sewing machine propelled the U.S. apparel industry to a world-status second to none. The industry's main advantage lay in the ability to reduce the cost of labor per shirt, which led, in turn, to a sharp decrease in the selling price of its product. The sewing machine had a profound structural impact on the organization of the workplace. It ultimately led to greater divisions of labor based on routinization and job specialization. Highly paid, skilled tailors were replaced by low-wage semi-skilled or unskilled laborers who arrived from Europe to work in U.S. factories.

Another milestone in the shirt industry occurred with the outbreak of the Civil War. Prior to the war, manufacturers and retailers of ready-made apparel had been hampered by the absence of standard clothing sizes. In order to facilitate its clothing orders for private manufacturers, the Union Army's Philadelphia Quartermaster collected body-measurement data on over one million recruits and conscripts. These measurements were organized into tables of standardized body proportions which could be easily applied to the manufacture of civilian garments.

In the early twentieth century, fashion began to have a greater influence on the direction of the men's and boys' shirt industry. Affluent, well-dressed men, for example, eschewed the soft shirts being offered by Sears, Roebuck and Co., in favor of the ''stiff-bosom'' shirt, a marker of mental, as opposed to manual, labor. Cluett Peabody's ''Arrow'' line of stiff-bosom shirts, for instance, came in 20 starch collar styles of the ''poke'' type: a plain standing collar without tabs. By 1906, fashion tastes had shifted from the poke-type detached collar to embrace the fold or turned-down collar style. Arrow promoted this new collar through the creation of the ''Arrow collar man,'' whose sex appeal over the next dozen or so years managed to drive the sales of Arrow's 400-plus detached-collar styles to the $32 million mark. In 1911, the notched detached-collar shirt was all the rage. Accompanying advertisements pointed to the shirt's numerous advantages, allowing the wearer to save time, money, and temper since it prevented buttonholes from ripping, didn't tear fingernails, and bypassed the use of metal collar boutonnieres.

In 1918, a new fashion wave swept across the United States: the soft-collar-attached shirt. During their tour of duty in World War I, many American men became impressed with the relative comfort of the soft-collar-attached khaki army shirt, especially when compared to its more irritating starched, collar-detached civilian counterpart. In fact, just prior to the widespread circulation of the collar-attached shirt in its various civilian guises, sales of military shirts, replete with regulation army cuffs, and pocket, collar, and sleeve insignias, were booming.

In 1920, John M. Van Huesen was credited with the introduction of a three-ply collar constructed in a one-piece arc. The collar incorporated the advantage of the starch collar's crisp appearance with the comfort of the soft collar. It also had the advantage of retaining its shape longer than other collars due to its construction. By 1925, the Van Huesen Shirt Company ran advertisements declaring it the "collar of the century," while incorporating the new collar into the design of their entire line of shirts.

Van Huesen also pioneered the development of a patented weaving process that introduced the industry to the one-piece collar that would become an industry standard. The collar's novel quality lay in its uniform thickness, designed and constructed without any lining so that, even after repeated wearings, it proved to be wrinkle-, blister-, and buckle-resistant.

World War II, as had been true of World War I, precipitated important changes in shirt production. First, the war-effort contributed to the economic integration of the southern- and northern-based apparel industries, whose prior operations had been largely conducted on a regional basis. In addition, the war introduced new synthetic materials which eventually spun-off into the apparel industry. Immediately following World War II, some shirt manufacturers began using nylon and other synthetic fibers. Though receiving enthusiastic support from the public, not all major shirt producers were willing to plunge headfirst into the nylon shirt fad. Cluett Peabody announced that no Arrow-label shirts would be produced from nylon. They, along with other traditional shirt producers, questioned whether synthetic fibers were an authentic "shirting fabric."

During the 1950s, three major technological changes occurred that had a great impact on the shirt industry. Concerns about the longevity of synthetic fibers were silenced when Du Pont became the first U.S. commercial producer of the manmade fiber polyester, marketed under the brand name Dacron. Consumers prized polyester for its wrinkle resistance; its ability to maintain its shape after repeated washing; for requiring little, if any, ironing; and for its ability to be treated with a permanent heat-setting process which helped to maintain pleats and guard against shrinkage and sagging. Polyester also offered a big advantage to manufacturers, because it could be readily blended with other fibers. Since its first appearance, polyester has undergone many significant product-enhancing modifications. Monsanto, for example, developed and commercially produced "Spectran" polyester, a brand which, among other things, is highly regarded for its superior stain release properties.

The year 1956 witnessed the introduction of wash-and-wear, all-cotton shirts. Thanks to a special resin treatment, apparel made of natural fibers was now able to withstand repeated laundering without losing its original shape or appearance. And in 1959, the longstanding problem of a garment's susceptibility to stains found a solution when apparel products began to be treated with numerous special finishing processes that allowed stains to be washed out with plain cold water. The "Scotchgard" process emerged during this period.

CURRENT CONDITIONS

The two major segments of the men's and boys' shirt industry were moving in opposite directions in the mid-1990s. In 1995, U.S. manufacturers shipped 1.13 billion knit shirts (including T-shirts, sweatshirts, and polo shirts), valued at $5.84 billion, up from $4.89 billion in 1992, and $3.92 billion in 1991. In fact, these gains were entirely due to a jump in shipments of T-shirts and tank-tops, which jumped from 565 million shirts at $2.09 billion in 1991, to 833 million shirts at $3.99 billion in 1995. These figures were expected to jump even more dramatically in 1996, due to the merchandising bonanza offered by the 1996 summer Olympics in Atlanta. Shipments of woven shirts (including dress, business and sports shirts) by contrast, declined steadily over the same period, from 105 million shirts at $1.11 in 1992, to 88.4 million shirts at $0.99 billion in 1995.

The very different fortunes of these two segments of the industry were attributable, at least in part, to the "casualization" of American clothing tastes, expressed in the trend toward corporate dressing-down, which hurt sales of dress and business shirts. By the mid-1990s dress-shirt manufacturers were responding to this trend by developing new lines of casual woven shirts, sometimes known as "Friday wear." T-shirt sales not only gained from this trend, but also benefited from the synergy between corporate merchandising campaigns and the desire of millions of Americans to express their loyalties to sports teams, rock groups, and other icons of popular culture on their chests and backs.

While these trends had very different impacts on the different branches of the U.S. men's and boys' shirt industry, both branches were feeling the effect of competition from overseas shirt manufacturers, producing cheap goods with cheap labor. Additional long-term uncertainties were thrown into the mix with the 1993 passage of the North American Free Trade Agreement, soon followed by the Agreement on Textiles and Clothing, which promised to dismantle the protection from imports currently enjoyed by the apparel industry.

How were shirt manufacturers responding to the challenges posed by competition from foreign manufacturers? One strategy involved a combination of downsizing U.S. operations by closing plants and laying off production workers, while sourcing an increasingly large portion of production to company-owned plants or contractors in Mexico or the Caribbean Basin. By sending cut fabric to these foreign plants for sewing and then shipping the finished garments back to the U.S., at preferential duties, U.S. companies could take advantage of the chance to manufacture shirts with cheaper labor than could be done in the U.S. Between 1991 and 1995, the value of such "807" imports of shirts by U.S. firms (a figure that included the value added in both the U.S. and abroad) rose from $183 million to $1.03 billion.

If offshore production provided U.S. companies with a chance to produce their goods with cheap labor, domestic production entailed its own set of advantages, especially proximity to the huge U.S. consumer market, and the opportunity to respond rapidly to shifts in consumer demand. One major shirt manufacturer, Hampton Industries Inc., estimated that the production cycle (the time from cutting the fabric to the product's arrival at the company's distribution center) for shirts produced in the Far East could be as long as six months; for shirts produced in the Caribbean Basin, about ten weeks; and for shirts produced in the U.S., just five weeks. In the 1990s, leading shirt manufacturers took steps to capitalize on this advantage of domestic production by pursuing a strategy of competition through flexibility, rather than cheap labor. This con-

sumer-driven "quick response" strategy integrates numerous dimensions of the production cycle with an eye toward shortening the cycle's duration, implementing productivity improvements, and shrinking inventory levels through the immediate transmission of consumer taste information back to manufacturers. A key component of quick response was manufacturers' investment in state-of-the-art communications systems, known as electronic data interchange (EDI) which linked manufacturers to retailers' computer-recorded sales information, allowing them to track changes in consumer preferences as they happened.

A second aspect of quick response strategies were attempts to reduce in-process inventories and accelerate production cycles, so that these changing preferences could be quickly translated into modified products. The most far-reaching attempt to accomplish these goals involved the abandonment of the bundle system of assembly, in place since the early twentieth century, in favor of "modular" production systems. In modular systems, teams of multi-skilled operators work together to produce a single garment, or a single part of a garment, such as a collar. Pay is based on the entire team's output, rather than an individual piece-rate, giving incentive for team-members to shift tasks when backlogs develop and to focus on maximizing the number of finished pieces produced by the whole team, rather than the number of individual operations performed. While individual labor productivity may not be quite as high as in the progressive bundle system, where each operator performs just one specialized task, inventory levels are reduced, and the production cycle for assembly of an entire garment is greatly accelerated. Although industry analysts, industry leaders and unions began to advocate for adoption of modular production as a key part of quick response strategies as far back as the 1980s, manufacturers were slow to undertake such a dramatic overhaul of their management and human resources practices. A study of firms from a number of different branches of the apparel industry in the early 1992 revealed that less than 10 percent of all garments were produced according to the modular system.

In addition to the quick response system, shirt producers directed major investments at computer-controlled automated machinery in order to effect increases in productivity. These investments targeted the areas of design, cutting, embroidery, sewing, finishing, ticketing, and various distribution operations. Independent of the particular area of operation, most apparel-industry investment projects were undertaken with the aim of reducing the labor-time component per unit of output.

When compared against the standards of other industries, the measure of labor intensity in apparel manufacturing remained excessively high and acted to inhibit productivity. In order to compete among themselves, as well as against other industries, the leading apparel firms took notice. For reasons related to their economies of scale and access to internally-generated funds, the larger shirt firms were better positioned to implement many high start-up-cost technological advances. With the passage of time, this was expected to result in an uneven pattern of technological change across the entire industry, further exacerbating the downsizing trend present throughout the industry.

INDUSTRY LEADERS

During the mid-to-late 1990s, the largest producers of men's dress shirts were Phillips Van Heusen Corp. ("Van Heusen" and "Geoffrey Beane" brand names); Cluett, Peabody Inc. ("Arrow"); Salant Corp. ("Perry Ellis" and "John Henry"; and the Warnaco Group Inc. ("Hathaway"). Phillips Van Heusen claimed the largest overall share of the dress shirt market, as well as the largest share of the designer dress-shirt market. In 1995, the company significantly expanded its sport shirt operations by purchasing the Apparel Group of Crystal Brands Inc., which includes the "Izod" and "Gant" brand-names. Phillips Van Heusen began marketing wrinkle-free dress shirts in 1994, which negatively affected earnings due to the high advertising and production costs associated with introducing a new product.

One of the most venerable brand-names in the shirt industry went through a tumultuous period in the mid-1990s. Warnaco's Hathaway division, founded in Waterville, Maine, before the Civil War, lost $5 million in 1995. Despite productivity increases by the Waterville plant's 500 plus workers, Warnaco threatened to close the plant in the summer of 1996. The plant was at least temporarily saved, however, when a group led by the state's former governor bought it from Warnaco.

WORK FORCE

Total employment in the men's and boys' shirt industry in 1994 was 73.6 thousand, among whom 66.8 thousand were production workers. These figures represented the results of the industry's long-term downsizing, as employment dropped more-or-less steadily since at least as far back as the early 1980s. Census-based projections, however, predicted a flat trend in employment from 1995 through 1998.

While total employment was declining, the average hours worked by production workers exhibited a modest but steady rise, going from 36 hours per week in 1981 to 37.1 hours per week in 1992. For the same period, these workers' average wage rose from $4.55 to $6.56 per hour. By 1994, average wages had reached $6.95.

Women accounted for 85.5 percent of overall employment in the industry. This percentage has remained fairly consistent since at least 1981. Nevertheless, the predominance of women in the industry has not translated into wage parity with men. According to data provided by the Bureau of Labor Statistics, the average hourly earnings of male production workers in 1987 stood at $5.50 while women within the same category received $4.86. Also significant in terms of the social composition of the industry's work force were results of a 1988 survey about the entire apparel industry conducted by the Amalgamated Clothing and Textile Workers Union. The survey concluded that African-American workers comprised 21.2 percent of the overall apparel work force, with the percentage of all minority workers falling in the neighborhood of 36 percent.

Occupational categories in the men's and boys' shirt industry fell within four production-related classifications: cutting, sewing, finishing, and miscellaneous departments. In 1987, occupational activities pertaining to the sewing function accounted for 72.7 percent of all production workers. The finishing area accounted for 15.7 percent of all production workers. Workers performing miscellaneous functions represented 6.4 percent of total production employees, while those working in the cutting room made up the remaining 5.2 percent.

The Bureau of Labor Statistics forecasted that most of these occupational categories would undergo a continuous state of decline through the year 2005. Assuming a continuation of the more-or-less forward momentum of the industry's productivity, in conjunction with the great number of workers in the category, employment of sewing machines operators was projected to experience the steepest decrease.

AMERICA AND THE WORLD

Since the end of World War II, the apparel industry has proven to be extremely susceptible to import competition and thus has frequently lobbied the U.S. government to impose tariffs and quotas. The share of imports in U.S. consumption of both knit and woven shirts rose substantially from the 1970s to the 1990s, although import penetration was much higher in the latter branch of the industry. In 1993, imports accounted for just over half of the roughly $12.7 billion dollar U.S. men's and boys' shirt market. In 1995, over

1.2 billion shirts were imported into the U.S., valued at $6.4 billion dollars. U.S. manufacturers exported 347 million shirts, valued at $642 million.

With the NAFTA and ATC international trade agreements of the mid-1990s, the U.S. shirt industry, like other branches of the apparel industry, was expected to face new pressures from foreign competitors. Since 1974, the Multifiber Agreement had regulated textile and apparel imports to the U.S., by establishing import quotas on most apparel items, including suits, on the basis of bilateral agreements with individual countries. ATC, which took effect on January 1, 1995, will accelerate the growth of the number of items allowed in to the U.S. under these quotas, and will phase out the quotas on shirts altogether in 2005.

RESEARCH AND TECHNOLOGY

Reducing the large number of sewing machine, assembly, and packaging operations necessary in the manufacture of a single dress shirt has been a hurdle the industry has been struggling to clear. According to Ernest Schramyr, president of Jet Sew, one key variable that factored into production cycle of a shirt batch—generally 1,500 shirts—was the length of time it took to move from one operation to the next. In an article in *Bobbin* Schramyr put forward an alternative shirt production system, which called for the installation of already available robotic units as a means of rationalizing many of the assembly operations. If implemented, Schramyr estimated that a typical shirt would require only 27 instead of 40 total operations.

The largest impact of the introduction of advanced technology, though, would come in the total number of critical path operations, which could be reduced from 20 to 14 with the use of robotics. While such advances in machinery were being made, attempts to automate segments of production were often considered unsuccessful because they failed to meet their expected rate of return on investment. The fact remained, however, that assembly operations, which accounted for nearly half of a firm's total stitching costs, still offered the greatest opportunity for potential cost savings.

As a second feasible alternative to the existing assembly operations method, Schramyr suggested the implementation of equipment used with the unit production system (UPS). Outside the shirt industry, performance results from the UPS reported productivity gains as high as 25 percent and also reductions in material "throughput time" equal to an eye-opening 80 percent. The most notable drawbacks associated with the UPS were its relatively high start-up expenditure and, according to traditional investment criteria, its tendency to generate a marginal return on invest-

ment. Schramyr remained critical of the conservative investment philosophy espoused by corporate financial officers to weight potential investment projects. According to Schramyr such an approach neglected to factor in a host of cost savings which included: reduced work-in-process-carrying costs; reduced inventory-carrying costs; significant direct labor savings through a downsizing of the labor force; and heightened capabilities to complement such concepts such as immediate product delivery based on customer preference, production based on orders and not speculation, and the avoidance of unwanted discount markdowns. With these in mind, Schramyr advocated the development of a new, "non-traditional investment criterion." Failing that, he feared that many technological advances applicable to the industry would go ignored.

FURTHER READING

Abernathy, Frederick H., et al. "The Information-Integrated Channel: A Study of the U.S. Apparel Industry in Transition." *Brooking Institute Papers on Economic Activity. Microeconomics,* 1995.

Arpan, Jeffery S., Jose de la Torres, and Brian Toyne. *The U.S. Apparel Industry: International Challenge, Domestic Response.* Atlanta: College of Business Administration, Georgia State University, 1982.

Bailey, Thomas. "Organizational Innovation in the Apparel Industry." *Industrial Relations,* Winter, 1993.

Corbin, Harry A. *The Men's Clothing Industry: Colonial through Modern Times.* New York: Fairchild Publications, 1970.

Darnay, Arsen, ed. *Manufacturing USA.* Detroit: Gale Research, 1996.

Dunlop, John T. and David Weil. "Diffusion and Performance of Modular Production in the U.S. Apparel Industry." *Industrial Relations,* July, 1996.

Economic and Demographic Indicators of 42 ACTWU Industries. New York: Research Department, Amalgamated Clothing and Textile Workers Union, 1988.

Forms 10-K filed with the U.S. Securities and Exchange Commission, for: Hampton Industries, Inc. (filed April 15, 1996); Phillips Van Heusen Corp. (filed May 1, 1995); Salant Corp. (filed March 26, 1996); and Warnaco Group Inc. (filed March 20, 1996). Available from http://www.sec.gov/cgi-bin/srch-edgar.

McGraw, Dan. "Dressing Down for Dollars." *U.S. News & World Report,* 13 May 1996.

1993 Focus: An Economic Profile of the Apparel Industry. Arlington, VA: American Apparel Manufacturers Association, 1993.

Popkin, Martin, E.. *Manufacture of Men's Clothing.* New York: Isaac Pittman, 1929.

Report of the General Executive Board. ACTWU and AFL-CIO Sixth Constitutional Convention, June 1993.

Schoeffler, O. E., and William Gale. *Esquire's Encyclopedia of 20th-Century Men's Fashions.* New York: McGraw-Hill, 1973.

Schramyr, Ernst. "Jets-In-Time: 13 Operation Can Go." *Bobbin,* May 1987.

Shelton, Linda and Robert Wallace. "World Textile and Apparel Trade: A New Era." *Industry, Trade, and Technology Review,* October 1996. Available from http://www.usitc.gov/ittr.htm.

U.S. Bureau of the Census. *Current Industrial Reports: Apparel,* MQ23A, 1992, tables 2B, 5; 1995, tables 2B, 6. Available from http://www.census.gov/cir/www/mq23a.html.

U.S. International Trade Commission. *Industry and Trade Summary,* publication 2853. Washington: 1995. Available from http://www.usitc.gov/ittr.htm.

U.S. Industrial Outlook 1993. Washington, DC: U.S. Department of Commerce, 1993.

Wingate, Isabel B.. *Textile Fabrics and Their Selection.* Englewood Cliffs, NJ: Prentice-Hall, 1976.

Zagorin, Adam. "Short-shirted in Maine." *Time,* 3 June 1996.

—Daniel King, updated by Jonathan Mogul

SIC 2322

MEN'S AND BOYS' UNDERWEAR AND NIGHTWEAR

This category includes establishments primarily engaged in manufacturing men's and boys' underwear and nightwear from purchased woven or knit fabrics. Knitting mills primarily engaged in manufacturing underwear and nightwear are classified in **SIC 2254: Knit Underwear and Nightwear Mills;** and those manufacturing men's and boys' robes are classified in **SIC 2384: Robes and Dressing Gowns.**

INDUSTRY SNAPSHOT

The first half of the 1990s were an up-and-down period for the men's and boys' nightwear and underwear industry. Two years of increases in the value of shipments of these products in 1992 and 1993 were followed by two years of decline, in 1994 and 1995. Results from the first three quarters of 1996 indicated, however, that shipments were once again on the rise.

While levels of output did not change dramatically in the first half of the 1990s, the conditions facing the industry and the structure of the industry itself were undergoing considerable changes. Starting in the early to mid-1980s the economic fortunes of the men's and boys' underwear and nightwear industry entered a period of sharp decline. By the late 1980s and then extending well into the 1990s, both the retail and wholesale levels of distribution had undergone a period of widespread shakeout and structural change. This led to the break-up of many established lines of distribution and sent producers scrambling in search of new outlet sources. Even in instances where these links were not severed, they were considerably transformed, which typically led to the implementation of "quick response" systems. Also, as the U.S. economy began to experience a period of economic recovery in the mid-1990s, the upward movement of apparel prices historically associated with upturns in economic activity failed to materialize. The expected price rises were held in check due to stiff price competition from both U.S. and foreign producers. As a result, some firms in the industry found themselves burdened with levels of excess capacity that were never before encountered during previous periods of economic recovery. Finally, the lingering overhang of takeover debt piled up to defend against hostile takeover threats, a frenzy which peaked in the late 1980s and subsided in the early 1990s, continued to exert a dampening effect on company profits and growth.

By the mid-1990s, a particularly important force shaping the U.S. nightwear and underwear industry was economic globalization. As foreign competitors' share of the domestic market expanded throughout the first part of the decade, U.S. firms adapted by basing an increasing share of their own production outside of the United States itself. The passage of the North American Free Trade Agreement (NAFTA) and the Agreement on Textiles and Clothing (ATC) seemed likely to provide further stimulus to both trends in the near future.

In addition, while the industry itself was staggering under economic difficulties, its larger firms continued to gain market share and were well positioned to invest internally generated funds in state-of-art technologies. These new technology investments were expected to result in a boost in productivity and lower unit costs of production. Under the prevailing economic circumstances, if the middle and lower tier firms in the industry failed to keep pace, some industry observers expected the gap related to productivity and unit cost differentials to widen, placing the continued existence of the less competitive firms in serious jeopardy.

ORGANIZATION AND STRUCTURE

In the early 1990s, approximately 90 U.S. establishments were involved in the manufacture of men's and boys underwear and nightwear. Of these, about 70 establishments operated with twenty or more employees. The industry was heavily concentrated in the southeastern U.S., with Georgia, Tennessee, South Carolina and Kentucky accounting for nearly three-quarters of all employment in the industry. Data available from 1992 indicated that the primary materials consumed by the men's and boys underwear and nightwear industry ranked in terms of cost were: knit fabrics ($222.6 million, or 67 percent of total costs) and broadwoven fabrics ($50.7 million, or 15 percent).

BACKGROUND AND DEVELOPMENT

Underwear. At the turn of the twentieth century underwear was designed with one purpose in mind: as apparel to be worn underneath more stylistic outer garments for the simple purpose of protecting the wearer against seasonal elements. During severe weather, a man could choose from several different styles and weights of either one- or two-piece long-sleeved and long-legged knitted wool underwear. For the summer months, the wearer changed to underwear that was lighter and cooler, though it was also designed in a long-sleeved and long-legged style. A popular two-piece outfit was made of French knitted balbriggan. It featured an undershirt complete with a fancy collarette neck, pearl buttons, ribbed close fitting cuffs and a fine silk-like finish. The matching drawers came with a sateen band and pearl buttons. It was available in the colors of either ecru or camel's hair. Though interest in silk underwear was growing on the margin, due not so much to its aesthetic or status-symbol value as to its superior drying quality, underwear made of knitted wool dominated throughout the first two decades of the twentieth century.

The early twenties witnessed the arrival of the one-piece union suit. The union suit featured an athletically tapered look and came with long or short sleeves. Made from knit of long staple combed cotton yarn and sewn with smooth flat locked seams, the union suit was specially designed to eliminate the feeling of tightness around the crotch area. The union suit was also tailored to fit different body lengths and was available in long, medium and short sizes.

The next innovation was "athletic underwear," which was cut very brief and was available in a variety of staple and fancy woven cloths. It came with a "trouser seat" designed so that when opened it made no contact with the body. The sleeveless athletic shirt, popular throughout the 1930s, was adapted from the top half of the tank swimsuit worn by U.S. men during the early years of the twentieth century. It was supplanted in the 1940s by the short-sleeve T-shirt worn by World War II servicemen. These soldiers found these garments so comfortable, they continued to wear them upon re-entering civilian life. By the 1950s, the T-shirt had been transformed into a popular outerwear garment. It was propelled into the national consciousness by rebellious movie idols such as James Dean and Marlon Brando, who wore T-shirts, as opposed to the more traditional sportshirt, with their blue jeans.

Perhaps the biggest sensation to hit the men's underwear scene was the 1934 arrival of "jock-type" underwear shorts. Advertisements proclaimed their virtues, noting that jock-type shorts, specially designed with the male figure in mind, featured a "No gap opening with gentle support, elastic fabric, no buttons, no bulk, and no binding." By 1936 lightweight jock-type underwear was available in open weave and netlike fabric, with very high porosity. During the early 1940s, boxer shorts, some of them made with grippers, continued to gain in popularity but never supplanted jock-type knitted underwear, which by 1946 was available with an inverted Y-front construction accompanied by advertisements which proclaimed them to be "scientifically perfected for correct male support."

Synthetic fabrics appeared in the 1950s. Nylon underwear took the spotlight and was soon followed by polyester and cotton blends in a variety of colors. Men's fashion critics dubbed the 1960s and early 1970s the "Peacock Revolution." During this period men's underwear fashions showed regard for style and color that had been historically reserved for outerwear apparel. Undershirts and shorts, for instance, were color coordinated and could be found in a broad assortment of colors, patterns, and fabrics.

Sleepwear. Until the 1920s, when central heating became more widespread, the standard boys' sleep apparel consisted of a one-piece body suit with attached feet. As for men, a muslin nightshirt designed as a collarless pullover with long sleeves and side vents was standard. It usually extended below the calf, had three buttons in the front and a chest pocket. Both men's and boys' nightwear were very warm.

By 1925, as central heat became increasingly commonplace, the switch from men's nightshirts to pajamas gathered full force as the warmth factor was no longer quite as paramount. *Men's Wear* magazine noted that the tendency to discard nightshirts in order to take up the wearing of pajamas was everywhere in evidence, and pajama manufacturers sought to portray the new product as a vastly preferable alternative to the staid old nightshirt.

At the close of the 1920s and into the early 1930s, broadcloth competed with sateen for the number one position among sleepwear fabrics. Large bold striped pajamas were the style of choice. By 1936 pajamas designed with extended waistbands and pleats for added comfort were, for the first time, promoted not just for sleepwear but also for at-home leisure activities.

In the early 1960s the distinction between sleepwear and men's leisure-wear grew even more blurred. Men's pajamas regularly incorporated fashions and designs from sportswear and dress shirts. By the 1970s the transformation of sleepwear into sporty leisure or lounge wear was complete. The leading sleepwear manufacturers were busy putting together mix-match coordinate packages of either similar or contrasting fabrics. Even the once-maligned nightshirt made a comeback as Pierre Cardin marketed a lightweight floral-striped version design especially for the holiday season. Marketing buzzwords such as ''Unjamas'' and ''Kimojamas'' were created to emphasize a pajamas' dual loungewear and sleepwear characteristics. During this time, the prevailing wisdom appeared to be that whatever proved popular in sportswear was to be immediately adapted to sleepwear.

CURRENT CONDITIONS

In 1995, Census Bureau statistics estimated the value of nightwear and underwear shipments (including robes) by U.S. manufacturers at $1.81 billion. This figure was up from the total of $1.67 billion in 1991, but below the peak of $1.84 billion in 1993. Throughout the 1990s, nightwear shipments made up a very small share of the total, just $119 million in 1995, or roughly seven percent. Of the $1.45 billion in men's and boys' underwear shipments in 1995, the two largest categories were knit shorts and briefs, at $562 million, and undershirts, at $510 million. The remaining shipments were made up of woven boxers ($205 million) and thermal underwear ($172 million).

INDUSTRY LEADERS

Two firms, Fruit of the Loom Inc. and Sara Lee Corp., dominated the U.S. men's and boys' underwear industry in the mid-1990s. In 1995, according to Fruit of the Loom, each company had about 35 percent of U.S. market share. Sara Lee sold underwear under the Hanes brand, and planned, in 1997, to introduce products under a license agreement with Polo/Ralph Lauren. Fruit of the Loom brands included Fruit of the

Loom, BVD, Munsingwear, Botany 500 and John Henry.

Downsizing domestic production and increased offshore production were prevalent trends in this industry in the mid-1990s. Fruit of the Loom, for example, closed six U.S. plants in 1995 and laid off 3,200 workers, about 12 percent of its U.S. work force. The company expected to move an increasing share of its assembly operations to Mexico and the Caribbean basin in the coming years. Joe Boxer Corp., a popular producer of boxer shorts, designed its products in the U.S. but contracted out all manufacturing to firms in the Far East.

WORK FORCE

Industry employment data from 1987 to 1994 reflected a trend of steady job losses. In 1987 the number of production workers stood at 16,200 and by 1994 had fallen to 10,100. Underlying this trend were automation in the industry and the tendency of U.S. producers to relocate apparel establishments abroad or to outsource to foreign locations work formerly performed within U.S. borders. Wages for production workers in the industry averaged $7.03 per hour in 1994, as compared to an average of $12.09 for all manufacturing industries.

When compared against the measures of employment by gender and race for the U.S. manufacturing sector as a whole, women and minority workers were a greater presence in the apparel work force than in most other manufacturing industries. In 1988 demographic data gathered from a survey taken by the Amalgamated Clothing and Textile Workers Union indicated that women workers made up 84.4 percent of the men's and boys' sleepwear and nightwear work force. African American workers accounted for 21.2 percent of the total apparel work force, while all minority workers accounted for a total of 36 percent of the employment in the industry.

AMERICA AND THE WORLD

Import penetration of the U.S. underwear market has traditionally been relatively low compared to other apparel sectors. One explanation that analysts have offered for this pattern is that underwear production by U.S. firms is highly automated and efficient, reducing the importance of the difference in hourly wages between U.S. establishments and foreign competitors. In the first half of the 1990s, however, the share of the U.S. underwear market (both women's and men's) captured by imports climbed steadily, from roughly 25 percent (by value) in 1991, to 40 percent in 1995. As barriers to imports continued to fall in the wake of the implementation of NAFTA and ATC in the middle of the decade, all signs indicated that competition with foreign manufacturers would continue to shape the U.S. nightwear and underwear industry.

RESEARCH AND TECHNOLOGY

By the mid-1990s, the most aggressive industry response to its economic condition was to step up its investment in state-of-the-art communication systems that facilitate the rapid transmission of sales information back to the producers, so as to immediately adjust production to consumer preferences. Referred to as the ''quick response'' system, this consumer-driven process more finely integrates various phases of the production cycle, shortening the duration of various production steps and reducing inventory levels to a bare minimum.

In addition to the quick response system, firms active in this industry directed major investments at computer controlled machinery. Such purchases were undertaken in an effort to increase productivity, to minimize waste, and to secure efficiencies in traditional apparel areas such as design, cutting, embroidery, sewing, finishing, ticketing and distribution operations. Independent of the particular area of operation, the overall investment goal was intended to reduce the amount of labor-time per task, which remained high when compared to other non-apparel group industry standards.

FURTHER READING

Arpan, Jeffery S., Jose de la Torres, and Brian Toyne. *The U.S. Apparel Industry: International Challenge, Domestic Response.* Atlanta, GA: Georgia State University, 1982.

Darnay, Arsen J., ed. *Manufacturing USA.* 5th ed. Detroit: Gale Research, 1996.

Economic and Demographic Indicators of 42 ACTWU Industries. New York: Research Department Amalgamated Clothing and Textile Workers Union, 1988.

Feder, Barnaby J. ''Fruit of the Loom to Close Six U.S. Plants.'' *New York Times,* 31 October 1995.

Lane, Randall. ''The Boxer Rebellion.'' *Forbes,* 12 September 1994.

Report of the General Executive Board. ACTWU and AFL-CIO Sixth Constitutional Convention, June 1993.

Schoeffler, O.E., and William Gale. *Esquire's Encyclopedia of 20th Century Men's Fashions.* New York: McGraw-Hill, 1973.

U.S. Bureau of the Census. *Current Industrial Reports.* Washington, 1996. Available from http://www.census.gov/cir/www/mq23a.html.

U.S. Department of Commerce. International Trade Administration. *U.S. Industrial Outlook 1994.* Washington: GPO, 1994.

U.S. International Trade Commission. *Industry and Trade Summary.* Washington, 1995. Available from http://www.usitc.gov/wais/reports/rptindex.htm?apparel.

—Daniel King, updated by Jonathan Mogul

SIC 2323

MEN'S AND BOYS' NECKWEAR

This category includes establishments primarily engaged in manufacturing men's and boys' neckties, scarves, and mufflers from purchased woven or knit fabrics. Knitting mills primarily engaged in manufacturing neckties, scarves, and mufflers are classified under **SIC 2253: Knit Outerwear Mills.**

INDUSTRY SNAPSHOT

About 130 establishments were engaged in the manufacture of men's and boys' neckwear in the United States in the early 1990s. All told, shipments of neckwear from these businesses in 1994 were just over $700 million, which represented a steady rise from the 1990 total of $500 million. A climate of uncertainty, however, surrounded the industry in the mid-1990s, in large part due to changing conditions of international trade, with the implementation of the North American Free Trade Agreement (NAFTA) and the Agreement on Textiles and Clothing (ATC). The progressive growth of the import share of the U.S. neckwear market during the 1980s and early 1990s generated considerable alarm and prompted calls for protectionism among members of the Neckwear Association of America (NAA), the principal trade association representing U.S. neckwear manufacturers. In the NAA's opinion, any further reduction in current import duties would only exacerbate a trend that had already wreaked havoc upon U.S. domestic producers.

ORGANIZATION AND STRUCTURE

According to U.S. Census Bureau figures, 138 establishments manufactured neckwear in the United States in 1993. Nearly half of these, 62, were very small operations, with less than 20 employees. Neckwear production was not heavily concentrated in any particular region: New York, California and North Carolina led the way, with, respectively, 32.0, 20.0, and 10.7 percent of total employment in the industry in 1992. The two most important material inputs in this industry were broadwoven fabrics and narrow fabrics, which accounted for 62 percent ($150 million) and 15 percent ($36 million), respectively, of total material costs. Woven neckties, especially from silk, made up the overwhelming majority of products in this industry; all other neckwear, including scarves, leather ties, and mufflers, accounted for less than 2 percent of the value of industry shipments in 1992.

BACKGROUND AND DEVELOPMENT

To a large extent, even before the advent of the "quick response" system, the emergence and eventual growth of the twentieth-century neckwear industry was predicated on consumer trends. An antenna-like ability to stay abreast of fashion and design construction changes proved to be a critical factor in determining whether or not a company survived as an industry leader. Other growth-related influences of comparable importance were: changing fashions and construction of shirts, for which neckwear apparel served as a complementary article of clothing; utilization of breakthrough technological processes, usually first emerging in non-neckwear apparel industries, which led to the progressive marginalization of handmade neckwear in favor of machine-made methods; and the development of a professional/managerial strata in the U.S. work force.

Fashion-Related Growth. Although it is impossible to account for every significant change in neckwear and shirt designs occurring over the course of the twentieth century, it is possible to note the influence exercised by a few dominant styles that, on a decade-by-decade basis, accounted for expansion of the neckwear industry.

At the turn of the century, the two most prominent styles worn with the popular wing collar shirt were the sailor's knot Teck and Joinville ready-tied neckwear. The Teck was available with both straight and pointed ends, while Joinville was a straight-end only model. According to a 1900 Sears, Roebuck & Co. catalog, Teck and Joinville ties 6 inches wide and 34 inches long were "the most popular and swellest gentleman's scarf ever produced" and were made from the purest of specially imported woven silk. Such ties were available in an assortment of more than 300 designs and in almost every color and shade.

During the 1910s, the last decade before the appearance of the collar-attached shirt, the white, starched-collar, high-band Belmont shirt was an instant hit. It was worn with a narrow tie whose small knot was conspicuously located at the bottom of the shirt's collar. Also meeting with wide acceptance was the Henley detached collar shirt worn with a wide-body necktie covering much of the shirt's front. Two other new forms of ties were introduced during this period: the butterfly bow and the long tie formed in a sailor's knot.

Around 1920, the civilian collar-attached shirt hit the scene and became an instant success, largely due to demobilized World War I veterans who had worn a version of the shirt in the military and found it noticeably more comfortable than its collar-detached alternative. At about the same time, a highly significant design breakthrough also occurred in the neckwear industry. A technique that incorporated a loose stitch method to sew a bias-cut wool interlining (a line cutting diagonally across a fabric's grain) made possible the development of ties which retained their original shape after being knotted and unknotted. These relatively resilient ties went on to become an industry standard.

In the mid-1920s, marked changes in neckwear colors and fabrics were introduced. Ties were designed to capture the attention of women shoppers, who made up the largest component of consumers responsible for the purchase of men's neckwear items. By the late 1920s, the silk-and-wool tie rose to prominence thanks to its ripple weave design, which imparted a three dimensional effect. Among the growing number of college students, ties had taken hold and become an everyday part of dress, even though preferred styles and fashions differed across geographic regions.

The Great Depression of the 1930s ushered in the first appearance of woolen ties, whose growing popularity threatened the then undisputed reign of silk fabric ties. During this time, the influence of British fashion was at its greatest in the United States, as witnessed by the rise in popularity of two British formal evening wear bow ties: the straight club bow and the satin butterfly bow tied in a narrow knot.

In 1936, improvements in the design and construction of the wash tie led to its gaining widespread acceptance. Wash neckwear worn in a sailor's knot tie or bow tie was now available in a twin-ply design that fortified fabric strength and wrinkle resistance. Other significant advances in the design and construction of wash ties came from the introduction of spiral seams, which increased durability; improvements in bias cut shapes, which permitted a more perfect-looking knot; and hand bar tacking, which eliminated the unraveling of loose stitching during laundering. Due to the popularity of the widespread collar shirt, the wash bow tie and the large knot tie, known as the Windsor knot, rose to prominence.

World War II diverted silk fabric into the manufacture of parachutes, and rayon quickly became the number one tie fabric while wool maintained its solid hold on second. Wool's persistence in the marketplace was a result of its relatively wrinkle-resistant qualities, along with the fact that it was considered extremely fashionable to sport a wool tie to go along with button-down shirt and single-breasted three-button suit. During the same period of the silkless tie, the highly idiosyncratic hand-painted tie, usually with sporting motifs, was introduced and proceeded to become a mainstay for the whole decade.

For the period from 1950 to 1960, three significant design and construction breakthroughs reverberated through the neckwear industry. Washable, nonwrinkle, and no-stretch Dacron knit ties hit the scene in the early 1950s. Next came wash-and-wear all-cotton ties, which, due to a special resin treatment process, retained their original shape and appearance after washing. Around 1957, a more opulent line of what fashion critics referred to as "elegant air" ties became popular. The trouble with these rather expensive ties was their inability to withstand stains. The solution arrived in 1959, when ties were treated with a special finish, namely Scotchgard, that permitted stains to be washed out with plain cold water.

Major Technological Manufacturing Changes. While the neckwear industry has probably never been in the forefront of major technological innovations, it has proven adept at integrating other non-neckwear apparel industry technologies into its production processes.

The appearance of the sewing machine in 1846 prompted a reorganization of the apparel industry in general, and neckwear in particular. The era of the sewing machine served as a bridge between the transformation of the neckwear industry from a handicraft to a form of machine-based mass production. The sewing machine's introduction tended to quicken the pace of the division of labor and job specialization trends spreading through the apparel industry. With the sewing machine serving as the critical operation point in the overall production process, work related to the handling of material prior to and after being sewn was radically overhauled in accordance with a division of labor based on job specialization. The productivity gains made from these changes were staggering.

Before long, technological progress in apparel manufacturing equipment began to take hold of the entire industry, leading to improvements not only in sewing machine technology but also in cutting and finishing operations. Electric-powered portable cutting knives, motor-driven cloth spreading machines, and gas-powered pressing machines displaced such devices as smaller hand-held irons.

Later manufacturing developments included a laser beam-directed cloth cutting process and the integration of computers used for pattern making, grading, and fabric utilization. In addition, the application of computers to other areas of manufacturing operations continued. To gain an appreciation of the impact technological change has had on productivity, a comparison of value added per production worker for the years 1940 and 1989 showed an increase from $10,000 and $44,857 per worker.

Rise of the Managerial/Professional Strata. One of the consequences of long-term economic change in the U.S. was the emergence and growth of a managerial and professional strata. The shirt-and-tie style of dress that was practically mandatory for white collar workers for much of the twentieth century provided a lasting and substantial source of demand for the neckwear industry. New trends at the end of the century, however, were casting doubt on the future stability of this demand.

CURRENT CONDITIONS

While neckwear shipments increased in the first half of the 1990s, there were two signs of trouble ahead for U.S. businesses in this industry. First, new international trade treaties promised to increase the pressure from imported goods on an industry that had historically been vulnerable to foreign competition. Second, relaxed dress-codes in U.S. corporations and a more casual approach to every-day dressing meant that American men were wearing ties less often.

The first half of the 1990s witnessed a major shift in tie styles. In the 1990s, American men preferred to wear ties, when they wore them at all, that made more personal and colorful statements. Out of fashion were the conservatively patterned yellow and red power ties which set the tone in the 1980s. 1990s ties tended to be wider and more brightly colored, and had bolder abstract patterns. Exemplifying these trends was the line of ties designed by the late Grateful Dead leader Jerry Garcia, which were introduced in 1992 and enjoyed record sales after his 1995 death. These ties, perhaps, were as appealing to women—who continued to buy the majority of ties sold in the U.S.—as to men.

INDUSTRY LEADERS

The leading U.S. neckwear manufacturer in the early 1990s was Wemco, Inc., based in New Orleans, Louisiana. Wemco, started in 1925 by the brothers Samuel and Emanuel Pulitzer, continued to be owned by the founders' heirs in the 1990s. At the beginning of the decade, the company had fallen behind fashion trends and began to lose orders from major department stores. A move to revamp the company in the early 1990s led to big new orders from Wal-Mart, as well as a comeback in department-store purchases. Wemco had a work force of about 900 people in 1995, and its sales were estimated at $69 million. All but five of the 27 leading companies engaged primarily in neckwear manufacture in 1995 were privately owned.

WORK FORCE

Employment in the men's and boys' neckwear industry, despite annual fluctuations, remained relatively flat for the period from 1982 to 1994. Total employment in the neckwear industry in 1994 was estimated at about 6,200 workers, approximately 4,600 of whom were classified as production workers. These figures were down considerably from 1992, when total employment stood at 7,500 total workers, and 5,800 production workers. Projections based on Census Bureau figures predicted an increase to 6,800 total workers in 1995, after which employment was expected to remain flat for several years.

The average hourly wage for production workers in the men's and boys' neckwear industry in 1994 was $9.21. This was a relatively high figure for the apparel industry as a whole, but still far below the average of $12.09 per hour for manufacturing industries in general.

AMERICA AND THE WORLD

International trade has long been a contentious issue for the U.S. neckwear industry. From 1974 until 1995, world trade in textiles and apparel was regulated under the Multifiber Arrangement (MFA). Yet only a portion of neckwear category types—not including most silk neckwear categories—were covered by this agreement, and no specific quota structures had been put into effect. For this reason, protectionist-minded U.S. neckwear producers turned to lobbying the U.S. government to impose tariff or import duties, and they met with success.

A trade agreement put into effect from 1981 through 1987, which specified a staged reduction in the level of neckwear tariff duties, highlighted the industry's import vulnerability. The overall results of a report prepared for the NAA by Economic Consulting Services Inc. were less than favorable. The U.S. neckwear industry experienced a sustained decline in the level of domestic profits, production employment fell from 5,300 to 4,800 workers, and, most strikingly, these negative trends occurred over a period when U.S.

consumption of neckwear was on the increase. During the same period, the amount of neckwear imported increased by 356 percent, going from approximately 373 thousand dozen to 1,698 thousand dozen units. The report indicated that Korean and Chinese neckwear manufacturers gained the most market share throughout the period.

The 1993 passage of the Uruguay Round of the General Agreement on Tariffs and Trade (GATT) meant that the provisions contained in the MFA were to be supplanted and phased out gradually over the course of ten years, from 1995 to 2005. Much to the displeasure of the NAA, the terms of the GATT called for a significant reduction in worldwide tariff duties. Difficult as it is to separate fact from speculation, in light of the less than positive results experienced by the industry during the previous period of falling import tariffs, the implementation of the provisions called for by GATT was not a source of optimism for U.S. manufacturers

One important response undertaken by U.S. neckwear manufacturers to counter the gains made by lower priced import competition was to take advantage of tariff provision 9802 (formerly 807), as set forth by the Harmonized Tariff Schedule of the United States (HTSUS). The provision allows foreign factories to assemble finished neckwear from U.S. components, which are then reimported into the U.S. domestic market with duty charged only on the foreign value added. In the past, Mexico and the Caribbean Basin countries were the largest recipients of HTSUS 9802 trade. With the passage of NAFTA, Caribbean Basin countries expressed concern that 9802 economic activity in their region would shift eventually to Mexico's advantage.

RESEARCH AND TECHNOLOGY

Beginning in the late 1980s, neckwear establishments, like all segments of the apparel industry group, invested heavily in state-of-the-art communications systems that rapidly transmit and respond to information about consumer preferences in the marketplace. These information technology systems, together with attempts to shorten the production cycle and reduce in-process inventories, formed a consumer-driven strategy, coined ''quick response,'' increasingly adopted by U.S. apparel manufacturers. The adoption of ''quick response'' systems was often a result of pressure from wholesalers and retailers, who were determined to accelerate shipments of hot-selling items and shorten the time required to respond to changing consumer preferences.

In addition to quick response systems, neckwear firms directed major investments at computer-controlled automated machines. Such efforts were undertaken in order to increase productivity and secure production efficiencies in the areas of design, cutting, embroidery, sewing, finishing, ticketing, and various distribution operations. Independent of the particular area of operation, most investment projects were undertaken with the intention of reducing the labor-time component per task, which remained excessively high compared to other nonapparel industry group standards. Typically, larger neckwear firms, because of their economies of scale and access to internal financing, were better positioned to implement high-cost technological advances. As a result, the pattern of technological change was anything but uniform across all neckwear establishments.

FURTHER READING

Arpan, Jeffery S., Jose de la Torres, and Brian Toyne. *The U.S. Apparel Industry: International Challenge, Domestic Response.* Atlanta: Business Publishing Division, Georgia State University, 1982.

Button, Graham. ''Tieing One On.'' *Forbes,* 23 October 1995.

Corbin, Harry A.. *The Men's Clothing Industry: Colonial Through Modern Times.* New York: Fairchild Publications Inc., 1970.

Darnay, Arsen J., ed. *Manufacturing USA.* 5th ed. Detroit: Gale Research, 1996.

Focus: An Economic Profile of the Apparel Industry. Arlington, VA: American Apparel Manufacturers Association, 1992.

Poole, Claire. ''Family Ties.'' *Forbes,* 26 April 1993.

Schoeffler, O. E., and William Gale. *Esquire's Encyclopedia of 20th Century Men's Fashions.* New York: McGraw-Hill, Inc., 1973.

Statement of the Neckwear Association of America, Inc., in Connection With the Uruguay Round Market Access Negotiations. Economic Consulting Services Inc., 1989.

U.S. Department Commerce. International Trade Administration. *U.S. Industrial Outlook 1994.* Washington: GPO, 1994.

—Daniel King, updated by Jonathan Mogul

SIC 2325

MEN'S AND BOYS' SEPARATE TROUSERS AND SLACKS

This category includes establishments primarily engaged in manufacturing men's and boys' separate trousers and slacks from purchased woven or knit fabrics, including jeans, dungarees, and jean-cut casual slacks. Establishments primarily engaged in manufacturing complete suits are classified in **SIC 2311: Men's and Boys' Suits, Coats, and Overcoats;** those manufacturing workpants (excluding jeans and dungarees) are classified in **SIC 2326: Men's and Boys' Work Clothing.** Knitting mills primarily engaged in manufacturing men's and boys' separate trousers and slacks are classified in **SIC 2253: Knit Outerwear Mills.**

INDUSTRY SNAPSHOT

During the first half of the 1990s, the value of shipments by U.S. companies making men's and boys' trousers and slacks rose steadily, while employment levels remained flat. If aggregate statistics suggested stable conditions, these years were in fact, however, a period of substantial transformation in this industry.

Pressures for change in the industry came from a number of different sources. First, shifts in the nature of consumer demand, especially a growing preference for casual clothes, led manufacturers to introduce new lines and new products in the early 1990s. Second, concentration in the U.S. retail industry meant that manufacturers of pants had fewer potential retailers with whom to deal, and this process, consequently, gave greater leverage to those powerful chains that remained. In response to retailers' demands for cheaper goods and faster replenishment, manufacturers invested in new communications technologies and developed new methods of production. Finally, U.S. manufacturers had to compete for space on retailers' shelves with cheaply produced imported pants—a trend that was likely to intensify in the aftermath of the implementation of new international trade agreements in the mid-1990s. One response to pressure from foreign competitors which U.S. firms adopted was to downsize domestic production and base an increasing share of production off-shore.

ORGANIZATION AND STRUCTURE

In 1992 approximately 424 establishments owned by 278 companies were engaged in the production of men's and boys' trousers and slacks. Despite the large number of enterprises, this was a relatively highly concentrated industry, as the four largest manufacturers produced 60 percent of industry shipments. The industry was concentrated geographically in the South and Southeast of the United States. Texas led the way with almost 20 percent of all industry employment, followed by Tennessee, Georgia, and Alabama, each with just over 10 percent.

Men's and boys' jeans (including jean-cut casual slacks) was the most important major product class for this industry, accounting for 64 percent of the value of industry shipments; men's and boys' separate dress and sport trousers, pants, and slacks accounted for 26 percent; and about 10 percent was accounted for by contract or commission work on various product categories. By far the most important material used in this industry was broadwoven fabric; this fabric made up 78 percent ($1.539 billion) of total material costs for the industry.

Establishments in this industry sold their goods to department stores, specialty clothing shops, mass merchandisers, and discount chains. In addition, a number of leading pants manufacturers were expanding their own network of brand-name retail outlets. In the late 1980s and early 1990s, there was substantial concentration among U.S. apparel retailers as a result bankruptcies and consolidation. Those remaining retail chains controlled a larger share of the market and enjoyed greater leverage in their relationships with manufacturers.

BACKGROUND AND DEVELOPMENT

In colonial America, the trousers worn by members of the elite classes were, in part, a means of denoting social status and wealth. Typically, these trousers, or breeches, as they were then called, were produced by highly skilled craftsmen. Although they had utilitarian function, no effort was spared in trying to embellish these slacks, which were made from the finest of fabrics and decorated with ornaments of distinction.

The outcome of the American Revolution thrust an emergent and growing middle class, composed of industrialists, merchants, storekeepers, and their various assistants or professionals, to the forefront of political and economic activity and had a profound impact on men's fashion. The fashions of the European nobility were quickly discarded, coming to be seen as the garb of counter revolutionaries. Gone were ornately designed trousers. Garments manufactured by U.S. producers gained prominence, while those woven from imported fabrics were looked upon with political disfavor. Simplicity and utility were central to what was regarded as "good taste" in dress. The day George Washington was inaugurated as the first president of the United States, he wore a suit coat and pants of fine dark brown broadcloth woven in one of the regional hotbeds of the American Revolution— Worcester, Massachusetts.

The taste among American men for utilitarian design contributed to new production and commercial methods in the industry. Tailors began to cut pants in batches and, after sewing them, store them as inventory on demand or display them on retailers' shelves. Advertisers attempted to drum up demand for these ready-made goods. In Boston, George W. Simmons made extensive use of newspaper advertising when, in 1842, he began to promote slacks using enclosed window displays rather than simply hanging or stacking trousers outside his shop. Simmons was also reported to have launched balloons announcing sales and to have established a successful mail order department. Similar efforts, using various novel forms of advertising meant to enhance brand recognition, were undertaken by Jacob Reed and Brooks Brothers.

Almost from the end of the American Revolution until 1860, the embryonic U.S. apparel industry, including the trouser business, was nurtured by a highly protectionist government policy. Until 1816, the duty for imported slacks stood at 25 percent. By 1828 it had reached 50 percent, where it remained until 1860. During the same period, an additional tariff was applied when imported trousers arrived on U.S. shores in foreign ships.

After 1860 U.S. producers believed they could hold their own against foreign competitors. More than one-half a century of protection had provided the industry with the necessary breathing space to mature and eventually enter the global marketplace with a world-class level of productivity. Confidence in the industry's second-to-none productivity level was warranted, due primarily to the introduction and diffusion of sewing machine technology by the late 1850s, which decreased labor time and, consequently, costs of finished garments.

From the standpoint of the workers however, the sewing machine's productivity-enhancing virtues were anything but a benefit. The widespread diffusion of the sewing machine quickly eliminated the need for highly paid skilled laborers performing hand sewing operations. At the same time it permitted the employment of semiskilled employees, whose wages gravitated towards a bare subsistence level. Whether employed in domestic tenement quarters or in factory sweat shops, working conditions were abysmal, health hazards went unchecked, and child labor was common. For the next couple of decades, the ranks of semiskilled workers grew, and working conditions became more miserable with each successive wave of immigration. It was not until the formation of apparel-based trade unions that such conditions began to be combated.

Until the outbreak of the Civil War, manufacturers and retailers of ready-made pants confronted a persistent problem—the absence of any reliable sizing standards to assure that mass-produced clothing would fit properly. The solution arrived from a study performed by the U.S. Army's Philadelphia Quartermaster Depot, which had collected body size measurement data on over a million recruits and conscripts. The depot organized these measurements into tables of standard body proportions and thus created a set of data that could be readily applied to the standardization of manufactured civilian garments.

Body sizing standards, coupled with the diffusion of sewing machine technology, radically transformed the clothing industry by increasing the division of labor. By 1895 these changes resulted in what came to be known as the "bundle system" of production, where one or more workers performed a single operation on a repetitive basis. Once the bundle limit was reached, the work in process was passed on to the next station of workers performing another distinct operation. This process would continue until the entire trouser garment was completed. The bundle system proved to be an enduring and flexible method of production, capable of undergoing refinement, modification and integration with new technologies. It was still in widespread use throughout the apparel industry in the mid-1990s.

The 1880s witnessed the first major improvement in the non-sewing processes, when the sword knife and slotted table were introduced into cutting rooms. Later came the electrically operated knife, which though immobile, proved to be the forerunner of the more modern, portable, electrically driven assortment of cutting tools. In turn, the widespread application of portable rotary and reciprocating electric knives would not have been possible without earlier advances in the construction of electric motors. In the late 1890s, pressing operations were transformed. Operations reliant upon gas- and coal-heated irons were replaced first by the steam pressing iron and later the steam pressing machine.

New technological developments late in the twentieth century featured a laser beam-directed cloth-cutting process along with the integration of computers utilized for pattern making, grading, and fabric selection. The extension of computer-aided job processes to most areas of trouser production was expected to continue. Such efforts were in step with the industry's drive to raise the level of productivity, a measure usually captured by changes in the value added per production worker.

CURRENT CONDITIONS

The value of shipments of men's and boys' trousers and slacks by U.S. manufacturers stood at $7.23

billion in 1994, according to Census Bureau statistics. This figure marked a substantial rise from 1990, when shipments were valued at $5.66 billion. By 1998 shipment values were expected to increase further to about $7.87 billion. In the longer run, growth in output appeared less impressive, as 1990 represented a lowpoint after several years of decline, from a total of $6.01 billion in 1987, the first year statistics were recorded for this category of apparel.

The two major product categories in this industry fared very differently over the early 1990s. Annual unit shipments of dress and sport trousers declined between 1991 and 1995, from 103 million to 92 million, while the value of these garments fell from $1.57 billion to $1.54 billion. Shipments of jeans and jean-cut casual pants, on the other hand, climbed steadily, from 237 million to 311 million units, and shipment values increased from $3.47 billion to $4.49 billion. These changes were the results of attempts by American pants manufacturers to adapt to the shifting clothing habits of American men, in a society where informal dress was increasingly common in both business and leisure contexts. This was a trend that showed every sign of continuing: a Levi Strauss Associates executive, for example, estimated that by the year 2000, one-half of all U.S. corporations would no longer require formal dress at all. In order to capitalize, major manufacturers like Levi Strauss and Haggar Corp. were planning to introduce new lines of pants in the mid-1990s that would straddle the division between casual and formal wear.

An important product innovation in the early 1990s was the introduction of wrinkle-free cotton pants. These pants, treated with a chemical finish to prevent wrinkling, were first marketed in 1989 by Farah Inc. By the mid-1990s all other major manufacturers had introduced their own wrinkle-free products, which according to 1993 estimates, represented the fastest growing segment of the domestic men's apparel market.

Apparent U.S. consumption of men's pants of all kinds —which includes shorts, sweatpants, and workpants not included in this industry classification—rose from $8.73 billion to $10.97 billion between 1991 and 1995. How were U.S. manufacturers striving to maintain their share of this market in the face of competition from foreign manufacturers? One widespread strategy was to take advantage of tariff provision 9802 (formerly 807), of the Harmonized Tariff Schedule of the United States (HTSUS). This provision allows U.S manufacturers to ship cut pieces offshore to Caribbean Basin countries, where they are sewn, either by outside contractors or in company-owned factories, and then re-imported to the United States with duty assessed only upon the value added outside the United States. The value of such "807" imports of men's and boys' pants more than doubled between 1991 and 1995, rising from $696 million to $1.7 billion. The other side of this process, of course, was the downsizing of U.S. manufacturing, involving closure of assembly plants and layoffs of workers. This trend was more pronounced for manufacturing of formal pants, which require considerably more labor than jeans. One major manufacturer, Farah Inc., had shifted all sewing and finishing operations offshore by 1996.

Some of the same manufacturers, however, were also developing strategies that pointed in the direction of increasing the competitiveness of domestic manufacturing operations. Known as "quick response," these strategies were aimed at enhancing the flexibility of manufacturers in responding to changing buying habits of consumers and changing demands of retailers. The most widely adopted quick response strategy was the development of state-of-the-art communications networks, known as electronic data interchange (EDI), which link the computer systems of manufacturers to retailers and allow manufacturers almost instant access to information about retail sales of their items. Manufacturers could immediately adjust production schedules and shipments in accord with this data.

Manufacturers were also attempting to speed-up the production-cycle, in order to take full advantage of their access to data about market conditions. A far-reaching, but not very widely implemented strategy for meeting this goal was the replacement of the long-standing bundle system with "modular" systems of production. In modular systems, teams of multi-skilled operators work together to sew an entire pair of pants. Pay is based on the entire team's output, rather than an individual piece-rate, giving incentive for team-members to shift tasks when backlogs develop and to focus on maximizing the number of finished pieces produced by the whole team, rather than the number of individual operations performed. While individual labor productivity may not be quite as high as in the progressive bundle system, where each operator performs just one specialized task, in-process inventory levels are reduced, and the production cycle for assembly of an entire garment is greatly accelerated. Although industry analysts, industry leaders, and unions began to advocate for adoption of modular production as a key part of quick response strategies as far back as the 1980s, manufacturers were slow to undertake such a dramatic overhaul of their management and human resources practices. A study of firms from a number of

different branches of the apparel industry in early 1992 revealed that less than 10 percent of all garments were produced according to the modular system. At least one major company in the trousers and slacks industry, however, Levi Strauss, adopted the modular production with enthusiasm in the mid-1990s.

INDUSTRY LEADERS

The leading U.S. manufacturers of men's and boys' trousers and slacks in the mid-1990s were Levi Strauss Associates (with its "Levi's" and "Dockers" brand names), V.F. Corporation ("Wrangler," "Rustler" and "Lee"), Haggar Corp. ("Haggar" and "St. James"), and Farah Inc. ("Savane," "Farah" and "John Henry"). V.F. Corp. had the largest share of the domestic jeans market, with 30 percent. Levi Strauss was second overall in jeans, although its Levi's brand was the best-selling individual brand. Levi Strauss led in casual pants, with its Dockers brand, followed by Haggar, which led in domestic sales of formal pants.

Levi Strauss, still owned by the descendants of its founder, was the largest brand-name apparel manufacturer in the world in the mid-1990s. The company hoped to complement its extremely successful Levi's and Dockers brand names by introducing a third major line of pants in late 1996, Slates, which were to compete in the "corporate casual" market. Levi-Strauss was clearly in a position to benefit from the turn towards more casual business clothing in the 1990s and successfully pressed its advantage by aggressively marketing its products via fashion shows, seminars, and video-tapes targeted at thousands of corporate employers. Another strong suit of the company was the prestige of its Levi's brand name among foreign consumers, which enabled it to sell blue-jeans as a fashion item at considerably higher prices than domestically. As a result of these factors, Levi Strauss's sales were strong throughout the 1990s, peaking at $6.7 billion in 1995. Levi Strauss also earned notoriety in the 1990s for its "values-based" approach to management, based on encouraging employee input in decision-making, diversifying management personnel, and applying ethical standards in foreign sourcing operations.

Both V.F. and Haggar also enjoyed strong sales in the mid-1990s. A key to VF's success was the performance of its quick response computer links to major retailers, such as J.C. Penney and Wal-Mart. VF's computer center received nightly data from these retailers about the day's sales and immediately set the process in motion to replenish the sold products. Replacements for a pair of jeans sold on a Tuesday were thus often on the retailer's shelf by Thursday. The effectiveness of this system was seen by some analysts as the cause of VF's growing edge in domestic jeans sales over Levi Strauss, which had begun implementing plans to emulate its competitor by the mid-1990s. Haggar's success in the first half of the 1990s was at least partly due to its aggressive marketing of wrinkle-free cotton pants. Both VF and Haggar, despite their strong sales, were in the process of downsizing domestic production in the mid-1990s.

WORK FORCE

Total employment in the men's and boys' trousers and slacks industry stood at 82,200 people in 1994, 71,900 of whom were production workers. These figures represented a continuation of the trend of flat employment levels through the first half of the 1990s, following a steep decline in the late 1980s. Projections for the second half of the 1990s, based on Census Bureau statistics, predicted a new round of sharp reductions in employment. Employment was expected to drop to 68,800 by 1998. Average hourly wages for production workers in this industry in 1994 were $7.03, up from $5.88 in 1987, but still far below the average of $12.09 for all manufacturing jobs. Wages were only expected to increase to $7.81 per hour by 1998. Major employers in this industry reported that only small minorities of their workers were covered by collective bargaining agreements.

AMERICA AND THE WORLD

Both imports and exports of men's and boys' pants—including shorts, sweatpants and workpants—climbed over the first half of the 1990s. In 1995 U.S. manufacturers exported 234 million pairs of pants valued at $882 million dollars. By contrast, 1991 exports were just 170 million pairs at $598 million. Exports have been aided by the strong brand-recognition enjoyed by U.S. makers in many parts of the world.

Import penetration levels, measured according to value, for men's and boys' pants rose slightly in the first half of the 1990s, from 30.3 percent in 1991 to 34.3 percent in 1995. This was a relatively low level compared to other sectors of the apparel industry, in which import penetration levels often approach or exceed 50 percent. Still, absolute levels of pants imports increased steadily in the 1990s at a slightly faster rate than overall consumption. In 1991, the United States imported 358 million pairs of pants valued at $2.65 billion; by 1995 these figures stood at 581 million and $3.76 billion.

With the passage of the North American Free Trade Agreement (NAFTA) and the Agreement on Textiles and Clothing (ATC) in the mid-1990s, competition from foreign manufacturers and pressures to

downsize domestic operations were likely to increase. The former lifted quotas and removed some tariffs on apparel imports from Mexico. The latter called for accelerated growth in quota levels for apparel imports from other countries and for the eventual elimination of quotas by the year 2005.

RESEARCH AND TECHNOLOGY

In addition to the quick response system, men's and boys' trousers and slacks firms directed major investments at computer-controlled automated machinery in an effort to increase productivity and secure production efficiencies in the areas of design, cutting, embroidery, sewing, finishing, ticketing, and various distribution operations. Independent of the particular area of operation, most investment projects were undertaken with the intention of reducing the labor-time component per task, which remained excessively high relative to other nonapparel industry group standards. Because of their economies of scale and access to internally generated funds, the larger trousers and slacks firms have been better positioned to implement technological advances. This has resulted in a pattern of technological change that is highly uneven across the entire men's and boys' slacks industry.

FURTHER READING

Arpan, Jeffery S., Jose de la Torres, and Brian Toyne. *The U.S. Apparel Industry: International Challenge, Domestic Response.* Atlanta: Business Publishing Division, College of Business Administration Georgia State University, 1982.

Canedy, Dana. "Struggling to Duplicate a Success." *New York Times.* 9 October 1996.

Corbin, Harry A. *The Men's Clothing Industry: Colonial Through Modern Times.* New York: Fairchild Publications Inc., 1970.

Darnay, Arsen J., ed. *Manufacturing USA.* 5th ed. Detroit: Gale Research, 1996.

Dunlop, John T., and David Weil. "Diffusion and Performance of Modular Production in the U.S. Apparel Industry." *Industrial Relations,* July 1996.

Focus: An Economic Profile of the Apparel Industry. Arlington, VA: American Apparel Manufacturers Association, 1992.

Forest, Stephanie Anderson. "Pumping No-Iron Slacks." *Business Week,* 7 February 1994.

Himmelstein, Linda, and Nancy Walser. "Levi's Versus the Dress Code." *Business Week,* 1 April 1996.

Lenzner, Robert, and Stephen S. Johnson. "A Few Yards of Denim and Five Copper Rivets." *Forbes,* 26 February 1996.

Popkin, Martin, E. *Manufacture of Men's Clothing.* New York: Isaac Pittman & Sons, 1929.

Russell, Mitchell. "Managing by Values." *Business Week,* 1 August 1994.

Schoeffler, O. E., and William Gale. *Esquire's Encyclopedia of 20th Century Men's Fashions.* New York: McGraw-Hill, Inc., 1973.

U.S. Bureau of the Census. *Current Industrial Reports: Apparel.* Available from http://www.census.gov/cir/www/mq23a.html.

U.S. Department of Commerce. International Trade Administration. *U.S. Industrial Outlook 1993.* Washington: GPO, 1993.

U.S. International Trade Commission. *Industry and Trade Summary.* Washington, 1995. Available from http://www.usitc.gov/ittr.htm.

Weber, Joseph. "Just Get it to the Stores on Time." *Business Week,* 6 March 1995.

—Daniel King, updated by Jonathan Mogul

SIC 2326

MEN'S AND BOYS' WORK CLOTHING

This category includes establishments primarily engaged in manufacturing men's and boys' work shirts, workpants (excluding jeans and dungarees), other work clothing, and washable service apparel. Establishments primarily engaged in manufacturing separate trousers and slacks (including jeans and dungarees) are classified in **SIC 2325: Men's and Boys' Separate Trousers and Slacks.**

INDUSTRY SNAPSHOT

About 225 establishments active in the manufacture of men's and boys' work clothing accounted for an inflation adjusted value of total product shipments of $1.2 billion in 1992. This figure, though up by 6.1 percent from the previous 1991, remained in line with the five year declining trend, which peaked during 1987 and 1988 and was some 13.2 percent below the peak period's level of performance. When viewed over a five year period covering 1987-1992, the annual percentage change in the inflation adjusted value of total product shipments fell by an average of 2.2 percent. Total product shipments reached $1.7 billion in 1994. In 1995, the industry employed roughly 26,500 individuals, down from 28,500 in 1994, and down even further from 30,000 in 1993.

In certain cases, attempts to note statistical trends past 1987 meet with difficulties as this was the year that the U.S. Department of Commerce's Bureau of

Census rearranged some of the apparel industries' categories. Prior to 1987, the men's and boys' work clothing was classified as SIC 2328 and included jeans and dungarees among its product classifications. In 1987 jeans and dungarees were excluded from men's and boys' work clothes and assigned to **SIC 2325: Men's and Boys' Separate Trousers and Slacks.**

Unlike other apparel industries, which are variously categorized within the apparel industry group according to gender, age, and body part specific garments, the men's and boys' work clothes industry produced apparel garments extending from the neck down to the feet. These included: work aprons, coveralls, work jackets and laboratory coats, institutionalized medical uniforms, work overalls and overall jackets, work pants, washable service industry apparel, work shirts, and non-tailored uniforms.

Following years of consecutive growth, the men's and boys' work clothing industry garnered a reputation for being the only recession-proof industry. This was in stark contrast to other industries within the apparel group who were highly susceptible to business cycle swings. Things changed when the work wear industry entered a protracted period of stagnant to falling growth beginning with the recession of 1981-1982. Well into the 1990s the industry had yet to regain the level of its former years of prosperity.

To a great extent the industry's woes were precipitated from its demand side. A steady and prolonged fall-off of its once core industrial and agricultural customer base left the industry in shambles. This resulted in considerable intra-industry price competition and a run-up in unused manufacturing capacity. These same economic forces were also responsible for the industry's downsizing and served to explain why the total number of manufacturing establishments went down from 255 in 1987 to approximately 225 in 1992, to a decline of 11.8 percent. In 1993, there were a total of 275 establishments engaged in some aspect the of men's and boys' work clothing industry, most of which had over 50 employees.

A glance at the movement of some of the industry's more dominant product categories for the period of 1981-1990 provided further evidence of stagnation and decline. In terms of consumer purchases of men's work pants, for 1986-1990 the average annual volume fell to 16.4 million units, declining by about 13.5 percent from the previous five years. For the category of men's overalls, during 1986-1990 the annual volume of consumer purchases averaged 6.7 million units, a decline of 18.3 percent from the previous five years. Finally, for the category of men's work shirts, for

1986-1990 the average annual volume of consumer purchases was 31.6 million units, a decline of 11.5 percent from the previous five years. In fact, it wasn't until 1992 that shipment value of men's and boys' work clothing began to reach levels comparable to those in 1987 and 1988. In 1993, the industry shipments surpassed $1.6 billion; in 1994 the value of shipment rose to $1.7 billion and in 1995 shipments reached nearly $1.8 billion.

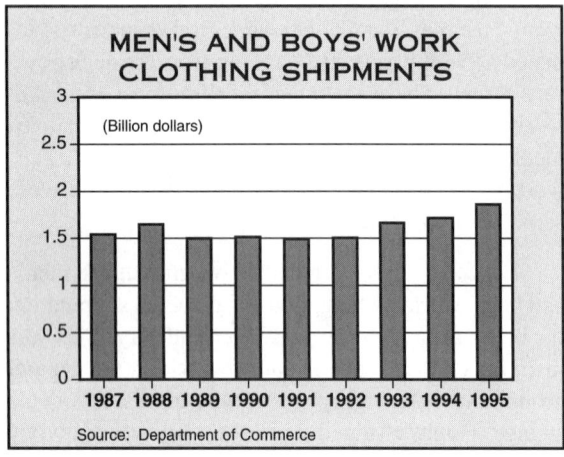

MEN'S AND BOYS' WORK CLOTHING SHIPMENTS

(Billion dollars)

1987 1988 1989 1990 1991 1992 1993 1994 1995

Source: Department of Commerce

Unlike what was happening in other apparel industries, the men's and boys' work clothing industry had remained relatively immune from the deluge of imports wreaking havoc on the domestic markets of their apparel counterparts. On the work wear industry's input side however, imports were playing an important role as more companies were turning to inputs to lower labor and material costs so as to reverse the long term slide in profit margins. To this end the "outsourcing" of work formerly performed within establishments to contractors outside U.S. borders had become an established trend.

One major demand-side development, which was expected to fill the void left by the fall-off in industrial/agricultural markets, was the ongoing structural shift toward a service based economy. Such a movement carried with it the potential for opening up a vast areas of untapped demand for washable nontailored uniforms in health care facilities, personal care services, fast food chains and other food preparation and service institutions. In addition, a trend towards the wearing of uniforms by corporations seeking to enhance their employees and company image was afoot. Viewed as a strategy to build customer recognition and loyalty, the wearing of corporate uniforms had already become an established trend among some airlines, banks, fitness centers, retail chain stores, and major hotels.

ORGANIZATION AND STRUCTURE

In 1993 approximately 275 establishments were active in the production and/or sales men's and boys' work clothing. The largest concentrations of the industry's establishments were located in the East South Central, West South Central, and South Atlantic regions of the United States.

In 1996, the industry's dominant companies were: VF Corp.'s Tennessee-based Red Kap Industries, with $420 million in sales and 6,000 employees; Missouri-based Angelica Uniform Group, with $170 million in sales and 3,000 employees; Georgia-based Riverside Manufacturing Co., with $240 million in sales and 2,400 employees; Florida-based Superior Surgical Mfg. Co. Inc., with $135 million in sales and 1,900 employees; and Missouri-based Unitog Co., with $214 million in sales and 3,100 employees. Founded in 1932, Unitog has experienced 63 years of consecutive growth.

Input data available from 1982 and 1987 indicated that the primary materials consumed by the men's and boys' work clothing industry when ranked by cost were: materials, parts, containers, and supplies; broadwoven fabrics; and knit fabrics. The primary sources of input supply were from imports, broadwoven fabric mills, apparel made from purchased materials, and knit fabric mills. For the same two years, the share of the industry's total output disaggregated by its major product category indicated that men's and boys' work shirts accounted for 23.5 percent; men's and boys' work clothing and washable service apparel registered 58.3 percent; contract and commission work on men's and boys' work clothing in general was 9.5 percent; and men's and boys' work clothing not specified by any kind accounted for 8.7 percent.

During the late 1980s and into the 1990s, the distribution network servicing the men's and boys' work clothing industry was undergoing a fundamental transformation. For articles like washable uniforms and service related apparel, laundry rental companies had historically been the major source of distribution to large companies. But when corporate demand for a more customized look requiring a greater assortment of new fabrics, styles, and colors started to reverberate through the industry, many of the industry's larger firms bypassed the traditional laundry rental channel and opened their own corporate accounts, through which they sold directly to the wearing customer. As a result, domestic fabric mills, who supplied materials to the work clothing industry, also began a closer working relationship with work wear manufacturers in a joint effort meant to better serve the industry's developing corporate accounts.

For individual purchases of work clothes, mass merchandisers and discount outlets accounted for the largest share of sales, followed by smaller specialty stores located outside of major urban areas. Catalog sales picked up noticeably during the late 1980s and 1990s and were expected to show continued strength into the future. A development of a more recent kind featured the appearance of farm/fleet stores. These were large stores located in rural areas which carried a wide assortment of work related items ranging from work clothes to farm equipment. The stores' core customer base consisted of farmers and truckers who wore functional work clothes for occupational reasons. Two major operators active throughout the Midwest were Blain Farm & Fleet and Mills Farm & Fleet.

BACKGROUND AND DEVELOPMENT

In a less spectacular manner, the origins of the ready-to-wear work clothes industry followed the historical trajectory of the more colorful mens' apparel industry. With the onset of the industrial era in the early nineteenth century spurring the transformation from rural to urban life, the social demand for working apparel soon surpassed the efforts of custom tailors and housewives. In their place developed the early manufacture of mass produced work clothes which, if possible, were typically shunned due to their inferior quality and wearing discomfort. As improvements in fabrics began to seize hold of the men's apparel industry, any notion of their reputed inferiority went to the wayside. During the same period, the widespread diffusion of sewing machine technology provided added impetus to the industry's emergence and boosted its output to unprecedented levels. During the Civil War, an extensive survey compiled on the height and chest measurements of more than one million soldiers provided the first mass of statistical data on the form and build of U.S. men. Immediately after the war these results were made available to producers of men's ready-made work clothes, providing a more scientific basis on which to improve their fit.

A milestone episode that dramatically accelerated the need for ready-made work clothes occurred with the Gold Rush of 1848. The prospect of getting rich drew thousands of men westward to pan or mine for gold. Figuring that these adventurers would need tents for shelter, Levi Strauss journeyed to California with a supply of heavy fabrics for tent making. Among these fabrics was a French material referred to as ''de Nime,'' which U.S. tongues later pronounced as ''denim.'' Aware that a need for durable work clothes was not being met, Strauss began to make workpants from denim that featured large back pockets to hold mining tools. By adding metal rivets to strengthen the durability of the pockets, Strauss hit on an idea that brought him almost instant success—and the men's work clothes industry started booming. The continued westward migration, not just in California but in the prairie and mountain states, developed into a steady market for ready-made work clothes for decades to come. To meet the growing demand, large work clothes manufacturing centers sprung up in Chicago and St. Louis.

Beginning near the early twentieth century, the steady growth of a work force comprised of semi-skilled and unskilled laborers engaged in various mass production-related occupations—across the entire range of manufacturing and agricultural industries—proved a boon to work clothes producers. After World War II, an unprecedented rise in the consumption of consumer durables was matched by the growth of a repair industry whose workers, more often than not, were outfitted with non-tailored work uniforms. To the envy of the non-work clothes apparel industries who regularly incurred the economic vicissitudes of the traditional business cycle, the work clothes industry proceeded along its expansionary path in a steady manner until the onset of its stagnation period commencing in the early 1980s.

CURRENT CONDITIONS

The highly anticipated salvation of the men's and boys' work clothing industry was expected to come in the form of the U.S. economy's structural shift to service producing industries and occupations where career/work apparel tended to be the norm. According to BLS employment projections, approximately nine out of every 10 new jobs were to be added in service providing industries such as transportation, communications, public utilities, trade, health care, finance, insurance, real estate, food handling and production, janitors, and government. At the same time, the increasing trend towards a cultural climate of corporate uniformed-employees—as a means to foster brand recognition and customer loyalty—was already breathing new life into the industry as well as holding out the promise of future growth.

A question remained as to whether the service economy rescue scenario would arrive in time to stem the industry's downsizing. Being the first to invest in the latest apparel technologies, the larger firms were better positioned to seize the day and offer a greater volume of high quality garments at lower cost than their lesser endowed rivals. No doubt the industry's future looked bright, but whether the larger firms would cast an obliterating shadow over their smaller competitors remained uncertain.

Third quarter 1996 figures revealed a decline in the productions of all segments of the men's and boys' work clothing industry. Production of work jackets fell 21 percent from third quarter 1995; production of work shirts dropped 7 percent; production of work pants declined 4 percent; and production of washable service apparel tumbled 10 percent.

A new World Trade Organization (WTO) was established in 1995, and the Multifiber Arrangement (MFA) which allowed importing countries to limit the flow of imports from lower cost, developing countries was replaced by the Agreement on Textiles and Clothing (ATC), which required the phasing out of MFA quotas over a ten-year period. According to Linda Shelton in an *Industry, Trade, and Technology Review* report, "The elimination of MFA quotas likely will have a significant impact on the U.S. textile and apparel sector given the level of protection that such restrictions have provided domestic producers over the past two decades." Since the U.S. has until 2005 to implement the ATC, the legislation's impact on the men's and boys' work clothing industry may not be realized for several years.

WORK FORCE

Total employment in the men's and boys' work clothing industry was 33,000 in 1987, of which 29,000 were classified as production workers. By 1992, total employment had fallen to 31,100, of which 27,300 were production workers. For the entire period total employment fell by 5.8 percent while production employment declined slightly more by 5.9 percent. From 1987-1992 industry real wages had fallen without interruption, while value added per production worker rose, though not in a dramatic manner, suggesting that productivity improvements and real wages were moving in opposite directions. In 1993, the number of individuals employed in the industry rose slightly to 32,500.

In 1990, the dominant occupational categories for the work clothes industry were: sewing machine operators; inspectors, precision inspectors, and testers; blue collar work supervisors; pressing machine operators; hand packers and packagers; and hand cutters and trimmers. Close to 56 percent of the work force was engaged in sewing operations, while the remaining categories individually fell within the 3.1 to 2 range. According to an occupational survey undertaken by the of Bureau Labor Statistics (BLS), all of the major occupational categories within the work clothes industry were forecasted to experience significant declines by the year 2005. Given the more or less forward trajectory of the industry's productivity trend, the decline in sewing machine operators was expected to encounter the steepest decline.

Compared to their employment rates in the overall manufacturing sector, the participation rates of women and Hispanic workers within the industry exceed their national counterparts, while the opposite is true for African American workers. In 1995 women comprised 70 percent of this industry's work force compared to a national average of 31.6 percent of women in manufacturing industries. Hispanic workers accounted for 24 percent of the industry's work force compared to a national average of 10.2 percent. The percentage of African American workers was 15 percent, slightly greater than the national average of 10 percent of African Americans in manufacturing industries. Taken collectively, over 1 million minority workers were active in the apparel industry's work force, while over 20 million worked in manufacturing industries in general.

FURTHER READING

Apparel Import Digest. Arlington, VA: American Apparel Manufacturers Association, 1997.

Apparel Industry Trends. Arlington, VA: American Apparel Manufacturers Association, March 1997.

Arnold, Pauline, and Percival White. *Clothes and Cloth: America's Apparel Business.* New York: Holiday House Publishers, 1961.

de Marly, Diana. *Working Dress: A History of Occupational Clothing.* New York: Holmes and Meier Publishers, Inc., 1986.

Fairchild Fact File: Men's Career/Work Wear. New York: Market Research Division, Fairchild Publications, 1987.

Focus: An Economic Profile of the Apparel Industry. Arlington, VA: American Apparel Manufacturers Association, 1993.

Focus: An Economic Profile of the Apparel Industry. Arlington, VA: American Apparel Manufacturers Association, 1996.

Greco, Monica. "63 Years of Growth." *Apparel Industry,* December 1995.

Jarnow, Jeannette, and Miriam Guerreiro. *Inside the Fashion Business.* New York: Macmillan Publishing Company, 1991.

Lehman Brothers. *The Clothes Line,* December 1993.

Manufacturing USA: Industry Analyses, Statistics and Leading Companies, 3rd Edition, Detroit: Gale Research Inc., 1993.

Schoeffler, O.E. and William Gale. *Esquire's Encyclopedia of 20th Century Men's Fashions.* New York: McGraw-Hill Inc., 1973.

Shelton, Linda and Robert Wallace. "World Textile and Apparel Trade: A New Era." *Industry, Trade, and Technology Review,* October 1996.

U.S. Industrial Outlook 1993. Washington: U.S. Department of Commerce, 1993.

Williams-Mitchell, Christobel. *Dressed for the Job: The Story of Occupational Costume,* Poole, United Kingdom: Blandford Press, 1982.

—Daniel King, updated by AnnaMarie Sheldon

SIC 2329

MEN'S AND BOYS' CLOTHING, NOT ELSEWHERE CLASSIFIED

This category includes establishments primarily engaged in manufacturing men's and boys' clothing, not elsewhere classified, from purchased or woven fabrics. These items include, but are not limited to, athletic clothing, bathing suits, down-filled clothing, shorts, nontailored sports clothing, sweaters, athletic uniforms, and windbreakers. Establishments primarily engaged in manufacturing leather and sheep-lined garments are classified in **SIC 2386: Leather and Sheep-Lined Clothing.** Knitting mills primarily engaged in manufacturing outerwear are classified under **SIC 2253: Knit Outwear Mills.**

INDUSTRY SNAPSHOT

Approximately 575 establishments were engaged in the manufacture of men's and boys' clothing, not elsewhere classified, in the early 1990s. As was true for much of the U.S. apparel industry, these establishments were generally small, family-run businesses that faced stiff competition from low-cost imports. In 1994, total industry shipments reached $2.8 billion. In 1995 and 1996, while production declined and import growth decelerated, men's and boys' apparel retail sales grew.

ORGANIZATION AND STRUCTURE

The industry was comprised of manufacturers, contractors, and jobbers. Contractors were independent manufacturers, hired by various, and often competing, manufacturers. Contractors specialized in sewing the garment from pieces provided them, and they were hired by producers that either did not have their own sewing facilities or whose own capacity had been superseded.

Jobbers were design and marketing businesses which were hired to perform specific functions, including purchasing materials, designing patterns, creating samples, cutting material, and hiring contractors to manufacture the product. After purchasing materials needed to produce the pieces, jobbers then sent the cut material to contractors for assembly.

In creating apparel from the purchased materials, manufacturers retained staffs either to produce designs or buy them from freelancers, as well as to purchase the fabric and trimmings. While cutting and sewing the garment was generally performed in the manufacturer's factories, outside contractors were hired when demand for an item exceeded the manufacturer's capacity or shipping deadlines could not be met. For the purposes of this entry, the term "manufacturers" will refer cumulatively to contractors, jobbers, and manufacturers.

BACKGROUND AND DEVELOPMENT

During the 1980s interest in men's fashions increased, augmented by the introduction of several new men's fashion magazines, which featured articles and advertisements centering on stylishly dressed men. During this time, office wear became more comfortable and less formal. Sales of the traditional tailored suit declined slightly as sweaters and sports coats became acceptable in some work environments. As the men's apparel industry grew and diversified, manufacturers and retailers began to target specific markets according to income, age, and education, a strategy already common in the women's fashion industry. Many retailers, from departments stores to mass merchandisers, expanded their men's wear departments, and the industry grew at a faster pace than women's wear throughout the 1980s. This trend continued throughout the 1990s.

As in other sectors of the apparel industry, increased consolidation and the strength of imported clothing were the industry's primary concerns in the early 1990s. Despite the increased competition, however, the value of shipments for men's and boys' clothing had increased from $1.6 billion in 1982 to an estimated $2.3 billion in 1992. Furthermore, employment in the industry had expanded from approximately 44,600 in 1982 to 53,300 in 1990. The economic recession of the early 1990s prompted manufacturers to step up production of moderately priced clothing lines. Many of these lines featured fleece in the form of sweat shirts, jackets, and pants, which offered consumers a particularly comfortable and inexpensive alternative in casual wear.

CURRENT CONDITIONS

The value of men's and boys' apparel production dropped 2 percent in 1996; however, retail sales of men's apparel climbed 7.3 percent, almost twice the growth in 1995, and retail consumption of boys' apparel grew 4.4 percent. While the production of sweat pants, shorts, and sweaters declined in 1996, the production of team sport uniforms grew slightly.

A new World Trade Organization (WTO) was established in 1995, and the Multifiber Arrangement (MFA), which allowed importing countries to limit the flow of imports from lower cost, developing countries, was replaced by the Agreement on Textiles and Clothing (ATC) which required the phasing out of MFA quotas over a ten-year period. According to Linda Shelton in an *Industry, Trade, and Technology Review* report, "The elimination of MFA quotas likely will have a significant impact on the U.S. textile and apparel sector given the level of protection that such restrictions have provided domestic producers over the past two decades." Since the U.S. has until 2005 to implement the ATC, the legislation's impact on the men's and boys' apparel industry may not be realized for several years.

INDUSTRY LEADERS

Russell Corporation, founded in Alabama in 1902, benefited from the trend toward leisure wear, and, in particular, the growing popularity of licensed sportswear. The largest U.S. manufacturer of athletic uniforms in the early 1990s, Russell Corporation was awarded the title of official supplier to major league baseball in 1991. As part of that agreement, Russell Corporation was given the exclusive rights to make and market a line of jerseys and pants—the Authentic Diamond Collection—for the general public. In 1996, Russell reported $1.1 billion in sales and employed approximately 16,800.

Another important presence in the industry was Oregon-based Nike, Inc. Although known primarily as a shoe manufacturer, Nike also began producing a line of sports wear in the late 1980s, which was bolstered by it's reputation as a trend setter in the athletic shoe industry. Spending a reported $233.3 million on advertising in 1991-92, Nike showed revenues of $3.93 billion in 1993. That year, approximately 14 percent of the company's domestic sales, and 25 percent of its international sales, were generated from its apparel lines. Roughly 57 percent of Nike's clothing was manufactured in the United States in the early 1990s, while the remainder was produced in Asia and South America. In early 1996, Nike was awarded a contract to supply jerseys to four National Hockey League teams during the 1996-97 season.

WORK FORCE

Most of those employed in this category (an estimated 49,124 in 1993) were production workers, approximately half of which were union members. The production work position consisted largely of sewing-machine operators, whose average wage in 1993 was $5.85 an hour. In 1995, the average wage for men's and boys' clothing production workers was $7.19. While many manufacturers in this sector of the apparel industry, as with the industry as a whole, were small, family-owned businesses, several large and growing establishments dominated the industry. The average number of employees per establishment in the early 1990s was 66.

A long-time center of the apparel business in the United States, New York was home to the majority of men's and boys' wear manufacturers in the early and mid-1990s. California, however, reported the greatest value of shipments at about $308.6 million. Tennessee reported having the highest number of employees in the industry at about 5,700. Alabama and Pennsylvania also had significant concentrations of workers in this category.

AMERICA AND THE WORLD

In the 1960s, the U.S. men's and boys' apparel industry began to lose significant market share to imports, which offered consumers lower prices and acceptable quality. This trend accelerated in the 1970s, and, by the 1990s, imports had reached all-time highs. Moreover, with U.S. manufacturers relying more heavily on off-shore assembly plants, the industry experienced further losses.

Manufacturers in the Far East represented a significant source of men's apparel. In the 1960s, U.S. apparel makers began moving their manufacturing operations abroad, focusing on Hong Kong, Taiwan, and South Korea, where labor cost was 10W. By the 1980s, however, labor costs in these countries had increased and operations were moved to Bangladesh, Thailand, Pakistan, Indonesia, Malaysia, Sri Lanka, and India. By the early 1990s China had replaced Hong Kong as the greatest supplier of imports to the United States. Hong Kong, Taiwan, and South Korea, as well as China, continued to lose market share to new players and represented only 28 percent of apparel imports in 1995. In the mid-1990's the largest gains in import market share belonged to the Caribbean countries and

Mexico. These countries increased their market share from 20 percent in 1992 to approximately 54 percent in 1996.

The North American Free Trade Agreement (NAFTA)—ratified in 1993 to create a free-trade zone between the United States, Mexico, and Canada by gradually eliminating tariffs over 15 years—was generally supported by executives in the men's apparel industry. While workers' unions sought to stem the loss of jobs among Americans in the industry by limiting the imports allowed in the country, the free-market philosophy ultimately triumphed in the passage of NAFTA.

During the early 1990s, increasingly more imports entered the United States under provision 9802 (formerly known as Section 807) of the Harmonized Tariffs Schedule of the United States. This provision allowed clothing assembled abroad—from pieces cut in the United States and then exported—to be reimported with duty paid for the value added abroad. This meant that the most labor-intensive part of the assembly process could be accomplished for lower wages. Many U.S. manufacturers took advantage of provision 9802, moving assembly operations to the Caribbean where they expected to reduce costs and more successfully compete against imports from Asia. While the process greatly decreased the turnaround time assembling more complex clothing items, its logistics sometimes proved cumbersome and time-consuming, as contractors in other countries managed the transportation, paperwork, and assembly required. Furthermore, the passage of NAFTA led some to expect that the Caribbean would largely be replaced by Mexico as a more desirable manufacturing location.

RESEARCH AND TECHNOLOGY

In the battle against imports, U.S. apparel makers tried a several strategies, including increased use of automation, delivering higher quality goods, and trying to more closely keep track of the consumer's needs and desires. Although the intrinsic "soft" quality of material made the extensive use of automated equipment difficult, most of the larger manufacturers continually sought to invest in newer machinery to improve efficiency. Nevertheless, apparel manufacture remained a highly labor-intensive industry.

Another new strategy involved "quick response," the idea that bringing apparel to the retailer more rapidly would shorten the production cycle, reduce inventories, improve productivity, and help manufacturers to avoid overstocking by providing them with more timely information regarding consumers' preferences. Using computers to track inventory, sales, and con-

sumer response, domestic manufacturers hoped to compete more effectively with importers. Department stores and manufacturers worked together to find ways to speed deliveries and increase efficiency.

FURTHER READING

Apparel Import Digest. Arlington, VA: American Apparel Manufacturers Association, 1997.

Apparel Industry Trends. Arlington, VA: American Apparel Manufacturers Association, March 1997.

"Ducks, Rangers, Blues to Suit up in Nike Togs." *Brandweek,* 15 January 1996.

Fairchild Fact File: Men's Clothing and Furnishings. New York: Fairchild Publications.

Focus: An Economic Profile of the Apparel Industry, Arlington, VA: American Apparel Manufacturers Association, 1996.

"Import Growth Slowing, AAMA Says." *Apparel Industry,* June 1996.

Shelton, Linda and Robert Wallace. "World Textile and Apparel Trade: A New Era." *Industry, Trade, and Technology Review,* October 1996.

Spruill, Sandy. "Staying Home." *Apparel Industry,* September 1996.

—Cheryl Collins, updated by AnnaMarie Sheldon

SIC 2331

WOMEN'S, MISSES', AND JUNIORS' BLOUSES AND SHIRTS

This category includes establishments primarily engaged in manufacturing women's, misses', and juniors' blouses and shirts from purchased woven or knit fabrics. Knitting mills primarily engaged in manufacturing outerwear are classified in **SIC 2253: Knit Outerwear Mills.** Establishments primarily engaged in manufacturing girls', children's, and infants blouses and shirts are classified in **SIC 2361: Girls', Children's, and Infants' Dresses, Blouses, and Shirts.**

INDUSTRY SNAPSHOT

More than 900 companies were engaged in the manufacture of women's and misses' blouses and shirts in 1992. This figure marks a considerable drop in the industry, for ten years earlier there were more than 1,800 companies engaged in this area of manufacturing. Much of the drop can be attributed to anemic product demand and the increased market share enjoyed by international competitors. In 1994 establishments in the industry accounted for an inflation-adjusted value of total product shipments estimated at $4.1 billion. In 1996 total product shipments for the industry had only increased to $4.4 billion. These figure were consistent with an overall declining industry trend which began in 1982 and has, with only minor aberrations, continued through the mid-1990s.

In addition to the loss of market share to foreign companies, the domestic industry had also felt the sting of a declining trend in middle class discretionary incomes. The decline was particularly important since in former times the personal consumption expenditures of this income strata were a cornerstone of the industry target market, responsible for a major portion of apparel purchases of all types. The lingering overhang of takeover debt accumulated from the takeover frenzy of the late 1980s also imparted a growth inhibiting effect on company profits. To a lesser extent, other significant factors contributing to the industry's decline included a stabilization in the number of women entering the work force, as well as a change in consumer buying habits to discounters and off-price stores.

One positive business trend in recent years for blouse and shirt manufacturers has been an increased ability to take advantage of overseas opportunities. The long term decline in the value of the dollar spurred the export sales of women's and misses' blouses and shirts. In the early 1990s industry watchers remained enthusiastic about the prospects for export growth as a cure for the industry's economic woes. Their optimism was further buoyed with the 1993 passage of the North American Free Trade Agreement (NAFTA) and the elimination of significant world trade barriers as specified under the General Agreement on Tariffs and Trade (GATT).

On another front, while the industry itself was continuing to reel from the downsizing trend, the industry's larger firms had managed to increase their market shares and were using internally generated funds to invest in state-of-art apparel-related technologies and industry-related acquisitions.

In 1996 the women's and misses' blouses and shirts manufacturing industry was led by New York-based Cygne Designs, the third largest women's wear maker in the U.S. with $516 million in sales and 5,000 employees. Other notable companies included California-based Capucci Creations Internationale with $474 million in sales; California-based Esprit de Corp. with nearly $450 in sales; and New York-based Bernaud Chaus Inc.

ORGANIZATION AND STRUCTURE

Because many establishments within the apparel industry group (including manufacturers of women's and misses' blouses and shirts) do not always manufacture the entire garment within the establishment's premises or across the company's factories, the U.S. Census of Manufacturers separates the industry into three broad producer classifications. Just where a company or establishment falls within the classifications depends on the degree of comprehensiveness of its production activities. Producers are classified as manufacturers if they buy fabric and undertake the design, patternmaking, grading, cutting, sewing, and assembling of their garments from within their own establishment or firm. Because of their integrated structure, wholly owned manufacturers operate in a manner that allows them to exercise a considerable measure of control over the production quality of their garments. Since they require relatively large investment expenditures, such operations fall outside the financial reach of the majority of the establishments active in the industry.

A firm or establishment that carries out all garment making processes minus its sewing and (sometimes) its cutting operations, deciding instead to contract out these operations to independently owned outside firms, is defined as an apparel jobber. Many apparel firms, independent of their size, contract out their sewing and cutting needs, along with other highly skilled production functions such as embroidery, quilting, and pleating, which are performed using specialized machinery.

A firm or establishment that is independently owned and uses its own machinery and employees to sew and cut garments from the designs, materials, and specifications supplied by the apparel jobbers is classified as a contractor. The contracting system actually began in the 1880s and was then referred to as the "cottage industry" where women sewed at home doing piece work. Eventually the system was transferred to privately owned factories. The contractor system's continued existence is due to the system's ability to accommodate seasonal production peaks without the apparel jobbers having to undertake investments that are subject to periods of intense activity and idleness.

In 1987, when ranked according to their density within census regions, the largest number of establishments engaged in this industry were located in the Pacific, Middle Atlantic, and South Atlantic regions. Alternatively, when ranked by the number of establishments per state, California was first with 485 and New York was second with 294, followed by Pennsylvania with 173 and Georgia with 76.

Input data compiled from the 1980s indicated that the primary materials consumed by the industry when ranked by cost arrived in the form of materials, containers, and supplies; broadwoven fabrics; and knit fabrics. The major economic sectors responsible for the share of the industry's input supply flowed from imports (29.1 percent); broadwoven fabric mills (20.2 percent); apparel made from purchased materials, (18.3 percent); and knit fabric mills, (8.6 percent).

The disaggregated share of the total output identified according to the category of its major product class indicated that women's and misses' knit shirts and blouses accounted for 30.1 percent of total sales, women's and misses' woven shirts and blouses represented 46.7 percent, contract work performed on women's and misses' blouses and shirts accounted for 16.5 percent, and about 6.7 percent went unspecified by kind.

BACKGROUND AND DEVELOPMENT

Up until the mid-nineteenth century, women's and misses' ready-made or ready-to-wear blouses and shirts were practically nonexistent. Dating back to early colonial times, U.S. women typically wore clothes that were made in the household. Popular women's magazines carried sewing instructions for making new patterns or styles. From the 1860s until the turn of the century efforts to manufacture women's ready-wear garments met with little success. What was available was usually of inferior quality and questionable design, despite the invention and diffusion of sewing machine technology. For the most part, domestically produced garments continued to dominate the scene; mass produced ready-wear women's clothes were spoken about in derogatory terms.

Things changed slowly during the first two decades of the twentieth century, but change they did as women's ready-to-wear clothes encountered wider social acceptance. The combined influence of several concurrent social and economic forces explained this shift. For instance, ongoing improvements in European and U.S. textile technologies transformed both the quality and availability of fabrics, enabling manufacturers to produce a more comfortable and style-conscious fit. Continuous upgrades in sewing machine technologies, cutting instruments, and pressing processes permitted the output of women's clothes to increase dramatically while their prices fell. Spurred on by the burgeoning women's movement, women were able to move beyond their traditional confines of home and family and participate more fully in social life. Women increasingly entered the work force, attended college, and became more active in sports and

politics. World War I found many women taking over jobs once performed by men. In sum, given their fuller participation in social affairs outside the home, women found the ready-to-wear clothes for themselves and their families a necessary convenience.

From the 1920s onwards, the women's apparel industry developed along the lines of small, privately-owned, single-product firms. By the late 1950s things began to change as larger publicly held multi-product firms started to move into the women's apparel industry. In most instances, their methods of gaining entry into the industry took the form of mergers with or acquisitions of existing firms. This growth in the industry continued unabated into the 1960s: there were only 22 publicly owned firms in women's apparel industry in 1959; by the close of the 1960s their number exceeded 100. The forward march of large, publicly-owned firms continued more or less without interruption until the mid-1980s when the trend reversed itself and large manufacturing firms began to "go private" again during the era of leveraged buyouts.

The progressive growth of import penetration into the domestic market for women's and misses' blouses and shirts was a significant factor in the domestic industry's protracted tailspin. As part of industry-wide efforts to lower production costs, U.S. producers participated in this import deluge through the processes of "outsourcing" and relocation by foreign investment. Beginning around 1982 and still in force by the 1990s, price competition from both foreign and domestic producers resulted in strong disinflationary pressures which in turn triggered a steep decline in the domestic industry's rate of capacity utilization. During the recession of 1981-1982, the percentage change in producer prices for women's apparel collapsed and then remained more or less flat for most the period covering 1983-1990. Though not as dramatic as the previous recession, disinflationary forces hit once again during the 1990-1991 recession, and then, most uncharacteristically, set out along the path of another steep decline despite being some two years into a recovery. During the past decade capacity utilization fluctuated erratically, moving up and down between the 83 to 79 percent range during the 1981-1982 recession. During the early years of the recovery it climbed upwards, peaking at the 89 percent mark in 1984. It then plummeted to settle at 76 percent in 1993, marking a drop of almost 15 percent in capacity utilization in the industry. As a direct consequence of the shakeout working through the industry's manufacturing sector, many traditional wholesale and retail linkages were sent into disarray or ruptured entirely, spawning a number of mergers and bankruptcy declarations.

During the 1980s another new trend arose in the form of manufacturer-owned retail stores that were usually located in prime retail areas and carried a large and complete stock of the firm's product lines sold at regular prices. Such outlets provided manufacturers with a wealth of consumer information that was used to determine whether the prospect of future sales warranted future production runs.

CURRENT CONDITIONS

According to the American Manufacturers Association, apparel imports grew only 10 percent in 1995. Imports of cotton apparel grew 1 percent; man-made fiber apparel imports increased 7 percent; and wool apparel imports rose 8 percent. Imports of fibers covered by the Multi Fiber Arrangement (MFA) fell 18 percent. In keeping with these overall industry trends, imports of women's knit shirts and blouses fell 12 percent in 1996, while import figures for women's shirts and blouses, not knit, remained similar those of 1995. Although import growth was down and domestic production dropped in 1996, U.S. apparel consumption grew 5.8 percent. Retail sales of women's apparel grew 5.1 percent in 1996 compared to a 1 percent growth in 1995.

A new World Trade Organization (WTO) was established in 1995, and the Multifiber Arrangement which allowed importing countries to limit the flow of imports from lower cost, developing countries was replaced by the ATC which required the phasing out of MFA quotas over a ten-year period. According to Linda Shelton in an *Industry, Trade, and Technology Review* report, "The elimination of MFA quotas likely will have a significant impact on the U.S. textile and apparel sector given the level of protection that such restrictions have provided domestic producers over the past two decades." Since the U.S. has until 2005 to implement the ATC, the legislation's impact on the women's apparel industry may not be realized for several years.

WORK FORCE

In 1982 total employment in the women's and misses' shirts and blouses industry stood at 92,300, of which 79,400 were classified as production workers. By 1991 total employment had fallen to 55,900, of which 46,900 were production workers. During those ten years total employment fell by 39.5 percent and production worker employment dropped by 41 percent. Over the same period the annual total value added by production workers either stayed about the same or increased as their average weekly hours steadily increased from 34 hours in 1982 to 36.4 hours in

1991. From 1982 to 1990 the industry's value added per production worker climbed almost continuously from $23,200 to $36,000. For the same period movements in the real wage indicated a mostly downward trend, suggesting that productivity gains were not being matched by increases in the real wage. In 1995, the industry's work force dropped 10 percent and wages increased to approximately $7.30 per hour for women's apparel workers.

Compared against the measures of employment by gender, race and Hispanic origin for the U.S. manufacturing sector as a whole, women, black, and Hispanic workers active in the apparel work force far exceeded their national counterparts. According to American Apparel Manufacturers Association estimates for 1995, women accounted for 70.1 percent of the apparel work force, a figure considerably higher than the overall manufacturing average of 31.6 percent. Black apparel workers accounted for 15 percent of the work force total—the total manufacturing average is 10.4 percent—and Hispanic workers accounted for 24 percent of the employee work force, compared to the national average of 10.2 percent.

AMERICA AND THE WORLD

Ever since the end of World War II, the domestic producers of women's and misses' blouses and shirts have been vulnerable to import penetration. As mentioned earlier, a particularly acute phase occurred during the period of 1983-1992. Although they still account for the largest share of U.S. imports, the market share of the "Big Four" countries, the People's Republic of China, Taiwan, Hong Kong, and Korea, actually declined during this period, dropping from 63 percent in 1984 to 41 percent in 1992. Shipments from all of these countries declined with the exception of China, which recorded an increase of more than 100 percent. The "Big Four" continued to lose market share to new players such as Bangladesh, Indonesia, and Thailand, and represented only 28 percent of apparel imports in 1995. This was due in part to increased implementation of "quick response" and U.S. apparel manufacturers ability to react more quickly to fluctuating consumer demands. By far the largest gains in import market share occurred were enjoyed by the Caribbean countries and Mexico. These countries increased their market share from 20 percent in 1992 to approximately 54 percent in 1996.

To an increasing degree, many U.S. garment makers actively participated in this import binge and contributed to the erosion of domestic employment in the industry through their emphasis on foreign outsourcing. With respect to the Caribbean countries, this was true as a matter of policy ever since 1983 when Congress, fearful that the spread of poverty in the Caribbean would attract large portions of its citizens to communist politics, passed the Caribbean Basin Initiative (CBI) program. The CBI permitted almost all apparel items which had been cut within the U.S. to be shipped abroad for further processing and then reenter the U.S. as manufactured or semi-manufactured goods. According to section 807 of the U.S. Tariff Code, the percentage of duty paid on the goods was equated to the value added abroad. And, as was often the case, this was set equal to the cost of foreign sewing labor, which was notoriously low when compared to the cost of U.S. workers. Among the countries participating in the program were Jamaica, the Dominican Republic, Haiti, Costa Rica, and, even though it was not a Caribbean country, Mexico. With the passage of NAFTA and GATT, trade relations between the U.S. and the rest of the world were supposed to be put on a more level playing field. Additional job losses in America, however, may well be one result. In discussing GATT's impact on the textiles and clothing industries, the *Christian Science Monitor* commented that ''the accord puts the textiles sector back under multi-lateral trade rules, after a 20-year hiatus during which bilateral accords reigned under the Multi-Fiber Agreement regime. Most tariffs and quotas in developed countries will be eliminated over the decade. Developing countries will take a growing share of textiles and clothing trade, worth $250 billion in 1992. Consumers should enjoy lower prices, while developed-world manufacturers, such as those in the United States, will continue to feel the heat.''

RESEARCH AND TECHNOLOGY

Despite being caught up in ongoing grip of establishment downsizing, major technological changes began to impact on the industry in the late 1980s that led to a closer integration between retailers and manufacturers. New labor saving and lower cost technologies were introduced at larger companies, which only served to widen the competitive cost differentials between themselves and the middle and lower tier firms in the industry. Unless rectified, this situation could also stoke the industry's downsizing trend.

A significant development in recent years between retailers and the industry's manufacturers has been the implementation of the quick response system, a computerized strategy that provides for the quick and precise replenishment of ''hot-selling'' garments. By means of electronic data interchange, participating apparel producers are privy to an instant and continuous flow of information concerning retail sales by styles, sizes, and colors, along with the level of retail inventory. With this information in their possession, manufacturers plan further production rounds on a more precise basis by discarding slow-moving styles and devoting their efforts towards fast selling items. As a result, they avoid costly markdowns and increase turnover. In most instances quick response systems have been formed between large volume manufacturers and retailers with the high level of funds necessary to purchase these costly systems.

Internal to the establishments, new automated technologies were being installed to speed up the manufacturing process and reduce the labor time required per garment. Examples included automated marker and patternmakers, computer inspection of fabrics, scanning and measurement of fabric width variance, and shade recognition apparatus, which have all become automated parts of a fully integrated quality enhancing system. New programmable sewing units that utilize microprocessors were also instrumental in reducing sewing labor costs. Prior to their introduction the sewing of a garment accounted for the largest portion of an article's labor cost, while anywhere from 70 to 80 percent of its in-process production time was spent handling and positioning a garment. To reduce in-process handling new automatic conveyor systems are being developed, along with robotics systems and automated warehouse facilities.

FURTHER READING

Apparel Import Digest. Arlington, VA: American Apparel Manufacturers Association, 1997.

Apparel Industry Trends. Arlington, VA: American Apparel Manufacturers Association, March 1997.

Arpan, Jeffery S., de la Torres, Jose, and Toyne, Brian. *The U.S. Apparel Industry: International Challenge, Domestic Response.* Atlanta, GA: Georgia State University, 1982.

Focus: An Economic Profile of the Apparel Industry. Arlington, VA: American Apparel Manufacturers Association, 1993.

Focus: An Economic Profile of the Apparel Industry. Arlington, VA: American Apparel Manufacturers Association, 1996.

''Import Growth Slowing, AAMA Says.'' *Apparel Industry,* June 1996.

Jarnow, Jeannette, and Guerreiro, Miriam. *Inside the Fashion Business,* New York: Macmillan Publishing Company, 1991.

LaFranchi, Howard, ''Looking Back: Accomplishments of the Uruguay Round.'' *Christian Science Monitor,* 23 December 1993.

Rose, Clare. *Children's Clothes Since 1750,* New York: Drama Book Publishers, 1989.

Shelton, Linda, and Robert Wallace. "World Textile and Apparel Trade: A New Era," *Industry, Trade, and Technology Review,* October 1996.

Statistical Abstract of the United States, Washington DC: U.S. Department of Commerce, 1996.

—Daniel King, updated by AnnaMarie Sheldon

SIC 2335

WOMEN'S, JUNIORS', AND MISSES' DRESSES

This entry describes establishments primarily engaged in manufacturing women's, misses', and juniors' dresses (including ensemble dresses), from purchased woven or knit fabrics, including woven or knit fabrics of paper, whether sold by the piece or by the dozen. Establishments primarily engaged in manufacturing girls', children's, and infants' dresses are classified in **SIC 2361: Girls', Children's, and Infants' Dresses, Blouses, and Shirts.** Knitting mills primarily engaged in manufacturing knit dresses are classified in **SIC 2258: Lace and Warp Knit Fabric Mills.**

INDUSTRY SNAPSHOT

There were more than 3,500 manufacturers of women's, juniors', and misses' dresses in the United States in 1993. In 1994, this industry generated over $6 billion in total shipments, representing nearly 25 percent of the $22 billion women's and misses' outerwear category. In 1995, women's, misses', and juniors' dress shipments reached nearly $6.2 billion.

Centered in New York and California, the industry has more than 3,600 manufacturers in those two states; however, manufacturers can be found in 27 other states stretching from Rhode Island and Pennsylvania to Texas and Hawaii. The size and scope of these dress manufacturers varied greatly from small manufacturers operating out of their homes or a single showroom to the industry leader Kellwood Co., which employed over 16,000 individuals and had sales of nearly $1.5 billion in 1996.

The clothing industry, particularly women's apparel, is sensitive to changes in economic conditions. In the 1980s, consumers were wearing designer labels and $100 jeans. The economic downturn in the early 1990s, however, caused consumers to look for value and savings. Consumer preferences shifted from fancy dressing to basic apparel at home as well as at work. As a result of this shift, manufacturers moved to the extremes of the industry: discounters and high fashion designers. Consequently, the number of women's apparel manufacturers declined. An increase in imports further increased the competition in this already volatile and difficult industry. Although imports increased by only 5 percent per year between 1988 and 1991, they jumped 15 percent in 1992, and again in 1993, slowing to 12 percent in 1994, 1995, and 1996. According to *Apparel Industry Magazine,* "Weak consumer demand (prompted by factors that include consumers' anxiety about their jobs, the tendency of Baby Boomers to spend more on furniture and less on clothing, and casual Fridays)" was to blame for sluggish apparel imports.

These events created increased competition and a reluctance on behalf of manufacturers and retailers to raise prices on apparel. Many small players were forced to close their doors, and the strength of the remaining manufacturers during the mid-1990s depended on an end to worldwide recessionary conditions. Between 1992 and 1997, average annual apparel employment decreased by 160,000 workers. In 1996, dress production fell 9 percent.

ORGANIZATION AND STRUCTURE

The American Apparel Manufacturers Association (AAMA) is the central trade association for the U.S. apparel industry. Throughout the 1990s, the AAMA represented three-fourths of the industry and provided its members with guidance and support through publications, statistical reports, and trade negotiations. In addition to the AAMA there are regional associations that focus on local issues and policies.

Business Centers. The industry's central business locations are New York City, Los Angeles, and Atlanta; each of these is supported by an apparel mart. These marts house showrooms in which manufacturers display their lines, and buyers and sellers converge at these marts to conduct the business of selling clothes. The selling periods for women's, misses', and juniors' dresses are typically condensed into monthly "market weeks." Retail buyers visit manufacturer showrooms to buy product for the coming season. In 1992, the women's apparel industry garnered retail sales of $64.5 billion. In 1995, domestic dress production reached $4.6 billion, and consumption of women's apparel grew by 1 percent; in 1996, consumption increased 5.1 percent.

The apparel industry operates under the principles of clustering. Clustering requires makers of similar products to congregate their operations in a small geographical location. This facilitates communication between buyers and sellers, increases the speed of innovation, and promotes a business culture that nourishes and supports an industry. Clustering is well-established in New York City and Los Angeles, thus ensuring their prominence as fashion centers for the United States.

Manufacturing Process. The manufacturing process requires an average of 6 to 8 months to move a particular line from design to sale. The process typically begins with a designer's sketch, which is turned into a pattern. Fabric is selected and a cost sheet is established to detail expenses. A wholesale price is determined by using the cost sheet as the base. The production department grades a pattern to accommodate the required size range and then cuts the fabric according to the patterns. The materials are then sewn and finished, and finally, the garments are pressed, then they packed or hung on racks for shipment to the retail customer. Across all manufacturers, only the first step, that of design, was uniformly handled in-house. The ability of a manufacturer to maintain control of the remaining processes was a function of its size and capital equipment. The most frequently outsourced process was sewing and finishing. This process was given to small contractors, typically employing immigrant labor in sweatshop-like factories. The nature of the contracting business has made the tracking of operating businesses and gross sales nearly impossible.

Financial Structure. According to *Bobbin* magazine, two-thirds of apparel manufacturers factored their receivables in the early 1990s. This accounting method entails a contract between manufacturer and factor regarding credit approval for retailers. The factor, essentially a lender, buys the manufacturer's receivables for 80 percent to 85 percent of value, and in turn sells them to a retailer. This allows manufacturers to decrease risk and increase capital turnover.

BACKGROUND AND DEVELOPMENT

The 1830s marked the emergence of the women's ready-to-wear dress industry in America. Manufacturers were able to keep pattern making and fabric cutting on their premises, typically in the tailor shop, with the pieces contracted to workers who would sew and finish the product in the home. By mid-century, several variables emerged that pushed this nascent business towards an industry of mass production: (1) strengthening of domestic textile manufacturing techniques (2) invention of a treadle-powered sewing machine by Isaac Singer (3) influx of large numbers of immigrants, and (4) methods developed during the Civil War for the mass production of garments.

The easy availability of cheap immigrant labor encouraged the development of large sweat shops typically housed in lofts. Not until the turn of the century

did the workers begin to mobilize and organize to promote better working conditions. Their actions resulted in the 1910 Protocol of Peace, which abolished home work, ended inside subcontracting, limited the workweek to 54 hours, and created an arbitration process for complaints. These benefits were granted at the expense of the workers' right to strike. The terrible images of 146 young women who died behind locked factory doors in the Triangle Shirt Waist fire of 1911 resulted in further reforms. By World War I, the International Ladies Garment Workers Union was one of the most powerful labor organizations in America.

New York City was the undisputed center of the women's ready-to-wear apparel industry. The city's dominance was secured during the 1920s when a group of New York developers consolidated the industry around a group of buildings along Seventh Avenue that were designed to house workrooms and showrooms for apparel manufacturers.

The apparel industry was not immune to the effects of the Great Depression of the 1930s. Many manufacturers ceased operations as a result of bankruptcy; however, the manufacturing boom during World War II quickly reversed the fortunes of the industry. There were tremendous profits to be earned in servicing the needs of a fully employed population.

The labor intensive aspect of garment manufacturing requires an ongoing search for cheap sources of labor. It was this requirement, in addition to the increasing congestion and expense of doing business in New York City, that began the movement of manufacturers away from New York towards the South and West. This period also saw the rise of large-scale manufacturing operations that could benefit from economies of scale not possible in the small spaces typically found in New York. This led to the wholesale manufacture of staple garments such as jeans.

The unending search for cheap labor eventually led to an increase in imported goods. Under the terms of Tariff Item 807, now called 9802, a U.S. company can send semi-finished garments overseas for incidental work, such as sewing and finishing. The company can then import the items back to the United States and pay duty only on the value-added portions of the garments. By the 1980s, the rise in imports was dramatic; 1985 imports were $15 billion, seven times that of 1972. By 1989, that number jumped to almost $24 billion. Manufacturers were pitted against retailers in their attempts to get protectionist legislation passed through Congress. The retailers argued that such legislation would result in an increase in domestic clothing prices. As a result, textile and apparel manufacturers established the Crafted with Pride in the USA Council, designed to encourage consumers to buy American products.

Consolidation. Changing consumer buying patterns and the continuing increase in imported goods contributed to a decrease of 800,000 apparel and textile jobs during the 1980s. They also forced the industry to consider the increased usage of automated manufacturing processes. Although the industry was still labor intensive, computer integrated manufacturing principles and the use of electronic data interchanges for "quick response" in inventory and ordering had become increasingly popular among manufacturers. However, the capital outlays required for the transition to a more automated environment and increased economies of scale were often too costly for smaller manufacturers.

This led to an atmosphere of consolidation wherein heavily capitalized companies introduced automation, expanded their operations, and increased their access to a wider strata of retailers through the acquisition of other labels. Consequently, small, independent companies were squeezed by the ever-increasing import market and these large, domestic apparel corporations. For example, Liz Claiborne, Inc. diversified its holdings by purchasing several brands from Russ Togs Inc., and continued to sell its garments to department stores while these new brands allowed the company to do business with such high growth mass merchandisers as Sears Roebuck and Co. and J.C. Penney Company, Inc.

Licensing. Brand licensing was a strategy employed throughout the industry to increase market share or avoid the necessity of automating a manufacturing process. Through licensing, the brand owner can reap the benefits of its name without the attendant problems of manufacturing or contracting out the goods themselves. Likewise, the licensee views a licensed brand as an opportunity to expand its line of offerings without the risk of financing a product launch. In a December 1992 *Bobbin* article, Craig Kalter, vice president of marketing and licensing for French Toast, noted that, "the advantage to the licensee is that it is able to benefit from a name that has a high degree of awareness and penetration in the marketplace."

NAFTA. The North American Free Trade Agreement (NAFTA) presented new challenges to the apparel industry. The agreement carried the possible threat of U.S. workers losing jobs to Mexico's cheaper labor source. However, the advocates asserted that businesses only moved to Mexico production that was no longer viable in the United States. In its study of NAFTA, the Office of Technology Assessment commented that "Mexico has so far been a minor supplier

of garments to the United States and will have difficulty dislodging established Asian producers. The threat to U.S. apparel jobs is global, not regional." Further, the American Apparel Manufacturers Association (AAMA), which supported NAFTA, argued that without NAFTA, such production would have moved to the Far East, thus completely eliminating U.S. involvement in the manufacturing process. A 1993 survey of AAMA membership indicated that despite NAFTA, only 3 percent of respondents expected an employment decline in the coming year. A full 50 percent expected no changes in their work force, while 46 percent of the manufacturers anticipated increasing their domestic employment.

The apparel industry in general, and women's and misses' dresses in particular, were very sensitive to economic and demographic changes. The economic conditions in the 1980s, boosted by the increase of women in the workplace, led to an average yearly business growth of 10 percent in terms of value of shipments for this category. During the recessionary climate of the early 1990s, however, the industry averaged only 2 percent growth. This sensitivity was further noted in the growth in sales for discount mass merchandisers at the expense of specialty boutiques and department stores. Manufacturers had to hold down costs and provide high quality garments to increasingly demanding and careful customers.

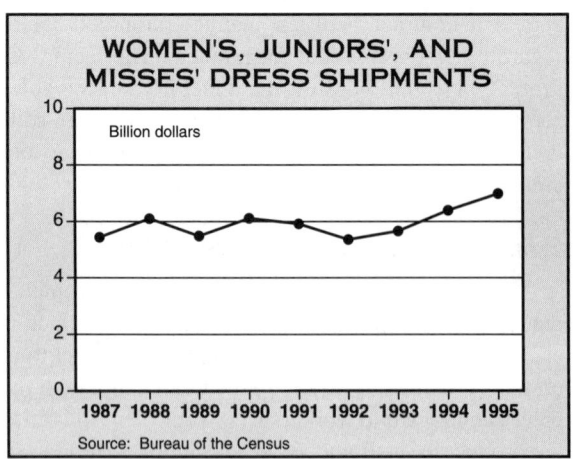

WOMEN'S, JUNIORS', AND MISSES' DRESS SHIPMENTS

Billion dollars

Source: Bureau of the Census

CURRENT CONDITIONS

A report issued by the U.S. Department of Commerce projected moderate growth for the U.S. apparel industry through the mid-1990s. This forecast, based on a favorable long-term outlook for consumer spending, housing starts, and new car purchases, also noted the increasingly competitive nature of the industry as foreign producers work to increase their share of the U.S. market.

Overseas markets had become increasingly important to U.S. apparel manufacturers, particularly in the developing markets of the former Soviet Union and Eastern Europe. An economic newsletter published by the American Apparel Manufacturers Association paid particular attention to trends in Asia that suggested opportunities for domestic apparel manufacturers. Japan, for example, had huge stores of foreign exchange but the public's living standard is below that of U.S. citizens. The cultural climate in Japan was changing in the early 1990s and Japan's citizens were beginning to enjoy more leisure time. It was anticipated that such time would lead to an increase in the consumption of personal goods and services. Likewise, the opening of trade doors to China and the increasing interest in Western goods offered tremendous growth opportunities for U.S. apparel manufacturers.

A new World Trade Organization (WTO) was established in 1995, and the Multifiber Arrangement (MFA), which allowed importing countries to limit the flow of imports from lower cost developing countries was replaced by the Agreement on Textiles and Clothing (ATC), which required the phasing out of MFA quotas over a ten-year period. According to Linda Shelton in an *Industry, Trade, and Technology Review* report, ''The elimination of MFA quotas likely will have a significant impact on the U.S. textile and apparel sector given the level of protection that such restrictions have provided domestic producers over the past two decades.'' Since the United States has until 2005 to implement the ATC, the legislation's impact on the women's apparel industry may not be realized for several years.

INDUSTRY LEADERS

Founded in 1976 and based in New York City, Liz Claiborne, Inc. has grown into one of the leading manufacturers in this industry. From 1982 to 1990, the company's sales grew from $166 million to $1.7 billion. Its acquisition of Russ Togs Inc., which included the Russ Togs, Villager, and Crazy Horse lines, increased sales to over $2 billion. This acquisition strategy allowed Liz Claiborne to gain access to lower-priced, mass merchandise retailers while retaining its Liz Claiborne line exclusively for department and specialty stores. Liz Claiborne Inc. is also an aggressive player in the outlet mall market, with over 31 stores across the country. In a Standard & Poor's Industry Survey, Jerome A. Chazen, chairman of Liz Claiborne Inc., called the outlet business excellent and projected that future stores would handle all surplus inventory.

Leslie Fay Companies, Inc., which include the Leslie Fay Classic, Leslie Fay Collection, Albert Nipon, and Nipon Boutique lines, was founded in 1946 and had sales of over $800 million in 1992. A New York-based publicly traded company, Leslie Fay responded aggressively to consumer demands for moderately priced, value-oriented fashion by cutting prices in several of its dress lines. This ''everyday value'' pricing strategy resulted in the company gaining the leading market share in the moderate-price dress category. Despite this market edge, the companies stock, which took a tumble in 1992, continued its downward trend, mirroring the sluggish women's apparel industry. In 1993, the company filed for Chapter 11 bankruptcy reorganization and continued its Chapter 11 operation through 1996.

Kellwood Co., the fifth largest apparel maker in the U.S., grew rapidly during the mid-1990s. Despite a stagnant retail environment in 1995, the company's women's wear division grew at 11 percent. Kellwood has acquired over 25,000 retail customers, including J.C. Penney, Wal-Mart Stores, Inc., and Sears, Roebuck & Co.

WORK FORCE

The apparel and textile manufacturing industries employed approximately 9 percent of the entire U.S. work force. More than one million workers were engaged in apparel manufacturing. The number of workers involved specifically in the manufacture of women's, juniors', and misses' dresses fell from a high of 122,000 in 1983 to less than 100,000 by 1993. In that same time period, average wages rose from $5.18 per hour to close to $7.00 per hour. In 1995, average wages reached $7.29 per hour.

In the early 1990s, New York and California each employed approximately 33,000 people in this industry, representing almost 30 percent of the industry's total work force. Pennsylvania employed 13,000 workers, and strong manufacturing centers in New Jersey, Florida, North Carolina, and South Carolina each supported between 1,500 and 5,500 workers. The largest percentage of workers were employed as sewing machine operators, followed by pressing machine operators and inspectors. With the exception of sales and machine mechanics, all other employment categories in the industry were anticipating work force reductions through the turn of the century.

Despite inroads into automation, the bulk of apparel manufacturing in the United States was still labor intensive in the early 1990s. Production workers in this industry made up 85 percent of the work force compared to only 68 percent for all other U.S. manufacturing. Wages in this sector were typically lower than in other manufacturing industries, resulting in an ongoing reliance on immigrant labor.

America and the World

Exports of apparel grew from 2 percent of total U.S. product shipments in 1987 to more than 7 percent in 1992. Total U.S. exports in that year were nearly $4 billion. Although much of this growth represented expansion of existing or new markets, a large portion of this gain was due to semi-finished garments sent abroad for finishing and then returned to the United States under the provision of Harmonized Tariff Schedule of the United States (HTSUS) code 9802, formerly 807. Although section 807 existed since the Tariff Act of 1790, it only gained importance during the 1980s, as apparel imports dramatically increased. In the decade from 1980 to 1990, apparel imports increased 202 percent.

The 9802 program allows a manufacturer to pay duty only on the value added to the garment abroad, not the total value of the product. In 1992, HTSUS 9802 trade was slightly more than 14 percent of total imports, and nearly $900 million worth of HTSUS 9802 imports were produced in the Dominican Republic. Mexico produced approximately $700 million, followed by Costa Rica with $400 million in apparel production.

Apparel trade is governed by the Arrangement Regarding International Trade in Textiles, also known as the Multifiber Arrangement (MFA). This agreement provides guidelines for member nations regarding international trade in textiles and apparel. Apparel is further controlled under the auspices of the General Agreement on Tariffs and Trade (GATT). The Uruguay Round of talks regarding GATT, begun in the late 1980s, were also expected to have an impact on the industry.

The largest suppliers of apparel to the United States were China, Taiwan, Korea, and Hong Kong, with almost $12 billion in sales for 1992. This represented nearly half of the $26 billion of all garments imported into the United States in 1992. Although labor costs in China, Pakistan, and India averaged only $.23 per hour, wages in Singapore, Hong Kong, and Taiwan were $3.25 per hour, significantly higher than the $1.17 average hourly wage paid in Mexico. In the mid-1990s conventional Far East importers lost U.S. market share to new players such as Bangladesh, Indonesia, and Thailand. The "Big 4" (China, Hong Kong, Taiwan, and Korea) represented only 28 percent of apparel imports in 1995. This was due, in part, to increased implementation of "quick response" and

U.S. apparel manufacturers' ability to react more quickly to fluctuating consumer demands.

Further Reading

Abend, Jules. "The Increasingly Common Denominator." *Bobbin,* December 1992.

Apparel Import Digest. Arlington, VA: American Apparel Manufacturers Association, 1997.

Apparel Industry Trends. Arlington, VA: American Apparel Manufacturers Association, June 1993.

Apparel Industry Trends. Arlington, VA: American Apparel Manufacturers Association, March 1997.

Barcomb, Amy. "License to Manufacture." *Bobbin,* December 1992.

Bonner, Staci. "Kellwood's Vision Pays Off." *Apparel Industry,* November 1996.

Feldman, Amy. "Consumer Nondurables." *Forbes,* 4 January 1993.

Focus: An Economic Profile of the Apparel Industry. Arlington, VA: American Apparel Manufacturers Association, 1996.

"Import Growth Slowing, AAMA Says." *Apparel Industry,* June 1996.

"Leslie Fay Seeks Post-Chapter 11 Lender Facility." *Women's Wear Daily,* 4 January 1996. Available from http://207.51.71.250/samples/archive/1996/000/069.htm.

Mattera, Philip. *Inside U.S. Business.* Homewood, IL: Irwin, 1991.

O'Rourke, Mary T. "Labor Costs - From Pakistan to Portugal." *Bobbin,* September 1992.

Pouschine, Tatiana. "Ridin' High." *Forbes,* 9 November 1992.

Shelton, Linda and Robert Wallace, "World Textile and Apparel Trade: A New Era." *Industry, Trade, and Technology Review,* October 1996.

Standard & Poor's Industry Surveys. New York: Standard & Poor's Corporation, 1993.

Struensee, Chuck. "Leslie Fay Cuts Moderate Dress Prices." *Women's Wear Daily,* 22 September 1992.

———. "Revamping at Leslie Fay." *Women's Wear Daily,* 1 September 1992.

U.S. Department of Commerce. *Statistical Abstract of the United States.* Washington: GPO, 1996.

U.S. Department of Commerce. International Trade Administration. *U.S. Industrial Outlook 1993.* Washington: GPO, 1993.

—Shula Malkin, updated by AnnaMarie Sheldon

SIC 2337

WOMEN'S, MISSES, AND JUNIORS' SUITS, SKIRTS, AND COATS

This category covers establishments primarily engaged in manufacturing women's, misses', and junior's suits, pantsuits, skirts, coats (except fur coats and raincoats), and tailored jackets and vests, from purchased woven or knit fabrics. These garments are generally tailored and usually lined. Establishments primarily engaged in manufacturing fur clothing are classified in **SIC 2371: Fur Goods;** and those manufacturing raincoats are classified in **SIC 2385: Waterproof Outerwear.** Knitting mills primarily engaged in manufacturing knit outerwear are classified in **SIC 2253: Knit Outerwear Mills.**

INDUSTRY SNAPSHOT

The U.S. apparel industry, especially the women's apparel industry, underwent dramatic change beginning in the 1960s. The increased automation of the industry, the profound surge in imports, and fundamental shifts in the retail industry all affected the manufacture of women's clothing in the United States.

Over 1,000 companies produced women's suits, coats, skirts, and jackets in 1993, and they employed 49,000 workers. Many industry establishments were small, family-owned and operated businesses, although there was a trend toward consolidation. By 1995, the industry employed only 40,400 individuals. The value of shipments of women's suits, coats, skirts, and jackets in 1995 fell to $3.92 billion from $3.93 billion in 1994 and $4.2 billion in 1993, continuing a decade and a half-long downward trend. Factors such as the increase in imports and a general shift toward more casual office wear had a negative impact on this segment of the U.S. market.

ORGANIZATION AND STRUCTURE

The apparel industry was composed of three types of producers: contractors, jobbers, and manufacturers. Contractors were independent firms performing specialized work, such as sewing a garment, for a number of competing firms. Contractors were hired by producers who either did not have their own sewing apparatus or whose own capacity had been exceeded. Contractors were not involved in the retail sale of merchandise. Over one-half of the plants making women's coats and suits were run by contractors.

Jobbers were design and marketing businesses that were hired to perform specific functions. For ex-

ample, jobbers might purchase materials, design patterns, create samples, cut material, and hire contractors to manufacture the product. Most jobbers, however, did not sew garments, but instead hired contractors to sew and finish the products. These contracted sewing-machine operators completed specific parts of the garment, which were provided by the manufacturer. Through this system of piece work, operators could work more quickly and efficiently because they did not have to switch or adjust their machines.

Jobbers often had their own design staffs to create seasonal lines, or they might hire free-lancers to do design work. A jobber bought the materials needed to produce the pieces, and then created the patterns for different sizes. The cut material was then sent to contractors to be sewn and finished. Orders were taken for the garments, and the finished garments were then shipped to retailers.

Manufacturers were those establishments performing all functions involved in creating apparel from purchased materials. The manufacturer had a staff that produced designs, or it bought work from free-lancers. It then purchased the needed materials (fabric and trimmings). Generally the cutting and sewing of the garment was done in the manufacturer's factories. However, when demand for an item exceeded the manufacturer's ability to supply it within shipping deadlines, outside contractors might be hired. The manufacturer's own sales and shipping staff took orders and sent them out.

When a manufacturer handled all stages of a garment's assembly, it clearly had greater control over the quality of the product. Nevertheless, the advantages to using contractors were numerous. For example, those companies without the capital to update machinery would find the system advantageous. Manufacturers who relied upon contractors also avoided the responsibility of hiring and training workers. And the contractor system was flexible—providing manufacturing capacity when needed at busy periods without having to meet payroll obligations at off-peak periods.

BACKGROUND AND DEVELOPMENT

The growth of the U.S. women's apparel business began in the mid-nineteenth century when certain garments that did not need to be fitted, such as cloaks and mantles, started to be mass-produced. Small quantities of women's suits and skirts were turned out in a limited number of factories, but most women still made their own clothing at home.

Early in the twentieth century, the number of apparel manufacturers grew as more women chose to buy their clothing. New York City became the center of the women's apparel business for a variety of reasons. For example, manufacturers were able to take advantage of the inexpensive labor found in newly arrived immigrants—most of those working in the industry were young Jewish and Italian women. New York City also formed an ideal location for the industry due to its position as a port city and its proximity to the textile mills in New England and the South.

Soon, many manufacturers began to outgrow their quarters in an industry that was expanding rapidly. A consortium of apparel makers, investors, and a real estate developer came up with the idea of moving to an undeveloped area of New York City. Between 1918 and 1921, approximately 50 clothing makers moved to the area along Seventh Avenue, which came to be known as the garment district.

Since the garment industry was unregulated, the employees in these days often worked in crowded, unsafe, and poorly lit "sweat shops" for low pay. Early efforts to organize the workers into unions were met with industry-wide resistance—as one shop became organized, business would then simply shift to an unorganized one.

The Triangle Shirtwaist Factory fire in 1911, in which 146 employees were killed, was a tragedy that galvanized the industry. After much resistance from business owners, industry-wide minimum standards for worker safety were put into place. In the 1930s and 1940s federal legislation made it easier for the unions to organize, and more labor standards were established. Two unions largely represented U.S. apparel workers, the International Ladies' Garment Workers' Union (ILGWU) and what eventually came to be known as the Amalgamated Clothing and Textile Workers Union (ACTWU). For many years they were able to negotiate contracts with yearly pay increases and benefits.

By the 1960s apparel manufacturers started to move their production facilities out of the United States to markets where the labor was plentiful and cheap. Apparel manufacturing became a global industry. Manufacturers from the United States first looked largely to Hong Kong and Taiwan, but as labor costs grew, manufacturers moved to other Asian nations and the Caribbean. Apparel imports into the United States increased from 9 percent in 1967 to 62 percent in 1992. The value of imports of women's suits, coats, skirts, and jackets reached $2.8 billion in 1995.

Another important development came in the 1960s, when many textile companies (which produced the materials) and retailers (which bought the finished products) grew into huge companies. The apparel manufacturers responded in kind, as many merged to create large, publicly owned corporations. Historically, women's apparel companies were small businesses, often family-run. Although the new corporations were large, they sometimes lacked the flexibility needed in the ever-changing fashion industry. However, the larger companies were armed with the capital needed to upgrade machinery and modernize equipment to compete more effectively with imports.

Another trend which led to profound change in the industry was the dramatic increase in the number of women in the work force, beginning in the 1970s. As a result, the demand for professional women's wear skyrocketed.

Personal-consumption expenditures on clothing nearly doubled during the 1980s, and women's apparel was an important part of that increase. As recession hit the industry in 1989, however, the spending splurge ended; manufacturers responded by cutting costs. While the women's apparel industry adjusted to the recession, the larger manufacturers grew stronger as the industry continued to consolidate. Some big manufacturers were able to take advantage of the weakened position of many smaller firms and strengthen their already-dominant positions.

Other factors changed the women's apparel industry as well. For example, manufacturers began to sell their own products as the line between manufacturer and retailer blurred. Manufacturers were often unhappy with the way the retailers displayed their products or with the performance of sales staff. By opening their own retail spaces—either complete stores or freestanding "shops" within department stores—manufacturers could exert direct control of the sales, service, and environment. Another popular tactic was for manufacturers to sell through catalogs, again jumping over the middleman and appealing directly to the consumer. By marketing their own goods, manufacturers could avoid retailers who were looking to increase their profit margin at the manufacturers' expense.

Manufacturers responded to the surge in imports in a variety of ways. Some sold off their manufacturing facilities, hiring contractors to make products to their specifications; others contracted for their apparel to be produced almost exclusively offshore and then reimported. By contracting out, manufacturers could reduce their overhead, and their inventories would be more flexible. Those who kept their facilities in the United States often stressed their reliability, on-time delivery, and quality.

CURRENT CONDITIONS

Retailers themselves sought to cut costs and become more efficient, as the market became more competitive. Retailers often looked to the larger apparel manufacturers that were providing merchandise that consumers recognized and respected. By limiting the number of manufacturers supplying them, retailers could reduce overhead expenses—thus favoring the larger manufacturers over the smaller ones.

The value of women's wear shipments declined gradually through the 1990s. One of the many reasons included a leveling-off of the number of women entering the work force. Historically, women's apparel accounted for half of all clothing sold, and it was sold primarily to working women, who by 1990 comprised 45 percent of the U.S. work force. In addition, office wear became more casual, and this particularly affected the sales of women's suits. And as the U.S. population aged, people often became less concerned with up-to-the-minute fashions than with saving for mortgage payments and children's educations. The market stabilized in 1996 and 1997 as manufacturers adjusted their lines to meet the demands of the more casual workplace. Nearly 63 million women were in the labor force in 1997, and they represented almost 50 percent of managerial and professional positions. As Anne D'Innocenzio reported in a *Women's Wear Daily* article, suits were expected to account for 10.8 percent of the tailored market in 1997, which meant the decline in women's suit sales had ceased. Blazers were expected to generate 27.7 percent of total tailored sales.

INDUSTRY LEADERS

Hartmarx Corporation designed, produced, and marketed both men's and women's apparel, and it was one of the largest manufacturers of women's suits. Hartmarx produced moderately priced women's clothing through its Women's International Division. It also sold clothing through the Barrie Pace Catalog division. Hartmarx grew considerably throughout the 1980s, mainly due to an aggressive acquisition strategy. Incorporated in 1911 and headquartered in Chicago, it employed 13,000 workers in the early 1990s. In 1992 it reported $1.05 billion in revenues. Sales grew 1.06 percent from first quarter 1995 to first quarter 1996.

Leslie Fay Companies, Inc. designed and manufactured women's sportswear, suits, and separates at a diverse range of style and price points. Leslie Fay grew during the 1980s into one of the dominant forces of the industry through strong sales of apparel aimed at working women and a string of acquisitions. In 1988 it bought Albert Nipon, Inc. and Mary Ann Restivo, Inc., and in 1989 it purchased Non-Stop Fashions, Inc. and NS Petites, Inc. Leslie Fay also adopted the retailing approach of Calvin Klein and Liz Claiborne by opening "shops" within department stores.

In April 1993 Leslie Fay Companies, Inc. declared bankruptcy after accounting irregularities were discovered, and the company was found to be losing money. The company had difficulty moving its merchandise, as its apparel was criticized as over-priced and old-fashioned. Leslie Fay always relied on department stores to distribute its clothing, but the larger retailers faced stiff competition from discount and outlet stores, especially when the recession took hold in 1989. The company continued its Chapter 11 operation through 1996.

Oxford Industries, Inc., based in Atlanta, Georgia, was one of the leading apparel manufacturers in the United States. It produced and distributed men's and women's apparel, including suits, skirts, and jackets, in a range of prices and styles. Oxford, like many other manufacturers, took advantage of the increased profits that came from the extended consumer spending spree of the 1980s to acquire a variety of labels and gain lucrative licensing agreements. With the recession in 1989, Oxford moved to shed its unprofitable lines and lower operating expenses.

Oxford reported sales of $573 million in 1993 and employed 9,300 workers. The Company sold its apparel to a variety of customers, including Eddie Bauer, L.L. Bean, Land's End, Target, and Wal-Mart. Two of its biggest customers were J.C. Penney and Sears, from which Oxford gained approximately a third of its sales in the fiscal year 1992-93. Oxford manufactured its clothing at its own factories in the United States and abroad, and it also used independent contractors. In 1991 approximately 50 percent of its apparel was manufactured domestically, while the other half was produced in 22 countries. The company was expected to shift more of its production overseas. In the first quarter of 1996, sales dropped 9.47 percent from the same period in 1995.

Founded in 1981, Norton McNaughton was another industry leader with sales of $228 million in 1996. Profit margins fell at the end of 1995 and the beginning of 1996 due to an excess of casual wear merchandise, an inability to compete with private label suits in the market, and high prices. Norton McNaughton responded by closing its young Kate McNaughton suit division, restructuring its Danielle Page casual division, evaluating pricing strategies, and increasing its career merchandise offerings. The company also increased its overseas production by 20 percent and added China, Hong Kong, and Turkey to its manufacturing network.

WORK FORCE

As imports increasingly replaced American-made clothing, the number of employees in the industry predictably declined. The International Ladies' Garment Workers' Union reported that from a peak in 1973, 34 percent of production worker jobs (nearly 25,000) were lost in 20 years in the women's and children's apparel industry, a process which accelerated in the 1980s.

There were approximately 40,400 workers involved in the manufacture of women's suits, coats, skirts, and jackets apparel in 1995, down from 45,900 five years earlier. The majority (approximately 30,900) were production workers. Wages averaged $8.09 an hour, up over $1 an hour from wages in 1990.

New York was the state with the largest number of employees in the women's apparel industry, while Pennsylvania, New Jersey, California, and Massachusetts also had significant concentrations of workers.

AMERICA AND THE WORLD

The U.S. women's apparel industry was dominated by imports by the early 1990s. Imports were attractive to consumers because they were often less expensive than domestically produced clothing, and they had increased in quality over time. The industry began to lose market share to imports in the 1960s. The process began to accelerate in the 1970s, and by the early 1990s, imports reached all-time highs. From 1980 through the early 1990s, apparel imports tripled when measured in square meters. Also contributing to the industry's decline in the United States was the reliance of manufacturers on off-shore assembly of pieces cut domestically.

Manufacturers in the Far East represented a significant source of women's apparel. When apparel makers started to move their manufacturing bases out of the United States in the 1960s, they first went to Hong Kong, Taiwan, and South Korea to take advantage of the cheap labor there. By the 1980s, however, labor costs had increased, and capital and experience from those traditional low-wage markets moved to lower wage countries such as Bangladesh, Thailand, Pakistan, Indonesia, Malaysia, Sri Lanka, and India, which became the sources for more of the imports entering the U.S. market. By the early 1990s, China replaced Hong Kong as the greatest supplier of imported clothing to the United States. The China, Hong Kong, Taiwan, and Korea represented only 28 percent of apparel imports in 1995.

The North American Free Trade Agreement (NAFTA), which created a free-trade zone between the United States, Mexico, and Canada by gradually eliminating tariffs over 15 years, took effect January 1, 1994. Since a similar agreement was already in effect between the United States and Canada, analysts expected NAFTA to increase trade with Mexico. Apparel-industry executives supported NAFTA. The ILGWU and the ACTWU, by contrast, sought to stem the loss of jobs in the apparel industry by limiting the imports allowed into the country. However, their arguments did not succeed in challenging the free-market philosophy that ultimately triumphed in the passage of NAFTA.

Any agreement to come from the negotiations of the General Agreement on Tariffs and Trade (GATT), started in 1986, would possibly have wide-ranging impact on the U.S. apparel industry. GATT was first established in the 1960s, and it created the Arrangement Regarding International Trade in Textiles, known as the Multifiber Arrangement (MFA). The MFA regulated apparel that was imported into the United States and other member nations, and it was renewed every three years. Proposals involved in the GATT negotiations would reduce the tariffs on imports into the United States by half over time, without guaranteeing U.S. products access to markets in other countries. Some countries that exported heavily into the United States—for example, China—did not allow corresponding access to their home markets. The MFA would be superseded by any agreement reached in the GATT talks, but if no agreement was reached the MFA would be extended. The textile industry estimated that one million U.S. textile and apparel jobs would be lost under the provisions of GATT.

More and more imports entered the United States under provision 9802 (formerly known as Section 807) of the Harmonized Tariffs Schedule of the United States. This provision allowed clothing assembled abroad—from pieces cut in the United States—to be reimported with duty paid for the value added abroad. Thus, the most labor-intensive part of the assembly process could be done at lower-wage rates. Many U.S. manufacturers took advantage of the provision and moved assembly operations to the Caribbean. They noted that they could reduce costs and more successfully compete against imports from Asia. More complex items could be assembled and turned around more quickly than if created in Asia. Disadvantages included sometimes cumbersome and time-consuming logistics considerations. By 1992, apparel assembled in the Caribbean comprised 14 percent of imports. The passage of NAFTA, however, led some observers to expect that the Caribbean would become less desirable as a manufacturing destination than Mexico.

U.S. women's apparel exports grew rapidly starting in the late 1980s. In 1995 exports of women's suits, coats, skirts, and jackets reached $259 million, over double the value of these exports in 1989. U.S. clothing seemed to grow in popularity in Europe, perhaps due to the adoption by European women of a lifestyle more in line with the easy-care, comfortable clothing purchased by women in the United States. The weak U.S. dollar helped increase shipments to Japan and Canada, as well as Europe and the Middle East.

A new World Trade Organization (WTO) was established in 1995, and the Multifiber Arrangement (MFA), which allowed importing countries to limit the flow of imports from lower cost, developing countries, was replaced by the ATC, which required the phasing out of MFA quotas over a ten-year period. According to Linda Shelton in an *Industry, Trade, and Technology Review* report, "The elimination of MFA quotas likely will have a significant impact on the U.S. textile and apparel sector given the level of protection that such restrictions have provided domestic producers over the past two decades." Since the U.S. has until 2005 to implement the ATC, the legislation's impact on the women's apparel industry may not be realized for several years.

RESEARCH AND TECHNOLOGY

The large firms in the women's apparel industry had the capital to invest in new technology, but many of the smaller firms, struggling against the tide of imports, were not in a position to do so. Nevertheless, the intrinsic "soft" quality of material made it difficult to use automated equipment widely, and apparel manufacture remained a highly labor-intensive industry.

One tool that was advocated to better meet the market's demands was "quick response"—the idea of bringing apparel to the retailer rapidly by shortening production cycles, reducing inventories, improving productivity, and relaying information regarding consumers' preferences quickly back to manufacturers. By using computers to track inventory and sales as well as consumers' responses to particular items, U.S. manufacturers could respond quickly to market demand—and thus get a jump on foreign producers. Department stores and manufacturers worked together to find ways to speed deliveries and increase efficiency. Mass merchandisers were among the first to implement the quick response concept.

FURTHER READING

"Apparel and Footwear Profiles for 1991." *KSA Perspective,* June 1992.

Apparel Import Digest. Arlington, VA: American Apparel Manufacturers Association, 1997.

Apparel Industry Trends. Arlington, VA: American Apparel Manufacturers Association, March 1997.

Brady, Jennifer L. "Analysts: Apparel on Slow Road to Recovery." *Women's Wear Daily,* 13 May 1996.

Conditions in the Women's Garment Industry. International Ladies' Garment Workers' Union, 27 January, 1993.

D'Innocenzio, Anne. "McNaughton: New Directions." *Women's Wear Daily,* 20 March 1996.

"Dresses Excel in Tailored." *Women's Wear Daily,* 8 May 1996.

Focus: An Economic Profile of the Apparel Industry. Arlington, VA: American Apparel Manufacturers Association, 1996.

"Leslie Fay Seeks Post-Chapter 11 Lender Facility." *Women's Wear Daily,* 4 January 1996. Available from http://207.51.71.250/samples/archive/1996/000/069.htm.

Shelton, Linda and Robert Wallace. "World Textile and Apparel Trade: A New Era." *Industry, Trade, and Technology Review,* October 1996.

U.S. Department of Commerce. *Statistical Abstract of the United States.* Washington: GPO, 1996.

"Women's Coats, Suits, Tailored Career Wear (Uniforms), Rainwear." *Fairchild Fact File,* 1987.

—Cheryl Collins, updated by AnnaMarie Sheldon

SIC 2339

WOMEN'S, MISSES', AND JUNIORS' OUTERWEAR NOT ELSEWHERE CLASSIFIED

This industry includes establishments primarily engaged in manufacturing women's, misses', and juniors' outerwear, not elsewhere classified, from purchased woven or knit fabrics. Knitting mills primarily engaged in manufacturing outerwear are classified in **SIC 2253: Knit Outerwear Mills.**

There were more than 1,700 manufacturers of women's, misses', and juniors' outerwear in the United States in 1993. In 1994, total shipments of women's, misses' and juniors' outerwear not elsewhere classified totaled $8.1 billion.

During the mid-1990's the industry was centered in California and New York. There were more than 1,100 manufacturers in those two states. The size and scope of these dress manufacturers vary greatly from small manufacturers operating out of their home or a single showroom to industry leading Liz Claiborne,

Inc., which employed over 8,000 individuals and had $2 billion in annual sales in 1996.

The women's apparel industry is particularly sensitive to changes in economic conditions. Consumer tastes shifted from a preference for designer labels during the 1980s to an increased interest in more casual, and inexpensive, apparel as the economic downturn of the early 1990s caused consumers to look for value and savings. This shift in consumer behavior resulted in a decrease in the number of women's apparel manufacturers. An increase in imports further increased competition in this already volatile and difficult industry. While imports increased by only 5 percent per year between 1988 and 1991, they took a jump of 15 percent in 1992. They jumped another 15 percent in 1993 and increased 12 percent in 1994. Growth slowed to 10 percent in 1995.

These events created increased competition and fostered a reluctance on behalf of manufacturers and retailers to raise prices on apparel. Many small manufacturers were forced to close their doors.

Women's, juniors', and misses' outerwear has been very sensitive to economic and demographic changes. This sensitivity was noted in the growth in sales for discount mass merchandisers at the expense of specialty boutiques and department stores. In the early 1990s, manufacturers attempted to hold down costs and provide high quality garments for increasingly demanding and careful customers.

Founded in 1976 and based in New York City, Liz Claiborne, Inc. has grown into one of the leading manufacturers in this industry. In 1989, with the retirement of founder Liz Claiborne, the company began a major slump caused by repetitive product lines, high prices, and outdated styles. When profits dropped from $223 million in 1991 to $83 million in 1994, the company hired Paul Charron from the V.F. Corporation to overhaul product lines, update designs, and cut costs. Due to these efforts, earnings in 1996 grew 69 percent from the previous year.

The apparel and textile manufacturing industries employed approximately 9 percent of the entire U.S. work force in the early 1990s. The number of workers involved women's, misses', and juniors' outerwear production fell from a high of 360,000 in 1980 to less than 222,000 in 1995. In that same time period, average wages rose from $4.61 per hour to $7.29 per hour.

More than 22,000 people, or over 20 percent of this industry's work force, were employed in California's 670 establishments engaged in women's, juniors', and misses' outerwear manufacturing in the mid-1990s. New York employed 12,800 people in this industry. The largest percentage of workers were employed as sewing machine operators, followed by pressing machine operators and inspectors. With the exception of sales and machine mechanics, all other employment categories in the industry were anticipating work force reductions through the turn of the century.

Despite inroads into automation, the bulk of apparel manufacturing in the United States was still labor intensive in the early 1990s. Wages in this sector were typically lower than in other manufacturing industries, resulting in an ongoing reliance on immigrant labor.

A new World Trade Organization (WTO) was established in 1995, and the Multifiber Arrangement (MFA), which allowed importing countries to limit the flow of imports from lower cost, developing countries, was replaced by the Agreement on Textiles and Clothing (ATC) which required the phasing out of MFA quotas over a ten-year period. According to Linda Shelton in an *Industry, Trade, and Technology Review* report, ''The elimination of MFA quotas likely will have a significant impact on the U.S. textile and apparel sector given the level of protection that such restrictions have provided domestic producers over the past two decades.'' Since the U.S. has until 2005 to implement the ATC, the legislation's impact on the women's, misses' and junior's outerwear industry may not be realized for several years.

FURTHER READING

Apparel Import Digest. Arlington, VA: American Apparel Manufacturers Association, 1997.

Apparel Industry Trends. Arlington, VA: American Apparel Manufacturers Association, March 1997.

Feldman, Amy. ''Consumer Nondurables.'' *Forbes,* 4 January 1993.

Focus: An Economic Profile of the Apparel Industry. Arlington, VA: American Apparel Manufacturers Association, 1996.

''Import Growth Slowing, AAMA Says.'' *Apparel Industry,* June 1996.

O'Rourke, Mary T. ''Labor Costs - From Pakistan to Portugal.'' *Bobbin,* September 1992.

Pouschine, Tatiana. ''Ridin' High.'' *Forbes,* 9 November 1992.

Rotenier, Nancy. ''Niki and Me.'' *Forbes,* 13 January 1997.

Shelton, Linda and Robert Wallace. ''World Textile and Apparel Trade: A New Era,'' *Industry, Trade, and Technology Review,* October 1996.

Standard & Poor's Industry Surveys. New York: Standard & Poor's Corporation, 1993.

U.S. Department of Commerce. International Trade Administration. *U.S. Industrial Outlook 1994.* Washington: GPO, 1994.

—Shula Malkin, updated by AnnaMarie Sheldon

SIC 2341

WOMEN'S, MISSES', CHILDREN'S, AND INFANTS' UNDERWEAR AND NIGHTWEAR

This category includes establishments primarily engaged in manufacturing women's, misses', children's and infants' underwear and nightwear from purchased woven or knit fabrics. Knitting mills primarily engaged in manufacturing underwear and nightwear are classified in **SIC 2254: Knit Underwear and Nightwear Mills.** Establishments primarily engaged in manufacturing women's and misses robes and dressing gowns are classified in **SIC 2384: Robes and Dressing Gowns,** and those manufacturing children's and infants' robes are classified in **SIC 2369: Girls', Children's, and Infants' Outerwear, Not Elsewhere Classified.** Establishments primarily engaged in manufacturing brassiere, girdles, and allied garments are classified in **SIC 2342: Brassieres, Girdles, and Allied Garments.**

INDUSTRY SNAPSHOT

About 340 establishments were engaged in the manufacture of women's, misses', children's, and infants' underwear in 1993. These establishments were collectively responsible for an inflation adjusted value of total product shipments estimated at $1.9 billion. This figure was in line with a long term declining trend which, beginning in 1984, had fallen without interruption. When tracked over the five year period covering 1987 1992, the annual percentage change in the value of the total product shipments averaged a negative 6.1 percent. The industry grew slightly from 1993 to 1995 with total product shipments for the industry valued at $2.2 billion in 1995.

Beginning from the early to mid-1980s, economic conditions in the women's apparel industry group turned from bad to worse, with the women's and children's underwear and nightwear being no exception. In 1982, for instance, there were approximately 604 establishments involved in manufacturing activities, and by 1989 their number had dropped to 383. During the same period total employment declined from 67,800 to 49,400. This trend continued in the early to mid-1990s, and by 1995 total employment had dropped to 31,200 workers.

The ongoing concurrence of several major economic trends sufficed to explain the industry's sagging fortunes. First, the decline in middle class income levels, a trend which began in the mid- to late 1970s and picked up a full head of steam during the 1980s, led to the withdrawal of a considerable amount of consumer purchasing power formerly directed at the purchase of apparel products in general.

Second, and partly as a consequence of the above, established lines of distribution at both the retail and wholesale levels were in the throes of a bankruptcy-induced crisis. Around the same period, these sectors were also undergoing widespread structural change, owing to the introduction of advanced communication systems which greatly enhanced the flow of integrated information across retail, wholesale and manufacturing levels.

Third, the change in women's apparel producer prices plunged during the recession of 1981-82. Then, to the further detriment of the industry, as the recession ended, prices never climbed back to their previous levels but were to remain more or less flat instead for the period covering 1983 into the first half of 1990s. With the onset of the 1990-92 recession, women's apparel prices took another nosedive. Intense intraindustry competition from both domestic and foreign producers had played an important part in generating the unfavorable price climate and contributed to a significant ten year decline in capacity utilization. After peaking in 1984 at 88 percent, capacity utilization began to plummet on an annual basis and stood at 78 percent in 1994. Finally, the lingering overhang of takeover debt, piled up from the late 1980s period of speculative merger-mania, had exerted a retarding effect on company profits and growth.

On the positive side, however, the steady decline in the value of the U.S. dollar had proved advantageous to export sales of women's and children's underwear and nightwear, although it bears mention that export sales have traditionally figured as a rather insignificant component of the industry's overall U.S. sales. For the period covering 1989-1992, the annual change in nominal exports averaged 27.1 percent. In 1993, the value of exports grew to $186 million, and in 1995 exports in the industry were valued at $267 million. At the same time, the value of U.S. imports of women's and children's underwear and nightwear grew to $1.1 billion in 1993 and $1.5 billion by 1995.

ORGANIZATION AND STRUCTURE

When tracking the density of establishments by their census region of concentration, the highest number of establishments were located in the Middle Atlantic, South Atlantic, and Pacific regions. When ranked by the number of establishments per state, New York led the way, followed by Pennsylvania, North Carolina, California, and New Jersey. In terms of the industry's total employment level per state, Pennsylvania was first, followed by New York, California, and New Jersey.

An article appearing in *Sales and Marketing Management* estimated that in 1987 large plants with 100 or more employees accounted for only 41 percent of the total number of establishments but were responsible for close to 87 percent of the industry's shipments. It noted that many of the smaller establishments survived by making specialized products to supply market niches.

Data available from the U.S. Bureau of the Census for the years 1982 and 1987 stated that primary materials consumed by the women's, misses', children's, and infants' underwear and nightwear industry ranked on a cost basis were: materials, containers, and supplies; knit fabrics; miscellaneous materials and parts; and broadwoven fabrics. The Census also reported that the major economic sectors responsible for input supply came from: imports; broadwoven fabric mills; apparel made from purchased materials; and knit fabric mills. When disaggregated, the total product share broken down by its major product classifications were: women's and children's underwear with 38.3 percent; women's and childrens' nightwear with 46.4 percent; and contract and commission work on the two combined categories was 12.2 percent. The principal economic sectors responsible for the purchase of the industry's output were: private personal expenditures with 82.7 percent; other manufacturers with 12 percent; exports with 1.5 percent; followed by the Federal Government with 1 percent.

BACKGROUND AND DEVELOPMENT

Women's underwear. The modern history of women's underwear produced for mass consumption more or less began in the 1830s to 1840s with the manufacture of ready-made undergarments. Stay stitchers and gorers using hand techniques were employed in factories or worked from home as "outworkers." Around the early 1860s, the widespread use of sewing machines pushed underwear output to unprecedented levels. Other complementary technologies, like the band knife, which enabled garment workers to slice through several layers of mate-

rial at once, proved instrumental in reorganizing the factory floor along the lines of the "batch" system.

During the 1870s, underwear was available in attractively packaged boxes with decorative and typically colored labels. Large-scale advertising campaigns trumpeting the virtues of underwear became commonplace by the end of the 1870s. Well into the 1880s, the marketing themes became more explicit in an attempt to match the luxury and erotic appeal of the undergarments. Underwear could be purchased from large department stores or by mail order from companies like Sears, Roebuck and Co. of Chicago or the Great Universal Stores located across the United States.

Fashion historians refer to the period of 1890-1913 as the "Belle Epoque." It was characterized as a period of extravagance and conspicuous consumption in women's dress in general, and in women's underwear in particular. Underwear was much lighter in appearance, feel, and weight, and compared to its lackluster mid-Victorian antecedents, more luxurious and glamorous in conception. New luxury underwear first became available in sets which included nightwear and were christened with the group name "lingerie," a term derived from the French word "linge," meaning linen. Earlier material mainstays such as cotton longcloth and flannel were replaced by cambrics, merino, and silks. The extravagance in tastes and materials continued to lead the underwear fashion charge until the economic slump of the 1930s, which ushered in the era of mass-produced machine made rayon lingerie.

The introduction in the nineteenth century, and the 1930s full-scale development of, elastene stretch fabrics exerted a tremendous influence on underwear production. And it was during the 1930s period, more than ever before, that the popularity of ready-made underwear began to seize the day. It supplanted the more upscale fabrics associated with the Belle Epoque.

During the 1940s, events surrounding World War II and its lingering after-effects, put changes in the underwear industry on a ten year hold as resources used throughout the apparel industry were diverted to wartime production. For instance, foundation wear finishing tape was used for cartridge belts, the production of hooks, eyes, and stocking supporters was supplanted by brass armaments manufacture, while lace machines were used for making camouflage nets. Nylon, invented in 1938, was used for glider tow ropes and parachutes and not until 1947 did it re-enter into the production of underwear.

During the 1950s nylon and other manmade fibers entered into the production of underwear and dominated the scene. At the time, nylon's chief drawback was its non-absorbent property, but later the fabric was somewhat modified and woven to obtain a more comfortable porous state. Another manmade material achieving popularity was rayon, which when mixed with cotton created a shiny and always "new" appearance. Other manmade 1950 notables were polyester and acrylic undergarments. In 1959 lycra, arguably one of the most important and versatile of man-made fibers, was introduced and was originally referred to as Spandex or elatomerics, only to be renamed elastene by the EEC in 1976. Containing no natural fiber at all, lycra was lighter, proved far more durable than rubber elastic, and remained a foundation wear mainstay well into the 1990s.

The decade of the 1960s and early 1970s ushered in a tumultuous period of great social and political upheaval. Television exerted a powerful influence, and Maidenform Inc. became the first U.S. company to advertise underwear on a national level. Magazines such as Vogue and other glossy women's magazines were highly attuned to promoting a version of what the beautiful woman looked like in terms of both her outer and innerwear garments. During this period, attitudes toward sex and the traditional woman's lifestyle, both outside and inside the house, were under assault, opening up new avenues for self-expression and lifestyle changes. Drowning in its wake were the more restrictive type of underwear previously equated with outdated notions of decency—and in their place came bikini-style briefs. The popularity of the briefs, which were available for men and women alike, rested on their comfort and usability.

The teenage apparel market first became a distinct entity during the 1950s and went on to become an institutional mainstay in the 1960s. The needs of younger girls (misses) for suitable and acceptable underwear reflecting their own stage of development and active involvement in various social activities was readily acknowledged. As a result, the U.S. company Lily of France introduced a special "Lilies" line of underwear for college-age girls along with a preteen collection called "Teenform," which was later imported into Britain by Berlei.

By the 1990s, the 30-year transformation of children's and infants' underwear had achieved significant results. Unlike the underwear that was worn up to the late 1960s, undergarments in the 1990s washed easier; were more attractive, lightweight, and durable; and were less prone to induce irritation. The comfort provided from t-shirts made from cotton and simple crop tops left a favorable impression on the mother or child able to recall the discomfort related to wearing undergarments made from knitted wool, liberty bodices, and burdensome knickers lined with breakable elastic during the 1940s, 1950s and early 1960s.

CURRENT CONDITIONS

The downsizing through elimination and mergers of the number of establishments comprising the women's, misses', children's, and infants' underwear and nightwear industry became a recognized trend by the late 1980s. By the mid-1990s things began to stabilize somewhat, yet it was not clear whether the trend had been entirely played out. The opening up of the countries of the former Soviet Union and Eastern Europe, where there resided a well-trained apparel workforce ripe for capitalist investment, also presented the industry with untapped opportunities that looked promising, even if they had not yet been fully explored. Further long term uncertainties were thrown into this mix with the 1993 passage of the North American Free Trade Agreement and (NAFTA), later that year, the General Agreement on Tariffs and Trade (GATT).

Well into the 1980s, the entire U.S. apparel industry group was negatively impacted by the erosion of middle class income earners who generally accounted for the overwhelming percentage of apparel purchases. At the same time, the industry's growing trend toward the foreign relocation of apparel establishments, or else the foreign outsourcing and re-entry into the United States of intermediate apparel-related work formerly performed within U.S. borders—under the auspices of the 9802 provision of the Harmonized Tariff Schedule of the United States—did not bode well for the industry's U.S. job growth prospects. The effect of apparel import competition leading to the progressive domestic market share deterioration of U.S. apparel manufacturers also indicated no sign of abating.

A new World Trade Organization was established in 1995, and the Multifiber Arrangement (MFA) which allowed importing countries to limit the flow of imports from lower cost, developing countries was replaced by the Agreement on Textiles and Clothing (ATC) which required the phasing out of MFA quotas over a ten-year period. According to Linda Shelton in an *Industry, Trade, and Technology Review* report, "The elimination of MFA quotas likely will have a significant impact on the U.S. textile and apparel sector given the level of protection that such restrictions have provided domestic producers over the past two decades." Since the U.S. has until 2005 to implement the ATC, the legislation's impact on the women's, misses', children's, and infants' underwear and nightwear industry may not be realized for several years.

INDUSTRY LEADERS

In 1996, the dominant firms in the women's, misses', children's, and infants' underwear and nightwear were: New York City-based Warnaco Incorporated, with sales of $560 million and 11,500 employees; Alabama-based Vanity Fair Mills Incorporated, with sales of $390 million and 8,500 employees; New York City-based Maidenform Inc., with sales of $400 million and 8,900 employees; and Georgia-based William Carter Co., with sales of $280 million and 6,000 employees. Both Warnaco Inc. and Vanity Fair Mills were registered as subsidiaries, while Maidenform and William Carter were privately owned companies. In 1996 Warnaco announced plans to acquire Lejaby, a $120 million European intimate apparel manufacturer. The acquisition allowed Warnaco to introduce its lucrative Calvin Klein underwear line in Europe.

WORK FORCE

In 1989 the average value added per production worker was $29,095—a figure considerably below an overall average of $105,881 calculated for 459 U.S. manufacturing industries. Efforts to redress this productivity gap have been consistently, though not uniformly, percolating throughout the industry for some time. These have variously taken the form of labor-management cooperation schemes, technology diffusion, mergers, periods of protectionism meant to provide the time necessary to restructure the workplace, and the ''outsourcing'' to other domestic or foreign firms of work formerly performed within a company's premises.

The industry's employment picture had indicated a sharp decline going back as far as 1982. For the period covering 1987-1991, the industry's total employment fell from 53,700, of which 46,700 were classified as production workers, to 45,800 with 39,200 classified as production workers. Comparison between the two years indicated that the level of total employment declined by 14.7 percent while the level of production workers fell 16.1 percent. Over the same period the real wage has fell while value added per production worker either stayed the same or rose, suggesting that productivity gains were not being matched with rising wages.

In 1995 the total number of individuals employed by women's and children's underwear and nightwear manufacturers fell to 31,200, with 27,100 classified as production workers. The average hourly wage in 1995 was $6.75, only $.24 more than the previous year and well below the industry average.

In 1990, the industry's major occupational categories were: sewing machine operators; precision inspectors, testers, and graders; pressing machine operators; and blue collar supervisors. Close to 56 percent of the work force was active in sewing machine operations. The remaining occupational categories accounted for approximately 3.1 percent of the total work force each. The U.S. Bureau of Labor Statistics had forecast that many of these occupational categories were expected to decline by the year 2005. Assuming no great deviations from the forward path of the industry's productivity trend, sewing machine operators were projected to experience the largest decline.

When compared to the measures of employment by gender and race for the U.S. manufacturing sector as a whole, women, Hispanic, black, and workers were disproportionately represented in the industry's work force to such a large degree that they dramatically exceeded their national average counterparts. In 1995, demographic data gathered from the American Apparel Manufacturers Association indicated that women workers comprised 70 percent of the industry's work force, Hispanic workers 24 percent, and black workers 15.2 percent.

RESEARCH AND TECHNOLOGY

To date, the most far-reaching domestic response to the deteriorating conditions impacting the industry was to invest in state-of-the-art communication systems which facilitate the rapid flow of information used to immediately react to, and determine, consumer preferences formed in the marketplace. This consumer driven process, which the industry refers to as the ''quick response'' system, integrates several dimensions of the production cycle with the intent of shortening the cycle's duration. Via the immediate feedback of consumer sales information from the retail to manufacturing level, producers are able to implement productivity improvements and shrink inventory levels and their associated costs to a bare minimum. To determine the changing direction of consumer tastes, the quick response system compiles the results of consumer surveys which express what consumers most likely will and will not purchase in the immediate future.

In addition to the quick-response system, the industry had also directed sizable investments at computer controlled automated machinery. With the intention of increasing productivity foremost in mind, these investments targeted the areas of design, cutting, embroidery, sewing, finishing, ticketing, and several distribution operations. In order to compete within their own industry as well as against other non-apparel industries, the industry's leading firms were the first to implement these investments to any significant degree. Their ability to finance high cost start-up technological advances was related to their economies of scale and access to internally generated funds. With the passage of time, if the middle and lower tier firms failed to respond by adapting these new technologies, then across the entire industry an uneven pattern of technological change would result and most likely exacerbate the downsizing trend active throughout the industry.

FURTHER READING

Apparel Import Digest. Arlington, VA: American Apparel Manufacturers Association, 1997.

Apparel Industry Trends. Arlington, VA: American Apparel Manufacturers Association, March 1997.

Arpan, Jeffery S., Jose de la Torres, and Brian Toyne. *The U.S. Apparel Industry: International Challenge, Domestic Response.* Atlanta: Business Publishing Division, College of Business Administration Georgia State University, 1982.

Carter, Alison. *Underwear: The Fashion History.* London: B.T. Batsford LTD, 1992.

Darnay, Arsen J., ed. *Manufacturing USA.* 5th Ed. Detroit: Gale Research, 1993.

Ewing, Elizabeth. *Dress and Undress: A History of Women's Underwear.* New York: Drama Book Specialists, 1978.

Fairchild Fact File: Women's Inner Fashions: Nightwear, Daywear, Loungewear. New York: Fairchild Publications, Market Research Division, 1989.

Focus: An Economic Profile of the Apparel Industry. Arlington, VA: American Apparel Manufacturers Association, 1993.

Focus: An Economic Profile of the Apparel Industry. Arlington, VA: American Apparel Manufacturers Association, 1996.

Jarnow, Jeannette, and Miriam Guerreiro. *Inside the Fashion Business.* New York: Macmillan Publishing Company, 1991.

Lehman Brothers. *The Clothes Line,* December 1993.

Rose, Clare. *Children's Clothes Since 1750.* New York: Drama Book Publishers, 1989.

Shelton, Linda, and Robert Wallace. "World Textile and Apparel Trade: A New Era." *Industry, Trade, and Technology Review,* October 1996.

U.S. Department of Commerce. International Trade Administration. *U.S. Industrial Outlook 1995.* Washington: GPO, 1994.

—Daniel King, updated by AnnaMarie Sheldon

BRASSIERES, GIRDLES, AND ALLIED GARMENTS

Establishments primarily engaged in manufacturing brassieres, girdles, corsets, corset accessories, and allied garments are included in this industry.

INDUSTRY SNAPSHOT

The U.S. bra and allied garment industry shipments were valued at $1.8 billion in 1995. During its century of existence, the industry saw a number of ups and downs, influenced by a variety of factors—only some of them style-based. During World War II, for example, the cotton, rubber, silk, and steel used to make women's undergarments were needed instead for the war effort. The bra and girdle industry was forced to develop new products that made use of synthetic fabrics.

Although the braless look of the 1960s caused concern among manufacturers, who saw their profits literally going up in smoke during the "burn the bra" movement, bras and girdles did reappear—in different fabrics, shapes, and colors—and the industry remained strong. Fashion trends changed the shape of the bra and technology altered its fabric content, but the garment remained a big seller. In a 1989 tribute to the centennial of the bra, *Life* magazine estimated that more than half a million undergarments of this type were sold daily in the United States. In 1996, nylon bras accounted for 54.3 percent of the market; polyester, 24.0 percent; and cotton, 14.4 percent.

BACKGROUND AND DEVELOPMENT

The first bra was developed in France in 1889 by the corsetmaker Herminie Cadolle. Designed to replace the restrictive whale-bone corsets that stylish women of the time were forced to wear, the bra supported a woman's breasts without constricting her diaphragm. Americans were introduced to the bra during the 1910s—the Flapper Era—when the ideal woman's silhouette was slim and boyish. An undergarment that would flatten a woman's breasts was an ideal accompaniment to the straight-cut, form-fitting flapper dress preferred by suffragettes and stylish debutantes in Europe.

The style was brought back to America, and in 1913 New York socialite Caresse Crosby designed a brassiere out of two handkerchiefs and silk ribbons. The patent for her design was registered in 1914. Shortly thereafter, it was purchased by the Connecticut-based Warner's Company for $1,500. Warner's, previously a corset company, became one of the first American manufacturers of the bra. Other companies followed, including the now-defunct Boyshform — the name of which encompassed all the new bra was supposed to do.

Until the 1930s, the bra was more or less a "one size fits all" product. Because of the manly styles of the 1920s, women did not want to emphasize the size or shape of their breasts; rather, they tried to conceal them. In the Depression era, however, fashion designers began to emphasize women's feminine form once again. Warner's introduced bras with fitted cups, ranging from A (small) to D (large) size, in 1935; other manufacturers quickly followed suit.

The rages of fashion shifted all the way from the World War I boyish look epitomized by the flappers, to the very womanly figure of such pin-up girls as Betty Grable and Jane Russell during World War II. Even though the fabrics used to make bras and girdles—silk, cotton, and rubber—were reserved for the war effort, designers still found ways to manufacture bras and girdles that emphasized the curvaceous look favored by sweater girls and soldier boys.

Anecdotal evidence claimed that Howard Hughes's aeronautics firm once designed a bra for Jane Russell, star of the 1943 movie classic *The Outlaw*. Made of metal, the bra was heavy and uncomfortable, according to Russell, who claimed that she never wore it. But the use of metal did play an important role in the next phase of bra silhouettes. In 1946, under-cup wiring was introduced. This engineering feat allowed bra designers to lift the bust even more, since the underwiring added extra support.

During the 1940s, bras were being manufactured by Maidenform Inc., founded in 1922; Playtex Apparel Inc., founded in 1932; Vanity Fair Mills Inc., founded in 1899; and other smaller companies including Bestform, founded in 1923; and Bali, founded in 1927.

Women's fashion took on a retro look in the postwar 1940s and 1950s, when returning soldiers reclaimed the workplace and many women returned to the role of homemaker. With sheath dresses that emphasized every curve of a woman's figure being shown in every fashion house in Europe and America, undergarment manufacturers introduced one-piece, constructed undergarments to hold in stomachs, nip in waists, and push up busts. Another fashion favorite, the tight-bodiced, full-skirted dress, also required undergarments to pull in the waist and emphasize the bust.

During the 1950s, bra manufacturers experimented with a new look, the push-up bra, in which the cup section was cut in half, leaving the cleavage exposed. Usually strapless, to be worn under the strapless formal dresses so popular in the 1950s, the push-up bra gave every woman who wore it an ample-looking, high-bosomed silhouette. Cone-shaped bras, which emphasized a pointy-busted look, were also popular in the 1950s, and were returned to popularity briefly by singer Madonna in the late 1980s.

While bras changed in shape throughout the forty-odd years they were manufactured by American companies, other undergarments also changed to keep up with the current styles. The Edwardian look of the last years of the nineteenth century and the first decade of the twentieth century involved the wearing of a firm foundation garment that pulled in the waist and supported the bust. Corsets of the 1920s flattened the figure, but they were often too long for the short dresses being worn by young women. In response, manufacturers developed corselettes—shorter corsets—as well as slide-on garter belts and other, even briefer, undergarments.

The technological innovations of the 1930s turned up in undergarments. "Living Lastex," one of the earliest of the stretchy, shape-holding textiles, along with narrow, dependable zippers, allowed manufacturers to sell undergarments that not only helped a woman maintain a womanly shape, but also let her move and breathe with at least a bit more comfort. Panty girdles—girdles that were shaped like underpants—were invented in the 1930s, to be worn under then more acceptable slacks and shorts.

Dior's "New Look" of the late 1940s and 1950s needed new-looking undergarments. To go with the cantilevered bras required by the new silhouette, women laced themselves into guepieres, or waist cinchers—a new back-laced corset. Also at this time the Merry Widow corset, an all-in-one bra and girdle combination that was popular at the end of the nineteenth century, was reintroduced. The industry giant Warner's was among the first manufacturers to make the new Merry Widow available to the masses by introducing a line of them in retail stores in 1952.

The pulled-in, pushed-up look of the 1950s became the pulled-apart look of the 1960s, as women's liberation swept across America. Bras were suddenly seen as harnesses rather than supports, which held women back rather than up. Women's libbers burned bras in city streets. At the Miss America pageant of 1968—the height of the women's movement—protesters threw bras, girdles, and other symbols of enslavement, such as curlers and *Cosmopolitan* magazine, into a garbage can. Bras were out, and many women appeared in public without undergarments.

Bra and girdle manufacturers were undoubtedly concerned about their profits shrinking in the tide of the braless revolution. They worked hard at developing "natural-looking undergarments"—bras that held a woman's breasts without changing their natural shape, and "barely there" girdles. But it was not the revolutionary bra style that forced women back into underwear. Rather, it was the concern voiced by the medical community that women who went braless for a long period of time ran the risk of stretching their breast ligaments to a point where the breast would look elongated and feel uncomfortable.

At the same time as bra manufacturers struggled to keep a reign on the top part of the industry, girdle manufacturers faced a revolution even more harmful than bra burning. It was the invention of pantyhose—all-in-one stockings and panties—that struck a blow from which some manufacturers took years to recover. Pantyhose did not require garters, garter belts, or girdles. Women's libbers—and in fact almost every woman in the country—adopted pantyhose faster than anyone could possibly have foreseen.

As women became more confident about appearing in public without the entrapments of constricting undergarments, bra and girdle manufacturers had to scramble to keep up. Luckily, however, another movement—the exercise and fitness phenomenon of the 1970s and 1980s—provided a new market for their wares.

Women and men throughout the United States became exercise fanatics, spurred on by such fitness gurus as Jane Fonda. Workout attire, such as sports bras, became popular. But for many women, especially those who suddenly found themselves part of the 24-hour-a-day corporate world, an exercise regimen was difficult to maintain on a regular basis. They needed help—and the bra and girdle manufacturers of America were prepared to support them with body suits, bras, body shapers (a synonym for "girdle"), and control-top underpants, all made of lycra, spandex, and other miracle synthetics, to pull in, push up, and smooth out a myriad of lumps, bumps, and ridges.

By the late 1980s, the bra and girdle industry came almost full-circle as tastes and styles changed once again. Bras, girdles, and even corsets were popularized by performers such as Madonna, who almost single-handedly revived the bustiere industry; movies such as *Dangerous Liaisons,* in which the female characters were laced up in tight corsets; and couturiers who put

their bras on the outside of dresses, rather than the inside.

Women's wear shipments, including bras and allied garments, were much lower than the industry average in 1992. Among the factors affecting the growth of the industry were demographic trends—apparel expenses became a lower proportion of total personal expenditures for the baby-boom generation. These consumers reached the point in their lives when other expenses—mortgages and their children's college tuition, for example—began to take precedence over clothing purchases.

As well, there was a shift in consumer buying habits. Instead of patronizing retail stores, a majority of shoppers began making regular visits to discounters and off-price emporiums, where they could find bargains. Bra and girdle manufacturers began offering discount lines; although there might still be a small market for luxury underclothes, most women wanted to spend less on a bra than on an evening meal.

The fashion splurge of the 1980s, when expenditures on clothes practically doubled, was replaced with frugal shopping by recession-stressed consumers who frequented Kmart and Wal-Mart more often than designer boutiques and department stores. According to Standard and Poor's *Industry Surveys* (1992), not only did the spending patterns of consumers change, but their buying patterns also took a new direction.

Basic apparel—T-shirts, sweatshirts, denims, and fleecewear—were in, as were moderately priced name brands like Fruit-of-the-Loom and Van Heusen. The major manufacturers of bras and girdles began producing basic styles at popular prices, and in that way they were able to keep up with this latest trend.

But manufacturers of bras and girdles also realized that undergarments were something that women—and men—would occasionally splurge on. Companies such as Victoria's Secret Stores and Gossard, manufacturer of the new super-uplift bra launched in 1994, continued to have success selling pure silk and lace undergarments for romantic occasions like Valentine's Day and honeymoons. They also served a number of women who desired a "little bit of femininity" under their business clothes.

Although the value of shipments of bras and allied garments increased 13 percent between 1987 and 1988, the industry remained fairly stagnant since then. The worst year was 1988-1989, when the industry saw an almost 16 percent decline in the value of its shipments. In 1989 to 1990, there was a modest 2 percent gain, offset by a 1 percent decline in 1990-1991.

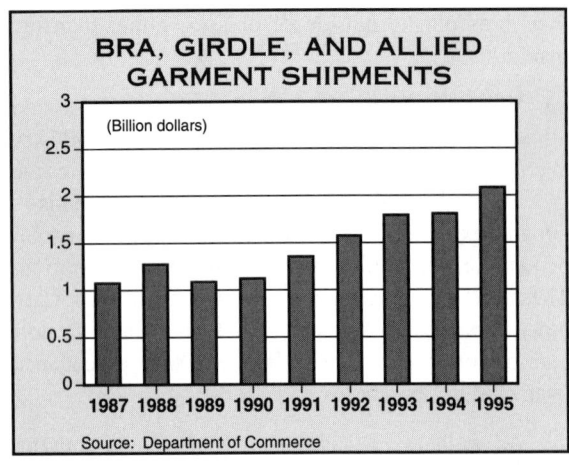

BRA, GIRDLE, AND ALLIED GARMENT SHIPMENTS

(Billion dollars)

Source: Department of Commerce

CURRENT CONDITIONS

As a result of the more frugal spending patterns of shoppers in the early and mid-1990s, discount stores held 30 percent of the bra market by 1997; bras were the most lucrative intimate apparel item of discounter. Chain stores accounted for 19.6 percent of the market, while department stores captured 18.7 percent. Between 1990 and 1997 bra sales at department stores increased 5 percent.

Mail order sales doubled from 1990 to 1997 due, in part, to the privacy afforded by mail order purchases. Catalog companies like Victoria's Secret depended on bras to generate 5.9 percent of catalog sales. By 1997, mail order chains accounted for 13.4 percent of the bra market.

As manufacturers adjusted to meet consumer demands, the bra and allied garment industry grew slowly but steadily from shipment values of $1.2 billion in 1990 to shipment values of $1.8 billion in 1995.

INDUSTRY LEADERS

One of the largest manufacturers of bras and related intimate apparel in the United States was New York City-based Warnaco, Inc., which posted sales of $560 million in 1996. During the same year, the company announced plans to acquire Lejaby, a $120 million European intimate apparel manufacturer. The acquisition would allow Warnaco to introduce its lucrative Calvin Klein underwear line in Europe.

Playtex Apparel Inc. of Stamford, Connecticut, a subsidiary of the Sara Lee Corporation, posted sales of $400 million and employed 7,800 individuals in 1996. Vanity Fair Mills Inc. of Monroeville, Alabama, a subsidiary of V.F. Corporation, had sales of $390 million and employed 8,500 people in 1996. Maidenform, Inc. posted 1996 sales of $400 million. Bestform Foundations Inc., a privately held company based in

Long Island, New York, had sales of $250 million in 1996.

Victoria's Secret Stores posted sales of $661 million for 1995. In 1996 the company introduced the Perfect Silhouette seamless bra. According to CFO Philip R. Mallot the seamless style became "the most successful, highest-margin product in the store." In the same year, the company planned to add 50 new stores and remodel 25 of its 671 existing stores.

WORK FORCE

Manufacturers of bras and allied garments employed approximately 14,100 workers in 1996, 10,500 of whom were involved in production activities. Employment within this industry declined steadily, from 13,800 in 1987 to 10,600 in 1991, but recovered slightly as the U.S. economy emerged from its recession. Average hourly earnings within the industry were projected at $8.15 in 1995, up from $7.22 in the previous year.

AMERICA AND THE WORLD

The value of exports of bras and allied garments has increased rapidly since 1988, as women in Europe and other markets faced busier lifestyles and responded by adopting some U.S. fashions. The value of industry exports increased nearly 20 percent to $252 million in 1992. By 1995 the value of exports increased to $387 million. At the same time, U.S. imports within the bra and girdle industry increased 15 percent, to $534 million in 1992. By 1995, imports increased to $902 million. Some U.S. manufacturers of basic apparel opened plants overseas, particularly in Europe.

RESEARCH AND TECHNOLOGY

Manufacturers of basic apparel, such as bras and girdles, were strong candidates for implementation of electronic data interchange (EDI) systems, which linked manufacturers with retailers via computer networks. Through these systems, retailers electronically scanned the bar codes on all merchandise as it was sold. Then product data—such as number, color, and size—was transmitted automatically to manufacturers. EDI allowed manufacturers to plan production more efficiently and respond more quickly to consumer demand. Many such systems also provided for "automatic replenishment," where manufacturers shipped replacement merchandise directly to retailers without the delay of processing paperwork. Manufacturers of basic apparel stood to gain most from EDI systems since their operations were more highly automated and less dependent upon fashion trends than other apparel manufacturers.

Environmental issues were another area of research that occupied bra and girdle manufacturers in the mid-1990s. The industry came under pressure to reduce the inks and dyes, fabric scrap, and packaging it used, which often ended up in landfills or water supplies. The industry responded by developing new production processes that reduced ink use and scrap, as well as reevaluating its packaging choices. Consumer preferences also shifted toward natural, organically grown fabrics, so bra and girdle manufacturers increasingly tried to incorporate these materials into their garments.

FURTHER READING

Apparel Import Digest. Arlington, VA: American Apparel Manufacturers Association, 1997.

Apparel Industry Trends. Arlington, VA: American Apparel Manufacturers Association, March 1997.

Bond, David. *The Guinness Guide to 20th Century Fashion.* Enfield, England: Guinness Superlatives Limited, 1981.

Brady, Jennifer L. "Analysts: Apparel on Slow Road to Recovery." *Women's Wear Daily,* 13 May 1996.

———. "Victoria's Secret Seamless Bra Sews Up Sales." *Women's Wear Daily,* 8 May 1996.

Dowling, Claudia Glenn. "Ooh-La-La! The Bra." *Life,* June 1989.

Focus: An Economic Profile of the Apparel Industry. Arlington, VA: American Apparel Manufacturers Association, 1996.

Garland, Madge. *The Changing Form of Fashion,* New York: Praeger Publishers, Inc., 1970.

Glynn, Prudence. *In Fashion: Dress in the Twentieth Century.* New York: Oxford University Press, 1978.

Gray, Mitchel, and Mary Kennedy. *The Lingerie Book.* New York: St. Martin's Press, 1980.

"Intimate Scores at Mass." *Women's Wear Daily,* 8 May 1996.

Lurie, Alison. *The Language of Clothes.* New York: Random House, 1981.

Reda, Susan. "Sweet Dreams (Brassiere Marketing)." *Discount Store News,* 3 May 1993.

Standard and Poor's Industry Surveys. November 1992.

U.S. Department of Commerce. International Trade Administration. *U.S. Industrial Outlook 1994.* Washington: GPO, 1994.

—Marcia K. Mogelonsky and AnnaMarie Sheldon

SIC 2353

HATS, CAPS, AND MILLINERY

This category includes establishments primarily engaged in the manufacture of hats, caps, millinery, and hat bodies. Establishments primarily engaged in manufacturing millinery trimmings are classified in **SIC 2396: Automotive Trimmings, Apparel Findings, and Related Products.** Establishments primarily engaged in manufacturing hats and caps of paper are classified in **SIC 2679: Converted Paper and Paperboard Products, Not Elsewhere Classified;** those manufacturing caps of rubber are classified in **SIC 3069: Fabricated Rubber Products, Not Elsewhere Classified;** those manufacturing caps of plastics are classified in **SIC 3089: Plastic Products, Not Elsewhere Classified;** and those manufacturing fur hats are classified in **SIC 2371: Fur Goods.**

INDUSTRY SNAPSHOT

Approximately 363 establishments were engaged in the manufacture of hats, caps, and millinery (the design, production, and sales of women's hats) in 1993. Altogether, these establishments were responsible for total product shipments estimated at $990 million. Between the years of 1987 and 1991, total industry sales rose from $663 million to $801 million. Since 1987, the industry had been experiencing a modest recovery, due in large part to the fad-driven popularity of team logo sports headwear. This came as a welcomed sign of relief to an industry whose fortunes had been steadily drifting downward since the early 1960s when there was a national trend toward hatlessness. For the 10-year period covering 1982-1992 alone, the number of establishments active in the industry fell from 420 to about 330, a 21.4 percent decline.

In addition to team logo sports headwear, the industry's output included straw harvest hats; jungle-cloth helmets; opera hats; Panama hats; and hat bodies made from fur-felt, straw, and wool-felt. To professional uniform services, the industry supplied chauffeur caps, police hats and caps (excluding protective headwear), and various other uniform hats and caps. In 1989, millinery establishments contributed an estimated $180 million to the industry's overall total product sales. A rather significant turnaround when compared to the $58 million mark achieved during the late 1970s.

In the mid-1990s, hats began to be seen once again as fashionable accessories. Department store hat sales increased by 5.5 percent, and in 1995 rose again by 2.9 percent to $720 million.

ORGANIZATION AND STRUCTURE

In 1989, about 380 establishments were engaged in the production of hats, caps, and millinery. The average establishment employed approximately 42 employees. In the same year, the average value added per production worker was $30,355, a figure that was considerably below an overall national average of $105,881 for 459 U.S. manufacturing industries. In terms of investment per production worker—usually a reliable indicator of inter-industry levels of productivity—the hats, caps, and millinery industry averaged $471, which paled significantly against the national average of $7,959.

According to the 1987 Census of Manufacturers, the largest concentration of the industry's establishments was located in the middle Atlantic region, followed by the South Atlantic and west north Central regions, respectively. In terms of the number of establishments per state, New York topped the others with 152, followed by California with 40, and Missouri with 39.

Industry leaders in 1996 included Texas-based Hat Brands Inc., with sales of $180 million and 1,000 employees; Pennsylvania-based Bollman Hat Co., with $35 million in sales and 700 employees; Denver-based Imperial Headwear Inc., with sales of $30 million and 400 employees; and Illinois-based American Needle and Novelty Co., with $23 million in sales and 200 employees. Although not among the top five companies, AJD Cap Corp. was a rising star in the segment of men's and boys' sports headwear.

Input data from 1982 and 1987 indicated that the major sources or sector of input supply entering into the production of felt-related headwear were from processed textile wastes, textile goods, motor freight transportation and warehousing, cyclic crudes and organics, petroleum refining, fabricated rubber products, plastic materials and resins, and electric services. On the other hand, the principal industrial recipients or sectors purchasing felt-related headwear were manufacturers of electrical machinery and general industrial machinery, exports, blowers and fans, surgical appliances and supplies, and photographic equipment and supplies.

In 1987, disaggregation of the industry's total output by its major product category indicated that cloth hats and caps, excluding millinery, accounted for a 50.8 percent share. Within this category, men's and boys' hats and caps dominated with 46.6 percent, followed by all other hats and caps with 3.8 percent. It is important to note that the fad-driven growth in the sales of sports headwear bearing the team logos from the National Basketball Association (NBA), the National Football League (NFL), Major League Baseball (MLB), and the National College Athletic Association (NCAA) also fell within this major product category and that midway into the 1990s their sales continued at a record pace.

The second major product category, accounting for 18.2 percent of the total output was hats, caps, and millinery not specified by kind. Close behind followed the classification of millinery products that accounted for 17.7 percent of the industry's total output. Shares accounted for within this classification were fur-felt and wool-felt millinery with 3.6 percent, millinery fabrics with 4.9 percent, all other millinery and hat frames with 3.5 percent, and millinery not specified by kind with 5.7 percent. The last major product category, responsible for 13.2 of the industry's total output, was hats and hat bodies, excluding cloth and millinery. Within this major category, the share accounted for by men's and boys' finished straw hats was 4.7 percent, by men's and boys' wool-felt hats with 3.9 percent, fur-felt finished hats with 2.3 percent, and hat bodies for 2.2 percent.

BACKGROUND AND DEVELOPMENT

Prior to the more recent era of hatlessness, which took root during the suburbanization wave of the 1950s and 1960s, no respectable man or woman would have thought of leaving the house without a hat. The question of whether the hat industry would survive or not was unheard of during this time. Instead, of vital concern to the successful firms competing in the industry was their ability to produce and market an unending procession of new styles or modified variations of current popular styles. Since the life of a hat as a fashion accessory was typically short, the faster a firm was able to get in and out of a hot-selling style proved the key to its success.

Although not totally isolated from historical forces of technological change sweeping through other apparel industries, up until the 1990s, opportunities to mechanize and automate the industry had proven difficult. As a result, production methods frequently required a great deal of handwork, therefore, labor-intensive manufacture has long remained the industry's norm.

Men's Hats. As the twentieth century began, most men living in urban areas of the United States wore hats. During the first decade, men could choose from a large variety of hats with each style purported to reflect the wearer's personality. One of the most prominent was the "princely" brown or black derby hat, which was available in three basic styles. At the time, most successful or aspiring businessmen sported the derby look. One of the more notables was the financier J.P. Morgan, who popularized a flat-topped version of the derby.

The manufacture of the derby was a time-consuming and labor-intensive process. Made from felt treated with repeated applications of a shellac solution, the material was heated and then allowed to cool. As it cooled, it took on it's stiffened state. Next came an oven process, which softened it to the touch, followed by an iron mold process. To press the hat into its distinctive derby shape, a rubber bag was inserted inside the hat into which cold water was forced. Finally, the hat's brim was curled through a highly skilled operation that required a set of specialized tools referred to as "shackles."

Almost as popular as the derby was the fedora, which was made from soft felt. Except for its shaping process, the fedora's manufacturing process mimicked many of the steps involved in producing a derby. The hat was available in black, brown, and gray and received its named from the popular drama *Fedora*, penned by Victorien Sardou.

Though derby and fedora hats were to remain popular U.S. favorites for decades to come, a challenge to their popularity arrived in the form of the Homburg hat. Made popular by King Edward's recreational visits to the town of Homburg in southern Germany, the Homburg hat was of Tyrolean origin and featured a small brightly colored feather in its side band's bow. By the time the hat achieved mass appeal, it was mostly available in black and was worn with an informal evening jacket.

During the 1920s, the U.S. men's fashion scene was heavily influenced by the British, particularly items connected to the pastimes of the Prince of Wales or associated with displays of wealth. For instance, in 1925, the English international tennis team showed up to play in Newport, Rhode Island, wearing brown snap-brim soft felt hats that the Prince, just a short time earlier, had been seen vacationing in. These hats became the rage with wealthy crowds frequenting tennis matches and then proceeded to gain mass U.S. appeal. As an emphasis on dressing in style for leisure events and travel to warmer climates of the United States became more popular, Panama hats, which were woven from such lightweight materials as oatmeal, coconut, and rice straws, increased in popularity. Bangkoks and Balibuntals, made from bamboo grasses or bamboo saplings growing wild in the Philippines, also became popular. Another lightweight favorite were Mi-

lan hats, made from Tuscan straw grown in Italy. Woven loosely, these hats offered protection from the sun and allowed for good ventilation.

Except for the affluent few, the era of the Great Depression knocked the demand out of the market for hats. Just the same, British fashion influences continued, as was evidenced by the sensation created by the "porkpie" hat's arrival in 1934. A low-crowned hat of the telescope type and made from felt, the porkpie was first worn by well-to-do men who frequented polo games and horse races. Within a short time, the porkpie hat was accepted as appropriate attire for either business or casual settings. After it's initial introduction in felt, the porkpie later became available in a variety of straws, including panamas, leghorns, and bangkoks.

Caps worn for purposes other than work also became popular during this decade. The checkered cap was deemed appropriate for golf and weekend motoring. For hunters, fishing enthusiasts, and country sports spectators, rough tweed caps were fashionable. Irrespective of whether it was worn for work or leisure purposes, the production process for cloth cap manufacture was practically the same. Cloth was cut by hand, usually with a manually operated knife, to ensure a precision pattern. The pieces were then sewn carefully to ensure that the cloth's design matched, with special attention paid to where the crown joined the visor. The cap was then steamed and ironed. Additional leather and linings were sewn in during the finishing stages. Should the cap be unlined, the crown seams were filled with tape so the threads did not appear on the outside of the cap.

With economic production geared toward military purposes, the war years of the 1940s witnessed little change in terms of style or material in men's hats. For the remainder of the decade, the war's aftershocks continued a dulling effect on the industry. By the early 1950s, the advent of man-made fabrics—many of which were washable and lightweight—dramatically transformed the material base from which most apparel garments were constructed. In turn, the reigning emphasis on lightweight materials translated into a boom for straw hats. Around the same time, the popularity of the low-crown porkpie hat increased and the wearing of the small-shape strip tweed cap outside of its more narrowly defined traditional sporting events boundaries was common. By the decade's end, hats made from man-made material, such as nylon, displaced straw hats as they proved lighter in weight and came with more ventilation and durability.

CURRENT CONDITIONS

As already indicated, the decline in the hats, caps, and millinery industry reaches back to at least the early 1960s, if not before, when a massive structural shift away from the wearing of hats took hold. The reversals in the industry's millinery branch appeared to be the most permanent. Although several short-lived, fad-driven waves have hit, these were hardly sufficient to restore millinery back to the level of its formative years in the 1950s, when over 400 companies supplied hats worn by the majority of U.S. women. By 1989, fewer than 80 companies produced millinery articles.

In the mid-1990s hats began to sell again as fashion accessories. To promote hats, ten independent Chicago hatmakers formed the Millinery Arts Alliance in 1995. As department store sales increased in both 1994 and 1995, the industry seemed to be turning itself around, although to what level was still speculative. By 1997, graduates of New York's Fashion Institute of Technology, the only domestic school with a two-year millinery program, reached 500, 20 times the number of graduates in 1987.

Men's and boys' team logo sports headwear was the only other area breathing life into the struggling industry. Coupled with the increase in sales of hats as fashion accessories, this may have been sufficient enough to warrant a more optimistic outlook for the industry as a whole since data tracking the value of the industry's shipments for the period of 1987-1994 had risen significantly. In 1994 some of the top U.S. firms with leading market shares in the sports headwear market were: American Needle, Starter, Logo 7, A.J.D Cap, Drew Pearson, and Apex. In an effort to eliminate the high cost of sewing labor, some firms were experimenting with heat applied techniques to join sports headwear fabrics. The result of these undertakings were mixed as some products proved to be of inferior quality.

As to what impact the market turnaround of the late 1980s and early and mid-1990s would have on the industry's domestic work force was uncertain. For the most part, the leading firms in the sports headwear market were becoming increasingly involved in foreign outsourcing, so that while the industry's U.S.-based firms might prosper, the same could not be said for its U.S. work force. Add to the mix the passage of the North American Free Trade Agreement and the trade stimulating accord reached in the 1993 round of the General Agreements on Tariffs and Trade and the near future domestic employment picture looked less than promising.

One pathbreaking technology figuring largely in all sports headwear firms' success came from the introduction of Quick Response (QR) systems. Seldom has a system been devised that was so in line with the apparel industry's business climate where rapid change, high stakes risk, and oftentimes fickle consumer behavior play so important a role. By design, Quick Response programs electronically link textile manufacturers, apparel producers, and retailers into a computerized information network analyzing consumer sales information. Its ultimate purpose was intended to considerably shorten the turnaround time it takes for hot-selling items to arrive in retail stores, minimize systemwide inventory levels, and reduce or eliminate slow-moving articles to prevent unwanted markdown. Other technological inroads were being forged through the application of computer aid design and manufacture and laser beams used to cut cloth.

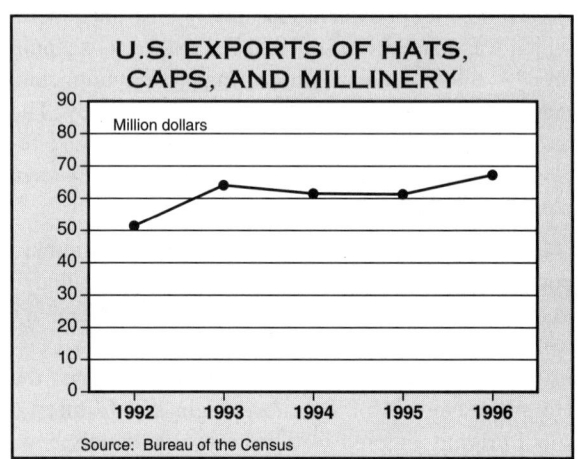

U.S. EXPORTS OF HATS, CAPS, AND MILLINERY

Million dollars

Source: Bureau of the Census

When the World Trade Organization (WTO) was established in 1995, and the Multifiber Arrangement (MFA), which allowed importing countries to limit the flow of imports from lower cost, developing countries was replaced by the ATC, which required the phasing out of MFA quotas over a ten-year period. According to Linda Shelton in an *Industry, Trade, and Technology Review* report, "The elimination of MFA quotas likely will have a significant impact on the U.S. textile and apparel sector given the level of protection that such restrictions have provided domestic producers over the past two decades." Since the United States has until 2005 to implement the ATC, the legislation's impact on the women's apparel industry may not be realized for several years.

WORK FORCE

In 1987, the industry's total employment was 17,200, of which 14,600 were classified as production workers. In 1993, the industry employed 19,355, over half of whom were employed at establishments with under 20 employees; the average number of employees per establishment was 53. Between these years, and despite the fact that total employment had fallen by 5.2 percent, there was little change in the level of production workers, which suggests that most of the job loss was confined to management personnel. During the same period, when compared to other apparel industries—most of which experienced higher levels of decline for the categories of total employment and production workers—the hats, caps, and millinery industry had fared rather well. To a large extent, the reversal of the industry's fortunes after several decades of decline can be attributed to the growing influence of team logo sports headwear sales and the resurgence of hats as fashion accessories in the mid-1990s.

For the period of 1987-1991, the value added per production worker had risen considerably. It climbed from $368 in 1987 to $459 in 1991, an increase of 24.7 percent. In 1994, value added per production worker reached $573. At the same time, the level of hourly real wages—which were only half the national average to begin with—either stagnated or slightly declined, indicating that the industry's productivity improvements and wages were moving in opposite directions.

According to the Bureau of Labor Statistics (BLS), sewing machine operators by far constituted the industry's largest occupational category accounting for 56 percent of all occupations. Several other occupational categories falling just slightly above or below the 3 percent level were: precision inspectors, testers, and graders; blue collar work supervisors; and pressing machine operators. Traffic, shipping, and receiving clerks accounted for 2 percent of all occupational categories. Based on the expectation that the industry continued along a moderate path of productivity growth, a BLS survey forecasting the growth of the industry's occupational categories until the year 2005 indicated negative growth for all categories, with sales-related occupations being the lone exception. Sewing machine operators were projected to be the hardest hit as improvements in sewing technologies and new stitch-free techniques would exercise a displacing effect.

The industry's work force demographics, especially in terms of its race and gender components, bore little relationship to their national average counterparts for the manufacturing sector taken as a whole. According to research conducted by the American Apparel Manufacturers Association in 1995, women made up 70 percent of the industry's work force against a na-

tional manufacturing average of 31.6 percent. Workers of Hispanic origin accounted for 25.7 percent of the industry's employment compared to a national manufacturing average of 10.2 percent. Blacks surprisingly comprised only 14.4 percent of the industry's work force. This figure stood was similar to the black participation rate for the apparel industry group as a whole, and was also only slightly above the national manufacturing average of 10.4 percent.

FURTHER READING

Arnold, Pauline, and Percival White. *Clothes and Cloth: America's Apparel Business.* New York: Holiday House Publishers, 1961.

Arpan, Jeffery S., Jose de la Torres, and Brian Toyne. *The U.S. Apparel Industry: International Challenge, Domestic Response.* Atlanta, GA: Business Publishing Division, College of Business Administration Georgia State University, 1982.

Chandler, Susan. "Heady Days for Milliners." *Business Week,* 13 January 1997.

Economic and Demographic Indicators of 42 ACTWU Industries. New York: Research Department, Amalgamated Clothing and Textile Workers Union, 1988.

Focus: An Economic Profile of the Apparel Industry. Arlington, VA: American Apparel Manufacturers Association, 1993.

Focus: An Economic Profile of the Apparel Industry. Arlington, VA: American Apparel Manufacturers Association, 1996.

Jarnow, Jeannette, and Miriam Guerreiro. *Inside the Fashion Business.* New York: Macmillan Publishing Company, 1991.

Lehman Brothers. *The Clothes Line,* December 1993.

Darnay, Arson J., ed. *Manufacturing USA.* 3rd ed. Detroit: Gale Research, 1993.

Schoeffler, O.E. and William Gale. *Esquire's Encyclopedia of 20th Century Men's Fashions.* New York: McGraw Hill Inc., 1973.

Shelton, Linda and Robert Wallace. "World Textile and Apparel Trade: A New Era." *Industry, Trade, and Technology Review,* October 1996.

U.S. Department of Commerce. International Trade Administration. *U.S. Industrial Outlook 1993.* Washington: GPO, 1993.

—Daniel King, updated by AnnaMarie Sheldon

SIC 2361

GIRLS', CHILDREN'S, AND INFANTS' DRESSES, BLOUSES, AND SHIRTS

This category covers establishments which are primarily engaged in manufacturing girls', children's, and infants' dresses, blouses, and shirts from purchased woven or knit materials. Knitting mills primarily engaged in manufacturing outerwear are classified in **SIC 2253: Knit Outerwear Mills.**

INDUSTRY SNAPSHOT

There were approximately 315 establishments that manufactured the items covered in this category in 1996—a drop from the 419 recorded for 1993. As was true for much of the U.S. apparel industry, these establishments tended to be small, family-run businesses, and they faced stiff competition from low-cost imports. Against this backdrop, the baby boomer generation was having children leading to its own mini-boom, and these parents were better educated and had more disposable income than their parents—factors influencing their purchasing decisions for their children's clothing. Also, children's clothing had become more fashionable and trendy than ever before.

ORGANIZATION AND STRUCTURE

Establishments that produced children's clothing are organized similarly to the rest of the apparel industry comprised of manufacturers, contractors, and jobbers. Contractors are independent manufacturers, hired by various, and often competing, manufacturers. Contractors specialize in sewing garments from pieces provided to them, and are hired by producers who either do not have their own sewing facilities or producers whose own capacity has been surpassed.

Jobbers are design and marketing businesses, hired to perform specific functions; for example, to purchase materials, design patterns, create samples, cut material, or hire contractors to manufacture the products. The cut materials are then sent to contractors to be assembled.

Manufacturers are those establishments that perform all functions, that is, creating apparel from purchased materials. Manufacturers have staffs that produce designs, or buy them from freelancers, and then purchase the materials (fabric and trimmings) needed. Generally the cutting and sewing of the garment is done on site. However, when demand for an item exceeds the manufacturer's capacity or if shipping deadlines could not be met, outside contractors would

be hired. Most manufacturers have their own sales and shipping staff.

Children's clothing sizes are divided into separate categories for specific age groups. Clothing for infants includes newborns up to age one; clothing for toddlers covers ages two to three; clothing for children covers ages three to six; and clothing for girls covers ages seven to fourteen.

Children's apparel manufacturers generally produce one line per season, typically creating four lines a year—winter, spring, summer, and fall.

BACKGROUND AND DEVELOPMENT

The children's wear industry developed early in the twentieth century around the same time as the women's apparel industry. Women turned away from making their own clothes, and they stopped making their children's clothing as well. Over time, children's clothing became more durable and the sizes became standardized.

A significant factor affecting development of children's wear was the growing importance of television in children's lives after World War II. Children could emulate what other children wore on television, and they could be appealed to directly through advertising. Children began to demand a greater influence over the clothing their parents purchased for them, and often asked for stylish and fashionable clothing. They became independent consumers themselves and were often very fashion conscious and brand-name aware.

CURRENT CONDITIONS

The number of workers employed in this industry dropped throughout the 1980s even as the value of shipments rose. As in other sectors of the apparel industry, increased consolidation and the strength of imported clothing contributed to this trend. The value of shipments grew from $1.4 billion in 1982 to an estimated $1.8 billion in 1996.

The recession that began in the apparel industry in the late 1980s particularly affected children's apparel producers. Domestic manufacturers were hard hit while imports slowed only moderately. Nevertheless, it was expected that children's apparel sales would continue to increase as parents, grandparents, and children themselves purchased clothing manufactured in this industry.

INDUSTRY LEADERS

Gerber Childrenswear Incorporated is a dominant force in the children's apparel industry. Gerber reported revenues of $200 million in 1995. Besides infantwear, Gerber Childrenswear manufactured sleepers, cloth diapers, bedding, underwear, knitwear, and vinyl baby pants.

Another leading manufacturer in this category is The William Carter Company, a private company founded in 1864 and acquired in 1996 by Investcorp. Its estimated revenues in the mid-1990 were $280 million. Willam Carter produces children's apparel under its own name as well as licensed apparel under several brands, including the Christian Dior and Cambell Kids labels.

WORK FORCE

The number of employees in this category declined throughout the 1980s. From 1982 to 1995, employment in this category fell from 38,000 to an estimated 19,900 in 1996. New York had the most establishments in this category, indicating the state's long history as the center of the apparel business in the United States. Approximately 78 such establishments, employing about 2,700 workers, were headquartered in the state in the early 1990s. California was home to fewer manufacturers (approximately 77) but a greater number of employees (about 3,500). Other states with noteworthy concentrations of workers in this category were South Carolina, Florida, and Pennsylvania.

AMERICA AND THE WORLD

The U.S. children's apparel industry began to lose significant market share to imports in the 1960s as did other sectors of the apparel industry; imports were attractive to consumers because of their lower prices and acceptable quality. The process began to accelerate in the 1970s and, by the 1990s, imports had reached all-time highs. Also contributing to the industry's decline in the United States was the reliance of manufacturers on off-shore assembly of pieces cut in the United States.

Asia-based manufacturers represented a significant source of children's apparel. When apparel makers started to move their manufacturing bases out of the United States in the 1960s, they first went to Hong Kong, Taiwan, and South Korea to take advantage of the cheap labor there. By the 1980s, however, labor costs had increased, and capital and experience from those traditionally low-wage markets moved to lower wage countries such as Bangladesh, Thailand, Pakistan, Indonesia, Malaysia, Sri Lanka, and India, which became the sources for more of the imports entering the United States. By the early 1990s, China replaced Hong Kong as the greatest supplier of imports to the United States.

The ratification of the North American Free Trade Agreement (NAFTA) was expected to increase imports from Mexico. Apparel-industry executives supported NAFTA even though the agreement was expected to have an adverse effect on U.S. garment manufacturers. Companies were expected to move existing plants to Mexico in search of cheaper labor and overhead.

Still more imports entered the United States under Provision 9802 of the Harmonized Tariffs Schedule of the United States (formerly known as Section 807). This provision allowed clothing assembled abroad—from pieces cut in the United States and then exported—to be reimported with duty paid for the value added abroad. Thus, the most labor-intensive part of the assembly process could be done at lower-wage rates but both import and export data were skewed. Many U.S. manufacturers were taking advantage of Provision 9802 and moving assembly operations to the Caribbean, noting that they could reduce costs and more successfully compete against imports from Asia. By 1992 garments manufactured in this manner comprised 14 percent of apparel imports. The passage of NAFTA, however, led some to expect that the Caribbean would be a less desirable manufacturing destination than Mexico.

The International Ladies' Garment Workers Union and other unions supported measures to stem the loss of jobs in the industry by limiting the number of imports allowed in the country. Their arguments did not succeed in defeating passage of NAFTA.

RESEARCH AND TECHNOLOGY

In the battle against imports, U.S. apparel makers tried a variety of stratagems, including increased use of automation, delivering higher quality goods, and trying to more closely keep track of the consumer's needs and desires. Although the intrinsic "soft" quality of material made the extensive use of automated equipment difficult, most of the larger manufacturers had tried to invest in newer machinery to improve efficiency. Nevertheless, apparel manufacture remained a highly labor-intensive industry.

One tool that was advocated to better meet the market's demands was "quick response": the idea of bringing apparel to the retailer rapidly by shortening the production cycle, reducing inventories, improving productivity, and sending information regarding consumers' preferences quickly back to the manufacturers, and thus avoiding overstocking. By using computers to track inventory and sales as well as consumers' responses to particular items, the ability to respond quickly to market demand—and thus get a jump on foreign producers often half a world away—domestic manufacturers could minimize their vulnerability to imports. Department stores and manufacturers worked together to find ways to speed deliveries and increase efficiency. Mass merchandisers were among the first to implement quick response systems.

FURTHER READING

Baby and Junior: International Trade Magazine for Children's Fashions. Bamberg, Germany: Meisenbach GMBH.

Conditions in the Women's Garment Industry. The International Ladies' Garment Workers' Union.

Earnshaw's Infants, Girls and Boys Wear Review. New York: Earnshaw Publications, Inc.

Fairchild Fact File: Children's Market, Infants', Toddlers', Girls', and Boys'—Apparel, Juvenile Products, Toys/Dolls. New York: Fairchild Publications, Inc.

—Cheryl Collins, updated by Jennifer Stong

SIC 2369

GIRLS', CHILDREN'S, AND INFANTS' OUTERWEAR, NOT ELSEWHERE CLASSIFIED

This category includes establishments primarily engaged in manufacturing girls', children's, and infants' outerwear, not elsewhere classified, from purchased woven or knit fabrics. This includes, but is not limited to, bathing suits, jeans, jogging suits, playsuits, shorts, skirts, slacks, and sweatsuits. Knitting mills primarily engaged in manufacturing outerwear are classified under **SIC 2253: Knit Outwear Mills.**

INDUSTRY SNAPSHOT

In 1994, 362 establishments were engaged in the manufacturing of clothing covered in this category. This number steadily declined throughout the 1980s, because, as with much of the U.S. apparel industry, manufacturers faced stiff competition from low-cost imports. Nevertheless, during this time a well-educated baby boomer generation, with more disposable income than their parents had, were themselves having children and spending increasing amounts on children's clothing. Consequently, children's clothing became more fashion-oriented and expensive. Total industry shipments totaled $2.156 billion in 1993.

ORGANIZATION AND STRUCTURE

Clothing lines in this industry include "infant wear" for babies up to one year in age, "toddlers

wear" for children from ages two to three, "children's wear" for ages three to six, and "girls' wear" for girls between the ages of seven and fourteen. Children's apparel manufacturers generally produce one new line of clothing per season; spring, summer, winter, and fall or four lines a year.

Establishments producing children's clothing were comprised of contractors, jobbers, and manufacturers. Contractors are independent manufacturers, hired by various—usually competing—manufacturers. Contractors specialize in sewing the garment from pieces provided to them, and are hired by producers who either do not have their own sewing facilities or producers whose own capacity has been superseded.

Jobbers are design and marketing businesses hired to perform specific functions, including purchasing materials, designing patterns, creating samples, cutting material, and hiring contractors to manufacture product. After purchasing materials needed to produce the pieces, jobbers then send the cut material to contractors for assembly.

When creating apparel from the purchased materials, manufacturers retained staffs either to produce designs or buy them from freelancers, as well as to purchase the fabric and trimmings. While cutting and sewing the garment is generally performed in the manufacturer's factories, outside contractors are hired when demand for an item exceeded the manufacturer's capacity or shipping deadlines cannot be met. For the purposes of this entry, the term "manufacturers" will refer cumulatively to contractors, jobbers, and manufacturers.

BACKGROUND AND DEVELOPMENT

Children's apparel production developed early in the twentieth century, concurrent with the emergence of the women's apparel industry. During this time, as women joined the professional work force in increasing numbers, they had less time for sewing their own or their children's clothing. Advances in the industry eventually lead to the production of more durable children's clothing available in standardized sizes.

The growing popularity of television during the 1950s, particularly among children, provided a boost to the children's apparel industry. Not only did young people begin to emulate fashions worn by their peers on television, but they were especially responsive to advertising. During this time, children assumed a greater role in choosing the clothing purchased for them by their parents. Moreover, they came to represent an independent consumer market, purchasing clothing themselves with the money they received as gifts or for allowances. In the 1990s practically every major character on television or in the movies had a line of clothing available.

CURRENT CONDITIONS

The number of employees in the industry dropped throughout the 1980s as the value of shipments rose. As in other sectors of the apparel industry, increased consolidation and the popularity of imported clothing contributed to downsizing in the industry. While the value of shipments grew from $1.3 billion in 1982 to an estimated $2.156 billion in 1993, employment fell from about 33,700 in 1982 to approximately 25,000 in 1993. Of the total amount of employees, 22,000 were production workers.

The economic recession of the early 1990s particularly affected children's apparel producers; domestic manufacturers were hard hit while imports only slowed moderately. Nevertheless, analysts expected sales of children's apparel to continue to increase as parents, grandparents, and children themselves purchased more clothing for the offspring of the babyboom generation.

INDUSTRY LEADERS

Oshkosh B'Gosh, Inc., which designed, manufactured, and marketed children's apparel, dominated the industry in the 1990s. Founded in 1895 and based in Wisconsin, the company employed approximately 6,500 people and saw revenues of approximately $444.8 million in 1996. Oshkosh's employment rate fell from 7,700 in 1993 due to the closing of domestic plants and the increase in foreign production. Oshkosh B'Gosh uses its own manufacturing facilities in the United States and abroad. The company also began exporting merchandise to Europe, a strategy that initially met with a disappointing response in the early 1990s. Oshkosh sells its merchandise to both specialty and department stores.

Another industry leader, Buster Brown Apparel, Inc., became a private company in 1993 when it was sold by Gerber Products Company. Originally founded in 1903, Buster Brown was once a highly profitable company, but leaner times necessitated Gerber's sale in an effort to cut costs. Its revenues in 1993 were estimated at $150 million, and it employed approximately 3,200 people.

WORK FORCE

Total employment for 1993 was 29,500 and most of those employed in this category (an estimated 24,600 in 1993) were production workers, approximately half of whom were union members. Production consisted largely of sewing-machine operators, whose average wage in 1993 was $5.66 an hour. While many manufacturers in this sector of the apparel industry, as with the industry as a whole, were small, family-owned businesses, there were a number of large and growing establishments dominating the industry. The average number of employees per establishment in the mid-1990s was around 110.

A long-time center of the apparel business in the United States, New York was home to the majority of children's wear manufacturers in the early 1990s. During this time, approximately 60 establishments, employing about 2,900 workers, were headquartered in New York. North Carolina and South Carolina retained fewer manufacturers (approximately 40 and 16, respectively) and more employees (about 5,500 and 5,400, respectively). Tennessee and Pennsylvania also had significant concentrations of workers in this category.

AMERICA AND THE WORLD

In the 1960s, the U.S. children's apparel industry began to lose significant market share to imports, which offered consumers lower prices and acceptable quality. This trend accelerated in the 1970s, and, by the 1990s, imports had reached all-time highs. Moreover, with U.S. manufacturers relying more heavily on offshore assembly plants, the industry experienced further losses.

Manufacturers in the Far East represented a significant source of children's apparel. In the 1960s, the U.S. children's apparel industry began moving manufacturing operations abroad, focusing on Hong Kong, Taiwan, and South Korea, where labor was cheap. By the 1980s, however, labor costs in these countries had increased and operations were moved to Bangladesh, Thailand, Pakistan, Indonesia, Malaysia, Sri Lanka, and India. By the early 1990s China replaced Hong Kong as the greatest supplier of imports to the United States.

The North American Free Trade Agreement (NAFTA)—ratified in 1993 to create a free-trade zone between the United States, Mexico, and Canada by gradually eliminating tariffs over 15 years—was generally supported by executives in the apparel industry. While the International Ladies' Garment Workers Union and other unions sought to stem the loss of jobs among Americans in the industry by limiting the imports allowed in the country, the free-market philosophy ultimately triumphed in the passage of NAFTA.

Throughout the 1990s, increasingly more imports entered the United States under provision 9802 (formerly known as Section 807) of the U.S. Harmonized Tariffs Schedule. This provision allowed clothing assembled abroad—from pieces cut in the United States and then exported—to be reimported with duty paid for the value added abroad. This meant that the most labor-intensive part of the assembly process could be accomplished for lower wages. Many U.S. manufacturers took advantage of provision 9802, moving assembly operations to the Caribbean, where they expected to reduce costs and more successfully compete against imports from Asia. While the process greatly decreased the turnaround time for assembling more complex clothing items, its logistics sometimes proved cumbersome and time-consuming as contractors in other countries managed the transportation, paperwork, and assembly required. Furthermore, the passage of NAFTA led some to expect that the Caribbean would largely be replaced by Mexico as a more desirable manufacturing destination.

RESEARCH AND TECHNOLOGY

In the battle against imports, U.S. apparel makers tried several strategies, including increased use of automation, delivering higher quality goods, and trying to track consumer's needs and desires more closely. Although the intrinsic ''soft'' quality of material made the extensive use of automated equipment difficult, most of the larger manufacturers continually sought to invest in newer machinery to improve efficiency. Nevertheless, apparel manufacture remained a labor-intensive industry.

Another new strategy involved ''quick response,'' the idea that bringing apparel to the retailer more rapidly would shorten the production cycle, reduce inventories, improve productivity, and help manufacturers avoid overstocking by providing them with more timely information regarding consumers' preferences. Using computers to track inventory, sales, and consumer response, domestic manufacturers hoped to compete more effectively with importers. Department stores and manufacturers worked together to find ways to speed deliveries and increase efficiency.

FURTHER READING

Baby and Junior: International Trade Magazine for Children's Fashions. Bamberg, Germany: Meisenbach GMBH.

''Conditions in the Women's Garment Industry.'' The International Ladies' Garment Workers' Union.

Earnshaw's Infants, Girls and Boys Wear Review. Earnshaw Publications, Inc.

Fairchild Fact File: Children's Market, Infants', Toddlers', Girls', and Boys' Apparel, Juvenile Products, Toys/Dolls. New York: Fairchild Publications, Inc.

Osh Kosh B'Gosh, Inc. Annual Report. Osh Kosh, WI: Osh Kosh B'Gosh, 1997.

U.S. Department of Commerce. *U.S. Industrial Outlook 1993.* Washington: GPO, 1993.

—Cheryl Collins, updated by Jennifer Stong

SIC 2371

FUR GOODS

This category covers establishments primarily engaged in manufacturing fur coats, and other clothing, accessories, and trimmings made of fur. Those establishments that are primarily engaged in manufacturing sheep-lined clothing are classified in **SIC 2386: Leather and Sheep-Lined Clothing**, and those that are engaged in dyeing and dressing of furs are classified in **SIC 3999: Manufacturing Industries, Not Elsewhere Classified.**

Furs were once considered a luxury that only a few could afford. The huge influx of women entering the work force in the 1970s, though, changed that perception forever. Their increased disposable income allowed many women to buy for themselves an item that historically had been purchased by men as gifts to their wives. From 1971 the U.S. fur market grew steadily, and by the 1980s furs had surged in popularity. In 1965 the average age of the first-time fur buyer was 50; by 1985 it was 26.

The popularity of fur goods exploded in the 1980s—fur sales increased an average of 10 percent a year between 1979 and 1986. However, the majority of those furs were mass-market priced (under $5,000) and of lesser quality, and most of those furs were imported from such places as South Korea and Hong Kong, where labor costs were low. By the mid-1980s, more than 50 percent of the furs sold in the United States were imported. The increased competition from imports kept the value of the goods shipped relatively constant so that, in spite of the increase in sales, the total work force in the U.S. fur industry declined. The increase of imports also led to a reduction in the number of small manufacturing establishments, and so a greater concentration of the share was held by the largest establishments.

A surplus of pelts on the international market, a slow U.S. economy, warm winters, and price battles among retailers contributed to lower profits in the late

1980s. By 1991, U.S. fur sales had declined 44% from a high of $1.8 billion in 1987. Over-production saw retail prices fall 40 percent below their peak of 1986. Animal rights groups, which had won much publicity in the 1980s with their advertising and public relations campaign against the fur industry, attempting to reduce the demand for fur, pointed to the declining numbers and claimed their campaign had been successful. Other analysts saw other factors—a series of mild winters, the slow down of the economy, and a glut of pelts on the market—as much more important. By 1992, pelt prices had begun to turn around and the following year sales increased by 13 percent. In the early 1990s lower prices helped increase the unit sales of furs, but dollar sales remained constant.

By the mid-1990s, there were approximately 100 companies that manufactured fur goods in the United States, down from 503 in 1982. The number of workers employed by U.S. fur manufacturers plummeted from 2,600 in 1983 to 500 in 1994. Over half of those employed were sewing-machine operators. The industry was concentrated in the state of New York, with almost 90 percent of manufacturers based there in 1987. The largest fur manufacturers were privately held companies; the top two, Mohl Fur Company, Inc. and Elika Ltd., were located in New York City. The two leading retailers in the fur industry were Furs by Weiss, based in Beachwood, Ohio and Revillon, Inc., headquartered in New York City.

By 1995, fur sales were back up to $1.2 billion, an increase of 10 percent over the previous year. Some industry analysts attributed the increase to a generally healthy economy and record snow falls in the Northeast. By the late 1990s, the fur industry saw a rise in worldwide fur prices, boding well for its future health. However, while it seemed to have survived the overproduction and the anti-fur campaigns of the 1980s, the U.S. fur industry headed into the late 1990s with serious questions raised by the European Union's threat to ban U.S.-produced fur in a controversy over U.S. use of leghold traps.

FURTHER READING

Agins, Teri. "Holiday Season Is Bringing Little Cheer to Furriers." *Wall Street Journal,* 19 December 1991.

Darnay, Arsen J., ed. *Manufacturing USA.* 5th ed. Detroit: Gale Research, 1996.

Feitelberg, Rosemary. "Furriers Lament Spotty Season." *Women's Wear Daily,* 10 January 1995.

Feitelberg, Rosemary. "The Sizzle is Back." *Women's Wear Daily,* 12 March 1996.

Hinge John B. "Fur Industry, Under Fire, Shows Its Claws." *Wall Street Journal,* 3 January 1991.

Munk, Nina. "Animal Magnetism." *Forbes,* 10 March 1997.

Reilly, Patrick M. "Furriers Hustle to Keep Sales Warm." *Wall Street Journal,* 21 September 1993.

Tamburri, Rosanna. "Fur Industry Warms to Rising Prices After Taking a Pelting in Late 1980's." *Wall Street Journal,* 24 January 1996.

Wilson, Eric. "Luxury Fever Feeds Furs." *Women's Wear Daily,* 18 February 1997.

—Cheryl Collins, updated by Merry McInerney

SIC 2381

DRESS AND WORK GLOVES, EXCEPT KNIT AND ALL-LEATHER

This industry includes establishments primarily engaged in manufacturing dress, semi-dress, and work gloves and mittens from purchased woven or knit fabrics, or from these materials combined with leather or plastics. Knitting mills primarily engaged in manufacturing gloves and mittens are classified in **SIC 2259: Knitting Mills, Not Elsewhere Classified;** establishments primarily engaged in manufacturing leather gloves are classified in **SIC 3151: Leather Gloves and Mittens;** those manufacturing sporting and athletic gloves are classified in **SIC 3949: Sporting and Athletic Goods, Not Elsewhere Classified;** and those manufacturing safety gloves are classified in **SIC 3842: Orthopedic, Prosthetic, and Surgical Appliances and Supplies.**

Glove manufacturers produce gloves for a variety of purposes, ranging from the functional to the purely ornamental. Because of their utility in work, industry, fashion and casual apparel, gloves have been a popular accessory for men, women, and children for centuries.

Gloves have been used since the fourteenth century BC. Linen gloves were found in the tomb of King Tutankhamen. These accessories have served many purposes for both men and women throughout history and once were among the costliest items of clothing. In 1834 Xavier Jouvin, a French glovemaker, invented a press that could cut six gloves simultaneously, bringing down the cost and increasing their popularity and availability.

The two major types of gloves are work or industrial gloves and casual or dress gloves. In 1995, there were a total of 344,132,000 dozen pair of gloves produced, up from 304,641,000 in 1994. Only 375,000 dozen pair or 0.1 percent of the total produced in 1995 were dress gloves. Work glove production numbered 343,757,000 dozen pair, up 12 percent from 304,220,000 in 1994. In 1994, there were 72 establishments producing dress and work gloves, up from 70 in 1993. The industry shipped more than $274 million worth of goods in 1995, over 90 percent of which consisted of gloves and mittens made from leather-fabric combinations.

Since industrial gloves are designed to provide protection, they are constructed of more durable materials, such as cotton, wool or leather. Some of the leading work glove manufacturers are Best Manufacturing, Wells Lamont, Pioneer, and Premier. These companies ship products directly to industries and retailers throughout the year. In 1995 Wells Lamont, an Illinois-based glove manufacturer, posted sales of $200 million and employed 2100 workers.

Between 1987 and 1992, there was a 19 percent decrease in employment in the dress and work glove industry, but 1993, 1994 and 1995 figures steadily increased. In 1995, this particular segment of the industry employed approximately 42,000 people, 36,000 of whom were in production work.

Nurseries, gardening stores, and hardware stores stock gloves made from synthetics, heavier cottons, leather, cowhide, deerskin, goatskin, and sheepskin. These are used by gardeners and shade-tree mechanics. While the natural skin gloves are very popular, the heavy cotton gloves are soft, cool, and absorbent, and protect hands against blisters, dirt, and grease. The cotton gloves are also relatively inexpensive.

However, rubber gloves make up the largest part of the entire glove industry. But, even though rubber glove production is nearly ten times that of fabric glove production, the 36,535,000 dozen pair of fabric gloves produced in 1994 were worth more than the 234,454,000 dozen pair of rubber gloves produced.

Casual and dress gloves are different from work gloves in many ways. Unlike their more durable counterparts, they are made from finer fabrics and weaves—including linen, silk, and fine weaves of cotton and wool. Their popularity as an accessory rises and falls according to the dictates of fashion. Isotoner, Inc., a division of Sara Lee Corporation, is one of the leading manufacturers of dress and casual gloves. In 1993, Isotoner employed approximately 200 workers and posted sales of $250 million.

FURTHER READING

"Glove Story." *Connoisseur,* February 1988, 65.

Kimber, Robert. "Tough, Supple Work Gloves." *Country Journal,* July-August 1992, 59.

McCauseland, Jim. "Matching Gloves to Garden Chores." *Sunset,* November 1993, 64.

U.S. Bureau of the Census. *1995 Annual Survey of Manufactures.* Washington: GPO, 1997.

U.S. Department of Commerce. *1994 County Business Patterns.* Washington: GPO, 1996.

U.S. Department of Commerce. *Current Industrial Reports: Gloves and Mittens 1995.* Washington: GPO, 1996.

U.S. Department of Commerce. *1992 Census of Manufactures.* Washington: GPO, 1992.

U.S. Department of Commerce. International Trade Administration. *U.S. Industrial Outlook 1994,* Available from http://sci.dixie.edu/BusinessInformation/Industryoutlooks/IndustryOutlooks.html.

—Joan R. Neubauer, updated by Paula Hartman Cohen

SIC 2384

ROBES AND DRESSING GOWNS

Establishments in this industry are primarily engaged in manufacturing men's, boys', and women's robes and dressing gowns from purchased materials and fabrics. This classification includes the manufacturing of bathrobes, caftans, housecoats, dusters, lounging robes, and men's smoking jackets. Companies primarily engaged in manufacturing girls', children's, and infants' robes from purchased fabrics are classified in **SIC 2369: Girls', Children's, and Infants' Outerwear, Not Elsewhere Classified.** Knitting mills which manufacture robes and dressing gowns are classified in **SIC 2253: Knit Outerwear Mills.**

In 1996 there were 13 leading companies in this industry yielding gross sales of $346 million and employing 6,000 workers. I Appel Corp ranked as the sales leader, with $110 million, followed by Movie Star, Inc. with sales of $103 million, and Marengo Mills (Division of Vanity Fair Corporation) with sales of $30 million. Remaining companies each had less than $24 million in sales in the mid-1990s.

In contrast with figures of 1993, this industry's sales decreased by $138 million, and the number of workers decreased by 30 percent in 1996. Imported robes and lounge wear competed for the domestic manufacturers' department-store market share, and some department stores had begun to contract with foreign mills to issue their own insignia bathrobes. In one instance in early 1997, this cost the Neiman Marcus Group almost $2 million in sales when 6,500 terry-cloth bathrobes were recalled at the request of the U.S. Consumer Products Safety Commission when the garments failed flammability tests, igniting upon exposure to flame.

In the mid-1990s, large leisure-wear manufacturers also began expanding to include robes and lounge wear for men and women, providing additional market competition for the dedicated robe and dressing-gown manufacturers in the United States. Famous athletic name-brand robes matching their shoes became available in large department store chains as well as specialty shops for lingerie, sporting goods, and mail-order catalogs. Sports and leisure apparel outside of this primary category have enjoyed a significant increase in sales throughout the 1990s due to their diversification. Robe manufacturers experienced increased business from hotel-chain orders, particularly where terry-cloth towels are also provided.

While exact figures are not available, employment in this industry has been on the decline since the late 1970s. In 1995, more than 82 percent of this industry's work force was comprised of production workers.

American companies manufacturing robes and dressing gowns have long been in competition with overseas manufacturing, mostly from China and Taiwan. In 1993, over half of the robes and gowns sold in America were imported. American exports of these products have traditionally been small; however, their numbers increased to 9 percent of U.S. products in this apparel sector. American exports are expected to be one of the main factors in increased production in this industry by the end of the twentieth century.

Technological advances have helped manufacturers of robes and dressing gowns improve efficiency in production and distribution of their goods. Three areas in particular have been improved in this industry with technological developments: computer-aided design, production, and communications; modular manufacturing systems; and ergonomics (workplace equipment designed with respect to worker health and safety).

FURTHER READING

"Consumer Watch: Women's Robes." *Chain Store Age General Merchandise,* November 1982.

Joyce, Katherine. "Relax in Style." *Stores,* November 1985.

Reda, Susan. "Robes: Tough Sell for Spring." *Stores,* November 1992.

U.S. Department of Commerce. *1995 Annual Survey of Manufactures.* Washington: GPO, 1997.

—Paola Trimarco, updated by Ariel Pennie

WATERPROOF OUTERWEAR

This category includes establishments primarily engaged in manufacturing raincoats and other waterproof outerwear from purchased rubberized fabrics, plastics, and similar materials. Included in this industry are establishments primarily engaged in manufacturing waterproof or water repellent outerwear from purchased woven or knit fabrics other than wool. Establishments primarily engaged in manufacturing men's and boys' oiled-fabric work clothing are classified in **SIC 2326: Men's and Boys' Work Clothing;** those manufacturing vulcanized rubber clothing and clothing made from rubberized fabrics produced in the same establishment are classified in **SIC 3069: Fabricated Rubber Products, Not Elsewhere Classified.**

Raincoats are the largest share of products produced by establishments classified in this industry. In 1997, these companies shipped goods with a total value of about $95 million. This shows a dramatic decrease in revenues, which were $333 million in 1987.

The 1990s brought a return of polyurethane-coated fabrics to the forefront of raincoat fashion. Polyurethane gives fabrics—the shiny look associated with rain slickers of the 1960s. The newer versions of the shiny raincoat have benefitted from improvements in the technology used to coat the fabrics. Softer fabrics—such as rayon, cotton, and polyester—can now be used to back a very thin layer of polyurethane, creating a much more comfortable garment than was previously possible. Technological improvements have also expanded the number of softer styles available; some use new microfibers, as well as sueded cotton and velvet, treated with water-repellent chemicals. These improvements in waterproofing techniques have given linens an important role in outerwear for the first time.

Although the rainwear industry experienced a steady decline in the 1980s and 1990s, with a short upturn in 1991 and 1992, industry professionals were becoming more optimistic in the late 1990s. One reason seemed to be that rainwear was becoming more of a fashion item. In 1996, Nicole Fischelis, vice president and fashion director at Saks Fifth Avenue told *WWD* that "Women aren't buying rainwear purely as a functional item anymore. They're buying it for lifestyle, as an alternative to other spring coats."

The most significant change in rainwear sales was due to the advent of the short coat into the market.

According to the *Daily News Record,* 34 to 37 inch coats (as opposed to the traditional 48 to 50 inch lengths) would make up 30 percent of the business for fall of 1997.

Another factor contributing to sales growth was the introduction of "high-tech" fibers and finishes that made raincoats wearable in all kinds of weather. Fibers include Tencel polynosics, suede and twill-weave polyester, and high-twist wools. The industry called this fashion trend "hybrid coats" because they are all-weather fashion garments. Frederick Stollmack, director of Weatherproof Garment Co., told the *Daily News Record,* "We don't say raincoats. We say bridge coats because of the multipurpose approach we take to rainwear/outerwear."

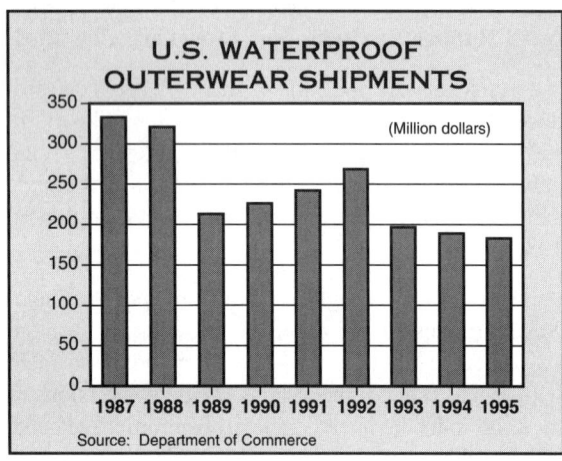

U.S. WATERPROOF OUTERWEAR SHIPMENTS

(Million dollars)

Source: Department of Commerce

Like many industries involving the manufacture of apparel, a large percentage of production jobs in the waterproof apparel industry have left the United States in recent years. The number of U.S. industry workers in 1997—1,400 —was 30 percent less than the number employed five years earlier and 60 percent less than the number employed in 1987. Employment in this industry is concentrated on the East Coast, particularly Maryland, Massachusetts, and New Jersey, which together account for about one-half of the industry's jobs. More than one-half of the establishments in the waterproof outerwear industry have fewer than 20 employees. In 1997, workers in this industry earned $39 million in wages.

The waterproof outerwear industry is dominated by Londontown Corp., which produces the well-known London Fog line of outerwear. The company also licenses the London Fog name to a wide range of products. The London Fog brand name is recognized by an amazing 98 percent of consumers. Londontown has estimated sales of $350 million—more than four times its nearest competitor. Londontown, founded in

1928, is based in Eldersburg, Maryland and has about 2,000 employees.

Other leading companies include Rainfair Inc., of Racine, Wisconsin, with $20 million in sales; Neese Industries Inc. of Gonzales, Louisiana, with $17 million in sales; and Chief Apparel Inc. of Amer, New York, with $16 million in sales.

FURTHER READING

Gellers, Stan. "Short Raincoats Long on High-Tech Fabrics." *Daily News Record,* 5 March 1997.

Pogoda, Dianne M. "Londontown: Refinanced and Ready to Grow." *Women's Wear Daily,* 21 August 1990, 6.

———. "Rainwear: Short and Slicker." *Women's Wear Daily,* 15 March 1991, 8.

Pogoda, Dianne M. and Arthur Friedman. "Finally, Some Sunshine for Rainwear." *WWD,* 16 April 1996.

Salfino, Catherine. "Outerwear Orders Rolling In." *Daily News Record,* 10 August 1993, 1.

—Robert R. Jacobson, updated by Sharyn Kolberg

SIC 2386

LEATHER AND SHEEP-LINED CLOTHING

This category consists of manufacturers of many types of leather and sheep-lined clothing, including coats, jackets, hats, pants, skirts, vests, and other garments. Companies that make leather gloves and mittens are included in **SIC 3151: Leather Gloves and Mittens.** Fur clothing is classified separately in **SIC 2371: Fur Goods.**

In the mid-1990s, there were about 110 establishments in the industry, down 18 percent since 1990. In 1995, the leather and sheep-lined clothing industry shipped about $193.3 million in products, a decrease of approximately 5 percent since 1990. Overall, retail sales of leather apparel have quadrupled since 1985. These increases reflected the end of a rising trend in the price of leather. The cost of leather relative to other clothing materials has proved to be a reliable indicator of the leather apparel industry's performance from year to year. As is the case in the apparel industry in general, patterns of consumption can change rapidly as customer demand is influenced by fashion developments. Leather clothing, which is both high-fashion and high-cost in the world of apparel, is particularly susceptible to both of these kinds of fluctuations in demand.

The leading U.S. company in the leather apparel industry is G-III Apparel Group, Ltd. New York, NY. The company had over $208 million in sales in 1995 and employed 400. Excelled Sheepskin & Leather Coat Corp., also of New York, NY, had over $50 million in sales and employed 250 in 1995. The entire industry employed 1.9 million that year, down 17 percent from 2.3 million in 1990.

Although demand for leather apparel is expected to rise slightly as the American economy improves, the market share lost to imports is expected to increase as well. In addition, American companies are moving more of their manufacturing abroad to reduce labor costs. These are the most severe challenges facing the industry at the turn of the century.

FURTHER READING

Friedman, Arthur. "Primed for a Revival." *Women's Wear Daily,* 23 March 1993, 12.

Pogoda, Dianne M. "New Plans for Leather." *Women's Wear Daily,* 25 June 1991, 8.

U.S. Bureau of the Census. *1995 Annual Survey of Manufactures.* Washington: GPO, 1996.

U.S. Department of Commerce. *County Business Patterns.* Washington: GPO, 1996.

U.S. Department of Commerce. *1992 Census of Manufactures.* Washington: GPO, 1992.

—Robert R. Jacobson, updated by Paula Hartman Cohen

SIC 2387

APPAREL BELTS

This category includes establishments primarily engaged in manufacturing apparel belts. Companies that produce all types of belts for clothing are grouped in this industry, regardless of the material from which the belts are made.

In 1995 shipments in this industry totaled $678 million. A surge in the popularity of leggings and stretch pants for women that took place at the end of the 1980s, and new trends such as the grunge look and natural soft flowing fabrics in the early to mid-1990s, created a slump in sales for makers of belts. In general, however, industry sales were quite strong for much of the 1990s in spite of generally poor showings throughout much of the apparel industry.

Since the early 1980s, the number of U.S. jobs in this category has been on a steady decline. In 1982 the industry employed 11,700 U.S. workers. By 1995 that number was 7,100. Four states provided over 70 percent of those jobs: New York, California, Texas, and Connecticut. Of the 245 companies operating in the industry, nearly two-thirds had less than 20 employees. The industry's employees earned a total of $150 million in wages that year.

Leather is by far the most important material for apparel belts, making up 67.5 percent of total shipments in 1995. Since the beginning of the 1990s, Nubuck suede has become an important material in the manufacture of apparel belts. Nubuck is a softened leather that is available in a variety of colors and textures. Nubuck first appeared as a footwear material, and soon began to show up in women's accessories. Men's belts, which have traditionally been closely linked to footwear in terms of leather trends, followed soon thereafter.

An important factor in the belt industry's success throughout the 1990s has been an increasing emphasis on casual styles, as epitomized by the workday casual movement adopted by many American businesses by the mid-1990s. The glossy look of 1980s accessories had given way to a more down-to-earth and practical flavor in belts. With the comeback of jeans, belt manufacturers were producing "jean friendly" belts—belts with wider widths, braided belts, belts with brushed textures—to work with the wider legs and roomier fit featured in many of the modern styles. Furthermore, the crossover market in men's belts continued to grow. What had until recently been mainly a replacement business had been spurred on by increasing attention paid to men by designers and manufacturers, and ever-changing fashion trends such as textured belts and updated buckles. On the women's side, the reappearance of the fitted look and a renewed emphasis on the waistline contributed to the health of the belt industry in the 1990s.

Tandy Brands Accessories Inc. of Arlington, Texas is the leader among companies primarily engaged in manufacturing apparel belts. Tandy, a public company, was founded in 1919. In 1996 the company had 733 employees and annual sales of about $68.4 million. Another important belt manufacturer is Harmal Industries Inc. based in Long Island City, New York. A subsidiary of publicly held Oak Hill Sportswear Corp. of New York, Harmal had 100 employees in 1996. The company had annual sales of $20 million.

FURTHER READING

"Beltin' It Out." *Women's Wear Daily Accessories Supplement,* January 1995.

Curan, Catherine. "Belts Won't Buckle Under." *Daily News Record,* 16 August 1996.

Curan, Catherine. "Denim Demand Paves Path for Jeans Belts." *Daily News Record,* 3 May 1996.

Darnay, Arsen J., ed. *Manufacturing USA.* 5th ed. Detroit, MI: Gale Research Inc., 1996.

Hart, Elena. "Nubuck Spells Big Bucks for Belts." *Daily News Record,* 3 June 1992.

"Total Women's Accessories." *Accessories,* January 1997.

—Robert R. Jacobson, updated by Leslie Joseph

SIC 2389

APPAREL AND ACCESSORIES, NOT ELSEWHERE CLASSIFIED

This industry consists of establishments primarily engaged in manufacturing suspenders, gaffers, handkerchiefs, and other apparel not elsewhere classified, such as academic caps and gowns, vestments, and theatrical costumes. Also included are establishments primarily engaged in manufacturing clothing by cutting and joining (for example by adhesives) materials such as paper and nonwoven textiles.

The apparel and accessories industry is made up of a wide variety of products. Ecclesiastical vestments and other clothing made up 12.5 percent of sales in 1992, a sharp drop from its 30 percent share in 1987; academic caps and gowns, costumes, and theatrical make up an increased share of sales in 1992, accounting for 41.5 percent of the total; garter belts made up 3.1 percent and apparel and accessories, not elsewhere classified, made up 25.4 percent. Other items in this category are: garters, hose supporters, arm bands, and suspenders, accounting for 7.0 percent; men's, boys', women's and children's handkerchiefs, which, combined with burial garments, accounted for 10.5 percent of total sales. Historically, burial garments have usually been responsible for about 2.0 percent of total sales in this category.

Industry output in this category is generally concentrated in the northeastern portion of the United States. But in 1992, some states that had trailed in recent years, moved to the top of the list. The top three states in 1992 were Pennsylvania, California, and New York. Pennsylvania was responsible for $94.1 million, or 17 percent of output; California registered $92.2 million, or 16.7 percent; and New York produced $61.4 million, or 11.1 percent. South Carolina and Florida were the two next-largest producers, but apparel and accessory production was also sizable in North Carolina, Virginia and Tennessee.

The modern manufacture of apparel and accessories within this listing is characterized by a high level of specialization, with some cross-item production. For example, industry leaders include specialty and product-specific manufacturers such as Art Stone Theatrical Inc., Oak Hall Cap and Gown Co., and Eaves and Brooks Costume Co. Multi-product manufacturers include I. Shalom and Company, Inc., which manufacturers both women's accessories and men's handkerchiefs, and White Knights, which manufactures disposable medical products, including hospital gowns.

Labor and occupations are specialized within this category. Sewing machine operators historically have constituted approximately 56 percent of occupations; garment inspectors, testers, and graders constitute 3.2 percent; and precision blue-collar worker supervisors constitute 3 percent. Other occupations include pressing machine operators, shipping and receiving clerks, hand packers and packages, helpers, laborers, and materials movers.

The number of establishments in the industry gradually increased during the early 1990s to 462 by 1994. The total value of shipments in 1995 was $893.9 million, up from $751.8 million in 1994. The United States imports nearly twice as many products in this category as it exports.

Employment has also been on the rise. The total number of employees in this industry has risen from 10,400 in 1992 to 12,900 in 1995. Production workers have consistently accounted for approximately 80 percent of the labor force. However, in 1992, average hourly earnings for a production worker in this industry were $6.93. In 1995, that figure was down to $6.80, which was $0.74 per hour less than the average hourly earnings for all production workers in the broader apparel industry.

The majority of goods manufactured within this industry are made for personal consumption. For example, it was recorded that, in previous years, 82.7 percent of the output of this industry is bought for personal consumption, followed by 12 percent for apparel made from purchased materials and 1.5 percent for exports. Others buying fractional amounts of the output of this industry include, in descending order: federal government purchases; pleating and stitching; knit outerwear mills; hospitals; laundry, dry cleaning, and shoe repair; government purchases for hospital and health; portrait and photographic studios; and government purchases for public assistance and relief.

FURTHER READING

Darnay, Arsen J., ed. *Manufacturing USA.* Detroit: Gale Research, 1996.

U.S. Bureau of the Census. *1992 Census of Manufactures.* Washington: GPO, 1995.

———. *1995 Annual Survey of Manufactures.* Washington: GPO, 1997.

———. *County Business Patterns.* Washington, 1996.

—Karyn Bober Kuhn, updated by Paula Hartman Cohen

SIC 2391

CURTAINS AND DRAPERIES

The establishments covered in this category are primarily engaged in manufacturing curtains and draperies from purchased materials. Those establishments that are primarily engaged in manufacturing lace curtains on lace machines are classified in **SIC 2258: Lace and Warp Knit Fabric Mills,** and those manufacturing shower curtains are classified in **SIC 2392: Housefurnishings, Except Curtains and Draperies.**

ORGANIZATION AND STRUCTURE

In the mid-1990s, there were 34 leading companies in this industry whose primary function was the manufacture of curtains and draperies. The value of shipments in this category has been steady since the late 1970s. The value of shipments of all manufacturers who produced curtains and draperies in 1977 was $1 billion, and the shipment value drifted up to $1.5 billion between 1986 and 1991.

Most curtains were manufactured in standard, ready-made sizes. Draperies included ready-made items as well as custom-made versions. These made-to-measure draperies were ordered from a showroom or a catalog and then produced by the manufacturer.

BACKGROUND AND DEVELOPMENT

Curtains and draperies were once considered the only options for dressing windows, especially in the home. Attitudes shifted over time, however, and by the 1980s, consumers wanted their homes to feel more comfortable and less formal. Spending on home furnishings grew throughout the 1980s as imports did not have much of an impact on this segment of the market. The decline in lined, pinched, and pleated draperies was tied to the increased popularity of one-inch miniblinds. Many of the manufacturers of traditional window treatments expanded into alternative treatments by the early 1990s, as many analysts saw the manufacture of formal draperies on a downward spiral.

CURRENT CONDITIONS

The value of shipments for all manufacturers making curtains and draperies reached $1.2 billion in 1995. Total sales from companies whose primary product was curtains and draperies was $537 million. According to the U.S. Census Bureau, manufacturers in this category spent $23.5 million to upgrade buildings and machinery in 1995.

INDUSTRY LEADERS

The majority of companies in this industry category were small—fewer than 100 employees—and produced custom-made draperies. However, most of the business in this category went to the larger companies. Two companies, whose primary product was curtains and draperies, led the industry in sales in the mid-1990s. The Arley Corp. of Taunton, Massachusetts, had an estimated $160 million in annual sales and employed 1,000 workers. Croscill, Inc. was second with $150 million in annual sales and 1,200 employees.

WORK FORCE

In 1995, the total number of employees working at establishments that manufacture curtains and draperies was 23,000—with about 17,000 of them being production workers who earned $7.48 per hour.

FURTHER READING

American Textile Manufacturers Institute. ''Press Release: U.S. Textile and Apparel Exports Increase in 1996. Mexico Surpasses Canada as Top U.S. Import and Export Market.'' American Textile Manufacturers Institute, 1997. Available from http://www.atmi.org/graphic/pr970221.html.

Home Textiles and Related Products. Fairchild Fact File, Fairchild Books.

Hoover's Online. ''Croscill, Inc.'' *Hoover's Company Capsule.* Hoover's, Inc., 1997. Available from http://www.hoovers.com.

Squire, Laurie. ''When Window Dressing is More Than Mere Window Dressing.'' *Newsday,* 26 January 1997.

U.S. Department of Commerce. *1992 Census of Manufactures.* Washington: GPO, 1992.

U.S. Department of Commerce. *1995 Annual Survey of Manufacturers.* Washington: GPO, 1995.

—Cheryl Collins, updated by Nancy Hammond

SIC 2392

HOUSEFURNISHINGS, EXCEPT CURTAINS AND DRAPERIES

This category covers those establishments primarily engaged in manufacturing housefurnishings—such as blankets, bedspreads, sheets, tablecloths, towels, and shower curtains—from purchased materials. Those establishments producing housefurnishings primarily of fabric woven at the same establishment are classified, according to fiber, in SIC 2211: Broadwoven Fabric Mills, Cotton; SIC 2221: Broadwoven Fabric Mills, Manmade Fiber and Silk; SIC 2231: Broadwoven Fabric Mills, Wool (Including Dyeing and Finishing); or SIC 2299: Textile Goods, Not Elsewhere Classified.

INDUSTRY SNAPSHOT

For many years, housefurnishings such as sheets, towels, and blankets functioned as basic household necessities. In the growing economy after World War II, however, these products were manufactured with new technology in an expanding palette of colors, prints, and styles—thus becoming more of an expression of personal taste. By the 1990s, it was easy and affordable for consumers to redecorate their rooms with coordinated bedroom and bath products offered by these companies.

ORGANIZATION AND STRUCTURE

In the mid-1990s, there were 97 leading companies with about 34,000 employees whose primary products matched this industry's description. The manufacture of sheets and towels was dominated by a few large corporations. Some of the other products covered in this category included tablecloths, pillows, boat cushions, laundry bags, shower curtains, slipcovers, and mattress pads. These were produced by a variety of small manufacturers, thus creating a very fragmented sector of the market.

BACKGROUND AND DEVELOPMENT

The housefurnishings market grew throughout the 1980s. Several factors contributed to the industry's relative strength. The home textile market was less penetrated by imports than other sectors of the textile industry. Also, home textiles were manufactured in a more automated process, with specialized machinery taking the place of the paid production worker. A large portion of the profits in this category were used to upgrade building and machinery. New capital expenditures—at $27 million in 1977—escalated to $81 million in 1995 as companies implemented new technologies at their manufacturing facilities.

CURRENT CONDITIONS

The top five companies with primary products in this category employed over 1000 workers each, while about half of the remaining companies employed fewer than 100 workers. The value of shipments of all products in these establishments, including but not limited to the primary products of the industry, grew from $2.3 billion in 1977 to $6.0 billion in 1995. Specifically, the value of shipments in the various market segments in 1995 were as follows: other housefurnishings at $3.5 billion; sheets and pillowcases at $1.0 billion; towels and washcloths at $622.0 million; bedspreads and bedsets at $560.0 million; and housefurnishings, not elsewhere classified and not specified by kind at $346.0 million.

INDUSTRY LEADERS

Companies in this industry earned $3.1 billion collectively. This category was dominated by the giant textile manufacturer Fieldcrest Cannon, Inc. This company was created in 1986 after Fieldcrest Mills purchased its competitor, Cannon Mills, thus merging the two largest U.S. manufacturers of sheets and towels. Its sales in 1996 reached $1.2 billion, and it employed close to 14,000 workers. In November of 1996, Fieldcrest and their closest competitor, Pillowtex Corp., of Texas signed an agreement giving Pillowtex access to the inventory of and the licensing to Fieldcrest's blanket division.

WORK FORCE

There were 44,000 production workers and 52,000 total employees in the housefurnishings business in 1995. Production workers earned an average of $8.08 per hour and worked an average of 38.3 hours per week.

Repetitive motion injuries, a common problem in the manufacturing industry, got some attention from Fieldcrest in 1992. James Overstreet, of *The Business Journal of Charlotte* reported that workers and management in all of Fieldcrest's manufacturing plants joined together to implement ergonomic programs. In 1993, a study at Fieldcrest's Georgia manufacturing plants reported 121 work-related injuries and 442 lost work days. In 1996, however, there were only 21 work-related injuries and 7 lost work days reported.

FURTHER READING

American Textile Manufacturers Institute. "Press Release: U.S. Textile and Apparel Exports Increase in 1996. Mexico Surpasses Canada as Top U.S. Import and Export Market." American Textile Manufacturers Institute, 1997. Available from http://www.atmi.org/graphic/pr970221.html.

Fairchild Fact File: Home Textiles and Related Products. New York: Fairchild Publications.

"Fieldcrest Cannon Inc. Sells Blanket Inventory." *Reuters,* 18 November 1996.

Hoover's Online. "Fieldcrest Cannon, Inc." *Hoover's Company Capsule.* Hoover's, Inc., 1997. Available from http://www.hoovers.com.

Hoover's Online. "Pillowex Corporation." *Hoover's Company Capsule.* Hoovers, Inc., 1997. Available from http://www.hoovers.com.

"Labor Snaps a Wet Towel at Fieldcrest." *Business Week,* 21 March 1994.

U.S. Department of Commerce. *1992 Census of Manufactures.* Washington: GPO, 1992.

U.S. Department of Commerce. *1995 Annual Survey of Manufacturers.* Washington: GPO, 1995.

"The Week in Business." *The Business Journal of Charlotte,* 25 November 1996.

—Cheryl Collins, updated by Nancy Hammond

SIC 2393

TEXTILE BAGS

This category includes establishments primarily engaged in manufacturing shipping and other industrial bags from purchased fabrics. Establishments primarily engaged in manufacturing plastic bags are classified under **SIC 2673: Plastics, Foil, and Coated Paper Bags;** those manufacturing laundry, wardrobe, shoe, and other textile housefurnishing bags are classified under **SIC 2392: Housefurnishings, Except Curtains and Draperies;** and those manufacturing luggage are classified under **SIC 3161: Luggage.**

ORGANIZATION AND STRUCTURE

This category produces textile bags (except laundry, wardrobe, and shoe bags). In the mid-1990s, there were 33 manufacturers whose primary products were textile bags. Fifty percent were small corporations that employed less than 100 workers. The other half of the companies had 200 to 500 employees with the exception of the industry leader, BHA Group, Inc. and its subsidairy, BHA Company, who together employed 1,100 workers.

BACKGROUND AND DEVELOPMENT

The value of shipments for textile bags was $341 million in 1982 and increased to $676 million in 1992. The value of shipments of all products these companies produced, including textile bags, was $422 million in 1982 and $779 million in 1992. The number of companies producing textile bags increased to 298 in 1992 from 211 in 1977. End-of-year inventories at these establishments increased substantially with $59 million in 1977 and $121 million in 1992. New capital expenditures went from $6 million in 1977 to $12 million in 1992 as manufacturers updated their machinery and buildings.

CURRENT CONDITIONS

The value of shipments for all manufacturers who made textile bags reached $871 million in 1995. This figure included the shipment of secondary products and total miscellaneous receipts as well as the shipment of textile bags. Thirty-three companies whose primary product was textile bags employed 4,600 employees in the mid-1990s and earned an estimated $407 million. New and used capital expenditures in this category were $25 million in 1995.

INDUSTRY LEADERS

The industry leader in this category in the mid-1990s was BHA Holdings, Inc. (formerly known as the BHA Group, Inc.). They were founded in 1975 and have corporate offices in Kansas City. They design, produce, and market filter bags and replacement parts and accessories for fabric filter air pollution control equipment. They produce filter bags and other baghouse related components at their manufacturing plant in Slater, Missouri. In 1996, sales reached $121.3 million. The estimated total sales for all companies whose primary product was textile bags was $407 million.

WORK FORCE

This category had an estimated 4,600 employees working at establishments primarily engaged in the making of textile bags. The total number of workers in this category, including companies who make textile bags as a primary product was 14,000 in 1995. Total employees of the major industry group of miscellaneous fabricated textile products was 229,000. Wages earned by all workers who produced textile bags totaled $150 million in 1995 while wages for all employees producing fabricated textile products reached $3 billion in 1995.

AMERICA AND THE WORLD

In 1993 the leaders of the United States, Mexico, and Canada agreed to implement the North American Free Trade Agreement (NAFTA) on January 1, 1994. This pact will gradually allow most goods made and sold in North America to be free from all tariffs and other trade restrictions. In a press release issued by the American Textile Manufacturer's Institute (ATMI) in February 1997, President James M. Fitzgibbons said that the United States was the biggest exporter to Mexico in 1996. Fitzgibbons said, "This rapid increase in trade between the U.S. and Mexico is evidence that preferential trading agreements, when done correctly, can greatly benefit the U.S. textile industry."

FURTHER READING

"BHA Group Holdings Inc." *Hoover's Company Capsules.* Hoover's Inc., 1997. Available from http://www.hoovers.com.

BHA Group Holdings, Inc. Website. Kansas City: BHA Group Holdings, Inc., 1997. Available at http://www.bhagroup.com.

"BHA Group, Inc. Changes Name to BHA Group Holdings, Inc." *Business Wire.* 19 February 1997.

Darnay, Arsen J., ed. *Manufacturing USA.* 5th ed. Detroit: Gale Research, 1996.

"LLDPE Fills Product Niches in Film Shipping Sacks." *Modern Plastics,* December 1991.

U.S. Bureau of the Census. *1992 Census of Manufactures.* Washington: GPO, 1992.

U.S. Bureau of the Census. *1995 Annual Survey of Manufacturers.* Washington: GPO, 1997.

U.S. Department of Commerce. International Trade Administration. *U.S. Industrial Outlook 1994.* Washington: GPO, 1994.

"U.S. Textile and Apparel Exports Increase in 1996: Mexico Surpasses Canada as Top U.S. Import and Export Market." *American Textile Manufacturers Institute,* 21 February 1997. Available from http://www.atmi.org/graphic/pr970221.html.

—David Kucera, updated by Nancy Hammond

SIC 2394

CANVAS AND RELATED PRODUCTS

This category covers establishments primarily engaged in manufacturing awnings, tents, and related products from purchased fabrics. Establishments primarily engaged in manufacturing canvas bags are classified under **SIC 2393: Textile Bags.**

ORGANIZATION AND STRUCTURE

Approximately one-half of the 60 companies primarily producing canvas and related products employed under 100 workers each in the mid-1990s. There were two corporations with more than 500 employees. The top canvas products are awnings, non-camping tents, fitted tarpaulins, camping tents, flat tarpaulin, and sails. An important new market is for truck trailers with flexible fabric sides, called curtainsiders.

Synthetic textiles that resemble canvas but are cheaper and easier to clean than true canvas entered the retail market. However, the more expensive true canvas was still offered as an upgrade of the lower-end, canvas-like product. This was made available for the consumer who desired a more durable product and was willing to pay the higher price for better quality.

BACKGROUND AND DEVELOPMENT

The canvas and related products industry has become more of a custom industry since the 1950s, offering more colors than the well-known khaki or green, according to Tim O'Brien of *In Amusement Business.* The value of shipments of canvas and related products—made from cotton, nylon, polyester, and other industrial products—was $991 million in 1992, up from $641 million in 1982. The value of shipments for all products made by the companies in this category was $487 million in 1977 and $1 billion in 1992. By 1995, the value of all product shipments in this category grew to $1.3 billion.

CURRENT CONDITIONS

In the mid-1990s there were 60 companies with about 3,800 employees who earned an estimated $338 million dollars manufacturing canvas and related products as their primary product. The majority of the companies were small firms employing under 100 workers. New and used capital expenditures spent on buildings and other structures, along with machinery and equipment, in this category were $30 million in 1995, up from $8.4 million in 1977.

INDUSTRY LEADERS

The top two firms in the canvas products industry in the mid-1990s, based on sales, were American Recreation Products, Inc. of St. Louis, and Outdoor Venture Corp. of Stearns, Kentucky. American Recreation had $70 million in sales and 600 employees. The firm was a subsidiary of the publicly held Kellwood Co., also of St. Louis. They manufactured canvas and related products, fabricated textile products, and sporting and recreational products. The Outdoor Venture Corp. had an estimated $36 million in sales, employed 200 workers, and manufactured military tents.

WORK FORCE

The canvas products industry employed about 16,000 workers in 1995, up slightly from 14,000 employees in 1977. Payroll for all employees in 1995 totaled $294 million. The 12,000 production workers in these establishments earned a total of $204 million in wages.

FURTHER READING

American Textile Manufacturers Institute. "Press Release: U.S. Textile and Apparel Exports Increase in 1996. Mexico Surpasses Canada as Top U.S. Import and Export Market." Available from: http://www.atmi.org/graphic/pr970221.html.

Darnay, Arsen J., ed. *Manufacturing USA*. 5th ed. Detroit: Gale Research, 1996.

"Fabric Sides Are Opening Up Trucking." *The New York Times,* 4 November 1992.

"North Woos Non-Marine Market." *Soundings Trade Only,* November 1991.

O'Brien, Tim. "Midways and Fairgrounds Are Seas of Multiple Colors Thanks to the Colorful Tents, Awnings, and Ballys." *In Amusement Business,* 14 March 1994.

U.S. Department of Commerce. *1992 Census of Manufactures.* Washington: GPO, 1992.

U.S. Department of Commerce. *1995 Annual Survey of Manufacturers Statistics.* Washington: GPO, 1995.

U.S. Department of Commerce. International Trade Administration. *U.S. Industrial Outlook 1994.* Washington: GPO, 1994.

—David Kucera, updated by Nancy Hammond

SIC 2395

PLEATING, DECORATIVE AND NOVELTY STITCHING, AND TUCKING FOR THE TRADE

The establishments covered in this category are those engaged in pleating, decorative and novelty stitching, and tucking for the trade. Establishments primarily engaged in performing similar services for individuals are classified in service industries. Establishments primarily engaged in manufacturing trimmings are classified in **SIC 2396: Automotive Trimmings, Apparel Findings, and Related Products.** Establishments primarily engaged in manufacturing Schiffli machine embroideries are classified in **SIC 2397: Schiffli Machine Embroideries.**

ORGANIZATION AND STRUCTURE

In the mid-1990s, most of the companies in this category were private corporations with 100 or fewer workers. Production workers at these establishments produced art needlework, quilted fabrics or cloth, Swiss loom embroideries, machine-made crochet ware, and sequined embroideries. Also covered are various products for the trade, including appliqueing, buttonhole making, eyelet making, hemstitching, looping, permanent pleating and pressing, pleating, ruffling, and scalloping.

BACKGROUND AND DEVELOPMENT

During the 1980s, 200 companies dropped from this industry. However, the industry rebounded in the early 1990s when establishments grew to 756 in 1992, from a low of 685 in 1988. Companies continued to spend money to upgrade their buildings and machinery to meet the increased demand for their products. New capital expenditures totaled $12 million in 1987 and climbed to $27 million in 1995.

CURRENT CONDITIONS

In the mid-1990s, there were 27 companies with an estimated 1,800 employees whose primary product was in this category. The value of product shipments of these establishments in 1995 was $700 million. More specifically, embroideries shipment value was $401 million, commission work on materials owned by others' value was $124 million, and pleating and stitching's value was $175 million.

INDUSTRY LEADERS

There were two leading companies in this category in the mid-1990s. Weiner Laces, Inc., a New York company, specialized in the manufacture of lace and embroidery products, and Kimberton Co. of Phoenixville, Pennsylvania, provided custom embroidery work.

AMERICA AND THE WORLD

In 1993, the leaders of the United States, Mexico, and Canada agreed to implement the North American Free Trade Agreement (NAFTA) on January 1, 1994. This pact will gradually allow most goods made and sold in North America to be free from all tariffs and other trade restrictions. In a press release issued by the American Textile Manufacturer's Institute (ATMI) in February 1997, President James M. Fitzgibbons said that the United States was the biggest exporter to Mexico in 1996. Fitzgibbons said, "This rapid increase in trade between the U.S. and Mexico is evidence that preferential trading agreements, when done correctly, can greatly benefit the U.S. textile industry.''

FURTHER READING

American Textile Manufacturers Institute. ''Press Release: U.S. Textile and Apparel Exports Increase in 1996. Mexico Surpasses Canada as Top U.S. Import and Export Market.'' American Textile Manufacturers Institute, 1997. Available from http://www.atmi.org/graphic/pr970221.html.

Darnay, Arsen J., ed. *Finance, Insurance, and Real Estate, U.S.A.* Detroit: Gale Research, 1993.

U.S. Department of Commerce. *1992 Census of Manufactures.* Washington: GPO, 1992.

U.S. Department of Commerce. *1995 Annual Survey of Manufacturers.* Washington: GPO, 1995.

U.S. Department of Labor. *Occupational Outlook Handbook 1992-1993.* Washington: GPO, 1992.

—Cheryl Collins, updated by Nancy Hammond

SIC 2396

AUTOMOTIVE TRIMMINGS, APPAREL FINDINGS, AND RELATED PRODUCTS

ORGANIZATION AND STRUCTURE

In the mid-1990s, 55 corporations with some 12,000 employees were primarily engaged in making products in this category. The largest earnings in this category came from companies that manufactured automotive trimmings, apparel findings, and related products, and those that specialized in printing on garments and apparel accessories (including silk screen printing), and stamped art goods. Other corporations classified under this industry made trimmings and bindings for hats, suits, and coats, as well as linings for purses, hats, luggage, and men's and women's clothing.

BACKGROUND AND DEVELOPMENT

As reported by William C. Smith in *Textile World,* automotive trimming suppliers in this category will need to restructure their corporations to better serve the needs of the changing automotive industry. Automotive companies are demanding that their suppliers become more involved in the preproduction process. Smith also reported that some automotive companies want these suppliers to offer a set of products instead of just one product, thus reducing the number of suppliers necessary to complete the automotive trimmings

in a particular automobile. Automotive companies have historically used different suppliers for overseas production but are starting to use domestic suppliers in this market.

CURRENT CONDITIONS

There were 55 companies that manufactured products primary to this category in the mid-1990s. As a whole they employed about 12,000 workers and earned an estimated $2 billion. The value of shipments in the various product classes in 1995 were as follows: automotive trimmings at $3.4 billion; printing on garments and apparel accessories (including silk screen printing) and stamped art goods at $2.1 billion, automotive trimmings, apparel findings and related products, not specified by kind, at $533 million; other trimmings and findings at $502 million; and mens' and boys' suit and coat findings, hatters' fur, and other hat and cap materials at $167 million. The total value of shipments of all of the above products classes was $6.7 million in 1995.

Smith reported that automobile trimming suppliers should recognize that each automobile company will have different needs and different ways they want those needs satisfied. In order to survive in this very competitive world market, automobile suppliers will need to anticipate and fully satisfy their customers needs.

The value of product shipments in this category grew from $4.6 billion in 1987 to $6.1 billion in 1995. New capital expenditures for this SIC in 1995 were $326 million with $61 million spent on buildings and other structures, and $266 million spent on machinery and equipment.

INDUSTRY LEADERS

The leaders in this category supplied products to the automotive industry. Prince Corp. of Holland, Michigan and Findlay Industries, Inc. of Findlay, Ohio manufacture automotive trimmings. In the mid-1990s, Prince reported annual earnings of $700 million and employed 4,000 workers; Findlay reported annual earnings of $465 million and employed 2,900 workers for the same time period.

WORK FORCE

Production workers in this category were the highest paid textile workers in this industry group with hourly earnings of $11. The number of employees making products for this category in 1995 was 65,000, up substantially from 44,000 in 1987.

AMERICA AND THE WORLD

In 1993, the leaders of the United States, Mexico, and Canada agreed to implement the North American Free Trade Agreement (NAFTA) on January 1, 1994. This pact will gradually allow most goods made and sold in North America to be free from all tariffs and other trade restrictions. In a press release issued by the American Textile Manufacturer's Institute (ATMI) in February 1997, President James M. Fitzgibbons said that the United States was the biggest exporter to Mexico in 1996. Fitzgibbons said, "This rapid increase in trade between the U.S. and Mexico is evidence that preferential trading agreements, when done correctly, can greatly benefit the U.S. textile industry."

RESEARCH AND TECHNOLOGY

Research and technology in fabricated textile manufacturing has focused on quality control. Recent achievements include computer-aided design (CAD), new modular manufacturing systems, and ergonomics.

FURTHER READING

Smith, William C. "Textiles in Automotives: the Market of Significance." *Textile World,* June 1996.

U.S. Bureau of the Census. *1992 Census of Manufactures. Industry Series: Miscellaneous Fabricated Textile Products.* Washington: GPO, 1995.

———. *1995 Annual Survey of Manufacturers: Industry Statistics.* Washington: GPO, 1995.

———. *1995 Annual Survey of Manufacturers: Value of Product Shipments.* Washington: GPO, 1997.

U.S. Department of Labor. *Employment, Hours, and Earnings, United States, 1988-1996.* Washington: GPO, 1996.

—Catherine Quagliana, updated by Nancy Hammond

SIC 2397

SCHIFFLI MACHINE EMBROIDERIES

Establishments primarily engaged in manufacturing Schiffli machine embroideries.

ORGANIZATION AND STRUCTURE

All of the corporations in this category whose primary business is Schiffli embroidery are privately owned. In the mid-1990s, there were four leading companies whose primary product was made with the Schiffli machine. Schiffli lace is produced by a machine with several hundred needles placed horizontally one above the other. With fabric held in a frame covering the full width of the machine, the needles move back and forth through the material. The yarn used to embroider the fabric is supplied from individual spools.

BACKGROUND AND DEVELOPMENT

Schiffli lace is a type of embroidery that once was made by hand using needles that were pointed at both ends. The lasting popularity of hand made lace led to the invention of lace-making equipment like schiffli machines. Many types of laces are machine made, frequently with geometrically shaped netting used as backgrounds. Once made only from cotton, schiffli lace, like other laces, can be manufactured from man made fibers.

According to the 1992 Census of Manufactures, there were 357 Schiffli machine embroidery companies with 6,000 employees in 1977 and 220 companies with 5,500 employees in 1992.

Following an almost continuous decline since 1988, employment in all of the fabricated textile industries increased in 1993. However, employment for machinery operators is expected to decline through 2005. Increased productivity created by more efficient machinery could be a major reason for the projected reduction in machinery operators.

CURRENT CONDITIONS

New capital expenditures were at an all-time high in 1992 with $7 million spent on new buildings and machinery—up from $3 million in 1977. In 1995, new capital expenditures totaled $1.4 million. Manufacturers have been investing in high-technology machinery such as computerized embroidery machines. As the textile industry continues to become increasingly automated, operators and setters will need to understand complex machinery and have sufficient computer skills.

The value of shipments in this category increased substantially in the last few years. The value of shipments in 1992 was $254 million and increased to $320 million in 1995.

INDUSTRY LEADERS

The top two companies both reported about $8 million in annual sales in the mid-1990s. Moritz Embroidery Works, Inc. in the Pocono Mountains of

Pennsylvania employs 100 workers who make embroidered letters, numbers, and Swiss inserts. These chenille products are made of 100 percent wool on felt. Schweizer Emblem Company, Inc., of Chicago, employs 50 people and specializes in emblem embroideries. Total sales in the mid-1990s for all four leading companies whose primary product is produced with the Schiffli machine is $18 million.

WORK FORCE

In the mid-1990s, about 200 workers were producing Schiffli embroideries as their primary product. The total number of people making Schiffli embroideries—including but not limited to the companies making them primarily—were 5,000 in 1995. Total earnings for all Schiffli workers for 1995 was $63 million.

AMERICA AND THE WORLD

In 1993, the leaders of the United States, Mexico, and Canada agreed to implement the North American Free Trade Agreement (NAFTA) on January 1, 1994. This pact will gradually allow most goods made and sold in North America to be free from all tariffs and other trade restrictions. In a press release issued by the American Textile Manufacturer's Institute (ATMI) in February 1997, President James M. Fitzgibbons said that the United States was the biggest exporter to Mexico in 1996. Fitzgibbons said, "This rapid increase in trade between the U.S. and Mexico is evidence that preferential trading agreements, when done correctly, can greatly benefit the U.S. textile industry."

FURTHER READING

"Moritz Embroidery Works, Inc." Pocono, PA: Moritz Embroidery Works, Inc., 1997. Available from http://www.qdtmoritz.com/moritz1.htm.

U.S. Department of Commerce. *1992 Census of Manufacturers.* Washington: GPO, 1992.

U.S. Department of Commerce. *1995 Annual Survey of Manufacturers.* Washington: GPO, 1995.

U.S. Department of Commerce. *U.S. Industrial Outlook 1994.* Washington: GPO, 1993.

U.S. Department of Labor. *Career Guide to Industries.* Washington: GPO, September 1992.

U.S. Department of Labor. *Occupational Outlook Handbook 1996-97.* Washington: GPO, 1991.

—Catherine Quagliana, updated by Nancy Hammond

FABRICATED TEXTILE PRODUCTS, NOT ELSEWHERE CLASSIFIED

This category covers establishments primarily engaged in manufacturing fabricated textile products, not elsewhere classified.

ORGANIZATION AND STRUCTURE

There were 74 companies in the mid-1990s whose primary product was in this category. They employed about 26,000 workers and reported an estimated $2 billion in sales. The top three companies in this category supplied textile products to the automotive industry. Other companies classified here include manufacturers of banners, flags, sleeping bags, cloth diapers, fishing nets, parachutes, aprons, horse blankets, seat covers, hammocks, pennants, and non-leather straps.

BACKGROUND AND DEVELOPMENT

The number of companies in this category has grown considerably in the last two decades. In 1977, the number of companies who manufactured products in this category (not necessarily as their primary product) was 845. In 1992, that number grew to about 1,100. The value of shipments from these corporations increased from $1.1 billion in 1977 to $3.2 billion in 1992.

CURRENT CONDITIONS

Approximate annual earnings for corporations producing fabricated textiles not elsewhere classified, as their primary product reached $2 billion in the mid-1990s. The value of shipments for products in this category was $4 billion in 1995. Companies tried to keep pace with technology by spending $105 million on new machinery and equipment in 1995.

INDUSTRY LEADERS

In the mid-1990s, the leader in this category was TRW Vehicle Safety Systems, Inc. located in Detroit. They reported annual sales of $1 billion—half of the $2 billion total earnings of the 74 companies with this SIC as their primary product. They employed 11,000 workers and manufactured automobile seat belts and air bags.

WORK FORCE

In 1995, there were 39,000 employees working in this category with 32,000 of them working in production. These numbers grew somewhat since 1977 when there were 31,000 total employees and 26,000 production workers.

AMERICA AND THE WORLD

In 1993, the leaders of the United States, Mexico, and Canada agreed to implement the North American Free Trade Agreement (NAFTA) on January 1, 1994. This pact will gradually allow most goods made and sold in North America to be free from all tariffs and other trade restrictions. In a press release issued by the American Textile Manufacturer's Institute (ATMI) in February 1997, President James M. Fitzgibbons said that the United States was the biggest exporter to Mexico in 1996. Fitzgibbons said, "This rapid increase in trade between the U.S. and Mexico is evidence that preferential trading agreements, when done correctly, can greatly benefit the U.S. textile industry."

FURTHER READING

U.S. Bureau of the Census. *1992 Census of Manufactures. Industry Series: Miscellaneous Fabricated Textile Products.* Washington: GPO, 1995.

———. *1995 Annual Survey of Manufacturers: Industry Statistics.* Washington: GPO, 1995.

———. *1995 Annual Survey of Manufacturers: Value of Product Shipments.* Washington: GPO, 1997.

—Catherine Quagliana, updated by Nancy Hammond

LUMBER & WOOD PRODUCTS, EXCEPT FURNITURE

SIC 2411

LOGGING

This category covers establishments primarily engaged in cutting timber and in producing rough, round, hewn, or riven primary forest or wood raw materials, or in producing wood chips in the field. Independent contractors engaged in estimating or trucking lumber, but who perform no cutting operations, are classified in non-manufacturing industries. Establishments primarily engaged in the collection of bark, sap, gum, and other forest products are classified in **SIC 0811: Timber Tracts**; **SIC 0831: Forest Nurseries and Gathering of Forest Products;** and **SIC 0851: Forestry Services.**

INDUSTRY SNAPSHOT

Logging, among the oldest of American industries, has become one of the most controversial. Environmentalists have severely attacked harvesting practices, and they have scored significant victories. Much of the dispute thus far has centered on protecting government forests in the Pacific Northwest to ensure the survival of the northern spotted owl. In August of 1990, the federal government listed the spotted owl as an endangered species. The net result was strict restriction: logging was prevented around a 2,000 acre radius around a known spotted owl nest, the largest trees in that zone had to be left uncut around a 500 acre area, and logging was prohibited within a 70 acre area around a nest. However, in April 1997 the Oregon Supreme Court allowed a logging company to sue for millions of dollars of compensation because it lost revenues from logging restrictions to protect the spotted owl—a precedent-setting decision that promises to continue the strife between the industry and its opponents.

The conflicts have already had a major impact on the geographic distribution of logging within the United States. The South and the Pacific Northwest have been the two traditional centers of U.S. logging. In the South, loggers have relied on private holdings, which account for some 90 percent of all timberland in the region. In the Pacific Northwest, however, much of the supply has come from federal forests. With harvesting of government-owned land down sharply, the Pacific Northwest has accounted for a shrinking portion of the nation's production. According to *Wood Technology,* about 62.9 percent of the forest in the Pacific Northwest was available for harvest at the beginning of 1997, and 28.9 percent was withdrawn mostly because the areas were designated as wilderness areas. In the 1960s and 1970s, the Pacific Northwest used to be the world leader for veneer based wood products. However in 1997, it dropped 80 percent in size. The plywood industry in the U.S. West Coast produced 6.2 billion board feet in 1990, but in 1997 the levels were expected to reach about a third of what it was in 1990. Restructuring has hit the industry, with smaller mills that failed to modernize and adopting to changing market conditions finding themselves out of business. Leadership in the industry thus continues to shift to the South.

The curtailment of harvesting on federal lands has had a disparate impact on firms in the wood products industry. In general, the major forest products companies performed poorly during 1991 and had mixed results in 1992, as the recession took its toll. In the first half of 1993, however, large firms that had extensive land holdings of their own recorded sharply higher earnings, as they benefited from the price increases that accompanied shrinking supply. Other companies, however, including many small sawmills without timber assets, faced increasing margin pressure as their raw material costs rose. 1995 and 1996 were two years in which wood product companies held their own in the face of continued flat prices. In 1996, the housing market grew to 1.5 million units according to *Forbes,* January 13, 1997 issue. This was an increase of 8 percent from 1995. After the Federal Reserve tightened credit from 1994 to 1995, the homebuilding market slowed. It picked up in 1995, but wood chip demand from the paper industry and a strong level of Canadian imports created an oversupply of lumber and held back a return to stronger conditions. However, the paper industry demand for chips dropped and an April 1996 Canadian lumber quota reduced the lumber supply. Along with a stronger construction level, the economic conditions leading into 1997 appeared stronger. What may set back a temporary recovery is that the housing cycle is fairly mature, and any efforts of the Federal Reserve to raise interest rates may hamper the housing market, and therefore the wood products industry.

ORGANIZATION AND STRUCTURE

A diverse group of economic entities and individuals are involved in logging. Among the participants are the giant, integrated forest products firms, like Weyerhaeuser and Georgia-Pacific, which may own millions of acres of private timberlands; small sawmills that may harvest relatively few trees on federal lands for their own use; and independent cutters, who are compensated according to the number of trees they are able to distribute to mills. Logging activities are thus distributed among different types of firms and individuals, but they can also be integrated with other operations within a single, large company.

According to the government, products and services sold by the logging industry in 1996 had an estimated value of $13.2 billion. Broad estimates of the total size of the forest products, and related industries, of which logging is but a small segment, run to about 4 percent of gross national product, or $220 billion. According to Home Improvement market, U.S. lumber production in billions of board feet by region is as follows: Western U.S., 17.47 (1994), 15.67 (1995); Southern U.S., 15.01 (1994), 14.80 (1995); Canadian imports, 16.02 (1994), 16.90 (1995); other, 1.62 (1994), 1.52 (1995).

BACKGROUND AND DEVELOPMENT

Wood was a commodity of great value in ancient Rome, and in Athens its export was banned—a harbin-

ger of the recent controversy over sending U.S. logs abroad to Asia. In the United States, of course, logging is older than the country itself, and wood products have played a central role in the economy's development.

The clearing and revival of the U.S. forest has been extraordinary. The land area of the coterminous United States is 1.9 billion acres. Between 822 and 850 million acres, or about 45 percent of the country's land area, was originally covered by commercial forest. By 1920, owing to agricultural clearing, lumbering, and other activities, the original cover had fallen to about 470 million acres, of which only 138 million acres were original forest (some 250 million acres were significantly disturbed through grazing, cutting, and burning and could not sustain second growth, while 81 million acres were both nonrenewable and non-restoring). By 1977, however, because of better management, the suppression of fire, replanting, and other factors, the trend had reversed itself: the commercial forest had grown to 483 million acres. The Forest Service estimates that there were 490 million acres of timberland in 1992.

Logging in the great forests of the Pacific Northwest was begun by the Hudson Bay Company at its Fort Vancouver trading post on the Columbia River in 1820. In 1825, the Royal Horticultural Society of London sent out a Scottish botanist, David Douglas, to the area; he returned to England with a sprig of what is now the most important commercial tree of these forests, the eponymous Douglas fir. Logging as an industry began in the region at the time of the Gold Rush, which produced a new market for timber in California. It was the timber barons from the East who saw the potential of the Pacific Northwest forests. Most famous among them was George Weyerhaeuser, who incorporated his company in 1900 in Tacoma, Washington; often a pioneer in the industry, Weyerhaeuser began the practice of hand-planting new trees on clearcuts in 1938. In the early 1990s, the firm had average annual sales in excess of $9 billion.

CURRENT CONDITIONS

The national recession during the early 1990s hurt the wood products sector badly, but as the recession waned the industry began to recover. Due largely to the strength of higher housing starts and firmer timber prices, the wood products operations of the major forest products companies did better in 1992 and 1993 than in 1991. In the first-half of 1993, profits at those companies that rely most heavily on wood products were up 179 percent from the same period in 1992, according to *Business Week.* Nevertheless, the prospect of sustained cutbacks in the timber supply raised significant questions about the long-term health of the industry. In 1996, merger and acquisition activity was strong, with 5 million acres of timberland changing hands, according to *Wood Technology,* December 1996. Most of the land that changed hands was located in the southern and western regions of the U.S. For perspective, this is about 7 percent of the estimated 68.6 million acres that is owned by the industry. The largest timber owner, International Paper Company, holds 6.4 million acres. Fifty percent of the 5 million acres that changed hands was in the South, 42 percent was in the West, and 8 percent was in the Northeast and Lake states. Lumber markets improved in 1996 due to tightened lumber supplies and better pricing for lumber products. Housing starts increased 5 percent in 1996, aiding wood products sales. Additional capacity in the industry is not expected to occur, and earnings growth for 1997 is expected to improve.

According to *Industry Week,* the last ten years of environmental constraints on logging have reduced by 75 percent the amount of timber harvested from national forests in the U.S., most of which has affected the Pacific Northwest markets. These logging restrictions have not had a major impact in most of the South, the Northeast, and North Central regions of the country. It is important to remember, however, that about half of the country's timber for wood products has come from the Pacific Northwest. The deterioration of the climate for timber harvesting in that region has been so dramatic that it has already had a significant impact on the nation's overall supply. More importantly, the political and social forces that have caused the industry such problems in the Northwest are expected to continue in the future.

Most of the nation's timber supply has come from softwoods, which are used predominately in housing construction; hardwoods, which have a variety of uses, are harvested primarily in the South. In 1987, approximately 35 percent of the nation's softwood lumber came from sales of timber on federal lands in the Pacific Northwest. By 1992, that contribution had dropped to 25 percent. Sales of timber from federal forests in the region have fallen from 6.0 billion board feet in 1987 to 1.5 billion in 1992.

In 1996, the industry also struggled against competing materials, namely steel for wood, in homebuilding. An increasing number of builders are using steel-frame housing, with 800 estimated to be built in 1992 versus 80,000 houses built in 1996. Industry experts expect this trend to continue as long as lumber prices for homebuilding remain steady.

It has been estimated that once the environmental controversies in the Northwest are settled, government timber sales in the West will be at about 40 percent of historical levels. Given that 35 percent to 40 percent of the U.S. timber supply has historically come from federal lands in the area, these curtailments would represent a 22 percent decline in the national timber harvest. A drop in the timber supply of that magnitude portends higher log prices, as well as narrower margins for wood products firms that do not own timber acreage.

The Spotted Owl Controversy. On June 26, 1990, the government listed the northern spotted owl as a threatened species under the Endangered Species Act. Unlike most other species protected by the Act, the spotted owl's habitat covers a much larger area: it ranges from southern British Columbia, Canada, to Marin County, California. Under the terms of the act, more than five million acres of forests were designated as conservation areas; these generally contained conifers of mixed varieties that were over 200 years old, i.e., old-growth forests.

Technically, logging was still allowed within the conservation areas as long as it did not threaten the spotted owl, but as a practical matter much of the owl's habitat was off-limits to loggers. The U.S. Forest Service reported that in total it sold 4.45 billion board feet of timber in fiscal 1992—less than half of its sales in 1990. The agency managed to sell only 20 percent of the Congressionally approved volume in the Pacific Northwest and 40 percent in California. Most if not all of this shortfall stemmed from measures taken to protect the spotted owl and other species. Loggers cut 61 percent more national forest timber in 1992 than was sold during the year.

Some observers believed that the timber industry had only itself to blame for its problems with the owl. They argued that the industry ignored the bird, and attempted to discredit research that showed the owl was truly endangered. They also said that the timber on the federal lands which the spotted owls inhabit represent public assets—assets that, in their view, have often been sold at below cost by the Forest Service and the Bureau of Land Management for the industry's benefit.

Many industry supporters, however, said there is much evidence that spotted owls of one subspecies or another are thriving on millions of acres of privately and publicly managed second-growth forests. They also noted that counts of the northern spotted owl have risen substantially over the past several years. They argued, additionally, that even if the spotted owl was indeed endangered, it did not provide sufficient reason to throw thousands of workers out of their jobs and destroy dozens of timber communities.

A shift in the battle between loggers and environmentalists may occur with a 1997 Oregon Supreme Court ruling. Boise Cascade was found to be able to seek reimbursement from the State of Oregon because the value of the 64 acres the company owned in Oregon dropped in value because of the environmental protections afforded the spotted owl from the Endangered Species Act. As reported in the *Oregonian,* Mark Rutzick, a Portland, Oregon attorney who represents many timber companies stated, '' . . . when private citizens' economic interests are hurt by environmental laws, they have the right to go to court . . . a lot of people will be looking at this very carefully.''

While the clash between the timber industry and environmentalists (or preservationists, the term the industry prefers) has centered on the survival of the northern spotted owl, campaigns to protect other species may affect the industry in the future. Timber executives are also worried about the impact of logging on salmon. Because logging often damages the streams in which salmon spawn, the species could eventually become federally protected and thus further limit the industry in the Northwest.

Some observers, both within the industry and the environmental movement, believe that efforts to save individual species are merely tactical devices in the battle to curtail logging. The environmental movement needed a weapon to shut down logging on federal lands, they say, and the Endangered Species Act merely happened to be conveniently at hand. Andy Stahl, an environmentalist, is quoted in the book *The Final Forest* as saying ''I've often thought that thank goodness the spotted owl evolved in the Northwest, for if it hadn't, we'd have to genetically engineer it.''

Environmentalists recognize that the total amount of woodland in the United States is not contracting—new plantings more than offset cuttings. Still, many are concerned that the way the nation's forests have been managed reduces biodiversity. When loggers cut down mixed forests with trees of different ages, they often replant with a single species (such as the Douglas fir, which reaches maturity in a relatively fast 50 years) of the same age. Some environmentalists argue that in a naturally regenerating forest, there are dead trees, clearings, old trees, and young trees, and each attracts its own group of plant and animal species. But when a forest consists solely of one tree type, all of the same age, only one set of species is attracted. Ecologists believe that this hurts the forest's ecosystem, and leaves it prone to pest infestations.

In rebuttal, the industry's supporters pointed to the expansion in total timberland over the last fifty years, and the millions of acres, including much old-growth (trees over 200 years old), in national and state forests that are protected from logging. They also called attention to the significant advances in forestry management over several decades. For example, after the volcanic eruption of Mount St. Helens on May 18, 1980, Congress, in 1982, established a 110,000 acre National Volcanic Monument. In this area nature would be allowed to take its course, and the land would be left undisturbed. On the acreage adjacent to it, Weyerhaeuser and other companies salvaged the downed trees and planted new seedlings. According to some observers, the result of this effort is a forest not significantly different from the original (pre-1980) cover below the slopes of the volcano. By 1992, many of the trees Weyerhaeuser had planted were already 25 or 30 feet high. Next door, the National Volcanic Monument was recovering much more slowly—but, some would argue, more completely.

Others in the industry said that the uncertainty that surrounded harvesting in 1993 would have long-term repercussions for the industry. In this regard, *The Economist* cited the words of a Weyerhaeuser economist: ''Planting trees is an act of faith.'' It takes some 80 or 90 years for a forest to regrow on its own after cutting, versus 50 to 60 years in a managed forest. So if timber firms lose confidence that they will be able to harvest the tree they have sown, they are unlikely to put much effort in expensive forest-management techniques.

In February 1993, news reports indicated that the Clinton administration was trying to modify the policies of the Department of Interior (DOI) so that ''national train wrecks'' (in the words of DOI Secretary Bruce Babbitt), like the one over the spotted owl in the Pacific Northwest, could be averted in the future. Instead of protecting single species, the DOI would seek preventive measures to insure long-term protection of whole ecosystems and all of their species. The theory behind such an approach is that both conservation and business interests are better served by preplanning the fate of entire ecosystems, before any single species is threatened.

Winners and Losers. Cutbacks of harvesting on federal lands has had a diverse impact on industry participants. Some believe that the largest companies—at least those with substantial timber holdings of their own—have been less than vigorous in fighting curtailments of logging on federal land. These firms have huge plantations of genetically improved trees, which afford them ample supply. Their reliance on federal sales of old-growth trees is relatively small, and the spotted owl doesn't appear to thrive on their own second- and third-growth forests. It has been argued, therefore, that these companies have been willing, and even happy, to accept restrictions on logging of federal lands.

Small, independent sawmill owners, on the other hand, have since World War II relied on public lands to supply the old-growth logs that can be turned into specialty products. The trees they used were often as much as five centuries old; consequently, they were often inhabited by the spotted owl. The trees that have been engineered by big corporations are but a tenth the age and only half the height of the old-growth trees. Often they are too small for the saws and conveyor belts of the old-time sawmills.

Lumber prices rose sharply in the first-quarter of 1993, and while they fell back in the spring, they were still significantly above 1992 levels. Prices continued to remain stable and increased somewhat through 1996. Meanwhile, however, smaller sawmill companies in the Pacific Northwest were hurt by contracting supply and continued to decline in number. Some observers argued that these companies have only themselves to blame, since they tended to disregard forecasts, dating back to the 1970s, of a looming timber shortage during the 1990s. They also suggested that at the rate the loggers were cutting, the Pacific Northwest would have had severe supply problems by the year 2000, regardless of the spotted owl endangerment controversy.

The South. Level terrain, frost-free winters, and numerous highways made logging much easier in the South than it was in the Northwest. Trees in the region grew faster because of the relatively warm winters. Since most of the South's acreage was logged years ago, there is little of the old-growth forest that has aroused such strong environmental opposition in the Northwest. Most notably, some 90 percent of Southern timberland is privately owned.

The conflicts between the environmentalists and timber interests that halted logging in much of the Northwest has been comparatively rare in the South. The two sides have actually worked together to balance environmental and economic concerns. Georgia-Pacific, which moved its headquarters from Portland, Oregon, to Atlanta in 1982 and has an important presence in the region, believes that it is successfully dealing with the red-cockaded woodpecker, which some see as a potential "spotted owl" of the South. Others, however, believe it is only a matter of time before the environmental movement begins to become more aggressive in opposing logging in the South.

In July of 1993 the Clinton administration issued a plan that would reduce timber harvests on national forests in the Pacific Northwest to 1.2 billion board feet per year, down 75 percent from peak levels in the mid-1980s. At the same time, the proposal made available $1 to $2 billion in funds to help retrain loggers and aid lumber communities. Both environmentalists and industry officials attacked the plan, and it was unclear whether it would offer a long-term solution to the controversy.

INDUSTRY LEADERS

The business operations of the large, integrated forest product companies were usually divided into three areas: paper, pulp, and packaging; wood and building products; and other miscellaneous activities. The three largest forest products companies— International Paper, Georgia-Pacific, and Weyerhaeuser—were notably larger than other firms, and each had more than $8 billion in sales in 1991. According to *Moody's Industry Review*, the industry leaders in order of 1995 revenues were the following: Georgia-Pacific Corporation ($14.2 billion), Weyerhaeuser Company ($11.8 billion), Mead Corporation ($5.2 billion), Willamette Industries ($3.9 billion), and Louisiana-Pacific Corporation ($2.8 billion).

Weyerhaeuser stands to benefit from any shortages in the timber supply. In 1991 the company had more than 5.5 million acres in timber holdings, so it had much to gain from any run-up in prices resulting from curtailed supplies. In fact, during the first six months of 1993, when lumber prices surged, the company's profits rose 100 percent. Still, the environmental movement has not been an unmixed blessing: logging on some 320,000 acres of its land is restricted because of federal and state rules protecting the spotted owl, and the company was worried about further restrictions on its supply. Further, the movement to restrict log exports to Japan and other countries could also hurt the company in the longer term.

In the 1980s Weyerhaeuser had embarked on a diversification program that was generally considered to have been ill-conceived. Among the failed operations were garden supplies, lettuce factories, mortgage banking, and dog food. As a result, while the timber industry as a whole posted a combined 18.5 percent return on equity in the 1980s, Weyerhaeuser posted just 10 percent. Although the proportion of "other activities" among all of its businesses was still higher than most of its competitors in 1992, it had slimmed down considerably and shed many of its extraneous operations. The company has been very aggressive in taking steps to maximize profitability. In 1995, the company concentrated on cutting costs, resulting into $200 million of savings. In 1997, the company was estimated to have saved another $400 million, according to *Industry Week*.

As logging on public lands in the Northwest came under increasing attack from environmental groups in the 1980s, Georgia-Pacific began to increase its holdings of fast-growing pine forests in the Southeast where it had logged extensively earlier in the century. Losses from the paper side of the business, which had been expanded significantly with the purchase of Great Northern Nekoosa in 1990, more than offset gains from logging in the early 1990s. The acquisition also saddled the company with debt. In 1992, however, operating profits from the building products division reached a record level of $691 million, more than double the 1991 total of $344 million.

WORK FORCE

In 1995, total employment in the lumber and wood products industries exceeded 764,000 workers. Of these, 81,800 persons were employed in logging. This figure was down from the late 1980s high of 88,000 for this industry.

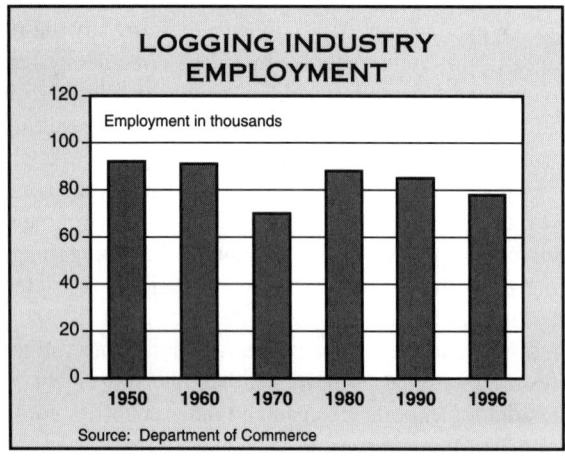

LOGGING INDUSTRY EMPLOYMENT

Employment in thousands

Source: Department of Commerce

Estimates of the number of jobs that would be lost due to federal protection of the spotted owl habitats varied widely. In early 1993, the U.S. Fish and Wildlife Service attempted to estimate cuts in timber-related employment if the level of owl protection remained at existing levels. They forecast that by 1995 about 32,000 jobs would be lost, including 6,500 in Washington, 21,600 in Oregon, and 4,300 in California. The Clinton administration estimated that under its plan introduced in July of 1993, 6,000 jobs would be lost. Still, some in the timber industry said that the number of lost jobs would be ten times that level.

Even without the threat of continuing job losses due to environmental concerns, employment in the industry was likely to decline because of increasing automation. Between 1979 and 1989, timber employment fell from 160,000 to 130,000 in Oregon and Washington, though the wood harvest in both years was roughly the same. Most of the decline had little to do with protecting rare species or setting aside old-growth, but rather was the result of increasing mechanization in the industry. In 1991, for the first time in decades, more people worked in the food industry in Washington state than in forest products. The number of forest workers had fallen to 36,500 from 41,000 in 1988, while food industry workers climbed from 33,100 to 37,400 during that period.

Some loggers have been successful in finding alternative sources of revenue within the industry itself or in related businesses. For example, loggers have sold pine cones and moss-covered sticks to floral designers, and they have found work harvesting herbs for use in the decorative, culinary, and medicinal markets. These activities, however, tend to pay less than cutting trees, and some loggers say they enjoy the work much less than logging.

Logging is in fact very dangerous work. Many workers within the industry have suffered serious injuries and have had friends and relatives killed on the job. These risks are apparent in workmen's compensation rates for loggers. In Maine, for example, they run about $37 for every $100 in salary, compared to an average of $12 for carpenters.

Some logging communities are now looking to the Clinton plan to revive their economic bases and enhance job opportunities. If the funds are approved by Congress, money would be available for retraining programs. Some ideas for economic regeneration on the Olympic Peninsula in Washington state, an area that has been hurt by logging restrictions, included docks for cruise ships, Indian cultural centers, and industrial parks.

AMERICA AND THE WORLD

Exports. Total log exports from Pacific Coast ports in 1992 were 2.73 billion board feet, down from approximately 3.15 billion feet in 1991. The drop continued the decline in log shipments since 1988, when exports peaked at 4,331 million feet. Log exports to Japan totaled 2.03 billion feet, or over 70 percent of total shipments. It is estimated that U.S. log exports in the first three quarters of 1992 represented 57 percent of all softwood imports in Japan. Other important destinations were China and South Korea, although exporters faced increasing competition from New Zealand for those markets.

The issue of log exports, especially to Japan, has become a source of controversy. It was estimated that about 40 percent of all logs felled in Washington state were being shipped overseas in the early 1990s, and sawmill operators complained that they were unable to get wood because of the large number of logs being sent abroad. While the export of logs from federal lands is prohibited, some mill operators said that companies substituted logs from private holdings for export and sawed the government logs for domestic use. Indeed, the issue has become embroiled with the spotted owl controversy, with environmentalists suggesting that overseas shipments were the reason for any lumber shortages, while major exporters attributed supply shortages to the impact of the Endangered Species Act.

Imports. In early 1996, a strong level of imports provided tough competition for the industry. Canadian lumber stood at 35 percent of the U.S. market, an increase from 28 percent in 1989. Almost all U.S. imports currently come from Canada, particularly the province of British Columbia. But the province's forests have been more aggressively cut than U.S. acreage, and Canada's environmentalists are trying to reduce harvests.

The former Soviet Union still had bountiful forests in the early 1990s, but it lacked the infra structure to make harvesting worthwhile. It would take billions of dollars in roads as well as a stable government for Russia to become a major producer. Moreover, some Russian acreage is believed to be infested with pests that could harm Northwest trees. Earlier attempts to process Russian logs in California were stymied by costly pesticidal treatments that had to be performed before the logs were allowed into the country.

Ironically, the first logs to be imported in quantity may be transplanted Californian natives. New Zealand and Chile have large plantations of radiata pine, and both countries already export large volumes of logs. The radiata is known as Monterey pine in its native California, where it is not grown commercially.

RESEARCH AND TECHNOLOGY

As a result of mechanization and automation, timber companies can now log more efficiently while doing less harm to the environment. Huge "feller-bunches" now often replace individual loggers in second-growth forests. These vehicles are built like tanks and have enormous "scissors" mounted in front; they

are able to snip mature trees and lay them down carefully to avoid smashing small, still-growing ones. Additionally, mechanized skidders that are used to haul logs out of the forest are being fitted with extra-wide tracks or oversized tires to spread their weight and reduce damage to the forest floor.

Timber companies are also experimenting with different forestry techniques. After harvesting, some loggers are leaving behind the odd mature tree, dead-sun-silvered trunks, and the usual litter of the woods. The hope is that, as new trees grow, their surroundings mimic what would follow a natural fire or windstorm, which a forest can survive.

Timber shortages and the possibility of higher lumber prices over the long-term are encouraging the creation of new offerings and the promotion of relatively inexpensive existing products. Forest products producers face a threat from the steel industry, which is promoting steel studs as replacements for wood in residential construction. To fend off this and other challenges to its products, the industry is focusing on promoting such engineered wood products as oriented strand board and particle board.

According to *Business Week,* a new engineered product called oriented strandboard, promises to be a profitable market for lumber companies to pursue. The new type of fiberboard is expected to grow up to 7 billion feet of oriented strandboard capacity in 1998, an increase from zero in 1988. L. Pendleton Siegel, CEO of Potlatch Corp, states that the market will be very competitive for this type of board, capturing approximately 50 percent of the fiberboard capacity.

FURTHER READING

Boise Cascade & American Forest and Paper Association. "Quick Facts About Our Industry." April 1997. Available from http://www.bc.com/indust.html.

Burrow, Clive. "Tech Notes: With Tall Trees in Short Supply. . . ." *New York Times,* 13 December 1992.

Chipello, Christopher "Paper, Lumber Are Diverging in Their Results." *Wall Street Journal,* 12 April 1993.

Clark, Earl. "When the Bullwhacker Reigned Supreme." *American Forests,* September/October 1991.

Conway, Richard S., et al. *The Forest Products Economic Study.* Olympia, WA: Washington Forest Protection Association, 1991.

"Corporate Scoreboard." *Business Week,* 16 August 1993.

Cory, M. James. "If a Tree Falls, etc., Market View, Editorial." *Home Improvement Market,* October 1996.

Dietrich, William. *The Final Forest.* New York: Simon & Schuster, 1992.

Egan, Timothy. "Thunder of Debate on Owls and Jobs Rings in Forests as Opponents Face Off." *New York Times,* 2 April 1993.

————. "The Things That Get Left Out in the Fight for the Wild Northwest." *New York Times,* 30 May 1993.

Flynn, Bob. "Filling The Wood Gap, U.S. Buyers Look Worldwide." *Wood Technology* (September 1994).

Forest Industries 1992-93 North American Factbook. San Francisco: Miller Freeman, 1992.

Forest Resource Fact Book. Memphis, TN: National Hardwood Lumber Association, 1993.

"Forest Service Issues Logging Restrictions to Aid Owl Species." *New York Times,* 15 January 1993.

"The Future of Forests." *The Economist,* 22 June 1991.

Ifill, Gwen. "Clinton Backs a $1 Billion Plan to Spare Trees and Aid Loggers." *New York Times,* 1 July 1993.

Killian, Linda. "Forest Products & Packaging." *Forbes,* 4 January 1993.

Knize, Perri. "The Mismanagement of the National Forests." *Atlantic Monthly,* October 1991.

McCoy, Charles. "Even a Logger Praised as Sensitive to Ecology Faces Bitter Opposition." *Wall Street Journal,* 1 April 1993.

"Wood Products." *Moody's Industry Review,* Spring 1996.

Norvell, Scott. "Southern Comfort for a Timber Giant: Georgia-Pacific Is Sitting Pretty Far from the Troubled Northwest." *New York Times,* 28 March 1993.

"Owlmageddon." *The Economist,* 4 May 1991.

Pacelle, Mitchell. "It Takes Guts Telling Paul Bunyan to Get Herbs, Spare Timber." *Wall Street Journal,* 27 November 1992.

Passell, Peter. "Economic Scene: The Pacific Timber Industry Isn't Really on the Endangered List." *New York Times,* 1 April 1993.

Pease, David. "Timber Shortages Will Encourage New Products." *Forest Industries,* July/August 1992.

Ray, Dixy Lee. "A Forest Rises From the Ashes, Privately." *Wall Street Journal,* 1 April 1993.

Rice, James Owen. "Where Many An Owl Is Spotted." *National Review,* 2 March 1992.

Richards, Bill. "Owls, of All Things, Help Weyerhaeuser Cash In on Timber." *The Wall Street Journal,* 24 June 1993.

Stevens, William. "Interior Secretary Is Pushing A New Way to Save Species." *New York Times,* 17 February 1993.

Suskind, Ron. "Guys Holding Axes and Chainsaws Get to Use Any Name They Like." *The Wall Street Journal,* 26 February 1993.

Taylor, John A. "The Ducks Are Flying." *Forbes,* 20 July 1992.

"The Timber Industry: Log On." *The Economist,* 9 November 1991.

"To the Dinosaurs." *The Economist,* 10 July 1993.

"U.S. Wood Industry Reshaped By Timberland Acquisitions." *Wood Technology,* September 1996.

Waker Jr., Donald. "A Logger's Story." *Wall Street Journal,* 15 May 1992.

Weaver, Jim. "Troubles for Timber." *New York Times,* 2 April 1993.

Williams, Michael. *Americans & Their Forests: A Historical Geography.* Oxford: Cambridge University Press, 1989.

"Year End Review - Paper and Pulp Industries." *Forbes,* 13 January 1997.

           —Bob Schneider, updated by Bill Bennett

SIC 2421

SAWMILLS AND PLANING MILLS, GENERAL

This industry includes establishments primarily engaged in sawing rough lumber and timber from logs and bolts, or resawing cants and flitches into lumber, including box lumber and softwood cut stock; planing mills combined with sawmills; and separately operated planing mills which are engaged primarily in producing surfaced lumber and standard workings or patterns of lumber. The industry also includes establishments primarily engaged in sawing lath and railroad ties and in producing tobacco hogshead stock, wood chips, and snow fence lath. Establishments primarily engaged in manufacturing box shook or boxes are classified in wood container manufacturing industries; those manufacturing sash, doors, wood molding, window and door frames, and other fabricated millwork are classified in millwork, veneer, plywood, and structural wood industries; and those manufacturing hardwood dimension and flooring are classified in **SIC 2426: Hardwood Dimension and Flooring Mills.**

INDUSTRY SNAPSHOT

The mid-1990s were the best and worst of times for sawmill owners. With the economy healthy and interest rates low, housing starts climbed upwards, and lumber demand was buoyant. But while strong demand led to higher prices, lumber quotes continued to be highly volatile. Moreover, the supply side of the equation remained perilous. Conservationists remained committed to restricting timber harvesting, and the tug of war for control of the nation's forests was as polarized as ever. Thus mill owners had to scramble to find adequate supplies of raw material.

Relatively small mills without their own timber holdings have come under increasing pressure as logging on federal lands has declined: between 1987 and 1995, the Western lumber industry lost almost half its mills. The major, integrated forest products companies that have large timber holdings of their own, however, have remained competitive. While the big firms are not insulated from losses related to environmental legislation, they are generally in a stronger position to benefit from the higher prices that follow restricted supplies.

There has also been a notable shift in lumber production away from the Northwest and toward the South, where most timberlands are privately owned. During the 1980s the seven largest forest products companies cut their mill capacity in the Pacific Northwest by 35 percent, while they increased it in the South by 121 percent. In the 1990s, lumber production continued to shift to the South, where softwood output was approaching that in the West.

ORGANIZATION AND STRUCTURE

According to the annual survey of North American producers in the trade publication *Forest Industries,* the 20 largest lumber producers in the United States cut a total of 22.5 billion board feet in 1994, or some 38 percent of total North American production. These 20 firms operated 252 mills—down from 283 mills in 1991. The 100 largest companies in North America cut about 43.0 billion board feet, or about 71 percent of the industry's total production.

Even without any impact from curtailments of logging due to the spotted owl controversy, there has been a general trend toward consolidation in this industry. One study completed on the lumber industry in Idaho noted that in 1956, the state had 311 sawmills, with 37 producing more than 10 million board feet. By 1990 the number of sawmills had fallen to 80, with 40 producing more than 10 million feet. In 1956, 73 percent of lumber production came from mills producing more than 10 million feet annually. In 1979, mills with yearly output of 10 million feet represented 93 percent of the state's lumber supply. In 1990, the forty mills in this category produced 98 percent of Idaho's 2.06 billion feet of lumber.

BACKGROUND AND DEVELOPMENT

The first sawmill in the United States is said to have been built in York, Maine, in 1623. Sawmills quickly became a common sight in frontier settlements. Most were small enterprises with just one or two workers, and nearly all of these mills were located on rivers, using running water as their power source. As railroads spread across the country in the nineteenth century, the best spot to put a sawmill became the bank of a log-driving stream where a railway

crossed it. With the shift from water to steam power, mills became larger and more complex. One mill on the Saginaw River produced 14 million board feet during the first half of 1874 and employed 150 men. Circular saws replaced the old-fashioned up and down saws in the 1860s, and the contemporary invention of a method for repairing worn or broken teeth greatly extended their useful lives. Electric power began to replace steam power in the early twentieth century, and by 1929 it accounted for 45 percent of all energy sources.

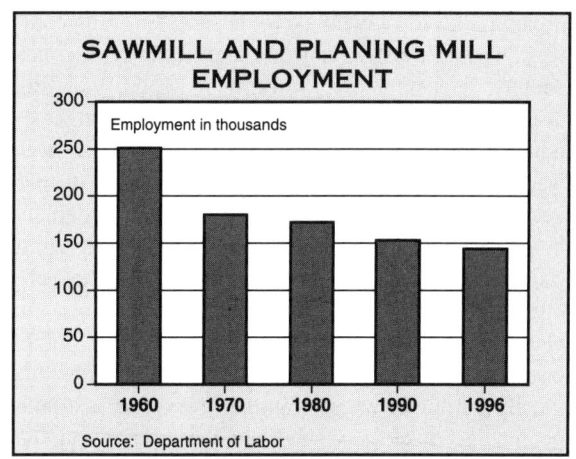

SAWMILL AND PLANING MILL EMPLOYMENT

Employment in thousands

Source: Department of Labor

CURRENT CONDITIONS

According to estimates of the Western Wood Products Association (WWPA), lumber consumption increased about 6 percent in 1996 to 50.5 billion board feet, compared with 47.7 billion feet the year before. Annual housing starts increased by 9 percent to 1.48 million units from 1.35 million units in 1995, and were about level with 1.46 million starts in 1994. Starts in the key single-family-home category rose 8 percent year over year to 1.20 million units (compared with just 0.90 million in 1991). Thus, the lumber market for new residential construction expanded a solid 9.5 percent from 1995 levels. Repair and remodeling also did well, rising 6.5 percent.

Pricing. Because of the rise in new home construction and the increasing restrictions on the lumber supply, lumber prices rose dramatically in 1993 to the area of $500 per thousand board feet. For most of 1994, lumber prices were still quite high, fluctuating in the $350 to $400 range. The high prices drove wood consumers to search for alternative materials, and the use of engineered wood and nonwood substitutes increased. In 1995, as prices eased further, the amount of lumber used per square foot of construction rose. In 1996, when prices again turned upwards, users once more considered lumber substitutes.

Wood Alternatives. Despite the frustration with lumber's price volatility, users were not rushing to buy other materials. As lumber prices climbed above $500 per thousand board feet in 1993 and future supplies became uncertain, steel producers envisaged a windfall of new demand from the construction sector. But the pot of gold never materialized. The immediate short-term reason was that lumber prices retreated in 1995. However, there were also significant, underlying impediments to switching over to steel. Building codes were written mostly for wood and masonry, and carpenters, accustomed to working in wood, had little desire to use steel. Thus steel's share of the market for home frames was just 2 percent in 1996. Still, users were not happy with the lumber situation. With harvesting of federal lands severely restricted and demand healthy, mill owners scrambled to find logs. High lumber prices did enable Western mills to pay the hefty quotes private owners demanded for their logs. But clear, blemish-free lumber comes from the mature trees of old forests, which environmentalists had mostly put under wraps; younger trees have a smaller percentage of clear wood. Thus the industry has become more sensitive to grade distinctions, with ''better'' (i.e., blemish-free) grades selling at a premium. Builders discovered that home buyers who watch their houses being built often demand this perfect lumber, even if other grades meet all structural requirements. But sometimes the difference in grades isn't purely cosmetic. Some of the wood of the faster-growing, younger trees that private tree farmers harvest is less strong, and thus more wood must be used to cover the same span. While this is usually not a crucial matter in a typical single-family home, for light commercial builders it had become an important issue. Thus builders continued to search for reliable alternatives.

Move to the South. The wood products industry began to shift from the Pacific Northwest to the South in the late 1980s and 1990s, primarily because of environmental legislation and regulations that limited harvesting of federal timber lands. Even relatively small sales of federal timber lands became tangled up in lawsuits and court actions. In 1987, almost 10 billion board feet of timber was harvested from federal forests, compared with about 2.2 billion board feet in 1995—a drop of 78 percent in just eight years. Overall, annual lumber production in the West fell by a third over the period. Meanwhile, production of lumber from southern pine (mostly on private lands in the South) rose by about one-fifth.

Many sawmills in the Pacific Northwest, particularly those that had relied on old-growth trees from federal lands for their logs, experienced dramatically reduced profit margins and struggled to survive. The Western lumber industry had 702 mills operating in 1987; at the end of 1995, there were just 357 left. While the trend toward consolidation has been evident for decades, the difficulty of obtaining adequate supply has certainly put increasing pressure on small mills.

INDUSTRY LEADERS

According to the annual *Forest Industries* survey, in 1994 the top lumber producer in North America was Weyerhaeuser, which had 35 mills and cut 3.5 billion board feet. In second place was Georgia-Pacific, with 41 mills that produced 2.6 billion board feet. Louisiana-Pacific came in third with 2 billion board feet, but it had the most mills of any producer, with 46 facilities.

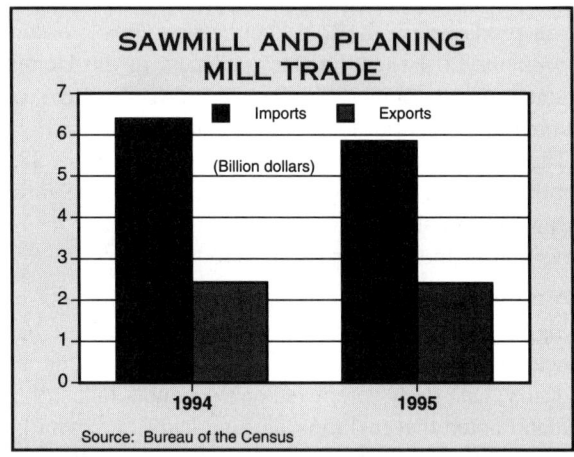

SAWMILL AND PLANING MILL TRADE

Source: Bureau of the Census

AMERICA AND THE WORLD

Based on 11 months of trade data, the Western Wood Products Association estimated that softwood lumber exports fell 3.2 percent in 1996 to 1.9 billion board feet. Exports to Europe and Japan were down 4 percent and 3 percent, respectively, while shipments to Australia and Mexico dropped 36 percent and 17 percent. In April 1996, Japan agreed to accept lumber grades that may have a few more imperfections but are still structurally sound. Lumber exporters hoped the agreement would shore up shipments to Japan, although some domestic users expressed concern that it would exacerbate lumber price inflation in the United States.

To meet expanding demand at home, the U.S. has increased its lumber imports. In 1994, softwood lumber imports, mostly from Canada, rose 16 percent to a dollar volume of $5.8 billion. To help even the flow of lumber between the two countries, on April 2, 1996, Canada agreed to restrict its softwood lumber exports to 14.7 billion board feet between April 1, 1996, and March 31, 1997. Lumber prices rose sharply after the agreement went into effect, and U.S. builders protested what they felt was the agreement's impact on lumber markets. However, the effect of the pact on prices was a subject of dispute—some in the lumber industry argued that strong demand and lower inventories importantly contributed to the short-term price changes.

RESEARCH AND TECHNOLOGY

New technology has greatly improved productivity in the industry. In the 1990s, mills were using computerized controls and laser scanners to maximize the amount of lumber obtained from a log. Automated graders were replacing humans. Waste materials were being used to fire boilers that provided mills with electricity.

Automation greatly improved the output of many companies. An industry trade magazine, *Wood Technology,* discussed the experience of one mill in Georgia that increased its productivity by upgrading its plant. Since logs accounted for 75 percent of its costs, the sawmill owners invested their money in developing techniques to get more lumber from the logs. In 1986 the company began an extended program to improve its facilities, which included adding sophisticated scanning systems and more efficient machine centers. The owners noted that over the five-year period they hadn't used any more logs, but their production had increased from between 10,000 and 12,000 board feet per hour to 18,000 to 20,000 board feet.

FURTHER READING

Blackman, Ted. "For a Look at High Tech, Head for Quebec Sawmills." *Wood Technology,* October 1996.

Dietrich, William. *The Final Forest.* New York: Simon & Schuster, 1992.

Forest Industries 1995-96 North American Factbook. San Francisco: Miller Freeman, 1995.

Holt, Shirleen. "No Knot, No Splinters, No Dice." *Oregon Business,* August 1996.

Keegan III, Charles A., et al. *Idaho's Forest Products Industry: A Descriptive Analysis, 1990.* Missoula: The University of Montana, 1992.

Kelly, Joseph. "Is More U.S. Lumber Bound for Japan?" *Home Improvement Market,* October 1996.

Little, Jane. "Land of the Pampered Plantation." *American Forests,* January/February 1991.

———"To Cut or Not to Cut." *American Forests,* Autumn 1996.

Shuster, Laurie. "Lumber Prices Continue to Climb." *Home Improvement Market,* October 1996.

———"Why Lumber Isn't What It Used to Be." *Home Improvement Market,* October 1996.

Western Wood Products Association. *Economic Services Forecast.* Portland, Oregon: Western Wood Products Association, 14 March 1997. Available at http://www.wwpa.org/.

Western Wood Products Association. *Lumber prices: A Question of Supply and Demand.* Portland, Oregon: Western Wood Products Association, November 1996. Available at http://www.wwpa.org/.

Williams, Michael. *Americans & Their Forests: A Historical Geography.* Oxford: Cambridge University Press, 1989.

—Bob Schneider

SIC 2426

HARDWOOD DIMENSION AND FLOORING MILLS

This classification consists of companies that primarily make hardwood dimension lumber and workings therefrom; and other hardwood dimension, semifabricated or ready for assembly; hardwood flooring; and wood frames for household furniture. Companies that primarily make stairwork, molding, and trim are classified in **SIC 2431: Millwork;** and those making textile machinery bobbins, picker sticks, and shuttles are classified in **SIC 3552: Textile Machinery.**

Hardwood flooring and furniture components made up the largest shares of output in this industry segment. The remaining output includes many items, such as skis, golf clubs, and tool handles. Wood blocks for bowling pins and textile machinery accessories, rounds or rungs for ladders, and spool blocks and blanks are also produced by this industry.

The total value of all products and services sold by the hardwood dimension and flooring mills industry was $2.91 billion in 1995, up significantly from $1.74 billion in 1990. This figure represented a steady increase through the 1990s. Since the health of this industry ties closely to housing starts in the United States, the healthier economy of the mid-1990s brought rising revenues. There were 1,354,100 housing starts in 1996, compared to 1,013,900 starts in 1991, during the economic lull of the Gulf War. The amount of hardwood flooring shipped in 1996 was more than 367 million board feet, compared to close to 200 million board feet in 1991.

Oak, beech, birch, maple, and pecan are the species most often used in furniture and flooring manufacture in the United States. Ash, cherry, poplar, and walnut are also frequently used. Four types of flooring are commonly made: strip, parquet, plank, and laminated. In 1996, the average housing start used 243.86 board feet of lumber, compared to 172.04 board feet in 1990.

Hardwood dimension and flooring generally account for 8 to 10 percent of hardwood lumber exports by value. Canada, Japan, and Taiwan are the most frequent destinations of dimension and flooring exported from the United States. About 12 percent of the dimension and flooring consumed in the United States is imported, with the biggest suppliers being Canada and Taiwan.

Triangle Pacific Corporation of Dallas, Texas, was the largest company in this category with 1996 annual sales of $534 million and nearly 5,000 employees. Triangle Pacific made hardwood floors under the brand names Bruce Hardwood Floors and Premier Wood Floors, in addition to a line of prefinished hardwood flooring called Natural Reflections. The company's cabinet division made wood cabinets for kitchens and bathrooms with brand names such as Ultrawood, Baseline, and Gemini. Crown Pacific Partners, L.P. of Portland, Oregon, was second in this category with 1996 annual sales of $401 million and 1,600 employees. The company owns mature forests in Washington, Oregon, Idaho, and Montana totaling over 207,000 acres, with a potential for 3.4 billion board feet of lumber.

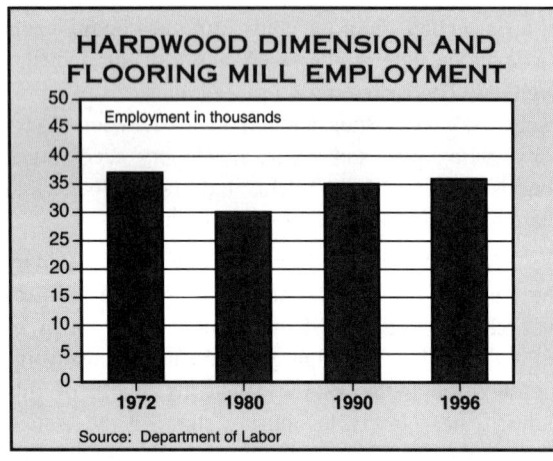

HARDWOOD DIMENSION AND FLOORING MILL EMPLOYMENT

Source: Department of Labor

In 1995, this industry employed 35,300 people, with approximately 31,400 working in production. This is a 30 percent increase from 1990, when the industry employed 24,600 production workers. Nationwide, there were approximately 730 companies in

this industry in the early 1990s. Of those, only 3 companies had more than 500 employees; 79 employed between 100 and 500 workers; 162 companies had 20 to 49 employees; and 178 companies had fewer than 5 employees.

Several issues may affect the hardwood dimension and flooring industry in coming years. Changes in logging and land management regulations could have a major impact, as well as legislation affecting lumber imports or exports. Those changes, coupled with stricter air pollution laws, may drive up the cost of lumber. The industry will most likely remain vulnerable to any change, good or bad, in the number of housing starts. An interesting future trend, due to environmental concerns, may be the refurbishing and marketing of "antique" floor and wall boards salvaged from condemned buildings.

FURTHER READING

"Flooring Shipments and Housing Starts, 1996." The National Oak Flooring Manufacturers Association, Memphis, Tennessee.

Hoover's Company Capsules. Austin, TX: Hoover's, Inc., 1997. Available from http://www.hoovers.com.

National Wood Flooring Association. Available from http://www.nwfa.com.

U.S. Department of Commerce. *1987 Census of Manufacturers.* Washington: GPO, 1987.

U.S. Department of Commerce. *1995 Annual Survey of Manufactures.* Washington: GPO, 1997.

—Robert R. Jacobson, updated by Dave Fagan

SIC 2429

SPECIAL PRODUCT SAWMILLS, NOT ELSEWHERE CLASSIFIED

This industry classification includes mills, not elsewhere classified, that make excelsior (wood shavings used for packing or stuffing), wood shingles, and cooperage stock; or mills that make special sawed products. This category also includes pads and wrappers made from wood excelsior, and makers of all types of wood shingles and shakes. Cooperage stock is the staves, headings, and hoops used for making barrels, although barrel construction is classified in **SIC 2449: Wood Containers, Not Elsewhere Classified.**

Special product sawmills shipped $153.5 million worth of goods in 1995, down from $211.3 million in 1990. The number of companies classified in this industry declined since the early 1980s, with about 200 firms operating in 1995. In the early 1990s, the majority of special product sawmills were small operations with fewer than five employees. The total annual payroll in 1995 for the industry's 1,700 workers was $30.6 million, and workers earned about $10.00 an hour on average. A large share of industry activity took place in Washington state, which accounted for 59 percent of industry employment in 1987.

Wood shingles and shakes (shakes are hand-split, thicker shingles) make up the largest share of the industry's products—nearly half of its output—as of 1994. The majority of shakes and shingles are made of red cedar, grown mainly in the Pacific Northwest. Red cedar shakes and shingles accounted for more than 47 percent of the industry's production in 1987. Other woods used for shakes and shingles were northern white cedar, bald cypress, and redwood.

Cooperage stock made up about 16 percent of the industry's output. This included stock for both tight (used to hold liquids) and slack (for nonliquid use) cooperage (including buckets), hot tubs, and storage vats, as well as barrels. Excelsior, also known as wood wool, accounted for another 7.5 percent of production.

American Excelsior Co., based in Arlington, Texas, was the leading specialty product sawmill operation in 1995. As its name suggests, the company specializes in making cushioning from wood fibers, such as animal bedding or poultry pads. Another use for wood fibers was in the company's Curlex Power-Stop archery targets. American Excelsior is a privately owned company employing almost 700 people. In 1995 it had annual sales of about $90 million.

The next largest company in the industry was Miller Shingle Co. of Granite Falls, Washington, with 200 employees and 1995 estimated sales of $36 million. Shakertown Inc., a private company located in Winlock, Washington, had 1995 sales of $24 million (estimated) and 200 employees. Shakertown specializes in a scallop-shaped wood siding often used in the restoration of Victorian buildings. A much larger Canadian company, Clarkson Group of Mission, British Columbia, owns Shakertown, and claims to be the largest producer of wood shingles and shake in North America.

During the early 1990s, the use of wood shingles came under attack in areas prone to fires. In California, several local governments banned new roofs made of wood products, due to the number of homes lost to fire during summer droughts. Aside from legislative threats, wood shingle producers may also be vulnera-

ble to competition from nonwood roofing materials, such as asphalt shingles.

FURTHER READING

American Excelsior Co. website. Available from http://www.amerexcel.com.

Clark Group company website. Available from http://www.clarkgroup.com/shakertown.

Groves, Martha. ''Wood Shingle Firms Halt Fire Safety Standard Fight.'' *Los Angeles Times,* 26 October 1991.

Spencer, Albert G. and Jack A. Luy. *Wood and Wood Products.* Columbus, OH: Charles E. Merrill Publishing Co., 1975.

U.S. Department of Commerce. *1995 Annual Survey of Manufactures: Statistics for Industry Groups and Industries.* Washington: GPO, 1997.

U.S. Industrial Outlook 1994. Washington: U.S. Department of Commerce, 1994.

—Robert R. Jacobson, updated by Dave Fagan

SIC 2431

MILLWORK

Establishments primarily engaged in manufacturing fabricated wood millwork, including wood millwork covered with materials such as metal and plastics. Planing mills primarily engaged in producing millwork are included in this industry, but planing mills primarily producing standard workings or patterns of lumber are classified in **SIC 2421: Sawmills and Planing Mills, General.** Establishments primarily engaged in manufacturing wood kitchen cabinets and bathroom vanities for permanent installation are classified in **SIC 2434: Wood Kitchen Cabinets.**

INDUSTRY SNAPSHOT

According to the U.S. Labor Department and the Bureau of the Census, over 3,000 mills in America employ 86,000 workers to manufacture products almost entirely for the construction industry. The 1993 Bureau of the Census reported the value of output for the industry at $9.6 billion in 1992. The composition of output shifted in the late 1980s as renovation and repair increased faster than new construction; new construction starts have increased significantly, however, in the early 1990s. Total construction spending in 1996 rose 5.3%, with residential construction increasing by 8.3% due to an 8.9% rise in housing starts, as reported in *Cahners Building & Construction Market Forecast.* A slight decline is predicted to start in 1997 and continue in 1998. Nonresidential construction is expected to grow in 1997. According to the Department of Commerce, mill output is primarily used in construction, specifically residential construction. Residential construction utilizes more than 60 percent of mill output, while non-residential construction accounts for approximately 15 percent.

Recent environmental legislation has put the industry under tremendous supply pressures, although the effect on employment has been minimal compared to the logging, sawmill, and plywood industries. Nevertheless, the pressures are shifting the direction of technological change and marketing techniques in the industry. Most establishments specialize in one product class, such as wood door units, stairs, or railings, and are concentrated primarily in the Pacific Northwest, the Midwest, and Texas.

ORGANIZATION AND STRUCTURE

Mills in this industry cut down raw logs or stock lumber to produce wood shapes for windows and door trims, baseboards, railings, window sashes, and other items. Wood pieces are also assembled with glass, vinyl, and aluminum cladding to make window sashes and frames. Often an inert gas such as argon fills the space between the glass panes to enhance insulation. Doors may be constructed out of solid pieces for high-end uses or, more commonly, consist of a frame, two-panels and filling. Exterior doors and interior apartment entrance doors often use steel to enhance security.

Over time the breakdown in the industry's dependence on new construction and repair, remodeling, maintenance, and home improvements has been shifting. During economic downturns, new construction subsides and repair work increases its share of construction activity. During the real estate boom of the 1980s, new construction outpaced repair work, especially in non-residential construction. However, through the 1990-1991 recession, repair work held steady while new construction plummeted.

According to 1993 reports of the Department of Commerce, the primary products produced by the millwork industry are doors (30 percent of total industry output), wooden windows and sashes (26 percent), and moldings (12 percent). Increasingly, doors and especially windows are clad with vinyl, aluminum or other metals. Energy concerns over the last two decades have led to the development of vinyl and aluminum windows. However, wood windows are regaining popularity because of their strength, beauty and natural insulating properties. Recent industry developments allow aluminum and vinyl clad wood windows to be produced in unlimited shapes and sizes. Solid wood doors, though, have lost market share in recent years to non-solid wood doors, steel, and steel-covered exterior doors.

CURRENT CONDITIONS

Forest product mills in the Pacific Northwest have taken a double beating in recent years. On the demand side, the 1990 economic recession resulted in a downturn in housing starts. However, housing starts have risen, with 1996 being the best year since 1988, according to Cahners. On the supply side, recent legislation over the spotted-owl has led to a reduction in timber harvests on federal lands. According to Tom Kenworthy of the *Washington Post,* the blow resulted in the closing of 132 mills and the loss of approximately 13,000 jobs between 1990 and April of 1993 in the larger logging industry. The impact on the profits for mill owners was mixed. Companies that had private sources of timber or were located away from spotted owl habitats such as those in southern locales benefited from the increased price of lumber.

For the millwork industry itself, the job impact has been minimal. Employment lost in the downturn and since the logging ban has been restored somewhat by the economic upturn of 1992 and 1993, and the increase in total construction spending. The mill industry is dependent, however, on the supply of wood. Some observers argue that the recent increase in construction doesn't guarantee the millwork industry unlimited success, however. Environmental and regulatory concerns regarding the industry's staple materials—Douglas fir and western pines—remain.

Wood Technology magazine noted in 1993 that some millwork plants have sought alternatives to western pines and Douglas fir, which are in short-supply and dwindling fast. Some of these alternatives are radiata pine imported from Chile and New Zealand, southern pine, hem-fir, sitka spruce, eastern white pine, and hardwoods. These new alternatives require mills to be flexible in their handling of woods. Each species requires its own methodologies of treatment, drying, and handling of imperfections. This is not only because of the unique characteristics of each kind of wood, but also because of the harvesting and storage practices of distant vendors, both in the United States and abroad. Good wood, or certified wood, is starting to make a name for itself in the industry. Forest owners are certified by an independent source as having sustainably managed their forest, i.e. no clear-cutting or other practices harmful to the long-term health of the forest. Companies view the use of good wood as a good Public Relations tool. Windows and door frames are good candidates for good wood.

Environmental Issues. The millwork industry is impacted by a variety of environmental issues. Logging restrictions on federal lands, due to concern for the future of the spotted owl and a general desire to leave remaining forestlands untouched, is a major environmental issue in the wood products industries. Boycotts and export restrictions on tropical wood affect imports and export markets. Concern over the health effects on workers and consumers of volatile chemicals have resulted in advances in wood treatment. Energy-loss concerns have led to major innovations in window and door production over the last 15 years.

Logging restrictions are a source of particular concern to the industry, as they directly influence the price and availability of millwork establishments' primary production materials. In 1989 environmental groups invoked the Endangered Species Act of 1973 to halt logging in many forests to protect the spotted owl. In 1993 the ban was extended to parts of California to protect the California spotted owl, which is listed only as a sensitive species, not endangered. The move has sparked debate about trading jobs for the environment. The effect of the logging restrictions on jobs has been devastating in the northwestern logging and wood products industries. With timber harvests reduced by 75% from national forests, however, forest-products companies are seeing healthier markets and improved pricing in 1996 and projected into 1997.

On April 2, 1993, President Clinton held a timber conference in an attempt to find common ground and compromise between environmentalists and forest product workers. The compromise plan allowed 1.2 billion board feet a year to be cut from federal forests. This was approximately one-quarter of the amount permitted at the height of the 1980s. The proposal also established spotted owl reserves and water system buffer zones to protect the owl from extinction and streams from erosion. The President also proposed the development of ten intermediary zones. Loggers can experiment with new harvesting techniques in these zones, while forest management and environmental effects are monitored.

Greater flexibility in applying the restrictions could also allow logging on land that is less important to the spotted owl and to allow the clearing of dead and dying trees. Partially to compensate for lost jobs, another proposal was to provide retraining and to employ forest product workers in environmental projects to rebuild the forests and protect watersheds.

INDUSTRY LEADERS

The privately-owned Anderson Corp., based in Bayport, Minnesota, is the leading window and door manufacturer in the industry. It utilizes high-profile marketing to promote its product to the end user and keeps cost down by producing a large variety of standard sizes.

Marvin Lumber and Cedar Co., with headquarters in Warroad, Minnesota, specializes in high-value custom production for replacement windows and doors and for unusual architectural arrangements on new construction

Morgan Products Ltd., of Williamsburg Virginia manufactures doors, windows, mouldings, stairways, and mantels for new and renovated structures, their 1995 sales topped $338 million.

Trus Joist International has developed a long-term market strategy of focusing on engineered woods to improve strength and conserve old growth timber. TJ International markets most of these products for structural uses such as beams and framing materials. However, 28 percent of its business is in windows and doors, which it produces and markets through its subsidiaries, Dashwood Industries, Laffamme & Frere, and Norco Windows. It has, however, begun marketing windows constructed with laminated strand lumber through these subsidiaries. Total sales of all TJ products for 1995 were $484 million.

Other leading companies in the millwork industry include Jeld-Wen Inc., of Klamath Falls, Oregon; Clopay Corp., based in Cincinnati, Ohio; Huttig Sash and Door Co., of Chesterfield, Missouri; and Pella Corporation of Pella, Iowa.

WORK FORCE

Safety issues. According to the United States Department of Commerce, the millwork industry has a high accident rate, 49 percent higher than for general manufacturing. The accident rate for millwork was also higher compared with related industries of wood kitchen cabinets, hardwood veneer and plywood, softwood veneer, and plywood, but lower than industries categorized in **SIC 2439: Structural Wood Members, Not Elsewhere Classified.** The rate of injuries sustained per 100 full-time workers was greater in large mills (defined as 20 or more workers) than in small mills.

The Labor Department's Bureau of Labor Statistics lists back strain and hand and finger injuries as the two highest types of injuries in the millwork industry. Back strain injuries were primarily the result of lifting heavy objects. Serious hand and finger injuries were received while operating stationary saws and other machinery. Other safety issues that have received attention in recent years include the respiratory effects on workers involved in sanding and the application of volatile materials such as polyurethane and formaldehyde. The Labor Department believes that many accidents are preventable through education and training and minor machinery enhancements.

Employment. The Bureau of the Census reported in 1996 that 223,000 people were employed in millwork and related industries in 1995, with an average hourly wage of $10.12. According to the Labor Department, despite the large number and variety of machines employed in the industry, it is quite labor intensive. For each dollar of value that mills add to raw materials, it uses 72 percent more production-worker hours than in manufacturing as a whole. According to Brad Knickerbocker, writing in the *Christian Science Monitor*, recent technical innovation has enabled the membership of the timber industry to record gains in productivity of as much as 40 percent; this has created a corresponding decline in timber industry employment. More recently, especially with the shortages of raw materials, technological innovation has taken a shift toward the maximization of materials savings, rather than labor savings.

A 1992 article in the *Christian Science Monitor* estimated that Oregon lost 12 percent of its work force employed in the timber industry because of logging restrictions and a weak market for construction. Employment in millwork has about evened out, with 86,000 workers employed in 1992 as opposed to 89,000 in 1987. Wisconsin, California, Minnesota, and Oregon are the leading states for these employees. According to the Commerce Department, employment in the millwork industry in particular was affected more by the recession than by the spotted owl crisis. The Bureau of the Census reported that employment began slipping in 1990. It plummeted nearly seven percent (6,200 jobs) between 1989 and 1991. However, employment climbed more than eight percent (6,900 jobs) between 1991 and 1992. Between 1992 and 1993 another 600 jobs were created in the industry, and Bureau of Labor Statistics predict a slight decline of 0.9% from 1994-2005.

AMERICA AND THE WORLD

Trade patterns in millwork and other wood products have undergone considerable change recently due to environmental pressures, the reduction of trade barriers, and the end of the cold war.

In the late 1980s, U.S. construction material trade, including wood products, nearly doubled. According to 1993 reports by the Commerce Department, trade

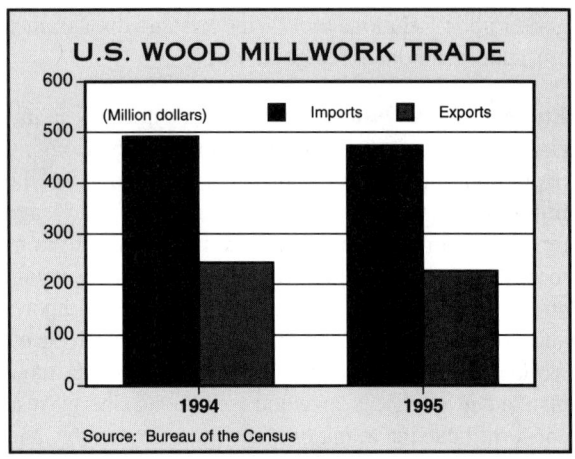

U.S. WOOD MILLWORK TRADE

(Million dollars) ■ Imports ■ Exports

Source: Bureau of the Census

liberalization in Canada and Mexico and a weak dollar led to the first trade surplus for millwork in the last 20 years. Millwork exports doubled between 1989 and 1991, from $102 million to $207 million. Then they jumped 40 percent from 1991 to 1992 and 25 percent from 1992 to 1993. Meanwhile, imports rose less than an estimated 10 percent between 1989 and 1993.

Developing countries have advantages in low-cost labor and raw materials when competing in international trade. They have utilized these advantages to develop wood-working industries and increase their exports of furniture and millwork products to America. Many industry observers expected U.S. imports of such products to increase as a result of the North American Free Trade Agreement (NAFTA) and the General Agreement on Tariffs and Trade (GATT). However, as a result of lobbying from the forest products industry, quotas were placed on Canadian imports, thus slowing down the number of board feet coming in from the north.

Environmental concerns have reduced the international supply of millwork's principal raw material—logs, although the U.S. Supreme Court reversal of a federal law restricting log exports has somewhat eased international supply. Indonesia banned the export of logs in the early 1980s to slow the consumption of its own forests while expanding employment in wood products industries. By doing so, the Indonesian government stimulated the development of wood processing industries such as milling and plywood. However, according to a report in *The Nikkei Weekly* plywood plants began shut downs in 1996 due to a lack of logs. Only 70% of mill demands were met in 1995. Malaysia also recently restricted its exports of raw logs to preserve its forests and develop its wood-working industries.

According to Jonathan Friedland, writing in the *Far Eastern Economic Review,* the reduction in the supply of raw logs, especially in East Asia, caused a crisis in the Japanese millwork, plywood, and construction industries. Prices of East Asian hardwood jumped 110 percent and prices of North America Douglas Fir climbed 60 percent. If these high prices are sustained, Japan may look to Russia for a greater proportion of its wood materials.

In the spring of 1995, Canada and the United States signed a timber pact which restricts timber imports by allowing only 14.7 billion board feet of Canadian lumber imported to the United States duty free. This reduces lumber supplies by about one-third, and, according to *Barron's* is sited as one of the causes of rising lumber prices. Mexico has also been reducing its tariffs since the mid- to late-1980s and will continue to do so under NAFTA. In recent years Mexico has attracted large amounts of foreign investment and lowered its tariff barriers. This inflow of capital raised foreign exchange income, which in turn allowed it to raise imports. As a result, Mexico has increased its importation of wood and wood products from the United States. According to 1993 Department of Commerce statistics, Mexico bought 26 percent of U.S. window exports and 48 percent of door exports in 1992. The passage of the NAFTA in the United States Congress is expected to quicken this flow of capital to Mexico and further reduce tariffs.

According to David A. Pease, writing in *Wood Technology* in 1992, extensive development of Russia's forestry industries may drive down bloated prices on the international market, but this will not happen soon. Russia's political turmoil and poor infrastructure in the areas with the largest forests will require large capital investments in a risky policy environment. Nevertheless, Korean and Finnish firms have already developed joint ventures with Russians to develop forestry products. The Korean industrial giant Hyundai ships logs from Russia's Pacific coast. The United States' largest forest products company, Weyerhaeuser, is also attempting to purchase logs from the same region. On the Atlantic side, Finnish concerns have established a joint effort with Russian concerns to produce wood products such as plywood.

RESEARCH AND TECHNOLOGY

Concerns about energy costs, maintenance requirements, and personal security have led to significant technological change over the last two decades in the millwork industry. Environmental restrictions on raw materials and worker safety are beginning to lead another wave of technical change in the present decade.

For both doors and window frames, the newest technological advances are coming in the area of materials conservation. Sustained high costs for woods such as Douglas fir, Ponderosa, and other western pines have spurred innovation in window frame and door production. Increasingly, composite materials are used as substitutes for solid wood parts, while window frames are increasingly produced from engineered woods. Trus Joist International, for example, produces window frames made from laminated strand lumber. This technology is still in its infancy. As the industry continues to substitute engineered woods such as laminated strand lumber for sawn wood, it will have to focus technological attention on worker safety issues such as exposure to dust, formaldehyde, and other volatile organic compounds. Currently the industry is developing a voluntary standard for formaldehyde levels.

FURTHER READING

Council of Economic Advisers. "Economic Indicators." *Economic Indicators,* 22 June 1993.

"Eastern German Housing to Boom." *Wall Street Journal,* 22 June 1993, A11.

Einhorn, Cheryl Strauss. "Behind the Inflation Fears: Are Lumber and Energy Prices Really So Strong?" *Barron's,* 9 September 1996.

Freeman, Emily N. "WWPA Spring Meeting Explains How to Go Green." *Wood Technology,* 120, no. 3, May/June 1993, 12.

Friedland, Jonathan. "Meany Greenies: Japan Faces Soaring Cost of Imported Timber." *Far Eastern Economic Review,* 4 March 1993, 43-44.

Grogan, Tim, et. al. "Third Quarterly Cost Report." *ENR* 13, (28 September 1992): 25-40.

Irland, Lloyd C. "Wood Producers Face Green Marketing Era." *Wood Technology,* March/April 1993, 34-36.

Kennedy, Kim. "Q1/97: Slower But Steady Gains Ahead." *Cahner's Building & Construction Market Forecast,* March 1997. Available from http://members.aol.com/cahners/bcmf.html.

Kenworthy, Tom. "The Owl and the Lumberjack: Can Clinton Break the Logjam?" *The Washington Post,* 2 April 1993: A4.

Knickerbocker, Brad. "Saving Endangered Jobs as Well as Owls." *Christian Science Monitor,* 5 March 1992: 17.

Schatz, Amy. "'Good Wood' Winning With the Green Crowd." *Wall Street Journal,* 17 May 1996, sec B, 10.

"Timber Shortages Cripple Some Indonesian Plymills." *Wood Technology,* May 1996: 53.

Pease, David A. "Joint-Venture Mill Taps Russian Forest Resource." *Wood Technology,* 6, November/December 1992: 13-15.

————, ''Millwork Producers Seek 'Other' Raw Material Sources.'' *Wood Technology,* 4, July/August 1993: 6.

Personick, Martin E., and Biddle, Elyce A. ''Job Hazards Underscored in Woodworking Study.'' *Monthly Labor Review,* 9, (September 1989): 18-23.

''Provinces Fight Over Lumber-Quota Shares.'' *Wood Technology,* 8 (1996).

Shaw, Robert M. ''World Trade in Building Projects.'' *Construction Review,* Winter 1993, vii-xvii.

Stanley, J. ''TJ International - Company Report.'' A.G. Edwards and Sons, Inc., 1992.

Statistical Abstract of the United States. Washington: U.S. Bureau of the Census, 1996.

Trumbull, Mark. ''Northwest Growth Leads Nation.'' *Christian Science Monitor,* 10 December 1992, A8.

U.S. Department of Commerce. Bureau of Economic Analysis. *The 1982 Benchmark Input-Output Accounts of the United States.* Washington, 1991.

U.S. Bureau of the Census. *The 1992 Census of Manufacturers: Millwork, Plywood, and Structural Wood Members.* Washington, 1995.

Verespej, Michael A. ''Surviving with Low Prices.'' *IW,* 2 December 1996.

Warren, Debra D. *Production, Prices, Employment, and Trade in Northwest Forest Industries, Fourth Quarter 1985,* Washington: U.S. Forest Service, 1986.

—Joseph Kirchner, updated by Angela Thor

SIC 2434

WOOD KITCHEN CABINETS

This industry includes establishments primarily engaged in manufacturing wood kitchen cabinets and wood bathroom vanities, generally for permanent installation. Establishments primarily engaged in manufacturing free-standing cabinets and vanities are classified in various furniture-manufacturing industries. Establishments primarily engaged in building custom cabinets for individuals are classified in **SIC 5712: Furniture Stores.**

In 1995 the Bureau of the Census reported the value of output for the wood kitchen cabinet manufacturing industry as $4.9 billion for 1992. The demand for wood kitchen cabinets is heavily dependant upon new construction, for more than 90 percent of the industry's output goes toward new construction. Of that total, the Commerce Department noted in 1991 that more than 85 percent went to residential new construction. Total construction spending in 1996 rose 5.3%, with residential construction increasing by 8.3%

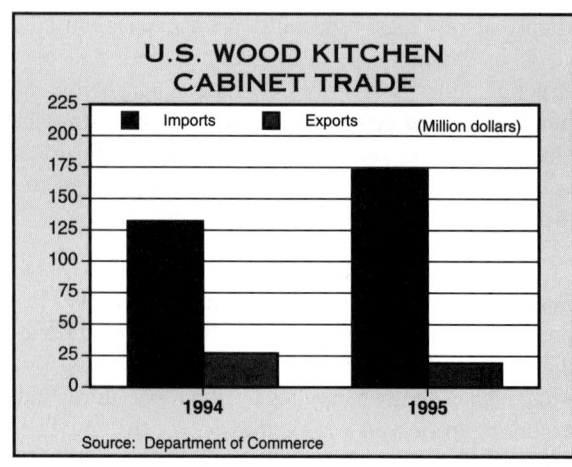

U.S. WOOD KITCHEN CABINET TRADE

Source: Department of Commerce

due to an 8.9% rise in housing starts, as reported in *Cahners Building & Construction Market Forecast.* A slight decline is predicted to start in 1997 and continue in 1998. The National Association of Home Builders (NAHB) predicts that remodeling expenditures will increase over the next several years at 2.5 percentage points over inflation, making the industry worth about $180 billion by 2005. Much of this remodeling will be in the kitchen and bathroom, which may help take up any slack caused by slower new housing starts.

Wood kitchen cabinets have been facing pressures from both the supply and demand side. On the supply side, plywood and composite board prices have been soaring in response to timber shortages in the Pacific northwest. On the demand side, the industry's dependance on the health of the larger construction industry resulted in a loss of output during the course of the 1990-1991 recession; this downward trend was alleviated, however, by the economic recovery of the mid-1990s, which saw a dramatic rise in housing starts, with 1996 being the best year since 1988.

According to 1995 Bureau of the Census statistics, more than 62,000 people were employed in the industry in 1992, with most of the labor force in the states of California, Pennsylvania, Texas, and Indiana. According to the United States Department of Labor, the wood kitchen cabinet industry had an injury and illness rate 32 percent higher than for general manufacturing in 1987.

Leading establishments in the wood kitchen cabinet manufacturing industry include Masco Corp. Cabinet Group with 1995 sales of $675 million, Aristokraft, Inc. with $230 million in 1995 sales, Schrock Cabinet Co. with $200 million 1995 sales, and American Woodmark Corp., with sales of $195 million in 1995. Other establishments include Triangle Pacific Corp. of Dallas, Texas, Omega Cabinets, Wood-Mode Inc., and

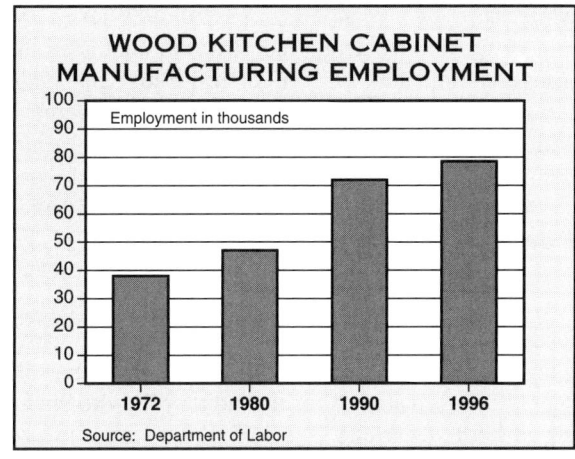

WOOD KITCHEN CABINET MANUFACTURING EMPLOYMENT

Employment in thousands

Source: Department of Labor

Canac Kitchens, all posting over $100 million in 1995 sales.

While the industry has seen few dramatic technological breakthroughs, several changes in the appearance of the industry have taken place in recent years. Raw material shortages are forcing some manufacturers to use more composite and engineered woods. Good wood, or certified wood, is starting to make a name for itself in the industry. Forest owners are certified by an independent source as having sustainably managed their forest, i.e. no clear-cutting or other practices harmful to the long-term health of the forest. Companies view the use of good wood as good public relations. Frameless cabinetry design, in which shelf space can be utilized right up to the cabinet wall rather than sacrificing one inch around to the frame, is also increasing. Finally, manufacturers are offering a greater variety of easy access storage designs.

FURTHER READING

Fried, Carla. ''The Safe and Sane Way to Make Your House Everything You Want.'' *Money,* April 1997.

Kennedy, Kim. ''Q1/97: Slower but Steady Gains Ahead.'' *Cahners Building & Construction Market Forecast,* March 1997. Available from http://members.aol.com/cahners/bcmf.html.

Lazich, Robert S. *Market Share Reporter-1997.* Detroit: Gale Research Inc., 1997.

Schatz, Amy. '''Good Wood' Winning With the Green Crowd.'' *Wall Street Journal,* 17 May 1996, 10.

Statistical Abstract of the United States. Washington: U.S. Bureau of the Census, 1993.

The 1982 Benchmark Input-Output Accounts of the United States. Washington: U.S. Department of Commerce, Bureau of Economic Analysis, 1991.

The 1992 Census of Manufacturers: Millwork, Plywood, & Structural Wood Members. Washington: U.S. Bureau of the Census, 1995.

U.S. Industrial Outlook 1993. Washington: U.S. Department of Commerce, 1993.

Personick, Martin E., and Elyce A. Biddle. ''Job Hazards Underscored in Woodworking Study.'' *Monthly Labor Review,* 9 September 1989: 18-23.

—Joseph Kirchner, updated by Angela Thor

SIC 2435

HARDWOOD VENEER AND PLYWOOD

This classification covers establishments primarily engaged in producing commercial hardwood veneer and those primarily engaged in manufacturing commercial plywood or prefinished hardwood plywood. This includes nonwood backed or faced veneer and nonwood faced plywood, from veneer produced in the same establishment or from purchased veneer. Establishments primarily engaged in the production of veneer which is used in the same establishment for the manufacture of wood containers, such as fruit and vegetable baskets and wood boxes, are classified in various wood container manufacturing industries.

INDUSTRY SNAPSHOT

Plywood manufacturing and related industries have been passing through hard times as the result of several challenges to the industry. Industry obstacles in recent years have included a shortage of available lumber, resulting in higher operating costs, and the general economic recession of 1989-1991, which resulted in numerous plant closings and lost jobs. Many small firms in the Pacific Northwest, dependent on timber from federal lands, have been particularly affected. Industry critic Paul Ehinger claimed in a 1992 issue of *Forest Industries* that an estimated 133 sawmills, plywood, and veneer plants—20 percent of the mills in the Pacific Northwest—closed in the region between January 1990 and May 1992. This is an acceleration of a trend that saw 145 mills close in the 1980s. On the other hand, plywood firms with access to timber unaffected by legislation designed to protect the spotted owl, such as those in the south or large firms with private sources of timber, have benefited from the soaring prices of plywood. According to a report of S.G. Warburg & Co. Inc., plywood prices rose 67 percent between 1991 and March 1993.

To cope with supply pressures, firms have developed new products such as engineered woods. Some observers expect this trend will continue to shift the composition of output in the industry. As a result, the plywood and veneer hardwood industry is losing market share to establishments involved in the manufacture of reconstituted panel products, which includes particleboard, medium density fiberboard, and oriented strand board (OSB), among other products. According to *Wood Technology,* the number of plywood plants decreased by 28 percent between 1987 and 1995 while OSB plants increased by 37 percent. An 8 percent decline is predicted for 1996. David L. Fleiner, vice president, structural panels for Georgia-Pacific Corp, predicts that in the future plywood mills will produce specialties and veneer for laminated veneer lumber (LVL).

Another challenge on the horizon for the industry membership is the cost of complying with growing environmental regulation of indoor pollutants. This regulation affects the production of composite boards and plywood itself. The industry has set voluntary formaldehyde emission standards; in the meantime, the U.S. Environmental Protection Agency (EPA) is collecting information on other forms of indoor pollutants.

The Bureau of the Census reported the value of output for the industry as $2.2 billion for 1992. According to 1991 Department of Commerce reports, the demand for veneer and plywood is heavily dependent upon construction, but not quite as dependent as is the millwork industry. Nearly one-half (48 percent) of veneer and plywood output goes to construction, mainly residential. Roughly a quarter of the output is used in other lumber and wood products industries, with another 11 percent used in furniture and fixtures. According to 1993 Department of Commerce statistics, plywood sales constituted 45 percent of the industry's total output for 1992, while hardwood veneer products constituted an additional 25 percent of output.

Veneer production peels layers of wood from logs. Plywood production glues these veneer sheets together, alternating the direction of the grain for each sheet. Typically, plywood sheets are four feet by eight feet. Veneer is also glued to lumber, fiberboard and medium density fiberboard. It is also used in the production of oriented strand lumber and other engineered woods.

CURRENT CONDITIONS

The Department of Commerce notes that plywood is dependent on construction for nearly 50 percent of its sales. Construction was hard hit in the 1990 recession and did not rebound as quickly as in past recoveries despite low interest rates. Residential construction did not recoup its 1989 levels until late 1993,

while the overall economy surpassed 1989 levels by mid-1992. Non-residential construction continued its recession well into 1993. Both residential and non-residential construction have advanced since then, with residential growth rising 8.9 percent in 1996 and non-residential construction growth at 5.4 percent, according to *Cahners Building & Construction Market Forecast.*

Environmental issues. Logging restrictions on federal lands coupled with export restrictions of tropical hardwoods are the major environmental issues affecting the supply of raw materials for the industry. Environmental concerns regarding levels of dust, formaldehyde, and noise in plywood and hardwood veneer production have also grown in recent years.

According to David A. Pease, writing in *Wood Technology* in 1993, this concern is not limited to American manufacturers. The Dutch have adopted strict dust level restrictions of 1.7 parts dust per million parts air (by weight). They set formaldehyde at .3 parts per million of air and noise exposure to 90 dbA with hearing protection. The Germans have implemented similar limits as well. The EPA is drafting a catalogue of indoor air pollutants such as formaldehyde and other volatile organic compounds that result from the production of plywood, particleboard, medium density fiberboard, oriented strand board, and other engineered wood products.

A nationwide industry investigation was begun by the EPA in the early 1990s of outdoor air pollutants. As a result, Weyerhaeuser Company has paid more than $1.5 million in state fines, and has agreed to install millions of dollars worth of controls in its plants. Louisiana-Pacific has pledged to install $70 million in control devices, and has paid $11 million in Federal fines. Georgia-Pacific, however, is lobbying to curtail the EPA investigation in order to avoid fines & costly upgrades. Company executives at Weyerhaeuser estimate that controls add an additional $1 million a year to plant operating costs.

The plywood industry is experimenting with several means of reducing these emissions. One is to use other chemicals to bond particleboard, plywood, and other products. Another possible solution is to treat the product with ammonia after it has been glued with traditional compounds. Further complicating these efforts to address these environmental concerns, however, is the increasing emphasis on engineered wood production; production of these goods require the use of volatile organic compounds.

INDUSTRY LEADERS

Leading companies in the industry include Georgia-Pacific, with $14.2 billion in 1995 sales; Weyerhaeuser with $10.4 billion in 1994 sales; Louisiana-Pacific with $3 billion in 1994 sales, and Ply Gem Industries, Inc., based in New York City, which posted sales in 1995 of more than $741 million. Other major producers include Plywood Panels Inc., headquartered in New Orleans, Louisiana; Darlington Veneer Company, Inc., based in Darlington, South Carolina, and Columbia Forest Products Inc., of Portland, Oregon.

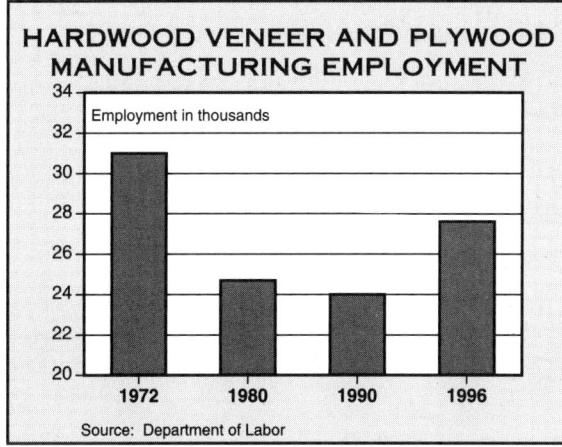

HARDWOOD VENEER AND PLYWOOD MANUFACTURING EMPLOYMENT

Employment in thousands

Source: Department of Labor

WORK FORCE

Worker-participation in management and ownership is prevalent in the plywood manufacturing industry. For nearly three-quarters of a century a large number of plywood mills in the Pacific Northwest have been operated by worker cooperatives. These firms are owned and controlled by worker-owners. Major decisions are made, policy is developed, and a board of directors is chosen democratically at the quarterly or semiannual meeting of the general membership. The board elects officers from its own ranks subject to approval from the membership.

Christopher E. Gunn notes in a study of Pacific Northwest plywood cooperatives published in *Economic Analysis and Workers' Management* that proceeds of the worker-enterprises are generally distributed according to work performed rather than on an equal basis or by capital stake. Members tend to prefer to forgo earnings rather than suffer unemployment. The enterprises tend to be efficient users of raw materials and are less capital intensive then conventional mills.

Worker-participation is not limited to worker-owned mills. Some of the conventionally owned mills are attempting to incorporate some of the ideas of worker participation in management. For example, as a 1991 *Forest Industries* article by Ted Blackman notes, Potlatch has introduced a new management style in which workers at the team level have decision making influence and responsibility in production, investment, and hiring new workers.

According to U.S. Department of Labor statistics, the hardwood veneer and plywood manufacturing industry has a high injury and illness rate— approximately 50 percent higher than for general manufacturing.

Employment varies considerably over time in hardwood plywood and veneer manufacturing establishments because of its dependence on the larger construction industry. The hardwood plywood and veneer industry in particular was affected more by the spotted owl crisis than by the recent recession. Department of Commerce statistics indicate that employment in the industry began slipping in 1989. Between 1989 and 1991 it plummeted 17 percent and only regained 4.2 percent in 1992, when most construction related industries saw a much greater surge in employment. In 1992 approximately 20,000 people were employed in the industry, at an average hourly wage of almost $10. The majority of these workers are employed in North Carolina, Indiana, Wisconsin, and Oregon.

AMERICA AND THE WORLD

International trade has been favorable for the United States plywood industry in recent years. According to the Commerce Department, between 1989 and 1993 imports grew only 1.5 percent while exports shot up 62 percent. The United States, Indonesia, and Japan were the three top plywood producers, according to recent FAO statistics, with Japan leading the pack in importing plywood products. However, a 1996 *Nikkei Weekly* report indicates that plywood plants in Indonesia have been shutting down due to a low supply of logs caused by overcutting.

In veneer production, China, Malaysia, and Canada were the leading producers during 1993. Chile is experiencing some growth in the veneer market with new startups by the Rio Itata group reported in 1995. The Chilean forestry industry in general, as well as the nation's economy, is growing due to an open economy. The reduction of trade barriers between Canada, Mexico, and the United States as a result of the North American Free Trade Agreement (NAFTA) will continue to shift international trade patterns. Due to an outcry from the industry, a timber pact was cut between Washington and Canada restricting imports by allowing only 14.7 billion board feet of lumber into the U.S. duty-free.

RESEARCH AND TECHNOLOGY

Technological change is shifting in emphasis from labor-saving innovation to material-saving innovation. In order to get more lumber out of a given amount of wood pulp, producers are developing engineered wood products such as laminated veneer lumber, particleboard, medium density fiberboard, and oriented strand board.

Laminated veneer lumber has the added advantage that it can be made wider, longer, stiffer, and stronger than traditional lumber products. Defects in the wood such as knots are reduced in size and redistributed through lamination. For lengths longer than eight feet, short lengths can be joined with finger joints. Laminated veneer lumber is produced in a manner similar to plywood except it is two inches thick and the grain is all in the same direction. Thick planks as wide and long as plywood are then cut down to standard lumber sizes.

The shift to particleboard, medium-density fiberboard and oriented strand board represents a shift out of this industry and into reconstituted panel products (see **SIC 2493: Reconstituted Wood Products.**)

FURTHER READING

Blackman, Ted. ''Adding Value: Chilean Mills Get Full Value From Forests.'' *Wood Technology,* January/February 1996, 34-35.

Blackman, Ted. '''Team Concept' Involves Crews in All Aspects of Mills.'' *Forest Industries,* 9 November 1991, 14-15.

''Computer Model Showed Way to Run Plant More Profitably.'' *Forest Industries,* September/October 1992, 28-29.

Einhorn, Cheryl Strauss. ''Behind the Inflation Fears: Are Lumber and Energy Prices Really So Strong?'' *Barron's,* 9 September 1996.

Engelberg, Stephen. ''Tall timber and the EPA.'' *New York Times,* 21 May 1995, Sec 3, 1.

Gunn, Christopher E. ''Plywood Co-operatives of the Pacific Northwest: Lessons for Workers' Self-Management in the United States.'' *Economic Analysis and Workers' Management,* XIV, no. 3 (1980): 393-416.

Keil, Bill. ''US Leads in Wood-Based Panel Output As Global Volume Rises To New Record.'' *Wood Technology,* January/February 1996.

Kennedy, Kim. ''Q1/97: Slower But Steady Gains Ahead.'' *Cahners Building & Construction Market Forecast,* March 1997. Available from http://members.aol.com/cahners/bcmf.html.

1982 Benchmark Input-Output Accounts of the United States. Washington: U.S. Department of Commerce, Bureau of Economic Analysis, 1991.

1992 Census of Manufacturers: Millwork, Plywood, and Structural Wood Members. Washington: U.S. Bureau of the Census, 1995.

''Panel Capacity Race Starts to Slow down.'' *Wood Technology,* September 1996.

Pease, David A. ''Board Plant Designers Set Environmental Pace.'' *Wood Technology,* 3, May/June 1993: 26-28.

———. ''Timber Shortages Will Encourage New Products.'' *Forest Industries,* 4, July/August 1992, 21-22.

Personick, Martin E., and Elyce A. Biddle. ''Job Hazards Underscored in Woodworking Study.'' *Monthly Labor Review,* September 1989, 18-23.

''Plywood Pact Paves Way to U.S.-Canada Duty Cuts.'' *Wood Technology,* January/February 1993, 25.

''Provinces Fight Over Lumber-Quota Shares.'' *Wood Technology,* 8 (1996).

''Timber Shortages Cripple Some Indonesian Plymills.'' *Wood Technology,* May 1996, 53.

''Wood Products Mirror Modest Economic Gains.'' *Wood Technology,* January/February, 1996.

—Joseph Kirchner, updated by Angela Thor

SIC 2436

SOFTWOOD VENEER AND PLYWOOD

Establishments primarily engaged in producing commercial softwood veneer and plywood, from veneer produced in the same establishment or from purchased veneer. Establishments primarily engaged in producing commercial hardwood veneer and plywood are classified in **SIC 2435: Hardwood Veneer and Plywood.** Establishments primarily engaged in the production of veneer used in the same establishment for the manufacture of wood containers such as fruit and vegetable baskets and wood boxes are classified in various wood container manufacturing industries.

The Bureau of the Census reported the value of output for the plywood and veneer (softwood) manufacturing industry as $5.4 billion for 1992. The demand for veneer and plywood is dependant upon construction. Nearly 48 percent of veneer and plywood output goes to construction, mainly residential. Roughly a quarter of the output is used in other lumber and wood products industries, with an additional 11 percent in furniture and fixtures.

As with other construction material producing industries, this industry suffered during the economic recession of 1990-1991, but has benefited tremendously from the surge in housing construction at the end of 1993. *Cahners* predicts continued slow advances in overall construction during 1997. Despite the positive economic situation entering the mid-1990s, however, the industry still is grappling with a troublesome shortage of materials.

Another challenge on the horizon is the cost of complying with growing environmental regulation of indoor pollutants. The industry has set voluntary formaldehyde emission standards and the United States Environmental Protection Agency (EPA) is collecting information on other forms of indoor pollutants.

A nation wide industry investigation was begun by EPA in the early 1990's of outdoor air pollutants. As a result, Weyerhaeuser Company has paid more than $1.5 million in state fines, and has agreed to install millions of dollars worth of controls in its plants. Louisiana-Pacific has pledged to install $70 million in control devices, and has paid $11 million in Federal fines. Georgia-Pacific, however, is lobbying to curtail the EPA investigation in order to avoid fines & costly upgrades. Company executives at Weyerhaeuser estimate that controls add an additional $1 million a year to plant operating costs.

Competition is also increasing from the Oriented Strand Board (OSB) industry. While OSB production gained 99% between 1987 and 1995, plywood production decreased 16% during that same time period, according to *Wood Technology*. David Fleiner, vice president, structural panels for Georgia-Pacific Corp, feels that in the future, plywood mills will produce specialties and Laminated Veneer Lumber (LVL).

Leading companies in the industry include Georgia-Pacific Corp., based in Atlanta, Georgia with 1995 sales of $14 billion; Champion International Corp.'s Forest Products Group, headquartered in Stamford, Connecticut with 1996 reported rood products income of $126 million, a drop from the $138 million reported in 1995 and attributable to decreased prices and shipments of plywood; and Roseburg Forest Products Co., based in Roseburg, Oregon.

Worker-participation in management and ownership is prevalent in the plywood industry. For nearly three-quarters of a century a significant number of plywood mills in the Pacific northwest have been operated by worker cooperatives. These firms are owned and run by worker-owners. According to the Labor Department, the softwood plywood and veneer industry's injury and illness rate is closer to the average for manufacturing than is that of other woodworking industries. In 1987, the softwood plywood and veneer industry's 13.2 injury and illness rate per 100 full-time workers was significantly closer to the overall manufacturing 11.9 rate per 100 than the 18.0 average rate posted by establishments engaged in millwork, wood kitchen cabinets, hardwood plywood and veneer, and miscellaneous structural wood product manufacturing.

According to the Commerce Department, total employment for the industry dropped 20 percent from 38,000 in 1987 to 31,000 in 1992. Average earnings for workers in the industry rose during that time span from just under $10 an hour to approximately $10.50 an hour. In the Pacific northwest and amongst smaller mills without access to private sources of timber, the employment situation is generally worse. Most employees are found in the states of Oregon, Louisiana, Texas, and Arkansas.

International trade has been favorable but volatile for the United States softwood plywood and veneer industry in recent years. The economic recession led to sharp declines in imports by 32 percent between 1989 and 1991. The gradual economic recovery, coupled with timber-cutting restrictions that arose out of environmental concerns and the liberalization of trade, resulted in a sharp reversal of this decline in imports. Between 1991 and 1993 imports soared 55 percent. Meanwhile exports surged as a result of trade liberalization, increasing 27 percent between 1989 and 1993, despite a drop of 16 percent between 1990 and 1991. Leaders in plywood production are the United States, Indonesia, and Japan. However, a 1996 *Nikkei Weekly* report indicates that plywood plants in Indonesia have been shutting down due to a low supply of logs caused by over-cutting. The Japanese remain the leading importer of plywood, and U.S. imports from Canada have been reduced due to restrictive quotas placed on duty-free sales of lumber.

In veneer production, China, Malaysia, and Canada were the leading producers during 1993. Chile is experiencing some growth in the veneer market with new start-ups by the Rio Itata Group reported in 1995. The Chilean forestry industry in general, as well as the nation's economy, is growing due to an open economy.

FURTHER READING

Blackman, Ted. "Adding Value: Chilean Mills Get Full Value From Forests." *Wood Technology,* January/February 1996, 34-35.

''Champion International Corporation Reports Earnings For Fourth Quarter and the Year.'' *Business Wire,* 16 January 1997. Available from http://biz.yahoo.com/news/cha.html.

Engelberg, Stephen. ''Tall Timber and the EPA.'' *New York Times,* 21 May 1995: Sec 3, 1.

Keil, Bill. ''US Leads in Wood-Based Panel Output as Global Volume Rises To New Record.'' *Wood Technology,* January/February, 1996.

Kennedy, Kim. ''Q1/97: Slower But Steady Gains Ahead.'' *Cahners Building & Construction Market Forecast,* March 1997. Available from http://members.aol.com/cahners/bcmf.html.

1982 Benchmark Input-Output Accounts of the United States. Washington: U.S. Department of Commerce, Bureau of Economic Analysis, 1991.

1996 Census of Manufacturers: Millwork, Plywood, and Structural Wood Members. Washington: U.S. Bureau of the Census, 1995.

''Panel Capacity Race Starts to Slow Down.'' *Wood Technology,* September 1996.

Personick, Martin E., and Elyce Biddle. ''Job Hazards Underscored in Woodworking Study.'' *Monthly Labor Review,* 9 September 1989, 18-23.

''Provinces Fight Over Lumber-Quota Shares.'' *Wood Technology,* no. 8, 1996.

Statistical Abstract of the United States. Washington: U.S. Bureau of the Census, 1993.

''Timber Shortages Cripple Some Indonesian Plymills.'' *Wood Technology,* May 1996, 53.

U.S. Industrial Outlook 1993. Washington: U.S. Department of Commerce, 1993.

''Wood Products Mirror Modest Economic Gains.'' *Wood Technology,* January/February, 1996.

—Joseph Kirchner, updated by Angela Thor

SIC 2439

STRUCTURAL MEMBERS, NOT ELSEWHERE CLASSIFIED

This classification covers establishments primarily engaged in producing laminated or fabricated trusses, arches, and other structural members of lumber. Establishments primarily engaged in fabrication on the site of construction are classified in Division C, Construction. Establishments primarily engaged in producing prefabricated wood buildings, sections, and panels are classified in **SIC 2452: Prefabricated Wood Buildings and Components.**

The Bureau of the Census reported the value of output for this industry as $2.5 billion for 1992. According to 1991 Commerce Department data, output is almost entirely used in new construction, with a fairly even distribution between residential and non-residential markets. Consequently, the industry is highly sensitive to the business cycle. While residential construction picked up in 1992 and surged in the latter part of 1993, non-residential construction grew at a sluggish rate due to the excessive building of the 1980s. *Cahners* predicts slow but steady gains in both non-residential and residential construction in 1997. *Wood Technology* states that home building is the fastest growth area for structural composite lumber, with single and multi family homes using over 80% of North American LVL. In the home improvement area, it is estimated that 28% of total expenditures go toward key wood-using categories, a hefty chunk of an industry that saw $115 billion spent in 1995. The National Association of Homebuilders (NAHB) predict that this market should grow steadily over the next decade.

The industry faces the same supply constraints as do the other wood working industries. This is the result of environmental pressures to save the endangered spotted owl in the Pacific northwest and to save tropical rain forests abroad.

Traditionally, mills in this industry cut joists, beams, and other structural members from logs of large dimensions. Recently the industry has developed several engineered wood products to save on raw materials and to strengthen structural members such as beams, trusses and joists. These engineered products are constructed by gluing veneer sheets or strands of wood with a compound, pressure, and heat. *Wood Technology* predicts an increase in demand and production of engineered wood products in 1997.

In 1995, there were 170 structural panel plants, 35 glulam plants, and 47 I-joist and other engineered wood plants with a total sales of approximately $8 billion. TJ International Inc. is the leader in engineered woods for structural members and framing materials. It has positioned itself on the cutting edge to take advantage of the current timber shortage and consequent price hikes. The company has two main product lines. Its Trus Joist MacMillan subsidiary makes engineered wood structural members and framing boards. Its other primary subsidiary in this area, its Western Division, produces windows and doors. Other notable industry establishments include Elk River Enterprises Inc., Shelter Systems Corp., and Trussway, Inc.

In order to capture the opportunities created by supply constraints, TJ International formed a joint venture with the Canadian-based MacMillan Bloedel Inc.

The new company, formed in September 1991, dominates the high tech and environmentally friendly end of structural and framing lumber. The venture, which is 51 percent owned by TJ International, has developed several new products that are as good or superior in quality to established lumber equivalents using fast-growing timber produced on tree farms. Total sales for TJ International were reported at $484 million for 1995.

A 1993 article in *Wood Technology* notes that Boise Cascade is also venturing into the production of these new technologies. It installed capacity to produce laminated veneer lumber for beams and joists. Sale of building products were reported as $1.4 billion for 1995. Universal Forest Products of Grand Rapids MI, a manufacturer of roof trusses and value added lumber products reported 1995 sales of $739 million.

According to the Bureau of the Census (1995), 24,000 people were employed in the industry in 1992. Florida, California, Oregon, and North Carolina are the leading states for employment in this industry. Labor Department statistics indicate that the industry has one of the highest accident rates of any manufacturing industry, and suffers from a higher accident/illness rate than posted by other woodworking industries.

Like other woodworking industries, the structural members industry is responding to the crisis in timber supply through innovative technology. The industry is developing engineered products that have the advantage of using fast-growing small dimension timber to produce products that are often superior to those created using sawn woods. Among the new products being developed are wooden I-joists, series joists, laminated veneer lumber (LVL), parallel strand lumber, and laminated strand lumber.

Glulam production rose from 259 million board feet in 1994 to 325 million in 1996, while LVL production, a glulam competitor in some applications, increased from 27.1 million feet in 1994 to 37 million in 1996. Due to greater acceptance in Japan, exports of glulam are forecast to increase.

Wooden I-Joists are so strong that they compete with steel I-beams in small buildings where building codes don't prohibit the use of wood. Engineered Wood Association (APA) formerly American Plywood Association reports an increase in production from 420 million lineal feet in 1994 to 580 million in 1996. Market share is predicted to increase from 17 percent of U.S. residential floors in 1996 to 35 percent in the year 2000, spurred on by an APA promotion for residential floor joists.

In Canada, building authorities are calling for an objective-based National Building Code, which, according to *Wood Leader* would allow for greater use of wood based structural members. Series joists, marketed under the trademark "Silent Floor" joists by Trus Joist Macmillan, are used to support floors or ceilings. They help to reduce squeaky floors because they are less prone to warping. Laminated veneer lumber is made from numerous layers of high grade thin veneer which are glued using an adhesive, heat, and pressure. Laminated veneer lumber is used for the flanges of I-joists and as beams. Japan is becoming a top importer of these wood products for use in seismic-resistant construction.

FURTHER READING

Adair, Craig. "Regional Production and Market Outlook For Structural Panels and Engineered Wood Products 1996-2000." Tacoma, Washington: APA-The Engineered Wood Association, 1996.

Bland, John D. "Quality Assurance Tops List at Parallel Strand Lumber Mill." *Forest Industries,* 2 March 1991, 15-18.

Kennedy, Kim. "Q1/97: Slower But Steady Gains Ahead." *Cahners Building & Construction Market Forecast,* March 1997. Available from http://members.aol.com/cahners/bcmf.html.

Moran, D. S., et. al. "TJ International, Inc. Company Report," Dillon & Read & Co., 1993.

1982 Benchmark Input-Output Accounts of the United States, Washington: U.S. Department of Commerce, Bureau of Economic Analysis, 1991.

1992 Census of Manufactures: Millwork, Plywood, and Structural Wood Members, Washington: U.S. Bureau of the Census, 1995.

Personick, Martin E., and Elyce A. Biddle. "Job Hazards Underscored in Woodworking Study." *Monthly Labor Review,* 9 September 1989, 18-23.

Statistical Abstract of the United States, Washington: U.S. Bureau of the Census, 1993.

U.S. Industrial Outlook 1993. Washington: U.S. Department of Commerce, 1993.

Walters, William R. "Planning an Expansion Into Engineered Wood?" *Wood Technology,* September 1996.

"Wood Products Mirror Modest Economic Gains." *Wood Technology,* January/February 1996.

"Year 2001Code Strategy Will Benefit Wood." *Wood Leader,* February 1996. Available from http://www.cwc.metrics.com/w1296p4.html

—Joseph Kirchner, updated by Angela Thor

SIC 2441

NAILED AND LOCK CORNER WOOD BOXES AND SHOOK

This industry classification includes companies that are primarily engaged in making nailed and lock corner wood boxes (lumber or plywood) and shook for nailed and lock corner boxes.

The nailed and lock corner boxes and shook classification covers the production of containers made wholly or partly of wood. Containers in this category include ammunition boxes, tool chests, wooden cigar boxes, and cases for packing produce. Shook refers to sets of box parts—sides, tops, bottoms, and ends—that are ready to assemble.

Unlike pallets and skids, the largest segment of the wood container industry, sales of wooden boxes did not rise much during the 1990s. Fierce competition came from non-wood containers, such as boxes made of corrugated paperboard. Nailed and lock corner wood box makers also lagged behind the pallets and skids industry in using new technology to improve efficiency. Because the variety of boxes made is so diverse, most production runs are too small to benefit from automation. Improved conveyors and material handling equipment increased productivity for companies whose markets required large numbers of one kind of box. Elsewhere, however, nail guns were the most high-tech tool for making boxes. Therefore, of the growth in output and productivity in the wood container industry between 1977 and 1995 (including **SIC 2448: Pallets and Skids** and **SIC 2449: Wood Containers Not Elsewhere Classified**, little came from sales of nailed and lock corner wood boxes.

The nailed and lock corner wood box and shook industry consists mainly of smaller companies. In 1987 only two percent of these businesses employed 100 or more workers, while 50 percent of the companies had less than 10 employees. As of 1995, the top 21 companies in this category were all small and privately owned. Industry leaders in 1995 included Seattle Box Co. of Kent, Washington (with $20 million in annual sales and 100 employees); Lane Container Co. of Dallas, Texas (with $10 million in annual sales and 100 employees); and Florin Box and Lumber Co. of Sacramento, California (with $9 million in annual sales and 100 employees). The entire industry employed approximately 5,600 people in 1995 (with 4,600 in production), and had a total payroll of $108 million. Production workers averaged $8.30 per hour in 1995.

In 1995, the industry shipped $483 million worth of goods. During the industry's peak in the 1970s, approximately one billion nailed wood boxes were made each year. The 1977 Census of Manufacturers estimated the value of nailed wooden boxes and box components shipped that year at $261 million. Adjusting for inflation since then, the industry lost some business to improved plastic and corrugated container technology. (Boxes from these materials cost far less to produce.) However, during the 1990s wood boxes appeared as a specialty packaging item that, marketers hoped, lent products an air of quality. Durability and reusability of wooden boxes supposedly made them more attractive to consumers.

Like the wood containers industry as a whole, wood boxes have not historically faced much competition from foreign manufacturers. This industry's future primary concern will likely be the expense of making wooden boxes compared to cheaper, non-wooden containers.

FURTHER READING

"The New Growth of Wooden Boxes." *Modern Packaging,* November, 1979.

Spencer, Albert G. and Jack A. Luy. *Wood and Wood Products.* Columbus, OH: Charles E. Merrill Publishing Company, 1975.

U.S. Department of Commerce. *1995 Annual Survey of Manufactures: Statistics for Industry Groups and Industries.* Washington: GPO, 1997.

York, James. "Productivity in Wood Containers." *Monthly Labor Review,* October, 1992.

—Robert R. Jacobson, updated by Dave Fagan

SIC 2448

WOOD PALLETS AND SKIDS

This classification covers establishments primarily engaged in manufacturing wood or wood and metal combination pallets and skids.

The manufacture of wood pallets and skids is the largest segment of the wood container industry. Pallets were made of platforms that are specially designed to allow heavy crates and boxes to be easily moved by forklift. Pallets play an important role in the shipping, handling, and storage of a huge variety of materials in an equally vast array of industries. In the United States, approximately 3,700 companies produce pallets. The industry is dominated by small firms with an average of 23 employees per operation. The largest concentration of these companies is in Ohio and California, with each state having at least 300 such firms. While many of these firms sell locally or regionally, a few pallet suppliers have nationwide coverage. These include: Pallet Pallet, First Alliance Logistics, CHEP USA, and PRANA.

Of all the pallets and skids produced in the United States in 1995, 97 percent were made of wood. The remaining pallets were made of wood composite, cardboard/corrugated, metal, plastic, or other materials. In 1995, about 411 million new wood pallets and skids were manufactured in the United States. Used and/or repaired pallets added an additional 208 million to this total. The per-firm annual production of pallets in the United States has doubled since 1980. The average firm produced 254,000 pallets annually in 1995, compared to an average of 112,000 pallets annually in 1980. The industry has grown at an annual rate of 5-7 percent since 1980.

Hardwood lumber, such as oak, was used for 62 percent of the wood in pallets in 1995. Other wood materials used in 1995 included stumpage, logs, and cants. Manufacturers used an average of 17.9 board feet of wood per pallet in 1995, up from 17.3 board feet in 1990. Waste materials are sometimes used by pallet manufacturers to make fuelwood, bedding, pulp, or charcoal, among other products.

The biggest pallet users are the food, paper and fiber, printing, steel and metal, and chemical industries. The most common pallet produced is the flushed stringer, double-face, nonreversible type measuring 48 by 40 inches, which is most often used by supermarkets. Since the 1980s, technology has played an increasingly important role in the pallet and skid industry, contributing to both production and design improvements. Most pallet manufacturers still used hand-held nailers and semi-automated equipment in 1980. By the 1990s, however, using fully automated assembly systems allowed two laborers to put together 1,200 pallets in a day, at least four times the rate of production that hand nailers allowed. The average firm, as of 1995, could produce up to 1,500 pallets per day at full capacity.

Computers have had a major impact on pallet design since about 1980. In the mid-1990s, a computer-assisted Pallet Design System (PDS) enabled manufacturers to better analyze the pallet needs of a particular product and to build pallets specifically tailored for that product. For example, a company dealing in a fairly light commodity could save money using pallets made from softer, less expensive wood.

In recent years, the pallet industry has incorporated recycling. Forty-one percent of all firms used some recycled pallets during production in 1995, with an average of 131,500 recycled pallets used annually per firm. Recycling has become a more common low-cost option for wood pallet companies as competition from nonwood pallet producers increases. The wood pallet industry has responded to this challenge with the development of "enhanced pallets," which are more resistant to fire and rot than conventional pallets. There is also a trend toward producing multiple-use pallets which can be leased by customers and returned when worn out.

Several trends were predicted to affect the pallet industry in coming years. In addition to growth in recycling and leasing pallets, and the use of nonwood materials, producers would probably continue automating the design and manufacturing process. Another expected trend was consolidation, in which larger firms buy out smaller firms, reducing the total number of competitors. A shrinking labor force and future Occupational Safety and Health Administration (OSHA) and environmental legislation could also affect the industry, as well as the chance of reduced access to federal forest lands.

FURTHER READING

"Alternatives to Wood Pallets Sparking Market Demand." *Chemical Marketing Reporter,* 28 September 1992.

McCurdy, D.R., and John E. Phelps. *The Pallet Industry in the United States, 1980, 1985, 1990, and 1995.* Southern Illinois University, Carbondale, IL: Department of Forestry Publication, 1996.

"The Pallet Industry at a Glance." *Tech Talk.* Fact sheet from The National Wooden Pallet and Container Association, February 1997.

Schwind, Gene. "Engineering Your Wooden Pallet Can Reduce Handling Costs." *Material Handling Engineer,* October 1981.

Spencer, Albert G., and Jack A. Luy. *Wood and Wood Products.* Columbus, OH: Charles E. Merrill Publishing Company, 1975.

York, James. "Productivity in Wood Containers." *Monthly Labor Review,* October 1992.

—Robert R. Jacobson, updated by Dave Fagan

WOOD CONTAINERS, NOT ELSEWHERE CLASSIFIED

This industry classification includes companies that primarily make wood containers, not elsewhere classified, such as cooperage, wirebound boxes and crates, and other veneer and plywood containers. Companies that primarily make tobacco hogshead stock are in **SIC 2421: Sawmills and Planing Mills, General** and those making cooperage stock are in **SIC 2429: Special Product Sawmills, Not Elsewhere Classified.**

This classification covers makers of nearly any wooden container that is not a pallet or a nailed or lock corner box. Many containers in this classification are made from staves, heads, and hoops—a group of products called cooperage. Containers made this way include barrels, storage vats, and buckets. Tight cooperage refers to containers used to store liquids, such as wine casks, beer barrels, or hot tubs. Containers built to hold solid materials are called slack cooperage. Cooperage is usually built in one facility from pieces constructed elsewhere.

The wood used for staves varies depending on the material to be shipped or stored. For instance, high quality white oak is used for aging bourbon, while seafood is often shipped in smaller kegs made of southern yellow pine. Hoops can be made from steel, wire, or wood.

Wirebound boxes are another part of this industry classification. About 60 percent of wirebound boxes are used for agricultural clients, such as fruit and vegetable growers. The military and private industry also use wirebound boxes. Unlike coopered container producers, wirebound box makers often process their own lumber or veneer. The technology for making wirebound boxes is relatively simple: box parts move down a conveyor belt, wire is stapled to the box, then a fastening machine binds the wire ends together.

Like other segments of the wood container industry, businesses in this classification are mostly small companies. Sixty-one percent of the establishments in this industry had less than ten employees in 1987. Compared to the other segments, however, a greater portion employed at least 100 workers. In 1995, this industry shipped $402 million worth of products and employed 5,900 people. The 1995 total payroll was $103.2 million, with the average production worker earning less than $8 per hour.

The largest companies in the industry in 1995 included: Calpine Containers Inc., a private company in Walnut Creek, California ($95 million in sales, 300 employees); Elberta Crate and Box Co. of Bainbridge, Georgia, also privately owned ($35 million in sales, 400 employees); and Napa Valley Box Co. of San Diego ($25 million in sales, 200 employees).

Although the wood container industry as a whole grew throughout the 1990s little growth came from miscellaneous wood containers. This is partly due to competition from containers made without wood, such as corrugated paperboard and plastic. Also, since the containers clients want vary in size and shape, their production could not be automated as easily as a standard-sized product like wood pallets. However, demand for quality wood containers probably will not fade, regardless of non-wood containers available. This, coupled with little foreign competition, hints at a positive future for the U.S. wood container industry.

FURTHER READING

Spencer, Albert G., and Jack A. Luy. *Wood and Wood Products.* Columbus, OH: Charles E. Merrill Publishing Company, 1975.

U.S. Department of Commerce. *1995 Annual Survey of Manufactures: Statistics for Industry Groups and Industries.* Washington: GPO, 1997.

York, James. "Productivity in Wood Containers." *Monthly Labor Review,* October 1992.

—Robert R. Jacobson, updated by Dave Fagan

MOBILE HOMES

This category covers establishments primarily engaged in manufacturing mobile homes and nonresidential mobile buildings. These units are generally more than 35 feet long, at least 8 feet wide, and often are equipped with wheels. Trailers that are generally 35 feet long or less, 8 feet wide or less, and with self-contained facilities are classified in **SIC 3792: Travel Trailers and Campers.** Portable wood buildings not equipped with wheels are classified in **SIC 2452: Prefabricated Wood Buildings and Components.**

INDUSTRY SNAPSHOT

In many ways, this industry has declined since its peak in unit shipments was reached in the 1970s. In 1996, for example, there were only 98 corporations shipping homes, compared to 261 companies in 1982.

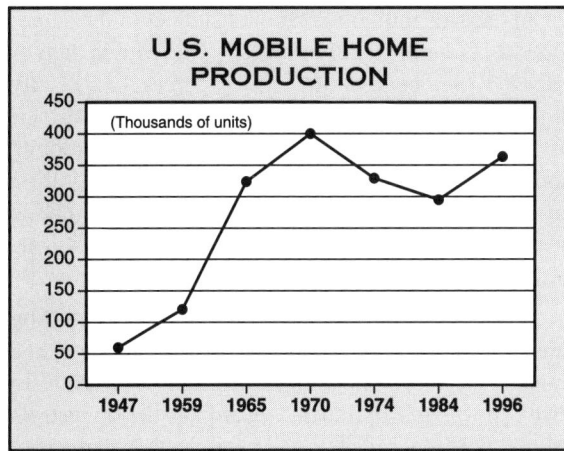

U.S. MOBILE HOME PRODUCTION

(Thousands of units)

Units shipped in 1996 totaled 363,411 homes, still well below the 400,000 mark that was exceeded in the 1970s.

However, in other ways the industry has entered a profitable period of rebirth. The 1996 unit shipments represented a 7 percent increase over 1995 shipments and a huge increase over the 197,000 units shipped in 1992. Industry revenues were estimated at $13.8 billion in 1996—far ahead of the less than $5 billion revenues of the mid-1980s. In 1996, the U.S. Census Bureau reported that one out of every four single-family housing starts (23.9 percent) and one out of three new single-family homes sold (32.6 percent) was a factory-built home.

This upbeat picture came about for several reasons, but perhaps the primary one is that the industry has virtually redefined its product in recent years. The old image of trailer parks, with metal-walled mobile homes and flat roofs, has been replaced, more or less, by an image of manufactured homes. Like the old mobile homes, a manufactured home is made in a factory, generally comes with wheels and chassis and is trucked to its destination. But as Carlos Tejada reported in the *Wall Street Journal,* "Today's multi-section manufactured home takes pains to hide those origins, with wood exteriors, wood-framed windows, porches and shingled, peaked roofs." Many manufactured homes are now indistinguishable from site-built homes. In pricing, too, the industry has gone further upscale. Where mobile homes sold for under $10,000 a couple of decades ago, today the average manufactured home sells for between $40,000 and $70,000. Indeed, even the name "mobile home" is something of a misnomer, because the vast majority manufactured homes are never moved after they have been installed on their site, according to the industry's trade group, the Manufactured Housing Institute.

Large multi-section homes (some with three bedrooms) accounted for nearly half of all 1996 industry shipments, compared with 15 percent in the early 1970s. Industry figures report that today there are 7.3 million manufactured homes in America, housing 18 million people, or about 7 percent of the nation's population.

Economics and demographics have both played a part in the growth of manufactured housing. Manufactured homes typically cost just 33 to 50 percent of what traditional site-built homes do. This price advantage helps to attract first-time buyers. A rise in apartment rental rates and a sharp drop in apartment construction has hastened the shift of many consumers to manufactured housing. Finally, with the number of retirees and "empty-nesters" on the rise, manufactured homes often gleam as an attractive option, either for a second vacation home or as a year-round residence.

For all these reasons, the surviving manufacturers, including a dozen or so of the top firms, were all enjoying solid financial performances in the mid-1990s. The industry leader is Fleetwood, which reported revenues of $2.8 billion in 1996. The company enjoys about a 19 percent share of the factory-built housing market. That figure marks a slight decline from Fleetwood's 21.6 percent share in 1994, which according to a January 1997 report in Barron's stemmed from the company's attempt to strengthen its dealer network by culling the less productive outlets.

Perhaps the most aggressive manufactured home maker in the mid-1990s has been Champion Enterprises, which came back from near-bankruptcy several years ago to close seven acquisitions of competing firms between 1994 and early 1997, including a merger with Redman Industries. The company was expected to report final 1996 revenues in the range of $1.6 billion (up from less than $300 million in 1992). Champion's chairman, Walter R. Young, told Barron's in early 1997 that he's "certainly not pessimistic" about the industry's short-term outlook and that in the long term he expects to see manufactured housing "taking a bigger piece of the housing pie."

Clayton Homes, another major manufacturer, reported revenues of $929 million in 1996. Skyline Corp. reported revenues of $646 million and Southern Energy reported revenues of $300 million in 1996.

BACKGROUND AND DEVELOPMENT

Due to the high costs associated with shipping mobile homes, which generally measure 14 by 70 feet in length or larger, the number of mobile homes shipped abroad represents only a negligible portion of the industry's business. (The same holds true for mobile home imports entering the U.S. market.) In fact, the 313 plants operating in 1996 generally were limited to markets located relatively close to their plants. Consequently, the industry's facilities dot the nation's landscape, with each manufacturing plant wedded, to a certain degree, to its surrounding market.

Geographically, the majority of facilities engaged in mobile home manufacturing were located in the South Atlantic region of the United States, although more than half of the nation's states contained mobile home manufacturing establishments. Wisconsin, Ohio, and Indiana formed the second largest regional concentration of facilities, while California, Oregon, and Washington composed the third largest regional concentration.

During the mobile home industry's beginning, its products answered the need of a small percentage of the American populace: temporary shelter primarily used by migrant farm workers and equally nomadic construction workers. Although these were not the only purchasers of mobile homes, they did account for the bulk of the industry's sales and, consequently, limited the potential of the industry's future expansion. Since both of these market niches composed a negligible portion of the nation's consumer base and any significant increase in their size—at least in proportion to the rate of population growth—appeared unlikely, the mobile home industry seemed destined to remain a relatively small industry, catering to customers without the aggregate purchasing power to launch manufacturers toward exponentially higher sales volumes.

This restrictive quality inherent in the industry's market would not inhibit mobile home manufacturers for long, however; once a product was manufactured and marketed that could attract a more diverse clientele and fulfill a need overlooked by the traditional construction industry, sales would increase. But during the 1920s, when mobile homes were first emerging, and into the 1930s, as the industry began to take shape, sales figures remained unsubstantial.

The onset of World War II provided an unexpected boost for mobile home manufacturers, infusing the industry with production orders for military personnel shelters (essentially miniature barracks on wheels) and mobile housing for defense workers. By the conclusion of the war, mobile home manufacturers had enjoyed several years of comparatively prodigious production levels, thanks primarily to defense contracts. Mobile homes had become, as a consequence of this war-related work, familiar fixtures in many encampments across the country. Moreover, once the war ended, America had, in effect, a standing army: a new

social class of military personnel subject to the sometimes itinerant demands of military life. Mobile homes afforded members of the armed forces—especially those with families—the housing flexibility that their frequent relocation orders required, supplying mobile home manufacturers with a new market niche for their products. Two years after the war, in 1947, the mobile home retail market neared $150 million in sales, garnered from the sale of 60,000 units.

The following year sales eclipsed $200 million and unit sales leapt to 85,000 as the mobile home industry began to show signs of dramatic growth. In 1949, however, optimism regarding the industry's growth potential faded. Retail sales for the year were a disappointing $122 million and unit sales plunged to 46,200.

As the industry entered the 1950s, it effected a recovery from the dismal showings of 1949, posting successive gains in annual sales until 1956, a year that would mark the beginning of a new era in the mobile home industry. Originally, the size of mobile homes varied in length, but always measured eight feet in width to conform to the maximum width permissible by law for vehicles on highways. These homes, after all, were intended to be mobile. But in 1956, manufacturers first introduced 10-foot-wide models, or "ten wides," which quickly became the industry standard. By 1958, ten wides accounted for 65 percent of the industry's shipments and two years later, represented over 85 percent.

It rapidly became apparent to manufacturers that mobility was not the primary asset mobile homes offered consumers. Instead, consumers were attracted by their affordability. To be sure, mobility was still an important feature, but mobile home owners moved their units on average only once every two and a half years, becoming for many a semi-permanent dwelling, and for some a house on wheels that never moved. Further, mobile homes came from the factory equipped with all the basic domestic appurtenances homeowners or renters of conventional houses ordinarily would have to purchase separately, a total package for the mobile home customer that came with a significantly lower price tag than a bare conventional home.

The magnitude of the mobile home industry had reached respectable proportions by relying solely on the production of eight-foot-wide models, reaching $462 million in retail sales from the sale of 111,900 units in 1955, the last year in which eight-foot-wide models represented 100 percent of the mobile home market. Although ten wides quickly dominated the market, their introduction did not initially spark an exponential increase in either unit production or in the industry's overall revenues. They did, however, provide the industry with a more stable and potentially rewarding foundation from which to build on in the future. Newly married couples and those over 50 years of age became two of the industry's largest market segments, attracted by the affordability and flexibility mobile home housing offered at a time when both these components of the American populace were growing faster than the rate of population growth as a whole.

Along with these favorable developments came the ills suffered by any industry whose target market has transformed into a more lucrative audience. For the mobile home industry these growing pains came in the form of increased competition during the late 1950s, as the low initial investment required to establish a mobile home manufacturing facility enabled hopeful entrepreneurs to enter the industry, causing the market to become quickly saturated. This influx of small, single-plant manufacturers created considerable turmoil in the mobile home market between 1960 and 1961, when a number of small manufacturers failed and their inventories entered the market at panic prices. Units shipments for the industry fell from 120,500 in 1959 to 90,200 in 1961, while industry revenues dropped by roughly $100 million to $505 million.

The anxiety caused by this decline led to a period of consolidation in the mobile home industry during the early 1960s, as a handful of publicly owned conglomerates wrested control of the market from a scattered group of small, privately owned manufacturers through mergers and acquisitions. On the whole, however, the industry continued to be populated primarily by small, independent companies (the high cost of shipping mobile homes made large, centralized manufacturing consortiums impractical), but for the first time the industry's leaders were primarily comparatively larger, publicly held companies, such as Elkhart, Indiana's Skyline Homes, Dryden, Michigan's Champion Home Builders, New York's Divco-Wayne Corp., and Redman Industries.

By 1963 the mobile home industry had fully recovered from the losses suffered during the decade's first two years. Retail revenues stood at $862 million and unit sales topped 150,000, surpassing for the first time the figures recorded in 1959. By the following year, mobile homes accounted for one of every nine housing starts, with approximately 220 companies competing for the burgeoning business occasioned by the advent of ten wides, which was finally coming to fruition six years later. Twelve-foot-wide mobile homes had been introduced two years earlier, in 1962,

as the inevitable offshoot of ten wides, garnering an encouraging 10 percent share of the industry's 1964 sales. "Double wides," the joining of two ten wides to form a single unit, were also widely popular as the industry entered the mid-1960s, giving owners up to 1,000 square feet of living space.

The consolidation of the previous years now left the five largest companies controlling 30 percent of the market, the demographics of which had changed considerably in the previous 20 years. Families in which the head of the household was older than 51 years of age represented 35 percent of all mobile home residents, but only 8 percent of these owners were retired. Nomadic construction and factory workers, once the mainstays of the mobile home market, accounted for 19 percent of mobile home ownership, yet were surprisingly outnumbered by professional and business people, who represented 25 percent of all owners.

Added to these changes in the composition of the mobile home market was the emergence of an entirely new market segment in the early 1960s—commercial and industrial customers. Businesses such as banks used mobile "offices" as temporary branch outlets, manufacturing companies requiring temporary additional space to execute contract work used mobile home structures, and school systems used mobile homes as portable classrooms. These mobile "home" structures were custom built, or converted from existing mobile home units, requiring the re-tooling of production machinery that many of the larger mobile home manufacturers found disruptive to their assembly lines. Consequently, the smaller manufacturers in the industry benefited from the majority of the commercial and industrial business, building each structure according to the specifications required for its particular application. Although industrial and commercial business accounted for only five percent of the industry's total sales during the early and mid-1960s, the market was just opening up and promised to develop into a lucrative component of the mobile home industry.

By 1965 mobile homes accounted for one out of every 6.5 housing starts, representing 324,050 unit sales for the year, while total revenues for the industry exceeded $1.2 billion. The industry also demonstrated encouraging independence from the traditional housing market in the mid-1960s, as it rapidly matured and began to stand on its own, rather than merely exist as an adjunct to the construction industry. When mobile home manufacturers suffered losses in the early 1960s, some of the difficulties stemmed from the proliferation of imprudent manufacturers, but the drop in unit sales and revenues also mirrored the curtailment of conventional housing construction. Once conventional housing construction resumed normal activity in 1962, mobile home unit sales tagged along, showing a rise as well. But in the mid-1960s, when decreased spending once again negatively affected housing construction, mobile home sales remained robust. Released, to a large extent, from its dependence on the cyclical housing market, the mobile home industry was instead buoyed by the deleterious economic conditions. Mobile home manufacturers reaped business from prospective home buyers unwilling to spend the amount of money required to construct new homes.

Toward the close of the 1960s, the optimism pervading the industry grabbed the attention of those outside the industry, leading to some fantastic and, in retrospect, starry-eyed predictions for the industry's future. Some of these futuristic visions were extrapolations of the diverse applications for which mobile homes were used during the late 1960s. One such use was as an alternative to low-cost housing, a housing need particularly well-suited for mobile homes, considering their affordability and mobility. In 1968 alone, three cities, Atlanta, Chicago, and Washington D.C., began employing mobile homes as temporary housing for individuals forced from their homes as a result of rehabilitation or redevelopment projects. Mobile homes, with their wheels removed, were also stacked on top of each other to form low-rise apartment complexes in Baltimore, Amherst, Massachusetts, and Michigan City, Indiana. From these utilizations, plans for mobile home ''skyscraper'' structures were born. Architects were swept up by the enthusiasm surrounding the industry, envisioning the creation of mobile modular homes that could removed and reinserted into high-rise structures, trailing the migratory travels of the owner. Although such structures never materialized, their creation, at least on paper, was indicative of the promising conditions characterizing the mobile home industry in the late 1960s.

Entering the 1970s, the industry had enjoyed a decade of prodigious growth, expanding at an annual rate of 20 percent throughout the 1960s and at 30 percent in the last two years of the decade. Unit shipments in 1970 topped 400,000, representing one mobile home for every 4.5 conventional housing starts, and revenues for the industry approached $3 billion.

At this point in the industry's history, several characteristics demonstrated by the industry augured increased growth for mobile home manufacturers, while some potentially hazardous market conditions loomed in the near future. On the favorable side, the average price for a mobile home had increased only negligibly, from $5,600 to $6,000, throughout the

1960s, while single family housing construction costs had risen sharply. This disparity was primarily due to the cheaper labor costs incurred by mobile home manufacturers than the wages construction contractors were obliged to pay, increasing the industry's grip on the under-$20,000 housing market. In fact, considering that mobile home units had increased in size since the introduction of ten wides in 1956, yet had increased only marginally in price during the intervening years, the price per square foot had actually declined. Additionally, financing a mobile home, a process resembling the financing of an automobile, was made easier through the enactment of the Housing and Urban Development Act of 1968, which permitted saving and loan associations to finance mobile home purchases.

The negative factors affecting the industry's future, however, were numerous. The most pressing was the decreasing space available for mobile homes. For the 400,000 units that entered the market in 1969, there were only an estimated 118,000 new mobile home park sites available, and the number sites for future mobile home parks were scarce. Almost entirely relegated to rural areas, mobile home parks, in which roughly 80 percent of all mobile homes were parked, were generally not well respected by urban residential neighborhoods and were often banned from existing alongside conventional houses through zoning restrictions. This left mobile home manufacturers unable to respond to the urgent need for low-income housing—a large segment of the under-$20,000 housing market from which manufacturers derived almost all of their earnings—during the early 1970s. This additional business could have offset, in part, the mounting competition that continued to plague the industry, making market saturation an imminent reality. In 1969 alone, 110 new manufacturers joined the industry, attracted by the robust growth demonstrated by the industry and the low capital investment required to establish a mobile home manufacturing facility.

Despite the development of these conditions, the industry posted the most successful year in its history in 1972, recording remarkable production and sales volumes that would stand as benchmark figures for the rest of the decade. Unit shipments totaled 575,940 for the year and sales reached the $4 billion plateau, quelling observations that the industry was headed for less prosperous years. Two years later, the two decades of solid growth that had been marred only by several minor economic came to a halt.

Unit shipments in 1974 plunged 42 percent from the previous year's level to 329,300. Sales plummeted to $2.5 billion as the industry quickly joined the nation in a recessive slide. The results from the next year's efforts were equally as dismal. Unit shipments dropped by an additional 35 percent from 1974's poor showing to 212,690, while revenues dropped only slightly to $2.4 billion. The less dramatic spiral of these dollar values, however, did not reflect the actual extent of the losses incurred by the industry during these two years; artificially buoyed by soaring inflation, revenues in reality were lower than they appeared.

Indeed, the losses suffered by the industry were severe and the reasons for the decline were manifold. Perhaps the single greatest contributing factor to the industry's demise was the economic downturn affecting the entire nation during this time. Unemployment rose and consumer income dropped, which threw a surfeit of repossessed mobile homes, over 100,000, on the market. This, in turn, made financing a mobile home purchase more difficult, as the tight money conditions combined with the increasing size and price of mobile homes extended loan payback terms from 5 to 10 years, to 10 to 20 years. Since mobile homes depreciated in value, rather than appreciating like conventional houses, lenders were reluctant to provide loans, rejecting 60 percent of all mobile home loan applications during the two-year slump. Compounding these difficulties was the growing popularity of condominiums, which impinged on the mobile home market, eroding manufacturers' customer base further.

As a result of the losses sustained during this period, the proliferation of manufacturing facilities that preceded the recession (a net total of 295 plants had sprouted up between 1969 and 1973) was halted, then reversed, when over 40 percent of the 550 firms involved in the market went bankrupt. Production capacity dropped by 43 percent from 1973 levels, nearly matching the increase in capacity during the four years leading up to the downturn.

To effect a recovery, several measures were taken—some which were initiated by the mobile home industry itself, while others came through federal intervention. Internally, mobile home manufacturers increased their output of larger mobile homes, concentrating on 14-foot-wide models and double-wides. Quality control was also a problem, engendered, in part, by unscrupulous manufacturers entering the field in the late 1960s and early 1970s. Many of these companies failed during the recession, solving part of the problem, but the more reputable companies also intensified their efforts toward producing higher-quality mobile units. To increase consumer confidence further, the federal government established uniform building codes and warranty standards, mandates that

made entry into the industry by unethical manufacturers somewhat more difficult.

In addition to these changes, the federal government eased mobile home financing by permitting federally chartered credit unions, which historically were short-term lenders, to provide longer-term credit to mobile home buyers. Also, the Veterans Administration increased the loan guarantee limits for mobile homes from 30 percent to 50 percent.

These ameliorations led to a slow recovery of the mobile home industry. Because of their expanded size and better workmanship, mobile homes began to appreciate in value after the mid-1970s, and began to increase their presence in conventional housing neighborhoods, as zoning restrictions eased. In 1976 unit shipments increased 16 percent to 246,120, still far below the level recorded in 1972, but, nevertheless, an improvement from the successive, precipitous drops suffered during the previous two years.

Also aiding the industry's recovery was the escalating price of conventional housing. Between 1974 and 1978, the average price of a new house rose 61 percent from $38,900 to $62,500, while the average price of a mobile home in 1978 was $15,900. Mobile homes had actually increased at greater rate than conventional houses during this period, leaping 71 percent from 1974's average price of $9,300, but the price disparity between the two housing choices was great enough to invigorate sales for mobile home manufacturers. In fact, the soaring costs of conventional houses attracted a new breed of mobile home customers by the end of the decade—middle class consumers.

Although these developments provided enough of an impetus to pull the industry out of its doldrums, a complete turnaround was not achieved, and growth of the industry remained stunted as it entered the 1980s. Unit shipments in 1980 were still well below half the total recorded in 1972 and even below the number of units shipped in 1976, the first year of the industry's recovery. After a 23 percent increase in 1983, unit shipments rose to 295,000, and topped 300,000 by the following year. Revenues during this period eclipsed the record year of 1972, peaking at $4.78 billion in 1983, and then dwindling down to just over $4 billion a year for the rest of the decade.

According to the Census Bureau, mobile homes were the fastest-growing type of housing during the 1980s, a distinction earned primarily from robust sales in the fist half of the decade. The late 1980s brought recessive conditions to the fore once again, causing unit shipments to decline, but mobile home manufacturers avoided significant losses, as mobile homes con-

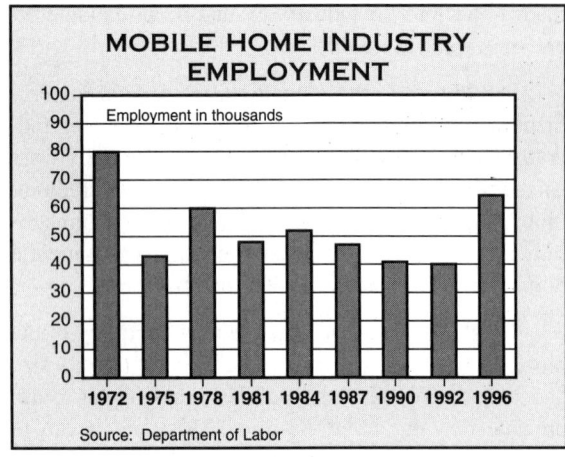

MOBILE HOME INDUSTRY
EMPLOYMENT

Employment in thousands

Source: Department of Labor

tinued to be the only housing alternative for many consumers.

CURRENT CONDITIONS

By the 1990s, the once-threatened industry was finding its new direction. However, locating a suitable site for permanent residence proved difficult for many mobile home owners due to zoning codes that excluded mobile home units, which, in turn, negatively affected mobile home manufacturers.

A large part of the industry's future growth depends on opening up additional areas for mobile home placement, a formidable challenge for the industry that requires shedding some of the stigma associated with mobile homes both in the eyes of potential customers and, more importantly, in the perceptions held by American society as a whole. While this may prove impossible, some headway has been made through legislation. By 1992, 22 states had outlawed "anti-mobile home" zoning restrictions, declaring them discriminatory. Further progress achieved in this direction should provide additional business to mobile home manufacturers as they look ahead to the mid-1990s. Meanwhile, the U.S. mortgage banking industry has begun to look more favorably than it had upon loans to purchases of manufactured homes.

FURTHER READING

Byrne, Harlan S. "No Laughingstock: Once a Joke, Manufactured Housing Has Gained Respect and a Bright Future." Barron's, 6 January 1997.

Darnay, Arsen J., ed. *Manufacturing USA*. Detroit: Gale Research, 1996.

Elliot, Richard J. Jr. "Long, Long Trailer: Mobile-Home Producers, Old and New Alike, Have Over-Expanded." *Barron's*, 23 February 1970, 3.

Jaffe, Thomas. "Mobile No More." *Forbes*, 14 September 1981, 140-144.

Johnson, Dirk. "Life in a Trailer Park: On the Edge, But Hoping." *New York Times*, 4 July 1992, 1.

"Just the Facts." The Manufactured Housing Institute. Arlington, VA, 1996.

King, Michael L. "Trailer Turnabout." *Wall Street Journal*, 1 August 1979, 1.

von Koschembahr, John C. "Mobile Homes: The Comeback That Died." *Financial World*, 1 December 1978, 37-39, 46.

"The Mobile Home Builders." *Financial World*, 5 August 1964, 7.

"Mobile Homes Take on New Forms for Low-Cost Housing." *Engineering News-Record*, 25 April 1968, 38-40.

Simonson, Robert. "The Mobile Home Industry." *Wall Street Transcript*, 16 March 1970, 19, 931-32.

Tejada, Carlos. "Today's Mobile Home May Have a Hearth." *The Wall Street Journal*, 14 June 1996.

Thomas, Dana L. "Road to Recovery: Makers of Mobile Homes Are Emerging from Their Slump." *Barron's*, 2 January 1978, 11, 27-28.

U.S. Industrial Outlook. Washington, DC: U.S. Department of Commerce, 1993.

—Jeffrey L. Covell, updated by John Gallagher

SIC 2452

PREFABRICATED WOOD BUILDINGS AND COMPONENTS

Companies that primarily make prefabricated wood buildings, sections, and panels make up the prefabricated wood buildings and components industry. Manufactured and mobile homes delivered to a site are not part of this industry. Companies that assemble panels and components on-site are classified in various construction sectors.

INDUSTRY SNAPSHOT

Modern prefabrication techniques date back to 1905. The use of gasoline-powered trucks and the U.S. housing boom after World War II built an identifiable prefabrication industry by the 1950s. By the early 1980s, this industry shipped more than $1 billion in goods and employed approximately 16,000 workers.

Healthy construction markets and greater demand for labor-saving prefabricated building products more than doubled the size of the industry during the 1980s. When housing starts fell during the late 1980s and early 1990s, prefab sales slipped. However, the advantage of productivity and quality assured a future for pre-made wood units.

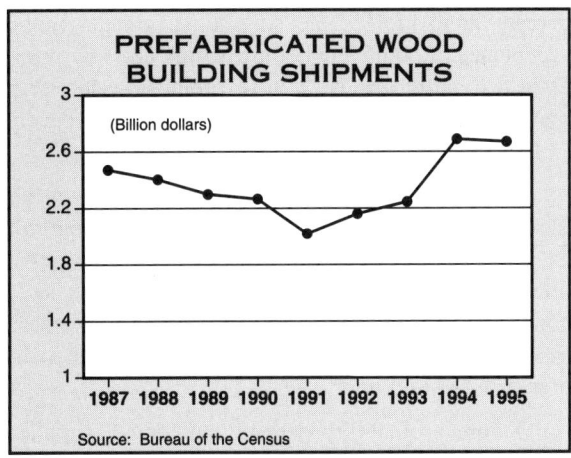

PREFABRICATED WOOD BUILDING SHIPMENTS

(Billion dollars)

1987 1988 1989 1990 1991 1992 1993 1994 1995

Source: Bureau of the Census

Going into the mid-1990s, producers benefited from more housing starts and renewed demand for prefabricated products. Low interest rates and economic growth boosted annual sales to $2.68 billion. Some industry niches, such as log homes, were even stronger.

ORGANIZATION AND STRUCTURE

The prefabricated wood components industry includes many products, including pre-made panels and sections for chicken coops, farm buildings, geodesic domes, marinas, sauna rooms, hotel rooms, and decks. The industry is fragmented and entrepreneurial, and is represented by a wide range of companies.

The advantage of prefabricated wood building products is they save builders money. Because large pieces of the structure come from a factory and are designed for quick and easy assembly on-site, builders reduce on-site costs, such as labor, workers' compensation, and insurance. Assembly-line production also allows prefab manufacturers greater quality control.

The cost advantage of prefabricated buildings shows in the price gap between site-built and manufactured homes, which come to the site completely built. The average site-built, single-family dwelling cost about $70 per square foot in the early 1990s, while manufactured homes cost about $23 per square foot. Most prefabricated homes fell somewhere within this range.

The largest segment of the prefab wood products industry is single-family homes, which made up about 65 percent of sales in the early 1990s. Homes built using prefab units are called component or prefabricated housing. Typical prefab housing products include roof trusses, wall frames, and floors. Many builders also use pre-made wall units complete with insulation, plumbing, wiring, ventilation systems, and

doors. Such builders use standard home plans with wall dimensions of 8 feet by 4 feet; and 8, 16, or 24 feet long. By doing so, they can order standard prefab units with a range of different window, door, and amenity configurations.

Builders of both detached and attached homes with prefab products use a systems approach to building, which is a hybrid of site-built and manufactured housing. The four types of systems-built housing include: pre-cut homes, for which all lumber and materials come to the site already cut; panelized homes, for which the main wall panels are shipped to the site, often with plumbing and wiring already installed; sectional homes, which are over 90 percent complete when they leave the factory and have cabinets and flooring already installed; and log homes, which are factory-made kit homes.

Markets. In the early 1990s, about one-third of prefab units produced were stationary buildings (i.e., those with floors and walls, and usually ceilings and roofs, attached in three-dimensional assemblies). About 17 percent of sales were stationary buildings sold as complete units but shipped as flat panels for assembly on-site; 16 percent of sales were from precut packages, such as log homes, sold as complete units but shipped in pieces and put together on-site; 17 percent of prefab products were individual components not sold as a complete unit. Miscellaneous parts and attachments made up the remaining 16 percent of sales.

Prefab units for single-family, detached-home construction, including remodeling, made up 50 percent of sales in the 1990s. Products used for apartment buildings were 10 percent of revenues, and prefab office building units made up 19 percent of shipments. The rest of the market was fragmented. Units used to build warehouses, for example, were about 3 percent of sales; as was farm construction. Other markets for wood prefab products included hotels, service stations, schools, and the armed forces. The remaining 3.2 percent of production was exported.

BACKGROUND AND DEVELOPMENT

Assembling wooden building components off-site has been practiced for centuries. The modern concept of prefabrication, which mass produces uniform panels and components, dates back to the early 1900s. Builders of that period, often the homeowners themselves, bought lightweight, pre-made frames and trusses to simplify construction. The use of gasoline-powered trucks early in the decade boosted sales of prefab products, and allowed manufacturers to build larger, heavier components.

The fledgling prefab industry grew during the post-World War II economic boom. As the economy and population grew, housing starts soared. Also, government housing programs, such as the Veteran's Administration Home Loan Guarantee Program of 1944, prodded demand for new construction. Single-family housing starts went from 139,000 per year in 1944 to 1.9 million in 1950.

Throughout the 1950s and 1960s, as the post-war economy thrived, families flocked to the housing market in a buying frenzy. Thousands of tract subdivisions were built on the edge of urban America, typically offering quality detached homes for less than $10,000 in the 1950s, with mortgage payments less than $100 per month. To keep up with demand, both residential and commercial builders sought more efficient production methods, including prefabrication.

New construction techniques and standard components made construction more viable during the 1950s, 1960s, and 1970s. New federal and state regulations were enacted, for example, mandating structural integrity and uniform building practices. Plywood, plastics, and aluminum, which all eventually went into wood prefab units, also increased sales. Although wood components held a minor share of U.S. construction, industry sales surpassed $1 billion in the early 1980s, and employment topped 16,500.

The 1980s and Early 1990s. Although demand for new construction remained high through the 1980s, several factors, including higher construction costs, slowed demand compared to past decades. As housing affordability and home ownership rates fell, many builders used component construction to cut costs. At the same time, higher quality components gave the industry a share of upscale markets. In addition, demand for heavy-duty commercial and industrial units rose.

Industry sales rose to nearly $2.5 billion by 1987, reflecting average annual growth of more than 12 percent between 1981 and 1987. Although commercial and residential construction markets stalled in the late 1980s and early 1990s, prefab industry revenues fell only marginally as the search for less-expensive production methods escalated. Sales slipped to about $2.3 billion in the early 1990s, but demand rose with better construction markets in the mid-1990s. The industry shipped goods worth $2.66 billion in 1995, down slightly from 1994.

CURRENT CONDITIONS

Industry sales rose in the mid-1990s. Shipments for single-family units, approached $3 billion. A 20 percent jump in 1992 housing starts, greater public acceptance of component construction, and low interest rates spurred sales in most prefab industry segments. Even lumber inflation, which stung producers in the early 1990s, receded by mid-decade.

The component construction trend boded well for the industry's future. Export markets seemed plentiful, as growing Third World nations wanted low-cost housing for swelling populations. Several savvy U.S. construction firms were already working in overseas markets, often through joint ventures and foreign manufacturing subsidiaries.

Future profitability depends on lumber supplies from the Northwest and other regions in the United States where environmental regulations limited logging in the mid-1990s. The use of wood substitutes, such as new high-performance synthetic resins, could also affect long-term wood component demand. Nevertheless, the industry outlook was positive through the 1990s.

Log Homes. Aside from more demand for prefabricated traditional homes, one large and growing segment of the industry was log homes. One estimate placed log home sales at about 12 percent of total industry revenues, though statistics are rare for this private company-dominated sector. Following a severe lag in the late 1980s, U.S. log home sales surged. At an average mid-1990s price of $67,000, ready-to-assemble log homes provided low-cost living.

Log home exports rose also. For example, New England Log Homes, Inc. of Connecticut shipped components to Israel, Europe, and Japan. Precision Craft, Inc. of Idaho, which began building log homes in 1992, had revenues over $4 million within six months—$1 million of which were from sales to Japan. Demand for U.S. log homes was also strong in Mexico, Jamaica, and South Korea.

Industry Niches. Besides prefab growth in single-family and log homes over 60 percent of industry revenues, other industry sectors offered solid growth in the 1990s, and new product launches expanded the breadth of the wood prefabrication business. Many utilities, for example, experimented with prefabricated power-control centers (PCCs) that came pre-wired and tested. Pre-made units offered reduced construction and maintenance costs, greater durability, and improved aesthetics.

One niche market in the mid-1990s was prefab units for building restaurant carts, kiosks, and drive-thrus. These are designed for fast, inexpensive assembly. Rally's, a hamburger drive-thru chain, built its modular units for thousands of dollars less than traditional brick buildings. Similarly, about 1,000 Checkers restaurants, also built with prefab components, were completed in 1995.

Interestingly, inventor Al Rice launched a chain of ultra-economy mini-motels in the mid-1990s. The pre-fabricated 140-square-foot hotel rooms feature a double bed, bathroom, television, and phone for less than $20 per night. The units could be assembled in groups of 10 to 30 and operated using a patented Autoclerk system. Guests check into the rooms electronically using a credit card. The Autoclerk provides wake-up calls and security, and allows the travelers to contact a manager at a remote site.

INDUSTRY LEADERS

About 650 companies participated in the prefabricated wood component industry in the mid-1990s. Because it is a localized industry by logistic necessity, most companies were small. Most of the top 50 competitors had sales of less than $25 million per year in the 1990s and employed fewer than 150 workers.

The largest U.S. supplier of wood building components in 1995 was privately held Guerdon Homes, Inc. of Lake Oswego, Oregon (with $1.2 billion in annual sales and 800 employees). Next was a public company, Skyline, Corp., of Elkhart, Indiana (with $642 million and 3,600 employees). In third place was another public company, Champion Home Builders of Auburn Hills, Michigan (with $250 million and 2,000 employees).

Alpine Log Homes, Inc. was more typical of firms in the prefab industry because it was small, entrepreneurial, and niche-oriented. The company was started by Ken Thuerbach, who left his job as a financier to build log cabins in Montana. Alpine built each log home in Montana, took it apart, and trucked it to a site for reassembly. It also built multimillion-dollar structures, such as the University of Montana's Entrepreneurial Center. Thuerbach reported annual revenues in the early 1990s of $9 million to $14 million per year.

WORK FORCE

For production, the industry employed many assemblers, fabricators, and woodworkers. In 1995, 21,000 people worked in this industry, with 15,700 jobs in production. Total payroll for 1995 was $497 million, of which $298 million paid production wages. While the industry grew rapidly during the 1980s (in contrast to other U.S. manufacturing industries) to more than 22,500, wages in the prefab industry lagged behind other manufacturing jobs in the mid-1990s.

U.S. PREFABRICATED WOOD BUILDING TRADE

Imports   (Million dollars)

Exports

1992   1993   1994   1995   1996

Source: Bureau of the Census

RESEARCH AND TECHNOLOGY

Most technological advances throughout the mid-1990s centered around prefab housing's advantages of low cost, ease of construction, and uniform quality. Prefab makers also developed products to compete with traditional construction markets, such as high-rise buildings. For instance, component makers in Japan marketed sections and panels for medium-rise apartment buildings as high as five stories.

Japanese companies were leading technological advances in other areas of the industry, as well. Shimizu Corporation's Smart System, introduced in 1993, was designed to cut the number of man-hours required to complete a 20-story office building by 30 percent. The Smart System uses a network of nine computer-controlled cranes that scale the frame of the building and attach components automatically.

U.S. home builder Land & Houses used direct mail to market its high-tech prefab units to consumers in Thailand. In 1993, it built a factory in that country to make prefabricated floors and walls that could be used to make low-cost housing on a massive scale.

Technological developments that competed with the wood component industry in the 1990s included advances in wood substitutes. Producers in Saudi Arabia, for example, mass-produced prefab aluminum houses and buildings. Similarly, manufacturers in Poland shipped prefab metal and reinforced plastic components. The panels and sections built retail kiosks to support the growing entrepreneurial population.

FURTHER READING

Al-Dohaim, Yasser A. and Abid Ali. "Using Work Design Techniques and Method Engineering to Enhance Productivity." *Industrial Engineering,* July 1993.

Bond, Helen. "Investor Eyes New Niche." *Hotel & Motel Management,* 7 June 1993.

Bretz, Elizabeth. "Busy Utilities Turn to Pre-Fab Control Buildings." December 1992.

"Exporting Pays Off." *Business America,* 24 August 1992.

Friedland, Jonathan. "Home Run: Thai Builder Pioneers Mass-Produced Housing." *Far Eastern Economic Review,* 8 November 1990.

Goldstein, Carl. "Tall Storey: Hong Kong's Top Contractor Is Dragages of France." *Far Eastern Economic Review,* 19 April 1990.

Harper, Doug. "Export Boom Gives Log Home Industry Badly Needed Boost." *Journal of Commerce and Commercial,* 9 November 1992.

Hooser, Dwane D. "Montana's Log Home Industry." *Montana's Business Quarterly,* Autumn 1990.

Joint Center for Housing Studies. *The State of the Nations Housing 1993.* Boston: Joint Center for Housing Studies, 1993.

Menzel, Thomas R. "Going Global from Scratch." *World Trade,* January 1993.

National Association of Home Builders. *50 Years of Housing—50 Years of NAHB.* Washington: National Association of Home Builders, 1992.

National Association of Home Builders, Public Affairs Division. *Housing Backgrounder.* Washington: National Association of Home Builders, 1993.

Normile, Dennis. "Building-By-Numbers in Japan." *Engineering News Record,* 1 March 1993.

Paliwoda, Stan. "Optimistic Report from Poland: Veteran Analyst Describes Changes, Investment Opportunities." *Marketing News,* 13 September 1993.

"Prefabricated Modular Buildings." *Communications News,* June 1991.

Standard & Poor's Industry Surveys. New York: Standard & Poor's Corporation, 5 August 1993.

Taras, Susan. "Easy to Log Quality Time in Homes of Good Timber." *Advertising Age,* 11 January 1993.

"Trade and Industry Briefs: Synthetic Fibers; Housing." *Mitsubishi Bank Review,* January 1992.

U.S. Department of Commerce. *1995 Annual Survey of Manufactures: Statistics for Industry Groups and Industries.* Washington: GPO, 1997.

Wallace, Don. "Leisure Class: The Creative Adventurer." *Success,* September 1991.

Walter, Kate. "Breaking With Brick." *Restaurant Business,* 1 September 1993.

—Dave Mote, updated by Dave Fagan

SIC 2491

WOOD PRESERVING

The wood preserving industry comprises establishments primarily engaged in treating wood—sawed or planed in other establishments—with creosote or other preservatives to prevent decay and protect against fire and insects. The industry also cuts, treats, and sells poles, posts, and pilings; however, establishments primarily engaged in manufacturing other wood products, which they may also treat with preservatives, are classified elsewhere.

People have been coating wood with crude preservatives, such as tar and pitch, for ages. Chemicals and processes developed during the nineteenth and twentieth centuries, however, have resulted in techniques for preserving wood for 35 years or more. Untreated wood exposed to the elements typically lasts about three years. Perhaps the greatest industry innovation during the 1900s was the high-pressure chemical treatment process, which accelerated wood's absorption of preservatives and increased the treatment's depth. In the early 1990s, 95 percent of all preserved wood was treated using that process.

Utility poles make up the single largest market segment for wood preservers and accounted for roughly 25 percent of sales in the early 1990s. Various residential, commercial, and institutional construction industries consume the bulk of industry output. Three-quarters of all wood products are treated with chromated copper arsenate. Pentachlorophenol and creosote account for the remaining one-quarter. In addition to utility poles, the most commonly treated wood products are lumber, plywood, timbers, posts, and railway ties. Southern yellow pine accounts for 75 percent of all treated wood; the remaining 25 percent includes spruce-pine-fir, hemlock, Douglas fir, cedar, inland species of Ponderosa pine, and Brazilian pine. Demand for treated hardwoods is meager.

Wood preservers have had to adjust to new environmental restrictions. In 1990 the Environmental Protection Agency (EPA) identified the byproducts of wood preserving processes as hazardous waste, and chose to begin regulating the industry in 1991. Naphthenate and other substitutes increasingly will offer viable alternatives to preservatives that spawn high-cost toxins. In 1996 industry leader, Koppers Industries, reported ongoing problems with site and groundwater contamination from wood preservatives, and EPA violations at many of their facilities. The company reported the possibility of having to install additional pollution control and monitoring devices at various facilities and participated in extensive cleanup operations.

In 1994 the wood preserving industry had revenues of approximately $3.4 billion from 474 companies employing 11,218 workers. By 1995, revenues increased to $3.5 billion, up from $2.6 billion at the beginning of the decade. The *Economic Census: Annual Survey of Manufacturers* predicted sales would increase to more than 3.9 billion by 1998.

In the mid-1990s, 15.4 percent of industry employees worked as assemblers, fabricators, and hand workers. Other occupations included sawyers; machine feeders; blue-collar supervisors and laborers; wood machinists; truck and tractor operators; freight and material movers; managers and executives; and coating, spraying, and painting workers. Despite the industry's growth in the 1980s and 1990s, employment is predicted to decline in the wake of productivity gains. Most occupations are expected to realize a work force reduction of 5 to 25 percent between 1990 and 2005, according to the Bureau of Labor Statistics.

Top companies in the industry in 1996 were Koppers Industries of Pittsburgh, Pennsylvania, which had sales of $465 million and 1,800 employees, and Fibreboard Corporation of Walnut Creek, California, which had sales of $364 million and 3,500 employees. Other leading companies included Tolleson Lumber Company, Walker-Williams Lumber Company, and Robbins Manufacturing Company.

FURTHER READING

Darnay, Arsen J., ed. *Manufacturing USA.* 5th ed. Detroit: Gale Research, 1996.

Koppers Industries 1996 Annual Report. Pittsburgh: Koppers Industries, 1997.

U.S. Department of Commerce. International Trade Administration. *U.S. Industrial Outlook 1994.* Washington: GPO, 1994.

U.S. Department of Commerce. *1994 County Business Patterns.* Washington: GPO, 1996.

U.S. Department of Commerce. *1995 Annual Survey of Manufacturers: Value of Product Shipments.* Washington: GPO, 1995.

—Dave Mote, updated by Joanne Wolf

RECONSTITUTED WOOD PRODUCTS

The reconstituted wood products industry comprises establishments primarily engaged in manufacturing hardboard, particleboard, insulation board, medium-density fiberboard, waferboard, and other panelized products made from wood chips and particles.

Particleboard is created from wood flakes, shavings, or splinters that are discharged when wood products are processed. The particles are bonded together under pressurized heat using resin and adhesives to make an inexpensive, durable wooden panel. Approximately 80 percent of all particleboard is used to make furniture, cabinets, and doors. A hardboard, or fiberboard, panel is made from wood fibers that are steamed, rubbed apart, and then compacted under pressurized heat. Unlike particleboard, only a small amount of resin or adhesive is used to bond the fibers. Hardboard has a smooth finish and is used primarily for exterior house siding, indoor cabinets, and fixtures.

LEADING U.S. RECONSTITUTED WOOD PRODUCER SALES

Louisiana-Pacific

Valcor

Masonite

Medile

(Million dollars)

0   50   100 150 200 250 300 350 400

Commercially useful wood particle panels resulted from the chemical industry's development of high-tech synthetic resins and adhesives, particularly during the 1960s, 1970s, and 1980s. The value of reconstituted panel shipments increased steadily during the 1980s and 1990s to an estimated $5.5 billion by 1996.

Although the early-decade economic recession caused industry revenues to drop slightly, improved economic conditions in the mid-1990s saw a surge in shipments of particleboard and medium-density fiberboard (MDF) from U.S. mills. U.S. consumption of particleboard was expected to reach 5.7 billion square feet by 1996, and MDF consumption was predicted at 1.7 billion square feet. The Asian furniture market has become a primary target for North American exports of particleboard; exports are forecast to exceed 565 million square feet by 1997, primarily to Pacific Rim countries.

Waferboard and oriented strand board (OSB) made up about 20 percent of industry sales in the early 1990s. Waferboard is similar to particleboard, but only three-inch, square wood flakes are used. OSB is a type of waferboard, but its flakes are layered and oriented in a way that makes it much stronger than waferboard, yet still less expensive than plywood.

OSB production capacity began to expand rapidly in the first half of the 1990s, and 27 new North American plants were slated for 1995. The OSB market was predicted to expand by 2 billion square feet between 1994 and 2000, and U.S producers targeted European markets to absorb excess capacity. Although the Engineered Wood Association predicted a downturn in panel production by the year 2000, it also predicted that OSB will account for 44 percent of total production, up from 28 percent of the market in 1994 and 31 percent in 1995. Canada's panel production is predicted to be 82 percent OSB by the year 2000, up from 62 percent in 1994.

Despite overall growth, opportunities in most occupations in the industry are expected to decline significantly between 1990 and 2005, according to the U.S. Bureau of Labor Statistics. Jobs for assemblers and fabricators, which accounted for 14 percent of the work force in the early part of the decade, are predicted to fall by more than 25 percent. Most positions, in fact, are expected to decline 5 to 20 percent by 2005.

The largest U.S. producers of reconstituted wood products in 1996 were Valcor of Dallas, Texas, and Louisiana-Pacific Corporation (L-P) of Hayden Lake, Idaho. Both had revenues of $350 million. Valcor had 5,300 employees and L-P employed 2,800 workers. Masonite Corporation of Illinois had sales of $250 million and Medite Corporation had revenues of $200 million.

FURTHER READING

Darnay, Arsen J., ed. *Manufacturing USA*. 5th ed. Detroit: Gale Research, 1996.

''Global Panel Industry Increases Growth Rate.'' *Wood Technology,* 122, no. 6 (September 1995).

U.S. Department of Commerce. *U.S. Industrial Outlook 1993.* Washington: GPO, 1993.

—Dave Mote, updated by Joanne Wolfe

WOOD PRODUCTS, NOT ELSEWHERE CLASSIFIED

This category includes establishments primarily engaged in manufacturing miscellaneous wood products, not elsewhere classified, and products made from rattan, reed, splint, straw, veneer, veneer strips, wicker, and willow.

The industry covers a plethora of wood products not categorized under other classifications, such as ship masts, dowels, rowboat oars, clipboards, rattan seat covers, shoe trees, tool handles, toothpicks, washboards, paint stirring sticks, and wooden ladders. Although the breadth of this industry is enormous, some categories account for a significant portion of overall sales. For example, wooden picture and mirror frames are by far the largest category, supplying 36 percent of industry revenues in the first half of the 1990s and garnering revenues of more than $1 billion by 1995.

Individuals, the largest consumers of miscellaneous wooden goods, accounted for about 22 percent of industry sales in the early 1990s. Office building owners and managers were the second-largest sector, representing about 4 percent of the market. Other major consumers of industry output were furniture manufacturers, makers of glass products, and paperboard mills. Exports accounted for 3.5 percent of production.

The industry is intangible and unstructured compared with most other industrial categories. The industry experienced wide swings in revenues during the 1980s, according to the U.S. Census of Manufactures. At that time 3,400 firms reported total sales of $3.4 billion. By 1992, the Census reported only 2,644 firms having $3.7 billion in total shipments of miscellaneous wooden items.

An estimated 52,705 workers served the industry in 1994; a slight increase since 1992, but an overall decline from the 61,000 workers reported in 1987. Production workers comprised 83 percent of employees. Significant occupations in this industry include assemblers and fabricators, machine operators, sawers, blue-collar work supervisors, and truck drivers. Seventy-nine percent of firms surveyed had fewer than 100 employees.

Long-term growth in industry sales and profits will depend on individual product segments. Overall employment is expected to decline significantly between 1990 and 2005, according to the Bureau of Labor Statistics. Assembler and fabricator jobs, for example, could plummet by more than 26 percent; positions for machine operators and bookkeepers also could decline. Most occupations, it is anticipated, will realize a 5 to 20 percent reduction in the work force as companies seek to automate and increase productivity. Sales and marketing professionals, in contrast, will see positions in this industry grow by nearly 20 percent.

The largest producer of miscellaneous wood products throughout the first half of the 1990s was Masonite Corp. of Illinois, although the company's revenues and number of employees declined sharply during that period. Masonite generated revenues of $264 million from its diversified operations in 1996 and employed about 3,000 workers, down from revenues of $535 million and a work force of 5,000 in 1991.

ABT Building Products Corporation, of Neehnah, Wisconsin, posted 1996 sales of $203 million with 1,400 employees. Other industry leaders include ABTCO of Troy, Michigan; Norco, of St. Paul, Minnesota; and Larson-Juhl, of Ashland, Wisconsin.

FURTHER READING

Darnay, Arsen J., ed. *Manufacturing USA*. 5th ed. Detroit: Gale Research, 1996.

Standard & Poor's Industry Surveys. New York: Standard & Poor's Corporation, 5 August 1993.

U.S. Department of Commerce. *1995 Annual Survey of Manufactures: Statistics for Industry Groups and Industries*. Washington: GPO, 1995.

U.S. Department of Commerce. *1995 Annual Survey of Manufactures: Value of Product Shipments*. Washington: GPO, 1995.

U.S. Department of Commerce. *U.S. Industrial Outlook 1993*. Washington: GPO, 1993.

U.S. Department of Commerce. *1992 Census of Manufactures*. Washington: GPO, 1992.

—Dave Mote, updated by Joanne Wolfe

Furniture & Fixtures

WOOD HOUSEHOLD FURNITURE

This classification consists of establishments engaged in manufacturing wood furniture commonly used in dwellings, with the exception of television, radio, phonograph, and sewing machine cabinets, which are classified in **SIC 2517: Wood Television, Radio, Phonograph, and Sewing Machine Cabinets**; also, millwork production is classified in **SIC 2431: Millwork**; wood kitchen cabinets are classified in **SIC 2434: Wood Kitchen Cabinets.** Cut stone and concrete furniture is classified in the major group for stone, clay, glass, and concrete products; laboratory and hospital furniture, except hospital beds, is in the major group for measuring, analyzing, and controlling instruments; photographic, medical, and optical goods; watches and clocks; and beauty and barber shop furniture is classified in the major group for miscellaneous manufacturing industries; and those engaged in woodworking to individual order or in the nature of reconditioning and repair are classified in non-manufacturing industries.

The market for wood household furniture has been estimated to be worth over $10.4 billion in 1996, and the industry employed over 125,000 people in the United States. Most furniture sold in this category (30 percent) was for the bedroom; with living rooms, dens, and libraries (20 percent) and kitchens and dining rooms (20 percent) accounting for large shares of the market as well.

The industry's leading company, Furniture Brands International, began as the International Shoe

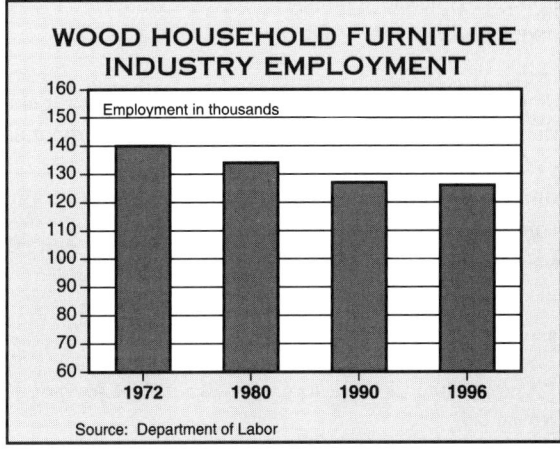

WOOD HOUSEHOLD FURNITURE INDUSTRY EMPLOYMENT

Employment in thousands

Source: Department of Labor

Company. Its purchase of Thomasville (the company also owns the well-known brands of Broyhill and Lane) made it the largest maker of wood household furniture. Sales in the mid-1990s were $1.1 billion for the company, which employed over 20,000. The second largest company in this industry, Kimball International Inc., had a turnover of $896 million; and the third, LADD Furniture Inc., $615 million.

Ready-to-assemble (RTA) furniture was extremely popular in the 1990s, partly due to an improvement in quality—the products no longer smacked of dormitory living. Typical products offered wood veneer finishes, and such details as rounded corners and beveled glass doors. A piece of RTA furniture can be assembled quickly, usually in less than an hour. O'Sullivan Industries has even utilized Velcro fasteners instead of screws to help speed up assembly. An average price for a ready-to-assemble desk was $225.00, 65 percent less than a factory-finished product. The low cost of RTA furniture and the ease of stocking it has made it popular among large mass merchandisers and warehouse-type stores, which had themselves become more popular among consumers.

Traditional furniture stores worked with vendors to introduce vendor-ship programs, with manufacturers shipping furniture directly to the customer, allowing the stores to carry less inventory and ensuring safe delivery of the products.

International Trade. Most exports of American wood household furniture went to Canada (39 percent), Mexico (12 percent), and Saudi Arabia (9 percent). Imports came from Taiwan (29 percent), Canada (14 percent), and Mexico (7 percent). International trade liberalization agreements such as GATT and NAFTA seemed poised to benefit U.S. exports of wood household furniture, though developing nations seemed poised to pursue aggressive forest management and export policies.

U.S. Environmental Protection Agency regulations attempted to reduce volatile organic compound (VOC) emissions from chemicals used in furniture finishes. However, the industry was able to postpone some environmental legislation.

FURTHER READING

"Acton Unit to Close Factory." *The Wall Street Journal,* 12 November 1992.

Adams, Larry. "Soft Landing Means Economy to Grow, But Slow." *Wood and Wood Products,* January 1996.

Agins, Teri. "Marketing—Home Furnishings." *The Wall Street Journal,* 22 November 1993.

Blumenthal, Robin Goldwyn. "Bassett Furniture Expects Increases in Fiscal '93 Results." *The Wall Street Journal,* 18 January 1993.

Drill, Larry. "Stop the Ax." *Modern Paint and Coatings,* August 1996.

Marks, Robert. "RTA Puts Together Prosperous '94." *HFN:The Weekly Newspaper for the Home Furnishing Network,* 20 February 1995.

"Stanley Furniture Co.: Restructuring Plan Gives Stake to Preferred Holders." *The Wall Street Journal,* 10 November, 1992.

"Study Links Component Purchases with Profits." *Wood and Wood Products,* July 1994.

"Textiles, Apparel, and Home Furnishings." *Industry Surveys,* 26 November 1992.

—Frederick C. Ingram

SIC 2512

WOOD HOUSEHOLD FURNITURE, UPHOLSTERED

This category covers those establishments primarily engaged in manufacturing upholstered furniture on wood frames. Shops primarily engaged in reupholstering furniture, or upholstering frames to individual order, are classified in Services, **SIC 7641: Re-upholstery and Furniture Repair,** or Retail Trade, **SIC 5712: Furniture Stores.** Establishments primarily engaged in manufacturing dual purpose sleep furniture, such as convertible sofas and chair beds, are classified in **SIC 2515: Mattresses, Foundations, and Convertible Beds,** regardless of the material used in the frame. Establishments primarily engaged in manufacturing wood frames for upholstered furniture are classified in **SIC 2426: Hardware Dimension and Flooring Mills.**

This industry is defined primarily by the materials with which the products are constructed, rather than the end product itself. All products feature wood frames and fabric or leather upholstery. Establishments within this industry produce a wide range of upholstered furniture for the home, including such upholstered living room furniture as chairs, rockers, couches, sofas, and recliners. Products manufactured in this industry include other household furniture as well as juvenile furniture.

Establishments in this industry produce goods that are sold to distributors or directly to retailers. Manufacturers produce goods for sale at a variety of price points and under a variety of brand names. *Standard and Poor's Industry Survey* estimated that approximately 44 percent of upholstered furniture is sold through furniture stores, 10 percent through department stores, and 44 percent through mass merchandisers. New retailing techniques are affecting the industry. Standard and Poor's noted a growing tendency among manufacturers to enter into agreement with a retailer to open a gallery devoted to the manufacturer's goods, a concept that has been "very successful in attracting customers and generating sales." The arrangement is mutually advantageous because the retailer has proprietary rights on the goods while the manufacturer gets a dedicated retail outlet for its merchandise.

According to *1995 Annual Survey of Manufactures,* establishments in this industry shipped an estimated $7.45 billion worth of products in 1994. This amount equaled approximately 30 percent of the total sales recorded by the household furniture manufacturing industry as a whole. Furthermore, the industry is an important source of jobs. Again, according to the *1995 Annual Survey of Manufactures,* the industry employs approximately 89,700 people and maintains a payroll of approximately $1.91 billion. The employment figures were up from the *1992 Census of Manufactures,* which reported employment of only 79,200 people, and from the previous 1987 data, which reported employment of 82,100.

Manufacturers of upholstered wood furniture benefited from an expanding market in the early 1990s, leading to approximately 5 to 6 percent growth between 1992 and 1993 alone. The industry is influenced by the rate of new home construction and the number of existing homes being remodeled. Standard and Poor's estimated that the upholstered wood household furniture industry will continue to expand through the mid-1990s due to changing demographics. Baby Boomers are "getting older and richer and will soon want nicer things to suit their more upscale lifestyles." The largest manufacturers in the industry in the mid-1990s were Masco Corp., the La-Z Boy Chair Company, Mohasco Corporation, and Klaussner Furniture Industries, Incorporated. The states with the highest percentage of people employed in this industry were North Carolina, Mississippi, Tennessee, and California. Between them, they accounted for 70 percent of the industry's employment.

FURTHER READING

Standard and Poor's Industry Surveys. New York: Standard and Poor's Corporation, 1997.

U.S. Bureau of the Census. *1995 Annual Survey of Manufactures.* Washington: GPO, 1997.

————. *Census of Manufactures.* Washington: GPO, 1990.

—Jim Cuene, updated by Kenneth R. Shepherd

SIC 2514

METAL HOUSEHOLD FURNITURE

This industry category includes establishments primarily engaged in manufacturing metal furniture of a type commonly used in dwellings.

Metal furniture dates back almost as far as the use of wrought iron, with society witnessing an extraordinary increase in the use of metal furniture by the end of the eighteenth century. By the beginning of the nineteenth century, both English and American craftsmen began constructing Windsor-style chairs in wrought iron. In 1851 at the Great Exhibition in London, England, the American Chair Company of New York exhibited a metal-framed, sprung, revolving chair, one of several styles with frames made largely of cast-iron, steel, or a combination of the two. And by the 1890s, metal beds had become one of the most popular selling furniture items in America.

With the development of steel and other innovations in metal production by American manufacturing companies during the 1920s and early 1930s, major impacts on furniture design were felt. The abundance of ready steel made it a popular and reasonably cheap material for furniture. One of the most dramatic new processes, discovered in the early 1920s by an American inventor named Mannesman, produced seamless tubular steel. This new material had the combined advantages of being light, strong, and modern.

The role that bent metal furniture played in the design culture of the 1920s and 1930s has never been equaled by any other material or at any other time in design history. The designs seemed to encompass an era. The development of modern tubular steel furniture can be seen in terms of the technical accomplishments of modern industrialization, with its improved methods of steel production, metal plating and welding—all of which helped to disseminate the new furniture to a wider market. But above all of this is the fact that steel furniture came from the world of modern art and architecture and its preoccupation with the idea and image of the machine.

For that reason the major drawback to metal furniture was that its look appealed to a small, sophisticated market that enjoyed what was, at the time, called the Modern style of design. For that same reason, there remained for several years a great deal of resistance to its use in the home, with many feeling that it was too impersonal for domestic use, but perfectly suitable for hospitals and offices. Then 1933 Chicago World's Fair exhibited a large number of pieces of tubular steel furniture. Seen as a symbol for modern life, the use of steel was advertised at the Fair as, "natural, therefore that the modern spirit should express itself in striking, radically different kinds of furniture—and that furniture should be of steel, for this is the age of steel, and steel sounds the keynote of practicability, energy, and strength which dominates our modern life." By the mid-1930s tubular steel furnishing was being more easily accepted into domestic use, with steel items coming out of American factories in ever-increasing, large numbers.

Companies, such as the Chicago and Grand Rapids Company of Michigan, immediately began producing large quantities of tubular steel furniture.

The American industrial designer, Donald Deskey, designed a line of metal furniture that was mass-produced around 1930 by the Ypsilanti Reed Furniture Company. A 1930 ad for the company pointed out that Ypsilanti Reed had pioneered steel furniture in America, "and in less than two years has assumed outstanding leadership in style and quality in this singular furniture."

By 1933 the Howell Company of Geneva, Illinois, began mass-producing tubular steel furniture, including the best-selling "Beta," a chrome-plated, tubular steel and upholstered chair, as well as other innovative chair forms, such as the "S" chairs, with their bent metal frames, that were produced and sold in high volume throughout the 1930s.

The famous industrial designer, Gilbert Rohde, was among the first American innovators who worked with bent metal to create innovative furniture designs. His earliest tubular steel design was manufactured by the Troy Sunshade Company of Troy, Ohio in 1931. Because the company had additional offices in Amsterdam and Rotterdam in the Netherlands, Rohde's designs were sold in Europe as well.

The Kroehler Manufacturing Company of Chicago, Illinois also employed Rohde, who designed furniture not only from tubular steel, but from stainless steel, aluminum, and chrome. Rhode's pieces were advertised by the company as "functional and modern" with "a hygienic quality (no nooks and crannies to conceal dirt) that reduced dusting to a minimum while retaining their luster without the drudgery of polishing."

By 1930 Gilbert Rohde moved on to take over the design leadership for the Herman Miller Furniture Company of Grand Rapids, Michigan. With Rohde at its helm, the company began an extensive program to produce modern furnishings, most of which incorporated the use of bent metal elements in many of their designs. In fact, throughout the decade leading up to World War II, the Herman Miller Company continued to increasingly produce bent metal furnishings designed by Gilbert Rohde.

Although metal furniture was seen as innovative to the American public, many American designers, like Gilbert Rohde, owed a great debt to their European counterparts during the decades between the two world wars. Many progressive European publications published designs for tubular steel furniture. In fact, some of the most copied modern tubular steel furniture designs belonged to Marcel Breuer, the avant garde designer, and were originally created while he was at

the Bauhaus, the German experimental design school, as early as 1925.

With the dissemination of European tubular steel designs to a wider, world market and manufacturers producing their own interpretations of bent metal furniture, the originality and inventiveness of design had largely ended by the early years of the 1940s.

After World War II, the profound changes in design and manufacturing moved the center of progressive development of metal furniture from Europe to the United States. Charles and Ray Eames, a husband and wife team of industrial designers, helped to develop new, and even more innovative, metal furniture designs for the Herman Miller Company in the 1940s and 1950s.

Research into new materials such as molded plywood, and the use of light metal alloys (especially aluminum and magnesium, which were developed during the War) provided an entire new range of possibilities for post-war furniture.

The American furniture manufacturer, Knoll International, produced such innovative designs as the 1952 metal "Grid" chair by the artist/designer, Harry Bertoia, as well as several other metal pieces. And, in the 1960s, Knoll produced the internationally acclaimed architect/designer Mies van der Rohe's last body of furniture designs of tubular and flat steel.

But by the end of the 1950s, metal was being used less and less frequently for innovative furniture designs. The Herman Miller Company and Knoll International continued to manufacture steel bent and tubular steel "design classics" from the 1930s, but with new and even more innovative materials, such as plastics, arriving on the scene, metal furniture was relegated to experimental, one-of-a-kind and limited edition pieces by artist/designers who did not look for mass production or wide audience acceptance.

The total 1993 sales for the entire furniture industry were $22.2 billion. Metal furniture accounted for 10 percent of the total amount. Ten percent of all furniture exports in 1994 were metal.

Because metal was the symbol of the machine age, it was quite natural for metal furniture's high point to coincide with the era of the "machine age," that of the 1930s. The bent metal furniture designed and manufactured during that period was never equaled again. Throughout the 1990's metal furniture is still prevalent in schools and hospitals, but rather scarce for home furnishings. With the popularity of daybeds and futons in the mid 1990's, certain metals have had a slight resurgence in the furniture industry. Metal chairs and tables are still being produced in the United States today. The newer, 1990's forms of furniture are geared towards works of art rather than functional pieces of furniture.

FURTHER READING

Wilson, Richard Guy, Dianne H. Pilgram, and Dickran Tashjian. *The Machine Age in America, 1918-1941.* New York: Harry N. Abrams, Inc., Publishers, 1986.

Sparke, Penny. *Design in Context.* London: Quarto Publishing, 1987.

Alvera, Allessandro, Dry, Graham, and Robert Keil et.al. *Bent Wood and Metal Furniture: 1850-1946.* New York: The American Federation of the Arts, 1987.

Lucie-Smith, Edward. *A History of Industrial Design.* Oxford: Phaidon Press Ltd., 1983.

Garner, Philippe. *Twentieth Century Furniture.* London: Adkinson Parrish Ltd., 1980.

U.S. Deaprtment of Commerce. *US Industrial Outlook 1994,* 1995.

—David Sprinkle, updated by Jennifer L. Stong

SIC 2515

MATTRESSES, FOUNDATIONS, AND CONVERTIBLE BEDS

This category covers establishments primarily engaged in manufacturing innerspring mattresses, box spring mattresses, and non-innerspring mattresses containing felt, foam rubber, urethane, hair, or any other filling material; and assembled wire springs (fabric, coil, or box) for use on beds, couches, and cots. This industry also includes establishments primarily en-

gaged in manufacturing dual purpose sleep furniture, such as convertible sofas and chair beds, regardless of the material used in the frame. Establishments primarily engaged in manufacturing automobile seats and backs are classified under **SIC 2531: Public Building and Related Furniture;** those manufacturing individual wire springs are classified under **SIC 3495: Wire Springs;** and those manufacturing paddings and upholstery filling are classified under **SIC 2299: Textile Goods, Not Elsewhere Classified.**

Establishments that manufacture mattresses, foundations, and convertible beds are part of the $22.2 billion household furniture manufacturing industry. According to the *1995 Annual Survey of Manufactures,* manufacturers within this classification sold approximately $3.5 billion dollars worth of products in 1995, an increase of about 8 percent over 1993 figures. The same survey showed that manufacturing establishments employed 25,700 workers, with a total payroll of $569.3 million. These numbers mark an increase of 2.0 percent over the 25,200 workers and 1.5 percent over the $560.8 million payroll reported in 1994.

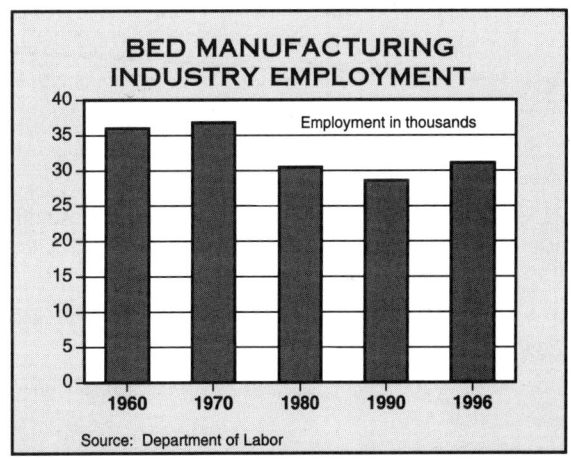

The industry is populated by smaller manufacturing facilities. Of the approximately 840 establishments in operation, about 500 had less than 20 employees. The industry employs approximately 24,000 people (including almost 18,000 as production workers) with a $508 million payroll. The states with the most people employed in the industry are California, Texas, New Jersey, and Florida.

Manufacturers create products to be sold under different brand names at a variety of price points. A high quality mattress can cost the retail consumer as much as $899 or more. Establishments in this industry distribute their goods to specialty stores that deal only in mattresses and foundations. According to the 1994 edition of *Standard and Poor's Industry Surveys,* 45 percent of bedding is sold through such stores, followed by discount stores and department stores, which sell 13 and 12 percent of manufacturer's goods, respectively.

According to *Ward's Business Directory of U.S. Private and Public Companies,* the largest manufacturer of mattresses and bedsprings in the mid-1990s was Legget and Platt, Inc. of Carthage, Missouri. Behind them is Sealy Corporation of Cleveland, Ohio, and the Simmons Company. Serta, Inc. and Restonic, Inc. are also among the industry leaders in sales and numbers of employees. In the early 1990s the states of California, Florida, Texas, and North Carolina were the leaders in the industry, accounting for about 35 percent of the industry's employment. Establishments of less than ten employees were not counted in the survey, but account for about 11 percent of total shipments.

FURTHER READING

American Furniture Manufacturers Association. High Point, NC.

Standard and Poor's Industry Surveys. New York: Standard and Poor's Corporation, 1994.

U.S. Bureau of the Census. *Annual Survey of Manufactures.* Washington: GPO, 1997.

U.S. Bureau of the Census. *1995 Census of Manufactures.* Washington: GPO, 1997.

U.S. Department of Commerce. International Trade Administration. *U.S. Industrial Outlook 1994.* Washington: GPO, 1994.

Ward's Business Directory of U.S. Private and Public Companies. Detroit: Gale Research 1997.

—Jim Cuene, updated by Kenneth R. Shepherd

SIC 2517

WOOD TELEVISION, RADIO, PHONOGRAPH, AND SEWING MACHINE CABINETS

This category covers establishments primarily engaged in manufacturing wood cabinets for radios, television sets, phonographs, and sewing machines.

Comprised of companies principally employed in manufacturing wood cases for audio and visual equipment, this industry produces such products as wooden speaker boxes, stereo cabinets, sewing machine cases, and television cabinets. It is part of the larger household furniture industry. About 60 percent of industry output in the early 1990s consisted of TV cabinets, or cases for combinations of TV, stereo, or radio. Stereo and radio cabinets constituted 20 percent of the market. Wooden sewing machine cases accounted for only 3 percent of industry sales, and miscellaneous items comprised the remainder of revenues. Radio and television manufacturers consumed nearly 85 percent of industry production in the early 1990s. Personal consumption expenditures represented less than 8 percent of sales.

A limited market existed for sewing machine cases and radio cabinets early in the twentieth century. Not until after World War II, however, did the U.S. wooden cabinet business emerge as a small industry. A consumer spending boom, boosted by a surging demand for television cabinets beginning in the 1950s, resulted in healthy industry growth throughout the 1950s, 1960s, and much of the 1970s. Indeed, by the early 1980s, television and radio cabinet producers were shipping more than $300 million worth of products per year and employing about 7,000 workers.

Although industry sales swelled to nearly $400 million in 1984, the industry was destined for failure. The two primary culprits of imminent demise were foreign competition and plastic. As imports of consumer electronics into the United States, particularly from Japan, ballooned throughout the 1980s, domestic demand for TV and radio cabinets plummeted. Even producers that kept factories in the United States were increasingly replacing wood with cheaper, more versatile plastic cabinets.

Wood cabinet sales tumbled at a rate of nearly 9 percent per year between 1984 and 1990, depressing industry revenues below a discouraging $250 million per year. As competitors scrambled to cut costs and increase productivity, the work force was mercilessly slashed by the early 1990s to less than half the size it had been in 1982. To make matters worse, a U.S. economic recession battered the business in the early 1990s, causing some competitors to exit. By 1992, the *Census of Manufactures* reported that the industry had total employment of only 4,500, a 24 percent decline from the 5,900 workers appearing in the 1987 census.

By the mid-1990s, the industry began making a slow recovery. The *1995 Census of Manufactures* reported a constant 4,500 workers in the industry in 1995, with a total payroll of $96.7 million. Although these numbers were about the same as 1992 figures, they nonetheless represented an increase of 4.6 and 7.6 percent, and over the 1994 figures of 4,300 workers and $89.8 million payroll.

Only about 30 producers competed in this industry in the early 1990s. The largest U.S. maker of TV

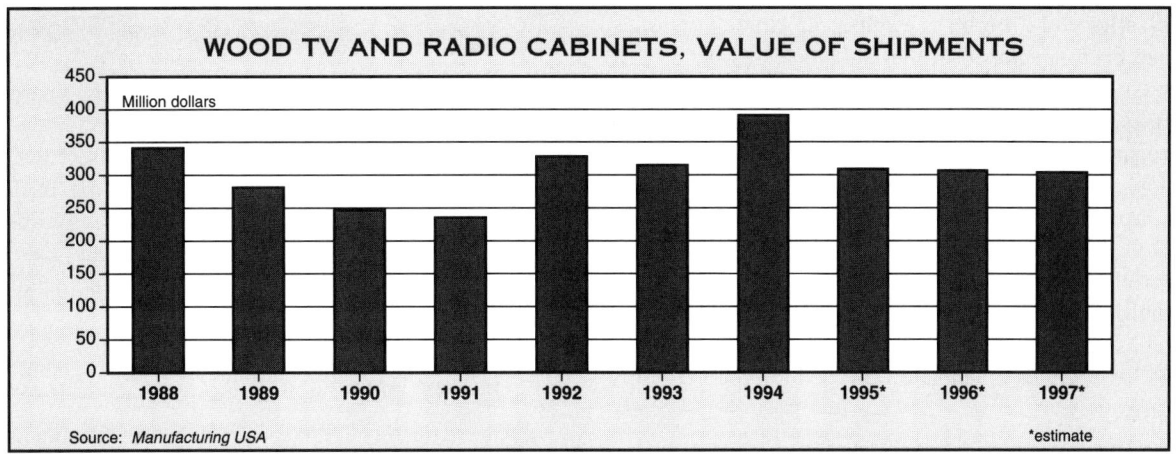

WOOD TV AND RADIO CABINETS, VALUE OF SHIPMENTS

Million dollars

Source: *Manufacturing USA*   *estimate

and radio cabinets was American Quality Manufacturing Corp. Of Arizona. American quality earned $10 million in revenues in the mid-1990s and employed a work force of approximately 400. Panex Corp. of Wisconsin was the second-largest rival, with sales of $4 million and 100 workers. Other industry leaders included Cabinet Co., Inc. of Arizona, and JT Parsons I and S Custom Cabinets Inc. of California. Companies with less than 10 employees were excluded from the 1995 census, but they accounted for only 6 percent of the total value of shipments for the industry.

FURTHER READING

Darnay, Arsen J., ed. *Manufacturing USA.* 5th ed. Detroit: Gale Research, 1996.

Standard & Poor's Industry Surveys. New York: Standard & Poor's Corporation, 1994.

U.S. Bureau of the Census. *1995 Census of Manufactures.* Washington: GPO, 1997.

—Dave Mote, updated by Kenneth R. Shepherd

SIC 2519

HOUSEHOLD FURNITURE, NOT ELSEWHERE CLASSIFIED

This industry category includes establishments primarily engaged in manufacturing reed, rattan, and other wicker furniture, plastics and fiberglass household furniture and cabinets, and household furniture not elsewhere classified.

INDUSTRY SNAPSHOT

In the mid-1990s, there were 187 establishments in the industry, an increase of 20 percent since 1990. In 1995, the industry shipped $494 million worth of products, an increase of 4 percent since 1990. There were 5,400 employees in the industry in 1995, a decrease of 29 percent since 1990.

BACKGROUND AND DEVELOPMENT

Wicker, Rattan and Reed Furniture. Wicker furnishings have been used in American households since the seventeenth century. The first known craftsmen to advertise wicker furniture were early nineteenth-century basket weavers. During that period, straw and willow were replaced by rattan, which was imported by the East India Company.

In the mid-nineteenth century wicker furniture, customarily styled with closely woven cane seats and looped reed backs and arms, became increasingly popular. Furniture frames were constructed from hickory and oak pieces that were steamed and bent into shape, then wrapped with split cane. At that time, construction of wicker furniture changed from craft to industry.

Between 1875 and 1910, wicker furniture reached the height of its popularity, in part because of its association with exotic, foreign countries. In 1917, Marshall B. Lloyd invented a wicker-weaving machine that used fiber material—the Lloyd Loom. Concurrently, many wicker manufacturers began to experiment with materials such as prairie grass and fiber. Wire grass, converted into a pliable twine and woven into furniture, was obtained from the prairie marshes of northwest America.

By the end of World War I, the skilled labor needed to weave wicker became scarce in the United States, and imports began replacing domestically manufactured goods. By the close of World War II, almost all wicker furniture sold in America was imported, a situation that continues to this day.

Plastics and Fiberglass Furniture. Although plastics had been developed in the late-nineteenth century, it wasn't until 1909, when the American chemist Leo Baekeland developed Bakelite, that plastics gradually began to replace metal for body-shells in industrial applications. Baekeland, along with two Westinghouse Corporation engineers, Harold Faber and Daniel O'Connor, developed a laminate originally intended for electrical insulation. The development of this formula in 1913, however, eventually resulted in the establishment of the Formica Corporation. By the mid-1920s Formica's laminate was used to produce furniture.

With the demands for light-weight seat furniture brought on by the aircraft industry during World War II, the development of plastics for furniture construction increased. Two early pioneers of American furniture design, Eero Saarinen and Charles Eames, began experimenting with molded polyester in 1941. Saarinen's "Womb" chair, the first fiberglass design to be mass-produced in America, was manufactured by Knoll Associates in 1946. The chair remained in continuous production for over four decades. In 1950 New York's Museum of Modern Art held an exhibition entitled "Organic Design in Home Furnishings." The prize-winning fiberglass armchair, designed by Charles Eames, was manufactured by the Herman Miller Furniture Company. Eames' molded plastic chair series, which also included a stacking chair, became one of the most basic and popular lines of American seating furniture.

INDUSTRY LEADERS

Krause's Furniture Inc. is one of the leading companies in the industry, with 1996 sales of $122 million. Other major players in the industry include O'Sullivan Industries, Inc. and Sealy Corporation.

FURTHER READING

Garner, Philippe. *Twentieth Century Furniture.* London, England: Adkonson Parrish Ltd., 1980.

Lucie-Smith, Edward. *A History of Industrial Design.* Oxford, England: Phaidon Press Ltd., 1983.

Menz, Katherine. *Nineteenth Century Furniture.* New York: Art & Antiques Books, 1982.

Pushkaf, Robert. "Cyrus Wakefield's Smart Idea." *Yankee,* June 1997, 56+.

Sparke, Penny. *Design in Context.* London, England: Quarto Publishing, 1987.

U.S. Department of Commerce. 1995 Annual Survey of Manufactures. Washington: GPO, 1997.

—David Sprinkle, updated by Kenneth R. Shepherd

WOOD OFFICE FURNITURE

This classification covers establishments primarily engaged in manufacturing office furniture made chiefly of wood, including benches, bookcases, cabinets, chairs, desks, filing boxes and cabinets, panel furniture systems, stools, tables, partitions, and modular furniture systems.

INDUSTRY SNAPSHOT

Approximately 2,300 wood office furniture manufacturers operated in this industry during 1996. This number has dropped slightly since the early 1990s, partly due to fierce competition in domestic and foreign markets as well as a flurry of mergers and acquisitions among some of the biggest names in the business. The majority of wood office furniture manufacturers—around 90 percent—posted sales of less than $5 million in the mid-1990s.

According to the Business and Institutional Furniture Manufacturers Association International (BIMFA), a leading trade group, shipments for the office furniture industry as a whole were worth $9.4 billion in 1995, the last year for which complete figures were available. Wood products consistently make up about one-quarter of this total. In 1995, that amounted to approximately $2.35 billion. This was up from an industry total of almost $8.8 billion in 1994 and $8.2 billion in 1993. Preliminary figures for 1996 indicated that U.S. office furniture manufacturers saw a 6.4 percent increase in shipments over 1995, pushing the total value of U.S. office furniture shipments to $10.04 billion.

While these increases were not as high as some of those posted in the late 1970s and early 1980s, when the office furniture industry enjoyed an annual average growth rate of 19 percent, they represented a slow but steady recovery from the recession of the early 1990s. In 1990, for example, office furniture shipments increased by only 0.5 percent to $7.87 billion. The following year saw shipments drop by 8.1 percent to $7.2 billion. Growth since then has remained in the vicinity of 6.5 percent, with the exception of 1994, when the value of office furniture shipments posted a gain of 8.5 percent.

ORGANIZATION AND STRUCTURE

West Michigan—most notably in and around the cities of Grand Rapids and Holland—is home to office furniture manufacturing giants Steelcase Inc. (whose product line focuses on non-wood rather than wood furniture), Haworth Inc., and Herman Miller Inc., as well as a number of other firms. As a result, the area can boast that its facilities produce about 65 percent of all office furniture manufactured in North America. This dominance can be attributed to two factors—an abundant supply of good quality hardwood in Michigan forests during the industry's early years and the availability of highly skilled woodworkers.

When wood was still the material of choice for most manufacturers, stationery stores and office equipment dealers handled sales of office furniture. The concept of "office design" was unheard of; companies purchased desks and other pieces as needed, setting them up in rows in big, open spaces, creating an office environment that very much resembled a classroom.

Later, as the demand for office furniture increased and the market became more specialized and sophisticated, the major manufacturers developed their own sales staffs and dealer networks to handle large-scale orders. In addition, the introduction of new products such as computer desks and "systems furniture" (consisting of panels and other pieces that could be easily moved and reconfigured to accommodate changing needs) generated a need for office designers. So the bigger firms began to offer design assistance to customers eager to get the most out of their furniture purchases. Smaller companies that were unable to support their own sales and design staffs turned instead to manufacturers' representatives to provide the same services to customers.

In the 1990s, while a few manufacturers still sold directly to customers, most relied on other means of distribution. For example, contract office furniture dealers—those specializing in large-scale orders placed with industry giants such as Haworth—handled nearly 65 percent of all office furniture sales in 1994, according to a joint survey conducted by BIFMA and Business Products Industry Association (BPIA). The remaining 35 percent of sales were divided fairly evenly among six other categories: budget to mid-market furniture dealers; office product dealers; superstores, warehouse clubs, and other mass merchandisers; wholesalers; government; and mail order, direct sales, and other channels. Superstores, warehouse clubs, and other mass merchandisers showed the strongest growth from 1993 until 1994, increasing from 2.8 percent of the total to 4.1 percent.

Office furniture manufacturers of all kinds showcase their newest products and services at a number of trade shows around the country, most notably the NeoCon World's Trade Fair. Held annually at the Merchandise Mart in Chicago, it is billed as North America's largest commercial interiors exposition.

BACKGROUND AND DEVELOPMENT

The wood office furniture industry first began to take shape in the late nineteenth century, a period of rapid industrial growth in the United States. This industrial growth—along with technical innovations such as the elevator, the typewriter, and the telephone—sparked a corresponding increase in the number of people working in offices. Manufacturers of residential furniture soon began to notice that more of their desks, tables, and bookcases were being put to use in a business setting. Some of them responded by designing and building pieces specifically suited to the needs of this new kind of employee, thus establishing office furniture as a separate segment of the overall furniture industry.

Wood dominated the market until the 1930s, when metal filing cabinets and desks became popular (and cheaper) substitutes for the old wooden models. The military's need for steel briefly interrupted this trend during World War II, but in the postwar years, metal office furniture once again reasserted itself as a serious threat to wood. Both sides responded by launching aggressive marketing campaigns emphasizing the advantages of their respective products.

The rivalry between the two camps gradually eased, however, as wood office furniture manufacturers began to incorporate steel parts in their designs, and metal office furniture manufacturers began to feature wooden tops. By the early 1960s, the distinctions between the two industries had blurred to the point where the wood furniture manufacturers dissolved the trade association they had originally established to distinguish themselves from metal office furniture manufacturers. In 1973, office furniture manufacturers of all types officially recognized their common interests and concerns by joining forces in a single trade organization, BIFMA International. By 1997, BIFMA represented over 140 North American office furniture-manufacturing companies located throughout the United States, Canada, and Mexico.

Growth was especially strong in the office furniture industry in the late 1970s and early 1980s, with average annual sales gains of 19 percent. Beginning in the late 1980s, however, significant white-collar downsizing in a number of Fortune 500 companies had a marked impact on office furniture manufacturers—fewer employees translated into less need for new desks, chairs, and other equipment. A recession in 1991-1992 added to the industry's troubles, resulting in a drop of 8.5 percent in the value of shipments in

1991 over 1990 figures. The picture began to improve a bit in 1993, with shipments of wood office furniture showing a slight increase. Virtually no one, however, was forecasting a return any time soon to the strong growth of the early 1980s.

CURRENT CONDITIONS

Industry analysts continued to be cautiously optimistic in their predictions for the office furniture manufacturing industry as the 1990s drew to a close. Steady interest rates, a moderately growing economy, and low inflation all seemed conducive to a sustained period of modest sales gains in the range of 4 to 5 percent. Nevertheless, many wood office furniture manufacturers began reassessing their markets in the middle of the decade, noting that the strongest demand for office furniture was coming from small companies with limited budgets and a desire to stretch their dollars as far as possible. The high-end products that large corporations typically purchased were simply out of reach for businesses with only a few dozen employees. A number of the major manufacturers responded to the situation by creating new lines of mid- and lower-priced furniture.

Wood office furniture manufacturers also began exploring new niche markets for their products during the 1990s. With an estimated 43 million people doing at least some work out of their homes as of 1996, companies looking for ways to expand their traditional customer base offered more and more pieces intended for home offices. Another growth market was ergonomically designed furniture, which client companies hoped would increase productivity, cut down on the number of repetitive strain injuries and backache (thus curbing health care costs), and reduce the threat of lawsuits from employees with work-related disabilities.

Industry observers also continued to express concern about the common practice of price discounting as much as 50 percent or more in a fiercely competitive market. Because it drains a manufacturer of financial resources, discounting was blamed for the rise in the number of buyouts and mergers that occurred in the office furniture industry during the 1990s. The small company with a foothold in a niche market that a larger competitor wished to enter proved to be especially vulnerable to this kind of takeover. Major acquisitions were made by HON Industries Inc. and Kimball International in 1992, for instance, and by Haworth in 1993 and again in 1995 and 1996. Many companies called for an end to discounting and price wars, listing them among the greatest challenges the industry faced in the 1990s.

In a related action, office furniture manufacturers also joined together to fight for legislation to eliminate the competitive advantage enjoyed by the Federal Prison Industries (FPI) over private companies. By law, whenever the federal government is in the market for office furniture, it must give preference to the FPI and its prison-made products, regardless of cost. As a result, U.S. manufacturers lose tens of millions of dollars in sales every year.

In addition, wood office furniture manufacturers expressed apprehension about the effect of ongoing environmental legislation on their bottom lines. In their factories, they have already incurred increased costs for disposing of hazardous wastes generated by the furniture-finishing process. They also must abide by strict rules governing wood dust levels. In the marketplace, they have faced mounting concerns about the effect of various pollutants on indoor air quality. Under the terms of the Clean Air Act Amendment of 1990, for example, various substances involved in the production of wood furniture are subject to regulation. Most commonly cited are the volatile organic compounds used in finishes and two types of adhesives, urea-formaldehyde resins and contact adhesives. To address these problems, some U.S. wood office furniture companies have switched to water-based finishes and alternative glues, although some of these substitutes performed poorly.

In the mid-1990s, the U.S. Environmental Protection Agency (EPA) launched two major studies of indoor air quality in order to gain a better understanding of the problem in both public and private buildings. Results were not expected until near the end of the decade at which time the EPA will use those findings to develop a set of proposed national guidelines and standards for acceptable levels of indoor air pollutants.

Other challenges office furniture manufactures faced as they headed into a new century included dealing with continued corporate downsizing, adjusting to the increasingly limited supply of wood and the subsequent rising price of wood and wood-based panels, and developing more products for home use in a market that was increasingly dominated by ready-to-assemble (RTA) furniture companies like O'Sullivan Industries, Sauder Woodworking, and Bush Industries. On the labor front, they were also concerned about the shortage of skilled workers (especially wood experts) and the need to work more efficiently to cut manufacturing costs.

INDUSTRY LEADERS

The nation's leading wood office furniture manufacturer is Haworth Inc., a private company that posted nearly $1.4 billion in sales in 1996, up from $1.2 billion in sales in 1995. It ranks as the second-largest general office furniture manufacturer behind Steelcase, which specializes in non-wood products. Teacher Gerrard Haworth started the firm in 1948 in his garage, enjoying modest success with his wood and glass office partitions. But it wasn't until his son Richard patented a prewired, movable office panel in 1975 that sales really began to climb. The innovation made it possible for customers to assemble and disassemble workstations to suit new office arrangements without having to call in an electrician. Before long, Haworth had vaulted into the top ranks of office furniture manufacturers. It has aggressively defended itself against patent infringements by competitors, winning millions of dollars in damages from both Herman Miller and Steelcase over its prewired office panel.

Since 1988, Haworth has pursued an ambitious policy of acquisition, buying up more than a dozen smaller companies at home and overseas to broaden its product base and distribution channels. At the same time, it has paid very close attention to the bottom line. As a result, Haworth enjoys a reputation for being one of the leanest and most profitable businesses in its category, with a solid manufacturing, marketing, and distribution presence throughout the world and a reputation for undercutting its rivals on price. The products manufactured and sold by its 9,000 employees include a full line of systems furniture, desk and guest seating, steel and wood casegoods (bookcases, cabinets, and other pieces that provide interior storage), files, tables, and desks. Haworth makes these items available in nearly all price ranges but is increasingly emphasizing its less expensive lines.

Publicly-traded Herman Miller Inc. holds the number two spot among wood office furniture manufacturers and comes in third among general office furniture manufacturers, with record sales in 1996 of nearly $1.3 billion, up from $1.01 billion in 1995. It began, however, as a residential furniture manufacturer founded in 1923 by D. J. De Pree. He used money borrowed from his father-in-law, Herman Miller, to buy the Star Furniture Company, which had been in existence since 1905. De Pree then renamed the firm in honor of its major shareholder.

Herman Miller struggled to compete with larger local manufacturers during the Depression, most of whom were turning out reproduction pieces. To make his company's offerings stand apart from everyone else's, De Pree introduced a collection of furniture with a distinctively modern flair. Innovative design soon became a hallmark of the Herman Miller line of office furniture, some pieces of which have been cre-

ated by notables such as Charles Eames and Isamu Noguchi.

In the mid-1960s, Herman Miller once again revolutionized the industry by introducing systems furniture. Its panels, storage units, and work surfaces made it simple to rearrange and customize open-plan office spaces. Since then, the company has also devoted considerable research and design efforts toward developing ergonomic seating and other components that fulfill the need for comfortable and multifunctional office furniture. Herman Miller has also branched out into manufacturing furniture for hospitals and other health-care facilities and has entered the residential office furniture market as well with a line called Herman Miller for the Home.

For almost its entire history, Herman Miller has also been known as an unusually progressive firm in terms of its treatment of employees. In 1950, for example, it became one of the first companies in West Michigan to institute a participative management program that made it possible for all workers to be involved in setting goals for the firm, making suggestions for cost-cutting and other improvements, and sharing in the profits. As a result, Herman Miller consistently ranks among the most admired companies in the United States.

The boom in office furniture sales in the 1980s led to record sales at Herman Miller in 1990. But recession hit the following year, and by 1992, the company had posted the first loss in its history. It then began restructuring in an effort to combat the negative impact of the recession and decreased demands for its high-end products. With seven subsidiaries and operations in some forty-five foreign countries that employ 7,000 people, Herman Miller has continued efforts to compete more effectively in the marketplace by cutting jobs (including many in the executive ranks) and shutting down plants that fail to meet performance expectations.

Another notable wood office furniture manufacturer is HON Industries Inc., with 1996 sales of $998 million, an increase of 11.8 percent over the 1995 figure of $893 million. It is a very diversified company that designs and builds mid-priced products for both office and home, including desks, chairs, file cabinets, credenzas, storage units, tables, bookcases, partitions, and panel systems. HON markets its wood office furniture lines under the Gunlocke Company brand name. It also manufactures metal office furniture. Nearly 6,000 people work for HON.

A trend that has traditional office furniture manufacturers looking over their shoulders is the boom in ready-to-assemble (RTA) furniture. A leading player in this particular market is O'Sullivan Industries Holdings Inc. It sells more than three hundred different kinds of business and residential products—including desks and tables, computer stands, credenzas, and cabinets—through office superstores, mass merchants, catalogs, and furniture specialty stores. It employs some 1,800 people and posted 1996 sales of nearly $292 million.

OFFICE FURNITURE INDUSTRY EMPLOYMENT

Employment in thousands

Source: Department of Labor

WORK FORCE

Since 1988, there has been a steady decline in employment in all sectors of the office furniture manufacturing industry, with the wood segment experiencing the most significant losses. After climbing steadily through the early and mid-1980s, the work force fell from 31,000 people in 1987 to 30,800 in 1988. It rose slightly in 1989 to 31,000 before falling to 28,200 in 1990. In 1991, it plunged to 22,500 as a result of the recession that began that year. Among production workers in particular, jobs fell from 24,600 in 1988 to 24,300 in 1989, 22,100 in 1990, and 17,000 in 1991. By the middle of the decade, total employment in the wood office furniture industry appeared to be stabilized at around 28,000.

Since then, the decline in employment has slowed somewhat, with job losses in the office furniture industry as a whole totaling about 2,200 from mid-1995 through mid-1996. The remaining work force consisted of nearly 61,000 people, almost 45,000 of whom were production employees. Average hourly wages for production workers in mid-1996 stood at $10.81.

It appears unlikely that all of the jobs lost in the office furniture industry since the late 1980s will be replaced. Instead, manufacturers are seeking to increase the productivity of existing employees. This disquieting loss of job security coupled with a new

emphasis on bottom-line issues helped spark unionization drives during the 1990s at several West Michigan office furniture manufacturers, whose employees have traditionally shunned unions. In 1993, for instance, the United Steelworkers tried to organize at both Steelcase and Haworth without much success. In 1997, however, the United Auto Workers mounted a campaign at Haworth that attracted far more attention and support.

AMERICA AND THE WORLD

With no rise in demand expected in the U.S. market any time soon, wood office furniture manufacturers have been looking overseas to increase their sales. Results have been lackluster at best; as of the mid-1990s, the major firms had yet to see much in the way of profits from their foreign divisions, often because of economic and political instability in certain markets.

The passage of the North American Free Trade Agreement (NAFTA) in 1993 opened the doors to anticipated heavier volume of office furniture imports and exports. Overall, however, imports and exports of wood and non-wood office furniture continued to make up a fairly small percentage of total industry shipments. According to BIFMA, U.S. office furniture imports in 1995 totaled $797 million, and exports totaled $299 million. Canada ranks as the country's main trading partner. In 1995, it received about 38 percent of all U.S. office furniture exports and provided more than 60 percent of all office furniture brought into the United States.

RESEARCH AND TECHNOLOGY

In response to management trends stressing teamwork, ongoing corporate downsizing, concerns about occupational-related injuries, and the increasing number of people working out of their homes, office furniture manufacturers are devoting many of their research dollars to the development of multifunctional, ergonomically-designed products. In larger offices, for example, cubicle clusters and movable panels are out in favor of a more open, less isolated environment that encourages people to work together and makes it physically easier for them to do so. Also growing in popularity are adjustable work surfaces and components that can serve many uses to accommodate workers whose jobs are no longer quite so narrowly defined as they might have been in the past. Designing all of these products to work better with rapidly-changing computer technology is also a top priority.

Ergonomics is in the forefront, too, as employers and manufacturers both seek ways to comply with federal mandates (some resulting from the 1990 Americans with Disabilities Act) and ward off lawsuits filed by workers suffering from job-related aches and pains. The emphasis is on adjustability, such as motorized tables with multiple height settings to accommodate a person who is standing or sitting and chairs that come in several sizes to fit a wide range of body types.

The need many people have for a comfortable and functional home office has also led to creative new products from the design centers of U.S. manufacturers. Flexibility and good looks are especially important to this market, given that office space may be very limited and any pieces must blend well with home furnishings. So manufacturers are putting work centers and other components on wheels for portability, inventing desks that fold out or swing open for working and then close up to hide office equipment, and creating adjustable tables that can do double-duty as coffee tables or typing tables.

FURTHER READING

Adams, Larry. "Blockbuster Deals Usher Out 1995." *Wood and Wood Products,* February 1996.

Adams, Larry. "Overall, Wood Industry Stronger in '93 Than '92: Industry Overview." *Wood and Wood Products,* November 1993.

"Adhesives are 'Last Minute' Inclusion in Reg-Neg." *BIFMA,* October 1993.

"Are You Suited Comfortably?" *Management Today,* January 1995.

"BIFMA Reflects on the Issues of the Day." *Wood and Wood Products,* February 1996.

BIFMA International web site. Available from http://www.bifma.com.

Blake, Laura. "Dealers Compete Against New Distribution Options." *Grand Rapids Business Journal,* 12 June 1995.

Blake, Laura. "Industry Forecast Shows 4 Percent Growth." *Grand Rapids Business Journal,* 12 June 1995.

Brown, Christie. "You Say 65 Percent Off, They Say 71 Percent." *Forbes,* 20 May 1996

Christianson, Rich, and Larry Adams. "Back on Growth Track." *Wood and Wood Products,* February 1995.

"Clean Air Negotiations Status Update: Reg-Neg Reaches Tentative Agreements." *BIFMA News,* December 1993.

Crook, David, and John Pierson. "New Products Bring Office Work Home." *The Wall Street Journal,* 15 November 1996.

Derning, Sean. "Economy Still Top Concern of Contract Furniture Manufacturers." *Wood and Wood Products,* February 1993.

"Furniture Mart Reels from Layoffs." *Purchasing,* 20 April 1995.

Ghering, Mike. "Cubicle Clusters Out, 'Teaming' Panels Up." *Grand Rapids Business Journal,* 28 October 1996.

Haworth Inc. web site. Available from http://www.haworth-furn.com.

Herman Miller Inc. web site. Available from http://www.hmiller.com.

Jackson, Maggie. "Doing Right Can Be Financially Rewarding." *Grand Rapids Press,* 23 February 1997.

Kleeman, Walter B., Jr. "One Hundred Years of Wood Office Furniture Design." *Wood and Wood Products,* Special Annual Issue, 1995.

Novack, Janet. "Ergonomical Correctness." *Forbes,* 24 October 1994.

Palmer, Keasha. "No Place Like Home Office." *Grand Rapids Press,* 9 February 1997.

Tunison, John. "Furniture Firms Get Help from Lawmakers." *Grand Rapids Press,* 22 February 1997.

Veverka, Amber. "Office Furniture Sales to Rise at Slower Pace." *Grand Rapids Press,* 26 January 1997.

Veverka, Amber, and Kyla King. "Union Drive Gets Serious at Haworth." *Grand Rapids Press,* 27 February 1997.

—Kerstan B. Cohen, updated by Deborah Gillan Straub

SIC 2522

OFFICE FURNITURE, EXCEPT WOOD

This category describes establishments primarily engaged in the manufacturing of office furniture, except furniture chiefly made of wood. Establishments primarily engaged in manufacturing safes and vaults are classified in **SIC 3499: Fabricated Metal Products, Not Elsewhere Classified.** The products manufactured by the industry include office benches, bookcases, chairs, cabinets, desks, filing cabinets, modular furniture systems, panel furniture systems, office partitions, stools, tables, and wall cases.

INDUSTRY SNAPSHOT

Approximately 900 office furniture manufacturers specializing in non-wood products were in business during 1996. Nearly 30 percent of these firms were large-scale enterprises with more than $5 million in annual sales during the mid-1990s, while industry leaders earned substantially more than that.

According to the Business and Institutional Furniture Manufacturers Association (BIFMA) International, a trade group that represents more than 140 North American office furniture manufacturing companies, shipments for the office furniture industry as a whole were worth $9.4 billion in 1995, the last year for which complete figures were available. Nonwood products consistently make up about 75 percent of this total. In 1995, that amounted to approximately $7.05 billion. This was up from an industry total of almost $8.8 billion in 1994 and $8.2 billion in 1993. Preliminary figures for 1996 indicated that U.S. office furniture manufacturers saw a 6.4 percent increase in shipments over 1995, pushing the total value of U.S. office furniture shipments to $10.04 billion.

While these increases were not as substantial as some of those posted in the late 1970s and early 1980s, when the office furniture industry enjoyed an annual average growth rate of 19 percent, they represented a slow but steady recovery from the recession of the early 1990s. In 1990, for instance, office furniture shipments increased by only 0.5 percent to $7.87 billion. The following year saw shipments drop by 8.1 percent to $7.2 billion. Growth since then has remained in the vicinity of 6.5 percent, with the exception of 1994, when the value of office furniture shipments posted a gain of 8.5 percent.

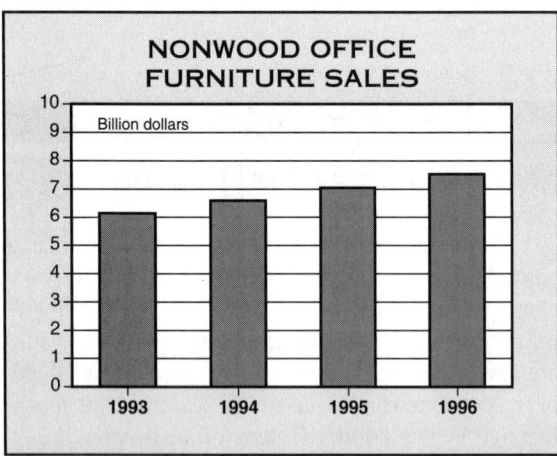

NONWOOD OFFICE FURNITURE SALES

ORGANIZATION AND STRUCTURE

West Michigan—most notably in and around the cities of Grand Rapids and Holland—is home to office furniture manufacturing giants Steelcase Inc., Haworth, Inc., and Herman Miller, Inc., as well as a number of other firms. (Product lines at both Haworth and Herman Miller tend to focus more on wood office furniture, although the companies do produce nonwood pieces as well.) As a result, the area boasts facilities that produce about 65 percent of all office furniture manufactured in North America.

When wood was still the material of choice for most manufacturers, stationery stores and office equipment dealers handled sales of office furniture. The

concept of "office design" was unheard of; companies purchased desks and other pieces as needed, setting them up in rows in big, open spaces, creating an office environment that very much resembled a classroom.

Later, as the demand for office furniture (including new nonwood products) increased and the market became more specialized and sophisticated, the major manufacturers developed their own sales staffs and dealer networks to handle large-scale orders. In addition, the introduction of new products such as computer desks and "systems furniture" (consisting of panels and other pieces that could be easily moved and reconfigured to accommodate changing needs) generated a need for office designers. So the bigger firms began to offer design assistance to customers eager to get the most out of their furniture purchases. Smaller companies that were unable to support their own sales and design staffs turned instead to manufacturers' representatives to provide the same services to customers.

In the 1990s, while a few manufacturers still sold directly to customers, most relied on other means of distribution. For example, contract office furniture dealers—those specializing in large-scale orders placed with industry giants such as Steelcase—handled nearly 65 percent of all office furniture sales in 1994, according to a joint survey conducted by BIFMA and the Business Products Industry Association (BPIA). The remaining 35 percent of sales were divided fairly evenly among six other categories: budget to mid-market furniture dealers; office product dealers; superstores, warehouse clubs, and other mass merchandisers; wholesalers; government; and mail order, direct sales, and other channels. Superstores, warehouse clubs, and other mass merchandisers showed the strongest growth from 1993 until 1994, increasing from 2.8 percent of the total to 4.1 percent.

Office furniture manufacturers of all kinds showcase their newest products and services at a number of trade shows around the country, most notably the NeoCon World's Trade Fair. Held annually at the Merchandise Mart in Chicago, it is billed as North America's largest commercial interiors exposition.

BACKGROUND AND DEVELOPMENT

Until the 1930s, wood dominated the office furniture market. Then metal filing cabinets and desks emerged as popular, cheaper substitutes for the old wooden models. The military's need for steel briefly interrupted this trend during World War II, but in the postwar years, the metal office furniture industry launched an aggressive marketing campaign touting the advantages of its products, emphasizing durability and safety (offices filled with wood furniture posed a fire hazard). The rivalry between the two camps gradually eased, however, as wood office furniture manufacturers began to incorporate steel parts in their designs, and metal office furniture manufacturers began to feature wooden tops.

As recently as the 1950s, American offices and office furniture were generally drab, stark, and purely functional. Beginning in the late 1960s and early 1970s, however, office design, layout, and furniture began to be influenced by modern ideas of worker productivity and the realization that a link existed between employee performance and the quality of the office environment.

From the late 1970s through the early 1980s, office furniture sales grew by an average of 19 percent annually, according to BIFMA. The boom was fueled by the rapid growth of the white-collar workforce, especially in the computer industry and other information-related fields. These sales were largely driven by the demand for ''systems furniture,'' or mix-and-match cabinets, desks, and wall panels or partitions. Changing work habits had created a need for such products. For example, the rise of computers and related hardware helped spawn new types of workstations, printer tables, and movable walls and partitions that made it easy to reconfigure office space. Prewired partitions, which first appeared in the mid-1970s, facilitated wiring and networking of computers.

Beginning in the late 1980s, however, the entire office furniture industry felt the impact of white-collar downsizing at many firms. A recession in 1991-92 also hit furniture manufacturers extremely hard. From 1986 until 1992, average annual sales growth stood at just under 3 percent. Shipments for the metal office furniture manufacturing industry fell from $6.2 billion in 1989 to $5.6 billion in 1991. Exports, which had doubled between 1988 and 1989 from $86.7 million to $170.8 million, fell during this period as well.

The recession led to even more layoffs among office workers as one company after another downsized. Office space, which had mushroomed during the boom years of the 1980s when demand was high, sat vacant. As a result, few new offices were built during the late 1980s and early 1990s, which meant less demand for new office furniture. Corporations desperately searching for ways to save money began to regard new office furniture as a luxury item rather than a necessity. The weak economy eventually forced some office furniture manufacturing companies out of business, especially those that specialized in high-end products. To remain competitive, surviving manufacturers were forced to reduce their own staffs and increase productivity.

The economic picture began to brighten a bit in 1993, when office furniture sales hit $8.1 billion, a 5.1 percent increase over the previous year's sales figure of $7.7 billion. The improved fortunes of office furniture manufacturers in the mid-1990s reflected an overall upswing in the economy, including a surge in nonresidential building starts and falling unemployment rates. No one, however, envisioned a return to the boom years of the early 1980s.

CURRENT CONDITIONS

As the 1990s neared an end, analysts expressed guarded optimism about the future prospects and performance of the office furniture manufacturing industry. Steady interest rates, a moderately growing economy, and low inflation all seemed conducive to a sustained period of modest sales gains in the range of 4 to 5 percent. Yet the industry continued to suffer from too many suppliers competing for increasingly few customers. In fact, manufacturers were routinely forced to discount their prices by as much as 50 percent or more on high-volume purchases in order to win lucrative contracts.

Because most manufacturers realized that they could not necessarily compete on product alone, they began coming up with ways to provide more services to their customers. Terms such as ''value-added partnering'' became part of the industry lingo. This was just one way that the higher-end manufacturers tried to distinguish themselves from their lower-end rivals.

Another change since the early 1990s focused on distribution. Many of the industry leaders, including Steelcase, Haworth, and Herman Miller, switched to dedicated dealers. Others, including HON Industries, moved in the opposite direction and distributed their products through office supply superstores and other discount outlets.

Another strategy that high-end manufacturers in particular adopted as they reassessed their market involved acquiring smaller companies that already had a foothold in growing niche markets. For example, with an estimated 43 million people doing at least some work out of their homes as of 1996, companies eager to expand their traditional customer base offered more and more workstations, chairs, shelving units, file cabinets, and other components designed for the home office.

Ready-to-assemble (RTA) furniture also captured the attention of some industry leaders. In late 1993, for example, Haworth purchased Globe Business Furniture, an RTA supplier specializing in partially assembled chairs. Globe's sales grew an average of 25 percent between 1981 and 1992, making it an attractive acquisition for a company like Haworth that was intent on broadening its product line to include lower-priced furniture. Industry experts expected the trend to continue, but they warned producers against moving to RTA as a quick-fix method for regaining market share, in part because RTA requires an entirely different cost structure than that used by traditional office furniture manufacturers.

Also lucrative was the market for ergonomically designed office furniture that offered maximum comfort and flexibility. As people became more aware of computer-related, white-collar occupational hazards such as repetitive strain injury, carpal tunnel syndrome, backache, and other ailments, they demanded furniture that will prevent or lessen the severity of these injuries. Office furniture manufacturers were at the forefront of the drive to design and produce ergonomic office furniture that their customers hoped would increase productivity, curb health care costs, and reduce the threat of lawsuits from employees with work-related disabilities.

Sales of high-end products, such as workstations that adjust to let users sit or stand while they work and position computer monitors and keyboards at various levels, helped to propel growth in the industry. Demand for less expensive ergonomic furniture was also strong. Small companies concerned about liability for their employees' work-related injuries were often unable to afford traditional high-priced ergonomic furniture. Companies responded to this dilemma by coming out with new mid- and lower-priced lines that offered some adjustability.

The major players in the office furniture industry diversified their operations in other ways as well. In 1994, Steelcase announced plans to establish a consulting and service management subsidiary called Tangerine that would help companies identify their workplace needs, both on- and off-site, and then cater to those needs. This move by the industry leader underscored its recognition of the changing nature of the workplace.

Among the more pressing issues faced by the office furniture manufacturing industry in the 1990s was the growth of Federal Prison Industries (FPI), a program that employs prisoners to make various kinds of products, including office furniture. By law, whenever the federal government is in the market for office furniture, it must give preference to FPI and its prison-made products, regardless of cost. As a result, U.S. manufacturers lost tens of millions of dollars in sales every year. With BIFMA, office furniture manufactur-

ers joined together to fight for legislation to end the competitive advantage enjoyed by the FPI over private companies.

In addition, office furniture manufacturers expressed apprehension about the effect of ongoing environmental legislation on their bottom lines. In their factories, they have already incurred increased costs for disposing of hazardous wastes generated by the furniture-finishing process. In the marketplace, they have faced mounting concerns about the effect of various pollutants on indoor air quality. Among the most common offenders are formaldehyde (from pressed wood products), adhesives, and paints and other finishes. To address these problems, some U.S. office furniture manufacturers switched to different kinds of finishes and alternative glues, although some of these substitutes performed poorly.

In the mid-1990s, the U.S. Environmental Protection Agency (EPA) launched two major studies of indoor air quality in order to gain a better understanding of the problem in both public and private buildings. Results are not expected until near the end of the decade. The EPA was to use those findings to develop a set of proposed national guidelines and standards for acceptable levels of indoor air pollutants.

Other challenges office furniture manufactures faced as they headed toward a new century included dealing with continued corporate downsizing and developing more products for home use in a market that was increasingly dominated by ready-to-assemble (RTA) furniture companies like O'Sullivan Industries, Sauder Woodworking, and Bush Industries. On the labor front, they were also concerned about the shortage of skilled workers and the need to work more efficiently to cut manufacturing costs.

INDUSTRY LEADERS

The top company in the U.S. office furniture manufacturing industry is Steelcase Inc., a privately owned firm that posted sales of $2.6 billion in 1996. This gave Steelcase a 25 percent share of the entire domestic office furniture manufacturing market that year. It has production and service facilities in 15 countries and employs 19,000 people worldwide. Although it specializes in nonwood office furniture, Steelcase also manufactures wood office furniture, panels and partitions, lighting systems, and customized millwork. It even produces computer software that aids in designing office environments.

Steelcase's chief rivals in the high-end office furniture industry are Haworth, Inc. and Herman Miller, Inc. In 1996, Haworth posted nearly $1.4 billion in sales and employed 9,000 people; that same year, Herman Miller reported nearly $1.3 billion in sales and employed 7,000 people. Other leaders in the metal office furniture market include HON Industries Inc., with $998 million in sales and 6,000 employees in 1996, the Knoll Group, HMK Enterprises, and Krueger International.

WORK FORCE

Since 1988, there has been a steady decline in employment in all sectors of the office furniture manufacturing industry, with the wood segment experiencing the most significant losses. When recession struck in the early 1990s, it forced the industry's corporate customers to rethink their priorities and postpone furniture purchases that could be considered luxuries rather than necessities. Office furniture manufacturers responded by targeting their own payrolls for cutbacks. Since then, increased automation and efficiency have also contributed to a reduction in the work force (especially in production), adding to the likelihood that those lost jobs will never be replaced.

At its peak in 1989, the office furniture industry as a whole employed 71,300 people. This fell to 68,000 in 1990, 62,600 in 1991, and 61,900 in 1992. Among production workers in particular, jobs dropped from 52,900 in 1989 to 50,600 in 1990, 46,100 in 1991, and 45,800 in 1992. By the middle of the decade, total employment in the metal office furniture segment of the industry appeared to have stabilized at about 33,500.

Since then, the decline in employment has slowed somewhat, with job losses in the office furniture industry as a whole totaling about 2,200 from mid-1995 through mid-1996. The remaining work force consisted of nearly 61,000 people, almost 45,000 of whom were production employees. Average hourly wages for production workers in mid-1996 stood at $10.81.

The disquieting loss of job security coupled with a new emphasis on bottom-line issues helped spark unionization drives during the 1990s at several West Michigan office furniture manufacturers, whose employees have traditionally shunned unions. In 1993, for instance, the United Steelworkers tried to organize at both Steelcase and Haworth without much success. In 1997, however, the United Auto Workers mounted a campaign at Haworth that attracted far more attention and support.

AMERICA AND THE WORLD

With little hope of a rise in demand for their products in the United States any time soon, the coun-

try's biggest office furniture manufacturers have bolstered their presence overseas. Results have been lackluster at best; as of the mid-1990s, the major firms had yet to see much in the way of profits from their foreign divisions, often because of economic and political instability in certain markets.

The passage of the North American Free Trade Agreement (NAFTA) in 1993 opened the doors to anticipated heavier volumes of office furniture imports and exports. Overall, however, imports and exports of nonwood and wood office furniture continued to make up a fairly small percentage of total industry shipments. According to BIFMA, U.S. office furniture imports in 1995 totaled $797 million and exports totaled $299 million. Canada ranks as the country's main trading partner. In 1995, it received about 38% of all U.S. office furniture exports and provided more than 60% of all office furniture brought into the United States.

RESEARCH AND TECHNOLOGY

In response to management trends stressing teamwork, ongoing corporate downsizing, concerns about occupational-related injuries, and the increasing number of people working out of their homes, office furniture manufacturers are devoting many of their research dollars to the development of multifunctional, ergonomically designed products. In larger offices, for example, cubicle clusters and movable panels are out in favor of a more open, less isolated environment that encourages people to work together and makes it physically easier for them to do so. Also growing in popularity are adjustable work surfaces and components that can serve many uses to accommodate workers whose jobs are no longer quite so narrowly defined as they might have been in the past. Designing all of these products to work better with rapidly changing computer technology is also a top priority.

Ergonomics is in the forefront, too, as employers and manufacturers both seek ways to comply with federal mandates (some resulting from the 1990 Americans with Disabilities Act) and ward off lawsuits filed by workers suffering from job-related aches and pains. The emphasis is on adjustability, such as motorized tables with multiple height settings to accommodate a person who is standing or sitting and chairs that come in several sizes to fit a wide range of body types.

The need many people have for a comfortable and functional home office has also led to creative new products from the design centers of U.S. manufacturers. Flexibility and good looks are especially important to this market, given that office space may be very limited and any pieces must blend well with home furnishings. So manufacturers are putting work centers and other components on wheels for portability, inventing desks that fold out or swing open for working and then close up to hide office equipment, and creating adjustable tables that can do double-duty as coffee tables or typing tables.

FURTHER READING

Adams, Larry. "Blockbuster Deals Usher Out 1995." *Wood and Wood Products,* February 1996.

Becker, Franklin. "The Ecology of New Ways of Working: Non-territorial Offices." *Site Selection,* February 1993.

"BIFMA Reflects on the Issues of the Day." *Wood and Wood Products,* February 1996.

Blake, Laura. "Dealers Compete Against New Distribution Options." *Grand Rapids Business Journal,* 12 June 1995.

Blake, Laura. "Industry Forecast Shows 4 Percent Growth." *Grand Rapids Business Journal,* 12 June 1995.

Brown, Christie. "You Say 65% Off, They Say 71%." *Forbes,* 20 May 1996.

Christianson, Rich, and Larry Adams. "Back on Growth Track." *Wood and Wood Products,* February 1995.

"Competition Hits Office Furniture: Office Products and Business Systems." *Purchasing,* 21 November 1991.

Crook, David, and John Pierson. "New Products Bring Office Work Home." *Wall Street Journal,* 15 November 1996.

Derning, Sean. "Economy Concerns Top Contract Furniture Makers." *Wood and Wood Products,* February 1992.

Derning, Sean. "Economy Still Top Concern of Contract Furniture Manufacturers." *Wood and Wood Products,* February 1993.

"Economic Use of Space, Equipment, and Energy Still Considerations." *Modern Office Technology,* January 1983.

"Furniture Mart Reels from Layoffs." *Purchasing,* 20 April 1995.

Garet, Barbara. "Offices To Go." *Wood & Wood Products Magazine,* August 1992.

Ghering, Mike. "Cubicle Clusters Out, 'Teaming' Panels Up." *Grand Rapids Business Journal,* 28 October 1996.

"High Point Furniture Industries: Nineties Point Furniture in a New Direction." *Managing Office Technology,* July 1993.

Marks, Robert. "Accent on Home Office: Furniture Manufacturers Targeting Market." *The Weekly Home Furnishings Newspaper,* 18 November 1991.

Marks, Robert. "More Demand for RTA Office Products Seen; Ready-to-Assemble Office Furniture." *The Weekly Home Furnishings Newspaper,* 7 January 1991.

Monroe, Linda. "Facilities Challenges in the Information Age." *Buildings,* May 1991.

Mumfor, Steve. "The Straight Facts About Human Factors." *Buildings,* March 1993.

Novack, Janet. "Ergonomical Correctness." *Forbes,* 24 October 1994.

Palmer, Keasha. "No Place Like Home Office." *Grand Rapids Press,* 9 February 1997.

Stepanek, Steven. "Dividing and Conquering with Walls and Partitions: Office Interiors Management." *Buildings,* July 1991.

"Traditional Furniture Manufacturers Buying RTA Vendors to Share in Sales Boom: Ready-to-Assemble Office Furniture." *Discount Store News,* 18 October 1993.

Tunison, John. "Furniture Firms Get Help from Lawmakers." *Grand Rapids Press,* 22 February 1997.

Veverka, Amber. "Office Furniture Sales to Rise at Slower Pace." *Grand Rapids Press,* 26 January 1997.

Veverka, Amber, and Kyla King. "Union Drive Gets Serious at Haworth." *Grand Rapids Press,* 27 February 1997.

—Kerstan B. Cohen, updated by Deborah Gillan Straub

SIC 2531

PUBLIC BUILDING AND RELATED FURNITURE

This category primarily encompasses establishments engaged in manufacturing furniture for public use in schools, theaters, assembly halls, churches, and libraries. Examples of such furniture include bleacher and stadium seating, church pews, library chairs and tables, and blackboards. The public building and related furniture category also includes seating for public conveyances such as automobiles, aircraft, and passenger trains. This category does not include manufacturers of stone furniture, which are classified under **SIC 3281: Cut Stone and Stone Products,** nor does it include those that manufacture concrete furniture, which can be found under **SIC 3272: Concrete Products, Except Block and Brick**

INDUSTRY SNAPSHOT

An estimated 500 establishments were involved in the production of manufactured goods falling under the category of public building and related furniture in the United States. The total value of shipments generated by the industry amounted to over an estimated $6 billion by 1997. The companies that comprised this category differed greatly in structure, marketing strategy, and fiscal health, due to the variegated nature of the classification. Nearly half were smaller firms with less than 20 employees on the payroll, while roughly ten percent were corporate subsidiaries. The majority of companies in the industry were "single establishment companies,'' which were not part of a larger parent corporation.

The variety of products manufactured by the public building and related furniture industry defies a general description of industry outlook. A smaller and less profitable segment of the industry involved the manufacture of church furniture, while providers of car seats to automobile manufacturers were more visible and fiscally sound. While earlier in the twentieth century much of the public seating furniture was made of wood, the incorporation of new technologies such as plastic have radically altered manufacturing processes in this category. Throughout the mid-1990s, many companies were compelled to re-market their products to meet changing demands and a tougher economic situation. Increasingly stringent government regulations in regard to consumer safety and access for the disabled have also forced period changes in the industry.

ORGANIZATION AND STRUCTURE

Most companies in the public building and related furniture industry were comprised of divisions responsible for different steps of the manufacturing process, including research and development, executive decision-making, manufacturing, marketing strategy, and customer support. Many of the products manufactured in the industry were marketed to other companies or institutions, rather than the general public. Automobile seats, for example, were sold to firms specializing in seat frames and exteriors, which, in turn, sold the completed seating unit to automobile manufacturers. Manufacturers commonly advertised in trade journals, such as *Automotive News, Library Journal,* and other publications aimed at executives, buyers, and other upper-level personnel.

During the economic recession of the early 1990s, many public building and related furniture manufacturers focused on customer satisfaction and product reliability as part of their plan to survive in the industry. This represented a particular challenge, as many public building and related furniture manufacturers marketed their products to other companies, rather than the ultimate consumer, making it difficult to gauge product satisfaction.

BACKGROUND AND DEVELOPMENT

Many of the firms engaged in manufacturing public building and related furniture date back to the late nineteenth century. During this period, the Industrial Revolution and the urbanization of America played a key role in the development and growth of the industry, as a variety of new demands for public-use furni-

ture developed. For example, when educational reform in the United States led to the replacement of the one-room schoolhouse with large school buildings in consolidated districts, the subsequent demand for school desks and blackboards was filled by newly formed firms in the industry. Furthermore, newly prosperous industrial magnates founded and endowed hundreds of colleges and universities, necessitating the development of firms that could manufacture and ship seats and desks all over the country. U.S. Steel founder Andrew Carnegie funded the construction of over 2,800 public libraries across the country, and a new niche in the market arose to meet the demand for librarians' desks as well as patron tables and chairs.

The Industrial Revolution was also responsible for major shifts in population from rural regions to larger urban centers and, later, suburban communities. The shift in demographics was compounded by waves of immigrants from Europe, necessitating the construction of new and larger churches to serve the needs of evolving communities. A demand for more interior furniture, such as church pews, accompanied the exponential growth of churches.

The increased popularity of leisure and entertainment activities in the United States also played a key role in the genesis of the public building and related furniture industry. The development of organized community and collegiate sports, such as baseball and football, necessitated the construction of stadiums and arenas able to seat spectators. Moreover, as plays and motion pictures gained popularity, theaters were built in all but the most rural of American cities, and many competed to provide patrons with the most luxurious interiors, including plush seating.

Perhaps most importantly, the development of new technology in the transportation industry augmented the public building and related furniture industry. The growth of a network of railroads in America gave rise to the popularity of passenger rail travel, and companies evolved to provide comfortable seating for the new long-distance traveler. The invention of the automobile and its rapid rise as a major form of transportation necessitated the evolution of a parallel supplier industry for interior automotive equipment, including seats. During the 1950s and 1960s, the increasing affordability of passenger air travel fueled a great demand for new aircraft, with cabin accoutrements and furnishings.

CURRENT CONDITIONS

The 1980s was a period of growth for the public building and related furniture industry. The value of shipments nearly doubled from $1.1 billion in 1982 to

$2 billion in 1987; by 1991 this figure had reached $3.1 billion but showed a small decline from the previous year. In 1995 sales were $2.35 billion for seats for public conveyance (bus, train, etc.), $482.6 million for school furniture, $268.7 million for airplane seats, $223.2 million for chairs and seats and $122.8 million for stadium and bleacher seats. The number of employees in this field jumped from 18,800 in 1982 to 21,800 in 1987, and by 1996 this figure had reached an estimated 33,000. The largest and most competitive companies in this industry were automobile and airline seat manufacturers, which had to possess the working capital and financial solvency to meet the high costs of developing specialty seats built to withstand accidents. Such companies had to invest large sums in research and development, attract well-qualified engineers for product design, and have the promotional budgets to capture greater market share.

INDUSTRY LEADERS

The companies that manufactured public building and related furniture were as diversified as their products. In the automotive industry, the main suppliers of car seats were Johnson Controls, Inc. and Douglas and Lomason Company. Johnson Controls, founded in 1900 and headquartered in Milwaukee, Wisconsin,was a major manufacturer of automobile seats, but was best known as a provider of electronic control systems that regulate heating, cooling and security for commercial buildings. Total sales for the auto segment were $5.31 billion in 1996 while total company sales were $10 billion. The international company employed 70,000. In 1991, Johnson Controls purchased Lahnwerk GmbH, a German company that supplied seat components and metal seat frames to the European auto industry. Two years later it acquired a similar Mexican firm, Grupo Summa. The company's 50 manufacturing plants involved in automotive seating were located in Michigan, Tennessee, and California, as well as in Portugal and Austria. In 1996 the company delivered more than 9 million seats for more than 100 car and truck models. Johnson Controls Automotive Division is the world's largest auto seating supplier for the major car companies. In October of 1996 the company acquired Prince Automotive, which had been a smaller, yet still viable competitor.

The other large supplier of seats to the American automotive industry was Douglas and Lomason Co., a suburban Detroit, Michigan, firm founded in 1902. Douglas and Lomason primarily manufactured stamping and conveyer equipment for the industry. The company's total sales in the early 1990s were $391.2 million, and it had 5,817 employees on its payroll.

Airline seats are an integral part of this industry as a whole. According to early 1990 statistics a row of seats in first class cost approximately $10,000 while a row of seating in coach cost $5,000. Aircraft cabin seating is the largest segment in this industry, and the largest market share was held by BE Aerospace, Weber Aircraft Inc., and Burns Aerospace Corporation. BE Aerospace, with over 2,700 employees, was the largest integrated supplier of aircraft cabin accessories, selling approximately 25 percent of the seat market according to early 1990 figures. Headquartered in Florida, the company was founded in 1987 and expanded in 1992 when it acquired the Connecticut-based aircraft cabin seat company PTC Aerospace. With other acquisitions of cabin supplier firms that produced such components as galley appliances and video monitors, BE Aerospace's sales went from $24 million in 1991 to nearly $233 million by 1996, providing the airline industry with all cabin products except for lighting fixtures and lavatories. Although the demand for new aircraft declined in the early 1990s, BE Aerospace remained a strong leader in the field. Second in sales of aircraft cabin seats was the California-based firm of Weber Aircraft, Inc., which reported 1992-93 sales of $80 million, controlling 19 percent of the market and employing 800. Burns Aerospace Corp., a subsidiary of Eagle Industries, Incorporated, employed 700 and posted sales of $80 million, representing 16 percent of the market.

The largest supplier of library furniture in the 1990s was Gaylord Brothers, a Syracuse, New York, firm dating back to the end of the nineteenth century. Gaylord was started by two brothers, bank clerks, who developed a gummed parchment that they marketed to libraries for use in repairing books. When the business turned a profit in 1909, the Gaylord brothers quit the bank and developed their company into a full-service provider for American libraries. Their products included book shelving systems, magazine display units, storage facilities, librarians' desks, and patron chairs and tables. Gaylord Brothers, which became a subsidiary of the Croydon Company, marketed its products by catalog. By 1997 the company boasted over 11,000 different items in its product line.

WORK FORCE

In the public building and related furniture industry, the majority of jobs were concentrated in the actual manufacturing process. In 1995 the total number of jobs was 42,000 for the industry, with production workers accounting for 33,400 positions in that figure. The average hourly earnings for production workers in the industry was $10.15.

AMERICA AND THE WORLD

In the public building and related furniture industry, seating for public conveyances such as automobiles and airline cabins represents the most common export. The costs for importing other types of furniture, such as classroom or stadium seating, proved prohibitive for many foreign manufacturers that already had successful domestic furniture industries. American automotive seat suppliers such as Johnson Controls faced domestic competition from Japanese firms such as Atoma and Toyo Seat USA, and have made acquisitions to expand into a lucrative foreign automobile market.

RESEARCH AND TECHNOLOGY

Government regulations have prompted the development of new technologies in the public building and related furniture industry, particularly in automotive and airline seat manufacturing. Minimum criteria for car seats, set by the National Highway Traffic Safety Administration (NHTSA), stipulated that seats not have parts that might injure drivers or passengers on impact and that the seat withstand the force of a crash up to a specified gravitational force, requiring seat frames made of particularly resilient material attached firmly to the car floor.

Auto seat manufacturers were also concerned with the seat's overall performance in terms of comfort, durability, and appearance. As changing demographic patterns engendered longer commuting times for many consumers, the average amount of time spent sitting in a car seat increased. In response, researchers measured the amount of lumbar support various types of seat cushions provided, developing two methods used in the suspension of automotive seats. The most common type of seat consisted of foam block, a combination of a polyurethane cushion and springs, while another featured a light platform supported by a system of springs.

Governmental regulations, issued by the Federal Aviation Administration (FAA) and the National Transportation Safety Board (NTSB), also affected the industry. Due to the potential for extremely high impact crashes in air travel, regulations on aircraft cabin seat construction was more stringent than for any other area of the public building and related furniture industry. Initially, the industry resisted modifications of cabin seating, complaining that heavier anchoring components used to bolt seats to the floor added too much weight to the aircraft. However, the development of new technology and materials in the 1980s allowed for seats that could withstand up to 9g in gravitational force. In 1988 the FAA ruled that all newly certified aircraft be outfitted with such seats, and

proposed that all seats aboard U.S. aircraft meet a 16g requirement by 1995. In accordance, most seat manufacturers, including Weber, had switched production to the 16g seats by 1990.

The fabric used in aircraft cabin seats was also regulated, ensuring cushions that were fire retardant and able to serve as floatation devices. Furthermore, regulatory officials continued to monitor the number and placement of seats on a given aircraft, a procedure that directly affected the profits of both the airline industry and the public building and related furniture industry. Some innovations in airline seating expected to be developed toward the end of the century included seats featuring attached shoulder harnesses, as well as seats that could rotate the passenger's legs upward and out of danger in the event of a crash.

FURTHER READING

Berry, John. ''The Past Defines the Present at Gaylord. '' *Library Journal,* 15 April 1991.

Edwards, Mary, and Elwyn Edwards. *The Aircraft Cabin: Managing the Human Factors.* Brookfield, VT: Gower Publishing, 1990.

Flint, Perry. ''BE Aerospace Breaks the Mold. '' *Air Transport World,* September 1993.

Johnson Controls Annual Report 1996. Available from http://www.jci.com/annual-report.

Lazich, Robert S. *Market Share Reporter.* Detroit: Gale Research, 1997.

''Measuring Seat Comfort. '' *Automotive Engineering,* July 1993.

Meier, Barry. ''Airlines Phasing in Safer Plane Seats. '' *New York Times,* 2 June 1990.

Ott, James. ''Seat Manufacturers Seek Ways to Meet New Criteria. '' *Aviation Week and Space Technology,* 23 November 1992.

—Carol Brennan, updated by Jennifer L. Stong

SIC 2541

WOOD OFFICE AND STORE FIXTURES, PARTITIONS, SHELVING, AND LOCKERS

This category covers establishments primarily engaged in manufacturing shelving, lockers, and office and store fixtures, plastics laminated fixture tops, and related fabricated products, chiefly of wood. It also includes prefabricated partitions made of wood if they are designed to be attached to floor; if they are designed to be free-standing or part of an office furniture panel system, they are classified under **SIC 2521: Wood Office Furniture.** This category excludes wooden refrigerated cabinets, showcases, or display cases, which are found under **SIC 3585: Refrigeration and Heating Equipment.**

INDUSTRY SNAPSHOT

As of the mid-1990s, more than 3,900 companies were engaged in the manufacture of wood shelving, partitions, and fixtures for commercial and residential use in the United States. The vast majority of them—nearly 80 percent—were firms of less than 20 employees. About 90 percent of the manufacturers in this category posted sales of less than $5 million in the mid-1990s.

The industry once manufactured many types of products that are now either obsolete or only rarely made, including butcher shop display cases and telephone booths. Other products have become prohibitively expensive both to manufacture and purchase due to the high cost of materials and labor. Nevertheless, many of the firms that supply wood partitions and fixtures are still thriving due to the increased demand for retail shelving and display units made of wood. The industry has also benefited from the development of laminated plastics coatings, which provide a much-used wood surface with increased durability.

ORGANIZATION AND STRUCTURE

Most companies in the wood partitions and fixtures industry were originally organized into divisions reflecting their potential customers. In general, they focused on assembling and retaining a staff of highly skilled woodworkers. Research and development, marketing, and customer support typically did not receive a high priority, especially among smaller firms. Even today, only the largest companies can afford in-house staffs to handle those responsibilities.

Manufacturers of wood partitions, shelving, and fixtures usually reach out to their markets by advertising in trade journals such as *Restaurant Hospitality, Chain Store Age Executive,* and other publications aimed at business owners and managers. They sell to a wide range of customers, including major wholesalers, contract hardware jobbers, display and fixture jobbers, specialty wholesalers, independent hardware distributors, export outlets, government agencies, original equipment manufacturers, national mass merchants, large home centers, and building supply outlets.

BACKGROUND AND DEVELOPMENT

The wood partitions and fixtures industry emerged in the late nineteenth century during a period of tremendous expansion in the U.S. economy. Rapid industrialization attracted large numbers of people to cities, which in turn sparked the development of major urban commercial districts. The proliferation of small specialty shops and large department stores required a huge supply of fixtures for the display of merchandise.

Although they are no longer manufactured, wooden telephone booths once represented a small but important part of the industry. The first one was installed in 1889 outside a bank in Hartford, Connecticut. Western Electric continued to manufacture wooden telephone booths until the late 1940s, when the more durable glass and steel model was invented and went into production. By the 1990s, wooden phone booths were considered collectibles, and some sold for as much as $3,000.

CURRENT CONDITIONS

The wood partitions and fixtures industry was hit hard by recession in the early 1990s, with the value of shipments declining from a 1990 peak of $3.1 billion to $2.8 billion in 1991. In addition to the economic downturn, this decline was attributed in part to the fact that many products became obsolete and simply were no longer manufactured. Furthermore, the growth in the market for plastic imitations of wood as well as the higher costs associated with fabricating real wood products had a significant impact on the overall health of the industry. By 1994, the shipment value increased to $3.4 billion and was expected to reach $4 billion by 1998.

The mid-1990s represented a time of increased prosperity for the nation's wood shelving and fixtures manufacturers. Among their commercial customers, for example, the slow but steady growth of the economy and highly competitive retail atmosphere encouraged merchants to invest in new store fixtures to keep their product displays attractive and up to date. Manufacturers saw increased demand for both customization and flexibility. Retailers wanted a distinctive ''look'' that set them apart from their rivals, yet they were not interested in fixtures that could not be moved or changed to accommodate different kinds of displays, new inventory, or changing seasons of the year.

Although metal fixtures gained popularity for their high-tech look and lower cost, wood was still the material of choice for those who preferred its warmer appeal. The market for combination wood and metal fixtures and shelving also grew during the 1990s, as did the demand for laminates. These gains came at the expense of all-wood products.

Among residential buyers of wood shelving and storage products, manufacturers noted more interest in their products as part of an upscale trend toward customized closet systems and other organizers. According to their research, home owners desired the attractiveness and perceived durability of wood over similar products made of wire, plastic, or other materials.

Sales of wood partitions, fixtures, and shelving are expected to remain strong as long as the economy is stable. Steady interest rates will prompt more retailers to expand their operations, thus creating more demand for products created to display merchandise. And the strong home-improvement market means more home-owners will be seeking out new shelving and storage solutions.

Manufacturers in this category faced a number of challenges as the century neared an end. One of their top concerns was the shortage of highly-skilled wood-workers. Without such workers, manufacturers found it impossible to keep up with production, a situation that in some cases proved to be an obstacle to growth. To help alleviate the problem, some companies started in-house training and apprentice programs.

Another barrier to growth was the increasingly limited supply of wood and wood panels. In particular, the industry's needs for particle board and fiberboard were not being met in the mid-1990s. This helped keep wholesale prices fairly high, but for the most part, manufacturers hesitated to pass along the rising costs to retailers because their customers were so price-conscious.

Health concerns and environmental regulations also affected manufacturers of wood shelving and fixtures. Working in the wood industry brings with it a number of serious risks, including injuries caused by saws and drills and illnesses brought on by wood dust and paint vapors. As a result, companies struggled with high health care costs and a growing number of workers' compensation claims. They also incurred mounting costs for disposing of hazardous wastes generated by the wood finishing process, and they had to abide by strict rules governing wood dust levels in their factories. In addition, manufacturers were subject to regulations aimed at improving indoor air quality, which can be adversely affected by fumes from finishes and adhesives. Yet some of the products that were developed as substitutes performed poorly, as evidenced by glues that failed to hold and less durable finishes.

Finally, wood shelving and fixtures manufacturers in the 1990s were concerned about discounting and low bidding on projects, a practice they believed hurt the industry as a whole. Companies that operated in northern states were especially concerned about what they perceived to be unfair competition from Canada. The favorable exchange rate during the 1990s made it possible for Canadian firms to submit bids on projects that were substantially lower than those of their U.S. rivals.

INDUSTRY LEADERS

One of the largest suppliers of wood partitions, shelving, and fixtures during the 1990s was Knape & Vogt Manufacturing of Grand Rapids, Michigan. Founded in 1906, it employed 1,056 people in 1996 at facilities in four states and two Canadian provinces. It reported sales of $163 million in 1996, a figure that not only included sales of wooden store fixtures and shelving but also those made from materials other than wood as well as drawer slides, hardware items, and miscellaneous furniture components. As a result, only about $80 million of their total sales could be directly attributed to the shelving systems part of their business.

This represented a 3.1 percent drop in sales from the previous year, when Knape & Vogt posted record sales of $168.2 million. The decline was due to a number of factors, including increases in the prices of both particle board and steel, resistance to promotional efforts on the part of mass merchant customers, and transitional problems resulting from a major company restructuring. Sales were expected to rebound in the late 1990s with the introduction of new products, including a wood storage, stacker, and closet system that was Knape & Vogt's first foray into the growing ready-to-assemble (RTA) market.

Another leading manufacturer of wood fixtures was Lozier Corp., based in Omaha, Nebraska. It had sales in the mid-1990s of around $190 million and employed nearly 2,000 people. Smaller firms engaged in the manufacture of wood shelving, panels, and fixtures were Stevens Industries of Teutopolis, Illinois, with 400 employees and mid-1990s sales of about $42 million; Dorfile Storage and Shelving Systems of Memphis, Tennessee, with 550 employees and mid-1990s sales of about $35 million; and Bernhard Woodwork of Northbrook, Illinois, with 70 employees and sales of about $9 million in the mid-1990s.

WORK FORCE

In 1995, 45,200 people were employed in the wood shelving and fixtures industry; this was slightly less than the previous year's total of 44,300. The average hourly wage for production workers in the industry as a whole (both wood and non-wood segments) in 1996 was $11.12.

FURTHER READING

Adams, Larry. "Survey Says: 1995 Looking Good. " *Wood and Wood Products,* March 1995.

Applefeld, Catherine. "Fixture Manufacturers Keep Up with Retailers to Stay Up-to-Date. " *Billboard,* 16 September 1995.

"Customization Enhances Retailer Identity. " *Chain Store Age Executive with Shopping Center Age,* July 1996.

"Finding Shelf Space. " *HFD: The Weekly Home Furnishings Newspaper,* 3 January 1994.

"Fixture Flexibility Is Key: Trend Toward Modular, Customized Units. " *Chain Store Age Executive with Shopping Center Age,* October 1995.

Hill, Dawn. "In Two Reports, Costs Put Drag on Net. " *HFN: The Weekly Newspaper for the Home Furnishing Network,* 15 May 1995.

Hillinger, Charles. "Welcome to the Phone Booth Capital of America. " *Los Angeles Times,* 30 September 1990.

"Knape & Vogt's Quarterly Profits Inch Up. " *HFN: The Weekly Newspaper for the Home Furnishing Network,* 20 February 1995.

Melaniphy, Margie. "Breaking into the RTA Storage Market. " *Wood and Wood Products,* December 1995.

Meyer, Nancy. "Knape Ready to Lead in All Shelving. " *HFD: The Weekly Home Furnishings Newspaper,* 28 March 1994.

—Carol Brennan, updated by Deborah Gillian Straub

SIC 2542

OFFICE AND STORE FIXTURES, PARTITIONS, SHELVING, AND LOCKERS, EXCEPT WOOD

This category covers establishments primarily engaged in manufacturing office and store fixtures, shelving, storage racks, lockers, and related fabricated products, chiefly of materials other than wood. This industry also includes prefabricated partitions if they are designed to be attached to the floor; those designed to be free-standing or part of an office furniture panel system are instead classified in **SIC 2522: Office Furniture, Except Wood.** Establishments primarily engaged in manufacturing refrigerated cabinets, showcases, or display cases, are classified in **SIC 3585: Air-Conditioning and Warm Air Heating Equipment and Commercial and Industrial Refrigera-**

tion Equipment. Companies engaged in manufacturing safes and vaults are classified in **SIC 3499: Fabricated Metal Products, Not Elsewhere Classified.**

INDUSTRY SNAPSHOT

More than 1,800 companies in the United States were engaged in the manufacture of metal shelving, partitions, and fixtures for commercial and residential use during the mid-1990s. About 62 percent of this total consisted of firms with less than 20 employees. Nearly 80 percent of the manufacturers in this category posted sales of less than $5 million in the mid-1990s. This is a thriving industry, due in part to an increased demand for unique store fixtures to showcase products for the burgeoning retail sector of the U.S. economy. By 1998, shipment values are expected to reach $4.3 billion.

BACKGROUND AND DEVELOPMENT

The growth of the metal partitions and fixtures industry in the United States is directly related to both the expansion of the retail segment of the economy and the development of new technology. After World War II, America's rapidly growing suburbs fueled the construction of large retail outlets such as supermarkets and shopping centers. Hand in hand with those changes came an increased demand for shelving and other fixtures to outfit all of those new stores. At the same time, new manufacturing processes made it possible to craft fixtures and partitions from lightweight blends of metal alloys. Soon these began to replace the standard wood fixtures. Metal shelves, cases, garment racks, and other products proved to be very appealing to retailers, who appreciated their affordability and the ease with which they could be moved.

Although manufacturers of nonwood shelving and fixtures experienced tough times in the early 1990s due to a recession, they have since enjoyed several successful years. The highly competitive retail market and steady growth of the economy encouraged merchants to invest in new store fixtures to keep their product displays attractive and up to date. This was as true for the large specialty "superstores," such as Office Max and Builders' Square, as it was for smaller outlets such as grocery stores.

Customization was a key word for retailers seeking a distinctive "look" to set them apart from their competitors. Flexibility was important, too, because few businesses were interested in buying fixtures that could not be moved or changed to accommodate different kinds of displays, new inventory, and changing seasons of the year. Metal wire emerged as a particular favorite because of its high-tech look, although combinations of wire and other materials (mostly wood and plexiglass) had their fans as well. Part of that appeal could be attributed to price—wood shelving and other fixtures tended to be more expensive due to higher costs for both materials and labor. Metal products, on the other hand, could be manufactured quickly and efficiently, often on highly automated assembly lines that relied on robots and the latest computer technology to keep production costs down.

Among residential customers for nonwood shelving, storage components, and fixtures, wire and wire combination products were extremely popular. They were routinely used in closets, kitchens, baths, laundries, and garages and were readily available at a wide variety of retailers. They offered a less expensive alternative to similar wood and laminated wood products, which appealed to a more upscale market.

Growth is expected to continue at a healthy pace in the nonwood shelving and fixtures industry as long as the economy remains stable. Steady interest rates will prompt more retailers to expand, thus creating more demand for products created to display merchandise. And the strong home-improvement market means more homeowners will be seeking new shelving and storage solutions.

INDUSTRY LEADERS

Industry leaders in nonwood shelving and fixtures manufacturing during the mid-1990s included L. A. Darling Co., headquartered in Paragould, Arizona. It posted sales of $165 million and employed 2,700 people. Another large firm was American Seating Co., a privately-owned company based in Grand Rapids, Michigan. During the mid-1990s, it posted sales of about $130 million and employed 1,000 people. St. Louis-based Lee/Rowan Co., a subsidiary of the housewares giant Newell Co., reported 1992 sales figures in the range of $70 million. Another player in this manufacturing category is Stanley-Vidmar, part of the Stanley family of tools and hardware. It employed about 500 people and enjoyed $100 million in sales in the mid-1990s. Cincinnati-based Schulte Corp. is best known as a primary supplier of epoxy-coated shelving units.

WORK FORCE

Employment in the industry remained steady throughout the 1970s. Data for 1977 showed 28,000 people worked in the industry, a number that remained unchanged in a 1982 survey. By 1987, that number increased to 33,500, but the recession and economic restructuring of the early 1990s led to a drop in the

industry's labor force to 31,000 in 1991. The number increased as business picked up again, rising to 35,700 in 1994 and 36,900 in 1995. The average hourly wage for production workers in the industry as a whole (both wood and nonwood segments) in 1996 was $11.12.

FURTHER READING

Applefeld, Catherine. "Fixture Manufacturers Keep Up with Retailers to Stay Up-to-Date. " *Billboard,* 16 September 1995.

"Customization Enhances Retailer Identity. " *Chain Store Age Executive with Shopping Center Age,* July 1996.

Darnay, Arsen J., ed. *Manufacturing USA.* 5th ed. Detroit: Gale Research, 1996.

Dykema, William N. "Successful Retailers Display High Shelf Respect. " *Chain Store Age Executive,* October 1991.

"Fixture Flexibility Is Key: Trend Toward Modular, Customized Units. " *Chain Store Age Executive with Shopping Center Age,* October 1995.

Gill, Penny. "Showers of Bath Storage Lines. " *HFN: The Weekly Newspaper for the Home Furnishing Network,* 13 January 1997.

Hill, Dawn. "Lee/Rowan Targets Mass Retailers. " *HFN: The Weekly Newspaper for the Home Furnishing Network,* 22 January 1996.

Hill, Dawn. "Schulte Adds Wood Laminate. " *Discount Store News,* 7 August 1995.

Hill, Dawn. "Taming the Last Frontier: Garages," *HFN: The Weekly Newspaper for the Home Furnishing Network,* 13 January 1997.

Palmer, Jay. "On the Shelf No More? The Outlook Improves for Knape & Vogt. " *Barron's,* 13 January 1992.

"Schulte Snares Spur Shelving Line Distribution. " *HFD: The Home Furnishings Daily,* 29 March 1993.

Sellers, Pamela. "Kitchen Storage on the Rise. " *HFN: The Weekly Newspaper for the Home Furnishing Network,* 13 January 1997.

"Shelf Makers Look to the '90s," *HFD: The Home Furnishings Daily,* 12 December 1988.

Stankevich, Debby Garbato. "Lee/Rowan Sees New Growth. " *HFD: The Home Furnishings Daily,* 20 September 1993.

—Carol Brennan, updated by Deborah Gillan Straub

SIC 2591

DRAPERY HARDWARE AND WINDOW BLINDS AND SHADES

This category covers establishments primarily engaged in the manufacture of curtain and drapery rods, poles, and fixtures, venetian blinds, horizontal mini-blinds, and vertical blinds in all materials except canvas. Establishments primarily engaged in manufacturing canvas window shades and awnings are classified in **SIC 2394: Canvas and Related Products.**

INDUSTRY SNAPSHOT

Companies engaged in the manufacture of drapery hardware and window coverings have witnessed an astounding demand for their wares since the 1980s, and have introduced many new types of products to satisfy consumer needs. However, U.S. manufacturers in this category face stiff competition from overseas companies that produce cheaper imitations for the consumer market. The trade gap for this industry is amongst the highest.

Drapery hardware sales comprise 17.7 percent of the market, with pleated shades making up an additional 17 percent of sales figures. Early 1990's sales figures show that mini-blinds comprise 38 percent of window-covering sales in the United States, followed by vertical blinds at 24 percent. Wood blinds round out the total at nearly 2 percent of sales. The value of shipments generated by this industry increased from $1.7 billion in 1991 to an estimated $2.3 billion in 1996, a clear indication of the growth in this industry. Correspondingly, the drapery hardware and window blinds industry employed 13,600 workers in 1977, but by 1996 the number of workers employed in the industry had increased to an estimated 20,800.

ORGANIZATION AND STRUCTURE

Many of the U.S. firms that manufacture and sell drapery hardware and window blinds are private companies, but some are subsidiaries of much larger publicly-traded home-furnishings conglomerates. Like other manufacturers, they are comprised of many specific divisions, but one of the largest concerns is in providing consumers with up-to-date and contemporary styles. For this reason research and development departments play an important role in companies engaged in manufacturing drapery hardware and window blinds. This division keeps an eye on general trends in consumer lifestyle patterns, home-furnishing expenditures, and overall color and pattern changes in the interior design industry. Design analysts in the research and development departments look for certain color groups and textures that they believe will appeal to the broadest range of consumers. For instance, in the 1980s dramatic changes in the American lifestyle and consumer spending patterns, with the burgeoning emphasis on high-tech products, refashioned the home environment. A new edginess to interior design was manifested in sharp angles and artificial colors such as mauve. A downturn in the economy in the late 1980s, combined with a growing awareness of the concept of the global village, brought a new palette of colors to the window coverings industry and encouraged the introduction of the wood mini-blind.

In the interior furnishings industry, window blinds fall under the category of home textiles, although they are not specifically textiles. Previously, curtains and drapes, geared to match furniture and bedspreads, were the dominant force in the category, but were replaced by the popularity of mini-blinds beginning in the 1980s and continuing through 1997. Consumers switched from buying pinch-pleated draperies and curtains to mini-blinds accessorized with a "top treatment"—a swath of fabric that matched some other component of the interior. In the industry, mini-blinds, vertical blinds, and pleated shades were first known as "alternative window treatments," to differentiate them from fabric-based draperies and curtains. Yet, by the early 1990s, this "alternative" category achieved retail sales figures of $2.78 billion dollars. Mini-blinds have become a standard in home furnishings. The lower-cost mini-blinds, available at discount and chain retailers have found a booming segment within the industry as a whole.

Manufacturers of mini-blind products are divided over the two segments of the market, vinyl and aluminum. Vinyl blinds cost less to manufacture, do not rattle in the wind, and won't develop bend marks. Yet vinyl blinds are susceptible to flapping on windy days, let a good deal of light through even when completely closed, can become discolored, and have a tendency to lose shape over time. They are popular with consumers, however, because of their low cost, range of standard sizes, relative ease of installation, and ultimate disposability. On the other hand, aluminum blinds are perceived as a much more durable investment. Heavier than vinyl, aluminum blinds do not flap in the breeze, keep out light more effectively, and their colors and finishes will last longer than plastic. Aluminum blinds may scratch a window, however, and can fall victim to dents and creases in its surface. Major manufacturers such as Hunter-Douglas and Levolor concentrate primarily on the custom-made aluminum blind market, and have left the vinyl blind market primarily to overseas manufacturers. However, some companies offer stock aluminum blinds in retail outlets, and may also sell custom-made vinyl blinds. In 1996 reports of unsafe mini blinds, particularly those manufactured overseas led to a massive recall. The mini-blinds were found to contain lead and thus deemed unsafe for home usage, especially those homes with small children. Every retailer took part in the recall by pulling the affected mini-blinds from the shelves and giving customers refunds.

Another large segment of the window coverings industry is newly geared to pleated shades to replace standard mini-blinds and curtains. The pleated shades owe their development in part to new manufacturing processes that produce versatile fabrics in lightweight weaves to allow a great deal of light through, yet also possess insulating properties. The new processes have also introduced a variety of textures. A leading brand in this new segment of the industry is Duette, a brand line manufactured by Hunter-Douglas. The product was introduced in 1985 and proved popular with consumers, in part because the pull cord could be hidden. The company has also introduced another version of the pleated shade under the brand name Silhouette. Wood blinds, with their natural appearance, also occupy a growing segment of the window covering market.

In the field of drapery hardware and window coverings, department stores are the primary retail outlets to consumers, led by the entrenched home-decorating departments of national chains such as J. C. Penney and Sears. However, the larger stores are being jostled in the home-furnishings market by such specialty retailers as Bed Bath and Beyond. These smaller national outlets provide consumers with either in-stock or custom-made window coverings in a large variety of styles, along with accompanying hardware.

BACKGROUND AND DEVELOPMENT

Prior to the mini-blind-dominated era in interior window coverings, there was a relatively limited range of styles and options for consumers. Drapery hardware was relatively standardized and available in a narrow range of styles. Venetian blinds were originally made of wood, but later an aluminum version became ubiquitous. The companies that produced venetian blinds primarily sold them to institutions such as schools and offices. Most interior window treatments in kitchens, bathrooms, and bedrooms consisted of curtains made of a lightweight fabric with a pull-down vinyl shade spanning the window. In living rooms, heavy pinch-pleated draperies were the most popular window coverings.

The popularity of the aluminum mini-blind helped fuel the tremendous growth of this sector of the U.S. consumer home-furnishings industry. Later, vertical blinds and window shades developed from stronger, light-emitting materials were also introduced. However, in the late 1970s, Taiwan restructured its polyvinylchloride (PVC) manufacturing industry to mass-

produce and import mini-blinds. This resulted in the flooding of the U.S. market with cheaper plastic versions of the aluminum mini-blinds. Manufacturers responded by diversifying their aluminum lines into a greater selection of colors and finishes, producing a competing stock line of more affordable vinyl blinds, and keeping a strong foothold in the custom-made aluminum mini-blind market. This has proven to be a popular segment of the window coverings industry— consumers can take their window measurements to a retail outlet, sift through catalogs of styles, and in a few weeks have their custom-crafted aluminum blinds installed throughout their home. These custom-made products accounted for 80 percent of the domestic mini-blind market in the early 1990s.

The drapery hardware segment of the industry has made a concerted effort to come out from behind-the-scenes. When long, heavy, pinch-pleated draperies were in vogue for many years, the accompanying hardware was designed to stay hidden. The poles, rods, and tieback elements served a basic functional need and were correspondingly utilitarian in design. However, the emerging popularity of top treatments for windows—swaths of fabric that added a decorative element to the mini-blind or pleat-shade covered window below—paved the way for a new emphasis on drapery hardware. These products are generally manufactured from a variety of metals, including steel, bronze, and brass, but some companies offer poles and rods in numerous wood finishes. Consumers may purchase drapery hardware in a variety of novelty styles. Drapery hardware products are made available in both traditional and contemporary styles, and many now have removable decorative elements that give them a greater versatility.

CURRENT CONDITIONS

The economic restructuring and recession of the late 1980s and early 1990s had a negative impact on the drapery hardware and window coverings industry. Sales dropped during these years and, as with other manufacturing industries, some budgetary restructuring and across-the-board layoffs took place.

The industry was also witness to changes in its overall corporate structure through acquisitions and mergers that took place during this period. Companies struggled to hold on to their segment of the consumer-durables market while also introducing products to fill new niches. Consumers became increasingly price-conscious and firms competed to offer the best dollar value among a range of similar products. Industry leaders began to introduce more upscale products, such as aluminum blinds with elegant finishes, that appealed to consumers yet were inexpensively priced.

INDUSTRY LEADERS

Many of the top U.S. companies engaged in the manufacture of drapery hardware and window coverings are major corporations. One of the largest is Hunter-Douglas, Incorporated of Upper Saddle River, New Jersey. It is a private company founded in 1963 that employs approximately 5,000 workers. Annual sales figures in the mid-1990s were $600 million. Another corporate giant is the Newell Company, a major housewares conglomerate that sells window shades and drapery hardware under the brand name Window Furnishings. Based in Freeport, Illinois, the company traces its roots back to 1903 and reported annual sales of $2.87 billion in 1996 (a figure that represents the total for all of its corporate holdings, which include glassware, cookware, and hardware companies). In 1993, Newell acquired the Levolor Corporation of San Jose, California. Levolor was founded by the Lorentzen family in 1911, but in recent years, its brand name became nearly synonymous with the mini-blind. At its peak, Levolor's sales neared $300 million, and Levolor held onto a 40 percent share of the market. But during the 1980s, the company was beset by internal squabbling and the company suffered from this diversion. Instead of cultivating and maintaining valuable accounts with industry distributors, it instead concentrated on selling directly to the consumer and subsequently lost some major distributor accounts to more aggressive competitors. Sales declined, and in 1988 the company was sold to an investment firm for only $135 million.

Other leading companies in the window coverings manufacturing industry include Springs Industries, a Fort Mill, South Carolina based company, which reported sales of $2.24 billion in 1996. Founded in 1938, it also exported its products overseas and provided jobs for 22,600 people. Home Fashions, Incorporated of Westminster, California, sells its products under the Del Mar brand name. The company employed 775 workers, and reported sales figures at $90 million. The leading manufacturer of drapery hardware is Kirsch, a company based in Sturgis, Michigan, followed by Graber Industries and Kenney Manufacturing.

WORK FORCE

The work force engaged in manufacturing drapery hardware and window coverings numbered 17,300 in 1991. The recession of the early 1990s had a negative impact on the drapery hardware and window coverings industry, as employment figures dropped precipitously from 19,000 in 1990, a decline of nearly 10 percent. However, since that time, the industry's employment figures have continuously increased reaching to approximately 21,000 by 1997. Among these 21,000 workers, approximately 14,000 were in the production sectors.

AMERICA AND THE WORLD

The relative ease with which window coverings can be manufactured by overseas companies, primarily in Taiwan, and exported into the U.S. market has negatively impacted the window coverings segment of this industry. The domestic drapery hardware business, meanwhile, has been invaded by a leading German manufacturer, Blome, which entered the U.S. market in 1991. The company has mainly distributed its products through intermediary outlets, but also planned to market its wares in upscale department stores.

RESEARCH AND TECHNOLOGY

Industry critics of vinyl blinds, which are primarily imported from Taiwan, have decried their saturation in the U.S. market and charge that the imported products are not subject to the same lead-content restrictions as U.S. manufacturers. Critics charge that the Taiwanese vinyl blinds are ecologically unsound, since they will eventually wind up in American landfills and take decades to disintegrate. Another problematic area for the window coverings industry has been the danger of the pull cords that raise and lower the blinds. Their looped construction has proven hazardous to both small pets and children since the product's introduction on the market. A 1981 Consumer Product Safety Commission report found that the cords were the leading cause of accidental child-strangulation deaths. However, in 1993, one of the largest manufacturers of mini-blinds, Hunter-Douglas, began manufacturing a patented ''Break-Thru Safety Tassel,'' which is a two-piece cord attachment designed to come apart at the slightest touch. Also in 1993, Hunter-Douglas entered into a venture with the baby-product giant Gerber. Gerber began marketing the device under its own name along with its other child-safety items, but Hunter-Douglas also made it a standard feature of one of its major product lines.

FURTHER READING

Bermingham, Geoffrey B. ''Aluminum vs. Vinyl: Mini Blind Battle Rages On.'' *HFD: The Home Furnishings Daily,* 24 August 1992.

———. ''Child-Safe Mini-Blind Cords.'' *HFD: The Home Furnishings Daily,* 31 May 1993.

———. ''Drapery Hardware: Out of Hiding, Into the Light. '' *HFD: The Home Furnishings Daily,* 16 December 1991.

———. ''Hard-Side Guys: Leading Suppliers of Alternative Window Fashions Cite the Challenges Facing Their Changing Industry. '' *HFD: The Home Furnishings Daily,* 24 August 1992.

———. ''The Nature of the '90s'. '' *HFD: The Home Furnishings Daily,* 16 March 1992.

———. ''Window Situation Cloudy: Industry Sectors Differ on the Role of Curtains and Draperies in the Market. '' *HFD: The Home Furnishings Daily,* 27 September 1993.

Byrne, Harlan S. ''Newell Co.: It Is Adding Products, Slashing Costs. '' *Barron's,* 12 April 1993.

McNamara, Michael D. ''Makers Set to Fuel Growth in 1990s. '' *HFD: The Home Furnishings Daily,* 5 February 1990.

Moody's Industrial Manual 1993. New York: Moody's Investors Service.

U.S. Census of Manufactures, 1992 Supplement. Washington: U.S. Department of Commerce, 1992.

Wendlinger, Lisa D. ''Curtain and Drapery Business: A Tough Sell. '' *HFD: The Home Furnishings Daily,* 17 June 1991.

U.S. Department of Commerce. International Trade Administration *U.S. Industrial Outlook 1994.* Washington: GPO, 1994.

—Carol Brennan, updated by Jennifer L. Stong

SIC 2599

FURNITURE AND FIXTURES, NOT ELSEWHERE CLASSIFIED

This classification covers establishments primarily engaged in manufacturing furniture and fixtures, not elsewhere classified, including hospital beds and furniture specially designed for use in restaurants, bars, cafeterias, bowling centers, and ships.

This highly fragmented category was valued at $2.86 billion in 1995, according to the U.S. Census Bureau. By product type, nearly 47 percent, or $1.3 billion, of the industry's shipments were such miscellaneous commercial furnishings as bowling alley, factory, and ship furniture, followed by commercial food-service fixtures at 40 percent, or $1.14 billion, and hospital beds at 12.8 percent, or $366 million. The industry's 1995 performance reflected a 66 percent increase in current dollar shipments over its 1985 results. Modest growth was expected to continue into the late 1990s, with total shipments anticipated to exceed $3 billion in 1997.

The manufacturing of furniture and fixtures in this category primarily arose to fill specific needs within the service industry market. For instance, after World War II, the rise of bowling as a recreational sport necessitated the construction of a plethora of alleys across the United States to satisfy a growing demand. The factories and manufacturing plants that sprouted up all across the country needed specific interior furniture for a wide variety of purposes also, so this industry filled the needs of the growing industrial economy of the United States. Later, as orders for factory furniture declined due to the drop in overall manufacturing, the furniture and fixtures industry accommodated other segments of the economy. Hospital furniture manufacturing firms met the increased demand for new beds as medical facilities were built to serve more populous suburban communities. The growing consumer willingness to spend more entertainment dollars on dining out during the 1970s and 1980s fueled the construction of restaurants and the corresponding need for sturdy yet attractive furniture to fill the interiors.

There were an estimated 1,400 establishments operating in this industry in 1997. This figure was up from an early 1990s low of only 881 establishments. Approximately 30,000 people constituted its work force in the mid-1990s, an increase of roughly 20 percent since the early 1990s. In 1995, the average wage for the broader miscellaneous furniture group was $9.91 per hour.

Kinetic Concepts Inc. was the largest company primarily engaged in furniture manufacturing not elsewhere classified, with 2,000 employees and $270 million in revenues in 1996. The San Antonio, Texas-based hospital bed manufacturer has felt more than one downturn in the market for its goods: from a sales peak of $278 million in 1992, the company's revenues dropped by 3 percent in 1993, recovered slightly in 1994, and dropped another 9 percent in 1995. Kinetic's 1996 sales, however, showed a 10 percent increase.

Hill-Rom, Inc., a subsidiary of Hillenbrand Industries, Inc., was another leading hospital bed firm and, as of 1997, claimed top sales in the electrically powered bed category. The Batesville, Indiana-based company employed approximately 3,700 persons and, together with Hillenbrand's other health care holdings, posted operating profits of $111 million in 1996—a 26 percent increase over 1995—while its actual health care sales of $234 million grew by only 2 percent. In 1995, Hill-Rom and its parent were the target of antitrust litigation brought by Kinetic Concepts and another firm for allegedly attempting to monopolize the hospital bed market through its pricing and product bundling policies. In return, Hill-Rom filed a counter-suit and a patent infringement suit against Kinetic in late 1996 because of Kinetic's alleged monopolization of the therapeutic bed segment.

Jasper, Indiana-based Kimball International, Inc. was one of several more diversified competitors in the miscellaneous furniture category with total revenues of $923.6 million and 8,723 employees in 1996. Along with office furniture and cabinetry, Kimball produced a variety of ready-made and custom-built furnishings for the health care and hospitality industries. In 1996 the firm reported sales growth in its hospitality product line.

Shelby Williams Industries, Inc. of Chicago was the leading contract seating manufacturer for the hospitality and foodservice industries in 1997. In 1996 the company reported that approximately 80 percent of its $172 million sales were to hospitality and foodservice firms, and only 13 percent were to health care and other institutions. In 1996 Shelby Williams employed 1,667 workers.

Falcon Products, Inc. of St. Louis was another leading company, posting sales of $111 million and employing 1,300 persons in 1996. In addition to furniture offerings outside this industry, this diversified manufacturer marketed furniture to foodservice and health care facilities. In the mid-1990s the company engaged in several acquisitions and consolidations to boost its revenues and market share, particularly in the hospitality and foodservice markets.

FURTHER READING

Darnay, Arsen J., ed. *Manufacturing USA.* 5th ed. Detroit: Gale Research, 1996.

Falcon Products, Inc. *Annual Report.* St. Louis, 1997.

Hillenbrand Industries, Inc. *Annual Report.* Batesville, IN, 1997.

Kimball International, Inc. *Annual Report.* Jasper, IN, 1996.

Kinetic Concepts, Inc. *Annual Report.* San Antonio, TX, 1997.

Shelby Williams Industries, Inc. *Annual Report.* Chicago, 1997.

U.S. Census Bureau. *1992 Census of Manufactures.* Washington, 1995.

U.S. Census Bureau. *1995 Annual Survey of Manufactures.* Washington: GPO, 1997.

—Carol Brennan

PAPER & ALLIED PRODUCTS

PULP MILLS

This category covers establishments primarily engaged in manufacturing pulp from wood or from other materials, such as rags, linters, wastepaper, and straw. Establishments engaged in integrating logging and pulp mill operations are classified according to the primary products shipped. Establishments engaged in integrated operations of producing pulp and manufacturing paper, paperboard, or products thereof are classified in **SIC 2621: Paper Mills** if primarily shipping paper or paper products; in **SIC 2631: Paperboard Mills** if primarily shipping paperboard or paperboard products; and in **SIC 2611: Pulp Mills** if primarily shipping pulp. Establishments primarily engaged in cutting pulpwood are classified in **SIC 2411: Logging.**

INDUSTRY SNAPSHOT

The U.S. pulp industry is by far the world's largest. In 1995, the United States produced 90 million metric tons of wood pulp, representing 53 4 percent of the 168.3 million metric tons produced worldwide. The next largest producer, Canada, produced 27.5 million metric tons. U.S. pulp mills make a wide variety of pulps for making paper and paperboard. Most of the pulp made in the United States is chemical pulp, which is produced by a chemical digesting process that converts wood chips into pulp by chemically liberating the cellulose fibers from the lignin that holds them together in the wood. Mechanical pulps are made with large "grinders" which physically shred the wood pulp into individual fibers. Some processes combine elements of mechanical and chemical pulping.

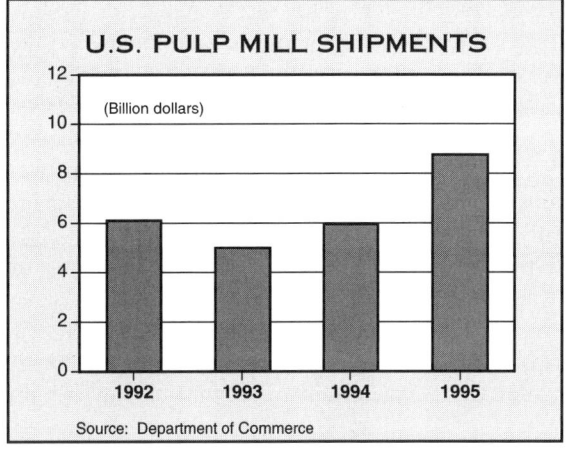

U.S. PULP MILL SHIPMENTS

(Billion dollars)

1992 1993 1994 1995

Source: Department of Commerce

After the wood chips are digested or ground, they are called wood pulp. This wood pulp is cleaned, screened and refined. If the pulp will be used for white paper, it is bleached (otherwise the pulp retains its natural brown color). At this point, the pulp is ready to be used in papermaking. Various grades of pulp can be made from softwood trees such as southern pine, hardwood trees such as oak, or from other sources that include recovered paper, rags, or agricultural products such as cotton linters, kenaf, bagasse, or straw.

In 1995, there were approximately 189 U.S. wood pulp mills producing a variety of pulps, about 7 percent fewer than in 1993. Most of this pulp was used in integrated pulp and paper mills, which means that the pulp mill and the paper mill were owned by the same company and operated in many cases at the same location. There were numerous smaller paper mills, however, that were not connected with a pulp mill; they purchased "market pulp" on the open market from other pulp producers. Some companies produced only market pulp; other companies sold the excess pulp that could not be used by their paper machines.

ORGANIZATION AND STRUCTURE

U.S. pulp mills maintain a dominant share of the U.S. market for pulp—92.5 percent in 1995—and are also very strong competitors in global markets. One reason for this market strength is good economic fundamentals: U.S. pulp mills have access to low cost and abundant raw materials, a highly trained work force, and they operate world-class plants and equipment.

In most cases, pulp mills need to be located near their raw materials— trees or wastepaper—to minimize transportation costs. The United States has a very large growing stock of pulpwood in several areas: the Pacific Northwest, the upper Midwest, the Northeast, and the Southeast. This, combined with an efficient manufacturing base, makes the United States the low cost producer of many grades of pulp throughout the world. However, by the mid-1990s, that position as low-cost producer was beginning to be challenged by a new generation of pulp mills, largely in South America and Southeast Asia. These mills have access to fast-growing hardwood and softwood fiber, which dramatically reduces operating costs. Many new, world-class pulp mills were built in South America and Southeast Asia in the early to mid-1990s, while virtually none were built in the United States and Canada. This new capacity made the global pulp market very competitive, and, consequently, increased the volatility of pulp prices.

While the pulping and papermaking processes are very energy intensive, the industry has become an efficient user of energy by burning its own waste by-products, such as tree bark and spent chemicals from the pulping process. In the mid-1990s, the pulp and paper industry generated well over half of the energy needed to run its mills. From the early 1970s to the early 1990s, the industry reduced oil consumption by nearly 66 percent and natural gas consumption by 10 percent while increasing production capacity by 60 percent. Some mills even generate excess power and sell it back to local utilities.

Pulp mills and paper mills use a large amount of water from lakes, rivers, and in some cases oceans. They must reuse and/or clean all of this water before it is returned to the body of water from which it came. In the early years of the industry, pulp mills would discharge untreated waste (effluent) back into the receiving body of water. Beginning in the late 1960s, however, the industry began operating under strict water use regulations which required primary, secondary, and in some cases tertiary treatment of wastewater.

These rules were tightened considerably during the following decades. Also, to cut down on treatment costs, mills reuse a large portion of the water they used elsewhere in the pulping and papermaking process. The process of cleaning and reusing water is commonly called "closing the mill."

In the early 1990s, it took 60 percent less water to make a ton of paper than it did about two decades earlier. The water that cannot be reused goes to large outdoor water treatment plants. The biochemical oxygen demand (BOD) of the treated water—a measure of environmental impact—has been reduced by 70 percent in 25 years, even though total paper production has gone up 50 percent.

Captive Pulp. The vast majority of pulp produced in the United States—about 85 percent in 1995—is considered "captive" because it is used in an integrated pulp and paper operation and is not sold on the open market. Market pulp sold on domestic and foreign markets accounted for the remaining 15 percent of total U.S. pulp production. While captive pulp accounts for the majority of pulp used in the United States, much more information and documentation is available for market pulp since it is bought and sold publicly.

While wood pulp production has been expanding in recent years, the percentage of virgin wood fiber used in paper and board production in the United States and other countries has been steadily declining. Wood fiber, as a percentage of total global paper and board production, dropped from about 75 percent in 1970 to just 60 percent in 1997.

This decline is explained by several trends. While virgin wood fiber has long been the fiber of choice in most advanced papermaking operations, it is coming under sustained challenge from other fiber sources. For example, the use of recovered (recycled) paper is increasing dramatically and has displaced large amounts of virgin wood fiber in the pulping market. The increased use of recovered paper has been driven partly by society's desire to reduce the amount of paper going to landfills, and partly by pulp producers realizing that virgin fiber will be increasingly hard to sustain in years to come.

North American paper producers have dramatically increased their use of recovered paper in recent years. The percentage of paper recycled in the United States rose from about 30 percent in 1990 to 40.3 percent in 1994. The American Forest and Paper Association, the Washington, D.C.-based trade association that represents the paper industry, has a goal of recycling 50 percent of all paper produced by the year

2000. In the mid-1990s, consumption of recovered paper was far out-pacing the underlying capacity growth at U.S. paper and paperboard mills. U.S. mill consumption of recovered paper rose 9.2 percent in 1996, or about two and a half times the rate of total paper and paperboard capacity growth. From 1997 to 1999, recovered paper consumption was expected to increase at an average rate of 2.9 percent, about twice the pace of paper and paperboard capacity growth during the same three-year period.

Virgin wood fiber also faces a challenge from the growing use of mineral coatings and inert fillers, mainly in printing and writing papers. Producers of these grades have completed a long-term shift from acid pulp to alkaline pulp. One reason for this shift is that paper produced from acid pulp becomes brittle and breaks up over time, while alkaline papers tend to last longer. The main reason, however, is that alkaline papermaking tends to be less expensive since it permits greater use of fillers, such as calcium carbonate, that replace a percentage of the wood fiber in the finished paper. In U.S. printing and writing papers, such as copy paper, the amount of filler can be 10 to 20 percent of the finished paper or higher. The cost of fillers is about one third that of wood pulp, so paper mills have a financial incentive to increase their use of fillers. Papermakers use filler not only to reduce the amount of wood fiber used, but also to increase the smoothness and opacity of their finished products. As techniques to use more filler are developed, wood pulp will be displaced.

While the percentage of wood pulp in finished paper products will continue to decline, the use of wood pulp will still grow—at least slightly—as the entire market for paper expands. Global production of wood pulp should grow about 2 percent per year for the next two decades worldwide. In the United States, wood pulp will probably grow more slowly since growth in recycled fiber will be strong. For example, U.S. wood pulp capacity was projected to rise just 0.5 percent per year between 1997 and 1999. However, foreign markets will likely absorb an increasing amount of U.S. market wood pulp.

Chemical Pulp. Within the overall market for wood pulp, the use of chemical pulp—mostly kraft pulp, which is produced using the sulfate process—is increasing. In 1995, chemical pulp accounted for 68.5 percent of all pulp produced throughout the world, up from 66 percent in 1970. This figure was expected to reach 70 percent in 1997. In the United States, chemical pulp accounts for an even higher percentage of wood pulp capacity—81.5 percent in 1995. Semichemical pulp accounted for about 6.2 percent

and mechanical pulp for 9.9 percent in 1995, with other grades accounting for the remaining 2.4 percent. The trend toward greater use of chemical pulp is driven by the need for greater strength as papermakers begin to blend less costly and weaker mechanical pulps and recycled paper fibers into the furnish they use to make paper.

As it has been for some time, kraft pulp was the primary product of the U.S. market wood pulp industry in the 1990s. In 1996, U.S. kraft market pulp mills had total capacity of 10.9 million tons. Market chemical pulp, with 1996 capacity of 9.69 million tons, accounted for 87 percent of that total, while market dissolving pulp, at 1.44 million tons, accounted for the remainder. The two primary market pulp grades in 1995 were bleached softwood kraft pulp, at 5.43 million tons, and bleached hardwood, at 3.81 million tons.

Overall, U.S. market wood pulp capacity was expected to remain flat through much of the 1990s. While some small fluctuations are expected, total market wood pulp capacity was expected to drop by 1 percent between 1995 and 1999, from 11.13 million tons to 11.01 million tons. The main reason for this decline is that major capacity increases are being concentrated in recovered paper market pulp, which is made from recycled paper. The capacity of U.S. recovered paper market pulp producers jumped from 959,000 tons in 1995 to 1.4 million tons in 1996, and was expected to reach 2 million tons by 1999.

The United States has almost 30 percent of the world's capacity to produce paper and paperboard and more than one-third of the world's capacity to produce wood pulp. As mentioned earlier, the majority of U.S. paper mills are integrated with captive pulp mills that do not sell pulp on the open market. Despite this fact, the United States is a major importer and exporter of market pulp. In 1995, the United States produced 9 million tons of market wood pulp, imported 3.75 million tons, and exported 5.79 million tons.

BACKGROUND AND DEVELOPMENT

Before the U.S. Civil War, paper was made exclusively from rags in the United States and around the world. Rag collection for papermaking was a major part of the U.S. economy. However, as the demand for paper continued to increase, the demand for rags began to outstrip supply.

This changed between 1851 and 1918, when wood pulp was invented, developed, and industrialized. The Civil War created a huge demand for both paper and rags; this helped spur research into using the fiber from trees for papermaking. This time period saw the development and commercialization of all the major wood pulping processes, including groundwood, soda, sulphite and kraft (sulphate). Wood pulp quickly reduced the cost of papermaking, allowing the use of paper in new applications and new products.

Soda pulping was invented by Burgess and Watt in England and was patented in 1854 in the United States. Groundwood became established in the 1860s. The first chemical wood pulp was manufactured in 1864 in Manyunk, Pennsylvania, and the first kraft pulp mill came on line in 1909. Kraft pulping had been invented in 1884 by German chemist Carl Dahl using sodium sulfate as the pulping agent. The pulp produced a strong brown paper, which was then described with the German word for strong: kraft.

While other materials were used for pulping—including bagasse cactus, cudweed, straw, cornstalks and even cow dung—wood pulp quickly became the preferred source of pulp. By the 1870s, pulp mills were springing up in heavily forested areas such as New York, Massachusetts, Michigan, Ohio, and Wisconsin. These areas continued to develop as key pulp and paper regions throughout the early 20th century and most remained so in the early 1990s.

The science of pulping continued to develop along with the growth of papermaking. Major pulping milestones included the invention of the recovery boiler, in which spent pulping chemicals are burned. This process recovers the energy in the chemicals and the chemicals themselves, which can then be reused. Another milestone was the development of the continuous digester, which replaced the slower batch digesting process.

More recently, in the 1980s, entire pulp mills were rebuilt to increase capacity and quality. Popular additions included new chip screening, handling and storage systems, new digester cooking controls, new washing systems, more screening and cleaning, new bleaching systems emphasizing oxygen, and better mixing. Pulp and paper mills also took advantage of process control to more closely control the process and produce better quality products.

CURRENT CONDITIONS

The U.S. pulp industry in the 1990s saw much price fluctuation. In the early to mid-1990s, low pulp prices and high levels of spending required to meet environmental demands depressed the U.S. pulp industry to such an extent that few if any pulp producers were profitable. By 1993, after factoring out inflation, the price of pulp was the lowest it had been in decades. However, in 1994, pulp prices began a meteoric rise

which saw prices double in less than two years. The price for northern bleached softwood kraft market pulp (NBSK), a common benchmark for pulp producers, averaged $566 per metric ton in 1994 (during the year, prices increased from a low of $440 per metric ton at the beginning of the year to $700 per metric ton at year end). In 1995, the price for NBSK averaged $871 per metric ton and many pulp producers reaped record profits (prices during the year increased from a low of $750 per metric ton at the beginning of 1995 to $910 per metric ton at year end). However, 1996 saw an steep fall in pulp prices. For the year, the average price for NBSK was $591 per metric ton, falling from a high of $860 per metric ton in the first quarter of 1996 to a low of $500 per metric ton in the second quarter. Prices recovered to $600 per metric ton at the end of 1996.

Water Regulations. Environmental pressure on pulp mills continues in three areas: water regulations, recycling, and timber harvesting. The most recent wave of water regulations have been spurred by the desire to eliminate or reduce to non-detectable levels the toxic chemical dioxin, which was discovered in small amounts in pulp mill water-borne effluent in the mid-1980s. Despite the lack of hard evidence that dioxin in minute quantities poses a human health risk, the paper industry voluntarily spent more than $1 billion to reduce dioxin discharges by over 90 percent by the mid-1990s.

In 1993 the Environmental Protection Agency (EPA) proposed new regulations further restricting dioxin emissions by pulp mills, among other toxic chemicals. These regulations resulted from research the EPA had begun in the late 1980s, when it formed a ''pulp and paper cluster group'' to coordinate regulatory actions involving the pulp and paper industry.

The EPA's pulp and paper cluster group focused on two major rule making efforts. The first involved issuing revised effluent guidelines mandated by the Clean Water Act and required by a consent decree signed by the EPA after being sued by environmental groups over dioxin discharges from pulp mills. The second area involved defining maximum achievable control technology (MACT) emissions standards for pulp and paper mills, which was required under the Clean Air Act Amendments of 1990.

The Clean Air Act Amendments dramatically changed the allowable types and amounts of emissions. Based on emissions such as ozone, carbon monoxide, and particulates, regions of the United States can be classified as ''nonattainment areas.'' These areas's pulp mills, like other industries, can be subject to severe restrictions.

While formulating new regulations, the EPA worked with the pulp industry through the "stakeholders" process. This allowed the pulp industry to develop new testing and process treatment methods; introduce scientific data and research; and offer advice on the environmental, economic, and industrial impact of EPA's findings. Through this cooperation, standards regulating chemical oxygen demand (COD), biochemical oxygen demand (BOD), color and adsorbable organic halides (AOX) were revamped and made less costly to the industry. After final regulations are issued, the pulp and paper industry then has up to three years to comply with the new regulations.

One controversy regarding pulp bleaching that arose in the early 1990s appeared to be resolved by the mid-1990s. Advocates of totally chlorine bleaching (TCF), in which no chlorine compounds are used to bleach pulp (including chlorine dioxide), argued that the process was environmentally superior to elemental chlorine free (ECF) bleaching, which uses chlorine dioxide. While the TCF process has some following in Europe, it has not appeared to catch on in the United States; no regulations have been passed requiring TCF bleaching. As a result, just two pulp mills in the United States were producing TCF pulp in 1996.

Recycling. The second major environmental trend affecting the pulp industry is recycling. Public interest in paper recycling, driven by concerns about a potential landfill crisis, began to build in the late 1980s and peaked in the early 1990s. Consensus on landfills does not yet exist, as studies in the mid-1990s suggested the landfill crisis to be less of a threat than previously reported.

Nonetheless, the push for recycling—primarily through federal and state legislation—continues and paper companies now are marketing a wide variety of new recycled grades. Much of the new pulping capacity being built or planned uses wastepaper instead of virgin fiber as its raw material. This change has had a major impact on traditional pulping of wood fiber.

Much of the impetus for recycling came from government, and various local state and federal government rules still regulate the recycling process. Many of these laws specify precise levels of "postconsumer" content (paper that has been used and discarded by a consumer) and restrict the amount of "preconsumer" wastepaper that can be used. Examples of preconsumer wastepaper might include trimmings from the printing or papermaking process, unsalable newspapers, or overprints of magazines. There is, however, considerable disagreement over where the line should be drawn between postconsumer and preconsumer.

Paper companies also face other recycling regulations, including: restrictions on products' use of "green labeling" claims; limits on permissible types of packaging; strict requirements on secondary fiber content; procurement preferences for certain kinds of recycled paper; and surcharges on paper products not meeting certain recycled standards. Consumers in some localities are required to collect and separate wastepaper for recycling.

Demand for recycled paper and recycling regulations are significant for pulp producers because they must manufacture the recycled pulp to be used in making the paper that meets the specifications. In the early to mid-1990s, the pulp and paper industry responded by building large numbers of recycled paper processing plants. However, while paper recycling is an important part of waste minimization, it is only part of what is needed to reduce the generation of solid waste. It should also be noted that recycling itself generates a considerable waste stream. In recycled newsprint pulp mills, for example, only 85 percent of incoming newsprint is usable as fiber. The rest is unusable sludge that must be cleaned out of the process and then burned or placed in landfills. In some recycled grades, sludge can be up to 50 percent of the incoming waste paper.

Timber Harvesting. The third major environmental challenge facing pulp mills in the 1990s is timber harvesting, which is used to create lumber products as well as pulpwood. Access to pulpwood is vital for all virgin wood pulp mills, but that access has been severely restricted in some areas—most notably the Pacific Northwest. Court decisions in the early 1990s reduced harvesting drastically in many national forests and other federal areas in the Northwest. Through the Endangered Species Act, environmental groups filed successful lawsuits restricting harvesting in order to protect the northern spotted owl, among other species. While the Clinton administration attempted to broker a compromise between timber interests and environmentalists in 1993, harvests in 1993 were at one-sixth the level of those in the 1980s. By 1996, small tracts of timber in the Northwest were being released for harvesting and special provisions allowed some "salvage" logging of timber damaged by fire and other natural phenomena. However, harvest rates still remained well below historic levels in the Pacific Northwest. The American Forest & Paper Association said that the unusually high number of U.S. forest fires in 1996 in that region was due to poor forest management on "locked up" federal lands that left large amounts of underbrush, dead and dying trees, and unthinned stands of trees as highly flammable fuel for forest fires.

This situation has led some pulp mills in the Northwest to close and others to seek raw materials from different sources, such as recycled paper and foreign wood chips. The long term effects are likely to permanently reduce tree harvesting and pulping in the Pacific Northwest, and pulp producers in foreign countries and the southern United States are likely to take up the lost volume.

Forest products companies and pulp and paper companies around the country still face pressure from environmental groups and government bodies to change their harvesting practices. Many groups want to eliminate clearcutting, which the industry argues is the most efficient harvesting method and is environmentally sustainable, provided that the clear cut is replanted. In the early to mid-1990s, the U.S. forest products industries—which include the pulp industry—planted more trees than they cut down. In 1995, over three and a half million acres of forestland were planted with over three billion seedlings. The net effect of tree planting on government, corporate, and private land is that the net amount of forested land in the United States is actually increasing. From the early 1980s to the early 1990s, forest growth has exceeded the volume of trees cut or burned in forest fires. From the early 1970s to the early 1990s, the number of trees growing in the United States increased by 20 percent. Even in areas where the pulp and paper industry has access to virgin fiber, however, there is concern that the industry is effectively using all the pulpwood that is currently available, and that in coming years there may be shortages of virgin fiber. That is one reason almost no new virgin pulp mills were being built in the U.S. during the mid-1990s. Pulp producers hope that by improving the growth rate of trees through genetic research, they will be able to increase the amount of wood grown on the same amount of land.

The Business Cycle. Aside from environmental challenges, in the early to mid-1990s U.S. pulp mills experienced volatile swings between profits and losses. When demand began to increase again in early 1994, there was little excess capacity to supply the new demand. Pulp prices surged dramatically and quickly, reaching $910 per metric ton by the third quarter of 1995. Market pulp producers again enjoyed record profits, and speculation centered on pulp prices remaining high into the next century. However, much of the run-up in pulp prices appeared to be caused by customers stocking up on inventory in anticipation of future price increases. When these customers stopped taking new shipments of pulp, prices dropped dramatically. Also, U.S. pulp producers were beginning in the mid-1990s to be affected by very large pulping capac-

ity additions in Asia and South America. These trends appear to have made U.S. pulp producers very cautious about future capacity increases. Total U.S. wood pulp capacity—including market pulp and captive pulp—is slated to rise slightly from 62.4 million metric tons in 1995 to 64.1 million metric tons in 1999, an average annual growth rate of just 0.7 percent.

INDUSTRY LEADERS

International Paper Company. Founded in 1898 by the merger of 18 northeastern pulp and paper companies, International Paper Company (IP), Purchase, N.Y., was the world's largest pulp and paper company in 1995. In that year, IP had total sales of $19.8 billion, which included $14.4 billion worth of pulp, paper and converted products sales. Worldwide, IP produced 1.8 million tons of market pulp in 1995 for the paper, packaging and specialty products industries. From the United States, IP exports market pulp to over 40 countries. Some of IP's market pulp grades include Supersoft fluff pulp for hygiene products; and dissolving pulp grades such as Estercell and Solvekraft, used for yarns, tow, films and plastics.

Georgia-Pacific Corporation. Atlanta-based Georgia-Pacific Corporation (G-P) has major interests in building products, pulp and paper, and paper chemicals. In 1995, G-P had total sales of $14.3 billion, including pulp, paper and converted product sales of $6.9 billion. In that year it employed 47,500 people at over 400 locations, and owned or controlled more than 5 million acres of timber and timberland in North America. In addition to many other products, G-P is the world's second largest producer of market pulp, owning six mills with a combined annual capacity of 2.1 million tons, about 18 percent of U.S. market pulp capacity. G-P produces southern softwood, southern hardwood and northern hardwood pulps for use in the manufacture of many paper grades. G-P is also a major supplier of fluff pulp (used in disposable diapers) and other specialty pulps. G-P exports 65 percent of its market pulp.

Weyerhaeuser Company. Based in Tacoma, Washington, Weyerhaeuser has several core businesses, including growing and harvesting timber and manufacturing and distributing forest products (including logs, wood chips, building products, pulp, paper and packaging products). In 1995, Weyerhaeuser had total sales of $11.8 billion and pulp, paper and converted product sales of $5.68 billion. In 1995, the company had 39,400 employees and owned 5.3 million acres of commercial forestland in the United States, with about half in the South and the other half in the Pacific Northwest. The company also has license arrangements on 18.9 million acres of Canadian forestland. In 1995, Weyerhaeuser completed modernization projects at three of its largest pulp and paper mills.

Champion International Corporation. In 1995, Champion International had total sales of $6.97 billion, which included pulp, paper, and converted product sales of $6 billion. The company employs more than 24,000 people at its paper and wood products facilities in North America and Brazil. At the end of 1995, Champion owned or controlled more than 5 million acres of U.S. timberlands and had the capacity to produce 6.3 million annual tons of paper, paperboard and market pulp. Champion's mills at Courtland, Alabama; Pensacola, Florida; Quinnesec, Michigan; and Sheldon, Texas, have a combined capacity to produce 552,000 tons of market pulp. The pulp is used for domestic and export markets, as well as for internal use at other Champion paper mills. Champion's Weldwood of Canada subsidiary operates a pulp mill in Hinton, Alberta, that can produce 452,000 tons of bleached softwood kraft pulp for export markets, primarily in the United States, and for use at other Champion mills. Weldwood's 50 percent interest in Cariboo Pulp and Paper Co. in Quesnel, British Columbia, accounts for another 176,000 tons of bleached softwood kraft market pulp.

James River Corporation of Virginia. This Richmond, Virginia-based company manufactures and markets consumer products as well as food and consumer packaging and has 98 manufacturing facilities and 27,000 employees in North America and Europe. It manufactures market wood pulp at mills in Marathon, Ontario; Old Town, Maine; and Pennington, Alabama, as well as well as market pulp made from recovered paper in Halsey, Oregon.

WORK FORCE

Total employment in the pulp, paper and converting industries was about 619,000 in 1996. The level of employment declined during the early to mid-1990s despite large capacity increases. Employee wage increases remained at or below the inflation rate in the 1990s, averaging about 2.5 percent. These increases were far below the average 7.5 percent annual increases recorded during the period from 1975 to 1985.

Like other manufacturing industries, the pulp and paper industry employs many unionized workers. However, the heaviest concentrations of union employees are in older mills which were organized years ago. Almost all new pulp and paper mills are nonunion operations, including mills constructed by companies with unionized mills in other locations. In general, the

wages and benefits provided by nonunion mills are comparable to unionized mills.

There has been relative labor peace in the paper industry during the 1980s and early 1990s. In exchange for salary increases, management was able to obtain work rules changes that allowed workers to perform more jobs in the mill and eliminate pay differentials for Sunday and holiday pay. There have been no major work stoppages in the pulp and paper industry in the 1990s.

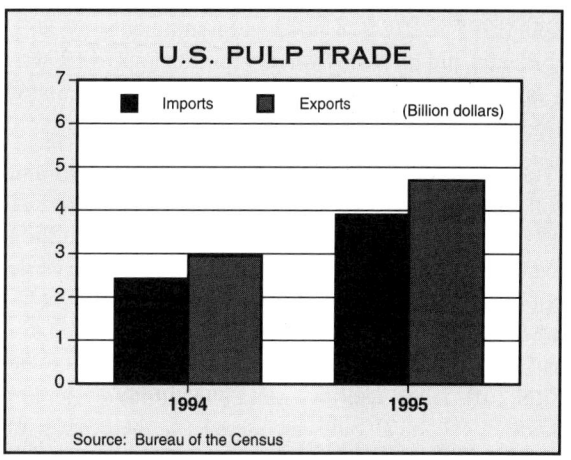

U.S. PULP TRADE

Source: Bureau of the Census

AMERICA AND THE WORLD

Market pulp is a truly global commodity, with prices changing quickly in response to capacity changes, inventory levels, and purchase levels. While market pulp is produced in about 25 countries, more than two-thirds of world output comes from five northern countries: the United States, Canada, Sweden, Finland, and Norway. Global demand for woodpulp totaled nearly 160 million metric tons in 1995, about 5 million tons more than in 1994. Nonwood pulp demand was about 20 million metric tons in 1995. Of the total 180 million metric tons, about 30 million metric tons (17 percent) was shipped as market pulp.

Southern Hemisphere pulp producers expanded their operations extensively during the mid-1990s. New, technologically advanced market pulp mills were built in China, Indonesia, Brazil, Chile, and Argentina. Some of these mills include North American pulp and paper companies as investors. One major advantage of mills in South America and Southeast Asia is access to incredibly fast-growing pulpwood trees, such as eucalyptus and radiata pine species. These trees reach pulping maturity in about seven years or less, compared to 30 years in some northern countries. Other advantages of these new pulp mills include lower operating costs, lower labor costs, and less costly environmental regulation. Established pulp producers will have to carefully control costs and increase productivity in order to compete with these new market factors.

Increased Foreign Demand. In the early to mid-1990s, production in the U.S. market wood pulp industry was relatively flat due to recessionary conditions in the early 1990s; flat or declining domestic markets; and growing use of secondary fiber. That situation was expected to continue from the mid- to late 1990s, with capacity expected to grow only 0.4 percent annually from 1995 to 1999. Market pulp shipments by U.S. producers did increase from 8.4 million tons in 1994 to 9 million tons in 1995, but a decline in shipments of around 5 percent was estimated for 1996.

U.S. wood pulp exports are a relatively small but still significant portion of total U.S. wood pulp production. In 1995, the United States produced 65.8 million ton of wood pulp and exported 7.43 million tons (while importing 5.86 million tons). Chemical pulp was by far the leading grade of pulp exported by the United States in 1995, accounting for 7.25 million tons out of the total of 7.43 million tons. Groundwood and thermomechanical pulp accounted for the rest, with just 183,000 tons exported. Japan and South Korea have traditionally been the largest U.S. market pulp customers.

Despite producing and exporting large volumes of market pulp, the U.S. pulp and paper industry still imports a substantial amount. In 1995, the United States imported 5.97 million tons of wood pulp with a value of $3.7 billion. These imports accounted for under 10 percent of total U.S. wood pulp consumption. Canada has traditionally been the leading U.S. supplier, accounting for around 85 percent of the total in 1995.

Reasons To Import. While the U.S. has the capacity to supply all the pulp it needs for domestic paper production, it still imports pulp in order to exploit the different properties of foreign market pulp. The domestic market pulp industry is largely based on southern pine and hardwood, and many U.S. mills prefer the special properties of other grades, such as NBSK, produced in Canada, and eucalyptus pulp produced in countries such as Brazil. At the same time, a large number of foreign paper mills covet the southern pine and hardwood market pulp produced by U.S. market pulp mills.

Despite sluggish growth and new foreign competition, the United States was expected to remain a strong global market pulp competitor throughout the 1990s. The combination of relatively low cost fiber resources, energy and water supplies and improvement in product technology and operating conditions will likely allow the U.S. pulp industry to remain the leader among world producers. However, competition for sales in the United States and overseas will intensify as foreign pulp and paper producers in developing regions such as Latin America, Asia, and Eastern Europe improve pulp quality and compete harder in major consuming markets in North America, Asia, and Europe. One major change in the global pulp market may be developing with the mid-1990s launch of various pulp futures markets, including the Helsinki Pulp Options Exchange and the OM Group's London Exchange. Futures markets, widely used to trade futures in commodity products such as copper, aluminum, sugar, and coffee, may bring more price stability to the pulp market and even out some of the extreme price fluctuations that have plagued the global market pulp industry.

RESEARCH AND TECHNOLOGY

Pulping processes, both chemical and mechanical, are likely to see continued improvement in research and technology. Pulp mills will focus on higher energy recovery, which can then be used in other mill processes. This will be essential to the future profitability of many mills facing competition from mills with lower cost structures. Energy is already a major cost for the pulp and paper industry, which is one of the largest industrial users of electricity. Other areas of improvement include: the use of additives to speed up the chemical digesting process to increase fiber yields; new technical and environmental processes to reduce air and water pollution; and increased process control, monitoring and automation. Similar measures to keep costs down and productivity high will be needed for the industry to remain competitive and expand its market share in world pulp consuming markets.

With more and more regulatory attention focused on pulp mill emissions, there has been more research devoted to the "effluent free" mill, also called the "closed mill." In theory, the closed mill perfectly balances all the "inputs and outputs" to the pulping and papermaking process, so that the mill reuses, recycles, or cleans all waste materials. This would mean that the mill produces no air or water pollution.

Widely regarded as impossible just a decade ago, this prospect appears to be feasible provided that current technology continues to develop and the cost of implementation decreases. For example, the Institute of Paper Science and Technology has been directed by its member companies to increase its research efforts on how heat and contaminants build up in closed pulping and papermaking systems; where the optimum "purge" points are in the process; and how to deal with the increased metal corrosion in closed systems. Many industry experts consider the truly closed mill to be a decade or two away. However, others argue that an effluent free mill, while feasible, may not be practical in that it will be too costly to implement. They argue that the industry should focus on the "minimum impact mill," which while producing some effluent, does not harm the environment in any substantial way.

Another major research area affecting pulp mills is in high yield forestry. The industry needs to reduce the time it takes to produce a mature pulpwood tree from 28 years to about 7 or 8 years. There are two reasons for this. One is to compete with pulpwood from countries such as Brazil, which today can produce a mature pulpwood tree in seven years. The other is to reduce the amount of forestland used for harvesting trees. There is a great deal of pressure on the pulp industry to minimize its harvesting operations, and if it can produce the same amount of pulpwood from a smaller amount of land, it may mollify some of its critics. However, this will require major investment in plant biology and other high-tech genetic research. This area in particular will require more extensive networking between the pulp and paper companies, research institutions, and government agencies. One of the major research initiatives involving the pulp industry is Agenda 2020, a cooperative research project involving the U.S. Department of Energy (DOE), pulp and paper research institutions, and leading paper companies. Agenda 2020 was prepared by the chief technology officers of major paper companies under the auspices of the American Forest & Paper Association. The development of the document was spurred by the DOE's "Industries of the Future" program, which seeks to fund research in specific manufacturing industries—including pulp and paper—that will reduce energy intensiveness and improve environmental performance. The DOE prepared a draft document on the "Pulp Mill of the Future," which the team of chief technology officers reviewed and modified to create Agenda 2020. It outlined six specific areas for R&D, including sustainable forest management; environmental performance; energy performance; capital effectiveness; recycling; and sensors and control. Many of the Agenda 2020 research projects involving pulping. For example, a research project underway at Auburn University and the Institute of Paper Science and Technology focuses on the bleachability of pulp. Bleach plant effluent loadings can be reduced by decreasing residual lignin and modifying the chemical structure of the residual lignin to make it easier to remove by bleaching. To make this process work,

operators will need simple predictors of how easy the pulp will be to bleach. Once these predictors are in place, mills will be able to develop shorter bleaching sequences which use less energy and fewer chemicals. This research may also make the use of pulping additives such as anthraquinone (AQ) more effective. Potential savings from this one research project in energy usage alone is estimated at $200 million per year, based on a projected 5.8 percent decrease in total energy usage for bleached and unbleached kraft pulping.

FURTHER READING

Biermann, Christopher J. *Essentials of Pulping and Papermaking.* San Diego: Academic Press, 1993.

"Market Pulp: Recent Collapse, Still Uncertain Demand Challenges Efforts to Return to Upcycle." *Pulp & Paper,* August 1996.

"Market Pulp: Is There a Cure for Volatility?" *PIMA's International Papermaker,* February 1997.

Paper, Paperboard, Pulp Capacity and Fiber Consumption. Washington: American Forest & Paper Association, 1996.

Thesaurus of Pulp and Paper Terminology. Atlanta: Institute of Paper Science and Technology, 1991.

U.S. Department of Commerce. International Trade Administration. *U.S. Industrial Outlook 1994.* Washington: GPO, 1994.

"U.S. Paper Industry Will See More Globalization, Slower Growth in 1997." *Pulp & Paper,* January 1997.

U.S. Trade and Industrial Outlook, 1997-1998. New York: McGraw-Hill, 1997.

"Vision 300: A Celebration of American Papermaking." *PIMA Magazine,* January 1991.

Wright, Helena. *300 Years of American Papermaking.* Washington: Smithsonian Institution, 1991.

—Alan Rooks

SIC 2621

PAPER MILLS

This category covers establishments primarily engaged in manufacturing paper from wood pulp, wastepaper, and other fiber pulp, and which may also manufacture converted paper products. Establishments primarily engaged in integrated pulping and papermaking are included in this industry if primarily shipping paper or paper products.

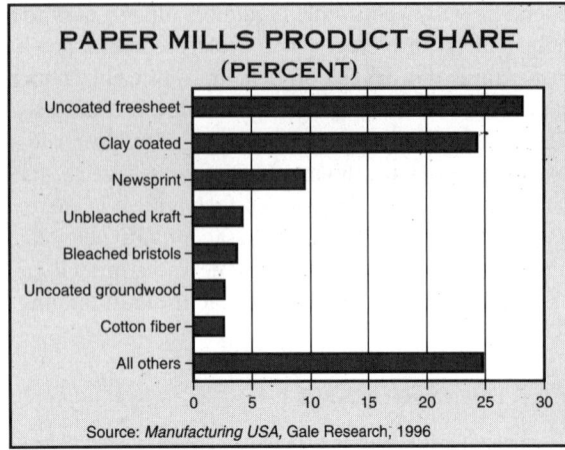

PAPER MILLS PRODUCT SHARE
(PERCENT)

Source: *Manufacturing USA*, Gale Research, 1996

INDUSTRY SNAPSHOT

The United States produces more paper and paperboard than any country in the world. It has maintained this position by consistently producing about one-third of total world production, far more than any other country. While the paper industry remains prosperous and relatively unscathed by foreign competition, competition is rising across the globe as new regions—notably Asia and Latin America—develop strong paper industries.

Domestic U.S. paper and paperboard mills—of which there were 527 in 1995—produce about 90 percent of the paper consumed in the United States. In 1995, these mills used a total of 1,135 paper machines to produce all U.S.-made paper and paperboard, a reduction of 81 machines from 1993. The 1995 total included 751 machines producing paper and 384 machines producing paperboard. Taken as a whole, the U.S. pulp, paper, and converted paper products industry is the eighth largest U.S. manufacturing industry in dollar sales. While imports—mostly from Canada—account for about 10 to 12 percent of the paper consumed each year in the United States, domestic manufacturers dominate most segments of the industry.

While paper mills are separate from pulp mills in the Standard Industrial Classification System, the two are, in reality, directly connected. About 70 percent of all paper is produced at mills that are "integrated" with a pulp mill at the same site, both of which are typically owned by the same company. Almost all high volume "commodity" paper and paperboard grades—such as newsprint, uncoated free sheet, and linerboard—are produced in this fashion. Some smaller paper mills producing specialty grades may not be connected with a pulp mill. They procure pulp from other mills owned by the same company or buy "market pulp" produced by other companies.

Converters of paper products, which are often owned by paper companies, add value to paper and distribute their products to consumers and industrial users. This sector is more widely distributed and includes firms that are directly integrated with paper manufacturers as well as firms that purchase paper, paperboard, and plastic film from manufacturers. Converters transform these materials into thousands of different finished products. The largest number of converters are fully independent operations. However, the converters that are directly owned by or connected to paper and board manufacturers tend to be very large and account for a disproportionate percentage of total industry sales.

While growth in domestic markets has slowed in recent years, the U.S. paper industry still produces a vast amount of paper and paperboard. In 1995, total production reached 89.3 million tons of paper and paperboard in 1995, with 42.7 million tons being paper and 46.6 million tons being paperboard.

While papermaking is an energy intensive industry—being the third largest U.S. industrial consumer of energy—the pulp and paper industry itself produces well over half of the energy it uses through cogeneration and burning of waste fuels, such as bark and spent pulping chemicals.

ORGANIZATION AND STRUCTURE

Papermaking starts where the pulping process leaves off. The first step in papermaking is piping the pulp to the headbox of the paper machine. At this point the pulp—now called the furnish—is 99 percent water and 1 percent fiber. At the headbox, the pulp is laid onto a large mesh belt made of plastic, which is called a wire or a forming fabric. This wire can be as wide as 33 feet. As the water drains out, the fibers bond to each other and form a strong web. This web is taken off the wire by a series of rolls and put into a press section, where more water is squeezed or vacuumed out of the web. Then the web enters a long series of dryer rolls which are heated by steam. As the web comes in contact with these rolls, the water flashes off. By the time it leaves the dryers, the web is three to four percent water. After the paper is wound on a reel at the end of the paper machine, many things can happen, depending on the grade. It can be slitted and shipped as a large roll, or converted into paper products at the same location.

Paper mills are organized by the type of paper they produce. For example, some paper mills produce only printing and writing paper, while others produce newsprint. Many paper mills produce "white" paper, in which brown wood pulp is bleached to remove color and other impurities. Many paperboard mills, which are discussed in **SIC 2631: Paperboard Mills,** manufacture unbleached "brown grades" of paperboard, some of which are used for making corrugated shipping containers. However, some paperboard mills produce "white" products, such as the bleached paperboard used to make folding cartons for products such as breakfast cereal boxes. And some paper mills produce unbleached brown paper for products such as grocery sacks.

Financial Structure. The paper industry is the most capital intensive of all basic U.S. manufacturing industries, requiring nearly continuous major investments for plant and equipment. According to one ranking, the pulp and paper industry is twice as capital intensive as any other major U.S. industry. This has led major paper companies to invest in enormous, high-speed machines that can use economies of scale to produce paper at the lowest possible cost.

The late 1980s and early to mid-1990s were a roller coaster for the U.S. paper industry. After paper companies enjoyed record profits in the late 1980s, the early 1990s saw a dramatic drop in paper prices and very difficult financial circumstances for many paper companies. Prices for most paper products started to drop in mid-1989 and remained low well into the 1990s. Despite low prices being paid for paper, many paper companies had embarked on major capital projects to build new paper machines and expand existing units. The twin conditions of new capacity coming on line and soft demand conspired to keep prices low even when demand began to recover in 1992 and 1993.

However, the spring of 1994 saw the beginning of one of the sharpest run-ups in paper prices ever. Supplies tightened, prices rose and customers began stocking unusually large amounts of inventory in anticipation of future price increases. The result was that average prices for all paper and paperboard rose 8 percent in 1994 and a whopping 41 percent in 1995. However, the boom in paper prices was destined to be one of the shortest on record. Customers began to take stock out of inventory in the fall of 1995 and prices began falling again. By mid-1996 prices of some grades had fallen by a third.

This business cycle has plagued the paper industry for years. Plans for big greenfield (new) mills and machine additions are usually made in the middle of an economic recovery, when paper company profits are rising. These projects involve complicated engineering and take about three to four years to complete. This means new or expanded mills tend to come on line in the middle of a recession, which is what happened in the early 1990s. Also, since paper is a largely non-

perishable product, both mills and customers can stock large amounts of paper in inventory. As a result, inventory adjustments can produce large swings in paper pricing.

After a burst of new mills and paper machines in the early 1990s, the mid-1990s saw relatively low growth in papermaking capacity. After increasing capacity at a 2.6 percent average annual rate from 1986 to 1995 and by 3.5 percent in 1996, paper and paperboard companies planned to add capacity at only a 1.5 percent rate during the period from 1997 to 1999. On a tonnage basis, U.S. paper industry capacity was expected to expand from 99.1 million tons in 1996 to 103.7 million tons in 1999—a three-year increase of 4.6 million tons.

In 1994, pulp and paper companies produced about 40 percent more tonnage with 4 percent fewer employees than in 1984. This was caused directly by paper companies' huge investment in higher capacity, heavily automated machines. For example, in 1995, the industry had the capacity to produce 95.7 million tons of paper and paperboard, up 5.6 percent more than 1993, while operating 6.7 percent fewer machines.

These large investments have created high fixed costs for paper companies. The expense of building and maintaining plants and equipment have become a much greater percentage of a paper company's total costs, while labor has become a lower percentage of costs. Because huge, automated mills need fewer people to run them, many in the industry assumed that paper companies could not adjust to lower demand by laying people off and taking capacity out for short periods. However, while that strategy appeared to be true during the paper industry's recession in the early 1990s, the industry used a completely different approach when prices began dropping during the last quarter of 1995. During that quarter and throughout 1996, many U.S. paper companies—particularly newsprint producers and linerboard producers—took extensive downtime to try to reduce both their own inventories and those of their customers.

BACKGROUND AND DEVELOPMENT

American papermaking began just over 300 years ago in Philadelphia. In September of 1690, an entrepreneur named William Bradford—a recent English immigrant—built the first American paper mill on the shore of Wissahickon Creek in Philadelphia. At the time, paper manufacturing had not yet become an important part of the colonial economy. The small amount of paper consumed in the colonies was produced in Holland and France.

However, economic growth in the colonies soon created a booming market for paper. Bradford and other papermakers were soon ready to produce products for this market. Bradford built his mill with the assistance of William Rittenhouse, an immigrant from Holland, and other financial backers. The mill produced about 20 pounds of pulp, paper, and board a day. While at the time there was some mechanization of papermaking, it was largely a handmade process.

After 1690, the population of the American colonies grew quickly and so did the number of U.S. paper mills. By the time of the American Revolution—in which printed materials played a key role—there were more than 45 mills producing about 300 tons of paper per year. This production was used by more than 50 printers throughout the new nation.

At the beginning of the 1800s, an event occurred that would revolutionize the paper industry throughout the world. A Frenchman, Louis-Nicolas Robert, invented a machine to produce paper. Eventually, the machine patents were purchased by two English papermakers, the brothers Henry and Sealy Fourdrinier. After modification, the fourdrinier machine began to catch on in England, and it later was produced in the United States as well. The name fourdrinier is still used today to describe certain paper machines. The development of the paper machine changed what had been a lengthy and time consuming handmade art into a manufacturing process.

The other event that forever changed papermaking occurred in the middle of the nineteenth century. After 1851, the preferred fiber source for papermaking began to change from old rags to wood pulp. This event, along with the invention of the paper machine, in effect created the modern paper industry (see ''Background and Development,'' **SIC 2611: Pulp Mills**). The size and speed of paper machines increased rapidly between 1850 and 1916. Paper use was booming by 1889, when the annual U.S. production of paper reached one million tons. This figure doubled in the next ten years.

At the end of World War I, the United States began a period of rapid economic growth and the paper industry grew along with the general economy. Several new associations, including the Paper Industry Management Association and the Technical Association of the Pulp and Paper Industry were founded and developed during this time. Paper containers and packaging, a growing use of corrugated medium and linerboard to make shipping boxes, and a host of new products—such as tissues and sanitary napkins—all emerged as major trends in the postwar era. It was during this time that Canadian mills became dominant

in newsprint manufacture, producing the majority of American newsprint. It is only recently that U.S. manufacturers have produced the majority of newsprint consumed in the United States.

Southern Growth. It was also during this period that the Pacific Northwest became a major pulp producer. The southern United States, however, saw the greatest growth. Prior to this time, it was difficult to use southern pine to make paper because of its high resin content. However, new processes were developed using southern pine to make bleached and unbleached kraft paper. Southern pine was ideal for this type of paper because its long fibers produced very strong paper and board. Kraft production in the South shot up from just 258 tons per day (tpd) in 1919 to 9,128 (tpd) a day in 1940. By the end of World War II, this total was up to about 13,000 (tpd).

The growth of southern paperboard mills—and other board mills around the country—was greatly enhanced by a 1914 Federal Trade Commission decision that legalized the use of corrugated medium packaging in shipping. Prior to that, wooden boxes were used for shipping goods around the country. Military development of paper packaging materials during World War I helped provide new technology and methods for producing superior paper packaging. Southern newsprint production also began during this time, due in large part to the talents of Charles H. Herty. Methods developed by Herty and his relentless promotion of southern papermaking helped create today's paper industry in the South.

While the Great Depression of the 1930s severely hurt other industries, it did not affect the pulp and paper industry as much since paper was being used in new ways throughout the economy. It was around 1930 that machine coated paper was first manufactured in the United States.

During World War II, the paper industry worked closely with the federal government to make sure that adequate supplies of paper were available both for domestic use and for the armed forces. Paper was one of the main materials used for shipping and storing military supplies. Recycling of paper reached a peak during the war years as well, with paper drives being common in many big cities.

Postwar Growth. After World War II, the paper industry continued growing. New pulping strategies and tree planting allowed the paper industry to develop the fiber sources it needed to meet the expanding demand. Prior to this time, paper companies tended to cut down trees and not replant. It was during this time that southern pine first began to be used to make white printing paper.

During the late 1940s, all areas of the paper industry were growing fast, but some new areas—such as milk cartons and drinking cups—saw exponential growth. Many of the growth trends were centered around the use of disposable paper products, a trend that had started in World War II.

In the 1950s and 1960s, paper machines grew wider and faster, which helped multiply the supply of paper and board. By 1970, however, the paper industry faced sustained challenges to its environmental practices. New clean air and water rules from federal and state governments in the early 1970s forced the industry to install expensive new treatment systems. Many other capital projects were put on hold and then frozen when the economy entered a severe recession in the early 1980s. However, in the mid- to late 1980s the paper industry initiated what has been called its greatest modernization ever. These capital intensive projects included millwide automation, technological innovations, mill modernization, environmental upgrades, and a push for total quality. The U.S. paper industry began competing more effectively in global markets during this time as well.

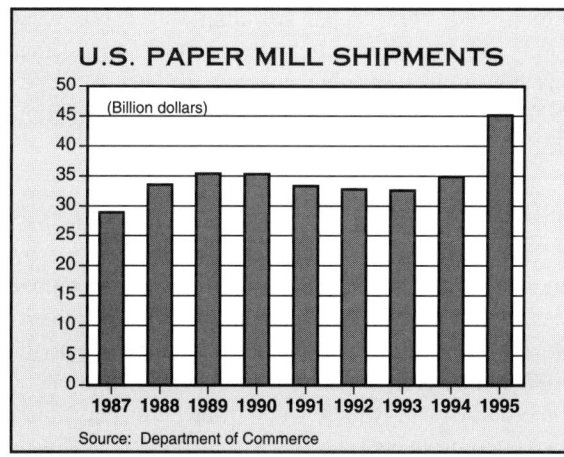

U.S. PAPER MILL SHIPMENTS

(Billion dollars)

Source: Department of Commerce

CURRENT CONDITIONS

The paper industry of the 1990s is highly competitive, both in domestic and foreign markets. It has a modern, efficient manufacturing base, labor peace, and strong markets. However, the industry faces several major challenges, including environmental compliance, recycling, and alternative media.

Environment. Environmental compliance has been a daunting—and expensive—challenge for the paper industry in the 1990s. There is sustained opposition from environmental groups and increased government regulation in nearly all steps of production. For example, the lumber industry in the Pacific Northwest has been drastically reduced in scale. Due to successful court challenges by environmental groups under the Endangered Species Act, tree harvests in the early to mid-1990s dropped to one sixth of harvesting levels in the mid-1980s. Despite the release of some lands for harvesting and permits for salvage logging issued in 1995, harvesting was still greatly reduced in the mid-1990s.

Pulp and paper mills in the Northwest dependent on the residue of lumber operations for raw material have had to look to new sources—even overseas—for sources of wood chips. Many northwestern U.S. mills have converted partially or completely to the use of recycled paper. Also, the pulping and bleaching of wood fiber was the focus of proposals for stringent and costly new federal regulation in the mid-1990s (see Current Conditions, **SIC 2611: Pulp Mills.**

Recycling. While paper recycling was a major environmental challenge in the early 1990s, the industry's quick response to recycle more paper has convinced many of its critics—both in the public and government—that the industry is serious about recycling. The U.S. paper industry reached an overall recycling rate of 40 percent in 1993 and is on track to reach a goal of recycling 50 percent of all paper produced in the United States by the year 2000.

Recycling of certain grades, such as newsprint and old corrugated containers, has traditionally been high, while recycling rates for other grades, such as printing and writing papers, are growing rapidly. For example, over 59 percent of all newsprint used in the United States was recovered in 1994, up from just 29 percent in 1980. In linerboard, almost all capacity increases in the early 1990s came from new recycled linerboard mills, and by 1994 over 62 percent of old corrugated containers—known as OCC in the business—were being recovered, up from 47.9 percent in 1986.

Recycling of printing and writing paper, while lower than other grades, has also increased dramatically, thanks in part to aggressive state and federal legislation in the early 1990s that sought to increase recycling rates in all grades. In 1993, President Clinton signed an executive order mandating higher levels of recycled fiber in paper purchased by the federal government. In 1994, the recovery rate from printing and writing paper stood at 34.1 percent, up from just 22.9 percent in 1986.

While highly touted as an environmental "silver bullet," recycling itself has some environmental liabilities. Most recycling mills generate a major waste stream and consume large amounts of purchased energy. With recycled newsprint, for example, only 85 percent of incoming newsprint is usable as fiber. The rest is unusable sludge that must be cleaned out of the process and then burned or placed in landfills. In some recycled grades, sludge can be up to 50 percent of the incoming waste paper. Considering that some mills make up to 2,500 tons per day of paper, sludge can become a major waste problem. Also, since recycling mills cannot burn bark or spent pulping chemicals to generate electricity on their own, they must purchase large amounts of power from local utilities.

In the mid-1990s, recycling began to change the geographic distribution of paper mills. So called "mini mills" began to crop up near major U.S. cities. These mini mills remove ink and recycle old newsprint and other grades of wastepaper and make new newsprint and linerboard on relatively small paper machines. Since they are close to where much of the country's wastepaper is collected—major cities—they are able to greatly reduce shipping costs.

Alternative Media. A third major challenge to the paper industry comes from the electronic display and storage of information. In the 1970s and early 1980s, some people predicted that computers would soon replace paper in the so called "paperless office." In reality, computers encouraged users to print out even more paper than ever before, fueling a boom in printing and writing papers.

Today, however, computers are being used more often to replace paper for the storage and transfer of information previously accomplished only on paper, such as the filing of legal papers with the Securities and Exchange Commission, which as of 1996 began to require electronic submissions of some corporate documents. Some observers feel that this may curtail the growth of paper. However, other observers point out that computers have vastly expanded the amount of information that can be stored. Even if a smaller percentage of this information is printed out, it is predicted that the use of paper should still grow. Several studies concluded that alternative media is not likely to affect consumption of paper until 2005, and that even then, only select grades are likely to be negatively affected by alternative media.

Financial Conditions. In the early 1990s, the paper industry produced more paper than ever before but was unable to maintain effective pricing. Paper prices fell in 1991 and 1992, before beginning a sharp recovery in 1994 that lasted through most of 1995. In fact, in 1994 and 1995 average paper prices were up more than 50 percent, with prices of some grades increasing at even higher rates. These high prices led to record U.S. paper

company profits in 1995. However, 1996 saw prices—and profits—plummeting once again, though not falling as low as they had in the early 1990s.

Operating rates are another key to profits in the paper industry. In general, operating rates—the percentage of time that mills are in operation—need to be at or over 90 percent for the mill to be profitable. This means most large mills operate 24 hours a day, 7 days a week. Operating rates dropped in 1990 and 1991, but rebounded to about 90 percent for paper producers and 95 percent for paperboard manufacturers in 1992. In 1993, the operating rate for all producers reached 93.7 percent and shot up to 96 percent in both 1994 and 1995. However, operating rates dropped dramatically in 1996 to about 89 percent as many producers took extensive downtime in an attempt to work off large inventories of pulp and paper products.

Another measure of paper industry economic health is capital expenditures for new plants and equipment. When paper companies are profitable, they tend to reinvest a large share of their profits into capital expenditures. Capital expenditures for the U.S. pulp and paper industry peaked in 1990, at about $18 billion, and stayed high in 1991 at about $17 billion. However, from 1992 to 1996, the rate of capital expenditures stayed within a range of $12 billion to $14 billion, and 1997 capital spending was expected to barely top $10 billion. Industry analysts suggest that this may reflect growing concern in the U.S. paper industry that domestic growth in paper consumption will remain low for some time.

INDUSTRY LEADERS

International Paper Company. Founded in 1898 by the merger of 18 northeastern pulp and paper companies, International Paper Company (IP), Purchase, New York, was the world's largest paper company in 1996. In that year, IP had total sales of $20.1 billion, of three-quarters of which were from pulp, paper and converted products sales. IP is one of the largest producers of printing and writing papers, marketing these products under its Hammermill, Springhill, Strathmore and Beckett brands, and through its Aussedat Rey, Zanders and Kwidzyn operations in Europe. IP is one of the industry's largest producers of kraft paper and packaging; containerboard and corrugated boxes; and folding boxboard. In 1995, IP made two major acquisitions: Carter Holt Harvey of New Zealand, and Federal Paper Board, a U.S. company.

Georgia-Pacific Corporation. Atlanta-based Georgia-Pacific Corporation (G-P) has major interests in building products, pulp and paper, and paper chemicals. In 1996, G-P had total sales of $13 billion. In that year it employed 47,500 people at over 400 locations, and owned or controlled more than 5 million acres of timber and timberland in North America. G-P produces containerboard and packaging, communications papers, market pulp and packaging products at 84 facilities in the U.S. and Canada. In 1995, G-P had the capacity to produce 8.9 million tons of pulp, paper and paperboard, about 8 percent of total U.S. capacity.

Weyerhaeuser Company. Based in Tacoma, Washington, Weyerhaeuser's main businesses are growing and harvesting timber; manufacturing and distributing forest products (including logs, wood chips, building products, pulp, paper, and packaging products); real estate development and construction; and financial services. In 1996, Weyerhaeuser had total sales of $11.1 billion and employed 39,700 workers. Weyerhaeuser owned 5.3 million acres of commercial forestland in the United States, with about half in the South and the other half in the Pacific Northwest. The company also has license arrangements on 18.9 million acres of Canadian forestland. In 1995, Weyerhaeuser completed modernization projects at three of its largest pulp and paper mills and acquired nine box plants from Westvaco.

Kimberly-Clark Corporation. Dallas-based Kimberly-Clark is a leading global manufacturer of products for personal, business and industrial uses. In 1995, K-C had total sales of $13.1 billion, all from pulp, paper and converted product sales, and employed 54,800 workers. K-C is best known for its Kleenex, Huggies, Scott, and Kotex brand consumer products. In December 1995, Kimberly-Clark completed a stock for stock merger with Scott Paper Co., a global producer of sanitary tissue products. The $9.4 billion merger made K-C the largest tissue manufacturer in the world. Following the merger, K-C operated manufacturing operations in 33 countries, with products available in 150 countries.

The Procter & Gamble Company. This consumer products giant markets a wide range of household products, including paper products, worldwide. The company operates in 58 countries, employs 103,000 people, and had total 1996 sales of $35.2 billion. The company's paper segment had net sales of $9.29 billion in 1995, up 12 percent from 1994, when sales were $8.28 billion. P&G completed the acquisition of the European tissue business of V.P. Schickendanz AG in 1995.

Stone Container Corporation. Chicago-based Stone Container Corporation is a major multinational paper company, specializing in pulp, paper and packaging products. With 1996 revenues of $5.1 billion, Stone is reportedly the world's leading manufacturer of unbleached containerboard and kraft paper. Since it competes in many commodity markets, Stone Container relies on a "value-added" approach to maintain its share of those markets. Stone is a 47 percent owner of Canada-based Stone-Consolidated Inc., which is the world's largest marketer of newsprint and groundwood paper. In 1995, Stone made several international acquisitions and also purchased certain assets of St. Joe Paper Co.

Champion International Corporation. In 1996, Champion International had total sales of $5.8 billion, most of which came from pulp, paper and converted product sales. The company employs more than 24,000 people at its paper and wood products facilities in North America and Brazil. Champion produces paper for business communications, commercial printing, publications and newspapers as well as pulp and building products. At the end of 1995, Champion owned or controlled more than five million acres of U.S. timberlands in the U.S. and had the capacity to produce 6.3 million annual tons of paper, paperboard and market pulp.

Fort James Corporation. Created by a 1997 merger between James River Corporation of Virginia and Fort Howard Corporation, this Richmond, Virginia-based company manufactures and markets consumer products as well as food and consumer packaging. The James River side of the business had revenues of $5.7 billion, 98 manufacturing facilities, and 23,000 employees in North America and Europe in 1996; the Fort Howard side had $1.5 billion in revenues and 7,000 employees. Fort James Corporation (FJC) was expected to retain the structure of James River's three major business units: North American consumer products; European consumer products; and food and consumer packaging. During the third quarter of 1995, James River spun off a large part of its communications papers business, along with the specialty paper-based portion of its packaging business, by creating Crown Vantage Corp., which is based in Oakland, California.

The Mead Corporation. Dayton, Ohio-based Mead Corp. is a forest products company with offices and operations in 30 countries. In 1996, Mead had total sales of $4.7 billion, all in pulp, paper and converted products. Mead produces more than 1.1 million tons of paper and 1.3 million tons of paperboard annually, as well as pulp products. It is a leading producer of coated paperboard, containerboard, and multiple packaging; a distributor of paper, packaging and supplies; and a leading manufacturer and distributor of school supplies in the United States and Canada. In 1995, Mead completed a $350 million stock buyback program and retired $269 million in debt following the sale of its

Mead Data Central business unit, which became Knight-Ridder's LEXIS-NEXIS online subscription database.

WORK FORCE

Total employment in the pulp, paper and converting industries was about 619,000 in 1996, down slightly from 627,000 in 1992. This continues a long term trend of stable or slightly declining employment in the industry despite large capacity increases. Employee wage increases remained at or below the inflation rate in the early 1990s, averaging about 2.5 percent. These increases were far below the average 7.5 percent annual increases recorded during the period from 1975 to 1985.

Like other manufacturing industries, the paper industry employs many unionized workers. However, the heaviest concentrations of union employees are in older mills which were organized years ago. Almost all new pulp and paper mills are non-union operations, including mills constructed by companies with unionized mills in other locations. In general, the wages and benefits provided by non-union mills are comparable to unionized mills.

There has been relative labor peace in the paper industry during the 1980s and 1990s. In exchange for salary increases, management was able to obtain work rules changes that allowed workers to perform more jobs in the mill and eliminate pay differentials for Sunday and holiday pay. One dramatic strike in the 1980s ended in failure when unionized workers at International Paper's mill in Jay Maine were permanently replaced by new workers. Only a handful of the original workers regained their jobs. Since that strike, there have been no major work stoppages in the paper industry.

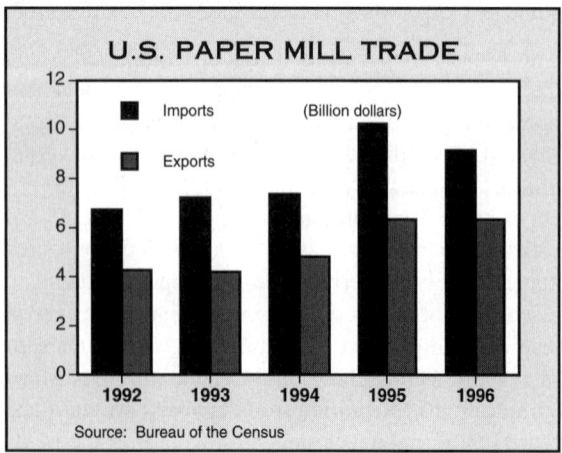

U.S. PAPER MILL TRADE

■ Imports   (Billion dollars)
■ Exports

1992   1993   1994   1995   1996

Source: Bureau of the Census

AMERICA AND THE WORLD

In 1995, the U.S. paper industry exported about 10.9 million tons of paper, paperboard, and converted products, over 11 percent of total industry production. During this same year, it imported 15.5 million tons of paper, paperboard, and converted products, mostly from Canada. Newsprint accounted for about half of these imports. (These figures do not include imports and exports of pulpwood chips and wood pulp, which are widely traded.)

Because of the large amount of market pulp and newsprint imported from Canada, the U.S. paper industry usually runs a trade deficit. For example, in 1995, the value of all U.S. paper, paperboard and converted product exports was $9.7 billion, while imports in these categories totaled $12.3 billion. This figure does not include about $1.56 billion for U.S. wastepaper exports in 1995, an area where the United States leads the world, with a large share of wastepaper exports going to the fiber-starved Asian countries. Japan and Korea are two of the leading Asian wastepaper importers.

Exports have played a key role in stabilizing the paper industry during the 1990s. As domestic sales of paper and allied products (including pulp) have only experienced slight growth from 1991 to 1996, at an average annual rate of 1.5 percent to 2 percent, exports increased 8.2 percent during the same period.

Overall, U.S. exports of paper and allied products—including wastepaper—were aided by the declining value of the U.S. dollar in the early 1990s and competitive pricing, though that advantage began to weaken in 1996 and early 1997 as the dollar continued to rise against most foreign currencies. Paperboard has long been a leading export product, and in 1995 the U.S. industry exported 6 million tons of paperboard. By contrast, a total of 3 million tons of paper was exported in 1995. Of the paper total, printing and writing paper accounted for 1.5 million tons.

While the U.S. paper industry exports products throughout the world, China has emerged as a major U.S. customer. In 1996, for example, China purchased $700 million worth of U.S. paper products, about 10 percent of all Chinese imports from the U.S.

Newsprint Growth. Newsprint is one of the major areas where U.S. producers have become more competitive in the global economy. Canadian newsprint, which until the early 1980s held a dominant 60 percent share of total U.S. consumption, has fallen on hard times. In the late 1980s, Canadian newsprint became significantly less competitive with U.S. newsprint because of higher production costs, new state government requirements for recycled newsprint, and growing U.S. newsprint capacity. In 1993, Canadian newsprint accounted for only slightly more than 40 percent of U.S. newsprint consumption, compared with about 52 percent in 1991. Many Canadian newsprint mills are located in rural Quebec, far from recycled fiber sources, and are old and have high production costs. As a result, many market observers expect the Canadian market share to decrease. However, some Canadian producers have made aggressive moves to obtain recycled fiber and build mills closer to urban areas in order to compete in the market for recycled newsprint.

The Japanese market remains a major challenge for U.S. producers. Despite major cost advantages, U.S. producers have a very small market share of the $70 billion Japanese paper and paperboard market, which is second only to the United States in size. This low market share has been attributed to structural impediments in the Japanese market and a general reluctance by Japanese customers to use imported products.

In 1992 the U.S. industry achieved a major breakthrough, when, after lengthy negotiations, a formal five-year agreement was concluded between the governments of the United States and Japan on measures designed to open Japan's paper market to foreign suppliers. The agreement requires the Japanese government to encourage Japanese paper distributors, converters, printers and other major consumers of paper products to use more imported paper and develop long-term buying relationships with foreign producers. Paper users in Japan are also expected to establish nondiscriminatory purchasing practices and develop purchasing guidelines that can be followed by both domestic and foreign suppliers of paper and paper products. Under the agreement, the two governments periodically review the implementation of the pact.

From 1992 to 1996, however, the U.S. share of the Japanese paper market increased by only 0.5 percent, from 3.6 percent to 4.1 percent. The United States contends that if all barriers were eliminated, Japanese imports of foreign paper products would increase fourfold. As a result of the lack of progress, in 1995 the U.S. Trade Representative placed the government of Japan on a Super 301 "Watch List," which allows the U.S. government to monitor trade activities of foreign country's markets in order to determine whether U.S. and other foreign suppliers are being discriminated against.

Prospects. While the global economy slowed considerably in the early 1990s and went into recession in some areas, most U.S. producers remained very competitive worldwide. The U.S. industry still maintains substantial raw material and energy advantages over many of its foreign competitors. The United States also employs a large, well-trained work force that has access to modern process control technology and scheduling software. Given these advantages, the U.S. paper industry should have a long-term competitive edge over other paper producers in Japan, Europe, and Scandinavia. However, Asian and Latin American producers invested large amounts of capital in the 1990s to build modern, world-class pulp and paper facilities. These mills, which use very low cost fiber largely from hardwood and softwood plantations, have emerged as formidable global competitors.

RESEARCH AND TECHNOLOGY

Traditionally, papermaking research has focused on making faster, wider machines that experience fewer paper breaks. To support these goals, research is continuing in every area of the paper machine: the forming section, the press section, the drying section, and the finishing and converting areas. Much of this research is being performed by supplier companies to the paper industry, which have traditionally assumed a much larger research role than the paper companies. However, paper companies—as well as suppliers— are expanding their support of cooperative research at the nation's pulp and paper schools, such as North Carolina State University, the University of Maine, and the University of Wisconsin-Stevens Point. They also support non-profit research groups such as the Institute of Paper Science and Technology, the Pulp and Paper Research Institute of Canada (PAPRICAN) and the Herty Foundation.

Recycled Research. Much of the research in the paper industry is focusing on how to effectively use more recycled fiber. This is particularly important as the paper industry works to meet its own challenge of recycling 50 percent of all paper produced by the year 2000 and government mandates such as President Clinton's 1993 executive order on recycled paper.

Much of this research will focus on improving the physical chemistry of the "flotation cells" of the deinking process. This technology uses air bubbles to literally "float" detached ink particles to the top of a mixture of ground up paper and water, where the inky froth is skimmed off. Improving the efficiency of this system would speed up production and lower costs.

Research will also focus on using new chemical processes to help produce recycled paper that matches virgin uncoated freesheet in quality. Uncoated freesheet, used in products such as copy paper, is one of the biggest grades of paper, and one of the most demanding in terms of quality.

One of the major initiatives involving the pulp and paper industry is Agenda 2020, a cooperative research project involving the U.S. Department of Energy, pulp and paper research institutions and leading paper companies. Agenda 2020 was prepared by the chief technology officers of major paper companies under the auspices of the American Forest & Paper Association, a trade association. The development of the document was spurred by the U.S. Department of Energy's "Industries of the Future" program, which seeks to fund research in specific industries—including pulp and paper—that will reduce energy intensiveness and improve environmental performance. The DOE prepared a draft document on the "Pulp Mill of the Future." That document was reviewed by the team of chief technology officers and modified to create Agenda 2020, which outlines six specific areas for R&D, including sustainable forest management; environmental; performance; energy performance; capital effectiveness; recycling and sensors and control.

In addition to research to complete Agenda 2020, there are hundreds of other ongoing research projects in the paper industry. The industry is seeking closer cooperation among all players—paper companies, suppliers, research institutions and government agencies, as it tries to improve on the complex art of making paper.

FURTHER READING

Biermann, Christopher J. *Essentials of Pulping and Papermaking.* San Diego: Academic Press, 1993.

Kline, James E. *Paper and Paperboard: Manufacturing and Converting Fundamentals.* San Francisco: Miller Freeman Publications, 1982.

Paper: Linking People and Nature. Washington: American Forest & Paper Association, 1992.

Paper, Paperboard, Pulp Capacity and Fiber Consumption. Washington: American Forest & Paper Association, 1996.

"Pima's Top 50 North American Paper Companies." *Pima,* June 1996.

Smook, Gary A. *Handbook of Pulp & Paper Terminology: A Guide to Industrial and Technological Usage.* Bellingham, WA: Angus Wilde Publications, 1990.

Thesaurus of Pulp and Paper Terminology. Atlanta: Institute of Paper Science and Technology, 1991.

Stanley, Gary. "Paperboard, Imports, and Exports to Fuel 1997 Growth." *TAPPI Journal,* January 1997, 56.

"Vision 300: A Celebration of American Papermaking" *Pima,* January 1991.

Wright, Helena. *300 Years of American Papermaking.* Washington: Smithsonian Institution, 1991.

—Alan Rooks

PAPERBOARD MILLS

This industry consists of establishments primarily engaged in manufacturing paperboard from wood pulp and other fiber pulp. Paperboard mills may also manufacture converted paperboard products. Establishments primarily engaged in integrated pulp production and paperboard manufacturing are included in this industry if they ship mostly paperboard or paperboard products. Establishments primarily engaged in manufacturing converted paperboard products from purchased paperboard are classified in Industry Group 265 or 267. Establishments primarily engaged in manufacturing insulation board and other reconstituted wood fiberboard are classified in **SIC 2493: Reconstituted Wood Products.**

INDUSTRY SNAPSHOT

U.S. paperboard mill production reached 46.6 million tons in 1995, a slight increase over the previous year, when production was 45.7 million tons. At this rate, paperboard out-paced production of paper in the United States in 1995, which checked in at 42.6 million tons.

The capacity of U.S. mills to produce paperboard is projected to grow from 52.9 million tons in 1997 to 54.3 million tons in 1999, a total increase of just 2.6 percent (paperboard production typically is about 88 percent to 98 percent of total capacity, depending on economic conditions). Of this increase, 39 percent will come from the construction of new machines and 61 percent from improvements to existing machines.

The most extensive use of paperboard is to make shipping containers, cartons, and packaging. The vast majority of paperboard consumed in the United States is manufactured by U.S. paperboard producers. In addition to dominating the domestic market, U.S. paperboard producers hold a strong position in the international market, with exports reaching 6 million tons in 1995, 12.9 percent of total U.S. paperboard production, which was 46.6 million tons.

Two grades of paperboard—corrugating medium and linerboard—are used to make corrugated shipping containers. These two grades account for the majority of paperboard produced in the United States. A third grade—solid bleached sulfate (SBS), used for folding cartons such as those used in retail stores—accounts for a large share of the remaining production. Paperboard grades are also distinguished between folding and non-folding grades. Folding grades have to be flexible enough so that when the board is folded to make a box—such as a cereal box—the surface will not split or crack.

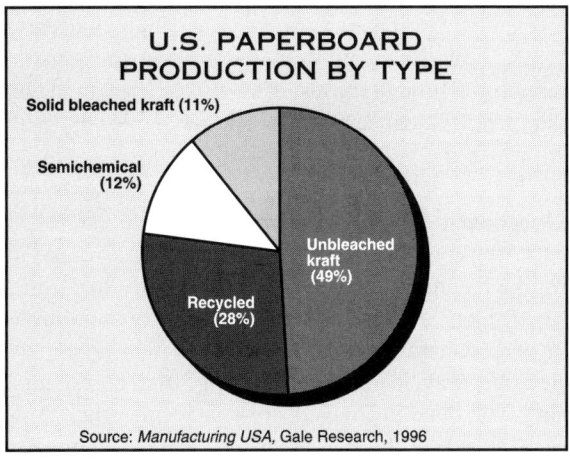

U.S. PAPERBOARD PRODUCTION BY TYPE

Solid bleached kraft (11%)

Semichemical (12%)

Unbleached kraft (49%)

Recycled (28%)

Source: *Manufacturing USA*, Gale Research, 1996

ORGANIZATION AND STRUCTURE

Paperboard production in the United States is divided into four major categories:

• Unbleached kraft paperboard, which is made from pulp containing not less than 80 percent wood fibers produced by the sulfate (kraft) process. Since it is unbleached, this type of paperboard retains a brown color. Unbleached kraft accounted for 49 percent of all U.S. paperboard production in 1995.

• Recycled paperboard, which is manufactured from a combination of recycled fibers from various grades of paper stock, with the predominant portion of the pulp being recycled fibers and a minor amount being virgin fibers. Recycled paperboard that contains no virgin fibers is commonly called 100 percent recycled paperboard. Recycled paperboard accounted for 28 percent of all U.S. paperboard production in 1995.

• Semichemical paperboard, which is made from pulp containing not less than 75 percent virgin wood fibers, the majority of which is produced by a semichemical process. Semichemical board accounted for 12 percent of all U.S. paperboard production in 1995.

• Solid bleached packaging paperboard, which is used in packaging and made from pulp containing not less than 80 percent bleached virgin wood fibers. This paperboard is white and is used for higher-end packaging applications, such as milk cartons and frozen food packaging. Solid bleached

kraft accounted for 11 percent of all U.S. paperboard production in 1995.

More paper and paperboard is used to make packaging than in any other single application. While most paperboard is still made from virgin fibers (trees), paperboard mills have traditionally used a large percentage of recycled fiber because of favorable economics. The use of recycled fiber in paperboard production is growing quickly, especially in products in which the reclaimed pulp does not need to be cleaned. Combination boxboard, for example, is used in cereal cartons where two white outside layers mask a recycled, gray inner layer.

Paperboard produced on cylinder board machines has commonly been made from recycled fibers. This is because cylinder machines form the paperboard web in separate layers, which are then pressed together. This makes it possible to hide a layer of recycled board, which can have poor appearance and lower strength in between two outside layers of virgin material.

Fourdrinier paperboard machines, which traditionally have made paperboard in a single web, are generally used to make virgin paperboard since it makes a superior web from one fiber source. Newer paperboard machines, however, include machinery that allow the formation of a single web from different fiber sources.

Kraft softwood has been the preferred pulp for making paperboard because of its superior strength characteristics. While most paperboard is unbleached, retaining the characteristic brown color of the pulp, bleached grades are often used where the consumer is likely to see the box—such as gift boxes and food and beverage packages. Besides food applications, cosmetics and other high-profit products use the more expensive bleached board because they can afford its higher cost.

Paperboard comes in a wide variety of styles and qualities, but can divided into two categories based on its use: containerboard, which includes all the materials used for making corrugated boxes; and boxboard, which includes all the materials used for making non-corrugated packaging such as food containers and department store boxes. Containerboard is divided further into two subcategories: corrugating medium, the inner fluted part of the box; and linerboard, which makes up the outer faces, or layers of the box. Corrugating medium—or just "medium," as it is often called in the trade—is made from both semichemical pulp and recycled fiber.

Boxboard is divided into three subcategories: folding boxboard, set-up boxboard, and milk carton/

food service boxboard. Total U.S. production of boxboard in 1995 reached 14.54 million tons, up 3.4 percent over the previous year. Most paperboard can be coated with a pigment such as clay to improve printing properties. Most grades of paperboard can also be made impermeable to air and liquids by using plastic coating and laminating. This is essential for products such as milk carton stock.

Corrugated Boxes. The universal use of corrugated containers for shipping manufactured goods by truck, train, or ship makes this grade one of the largest in the paper and board industry. There are a large number of converting plants located throughout the country that use corrugating medium and linerboard, which are glued together to make boxes. These converting plants are located close to users of the containers and are often owned by the same company that manufactures the linerboard and medium.

The main raw material used to make corrugating medium is semichemical hardwood pulp. Hardwood pulp, which is made from deciduous trees such as oak and maple, is used rather than softwood pulp, made from conifers such as southern pine. Hardwoods are used because they are less costly and help make the corrugating medium stiff since they are less flexible than softwood fibers.

Unlike the pulp used in other types of paper and paperboard, the pulp used for making medium still contains some lignin, the chemical ''glue'' that holds fibers together in the tree. This is because medium pulp is not washed as intensively as pulps used in making other grades. As a result, the lignin and other wood by-products are left in the pulp and formed into the web of paperboard. When the paperboard web goes through the corrugator, the remaining wood by-products help form the rigid fluted shape.

Growth of Recycling. Like other predominantly virgin paper and paperboard grades, semichemical medium has seen its share of total capacity decline as a result of increased production of recycled products. Semichemical medium's share of total medium production declined to 61.4 percent in 1995 from 79 percent in 1980, while recycled medium's share grew to 38.6 percent. In the mid-1990s, the shift away from semichemical was dramatic. For example, production of semichemical corrugating medium in 1995 was 5.5 million tons, down 5.2 percent from the previous year, while production of recycled corrugating medium was 3.5 million tons, up 17.4 percent over 1994.

While there are many basis weights for both semichemical and recycled medium, including 22, 26,

33, 36, and 40 pound, the standard weight is 26 pound. It accounts for nearly 80 percent of all production.

Medium production is directly related to U.S. corrugated box shipments. In the late 1980s and early 1990s, box shipments grew faster than the general economy. Through the rest of the 1990s, growth in box shipments is expected to track more closely with growth in the general economy.

Linerboard. Total U.S. linerboard production reached 19.77 million tons in 1995, up 2.4 percent over 1994. Unlike medium, linerboard is made mostly from softwood fibers. However, linerboard may contain up to 20 percent hardwood pulp or recycled fiber. The recycled fiber may be made from cuttings from corrugating plants or other recovered corrugated material. Softwood is needed to give linerboard adequate strength. Most softwood pulp for linerboard is produced using the kraft pulping process. To suit the varied packaging needs of box consumers, bleached kraft linerboard is made in many different basis weights. The standard variety is 42 pound, but other major grades include 26 pound, 33 pound, and 69 pound. While production of recycled linerboard is significantly less than virgin linerboard, 100 percent recycled linerboard grew very fast in the United States from the late 1980s through the mid-1990s, and was projected to grow even faster during the late 1990s.

SBS. Solid bleached sulfate (SBS) is a top-quality paperboard made from pulp that includes at least 80 percent bleached virgin fiber. Most U.S.-produced SBS is coated with a clay solution to improve its surface for printing. SBS used for food packaging—such as milk carton stock—is often coated with polyethylene. Basis weights for SBS range from 40 to 100 pounds. SBS is also used for products such as disposable cups and plates and as linerboard for corrugated boxes and displays that need an outside surface for high-quality, four-color printing. In 1995, the capacity of U.S. mills to produce SBS reached 5.37 million tons per year (tpy). By 1999, capacity was expected to grow to 5.79 million tpy. In 1995, actual SBS output increased 6 percent to 5.3 million tons compared with 1994, fueled by higher demand in the domestic folding carton segment and higher export growth.

Another product made by some mills that produce SBS is bleached bristol. This product, usually a lightweight grade, is used for greeting cards, paperback book covers, and telephone directories, among other products. Bristol is usually classified under paper production, rather than paperboard.

BACKGROUND AND DEVELOPMENT

Since the majority of paperboard capacity is used to make materials for corrugated boxes, the background and development of paperboard mills tends to mirror growth in the use of these boxes.

Before corrugated containers became the accepted standard for domestic and international shipping, wooden crates and boxes were the preferred method. However, this began to change dramatically after the U.S. Federal Trade Commission, in the 1914 Pridham decision, legalized the use of corrugated packaging in shipping. Also, during World War I, the U.S. military spurred research and development of corrugated packaging to ship military supplies.

As new methods helped improve the strength and durability of corrugated containers, their use in the general economy increased dramatically. For example, between 1935 and 1942, 29 new paperboard machines came on line. Collectively, these machines produced 15,545 tons per day. During World War II, military needs fostered improvements in corrugated shipping containers, including water and temperature resistance. In the postwar years, the growth of corrugated containers more than kept pace with the general economy, which itself was growing rapidly. Also, the development of more disposable containers for products such as food and beverages fueled solid increases in the production of SBS board. Paperboard accounted for slightly more than half of the overall production of paper and paperboard in the United States in 1995.

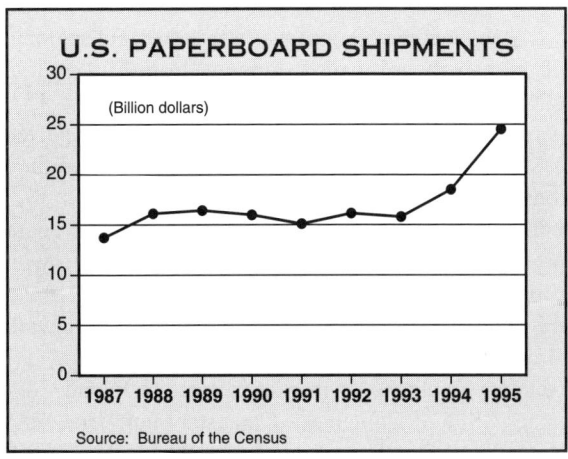

U.S. PAPERBOARD SHIPMENTS

(Billion dollars)

Source: Bureau of the Census

CURRENT CONDITIONS

Like other sectors of the U.S. pulp and paper industry, the 1990s have been volatile for U.S. paperboard mills. The industry saw depressed conditions in the early 1990s; booming demand and huge prices

increases in 1994 and 1995; and falling prices in 1996. For example, year-end transaction prices for 42-pound kraft linerboard were $315 per ton in 1993 before shooting up to $430 per ton in 1994 and $480 per ton in 1995. However, this huge run-up was followed by a huge drop in 1996, to $360 per ton. One of the reasons prices for linerboard—and other paperboard grades—fell hard in 1996 was that capacity increases far outpaced demand for the product, which was in some cases falling as customers worked off large amounts of inventory they had purchased in anticipation of future price increases. Some recovery was expected in 1997, with prices expected to reach $410 per ton.

Predictably, the U.S. paperboard industry—after expanding capacity dramatically in 1996—planned only modest capacity increases for the rest of the decade. The total capacity of U.S. mills to make paperboard increased 2.5 million tons in 1996, a 5.1 percent increase over the previous year. Within the overall paperboard category, containerboard grades had a very large (6.1 percent) capacity increase in 1996, up by 2.1 million tons, and boxboard capacity was up 4.1 percent in 1996, by 419,000 tons. However, from 1997 to 1999, growth in U.S. paperboard production was expected to drop down to just 1.7 percent on an annual basis, with containerboard holding to 1.7 percent annual increases. Boxboard capacity growth was expected to be somewhat higher during the period, at 2.3 percent, but the ''all other'' paperboard category was expected to barely grow at all, with just a 0.8 percent rate of annual increase. A 1.7 percent average annual growth in U.S. paperboard capacity from 1997 to 1999 was expected to increase capacity from 51.6 million tons to 54.3 million tons during the period.

Most of the growth in boxboard was forecast to come from one grade: unbleached kraft folding board, which is used to make beverage carrier board for six-packs of bottled beverages, 24-packs for canned beverages, and many other applications. Produced by just four mills, unbleached kraft folding capacity was projected to jump from 2 million tons in 1996 to 2.4 million tons in 1999, an increase of 6.4 percent annually. The increase will be generated by companies that convert machines previously used to produce linerboard to unbleached kraft folding grades.

Capacity to produce containerboard grades—a group that includes linerboard and corrugating medium made from both virgin and recycled furnish—grew 2.1 million tons in 1996, a 6.1 percent gain over the previous year. However, that growth was expected to taper off, and containerboard capacity was expected to rise by a total of just 1.8 million tons from 1997 to 1999, an average growth rate of 1.7 percent per year over the three-year period. Eight new containerboard machines were responsible for most of the expansion from 1996 to 1999, and four of the eight were said to be producing paperboard by the end of 1996. This accelerated schedule explains why containerboard capacity shot up in 1996 and was expected to rise another 3.2 percent in 1997 before the growth tapers off.

Solid bleached paperboard also had a healthy year in 1996, with capacity expanding 3.8 percent. This grade was expected to grow more slowly, at 1.3 percent per year, from 1997 to 1999. Within the solid bleached paperboard category, bleached folding boxboard capacity increased 2.4 percent in 1996 and was expected to rise 1.5 percent annually through 1999. U.S. capacity to manufacture milk carton and food service stock was up a strong 5.9 percent in 1996, but that level of growth was anticipated to fall sharply to just 1.7 percent per year from 1997 to 1999.

U.S. capacity to produce recycled folding boxboard rose 2.5 percent (75,000 tons) in 1996. That growth was expected to drop by half from 1997 to 1999, just 1.2 percent annually. With no new machines planned for this category, the entire increase was expected to come from productivity improvements.

While capacity, demand, and prices are the key elements determining the current status of the U.S. paperboard industry, other factors have also come into play. U.S. linerboard is recognized worldwide as being the highest quality and best performing linerboard for most packaging applications. One of the major changes in linerboard occurred in the early 1990s when ''Rule 41, Item 22'' of the freight classifications was changed to emphasize ''ring crush,'' which measures resistance to compression, instead of bursting strength. This change allowed U.S. manufacturers to begin making more ''high performance'' linerboard, which is lighter in weight than traditional liner but still useful for shipping. As a result, U.S. producers have developed a number of high performance bleached and unbleached linerboard grades.

INDUSTRY LEADERS

Major paper companies produce large quantities of both paper and paperboard, thus the industry leaders are many of the same companies listed under **SIC 2621: Paper Mills.** However, some large companies such as Stone Container Corp., Tenneco Packaging, Temple-Inland Inc., and International Paper have much larger interests in paperboard than other companies in the industry.

Different companies lead in production of individual grades of paperboard. For example, in corrugating

medium, Stone Container is the industry leader, with 990,000 tons of annual production capacity in 1995 and about 10.3 percent of total capacity; they are followed closely by Weyerhaeuser Co., with 9.3 percent, and Georgia-Pacific, with 9.1 percent. Other significant companies in this grade include Tenneco Packaging, Temple-Inland, and Jefferson Smurfit Corp.

In bleached paperboard, International Paper Company dominates the market, with 2.62 million tons of annual production capacity in 1996, good for 36.6 percent of all U.S. capacity in this grade. International Paper achieved this position by acquiring Federal Paper Board in 1996, another major bleached board producer. Second place is occupied by Westvaco, which had annual capacity of 965,000 tons in 1996 (13.5 percent of capacity), followed by Temple-Inland with 11 percent and Potlatch with 8 percent. Other leading companies include Georgia-Pacific, Champion International, and James River Corp. This category is dominated by a few large players, with the top ten companies holding nearly 88.8 percent of production capacity in 1996.

In linerboard, the three top manufacturers together controlled over 32 percent of U.S. capacity in 1995, with Stone Container holding 14 percent (3.44 million annual tons), International Paper 9.3 percent (2.28 million annual tons), and Georgia-Pacific 9 percent (2.22 million tons). Other significant players in 1995 included Temple-Inland (8.1 percent); Union Camp (7.4 percent), Jefferson Smurfit/CCA (7.1 percent); and Weyerhaeuser (7.2 percent).

Recycled paperboard was a fast growing segment of the paperboard market, jumping from 13.9 million tons in 1995 to 16.1 million tons in 1996, a 15.8 percent increase. However, this growth was expected to slow somewhat, with capacity reaching 16.9 million tons in 1997, 17.4 million tons in 1998, and 17.6 million tons in 1999. The leading recycled paperboard producer in 1996 was Jefferson Smurfit Corp., with capacity of 1.3 million tons, which represented about 8.2 percent of the market. It was followed by Newark Group (7.1 percent) and Sonoco Products Co. (5.7 percent). Other major market factors are Inland Container, Stone Container, Caraustar Industries and Rock-Tenn Co. The Cedar River Paper Co., a new company on the market, was number nine in 1996, with 3.9 percent of the market.

AMERICA AND THE WORLD

Paperboard—particularly linerboard—is one of the strongest export products for the U.S. pulp and paper industry. U.S. linerboard mills, mostly in the southern United States, have traditionally been among the world's lowest-cost producers. In 1995, U.S. mills produced 6.04 million tons of paperboard for export with a value of $3.45 billion. Those exports represented 13 percent of total U.S. paperboard production.

Paperboard is a leading export product, accounting for just under 60 percent of all paper, paperboard, and converted product exports in 1995. By contrast, the United States imported a relatively small volume of paperboard in 1995, just 1.4 million tons, with a value of $810 million.

Linerboard exports tend to increase and decrease sharply due to global economic trends, though the long-term trend has been upward. Prospects for paperboard exports remain strong, but are subject to currency and price fluctuation.

RESEARCH AND TECHNOLOGY

Many of the research trends affecting paperboard mills are shared by paper mills (see **SIC 2621: Paper Mills.** However, there is some interest in using new concepts such as stratification in making paperboard. Stratification involves using a special headbox that can produce three or more layers simultaneously from different fiber sources. In this way, a layer of recycled fiber or some other lesser quality fiber source could be sandwiched between layers of better quality fiber. With newer model headboxes, these layers can be extremely thin.

Like other grades, much of the effort in research and technology in paperboard is to create machines that will produce a wider web of paperboard at higher speeds. In this way, paperboard mills can run their mills more productively. Also, as in other grades, mill processes are becoming more automated and less subject to product variation. This, and continual improvements in paperboard quality, are the main reasons that U.S. paperboard mills can continue to lead the world both in price and product quality.

FURTHER READING

Biermann, Christopher J. *Essentials of Pulping and Papermaking.* San Diego: Academic Press, 1993.

Kline, James E. *Paper and Paperboard: Manufacturing and Converting Fundamentals.* San Francisco: Miller Freeman Publications, 1982.

"Linerboard: Weaker Market Outlook Caused by Surge of New Capacity." *Pulp & Paper,* January 1996.

Paper, Paperboard, Pulp Capacity and Fiber Consumption. Washington: American Forest & Paper Association, 1996.

"Recycled Paperboard: Market Pricing Reacts to Weaker Demand and Lower Wastepaper Costs." *Pulp & Paper,* June 1996.

Thesaurus of Pulp and Paper Terminology. Atlanta: Institute of Paper Science and Technology, 1991.

"U.S. Mills Looking for a Turnaround in 1997." *PIMA's North American Papermaker,* January 1997.

U.S. Trade and Industrial Outlook, 1997-1998. New York: McGraw-Hill, 1997.

"Vision 300: A Celebration of American Papermaking." *PIMA,* January 1991.

—Alan Rooks

SIC 2652

SETUP PAPERBOARD BOXES

Establishments in this industry manufacture setup (rigid) paperboard boxes from purchased paperboard. This classification includes setup paperboard boxes, paperboard filing boxes and metal-edged newsboard boxes. These products differ from other paperboard boxes in that they are not folded down, like corrugated boxes, and are shipped to customers in their final form.

Setup paperboard box manufacturers comprise one of the smaller paper and board products industries. The value of setup paperboard box product shipments grew 18 percent over the ten years from 1984 to 1991, from $466.1 million to $554.9 million. While the average annual growth rate over this period was 1.8 percent, the setup paperboard box industry's sales performance was uneven. Sales tended to spike up and down throughout the 1980s. For example, after rising to $552 million in 1986, sales dropped dramatically the next year, to $436 million, before rising to a peak of $565.1 million in 1990. With the pulp and paper industry in recession in the early 1990s, the value of shipments of setup paperboard boxes dropped back to $430.3 million by 1993.

Since this is a small industry, some of the spikes in shipment values may be explained by changes in customers' inventory levels. If customers hold more product in inventory one year, they tend to purchase less the next year, even if their consumption rate is steady. However, an even more important factor is the price of the product, which tends to swing widely. The cost of materials rises and falls with the market price for paperboard, which during 1994 and 1995 rose as much as 50 percent before dropping back in 1996. These wide price swings help explain the volatility of the value of shipments in the setup paperboard box industry.

The production of setup paperboard boxes is concentrated in the Eastern half of the country, with the three largest production states being New York, New Jersey, and Pennsylvania. The other area combined Northeast and the North Central states, including Wisconsin, Illinois, Ohio, Michigan, and Indiana.

Customers of the setup paperboard box industry are divided among several different product groups. Setup boxes used by department stores and other retailers accounted for 13.94 percent of the market in 1992, while those used for textiles, wearing apparel, and hosiery accounted for 12.57 percent. Candy products manufacturers used 10.11 percent of the total and setup boxes used for cosmetics (including soap) another 6.56 percent. Stationery and office supply manufacturers accounted for 6.3 percent and hardware and household supplies another 2.24 percent. Setup paperboard boxes are used for a wide variety of other products, accounting for 30.63 percent of the market in 1992.

The value of shipments in the setup paperboard box industry is expected to remain flat throughout the late 1990s. While this is a "mature" industry with little chance for exponential growth, it appears to be a stable one. Since setup paperboard boxes are, by definition, rigid packaging, they face little competition from alternative materials—such as plastic— that cannot provide rigidity without undue cost. Also, the recyclability of setup paperboard boxes is seen as an environmental plus, and they can be easily made from recycled materials.

Most of the companies in this industry are smaller, "niche" manufacturers. All but one had annual sales under $100 million in the early 1990s. Caraustar Industries, of Austell, Georgia, is the largest manufacturer in this industry, but it makes products in other industries as well. Other leaders in the setup paperboard box industry include Old Dominion Box Co., of Lynchburg, Virginia; Ward Paper Box Co.; Schiffenhaus Industries Inc., of Newark, New Jersey; and FN Burt Co., of Buffalo, New York.

In 1993 setup paperboard box plants employed about 6,700 people nationwide with an annual payroll of about $134.5 million. Production workers accounted for about 5,300 of that total and put in 11.6 million man hours. Total employment in this industry has been trending downward for years. Total employment in 1993 was a little over half of what it was in 1983, when the industry employed 12,300 people.

FURTHER READING

Darnay, Arsen J., ed. *Manufacturing USA.* Detroit: Gale Research, 1996.

Paper, Paperboard, Pulp Capacity and Fiber Consumption. Washington: American Forest & Paper Association, 1996.

Smook, Gary A. *Handbook of Pulp & Paper Terminology: A Guide to Industrial and Technological Usage.* Bellingham, WA: Angus Wilde Publications, 1990.

U.S. Department of Commerce. *U.S. Industrial Outlook 1994.* Washington: GPO, 1994.

—Alan Rooks

SIC 2653

CORRUGATED AND SOLID FIBER BOXES

This category covers establishments primarily engaged in manufacturing corrugated and solid fiber boxes and related products from paperboard or fiber stock. Important products of this industry include corrugated and solid fiberboard boxes, pads, partitions, display items, pallets, single face products, and corrugated sheets.

INDUSTRY SNAPSHOT

The United States is the world's largest producer of corrugated and solid fiber boxes, and as of the mid-1990s accounted for over a third of total world volume. Corrugated paperboard products are used to ship almost all of the nondurable goods manufactured in the United States and a majority of the durable ones as well. They face relatively little competition from alternative shipping methods. The total value of corrugated paperboard and solid fiber box shipments in 1995 reached $23.8 billion.

The corrugated and solid fiber box industry employed 119,000 people in 1994 with an annual payroll of $3.7 billion. Of that total, 89,000 were production workers putting in 190 million man hours for wages of $2.25 billion.

Corrugated paperboard products have long accounted for the majority of American paperboard container shipments, holding over 60 percent of the total paperboard container market in the mid-1990s. During that period, corrugated product shipments also held about 25 percent share of the overall domestic U.S. packaging market—which includes packaging made from wood, paper/paperboard, plastic, metal, glass, composites, and other materials.

The United States is a major consumer as well as a major producer of corrugated products. In the early to mid-1990s, annual per capita U.S. consumption of corrugated products was the highest in the world—topping 80 kilograms (kg). Japan was the second leading consumer, at just under 70 kg. European nations make up the remaining per capita consumption leaders, with Germany at just under 50 kg, Italy at 45 kg, Spain at 40 kg and the United Kingdom at 30 kg.

Variations in End-Use Markets. The vast majority of corrugated products are used to package nondurable goods, such as food products. In 1993, for example, just under 80 percent of corrugated products were used to package nondurable goods. The percentage of corrugated products directed toward nondurable goods tends to rise during recessions since the number of high-ticket durable goods shipped—such as stoves and refrigerators—decreases. For example, by 1993 the slow-paced U.S. economic recovery had reduced the proportion of corrugated products used for durable goods to 20 percent from about 25 percent in 1989.

Shippers and packagers of food products, the largest market for corrugated products, are likely to be the highest growth market for the corrugated industry in the 1990s. Also, shippers are using more corrugated pallets to replace wooden ones because of concerns over costs and recycling.

One of the key trends in corrugated boxes is recycling. This affects both the material used to make the boxes and how they are disposed of after use. Corrugated boxes are easily recycled and are biodegradable, which tends to help them compete well against plastic products among ''green'' consumers. Most corrugated products are unbleached, which exempts them from recent controversy surrounding bleaching processes in the paper industry. In 1994, 62.5 percent of corrugated products were recovered for recycling into new boxes or other paperboard products. That represents the second highest recovery level of any major consumable material (aluminum cans are first). Increased collection of corrugated boxes—including those coming from the homes of consumers—was expected to increase gradually each year through the 1990s until it nears 70 percent by the year 2000.

ORGANIZATION AND STRUCTURE

The corrugated box market is about 80 percent integrated. This means that 80 percent of all containerboard (the linerboard facing and corrugated fluting that together make a corrugated box) is not sold on the open market. Instead, it is delivered from containerboard mills to corrugated box plants owned by or affiliated with the same organization. The remaining 20 percent is sold by containerboard producers to independent box plants.

The value of corrugated and solid fiber box shipments reflect both the economic activity of the products shipped in them and the prices paid for boxes, which are typically pegged to the price of raw materials. These raw material prices tend to fluctuate widely. For example, the value of corrugated box shipments were up a strong 10.7 percent in 1994 to $22.8 billion, reflecting the recovery in the general economy, higher demand for corrugated boxes, and higher prices for boxes. That growth continued in 1995, as the value of shipments reached $23.8 billion, but in 1996 the value of shipments fell sharply, to $21.7 billion, as slackening demand, drawing down of inventories by customers, and sharp drops in raw material prices led to lower unit sales volumes and lower box prices. Unit volume growth was negligible in both 1995, which saw an actual decline in shipments of 0.5 percent, and 1996, in which unit shipments rose 1 percent.

Still, the 1 percent increase in box shipments in 1996 pushed U.S. corrugated product shipments to an all-time high: 376.2 billion square feet (bsf). This topped the 1994 record of 374.8 bsf. Corrugated box and container product shipments accounted for 99.5 percent of the industry shipment total in 1996, while solid fiber boxes made up the small remainder.

Making corrugated board. Corrugated medium and linerboard are made into corrugated board at box plants. In 1995 the value of the corrugated board market in the United States was more than $8.5 billion. Many weights, thicknesses, and combinations of liners and corrugated medium are used to make different types of corrugated board. In this process, flat corrugated medium board is softened with heat and moisture and passed between a set of corrugating rolls to form it into flutes. Adhesive is applied to the flute tip on one side of the medium. A separate, single face linerboard is then brought into contact with the fluted medium under heat and pressure to produce a single facer web.

This web is conveyed to the double backer station, where adhesive is applied to the exposed flute tips and the double back liner is applied. The combined corrugated board is then passed over a series of hot plates to set the adhesive. Modern corrugating machines run at a variety of speeds, ranging from as low as 100 feet per minute (fpm) to as high as 1,000 fpm, depending on the type of corrugated board under production.

After this, the corrugating board is cut into individual sheets, or blanks, on a trimmer-cutter. The blanks are then fed to a printer-scorer-slotter or some other device, which turns the blank into a flat box that can then be opened and glued by the end user.

Recycled Corrugated. Corrugated boxes have the image of being "environmentally correct" because they can be recycled into new boxes and other products. That image is to a large extent justified, since the recycled fiber content of corrugated is generally the highest of any paper product: as of 1994 it was 62.5 percent and still climbing. While corrugated products are often reused and the majority are recycled, some corrugated boxes do end up as waste in landfills.

To produce recycled linerboard and recycled corrugating medium, many paperboard mills use both preconsumer and postconsumer old corrugated (OCC). Preconsumer waste is corrugated materials such as off-rolls and trimmings from box plants. Postconsumer waste includes boxes that have been used for shipping and subsequently discarded. In 1994, pulp and paper producers used 14.5 million tons of old corrugated containers (OCC) to make new containers, while another 3.4 million tons of OCC were exported.

Standard corrugated boxes are fairly easy to recycle since they are printed lightly and require little or no de-inking. The pulp made from OCC needs little cleaning and does not have to be bleached. Unlike many grades of recycled paper, OCC suffers a minimal loss in fiber strength and other physical properties. However, there is a limit to how many times fibers can be recycled. For example, Asian corrugated boxes, which have been recycled many times due to chronic virgin fiber shortages in those countries, tend to be weaker and less resistant to water than U.S. corrugated boxes. The fiber quality of Asian OCC is so low that many American recycling mills exclude it from their processes.

CURRENT CONDITIONS

At the end of 1995 the domestic corrugating industry consisted of 1,468 box plants. Of that total, 899 were independent operations (not associated with a paperboard mill that produces linerboard and corrugating medium) and 569 were fully integrated plants (where there is a paperboard mill, a corrugated plant, and a sheeting plant). Of the 899 independent operations, 167 were corrugated plants (which take corrugating medium and linerboard and make it into containerboard) and 732 were sheeting plants (which take finished containerboard and make it into boxes). By comparison, of the 569 fully integrated operations, 450 were corrugated plants and 119 were sheet plants. The total number of U.S. box plants continued to decrease in the mid-1990s, as downsizing and merger activity

helped consolidate the industry and eliminate some smaller operations.

The Southeast and West Central regions of the United States have been among the fastest growing areas for the production of corrugated packaging. In the mid-1990s these regions accounted for more than 40 percent of total U.S. corrugated shipments. The Southwest has also been an area of significant growth.

The leading use of corrugated packaging is for food and other grocery products that are shipped to the nation's supermarkets and other retail outlets. In 1997, manufacturers of food, meat, dairy and kindred products were expected to be the largest user of corrugated boxes, accounting for 39 percent of all box deliveries used for nondurable goods. This was down slightly from a 40 percent share in 1992. In this same nondurable category, the paper industry is its own second-best customer, with paper and allied products estimated to use about 22 percent of the nondurable total in 1997.

The durable goods market for corrugated products is considerably more fragmented, with toys and sporting goods leading the corrugated box users market in this category with just 5 percent of shipments.

One significant change for boxmakers in the early 1990s was the modification of Rule 41 and Item 22 of the freight classifications. These standards specify corrugated box design criteria, and after the modification they now stress performance-based edge compression tests rather than the old mullen/burst strength-based test. This allows boxmakers to design lighter weight containment packaging. The revised classifications also create wider opportunities for the use of other types of corrugated boxes that use high performance linerboard (often with a predominantly virgin fiber furnish) and standard liners (usually having a fairly high recycled fiber furnish).

Industry Growth Predicated on Other Industries. The fortunes of the corrugated and solid fiber box manufacturing industry have historically risen and fallen with the shipping needs of other industries. In fact, some financial analysts use corrugated packaging as an indicator of overall economic activity. Corrugated container shipments were expected to continue to track with growth in the general economy throughout the 1990s. For example, in 1991, while the United States was struggling to emerge from recession, corrugated container shipments grew just 0.6 percent to a total of 320.1 billion square feet (bsf). In 1992, however, as the economic recovery picked up steam, shipments were up 4.8 percent to 335.7 bsf, and in 1993 shipments rose again, by 2 percent, to 344.1 bsf. In

1994, shipments shot up sharply, reaching 374.8 bsf, before falling slightly in 1995. However, in 1996 shipments hit a new high of 376.2 bsf.

Pricing of U.S. box production generally reflects the pricing of its underlying materials—mostly linerboard and corrugating medium. In the early 1990s, domestic prices of corrugated boxes and their raw materials were quite low, shackled by the unusually long U.S. economic slowdown in the late 1980s and early 1990s, too much box making capacity, and lower demand for boxes. The average price for corrugated boxes dropped from a 1989 high of $47.72 per thousand square feet (msf) in 1989 to $46 per msf in 1990 and $44.08 in 1991, before recovering to $45.03 per msf in 1992. Prices of corrugated boxes continued to rise in 1994 and 1995 along with prices of linerboard (which rose from $315 per ton in 1993 to $430 per ton in 1994 and a record $480 in 1995) and corrugating medium (which were $295 per ton in 1993, $425 per ton in 1994, and $470 per ton in 1995). However, 1996 saw significant downward pressure on corrugated boxes as customers worked off large amounts of inventory accumulated in anticipation of price increases during the intense price runup in 1994 and 1995.

Preprinted Linerboard. One of the major recent changes in the corrugated box industry has been the fast-growing use of preprinted linerboard. This product is used to make boxes with a white enamel surface that can be printed on with four-color graphics, while the rest of the box remains the same unbleached brown color. The main reason for the growth of preprint has been the growing belief by manufacturers that an attractive box can influence consumer buying decisions at the "point of purchase" in the store. Simply put, an attractively packaged product is more likely to be purchased than one in a brown box. Some studies have shown that up to 80 percent of buying decisions are made at the point of purchase, so the additional "advertising" from a colorful box can help influence that decision. Shipments of value-added, highly graphical boxes made from preprinted linerboard are expected to increase at a rate of 6 to 7 percent a year through much of the 1990s, compared with growth of 2 percent for all corrugated packaging products.

Competitors. One of the market threats to corrugated packaging is flexible plastic films. These products— mostly stretch and shrink wraps—are likely to become more competitive with corrugated products throughout the 1990s, at least in domestic markets.

However, the corrugated container industry has responded to these kinds of market threats by producing lighter weight, higher strength products that reduce shipping costs for box users. In addition, features such

as visual appeal (of boxes made from preprint linerboard) and improved resistance to moisture should help corrugated boxes compete in other areas.

INDUSTRY LEADERS

The industry leaders in this category tend to be the same as the leaders in the production of containerboard since so much of box production is fully integrated. Some of the leading corrugated and solid fiber box producers include: Boise Cascade, Tenneco Packaging, Jefferson Smurfit Corp., Weyerhaeuser Co. and Temple-Inland Inc. Other significant players include Union Camp Corp., Willamette Corp., Packaging Corporation of America, Sonoco Products Co., and Stone Container Corp.

AMERICA AND THE WORLD

The United States is a major player in the global market for corrugated products, both as a producer and as an exporter. Strong export demand for American corrugated products in the 1990s, in fact, helped keep the U.S. industry healthy. For example, in 1996 U.S. exports of corrugated products increased 24 percent in volume, to 702,374 metric tons, and 19 percent in value, to $803.2 million. Both figures represented all-time export records for the U.S. corrugated box industry. It is expected that U.S. exports will continue to rise through the rest of the 1990s at a 10 percent annual clip. In the mid-1990s U.S. exports of value added corrugated products were shipped mainly to nearby markets in Mexico (69 percent) and Canada (16 percent). However, sustained growth in markets in Latin America, Eastern Europe and Asia-Pacific markets bodes well for U.S. exports.

The value of imports of corrugated products into the U.S. was comparatively small in 1996, at $138 million. However, this was more than double the 1993 total of $67.2 million. Principal suppliers of corrugated products to the U.S. in 1996 were Canada and Mexico, which accounted for about 80 percent and 6 percent of all imports, respectively.

The nations of the European Union are significant competitors for U.S. corrugated products. In 1992, the EU had nearly 550 corrugator plants operating, and these plants shipped a total of about 240 billion square feet of corrugated products. Japan, another large producer of corrugated products, shipped almost 140 billion square feet from 335 converting plants in 1992.

International Competitiveness. Since U.S. containerboard producers are often the low-cost producer in world markets, U.S. corrugated products tend to be very competitive in global markets. When the U.S.

dollar is low against foreign currencies, U.S. corrugated products are even more competitive. This was the case in the early to mid-1990s, when U.S. corrugated exports boomed. However, by 1996 the combined effect of Mexico's fiscal crisis and the rising value of the dollar threatened to erode some of these export gains, since Mexico's ability to purchase corrugated products was damaged and the rising dollar raised the effective cost of U.S. products in foreign markets.

Worldwide shipments of corrugated packaging reached $50 billion in 1993 and are expected to grow as fast as four percent annually through much of the 1990s. As the global low-cost producer, the U.S. is likely to maintain its 35 percent share of the total number of boxes produced from 1994 to 1998. That share amounts to over 25 million metric tons. Growing economies in Asia, Eastern Europe and South America may become more important to the U.S. industry if they are unable to satisfy domestic needs for packaging and shipping containers. However, pulp and paper facilities are being constructed at a rapid pace in many of these markets—particularly in Asia— and many nations may be able to satisfy their domestic demand for corrugated packaging more quickly than was once thought.

Although the U.S. corrugating industry is the world's largest, it needs to continue to increase the productivity of its corrugator and sheet plants by staying competitive on labor and operating costs. The industry will also have to do a better job of responding to customers by developing or implementing new graphics, coatings, inks and dyes. Through computer technology, the industry will also have to streamline the process of ordering, producing, and transporting corrugated products, both domestically and around the world.

RESEARCH AND TECHNOLOGY

Much of the research and technology in corrugated box production in the 1990s will focus on improved process control and computerized order entry and production scheduling.

One area of concern to researchers is twist warp—the loss of flatness—in linerboard when it is converted into corrugated board. This problem was relatively unknown until the past few years, when corrugating machines began to run at faster speeds—around 1,000 feet per minute. At these speeds, linerboard with twist warp can cause malfunctions on the corrugator. While paperboard producers are currently focusing on making operating changes to minimize the problem, more research is needed into the fundamental reason for twist warp in order to help solve the problem.

Another promising research area for corrugated products manufacturers involves recycling. Traditionally, manufacturers of boxes for applications where the box becomes wet (such as for shipping produce) have used corrugated materials treated with chemical wet-strength agents. These agents make the box resistant to moisture, but also make it almost impossible to recycle since it will not break down during the recycling process. However, a paper chemical manufacturer, Georgia-Pacific Resins Inc., has researched and developed a wet strength agent that will break down during recycling. It is expected that this will expand the recyclability of many old corrugated containers.

Other research efforts will focus on how to maximize quality and minimize cost as the U.S. corrugated box industry attempts to preserve its strong market advantages into the next century.

FURTHER READING

Paper, Paperboard, Pulp Capacity and Fiber Consumption. Washington, DC: American Forest & Paper Association, 1996.

Snook, Gary A. *Handbook of Pulp & Paper Terminology: A Guide to Industrial and Technological Usage.* Bellingham, WA: Angus Wilde Publications, 1990.

U.S. Department of Commerce. *U.S. Industrial Outlook 1994.* Washington: GPO, 1994.

"U.S. Mills Looking for a Turnaround in 1997." *PIMA's North American Papermaker,* January 1997.

"U.S. Paper Industry Will See More Globalization, Slower Growth in 1997." *Pulp & Paper,* January 1997.

U.S. Trade and Industrial Outlook, 1997-1998. New York: McGraw Hill, 1997.

—Alan Rooks

SIC 2655

FIBER CANS, TUBES, DRUMS AND SIMILAR PRODUCTS

Establishments in this industry are primarily engaged in manufacturing fiber cans, tubes, drums, cones, and similar products from purchased paperboard. These products can be made with or without metal ends. This industry segment produces a wide variety of products, including paper fiber bottles, fiber bobbins, composite cans, all-fiber cans, fiber drums (metal-end or all fiber), fiber cores, mailing cases and tubes, and tubes for chemical and electrical use.

Fiber can and drum manufacturing is a mature industry, with growth at or below the rate of increase in the U.S. gross domestic product (GDP). From 1984 to 1995, the value of this industry's product shipments increased 18 percent, from $1.69 billion to $2 billion. With an annualized growth rate of just 1.8 percent, this industry ranks among the slower growing paper products industries. In the late 1980s and early to mid 1990s, the fiber can and drum industry plateaued, with the value of shipments inching up each year from $1.83 billion in 1989 to $1.92 billion in 1992 and $2 billion from 1993 to 1995. Projections for the remainder of the 1990s show steady if unspectacular growth: the value of shipments was expected to rise from $2.05 billion in 1996 to $2.17 billion in 1998.

The number of establishments in the industry in the mid-1990s was 301, a 5 percent increase since 1990. In the mid-1990s, this industry employed 13,000 people with an annual payroll of $341 million. Of that total, 11,000 were production workers who put in 23 million hours for wages of $247 million.

The manufacture of fiber cans, tubes, and drums is concentrated east of the Mississippi River. The top three producing regions, in terms of total shipments, are the north central, the southeast/mid-Atlantic, and the northeastern regions of the United States. In the early 1990s, Ohio was the leading producer of fiber cans and drums, with 25 establishments producing 9.7 percent of all U.S. shipments. Wisconsin was second, producing 6.9 percent; and New York state was third, with 6.5 percent.

Fiber cans, tubes, and similar products are by far the largest category of products produced by this industry, accounting for 72 percent of all product shipments in 1995. Paperboard fiber drums, a larger-sized product, accounted for 18 percent of total fiber cans, drums, and similar product shipments in 1995. The remaining 10 percent of shipments consisted of other products not specified by kind.

Paper and paperboard (not including boxes and containers) represented the single largest category of materials consumed by the fiber can, tube, and drum industry in the early 1990s, accounting for $424 million (40 percent) of the total $1.06 billion worth of materials consumed. Sheet steel and strip claimed another $182.7 million while all other materials and components, parts, containers, and supplies cost $265.6 million.

Like other paper product producers, the makers of fiber cans, tubes, and drums have been using more recycled paperboard and less virgin paperboard in order to satisfy end user demands. In the mid-1990s, this industry appeared to benefit from the desire by consumers and the government to use more products made from recycled materials or materials that were more recyclable than competing products. This environmental factor was a distinct advantage for industry manufacturers as many competing products are made from plastic, which is perceived to be a less recyclable product.

The paper industry is a good customer as well as a supplier for the fiber can, tube, and drum industry. Many mills use heavy-duty fiber cores to wind their paper and paperboard rolls. These cores are either shipped in long lengths and cut at the mill or pre-cut by the core manufacturer. This market shows little sign of moving toward alternative products, such as steel cores.

Drum Declines. The fiber drum has seen its market share decline as many industrial users are trying to eliminate the use of disposable containers. For example, for regulatory reasons, the chemical industry is moving away from using drums of any kind, including fiber or metal. Instead, they are using more portable chemical feed containers that are dropped off by the chemical manufacturer and then picked up to be reused when empty.

Some of the industry leaders in this category are integrated manufacturers, in that they produce fiber cans, drums, and tubes, as well as the paperboard from which they are made. Other fiber can, tube, and drum manufacturers are independent converters of purchased paperboard. One of the leading companies in this industry, Sonoco Products Co. of Hartsville, South Carolina, is an integrated producer. Other leaders in this industry include Greif Bros. Corporation of Delaware, Ohio; Star Paper Tube Inc. of Rock Hill, South Carolina; Anvil Cases Inc. of Hacienda Heights, California; and Niemand South Inc. of Marion, Alabama.

FURTHER READING

Darnay, Arsen J., ed. *Manufacturing USA*. 5th ed. Detroit: Gale Research, 1996.

Paper, Paperboard, Pulp Capacity and Fiber Consumption. Washington: American Forest & Paper Association, 1996.

Smook, Gary A. *Handbook of Pulp & Paper Terminology: A Guide to Industrial and Technological Usage*. Bellingham, WA: Angus Wilde Publications, 1990.

U.S. Department of Commerce. International Trade Administration. *U.S. Industrial Outlook 1994*. Washington: GPO, 1994.

U.S. Trade and Industrial Outlook, 1997-1998. New York: McGraw-Hill, 1997.

—Alan Rooks

SIC 2656

SANITARY FOOD CONTAINERS, EXCEPT FOLDING

This category includes establishments primarily engaged in manufacturing non-folding food containers from special foodboard. Industry products include paperboard beverage cartons, round and nested food containers, paper cups for hot or cold drinks, and stamped plates, dishes, spoons and similar products. Establishments primarily engaged in manufacturing similar items from plastic materials are classified in Industry Group 308; those making folding sanitary cartons are classified in **SIC 2657.**

Sanitary food containers have been a strong growth market for the paper industry. Despite increasing consumer interest in reducing usage of disposable products, the convenience of disposable paper products has continued to appeal to growing numbers of consumers. Also, the use of paperboard milk cartons in alternative, nonfood markets has given that part of the industry a healthy boost.

In the early to mid-1990s, the value of U.S. sanitary food container product shipments rose and fell, largely in concert with the fortunes of the paper industry, which produces the raw materials from which these products are made. When paper prices dropped, as they did in the early 1990s, so did the value of sanitary food container products shipments. When paper prices recovered in 1995 and 1996, sanitary food containers did likewise. For example, in 1991 the value of shipments reached a record $2.72 billion, but dropped back sharply in 1992, to $2.49 billion, and dropped again in 1993, to $2.46 billion. However, the value of shipments of sanitary food containers recovered in 1994, and was projected to increase for the rest of the decade, from $2.76 billion in 1996 to $2.87 billion in 1998.

Cups and liquid-tight paper and paperboard containers comprised 44 percent ($1.24 billion) of all shipments in 1995. Other sanitary paper and paperboard food containers, boards, and trays, except folding made up 29 percent ($757.5 million) of shipments; milk and milk-type paperboard cartons, 26 percent ($671.8 million); sanitary food containers, except folding, not specified by kind, 1 percent ($26.5 million).

Sanitary-food-container manufacturers employed 15,471 people in the mid-1990s, down slightly from15,700 in 1990. There were 86 establishments in the industry in the mid-1990s, which is approximately the same number there were in 1990. Annual payroll was $402 million, up 3 percent from $392 million in 1990.

The market for paper cups, plates, and other disposable paper products appeared healthy in the mid-1990s. Despite the fact that these products are relatively difficult to recycle—most are contaminated with food after use—the category continued to grow throughout the decade. In the mid-1990s, manufacturers of sanitary food containers were able to answer some of their environmental critics by including recycled fiber in their products. This was made possible when the Food and Drug Administration issued guidelines for the use of recycled paper in products that come in contact with food. Also, the increased strength and grease resistance of paper products, particularly plates, allowed for their use in an increasing number of applications. Household use of paper cups showed no signs of abating.

Paperboard milk cartons have a formidable competitor in milk jugs made from high density polyethylene (HDPE). These plastic milk jugs captured a growing share of the milk market in the 1970s and 1980s, most particularly in the gallon size, but also in the half-gallon size. However, an extended decline in sales of paperboard milk cartons began to slow and even stop in the 1990s when it became widely known that paperboard milk cartons retain vitamins better than their plastic counterparts (fluorescent lights in dairy cases leech vitamins from milk in translucent plastic jugs). This knowledge led some dairies and consumers to once again favor paperboard. Also, major efforts to promote the recycling of milk cartons by milk carton manufacturers, notably International Paper Co., helped improve the appeal of this type of packaging. Product innovations, such as adding spouts with resealable caps to paperboard orange juice cartons, have also helped increase the use of carton packaging.

Because of paperboard milk-style carton's ease of storage and ability to withstand repeated access, additional domestic uses for it were developed. These included packaging for nondairy flavored drinks, fruit juices, dry pet foods, laundry detergents, candy, and hardware. Such alternative uses helped increase the sale of milk cartons: In 1980, nondairy carton tonnage accounted for only 13 percent of all milk-carton sales. By 1994, that percentage had topped 30 percent.

Leaders in this industry have included a mixture of major paper companies and independent converting companies. One of the leading companies is James River Corporation of Virginia, manufacturer of Dixie Cups and other sanitary paper products. Other key market players include International Paper Company and Champion International Corporation—both of which manufacture milk carton stock—Solo Cup Company, Sealright Company, Inc., Keyes Fibre Company, and Imperial Bondware Inc. While many of these leading companies produce brand products, sales of private label products are very strong in key categories, such as disposable dishes. For example, private label products accounted for 46.4 percent of the disposable dish market (including paper and plastic) in 1995. The leading paper disposable dish brand was James River's Dixie Livingware, at 17.6 percent of the market, followed by Keyes Fibre's Chinet brand, at 9.8 percent.

FURTHER READING

Darnay, Arsen J., ed. *Manufacturing USA.* 5th ed. Detroit, Gale, 1996.

Lazich, Robert S., ed. *Market Share Reporter.* Detroit: Gale Research, 1997.

Paper, Paperboard, Pulp Capacity and Fiber Consumption. Washington: American Forest & Paper Association, 1996.

Smook, Gary A. *Handbook of Pulp & Paper Terminology: A Guide to Industrial and Technological Usage.* Bellingham, WA: Angus Wilde Publications, 1990.

U.S. Trade and Industrial Outlook, 1997-1998. New York: McGraw-Hill, 1997.

—Alan Rooks

SIC 2657

FOLDING PAPERBOARD BOXES, INCLUDING SANITARY

Establishments in this industry are primarily engaged in manufacturing folding paperboard boxes from purchased paperboard, including folding sanitary food boxes or cartons (except milk cartons). Products include folding paperboard boxes such as cereal boxes; folding cartons; frozen food containers; ice cream containers; folding sanitary food pails such as those used for takeout food from restaurants; and paperboard backs for blister packages.

INDUSTRY SNAPSHOT

While the folding paperboard box industry demonstrated sales growth for most of the early to mid-1990s, it encountered some difficulties in the middle part of the decade. The value of folding paperboard box shipments grew from $7.93 billion in 1992 to $8.63 billion in 1995. While the value of shipments slipped slightly in 1996, to $8.49 billion, it was projected to continue growing again in 1997 and reach a high of $9 billion in 1998.

Initial estimates showed that 1996 shipments of folding paperboard boxes and cartons dropped 2.8 percent in constant dollars (adjusted for inflation) over 1995, the second consecutive decline in constant dollar product shipments. While slow growth in domestic demand contributed to these declines, another major factor was that many customers cut back on purchases of folding paperboard boxes as they used up large volumes of inventory they had accumulated in anticipation of future prices increases.

Food products represent some of the best markets for the folding paperboard box industry, with strong growth reported in packaging materials for beverages, dry bakery goods, and cereals during the mid-1990s. Other non-food markets reporting good growth rates included toys, sporting goods and textiles.

The production of folding paperboard boxes is divided fairly evenly across a wide range of food and non-food consumer products. In 1995, dry food was the single biggest application for folding paperboard packaging, accounting for 14 percent of the $8 billion spent on folding cartons in the United States. Wet food accounted for 12 percent while beverage carriers (such as those used for 24-packs of canned soft drinks) took another 11 percent. Other significant users included medicinal/cosmetic products (9 percent); paper goods (7 percent); hardware (6 percent); and tobacco (6 percent).

ORGANIZATION AND STRUCTURE

In the mid-1990s, the U.S. folding paperboard box industry was made up of about 445 companies operating 600 establishments. Shipments by the U.S. folding carton industry were concentrated in four main regions: North Central, Eastern, Southern and Pacific. In 1996, the North Central region led the United States in folding carton shipments, with 41 percent of the total, followed by the Eastern and Southern regions, which each had 25 percent of the total. The North Central region lost share compared with 1992, when it held 45 percent of the total. The Pacific region, while holding just 9 percent of the total, was the fastest growing region in terms of folding paperboard box shipments, with this growth being attributed to improved economic performance in the region's agricultural, aerospace, construction and manufacturing industries.

The growth of food-related packaging and other retail applications has helped expand the retail market for folding paperboard boxes. The growing use of folding boxes as beverage carriers has also helped fuel growth in folding-paperboard-box sales. Both beer and soda bottlers were using 24-can "cases" as promotional vehicles in the mid-1990s. As a result, more of those products were being sold in folding paperboard boxes and fewer in the traditional six-packs held together by plastic carriers.

In the mid-1990s, folding box manufacturers were expanding production of high-quality, high-whiteness boxes suitable for four-color-process printing. Better visual appeal of such packaging often translates into higher "impulse" purchases by consumers, and folding boxboard customers often will pay a premium price for goods so boxed.

However, unlike its corrugated container cousins, the folding paperboard box has faced direct competition from alternative materials, principally the bewildering array of plastics. The growth of flexible bags, pouches, and wraps, as well as rigid carriers and containers made from plastics, has created a serious challenge to the dominance of the folding paperboard box in the packaging marketplace.

Folding paperboard boxes have also faced competition from some other paperboard products. In some retail applications, corrugated products and carded "blister packs" (paperboard backings that hold a molded plastic insert) have been used as a substitute for paperboard boxes.

CURRENT CONDITIONS

While still facing formidable competition from alternative packaging, the folding paperboard box industry was expected to grow through much of the 1990s. Improved strength and lighter weight folding boxboard helped to improve the competitive position of folding paperboard boxes in the packaging marketplace. Folding paperboard boxes also benefited from the fact that they are recyclable and contain recycled fiber. Both of these attributes were actively promoted on retail packages.

Paperboard's recyclability is significant since packaging in general has garnered a reputation for increasing the amount of solid waste produced in the United States each year. In the early 1990s, recycling was a important issue and there was much public discussion of the "landfill crisis," which presumed that the United States was running out of landfill space. The use of paperboard packaging (and other forms of packaging) was criticized as being inherently wasteful.

Manufacturers were encouraged to reduce or eliminate packaging for their products.

The folding boxboard industry and other sectors of the paper and paperboard industry responded by increasing the amount of recycled fiber used in their products. This successful campaign should lead to the paper industry recovering a full 50 percent of the paper and paperboard produced in the United States by 2000, up from just 28 percent in 1986. Also, the landfill crisis turned out to be more imaginary than real, with major amounts of new landfill capacity coming on stream in the mid-1990s. The combination of these two developments helped curtail pressure to reduce the use of paperboard packaging, and shipments of folding paperboard boxes were expected to increase—not decrease—through the end of the 1990s.

Production of the raw material for folding paperboard boxes—folding boxboard—was growing steadily in the mid-1990s. The United States produced 6.38 million tons of folding boxboard in 1995, up 3 percent over 1994, when production was 6.18 million tons. That came on top of a 5 percent increase in 1994 over the previous year.

There are three grades of U.S. folding boxboard: solid bleached sulfate (SBS), which is bleached white for high brightness; unbleached kraft, which retains the natural brown color of paperboard; and recycled. Of the 6.38 million tons of folding boxboard produced in 1995, 2.86 million tons were recycled folding boxboard (45 percent); 2.07 million tons were SBS (32 percent) and 1.45 million tons were unbleached kraft (23 percent).

SBS is favored by manufacturers of folding paperboard boxes for the packaging of cigarettes, frozen and wet foods, meats, non-prescription drugs, bakery foods, and cosmetics. These manufacturers appreciate its superior visual and performance characteristics. Throughout the 1980s and early 1990s, SBS accounted for about 35 percent of the folding boxboard used by the domestic folding paperboard box industry.

In the early 1990s, SBS was challenged by two market forces—competition from lower cost alternatives and the growth of recycling. As the quality of lower-cost kraft- and recycled-board grades increased, some boxmakers opted for the cost savings those grades could provide. Also, many companies purchasing folding paperboard boxes wanted to demonstrate environmental awareness to their retail customers by providing the ultimate end-user with products encased in recycled packaging.

However, in the mid-1990s SBS staged something of a comeback, and in 1995 production of SBS increased—to 2.07 million tons from 2.02 million tons the previous year—while production of recycled folding boxboard declined slightly, to 2.86 million tons from 2.87 million tons. Growing demand for SBS can be attributed to demands by domestic packagers for better graphics on their packages and growing export demand for SBS.

While production of recycled folding boxboard declined slightly in 1995, it is still the leading folding boxboard grade—and an environmental success story for the industry. The success of this grade is due to several reasons. Obviously, the tremendous interest in recycling has helped. But most industrial users would be unwilling to accept an inferior product simply because it was more environmentally friendly. Better recycling procedures and improvements in strength, formation, and surface coating have allowed quality recycled clay-coated board to compete in several markets from which it was previously excluded.

The capacity to produce all three grades of folding boxboard was expected to increase continuously throughout the late 1990s. Unbleached kraft folding capacity was expected to increase the fastest, from 2 million tons in 1996 to 2.4 million tons in 1999, an average annual increase of 6.4 percent. SBS folding boxboard capacity increased 2.4 percent in 1996 and was expected to rise 1.5 percent a year through 1999. Capacity to produce recycled folding boxboard was up 2.5 percent in 1996 and was expected to grow an average of 1.2 percent per year through 1999.

In the mid-1990s, folding paperboard box volume shipments tended to mirror the general economy, growing only as fast as gross national product (GNP). However, since these figures are based on tonnage, it must be taken into account that today's folding paperboard box manufacturers are producing lighter weight boxes that still meet existing strength tests and other industry standards. As a result, lighter boxes—which reduce industry tonnage—are replacing heavier products.

Folding paperboard box plants employed 52,000 people in 1996. Just over 42,000 of those were production workers with average hourly earnings of $12.61.

INDUSTRY LEADERS

The folding paperboard box industry is highly integrated. This means that the leading producers of folding paperboard boxes also produce the folding boxboard used to make the product. Leading producers of folding paperboard boxes include Georgia-Pacific Corporation; James River Corporation of Virginia; Jefferson Smurfit Corp.; Westvaco Corp., Packaging

Corporation of America; and Rock-Tenn Co. Other leading companies include Field Container Corp.; Green Bay Packaging Inc.; Waldorf Corp., and Gulf States Paper Corp.

AMERICA AND THE WORLD

The folding paperboard box industry has traditionally imported more than it has exported, even though the difference is relatively small. Exports in this category are divided into two subcategories: sanitary food and beverage containers of non-corrugated paper and paperboard; and folding cartons, boxes and cases of non-corrugated paper and paperboard. In 1996, U.S. exports in these two categories combined amounted to 138,400 metric tons, valued at $238 million. This represented a record in terms of both quantity and value. Within this total, exports of sanitary food and beverage containers were projected to be 51,606 metric tons, valued at $98.2 million, a 27 percent increase in volume and a 18 percent increase in value over the previous year.

In 1996, U.S. imports of folding paperboard boxes did not equal exports in quantity, but did exceed them in value. When the two trade categories are combined, the U.S. imported a total of 127,536 metric tons, valued at $293 million. Within this total, finished folding cartons accounted for 103,036 metric tons (valued at $249.8 million) and sanitary food and beverage containers accounted for 24,500 metric tons (valued at $43.2 million). The leading supplier to the U.S. market, by far, is Canada, which shipped 86 percent of the imported products in both categories.

While exports of folding paperboard boxes have continued to grow, they are still a relatively small portion of total production. In 1996, for example, exports accounted for just 3 percent of total folding paperboard box production. It usually makes the most economic sense to export folding boxboard in sheets or rolls and then convert them into boxes locally. Many U.S. folding paperboard box manufacturers possess sites for foreign conversion for this reason. As a result, exports of unconverted folding boxboard were roughly three-and-a-half times the size of finished folding paperboard box exports in the mid-1990s.

Foreign trade was expected to continue to play a minor but growing role in total industry shipments through the end of the 1990s. With exports to Mexico, other Latin American countries, and Pacific Rim countries expected to increase, folding carton product shipments were anticipated to increase 11 percent in value in 1997 and 8 percent in 1998. The domestic market will likely remain the central focus of folding paperboard box manufacturers. The historically high U.S.

per capita consumption of folding paperboard boxes—approaching 40 pounds per year—will help maintain that focus. By comparison, western European per capita consumption has been documented as only about half that of the United States.

FURTHER READING

Darnay, Arsen J., ed. *Manufacturing USA: Fifth Edition.* Detroit: Gale Research, 1996.

Lazich, Robert S., ed. *Market Share Reporter 1997.* Detroit: Gale Research, 1997.

Paper, Paperboard, Pulp Capacity and Fiber Consumption. Washington, DC: American Forest & Paper Association, 1996.

Smook, Gary A. *Handbook of Pulp & Paper Terminology: A Guide to Industrial and Technological Usage.* Bellingham, WA: Angus Wilde, 1990.

U.S. Trade and Industrial Outlook 1997-1998. New York: McGraw-Hill, 1997.

—Alan Rooks

SIC 2671

PAPER, COATED AND LAMINATED PACKAGING

This classification covers establishments primarily engaged in manufacturing coated or laminated flexible materials made of combinations of paper, plastics film, metal foil, and similar materials (excluding textiles) for packaging purposes. These are made from purchased sheet materials or plastics resins and may be printed in the same establishment. Establishments primarily engaged in manufacturing coated or laminated paper for other purposes are classified in **SIC 2672: Coated and Laminated Paper, Not Elsewhere Classified,** including establishments manufacturing all gummed or pressure sensitive tape. Those establishments that manufacture unsupported plastics film are classified in **SIC 3081: Unsupported Plastics Film and Sheet.** Establishments manufacturing aluminum foil are classified in **SIC 3497: Metal Foil and Leaf,** while those manufacturing paper from pulp are classified in **SIC 2621: Paper Mills.**

The paper, coated and laminated packaging industry is one of the smallest segments within the paper industry group, but was also one of its faster growing segments in the mid-1990s. In 1995, the value of shipments for this segment were estimated at $4.14 billion, and that value was expected to jump 15.5 percent to $4.78 billion by 1998, more than 5 percent

per year. Nonetheless, industry shipments totalled less than 3 percent of the combined paper and allied products SIC group.

The industry is more fragmented than most other paper industries, with a number of small players competing either in highly specialized product niches or regions. A company might, for example, have a leading position in one segment but have no products in any of the other segments. A distinguishing feature of the industry is the fact that an inordinately high percentage (approximately 20 percent) of potential clients such as manufacturers package their own goods. This means that firms within the industry are often competing with potential clients.

Companies in this industry are located primarily in the Midwest, with Wisconsin home to the most establishments (24), producing 24.5 percent of all U.S. shipments in 1992. Illinois was a distant second, with 17 establishments producing 7 percent of the total. Other leading states in this industry include Georgia (producing 6.5 percent of all U.S. shipments in 1992); Tennessee (5.8 percent); and Pennsylvania (5 percent). The concentration of this industry in the Midwest is not surprising given the fact that some of the principal users of products in this industry are food processors, many of which are located in the Midwest.

The paper, coated and laminated packaging industry, while small, has been resilient for much of the 1980s and 1990s, producing a gain in the value of shipments even during recessions. Since 1987, the value of shipments for this industry has increased every year. This growth should continue throughout the late 1990s: In 1998, the value of shipments is expected to be 36 percent greater than it was in 1992. A stronger national economy in the mid to late 1990s, more emphasis on research and development, and the expansion of niche markets appear to driving this industry toward increased sales and new markets. That may be one of the reasons that demand for all types of plastic film—one of the key raw materials used by this industry—was expected to increase 17 percent (in volume) between 1993 and 1998, moving from 10.66 million pounds in 1993 to 12.44 million pounds in 1998.

Some of the more notable changes the industry has experienced include: new materials, environmentally conscious products, specialization, and technological innovation. The industry has experimented with new materials as customers have demanded lighter weight, stronger materials for packaging. Some of the new materials include lighter-weight, high-tech plastics and reinforced paper. The increased popularity of the microwave, for example, has produced a growing need for a wider range of uses for existing and new materials. Also, very high prices for paper products in 1994 and 1995 encouraged some manufacturers to substitute more plastic materials, which became comparatively less expensive.

Biodegradable, recyclable, and recycled materials have become essential in the packaging industry. Packaging accounted for over 30 percent of U.S. solid waste in the mid-1990s. In response to environmental pressures as well as to higher prices for landfill usage, producers have incorporated "green" products and recycled raw materials into their packaging. However, there is some doubt about whether or not "green" products are commercially viable. While in surveys consumers often they say they want to buy more environmentally friendly products, when asked to pay more for them, they usually decline.

With manufacturers demanding more from packaging, producers have had to incorporate new skills and materials into producing packages. This has led to specialization and technological innovation. An example of such innovation is razor packaging, which has been made to simulate the look of a mirror.

Bemis Corporation of Minneapolis, primarily active in flexible film packaging, is one of the leading companies in this industry with 1996 sales of $1.23 billion. Consolidated Papers Incorporated, a major paper manufacturer of paper and converted paper products, is also very active with 1996 sales of $1.03 billion. Printpack Incorporated, Atlanta; Instrument Systems Corporation, Jericho, New York, and Minnesota Mining & Manufacturing (3M), St. Paul, Minnesota are other leading companies in the industry.

FURTHER READING

Darnay, Arsen J., ed. *Manufacturing USA.* 5th Ed. Detroit: Gale Research, 1996.

"Markets Increase, Expand for Converters' Products," *Paper, Film & Foil Converter,* September 1994, 81.

Paper, Paperboard, Pulp Capacity and Fiber Consumption, Washington, DC: American Forest & Paper Association, 1996.

Sacharow, Stanley. "Package Converting: Educate the Consumer to Become a Better Customer." *Paper, Film & Foil Converter,* July 1995, 52.

Smook, Gary A. *Handbook of Pulp & Paper Terminology: A Guide to Industrial and Technological Usage.* Bellingham, WA: Angus Wilde, 1990.

U.S. Trade and Manufacturing Outlook, 1997-1998. New York: McGraw-Hill, 1997.

—Andrew Ballard, updated by Alan Rooks

SIC 2672

COATED AND LAMINATED PAPER, NOT ELSEWHERE CLASSIFIED

This industry covers establishments primarily engaged in manufacturing coated, laminated, or processed paper and film from purchased paper, except for packaging. Also included are establishments primarily manufacturing gummed paper products and pressure sensitive tape with backing of any material other than rubber, for any application. Establishments primarily engaged in manufacturing coated and laminated paper for packaging are classified in **SIC 2671: Packaging Paper and Plastics Film, Coated and Laminated**; those manufacturing carbon paper are classified in **SIC 3955: Carbon Paper and Inked Ribbons**; and those manufacturing photographic and blueprint paper are classified in **SIC 3861: Photographic Equipment and Supplies.**

INDUSTRY SNAPSHOT

This classification incorporates a wide variety of products and companies. By 1998, the value of shipments for the laminated and coated paper industry is expected to reach $9.96 billion, up from $8.87 billion in 1994. Overall, this industry accounts for a little over 6 percent of the paper industry group **SIC 2600** as a whole. Industry establishments employed approximately 33,900 workers in 1996, including 23,200 production workers. The value of shipments in this industry grew 51 percent between 1987 and 1994, an annual growth rate of 7 percent, well above the 2.5 percent annual growth in the overall paper industry group. Moreover, the industry grew every year from 1987 to 1994, while other segments in the group experienced peaks and valleys in the value of shipments.

ORGANIZATION AND STRUCTURE

Most companies in this industry limit their activities to the coating of paper or other materials, but produce diverse products from this process. Of the many products in the industry, the vast majority of industry shipments come from one of two sectors: pressure-sensitive products and "other" coated and laminated paper. The pressure-sensitive products group includes cellophane tape, almost all labels, and a variety of other pressure-sensitive adhesives (PSAs), but does not include gummed tape. Other coated and laminated paper products include paper that is treated or coated to enhance the paper's utility. PSAs are by far the largest class of product produced by this industry, accounting for 64.1 percent of all shipments in

1992, according to the U.S. Economic Census. The next largest category is other coated and processed papers, which garnered 20.4 of all shipments. The remaining shares were held by gummed paper products (3.2 percent); printing paper coated at establishments other than where the paper was produced (3.2 percent); and "all other" products (9.1 percent).

Pressure-Sensitive Products. Even within this subsegment of the industry, there is a great deal of diversity. Pressure-sensitive products range from cellophane tape to shrinkable labels to sealing tapes. Advances in adhesive technology and continuing development work by manufacturers of pressure-sensitive adhesives (PSAs) have led to increases in the applicability and quality of PSAs, and their market share in this industry has continued to climb. Lighter weight products offering greater flexibility and lower cost than traditional materials have allowed some types of adhesives to be used in place of rivets, bolts, and chemical compounds in assembly processes. Even heavy industrial processes such as engine manufacturing and truck frame assembly have found applications for PSAs.

To produce PSAs, manufacturers use paper, plastic films, non-woven cloth, or polyethylene as a base. A chemical solvent or waterborne acrylic, which provides the adhesive necessary for the PSA to stick, is applied to the base, usually to one side. PSAs can be measured on three different criteria: tack, or how well the PSA bonds with a given surface; peel, or how difficult it is to remove the tape from the surface; and shear resistance, or how well the PSA responds to "creep" over time. The type of adhesive that coats the film depends on the PSA's desired application.

A common application of PSAs is found in the large pressure-sensitive label market (excluding office labels), which was expected to reach sales of $4.4 billion in 1997, up from $3.1 billion in 1993. Between 1993 and 1997, the label market grew at a 9 percent annual rate, an above average growth rate in this industry. Labels can be made of paper, polystyrene, film, or other materials, but the defining feature of a label is its mode of application.

Competing Technologies. Pressure-sensitive labels face competition from several other technologies, the two most common being wet glue and shrink sleeve. Wet glue applications affix a paper or plastic label via a pre-applied adhesive. Beverages and foods in glass containers often use wet glue labels. Glue-applied labels are the leading labeling method, holding an estimated 54 percent share of the total label market in the mid-1990s, compared to about 36 percent for

PSAs. All other technologies hold about 10 percent of the market.

Shrink sleeve applications, in which the label is wrapped around the product and then shrunk directly on to it to form a bond, are most common on batteries and film products. Other competing technologies include heat transfer; heat seal; and in-mold labels. Gummed labels, which held about 25 percent of the label market in the 1960s, have dropped to about 2 percent and are not a significant competitor. Most of the erosion in the gummed label market has been linked to increased use of pressure-sensitive labels.

Other Coated and Laminated Papers. The products produced through the coating and laminating process range from specialty papers to wax paper, carbonless, and thermographic business papers. This category does not include the vast majority of coated paper produced in the United States, which is produced on-site at paper mills (see **SIC 2621**). Most coated paper manufacturers have off- or on-papermachine coaters which can be set to coat the paper (or be left off to produce un-coated paper) as it leaves the production line. Paper produced in this fashion (coated on site) is classified under **SIC 2621**. The coated and laminated paper that is included in **SIC 2672** is produced by companies that purchase "base stock" paper from paper mills, and then coat or laminate it. In fact, three-fourths of the "other coated and laminated papers" category in **SIC 2672** is accounted for by carbonless paper coated at establishments other than where the paper was produced. It is very likely that this segment will drop dramatically in the next Economic Census, since most of that carbonless paper was produced by one company—Appleton Papers in Appleton, Wisconsin—which dramatically reduced its use of outside base stock when it installed a new paper machine in 1994 to produce almost all of its own base stock. By doing so, it moved a large share of its production volume to **SIC 2611**.

Likewise, the value of coated printing paper included in **SIC 2672** (paper coated at establishments other than where the paper was produced) is extremely small, compared with the value of the entire coated printing paper market, which is included in **SIC 2611**. For example, U.S. shipments of paper coated at establishments other than where the paper was produced had a 1992 value of $247 million, compared to the value of coated printing paper produced at U.S. paper mills, which amounted to $4.89 billion.

Some of the factors involved in coating papers include the printing process (offset, rotogravure, non-impact, etc.), the type of ink used (colored, black and white, thickness), and environmental considerations.

Coating must take into account the uniformity of the coating application, the evenness of the coat weight, and the smoothness and uniformity of the coat. Coated papers are broken down into five grades, with number one being the heaviest and generally the highest quality.

Paper is coated with pigments, which can consist of either chemical solutions or clay compounds. Titanium dioxide has long been a favorite coating material because of its opacity, though substitutions are usually sought since titanium dioxide is fairly costly. Other popular coatings include calcium carbonate and kaolin (clay), a naturally occurring mineral.

Within the coated and laminated paper sector, converters might apply any number of coatings to change the function or quality of paper. Gummed resins might be applied to make flypaper or gummed adhesive tape; cloth or fluids might be incorporated into the papermaking process to produce cloth-lined or porous impregnated papers. The carbonless paper segment of this industry saw continuing growth in the 1990s. This type of paper is manufactured by weaving small beads of ink into the paper fiber itself. When pressure is applied, the beads are broken and ink darkens the paper to emulate the pen strokes of the writer.

BACKGROUND AND DEVELOPMENT

Technological advances in coatings, paper manufacturing processes, and adhesives have long been the driving force behind developments in the coated and laminated paper industry. One clear event that prodded the growth of the label industry was the development of the self-adhesive label by Stanton Avery in 1935. From this initial product line came a whole range of self-adhesive (now called pressure-sensitive) products, including thermal films, airline bag tags, computer imprintable films, and thermal transfer self-adhesives. A wide range of industries now make extensive use of pressure-sensitive labels, including airlines; automotive; consumer durables; food and beverages; health and beauty aids; chemicals; pharmaceuticals; retailing; and transportation.

CURRENT CONDITIONS

The coated and laminated paper industry is generally characterized by small firms that have sought to stake out dominant shares in niche markets. However, there is one industry giant (3M Corporation) and several other relatively large companies (Appleton Papers, Nashua Corporation and Mosinee Paper Corporation) that hold commanding positions in this industry segment.

Coated Paper Markets. Along with much of the rest of the paper industry, the coated market experienced slow growth through the downward business cycle of the early 1990s. However, coated paper prices shot up dramatically in 1994 and 1995 as demand surged and supplies remained tight. While prices retreated in 1996, they remained at relatively high levels. One trend, however, may have changed the long-term market for coated papers. Publishers faced with enormous price hikes during the 1994-1995 period (as much as 75 percent in a 12-month period) found themselves cutting back on the number of magazine or catalog pages they printed, or dramatically trimming circulation in order to conserve on paper. Even though prices eased following this period, some publishers may have learned to "live with less" coated paper.

One problem facing producers of coated papers in the early 1990s—demands for more recycling—has begun to ease for two reasons: manufacturers are now producing more coated papers made at least partially from recycled paper, and magazines and catalogs printed on coated paper are being recycled in greater volumes. While paper recyclers once shunned coated paper because of the coating materials used on them, recycling operations have learned how to process this type of paper. Still, coatings and fillers typically account for a large part of the paper. When the paper is recycled, these materials have to be separated, removed from the process, and landfilled. Some coated papers can consist of as much as 50 percent coating and filler, which greatly reduces the amount of recoverable paper fiber. As a result, most recycling operations tend to mix a small amount of coated papers with much larger volumes of uncoated paper.

Growth in Pressure-Sensitive Products. Applications for pressure-sensitive products have been driven by the bewildering array of technology options available to manufacturers and new products targeted toward the consumer sector. Removable adhesives—such as those found in Post-It notes—have driven growth, as have new applications of traditional products. For example, the U.S. Postal Service is in the process of converting most of its stamp products to PSAs.

Label markets grew faster than the U.S. gross domestic product (GDP) in the mid-1990s, and this segment continues to be one of the fastest growing within this classification. Some of the factors contributing to the growth of this sector include: increased use of bar codes at end point-of-sale processors (such as supermarket deli counters); legislation requiring food manufacturers to disclose an increased amount of information on food labels; and advances in application and material technologies, which have allowed manufacturers to increase the use of labels.

In terms of the "face stock" used to produce pressure-sensitive labels, the fastest growing segment is sheeted laser paper, reflecting the increase of in-house printing of information by label users. Laser paper usage was growing at a rate of 20 percent annually in the mid-1990s, and in 1996 accounted for just over 10 percent of the face stock used by pressure-sensitive label manufacturers. General paper is the largest single face material used, and accounted for just over 50 percent of the market in 1996. General paper is said to be growing more slowly than the market as a whole, reflecting displacement by film face stock in some applications. Film prices are declining and have approached high-end paper grade prices. Film accounted for just under 25 percent of the market in 1996.

While the use of pressure-sensitive labels is growing, they face increased competition from other technologies. For example, the use of shrink sleeve and in-mold labels was growing fast in the mid-1990s. Shrink sleeve labels, which dominate much of the plastic beverage bottle market, were said to be growing at a 7 percent annual clip in the mid-1990s. In-mold labels, used on blow-molded plastic containers, have a high penetration rate in the health and beauty products and household chemicals markets, and were growing at a rate of 10 percent in the mid-1990s.

INDUSTRY LEADERS

The fragmented and specialized nature of the coated and laminated paper industry makes true dominance across all sectors a virtual impossibility. Certain firms, however, have managed to carve out strongly defensible niches and have consistently maintained innovation and expertise to keep a strong position in their particular sector. Until 1994, the largest firm by revenues in the industry was Appleton Papers, Incorporated, a division of the UK firm Arjo Wiggins Appleton (AWA). Appleton is a market leader in carbonless and thermographic papers and made several major moves to expand its presence in the coated freesheet market in 1996. However, because the company is now producing most of its own carbonless base stock, much of its production will be transferred outside this industry.

Among the notables in the pressure-sensitive products area is the Minnesota Mining & Manufacturing Company (3M). 3M pioneered cellophane tape and manufactures some of the best-known brand names in the industry with its Scotch tape and Post-It notes. 3M manufactures only part of its products within this in-

dustry, but still has a sizeable representation within the industry leaders.

WORK FORCE

Because of the extremely specialized nature of the industry, those who work with coated and laminated papers tend to be more specialized than workers within the rest of the paper industry group. At the same time, the wide array of activities within the classification tends to minimize variance of wages; wages within the industry averaged $14 per hour in the mid-1990s, roughly on par with the rest of the paper industry. Because of the dispersion and fragmentation of the industry, organized labor tends to be less represented.

AMERICA AND THE WORLD

A high value-to-weight ratio along with the unique nature of many of the products within the industry have contributed to a globalization of the industry. Since technologies are often proprietary, few barriers exist to stop products from migrating from one market to another. A list of the world's leading thermal coaters, for example, would list few U.S. firms. Another factor hindering the United States' growth in the sector is the fact that many of the advances in coating equipment technology have come from overseas. This has meant a delay in the diffusion of technology to the United States and a subsequent lag in U.S. competitiveness in certain sectors. Continuing advances in specialty coatings, material technology, and environmental friendliness will dictate the success of firms in the United States throughout the 1990s.

FURTHER READING

Bottiglieri, Janice. "The Future Is Clear for Coating Technology." *PIMA Magazine,* May 1996, 41.

Darnay, Arsen J., ed. *Manufacturing USA.* 5th Ed. Detroit: Gale Research, 1996.

Klein, James E. *Paper & Paperboard Manufacturing and Converting Fundamentals.* 2nd Ed. San Francisco: Miller-Freeman, Inc., 1991.

1997 North American Pulp & Paper Factbook. San Francisco: Miller-Freeman, Inc., 1996.

1996 Pressure Sensitive Label Market Research Study. Chicago: Tag & Label Manufacturers Institute, Inc., 1996.

Stratton, William M., and Richard T. Glackin. "Getting Acquainted with Pressure-Sensitive Adhesive Tapes." *Machine Design,* 21 May 1992.

Rooks, Alan. "Training's the Ticket for Locks #7 (Appleton Mills)." *PIMA Magazine,* September 1994, 37.

—Alan Rooks

SIC 2673

PLASTICS, FOIL AND COATED PAPER BAGS

This category covers establishments primarily engaged in manufacturing bags of unsupported plastic film, coated paper, metal foil, or laminated combinations of these materials. These bags can be printed or unprinted. Establishments primarily engaged in manufacturing un-coated paper bags and multi-wall bags and sacks are classified in **SIC 2674: Un-coated Paper and Multi-wall Bags;** those manufacturing textile bags are classified in **SIC 2393: Textile Bags;** and those manufacturing garment storage bags, except of plastics film and paper, are classified in **SIC 2392: Housefurnishings, Except Curtains and Draperies.**

The performance of the plastic, laminated, and coated paper bag industry was somewhat erratic in the early 1990s, but the industry made steady gains in its value of shipments in the mid-1990s. Projections call for continued growth through the late 1990s. After reaching an all-time high of $5.65 billion in 1989, the value of industry shipments decreased two years in a row, to $5.5 billion in 1990 and $5.08 billion in 1991. However, from that point on, the plastic, laminated, and coated paper bag industry produced steady sales gains, rebounding to $5.71 billion in 1992, $5.81 billion in 1993 and $6.02 billion in 1994. Projections call for the industry to reach $6.48 billion in 1997 and $6.64 billion in 1998. From 1991 to 1998, this industry will have grown at an annual rate of 4.4 percent. The outlook for the industry is generally thought to be quite positive, as more retail outlets convert to plastic merchandise bags and as other applications are developed.

While this industry is classified under paper and allied products, the industry uses very little paper in its products, and even that small percentage is declining. The vast majority of products in this industry are made exclusively from plastic.

Products found in this industry include merchandise bags, trash bags, waste bags, frozen food bags, garment storage bags, and wardrobe bags. The vast majority of products manufactured in this sector are specialty bags and liners made from polyethylene single-web film. This segment accounted for 77.37 percent of total industry shipments in 1992, up from 58 percent in 1987. Within the polyethylene single-web segment, refuse bags are by far the largest component, accounting for 27.2 percent of total shipments in this industry, while grocery and variety bags account for another 17.38 percent. Both of these bag types increased their share of market from 1987.

Other significant industry products include multi-web bags and liners, which accounted for 9.03 percent of industry shipments in 1992. Another category, specialty bags and liners made from coated single-web paper, appears to be on the decline. Products in this category accounted for just 4.81 percent of industry shipments in 1992, down from 10 percent in 1987.

The biggest purchaser of plastic, laminated, and coated paper bags continues to be retail trade outlets (not including eating and drinking establishments). These retail outlets purchased about 60 percent of all bags produced in this category in 1992. Personal consumption accounted for 8.5 percent of the output, and wholesale trade another 6.7 percent. The remainder of product shipments were purchased by a wide variety of other sectors of the economy, mostly in manufacturing.

The vast majority of products in this classification are made from plastic resins or sheets. Plastic resins used in granule, pellet, powder, or liquid form accounted for $1.2 billion of the $2.57 billion worth of materials consumed by this sector in 1992. Plastic products used in the form of sheets, rods, tubes, and other shapes accounted for another $325.3 million. By contrast, paper accounted for just $107 million of industry purchases. Other significant raw materials for this category include printing ink ($69.8 million), paperboard containers, boxes and corrugated paperboard used to ship finished products ($182.6 million), and glues and adhesives ($39 million).

Several different types of companies are leaders in this industry. Mobil Chemical Co., of Fairfax, Virginia, a division of Mobil Corporation, is one of the leading companies, as is First Brands Corporation, of Danbury, Connecticut, which manufactures a wide variety of trash bags, among other consumer products. Other leaders include Cryovac, of Duncan, South Carolina; Scholle Corp. in Northlake, Illinois; and Graphic Packaging Corp., of Paoli, Pennsylvania. This industry segment employed 38,100 with a payroll of $1.05 billion in 1994. The average hourly wage for production workers was $10.68.

A large portion of this industry's output is in branded products, with trash bags being one of the leading products. Of the total U.S. trash bag market in 1995, private label products held a 20.5 percent share of the market, equal to the leading national brand, Glad, which also held a 20.5 percent share. Other leading brands include Hefty Cinch Sak (8.2 percent); Hefty (4.6 percent); and Glad Stress Flex (2.1 percent).

The plastic, foil, and coated paper bag industry has made extensive use of new plastic materials to make products that are both lighter and stronger. For example, the use of high-density polyethylene by all manufacturers was expanding at a healthy 5.7 annual rate in the mid-1990s and is expected to reach 1.7 billion pounds in 1998. High-molecular weight resins will offer major performance improvements over linear-low density polyethylene. While the primary application for this product is retail plastic bags, trash bag manufacturers are using this material as well to take advantage of its strength, toughness, and printability.

FURTHER READING

Darnay, Arsen J., ed. *Manufacturing USA,* 5th ed. Detroit: Gale Research, 1996.

Lazich, Robert S. *Market Share Reporter.* Detroit: Gale Research, 1997.

''1997 Converting Business Forecast.'' *Paper, Film, & Foil Converter,* September 1996.

U.S. Trade and Industrial Outlook, 1997-1998. New York: McGraw-Hill, 1997.

—Alan Rooks

SIC 2674

UNCOATED PAPER AND MULTIWALL BAGS

This classification includes establishments primarily engaged in manufacturing uncoated paper bags or multiwall bags and sacks, whether or not coated or containing plastics film or metal foil. Establishments primarily engaged in manufacturing bags from plastics, unsupported film, foil, coated paper, or laminated or coated combinations of these materials, are classified in **SIC 2673: Plastics, Foil, and Coated Paper Bags.** Those establishments manufacturing textile bags are classified in **SIC 2393: Textile Bags.**

INDUSTRY SNAPSHOT

The uncoated paper and multiwall (three-ply or more) bag industry is not a fast-growing one, largely because it faces sustained and intense competition from rival products made from plastic. Despite this threat, the industry's sales were stable in the 1990s as the industry expanded sales of shipping sacks and multiwall bags while its grocery bag market declined. The value of shipments in this industry remained relatively static from the early to mid-1990s, moving from $2.75 billion in 1990 to $2.85 billion in 1992 before decreasing slightly to $2.77 billion in 1994. The value of shipments is projected to increase moderately to $2.95 billion in 1997 and $2.98 billion in 1998.

In all uncoated paper and multiwall bag applications, the package must contain and protect the product or contents. Paper is used because of its ability to contribute strength and stiffness or rigidity to the container. Plastics may also offer strength, but paper is more resilient than plastics over a wider temperature range. Paper is more easily printed on than other materials. However, in many applications paper bags must be coated with waxes or plastics, or laminated to plastic films or foil to develop effective barriers to water, vapor, gases, or odors.

Market shares. The uncoated paper and multiwall bag industry is split between two categories. Shipping sacks and multiwall bags accounted for 55.57 percent of the industry's value of shipments in 1992, up from 50.71 percent in 1987. Grocers' bags, sacks, variety and shopping bags held 43.08 percent of the market in 1992, down from 48.34 percent in 1987. A small ''not specified by kind'' category accounts for the remainder of shipments. The gap between the two large categories will likely continue growing throughout the 1990s as the grocers' bag market continues to decline.

In the shipping sack and multiwall bag subcategory, the dominant product is multiwall shipping sacks and bags, holding about 81 percent of production in the subcategory, with single- and double-wall sacks and bags a distant second at 16.7 percent. In 1996, U.S. manufacturers produced 3.69 billion multiwall bags. Of this total, 1.75 billion were used in agriculture and food; 665 million in building materials; 615.3 million in chemicals; 366 million in minerals; and 294.7 million for all other applications.

In the uncoated paper grocers' bags, variety and shopping bags subcategory, the leading product is still uncoated paper grocer's sacks, with 68 percent of shipments, followed by uncoated shopping bags at 9.8 percent and uncoated paper merchandise bags at 8 percent.

In the industry's terminology, paper sacks refer to the large bags used to hold customers supermarket purchases. The 1/6th barrel sack is the standard paper sack used in supermarkets. It is called that because in the early 1900s, when paper bags were gaining in popularity, they were used to hold 1/6th of a barrel of flour. Another popular size is the 1/8th barrel sack.

Paper sacks come in a variety of basis weights. Single-ply bags range in basis weight from 60 pound to 80 pound. Some stores prefer a double-ply bag, made of two 40-pound basis weight bags, since it can hold heavier items. Stores using this double-ply bag can avoid the ''double bagging'' common at checkouts of supermarkets using single-ply bags.

The bag industry refers to smaller, lighter weight bags as "grocery bags." These bags are used in outlets such as convenience stores and fast food restaurants. They come in a variety of sizes, from 1/2-pound bags to 25-pound bags. These weights also are based on early 1900s terminology, when paper bags were graded by how much sugar they could hold. For example, a 1/2-pound bag could hold 1/2 pound of sugar. Retail trade establishments remain this manufacturing industry's primary customer.

In 1994, U.S. producers shipped a total of 39.4 billion paper sacks and bags, including 25.3 billion sacks (large), 10.1 billion bags (small) and 4 billion merchandise bags.

ORGANIZATION AND STRUCTURE

The uncoated paper and multiwall bag market was a steadily growing and relatively stable industry into the 1970s. Paper accounted for the vast majority of bags produced for retail outlets, such as supermarkets. However, in the 1970s, plastics manufacturers began to perfect the single ply polyethylene shopping bag, which could compete effectively with the traditional paper sack. While lacking some of the characteristics of the paper sack, such as stiffness, the plastic sack had one big advantage—lower cost. Today, individual plastic bags cost about one-third as much as the average paper sack. This price advantage increased when kraft paper prices skyrocketed along with other grades of paper in 1994 and 1995. For example, the price of 70-pound grocery sack paper rose from $320 per ton in 1993 to $490 in 1994 and $530 in 1995, before falling back to about $410 per ton in 1996. With supermarket net profits averaging about one cent for every dollar of sales, these retailers have been quick to convert to plastic bags. While most supermarket chains still stock paper bags for customers that ask for them, many have stopped asking the question "paper or plastic" at the checkout, leading to increased use of plastic bags.

Prices prevalent in the mid-1990s clearly demonstrate the cost differential. For example, the average paper grocery sack cost $34-$36 per 1,000, or 3.4-3.6 cents each, while the typical high density, 1/2 mil polyethylene sack cost $12-$14 per 1,000, or 1.2 cents-1.4 cents each. While plastic bags do not hold as much as comparable paper bags, supermarket chains still see substantial cost savings in using plastic bags. While a few supermarket chains use paper sacks extensively, and others still stock paper bags, that has not stopped the steady erosion of paper's market share. Also, other retail outlets, such as mass merchandisers, use plastic bags exclusively. Kmart Corporation converted from paper in the 1980s. This led Union Camp Corporation,

formerly a major supplier of paper sacks to Kmart, to invest in plastic bag manufacturing in order to continue supplying Kmart. In the early 1990s, Wal-Mart Stores, Inc., the nation's largest retailer, converted to using plastic bags exclusively. In the mid-1990s, Union Camp scaled back its production of paper bags and sacks, and closed its flagship Savannah, Georgia mill.

Multiwall market stronger. Multiwall paper bags, which use three or more plies of paper, are used heavily in industrial applications for the transport and sales of products such as seed and fertilizer. They have continued to expand their share of this market at the expense of paper sacks. Multiwall bags are used for many business-to-business transactions, such as the sale of fertilizer to farmers, and also for consumer transactions, such as pet food. As a result, multiwall bags are sold in a variety of shapes, sizes, and constructions, from the plain brown bags used for cement mix to the high quality, four-color, plastic-lined packages used for pet food or lawn fertilizer.

Multiwall bag producers divide their market into two categories: paper multiwall packaging, designed for products weighing 20 pounds and over; and consumer packaging, designed for products weighing five to ten pounds, such as pet food and charcoal.

The number of packaging layers depends on the application. For example, multiwall bags for products being shipped overseas may have as many as five or six layers to withstand severe handling and extreme temperature conditions. Pet food bags, on the other hand, may have just three layers, with one being a grease-resistant paper. Cement bags usually include a polyethylene liner to keep the product's moisture away from the outer paper layers. However, some bag manufacturers, in order to make their bags more "environmentally friendly" and recyclable, are looking for ways to eliminate the plastic film inner layer by using specially-treated paper instead.

BACKGROUND AND DEVELOPMENT

Paper bags have been a major product for the paper industry for more than 100 years. One of the earliest bag makers, Union Paper Bag Machine Co. (now Union Camp), was founded in 1861 in Bethlehem, Pennsylvania, to make and sell machines for manufacturing paper bags. In the late 1800s and early 1900s, the use of paper bags continued to grow along with the economy. The bag market received a major boost from the invention and development of self-serve grocery stores in the early 1900s. As self-serve stores continued to expand in other retail environments, the use of paper bags boomed.

CURRENT CONDITIONS

The big issue for the uncoated paper and multiwall bag industry continues to be the penetration of plastic bags into markets previously dominated by paper. The depth of this problem is illustrated by the long-term decline in production of the kraft paper from which bags and sacks are made. The long-term decline in demand for unbleached kraft packaging papers, particularly for grocery bags and sacks, caused paper producers to reduce production capacity by 40 percent from 1985 to 1995, from about 3.9 million tons in 1985 to 2.5 million tons in 1995. In 1996, production was down another 80,000 tons, following a decline of 300,000 tons in 1995.

However, the damage that plastics have done to the paper bag market varies greatly by category. In the paper sack market, plastics had taken over 75-80 percent of the market in the mid-1990s. That was a dramatic reversal from the early 1980s, when paper sacks accounted for the majority of the market. Paper is expected to "bottom out" and hold on to the 20-25 percent market share it held in the mid-1990s, since many customers still prefer the paper sack in supermarkets. However, much of those sales depend on supermarkets being willing to continue stocking two types of sacks.

In the grocery bag market, plastics penetration has been far less pervasive. In the mid-1990s, paper still accounted for 70 percent of the market. Much of the strength in this market is accounted for by the growth of the fast food marketplace. Fast food chains such as McDonald's Corporation and Burger King use a very high volume of small bags to package customers' orders. Plastics have almost no penetration in this particular market segment. The main reason is that plastics have no rigidity, a real problem when food, drinks, and other items are placed in one bag. Also, these chains use the high-quality printing surfaces of the bags for promotions and advertising.

The product mix in the fast food bag segment changed radically in the early to mid-1990s as demand for recycled products grew. For example, the McDonald's chain converted from a bright white bleached bag made from virgin fiber to a 100 percent recycled, unbleached brown bag. Other chains, such as Burger King, soon followed with other types of bags made from recycled paper. Changes demanded by large customers such as McDonald's are highly significant. For example, in 1985, McDonald's used 285,000 tons of packaging materials (much of that in bags), with 86 percent being paper and 14 percent being plastic. The average recycled content in McDonald's packaging increased from 17 percent in 1990 to 42 percent in 1995.

Also, some "high-quality" retailers use paper bags to promote store image, since plastic bags tend to be associated with discount outlets. For example, Starbucks Coffee was using a highly printed, intricately patterned brown paper bag at its retail outlets in the mid-1990s.

The "notions and millinery" sector includes the flat bags (without folded bottoms) used to hold customer purchases in variety stores and department stores. Plastic has made heavy inroads into paper's market share in this category, accounting for about 75 percent of this market in the mid-1990s. However, paper appeared to be holding on to its 25 percent of the market as of 1995.

The only paper bag product line seeing any real growth in the mid-1990s was heavy duty, cord-handled shopping bags used by many department store chains. Many retail outlets use these bags for marketing purposes, since they can be made from high-quality, bleached, clay-coated paper for four-color printing. Many stores use these bags as a customer service—often charging for them—so that customers can consolidate their purchases from different areas of the store.

Slow growth in multiwall. The multiwall bag market was growing at an annual rate of 1.5-2 percent per year in the mid-1990s. Some of this slow growth is attributed to inroads made by low-density plastic bags and wraps. One of the fastest growing bag applications, for example, is multilayer industrial plastic film bags, which are replacing multiwall paper bags for products such as herbicides, pesticides, and fertilizers.

By the mid-1990s, plastics had claimed 25 percent of the market previously held exclusively by multiwall paper bags. For example, plastic bags are often used for high-moisture products, such as bark chips.

Manufacturers are also producing combination bags, which include several outer layers of paper and inner liners made of plastic. This hybrid bag combines the barrier properties of plastic with the rigidity and strength of paper. Also, manufacturers have found that layers of different materials, such as paper and plastic, can provide a better odor barrier in some instances than either material alone.

However, some multiwall bag applications have been converted to 100 percent plastic. Plastic resin for industrial applications is now contained in bags made from that same resin, so that when the product is needed, the entire bag is used. Also, some 100 percent plastic bags are being made with three or more layers of different plastics to accommodate specialized packaging processes. For example, some products are packaged with a "hot fill" process, where the product is put into the package while still hot. The inner plastic layer can handle the hot product while the outer layers are designed to protect the product in transit.

INDUSTRY LEADERS

Major manufacturers of uncoated paper and multiwall bags include Stone Container Corporation, Duro Bag Manufacturing Co., International Paper Company, Gaylord Container Corporation, and Union Camp Corporation. The top three manufacturers—Stone, Duro and Gaylord—held 80 percent of the paper sack market in the mid-1990s. Two of these producers, Stone Container and Gaylord, merged their retail bag operations in 1996, a move that was expected to help the firms compete more effectively against producers of plastic bags. Of the five manufacturers listed above, both Duro and Union Camp are heavily integrated, in that they produce both plastic and paper bags. These same companies are also leaders in the production of multiwall bags.

The uncoated paper and multiwall bag industry employed 17,900 people with a payroll of $430.7 million in 1994. The industry employment total includes 15,000 production workers who put in 31.7 million total hours at an average pay rate of $10.17 in 1994.

FURTHER READING

Biermann, Christopher J. *Essentials of Pulping and Papermaking.* San Diego: Academic Press, Inc., 1993.

Darnay, Arsen J., ed. *Manufacturing USA.* 5th ed. Detroit: Gale Research, 1996.

"Kraft Paper: Low Operating Rates and Price Levels for Kraft Paper Mills." *Pulp & Paper,* November 1996, 13.

Paper, Paperboard, Pulp Capacity and Fiber Consumption. Washington: American Forest & Paper Association, 1996.

"PIMA Conference Coverage." *PIMA Magazine,* September 1996, 38.

Thesaurus of Pulp and Paper Terminology. Atlanta: Institute of Paper Science and Technology, 1991.

U.S. Trade and Industrial Outlook 1997-1998. New York: McGraw-Hill, 1997.

—Alan Rooks

SIC 2675

DIE-CUT PAPER AND PAPERBOARD AND CARDBOARD

Establishments in this industry are primarily engaged in die-cutting purchased paper and paperboard and in manufacturing cardboard by laminating, lining or surface coating paperboard. Establishments primarily engaged in laminating building paper from purchased paper are classified in **SIC 2679: Converted Paper and Paperboard Products, Not Elsewhere Classified.**

Products in this industry classification include pasted chip board; bottle caps and tops; cardboard foundations and cutouts; pasted, laminated line and surface coated paperboard; plain paper cards; tabulating cards; die-cut paper and paperboard; egg cartons and egg case fillers and flats; and filing folders, index cards, and paperboard library cards.

The performance of the die-cut paper and board industry was erratic in the early to mid-1990s. The value of shipments reached an all-time high of $2.29 billion in 1991, but fell sharply the following year to $2.01 billion, before recovering to $2.02 billion in 1993 and $2.24 billion in 1994. Projections called for very modest growth in the late 1990s, with the value of shipments expected to reach $2.44 billion by 1998. The slow growth experienced by this industry reflects the fact that the market for many of its traditional products is a mature one.

Most of this industry's products are office supplies. Die-cut paper and board office supplies accounted for 47 percent of industry shipments in 1992, down sharply from 53 percent in 1987. Pasted, lined, laminated or surface coated paperboard was the next largest category, with 37.6 percent of the total in 1992, up dramatically from 27.6 percent in 1987; all other die-cut products accounted for the remaining 15.4 percent. Die-cut paper and board manufacturers tend to be located in areas where business activity is highest. As a result, industry activity is greater in such states as Illinois (which accounted for 10.8 percent of industry shipments in 1992); California (9.2 percent); New York (7.5 percent); Georgia (5.4 percent); and New Jersey (4.9 percent).

This industry manufactures a wide variety of products and yet is closely linked to the production of corrugated boxes, since many of its products are used as box inserts. Also, many products are made from recycled fiber—often 100 percent recycled fiber. The desire by consumers and businesses to buy products made from recycled materials appears to have increased demand for products from the die-cut paper and board industry.

Die-cut paper and board industry leaders tend to be independent converters; there are few major paper companies with holdings in die-cut paper and paperboard. Some of the leading companies include Esselte Pendaflex Corp., Garden City, New York; Fleer Corp., Mount Laurel, New Jersey; Book Covers Inc., Newark, New Jersey and Advertising Display Co., Englewood Cliffs, New Jersey. Chesapeake Corp. is one of the few paper companies with a large market share in this industry through its Chesapeake Display Co. in Winston-Salem, North Carolina.

The die-cut paper and board industry employed a total of 16,000 employees in 1994, including 12,800 production workers. The average hourly wage was $10.40, up from $8.24 in 1987.

FURTHER READING

Darnay, Arsen J., ed. *Manufacturing USA,* 5th ed. Detroit: Gale Research, 1996.

Paper, Paperboard, Pulp Capacity and Fiber Consumption. Washington: American Forest & Paper Association, 1996.

Smook, Gary A. *Handbook of Pulp & Paper Terminology: A Guide to Industrial and Technological Usage.* Bellingham, WA: Angus Wilde Publications, 1990.

U.S. Trade and Industrial Outlook 1997-1998. New York: McGraw-Hill, 1997.

—Alan Rooks

SIC 2676

SANITARY PAPER PRODUCTS

This classification covers establishments primarily engaged in manufacturing sanitary paper products from purchased paper, such as facial tissues and handkerchiefs, table napkins, toilet paper and paper towels, disposable diapers, and sanitary napkins and tampons.

INDUSTRY SNAPSHOT

The sanitary paper products industry manufactures paper into finished products with sanitary applications. The value of shipments in the sanitary paper industry was approximately $16.2 billion in 1994 (about 11.2 percent of the paper and allied products industry group as a whole). Projections indicate a steady increase through the rest of the decade, including $18.55 billion in 1997 and $19.17 billion in 1998.

A large majority of the products contained in this classification are branded consumer products sold in many different retail outlets, so the sanitary paper industry spends more on advertising than any other part of the paper industry.

There are three broad subcategories within the sanitary paper products industry: sanitary tissue products, which accounted for 59.5 percent of the value of industry shipments in 1992; disposable diapers (27.8 percent); and sanitary napkins and tampons (11.2 percent). A small "not specified by kind" segment accounted for the remaining 1.5 percent.

Many of the products contained within this classification are considered non-discretionary and as a result, sales within this classification have tended to follow different business cycles than those of more commodity-oriented paper lines. While new sanitary products, such as adult incontinence products, have helped to expand the market, this industry tends to grow only as fast as the overall gross domestic product (GDP). As in many mature markets, competition for customers is fierce. For example, tissue manufacturers continually seek to lower production costs since small gains can lead to major gains in either profit margins or market share. In order to maintain growth, firms have begun to focus on expansion abroad while at the same time continuing to segment the market and introduce new products domestically. Production of sanitary paper products is one of the few areas of the paper industry where major global corporations—notably Kimberly-Clark Corporation, The Procter & Gamble Company, and Fort James Corporation—operate manufacturing facilities in many locations around the world.

Most of the major companies in the sanitary paper products industry are integrated, in that they produce the raw materials for finished products, such as parent rolls of tissue at large paper mills, as well as the converted sanitary paper products, such as packages of bathroom tissue.

ORGANIZATION AND STRUCTURE

The majority of sanitary paper products are made from pulp or paper, though a significant percentage are made using the "nonwoven" process in which natural or synthetic fibers are bonded together by cohesion, friction, and/or adhesion. Sanitary paper products are usually broken down into two sectors: consumer and commercial and industrial (C&I). Customers in the C&I category of sanitary paper might be schools, hospitals, or offices. C&I shipments comprise about one-third of sanitary tissue sales and a much smaller percentage of nonwoven sales.

Sanitary Tissue. Sanitary tissue products, the largest segment of this industry, is broken down into several different subcategories. The largest of these is retail toilet tissue, which accounted for more than 29 percent of all sanitary tissue product shipments (by value) in the mid-1990s. Commercial and industrial toilet tissue accounted for about 11.5 percent of shipments. Retail paper towels is another large subcategory, accounting for more than 22 percent of sanitary tissue product shipments, while industrial paper towels were another 10 percent of the market. Facial tissues were 8.7 percent while industrial paper napkins (hand towels) accounted for 7.9 percent. Retail paper napkins held 4.1 percent of the market. All other sanitary tissue products accounted for nearly 7 percent of the market.

The processes used to make sanitary tissue products are very similar to those used to create other types of paper. In the standard papermaking process, wood fibers are stripped from wood chips in either a chemical or mechanical process to produce wood pulp. This pulp, a combination of wood fibers and water, is then spread on a continuous fine screen. The resulting mat is then passed over vacuum boxes (to remove some water) and run through successive drying and pressing processes until the finished paper product is achieved.

The major differences between general paper manufacture and tissue manufacture lie in the type of raw material used and the converting processes. Because of the relationship between the softness of the raw material and the softness of the final product, lightly refined softwood fibers are generally preferred for consumer-oriented products. These fibers come both from virgin fiber (wood) and from recycled fiber. In fact, the sanitary tissue products industry is one of the largest recycling industries in the United States. As of 1995, 42 percent of all U.S. tissue was produced with fiber from purchased wastepaper (recycled paper), and 21 percent was produced from purchased virgin pulp. The remaining fiber was produced on-site at integrated pulp and paper mills. Products for the C&I market typically place a higher premium on strength as opposed to softness, and are made from a coarser grade of wood.

Once the tissue paper is formed, producers convert it into consumer products on-site. Depending on the type of product, dyes and perfumes may be added and the paper may be embossed. The tissue is then prepared for market—facial tissues are folded and boxed, and bathroom tissue is rolled and prepared for shipment.

Nonwoven Sanitary Products. A second segment of the sanitary paper market consists of products which incorporate nonwoven fabrics in their manufacture.

Nonwoven products include: disposable diapers/training pants, feminine hygiene products, adult incontinence products (including consumer and institutional adult pads and bed pads), and pre-moistened tissues (including baby wipes). Advances in nonwoven technology have increased the number of nonwoven applications and enhanced the use of nonwovens in existing applications.

Nonwovens are so named because the fibers (synthetic or wood pulp) used in their fabrication are bonded together instead of woven, as they would be in textile-type products. This bonding can take the form of an adhesive applied to the fiber mat before or after forming, or it can be the result of a chemical reaction. The typical nonwoven product incorporates many steps into its fabrication. A diaper, for example, will begin with a polyethylene outer shell. Bonded to the shell will be dry formed wood pulp (fluff pulp) within layers of impervious nonwoven fabric. Glues, resins, and adhesives will be used to bind the various components to one another. The typical adult incontinence pad, sanitary napkin, and tampon will incorporate many of the same steps into its manufacture.

In the manufacturing process, nonwovens are often treated with super-absorbent polymers (SAPs) which can absorb as much as 70 to 80 times their weight in liquid. A further distinguishing feature of SAPs is that, unlike a sponge or other woven absorbent products, SAPs retain water even when squeezed. A sponge, for example, retains water in channels or pores. SAPs chemically bind with the fluid to form a gel. Under extremely heavy pressure, SAPs might release a type of gel, but most liquids remain in their chemical compound.

Aside from sanitary applications, nonwovens can also be found in other applications either as a substitute for cloth or in applications requiring a high degree of absorbency (filters, car covers, durable shop towels). Since most producers of nonwoven sanitary products are also producers of nonwoven fabrics, the strength of these related industries can also have an impact on these companies' results.

Marketing. After the final product is ready, the process moves from manufacturing to marketing. The need to market effectively drives two additional defining features of the industry. First, there is the need for extensive promotion: companies within the sanitary paper industry spend the highest percentage on advertising of any paper-producing industry. Secondly, companies have also recognized the need for sophisticated marketing techniques. Increased segmentation and "database marketing"—using elaborate information banks to determine lifestyle predictors for a target segment—have become important success factors in the industry.

Establishment Size and Distribution. Unlike other grades of paper, many sanitary paper products—notably tissue products—are bulky, and as a result it is not cost effective to ship them long distances. As a result, sanitary product converters have traditionally been located close to their end use markets. This is especially true for more commodity-oriented product lines such as bathroom tissue and household towels. This is one of the reasons sanitary paper product manufacturers have developed a global network of manufacturing plants. For higher value added products such as tampons and ultrathin pads, or niche products such as pre-moistened tissues and baby wipes, producers typically supply markets from only one or two manufacturing facilities.

The twin requirements of converting massive amounts of raw materials and a highly-competitive consumer marketplace have led to a high degree of concentration in the sanitary paper products industry. In 1996 five firms—Kimberly-Clark, Procter & Gamble, James River, Georgia-Pacific Corporation and Fort James Corporation—controlled 77 percent of the U.S. retail tissue market, with the top two firms controlling more than half. Kimberly-Clark, following its 1995 merger with Scott Paper Company, held 29 percent while Procter & Gamble controlled 23 percent. They were followed by James River with 16 percent and Fort Howard and Georgia-Pacific, each with 10 percent.

In the disposable diaper segment, market concentration is even more pronounced. The two leading firms, Kimberly-Clark and Procter & Gamble, shared 77.2 percent of the market in 1996, with nearly equal shares. Private label products accounted for 17.3 percent while other brands held 5.3 percent of the market.

BACKGROUND AND DEVELOPMENT

The development of the sanitary paper market in the United States has parallelled the development of two broader categories the market represents, the paper and consumer products industry groups. The advances made in paper production technology from the latter half of the nineteenth century to the early part of the twentieth century that had an impact on the paper industry as a whole also had an impact on the sanitary paper industry.

Sanitary Tissue Products. As with most of the paper industry, the sanitary tissue sector owes much of its growth to advances in automation and wood processing made in the last century. The development of the

fourdrinier paper machine in the first half of the nineteenth century allowed greater volumes of paper to be produced at a lower price. This process is particularly relevant for sanitary tissue since it is still the ideal process for lighter weight grades in general and tissue manufacture in particular.

Since 1850, ongoing developments in wood processing have provided paper manufacturers with a cheap, reliable source of raw materials. Prior to these discoveries, the main raw materials for paper production were rags, cloth, and straw. By the 1850s, mechanization had already substantially reduced the costs of producing paper, but constraints on the supplies of raw materials limited paper production to specific applications. Once a process was developed for wood fiber to be converted into pulp, greater applications for paper became possible and the sanitary paper industry was born. Paper began to find its way into more and more households and assumed the roles previously held by towels, leaves, and rags.

The marketing of sanitary paper products did not assume its current importance until the early part of the twentieth century. Prior to that, competition in the industry seemed to be oriented toward consolidation and acquisition. The United Paper Company made a series of acquisitions in the 1890s in an attempt to form a "tissue trust," but the trust was broken and the company forced into bankruptcy when other paper producers switched to tissue production and undercut the trust's position.

From the early part of the twentieth century, developments in the sanitary sector were not so much technology- as consumer-driven, and the role of the sanitary paper producer switched from being a provider of specific products to responding to consumer needs. The development of one company, Scott Paper Company, reflects many of these changes. In 1902, the company introduced Waldorf, one of the first branded bathroom tissues, and moved quickly into a position of dominance in this product line. Scott's invention of paper towels in 1907 further consolidated the company's position. By the 1950s, Scott held more than 50 percent of the sanitary tissue market. Over time, however, new product introductions and sustained marketing efforts by competitors reduced Scott's market dominance.

Perhaps it was Kimberly-Clark's long experience with marketing that allowed it to gain some of Scott's market share. In 1915, Kimberly-Clark developed Cellu-cotton, an absorbent wadding that was later used in feminine hygiene products. In 1924, Kimberly-Clark introduced one of the most ubiquitous brand names in America: Kleenex. Originally developed as a tissue for removing cold cream, the company found that it sold better as a disposable handkerchief; due to technological innovations in folding and packaging, Kimberly-Clark was able to market it as such.

Since these developments, the sanitary tissue sector has been marked more by evolutionary realignments than revolutionary innovations. The basic product offerings of the major producers in the sector have remained essentially the same, but improvements in quality, strength, and packaging, have been the driving forces in the market. Since the 1960s, the sanitary paper market has witnessed intensified competition among a number of strong competitors. Low-cost producers have captured large segments of the low-end market, while marketing and consumer product giants have gained substantial market share in the premium branded segments. James River Corporation of Virginia, founded in 1969, used acquisitions and joint ventures to expand its activities rapidly. James River evolved from a start-up operation in the early 1970s to the third largest tissue producer in the United States in the mid-1990s.

Nonwoven Sanitary Products. The nonwoven sector, with its emphasis on consumer goods, reflects the development of the power of marketing on American lifestyles. At the same time, the technological innovations in super-absorbent polymers and nonwoven fabrics have marked advances in the sector.

Disposable diapers comprise the largest sub-segment in the nonwoven product group, generating sales of nearly $5 billion in 1996. Procter & Gamble introduced disposable diapers with the Pampers brand in 1961. Since that time, the market has exhibited steady growth based mainly on increasing penetration rates. Continuous product enhancements and forceful marketing by the two main players in the disposable diapers field—Procter & Gamble and Kimberly-Clark—led to high usage rates. Annual new product introductions have kept competition high and have continuously improved the image of disposable diapers. Advances in nonwoven technology have led to improvements in absorbency and size reductions, therefore enabling producers to achieve savings in transportation and packaging. The next generation of diapers is expected to allow for even greater absorbency, so as to stay dry even through multiple wettings.

Sanitary napkins and tampons are the second-largest component within the nonwoven product group, generating $2 billion in total sales in 1996. Kimberly-Clark first entered the consumer products segment in the 1920s with a sanitary napkin called Kotex. At first, societal norms prevented feminine care products from being publicized and displayed. Many magazines refused to carry advertising for feminine care products, and stores were reluctant to stock them. However, despite these barriers and the relatively high prices, consumer acceptance of the products was high.

CURRENT CONDITIONS

The sanitary paper market experienced steady growth in the mid-1990s. The non-discretionary nature of many of its product lines seems to ensure a strong demand base. At the same time, many producers see limited growth opportunities in the domestic market. The aging of the American population, the relatively stable birth rate, and increasing competition all pose significant challenges for this industry.

Perhaps the biggest change in the U.S. sanitary paper products industry was the 1995 merger of Kimberly-Clark Corporation and Scott Paper Company. The merger of these two industry giants was valued at $9.4 billion, with Kimberly-Clark being the surviving corporation. The new K-C is a massive presence in the sanitary paper products industry, controlling nearly 30 percent of the sanitary tissue market and more than 38 percent of the disposable diaper market. The U.S. Justice Department, concerned about excessive market concentration, reached a consent decree with K-C before it approved the merger. Under the decree, K-C agreed to sell the Scotties facial tissue brand and its Fort Edward, New York tissue mill to Irving Tissue Inc., It also sold the former Scott wipes plant to its leading competitor, Procter & Gamble. The latter sale gave P&G a one-third share of the baby wipes market.

While the massive K-C/Scott merger might inspire other leaders in the market to consider similar action, most industry observers believe that the U.S. Justice Department will not approve of any further concentration in this industry. For example, K-C and Procter & Gamble hold more than half of the retail tissue market, and K-C and Fort Howard Corporation control nearly half of the commercial and industrial tissue market.

In April 1997, antitrust enforcers at the Justice Department were beginning to look into Procter & Gamble's decision to buy Tambrands Inc. for $1.85 billion. Regulatory officials needed to examine this deal to make sure it would not give Procter & Gamble too much control over the market. Procter & Gamble already held a 20 percent share of the sanitary-care market, and with this acquisition they add Tampax, the world's best selling tampon, to their portfolio.

Two of the major U.S. sanitary paper products producers moved away from vertical integration in the mid-1990s. Both Procter & Gamble and Kimberly-Clark sold much of their pulp making capacity, in order to establish long-term agreements with independent pulp producers. Both companies cited the need to put more money into their core marketing, operations, and R&D units as reasons for the divestitures.

Since production of tissue and tissue products is highly integrated, one of the major factors affecting the financial performance of the industry is the capacity to produce tissue. If there is excess capacity, prices of tissue tend to drop—as do retail prices for tissue products. When demand exceeds growth in capacity, tissue prices can rise sharply, as they did in 1994 and 1995. U.S. tissue manufacturing capacity in 1996 was estimated at 6.65 million tons, up 1.4 percent from 6.55 million tons in 1995. Tissue capacity is expected to increase at an average annual rate of 2 percent between 1997 and 1999, for a total three-year increase of 413,000 tons. Much of the growth reflects the anticipated start-up of seven new tissue machines. By 1999, total U.S. tissue production capacity should reach 7.1 million tons.

Sanitary Tissue Markets. While unit volume of sanitary tissue products grew steadily at about 2 percent in the early to mid-1990s, the value of shipments was somewhat erratic, largely due to low underlying prices of tissue. However, the value of shipments began increasing again in 1994 and 1995 as major producers raised prices in response to dramatically higher prices for tissue paper and the wood pulp and wastepaper it is made from.

In 1996, however, sharp drops in wood pulp and wastepaper prices helped increase profitability for major sanitary tissue product producers. These lower raw material prices allowed manufacturers to reduce prices modestly while still maintaining profitability. For example, Procter & Gamble instituted a 5-8 percent price cut in early 1996 for various consumer tissue products.

Despite a sharp drop in pulp prices in late 1995 and early 1996, the overall decline in tissue pricing was only 3 percent in 1996. Steady demand, rising operating rates, and an expected increase in pulp prices during 1997 were expected to drive prices up modestly. In late 1996, the three largest commercial tissue producers—K-C, James River, and Fort Howard—announced price increases on their commercial and industrial lines. Traditionally, retail prices have followed those in the C&I market.

Producers have seen slow but steady growth in the disposable diaper market since the product's introduction. Total manufacturers' sales were estimated at $4.77 billion in 1995, up from $3.9 billion in 1992. Growth in the domestic diaper industry reached a plateau in the late 1980s and early 1990s with a decline in net births and stabilization of market penetration. Much of the sector's growth can be accounted for by increased market penetration and higher usage rates as the product has improved, yet marketers view opportunities for domestic growth as limited.

As diaper penetration rates have stabilized, makers of disposable diapers have tried to use their capabilities to introduce products for market segments exhibiting increasing growth. Some of these products include training pants (for children making the transition from diapers) and adult incontinence products. The adult incontinence segment is considered one of the fastest-growing in the country, albeit from a small base.

In the feminine care sector, sanitary napkin usage continued to decline in the mid-1990s in favor of tampon usage. The total sanitary napkin and tampon market was estimated at $1.93 billion in 1995. Feminine pads held 60 percent of the feminine care market in the mid-1990s, with tampons accounting for the remaining 40 percent. The share of tampons peaked at around 50 percent in the late 1970s, but declined in the 1980s, due to adverse publicity associated with toxic shock syndrome. Since then, medical improvements in tampon manufacture have led to increased acceptance of these products, and the tampon market has rebounded.

Environmental Concerns. In the early to mid-1990s, environmental concerns and long-term access to fiber were two of the top issues facing the paper industry group. Restrictions on timber-cutting, new environmental regulations, and potential long-term fiber shortages are all concerns for many sectors of the industry. However, timber-cutting restrictions in the Northwest, which were expected to continue throughout the 1990s, have had less of an impact on sanitary paper products industry, largely because a large proportion of the industry's fiber base is in recycled paper.

Manufacturers of tissue, like other producers of bleached paper products, faced stricter air and water regulations under the Environmental Protection Agency's "Cluster Rule," which was due to be issued in 1997. This rule was expected to further limit air and water discharges from bleached kraft pulp mills and other paper industry facilities, focusing on limiting discharges—particularly of dioxin, chloroforms, and other chlorinated organics arising from the pulp manufacturing process. Mills also faced new regulations promulgated by the EPA under revisions to the Clean Air Act of 1970 and Clean Water Act of 1972. However, mills that use recovered paper were expected to be less affected by these new rules than mills using wood pulp. This is significant for the sanitary paper products industry since nearly half of all tissue produced in the United States is made from recycled paper.

Producers of nonwovens have had other concerns to deal with. In the early 1990s, environmental pressure about disposable diapers in landfills caused some concern among producers. It even prompted Procter & Gamble to create a program to compost used diapers, although the experiment was eventually discontinued. However, diapers account for just 2 percent of solid waste in the average municipal landfill, and concern over was this issue dying down at the same time that the landfill "crisis" was easing. By the mid-1990s, new landfills were being opened and it was discovered that available landfill space had been drastically underestimated.

While the United States is still an enormous market, most producers see their greatest opportunities for growth in the sanitary paper markets in overseas expansion. The relatively large size of U.S. producers compared to their foreign counterparts, the marketing strength of U.S. companies, and relatively low levels of penetration of sanitary products in developing nations indicate continued globalization efforts.

INDUSTRY LEADERS

The largest companies within the sanitary paper segment are Kimberly-Clark Corporation, The Procter & Gamble Company, James River Corporation of Virginia, Georgia-Pacific Corporation and Fort Howard Paper Company.

Since its merger with Scott Paper Company, Dallas-based Kimberly-Clark Corporation is clearly the leading company in this industry, and one of the leading consumer products marketers in the United States. In 1995, K-C's sales were $13.79 billion, all of it in pulp, paper, or converted paper products. This made K-C the second largest U.S. paper company according to PIMA Magazine's annual ranking survey. K-C is a global manufacturer and marketer of products for personal, business and industrial uses. Nearly all of its products are made from natural and synthetic fibers. K-C now operates manufacturing operations in 33 countries, with products available in 150 countries.

Kimberly-Clark holds commanding market shares in many segments of the sanitary paper products industry. Its diaper brands accounted for a leading 38.7 percent share of the market in 1996, and its Kleenex facial tissues garnered 46.6 percent of that market in

1995. K-C also dominates the adult incontinence products market, with 53.1 percent in 1995. Areas where K-C is not as dominant include tampons, where its Kotex brand had a 10.7 percent share in 1995; and toilet paper, where it held 7 percent of the market as of December 1995.

Procter & Gamble of Cincinnati, Ohio is one of the world's largest consumer products companies with revenues of $33.4 billion and 99,200 employees in 1995. Procter & Gamble had pulp, paper, or converted product sales of $9.29 billion, which ranked it third on PIMA Magazine's listing of top paper companies. P&G operates in 58 countries and in the mid-1990s greatly expanded its overseas operations with the acquisition of the European tissue business of VPS-AG.

Procter & Gamble dominates the U.S. toilet paper segment, holding 32 percent of the market in 1995, well ahead of second place James River, which held 14 percent. With 38.5 percent of the disposable diaper business in 1996, P&G battles with Kimberly-Clark, which held a slight advantage with 38.7 percent of the market. P&G held a 32.1 percent share of the facial tissue market in 1995, well behind Kimberly-Clark.

Founded in 1969, James River is the youngest of the industry's stronger competitors. James River expanded rapidly in the 1970s and 1980s by acquiring mills considered obsolete and re-tooling them for efficient use. Its purchase of Dixie-Northern in 1982 made the company a serious competitor in the bathroom tissue market. James River's 1995 sales were $6.16 billion, all in pulp, paper, or converted products. The company has three main business units: consumer products, North America; consumer products, Europe (Jamont); and food and consumer products. In 1995, James River spun off its communications papers business and its specialty paper-based packaging unit.

Green Bay, Wisconsin-based Fort Howard Corporation manufactures paper towels, bath tissue, napkins, facial tissues, wipes, and specialty nonwovens. It operates three tissue mills in the United States. In 1995, its sales were $1.62 billion, all in pulp, paper, or converted products. Total employment was 6,800. The vast majority of its products are made from recovered wastepaper. The company holds a 28 percent market share of the U.S. C&I tissue market, and a 10.5 percent share of the U.S. consumer tissue market. It is also the leading supplier of private label tissue products. In 1995, the company went public with an offering of common stock.

The feminine hygiene market contains a number of other players: Tambrands Inc. (acquired by Procter & Gamble in 1997) holds a dominant share of the tampon market, with 44.3 percent in 1995, followed by Playtex Products Inc. with 25.1 percent. Other leaders in this market include Kimberly-Clark, with 20 percent and Johnson & Johnson with 8.6 percent.

WORK FORCE

A typical manufacturing plant will employ machinists, millwrights, mechanics, paper-machine tenders, hands (who assist in removing finished paper rolls from paper machines), guards, and janitors. The sanitary paper products industry employed 40,400 people in 1995, including 33,400 production workers. Wages in this industry are much higher than other industries in the paper and allied products group, averaging $17.08 per hour in 1995. That hourly average was expected to climb to $18.27 per hour by 1998.

AMERICA AND THE WORLD

The capital-intensive nature of paper manufacturing means that cheaper overseas labor has less of an impact on manufacturing costs than in other, more labor-intensive industries. U.S. manufacturers face little threat from abroad; only one foreign paper manufacturer, Finland-based Molnlycke, has established a significant presence in U.S. sanitary markets. The internationalization of the sanitary paper industry has meant U.S. firms going abroad. Superior product quality and marketing ability has given the United States a competitive advantage in a number of foreign markets.

For most sanitary paper producers, Europe is viewed as particularly promising: the European Community contains 5 percent of the world's population, but consumes only 25 percent of the world's sanitary tissue. This compares with 3 percent and 40 percent, respectively, in the United States. This is one of the factors behind Procter & Gamble's acquisition of VPS AG, a major European tissue manufacturer, in 1995. Through the early 1990s, nearly all of the large U.S. producers, except Fort Howard, had secured market positions in the European Union.

The prospects of greater access to global markets was one of the key elements behind the merger of Kimberly-Clark and Scott Paper in 1995. Scott Paper had more extensive European operations than K-C, and the combination of the two made K-C a powerful competitor in Europe. In fact, before the deal was allowed to go through, governing bodies of the European Union required significant divestitures, including selling the Kleenex tissue and towel lines in Europe, Scotties boxed facial tissue, and Handy Andies facial tissue in the United Kingdom and Ireland. K-C was also forced to sell its Prudhoe, England tissue mill. In 1996, K-C was the leading European producer of con-sumer tissue products, holding 25 percent of the market.

In Asia, U.S. sanitary paper producers have had limited success penetrating the Japanese market but much more success in the rest of Asia. While the Japanese market is highly fragmented and thus viewed as vulnerable to the sophisticated marketers of U.S. products, intricate supplier-retailer relationships have thus far prevented any U.S. producer from establishing a significant presence.

However, U.S. companies' penetration of the fast-growing "rest of Asia" market is much greater. For example, Kimberly-Clark holds a strong position in Taiwan, Korea, and the Philippines. K-C joint ventures in Indonesia, Malaysia, and China are also generating strong sales growth.

RESEARCH AND TECHNOLOGY

Changes in the manufacture of paper have historically been evolutionary rather than revolutionary. The same processes used to manufacture paper from rags in the middle of the nineteenth century are in many forms still used today. Much of the research and technology in this industry is focused on lowering incremental manufacturing costs, since the ability to be the low-cost producer can translate into a strong market advantage. Also, the ability to produce softer and stronger paper is a significant focus of sanitary paper products research and development. Because companies in this industry are highly competitive, their R&D programs are tightly guarded secrets. Many companies will not allow tours of their tissue-making operations for fear of industrial espionage.

FURTHER READING

Darnay, Arsen J., ed. *Manufacturing USA* 5th ed. Detroit: Gale Research, 1996.

Four Men and a Machine: Commemoration of the 75th Anniversary of the Kimberly-Clark Corporation. Neenah, WI: Kimberly-Clark Corporation, 1947.

Klein, James E. *Paper & Paperboard Manufacturing and Converting Fundamentals,* 2nd ed. San Francisco: Miller-Freeman, Inc., 1991.

Lazich, Robert S., ed. *Market Share Reporter 1997.* Detroit: Gale Research, 1997.

Narisetti, Raju and Brian Gruley. "P&G Is Likely to Face Antitrust Scrutiny on How Feminine-Care Market Is Seen." *The Wall Street Journal.* 10 April 1997, A3.

"Outlook 1997: U.S. Paper Industry Will See More Globalization, Slower Growth in 1997." *Pulp & Paper,* January 1997, 55.

"PIMA's Top 50 Paper Companies." *PIMA Magazine,* June 1996, 32.

"Tissue: Industry Undergoes Massive Consolidation but Outlook Bright." *Pulp & Paper,* February 1996, 13.

United States Trade and Industrial Outlook 1997-1998. New York: McGraw-Hill, 1997.

Weeks, Lyman Horace. *A History of Paper-Manufacturing in the United States, 1690-1916.* New York: Burt Franklin, 1916, reprinted 1969.

—Andrew Ballard, updated by Alan Rooks

SIC 2677

ENVELOPES

This category includes establishments primarily engaged in manufacturing envelopes of any description from purchased paper and paperboard. Establishments primarily engaged in manufacturing stationery are classified in **SIC 2678: Stationery, Tablets, and Related Products.**

INDUSTRY SNAPSHOT

The envelope category is classified as a converting operation, since it transforms a finished product—rolls and sheets of paper and paperboard or synthetic materials—into envelopes. In 1995, U.S. envelope manufacturers shipped 168 billion envelopes worth $2.82 billion. Of that total, commercial envelopes accounted for about 70 percent of the total, for a value of $1.97 billion. The envelopes in this category can be white or colored, but do not include clasp or string-and-button envelopes. The next largest category is "all other" commercial envelopes, a category that includes padded shipping envelopes. This sector accounted for 13 percent of industry shipments, which amounted to $300 million in 1995. The envelope market is rounded out with commercial kraft mailing envelopes, with 11 percent of the market and commercial clasp and string-and-button envelopes with 5 percent.

The envelope industry is obviously a major consumer of paper. In 1992 envelope converters consumed $788.3 million worth of paper and paperboard in their manufacturing processes, mostly uncoated freesheet and kraft paper. These converters also used $72 million worth of paperboard containers, boxes, and corrugated paperboard, used primarily to ship their products. Converters also used $36.5 million worth of glues and adhesives; $34.6 million of plastics film and sheet; and $17.1 million of glassine film. The industry also used $325.2 million worth of other materials.

The envelope industry is clearly not a growing industry. At best, it can be considered a static industry—neither growing or declining rapidly. Envelope shipments ranged between 166 billion units and 174 billion units from 1988 to 1995, with small increases or declines each year. The value of shipments is also relatively static.

The chief threat to the envelope industry is alternative means of transmitting information, from such mediums such as fax machines, voice mail message systems, electronic mail, and other electronic communications systems. However, despite these threats some industry observers point out that new technologies rarely eliminate "old" technologies—they simply move them into new applications. Just as television did not eliminate radio broadcasts, electronic communications are not likely to eliminate or severely diminish the use of "old-fashioned" mail. While fewer envelopes may be used for personal communication, for example, more will probably be used for marketing purposes.

ORGANIZATION AND STRUCTURE

Envelope manufacturing is widely distributed throughout the United States and basically involves folding, gluing, and printing on high-speed converting equipment. There are many companies involved in envelope manufacturing, including numerous small producers. As in other industries, though, the envelope industry is consolidating as larger, more efficient producers buy up smaller entities or force them out of business.

The domestic envelope sector continued to suffer from overcapacity, low capacity utilization rates, and flat or declining prices in the mid-1990s. In simple terms, there was too much envelope-folding machine capacity compared to total envelope demand. Many converters reacted by scrapping older, less-efficient equipment or even closing some plants. Few new plants are expected to be built in the late 1990s, as converters instead pursue a strategy of rebuilding or refurbishing older machines so that they can compete more effectively with new equipment.

As a result of overcapacity and flat demand, the value per thousand envelopes shipped was declining in the mid-1990s, from about $20 per thousand in 1995 to about $18.50 per thousand in 1996, according to the Envelope Manufacturers Association. The value per thousand was expected to stabilize at about $18.00 per thousand in 1997.

While standard business and commercial stationery envelopes still account for the majority of envelopes produced in the United States, the specialty envelopes sector has been the fastest growing in recent years. This growth has been spurred by several factors, including the proliferation of specialty "quick print" shops and home-based envelope printing. Many quick print shops use personal computers and laser printers to create custom-printed business forms, stationery, and envelopes.

Envelopes for the specialty envelope market must be able to accept the output of laser printers, which use dry plastic toner ink that is fused to the paper in a heating process similar to that of copier machines. Specialty envelopes also require special adhesives and cannot use windows, snaps, buttons, or clasps. They must also be made of paper, since nylon, plastics, and olefin cannot accept the dry ink process.

Another growing market for specialty envelope converters is the overnight parcel delivery industry. Providers of these services—such as Express Mail, Federal Express, and United Parcel Service—offer shipping envelopes free to their customers. These envelopes are made from several materials, including paper, paperboard, spunbonded olefin, and plastic. The overnight package delivery industry, begun in the 1970s, was delivering more than 4 million packages daily in the mid-1990s.

Mailing and in-house envelopes, which use adhesive seals, metal clasps, or string-and-button closures, are another important segment of the industry, as are heavy-duty padded shipping envelopes and mailers. Catalog services, which proliferated in the 1980s and early 1990s, are a major market for shipping envelopes. Aided by the vast expansion of credit cards and toll-free telephone numbers, catalogs exist for every imaginable consumer need. Each catalog order must be shipped in envelopes or paperboard boxes.

In addition to catalogs, telemarketing and television shopping networks, such as the Home Shopping Network, are major users of shipping envelopes and mailers. Also, consumers responding to direct mail solicitations often trigger an avalanche of paper use, including the paper and envelope for the solicitation, the paper and return envelope containing the order, and the envelope or box in which the product is shipped to the consumer. Envelopes and mailers for catalog and direct mail orders must meet strict shipping requirements and thus are heavier and more expensive than other envelopes. They come in a wide range of shapes, sizes, and combinations of base construction materials.

While paper envelopes have traditionally been made from 100 percent virgin fiber, many converters have reacted to public demand for more environmentally friendly products by introducing standard business and specialty envelope products that contain varying amounts of recycled materials. Since the products themselves can be recycled, they hold an advantage over newer plastic and olefin envelopes. In fact, some municipal collection programs have begun collecting "junk mail," giving paper-based envelopes an environmental plus.

Postal Service Is Key. While overnight parcel services are a growing market, the U.S. Postal Service (USPS) remains the dominant carrier of envelopes. In 1995, the USPS handled about 95.3 billion pieces of first-class mail and 71.1 billion pieces of third-class mail, which translates into an enormous demand for a wide variety of envelopes, particularly plain, unprinted envelopes. The volume of both first-class mail and third-class mail was up from 1992, when volumes were 90.1 billion and 62 billion units respectively.

A major portion of envelope production is sold directly to individual consumers and the business community. Another large portion of the plain envelope market is consumed by printing and publishing operations for customized business and personal envelopes. As discussed earlier, the personal computer and high-quality printers have enabled many users to print their own stationery and envelopes, bypassing traditional offset printers.

Third-class, direct mail advertisers are another major market for envelope converters. Direct mail experienced an enormous boom in the 1980s and early 1990s, despite perceived negative consumer perceptions about the practice. While costly, direct mail allows manufacturers to target their marketing efforts directly to consumers most likely to purchase their products, avoiding the "waste" of traditional mass media, where many consumers reached by an ad are unlikely to buy the product or service it promotes. The expansion of consumer databases and the ability by marketers to more closely define certain market "niches" has allowed marketers to fine tune their direct mail solicitations, leading to long-term growth in this advertising and marketing vehicle.

One of the major costs of direct mail advertising is postage. Postal rates have been rising far faster than inflation as the USPS attempts to come closer to recouping its actual costs for each class of mail. Direct mail advertisers were aware that the major postal rate hike in 1994 would be followed by others, so they were looking for ways to reduce the cost of each mailing. One way of reducing costs is by "lightweighting" envelopes, using envelopes made with either lighter paper or with lightweight plastics or composites. Envelopes made from nontraditional materials are more resistant to tearing and puncturing and are more resistant to water. However, traditional paper envelopes still dominate both the standard and specialty envelope sectors because of their low cost and other properties, such as high strength, rigidity, and resistance to curl and fold.

Most paper envelopes are made from uncoated freesheet, one of the largest grades produced by U.S. paper mills. In 1995, envelope grades accounted for about 10 percent of the 12.8 million tons of uncoated freesheet produced by U.S. mills. Production of this grade was expected to climb to 13.5 million tons in 1996.

CURRENT CONDITIONS

Envelope consumption is sensitive to overall economic conditions, and like the rest of the paper and allied products industry, envelope manufacturers suffered from sluggish demand and overcapacity in the early 1990s. In the early to mid-1990s, the value of shipments in the envelope industry was highly erratic. However, in the mid-1990s the value of envelope shipments appeared to stabilize at about $2.8 billion per year. The continued growth in third-class advertising, better known as "junk mail," and new applications for specialty envelopes helped support stabilization in this industry.

In the mid-1990s, specialty envelopes emerged as the fastest-growing segment of the envelope industry. Its existing markets expanded rapidly and new markets were opened. The standard business envelope market is considered to be "mature" and is expected to decline slightly in unit volume. As a result, many envelope converters are concentrating their development efforts on the specialty envelope sector. Some of these envelopes are made from paper, but many others are made from unconventional materials such as nylon, plastic and plastic resin, and combinations of different materials.

For the rest of the 1990s, the envelope industry is expected to sustain very modest growth, with sales increasing from $2.86 billion in 1996 to $2.88 billion in 1997 and $2.89 billion in 1998. If projected figures are correct, the envelope industry in the 1990s will only have sustained an average annual growth rate of 0.37 percent. Considering inflation, the industry actually will have lost sales (in real dollars) of about 1.5 to 2.5 percent per year in the 1990s. However, many industry observers consider that to be something of an achievement for an industry that still embraces the "old technology" of mailing, as opposed to new electronic communications. The envelope industry may have even more "breathing room," according to several studies of the effect of electronic communications on the paper industry. According to one of these studies, by Jaakko Pöyry Consulting, Tarrytown, N.Y., electronic media will have almost no effect on the consumption of most paper products, including envelopes, until 2005. However, other factors, such as higher mailing costs, may still have a deleterious effect on the industry.

In the late 1990s the U.S. envelope industry is expected to improve operating efficiency and reduce heavy overcapacity in converting equipment. This strategy should boost the relatively low operating rate—the percentage of time equipment is operating—that plagued the industry in the early 1990s. As less efficient converters with aging plants become uncompetitive, more plant closures and layoffs are expected in the envelope industry. In fact, employment of production workers in envelope converting slipped from a high of 21,100 in 1989 to 17,900 in 1995, and is expected to shrink further, to just 16,700 by 1998.

By the mid-1990s, many envelope manufacturers had dramatically increased their purchases of envelope stock containing recycled fiber in order to accommodate increased consumer demand for recycled products. (Paper used to make "recycled" envelopes typically contains a mix a recycled fiber and virgin fiber.) Federal agencies and state government are required by law to choose recycled paper products, including envelopes, if they are available. As a result, converters have developed and aggressively marketed new recycled/recyclable envelopes and mailers.

INDUSTRY LEADERS

Unlike other paper categories, where paper manufacturers also control most of the converting operations through integrated subsidiaries, almost all of the leading envelope converters are independent of paper producers. Leading companies in this category include American Business Products, Atlanta, Georgia; Mail-Well Envelope, Englewood, Colorado; New York Envelope, Long Island City, New York; and Tension Envelope, Kansas City, Missouri.

WORK FORCE

The envelope segment employed 22,800 people in 1995 with a total payroll of $663 million. Production workers earned hourly wages averaging $11.84. The number of people employed by envelope converters has been dropping as the industry decreases the total number of plants producing envelopes and invests in more heavily automated operations.

U.S. ENVELOPE TRADE
(MILLION DOLLARS)

Source: Bureau of the Census

"slip," causing runnability problems. Recent research, though, has prompted the development of new sizing products that allow envelope manufacturers to use alkaline paper without concerns about runnability. Such innovations will help improve efficiency and keep the industry competitive.

While it is true that envelope converters face competition from electronic personal communications and electronic data interchange, the industry was not expected to experience undue harm. While envelopes may be the carriers of a smaller percentage of the total market for "communications," their use will continue as the entire market grows even faster. In addition, the fact that envelopes are still a very low-cost, attractive way to send information means that the envelope market will remain stable for the foreseeable future.

AMERICA AND THE WORLD

International trade in envelopes is relatively small, since envelopes tend to be manufactured close to where they are ultimately used. Nonetheless, U.S. converters have expanded their exports, mostly to nearby trading partners such as Canada and Mexico. The North American Free Trade Agreement (NAFTA) with Mexico and Canada, ratified by the United States in 1993, was expected to help expand the exports of efficient U.S. converters.

RESEARCH AND TECHNOLOGY

Much of the research and technology in envelope manufacturing has focused on improving converting equipment, which allows envelopes to be produced faster and with better quality. Indeed, slower pre-1970 equipment is slowly going out of production, since capacity utilization on this equipment has dropped from 57 percent in 1994 to 48.9 percent in 1996, while capacity utilization of higher-speed, post-1970 equipment remained high, at 84.9 percent in 1994 and 85.1 percent in 1996, according to the Envelope Manufacturers Association.

As the speed of the envelope converting equipment increases, however, new problems emerge. Previously, for example, most paper was produced using an acid process. However, due to the desire to reduce costs and improve the life of paper products, the majority of mills producing fine paper, which is used in many envelopes, have converted to the alkaline process.

Alkaline paper is usually produced with a synthetic "sizing" product, such as alkylketene dimer (AKD), to improve the surface of the paper. AKD is used to produce many fine paper grades, including envelope paper. On newer, high-speed precision converting equipment, AKD paper has been known to

FURTHER READING

Darnay, Arsen J., ed. *Manufacturing USA*. 5th ed. Detroit: Gale Research, 1996.

Envelope Manufacturers Association Fact Sheet. Alexandria, VA: Envelope Manufacturers Association, 1996.

Outlook for Envelopes, 1997. Alexandria, VA: Envelope Manufacturers Association, 1996.

Paper, Paperboard, Pulp Capacity and Fiber Consumption. Washington, DC: American Forest & Paper Association, 1996.

Smook, Gary A. *Handbook of Pulp & Paper Terminology: A Guide to Industrial and Technological Usage*. Bellingham, WA: Angus Wilde Publications, 1990.

Thesaurus of Pulp and Paper Terminology. Atlanta: Institute of Paper Science and Technology, 1991.

"Uncoated Free-Sheet: Sliding Prices Close to Bottom, Producers Hope." *Pulp & Paper*, April 1996, 13.

U.S. Trade and Industrial Outlook 1997-1998. New York: McGraw-Hill, 1997.

—Alan Rooks

SIC 2678

STATIONERY, TABLETS, AND RELATED PRODUCTS

Establishments in this industry are primarily engaged in manufacturing stationery, tablets, loose-leaf fillers, and related items from purchased paper. Products include correspondence-type tablets, paper desk pads, loose-leaf filler paper, memo books, newsprint tablets and pads, notebooks, stationery, and various other padded paper products.

The stationery products industry turned in an erratic performance in the mid-1990s, although projections call for modest growth in the latter part of the decade. After reaching a high of $1.48 billion in 1993, this industry's value of shipments fell back to $1.47 billion in 1994, before climbing to $1.53 billion in 1995. Projections call for the industry's value of shipments to reach $1.6 billion in 1997 and $1.64 billion in 1998. If those projections are correct, the industry will have grown at an annual rate of about 2.9 percent in the 1990s, which means it kept up with inflation, but did not grow sharply in real (inflation adjusted) dollars.

The stationery products industry consists of three categories: stationery; tablets, pads, and related products; and stationery, tablets, and related products not specified by kind (NSK). Tablets and pads accounted for a large majority of industry products in 1992, with 64.1 percent of industry shipments (by value), followed by stationery with 26.1 percent. The NSK category accounted for the remaining 9.8 percent of industry shipments. These market share figures were virtually unchanged from 1987.

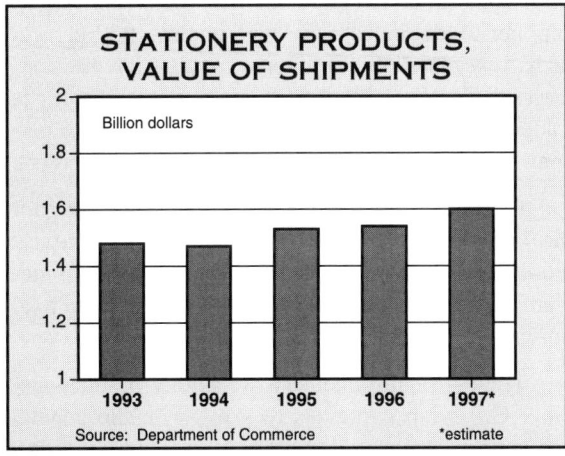

STATIONERY PRODUCTS, VALUE OF SHIPMENTS

Billion dollars

Source: Department of Commerce   *estimate

Within the tablet and pad category, the leading product category is bound notebooks, followed by tablets and pads and looseleaf paper fillers. The two leading products in the stationery category are boxed stationery and portfolios, and wedding and social announcements.

Stationery products are produced by a wide range of companies. Some of the larger paper manufacturing companies have divisions that convert and distribute their own brands of stationery products. Smaller independent stationery converters have also managed to survive and thrive in this market.

Consumers account for the majority of stationery products purchased, at just over 50 percent. The remaining customers for stationery products comprise a wide range of businesses and government agencies, including retail trade, water supply and sewage system operators, wholesale trade, and doctors and dentists.

School supplies are a vital part of the market for this industry. For example, sales of stationery at discount stores (which include products not classified in **SIC 2678**) amounted to $5.32 billion in 1996. Of these sales, 31 percent were accounted for by back-to-school products; 30.5 percent by greeting cards; 19 percent by office supplies; 6.2 percent by party goods; and 13.3 percent by other products.

As one might expect, the largest supplier to the stationery products industry is paper mills, providing almost 57 percent of all product inputs. Other suppliers of products and services include the wholesale trade; paperboard mills; motor freight transport firms; and railroads.

The stationery products industry is considered a mature industry, meaning that sales increases are likely to track closely with general growth in the economy. The industry has been negatively impacted by the increased use of personal computers for home and office use, which has reduced the demand for a wide variety of stationery products. While computer printers have increased the use of paper in general, such increases have come in the use of continuous-form computer paper and laser printer paper, which are not included in this classification. Also, extensive downsizing at many U.S. companies in the mid-1990s negatively affected the use of all office paper products, including stationery. The trend toward home-based offices, however, has been a bright spot for stationery product manufacturers.

One major change in the stationery products industry has been the manner in which its products have been marketed to consumers. While stationery products were once sold primarily by small, independent stationery stores, much of that sales volume has been captured by office product "superstores" such as OfficeMax, Inc. and Office Depot, Inc. which, because of their size, have been able to force smaller retailers out of the marketplace and drive wholesale prices down.

Several large paper companies are leaders in the stationery products industry, including International Paper Company, Purchase, New York; Georgia-Pacific Corporation, Atlanta, Georgia; and Mead Corporation, Dayton, Ohio. However, there has remained room for some mid-sized independent converters such as Smead Manufacturing Co., Hastings, Minnesota.; Ampad Corp., Dallas, Texas; Demco Inc., Madison,

Wisconsin; and Roaring Spring Blank Book Co., Roaring Spring, Pennsylvania,

The stationery products industry employed 8,900 people in 1995, down about 11 percent from 1991. That included 6,500 production workers who earned average hourly wages of $11 per hour, comparable to other industries in the paper and allied products group.

FURTHER READING

Darnay, Arsen J., ed. *Manufacturing USA*. 5th ed. Detroit: Gale Research, 1996.

Lazich, Robert S., ed. *Market Share Reporter*. Detroit: Gale Research, 1997.

Paper, Paperboard, Pulp Capacity and Fiber Consumption. Washington: American Forest & Paper Association, 1996.

Smook, Gary A. *Handbook of Pulp & Paper Terminology: A Guide to Industrial and Technological Usage*. Bellingham, WA: Angus Wilde Publications, 1990.

U.S. Trade and Industrial Outlook 1997-1998. New York: McGraw-Hill, 1997.

—Alan Rooks

SIC 2679

CONVERTED PAPER AND PAPERBOARD PRODUCTS, NOT ELSEWHERE CLASSIFIED

Establishments in this category are primarily engaged in manufacturing miscellaneous converted paper or paperboard products, not elsewhere classified, from purchased paper or paperboard. Products in this classification include gift wrap, pressed and molded pulp goods, laminated building papers, cigarette paper, fiber conduits, crepe paper, pressed and molded pulp cups, pressed and molded dishes, molded pulp egg cartons, and converted filter paper.

In the early to mid-1990s, the value of shipments in this industry grew steadily from $4.13 billion in 1990 to $4.95 billion in 1993 and $5.16 billion in 1995. The value of shipments was projected to continue rising through the end of the decade, to $5.55 billion in 1997 and $5.75 billion in 1998. These estimates signal an annual growth rate for the industry of 4.9 percent in the 1990s, ahead of inflation and above average for the paper and allied products group.

The paper products in this classification are best described as specialty products because of their diversity. The largest product category in this industry is "other converted paper and paperboard products," accounting for 40.3 percent of the value of industry shipments in 1992. This category includes such diverse products as paper party and holiday goods; cellulose insulation; paper doilies; and paper coffee filters, among other products. Gift wrap paper was the second largest category, at 14.5 percent, followed by wallpaper at 11.1 percent and paper supplies for business machines (which includes thermal fax paper) at 10 percent. Molded pulp goods (such as egg cartons) were 8.5 percent of shipments while all other converted paper products not specified by kind accounted for the remaining 15.7 percent.

The total value of raw materials used in converted paper and paperboard products not elsewhere classified in 1992 amounted to $1.98 billion in 1992. Of this total, paper and paperboard was the largest raw material category, at $863.5 million. Other leading raw material categories include wastepaper at $57.2 million; paperboard containers, boxes, and the corrugated paperboard at $49 million; and printing inks at $46.3 million. The raw materials not specified by kind (nsk) category accounted for a rather large portion of the total, at $503.4 million.

Paper mills have traditionally been the largest supplier to this industry, providing almost 30 percent of its raw materials. Imports accounted for the next-largest volume, at 21 percent, followed by wholesale trade with 9.2 percent; paperboard mills with 6.6 percent; and plastics materials and resins with 2.5 percent.

Personal consumption expenditures account for the largest share of purchases from the industry, at close to 30 percent of the total. The wholesale trades were the next-largest customer, with 11 percent of total purchases.

Trends for this industry are highly product-specific. Gift wrap continues to grow with the general economy, despite admonitions by environmental groups for consumers to cut down on or eliminate the use of gift wrap. Sales of gift paper are directly related to the level of gift purchasing in the United States. After several mediocre years during the recession in the early 1990s, gift paper enjoyed an upward sales trend in the mid-1990s as gift buying—particularly during the key Christmas period—accelerated along with the general economy.

Wallcoverings enjoyed a boost in the mid-1990s as a result of the acceleration in new home construction, which remained strong as the economic recovery that began in 1992 continued well into 1997. Molded pulp products—primarily egg cartons—enjoyed a resurgence in the early to mid-1990s due to public interest in recycling. These gray cartons, often made of recycled newsprint, lost share in the 1980s to molded plastic products. But as consumers began to express some displeasure with hard-to-recycle plastic cartons, some egg producers responded by moving back to molded pulp products. Schools and fast food outlets also stepped up their use of molded food trays in the mid-1990s.

Another significant product in this category, cigarette paper, suffered as a result of the general downturn in domestic cigarette consumption that began in the mid-1980s. The combination of high excise taxes on cigarettes and increased restrictions on public smoking contributed to large-volume decreases in domestic cigarette consumption. Losses in the U.S. market were at least partially offset by increases in the export market for cigarettes, but cigarette paper sales remained at best stagnant in the mid-1990s. In 1995, one major manufacturer of cigarette paper, Kimberly-Clark Corporation, spun off this part of its operations as a new company, Schweitzer-Maudit International, Alpharetta, Georgia. This move was prompted in part by demands by shareholders for K-C to divest operations related to cigarette manufacturing.

The converted paper products not elsewhere classified industry employed 32,400 people in 1995, up slightly from the early 1990s. Of that total, 24,500 were production workers, earning an average hourly wage of $11.02 and working 51.2 million man hours.

FURTHER READING

Darnay, Arsen J., ed. *Manufacturing USA*. 5th ed. Detroit: Gale Research, 1996.

Lazich, Robert S., ed. *Market Share Reporter 1997*. Detroit: Gale Research, 1997.

Smook, Gary A. *Handbook of Pulp & Paper Terminology: A Guide to Industrial and Technological Usage*. Bellingham, WA: Angus Wilde Publications, 1990.

U.S. Trade and Industrial Outlook 1997-1998. New York: McGraw-Hill, 1997.

—Alan Rooks

PRINTING, PUBLISHING, & ALLIED INDUSTRIES

NEWSPAPERS: PUBLISHING, OR PUBLISHING AND PRINTING

This category includes establishments primarily engaged in publishing newspapers, or in publishing and printing newspapers. These establishments carry on the various operations necessary for issuing newspapers, including the gathering of news and the preparation of editorials and advertisements, but may or may not perform their own printing. Commercial printing is frequently carried on by establishments engaged in publishing and printing newspapers, but even though the commercial printing may be of major importance, such establishments are included in this industry. Establishments not engaged in publishing newspapers, but which print newspapers for publishers, are classified in **SIC 2759: Commercial Printing, Not Elsewhere Classified.** News syndicates are classified in **SIC 7383: News Syndicates.**

INDUSTRY SNAPSHOT

Since the 1960s, newspaper management has undergone a transformation from essentially family-run companies to the concerns of multimedia corporations. According to Ellis Cose, author of *The Press,* 1963 brought the first sign that the newspaper industry was in for a change. That year, the Chandler family, owner of The Times Mirror Company, the chief holding of which was the *Los Angeles Times*, listed the company on the New York Stock Exchange. Soon other newspapers went public, making their actions accountable to shareholders and not just the families that ran them. This trend led to the growth of newspaper chains and the proliferation of a corporate culture, which stressed profits and growth over conventions of journalism. By 1989 five companies—Washington Post Company, Times Mirror Company, The New York Times Company, Gannett Co., Inc., and Knight-Ridder Inc.—were responsible for one-fourth of the newspapers read each day in the United States. In keeping with the transformations of the industry, corporations that controlled newspapers began to branch out into other related ventures such as book publishing and marketing, and as a result their newspapers became part of entire communications systems, rather than self-contained enterprises.

The newspaper industry has been feeling pressure since the late 1980s. Many papers with long histories have been forced to shut down, and many others have reported financial losses. To counteract this crisis, publishers reduced editorial and production staffs through layoffs and hiring freezes, raised newspaper prices and advertising rates, experimented with new layouts, and increased automated processes. The industry's advertising revenues rose more than $2 billion to $38 billion in 1996. This was a 5.8 percent increase from 1995. Circulation contributed another $7 billion, making this a $45 billion industry. Even so, circulation figures keep declining. The Newspaper Association of America has responded to this challenge by hiring an advertising agency to promote newspaper reading. This three-year, multimedia campaign will attempt to draw in more advertisers and readers, including children. The promotion is set to begin in the fall of 1997 and will cost $18 million.

ORGANIZATION AND STRUCTURE

A variety of publications could be called newspapers. The most common format is the gatefold, which is divided into individual sections. Pagination in a gatefold restarts in every section. The other major format, the tabloid, is read like a book or a magazine. Tabloids usually have fewer articles than gatefolds, and are paginated without interruption from beginning to end. Traditionally, the content of tabloids has been considered less serious and less comprehensive than gatefolds.

Frequency of publication is another variable among newspapers. The papers with the greatest circulation are dailies; most of these issue a denser, more expensive Sunday edition. There are far more weeklies in operation, though their circulation is smaller. The two most common types of weeklies are the community newspaper and the alternative newspaper. The community newspaper highlights local current events such as education, sports, and politics. The alternative newspaper provides coverage of news items and arts-related activities that are often overlooked by the mainstream press. Since advertising provides the bulk of revenue for weeklies, these newspapers are often free.

Advertising. Most newspapers rely on circulation and advertising to finance their operations. Measured in linage, advertising amounts to about 80 percent of an average newspaper's income. Placement of advertisements is a significant factor; the section and page of an ad, as well as its size, will determine its price. Department stores traditionally have been a major source of advertising dollars, filling pages with pictures of their merchandise. Classified advertising is also a reliable and profitable endeavor for newspapers, adding up to 37 percent of total advertising income. This type of advertising is sold by the word.

One recent and controversial development in newspapers is the "advertorial," or paid announcement on the opinion page or in another section where the advertiser expects to gain from its context. Other advertisements of this type consist of multi-page inserts or theme magazines distributed with papers. Paid announcements are labeled as such to avoid confusion, however, many editors feel the ads jeopardize the integrity of the newspaper.

Circulation. Newspapers are sold in vending machines and privately owned newsstands, or by subscription, which allows customers to pay a reduced rate per issue and have the paper delivered to their home or business. Newspapers profit from subscribers because they mean guaranteed, consistent sales. In determining a price for newspapers, publishers have to weigh the potential earnings from sales against what readers are willing to pay. If the price is too low, circulation might be healthy, but profits could decline. If the price is too high, circulation could drop.

Averaging 50-60 percent of total costs, personnel represents the largest expenditure for newspapers. Departments include management, editorial, advertising, circulation, and production. Within the editorial department, the staff is divided according to paper sections, which may include: local and national news, sports, entertainment and the arts, business, opinion, and others, depending on the paper's size and focus.

Newsprint was the second-highest expenditure, averaging one-quarter of total costs. The United States consumes more than one-third of the world's newsprint, most of that going for the nation's newspapers. A dip in newsprint costs can save a newspaper during hard times, and since a failed newspaper means loss of business for the newsprint manufacturer, most offer substantial discounts from list prices. However, publishers such as the New York Times Company and the Tribune Company also own paper mills, and consequently suffer when newsprint sells at a low cost. Equipment such as printing presses and cameras represents the third-largest expense for newspapers.

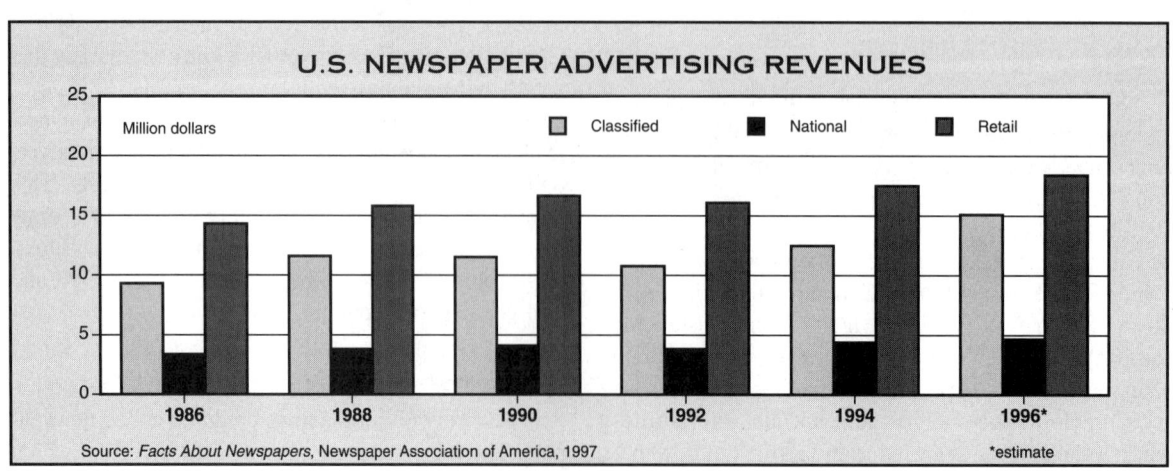

U.S. NEWSPAPER ADVERTISING REVENUES

Source: *Facts About Newspapers*, Newspaper Association of America, 1997   *estimate

BACKGROUND AND DEVELOPMENT

Newspapers served to inform the public of events and circumstances pertaining to society, government, and commerce. The providers of information were expected to be reliable and current, without neglecting their other function of entertaining the literate population. The Acta Diurna of the Roman empire and the Chinese gazettes of the first century A.D. are the distant ancestors of today's newspapers. The first modern newspapers appeared in Europe in the sixteenth century.

Newspaper reporters had a responsibility to act as watchdogs against injustice, corruption, and impropriety; the right to expose these qualities in public figures is protected in the First Amendment to the Constitution of the United States. The first great moment in American journalism came in 1735 with a court case deciding the issue of freedom of the press. Editor John Peter Zenger was brought to trial on charges of seditious libel for printing articles that were critical of colonial governor Sir William Cosby. In his successful defense of Zenger, Alexander Hamilton invoked the Magna Carta and stressed that opposition to the establishment was a basic civil liberty, thus creating the foundation on which the American press was built.

An overriding objective for American newspapers was to reach as many readers as possible. One early manifestation of this aim could be seen in the *New York Tribune,* founded by Horace Greeley in 1841. Priced at one penny, the paper was written by Greeley and other advocates of social change in a style that was described as simple but not condescending. It boasted a tremendous readership throughout the country, which led to enthusiastic support from its advertisers. The populist instincts that Greeley embodied eventually evolved into "Yellow Journalism," a term originally referring to the practices of many of the New York daily newspapers during the late 1800s. Joseph Pulitzer, editor of the *New York World,* and William Randolph Hearst, editor of the *New York Journal* strove to increase circulation through a variety of aggressive tactics, such as reporting sensational stories, setting headlines in extremely large type, making extensive use of pictures, and issuing Sunday supplements with color comics.

Telegraph lines, which by the turn of the century reached points all over the United States and crossed the Atlantic Ocean, were essential to the dissemination of news, and they facilitated the rise of cooperative news gathering. The Associated Press, originally formed by the morning newspapers of New York City, allowed member newspapers to run each other's sto-ries. England's Reuters news service and other similar European agencies established reciprocal agreements with the Associated Press, fostering the potential for newspapers to run stories from around the world. The United Press and the International News Service were established to compete with Associated Press during the 1920s. In 1958, these two services merged to form United Press International.

In the early twentieth century, newspapers began to contend with the rise of new media that was capable of quickly bringing more information into American homes. The formation of the Radio Corporation of America (RCA) in 1919 represented the first of these challenges. In 1929, advertising revenues at newspapers were still far ahead of those of radio, but the newer medium was quickly growing. The Depression, which left the newspaper industry with barely more than half of its advertising income, had little effect on radio advertising, which doubled in the years from 1929 to 1933. A second news forum arose in the 1930s— the newsreel, which was shown between features at movie theaters.

The 1950s brought another challenge for print journalism. Television captured the imagination and leisure time of many Americans. As it quickly became the medium of choice, television siphoned advertising dollars away from newspapers. Network television news became more readily identified with major events, such as the assassination of President John F. Kennedy. The 24-hour Cable News Network (CNN) debuted in 1980, and its phenomenal growth contributed to the sense that newspapers were becoming an outmoded form of transmitting breaking stories. The late 1980s and early 1990s saw an even greater expansion of cable television, and American viewing habits changed accordingly. By 1995, the average adult spent approximately 1,580 hours watching television—30 hours per week. During the same time period, newspapers across the country were battling circulation losses. As a result, the number of daily newspapers dropped from 1,745 in 1980 to 1,533 in 1995.

CURRENT CONDITIONS

The economic recession at the end of the 1980s brought heavy losses in advertising and circulation revenues. The effects were even felt by new publications. The *St. Louis Sun,* a tabloid created by Ralph Ingersoll II with money from junk bonds, debuted in September 1989 and closed the following August. Another new publication, *The National,* a nationwide sports daily, ran only eighteen months before folding in June 1991. By 1991, papers with long histories, many of which had survived the Depression, were beginning to shut down as well. These included *The State-Times* of Baton Rouge, Louisiana, and the *Dallas Times Herald*. The latter closing left 900 people unemployed and made that city the largest in the country with only one daily paper. In 1991, United Press International filed for bankruptcy for the second time in six years.

One solution to these dire conditions was the Joint Operating Agreement (JOA). Under the Newspaper Preservation Act of 1970, newspapers were largely exempt from antitrust suits. In a JOA, two or more newspapers are allowed to share the costs associated with operations, while maintaining separate editorial departments. However, the papers must prove that one would not survive if not for a JOA. One of the most substantial and controversial agreements, between Knight-Ridder's *Detroit Free Press* and Gannett's *Detroit News,* was finalized in November 1989 after a lengthy court battle. While similar agreements have saved newspapers in other cities, both of these papers continued to lose money and circulation.

In terms of advertising, 1990 and 1991 were two of the worst years ever for the newspaper industry. For the first time since the Depression, there were back-to-back losses in annual advertising revenues as national, retail, and classified linage all shrunk. In response, advertising departments began to experiment with nontraditional solutions. Where they once aimed at reaching the greatest number of readers, they now refined their methods to reach geographically and demographically desirable readers with special sections and zoned editions. They also adapted classified advertising, such as automobile announcements and personal ads, for telephone use. Other ventures into nonprint areas of communication included voice information lines for late-breaking news, sending news updates by facsimile, and videotex, which allowed subscribers to receive the news by modem and read it on the screen of their personal computers.

Ad revenues saw a decided turnaround in the mid-1990s, with revenues of $39 billion in 1996. This was a 7.7 percent gain from 1995, and a $5 billion increase from 1994. These increases followed a 5.2 percent gain in 1993 and a 3.9 percent gain in 1992. The recovery was broad-based, spreading across all media and market categories. The largest increases were attributed to political elections and the 1996 Summer Olympics.

One major concern of the newspaper industry has been readership. Through academic studies and marketing surveys, publishers attempted to discover who was reading the newspaper with regards to such factors as age, sex, and financial status; frequency and dura-

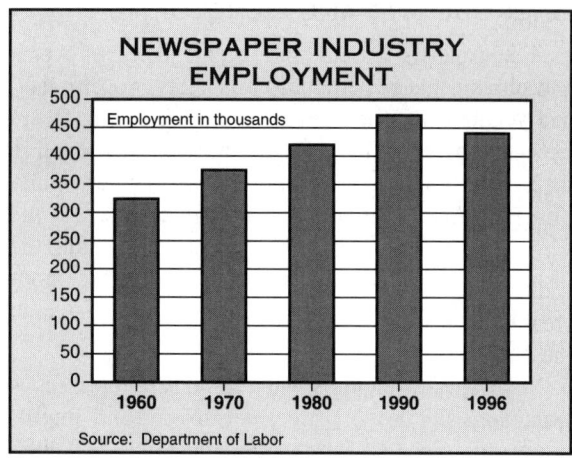

NEWSPAPER INDUSTRY EMPLOYMENT

Source: Department of Labor

tion of an average read; the instances where one newspaper was shared by two or more readers; and the sections of the newspaper that were read or ignored. In most cases these inquiries yielded discouraging results. A study by journalism professor Gerald Stone determined that between 1967 and 1989, the number of people aged 18 to 29 who read a daily paper declined 35 percent. According to Stone, this was due to parents passing on to their children their disinclination for newspaper reading, resulting in an ever-deepening alienation from the publications. The trend was linked to a pervasive apathy towards current events. A study by the Times Mirror Center for the People and Press found that merely 42 percent of those under age 30 showed an interest in the fall of the Berlin Wall, an event given a great deal of attention by newspapers.

USA Today was the industry's most revolutionary gesture towards appealing to a mass readership. Pioneered by Gannett's Allen Neuharth in 1982, *USA Today* modified the approach of other newspapers aiming at the entire nation—the *New York Times, The Wall Street Journal,* and the *Christian Science Monitor.* The paper was printed in regional plants via satellite transmissions from its editorial centers. Aware that advertisers and readers tended to regard the average daily newspaper as visually bland and difficult to navigate, designers of *USA Today* incorporated such features as an easily read index on the front page, bold graphics featuring statistical information related to the day's events, and a large color weather map. The newspaper was even sold in vending machines designed to resemble television sets. Neuharth limited the number of sections in his paper to four: a news section emphasizing the positive side of current events; a ''Money'' section devoted to business coverage with a strong consumer orientation; an extensive sports section providing many pictures and ample statistical data; and a ''Life'' section encompassing health, education, and entertainment. By early 1996, *USA Today* had become the most widely circulated newspaper with nearly two million readers, though it had yet to turn a profit.

Readership continues to be the primary problem facing the industry. According to a 1996 American Opinion Research poll, only half of those in the industry said that it would be "healthy" in ten years. In addition, concern about the growth of the Internet increased from 1995 to 1996 by more than 50 percent— the largest increase for any issue.

INDUSTRY LEADERS

Gannett Co., Inc., ranked first in daily circulation in 1996, reached 6.5 million readers with its 90 dailies. Founded by Frank Gannett in 1906, the company began acquiring newspapers throughout New York State. It owned 22 dailies by 1947, the year he died. Allen Neuharth joined the company in 1963, and he is credited for making it a major force in the industry. After going public in 1967, Gannett absorbed small newspapers all over the country, bringing to them exacting management requirements and transforming them into profitable enterprises. Additionally, Gannett augmented its holdings with radio and television stations, and entered the field of billboard advertising. The birth of *USA Today* in 1982 was facilitated by the fact that Gannett's reporters, editors, and technology were established in every region of the nation. In 1996, Gannett had an operating revenue of $4.4 billion, an 18.1 percent increase from 1995. This Arlington, Virginia-based company has 37,200 employees.

Knight-Ridder, Inc., with the second-largest daily circulation at 3.8 million, resulted from the 1974 merger of the Knight and Ridder newspaper chains. In addition to owning such respected newspapers as the *Philadelphia Inquirer, Miami Herald,* and *Detroit Free Press,* Knight-Ridder became a leader in the related field of information services, acquiring Dialog Information Services in 1988. In late 1996, Knight-Ridder announced a joint venture with Financial Times Information and Dow Jones & Company, Inc. for the co-development of a global electronic news resource for corporate, research, government and academic customers. The information resource was slated to be distributed independently through the companies' respective electronic information services beginning in mid-1997. However, in early 1997, Knight-Ridder announced that it intended to refocus on the newspaper industry. The company acquired several newspapers from Walt Disney Co., and said it would sell its online division. Knight-Ridder's revenues for 1996 were $2.77 billion. First-quarter 1997 revenues were $697.7

million, an increase from 1996's first-quarter figure of $679.3 million. The company is based in Miami, Florida and has 24,000 employees.

In 1996, The Times Mirror Company of Los Angeles, California boasted the fourth-largest daily circulation at 2.8 million. Unlike Gannett and Knight-Ridder, which own a great number of small newspapers, Times Mirror's holdings are concentrated on large city dailies, including the *Los Angeles Times* and *New York Newsday.* In 1996, the company had revenues of $3.4 billion. The first quarter of 1997 generated $773.9 million, of which $514.7 million came from newspaper publishing. The company has 20,600 employees.

The New York Times Company is publisher of the *New York Times,* third in circulation behind *USA Today* and the *Wall Street Journal.* The *Times* has been a longtime stronghold of journalistic standards, beginning when Adolph Ochs and his son-in-law Arthur Hays Sulzburger emphasized comprehensive coverage and news writing of the highest order. In 1996, the New York Times Company owned 22 other newspapers, including the *Boston Globe,* and had revenues of $2.6 billion. Revenues for the first quarter of 1997 were $692.5 million, up from $622.5 million during the same period in 1996. In 1996, the company employed 12,600 people.

WORK FORCE

The newspaper industry employed 4.4 million people in 1996, including more than two million women. Production workers accounted for 34 percent of total employees, earning an average hourly wage of $12.39. In light of the changes in newspaper management and production during the late 1980s and early 1990s, those working in the industry were obligated to learn new skills and take on new duties. Foremost among these were related to the computer revolution, as word processing programs and developments in page design proliferated in newsrooms. Some of the tasks that previously belonged to production departments, such as typesetting, either were made obsolete or were dramatically altered with technological developments. In addition, some departmental differences began to disappear, meaning that former specialized positions now required proficiency in many areas, as well a general knowledge of all newspaper operations.

RESEARCH AND TECHNOLOGY

In the early 1990s, some newspapers began to move toward becoming electronic information suppliers. They made their databases available to subscribers, creating special editions and enhancing their classified ads. The five newspapers with the highest circulation—*Wall Street Journal, USA Today, New York Times, Los Angeles Times,* and the *Washington Post*—all have online versions. By early 1997, 18 of Gannett's newspapers were online.

Despite being touted as the most important development in the industry since the invention of the printing press, online publications pose some challenges. Creating an online newspaper is both expensive and labor intensive. Since reading an on-screen publication is different than reading a newspaper, design and graphics are even more important—content must be adjusted accordingly. If an online newspaper has no subscription fee, advertisers will have to absorb the costs. If those advertisers support an online version, they may pull their dollars from the print. Finally, it is not clear if there are enough potential readers. Currently only 15-20 percent of U.S. households have computers with modems. How much this market will grow is unknown.

The advent of online services has had a decided impact on the newspaper industry. A 1996 survey by American Opinion Research indicated that while 45 percent of editors felt that the online services would hurt them in the long term, 44 percent said they would help. There is some agreement, however—80 percent felt that online services will continue to be an important factor in the communications industry.

FURTHER READING

Cose, Ellis. *The Press.* New York: Morrow, 1989.

''Editor & Publisher Interactive.'' New York: The Editor & Publisher Co., 1997. Available from http://mediainfo.elpress.com.

Emery, Edwin and Michael. *The Press and America: An Interpretive History of the Mass Media.* Englewood Cliffs, NJ: Prentice-Hall, 1984.

Foroohar, Kambiz. ''Chip off the Old Block.'' *Forbes,* 17 June 1996.

Fost, Dan. ''Newspapers Enter the Age of Information.'' *American Demographics,* September 1990.

Lazich, Robert S., ed. *Market Share Reporter.* Detroit: Gale Research, 1997.

Taylor, John H. ''Betting on the Wrong Horses.'' *Forbes,* 12 April 1993.

''Welcome to the Newspaper Association of America.'' Vienna, VA: Newspaper Association of America, 1997. Available from http://www.naa.org.

''Welcome to Hoover's Online.'' Austin, TX: Hoover's, Inc., 1997.

Ziegler, Bart. ''Stop the Presses: Publishers Scramble into On-line Services, but Payoff is Unclear.'' *Wall Street Journal,* 26 April 1995, 1.

—Mark Swartz, updated by Lin Grensing-Pophal

SIC 2721

PERIODICALS: PUBLISHING, OR PUBLISHING AND PRINTING

This category covers establishments primarily engaged in publishing periodicals, or in publishing and printing periodicals. These establishments carry on the various operations necessary for issuing periodicals, but may or may not perform their own printing. Establishments not engaged in publishing periodicals, but which print periodicals for publishers, are classified in commercial printing industries.

INDUSTRY SNAPSHOT

The first American magazines appeared in 1741, but like many of their successors, were doomed to swift failure. This inauspicious start notwithstanding, the periodicals industry burgeoned steadily over the following 250 years, employing an estimated 131,000 Americans by 1996, distributing upward of 11,000 publications, and generating annual revenues of more than $24.786 billion. Indispensable to Americans as a source of entertainment and information, magazine publishing also provides an essential advertising medium for other industries.

In the first half of the twentieth century the magazine publishing industry progressed steadily, without meteoric rises until the early 1980s, when new production technology, positive demographic trends, and an accelerated need for information all came together to spur a doubling in revenues over the span of the decade. Unfortunately this growth spurt did not last. A widespread recession started in the late 1980s, just when periodical markets were starting on a disturbing tendency towards maturity and saturation. In response, major advertisers hastened to slash their budgets, bringing diminished revenues and dwindling profits to the publishing industry generally.

The challenges produced by these two important problems found magazine publishers scrambling both to reduce costs and retain their share of U.S. advertising expenditures. To keep advertisers interested, many companies introduced niche periodicals. New magazines like Milwaukee-based *Reunions Magazine* and *Chicagoland Gardening* catered to smaller audiences, but offered their advertisers useful, tightly focused audiences. This eased the advertising situation somewhat, but also split the magazine market into highly-fragmented target areas.

ORGANIZATION AND STRUCTURE

Periodical publishers earn money either by selling advertising space in their pages to companies wanting display areas for their products or by charging readers for subscriptions or individual issues. Thus the periodical's content is essentially a tool which can be fine-tuned in order to boost sales and ad revenues. Many publishers also generate income thorough database marketing techniques, such as selling subscriber lists or marketing "back-end" products and services to their customers.

Periodicals sales and ad revenues each account for about 50 percent of the average publisher's receipts. Although 80 percent of all periodicals are purchased through mail-order subscriptions, 30 percent of sales dollar volume is garnered through newsstand sales. As is the case with most items, the prices of magazines have risen during the 1990s. In 1992 the average annual subscription price of a U.S. periodical was about $27, while the typical newsstand price per individual issue was about $2.85. By the end of 1996, however, newsstand prices averaged $2.93, and subscription rates had risen to an average $29.42.

Markets. In 1988, according to McCann-Erickson, magazines received a 5.1 percent share of the print-media advertising market. By the end of 1996, their share had risen to 5.3 percent. This prompted publishers to find innovative ways to attract more advertising dollars. Some, like top-ranked *TV Guide*, cut their ratebases to advertisers, making up the difference in revenues by boosting the newsstand price of the magazine. Others started custom publishing magazines tailored to the needs of specific clients. In November 1996 *Business Week* noted two interesting examples. One, a richly illustrated Conde Nast publication, advertised only the expensive watches specified in its title, *Patek Phillipe;* the other, from Hachette Filipacci Magazines, was *Mercedes Momentum,* launched in 1995 specifically to attract more female purchasers to the Mercedes Benz automobile.

A second way to multiply advertising dollars is by paying close attention to previously skirted markets. Notable in this regard is Essence Communications, publishers of the highly successful *Essence,* a magazine for African-American women. Sparked by its own considerable experience, the company backed *Latina,* a bilingual Spanish-English magazine which made its debut in May 1996. Another trendsetter in the advertis-

ing revenue field is Hachette Filipacci CEO David Pecker, who has introduced the practice of combining ads for two ostensibly unrelated products which are aimed at the same consumer. One notable company success was an ad in *Car and Driver,* which was targeted in tandem with a Liz Claiborne fragrance to the young female customer. As Joshua Levine noted in *Forbes* of June 3, 1996, "advertising, not editorial, is Pecker's big interest." Other strategies have included "licensing" the name of a magazine to a different product, as *Playboy* has done with recreational clubs.

Aside from general merchandise, the industrial sectors that purchase the greatest amount of advertising from periodical publishers are transportation and agricultural, which contributed about 20 percent of all ad dollars in early 1994, the auto and truck industry alone contributing about $70 million per month for ad space. Business and financial products and services represented about 18 percent of magazine ad sales, and drug and toiletry industries purchased about 14 percent of advertising space; food and beverage products represented 11 percent of ad receipts. Cigarette ads alone accounted for over $20 million per month of sales in that category.

By the end of 1996, though, things were not quite the same. While still in first place, the auto industry sliced 2.2 percent off their magazine-ad budgets, having spent large parts of their annual budgets on television advertising during the Olympics. Cigarettes and tobacco, formerly one of the country's top ten advertisers, had now slipped to 12th place as a result of FDA disapproval. On the plus side, however, pharmaceutical products added 22 percent to their magazine advertising during the year.

Competition. Approximately 11,000 American magazines are published each year, yet there are a few publishing companies which dominate the industry. In 1995, according to Standard & Poor's Industry Survey for 1996, the 10 largest consumer magazines generated 23 percent, or $4.8 billion of the total $24.7 billion in magazine revenues. Leading the pack in 1995 was *TV Guide,* ($1.1 billion) followed by *People, Sports Illustrated,* and *Time.*

Because competition for ad and circulation dollars is intense, the turnover rate of publications is enormous—particularly for start-up periodicals. In 1995 alone, 838 magazines debuted, but indications are that 50 percent of them are doomed to failure. Low barriers to entry—in comparison to most other industries—contribute to the high failure rate, because anyone with several thousand dollars and an idea can start a new periodical. Poor business planning and inadequate market research, however, usually accompany such endeavors.

BACKGROUND AND DEVELOPMENT

Periodicals evolved from book notices that were inserted in European newsbooks published during the early 1600s. By the 1640s publishers were beginning to include critical commentary, and by the 1650s, the notices began appearing as regular features of newsbooks and papers. About the same time that book notices were developing, digests and abstract journals began appearing. These periodicals provided summaries of published books, biographies, and reports on important philosophical, literary, and scientific matters of the time. The *Journal des scavans,* first issued in Paris on January 5, 1665, is recognized as the parent of the modern periodical industry.

Throughout the remainder of the seventeenth century, several publishers, mostly in Great Britain, began to produce periodicals offering opinion, news, and entertainment. Next, early in the 1700s, journals of political opinion became particularly popular. Great Britain's *Spectator,* for example, achieved a circulation of 4,000. Other well-received British journals during the eighteenth century included *Farmer's Magazine, Gentlemen's Magazine,* and *London Review.* During the nineteenth century as the European industry evolved, journals appealing to a broad range of interests emerged. Great Britain's *Westminster Review,* Italy's *Scena Illustra,* and Russia's *Russky Vestnik* were popular, as were new magazines targeting special interest groups such as children, physicians, and women.

The first American periodicals were Andrew Bradford's *American Magazine* and Benjamin Franklin's *General Magazine,* both of which started and failed in 1741. Other early efforts included *The Columbian* and Thomas Paine's *Pennsylvania Magazine.* In all, about 100 magazines were eventually started in the colonies; most of them failed within a few years. After numerous duds and over 500 new periodical start-ups during the early 1800s, by 1825 about 100 magazines and journals were circulating on U.S. soil. Spurred by a demand for weekly literary journals, as well as children's, women's, religious, and political periodicals, the total number of magazines in circulation rose to 600 by 1850. Two famous titles of that time were *North American Review* and *Southern Literary Messenger.*

With the 1850s came a new era for the periodicals industry. It began with *Harper's New Monthly Magazine,* a richly illustrated periodical that which spurred a horde of highly successful imitators. *The Nation, Outlook, Scribner's Magazine,* and *Christian Union*

were a few of the titles that rocketed the number of U.S. periodicals to 1,200 in 1870, 2,400 in 1880, and nearly 3,000 by 1890. In the 1890s, moreover, low-priced illustrated monthlies were introduced that cost only 15 cents per copy, compared to the 35 cents charged by their predecessors. Many of these magazines were "muckrakers" that exposed government corruption.

The number and circulation of periodicals continued to proliferate rapidly during the early twentieth century. Among the most popular publications were *Good Housekeeping* and *Ladies' Home Journal,* which were joined by *Life* in 1923, and *Newsweek* ten years later. *Reader's Digest,* founded in 1922, became a classic American success story, its circulation soaring to a stunning 21 million during the 1950s. *Life* and a similar publication called *Look,* waited until the 1960s for success, but finally reached combined sales of 7 million dollars.

The periodical publishing industry found itself facing new challenges during the 1950s and 1960s. Most visible was the immediate popularity of television. In company with radio, television altered American reading habits and allowed periodical publishers an increasingly smaller proportion of overall advertising expenditures. Augmenting this trend were diminished profit margins caused by growing production expenses and higher postal rates, though media competition and rising costs could not suppress strong circulation growth throughout the middle years of the century. Publications like *Playboy* and *Seventeen* opened up entirely new, and massive, market segments. Likewise, a plethora of trade and business journals boosted industry breadth and earnings. In addition, entire sub-industries sprang up during the 1970s to serve automotive enthusiasts, fashion fans and other niche readers. New marketing channels, such as the Publisher's Clearinghouse Sweepstakes, also spurred growth. By the end of the 1970s, the periodicals industry was grossing more than $10 billion in sales and employing a work force of over 90,000.

The periodicals industry continued to expand steadily during the 1980s, a general increase in the demand for all types of current information and escalating advertising expenditures helping to boost circulation. Other stimulants came from burgeoning electronics technology, spurring a $275 million market niche for computer and office equipment magazines which had not existed at the beginning of the decade. Other industries which significantly increased their magazine ad expenditures included apparel and travel.

As periodical demand rose and ad revenues climbed, the number of periodical titles increased from

10,700 in 1982 to about 11,000 by 1990. During the same period, total industry sales jumped from $11.5 billion to $23.1 billion, representing an average annual growth rate of more than 7 percent. Some of the readership niches that offered the best opportunities were newsweeklies, women's, men's sports, and travel.

Periodical prosperity waned in 1989 and the early 1990s. A U.S. and global economic recession blasted ad revenues, stalled subscription growth, and slashed newsstand sales. In addition, some analysts believed that the market was becoming saturated and mature, thus offering fewer profit opportunities. Finally, periodical producers were slowly losing their share of U.S. ad dollars to other media, such as direct mail and catalogs.

Total magazine advertising revenues rose less than 2.5 percent in 1990 before plummeting almost 5 percent in 1991. Factoring in discounts and incentives that publishers offered to advertisers, however, those figures are probably optimistic. Total industry receipts, adjusted for inflation, actually fell 0.4 percent in 1989, 3.6 percent in 1990, and 4.7 percent in 1991. As publishers scrambled to compete for scarce ad and sales dollars, the number of periodical titles slipped from 11,556 in 1989 to only 11,092 in 1990.

Interestingly, start-up magazine publishers seemed undaunted by the industry slump. In 1989, 599 new magazines were launched, with 553 following hot on their heels in 1990. By 1996, the number of new periodicals was expected to top 900, after reaching a high of 838 in 1995.

CURRENT CONDITIONS

According to the *Standard Directory of Advertisers,* the top advertisers in consumer magazines for 1995 were General Motors Corporation, which spent $428,393; Philip Morris Companies, with $381,306; and Chrysler Corporation, whose magazine budget ran to $271,114. The Procter & Gamble Company was fourth, with a budget of $267,994, followed by Ford Motor Company, at $266,040.

Besides ad revenues, publishers also enjoyed a slight reprieve from lackluster circulation sales—a relief to advertisers, who place their ads according to circulation figures. Receipts grew by about one percent in 1992 and rose at a slightly faster rate in 1993. Subscription sales rose about 1.2 percent in 1992. The rise in subscription price, moreover, was accompanied by a reduction in the average number of annual issues, which had fallen from 12.2 in 1988 to 11.8 in 1993.

Overall gains in circulation revenues, however, were partially offset by postal rate increases.

Besides subtly reducing the number of annual issues, publishers were also trying to reduce costs through other strategies. For instance, by presorting mail and including four-digit zip code suffixes to address labels, some producers were able to cut second-class postage costs by as much as 5 percent. Other publishers were switching to lightweight paper and trucking magazines to regional distribution centers. Many producers were also increasing their database marketing efforts and striving to garner follow-up retail sales from their subscribers. The largest gains, though, were being accomplished through layoffs, salary freezes, and benefit cutbacks.

Winners and Losers. In the face of slow overall growth, publishers were jockeying to take advantage of a few healthy industry niches. Regional magazines, for example, realized an increase in successful titles of 38 percent between 1988 and 1993. The number of not-for-profit periodicals, which make up about 18 percent of total consumer magazine circulation, jumped as well, by 22 percent. Two American Association of Retired Persons (AARP) periodicals with combined circulation of over 22 million lead not-for-profit growth. Rapid sales growth also occurred in travel, golf, camping, and pet publications.

Erotic and pornographic titles continued to lead new magazine start-ups: 66 such periodicals entered the market in 1991, though the number of new entrants dropped to 44 by the end of 1994. Gay and lesbian publications were also showing strong growth, as 22 new titles appeared in 1992, compared to only ten in 1990. Other growing niches related to crafts and games, fishing and hunting, comics, military, and computers.

The most rapid declines in 1993 were taking place in periodicals related to airline flight, television and radio, all of which had previously offered solid gains. Boating, dancing, gardening, and dressmaking segment revenues were declining more slowly, as were magazines about horses, and boating. Declining numbers of titles in the early 1990s were occurring in subjects related to health, men, motorcycles, and lifestyle. Some well-known periodicals that ceased circulation in the early 1990s were *Ovation, Christian Herald, HG, NY Woman, Motorboat, Trumps Business Month,* and *Fame.*

As the 1990s progressed, however, certain categories regained in popularity, and new ones arose to plump revenues still further. Gardening, for example, became such a popular pastime across the country that periodicals like *Martha Stewart Living,* which also incorporates home decorating and other domestic arts, found an ever-broader market niche. Others, like *Modern Dad,* (circulation 100,000) are more tightly focused, catering for more specialized consumers.

The Future. Although U.S. media advertising expenditures grew by 5.4 percent between 1986 and 1996 (in inflation adjusted dollars), total periodical industry receipts were expected to rise by only 1 to 2 percent above inflation in the late 1990s. As a result, publishers will concentrate on growing revenues and profit margins associated with circulation sales. As markets mature, moreover, periodical manufacturers will increasingly seek additional revenues from back-end sales to their subscriber database. Many publishers had already initiated aggressive campaigns to sell products and materials that complement their publications.

In the late 1990s magazines are increasingly turning to online services, which offer benefits such as decreased dependence on advertisers. Many well-known magazines have offered electronic versions on consumer online services such as America Online and Compuserve. With the popularity of the World Wide Web, publishers have also begun hosting their own sites that often include back issues and other special features. There have also been numerous Internet-only publications, sometimes called e-zines, that offer similar content and format as their print-based competitors. This does not mean that publications in print form are on their way out. There are many situations, such as when traveling, when consumers may not have access to their computers, and therefore turn to printed magazines. Also, there are still millions of households across the country which do not have computers. In an effort to pursue ever-greater advertising revenues, magazines will begin offering different ads and editorial sections for the same publication, so that different customer segments will receive issues tailored to their demographic profile.

Environmental considerations will receive growing industry attention entering the twenty-first century. In the early 1990s, government and special interests were already prodding publishers to reduce their use of hazardous inks and to utilize more recycled materials in their production processes. However, problems associated with quality, price, and availability of recycled stock plagued recycling efforts. As Congress threatened to legislate the mandatory use of recycled paper, the number of publishers using at least some recycled materials rose from 24 percent in 1991 to 35 percent in 1992.

INDUSTRY LEADERS

Counting purely by magazine revenues, Time Warner was the industry leader in 1996, with sales of almost $10 billion. Next came Hearst, with sales of $2.5 billion, up from $2.3 billion in 1995.

McGraw-Hill, Inc., of New York was the third largest periodical publisher, with 1996 sales of more than $3 billion and about 16,000 employees. It was followed closely by New York's Reader's Digest Association Inc., which grossed about $3 billion in 1996 receipts and employed over 6,000.

The company that garnered the most magazine advertising revenues in 1992 was Time Warner Inc., (formerly Time Inc.), which captured over 19 percent of all industry ad revenues in 1992. Hearst Magazines placed second in order of ad revenues, with about eight percent of the market. Conde Nast Publications, Inc., a major supplier of travel magazines, captured over 7 percent of industry ad dollars. Parade Publications, The New York Times Company, and Hachette were other top ad sellers. By 1995, *Parade,* a weekly newspaper insert, led the field with more than $515 million in advertising revenues. Next came *People,* with $438 million.

The same contenders had been present in 1992, though the top ad-generating periodical in the United States in 1992 was *TV Guide,* which sold over $822 million worth of ad space and circulated 15 million copies weekly. *People,* the second greatest ad earner, had advertising revenues of $562 million in 1992. Other ad leaders included *Time* ($446 million in 1992 ad sales), *Sports Illustrated* ($437 million), *Reader's Digest* ($428 million), *Parade* ($328 million), and *Newsweek* ($310 million).

In 1992 the largest magazine by total number of issues circulated was *Parade,* which boasted a weekly circulation of over 36 million. Other major periodicals, by circulation totals, were *Modern Maturity* (with 22.6 million subscribers in 1992), *Reader's Digest* (17 million), *USA Weekend* (15.8 million), and *National Geographic* (9.9 million).

By the end of 1995, the order had changed somewhat. *TV Guide* won the laurel wreath with $660 million in combined newsstand and subscription sales, with *People* next in line, showing about $360 million.

Of the top 100 U.S. magazines, in 1992 the fastest growing periodical, by circulation, was *Parenting,* which boosted its circulation 31 percent in 1992 to 921,000 per month. *Vanity Fair* unit sales jumped 23 percent, past one million per month, and *Conde Nast Traveler* circulation rose 21 percent, to 870,000. The largest declines were experienced by *Barron's* (with a circulation drop of 23 percent in 1992), *Computerworld* (20 percent), and *The Cable Guide* (17 percent).

WORK FORCE

The periodical industry employed roughly 131,000 workers in 1996, according to the Magazine Publishers of America. Workers in the industry are relatively well paid and work fewer hours than the average manufacturing industry employee. The average production worker earned $13.42 per hour in 1995, compared to the manufacturing average of $12.37. Furthermore, the average work week in this industry was only 37.1 hours in 1995, compared with 41.6 hours for all other manufacturing sectors.

The industry is a major employer of writers, editors, and technical writers, which together constitute 13 percent of its work force. Many employees begin as copywriters, copyeditors, or production editors, and work their way up to various editorial management positions. Senior editors, for example, traditionally write copy and may also manage other editorial employees or freelancers. But a salary survey presented in August 1996 by *Folio* pointed to an increased workload for senior editors, as a result of the corporate downsizing that has taken place during the 1990s. The average senior editor's salary, $43,400 in 1993, rising through the top third averaged $62,600, according to a survey with 404 respondents in the August 1, 1993 issue of *Folio*. By 1996, salaries had risen considerably. The average senior editor on a business publication could now expect to earn $49,900 per year, while consumer magazines offered an average annual salary of $63,300, with the top third yielding $81,200 on average.

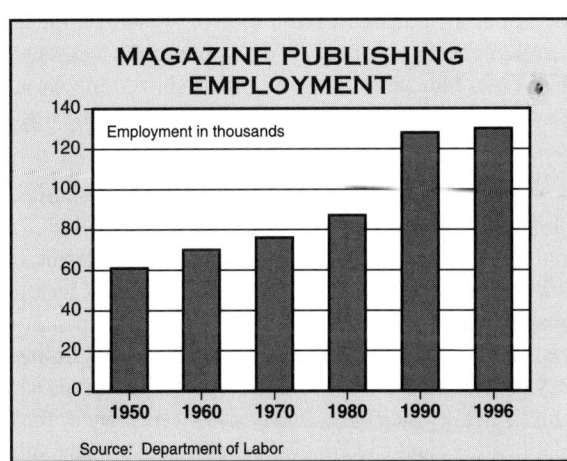

MAGAZINE PUBLISHING EMPLOYMENT

Employment in thousands

Source: Department of Labor

Managing editors coordinate the editorial, art, and production departments of a publication and oversee proofreading and copywriting functions. Salaries for this job averaged $41,000 in 1993 and $48,500 by 1996, with business magazines paying an average $48,100 and consumer publications slightly more, at $48,900 per year. Editors, who are responsible for directing the content of a publication, averaged $47,000 in 1993, though the top one-third of survey respondents earned over $70,000. By 1996, however, the average was $65,100, with the top third earning $102,700. Editorial managers, who may be called publishers, are responsible for setting editorial policy and managing operations. The average salary for this function was $66,400 in 1993, with the top third of the group earning more than $100,000. By 1996, the average for this position was $73,400, while top wages averaged $112,700. Base salaries as well as bonuses for all positions vary primarily according to the circulation volume of each periodical, by the frequency of its appearance, and by the number of pages in each issue.

Periodical producers also employ a large number of ad salespeople, who make up 12 percent of industry employment. According to a *Folio* survey, the average director of ad sales earned $90,208 in 1993. When the same survey was repeated in 1996, the top one-third of the directors, averaged $137,310. Branch and regional ad sales managers averaged $72,000, with the top salary reaching $122,000. Also included in this group were ad salespeople, whose average salary, in 1996, was $46,000 for business publications, and $41,000 for consumer magazines; the highest salary was $110,000.

Although overall compensation slumped in the early 1990s, the long-term employment outlook for the periodicals industry was very positive going into the mid-1990s. Jobs for writers and editors were expected to increase by over 50 percent between 1990 and 2005, according to the Bureau of Labor Statistics. Sales and related positions, moreover, were expected to grow by over 65 percent. Indeed, almost every occupation in the industry was forecast to jump by over 30 percent. Jobs for executives, for example, should rise 28 percent, and administration and support staff will likely grow by over 30 percent. Opportunities for computer programmers should bound nearly 80 percent by 2005.

AMERICA AND THE WORLD

In an effort to boost earnings in slow domestic markets, many periodical publishers in the early 1990s were seeking growth overseas. Although total industry exports amounted to only 3.5 percent of receipts in 1993, cross-border shipments had grown almost 100 percent since 1989 and were expected to increase at a rate of 5 to 10 percent annually through the turn of the century. Furthermore, U.S. publishers had a stranglehold on domestic markets, as imports amounted to less than $170 million in 1993 and the industry's trade surplus topped $600 million.

Canada consumed about 78 percent of all periodical exports in the early 1990s, but other countries were exhibiting solid market growth. The United Kingdom, for example, purchased 6 percent of periodical exports, and Mexico and the Netherlands each purchased 3 to 4 percent. Consumer and farm magazines were the greatest sellers. Helping to increase foreign sales in the early 1990s were U.S. joint ventures with overseas publishers that were directing local marketing and publishing efforts. For example, IDG, a global computer-related publisher, entered a joint venture in China to publish *Electronics International,* while 1996 brought a joint venture between *Newsweek* and a Russian banking, real estate, and communications conglomerate called Most, to produce *Itogi,* a newsmagazine aimed at the emerging highly educated new middle class in Russia. Top magazine circulations in Russia may run as high as 2 million, *FIPP Magazine World* claimed in January 1997.

While the majority of magazine exports have traditionally gone to English speaking foreigners, U.S. publishers began significant efforts during the 1980s and early 1990s to establish foreign editions of their publications. Some of these efforts were quashed by the global recession of the early 1990s.

Other companies that had successfully invaded foreign periodical markets in the early 1990s included Miller Freeman, Inc., of California, PennWell Publishing of Texas, Advanstar Communications of Ohio, and several others. Cahners Publishing, of Illinois, for example, was selling 38 percent of its 58,000 monthly circulation of *Hotels* to overseas readers in 1993. Likewise, Paisana Publications was shipping over 68,000 issues of the semimonthly *Easyriders,* a Harley Davidson motorcycle enthusiasts magazine, to foreign customers. *Surfing,* published monthly by California's Western Empire Publishing had about 13,744 overseas subscribers in 1993, and by the end of the same year *Scientific American* was selling 113,000 copies of a total 663,000 overseas, and *Fortune* magazine introduced a new Chinese-language edition at the end of 1996.

Despite some overseas success, the export potential for U.S. periodicals remained limited by multiple factors going into the mid-1990s. Most important, postal rates in most European and Asian countries are much higher than U.S. rates. This severely restricts subscription sales. U.S. publishers also often incur great difficulty obtaining effective mailing lists which they can use to market their publications. The U.S. list industry is highly advanced by comparison. Furthermore, some important markets like Germany have strict environmental and privacy regulations that limit periodical sales through the mail.

U.S. exporters will likely experience little relief from foreign regulations in the near future, depending on revisions to the European Union's law on privacy and data protection, which threatened to make it very costly for U.S. publishers to acquire customer lists. Nevertheless, Europe, as well as Asia and Latin America, will remain the focus of joint ventures and licensing arrangements aimed at boosting overseas sales. The North American Free Trade Agreement (NAFTA), signed in 1994, was expected to have a negligible impact on industry participants.

RESEARCH AND TECHNOLOGY

After losing ground in 1990 and 1991, periodical publishers realized a modest recovery in 1992 and 1993 that seemed to be accelerating as they entered 1994. Gross receipts climbed an encouraging eight percent in 1992 as inflation remained low. Furthermore, employment jumped about 2,000 after dipping to 110,000 in 1991. A slow U.S. economic recovery and an upsurge in new product introductions helped to revive sales and profit growth.

Ad revenues climbed 7.1 percent in 1992 based on published advertising rates; real ad revenue growth was estimated at a tepid 2 percent. Leading ad sales were increases in advertising spending on drugs and remedies, which swelled 66 percent in 1992, and computers and office equipment, which leapt over 20 percent. Toiletries and cosmetics expenditures also grew, by about 12 percent, as automotive ad sales climbed ten percent. Sales of tobacco ads plunged 15 percent, however. Magazine categories that realized the strongest ad growth were women's, fashion, national business news, outdoor, sport, and automotive.

The growth in revenues resulted from a combination of higher rates and greater volume. Indeed, published magazine ad rates grew about six percent in 1993, as total ad volume jumped five percent. Overall, magazines' share of total U.S. media ad spending remained at 5.2 percent. To retain this share, publishers in 1992 and 1993 offered increased incentives and multi-media packages. Many also redesigned their publications and tried to eliminate marginal readership that diluted advertisement impact.

In 1993 a data-gathering service called Periodical Retail Information Management (PRIM) was introduced. The system was designed to provide timely and accurate data to retailers, wholesalers, and publishers. The system was expected to eventually assist with the distribution of more than 3,000 titles to more than 189,000 retailers each month, and would keep close track of title data related to each retailer's sales, including promotion and discount information.

In the long term, periodical publishers will start to view their role as providers of information services, rather than just product publishers. This will occur as electronic and digital publishing proliferates, and as publishers seek to enhance revenue streams through advanced media options. Many publishers were already experimenting with multimedia markets in the early 1990s, and several had been offering their periodicals on CD-ROM or online since the 1980s. Some analysts believed that electronic publishing, in some form, would dominate the industry by the 2010s, with paper publishing used only as a side or specialty media.

Indeed, as the number of American households with a modem-equipped personal computer rose from 13 percent in 1993 to an estimated 25 percent by 1995, publishers were increasingly striving to take advantage of this media.

Evidencing the trend toward electronic media was a partnership formed in 1993 by Jeffrey Dearth, president of the *New Republic,* and Rob Raisch, president and founder of The Internet Co. Their online partnership, The Electronic Newsstand Inc., was designed to give print publishers a ''point of presence'' on the Internet. More than 50 magazines were represented on The Electronic Newsstand by 1994, including such titles as *Arthritis Today* and *New Yorker.* By the end of 1996, this number had soared dramatically, with *Publisher's Weekly* counting some 800 magazines on line. In November of 1996, *Folio* reported that on-line publishers had joined with members of other businesses to form a trade association called the Internet Advertising Bureau. Adweek Magazines, Hearst, and Time Warner Inc. New Media were among 70 others who paid their first annual $70,000 fee, in order to join discussions of such topics as advertising to children and agency and marketer relations.

FURTHER READING

Alexander, Bob. ''The State of the Newsstand.'' *Folio: Special Sourcebook Issue 1994,* January 1994.

Angelo, Jean Marie, and Rachel Drucker. ''Editors Report Stalled Earnings.'' *Folio,* 1 August 1993.

Angelo, Jean Marie. ''Ad Sales Salary Survey.'' *Folio: Special Sourcebook Issue 1994,* January 1994.

''Circ City: Here We Come!'' *Folio,* 1 July 1996.

Forbes, Thomas. ''Testing the Waters Online.'' *Folio,* 1 December 1993.

Hovey, Susan. ''Away From Home.'' *Folio,* 15 June 1993.

Huhn, Mary. ''In a Tight Spot.'' *Brandweek,* 13 September 1993.

''The Latina Link in Two Languages.'' *Folio,* 1 September 1996.

Levine, Joshua. ''Go Break a Leg.'' *Forbes,* 3 June 1996.

Kaplan, Michael. ''The Resurrection of Larry Flint.'' *Folio,* 15 June 1993.

Kobak, James B. ''Magazine Trends.'' *Folio: Special Sourcebook Issue 1994,* January 1994.

''Market Trends: Magazines.'' *MEDIAWEEK,* 10 January 1994.

McDougall, Paul. ''The Best and the Biggest.'' *Folio,* 15 September 1993.

''Newsmagazines Take Hold in Russia.'' *Folio,* 1 November 1996.

Pace, Charles L. ''New Directions for the U.S. Postal Service.'' *Folio: Special Sourcebook Issue 1994,* January 1994.

Pogrebin, Robin. ''Magazines Multiplying As Their Focuses Narrow.'' *New York Times,* 2 January 1997.

''Production Salaries Post Moderate Gains.'' *Folio,* 1 June 1966.

''Read All About It.'' *Business Week,* 18 November 1996.

Saffo, Paul, John Warnock, Brenda Laurel, and Perry Barlow. ''It's 2013: Do You Know What Your Magazine Looks Like?'' *Computer Pictures,* May/June 1993.

Silber, Tony. ''Outpacing Inflation . . . And Then Some.'' *Folio,* 1 August 1996.

Standard & Poor's Industry Surveys, New York: Standard & Poor's Corporation, 1996.

''Trade Group Forms for Online Publishers.'' *Folio,* 1 November 1996.

—Dave Mote, updated by Gillian Wolf

SIC 2731

BOOK PUBLISHING

This category includes establishments primarily engaged in publishing, or in publishing and printing, books and pamphlets. Establishments primarily engaged in printing or in printing and binding (but not publishing) books and pamphlets are classified in **SIC 2732: Book Printing.**

INDUSTRY SNAPSHOT

The book publishing industry experienced extraordinary growth over the past three decades, with annual book sales of $1.68 billion in 1963 rising to $17.17 billion by 1993. At the beginning of the 1990s, the industry published just under 50,000 new titles and at least 800,000 books were in print, with about 70 million adults in the United States reportedly purchasing books on a regular basis. A study conducted by the NPD Group, Inc. revealed that approximately 1.5 billion books were bought by American consumers in 1995, with 500 million of these being juvenile titles. Areas of strongest sales growth tended to include children's books, professional/technical books, and religious books—particularly sacred texts. As reported by Jim Milliot of *Publisher's Weekly,* a study by Veronis, Suhler and Associates found that consumers spent close to $24 billion on books in 1994 alone. That figure approached $25 billion in 1995. In a 1996 report, the American Booksellers Association indicated book purchasing rose by over 30 percent between 1991 and 1994. Women, according to Mediamark Research, Inc., were the primary purchasers of books domestically, representing almost 59 percent of all book buyers. The leading metropolitan areas for book sales included Los Angeles, New York, Chicago, Boston, and Washington D.C.

Part of the increase in the early 1990s was attributed to the proliferation of large retail bookstore chains. By offering conveniences such as comfortable browsing areas and coffee bars, and special events such as book-signings, author readings, and children's story hours, these chains created "superstores" that provided an enjoyable atmosphere for consumers while expanding the overall market for books. In the mid-1990s the two biggest players in this arena were Borders Group Inc. and Barnes & Noble Inc. Another factor that influenced growth was the move by many publishers toward the creation of "book" products in electronic formats and the introduction of more general entertainment products for use on personal computers. Electronic publishing exposed book publishers to unprecedented competition from software and communications companies, which resulted in significant new pressure on the bottom line.

ORGANIZATION AND STRUCTURE

In some respects, book publishing appeared to be a fragmented industry, with over 20,000 companies participating in the United States in the early to mid-1990s. In reality, however, the industry was dominated by several giant publishing houses. According to *Trade Book Publishers, 1996: Analysis by Category,* as quoted in *Media Daily,* the top dozen trade book publishers accounted for nearly 85 percent of the overall U.S. book publishing market. These large publishers consolidated many of their smaller imprints in the early 1990s in order to cut costs and reposition themselves for the onset of electronic publishing. According to Malcolm Jones of *Publishers Weekly,* most of these companies considered themselves to operate within "the publishing aspect of the communications industry." However, this concentration of power among relatively few publishers led to criticism regarding the quality and diversity of materials published. Industry observers saw an increasing role for small presses to publish works of literary quality that did not necessarily have enormous sales potential.

Products within the book publishing industry could be divided into six major categories: adult trade; juvenile trade; mass market; professional, technical, and reference; university press; and religious books. Trade books, representing the largest share of the book market, encompassed all general-interest publications, such as adult and juvenile fiction, nonfiction, advice, and how-to books. In 1995, the adult trade category alone, covering both hardcover and trade paperback, posted publishers' net dollar sales of over $4.3 billion according to *Book Industry Trends 1996,* a study sponsored by the Book Industry Study Group. In the mass market paperback category, publishers' net dollar sales approached $1.35 billion for 1995; net dollar sales for professional titles reached almost $3.87 billion. The same study revealed that American consumers spent in excess of $14.29 billion on books for pleasure in 1995 (including all trade, mass market paperback, book club, and religious book purchases) while combined sales of all educational, professional, and reference titles exceeded the $10 billion mark. The expansion of large chain bookstores and the population growth among school-age children and high-income adults were among the factors that contributed to the growth of these sales. According to Veronis, Suhler & Associates' study, the compound annual growth rate of spending on books increased by 5.7 percent in the period from 1989 to 1994 and was expected to continue to grow at an even higher rate through 1999.

The book publishing process was fairly similar across these product categories. Most books originated as a concept or idea, which was either submitted by an outside author or generated internally by the publisher. The concept was usually refined using market analysis, and the final decision to proceed resulted from a comparison of the product's expected costs and potential revenues. Such decisions were increasingly made by committee consensus versus the decree of one individ-

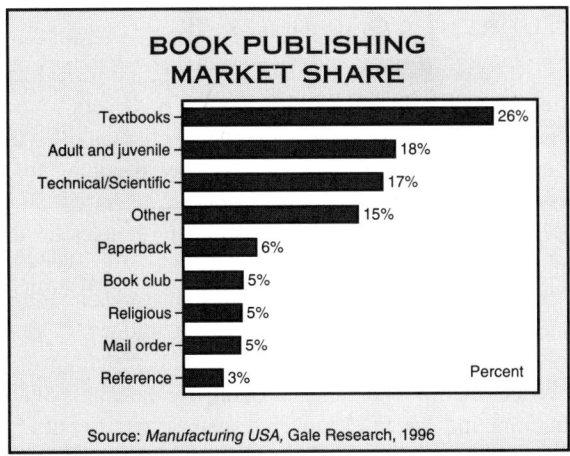

BOOK PUBLISHING MARKET SHARE

Textbooks — 26%
Adult and juvenile — 18%
Technical/Scientific — 17%
Other — 15%
Paperback — 6%
Book club — 5%
Religious — 5%
Mail order — 5%
Reference — 3%

Percent

Source: *Manufacturing USA*, Gale Research, 1996

ual editor. Next came the actual compilation of the book's content, followed by editorial work to ensure its quality and tailor it specifically to a target market. Meanwhile, the marketing and art departments designed the finished product, including type style, page size and layout, presentation of graphics, and appearance of the cover. Then the book was typeset (set in final, camera-ready form for printing), either by an outside vendor or with an in-house desktop publishing system. Finally, the book was transformed into plates, printed, and bound, usually by an outside vendor or affiliated company rather than the publishing house.

According to *Standard & Poor's Industry Surveys* for July 1996, the viability of the book publishing enterprise was "a function of volume," thus making the size of the print run a main factor. Non-educational publishers normally held first hardcover runs to 5,000-50,000 copies while new books by bestselling authors may have merited first runs of over 300,000 copies. Per unit fixed costs were a function directly related to the size of the print run. The American Association of Publishers indicated that the typical manufacturing costs for a mass-market paperback were less than 10 percent of gross sales, while the average for all books was approximately 25 percent.

Returned books represented a substantial cost to publishers, and one that rose ominously throughout the mid-1990s. The cost of returns included "handling, processing, and disposal," and, according to *Standard & Poor's,* such costs cut heavily into publishers' pretax profit margins. The *New York Times* noted the following in August 1996, "Returns are the most significant barometer of the financial success of a book, a measurement more critical than a ranking on a bestseller list because rejects cut directly into profits. Historically, publishers have agreed to take back returns and absorb the loss to entice bookstores to stock their titles." According to the American Association of

Publishers, from 1990 to 1995, industry losses on returned hardcover books rose by 60 percent to over $530 million; as a point of contrast, gross sales grew during the same period by 47 percent.

Book publishers sold their products to the following primary markets: chain and independent retail bookstores; college bookstores; elementary and high schools; libraries, universities, and other institutions. Among these markets, large chain bookstores proliferated and gained importance in the early 1990s—making book-buying into a form of entertainment and siphoning sales away from mail order and book clubs. In addition, the library market, though small, was considered crucial in that it guaranteed publishers a minimum number of sales and, traditionally, required comparatively little in terms of marketing attention. Online bookselling, the newest and fastest growing retail format, provided consumers with relatively quick access to over one million titles purchasable via the Internet.

BACKGROUND AND DEVELOPMENT

The U.S. book publishing industry grew after the Civil War, as the country moved from an agrarian to an industrial society and people increasingly sought information about emerging technology. World War I increased demand for engineering manuals, especially with regard to radio communication, aviation, construction, and aerial photography. During World War II, training manuals gained importance as factories had to hire untrained people to replace soldiers. Publishers who could provide this information quickly received special allocations of paper, which was scarce during wartime.

Beginning in the mid-1800s, publishing houses provided gathering places for literary talent of the time, especially in London and New York City. Most writers formed relationships with particular editors—who often became well-known public figures in their own right—and followed them from one publishing house to another. Several publishing houses became prominent in the fight against censorship in the early twentieth century. One celebrated case occurred in the 1930s when Bennett Cerf, one of the founders of Random House, intentionally notified U.S. Customs about the arrival of James Joyce's allegedly obscene novel *Ulysses* from Paris. Cerf wanted Customs to confiscate the book so that he could fight the censorship in court. Publishing houses that supported freedom of speech often attracted the top literary and editorial talent.

Paperback books first appeared in the United States in the 1770s, but they did not gain a wide audience until Simon & Schuster introduced its line of Pocket Books in 1939. These early softcover editions sold for 25 cents each and met with great success—over 25 million copies were shipped overseas during World War II. Public acceptance of paperbacks increased the overall market for books and made it necessary for publishers to adopt high-volume, low-cost production methods.

In *Publishers Weekly,* John F. Baker called the 1940s and the 1950s "the golden age of publishing," when the industry was a "comparatively small business producing a comparatively limited number of books for a dozily elite readership whose access to bookstores was limited by geography." As the U.S. population grew and became more educated, however, book publishing boomed. This rapid growth culminated in what Baker described as "the decade of the Great Communications Conglomerate Takeover" in the 1960s. Many publishing houses either acquired one another or joined forces with communications conglomerates that held interests in newspapers, magazines, television, and motion pictures. By the early 1970s, the industry was dominated by about 15 giant companies. The consolidation of power continued into the early 1990s, when about seven publishers controlled the industry.

Many of the challenges facing the book publishing industry were reflected in the children's literature boom of the late 1980s. Children's books traditionally represented a quiet, consistent segment of the market, and were virtually ignored by most large houses except for the revenue generated by the classics year after year. However, sales of children's books exploded during the "baby boomlet"—a result of the financially secure baby-boom generation reaching child-bearing age—from $336 million in 1985 to $1.1 billion in 1992. As more publishers jumped on the bandwagon and expanded their children's divisions, annual output grew from 3,800 titles in 1985 to over 5,000 in 1991 and the number of children's-only bookstores doubled. However, such rapid expansion led to an oversaturation of the market with books of mediocre quality, which was compounded by the recession and decreases in library budgets. As a result, sales growth suddenly dropped by half, retailers returned unprecedented numbers of unsold books, and many publishers were forced to reevaluate their approaches in the face of fierce competition. According to M. P. Dunleavy in *Publishers Weekly,* "the publishing of children's books has not only grown up but completed an odyssey," and the industry learned in the process that it must adopt a longer-term outlook in order to survive.

CURRENT CONDITIONS

The book publishing industry faced a transformation entering the mid-1990s. Many observers noted that the industry, which once could be characterized as gentlemanly and literary, had quickly become more cutthroat and businesslike. *National Review* cited as evidence the trend for large publishing houses to replace long-time chief executives, best known for their "literary sensibilities," with industry outsiders steeped in "modern management techniques." As a result, many employees within the publishing industry shifted their focus from building relationships with authors and carefully tailoring manuscripts to cutting costs and analyzing profit and loss statements. Former Pantheon managing director Andre Schiffrin noted in *The Nation* an increasing trend among modern day publishing houses to set higher and higher profit targets, which often ranged from 12 to 15 percent in 1996; this figure contrasted starkly with the typical 1920s publishing company's average profit of four percent. Rising overheads also contributed to the financial strain placed on publishers in the mid-1990s, making many companies even more vulnerable.

Some analysts felt that this shift toward modernization was overdue, since book publishing faced challenges on a number of fronts yet lagged behind other industries in seeking efficiencies in production, distribution, and marketing. One problem addressed by many large houses was their overproduction of titles, which resulted in an average of 30 percent of trade books (and up to 48 percent of paperbacks) being returned unsold for credit. Retailers tended to over-order some titles to attain volume discounts and hopefully predict the next best-seller. In response, some publishing houses utilized new technology to make shorter production runs more profitable, and their average first-runs dropped significantly in the late 1980s. In addition, several publishers began experimenting with "no-return" policies with the goal of encouraging booksellers to make more realistic orders.

Another factor affecting the book publishing industry was the proliferation of large, influential retail bookstore chains. While these chains expanded the overall market for books, they also had the power to limit pricing and affect the selection of books that publishers could offer profitably. Some critics argued that by catering to a mass market, chains caused publishers to create books of broad appeal, but low quality. For example, the early 1990s saw many publishers adopt genre publishing—focusing on books with similar themes in order to limit their risk. One highly criticized result of this trend was the battle to attain publishing rights for headline-grabbing, "true-life" stories of questionable literary value, such as celebrity scandals and lurid crimes. Some analysts also worried that chains would disrupt the business of independent booksellers, who were often closely linked to tastes within their communities and provided a market for more eclectic books. *The Nation* noted in 1996 that, "In a series of lawsuits brought by the American Booksellers Association, the independents have charged that the large publishers favor the chains through unfair practices." The argument was that the big publishers allegedly paid generously to have their bestsellers prominently displayed and advertised within the stores while the smaller publishers did not have the means to compete in such a system.

The two biggest retail bookselling chains, Borders Group Inc. and Barnes & Noble Inc., expanded aggressively throughout the United States, opening outlets reaching from New York's World Trade Center to the west coast. In 1995, Borders boasted sales of $1.75 billion while Barnes & Noble posted a total revenue figure of $1.97 billion. In 1996, the potential for such giants to continue their expansion efforts was unhindered, with over 140 U.S. metropolitan markets still without one of their "superstores." *The Wall Street Journal* offered analyst Amy Ryan's assertion that the expansion could go on "through the year 2000 and . . . the U.S. can support 1,500 such outlets."

Book publishers also faced a challenge to their continued profitability due to the 1980s legacy of offering huge cash advances to prominent authors. Examples of this included HarperCollins' highly publicized 1994 offer to pay Congressional House Speaker Newt Gingrich an advance of $4.5 million for future writings, and—in 1996—an offer by Random House of $2.5 million to former Clinton administration political strategist Dick Morris. Some industry executives likened the impact of this trend to mass suicide by publishers, since it meant that only one in five products were successful enough to turn a profit. In addition, large advances were criticized within the industry for preventing publishers from nurturing talented, yet less well-known authors. However, other industry observers argued that the proceeds from one best-seller could often support a number of "more literary" releases. Overall, many publishers expressed their intention to limit future advances.

Book publishers also faced keen competition for the leisure time of their traditional customers from cable television, VCRs, video games, multimedia products, and the Internet. On a positive note *Publishers Weekly* cited a study in 1996 that indicated "spending on reading material by households with computers is at least as high as spending on such material by those without." In addition, the recession of the early 1990s led to cutbacks in education and library funding, with subsequent reductions in book purchases by these markets. These trends reinforced industry concerns about declining literacy rates in the United States, and led several publishing houses to participate in programs to encourage a more book-oriented culture. Many publishers also faced shrinking profit margins in key areas. For example, author royalties generally accounted for 10 to 15 percent of the cover price of trade books, which left publishers with an average margin of 9.5 percent. For textbooks and professional books, however—which were less expensive to produce and usually sold in larger quantities—houses obtained an average margin of 20 percent. Many book publishers responded to these challenges by cutting costs, streamlining operations, adopting new technologies, and investigating the marketing potential of electronic products such as CD-ROMs and on-line information delivery.

As John F. Baker explained in *Publishers Weekly,* "Publishing is changing quite markedly, to the extent that there's more caution, a much greater sense of the potentials, up and down, of the market, and a determination to focus more sharply, among the big houses; new skills, better distribution, and a real sense of a significant role to play, among the smaller ones." As the U.S. economy began to recover in the mid-1990s, the outlook for the book publishing industry also began to improve. Shifting demographics pointed toward higher enrollment levels in schools and colleges, while the Clinton administration appeared likely to increase funding for libraries and the arts. Many publishers expected growth among medical and health care-related titles to correspond with concerns of the aging U.S. population, as well as growth in professional and technical titles to support rapid changes in office technology. In 1995, the latter expectation was born out and evidenced in part by an 82 percent increase in revenues from the sale of computer books for that year alone.

Also in 1995, the market for juvenile trade books had begun to rebound. Sales in that category reached $1.35 billion and *Book Industry Trends 1996* projected that domestic consumer expenditures on children's books would nearly double to $2.67 billion by the year 2000. According to the American Association of Publishers, 500 million children's books were purchased domestically in 1995, as the juvenile publishing segment posted a gain of 4 percent over the previous year.

INDUSTRY LEADERS

The leading trade book publishers for 1995, according to *Book Publishing Report*, in terms of revenue and market share were: Random House, Inc. with $1.25 billion, and a 22 percent market share; Simon & Schuster Inc. with $832 million and 14.7 percent; Bantam Doubleday with $670 million and 11.8 percent; Time Warner Inc. with $325 million and 5.7 percent; HarperCollins Publishers, Inc. with $317.2 million and 5.6 percent; Penguin USA with $317.0 and 5.6 percent; Putnam Berkley with $300 million and 5.3 percent; Holtzbrink (includes St. Martin's Press; Henry Holt & Co.; and Farrar, Strauss, and Giroux) with $267 million and 4.7 percent; Hearst Book Group with $160 million and 2.8 percent; Thomas Nelson with $145.7 million and 2.6 percent; Andrews & McNeel with $92.4 million and 1.6 percent; and Houghton Mifflin Company with $87.2 million and 1.5 percent in market share. Total 1995 revenues for the trade book market exceeded $5.65 billion.

Random House, Inc., the largest American trade book publisher, became a subsidiary of Advance Publications (formerly Newhouse Publications) in 1980, when it was acquired for $70 million. Random House was founded when Bennett Cerf and Donald Klopfer purchased the Modern Library series—popular books in an inexpensive format—in 1925. The founders decided to publish luxury editions "at random" in 1928, and named their company Random House. Over the years, the company retained such prominent authors as Eugene O'Neill, Robinson Jeffers, Dr. Seuss, Willa Cather, John Updike, and James Joyce (whose books were the cause of celebrated legal battles). Random House merged with Knopf in 1960 and Pantheon in 1961, became an independent subsidiary of RCA in 1966, and acquired Ballantine paperbacks in 1973 to become a full-line book publisher.

Simon & Schuster Inc. was founded in New York City in 1924 by Richard L. Simon and M. Lincoln Schuster, who began their careers by publishing highly popular books of crossword puzzles. Some of the company's most famous publications over the years included Leon Trotsky's *History of the Russian Revolution,* Felix Salten's *Bambi,* Dale Carnegie's *How to Win Friends and Influence People,* Dr. Benjamin Spock's *Baby and Child Care,* and Bob Woodward and Carl Bernstein's *All the President's Men.* In 1939 the company introduced Pocket Books, which created the market for inexpensive, paperback books. In 1942 Simon & Schuster followed this effort with the equally successful introduction of Little Golden Books, aimed at the children's market. The company went public in 1966 and was acquired by Gulf + Western in 1975.

Simon & Schuster expanded aggressively during the 1980s by launching a dozen new imprints and acquiring interests in textbooks and software. In 1993, Simon & Schuster acquired the 150 year old Macmillan, Inc. from the estate of British media mogul Robert Maxwell.

Bantam Doubleday Dell was a subsidiary of German conglomerate Bertelsmann A.G. Bertelsmann was founded in 1835 as a family publisher of evangelical materials, and grew to become the largest media group in Europe. The parent acquired Bantam Books in 1980, then combined it with Doubleday in 1986.

Time Warner's book publishing companies in 1996 included Warner Books, Little, Brown, and Co., Time-Life Books, and Book-of-the-Month-Club.

HarperCollins was a subsidiary of Rupert Murdoch's News Corporation Limited. Murdoch was born in Australia in 1931 and spent several decades building a newspaper empire in the United Kingdom. He purchased controlling interest in British publisher William Collins and Sons in 1981, then added American house Harper & Row in 1987, and combined the two along with other publishing companies (including Basic Books, T.Y. Crowell, and Scott Foresman) to form HarperCollins in 1989. Besides one of the largest English-language publishers in the world, News Corporation also owned Twentieth Century-Fox studios and the Fox Broadcasting network. In 1996, Harper-Collins sold off its educational publishing division to Pearson PLC for $580 million; planned the development of HarperEdge, a new imprint focused on high technology titles; detailed its intention to open an office in Los Angeles; announced a restructuring of its trade, mass market, and audio book sales areas; and chose to discontinue its activity in the adult CD-ROM market by selling the rights to its 14 adult CD-ROM titles to Multicom.

Penguin USA was a subsidiary of London-based holding company Pearson PLC, which also owned controlling interest in Addison-Wesley and Longman. The Pearson conglomerate originated with holdings in construction and oil, began acquiring banks and newspapers in the 1920s, and expanded into book publishing throughout the 1980s. Under the Pearson umbrella, Longman (acquired in 1982) became a major publisher of professional, educational, and general reference books; Penguin (acquired in 1985) became prominent in both hard and softcover fiction; and Addison-Wesley (acquired in 1987) contributed a strength in textbooks. Books accounted for 44 percent of Pearson's revenues in 1992. The parent had 28,000 employees and operated in every country of the world.

The leading publishers of children's trade books for 1990-1995, according to *Youth Market Alert,* included: Western Publishing (by 1996, reorganized as Golden Books Family Entertainment); Random House; HarperCollins; Simon & Schuster; Scholastic; Putnam; Penguin USA; Bantam Doubleday Dell; Disney Publishing; Hearst (Morrow/Avon); Dorling Kindersley; Houghton Mifflin; Harcourt Brace; Little, Brown; and Henry Holt.

Outside of general trade publishing, McGraw-Hill, Inc. ranked among the leading publishers of multimedia products for the business, industry, professional, education, and government markets. The company was formed in 1909 through the combination of two competing publishers of railroad and technical magazines. It benefitted from the increased interest in technical and engineering manuals and expanded rapidly during wartime. In the late 1970s, McGraw-Hill became one of the first companies to enter electronic publishing. By the 1990s, it implemented an electronic textbook publishing service, which allowed teachers to custom design books and see the results within 48 hours.

In the 1980s and 1990s, some critics argued that the consolidation of book publishing among few large corporate groups meant that the materials published would become less diverse and have a bland influence on American culture. However, other analysts viewed the situation as an ideal opportunity for small publishers to fill the gap. "Small presses do constitute one of the bright spots in American publishing," Malcolm Jones claimed in *Publishers Weekly.* "These diverse grass-roots efforts act as a natural corrective to the concentration at the top." In 1996, this opinion of the small independents was cautiously confirmed by Andre Schiffrin in *The Nation.* He wrote, "In a vast cultural desert, the combined effort of all the independent presses does succeed in making a few flowers bloom. But only a few. The share of the market of these presses is minuscule, at most 1 percent of total book sales." Schiffrin went on to applaud the efforts of "a new generation of young publishers" whom he described as willing to publish books of quality despite their limited commercial potential.

WORK FORCE

In an assessment for *Black Enterprise,* Lolis Eric Elie called book publishing "an industry that rewards creativity, treasures personal taste, and provides opportunities to combine work with a socially responsible endeavor." In addition to editorial work, publishing offered career potential for individuals with backgrounds in business, marketing, sales, graphic de-

sign, and computer applications. Traditionally, however, "low entry-level salaries, long hours, and slow advancement have deterred those who tried their hand in the field," Elie continued.

Total employment in the book publishing industry increased slightly to reach 73,000 in 1992, after declining for the previous two years. According to a 1992 *Publishers Weekly* survey, the average publishing company showed annual revenues of $9 million and had 63 employees. Almost half of the companies in the book publishing industry reported no change in their level of employment from 1990 to 1991, while 36 percent increased and 15 percent decreased their staffing levels. According to a 1995 *Publishers Weekly* survey, hourly earnings in the publishing industry rose by 1.6 percent in 1994 and were expected to rise another 3.5 percent for 1995. Total employment increased to 85,000 in 1994 with expectations for another increase of 2.4 percent in 1995.

The 1992 survey indicated that publishing company presidents earned the highest average annual salaries in the industry at $94,634, which ranged from an average of $31,102 at small publishing firms (those with 1990 revenues less than $250,000) to an average of $165,800 at large houses (with revenues greater than $10 million). The average head of an editorial department made just under $50,000, while an entry-level editorial assistant's salary was less than $19,000. The heads of marketing and sales departments earned an average salary between $65,000 and $70,000, while entry-level employees in these areas made about $20,000 annually. Other areas commonly found within publishing companies included production departments, where salaries ranged from $52,000 for a vice president to $19,000 for an entry-level employee; art departments, which paid over $43,000 for a vice president and over $19,000 at the entry level; and rights and permissions departments, which offered over $40,000 for a vice president and $21,000 for an entry-level employee. According to the U.S. government's *Occupational Outlook Handbook,* beginning salaries for writers and editorial assistants averaged $18,000 annually in 1994, while those with at least five years of experience could expect an average of $30,000.

Some industry observers predicted that technology would redefine the roles of everyone in the publishing industry in the late 1990s. As Susan Trowbridge, vice president of publishing technology at Addison-Wesley, explained in *Publishers Weekly,* "the new technological capabilities are causing us to re-examine the roles and procedures of all the publishing participants, from author to editor to designer to manufacturer." Trowbridge foresaw desktop publishing technology moving upstream into editorial functions as well as downstream to manufacturers; a more coordinated focus on the development of multimedia products, involving teamwork between editorial, marketing, and technical experts; and increased automation of administrative processes, such as scheduling and cost-tracking. Employees in all sectors of the publishing industry increasingly required knowledge of computers in order to be successful in their careers.

AMERICA AND THE WORLD

The U.S. publishing industry was by far the world's leading exporter of books. Exports accounted for nearly 10 percent of U.S. publishers' shipments in 1993, or about $1.7 billion. According to the U.S. Department of Commerce, book exports reached $1.76 billion in 1995 (displaying a 4 percent increase over 1994) while unit sales increased to over 885 million. Half of U.S. exports were textbooks or professional and technical products. The major markets for U.S. book exports were Canada, the United Kingdom, Japan, Australia, Germany, and Mexico. In 1995, the biggest increase was in exports to South Korea. The predominance of U.S. exports was explained in part by the increasing numbers of people worldwide who used the English language to conduct business. Total U.S. imports of books reached $1 billion in 1992, an increase of 13 percent over the previous year. By 1995, 530 million books worth $1.2 billion entered the U.S. with the largest increases coming from Canada, Mexico, China, and Italy according to *Publishers Weekly.* The United Kingdom, Hong Kong, Japan, Thailand, South Korea, and Canada were the sources for most imported books, although the figures also included shipments of books manufactured abroad for U.S. publishers.

Industry analysts in the early 1990s expected international sales of U.S. books to continue to improve, particularly in emerging markets such as the former Soviet Union, Mexico and Latin America, and the Asia. U.S. publishers faced some challenges in international sales, however, due to inconsistent application of copyright, or intellectual property right, laws overseas. Publishers of audio books and electronic products, in particular, were displeased with the lack of specific protection afforded by the General Agreement on Tariffs and Trade (GATT) when it concluded in late 1993.

RESEARCH AND TECHNOLOGY

The traditional, printed book might never disappear completely, but new technology revolutionized production, distribution, and nearly every other aspect

of operations in the publishing industry in the 1990s. As *Publishers Weekly* predicted, "The definition of 'publisher' will change. It won't just refer to a person who makes books, but a person who holds information or intellectual property, and disseminates that information in any way he or she can benefit from it." Most publishers began to store information in digital form on computer systems so that it could be readily translated into a variety of electronic product formats. While the conversion to the new technology was often difficult and costly for publishers, most electronic products essentially repackaged information the publishers already owned and thus offered higher margins than print products.

The advent of new technology raised a number of interesting issues within the publishing industry. Publishers faced unprecedented competition from software and communications companies entering the electronic publishing market. These industries began to converge—through partnerships and acquisitions—into something analysts called "the new media." Authors and publishers disagreed about who owned electronic publication rights, and significantly more complex contract negotiations became the norm. Additionally, some confusion arose about which channels of distribution would be most appropriate for electronic products, since bookstores, software stores, on-line subscriptions, and direct mail all formed possible outlets. Many publishers were concerned about what would emerge as the dominant technological platform for electronic publishing. Libraries initiated the movement toward electronic publishing by purchasing reference products in on-line and CD-ROM formats. However, since millions of American homes were equipped with personal computers in the mid-1990s, this presented a formidable market for entertainment and educational products on CD-ROM or diskette. In addition, small, hand-held electronic books such as the Sony Data Discman and the Philips CD-Interactive, which sold for $400-600 each, gained acceptance as their prices fell. Some observers predicted that CD-ROM drives might become standard accessories on television sets in the near future, while others claimed that telecommunications would provide the next mass-distribution medium for electronic publishing. Finally, all of these issues had strong implications for the current organization and future staffing of book publishers. They had to become more flexible and technologically adept in order to compete.

By 1996, many publishing companies had to make the decision of whether or not to abandon their fledgling efforts in the CD-ROM market. According to *Multimedia Business Report,* "One of the biggest problems for many book publishers is that the CD ROM publishing model is moving away from the book model. Three or four years ago, a CD ROM title could be published for not much more than it cost to publish a book, and marketing costs were minimal. Today, CD ROM budgets are headed in the direction of movie budgets. Text is the forgotten media, compared to video, audio and animation.''

Accessing information electronically offered a number of advantages for consumers. For example, CD-ROM products allowed easy sorting of information from a wide variety of databases, as well as made it possible to combine text, graphics, sound, and animation. Some examples of innovative CD-ROM products included a dictionary that could pronounce words, an encyclopedia that could show video clips about entries, and a book that could help a child learn to read. Another common format for electronic information was on-line through computer subscription services and via the Internet. On-line materials were less expensive for publishers to distribute than paper, easier—in some cases—for users to search, and also provided quick publication for time-sensitive information such as medical advances.

Computers also had a significant impact on book production technology. Desktop publishing systems— which featured sophisticated yet simple graphic design software to manipulate digitized text and images into publishable form—made many operations quicker and less expensive for publishers. For example, desktop publishing made it possible for houses to reprint fewer copies of books more often, and thus avoid inventory costs. In addition, the technology allowed publishers to save up to 70 percent in typesetting and other production costs. However, since publishers performed more operations themselves, desktop publishing led to significant changes in the roles of suppliers. In response, many typesetters and printers offered creative services—such as 24-hour turnaround, consulting and training in the use of electronic systems, and management of huge amounts of data—in order to continue to add value.

Technology also began to impact distribution and marketing within the book publishing industry. In the early 1990s, one such system was PUBNET, an electronic book-ordering system that linked 65 publishers with 2,400 bookstores. PUBNET had the capacity to provide publishers with timely, in-depth sales information, which they hoped to better incorporate into upstream decisions.

By the mid-1990s, the Internet was being used by hundreds of publishing companies and distributors alike not only as a vehicle to advertise their goods and display product catalogs online, but also as a means to sidestep the middleman in sales transactions. By 1996, the leading on-line book provider was Amazon.com, a company founded only two years earlier in a garage. Owned by Jeff Bezos, the firm employed 85 people, had estimated sales of $5 million, boasted a stock list of over one million titles, and was experiencing extraordinary sales growth. According to Steve Potash, as quoted in *Publishers Weekly,* "After software, books are the most popular type of product sold on the Internet. The most popular electronic-book categories on the Web are reference, professional and self-help." Though bookselling sites have burgeoned on the World Wide Web, insiders cautioned publishers and booksellers not to expect the Internet to take the place of bookstores but to view the new online marketplace as yet another avenue for reaching consumers.

Several industry analysts predicted that environmental issues would gain importance within the publishing industry. For example, some consumer groups demanded that books, especially paperbacks, be made recyclable. Publishers cooperated with printing and binding companies to make book-binding processes and cover materials more environmentally sound, and some products were developed that could be unbound easily. In 1995, the Environmental Protection Agency announced, as part of its 1994 Common Sense Initiative, an air toxics rule for the printing and publishing industry that would cut dangerous air emissions resulting from printing and package production processes. The proposal was expected to impact 127 existing printing and publishing facilities in the U.S. and any future facilities to be built.

FURTHER READING

Baker, John F. "Anxieties and Openings." *Publishers Weekly,* 4 January 1993.

———. "Hard Times, Hard Choices." *Publishers Weekly,* 4 January 1993.

———. "Rates of Pay in Publishing." *Publishers Weekly,* 6 January 1992.

———. "Reinventing the Book Business." *Publishers Weekly,* 14 March 1994

"Bibles Top All Industry Categories in June '95 Sales Growth." *Book Publishing Report,* 21 August 1995.

Book Industry Trends 1996. New York: Book Industry Study Group, Inc., 1996.

The Business of Publishing: A Publishers Weekly Anthology. New York: Bowker, 1976.

Carvajal, Doreen, "Returns are Swamping the Publishing Industry," *The New York Times,* 1 August 1996.

"The Changing Role of Suppliers." *Publishers Weekly,* 14 September 1992.

"Computer Books Fastest Growing Sector—Study." *Media Daily,* 18 July 1996.

"Do Not Panic: How Emphasis on Business Has Changed Book Publishing." *National Review,* 5 February 1990.

Dunleavy, M. P. "The Crest of the Wave?" *Publishers Weekly,* 19 July 1993.

Elie, Lolis Eric. "Industry Overview: A Career You Can Make Book On." *Black Enterprise,* February 1991.

"Harper Sells its CD-ROM Rights." *Publishers Weekly,* 21 October 1996.

"HarperCollins' Cutting 'Edge' to Focus on High-Tech; Sales Force Realigns." *Book Publishing Report,* 29 July 1996.

"HarperCollins Reorganizes Operations, Announces Plans for L.A. Office." *Book Publishing Report,* 20 May 1996.

Hilts, Paul. "The American Revolution in Book Publishing." *Publishers Weekly,* 14 September 1992.

Industry Surveys. Standard and Poor's Corporation, July 1995.

"Innovations in Binding." *Publishers Weekly,* 14 September 1992.

International Directory of Company Histories. Detroit: St. James Press, 1991.

Jones, Malcolm. "The New Publishers' Row." *Newsweek,* 21 February 1994.

Langstaff, Margaret. "Selling the New Media." *Publishers Weekly,* 10 May 1993.

"Lean, Green, and on the Screen: Book Publishers Look to the Advantages of CD-ROM Publishing." *Economist,* 13 July 1991.

Milliot, Jim. "Veronis, Suhler Study Sees Positive Outlook for Books." *Publishers Weekly,* 7 August 1995.

Milliot, Jim, and Sally Taylor. "Book Exports Slightly Up in '95." *Publishers Weekly,* 25 March 1996.

"The Market for Children's Books Is Still Large, But It Is Changing Significantly," *YouthMarkets Alert,* 1 June 1996.

Moran, Susan. "Amazon.com Forges New Sales Channel." *Webweek,* 19 August 1996.

"Multimedia Future Uncertain for Many Book Publishers." *Multimedia Business Report,* 7 June 1996

Mutter, John. "The Bookstore of the 21st Century." *Publishers Weekly,* 22 July 1996.

———. "Heated Competition Gets Hotter." *Publishers Weekly,* 4 January 1993.

"New Roles for Publishers in an Electronic World." *Publishers Weekly,* 14 September 1992.

"Quarterly Financials: Time Warner; McGraw-Hill." *Book Publishing Report,* 22 July 1996.

"Random House Top Trade Book Publisher in '95, SIMBA Report Says." *Book Publishing Report,* 15 July 1996.

Reilly, Patrick M. "Street Fighters: Where Borders Group and Barnes & Noble Compete, It's a War." *The Wall Street Journal,* 3 September 1996.

"Reshaping the Flow of Production." *Publishers Weekly,* 14 September 1992.

Reuter, Madalynne, and Calvin Reid. "State of the Business." *Publishers Weekly,* 29 September 1989.

Robinson, Carol. "Publishing's Electronic Future." *Publishers Weekly,* 6 September 1993.

Schiffrin, Andre. "The Corporatization of Publishing." *The Nation,* 3 June 1996.

"63% of Heaviest Book Buyers are Women." *About Women and Marketing,* 1 July 1996

"Slow Growth in Consumer Book Purchases Last Year, New Study Shows." *American Association of Publishers Monthly Report,* September 1996. Available from http://www.publishers.org/news/releases/9610.html.

"U.S. Book Exports Edge Up 1.5%." *Publishers Weekly,* 9 September 1996.

SIC 2732

BOOK PRINTING

This category includes establishments primarily engaged in printing, or in printing and binding, books and pamphlets, but not engaged in publishing. Establishments primarily engaged in publishing, or in publishing and printing, books and pamphlets are classified in **SIC 2731: Books: Publishing, or Publishing and Printing.** Establishments engaged in both printing and binding books, but primarily binding books printed elsewhere, are classified in **SIC 2789: Bookbinding and Related Work.**

INDUSTRY SNAPSHOT

The earliest printing techniques were developed in China in the second century A.D. The printing industry was inaugurated in the Western world when Johannes Gutenberg, Johann Fust, and Peter Schöffer invented moveable type and the printing press, producing the first printed books in the Western world with newly developed equipment around the middle of the fifteenth century. Printing came to the United States with some of the earliest English immigrants; the first book printed in the new world was the Bay Psalm Book, printed by Steven Day in 1640. Since that time, design improvements and new inventions have made the process quicker and less costly. Almost from the beginning, printing and publishing were separate enterprises. Today, publishers decide what to print and how it will look, and printers put the words on the page to the publisher's specifications.

Continued movement toward automation, computerization and new technologies are precipitating changes in the industry. Desktop typesetting and formatting at point of origin (the author), digitized color scanning and imaging, electronic publishing over the World Wide Web, and new media formats for the conveyance of information are some of the driving forces of the industry.

ORGANIZATION AND STRUCTURE

An overview of the major segments of the industry is provided through the various affiliates and sections of the Printing Industries of America: Electronic Prepress, Graphic Arts Marketing and Information Service, Graphic Communications Association, International Thermographers, Label Printing Industries of America Printing Industry Financial Executives, Sales & Marketing Executives, the Web Offset Association and the Non-Heatset Web Section. In addition, the Printing History Association and Research and Engineering Council of the Graphic Arts Industry help preserve the heritage of printing and coordinates production techniques and new technologies.

Historic book categories are trade, mass market paperback, textbooks, scientific, technical, reference and professional books. These have been marketed through traditional bookstores, super or mega bookstores, book clubs and via direct mail order. Several companies are now also adding Web site marketing.

The book printing industry is a function of several things: the publishing industry in general with its mass and specialized book marketing, thus the economy at large, and technological innovations particularly those relating to increased quality or production.

The publication of books in the United States is characterized by a clear division of labor between book printer and book publisher. The publisher selects the books to be printed, makes all of the decisions regarding the appearance of the final product, from page layout and illustrations to type font and paper quality, and finances the production. The printer takes the camera-ready copy or the film negative and reproduces them in the quantities required by the publisher, on the paper specified and often already purchased by the publisher. The printer's role in the publishing process is one of reproduction rather than production.

Depending on whether the publisher supplies the camera-ready copy, a phototypeset film negative, or a computer text file, the printer's job begins either with making film negatives of each page or printing plates. In some cases, graphic artists working for the publisher take the corrected typeset hard copy of the text and lay out each page with any necessary graphics. These camera-ready pages, called mechanicals, are then sent on to the printer. The printer then photographs these mechanicals to produce the film copy necessary in the plate-making process. With recent advances in computer graphics capabilities many computer systems can bypass both the lay-out process and the photographing process. Computer programs can combine text and graphics, so page layout can be done on a computer rather than the drafting table. Hardware peripherals can generate output in the form of a film, ready for platemaking.

Metal, paper, or plastic plates are what actually put the images of the text onto the paper. Using photochemical processes, the image to be printed is transferred from the film negative onto the plate. The prepared plate has image areas that chemically accept ink and can therefore pass the ink onto a piece of paper, and non-image areas that chemically repel ink and therefore pass nothing onto the paper, leaving spaces between the letters, images, and lines.

Having made the plates, the printer can begin the reproduction process. Most printing is offset. The inked plates pass a reverse image onto a rubber sheet, which then passes a positive image onto the paper; offset tends to produce a clearer image than direct printing. Black and white graphics, and text only pages, need only pass through the machine once to produce the complete image. Color pictures complicate the process, however, and are usually sent through several times for different colored inks. After the actual printing, some print shops also bind the books while others ship the product back to the publisher or on to the bindery unbound.

BACKGROUND AND DEVELOPMENT

It is thought that the Chinese invented the earliest printing. During the second century A.D., they carved religious texts and images into marble columns around their temples; devotees and pilgrims would ink the columns and press paper to it to make their own copies of the text. Small seals were carved for similar purposes, and by the sixth century, artisans carved wood blocks with which to make prints as well. The oldest known printed works were made with wood blocks in Japan in the eighth century. A million Buddhist charms were printed on paper and distributed to followers around 770 A.D. One of the oldest printed books now extant, the *Diamond Sutra* (a Chinese version of the

Buddhist scriptures), was printed in 868 A.D. using wooden blocks on seven sheets of paper attached at the top and bottom ends to form a single sixteen foot roll. Although moveable clay block type had been invented nearly 400 years earlier, it took the rebirth of knowledge, an abundant paper supply, ink that could be applied to metal and transferred to paper, a wooden press and the availability of an alphabet to allow printing to become a major force in communication.

The geographical containment of Europe and sociological needs of the Renaissance along with four essential elements (paper, ink from painters, a press from the olive and grape vine yards and metal casting from the goldsmiths) and the synthetic genius and tenacity of Gutenberg set the stage for typography. It took yet another 500 years for the age of automated typesetting and computer generated camera ready copy to arrive.

Paper making, a necessary predecessor to printing, came to Europe via the Arabian presence in Spain between the twelfth and the thirteenth centuries. Wood-carving prints survive from the fourteenth century, but the printing industry really started in Germany in 1455 with the invention of metal moveable type and a printing press by Johannes Gutenberg. Gutenberg made molds of individual letters which then could produce many type pieces of the same letter, all identical. The printer then arranged the pieces in a composing stick in the proper order, and fastened each stick onto the press, which could print many copies of each page. Type pieces could then be removed from the composing stick and revised for the next page.

In the first century of printing, printers were publishers and publishers were printers: the printer decided what to print and provided the initial financial investment. In the sixteenth century, as the church and different governments gained control over the trade and determined what would and would not be printed, they granted licensing rights to only a small number of men to produce a small number of politically acceptable books. In England, booksellers were granted these rights rather than the printers, so the printers lost the power to decide what to print, and the publishing industry was born. The English booksellers' guild, called the Stationers' Company, had the authority to inspect any printing office and destroy unauthorized publications, so the members of the company became the sole (legal) publishers in the country, and law-abiding printers worked on commissioned jobs.

Printing and publishing have always been separate ventures in the United States. The Reverend Jose Glover, who might rightfully be called the father of printing in the United States, brought the first printing press from England to America in 1638, and hired Stephen Day, a locksmith, to do the printing. Glover died during the voyage; the press passed to his wife, who brought the press to the newly-established Harvard College. The first president of Harvard, Henry Dunster, oversaw the printing in 1641 of the first book in this country, *The Whole Booke of Psalmes Faithfully Translated into English Meter,* by Stephen Day and his son, Matthew.

The history of the U.S. printing industry is essentially the history of the technology. Minor improvements have driven continuous improvements in the speed and efficiency of the presses, and major new inventions have periodically altered production. In the process of stereotype, molds were made for each page before printing to free the type pieces before the printing process and allow more than one press to be used simultaneously. By the end of the next century, photography was applied to the process, and photoengraving was invented. This process used film, light, and chemical reactions to engrave the text on a thin plate which was then used for printing. New desktop publishing capabilities have demystified the jargon of printing. Now authors are familiar with various type styles, point sizes, and page formats and adapt their computer-generated text at the point of origin to the styles required by publishers.

Composition, the process of setting the type, also underwent several changes. By the late nineteenth century, the invention of the linotype and monotype machines improved typesetting speeds over hand composition. The first quarter of the twentieth century was characterized by innovative and creative breakthroughs in typography driven by consumer needs rather than artistic design, such as sans serif type. In the middle of the twentieth century, the invention of computers revolutionized typesetting once again. Today, the computer is used to set the type, and can either produce a hard copy on paper that is then photographed to make the plates, or can generate the image on film rather than paper to be used immediately to produce a plate; some of the newest machines can even make plates directly from the computer file, sidestepping the film stage completely.

The medium for printed matter is rapidly changing. CD-ROMs, the World Wide Web with its ability to transmit text, color images and even full-motion color video is providing new media for the printed word. Once data or text are entered into a computer for book production, it is an easy step to transmit this data over the wire to a publisher or a consumer.

CURRENT CONDITIONS

The printing industry has been effected predictably by general economic trends. In the economic growth years of the early 1980s the industry grew tremendously. The recession of the early 1990s slowed business dramatically, but a modest recovery was under way by the mid 1990s. School and library budgets were cut, affecting a large part of the market. Like other manufacturers, printers became cautious about adding new equipment and employees, and concentrated on cutting waste and becoming more efficient. The recovery which began in 1992 by and large continues. The publishing industry saw an increase of 2.9 percent in sales, which reached $17.1 billion. In 1995 printers averaged 3 percent in profits, down just slightly from 1994. The leveling off and even discounting of paper prices in 1996 ameliorated a three year trend and made book printing more viable.

The global book market was estimated to be over $80 billion in 1995 representing an 8 percent increase over the previous year. The U.S. book market was placed at $25 billion. After a mid-summer slump in 1996, book sales rebounded in December to finish ahead of 1995 sales in 9 out of 14 categories according to the Association of American Publishers. Increases ranged from 2.3 percent to 21.9 percent, with religious books and juvenile books among the leaders.

The adult trade market momentarily came to a dramatic halt in 1995 when the total number of books dropped significantly due to changes in the adult population and the economy in general. Presidential elections and the Summer Olympics boosted book printing in 1996. However, the restructuring and re-engineering of printing operations, greater variability in sales and profits, technological changes driving the graphic arts industry and a general breakdown in traditional industry boundaries are areas of concern according to Ron Davis, chief economist for Printing Industries of America in the *American Printer*.

The year 1996 saw mixed performance with heavy discounting, an exceptionally large amount of returns, and a decrease in the number of releases. After Amazon's Web marketed book sales went from virtually zero to $15 million dollars in 1996, several book publishers are getting on the electronic highway. Barnes and Noble plans to establish an online supermall on AOLs Marketplace featuring a million titles with substantial reductions for direct online orders. Some corporations experienced a turn around from a losses in 1995 to net income in 1996. Superstores Barnes & Noble, Borders Groups, Crown Books and Books-A-Million combined sales increased from $2.7 billion to $3.2 billion.

Book publishers have expressed concerns about the over expansion of superstores (expected to grow from 800 in 1996 to 1,500 stores within the next few years), the distraction of the Net, a confused market and changing life styles. Barnes & Noble is currently the largest chain with 440 of the superstores, followed by Borders Books & Music, and Crown Books. In the first three quarters of 1996 sales of the top four superstore chains grew to $3.2 billion. Media Play, a division of Musician is closing 29 of its 98 stores. Media Play, On Cue and Books-A-Million are likely to close, merge or cutback according to *Publishers Weekly*.

Acquisitions and mergers in the printing industry have continued to grow. Graphic Industries and Consolidated Graphics were two of the leading acquirers. Of the 59 total number of mergers in the printing, publishing and allied services industry in 1994, four were U.S. companies acquiring foreign companies and only one was a foreign company acquiring a U.S. company. More than one-half of the top printing companies were involved in acquisitions in 1995/96 reflecting an ongoing trend. Mergers and acquisitions are now demanding closer scrutiny of operations with a bottom-line orientation in order to satisfy their investors.

The value of book shipments was placed at $24.1 billion in 1994. The value of shipments for book printing alone was $5.1 billion in 1995 compared to $20.9 billion for all book publishing. U.S. Book exports were up the first 6 months of 1996 by 1.5 percent. Book title output in 1995 was estimated to be down from the previous year by approximately 6,000, an estimated 44,857.

New media formats are redefining the word printing to at least include CD-ROMs, electronic publishing, etc. Many reference books and technical manuals are now sold with a CD-ROM in their pocket. The number of CD-ROM book titles continues to rise rapidly from 956 in 1994 to 1,131 in 1995 with average prices hovering around $1,900 per title compared to the average price of $44.66 per volume (1995 preliminary) for U.S. hardcover books. The compound annual growth rate of spending on books is projected to remain fairly constant from 5.5 percent during 1990-1995 to 5.3 percent during the period from 1995 to 2000. Personal consumption of books and maps was up slightly from $19.1 billion in the previous year to $19.4 billion in 1995.

The hours per person per year consumers spend reading books continues to rise from earlier years and is projected to become 105 in 1999. Correspondingly the number of dollars spent for consumer books per year is projected to rise to $107.19 in 1999. The number of hours spent reading daily newspapers and consumer magazines is expected to decline over the same time period. Consumer spending for books per person in 1994 was second only to basic cable in the communications industry which also includes home video, recorded music, newspapers and magazines.

The perception of the industry is changing as the diversification of media for transmitting information increases. There is a growing tendency for the industry to view itself as being in the information business and to provide the message regardless of the medium using alternative media. Increased attention is being paid to the marketing end of the printed or produced product, to digital technology, and to establishing a place on the information highway via whatever process is necessary.

Some major trends that could impact the growth of the printing and publishing industry are general business investment levels, high consumer debt and inflation due to increased wage demands. Print as a mass medium is expected to top out in 1997. Although the industry will not decline, it is expected to fragment along the lines of technologies and be absorbed by online services and publishing.

INDUSTRY LEADERS

The top seven printing firms in 1996 according to *Graphic Arts Monthly* in its GAM 101 Official Ranking list were R.R. Donnelley & Sons, Quebecor Printing, Moore Corporation, World Color, Deluxe Corporation, Banta Corporation and Quad/Graphics. This list includes commercial, book, business forms and other printing categories.

A few large corporations dominate the book printing industry. Some are part of large conglomerates that also own publishing houses. Bertelsmann USA, the American branch of a German media conglomerate, includes Bertelsmann Printing and Manufacturing Corporation, but also the Bantam Doubleday Dell publishing group. Bertelsmann's book product group, now its second largest segment, rose to $4.59 billion in fiscal 1996 and its printing, paper and other technical services rose to $2.36 billion.

The largest printing companies have subsidiaries all over the country and the world. R.R. Donnelly and Sons, headquartered in Chicago and considered by *Graphic Arts Monthly* to be the largest printer in the United States has operations in over 80 sites around the world, with facilities in Iowa, Virginia, North Carolina, and Arizona, as well as London, Tokyo, Barbados, and Ireland.

The three largest American printing companies began to see healthy sales at the beginning of the economic recovery. Sales for R.R. Donnelly and Sons, which prints books, magazines, catalogs, directories, and newspapers, reached $6.5 billion in fiscal 1996. Quebecor Printing, a Canadian firm with American subsidiaries that prints books, directories, magazines, and catalogues, had $3 billion in sales in 1995/96. Quebecor had an average compound growth rate of 19 percent from 1990 to 1995 driven in part by U.S. and European acquisitions. When it completed its acquisition of Arcata Corp in 1994 at an estimated 192 million dollars, it added a distribution facility and five book manufacturing plants.

Arcata Graphics Company was the third largest book printing firm in the country, began as a lumber business, and entered into printing with their acquisition of plants in Tennessee and Massachusetts in 1969. In the early 1990s they owned 10 plants and employed 6,200 people. Their clients had included Random House, Crown Publishers, Harper and Row, and Farrar, Strauss, and Giroux.

Arcata's book plants offered full service facilities with composition computers for the initial steps and bindery operations for the final ones. They printed medium to large size runs, producing anywhere between 10,000 and 1,100,000 books in a single run. In December of 1992, the company had already sold three of their non-book printing plants to Quebecor. It concentrated on book printing in part, at least, because of their belief that, as Ed Owens of Arcata Graphics told *Publisher's Weekly,* "I can not see any reason the American Public is going to quit buying books." Banta Information Services Group expanded its overseas operations in 1994.

BookCrafters, a vertically integrated company that is now 32 years old, has emerged to a fulfill special niche by printing, storing and shipping books for publisher in specialized markets as well as self-publishers. It uses 21 presses, web, belt roll-fed and color sheet feed presses in addition to its own in-house bindery.

One example of short run printers is the Thomas-Shore company of Dexter, Michigan. It is a small company, but a leader among short run printers. It was founded by Ned Thomson and Harry Shore, both of whom worked for another Ann Arbor, Michigan small press, left their jobs and started their own company with their own business philosophy. Decisions were made by committees of employees, who own one third of the company. They employ no sales force. "Customers come to us, and we've made our entire effort based on the idea that quality would sell for us if we did better than our competition."

After almost twenty years of just printing books, Thomson-Shore began to branch out into pre- and post-press activities. They added a bindery operation and a page-making program for their computers with an eye towards eventual composition work. They specialize in short runs. Reprint costs are considered cheaper than carrying long-term inventories. Thomson-Shore's average runs are between 300 and 5000 copies.

WORK FORCE

Printing companies employ skilled technicians, mid-level management, and high-level management. The actual production is carried out by skilled workers using highly complex machines. Vocational and technical colleges offer training, as do some high schools and two year colleges. Workers can often rise to mid-level management jobs, such as foreman or production control. A college education is frequently required for the higher-level management positions. A few schools offer degrees in printing technology, but science, art, or business degrees can also be helpful.

Printing occupations are divided into three main stages: prepress, press and binding or post-press. The industry is rapidly moving to "digital imaging" or direct conversion of customer submitted computerized text to printing plates. Typesetting and layout is frequently done prior to coming to press and increasingly at the source. Authors now produce their product on a pre-formatted computerized layout that is transmitted directly to the publisher via e-mail or disk. Hot type composition has been replaced with electronic type or computer-to-plate technology.

According to the 1996-97 *U.S. Occupational Outlook Handbook* there were 169,000 prepress workers in 1994 of which 25,000 were prepress machine operators. An overall decline in prepress worker positions is expected through 2005. Hourly wages ranged from $17 to $21 per hour in 1995. The increase in at-source typesetting and layout is likely to eliminate many jobs in this area, even though the demand for printed products is anticipated to grow. Smaller presses will provide the best opportunity for new entrants.

The 244,000 printing press operators in 1994 were expected to grow in number through 2005 but at a slower rate than other occupations. New jobs will result from U.S. expansion into foreign markets and more direct mail advertising. Hourly wages for printing press operators in 1994 (the latest available rates) ran from $11 to $19 per hour. Average hourly earnings of non-supervisory workers in the printing and publishing at large has remained relatively stable over the past several years and was between $12 and $13 per hour in 1996.

Book printing is largely dependent on the publishing industry. The printing and publishing industry combined experienced a growth in employment from 1.2 million workers in 1983 to 1.5 million in 1994 or annual growth rate of 1.6, with a projected growth rate of 0.5 to 1.6 million workers from 1994-2005. The total number of employees in the book printing industry alone rose from 121,000 to 123,000 from 1990 to 1995, while production workers dropped slightly from 66,000 to 65,000. The average hourly earnings of production workers rose from $10.10 to 11.57 per hour during the same period.

AMERICA AND THE WORLD

Historically, printing has been a national business. American copyright laws have kept foreign printers from American publishers, and American printers have been kept busy with the domestic market. In the early 1990s, however, American printers began to take on more international business. Long-standing disadvantages to overseas work include language barriers, shipping costs, cultural differences, and periodically fluctuating exchange rates. As the Eastern Block countries began to open up, however, American technology and supplies, far superior to those available in many other countries, became increasingly in demand. Some companies, like R. R. Donnelly, have subsidiaries overseas as well. Exports in the printing and publishing industries grew steadily in the 1990s.

A favorable balance of trade exists in the book industry in spite of a surge in U.S. imports due to the strength of the dollar in 1995, with a ratio of exports to imports of 1.41 in 1995, though down slightly from previous years. The value of all U.S. book exports totaled $1.7 billion in 1995 and 885.5 millions of copies shipped. This represented a 4 percent increase in exports from 1994 to 1995. Japan and Columbia who had the largest number of printing contracts experienced a 10 percent decline in contracts. China and Mexico absorbed some of these contracts. In 1994 NAFTA impacted the book printing industry by heating up the Mexican market where U.S. printers are competing for Mexican work. Pesano Printing of San Francisco has opened offices in Mexico. Book imports totaled $1.2 billion.

After experiencing a rapid growth rate, Japan's printing related industries experienced a downward trend in 1996. This was documented in the reduction in the production of printing machines, plate-making machines and bookbinding machines, in part reflecting export reactions to changes in the yen. Book printers in Hong Kong are migrating to mainland China.

RESEARCH AND TECHNOLOGY

Book printers are becoming increasingly responsive to the needs of their different customers. Publishing firms that need large quantities of best sellers are only one segment of their market. Today there are increased demands for shorter runs, quicker turn around in a computer environment. The printing industry has sought new technology to meet these needs.

Small publishers, and publishers producing books with limited appeal, such as university presses and the scholarship they support, frequently do not want large runs of books. Usually, the fewer the books printed at one time, the more each book costs to make, primarily because of the time needed for composition. Because more and more publishers are gravitating toward shorter runs, to cut down on storage costs and to realistically reflect the market, book printers are beginning to specialize in smaller runs, with new computer composition techniques. Computer graphics produce illustrations more efficiently than draftsmen. New machinery has introduced new methods of plate production directly from a computer file without the middle step of a film. Each reduction in the time and cost of composing reduces the cost and increases the efficiency of shorter book runs. Some companies can produce any number of books—from 25 to 5000—cost effectively.

Newer formats, such as CD-ROMS and Web publishing, can demand new skills but increase profitability. Printing on demand is also becoming popular and necessary. Computer storage and laser technology means that books need never be out of print. On demand and short-run color printing bypasses film intermediaries, creates printed images directly from data and is growing twice as fast as conventional printing. Digital printing systems are impacting on printing. The definition of a digital color press varies although most use electrophotographic imaging. E-Print 1000, Xeikon, or Agfa Chromapress represent some of this new equipment. CTP (Computer-to-plate) such as Linotype Hell's Gutenberg, was suggested in 1995 as a major trend in the next 5 years. Over 1,600 shops planned to buy this technology as early as in 1995. This digital electronic printing is expected to grow to a $2 billion dollar industry by 1998 according to James Vanderslice of Pennant, the IBM Printing Systems, Company in *Marketing News.*

Many large industrial or technological firms need to produce manuals for their employees and consumers, but do not want to get into the printing business. Companies, such as Corporate Publishing Ser-

vices of Freemont, California, were established to fill their needs. Its goal was to take data from their clients, usually in the form of computer files, and with their high-quality computer printers, xerographic copying machines, and in-house bindery presses, provide custom quantities of publications within hours. Recent advances in computer laser printing and computer composition have made this realistic and economically feasible. An overall increase in the book buying population, the NAFTA (North American Free Trade Agreement) which should favor increased exports, the GATT (General Agreement on Tariffs and Trade) which should increase royalties through better protection of copyrights, and improved technology should favor the industry. The biggest challenges facing the industry will be to increase productivity while keeping up with new technological developments and new media formats.

FURTHER READING

Adams, J. Michael, David D. Faux, and Lloyd J. Rieber. *Printing Technology.* 3rd ed. Albany, NY: Delmar Publishers, 1988.

Baker, John F. "Big Changes Seen for Arcata, Quebecor." *Publishers Weekly,* 7 December 1992.

———. "Whatever Happened to the Book Market?" *Publishers Weekly,* 6 January 1997.

"B&N Will Launch Online Bookstore on AOL." *Publishers Weekly,* 3 February 1997.

The Bowker Annual Library and Book Trade Almanac. 41st ed. New Providence, NJ: R.R. Bowker, 1996.

"The China Syndrome." *Publishers Weekly,* 26 September 1994.

Cross, Lisa. "The GAM 101: Official 1996 Ranking of the Industry's Top Printing Firms." *Graphic Arts Monthly,* August 1996.

Delano, Daryl. "Economic Outlook: Rollin' But Slowin'." *Graphic Arts Monthly,* December 1996.

Dilger, Karen Abramic. "Pressing On." *American Printer,* October 1996.

Ducey, Micahel J. "Newsprint Prices Take a Dive." *Graphic Arts Monthly,* September 1996.

Encyclopedia of Associations. 32nd ed. Detroit: Gale Research, 1997.

Encyclopedia of Associations: International Organizations: 1997. 31st ed. Detroit: Gale Research, 1996.

Ferris, Fren. "Book Smart." *American Printer,* September 1992.

"Foreign Trade." *American Printer,* November 1991.

"The Foremost Ranking of Top Printing Companies." *American Printer,* July 1992.

Goddard, Connie. "Working Smarter, Not Harder." *Publishers Weekly,* 31 May 1991.

Greenfeld, Howard. *Books: From Writer to Reader.* New York: Crown, 1976.

Hilts, Paul. "Arcata/Kingsport Turns 70 Years Young." *Publishers Weekly,* 13 July 1992.

Jeffrey, Noel. "Globe-trotters." *American Printer,* October 1994.

Lottman, Herbert R. "Bertelsmann Sales Rise 5% in Fiscal '96; Books Now No. 2." *Publishers Weekly,* 9 September 1996.

McMurtrie, Douglas. *The Book: The Story of Printing & Bookmaking.* New York: Oxford University Press, 1976 [c1943.

Millardi, Vincent. "Hot Markets for 1997." *American Printer,* December 1996.

———. "Trading Partners." *American Printer,* September 1994.

Millot, Jim. "New Study Puts Global Book Market at $80 Million." *Publishers Weekly,* 14 October 1996.

———. "Trade Sales Jump in December, But Year-End is Soft." *Publishers Weekly,* 17 February 1997.

Mutter, John. "One Size Doesn't Fit All." *Publishers Weekly,* 6 January 1977.

Peterson, Debbie. "Be a Best Seller." *American Printer,* September 1992.

———. "The State of Plates." *American Printer,* February 1992.

Piechowski, Rod. "From Cover to Cover." *American Printer,* June 1990.

"Print Down, Not Out." *American Printer,* September 1996.

"Print Markets and the Recession." *American Printer,* January 1993.

"Quebecor Finalizes Arcata Deal." *Graphic Arts Monthly,* August 1994.

"Quebecor Printing, Inc.: Pressing All the Right Buttons." *Canadian Shareowner,* March/April 1996.

Rosen, Robert H. "Coping with a Changing Industry." *American Printer,* August 1991.

Roth, Jill. "Modest Expansion." *American Printer,* December 1996.

———. "Open Borders." *American Printer,* July 1995.

———. "Tracking the Trends." *American Printer,* July 1995.

Sharples, Hadley. "Innovators Sculpt and On-Demand Market." *Graphic Arts Monthly,* September 1994.

———. "New Technologies Divide Short-Run, On-Demand." *Graphic Arts Monthly,* September 1995.

Shirai, Hiroshi. "Developments in Japan's Printing-Related Industry." *Japan 21st,* April 1996.

Taylor, Sally. "Bertelsmann Targets a New World in Publishing." *Publishers Weekly,* 12 July 1991.

"Technology Update." *American Printer,* July 1995.

"Tracking the Trends." *American Printer,* July 1996.

"U.S. Book Exports Edge Up 5.5%." *Publishers Weekly,* 9 September 1996.

U.S. Department of Commerce. Economics and Statistics Administration. Bureau of the Census. *Statistical Abstract of the United States 1996.* 116th ed. Washington: GPO, 1996.

U.S. Department of Commerce. Economics and Statistics Administration. Bureau of Economic Analysis. *Survey of Current Business.* Washington: GPO, 1997.

U.S. Department of Labor. Bureau of Labor Statistics. "15. Average Hourly Earnings of Production or Nonsupervisory Workers on Private Nonfarm Payrolls, by Industry." *Monthly Labor Review,* November 1996.

U.S. Department of Labor. Bureau of Labor Statistics. *Occupational Outlook Handbook.* Washington: GPO, 1996.

U.S. Industry Profiles, Detroit: Gale Research, 1995.

"Veronis, Suhler Study Sees Spending on Books Slowing." Includes chart: "Compound Annual Growth Rate of Spending on Books." *Publishers Weekly,* 19 August 1996.

Vincour, Richard M. "What's Behind the Urge to Merge?" *American Printer,* November 1996.

—Robin Armstrong, updated by David C. Genaway

SIC 2741

MISCELLANEOUS PUBLISHING

This classification includes establishments primarily engaged in miscellaneous publishing activities, not elsewhere classified, whether or not engaged in printing. This includes the publishing of atlases, business service newsletters, calendars, catalogs, directories, guides, maps and map globe covers, paper patterns, race track programs, racing forms, sheet music, shopping news, technical manuals and papers, telephone directories, and yearbooks, as well as the activity of micropublishing.

INDUSTRY SNAPSHOT

Miscellaneous publishers tend to be specialized within their respective categories. However, in addition to independent publishing companies, some book and periodical publishers also have divisions or departments engaged in miscellaneous publishing. The industry spans a range of some of the largest companies in publishing down to sole-proprietorship enterprises. The activities of some miscellaneous publishers more closely resemble book publishers, while others more closely resemble periodical publishers.

ORGANIZATION AND STRUCTURE

The largest category within miscellaneous publishing, comprising about a third of the industry's revenues, is telephone directory publishing. There are over 6,000 telephone directories published in the United States annually by approximately 200 publishers. This includes both telephone companies or their subsidiaries and independent publishing companies. There are several kinds of telephone directories. The utility, or core directory, is the standard directory provided by telephone companies for their service areas, with an edition distributed free to the owner of each phone line. Directories for smaller regional areas, such as a specific town, neighborhood, or larger regions than the core directories cover, may be published by either a telephone company or an independent publisher. Telephone company publishers also publish business-to-business directories whose listings include establishments that would be of interest to other businesses. Finally, there are independent companies that publish special interest directories, such as those targeted at specific ethnic groups.

The telephone directory publishing industry is often synonymous with the term yellow pages publishing, because the same companies publish both comprehensive alphabetical telephone listings and categorized paid advertising listings known generically as yellow pages. Even if certain directory editions do not contain classified business listings, their publishers earn their revenues from the yellow pages that they publish, whether as part of a directory or in a separate volume. Telephone directory publishing is thus an unusual industry, because the bulk of its revenues are earned through advertising services and not the selling of the publications. The yellow pages account for 85 percent of the directory printing market.

Directories. Directories that do not base their revenues on selling advertising space usually provide more comprehensive information on their entries than merely the telephone number and street address—and list individuals or organizations based on a common specialization. These directories are published by a different category of publishers than the telephone directory publishers. These publishers typically create and own their own databases of information to be published. Directory publishers may be primarily publishers of periodicals, such as trade journals, and publish directories focused on their journals' specialization. Other comprehensive directories, which provide substantive additional information, are published by

reference book publishers. Directories are also published by nonprofit organizations, such as professional or trade associations.

Two new revenue streams are emerging for directory publishers: as reference works and as sources of names and addresses for new business purposes. Beardsley Ruml began producing medical directories in 1995, recognizing a market for publishing directories of physician practices. This Medical Support Systems group, which started in the early 1990s was predicted to gross over $5 million in before-tax revenues in 1996. Demand for these directories was attributed to the growing retirement population and the emergence of managed care operators.

Catalogs. The catalog industry is primarily a printing industry, because catalogs are usually produced on contract for manufacturing, wholesale, or retail companies for the marketing of their products. In some cases, however, publisher-printers create catalogs on their own as a business initiative.

Business Service Newsletters. Newsletters became a billion dollar-plus business in 1995, and the field is crowded with more than 5,000 publications. Nearly half of their income is from related products and services, as these publications depend heavily on revenues from advertising. Profitability is also tied to the cost of postage.

The distinction between business service newsletters and regular periodical publishing is often blurred. In general, business service newsletters contain no advertisements, charge high subscription rates, are narrowly focused, and contain articles, tables, or graphs oriented toward data rather than commentary. Such newsletters are often available in electronic form in addition to or instead of print. Companies in this industry may be independent firms, but the largest publishers are often divisions or subsidiaries of market research or financial information services firms. Other business service publications besides newsletters are sometimes grouped with this category; these would include such publications as bibliographic databases.

Relatively new is fax publishing, which is usually done on demand. By the mid-1990s, the total newsletter business had become more than a billion dollar business. While there were some concerns about postal rates, many publishers cut costs by reducing paper weight, and more accurately targeting their audiences.

Sheet Music. Like trade book publishers, publishers of sheet music publish, market, and hold existing copyrights to creative works of independent composers and lyric authors. Many music publishers, however, derive the majority of their revenues from sources other than sheet music, namely from performance royalties or recorded music royalties for the music to which they own the copyrights. Thus, these publishers are categorized instead under the financial industry for patent and trademark owners and lessors. Publishers that gain most of their business from printed sheet music publishing, and thus are part of the miscellaneous publishing industry, tend to be publishers of classical music, in which most of the written music is in the public domain and no royalties are paid. Sheet music publishers may also publish collections of their music as books.

Maps and Atlases. Map and atlas publishers create maps with their own copyright, using data from public domain geographic surveys. The publishers' cartographers draw up their own maps according to these surveys, altering the map sizes and adding or deleting data to the maps. Major publishers publish their maps both in book form as atlases and as free-standing poster-style maps. Smaller map publishers create local and regional maps for their local market. Smaller cartographic companies draw up maps on request for clients, which are typically book publishers and advertising agencies. Other book or periodical publishers may also publish atlases as a secondary activity.

Trading Cards. The trading card industry is dominated by baseball cards, but also includes the publishing of other sports cards and entertainment cards, depicting personalities or scenes from films, television shows, and music. Companies may publish a full range of cards or they may specialize. In the early 1990s, 60 percent of the trading card publishing business was in baseball cards, with about 81 billion cards produced annually; 11 percent of the cards were for football, 8 percent for basketball, 3 percent for hockey, 3 percent for other sports, and 15 percent for entertainment cards. Sport trading card publishers have licenses from the professional sports leagues and pay royalties to the players or teams pictured. There are approximately 100 companies in the sports and entertainment trading card business. Sport cards were originally sold with bubble gum, but are increasingly sold separately and marketed toward adult collectors. Trading card publishers are often categorized under the printing industry instead of publishing. The value of individual cards after time has been proven by such instances as a single 1910 baseball card, which was sold for $640,500 in 1996—and was immediately advertised for sale for $1 million.

Calendars. Approximately 200 companies published calendars in the United States in the mid-1990s. These comprise both specialized calendar publishers and those with other publishing or non-publishing activities. The industry does not include the multitude of companies that have calendars produced in their name as marketing devices. The Millennium Planner, the first full column calendar for the year 2000, was published by Viking Studio Books in 1995. Calendars are among the most effective conventional ways to boost business.

Micropublishing. Micropublishing comprises microfilm and microfiche publishing, known collectively as microform. Publishing on microform typically involves the reproduction of printed material, especially periodicals, for distribution primarily to libraries. Microform publishers usually are not the original copyright holders of documents, but must obtain licenses from the original print publishers to publish microform editions. Newspapers and magazines are usually reproduced on reels of microfilm, whereas government documents and telephone directories are the texts most commonly published on microfiche. Some print publishers, such as The New York Times Company, publish their own microform versions.

UMI, a Bell & Howell company, has been aggressively acquiring business information service providers such as Data Times, establishing cooperative relationships with index producers, and making the Worldwide Web central to its strategy. Both text and images from more than 3,000 journals, magazines, and other titles were available from Telnet, CD-ROMs, or the Web using its ProQuest Direct services and Z39.50 compliant servers. Selected articles indexed in ABI/Inform and Periodicals Abstracts are provided directly to library users in seconds upon their request from any terminal they are using. OCLC, the largest provider of library services, has agreed to make such access available via its Web site. Electronic, on demand publishing, and delivery of archived articles will continue to make UMI a viable force. The foremost publisher of microfilm for other newspapers, magazines, and academic dissertations is University Microfilms International. Microforms have not yet been completely replaced with electronic, digitized formats, however.

BACKGROUND AND DEVELOPMENT

Telephone Directories. The first telephone directory, which listed 50 names, was published in New Haven, Connecticut, in 1878, just two years after Alexander Graham Bell invented the telephone. The first directory with classified business headings was published in 1883. It is said that the first yellow pages were printed in 1883 when a printer in Cheyenne, Wyoming, ran out of white paper and had to use yellow sheets instead. Telephone directories were originally produced as a service for telephone users, and the business of taking in revenues from advertising developed later.

The telephone company American Telephone and Telegraph (AT&T), a major phone company in the United States, became the largest directory publisher, earning more than $1.5 million from its yellow pages business in the late 1970s. AT&T had introduced the name Yellow Pages and the famous walking fingers logo, but chose not to trademark either name or logo, which have since been adopted by numerous publishers. When AT&T divested its Bell companies in 1984, the directory publishing business was also divided among the seven new regional holding companies, resulting in a publishing subsidiary or division for each company. This led to greater competition for advertisers, as the regional Bell companies introduced directories for regions beyond their own service areas. Meanwhile, independent yellow pages publishers had existed for decades.

The yellow pages industry grew rapidly in the 1980s from revenues of $2.9 billion in 1980 to $8.9 billion in 1990, including non-publishing marketing and advertising service sales. The number of directory editions published increased steadily to a peak of 6,500 in 1986, when the number began to decline somewhat. The regional Bell companies withdrew to publishing for only their own territories in response to consumer confusion and advertiser complaints over multiple yellow pages for the same region. Also, some niche publications, such as one by Southwestern Bell that targeted the elderly, were unsuccessful. Although traditionally considered a recession-proof industry, yellow pages advertising sales slowed, but did not decline during the recession of 1990-92.

Several trends affected yellow pages publishing in the early 1990s. Publishers are increasingly relying on third-party marketing agencies. The industry was working toward a standardized advertising menu in 1993. Targeted niche marketing is being further developed. The growth of 800 numbers has led to an increase in national advertising whereby a company chooses to advertise in various yellow pages throughout the country. Recently, audiotex services were being introduced in some areas. Sometimes referred to as "talking yellow pages," voice information services permit callers to enter in codes for information on the advertised product or service. Yellow pages publishers, both independent and utility, are teaming up with newspaper publishers to offer these information services. Another trend among telephone directory publishers is a greater dedication to community service with the publishing of community-oriented information pages. Recently efforts were made to overcome the old dusty image and to consider the yellow pages as the first place to shop. Directories rating World Wide Web sites for beginners and listings or evaluations of CD-ROMs are also being published.

CURRENT CONDITIONS

The total value of shipments for miscellaneous publishing as a whole was $12.3 billion in 1994, up from $8.4 billion in 1992, and was projected to reach $13.3 billion in 1995.

Tourism is boosting sales of atlases and maps and foreign language phrase books by providing new markets. Duty-free atlases, calendars, and catalogs have been eagerly exported to Mexico's print hungry market since the passage of the North American Free Trade Agreement (NAFTA).

About 60 percent of the catalog producers expect to use more paper in 1996, reflecting confidence in the stability of paper prices. The *Catalog Age Benchmark Report* expressed concerns about postal rate increases that have led to static page counts among 55 percent of the catalog producers; however, 33 percent actually planned to increase page counts. Fewer catalog printers plan to print their primary catalog on recycled paper, down to 25 percent as compared to 67 percent two years ago. There is a rapid movement toward electronic cataloging and consolidating design and prepress operations to bring them in-house.

Revenues for telephone directories in 1995 were $5.4 billion. The yellow pages industry as a whole, which includes advertising-related services, had much higher revenues, totaling more than $10 billion in 1996. Directories received a 10.5 percent market share of press advertising expenditures, ahead of consumer magazines, which accounted for 8.5 percent. With the passage of the new telecommunications law, yellow pages ad agencies foresaw new growth for the $10 billion directory advertising market. Amid the emergence of local phone competition and Internet yellow pages, industry advertising revenues were projected to increase 5.9 percent in 1997.

Sheet music publishing generated global royalty revenues of $604.12 million, or 10 percent of all royalty revenues, in the mid-1990s, according to the National Music Publishers' Association. This figure includes $68.91 million from rentals and public lending. The United States led this category with $187.30 million or 31 percent of worldwide total printed music sales. A total of $5.83 billion for all revenues in 1994 made up largely of royalty payments for the entire music publishing industry compares with gross revenues of $1.10 billion in 1991. Growth in sheet music publishing revenues is limited by the tendency toward copyright violations. Since sheet music is usually only a few pages long, it is easily photocopied illegally.

Sheet music publisher Warner/Chappell Music, Inc. acquired CPP Belwin, the second largest printed music company in the United States in the mid-1990s. Warner/Chappel is a unit of Time Inc.'s Warner Music. The combined company will operate under the Warner Brothers Publications, Inc. umbrella.

The trading card industry has had to adapt to survive a shaken market that resulted from the baseball strike, experiencing a 22 percent loss in supermarket sales in 1994, after a 25 percent loss in 1993. The trading card category of supermarket sales represented $1.4 billion in 1996. Sports fans showed a renewed interest, and a 5 percent increase in trading card sales was predicted for 1996. In addition to separate trading card stores, Pinnacle Brands has promoted displays in supermarkets to market cards. Meanwhile, the secondary market of dealers and collectors has been growing recently due to increases in sales to adults, sophistication in marketing, and the use of nonexclusive licensing contracts by professional sport leagues as a means of improving their images and marketing their players and teams.

Alliances with Kodak, MCA, Marvel Entertainment Group, and the like were tapped to promote card sales. Fleer Ultra, Upper Deck, Topps Stadium Club, and SkyBox Premium companies were brought together for a point-of-purchase promotion in 1996. One of the challenges was to keep up with the increasing number of brands, since there were as many as 40 brands in the late 1990s.

Globe publishing began with Johann Schiner, a German mathematician, who was the first to produce globes in quantity in 1515, shortly after the appearance of the printing press. Antique globes are now attracting the attention of collectors, and auction prices for eighteenth century versions have brought up to $20,000.

The super graphics segment of the industry (oversized posters, murals, banners, signs, and maps) has been expanding into new markets such as ''tied'' formats in large collages and historical exhibits. Using new technology, they then print on transfer paper to vinyl, textiles, canvases, and even wood. Large-format output is one of the largest areas of anticipated growth.

INDUSTRY LEADERS

The major telephone directory publishers are the seven regional Bell companies—Bell Atlantic Corporation, Bell South Corporation, Pacific Telesis Group's Pacific Bell Directory subsidiary, Nynex Corporation,

U.S. West Incorporated, Southwestern Bell Corporation, and Ameritech Corporation—as well as GTE Corporation, United Telecom, Sprint, Reuben H. Donnelley Corporation, and DonTech (a joint venture of Ameritech and Reuben H. Donnelley).

U.S. West acquired Thomson Directories, U.K. competitor to the Yellow Pages directory, from Dun & Bradstreet Corporation and Thomson Corporation in 1994. Banta Corporation has expanded into non-traditional media such as CD-ROMs in addition to its catalogues and educational materials. CDs have the advantage of low costs, compact size, and standardization and are an ideal publishing format for business consumers. Florida Directory Publishing ceased publication of its yellow pages in selected areas. GTE Directories consolidated two publications of two neighboring cities in adjacent states into one to save the cost of dual ads for advertisers.

The leading business service publishers include Dow Jones and Company Incorporated; Dun & Bradstreet Corporation and its Moody's Investors Service subsidiary; Thomson Information Publishing Group; Value Line Incorporated; and Disclosure Incorporated.

The largest music publishers include Hal Leonard Publishing Corporation, EMI Music Publishing Worldwide, and CPP/Belwin Incorporated. The biggest catalog publisher-printer is R.R. Donnelley and Sons Company. Another leader is World Color Press Incorporated.

The leading publishers of sports cards, based on mid-1990s market share, were Upper Deck, with 24 percent of the market, Topps Company Incorporated—historically the market leader—with 22 percent, Marvel Entertainments Group Incorporated's Fleer with 22 percent, Score Group Incorporated with 10 percent, and Leaf Incorporated's Donruss division with 8 percent.

The top map publisher was Rand McNally Company, which sells more than 10 million road atlases annually, accounting for 12 percent of its estimated $439 million in revenues in the mid-1990s. The U.S. subsidiaries of Munich-based Langenscheidt are second in sales combined. Third was Simon & Schuster, which owns Mobil Road Atlas and H.M. Gousha, and fourth was Hammond Incorporated. The nonprofit National Geographic Society was also a major publisher of maps and atlases. Thomas Brothers, a privately owned producer of street maps, grossed $21 million in sales in 1994 and was working on a digital mapping of all its guides. In 1995, maps and guides maintained their traditional importance in the incentives market despite high-tech alternatives.

The leading school yearbook publishing and printing companies were Taylor Publishing Company and Jostens Incorporated. The largest clothing patterns manufacturer was Butterick Company Incorporated with sales of $130 million.

WORK FORCE

The miscellaneous publishing industry was one of the top 20 industries at the three-digit SIC level for rate of employee growth during the 1980s. Its work force increased 79.6 percent between 1979 and 1989. The work force in all categories of miscellaneous publishing was approximately 84,100 in 1995, of which 49,100 were women and 39,700 were production workers. In 1995 the production worker's wage rate averaged $11.68 per hour. While the industry's work force is not expected to maintain the high growth of the 1980s, it is predicted to be the fastest growing category of the publishing and printing industries, to reach around 1.13 million workers in the year 2000.

AMERICA AND THE WORLD

Had it not been for the breakup of AT&T, the United States might have had the largest yellow pages publisher in the world, but that honor goes to Bell Canada's subsidiary Tele-Direct Publications. Tele-Direct and U.S. publishers both have expanded their operations overseas in countries where no large-scale yellow pages had existed. While local and national telephone utilities continue to publish the alphabetical directories, the commercial market has been left wide open for experienced North American publishers. Tele-Direct has been actively publishing yellow pages through joint ventures, especially in the Middle East. More recently, U.S. publishers have won contracts to publish directories in Eastern Europe and Russia as those countries move to a free-market economy. In 1992, Nynex Information Resources Company won the contract for publishing the Prague yellow pages in the Czech Republic. An international yellow pages publisher can also offer international advertising exposure to its advertising clients within a common commercial region of more than one country.

Sheet music publishing is a lucrative international business, along with music publishing as a whole. Publishers contract with licensed distribution agents in each country or region in which they distribute their music. In printed music, the United States is the world leader. The revenues of U.S. music publishers have been growing faster internationally than domestically. The United States is followed by Germany with 21.4 percent of the world market share, while companies located in the United Kingdom command 12 percent of the market.

Business service publishers are increasingly marketing their publications internationally to serve business people interested in market conditions in different countries. Newsletters are much lighter than business magazines and therefore ship well by airmail. Whether companies are sending articles, bibliographic or directory databases, or numeric tables, business service publications in electronic formats are by far the easiest to ''export.''

RESEARCH AND TECHNOLOGY

More so than the other publishing industries, miscellaneous publishing is rapidly being transformed by the adoption of electronic media, such as CD-ROM and online services. Many publishers of printed material have begun publishing versions of their books or periodicals on CD-ROM, while others license their data to specialized CD-ROM publishers and online vendors. A wide range of miscellaneous publishing exists on CD-ROM: telephone directories, other directories, maps, business service publications, business newsletters, guides, and even forms of catalogs and yearbooks. Some business service publishers now publish more information in electronic form than either print or microform. Fax and online information services are being utilized especially by business newsletter publishers, who need to provide speedy delivery of information.

CD-ROMs have the physical attributes, low production costs, and standardization necessary to make it an almost ideal medium for publishing, data distribution and archival material for the business consumer. Computerized maps of the entire United States with adjustable scales now fit on one CD-ROM. Rand McNally, along with several other map producers, have expanded into the CD-ROM market. One CD-ROM can contain maps of the entire United States. Leading products are produced by DeLorme, Adept Computer Solutions, and Rand McNally. McNally's Tripmaker edged out Microsoft's Automap in 1995. New products and markets include outsized posters, banners, and maps for exhibits or murals and a variety of surfaces. In 1995, there were in excess of 9,500 CD-ROM titles. CD-ROM copies of many reference books and technical manuals now accompany them. CD-ROMS are increasingly used for technical manuals because of their ease of indexing and compactness. The manufacturing industry at large still relies heavily on paper technical manuals, however.

Some might categorize CD-ROM (compact disc read-only memory) the newest category of miscellaneous publishing in the micropublishing industry. Indeed, an entire industry has emerged since the last revision of the Standard Industrial Classification system. Since CD-ROM is merely a medium for data, it is the type of data written on it that best determines the classification of its producers. If the data are principally text, then the CD-ROM producer is classified under the appropriate publishing industry. Although all CD-ROMs contain some computer software, if the software is the primary feature of the CD-ROM product, such as in an interactive game, then the producer would be classified under the computer software industry. New DVD (digital video discs) will provide specialty multimedia opportunities.

Recent innovations in trading cards includes SpaceMark's talking cards with 90 seconds of permanently stored voice recordings with musical accompaniment. Several companies are producing other high technology cards, for example Upper Deck's Holoview line of holographic images that seem to make players come to life.

FURTHER READING

1990-91 International Survey of Music Publishing Revenues. New York: National Music Publishers' Association, 1992.

"A Deal in Printed Music." *New York Times,* 11 August 1994.

Andrews, Edmund L. "Changing Shopping Habits Keep Those Fingers Walking." *New York Times,* 1 July 1990.

Athineos, Doris. "As the World Turns." *Forbes,* 20 May 1996.

Basch, Reva. "UMI." *Link-Up,* January/February 1996.

Behrens, John C. "Good Newsletters Defy Postal Hikes." *American Printer,* March 1995.

"Bell Atlantic Offers Interactive Yellow Pages." *Editor & Publisher,* 18 November 1995.

Belsky, Gary. "Trading Up." *Money,* May 1991.

Beradinis, Lawrence A. "New Chips Hold Voices from the Past." *Machine Design,* 24 October 1996.

Bowles, Elena. "East Europe Entices Publishers." *Advertising Age,* 16 March 1992.

Brightman, Joan. "Yellow Pages Change with the Times." *American Demographics,* March 1995.

Byrne, Harlan S. "Banta Corp.: A Power of the Press." *Barron's,* 20 March 1995.

Camillo, Jay. "Mexico's Surging Economy Lures U.S. Commercial Printers." *Business America,* May 1994.

"Caution Rules in Production." *Catalog Age,* 15 October 1996.

"Compact Discs: Tearing up Phone-Books." *Economist,* 14 January 1995.

Croft, Martin. "Direct Challengers." *Marketing Week,* 24 November 1995.

DeWitt, John W. "CAD Dreams Come True." *Apparel Industry Magazine,* April 1994.

Doebele, Justin. "Madison Avenue Refugee." *Forbes,* 10 April 1995.

Dowling, Melissa. "Daring to Try a Desktop." *Catalog Age,* November 1995.

"Duplicators: Two Firms are Doing Big Jobs Fast." *Managing Office Technology,* August 1996.

Edelmann, Eric. "The Calm Before the Storm?" *Catalog Age,* 15 October 1996.

Emmons, Sasha. "Yellow Pages Bounce Back: Bell South on Top." *Advertising Age,* 19 August 1996.

Encyclopedia of Associations. Detroit: Gale Research Inc. 1996.

Ettore, Barbara. "Simplicity Cuts New Pattern." *Management Review,* December 1993.

Fitzgerald, Mark. "Aligning with Yellow Pages in Audiotex Ventures." *Editor & Publisher,* 28 October 1995.

———. "Newspaper Alliances with Yellow Pages: Thing of the Past." *Editor & Publisher,* 7 October 1995

Gaetan, Manuel. "Lectra Launches TAS." *Bobbin,* March 1996.

Gleason, Mark. "Yellow Pages Shops Brace for Expected Boom in Directories." *Advertising Age,* 19 February 1996.

Goldman, Debra. "Apocalypse Now." *Adweek,* 6 March 1995.

Hawn, Carleen. "Timing the Embargo." *Forbes,* 21 October 1996.

Hilts, Len. "Maps that Fill a Gap." *Publishers Weekly,* 27 January 1992.

Klemm, Alisa. "Trading Up." *Sporting Goods Business,* June 1996.

Knight, Doug. "Direct Marketing Campaign Sparks Interest, Spurs Action." *Direct Marketing,* September 1996.

Koshy, Thomas T. "Application of Hypertext Technology to Assist Maintenance on the Shop Floor." *Computers & Industrial Engineering,* April 1996.

"Lectra System's Total Apparel System 2000." *Apparel Industry Magazine,* September 1996.

Levy, Clifford J. "So Long, Grim Slugger: It's a New Card Game." *New York Times,* 18 March 1992.

Martina, Nita L. "Fax Publishing—Fast Facts." *Communication World,* September 1995.

Mathews, Ryan. "Category Management: It's in the Cards." *Progressive Grocer,* April 1996.

Matzer, Marla. "A Digitized Future." *Forbes,* 24 April 1995.

Miller, Rachel. "Rank by Name and Number." *Marketing,* 1 February 1996.

International Survey of Music Publishing Revenues. New York: National Music Publishers' Association, 1996.

"New Directory Shows Prolific Community Press." *Editor & Publisher,* 9 November 1996.

"More Than a Contractor." *Apparel Industry Magazine,* December 1996.

Oberndorf, Shannon. "Reluctant Recyclers." *Catalog Age,* 15 October 1996.

Oliver, Suzanne. "Peddle or Perish." *Forbes,* 23 October 1995.

Owen, Tim. "Business Information in the UK: 1996 Market Review." *Business Information Review,* December 1996.

Radice, Carol. "Trading Cards: Managing a Post-Peak Category." *Progressive Grocer,* February 1996.

Rebello, Kathy. "The Ultimate Photo Op?" *Business Week,* 23 October 1995.

Rudich, Joe. "Cybermapping." *Link-Up,* September/October 1996.

———. "CD-ROM Telephone Directories." *Link-Up,* July/ August 1996.

"St. Pete Kills Yellow Pages." *Editor & Publisher,* 24 August 1996.

Schifrin, Matthew. "The Message, Not the Medium." *Forbes,* 11 September 1995.

Scussel, Patricia A. "Viking Office Products." *Catalog Age,* September 1996.

Seal, Kathy. "Industry Discovering the Power of Newsletters." *Hotel & Motel Management,* 18 September 1995.

Stein, M. L. "Perfect Together?" *Editor & Publisher,* 12 November 1994.

Steinhauer, Jennifer. "With Computers, Mapmakers Are Redrawing the World." *New York Times,* 2 December 1990.

Strand, Patricia. "Yellow Pages: Industry Bumps Ante and Rolls the Dice in Bid for National Ads." *Advertising Age,* 27 September 1993.

Toth, Debora. "Supergraphics: High, Wide & Profitable." *Graphic Arts Monthly,* August 1996.

U.S. Department of Commerce. Economics and Statistics Administration. Bureau of the Census. *Statistical Abstract of the United States 1996.* 116th ed. Washington: GPO, 1996.

U.S. Department of Labor. Bureau of Labor Statistics. *E&E: Employment and Earnings,* November 1996.

Wise, Robert. "Volume Grouping Allows Many CDs to Exist as Directory Entries Under a Common Root Directory." *Computer Technology Review,* Summer/Fall Supplement 1995.

Yellow Pages: Meet the Industry Behind the Books. Troy, MI: Yellow Pages Publishers Association.

Yellow Pages: Industry Facts Booklet 1992-93 Edition. Troy, MI: Yellow Pages Publishers Association, 1992.

—Heather Behn Hedden, updated by David C. Genaway

SIC 2752

COMMERCIAL PRINTING, LITHOGRAPHIC

This category includes establishments involved primarily in printing by various processes involving lithography. It includes printers using both web and flat sheet technologies. Terms describing the processes include offset printing, photo-offset printing, photo-lithography, and planography.

Most of this industry's work is done on a custom-job basis. Typical products include advertising posters, circulars, coupons, and labels. In addition, some products such as calendars, maps, posters, and de-calcomanias are bulk manufactured and offered for sale. Greeting card printers, however, are classified in **SIC 2771.**

Lithographed newspapers and periodicals manufactured by printing companies which are not publishers are also included in this industry. Establishments primarily involved in printing books are classified in **SIC 2732.** Newspaper, periodical, and book publishers are classified in **SICs 2711, 2721,** and **2731,** respectively.

Establishments primarily involved in preparing plates and related prepress services are classified in **SIC 2796.** Establishments offering photocopying services are classified in **SIC 7334.**

INDUSTRY SNAPSHOT

"Lithography" describes the printing process in which ink is transferred from a plate with a level surface that has been chemically treated to make some areas ink-receptive and others ink-repellent. The term "offset lithography" was coined to describe the process by which an image is transferred from a lithographic plate onto a rubber blanket cylinder and then pressed from the cylinder onto paper or other substrates. About half of all the printing done in the United States is accomplished by lithography.

In 1996, the offset lithography industry pulled approximately $55 billion in shipments and employed 500,000 workers. Advertising printing continued to be its largest single category in 1996, counting for 31 percent of all production. Examples of advertising products were direct mail circulars, letters, pamphlets, mailing inserts, and brochures. Other large categories included periodical printing and general business paperwork printing.

Offset lithographers as a whole reported an average of 6 percent growth in sales in 1996, but of that category, commercial offset "quick printers" reported 19 percent growth in sales, with their biggest category being multicolor jobs. Quick printers are geared to turn work around in less than a week.

Industry prognosticators expected stable growth for the entire industry at 2-3 percent annually through the turn of the century. Commercial printing continued to be challenged by the relative scarcity of electronically savvy employees, greater expenditures for pollution management and Occupational Safety and Health Administration (OSHA) compliance, and fluctuating paper cost and supply—but the impact of these factors would be lessened by U.S. population growth increase, the rising new business starts, and the increasing demand for English-language publications internationally.

BACKGROUND AND DEVELOPMENT

The term "lithography" comes from two Greek words: *lithos,* meaning "stone," and *graphien,* meaning "to write." The process was developed by the German inventor Aloys Senefelder, who discovered that by treating limestone with gum arabic, nitric acid, and a mixture of soap and tallow he could make parts of the stone repel printing ink and parts of it repel water. In 1798, he perfected his process for use in printing.

Early lithographic plates were made from limestone, and presses were made of wood. During the first two decades of the 1800s, technical advances were made. Cast iron platens helped improve impression quality, and steam-driven cylinder presses increased operating efficiency. The ability to print in color was developed in 1837. Publishers of popular travel books were among the first to replace the more expensive methods of etching and engraving with lithography. A typical nineteenth century press could print approximately 600 impressions per hour.

The twentieth century brought innovations to increase press speeds and improve image resolution. Ira W. Rubel and Caspar Hermann, both of New Jersey, developed thin metal plates in 1904. Their success enabled the development of rotary lithography, a procedure in which the plate was mounted on a cylinder. By the late 1980s, advances in offset rotary press technology had produced presses capable of making 30,000 impressions per hour, printing on both sides of the paper, and receiving paper in sheets or from large rolls called "webs."

Despite its widespread use, many people find lithography more difficult to understand than other printing processes. Unlike methods in which printing plates contain raised or etched images, lithographic plates are flat. To create a lithographic plate, a plate maker begins with a thin piece of metal coated with an oil-based emulsion. A photographic negative of the image to be printed is placed over the plate, which is then exposed to a bright light. The light reacts with the uncovered emulsion so that when the plate is chemically washed the emulsion remains only in the image area. During the printing process, water is used to wet the bare metal, non-image areas of the plate. Printing ink, an oil-based product, is able to adhere only to the emulsion in the image area.

According to the U.S. Department of Commerce, commercial printing by lithography drew in receipts totalling $32.7 billion in 1987. Of this amount, $30.0 billion represented products considered primary to the industry. These statistics yielded a specialization ratio of 94 percent for 1987, an increase over the 91 percent reported in 1982. The combined value of commercial printing by all methods in 1987 was estimated at $44.7 billion.

By 1991, the commercial printing industry had grown to $55.7 billion, however, profit margins for many establishments were down as a result of intensified price competition during the national recession.

According to figures published by the National Association of Printers and Lithographers, commercial printing represented the fifth largest manufacturing industry in the United States. During the early 1990s, government statistics indicated that commercial printing was growing faster than general manufacturing in all 50 states. The industry continued striving toward faster presses, quicker set-up, improved color reproduction, and better material handling procedures. One noted trend was toward shorter but more numerous press runs. Industry analysts attributed this to "just in time" inventory systems and to advertisers' ability to target markets with greater precision. Six-color systems became the new industry standard.

Compliance with national, regional, and local environmental regulations posed a challenge to the industry. Commercial lithography depended on the use of solvents, volatile organic compounds (VOCs), and other substances classified as toxic. The printing process also generated waste materials which were considered hazardous. In addition, some environmental groups criticized the industry for its mass production of newspapers, periodicals, catalogs, and direct mail items which used paper resources and congested the nation's landfills.

Another observed trend was increased use of color. Previously, four color presses were considered the industry standard for reproducing photographic images. Four-color process printing created shades and tones of color by employing a technique called color separation, which involved filtering an image through a screen to produce a series of single-color plates, each containing an image comprised of tiny dots. Six- and eight-color presses enabled printers to exactly match distinctive colors, take advantage of special effects such as the application of metallic inks, and apply coatings or other finishes.

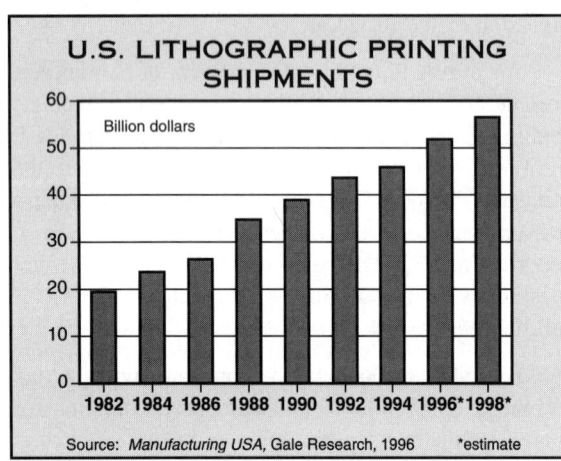

U.S. LITHOGRAPHIC PRINTING SHIPMENTS

Source: *Manufacturing USA*, Gale Research, 1996   *estimate

CURRENT CONDITIONS

According to a July 1996 article in *American Printer,* a survey of the top fifth of domestic printing firms indicated more than half were involved in mergers or acquisitions. The larger the company, the more likely the chance of merger. In February 1997, *Publishing & Production Executive* suggested that the consolidation trend was fueled by the printing customer's demand for a one-stop shop. The huge capital investments required to stay competitive in the industry were also a factor.

The National Association of Printers & Lithographers identified seven key industry trends in a November 1996 report published in *GATF World,* the magazine of the Graphic Arts Technical Foundation. The trends, in order of importance, were: more color, graphics, and complex designs; shorter run-lengths; paper and material cost inflation; severe price competition among printers; much quicker turn-around times; black and white printing now going to copying ma-

chine technology; and, clients insisting on higher quality.

An increasingly pressing challenge for the industry was training and retaining qualified employees. The industry was revamped during the 1980s and 1990s, and traditional mechanical printers' skills were not sufficient in leading shops. From electronic prepress to digital presses, the new standard of commercial printing equipment was redefining the craft in terms of the electronic era. New technology was a two-edged sword. According to a 1996 study by the National Association of Printers and Lithographers, the cost of staying "state-of-the-art" with regard to new software and hardware was the leading threat to overall profitability for the industry. Interestingly, the same survey identified the key strength of the industry as having state-of-the-art equipment that could handle a broad range of work. The second most serious "threat to profitability" was closer kin to it—the learning curve of keeping current with new technology and converting to new systems.

The mid-1990s was a trying time for many in the industry. Rising postage costs, rising paper costs, and threats of recession kept many companies lean. Aggressive competition among printers cut profit margins close. The "hot" markets for the turn of the century, said Ron Davis of the Printing Industries of America (PIA) would be "general marketing and promotional." The PIA predicted that the industry would do well into the late 1990s, seeing a growth in sales of approximately 6 percent. The driving trends were toward more color, faster color, digital proofing, and a preference among customers for shops that could combine all-in-one digital proofing, printing, fulfillment, and delivery service.

On the horizon in the late 1990s, the dominance of 6-color presses was being challenged by 8-color sheetfed "perfectors" that could print both sides of a sheet of paper during one pass through the press. At prices ranging from $2.7 to $4 million dollars, these behemoth machines were considered expensive, but incredibly productive—and a sure contender for the wave of the future. By 1997, they were already widely adopted by printers in Europe.

Another important development within commercial lithography was the growing impact of environmental regulations. Systems used to produce proofs (samples made before printing to exactly depict the finished product) were criticized because of their reliance on solvents associated with air and water pollution. Many local ordinances controlled waste water discharges from printing establishments by defining acceptable pH levels, restricting the discharge of ignitable substances, and banning the presence of heavy metals. Worker safety regulations mandated chemical exposure limits, and the storage and handling of hazardous substances were controlled by legislation. The Clean Air Act Amendments of 1990 required companies to obtain permits for press equipment, and some states also ordered permits for vented prepress equipment. In some places, local governing authorities restricted the number of hours a day certain types of presses were allowed to run and limited the acquisition of additional printing capacity.

INDUSTRY LEADERS

One of the largest commercial printers operating in the United States during the 1990s was Quebecor Printing (USA) Corporation. Quebecor USA maintained its headquarters in Boston, Massachusetts. The company's parent organization, Quebecor Inc., was founded in 1965, and its corporate headquarters are located in Montreal, Canada. In 1997, Quebecor operated 48 printing and related service plants in the United States, mostly concentrated in the Northeast. The company reported annual sales of $2 billion and employed 16,000 workers in North America.

Quebecor's principal products included advertising inserts, circulars, flyers, magazines, catalogs, and books. Divisions producing these items provided more than 77 percent of the company's revenue in 1992. Other divisions included specialty printing, directory printing, securities printing, newspaper printing, and other printing services such as prepress support, circulation fulfillment, and list management.

A home-grown industry leader is Quad/Graphics, Inc., founded in 1971 by entrepreneur Henry Quadracci in Pewaukee, Wisconsin. In the late 1990s, Quad/Graphics was the largest privately held printing company in North America, with annual sales in excess of $1 billion dollars and 8,500 employees. Quad/Graphics also operates extensive digital design, gravure, book publishing, mailing and fulfillment centers.

Other industry leaders in the mid- to late 1990s included R. R. Donnelly & Sons Company, a Memphis-based printing giant founded in 1866, with annual sales of $6.5 billion; Banta Corporation, out of Menasha, Wisconsin, with annual sales of $1 billion, and Moore Graphics of Minneapolis, with yearly revenues of $215 million.

WORK FORCE

In 1994, the U.S. Bureau of Labor Statistics noted that there were 79,000 offset lithography press opera-

tors, out of a total of 244,000 press operators national wide. The jobs were well distributed through the country, with only slightly heavier concentrations in New York, Los Angeles, Chicago, Philadelphia, Washington, D.C., and Dallas.

Workers within the commercial printing industry were facing rapid changes as new production methods and materials were adopted. Some, critical of the innovations, claimed that craftsmanship was being replaced with technology; others claimed that technological improvements enhanced traditional craftsmanship. Changes resulted in the elimination of some job classifications but created shortages of experienced labor in others. The prepress and postpress areas were expected to yield the greatest gains in employment opportunity, while traditional jobs such as those of "strippers" were being eliminated by computerized prepress.

According to U.S. government statistics, approximately 37,000 establishments were involved in commercial printing during 1991. The National Association of Printers and Lithographers stated that "Though commercial printing is a huge industry, it is an industry of numerous small businesses, embodying the U.S. entrepreneurial spirit." Forty-three percent of commercial printing establishments employed fewer than four employees; 66.2 percent employed fewer than ten; 85 percent fewer than 20; and 93.4 percent of the nation's commercial printers employed fewer than 50 employees.

In the mid-1990s, the median weekly wage for a press operator was $432, according to the U.S. Bureau of Labor Statistics. Employment in this sector was expected to grow slowly through 2005, because although demand for the printed product will increase, technology will enable one professional offset press operator to print more quickly and more efficiently than several were able to do in the past.

RESEARCH AND TECHNOLOGY

Evolving technology played a vital role in the development of the commercial printing industry. Analysts estimated that printers invested more than $2 billion in new technology during 1991 to maintain their competitiveness. The development of high-quality copying machines drove printers to adopt presses capable of offering more benefits. Innovations brought improvements in color capacity, press speeds, and automation.

As press speeds approached 2,500 feet per minute, automated equipment became increasingly important because of human physical limitations. New methods of feeding paper into the press and taking printed matter away from the press were developed. Researchers designed computers to help achieve optimal results by automatically monitoring press temperatures, plate register (how images fit together), and web tension. One device that facilitated the development of higher speed presses was a densitometer. A densitometer was a device used to insure color integrity throughout an entire press run by automatically making adjustments to the ink fountains. Prior to the development of densitometers, ink fountain adjustments were made by an experienced pressman based on visual perception.

Other technological changes were aimed at improving the ability to quickly set up a press and to reduce paper waste. One area under study was the automatic setting of press variables from prepress operations. For example, if computerized color separations could be used to directly set press ink keys, exact color reproductions could be made without wasting time and paper in experimental attempts to duplicate the required visual results. Other evolving technologies included faster plate changes, reductions in the amount of blank space required to lock plates onto press cylinders, additional in-line finishing capabilities, optimized material handling at the end of the press run, and better photographic reproductions.

One system gaining acceptance was called dry lithography. Dry lithography used waterless ink systems. In traditional lithography, water was necessary to dampen the plate. A precise ink/water balance was essential for superior quality. Systems printing without water achieved higher-quality results and operated more efficiently. Waterless printing also enabled printers to work with higher resolutions. For example, commercial printers traditionally reproduced photographs using screens of 150 lines per inch. Using waterless technology, printers could employ screens of 300 to 500 lines per inch. The investment required to "retro-fit" presses for dry lithography, however, delayed the penetration of this technology into the market. The technology required special inks and special plate materials able to repel the inks from non-image areas. In addition, press temperatures were more difficult to control. Using traditional water systems, the water served not only to keep ink away from non-image areas, but also to cool the press. Waterless systems required chilling rolls to carry off excess heat or ink adjustments to compensate for higher temperatures.

FURTHER READING

"1997 Technology Forecast." Special pull-out section. *GATF World,* January/February 1997.

"A Colorful Explanation." *Indiana Business Magazine,* April 1991.

Borowsky, Irvin J. *Opportunities in Printing Careers.* Lincolnwood, IL: NTC Publishing Group, 1992.

Borowsky, Mark. "Skill Hard to Find in New Technology." *Memphis Business Journal,* 15 January 1990.

Cross, Lisa. "Eco Impact on Proof Systems." *Graphic Arts Monthly,* March 1993.

———. "Waterless Ignites Renewed Interest." *Graphic Arts Monthly,* April 1992.

Dun's Business Rankings. Bethlehem, PA: Dun & Bradstreet, 1996.

"Eight Is Enough: Printers Look to Eight-Color Perfectors . . ." *American Printer,* February 1997.

Esler, Bill. "The Quick Print Giants." *Graphic Arts Monthly,* December 1996.

Ferris, Fred. "A Step Ahead of the Crowd: Short-Run Digital Color Requires a Fresh, Aggressive Marketing Approach." *American Printer,* April 1996.

Koeslka, Rita. "How to Print Money." *Forbes,* 24 December 1990.

Koren, Michael. "Keep Your Balance." *American Printer,* September 1992.

Lorenzi, Neal. "Web Offset Moves into the 1990s." *American Printer,* May 1989.

Merkli, Werner. "Landmarks in Printing." *UNESCO Courier,* July 1988.

Milburn, David L. "Connects Pixels to Paper—1996 Technology Forecast." *GATF World,* March/April 1996.

Petersen, Debbie. "In Search of Excellence." *American Printer,* October 1989.

———. "A Dry Run: Waterless Technology for Web Offset Printing." *American Printer,* May 1996.

"Printer's Perspective: 1996 in Review." *Publishing & Production Executive,* February 1997.

"Printers' Profits Remain Healthy Despite Drop." *GATF World,* July/August 1996.

"Quebecor Printing (USA) Company Overview." Boston: Quebecor, 1997. Available from http://www.quebecorusa.com/facilityglb.htm.

Rasie, Lawrence, ed. *Directory of Business Information.* John Wiley & Sons: New York, 1995.

"The More Complete Sheet." *Printing Impressions,* February 1997.

Toth, Debbi. "Multicolor Sheetfeds: In a Quick Tournabout, Six-Colors Rule the Market." *Graphic Arts Monthly,* March 1989.

"Tracking the Trends: Merger Activity in Top Printing Firms." *American Printer,* July 1996.

U.S. Bureau of Labor Statistics. *Occupational Outlook Handbook.* Washington: GPO, 1996. Available from http://stats.bls.gov/oco/ocos231.htm.

U.S. Department of Commerce. *Census of Manufactures.* Washington: Bureau of the Census, 1990.

"Who Are We?" Company brochure. Pewaukee, WI: Quad/Graphics, 1997. Available from http://www.qg.com/who.html.

—Karen Bellenir, updated by Lisa Calhoun

SIC 2754

COMMERCIAL PRINTING, GRAVURE

This category includes establishments primarily engaged in commercial printing using the gravure process. Other terms often used to describe current methods of gravure production are "photogravure," "rotogravure," and "intaglio." Examples of products in this industry include magazines, postage stamps, dollar bills, calendars, fine art prints, wallpaper, catalogs, coupons, directories, newspaper advertising inserts, playing cards, postcards, gift wrap, and product packaging and wrappers.

INDUSTRY SNAPSHOT

Gravure is a form of intaglio printing. The word "intaglio" comes from an Italian word meaning "to engrave;" the word "gravure" is taken from the French and has the same meaning. Intaglio printing methods were developed by carving or engraving an image in stone or metal. In contemporary commercial gravure printing, a reversed image is cut into a thick metal plate wrapped around a cylinder. Ink, applied to the plate and wiped off the surface with a blade, remains in the incised image cells so that when paper is placed against the plate it absorbs the ink and produces a crisp copy of the image.

The contemporary gravure printing process has generally been used for very long press runs on projects requiring superior color accuracy and clarity on thin papers. Gravure is preferred in runs over 300,000 copies, like printing weekly or monthly magazines or mass-distributed catalogs. Gravure's primary advantage over other forms of printing is its ability to produce millions of impressions without suffering any image deterioration. Gravure can also print a superior image on light papers than other printing methods can, since gravure lays down wet ink over dry. Other commercial printing methods lay wet ink over wet ink, which causes the image to degrade more quickly.

Gravure's disadvantages include generally higher costs and increased press set-up time.

According to executive director of the Gravure Association of America (GAA), Cheryl Kasunich, in 1997 gravure comprised 20 percent of the entire commercial printing market. From 1989 to 1997, the industry employed between 90,000 and 80,000 people, a number slowly and steady declining over that period of time and anticipated to decline still more. Gravure printing shipments in 1996 were estimated at just under $4 billion—a relatively static figure since 1990.

Catalog and directory printers represented a substantial segment of the gravure market. Twenty percent of the catalogs and 15 percent of the newspaper inserts published domestically were gravure, according to the GAA. Roughly 26 percent of the gravure industry was devoted to the category of catalog and directory printing, which also included direct mail catalogs and telephone and business directories.

Approximately 16 percent of the gravure printing industry was devoted to magazine printing in the late 1990s. Roughly one-third of all consumer magazine circulation was gravure, and more than 90 percent of Sunday magazines. In the late 1990s, according to the GAA, 30 magazines were printed gravure, including *Family Circle, McCalls, Better Home & Garden, Reader's Digest, Parade,* and *TV Guide.* These magazines were all in the top 25 magazines in 1996, ranked in *Ad Age* by gross revenue. Another 27 percent of the gravure industry profited from producing advertising flyers, leaflets, and direct mail ad campaigns.

Gravure is also used for packaging designs, such as the printed plastic wrapping around many perishable foods or around beverage containers. Fifteen percent of the gravure's printing market in the mid- to late 1990s was devoted to printing labels and wrappers.

BACKGROUND AND DEVELOPMENT

The gravure printing process developed from copperplate engraving techniques employed during the fifteenth century. Early plates were flat and had to be hand engraved. The development of engraved cylinders to replace flat plates led to rotary gravure, called "rotogravure." Rotary gravure presses operate by squeezing paper between the image cylinder and a second cylinder called an impression cylinder. Rotary technology enabled the development of presses with increased printing speeds. A process by which rotary gravure presses were able to print on both sides of the paper was patented in 1860 by Auguste Godchaux, a publisher located in Paris. A photographic etching technique developed in 1878 by a Czech painter helped simplify platemaking procedures.

Gravure printing was further refined in 1908 when two German textile printers, Ernst Rolffs and Eduard Mertens, developed the "doctor blade." Gravure printing techniques relied on creating height differences between the image and non-image areas of the plate. An image was formed by making small recessed ink cells. The doctor blade assured the removal of excess ink from the surface level and enhanced the quality of reproductions.

One of the most popular items reliant on gravure technology was the Sunday newspaper magazine section. Many magazine sections even used the term "rotogravure" as part of their name. Although gravure newspaper supplements were not suited for up-to-the-minute reporting because of their lengthy preparation requirements, they made color advertising possible.

Despite advances made in gravure technology during the early twentieth century, plate engraving expenses and the length of time required to set up press runs remained problematic. The industry responded with efforts aimed at increasing gravure's efficiency. According to a study conducted by the Gravure Research Institute in 1969, 38.5 man-hours were required to complete the necessary pre-press work for each color page printed using available gravure technology. By 1986, improvements including computer assisted imposition—arranging the pages of a publication into their proper configuration for the press—and computer-to-plate (CTP) techniques had cut the pre-press time drastically. Lithography printing and gravure printing were practically equal in the late 1990s in terms of pre-press time. However, the costs associated with gravure were still higher, including costs to engrave and handle the heavy gravure press cylinders.

In comparison with offset lithographic presses, gravure presses tended to be larger, faster, and more expensive. A gravure press during the late 1980s could cost as much as $10 million, not counting the costs associated with other equipment such as engraving devices, cylinder handling systems, ink, and paper rolls. By the mid-1990s, the cost of an average no-frills American-made gravure press hovered around $10 million dollars, not including additional thousands of dollars spent in buying impression rollers, safety cages, and expert on-site installation. Other costs associated with the purchase of a new gravure press include "extras" that most shops find to be necessities, such as cylinder-loading, viscosity, plumbing, and duct systems. Gravure presses were, at the time, often as much as three meters wide and as much as four and a half meters long.

During the early 1990s, analysts noted uncertain conditions within the commercial gravure industry. Among catalog and directory printers, gravure held approximately one fourth of the market share, and growth in gravure print orders for catalogs was growing at a faster rate than the overall growth rate for catalog printing.

In other areas, however, gravure printers were experiencing decreasing demand as publishers and advertisers turned to other print processes. According to figures released in 1989 by the GAA, annual increases in gravure advertising totaled only 6 percent during the 1980s while offset advertising print orders had increased at an annual rate of 13.6 percent. In addition, gravure's market share for inserts had dropped to 8.5 percent from 19 percent recorded in 1982. Among magazine printers, annual increases in page production fell short of increases in print capacity and productivity. This led to increased competition and reduced profit margins.

According to statistics gathered by the GAA, gravure Sunday magazine production was 12 percent higher in 1988 than in 1987 but the total number of individual magazines produced had dropped. By the end of the decade, they numbered less than 50, and the 1990s reduced their numbers further. Discontinued magazines included publications offered by the Des Moines *Register, Denver Post, Oakland Press, Sacramento Union,* New York *Daily News,* and *Newsday.*

The fact that total production had not also fallen was attributed to two growing national Sunday supplements, *Parade* and *USA Weekend,* both gravure products.

In addition to competition among gravure printers, the commercial gravure industry as a whole faced competition for advertising dollars from television and other printing processes. Trends toward shorter press runs to produce demographic editions of large-circulation magazines and similar trends among catalog publishers toward smaller specialty catalogs lessened the economic advantages offered by gravure's long run capability. At the same time, improvements in the ability of competing print processes to achieve high-quality photographic reproductions further eroded gravure's traditional advantages.

CURRENT CONDITIONS

In the 1990s, the entire commercial printing industry experienced a period of discomfort caused by a series of large acquisitions and mergers, an increase in the cost of paper supplies, and postage rate increases. Gravure as a subset of the industry felt these changes keenly, since its profit margin relied on an affordable paper supply. In the July 1996 issue of *American Printer,* 50 percent of the country's top 20 printing firms were involved in a merger. Gravure printers and heatset web plants (another kind of printing used primarily for magazines) were the most aggressive in seeking mergers.

Trends within the industry toward shorter print runs aimed at more focused markets lessened gravure's advantages and brought increased competition from other print technologies, especially offset. During the mid-1990s, computer magazines, weekly magazines, and direct mail prospered, all contributing to a steady overall profitability for the gravure—albeit with little significant growth. In early 1997, the industry hoped to take advantage of strong magazine starts. Lawrence Rasie's 1995 Directory of Business Information indicated a magazine industry sales increases of 1-2 percent per year until 2000—a fortuitous sign for gravure.

The Printing Industry Association (PIA) predicted a 6 percent rise in sales throughout the commercial printing industry in 1997-1998, a growth rate that included the gravure industry. Some industry prognosticators foresaw more consolidation and merger activity among printers, as well as a continuing challenge for gravure to remain viable in the face of competition from the more flexible and often more cost-effective offset printers.

By the late 1990s, gravure had made tremendous strides to overcome its high cost of set-up, lengthy cylinder engraving process, and environmentally unsound ink solvents; however, offset presses—the competition—improved quality, turn-around time, and ability to print longer runs with better quality. Prepress costs were about equal for offset and gravure process by the late 1990s, but gravure cylinders were still substantially more expensive. Plates for an offset press can cost as little as $200, while a typical gravure cylinder cost $1,000-$1,200. The future of gravure technology within the publication industry is unsure. Gravure technology may move away from traditional commercial printing and become reserved for operations in which it is undisputed master—like decorating vinyl wall and floor covers.

INDUSTRY LEADERS

Foreign-Owned Giants. One of the largest gravure printers operating in the United States was Quebecor Printing, Inc., a multi-billion dollar Canadian firm whose U.S. headquarters were located in Boston, Massachusetts. In the late 1990s, Quebecor had annual sales (including non-gravure commercial printing) of $2 billion, 48 plants, and 16,000 employees. Quebecor produced Sunday newspaper magazines—including *Parade* and *USA Weekend*—and retail inserts. The company's major advertising clients included Sears, Dayton-Hudson, Montgomery Ward, Radio Shack, and Woolco-Woolworth. Quebecor also printed magazines including *Time, Reader's Digest,* and *People.*

In late 1994, Quebecor signed an additional agreement with *USA Weekend* magazine to print 17 million copies a week of its regional editions until July 2004. Despite its heavy involvement in gravure printing, however, Quebecor's primary classification was under **SIC 2752: Commercial Printing, Lithographic.**

Lawson Mardon Packaging, formed in 1994 as the offspring of Swiss multinational Alusuiise-Lonza, operated 70 gravure presses and printed on the typical media used in packaging: paper, film, foil, and various grades of cardboard. The company, whose packaging customers included Philip Morris, Unilever, Procter & Gamble, and RJR Nabisco, also operated over 40 litho presses. Lawson's Marcel J. Pilon, in a presentation at the GAA's 1996 Annual Convention, pointed out the gravure is the process of choice—and had better results than other methods of printing—when the job required a lot of florescent ink, extremely tight registration, printing on foil, or extremely long runs. In these areas, gravure still had an edge on litho, but industry reports at the end of the 1990s indicated that competing processes were certainly closing the gap.

Native Gravure. Founded in 1971 in Pewaukee, Wisconsin, by entrepreneur Harry Quadracci, Quad/ Graphics was the largest privately held printing company in North America, with ten plants, 9,000 employees, and over a $1 billion in annual sales. Quad/ Graphics, in the late 1990s, operated 12 Cerutti-built gravure presses in 2 all-gravure printing plants—one in Lomira, Wisconsin, and the other in Martinsburg, West Virginia. Both shops were 100 percent direct-digital engraving.

AMERICA AND THE WORLD

Gravure's popularity was increasing faster in Europe during the late 1980s than in the United States. Large gravure presses capable of "all-at-once" production were used to print entire magazines in a single print pass. Popular weekly news magazines featuring topical issues, televisions listings, and celebrity news required regular press runs of several million copies. In Europe, gravure was successfully used to print much shorter pressruns of only 150,000 copies, as opposed to the 300,000-500,000 copy minimum practiced in the United States. Analysts noted that the European gravure market did not have to weather the same bottom-line, cost-conscious mentality as many American companies.

Some industry watchers note that U.S. printers and publishers were poised to succeed as agreements such as the North American Free Trade Agreement (NAFTA) and the Uruguay Round of the General Agreement on Tariffs and Trade (GATT) increased the viability of exporting U.S. printing abroad and increased U.S. copyright protection. Also, U.S. printers looked forward to reaping the advantage of having American English as the world's standard language of trade, science, and commerce.

RESEARCH AND TECHNOLOGY

Digital Process. By the late 1990s, digital engraving technology was helping to overcome one of gravure's traditional problems—lengthy cylinder engraving time. Direct digital engraving methods used laser technology to etch cylinders without making an intermediate film copy of an image. Reportedly, by the mid-1990s all gravure shops used digital engraving for some portion of their work. Getting rid of the film step in the printing process removed a large cost component, saved time, and also reduced waste and environmental impact of the manufacturing process. Max Daetwyler Corp. (Huntersville, North Carolina) developed one of the first complete digital systems, using a laser to engrave on a non-reflective metal alloy. Lasers could cut 25,000-30,000 image cells per second.

Environment. The 1990s saw a great deal of research into improving the environmental impact of gravure because of U.S. Occupational Safety and Health Administration (OSHA) compliance issues, the Pollution Prevention Act of 1990, and the Clean Air Act Amendment. Traditional toluene-based inks, which were strictly regulated and rated by the U.S. Environmental Protection Agency as both VOCs (Volatile Organic Compound) and HAPs (Hazardous Air Pollutants), were slated to be phased out by water-based inks. However, the technology was still in a developmental stage. Promising developments included mixing acetone, a non-hazardous but flammable substance, with water to increase ink drying time, and multicolor pressruns that used a waterbased ink as only one of the colors. One study noted that, in a typical four-color (cyan, yellow, magenta, and black) printing run, if a water-based ink were used just for the yellow component, toluene emissions would be reduced 35 percent. Full color water-based printing was not a reality by the mid- to late 1990s.

Competition Online. Many short-run publications were complemented by material on CD-ROM or on a website. Referenced in the February 1997 *Publishing & Production Executive*, a study of 1,000 U.S. consumers commissioned by the Printing Industries of America (PIA) found that only 21 percent of those surveyed thought that electronic media would replace print. Many felt that electronic and print media would remain independent methods of information. The advance of electronic media into the short-run market, however, could be a driver to encourage printers to expand into electronic publishing, or to take over increasingly large segments of what has been traditionally gravure's domain—long, multicolor press runs.

Going into the late 1990s, industry leaders appeared in agreement that long-run magazine and catalog publishing was unthreatened by electronic publishing—at least for the next decade. Many industry giants, like Quebecor and Quad/Graphics, welcomed digital publishing by advertising their services online and using webpages as marketing tools.

FURTHER READING

"A Commitment to Gravure Excellence." *Gravure,* fall 1996.

"Austrian Machine Corporation." Cranston, RI: Austrian Machine, Inc., 1997.

Borowsky, Irvin J. *Opportunities in Printing Careers.* Lincolnwood, IL: NTC Publishing Group, 1992.

Chorvat, Bill, et al. "Waterbased Inks: What Are the Real Issues?" *Gravure,* fall 1996.

Darnay, Arsen J., ed. *Manufacturing USA.* 5th ed. Detroit: Gale Research, 1996.

"Electronic Media Not Likely to Replace Print." *American Printer,* July 1996.

Fitzgerald, Mark. "Ironic Victims of Newspaper Color." *Editor and Publisher,* 28 September 1991.

Gravure Association of America. "The Gravure Industry Today." Rochester, NY, 1994.

Hobson, Garnett. "Package Printing Technology Change with the Times." *Gravure,* winter 1996.

Hunter, Margaret. "Direct Digital Color Proofing (DDCP)." *Folio,* July 1990.

Johnston, Peter. "The Gravure Forecast: Partly Cloudy." *Graphic Arts Monthly,* June 1989.

———. "Gravure Revisited." *Graphic Arts Monthly,* April 1987.

Kirby, Gretchen A. "1996: Looking Back—The Year in Review." *Publishing & Production Executive,* February 1997, 18-21.

Lessner, Ivy. "Gravure Update." *American Printer,* March 1989.

Merkli, Werner. "Landmarks in Printing." *UNESCO Courier,* July 1988.

Peterson, Debbie. "Gravure Gets Going." *American Printer,* March 1994.

"Quad/Graphics Breaks Ground in Martinsburg, WV for First All-Digital Gravure Printing Plant." *Gravure,* winter 1995.

Quad/Graphics. "Quad/Graphics: Who Are We?" Company brochure. Pewaukee, WI, 1997. Available from http://www.qg.com/who.html.

Quebecor Printing USA Corp. "Quebecor Printing USA Corp. Company Overview". Boston: Quebecor Printing USA Corp., 1997. Available from http://www.qubecorusa.com/facilglb.htm.

"Quebecor Will Print USA Weekend." *Gravure,* winter 1995, 11.

Rasie, Lawrence, ed. *Directory of Business Information.* New York: John Wiley & Sons, Inc., 1995.

Robbins, Scott. "Gravure and the Environment." *Gravure,* fall 1996

Standard & Poor's Industry Surveys. New York: Standard & Poor's Corporation, July 1996.

"Top 300 Magazines: 1-100, ranked by gross revenue." *Ad Age,* 1997. Available from http://adage.com/dataplace/archives/dp085.html.

"Tracking the Trends." *American Printer,* July 1996.

U.S. Department of Commerce. U.S. Census Bureau. *1987 Census of Manufactures.* Washington, March 1990.

U.S. Department of Commerce. International Trade Administration. *U.S. Industrial Outlook 1994.* Washington: GPO, 1994.

—Karen Belliner, updated by Lisa Calhoun

SIC 2759

COMMERCIAL PRINTING, NOT ELSEWHERE CLASSIFIED

This industry classification is comprised of diverse establishments involved in commercial or custom-job printing not categorized elsewhere. Example products include newspapers and periodicals printed on behalf of publishers, engraved announcements, circulars, maps, tags and labels, directories, stock certificates, and currency. Procedures include screen printing, flexography, letterpress, digital printing, embossing, engraving, debossing, and thermography on substrates such as paper or plastic, but not textile. For information on commercial lithographic printing, see **SIC 2752.** For commercial gravure printing, see **SIC 2754.**

INDUSTRY SNAPSHOT

In 1996, receipts for this industry totaled $9 billion, a rather steady figure for most of the decade, and one that is not expected to fluctuate significantly in the future. More than 100,000 people were employed in the industry, a figure that was expected to decline as more processes become automated. Flexographic label and wrapper printing held 21 percent of the market in 1996, the largest single share. Screen printing, for items like signs, posters, and bumper-stickers, came in second, with 20 percent of the market. The third largest single category was letterpress general job printing at 10 percent, which included products like scientific chart paper, letterpress newspapers, and tags. A great deal of excitement was generated in the late 1990s by an emerging technology that relied solely on an electro-chemical reaction to produce an image. This dynamic plate-less and film-less process still had no firm nomenclature in early 1997, but one of the developing companies, Elcorsy Technology of Montreal, registered the name "elcography." Images could be changed or manipulated in real time, while the press was still running. A memory buffer in the system allowed another job to be "moved into line" while the press was still printing a previous piece. The transition from job to job was accomplished seamlessly, with no need to recalibrate the press.

ORGANIZATION AND STRUCTURE

Letterpress and flexography are two common relief printing methods. In relief printing, plates are cast or engraved to produce a raised image. The image is transferred by applying ink to the plate's surface and pressing it against paper or other substrates. Letterpress and flexographic technologies are similar, except that letterpress plates are made from metal and flexographic plates are made from rubber or photopolymer materials. As a result of its different plate composition, flexographic processes require special inks to avoid plate damage.

Screen printing (sometimes called porous printing or silk screening) employs a screen stencil. The image area is left open and nonimage areas are sealed using a substance called "resist." Ink is applied to the screen and forced through its mesh onto paper or other substrates such as glass, plastics, and metal (including highway signs). Screen printing is commonly used for limited quantity outdoor posters such as billboards and point-of-purchase advertising displays. Screen printing is unique in that it allows printing onto uneven, oddly shaped, or extremely large substrates.

Thermography, also called raised printing, is used primarily for business cards, social invitations, and stationery. The raised effect is achieved by applying a colorless resin powder to the wet ink. The powder then assumes the color of the underlying ink and, when heated, it bubbles and bonds to the paper. Some printers use pearlescent and glitter powders to create special effects.

BACKGROUND AND DEVELOPMENT

Human interest in making multiple copies of art and documents dates back many centuries. The Chinese, credited with the invention of paper, designed a kind of wooden movable type based on Chinese characters. Modern print methods, however, trace their beginnings back to the early 1400s when Johannes Gutenberg, a German publisher, developed movable metal type based on alphabetic characters. Gutenberg created molds for individual letters and cast them using a metal alloy made of lead, antimony, and tin. He hand-assembled text, letter by letter, from pieces of type which were kept in a special "type case" with compartments for each letter, accent mark, and punctuation mark. To print, Gutenberg locked the type in a frame and placed the frame in a fixed position on a hand-operated wooden press. He spread ink made of soot and linseed oil on the surface of the type and pressed paper against it with a movable flat platen.

Wilhelm Haas, a Swiss type maker, developed a metal hand press in 1787. Haas's press produced higher quality impressions than previously existing wooden presses. Further print improvements came during the early 1800s, when flat platens were replaced with steam-driven "impression cylinders." Because an impression cylinder rolled over a plate, it created even pressure across the entire surface and required less energy to operate. The first press to replace its flat platen with a metal cylinder was constructed in the United States by Richard Hoe in 1844.

A major innovation in typesetting technology occurred in 1884 when Ottmar Mergenthaler, a German immigrant to the United States, invented the Linotype machine. It operated by casting lines of type rather than individual letters. A Linotype machine stocked engraved letter dies in a storage area. The letters were released by typing on a keyboard. The machine ordered them, along with punctuation marks and spaces, into entire lines which could then be cast into metal bars. After lines were cast, the individual letters were routed back into storage for future use. The metal bars of type were used to make printing plates. Prior to the invention of the Linotype machine, typesetters could set approximately 1,400 characters per hour. A Linotype machine could set 6,000 characters per hour.

Other typesetting refinements included the Monotype machine, which was invented in 1897. The Monotype machine produced a perforated paper tape to control typecasting equipment. Photographic typesetting techniques were developed by René Higonnet and Louis Moyroud during the 1940s. During the 1950s, computer technology began to be employed. Further progress over the next several decades brought additional improvements in typesetting capabilities through the advancement of Optical Character Recognition and digital scanning. Prior to the development of offset lithography during the early twentieth century, letterpress was the most common form of printing in the United States and other developed nations. Even during the latter twentieth century it remained the most popular printing method in economically developing nations.

CURRENT CONDITIONS

Because of advances in offset lithography, some predicted that letterpress and flexography would fall into disuse. Enhanced technologies emerged, however, and brought increased interest in flexo. A 1992 article in *Graphic Arts Monthly* claimed that nearly all telephone directories and full-color newspaper comics were being printed by flexography and that the volume of regular newspaper sections printed by flexography had doubled within the previous few years. The report anticipated that the future availability of better paper grades and improved inks would also bring increased use among magazine printers. Many current letterpress operations looking to upgrade may look to flexo as well, since flexo is a less expensive printing process and is being technologically developed more quickly.

The flexo trend among newspapers continued into mid-1990s because flexo continued to offer several advantages over other printing methods, including water-based, environmentally-friendly inks that don't rub off, brighter colors, an enhanced ability to print on light paper stocks, and competitive make-ready time. According to Dr. Gregory D'Amico, publisher of Flexo Today and quoted in a 1997 GATF World, nearly 47 daily North American newspapers are printed at least partially with flexography, and another 75 are poised to begin flexographic production. The Pittsburgh Post-Gazette, for example, began flexo printing in 1996. Quoted in Flexo Today, Robert Higdon, general manager of the newspaper, said they made the switch because of environmental impact issues, ease of production, and quality.

Screen printers also benefited from four-color-process work refinements, computerized design, increased press speeds, and environmentally responsive improvements. In anticipation of governmental regulations mandating cuts in solvent use, screen printers began turning to water-based inks cured with ultraviolet (UV) light. Traditional inks contained solvents to aid in drying; UV inks were dried with UV light.

According to *American Printer,* the screen printing industry was previously a secretive and "unwieldy group of individualistic entrepreneurs." Screen printers put images on everything from highway signs to pens and computer components. The market's four leading categories were decals and labels, electronic components, point-of-purchase displays, and signage.

To meet future challenges, the Screen Printing Association International, headquartered in Fairfax, Virginia, established the Screen Printing Technical Foundation in 1985. The nonprofit foundation was charged with the responsibility of developing guidelines, testing methods, and uniform practices. Specific areas under study included ink opacity, weather exposure, process colors, ink drying techniques, and ways to eliminate *moiré,* a problem pattern caused by improper screen alignment. Screen printers hoped that standardization would help the process become more conventional and result in increased sales.

In the mid-1990s, a new kind of printing technology emerged that allowed digital files to be uploaded into the memory of an elcographic press. No film and no plates were used; rather, the image in the memory was translated into a series of electrical pulses. A special ink—a waterbase with pigment polymers and salts to enhance conductivity—coagulated in response to the pulses, and was cold-offset onto the paper. This new process was first utilized in short-run, high-speed markets, and industry prognosticators expected it to grow quickly into the high-speed publishing arena.

INDUSTRY LEADERS

One of the largest organizations in the industry was the Deluxe Corporation. Deluxe was the largest check printer in the United States in the mid-1990s, with more than half the marketshare, 20,000 employees, and nearly $2 billion in annual sales. Through its divisions, Deluxe provides short-run computer forms, business forms, electronic tax filing services, and screen-printed promotional items like pens and coffee mugs. Deluxe's subsidiary, Current, Inc., is the nation's largest direct-mail marketer of specialty products.

The American Banknote Corporation, formerly the United States Banknote Corporation, was one of the largest security printers in the world. In 1995, the company reported sales of $206 million. In 1993, the company expanded into Brazil, and in subsequent years the ABN-Brazil division accounted for 38 percent of the company's sales. ABN produced a wide variety of security items for corporate and commercial customers. These included products such as stock and bond certificates, travelers checks, gift certificates, promotional coupons, dividend checks, union benefit stamps, certificates of deposit, and motor vehicle certificates of origin. ABN also supplied certificates for the emerging stock and bond exchanges in Eastern Europe and some of the former Soviet Republics. In 1994, the company lost the annual U.S. postage stamp contract. However, ABN is growing aggressively in other areas, including its holographic division, which is the world's largest. During the 1990s, Mastercard™, VISA™, Discover™, And EuroPay™ all carried a holograph made by ABN.

One of ABN's fastest growing products was currency printed for foreign governments. The company's customers include Lithuania, Estonia, Malaysia, Haiti, and Venezuela. Under normal usage, paper currency is generally replaced after approximately 15 months in circulation, however, the political turmoil experienced around the globe during the early 1990s resulted in more frequent changes. Changing political regimes caused some nations to redesign their money; newly independent countries sought to establish their own national currency; and countries experiencing rapid inflation required increased amounts of currency and changes in its denominational units. According to a report published in the *New York Times,* an ABN spokesperson estimated the cost of money was between $26 and $45 per thousand bills regardless of the denomination. Price variables depended on features employed against potential counterfeiting and other options.

RESEARCH AND TECHNOLOGY

The entire commercial printing industry has relied on continuously improving technology to remain competitive. One area under study during the late 1980s and early 1990s, was the development of better flexographic inks containing higher levels of pigment solids to improve drying and color density. Letterpress operators investigated keyless inking systems. One such system, the Civilox system, employed an ink-carrying drum to provide a continuous, evenly distributed and automatically monitored ink supply. Advocates of Civilox technology noted that converting letterpress equipment would cost an estimated $100,000, much less than the $1 million to an offset press.

Another innovation developed during the early 1990s was a hybrid of web-fed technology and plateless printing, in which a special light-sensitive drum was used to print variable information for each impression made during a press run. This computer enhanced system enabled its operators to offer personalized, mass-printed output. One industry analyst predicted that as computer and printing technologies advanced, future recipients of documents would be unable to tell the difference between an item printed on a printing press and one individually generated with a computer.

The most significant technological strides in flexography surrounded direct-to-plate (DTP) flexo technology, which was fully realized for the first time in 1996. The Illinois *Decatur Herald & Review* was the first of several newspapers to commercially use DTP in every section of the full-color newspaper. Other flexographers were moving toward DTP technology, which is advantageous because of time, resource, and environmental savings.

One recently-discovered, unexpected environmental bonus for flexo is that a mixture of baking soda effectively cleans press rollers. Previous roller cleansers were hazardous to the environment, whereas the Environmental Protection Agency considers baking soda nontoxic. Printers also found that the baking soda mixture is gentle to the rubber-composition rollers, and thus preserves the life of expensive equipment better than harsh cleaning agents did.

By the mid-1990s, researchers at institutes like the Graphic Arts Technical Foundation were still looking for ways to address optimum ink control on flexographic presses. Of special concern was the fact that barcodes were difficult to reproduce well, and the consequences of a finished job with defective barcoding were, of course, disastrous. A new procedure called "echotopography"—a computerized schematic of press capabilities in a given situation—was in development and would allow printers to determine exact ink density for specific kinds of paper.

FURTHER READING

"American Banknote 1995 Annual Report." American Banknote Corporation: New York, 1996.

Berreby, David. "The Companies that Make Money from Making Money." *The New York Times,* 23 August 1992.

Borowsky, Irvin J. *Opportunities in Printing Careers.* Lincolnwood, IL: NTC Publishing Group, 1992.

Castegnier, Pierre. "Elcography: a New Digital Printing Alternative." *GATF World,* January/February 1997.

Annual Report. Deluxe Corporation: Shoreview, MN, 1997. Available from http://www.hoovers.com.

"Delving into Digital Proofing." *Graphic Arts Monthly,* July 1992.

Falkman, Mary Ann. "Bio-Lab Makes a Splash with Inhouse Bottle Decorating." *Packaging Digest,* September 1996.

"High-speed Hot Stamp is For In-line Decorating." *Plastics World,* September 1996.

Karol, Michael. "UV Inks Put Bally in the Game." *Graphic Arts Monthly,* April 1993.

Kendra, Erika. "1997 Technology Forecast—Flexography." *GATF World,* January/February 1997.

———. "1997 Technology Forecast—Screen Printing." *GATF World,* January/February 1997.

Keuny, Barbara. "Presses at Milwaukee-area Printers Ready to Roll Out of Recession." *The Business Journal Serving Greater Milwaukee,* 27 May 1991.

Lustig, Theodore. "Flexography: Growing and Changing." *Graphic Arts Monthly,* July 1992.

Morris-Lee, James. "New Technology Helps Marketers Get Personal." *Direct Marketing,* February 1992.

Rosenberg, Jim. "Not Just for Offset Anymore." *Editor & Publisher,* 28 September 1991.

———. "Single Width, CTP for Flexo, Too." *Editor & Publisher,* 4 May 1996.

Darnay, Arsen J., ed. *Manufacturing USA,* 5th ed. Detroit: Gale Research, 1996.

—Karen Bellenir, updated by Lisa Calhoun

SIC 2761

MANIFOLD BUSINESS FORMS

This category covers establishments primarily engaged in designing and printing, by any process, special forms for use in the operation of a business, in single and multiple sets, including carbonized or interleaved with carbon or otherwise processed for multiple reproduction.

The status of the manifold business form industry is directly tied to the overall health of the business sector in the United States. A bustling economy, with established businesses reporting growth and new enterprises entering the field and surviving during their first years of operation, breeds a demand for business products. The establishments engaged in printing and manufacturing manifold business forms generally limit their product lines to such forms. The number of these establishments has grown steadily throughout the 1970s, 1980s, and 1990s. Dun & Bradstreet reported 941 establishments as of 1996, an increase of approximately 100 establishments over the course of a decade. The value of shipments for 1996 topped $7.8 billion, up from $7.4 billion in 1992. Industry leaders into the late 1990s are Standard Register Co., of Dayton, Ohio; New England Business Service, Inc., of Groton, Mass.; and Shade/Allied, Inc., of Green Bay, Wis.

While revenues and the number of establishments have continued to increase, the number of people employed by the industry began to decrease in the early 1990s. In 1987, for instance, the industry employed 53,000 people, of which production workers accounted for 37,100. As of the mid-1990s, however, the industry employed only 45,000 people, with production workers accounting for only 32,000. This decline is partly due to the growing use of computers in businesses of all sizes. Affordable laser printers can easily produce mass-volume custom business forms of all types, rendering unnecessary the need to purchase standard manifold forms. The proliferation of electronic financial transactions has also hurt the industry, resulting in a reduced demand for standard commercial checkbooks. In addition, many companies and government facilities have begun to make their forms available for download over the Internet. While widespread use of laser printers for on-demand forms, along with other industry-related factors (such as increasing paper prices), suggests a challenged industry, the continued increase in revenues shows every indication of stability, albeit with a smaller workforce.

Manifold business forms are printed by commercial printing establishments and then sold to other businesses for use in all manner of transactions. Many of the establishments in this industry are regional in scope, gearing their sales and distribution efforts to a limited area. Such companies may market their products through an in-house sales team that targets area businesses, or they may sell their wares through retail office supply outlets or local printing shops. The products can be classified into two sub-categories: custom and stock. Custom forms are printed to a specific enterprise's particular needs, while stock forms can be sold to and used by a wide range of establishments. Stock manifold business forms include sequentially-numbered tickets, cash receipt journals, message memo pads, invoice books, and spreadsheet books. Blank standard legal documents, such as lease agreements for landlords and incorporation forms, are also a vital component of the manifold business form industry. Most Americans encounter manifold business forms in a variety of daily public transactions, but their use is often vital to behind-the-scenes business operations as well.

FURTHER READING

1987 Census of Manufactures, Washington: United States Department of Commerce, 1989.

1992 Census of Manufactures, Printing and Publishing U.S. Census Bureau. Available from http://www.census.gov/epcd/www/mc92ht27.html], 1996.

''American Business Products.'' *Wall Street Transcript,* 2 January 1989.

''Bowater to Sell Star Forms Business Unit.'' *Pulp & Paper,* 70 no. 11 November 1996.

Current Industrial Reports: Business Forms, Binders, Carbon Paper, and Inked Ribbons 1986, Washington: United States Department of Commerce, September 1987.

Dun's Census of American Business 1996, Bethlehem, PA: Dun & Bradstreet, 1996.

Employment, Hours, and Earnings, United States, 1990-95, Washington: United States Department of Labor, Bureau of Labor Statistics, September 1995.

''Illinois Offers Forms On-line,'' *St. Louis Post-Dispatch,* 11 May 1996.

''Legal Kit Sales Hold Steady.'' *Discount Store News,* 6 January 1992.

Market Share Reporter, Detroit: Gale Research, 1997.

''Paying Taxes Gets Cleaner Due to ADP Form Change.'' *Wall Street Journal,* 4 December 1989.

United States Industrial Outlook 1992, Washington: United States Department of Commerce, January 1992.

United States Industrial Outlook 1994, Washington: United States Department of Commerce, January 1994.

Wandyez, Katarzyna. ''Limited Options.'' *Forbes,* 27 November 1989.

—Carol Brennan, updated by James P. Dee

SIC 2771

GREETING CARDS

This category includes establishments which publish and/or print greeting cards for all occasions. Producers of hand-painted greeting cards are classified in **SIC 8999: Services, Not Elsewhere Classified.**

INDUSTRY SNAPSHOT

In 1994 just over 160 establishments made up the U.S. greeting card industry. Two manufacturers dominate the business: American Greetings Corporation, the largest publicly owned greeting card manufacturer in the world, and Hallmark Cards, Inc., the largest privately owned manufacturer. Together, these two companies entered the 1990s controlling 75 percent of the $5.6 billion in annual U.S. greeting card sales. Gibson Greetings, Inc. was a distant third with 10 percent of industry sales. By 1996, according to *Adweek,* American Greetings commanded a 36 percent share of the market, and Hallmark claimed 42 percent.

Throughout the latter part of the twentieth century, this industry has grown annually by roughly 1 percent, based on sales revenues. However, the Greeting Card Association has predicted an annual growth rate of 5 percent by the start of the twenty-first century due to developments in marketing and technology. *Progressive Grocer* reported that 1995 greetings card sales in supermarkets alone reached $1.9 billion. Representing a 4 percent rise in this category over 1994, this one year growth pattern shows hefty progress in what is a $3.6 billion industry.

ORGANIZATION AND STRUCTURE

Greeting card companies run their establishments on two structural models. Larger establishments have in-house creative staff, including graphic artists, designers, creative consultants/directors, and writers. Smaller companies typically use freelancers to provide these services. Generally, printing is done in-house by both large and small establishments; the notable exception to this, however, is Hallmark Cards, Inc., which has used an outside printer since the late 1940s. Common to both types of establishments is the emphasis on marketing. Leaders in this industry have highly developed distribution and marketing research and promotion systems.

Distribution. Since greeting cards formerly appeared mainly in drug and grocery stores in relatively small quantities, manufacturers relied heavily on small-package delivery services. Hallmark Cards, Inc. used long-haul trucks and trains to ship cards from their distribution centers in Liberty, Missouri and Enfield, Connecticut to distribution points throughout the country. From there, smaller courier services handled regional distribution. But since 1995, reports *Material Handling Engineering,* Hallmark has handled all phases of its own distribution from its Research Distribution Operations division in Kansas City, a 226,000 square foot facility that uses ergonomic operator workstations, high-tech carousels, and a state-of-the-art tracking system to triple its throughput.

Other manufacturers, however, rely heavily on their relationship with couriers, notes *Distribution.* Because of the seasonal nature of most greeting cards, companies require timeliness of shipments and a courier that is able to handle the returned unsold cards at the end of a season. Moreover, throughout the year unsold cards need to be returned and replaced speedily as part of this industry's marketing strategy.

Marketing Research and Promotion. Manufacturers have structured their marketing divisions to engage in marketing research and promotion at two levels. One level addresses retailers and works with each store or regional chain to create a product mix and display specific to each retailer's sales record. The other level addresses customers directly by using consumer-specific research. The industry uses demographic studies and surveys of consumer tastes and purchasing behaviors extensively.

BACKGROUND AND DEVELOPMENT

Louis Prang, a German-born immigrant who founded a lithography business in Boston, made the first commercially printed greeting cards in America during the Christmas season of 1874. His folded cards contained messages inside, copying the newly formed tradition of Victorian English Christmas cards. Since Americans were not accustomed to purchasing greeting cards, Prang's first year of business went exclusively to England. He put his cards on the American market the following year and soon added birthday and Easter cards to his product line. But sales were slow, and by 1890 he had stopped producing cards. In *The Romance of Greeting Cards,* Ernest Dudley Chase suggests that Prang's lack of success with the American market was due in large part to the popularity of less expensive German-made greeting cards, which were closer in appearance to postcards than greeting cards. Prang's cards were also more costly to produce due to their use of colors.

Joyce C. Hall, founder of Hallmark Cards, entered the greeting card industry in the early 1900s by producing postcards similar to the German-made cards. Hall had predicted that the postcard craze would not last because he felt that postcards were an inadequate means of personal communications. Hall's prediction was realized at the onset of World War I. At this time greeting cards, as known from the Victorian era, were reintroduced to the American consumer because the war curtailed postcard shipments from European manufacturers and because greeting cards filled a niche by providing sentiments and "morale boosters" to send to soldiers.

World War II saw another increase in card sales, as greetings were again sent to soldiers overseas. But this time, card sales continued to grow in post-war America as more people moved across the country and corresponded more by mail. Also, the industry grew with increased competition; at the end of the war, American Greeting Publishers (later American Greetings Corp.) entered the market and by the mid-1950s proved to be a major competitor for Hallmark. The competition between these two industry leaders and the increase in television advertising evolved into the marketing-oriented greeting card industry of the late twentieth century.

Sales Trends. From the 1970s to the early 1990s marketing underwent major changes within this industry. At the retail level, sales to chain variety stores and drug and grocery stores increased while sales to card shops decreased. This shift from card shops to departments of other retail stores resulted in large part from changes in consumer habits, for people wished to purchase cards at the same store where they made their other purchases. In the mid-1980s, this shift was fueled by a price war among industry leaders which dramatically reduced prices for retailers while retaining the same pre-printed prices for consumers.

Marketing directed at consumers has been historically difficult for this industry. According to *Drug Topics,* studies have revealed that card shoppers (90 percent of whom are female) do not tend to purchase cards on the basis of brand names. One approach to this marketing problem has been to attract customers through messages available in greeting cards, which reflect trends in consumer interests and lifestyles. In *Discount Merchandiser,* Ela Schwartz observes that "when it comes to responding to shifts in consumer behavior or picking up on the latest trends, greeting-card vendors are in the forefront."

The 1980s marked a departure from tradition for card manufacturers as they responded to changes in consumer behavior with "alternative" or "non-occasion" cards. The demand for such cards emerged from changes in letter-writing habits and in personal relationships. As Karen Durand, product manager at Gibson Greetings, explained to *Discount Merchandiser,* "The customer doesn't want to spend 20 minutes writing a letter, but they will spend ten to 20 minutes finding the right card." The alternative cards assist personal communications by dealing with such topics as drug and alcohol addiction. These cards have also responded to changes in personal relationships with messages addressing topics such as coping with a divorce or living with a step-parent. Alternative cards grew in sales by nearly 10 percent per year in their first few years of production.

Another notable shift in the types of messages in greeting cards has been movement away from the more traditional poetry to conversational verse and prose. Marketing research for alternative cards showed consumers wanted straightforward messages written in a straightforward style. An exception to this trend for prose messages has been in religious cards. All of the industry leaders produce a religious or inspirational line of cards, which experienced an increase in sales at the beginning of the 1990s.

By the mid-1990s the concept of market segmentation had evolved further. *Progressive Grocer* noted in August 1996 that Hallmark had developed an ethnic line with Mahogany, a highly successful selection of cards for the African American market, and that specially-designed Tree of Life cards were enjoying growing popularity with Jewish customers.

Innovations and Developments. The mid-1980s and early 1990s brought on significant developments in the greeting card industry in the areas of production and distribution. In the mid-1980s an innovation in printing added to the many printing processes used by greeting card manufacturers. A process called Prismatic Imaging stamps a card with a silver dye and then prints on top of the stamping. By 1991, the House of Gold, New Jersey, which has exclusive license on the process, stamped 40 million cards annually for the greeting card industry.

In 1991, Gibson Greetings introduced a line of recyclable cards. At that time, Hallmark Cards and American Greetings had started using recyclable paper to a lesser extent in some of their products. Gibson Greetings also began using other environmentally sensitive materials in production, such as organic dyes, inks, and cleaning solutions.

A significant development in the distribution of greeting cards emerged with the use of electronic ordering and inventory control systems, known as electronic data interchange (EDI). Replacing the use of the postal service, EDI systems allow retailers to order cards through a computer directly linked with manufacturers and independent distributors. This has facilitated speedier ordering and more accurate inventory controls.

In 1992, Hallmark and American Greetings introduced self-access personalized greeting cards which customers were able to produce personally at an in-store computer kiosk. A variety of designs, colors and typefaces made it possible to buy cards which were far more original than mass-produced ones, and personally-added messages expressed their senders' personalities even further.

While the idea was potentially profitable, the path of the computer kiosks was not a smooth one. Since several companies chose to introduce them almost simultaneously, there was a controversy over patent rights. In 1992, Hallmark filed a claim against American Greetings, claiming that Hallmark had marketed the concept first with its Touch-Screen Greetings, patented in July 1991 while American Greetings patented CreataCard in October 1991. Also heavily involved in the dispute was Custom Expressions, Inc., the company which had invented the technology behind these kiosks.

Nevertheless, Morry Weiss of American Greetings predicted that his company's CreataCard kiosks would generate nearly $500 million in annual sales by the end of the century, according to *Industry Week.* His reasoning, given the fact that customers were now able to express their own personal taste, was that the kiosks would not only encourage more card-buying by younger shoppers and by men, but would also make it easier for market researchers to gauge the tastes of the buying public. However, as the *Kansas City Star* noted, these kiosks did not fulfil their early promise. By June 1995, Hallmark was expected to close 1,500 of its 2,700 centers, based on a two-year survey of sales.

Other innovations of the mid-1990s come from Hallmark and American Greetings, both of whom routinely provide card-shopping service through online services America Online and CompuServe. Special occasion greetings, cards for gay and lesbian shoppers, and mail-out services are featured. Another trend ties cards to the movies. In July 1995 *Chain Drug Review* reported that Hallmark had made licensing arrangements with Disney and Warner Brothers to produce theme cards based on popular movies.

INDUSTRY LEADERS

Founded in 1910 as Hall Brothers, Hallmark Cards, Inc. has become the leading producer of greeting cards sold in the United States, with 1996 sales of $3.6 billion. Along with the other industry leaders, American Greetings Corporation ($2.2 billion in 1996 sales) and Gibson Greetings, Inc. ($390 million in 1996 sales), Hallmark also manufactures wrapping paper and other gift and novelty items. By the early 1990s, only 52 percent of Hallmark's sales came from greeting cards.

In 1996, the privately held Hallmark employed 20,100 workers, with roughly 5,000 working in production (printing, lettering, die-cutting and related jobs) and 700 in writing and designing. Up until the early 1990s, staff developing new cards worked independently within their own department. Hallmark reengineered this process so that a team of mixed-occupation personnel (artists, writers, lithographers, merchandisers and administrators) worked on a single holiday. This system is not expected to completely replace departments, but "should cut cycle time in half, which will not only save money, but will also

make the company more responsive to changing tastes," according to *Fortune.*

Due to the slow growth of this industry, Hallmark and other industry leaders have diversified into new markets. By 1992, Hallmark owned over nine Spanish language television stations, a cable television company and Binney and Smith, which produces Crayola crayons. At this time Hallmark also investigated selling the remaining 170 Hallmark Card Shops that they still owned. Of the more than 10,000 shops which exclusively sell Hallmark products, the majority are now privately owned.

In the mid-1990s, drugstores and supermarkets continue to be among the most important outlets for greetings cards. Since card suppliers maintain these card displays, a store rarely carries more than one brand, and often works in tandem with the manufacturer to maximize its profits. The Copps supermarket chain based in Stevens Point, Wisconsin, advertises its American Greetings cards about 15 times per year, centering efforts round seasonal events. Each store also cross-markets by displaying birthday cards in the bakery department, Thanksgiving cards alongside turkeys, and get-well cards in the in-house drugstore. According to *Progressive Grocer* of January 1996, these efforts have paid handsome dividends for Copps. The 17 corporate stores selling greetings cards have enjoyed a 20 percent rise in revenues since their promotions began.

Upon entering the 1990s, Hallmark, like other commercial publishers and printers, was concerned about regulations on the use of solvents, which are primarily employed for cleaning printing presses. According to Jennifer Hicks of *American Printer,* Hallmark might have to change its use of solvent-laden cleaning cloths as a result of legislation in Kansas against such solvents. This legislation could reverse the use of time-saving cleaning techniques, which have taken years to develop.

WORK FORCE

In the United States, greeting card manufacturers employ an estimated 60,000 workers. Administrative and marketing staff make up 50 percent of the workers; additional marketing and public relations agencies frequently provide temporary personnel. Printers and production specialists make up nearly 40 percent of this work force. Graphic artists and writers account for only ten percent, but their numbers are expected to increase with increased production of alternative cards.

AMERICA AND THE WORLD

According to the Greeting Card Association, this industry has virtually no competition from foreign manufacturers selling in the United States. As exporters of greeting cards, the American industry has limited its business due to the high cost of small shipments. American exporters primarily license foreign printers to print their cards. Canada and the United Kingdom are the largest importers of American-made greeting cards.

FURTHER READING

"American Greetings Corp." *Wall Street Journal,* 12 August 1992.

"Among Greeting Cards Shoppers, Brand Switching Is Commonplace." *Discount Store News,* 15 October 1990.

Appelbaum, Cara. "Gibson Greetings Goes Green." *AdWeek's Marketing Week,* 11 February 1991.

Bowman, Robert. "Casebook: Hallmark Cards." *Distribution,* May 1990.

———. "Casebook: Hallmark Cards." *Distribution,* June 1992.

Butcher, Lola. "Log On, Type: Zap! Greet 'Em Yourself." *Kansas City Business Journal,* 15 May 1992.

———."Carousels Drive Hallmark's New Selection System." *Material Handling Engineering,* November 1995.

Cohen, Jeffrey. "It's in the Cards." *Progressive Grocer,* January 1996.

Gordon, Jay. "Managing Small Shipments Is Big Business at Hallmark." *Distribution,* September 1989.

"Greeting Cards." *Progressive Grocer,* August 1992.

"Greeting Cards." *Progressive Grocer,* August 1996.

"Greeting Cards: Party On." *Progressive Grocer,* June 1996.

"Hallmark Keeps Close Eye on Emerging Market Trends." *Chain Drug Review,* 3 July 1995.

"Hallmark Shifts Card Strategy." *Kansas City Star,* 21 June 1995.

"Hallmark Takes to the Net and Sentiments Go E-Mail." Kansas City Business Journal, 15 November 1996.

Hicks, Jennifer. "A Clean Sweep." *American Printer,* August 1991.

Johnson, Gregory S. "Data Link Keeps It All in Order." *Journal of Commerce,* 18 November 1991.

Kiley, David. "Hallmark's Cards Address Modern Family Problems." *AdWeek's Marketing Week,* 27 March 1989.

McCormack, Kevin. "Greetings from Hallmark." *Adweek,* 11 November 1996.

McKenna, Joseph F. "From JIT, with Love: American Greetings Sends a Trump Card to Competitors by Way of Do-It-Yourself Retailer." *Industry Week,* 17 August 1992.

"Mix-and-Match Sentiments." *New York Times,* 29 July 1992.

Mooney, Barbara. "American Greetings Shopping for CreataCard PR Aid." *Crain's Cleveland Business,* 10 August 1992.

Much, Marilyn. "Hallmark Pursues Best Customers." *Direct,* August 1992.

Oliver, Suzanne. "Christmas Card Blues." *Forbes,* 24 December 1990.

Pyle, Diane L. "How to Interview Your Customers." *American Demographics,* December 1990.

Rouland, Renee Covino. "Micromarketing and Best Wishes." *Discount Merchandiser,* July 1992.

Schwartz, Ela. "The Next Cycle in Greeting Cards." *Discount Merchandiser,* July 1990.

"Slow Economy Helps Boost Sales of Greeting Cards." *Drug Topics,* 20 July 1992.

Stern, Ellen Stock. *The Very Best From Hallmark: Greeting Cards Through the Years.* New York: Abrams, 1988.

Stern, William M., "Loyal to a Fault," *Forbes,* 14 March 1994.

Stewart, Thomas A. "The Search for the Organization of Tomorrow." *Fortune,* 18 May 1992.

Toth, Debra. "Cards Compete in New Outlets." *Graphic Arts Monthly,* December 1991.

Touby, Laurel. "Congratulations on Your Big Earnings Increase!" *Business Week,* 17 August 1992.

Wandycz, Katarzyna. "Love Means Never Having to Say Anything." *Forbes,* 1 April 1991.

—Paola Trimarco, updated by Gillian Wolf

SIC 2782

BLANKBOOKS, LOOSELEAF BINDERS AND DEVICES

This industry consists of establishments primarily engaged in manufacturing blankbooks, including checkbooks and books with ruling paper, and looseleaf binders. Other items included in this industry are albums, ruled chart and graph paper, and record albums.

In 1996, the three largest U.S. companies in terms of sales for blankbooks and looseleaf binders were Safeguard Business Systems, Inc., ACCO USA, Inc., and Holson Burnes Group, Inc., totalling approximately $480 million in sales for that year. According to a Dun & Bradstreet study, there were 851 establishments within this category in 1996, with the value of shipments estimated at $4.3 billion, up from the 1994 figure of $3.9 billion. As of the 1994 Census of Manufactures, the industry employed more than 37,000 people, a figure unchanged since the previous Census of 1987.

While blankbooks have been produced since the advent of the first printing presses, the modern-day concept of the looseleaf binder is less than 50 years old in the United States. The production of blankbooks, which includes checkbooks, ledgersheets, accounting books, and diaries, has changed little in its U.S. history, until recently. Modernization has replaced letterpress with offset printing for the small amount of actual printing involved in blankbook manufacturing.

The largest checkbook producers looked to product diversification for increased profits in the early 1990s, but mid-size checkbook companies in the late 1990s are reportedly focusing on improving existing check printing systems to meet the ever-growing volume of checks written in the United States each year. One report stated that 61 billion checks were written in 1995, a figure that is increasing in the late 1990s by about 2 percent per year.

The looseleaf binder manufacturers have seen growth through innovation and diversification within their product lines. According to Fred Ferris of *American Printer,* the "most exciting development" in this sector of the industry in recent years has been the use of 4-color lithograph on vinyl. This has greatly eased the majority of the industry's manufacturing, which entails the production of custom-designed binders with company logos and other artwork.

Another major development for looseleaf binder manufacturers has been the introduction of new flexible vinyls for binder covers; these vinyls are more durable and tighter fitting than their predecessors. However, these new vinyls have posed problems for the industry because they are harmful to the environment; the vinyl does not decompose in landfills and releases a hazardous chemical when incinerated.

Competition among manufacturers is generally concentrated in the area of accessories, such as supplementary pockets and slots designed to carry additional awkward items. From the mid-1980s, binders with accessories have remained in strong demand with the advent of organizers—looseleaf datebooks with inserts, such as foldout maps and charts. For looseleaf binder manufacturers involved in the production of organizers, diversification has also been realized with profits derived from the sale of a large variety of insert refills.

Despite recurring predictions that blankbooks and looseleaf binder manufacturers would suffer as a result of the emergence of the computer industry, the industry has experienced considerable growth during the 1980s and 1990s. In fact, with the increase of computer use, this industry has increased its production for computer-related products.

FURTHER READING

1992 Census of Manufactures, Printing and Publishing U.S. Census Bureau. Available from http://www.census.gov/epcd/www/mc92ht27.html, 1996.

"Checks: Still Second Only to Cash." *Chain Store Age Executive with Shopping Center Age,* 70, no. 9, September 1994.

Chithelen, Ignatius. "Printing Money." *Forbes,* 18 March 1991.

"Custom Binders Do More Than Capture Paper." *American Printer,* February 1989.

Dun's Census of American Business 1996, Bethlehem, PA: Dun & Bradstreet, 1996.

Employment, Hours, and Earnings, United States, 1990-95, Washington: United States Department of Labor, Bureau of Labor Statistics, September 1995.

Ferris, Fred. "Loose Talk." *American Printer,* March 1991.

Slovak, Julianne. "Companies to Watch: John H. Harland." *Fortune,* 27 March 1989.

Tenner, Edward. "The Right Organizer Can Make Your Day." *Money,* December 1985.

"Two Midsize Check Printing Firms Put Their Bets on High-Tech Gear." *American Banker* 161, no. 39.

—Paolo Trimarco, updated by James P. Dee

SIC 2789

BOOKBINDING AND RELATED WORK

This industry covers establishments providing edition, trade, job, and library bookbinding and related services, such as paper bronzing, gilding and edging, and mounting of maps and samples. The classification covers only establishments primarily binding books printed elsewhere; establishments binding books printed at the same establishment are classified in **SIC 2731: Books: Publishing, or Publishing and Printing** and **SIC 2732: Book Printing.**

The total value of bookbinding shipments increased from $1.258 billion to $1.379 billion from 1993 to 1994. Shipment value in 1995 was estimated at $1.50 billion, and it was expected to increase to $1.66 million by 1998. In 1996 approximately 1,100 binderies were in operation in the United States. In the early 1990s the two leading binders in America were

Hart Graphics, Inc. and Nicohstone, Inc. The majority of small to medium binderies were subsidiaries of the commercial printing industry.

There were three major associations concerned with bookbinding: Book Manufacturers Institute, Binders' Guild, and the Society of Bookbinders.

Bookbinding falls into several categories: edition (large runs), job binding (short runs), library, pamphlet, manifold (business forms or ledgers) and blankbook binding. Highly specialized preservation bookbinders usually attempt to restore original bindings of old books.

Until the 1980s, few developments were made in the binding process, although more establishments emerged in response to the demand for more magazines and books. In 1988 Otava Publishing in Finland introduced America to a binding process called Otabind, which enables books to stay open and lie flat without damaging the spine of the book. The process was developed in 1980 and has since been used increasingly throughout Europe. Otabind has proven highly valuable to trade printers who produce computer manuals, previously made with costly spinal binders. The predecessors to Otabind were the centuries-old casebinding, wherein cases (folded sheets of paper) were stitched together, and perfect-binding, a modern innovation that applied durable adhesives directly to the edge of unfolded paper, replacing the time-consuming folding and stitching process.

Given the expense of new machines and adhesives needed to implement the Otabind process, it was slow to gain popularity with binders. In order to justify costs, binders needed to take on large runs using Otabind. This problem was reduced with the introduction of RepKover—meaning reinforced paperback cover—which uses cloth strips for pre-assembly of covers, allowing printers to send partially bound books to a binder for Otabinding. This has enabled binders to accept numerous small orders, adding up to a large run.

By 1992 the inventors of Otabind had issued 29 licenses to U.S. binders to use their process. However, American versions of this process were beginning to emerge in the early 1990s, and more versions are expected to be developed by the end of the century.

New equipment to improve binding included Xerox's ChannelBind System that provided 2.5 tons of clamping force; the Muller Martini Trendbinder; the BQ-440 perfect binder; and the Profinish CT-1000 casing machine that doubled the amount of hand production from 50 to 100 per hour. Bindery equipment manufacturers all emphasized equipment that utilized digital technology to integrate components, simplify set-up steps, and boost productivity. In 1994 new saddle-stitching systems were introduced, among them the Stahl USA ST-90 with the capability of converting untrimmed signatures into completed books.

Other significant innovations in this industry have come from the use of new adhesives and less labor-intensive machines. Polyurethane resin (PUR) added durability to bindings, and Polyvinyl acetate (PVA) added flexibility. PVA proved valuable in manufacturing because it can be applied cold. Less labor-intensive machines have also appeared in binderies in response to employee health problems, such as carpal tunnel syndrome—a result of hand gathering and feeding.

While Japan's printing industries achieved a faster growth than the average for all industries, its production of bookbinding machines fell 25 percent from 1990 to 1994.

WORK FORCE

The total number of employees in blankbooks and bookbinding in 1995 was over 70,000, of which 54,000 were production workers. The majority of jobs were in commercial printing plants. Bindery workers had median weekly earnings of about $396 in 1994, with a range from $205 to $673 weekly. Production workers earned an average of $9.68 per hour that same year.

The demand for bindery workers is expected to grow slower than for all other occupations through the year 2005. Demand for printed material is expected to increase, but productivity through greater efficiencies and increased mechanization is also expected to increase, accounting for the stabilization of employment in the industry.

Arandell Corporation, Quebecor Printing, and R.R. Donnelly & Sons used new software to create the most automated binderies in the United States. New "in-line" equipment performs operations in sequence from beginning to a finished product.

Other binderies rely on niche marketing for viability. Reindl Bindery designs, engineers, and builds its own equipment to create a special product for a client. It recently installed a Kolbus perfect binding system and doubled the number of perfect-bound books it processed in one year and increased run lengths from 10,000 to 100,000. How Booklet Binding, Inc. has successfully resorted to hiring a sales force, something most binderies are reluctant to do. Starting with $20,000 in 1976, the company grew to an anticipated $23 million sales revenue in 1996.

BookCrafters grew so fast in one year that it outgrew its building. Using a total of 21 presses,

Otabind, Smythe sewing, and other equipment, it offers a variety of bindings such as: case, spiral wire, and saddle-stitch. The company provided binding and printing services and now offers a full line of book production services to niche publishers.

Changes are occurring both in the processing and the promotion of bindery products and services. Targeted advertising and increased distribution costs are two of these. General binding and finishing were among the top services provided in-house at many small commercial and quick printers. Guillotine cutters found a home as an accessory for on-demand color printers and direct-imaging presses.

As the industry entered the 1990s, new concerns arose over the education and safety of employees. The rapid technological changes in the industry required employee training and specialized education. Employee safety became increasingly important with discoveries that the new adhesives were hazardous to air quality. This factor also gained the attention of customers, who were concerned about the contents of the chemicals used in the binding process and the environmental consequences of getting rid of bound materials. There was some concern regarding recycling ethylene-vinyl acetate (EVA)—a hot-melt adhesive preferred for its excellent adhesion to a variety of paper and cardboard stocks. Water dispersable hot melt adhesives were the only type that could be repulped.

FURTHER READING

"Bound For Change." *Graphic Arts Monthly,* May 1990.

Burke, Steven. "Prospering in a Changing Bindery." *American Printer,* May 1994.

Dilger, Karen Abramic. "Pressing on." *American Printer,* October 1996.

Ferris, Fred. "Bound to No Rules." *American Printer,* March 1995..

———. "High-Tech Ending." *American Printer,* September 1995.

———. "The State of the Bindery." *American Printer,* June 1991.

Hilts, Paul. "New Developments in Otabind: A Better Mousetrap Gets Better." *Publishers Weekly,* 28 June 1991.

Hyatt, Joshua. "Hot Commodity." *Inc.,* February 1996.

Jarvis, Neil R. "Impact of EVA Based Hot Melts on Paper Recycling." *Adhesives Age,* November 1995.

Lynch, Terrence. "Cam Mechanism Powers Desktop Book Binder." *Design News,* 7 March 1994.

Owens, James Joseph. "Commercialization of Hot Melt Adhesives." *Adhesives Age,* November 1993.

"Packaging, Binding, Design Top Services." *Graphic Arts Monthly,* July 1995.

"Product Trends Chart Future Course." *Graphic Arts Monthly,* April 1996.

Shirai, Hiroshi. "Developments in Japan's Printing-Related Industry." *Japan 21st,* April 1996.

Spear, Robert C. "In-line Binding: Toward More Perfect Postpress." *Publishers Weekly,* 25 October 1993.

"Stahl USA Automates Stitching with the ST 90." *American Printer,* May 1994.

"Three Printers Choose Software to Update Bindery." *Graphic Arts Monthly,* November 1996.

Toth, Debbie. "Cutters Mend a Vital Link." *Graphic Arts Monthly,* April 1996.

Toth, Debora. "Adhesive Binding Widens Its Reach." *Graphic Arts Monthly,* October 1992.

U.S. Bureau of the Census. *Statistical Abstracts of the United States 1996.* 116th ed. Washington: GPO, 1996.

U.S. Department of Labor. Bureau of Labor Statistics. *Occupational Handbook.* 1996/97 ed. Washington: GPO, 1996.

—Paola Trimarco, updated by David C. Genaway

SIC 2791

TYPESETTING

This classification includes establishments primarily engaged in typesetting for the trade, including advertising typesetting, hand or machine composition, photocomposition, phototypesetting, computer-controlled typesetting, and typographic composition.

INDUSTRY SNAPSHOT

By the 1990s, the typesetting industry had been revolutionized by electronic technology, resulting in frequently upgraded equipment, redefined job functions, retraining of workers, and expansion of services provided to clients. New technology allowed faster turnaround on jobs, and typesetting companies were under pressure to continue to improve their equipment for even faster results.

The growing popularity of desktop publishing allowed many of typesetting's traditional clients to produce their own newsletters, advertising, and other print materials instead of contracting with typesetters for the work. Many organizations and businesses, however, elected not to become their own publishers and continued to contract with typesetters and other preprint services. With the burst of personal computers at home and in businesses, many producers of printed materials used a combination of their own computer-based technology and outside typesetting services. Typesetting remained in the 1990s a vital service industry for book publishers, magazine publishers, advertising agencies, catalog companies, and other large and small businesses.

ORGANIZATION AND STRUCTURE

The typesetting industry includes large, multi-million dollar shops with several hundred employees as well as small shops with only a few employees. Many of the larger companies offer related services, including printing, bookbinding, development, and sales of custom computer systems for desktop publishing or typesetting to client companies. Many large typesetting companies have areas of specialization as well, producing catalogs for car parts companies, textbooks, trade paperbacks, and so on.

Jobs that come into typesetting establishments must be compatible with the typesetting system. Creating this compatibility can be complex. Typesetting companies accept word processing disks from clients and convert them for use on their own systems. With the new flexibility—but potential incompatibility—of increasingly sophisticated systems, software, and hardware, the typesetting shop may enter the publishing process sooner than it has in the past. With electronic capabilities, the client and typesetting shop may test various formats and styles before actually doing the typesetting job to make sure that the two systems will work together without glitches and to be sure that the client's word processing control codes can automatically be converted to phototypesetting control codes. Most of the code conversion can be done automatically, with the typesetting operator making few decisions other than those concerning hyphenation, justification, and final output.

Desktop systems offer "what you see is what you get" technology. That is, the screen displays the text and layout exactly as it will appear on the finished page. Commercial digitized typesetting equipment also offers this electronic pagination. Once material is input, the page can be automatically arranged according to batch page processing, or an operator can manipulate the elements on the page. Because the material can be altered on screen before any hard version has been produced, changes are less expensive and time-consuming.

Large companies, such as Black Dot Graphics in Crystal Lake, Illinois, expanded their services to a point where they are considered "electronic prepress service bureaus." They provide technical assistance as well as typesetting to their clients. According to *Pub-*

lishers Weekly, these companies "are at the forefront of technical innovation in a field where technology is advancing at a breathless rate." When Black Dot began in the 1960s, it provided photocomposition services to book publishers. By the 1990s, Black Dot and other typesetters were providing a broad range of services for both color and black-and-white jobs, from initial input of data to output of printing plates or final page proofs, or any services in between, including illustration, pagination, and integration of words and graphics.

BACKGROUND AND DEVELOPMENT

Typesetting changed drastically during the last 40 years of the twentieth century. For hundreds of years, type was set with metal printing elements; this was called "hot type" because molten lead was used to manufacture individual letters, which were then set into complete words, sentences, and paragraphs. At first, the molten lead letters were set by hand, one letter or space at a time. The letters were mirror images of actual letters so that, when printed, they would read correctly. The set type was locked into a frame and ink applied to it, and the paper was printed directly from the type.

In 1886, Ottmar Mergenthaler invented a typesetting machine, which became known as a Linotype machine. This was also a hot type method, but it sped up typesetting considerably. Typesetting machines became faster and more sophisticated for the next 80 to 90 years, but operated on the same principle as the one Johann Gutenberg used in the 1400s when he invented movable type.

Unlike hot type, which is three-dimensional, "cold type" is two-dimensional. Cold type is generally regarded as any of a variety of methods in which photographic principles are used to create an image on specially treated paper. It came into widespread use in the 1970s. As a typesetter keyed in the letters, the machine made photographic images of them and reproduced those images on photosensitive paper or film. The images were arranged on a layout sheet and the printer photographed it to make a film negative from which a printing plate was then made.

Cold type has undergone several generations of change in both data storage and output. They all begin with keying in the text on a keyboard like that of a typewriter. That data input may be done by a typesetter, but generally that is now done by authors as they compose with word processors.

The first phototypesetting equipment stored the text on paper tape. The tape was punched using a special keyboard, and this specially-punched encoded tape drove the typesetting equipment, sending instructions about typeface, size, and appearance of the set type.

The next development in phototypesetting brought equipment with powerful software, photo fonts, and magnetic data storage. This was actually the first true phototypesetting machinery, and in the 1990s, was still in use in many typesetting operations.

The next generation of cold type created characters from digital information instead of a photo negative. Output is produced on photosensitive paper or film. This equipment became the standard in the 1980s. Subsequent generations of equipment employed various laser technologies for output. This is not phototypesetting since it does not employ photographic technology and output is on regular paper rather than photosensitive paper.

CURRENT CONDITIONS

The application of electronics and computers moved the industry to digitized imaging in which material is printed directly from the computer to paper or a printing plate. More typesetting companies are offering extensive preprinting services, including digital color scanning with electronic dot generation, electronic color page composition, electronic page layout, and off-press color proofing. Although many typesetting shops were still using traditional phototypesetting equipment in the early 1990s, digital typesetting is likely to make such methodologies obsolete in years to come.

Digitized typesetting opened up a world of possibilities for interface technology, the ability of two computers to communicate with one another. Some experts in the typesetting industry were predicting that by the year 2000, 50 to 75 percent of typesetting would be accomplished via interface technology.

Data may be transferred through direct or remote interfacing. Direct interface includes a cable connection with other computers such as word processors or personal computers; optical character recognition by means of scanners; media conversion (conversion of word processing program on disk to typesetting software; or reading magnetic or paper tape). Remote interfacing refers to telecommunication through a modem.

Interfacing, regardless of the method, however, requires appropriate software for conversion from word processing to typesetting equipment. Not all word processing programs and typesetting equipment, however, are compatible, requiring client and typeset-

ter to coordinate their work in advance of transmission. Typesetters do not ordinarily have the capability to convert all of the hundreds of word processing programs to their typesetting programs; however, a third-party service bureau can handle most conversions.

Such varied technological advances, however, allowed publishers to transmit manuscripts to keyboarders or typesetters in other countries with lower wages, thereby cutting publishing costs. Use of satellite and other technology is expected to further expand publishers' options.

The role of typesetting is expected to expand to include some layout or ''paste-up'' work as well. Desktop publishing systems offer this capability, and its use in commercial typesetting is growing. While in the past, typeset copy was passed on to an artist who arranged the various graphic and textual components on the page and then pasted them up on a layout sheet, components can now be arranged on the computer screen and corrections made before anything is printed out on paper or film. Even photographs or illustrations can be inserted on screen by use of digital scanners. Once the layout is complete, it is transmitted for reproduction onto paper, film, or even directly onto a plate for printing.

INDUSTRY LEADERS

The typesetting industry was led throughout the 1990s by Merrill Corporation, a public company based in St. Paul, Minnesota, that boasted annual sales in 1996 of around $237 million. Other typesetters of note include the Black Dot Group, headquartered in Crystal Lake, Illinois; York Graphic Services Incorporated, based in York, Pennsylvania; and Composing Room, Incorporated, based in Pennsauken, New Jersey.

WORK FORCE

There were more than 6,000 U.S. typesetting establishments as of 1996, more than 4,000 of which had fewer than five employees. The U.S. Census Bureau reported a 31 percent decrease in the number of employees in this industry between 1987 and 1992—from 37,600 to 26,100.However, while it may be true that technology tends to reduce the labor needed to attain the same results over time, the typesetting industry may see improvements in their employment statistics as the need arises for typesetting for electronic publications such as web sites. Adobe Systems, for instance, a leader in providing software to the typesetting industry, began in the mid-1990s to offer software for creating Internet documents. Indeed, several of the typesetting software leaders, such as Corel Corporation and Microsoft Corporation, began to incorporate

Internet publishing tools within their already popular typesetting packages.

Electronic technology changed the nature of work that typesetters do, requiring knowledge and familiarity with computers and a multitude of software programs. In typesetting, as in other prepress functions, technology required constant upgrading of skills and retraining of the work force as more and more functions become computerized.

FURTHER READING

"Computers:Software." *Standard & Poor's Industry Surveys.* New York:Standard & Poor, 10 October 1996.

"Disk-to-Disk Conversion System to Expand In-House Services." *Graphic Arts Monthly,* March 1988, 60-3.

Dun's Census of American Business 1996. Bethlehem, PA:Dun & Bradstreet, 1996.

"Expertise Pays Off." *Graphic Arts Monthly,* March 1987, 98-100.

Frank, Jerome P. "Changes in Typesetting Create Faster Turnaround." *Publishers Weekly,* 5 February 1988, 67-69.

Hilts, Len. "Avoiding Potholes in the Desktop Publishing Road." *Publishers Weekly,* 18 October 1991, 34-36.

McCollum, Tim. "In-House Publishing, Professional Results." *Nation's Business,* November 1996.

Negru, John. *Computer Typesetting.* New York: Van Nostrand Reinhold Company, 1988.

Parnau, Jeff. "The Short Life of Typesetting Equipment." *Folio,* March 1986.

Perenson, Melissa. "Do-It-Yourself Publishing." *PC Magazine,* 21 January 1997.

Rosenberg, Jim. "Technology Progress '95." *Editor & Publisher,* January 1996.

Sucov, Jennifer. "Invested Interest." *Folio,* 15 October 1996.

U.S. Bureau of the Census. *1992 Census of Manufactures.* Washington: GPO, 1996. Available from http://www.census.gov/epcd/www/mc92ht27.html.

U.S. Department of Labor. *Employment, Hours, and Earnings, United States, 1990-95.* Washington: GPO, 1995.

Ward's Business Directory of U.S. Private and Public Companies. Detroit: Gale Research, 1997.

—Wendy Stein, updated by Jim P. Dee

SIC 2796

PLATEMAKING AND RELATED SERVICES

This category covers establishments primarily engaged in making plates for printing purposes and in related services. Also included are establishments primarily engaged in making positives or negatives from which offset lithographic plates are made. These establishments do not print from the plates they make, but prepare them for use by others. Engraving for purposes other than printing is classified in **SIC 3479: Coating, Engraving, and Allied Services, Not Elsewhere Classified.**

INDUSTRY SNAPSHOT

The platemaking and related services industry was comprised primarily of companies that made printing plates used in offset lithographic printing processes. It also encompassed platemaking for numerous miscellaneous printing processes, such as gravure and letterpress. Lithography was introduced in 1796 and became popular during the 1900s. Offset printing, first applied in 1902, came to represent about 40 percent of all U.S. printing.

Steady demand growth for lithographic and related printing boosted platemaking service industry revenues to about $2.4 billion in 1987, the first year in which this industry was separately classified. Steady growth in printing markets pushed platemaking industry sales steadily upward to nearly $3.5 billion by the mid-1990s. Likewise, sales and employment are forecast to continue growing through the early 2000s, bolstered by new printing technologies and greater demand.

ORGANIZATION AND STRUCTURE

Most companies in the platemaking industry served lithographic printers. Lithography was a printing process whereby ink was applied to a flat printing surface (plate) that was treated with grease. Blank, or nonimage, areas of the surface repelled the ink, while the greased areas held it. The inked surface could then be transferred directly to paper by means of a press. In the popular offset (planographic or litho-offset) process, the inked image was first printed on a rubber cylinder and then transferred to other materials.

Platemaking companies created the templates that printers used to transfer images to the rubber cylinder or other printing media. The plate cylinder was usually zinc, aluminum, or a special alloy. Its porous surface was coated with a photosensitive material. When exposed to an image, the coated area hardened and the coating on the nonimage areas was washed away. Ink, which was continually deposited on the plate cylinder by inking rollers, was accepted by the greasy image on the plate. Modern offset printing plates were usually cylindrical, allowing them to provide a continuous transfer of ink to a rubber-covered, or blanket, cylinder.

A variety of plates were used for different offset printing processes and print jobs. Basic monometal plates were made of zinc or aluminum and functioned as described above. The plate was usually exposed to an image by covering it with a negative of text or illustrations and exposing it to intense light, after which the coating on the unexposed areas was washed away. A slight variation was the presensitized plate, which had a coating with a longer life span and could be made of paper or plastic for short print jobs.

Deep-etch plates, in contrast to monometal, exposed the plate to a positive of the text or illustration. The nonprinting areas were hardened and the printing areas were washed away. A mild acid bath etched the metal of the printing areas. The plate was then treated with an ink-receptive lacquer. Deep-etch plates were used for longer print runs of 250,000 or more copies. Bi-metal and tri-metal plates were more durable, and could dependably endure runs of 500,000 copies or more. They were created using two or three metal plates, one or two of which covered the primary plate as a microscopic film. A photoengraving process partly removed the thin metal layers.

In addition to conventional offset plates were several other platemaking processes. Electrostatic (xerographic) plates, for example, were electrically charged plates that absorbed images. A negatively charged powder stuck to the positively charged image, was heated and hardened, and acted as the ink-receptive printing surface. Similarly, immediate offset plates incorporated a polymer layer that responded to heat, as opposed to light.

In addition to lithography, other types of printing processes used plates. Rotogravure, for example, transferred fluid ink contained in the cells of the printing cylinder, or plate. Nonprint areas of the plate were kept ink-free through constant wiping. Rotogravure plates were made in a process that utilized carbon tissue paper soaked in an emulsion and exposed to an image. The carbon-imprint was then transferred to a (usually copper) cylindrical plate. Rotogravure was often used to produce high-quality color illustrations. In addition to plates for rotogravure printing were plates for collotype printing, which generated high-quality color photo reproductions; flexographic printing, used for large-scale commercial printing (e.g., newspapers and magazines); and other miscellaneous processes.

BACKGROUND AND DEVELOPMENT

During the second century A.D., the Chinese were capable of printing on paper using ink on stone surfaces with carved impressions, precursors to modern day printing plates. In about 1040, Chinese alchemist Pi Sheng designed a crude printing plate consisting of an iron plate coated with a mixture of resin, wax, and paper ash. Other rough printing plate forms were used in subsequent print processes, such as xylography (fourteenth century), metallographic printing (1430), typography (fifteenth century), and stereotypy (eighteenth century).

Czechoslovakian Alloys Senefelder envisioned the lithographic printing process in 1796. The first mechanized lithographic printer, complete with a plate cylinder, was constructed in 1850. Importantly, technological advancements during the early 1800s related to etching and photosensitivity made Senefelder's design possible. Gravure and rotogravure platemaking processes were first used in the 1890s.

It was not until the early 1900s that lithographic platemaking became widespread. The popularity of lithography, and even of modern day printing techniques, was largely a result of American Ira W. Rubel's discovery of offset printing in 1902. Rubel accidentally transferred an image from a plate cylinder to a rubber blanket, discovering that the rubber offset produced a superior image to that of the metal plate. The popularity of offset lithography spawned a flurry of advancements during the middle 1900s in the area of chemical etching, electroplating, and other technologies that were integrated into the printing and platemaking process.

Besides general economic expansion during the 1960s, 1970s, and 1980s, new inks and printing processes bolstered platemaking industry revenues. By 1987, the first year in which this industry was separately classified, platemaking companies garnered about $2.4 billion annually and employed a work force of more than 30,000. Despite the U.S. and global recession during the late 1980s and early 1990s, moreover, industry sales expanded to more than $3 billion annually by the early 1990s, and have continued to increase into the mid-1990s.

CURRENT CONDITIONS

The continual increase in revenues is stimulated by a general increase in demand for printed materials as well as technological advancements that increased the use of plate printing processes. For example, markets for several types of printed packaging ballooned, as did demand for direct mail and catalog printing.

And higher quality, faster, and less expensive printing processes, such as waterless sheetfed printing, boosted demand. Likewise, new computer technologies improved the platemaking process. Advanced desktop publishing software, for example, was integrated into digital platemaking processes to quickly produce relatively inexpensive, high-quality plates.

In the 1990s, lithographic platemaking services accounted for about 57 percent of industry sales. Color film platemaking represented the large majority of the lithographic segment, followed by various noncolor plate services. Deep-etch metal plates accounted for less than .5 percent of industry receipts, as did multi-metal plate processes. Aside from lithography, gravure cylinders made up almost six percent of industry revenues, and flexographic plates represented about 3 percent. Miscellaneous services, such as letterpress and electrostatic platemaking, comprised the remainder of sales.

Commercial printers of consumer packaging, marketing materials, and a plethora of other media accounted for roughly 75 percent of the demand for platemaking services in the early 1990s. The balance of the market was comprised of newspaper publishers, book printers and publishers, magazines, and numerous smaller markets.

The mid-1990s saw an exciting development in the platemaking industry. Computer-to-plate systems, dubbed ''CTP'' by insiders, had taken over the industry spotlight. CTP promises a quantum leap in productivity for printers. It requires fewer materials and less labor while offering enhanced quality and faster turnarounds. However, the change from conventional methods will be slow. DuPont Printing & Publishing projects that, by 2003, the percentage of pages printed via conventional means will fall only 30% from its 1996 level of 95%. As of late 1996, *Graphic Arts Monthly* reported plate manufacturer expectations that CTP will account for 15% of all printing plates by 2001, and that conventional plates won't disappear for ''some time.''

INDUSTRY LEADERS

More than 1,700 U.S. companies provided platemaking services in 1996. The industry was highly fragmented, consisting mostly of small, localized manufacturers with just a few employees. Polychrome Corp. of Fort Lee, New Jersey, was the largest industry participant, with $500 million in sales and about 1,700 workers in 1996. Eastman Kodak followed with 1996

sales of $260 million from platemaking services. Other industry leaders included Matthews International Corp. of Pennsylvania, and Techtron Graphic Arts Inc. of Illinois, which had sales of $150 and $100 million, respectively, in 1996.

WORK FORCE

Contrary to employment prospects for most U.S. manufacturing industries, job growth in printing trade services was expected to be robust between 1990 and 2005, according to the Bureau of Labor Statistics. Overall employment for platemaking laborers was forecast to rise 30 percent by 2005, despite anticipated productivity gains resulting from automation. Even positions for general managers and executives should rise an estimated 20 percent.

FURTHER READING

1992 Census of Manufactures, Printing and Publishing U.S. Census Bureau. Available from http://www.census.gov/epcd/www/mc92ht27.html], 1996.

Cross, Lisa. ''Litho Plate Technology Meets Productivity, Eco-Challenges.'' *Graphic Arts Monthly,* June 1993.

Darnay, Arsen J., editor. *Manufacturing USA; Industry Analyses, Statistics, and Leading Companies,* Detroit: Gale Research, 1993.

Dun's Census of American Business 1996, Bethlehem, PA: Dun & Bradstreet, 1996.

Esler, Bill. ''Conventional Plates Hold Their Ground.'' *Graphic Arts Monthly,* 68, no. 7, July 1996.

Employment, Hours, and Earnings, United States, 1990-95, Washington: United States Department of Labor, Bureau of Labor Statistics, September 1995.

Hilts, Paul. ''CTP for the Rest of Us.'' *Publishers Weekly,* 15 April 1996.

Johnston, Peter. ''CTP: Poised on the Brink of Success.'' *Graphic Arts Monthly,* 68, no. 4, April 1996.

''Redesigned Lith-Laminator Ideal for Specialty Packaging.'' *Paperboard Packaging,* February 1994.

Shepherd, Gary. ''Pre-Press House Skips a Generation, Goes Digital.'' *Tampa Bay Business Journal,* Available from http://www.amcity.com/tampabay/stories/072296/mewscolumn4.html], 22 July 1996.

Wards Business Directory of U.S. Private and Public Companies, 5, New York: Gale Research, Inc., 1996.

Wong, Michael, ''Adobe Systems Announces Adobe Brilliant Screens Technology for High-End Color Printing.'' *Business Wire,* 22 March 1994.

—Dave Mote, updated by James P. Dee

CHEMICALS & ALLIED PRODUCTS

ALKALIES AND CHLORINE

This industry classification includes establishments engaged in manufacturing alkalies and chlorine. Examples of products include compressed or liquefied chlorine, sodium or potassium hydroxide, sodium bicarbonate, and soda ash (not produced at mines). Alkalies produced by mining are classified in **SIC 1474: Potash, Soda, and Borate Minerals.**

INDUSTRY SNAPSHOT

The two primary commodities offered by the alkalies and chlorine industry are chlorine and sodium hydroxide (caustic soda). Together they represent about 82 percent of all shipments. The third largest commodity, soda ash, which is an alkali product used in glass making, water treatment, pulp bleaching, and detergent manufacturing, accounts for only 14 percent of shipments. Other remaining products account for 4 percent.

Chlorine and caustic soda have consistently appeared on lists of the top ten U.S. chemicals according to production weight. They are both co-products of the same chemical process. This means they are created at the same time and that the production of one results in the production of the other. Although there are several modern procedures used to produce chlorine and caustic soda, most rely on a technique called electrolysis. As electricity is passed through brine (a salt water solution), the brine's components, salt (sodium chloride) and water (made up of hydrogen and oxygen), recombine to form chlorine and sodium hydroxide (caustic soda) in approximately equal amounts. Some hydrogen gas also results from the process.

Organic chemical manufacturers are the primary chlorine users in the United States. Some examples of chemicals produced with chlorine are ethylene dichloride, carbon tetrachloride, and methylene chloride. These and other chlorinated organic chemicals are used to make many products including flame retardants, herbicides, solvents, refrigerants, polyvinyl-chloride (PVC) pipe, and pigments. The second largest chlorine user is the pulp and paper industry, which uses chlorine as a bleaching agent. Chlorine products are also used as raw ingredients in household and commercial bleaches, scouring powders, and automatic dishwashing compounds. Other chlorine uses include water treatment, sewage treatment, sanitizing, and metal extracting.

Caustic soda has a wide range of industrial applications. It is used in petroleum exploration and by water treatment facilities, tanneries, and the textile industry. It also plays a role in food processing, metal fabrication, and chemical manufacturing. Caustic soda is also used in industrial complexes to remove boiler scale.

According to U.S. Department of Commerce statistics, shipments within the alkalies and chlorine industry totaled $3.3 billion in 1995. In current dollars, the industry more than doubled since 1987 when it shipped $1.5 billion worth of products. Growth patterns of the various industry segments varied. Although overall growth within the chlorine and alkalies industry was expected to increase at a rate of 2 percent to 3 percent through the mid-1990s, some industry forecasters predicted the slowest growth would occur within the chlorine segment.

During the late 1980s, chlorine production increased, but by the early 1990s demand and production declined. The shift was attributed to economic and environmental conditions. As the national economy suffered during the recession of the late 1980s and early 1990s, construction slowed and demand for PVC products fell sharply. At the same time, pulp and paper manufacturers were turning away from chlorine-based processes because of concerns about the toxicity of dioxins, which were formed from the combination of chlorine and residue organic compounds. Other major chlorine products such as chlorofluorocarbons (CFCs) and chlorinated solvents were also under increasing criticism because of their damaging effects on the environment.

Dropping demand led to an oversupply, which consequently reduced chlorine prices. Chlorine sold at $145 per ton in 1986 and fell to about $50 per ton in 1991. Conditions within the chlorine segment of the industry affected other products. Because chlorine and caustic soda were co-products of the same chemical process, cuts in chlorine production led to shortages and higher prices within the caustic soda market. The price of caustic soda rose from approximately $120 per ton in 1986 to $300 per ton in 1991. High caustic soda prices led to increased demand for alternative products such as hydrogen peroxide and soda ash.

Although historically soda ash has been manufactured synthetically from the evaporation of brines, it is primarily produced from trona, a mined product. The last synthetic soda ash facility in the United States closed in 1986, idling 700,000 tons of capacity. Operators closed the plant because it could not produce soda ash at prices low enough to compete with the trona-reliant process. Almost half of the domestic production of soda ash is used by glass makers.

ORGANIZATION AND STRUCTURE

Approximately 99 percent of the chlorine and alkali chemical manufacturers in the United States and Canada belong to the Chlorine Institute. The Chlorine Institute was founded by ten industry leaders in 1924. Although their original purpose was to further the demand for chlorine, their focus shifted to providing the industry with supervision and direction following a destructive hurricane in 1926. The hurricane wrought havoc on Florida's water treatment facilities. Thousands of chlorine cylinders were shipped to the state to aid in restoring safe water supplies, but many could not be used because the industry had not previously adopted standardized fittings. The emergency chlorine supply sat idle until adaptors and valves could be obtained.

As a result of the experience, the Chlorine Institute initiated a study of valve and fitting designs. Following its recommendation, producers voluntarily adopted a standard. Federal officials later relied on information from the Chlorine Institute in establishing standards for all compressed gases.

The Chlorine Institute also began working on programs to improve the safety record of the industry. In the 1930s, an informal policy was established for responding to emergencies. Later the institute developed a formal program called CHLOREP (Chlorine Emergency Plan). CHLOREP consisted of volunteer teams who were available to respond to chlorine emergencies 24 hours a day, seven days a week. By 1991, the Chlorine Institute had trained 250 CHLOREP teams comprised of members from more than 40 companies, and they were placed at more than 100 locations throughout the United States and Canada.

In addition to establishing standards and emergency response programs, the Chlorine Institute published a wide range of manuals, pamphlets, and audiovisual materials to provide technical and safety information. The institute also worked on behalf of its members with the government agencies responsible for regulating various aspects of chemical production and shipment such as the Department of Transportation (DOT), the Interstate Commerce Commission (ICC), the Coast Guard, and the Occupational Safety and Health Administration (OSHA).

BACKGROUND AND DEVELOPMENT

The use of chlorine compounds in chemical processes dates back to at least 77 A.D., but the isolated element itself was not produced until 1774. Although chlorine is a common element, in nature it exists only in compounds because it reacts readily with other substances, both organic and inorganic. For example, salt, or sodium chloride, is made from chlorine and sodium.

A Swedish chemist, Karl Scheele, is acknowledged as the first person to create and identify chlorine. Scheele (who also discovered oxygen) generated a greenish-yellow gas during experiments with sea water. He called it "dephlogisticated marine acid air." The word "dephlogisticated" referred to the fact that it was not susceptible to combustion. The phrase "marine acid air" identified the new gaseous material produced from the acid obtained from marine brine. The name chlorine was not bestowed until the early 1800s when Sir Humphry Davy used electricity to demonstrate that the gas was an element. Davy borrowed a word from the Greek language referring to the gas's greenish-yellow hue and renamed it "chlorine."

The bleaching effects of chlorine were first put to commercial use by textile makers in France near the end of the eighteenth century. Natural cottons and linens were light brown and had to be bleached before they could be dyed with light or bright colors. Under traditional practices, bleaching was accomplished by spreading the fabrics out and exposing them to the sun. Bleaching cotton had taken up to three months and linen as long as six months. Chlorine bleaching compounds enabled textile manufacturers to keep up with fast-paced increases in production following improvements in spinning and weaving methods.

Chlorine products were greatly improved by technology during the late eighteenth and early nineteenth centuries. In 1792, a process for bleaching rags used in paper making was developed. Bleaching powder, or calcium hypochlorite, was first introduced in 1799. The ability to transport chlorine to markets distant from manufacturing plants was achieved through the formation of potassium hypochlorite, a liquid product created with chlorine and caustic potash.

The development of chlorine production based on electrolysis lowered chlorine prices and increased the chemical's popularity. Electrolysis methods evolved through the mid-nineteenth century and by the century's close had become commercially viable in areas with low cost electricity. The first commercial plant in the United States opened in Rumford, Maine in 1893.

As the twentieth century began, chlorine was being used for an increasing number of purposes. Jersey City, New Jersey was the first city to use chlorine to disinfect drinking water supplies. Its chlorination efforts began in 1908 and were soon followed by other major cities, including New York. Sewage treatment methods based on liquid chlorine were first adopted in Altoona, Pennsylvania in 1913. The use of chlorine by water and sewage treatment facilities helped virtually eliminate diseases such as cholera, typhoid, and dysentery.

Not all chlorine's uses, however, were benevolent. During World War I, chlorine gas, an extremely poisonous substance, was used as a weapon against the Allies. Despite the horrors associated with chlorine gas, the U.S. chlorine production industry benefited from the war. Imports of chemicals from Europe were sharply curtailed because of submarine warfare. As a result, domestic production tripled and continued to grow after the war. Chlorine has also played a role in the development of insecticides, anesthetics, dry cleaning fluids, and fire fighting compounds. The fledgling plastics industry relied on chlorine to make its vital vinyl chloride products. Between 1955 and

1970, chlorine usage grew approximately 5.8 percent per year.

The 1970s ushered in an era of changes. Although the decade closed with chlorine production at its historic high, growth stagnated. Environmental questions hampered producers and economic woes diminished demand by users. By the early 1990s, chlorine production and demand were still less than they had been in 1979.

Despite improvements ameliorating the environmental impact of chlorine and caustic soda production, the industry continued to suffer from adverse publicity concerning chlorine use. Chlorine compounds reacted with organic substances to form dioxins, which were suspected carcinogens and posed potential health hazards including birth defects and damage to the body's skin, liver, neuroendocrine system, and immune system.

Controversy about dioxins affected usage by pulp and paper producers, one of the largest chlorine-consuming industries. Chlorine was traditionally used to bleach pulp and create white paper products. Increasingly, manufacturers were turning to innovative oxygen and hydrogen peroxide bleaching technologies. Analysts estimated that the pulp and paper industry used only about 9 percent of the domestic chlorine production in 1994, a drop from the 15 percent recorded in 1990.

Environmental groups increasingly protested the use of chlorine in other areas as well. Chlorofluorocarbons (CFCs) were suspected of damaging the ozone layer of the earth's upper atmosphere. Chlorinated solvents were considered a source of air pollution because of their emissions. In addition, some water treatment facilities began turning away from chlorine to other methods of water purification. According to the Chlorine Institute, however, calls to eliminate chlorine were unreasonable, citing the heavy financial burden of meeting such restrictions.

Despite the problems associated with chlorine and its declines in traditional markets, industry analysts anticipated overall demand to grow and prices to increase as much as 15 percent by 2002. Vinyl exports and PVC use in new construction and in remodeling were expected to make up for the declines in other areas.

CURRENT CONDITIONS

Modern methods of chlorine production were developed around electrolysis. The three most often used technologies, diaphragm cells, mercury cells, and membrane cells, all produced chlorine and caustic soda by decomposing brine (salt water). Combined, they accounted for 97 percent of U.S. chlorine production in 1997. Other methods in operation in 1997 included electrolysis of either molten magnesium chloride or molten sodium chloride; electrolysis of hydrochloric acid, and non-electrolytic processes. The brine used as a raw material was obtained from natural deposits under the earth's surface or was made from salt and water.

Diaphragm cells, the oldest and most widely used of the modern methods, produced more than three quarters of the nation's chlorine. They used direct current to separate salt and water into chlorine, hydrogen, and sodium hydroxide (caustic soda). An internal asbestos fiber-coated device called a "diaphragm" helped keep the chlorine and caustic soda separate. Manufacturers relied on additional evaporation and drying procedures to create products in marketable concentrations.

Mercury cells accounted for 12.1 percent of the U.S. chlorine production in 1997. They employed a different technique for keeping manufactured chlorine and caustic soda separate. Because of the presence of mercury during the application of the cell's electric current, the sodium could be isolated and dissolved into the mercury. A secondary process recaptured the mercury and released the sodium to form sodium hydroxide (caustic soda). During the early 1990s, producers were moving away from mercury cells because of environmental concerns surrounding the mercury content of plant waste water.

Membrane cells, the most rapidly growing form of production, accounted for only 9.5 percent of U.S. chlorine production in 1997. They employed an ion exchange membrane to separate the chlorine and caustic soda. Membrane technology required less electricity and produced grades of chlorine and caustic soda with higher purity than other methods.

The remaining 2.6 percent of U.S. chlorine capacity was contributed by alternate methods. By comparison, in Canada, diaphragm cells retained their role in 85.3 percent of the production capacity, with membrane cells at 11.9 percent and mercury cells at 2.8 percent of the total.

It is of interest to note that in both nations during the period 1988-97, there was a decrease in the percentage of total chlorine production capacity contributed by mercury cells, with corresponding increases in the percentage of membrane cells in operation. This change was most dramatic in Canada, where the decrease was 12.5 percent. The decreases reflected continuing concerns about the hazards involved in use of

mercury and its potential adverse environmental impact. The relative contribution of diaphragm cells remained virtually unchanged in the United States and slightly increased in Canada (4.6 percent).

Chlorine Packaging Plants in the United States. In 1997, there were 27 different companies in the United States operating a total of 86 chlorine packaging plants. One additional plant was shut down in November of 1996—that operated by Jones Chemical in Henderson, Nevada. In contrast, there were only three such companies in Canada operating a total of seven plants, and four in Mexico, each operating one plant.

Chlorine and Caustic Soda Producers. In 1997, there were 24 companies in the United States operating 45 chlorine production plants with a total production capacity of 39,558 tons per day. By comparison, the seven operating Canadian plants had a daily production capacity only 11 percent of the U.S. value (3,561 tons per day), while the five operating Mexican plants were at 1.3 percent of U.S. capacity (529 tons per day).

Five companies either completed or were engaged in plant expansions and modernizations in the U.S. as of late 1996—Dow Chemical, Occidental Chemical, Formosa Plastics, and a joint venture between Olin Corporation and GEON.

Figures released by Dow Chemical for 1996 showed their global chlorine production capacity at 11.5 billion pounds per year and global caustic soda production capacity at 12.5 billion pounds per year. About 50 percent of the caustic soda produced was sold, generating global sales of $500 million in 1996. A plant expansion in Freeport, Texas in late 1996 increased Dow chlorine production capacity by 440 million pounds (200,000 metric tons) per year. The company heralded its first ever commercial use of membrane cell technology in its plant expansion in Stade, Germany, which added additional capacity of 260 million pounds (118,000 metric tons) per year. These increases were earmarked for the company's internal chlorine demand, which consumed over 95 percent of the chlorine generated.

Of Dow Chemical's total chlorine production in 1996, approximately one-third was directed towards production of 10 billion pounds of ethylene dichloride (EDC), which in turn was used for synthesis of vinyl chloride monomers (VCM). The latter were sold to other companies principally for production of polyvinyl chloride (PVC). An additional one-third of the chlorine production was directed towards synthesis of propylene oxide, with production of 3 billion pounds per year reported in 1996. Roughly 25 percent of this was destined for synthesis of propylene glycol, important in products such as aircraft deicing fluids. The remaining one-third of Dow's chlorine production was used for production of other chlorinated compounds.

Occidental Chemical, the second largest producer, but largest merchant marketer of chlorine and caustic soda, reported that it had completed expansions and improvements at several of its chlor-alkali facilities, noting that since 1993, Oxychem's U.S. chlorine production capacity was increased by 400 tons per day with plans to add 600 tons per day additional capacity at three Gulf Coast plants where the bulk of its production is concentrated by the end of 1998. This was slated to bring the total domestic capacity to roughly 9,000 tons per day. About 60 percent of the company's chlorine production in 1996 was directed towards its vinyls product chain—including EDC and VCM, ultimately used to manufacture PVC. The vinyls chain was the largest and most rapidly growing market for Oxychem's chlorine.

According to the U.S. Department of Commerce, chlorine capacity remained fairly stable from 1991 through 1996, with a general upward trend beginning in 1995. By 1996, the U.S. capacity (38,416 short tons per day) had slightly surpassed the 1985 value (38,298 short tons per day), but not yet returned to the 1980 level (39,391 short tons per day).

Statistics released by the Chlorine Institute revealed an overall trend towards increased domestic U.S. production of chlorine gas (and its alkali co-product) as well as the amount liquefied from 1991 through the start of 1997. Chlorine production for 1991 and 1996 was, respectively, 11,489,896 and 13,168,384 short tons. Equivalent values for liquefied chlorine were, respectively, 9,340,125 and 10,179,100 short tons. For the same period, liquid sodium hydroxide production was 12,151,285 and 13,856,531 short tons per year, respectively. The amount of dry sodium hydroxide produced during these years, although only a small percentage of the total, actually decreased from 266,137 short tons per year in 1991 to a value of 183,062 in 1996, a low of 173,925 short tons having been reached in 1995. By comparison, dry sodium hydroxide production was considerably greater in 1980 at 418,178 short tons. For the first two months of 1997, there were slight increases over the same two months of 1996 in production of chlorine and both liquid and dry sodium hydroxide.

Figures released by the U.S. Bureau of Census for the chlor-alkali industry in 1995 showed domestic total production at $3.3 billion in shipments, with contributions to this total from chlorine (compressed or liquefied) at $849.7 million, sodium hydroxide or caustic soda at $2.06 billion, and other alkalies at $382.3 million.

Prices for chlorine increased by $25 to $40 per ton at the end of 1996 and again in early 1997, by Dow, Occidental, and Vulcan. Increases were due to: previous expansions in downstream production of chlorine derivatives not having been matched by corresponding expansions in chloralkali plants, demand thus exceeding supply; failures at two Dow chloralkali rectifiers (Freeport, Texas), with resultant production delays due to repairs; a 30 day loss of production at LaRoche Industries' Gramercy, Louisiana plant, due to a fire that caused a daily 50 percent reduction in the normal 300 tons per day output; with an additional possibility being the seasonal spring increase in homebuilding, with its attendant increase in demand for PVC products.

During the first quarter of 1997, caustic soda prices continued to decrease with prices reported in February at about $95 per ton on the Gulf. Although caustic soda prices dropped $100 per ton in the year from early 1996 to early 1997, it was believed by April 1997 that prices had bottomed out. Severe flooding in the Midwest, limited transport on the Mississippi River due to elevated levels, the Dow and LaRoche production problems, and other unforeseen difficulties during the first quarter helped to stabilize prices in part by their effects on caustic soda inventories.

EPA Limits On Toxic Pollution. In 1994 the Environmental Protection Agency announced that chemical companies in the United States would have to cut their manufacturing plants' toxic air pollution by almost 90 percent from 1990 levels. The rule, noted the *Detroit Free Press,* "requires the companies . . . to install equipment to better prevent evaporation and leaks of 112 toxic chemicals. . . . About 370 chemical plants in 38 states will be forced to cut toxic air pollution by a total of 506,000 tons, an EPA statement said." While the new rules, instituted as a part of the 1990 Clean Air Act, would involve significant expenditures on capital improvements for the affected companies, regulators noted that chemical companies have already taken significant steps to address the new requirements in anticipation of the announcement.

Hydrogen Peroxide. Environmental issues continued to affect the worldwide chlorine industry in 1997, matters that were clearly reflected in the peroxide market, which is linked to the pulp and paper market. Due to excessive pulp inventories in 1996, pulp prices declined. Prior to the crash, peroxide growth was forecast at 10-12 percent annually through 2000, but afterward, at only 5-8 percent.

The initial impetus for increased hydrogen peroxide demand in the pulp and paper industry was conversion of pulp mills from elemental chlorine use due to new EPA regulations, to either chlorine dioxide (which may be generated, in turn, from sodium chlorate) or hydrogen peroxide.

By the beginning of 1997, most U.S. pulp plants had stopped using elemental chlorine for bleaching and substituted chlorine dioxide to eliminate dioxin production. During the same period, a bill was introduced in Congress to force U.S. pulp plants to use totally chlorine free (TCF) bleaching processes, a move favored by many environmentalists as a means to reduce dioxin pollution. The EPA was therefore debating between two possible rules—to either allow chlorine-based plants to substitute chlorine dioxide or to require partial substitution of chlorine dioxide with oxygen. The Chlorine Chemistry Council and paper workers' unions supported the shift to chlorine dioxide, arguing that partial substitution of oxygen would be very costly (perhaps $1 billion) and potentially eliminate thousands of jobs.

The Canadian pulp industry was believed to be at 89-90 percent elemental chlorine-free (ECF) substitution, with the United States lagging behind at perhaps only 45 percent as of early 1997. Worldwide, Scandinavian pulp producers adopted total chlorine free (TCF) substitution due to pressure from the Green Movement in Europe. Of related interest in 1997 were proposals to the European Commission by EURO-CHLOR for new air and water emissions standards for mercury-based chlor-alkali production processes. Proposed limits for air and water were 1.9 grams of mercury per metric ton of chlorine produced. Final legislation would take effect in 2005.

The trend away from chlorine use was highly beneficial for the peroxide market, and by 1996 the six producers in North America (DuPont, Solvay, Degussa, Chemprox, FMC and Eka Nobel) were gearing up for plant expansions to increase North American capacity to roughly 2 billion pounds by 1998, an increase of more than 800 million pounds over previous levels.

Despite the efforts to reduce or eliminate elemental chlorine use, strong growth was predicted in 1997 for both chlorine and non-chlorine bleaching agents in foreign markets—principally Latin America and Asia. Growth was also predicted for the U.S. domestic market for both oxygen and chlorine-containing bleaches, up from the 1996 estimated 10.4 billion pounds valued at about $2.9 billion. Forecasts were for annual market growth of 5.1 percent, reaching a value of $3.5 billion by 2000 with pulp bleaching accounting for about 66 percent of the total value, followed by water treatment, and finally by cleaning compounds.

WORK FORCE

The U.S. Department of Commerce reported that the chlorine and alkalies industry employed 7,600 workers in 1994. This figure was up to 25 percent from the mid-1980s. Four states: West Virginia, Louisiana, Texas, and Alabama, accounted for more than half of the industry's employment.

AMERICA AND THE WORLD

Chlorine production in the United States accounts for almost 30 percent of the world's capacity, but there is little international movement of chlorine because of difficulties related to its transportation and storage. Producers generally prefer to erect production facilities in regions where demand exists.

In 1992, analysts predicted that worldwide chlorine demand would grow at a rate of less than one percent per year, but they forecast wide regional fluctuations. Japan, Europe, and Canada were expected to experience declining demand for chlorine. High demand growth rates, however, were predicted for the Middle East, where annual increases of about 9 percent were expected. Other regions with potentially rapid growth rates were the Asian Pacific, Latin America, and Africa.

The overall slow growth experienced with chlorine demand resulted in an increased demand for soda ash. Pulp and paper manufacturers and water treatment facilities were among those using soda ash as a chlorine substitute. The global soda ash industry included many non-U.S. companies. For example Solvay, the world's largest soda ash producer (headquartered in Brussels), purchased Tenneco's soda ash division in 1992. As a result of the acquisition, Solvay controlled almost half of the U.S. soda ash production and was positioned to expand in the Asian Pacific and Latin American markets. By 1997, a Korean company, OCI, also became part of the U.S. soda ash production landscape, operating the Big Island Mine and Refinery in Green River, Wyoming.

Humanitarian Aid. In early 1997, PPG Industries donated 11 million metric tons of calcium chlorite, and Olin Corporation donated an additional 1 million, for a total of 12 million metric tons to help residents of Cuba still recovering from the effects of Hurricane Lili, which struck the island in October of 1996. The calcium chlorite was for use in disinfecting drinking water.

FURTHER READING

Brand, Tony. "Bleaches Brighten Abroad." Special Report, *Chemical Market Reporter,* 27 January 1997.

"Chloralkali Industry Sees Changes." *Chemical Marketing Reporter,* 21 September 1992.

Chlor-Alkali Chemicals and the Chlorine Institute. Washington: Chlorine Institute, 1991.

"Chlorine Surge to Taper Off, But Long-Term Growth is Seen." *Chemical Marketing Reporter,* 11 January 1993.

"CI Industry Aids Victims." *Chemical Market Reporter,* 27 January 1997.

"Dioxin Battle Flares Anew in Capital." *Chemical Marketing Reporter,* 15 June 1992.

Fairley, Peter. "Zero Discharge Bill Introduced." *Chemical Week,* 2 April 1997.

Johnson, Dexter. "Chlorine Makers Hike Prices Again As Plant Outages Tighten Up Market." *Chemical Market Reporter,* 24 February 1997.

Johnson, Dexter. "Hydrogen Peroxide Outlook Strong, Despite the Effect of Cluster Rules," *Chemical Market Reporter,* 3 February 1997.

———. "Sodium Chlorate Market Doing Well Despite Still Flagging Pulp Business." *Chemical Market Reporter,* 13 January 1997.

Kirschner, Elisabeth. "Total Chlorine Phaseout Would Cost $102 Billion/Year, Says CI." *Chemical Week,* 28 April 1993.

Martorella, Maurice, and Ian Young. "Soda Ash: Still a Steady Player." *Chemical Week,* 29 July 1992.

Mullin, Rick and Emily Pilsher. "Bit Ticket Changes in Store for North American Pulp and Paper." *Chemical Week,* 21 April 1993.

North American Chlor-Alkali Industry Plants and Production Data Report - 1996. Washington: The Chlorine Institute, 1997.

Roberts, Michael. "Structural Changes in Chlor-Alkali." *Chemical Week,* 4 November 1992.

Scott, Alex. "Chlor-Alkali Standards Proposed." *Chemical Week,* 12 March 1997.

Westervelt, Robert. "Caustic Market Starts to Settle." *Chemical Week,* 2 April 1997.

Williams, Mike. "EPA Sets New Limits on Toxic Pollution." *Detroit Free Press,* 2 March 1994.

U.S. Bureau of the Census. *1995 Annual Survey of Manufacturers.* Washington: GPO, 1997.

—Karen Bellenir, updated by Larry Fishel

INDUSTRIAL GASES

This industry classification contains establishments primarily involved in manufacturing industrial gases (organic as well as inorganic) which may be sold in compressed, liquid, or solid forms. Industrial gases include acetylene, argon, carbon dioxide, helium, hydrogen, neon, nitrogen, nitrous oxide, and oxygen. Fluorocarbon gases are covered under **SIC 2869: Industrial Organic Chemicals, Not Elsewhere Classified.** Industrial gas distributors, including liquid oxygen shippers, are classified in **SIC 5169: Chemicals and Allied Products, Not Elsewhere Classified.**

INDUSTRY SNAPSHOT

In the United States, industrial gases touch virtually every facet of twentieth-century life. The three major atmospheric gases, oxygen, nitrogen, and argon, are used in steel production. Oxygen enhances kiln firing to reduce brick making costs. Liquid oxygen and liquid hydrogen fuel rockets. Nitrogen is used in brewing beer, recycling tires, and applying metallic finishes on toys. Liquid nitrogen and liquid carbon dioxide are used to make plastic fittings for moldings, enhance oil recovery from wells, and enable solvent recycling. Argon contributes to stainless steel manufacturing and serves as a component in fluorescent tube lighting.

The industrial gas industry differs from many other types of manufacturing because its raw materials are primarily extracted from the atmosphere. The two principal gases produced by the industry are nitrogen and oxygen. Dry air is composed of 78.1 percent nitrogen, 20.9 percent oxygen, and just under 1 percent argon. All other atmospheric gases, often called rare gases, make up the remaining one-tenth of a percent. Additional industrial gases such as hydrogen, acetylene, and carbon dioxide are obtained as co-products or by-products from other operations. Production costs within the industry are divided fairly evenly among labor, energy, and distribution.

The industry uses three different techniques to separate gases from the atmosphere. Cryogenic methods are the oldest and most widely used. Cryogenic separation relies on cooling and pressurizing the air until it becomes liquid. Oxygen, when held at a pressure of 80 pounds per square inch, liquefies at minus 274 degrees Fahrenheit; nitrogen liquefies at a colder temperature. As the atmospheric gases liquefy, they are extracted by means of a distillation process. Additional distillation steps are necessary to produce argon and other rare gases such as krypton and xenon. Helium liquefies only at temperatures approaching absolute zero. As a result, cryogenic production is not economically feasible for helium. Most commercially available helium is derived from natural gas rather than from the atmosphere.

Two non-cryogenic gas production methods are membrane separation and pressure swing absorption (PSA). Membrane separation uses hollow fibers, most frequently made of organic polymers, to recover gases such as hydrogen from oil refineries or carbon dioxide from natural gas supplies. Pressure swing absorption (PSA) relies on a molecular sieve material that selectively absorbs atmospheric components at specific temperatures and pressures.

According to the U.S. Census Bureau, the industrial gases industry shipped products valued at $3.6 billion in 1995. Although industry sales declined in the late 1980s, growth was achieved during the early and mid-1990s. In 1996, U.S. oxygen production was estimated at 668 billion cubic feet; nitrogen production at 1.03 trillion cubic feet; hydrogen production at 271 billion cubic feet; and argon production was approximately 18 billion cubic feet. The United States likewise produced more than 5 million short tons of liquid carbon dioxide and 235,000 short tons of solid carbon dioxide.

In addition to its major products, the industry produced almost 100 different specialty gases such as krypton, xenon, and neon. Many specialty gases were used for medical, communications, electronics, aerospace, laser, and special lighting applications. Although specialty gases accounted for only about 8 percent of the industry's total production in 1992, they accounted for 29 percent of its revenues.

ORGANIZATION AND STRUCTURE

The industrial gas industry is divided into two major segments. The first, called the "tonnage" or "supply scheme" market, is comprised of large volume users who usually receive gas directly from an on-site production facility via pipeline. Under typical on-site contracts, a gas supplier constructs a production plant at or adjacent to a gas user's facility. The gas supplier owns and operates the plant for the benefit of the gas customer. Long-term contracts dictate that the customer take a specified volume of gas, often the entire amount produced. Many contracts contain adjustment clauses to account for increasing energy prices, variances in productivity, or changes in labor costs. Within this market segment, gas sold is measured in terms of tons per day. Examples of customers who routinely purchase industrial gases on the tonnage

market include chemical, petroleum, electronics, and steel manufacturers.

The other major market segment is known as the "merchant" or "bulk liquid" market. Customers within this market generally have fluctuating demand rates or operate multiple facilities in scattered locations. They often purchase gas products under short term contracts of less than five years in duration. Suppliers deliver liquid gas in cryogenic tanker trucks or by rail. Gases are shipped and stored in liquid form because of volume constraints. For example, liquid oxygen takes up less than one percent of the space required to contain the same amount in a gaseous state. Examples of customers in this category include the metal, food processing, electronics, chemical, aerospace, plastics, medical, glass, and paper industries.

A third, but much smaller market segment, consists of cylinder gas deliveries. Cylinder gas shipments are generally limited to expensive specialty gases and mixtures. A typical tanker truck carries the equivalent of 1,600 large cylinders. A train of ten cars, carries the equivalent of 57,000 cylinders.

BACKGROUND AND DEVELOPMENT

The gases that make up the multi-billion dollar industrial gas industry were discovered by various researchers living in several different countries beginning in the later half of the eighteenth century. One year before the United States declared its independence from England, oxygen was discovered by two chemists working independently in Europe. During the later part of the 1800s, it was used for medical purposes and put to use commercially in welding. Oxygen was also used to generate limelight for theaters and music halls.

Acetylene was discovered in 1863 and first produced commercially in 1892. In 1897, Georges Claude, a French researcher, developed a method of dissolving acetylene in acetone at low pressures. Claude's process enabled the development of methods which allowed the movement of the gas via transportation cylinders. The first acetylene-burning torches were developed around the turn of the century.

In 1902, two researchers, one in France and one in Germany, developed similar processes for the fractional distillation of liquid air. This procedure made it possible to produce large volumes of oxygen economically. In 1903, the Linde Air Products Company constructed the first commercial oxygen plant in the United States.

Events of the early twentieth century demanded increasing amounts of industrial gases. World War I required large amounts of oxygen and acetylene for welding; pilots of high-altitude aircraft during World War II needed oxygen for their flights. Following the wars, researchers put inert gases such as argon and helium to use in electric arc welding.

Growing industrialization in the Western World brought rapid expansion to the gas industry. Oxygen demand continued growing through the 1950s as steel manufacturers turned to the gas to improve production methods. Maturing uses for nitrogen, previously considered a waste material, developed during the 1960s along with advances in the uses of helium and argon. The 1970s brought large scale expansions in the nation's capacity to produce industrial gases. The decade also saw growth in the use of specialty gases by the electronics industry. By the mid-1980s, the electronics industry used an estimated 15 percent of the nation's nitrogen output.

CURRENT CONDITIONS

Although demand for nitrogen in 1960 had been practically nonexistent, by the early 1990s nitrogen sales surpassed the sales of all other industrial gases. Nitrogen and oxygen sales combined accounted for approximately two-thirds of the industry's sales in 1995. Carbon dioxide, hydrogen, and argon sales ranked a distant third, fourth, and fifth, respectively.

Because nitrogen does not readily react with other materials, several industries use it as a "blanketing agent," which is a compound able to prevent unwanted reactions. For example, when nitrogen is used as a blanketing agent with embers, it prevents them from igniting. Nitrogen is therefore used to ensure product quality and improve plant safety. Oil producers use nitrogen to stimulate and pressurize wells. The gas also finds use in steel processing, food production, cooling, refrigeration and freezing systems, solvent recovery, chemical and glass production, and in the electronics and aerospace industries. Nitrogen production rebounded in 1996 after a decline in 1995.

Measured in terms of sales volume, the second most significant industrial gas in the 1990s was oxygen, which is used to intensify or control combustion in a variety of industries. Its other uses include speeding fermentation, providing life support, and controlling odors. Chemical manufacturers, brick makers, and metal fabricators all rely on oxygen. Innovative uses include processes aimed at restoring or maintaining environmental integrity. Oxygen is used in hazardous waste cleanup efforts, waste water treatment facilities, and coal gasification systems (a process designed to reduce the hazardous emissions associated with burning coal). One of the fastest growing areas of oxygen use in the 1990s, however, was as a replacement for chlorine in bleaching, especially by pulp and paper manufacturers because the oxygen process pollutes less.

Another gas with a rapidly growing demand in the early 1990s was helium. Helium, traditionally used in welding, balloons, and leak detection, was finding new applications in cryogenic cooling. Liquid helium was the only gas known to get cold enough for use in the superconducting magnets used in body scanners. By 1991, the cooling requirements of superconductive magnets such as those used by magnetic resonance imaging (MRI) diagnostic equipment accounted for more than one-fourth of the world's demand for helium. The United States produced 3.4 billion cubic feet of helium in 1995.

Demand for specialty gases such as krypton, xenon, and neon was also growing. Low power lamps relied on krypton, high-intensity filament lamps and CAT scanners depended on xenon, and neon was necessary for lasers, display lighting, and bar code scanners. All three rare gases were used to develop radial-keratotomy, a form of laser surgery for eyes.

INDUSTRY LEADERS

In the mid-1980s Union Carbide was the largest industrial gas supplier in the United States. It provided approximately one third of the nation's merchant gas. In 1985, the company opened six new nitrogen plants with most of its production capacity aimed at the fast-growing high-tech market. In 1992, Union Carbide's industrial gas unit was spun-off to become an independent entity, Praxair, Inc., which had revenues of $4.4 billion in 1996.

Another major producer was Air Products and Chemicals, Inc. Founded in 1940, Air Products pioneered on-site industrial gas manufacturing. In 1991, the company introduced small volume, low cost, non-cryogenic nitrogen for use by metal heat-treating firms. In 1996, Air Products employed more than 15,200 workers and its global sales exceeded $4 billion, of which more than $2.3 billion was derived from industrial gas sales. The firm's industrial gas segment was growing less rapidly than its chemical and related businesses.

Liquid Air Corporation, a subsidiary of the French company L'Air Liquide, entered the U.S. market in 1968. By the mid-1980s, L'Air Liquide operated in 66 countries. Liquid Air is the company's headquarters for its operations in North and South America. It supplies products including oxygen, nitrous oxide, hydrogen, nitrogen, specialty gases, chemical gases and rare gases to a wide variety of industrial users. Big Three Industries, another L'Air Liquide unit, sells most of its production to chemical and petroleum producers via a pipeline system located in the Gulf Coast region.

Another international gas producer with a strong presence in the U.S. market was the BOC Group., which derived more than half of its worldwide sales in 1996 from industrial gases. The BOC Group originated in England with the incorporation of the Brins Oxygen Company Limited in 1886. BOC acquired the American company Airco in 1978. By the mid-1980s Airco provided 20 percent of the U.S. domestic merchant gas. BOC's expansion continued and by the early 1990s the company operated units in North and South America, Europe, India, Australia, Japan, and other locations around the Pacific Rim.

WORK FORCE

In the United States, the Department of Commerce reported that the industrial gases industry employed a total of 7,700 workers with payroll of more than $300 million in the mid-1990s. The statistics show a continued reduction in industry employment since the early 1980s. The three leading states by employment were Texas, California, and Ohio.

AMERICA AND THE WORLD

The global market for industrial gases was estimated at $20 billion in 1992. Because of problems related to the transportation and storage of gas products, most production occurred close to its point of use. There was, therefore, very little international trade in industrial gases. Instead of transporting products, large international corporations functioned by operating production facilities in many countries.

The types and volumes of gases provided in an area depended on the development of the region's economy. Regions with emerging economies typically required high volumes of oxygen, whereas countries with economies based on high-technology and service, needed greater amounts of nitrogen. According to the BOC Group, the ratio of nitrogen sales to oxygen sales could be used as a measurement of a nation's industrial development.

RESEARCH AND TECHNOLOGY

During the early 1990s, pollution abatement was one of the most rapidly developing areas of study within the industrial gases industry. Researchers were examining methods of improving waste water treatment by oxygen injection. Recovery systems using nitrogen to condense and recapture solvents and chem-

ical vapors helped manufacturers come into compliance with the Clean Air Act Amendments of 1990. An innovative technology based on carbon dioxide offered promise for reducing the environmental impact of solvent use within the paint and coatings industry. Additionally, carbon dioxide-based refrigeration systems were introduced to replace systems that relied on chlorofluorocarbons (CFCs).

Research into new or refined uses for industrial gases also continued. Liquid nitrogen was being considered as a possible aid in reducing problems associated with cracking in structural concrete. Xenon provided sun-like brightness to meet the special lighting needs of airports, stadiums, the motion picture industry, and copying machine manufacturers. Other rare gases were also being developed for use in diagnostic technologies and pharmaceutical applications.

FURTHER READING

Agoos, Alice. "Industrial Gases Travel an Upward Road." *Chemical Week* , 1 January 1986.

Air Products and Chemicals, Inc. *1996 Annual Report.* Allentown, PA, 1996.

Banov, Abel. "Revolutionary Technology Unveiled: Union Carbide Process may Reduce Solvent Content 30 - 70%." *American Paint & Coatings Journal,* 24 July 1989.

Deal, Richard, Richard Hendrickson, and William Lewis. "Onsite Oxygen Plants Can Reduce Pulp Mill Costs for Volume Users." *Pulp and Paper,* September 1991.

Greek, Bruce F. "Rising Demand for Industrial Gases Paves Way for Price Increases." *Chemical & Engineering News,* 2 December 1991.

"Liquid CO2—An Alternative to Freon (CFCs) for the Frozen Food Shipping Industry." *Frozen Food Digest,* October 1992.

Loesel, Andrew. "Inert but Growing." *Chemical Marketing Reporter,* 9 December 1991.

Taub, J. S. "Liquid Air Finding New Markets for Its Industrial Gases." *San Francisco Business Journal,* 3 March 1986.

U.S. Bureau of the Census. *1992 Census of Manufactures.* Washington: GPO, 1995.

U.S. Bureau of the Census. *1995 Annual Survey of Manufactures.* Washington: GPO, 1997.

U.S. Bureau of the Census. "Industrial Gases." *Current Industrial Reports.* Washington: GPO, 1997.

Wood, Andrew. "Making Acetylene Competitive." *Chemical Week,* 21 February 1990.

—Karen Bellinir, updated by Beaird Glover

SIC 2816

INORGANIC PIGMENTS

This industry classification is comprised of establishments engaged in manufacturing inorganic color pigments, white pigments, and black pigments, including animal black and bone black. Carbon black is classified in **SIC 2895: Carbon Black.** Organic color pigments are classified in **SIC 2865: Cyclic Organic Crudes and Intermediates, and Organic Dyes and Pigments.**

INDUSTRY SNAPSHOT

Inorganic pigments serve the purpose of imparting color to various compounds. They also add properties such as rust inhibition, rigidity, and abrasion resistance. Pigments are insoluble substances that can be incorporated into a material to selectively absorb or scatter light. Depending on the specific pigment used, different visual effects are produced. Inorganic pigments may be obtained from a variety of naturally occurring or synthetically produced mineral sources. The counterpart, organic pigments, are carbon compounds derived from petroleum sources.

In comparison with organic pigments, inorganic pigments are generally better able to withstand the affects of sunlight and chemical exposure. They provide superior opacity, which means they can render a substance or object opaque by prohibiting light from passing through it. Inorganic colors, however, tend to be less bright, pure, and rich than their organic counterparts. Because inorganic pigments possess less tinting strength, more pigment is needed to produce the desired effect. This generally makes them more durable. Almost all inorganic pigments are completely insoluble; consequently, they do not bleed or leach out of coatings, inks, or plastics. In addition, inorganic pigments are usually less expensive than similar organic colors.

Pigments differ from dyes as a result of their distinctive chemical natures. Dyes are soluble, and to impart color they are dissolved in a carrier and applied by a process that involves chemical changes. Pigments, however, remain unchanged physically and chemically. They function without altering their crystalline, particulate, or metabolic structures.

Inorganic pigments are classified as single-metal oxides, mixed-metal oxides, and earth colors. Single-metal oxides include pigments made from titanium, zinc, cobalt, and chromium. Mixed-metal oxides include pigments such as cobalt aluminate blue, which is used in ceramic glazes, and nickel antimony titanate, manganese antimony titanate, and chromium antimony titanate, which are used for outdoor coatings and plastic siding. Earth colors, including siennas, ochers, and umbers, are generally made from iron oxides and lead chromates. A method of high-temperature firing called calcination is used to produce pigments with improved heat resistance.

Pigment manufacturers supply inorganic colors in a variety of forms such as powders, pastes, granules, slurries, and suspensions. Pigment users include manufacturers of paints and stains, printing inks, plastics, synthetic textiles, paper, cosmetics, contact lenses, soaps and detergents, wax, modeling clay, chalks, crayons, artists' colors, concrete and masonry products, and ceramics.

Within the inorganic pigments classification, the largest selling individual pigment is titanium dioxide (TiO_2), a white pigment with opacifying characteristics. Titanium dioxide is by far the most widely used white pigment in the world. It is a solid that melts at over 1800 degrees Celsius. It has a higher refractive index than everything except diamonds. It is polymorphous and exists in three crystal structures: rutile, anatase, and brookite. To utilize titanium dioxide's special properties, it must be developed to an ideal particle size. Most often, the particle size is one half the wavelength of visible light or about 0.3 microns.

BACKGROUND AND DEVELOPMENT

The use and exploitation of color dates back to the prehistoric era. Pigments were made by grinding naturally colored materials into minute particles and then mixing them into a binder material. Some of the substances used to produce paintings on cave walls were still used during the twentieth century. For example, the reds used to produce the drawings in the Lascaux caves of southern France were made from red iron oxide.

During the early part of the twentieth century, the pigments industry relied heavily on lead-based ingredients. One ingredient, lead carbonate (white lead) was known to be toxic as early as the late nineteenth century, and although some countries began imposing restrictions on its use in the 1920s, the United States was not among them. The toxicity of lead carbonate, especially to children who ate paint chips, received increasing publicity. By the mid-1960s paint manufacturers were required to begin phasing out its use.

According to industry researchers, lead carbonate caused lead poisoning because of its solubility. The solubility enabled it to interfere with the human body's biochemical system. Investigators claimed that other lead pigments suffered from non-specific adverse publicity resulting in regulations that failed to differentiate between soluble and insoluble lead compounds. A reduction in the use of lead chromate pigments during the 1970s resulted in increased costs of more than $1 billion because available replacements were inferior. Into the late 1990s, this problem still existed and lead carbonate was still in use to some degree; advancements in the industry continued to make substitutes that were economically feasible and comparable in color strength.

To address issues such as environmental matters, tariffs, toxicity, and worker health, the Dry Color Manufacturers Association (DCMA) was formed. Originally organized in 1925 and headquartered in New York City, the trade association moved to New Jersey and then to Washington, D.C. In 1993, the organization changed its name to the Color Pigments Manufacturers Association, Inc. (CPMA) and as of 1997, it was located in Alexandria, Virginia.

Growth in production and demand for titanium dioxide increased rapidly through the 1980s. By 1989, production was 67 percent above the 1982 level. Although demand declined in 1990, industry analysts predicted annual domestic growth within the titanium dioxide market of about 2 percent during the mid-1990s. Globally, demand was expected to increase about 3 percent per year. Almost half of the titanium dioxide produced in the United States was used by paint and coatings manufacturers. Other users included the plastics, rubber, printing inks, floor coverings, ceramics, textiles, cosmetics, and paper industries.

According to figures released by the U.S. Department of Commerce, shipments of inorganic pigments were valued at $2.4 billion in 1987. Of this amount, $2.2 billion represented products considered primary to the industry. The largest end user was the paint and coatings industry.

CURRENT CONDITIONS

As the inorganic pigments industry entered the 1990s, the largest single product produced was titanium dioxide. Titanium dioxide production relied on two different raw materials containing titanium: ilmenite and natural rutile. Both minerals were primarily mined in Australia and South Africa. Ilmenite contained less titanium than rutile, but it was more plentiful and less expensive.

The industry implemented several price increases in 1995, and 1996 saw a downturn in the market for titanium dioxide. The worldwide price index dropped

several cents per pound. Pigments in general showed a moderate growth, indicating a mature market.

Demand for titanium dioxide is expected to grow from 2 to 4 percent annually to the year 2000. The U.S. market is slightly lower, with an expected growth rate of 1.8 percent per year. In 1996 the North American market for titanium dioxide was about 1.239 million metric tons per year and was expected to reach 1.538 metric tons by the year 2000. In 1996, the average selling price for titanium dioxide was $1940 per metric ton, and the global average price was $1,947 per metric ton or roughly $1 per pound.

DuPont, the world's largest titanium dioxide producer, planned to raise prices on titanium dioxide in Europe, the Mideast, and Africa in early 1997. Entering 1997, titanium dioxide prices were at $1,600 per metric ton in the Mideast, and $1,950 per metric ton in Europe.

Manufacturers used two basic processes to make titanium dioxide. The sulfate process, which produced slightly less than half of the world's supply of titanium dioxide, was the older method. It used sulfuric acid to dissolve the titanium dioxide. Further refinement was required to produce different grades of the finished product.

The newer method, called the chloride process, centered around the use of chlorine and accounted for 51 percent of the world's titanium dioxide capacity. By this method, chlorine was reacted with titanium-containing minerals to produce titanium tetrachloride. The titanium tetrachloride was reacted with oxygen to form titanium dioxide and recyclable chlorine. Advantages of the chloride process included its ability to create higher grades of titanium dioxide without additional handling, its use of less labor and equipment, and its ability to produce in a continuous, as opposed to a batch, process.

The chloride process also produced a smaller volume of waste by-products. Up to 12 tons of waste material were generated when the sulfate process was used in making one ton of titanium dioxide from ilmenite. The chloride process generated four to five tons of waste in producing the same amount of titanium dioxide. A large part of the wastes generated by the chloride process, however, consisted of iron chloride. Disposal of iron chloride created controversy because of its acidic properties and hazardous nature. To reduce the amount of iron chloride waste, manufacturers were forced to rely on higher priced rutile or other purified forms of titanium-containing raw materials. High grade rutile generated only about 70 pounds of iron chloride to yield one ton of titanium dioxide.

Titanium dioxide was also being used to create synthetic pearlescent pigments. Pearlescent pigments, a twentieth century innovation, were developed in an attempt to create the visual sense of depth associated with natural pearls. Initial pearlescent pigments were made from crystals obtained from fish scales. Rosary bead manufacturers were among the first users of these products.

Researchers identified two chemical compounds with similar light reflective properties. One of these, carbonate white lead, was withdrawn because of its toxicity. The other bismuth oxychloride found wide use in applications such as cast polyester buttons, automotive paints, fingernail enamels, cosmetics, wall papers, and plastics.

Synthetic pearlescent pigments, however, failed to exactly duplicate those of fish scales. The search for other synthetic pearlescent pigment compounds led to the use of such minerals as mica. Mica, when coated with titanium dioxide, was judged to reflect light in a manner suitable for use in pearlescent pigments.

The second largest family of pigments was iron oxides. Although iron oxides produced pigments in a wide range of colors, reds accounted for almost half the consumption. By the early 1990s, synthetic iron oxides had captured two-thirds of the market. Industry forecasters expected increased interest in synthetic iron oxide pigments because they offered improved color strength over naturally occurring ores. The primary users of iron oxide pigments were paint and coatings manufacturers.

Lead chromates represented the third largest family of pigments. By the early 1990s, approximately 42 million pounds of these pigments were still being sold annually. Nearly 18 million pounds of these pigments were used by traffic paint manufacturers. Despite their popularity, lead chromates were being subjected to increasing Congressional scrutiny because of concerns about lead toxicity and environmental integrity.

Questions about environmental degradation and the toxicity of heavy metals challenged the inorganic pigment industry throughout the 1980s and early 1990s. Heavy metals such as lead, cadmium, chromium, and mercury were associated with ailments including cancer and liver disease. Both the Congress and the Environmental Protection Agency (EPA) considered legislative and regulatory initiatives to control, limit, and in some cases ban, the use of several of the industry's essential raw materials. Some manufacturers responded by backing away from heavy-metal pigments. Others defended their formulations and offered

evidence that if raw materials were banned, certain colors would become unavailable.

In addition to struggling with direct toxicity problems, pigment manufacturers faced charges claiming that their disposal of heavy-metals used in pigments were threatening the nation's water supplies. Products undergoing incineration or degradation in landfill sites created a potential hazard as heavy metals were released into the environment. As a result of this growing environmental concern, the Conference of North East Governors (representing nine northern states) and the legislatures in several other states, began working toward bans on heavy metals in packaging materials. During the early 1990s, industry watchers expected the number of environmental regulations regarding the use of heavy metals in pigments to increase.

Many inorganic pigment formulas relied on heavy metals. Some colors were not even achievable without their traditional raw materials. In other cases, colors could be matched using organic ingredients but the resulting pigment suffered from decreased light stability, poor opacity, and an inability to withstand high-temperature processing. Acceptable organic pigment substitutes were often more expensive than the inorganic pigments. Analysts suggested that switching to organic pigments could increase the price of a color concentrate by as much as 300 percent.

An often cited example of the difficulties faced by industries forced to switch away from heavy metal inorganic pigments was the problem of the Pennzoil oil bottle. The Pennzoil oil bottle, fabricated from an identifying bright yellow plastic, depended on yellow lead chromate. During the early 1990s yellow lead chromate cost between $1.00 and $1.50 per pound, but as legislation was likely to continue to limit the use of lead chromate, the company was forced to look for substitutes for the ingredient. One commonly used substitute cost between $6.00 and $7.00 per pound and other organic yellows cost up to $30.00 per pound. Facing a similar situation, Caterpillar (a manufacturer of heavy equipment) switched from its traditional color to a less bright yellow.

INDUSTRY LEADERS

The largest U.S. corporation producing inorganic pigments in 1997 was Ferro Corp. of Cleveland, Ohio, Ferro began operating in 1919 as a frit manufacturer. Frit is a special glass material used to produce porcelain enamel and ceramic glaze. Color pigments for the ceramics and coatings industries were added to the company's product line in 1939. The company began supplying pigments to the plastics industry in 1947. By

1993, Ferro operated 12 color production facilities and sold its products in more than 100 countries.

Ferro's line of inorganic mixed metal oxide pigments are used primarily to color vinyl siding, window profiles, appliance housings, garden tools, and automotive components. The company's ultramarine blue and violet pigments are manufactured in Spain from sodium aluminum sulfosilicate complexes. They find use in thermoplastic resins, rubber compounds, paints, printing inks, artists' colors, and roofing granules. A third line of colors, called complex inorganic color pigments, are man-made minerals that are heat-stable, light-stable, and weather resistant. According to the manufacturer, they are the most chemically resistant pigments known to exist. They are recommended for use in exterior building applications and engineering plastics.

The other largest inorganic pigments companies in the United States in 1997, according to *Ward's Business Directory of U.S. Private and Public Companies,* were NL Industries Inc. of Houston, Texas; Kronos Div. of Houston, Texas; SCM Chemicals Inc. of Baltimore, Maryland; and Zinc Corporation of America, located in Monaca, Pennsylvania.

SCM Chemicals began its involvement in titanium dioxide production in 1933, and by 1992 it was the third largest producer of titanium dioxide in the world. SCM operated eight plants in the United States, England, and Australia and reported an annual production of 446,000 metric tons in 1992. In 1996, SCM implemented a program to reduce sulfate-process manufacturing capacity. They also announced a delay in chloride-process expansion projects and an increase in their selling prices for titanium dioxide products around the world.

AMERICA AND THE WORLD

In 1990, estimates suggested that titanium dioxide accounted for about 30 percent of global pigment sales, and demand for the white pigment was expected to grow at approximately 3 percent per year. Industry forecasters expected new global production capacity, estimated to add 850,000 tons between 1990 and 1995, to result in a slight over-supply and keep prices down.

Western Europe, however, was expected to see reduced production. Approximately 73 percent of the region's existing capacity was based on the sulfate process, which was subject to increasing criticism from environmental groups. A European Union directive to stop ocean dumping of wastes, slated to take effect at the end of 1993, was expected to increase operating expenses by about 15 percent and force older plants out of the global market.

Heavy metal pigment manufacturers were also facing difficulty in some parts of the world. In Japan, cadmium was replaced in 1980. European manufacturers began phasing it out several years later. By 1990, an estimated 50 to 60 percent of European cadmium production had been eliminated. Some industry observers suggested that the banning of heavy metal pigments resulted in an increased reliance on duller colors.

DuPont, the world's largest titanium dioxide producer, planned to increase its worldwide capacity by 185,000 tons in 1997. This would raise its capacity by about 25 percent, to almost one million tons a year.

RESEARCH AND TECHNOLOGY

Much of the developing technology within the inorganic pigments industry attempted to lessen the risks such pigments presented to humans and the environment. One innovation, called silica encapsulation, involved encasing pigment particles or crystals within a shell of silica (a glass like substance). Researchers claimed that encapsulated lead chromate pigments were protected from chemical, photochemical, and thermal degradation. The encapsulation process also reduced their toxicity by making them less able to be absorbed by the body. Researchers also claimed that silica encapsulation improved the brightness and intensity of the pigments, making them better suited for use in high-temperature applications such as plastic manufacturing.

Other researchers were examining methods of producing low dust, low soluble cadmium pigments. One newly developed product line contained less than one part per million of soluble cadmium, falling under the threshold defined by the EPA to identify a hazardous waste material. Low dust products also helped industry manufacturers to meet the standards set by the Occupational Safety and Health Administration (OSHA).

As paint formulas became more standardized around the world, new and existing grades of titanium dioxide were made more similar to each other. Slight regional differences, such as particle size or degree of opacity, were being phased out by the industry. Leaders in this trend, as of 1996, were DuPont's R-706 multi purpose pigment for coating applications and SCM's RCL535. Kronos and Kerr-McGee were also working on similar products.

Rare-earth-based red and orange pigments were scheduled for production in the 3rd quarter of 1997 when Rhone-Poulenc SA planned to start its 500 metric ton per year operation at La Rochelle, Les Roches-Roussillon and Clamecy. This inorganic pigment, trade-named Neolor, would be an environmentally friendly alternative to cadmium and lead-based paint types.

In 1996, an advance in the making of complex inorganic color pigments by Englehard Corp., brought about the reddest pigment of it kind for use in PVC, nylon and other engineering plastics. Meteor Plus 9384 had 70-80 percent greater color strength than the next closest complex inorganic color pigment with a red value.

FURTHER READING

Alperowicz, Natasha, and Ian Young. "DuPont to Raise Prises; SCM Plans to follow Suit." *Chemical Week* 158, no. 48, (11 December 1996) 20.

Armanini, Louis. "Ah, the Beauty of a Pearl." *Industrial Finishing,* April 1992.

"Chemicals." *Standard & Poor's Industry Surveys.* New York: Standard & Poor's Corporation, 1993.

"Colorants and Pigments." *American Paint and Coatings Journal,* 8 June 1992.

Dry Color Manufacturers' Association. "Pigments—A Primer." *American Ink Maker,* June 1989. Reprinted by Color Pigments Manufacturers Association, Inc. (formerly DCMA).

Ferro 1992 Profile. Cleveland, OH.: Ferro, 1992.

Ferro. "Geode: Complex Inorganic Color Pigments." Cleveland, OH.: Ferro, nd.

"The Freedonia Group - Inorganic Chemicals." 1996. Available from http://www.freedoniagroup.com/737.htm.

Gray, Donald. "Putting Risk Into Perspective." *American Paint and Coatings Journal,* 24 September 1990.

———. "Inorganic Mixed Metal Oxide Pigments." Cleveland, OH.: Ferro, nd.

"Inorganic Pigments." *Standard & Poor's Industry Surveys.* New York: Standard & Poor's Corporation, 1997.

Kiesche, Elizabeth S. "Pigments and Dyes Adapting to New Environments." *Chemical Week,* 3 October 1990.

Loesel, Andrew. "Color Concentrate Makers Will Phase Out Heavy Metals." *Chemical Marketing Reporter,* 11 June 1990.

Loesel, Andrew. "Color Me Bleak." *Chemical Marketing Reporter,* 19 October 1992.

Loesel, Andrew. "Lead Chromate Makers Worry About Lead Ban." *Chemical Marketing Reporter,* 18 June 1990.

Loffredo, Douglas. "Pigment Producers Face Tougher Times." *Chemical Marketing Reporter,* 29 October 1990.

MacDonald, Cindy. "New Technologies Boost Performance." *Canadian Plastics* 54, no. 2 (February 1996) 15-21.

Maty, Joe. "Suit Seeks Lead Cleanup Help: Companies Face Specter of Millions in Abatement Costs." *American Paint and Coatings Journal,* 26 November 1990.

Parkingson, Gerald. "Rhone-Poulenc Will Commercialize 'Friendly' Pigments. *Chemical Engineering* 103 no. 10 (October 1996) 21.

"Pigment Makers Seek Stay of OSHA Cadmium Rule." *American Paint and Coatings Journal,* 11 January 1993.

"Production By the U.S. Chemical Industry: Production Growth Sputtered in Most Sectors." *Chemical and Engineering News* 74, no. 26 (24 June 1996) 40-46.

SCM Chemicals. *Titanium Dioxide in Today's Environment: A Responsive and Responsible Industry.* Baltimore, MD.: SCM, nd.

"SCM to Reduce TiO2 Capacity, Hike Prices." *Modern Paint and Coatings* 86, no. 9, (September 1996) 8.

Shearer, Brent. "Pigments Fade." *Chemical Marketing Reporter* 250, no. 17 (21 October 1996) SR12-SR13.

Singletary, Lynda. "Black and White." *Chemical Marketing Reporter,* 4, November 1991.

———. "Ultramarine Pigments." Cleveland, OH.: Ferro, nd.

U.S. Bureau of the Census. *1987 Census of Manufactures.* Washington: GPO, 1990.

U.S. Department of Commerce. *U.S. Industrial Outlook '92.* Washington: GPO, 1992.

Wallace, David. "Paint Suit May Yield Thousands of Plaintiffs." *Philadelphia Business Journal,* 8 July 1991.

———. *World View.* Baltimore, MD.: SCM, 1993.

"What Is Titanium Dioxide?" Kronos. Available from http://www.nl-ind.com/kronos/titanium/html.

Wriede, Peter A., and Donald Gray. "Heavy-Metal Based Pigments: Putting Use Risks in Perspective." *American Paint and Coatings Journal,* 6 January 1986.

—Karen Bellenir, updated by Beaird Glover

SIC 2819

INDUSTRIAL INORGANIC CHEMICALS, NOT ELSEWHERE CLASSIFIED

This category includes establishments primarily involved in manufacturing industrial inorganic chemicals not elsewhere classified. A few examples are alum, ammonium compounds (except for fertilizer), industrial bleaches (sodium or calcium hypochlorite), chemical catalysts, hydrazine, hydrochloric acid, hydrogen peroxide, inorganic sodium compounds, and sulfuric acid.

Establishments primarily engaged in mining, milling or otherwise preparing natural potassium, sodium, or boron compounds (other than common salt) are classified in **SIC 1474: Potash, Soda, and Borate Minerals;** establishments primarily engaged in manufacturing household bleaches are classified in **SIC 2842: Specialty Cleaning, Polishing, and Sanitation Preparations;** those manufacturing phosphoric acid are classified in **SIC 2874: Phosphatic Fertilizers;** and those manufacturing nitric acid, anhydrous ammonia, and other nitrogenous fertilizer materials are classified in **SIC 2873: Nitrogenous Fertilizers.**

INDUSTRY SNAPSHOT

The inorganic chemicals industry makes up the bulk of basic chemical production. Inorganic chemicals are those derived from inanimate earth materials such as minerals and the atmosphere. They are differentiated from organic chemicals, which are derived from plant and animal sources. Organic chemicals are based on carbon; inorganic chemicals are based on all other naturally occurring and synthetically produced elements.

The major chemicals within this classification are known as "basic" chemicals. They are also sometimes referred to as "heavy," "bulk," or "commodity" chemicals. Manufacturers typically produce them from ores or brines, or as co-products or by-products of other processes. They serve industrial users who put them to work in the creation of other products. Some common applications include their uses as processing aids and chemical catalysts. Inorganic chemicals are also used as ingredients in non-chemical products. The primary markets for chemical products are paper, housing, automobiles, water treatment, fertilizer, petroleum refining, steel production, manufacturing, and soap and detergent production.

Sulfuric acid is by far the largest volume inorganic chemical. It is used primarily as a chemical reagent in a variety of industrial processes with a largest end use in fertilizer production. About three-fourths of domestic sulfuric acid is used for phosphate fertilizer.

Hydrogen peroxide is a rapidly growing sector of the inorganic chemicals industry. Pulp and paper manufacturing account for more than half the demand for hydrogen peroxide, as it becomes a more viable option than chlorine for the chemical bleaching of paper. It is also used to de-ink paper before the recycling process. Other uses for hydrogen peroxide are in water and waste treatment and for bleaching textiles.

ORGANIZATION AND STRUCTURE

Chemical producing companies range in size from small establishments providing a single chemical to multi-national corporations offering an array of a thousand or more different chemical products. The Chemical Manufacturers Association (CMA) was established to represent the industry's interests in local, state, and national affairs. In 1978, the CMA (formerly the Manufacturing Chemists Association), adopted an Advocacy Charter to define its lobbying role. According to the CMA's 120th Annual Report covering the fiscal year 1991-1992, one of the organization's goals was to become "a positive and proactive force for the industry." The CMA's stated challenge was "to balance industry's interests with those of its many publics—legislators, regulators, the courts and, especially, employees and neighbors."

To help it achieve these goals, the CMA reported that by 1992, its members were making progress fulfilling the program's practices despite the economic difficulties facing the industry. The organization was also in the process of adopting ways to measure the program's success.

Historically, efforts made by chemical producers to address hazards included plant safety considerations and voluntarily withdrawing dangerous products from the market. In addition, several governmental agencies existed to regulate specific facets of the industry. For example, regulations covering railroad shipments of hazardous materials were instituted following the Civil War; and during the closing years of the 1800s, the Bureau of Chemistry (within the U.S. Department of Agriculture) was responsible for overseeing the safety of chemicals used in foods and drugs.

Governmental efforts to ensure product safety, establish worker safety laws, and protect the environment intensified during the 1970s, beginning with the establishment of the Environmental Protection Agency (EPA) in 1970. The decade brought along the following host of new regulations: revisions of the Clean Air Act (1970 and subsequent amendments), the Occupational Safety and Health Act (1970), the Resource Recovery Act (1970), the Federal Water Pollution Control Act (1972), the Safe Drinking Water Act (1974), amendments to the Federal Insecticide, Fungicide, and Rodenticide Act (1972), the Resource Conservation and Recovery Act (1976), and the Toxic Substances Control Act (1976). The 1980s opened with the passage of the Comprehensive Environmental Response, Compensation, and Liability Act (also known as the "Superfund" Act).

Federal regulations mandated that new chemicals be evaluated for safety before use, that new uses of existing chemicals be evaluated, and that all chemicals meet specific safety and health standards. In addition, governmental bodies regulated by-products and co-products, controlled transportation, and monitored waste disposal. In her 1984 work *Toxic Substances Controls Primer* Mary Devine Worobec noted, "Virtually every chemical and substance used in the United States is subject to some type of control. During manufacture, workers who are exposed must be monitored. During use, by-products are created that must be treated in specified ways and when use of a substance is completed, the wastes that remain must be disposed of in approved ways. And at each juncture, the chemical must be transported to the site of the next stage in a proper manner."

BACKGROUND AND DEVELOPMENT

The first attempt to identify the "elements," basic indivisible materials, resulted in a list of four substances: earth, air, water, and fire. The ancient Greeks identified nine modernly recognizable elements: gold, silver, mercury, copper, lead, tin, iron, sulfur, and carbon. As elements and compounds were identified and understood, they were put to work. Early uses for chemicals included dyeing, bleaching, tanning, brewing, embalming, baking, mining, and cleaning. Chemicals were also important to the development of art and medicine.

One of the first products of the chemical industry was borax. Borax, a naturally occurring compound containing sodium, boron, and oxygen, was known to the Babylonians and Egyptians. Marco Polo inaugurated trade in borax between the Far East and Europe. Another early product (still traded in modern times) was alum. Alum was used during the fifteenth century to stop bleeding, and served as an additive to dyes to improve their ability to adhere to fabrics.

The modern inorganic chemicals industry has its roots in the discovery of the elements. The first element discovered since the time of the ancient Greeks was phosphorous. A German alchemist, Henning Brand, discovered it in 1669 during his attempts to make gold. Modern applications of phosphorous include matches (invented in 1831) and tracer bullets.

During the 1700s, a Dutch chemist decomposed borax to make boric acid. French chemists further decomposed the boric acid and discovered the element boron. Uses of boron compounds in the twentieth century have included water softeners, cleansers, fiberglass, gasoline additives, rocket fuel, fire proofing and fire fighting compounds, cosmetics, pharmaceuticals,

and soldering flux. One of the most well-known products is Pyrex glass. Pyrex glass is made with boron oxide to reduce the amount of expansion that occurred upon heating. As a result, unlike regular glass, Pyrex is not susceptible to cracking during heat changes. Boron has also been used as a neutron-absorbent material to help control nuclear energy during power production.

In 1730, innovative procedures led to the production of sulfuric acid on a commercial scale. The corrosive substance had been used since the eighth century for a variety of purposes including tanning, tin-plating, brass-founding, and hat and button making, but the time-consuming methods employed created only weak acid. Changes introduced by Joshua Ward and improved upon by John Roebuck during the eighteenth century led to the industry's ability to produce stronger acid in greater volumes. By the end of the twentieth century, sulfuric acid topped the list of the most widely sold inorganic chemicals.

Other eighteenth-century discoveries included Georg Brandt's identification of cobalt, Axel Cronstedt's discovery of nickel, and Nicolas Vauquelin's identification of chromium. Cobalt chloride achieved popularity as an invisible ink, and in 1948 cobalt-60, a radioactive isotope, was found to be helpful in treating cancer, preserving foods, and sterilizing medical supplies. Nickel, previously thought to be a form of copper, was used to strengthen gold, silver, and copper. Twentieth-century applications have included use in high-strength magnets and household appliances. A chromium compound developed in 1913 by Harold Brearely, an English metallurgist, became widely known as "stainless steel." By the late eighteenth century, 30 elements were known.

During the early nineteenth century, researchers learned more about separating the components of naturally occurring compounds. It was a time of rapid discovery, and many more ingredients used by the modern inorganic chemicals industry were identified. For example, Sir Humphry Davy, an English scientist, discovered sodium, potassium, magnesium, calcium, barium, and strontium. A French chemist, Bernard Courtois, accidentally discovered iodine during experiments with seaweed in which he was trying to produce sodium nitrate to make gunpowder for Napoleon's army. Antoine Balard, another French chemist, discovered elemental bromine. Although pure bromine was poisonous, compounds have been used as sedatives and in synthetic dyes. Silver bromide, a light-sensitive compound, is a critical component used to produce photographic film. In gasoline, bromine serves as an anti-knock additive. Johann Afrwedson, a Swedish chemist, discovered lithium. Lithium, a light alkali metal, weighed only one fifth as much as aluminum and burned when exposed to air. Copper and steel manufacturers exploited this tendency and used lithium to eliminate gas pockets that occurred during metal fabrication. Lithium compounds were also used during World War II to lift emergency radio antennas. They have also served as solid rocket fuels.

In 1860, German chemists Robert Bunsen and Gustav Kirchhoff discovered cesium. Cesium was the first element to be found with a light spectroscope, a device used to measure the light given off from a heated material. According to spectroscopic theory, no two materials emitted the same light pattern, each element had its own "fingerprint." Cesium, an element that easily releases its electrons when exposed to light, was later used in the development of television and space technologies.

Another discovery made during the 1860s was the creation of elemental fluorine by the English chemist George Gore. Gore succeeded in creating only a small amount of fluorine, however, which spontaneously exploded. In 1886 Henri Moissan, a French chemist, developed a way to produce fluorine in platinum vessels without explosive results. In the twentieth century, fluorine has been used in the separation of uranium for atomic weapons, as a component in liquid rocket fuel, and in combination with carbon to make fluorocarbons. Fluorocarbons have been used to replace ammonia in refrigeration systems and as propellants in aerosol cans (before they were banned due to their damaging environmental impact). Fluorine has also been used as a water additive to prevent tooth decay.

The 1860s also brought the development of synthetic dye manufacturing in Germany. The German synthetic dye producers evolved into world chemical production leaders. BASF (Badische Anilin und Soda Fabrik), for example, was established in 1861 originally as a manufacturer of alkali and related products. A BASF chemist enabled the company to expand by developing a method to produce alizarin (a yellowish-red compound) on a commercial scale. Other large German dye companies were Hoechst and Bayer. By the early twentieth century, the German companies held almost 90 percent of the world's dye production ability.

The Dow Chemical Company, founded in 1897, originally sold bromine and chlorine. The first additions to its product line included chloroform, sodium, magnesium, and calcium. Soon after, other corporations joined the roster of chemical manufacturers. They included the Hooker Electrochemical Company (1905), American Cyanamid (1907), Shell Chemical (1912), and Occidental Chemical (1920).

One of the biggest influences on the early twentieth century chemical industry was World War I. During this period, governments sponsored research and guaranteed purchase contracts for finished products. As a result, chemical companies developed new products more quickly than would have been economically possible during times of peace. Following World War I, the German chemical companies regrouped and formed IG Farben, the largest chemical group outside the United States. According to one estimate, IG Farben employed one out of three chemical workers in Germany by 1928. After World War II, IG Farben was divided back into the three largest companies that had merged for its creation: BASF, Bayer, and Hoescht.

In the United States, DuPont invested its war profits by expanding into production areas of rayon, plastics, ammonia, heavy chemicals, insecticides, electrochemicals, paints, pigments, and varnishes. American Cyanamid, originally a producer of fertilizers, also expanded. New areas included chemicals and chemical catalysts.

During the 1920s, mergers and acquisitions expanded the political influence held by U.S. chemical companies. Allied Chemicals was formed in 1920 through the merger of five previously existing chemical companies. Allied specialized in heavy inorganic chemicals and dyes. Union Carbide was founded in 1920 from three previously existing firms. Domestic chemical producers benefited from reduced foreign competition in the years between World War I and World War II. The Fordney-McCumber Act of 1922, for example, required that imported chemical products be sold at the same price as domestically produced chemicals. As a result, the chemical industry was one of the fastest growing industries in the country. By 1935, the combined value of the 26 U.S. chemical companies was estimated at $1.7 billion.

World War II brought increased demand for chemical products. These included chemical weapons, bombs, and incendiary devices, as well as a host of new products designed to meet the demands of developing technologies such as aviation. Other products developed by the industry included flameproofing and waterproofing materials. From 1947 to 1978, U.S. chemical production increased 900 percent. During the 1970s, however, environmental issues came to the forefront of the nation's conscience and challenged the safety of many products produced by the inorganic chemicals industry. The Environmental Protection Policy Act of 1970 established the Environmental Protection Agency (EPA), and subsequent legislative and regulatory efforts had far reaching effects on the industry. For example, the Toxic Substances Control Act of

1976 gave the EPA authority to regulate chemicals posing a risk to the environment or to human health.

Nevertheless, expansion continued. By the mid-1980s, approximately 60,000 chemicals were being used in the United States, and new industrial chemicals were being developed at a rate of about 1,000 per year. Concerns about safety also escalated, and waste disposal methods were criticized. In 1984, Lee Niedringhaus Davis, a writer specializing in the social impact of high technologies, wrote, "Each person now contains within his or her body a mixture of poisonous chemicals that no generation throughout humankind's entire history ever accumulated. Their long-term consequences we can only guess at."

Chemical-producing companies employed the following methods to reduce the amounts of waste generated: recapturing and reusing materials previously discharged, using wastes as raw materials for other products, increasing the efficiency of chemical reactions, using waste materials as energy sources, and processing wastes into products by finding innovative uses for them. As companies began to change their views about waste materials, terminology changed. According to Davis, the increasing popularity of the term "co-product" reflected a changing attitude where substances previously discharged as polluting wastes were instead viewed as potential products.

In 1987, the U.S. Department of Commerce reported that the value of shipments within the inorganic chemicals industry totaled $13.2 billion. Products were provided by approximately 700 establishments. About half of these firms were small companies that produced small volumes of specialty chemicals. These types of establishments accounted for only 4 percent of the industry's total shipments, but according to government projections, demand for specialty chemicals was expected to grow faster than demand for commodity chemicals.

The 1990s brought more questions about pollution and environmental and health concerns to the drawing board. One chemical under increasing criticism is hydrofluoric acid (HF). Overall demand for HF, an ingredient in the manufacture of chlorinated fluorocarbons (CFCs), was falling during the early 1990s as a result of CFC phaseouts. Some industry analysts expected demand for the chemical to continue declining, but others anticipated a rebound as CFCs were replaced with chemicals containing greater percentages of HF.

HF, however, has many other uses. It has been commonly used for the manufacture of other chemicals, aluminum production, stainless steel pickling, and as an octane booster in the petroleum industry.

Some well-known end products created with HF technology included computer screens, fluorescent light bulbs, semiconductors, and fluoride toothpaste. Despite its widespread use, *Audubon* magazine called HF "the most dangerous chemical in town." HF, a hazardous material, boils at 68 degrees Fahrenheit. As a result, spills of the chemical form dense, low-lying toxic clouds. One accident in 1987 sent more than 1,000 people to the hospital.

A legal action against Mobil Oil Company in California led to the issuance of a consent decree in 1990 requiring all refineries in the state to stop using HF by the end of 1997. Industry watchers estimated that nationwide consumption of HF by gasoline refineries totaled 40 million pounds per year. Nevertheless, only half the gasoline refineries in the country depended on HF; the rest relied on sulfuric acid. According to Mobil, expenses related to switching from HF to sulfuric acid were expected to approach $100 million. Sulfuric acid, although still considered a hazardous chemical, posed less danger than HF. Sulfuric acid had a much higher boiling point, 625 degrees Fahrenheit, and as a result, remained in a liquid state if spilled. Because sulfuric acid does not boil at naturally occurring ambient temperatures, it poses no threat of hard-to-control toxic cloud formation.

Since the early 1990s, the largest single chemical produced within the industry has been sulfuric acid. In 1991, producers generated 43 million tons of the chemical. Although some sulfuric acid was manufactured as a by-product of smelting operations and some was regenerated from previously used acid, most was created through the oxidation of sulfur.

Annual demand for sulfuric acid was expected to top 45 million tons by the mid-1990s. As the petroleum refining industry turned away from HF, some industry watchers predicted increased domestic demand for sulfuric acid. Others, however, expected no overall demand increase because of its reduced use in historically important markets, such as rayon production. Sulfuric acid has been used in phosphate and nitrogen fertilizers, ore processing, inorganic pigments, inorganic and organic chemicals, pulp and paper manufacturing, synthetic rubber production, plastics, water treatment, and soaps and detergents.

In the 1990s, hydrazine faced environmental and safety challenges. Approximately 40 percent of the hydrazine produced in the United States is used as an anticorrosion agent in boilers; however, users began turning to alternative products after hydrazine was identified as a carcinogen. Some hydrazine producers began promoting closed handling systems to permit customers to continue using hydrazine without exposing their workers to dangerous concentrations of the chemical.

One chemical product benefitting from the increased emphasis on environmental safety has been hydrogen peroxide. Although production volumes fell short of other products in the early 1990s, its growth rate and potential were notable. A report published in 1993 suggested that the North American hydrogen peroxide market was expanding at a rate of about 10 to 12 percent annually. One of its primary uses has been as a substitute for chlorine in the pulp and paper industry. Other areas of anticipated growth include the detoxification of cyanide used in gold mining, laundry and cleaning products, chemical manufacturers, water treatment facilities, and pollution control. More potential users of hydrogen peroxide are in the textiles industry, by suppliers of laundry products, electronics manufacturers, and food processors.

EPA Limits on Toxic Pollution. In March 1994 the Environmental Protection Agency announced long-expected regulations regarding toxic air pollution as part of the 1990 Clean Air Act. Under the rule, ''The nation's chemical companies will have to cut their plants' toxic air pollution by almost 90 percent from 1990 levels,'' according to the *Detroit Free Press.* ''The rule requires the companies . . . to install equipment to better prevent evaporation and leaks of 112 toxic chemicals.'' Environmental Protection Agency Administrator Carol Browner called it the most far-reaching effort ever taken to reduce air toxins. Prior to the new regulations, only 13 air toxins were federally regulated, with others regulated in varying fashions at the state level. To meet requirements, the EPA estimated that approximately 370 chemical plants across the nation would be forced to cut toxic air pollution by a total of 506,000 tons. *The Detroit Free Press* pointed out that ''the chemical industry will have to spend $450 million on capital improvements and another $230 million a year in ongoing costs to satisfy the requirements, which will go into effect in most cases within three years.'' The *Free Press* noted that chemical companies have, in many cases, already initiated efforts to improve their pollution emissions in anticipation of the EPA ruling. Company spokespersons for Dow Chemical and Upjohn, for instance, say that both companies have reduced air pollution levels at their plants by more than 50 percent in recent years.

According to the 1993 edition of *Standard and Poor's Industry Surveys,* the chemical industry as a whole was experiencing a slow recovery after a national economic slowdown during the early 1990s. Forecasters expected the overall industrial inorganic

chemicals industry to grow at a rate comparable to the nation's economic growth rate.

CURRENT CONDITIONS

The outlook for inorganic chemicals in 1996 was mixed. The hydrogen peroxide commodity was sold out and prices were expected to remain the same until more product became available. Chlorine and sodium chlorate were expected to drop slightly from their strong 1995 levels, and sodium bicarbonate sales would reflect growth in gross domestic product.

The demand for hydrogen peroxide was 1 billion pounds in 1994, 1.1 billion pounds in 1995, and was expected to be 1.55 billion pounds in 1999. The expected growth rate of 8 to 10 percent would fall short in 1996, when the pulp market crashed. As the pulp market used 60 percent of all hydrogen peroxide in North America, the pulp and paper industries dictated, to a large degree, the livelihood of hydrogen peroxide. The market had been going so well up until then, that hydrogen peroxide makers were not incredibly hurt by the sudden decrease in activity, and some manufactures were even relieved for the opportunity for maintenance.

Gains in the fertilizer market caused the demand for sulfur to increase 5 percent from 1993 to 1994. Another healthy gain occurred in 1995 due to increased fertilizer consumption. Sulfur sales were expected to remain closely tied to U.S. and world fertilizer demand.

Sulfuric acid recovered well in 1995 from reduced levels of 1993 and 1994. In March of 1994, the industry hit bottom with prices falling to $8 and $9 per ton. By 1995 sulfuric acid was up to $35 per ton. This was beginning to approach the $50-per-ton record high of the late 1980s.

The better market of the mid-1990s was due to an increase in demand for phosphate fertilizers and more use by the copper industry. As copper prices doubled in the first two months of 1995, more sulfuric acid was suddenly needed as copper miners tried to extract as much copper as quickly as possible. Another contributing factor was that imports of sulfuric acid from non-Canadian sources were almost nonexistent in 1995. The import rate had dropped from 684,000 metric tons in 1993 to 333,000 metric tons in 1994. Shipping prices from Germany, for example, were more expensive per ton than the sulfuric acid was worth.

INDUSTRY LEADERS

The leaders of the inorganic chemical industry were E.I. DuPont de Nemours and Co. of Wilmington,

Delaware; Dow Chemical Co. of Midland, Michigan; Hanson Industries Inc. of Iselin, New Jersey; Eastman Chemical Co. of Kingsport, Tennessee; and FMC Corp. of Chicago, Illinois.

In 1997, E.I. du Pont de Nemours and Co. was the largest company in the entire chemicals industry. It showed revenues of $43.8 billion and a net income of $3.6 billion in 1996. In 1996, half the company's sales were outside the United States. Exports from the United States were $3.8 billion, making DuPont one of the largest U.S. exporters. In 1996, DuPont employed nearly 100,000 people, with 65 percent of them working within the United States. The company operated in about 70 companies worldwide with 175 manufacturing and processing facilities.

The Dow Chemical Company was founded in 1897 by Herbert Henry Dow, and its first two products were bromine and chlorine. Other products added during the company's early years included sodium, magnesium, calcium, synthetic dyes, chemical fertilizers, food preservatives, solvents, and caustic soda. Throughout the twentieth century, Dow acquired other companies and diversified into many areas including chemicals, plastics, hydrocarbons, energy, pharmaceuticals, and consumer products.

Dow was an early pioneer in toxicology work. The company established its first toxicology laboratory in 1933 following the deaths of workers from chemical exposure. Dow was also working to reduce the environmental impact of its products and manage solid wastes in a more responsible manner. In 1991, Dow created a Corporate Environmental Advisory Council, the first of its kind in the industry. The Council was comprised of professionals from the government, education, environmental protection, and scientific communities who met together to discuss issues concerning environment, health, and safety.

In the late 1990s, Dow was the fifth largest chemical company in the world, measured in terms of sales. Dow's sales totaled $20 billion, a slight increase over 1992; however, because of falling prices due to recession of the global economy, the increased sales brought reduced profits. Dow manufactured its products at 178 facilities in 33 countries and offered a product line of more than 2,000 goods and services. Global employment reached 61,000. The company boasted that in 1992, its researchers received 335 U.S. patents and 1,385 international patents.

Another leading company involved in the production of industrial inorganic chemicals was W.R. Grace and Company. In the mid-1990s Grace reported annual sales in excess of $3.5 billion. The company was active in 48 states and 50 countries. Grace, the world's largest specialty chemicals company and largest manufacturer of catalysts, also supplied products to the construction and water treatment industries. Grace additives provided fireproofing, waterproofing, insulation, and anti-corrosive benefits.

The company's Grace Dearborn Division provided products for wastewater treatment and industrial cooling and boiler water systems. The division also supplied chemicals to the paper, oil, and petrochemical industries. In 1992, Grace Dearborn finished a $1.7-million expansion of its research facility in Antwerp, Belgium, in order to better serve increasing global demand for water treatment products.

In 1992, Grace introduced Grace Emission Control Products, a new line aimed at the environmental market. One example in this innovative category was a system designed for use by industrial customers attempting to reduce their emissions of volatile organic compounds. Grace reported its own annual expenditures to meet and surpass environmental, health, and safety standards totaled $150 million.

The FMC Corporation reported sales of $4 billion in 1992. Approximately 45 percent of the company's total sales represented foreign trade. FMC divisions held top positions in several segments of the inorganic chemicals market. Its Lithium Division, the world's largest producer of lithium chemicals, served a wide range of customers including manufacturers of aluminum, ceramics and glass, lubricating greases, textiles, air conditioning, and pharmaceuticals. The company's Peroxygen Chemicals Division was one of the world's largest producers of hydrogen peroxide and served such customers as the pulp and paper, textile, detergent, electronics, and environmental industries. FMC Foret, S.A., the company's European division, supplied products to a variety of users including other chemical manufacturers and the detergent industry.

Like many of its competitors, FMC has been heavily affected by environmental legislation. The company reported that its waste releases were decreased by 30 percent between 1987 and 1992. In addition, FMC voluntarily participated in an Environmental Protection Agency (EPA) program to reduce its emissions of specific hazardous chemicals.

WORK FORCE

According to government statistics for 1992, the inorganic chemicals industry employed 88,000 workers. This figure reflects a steady level in the employment picture for this industry. By 1995, however, the number of employees dropped to 73,700. In 1981, U.S.

Department of Labor statistics indicated a total work force in the industry of more than 107,000 employees; by 1987 the number of workers had fallen to 87,000, but the industry has held steady at about that figure since that time. Four states accounted for more than half the employment within the industry: South Carolina, Tennessee, Washington, and Ohio. Of the almost 700 companies classified in the industry, about 50 percent employed fewer than 20 people.

One of the major issues confronting the industry's labor force was worker health and safety. The chemical industry has had a long history of exposing its workers to hazardous situations. For example, in the latter half of the 1800s, the Leblanc method of reacting sulfuric acid on salt to produce alkali created hydrochloric acid gas as a by-product. The hydrochloric acid gas rotted workers' teeth, led to chronic bronchitis, and caused skin ailments. Moreover, industrial accidents involving chemicals often resulted in greater harm to workers and the environment than accidents in other industries.

To address the needs of workers, Congress passed the Occupational Safety and Health Act of 1970. The Act created the Occupational Safety and Health Administration (OSHA) within the U.S. Department of Labor. OSHA's responsibilities include establishing safe standards for chemical exposure and keeping workers informed of potential risks. Chemical companies also began to address safety needs with greater vigor and introduced increasing numbers of voluntary measures to help ensure employee and public safety.

RESEARCH AND TECHNOLOGY

As the chemicals industry evolved during the twentieth century, the cost of investigating and developing new products was very high. Many new compounds studied by researchers were rejected because they failed to meet expectations, were too expensive to produce, or posed safety problems. Another related problem was rapid obsolescence of products and related manufacturing methods. Because technologies changed so quickly, new products were sometimes outdated before their developing companies could recapture costs associated with research and development. Additionally, as technologies changed, many manufacturing methods also became obsolete.

By the 1990s, many products within this industrial classification were considered basic commodities. As a result, research activities to develop new products were conducted with less vigor than in other segments of the chemical industry. Instead of focusing on new product development, most research focused on ways to reduce production costs by reducing labor costs, cutting energy needs, improving process efficiencies, and finding new applications for existing products. Researchers also investigated ways to meet environmental mandates by curtailing emissions, putting waste products to work, recapturing materials, and rendering hazardous substances inert.

A new use for sulfuric acid, called the Santa Cruz In Situ Mining Research Project, was experimented with in 1996. This project demonstrated the environmental, technical, and economic feasibility of in situ, or "in place" mining. The goal was to reach copper that was buried too deeply and was of too low a grade to be mined by conventional methods. A dilute solution of sulfuric acid was injected nearly 1,600 feet below the earth's surface into undisturbed granite bedrock containing soluble copper oxide minerals. The solution was then recovered through wells and pumped to the surface where it was processed and re-injected to the mining zone in a closed loop.

FURTHER READING

Busch, Gretchen. "HF Future Tied to CFC Phaseout." *Chemical Marketing Reporter,* 13 July 1992.

Chapman, Peter. "Chemical Outlook '96: Inorganic Chemicals." *Chemical Marketing Reporter* 249, no. 3 (15 January 1996): 14.

———. "Peroxide Producers Jolted by Pulp Crash." *Chemical Marketing Reporter* 249, no. 8 (19 February 1996): 3, 23.

———. "Sulfuric Acid Market Regains its Strength." *Chemical Marketing Reporter* 248, no. 11 (11 September 1995): 3, 24.

Chemical Manufacturers Association 1991 - 1992 Annual Report. Washington: Chemical Manufacturers Association, 1992.

"Chemicals." *Standard & Poor's Industry Surveys.* New York: Standard & Poor's Corporation, 1993.

Coeyman, Marjorie, and Natasha Alperowicz. "Future Stays Bright for H2O2 Despite Slower Growth, Overcapacity in 1992." *Chemical Week,* 17 February 1993.

Davis, Lee Niedringhaus. *The Corporate Alchemists: Profit Takers and Problem Makers in the Chemical Industry.* New York: William Morrow and Company, 1984.

Dow At a Glance, Midland, MI: nd.

The Dow Chemical Company. Available from http://www.dow.com/index2.html.

Dow 1992 Annual Report. Midland, MI: 1993.

"DuPont At a Glance . . . " Available from http://www.dupont.com/corp/gbl-company/overview.html.

Flaschen, Steward S. *Search and Research: The Story of the Chemical Elements.* Boston: Allyn and Bacon, 1965.

FMC 1992 Annual Report. Chicago: FMC, 1993.

Gallagher, Matthew. "Sulfuric Acid Aided By 'Diverse Factors'." *Chemical Marketing Reporter* 247, no. 13 (27 March 1995): 5, 18.

"Grace Fact Sheet." Boca Raton, FL: W. R. Grace, 1993.

Grace, W. R. & Company Annual Report 1992. Boca Raton, FL: 1993.

Hunter, David. "Hydrazine: An Uproar Over New Projects." *Chemical Week,* 8 February 1989.

"Hydrofluoric Acid." *Chemical Marketing Reporter,* 29 July 1991.

"Hydrogen Peroxide." *Chemical Marketing Reporter* 248, no. 21 (November 1995): 20, 36-37.

"Inorganic Chemicals." *Standard And Poor's Industry Surveys.* New York: Standard and Poor's Corporation, 1997.

"New Use For Sulfuric Acid?" *Chemical Marketing Reporter* 249, no. 10 (4 March 1996): 5.

Peterkofsky, David. "Running Hot and Cold." *Chemical Marketing Reporter,* 13, April 1992.

Santos, William. "Sulfuric Acid Oversupply Keeps Prices in Abeyance." *Chemical Marketing Reporter,* 19 April 1993.

Selcraig, Bruce. "The Most Dangerous Chemical in Town." *Audubon,* November-December 1992.

Sternberg, Ken. "Use of Hydrofluoric Acid Comes Under the Gun in California." *Chemical Week,* 31 October 1990.

"Sulfuric Acid." *Chemical Marketing Reporter.* 16 September 1991.

Trost, Cathy. *Elements of Risk: The Chemical Industry and Its Threat to America.* New York: Times Books, 1984.

"U.S. Chemicals Challenged in Global Marketplace." *Chemical Marketing Reporter.* 5 April 1993.

U.S. Department of Commerce. International Trade Administration. *U.S. Industrial Outlook 1994.* Washington: GPO, 1994.

U.S. Department of Labor. *Employment, Hours, and Earnings, United States, 1988-96.* Washington: GPO, 1996.

Ward's Business Directory of U.S. Public and Private Companies. Detroit: Gale, 1997.

Williams, Mike. "EPA Sets New Limits on Toxic Pollution." *Detroit Free Press,* 2 March 1994.

Woodburn, John H. *Opportunities in Chemistry Careers.* Chicago: National Textbook Company, 1987.

Worobec, Mary Devine. *Toxic Substances Controls Primer.* Washington: Bureau of National Affairs, Inc., 1984.

—Karen Bellenir, updated by Beaird Glover

SIC 2821

PLASTIC MATERIALS AND RESINS

The plastic materials and resins industry is comprised of companies primarily engaged in manufacturing various resins and plastics for sale to other industries that create plastic sheets, rods, films, and other products. Information on related products can be found under **SIC 2822: Synthetic Rubber, SIC 2823: Cellulose Manmade Fibers,** and **SIC 2824: Organic Fibers—Noncellulosic.**

INDUSTRY SNAPSHOT

Synthetic plastic was invented late in the eighteenth century and did not reach widespread use in the United States until the 1900s. Swift advances in chemical and manufacturing technologies during the twentieth century, however, made plastic one of America's most important manufacturing materials. Massive demand for plastic had propelled the industry past $43.5 billion in annual sales by 1995. Plastic manufacturers employed over 69,000 workers in 1995 and exported more than $4 billion worth of material.

The industry realized a healthy average growth rate of about 6 percent during the 1980s, as plastics increasingly invaded markets formerly dominated by wood, metal, glass, and paper products. Moreover, growth was spurred by the development of new and better plastics that spawned new uses for industry output. Although an economic recession in the early 1990s caused growth to lag, the long-term outlook for plastics was optimistic in the mid-1990s.

Consumption of acrylic resins and plastics is highly dependent upon the economic conditions of each region. From 1994 to 1997, consumption of acrylic resins and plastics worldwide was expected to increase at a rate of 3.7 percent per year, reaching 1.45 billion pounds (658 thousand metric tons) in 1997. New technology and increased demand were expected to boost production and profits throughout the decade and into the twenty-first century.

ORGANIZATION AND STRUCTURE

Plastics provide an important alternative to natural materials for a plethora of applications. One of the most important distinguishing factors between plastic and other materials is plastic's ability to "creep" under load, or gradually stretch or flow when subjected to stress. While metals and ceramics exhibit this property as well, they do so only at much higher temperatures. Plastics also resist erosion and do not require a coating to protect them against inorganic acids, bases, and water or salt solutions. Perhaps the greatest advantage that plastics offer, however, is their ability to be molded into any shape and to be processed to exhibit any of a massive number of physical characteristics.

Competition and Market Structure. The synthetic materials industry is considered a segment of the overall chemical industry; synthetic materials manufacturers represent about 20 percent. The plastics industry comprises about 70 percent of the entire synthetic materials industry, which also encompasses rubber and manmade fibers. Manufacturers produce about 500 different types of resins and compounds. Each of these products is available from various suppliers in multiple grades, each grade offering varying physical properties and prices.

Production. Plastics are giant polymers, or long-chain molecules that contain thousands of repeating molecular units. When combined with other ingredients called additives, the polymers can be shaped and molded under heat and pressure into a resin. Resin usually takes the form of pellets, flakes, granules, powder, or liquid. Most resins are not used in their natural state, but are instead combined with other materials by mixing or melt-state blending. The end result is a plastic compound, still in the form of pellets, granules, or powder, that is ready to be delivered to a processor.

The physical properties of the final plastic product can be altered at various stages of the polymerization and production process. The most versatile method of varying properties is by compounding. With this method, additives—such as colorants, flame retardants, heat or light stabilizers, or lubricants—may be added to the resin to achieve a desired result. Fillers or reinforcement—such as glass fibers, particulate materials, or hollow glass spheres—may instead be added to the resin, as may other polymers, which form a polymer blend or alloy.

Plasticizers are the most common additives used to alter plastic resins. Plasticizers increase a resin's flexibility and are often used to make polyvinyl chloride resins used in construction products. Impact modifiers are an additive used to boost a plastic's resistance to stress. Similarly, antidixodiants retard the oxidation and breakdown of plastics, and heat stabilizing additives help resins to maintain their physical structure during processing. Light stabilizers filter out radiation that can cause a plastic to deteriorate as a result of exposure to sunlight, and flame retardants enable resins to resist combustion. Colorants are another major additive used in the compounding process.

Four major commercial divisions of plastic resins are manufactured. Commodity resins, which represent the bulk of industry production, are low-tech plastics available in standardized formulas from many companies throughout the world. Intermediate resins are generally considered more advanced and somewhat specialized in comparison to commodity resins. Similarly, engineering resins generally exhibit more advanced performance characteristics and are produced on a smaller scale than other types of resin. Finally, advanced resins are generally those most capable of withstanding impact and high heat, carrying loads, and resisting attacks by chemicals and solvents.

Thermoplastics. The two main classes of plastic are thermosets and thermoplastics. Thermoplastics accounted for about 83 percent of industry output. They solidify by cooling and may be remelted repeatedly to form new shapes. Examples of thermoplastic resins are polyethylene, polypropylene, and polystyrene. Polyethylene is the highest volume plastic, accounting for about 40 percent of thermoplastic production, and is used primarily to create packaging, though many consumer and institutional products are made as well. About 20 billion pounds of polyethylene were produced in 1991. Major manufacturers of this resin include Quantum Chemical, Union Carbide, and Dow Chemical Co.

Polyvinyl chloride (PVC) makes up the second largest share of the thermoplastics segment. It is used primarily to make gutters, pipes, siding, windows, and other products used by construction and building industries. About 11.2 billion pounds of PVC were shipped in 1991. Major producers include Occidental Petroleum, Shintech, and Formosa Plastics. Polypropylene, another thermoplastic, accounted for about 8.3 billion pounds of production in 1991. This resin is used mainly in the creation of fiber and filaments, as well as in the production of packaging and molded consumer products.

Polystyrene, a fourth major thermoplastic product, represented about 5 billion pounds of production in the early 1990s. This resin is used to make disposable packaging, furniture finishings, and miscellaneous consumer products. Other thermoplastics segments include polyamide resins, styrene-butadiene, and some polyesters.

Thermosets. Thermosets, the other division of the plastics industry, account for about 17 percent of output. Unlike thermoplastics, thermosets harden by chemical reaction, and cannot be melted and shaped after they are created. Thermosets are also considered the more mature and less dynamic segment of the industry.

Typical thermosets include phenolics, urea-formaldehyde resins, epoxies, and polyester. Phenolics, which account for over 50 percent of all thermoset production, are used principally for construction products. Such materials include plywood adhesives, insulation, laminates, moldings, and abrasives. Urea, the second largest segment of the thermoset division, is also used as an adhesive for plywood and particle board. Other uses of this resin include protective coatings and textile and paper treating and coating.

Thermoset polyesters are used to create plastics that are reinforced with glass fiber and other materials. They are also used to make various construction supplies such as boat and marine equipment, transportation products, and electronics. Epoxy is primarily used as a protective coating for metal goods, but is also used in multiple construction applications. In 1991, 530 million pounds of epoxy was produced.

BACKGROUND AND DEVELOPMENT

The first plastic used in the United States was a natural material known as Keratin, which was made from animal hooves, horns, feathers, and hair. Keratin was used as a fabricating material to make lantern windows and other items as early as 1740. In the late 1800s, Americans copied a technique observed among Malayan natives, who molded a plastic made from gutta percha, or gum elastic, into knife handles and other articles. This technique had a variety of applications in the United States, from ocean cable insulation to billiard balls. Samuel Speck, regarded as the first American to mold plastics, helped to introduced shellac plastics in the 1850s. By then, different types of natural plastics were being used to produce such items as checkers, buttons, picture frames, and insulators.

''Parkesine,'' the first synthetic plastic, was invented in 1862 by Alexander Parkes, an Englishman. Recognizing the important plasticizing effect in the Parkesine production process, American John Wyatt renamed the substance celluloid in 1870, and was credited with originating the production of synthetic plastics in the United States. Celluloid, despite its inflammability, was used to make carriage and automobile windshields and motion picture film.

Dr. Baekland, also an American, invented the world's first moldable plastic material in 1909. Baekland's thermosetting phenolformaldehyde resin provided a tremendous impetus for other inventors, who began developing molding techniques and adding resins to paints and varnishes. Baekland's resin, later called ''bakelite,'' was also used in the electrical industry to make some of the first molded synthetic plastic components. The first colorless resin, urea-formaldehyde, was invented in 1918 and sold commercially in 1928.

Plastics research and development began to proliferate in the 1920s and 1930s. The Germans pioneered the creation of many new thermosetting resins, while Americans and several Europeans made significant contributions in the area of plastic molding and extrusion machines, and later in the advancement of thermoplastics. During World War II, the plastics industry realized significant advances, as warring nations hurried to develop new and better materials for their war machines.

Postwar economic expansion augmented the development of the plastics industry. As demand for all types of consumer, commercial, and institutional products soared, plastics producers scrambled to keep pace with expanding markets. Successive breakthroughs in chemical technology and production techniques opened up vast new markets for manufacturers. Most importantly, however, producers in other industries began to realize the advantages of substituting plastics for more expensive, less flexible, natural materials. By the 1970s the plastics industry was shipping more than $10 billion worth of resins per year. U.S. producers also controlled a major share of aggregate world exports.

Sales of all types of plastic resins continued to multiply throughout much of the 1980s. A variety of factors, such as excess capacity and high petroleum costs, contributed to brief periods of slow production or decreased profits. In general, however, industry participants benefitted from several factors. Growth in exports, for example, contributed to the industry's success; although U.S. chemical firms lost world market share, exports more than doubled from $2.7 billion in 1980 to $6.3 billion by 1990.

New additives and plastic alloys also increased in demand, opening entirely new markets for resins and prompting other industries to substitute plastic for more expensive, less flexible organic products. Furthermore, as many segments of the industry matured and became more competitive, falling prices allowed plastics to penetrate a number of metal, glass, and wood markets. Reinforcing downward pricing pressures were massive industry investments in research, development, and more efficient production facilities, allowing producers to remain extremely competitive domestically.

Automobile and truck makers, for example, became a vital market for resins during the 1980s as those manufacturers increasingly sought advantages related to cost and the physical properties of plastics.

Similarly, electronic equipment makers, appliance producers, and other consumer products industries significantly increased their use of various resins. Packaging markets grew as well during the 1980s as disposable items, microwave foods, beverage containers, and other products that were suited to plastic gained in popularity. Importantly, a boom in U.S. construction inflated demand for resins in that important segment.

Between 1982 and 1989, plastic industry shipments rocketed from $15.8 billion per year to over $33 billion—representing average annual growth of about 8.8 percent per year. Despite massive productivity gains, moreover, employment crept upward from 54,000 in 1982 to about 62,000 by 1989. Profits surged in the late 1980s as shipments rose and manufacturers began reaping the rewards of earlier capital investments.

An economic recession in 1989, which lingered through 1993, stabilized the demand for plastics. Transportation, consumer and industrial, and packaging sectors all temporarily scaled back their consumption of resins. The construction industry, which had plunged into a virtual depression by 1990, proved a major detriment to sales growth for all types of plastics. Revenues slipped nearly $2 billion in 1990, to $31.3 billion. Correspondingly, employment shrank nearly 3 percent the following year, to about 61,000. Buoying earnings, however, was a 30 percent growth in 1991 exports—largely a result of a weak U.S. dollar.

Despite a lull in prices, profits, and revenues throughout 1991 and much of 1992, the industry showed signs of renewed growth. Prices and production picked up, and the U.S. economy as a whole began to improve. Although employment continued to decline, analysts remained optimistic, citing newly developed additives and compounds as boding well for the industry's continued success.

About 500 manufacturers competed in the plastics industry in the early 1990s, making it highly concentrated in comparison to most other U.S. manufacturing businesses. The average revenue per plastics establishment during this time was over $65 million—about eight times greater than the average for all other U.S. industries. The top eight producers controlled 40 percent of the market in 1987, while the top 20 firms accounted for 66 percent of production. Like many other capital intensive and concentrated industries, high barriers to entry, such as large start-up costs and technical competency, discourage potential entrants from vying for market share.

The largest consumer of plastics in the early 1990s was the packaging industry, which created bags, bottles, food containers, and related items. That sector purchased about 30 percent of all plastics shipped. Building and construction supply manufacturers, which made plastic pipe, conduit, geotextiles, and other materials, represented about 20 percent of the plastics market. Exports accounted for an impressive 20 percent of industry output, while the remaining 30 percent of shipments were consumed by various commercial, institutional, and consumer markets. Electrical appliance and electronic component manufacturers, for instance, bought about 5 percent of all plastics in 1991.

Although 1992 profits were disappointing for most competitors, they represented an improvement over figures for 1991, prompting optimism among participants in the synthetic plastic and resin industry. Sales topped $32.7 billion in 1992, and were forecast to rise 3 percent in 1993. Demand also seemed to be growing in 1993, particularly in awakening automobile and construction sectors. Prices remained relatively weak, however, following a four-year slide that ended in 1992. Although profits for the largest competitors slipped as well in 1992, smaller and mid-sized firms had stable earnings.

In the mid-1990s, many producers began to realize the benefits of cost reduction efforts implemented over the past several years. Such efforts included reducing employment, restructuring management, and closing some production facilities. Growth in emerging foreign markets, as well as solid expansion of various niches of the resin market, also encouraged competitors. Continuing development of new compounds, spurred by ever-increasing expenditures on research and development, were boosting the industry's overall share of the U.S. economy.

CURRENT CONDITIONS

Industry Segment Performance. Thermoplastic resins, which led industry gains throughout the 1980s, continued to experience demand growth in the mid-1990s, particularly in the area of high-grade, low-volume resins that could serve niche markets. High-tech applications in the auto and aerospace industries for engineering and advanced resins, for example, were proliferating. Intermediate and commodity products were showing gains too. After posting an average annual production growth rate of 7 percent between 1982 and 1991, thermoplastics advanced 6 percent in 1992 and were forecast to rise by 7 percent or more in 1993.

The important polyethylene segment, which accounted for over 40 percent (22 billion pounds) of total thermoplastic output, grew slightly less than 6 percent in the mid 1990s. Demand for high-density polyethylene, which made up 50 percent of that segment, increased at a rate of 7 percent in 1993. Prices in this category had stabilized by 1993. New technology promised several advances in polyethylene resins in the late 1990s. New compounds were being marketed in 1993, for instance, that allowed producers of shrink-wrap, carpet wrap, liner, and other film products to reduce the thickness of their material by 30 percent without compromising strength.

PVC resin production grew 7 percent in 1992 to about ten billion pounds—a disappointing figure compared to the 9 percent increases between 1982 and 1991. Recessed growth was largely a result of environmental restrictions implemented by both domestic and international governments. Switzerland, for example, instituted a ban on PVC water bottles in 1992 while the Netherlands contemplated similar actions. In Austria, European producers were embroiled in a lawsuit against the environmental activist group Greenpeace, which ran an advertising campaign equating PVC with poison in 1991.

Polypropylene, the third major thermoplastic, grew an encouraging 9 percent in 1992 to 8.4 billion pounds produced, up from 1 percent annual growth between 1982 and 1991. Aided by new technological improvements and strong demand overseas, this resin was expected to realize solid gains. Prices remained weak in 1993, however—a result of global production overcapacity. Prices have increased in 1996 in an effort to restore profits, and a 10 percent growth was predicted. High-tech resins used in car interiors and appliances were leading this segment.

Smaller thermoplastic segments posted the greatest advances in the mid-1990s. Production of styrene-butadiene, polyamides, and thermoplastic polyester grew about 15 percent in 1992. These three categories represented a combined output of about 5.7 billion pounds. Improved additives, particularly colorants, were boosting styrene-butadiene sales, though long-term growth of that resin was in question. While sales of polyester suffered due to environmental concerns, the material was becoming a viable substitute for telephone and light poles, steel and concrete, and other construction materials.

While thermosetting resins lagged behind thermostats during the 1980s, they were posting solid gains in the mid-1990s. Total thermoset output jumped 7 percent to 6.3 billion pounds in 1992, contrasting with average annual gains of just 4 percent between 1982 and 1991. Phenolics, the largest thermoset segment, increased 10 percent in 1992 to 2.9 billion pounds.

New applications for transportation and other high-volume markets, improved additives and compounds, and low prices all contributed to the surge. Thermoset polyesters gained 9 percent in 1992, while urea production swelled a less impressive 5 percent. Epoxy resins, which accounted for only 4 percent of thermoset production by weight, realized output growth of 18 percent.

Environment. In 1993, the chemical industry as a whole was the largest polluting industry in the United States, producing more than three times as much hazardous waste as the second greatest offender. The industry also spent more on pollution control and clean-up than any other business sector. In 1992, for example, all chemical industries spent more than \$4.9 billion on pollution abatement efforts. Furthermore, over 20 percent of all capital expenditures in the industry went toward pollution control projects in 1992.

Government efforts to counter the effects of dangerous pollutants were stepped up in the 1980s and began to pay off in the early 1990s. Chemical industry emission of toxic waste was down 4 percent in 1991 from 1990 levels, having declined 34 percent since 1988. Nevertheless, new regulations were forcing producers to further reduce pollution and clean up the environment. The 1990 Pollution Control Act, for example, expanded the reporting requirements for resin producers and required recovery and reuse of some production materials. Another major development in this area was the announcement in March 1994 of a new federal government rule devised as part of the 1990 Clean Air Act. As a result of the new rule, ''the nation's chemical companies will have to cut their plants' toxic air pollution by almost 90 percent from 1990 levels,'' observed the *Detroit Free Press.* ''The rule requires the companies . . . to install equipment to better prevent evaporation and leaks of 112 toxic chemicals. . . . Under the 1990 Clean Air Act, the EPA was supposed to issue regulations curbing industrial toxic chemical releases by November 1992, specifically requiring chemical manufacturers to install the best available technology to capture the releases. Environmentalists accused the Bush administration of delaying action because of industry pressure and filed suit.'' The new ruling by the EPA is aimed at meeting that federal judge's ruling. The Environmental Protection Agency calls the new regulations the most comprehensive effort ever taken to reduce toxic air pollution, while representatives of the chemical industry point out that many chemical companies have already drastically reduced their toxic pollution emissions in anticipation of the new rule. They argue that EPA estimates (\$450 million on capital improvements and

$230 million annually in ongoing costs) of the cost of satisfying the requirements are far too low.

Environmental regulations also affected the businesses of resin buyers. Packaging producers, for example, struggled to find ways of reducing their contribution to overburdened landfills. Auto and truck makers met with some success in developing recyclable vehicle components—often with the help of plastics companies. Similarly, many plastic products were being used to solve environmental problems. Advanced geotextiles, for example, were used to develop cleaner and more efficient landfills, and recycled plastic was used in the manufacture of a wide variety of consumer goods, including outdoor furniture and parking bumpers.

Environmental concerns continued to fuel major research efforts. Low-styrene emission products, which limited volatile organic compound emissions during production, were receiving much attention in the mid-1990s, as were polyester composites that could be used to enhance corrosion resistance properties. Hastening to conform with new chlorinated fluorocarbon (CFC) emissions standards, foam producers learned to use resins to create carpet padding and packaging foams, for example, that emitted little, if any, CFC.

In 1992 and 1993 many industries including the plastics materials and resins industry, which were sailing in a mature economy, started slowing down. To set the recovery in motion, the industry started contending with capacity constraints and longer lead times. Production for all plastics by U.S. producers was up by about 3.4 percent over 1994.

In 1996 there were about 410 operating companies in the U.S. whose primary products fell under the umbrella of plastics materials and resins. The plastics industry continued to be one of the strongest performers in the U.S. economy, growing by an annual average of 4.8 percent since the late 1960's.

Plastics were considered cost-efficient, durable, and chemical resistant materials, that provided design flexibility in appliance manufacturing. Fifty-five percent of the annual plastic demand was utilized by major appliance manufacturing companies. The annual demand for plastics in the appliance manufacturing industry was predicted to be 4.6 percent, with the estimated totals for the year 2000 amounting to 2 billion pounds. The demand for plastics among small electric manufacturers also increased by 5 percent annually. Producers of automotive plastics had increased sales by 10 to 20 percent, in 1994, because of increased manufacturing of automobiles.

From 1996 to 1997, consumption of plastics in North American-built cars and light duty trucks was expected to decline nearly two pounds per vehicle as a result of materials conversions by the automakers; steel was expected to become the principal beneficiary of these conversions. For the first time small to medium size auto components made in plastics suffered an average net decline per vehicle of 1.8 to 2 pounds. However, interior applications for plastic trim and panel components was expected to expand somewhat in 1997 because of increasing vehicle dimensions and interior space.

In 1997, plastics manufacturers tried to displace the use of metals in the auto industry in underhood components. Dupont Automotive Co., Siemens, Bayer Polymers were prominent players in this effort. Plastics makers predicted that use of plastics such as nylon for underhood automobile parts would continue to replace metals.

INDUSTRY LEADERS

The largest U.S. company actively producing synthetic resins, plastics materials, and nonvulcanizable rubber in 1996 was Dow Chemical Company of Midland Michigan. This diversified company employed over 39,500 and generated $20 billion in sales in 1996. Allied Signal of New Jersey, came second with annual sales revenue of $14.34 billion and 88,500 employees.

Ashland Inc. was the third largest with a 1996 sales revenue of $12 billion. Dow Chemical U.S.A., with 1996 revenue of $9.5 billion, Monsanto Co. of St Louis, Missouri, with revenue of $8.9 billion, and Exxon Chemical Co. of Houston, Texas, with 1996 sales revenue of $7.4 billion ranked fourth, fifth, and sixth in the United States.

Hoechst Celanese Corp., of New Jersey, was the seventh largest competitor in the industry in 1996 with revenues of about $7.4 billion and 26,200 employees. Other large competitors included Union Carbide Corporation, of Connecticut, with $5.8 billion in 1996 sales, Occidental Chemical Corporation of Texas, with 5.4 billion in sales, and Eastman Chemical Co., of Tennessee, with $5 billion in sales.

WORK FORCE

In 1995, about 75,100 workers were employed in the plastics industry. This represented a slight decline since 1990, when employment hit a peak of 62,400. Despite solid increases in the bulk weight of resins produced, producers hesitated to hire more workers, echoing a trend that prevailed throughout the 1980s, during which the value of production rose over 100 percent while total employment grew only 13 percent. The reduced work force resulted from massive increases in productivity, attained through elimination of managers, automation of manufacturing facilities, and the displacement of support staff by computer and information systems. Furthermore, decreased employment figures reflected the fact that established workers were putting in more hours.

Despite stagnant job growth, the plastics industry offered opportunities for qualified individuals in the mid-1990s. Production workers, which made up about 60 percent of the industry work force, were among the highest paid industrial workers in the United States. The average 1995 production wage of $17.93 was 69 percent greater than the average for all other U.S. manufacturers. Manufacturing positions were on the decline, however, and fell 5 percent in 1992 alone.

The industry remained a major supplier of high-paying jobs for those specializing in science, particularly chemists. The average chemist's annual salary in 1994 was $45,400. Chemists with master's degrees averaged $53,500, while those holding doctorates earned an average of $66,000. Opportunities for such highly educated workers decreased only slightly in the early 1990s. Nevertheless, unemployment among chemists was at its highest level since 1983, and despite salary increases of more than four percent in 1992, unemployment grew to 7.2 percent.

Although industry output and profits were expected to rise steadily, jobs for production workers were likely to drop by 10 to 20 percent on average between 1990 and 2005, according to the Bureau of Labor Statistics. Experts estimated that opportunities for machine operators would realize the greatest decline—over 25 percent—and that mechanic and equipment controller jobs would fall 15 percent or more. Increases in work force were expected to affect positions related to sales, marketing, and advertising as well as engineering, mathematics, and science.

AMERICA AND THE WORLD

The U.S. plastics industry, by far the largest and most advanced in the world, was heavily dependent on exports in the mid-1990s. Overseas sales accounted for about $8.5 billion, or over 20 percent of U.S. resin output in 1994. Plastics accounted for about 25 percent of total U.S. chemical exports, and U.S. resin producers accounted for an estimated 36 percent of total world production in 1992. Japan, the next largest producer, manufactured less than half that amount, at 16 percent of world output, and Germany placed third with a 9 percent share of the market.

European and Japanese suppliers suffered setbacks even worse than those faced by U.S. manufacturers in the late 1980s. Overcapacity and relatively low productivity plagued European community producers. Moreover, after realizing chemical industry profits of over $2 billion per year in both 1988 and 1989, Japanese plastics producers were hammered in the early 1990s by weak foreign and domestic demand. Net profits plunged to just over $1 billion per year in 1992 and 1993, as exports and revenues declined, and the country remained mired in a severe recession.

Although U.S. plastics exports doubled during the 1980s and continued to grow rapidly in the early 1990s, the United States was steadily losing its share of the global market. Expanded overseas production, particularly in the Far East, was displacing U.S. sales. Nevertheless, burgeoning foreign markets offered promising prospects for growth to savvy U.S. exporters. Furthermore, U.S. technology and productivity had succeeded in protecting domestic market share. The U.S. plastics industry maintained a combined trade surplus of about $5.2 billion in 1994. Plastic imports, moreover, accounted for only $1.8 billion of the domestic market.

The largest buyer of U.S. plastics was Canada, which purchased 16 percent, or $1.2 billion, of total U.S. exports in 1991. Mexico, the second largest customer, accounted for about 8 percent, or $588 million, of exports. Belgium purchased 7.1 percent of overseas shipments, while Japan and the Netherlands each consumed about 6.9 percent of resin exports. Canada was also the largest exporter of chemicals to the United States, with 33 percent of all foreign sales. Japan held a 17 percent share of the U.S. import market, while Germany followed with 14 percent. The United Kingdom and France each represented about 5 percent of plastic imports.

Although U.S. exports were expected to rise 2 percent in 1993, observers had initially hoped for a much greater increase. Weak European and Asian markets were primarily to blame; many Asian consumers were beginning to rely on new domestic sources of resins and plastics, while the European community was simply mired in a recession. Latin American markets, in contrast, were proving surprisingly vital. Shipments to Mexico, for instance, nearly doubled between 1988 and 1992, explaining the industry's strong support for the North American Free Trade Agreement (NAFTA). Industry participants in 1993 were also strongly supportive of the pending General Agreement on Tariffs and Trade, an agreement that promised to significantly boost sales in Europe.

Unable to significantly penetrate U.S. markets, foreign companies participated in U.S. plastics markets primarily through direct investment during the 1980s and early 1990s. Overseas investment in the overall chemical industry climbed from just $14.4 billion in 1982 to $45.6 billion in 1990, and to $49.1 billion by 1991. Foreign chemical companies that invested in U.S. companies sought access to U.S. technology, markets, and research and development. Such investment was expected to continue throughout the 1990s, though on a smaller scale.

In 1996, makers of masterbatches or plastic concentrates with pigments and additives already mixed in were increasingly considering acquisitions as global competition gradually took over the industry. North America accounted for 35 percent of masterbatch sales, Europe accounted for 33 percent, and Asia for 27 percent. "Consolidation and globalization are the overriding themes in the 2.9 billion pound masterbatch business," said the *Chemical Marketing Reporter.*

In 1996, five acrylic resins and plastics producers held 71 percent of the total capacity in North America, Western Europe and Japan. AtoHaas and ICI were the largest producers accounting for 23 percent and 20 percent respectively, of the total volume.

RESEARCH AND TECHNOLOGY

The plastics industry invested a major portion of its resources in research and development. In the early 1990s, industry participants were making capital investments of over $2.5 billion annually, amounting to about 8 percent of total revenues. The industry invested about six times more per employee than did the average U.S. manufacturer in 1992. While many investments in the 1980s were used to expand production capacity and develop new products, producers in the early 1990s emphasized investments in productivity gains rather than capacity.

Research and development related to new products focused on the creation of specialty materials for niche markets, designing high-performance resins, and upgrading the properties of commodity thermoplastics. Thermoplastic research and development also concentrated on formulating resins that could compete with lower-priced materials. New additives and alloys played an important role in such advancements. However, emerging polymerization technology also offered strong growth potential for cutting-edge manufacturers. For instance, numerous and promising breakthroughs in bimodal resins, which typically combined two polymer types, were helping to enhance the balance of properties and processability of plastics.

Technological advancements occurring in other industries also promised to boost plastics sales. Resin processors, for instance, had developed new extrusion and molding devices, allowing manufacturers to maximize the benefits of new compounds and alloys. Such compounds held promise for makers of cars and appliance manufacturers, which sought stronger, lightweight materials. Similarly, processing techniques that complemented lighter, stronger, and thinner plastics promised to boost the use of plastics in all types of packaging applications.

New biodegradable plastics, including weak-link and bacterial polymers, also offered growth opportunities in the industry. Although the price of many biodegradable plastics in the mid-1990s was between 2 and 25 times greater than traditional resins, prices were expected to fall as the technology was refined. Biodegradable plastics were considered important for reducing the volume and longevity of waste in landfills; in the early 1990s, plastics accounted for about 10 percent of all solid waste.

One of the most interesting discoveries occurred in 1993, when Maurice Ward unveiled a new polymer that withstood heat, lasers, and flames with little or no damage, and let off virtually no toxic fumes in the process. "Starlite," as the new plastic was called, was intended to serve as a flame retardant material, though its uses could be widespread.

FURTHER READING

Anderson, Earl V. "Foreign Trade: U.S. Chemical Trade Surplus Declines." *Chemical & Engineering News,* 13 December 1993.

———. "Japan: Once Booming Economy Struggles Through Times." *Chemical & Engineering News,* 13 December 1993.

Cavanaugh, Tim. "Along for the Ride." *Chemical Marketing Reporter,* 14 November 1994.

"Chemical and Additives." *Modern Plastics,* September 1993.

Chemical Economics Handbook. SRI Consulting, 1996.

Dagani, Ron. "Wonder Plastic Resists Lasers, Nuclear Heat." *Chemical & Engineering News,* 26 April 1993.

Dubois, J. Harry. *Plastics,* New York: Van Nostrand Reinhold Company, 1974.

"Facts & Figures for the Chemical Industry." *Chemical & Engineering News,* 28 June 1993.

"4.6% Annual Growth Predicted." *Appliance Manufacturer,* August 1996.

"Global Forecast 1996." *Chemical Week,* 3 January 1996.

Heylin, Michael. "Job Market for Chemists Remains Depressed, Salaries Gain 5%." *Chemical & Engineering News,* 12 July 1993.

Layman, Patricia. "Europe: Definite Though Modest Recovery Forecast for 1994." *Chemical & Engineering News,* 13 December 1993.

Loesel, Andrew. "Now You See It . . . Degradable Plastics May Be Gaining a New Life as a Second Generation of Polymers is Taking Shape." *Chemical Marketing Reporter,* 6 July 1992.

Palmisano, Anna C., and Charles H. Pettigrew. "Biodegradability of Plastics." *BioScience,* October 1992.

Phelan, Mark. "Plastics Suppliers Take the Battle Underhood." *Automotive Industries,* January 1997.

Pittman, Robert H. "Industry Review: Plastics Defies Sun belt Location Strategy to Stay a Long Term Winner." *Site Selection,* December 1995.

Rawis, Rebecca L. "Salaries." *Chemical & Engineering News,* 25 October 1993.

"Resins 1993: What's in the Pipeline?" *Modern Plastics,* January 1993.

Shearer, Brent. "Masterbatch Resin Business Turning Regional to Global." *Chemical Marketing Reporter,* 26 August 1996.

Storck, William J. "United States: Chemical Industry Lackluster This Year." *Chemical & Engineering News,* 13 December 1993.

Tuczal, Eva, and Frank Cortolano. "Reformulating PVC to Eliminate Heavy Metals and Protect Performance." *Modern Plastics,* October 1992.

Williams, Mike. "EPA Sets New Limits on Toxic Pollution." *Detroit Free Press,* 2 March 1994.

Wood, Bill. "Bouncing Back but How High." *Plastics World,* August 1994.

Wrigley, Al. "Steel Wins back Auto Parts from Plastics." *American Metal Market,* 9 September 1996.

—Dave Mote, updated by Visi Tilak

SIC 2822

SYNTHETIC RUBBER (VULCANIZABLE ELASTOMERS)

This category covers establishments primarily engaged in manufacturing synthetic rubber by polymerization or copolymerization. An elastomer, for the purpose of this classification, is a rubber-like material capable of vulcanization, such as copolymers of butadiene and styrene, or butadiene and acrylonitrile, polybutadienes, chloroprene rubbers, and isobutylene-isoprene copolymers. Butadiene copolymers containing less than 50 percent butadiene are classified in **SIC 2821: Plastics Materials, Synthetic Resins, and Nonvulcanizable Elastomers.** Natural chlorinated rubbers and cyclized rubbers are considered as semifinished products and are classified in **SIC 3069: Fabricated Rubber Products, Not Elsewhere Classified.**

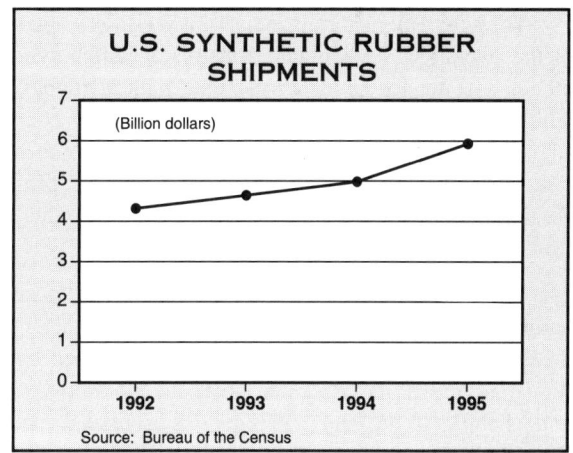

U.S. SYNTHETIC RUBBER SHIPMENTS

(Billion dollars)

Source: Bureau of the Census

INDUSTRY SNAPSHOT

Production of synthetic rubber on a commercial scale began in the United States during the 1930s, though natural rubber has been used since the early 1800s for multiple applications. The United States assumed an early lead in the development and production of vulcanizable elastomers—a position that it maintained throughout the twentieth century. Indeed, by 1997 the more than 100,000 employed in the industry were churning out about 2.7 million metric tons of synthetic rubber. The value of shipments increased from $4.74 billion in 1994 to $4.98 billion in 1995, and were expected to reach $5.36 billion by 1998.

Rubber manufacturers were limping into the mid-1990s, following a gradual industry decline during the 1980s. Product maturity, stagnant demand growth, and increasing foreign competition were the dominant factors suppressing industry profitability. Although producers tried to counter this downward momentum with increased productivity and the development of new rubbers, falling prices and a sluggish world economy in the early 1990s proffered little reason for optimism. Ironically, past industry successes contributed to the industry's malaise. Long-lasting rubbers, for instance, reduced demand in large market segments such as the tire industry. Competitors were looking to new rubbers for growth in the 2000s.

ORGANIZATION AND STRUCTURE

The synthetic rubber industry represents about 8 percent of the entire U.S. synthetic materials manufacturing sector. Plastics (**SIC 2821: Plastics Materials, Synthetic Resins, and Nonvulcanizable Elastomers**) and manmade fibers (**SIC 2824: Manmade Organic Fibers, Except Cellulosic**) are the other synthetics.

The synthetic materials industry is considered part of the overall U.S. chemical industry, of which synthetics account for about 25 percent. Natural rubber, which represents about 20 percent of all rubber consumed in the United States, is derived from rubber trees and other organic sources. Production and processing of natural rubber is not included in this industrial classification.

Synthetic rubber offers important advantages over natural materials. Among its most beneficial characteristics are its great resistance to corrosion caused by fluids and gases, its very poor electrical conductivity, and its ability to flex and then regain its original shape. Because of the endless variety of compounds that can be created, synthetic rubber has increasingly been used as a substitute for more expensive, lower performance natural materials. Besides displacing woods, metals, and ceramics in many traditional applications, rubber has allowed the creation of completely new products.

The synthetic rubber industry shipped $4.98 billion worth of material in 1994, which was equivalent to about one quarter of the value of sales by U.S. tire and inner tube manufacturers. By 1997, this number was expected to increase to $5.21 billion. Despite its relative economic insignificance, however, the industry supplied billions of pounds of material and has been an integral part of the U.S. and global industrial machine. Rubber serves a vital role in transportation industries, but is also an important production material for medical supplies, packaging and sealing devices, construction equipment, and other goods. Furthermore, U.S. producers supply about one quarter of total world rubber consumption.

Competition and markets. The industry is highly consolidated, with only about 75 firms competing in the mid-1990s. The average number of workers per company, for example, is nearly three times greater than the average for all other U.S. manufacturers. The top five establishments in the industry enjoyed combined revenues from diversified operations of over $2 billion per year in the mid-1990s—equal to about 50 percent of all rubber sales. They also employed an average of 2,000 workers. In contrast, the majority of even the top 40 competitors employed fewer than 100 workers. Most industry participants generate less than

$1 million per year in sales. High start-up costs, low profit margins, and established market leaders discourage potential entrants to the business.

Tire and inner tube manufacturers consumed about 30 percent of industry output in the mid-1990s. The remainder of the rubber market, though, is highly fragmented and is represented by a vast array of fabricated rubber products. Paper mills and floor covering producers each use about 5 percent of all rubber absorbed domestically, while about 3 percent of output is required to make hoses and belts. Adhesives, gaskets, sealants, and packing devices also consume about 5 percent of production. Other popular uses of rubber include the manufacture of sporting goods, medical supplies, footwear, paint, printing ink, chemical preparations, communication equipment, batteries, and cord. Outside of North America, tires and inner tubes represent about 60 percent of rubber demand.

Rubber production. Synthetic rubber is produced by first chemically rearranging molecules in a process called polymerization, during which the molecules are made to link up in very long chains. The polymer exists as a soft, tacky thermoplastic, which can be remelted and manipulated. The thermoplastic resin is then treated with heat and chemicals to create a thermoset, a compound that cannot be remelted and formed. This process, called vulcanization, is what contributes to the resilience and elasticity of rubber compounds—physical properties that have earned rubbers the name elastomers. Most elastomers are made using petroleum, although potatoes and grains, coke (made from coal), limestone, salt, or sulfur may also be used.

Endless varieties of rubbers are produced, each of which offers different physical properties and comes in a variety of grades. Different rubbers are created during the production process, for instance, by integrating additives, adding processing chemicals, or by creating alloys with natural rubber or other thermoplastics. Numerous chemical processing agents include accelerators, activators, vulcanizing agents, antidegradants, antioxidants, flame retardants, and stabilizers. Additives include reinforcement fibers, fillers, colorants, and catalysts, such as carbon black and sulfur.

The two major elastomer divisions are commodity and specialty. Commodity elastomers, which account for the bulk of industry sales, are available at relatively low prices from several manufacturers. The most popular commodity rubber is styrene butadiene rubber (SBR), which represented about 40 percent of total output in the mid-1990s. SBR is used primarily in tires and inner tubes, though it is also found in industrial applications such as carpet backing, nonwoven materials, and paper coatings. Major manufacturers of this compound include Uniroyal, Goodrich Tire Company, and Goodyear.

Polybutadiene, the second largest industry segment at about 20 percent of sales, is also used mostly to create tires and treads. In addition, it is an important production material for hoses and belts. Ethylene-propylene elastomers (EP) accounted for approximately 10 percent of shipments in the mid-1990s. This compound is used in the construction supply industry for such products as roof membranes and foundation sealants. It is also used as an impact modifier for plastic resins. Other uses include oil viscosity additives and various auto parts, such as gaskets and seals, hoses, belts, and tubing. Other commodity thermoset elastomers include nitrile, butyl, polyisoprene, polychloroprene, and silicone.

Specialty elastomers, the second division of the synthetic rubber industry, represented about 8 percent of sales in the mid-1990s. Specialty elastomers offer enhanced performance characteristics, are typically more expensive, and are sold by fewer competitors than are commodity elastomers. The two main categories of specialty rubbers are silicones and fluorocarbons. Silicones are used to make vehicle mechanical parts and sealants, adhesives for construction, and electronic products. Fluorocarbons are used for O-rings, seals, and gaskets and for high-tech aerospace, automotive, electrical, and petrochemical applications.

In addition to thermosets, the specialty category also encompasses a relatively new category of rubbers called thermoplastic elastomers (TPEs). TPEs are often more economical to produce and easier to process than are thermosets. TPEs can be categorized as styrenics, polyolefins, elastomeric alloys, polyurethanes, copolyesters, and polyamides. They are often used to create high-performance adhesives, to modify plastics during the production process, and in various consumer goods applications. TPEs provide benefits associated with recycling, and typically offer greater durability, hardness, and chemical resistance.

BACKGROUND AND DEVELOPMENT

Natural rubber has been in use since at least the fifteenth century. Christopher Columbus, for one, witnessed Haitian natives playing games with balls "made of the gum of a tree." The first record of rubber used for purposes other than recreation was made by explorer F. Juan D. Torquemada in 1615. He saw Indians brush rubber on their cloaks as waterproofing, and also witnessed them compressing rubber in earthen molds to create footwear and bottles. Rubber was brought to Europe in the eighteenth century from the East Indies and used to rub out lead pencil marks—hence the term "rubber." Rubber was later transported to Europe to make raincoats and rubber thread.

A recognizable natural rubber industry evolved in the United States by the 1830s, as numerous factories sprouted along the eastern seaboard. U.S. producers pioneered many important processing machines that furthered industry growth. For example, Edward M. Chaffe invented a rubber milling and rolling machine in 1836. Chaffe's machine, which was nicknamed "The Monster," was completed in 1837 at a cost of $30,000 and a weight of 30 tons. In another important industry breakthrough of the late 1830s, rubber's tendency to soften with heat and harden with cold was mitigated. Indeed, Charles Goodyear's discovery of vulcanization in 1839 lead to the use of rubber in many demanding mechanical applications.

Realizing the potential benefits of creating a synthetic replacement for natural rubber, scientists had been searching for a formula since the early 1800s. In 1826, Michael Faraday, an English scientist, was one of the first to successfully chemically analyze rubber. It was not until 1910, however, that S.V. Lebedev, a Russian, polymerized butadiene to produce the first synthetic rubber. This breakthrough, combined with processing and vulcanizing technologies developed during the 1800s, initiated a new era for the rubber industry.

By the 1930s, synthetic rubbers were being produced on a commercial scale only in Russia and Germany. World War I and World War II both pushed synthetic advances, as countries on all continents sought to sever their dependency on foreign natural rubber supplies. The United States, traditionally dependent on South American suppliers for natural rubber, shifted into overdrive during World War II in its quest for an inexhaustible synthetic supply. Between 1939 and 1945, in fact, U.S. production of synthetic rubber rose from a negligible experimental yield to about 820,000 tons per year.

World War II era. World output of synthetic rubber was estimated at 10,000 tons in 1935, and 72,000 tons by 1939. Germany and Russia produced all but a small fraction. By the end of World War II, though, global production had skyrocketed to well over one million tons per year, of which the United States supplied the lion's share. Correspondingly, the share of U.S. rubber consumption served by natural rubber declined during the 1940s. In 1939, about .3 percent of all rubber used in the United States was synthetic. By 1950 that share had grown to 43 percent, and the United States was devouring a whopping 55 percent of total global elastomer output.

Although large quantities of synthetic rubber continued to be produced after World War II, natural rubbers still dominated the market because of their superior physical characteristics. Advances in the use of recycled natural rubber boosted its popularity. In 1953, however, German chemists Karl Ziegler and Giulio Natta discovered a polymerization process that resulted in a synthetic rubber virtually identical in molecular structure to that of natural rubber. Commercial production of cis-1,4-polyisoprene was immediately undertaken in the United States, which became the dominant supplier for many war-ravaged European countries.

Augmenting the proliferation of synthetic rubber in the 1950s and 1960s was the development of new additives. New reinforcing materials allowed manufacturers to strengthen synthetics and reduce production costs, while at the same time achieving advanced performance. Asbestos, hard clay, limestone, and carbon black were among these fillers. Similarly, plasticizers and softeners allowed producers to develop synthetics with physical properties superior to many natural rubbers. Curing and vulcanizing agents, accelerators, and age-resistors all lead to the substitution of synthetics for natural rubbers and other organic materials.

Besides advances in quality and variety, synthetic rubber also benefitted from simultaneous breakthroughs in processing and molding technology used in other industries. Furthermore, the postwar U.S. economic expansion generated huge demand growth. Most importantly, the staggering growth of the automobile and truck industries during the 1950s and 1960s resulted in a vast market for tires, inner tubes, belts, and hoses. Construction and consumer markets ballooned as well. By 1960, global production of synthetic rubber stood at more than 2 million tons per year. The United States alone produced about 1.5 million tons and devoured more than 40 percent of global output. Although natural rubber still held over 50 percent of the world rubber market by 1960, synthetics supplied about 70 percent of U.S. rubber demand.

While it continued to realize growth during the 1960s and 1970s, the rubber industry had clearly surpassed its stage of rapid expansion by the 1970s. Even the 1960s showed evidence of industry maturation, such as consolidation. The number of competitors manufacturing tires, for instance, plummeted from about 60 in the late 1940s to just a handful of big producers by the 1970s. Spiraling petroleum prices during the late 1970s, moreover, dampened industry profitability. Furthermore, popular synthetics that were once cutting edge materials, such as styrene-butadiene,

became low-margin commodities. Foreign competition, too, began eating away at U.S. global dominance.

The 1980s. By 1980, U.S. synthetic rubber output was about 1.8 million metric tons per year. This represented a relatively slight increase over production levels of the late 1960s and early 1970s. Falling energy prices and an uptick in demand during the early 1980s, however, boosted industry output and profitability. Although the value of shipments jumped less than 1 percent between 1982 and 1983, the cost of production materials fell by about 3 percent as output jumped nearly 8 percent. In 1984, moreover, output value leapt over 8 percent as demand climbed steadily, causing revenues to surpass $3.4 billion.

After 1985, overall U.S. rubber output stagnated. Despite a healthy economy, U.S. synthetic rubber manufacturers were hurt by several factors, including: increased imports of automobile, tire, and rubber products; the trend toward smaller cars that used smaller tires; and the increased use of long-lasting radial tires. Exports from southeast Asia, as well as other regions of the world, were also cutting into demand from other market segments. Between 1982 and 1990 total industry output grew just 22 percent, from about 1.8 million to 2.2 million tons.

Despite sluggish demand in traditional commodity synthetic rubbers, such as SBR, the industry managed to maintain a fairly strong revenue growth rate of about 5 percent during the 1980s. This was accomplished through the development and sales of improved compounds and specialty rubbers. Production volumes of polybutadiene and ethylene-propylene, for instance, advanced 44 percent and 89 percent, respectively, between 1982 and 1991. Specialty TPEs, moreover, grew from a negligible share of the market in the early 1980s to account for about 8 percent of domestic industry consumption by 1991.

Although their share of the world rubber market declined in the 1980s and early 1990s, industry participants enjoyed solid export growth as foreign consumption of rubber slowly, but steadily escalated. Despite sluggish domestic markets, exports grew between 3 percent and 5 percent per year in the late 1980s and early 1990s. The demand for proprietary high-tech rubbers by overseas consumers was particularly strong.

Synthetic rubber manufacturers were able to buoy earnings throughout the early 1990s. Unfortunately, though, a domestic and global economic recession that began in 1989 and lingered through 1993 put the squeeze on industry profitability. Shipment volume declined .03 percent in 1989, .07 percent in 1990, and over 4 percent in 1991, while plant utilization dipped to a depressing 68 percent. Industry revenues grew about than 1 percent per year in 1987 dollars during that period. Although output jumped a surprising 9 percent in 1992, revenues gained only 4 percent, rising to about $4.4 billion, and an industry profit slump persisted.

A tepid economic recovery helped to boost industry expectations in 1992 and 1993. Analysts were discouraged, however, by fundamental weaknesses in rubber markets. Importantly, demand by the auto industry, which consumes 70 percent of SBR, was recessed. Overall production of SBR, in fact, had slipped from 876,000 tons to about 850,000 by 1992. Although shipments to tire producers rose about 8 percent in 1992, long-term growth in that segment was expected to remain weak.

Boosted by surging exports, SBR consumption was expected to grow by about 2 percent annually between 1993 and 1996, according to the International Institute of Synthetic Rubber Producers (IISRP). This growth rate was expected to fade, however. A continuing preference for other synthetic polymers in non-tire applications was expected to contribute to slack price and demand growth.

Although commodity polybutadiene and ethylene-propylene elastomers generally outperformed SBR during the 1980s and early 1990s, continued expansion of these segments was in question. As it entered a phase of maturity, polybutadiene was expected to offer a tepid growth rate of only 2 percent through the mid-1990s. Commodity ethylene-propylene markets were already recessing in the early 1990s, following a rapid rise during the early and mid-1980s. Although sales surged slightly in 1992, weak auto and construction markets were expected to restrain demand for this thermoset.

High-tech and thermoplastic opportunities. To sustain profits going into the mid-1990s, producers were looking to smaller industry segments for expansion. The greatest opportunities for profits in the mid-1990s were expected to be in TPEs. Besides their recyclability and often lower production costs, thermoplastics combined the rubber-like flexibility characteristic of thermoset rubbers with the heightened processing versatility of plastic. As a result, TPEs were expected to grow by 7 percent or more per year throughout the 1990s. Furthermore, worldwide consumption of TPEs should rise from 680,000 tons in 1992 to more than 1.1 million tons by the year 2000.

Besides cannibalizing market share held by thermoset rubbers, TPEs were creating entirely new markets for the industry. Styrenic TPEs, for example, offered significant potential for use as an asphalt modifier to keep roofing and roadways from cracking. High-tech niche TPEs were making inroads into industries such as medical, construction, and food packaging. New TPEs, for example, were being used in the plumbing industry to deliver drinking water that could meet strict new federal standards. Other TPEs were being developed to make everything from ski boots and swimwear to auto body panels that could be painted without a primer coat.

Like TPEs, high-performance thermosets also promised to buoy the earnings of the most savvy producers. Growth rates for some specialty ethylene-propylene elastomers, for instance, were expected to exceed 15 percent in the mid-1990s. High-performance nitrile rubbers were finding use in applications that required heat, chemical, and abrasion resistance. Some nitrile rubbers were forecast to realize 15 percent to 35 percent growth during the mid-1990s.

Environment. One of the greatest obstacles to success for synthetic rubber producers in the mid-1990s was environmental controls. The overall chemical industry was by far the largest polluting industry in the United States, and rubber producers contributed significantly to that reputation. Besides emitting large doses of hazardous chlorofluorocarbons (CFCs) into the air during the production process, rubber producers were also charged with creating end-user products that would not degrade. Furthermore, rubber manufacturers suffered from environmental controls that affected their consumers, such as fuel efficiency and emissions standards that were encouraging the production of smaller cars (and tires).

New environmental mandates (see **SIC 2821: Plastics Materials, Synthetic Resins, and Nonvulcanizable Elastomers**) were forcing manufacturers to bring their production facilities into compliance with federal and state rules. Such retrofitting was costing many companies millions of dollars. ''We're faced with an immense amount of cost considerations and capital investment, and a severe loss in revenue generating power for the business,'' said Glen Steady, vice-president of Industrial Business at Copolymer Rubber & Chemical, in the November 2, 1992, issue of *Chemical Marketing Reporter*. ''All this finds its way onto the balance sheet.''

Partially in an effort to allay criticism of nondegradable rubber waste, the Rubber Manufacturer's Association (RMA) had taken a lead role in reclamation and recycling efforts during the 1980s and 1990s. Although thermoset elastomers cannot be truly recycled, efforts were underway to convert rubber waste to other uses in the mid-1990s, such as highway asphalt production and fuel for energy plants. Tires, which consume about 60 percent of all elastomer output, were a focal point of such endeavors. In 1990, about 8 percent of the 240 million tires discarded annually were reused. By 1992, this percentage had jumped to 24 percent. By the mid-1990s, the RMA's Scrap Tire Management Council estimated that figure to double to nearly 50 percent.

CURRENT CONDITIONS

Several years of sluggish demand resulted in consolidation of the synthetic rubber industry and its suppliers. One of the biggest resulting mergers was that of Monsanto Company and Akzo Nobel's rubber chemicals business into a new company Flexsys. The synthetic rubber business was expected to grow no more than 1 to 2 percent per year in industrialized nations and 2 to 3 percent per year worldwide. The world demand for TPE's on the other hand was expected to increase from 823,000 metric tons in 1994 to over 1 million metric tons in 1999, an increase of 5.5 percent per year.

In 1996, there were 74 operating companies in the United States whose primary SIC code was 2822, Synthetic Rubbers. Consumption of synthetic rubber decreased faster than natural rubber consumption in global marketplaces between 1986 and 1995. The major increases in synthetic rubber consumption were in Asia, central Europe, and eastern Europe.

There were two contradictory trends prevalent in the synthetic rubber industry. While consumption was increasing, producers were unable to increase prices to make up for the increasing raw materials prices. The economic recovery of industrialized nations, upsurge in automobile production and the related demand for tires, belts and hoses were the causes for the increased demand and consumption for synthetic rubber. Even though a 4 percent annual global increase in synthetic rubber consumption was predicted from 1994 to 1999, the declining price of natural rubber was expected to have a dampening effect on synthetic rubber prices.

Stocks in the tire and rubber industry, which showed average performance in the mid-1990s, were expected to appreciate significantly out to 1998-2000, because of aging auto fleets and the promising market for replacement tire sales worldwide.

INDUSTRY LEADERS

The largest company competing in the synthetic rubber industry in 1996 was Shell Chemical Company of Houston, Texas, with a sales revenue of $3.2 billion.

Dow Corning of Midland, Michigan, ranked second with a 1996 sales revenue of $2.2 billion. Hoechst Celanese Corporation's Advanced Materials Division, with a sales revenue of $1.4 billion, ranked third.

The fourth place was held by Uniroyal Chemical Co. Inc. of Connecticut, which generated $1.08 billion in 1996 sales revenue and employed nearly 3,000 workers. Uniroyal Chemical Corporation, also of Connecticut, ranked fifth with a sales revenue of $946.5 million.

The sixth largest competitor in this highly consolidated industry was GenCorp Polymer Products of Ohio. GenCorp employed about 3,000 workers and had a sales revenue of $569 million in 1996.

Other big players were Duriron Co., Inc. of Ohio, with a sales revenue of $532.7 million; Texas Petrochemicals Corporation with a sales revenue of $400 million; Park-Ohio Industries with a sales revenue of $371.4 million; and Polysar Rubber Division of Akron, Ohio, with $270 million in sales revenue.

WORK FORCE

The economic stability of some of the larger players in the industry was largely the result of actions taken during the 1980s and early 1990s. To combat downward profit pressures, manufacturers attempted to cut costs and boost productivity. A large portion of the massive capital investments made by the industry during the 1980s, in fact, was used to automate production facilities and improve information systems. Many companies also realigned their management structure and moved production facilities to foreign countries. The end result of such efforts was stagnant employment growth. Despite production increases, the number of U.S. workers employed in the industry actually declined between 1982 and 1992, from 11,800 to 11,100.

Regardless of work force cutbacks, the synthetic rubber industry, like most chemical businesses, remained a high-paying haven for most of those fortunate enough to find jobs. The average rubber production worker, for instance, earned about $36,000 per year in the early 1990s, which compared favorably to the national production worker average of about $21,000. Workers in this industry averaged about 2.5 more hours of work per week, however. Overall, the average payroll per employee was about $40,000 in the early 1990s, or about 50 percent higher than the average for all other U.S. manufacturers.

Slight productivity gains combined with stagnant output growth forecasts for the 1990s and early twenty-first century bode poorly for future employment in the synthetic rubber industry. Jobs for most machine operators, which account for about 10 percent of the work force, should decline by more than 25 percent between 1990 and 2005, according to the U.S. Bureau of Labor Statistics. Positions for chemical equipment controllers, which make up 7 percent of the work force, will fall by over 15 percent. Indeed, most blue-collar jobs will dwindle by at least 5 to 10 percent. On the bright side, occupations related to sales and marketing will leap by more than 15 percent, and work for systems analysts and computer scientists will increase by a hearty 37 percent.

The synthetic material industries are major employers of chemists and engineers. Jobs for these professionals in the rubber industry will likely grow by 10 to 15 percent by 2005. For more information about chemical and engineering employment in this industry, see **SIC 2821: Plastics Materials, Synthetic Resins, and Nonvulcanizable Elastomers.**

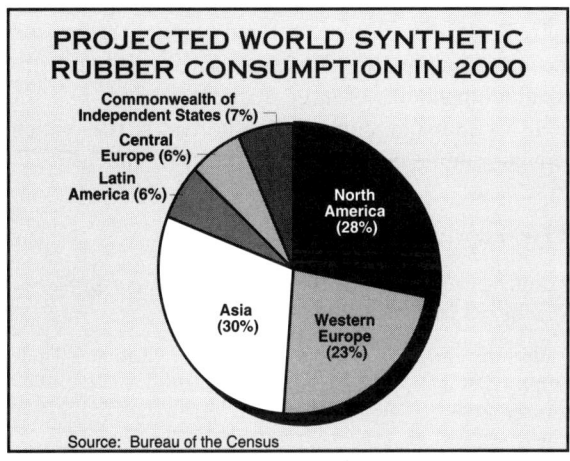

PROJECTED WORLD SYNTHETIC RUBBER CONSUMPTION IN 2000

Commonwealth of Independent States (7%)
Central Europe (6%)
Latin America (6%)
North America (28%)
Asia (30%)
Western Europe (23%)

Source: Bureau of the Census

AMERICA AND THE WORLD

The United States has gradually lost dominance of world rubber markets that it enjoyed in the 1950s, when U.S. synthetic rubber producers supplied more than 50 percent of global demand. Nevertheless, the U.S. elastomer industry remains the largest, most advanced, and most productive in the world. The United States produced about 23 percent of total global output in the early 1990s—far more than any other nation. It also exported over $1 billion worth of rubber and maintained a hefty trade surplus of about $450 million.

U.S. exports rose approximately 17 percent in 1995 and were expected to continue rising. Capital investments made during the 1980s that helped domestic producers become more competitive globally were partially responsible for export growth. Canada, the largest buyer of U.S. elastomers, accounted for about

19 percent of total U.S. exports in the early 1990s. Belgium consumed 18 percent of overseas shipments, while Brazil and Mexico each purchased about 7.5 percent of U.S.-produced exports. Japan, the fifth largest importer of U.S. rubber, demanded about 6 percent of shipments. The European Community accounted for 35 percent of U.S. exports in the early 1990s.

U.S. consumers purchased about $725 million worth of overseas elastomers per year in the mid-1990s. Canada supplied the majority of these imports, while Japan and France each delivered approximately 12 percent. The European Community sold approximately 43 percent of all U.S. rubber imports. Imports grew about 11 percent in 1995. Imports to the United States were expected to grow at a rate slightly greater than that of U.S. exports in the mid-1990s.

Notwithstanding increased use of rubber by many emerging industrial nations, overall global demand for rubber was expected to rise by only 2 to 3 percent per year during the 1990s. This sluggish growth will result from depressed demand for commodity rubbers in some European and Asian markets, caused in part by longer lasting rubber products.

In the mid-1990s, global demand for both natural and synthetic rubber was being repressed by feeble European and Japanese markets. Central Europe, for instance, registered a decline in demand of more than 15 percent in 1992, as it battled prolonged economic malaise. The Commonwealth of Independent States saw a similar decline in demand of about 10 percent. Likewise, consumption in Latin America and Africa slipped by 3 and 5 percent, respectively. Demand in Asia dropped 1 percent, though much of this was attributable to a deep recession in Japan— consumption in China, North Korea, and Vietnam expanded 6 percent. These figures contrasted with a rebound in total North American consumption of 11 percent in 1992.

Despite stalled growth for the overall synthetic elastomer industry, consumption of high-tech and specialty rubbers, such as TPEs, will grow at a pace of about 6 percent per year through the mid-1990s. Furthermore, uses of nontire rubber should grow about 40 percent faster than tire applications. Because the United States is a leader in the production of many niche elastomers, it should benefit disproportionately from global trends.

Regions of greatest demand growth in the mid- and late 1990s will include Southeast Asia and South America. Emerging industries in these regions should buoy demand for manufacturing and automobile applications. The United States will be increasingly forced to compete with low-cost domestic producers in those regions, however. American firms active in this industry will significantly benefit from the North American Free Trade Agreement (NAFTA).

Through the year 1999, the International Institute of Synthetic Rubber Producers (IISRP) projected growth of about 2.4 percent per year worldwide, with just 1.0 percent per year growth for North America, 2.2 percent per year for western Europe, 3.9 percent per year for Asia-Oceania, and 4.7 percent per year growth for Latin America.

While Asia accounted for the majority of rubber producing nations, Japan, North America, and Europe account for more than half of the world's total consumption of rubber.

RESEARCH AND TECHNOLOGY

Companies in the synthetic rubber industry are heavily dependent upon research and development to maintain competitiveness. The average rubber manufacturer in the late 1980s, for instance, invested over four times more money per employee in research and development than did the average U.S. manufacturer. This amounted to 5 to 7 percent of total industry sales. In 1990, moreover, the industry funneled a full 9 percent, or $380 billion, of total revenues into capital investments.

Technological advances in regulatory compliance were essentially a reaction to the 1990 Pollution Prevention Act, the Clean Air Act, and a multiplicity of other state and federal controls. Although producers were making large investments in new equipment and compounds that would allow them to produce rubber with fewer hazardous emissions, they were also focusing on the development of new recyclable rubbers that would result in less after-market waste. The most important of these was recyclable TPEs. Besides offering many advantageous physical characteristics, TPEs were increasingly being used as a substitute for many nondegradable thermoset rubbers.

Progress in the recovery of thermoset rubber waste was progressing, though at a relatively slow pace. Industry participants were still searching for economically viable uses for the nondegradable compounds. Besides asphalt modification and waste-to-energy applications, elastomer refuse was being used in several civil engineering functions. It was being utilized, for example, to create road embankments, artificial reefs, and as a replacement for gravel in water cleansing systems. Some recycled rubber was also being used as a filler for tires, and to make low-tech items like mud guards for trucks.

In addition to demands for more environmentally friendly rubber products, elastomer manufacturers were constantly under pressure to create new high-performance, cost-efficient products. While huge breakthroughs in tire longevity had been achieved throughout the 1960s, 1970s, and 1980s, producers in the early 1990s were introducing much better products. In 1991, for example, Michelin, the French tire company, introduced a cutting edge tire called the XH4. The company guarantees the tire to last 80,000 miles—longer than most people own their car. Michelin also introduced a tire in Europe in 1993 called the MXN. It delivers 4 to 5 percent better gas mileage than competing tires.

Many breakthroughs were occurring in the area of specialty elastomers in the early 1990s. One such example was hydrogenated nitrile, a product for which demand was expected to grow by 15 to 35 percent per year in the mid-1990s. Besides allowing manufacturers to more easily meet environmental emissions requirements, the substance offered superior thermo and mechanical properties. Hydrogenated nitrile can withstand temperatures of more than 300 degrees Fahrenheit, for example, compared to normal nitrile, which remains stable only to 212 degrees Fahrenheit.

FURTHER READING

Adam, Peter S. "Slow Growth Mode." *Chemical Marketing Reporter,* 2 November 1992.

Anderson, Earl V. "Foreign Trade: U.S. Chemical Trade Surplus Declines." *Chemical & Engineering News,* 13 December 1993.

Caney, Derek J. "Battles Brewing." *Chemical Marketing Reporter,* 2 November 1992.

"Chemical and Additives." *Modern Plastics,* September 1993.

"Facts & Figures for the Chemical Industry." *Chemical & Engineering News,* 27 June 1993.

Gibson, David W. "Depth and Diversity." *Chemical Marketing Reporter,* 2 November 1992.

Heylin, Michael. "Job Market for Chemists Remains Depressed, Salaries Gain 5%."

Ita, Paul A., and Gross Andrew C. "Industry Corner: World Rubber and Tire." *Business Economics,* January 1995, 58.

Loesel, Andrew. "Fuel of Filler." *Chemical Marketing Reporter,* 2 November 1992.

Lusk, Eric B. "Tire and Rubber Industry." *The Value Line Investment Survey (Part 3-Ratings and Reports),* 16 December 1994, 123.

Naude, Alice. "Down to the Bone." *Chemical Marketing Reporter,* 2 November 1992.

Rawis, Rebecca L. "Salaries." *Chemical & Engineering News,* 25 October 1993.

"Record Consumption for Rubber in 1995." *Rubber World,* March 1996, 14.

Reisch, Marc S. "Rubber Consumption Is Rising But Producers Profits Are Squeezed." *Chemical and Engineering News,* 14 August 1995, 11.

———. "Rubber: Slow Growth Ahead." *Chemical & Engineering News,* 10 May 1993.

Springer, Neil. "Signs of Life." *Chemical Marketing Reporter,* 2 November 1992.

"SR Consumption up 5% in 1995, 1996 Forecast Increase to Be 3.2%." *Rubber World,* June 1996, 12.

Standard & Poor's Industry Surveys. New York: Standard & Poor's Corporation, 31 December 1993.

Storck, William J. "United States: Chemical Industry Lackluster This Year." *Chemical & Engineering News,* 13 December 1993.

Topfer, Kurt. "Opening New Doors." *Chemical Marketing Reporter,* 2 November 1992.

U.S. Department of Commerce. International Trade Administration. *U.S. Industrial Outlook 1993,* Washington: GPO, 1993.

U.S. Department of Commerce. International Trade Administration. *U.S. Industrial Outlook 1994.* Washington: GPO, 1994.

Wood, Andrew and Breskin Ira. "Demand Keeps Improving, But Outlook Is Uncertain." *Chemical Week,* 26 April 1995, 36.

—Dave Mote, updated by Visi Tilak

SIC 2823

CELLULOSIC MAN-MADE FIBERS

The cellulosic manmade fiber industry is comprised of establishments primarily engaged in manufacturing rayon and acetate fibers in the form of monofilament, yarn, staple, or tow. These fibers are suitable for further manufacturing in other industries on spindles, looms, knitting machines, or other textile processing equipment. Synthetic fibers, which represent about 90 percent of all U.S. manmade fiber output, are classified in **SIC 2824: Manmade Organic Fibers, Except Cellulosic.**

Cellulose fibers are made from modified wood pulp that has been dissolved in a liquid and treated with chemicals. The solution is forced through small holes called spinnerets; the extrusion dries into a hard filament. The shape and physical properties of the fiber can be modified during extrusion and processing to yield numerous fiber types and grades.

In the early 1990s, over 90 percent of industry output was rayon. This fiber is used to make apparel, home furnishings, nonwoven products, tires, and industrial goods. Less than 10 percent of production in the early 1990s was acetate, which is primarily used to create apparel, home furnishings, and cigarette filters. In the mid-1990s, health concerns and "sin" taxes were expected to reduce the demand for cellulose cigarette filter tow. According to *Market Share Reporter 1997,* a shift in production did occur in 1995, and rayon accounted for only 55.8 percent of the market.

The largest consumer of rayon and acetate was the broadwoven fabric industry, which consumed over 40 percent of total production. Apparel linings accounted for a large portion of the market, along with special occasion apparel and acetate/spandex blended fabrics. Knit fabric manufacturers accounted for 20 percent of the U.S. market, and 3.5 percent of industry revenues were garnered from exports.

The fibers, when made into fabrics, are identified by generic classifications that were established by the Textile Fiber Products Identification Act of 1960, and generic names were assigned by the Federal Trade Commission. The Identification Act also states that products must be labeled with the manufacturer's name and country and list the percentage of fiber content.

The first patent related to the manufacture of cellulose fibers was granted in 1855. In 1883 Sir Joseph Wilson Swan, a British scientist, created the first non-flammable cellulose fiber. Commercially viable rayon fibers were invented during the 1890s. Acetate filaments were developed in the late 1800s as well, but did not receive commercial acceptance until the 1920s. During both world wars, particularly World War II, fiber development and production ballooned as warring nations sought inexhaustible supplies of apparel and textile fibers.

Rayon increased in popularity during the post-World War II U.S. economic expansion. In fact, by 1980 U.S. companies were generating more than 580 million pounds of fiber each year. Despite past growth, however, cellulose fibers were quickly losing favor to newer and better synthetic fibers, such as polyester and nylon. Between 1970 and 1990 the percentage of U.S. fibers (including organic filaments) made from cellulose declined from 28 percent to 6 percent. The industry was coping with environmental concerns and standards while trying to improve quality.

The industry suffered stagnation and decay during the 1980s. Besides the increasing popularity of synthetic fibers, foreign competition battered industry participants. In 1992, developing countries claimed 55 percent of manmade fibers. Total cellulosic fiber production slipped to less than 540 million pounds per year in 1992, as industry profit growth stalled. But in 1994, *U.S. Industrial Outlook* noted the industry as having the capacity to produce 612 million pounds of cellulosic fiber, with developing countries accounting for 63 percent of this capacity. In 1995, the industry was producing 500 million pounds.

Revenues lagged behind inflation with an average growth rate of less than 1 percent per year, and industry employment fell from over 14,000 in the early 1980s to about 11,000 by 1992. The employment rate was continuously falling from approximately 7,500 in 1995 to 6,400 in 1997. In 1998, employment rates were projected to plummet further to 5,900. The number of establishments was also declining from 18 in the mid-1980s to nine in 1995, and then approximately seven in 1998. The three leading cellulosic manmade fiber companies in the mid-1990s were Buckeye Cellulose Corporation with sales over $400 million, American Filtrona Corporation with sales over $175 million, and Lenzing Fibers Corporation with sales of about $120 million.

In the mid-1990s, the nine U.S. cellulose fiber producers were hoping that lyocell, a new fiber, might spare the gasping industry. Two of the largest competitors, Courtaulds Textiles PLC and Lenzing Fibers Corp., were vying for domination of this new market segment. Lyocell offered superior performance compared to rayon and could be manufactured with fewer emissions of hazardous wastes. Fiber makers were also hoping to benefit from massive capital investments made during the 1980s to improve productivity and develop better fibers.

Despite manufacturer's efforts, the long-term industry outlook remained bleak. Producers in emerging industrial nations, such as China and Malaysia, would likely devour greater global market share. More stringent environmental regulations would also take their toll on U.S. competitors (see **SIC 2824: Manmade Organic Fibers, Except Cellulosic**). Employment by cellulosic fiber production workers was forecast to continue falling by 15 to 25 percent between 1990 and 2005, according to the Bureau of Labor Statistics. Even high-paying research and engineering jobs were expected to increase only slightly during that period.

FURTHER READING

"Cellulose Acetate and Triacetate Fibers." *Chemical Economics Handbook,* May 1994. Available from http://piglet.sri.com/CIN/94/may-jun/article05.html.

Darnay, Arsen J., ed. *Manufacturing USA.* 5th ed. Detroit: Gale Research, 1996.

Duncan, Beth. "Fiber Facts." Mississippi State University, 10 April 1996. Available from http://www.ces.msstate.edu/pubs/is1250.htm.

"Facts & Figures for the Chemical Industry." *Chemical & Engineering News,* 28 June 1993.

Layman, Patricia. "Developing Nations Lead in Fibers Production." *Chemical & Engineering News,* 5 April 1993.

Lazich, Robert S., ed. *Market Share Reporter.* Detroit: Gale Research, 1997.

McNamara, Michael. "Courtalds, Lenzing Duke it Out Over Lyocell Turf." *WWD,* 6 July 1993.

Standard & Poor's Industry Surveys. New York: Standard & Poor's Corporation, 31 December 1993.

U.S. Department of Commerce. International Trade Administration. *U.S. Industrial Outlook 1993.* Washington: GPO, January 1993.

U.S. Department of Commerce. International Trade Administration. *U.S. Industrial Outlook 1994.* Washington: GPO, January 1994.

SIC 2824

ORGANIC FIBERS—NONCELLULOSIC

Establishments primarily engaged in manufacturing noncellulosic, or synthetic, fibers comprise the manmade organic fibers industry. The fibers are created in the form of monofilament, yarn, staple, or tow suitable for further manufacturing on spindles, looms, knitting machines, or other textile processing equipment. Textile glass fibers and cellulosic manmade fibers, such as rayon and acetate, are classified elsewhere.

INDUSTRY SNAPSHOT

Although experimental organic fibers existed as early as 1913, the first commercially viable synthetics were invented during the 1930s and 1940s. Explosive industry growth occurred mid-century as new fibers, such as polyester, made synthetic materials a strong part of American life. In the early 1980s, U.S. industry participants were generating over 3.5 million tons of fibers annually, worth more than $8 billion. By 1995, the worldwide production of synthetic fibers was 23.2 million tons. The fibers had a wide variety of applications and were used in the manufacture of such diverse products as underwear and truck tires.

Rapid industry expansion subsided in the 1980s, as important sectors of the fiber business matured. Although production tonnage and revenues increased slightly throughout the decade, profit margins were confined by stagnant export growth and a rising tide of imports in the form of apparel and textiles. Environmental regulations and economic recession in the late 1980s and early 1990s suppressed profits further as manufacturers scrambled to consolidate and reduce costs.

The industry seemed to be entering a stage of modest recovery in 1992. Production increased for the first time in four years, and prices surged. Nevertheless, producers still faced stiff foreign competition and sluggish market growth, which they sought to combat by taking advantage of new technologies that allowed productivity gains and the development of new types of fibers.

ORGANIZATION AND STRUCTURE

Manmade fibers offer a less expensive substitute for many natural fibers, such as cotton, wool, and silk. In addition, many synthetic fibers have greater durability, hold their shape better, and are more uniform than natural fibers. Products created with manmade fibers typically afford greater resistance to aging and breakdown as a result of exposure to the elements. Because they can be modified to create a great variety of filaments with different physical properties and grades, synthetics provide great flexibility for manufacturers of apparel and textiles.

The two categories of manmade fibers are cellulosic and synthetic. Cellulosic fibers include such products as rayon, acetate, and triacetate, which are derived from modified wood pulp that has been dissolved in a liquid. Synthetic fibers are derived from molecules containing various combinations of carbon, hydrogen, nitrogen, and oxygen. Examples of products in this group are nylon, olefin, polyester, and spandex.

Synthetic fibers accounted for about 90 percent of U.S. manmade fiber output in 1993. Manmade fibers constituted approximately 25 percent of the larger U.S. synthetic materials industry, which also encompassed plastics and rubbers. Synthetic materials, in turn, represented about 25 percent of the overall $300 billion per year U.S. chemical industry.

About 70 U.S. firms competed in this highly consolidated industry during the early 1990s. Even among the handful of competitors, earnings were top-heavy; the combined revenues of the top five firms in the

business, for example, were nearly four times greater than the aggregate sales of the next five largest companies. Moreover, the majority of the largest 20 establishments employed fewer than 200 workers—compared to between 10,000 and 20,000 employed by the top few companies. Extremely high start-up capital requirements, entrenched market leaders, and proprietary technology necessary to produce high-margin fibers discouraged potential market entrants to this exceptionally competitive business.

The largest U.S. market for synthetic fibers during the early 1990s was floor covering manufacturers. This sector consumed 32 percent of fiber output to create carpeting for commercial, institutional, and consumer applications. Apparel producers commanded about 25 percent of industry production during this time, and makers of various home textile products controlled 10 percent of output. Industrial products and miscellaneous consumer goods, representing 30 percent of consumption, included such items as tire reinforcements, rope, surgical and sanitary supplies, fiberfill, electrical insulation, and plastic reinforcements. About 4 percent of total output was shipped to other countries.

Production Process. Synthetic fibers are extremely long, threadlike molecules composed of hundreds of thousands of atoms strung together in chains. They typically originate from petroleum-based chemicals, which must first be converted into a liquid state by either being dissolved into a solution or by melting. The free-moving molecules that form the liquid are then extruded through small holes called spinnerets. The fine strands of liquid that emerge from the spinnerets are hardened to form long, silk-like filaments.

The three most popular spinning processes are known as dry, wet, and melt. In dry spinning, the fiber-forming substance is dissolved in a solvent, extruded through a spinneret, and then exposed to hot air. The heat causes the solvent to evaporate from the fiber, leaving a solid filament. Wet spinning works in a similar manner, except that the extrusion is jettisoned into a coagulating bath, which causes the fiber to harden as a result of chemical or physical change. Melt spinning is accomplished by simply melting and extruding a substance that dries upon contact with the air.

During the spinning process, the filament can be manipulated to result in various physical properties and forms. This manipulation determines such attributes as drapability, softness, elasticity, perceived coolness or warmth, stiffness, roughness, and resilience. Fibers that are formed to have a dog-bone or lobed cross-section, for instance, result in fabrics with greater density, while flat fibers give fabrics a rough feel.

After spinning, fibers go through a stretching and orientation process. During this procedure, the long molecules that constitute the fiber are pulled into alignment along the longitudinal axis of the filament. Through various techniques, the molecules can be aligned, packed, and manipulated to result in a variety of different physical characteristics. Tensile strength, dyeing properties, stretching ability, water penetrability, and resistance to breakdown are a few of the attributes that are influenced through stretching and orientation of the molecules.

Finished fibers are usually formed into monofilament, yarn, staple, or tow that can be used by other manufacturing sectors. Monofilaments are single, long strands of fiber used to create items such as nylon stockings and toothbrush bristles. Staple consists of fibers that have been cut into short lengths, usually between one and six inches. Staple can be mixed with other natural or manmade fibers to create yarns and fabrics. Tow is a fiber that is spun with hundreds of thousands of filaments bundled together into a loose rope and wound onto a spool. Tow is used like staple, but the cutting is done at a later stage to ensure that the filaments remain parallel to one another.

Products. Polyester fibers, the largest industry segment by production tonnage, constitutes about 40 percent of inorganic fibers shipments. Among other qualities, polyester sports low moisture retention, good electrical insulation characteristics, and high resistance to solvents. Nearly 80 percent of polyester fibers were used to produce textiles, apparel, and home furnishings. Eight percent of this segment was purchased by the tire industry to be used as rubber reinforcements, 7 percent was used for other industrial applications, and 5 percent went towards the production of carpeting. The majority of polyester was sold in the form of either yarn or staple. Tow represented a relatively small share of segment sales.

The second most popular synthetic fiber is nylon. This fiber, which comes in a multitude of characteristics and grades, accounts for nearly 30 percent of industry output. Nylon's advantages include a high strength-to-weight ratio, excellent recovery from deformation, and high abrasion and flex resistance. Seventy percent of nylon output was used to make carpeting, while about 20 percent was integrated into apparel and non-carpet home furnishings. Manufacturers of industrial products, such as tires and rope, represented the remaining 10 percent of this market. Most nylon was sold as yarn, though a substantial share of output took the form of tow.

Much of the remaining 30 percent of synthetic fiber revenues were derived from the sale of olefin and acrylic fibers. Olefins, which were the fastest growing segment of the industry in the early 1990s, are used to create durable carpeting and other textiles. Acrylic, the smallest volume synthetic fiber at about 5 percent of the market, is used to make clothing and home furnishings, such as blankets.

BACKGROUND AND DEVELOPMENT

Evidence suggests that hemp, presumably the oldest cultivated fiber plant, was grown in China as early as 4500 B.C. Furthermore, Egyptians were already weaving and spinning linen by 3400 B.C. The spinning of silk, which provided a major impetus for the creation of artificial fibers, dates back to 2640 B.C. Flax and wool fabrics dating back to the sixth and seventh centuries B.C. have been excavated in Switzerland.

English physicist Robert Hooke was one of the first scientists to explore the possibility of extruding artificial silk, proposing a mechanical device that mimicked the silkworm. Louise Schwabe, an English weaver during the nineteenth century, was the first to successfully produce filaments from molten glass. He forced the liquid through nozzles, which caused a strand of glass to protrude and harden into a fiber. These early experiments initiated the discovery and development of manmade cellulose filaments (see **SIC 2823: Cellulosic Manmade Fibers**).

Chemists carried out the first extensive research into possible methods of creating synthetic fibers after World War I. Finding that many polymers (long chains of molecules) could be dissolved in solvents, they began extruding different polymers in spinnerets. Their initial goal was to imitate rayon, a cellulosic fiber. Breakthrough synthetic fibers were produced by German chemists in 1913 and through the 1920s. Important advances occurred in 1928, for example, when vinyl chloride and vinyl acetate were used to produce fibers. This breakthrough lead to the development of the first commercially viable synthetic textile fibers in 1936.

The synthetic industry got its practical start in 1935, when American Wallace H. Carothers, working at E. I. DuPont de Nemours & Company, developed the first nylon fiber. This important discovery prompted intense research during and after World War II that resulted in many new classes of commercially useful synthetic textile filaments. The first polyester fiber, for example, was invented in 1941 by British researchers. Eastman Chemical Products Inc. of the United States introduced a vastly improved and more marketable version of that fiber in 1958. Acrylics and other polyvinyl-based fibers were developed during the 1950s.

Rapid technological advances during and after World War II paved the way for a massive synthetic fiber industry expansion during the 1960s and 1970s. Although polyester and vinyl fibers had existed for several years, public acceptance of textiles and apparel created with artificial filaments lagged behind technology. During the 1960s, however, fiber producers began making a wide variety of different products. Furthermore, they opened new markets and persuaded every feasible manufacturing sector to consider their products.

Nevertheless, the fiber industry was still dominated by cotton and other natural materials. Increased public acceptance of synthetics, combined with other influences, began to change this situation during the 1970s. For instance, pivotal synthetic fiber technology was developed for the space program, as well as for the military during the Vietnam era and the Cold War. These advances inspired new products that found favor in civilian markets. Most importantly, new production and processing techniques evolved, such as texturizing and chemical crimping, that allowed competitors to vastly improve the quality, look, and feel of their fibers.

In the early 1950s, manmade fibers accounted for about 13 percent of worldwide fiber production—synthetic fibers represented a negligible share of this total. By the late 1960s, however, manmade fibers met over 30 percent of global fiber demand, and synthetics were quickly displacing their cellulosic cousins. Boosted by postwar economic expansion, worldwide manmade fiber production rocketed from just 4.6 billion pounds in the early 1950s to over 16.2 billion pounds by 1970. Furthermore, the United States supplied a major share of global exports in this new, high-tech industry.

Continued technological advances prompted expansion of the synthetic fiber industry throughout the 1970s. While no completely new apparel and textile fibers were invented during that decade, modifications and processing advancements were numerous. Du Pont developed Antron nylon, as well as extremely light-weight, thin polypropylene fibers. Similarly, BASF introduced conductive nylon carpet fibers that reduced static. Popular anti-cling nylons were developed as well. "Pluscious" brushed nylon, created by Dow Chemical Co., became the preferred fiber for women's and children's sleepwear. Moreover, new polypropylene fibers with improved pigments and ultra-violet light inhibitors became popular in automotive and outdoor markets.

As industry revenues and output skyrocketed, the synthetic fiber industry adopted a more consolidated structure. The industry consisted of a multitude of innovators attempting to establish themselves as leaders in this new high-tech industry. However, commercial development of synthetic fibers proved to be an extremely capital-intensive endeavor, and research and development costs, plant construction, and ongoing fiber improvement expenditures became more than many companies could bear. As a result, many fiber making companies merged.

Polyester and nylon fabrics became more and more popular throughout the 1970s, and the industry surged ahead. By 1979, polyester accounted for 50 percent of all shipments by weight, while nylon held a 30 percent share of the market, and olefin and acrylic fibers each comprised 10 percent. Overall synthetic fiber output peaked at about 6.5 billion pounds in 1979.

Despite this impressive expansion, industry growth stalled in the 1980s. High petroleum prices helped to depress profits during the early part of the decade, and the industry faced more fundamental and long term obstacles as well. Specifically, the major innovations that had propelled growth during the previous 20 years were no longer new, and the synthetic fiber industry was entering a stage of maturity.

The declining market for polyester, the industry's mainstay, was of primary concern for struggling manufacturers in the 1980s. U.S. production jumped an encouraging 11 percent in 1983, but slipped for four consecutive years to only 3.3 billion pounds by 1986. Total production in this important segment climbed only 1 percent annually between 1982 and 1991. The other major class of fibers, nylon, reflected a similar growth pattern. From 1.9 billion pounds of output in 1982, demand rose an average of just 2 percent per year through 1991, to 2.5 billion pounds.

Olefin fibers continued to realize strong demand. That segment grew an average of 11 percent per year during the 1980s, topping 1.8 billion pounds per year by 1990, when olefin fibers accounted for over 20 percent of industry shipments. Acrylic fibers, by contrast, plummeted from 624 million pounds sold in 1982 to just 454 million by 1991, exhibiting an average annual decline of 4 percent. Consumer preference for cottons and polyester served to reverse expansion in this sector.

During this time, stiff foreign competition in commodity fiber markets emerged. The U.S. fiber makers faced a serious challenge from Europe, Japan, and emerging industrial nations. Taiwan and Korea became particularly aggressive competitors during the decade, and significant additions to the market also came from low-cost producers in Indonesia, Bangladesh, and Malaysia.

U.S. synthetic fiber imports reached over $900 million per year by 1992, approaching 10 percent of domestic sales. Besides cutting into domestic profits, foreign filament producers were quickly capturing global market share. As U.S. apparel and textile manufacturers moved their production facilities overseas, they often turned to cheaper foreign fiber suppliers. By 1990, the total U.S. share of global industry output fell to 18 percent, down significantly from the over 50 percent the country held in 1950.

In an effort to combat downward price and profit pressures exerted by foreign competitors, U.S. companies scrambled to cut costs and improve their products. Massive capital investments made during the early 1990s were used to update manufacturing facilities, increase automation, and integrate new information management systems. Investments also were used to create thinner, lighter, stronger, and more versatile fibers. Despite these efforts, however, industry sales climbed an average of only 4 percent per year between 1982 and 1990, to about $11.5 billion. Total output during that period remained stagnant at about 3.2 billion pounds. Only gains in productivity helped to buoy profits for many struggling competitors.

As if heightened competition and stagnant demand were not enough of a challenge for U.S. synthetic fiber manufacturers, the country experienced economic recession from 1989 through 1991. Output slipped about 1 percent in 1989 before plunging 4 percent in 1990. Revenues fell 4 percent as well. Sales slipped again in 1991 by less than 1 percent, disappointing many who had anticipated a significant recovery. Besides increased imports of apparel and textiles, fiber makers were hit particularly hard by a depression in the construction industry, a major consumer of carpet fibers.

Supported by overall improvement in the U.S. economy, American synthetic fiber markets began to show definite signs of recovery in 1992 and 1993. The value of shipments rose 4.0 percent (2.0 percent in inflation adjusted dollars), and output climbed 3.6 percent.

CURRENT CONDITIONS

The synthetic fibers industry had a mixed year in 1995. Unfortunate events in western Europe and the United States caused strains and negative shifts on the market. In Europe, synthetic fiber consumption dropped 20 percent from the 1994 level, and in the

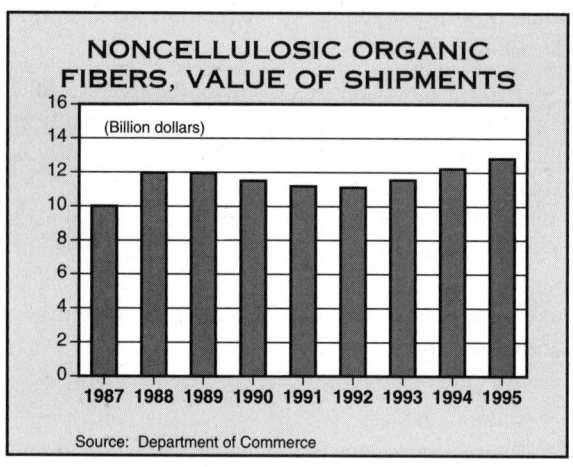

NONCELLULOSIC ORGANIC FIBERS, VALUE OF SHIPMENTS

(Billion dollars)

1987 1988 1989 1990 1991 1992 1993 1994 1995

Source: Department of Commerce

United States, the textile industry fared poorly, causing a lower demand for manmade organic fibers. Worldwide production was up 23.2 million tons, but growth dropped from its 8 percent level in 1994 to 3 percent. Nevertheless, synthetic fibers kept their 53 percent market share of the 43.5 million ton worldwide fibers market.

Even though the U.S. market was not doing exceptionally well in 1995, it was still doing better than markets in most parts of the world. This gave U.S. companies a chance to increase exports while imports were at a minimum. Probably more than at any other time, the worldwide fiber market was affecting the U.S. textile market. When Chinese and Pakistani cotton crops failed in 1995, the worldwide cotton price went up and this affected the synthetic fiber business as well. Raw material costs were soaring, and U.S. synthetic fibers makers were passing the costs to the mills.

Into the 1990s, manufacturers of polyester were benefitting from management and production restructuring, as well as from a slowdown in the growth of apparel imports that occurred in the late 1980s. Demand for polyester was also increasing from producers of high-performance tires and nonwoven products, such as disposable medical garments. Market demand for new polyester microfibers, which give polyester the feel of silk, encouraged manufacturers as well. In the first four months of 1995, export shipments of polyester filament were at about 29 million pounds, up 32 percent over that period of 1994.

Nylon producers expected to benefit from an increase in carpet demand in the mid-1990s. Despite generally weak markets, nylon fiber makers were scrambling to fill surging demand in the automotive air bag market, a lucrative niche expected to grow 15-fold between 1990 and 2000. Overall nylon production grew less than 1 percent in 1992, to 2.5 billion pounds.

U.S. producers maintained a 28 percent share of global nylon fiber production in the mid-1990s.

In 1996, U.S. production of nylon fibers was 2.8 billion pounds, an increase over the 2.7 billion pounds in 1995. Nylon fiber prices increased while capacity remained the same in 1996. Du Pont, the largest manufacturer of nylon fiber in North America, planned to begin a reorganization and price increase in 1997.

Olefin fibers continued to lead industry growth in the 1990s. Output jumped 7 percent in 1992 to about 2 billion pounds. Olefin producers were encouraged by a growing demand from carpet makers and by the new uses found in nonwoven products such as disposable garments. Amoco, for example, began marketing a new olefin fiber carpet for residential use, which was advertised as being highly resistant to the matting and crushing characteristic of nylon products.

Output of acrylic fibers remained stagnant in the early 1990s, and output dropped to 439 million pounds in 1992. In the beginning of 1995, the domestic market was still weak, with domestic shipments down nearly 13 percent from the levels of 1994. But exports were up, more than 51 percent. In the first four months of 1995, 49 million pounds of acrylic staple were exported, more than half as much as total domestic shipments. As with polyester, the high costs of raw materials hit the acrylic side of the industry, causing acrylic fibers to be in short supply.

The long term health of the U.S. synthetic fiber industry was questionable in the mid-1990s. Opportunities for impressive productivity gains seemed limited. Most competitors were already operating at low costs compared to foreign producers—particularly those in Europe and Japan—and gains allowed by automation and information technology had been largely exhausted.

Industry analysts expected the United States to realize a continued decline in its share of the global market. Fiber producers in such newly industrialized countries as South America and Asia were likely to dominate those regions, exerting downward pressure on global fiber prices as they competed in markets around the world. Also, increasingly stringent environmental rules and regulations reduced U.S. profit margins. To reduce toxic emissions, federal and state governments began requiring producers to meet strict manufacturing regulations (see **SIC 2821: Plastics Materials and Resins.** In order to comply, U.S. companies were spending millions of dollars retrofitting their factories and searching for cleaner production technologies.

INDUSTRY LEADERS

The largest company competing in the synthetic fibers industry in the early 1990s was E. I. du Pont de Nemours of Delaware. This diversified conglomerate increased its revenues 1.1 percent in 1992 to more than $15.5 billion. Its operating profits, however, jumped 9.6 percent to $1.38 billion. Du Pont, the inventor of nylon, remained the world's largest producer of that fiber, controlling about 36 percent of the nylon carpet fiber market in 1992, and 21 percent of the market for polyester staple fibers.

While Du Pont reduced its toxic emissions substantially since the late 1980s, the company released over 250 million pounds of waste in 1991 (as classified under federal toxic release inventory guidelines). Therefore, in July 1991, Du Pont announced plans to invest $300 million to modernize its polyester production facilities by 1994 and to expand filament capacity by 20 percent, a plan that would eliminate 1,000 jobs. In 1993, the company announced further plans to cut 1,600 jobs from its nylon business unit as part of an overall 4,500 company wide workforce reduction, which the company hoped would cut its fixed costs by 20 percent. This acquisition would result in a fiber behemoth, with nylon sales of $4.5 billion annually.

Though Du Pont did not rank as one of the top five producers of organic fibers specifically in 1997, it was still the largest producer of nylon in North America. Also, Du Pont was the largest company in the entire chemicals industry. It showed revenues of $43.8 billion and a net income of $3.6 billion in 1996. In 1996, one half of the company's sales were outside the United States. Exports were at $3.8 billion, making Du Pont one of the largest U.S. exporters. In 1996, Du Pont employed nearly 100,000 people, with 65 percent of them working within the United States. The company operated in about 70 countries worldwide with 175 manufacturing and processing facilities.

The second largest manufacturer of synthetic fibers in the early 1990s was Hoechst Celanese Corp., based in North Carolina. This competitor earned operating profits of $42 million in 1992 from revenues of $6.5 billion. Sales rose 2.4 percent over 1991, though profits slipped by more than 9 percent. Hoechst Celanese was the largest producer of polyester staple fiber—with over 31 percent of the world market—and the second largest manufacturer of polyester. The company spent $300 million in the early 1990s to upgrade its production facilities and add 100 million pounds of capacity.

Two of the next largest producers in the industry, Allied Signal Inc. of New Jersey, and BASF Corp.,

Fibers Division of Virginia, announced plans in 1993 to merge their nylon operations. By increasing their production capacity to 850 million pounds per year, this merger would displace Monsanto Corp. of St. Louis, as the second largest manufacturer of nylon fiber. Allied Signal reported profits of $249 million in 1992 from sales of $2.6 billion, while BASF had 1991 sales of $4 billion from its diversified operations.

In 1997, the industry leaders were Hoechst Celanese Corp. of New York, New York; Wellman Inc. of Shrewsbury, New Jersey; Alice Manufacturing Company Inc. of Easley, South Carolina; Texas Olefins Inc. of Houston, Texas; and Lydall Inc. of Manchester, Conneticut.

WORK FORCE

About 48,000 workers were employed in the U.S. synthetic fiber industry in the early 1990s. This reflected an employment decline of over 20 percent since 1982, when over 60,000 workers served the industry. Although many jobs had moved overseas to factories in low cost regions, workforce reductions were largely a result of huge productivity gains. Heavy investments in labor saving automation, for instance, resulted in the elimination of many production workers. Similarly, new information systems reduced the demand for managers and support staff.

Employment increased slightly during 1992 in response to slowly recovering markets. Employment prospects for the long term, however, remained discouraging. Most chemical equipment controllers and machine operators, which accounted for approximately 20 percent of the industry's labor force, were likely to see their positions decline in number by 15 to 25 percent between 1990 and 2005. Nevertheless, high-paying jobs for chemists, engineers, and scientists were expected to increase by 5 to 15 percent by 2005. Moreover, experts projected that positions related to sales and marketing would surge about 17 percent. The greatest opportunities would likely arise in the fields of systems analysis and computer science, with a potential increase of over 35 percent by 2005.

Despite unenthusiastic expectations for workforce growth, those established in the industry were relatively well paid. In 1989, for example, the average production worker earned $13.84 per hour—about 32 percent higher than the average for all other U.S. manufacturing sectors. Furthermore, the average annual payroll per employee topped $32,000, compared to $21,000 for workers in other manufacturing industries.

The highest paid workers in the business were generally scientists and engineers, particularly highly educated chemists involved with management or research and development. Salaries for these professionals averaged between $60,000 and $90,000 in 1993, depending on education level. For more information on chemical engineering jobs in the synthetic materials industries, see **SIC 2821: Plastics Materials and Resins.**

AMERICA AND THE WORLD

U.S. fiber manufacturers served 18 percent of global demand in 1992—more than all western European producers combined. Taiwan was the second largest producing nation, with 11 percent of the world market in 1992. Japan followed closely with 10 percent. Other major producers included Austria, Germany, Canada, the United Kingdom, Korea, China, and several developing countries.

U.S. producers held over 90.0 percent of the domestic market. With exports over $1.7 billion in 1992, the U.S. synthetic fiber industry produced a trade surplus of about $800 million. Canada was the largest importer of U.S. fibers, consuming over 14.0 percent of U.S. exports in the early 1990s. Belgium was the second largest customer at 10.0 percent. China absorbed 8.0 percent of U.S. exports, while Hong Kong accounted for 7.0 and Japan 4.5 percent. The European community purchased about 26.0 percent of U.S. exports and East Asia (excluding China) purchased a similar amount.

Importers were quickly eliminating the U.S. trade surplus in the mid-1990s. Canada supplied about 28 percent of all fiber imports into the United States, while Germany and Japan each accounted for about 12 percent of imports. The United Kingdom sold 10 percent of U.S. imports, while South Korea captured about 5 percent. The United States bought 33 percent of its fiber imports from the European community.

Although they held a small share of the U.S. market, fiber producers in southeast Asia were making the greatest gains in capturing worldwide and U.S. market share. Pacific Rim countries were expected to increase their portion of the world synthetic fiber market to 40 percent by 2001. All developing nations combined produced about 11 million tons of manmade fibers in 1992, or about 54 percent of total global output.

In 1996, prices of polyester in Hong Kong were lowest at $700 per ton and increased to $900 per ton by the year's end. Analysts were afraid that this rise in price was temporary and would drop again when Chinese stocks returned to normal levels. At $900 per ton, the selling and manufacturing cost of polyester was so nearly the same that another drop would seriously injure the field.

India was struggling with overcapacity problems in 1996 as global prices for polyester fibers fell almost 50 percent since the beginning of that year. Although the demand for polyester staple fiber (PSF) and polyester filament yarn (PFY) was growing at 13 to 15 percent per year, capacity was increasing much more than that. From 1995 to 1996, India's fiber capacity increased from 500,000 metric tons to 600,000 metric tons, and was expected to increase to 1 million metric tons during 1997. Prices were extremely low and small companies were having difficulties in making a profit.

As production in many developing nations escalated in the mid-1990s, synthetic fiber output in most leading industrialized countries stagnated. Global nylon production, for example, was forecast to grow 6 to 8 percent per year throughout the 1990s. Asian nylon production, however, was expected to grow by 9 to 12 percent. While U.S. production seemed to have stabilized in 1992 and 1993, demand for fiber in Japan and western Europe continued to decline. Japanese producers were scrambling to overcome slack demand and increased competition from neighboring nations. Similarly, western European producers were battling an ongoing regional recession, environmental problems, and an influx of inexpensive fibers from eastern Europe and the Commonwealth of Independent States.

As global competition became severe, and the growth rate hovered around 2 to 5 percent in the 1990s, U.S producers had to search for high-tech products that would help in overseas markets. They were also looking forward to sales growth as a result of the North American Free Trade Agreement (NAFTA). NAFTA would remove import quotas on polyester fibers and was expected to increase demand for U.S. fibers from Mexican textile and apparel manufacturers. The General Agreement on Trades and Tariffs (GATT), in 1994, was forecast to produce similar results for U.S. fiber makers in the European market.

Italy was on the cutting edge of technology in the organic fibers business in 1995. According to the *Daily News Record,* their ''Modem manufacturing techniques blended with old world artisanship continue to supply the world with an endless variety of new age fabrics.'' As of 1995, Italy's Montefibre produced about 500,000 tons of synthetic fibers annually in its 8 plants, making it the world's top fabricator of acrylic fibers and a European leader in polyester fibers. In 1994, the United States imported $49.41 million worth of synthetic fibers from Italy, up 28.1 percent from 1993.

RESEARCH AND TECHNOLOGY

Significant capital investments were made during the 1980s and 1990s to increase productivity and reduce hazardous manufacturing emissions. In 1990, synthetic fiber makers invested over $800 million, or about 10 percent of total revenues, back into their businesses, a figure roughly equal to three times the investment per employee of the average U.S. manufacturer and double the amount spent by the industry less than ten years earlier.

U.S. producers sought to develop cutting-edge fibers that could deliver high profit margins and displace commodity fibers increasingly supplied by emerging industrial nations. One significant product introduction during the early 1990s included Hoechst Celanese's Polarguard high void continuous filament (HV), which provided greater warmth from lightweight, outdoor polyester fiberfill products. Similarly, the company introduced a 100 percent recyclable, all-polyester carpet system in 1993.

Also in 1993, DuPont was improving its Micromattique MX, intended as a substitute for cotton in sportswear. Furthermore, DuPont revealed plans to develop nylon recycling technology. Planning to market recyclable fibers by 1997, the company hoped to eventually command 85 percent of the used nylon market. Seeking to revive the struggling acrylic sector, American Cyanimid Corp. introduced MicroSupreme, a microfiber product that offered superior softness and strength as well as greater wicking and heat barrier characteristics.

Promising technological breakthroughs were also occurring outside of the private sector. Researchers at the University of Minnesota developed a method of growing poly fibers in a vertical glass tube. The system, which allowed the shape and diameter of the fiber to be altered, offered an alternative to the traditional extrusion process.

For more information about capital spending to increase productivity and to meet environmental regulations in the synthetic chemical industry in general, see **SIC 2821: Plastics Materials and Resins.**

FURTHER READING

''AlliedSignal, BASF Join Their Nylon Fiber Lines.'' *Chemical Marketing Reporter,* 18 October 1993.

Anderson, Earl V. ''Foreign Trade: U.S. Chemical Trade Surplus Declines.'' *Chemical & Engineering News,* 13 December 1993.

———. "Japan: Once Booming Economy Struggles Through Times." *Chemical & Engineering News,* 13 December 1993.

Chapman, Peter. "Nylon Producers Completing Year of Record Output." *Chemical Market Reporter,* 6 January 1997, 1.

"Chinese Purchasing Buoys Fibres Markets." *ECN-European Chemical News,* 4 November 1996, 12.

"DuPont Looks at Used Nylon for Recycling." *Journal of Commerce and Commercial,* 14 October 1992.

"Facts & Figures for the Chemical Industry." *Chemical & Engineering News,* 28 June 1993.

Garcia, Carmen. "Mixed Bag for Man-made Fibres." *ECN-European Chemical News,* 20 May 1996, 15.

Heathcote, Mary. "NAFTA Set to Free the Flow of Fibres." *ECN-European Chemical News,* 9 August 1993.

Hirano, Koju. "Japanese Firms Count on Microfibers to Shore Up Sagging Sales." *Daily News Record,* 24 June 1993.

Layman, Patricia. "Developing Nations Lead in Fibers Production." *Chemical & Engineering News,* 5 April 1993.

———. "Europe: Definite Though Modest Recovery Forecast for 1994." *Chemical & Engineering News,* 13 December 1993.

"Market Outlook: Fiber Markets Also Stay Sluggish." *Textile World,* August 1993.

Maycumber, S. Gray. "Du Pont to Slash 4,500 Jobs; 1,600 Are in Nylon." *Daily News Record,* 14 September 1993.

———. "New Du Pont Microfiber Development, Called MX, May Be Rx for Market." *Daily News Record,* 24 June 1993.

———. "Manmade Fibers Suffer Summer '93 Shipment Chill." *Daily News Record,* 2 September 1993.

———. "U.S. Fiber Prices - The Good and the Bad Sides." *Daily News Record,* 1 June 1995, 8.

"PP Stakes Claim as Asia Dominates Fibres Sector." *ECN—European Chemical News,* 5 July 1993.

Rawis, Rebecca L. "Salaries." *Chemical & Engineering News,* 25 October 1993.

Reisch, Marc S. "Many Nylon Fiber Producers Moving to Consolidate." *Chemical & Engineering News,* 2 August 1993.

———. "Plastics, Synthetic Fibers Output Increases." *Chemical & Engineering News,* 12 April 1993.

Rzadzki, John. "Nylon Makers Head East in Search of High Growth." *Chemical Marketing Reporter,* 19 July 1993.

Storck, William J. "United States: Chemical Industry Lackluster This Year." *Chemical & Engineering News,* 13 December 1993.

Sudershan, O.P. Kharbanda. "Fibers and Intermediates Makers Lose Their Shirts; Overcapacity Drowns Strong Demand." *Chemical Week,* 11 September 1996, 52.

"Synthetics Climb to Summit of Success." *Daily News Record,* 30 October 1995, 8.

Thomas, Marita. "Fibers: Enhanced in the Last Quarter Century." *Textile World,* September 1993.

Walker, Marjorie. "Europe Loses the Thread." *ECN Chemscope,* December 1993.

—Dave Mote, updated by Beaird Glover

SIC 2833

MEDICINAL CHEMICALS AND BOTANICAL PRODUCTS

This classification covers establishments primarily engaged in manufacturing bulk organic and inorganic medicinal chemicals and their derivatives and processing—grading, grinding, milling—bulk botanical drugs and herbs. Included in this industry are establishments primarily engaged in manufacturing agar-agar and similar products of natural origin, endocrine products, manufacturing or isolating basic vitamins, and isolating active medicinal principals from botanical drugs and herbs.

INDUSTRY SNAPSHOT

Companies in this drug industry segment furnish the active ingredients used by pharmaceutical firms to manufacture their finished products, called pharmaceutical preparations. (See **SIC 2834: Pharmaceutical Preparations.**) Active ingredients are the portion of a finished drug that create the desired effect—therapeutic or preventive—for humans and animals. Extracts of crude drugs (not yet processed) derived from plant or animal sources are important examples of the components produced by this industry sector. By the 1960s synthesized chemicals—either a manufactured copy of an organic or inorganic substance, or a new chemical entity (NCE)—had become common active ingredients in pharmaceuticals, from vitamin pills to hormones. Meanwhile, the biotechnology revolution, beginning in earnest in the 1980s, resulted in ways of inserting genetic material into small microorganisms. This made them miniature factories for the production of active drug ingredients like insulin and in the process created patentable new molecular entities (NME's).

In the 1990s technological advances and shrinking resources created a new interest in natural products and plant-derived drugs. But, by the middle of the decade, experts had mixed reactions. One executive noted that the trend would not continue if significant

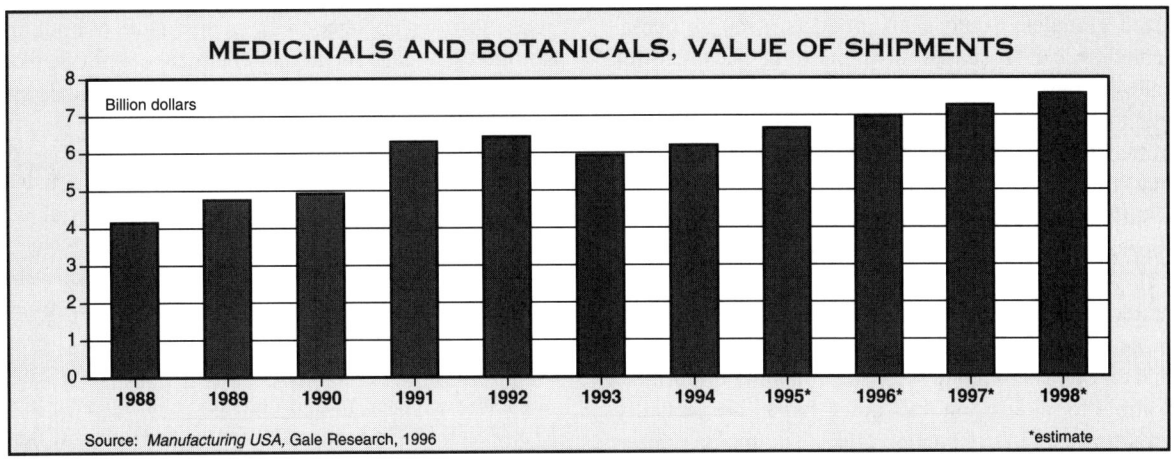

MEDICINALS AND BOTANICALS, VALUE OF SHIPMENTS

Billion dollars

Source: *Manufacturing USA*, Gale Research, 1996   *estimate

drug discoveries did not occur in the latter half of the decade.

ORGANIZATION AND STRUCTURE

There were an estimated 234 establishments in the medicinals and botanicals industry in 1997. A large amount of these were divisions or subsidiaries of other firms, including pharmaceutical industry giants such as Merck and Hoffman-La Roche. Parent firms that have developed in-house active ingredient suppliers are said to be "back-integrated," and their chemical products are referred to as "captive," dedicated to the parent firm. Chemicals produced by firms independent of the final purchaser are called "merchant."

Many "fine" chemical companies producing for the merchant market are contracted to large pharmaceutical companies to supply custom, or specialty chemicals, while others produce and sell them on the open market. The latter often manufacture well known bulk pharmaceutical compounds, like those used in the production of aspirin. Custom and specialty chemicals are produced in smaller quantities than bulks and frequently combine several different chemical compounds called intermediates which are more expensive. Traditionally, "fine" chemicals were those with fewer impurities than industrial chemicals not intended for human consumption.

Both the back-integrated firms and the independent fine chemical companies are involved in the complex process of producing extracts of natural substances, synthetic inorganic and organic chemicals, or combinations of any or all of these, that go into most modern medicines. The specific formulas for these substances can be found in academic monographs or in the official U.S. Pharmacopeia (USP) and the National Formulary (NF). If they have not yet been manufactured on an industrial scale or are entirely new compounds (NCE's or NME's), the pharmaceutical firm creates a document as a reference for its own in-house producers or as a guide to firms contracted to supply active ingredients. These references provide manufacturers with the acceptable legal standards of purity and potency for their products. A new manufacturing process, as well as an NCE or NME, is patentable in the United States.

Active ingredients from natural sources start as crude drugs. According to the standard text on drug extraction from natural sources, *Pharmacognosy,* crude drugs from vegetative or animal—even insect—origins are "natural substances that have undergone only the processes of collection and drying." Natural substances are those "found in nature . . . that have not had changes made in their molecular structure." The sources of these substances, medicinal plants or the animals from which glands and organs are needed, can either be raised commercially or collected in the wild. But environmental concerns tended to support the former in the 1980s and 1990s. Especially with plants, it is of vital importance that the correct species is identified before collection. Once a crude drug has been collected and the needed portions separated and cleaned, it must be safely stored or immediately processed, according to how quickly the active ingredient might spoil on lose its potency. Plants are often stored over long periods to help decompose unwanted plant components while leaving the desired portions intact. Animal glands and organs, however, are generally processed quickly to avoid deterioration.

If the crude drug is a plant, the active constituent—the ingredient desired for the final drug product—must be extracted. The first step in this procedure is grinding and mincing the appropriate plant parts, such as the leaves or the seeds. Production facilities in this industry house hammer mills, knife mills, and teeth mills designed to reduce leaves, stems, seeds, or roots to a manageable powder composed of evenly sized granules. Some plant products, such as herbal remedies, can be sent at this point to be packaged for sale or combined into other preparations. For most plant-derived drugs, the powdered plant must be submitted to a series of solvent baths (a process called maceration), such as alcohol or ether, or a series of distillation procedures (in the case of volatile oils), that separate the desired ingredient from the crude material. Animal glands or organs are also minced, then mixed with a solvent that aids extraction and often preserves the substance. After centrifugation, the animal extract is filtered to separate remaining impurities. Antibiotic molds, on the other hand, are actually grown in large fermentation tanks. The molds release their medicinal yield into a fermenting medium or solution. These fluid mixtures of either mold, plant, or animal materials are submitted to ''precipitation,'' which involves the application of either heat or freezing cold or the addition of salts or some other compound that separates or isolates the target active ingredient from the fluid. Isolates are then sent to the customer in either powdered or fluid form to be assembled into a marketable drug.

Manufacturers of active ingredients ship their finished products in ''batches'' to the preparation firm awaiting them. The chemical composition of these shipments must match a parent batch to ensure purity and strength and must meet with the approval of the U.S. Food and Drug Administration (FDA) as well as the client company. Firms that desire a regular supply of high-quality materials will often inspect manufacturing plants before assigning a production contract for active ingredients. Besides comparing active ingredients to the gold standard, the FDA is responsible for assuring that every step in the process of pharmaceutical raw material production meets specific production standards.

BACKGROUND AND DEVELOPMENT

Raw material suppliers for pharmaceutical companies, in the form of fine chemical producers, actually predated the pharmaceutical industry. Until well into the nineteenth century, doctors and apothecaries—pharmacists—collected and processed their own botanical remedies and compounded their own medicinal chemicals. Drugs in the limited and non-standardized pharmacopeia were herbal remedies whose provenance dated back centuries and could be prepared simply. Pharmacists could produce what chemical treatments there were in their drugstores using comparatively unsophisticated equipment. Because of the similarity of pharmaceutical chemicals to the processes for making industrial chemicals, small scale

producers often engaged in the manufacture of both. In fact, many modern medicinal chemical suppliers, like Dow and Hoechst, produce industrial chemicals as well.

An increase in the scientific study of chemistry and botanical extracts in the nineteenth century yielded a whole range of new chemicals and isolates with pharmaceutical potential. Included among these were the anesthetics ether and morphine. These new drugs required a greater degree of standardization and production expertise than earlier treatments. Their efficacy also increased public demand. Pharmacists, like H.E. Merck in Germany, as well as doctors and fine chemical producers, started developing and building the manufacturing capacity to meet these needs. The new pharmaceutical firms called themselves ''ethical'' manufacturers in order to differentiate themselves from the ''patent'' medicine producers, who bottled popular concoctions with broad therapeutic claims but dubious medicinal value. The makers of ethicals clearly labeled the contents of their products and promoted the therapeutic strength and purity of their medicines.

Many of the early active ingredient suppliers for both the American ethical and patent producers were European fine chemical companies. But such events as the War of 1812, the Civil War, and World War I tended to disrupt European supplies and spur American companies to increase their capacity for domestic chemical manufacture. American companies like Squibb—which became Bristol Myers-Squibb Company—established themselves by supplying medicines for the Union armies.

By the first decades of the twentieth century, breakthroughs in understanding the bacteriological basis of many diseases by Louis Pasteur and the effect of chemicals on certain parts of the body by Paul Ehrlich led to a new era in pharmaceutical science in which specific compounds could be screened for their effectiveness against known disease organisms. The discovery of such ''wonder drugs,'' like the anti-infective sulfanilimides and various vaccines, increased the demand for reliable new drug treatments. Most drugs, however, with the exception of injectables, still did not reach the physician or pharmacist in finished form. Pharmaceutical firms still purchased fine chemicals from companies like Pfizer Inc. or Merck and Co., Inc. and compounded them into pharmaceutical mixtures for distribution to hospitals and pharmacists. Pharmacists mixed these bulk ingredients into finished form in the drugstore. However, it is important to note that these treatments did not displace botanical products as the dominant form of drug treatment until after World War II.

With its emergency demand for the new anti-infectives like the antibiotic penicillin as well as sulfa drugs, World War II changed the structure of the pharmaceutical industry. Bulk suppliers like Pfizer Inc. and Merck and Co., Inc. found themselves producing drugs on a massive scale in both finished and bulk form. After the war, these companies stayed in the profitable ethicals business, making prescription-only pharmaceutical preparations. With a high public demand for new life saving or extending medications, companies began to finance enlarged research and development departments to discover and develop important—and profitable— new therapies. A vast array of new drugs resulted in the 1940s, 1950s, and 1960s, including tranquilizers, steroids, vaccines, and more antibiotics. Many of these drugs were derived from the laboratory screening of botanicals and animal products, like steroids from yams used to make a cortisonal treatment for arthritis, and insulin from animal pancreas extracts, used to control diabetes. The limits of natural supply, however, prompted many pharmaceutical companies to synthesize the active ingredients in these medicines.

Meanwhile, new federal regulatory requirements slapped tight new restrictions on the production of drugs after 1962, when a popular European sleeping pill, Thalidomide, was found to cause severe birth defects in some newborns. In response, Congress passed the 1962 Kefauver-Harris Amendments to the 1938 Food, Drug, and Cosmetic Act. The legislation required FDA licensing and oversight of all pharmaceutical manufacturing facilities and processes, including those of bulk pharmaceutical suppliers. Similar production controls had already been instituted after 1949 for "batches" of bulk penicillin.

Kefauver-Harris reinforced trends in the industry toward in-house production of active ingredient supplies for pharmaceuticals. Because the pharmaceutical company was ultimately responsible for the purity of its product, even if an outside supplier provided ineffective or dangerous compounds, companies thought it safer to have internal oversight and production control. Perhaps as important to major firms was a desire to maintain command of active ingredient supply even after patents had run out on new medications. In his history of the pharmaceutical industry titled *The Structure of American Industry,* Walter S. Measday cited a situation in which "upwards of 150 companies" offered Vitamin C in dosage form while "the entire output of the vitamin itself is produced by Merck, Pfizer, and Hoffman-La Roche, Inc." If ethical pharmaceutical companies could control bulk supplies for more advanced medications than Vitamin C even after product patents ran out, they would effectively extend their patent period—and associated high profits— indefinitely.

CURRENT CONDITIONS

In the late 1980s and early 1990s, pharmaceutical firms began to reverse their trend toward the in-house production of active ingredients in favor of a more complex combination of captive production and long-term contracts with outside custom suppliers. Among the factors fueling this trend were the 1992 economic recession and excess world chemical capacity, the increasing costs in both time and money to negotiate regulatory hazards, the complexity of new drug compounds, and the desire to avoid tying up too much capital in supply factories. Pharmaceutical firms in the 1980s had found themselves spending 7 to 10 years of their 17 year patent period on new drugs going through clinical trials and awaiting subsequent FDA approval. By looking more to outside fine chemical suppliers, drug companies could, as the *Chemical Marketing Reporter* put it in 1992, be "spared the cost of planting steel in the ground to produce a substance that may still require government approvals and has yet to prove commercially viable." For those companies lucky enough to sign on with a major pharmaceutical manufacturer on a long term supply contract, they could be assured of a 7 to 10 year market for their products. But, for the others, the competition in the open market promised to get tougher, suggesting consolidations might accelerate in the latter half of the 1990s.

Meanwhile, the highly politicized drive for healthcare reform in the late 1980s and early 1990s created downward pressure on the prices the big pharmaceutical firms could charge for their prescription drugs, even for new "breakthrough" treatment therapies costing considerable amounts of money to develop. The immediate winners in this contest over drug prices seemed to be the smaller independent generics companies. Generics, markedly cheaper therapeutic and chemical equivalents of prescription patented medicines, went into production once the patent protection on a prescription drug expired. Generics companies could manage cheap prices because they only had to copy—not research and develop—the drugs they produced.

Because of this, however, the active ingredients in generics accounted for almost one-half of their sale price—a ratio three to four times greater than prescription versions of the same drug. This made the generic companies susceptible to changes in the supply of active ingredients worldwide. When, as *Drug Topics* reported in 1994, the European Economic Community temporarily "outlawed the exportation of bulk/fine chemicals," generics companies were faced with a 85 percent cutoff of their supply. At the same time, the prescription pharmaceutical firms controlled the current capacity on the active ingredients in their drugs coming off-patent. Combined with a wave of takeovers or start-ups of generics firms by large pharmaceutical producers, the cutoff in supplies threatened to squeeze independent generic producers out and effectively extend prescription patents and higher drug prices much longer than healthcare reform advocates desired.

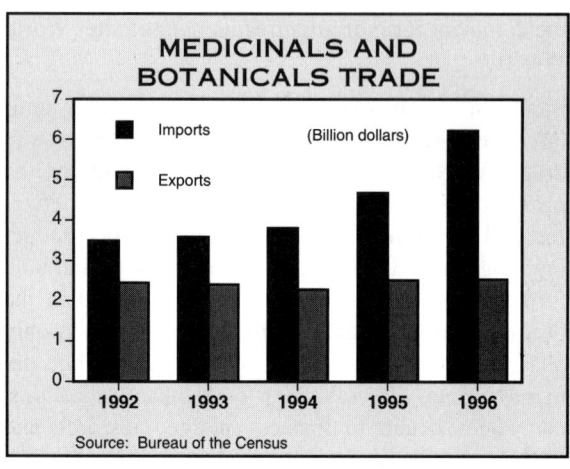

INDUSTRY LEADERS

In the 1990s, Merck & Co. Inc. continued to dominate the market with its broad range of human and animal health products and services. In 1994, the company brought in total sales of nearly $15 billion—by 1996, this number had increased by about 33 percent to $19.8 billion in sales. The company's best selling products in 1996 included elevated cholesterol products, hypertension and heart failure products, and anti-ulcerants. The company spent approximately $1.5 million in 1996 in research and development programs. In March of that year, the U.S. Federal Drug Administration cleared a new Merck product, crixivan, for the treatment of HIV infection in the United States. A new vaccine for the prevention of hepatitis A, Vagta, was also cleared for marketing in April 1996. By early 1997, the company employed 49,100 worldwide with more than 30,000 employed in the United States and Puerto Rico.

Roche Holding AG, of Switzerland, generated 1996 sales of approximately $13.7 billion—an 8 percent increase over the previous year. The company's pharmaceutical products comprise two-thirds of its sales. Roche manufactures the antibiotic Rocephin; the AIDS drug Invirase; and Cell Cept, for use in transplant medicine; along with other pharmaceutical products, diagnostics, fragrances, and flavors. The company has plans to launch several new products in 1997—including Posicor, a cardiovascular agent, and Xenical, for the treatment of Parkinson's disease. As of early 1997, Roche employed approximately 50,500 people worldwide (28 percent in North America).

AMERICA AND THE WORLD

Despite the twentieth century revolution in chemical pharmaceuticals, it was reported in *The Medicinal Plant Industry* that "50 percent to 80 percent of the developing world depends on traditional therapies for

their health care," namely plant-derived remedies. In China and Southeast Asia, indigenous industries process and package plant-based remedies based on ancient recipes. Some processors utilize the same machinery and manufacturing expertise as American companies, while others are extremely small and use traditional methods. This system of traditional active ingredient production for drugs, except to the extent that Western-style medicines were adopted or locally produced for export to the West, remained relatively untouched by American corporate influences.

Suppliers of fine chemicals for American pharmaceuticals, however, have never been limited to the country's borders. European chemical companies, except for temporary alterations during various wars, have always had—and continued to have in the late twentieth century—a large presence in the American market. The *Chemical Marketing Reporter* noted in 1992 that the U.S. share of the fine chemicals market only totaled about 30 percent, while European companies controlled more than 50 percent. American producers, however, more than held their own in domestic markets. In the 1990s industry leadership remained in European and American hands, which, with the addition of Japan, were estimated to control almost 90 percent of the market. A growing threat to this Western fine chemical hegemony were Asian and Indian producers, who do not have the strict Western environmental codes applied to U.S. producers. Asian producers showed themselves particularly competitive in the bulk pharmaceutical and intermediates classes.

FURTHER READING

"About Roche." F. Hoffmann-LaRoche Ltd., 1997. Available from: http://www.roche.com.

Akerele, Olayiwoia. "Summary of WHO Guidelines for the Assessment of Herbal Medicines." *HerbalGram,* 1993.

Begley, Ronald, and Emma Chynoweth. "Facing the Era of Post-Health Care Reform." *Chemical Week,* 31 March 1993.

De Sain, Carol. *Drug, Device and Diagnostic Manufacturing.* Buffalo Grove, IL: Interpharm Press, Inc., 1991.

"The Generic Industry '94: It's a Jungle Out There." *Drug Topics Supplement,* 1994.

Gibson, W. David. "Rising Prominence: Intermediate Chemicals '92, Custom Manufacture." *Chemical Marketing Reporter,* 7 September 1992.

Harvey, Alan L. *Drugs from Natural Products.* New York: Ellis Horwood, 1993.

"Hoover's Company Capsules." Hoover's, Inc., 1997. Available from: http://www.hoovers.com.

International Directory of Corporate Histories. Vol. I. Chicago: St. James Press, 1990.

Liebenau, Johnathan. *Medical Science and Medical Industry.* Baltimore, MD: Johns Hopkins University Press, 1987.

Mahoney, John. *The Merchants of Life.* New York: Henry Holt and Company, 1992.

Mattera, Philip. *Inside U.S. Business.* Homewood, IL: Business One Irwin, 1991.

World Class Business. New York: Henry Holt and Company, 1992.

Measday, Walter S. "The Pharmaceutical Industry." *The Structure of American Industry.* New York: Macmillan, 1971.

Morris, Gregory D.L. "Rx Intermediates: Business Booms." *Chemical Week,* 8 April 1992.

Moskowitz, Milton et al, eds. *Everybody's Business.* New York: Doubleday, 1990.

Mullin, Rick et al. "Manufacturers Head for Technology's High Ground." *Chemical Week,* 2 February 1994.

Nielsen, Robert. *Handbook of Federal Drug Law.* Philadelphia: Lea and Febiger, 1992.

Plishner, Emily S., and Debbie Jackson. "Generics Set to Take Off." *Chemical Week,* 12 August 1992.

Shon, Melissa. "Growing Pains, Bulk Actives." *Chemical Marketing Reporter,* 7 September 1992.

Spilker, Bert. *Multinational Drug Companies: Issues in Drug Discovery and Development.* New York: Raven Press, 1989.

Springer, Neil. "The Big Question." *Chemical Marketing Reporter,* 7 September 1992.

Stinson, Stephen C. "Custom Chemicals." *Chemical and Engineering News,* 31 January 1994.

Tilton, Helga. "For the Nimble." *Chemical Marketing Reporter,* 7 September 1992.

Tyler, Varro et al. *Pharmacognosy.* 8th ed. Philadelphia, PA: Lea and Febiger, 1981.

U.S. Department of Commerce. *1987 Census of Manufactures: Drugs.* Washington: GPO, 1990.

Wijesekera, R.O.B. *The Medicinal Plant Industry.* Boca Raton: CRC Press, 1991.

—J. Jacob Jones, updated by Gertrude Mandeville

SIC 2834

PHARMACEUTICAL PREPARATIONS

This industry includes establishments primarily engaged in manufacturing, fabricating, or processing drugs in pharmaceutical preparations for human or veterinary use. The greater part of the products of these establishments are finished in the form intended for final consumption, such as ampoules, tablets, capsules, vials, ointments, medicinal powders, solutions, and suspensions. Products of this industry consist of two important lines, namely: pharmaceutical preparations, promoted primarily to the dental, medical, or veterinary profession; and pharmaceutical preparations promoted primarily to the public.

INDUSTRY SNAPSHOT

According to *Fortune,* "Drugmakers live in what seems like profit paradise; they are consistently among the highest-earning industries, and last year [1995] kept an average of 15 cents from every dollar of sales—tops among all industries on our global list." According to the U.S. Census Bureau's *Current Industrial Reports,* the pharmaceutical preparations industry shipped $49.5 billion worth of product in 1995, up from $37.49 billion in 1994. Average returns make this one of the world's most profitable enterprises.

Since World War II, which established the American drug industry on a permanent footing, pharmaceutical firms have enjoyed a high level of profitability. The discovery and development of dozens of life-saving medications in company research labs created enormous demand for pharmaceuticals, while patent protection and sophisticated marketing structures maintained sales and profits. The high cost of drug development and marketing, though, tended to concentrate industry earnings in several large firms. In fact, the ten largest businesses accounted for over 50 percent of annual U.S. pharmaceutical sales in 1995. Even with strict regulatory oversight and periodic crises, like the Thalidomide scare of 1962, the American pharmaceutical industry, or at least its major players, managed to remain both profitable and beneficial to world health, while avoiding the price controls commonplace in other industrialized nations.

ORGANIZATION AND STRUCTURE

Pharmaceutical production and employment was concentrated in the northeast states of New Jersey, Pennsylvania, and New York. About 20 percent of the nation's drugs were shipped from New Jersey, home to industry leaders American Home Products Corp., Johnson & Johnson, and Merck and Co., Inc. Other states with high concentrations of drug companies were California, Illinois, Texas, Indiana, and Florida.

Companies marketing pharmaceutical preparations, or finished-form drugs, maintained their traditional leadership of the industry into the mid-1990s, earning approximately 60 percent of pharmaceutical sales in 1994. Companies in the this sector share similar manufacturing techniques: they combine active medicinal ingredients, chemicals, or natural products with excipients (i.e., buffered powders) or sterile water to produce the finished, or dosage, drug form. The most common dosage forms are oral (tablets, liquid suspensions, etc.), parenteral (by injection), or solid (suppositories and ointments). More novel drug delivery systems appeared in the 1980s and 1990s, including polymer implants, transdermal patches, and controlled-release sponges inside tablets.

Preparations firms also concentrated on the development, production, and marketing of therapeutic agents—drugs designed to treat, cure, or prevent specific diseases (antibiotics); suppress symptoms (analgesics); or supplement deficiencies (vitamins). Meanwhile, other industry segments concentrated on making drugs to create immunities (vaccines) or aid in diagnosis (radioactive iodine for X-rays). Within the general area of therapeutics, pharmaceutical companies developed expertise in one or more of the eight therapeutic classes of drugs, such as cardiovasculars, or even a specific disease, such as hypertension. Industry leaders generally manufactured and marketed drugs in several therapeutic categories, while some small companies produced only one drug.

All companies in the pharmaceutical industry operate within a strict regulatory environment. Because these companies manufacture potentially harmful, yet socially necessary products, but must also make a profit, the pharmaceutical industry has had a complex relationship with government regulators. These regulators are charged with protecting the public and encouraging business growth at the same time. Major incidents of adverse or fatal reactions from drugs, evidence of collusion or corruption within the industry, and the government's desire to move the industry in a particular direction have historically prompted new regulation. From the Food and Drug Administration (FDA) to the Federal Trade Commission (FTC), pharmaceutical companies and the federal government are linked at all stages, including development, production, and marketing.

Division and segmentation also characterized the industry. Some of this was the result of federal regulation, while the pressures of a highly competitive marketplace were responsible for the rest. One point of division for regulatory agencies was that between "ethical" and over-the-counter (OTC) drugs. Ethical drugs require a prescription from a physician before being dispensed to the patient, while consumers can purchase OTC medications (such as aspirin and antacid) without a doctor's prescription. Ethical drugs represented 60 percent of sales among preparations companies in 1995, while OTCs accounted for the remainder.

The ethical drug segment of the industry is further subdivided into "patented" and "generic" prescription drugs. Patented drugs are therapies developed by pharmaceutical companies whose formulas, production processes, and trade names (often called branded prescription drugs) enjoy 17-year protection under U.S. patent laws. Patented prescription drugs were the driving force behind pharmaceutical industry sales after World War II and continued market domination into the mid-1990s. Branded prescriptions included almost all of the major breakthrough therapies developed in drug research labs since the 1940s, continuing the drug industry's unusual combination of health- and profit-driven research. Meanwhile, an alternative to some of the most popular remedies were generics, markedly cheaper chemical and therapeutic equivalents of patented prescription drugs that go into production once brand name therapies have come "off-patent." Generics' share of the prescription drug market was expected to increase from 22 percent in 1985 to over 66 percent by the turn of the century.

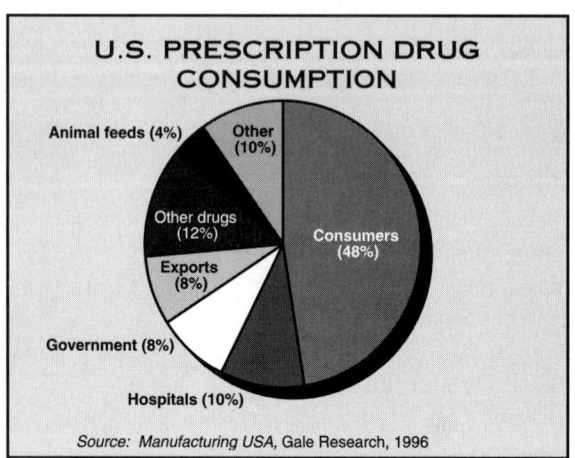

U.S. PRESCRIPTION DRUG CONSUMPTION

Animal feeds (4%)
Other (10%)
Other drugs (12%)
Exports (8%)
Government (8%)
Hospitals (10%)
Consumers (48%)

Source: Manufacturing USA, Gale Research, 1996

In addition to drugs for human consumption, pharmaceutical companies produce drugs for the veterinary market. Accounting for a relatively small percentage of overall industry sales—nearly $1.6 billion in 1995, according to the U.S. Census Bureau's *Current Industrial Reports*—many drug industry leaders either maintained specific animal health divisions or were involved in the animal health care industry. In 1995, Pfizer moved ahead of Merck and American Home Products in this segment with its acquisition of SmithKline Beecham's animal health operations.

Beginning in the early 1980s a new force entered the pharmaceutical arena—biotechnology. From the discovery of DNA structure in 1953 and new knowledge of "genetic blueprints" that direct protein growth by messenger RNA, scientists were able to clone proteins in the laboratory. Knowledge of a specific protein's function in the body—to stimulate infection-fighting cells or block a destructive internal process, for example—allowed physicians to induce desired reactions in patients by injecting biotechnology-produced cloned proteins, "Magic bullets" as they were called, into the body. Though biotech companies managed to create and patent many exciting new treatments in the 1980s, they were generally inconsequential, lacked marketing structure, consumed vast amounts of research capital, and created little profit compared to those offered by the industry leaders. Nevertheless, because of the potential to continue providing "breakthrough" treatments and vaccines for some of our most stubborn diseases, biotechnology companies were the target of buyouts, mergers, and joint ventures in the 1980s and 1990s. In one such move, industry giant Roche purchased controlling interest in biotechnology pioneer Genentech in 1990. The biotechnology industry is discussed in full under the separate article **Biotechnology.**

BACKGROUND AND DEVELOPMENT

Prior to the late nineteenth century, the American pharmaceutical industry barely resembled its current structure. Simple chemical compounds such as iodine chlorate, along with plant extracts such as quinine, constituted the prime ingredients of available remedies. However, these drugs lacked specific scientific formulas. Thus a doctor's order for a medication might not yield the product intended. To offset this problem, doctors often dispensed medicines in addition to prescribing them. But they did not have a monopoly on medical advice or drug selection for patients. Given the uneven quality of medical care before the twentieth century, patients often chose to dose themselves with "patent" medicines or to describe symptoms to the

druggist, who would obligingly offer his own remedy for purchase. Some traditional treatments, like digitalis, remain part of the pharmacological arsenal.

The War of 1812 and the Civil War stimulated an increase in domestic pharmaceutical manufacturing capacity. Both events temporarily disrupted the supply of fine chemicals (those with a purity level high enough for human consumption) from Europe with which pharmacists and doctors produced what few chemical medicaments they knew. Advances in the isolation and creation of new chemical substances, such as the 1840 discovery of the medicinal applications for nitrous oxide (laughing gas) by an American dentist, Horace Wells, stimulated demand for more fine chemical capacity. During the Civil War, American firms like Squibb were able to establish themselves profitably by providing advanced machinery and quality products to the Union Army.

As the century progressed, other companies turned to the production of "ethical" drugs for physicians and hospitals. These drugs had clearly labeled and pharmacologically reliable contents (and were thus termed "ethical"). They were intended to supply drugs of standardized quality. Brand name ethicals were also promoted as alternatives to the wide variety of other proprietaries, mainly bottled "patent" medicines. These extremely popular elixirs claimed great therapeutic value while the contents—often only colored water, alcohol, and opiates—were generally ineffectual and occasionally dangerous. The reliability of the new ethical suppliers, on the other hand, induced doctors to begin requesting branded pharmaceuticals in prescriptions by the end of the century.

Following scientific breakthroughs in understanding the causes and potential treatments for many of the diseases that had long been the scourge of mankind, demand for these reliable drugs and vaccines soon increased. The germ theory of disease, based upon the research of bacteriologists like Pasteur, revolutionized medicine and drug therapy in the 20 years immediately before and after World War I. Laboratory isolation of disease organisms meant that physicians could diagnose patients by tracing illnesses to specific infectious organisms, while drug researchers finally had a clear therapeutic target. New knowledge of the manner in which chemical treatments operated in the body, based upon the research of the German scientist Paul Ehrlich, opened up pathways of attack against these disease organisms. By World War I, "medical science," as this marriage of disease and therapeutic research came to be called, had created significant breakthroughs, especially in the development of vaccines and what Ehrlich called "chemotherapy."

Larger pharmaceutical companies like SmithKline expanded clinical departments in response to the popularity and promise of medical science. They increased research into new drug therapies and quality control activities. On the eve of World War I, however, these companies lagged far behind German manufacturers like Bayer in the development and patenting of new therapies. German companies had a long history of combining basic bacteriological research with the applied science of drug development. And, unlike American firms, they had no compunction about creating exclusive markets for therapeutic inventions by patenting drugs in the United States and Germany. Novel treatments, such as the popular antisyphilitic arsenical drug, Salvarsan, discovered by Ehrlich and produced by chemical giant Hoechst, illustrated the potentially large new markets for "scientific" pharmaceuticals. When, during the war, most German companies had American patent rights suspended, American pharmaceutical firms began manufacturing patented drugs invented in Germany (like Salvarsan and Bayer aspirin) and reaping the profits.

In the time between the two world wars, American firms copied the research orientation and patenting habits of German counterparts. Merck and Squibb opened direct ties with academic research institutions, financing research fellowships, laboratories, and institutes in the natural sciences. Drug companies hired academic research leaders to head or staff in-house labs. Firms developed some interest in basic research, but the major concern was using expanded research and development area capabilities to create new drug products for the expanding market. Major companies like Squibb, Merck, Abbott, and Upjohn all had research staffs of about 20 with budgets of at least $100,000 by World War II. Nevertheless, the discovery of the two major drug treatments of the war years, the sulfanilimides and the antibiotics, both resulted from European research. The sulfa drugs, chemotherapeutic anti-infectives derived from coal tars, were first developed at Bayer in 1935. One of the most important drug therapies of the twentieth century, mold-derived anti-infective penicillin, was first isolated and described by Alexander Fleming in England in 1928. Both the sulfa drugs and antibiotics became cornerstones of the American pharmaceutical industry from the 1930s to the 1950s.

Patent protection for the sulfas expired in the 1930s, and American companies, including Merck and American Cyanimid, began domestic manufacture of the anti-infectives. Meanwhile a grant by the Rockefeller family brought penicillin to America, where, in a Peoria, Illinois lab in 1941, scientists discovered how to mass produce penicillin mold by deep fermentation (as opposed to the slower surface culture). Several drug companies, including Pfizer, Squibb, and Merck, quickly geared up to produce marketable quantities of the "wonder drug" for use by armies and general populations. By 1945, the American manufacturing capacity for drugs had expanded so quickly that penicillin prices fell from $20 to $1 per dose, less than the labeled bottle containing it. This vastly expanded productive capacity on the part of pharmaceutical companies, an awareness of the potential market for antibiotics, and led to American domination of world markets after the war. Those factors resulted in the establishment of American pharmaceutical firms as research, manufacturing, and marketing powerhouses.

The first important federal law governing drug production came in 1902 with a law requiring the inspection and licensing of biologicals (e.g., vaccines and antitoxins) by a new federal agency, the Hygienic Laboratory, precursor of the National Institutes of Health (NIH). Soon thereafter, public outcry over the dangers of adulterated foods after the publication of Upton Sinclair's *The Jungle* secured passage of the second major piece of legislation covering therapeutic drugs, the Pure Food and Drug Act of 1906. This act prohibited adulterated or misbranded food or drugs from interstate commerce and granted authority to ban dangerous drugs.

In 1937, an American sulfanilimide producer, the Massengill Company of Tennessee, marketed a sore throat remedy that dissolved the sulfa drug in diethylene glycol, now the main ingredient in radiator antifreeze. Apparently, the manufacturer chose this particular solvent because of its pretty red color and sweet taste. No clinical trials for toxicity were performed. Over 100 reported deaths from kidney failure resulted from its ingestion before investigators determined the source of the fatalities. Public clamor over this incident led to the passage of the Food, Drug, and Cosmetic Act of 1938. This legislation required that all drugs must submit to tests for proof of safety by the newly-created Food and Drug Administration (FDA). Packaging was required to carry labels clearly describing the contents of the drug, how it should be administered, and possible side effects. Attendant legislation gave the Federal Trade Commission responsibility for ensuring valid drug advertising. Experience showed, however, that most consumers did not bother to read the extensive labels on medication. As a result, the Durham-Humphrey Amendment of 1951 exempted prescription drugs from full labeling requirements. These drugs, to be dispensed only by a licensed pharmacist under written direction of a physician, need only carry a "legend'' label, which read, "Caution: Federal law prohibits dispensing without a prescription." Legend drugs thereafter became another name for prescription or ethical drugs.

Despite regulatory hurdles, World War II and America's sustained postwar economic dominance secured the foundation for phenomenal growth in the pharmaceutical industry. The desire to find new drugs, especially antibiotics, led companies to sometimes absurd extremes. Pfizer requested that people- send them samples of dirt from all corners of the world on the chance that some might contain new molds from which to extract antibiotics. In fact, a Pfizer employee did find a profitable new treatment, terramycin, in a sample of dirt outside a company plant in Indiana. This and other "broad-spectrum" antibiotics, effective for a wide range of illnesses, provided revolutionary therapeutic regimens for physicians after the 1940s. Other breakthrough medications in the 1950s included Jonas Salk's polio vaccine, and tranquilizers and amphetamines, like Librium and Dexedrine, which promised to significantly aid patients suffering from mental illness. According to the Pharmaceutical Manufacturers Association (PMA) in its 1980 *Factbook,* new drug introductions increased from an annual average of 10 to 30 in the 1940s, to an average of 30 to 50 in the 1950s.

The array of new products available meant that individual physicians and pharmacists could not know all the available treatments at any one time. Pharmaceutical companies began to send out sales representatives, or "detail" men, as both educators in new therapies and promoters of company brands. Spending large sums on free physician samples and advertising in professional journals led to increased brand loyalty on the part of doctors. This marketing structure was expensive, but also supported high profits. Trained to think only of treatment regimens, doctors, often unaware of drug prices, prescribed medication where cheaper and equally efficacious therapeutic alternatives existed. Even if pharmacists wanted to substitute a cheaper generic for a doctor's prescription, doing so made little sense for a drugstore's profitability, might anger the physician, and was illegal in some states. The relationship established in the 1940s and 1950s between drug companies, pharmacists, and doctors, therefore, tended to perpetuate itself.

Fallout from another scandal, the Thalidomide crisis of 1962, however, placed more pressure on the industry. A popular European sleeping pill, Thalidomide was under investigation in 1962 by an American firm, the William S. Merrell Company, that wanted to start U.S. sales of the drug. The company's tests re-

vealed that the drug could cause severe birth defects in babies if taken by a pregnant mother. Despite the fact the drug was never sold in the United States, its inadequate premarket testing in Europe and its near-entry into the American market revealed that a thin line of regulation was all that stood between dangerous drugs and the general public. As James Nielson wrote in *The Handbook of Federal Drug Law* in 1992, the Thalidomide disaster made it clear "that people were taking drugs" for which "neither the prescriber nor the manufacturer had a clear knowledge of their effects." The Thalidomide crisis, along with public dissatisfaction with exorbitant drug-company profits, meant "drugs never again received the universal public acceptance they had previously enjoyed."

The federal government responded to the uproar over the Thalidomide crisis by passing the Kefauver-Harris Amendments of 1962. These amendments to the Food, Drug and Cosmetic Act of 1938 required pharmaceutical companies to prove both safety and efficacy before a drug entered the marketplace. Formal procedures for new drug applications (NDAs) to the FDA and for the clinical investigation of potential therapies were established. All adverse drug reactions in clinical studies would have to be fully reported, and human clinical subjects had to be informed of the dangers of involvement in trials before giving consent. Additionally, the new act required that drugs must follow specific production guidelines, called Good Manufacturing Practices (GMP). Manufacturing plants became subject to both registration and inspection procedures. Finally, advertising for prescription drugs was placed under FDA supervision, while OTC drug advertising continued under FTC oversight. The price controls for pharmaceuticals included in Senator Kefauver's original legislative proposal were dropped along the way.

The immediate effect of the Kefauver-Harris amendments was to drastically slow the rate at which pharmaceutical manufacturers introduced new drugs to the market. According to the Pharmaceutical Manufacturers Association (PMA), drug introductions fell from 45 to 24 annually between 1961 and 1962 alone. In the 1970s, they stayed below 20 in most years. Despite this slump, by the 1980s reinvigorated research efforts using advanced techniques in "molecular biology and biochemistry were promising a new generation of highly effective drugs for specific ailments, or magic bullets." One of the magic bullets was SmithKline Beecham's Tagamet, an anti-ulcer medication that quickly became "one of the most widely prescribed pharmaceuticals in the world" and prompted an increase in the research investments of pharmaceutical companies from "$1 billion in 1976 to $4 billion in 1985."

These larger research budgets yielded a whole crop of profitable new drug therapies in the 1980s, including drugs for hypertension (Merck's Vasotec), cholesterol treatment (Lopid from Warner-Lambert and Mevacor from Merck), and blood-clot dissolvers for heart-attack victims (Genentech's TPA). Meanwhile, Ortho Pharmaceutical's (owned by Johnson & Johnson) anti-acne Retin-A, and Upjohn's baldness treatment Rogaine, created new markets for cosmetic drugs. Even standbys like aspirin enjoyed increased sales as a result of studies that showed its potential to avert some heart attacks.

Despite some victories, by the end of the 1980s the prospects for the preparations industry did not look bright. Decades of expensive applied research, a wide patent umbrella, strong overseas sales, and aggressive marketing had sustained high profit and growth in the American prescription pharmaceutical industry since World War II. The system produced important new therapies that prolonged lives, banished ancient diseases, and made the aches and pains of modern existence easier to bear for those who could afford to purchase these new medications. But the highly structured corporate research, manufacturing, and marketing systems of industry leaders also required that wonderful new medications carry, what seemed to many, improperly inflated price tags. Some analysts felt that price was determining costs rather than the other way around. This trend continued into the 1980s. Thus, some industry critics claimed that the big brand pharmaceutical companies were charging unjustifiably high prices for drugs while spending more money on advertising, brand support, and lobbying efforts than they did for research and development. The prices of drugs were less related to cost inputs, therefore, than to companies' needs to maintain corporate structures. Meanwhile, the soaring costs of health care in general in the 1980s and early 1990s added fuel to demands for drug price control policies similar to those in Europe. Medications sold in Europe and America were reported to have price differentials exceeding 50 percent. Meanwhile, continued reports of industry profits added fuel to reform fires. According to industry analyst Robert Helms, quoted in a 1992 *Drug Topics,* "profits for the top ten drug companies averaged 15 percent of sales, compared to 4 percent for all other industries."

In 1991 legislation allowed state-funded Medicaid insurance programs to demand rebates from drug manufacturers for medications purchased by program recipients that resulted in downward price pressures. Standard and Poor's reported in its 1994 *Industry*

Surveys that Medicaid accounted for about 15 percent of all U.S. pharmaceutical sales. Similar programs for the federal government's Medicare program were included in President Clinton's 1993 health care reform proposals. Downward pressures on drug prices also resulted from the advent in the 1980s and 1990s of private managed care organizations such as health maintenance organizations (HMOs). Standard and Poor's estimated that HMO enrollment alone may top 50 percent of the population by the year 2000. These organizations increasingly adopted restrictive drug formularies (lists of drugs that could or could not be purchased by an organization) that stressed economical medication in therapeutic groups, often demanding discounts from manufacturers and the use of cheaper brands or generics to treat illness. Both of these movements created what one industry analyst, Paul Hanson, in an April 1994 *Chemical Week* article called a "strategic shift in power in pharmaceuticals from suppliers to consumers."

The price- and consumer-oriented generics and over-the-counter (OTC) segments, in fact, were poised to benefit from the health care reform movement. At least since the passage of the Drug Price Competition and Patent Term Restoration Act of 1984 (commonly called the Waxman-Hatch Act), the federal government attempted to increase industry competition and help supply cheaper drugs for the public by aiding the generally smaller and independent generics manufacturers. The act allowed generics companies to present a shorter version of the standard New Drug Application (NDA) to the FDA's anti-ulcer Zantac, which reached the open shelves of drugstores and groceries in the 1990s. Like generics, OTCs represented a significant price advantage over branded prescriptions. In addition, patients were more likely to diagnose and treat themselves with the drugs than to visit a doctor and receive a prescription. Fueled by these factors, sales of OTC drugs increased at a compound annual rate of 6 percent from 1985 to 1995. The OTC segment was expected to grow by more than 45 percent from $9.6 billion in 1995 to $14 billion by the year 2000.

U.S. drugmakers also faced the threat of increased regulation—including price controls—in the early 1990s. While it was defeated in 1994, the Clinton administration's health care proposal did have an indirect affect on the industry, inspiring wholesale belt-tightening and a rash of mergers and acquisitions. Furthermore, the industry's earnings growth slowed from an annual average of 18 percent from 1987 to 1992 to 9 percent from 1991 to 1993. Downsizing helped boost the earnings growth rate to 12 percent by 1995.

CURRENT CONDITIONS

The pharmaceutical preparations industry continued to be dominated by existing large branded firms in the mid-1990s. Through buyouts and in-house start-ups, as well as a continuation of the merger movement begun in the late 1980s, large companies adjusted to both market changes and reform movements. Many of the bigger companies, including industry leaders Marion Merrell Dow and Hoescht moved swiftly to buy or create generics divisions in the early 1990s. Industry sources estimated that approximately 40 percent of the generics market was already controlled by the leading branded pharmaceutical companies in 1992. Meanwhile, most major OTC companies were also prescription producers, and the majority of Rx to OTC switches could easily be carried out within these companies. As Roche did with Genentech, the majors also moved to purchase smaller competitors or start their own innovative biotechnology companies. Along with a number of new and important breakthrough drugs coming out of the majors' drug research pipelines, an aging population with greater drug demand, and what Standard and Poor's *Industry Surveys* called the "recession-resistant nature of the business" boded well for at least some of the industry's large companies.

While the pace of mergers and acquisitions slacked off by the mid-1990s, industry contraction (in terms of the number of companies) was expected to continue through the decade. As Jonathan Goldman noted in the December 1996 issue of *Institutional Investor,* "with no single drug company commanding more than a five percent share of the global marketplace, there is ample room for further consolidation."

INDUSTRY LEADERS

Hundreds of companies are involved in the pharmaceutical preparations industry, but the top five companies typically account for over 30 percent of American sales. Buyouts and competition among the major pharmaceutical companies continued to shift the rankings from year to year, but a handful of giants provided consistent leadership in both the ethical pharmaceutical and OTC segments of the field.

Merck and Co., Inc., a traditional industry leader in prescription drug research, had sales of $19.8 billion in 1996, more than double those of $8.6 billion in 1991. Merck controlled 6.7 percent of the global market in 1995, while maintaining a production and research presence on three continents. Under the leadership of CEO Raymond V. Gilmartin since 1994, the company reaffirmed its primary focus on research, as opposed to mergers and acquisitions.

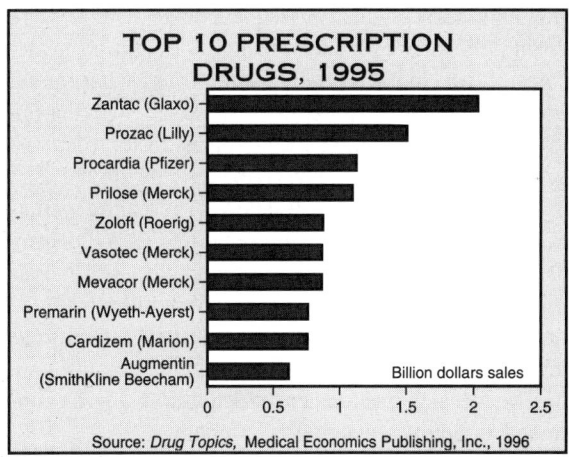

TOP 10 PRESCRIPTION DRUGS, 1995

Source: *Drug Topics,* Medical Economics Publishing, Inc., 1996

Merck originated as a German apothecary shop, and the family name was associated with pharmaceutical manufacturing for over 300 years in that country. In 1891, George Merck began American operations. In World War I, Merck avoided confiscation by giving the majority of its stock to the U.S. government, which sold it after the war to start American Merck. In the 1930s and 1940s Merck created a name for itself by making breakthroughs in the discovery and synthesis of vitamins, including B12 in 1948. Outside the drug area, Merck's *Manual of Diagnosis and Therapy* became a medical standard. Merck scientists also led in the synthesis of steroids and funded research that resulted in the discovery of streptomycin in 1943. Five Merck scientists received Nobel Prizes in the 1940s and 1950s for these and other pharmaceutical breakthroughs.

Merck's drug pipeline fell to a trickle and company fortunes slumped in the 1960s. But renewed commitment to research and development (R&D), started by new Chairman John Horan (1976) and continued by his biochemist successor Roy Vagelos (1985), yielded important new therapies. Two of these, Vasotec, an anti-hypertensive, and Mevacor, which lowered cholesterol levels, reached annual sales of $1 billion apiece. One of the few large companies to take advantage of biotechnology breakthroughs, Merck began marketing the first genetically-engineered human vaccine for hepatitis B late in the decade.

Rather than join the merger and buyout trend of the late 1980s and early 1990s, Merck sought to complement its industrial leadership in ethical pharmaceuticals by moving into joint ventures with companies like chemical industry leader DuPont in 1991, and OTC leader Johnson & Johnson. However, Merck did buy mail-order drug distributor Medco Containment Services for $6.6 billion in 1993. This, and new supplier agreements with Managed Care Organizations

(MCOs), showed that even giants like Merck were girding themselves for the changes wrought by health care reform. In 1992, Merck established what would become known as "the Rahway pledge," vowing not to increase prescription drug prices faster than the general inflation rate. Though plagued by slower than expected sales for its prostrate drug Proscar as well as pricing and distribution issues regarding its AIDS drug Crixivan, the company had several reasons for optimism as it entered the late 1990s. With older patented drugs maintaining profitability, a number of new drugs in the approval pipeline, and a continuing commitment to research and development expenditures, Merck continued to enjoy a position of strength.

With 1996 revenues of $15.06 billion, Bristol-Myers Squibb Company is a diversified firm with interests in medical devices and household products as well as pharmaceutical preparations, which comprised more than half of company sales. First quarter 1997 sales were $4 billion, up 10 percent from the first quarter of 1996. Pharmaceutical sales increased by 20 percent in the first quarter of 1997, with sales of Pravachol alone increasing 48 percent. The company's top ethical drugs in the early 1990s were Capoten, a hypertension treatment, and Pravachol, a cholesterol-lowering drug. Bristol-Myers Squibb also sells health and beauty aids under the Clairol and Matrix Essentials brands.

Bristol-Myers Squibb was formed via the 1989 acquisition of Squibb by Bristol-Myers for $12.7 billion. Named for founder Edward Squibb, the older of the two companies traced its roots to a New York City firm that specialized in such anesthetics as pure ether and chloroform. William Bristol and John Myers launched the firm in 1887 and initially named it for its hometown, Clinton, New Jersey. After the merger, the company shed many of its consumer products to concentrate on pharmaceuticals, especially anti-cancer and high blood pressure drugs. In the late 1980s, the company's Oncogen subsidiary began testing DDI, an AIDS treatment. When the drug won FDA approval in 1991, it was released under the brand name VIDEX. In 1996, the company formed an alliance with drug delivery company Sano Corp. to offer Bristol-Myers Squibb's anti-anxiety drug BuSpar in a transdermal patch.

One of the largest pharmaceutical firms in the world, Johnson & Johnson, also was an industry leader in OTC sales in the mid-1990s. About $6.3 billion of its $18.8 billion sales in 1995 came from pharmaceutical drugs. And overall sales for the first half of 1996 were $10.7 billion, up 15.7 percent from the first half of 1995 ($9.3 billion). Rx to OTC switches for its

popular yeast infection treatment, Monistat 7, and its antidiarrheal Immodium promised to improve its OTC position even further. Johnson & Johnson had also managed to bring Tylenol back to its position as the best-selling nonprescription drug in the country in the 1990s. According to the 1994 *Standard and Poor's* report, Tylenol represented about "one-quarter of the $2.8 billion dollar analgesic market." Other familiar OTC products from Johnson & Johnson include the athlete's foot medication Micatin and the sinus medication Sine-Aid.

Headquartered in New Brunswick, New Jersey, Johnson & Johnson got its start when founder Robert Wood Johnson decided to begin the production and distribution of plaster wound dressings he observed during the Civil War. High-quality sterile dressings, including the world famous Band-Aid, made the familiar Johnson & Johnson red cross logo ubiquitous in hospitals and bathroom medicine cabinets. The company also successfully promoted the placement of first-aid kits in homes, railroad cars, and businesses. Beyond Band-Aids, Johnson & Johnson became best known for its familiar line of baby-care products, like shampoos. The purchase of McNeil labs in 1959 expanded Johnson & Johnson's product line into prescription drugs like sedatives, muscle relaxants, and eventually the analgesic Tylenol, which went to OTC status in the 1960s. Other successful prescription introductions for the company have included the acne treatment Retin-A and the Ortho-Novum group of oral contraceptives.

Abbott Laboratories was another leader in the pharmaceutical industry in 1996, with net sales of $11.01 billion. Of that, $6.30 billion came from Abbott's Pharmaceutical and Nutional Products division. Abbott's latest development's in 1997 were Similac, a new formula designed to provide infants with more of the nutrients found in breastmilk, and Norvir, a treatment for children with HIV and AIDS. Abbott marketed products in more than 130 countries and employed 52,000 people in 1996. Of those, 5,000 were scientists engaged in research and development, on which Abbott spends approximately $1 billion each year. Research areas the company focuses on include: immunoscience, anti-infectives, neuroscience, and aging and degenerative diseases. Abbott was founded in 1888 by Dr. Wallace C. Abbott. His "dosimetric granules," which enabled precise measurement of drug dosages, revolutionized the industry.

Other industry leaders included Pfizer, with $11.30 billion in 1996 sales and 47,000 employees. Eli Lilly, headquartered in Indianapolis, Indiana, had $7.34 billion in 1996 sales and was the maker of

Prozac, on the market for ten years as of 1997. Also as of 1997, more than 24 million patients had been prescribed Prozac as a remedy for depression. American Home Products, had estimated $6.4 billion in pharmaceutical sales (of $10.6 billion total).

More than 20 companies were merged over its history to form industry leader Pharmacia & Upjohn, the largest of which were those between KaviVitrum and Pharmacia in 1990, between Kabi Pharmacia and Farmitalia Carlo Erba in 1993, and between Pharmacia and Upjohn in 1995. Net sales for Pharmacia & Upjohn in 1996 were $7.2 billion, a 3.3 percent increase over 1995 sales of $6.9 billion. The company is a global leader in areas such as infectious diseases, metabolic diseases, women's health, and ophthamology. Between 1995 and 1998, Pharmacia & Upjohn expected to launch at least 25 new products, including rescriptor, an antiviral drug to fight AIDS. OTC medications manufactured included Cortaid, Kaopectate, and Motrin IB. The company also manufactured Nicorette/Nicotrol and Rogaine.

WORK FORCE

Work in the preparations segment of the pharmaceutical industry is concentrated in the largest companies. Unlike other manufacturing sectors, employment in the pharmaceutical industry grew 45 percent from 1980 to 1992. About 43 percent of the estimated 141,400 people employed in the industry nationwide worked in production, while research, marketing, and administration accounted for the remainder. Merck and Squibb have been described as fulfilling places to work because of their aggressive research departments. Merck did, however, endure a 15-week strike by its unionized workers in 1985. Johnson & Johnson has also enjoyed a solid reputation as an employer, offering progressive child-care and maternity leave policies.

Even though the health care reform movement of the early 1990s failed, employees of the pharmaceutical industry faced large scale layoffs. The rise of MCOs and chain hospitals reduced the need for the large sales staffs major companies traditionally employed. Competitive pressures exacted a heavy toll on drug company employment in the mid-1990s, with an estimated 60,000 positions cut from 1993 to 1996. Most of the cuts were coming from marketing and promotion personnel rather than vital research and development employees. Industry observers noted that ongoing rationalizations of overcapacity would put "thousands more" out of work before the end of the decade.

AMERICA AND THE WORLD

The U.S. Department of Commerce estimated in 1994 that American pharmaceutical manufacturers produced nearly half of the major pharmaceuticals marketed worldwide, while the domestic market consumed approximately 65 percent of this output. Nevertheless, exports accounted for over 30 percent of sales for several major American drug companies in 1992, including Merck, Pfizer, and Johnson & Johnson. Europe, alone, consumed half of American pharmaceutical shipments, though sales to European Union (EU) countries and Japan slumped in 1993 because of world-wide recession and new price controls in many European nations. The finalization of the EU economic union in 1993, along with the passage of the North American Free Trade Agreement (NAFTA) in 1994 promised to improve the competitive position of American pharmaceutical companies overseas.

The formal economic integration of European Union countries did not immediately fulfill industry expectations. Before unification, American companies selling or producing in Europe navigated a mine field of conflicting national price controls (most European countries have national health care systems that control costs), quality standards, and approval requirements for each new drug introduction, while also worrying about adequate patent protection. Similar problems faced U.S. pharmaceutical companies in Japan, the country with the highest per capita consumption of pharmaceuticals in the world with over 20 percent of the global market.

The importance of international relationships illustrated the traditionally global character of the pharmaceutical industry. Like European and Japanese counterparts, American companies historically produced, manufactured, and marketed in each other's backyard. Rather than directly investing in full-scale overseas operations, many formed joint licensing agreements or joint ventures with home companies overseas to manufacture and market products in other countries. In the 1990s American OTC leader Warner-Lambert started a joint venture with British Glaxo to develop and market an OTC version of Glaxo's blockbuster anti-ulcer drug Zantac. Many American pharmaceutical firms, including Warner-Lambert, however, continued to have overseas production and marketing networks under their own control. Giants such as Merck, American Home Products, and Eli Lilly operated worldwide, while many European firms maintained extensive U.S. operations.

RESEARCH AND TECHNOLOGY

Though the federal government and academic institutions pursue both basic and applied research that often directly affects drug development, approximately 90 percent of new drugs come from the drug industry. However, analysts emphasize the importance of researchers financed by the National Institutes of Health (NIH) in initiating path-breaking drug developments, and the role of academic researchers (often with both NIH and drug company financing) in revolutionary cell-receptor research as well as initial chemical trials cannot be denied.

The Pharmaceutical Manufacturers Association (PMA) estimated in 1993 that its member companies invested, as an annual average, between 11 percent and 16 percent of the value of pharmaceutical sales in the research and development of new drugs between 1970 and 1992. Meanwhile, Standard and Poor's reported in its 1994 *Survey* that the drug industry's "ratio of research-to-sales ranks as the highest of all major domestic industrial groups." Competitive pressures did exert some downward force on this, the lifeblood of the business, in the mid-1990s, as average annual increases in industry wide investment slid to 9.3 percent in 1994. According to *Chemical Marketing Reporter,* it was "the first single-digit increase since 1977."

For patented prescription producers, the actual research and development of new drugs, especially after the adoption of the 1962 FDA regulatory guidelines, had always been an intricate process, sometimes referred to as "playing chess with nature." Company researchers began by screening or developing any number of New Chemical Entities (NCE's) that showed promise in a therapeutic class, on a specific disease, or with a specific cell receptor. Once one of these showed therapeutic potential, the company proceeded to move the new compound through a series of preclinical trials with animals to determine its toxicity at various doses. After initial testing, the research company generally patented its new chemical and announced to the FDA its intention to begin human trials. The potential drug then moved through three distinct phases of human clinical trials, often taking seven years. The process was designed to expose possible adverse reactions, determine safe and effective dosages for humans, and test treatment. Once an NCE successfully survived these trials, and 19 of 20 did not because of ineffectiveness or toxicity, the company submitted a completed New Drug Application (NDA) to the FDA seeking final market approval for the new therapy. Even after market approval, a fourth phase could result in a recall or new label warnings if the

drug showed adverse reactions in the larger population.

By its own regulations, the FDA was supposed to complete an NDA review within six months. By the 1990s though, review time in the understaffed agency had risen to over two years. Thus, by the time a company's new drug reached market, almost ten of its 17 years of patent exclusivity had disappeared, a point drug companies used to justify high prices. To address this problem, and to raise more revenue in order to add review staff to the FDA, Congress passed the Prescription Drug User Fee Act in 1992. This legislation generated over $325 million in five years and helped speed average NDAs by ten months. In fact, the FDA was expected to approve a record-breaking 30 new molecular entities in 1996. Drug delivery systems and biotechnology were two particularly active areas of research and development in the mid-1990s. Seeking ways to improve the therapeutic and economic performance of their products, pharmaceutical companies began to expand beyond the traditional delivery systems to inhalation, transmucosal, transdermal, and implantation methods. Examples include: timed-release capsules, implantable pumps, computerized inhalers, and "lollipop" sedatives.

FURTHER READING

"About Pharmacia & Upjohn." Available from http://www.pharmacia.se/about/history.html.

Ballance, Robert et al. *The World's Pharmaceutical Industries.* Brookfield, VT: Edward Elgar Publishing, 1992.

Borman, Stu. "Growth of Drug R&D Spending Slow in '94." *Chemical and Engineering News,* 17 January 1994.

Conlan, Michael. "OTA Undermines Industry R&D Case, but PMA Cries Foul." *Drug Topics,* 5 April 1993.

The Contribution of Pharmaceutical Companies: What's at Stake for America. Boston: The Boston Consulting Group, September 1993.

Darnay, Arsen J., ed. *Manufacturing USA.* 5th ed. Detroit: Gale Research, 1996.

"Drug R& D Spending Increasing Slowly." *Chemical Marketing Reporter,* 17 January 1994, 5.

Flynn, Julia et al. "A Shot in the Arm for Drugmakers." *Business Week,* 21 September 1992.

Goldman, Jonathan. "Pharmaceuticals Are Looking Good." *Institutional Investor,* December 1996.

Higby, Gregory, and Elaine Stroud, eds. *Pill Peddlers.* Madison, WI: American Institute of the History of Pharmacy, 1990.

Hoover's Handbook of American Business. Austin, TX: Hoovers Inc., 1997.

Inside U.S. Business. Homewood, IL: Business One Irwin, 1991.

"Internal Biotechnology Units Offer Growth for Pharmaceutical Firms." *Chemical and Engineering News,* 6 December 1993.

International Directory of Company Histories. Chicago: St. James Press, 1990.

Lerner, Matthew, and J. Robert Warren. "Delivering the Goods." *Chemical Marketing Reporter,* 5 August 1996.

Liebenau, Jonathan. *Medical Science and Medical Industry.* Baltimore: Johns Hopkins University Press, 1987.

"Mr. Nice Guy with a Mission." *Business Week Industrial Edition,* 25 November 1996, 132.

"New Pfizer Animal Health Becomes Industry Giant." *Agri Marketing,* September 1995, 48.

Nielsen, Robert. *Handbook of Federal Drug Law.* Philadelphia: Lea and Febiger, 1992.

"Pharmaceutical Results Improve Helped By New Product Launches." *Chemical Market Reporter,* 27 January 1997, 15.

"Pharmaceuticals '93, a CMR Special Report." *Chemical Marketing Reporter,* 8 March 1993.

Prescription Drug Industry Fact Book 1980. Washington: Pharmaceutical Manufacturer's Association, 1980.

Schonfeld, Erick. "Yum! The New Treat In Biotech." *Fortune,* 14 October 1996, 293-294.

Serwer, Andrew E. "Layoffs Tail Off-But Only For Some." *Fortune,* 20 March 1995, 14.

Shon, Melissa. "Industry, Heal Thyself: Pharmaceuticals '94, a CMR Special Report," *Chemical Marketing Reporter,* 7 March 1994.

Spilker, Bert. *Multinational Drug Companies: Issues in Drug Discovery and Development.* New York: Raven Press, 1989.

Standard & Poor's Industry Surveys. New York: Standard & Poor's Corporation, 29 August 1996.

Sterne, Diana. "How Come Drug Prices Are So High? Conference Hears Answer." *Drug Topics,* 20 April 1992.

Thayer, Ann M. "Biopharmaceuticals Overcoming Market Hurdles." *Chemical and Engineering News,* 25 February 1991.

Trends in U.S. Pharmaceutical Sales and R&D. Washington: Pharmaceutical Manufacturers Association, 1993.

U.S. Department of Commerce. International Trade Administration. *U.S. Industrial Outlook 1994.* Washington: GPO, 1994. Available from http://sci.dixie.edu/Business Information/IndustryOutlooks/IndustryOutlooks.html.

Weatherall, M. *In Search of a Cure.* Oxford: Oxford University Press, 1990.

Wechsler, Jill. "The Accelerating Assault on Rx Marketing." *Pharmaceutical Executive,* November 1994, 16.

—J. Jacob Jones, updated by April Dougal Gasbarre

SIC 2835

IN VITRO AND IN VIVO DIAGNOSTIC SUBSTANCES

This category covers establishments primarily engaged in manufacturing in vitro ("in glass," such as a test tube) and in vivo ("in the body") diagnostic substances, whether or not packaged for retail sale. These materials are chemical, biological, or radioactive substances used in diagnosing or monitoring the state of human or veterinary health by identifying and measuring normal or abnormal constituents of body fluids or tissues.

According to data compiled by the U.S. Department of Commerce, shipments made by establishments classified in **SIC 2835: In Vitro and In Vivo Diagnostic Substances** during 1990 were valued at $2.46 billion, an increase of 5.9 percent over figures for 1989. In 1993 shipments were valued at $5.2 billion, a 5 percent increase. Also in 1993, exports reported a 9 percent jump to reach $1.5 billion. By 1995 total diagnostic product sales surged to $8.9 billion. The primary market for these diagnostic substances has been hospitals and laboratories, but sales to physicians and individual consumers have seen considerable growth.

Government analysts predicted that the market for medical diagnostic products would increase. Projections for long-term growth were modest at 2 percent per year. Early in the 1990s, however, industry watchers expected a reduction in the number of establishments as a result of industry consolidation. Overall prices of IVD substances only increased 1.8 percent in 1995 and made up less than 1 percent of the total U.S. spending on healthcare. Areas within the industry that are expected to see the most expansion are establishments providing diagnostics for sexually transmitted diseases, diabetes, and cellular disorders.

Many of the products produced by the in vitro and in vivo diagnostics industry are regulated by the U.S. Food and Drug Administration (FDA). In 1989 the FDA gave its approval to new non-ionic (having no electrical charge) contrast media for use with innovative X-ray technologies including computed tomography (CT) and magnetic resonance imaging (MRI). These "in vivo" (used in the body) non-ionic products were able to disperse more readily and created fewer side effects such as nausea, pain, and allergic reactions.

The current trend in the industry is to miniaturize the machinery and make them more portable. This point-of-care (POC) testing is expected to present the greatest growth area in the near future for IVD. Already, the technology has found its way into hospitals and medical centers, and will soon be available in the home health care field. FDA approval of other products, such as an imaging agent for use with ultrasound technology, is expected to help bolster the industry. Yet, as the industry has grown, FDA approval time has slowed and more stringent governmental regulations have been enacted.

One of the leading companies classified in **SIC 2835: In Vitro and In Vivo Diagnostic Substances** was Bio-Rad Laboratories, Inc. Based in Hercules, California, Bio-Rad supplied more than 4,500 different products for laboratory and medical research including chemicals and instruments to diagnose and monitor diseases such as anemia, diabetes, and AIDS. The company developed clinical diagnostics test kits and analytical instruments, including a blood glucose analyzer. Established in 1957 with four employees, by 1995 Bio-Rad employed 2,460 workers in the United States and abroad. In 1995, sales were reported to be $396.6 million. The company's 25,000 customers, located in seventy countries, included universities, pharmaceutical companies, biotechnology firms, medical laboratories, and government agencies. In 1995, Bio-Rad and Hewlett Packard signed an exclusive licensing agreement that transferred HP's HP5965B infrared detector (IRD) technology and assets to Bio-Rad's Digilab Division. The two companies also planned to work on developing new technology in this field.

FURTHER READING

"Bio-Rad laboratories, Inc." *San Francisco Times,* 6 August 1993.

Health Industry Manufactures Association. "In Vitro Diagnostics: Medical Tests that Save Lives and Reduce Health Care Costs." Available from http://www.himanet.com/about/ivdfactsheet.html.

Kleinfield, N. R. "The Do-It-Yourself Armamentarium." *New York Times Magazine,* 3 October 1993.

Lipold, John. "Diagnostics Leap into the Future." *Chemical Marketing Reporter,* 20 March 1989.

Rauber, Chris. "High-Tech Outfit Tends Low Profile." *San Francisco Business Times,* 6 December 1991.

Scheck, Anne. "Plucking the Point-of-Care Plums." *IVDT Industry News* January/February 1996. Available from http://www.concom.com/ivd/jan96/toc.html.

Thompson, Bradley Merril. "In Vitro Diagnostics." *Medical Device & Diagnostic Industry,* May 1993.

U.S. Department of Commerce. International Trade Administration. *U.S. Industrial Outlook 1994.* Washington: GPO, 1994.

—Karen Bellenir, updated by Nancy Hatch Woodward

SIC 2836

BIOLOGICAL PRODUCTS, EXCEPT DIAGNOSTIC SUBSTANCES

This category covers establishments primarily engaged in the production of bacterial and virus vaccines, toxoids, and analogous products (such as allergenic extracts), serums, plasmas, and other blood derivatives for human or veterinary use, other than *in vitro* and *in vivo* diagnostic substances. Included in this industry are establishments primarily engaged in the production of microbiological products for other uses. Establishments primarily engaged in manufacturing *in vitro* and *in vivo* diagnostic substances are classified in **SIC 2835: In Vitro and In Vivo Diagnostic Substances.**

INDUSTRY SNAPSHOT

According to statistics compiled by the U.S. Department of Commerce, establishments classified in **SIC 2836: Biological Products, Except Diagnostic Substances** shipped products valued at $2.16 billion in 1990. By 1996, shipments had reached an estimated $6.15 billion, an increase of almost 10 percent over 1995. Exports stood at $1.56 billion in 1995, while imports totaled $613 million, up 10 percent over 1994. The largest class of products within the industry were blood and blood derivatives. They accounted for 33.3 percent of sales. Other major product classifications were vaccines, toxoids, and antigens (24.9 percent); biological products for veterinary, industrial and other uses (21.7 percent); and antitoxins, antivenins, immune globulins, therapeutic immune serums, and allergic extracts (9.8 percent). Other biological products (except diagnostics) not specified by kind accounted for the remaining 10.3 percent.

Government forecasters anticipated that sales of products derived from biotechnology would experience annual increases of 15 to 20 percent between 1992 and 1997. In 1996, this estimate was changed to reflect only a modest gain of 2 percent annually. The greatest growth was expected in medical products, but analysts warned that their development could be restrained as a result of changes in national health care priorities, strategies, and payment practices. Advances made in the evolution of non-medical biotech products were expected to be limited because of price constraints and uncertain public acceptance of genetically engineered foods and products.

BACKGROUND AND DEVELOPMENT

Biological products were created with biotechnology, the scientific and engineering procedures involved in manipulating organisms or biological components at the cellular, subcellular, or molecular level. These manipulations were carried out to make or modify plants and animals or other biological substances with desired traits. Although examples of primitive biotech processes dated back to ancient times (such as the use of fermentation in brewing and leavening agents in baking), their use in medical and pharmaceutical applications was an innovation of the latter decades of the twentieth century. Some analysts compared the biotech industry's impact on global medical care with the computer industry's impact on communication.

Biotech researchers produced products in essentially three ways: by developing ways to achieve commercial production of naturally occurring substances; by genetically altering naturally occurring substances; and by creating entirely new substances. Some of the tools used by biotech researchers included recombinant DNA and monoclonal antibodies. Recombinant DNA involved the ability to take the deoxyribonucleic acid (DNA) from one organism and combine it with the DNA from another organism thereby creating new products and processes. By using recombinant DNA techniques researchers were able to select specific genes and introduce them into other cells or living organisms to create products with specific attributes. Monoclonal antibodies were developed from cultures of single cells using cloning techniques. They were designed for use in attacking toxins, viruses, and cancer cells.

The U.S. Food and Drug Administration (FDA) required extensive scrutiny of products developed by biotech researchers before they could be offered for sale. Because the biological products presented for approval often involved new technologies or innovative therapies for diseases that had not been previously treated successfully, the approval process frequently proved to be long and costly. Many companies struggled financially through the 1980s waiting for an FDA determination.

One of the earliest biological products introduced to the U.S. marketplace was a blood protein first sold in 1966. The blood protein, called Factor VIII, was used by patients with hemophilia A to control bleeding episodes. Factor VIII, the blood factor responsible for normal clotting action, was manufactured from human blood received from donors. It was followed by the development of Factor IX for patients with hemophilia B.

During the early 1980s, problems arose as a result of AIDS contamination in the blood supply used to produce blood clotting factors. In 1984 manufacturers began using a heat treatment process to guard against future contamination, but, according to a report in the *Wall Street Journal,* approximately half of the nation's 20,000 hemophiliacs contracted AIDS, primarily through the use of Factors VIII and IX.

The earliest FDA approval for a modern biotech product designed for human therapeutic use was given to human insulin in 1982. Human insulin was used for treating patients with diabetes. Other product approvals followed in subsequent years. In 1984 the FDA approved an agricultural vaccine against colibacillosis (a disease commonly called scours, which causes diarrhea or dysentery in newborn animals). Approval was given in 1985 to a human growth hormone (HGH) for the treatment of dwarfism.

The first genetically engineered vaccine approved for use in the United States was a vaccine against hepatitis-B. It received approval in 1986. The vaccine had been created by inserting part of a hepatitis-B virus into yeast cells. Although the portion of the hepatitis-B virus used was not infectious, it caused an immune reaction against infection from the entire hepatitis-B virus.

Other firsts occurring in 1986 included the approval of therapeutic monoclonal antibodies (MABs) and alpha interferon. MABs were approved for use along with immunosuppressive drugs to help prevent kidney rejection in transplant patients. Alpha interferon's first approved use was in the treatment of hairy cell leukemia. Other approved uses for alpha interferon followed: for Kaposi's sarcoma in 1988, venereal warts in 1988, non-A/non-B hepatitis in 1991, and hepatitis-B in 1992. A product to dissolve blood clots in patients with acute myocardial infarction (heart attack) was approved in 1987. An agricultural vaccine to protect against pseudorabies won FDA approval the same year.

Erythropoietin (EPO), which was to become the largest single biotech product, received its first FDA approval in 1989. EPO, a protein that stimulates production of red blood cells, won initial approval for use with anemia associated with kidney disease. In the same year, the Health Care Financing Administration agreed to pay for EPO given to dialysis patients under the Medicare program. Within a few years, EPO was being used by approximately 82,000 dialysis patients in the United States. In 1991 the FDA gave additional approval for its use in treating AIDS-related anemia.

Advances continued during the 1990s. As the industry matured, cooperation between product developers and government regulators improved. The steps in the approval process became more predictable, and a shift in technology was also noted. The primary products of the 1980s had involved the use of recombinant DNA proteins without further alterations. During the early 1990s, researchers turned their attention to products requiring more extensive genetic modification and to more obscure applications.

During the first few years of the 1990s, the FDA granted approval for several products with uses targeting human conditions. These included a treatment for chronic granulomatous disease (a genetic abnormality affecting the immune system and resulting in severe or life-threatening infections), for acute pulmonary embolism, to aid in chemotherapy and bone marrow transplants, and for kidney cancer. Products wining FDA approval for veterinary use included a vaccine against feline leukemia and a treatment for canine lymphoma.

CURRENT CONDITIONS

By the end of the 1980s, sales of products developed around recombinant DNA technology exceeded $1 billion according to a study done by Consulting Resources and reported in *Chemicalweek.* Consulting Resources expected such sales to reach $4.29 billion by 1995 and to more than double again by the end of the century. The industry surpassed those estimates in 1994 by having $4.39 billion in sales—and in 1996 the value of shipments were estimated to have reached $6.15 billion.

Some industry watchers predicted that most of the pharmaceutical products developed during the 1990s would result from ongoing biotechnical research. The *U.S. Industrial Outlook 1993* reported that recent FDA approvals for vaccines against rabies, tetanum toxoids, and pertussis had been made. According to government statements, vaccines were one of the most effective and cheapest ways to eradicate some diseases. Concern about health care costs during the early 1990s focused the national spotlight on the pharmaceutical industry and questions were raised about the high cost of biological products.

INDUSTRY LEADERS

In 1996 there were over 70 companies with more than 7,300 employees engaged in the production of

biological products. One of the leading establishments classified in **SIC 2836: Biological Products, Except Diagnostic Substances** was Genentech, Incorporated. Headquartered in San Francisco, Genentech pioneered the development of first-generation biotech products. In 1988, the FDA approved the company's application for Activase, which was used to dissolve blood clots in heart attack patients. Approval, however, came only after a lengthy regulatory review and initial sales failed to meet projections. These difficulties left the company financially unstable. Roche Holdings Limited, a Swiss pharmaceutical maker, acquired majority ownership of Genentech in 1990. Under Roche's umbrella, Genentech continued to make significant contributions to the industry.

According to a report in *Chemical and Engineering News,* 5 of the 12 biopharmaceuticals on the market in the early 1990s were products developed by Genentech. The company's human growth hormone (HGH) was used to treat patients with pituitary growth hormone deficiencies. During the 1990s, other uses of HGH were under study including a treatment for Turner's syndrome (a genetic abnormality associated with the absence of a second sex chromosome often resulting in short stature and lack of some aspects of sexual development after puberty), pediatric burns, and growth retardation related to kidney disease. In 1990 sales of HGH by Genentech were reported to be $155 million; by 1994, sales had skyrocketed to $544 million, and the company employed over 2,300 employees.

In 1993 the FDA granted Genetech's request for approval of Pulmozyme, the first drug treatment developed for cystic fibrosis, a genetic disease associated with lung infections and life-threatening mucous secretions in the lungs. Pulmozyme was also being studied for its effectiveness in treating chronic bronchitis. Other products in various stages of research and development included substances to treat kidney cancer, AIDS wasting syndrome, diabetes, breast cancer, and ischemic stroke. Genetech's researchers were also working to develop a vaccine against the HIV virus and on substances to aid in immunotherapy for HIV-infected patients. Another drug developed by Genentech during the 1990s was Acctimmune, used for the management of chronic granulomatous disease.

In October, 1992, Genentech opened a 275,000 square-foot, $85 million facility, hailed as the world's largest research facility for biotechnology. The company followed in 1995 with a $62.5 million Process Science Center. In 1996, the company held over 1,500 patents worldwide, and had more than 1,200 pending.

The second largest company in this industry is Alpha Therapeutic Corporation with $380 million in sales in 1996 and 2,500 employees. The company, which has its headquarters in Los Angeles, was incorporated in 1978 by the Green Cross Corporation of Osaka, Japan. Alpha Therapeutic provides home infusion products and services, with their top products including Venoglobulin, AlphNine, Alphanate, Albutien, and Plasmatein. In 1996, the company was in the midst of a four-year $45 million facility expansion.

Another industry leader, Baxter Healthcare Corporation, Hyland Division, was headquartered in Glendale, California. The company had approximately $300 million in sales in the mid-1990s and employed more than 900 workers. In December of 1992, Baxter received approval from the FDA to sell Recombinate, the first genetically engineered drug to be used in the treatment of hemophilia A. Although Recombinate was expected to be more expensive than blood-derived Factor VIII, it did not carry the risk of transmitting the AIDS or hepatitis viruses, and its supply was not constrained by blood shortages.

In 1994, Baxter withdrew one of its products, Gammagard, from the market because of possible contamination with hepatitis-C, a virus potentially leading to chronic hepatitis or liver disease. Gammagard, an intravenous immune-globulin product used to treat inherited immunological disorders and to aid in bone-marrow transplants, was made with concentrated human proteins derived from donated blood plasma. Although no approved diagnostic test was able to directly test for the presence of hepatitis-C, the company screened all donated blood for hepatitis-C antibodies. According to a report in the *Wall Street Journal*, Baxter stated that 14 patients being treated with Gammagard had contracted hepatitis-C, but it was uncertain if other risk factors may have been involved.

Genzyme Corporation, with headquarters in Cambridge, Massachusetts, is another major producer of biological products. The company's researchers produced products in niche markets, especially those targeted at genetic diseases. Genzyme's product line had an estimated potential worldwide market of about $2 billion in the mid-1990s. The *New York Times* called Genzyme "one of a handful of biotech companies that can boast of being in the black." In 1991 the company announced a decision to build a $75 million biopharmaceutical production facility in Massachusetts. By the mid-1990s, Genzyme's sales had reached $219 million, and they employed 1,500 workers.

One of the best known Genzyme products was Ceredase, which was used to treat Type 1 Gaucher's disease. Gaucher's disease, an incurable metabolic dis-

order most common among people of Eastern European Jewish ancestry, affects between 2,000 and 3,000 people in the United States. The *Wall Street Journal* reported that Ceredase sales accounted for about half of the company's revenues during the first nine months of 1993. Although successful from an economic point of view, Ceredase was considered controversial because of its cost, which varied depending on age, weight, and severity of the disease, but averaged around $140,000 per year. In 1994, the company received approval for Cerezyme, which was also used to treat Type 1 Gaucher's disease.

In addition, Ceredase was made from GCR, a human placental product available only from one supplier in France, Pasteur Merieux. Following problems with contaminated blood, the French health ministry issued a ruling in 1993 ordering Pasteur Merieux to stop the production of human albumin from placentas. Although Ceredase did not contain human albumin, the cost of extracting its ingredient (GCR) had previously been shared with the costs of extracting human albumin. With extraction costs falling exclusively on GCR production, Genzyme's annual costs to make Ceredase were expected to increase up to $22 million.

AMERICA AND THE WORLD

Exports by U.S. biotech companies exceeded imports. According to government statistics, exports totaled $973 million in 1990, $1.19 billion in 1992, and $1.56 billion in 1995. Imports totaled $271 million in 1990, $420 million in 1992, and $613 million in 1995.

Although U.S. biotech companies pioneered the development of the industry, other countries were making significant progress. For example, research for an AIDS vaccine led to increased understanding of therapeutic vaccines in Switzerland. Industry watchers also noted that Japanese scientists were making gains. Some feared that future market domination by the Japanese could parallel the earlier experience of the electronics industry.

RESEARCH AND TECHNOLOGY

In 1987, the U.S. Patent and Trademark Office announced that it would issue patents on non-naturally occurring nonhuman animals, thus opening the door for patenting biotech-engineered animals. Although some hailed the decision as a boon to biotechnical research, others objected on ethical and religious grounds. The decision also drew protests from animal rights activists and environmental groups.

Products expected to be considered for FDA approval during the mid-1990s included a herpes simplex II vaccine, an insulin-like growth factor, an antitumor necrosis factor, and a product using a toxic protein to combat septic shock. In addition, biotech researchers were studying ways to combat bacterial diseases resistant to antibiotics such as drug-resistant tuberculosis.

AIDS research also received considerable attention throughout the 1990s. Recombinant DNA techniques had been used to demonstrate the life cycle of the human immunodeficiency virus (HIV) and show how the virus caused AIDS. Recombinant DNA techniques were also being used in the search for vaccines and therapeutic agents for AIDS treatment. Other areas of ongoing research in ways to use DNA focused on heart disease, cancer, Parkinson's disease, and bone marrow recovery in patients following transplantation.

FURTHER READING

"Baxter Withdraws Gammagard, Citing Hepatitis C in Users." *Wall Street Journal,* 25 February 1994.

"Biotech Booms in Boston." *Barron's,* 13 April 1992.

Burton, Thomas M. "Hemophiliacs Sue Firms, Foundation Over AIDS in '80s." *Wall Street Journal,* 1 October 1993.

Darnay, Arsen, ed. *Manufacturing USA.* 5th ed. Detroit: Gale Research, 1996.

Fisher, Lawrence M. "Rehabilitation of a Biotech Pioneer." *New York Times,* 8 May 1994.

Genentech. "The Biopharmaceuticals: FDA-Approved Biopharmaceutical Drugs and Vaccines." Access Excellence. 1997. Available from http://www.gene.com.ae.

Genentech. "Genentech, Inc. Scientific Achievements." Access Excellence. 1997. Available from http://www.gene.com.ae.

"Genzyme Gets Patent on Second Treatment for Gaucher Disease." *Wall Street Journal,* 31 August 1993.

Heller, Karen. "For Investors, It's More Than Just Hope Now." *Chemicalweek,* 17 January 1990.

"Hemophilia Drug Approved." *New York Times,* 11 December 1992.

Hunter, David and Gregory Morris. "Biotech Grows Up" and "New Techniques Drive Drugs to Market." *Chemicalweek,* 17 January 1990.

Matveld, H. Edward and Karen L. White. "Alpha Therapeutic Corporation." 1997. Available from http://www.biospace.com/exhib_script/exhibitors/AlphaTherapeuticCorporation.cfm.

"Recent Trends in Drugs." U.S. Department of Commerce. Bureau of the Census. 1996. Available from gopher://gopher.umsl.edu/oo/library/govdocs/usio0048.

Rotman, David. "States Fight Inertia in Biotech Regs." *Chemicalweek,* 17 January 1990.

"Ruling May Push Up the Price of Ceredase, Genzyme's Key Drug." *Wall Street Journal,* 3 December 1993.

Swarbrick, James, and James C. Boylan, eds. *Encyclopedia of Pharmaceutical Technology.* Vol. 2. New York: Marcel Dekker, July 1989.

Thayer, Ann M. "Biopharmaceuticals Overcoming Market Hurdles." *Chemical and Engineering News,* 25 February 1991.

U.S. Department of Commerce. International Trade Administration. *U.S. Industrial Outlook 1993.* Washington: GPO, 1994.

Ward, Leah Beth. "Play-It-Safe Genzyme Defies the Biotech Stereotypes." *New York Times,* 24 January 1993.

—Karen Bellenir, updated by Nancy Hatch Woodward

SIC 2841

SOAP AND OTHER DETERGENTS, EXCEPT SPECIALTY CLEANERS

This category includes establishments primarily engaged in the manufacture of soap and detergents. It includes companies who make crude and refined glycerin products from fats, or synthetic detergents such as laundry detergents, dishwashing compounds, and personal cleansing bars. Establishments primarily involved in the manufacture of specialty cleaning products are classified in **SIC 2842: Specialty Cleaning, Polishing, and Sanitation Preparations.** Establishments primarily involved in the manufacture of shampoos and shaving products are classified in **SIC 2844: Perfumes, Cosmetics, and Other Toilet Preparations.**

INDUSTRY SNAPSHOT

The soap and detergents industry's $3.9 billion marketplace in the United States faced increasing competition entering the late 1990s. Having to contend with increasing globalization, the U.S. market expanded 3.7 percent in 1995. High performance formulations that omitted bleach were the largest growing segments of this industry. In addition to environmental and health questions, societal transformation propelled changes in the soap and detergent industry during the late 1990s. Among the numerous factors presenting challenges to detergent formulators were: the need for improved sanitation; the increasing numbers of women working outside the home; the development of time-saving appliances; the trend towards using less energy by lowering wash temperatures; the need to conserve water; and changes in textiles and other cleanable surfaces.

Detergent modifications were also spurred by technical innovation, such as bleach additives, better optical brighteners, and improved technologies to release soils. Marketers packaged products differently to meet the needs of specialized users such as households with infants or with men performing tasks traditionally associated with women's roles. To meet the needs of various market segments, the industry saw a proliferation of brands and varieties. For example, a typical large supermarket might contain more than forty varieties of laundry detergents including both liquids and powders.

Industry trends for the late 1990s included the environmentally friendly "Ultra" or concentrated detergents and liquid soaps. However, analysts claimed that the increasing popularity of liquid soaps would not affect the sales of bar soaps in any way. Another popular trend was the consumers' growing interest in small soaps and detergents shops, such as Crabtree and Evelyn and The Body Shop, which used herbal and natural materials in their products.

BACKGROUND AND DEVELOPMENT

The soap and detergent industry's origins are obscured in antiquity. Michael C. Crossin, writing for *Soap, Cosmetics, Chemical Specialties,* stated "the caveman who fell into the river with his fur still on quickly learned that water is an excellent aid in the removal of soils and odors from garments." Crossin calls this find "the single most important discovery in laundry history."

Water alone, however, was not sufficient for all cleaning needs. The next important breakthrough was the development of soap. Different accounts place its invention between 2500 B.C. and 300 B.C. The word "soap" may have been derived from Mt. Sapo, near Rome, a place where burnt offerings were made to the gods. People discovered that the fat and ash residue from the offerings had cleaning properties.

By definition, soap is a cleansing product created through the chemical process of combining a fat or natural oil with an alkali (such as wood ashes or lye) under controlled conditions. Soap-producing factories developed in France and Italy, where olive oil was plentiful and used as the main ingredient, throughout the sixteenth, seventeenth, and eighteenth centuries. In the nineteenth century, palm oil began to replace olive oil in formulations. By the turn of the twentieth century, many people still made soap by boiling fats and lye to produce solid cakes.

In the United States, the soapmaking industry marks 1837 as an important year. In that year, William Procter and James Gamble established a candle and soapmaking business. Their company, Procter and Gamble, went on to become one of the foremost soap and detergent makers in the country. Procter and Gamble's famous "Ivory" soap bar was first introduced in 1882. Lever Brothers, another major soap and detergent company, offered "Lifebouy" and "Sunlight" soap bars in 1895.

Procter and Gamble introduced Oxydol, a flaked laundry soap, in 1924. Oxydol was followed in 1933 by Dreft, the nation's first synthetic household detergent. Instead of soap, Dreft's formula was based on alcohol sulfates. Alcohol sulfates were the first type of surfactants to make a significant impact in the formulation of cleaning products.

The term "surfactant" comes from shortening the phrase "surface active agent." A surfactant is a type of chemical capable of changing the surface properties of a liquid. As a result of their chemical nature, surfactants help wash-water wet the surface to be cleaned quickly and thoroughly. When water and mechanical action combine to remove soils from a surface, surfactants also help keep the soil suspended in the liquid so that it does not redeposit on the item being cleaned. Surfactants are basic ingredients in most products intended for use in washing clothes and dishes.

The first synthetic detergents based on sodium dodecylbenzene sulfonate were developed in 1939. They were followed by detergents based on alkylbenzene sulfonate (ABS), which provided better cleaning and more suds than traditional soaps at lower prices. ABS grew in popularity and its use expanded with the introduction of front-loading drum washing machines.

In addition to surfactant technology, the 1930s brought the introduction of "built" soap powders and detergents. "Builders" were materials used to enhance the efficiency of a cleaner. Although they had several purposes, such as providing alkalinity to aid cleaning, keeping removed soil from redepositing, and helping to emulsify oil and grease, one of their primary functions was to overcome problems associated with water hardness. Water hardness is a measurement of the soluble metal salts (primarily formed from calcium, magnesium, iron, or manganese) in the water supply. According to the U.S. Geological Survey, water is termed "soft" when it is relatively free of soluble metal salts. It is termed "moderately hard," "hard," or "very hard" based on the amount of hardness chemicals present.

When soap products were used in hard water, a substance called ''soap curds'' or ''lime soap'' formed. The lime soap precipitate, which would not dissolve, formed in the water and stuck to surfaces causing films and deposits. Builders were used to help counteract these problems. Several types of builders were developed and they worked in different ways. Sodium carbonate, a precipitating builder, caused the water hardness materials to precipitate from the wash solution. Sodium aluminosilicate, another type of builder, inactivated water hardness materials by a chemical process called ion exchange. The most commonly used builders, complex phosphates, worked by holding water hardness materials in the wash solution through a process called sequestration.

By the late 1930s, built soaps and soap in granular form had virtually replaced laundry bar soaps. A decade later, built detergents were becoming popular. The shift from soap to detergent formulations was driven primarily by efforts to overcome problems associated with water hardness.

Detergents, although similar in function to soaps, differed from them chemically. Detergents were made from other raw materials including petroleum products and fatty acids. They often contained additional ingredients such as fluorescent whitening agents, antiredeposition agents, corrosion inhibitors, suds control agents, non-chlorine bleaches, colorants, fragrances, enzymes, blueing, and processing aids.

Built detergents, like built soaps, also contained builders to help improve cleaning efficiency. The first and most widely used builder was sodium tripolyphosphate (STPP). Formulators found STPP effective and relatively easy to process in granulated detergent. Although most built detergents were designed for laundry use, some were adapted for non-laundry household chores. Typically these adapted formulas were high sudsing detergents and could be used for tasks such as hand dishwashing or floor care.

In 1946, Procter and Gamble test marketed their new phosphate-built Tide. Tide was launched nationally in 1947 and gained widespread acceptance. Built detergents based on surfactants continued to increase in popularity and by 1953 the poundage of surfactant products sold exceeded that of soaps. The rapid expansion of synthetic detergents, however, led to problems. Reports of foaming in streams and wastewater treatment plants were first heard in the late 1940s, and by the early 1950s scientific evidence identified synthetic detergents as the cause. ABS, the most widely used surfactant, was not biodegradable and led to water contamination.

In 1951, the Association of American Soap and Glycerine Producers, predecessor to the Soap and Detergent Association, began to study the industry's environmental concerns and search for biodegradable surfactants. The federal government also investigated the environmental impact of detergents and began to address national concerns with the Federal Water Pollution Control Act of 1956.

During the early 1960s, chemists developed a new form of ABS with a different molecular structure. The new surfactant, called linear alkylbenzene sulfonate (LAS), possessed the appropriate characteristics necessary for biodegradability. In 1965, U.S. detergent manufacturers switched from ABS to LAS in household laundry detergents. Within a few years the number of foaming incidents had dropped and the amount of surfactants in the nation's waterways had been reduced.

Foaming in waterways and treatment facilities, however, was only one problem with early synthetic detergents. Another was ''eutrophication.'' Eutrophication refers to the process of adding nutrients to bodies of water. Excess nutrients caused excessive algae growth, and when the algae decayed, oxygen levels in the water decreased. With diminished levels of oxygen, water bodies were unable to support their fish populations.

Although eutrophication occurs in nature, it takes place over thousands of years. Accelerated eutrophication of water bodies, sometimes referred to as cultural eutrophication, occurred when wastewater carrying nutrients such as phosphorous and nitrogen was dumped into lakes and streams. The phosphate builders used in synthetic laundry detergents were one source of phosphorous in the nation's wastewater.

How much laundry detergents contributed to cultural eutrophication was a controversial question. Proponents of phosphate bans cited studies indicating that 25 to 30 percent of wastewater phosphorus came from laundry detergents. Those opposing phosphate bans claimed that detergents contributed only three percent of the phosphorus entering the nation's surface water, and that most eutrophication could be attributed to agricultural practices.

In the early 1970s, the United States faced rising concern about environmental issues and the problems associated with phosphates. Initial phosphate bans were enacted during the early 1970s. By 1992, statewide phosphate bans for household laundry products were in effect in Georgia, Indiana, Maryland, Michigan, Minnesota, New York, North Carolina, Pennsylvania, Vermont, Virginia, and Wisconsin. Additionally, the city of Washington, DC and parts of Idaho, Illinois (including Chicago), Montana, New Hampshire, Ohio, Oregon, and Washington had instituted similar bans. The states of Connecticut, Florida, and Maine, while not banning phosphates outright, limited their use.

Industry analysts differed in their predictions over future demand for phosphate-built products. Some predicted steady or expanded use. They noted that by the early 1990s the rate at which bans overseas were being enacted had dropped, and that in 1991 the United Kingdom refused to institute a ban. They expected domestic demand to remain stable and demand for exports, particularly to Mexico and South America, to increase. Others, however, predicted that phosphates would be completely replaced in laundry products as alternatives were developed. Citing distribution problems associated with meeting varied local regulatory requirements and prevalent consumer perceptions connecting phosphates with environmental jeopardy, they anticipated phosphates would be phased out by the end of the century.

In the United States, phosphate bans helped encourage the development of liquid laundry detergents which were formulated without phosphates. Liquids began to achieve popularity by the mid-1970s and by the close of the 1980s had captured about half the market.

The Early 1990s. The early 1990s also saw a move away from premium pricing for name brands as customers became more value conscious. Although exceptions existed, many soaps and detergents were seen as undifferentiated commodity items. In 1992, reduced value pricing was being used by approximately 40 percent of detergent manufacturers. Typically, a value-priced product cost $1 or more less than a premium-priced product.

A similar trend brought the increased popularity of "value added," multi-purpose products. These included items such as detergent with bleach or fabric softener and three-in-one personal cleansing bars. Moisturizing, deodorant, and anti-bacterial multi-benefit synthetic detergent (also called syndet) bars and soap/syndet combination bars became popular following the introduction of Lever 2000 in 1990. Analysts expected multi-benefit bars to capture 10 to 20 percent of the soap market by the mid-1990s.

The automatic dishwashing detergent (ADD) market was also undergoing transformations. Although customers had rejected first-generation ADD liquids because they separated and were difficult to get out of their bottles, gels were gaining acceptance. ADD gels,

first introduced in 1991, were easier to dispense than their liquid predecessors and maintained product consistency. By the beginning of 1992, gels accounted for 35 percent of the ADD market.

While the ADD market was not as directly impacted by the growing concern over environmental issues as was the laundry detergent market, it was influenced. ADD formulas contained four basic types of ingredients: builders, bleaching agents, surfactants, and fragrances. The builder most often used was sodium tripolyphosphate (STPP). During the early 1990s, an estimated 250 million pounds of STPP were used annually in ADD products.

By 1992, phosphate use in ADD products had not been banned as it had been for laundry detergents, and no acceptable alternative for widespread use in household, institutional, and industrial applications had been discovered. In some jurisdictions, however, phosphate use had been limited, typically to 8.7 percent of the product by weight. Even in areas unaffected by such restrictions, manufacturers often reduced the phosphate content of their products from previous levels of 14 to 16 percent to 8.7 percent for the purpose of simplifying the national distribution of their merchandise.

By the end of 1992, Shaklee Corporation was the only U.S. company having a no-phosphate ADD product on the market. Industry analysts expected consumer demand for environmentally safe products to stimulate other manufacturers in their efforts to develop additional no-phosphate ADD alternatives. Environmental concerns were also expected to move the ADD market toward concentrated formulations. The ability to produce concentrated automatic dishwashing detergents was expected to be more difficult than reformulating laundry detergents had been because ADDs do not have as many inert fillers.

Within the laundry detergent segment of the industry, environmental concerns remained primary. Along with environmental issues came an emphasis on "natural" products because they were perceived by consumers to be better for the environment. Formulations were developed for detergents without added fragrances or colors to reduce the number of chemicals used. Manufacturers also promoted "mildness" because it was seen as less harsh for the environment.

The environmental movement led to the promotion of "green" products, products said to be "earth friendly." In contrast to general trends toward value pricing, U.S. consumers demonstrated a willingness to pay slightly higher prices for environmentally friendly products. U.S. consumers, however, were not willing to accept "green" products that were inconvenient to use or those with diminished performance capabilities.

Concern for the increasing amounts of solid waste in U.S. landfills also factored into the development of concentrated detergents. The nation produced 90 million tons of garbage annually in 1960; by the 1990s that amount had risen to 160 million tons, and some forecasters expected it to reach more than 190 million tons by the year 2000. Manufacturers discussed the nation's growing problems with solid waste management experts and developed responses. Concentrates used smaller volumes of some chemicals, required less packaging, and reduced transportation expenses. The percentage of plastic in the nation's garbage had been less than three percent in 1970, but was expected to reach nine percent by 2000. To emphasize their proactive environmental policies, manufacturers promoted the waste-reduction benefits of cartons made from recycled paper, measuring scoops made from recycled plastics, and containers that were recyclable.

The use of phosphates continued to be controversial. By 1990, phosphate usage in laundry products for household use had been banned in all the Great Lakes states and in many states draining into the Chesapeake Bay. The issue was still politically alive in the Pacific Northwest, and the industry continued its search for cost-effective, high-performance alternatives. Industry watchers expected major manufacturers to turn more heavily to non-phosphate detergents even in areas unaffected by bans because of distribution problems associated with supplying different formulas to different regions.

In addition to environmental questions, another area of concern for manufacturers involved the use of animal testing. During the 1970s and 1980s, animal testing had been widely used as a tool in investigating the safety of detergent ingredients. Animals were used to determine the likelihood of human reactions, the severity of possible injuries, and the time necessary for healing. Rabbits and monkeys were frequently used to discover if certain chemicals or combinations of chemicals would cause eye irritation. Animal rights organizations promoted bans on certain kinds of tests and favored regulations which would require labels to state if animal testing had been used in developing a product. The soap and detergent industry responded with claims that it was working on developing alternatives but some animal tests were still required. One promising alternative was the development of "in vitro" (meaning "in glass") tests.

According to Keith A. Booman, Technical Director for the Soap and Detergent Association, the use of animal testing was reduced by 64 percent between 1980 and 1988. In 1989, Booman wrote in *Soap, Cosmetics, Chemical Specialties* , "Further reductions in animal testing by the detergent industry at this time would impair its ability to evaluate the safety of new products for consumers." He predicted, however, that with further research the causes of chemical-induced injuries would be better understood. The results would thus assist researchers in their efforts to develop batteries of non-animal tests to help further reduce reliance on animal testing.

In 1991, the soap and detergent industry's shipments were valued at $14.4 billion. The amount represented an increase of 3.2 percent over figures from 1990, but the rate of growth was smaller than in previous years. Officials with the U.S. Department of Commerce attributed the slowing growth to the overall national economic picture. Among the factors negatively impacting demand for cleaning products, government analysts cited industrial cost-cutting measures and reduced consumption by hotels, schools, restaurants, hospitals, and other institutional users. International demand, however, was growing. In 1991, U.S. exports of soap and detergent products increased by 25 percent, totaling $487 million. At the same time, imports dropped four percent.

The household detergent segment of the market totaled $3.2 billion, which was split between powders ($1.9 billion) and liquids ($1.3 billion). The U.S. household market also consumed approximately 500 million pounds of automatic dishwashing detergent. An additional 300 million pounds of automatic dishwashing detergents were sold to the industrial and institutional markets.

The bar soap market, which had grown at an average rate of about 4.1 percent annually in the early 1980s, entered the 1990s with a growth rate of about 4.9 percent. Industry analysts attributed the increase to the introduction of body soaps and multipurpose bar soaps. Beauty bars comprised the fastest growing segment of the bar soap market, with sales increasing at a rate of about 7 percent per year.

Many of the companies in this classification also shipped secondary products. In 1987, for example, establishments in this category shipped $11.6 billion in products; $8.6 billion represented products considered primary to the industry, and $2.1 billion represented secondary products (The remaining $778.1 million represented miscellaneous transactions). These figures indicated a specialization ratio of 80 percent, a drop from 1982's ratio of 84 percent. The trend toward decreased specialization was seen in the expansion and diversification efforts of many industry leaders.

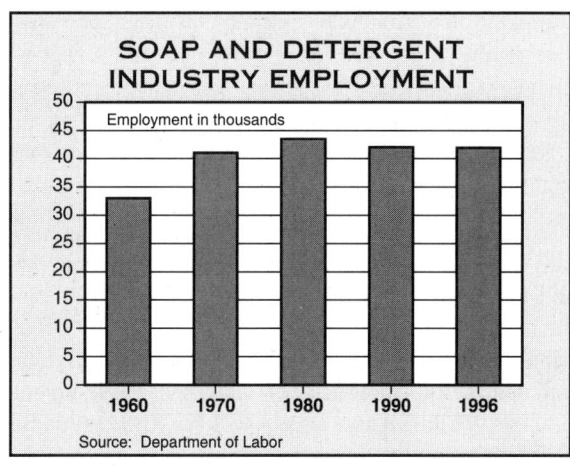

SOAP AND DETERGENT
INDUSTRY EMPLOYMENT

Employment in thousands

1960 1970 1980 1990 1996

Source: Department of Labor

One of the most significant challenges facing the soap and detergent industry during the early 1990s was a growing concern over environmental issues. Consumer demand and government regulations combined to push producers toward reformulating products with an emphasis toward "earth friendly" materials. As a result, manufacturers intensified their efforts to develop detergent formulas capable of meeting environmental concerns without sacrificing product performance or convenience.

The development of concentrated and super-concentrated formulas was an important step in these efforts. Concentrates and super-concentrates required fewer filler materials and chemicals than standard formulations. Their smaller size reduced transportation costs and decreased the volume of packaging materials required. Producers highlighted their environmental emphasis by offering many of the new formulations in recyclable packages made of recycled materials containing post-consumer waste. Despite the heavy emphasis on advertising environmental benefits, some industry watchers reported that consumers placed safety, cost, and performance ahead of environmental issues. Melinda Sweet, director of environmental affairs at Lever Brothers, told *Soap, Cosmetics, Chemical Specialties* that confusion about recycling caused some people to think that recycled products were used products. As a result, some customers thought that products in recycled packages ought to be cheaper.

CURRENT CONDITIONS

Consumers in the mid- to late 1990s market were very demanding, and value minded. They weighed many factors before buying any products. According to *Soap, Cosmetics, Chemical Specialties,* aging baby-boomers were looking for milder, less irritating products. Soaps using vegetable-based fats, with no animal fats or animal testing, were also in demand. Other popular items included loofahs, oatmeal products, and chamomile leaves. In general, customers demanded performance and value in all their soap, shampoo, and detergent products, which were the driving factors behind the soap and detergents industry at the turn of the century. Sales of body washes tripled in 1995 and were expected to double in 1996. Nevertheless, liquid and bar soaps did not lose their market share. In fact, liquid soap sales grew 5 percent to $233 million in 1994. Commodity bar soaps remained, however, the market share leader for this segment with sales growing 2 percent to $138 billion in 1994. Top brands in the segment were Neutrogena, Elizabeth Arden's One Great Soap, Beiersdorf's Basis, and Johnson and Johnson's Purpose.

Even though the laundry detergent market was typically slow and steady, U.S. detergent sales increased 4.2 percent for the period ending October 1996. However, according to the *Chemical Marketing Reporter*, "Ultra" product formulations cannibalized other detergents. Liquid detergents comprised the largest segment of the industry, with sales increasing 9.1 percent to $1.7 billion for the year ending August 1995.

The dishwashing detergent sector grew 3.2 percent in 1995 to $1.2 billion. Sales in the automatic dishwashing detergent (ADD)/additive sector reached $540 million, up .8 percent. With the U.S. detergent market becoming mature and gaining less than 1 percent each year, detergent manufacturers were attempting to decrease costs and increase sales.

INDUSTRY LEADERS

One of the oldest and largest companies in this industry is Procter and Gamble (P&G). Headquartered in Cincinnati, Ohio, P&G reported sales revenue of $33.434 billion and employed 99,200 people in 1996. Founded in 1837 by two brothers-in-law, the company originally made soap and candles. By 1992, P&G provided more than 100 brands to 140 countries. Its product list included laundry and cleaning products (Tide, Mr. Clean, Downy, Spic and Span), health and beauty aids (Noxzema, Clearasil, Head & Shoulders, Secret, Ivory), paper products (Charmin), and even foods and beverages. In the worldwide market, P&G's laundry detergents held the largest share and overseas trade represented P&G's fastest growing market. In Europe alone, sales topped $8 billion.

One of P&G's biggest competitors in the United States and abroad, and the second largest company in the industry, was Unilever, with sales revenue of $9.5 billion. Headquartered in New York, Unilever employed 24,000 people. Although P&G had entered the

European continental market in 1954, Unilever had already begun marketing a synthetic detergent, OMO, in Italy in 1951. In the United States, Lever Brothers (a Unilever unit) and P&G faced off in several areas. One market in which they both competed was automatic dishwashing detergents. Between them, they held the top two leading automatic dishwashing detergents. P&G's Cascade was the nation's best seller; Lever's Sunlight was number two.

Another area in which the two companies competed was the bar soap market. Industry analysts estimated Lever's market share to be 31 to 34 percent and P&G's market share to be about 32 percent. In 1990, Lever Brothers introduced a new three-in-one moisturizing, deodorant, and anti-bacterial cleansing bar called Lever 2000. Lever 2000 competed with several P&G products such as Safeguard, Coast, and Zest. Another Lever product, Dove, climbed to the top selling position, supplanting Dial, which had been the historic market leader in bar soaps. Dial continued to hold its position, however, in the liquid soap category.

Following Unilever, holding third place among soap manufacturers, was Colgate-Palmolive with sales revenue of $8.358 billion and 37,300 employees. In an attempt to be more competitive, Colgate-Palmolive replaced its original Palmolive soap with Palmolive Gentle Skin Bar. In liquid soaps, the company's SoftSoap made gains, but by 1992 was still behind Dial Liquid in market share. Colgate-Palmolive's total assets and net sales, however, exceeded those of Dial and the company held third place in automatic dishwashing detergents (followed by Benckiser's Electrasol).

In addition to providing products in the soap and detergent industry, Colgate-Palmolive manufactured oral and personal care products such as toothpastes, toothbrushes, oral rinses, and shampoos. The company also operated divisions in specialty fabric care products and in pet dietary care products. Colgate-Palmolive's domestic sales made up only 36 percent of its net sales in 1992. European sales accounted for 31 percent; sales in Latin America equaled 19 percent; and the Asian and African markets combined to total 14 percent.

Other large companies in the industry included Amway Coporation ($6.3 billion), Monsant Co. Chemical Group ($3.726 billion), S.C. Johnson and Son Inc. ($3 billion), and Clorox Co. ($2.217 billion). Dial Corporation, another example of a diverse, global company, reported 1996 revenues of $3.575 billion. Its products included bar soaps (Dial, Tone, Pure & Natural, Mountain Fresh, Spirit, Fels Naptha), Liquid Dial, Purex laundry products, and Brillo scouring pads. The

company also produced specialty cleaners, personal care products, and food items, and operated divisions in transportation manufacturing and service companies.

WORK FORCE

In 1987, soap and detergent establishments employed 31,700 workers, two percent less than in 1986 and ten percent less than in 1982. By 1992 employment had risen to more than 40,000 workers. Sixty-five percent were production workers. As the industry automated, worker productivity increased. Government officials attributed the ability to keep U.S. products competitive on the overseas market to the industry's high level of automation. States with the highest employment in the industry were Michigan, California, Ohio, and Illinois.

AMERICA AND THE WORLD

The soap and detergent industry is an international industry, and during the early 1990s world demand for its products increased one to three percent per year. Many of its participants competed on a global basis. Analysts, noting a firm correlation between a nation's standard of living and its usage of soap and detergent products, expected the market to continue growing in both industrialized and developing nations.

U.S. companies involved in foreign trade found the markets in Western Europe, Japan, and East Asia to be about the same size as the U.S. market. In Japan and Europe, demographic shifts toward older populations and smaller households were similar to the U.S. situation. Forecasters expected the greatest future export opportunities to occur in the developing economies of Eastern Europe. Eastern Europe was also considered a good location for new manufacturing plants.

One of the world's largest non-U.S. soap and detergent manufacturers was the Kao Corporation. Kao, an industry leader in Japan, supplied a broad range of products including laundry detergents, dishwashing detergents, cleaners, toilet soaps, and personal care products. In 1988, Kao entered the U.S. market through its acquisition of the Andrew Jergens Company. By the early 1990s, its global network included several Asian and Pacific nations and the company planned to expand into Australia.

Japanese and other foreign marketers, like their U.S. counterparts, struggled with environmental issues. For example, by 1990 superconcentrates had captured 80 percent of Japan's powdered detergent market, and Kao was switching its formulations to natural-based surfactants. In Europe, environmental efforts resulted in regulations stricter than many enacted in the United States. Refillable containers, which were considered innovations in the United States in 1992, were already popular in Holland and Germany. In addition, German consumers were required to return all outside packaging. Issues of water consumption and energy use were also prompting changes in overseas markets faster than in domestic markets. Some industry analysts expected that trends toward washing with room temperature water and with less water would eventually spread to the United States.

The controversy over phosphates affected soap and detergent marketers on virtually every continent. Sodium tripolyphosphate (STPP) use increased in some areas but fell in others. In Canada during the fall of 1990, a brand war emphasizing the environmental benefits of phosphate-free detergents caused phosphate detergents to drop from 90 percent of the market to 40 percent in only six months. In 1991, however, forecasters expected phosphate sales to increase in Eastern Europe and Asia. Industry analysts also predicted continued growth in phosphate usage within the industrial and institutional segment of the market and in automatic dishwashing detergents.

RESEARCH AND TECHNOLOGY

The need to meet environmental regulations both in the United States and abroad drove many of the research efforts undertaken by the soap and detergent industry during the early 1990s. Zeolite, sodium citrate, sodium carbonate, and sodium nitrilotriacetate were under investigation as possible builders to replace phosphates. Other questions being addressed included product safety, water quality, chemical disposal, the ability to wash in unheated water, and indoor air quality.

Although technological developments and an expanding understanding of chemical processes had improved the industry's ability to restore soiled garments and other objects to their pre-soiled condition, available soaps and detergents still failed to achieve perfect results. Chemical scientists, therefore, continued to work on developing innovative laundry additives such as new enzymes and oxygen bleaches.

FURTHER READING

Ainsworth, Susan J. "Soaps & Detergents." *Chemical and Engineering News,* 20 January 1992.

Artzt, Edwin L. "Whither Procter & Gamble in the Cosmetic Business?" *Drug and Cosmetic Industry,* February 1992.

Booman, Keith A. "Animal Testing Alternatives." *Soap, Cosmetics, Chemical Specialties,* October 1989.

Brenner, Theodore E. "Some Current & Future Issues Facing the Detergent Industry." *Soap, Cosmetics, Chemical Specialties,* November 1989.

Caney, Derek J. "STPP Market Improving Despite Bans." *Chemical Marketing Reporter,* 13 January 1992.

Carsch, Gustav. "Making Scents of Detergents." *Soap, Cosmetics, Chemical Specialties,* January 1993.

The Colgate-Palmolive Company. *Colgate-Palmolive Company 1992 Annual Report.* New York: Colgate-Palmolive, 1993.

Colwell, Shelley M. "Super Suds: Updating the Bar and Liquid Soaps Market." *Soap-Cosmetics-Chemical Specialties* , October 1995.

Crossin, Michael C. "Second Generation Detergent Protease Offered for Today's Multifunctional Laundry Detergents." *Soap, Cosmetics, Chemical Specialties,* August 1987.

D'Amico, Esther. "Soaps and Detergents the Push to Perform." *Chemical Week* , 24 January 1996.

The Dial Corporation. *The Dial Corp. 1992 Annual Report.* Phoenix, AZ: Dial, 1993.

Donohue, Janet. "Cleaning Products." *Soap, Cosmetics, Chemical Specialties,* January 1989.

Ecolab. *Ecolab 1992 Annual Report.* St. Paul, MN: Ecolab, 1993.

Fitzgerald, Patrick. "Ultra's in the Drivers Seat: Liquids Are the Growth in the Detergent Market." *Chemical Market Reporter* , 22 January 1996.

Gerry, Roberta. "Cleaning Up the Body and Spirit: Soap Market is Bubbling with New Body Washes Gaining Significant Market Share." *Chemical Marketing Reporter,* 22 January 1996.

————. "Stain, Stain Go Away." *Chemical Marketing Reporter* , January 27, 1997.

Hunter, David and David Rotman. "Phosphate Use Continues to Take Its Lumps." *Chemical Week,* 30 January 1991.

Kilburn, David. "How Kao Rules Japan." *Advertising Age,* 10 April 1989.

Kilburn, David, and Laurie Freeman. "Kao Angles Its Way Onto the U.S. Stage." *Advertising Age,* 10 April 1989.

Kintish, Lisa. "Laundry Detergents: The Golden Years." *Soap Cosmetic Chemical Specialties,* January 1992.

Mullin, Rick. "Japan's Market Under Pressure: Kao Moves on Asia/Pacific." *Chemical Week,* 27 January 1993.

Naude, Alice. "Family Resemblance: The Automatic Dishwashing Detergents Market is Beginning to Look More Like Laundry Detergents." *Chemical Marketing Reporter,* 25 January 1993.

The Procter & Gamble Company. *The Procter & Gamble Company 1992 Annual Report.* Cincinnati, OH: P&G, 1992.

Singletary, Lynda. "No-Soap Soaps Up: Bar Soaps, No Longer in the Doldrums of Maturity, Are Getting a Big

Boost from Syndets and Liquids.'' *Chemical Marketing Reporter,* 27 January 1992.

Sivak, Andrew. "LAS: A 25-Year Success Story." *Soap, Cosmetics, Chemical Specialties,* April 1988.

Soap and Detergent Association. *A Handbook of Industry Terms.* New York: SDA, 1987.

Soap and Detergent Association. "Types of Laundry Products," New York: SDA, 1991.

U.S. Department of Commerce. *1987 Census of Manufactures.* Washington, DC: Bureau of the Census, February 1990.

U.S. Department of Commerce. *U. S. Industrial Outlook 1992.* Washington, DC: Department of Commerce, 1992.

Van Raalte, John A. "Tale Ends." *Soap, Cosmetics, Chemical Specialties,* April 1988.

Zahodiakin, Phil. "Phosphate Bans Not Washed Up Yet." *Chemical Marketing Reporter,* 30 January 1989.

—Karen Bellenir, updated by Visi Tilak

SIC 2842

SPECIALTY CLEANING, POLISHING, AND SANITATION PREPARATIONS

This category includes companies that primarily make specialty cleaning products (those designed for specific surfaces such as bathroom, oven, drain, carpet, and upholstery cleaners), polishes and waxes (such as for furniture, metal, flooring, and glass), and other sanitation preparations including disinfectants and deodorizers. This category also includes companies making products such as household bleaches and ammonia, laundry starches, and fabric softeners. Companies that primarily make industrial bleaches are in **SIC 2819: Industrial Inorganic Chemicals, Not Elsewhere Classified.** Companies that primarily make household pesticides are in **SIC 2879: Pesticides and Agricultural Chemicals, Not Elsewhere Classified.**

INDUSTRY SNAPSHOT

In 1987, the specialty cleaning, polishing, and sanitation preparation industry shipped goods worth $5.6 billion. Of this total, $3.9 billion were considered primary to the industry and $1.5 billion were secondary products. Miscellaneous transactions made up the remaining $227.9 million. Based on these figures, the industry's specialization ratio was 73 percent, dropping 1 percent from 1982. The industry grew modestly during the late 1980s. By 1991, shipments totaled $6 billion, rising 2.7 percent over 1990. Exports of $455 million exceeded imports, which totaled $175 million.

Government forecasters predicted the industry would grow 2.5 to 3.0 percent during the mid-1990s. By 1995, sales reached $8.7 billion, even better than projected.

Industry goods sold were often classified as commodity cleaners or specialty cleaners. Commodity cleaners were usually sold in bulk for lower prices. Specialty cleaners were sold in smaller quantities at higher prices. About 65 percent of products were sold to the industrial and institutional (I&I) market. The I&I included: contract cleaning firms, office buildings, restaurants, hospitals, schools, and hotels. Analysts expected the I&I market to grow 1 to 3 percent per year. The nursing home market, which rose 7.5 percent in 1992, held the most promise for future growth.

Fabric softener sales rose 2 to 3 percent in the early 1990s. Sales of fabric softeners for use in dryers rose faster than sales of traditional liquid softeners made to be added during the washing machine's rinse cycle. Sales of detergents with added softeners declined.

BACKGROUND AND DEVELOPMENT

The specialty cleaning, polishing, and sanitation preparation industry makes hundreds of products, each serving specific cleaning needs of consumers in different markets. Products developed as a response to changes in technology, consumer need, government regulation, and other factors. This makes it hard to generalize about the industry's development as a whole. The development of fabric softeners, however, demonstrates certain factors affecting the industry.

Fabric softeners were introduced during the early 1950s, after synthetic laundry detergents became more popular. Because detergents stripped natural oils out of fabrics as they cleaned, clothes came out scratchy and often developed negative ionic charges (static cling) in the dryer. The first fabric softeners were liquids designed for adding to the wash during the rinse cycle. In the 1970s, fabric softeners for use in the dryer were developed, made of porous foam sheets doused with softener. Other types of dryer-added softeners included sprays and dispensing bars. The 1980s brought all-in-one detergents with fabric softeners designed for use during the wash cycle.

New developments in fabric softener followed as manufacturers worked to improve the product. One side effect of softener usage was material fibers began to appear dingy due to the softener's coating action. To counteract this problem, the industry invented optical brighteners, also called florescent whitening agents (FWAs). FWAs were chemical compounds that made fabrics appear brighter by converting ultraviolet light into visible blue light.

Fabric softeners made fabrics fluffy by coating fibers with fatty compounds. They eliminated static cling using "cationic surfactants," chemicals added to liquids to allow the wetting, foaming, dispersing, emulsifying, or penetrating actions of the solution on a fabric while adding positive charges to offset the negative ionic charges from static electricity. In addition to cationic surfactants, which did not clean effectively when used alone, the industry developed other surfactants. These included anionic, nonionic, and amphoteric surfactants. Anionics, the most widely used surfactants, carried negative charges and were typically high sudsing. Nonionics carried no functional ionic charges worked against oily soils. Amphoterics might be either positively or negatively charged depending on water conditions.

CURRENT CONDITIONS

A national trend toward mild, natural, and environmentally safe products affected fabric softener development through the mid-1990s. Historically, customers wanted softeners to add fragrance, but an emphasis on using fewer chemicals led to new formulas. Procter & Gamble, for example, introduced Bounce Free, which had no perfumes, inks, or extra additives. The environmental movement's campaign to reduce packaging waste led to the development of concentrates and refills. In 1990, Procter & Gamble introduced Downy Refill. Downy Refill, which customers mixed with water to make full strength, required 75 percent less packaging than the original 64-ounce bottle. By mid-1991, refills made up 40 percent of Downy's sales.

Environmental concerns also affected polishes and waxes. Few ingredients and industry by-products were biodegradable. The Clean Water Act challenged floor wax makers to meet product disposal requirements. Regulations concerning volatile organic compounds led some makers to phase out solvent-based products and increased use of water-based systems. Since zinc harmed sewage treatment facilities, the Environmental Protection Agency regulated zinc emissions. Also, many states and municipalities enacted their own zinc regulations.

During the early 1990s, the market for household polishes and waxes declined. The popularity of no-wax floors and a desire for more convenient products lowered demand for floor wax. Within the industrial and institutional market, improvements in maintenance technology, such as high-speed floor buffers,

reduced the need for floor wax. New acrylic floor materials also required less maintenance.

In other areas related to floor care, however, demand increased. The growing popularity of mineral surfaces, such as marble, terrazzo, quarry tile, and ceramics, brought a need for new types of cleaners. In addition, old asbestos flooring required constant care to keep it sealed and polished.

Carpet cleaner sales grew in 1990 as manufacturers introduced products with deodorizers. Although their growth stabilized the following year, specialty products (such as those formulated for pet owners) continued to do well. The carpet care industry also reacted to environmental concerns about indoor air quality. Formulas that were less harsh, non-toxic, and pleasant smelling were emphasized, while some companies promoted all-natural formulas. Packaging moved away from aerosols and favored plastic bottles with trigger delivery systems. More communities were able to recycle plastic than steel, so plastic was seen as a better choice for the environment. In addition, aerosols were seen as environmentally dangerous, even though CFCs (chlorofluorocarbons) had been banned since 1978.

Within the household bleach market, environmental concerns had less impact. Although perborate bleaches (the most widely used type of non-chlorine bleach) seemed safer for the environment and gentler on clothes than chlorine-based bleaches, consumer acceptance of perborates was not as strong as analysts anticipated. These bleaches performed poorly at the low wash temperatures preferred by many Americans. In Europe, where higher wash temperatures were popular, perborates captured 80 percent of the bleach market. In 1992, U.S. industry analysts expected chlorine-based bleaches to remain in the forefront with combined liquid and dry formulas capturing up to 90 percent of the market. One product expected to bring increased acceptance of perborates was Tide with Bleach. Tide with Bleach contained a patented low-temperature activator called sodium nonanoyloxbenzene sulfonate (SNOBS).

Another trend during the early 1990s was concern about the spread of infectious diseases. This brought an interest in disinfectants, especially those effective against HIV, the virus connected to Acquired Immuno-Defiency Syndrome (AIDS). Primary disinfectant users within the industrial and institutional market were hospitals, clinics, schools, building service contractors, and hotels. The overseas market also grew as developing countries used more disinfectants. For example, in South America, disinfectants were used to fight cholera.

The disinfectant industry came under scrutiny in 1990 following a report by the U.S. General Accounting Office. The report stated as many as 20 percent of disinfectants sold were ineffective and the Environmental Protection Agency could not ensure consumers that registered disinfectants worked according to their claims. The Chemical Specialties Manufacturers Association (CSMA) responded to this criticism by developing plans to monitor test data quality and check disinfectants worked on the market. The CSMA's Laboratory Accreditation Program evaluated laboratories' ability to perform accurate testing. Its Post-Registration Product Efficiency Testing program conducted random product reviews, first testing hospital disinfectants. According to the CSMA, U.S. disinfectants worked and passed the most stringent testing in the world.

Disinfectant registration brought contention within the industry. Industry leaders complained registration took too long and made it too costly to create new products. They claimed the process was further complicated by individual state requirements, which were often different from EPA requirements. CSMA favored standardized regulations to apply nationwide.

Another problem involved products for stopping the spread of HIV and Hepatitis. Occupational Safety and Health Association (OSHA) regulations required health care employees to work assuming all body fluids were infected with HIV or Hepatitis. Disinfectant makers complained the EPA measured disinfectant strength according to its ability to kill bacteria responsible for tuberculosis. According to the industry, the efficacy tests were not comparable because tuberculoides were airborne and most disinfectants used against HIV and Hepatitis were designed for surface use.

The disinfectant industry also came under scrutiny by the environmental movement. As a result, formulators looked for ways to make safer products by reducing volatile organic compounds and making products more biodegradable. In addition, marketers turned to packaging made of recycled post-consumer waste.

Another industry segment questioned by the environmental movement was dry cleaning preparation. These chemicals were often improperly discarded or leaked from faulty equipment and seeped into the ground, contaminating wells and aquifers. One of the biggest offenders was perchlorethylene (PCE, also called perc). More than 80 percent of U.S. dry cleaners used perc, and approximately 500 million pounds of perc were produced in the United States every year. The Clean Air Act of 1990 listed Perc as a hazardous pollutant that could cause dizziness and headaches.

Some studies also linked perc to miscarriage and cancer. The Environmental Protection Agency proposed that dry cleaners reduce perc emissions 13 to 26 percent by 1996.

INDUSTRY LEADERS

The number one company in this category as of 1995 was SC Johnson Wax, a private multinational company based in Racine, Wisconsin ($3 billion annual sales, and 13,600 workers). Their best-known consumer products included Glade air freshener, Shout laundry stain remover, Pledge furniture polish, and Windex glass cleaner. The company also sells equivalents of these products for the industrial and institutional market.

The second largest company in the industry was Clorox Co. of Oakland, California ($1.8 billion annual sales, with 4,900 employees). Clorox, a former division of Procter & Gamble, became independent in 1969 due to antitrust regulations. By 1992, the company offered 24 national retail brands in 94 countries. In addition to Clorox brand bleaches, products included top sellers such as Formula 409, Soft Scrub, and Liquid Plumr. The company bought out Pine-Sol, the nation's best selling dilutable cleaner, in 1990.

Number three for this industry in 1995 was Dowbrands, LP of Indianapolis, Indiana ($930 million annual sales, 4,900 employees). This was a consumer products division of Dow Chemical Co. ($20 billion annual sales), the fifth largest chemical maker in the world. Dow cleaning products included: branded bathroom cleaner with scrubbing bubbles, Glass Plus, Fantastik smart cleanser, Spray N' Wash laundry stain remover, Vivid color-safe bleach, and Yes laundry detergent.

WORK FORCE

According to the U.S. Department of Commerce, in 1995 the industry employed 23,000 people (14,000 of those in production), up from 21,700 people in 1991. The total payroll in 1995 was $702.3 million, with $318.2 million paid to production workers.

RESEARCH AND TECHNOLOGY

In 1992, government forecasters predicted changing regulations and environmental concerns would bring more "earth friendly" technologies and products. One new development was packaging using resin from recycled products. Clorox, for example, increased its use of post-consumer waste in containers. Some Clorox bleach bottles may contain 20 percent; popular sizes of Soft Scrub and Formula 409 should contain 25 percent; and bottles of dilutable Pine-Sol should be made from 100 percent recycled polyethylene terephtalate. Clorox claimed its efforts saved 8 million pounds of virgin plastic, glass, and corrugated paper board in 1992. Other efforts to reduce packaging materials included making caps and labels smaller and eliminating exterior packaging.

Product formulators were challenged to make safer cleaning products without losing performance or convenience. Manufacturers explored ways to reduce volatile organic compounds use in solvent-based formulas, make products more biodegradable, and lessen products' impact on sewage treatment plants. Some efforts toward producing products with lessened environmental consequences came from evolving federal and state regulations. Other efforts were market driven. Some industry analysts predicted innovations in ''environmentally friendly'' formulas would come from small suppliers.

FURTHER READING

Binenstock, Alan. ''Floor Care Products.'' *Soap Cosmetics Chemical Specialties,* June 1989.

''Cleaner Dry Cleaners.'' *Time,* 30 November 1992.

The Clorox Company. *The Clorox Company 1992 Annual Report.* Oakland, CA: Clorox, 1992.

''Disinfectants Under Attack.'' *Soap, Cosmetics, Chemical Specialties,* November 1990.

''Downy Refill Reduces Waste.'' *U.S. Distribution Journal,* 15 November 1990.

Eastman Kodak Company. *Eastman Kodak Company 1991 Annual Report.* Rochester, NY: Eastman Kodak, 1992.

Hoffman, John. ''Less Than Bright.'' *Chemical Marketing Reporter,* 25 January 1993.

Johnson, Bradley. ''Clorox's Identity Crisis.'' *Advertising Age,* 6 May 1991.

Kintish, Lisa. ''Disinfectants in Distress.'' *Soap, Cosmetics, Chemical Specialties,* November 1992.

National Service Industries, Inc. *National Service Industries, Inc 1992 Annual Report.* Atlanta, GA: NSI, 1992

Pellicano, Mary. ''Toward a Softer, Static-Free World.'' *Soap, Cosmetics, Chemical Specialties,* August 1991.

Perrault, Mike. ''Dry Cleaning Can Be Dirty Business.'' *Orlando Business Journal,* 3 April 1992.

''Polishing Up Their Act.'' *Soap, Cosmetics, Chemical Specialties,* September 1991.

Singletary, Lynda. ''Some Open Doors: Additives Producers are Responding to Emerging Opportunities in the Wake of Technology Changes.'' *Chemical Marketing Reporter,* 25 January 1993.

Soap and Detergent Association. *A Handbook of Industry Terms.* New York: SDA, 1987.

Springer, Neil. ''No Recession Here.'' *Chemical Marketing Reporter,* 25 January 1993.

Strandberg, Keith W. ''The Carpet Care Market.'' *Soap & Cosmetic Chemical Specialties,* February 1993.

———. ''Floor Waxes and Polishes Update.'' *Soap, Cosmetics, Chemical Specialties,* September 1992.

U.S. Department of Commerce. *1987 Census of Manufactures.* Washington: GPO, 1990.

U.S. Department of Commerce. *1995 Annual Survey of Manufactures.* Washington: GPO, 1997.

U.S. Department of Commerce. International Trade Administration. *U.S. Industrial Outlook 1992.* Washington: GPO, 1992.

—Karen Bellenir, updated by Dave Fagan

SIC 2843

SURFACE ACTIVE AGENTS, FINISHING AGENTS, SULFONATED OILS, AND ASSISTANTS

This industry classification includes establishments primarily involved in making compounds that, when dissolved in water, reduce the water's surface tension. Products include preparations such as wetting agents, emulsifiers, and penetrants. These ingredients are raw materials for soap and detergent manufacturers. This industry classification also includes establishments primarily involved in producing sulfonated oils and fats and related products.

In 1995, the surfactant (shortened form of surface active agent) industry shipments were valued at $4.68 billion, a growth of about 2 percent since 1991. Since 1987, the number of establishments has decreased about 11 percent to 196 in 1996. There were about 8,000 employees in the industry in 1995, one-half of them in the production sector. Wages for production workers were about $17 per hour in 1995, an increase of around 22 percent since 1990.

Customer demand and legislative requirements combined to bring changes to the surfactant industry during the early 1990s. Manufacturers worldwide focused on the development of milder products, increased use of natural ingredients, and emphasized environmental safety. In 1992, *Soap, Cosmetics, Chemical Specialties* quoted Ed Tobey, vice president of national accounts for Stepan Company, as saying, ''There isn't any product that hasn't changed in the past 12 months.''

One of the most profound changes was the shift to concentrated and superconcentrated formulas, not only within household products but also in the industrial and institutional markets. Some industry analysts feared that the increasing demand for superconcentrated surfactants produced by large manufacturers would impede the development of small companies because the formulas were difficult for smaller manufacturers to reproduce.

Environmental regulations also called for formulation changes. Personal care product manufacturers required solutions with less alcohol, makers of specialty cleaners were shifting from solvents and volatile organic compounds to water-based systems, and some communities upgraded biodegradability standards. Environmental concerns were affecting the European surfactant industry even more profoundly. Industry watchers expected some classes of surfactants to be banned in the 1990s because of problems with wastewater treatment facilities.

An international phenomenon affecting the industry in the 1990s was consolidation. As large global corporations bought smaller national companies, fewer independent manufacturers remained. Although the trend toward fewer, bigger corporations was expected to continue, the rate of industry consolidation was expected to subside.

The Stepan Company, founded in 1932 and headquartered in Northfield, Illinois, is one of the nation's largest producers of surfactants, polymers, and specialty chemicals. In 1996, the company reported net sales of $536 million, 75 percent from its surfactants line. Stepan's customers included detergent, shampoo, lotion, toothpaste, cosmetic, and other manufacturers. Stepan entered the foreign market in 1976 with its acquisition of a firm in France and the company continued to expand its global presence throughout the 1980s.

FURTHER READING

Darnay, Arsen J., ed. *Manufacturing USA.* 5th ed. Detroit: Gale Research, 1996.

Richards, David. "Going Natural." *Chemical Marketing Reporter,* 25 January 1993.

Shaw, Anita Hipius. "Surfactants:Evolution or Revolution?" *Soap, Cosmetics, Chemical Specialties,* September 1992.

Soap and Detergent Association. *A Handbook of Industry Terms.* New York: SDA, 1987.

Stepan Company. *Stepan 1996 Annual Report.* Northfield, IL, 1996.

U.S. Department of Commerce. *1987 Census of Manufactures.* Washington: GPO, 1990.

U.S. Department of Commerce. *1995 Annual Survey of Manufactures.* Washington: GPO, 1996.

SIC 2844

PERFUMES, COSMETICS, AND OTHER TOILET PREPARATIONS

This category includes establishments primarily engaged in manufacturing perfumes, cosmetics and other toilet preparations. Manufacturers of shampoos, shaving products, personal deodorants, hair preparations, suntan lotions and oils, talcum powders, toothpastes and powders, mouthwashes, and premoistened towelettes are included.

There were approximately 770 establishments in the toilet preparations industry in 1996, employing an estimated 60,000 workers. The total value of industry shipments totalled $19.7 billion in 1994—by 1997, this number had increased to an estimated $22.8 billion. California and New Jersey had the largest number had increased to an estimated $22.8 billion. California and New Jersey had the largest number of establishments in the 1990s, with approximately 140 and 105, respectively.

INDUSTRY SNAPSHOT

The nation's economic condition during the 1980s and early 1990s brought about changes in the industry's distribution patterns. Traditionally, retail products had been classified as upscale, mid-level, or low-scale, depending on where they were sold and their pricing structure. Upscale product lines were typically sold in major department stores or specialty boutiques; mid-level product lines were sold in department stores at lower prices; and low-scale product lines were sold in drug stores or through catalogs. Industry analysts reported that customers were turning away from upscale products and switching to lower priced brands which were increasingly being sold in mass market outlets. Department stores had sold almost 20 percent of upscale cosmetics in 1985, but by 1991 the figure had dropped to 12 percent, according to a study conducted by Business Trend Analysts reported in *Drug and Cosmetic Industry.*

Due to a mature and stagnant market in the United States, manufacturers met with global success in the mid-1990s in Europe and emerging markets such as Asia and Latin America. A leader in this market,

Gillete has the largest international market base with nearly 70 percent of its sales from foreign customer accounts. Procter & Gamble expects to boost its international sales which in 1996 accounted for about 50 percent of the total.

ORGANIZATION AND STRUCTURE

Many participants in the cosmetics, fragrances, and personal care products industry were members of the Cosmetic, Toiletry and Fragrance Association (CTFA). The CTFA, which was founded in 1894, represented manufacturers and distributors as well as industry suppliers. It provided scientific, legal, regulatory, and legislative services. According to a report published in *Soap, Cosmetics, Chemical Specialties* summarizing the events at CTFA's 97th Annual Meeting in Boca Raton, Florida, the organization's mission was "to provide an environment free of unnecessary government regulation."

The federal agency most often involved in regulatory encounters with the industry was the Food and Drug Administration (FDA). The FDA required that color additives be tested and approved prior to use. It banned or restricted the use of some specific ingredients including mercury compounds, chloroform, and methylene chloride. Other regulations dictated that cosmetics contain no poisonous or harmful substances, no filthy, putrid, or decomposed substances, and that they must be manufactured and held under sanitary conditions. The FDA also instituted labeling requirements which compelled manufacturers to list cosmetic ingredients in descending order according to the quantity used, with some flexibility allowed for the protection of trade secrets. The FDA also had the authority to take legal action against cosmetic companies if problems developed with the safety of products already on the market. In order to do so, the agency was required to prove in court that the product was harmful or misbranded.

The FDA, however, did not require the same type of pre-market approval for cosmetics as was required for drugs. According to a report published in *FDA Consumer*, cosmetics were legally defined as "articles other than soap which are applied to the human body for cleansing, beautifying, promoting attractiveness, or altering the appearance." The FDA recognized 13 categories of cosmetics: skin care products, fragrances, manicure products, eye makeup, makeup other than eye makeup, hair coloring preparations, shampoos and other hair products, deodorants, shaving products, baby products, bath oils and bubble baths, mouthwashes, and sunscreens.

The distinction between cosmetics and drugs was sometimes vague. According to FDA guidelines, products claiming to offer medical benefits or physiological effects were over-the-counter (OTC) drugs. Examples of items with controversial classifications included antiperspirants, which were classified as OTC drugs in the late 1970s, sunscreen products that listed a Sun Protection Factor (SPF) number, hair care products claiming to protect or restore hair, and shampoos professing to cure or remove dandruff. If the FDA deemed a cosmetic product to be an OTC drug, it was regulated as a new drug. The manufacturer was then required to demonstrate product safety and efficacy in order to gain FDA approval.

The cosmetic industry, under the sponsorship of CTFA, developed the Cosmetic Ingredient Review (CIR) in the mid-1970s in order to gather information about ingredient safety and make the information available to manufacturers. Reviews were conducted by a panel of scientific and medical experts. One report claimed that by 1988, 85 percent of the most frequently used 700 cosmetic ingredients had been reviewed, were under review, or were being regulated or studied by other procedures such as the FDA's process of reviewing over-the-counter drugs. Another report claimed that a review performed by the National Institute of Occupational Safety and Health found that 884 of the 2,983 chemicals used as ingredients in cosmetics were toxic substances. The CTFA refuted the claim and maintained that scientific and medical studies demonstrated the safety of ingredients used within the industry.

The fragrance segment of the industry organized the Research Institute for Fragrance Materials (RIFM) in the mid-1960s to independently test and certify the safety of natural and chemical aromatics. During its first 25 years of operation, the RIFM tested approximately 1,400 different materials. The studies resulted in recommendations to restrict or prohibit about 100 of the ingredients reviewed.

In an effort to further cooperation between cosmetic and fragrance manufacturers and the FDA, the regulatory agency instituted a voluntary registration program in which manufacturers participated in monitoring adverse reactions to products. The program provided for information exchanges among participants and with the government. By 1991, more than 165 companies had registered and the FDA planned to expand the program to include a larger percentage of eligible participants and to provide more useful services.

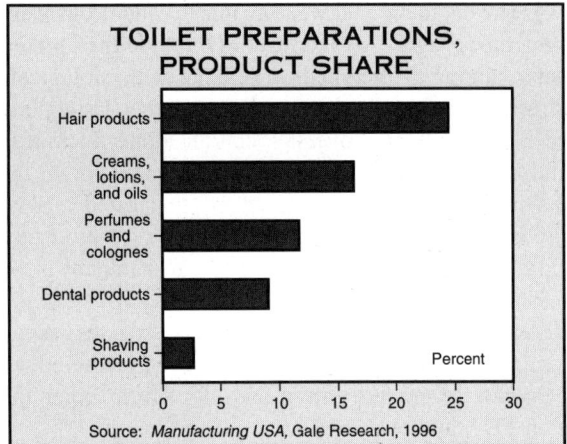

TOILET PREPARATIONS, PRODUCT SHARE

Hair products

Creams, lotions, and oils

Perfumes and colognes

Dental products

Shaving products

Percent

0   5   10   15   20   25   30

Source: *Manufacturing USA,* Gale Research, 1996

BACKGROUND AND DEVELOPMENT

The use of cosmetics, fragrances, and personal care products can be traced back to human's earliest days. Neanderthal man painted his face with reds, browns, and yellows derived from clay, mud, and arsenic. Bones were used to curl hair. Makeup, tattoos, and adornments conveyed necessary social information. The ancients also used fragrances. Some believed that a flower's aroma contained the presence of a deity, while others burned incense during religious rites. Different fragrances often had symbolic meanings and ceremonial oils were used for anointing.

During the reign of the Pharaohs, Egyptian aristocrats wore cones of solidified perfume that would melt under warm temperatures to provide cooling and mask odors. A mineral called hematite was applied as rouge and faces were painted with white lead. Black kohl encircled eyes. Egyptians curled their hair with sticks or straightened their hair with iron bands and weights. Aloe vera was known as an anti-irritant.

Greek women also painted their faces white and put red circles on their cheeks. Galen, an ancient Greek physician, invented cold cream. The Romans used oil-based perfumes on their bodies, in their baths and fountains, and applied them to their weapons. In the ninth century, Arabs developed alcohol-based perfumes. Crusaders of the thirteenth century brought fragrances back to Europe from the Far East.

The perfumes developed during the sixteenth century were powders or gelatinous pastes. They could be applied to scented fans or carried in jewelry with fragrance compartments. The ability to create new fragrances by blending ingredients was developed during the seventeenth century in France. A person who developed new perfume scents by blending ingredients was called a ''nose.'' Some of the compounding establishments developed in France during the eighteenth

and nineteenth centuries were still operating at the close of the twentieth century. America's first cologne water, Caswell-Massey's Number Six, was a blend of 27 ingredients and was said to have been a favorite of George Washington.

Natural perfumes were made from a variety of ingredients containing aroma. These included: essential oils, which were found in flowers, roots, fruits, rinds, or barks depending on the type of plant; resinoids, which were gums or resins that were purified with a solvent; and absolutes, which were aromas extracted with solvents existing in viscous liquid form. Natural perfumes were expensive, primarily because of the labor involved in gathering ingredients. For example, *Smithsonian* magazine reported that a pound of jasmine flowers contained approximately 5,000 blooms, and one pound of the flowers yielded only 1/800th of a pound of jasmine absolute.

Chemical formulations developed during the nineteenth century began to replace expensive natural ingredients and make perfumes more widely available. Early synthetic fragrances included vanilla and violet. In the United States, Francis Despard Dodge developed citronellol and citronellal with various floral scents.

The nineteenth century also brought changes in facial makeup. Ceruse, a cosmetic that had been widely used in Europe since the time of the second century, was replaced by a powder made from zinc oxide. Ceruse, made from white lead, was discovered to be toxic. It was blamed for causing physical problems such as facial tremors, muscle paralysis, and even death.

Antiperspirants and deodorants were developed during the 1890s. Aluminum chloride, the original active ingredient, frequently caused skin irritation and damage to clothes. These difficulties were overcome during the 1940s when aluminum chlorohydrate was developed. Although additives were subsequently produced to improve antiperspirant activity, aluminum chlorohydrate remained the primary ingredient in antiperspirants for the remainder of the twentieth century.

Cosmetics played a role during World War II. Leg makeup was developed in response to shortages of stockings. In Germany, women sacrificed lipstick, but U.S. officials judged it vital and necessary. Following the war, biological ingredients began to receive attention. Human placental products were first used in cosmetics during the 1940s. Cosmetic makers claimed that they stimulated tissue growth and removed wrinkles. The FDA ruled that such claims were medical in nature, and as a result classified these products as drugs and declared them ineffective. Placental products later reappeared in cosmetics but were listed only as a source of protein. Other biological ingredients (derived primarily from cows) included amniotic liquid, collagen (a protein substance), and cerebrosides (fatty substances with carbohydrates produced at the deepest layer of skin).

Fashion trends continued to bring new innovations. Artificial skin tanning aids were developed during the late 1950s. False eyelashes became popular during the 1960s. The 1960s also saw the introduction of "natural" products based on botanical ingredients such as carrot juice and watermelon extract. During the 1970s, the growing environmental movement brought challenges to the cosmetic and fragrance industry. The use of some popular ingredients was banned following the enactment of endangered species protection legislation. Some examples included musk (from Himalayan deer, Ethiopian civet, and certain types of beaver) and ambergris (taken from sperm whales).

Concerns about contaminated makeup emerged during the late 1980s. An FDA report in 1989 found that over five percent of samples collected from counters in department stores were contaminated with molds, fungi, and pathogenic organisms. Such contamination was supposed to be controlled by preservatives in the cosmetics. Preservatives, however, proved ineffective against the microorganisms responsible for causing product contamination when they lacked stability or when a particular product was kept longer than the shelf life of its preservative system.

Although cosmetic products seldom caused serious injury, some problems did occur. Most common among them were eye infections (caused by scratching the eyeball with a contaminated mascara wand) and allergic reactions. Fragrance additives were often blamed as a source of allergic responses. Two fragrances, acetylethly tetramethyltetralin (AETT) and 6-methyl coumarin (6-ME), caused sufficient numbers of adverse reactions for the FDA to take action against them. AETT, a neurotoxic, caused flushing, dizziness, nausea, and other reactions. 6-ME, which was frequently used in sunscreens, was photo-toxic and interacted with UV radiation occasionally leading to irreversible skin depigmentation and/or hyperpigmentation.

Manufacturers began to offer products labeled "hypoallergenic" or "natural." The term "hypoallergenic" meant a product was considered by its manufacturer to offer less potential for allergic reaction. Some makers conducted clinical tests to determine the likelihood of allergic responses. Others merely reformulated products without adding fragrances. An effort

by the FDA to regulate a precise meaning for the term "hypoallergenic" was overturned in the courts. The industry used the word "natural" to refer to any ingredient that was not synthetically produced. It had no regulated meaning implying "pure" or "clean."

Controversy continued into the 1990s over cosmetic ingredients and claims. Some popular materials were Nayad, liposomes, and vitamins. Nayad (a trade name) was a yeast extract said to make the skin look and feel smoother by reducing lines and wrinkles. Liposomes were round, microscopic sacs made of fatty substances which cosmetic makers claimed could penetrate the skin's surface to deliver other ingredients into deeper skin layers. Vitamins were listed on display labels to imply that their usage would nourish the skin. The FDA, however, prohibited manufacturers from making therapeutic claims based on the vitamin content of skin care products.

CURRENT CONDITIONS

As the perfume, cosmetic, and toiletry preparations industry entered the 1990s, it faced many challenges including regulatory changes, product safety concerns, calls for scientific data to document product claims, increasing environmentalism, and pressure from the growing animal rights movement. Congress began investigating possible revisions to the traditional "drug" and "cosmetic" definitions established under the Food, Drug and Cosmetic Act. A report titled *Classification and Regulation of Cosmetics and Drugs: A Legal Overview and Alternatives for Legislative Change* included provisions for a third category of "cosmeceuticals" to include products like sunscreens that fell in the gap between "drugs" and "cosmetics." Some industry analysts welcomed legislative changes to clarify product distinctions but doubted whether manufacturers would accept proposals that would require safety and efficacy testing to substantiate label claims.

The FDA continued compiling complaints from customers about neurological reactions to perfumes including symptoms such as burning of the eyes, nose and throat, flushing, dizziness, nausea, difficulty in breathing, memory loss, and drowsiness. Some hospitals banned the use of perfumes by operating room nurses. A group calling itself the National Foundation of the Chemically Hypersensitive wanted to ban the use of fragrances in public meeting places.

Some spokesmen within the fragrance and cosmetic industry claimed that, because no one had ever been killed or seriously injured as a result of fragrance use, the FDA's resources would be better spent on bigger health problems. They advocated individual avoidance of offending ingredients as a solution to skin irritations and allergic responses. Although the industry's safety record prior to the 1990s had been good, some seasoned industry watchers expressed concern about continued safety as many small, new companies emerged.

Growing concern about environmental issues also impacted the industry. Several surveys demonstrated increased awareness of pollution and related issues. In 1976, 64 percent of one survey's respondents favored banning products that polluted the environment; by 1988, 73 percent supported such a ban. In another survey, 82 percent of respondents claimed to have changed purchasing decisions as a result of environmental concerns; 77 percent said that the environmental reputation of a company was important to them when making brand decisions; and 56 percent had refused to buy a product during the previous year because of environmental concerns. In 1990, Find/SVP (a New York survey group) estimated that 18.8 million U.S. households were environmentally interested shoppers. These consumers, called "Green consumers," accounted for about 20 percent of the U.S. population and their number was expected to increase. In a report on Green consumers, Find/SVP cited three main concerns: animal rights and species preservation, availability of clean air and water, and waste management.

One of the most controversial environmental matters facing the fragrance industry was pressure to reduce its use of volatile organic chemicals (VOCs). The most popularly used VOC was ethyl alcohol, which functioned as a solvent. The industry claimed that water was not a good substitute for ethyl alcohol because many fragrance ingredients were not water soluble. Ingredients designed to help materials dissolve in water affected product texture and also presented possible safety concerns. Propellants and many other ingredients used within the industry were also VOCs.

VOCs were blamed for contributing to ground-level ozone. In California, VOC emissions from colognes, perfumes, toilet water, aftershaves, and body splashes were estimated at almost 1,700 pounds per day. Consequently, in the early 1990s, California proposed limits on VOC usage in fragrances. New York and other states were expected to follow. In California, the proposed regulations scheduled to take effect on January 1, 1995 limited VOCs to 70 percent of perfumes, colognes, and toilet waters; 60 percent of aftershaves; and 50 percent of other fragrances. Industry negotiators and the California Air Resources Board agreed to exempt colognes, perfumes and toilet waters

that were on the market before the regulations took effect.

In addition to planned compliance with VOC regulations, many fragrance and cosmetic companies brought "green" products to the market place. Estee Lauder introduced its Origins Natural Resources line of skin care, body products, aromatherapy, and makeup. The line was promoted as natural and non-animal tested. Items were sold in recyclable containers. Revlon brought out New Age Naturals, skin care products made of all degradable ingredients, and Pure Skin Care, a line of products developed without animal testing. Mary Kay Cosmetics' Countryside Colors line emphasized its use of recyclable packaging made from recycled materials. Mary Kay also eliminated most external packaging on men's skin care products. As some companies eliminated, reduced, or refrabricated outer packaging to emphasize their concern about waste disposal problems, others, particularly fragrance manufacturers, expressed concern about the trend because packaging contributed to their image.

Critics claimed that many of the environmental efforts advertised by cosmetic and fragrance manufacturers were exaggerated, false, or meaningless. For example, "biodegradable" packages were incapable of degrading under conditions present in most landfills. Some products were labeled "ozone friendly" because they did not contain chlorofluorocarbons (CFCs), but CFCs had been banned since the late 1970s. "Recyclable" notations on plastic containers were meaningless when recycling plants for particular plastics (like polystyrene) were not available.

Along with increased environmental awareness came concern for healthy products. Items seen as safe for the environment were perceived as healthy for users. This philosophy drove a trend toward increased use of natural products containing ingredients such as proteins and vitamins. It also brought expanded use of botanical ingredients such as aloe, cucumber, and berry extracts. In perfumes, the trend led to the increasing popularity of discreet scents, floral freshness, and sea smells. In makeup, consumers began turning to functional products. Cosmetics were expected to do more than add color and cover skin imperfections. Buyers wanted products to contain ingredients such as sunscreens and emollients to nourish and protect their skin. The focus on natural products also led to more realistic product claims.

The emphasis on natural ingredients, however, extended only to plant sources. Animal products were shunned and animal-testing fell into disfavor. Many companies promoted cosmetic lines that were developed without animal testing. One example was SafeBrands Inc, which prohibited the use of animal testing in the development of its products and by its raw ingredient suppliers.

The Cosmetic, Toiletries, and Fragrance Association (CTFA) remained firm in its support of some animal testing, however. According to the CTFA, even products that claimed to use non-animal test methods relied on models that were acquired as a result of animal testing. The organization believed that human health and safety were more important than animal rights. The CTFA reported that 74 percent of Californians polled opposed legislation that would prohibit animal testing to insure product safety.

The most widely used animal test, and perhaps the most controversial, was the Draize Eye Irritancy Test. The Draize test involved putting drops in the eyes of albino rabbits so investigators could note redness, swelling, cloudiness, and opacity. Also of importance was the eye's ability to recover from any injuries sustained.

In addition to the social and political concerns surrounding animal testing, environmentalism, and product safety, the industry was also impacted by the nation's economic situation. The perfume, cosmetic, and personal care products industry had established a "recession proof" image when sales of inexpensive cosmetics had outsold mid-priced food items and clothing during the depression of the 1930s. Cosmetics also did well during the recessions of the 1960s and 1980s. The recession of the early 1990s, however, brought new challenges. Counterfeit products were offered at low prices. Customers resisted high prices and demanded value. The numbers of distribution channels for upscale lines decreased as traditional department stores closed. Costs associated with product promotion increased and marketers turned more often to expensive strategies such as giving free complementary products.

In an effort to move away from traditional department store cosmetic counters, upscale manufacturers turned to self-serve packaging and sold greater volumes to discounters. This enabled retailers to place items on sale. Depressed pricing, however, sometimes diminished a product's image. Bridge brands increasingly aimed at a niche between the upscale and mass markets. Mass marketers focused on increasing volumes to generate more profit.

INDUSTRY LEADERS

One of the largest companies involved in the perfume, cosmetic, and toilet preparations industry was Procter & Gamble (P&G), which posted total sales in 1996 of $35.3 billion (including some noncosmetic items). In the early 1990's P&G's Cover Girl held 59 percent of the makeup market; Oil of Olay was the leader in mass-market skin care with a 29.7 percent share; and in men's products, Old Spice was a best seller. In order to expand Old Spice's appeal to younger men, P&G developed a new marketing campaign, which focused on sports and action.

P&G increased its involvement in the global cosmetics market through the purchases of Beatrix and Max Factor. Beatrix, a German-based cosmetic manufacturer, had annual sales estimated at $200 million. Max Factor's sales were estimated at $600 million per year. Domestic sales accounted for only 25 percent of the total. Japan and the United Kingdom were the largest overseas customers.

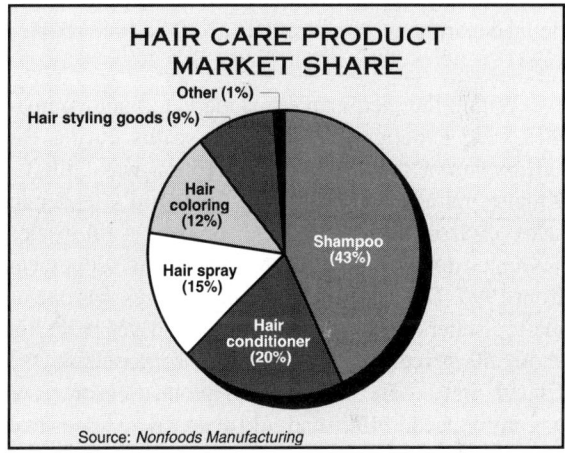

HAIR CARE PRODUCT MARKET SHARE

Other (1%)
Hair styling goods (9%)
Hair coloring (12%)
Hair spray (15%)
Shampoo (43%)
Hair conditioner (20%)

Source: *Nonfoods Manufacturing*

Max Factor, the company, took its name from the Hollywood makeup artist Max Factor. In 1914, Factor began making cosmetic products according to the demands of the technologically evolving film industry. One Factor creation, Pancake makeup, first appeared on the screen in 1937. Max Factor continued to develop new formulas to meet the needs of Technicolor movies and color television. In 1990, the company introduced a new makeup designed to meet the demands of high density television in Japan. New Definition Perfecting Makeup used four times more pigment dots than other products. Max Factor was also a leader in cosmetic development outside the film industry. In 1988, the company introduced the "no makeup look" with a no-color mascara and "Invisible Makeup," made of light-diffusing ingredients to blur skin imperfections. The "Transparencies" line, introduced in 1991, used a new combination of color pigments to avoid heaviness or opacity.

Johnson & Johnson, a diversified healthcare product manufacturer, was involved in producing consumer toiletries as well as pharmaceuticals and professional medical products. In 1996, the company brought in sales of more than $21.6 billion and employed 89,300 workers.

Within the fragrance segment of the industry, The Estee Lauder Group of Companies was one of the nation's largest companies. Estee Lauder first began marketing skin products in 1946. Lauder's earliest perfume, called Youth Dew, was introduced in 1953. Since then, other perfumes were developed including Estee, Cinnabar, and Beautiful. Lauder's marketing efforts presented American women with the idea of wearing perfume all day long, not just on special occasions. During 1996, Lauder's estimated world sales totaled $3.2 billion, most of which was in prestige markets. Industry analysts expected the company to be heavily impacted by a trend away from traditional department store cosmetic and fragrance counter sales.

Within the men's toiletries market, many companies were experiencing declining profits during the early years of the 1990s. An exception was Gillette. Gillette, founded in 1901, was the world's leader in sales of razors and blades. The company's 1996 sales amounted to $9.7 billion, an increase of 43 percent from 1995. The company's line of toiletries was one of the top sellers in the United States, and yet pulled in about 60 percent of its revenues from outside the United States. The innovative Gillette Sensor razor was introduced in 1990 and sold at premium prices that helped bolster the company's bottom line. As a result of the Gillette Sensor's success, the company expanded efforts to upscale some of its lines and aim them at a market niche between mass market items and upscale products. Gillette was also working toward encouraging retailers to group men's grooming products together in a single section containing shaving supplies as well as men's fragrances.

WORK FORCE

Although industry shipment figures demonstrated overall growth during the 1980s and the early 1990s, employment figures fell. In 1988, the toilet preparation industry employed 72,200. In 1991, several manufacturers including Colgate-Palmolive, Gillette, Revlon, Procter & Gamble, and American Cyanamid closed plants or announced future plant closings. In 1995, the industry employed 68,400.

Mergers, corporate acquisitions, and takeovers restructured the industry. Major participants like Faberge, Max Factor, Almay, Halston, Germaine

Monteil, Shulton, and Yardley changed owners. Consolidation and cost cutting measures eliminated less profitable products and resulted in the loss of many blue and white collar jobs. A few companies, such as Amway and Kao's Andrew Jergens Division, were expanding employment opportunities but not at a pace sufficient to counteract the shrinking work forces at other organizations.

AMERICA AND THE WORLD

In the early 1990s, the United States was a net exporter of perfumes, cosmetics, and toilet preparations. Canada, the United Kingdom, Japan, and Mexico were major purchasers of U.S. goods. About 55 percent of the nation's imports were received from France. Other countries supplying products to the U.S. market included the United Kingdom, Japan, and Mexico. The world wide fragrance market was estimated at $10 billion. Within this segment, U.S. demand represented the largest national market in the world, only slightly smaller than the entire European market. Demand in Japan was estimated to be about one third the size of the U.S. market.

As the industry moved increasingly toward globalization, new markets were developing in Latin America, Eastern Europe, and the Pacific Rim. While American companies like Procter & Gamble increased their penetration in overseas markets, foreign companies increased their involvement in American markets. Globalization brought efforts to adopt common terminology, particularly in describing ingredients. The Cosmetic, Toiletries and Fragrance Association (CTFA) expected wider use of the CTFA Ingredient Dictionary.

RESEARCH AND TECHNOLOGY

During the 1990s, research and technological improvements within the industry focused on reformulating products to move away from synthetic chemicals and to rely on natural products. Within the class of natural products, the primary emphasis was on vegetable and plant materials. Chemists also sought to meet customer demands for mildness and reduced toxicity. Within the growing sun-care segment of the industry, scientists researched products with improved protection, especially against year-round ultraviolet rays. Color market formulators worked to develop new silicon-based products which promised better color retention and improved waterproofing capabilities.

According to a report published in *Seventeen* magazine, Tony Barone, vice president of Barone Cosmetics, predicted further changes within the cosmetic industry. He guessed that as Americans shunned the sun because of health concerns, paler faces would become more fashionable. He speculated that modern habits of living in controlled environments would lead to a loss of body hair including diminished eyebrows and less head hair. Barone considered the advancement of medical cosmetics, where beauty doctors would tattoo permanent makeup in place and perform routine cosmetic surgery, a possible future development.

FURTHER READING

Abrutyn, E.S., B.C. Bahr, and S.M. Fuson. "Overview of the Antiperspirant Market: Technology and Trends." *Drug and Cosmetic Industry,* August 1992.

"The Big Picture: Cosmetic Figures Strong, Despite Recession Worries." *Drug and Cosmetic Industry,* June 1992.

"Can the Queen of Cosmetics Keep Her Crown?" *Business Week,* 17 January 1994.

Carsch, Gustav. "The Safety of Fragrance Ingredients." *Soap, Cosmetics, Chemical Specialties,* July 1992.

Christiansen, Suzanne. "Regulations Cast Cloud Over CTFA." *Soap, Cosmetics, Chemical Specialties,* April 1991.

"Cosmetics (Perhaps Too Many) for Women of Color." *Drug and Cosmetic Industry,* November 1992.

"Cosmetics Use Both Praised and Criticized." *Chemical Marketing Reporter,* 19 September 1988.

"CTFA Scientific Conference: VOC Limits for Fragrances, Coming Sunscreen Monograph." *Drug and Chemical Industry,* December 1991.

Darconte, Lorraine. "New Naturals." *Soap, Cosmetics, Chemical Specialties,* May 1991.

Darnay, Arsen, ed. *Manufacturing USA,* 5th ed. Detroit; Gale Research, 1996.

Davidowitz, Esther. "The History of Makeup." *Seventeen,* March 1987.

Davis, Donald A. "Anticipated Problems." *Drug and Cosmetic Industry,* September 1992.

———. "Cosmeceuticals Come Into Vogue." *Drug and Cosmetic Industry,* October 1990.

———. "The 'Green' Movement Comes to Cosmetics." *Drug and Cosmetic Industry,* June 1990.

Eiermann, Heinz J. "Regulating Cosmetics Can Be Done More Uniformly Worldwide." *Soap, Cosmetics, Chemical Specialties,* February 1988.

"Even Pharaohs Had Facials." *Newsweek,* 11 December 1989.

Foulke, Judith E. "Cosmetic Ingredients: Understanding the Puffery." *FDA Consumer,* May 1992.

"Fragrance Flashback!" *Teen,* April 1986.

Garrett, Anne Wolven. "Skin Deep." *Drug and Cosmetic Industry,* October 1989.

The Gillete Company. *The Gillete Company 1992 Annual Report.* Boston: Gillete, 1993.

Goldemberg, Robert L. "Fragrance-Free Zones." *Drug and Chemical Industry,* December 1991.

Green, Timothy. "Making Scents is More Complicated Than You'd Think." *Smithsonian,* June 1991.

Kintish, Lisa. "Making Sense of Male Scents." *Soap, Cosmetics, Chemical Specialties,* December 1990.

Lord, Shirley. "Makeup—The Modern Interpretation of Face Paint—Is Still Evolving." *Vogue,* February 1990.

Michelow, Raizel. "In Search of the Fountain of Youth."

"Overseas Consumers Flock to U.S. Household and Personal Care Brands." *STREETnet* , 26 July 1996. Available from http://www.streetnet.com.

"Rapid International Growth." *STREETnet,* September 1996. "Pretty and Practical." *STREETnet,* 30 July 1996. Available from http://www.streetnet.com.

Roach, Virginia. "Green is Beautiful." *Drug and Cosmetic Industry,* February 1991.

Stehlin, Dori. "Cosmetic Safety More Complex Than at First Blush." *FDA Consumer,* November 1991.

Strandberg, Keith. "Men's Toiletries: An Overview." *Soap, Cosmetics, Chemical Specialties,* December 1992.

Tilton, Helga. "Global Makeup." *Chemical Marketing Reporter,* 22 July 1991.

U.S. Department of Commerce. *1987 Census of Manufactures.* Washington, DC: Bureau of the Census, February 1990.

U.S. Department of Commerce. *U.S. Industrial Outlook '92.* Washington: Department of Commerce, 1992.

—Karen Bellenir, updated by Gertrude Mandeville

SIC 2851

PAINTS, VARNISHES, LACQUERS, ENAMELS, AND ALLIED PRODUCTS

This industry category includes establishments primarily engaged in manufacturing paints (in paste and ready-mixed form); varnishes; lacquers; enamels; shellac; dry powder coatings; putties, wood fillers, and sealers; paint and varnish removers; paintbrush cleaners; and allied paint products.

Establishments primarily engaged in manufacturing carbon black are classified in **SIC 2895: Carbon Black**; those manufacturing bone black, lamp black, and inorganic color pigments are classified in **SIC 2816: Inorganic Pigments**; those manufacturing organic color pigments are classified in **SIC 2865: Cyclic Organic Crudes and Intermediates, and Or-**

ganic **Dyes and Pigments**; those manufacturing plastics materials are classified in **SIC 2821: Plastics Materials and Resins**; those manufacturing printing ink are classified in **SIC 2893: Printing Ink**; those manufacturing caulking compounds and sealants are classified in **SIC 2891: Adhesives and Sealants**; those manufacturing artists' paints are classified in **SIC 3952: Lead Pencils, Crayons, and Artists' Materials**; and those manufacturing turpentine are classified in **SIC 2861: Gum and Wood Chemicals**.

INDUSTRY SNAPSHOT

According to the U.S. Census Bureau's *Current Industrial Reports,* U.S. manufacturers shipped about 1.4 billion gallons of paint, valued at $15.9 billion. About 700 firms produced paint in the United States in the mid-1990s, down from over 900 early in the decade. The paint and coatings business was considered a mature industry, with growth projected at about 1-2 percent annually.

Historically, paint remained a comparatively small, yet influential industry into the mid-1990s. Despite its relatively minor revenues, the industry's products affected virtually every aspect of modern life. From cars and homes, to containers for food and beverages, to appliances and furniture, paints and coatings protected, personalized, and beautified our surroundings. Some economists consider it a leading economic indicator.

The paint industry has become essential to nine major manufacturing industries, including: automobiles, trucks and buses, metal cans, farm machinery and equipment, construction machinery and equipment, metal furniture and fixtures, wood furniture and fixtures, major appliances, and coil coating (high speed application of industrial coatings to continuous sheets, strips, and coils of aluminum or steel). Additionally, paint manufacturers influence the wider chemicals industry via their purchase of billions of dollars worth of raw materials. Paint and coatings were also an integral contributor to the new and resale housing industry.

The paint industry underwent significant changes in the early 1990s, including a gradual expansion of specialized end-user markets, progressively stricter environmental regulations, an increase in foreign corporate ownership, and an accelerating pace of consolidation. But in the mid-1990s, as raw material prices eased and demand in two key markets (automotive and housing) surged, paint manufacturers experienced an increase.

ORGANIZATION AND STRUCTURE

The paint industry's first national professional organization, the National Paint, Oil, and Varnish Association, was founded in 1888 in Saratoga, New York. Industry associations proliferated in the early twentieth century until the Great Depression, when government officials and top paint company executives urged the creation of a single national organization. The National Paint, Varnish, and Lacquer Association was formed in 1933, and was later renamed the National Paint and Coatings Association (NPCA).

The NPCA's membership constituted over 75 percent of the entire paint industry in the 1990s. The organization existed to represent the industry to government regulators and the general public. Its public relations and educational programs focused primarily on the technical and aesthetic qualities of architectural paint. The group's annual ''Clean-Up, Paint-Up, Fix-Up'' campaign, which encouraged neighborhood pride through house painting, was first undertaken in 1912 and lasted through the early 1970s. In the 1990s, campaigns countered paint's persistently bad image as a noxious, but necessary, maintenance product. Following the lead of such successful ''category marketers'' as the cotton and milk industries, the NPCA promoted paint as a versatile decorating tool.

Competitive Structure. Numerous mergers, the high cost of regulation, and increasingly expensive, complex manufacturing processes began to have a cumulative effect on industry composition in the mid-1990s. Mergers and acquisitions reduced the number of companies in the industry from more than 900 to about 700 over the course of the early 1990s. By that time, the top three producers accounted for about 45 percent of U.S. shipments, up from less than 30 percent in 1990. The ten largest manufacturers comprised nearly two-thirds of the market. Industry observers expected consolidation to eliminate another 300 companies by the year 2000.

The geographic dispersal of paint manufacturers was historically dictated by the high transportation costs associated with paint distribution. The weight of prepared paint encouraged the development of a regionalized structure of small manufacturers by the end of the nineteenth century. Paint companies gravitated toward major population and industrial centers like Cleveland, New York, St. Louis, and Chicago. This arrangement dominated the industry until the 1940s and 1950s, when the leading paint manufacturers began to consolidate paint plants and develop wider distribution networks.

By the early 1960s, however, that trend reversed, and smaller branch plants were built to lower freight costs, avoid some state taxes, and facilitate more personalized service. In 1967, about 66 percent of paint was consumed within 500 miles of its manufacture. Decentralization persisted through the 1990s, represented by the industry segment of tenacious small-to medium-sized paint manufacturers who served limited regional markets.

Market Segments. Three basic segments existed within the industry: architectural coatings, Original Equipment Manufacturer (OEM) product coatings, and special purpose coatings.

Architectural coatings, known in the industry as trade sales paint and commonly referred to as house paint, comprised the largest segment, contributing 44 percent of annual gallonage and 38 percent of revenues in 1995. About 60 percent of the 617.5 million gallons of architectural coatings sold in 1995 were interior paints. Exterior paints contributed 36 percent (225.1 million gallons), and lacquers and all others accounted for the remainder of architectural paint shipped. Water-based, or latex, paints contributed for 76 percent of trade sales in 1996, up slightly from 73 percent in 1990.

The bulk of architectural coatings were distributed through wholesale and retail outlets. Marketing these paints encompassed both formulation and aesthetic factors. Safety, durability, consistency, washability, and convenience were some common consumer concerns with regard to formulation. But color and appearance were also important, so paint manufacturers were often obliged to keep up with decorating trends.

Sales in this industry segment were keyed to weather (which could limit the application of exterior paints), new housing starts, sales of existing homes, and to a lesser degree, commercial and industrial construction. Architectural coatings were subject to competition from vinyl siding, wallpaper, wood paneling, and glass. Major producers for this segment included Sherwin-Williams Co., PPG Industries, Inc., Grow Group, Valspar Corp., Glidden Co. (a subsidiary of Great Britain's ICI Paints), and Benjamin Moore and Co.

OEM paints constituted about 28 percent of industry gallonage in 1995. These products were often custom formulated in consultation with the end-user and applied during manufacturing. These coatings were used in such durable goods markets as automobiles, aircraft, appliances, furniture, metal containers, sheet and coil metals, and industrial equipment. Dollar shipments for this industry segment in 1995 were a record

$5.3 billion, up more than 25 percent from 1990. Strong automobile and consumer durables markets helped fuel volume growth as well, which rose from 339 million gallons in 1990 to 389.6 million gallons in 1995.

One major challenge facing OEM producers in the early 1990s was the increased use of plastics in automobiles and appliances, which created the need to match the paint finish of metal panels with plastic panels that were painted separately. Development of new applications technologies was another primary concern. Major companies with interests in OEM markets included E. I. DuPont de Nemours, PPG Industries, Inc., Grow Group, and Glidden Co.

Special purpose or industrial coatings, which largely developed after World War II, accounted for less than one-fourth of industry volume in 1994. While similar to architectural coatings in that they could be classified as stock or shelf goods, special purpose coatings were formulated for specific applications or environmental conditions, and were often sold directly to the end user. Primary markets for these products included automotive and machinery refinishing, industrial maintenance (including factories, equipment, tanks, utilities, and railroads), bridges, traffic markings, metallic coatings, and marine coatings. Having declined both in terms of volume and revenues in 1991 and 1992, this industry segment rebounded to sales of $3.1 billion in volume of 194 million gallons by 1994. E. I. DuPont de Nemours, PPG Industries, Inc., Sherwin-Williams Co., RPM Inc., Courtaulds Coatings, Inc., Glidden Co., Akzo Coatings, Inc., and Valspar Corp. were all important producers of specialty coatings.

BACKGROUND AND DEVELOPMENT

Industry Origins. The first recorded paint mill in America was established in Boston in 1700 by Thomas Child, who had emigrated from England. His business manufactured the components of paint in a paste form During most of the nineteenth century, professional painters mixed their own paints from linseed oil, white lead, turpentine, and pigments. Their formulas were inconsistent, and the paint they produced had virtually no shelf life.

In 1867, D. R. Averill, an Ohioan, patented ready-to-use paint. But early factory-made paints were notorious for their poor quality and unreliable performance. It was not until the 1880s that quality ready-mixed paints were produced. By 1888, the paint industry generated about $45 million in annual revenues.

During World War I, paint and varnish were vital to the U.S. military effort for protection and camouflage of equipment and personnel. The war exposed the industry's dependence on imported raw materials, and frequent shortages encouraged the development of domestic and synthetic replacements. By 1922, annual industry volume neared $300 million.

Paint and coatings were vital to the Allied effort during World War II, as the products once again preserved and camouflaged virtually everything. The unique needs of the military compelled the development of specialized paints and coatings. There were acid-proof, corrosion-proof, and waterproof coatings; fire-retardant, ice-repellent, fungus-resistant, weather-resistant, and water-resistant compounds that enhanced fabrics; and phosphorescent and florescent paints that proved strategically vital. The NPCA's "Paint Protects America" slogan summed up the industry's wartime contributions.

A Maturing Industry. After more than quadrupling from 1933 to 1947, it took the paint industry 17 years to increase from $1.25 billion to $2 billion. The American market was nearing saturation, and the same high transportation costs that prevented the consolidation of paint plants impeded expansion into overseas markets.

Overcapacity, increased competition, and rising expenses also plagued the paint industry. The U.S. Department of Defense reported on overcapacity in the paint industry during World War II, noting that "only 100 of the then 1400 paint manufacturers, working only one shift, could meet any emergency needs of the entire country." By the 1960s, alternatives like aluminum siding, concrete, and stucco for exterior application, and vinyl, wood, and paper wallcoverings for the interior, entered the already-crowded market. Paint producers began to sacrifice their profit margins in an attempt to maintain market share.

At the same time, labor, packaging, and distribution costs rose dramatically. From 1965 to 1970, wage costs rose 33 percent, but the dollar value of industry-wide shipments rose only 26 percent and productivity increased only 2 percent—not enough to account for the difference. By 1970, the industry's average return fell to 6.2 percent, compared to a 10.1 percent average for all industries.

As the growth and profits of the paint industry trailed the rest of the economy, top paint manufacturers diversified into everything from fertilizer to foods to garner profits. But promotional sales exacerbated the profit squeeze during the 1970s. Many in the industry blamed mass merchandising of paint. Discounters could afford to slash margins and even take a loss to capture market share. Paint manufacturers were forced to follow suit to hang onto their share. Another factor that emerged during the 1970s was the oil crisis, which caused the price of many of the industry's raw materials to rise rapidly.

As the paint industry matured and profit margins decreased, many firms merged to consolidate their resources and achieve economies of scale. In 1960, there were about 2,000 companies in the industry. Between 1963 and 1968 alone, 71 paint companies changed hands, often merging several smaller businesses into one substantial company. The larger, more powerful companies sought increased market share and the higher sales.

Rebound. The paint industry endured a recession in the early 1980s along with the rest of America, but from 1983 to 1990 growth was buoyed by strong construction and durable goods markets. Volume increased dramatically, from less than 420 million gallons shipped in 1982 to over one billion gallons in 1990. The physical increase was accompanied by a leap in dollar sales, from about $3.1 billion in 1982 to about $9.3 billion in 1985 and over $11.7 billion in 1990. Consolidation of the paint companies continued during the 1980s. By the end of 1992, less than 900 companies remained, down from 1,100 in 1984. Manufacturers also sought to increase their profit margins through applied research and development directed at refining existing technologies.

After decades of practice, paint and coatings companies anticipated environmental regulation and tried to prepare for it in advance. So when the Environmental Protection Agency estimated that coatings solvents were responsible for 8 to 10 percent of all Volatile Organic Compounds (VOCs) released in the United States, coatings formulators stepped up their efforts to produce high-performance, low-VOC paints before solvents were banned.

Government and independent analysts agreed that foreign investment in the U.S. paint industry was likely to continue in the 1990s, due to high currency values and low interest rates. And although consolidation within the industry was also expected to continue, some savvy smaller companies were able to hold their own by capitalizing on technical expertise, new products, and quick customer service.

Sales volumes in the paint and coatings industry fell 4.9 percent to about $11.39 billion in 1991, largely due to the recession's impact on the architectural and special purpose segments. From 1988 to 1991, raw materials prices increased 24 percent, but paint prices increased only 12 percent.

The financial picture brightened in 1992 and 1993, as sales of existing homes increased due to low interest rates. Some analysts noted that owners of offices and light manufacturing buildings purchased more paint to maintain their properties as well. These factors kept the paint industry growing slowly at an annual rate of about 2.9 percent from 1987 to 1992.

CURRENT CONDITIONS

In the 1990s, paint manufacturers' primary concerns centered on progressively stricter environmental regulations, increasing foreign ownership, greater likelihood of mergers and acquisitions, and accelerating technological advances.

Growth in manufacturing, especially autos and construction in the mid-1990s, fueled healthy expansion of the paint industry. Paced by double-digit volume gains in the water-based exterior coatings segment, dollar volume advanced 9 percent from 1993 to $15.9 billion in 1995. This trend accelerated into the first half of 1996, when volume increased 12.5 percent to 685 million gallons over the first half of 1995 and value jumped 16.4 percent to $8.3 billion in the period. The Freedonia Group forecast that domestic sales of paint and coatings would expand at an average annual rate of almost two percent, reaching $18 billion on volume of 1.3 billion gallons by the year 2000. Industrial coatings, especially powder and radiation-cured types, were expected to account for a significant portion of the growth.

INDUSTRY LEADERS

Mergers and acquisitions modified the upper ranks of the U.S. paint industry in the mid-1990s, bringing an end to longtime leader Sherwin Williams' dominance and adding new names to the list. Ongoing industry consolidation guaranteed that the standings would continue to change in this close-run horserace.

PPG Industries Inc. Formerly known as Pittsburgh Plate Glass, this company was founded in 1883. As its name implied, paint was historically not its primary product: in the late 1960s, coatings constituted less than 20 percent of PPG's annual sales. By the mid-1990s, however, PPG had expanded its paint interests to become its primary division with over $2.8 billion in annual revenues. A spate of acquisitions in the mid-1990s vaulted the company over Sherwin-Williams to make it the top manufacturer in the industry. Its key brands of architectural coatings included Lucite house paint and Olympic wood stain, both acquired from Clorox in 1989. By 1995, the company had also captured a leading share of the global automotive paint segment.

Sherwin-Williams Co. One of the founding firms of the American paint industry, Sherwin-Williams celebrated its 130th anniversary with estimated paint sales of $1.4 billion in 1995. The Cleveland-based company was America's largest paint manufacturer from 1905 until the early 1990s, when it relinquished its standing to PPG Industries. Its vertical integration, which extended from raw materials and packaging to retail stores, helped the company become a low cost manufacturer and the broadest distributor of architectural coatings in the United States. By 1995, retail operations had surpassed paint manufacture as Sherwin-Williams' largest business segment, with over $2 billion in annual revenues.

Sherwin-Williams always emphasized architectural coatings, offered under the company's namesake brand and its acquired Dutch-Boy label, but by the early 1990s also produced industrial finishes for the automotive after-market and painting accessories. In 1990, Sherwin-Williams acquired Krylon brand aerosol paint and DeSoto, a major producer of architectural paints. In 1995, it merged with Pratt & Lambert United Inc., formerly two mid-sized companies that merged in 1994.

Two other Cleveland-area companies battled for the number three spot in the mid-1990s: the Glidden Co. and RPM, Inc.

The Glidden Co. Founded in 1875, Glidden was a subsidiary of ICI Americas, Inc., and a division of the world's leading paint manufacturer, Great Britain's ICI Paints. Glidden's overall sales totaled an estimated $1 billion in 1995, and the company pioneered no-VOC paints in 1992.

RPM Inc. Founded in 1947 as Republic Powdered Metals, RPM Inc. boasted an unbroken record of rising sales through fiscal 1996. Having grown primarily through acquisitions—over 40 from 1971 to 1997—the company more than doubled its sales in the early 1990s to enter the upper echelons of the coatings industry. Its most significant paint purchase was Rust-Oleum Corp., best known for its spray paints. RPM's revenues surpassed the $1 billion mark in 1995 and totaled $1.2 billion in 1996.

Other key players included Courtaulds United States (a subsidiary of the UK's Courtaulds plc), Valspar Corp., and Benjamin Moore and Co.

WORK FORCE

The paint and coatings industry employed an estimated 50,500 Americans in 1996, down from about 61,800 in 1990. Production workers comprised about 50 percent of that total. Another 25 percent of the industry's employees were managers and administrators, and 20 percent were professional chemists and sales representatives.

Production workers operated and fixed machinery, moved raw materials, and monitored the production process. High school graduates qualified for entry-level production jobs, and advancement into better-paying jobs requiring higher skills or more responsibility was possible through on-the-job experience or additional vocational training at a two-year technical college. Hourly earnings for paint production workers averaged nearly $13.50, approximately 20 percent higher than the national average for manufacturing production jobs.

Most administrative and management positions required a bachelor's degree and experience in the industry. Support workers often held two-year technical degrees or some college, but these were not required.

Research and development specialists in the paint industry included chemists and chemical engineers. They typically conducted research and experimented with new products and processes. Advanced degrees were often essential for these positions. Some senior chemists were promoted to management positions.

Marketing and sales representatives promoted sales of their companies' products by developing new products, creating plans to market them, and advertising them to retail and industrial customers. These positions often required a degree in marketing, chemistry, or chemical engineering.

Employment in the paint and coatings industry was projected to continue its steady decline through the year 2005, with machine operators bearing the brunt of the cuts. Those positions were expected to decline by 29 percent. In line with the industry's strong emphasis on research and development, the number of chemists employed was expected to increase by over one-fourth by 2005. More efficient production processes, increased plant automation, growth of environmental awareness, health and safety concerns, and rising foreign competition were all expected to influence paint and coatings employment significantly and negatively.

AMERICA AND THE WORLD

Due to prohibitive shipping expenses, overseas trade historically did not contribute significantly to the U.S. paint market. Nevertheless, the United States dominated what global paint trade did exist after World War I, when Germany relinquished its top position in chemicals. But after World War II, foreign countries grew increasingly self-sufficient.

The United States dominated the global paint industry in the mid-1900s, accounting for 40 percent of the $5.2 billion value and 50 percent of the supply. West Germany ranked a distant second with revenues of about $460 million, and Great Britain, France, and Italy followed suit.

In 1960, the industry's total export business constituted less than 2 percent of total production. During this decade tariffs, quotas, licensing and exchange restrictions, and special import fees hamstrung U.S. coatings manufacturers' world trade. Trade barriers encouraged some paint producers to enter into joint ventures with their foreign competitors so that they could market their products overseas.

Trade liberalization and reductions in transportation costs in the 1990s encouraged international trade. By mid-decade, foreign sales represented a small, but growing percentage of total domestic revenue, with exports doubling from 1989 to 1993. More than half of goods went to Canada and Mexico. While the U.S. paint industry maintained a positive balance of trade in the early 1990s, Canada, Germany, Japan and Belgium had become the most significant importers.

Globalization. Globalization of the paint industry occurred as U.S. companies followed their primary OEM customers from America to the Far East and other lower-cost areas. Economic liberalization drew many of the world's leading paint manufacturers to China, where joint ventures promised a piece of double-digit sales growth. At the same time, foreign producers sought growth through acquisition of U.S. paint companies. These international movements enabled some large corporations to capitalize on their technological advantages in new markets.

Imperial Chemicals Industries was an aggressive acquirer of U.S. paint companies, purchasing the Glidden paint operations of SCM Corp. in 1986 and both Grow Group and Fuller-O'Brien Paints in 1995. The Glidden acquisition marked ICI's entry into the U.S. paint industry and made the British conglomerate the world's largest paint company.

By 1995, ten multinational companies held an estimated 60 percent of total world production, compared with one-fifth in 1980. By that time, the top five companies worldwide were ICI, Akzo-Nobel, PPG Industries, Sherwin-Williams, and Kansai. The Europeans and Japanese, historically the stiffest competitors of the United States, emerged in a particularly strong position internationally.

RESEARCH AND TECHNOLOGY

As of the 1990s, paints and coatings incorporated a myriad of chemical compounds uniquely formulated to fulfill the varied requirements of hundreds of thousands of applications. The need for regulatory compliance helped make research and development a paramount concern—and a major budget item. But the industry was not always so technically inclined.

From its inception in 1700 until the mid-1900s, paint formulation remained relatively unchanged. The switch from paste to ready-mixed paint in the 1860s and the mechanization of the manufacturing process in the mid-1880s were two significant innovations. But for the first half of the twentieth century, the manufacture of paint was a relatively simple process of mixing and grinding oils and pigments using "secret" recipes usually concocted by trial and error.

As previously mentioned, World War II inspired many innovations in paint formulation. One observer noted that there was more technological progress in the paint industry from 1947 to 1967 than in the previous 1,000 years. Product developments occurred so quickly that an estimated 90 percent of 1960's trade sales consisted of items that did not exist a decade before.

Most of the raw materials used in the contemporary paint industry were developed during the postwar era. They were derived from petroleum, then mixed in varying proportions with specific chemical agents to produce such distinct characteristics as durability, elasticity, and chemical and thermal resistance. By the mid-1960s, the major industrial paint manufacturers offered as many as 20,000 different products.

The 1980s and 1990s brought the industry's most significant and rapid changes. As one industry executive told *Industrial Paint & Powder* in 1994, "Technology has changed more in the last eight years than in the previous 80 years of our coatings business."

Color. During the late 1950s, some manufacturers of architectural paint offered an increased selection of colors to consumers by shipping a white base paint to retailers with separate oil or powdered pigments. The desired paint color would be mixed at the point of sale upon the customer's request. This system gave the customer a wider choice of colors (over 1,000 in some cases) and reduced the retailer's risk of overstocking an unpopular color. By 1960, these "custom" systems constituted about 5 percent of retail paint sales.

The Latex Revolution. The architectural paint market, and eventually the entire industry, was revolutionized by the introduction of waterborne, or latex, paint. Unlike its oil-based predecessors, latex paint required no ventilation, was non-flammable and scrubbable, gave a good finish, was easy to remove from brushes, and dried in about 20 minutes.

Latex ascent began in the industry in the 1950s. Before that time, solvent- or oil-based products dominated gallonage consumption, while waterborne, high-solids, and powdered coatings constituted only 10 percent of industry volume. By the early 1990s, water-based paints alone constituted over 75 percent of gallonage. Convenience was clearly a factor in the widespread commercial acceptance of water-based paints, but in the 1970s, another strong influence drove their industrial acceptance: government regulation.

Government Regulation Drives Innovation. Regulation of the industry accelerated dramatically during the environmentally conscious 1970s, when federal clean air regulations were adopted to encourage the production of less-polluting, less-toxic paints. By the beginning of the 1980s, nearly every aspect of the paint business was regulated. The Occupational Safety and Health Administration (OSHA) monitored the workplace. The Environmental Protection Agency regulated the introduction, generation, transportation, treatment, and disposal of hazardous materials used in or produced by the coatings industry. The Consumer Product Safety Commission protected paint customers by controlling what could be bought and sold.

Although many in the paint industry resisted government efforts to monitor the business, state and federal regulation actually encouraged several technological advances. An early example of this phenomenon occurred just after the turn of the century, when legislation was enacted in North Dakota requiring formula labels on house paints. The idea gained popularity among consumers and congressmen throughout the country. But paint manufacturers feared revealing their "secret formulas," and warned that the new law would inhibit research on new formulations. In hindsight, the rules encouraged the use of quality ingredients and fostered more scientific formulations.

Lead. Once a primary component of paint, lead ranked as the top environmental threat to children's health in the 1990s. Lead poisoning affected the nervous system, the gastrointestinal tract, and the blood-forming tissues, and was especially harmful to children. The deleterious effects of lead—which was also used in gasoline, ceramic finishes, plumbing, and many other products—were discovered in the 1930s. White lead pigments were essentially eliminated from architectural paints in the 1940s, but it was not until 1977 that the use of lead-based paints was outlawed in the United States.

Government and medical reports published in the late 1980s and early 1990s revealed evidence that lead poisoning could occur with much lower doses than was previously thought, so the lead problem was more pervasive than earlier believed. Some public health officials estimated that there could be accessible lead paint in up to 42 million homes and apartments housing 12 million children.

In the increasingly litigious American society, paint manufacturers rightly feared a wave of lawsuits. Some analysts predicted that lawsuits involving lead-paint poisoning could eventually eclipse asbestos suits. And in 1993, all paint manufacturers in California were assessed special fees under that state's Childhood Lead Poisoning Act of 1991. Paint industry spokespersons contended that the fines unfairly punished manufacturers and sellers that may not have been in business when the lead paint was sold, and that parents, contractors, and property managers should share the blame and the cost.

Superfund. In addition to the environmental concerns of producing and applying paints and coatings, manufacturers increasingly bore responsibility for disposal. Proposed in 1979, Superfund legislation mandated the accumulation of a multi-million dollar fund to pay for the cleanup of oil and hazardous waste spills and disposal sites. The fund would be amassed through fees assessed to businesses, municipalities, and individuals who were designated as Potentially Responsible Parties in the pollution of the sites. Since the Resource Conservation and Recovery Act (RCRA) had already classified paint wastes as hazardous materials, virtually all paint manufacturers found themselves subject to fee collection under Superfund. Representing the paint industry, the National Paint and Coatings Association argued that it was unfair to single out certain industries for problems created by the entire society.

Volatile Organic Compounds. Organic solvents, the oils that liquefied many paints, were blamed for some air pollution. As paint dried, the liquid portion evaporated. When the liquid was an organic solvent, volatile organic compounds (VOCs) were released in the drying process. VOCs reacted with sunlight to contribute to smog. State VOC regulations started to proliferate in the wake of 1977's Clean Air Act and subsequent Amendments, which required states to regulate geographic areas that failed to meet ambient air quality standards. Control of VOCs was a significant aspect of compliance. California was one of the first, and most stringent, state-level regulators.

Rather than resisting these state laws, the NPCA called for uniform federal guidelines, as opposed to the confusing array of state and local initiatives that cropped up. The NPCA supported the ''bubble concept'' of plant compliance, which allowed individual factories to develop plant-wide emission reduction plans using an average emission level of VOCs. Some companies went further, aiming for ''zero-waste generation:'' the elimination of plant emissions and reuse and recycling of materials.

Four basic coatings designed to save energy and pollute less were developed. For the most part, they exemplified different strategies to achieve the same purpose: to reduce the proportion of toxic solvents in paint. One industry executive predicted the eventual eradication of solvents from coatings. The development of water-soluble paint, for example, reduced the use of petroleum-based solvent in paints by about 90 percent. High solids paints contained more resins and pigments than solvents. Accelerated cure coatings were dried by ultraviolet light or an electron beam. Powdered coatings, which contained virtually no organic solvents, also sidestepped the VOC problem. New application processes also helped reduce the volume of paint required to perform a particular function. Most of these products were intended for industrial use.

The Glidden Co. became the first paint manufacturer to introduce major architectural paint lines containing no VOCs in 1992. Although consumers in the 1990s were clearly interested in environmentally sound products, zero-VOC paints had several drawbacks, including a reduced range of colors and lower performance.

Polyurethane automotive coatings for OEM and refinishing application offered durability and enhanced beauty at the same time. These included water-based coatings for cans, prefinished wood, and flat board.

Powder and radiation-curable coatings were considered two of the more exciting new developments, with a growth rate of 12.5 percent from 1990 to 1992. Industry analysts pegged growth at 15 percent through 1999. Powder coatings were sprayed on dry and electrically adhered to the surface. Major markets for powder coatings in the mid-1990s were metal finishing, appliances , automobile applications, and architectural products. Radiation-curable coatings, intended for use on vinyl flooring, wood furniture and paneling, paper, and metals, were hardened by ultraviolet light or electronic beam energy. Although the conversion to these new techniques was costly, factors like increased material utilization, reduced energy and lab costs, and the elimination of solvent emissions promised to more than offset the initial cost disadvantages. Growth in the powder and radiation-curable coatings segments outstripped that of more traditional paints and coatings. These products were expected to eventually replace many conventional solvent-based coatings.

FURTHER READING

Avery, Susan. "The Perils of Purchasing Paint." *Purchasing,* 21 March 1991, 56-69.

Babyak, Richard J. "Painting Plastics." *Appliance Manufacturer,* April 1991, 32-33.

Bailey, Jane M. "Where Paint Meets the Environment." *Industrial Paint & Powder,* October 1994, 14-15.

Bourguignon, Edward W., "Paint Industry Enjoys Strong First Half 1996." *American Paint & Coatings Journal,* 11 November 1996, 19.

"Building Downturn Hasn't Hit the Paint Companies." *Financial World,* 7 December 1960.

"Coatings Business Lively This Year After a Long Lull." *Chemical Marketing Reporter,* 14 August 1972.

Colgan, Kevin. "Coatings Makers Enter '80s Facing U.S. Regulatory Burden. *Chemical Marketing Reporter,* 27 October 1980, 36-37.

"Concentrating on the Home." *Economist,* 9 July 1960, 200.

Darnay, Arsen J., ed. *Manufacturing USA.* Detroit: Gale Research Inc., 1996.

Dickstein, George. "Paint Industry Is Using Spruced Up Ad Approach to Dispel Odorous Image." *Advertising Age,* 6 June 1966.

Dill, Larry. "California Paint Makers Face $1.8 Million Fee." *Modern Paint & Coatings,* May 1993, 13-16.

Fattah, Hassan. "Paints and Coatings: Mergers Create an Altered Image." *Chemical Week,* 23 October 1996, 33-34.

Gautier, Tom and Julie Larson Bricher. "Lead Paint: Old Coats Lead to New Suits." *Business & Society Review,* Fall 1991, 10-21.

"'Home Fever' Spurs New Paint Promotions." *Chemical Week,* 5 November 1980, 14-15.

Jacobs, David E. "Abating Lead-Based Paint." *Journal of Property Management,* March/April 1991, 32-34.

Jones, Sally. "A Bright Picture Waiting to Happen." *ECN-European Chemical News,* 11 July 1994, 21.

Kalkbrenner, Eric J. "Environment, Worker Safety Dominate Washington's Mind" *Chemical Marketing Reporter,* 29 October 1979, 48.

Kearney, Stephen. "Superfund Has Full Attention of Paint and Coatings Makers." *Chemical Marketing Reporter,* 4 November 1985, 39.

Kemizis, Paul. "Wait-and-See Stance Taken on Zero-VOC Architectural Paints." *Chemical Week,* 14 October 1992, 52-53.

Krizan, William G. "Regulators Putting the Lid on Paint." *ENR,* 5 October 1989, 30-33.

McGowan, Owen P. "Deflecting Liability in Lead-Poisoning Suits." *Best's Review,* February 1993, 62-63.

"More New Paints Counted On to Offset Slowing Growth." *Industry Week,* 15 December 1975.

"The New Gloss at Sherwin-Williams." *Business Week,* 15 July 1967, 154-156.

"NPCA Proposes Lead Regulation for Home Paints." *Chemical Marketing Reporter,* 20 September 1976.

Padow, Mark. "Sherwin-Williams, ICI, Others Were 'Serious' About Acquisitions in '95." *American Paint & Coatings Journal,* 29 April 1996, 14-15.

Padow, Mark. "Not a Bad Year, Most Say, All Things Considered." *American Paint & Coatings Journal,* 16 December 1996, 17-18.

"Paint Industry Outlook for the New Year." *Modern Paint & Coatings,* January 1993, 28-32.

"The Paint Makers." *Financial World,* 25 August 1965.

"Paintmakers Scrap for Sales." *Chemical Week,* 18 November 1961, 25-30.

"Paintmakers View the Big Picture." *Chemical Week,* 2 November 1977, 26-28.

"Paints, Coatings Manufacturers Sales Highest in Decade." *American Paint & Coatings Journal,* 15 January 1996, 11.

"PPG Industries: Deemed to be One of the Biggest Makers of Automotive & Industrial Coatings in the World." *Paint and Coatings Industry,* July 1996, 49.

Randel, Susan. "The Countertrend of House Paints." *Chemical Business,* October 1992, 6-9.

"RPM Inc. Increases Sales By Acquiring Rust-Oleum." *Modern Paint and Coatings,* August 1994, 8.

"'Sales' Buy Trouble for Paintmakers." *Chemical Week,* 26 April 1978, 23-24.

Sobrino, Frank. "Paint Firms Jockey for Share of Big $4 Billion U.S. Market." *Chemical Marketing Reporter,* 22 October 1984, 41.

Standard & Poor's Industry Surveys. 8 February 1996, C51-C54.

Trigg, Ernest T. *Fifty-five Colorful Years; The Story of Paint in America.* Stonington, Connecticut: Pequot Press, 1954.

U.S. Census Bureau. "Current Industrial Reports, Paint, Varnish and Lacquer - 1995." Available from http://www.census.gov/industry/ma28f95.txt.

"U.S. Paint Industry Faces Reduced Growth." *Modern Paint & Coatings,* May 1991, 10-16.

—April Dougal Gasbarre

GUM AND WOOD CHEMICALS

The gum and wood chemicals industry is comprised of establishments primarily engaged in manufacturing hardwood and softwood distillation products, natural dyes, tanning materials, and related products. Companies that make synthetic organic tanning materials and synthetic organic dyes are classified in **SIC 2869: Industrial Organic Chemicals, Not Elsewhere Classified** and **SIC 2865: Cyclic Organic Crudes and Intermediates, and Organic Dyes and Pigments,** respectively. Gum and wood chemical producers are part of the larger, industrial organic chemical industry.

Like organic chemicals derived from petroleum and natural gas, thousands of different natural chemical products can be distilled from wood. Turpentine, for example, is extracted from pine gum and pine wood. Numerous oils and finishes can also be obtained from pine, or other woods, as can many dyes, fuels, and resins.

INDUSTRY SNAPSHOT

According to *Chemical Marketing Reporter,* in 1996 the industry experienced a substantial drop in prices and reached levels not seen in years. However producers and suppliers continued to be very optimistic about the future.

In 1995 weak demand, low prices, stiff competition, and the changing fashion industry brought the U.S. dyes industry to a ten year low. U.S. manufacturers were losing out to cheaper, albeit lower quality products from Asia according to *Chemical Week* magazine.

BACKGROUND AND DEVELOPMENT

Popular industry products in the early 1990s included methanol (wood alcohol), charcoal, tar and tar oils, tanning extracts, pitch, and dyes. About 40 percent of industry revenues came from sales of hardwood charcoal briquettes. Hardwood distillates, such as oak extract, accounted for about 30 percent of industry output. Softwood distillates, like resin and turpentine, represented 17 percent of sales in the early 1990s.

The largest buyers of products in this industry are individual consumers, who primarily purchase charcoal, turpentine, and other products for home use. Manufacturers of plastics used 11 percent of production in the early 1990s to create base resins and addi-

tives. Distillates and extracts were consumed by other industries in the manufacture of soaps and detergents, paperboard, drugs, paints, printing ink, leather tanning chemicals, rubber, adhesives, sealants, and many other goods. About 12 percent of production in the early 1990s was exported.

U.S. industry shipments realized the strongest growth following World War II. Construction industries, for example, generated a demand for wood treatment chemicals, adhesives, and sealants. Growth in the popularity of outdoor barbecue grills during the 1950s and 1960s especially boosted sales of charcoal briquettes. Demand for ink dyes and tanning chemicals also grew during the post-war U.S. economic expansion.

By the early 1980s, the gum and wood chemicals industry was shipping over $600 million worth of products and employing about 3,500 workers. Revenues and profits recessed during the 1980s, however, for several reasons. Most important, synthetic chemicals displaced many natural wood and gum chemicals in everything from dyes to sealants. In addition, state and local environmental laws that restricted the burning of charcoal went into effect and cut into profits. Total revenues fluctuated around $600 million per year through the early 1990s, as productivity gains and cost-cutting measures reduced the work force to below 2,500.

Going into the mid-1990s, industry participants were hoping to benefit from a trend toward the use of natural chemicals, such as dyes and fuel additives, in response to environmental concerns about synthetics. Despite these hopes, the industry was expected to realize negligible growth through the turn of the century. Employment opportunities for most positions, in fact, were expected to decrease by 5 to 30 percent between 1990 and 2005, according to the U.S. Bureau of Labor Statistics.

INDUSTRY LEADERS

The largest competitor in this business in early 1997 was Hercules Incorported, based in Wilmington, Delaware, with sales revenue of $2.4 billion and 7,892 employees. Second place was held by Georgia Gulf Corporation of Atlanta, Georgia, with sales revenue of $1.1 billion and 1,143 employees. BASF's Coatings and Colorants Division came third with $982 million in sales revenue and 3,100 employees.

Westvaco Corportion's Kraft Division was fourth with sales revenue of $520 million and 1,400 employees. Koppers Industries Inc. of Pittsburgh, Pennsylvania. stood at fifth with sales revenue of $465 million and 1,800 employees.

FURTHER READING

Encyclopedia Britannica. Chicago: Encyclopedia Britannica, Inc., 1980.

Darnay, Arsen J., ed., *Manufacturing USA.* 5th ed. Detroit: Gale Research, 1996.

"Facts & Figures for the Chemical Industry." *Chemical & Engineering News,* 28 June 1993.

Foroohar, Kambiz. "A Tough Market Forces Dyes Suppliers to Realign." *Chemical Weeks,* 2 August 1995 p27.

Lerner, Mathew. "Gum Arabic Price Decrease Makes Suppliers Optimistic." *Chemical Marketing Reporter,* 17 June 1996, p14.

Reisch, Marc S. "Top 50 chemicals Production Recovered Last Year." *Chemical & Engineering News,* 12 April 1993.

Standard & Poor's Industry Surveys. New York: Standard & Poor's Corporation, January 20, 1994.

U.S. Department of Commerce. International Trade Administration. *U.S. Industrial Outlook 1994* Washington: GPO, 1994.

—Dave Mote, updated by Visi Tilak

SIC 2865

CYCLIC ORGANIC CRUDES AND INTERMEDIATES, AND ORGANIC DYES AND PIGMENTS

This industry covers establishments primarily engaged in manufacturing cyclic organic crudes and intermediates, and organic dyes and pigments. Important products of this industry include: (1) aromatic chemicals, such as benzene, toluene, mixed xylenes naphthalene; (2) synthetic organic dyes; and (3) synthetic organic pigments.

INDUSTRY SNAPSHOT

Organic chemicals contain carbon; are usually combustible; mostly insoluble in water; take the form of liquids or solids; and have relatively low melting points. Aromatics are included in a group called *basic organics,* which also includes aliphatics and methanol. These substances are obtained directly from raw materials, primarily crude oil and natural gas. Intermediates are often grouped with solvents and are made from basic chemicals for the express purpose of making other chemicals and chemical products.

U.S. manufacturers produced $11 billion worth of fine chemicals in 1993, or about 25 percent of global output. The 180 U.S. companies employed 23,000 workers and exported almost $1.4 billion worth of products per year in the early 1990s. Industry output provided an important supply of base manufacturing material for pharmaceutical, dye, fuel, and agricultural sectors.

Industry sales surged throughout the 1980s, as revenue jumped from about $7 billion to over $11 billion by the end of the decade. Prices declined in the early 1990s because of large capacity additions that came into effect. During the early 1990s, temporary price upswings caused by the war in the Persian Gulf were the only relief periods for the industry. Sales improved again by 1994, and into 1995, as prices and margins began to rise. This period was the industry's best financial performance since the late 1980s. By mid-1995, prices fell again. In 1996, varying levels of growth were observed in all major segments of the industry. One reason for the instability of the industry was the inability to predict the supply and demand for organic materials.

For example, benzene, styrene, and mixed xylenes saturated the market from July through December of 1996, while cyclohexane and phenol were not being produced quick enough to meet demands. Demand for some organic products, such as toluene fluctuated from year to year making it difficult to gage production.

ORGANIZATION AND STRUCTURE

Industrial organic chemicals are created from substances that contain carbon, such as petroleum, coal, and natural gas. Though inorganic chemicals may also contain carbon, they originate from inanimate materials within the earth's crust. The aromatics classified in this industry are separated from other organics by a closed-ring molecular structure. This structure allows them to be combined with other chemicals, including inorganics, to make a vast array of intermediate compounds. Intermediates are consumed by other industries for the production of plastics, pharmaceuticals, and fertilizers.

In 1992, chemicals classified in this industry constituted 20 percent of the $53 billion U.S. industrial organic chemical industry, which also includes gum and wood chemicals and industrial organics not elsewhere classified. Industrial organic chemicals, in turn, comprised 66 percent of the overall chemical industry, which includes inorganic and agricultural chemicals. The encompassing chemical and related products industry represents a $230 billion business, of which organics account for about one-third. Many products and compounds generated in the fine chemicals industry, however, are used to produce other chemicals and related goods.

In the early 1990s, 20 percent, or about $2.2 billion, of the $11 billion worth of aromatic, intermediate, and synthetic dye output was consumed by manufacturers within the industry to produce other fine chemicals. For example, an aromatics producer might sell benzene to a company that makes the intermediate chlorobenzene. Plastics materials and resin manufacturers demanded 13 percent of U.S. production, as did the organic synthetic fiber industry. Though they each accounted for less than 3 percent of the fragmented market, other major customers included petroleum refiners, pharmaceutical companies, paint and coating manufacturers, and semiconductor producers. Exports made up 13 percent of industry shipments. during the early 1990s.

The three primary aromatic chemicals used to create intermediates are benzene, xylene, and toluene. These three chemicals represent about 10 percent of U.S. industry output. Intermediates created using these base organics, however, account for an additional 70 percent of total production. Benzene, the simplest and most widely used aromatic, is combined with sulfuric acid and other chemicals to create many intermediates. U.S. manufacturers generated over 1.6 billion gallons of benzene in 1993. Benzene intermediates are used to produce plastic resins, epoxy, nylon, polyurethanes, synthetic rubber, and detergents.

The most common derivative of benzene is ethyl benzene/styrene, which accounts for 50 percent of demand for this aromatic. Nearly 21 billion pounds of ethyl benzene and styrene were produced in 1992. Styrene is a major ingredient in plastics and synthetic rubber. Cumene/phenol and cyclohexane represented 21 and 14 percent, respectively, of benzene derivative sales. Phenol is used to produce adhesives and high-grade plastics and epoxies. Other major intermediates in this category include: nitrobenzene/aniline (6 percent), alkybenzene (2 percent), and chlorobenzene (2 percent).

Xylene is primarily utilized as a gasoline additive and a solvent. It is separated into three commercial substances: paraxylene, orthoxylene, and metaxylene. Paraxylene derivatives are used to make polyester fiber and films, beverage bottles, and specialty engineering resins. Consumption of this chemical topped 5.6 billion pounds in 1992. Also in 1992, 918 million pounds of orthoxylene were generated. Orthoxylene is required to make intermediates that can be utilized in the production of plasticizers (plastic additives) and poly-

ester resins. Metaxylene has limited uses in the manufacture of coatings and plastics.

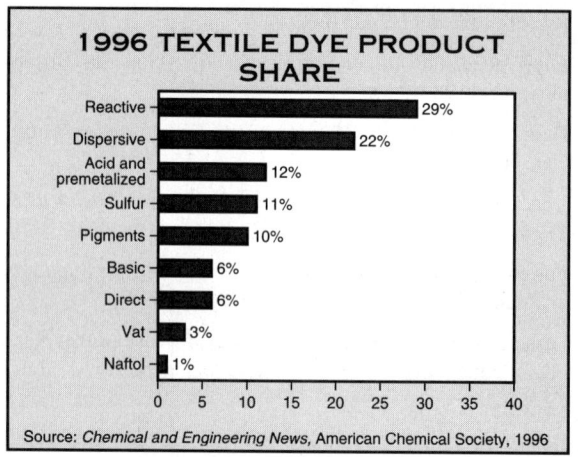

1996 TEXTILE DYE PRODUCT SHARE

Reactive	29%
Dispersive	22%
Acid and premetalized	12%
Sulfur	11%
Pigments	10%
Basic	6%
Direct	6%
Vat	3%
Naftol	1%

Source: *Chemical and Engineering News*, American Chemical Society, 1996

The last primary aromatic chemical is toluene. In 1992, the industry produced 833 million pounds of toluene. This aromatic is used to create benzene. End markets for toluene also include manufacturers of adhesives, solvents, photographic film, textiles, pharmaceuticals, inks, and coatings.

Besides aromatics and their intermediate offspring, organic dyes and pigments each make up about 8 percent of industry sales. Tar and pitch compounds round out industry offerings capturing 4 percent of sales revenue. Approximately 245 million pounds of synthetic organic dyes and pigments, valued at $761 million, were shipped by U.S. manufacturers in 1991. Two-thirds of dye and pigment production was consumed by textile industries. Dyes are typically obtained from petroleum through lengthy chemical processes and must conform to rigid safety standards before they can be used to color food, clothing, and other goods.

BACKGROUND AND DEVELOPMENT

William Henry Perkin, an Englishman and the father of the organic chemical industry, was the first chemist to synthesize an organic chemical for commercial use. In 1856, Perkin accidentally created mauve, a synthetic dye, from a piece of coal tar. Friedreich Von Kekule was the first to explain Perkin's invention when, in 1865, he proposed his breakthrough theory of the benzene ring. During the remainder of the nineteenth century, German chemists developed most of the dye classes, and many of the individual dyes, that were still being used in the early 1990s.

The advancement of aromatics, intermediates, and dyes, in the wake of Kekule's discovery, were considered relatively unimportant outside of Germany. It wasn't until World War I that Great Britain, France, and the United States frantically developed an organic chemical industry. World War II also brought massive industry expansion, especially as producers learned to derive aromatics from petroleum rather than coal tar. By the end of World War II, the United States was the major global supplier of aromatics and intermediates. Industry growth was rampant during the postwar U.S. economic expansion.

The aromatic, intermediate, and synthetic dye industry grew at a healthy rate of 5 percent per year between 1982 and 1990. Though this reflected a decline in growth rates compared to the 1960s and 1970s, it exceeded gains achieved by most other U.S. manufacturing sectors. Sales rose from $7.1 billion in 1982 to $10.9 billion by 1990. The demand for new high-performance intermediates, particularly by pharmaceutical and agricultural sectors, drove this sales growth.

In addition to revenue gains, producers also benefitted from increases in productivity and the development of new processing techniques during the decade. Productivity gains of approximately 4 percent per year during the 1980s were the result of massive capital investments in automation and information systems. These investments allowed manufacturers to eliminate both production workers and managers. Indeed, as production volume steadily rose throughout the 1980s, industry employment gradually shrank. The work force declined from over 27,000 in the early 1980s, to about 23,000 by the early 1990s. In addition to keeping the lid on labor costs, many manufacturers were able to reduce productions costs through advanced processing techniques.

Despite massive capital investments surpassing $43 billion during the 1980s, productivity and manufacturing gains were substantially offset by changing dynamics in the global organic chemical industry. Two primary factors stunting profit growth in the 1980s—and into the 1990s—were increased foreign competition and environmental regulations. In addition, regulatory intervention in important end markets, such as pharmaceuticals, were hindering competitors. Also hurting industry participants in the early 1990s was a U.S. and global economic recession. Overcapacity, a result of slower-than-expected growth in the early 1990s, was causing severe price suppression and reduced profits for most companies. Even as the United States experienced a modest recovery in 1992 and 1993, overseas markets remained flat.

During the mid-1990s, aromatic, intermediate, and dye producers continued to suffer from downward price pressures due to over supply. For example, while the demand for styrene grew about 13 percent between 1990 and 1993, excess production capacity in the United States crushed price growth in that segment. Many benzene derivatives were suffering a similar scenario, as were the xylenes. Only phenol dodged the burden of oversupply. In 1993, U.S. prices and demand recovered slightly, but primary global markets remained recessed.

Besides slack markets, increasingly stringent environment regulations were also taking their toll in the mid-1990s. A string of new rules implemented during the 1980s to cap hazardous waste emissions were heavily impacting manufacturers. The Clinton Administration supported efforts to reduce waste from this high-polluting industry. The Clean Air Act Amendment of 1990, the Environmental Protection Agency's (EPA) Toxic Inventory Release (TIR) program, the federal Emergency Planning and Community Right-to-Know Act, and voluntary Chemical Manufacturers Association (CMA) programs were just a few of the initiatives expected to cost the industry millions of dollars during the mid-1990s.

Perhaps the greatest challenge for most intermediate and dye producers in the mid-1990s was growing foreign competition. Although the European Community, Japan, and the United States remained the primary global suppliers for this industry, emerging industrial nations posed a real threat to their dominance. East Asian nations, excluding Japan, were capturing market share, as were producers in South America, Eastern Europe, India, and other developing regions.

Access to cheap labor and freedom from strict environmental regulations were expected to help manufacturers in these nations advance rapidly in the mid-1990s. For example, the average Chinese worker cost a company $1,000 per year in 1992. Conversely, the average U.S. aromatic production worker received over $35,000 in salary alone. As a result, dye imports to the United States almost doubled between 1981 and 1991 as the total value of U.S. dye production fell. Although intermediates had fared much better than dyes, U.S. global organic market share diminished from 30 to 25 percent between 1988 and 1992.

CURRENT CONDITIONS

Benzene. From 1982 to 1997, global demand for benzene doubled, and steady growth was predicted to continue at about 5 percent through the year 2000. Demand in 1996 was more than 27.0 million metric tons and was expected to increase to about 28.5 metric tons in 1997. The top U.S. benzene producers, including Amoco, Dow, Exxon, and Shell, controlled roughly half, or one billion gallons, of the total 2.4 billion gallons of U.S. benzene production.

Cyclohexane. Demand for cyclohexane was expected to grow from its 1.0 million metric tons in 1996 to approximately 1.1 million tons in 1997. No new cyclohexane plants were expected to come into operation until 1999, when Chevron planned to open a 75-million-gallon Saudi facility. The market will have little impetus to change until this Facility is built.

Toluene. The end of 1996 saw toluene at its highest price levels since early 1995. This increase was because toluene was the aromatic of choice for blenders who were adding octane to their gasolines.

Xylenes. Nineteen ninety-six saw an increase in crude prices and a drop in chemical prices. Many producers had to operate reformers at minimum levels, which significantly cut the production of mixed xylenesl. After reducing inventories and production levels, the supplies of mixed xylenes were decreased allowing prices to rise again.

Styrene. Worldwide demand of styrene was approximately 17 million metric tons in 1996. With annual growth at 4.5 percent, demand should approach 18 million metric tons in 1997.

Phenol. In 1996, the U.S. demand for phenol was more than 4.1 billion pounds. By the year 2000, if growth remained at 3 percent, it was expected to be over 4.7 billion pounds.

Dyes and Pigments. Demand for synthetic organic pigments and dyes will increase, but U.S. production will likely remain stagnant, or decline, as exports flood the market. Pharmaceutical intermediates and fuel additives will offer some of the greatest profit potential, as will environmentally safe compounds. In order to remain competitive in the global markets of the 1990s, U.S. producers have been forced to focus their efforts on the development of high-tech, high-margin specialty intermediates and dyes. Consumers of large-volume, low-tech, commodity-like aromatics, intermediates, and dyes will continue to seek low-cost producers in emerging nations.

INDUSTRY LEADERS

The fine chemicals industry is consolidated in comparison to most other U.S. manufacturing industries. There were only 180 U.S. companies competing in the early 1990s. The top five companies generated a combined revenue of approximately $1.7 billion. The majority of the top 25 firms, moreover, had sales of over $50 million and employed more than 300 workers. By contrast, the bottom 140 competitors each generated revenues of less than $1 million and employed fewer than 100 people.

In 1997, the largest company in the industry was First Mississippi Corp. of Jackson, Mississippi. It had total sales of $645 million and employed 1,600 people. Crompton and Knowles Corp. of Stamford, Connecticut, was the second largest with sales of $590 million and employing 2,700. Clariant Corp. of Charlotte, North Carolina, had sales of $400 million and employed 1,200 people. Systems Bio-Industries Inc. of Trevose, Pennsylvania, had sales of $300 million and employed 600. Warner-Jenkinson Co. of St. Louis, Missouri, had sales of about $140 million and employed 300 people. Major aromatics and intermediates producers primarily active in other industries included Exxon, Dow Chemical, Shell, Occidental Petroleum, Amoco, and Lyondell Petrochemical.

WORK FORCE

Into the mid-1990s, there were limited job prospects in the industry. Opportunities were being depleted as a result of productivity gains at the expense of the labor force; movement of production facilities overseas; and increased competition. Positions for chemical equipment controllers, which account for about 9 percent of the work force, are predicted to plunge by 25 percent between 1990 and 2005. Similarly, opportunities for machine operators and laborers will decrease. Among the last job positions expected to decrease are for general managers, top executives, and support staff, which will plummet by about 20 percent. On the other hand, jobs in sales and marketing should rise by about 5 percent, and engineering positions should increase by 1 to 4 percent.

AMERICA AND THE WORLD

In the early 1990, with sales of about $11 billion per year, U.S. producers accounted for roughly 25 percent of global fine chemicals output. The European Community met 40 percent of worldwide demand, and Japan represented 20 percent of production. Like the United States, which shipped $1.4 billion of its output overseas in 1992, Japan and the European Community were major chemical exporters within the global marketplace. These three regions also represented most of the world's chemical consumption.

In the mid-1990s, market share held by all major producers was steadily eroding. For example, in 1993, Eastern European and South American manufacturers generated approximately $2 billion and $1 billion worth of product respectively. At the same time, they were striving to boost exports. Also, East Asia, which sold $2 to $3 billion of aromatics and intermediates in

1992, was growing its output by 8 to 10 percent per year.

Two of the fastest growing export nations were China and India. China exported $800 million worth of intermediates in 1992, while India shipped approximately $500 million. Both countries were expected to surpass U.S. exports by the turn of the century. "China is in a major, major buildup," said Joshua Pratter, manager of technical marketing and planning at ICG, a California-based intermediates producer, in the August 30, 1993 issue of *Chemical Marketing Reporter.* "They're buying a lot of technology."

Another trend taking place in the early 1990s was the movement of U.S. production facilities overseas. Dow Chemical Co., for example, received a license in 1992 to build a polystyrene plant at Map Ta Phut, Thailand. This plant would be its fifth in that country. Many other producers were moving production to Mexico, Singapore, and other developing regions.

RESEARCH AND TECHNOLOGY

U.S. manufacturers were making capital investments during the early 1990s of more than $5.5 billion per year. This represented an investment, per employee, about five times greater than the average U.S. manufacturer. Indeed, the United States maintained the most productive and technologically advanced intermediates industry in the world. In the 1980s and early 1990s, the industry spent billions of dollars attempting to raise productivity through automation and information systems; grow capacity; and comply with environmental laws. By the mid-1990s, new product research and development was the primary investment focus.

Intermediate and dye manufacturers were scrambling to develop high-tech molecules and compounds to open new markets and battle foreign commodity producers. For example, advances in intermediates used to make pharmaceuticals, allowed the most savvy producers to reap significant rewards. Also in demand were high-performance intermediates that could be used to make cleaner fuel additives; new resins and fibers; better rubber and environmentally friendly chemicals. "Customers are needing more sophisticated molecules, which are more expensive and smaller in volume," said Jim Cornell, manager of business development at Eastman Fine Chemicals, in the August 30, 1993 issue of *Chemical Marketing Reporter.*

In the early to mid-1990s, numerous breakthroughs were occurring throughout the industry. In 1993, Monsanto Corp. was perfecting a method for producing aromatics using an environmentally safe process. The development offered potentially major commercial consequences.

An important growth area predicted for the late 1990s is peptide intermediates. Drugs using peptides were already being developed in the early 1990s. These drugs can be used to cause chemical changes in the human body that fight off diseases. Peptide-based drugs offered potential therapy for cancer, AIDS, and other major afflictions.

FURTHER READING

Alperowicz, Natasha. "Thailand: Dow Plans Polystyrene, Aromatics Project Reviewed." *Chemical Week,* 15 April, 1992.

Anderson, Earl V. "Developing Nation's Chemical Exports Surge." *Chemical & Engineering News,* 2 August, 1993.

———. "Foreign Trade: U.S. Chemical Trade Surplus Declines." *Chemical & Engineering News,* 13 December, 1993.

———. "Japan: Once Booming Economy Struggles Through Times." *Chemical & Engineering News,* 13 December, 1993.

Bahner, Benedict. "Intermediates '93: Hanging in There." *Chemical Marketing Reporter,* 30 August, 1993.

Brand, Tony. "Aromatics: A Mixed Review." *Chemical Market Reporter* 251, no.2 (13 January 1997).

"Chemical Industry R&D Rose 7 percent in 1992." *Chemical & Engineering News,* 23 August, 1993.

"Facts & Figures for the Chemical Industry." *Chemical & Engineering News,* 28 June, 1993.

"Industrial Organic Chemicals: Growth Projected for Organics." *Standard and Poor's Industry Surveys.* New York: Standard and Poor's Corporation, 1997.

Layman, Patricia. "Europe: Definite Though Modest Recovery Forecast for 1994." *Chemical & Engineering News,* 13 December, 1993.

Loesel, Andrew. "Intermediates '93: Getting Smarter." *Chemical Marketing Reporter,* 30 August, 1993.

Naude, Alice. "Intermediates '93: Waiting for Harvest." *Chemical Marketing Reporter,* 30 August, 1993.

Reisch, Marc S. "Top 50 Chemicals Production Recovered Last Year." *Chemical & Engineering News,* 12 April, 1993.

———. "New Woes May Trigger Another Shakeout for U.S. Dye Producers." *Chemical & Engineering News,* 5 July, 1993.

Rzadzki, John. "Intermediates '93: Region on the Rise." *Chemical Marketing Reporter,* 30 August, 1993.

Shon, Melissa. "Intermediates '93: Shakeout Time." *Chemical Marketing Reporter,* 30 August, 1993.

Springer, Neil. "Intermediates '93: Looking Outward." *Chemical Marketing Reporter,* 30 August, 1993.

Standard & Poor's Industry Surveys. New York: Standard & Poor's Corporation, 20 January, 1994.

Storck, William J. "United States: Chemical Industry Lackluster This Year." *Chemical & Engineering News,* 13 December, 1993.

Tomasula, Dean. "Cumene Yet to Benefit From Economic Recovery." *Chemical Marketing Reporter,* 3 January, 1994.

U.S. Department of Commerce. International Trade Administration. *U.S. Industrial Outlook 1993.* Washington: GPO, 1993.

—Dave Mote, updated by Beaird Glover

SIC 2869

INDUSTRIAL ORGANIC CHEMICALS, NOT ELSEWHERE CLASSIFIED

The Industrial Organic Chemicals, Not Elsewhere Classified (NEC) Industry is comprised of companies primarily engaged in the production of organic chemicals used by other manufacturing industries. It encompasses the majority of U.S. organic chemical output and represents the single largest segment of the overall chemical industry. Materials created using these chemicals, such as plastic and fiber, are classified in their respective industries.

INDUSTRY SNAPSHOT

Scientists began producing synthetic organic chemicals in the 1850s. Not until the 1900s, however, did production grow to surpass inorganic output. Rapid expansion during the twentieth century made the overall chemical industry one of the largest businesses in the United States and the biggest exporting sector of the American economy. In 1992, U.S. organic chemical manufacturers sold $54 billion worth of materials and employed 100,000 workers. They shipped almost $11 billion worth of exports and accounted for about 25 percent of global organic chemical output.

The industry realized healthy revenue and profit growth during the late 1980s. Production volume and sales continued to climb in the early 1990s. However, overcapacity and a weak global economy diminished manufacturers' earnings. As they entered the mid-1990s, producers faced other roadblocks as well. To combat these negative influences, manufacturers were increasing their productivity, focusing on high-margin specialty chemicals, and restructuring their organizations.

The 1990s saw massive efforts to reduce waste to the environment. Between 1988 and 1994, toxic chemical emissions were reduced 60 percent, according to materials submitted to the Environmental Protection Agency (EPA) in 1996.

Gradual increases were seen in the major products of this industry, along with plans for new plant construction and operation to take place by 2000.

ORGANIZATION AND STRUCTURE

The chemical industry is divided into organic and inorganic substances. Inorganic chemicals—which are derived from the inanimate material of the earth's crust—include compounds such as sulfuric acid, sulfur, phosphoric acid, and hydrogen peroxide. Organic chemicals are so named because in the industry's early days they were obtained from living organisms. Today they are derived from substances that contain carbon—such as petroleum, coal, and natural gas. Petroleum-based chemicals, or petrochemicals, account for about 80 percent of industry output by weight and 50 percent of production by value.

Organic chemicals, particularly petrochemicals, play an indispensable role in modern society. They are essential ingredients to plastics, synthetic fibers, rubber, fertilizers, and chemical intermediates, which are converted into a plethora of consumer and industrial products. They are the primary building blocks of important materials supporting health, food, transportation, and communication industries. Organic substances have also made possible many important specialty items—such as protective clothing and materials used for space exploration.

Organics constituted about 66 percent, or $54 billion, of the $81 billion chemical industry in 1992. Inorganic and agricultural chemicals made up the remainder of production. Likewise, the chemical industry represented about 46 percent of the overall chemicals and related products industry. Other segments of the general industry include synthetic materials—such as plastic and fibers—and chemical products—like paint, drugs, and soap.

Because organic chemicals are used to make so many products within the overall chemical and related products divisions, the industry eludes clear definition. Most industrial organic chemicals, in fact, are consumed by chemical-related businesses. For instance, companies that produce cyclic crudes and intermediates, such as aromatics and dyes (see **SIC 2865: Cyclic Organic Crudes and Intermediates, and Organic Dyes and Pigments**), purchased about 20 percent of industry output in the early 1990s. Plastic resin manufacturers (see **SIC 2821: Plastics Materials, Synthetic Resins, and Nonvulcanizable Elastomers**) consumed 13 percent of production. Synthetic fiber producers (see **SIC 2824: Manmade Organic Fibers, Except Cellulosic**) accounted for about 6 percent of industry revenues, and elastomer companies (see **SIC 2822: Synthetic Rubber (Vulcanized Elastomers**) absorbed 3 percent of production. Another 13 percent of organic chemical sales were garnered from exports.

The remaining 45 percent of organic output was used by numerous manufacturing sectors. Steel and aluminum mills, paper mills, semiconductor manufacturers, drug companies, carpet mills, and battery producers were relatively large customers. Other chemical uses included the production of items such as pipe, photographic equipment, electrical insulation, and food containers.

Production. The organic chemical industry serves one primary purpose: to take a relatively few fundamental raw chemicals that contain carbon and combine and transform them into new substances with desirable physical properties. Using carbon as a basic building block, chemists are able to unite other elements—such as nitrogen, hydrogen, oxygen, sulfur, and chlorine—to generate a multitude of different compounds. Furthermore, each resultant compound can be manipulated, with heat or additives to produce an infinite variety of characteristics and grades.

The most common category of organic chemicals are Aliphatics, or Olefins, which are straight-chain hydrocarbons. Olefins can be made using petroleum or natural gas, though most U.S. manufacturers use the latter. To produce Olefins, natural gas is separated into ethane, propane, and butane. From these gases, smaller percentages of marketable ethylene, propylene, and butadiene are extracted. These three substances are the basic building blocks for most organic chemicals and synthetic materials. Major producers of aliphatics include Dow Chemical, Union Carbide, Lyondell Petrochemical, Occidental Petroleum, and Quantum Chemical.

Ethylene is the largest volume organic chemical produced in the United States. Approximately 75 percent of all ethylene is utilized to produce plastics such as polyethylene, polyvinyl chloride, and polystyrene. It is also widely used to make antifreeze, synthetic fibers, rubber, solvents, and detergents. Derivatives of ethylene represent a significant share of total industry output as well. Nearly 16 billion pounds of ethylene dichloride, for example, were sold in 1992.

The second largest olefin by production volume is propylene. The industry churned out more than 22.5 billion pounds of this organic chemical in 1992. Forty percent of propylene is used to make polypropylene, which in turn is utilized to manufacture film, packaging, foams and coatings, solvents, gasoline, and fibers. In addition, propylene is used to make other popular chemicals, such as acrylonitrile, propylene oxide, isopropanol, and cumene. Over 4.5 billion pounds of cumene, were produced in 1992.

Butadiene, the third most popular olefin, is employed primarily in the manufacture of synthetic rubber. The remaining one-third of butadiene production is consumed by makers of latex, resins, and nylon fibers. In 1992, about 3.2 billion pounds of this compound were produced in the United States.

Aside from olefins and their offspring, synthetic methanol accounts for a large share of industry output—more than 8.7 billion pounds in 1992. Important derivatives of methanol include formaldehyde, acetic acid, methyl methacrylate, and various solvents. About 50 percent of all methanol is utilized in the production of adhesives, fibers, and plastics. In addition, it is an important ingredient in antifreeze and gasoline additives. Methyl tert-butyl ether (MTBE), a methanol derivative, is used as an oxygenate in automobile gasoline.

Environmental Impact. Laws and initiatives regarding hazardous emissions generated during organic chemical production and use are important dynamics that shape the industry. The chemical business is by far the largest polluting U.S. industry—generating at least three times more pollution than the second greatest offending industry.

In 1991, chemical producers released more than 1.5 billion pounds of toxins—as defined by the Environmental Protection Agency's (EPA) Toxics Release Inventory (TRI). This figure represented a full 46 percent of all U.S. industrial toxic emissions. Forty percent of this waste was dumped into the air, 40 percent into underground wells, and the remainder was released into water and land.

To minimize the detrimental effects of chemical industry pollutants, multiple local, state, and federal laws govern producers. The federal Emergency Planning and Community Right-to-Know Act (EPCRA), for example, requires many manufacturers to submit detailed emissions data to the EPA. Similarly, the Pollution Prevention Act (1990) requires those same companies to report their waste management and pollution reduction activities.

Other federal regulations impacting producers include the Safe Drinking Water Act, the Clean Air Act Amendments of 1990, and other laws that restrict hazardous wastes. In addition to legal restrictions, both the EPA and the Chemical Manufacturers Association (CMA) sponsor successful voluntary pollution reduction programs that encourage environmental sensitivity.

In an effort to comply with voluntary and mandated measures, chemical companies spent nearly $5 billion in 1992 on pollution abatement. Expenditures were used primarily to create cleaner production facilities and to research and develop new methods of reducing hazardous wastes.

BACKGROUND AND DEVELOPMENT

Ancient Egyptians and Chinese were the first to experiment with chemical processes in carrying out dyeing, leather tanning, and glassmaking activities. It was not until 1790, however, that Nicolas Leblanc, a Frenchman, gave birth to the chemical industry. He is credited with being the first person to successfully carry out a deliberate plan to convert one or more chemical products into one wholly different substance, keeping in mind not only the end product but also the economics of the process. Leblanc was inspired by a reward of 12,000 francs offered by the French Academy of Sciences to anyone who could devise a method for making inexpensive alkali.

While Leblanc's discovery was neglected in France, it became extremely important in England in the soap and textile industries. As British alkali producers advanced the inorganic chemical industry during the 1800s, they laid the foundation for organic chemistry. Although organic compounds had been known to man for centuries, it was not discovered until early in the nineteenth century that they all contain carbon. Once scientists realized they could unite carbon with other common elements, they quickly began to create their own substances. At first chemists sought to create elements that imitated natural, known substances. Later, though, they learned how to create a vast variety of unknown compounds.

The first chemist to synthesize an organic chemical for commercial use was Englishman William Henry Perkin, the father of the organic chemical industry. At 18 years old, Perkin, working in his father's house in 1856, accidently created a synthetic dye using a piece of coal tar. Although he received knighthood for his efforts, it wasn't until 1865 that the chemical structure of Perkin's dye was understood. In that year, Friedreich von Kekule announced his breakthrough theory of the benzene ring. Using Kekule's theory,

chemists were able to build millions of new organic chemicals during the nineteenth and early twentieth centuries, many of which displaced natural materials and dyes.

Chemists did not begin synthesizing petroleum and natural gas to create petrochemicals on a commercial scale until the 1920s. A huge demand for gasoline, rubber products, textiles, detergents, and plastics that could be created with petrochemicals in the 1920s and early 1930s boosted industry growth. It was World War II, however, that launched the organic chemical industry to national prominence. During this period, a shortage of natural and manmade materials that had previously been supplied by other sources resulted in rapid industry expansion. Production of synthetic rubber, for example, bolted from just 72,000 tons in 1939 to more than 800,000 tons in 1945.

Organic chemical sales continued to balloon after WWII as the post-war U.S. economy expanded. The explosion in automobile production during the 1950s, 1960s, and 1970s, for example, created a massive demand for chemicals utilized in the production of rubber, paint, and gasoline. Importantly, commercial and residential construction booms generated a huge need for paneling, roofing, insulation, carpet, draperies, upholstery, varnishes, and other chemical-based building materials. Likewise, the call for clothing created from organic chemicals ballooned as a rising population sought viable alternatives to costly natural fibers. Defense and consumer products markets grew as well. Besides meeting demand in domestic markets, moreover, the United States became a major chemical supplier to European countries that had been devastated by war.

As organic chemical revenues blossomed throughout most of the period between the 1950s and 1970s, overall chemical industry sales, including inorganics, reached approximately $50 billion. Production volume of ethylene and propylene, combined, topped 30 billion pounds, while total organic output climbed past 120 billion pounds. Heading into the 1980s, industrial organic chemical producers were employing more than 120,000 workers and shipping more than $5 billion in exports.

In the early 1980s, organic producers were battered by high petroleum prices and a deep U.S. economic recession. As sales stalled throughout the early years of the decade, inventories swelled and profit margins collapsed. Demand started recovering in 1983, however, pushed by a revival in housing starts and automobile markets. The demand for organics used to create plastics and textiles was especially strong, and consumption by paperboard and furniture markets recuperated. Sales climbed 9 percent in 1983—from $30.4 billion to $33.3 billion—and about 8 percent in 1984—to $35.8 billion.

Despite a temporary downturn in 1985 and 1986, industry expansion accelerated during the late 1980s. Sales rose to $42 billion in 1987 before jumping 16 percent to $49.1 billion in 1988. Prices and profits also improved following stagnation throughout most of the decade. Overall chemical industry profits, for example, rose to $4 billion in 1987, from just more than $2 billion per year between 1982 and 1985. Profit margins climbed from 4 percent in 1985 to a peak of almost 10 percent in 1988, boosting overall earnings past an annual rate of $7 billion in early 1989.

Production volume of many organics mushroomed during the 1980s. Propylene output, for example, rocketed from 12.5 billion pounds in 1982 to 21.8 billion by 1990, representing annual growth of more than 6 percent. Consumption of butadiene rose similarly, to about 3 billion pounds by 1990. Ethylene production climbed at an annual rate of more than 5 percent, from 24.5 billion pounds in 1982 to 36.5 by 1990. More importantly, however, many derivatives of the three major olefins realized average annual growth rates in excess of 10 percent throughout the decade. In anticipation of continued growth, producers responded in the late 1980s by making heavy capital investments to increase their production capacity.

Notwithstanding a surge in the latter years of the decade, chemical market growth during the 1980s was modest in comparison to the expansion enjoyed during the previous three decades. Indeed, many organic chemical producers realized that the industry was entering a new stage of maturity. The massive growth opportunities of the mid-twentieth century, propelled by economic expansion and uncontested global dominance, had diminished significantly even by the late 1970s.

Particularly disconcerting to producers of commodity-like organics was the steep rise of foreign competition that occurred in the early 1980s. Besides expanded output by Japan and the European Community, U.S. producers were also being challenged by low-cost producers in Korea and Singapore. Despite overall export growth by domestic chemical manufacturers in the mid-1980s, the U.S. share of the world chemical export market plummeted from about 17 percent in 1984 to less than 14 percent in 1987. Although inorganic commodity chemicals represented much of this decline, the share of U.S. exports represented by organic chemicals slipped from more than 30 percent in the mid-1980s to about 25 percent by the early

1990s. The U.S. global chemical export market share recovered slightly in 1989, to about 15 percent.

To combat long-term downward profit pressures exerted by relatively flat market growth and increased competition, many producers in the early 1980s began cutting costs, consolidating operations, increasing research and development spending, and implementing cost-saving automation and information systems. Most producers who were slow to implement such initiatives had climbed aboard the bandwagon by the late 1980s, and these efforts were evidenced by a decline in employment. Even as organic manufacturers scrambled to boost their productivity during the 1980s, employment fell from 111,000 in 1982 to about 100,000 by 1990. This occurred despite steady growth in production volume.

CURRENT CONDITIONS

After steady growth through 1989, industrial organic chemical manufacturers suffered serious setbacks in the early 1990s. A U.S. and global economic recession stumped profit growth, as the value of petrochemical and related products sales dropped 1.5 percent in 1990 to $54.1 billion. Sales rose just 1 percent in both 1991 and 1992 (using inflation adjusted dollars), and overall organic chemical output rose only slightly between 1990 and 1992. Moreover, this tepid growth, was offset by stagnant prices and declining profits. From its peak of nearly 10 percent in 1988, chemical industry profit margins sank to about 5 percent in 1992.

Compounding industry woes in the early 1990s was excess production capacity, the result of expansion in the previous half decade. Oversupply was still depressing organic prices into the mid-1990s, thus eliminating profit growth. Despite ongoing successful efforts to increase productivity and improve products, U.S. competitors were unable to overcome the effects of the latest downturn. Even a slow but steady increase in organic exports did little to alleviate the impact of sluggish domestic markets. After all, U.S. imports rose at a rate about 15 times greater than U.S. exports in 1992, augmenting downward price pressures.

In an effort to buoy earnings, domestic competitors continued restructuring in the 1990s. Companies were cutting costs out of every phase of the production process, often leading to massive lay-offs. DuPont, for example, announced a work force reduction of as many as 4,500 employees in late 1993, adding to about 5,500 lay-offs made by that company since 1991. Likewise, Dow Chemical eliminated 4,700 jobs in 1993, and Air Products reduced its work force by 1,300. Many companies were also restructuring by selling unprofitable operations and focusing on their core competencies.

While revenues improved and prices gained slightly in 1993, overcapacity and weak markets persisted into 1994. Industry shipments grew between 1 and 2 percent in 1993, and were expected to increase similarly in the near term. This growth was expected to eventually reduce overcapacity, however, allowing manufacturers to raise prices slightly. The effects of a reduction in oversupply may be offset by the diminished stature of U.S. producers in the global marketplace. U.S. firms will increasingly be forced to shift production from high-volume commodity-like organics to low-volume specialty and high-tech compounds that demand higher prices.

Ethylene. Shipment growth rates of ethylene were expected to be at 3 to 4 percent through the year 2000. Ethylene output was 47 billion pounds in 1995, an increase of 5.3 percent from the 44.6 billion pounds of 1994. Production was up 6 percent in 1994, even though there were supply problems. In 1995, the industry operated at 94.5 percent capacity, versus 93.1 percent in 1994. In 1992, domestic competitors made about 41 billion pounds of ethylene valued at over $8 billion—more than 15 percent of industry revenues. As ethylene demand continues to grow, the industry must increase capacity. At the expected growth rate of 3 to 4 percent, the industry will need to add a new facility each year to prevent a material shortage. However, no new major plants are expected to be built until 1998. Exxon Corp. plans to open an ethylene plant in Texas in 1998 to produce about 1.5 billion pounds of ethylene per year.

A joint venture involving Lyondell Petrochemical, Union Carbide Corp., and Quantum Chemical is also expected to open a new Texas operation in 1998. This plant will also produce about 1.5 billion pounds of ethylene per year. These three companies combined produce and use about 25 percent of the U.S. capacity of ethylene, and they intend to use the new plant for their own needs.

Propylene. Production of propylene rose 7.3 percent in 1995, and at year's end, inventories of propylene were twice those of 1994 and above average historical levels. Selling prices dropped from the mid-1995 high of 23.75 cents to 16.25 cents per pound. Long-term propylene demand is expected to rise at about 3.5 percent per year through the year 2000.

Butadiene. Though the United States produces more than 3 billion pounds of butadiene per year, it has historically imported most of its butadiene from Europe. Butadiene production rose about 7 percent in

1994 and 9 percent in 1995. At the end of 1995, the industry inventory was at a relatively high level of 271 million pounds—12 percent higher than 1994. Therefore, lower prices were expected in 1996.

Methanol. The price of methanol almost tripled in 1994 reaching $1.55 per gallon, but by the end of 1994, it was back down to 42 cents. Methanol production in 1995 was slightly higher than the previous year with the largest producers being Methanex Corp., Terra Industries, Borden Chemical and Plastics, Lyondell Petrochemical, Quantum Chemical, Hoechst-Celanese, Georgia Gulf, and Ashland Petroleum.

Methyl Tert-butyl Ether. MTBE production topped 10.5 billion pounds in the early 1990s as prices were driven up by the Clean Air Act Amendments of 1990 which required the use of gasolines containing oxygenates such as MTBE. Beginning in 1992, the sale of oxygenated fuels was required during the winter months in 37 U.S. metropolitan areas that did not meet the federal air standards for carbon monoxide. In January 1995, year-round use began in nine regions as dictated by the Clean Air Act. The demand of MTBE was not as high as expected in 1995, though, as some states were able to get out of the program. Also, higher methane costs made it less desirable than other octane enhancers. Prices were expected to return to pre-1994 levels to finish the 1990s. Major producers of methanol included Beaumont Methanol, Borden, Lyondell Petrochemical, Quantum Chemical, and Georgia Gulf.

Regulatory Impacts. While increasing federal and state regulations posed an ongoing challenge to chemical industry participants, positive signs indicated that the industry was successfully clearing these hurdles and was even benefiting from some laws. The overall chemical industry reduced its emissions of TRI wastes by 34 percent between 1988 and 1991 and expected to display similar reductions in 1992 and 1993. Water and air emissions were down by 19 and 29 percent, respectively, between 1988 and 1991, while underground injections had fallen a significant 34 percent. During the same period, moreover, total industry production climbed 11 percent.

Despite industry gains, chemical pollutants remained a major concern for regulators, and President Bill Clinton's administration planned to step-up efforts to reduce toxic emissions. Some regulations, though, were expected to boost industry profits. The Clean Air Act Amendments of 1990, for example, required automobile carbon-monoxide emissions to fall below certain levels by 1995. As a result, the demand for organic gasoline additives that allow such reductions was forecast to balloon.

Besides environmental restrictions, manufacturers were also burdened with increased costs related to new safety initiatives. The EPA's proposed risk management rule, for example, was pending in 1994. This law was designed to prevent, detect, and respond to the release of extremely hazardous substances from chemical plants that affected neighboring communities. Companies would be required to develop emergency response plans and implement new prevention programs under the proposal.

A similar Occupational Health and Safety Administration (OSHA) law, passed by Congress in 1992, was aimed at preventing accidents in the work place. OSHA estimated that its new law would cost about $863 million per year between 1992 and 1997. The EPA rule, according to government estimates, would cost $503 million in the first year but would save $890 million in environmental damage and response costs. Organic chemical producers also anticipated expenses starting in 1994 as a result of a CMA initiative. The CMA's Responsible Care Program would require its members to file safety incident reports for manufacturing mishaps.

Information submitted to the EPA in 1996 showed that emissions of toxic chemicals had decreased more than 60 percent between 1988 and 1994. Member companies of the Chemical Manufacturing Association (CMA) cut releases to the water, air, and land by more than 400 million pounds.

The Toxic Release Inventory of 1994 showed that 49 percent of the chemicals on the inventory were recycled or recovered for energy, 44 percent were treated, and 7 percent were released to the environment. Due to the industry's pollution prevention efforts, air releases were cut from 546 million pounds in 1988 to 230 million pounds in 1994—a 58 percent reduction. Surface water discharges were reduced to 7 million pounds in 1994—an 87 percent improvement over the 53 million pounds released in 1988. Land disposal declined 43 percent, from 77 million pounds to 28 million pounds.

The EPA considered underground injection wells "safer than virtually all other waste disposal practices." To dispose of highly diluted wastes, they were injected into EPA-permitted wells, drilled deep into special geologic formations that contained, and in some cases neutralized the waste. This remained the largest waste disposal system reported to the TRI, and CMA companies cut the annual amount of waste disposed this way by nearly 1 billion pounds since 1988—a 76 percent reduction. CMA members reduced the emissions and off-site transfers of 17 high

priority chemicals in 1994, ahead of the deadline set by the EPA for 1995.

In 1994, the EPA added 286 chemicals to its inventory list, nearly doubling its size. The CMA contended that some of these were innocuous, and the EPA stood the risk of confusing the public with what was truly hazardous and what was not.

INDUSTRY LEADERS

About 650 companies participated in the industrial organic chemical industry in the early 1990s. The top 15 competitors had sales of more than $1 billion from various businesses— and most of them employed several thousand workers. Most of the top 75 firms in the industry—though, had fewer than 500 workers and generated revenues of less than $200 million per year. The industry is highly consolidated in relation to most other U.S. manufacturing sectors. High start-up costs, technical expertise, and entrenched segment leaders discourage new competition. By 1997, only the top eight companies were making more than $1 billion per year

In 1997, the world's largest supplier of organic chemicals—and the largest U.S. producer—was Bayer Corp., of Pittsburgh, Pennsylvania, a subsidiary of Bayer AG. Bayer's product program consisted of about 750 organic intermediate and finished products and many fine and special chemicals. In 1997, Bayer had total sales of $11.389 billion and employed 23,500 people.

The second largest firm in the industry was Union Carbide Corporation, of Dansbury, Connecticut. Sales in 1992 of $4.8 billion earned this diversified producer chemical operating profits of $316 million. Union Carbide announced a major cost-cutting effort in 1993. By 1997, total sales were up to $5.888 billion. Union Carbide employed 11,500 people.

The third largest company was Dow Corning Corp. of Midland, Michigan. Herbert Dow started Canton Chemical in 1890, but it failed. He quickly rebounded, however, by starting the Dow Chemical Company, which achieved $4 million in sales by 1920 and $15 million by 1930. Dow's research and development strength helped it serve U.S. needs during WWII, when it took a leading role in providing butadiene for synthetic rubber production. Sales quadrupled from $200 million in 1949 to over $800 million by 1960 and grew at a rate of over 10 percent per year through the early 1970s. The chemical giant earned 1992 chemical operating profits of $592 million from sales of $12.9 billion. Its revenues slumped 2.7 percent in 1992 as profits rose 4.6 percent over 1991 levels. Dow employed 18,000 workers in its diversified operations in 1991. By 1997, Dow had total sales of $2.205 billion, but employment had dropped to about 6,000 people.

The next largest company in 1997 was Witco Corp., of Greenwich, Connecticut. Witco had total revenues of $2 billion and 800 employees. The fifth largest company was Lubrizol Corp., of Wickliffe, Ohio, with sales of $1.664 billion and 460 employees.

WORK FORCE

Approximately 100,000 workers served the industrial organic chemical industry in 1992. This represented a decline of about 10 percent since the early 1980s. Production workers accounted for about 76,000 of this group. Their numbers declined 6 percent in 1992 and averaged an annual reduction rate of 1 percent between 1982 and 1992. Largely to blame for cutbacks in both white and blue collar jobs were productivity increases achieved by manufacturers. Efficiency gains in the overall chemical industry averaged about 4 percent per year between 1983 and 1992, which was more than enough to offset gains from increased output. Furthermore, productivity jumped an impressive 6.4 percent in 1992, compared to average gains of just 2.9 percent in all other U.S. manufacturing businesses.

Employment growth in the organic chemical industry is expected to remain weak, and future employment prospects are bleak. Although output was rising going into 1994 and some firms were adding production workers, major producers continued to announce lay-offs, particularly of white collar management employees. Blue collar workers that will suffer most from long term trends, however. Positions for chemical equipment controllers, which account for a full 9 percent of the organic chemical industry work force, will fall by 25 percent between 1990 and 2005, according to the Bureau of Labor statistics. In fact, jobs for most production workers—such as technicians, supervisors, and machine operators—are expected to plummet by 5 to 35 percent by 2005.

Jobs for white collar workers and support staff will also fall. The demand for administrators and managers will decline 14 percent between 1990 and 2005, and clerical jobs will plunge almost 25 percent. General management and top executive positions will drop by 18 percent. Even chemists will see opportunities erode by about 6 percent. On the bright side, some engineering jobs will rise 3 percent. Sales and marketing positions, moreover, will jump 5 percent. The need for systems analysts and computer scientists in this industry are expected to increase by 22 percent by 2005.

A primary factor driving work force cutbacks in the 1980s and early 1990s was high wages. Indeed, workers in the organic chemical industry are among the highest paid manufacturing employees in the United States. The average organic chemical production worker, for example, earned $17.23 per hour in 1992, compared with the average of just $10.49 for all U.S. manufacturing laborers. For the entire organic chemical industry, payroll per employee topped $40,000 per year in 1992—about $14,000 more than the average for other U.S. manufacturers. Industry wages rose 4.2 percent in 1992 and 3.6 percent in 1991.

The best paying jobs in the industry go to highly educated chemists involved in research or management; they earned about $90,000 per year in 1992. The average staff chemist's annual salary, in contrast, was $56,000. Chemists with master's degrees averaged $58,000 while PhDs earned an average of $75,000. However, unemployment among chemists was at its highest level since 1983. And, despite salary increases of more than 4 percent, joblessness among chemists grew to 7.2 percent in 1992.

Graduates entering the chemical industry in 1993 could expect to earn $25,000 per year at the undergraduate level, $33,000 with a graduate degree, and about $50,000 with a doctorate. Twenty-five percent of graduating chemical engineers in 1992, however, were still seeking employment eight months after graduation. Even among chemists employed by the industry in 1993, surveys showed that one out of 25 had experienced joblessness during the past year.

AMERICA AND THE WORLD

The U.S. industrial organic chemical industry is a large part of a global industry and was shipping over $11 billion worth of output overseas going into the mid-1990s. American manufacturers produced more than 25 percent of global organic output in the early 1990s and accounted for one-quarter of all U.S. chemical exports. Chemical exports, in turn, represented 10 percent of total U.S. merchandise exports. The U.S. organics industry remains the largest and most technologically advanced in the world. Its supremacy has waned considerably since the 1950s, however, when U.S. organic producers supplied more than 50 percent of global output.

The largest foreign buyer of U.S. petrochemicals in 1991 was Canada, consuming 11.3 percent of exported shipments. Japan, the second largest importer, purchased 9.6 percent of all petrochemical exports, while China represented 8.7 percent of the foreign market. Taiwan and Belgium each bought about 7 percent of U.S. exports. East Asia was the largest region of U.S. organic consumption, constituting 25 percent of overseas orders. The European Community represented a combined 23 percent of foreign demand.

Despite the strength of the U.S. organic industry, foreign competition continued to erode its comparative might. Although American companies managed to boost organic exports again in 1992 by about 1 percent, imports advanced 15 percent, and the industry's trade surplus slipped to about $1.6 billion; three years earlier the surplus had exceeded $2.3 billion. Indeed, as the percentage of U.S. chemical exports represented by organics declined from 30 percent in the mid-1980s, the proportion of U.S. imports made up of organics climbed to 33 percent.

Economic stagnation in key export markets—such as Japan, the European Community, and recovering U.S.—demand helped importers increase their share of the U.S. market in the early 1990s. However, long-term structural changes in global chemical markets were also at work. Importantly, producers in emerging economies were increasingly challenging U.S. suppliers for both domestic and export sales. In fact, overall chemical exports by developing nations rocketed nearly 400 percent during the 1980s—from $10.5 billion in 1980 to $38.8 billion in 1991. East Asian countries, particularly, were increasing production. Of 28 new ethylene producers preparing to begin operation in the mid-1990s, for instance, 18 were in the Far East, and only 1 was in Japan. Likewise, 46 percent of new global styrene capacity scheduled to be added by 1995 was in the Far East. New competitors in South America, Africa, and the Middle East also threatened to depress both global and domestic prices and reduce U.S. market share.

The largest importer of petrochemicals to the United States in 1991 was Canada, supplying nearly 15 percent of imports. Germany and Japan supplied 14.3 and 12.7 percent, respectively, of all cross-border purchases by Americans. The United Kingdom held about 9 percent of the U.S. import market, and France captured 6.3 percent. The European Community supplied 43 percent of U.S. petrochemical imports. Although Mexico supplied only a small share of imports in the early 1990s, that country's import activity was expected to rise substantially throughout the decade in the wake of the North American Free Trade Agreement (NAFTA) passed in 1993. NAFTA eliminated tariffs on cross-border chemical sales.

In the long term, growing foreign organic chemical production will result in fierce competition and reduced opportunities for U.S. manufacturers. The United States, Europe, and Japan will remain the key producers, but much of the market for high-volume, commodity-like organics will be surrendered to emerging powers. To sustain profitability, U.S. competitors will be forced to boost their production of high tech compounds that will outperform existing chemicals and open new markets.

RESEARCH AND TECHNOLOGY

The organic chemical industry continues to invest a major share of its revenues in research and development. Most expenditures are used to increase productivity and meet stringent environmental regulations, as discussed previously. The average organic manufacturer made capital investments equivalent to $35,589 per employee in 1989—about 7 times more than the average U.S. manufacturer.

Total research and development expenditures by organic chemical manufacturers rose 7.4 percent in 1990 to $4.3 billion. Investments leveled off in 1991 and 1992, increasing 2 percent per year; nonetheless, total capital spending had increased significantly since the early 1980s when disbursements fluctuated between $1.6 and $2.5 trillion. In 1994—the chemical and related products industries employed 12 percent of all U.S. industrial scientists and engineers.

FURTHER READING

"Chemical Industry R&D Rose 7% in 1992." *Chemical & Engineering News,* 23 August 1993.

Darnay, Arsen J., ed. *Manufacturing USA.* 5th ed. Detroit: Gale Research Inc., 1993.

"Facts & Figures for the Chemical Industry." *Chemical & Engineering News,* 28 June 1993.

Hast, Adele, ed. *International Directory of Company Histories, Volume III.* Chicago: St. James Press, 1991.

Hess, Glenn. "Toxic Emissions Decline." *Chemical Marketing Reporter,* 7 October 1996.

Heylin, Michael. "Job Market for Chemists Remains Depressed, Salaries Gain 5%." *Chemical & Engineering News,* 12 July 1993.

Illman, Deborah L. "New Initiatives Take Aim at Safety Performance of Chemical Industry." *Chemical & Engineering News,* 29 November 1993.

"Organic Chemicals." Available from http://www.bayer.de/bayer/english/2xxxarb/2200/2210/2210.htm.

Rawis, Rebecca L. "Salaries." *Chemical & Engineering News,* 25 October 1993.

Reisch, Marc S. "Top 50 Chemicals Production Recovered Last Year." *Chemical & Engineering News,* 12 April 1993.

Standard & Poor's Industry Surveys, New York: Standard & Poor's Corporation, 8 February 1996.

Standard & Poor's Industry Surveys. New York: Standard & Poor's Corporation, 20 January 1994.

Storck, William J. "United States: Chemical Industry Lackluster This Year." *Chemical & Engineering News,* 13 December 1993.

Thayer, Ann M. "Growing Exchange of Information Spurs Pollution Prevention Efforts." *Chemical & Engineering News,* 26 July 1993.

U.S. Department of Commerce. *U.S. Industrial Outlook 1993.* Washington: GPO, January 1993.

—Dave Mote, updated by Beaird Glover

SIC 2873

NITROGENOUS FERTILIZERS

This category includes establishments primarily engaged in manufacturing nitrogenous fertilizer materials or mixed fertilizers from nitrogenous materials produced in the same establishment.

The main source of nitrogen for fertilizer production is atmospheric nitrogen, of which there is abundant supply; it has been estimated that there are about 35,000 tons of nitrogen over every acre of land. In order for plants to utilize this element, however, it must first be combined with either oxygen or hydrogen in a process called "fixation."

The primary ingredient of most nitrogenous fertilizers is anhydrous ammonia, which the fertilizer industry typically forms by fixing atmospheric nitrogen with the hydrogen found in natural gas—methane. The resultant compound is a gas that is 82.25 percent nitrogen. This gas is stored in containers that are pressurized and usually refrigerated, and it may be directly applied as a fertilizer beneath the soil surface with the use of injection equipment. Anhydrous ammonia is the least expensive and one of the more common nitrogenous fertilizers used for direct application in the United States.

Anhydrous ammonia may be reacted with nitric acid to produce ammonium nitrate. While it is an excellent fertilizer, ammonium nitrate is also highly combustible. Once the world's leading directly-applied nitrogenous fertilizer, it appeared to be giving way to urea. Produced by reacting anhydrous ammonia with carbon dioxide, urea has a higher nitrogen content and is easier and safer to store and handle than ammonium nitrate. In 1995, the total production of ammonium nitrate was valued at $8.491 million while urea was valued at $8.126 million.

The cost of ammonia production is closely tied to the cost of natural gas. As the cost of natural gas has risen in the United States, so has the cost of ammonia and nitrogenous fertilizers. About 35,000–40,000 cubic feet of gas are needed to create one ton of anhydrous ammonia. In the second half of 1992, natural gas prices shot upwards and accounted for between 70 and 85 percent of total ammonia production costs. This put the United States at a cost disadvantage compared to countries such as Russia, Canada, and Mexico, which have abundant and lower-priced sources of natural gas. In terms of production volume, the United States lags behind Russia and China and may be facing persistent erosion of world market share.

In 1994-95, the industry experienced growth due to a 1.3 percent increase in production and a 1.5 increase in consumption. Imports showed a growth of 3.6 percent; exports had grown 6.5 percent.

Two of the major producers of fertilizers in the United States, Arcadian Partners, LP and Terra Industries, took steps in 1993 to increase their production capacity for nitrogenous fertilizers. In March, Arcadian acquired both the Fertilizers of Trinidad and Tobago Limited and the Trinidad and Tobago Urea Company Limited. These two acquisitions both have top-notch ammonia and granular urea production facilities, as well as access to ample and low-cost natural gas. The following month, Arcadian acquired the nitrogenous fertilizer business from BP Chemicals Inc., a unit of British Petroleum Co. The deal gave Arcadian a multi-plant production facility in Lima, Ohio with capabilities for producing ammonia, urea, and nitric acid. Also in April, Terra Industries acquired a nitrogenous fertilizer manufacturing plant, regarded by many in the industry as one of the most efficient plants at converting natural gas to ammonia, from ICI Canada. The plant is located in Canada, and in 1992 its product sales were over $110 million (Canadian). In 1996, fertilizer users in Canada were 80 percent farmers, 17 percent commercial landscapers, and 3 percent consumers.

According to the 1996 *Manufacturing USA,* the 37 leading companies in the industry generated sales of $7.517 billion. Some sales leaders were Iowa-based Terra Industries, CF Industries Incorporated of Illinois, and Arcadian Corporation of Tennessee.

Overall, the industry was fairly stable. The number of establishments was growing from 166 in 1993 to about 168 in 1995. In 1997, approximately 173 establishments existed, and that was estimated to grow to 176 in 1998. The value of shipments decreased, though, from $4.246 billion in 1994 to about $3.483 billion in 1996. In 1998 shipments were expected to be valued at $3.568 billion. Employment also fell from 8,000 in 1994 to about 6,300 thousand in 1996. The total number of employees was expected to fall to 6,000 in 1998.

FURTHER READING

"Arcadian Acquires Nitrogen Fertilizer Business of BP Chemicals Inc." *PR Newswire,* 11 May 1993.

"Arcadian to Acquire Fertrin and TTUC Caribbean Nitrogen Fertilizer Businesses." *PR Newswire,* 25 March 1993.

"Fertilizer Materials-1995." Current Industrial Report. September 1996. Available from http://www.census.gov/industry/ma28b95.txt.

Darnay, Arsen J., ed. *Manufacturing USA.* 5th ed. Detroit: Gale Research, 1996.

Farm Chemicals Handbook 1992. Willoughby, OH: Meister Publishing Company, 1992.

Follet, Roy Hunter, Larry S. Murphy, and Roy L. Donahue. *Fertilizers and Soil Amendments.* New Jersey: Prentice-Hall, 1981.

Lazich, Robert S., ed. *Market Share Reporter.* Detroit: Gale Research, 1997.

"Nitrogenous Fertilizers." *Fertilizer Statistics-Summary Table 1994-1995.* Available from http://www.fao.org/WAICENT/faoinfo/economic/ferstat/nitr_gr.htm.

Soil Improvement Committee, California Fertilizer Association. *Western Fertilizer Handbook.* Danville, IL: The Interstate, 1985.

Standard & Poor's Industry Surveys. New York: Standard & Poor's Corporation, 1993.

"Terra Industries Completes Acquisition." *PR Newswire,* 8 April 1993.

Tinsdale, Samuel L., Werner L. Nelson, and James D. Beaton. *Soil Fertility and Fertilizers.* New York: MacMillan, 1985.

U.S. Department of Commerce. International Trade Administration. *U.S. Industrial Outlook 1993.* Washington: GPO, 1993.

Welch, C. D. "Energy Efficient Fertilization Practices." Texas A & M University. Available from http://leviathan.tamu.edu:70/Oh/pubs/agronomy/1-2035.html.

SIC 2874

PHOSPHATIC FERTILIZERS

This category includes establishments primarily engaged in manufacturing phosphatic fertilizer materials, or mixed fertilizers from phosphatic materials produced in the same establishment.

Although the original sources of phosphorus for plant fertilization were guano—bird and bat excrement—and ground bone, a more plentiful source came to be found in phosphate rock, which was the only commercially important source of fertilizer phosphorus in the 1990s. Chief sources of the world supply of phosphate rock are the United States —principally Florida and North Carolina—the Kola Peninsula in Russia, and Morocco. After mining, the phosphate rock must be refined and concentrated for use as fertilizer. Sometimes, finely ground phosphate rock is applied directly to soil, but usually it is converted, using sulfuric acid, into a more water-soluble form. The United States is the world's leading producer of phosphatic fertilizers. But Morocco, which actually has four times the phosphate rock deposits of the United States, is expected to overtake the United States in fertilizer phosphates production by the end of the twentieth century.

Florida had a multibillion dollar phosphate industry. In 1995, Jackonsville exported 293,000 tons of phosphate rock, while Tampa exported 3.44 million tons and shipped 6.6 million tons within the United States. Tampa also shipped 9.6 million tons of fertilizer in 1995.

In the early 1990s, the most widely used of the phosphatic fertilizers was diammonium phosphate (DAP). During the crop year which ended in the summer of 1991, about one-fifth of the 10.7 million tons of DAP exported by the United States went to India, and nearly one-half went to China. The forecast entering 1992 was for increased DAP demand, coupled with lower costs for sulphur, an expensive raw material. Optimism for a boom year in the industry, however, was followed by disappointment. Manufacturers, having increased DAP inventories in anticipation of an increase in demand, faced a DAP glut as both domestic demand and the market for exports weakened. Prices for DAP fell to the lowest point in nearly 15 years. According to the 1997 *Market Share Reporter,* phosphate rock was used more than two times as frequently as DAP, so the decline was continuing.

The result of these earlier economic difficulties was that IMC Fertilizer, Inc., one of the larger U.S. producers of phosphatic fertilizers, was forced in the first quarter of 1993 to indefinitely close a phosphate mine and DAP plant, both in central Florida. The following summer, IMC and Freeport-McMoRan Resource Partners LP formed a joint venture, called IMC-Agrico Co., through which the two companies combined their phosphatic fertilizer business. The industry consolidated further in May of 1993 when Cargill Fertilizer, Inc. bought the phosphate mining and phosphate fertilizer production assets of Seminole Fertilizer Corporation. This consolidation transformed Cargill Fertilizer into a major U.S. producer of phosphatic fertilizers.

In 1995, the industry had approximately 61 establishments. This number declined to 53 in 1997, and was expected to fall to 49 in 1998. The three leading companies in the industry were Louisiana-based Freeport-McMoRan Resource Partners LP with sales of about $765 million, Florida-based Cargill Fertilizer Inc. with sales of $500 million, and Ohio-based LESCO Inc. with sales over $205 million.

The depressed state of the industry in mid-1993 was a cyclical trough. About 45 percent of the phosphatic fertilizer produced in the United States is used on its domestic corn crop, so corn acreage is one determinant of domestic demand; other determinants are grain prices, the ability of U.S. farmers to compete globally, and the weather. Short term fluctuations in the domestic market are thus difficult to predict, but prices were expected to rebound by the mid- to late-1990s. The export market also held some promise for the long term, given the U.S. industry's cost advantage over many foreign producers with respect to phosphate rock and sulphur, two key raw materials.

In 1994-95, phosphate fertilizer production experienced a 3.2 percent growth rate. Exports grew 10.9 percent, and consumption was up 2.2 percent. Phosphatic fertilizer shipments were valued at $5.165 billion in 1995.

Overall, employment in the agricultural chemicals industry had been declining since the early 1990s. In 1996, approximately 5,200 were employed with an average hourly wage of almost $16. This rate was expected to drop to about 5,100 in 1998. Along with employment, production was also varying. In 1996, the cost of materials was approximately $2.949 billion with a shipment value of $4.508 billion. It was estimated that in 1998, material cost would be $2.998 billion with a shipment value of $4.583 billion.

FURTHER READING

"Cargill Completes Seminole Purchase." *PR Newswire,* 4 May 1993.

Cristy, Matt. "Phosphate Treasure Draws Little Interest." *Jacksonville Business Journal,* 31 March 1997. Available from http://www.amcity.com/jacksonville/stories/033197/story3.html.

Darnay, Arsen J., ed. *Manufacturing USA.* 5th ed. Detroit: Gale Research, 1996.

Farm Chemicals Handbook 1992. Willoughby, OH: Meister Publishing Company, 1992.

"IMC Fertilizer Joint Venture Formed." *Reuters News Service,* 1 July 1993.

"IMC Fertilizer to Close Fertilizer Plant Due to Deteriorating Prices." *PR Newswire,* 19 March 1993.

Lazich, Robert S., ed. *Market Share Reporter.* Detroit: Gale Research, 1997.

McMurray, Scott. "'Fertilizer Firms' Hopes for Turnaround Are Frustrated." *The Wall Street Journal,* 12 December 1993.

"Phosphate Fertilizers." *Fertilizer Statistics-Summary Table 1994-95.* Available from http://www.fao.org/WAICENT/faoinfo/economic/fertstat/PHOS_gr.htm.

Soil Improvement Committee, California Fertilizer Association. *Western Fertilizer Handbook.* Danville, IL: The Interstate, 1985.

Standard & Poor's Industry Surveys. New York: Standard & Poor's Corporation, 1993.

Tinsdale, Samuel L., Werner L. Nelson, and James D. Beaton. *Soil Fertility and Fertilizers.* New York: MacMillan, 1985.

"Tosco Completes Sale of Subsidiary." *PR Newswire,* 4 May 1993.

U. S. Department of Commerce. International Trade Administration. *U.S. Industrial Outlook 1993.* Washington: GPO, 1993.

U.S. Department of Commerce. *Statistical Abstract of the United States.* Washington: GPO, 1996.

U.S. Department of Commerce. "Value of Product Shipments." *Annual Survey of Manufactures.* Washington: GPO, 1995.

U.S. Department of Labor. *Employment, Hours, and Earnings, United States, 1988-96.* Washington: GPO, August 1996.

SIC 2875

FERTILIZERS, MIXING ONLY

This category covers establishments primarily engaged in mixing fertilizers from purchased fertilizer materials. In the industry, "fertilizer materials" refers specifically to fertilizers which have no more than one of the three primary plant nutrients (nitrogen, phosphorus, and potassium). This category also includes manufacturers of compost and potting soil; these products condition the soil to promote plant growth but contain relatively small amounts of plant nutrients.

There are three major types of mixed fertilizers: homogeneous mixtures, bulk blends, and fluids. A key process performed by producers of homogeneous mixtures, as well as by producers of fertilizer materials, is granulation. Before the granulation process, nongranulated dry fertilizer powders had a tendency to form hardened cakes, which made the product difficult to handle. The hardened cakes were not always broken up easily, and explosives were sometimes used to break up these cakes on heaps of stored fertilizer. Another problem with fertilizer mixes before the granulation process was the propensity for the component fertilizer materials to segregate, according to particle sizes, during transport and handling. Granulation addresses the problem of caking and segregation by forming the constituent parts of the fertilizer mix into larger granules which are relatively equal in size and which each have the same nutrient analysis. The manufacture of this type of mixed fertilizer is a complex process requiring sophisticated equipment.

Bulk blending plants, by contrast, do not perform granulation or any chemical processes and their basic equipment needs are rudimentary (i.e., bins, front-end loaders, mixers, and scales). They keep an assortment of fertilizer materials on site, from which they select desired proportions for mixing together, often to suit the specific nutrient needs of the customer. The mix may be bagged, or it may be taken directly to the customer's field and applied.

Fluid mixed fertilizers have the smallest share of the mixed fertilizer market. They are generally made by either the hot-mix or cold-mix process. Hot-mix plants combine ammonia with phosphoric acid, a reaction which releases considerable heat. The cold-mix process usually does not involve heat-producing chemical reactions, and the equipment needs for cold-mix plants are simpler than those for hot-mix plants.

The commercial usage of multi-nutrient fertilizers is somewhat controversial. Some governments have argued against the practice on the grounds that optimal results are obtained when farmers tailor their fertilizer usage to their specific crop/soil combination, and that this is best done with the use of single-nutrient fertilizers applied in the proper proportions. Research results have supported that argument, and advances in soil nutrient analysis technique have made it easier to determine which specific nutrient a particular plot of land may need. The result of the arguments has been a trend away from the use of mixed fertilizers. Data for fertilizer consumption in the United States, covering the period between 1955 and 1980, indicates that beginning in 1955 the use of mixtures was roughly twice that of direct application fertilizer materials. Over the subsequent years the use of single-nutrient fertilizers grew, both in absolute terms and relative to mixtures, and in the early 1970s surpassed the use of mixtures.

However, the manufacture of mixed fertilizers remains a major agricultural industry.

The total number of establishments in this industry was 413 in 1993. By 1996, the number fell to about 328, and it was estimated to fall even further to 298 in 1998. With 42 establishments, Florida had the highest number in the United States. The three leading companies in 1997 were not based in Florida, though. The Minnesota-based Cenex/Land O'Lakes Ag Services was the leader with sales of about $2.2 billion. Tennessee Farmers Cooperative was far behind with sales of $372 million, and Royster-Clark Incorporated of North Carolina reported sales of $209 million.

Although the employment rate was estimated to be 5.8 thousand in 1998, down from approximately 6.2 thousand in 1996, the value of shipments was increasing. In 1995, the industry's shipments were an estimated $2.233 billion, and they were expected to increase to $2.345 billion in 1998.

FURTHER READING

Farm Chemicals Handbook 1992. Willoughby, OH: Meister Publishing Company, 1992.

Darnay, Arsen J., ed. *Manufacturing USA.* Detroit: Gale Research Inc., 1996.

Soil Improvement Committee, California Fertilizer Association. *Western Fertilizer Handbook.* Danville, IL: The Interstate, 1985.

Tinsdale, Samuel L., Werner L. Nelson, and James D. Beaton. *Soil Fertility and Fertilizers.* New York: Macmillan, 1985.

Ward's Business Directory of U.S. Private and Public Companies. Detroit: Gale Research, 1997.

SIC 2879

PESTICIDES AND AGRICULTURAL CHEMICALS, NOT ELSEWHERE CLASSIFIED

This category includes establishments primarily engaged in the formulation and preparation of ready-to-use agricultural and household pesticides from technical chemicals or concentrates, and the production of concentrates which require further processing before use as agricultural pesticides. This industry also includes establishments primarily engaged in manufacturing or formulating agricultural chemicals, not elsewhere classified, such as minor or trace elements and soil conditioners. Establishments primarily engaged in manufacturing basic or technical agricultural pest control chemicals are classified in industries that manufacture industrial organic or inorganic chemicals.

INDUSTRY SNAPSHOT

During the 1980s, the pesticide industry faced increased economic pressures due to governmental regulations aimed at addressing environmental and food safety issues. The regulation led to a dramatic increase in research and development costs, as companies were forced to conduct exhaustive toxicology tests for pesticide effects on the environment, fish, and wildlife, as well as on human life. In 1988, the Environmental Protection Agency (EPA) began a program to re-register all agricultural pesticides, a procedure which pesticide manufacturers claimed, is both time-consuming and costly for the registrant. Faced with increased costs and a mature domestic market for their product, the industry rationalized and consolidated. The result was that the number of pesticide manufacturing firms fell from 286 companies in 1986, to about 238 in 1991.

Adjuvants are a wide range of inert additives, which are designed to make pesticides more effective. Examples are attractants, defoaming agents, extenders (which prolong the active life of the pesticide by screening out ultraviolet light), stickers (which prevent pesticides from washing off the treated crop in the rain), and surfactants. The market for these products is much smaller than the market for pesticides, but may benefit from the same regulations, which plague the pesticide industry because adjuvants serve to lower pesticide dosage requirements and do not need to be registered with the EPA.

Pesticides are typically manufactured in a concentrated form, and need to be mixed with adjuvants before they are of practical use to the consumer. This mixing process is called "formulation," and some establishments, which do not manufacture the concentrated form, may formulate the pesticide for the end user who may be a commercial farmer or just a homeowner with a lawn or garden. Manufacturers of the principal adjuvant ingredients supply their product to adjuvant formulators/distributors, who prepare the product and market it for sale to pesticide manufacturers.

About 85 percent of domestic pesticide sales are to the agriculture industry, with the remainder going to residential users. The largest of the pesticide subgroups is herbicides, which accounted for 64 percent in domestic sales in 1991, followed by insecticides at about 23 percent, and fungicides at 8 percent. The largest crop for pesticide application in 1991 was corn, followed by soybeans and cotton.

BACKGROUND AND DEVELOPMENT

Prior to World War I, pesticide use in the United States was limited. The Insecticide Act of 1910 imposed some regulations on pesticide manufacturers, but was mainly concerned with product effectiveness rather than public safety. After World War II, pesticides became more sophisticated, and their use more widespread. In 1947, Congress updated the Insecticide Act with the more comprehensive Federal Insecticide, Fungicide, and Rodenticide Act (FIFRA). The new legislation required pesticides, which were distributed across state lines, to be registered with the U.S. Department of Agriculture (USDA). However, the emphasis was on proper labeling and product efficacy.

It was not until 1954 that public health concerns were addressed by legislators. In that year, Congress amended the Federal Food, Drug, and Cosmetic Act (FDC Act) with a section (408) that directed the Food and Drug Administration (FDA) to set residue tolerance levels (i.e., maximum allowable pesticide residue) for pesticides used on raw produce. These tolerance levels were set using a risk/benefit analysis, whereby public health risks were weighed against benefits to the food supply. Four years later, in 1958, Congress added the controversial Delaney Clause, requiring pesticides, which may remain in processed foods in amounts that exceed their tolerance for raw produce, and have been found to cause cancer in laboratory animals, not be approved for any use on food crops, regardless of any countervailing benefit of those pesticides. In 1970, the newly created Environmental Protection Agency (EPA) was given responsibility for setting residue tolerances. Enforcement of the EPA pesticide tolerances remained the responsibility of the FDA.

In 1972, Congress amended FIFRA with the Federal Environmental Pesticides Control Act. The new act required all pesticides manufactured in the United States to be registered with the EPA. It also provided for civil penalties of up to $5,000 for each violation and criminal penalties of up to $25,000, plus one year in prison. In 1976, Congress enacted the Toxic Substances Control Act, which required the EPA to monitor the production of chemical substances, including pesticides, and to impose testing requirements on the manufacturers of those chemicals to determine any threat to the environment or to public health that those substances may present. In 1988, Congress amended the FIFRA to require the reregistration of all pesticides previously registered before November 1, 1984.

Controversy. The EPA struggled to find the best interpretation for administering the Delaney Clause. In 1988, it announced it would grant exceptions to the

Delaney Clause when the pesticide in question posed only a minimal risk of cancer in processed food. However, in July 1992, a decision by the U.S. Ninth Circuit Court of Appeals ruled such exemptions were contrary to the legislation. The decision, however, was controversial. This "zero risk" criterion was considered to be unreasonable by many in the agrochemical industry, and in the spring of 1993, two members of the U.S. House of Representatives introduced the Food Quality Protection Act in an attempt to loosen the EPA's pesticide tolerance-setting criteria. Both the National Association of State Departments of Agriculture and the National Food Processors Association supported the proposed act. But any lessening of pesticide regulations would receive opposition from environmental groups, especially in light of a National Academy of Science study released in June 1993, which charged that federal regulators were not adequately protecting children from pesticide poisoning.

Prior to passage of the Food Quality Protection Act, the Delaney Clause applied to pesticides in processed foods, but only when residues of a cancer causing pesticide increased during processing. The Delaney Clause never applied to fresh produce, or to crops the EPA did not consider processed, such as frozen vegetables. In fact, the Delaney Clause had minimal impact on pesticides precisely because the overwhelming majority of pesticide residues decrease or remain at the same levels when fresh food is processed.

Processed baby food best illustrates the limitations of the Delaney clause. In 1995, the Environmental Working Group and the National Campaign for Pesticide Policy Reform commissioned a food industry lab to test baby food for pesticides. The pesticide found most often was iprodione (trade name Rovral), classified by the EPA as a probable human carcinogen. The pesticide slipped past regulations noted in the Delaney Clause because the levels in the baby food were lower than those in the raw food from which the baby food was made.

The argument over pesticide regulation extended further than the Delaney Clause. In 1992, the U.S. Supreme Court ruled that state and local governments have the right to enact pesticide regulations, which are more stringent than those required by the federal government, as about 12 states had done. In response, Congress began considering passage of the Federal-State Pesticide Regulation Partnership Act, which would prohibit local regulation of pesticides. In a 1993 report, the Industrial Biotechnology Association anticipated that a compromise form of the act would be passed eventually.

CURRENT CONDITIONS

On August 3, 1996, President Clinton signed the Food Safety Protection Act, fundamentally improving the way pesticides are regulated in food. Under the new law, all exposures to pesticides must be shown to be safe for infants and children, with a clear consideration of the sensitivity of the young to these chemicals. In addition, when determining a safe level for a pesticide in food, the EPA must explicitly account for all infant and child exposures to other pesticides and toxic chemicals that share a common toxic mechanism.

Further, under prior law, farmer profits could justify risks that would otherwise be deemed unacceptable, and no explicit protection of infants and children was required. This framework was largely repealed, and replaced by a uniform standard of safety, with very narrow exceptions. And, when exceptions to the new health standard are granted for a specific pesticide, the public is informed in supermarkets of all foods treated with that pesticide.

In general, the political climate in the 1990s did not favor the domestic pesticide industry. The Clinton Administration announced a program to reduce the use of agricultural pesticides in the United States, and appeared to support the proposed Circle of Poison Prevention Act, which would prohibit U.S. manufacturers from exporting those pesticides that are banned in this country. The "circle of poison" refers to the U.S. export of pesticides, which are banned domestically, and the subsequent use of those pesticides on crops in foreign countries, which are then imported back into the United States. The pesticide industry argued that the proposed bill will inappropriately apply U.S. risk/benefit criteria to countries where the benefits may outweigh the risks, thereby depriving those countries of needed improvements to their food supply; will fail to distinguish between pesticides that have been refused registration by the EPA for public health reasons from those pesticides that the manufacturers have decided not to register in the United States due to a poor domestic demand; and will simply allow competitors from other countries to gain global market share by selling identical pesticides to the same countries. The combination of industry-adverse regulation in the United States and the proposed export restraint on pesticides is the impetus for the trend among pesticide manufacturers to send research and development and production operations overseas.

INDUSTRY LEADERS

Leading U.S. establishments in this category are DuPont Agricultural Products, Monsanto Company, and FMC Corp. Some of the larger foreign manufacturers have U.S. subsidiaries. Leading foreign companies include Ciba-Geigy AG (Switzerland), which is the world's largest agrochemicals company, Rhône-Poulenc Inc. (France), Imperial Chemicals PLC (Britain, whose U.S. subsidiary is ICI Americas, Inc.), Bayer Group (Germany, whose U.S. subsidiary is Miles, Inc.), BASF Group (Germany), and Hoechst AG (Germany).

Although E.I. Du Pont de Nemours, the parent company of Du Pont Agricultural Products, reported sales of $3.29 billion in 1995, versus $2.73 billion in 1994, almost $114 million was recorded as a loss, principally from costs associated with product liability litigation. In June of 1993, the company paid out $500 million in out-of-court settlements to 2,000 farmers who used the product and then claimed that it adversely affected their flowers and shrubs. These payments caused a 7.5 percent reduction in Du Pont's 1991 net income, and a 8.3 percent reduction for 1992. After Du Pont scientists purportedly found evidence that the Benlate DF was not at fault, the company discontinued its policy of settling the claims.

Another problem is Du Pont's pesticide, bromacil. In June 1993, a study was released jointly by the National Coalition Against the Misuse of Pesticides (NCAMP) and the United Mine Workers of America (UMWA), which charged that bromacil was causing widespread contamination of ground water. The groups asked the EPA and other regulators to stop the use of this pesticide.

Monsanto Company, which includes Ortho Consumer Products Division, reported sales earnings of $9.26 billion in 1996, up from $8.96 billion in 1995. In 1996, Monsanto Company's board of directors approved a plan to spin off the company's chemical businesses and form two new separately traded, publicly held companies— a life sciences company with $5 billion in sales that serves the agriculture, food, and health care markets, and a chemical company with $3 billion in revenues that makes and markets an array of high-performance, chemical-based products.

FMC Corp., whose 1996 pesticide/agricultural-related sales were $685 million, agreed in 1992 to a long-term plan for cleaning up its 30-acre hazardous waste landfill in the state of New York. It is estimated that the plan, crafted by the EPA and the New York State Department of Environmental Conservation and finalized in 1993, will cost the pesticide manufacturer a total of $8.4 million. 1997 also saw the release of Authority Broadleaf, the new pre-emergence soybean herbicide manufactured by FMC, registered by the Environmental Protection Agency for the 1997 growing season.

WORK FORCE

Employment levels in the pesticide industry, as well as the agricultural chemical industry in general, exhibited a slight downward trend during the 1980s, a trend projected by the Bureau of Labor Statistics to continue to the year 2000. Statistics for 1986 indicate that the average number of employees per establishment was 54, 32 of whom were production workers. Occupations utilized by the industry include chemical equipment controllers, chemical plant and system operators, maintenance repairers, truck drivers, secretaries, mechanics, chemists, electricians, warehouse workers, shipping clerks, and office workers.

AMERICA AND THE WORLD

The United States is the world's largest manufacturer of pesticides, followed by Germany and Japan, and enjoyed a favorable pesticide trade balance with the rest of the world into the 1990s, even though the ratio of exports to imports fell from 2.3 to 1.9 during the first three years of the 1990s. The largest market for U.S. exports of pesticides is Japan, which accounted for about 10 percent in 1996. Although the world market for pesticides, which was $22.5 billion in 1992, had been forecasted by the U.S. Department of Commerce to grow at a rate of about 2.5 to 3.0 percent per year, a drop of about 12.0 percent in the European Community market and increased price competition in the United States pulled the world market for pesticides downward in 1992. In 1996, however, the world market for pesticides skyrocketed up from the decline to $30.6 billion, with a projected increase in sales of 5.5 percent for the future.

RESEARCH AND TECHNOLOGY

Research and development costs have risen to high levels and are expected to continue to rise as regulatory requirements for more environmentally safe pesticides increase. The 1990s ushered in a trend among agrochemical manufacturers to develop low-dosage pesticides as a means of reducing the amount of chemical residue left on crops. Monsanto, for example, has a policy that any new pesticides that it develops must be designed for low-dosage application, must have low toxicity, and must be have low impact on the environment.

Another area which holds promise for the industry is biotechnology. Biotechnology involves the genetic engineering of plants to make them resistant to diseases, insects, drought, pollution, and herbicides, in addition to the use of bacteria and viruses to create biological insecticides. One especially promising group of viruses for use as ''bioinsecticides'' is the baculoviruses. These viruses are naturally occurring and only attack specific insects; they pose no threat to humans, wildlife, or non-targeted insects. In 1992, American Cyanamid Co.'s Agricultural Research Division signed an agreement with the University of Georgia Research Foundation Inc. to develop ways to make these viruses more effective.

FURTHER READING

Abrahams, Paul. "EC Reforms Hurt Agrochemicals—Schering's Mooted Deal with Hoechst." *Financial Times,* 13 May 1993.

"American Cyanamid Signs Research Agreement with the University of Georgia Research Foundation." *Business Wire,* 24 February 1992.

Bahner, Benedict. "The Stage Is Set for Change: Market for Agricultural Chemical Adjuvants Is Changing." *Chemical Marketing Reporter,* 17 May 1993.

Commins, Patricia. "Pesticide Makers Focus on Low-Dose Chemicals." *Reuters,* 2 July 1993.

Darnay, Arsen J., ed. *Manufacturing USA.* 5th ed. Detroit: Gale Research, 1996.

DuPont Homepage. Available from http://www.dupont.com.

"Du Pont Pesticide Shown to Contaminate Ground Water, According to Study." *PR Newswire,* 30 June 1993.

"$8.4 Million Cleanup Selected for the FMC Dublin Road Superfund Site in Orleans County, New York." *PR Newswire,* 12 April 1993.

EPA Homepage. Available from http://www.epa.gov.

Farm Chemicals Handbook 1992. Willoughby, OH: Meister Publishing Company, 1992.

"Global Pesticide Market Grows in 1996." Available from http://www.corpwatch.orgtrac/corner/worldnews/other/other26.html.

"Guide to the Global 500." *Fortune,* 26 July 1993.

Miller, Marshall Lee. "Pesticides and Toxic Substances." *Environmental Law Handbook.* Bethesda, MD: Government Institutes, Inc., 1975.

Monsanto to 1996 Report. Available from http://www.monsanto.com.

"Monsanto Co.—Acquisition Completed." *Regulatory News Service,* 17 May 1993.

Moody's Industrial Manual. Moody's Investor Services, Inc., 1992.

1996 National Trade Estimates—Japan. Available from http://www.ustr.gov/reports/nte/1996/japan.html.

"Pesticide Bill Draws Fire from Industry; Food Threat Seen." *Chemical Marketing Reporter,* 23 September 1991.

Regulating Pesticides in Food: The Delaney Paradox. Washington: National Academy Press, 1987.

Rhein, Reginald. "Five Biotech Bills Signed into Law, New Congress Ponders Many More." *Biotechnology Newswatch,* 4 January 1993.

"Shell to Sell Agro-Chemicals Division to American Cyanamid." *European Report,* 30 June 1993.

Standard and Poor's Industry Surveys. New York: Standard and Poor's Corporation, 1993.

U.S. Department of Commerce. International Trade Administration. *U.S. Industrial Outlook 1993.* Washington: GPO, 1993.

U.S. Exports Database. Available from http://maindoor.mangate.net/us-exports/index.htm.

Weber, Joseph, Gail DeGeorge, and Mary Beth Regan. "So Much for Making Nice." *Business Week,* 28 June 1993.

"World Wildlife Fund Calls for Ban on Carbofuran Pesticide Toxic to Threatened Burrowing Owl and Other Wildlife." *Canada News Wire,* 24 March 1993.

—Jeffrey T. Wingett, updated by Holly L. Day

SIC 2891

ADHESIVES AND SEALANTS

The adhesives and sealants industry consists primarily of manufacturers of industrial and household adhesives, glues, caulking compounds, sealants, and linoleum, tile, and rubber cements from vegetable, animal, or synthetic plastics materials, purchased or produced in the same establishment. Establishments primarily engaged in manufacturing gelatin and sizes are classified in **SIC 2899: Chemicals and Chemical Preparations, Not Elsewhere Classified,** and those manufacturing vegetable gelatin or agar-agar are classified in **SIC 2833: Medicinal Chemicals and Botanical Products.**

INDUSTRY SNAPSHOT

The adhesives and sealants industry includes two chemically similar but functionally different groups of formulated products, adhesive and sealants. Adhesive products are used to create a bond between two different or similar materials. Sealants are used to create an impenetrable barrier to gas or moisture. Adhesives and sealants are made from precise blends of petroleum-derived plastic resins, synthetic rubber elastomers, and agents or additives used to enhance certain characteristics. The final formulation ultimately depends on the end use. Industries that typically use adhesives and sealants include construction, consumer products, assembly, packaging, labeling, and transportation.

As the adhesives and sealants industry moved into the 1990s, manufacturers experienced flat markets. The commercial construction segment of the industry fared the worst and manufacturers found themselves increasingly dependent on the renovation and do-it-yourself markets.

Manufacturers contend that a resurgence in the structural markets and relatively recession-resistant packaging segment may translate into overall improvement for the $5.4 billion industry, which has typically seen growth rates exceeding the gross national product by 2 percent. Concurrent with these developments, stricter environmental regulation accelerated the development of new technologies in the industry.

Packaging holds the biggest share of the manufacturing adhesives market with $1.1 billion in annual sales and a growth rate of 1.5 percent. Construction-related sectors, including forest products and woodworking, are estimated at $675 million annually. The construction original equipment market claims about $430 million in annual sales.

Overall, the growth rate of the formulated adhesives market should be 4 percent throughout the decade according to some industry analysts. The waterborne adhesives market was estimated at about 64 percent of the total adhesives market and should post a 4 percent increase. For hot melts, representing about 18 percent of the total market, a growth rate of 5 percent is projected. The solvent-based sector of the manufacturing adhesives market claimed about 12 percent of the total and was expected to have flat growth. Specialty technologies, including reactives, experienced a growth rate of less than 10 percent.

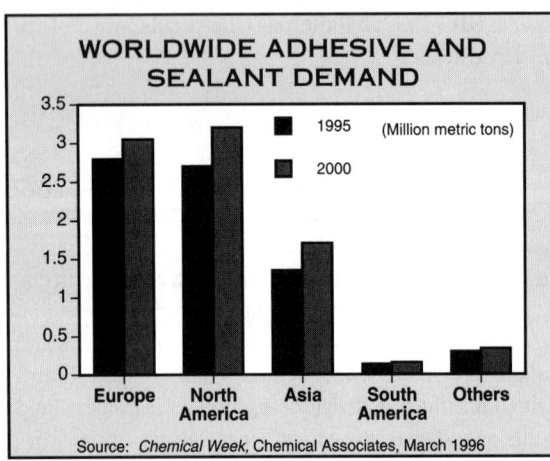

WORLDWIDE ADHESIVE AND SEALANT DEMAND

Source: *Chemical Week*, Chemical Associates, March 1996

Compound manufacturers are charting a new course as their customers change priorities and plastics

recycling continues to emerge as a major factor in this regard. Combined with recyclability, customers have tightened quality requirements. New specifications are forcing manufacturers of compounds toward more complex processes and more advanced equipment. Indeed, compounds themselves have become more complex because they combine difficult-to-mix components, as in the case of stainless steel reinforced compounds. This type of high technology manufacturing drives capital requirements higher and makes it more difficult for small, entrepreneurial ventures to stay profitable.

ORGANIZATION AND STRUCTURE

The industry serves two broad markets: the captive market of firms that formulate products for their own use and the merchant market that formulates products to sell to final consumers. The merchant market comprises about two-thirds of total shipments. In 1996 total product shipments reached an estimated $6.8 billion, an increase of 26 percent over 1990 figures.

The aerospace industry is an important sealant market. Because this market contracted in the 1990s, manufacturers aggressively sought new markets and product applications. About 60 percent of the industry's business in the aerospace market is dependent on commercial aircraft. The remaining 40 percent of the market depends on military spending, a sector in decline in the early 1990s because of the end of the Cold War.

The aerospace sealant market is dominated by polysulfide, which constitutes 80 percent of the products sold. This is a diverse market, with numerous varieties of polysulfide sealants and about 1,500 products.

BACKGROUND AND DEVELOPMENT

The adhesives and sealants industry's development can best be explained by the economy-wide transition from conventional materials (glass, stone, wood, and metal) to lighter and more economical resources, mainly petroleum-based plastics. These new materials mandated new methods of assembly, and suitable bonding components. A generation of new products emerged to service this rapid growth area.

Adhesive manufacturers have been hurt by the downturn in the automotive industry. Yet, concurrent with this trend, a rapidly changing business climate caused U.S. automakers to become more competitive. The net result was that adhesive manufacturers were being challenged and industry observers expected business in this area to improve. For structural adhesives, the greatest adjustments were in bonding new body panel materials. Environmental and worker safety regulations also played an equally important hand in the evolution of systems.

The market for reactive adhesives grew because the automotive industry was moving away from mechanical fasteners. At the same time, packaging applications for reactives were on the rise, adding buoyancy to the adhesives industry. The reactives sector of the industry was dominated by epoxy and polyurethane systems. Urethanes commanded a significantly larger portion of the market. About 100 million pounds of urethane resin went to adhesive and sealant applications in the early 1990s, compared to 28 million pounds of epoxy resin. Stronger performance for polyurethanes was attributed to their broader range of adhesive applications. Some applications experienced very rapid growth. Urethanes are most often used with flexible materials in high impact applications, while epoxies are known for their hardness and are used with more rigid substances.

The development of epoxy/urethane hybrids attracted particular interest because of the broad range of demands placed on adhesives used in the automotive industry. Both manufacturers and users of these products were looking for the best of both worlds: combining high tensile strength and compatibility with flexible materials. The problem was that a sacrifice was usually made in shelf life, toughness, or curing flexibility; the development of these hybrids minimized the number of sacrifices required.

Developments in reactive adhesives for the auto industry brought benefits to other industrial sectors. For example, appliance manufacturing was an area that took cues from adhesive formulations originally developed for the automotive industry. At the same time that these developments were taking place, there were new areas of application that were seeing growth from a small base. As an example, solvent replacement in the lamination of packaging films was one that was contributing to the overall high growth rate of urethanes.Industry experts believe that two-component systems based on polyurethanes meet the performance criteria, but require costly special application equipment.

CURRENT CONDITIONS

In the latter half of the 1990s, the sealants industry continued to suffer from the vagaries of the construction market, especially in maintenance and repair. Growth was expected to continue at 3 percent per year, especially if the construction market continued to pick

up as predicted. Automobile manufacturers continued to show an interest in using corrosion-resistant adhesives to replace welding. Additional capacity and a soft market stabilized adhesive prices.

Having undergone some fundamental changes the adhesives and sealants industry matured with adhesives having penetrated the mechanical fasteners markets. The development of environmentally acceptable alternatives to products containing high levels of volatile organic compounds represented a growth opportunity for the industry.

Despite raw materials pricing and environmental pressures, producers expected the adhesives industry to grow by about 4 percent per year through the year 2000. Theadhesives industry struggled to contain costs in spite of strong sales. The North American pressure sensitive adhesives market valued at $1.86 billion per year was expected to grow at 5.4 percent per year through 2000. The nonpressure sensitive adhesives industry valued at $7.5 billion was expected to climb by 3.7 percent per year.

INDUSTRY LEADERS

In 1996, the adhesives and sealants industry was comprised of more than 700 U.S. establishments employing approximately 12,000 people. Borden Incorporated located in Ohio, with sales of $5.77 billion, was the largest adhesive and sealant manufacturer in the second half of the 1990s. Borden employed about 20,000 people in 1996.

Illinois Tool Works Incorporated came second with sales of $4.15 billion and 21,200 employees. Other key organizations in the industry include Chicago-based Morton International, which ranked third with sales of $3.61 billion and 14,100 employees.

With more than $3.11 billion in annual sales and 15,500 employees, Avery Dennison Corporation was the fourth leading manufacturer of pressure sensitive adhesives and materials. In 1990, Avery International and Dennison Manufacturing Companies were combined to form the present company. Its three operating divisions include pressure sensitive adhesives and materials, office products, and product identification and control systems.

Other key players among the top 10 companies in the United States were Sonoco Products Co. of South Carolina with $2.70 billion in revenue, Hercules Incorporated of Delaware with $2.42 billion in revenue, B.F. Goodrich Company with $2.40 billion in revenue, Borden, Inc.'s Packaging and Industrial Products Division with revenues of$1.95 billion, M.A. Hanna Company of Ohio with $1.90 billion in revenue, and National Starch and Chemical Company of New Jersey with revenues of $1.80 billion.

AMERICA AND THE WORLD

The 1990s began with demand for global compounds of 700,000 metric tons annually, and a relatively flat growth rate of one to 1.5 percent. Industry experts estimate that worldwide annual growth rates of 6 to 7 percent will prevail through the middle of the decade and product demand will grow to an estimated one million tons during this time period. By the end of the century, total global demand is estimated to reach 1.3 million tons annually.

Numerous mergers and acquisitions indicated higher levels of foreign participation in the domestic industry in recent years. As industry-wide restructuring drew to a close in the United States, however, consolidation of the European industry continued, with a few highly diversified multinational corporations purchasing small privately-held firms. Companies in Japan, the United Kingdom, and Germany have emerged as major competitors of U.S. firms in the world arena.

RESEARCH AND TECHNOLOGY

Adhesives and sealants manufacturers are counting on proactive research and development to keep them one step ahead of environmental regulators and market demands. Among the challenges faced are regulations aimed at reducing volatile organic compound emissions and bolsteringpollution prevention measures.

Technological advances have contributed to the growing use of adhesives used by car makers to build lighter and more fuel-efficient vehicles. Corporate Average Fuel Economy (CAFE) standards have driven the weight of automobiles down. To lighten automobiles, adhesives are replacing mechanical fasteners and are increasingly taking the place of spot welds. They are also reducing the corrosion problems associated with traditional bonding methods.

The biggest growth area for adhesive technology has come as a result of changes in the materials used in auto body parts. The most significant of these new materials is the sheet molded compound (SMC). Many opportunities for weight reduction with sheet molded compounds have not been fully explored yet, so this remains a developing technology.

Newer areas of technological challenge in terms of bonding are glass-reinforced polyesters. One emerging plastic technology is resin transfer molding (RTM). This is a polyester material, based on resin, that is being used in lower volume auto and truck applications such as sporty or upscale car models.

A growing number of players in the adhesives and sealants industry have expressed a desire to move away from the use of primers in adhesive systems because of their flammability and volatility. Such a change, however, presents difficulties in getting the right adhesion to certain materials. Physical and chemical changes can be made to the surface of these materials, but the focus of new development is to make adhesives and sealants that will incorporate the function of a primer. Environmental mandates on chlorofluorocarbons, volatile organic compound emission standards, and other ecological considerations are thus forcing adhesive formulators to nudge solvents out of their products and find alternatives. Research continues on meeting high-performance parameters such as water resistance, durability, and humidity resistance without using such solvents.

In addition, a number of large users of solvent-borne adhesives have already installed equipment to recapture and recycle, or properly incinerate solvent, and are less likely to change to solventless products. Already, adhesive manufacturers have moved production of industrial adhesivesaway from solvents to 100 percent solids, epoxies, and urethanes. With respect to pressure sensitive adhesives such as duct tape and heavy duty industrial tapes, manufacturers have raised solid content to 65 percent, from as low as 35 percent.

FURTHER READING

Caney, Derek. ''Sticking to Their Guns.'' *Adhesives,* 27 July 1992, SR 14.

D'Amico, Esther. ''Squeezing Out Profits: Adhesives Makers Get Set For Growth.'' *Chemical Week,* 27 March 1996, 24.

Kirschner, Elisabeth. ''Formulators Pace Environmental Laws.'' *Chemical Week,* 11 March 1992, 34-35.

Loesel, Andrew. ''Plugging Along.'' *Chemical Marketing Reporter,* 27 March 1992, SR 19.

Mullins, Rick. ''A Quintessential Specialty Returns to Steady Growth.'' *Chemical Week,* 9 March 1994,30.

Murphy, Elena Epatko. ''Soft Market Unglues Possibility of Price Hikes.'' *Purchasing,* 9 November 1995, 81.

Naude, Alice. ''Renovating Growth.'' *Adhesives,* 27 July 1992, SR 22.

Naude, Alice. ''Rolling With the Punches.'' *Automotive Chemicals,* 17 February 1992, SR 18.

Shon, Melissa. ''A More Measured Pace.'' *Chemical Marketing Reporter,* 15 February 1993, SR 12-13.

''Specialty Recovery Still Coming.'' *Chemical Marketing Reporter,* 26 July 1993.

Springer, Neil. "Solvent-based Disappearing Act." *Chemical Marketing Reporter,* 27 July 1992, SR 9-10.

Tilton, Helga. "Sticking to Basics." *Chemical Marketing Reporter,* 27 July 1992, SR 3-8.

U.S. Department of Commerce. International Trade Administration. *U.S. Industrial Outlook 1994.* Washington: GPO, 1994.

U.S. Department of Commerce. *Statistics for Industry Groups and Industries, 1991.* Washington: GPO, 1991.

U.S. Department of Commerce. *Value of Product Shipments, 1991.* Washington: GPO, 1991.

—Garth K. Daniels, updated by Visi Tilak

SIC 2892

EXPLOSIVES

This industry covers establishments primarily engaged in manufacturing explosives. Establishments primarily engaged in manufacturing ammunition for small arms are classified in **SIC 3482: Small Arms Ammunition,** and those manufacturing fireworks are classified in **SIC 2899: Chemicals and Chemical Preparations, Not Elsewhere Classified.**

Historically, the explosives industry has been closely aligned with the coal mining industry. According to *Chemical Week* the coal industry consumed 65 percent of explosives manufactured in the United States in 1996. Explosives such as black powder were introduced in the metal industry as early as 1627 and these were soon utilized by coal miners. Before Alfred Nobel invented dynamite in 1866, blasting for engineering purposes was conducted with gunpowder.

In 1905, E.I. DuPont de Nemours & Company supplied 56 percent of the production of explosives in the United States and stood as one of the largest U.S. companies. DuPont continued to strengthen its hold on the market, and, in 1907, the U.S. government began antitrust proceedings against the company. In 1912 DuPont was forced to divest segments of its businesses, which resulted in Atlas Chemical Industries and Hercules Powder Company. Later, Atlas was purchased by Imperial Chemical Industries PLC, DuPont's explosives division was sold to Explosives Technologies International, and Hercules' explosives division was sold to Dyno Nobel, Inc.

In the early years of the industry, the volatile nature of explosives played a significant role in the organization of explosives manufacturers. Companies operated numerous small plants to ensure that their entire business would not be wiped out in the event of an explosion. In addition, plants were located near the consumer rather than the raw materials sources because of the danger in transporting the product.

Products of the explosives industry have changed dramatically over the years. ANFO, or ammonium nitrate mixed with fuel oil, was invented in 1953. Since 1959, it has become the most widely utilized explosive in surface coal mining. By the early 1990s, ANFO held 75 percent of the market. Dynamite has declined in importance from about one billion pounds in the mid-1950s to approximately 100 million pounds in 1993. Because of the drastic decline in the use of dynamite, manufacturing plants for that product have decreased from 30 in the 1950s to just one in 1993, which was owned by Dyno Nobel. Emulsions have gained popularity in the 1990s because of their water resistance and low density.

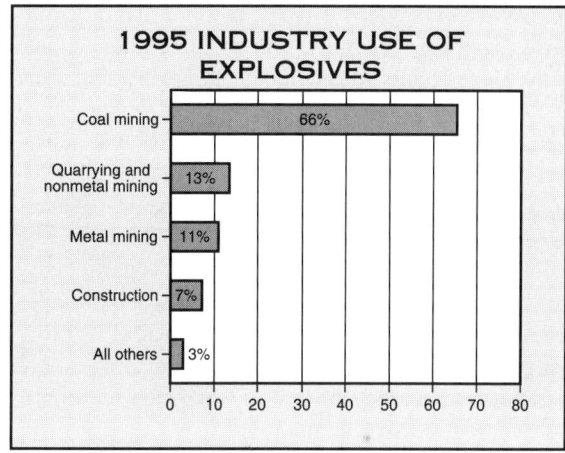

In 1991 approximately 125 establishments employing 13,600 people were in operation in the explosives industry. In 1995, 2.58 million short tons of explosives were sold in the United States. This was slightly up from the 2.56 million short tons sold in 1994. The coal industry continued to be the largest domestic user accounting for 1.65 million short tons of explosives. The rest of the explosives production was distributed among the quarrying and nonmetal mining industry (339,000 short tons), metal mining industry (275,000), construction industry (182,000), and miscellaneous activities (75,000). Ammonium nitrate-based explosives accounted for nearly 98 percent of production or approximately 2.24 million tons.

Although 1995 was a good year for the explosives industry sales volume is expected to decline through the end of the century. Coal mining, the largest domestic user of explosives, is gradually shifting in the United States from the East and Midwest to the West. Western surface mines have less overburden rock thus requiring less explosives to reach the coal. It is estimated that in the East ten pounds of explosives are needed to mine one ton of coal, while in the West only one pound of explosive is needed to mine the same amount of coal.

Because of the 1993 World Trade Center bombing in New York City and the 1995 bombing of the Federal Building in Oklahoma City there has been a push at the federal level to require that all explosives and potential explosive components such as fertilizer to be manufactured with taggants, which are color-coded, multilayered particles bearing a unique signature and can be seen under a microscope providing identification of the manufacturer's batch lot. Taggant legislation, however, has been stalled by manufacturers who claim that there are concerns over quality, stability, and effect on the environment. Many industry insiders believe that opposition to taggants is based more on liability concerns than product quality. Given the litigious climate in the United States today manufacturers fear that if the explosives used in a terrorist bomb could be traced to a specific manufacturer massive lawsuits and subsequent settlements might ensue. The manufacturers' argument that quality will suffer because of taggants may be muted by a new product being developed by Isotag of Houston. This taggant, which is particularly effective with ammonium nitrate explosives, provides labeling at the molecular level. Isotag claims its product replaces some of the explosive's atoms with nonstandard and unique isotopes allowing easy identification without decreasing quality.

FURTHER READING

"Custom Designed Explosives for Surface and Underground Coal Mining." *Mining Engineering,* October 1993.

"The Debate About Invisible Detectives." *U.S. News & World Report,* 16 September 1996.

"Producers Face a Blast of Litigation." *Chemical Week,* 11 September 1996.

"Product Liability Could Be the Real Issue With Taggants." *Chemical & Engineering News,* 26 August 1996.

"Taggants Become an Issue." *Coal Age,* December 1996.

"Tagged Out." *Science News,* 14 September 1996.

—Garth K Daniels, updated by Michael E. Knes

PRINTING INK

This classification includes establishments primarily engaged in manufacturing printing ink, including gravure ink, screen process ink, and lithographic ink. Establishments primarily engaged in manufacturing writing ink and fluids are classified in **SIC 2899: Chemicals and Chemical Preparations, Not Elsewhere Classified.** Those establishments manufacturing drawing ink are classified in **SIC 3952: Lead Pencils, Crayons, and Artists' Materials.**

The printing ink industry is one of America's oldest, dating back to the pre-Revolutionary War days. After more than 200 years of similar operating procedures, there was little change in the structure of the industry entering the 1990s. The top domestic manufacturers included Sun Chemical Corporation, Flint Ink Corporation, Inx International Ink Company, United States Printing Ink Corporation, and BASF.

The biggest ink manufacturers still remained profitable, but with reduced margins. The smaller ink companies were suffering most, with a number of them being bought by larger companies, forced to merge, or simply closing up entirely. Concurrent with these developments, there were segments of the market where new ink companies were emerging.

Overall, total 1996 shipment values for printing inks consumed in the United States was about $3.7 billion, an increase of approximately $200 million over the previous year. The total included domestic commercial and captive ink production plus imports, but excluded exports.

A concern in the domestic printing ink industry was the high percentage of foreign ownership of American corporations, between 40 percent and 50 percent. Very few of the larger ink companies remained independent. Even these companies were candidates for purchase or merger.

The Clean Air Act began to change the industry, and The Vegetable Ink Printing Act of Congress, passed in 1994, mandated that printers with government contracts use vegetable oil-based inks instead of volatile petroleum-based inks whenever possible. The main concerns were due to the hazardous effects of using crude oil as the ink base, as was done for most of the history of printing inks. Emissions from volatile organic compounds (VOCs), and emissions of hazardous air pollutants (HAPs), had to be controlled. Printing inks also had to be developed to make the deinking and recycling of paper easier. Printers wanted inks that stuck to paper, and recyclers wanted inks that could be easily removed.

During the recession at the beginning of the 1990s, raw material prices stabilized considerably. Purchasing experts in the ink industry found that there were only a few areas where upward price pressure could continue throughout 1990. The major factor affecting prices was the stable price of crude oil, from which more than 75 percent of the raw materials for ink was derived. The industry's membership sought to take full advantage of the relatively low raw material costs, resisting any price increases from raw materials suppliers unless they were fully justified. In some product areas, the companies were able to negotiate price reductions, which helped the industry hold the line on its own prices.

The printing ink industry has made efforts to reduce the environmental burden of its products. Before passage of the Clean Air Act, printing ink manufacturers were developing water-based ink systems to replace inks containing volatile organic compounds (VOCs). Many years before the first "CONNEG Law" was passed to reduce heavy metals in packaging, the printing ink industry had been reducing the use of lead-bearing pigments in packaging inks.

Growth in vegetable-based inks leveled off in 1996 as most of the users with environmental concerns switched to newer inks. Another increase in vegetable and water-based inks will only be likely if environmental pressure increases again.

Growth in the printing ink industry in general was down several points, from around 8 percent in the 1980s, to between 5 and 6 percent from 1990 to 1996. After 1994, a very successful year for the printing ink industry, 1995 and 1996 were less fantastic. By the year 2000, growth should be up to 6 percent, a small gain in what is already a mature market. The biggest ink manufacturers still remain profitable, but with reduced margins. Flint Ink bought BASF in 1996 and smaller companies either had to hold niche markets or merge with larger companies.

Ultraviolet (UV) and electron beam (EB) inks grew faster in the mid-1990s than any other niche of the printing ink market. These only constitute 5 percent of the total printing ink spectrum, but appear to have a greater growth potential than the other alternative inks: water-based or vegetable-based inks. Yellow pigment for printing ink used in consumer packaging is the other niche that is rising quickly. This ink is used on boxes and packages that have a very short shelf-life and then are thrown away or recycled.

According to *Ward's Business Directory of U.S. Private and Public Companies* in 1997, the industry leaders were Sun Chemical Corp. of Fort Lee, NJ; Flint Ink Corp., of Detroit, MI; Inx International Ink Co. of Elk Grove Village, IL; Lawter International Inc., of Fort Mill, SC; and Wikoff Color Corp. of St. Louis, MO.

FURTHER READING

"Europe's Printing Ink Makers Seek to Weather Realignment." *Chemical Marketing Reporter* 243, no. 23 (7 June 1993): 16.

"FlintINK Research Center." Detroit: FlintInk Corporation, 1997. Available from http://www.flintink.com/research.html.

Gentile, Deanna M. "Ink Outlook: Steady Growth and Evolving Technologies." *Modern Paint & Coatings* 86, no.7 (July 1996): 40-42.

Graphic Arts Monthly 64, no. 2 (February 1992): 40.

Lustig, Ted. "Outlook for Printing Inks, '95." *Graphic Arts Monthly* 67, no. 3 (March 1995): 60-66.

Lustig, Theodore. "Ink Suppliers Seek Rebound in 1996." *Graphic Arts Monthly,* March 1996, 68.

McConville, Daniel J. "Getting Bigger by Staying Small." *Chemical Week* 158, no. 17 (1 May 1996): 58-59.

Miceli, Donna L. "Alternate Inks Mark the Spot." *Chemical Marketing Reporter* 250, no. 9 (26 August 1996): 5R6.

Poirier, Mark. "Expect Another Ink Price Hike." *Catalog Age.* 12, no.7 (July 1995): 65, 68.

Scarlett, Terry. "The Truth About Inks." *Folio: the Magazine for Magazine Management,* 1994, 227.

U.S. Department of Commerce. International Trade Administration *U.S. Industrial Outlook 1994.* Washington: GPO, 1994.

Ward's Business Directory of U.S. Private and Public Companies. Detroit: Gale Research, 1997.

—Garth K. Daniels, updated by Beaird Glover

SIC 2895

CARBON BLACK

This category covers establishments primarily engaged in manufacturing carbon black (channel and furnace black). Establishments primarily engaged in manufacturing bone and lamp black are classified in **SIC 2816: Inorganic Pigments.**

INDUSTRY SNAPSHOT

Carbon black is essentially an oil by-product used to strengthen rubber. It is made by shooting a hot mist of oil particles into a flame, a very expensive process that has limited the number of competitors in the industry. Carbon black is a general name for a variety of trade name products such as acetylene black, attrited black, channel black, flame black, furnace black, lamp black, and thermal black. Carbon black production requires large amounts of heat. In addition to its main use in tires, the powdery reinforcing agent is used to make inks and other everyday products.

In 1996, the U.S. carbon black capacity was 3.4 billion pounds, and carbon black sold at prices between 28 and 50 cents per pound, depending on the grade. Approximately 50 to 70 percent of all carbon black manufactured in the United States, goes to rubber and tire manufacturing companies.

ORGANIZATION AND STRUCTURE

Carbon black is largely a homogenous product with many trade names. It is essentially an oil by-product used to make tires, inks, and other products. The principal economic industries responsible for the purchase of carbon black were domestic manufacturing industries, which purchased nearly 95 percent of the industry's shipments. A 1994 ranking of purchased carbon black output found these industries responsible for carbon black usage: tires and inner tubes, which purchased 51.8 percent of the industry's shipments; fabricated rubber products, which purchased 13.5 percent; and the chemical preparations industry, which purchased 8.2 percent.

In 1996, approximately 21 establishments were engaged in the production of carbon black. These establishments employed approximately 1,800 workers. In the 1990s, the U.S. carbon black industry was located primarily in southern states. Eight companies were established in Texas and five were founded in Louisiana.

BACKGROUND AND DEVELOPMENT

The Cabot family was involved in carbon black production from the industry's outset. In 1882, Godfrey Cabot built a carbon black plant in Buffalo Mills, Pennsylvania. At the time, carbon black was made by impinging a gas flame against steel. After World War I, it was discovered that carbon black had properties for reinforcing rubber products. It was this innovation that fueled the industry's growth.

As early as 1864, carbon black was used as a printing ink and is still employed in the 1990s. The most revolutionary application developed for the rubber industry, which discovered that carbon black made tires tougher. In 1920, the rubber industry consumed only 40 percent of the carbon black produced. Today, the rubber industry is the largest market for carbon black.

By 1972, carbon black prices were deteriorating because production capacity was greater than production. Production was three billion pounds per year, while production capacity was about four billion pounds per year. In addition, the cutback in gasoline usage that followed the oil embargo of 1973 took a heavy toll on carbon black demand. At that time, 95 percent of carbon black use was associated with automobile applications; 70 percent went into tire production alone. Higher costs were also having a detrimental effect on the industry. As carbon black prices increased, demand for the industry's products was reduced. By the late 1970s to the early 1980s carbon black production capacity fell from an estimated 4.21 billion pounds in 1979 to 3.38 billion pounds in 1981. The decline in 1978 and 1979 mirrored the downturn in the U.S. automotive industry, but export business buoyed the industry.

By the 1980s, with four or five years of increasing prices behind it, relative stability had returned to the carbon black market. Prices for carbon black generally followed oil prices. As oil prices stabilized, so did prices for carbon black.

The total value of industry shipments increased 21 percent from $570 million in 1987 to $692 million in 1990. This number declined to a decade low of $604 million in 1991, but continually rose to $800 million by the mid-1990s. Despite the increase in carbon black shipments, leading producers in the fierce price competition and lagging auto sales in the United States compelled producers to enter overseas markets. In the early 1990s, U.S. producers established operations in Europe and in Japan. The leading U.S. producer was Cabot Corporation, with total mid-1990s sales of $1.69 billion, recorded negligible profits in the United States, but generated huge profits abroad.

Leading companies, including Cabot Corporation, continued to expand into international markets in the early 1990s. In 1992, Cabot opened a new carbon black plant, Cabot Kashima, in Jashima, Japan, which produced special grades of carbon black. Many in the industry were also expanding into the budding capitalist societies of eastern Europe. Also during this time of exploration into international markets, new low cost production processes were developed and recycling efforts in the rubber and tire industries were encouraged. All these improvements within the carbon black industry were implemented to enable U.S. producers to compete against international export companies.

CURRENT CONDITIONS

As the carbon black industry entered the mid-1990s, U.S. producers were facing stiff competition from traditionally import-oriented countries. U.S. producers were seeking new markets in developing economies such as China. The demand for carbon black in China was expected to grow 6.6 percent per year during the 1990s. U.S. consumption of carbon black was also projected to increase an average of 2.7 percent annually to $640 million in 1997. This projection was predicated on the gradual recovery of the auto industry.

By March of 1995, U.S. demand for carbon black caused a 10 percent increase in price. This dramatic increase was not to be repeated the following year. In 1996, operating rates were high and pricing was weak as carbon black sold for 28 to 50 cents per pound. Industry leaders attempted to raise prices 5 percent, but were unsuccessful. Tire manufacturers who purchased 70 percent of U.S. produced carbon black, resisted the price increase.

INDUSTRY LEADERS

In 1992, Cabot Corporation, of Boston, Massachusetts, accounted for over half of total industry sales. The Cabot Corporation was a conglomeration of specialty metals, chemical, and energy businesses. When the carbon black market staggered in the early 1980s, Cabot expanded into fields such as high-technology ceramics. Cabot also kept effective control over the slow growth carbon black segment of its market through restructuring efforts, including drastic reductions in unit costs to counter the heavy fixed capital investment required for carbon black production.

In 1996, Cabot bought a plant in Merak, Indonesia. The plant was expected to double its capacity to 60,000 metric tons per year. Also in 1996, Cabot instituted a system to measure the performance of its 71 carbon black plants, and demonstrate that performance to all plant managers. If Cabot achieved the 20 percent return on its investment that was expected, it would generate an operating profit and a return on fixed capital at two or three times that of producers making tire-tread black. Cabot was able to stay ahead of competitors and quadruple earnings per share through cutting costs, modernization, and restructuring.

In 1997, the second largest company involved in carbon black production was Columbian Chemicals Co. of Atlanta, Georgia. In 1996, Columbian was undergoing a 25 percent expansion that would increase their global capacity by 180,000 tons by 1998. Three North American production sites would produce 100 tons of carbon black, and the rest would be produced in facilities located in Europe and Asia. This restructuring cost approximately $60 million. The company operated 11 plants in 8 countries. Columbian's total sales were $260 million in 1997, and they employed 1,400 people.

Another major industry player was Degussa's Carbon Black Division of Ridgefield Park, New Jersey, with $150 million in sales and 300 employees. Another was JM Huber Corporation Engineered Carbons Division (bought by Gantrade Corporation in 1995) of Borger, Texas, with $84 million in sales and 300 employees. Norit Americas Inc. of Atlanta, Georgia, had sales of $48 million and employed 300 people.

WORK FORCE

From 1987 to 1990, total employment growth in the carbon black industry was flat. Throughout the decade, the industry employed approximately 1,900 workers. During this same time period, production worker positions actually declined, from 1,400 workers to 1,200 workers.

The U.S. Bureau of Labor Statistics forecasted that most of the industry's occupational categories were expected to increase until 2005, reflecting the projected growth in demand for the industry's products. However, many of the occupations expected to grow most rapidly were non-production jobs, such as sales workers and highly skilled professional positions.

RESEARCH AND TECHNOLOGY

In 1996, Degussa AG, an industry leader, researched the effects of carbon black in relation to workplace exposure, and found it safe. This study was completed after reports from the International Agency for Research on Cancer (IARC), of the World Health Organization (WHO), indicated that carbon black could cause tumors in rats. IARC found that long-term exposure to fine dusts, including carbon black, could cause lung cancer and respiratory diseases. They wanted to reclassify carbon black as a carcinogen. Degussa countered with evidence that only rats exposed to massive amounts of dust were effected. They concluded that there was no evidence to show that mice, hamsters, or humans were significantly bothered by the dust.

In 1996, Texas Department of Transportation officials were researching the possible uses of carbon black to improve roads. Carbon black was to be combined with styrene, from discarded printer and copier cartridges, then added to asphalt. Test paving was scheduled for 1997.

FURTHER READING

"Blend Targeted at Static-Sensitive Uses." *Plastics News,* 27 April 1992.

"Cabot Opens Japanese Carbon Black Plant." *Plastics Industry Europe,* 31 January 1992.

"Carbon Black Faces Unsteady Future." *Ceramic Industry,* May 1993.

"Carbon Black Poses No Threat Degussa Says." *Chemical Marketing Reporter,* 5 August 1996.

"Carbon Black Stability Is Stressed." *Journal of Commerce,* 27 January 1980.

"Carbon Black Takes Road to Recovery." *Chemical-Marketing-Reporter,* 8 February 1993.

Cho, Aileen. "Waste Toner May Beef up Asphalt." *ENR,* 30 September 1996.

"Columbian Has Details on Hike in Carbon Black." *Chemical Marketing Reporter,* 22 April 1996.

"Consumption of Dyes, Carbon Black, Organic Pigments to be up 6.1%/year by 1997." *Chemical Week,* 22 September 1993.

Darnay, Arsen J., ed. *Manufacturing USA.* 5th ed. Detroit: Gale Research, 1996.

"Deza Together With Cabot." *Mlada-Fronta,* 2 April 1992.

Earle, Beth Ann. "Witco Restructuring Divisions." *Rubber and Plastics News,* 4 January 1993.

Hammonds, Keith. "Can Cabot Go Home Again." *Business Week,* 10 December 1990.

Henry, Brian. "Cabot Using Technology to Transform Carbon Black." *Chemical Marketing Reporter,* 21 October 1996.

Jenkins, Gilbert. *Oil Economists' Handbook 1985.* London: Elsevier Applied Science Publishers, Limited, 1985.

Kokish, Brian. "Demand Creating Carbon Black Shortage: Auto Industry Recovery Contributes to North America Carbon Black Shortage." *Rubber and Plastics News,* 3 May 1993.

"A Low-Ash Carbon Black From Coal: Carbon Black has Been Produced From Coal with Ash Content of up to 14%." *Chemical Engineering,* December 1991.

Mantell, Charles L. *Carbon and Graphite Handbook.* Huntington: Robert E. Krieger Publishing Company, 1979.

"Market Newsletter." *Chemical Week,* 11 November 1972.

Morris, Gregory DL. "Columbian Details Expansions." *Chemical Week,* 24 April 1996.

"Organic Dyes and Pigments See Market Growth." *Chemical-Marketing-Reporter,* 20 September 1993.

"Rebuilding the Cabot Legacy." *Forbes,* 14 April 1980.

Shearer, Brent. "Carbon Black Makers Adding New Capacity." *Chemical Marketing Reporter,* 23 September 1996.

———. "Carbon Blacks in a Good Year." *Chemical Marketing Reporter,* 9 October 1995.

"Sun Chemical Develops Carbon Black for Newsprint Inks that Rub Off Less on Readers of Newspapers." *American-Ink-Maker,* August 1993.

"Top 50 Chemicals Production by Volume, Part 2." *U.S. Chemical Industry Statistical Handbook.* 1992.

Tuthill, Mary. "Louis Cabot: He Made Room at the Top." *Nation's Business,* December 1980.

U.S. Department of Commerce. Bureau of the Census. *Census of Manufactures.* Washington: GPO, 1990.

U.S. Department of Commerce. International Trade Administration. *U.S. Industrial Outlook 1994.* Washington: GPO, 1994.

Warren, J. Robert. "Cabot Sees Strong Asian Markes for Carbon Black." *Chemical Marketing Reporter,* 25 March 1996.

—John A. Sarich, updated by Beaird Glover

SIC 2899

CHEMICALS AND CHEMICAL PREPARATIONS, NOT ELSEWHERE CLASSIFIED

This industry consists primarily of establishments engaged in manufacturing miscellaneous chemical preparations, not elsewhere classified, such as fatty acids, essential oils, gelatin (except vegetable), sizes, bluing, laundry sours, writing and stamp pad ink, industrial compounds, such as boiler and heat insulating compounds, metal, oil, and water treating compounds, waterproofing compounds, and chemical supplies for foundries. Establishments primarily engaged in manufacturing vegetable gelatin are classified in **SIC 2833: Medicinal Chemicals and Botanical Products;** those manufacturing dessert preparations based on gelatin are classified in **SIC 2099: Food Preparations, Not Elsewhere Classified;** those manufacturing printing ink are classified in **SIC 2893: Printing Ink;** and those manufacturing drawing ink are classified in **SIC 3952: Lead Pencils, Crayons, and Artists' Materials.**

As the specialty chemical industry entered the 1990s, many corporations implemented organizational restructuring coupled with cost reduction measures. Based on these management decisions, the industry appeared to be in the beginning of a business recovery from the cyclical downturn experienced during the last portion of the 1980s. However, the pickup was more difficult and slower than expected, in part because of the continued sluggishness of foreign economies. This factor reduced the export demand for chemicals and, consequently, the industry's trade surplus.

The growth of miscellaneous chemicals, such as sodium chlorate, posted double-digit growth since the late 1980s. Sodium chlorate is used in the form of chlorine dioxide as a substitute for traditional chlorine in pulp and paper bleaching. While the substitution of this chemical has been greater in Canada than the United States due to greater environmental concerns over chlorine, the use of the chemical in the United States is expected to continue increasing. About two-thirds of the North American production capacity of sodium chlorate was located in Canada. Considering the dramatic growth prospects for sodium chlorate, major producers have made sizeable capacity expansions in recent years.

In 1995, the segment with the lowest value of product shipments was gelatin. The most valuable segment of the industry was essential oils, automotive chemicals, and water treating compounds. Producers knew, though, that the biggest consumers of basic chemicals were the industrial and agricultural economic sectors.

Demand for basic chemicals strengthened in response to the prolonged economic expansion of the 1980s. Output in the early 1990s, as measured by the Federal Reserve Board (FRB) Basic Chemicals Production Index, was at its highest level since the prior peak reached in the late 1970s. Over the long run, the demand for basic chemicals was expected to pace the rise in real (inflation-adjusted) Gross Domestic Prod-

uct (GDP), with the automobile, housing, export, agricultural, and paper markets, in particular, holding sway.

As the demand increased, production levels increased. The shipment value for the industry increased from $9.965 billion in 1992 to approximately $11.777 billion in 1996. Shipments are estimated at $12.582 billion 1998. Establishments have been slowly increasing in number. In 1994, the industry had 1,407 establishments; this number rose to about 1,409 in 1995, and it was expected to reach 1,417 by 1998.

Employment in this industry has remained fairly constant. The number of employees was 36.5 thousand in 1994. It employed about 37.2 thousand in 1996 and an estimated 36.9 thousand in 1998.

Major United States corporations that produce specialty chemicals include Betz Laboratories Incorporated, R P Scherer Corporation, Morton Salt Division, Akzo Nobel Salt Incorporated, and Petrolite Corporation. The three leading companies in 1997 were Nalco Chemical Company of Illinois with sales of $1.215 billion, New Jersey-based GAP Corporation with sales of an estimated $1.030 million, and Henkel Corporation of Pennsylvania with sales of $1 billion.

FURTHER READING

Darnay, Arsen J., ed. *Manufacturing USA*. Detroit: Gale Research, 1996.

Standard and Poor's Industry Surveys. Standard & Poor's, July 1993.

U.S. Department of Commerce. International Trade Administration. *U.S. Industrial Outlook 1994*. Washington:GPO, 1994.

U.S. Department of Commerce. "Value of Shipments." *Annual Survey of Manufactures*. Washington: GPO, 1995.

Ward's Business Directory of U.S. Private and Public Companies. Detroit: Gale research, 1997.

PETROLEUM REFINING & RELATED INDUSTRIES

SIC 2911

PETROLEUM REFINING

This category covers establishments engaged primarily in producing gasoline, kerosene, distillate fuel oils, residual fuel oils, and lubricants, through fractionation or straight distillation of crude oil, redistillation of unfinished petroleum derivatives, cracking, or other processes. Establishments primarily engaged in producing natural gasoline from natural gas are classified in mining industries. Those manufacturing lubricating oils and greases by blending and compounding purchased materials are classified in **SIC 2992: Lubricating Oils and Greases.** Establishments primarily engaged in manufacturing cyclic and acyclic organic chemicals are classified in various chemicals and allied product manufacturing industries.

INDUSTRY SNAPSHOT

In the mid- to late 1990s the petroleum refining industry was engrossed in implementing day to day micromanagement strategies to remain profitable in the face of long-term environmental restrictions and short-term market volatility. Consistently flat market demand for gasoline combined with growing capitalization costs and the high number of companies competing in the industry required refiners to establish market niches and to expand their downstream operations to remain profitable.

Mergers and acquisitions were also a strong trend of this period. According to Journal of Commerce and Commercial, experts agreed that the trend towards mergers and acquisitions, especially in the heating oil

industry, was not likely to slow down soon. The eroding share of oil in the home heating market continued to drive increased merger activity. Consolidations in the petroleum refining industry is primarily driven by the fact that the industry has arrived at a mature market state with little opportunity for growth except through mergers and acquisitions.

According to the *Pipeline and Gas Journal* forecasts, the industry was headed towards a shortage in petroleum products due to domestic refining undercapacity. However, those predictions were not likely to materialize as the country's refining sector was instead expected to restructure and rationalize operations to become more competitive and increase capacity.

As many as 800 companies participated in the aroma chemicals, flavors, and fragrances business worldwide, a derivative of the petroleum refining industry. In 1992, the United States and western Europe accounted for more than 70 percent of the value of all aroma chemicals. Total world consumption is estimated at $1.2 billion. Between 1988 and 1992, demand for aroma chemicals grew by an estimated 4 percent annually in volume.

Consumption of flavors and fragrances products was estimated at more than $9.5 billion worldwide in 1995. The average growth rate for the industry was 5.7 percent between 1990 and 1995. Annual growth of 3.5 to 4.0 percent is projected through 1999, when consumption of flavors and fragrances products is expected to exceed $11 billion. The United States and western Europe together account for 62 percent of flavors and fragrances consumption.

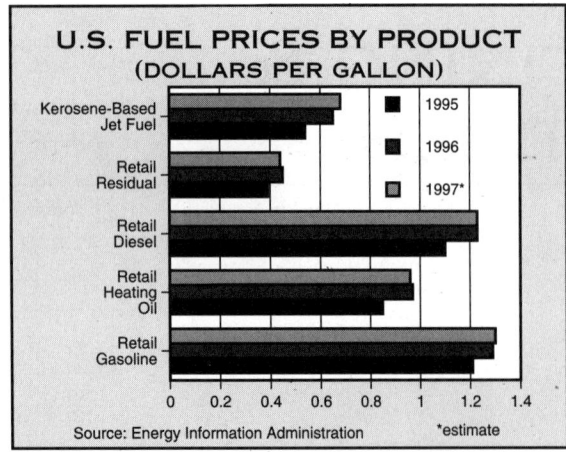

U.S. FUEL PRICES BY PRODUCT
(DOLLARS PER GALLON)

Source: Energy Information Administration   *estimate

ORGANIZATION AND STRUCTURE

Downstream. The process of turning crude oil into refined products, the "downstream" side of the oil business, involves several key participants and cannot be fully understood without a rudimentary knowledge of the "upstream" side of the oil business, the process of obtaining crude oil. Upstream operations consist of exploration, geological evaluation, and the testing and drilling of potential oilfield sites, that is, all of the procedures necessary to get oil out of the ground (see **SIC 1311: Crude Petroleum and Natural Gas.**) Downstream operations include pipelining crude oil to refining sites, refining crude into various products, and pipelining or otherwise transporting products to wholesalers, distributors, or retailers.

Because many downstream companies are subsidiaries of conglomerates that also maintain upstream subsidiaries, the sale of raw materials to refiners is often essentially a transfer of products between different operating units of the same corporation. Petroleum refiners, therefore, often depend on the upstream arms of their parent corporations for supplies of crude, and, in turn, supply wholesalers (who then sell to independent retailers) and retailers (company-owned gasoline stations, for example) who are also part of the same corporation. All major oil operating in this system are known as "integrated oil companies' non-integrated companies are often referred to as "independents."

This tendency toward massive, integrated supply systems affects the oil industry and refiners in that any shift in condition at any point in the crude-to-product chain is felt equally at all levels; economic trickle-down, as it exists in other industries, offers no stabilization.

Processes and Terms. Petroleum refineries turn crude oil into a variety of products, which are used in a wide range of products from asphalt to plastics. All products

begin in much the same way: with the distillation, or vaporization, of crude. Distillation begins when crude oil boils; components within crude condense at different rates, and so are extracted at progressive points along a time/temperature continuum. Lighter, high-value products—propanes, butanes, gasoline, jet fuel—condense at lower temperatures while heavier compounds require high temperatures or a special extraction method to be transformed into such products as diesel fuels, heavy fuel oil, and asphalts. The components of distilled crude vary according to the make-up of the raw crude, with some batches containing large amounts of sulfur, for example, while others may be bituminous and full of heavier compounds.

Prior to distillation, crude is stored in groups or "farms" of steel tanks. Distillation then occurs in a fractionating tower, in which the various fractions, or portions, of the crude are separated. The "straight runs" obtained in the fractionating tower are treated in secondary stages to create final products.

Some secondary processing involves simple heat and pressure manipulations, while others include complex chemical reactions. Thus not all refineries are capable of all processing techniques. Some of the most common processes include coking, which creates gasoline and gas oils from the heaviest molecules of the crude. Catalytic cracking uses heat, pressure, and a chemical catalyst to double the gasoline yield in a barrel of crude by converting heavy cuts to lighter products. Hydrocracking uses hydrogen to make 100 percent gasoline from the light gas oils which catalytic cracking and coking produce. Hydrofining removes sulfur from the crude, making a cleaner-burning base fuel and allowing the sulfur to be sold as a byproduct. Reforming rearranges molecules in a low-octane gasoline to produce a higher octane. Alkylation enlarges propane and butane molecules, allowing them to be mixed with gasoline.

From these processes emerge products which can be sorted into three main headings. Gas and gasoline, or "white" products, which comprise the lighter end of the barrel, usually about 20 percent of the total yield, are used for automobile gas, aviation fuel, and feedstocks for petrochemicals. Middle distillates, the middle quarter of the barrel, yield kerosene and light gas-oil, heating oil, diesel oils and waxes. Fuel oil and residuals, comprising the heaviest, bottom 55 percent, make up heavy fuel oils—for use in power stations and ship furnaces—asphalt, and bitumen.

Petroleum products have a wide variety of uses. Solvents, for example, go into ink, oil-base paints, dry cleaning solutions, rubber cement, and metal cleaners. Sodium hydrosulfide improves paper pulp and tans leather, while organic chemicals serve an entirely, separate spectrum of uses as petrochemicals.

Ethylene, the largest-volume organic produced in the United States, goes mostly into fabricated plastics but is also used in antifreeze, synthetic fibers and rubbers, and detergents. Propylene has several chemical offshoots which are used mainly in film, packaging, and fibers. Butadiene goes primarily into synthetic rubber, but is also used in ABS resins, latexes, and nylon fibers.

Aromatics, including benzene, toluene, and the xylenes, are primarily useful as blending agents in gasoline, as well as in increasing the octane rating of unleaded gas. Methanol is traditionally used in formaldehyde, acetic acid, solvents, and polymers for adhesives, fibers, and plastics. But in years to come, methanol is likely to be in greater demand to make the oxygenate MTBE (methyl tertiary-butyl ether). MTBE, used since 1979 when lead additives began to be phased out, is slated as a component of reformulated gasolines in cities designated by the Clean Air Act of 1990. Some projections indicate that demand for MTBE may triple by 1995.

Product yields per barrel have shifted with demand. In 1981, 10.4 percent of a barrel went toward residual fuel oils, only 6.7 percent was used in such fuel oils in 1991. Moreover, while 7.6 percent of a 1981 barrel went for jet fuel, 10.3 percent of a 1991 barrel was used in jet fuel. This trend should continue, and may become more pronounced, as various emissions regulations are adopted. Federal requirements for low sulfur diesel fuel and reformulated gasoline should change the yield of a barrel of crude; at the same time, wastewater and toxic solids limitations will change the methods of obtaining yields.

Financial Structure. Once crude oil has been refined, its products may be sold as raw materials to other manufacturers, such as plastics or pharmaceutical companies. Other products may be in a final, packaged form and destined for retail sale in service stations or chemical companies.

Within an integrated oil company, a refinery's profits then are part of the total profits made on the front-end. Its ability to compete depends entirely on efficient production without excessive expenditures, so that retail prices can remain low. Like the supply side interdependency of integrated oil companies, integrated profit margins are cumulative. They must absorb the costs of every aspect of the oil business, including geological research, refining procedures, and trucking the finished product, to show real net gain.

For refiners operating independently, turning a profit traditionally rested in purchasing crude at low enough rates to allow final product levels to match those of the integrated oils. Free from the overhead of exploration and test drilling, independents were able to compete effectively for years simply by taking advantage of plentiful, cheap supplies of crude. However, the increasingly stringent environmental requirements of the 1980s and 1990s put independents at a distinct disadvantage. Even with low crude prices, facility upgrading cut deeply into revenues and forced profit margins to fall.

Competitive Structure. Integrated international oil companies, integrated domestic oil companies, and independent domestic refining/marketing companies comprise the petroleum refining industry in America. Like the oil business in general, refining was dominated in the early 1990s by integrated internationals, specifically a few large companies such as Exxon Corporation, Mobil Corporation, and Chevron Corporation—all of which ranked in the top ten of Fortune's 500 sales ranking.

Of the nonintegrated refining companies—independents that focused exclusively on refined goods production and marketing—Ashland Oil, Inc., Diamond Shamrock, Inc., and Total Petroleum of North America stood out as major players. However, no independent companies competed on the same level as any integrated international in terms of net profits or refined goods sold.

Capacity also distinguished leading refiners as arms of integrated oils. Chevron and Exxon had over one million barrels per day capacity, with Amoco, Shell, Mobil, and BP America trailing them closely. A further 26 companies had over 100,000 barrels per day capacity, and the smallest 44 had less than 100,000.

As the costs of upgrading refineries escalates, the difficulties of small refining operations will probably intensify. Only with mass infusion of capital can existing refineries remain viable through the 1990s, and only large integrated oils have cashflow to divert. Even the majors struggled; Chevron, for example, put two of its refineries on the market in 1992, and downsized several others. Analysts speculated that upgrading and compliance costs may continue to shift the competitive structure of the American refined petroleum products market toward a monopoly by integrated internationals.

BACKGROUND AND DEVELOPMENT

The use of semi-refined fossil fuels dates back several millennia B.C. Six thousand year-old inscriptions in Mesopotamia include descriptions of oil and asphalt use as waterproofing materials. Egyptians embalmed their dead in asphalt, and Romans wrote by the light of oil lamps and drove chariots with wheels lubricated by crudely refined greases.

The invention of the kerosene lamp by Dr. Abraham Gesner of Pittsburgh prompted the formation of the Pennsylvania Rock Oil Company in 1854. During this time Americans sought alternative lamp fuels in response to a shortage of whale oil. Dr. Gesner extracted his "improved illuminating oil" from coal, but his methodology proved invaluable to petroleum refining's founding father, Benjamin Silliman, Jr., who wrote a treatise on the chemistry of petroleum in 1855 and then promptly figured out how to distill it. Steam was introduced into the distillation process in 1858. In 1860, the first semi-continuous refining system, operating in a battery of stills, was patented by D.S. Stombs and Julius Brace of Virginia. Luther Atwood cracked petroleum later that year, and Jean Lenoir then produced a three horsepower motor, which ran on benzene. The first full-fledged refinery began production in 1861 near Titusville, Pennsylvania, adjacent to the site where Edwin Drake and W.A. Smith had discovered the first producing oil field in the country at Oil Creek. The refinery churned out little except kerosene; contemporaneous demand for lubricating oils and greases wasn't high enough to keep anyone in business, and petroleum as a transport fuel was still several decades away.

Julius Hock's invention of the noncompression petroleum engine in Vienna in 1869 perhaps marked the beginning of the modern refining process, as engine fuel would become the primary vehicle for petroleum markets worldwide. "Horseless carriages"—powered by burning hay, steam, or electricity until Frank and Charles Duryea built the first gasoline-powered automobile in 1892—eventually became the channel through which refined petroleum captured public attention. The internal combustion engine, invented early in the twentieth century, and then Henry Ford's production of the Model T, suddenly brought petroleum to a pinnacle of economic significance.

In the early part of the twentieth century new technology was developed in petroleum-driven locomotion; automobiles, airplanes, and military vehicles proliferated as petroleum exploration and refining outpaced itself annually. Intense demand for petroleum products during World War I led to production facilities that would continue to produce innovations even after the war; solutions to agricultural, industrial and transportation problems came with each new piece of understanding about the capabilities of a barrel of crude. Even food supply was drastically affected, as gasoline powered tractors enabled farmers to increase their productivity, and asphalt surfaces on highways allowed diesel-powered trucks to speed goods to market.

World War II also prompted an upsurge in refining capacity, yielding subsequent massive peacetime productivity. American consumers during the 1950s demanded large, stylish automobiles, warm houses, and air travel. For nearly three decades, Americans found uses for more refined petroleum. The "more is more" credo became refining's byline; a constant, steadily increasing demand for new products was met by the constant, steadily increasing supply of new crude oil supplies. Unfettered by environmental controls or financial limits, refiners expanded and enjoyed a long, golden age of prosperity.

Then, in 1973, a political crisis in the Middle East spurred a severe recession and highlighted the extent to which America had become dependent of foreign oil supplies. Furthermore, the fall of the Shah of Iran in 1979 precipitated a series of supply interruptions and price increases. Overcompensating for the shortages brought on by Iran's domestic turbulence, refiners misjudged the oil demand for the early 1980s. While worldwide refining capacity increased tenfold between 1938 and 1981, "more is more" no longer held true, and in the 1980s refiners faced a loose market with substantial excesses in place.

Refiners entered the 1990s burdened by unpredictable supply and demand factors and the potential business consequences of the burgeoning environmental movement. Such issues as recycling, the hole in the ozone layer, and water pollution became an increasingly more important part of America's legislative agenda. Consequently, the business strategy of refiners shifted to finding cleaner-burning, more efficient fuels for smaller cars, as well as finding more environmentally friendly ways in which those fuels could be created.

There were more than 180 operating petroleum refineries in the United States in 1992, generating approximately $1.5 billion in products. These products included 7.24 million barrels per day (b/cd) of motor gasoline, 1.5 million b/cd of jet fuel, 3 million b/cd of distillate fuel oil, 1.12 million b/cd of residual fuel oil, and 4.03 million b/cd of other products. Output reflected a utilization rate of approximately 85 percent.

A mild recovery in demand for refined goods could not alleviate the strain refiners experienced in the early 1990s due to unimproved profit margins. Reduced operations, refinery closures, and low sales characterized a gloomy market. The 1991 recession had taken its toll, and the industry was braced in anticipation of new federal manufacturing standards. These new standards, prompted by a growing concern for the environment, meant that depressed market conditions were compounded by rigorous, expensive mandatory upgrading. Of paramount impact, however, is the low price of oil due to the world surplus supply. *Forbes* observed in 1994 that the price of oil at that time was near 20-year lows because world oil consumption actually fell by a miniscule amount in 1993 while "while oil supply exceeded world demand by about half a million barrels a day, swelling inventories."

CURRENT CONDITIONS

Petroleum refining, like the rest of the oil industry, saw profits dwindle to a five-year low in 1992, while spending on refining simultaneously rose 8.3 percent in an effort to meet costs of upgrading and research into alternative processing. Moreover, the 1991 economic recession had prompted shutdowns totaling 114,850 b/cd capacity and had dampened domestic refined product consumption. Though most integrated firms diversified as protection against unpredictable commodity prices, diversification was not enough to keep commodities and refined products from falling in 1991.

In 1992, due to intense gasoline price competition, profit margins at service stations dwindled. Furthermore, surplus production capacity dropped the price of petrochemicals, and the weak economy sabotaged demand. Widespread domestic downsizing, along with massive staff reductions and much asset stripping, resulted in low morale in the industry.

Added pressures in 1993, from excess fuel oil stocks at the beginning of the year and costs of regulatory compliance, kept refined product margins and refiner profitability low. Surplus oxygenates and gasoline dragged gasoline prices down despite a 2.5 cents per gallon rise in crude oil prices.

1996 sales by integrated international refineries went from a five-year average decline of 4.8 percent to a 12 month decline of 6.0 percent with total shipment valued at $110 billion, the lowest figure in 15 years. The list of petroleum product casualties in the domestic arena was extensive. The meager 1.2 percent increase in demand for motor gasoline in 1992 was projected to increase by only 1 percent in 1993 and 1994; record import levels would be necessary even to accommodate this demand as refinery capacity dropped. Jet fuel demand was down 1.4 percent in 1992, demand for residual fuel oil hit its lowest point in decades, and distillate fuel oil demand grew only modestly. The sole increase reported in the industry was in minor petroleum products, which went up by 5.9 percent in 1992.

By 1993, *Forbes* noted, "oil supply exceeded world demand by about half a million barrels a day, swelling inventories. . . . After hovering around $18 a barrel since the end of the 1991 Gulf war, benchmark crude prices dove in November [1993] to below $15; adjusted for inflation, oil now sells for what it did in 1973. That's particularly devastating to the big oil companies because so much of the investment on their books was made based on oil prices $3 to $4 higher than reality. Falling prices have made a mockery of much of the oil industry's elaborate exploration projects."

Profit margins for refineries decreased in 1994 because of increased gasoline imports, the introduction of reformulated gasoline, and the higher cost of crude oil. Margins averaged $2/bbl in 1994. The total distillate sales for 1994 was 48,477,157 gallons. Total kerosene sales for 1994 was 750,330 gallons in 1994. Re-

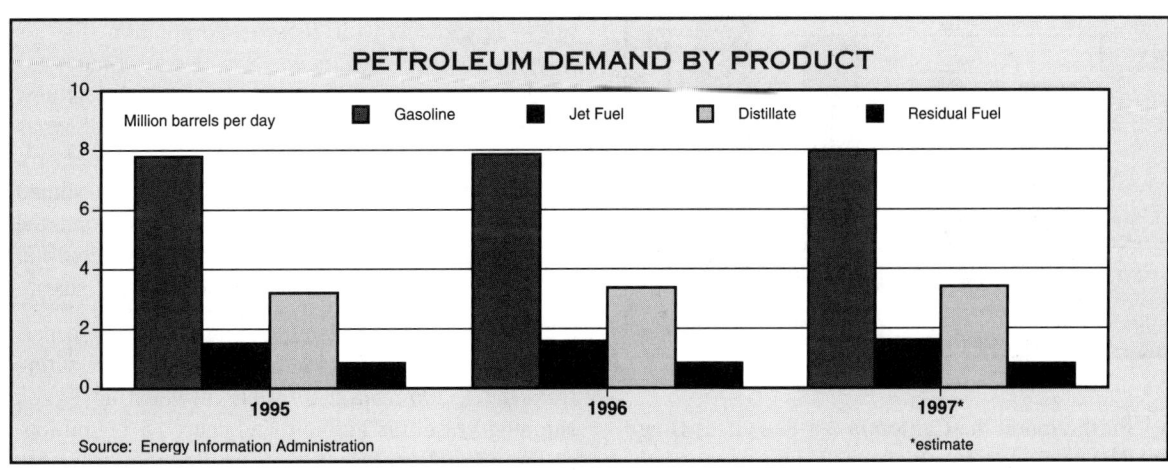

sidual fuel oil sales totalled 15,648,653 gallons in 1994.

Petroleum refining and marketing companies did not do very well financially at the end of 1996. High crude oil prices resulted in low profits for downstream oil companies in North America, the Far East and Europe. Gulf Coast reformulated gasoline prices were expected to have been the worst, according to The Oil daily.

Environmental Factors. One legislative package designed to address environmental pollution has had a significant impact on the industry. 1990's Clean Air Act requires that America's 39 smoggiest cities substitute oxygenated gasoline for winter use beginning in November 1992. By 1995, the country's nine smoggiest cities—Baltimore, Chicago, Hartford, Houston, Los Angeles, Milwaukee, New York, Philadelphia, and San Diego—were to have implemented its Phase I specifications. Phase I stipulated that oxygenates (MTBE) be substituted for aromatics (which do not burn completely) in octane enhancers, essentially prescribing complete reformulation of automotive gasoline.

This new gasoline must have a minimum oxygen content of 2 percent by weight, a maximum of 1 percent benzene by volume, a maximum aromatics content of 25 percent, and no heavy metals. It must not cause an increase in nitrogen oxide emissions and must create less tailpipe emissions of volatile organic compounds and toxic air pollutants (relative to a baseline of 1990 summertime gasoline). The cost to refiners of implementing substitutions and reformulations prescribed in Phase I was estimated to run $3 billion to $5 billion.

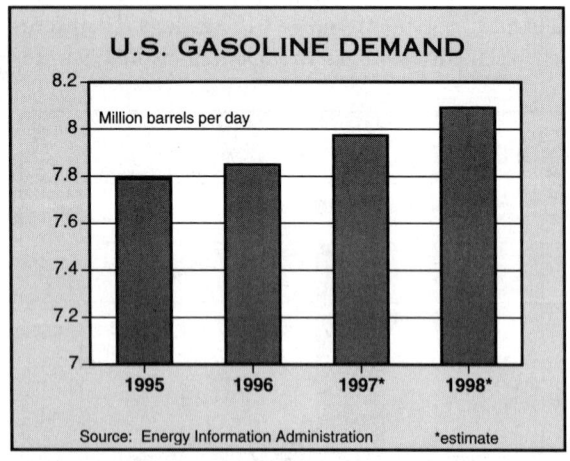

U.S. GASOLINE DEMAND

Million barrels per day

| | 1995 | 1996 | 1997* | 1998* |

Source: Energy Information Administration   *estimate

Furthermore, the California Air Resources Board (CARB) instituted standards exceeding those of the

Clean Air Act, requiring them to be met by 1996. Some analysts predicted the CARB standards would eventually replace Clean Air standards nationwide.

Costs of compliance prompted a spate of refinery closures in the early 1990s, including five smaller company sites in 1992, representing a total of 145,00 b/cd capacity lost. More streamlining was required of major companies, particularly Chevron. Chevron drastically scaled back operations at its Port Arthur, Texas, refinery (140,000 b/cd lost) and cut its Richmond, California, refinery capacity by 40,000 b/cd.

Estimates for upcoming compliance costs for U.S. refiners fall within the $20 billion range, as four more major amendments of the Clean Air Act come into play. In October 1993 ultra low-sulfur diesel fuel (.05 percent by weight) was to be required nationally. January 1995 marked the deadline for nationwide Stage I gasoline reformulation, and Stage II should have been met by January 1997, requiring adherence to a "complex" model as opposed to Stage I's "simple" model. January 2000 will see an additional ten percent reduction in organic compounds and air toxics from the 1990 baseline fuel, with no increase in nitrogen oxides.

INDUSTRY LEADERS

The largest refiner in the United States by sales revenue was Exxon, with $123 billion in the mid-1990s. Exxon, which had 82,000 employees, was formed in 1934, with the merger of Standard Oil Company of New Jersey and Anglo-American Oil Company Ltd. In 1992, it was the giant of integrated internationals, with gross operating revenues of $117 billion.

Exxon's vast international holdings allowed it to focus almost exclusively abroad for its refined product markets, and to write off the future of its U.S. refining as "mature." While expanding refineries abroad, Exxon streamlined domestic capacity and reached a sales agreement with Tosco Corporation for its Bayway Refinery in Linden, New Jersey. Exxon expanded refinery capacity in eastern Germany as new markets became open there. Other European refineries received cash infusions to increase production of profitable lines. Exxon's Sriracha Refinery in Thailand benefitted from a $750 million expansion, and the company stressed the Asia-Pacific region as its center for future growth potential in refined product sales.

While Exxon continues to enjoy financial prosperity, it has been unable to shake the fallout resulting from the *Exxon Valdez* disaster, in which an Exxon shipping vessel ran aground and caused a 11-million-gallon oil spill in Prince William Sound, Alaska, on

March 24, 1989. The disaster caused significant environmental and economic harm to the region (though Exxon has pointed to the millions of dollars it has spent in clean-up efforts), and in mid-1994, a jury blamed recklessnessness by Exxon Corp. and *Exxon Valdez* Captain Joseph Hazelwood for the disaster, allowing victims of the nation's worst ever oil spill to seek $15 billion in damages. Plaintiffs in the federal lawsuit included more than 10,000 Alaskan natives, property owners, and commercial fishermen who claimed they suffered economic harm as a result of the spill. The ultimate impact of the disaster on Exxon is yet to be determined. In 1996 Exxon posted profits of $7.51 billion on total revenue of $134 billion.

The Mobil conglomerate headquartered in Fairfax, Virginia was the next leader in the industry. Mobil Corp. ranked second, with $75.4 billion in sales revenue and 50,400 employees; Mobil Oil Corp., ranked third with a sales revenue of $51.7 billion and 39,100 employees in the mid-1990s. E. I. DuPont de Nemours and Co. ranked fourth with a sales revenue of $43.3 billion and 105,000 employees. Chevron Corp. ranked fifth, with a sales revenue of $37.1 billion and 43,019 employees.

WORK FORCE

Refiners employed 103,800 people in the United States in 1995. Employees earned an average of $21.44 per hour doing a variety of tasks centering on keeping technical processes functioning smoothly.

Within refineries, operators and craftsworkers monitored products via computers. They analyzed data and made adjustments to machinery to ensure optimum yields, repair faulty equipment, and make statistical reports on output. Mechanical engineers worked closely with operators, developing new machinery and making improvements whenever possible. These highly skilled technicians and scientists comprised the core of all refineries' staffs.

As refiners streamline staffs and close some operations altogether, employment prospects in petroleum refining during the 1990s weren't encouraging. Large numbers of experienced workers may be laid off as domestic refining capacities shrink and majors shift operations overseas.

Labor Negotiations. In 1993 the major oil refining outfits reached agreement with the Oil, Chemical and Atomic Workers on a new three-year contract that, according to the *Monthly Labor Review,* "struck a balance between the union's goal of improved wages and benefits, safety concerns, and a national health care program and the companies' desire to contain

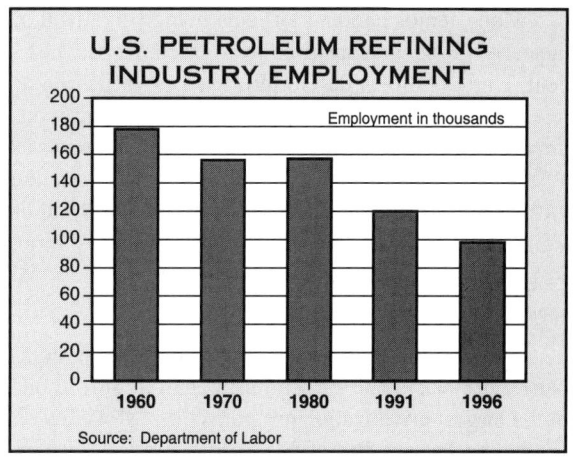

U.S. PETROLEUM REFINING INDUSTRY EMPLOYMENT

Source: Department of Labor

costs and retain operational flexibility." Labor goals in the petroleum refining industry have traditionally been articulated at the national level through the Oil, Chemical and Atomic Workers, while the actual negotiations take place at the local level. As *Monthly Labor Review* observed, "the first [local] settlement serves as a pattern, with the terms of the new contract reached with the leadoff oil company being matched by most other oil companies." The trendsetting settlement in 1993 was reached with Amoco Oil Co. and covered 4,500 Amoco employees. This agreement set the tone for subsequent agreements covering another 26,000 workers in the industry.

AMERICA AND THE WORLD

America was a pioneer in petroleum refining, perfecting most technical procedures earlier than other nations, and developing synchronized upstream and downstream supply lines early. U.S. petroleum refiners are still regarded as the world leaders, with an average yield of 52 percent gasoline from every barrel of crude oil, as opposed to 25-30 percent for foreign equivalents. The main difference between American petroleum refiners and refiners elsewhere lies in the country's free market operations. In no other country has petroleum production and refining developed with such complete autonomy from government.

This autonomy has led to minor competitive disadvantages for Americans selling in nationalized markets in that, unlike foreign refinery products, no correlative subsidies or guarantees existed for American goods. However, global economic stagnation and widespread failure of centrally planned economies catalyzed a surge in privatization in markets during the early 1990s, as nationals went private in the petroleum industry worldwide, a trend anticipated to continue throughout the decade.

Many major national systems being privatized in the early 1990s were inspired by Mexico, whose president, Carlos Salinas de Gortari, used privatization as one method to turn around his country's flagging economy. The Mexican example was held by economists as a lesson in the ills of planned economies and the virtues of market controls, a lesson particularly applicable to republics of the former Soviet Union, struggling with the absolute collapse of their national systems.

In 1993, the Italian state petroleum holding company Ente Nazionale Idrocarburi began to unfold one of the largest privatization programs ever. Most key oil producing nations in Latin America, growing economies in the Asia Pacific region, and much of western Europe were all in various stages of privatization in the early 1990s, depending on freer markets to sustain their national economies.

Members of the European Community faced challenges in both their individual privatization efforts and their collective energy legislative programs. For example, when EC efforts to reduce excess capacities required that England streamline some operations, the English public protested, claiming that mass unemployment in already-depressed areas would follow. Government systems were thereby forced to continue supporting unprofitable operations.

The situation in England highlighted the reason that nationalized petroleum may become an industry of the past: because of the decidedly global nature of petroleum markets, national systems might not be able to compete, once a majority of producer/refiners become private industries. As more organizations adopt efficient, profit-motivated structures, the standards for products worldwide may begin to resemble those in the United States in terms of stringent environmental standards. If so, the American market may become accessible to foreign competition.

There has already been a long history of joint venture and investment in the United States by refiners based overseas, and some of the integrated internationals which dominate in the United States are based in foreign countries, such as the Royal Dutch/Shell Group and British Petroleum.

The state energy companies of several OPEC countries, particularly Kuwait, Saudi Arabia, and Venezuela, invested heavily in U.S. downstream capacities in the early 1990s. Petreolos de Venezuela S.A. (PDVSA, the state petroleum company of Venezuela and Saudi Arabia) acquired the remaining 50 percent interest in Citgo Petroleum in 1991, becoming the full owner of this subsidiary. Star Enterprise, a 50/50 pe-

troleum refining and marketing joint venture between Saudi Arabia's ARAMCO and Texaco, began operating in 1989. And Delta International, another state-owned Saudi company, began negotiating a joint venture with Fina Oil and Chemical, the U.S. subsidiary of Petrofina, a Belgian firm, for its U.S. refining and marketing operations. Furthermore, the as yet unprivatized Pemex Corporation of Mexico acquired a 50 percent interest in Shell Oil's Deer Park, Texas, refinery and began negotiations with other Gulf Coast refiners.

The increasingly complex subsidiary networks of integrated internationals should link many refineries in the United States in the next decade. As the global economy shrinks and ties between nations become stronger, the already cosmopolitan arena of petroleum refining will know increasingly fewer political borders. Consequently, American refiners may compete more directly with foreign firms for markets both at home and abroad.

RESEARCH AND TECHNOLOGY

Although new advances in reformulating gasoline, substituting cleaner fuel bases, and eliminating production waste represent significant innovations in the industry, perhaps the most important revolution in petroleum refining technology involved the implementation of computers. In the early 1990s, distilling and manufacturing industries relied on mainframes that could record, compile, and recall data on all elements, from viscosity to sulfur levels, in any given barrel of crude. Everything from measuring proportions of ingredients to monitoring chemical reactions could be performed with computers, and engineers relied as much on three-dimensional graphic and diagramming software as on actual valves and gages to determine improvements in processes.

With upstream technology breakthroughs such as 3-D seismography, horizontal and directional drilling, and enhanced oil recovery (EOR) helping to ensure that every drop of oil was pumped from the ground, the impetus to utilize every drop of oil at maximum efficiency had never been stronger. Computers allowed such efficiency not only by storing and retrieving data in a central, accessible medium, but also by cutting the time required for compilation and computation. Moreover, by implementing self-cleaning machines monitored by more sophisticated computers, petroleum refiners should be able to produce the low-toxicity fuels in demand, and eventually find new areas for growth.

Nevertheless, patience, thrift, and ingenuity will be paramount to survival in the refining industry. Demand for petroleum products is forecast to grow at only half the rate of the U.S. economy. New regulations will limit the use of products which once had diverse applications, restricting them by season, geographical area, applications, and production costs. Federal standards requirements are likely to continue to proliferate, absorbing time and capital and man for research and experimentation. A restructuring of the industry will likely occur and continue beyond the 1990s into the next century.

FURTHER READING

Anderson, Robert O. *Fundamentals of the Petroleum Industry.* Norman: University of Oklahoma Press.

Basic Petroleum Data Book. Washington: American Petroleum Institute.

Bremner, Brian, et al. "Ho, Ho, Ho Chi Minh, Corporate America Rushes In." *Business Week,* 11 January 1993.

Cimini, Michael H., Susan L. Behrmann, and Eric M. Johnson. "Labor-management Bargaining in 1993." *Monthly Labor Review,* January 1994.

Economist Newspaper. New York: Economist & Newspaper Ltd.

Energy Information Administration. *Short Term Energy Outlook, Second Quarter 1993,* Washington: GPO, 1993.

"The Fortune 500." *Fortune,* 18 April 1994.

"Fuel Oil." *National Petroeum News* 88, no. 8, August 1996, 56.

Guthrie, Virgil B. "Petroleum Products." *The Petroleum Processing Handbook.* Edited by William F. Bland and Robert L. Davidson. New York: MacGraw Hill, 1963.

Kovski, Alan. "Refiners Endure Tough Quarter Burdened by High Crude Prices." *The Oil Daily* 46, no. 2157, 12 November 1996.

Kovski, Alan. "Specialists Predict Upswing n Profits for Refiners in 1995." *The Oil Daily* 45, no. 29, 13 February 1995, 6.

Mack, Toni, James R. Norman, Howard Rudnitsky, and Andrew Tanzer. "History Is Full of Giants That Failed to Adapt." *Forbes,* 28 February 1994.

OPEC's Joyride Was Great While It Lasted. *Business Week,* 3 June 1996, 52.

Petroleum Intelligence Weekly, New York: Intelligence Weekly, Inc.

Petroleum Outlook, Greenwich, CN: Herald, Inc.

Rosenberger, Gary. "Merger Trend Called Irreversible." *Journal of Commerce and Commercial* 408, no. 28714, 1 May 1996, 7B

Sinclair, Stuart. *The World Petroleum Industry.* New York: MGB.

"Sixty Percent of Oil Companies Show Declines in Asset Values." *National Petroleum News,* Mid-June 1993.

Standard and Poor's Industry Surveys. New York: Standard and Poor's Corporation, 1993.

Steedley, Gilbert. "Who's Where in the Stock Market." *Forbes,* 4 January 1993.

U.S. Bureau of the Census. *Monthly Labor Review.* Washington: GPO, July 1993.

U.S. Bureau of the Census. *1992 U.S. Statistical Abstract,* Washington: GPO, 1992.

U.S. Department of Commerce. *U.S. Industrial Outlook 1993,* Washington: GPO, 1993.

U.S. Department of Labor. *Occupational Outlook Handbook, 1992-1993 Edition,* Washington: GPO, 1992.

U.S. Refiners Home in on Profits Amid Near Term Uncertainities. *The Oil and Gas Journal* 94, no. 27, 1 July 1996, 27.

Woodburn, John H. *Opportunities in Energy Careers.* Lincolnwood, IL.: NTC Publishing Group.

Zellner, Wendy. "Now, They're Cooking with Gas." *Business Week,* 11 January 1993.

—Shannon Summers, updated by Visi Tilak

SIC 2951

ASPHALT PAVING MIXTURES AND BLOCKS

This category describes companies principally employed in manufacturing asphalt and tar paving mixtures, and paving blocks made of asphalt mixed with other materials.

INDUSTRY SNAPSHOT

Asphalt is a blackish-brown material with a consistency ranging from a viscous liquid to a glassy solid. Most asphalt is obtained as a byproduct of the distillation of petroleum or other natural materials. Natural asphalt, rarely used by the 1990s, is formed during the early stages of the breakdown of organic marine deposits into petroleum.

Asphalt is used most often in the construction of roads, parking lots, walkways, and other paved surfaces. Of the 2.27 million miles of paved road in the United States, 94 percent of them are surfaced with asphalt, including 65 percent of the interstate system.

Asphalt is also commonly utilized in reservoir linings, dam facings, and other harbor and sea applications. Highway and street constructors purchased about 45 percent of industry output in the early 1990s, and an additional 25 percent or more was used in the construction of parking lots and walkways for commercial buildings. The remainder of the asphalt market is fragmented.

The primary advantages of asphalt—over concrete—are cost and flexibility. Because it softens when heated and is comparatively elastic, asphalt offers a high degree of adaptability in construction applications. Its physical properties also make it less susceptible to cracking and weathering. Furthermore, asphalt is easier to remove and costs much less than either concrete or natural paving materials.

BACKGROUND AND DEVELOPMENT

Historic uses of asphalt date back to 3000 B.C., when natural asphalt was used to seal a reservoir at Mohenjo-Daro, Pakistan; it was later used throughout the Middle East to pave roads and seal waterworks. Pitch Lake on the Island of Trinidad was the first large commercial source of the material. The development of petroleum-based materials such as asphalt during the eighteenth, nineteenth, and twentieth centuries gradually replaced natural supplies.

The demand for asphalt that accompanied the post-World War II economic expansion in the United States drew primarily on petroleum-based supplies. By the early 1990s, asphalt paving mixture producers used over 50 million barrels of asphalt per year, selling more than $4 billion worth of mixtures and blocks annually.

Asphalt sales benefitted from a period of growth in industry revenue from about $3.0 billion in 1982 to more than $4.5 billion by 1988. Unfortunately, a slump in construction reduced the demand for asphalt mixtures as sales dipped 12 percent in 1989 and recuperated only slightly by 1990. Growth in demand stagnated in 1991.

CURRENT CONDITIONS

By 1992, asphalt sales were back to $4.45 billion, and by 1996, sales were at nearly $5.0 billion. From 1987 to 1996 sales increased 12 percent. The average hourly wage for asphalt workers in 1996 was $15.86, an increase of 24 percent over the $12.76 average wage of 1987.

The asphalt paving mixture industry employed about 14,000 workers in the early 1990s—down from 15,000 a decade earlier. Most employees were blue-collar laborers, such as truck drivers and machine operators. By 1996, 13,500 people were employed, which represented a decrease of 7 percent from the 1987 level.

The total number of paving, surfacing, and tamping equipment operators in the United States in 1994 was 73,000. The *Occupational Outlook Handbook,* published by the Bureau of Labor Statistics, projected the employment change to be faster than usual from 1994 to 2005, with most occupations decreasing.

The main asphalt paving product is hot mix asphalt; the hot mix asphalt (HMA) Industry employed about 300,000 people in 1996. Another 600,000 jobs revolved around the HMA Industry. Organizations involved in this industry are the National Asphalt Pavement Association (NAPA) of Lanham, Maryland, and the Asphalt Institute's National Asphalt Training Center II in Lexington, Kentucky.

A concern to the asphalt industry, revealed in 1992 by the U.S. Department of Labor's Occupational Safety and Health Administration (OSHA), was 500,000 workers were potentially exposed to asphalt fumes that could cause headache, skin rash, fatigue, reduced appetite, throat and eye irritation, and cough. OSHA was developing an action plan to reduce exposures to this hazard but had not initiated any further action.

INDUSTRY LEADERS

Over 1,000 companies competed in this highly fragmented industry in the early 1990s. One of the most innovative competitors was Granite Rock Co., which received a Malcom Baldridge National Quality Award in 1992. The majority of the top 50 firms in the industry earned less than $40 million and maintained an average of less than 200 employees.

In 1997, the largest company in the industry was Spectrum Construction Group Inc. of Virginia Beach, Virginia, with total sales around $4 billion and about 4,000 employees. The second largest was VEBA Corporation, of New York, New York, with approximately $3 billion in sales and 8,000 employees. The next largest company was CalMat Co. of Los Angeles, California, with an estimated $370 million in sales and 1,700 employees. Other industry leaders included Tilcon Inc., of New Britain, Connecticut, with approximately $230 million in sales and 1,400 employees, and Reilly Industries Inc., of Indianapolis, Indiana, with over $150 million in sales and about 900 employees.

RESEARCH AND TECHNOLOGY

Among the most prominent technological breakthroughs in the industry in the 1990s was stone mastic asphalt (SMA). Developed in Europe, SMA incorporates cellulose fibers that make it stronger than conventional asphalt. Efforts to use recycled rubber tires as an asphalt ingredient were encouraged by 1991's Intermodal Surface Transportation Efficiency Act (ISTEA), which mandated the use of scrap tires in federally funded state roads.

In 1996, Superpave also presented a breakthrough in asphalt technology. This breakthrough was a method of custom-designing asphalt cements, which are used to mix hot mix asphalt and was expected to be in steady use by the year 2000.

FURTHER READING

Blumenthal, Michael H., and John R. Serumgard. "Scrap Tires Find Future on the Road and in the Tank." *World Wastes,* August 1992.

Darnay, Arsen J., ed. *Manufacturing USA.* 5th ed. Detroit: Gale Research, 1996.

Green, Peter. "U.S. Road Builders Look to Europe." *Engineering News Record,* 12 August 1991.

Kendrick, John J. "Granite Rock Co." *Quality,* January 1993.

"Reshaping the Basics of Hot Mix Asphalt: Wholesale Change Readies HMA for the Twenty-first Century." *ENR.* 2 December 1996.

U.S. Department of Commerce. *U.S. Industrial Outlook 1993.* Washington: GPO, 1993.

U.S. Department of Labor. "Paving, Surfacing, and Tamping Equipment Operators." *Occupational Outlook Handbook.* Washington: GPO, 1994. Available from http://stats.bls.gov/oco/oco20057.htm.

U.S. Department of Labor Occupational Safety and Health Administration. "Asphalt Fumes." Available from http://www.osha/gov/oshinfo/priorities/asphalt.html.

—Dave Mote, updated by Beaird Glover

SIC 2952

ASPHALT FELTS AND COATINGS

This category is comprised of establishments that manufacture asphalt in roll or shingle form, either smooth or faced with grit, and roof cements or coatings. Examples of products include asphalt brick siding, tar coating compounds, roofing fabrics, pitch, shingles, and tar paper. Manufacturers of asphalt paving mixtures and blocks are described in **SIC 2951: Asphalt Paving Mixtures.**

Asphalt is a compound made of hydrogen and carbon, with minor proportions of nitrogen, sulfur, and oxygen. It exists in forms ranging from a black liquid to a glassy solid. Most asphalt is obtained as a byproduct of the distillation of petroleum or other natural materials. Some natural asphalt, however, is extracted from organic mineral deposits in the early stages of their breakdown into petroleum.

When formed into felts and coatings, asphalt provides a reliable protectant and sealant. It is extremely water-repellent, tolerates temperature fluctuations, and resists the breakdown and decay caused by exposure to the elements. These characteristics make asphalt ideal for roofs, coatings, floor tilings, and waterproofing. Asphalt coatings and sheets are also popular sound-proofing materials. Roofing shingles represented 40 percent of the total industry output in the early 1990s, and all roofing and siding fabrics combined made up 75 percent of production. Roofing cements and coatings accounted for an additional 15 percent of sales.

Although asphalt was used to line reservoirs as early as 3000 B.C., it didn't achieve widespread commercial application until the twentieth century. Aided by technological advancements in petroleum-based materials during World War II, the U.S. asphalt felt and coating industry mushroomed during the post-war economic expansion. Specifically, residential and commercial construction booms launched the industry to nearly $3 billion in sales by the late 1970s.

Industry growth stalled during the 1980s, as a reduction in the number of housing starts and competition from new synthetic materials cut into producer's profits. Sales rose from $3.3 billion to $3.6 billion between 1983 and 1990, lagging behind the rate of inflation. By 1996, sales were at $3.8 billion.

Likewise, industry employment declined from about 14,000 to 12,400 by 1990, and to 10,900 by 1996 as manufacturers boosted productivity through automation and layoffs. Depressed construction markets in the late 1980s and early 1990s further reduced earnings. The average hourly wage in 1987 was $11.75, which increased 30 percent to $15.24 by 1996.

As profitability declined during the 1980s and early 1990s, the already consolidated industry became more concentrated. The number of industry participants declined from 273 in 1982 to 245 in 1992, and to 242 in 1996. The combined revenues of the top ten companies in 1996 were over half of total industry sales.

The largest company in the industry in the mid-1990s was CertainTeed Corporation of Valley Forge, Pennsylvania, with total sales of $1.13 billion and a workforce of 6,000. In conjunction with the National Association of Home Builders (NAHB) Research Center, CertainTeed was making efforts to help its subcontractors develop quality programs to minimize employee turnover and reduce job call-backs. As of 1996, the program had certified more than 50 contractors in 20 states.

Another leading company in the industry was Firestone Building Products Co. of Carmel, Indiana, with sales of $420 million and 800 employees. The third largest was Tamko Asphalt Productions Inc. of Joplin, Missouri, with $240 million in sales, and 1,300 employees. Other industry leaders included Celotex Corporation Roofing Division of Tampa, Florida, with about $180 million in sales and 1,000 employees, and Bird Corporation, of Norwood, Massachussetts, with $168 million in sales and 500 employees. Only 15 of the top 50 companies made more than $20 million in sales, and most employed fewer than 100 workers.

Future employment prospects in this industry were predicted to be poor due to increased automation and a decrease in the growth of demand for asphalt-based products. Positions in the majority of occupations for this mostly blue-collar workforce were expected to decline by 10 to 20 percent between 1990 and 2005, according to the U.S. Bureau of Labor Statistics.

FURTHER READING

CertainTeed Corp. ''CertainTeed Offers Quality Program to Contractors.'' *Professional Builder (1993),* no. 6, April 1996, 61.

Darnay, Arsen J., ed. *Manufacturing USA.* Detroit: Gale Research, 1996.

''Journal of Housing LAB: Roofing.'' *Journal of Housing,* November/December 1993.

Sanders, Russell. ''Selecting the Best Roofing Options.'' *Journal of Property Management,* September/October 1993.

U.S. Department of Commerce. International Trade Administration. *U.S. Industrial Outlook 1993.* Washington: GPO, 1993.

—Dave Mote, updated by Beaird Glover

SIC 2992

LUBRICATING OILS AND GREASES

This category includes establishments primarily engaged in blending, compounding, and re-refining lubricating oils and greases from purchased mineral, animal, and vegetable materials. Petroleum refineries engaged in the production of lubricating oils and greases are classified in **SIC 2911: Petroleum Refining.**

Slow growth characterized the mature U.S. lubricating oils industry in the 1990s. The industry's esti-

mated 380 establishments shipped $5.33 billion worth of product in 1995, an increase of less than 1 percent over the previous year. From 1992 to 1995, total current dollar growth was 8.4 percent. Manufacturers of lubricating oils and greases employed roughly 11,800 people in the 1990s and produced some 57 million barrels of finished compounds annually. Lubricating oils made up approximately 83 percent of the industry's output, while greases amounted to 7.7 percent of shipments and miscellaneous lubricants constituted the remaining 9.3 percent. The single largest market for lubricating oils in the 1990s was the consumer market, which accounted for about 25 percent of the industry's shipments. Overall, synthetic lubricants were the fastest growing product in the industry in the mid-1990s because they were longer lasting and less toxic than conventional lubricants.

Manufacturers in this industry competed directly with petroleum refiners in many instances. However, the increasing degree of specialization required within the lubricants market gave lubricant manufacturers an edge over general refiners in that specialized equipment and multiple blending agents were more difficult to maintain in an integrated refining plant than in a lubricants plant.

The several thousand different lubricant products that were manufactured in the United States in the 1990s fell into three categories: automotive lubricants, industrial lubricants, and greases.

Within the automotive category, the three main types of lubricant included crankcase oils, transmission and axle lubricants, and fluids for hydraulic torque converters and fluid couplings used in automatic transmissions. Each category had subdivisions based on viscosity, or resistance to molecular rearrangement or flow. Automotive lubricants kept various parts of auto bodies and engines running smoothly by cushioning adjacent metal pieces, oiling moving parts, and keeping dirt out of combustion chambers.

Industrial lubricants range from machine oils to steam-turbine oils. These products serve similar purposes as automotive lubricants, with added endurance capacity, which allows them, for example, to prevent rust from high-temperature steams. Viscosity represents the main difference between lubricant uses. In 1997, the U.S. market for industrial lubricants, including those produced by manufacturers primarily engaged in other activities, was worth approximately $3 billion. Growth of industrial lubricants was expected to remain lower—less than 1 percent annually—than other segments of the industry through the late 1990s.

A lubricating grease is a solid or semisolid lubricant composed of a fluid lubricant with an added thickening agent. Generally the fluid base is petroleum derived, while the thickening agent usually consists of soap made from aluminum, barium, calcium, lithium, sodium, or strontium. Sometimes, if wide temperature variations will be encountered in usage, the fluid base is a synthetic, such as silicone or polyalkylene glycol. In some instances, non-soap thickeners such as modified clay or fine silica may be used. The trend in grease manufacturing in the late 1990s was toward longer lasting products.

Valvoline Company of Lexington, Kentucky, was one of the largest players in the industry. A division of oil refining giant Ashland Inc., Valvoline produced automotive and industrial lubricants and maintained a sizable presence in the consumer market. In 1996, the firm posted sales of $1.2 billion and employed approximately 3,500 workers. Like Pennzoil, Valvoline was increasingly involved in the quick oil change service industry in the mid-1990s.

Pennzoil Products Company, a subsidiary of Pennzoil Company, was another leading manufacturer of automotive lubricants with sales of $438 million in 1996. The company pursued several acquisitions of other oil manufacturers as well as initiating joint ventures with other oil-related companies in the mid- to late 1990s.

Quaker Chemical Corporation of Conshohocken, Pennsylvania was a leading manufacturer of industrial lubricants, particularly for the steel manufacturing industries. Quaker employed 835 people and produced revenues of $240 million in 1996, a 5.7 percent increase over 1995. More than half of the company's 1996 sales came from markets outside the United States.

FURTHER READING

Ashland, Inc. *Annual Report.* Russell, KY, 1997.

Darnay, Arsen J., ed. *Manufacturing USA.* 5th ed. Detroit: Gale Research, 1996.

Pennzoil Company. *Annual Report.* Houston, TX, 1997.

Quaker Chemical Company. *Annual Report.* Conshohocken, PA, 1997.

U.S. Census Bureau. *1995 Annual Survey of Manufactures.* Washington: GPO, 1997.

SIC 2999

PRODUCTS OF PETROLEUM AND COAL, NOT ELSEWHERE CLASSIFIED

This category includes establishments primarily engaged in manufacturing packaged fuel, powdered fuel, and other products of petroleum and coal not elsewhere classified. Products in this industry include calcined petroleum coke, regular petroleum coke, fireplace logs, fuel briquettes, or petroleum waxes, independently of petroleum refineries.

This small composite industry shipped $869.4 million worth of products in 1995, a 3.7 percent increase over 1994, according to the U.S. Census Bureau. Only slow sales growth was anticipated into the late 1990s. Exports made up 32.9 percent of the industry's output. In 1997, approximately 80 establishments employing a total of 2,100 workers comprised the miscellaneous petroleum and coal products industry. More than 50 percent of production was concentrated in the states of Louisiana, Texas, California, and Pennsylvania.

Raw materials for companies grouped in this area are procured from petroleum refineries or coal processors, while goods produced are shipped either to distributors for the retail market or to other manufacturers. Solid, packaged fuels, including fireplace logs and fuel briquettes produced by companies are sold for general consumer use.

Petroleum waxes and coke are often side business generated by such leading U.S. oil refineries as Pennzoil Company, Mobil Corporation, Shell Oil Company, and Exxon Corporation, which are classified under **SIC 2911: Petroleum Refining.** Smaller firms that are primarily classified in this industry hold a relatively small market compared to the oil giants. However, niche markets that demand specialty wax applications require blending capacities that are regarded as too costly for major refiners to install and maintain.

Petroleum Coke. A by-product from the thermal cracking of reduced crudes and residuums, coke serves as a domestic and industrial fuel. Used primarily in its refined form for heating on the east coast where most of its manufacturers are based, petroleum coke is used in aluminum anodes, furnace electrodes and liners, carbonaceous pastes and cements, as well as various carbon and graphite products. Highly purified graphite derived from petroleum coke can be used for construction materials in nuclear plants. In the 1990s petroleum coke accounted for 54.8 percent of this industry's shipments.

Petroleum Waxes. In general, waxes made up 19.3 percent of industry production during the 1990s. Driven by high demand, U.S. manufacturers produced roughly 2.4 billion pounds of petroluem waxes in 1996, up 8.2 percent from 1995. These waxes, which include paraffin wax and petrolatum, are used primarily in paper manufacturing; both the manufacture of paper and the coating and impregnating of paper and paperboard for protective wrapping of foods require petroleum wax. In the manufacture of rubber tires, petroleum waxes serve as an anti-ozonant, while in PVC manufacturing, the waxes serve as internal lubricant. Paraffin wax is used in making candles, cosmetics, and pharmaceuticals.

FURTHER READING

Darnay, Arsen J., ed. *Manufacturing USA.* 5th ed. Detroit: Gale Research, 1996.

U.S. Census Bureau. *1992 Census of Manufactures.* Washington, 1995.

U.S. Census Bureau. *1995 Annual Survey of Manufactures.* Washington: GPO, 1997.

Rubber & Miscellaneous Plastics Products

TIRES AND INNER TUBES

This category covers establishments primarily engaged in manufacturing pneumatic casings, inner tubes, and solid and cushion tires for all types of vehicles, airplanes, farm equipment, and children's vehicles; tiring; camelback; and tire repair and retreading materials. Establishments primarily engaged in retreading tires are classified in **SIC 7534: Tire Retreading and Repair Shops.**

INDUSTRY SNAPSHOT

The tire industry developed in the twentieth century as a major supplier to the manufacturers of automobiles and other vehicles and to consumers seeking replacement tires. The tire and rubber industries have traditionally been based in Akron, Ohio, where most tire and rubber companies' headquarters were located.

The tire industry is a highly competitive commodities business dominated by a few tightly run global players. Annual sales were estimated to have exceeded $12.5 billion in 1996, when the industry employed about 64,000 workers. According to the Rubber Manufacturers Association (as quoted in *Rubber World,* January 1995), 1994 tire shipments established a new record, at 170 million replacement units and 58.2 million original equipment units.

Tire Types and Characteristics. Though a small number of tires sold consist of solid rubber, practically all are pneumatic, or inflated with air. The pneumatic tire was developed in the late 1800s for use in bicycles, just prior to the onset of the automobile industry. Later, thousands of sizes and types of pneumatic tires were made available for passenger cars and other vehicles, including trucks, buses, tractors, motorcycles, airplanes, and construction vehicles. Tire sizes range from under two pounds to over three tons for earth-moving equipment.

Tire casings are made from layers of rubber compounds and synthetic fibers or steel wire. The design and arrangement of these layers, or plies, affect qualities like cornering ability, vibration absorption, and durability.

Changes in Ownership. Like the automobile industry, tire manufacturing developed in the early part of the 1900s and was dominated by U.S. enterprises. In the later part of the century, however, foreign companies purchased several major U.S. tire producers, and most of the largest tire manufacturers fell under foreign ownership.

ORGANIZATION AND STRUCTURE

Most tires are manufactured by relatively large companies that produce a wide range of types and sizes; smaller tire producers tend to limit output to specialized product groups. While a major portion of sales in the industry are to vehicle manufacturers for installation as original equipment, a larger share are sold as replacements through various distribution channels.

The tire and inner tube industry depends chiefly on rubber suppliers for raw materials and automobile manufacturers for sales. Well over half of the world's production of rubber goes into the manufacture of automobile tires. The tire and inner tube industry is the largest element of the rubber industry group as a whole, constituting over 40 percent of that group's product sales. The rubber industry group is represented by the Rubber Manufacturers Association (RMA). RMA members make up more than three-fourths of the dollar sales of the rubber industry group as a whole. One effort of the RMA has been the establishment in 1990 of a Scrap Tire Management Council to promote environmentally proper disposition of scrap tires.

In the late 1980s, the tire and inner tube industry changed from one in which most leading companies were domestically owned to one in which three of the four largest companies were owned by French, Japanese, and Italian nationals. British interests have attempted, unsuccessfully, to acquire control of remaining leading American tire producers. Competition has become more severe and more international in scope. These ownership changes have been a part of a trend toward mergers of many of the major companies, resulting in larger but fewer independent companies in the top structure of the industry. An important influence encouraging the purchases of American tire companies by foreign organizations has been the weaker dollar, which eliminated the price advantage for foreign companies when the dollar was stronger.

BACKGROUND AND DEVELOPMENT

The History of Rubber. Christopher Columbus noted the existence of rubber on his second voyage to the New World when he observed Indians playing with balls they had made from a liquid obtained from a tree. Practical uses of rubber products began in earnest in the early 1800s, particularly with the use of rubber in clothing as a means for waterproofing. However, widespread applications were limited because the rubber material was somewhat sticky, odorous, and easily affected by shifts in temperature.

An American inventor, Charles Goodyear, developed the vulcanization process of rubber in 1839. By incorporating lead and sulfur with rubber and applying heat, Goodyear created qualities of durability and stability, which facilitated the use of rubber in many practical and beneficial products, particularly tires.

In 1876, Sir Henry Wickham planted some rubber trees in Kew Gardens from rubber tree seeds he brought from Brazil. These trees were transferred to Ceylon (Sri Lanka) and the Malay Peninsula where a rubber plantation industry developed that produced almost 3 million tons a year. Some of the larger tire producers later acquired and managed their own rubber plantations.

Tire Design Developments. The pneumatic principle was first developed in 1845 by a British engineer, Robert William Thomson, who applied it with modest success to carriage tires. However, solid rubber tires remained more popular until John Boyd Dunlop patented a more practical pneumatic tire in 1888. Dunlop's tire consisted of a vulcanized rubber and canvas tube with a valve attached to a solid wood wheel.

In 1890 further tire design refinements were developed by Charles Kingston Welsh and William Erskine Bartlett. A design featuring a detachable pneumatic tire, created and patented by Welsh, continued to be used in the twentieth century. Bartlett developed the beaded edge for the tires so that the tire's edge could be hooked securely to the wheel's rim and remain firmly attached by compressed air in the tire.

Synthetic Rubber. The early 1900s saw the growth of the automobile and tire industries. The business increased when the steel wheels of agricultural tractors were replaced with rubber tires. All tires were made from natural rubber until the 1940s when the supply of natural rubber was cut off from Asian plantations as a result of World War II hostilities. Out of necessity, a synthetic rubber was quickly developed and remained an important raw material in the industry. In the 1960s, synthetic rubber sales equaled that of natural rubber as a raw material for tires, and synthetic rubber eventually became the preferred material.

Tire Structure and Features. Tires are manufactured by assembling plies of rubberized fabric on a cylindrical drum. Various materials may be used in the plies, including cotton, rayon, nylon, and polyester. Steel wire or glass fiber is incorporated in radial tires, perpendicular to the direction of the tire's motion, providing more stability.

Radial tires were first sold in the United States after World War II by France's Michelin. They were not produced extensively by U.S. tire manufacturers until the Lincoln Continental adopted Michelin radials as standard for its 1968 model. Radials eventually became the most popular tire, comprising over 90 percent of the passenger car tires and 65 percent of truck tires purchased in 1990.

The performance of tires has improved greatly over the years. Manufacturers have improved durability, traction, cornering, shock absorption, and ease of mounting. Designs for tires with greater width and lower height have given vehicles greater contact with the road, lowering the center of gravity.

Changes in Facilities, Employment, and Shipments. A 1992 report issued by the U.S. Bureau of the Census showed that the number of companies in the industry decreased from 115 in 1987 to 104 in 1992, and the number of production facilities decreased from 163 to 152 in that period. Employment dipped slightly from 65,400 to 64,600 but increased again to 65,700 by

1995. The dollar value of the tires and inner tubes shipped increased from $10.42 billion to $11.81 billion and rose to $14.07 billion by 1995. The industry's total payroll went from $2.50 billion in 1992 to $2.71 billion in 1995.

Relationship with the Auto Industry. The tire and inner tube industry has always been heavily dependent upon the automobile industry. Competition among the tire manufacturers has been fierce, particularly competition for status as original equipment for automakers. Since car buyers tend to purchase replacement tires of the same brand originally sold on the car, it behooves a tire producer to cut prices and induce auto producers to select its brand. For each tire included as original equipment, an average of three replacement tires will be bought.

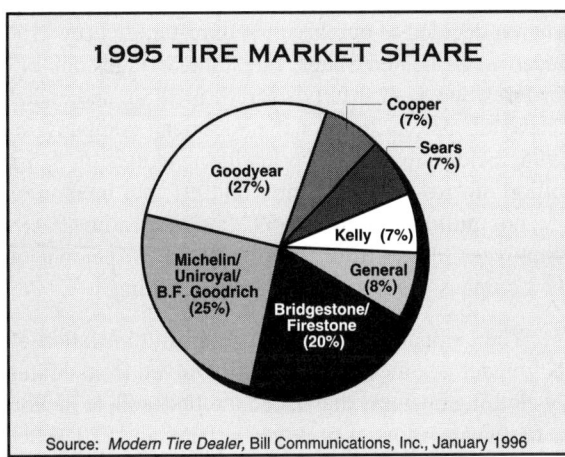

1995 TIRE MARKET SHARE

Source: *Modern Tire Dealer*, Bill Communications, Inc., January 1996

CURRENT CONDITIONS

According to *Modern Tire Dealer*, less than 20 firms were producing tires in the United States in the mid-1990s. Industry-wide employment was estimated at 63,900 in 1996, with about 80 percent of these involved in production. Total tire shipments were estimated at $12.8 billion in 1996, up from $11.9 billion in 1990.

The tire business is reasonably assured of stable sales. While the demand for vehicles can fluctuate with changing economic conditions, the purchase of replacement tires cannot be long deferred, giving a relative evenness to the rate of tire purchases. Unfortunately, however, the increased durability of tires, because of technical improvements, has decreased the rate of replacement purchases.

Market Share Competition. The industry's strength and stability belies an undercurrent of competition and economic issues that have changed the industry's

structure and led to abandonment of plants, reductions of employees, and limited profitability.

The tire industry's vigorous competitive atmosphere has hindered opportunities to improve profits through price increases. The tire manufacturers' Producer Price Index increased only 7.6 percent between 1982 and 1992, while manufacturing prices in general increased an average of 21.1 percent during that period.

Changing Company Ownership. Except for French-owned Michelin, technically and commercially successful since the late 1800s, the tire market was dominated by well-known U.S. company brand names such as Goodyear, Goodrich, Uniroyal, Firestone, Dunlop, General, and Armstrong. However, producers of most of these brands were purchased by foreign companies between 1985 and 1993.

A major reason for the purchase of U.S. tire companies by foreign firms was the decreasing value of the dollar. Furthermore, due to the weak economy, U.S. tire companies and foreign-owned companies operating in the United States were unable to overcome the fact that more tires have been imported to than were exported from the United States between 1971 and 1993. Nevertheless, three of the top tire companies planned modest price increases, and some considered plant expansion and further hiring in 1993.

INDUSTRY LEADERS

According to *Modern Tire Dealer*, Goodyear led the passenger tire market in 1995 with over 40 percent of sales. Michelin ranked second, with 17 percent, followed by Firestone (which was owned by Bridgestone) with 15.4 percent. Cooper Tire & Rubber Co. is mentioned in this essay as a unique example of a highly profitable, American-owned firm.

Goodyear Tire & Rubber Co. Based in Akron, Ohio, traditionally the global center of the tire and rubber industries, Goodyear has for years made more tires than any other tire producer. Since most of Goodyear's domestic tiremaking competitors were acquired by foreign firms by the mid-1980s, Goodyear became the only leading tire producer headquartered in the United States. In 1995, Goodyear had revenues of $13.2 billion, $11.3 billion of which was generated by tire sales, net income of $611 million, and 87,930 employees.

Goodyear was founded in 1898 by Frank A Sieberling, who named the company after Charles Goodyear, inventor of the vulcanization process. By World War I, after making a variety of technical and practical design improvements, Goodyear had the largest tire sales volume of any company. Between the two world wars, the company survived some financial difficulties, developed production operations in four other countries, owned and managed rubber plantations, and created the famous Goodyear blimp as a promotional tool. After World War II, Goodyear set up production facilities in six more countries and promoted the development of synthetic rubber. Goodyear addressed tough competition from Michelin's radial tire by developing its own design innovations, creating a new all-weather tire, and expanding its interests into the field of gas and oil pipelines.

In 1986, a British financier attempted to buy Goodyear. To fend off this move, Goodyear sold its cotton-growing and aerospace businesses, including its blimp manufacturing activity. Using those resources and heavy borrowing, Goodyear bought back $2.6 billion of its stock. When in 1991 the commune suffered its first year-end loss in decades, the board of directors selected a new chief executive, Stanley Gault, to strengthen the company and surmount the burden of its heavy debt load. The highly-praised leader successfully pegged Goodyear's fortunes on innovative new products like the Aquatred premium-priced tire, renewed emphasis on the replacement market, distribution through mass retailers, and expansion into the emerging markets of Latin America and Asia. Under Gault, Goodyear's sales increased from $11 billion in 1991 to over $13 billion in 1995, and its net income increased sixfold, from $96.6 million to $611 million. Stanley Gault was succeeded by CEO Sam Gibara in 1996.

Compagnie Generale de Establissements Michelin. Michelin was one of the earliest producers of tires for bicycles and carriages and has become the world's largest maker of tires for automobiles and other vehicles. In 1863, two brothers who had operated a rubber products business for some 30 years formed a new company, developing a detachable pneumatic bicycle tire in 1891, and producing similar products for carriages and then automobiles.

In the early 1900s, Michelin pioneered tire design improvements including the first tubeless tire and a low profile shape. The company soon added plants in Italy and the United States to its French production facilities. Michelin marketed the first radial tire, which significantly helped tire traction and wear, in the 1930s. U.S. tire producers did not follow Michelin's lead in radials until decades later.

Always a leader in Europe, Michelin broke into the United States market by selling its innovative radials to Ford and other automakers in the 1960s. By 1980, Michelin had four tire facilities in the United States. In 1989 Michelin bought the Uniroyal-Good-

rich Tire Company, a firm formed when two struggling tire companies merged in the mid-1980s. Absorbing these troubled organizations, along with a highly competitive tire market, resulted in heavy losses for Michelin in 1991. In 1995, Michelin had revenues of $13.5 billion in worldwide sales, up from $13.1 billion in 1991; net income of $570 million, up from a net loss of $195.6 million in 1991; 114,397 employees, down from 131,976 in 1991, and a unique logo, the Michelin Tire Man, a cartoon of a man made of a stack of tires. About $11.4 million of its global sales were generated by tires, with the remainder coming from travel guides and other products. Furthermore, about $3.8 billion of its total sales were made in the United States.

Bridgestone. Bridgestone is a leading Japanese tire manufacturer, as well as a producer of bicycles, sporting goods, and various rubber industrial products, when it decided to purchase the third-ranking tire producer in the United States, Firestone. Bridgestone bid for Firestone against Italy's Pirelli in 1988, and ended up paying $2.6 billion for the American company. In 1995, Bridgestone had worldwide revenues of $16.3 billion, up from $14.1 billion in 1991; net income of $523.6 million, up from $59.8 million, and 89,418 employees, down from 95,276. About 76 percent of the company's sales come from tiremaking.

The company's name is an English translation of its founder's name. The company evolved from a family clothing business that added a rubber sole to its line of footwear. A line of tires was initiated in 1923. After the Korean War, Bridgestone established tire plants in Singapore, Thailand, and Indonesia, and also formed a collaborative effort with Spaulding in the United States for making golf balls. In the 1980s, Bridgestone began tire production at a Firestone plant it acquired in Tennessee and a few years later purchased the entire Firestone company.

Firestone was formed in Akron, Ohio, by Harvey S. Firestone in 1900, and Ford was one of its early and regular customers. Later Firestone encountered several problems, including defects in its steel-belted radial tires, as well as alleged tax violations and illegal campaign contributions. These problems led to a period of retrenchment during which plants closed, employment dropped, and several businesses were sold.

Shortly after Bridgestone purchased Firestone, General Motors dropped the company as a supplier. Such difficulties produced a period of losses for Firestone's operations, which reduced Bridgestone's profitability significantly. Nonetheless, Bridgestone planned to invest an additional $1.4 billion to build up its Firestone operation.

Cooper Tire & Rubber Co. This company has distinguished itself from many of its competitors with a unique strategy and clean balance sheet. Rather than striving for market share by cutting prices of tires sold to automobile manufacturers, it has targeted the replacement tire market and a more ample gross margin. Instead of growth, Cooper has focused on return on investment. In 1995, Cooper had revenues of $1.5 billion, up 50 percent from 1991; net income of $112.8 million, up from $79.4 million; and 8,284 employees, up from 6,545.

Although the replacement market was dampened by increasingly longer lasting tires, cars also lasted longer and consumers were driving more miles per year than ever before, giving the total market a modest growth rate. Cooper has been distributing about half its tires via independent distributors and the other half as private brand labels through oil company retail systems.

Cooper has also saved by eliminating most research and development. Rather than develop unique designs, the company adopts the features of its competitors' tires, which have proven successful in the marketplace. The company's profitability was also attributed to its dedicated work force, motivated by a variety of pay incentives and leading to an unusually low turnover. Many employees achieved substantial gains from company stock purchases, since the stock made a remarkable rise of 6,800 percent in the 1980s. Fifteen percent of the company's shares are owned by its employees.

WORK FORCE

In 1996, the tire and inner tube industry employed an estimated 64,000 workers, of whom 80 percent were production workers. This was a 6 percent decline from 1990, a trend that was expected to continue throughout the remainder of the decade. The most plentiful jobs in the industry were in the production and maintenance areas. More technical activities are in the research and development, production planning and control, accounting and finance, and information systems functions. Career paths can proceed from production operator to supervisor, department head, and plant manager. Such lateral moves can be made as from production supervisor to production control technician.

Opportunities for careers in the industry have generally been fewer than in other industries, largely because of severe competition resulting from many mergers and acquisitions, excess capacity, and the efforts of most companies in the industry to keep prices low to gain or maintain market share. Conse-

quently, tire companies have sought to cut costs, eliminate plants, and resist pay increases. Nevertheless, some companies planned to increase prices and production capacity. Furthermore, at the top levels, opportunities have been created for business leaders to help organizations overcome losses or unsatisfactory profit margins. In 1996, the average tire industry production worker earned an estimated $19.74 per hour, up from $17.70 in 1991.

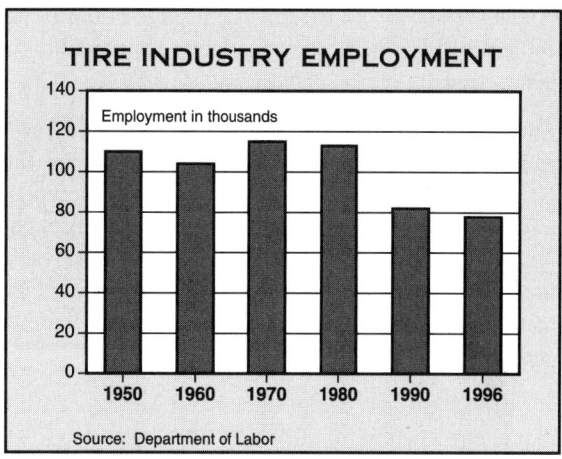

TIRE INDUSTRY EMPLOYMENT

Employment in thousands

Source: Department of Labor

Unions. The United Rubber Workers (URW) have represented employees at American tire companies since the 1930s and 1940s. Firestone's union workers endured long strikes in 1936 and 1976; in 1981 its URW members agreed to wage reductions. The URW instituted ''pattern bargaining'' to negotiate contracts in 1946. Having won modest concessions from the URW in the 1980s to help meet its competitive challenges, Goodyear came to a relatively generous agreement with the group in 1994. The URW expected Goodyear's largely foreign-owned competitors with U.S. operations and subsidiaries to follow suit, but many, including Michelin (whose anti-union stance is well-known) and Bridgestone, balked at the demands. In 1995, Bridgestone hired 2,000 replacements for striking workers, prompting the URW to seek strength in numbers via a merger with the United Steel Workers.

AMERICA AND THE WORLD

Most of the leading companies had tire plants in several countries and sold their products in international markets. Since the latter part of the 1980s, the tire industry has also become much more multinational in ownership as many of the top tire companies in the United States were bought by foreign concerns. In fact, the multinational mergers and acquisitions have left few tire companies in the United States unaffiliated with foreign firms. Imports shrunk 9 percent from a high of 56 million units in 1995.

RESEARCH AND TECHNOLOGY

Research and technology's emphasis has been on creating and improving the design and specifications of tire products to meet customers' needs and wishes. Though technical skills have always been applied to production methodology and cost controls, operating efficiency has been a dominant objective in the 1980s and early 1990s because of the intense competition in that period.

Tire Design and Specifications. Historically, research and technology have been used to design better tire products for the purpose of developing strong competitive positions in the marketplace. Major breakthroughs included pneumatic tires for cushioning, removable tires for convenience, synthetic rubber to overcome material shortage, and radials to enhance durability and performance.

Goodyear and Bridgestone have developed a tire that can run safely for 200 miles after a flat, eliminating the inconvenience and dangers in changing a tire on the roadside. Goodyear also has been working on microprocessors to monitor the tire's air pressure, temperature, and wear, which might extend a tire's life by 15 percent. Other research involves extending tire life, enhancing traction in adverse conditions, and increasing fuel efficiency and lowering auto emissions by reducing rolling resistance.

Environmental Concerns. The tire industry's environmental efforts have focused primarily on the reuse, recycling, and safe disposal of scrap tires. Reuse programs include retreading, a well-established niche of the tire industry, as well as newer anti-erosion programs. Recycled tires have been used in asphalt-based road coverings, shoes, household items, and even new tires. But in spite of all these programs, well over half of the country's 250 million tire discards went to landfills in the mid-1990s.

Manufacturing and Cost Controls. Since the mid-1980s especially, when merger and acquisition activities have dominated the industry, the intensified competition has encouraged or required the tire producers to reduce costs so they could trim prices and survive with slimmer profit margins. To cut costs, producers have engaged in re°engineering or ''downsizing,'' eliminating inefficient plants, and streamlining operations. These cost improvement activities have required the companies' technical staffs to design better production methods and apply computer techniques to save workers' time, speed processes, and improve quality.

FURTHER READING

1992 Census of Manufacturers, Rubber Products, Washington: U.S. Bureau of the Census, 1990.

Bernstein, Aaron. ''Rubber Workers With Nerves of Steel.'' *Business Week,* 18 December 1995, 44.

Darnay, Arsen J., ed. *Manufacturing USA: Industry Analyses, Statistics, and Leading Companies.* Detroit: Gale Research, 1996.

French, Michael J. *The U.S. Tire Industry: A History.* Boston: Twayne, 1991.

Mattera, Philip. *World Class Business.* New York: Henry Holt and Company, 1992.

''OE Market Share.'' *Modern Tire Dealer,* January 1996, 34.

Pook, Jane. ''P-D, Goodyear Team for Tire Dam Venture.'' *American Metal Market,* 30 July 1996, 6.

''Replacement Tire Shipments to Rebound, OE to Decline.'' *Rubber World,* January 1995, 13.

Slavens, Roger A. ''Survival of the Fittest.'' *Modern Tire Dealer,* September 1994, 35-36.

''Tire Shipments Set Record.'' *Rubber World,* January 1995, 13.

Stoyer, Lloyd. ''Setting Sights on First Place: Goodyear's Bullish on Growth.'' *Modern Tire Dealer,* May 1996, 52.

Stoyer, Lloyd. ''Michelin's Set to Roll in '95.'' *Modern Tire Dealer,* March 1995, 49-51.

''Tire Shipments Set Record.'' *Rubber World,* January 1995, 13.

U.S. Bureau of the Census. *1995 Annual Survey of Manufactures.* Washington: GPO, 1995.

Ward's Business Directory. Vol. 5, Detroit: Gale Research, 1997.

—Douglas Hoyt, updated by April Dougal Gasbarre

SIC 3021

RUBBER AND PLASTICS FOOTWEAR

This category covers establishments primarily engaged in manufacturing fabric-upper footwear having rubber or plastic soles vulcanized, injection molded, or cemented to the uppers, and rubber and plastics protective footwear. Establishments primarily engaged in manufacturing rubber, composition, and fiber heels, soles, soling strips, and related shoe making and repairing materials are classified in **SIC 3069: Fabricated Rubber Products, Not Elsewhere Classified**; those manufacturing plastic soles and soling strips are classified in **SIC 3089: Plastics Products, Not Elsewhere Classified**; and those manufacturing other footwear of rubber or plastics are classified in **SIC 3140: Footwear, Except Rubber.**

This industry consists primarily of two product areas. One area includes the waterproof footwear worn over shoes to protect them from inclement weather. Such products are often referred to as overshoes, rubbers, galoshes, and arctics. Also included in this area are rubber boots which are not worn over shoes but protect the feet from mud and water. The second area consists of rubber soled canvas shoes, generally known as sneakers. While other athletic shoes featuring rubber soles and a fabric upper are considered in this category, those with leather uppers belong to other SIC classifications.

The rubber footwear industry is largely based on the ability of rubber to protect against water and rain. An early breakthrough was made around 1920 by a Scottish chemist, Charles Macintosh, who developed rubberized waterproof cloaks which became known as ''mackintoshes.'' Later, Macintosh's associate, Thomas Hancock, devised ways to process rubber so that it could be used as a material for footwear. By the 1990s, the manufacture of footwear required more rubber than that of any other product except tires. The sewing of uppers to rubber soles had been superseded by the use of adhesives or vulcanizing directly.

The rubber and plastics footwear industry in 1995 was made up of 62 companies with a total of 9,600 employees. Some of the companies manufactured rubber plastic footwear exclusively, while others maintained it as a modest or minor product line. By the year-end of 1995, 63,505 pairs of rubber or plastic-soled, fabric-upper shoes had been manufactured with an overall shipment value of $521,866. Rubber or plastic protective footwear for that year saw 16,876 pairs of shoes produced at a shipment value of $253,792. By contrast, 1994 saw 61,280 pairs of fabric, rubber or plastic-soled shoes produced and shipped at a value of $599,154; 18,796 pairs of rubber or plastic protective footwear were produced and shipped at a value of $276,956. By the end of 1996, shipments and subsequent shipment valuation decreased for both classes of footwear, with rubber or plastic-soled, fabric-upper shoes valued at $404,081 for 60,757 pairs, and rubber or plastic protective overshoes valued at $212,601 for 14,866 pairs shipped.

Companies devoted exclusively to rubber and plastic footwear in 1996 included Deckers Outdoor Corporation of Goleta, California, with sales of $102.33 million, and 200 employees; Vans Inc. of Orange, California, with sales of $88.10 million and 1,100 employees; Thermwell Products Co. of Paterson, New Jersey, with sales of $60 million and 100 employees; and Bata Shoe Company Inc. of Belcamp, Maryland, with $20 million in sales and 200 employees.

Lacrosse Footwear, Inc. of La Crosse, Wisconsin, yielded sales of $98.5 million in the manufacture of rubber and vinyl protective footwear. Converse Inc. Of North Reading, Massachusetts, was primarily but not exclusively engaged in the manufacture of rubber and plastics footwear. It reported annual sales of $407 million in 1996. Biltrite Corporation of Waltham, Massachussets, was similarly engaged in the manufacture of rubber and plastics footwear and posted annual sales of $85 million from rubber plastics footwear in 1996.

Although these companies represented the leading manufacturers of rubber and plastics footwear in the United States, the leaders in the wholesale sneaker market in 1995 produced well-known brand-name products using facilities outside of the United States. Of the American sneaker market, NIKE controlled 33 percent, and Reebok held 16 percent, controlling almost half of the market. Other manufacturers using international facilities comprised 51 percent of this market, and none controlled more than 5.56 percent, the proportion held by Fila.

Much of the rubber and plastic footwear sold in the United States has been produced in other countries, largely due to lower production costs. Although sneakers represented a $5.5 billion industry in the United States in 1990, the value of rubber or plastic-soled footwear produced and shipped within the United States was estimated at only $561 million for that year. In 1996 and 1997, 80 percent of the sneakers that Nike produced were made in China, Indonesia, or Vietnam. NIKE received worldwide criticism because of substandard conditions and harsh treatment of workers at its factories in both Indonesia and Vietnam. The firm hired the Goodworks International Group in early 1997, headed by former United Nations ambassador and mayor of Atlanta, Andrew Young, to review a new code of conduct for its overseas factories. NIKE also expanded its United States advertising team, adding Goodby, Silverstein & Partners to help counteract the bad publicity. By the end of the first quarter of 1997, profits for Nike were up 77 percent.

U.S. employment in the industry decreased by 65 percent, between 1972 and 1987, caused in part by moves to lower cost suppliers overseas. Total employment had risen from 10,900 in 1987 to 11,700 in 1991, but continuously declined throughout the decade to an estimated low of 9,600 in 1996.

The Footwear Industries of America (FIA), a trade association founded in 1869 for footwear producers, marketers, and suppliers, provides support for the industry's activities and interests. FIA is based in Washington, D.C. Furthermore, the Shoe and Allied Trades Research Association (SATRA) maintains a Footwear Technology Centre in England. This group of 170 scientists, technicians, and support staff assists its 1,100 members in 40 countries by helping to control manufacturing costs and improve quality. Its members are footwear manufacturers, material and machinery suppliers, repairers, and retailers.

SATRA has done a great deal of pioneering research, providing industry members with technology too costly for the smaller companies in the footwear business to develop on their own. For example, SATRA has developed beneficial concepts in the areas of ergonomics, color durability, the environment, materials standards, quality control, and computer applications like CAD/CAM, robotics, and bar coding.

FURTHER READING

Clifford, Mark J., Michael Shari, and Linda Himelstein. "Pangs of Conscience: Sweatshops Haunt U.S. Consumers," *Business Week,* 29 July 1996.

Darnay, Arsen J., ed. *Manufacturing USA,* 5th ed. Detroit: Gale Research, 1996.

Dun's Million Dollar Disc, Fourth Quarter 1996, Dun & Bradstreet, Inc.

Lazich, Robert S., ed. *Market Share Reporter,* Detroit: Gale Research, 1996.

Standard & Poor's Industry Surveys. New York: Standard & Poor's Corporation, 1996.

U.S. Census Bureau. *Current Industrial Reports.* Washington GPO, 1996. Available from http://www.census.gov/cir/www/mq31a.html.

U.S. Department of Commerce. *1995 Annual Survey of Manufactures.*

—Douglas Hoyt, updated by Ariel Pennie

SIC 3052

RUBBER AND PLASTICS HOSE AND BELTING

This category covers establishments primarily engaged in manufacturing rubber and plastics hose and belting, including garden hoses. Establishments primarily engaged in manufacturing rubber tubing are classified in **SIC 3061: Molded, Extruded, and Lathe-Cut Mechanical Rubber Goods** and **SIC : 3069: Fabricated Rubber Products, Not Elsewhere Classified.** Those companies manufacturing plastics tubing are classified in **SIC 3082: Unsupported Plastics Profile Shapes.** Those establishments manufacturing flexible metallic hoses are classified in **SIC 3599: Industrial and Commercial Machinery and Equipment, Not Elsewhere Classified.**

INDUSTRY SNAPSHOT

More than 125 companies make hoses and belting in the United States in a market that approached the $3 billion-a-year range entering the mid-1990s. Manufacturing companies range from a myriad of small shops filling niche markets all the way up to several firms producing broad product lines with sales approaching or exceeding $1 billion a year.

The number of companies in the industry, however, actually dropped off from the late 1980s to the early 1990s because of the effects of restructuring and a move toward automation. These actions, though, helped the remaining players be more productive.

Hose and belting products find usage in a wide variety of industries. Hoses are used in such varied markets as automobiles, construction, and oil and gas. Transmission belting is used to help power cars, industrial machinery, agricultural equipment, household appliances, and construction equipment. Flat belting, commonly known as conveyor belting, finds usage from traditional markets such as mining and material handling as well as in lighter weight applications such as food handling and airline luggage conveyor systems.

Economies of scale are difficult to achieve except for some of the larger firms because a large number of products need short runs, and many of the lines have differences in chemical compounds and machinery needs. States with the greatest volume of hose and belt production include Colorado, Nebraska, North Carolina, and Ohio.

Rubber remains the predominant material in the market, accounting for between 70 and 80 percent of the products. For example, rubber is the main material for hoses, except in garden hoses, where plastic takes the majority of the share. Other materials, though, are expected to make some inroads as higher performing products are needed.

ORGANIZATION AND STRUCTURE

Much of the structure of the hose and belting industry is organized around how the product gets to its end user—either in the original equipment (OE) or replacement market. Looking at the automotive market, the OE market is much more straightforward, as most of the products are sold directly to the auto makers.

Sales to the aftermarket, though, are a bit more complicated, going through either a three-step or two-step distribution process. In the three-step process, the manufacturer sells his hose or belting to a wholesale distributor that handles automotive parts lines. The distributor in turn sells the product to what is known as a jobber, an example of which would include the NAPA store chain. The final step is for the jobber to sell the hose and belting to the installer—the repair shop that does work on automobiles, for example. Some manufacturers have increasingly tried to shorten the process by skipping the initial step and selling directly to the jobber.

Historically, this has been the most efficient way to get to market, ensuring that there is plenty of inventory in the aftermarket so that people can get the necessary parts for their car at almost any time. Hose and belt manufacturers, however, have had to shift with the times as the places where people get their automobiles serviced have evolved. While the total number of outlets for repair service has remained virtually unchanged, the make-up has changed considerably.

Prior to the growth in popularity of self-serve gasoline stations, about 150,000 gas stations in the United States also offered automotive service. By 1990, however, that number had declined to approximately 100,000. Conversely, the number of repair-only shops had grown from 110,000 to 140,000. Moreover, import car owners used to be much more likely to get their automobiles fixed at the dealer; but that has changed as repair shops have become more attuned to repairing imports. The number of retail auto stores also increased, from about 27,000 in 1980 to 40,000 a decade later, taking additional volume away from the jobbers.

Through all these changes, the hose and belt makers have had to ensure that their distribution system is getting the parts to the proper outlet in a timely fashion. Distribution also plays an important role in the industrial hose and belt markets. Many of these distributors also serve as fabricators, placing needed attachments and accessories onto the basic hose and belts for their final usage. The distributors in this sector also are more likely to play a role in OE accounts, especially for an account that needs to have local inventory. As for the aftermarket, a major portion of the business is sold through distribution sectors, although some hose and belt makers do sell some product directly to the end user.

Distributors also play a major role in times of overcapacity. While only four to five firms make broad lines across many industries, there are enough niche manufacturers to ensure stiff competition in all product areas. This situation gives the distributor an advantage in getting a lower price on products.

Types of Products. A hose is a flexible pipe or conduit that is intended to serve as a means to move material from one place to another. The three basic elements of a hose are the tube, carcass, and cover. The tube is the part of the hose that comes in contact with the fluid and therefore must be resistant to the material. The carcass gives the hose strength to withstand any forces, external or internal, that might be encountered, while the cover protects the product from environmental forces.

Although hoses can be referred to by their usage—such as gasoline, air, or garden hoses manufacturers and users generally classify the products by the method of reinforcement. The common hose types include:

Knitted Hose. A flexible product knitted in an open-loop manner. The garden hose is a typical example of this kind of product. This type generally is subjected only to low pressure.

Braided Hose. One of the more common hose types, it is produced when a single or multiple ends of yarn cord or wire are woven over the tube. The size and type of reinforcement material, as well as the angle, help establish the strength of the hose. These hose types find a variety of usage, from air, water, garden, spray, or low-pressure liquid transfer, to more demanding applications like hydraulic, steam, and high-pressure transfer of liquid and gases.

Wrapped Fabric Hose. This type of hose is reinforced with an impregnated woven fabric that can be applied by hand or machine. This makes for a stiff, bulky hose that is commonly used in suction or vacuum applications.

Wire Spiraled Hose. Used for hose facing high-impulse pressures, wires are placed in opposite directions to counter the twisting effect of applying the spiral wire.

Woven Jacket Hose. Looms are used for circular weaving of jackets for the hose; often used for fire hoses. The design allows the hose to lie flat when not transporting water, for more efficient storage.

Hand-Built Hose. Used to make the large hose that needs great strength and excellent crush resistance. Uses include rotary drill hoses and oil suction and discharge hoses.

Belting. Power transmission belts are more commonly known as V-belts. Given their name because they transmit power and motion between V-shaped sheaves, the belts are made in numerous sizes and lengths. V-belts are preferred where there is limited space. Major applications are in automotive, industrial, agriculture, fractional horsepower, and recreational uses. In automotive use, though, a poly-V, or serpentine belt, has become much more popular in newer car models.

Flat belting also is used in some limited power transmission applications, but the overwhelming use for these products is in conveying uses. Basic components of conveyor belts include the carcass, which bears the load and is usually made of several piles of rubber-coated textile fabric or a single layer of steel cable; the rubber cover, which must resist wear, cracking, and element pressures; the breaker, which improves adhesion between the carcass and cover; and the skim coating, used to hold the load-bearing plies together.

Conveyor belts are used for a variety of purposes, from the grocery market check-out stand, to coal mines where coal is conveyed from deep within the mine, to growing applications in recycling and waste management programs.

BACKGROUND AND DEVELOPMENT

This industry has undergone significant change over the past several decades. In the automotive market—the top market for hose and transmission belting—a catalog of about 50 V-belts and 100 hoses covered most of the cars on the road shortly after World War II. Cars became more complicated, however, and smaller cars that required smaller engine compartments assumed increased market share ever since the 1970s and 1980s. Hose and belt manufacturers responded with products that conformed to the new size and weight demands of the automotive market.

The serpentine belt also made great inroads over the years. While designs at one time had several V-belts in the engine compartment, producers discovered that one serpentine belt could drive a number of accessories simultaneously, resulting in weight and space savings. In 1982, there were approximately 50 sizes of serpentine belts; a decade later that number had increased to up to 250.

Belts and hoses also last much longer in the modern era of manufacturing. Such products used to last 10,000 miles. In the modern era, however, hoses and belts commonly last for 40,000 miles or more of use.

CURRENT CONDITIONS

Rubber hose shipments were expected to increase 3.5 percent a year from 1991 to 1996, rising to $1.54 billion per year because of an increase in motor vehicle production and growth in other industrial and construction products. While showing steady growth, a lack of new applications and penetration by alternate materials were expected to keep the growth of rubber hose below the increases made by general industry. Imports, which have been felt in other rubber product markets, could limit growth in this industry sector as well. Commodity hose lines are the most likely to be affected by imports from southeast Asia. Conversely, domestic hose makers are projected to raise their export sales.

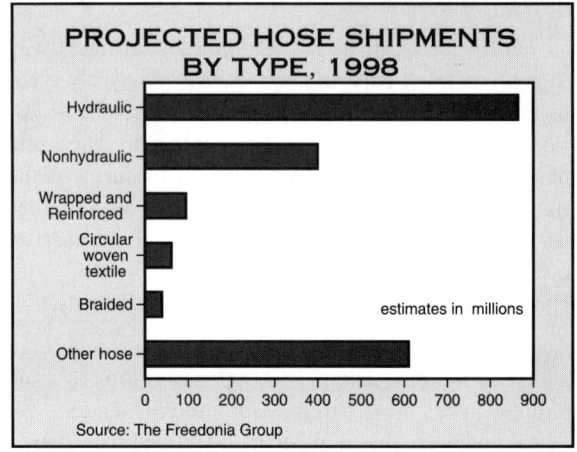

PROJECTED HOSE SHIPMENTS BY TYPE, 1998

Source: The Freedonia Group

Hydraulic hose shipments were projected to spur much of the industry's growth. In 1991, hydraulic hoses accounted for 44 percent of the industrial hose market. But because of the specialty uses of the sector, they are less susceptible to imports and allow for better margins on the pricing side.

The rubber belt market was expected to reach $1.1 billion by 1996. Factors inducing growth were projected to include automobile sales and a growth in the sales of industrial equipment, two major belting markets. Both flat belting and V-belts were projected to enjoy robust growth in the mid-1990s. The latter category made up nearly two-thirds of belt sales and was expected to grow 4.5 percent a year to $735 million annually. Automobiles will continue to be the largest market, but because rising sales of serpentine belts will hold down growth in this sector, some observers expect the percentage growth in industrial applications to nearly double that of the motor vehicle segment.

Flat belt growth was forecast to be 5.1 percent annually for the five-year period ending in 1996, which would bring the market to $433 million per year. The sector was projected for more growth because of expected new uses in waste recovery and handling systems and food handling equipment, where there is a movement toward increased automation.

Heavy duty conveyor belt shipments to North America reached $270 million by 1995, a 2.9 percent increase over 1993 sales of $210 million. This projected growth is expected because of a slow but steady growth in the mining industry. Since servicing the belts is as important as the initial sales, imports won't play a major role in U.S. markets. Most imports tend to be low-grade generic belting that most U.S. companies are not equipped to service properly. The newest trend in heavy-weight conveyor belting is increasing the tensile strength of the belt while making the belts as thin as possible.

Replacement belt and hose sales are estimated to grow 2.4 percent from 1995 to 2000 as sales from these products are expected to steadily increase in that time period. By 1997, the replacement belt industry should reach $300 million and top out at $340 million by the year 2000.

INDUSTRY LEADERS

Gates Rubber Company, Dayco Products Incorporated, and Goodyear Tire & Rubber Company generally are considered the top three hose and belt manufacturers in the United States.

Founded in 1911, Denver-based Gates had 10 hose and belt plants in the United States, two in Canada, and three in Mexico, as well as another 15 facilities around the world in the mid-1990s. The firm has a major presence in automotive, industrial, and hydraulic markets, and posted worldwide 1995 rubber product sales—mainly from belts and hoses—of $1.19 billion.

Dayco, headquartered near Dayton, Ohio, is the largest operating unit of publicly held Mark IV Industries Inc. Dayco had 27 production facilities worldwide, including 14 in the United States, and had annual sales of about $900 million, a tremendous increase over its sales of $320 million in 1986. This surge has been accomplished through both internal growth and two major acquisitions—hose maker Anchor Swan in 1990 and the power transmission belting business of Italy's Pirelli S.p.A. in 1993.

Goodyear, the leading U.S. tire maker, also operates 10 North American hose and belt plants. Although it does not release its hose and belt sales figures, the Akron, Ohio-based firm has major market shares in automotive hose and belts, industrial hose and belts, and heavy-duty conveyer belting.

WORK FORCE

Total employment in the industry was estimated at 20,000 in 1995 and was expected to remain steady through 1998. Of these, about 16,200 were production workers earning about $12.08 an hour, according to government figures. Other occupations include chemists, product designers, engineers, and sales people.

The average number of workers per factory has decreased over the years because of increased productivity traceable to improved processes and automation. In 1972, 19 hose and belt plants in the United States—about 21 percent of facilities—accounted for 76 percent of employment and 75 percent of shipments. A decade later, just 9 plants employed 500 workers or more, accounting for 44 percent of employment and 39 percent of shipments. The average number of workers per plant dropped from 354 in 1972 to 124 in 1987 to just 100 in 1995.

AMERICA AND THE WORLD

Importers generally compete more easily in commodity lines than specialty ones, putting pricing pressure on U.S. firms. One trend that increased competition in the United States in this industry was the emergence of transplant automakers, especially from Japan. As these Japanese firms began production in the United States, it was not uncommon for their traditional domestic suppliers to follow them to America. Examples include power transmission belters MBL (USA) Incorporated, located in Illinois, and Bando Manufacturing of America, which built its plant in Kentucky. There also was an increase in the number of joint ventures between Japanese and U.S. firms to supply the transplant car firms.

Global expansion is also an important force driving leading companies in the industry. "Much of the logic behind the current activity is to supply the global automotive industry," according to the *European Rubber Journal*.

In July 1995, Britain's Tomkins PLC purchased Gates Rubber Company for $1.16 billion in preferred stock. In return, Gates received a 15.7 percent stake in Tomkins, giving Gates an ever-increasing presence in Europe. Gates is also expanding eastward with two new plants in China and one in India. According to Lo Estenfelder, president of Gates Europe NV, "1996 sales for Gates Europe increased about 4 percent over 1995, which in turn was about 40 percent higher than 1994."

Mark IV, the parent company of Dayco, also plans to expand globally. Mark IV plans to double turnover by 2001 from about $1 billion, split 65/35 OE/aftermarket to about $2 billion splitting sales 50/50 U.S./rest of the world, according to Kurt Johansson, the president of Mark IV's automotive business. Pointing out Mark IV's joint venture in India and its manufacturing plant in Australia, Johansson commented that most hose and belt suppliers are interested in Asia.

RESEARCH AND TECHNOLOGY

Rubber hoses, while still used in the overwhelming majority of industrial hose products, will face increased competition from other materials. Driving the need for new materials are a number of factors, such as the evolution of some of the traditional applications of the product. For example, alternate fuels and higher operating temperatures bring different requirements for hose products. When states begin to require higher alcohol content in fuel in order to reduce emissions, the hose materials must change as well. Specialty rubbers, plastic, Teflon, and nylon are among materials expected to challenge commodity rubber.

Like hoses, belts will be impacted by the shrinking of auto engine compartments. Because of hotter temperatures, belt makers will be forced to turn to new materials that will withstand the environment in which it is used. Some of the commodity types of rubber also will face competition from specialty rubbers and plastics.

FURTHER READING

"Activity Intensifies in Hose Y Belt." *European Rubber Journal,* December 1996.

Babington, Mary. *Freedonia Study No. 416, Industrial Rubber Products.* Cleveland: Freedonia Group Inc., 1992.

"Belt Makers, Distributors Better Partners." *Rubber & Plastics News,* 22 June 1992.

Darnay, Arsen, ed. *Manufacturing USA.* 5th ed. Detroit: Gale Research, 1996.

"Dayco Chief Touts Teamwork." *Rubber & Plastics News,* 7 June 1993.

"Gates' Sales Increase 2.2%." *Rubber & Plastics News,* 21 February 1994.

"Heavy Duty Belting Digs Up Growth: Mining Stirs Steady Rise For Firms." *Rubber Plastics News,* June 1996.

"Hose, Belts to Expand 9-3." *Rubber & Plastics News,* 20 January 1992.

Long, Harry, ed. *Basic Compounding and Processing of Rubber.* Akron, OH: American Chemical Society Inc., 1985

"Plant Sites for U.S.-based Hose, Belt Makers." *Rubber & Plastics News,* 7 June 1993.

Plehwe, Dieter. *Change and Concentration in the World Rubber Industry.* Brussels, Belgium: International Federation of Chemical, Energy and General Workers' Unions.

"Study: Gaskets, H&B Markets to Grow: Replacement Engine Seals to Cool Down." *Rubber & Plastics News,* February 1995.

U.S. Department of Commerce. *1987 Census of Manufacturers,* Washington: GPO, 1987.

"U.S. Dominates Auto Belt Market." *European Rubber Journal,* January 1994.

The Vanderbilt Rubber Handbook. Norwalk, CT: R.T. Vanderbilt Co. Inc., 1990.

—Bruce Meyer, updated by Luann Brennan

SIC 3053

GASKETS, PACKING, AND SEALING DEVICES

This category covers establishments primarily engaged in manufacturing gaskets, gasketing materials, compression packings, mold packings, oil seals, and mechanical seals. It includes gaskets, packing, and sealing devices made of rubber leather, metal, asbestos, and plastics.

INDUSTRY SNAPSHOT

By definition, a seal is a "device for eliminating or controlling the leakage of liquids and/or gases while preventing the entrance of external contaminants such as dust and dirt," according to John J. Carr in the *Vanderbilt Rubber Handbook.*

Seals are divided into two classifications: static or dynamic. Static seals are used on surfaces where there is no relative motion between the surfaces. An example of a static seal would be an engine cylinder-head gasket. Dynamic seals are used wherever relative motion exists between two surfaces, either intermittently or continuously. Examples are engine crank-shaft seals and hydraulic cylinder-rod seals.

There are several basic types of seals. Cup-packings are mainly used as piston-head seals. Previously made from leather, elastomers are now used for low-pressure, smaller-sized cups, while an elastomer/fabric blend is used for high-pressure applications. Cup-packings are particularly effective where clearance between surfaces to be sealed is excessive—for example, when sealing rough metal surfaces.

Gaskets typify the compression-sealing method. They are made from a wide variety of materials, often times used in combination with one another. For example, cork and elastomers are a popular combination in automotive usage because cork's compressibility and rubber's resiliency combine to give excellent results in such uses as engine gaskets. Gaskets can be molded or cut from a sheet. They are installed between two surfaces, and pressure from bolting or clamping provides the sealing force.

Elastomeric gaskets are the most common type of non-metallic gasket. They can be made of synthetic rubber or thermoplastic elastomers (TPEs)—materials that have properties similar to rubber but are processed like plastics. Elastomeric gaskets are produced in a variety of sizes, colors, and finishes. They also can be produced to be especially resistant to such things as temperature, oil, chemicals, weathering, aging, and abrasion. With all these variations, as well as the variety of elastomers available, the applications vary tremendously. Simple applications would include such things as plumbing gaskets, while other, more sophisticated gaskets find advanced applications in aerospace products.

The simplest and most common sealing device, O-rings are used in numerous systems. They can be used in static and dynamic applications, depending on the proper design. Among their primary uses are as components in automotive steering and brake systems, off-road heavy equipment, aircraft, and other industrial and household items.

Mechanical face seals are a multi-component sealing device used to create a leakage-free seal between a rotating shaft and a member through which the shaft passes. They are used in automotive water pumps and in the chemical process industries.

Molded packings and seals are mainly used in such things as fluid handling pumps, valves, cylinders, piston-type accumulators, and other equipment. They can be used as seals on the rod, ram, piston, plunger stem, or spool to develop and maintain hydraulic working power. They find their main applications in static sealing uses. Molded seals include squeeze-type ring seals and lip types. Squeeze seals are used in low-pressure applications, with lip seals finding more usage in high-pressure needs.

Radial lip seals are used in dynamic, low-pressure applications. Many are available in standard sizes but the trend is to customized production.

U-packings are pressure-activated sealing devices commonly used in low to moderate dynamic sealing applications. They can be found in such things as pneumatically or hydraulically activated door openers.

Three or more seals are often used together in the low-speed, high-pressure dynamic applications common to V-packings. In one of this type of seal's many end-product uses, V-packings are found in heavy-duty hydraulic cylinders of off-road earth-moving equipment.

Gaskets and seals are vital to the operation of many types of equipment. Three markets—transportation equipment, industrial equipment and machinery, and electrical equipment—account for more than 90 percent of total demand. Of this, sales to original equipment manufacturers (OEMs) account for about 40 percent of revenue, and aftermarket sales an additional 60 percent.

Transportation equipment, including automobiles, is the largest OEM customer, accounting for 40 percent of total sales. The cyclical nature of the market resulting from such dependency on automobile sales has been offset by the relative stability of aftermarket demand for industry products.

By 1996, U.S. shipments in the seals and gasket industry were estimated at $4.23 billion, about 72 percent higher than a decade earlier. Gaskets held the greatest share, at $1.38 billion, followed by molded seals, $801 million; shaft seals, $568 million; and compression packings, $116 million.

ORGANIZATION AND STRUCTURE

This industry supports varied manufacturing and other industries, gaining its existence from the end use of its products rather than from the products themselves. Because of the industry's dependency on the health of the economy in general, the demand for gaskets, seals, and packings mirrors the cycles experienced by the makers of the durable goods that utilize such supplies.

Makers of gaskets and seals are also influenced by their customers in areas such as product development, production processes, marketing, and pricing. With the large number of suppliers available, end users can bargain not only for better pricing, but for better service as well.

Other variables outside the control of U.S. gasket and seal manufacturers combine to affect the market. For example, since the early 1980s the industry saw a rise not only in the amount of gaskets and seals imported into the U.S., but also in the variety of types of machinery in which such products were used. Varying levels of industrial production have also impacted the market.

Among the three major markets, transportation equipment uses accounted for 46 percent of gasket and seal demand in 1992. The transportation sector used more than $1.38 billion worth of product, nearly double the amount used a decade before. Industrial equipment and machinery accounted for 27 percent of applications, totaling $820 million in 1992. The final major end use, electrical and electronic equipment, took up $577 million, or 19 percent of gasket and seal sales in l992. A fourth market, instruments, accounted for the remaining 8 percent posting $91 million in sales in 1992.

Although sales to OEMs were predicted to grow at a faster pace than aftermarket sales, from 1987 to 1992 the aftermarket gained on OEMs as durable goods production was depressed by an economic slump. Traditionally, when economic times are tough, the replacement market generally shows greater increases because companies delay purchases of new equipment and spend money instead on maintenance of existing machinery. But when the economy goes up, this is reversed and OEM sales rise quicker as more new equipment is purchased.

BACKGROUND AND DEVELOPMENT

Historically, a number of different types of seals have been used in general applications. They are: gaskets, U-packings, V-packings, cup packings, and O-rings. In time, the uses for seals have multiplied and improvements in materials and technology have allowed seal manufacturers to offer a product with extended life and better performance.

The sealing industry encountered many challenges during the 1980s and 1990s as applications for sealing products became more complex. Aeronautical and oil-field consumers were among the first to push for more demanding requirements. Elastomeric seal chemists and engineers were forced to advance technology from a "so-called art," to an "engineering science," according to Kerry O. Smith in *Rubber & Plastics News.*

Traditional materials such as cork, rubber, paper, and felt soon began to give way to specialty materials. For example rubber gaskets used to be found in low-pressure and temperature uses. However, rubber is not always the material of choice for gaskets, because contact with oil and grease negatively impact its performance in such uses as the automobile aftermarket. The success of rubber in such usage is dependent on proper installation. Higher engine temperatures also negatively impact the selection of rubber for automobile gaskets. Specialty rubbers and TPEs more easily met the newer, more demanding standards and allowed the number of possible gasket applications to grow.

The synthetic rubber category can be broken into three sub-categories: commodity rubbers, medium performance rubbers, and specialty rubbers. The commodity types generally cost the least, but offer less in the area of performance. In the past, these types generally took the largest percentage of elastomeric gasket usage. More recently the trend has been toward the medium-performance and advanced rubbers. Among medium performance types, ethylene-propylene rubber, commonly known as EPDM, has found greater acceptance because it offers better weatherability and abrasion resistance.

Specialty rubbers are usually available in low volume and give the best performance, but at a markedly higher cost. These advanced materials have seen wider applications in head gaskets, manifold gaskets, and oven-door and other appliance gaskets. A number of these elastomers offer higher heat resistance, along with high fuel and oil resistance. Silicone rubber, especially, is being used more and more in aerospace applications.

Various TPEs find gasketing applications because they are resistant to oil and other engine fluids, are light-weight and offer superior durability. But TPEs haven't achieved greater market share because their heat resistance has not been comparable to some of the specialty rubbers. TPEs are expected to continue to gain in non-critical uses and will grow into more critical areas after their heat resistance is improved.

About 80 percent of the elastomeric gaskets manufactured have been made of various synthetic rubbers, with TPEs accounting for the remainder. Since the early 1980s, however, TPEs have increased their share. By the end of the 1990s, specialty synthetic rubbers are projected to once again show the highest percentage growth.

Examples of increasingly demanding design- and life-requirements in automotive applications have included the ability to seal the non-chlorinated refrigerants that began replacing the chlorofluorinated refrigerants (CFCs) that were historically used. Automakers looked for near-zero permeation but also expected seals to last up to 150,000 miles in engines operating at increasingly higher temperatures.

CURRENT CONDITIONS

The transportation equipment sector projected an annual growth rate of 6.6 percent through the end of the 1990s. Industrial equipment and related machinery was expected to have the highest growth, 7.2 percent, with sales forecast to hit $1.6 billion by 1997. The third major market sector, electrical and electronic

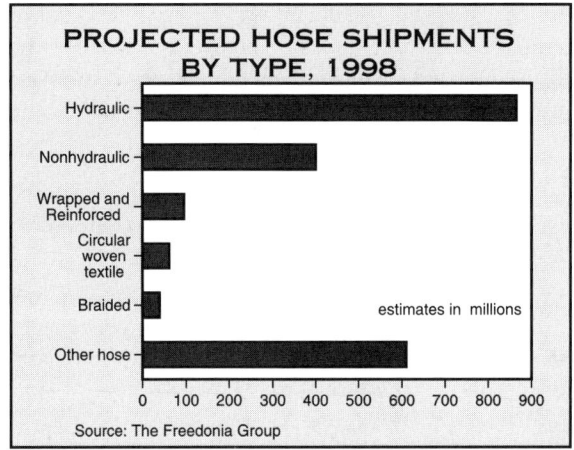

PROJECTED HOSE SHIPMENTS BY TYPE, 1998

Hydraulic
Nonhydraulic
Wrapped and Reinforced
Circular woven textile
Braided
Other hose

estimates in millions

0 100 200 300 400 500 600 700 800 900

Source: The Freedonia Group

equipment, expected to attain annual growth of 6.5 percent over the same period.

Such increases were expected to be fueled by better sales of cars and industrial equipment. The shift toward more specialty materials, such as carbon and aramid fibers, fluoroplastics, and expanded graphite, were predicted to increase the value of shipments relative to actual unit demand. Advances in auto engineering that resulted in greater engine temperatures also helped such specialty materials gain favor.

Manufacturers of molded seals, gaskets, and packings forecast the fastest growth—shipments totaled $801 million in 1992—because of the service the products provide in both static and dynamic sealing applications. Growth projections for molded seals alone called for annual increases of 7.1 percent, which would make it a $1.1 billion market by 1997. The advantages molded seals have over other seal types and an increase in durable goods production were seen as factors in growth potential. Also contributing to the growth was an effort underway to enact stricter fluid controls in the chemicals and petroleum industries.

Gasket shipments have declined over the years and will continue to decline according to a study by Frost and Sullivan, Inc. In 1992, 82.2 million gaskets were shipped by manufacturers, and that number dropped to 79.2 million in 1994. This rate of decline will continue through 1996 when 77.5 million units are expected to be shipped. This number will decrease even more until the year 2000 when the number of shipments is expected to reach 74.7 million. Frost and Sullivan attribute this decline to the slower growing number of automobiles. Also, today's vehicles are of better quality and experience fewer breakdowns. This can also be attributed to more ''technically advanced gaskets with longer life expectancies.''

O-rings and other ring seals continued to be the most commonly used products in this segment. O-rings and other ring seals accounted for $374 million of the $801 million in molded seals usage in 1992.

OEM sales were projected to increase 7.3 percent a year through 1997, bringing this segment to $1.8 billion in sales. Replacement sales were expected to climb to $2.5 billion in 1997, projecting an annual 6.4 percent increase annually. Areas expected to receive growth were transportation equipment servicing, manufacturing markets, and the utilities market. Though OEM sales were projected to grow at a more rapid pace, the aftermarket would still provide the majority of sales because of the broad base of existing machinery and equipment that would be serviced.

Revenues for automotive replacement gaskets alone hit $433.6 billion in 1994 and is expected to topple $515 billion by the year 2000 according to Frost and Sullivan, Inc.

Replacement engine seals, representing 5 percent of internal engine revenue, has remained steady because of hub assemblies eliminating the need for individual seals. Seal sales for 1994 were $52.1 million, the same as for 1993. Rates should increase slowly through 1998 and then start to decline after that. By the year 2000, income from seal revenues should reach $53.3 million.

Specialty materials were expected to see higher growth than traditional commodity materials such as cork and rubber. Because of new applications, studies projected elastomeric gasket usage to rise 7.7 percent a year to $511 million by 1997. Much of the increased usage was expected to involve these higher performing elastomers. By contrast, overall gasket usage was expected to climb just 6.9 percent a year.

INDUSTRY LEADERS

Freudenberg-NOK of Plymouth, Michigan, Detroit-based Federal-Mogul Corp., and CR Industries Inc. in Elgin, Illinois, were among the U.S.-based leaders in this industry. As these firms also derived revenue from other sources, It is difficult to pinpoint their exact sales in this category.

Other firms with a significant presence in the Industry include Cleveland-based Parker Hannifin Corp.; Wynn's Precision Inc. of Lebanon, Tennessee; John Crane Inc. in Vandelia, Illinois; and Coltec Industries' Garlock Mechanical Packing Division in Palmyra, New York.

WORK FORCE

Total employment in 1994 in the industry was about 35,100 according to the latest figures available from the U.S. government. The leading states in terms of employment were California, Illinois, Ohio, and Texas. The range of employment varied extensively, from factory workers producing the products, to chemists and engineers who develop the compounds and design, to the sales force that deals with OEM and aftermarket accounts.

Projected employment for 1995 was 38,000 workers. This was expected to increase by approximately 5.4 percent to reach an employment level of 37,000 by 1998. Of these 38,000 employees, 25,000 were production workers earning an average of $11.41 per hour in 1995. In 1998 the number of production workers is expected to increase by 5.2 percent to 26,300 employees earning and average of $12.23 per hour, and increase of 5.2 percent over the 1995 projected figures.

RESEARCH AND TECHNOLOGY

In response to increasing imports, many makers of gaskets and seals took a proactive stance: cutting manufacturing costs, going to advanced production concepts such as computer-aided design, and after-uses that had the opportunity to provide greater than average growth. Examples of such applications are non-asbestos gasketing, or seals designed to reduce emissions in process industries. Industry participants also spent to improve product design. These actions helped the industry maintain steady growth since the early 1980s.

Despite their uses in highly complex applications, gasket and seal technology itself is more defined. Developments have come in the form of the new materials being used and demands from customers for longer lasting materials. Capital costs aren't immense, but investment has been needed to keep up with these continuing shifts.

One new type of material is an oil-resistant liquid-silicone-rubber (LSR) introduced by Dow Corning STI in Plymouth MI. Typical applications of this product are gaskets, O-rings, grommets, rollers and electrical components. These new silicones should extend "hot-oil performance and high speed processing to manufacturers of automotive, off-highway, and industrial equipment"; according to *Mechanical Engineering*. The automobile industry demanded a new type of silicone due to rising temperatures in engine compartments, and the need for longer service-life in the automobile industry.

Firms in the gasket and seal industry that looked ahead at long-term industry prospects needed to be focused toward customer demands and ready to invest in new technology and product development.

FURTHER READING

Ita, Paul. *Freedonia Study #516: Gaskets & Seals.* Cleveland: Freedonia Group Inc., 1993.

Carr, John J. *The Vanderbilt Rubber Handbook.* Norwalk, CT: R. T. Vanderbilt Co. Inc., 1990.

Smith, Kerry C. "Seal Industry Rediscovers Stress Relaxation." *Rubber & Plastics News,* 31 January 1994.

1987 Census of Manufacturers. Washington: U.S. Department of Commerce.

Kokish, Bryan "Study: Gaskets, H&B Markets to Grow: Replacement Engine Seals to Cool Down." *Rubber & Plastics News,* 27 February 1995.

Darnay, Arsen J., ed. *Manufacturing USA.* 5th ed. Detroit: Gale Research, 1996.

"Technology Focus: Oil Resistant Silicone." *Mechanical Engineering,* September 1996.

—Bruce Meyer, updated by Luann Brennan

SIC 3061

MOLDED, EXTRUDED, AND LATHE-CUT MECHANICAL RUBBER GOODS

This category covers establishments primarily engaged in manufacturing molded, extruded, and lathe-cut mechanical rubber goods. The products are generally parts for machinery and equipment. Establishments primarily engaged in manufacturing other industrial rubber goods, rubberized fabric, and miscellaneous rubber specialties and sundries are classified in **SIC 3069: Fabricated Rubber Products, Not Elsewhere Classified.**

INDUSTRY SNAPSHOT

Molded, extruded, and lathe-cut goods are used in various machinery and equipment. End uses for these products exist in automobiles, oil and gas equipment, appliances, farm equipment, and construction machinery. About 600 firms in the United States make molded, extruded, and lathe-cut goods. The market is fragmented due to the diversity of end uses and no single company has dominated the industry. The sector also faces strong foreign competition. The U.S. and Canadian market alone was estimated at $5.1 billion in 1993, with sales of about $5.8 billion by 1997. Total

U.S. employment industry-wide is in the area of 50,000 people.

Much of the products in this segment have been custom-made to various end-user specifications. As such, manufacturers often sell them with a higher profit margin. Such customer orders have helped this sector show a higher rate of growth in shipment value than other industries.

Entering the mid-1990s, the recovery of the U.S. automobile industry was projected to fuel growth in industrial rubber products, which find more than half their end uses in cars. Other areas of growth were expected to be manufacturing, mining, construction, oil and natural gas, appliances, and agriculture.

Competition from imports and other materials such as plastics, which cut processing time by eliminating the curing step necessary to rubber production, were expected to hold back overall growth. As automakers continue to ask for just-in-time delivery to decrease inventories, the advantage of plastics provides a competitive edge in some uses.

BACKGROUND AND DEVELOPMENT

The term "molded goods" encompasses a wide-ranging group of products whose shape is determined by the mold in which they are produced. Markets using molded goods include automotive and other types of transportation, appliances, oil and gas fields, off-highway machinery, and equipment used in such industries as construction, farm, lawn and garden, and mining. Benefits of molded goods include resiliency, insulation, cushioning, flexibility, and vibration or noise dampening.

Among the myriad of products produced in this segment of the industry are automotive and off-highway air springs; chassis bumpers; engine and truck mounts; automotive vibration dampers; weatherstripping; wiper blades; pedals and pedal pads; rubber marine bearings; bellows, grommets, and mounts used in appliances; drill pipe protectors; shock absorber mounts; conveyor wheels; pool table bumpers; and railroad-crossing pads.

The rubber mold, normally made from steel, is the most important component in the molding process, giving the part its geometry and ensuring that it has the proper dimensions, look, and functions. The choice of molding process—compression, transfer, or injection—takes into account many variables because none of the three main methods can handle all applications. Some hybrid processes, combining two of the three molding techniques, have become popular in some uses.

Compression molding is the most widely used technique due to its relative simplicity. The material is placed in the mold and compressed using hydraulic clamp pressure. When the cycle is completed, the clamp is released and the product removed from the mold. The mold can be virtually any size as long as sufficient clamping pressure exists. This process generally has the least-expensive mold and yields minimal amounts of waste rubber. Drawbacks include having the longest cure time, the cycle it takes for the product to be formed; the number of finishing operations necessary to render the product usable; and the lack of control over meeting exact customer specifications.

Transfer molding is a more precise process. The material is transferred from a pot, normally located above the mold cavities, down to the mold at the desired time. The technique gives better tolerance control; ensures the mold is closed before rubber is introduced to eliminate exposure to the environment; can be used when other items are to be inserted into the rubber product; and offers a sometimes substantially shorter curing time. Transfer molding, however, leaves more waste, requires moderate secondary operations, and requires a more expensive mold.

Injection molding requires the most expensive press and molds, but often yields the lowest overall cost to produce the part, as it gives more options for automation. Material is injected into a closed mold from an injection barrel. One injection system can be used to feed material into several molds, either by having the injector automatically moved to different molds, or by having several molds rotate to a fixed injection unit. The part removal operation is also a good candidate for automation. Other benefits include high-precision parts; lowest rubber prepping cost; shortest cycle times; and minimal exposure to the environment during the molding process. Drawbacks to injection molding include expensive tooling and the potential for large amounts of waste if proper precautions aren't taken.

An extruder is a power-driven screw enclosed in a cylinder. In the extruded molding process, material goes in one end and is sent through the cylinder by a rotating screw. At the other end, the material is fed through a die, which is a steel mold designed to produce the desired shape of the product being made. Among the products made using extrusion are cables; wire insulation; door and deck automotive lid seals; window and glass channels in cars; wiper blades; and rubber tubing used in medical, automotive, and appliance applications.

Extruders have been in use for more than 150 years in industry. Originally, the rubber going into the extruder had to be prewarmed so it could be conveyed through the extruder. This hot-feed extrusion method was time-consuming and required great amounts of labor to complete the warming process.

Earlier in the twentieth century, however, cold-feed extruders were developed. These machines accept material at room temperature and include components designed to warm and soften the material for final forming. These machines are sometimes three times longer than hot-feed extruders, but they result in faster cycles, lower labor costs, and more uniform products. Extruded goods are flexible and good for sealing. They offer the advantage of low-cost permanent tooling and high production rates. Extrusion dies to make proto-types can be produced swiftly and for little cost. Recent studies have emphasized new designs for more effective self-feeding of the material and higher output rates.

Lathe-cut goods are by far the smallest segment of the category, accounting for just more than $50 million in business in the United States in the early 1990s. Automotive is by far the largest category, accounting for 80 percent of usage. Lathe-cut products in the automotive industry include oil filter washers; fuel system components; disc brake washers; and electric and electronic parts. Other areas using these goods are agriculture, communications, filtration, material handling, printing, and pumps and valves used in water systems.

CURRENT CONDITIONS

As automakers remain the single largest customer of molded, extruded, and lathe-cut products, their demands have a large impact on the industry. During the 1990s, for example, it was common for manufacturers to reduce their supplier base. While in the past an automaker may have bought a single part from many firms, he is now more selective in vendor selection, buying parts from fewer and fewer vendors. Auto companies became more stringent in their requests for high quality, on-time delivery, quick response to requests and, as always, competitive pricing.

Automakers also began to ask suppliers of these products to supply the technical capability to develop a component from conception to finished product. This enabled vehicle manufacturers to cut their own development overhead and leave certain design work to companies with expertise in that particular discipline. Full-service molders and extruders, therefore, were expected to make the most gains.

While there have been an increasing number of companies in this industry gaining size, industry exec-utives agree that there will always be a place for the so-called "job shops," which do custom work on products that often are short-run. These firms offer quick turnaround on prototypes and fill niche markets that larger molders can't service cost-effectively. Job shops are often run by entrepreneurial types, carry lower overheads, and are highly flexible. One government study found that single-establishment companies with up to 20 employees accounted for 7 percent of the total value of shipments in this category.

Growth prospects for U.S. consumption of molded goods was projected in one study at 7.1 percent a year for the five years leading up to 1996, bringing the U.S. market to $3.8 billion, more than $1.1 billion higher than 1991.

Areas of strong growth were expected to be transportation, off-highway machinery, appliances, and other miscellaneous applications—all above 6 percent a year. Off-highway machinery parts were projected to reach $290 million in 1996; appliance applications were forecast to rise to $190 million in 1996; and other applications were slated to rise to $1.17 billion. Such gains were forecast based on the assumption that capital spending in these areas would grow following the recession of the early 1990s.

Growth in molded products for oil and gas machinery was expected to lag behind, at just 2.1 percent a year. The sector was projected to climb slowly to $92 million in 1996, due to a drop in U.S. oil production. Also, natural gas production was expected to go up only slightly.

Strong growth in certain niche markets, including wiper blades and vibration control products, was expected. Use of molded products in the latter area mirrored automaker's efforts to try to provide smoother-riding vehicles.

Extruded rubber products shipments in the United States were forecast to grow 10.7 percent, jumping to $1.38 billion by 1996. Strong growth of end-use markets was expected to bring extruded product growth above 10 percent on all markets. These products were also likely to benefit from solid niche markets and good performance and processing characteristics.

Automotive extrusions, not including tubing, were projected to grow 39.9 percent to $700 million in 1996; tubing was forecast to grow 40 percent to $285 million in 1996. Extrusions for appliances were expected to nearly double to $150 million in 1996. Miscellaneous markets were expected to account for $245 million in business by 1996.

One niche market expected to rise quickly was weather-stripping, which was used both in automobiles and other markets. The product found favor with consumers and manufacturers alike because of its ability to reduce noise and keep out the elements. Another growing specialty niche was foam rubber for automobile cushioning, which was predicted to rise because of the ever-growing concentration on safety and comfort.

Shipments of lathe-cut goods were forecast to increase 5.7 percent a year, reaching $120 million in 1990. The segment also was expected to benefit from a stronger automotive market and rising spending on industrial equipment. Growth was, however, predicted to be confined by competition from other materials and imports.

Technology is evolving, though, to a future in which cars will have adaptive or active vibration control systems. Computer-controlled actuators and sensors will be used in conjunction with the rubber mounts, allowing the product to adapt to numerous frequencies.

INDUSTRY LEADERS

Because of the fragmented nature of the industry, no one firm or small group of firms dominate. Several companies do, however, have a substantial presence.

Akron, Ohio-based GenCorp Inc. had approximately $1.5 billion in total sales in 1996, a decrease from $1.8 billion in 1995. Employing about 8,950 workers, the company produces aerospace and defense products in addition to molded and extruded goods for the automotive market. Cleveland-based Standard Products Inc. reported total sales of $1.1 billion in 1996 and employed approximately 10,000 people. A good portion of the company's sales came from automotive sealing and other molded and extruded goods. In addition, Cooper Tire & Rubber Co. in Findlay, Ohio, continued to be a major presence in molded goods for automotive vibration controls, reporting 1996 sales of $1.6 billion.

Michigan-based Freudenberg-NOK General Partnership— a joint venture between a Japanese and a German firm—had $300 million in rubber product sales with production of molded goods at about ten factories in North America. Lord Corp. of Erie, Pennsylvania, posted $140 million in rubber product sales, with most of that in molded mounts and other goods. Clevite Elastomers of Milan, Ohio, and Goshen Rubber Co. Inc. in Goshen, Indiana, also posted annual sales in these areas of about $100 million.

WORK FORCE

The mechanical rubber goods industry employed an estimated 51,400 workers in 1996. This was expec-

ted to reach an employment level of 52,200 by 1998. Of these 51,400 employees, 40,600 work in production and earn an average of $10.78 per hour. In 1998, the number of production workers is expected to increase by 4.2 percent to 41,700 workers earning $11.10 per hour, an increase of 4.5 percent over the 1995 projected figures.

AMERICA AND THE WORLD

Imports from Europe and the Far East have played a significant role in the market. Some U.S. firms, in turn, explored service niches or specialty markets that have traditionally been harder for imports to penetrate than markets for commodity products.

Joint ventures, especially with Japanese-owned companies, also became prevalent. These helped U.S. firms gain business with both foreign automakers as well as transplant companies that make cars and other products in America.

RESEARCH AND TECHNOLOGY

Plastic products are expected to continue to challenge rubber for end-product applications that require more stringent characteristics. As automakers design smaller engine compartments in an effort to improve fuel efficiency and work in conjunction with front-wheel drive systems, they will demand better-performing products. As smaller compartments lead to hotter engine temperatures, automotive components will need to be made of materials with higher heat tolerances.

While traditional rubbers have continued to be used, other materials have been tested. Specialty elastomers, a synthetic rubber made for such specific uses, and thermoplastic elastomers, a material that is processed like a plastic but has the properties of rubber, are among the materials vying for increased usage. New fuels, mandated to reduce harmful emissions into the air, will also factor into material selections in the future.

A resin in demand is polyethylene terephthalate or PET. North American demand for PET is expected to grow annually by 4.4 percent for extruded products and by 6.0 percent for injection molded projects through the year 2000, according to a study by the Freedonia Group Inc. Although mostly in demand for blown molded bottles, engineering grades of injection molded PET are expected to be used in smaller quantities in the electronic and automotive industry.

New techniques will continue to evolve. One such predicted growth area is liquid injection molding (LIM) using silicone rubber. This process was unveiled in the late 1970s amid much hype as to how it would simplify life for molders. According to early literature, the liquid material went directly into the machine and the finished product came out—supposedly eliminating the need for several secondary operations necessary with traditional rubber molding.

While the reality of LIM didn't quite meet its promise when it was first introduced, improvements in its technology in the early 1990s increased its popularity. Molders of components for medical devices, especially, adopted the process, with many adding or expanding LIM capability. The draw for medical molders has been the ability to make a clean product—the finished component emerges virtually untouched—that meets tight tolerances.

Cellular manufacturing has also gained in prominence. In this process, molding and secondary finishing operations all take place in one "cell," eliminating the necessity for the product to be moved to different areas of the plant. This improves quality, product flow, and efficiency, and helps reduce staffing requirements as well.

A new fully integrated system for high-yield molding of trimless/flashless parts is the industry's newest technology, developed by Hull/Finmac Inc. in Warminster, Pennsylvania, and Trimless/Flashless Design Inc. (TFD) in Chantilly, Virginia. The system is a combination of a 35-ton compression press and a unique modular mold, a first for the rubber industry. The system will reduce scrap rates and should eliminate most deflashing operations, improving speed and quality in molding natural or synthetic rubber. According to Bob Huss, Vice President, Design for TFD, "The new equipment represents a step to truly wasteless molding." This new system should also speed up the mold fabrication time by 50 percent.

Industry products themselves are expected to continue to evolve. One such area is in the field of vibration control products for automobiles, which have traditionally been passive systems. With use of a rubber mount, engineers can control a single frequency that causes noise or motion of the vehicle. More advanced mounts have been designed to control two frequency-related problems.

Technology is evolving, though, to a future where cars will have adaptive or active vibration control systems. Computer-controlled actuators and sensors will be used in conjunction with the rubber mounts, allowing the product to adapt to numerous frequencies.

FURTHER READING

"Advanced Elastomer Introduces New TPE." *Rubber and Plastics News.* 13 November 1995.

Babington, Mary. *Freedonia Study No. 416, Industrial Rubber Products.* Cleveland: Freedonia Group Inc., 1992.

Darnay Arsen J., ed. *Manufacturing USA.* 5th ed. Detroit: Gale Research, 1996.

Freedonia Study No. 754, PET Resins in America, 2 February 1996.

"Hot Ticket: Molders Scramble to Expand LIM Capacity." *Rubber & Plastics News,* 15 February 1993.

"Job Shops: Is Bigger Better?" *Rubber & Plastics News,* 23 November 1992.

Long, Harry, ed. *Basic Compounding and Processing of Rubber.* Akron, OH: American Chemical Society Inc. Rubber Division, 1995.

"PMA Projects Slow Growth through 1987." *Rubber & Plastics News,* 23 November 1992.

Smith, Maurice, and James F. Walder, contributors. *The Vanderbilt Rubber Handbook.* Norwalk, CT: R.T. Vanderbilt Co. Inc., 1990.

"Technology Focus: Integrated System for Rubber Molding." *Mechanical Engineering,* September 1996.

U.S. Department of Commerce. *1987 Census of Manufacturers.* Washington: GPO, 1987.

"U.S. Rubber Industry's Top 50." *Rubber & Plastics News,* 5 July 1993.

—Bruce Meyer, updated by Luann Brennan

SIC 3069

FABRICATED RUBBER PRODUCTS, NOT ELSEWHERE CLASSIFIED

This category covers establishments primarily engaged in manufacturing industrial rubber goods, rubberized fabrics and vulcanized rubber clothing, and miscellaneous rubber specialties and sundries, not elsewhere classified. Included in this industry are establishments primarily engaged in reclaiming rubber and rubber articles. Establishments primarily engaged in the wholesale distribution of scrap rubber are classified in **SIC 5093: Scrap and Waste Materials.** Establishments primarily engaged in rebuilding and retreading tires are classified in **SIC 7534: Tire Retreading and Repair Shops;** those manufacturing rubberized clothing from purchased materials are classified in **SIC 2385: Waterproof Outerwear;** and those manufacturing gaskets and packing are classified in **SIC 3053: Gaskets, Packing, and Sealing Devices.**

INDUSTRY SNAPSHOT

This industry includes more than 100 rubber products not classified in other rubber products industries. The total value of U.S. shipments for these products was $7.7 billion in 1995, up 15 percent since 1990. There were 1,217 establishments in the industry in the mid-1990s, an increase of 22 percent since 1990. About 55,976 people were employed by U.S. companies in this industry in the mid-1990s, a decrease of 3 percent since 1990.

ORGANIZATION AND STRUCTURE

The main reason for shipment increases was the growing demand among manufacturers for rubber products, although higher consumer spending was also a major. Demands for items used in automobiles and those related to health protection were forecast to show larger than average percentage increases. With a large number of players in these market segments, firms must continue to focus on improved customer service, product design, and delivery. U.S. firms export a good deal of products to industrialized countries, but also import a considerable amount of low-cost products from developing nations. Manufacturers are expected to continue focusing on flexible, customer-oriented production. Developments of new materials also are forecast to help improve product quality and durability.

CURRENT CONDITIONS

Because this classification includes such a wide range of products, such as toy balloons, rubber brake linings, rubber rafts and pontoons, and many others, it is not possible to make broad generalizations covering the entire category. What follows is an explanation of some of the products, along with an exploration of some segments that were showing the most activity going into the mid-1990s.

Gloves and Condoms. With the AIDS crisis escalating throughout the 1980s and continuing into the 1990s, more attention has been focused on latex gloves and condoms than on any other fabricated rubber products. Both products are made by a dipping process in which a form in the shape of the product desired (such as a hand) is dipped into latex.

Latex condoms have been identified as the best way to prevent the passing of the AIDS virus from one person to another during sexual intercourse. The campaign to increase condom usage has included a plea from a former U.S. surgeon general, along with public service announcements on television featuring sports and entertainment personalities. One study indicated that, because of the sex education campaign, women are buying a larger share of condoms—as many as 20 percent of condoms in 1993.

According to the American Psychological Association and based on scanner data from retail outlets, between 1991 and 1994, condom sales fell. The top U.S. condom firms are Carter-Wallace Inc.; Schmid Laboratories Inc., which is owned by London International Group PLC; Ansell Inc.; and Aladan Inc.

But while condoms may have received the bulk of public attention, the role of latex gloves has been perhaps equally as important in the fight against AIDS. The gloves, used in examinations and surgery, are now used by virtually all health-care personnel when performing a task that requires contact with a patient. Besides physician's exams, the gloves also are widely used in dental procedures. Despite high expectations, however, neither the glove or condom markets reached the enormous proportions by the mid-1990s that were projected in the 1980s. Exam gloves, for example, were hit by a case of reality not meeting expectations. When demand began to grow to help protect workers from exposure to AIDS, many more plants went into operation than could be supported by the growing use. One official at a glove firm said that from 1986 to 1990 the demand for latex examination gloves may have doubled, but the capacity quadrupled. The situation was not helped by medical institutions that, trying to ensure delivery, placed duplicate orders with multiple distributors, helping to unrealistically raise apparent demand. This situation led to a consolidation in the glove industry, with many start-up firms going out of business and larger, multi-national firms scaling back production.

Ansell International, the world's largest exam glove firm, closed a plant in Arizona and shifted much of its production to its Asian facilities. Ansell still maintained two U.S. medical glove facilities, and had two such factories in Malaysia, and one in Thailand. Another multi-national, Smith & Nephew PLC., closed an exam glove plant in Ohio, and decided to concentrate on the more regulated surgical glove market.

Firms that produce examination gloves in the United States face stiff competition from overseas companies, much of it economically driven. Many companies locate plants in Malaysia because of the country's readily available supply of latex. Also, the Malaysian government places duties between five to ten percent on exported liquid latex, but none on exported finished gloves. Malaysia also offers economic incentives and cheaper labor than that found in the West. But even glove firms in Malaysia were hurt when demand did not meet expectations. From 1987 to 1990, the government issued 300 permits for glove factories. By late 1988 only 90 had begun operating and by the end of 1990 only 30 plants remained.

Entering the mid-1990s, glove and condom makers began studying a new problem: the use of alternate materials for those allergic to latex. Reactions to it range from relatively minor problems, such as localized contact dermatitis, to much more severe difficulties like systemic dermatitis and anaphylactic shock, which can be life-threatening. From October 1988 to April 1992, there were 1,036 severe reactions and 15 deaths related to latex allergies that were reported to the U.S. Food and Drug Administration. Studies showed that employee groups most exposed to latex, such as operating room nurses, were more susceptible to latex allergies.

To counter these problems, glove and condom makers are producing and testing more hypoallergenic latex products. By the mid-1990s, a few companies in North America began making gloves of thermoplastic elastomers, a material with the characteristics of rubber but processed like a plastic. Relatedly, in 1993, the FDA approved a condom made of polyurethane by London International, and approved a polyurethane condom for women that was produced by Pharmacal of Wisconsin. None of the nonlatex products, though, had made a major impact on the glove and condom market by the mid-1990s.

Single-ply Rubber Roofing. This is another market that was expected to grow tremendously yet never quite fulfilled the predictions made for it. The most common type of rubber roofing, which is used in commercial building, was developed in 1963 by DuPont. Two reasons this type of roofing evolved are the poor weather durability of other forms of roofing materials and the energy crisis of the 1970s, which resulted in higher material costs for asphalt-based roofs. Roofers were looking for a layer that would be flexible and have superior weather and water resistance over long periods of time. Rubber roofing increased in popularity because it could accommodate movement, was functional at high and low temperatures, resisted environmental elements, and was not subject to the effects of ponded water.

From a small 1980 base of $70 million, rubber roofing demand in the United States quadrupled by 1985 to $287 million, and then doubled by 1991 to an estimated $608 million. Annual growth of 11.1 percent from 1991 to the late 1990s is expected, which will allow rubber roofing to exceed $1 billion. But growth of rubber roofing staggered early in the 1990s, according to the Rubber Manufacturers Association (RMA), which represents rubber product firms. Single-ply roofing hit a peak in 1990 and stagnated for the next several years.

The RMA reported that 1990 usage at one billion square feet, but said the market fell to 850 million square feet in 1991 because of a drop in the U.S. economy. Shipments recovered to 910 million square feet in 1992 and 968 million square feet in 1993. The RMA forecast for the mid-1990s market is about one billion square feet, still short of 1990 demand.

The rubber roofing market has seen much consolidation, with many firms entering the fray but later dropping out, especially after a 1983 price war that virtually wiped out profits for many companies. The two leading firms in the United States are Carlisle SynTec Systems, which pioneered the product's usage, and Firestone Building Products Company, which is owned by tire maker Bridgestone/Firestone Inc. Both of the leaders made major acquisitions in 1993. Carlisle bought the roofing business of Goodyear Tire & Rubber Company after making the product for Goodyear for two years under a private-label arrangement. Firestone purchased the roofing operations of Colonial Rubber Works Inc.

Rubber-covered Rollers. Rubber covered rolls consist of three parts: a metal core, a rubber bonding adhesive applied to the core, and a rubber cover. The largest market for these products is the graphic arts industry, which uses rolls in printing presses to convey the ink onto the printing plate. Other applications are in paper making, plastic film production, printing, steel fabricating, textile manufacturing, metal coating and leather processing. In the paper industry, the rolls are used to squeeze water out of newly formed paper web so it compresses to the correct thickness. Steel mills use rolls in many strip processing lines as the rubber coverings reduce noise, provide traction, give a wringing action between processes, and protect the metal from corrosion.

Growth of rubber covered rolls has been gradual since 1980. U.S. usage was at $189 million in 1980, growing to $232 million in 1985. Growth slowed a bit as the market was estimated at $244 million in 1991. But shipments were expected to begin climbing faster, as the sales forecast for the late 1990s was $318 million.

Sheet Rubber. This rubber product is made using a machine called a calender. A strip of material fed into one side of the machine is flattened and emerges as a rubber sheet, which is used in various industrial applications like packing and lining. The process makes sheet goods in various widths and thicknesses. U.S. consumption of sheet rubber goods has varied since 1980. At that time, shipments were valued at $119 million, a figure that rose to $153 million in 1985. By 1991, though, demand had dropped to $142 million. Usage, however, was projected to pick up by the late 1990s, with a market forecast of $162 million.

Sponge Rubber Products. Sponge rubber goods are classified as either open- or closed-cell. Open-cell sponge rubber derives its name from natural occurring sponge. It is, by definition, ''an elastic mass made porous by interconnecting cells,'' G.R. Sprague of Colonial Rubber Works wrote in the *Vanderbilt Rubber Handbook.* Typical open-cell products include carpet underlay, mattress and upholstery filling. Closed-cell sponge is different because the cells do not connect. Applications of this type of sponge rubber include insulation, automotive weatherstripping, architectural gaskets, swimsuit material, pipe insulation, and mattress and upholstery filling.

Hard Rubber Products. Rubber products usually can stretch to at least twice their dimensions when stress is applied, and then return to their original form once the stress is removed. Hard rubber products are made so as to not follow this guideline, although the goods do retain many of the qualities of rubber. Typical hard rubber products include steering wheels, caster wheels, electrical insulation, battery boxes and bowling balls.

Rubberized Fabrics. The making of rubberized fabric is one of the oldest forms of rubber manufacturing. When latex was discovered, it was spread on a fabric and placed in the sun. When the water evaporated, the resulting product was a type of coated material. Historically, makers of rubberized fabrics considered their processes an art and kept such production methods secret. This created a situation in which only a few manufacturers could make products, and what they created was highly specialized. More recently, the technology for making coated fabrics has evolved from an art into a science, and the information has been spread through the industry so that the number of applications has grown tremendously. The process is used to create polyurethane coatings to simulate leather coatings, especially in the apparel, shoe, and upholstery industries Rubber fabric products include inflatable safety equipment, such as life vests, life boats, and escape slides carried on aircraft.

INDUSTRY LEADERS

Leading companies in the industry include Plumley Companies, Inc., Gates Corporation, and Foamex International, Inc. Plumley is a manufacturer of molded products, including hoses, tubing, and extrusions for home and industry, and had 1996 sales of $7.6 billion. The Gates Corporation produces belts and hoses for automotive and other industrial uses, batteries, formed fiber products, and other automobile accessories. Gates had 1996 sales of $1.46 billion. Foamex manufactures flexible polyurethane foam and foam products. Its 1996 sales totalled $1.2 billion.

FURTHER READING

''After the Gold Rush.'' *Rubber & Plastics News,* 19 August 1991.

''Ansell to Close Arizona Medical Glove Plant.'' *Rubber & Plastics News,* 17 September 1990.

''Assorted Lines to Post Gains.'' *Rubber & Plastics News,* 22 January 1990.

Babington, Mary. *Freedonia Study #416, Industrial Rubber Products.* Cleveland: Freedonia Group Inc., 1992.

Darnay, Arsen J., ed. *Manufacturing USA.* 5th ed. Detroit: Gale Research, 1996.

''Experts Seek Solution to Rising Latex Allergies.'' *Rubber & Plastics News,* 23 November 1992.

''Fabricated Goods to Rise 3 Percent.'' *Rubber & Plastics News,* 17 January 1994.

''Fabricated Goods to Rise 3 Percent.'' *Rubber & Plastics News,* 18 January 1993.

''Firestone to Buy Colonial Roofing Unit.'' *Rubber & Plastics News,* 22 November 1993.

''Goodyear to Cut 1,000 Worldwide in '92.'' *Rubber & Plastics News,* 1 February 1993.

''Latex Allergies Spawn Glove, Condom Maker.'' *Rubber & Plastics News,* 14 February 1994.

Long, Harry, ed. *Basic Compounding and Processing of Rubber.* Akron, Ohio: American Chemical Society Inc., 1985.

Plehwe, Dieter. *Change and Concentration in the World Rubber Industry.* Brussels, Belgium: International Federation of Chemical, Energy and General Workers' Unions, 1991.

''RMA Sees 6.5 Percent Rise in Roofing.'' *Rubber & Plastics News,* 23 August 1993.

''Smith & Nephew Axing Glove Line, Closing Plant.'' *Rubber & Plastics News,* 3 September 1990.

''Tactyl Adding Output for Latex-free Gloves.'' *Rubber & Plastics News,* 6 July 1992.

''Today's Roofing Market Flat As a Board.'' *Rubber & Plastics News,* 29 April 1991.

The Vanderbilt Rubber Handbook. Norwalk, CT: R.T. Vanderbilt Co. Inc., 1990.

"Single-ply Rubber Roofing." *Rubber & Plastics News,* 7 August 1989.

"U.S. Latex Glove Makers Struggle to Keep Up." *Rubber & Plastics News,* 1 October 1990.

"Unexplored Niche for Condoms." *Rubber & Plastics News,* 14 February 1994.

U.S. Bureau of the Census. *1994 County Business Patterns.* Washington: GPO, 1996.

U.S. Bureau of the Census. *1995 Annual Survey of Manufactures.* Washington: GPO, 1997.

"View from Above." *Rubber & Plastics News,* 19 August 1991.

SIC 3081

UNSUPPORTED PLASTICS FILM AND SHEET

Establishments primarily engaged in manufacturing unsupported plastics film and sheet from purchased resins or from resins produced in the same plant are classified in this industry. Establishments primarily engaged in manufacturing plastics film and sheet for blister and bubble formed packaging are classified in **SIC 3089: Plastics Products, Not Elsewhere Classified.**

INDUSTRY SNAPSHOT

The value of shipments in the plastics film and sheet industry in 1996 was $12.9 billion, up from $12.6 billion in 1994. About 800 establishments operated in the industry, and 62 percent of these establishments had 20 or more employees. The average firm size as measured by the number of production workers per establishment was 34 percent larger than that for the manufacturing sector as a whole.

The plastics film and sheet industry employed approximately 58,000 workers in 1996, 42,300 of which were production workers. This was roughly double the number employed in 1987. The industry was highly capital-intensive, having over 16 percent as much investment per production worker as that for the manufacturing sector as a whole. The industry's annual hours and hourly wages for production workers came in slightly higher than those in the manufacturing sector at large. In the mid-1990s, consumption of specialty films in the United States, western Europe, and Japan totaled almost 790,000 metric tons valued at approximately $5 billion. The United States fabricates and consumes the largest total volume of specialty

films. In 1993, the U.S. International Trade Commission estimated that over 70 billion pounds of plastics and resins were produced in the United States, valued at over $34 billion. In 1994, overall plastics production was estimated to have increased 11 percent over the previous year. World consumption of the commodity thermoplastics, polyethylene, polypropylene, polystyrene, polyvinyl chloride, and ABS/SAN resins approached 85 million metric tons in the mid-1990s, and demand was forecast to grow more than 4 percent per year until 1998.

ORGANIZATION AND STRUCTURE

Of the top 15 firms by sales in the plastics film and sheet industry, 2 were private independents, 3 public independents, and the remaining 10 were subsidiaries and divisions of larger firms. All of these 15 firms had greater than $100 million in sales. Of the remaining 60 firms ranking among the top 75 by sales, 50 percent were private independents.

The states ranking in the top 10 by value of shipments were, in order of descending value: Massachusetts, Texas, South Carolina, Ohio, Virginia, New Jersey, California, Illinois, Indiana, North Carolina, and Pennsylvania. Together, these states accounted for 60 percent of total shipments and 61 percent of total employment for the industry. The average number of employees per establishment varied widely across these states. South Carolina and Virginia, the states with the highest number of employees per plant, had between five and ten times as many employees per plant on average, as did New York and California.

The industry was served by the Chemical Fabrics and Film Association, headquartered in Cleveland, Ohio. The association, formerly known as the Plastic Coatings and Film Association, was founded in 1927 and had 23 members. The association published industry standards and an annual directory and also organized an annual convention. The most important industry periodical was the *Journal of Plastic Film and Sheeting.*

BACKGROUND AND DEVELOPMENT

Although the terms are sometimes used interchangeably, plastics films are generally defined as being less than 0.010 inches in thickness, whereas plastics sheet is thicker. The plastics film and sheet industry had its origins in the rapid growth of the organic chemical industry in the late-nineteenth century. The first commercially successful plastics film was cellulose nitrate. Although this film had many desirable properties, its flammability limited the scope of its use. In his book *Plastic Films*, John Briston called regenerated cellulose, or cellophane, "the most important development in films." The commercialization of this film followed the development of continuous-process film production machinery for which the Swiss chemist J.E. Brandenburger received his first patents in 1911. Cellophane was initially used for the packaging of luxury and semi-luxury goods, but its use expanded rapidly thereafter.

Plastic Films: Technology and Packaging Applications, Osborn and Jenkins summarized the growth of the industry as follows: "The commercialization of cellophane in the 1920s revolutionized the flexible packaging of consumer goods. For the first time, the buyer could see the contents of the package through a film that protected the packaged items from dirt, moisture, and atmospheric gases. Countless items previously packaged in heavy metal or fragile glass containers began to appear in this safe, convenient, light weight film. As a result, the flexible packaging industry grew from a small, paper-based operation into the . . . giant it is today."

Cellophane remained the dominant film in the industry until the commercialization of polyethylene film in the 1950s. One of the key advantages of polyethylene film was its lower cost, which made it possible to use for large tonnage packaging applications. As of 1987, cellulose films made up only 7 percent of the industry's product share, compared to 29 percent for polyethylene films. The rapid growth of the pre-packaged food industry in the post-World War II period provided an ever-growing demand for polyethylene films. The use of polyethylene films expanded to the packaging of textiles and toys, as well as heavy sacks for industrial and agricultural uses.

The industry introduced polypropylene films in 1959. This film was stiffer than polyethylene film, and thus, readily lent itself to packaging with high-speed machinery. Polypropylene film made up 7 percent of the industry's product share in 1987, and was expected to grow more rapidly in use than polyethylene films.

As of 1989, 28 percent of polyethylene and polypropylene film was used for merchandise bags, 25 percent for non-food packaging and trash and can liners, 24 percent for food packaging, 7 percent for shrink and stretch wrap, and the remainder for other non-packaging purposes.

The rapid market growth of plastics films was enabled in part by ever-lowering costs. This changed to some extent after the Oil Crisis of 1972, which slowed the growth of the industry. Nonetheless, plastics film continued to grow at the expense of cellophane and other traditional, flexible packaging materi-

als. In *Plastic Films: Technology and Packaging Applications*, Osborn and Jenkins considered the effects of rising energy costs on the plastics film industry. Noting that the production of aluminum foil was up to four times as energy-intensive as the production of plastics film, the authors wrote, "Rising energy costs will continue to favor flexible over rigid packaging, plastics films and paper over foil, and may cause a minor shift in the paper/plastics balance in the favor of paper. The latter effect can not be large, since paper has only a few of the many packaging-friendly attributes of plastics." The authors conclude that the diminishing supply of oil and gas will not significantly affect the production of plastics films for two reasons. First, of products produced with oil and gas, plastics have the highest value added in the production process. Second, plastics packaging used only one-half percent of all oil and gas consumed in the United States.

One of the relatively new important markets for plastics films was agricultural production. The agricultural industry used plastics films for greenhouses, row covers, irrigation channels, and mulches. Plastics mulches reduced weeds, fungi, and insects, and held in ground moisture. The use of plastics mulches resulted in yield increases of up to 250 percent in certain field tests.

CURRENT CONDITIONS

The value of shipments in the plastics film and sheet industry increased by 42 percent from 1987 to 1995, which exceeded projections by 14 percent. Capital investments increased by 17 percent over this same period, with 1992 a peak year, when $592.3 million in new capital investments were made.

The TPC Business Research group published a report on thermo-formed plastics films, entitled "High-Performance Films in the United States." The report projected an annual average growth rate of 3.8 percent for these films through 1997, implying $2.6 billion in sales by that year. While polyester made up 75 percent of such films in 1993, films made from polycarbonate, nylon, and polyolefin-based resins were expected to grow more rapidly. The use of stretch film was expected to continue growing at double-digit rates.

Employment of production workers was stable from 1987 to 1991. There was an 8 percent growth between 1991 and 1992. Employment has remained stable since then, but projections indicate that there will be a modest increase of 9 percent between 1993 and 1998. The U.S. Bureau of Labor Statistics made employment forecasts at the **SIC 3080** level for 30 occupational categories. Based on projected changes from 1990 to 2005, employment was expected to increase in all 30 occupations, with double-digit increases projected for 26 occupations. Projections made for the plastics film and sheet industry alone would have varied from these figures. Yet aside from **SIC 3089: Plastics Products Not Elsewhere Classified**, the plastics film and sheet industry was largest of the industries making up **SIC 3080**, comprising 13 percent of total shipments at the **SIC 3080** level.

One of the important challenges facing the plastics film and sheet industry was the development and use of more environmentally friendly products and processes. Two researchers at Cornell University published a study that addressed the issue of the biodegradability of plastics films. The researchers tested 12 films claimed by their manufacturers to be biodegradable and judged that only one of these films, produced by E.I. DuPont de Nemours & Company (DuPont), was truly biodegradable. This film was relatively expensive and may not be economically feasible for such applications as trash bags. Among other films claimed to be biodegradable, the best of them simply broke into small pieces.

Demand for biodegradable and recycled plastics was expected to have a lasting impact on the industry. In an early 1990s conference titled ''Greener and Better: Packaging Challenges for the 1990s,'' the subject was addressed by Richard Mayer, CEO of Kraft General Foods. The *Journal of Plastic Film and Sheeting* summarized his keynote speech as follows: ''Mayer emphasized that unity and partnership are needed by material producers, converters, packagers, wholesalers, and retailers if the industry is to meet the consumer's challenge for better and lighter packages, which use much recycled material. Since consumers are demanding legislative action to obtain source reduction, reuse of packages, and minimum recycling requirements, it is becoming increasingly important that the packaging industry respond with both action and education.''

INDUSTRY LEADERS

The four largest firms in the plastics film and sheet industry were: Borden Chemicals and Plastics Limited in Geismar, Louisiana; Envirodyne Industries, Inc. of Oak Brook, Illinois; ICI Americas, Inc. Films Group of Wilmington, Delaware; and CYRO Industries of Mount Arlington, New Jersey. Together these firms accounted for about 30 percent of total sales for the industry.

Borden Chemicals and Plastics Limited is a limited partnership that was formed in 1987 to acquire and operate chemical plants in Louisiana and Illinois that

were previously owned by Borden, Inc. In addition to plastics film and sheet, the company produces other PVC polymer products (which made up 65 percent of its 1996 revenues); methanol and derivatives (21 percent of revenues); and nitrogen products (14 percent of revenues). Total company revenues in 1996 totaled $709.2 million, a 4 percent decrease from 1995. The company employed approximately 800 workers in early 1997.

Envirodyne Industries was founded in 1970, and had $651.4 million in sales and 4,900 employees in 1996. Producing shrink wrap and plastics film for food packaging, the firm was a subsidiary of the privately held Emerald Acquisition Corporation, also of Oak Brook. Envirodyne acquired its plastics production facilities in its 1986 purchases of Union Carbide Corporation's film packaging business and of Filmco International Limited.

The ICI Films Group had approximately $300 million in sales and 1,000 employees in 1995. The group was a division of ICI Americas, Incorporated, a subsidiary of the publicly held Imperial Chemical Industries PLC, a U.K.-based firm. The firm had long been one of the main technical innovators in the plastics film industry. Among its key developments was low-density polyethylene in 1933. ICI Films started up a new $18 million plant in the United Kingdom in 1992, and announced in 1993 that it was tripling its capacity for the production of a new polyester film called Kaladex. The demand for Kaladex resulted from the film's great imperviousness to moisture and oxygen.

CYRO Industries had nearly $200 million in sales and 1,000 employees in 1995. The firm was founded in 1976 as a joint venture with the publicly held American Cyanamid Co. CYRO announced in the early 1990s that it would expand its capacity of continuously manufactured plastics sheet by 25 percent.

RESEARCH AND TECHNOLOGY

Plastics film and sheet was produced by feeding molten plastics through either a flat or tubular die. After being shaped, the film was cooled or ''quenched,'' either by coming into contact with a cooled roller or by being immersed in water. Water quenching more uniformly cools films and was preferred, especially when film clarity was a consideration.

One of the most important outputs of the industry was laminated plastics films. Lamination enabled a film that combined the optimal characteristics of each of the component materials, whether that characteristic be imperviousness, stiffness, clarity, strength, or wrinkle-resistance. Laminates were produced either by adhesive bonding of separately produced films or by the newer process of coextrusion. In coextrusion, two or more films were simultaneously formed and heat-bonded either by a set of adjacent dies or by a manifold die. By creating laminated plastics films in one continuous process, coextrusion greatly reduced their cost. One of the disadvantages of coextruded films is that it was not possible to print on their protected inside surface, since component layers are formed and bonded almost simultaneously. The quality of print was of great importance for the marketing of packaged food products. New developments in surface printing were underway to address this problem.

The industry developed a number of new products and processes in the 1990s to address the issue of environmental safety. A project undertaken by Dow Plastics and Advanced Environmental Recycling Technologies of Rogers, Arkansas, created a new process to remove dirt and other wastes from recycled polyethylene grocery sacks and stretch film. Grocery and merchandise bags constituted the bulk of recycled plastics film products. DuPont developed a new polyester film, Mylar OL, that enabled dependable seals for packaging with the use of adhesives, making the film more readily recyclable.

The Exxon Chemical Company started up a new film production line in 1993 that was capable of producing seven million pounds of plastics film a year, using up to 50 percent post-consumer plastics. Mobil Chemical developed a new low-density polyethylene called 'Super Strength' that enabled films to be produced that were 30 percent thinner, yet just as strong as conventional plastics films. Highly impervious silica-coated plastics films began to be commercialized in the United States in the 1990s after having been developed in Japan in Europe. Aside from their desirable packaging properties, silica-coated films more readily lent themselves to recycling than laminates containing vinyl-based resins.

Airco Gases of Murray Hill, New Jersey, developed a new cooling technology known as cryogenic bubble cooling. This process eliminated a long-standing bottleneck in the production of plastics films and enabled output increases of up to 60 percent.

FURTHER READING

"24th National Agricultural Plastics Congress." *Journal of Plastic Film and Sheeting,* January 1994.

Benning, Calvin. *Plastic Films for Packaging.* Lancaster, PA: Technomic Publishing Co., 1983.

"Biodegradability of Modified Plastic Films in Controlled Biological Environments." *Environmental Science and Technology,* January 1992.

Briston, John H. *Plastic Films.* 2nd ed. Harlow, England: Longman Scientific and Technical, 1983.

"Critical Issues: Broader Scope for TAPPI." *Journal of Plastic Film and Sheeting,* October 1993.

"Cryogenic Bubble Cooling Could Increase Film Output By Up to 60 Percent." *Modern Plastics,* August 1992.

"CYRO Begins Growth Project." *Glass Magazine,* August 1992.

Darnay, Arsen J., ed. *Manufacturing USA.* 5th ed. Detroit: Gale Research, 1996.

"Demand for High-Performance Films." *Paper, Film and Foil Converter,* September 1992.

"Donald Kelly Gets Egg on His Face." *Business Week, Industrial Edition,* 24 February 1992.

"Environmental News." *Journal of Plastic Film and Sheeting,* January 1993.

"Exxon Adds Post-Consumer Film Capacity." *Plastic News,* 11 January 1993.

"Marketing Reports." *Journal of Plastic Film and Sheeting,* January 1994.

"Mobil Chemical Makes New Polyethylene Resin." *Journal of Commerce,* 10 April 1992.

Moody's Industrial Manual. New York: Moody's Investors Service Inc., 1993.

"New Films." *Journal of Plastic Film and Sheeting,* January 1993.

Osborn, Kenton and Wilmer Jenkins. *Plastic Films: Technology and Packaging Application.* Lancaster, PA: Technomic Publishing Company, Inc., 1992.

"PEN Film Business Emerges as ICI Slates Production." *Chemical Marketing Reporter,* 16 March 1992.

"Plastic Film Demand to Hit 11 Billion Lb by '96." *Packaging U.S.,* August 1992.

"Plastics Units Fuel Envirodyne in Hard Times." *Plastic News,* 15 February 1993.

"Process Efficiencies Bolster Stretch Film." *Modern Plastics,* December 1991.

"Silica-Coated Plastics for Thin Films, Bottles on Edge of U.S. Market." *Paper, Film and Foil Converter,* August 1992.

Sweeting, Orville. *The Science and Technology of Polymer Films.* New York: John Wiley and Sons, Inc., 1968.

U.S. Census Bureau. *Annual Survey of Manufactures.* Washington: GPO, 1992.

U.S. Department of Commerce. *U.S. Industrial Outlook.* Washington: GPO, 1994.

—David Kucera, updated by Arthur G. Sharp

SIC 3082

UNSUPPORTED PLASTICS PROFILE SHAPES

This industry covers establishments primarily engaged in manufacturing unsupported plastics profiles, rods, tubes, and other shapes. Establishments primarily engaged in manufacturing plastics hose are classified in **SIC 3052: Rubber and Plastics Hose and Belting.**

The value of shipments in the plastics profile shapes industry in 1995 was $4.2 billion, up from $3.9 billion in 1994, according to the *1995 Census of Manufactures*. The industry employed 27,600 production workers in 1995, up from the 27,000 employed in 1994 and above the previous peak of 21,300 in 1989. The states that in 1992 dominated the industry in numbers of residents employed were Ohio, Illinois, California, and Pennsylvania.Together these states account for about 33% of total value of shipments.

The top three firms in the plastics profile shapes industry in the mid-1990s were Crane Plastics Company LP of Columbus, Ohio; Venture Industries Inc. of Grand Rapids, Michigan; and Laird Plastics Inc. of West Palm Beach, Florida. Crane Plastics founded in 1947, had $113 million in sales and 650 employee, Venture had $59 million in sales and 500 employees, and Laird Plastics had $57 million in sales with 500 employees also.

The top products by share in the industry are those made from vinyl (16 percent), polyethylene (16 percent), polypropylene (12 percent), polystyrene (10 percent), nylon (4 percent), acrylates (4 percent), and styrene copolymer (1 percent).

FURTHER READING

Darnay, Arsen J., ed. *Manufacturing USA.* 5th ed. Detroit: Gale Research, 1996.

U.S. Bureau of the Census. *1995 Census of Manufactures.* Washington: GPO,1997.

U.S. Department of Commerce.International Trade Administration. *U.S. Industrial Outlook 1994.* Washington: GPO, 1994.

—David Kucera, updated by Kenneth R. Shepherd

SIC 3083

LAMINATED PLASTICS PLATE, SHEET, AND PROFILE SHAPES

This category covers establishments primarily engaged in manufacturing laminated plastics plate, sheet, profiles, rods, and tubes. Establishments primarily engaged in manufacturing laminated flexible packaging are classified in industry group 267 (Converted Paper and Paperboard Products, Except Containers and Boxes).

INDUSTRY SNAPSHOT

Establishments engaged in the manufacture of plastic plates, sheets, and related products shipped goods valued at $2.26 billion in 1993 (not adjusted for inflation). This figure remained in line with a generally flat trend in the industry in recent years. The total value of shipments increased by 5 percent from 1987 to 1990. The industry lagged behind the growth of plastics products in general, which experienced growth in shipments of over 17 percent during the same period. By 1996 the value of shipments increased to about $2.31 billion. Projections for 1998 did not reflect a substantial increase—$2.33 billion.

The relatively flat trend in laminated plastic plate and sheet production has been attributed to several economic forces. Continuing weakness in the manufacturing sector due to the prolonged economic recession undoubtedly contributed to the stagnation in the demand for the industry's products during the late 1980s and early 1990s. On the positive side, however, laminated plastic makers have been able to maintain an advantage over competitors in nonplastic plate and sheet. In addition, research and development has resulted in better products and cheaper methods of production. Continuing advancements in processing technology are opening new markets throughout the world, most notably the recycling market.

ORGANIZATION AND STRUCTURE

In 1996 approximately 328 establishments were engaged in the production of laminated plastic plate and sheet. That number was projected to increase by approximately 20 percent by 1998, while the number of production workers was projected to decrease by 10 percent. The existing 1996 establishments employed 14,600 workers, 10,800 of which were production workers. During 1994, the average value added per production worker was $105,925—a figure which compared less than favorably with an overall average of $134,084 for all U.S. manufacturing industries.

In terms of geographic concentration, the largest number of establishments was located in the East North Central region of the United States, followed by the Middle Atlantic region and then the Pacific region, including Alaska and Hawaii. Alternatively, when ranked by the number of establishments per state, California was first with 44, followed by Ohio with 28, Illinois with 20, and Pennsylvania with 17. Ohio's establishments generated the most money from shipments—$307 million.

Market concentration was relatively high in the laminated plastics plate and sheet industry. In 1992 it was estimated that the largest eight companies accounted for approximately two-thirds of the industry's $2.8 billion in sales. In descending order of market share, the dominant companies in the laminated plastic plate and sheet industry in the mid-1990s were: James River Corporation, with a 22 percent market share; Ralph Wilson Plastics Company, (10 percent); Allied-Signal Incorporated (8 percent); Spartech Corporation (6.2 percent); Uniroyal Plastics Acquisition and Formica Corporation (each with 6 percent); Wolverine Technologies, Inc. (4.8 percent); and Nevamar Corporation (4 percent). Many of these companies were diversified though. While three of the largest companies in the industry, including the James River Corporation, were divisions of larger companies, most of the leading companies were subsidiaries. Only one company in the top ten, Spartech Corporation, was publicly traded.

The primary materials consumed by the laminated plastic plate and sheet industry, when ranked by delivered costs (not adjusted for inflation) were: materials, ingredients, containers, and supplies of various kinds, valued at $993.6 million in 1992; paper and paperboard products, except paperboard boxes, containers, and corrugated paperboard ($233.4 million); and other materials and components, parts, containers and supplies ($168.5 million).

The major sources of input for the plastics industry were overwhelmingly from the manufacturing sector, which accounted for nearly 63 percent of sector input. The single major input was plastic materials and resins, which comprised 36.2 percent of inputs. Wholesale trade accounted for 8.5 percent of inputs, while imports—undifferentiated by industry sector—contributed 5.8 percent of sector input.

If disaggregated by total product share, the industry's output was divided among the following product classes: thermosetting products were approximately 38 percent of the industry's total output in the early 1990s; thermoplastics were 29 percent; and other laminates were 28 percent. Plastic laminates (excluding flexible packaging), laminated plastics plate, and sheet and profile shapes accounted for the remaining 5 percent.

In the mid-1990s, the principal sectors responsible for the purchase of miscellaneous plastics products were hospitals, which bought 5.6 percent of sector output, followed by electronic components with 5.2 percent, and personal consumption with 4.3 percent. Exports made up 4.0 percent of total product sales.

BACKGROUND AND DEVELOPMENT

Laminated plastic plate and sheet products are defined, in rather technical terms, as plastic materials consisting of superimposed layers of synthetic resin-impregnated or coated filler which have been bonded together by means of heat and pressure to form a single piece. Plastic sheet is distinguished from plastic film by its thickness—sheet is more than 0.010 of an inch in thickness. Sheet is known for its resistance to corrosion and is used in applications from building construction to production of appliances and other consumer durables. When discrete separate layers of plastics are joined together by an adhesive, heat, or other method, the finished product is called a laminate. The term "composite" is used to describe sheets that result when two or more plastics are combined.

The history of laminated plastics can perhaps be best understood in the context of the development of the plastics industry in general. Some have referred to the twentieth century as the "plastic century," when plastics technology applications were thought—at the time of their inception—to be virtually limitless. In some respects this optimism was justified as plastic in general began to make vast inroads as a lighter replacement for steel and other natural materials. With the boom in consumer spending following World War II, the idea of what some referred to as a "plastics utopia" was not all that far-fetched. After the mid-1950s, laminated plastic was everywhere, with applications proliferating at an unprecedented rate.

One of the earliest and most famous names in laminated plastics history is Formica, the trade name developed by the Formica Corporation (Formica Laminate) over 80 years ago, spawning a vast array of products. It was during the 1950s that Formica took on its most characteristic use as kitchen counter tops. Formica was sold as a durable nonporous material that required only the wipe of a damp cloth to clean the surface. Eventually, Formica surfaces would be able to imitate any type of surface.

Formica laminate was perfected by two former Westinghouse employees—Daniel J. O'Conor and Herbert A. Faber. They developed a process for making rigid laminated sheets which could be cut into various shapes. The Formica Insulation Company started in Cincinnati in 1913 as a venture of these two enterprising former Westinghouse employees. The new product was called "Formica" to distinguish it from other products such as Westinghouse's "Bakelite-Micarta," which had distinguished itself from the previous "Micarta." While early laminates were dark in color and homogeneous, it wasn't long before Formica's surface could hold any color, pattern, or texture including stone, wood, and textile. Other companies, such as Redmanol Company and Bakelite, founded by plastics pioneer Leo Baekeland, as well as smaller companies such as Continental Fibre and Diamond State Fibre, were all selling virtually the same product in the 1920s and 1930s. Sales of laminates boomed as laminate panels covered interiors of railroad cars, decorative laminates covered lobbies of many buildings, and Formica laminate even lined the Queen Mary.

By the 1950s, technological change, lower resin prices, and new thermoplastic materials derived from petroleum led to a massive proliferation of laminates. Technological applications in the consumer appliance industry—including washing machines, vacuum cleaners, and refrigerators—all benefitted from Formica parts. During this time, Formica took on its most characteristic use as kitchen counter tops. Shortly afterward, the company was making dinette tops and chairs. Industry competition became fierce. By 1950 weekly production of Formica dinette sheets was 55,000 units, compared with just 28,000 units two years earlier.

In the 1950s the plastics industry expanded at an astounding rate—more rapidly than most other American industries. Plastic laminate applications boomed as well, especially in consumer industries. In 1969 Formica ceased production of industrial grade laminate, one of its first applications. And in 1971 they received a patent for the development of a heavy-ink process used as another surface texturing technique. One year later a metallic laminate line was produced. In 1982, Formica laminate went three-dimensional by way of ColorCore, a surfacing material that made it possible to achieve volumetric as well as intaglio or cameo effects.

CURRENT CONDITIONS

Since the applications of products in the laminated plastics plate, sheet, and profile shapes industry are widespread, the outlook for the industry depends on the state of the national and global economy. The outlook for the export market for laminated plastics products is relatively optimistic when compared with the rest of the plastics industry. More specifically, while during the 1980s imports of all plastics categories grew six-fold, laminated plastics continued to account for the bulk of industry exports. Most exports go to Canada and Mexico and are expected to increase with the removal of tariffs and taxes as part of the North American Free Trade Agreement (NAFTA), which went into effect at the beginning of 1994. Meanwhile, the world laminates market in 1990 was increasing at a rate of 20 to 25 percent annually. Predictions for 1995 from some European experts indicate a world market worth $5 billion.

WORK FORCE

While following a cyclical pattern, total employment in this industry remained relatively flat between 1987 and 1990. Total employment was 17,300 in 1987, rose 8 percent to around 18,600 in 1988, then dropped to 17,600 in 1990, for an overall increase of only 2 percent for the entire period. Production worker employment followed roughly the same trend, rising from 12,900 in 1987 to 14,000 in 1988, and falling to only 13,400 for an overall increase of 4 percent over the entire period. Employment dropped slightly to 16,000 workers in 1994—12,000 of which were production workers.

Average hourly earnings of production workers in laminated plastics was $12.11 in 1994—which is high relative to other plastics industries. Hourly wages were expected to increase to $13.22 by 1998. Regional differentials in average wages per hour for production workers ranged from a high of $13.39 in Ohio to a low of $7.40 in Indiana.

RESEARCH AND TECHNOLOGY

U.S. producers were continually developing new products and processes. This effort was reflected during the early and mid-1990s through the computerization of nearly all aspects of the laminated plastics production cycle, including design, manufacture, and distribution. Specifically, this has meant increased applications of computer-aided design and computer aided manufacturing. At the sales level, these innovations include individualized customer design which will lead to shorter delivery times and better quality control. By allowing manufacturers to determine precise product demand, these new methods of production and delivery will allow users of these techniques to achieve quick delivery and short turnover times.

Of course, all of these innovations, while increasing productivity and reducing unit costs, involve major investments in computer automated machinery. As a result, firms have tried to reduce relative labor costs, which remain high relative to other plastics industry groups. With their economies of scale and access to internally generated funds, the larger companies will be better positioned to implement these expensive, large capital commitment operations. This will undoubtedly lead to a pattern of technological change which is anything but uniform across firms in the industry.

Finally, most firms in the industry recognized the trend toward recycling and are devoting considerable research efforts to developing recyclable materials and technologies which hold potentially profitable applications.

FURTHER READING

Darnay, Arsen J., ed. *Manufacturing USA.* 5th ed. Detroit: Gale Research, 1996.

Dubois, Harry. *Plastics History U.S.A.* Hanover, MA: Halliday Lithographic Company, 1972.

Lewin, Susan Grant, ed. *Formica & Design: From the Counter Top to High Art.* New York: Rizzoli International Publications, 1991.

Pasquale, John A. ''Laminating.'' *Modern Plastics Encyclopedia: Modern Plastics,* October 1991.

Rosato, Dominick V., William K. Fallon, and Donald V. Rosato. *Markets for Plastics.* New York: Van Nostrand, Reinhold Co., 1969.

U.S. Bureau of the Census. *1995 Annual Survey of Manufactures.* Washington: GPO, 1997.

————*1994 County Business Patterns* Washington: GPO, 1996.

U.S. Department of Commerce. International Trade Administration. *U.S. Industrial Outlook 1994.* Washington: GPO, 1994.

—John A. Sarich, updated by Arthur G. Sharp

SIC 3084

PLASTICS PIPE

This category covers establishments primarily engaged in manufacturing plastics pipe. Establishments primarily engaged in manufacturing plastics pipe fit-

tings are classified in **SIC 3089: Plastics Products, Not Elsewhere Classified.**

INDUSTRY SNAPSHOT

Establishments manufacturing plastics pipe produced a total of approximately $3.85 billion dollars worth of product in 1995. This figure marked a significant increase of approximately one-third in the total value of shipments from 1990. The industry lagged behind the growth of plastics products in general, which experienced growth in shipments of over 17 percent during the same period.

In recent years, however, plastics pipe as a commodity has, in general, been able to maintain a large advantage over competitors in nonplastics piping. Although markets stagnated in the 1980s and early 1990s, plastics piping markets grew at a rate four times faster than that of nonplastics markets. In addition, research and development spurred new products and cheaper methods of production. The continuing advancements in processing technology are opening new markets and applications throughout the world.

ORGANIZATION AND STRUCTURE

In 1995, approximately 275 establishments were engaged in the production of plastics pipe. Each establishment employed an average of approximately 61 employees, 46 of which were production workers. In 1994, the average value added per production worker was $119,330. This figure compared less than favorably with an overall average of $134,084 calculated for all U.S. manufacturing industries.

In terms of major area of geographic concentration, the largest number of establishments were located in the Pacific region of the United States—including Alaska and Hawaii—followed by the West South Central region. Alternatively, when ranked by the number of establishments per state California was first with 31; followed by Texas with 27; Ohio with 13; Florida with 12; Alabama and Iowa each with 10; and Indiana, North Carolina, and Pennsylvania, each with nine.

Market concentration was relatively high in the plastics pipe industry. In 1992, it was estimated that the largest 25 companies accounted for approximately $1.3 billion, or over 90 percent of the entire industry's sales. In descending order of market share, the dominant companies in the plastics pipe industry were: Lamson and Sessions Company's Home Products Division, with approximately 18.3 percent of the market; Phillips Driscopipe, Inc., with 9.9 percent; Advanced Drainage Systems, with 7.1 percent; Pacific Western Extruded, with 6.4 percent; H & W Industries, with 5.3

percent; Harsco Corporation's Cantex Division, with 4.9 percent; National Pipe Company, with 4.2 percent; and Smith Fiberglass Products Inc., Cresline Plastic Pipe Company, Inc., Diamond Plastics Corporation, and Ameron, Inc.'s Fiber Glass Pipe Division, each with 3.5 percent. Many of these companies were diversified companies, though. While the largest companies in the industry, including Lamson and Sessions Company's Home Products Division, were divisions of larger companies, most of the leading companies were private companies. In fact, 26 of the top 48 companies were private companies.

Data available from the input-output tables assembled by the Commerce Department from 1977, 1982, and 1987 indicated that the primary materials consumed by the plastics pipe industry when ranked by delivered costs—not adjusted for inflation—were: materials, parts, and containers of various kinds with $1.58 billion; and plastics resins consumed in the form of granules, pellets, powders, liquids, $940.8 million. The major sources of input supply were overwhelming from the manufacturing sector, which accounted for nearly 63 percent of sector input. The major input was plastics materials and resins which comprised 36.2 percent of inputs. Wholesale trade accounted for 8.5 percent of inputs, and imports accounted for 5.8 percent of sector input.

If desegregated by total product share, the industry's output was divided among the following product classes: water piping was 32.92 percent of the industry's total output; drain, waste, and vent pipe was 22.8 percent of output; sewer pipes were 16.1 percent, while industrial and mining, oil and gas piping, and other plastics piping accounted for the remaining 28 percent. The principal economic industries responsible for the purchase of plastics pipe were hospitals, which bought 5.6 percent of sector output; electronic components, which accounted for 5.2 percent; and personal consumption at 4.3 percent. Exports made up 4 percent of total product sales.

BACKGROUND AND DEVELOPMENT

Plastics pipe was first manufactured commercially in the United States in 1940, when the Southern California Gas Company used a type of plastics pipe, butyrate pipe, to distribute natural gas. Prior to that time, polyvinyl chloride (pvc) pipe had been used in Germany as early as 1930. Then, plastics pipe was being produced as well by several U.S. companies for use in chemical services. Plastics pipe production in the U.S. commenced in 1948 with the development of polyethylene pipe for water services. Initial applica-

tions of the new pipe included use on farms for drainage and various applications in the petroleum industry.

Plastics pipe and tubing is the final stage of value added production into consumer or industrial products. In general, plastics manufacturing is as follows: plastics materials (monomers) are chemically altered to produce polymers, which are then mixed with certain materials to impart certain characteristics such as durability, flexibility, and chemical resistance. Then, other manufacturing processes are used to produce final products such as plastics pipe. The production processes specific to plastics pipe manufacturing—processes including a variety of methods such as coating, extrusion, molding, and laminating—allow for continuous production of piping. Plastics pipes have various functions for long and short distance transportation of fluids. Also, plastics pipes have various intermediary purposes for final use in building construction.

Plastics soften but do not melt when heated, thereby allowing them to change shape without losing cohesion. Before the 1930s, industrial products were largely based on coal as the basic chemical feed stock. The surge and rapid expansion of the production and consumption of plastics was directly related to the advent of petroleum as the main chemical feedstock. Thus, the petroleum and plastics industry are intrinsically related, and petrochemicals provide the basis for mass production of plastics, and conversely, plastics provided petroleum with their main downstream market.

The boom in plastics piping in the post World War II period is intertwined with the boom in plastics manufacturing which has a close relation to the advancement of consumer society in the United States, most notably the substitution of plastics material for other materials such as copper, aluminum, and steel. This enabled the use of plastics products to seriously challenge metal or alloy applications in such fields as aerospace, transportation, electricity, and engineering industry. In general, the plastics industry is the single, most-important ''downstream'' industry in the petrochemicals value-added chain. Plastics products are produced by various chemical processes that allow the formation of usable products by heating, milling, or extrusion.

Retail sales of plastics pipe for various applications were up to $500,000 by 1948 and annual sales volume grew to $10 million by 1952. The new major classes of rigid thermoplastics pipe, namely acrylonitrile-butadiene-styrene (ABS) and polyvinyl chloride (PVC) were introduced in 1949 and 1950, respectively, and became widely used in new markets, competing effectively with other materials such as steel and copper piping. Plastics piping became widely used in drain, waste, and vent applications; natural gas distribution; and in the chemical industry. By 1956, styrene rubber pipe for sewer and drainage services became common pipe material by around 1956. This was followed by other successful materials—thermoplastics piping, acetal, polypropylene, and polyvinyl dichloride. Sales grew to $25 million in 1957, $75 million in 1963, $100 million in 1964, and $120 million in 1965.

Applications became very wide-spread in construction and building, as piping of all sizes pervaded the economic development of the post World War II period in the U.S. New standards for municipal building codes were being written, and new standards were adopted to provide for the now dominant use of plastics pipe. In addition, the competitive effect on other materials products, such as steel and copper pipe producers, was such that manufacturers sought to protect their markets by acquiring manufacturers and distributors. This was especially important in oil piping where hundreds of miles of tubular goods are involved.

Plastics pipe's competitive advantage over various metals was the result of many factors, not the least of which was low cost. In addition, plastics pipe offers other advantages to users in that it is lightweight and resistant to varying environmental conditions. It is also relatively easy to install, minimizes solid deposits, has low frictional losses, and has self-insulating characteristics. Its only drawback is its temperature and pressure characteristics where various metal pipes sometimes enjoy an advantage.

Specific among plastics pipe's many applications developed are as follows: water supply and distribution, including water utilities, municipal water treatment plants, chemical feed lines, sludge lines, and water distribution; natural gas distribution; drain, waste, and vent services, where plastic is resistant to chemicals; industrial uses, including food and beverage piping, acid and corrosive drain lines, chemical, electric and communication conduits, water and gas service, and general drainage; and irrigation of farm and ranch systems, including movement of water and gas, fertilizer and insecticide.

In any case, the 1960s and 1970s were boom times for plastics in general and plastics piping in particular. Approximately 55 companies were engaged in the manufacture of plastics pipe by the mid-1970s. From 1964 to 1970 total sales more than doubled from 150 million pounds to 345 million pounds. In 1967, sales were 320 million pounds valued at $240 million dollars. By 1969, plastics pipe accounted for 1 to 2 percent of the $5 billion per year total pipe market, and was growing at a rate of about 15 percent per year, about two times as fast as the growth of the chemical industry. The $240 million plastic pipe industry in 1967 topped the $500 million mark by the mid-1970s. Steel would lose 5 percent of its market to plastic pipe—over $100 million sales—while copper lost 50 percent, and aluminum lost 20 percent.

CURRENT CONDITIONS

Overall, the plastics products market is expected to decline at a rate of 4 to 5 percent per year through the late-1990s, in real terms, according to U.S. industry projections. Plastics applications in building and construction—a category which includes not only piping, but also conduits and pipe fittings—comprise the second largest category of consumption at 21.1 percent; the largest category is packaging, which has 29.6 percent of total plastics markets. The underground piping market is the largest use segment of plastics pipe—water, drain, waste, vent, sewer and drain, gas, irrigation, conduit and pressure—and remains the largest market for plastics piping not only in the United States but in the world.

Significant recycling advances have been made in the industry but the portion of total plastics recycled remains low compared with total production or consumption. The industry is responding to public pressure to develop environmentally safer products and to advance recycling into all of its product areas. Efforts are underway between the industry and federal, state, and local governments to evaluate the merits of various policies.

While new technologies will further the trend toward the replacement of non-plastics materials with plastics, there is some concern over the feasibility of plastics recycling which may lead some to shift back to older materials such as aluminum, copper, and other metals. From the production side, industry efforts to implement computer-aided design and manufacture (CAD/CAM) is expected to lead to drastic reductions in costs, reductions in turnover time, and decrease some of the environmental concerns by minimizing material waste. These continuing advancements in process technology remain the key factors behind the plastics piping products' success and future growth.

WORK FORCE

Throughout 1990 to 1994, total employment in the plastics pipe industry rose by 22 percent—from 8,484 to 10,944 people. Production worker employment grew 17 percent over the same period, rising from 9,800 in 1990 to 11,800 in 1995. Projections indicate those numbers will remain approximately unchanged at least until 1998.

In 1990, the major occupational categories for the entire plastics products industry were: plastics molding machine operators, who made up 17.8 percent of total employment; assemblers and fabricators who made up 8.6 percent; and packers and packagers, which comprised 4.8 percent. Approximately 8.7 percent of occupations were involved in some type of managerial or supervisory function while 6.2 percent were engaged in some type of clerical, transportation, and accounting/financial tasks. The remainder were engaged in some type of production activity.

The Bureau of Labor Statistics has forecasted that all of these occupational categories are expected to grow by the year 2005, reflecting the projected growth in demand for the industry's products. However, the occupation that made up the bulk of the industry's employment in 1987, plastic molding machine operators, is projected to grow 29.5 percent by 2005, trailing 12 other categories in projected job growth. The percentage of production workers within total employment has drifted downward slowly since 1972—to about 78 percent in the late 1980s from 80 percent in 1972.

The job categories with the largest projected growth ranked by projected percentage growth to 2005 were largely nonproduction jobs: sales and related workers were projected to grow by 69 percent by 2005; industrial production managers have a projected growth of 64.2 percent; industrial machinery mechanics are expected to increase by 50.9 percent; tool & die makers have a projected growth of 44.9 percent. Blue collar worker supervisors; hand packers and packagers; inspectors, testers, and graders; freight, stock, and material movers; and extruding and forming machine operators occupations were forecast to grow by 35.8 percent.

While average hourly earnings of production workers in plastic pipe production rose from $3.27 in 1972 to $9.14 in 1987, the purchasing power of these money wages actually declined by 10 percent over the same period. General payroll per employee, adjusted for inflation, fell from an average of $18,215 to $17,903 over this same period. From 1987 to 1994, average hourly earnings rose by about 13 percent to $10.59, which, in real terms, translated into a decline of almost 9 percent.

In terms of value added per production worker, money wages per hour rose about two-and-one-half times while the value added per hour by these production workers increased over three times, indicating a

shift in income distribution away from wages and toward profits. (When comparing industry figures for plastic piping over time, plastic piping was included as part of **SIC 3079: Miscellaneous Plastics Products** in 1972, and the work force figures were calculated on the 1972 SIC basis.)

FURTHER READING

Chasis, David A. *Plastic Piping Systems.* Industrial Press, Inc., 1988.

Darnay, Arsen J., ed. *Manufacturing USA.* 5th ed. Detroit: Gale Research, 1996.

Dubois, Harry. *Plastics History U.S.A.* Hanover, Massachusetts: Halliday Lithographic Company, 1972.

Penn, W.S. *PVC Technology.* New York: Wiley Interscience, 1972.

Rosato, Dominick V., William K. Fallon, and Donald V. Rosado. *Markets For Plastics.* New York: Van Nostrand, Reinhold Co., 1969.

United Nations Centre on Transnational Corporations, United Nations. *Transnational Corporations in the Plastics Industry.* New York: United Nations, 1990.

U.S. Bureau of the Census. *1995 Annual Survey of Manufactures.* Washington: GPO, 1997.

———*1994 County Business Patterns.* Washington: GPO, 1996.

U.S. Department of Commerce. International Trade Administration. *U.S. Industrial Outlook 1994.* Washington: GPO, 1994.

Walker, Robert, P.E. ''The Early History of PVC Pipe.'' *Uni-Bell PVC Pipe News,* Summer 1990.

—John A. Sarich, updated by Arthur G. Sharp

SIC 3085

PLASTICS BOTTLES

Included in this category are establishments primarily engaged in manufacturing plastics bottles.

INDUSTRY SNAPSHOT

In 1995 U.S. producers shipped $6.3 billion worth of plastic bottles, a 70 percent increase over the 1990 level of $3.7 billion. Imports into the United States reached $162 million in 1995, while exports totaled $220 million. In the mid-1990s, there were 405 establishments in the industry, an increase of 42 percent since 1990, when there were 284 establishments.

ORGANIZATION AND STRUCTURE

This industry is dependent on nine separate plastic bottle markets: soft drink, milk, medicinal, household chemical, toiletry and cosmetic, automobile and marine, juice and water, food (excluding milk), and industrial. All of these markets had moderate and steady growth over the last ten years. The use of plastic in bottles has been steadily replacing the use of aluminum and glass because of its convenience and cost effectiveness.

BACKGROUND AND DEVELOPMENT

In 1990, plastic bottles comprised 22.7 percent of the container market by material shipments, metal cans were 59.1 percent, and glass containers were 18.2 percent. A report by the Freedonia Group entitled "Beverages & Containers: Markets & Materials" claimed that metal will remain the dominant packaging material for beverages, but plastic will continue to gain market share at the expense of glass throughout the 1990s.

At the heart of this growing industry are the suppliers of plastic resins, which, for the majority of plastic bottles, are one of three types—polyethylene terephthalate (PET), high density polyethylene (HDPE), and vinyl.

Bottle demand for PET in the United States was 1.3 billion pounds in 1992, about 70 percent of the total PET market. The largest market for PET is carbonated soft drink containers at 910 million pounds. Single serving carbonated soft drink containers in 12, 16, and 20 ounce sizes are now a 225 million pound market that is growing 25 percent annually.

PET resin producers supply the bulk ingredient to make plastic bottles, and their production in 1991 capacity rose to only 68,000 tons, while demand shot up to 206,000 tons. By 1992 demand had increased to 219,000 tons, while new capacity more than doubled, reaching 140,000 tons. Plants worldwide should be reaching capacities of upwards of 93 percent. Eastman Company expanded domestic resin production by 300 million pounds in 1993, and 1994, and 250 million pounds in 1995. In early 1992, PET resin stood at 65-67 cents per pound and fell at the end of 1992 to 62-64 cents per pound. Prices should rise with increased demand for PET resin. Technology Forecasts of Westport, Connecticut, projects an 8 percent annual growth rate in PET resin use through 1997.

In 1992, PET resin demand from the soft drink industry topped 900 million pounds, and by 1997 it could approach to 1.4 billion pounds. With PET resin bringing higher prices and worldwide demand exceed-ing supply, lightweighting of plastic bottles is PET manufacturer's highest priority. Environmental and pricing pressures are prompting PET producers to investigate methods for reducing the weight of the two liter bottle below its current weight of 55 grams. A one-gram reduction of PET from the current container would be a 22 million pound savings to the beverage industry and a cost savings of about $15 million per year. One way to achieve this goal is to make all PET bottles with plastic closure finishes instead of aluminum closures. The removal of basecups is also another potential solution. One-piece PET bottles in the United States could then fall to 50.5 grams. In Europe, PET producers are marketing a one-way PET bottle that weighs between 48 and 49 grams.

The recycled version of HDPE, the second type of plastic resin, had previously cost more than its virgin plastic, and many packagers have been using recycled HDPE to satisfy environmental concerns. But in 1994, there were indications that the gap between these plastics has significantly narrowed or, in some cases, disappeared. Important variables between these markets are the availability of high quality, well-sorted HDPE and the degree to which collection is subsidized by municipalities. As state lawmakers and major retailers insist on recycled content packaging, demand will rise for this resin.

Vinyl, the third type of plastic resin, is used mostly for packaging household chemicals, liquid soap, shampoo, edible oils, and bottled water. In Europe, vinyl is the leading packaging material for bottled water, and 36 percent of U.S. and Canadian water bottlers reported that they used one or more sizes. For clean, one-gallon water bottles, vinyl is the leading material. The amount of vinyl bottles produced annually was expected to grow to 270 million by the late 1990s.

CURRENT CONDITIONS

According to the Freedonia Group report, blow molded bottles likely will present the greatest opportunities for growth, particularly in small contoured carbonated soft drink bottles and hot-fill bottles, where the material has cost and performance advantages over metal and glass. While the strongest growth in volume terms will occur in the United States, the polyethylene terephthalate (PET) market will grow at a faster pace in Canada and Mexico. An expected growth rate of 18 percent in Mexico is attributed to the country's status as the second largest per capita consumer of soft drinks, poor tap water quality, hot climate, and PET advantages over glass.

The market research firm SRI International of Menlo Park, California, projects U.S. consumption of recycled PET will increase 12 percent annually through the late 1990s, due mostly to the success of curbside collection efforts. There are now 3,100 community programs in the United States that accept PET in their recycling bins, up from 575 in 1990. Approximately 3.7 billion PET bottles were recycled in 1992. The major soft drink manufacturers now use PET bottles that contain a percentage of recycled resin. Some 19 percent of all plastic bottles were recycled in 1992, led by the 41.5 percent recycling rate of soft drink bottles. In 1991, 14 percent of all plastic bottles were recycled, also led by the 36 percent recycling rate of soft drink bottles.

INDUSTRY LEADERS

In 1995, Crown, Cork, and Seal of Philadelphia, Pennsylvania, was the industry leader with 31.5 percent market share. Other major players include Johnson Controls Inc., Coca-Cola Co-ops, and Continental PET Technologies, which had 19.4, 14.6, and 9.7 percent of market share respectively. Crown, Cork, and Seal had 1996 sales of $5.05 billion; Johnson Controls, $8.3 billion.

WORK FORCE

In 1995, 31,900 employees worked for an estimated 430 companies in the plastic bottle industry, up 21 percent from 25,100 employees in 1987. In 1995 27,500 were production workers. Average wages in 1995 were $11.12 per hour, up 21 percent from the $8.74 per hour wage in 1987. Payroll in 1995 reached $666.9 million, up 25 percent from the level in 1987. In 1995, production hours reached 64.9 million, up 20 percent from 52.1 million production hours in 1990.

California is the largest plastic bottle manufacturing state in the United States, with 36 companies shipping more than $340 million worth of bottles. It accounts for 12 percent of industry shipments and employs approximately 3,000 workers. Other states in the top five are Ohio, with 26 companies shipping $319 million and employing 3,200; New Jersey, with 23 companies shipping $282 million and employing 2,700; Texas, with 22 companies shipping $216 million and employing 1,500; and Illinois, with 22 companies shipping $200 million and employing 2,100. The bulk of the nation's plastic bottles come from the Great Lakes region, which represents about 40 percent of total industry shipments.

AMERICA AND THE WORLD

Outside the United States, PET containers are battling glass for market share in the refillable-container soft drink market, especially in Europe where refillable PET is being driven by regulations and in Latin America where it is cost effective to use. Beverage containers account for 80 percent of the PET used in Europe, and just 4 percent was recycled in 1992. A Pan-European association called Petcore, which was formed by PET resin producers and bottle converters, is aiming to reach a recycling target of at least 15 percent, which would be in line with the European Packaging and Packaging Waste Directives. Petcore will work with public sector groups and industry to increase the recycling of blow-moulded PET containers up to five liters in size. Petcore wants to achieve a recycling target of 30 percent. Petcore's U.S. counterpart, NAPCORE, reached a 27 percent recycling level in 1992. "Reaching 15 percent in five years will be tough. The problem is not recycling capacity, but getting the PET back from the customer," states Dr. Vince Matthews, coordinator of Petcore.

Since 1991, German law has required manufacturers, distributors, and retailers to take back product packaging. Though 64 percent of all plastics were to be recycled by the mid-1990s, only 4 percent is recycled now in Germany, but an industry consortium called Duales System Deutschland (DSD) wants to improve that level. All costs of DSD systems are internalized and passed along to the consumer, and the estimated yearly per capita cost is $33. By weight, nearly 80 percent of the food and beverage container market in Germany is glass, approximately 18 percent is metal, and 2 percent is plastic. The program cost $6 billion to start and $2.6 billion annually, and it has come under criticism from German citizens. A comparable program in the United States could cost $18 billion annually.

RESEARCH AND TECHNOLOGY

Two University of Pittsburgh scientists are designing plastic that can be made without toxic by-products and recycled with help from an enzyme. If the technology can be developed in an economically feasible manner, it could aid in efforts to recycle plastic bottles. Drs. Alan Russell and Eric Beckman are working on developing "bioplastic"—instead of being made with organic solvents it is made with carbon dioxide. Carbon dioxide fluid can chemically sort out mixed batches of melted plastic, enabling recyclers to shred plastic and dump the pieces into a high pressure tank of supercritical carbon dioxide. The same type of plastic, usually the lightest, floats to the top of the tank.

Several companies are considering licensing the technology.

To aid in the recycling of plastic bottles, plastic labels are being widely produced in the same polymer type as the plastic bottle, and closures are also being made increasingly compatible. The packaging market for stretch blow-molded plastic bottles may also expand. Favorable market potential is attributed to a new thermoplastic polyester resin and a number of new process technologies.

FURTHER READING

"Crystallized Neck Thread Finish Stymies Heat Distortion: Makes Hot-Filled PET Alluring to More Beverage Processors." *Food Processing,* December 1992.

Humer, Caroline. "Shining Star: Polyethylene Terephthalate Use Increases in Plastic Container Industry." *Chemical Marketing Reporter,* 15 February 1993.

Jabbonsky, Larry. "Some Pretty Diverse Units; Beverage Packaging Industry Statistics." *Beverage World,* June 1993.

Lazich, Robert S., ed. *Market Share Reporter.* Detroit: Gale Research, 1997.

Predicasts Basebook. Cleveland, Ohio: Predicasts.

Prince, Greg. "Recycling from A to Z: An Alphabetic Guide to Recycling Issues." *Beverage World,* June 1993.

Pringle, David. "Petcore to Scan Europe for Waste PET Containers: Pan-European Association Formed by Polyethylene Terephthalate Resin Producers and Bottle Converters." *Packaging Week,* 6 January 1994.

"Recycled/Virgin Cost Gap Shrinks for HDPE Bottles." *Packaging,* January 1994.

Reiter, Jeff. "Recycling Bottleneck: Promoting High Density Polythylene Bottle Recycling." *Dairy Foods Magazine,* July 1992.

Rigdon, Joan. "Technology—In the Lab: Scientists Design Greener Plastic for Recycling by Using Enzymes." *Wall Street Journal,* 26 August 1993.

Sfiligoj, Eric. "Answering the Critics, Recyclable Polyethylene Terephthalate Beverage Containers Are Replacing Glass Bottles." *Beverage World,* June 1992.

Stack, Gifford. "Green Dot Not for U.S.: Germany's Packaging Law Doesn't Make Sense Here." *Beverage Industry,* September 1993.

—William A. Bennett, updated by Arthur G. Sharp

SIC 3086

PLASTICS FOAM PRODUCTS

This industry covers establishments primarily engaged in manufacturing plastics foam products.

INDUSTRY SNAPSHOT

Approximately 1,300 establishments were engaged in the manufacture of plastics foam products in 1996. In the mid-1990s, the industry manufactured products estimated at $10.1 million dollars. This figure remained in line with a generally upward production trend in the industry since 1987. Total value of shipments increased by over 31 percent from 1987 to 1993, higher than the increase in plastics products in general, which grew at a 17 percent rate over the same period. By 1996, the value of shipments was estimated to have increased another 15 percent to $11.8 billion.

This upward trend in plastics foam products production was due to several economic forces and to new applications for foam products. Consumer spending, especially for durable goods, construction, and health care products, which together make up the bulk of product demand, is expected to grow.

ORGANIZATION AND STRUCTURE

In 1996, approximately 1,300 establishments were engaged in the production of plastic foam products. These businesses employed approximately 49 employees per establishment, of which 34 were production workers. The average value added per production worker was $72,991, a small figure compared to an average of $93,930 calculated for the average of all U.S. manufacturing industries.

The largest number of plastic foam products establishments were located in the east north central region, followed by the middle Atlantic region and the Pacific region. However, when ranked by the number of establishments per state, California was first with 171, followed by Texas with 83, North Carolina with 70, Ohio with 62, Pennsylvania with 60, and Michigan with 59. It was estimated that the largest five companies producing plastic foam products accounted for approximately $2.6 billion, or more than 59 percent of the entire industry's sales. In descending order of market share, the dominant companies in the plastics foam products industry were: Lamson and Sessions Company's Home Products Division, with approximately 18.3 percent of the market; PMC Inc., with about 22 percent of the market; Dart Container Corporation, with 12.3 percent; E.R. Carpenter Company Inc., with 11.1 percent; Sealed Air Corporation, with 9.2 percent; and Amoco Foam Products Company, with 4.5 percent. Of the top five companies, only Sealed Air Corporation was publicly traded; the vast majority of the top 100 companies were privately held.

The industry's output was divided among various product classes as follows: furniture and furnishings plastics foam products (including carpet underlay; carpet and rug cushions; and formed and slab stock for pillows, seating, and cushioning), led with 25.25 percent of the industry's total output; consumer and institutional plastics foam products (including cups, plates and bowls, cooler chests, and trays) followed with 18.97 percent; transportation plastics foam products and packaging plastics foam products each comprised approximately 15 percent of the output. Building and construction foam products and other plastics foam products not elsewhere classified accounted for the remaining 26 percent. The principal industries responsible for the purchase of plastics foam products were hospitals, buying 5.6 percent of sector output; and electronic components makers, buying 5.2 percent. Personal consumption accounted for 4.3 percent.

BACKGROUND AND DEVELOPMENT

Plastics foams, sometimes called expandable plastics, are versatile materials that were first used in the post-World War II plastics boom. Plastic foam products are used both as original and replacement materials in industries. Foam products emerge out of a unique chemical process. Foamed plastic is an expanded material with a distinct cellular structure that can be either rigid or flexible. Rigid foam consists of spherical, hollow spheres attached together, while flexible foam has its cells connected, thus giving it a spongy structure. Polystyrene and polyurethanes are used for rigid foams and vinyls and cellulose acetate. Linear polyurethanes have been traditionally used in flexible foams. By 1969, flexible urethane dominated the market with polystyrene running second, rigid urethane third, and polyvinyl chloride fourth.

Following World War II, plastics foam consumption in the United States grew tremendously, increasing more than ten-fold from 1955 to 1970. By 1967, total consumption of plastics foam products rose to 700 million pounds or $60 million, and by 1970, output weight was one billion pounds. It took only five years for this figure to double. More than 700 companies in the 1970s were in some way involved in the production of plastics foams, including most major chemical companies, rubber and tire companies, textile mills, and drug companies.

By the end of the 1960s, the threat of oversupply prompted the industry to step up research and development to improve materials and develop new market outlets, notably tires, sporting goods, advanced military equipment, and highway safety barriers. Rigid urethane and polystyrene were used for industrial purposes such as industrial walls and cold storage insula-

tion. The foams came in many forms—slabs, logs, sheets, rods, tubes, and particles.

In general, plastics are manufactured as follows: plastic materials (monomers) are chemically altered to produce more complex materials called polymers, which are then mixed with certain materials to impart characteristics such as durability, flexibility, and chemical resistance. Subsequent manufacturing processes produce final products such as the rigid and flexible foam used in consumer durable goods, buildings, and refrigerated transport. Foam production processes involve a variety of methods, and the output takes the form of slabs, blocks, boards, sheets, molded shapes, and extruded insulation. Foam can also be produced onsite for building insulation and cushioning applications. Most grades of foam are produced by extrusion and injection molding. More than half of foamed plastic is polyurethane, and the rest consists of expandable polystyrene and vinyl, phenolic, epoxy, urea, and silicone.

The post-World War II boom in plastics foam products was intertwined with the growth in general plastics manufacturing, growth stemming from a burgeoning U.S. consumer base and from the substitution of plastics for materials such as copper, aluminum, and steel. Plastic products seriously challenged metals and alloys in the aerospace, transportation, electricity, and engineering industries. In general, the plastics industry is the single most important "downstream" industry in the petrochemicals value-added chain. Plastics are produced by various chemical processes that allow forming end-products through heating, milling, or extrusion. Plastics soften but do not melt when heated, thereby allowing them to change shape without losing cohesion. Before the 1930s, industrial products were largely based on coal as the basic chemical feed stock. The surge in production and consumption of plastic was directly related to the availability of petroleum—plastic's main chemical feedstock. The petroleum and plastics industry are linked; petrochemicals provide the basis for mass production of plastics and, conversely, plastics provide petroleum with their main downstream market.

Total plastics foam production tripled from 1970 to 1980. Increased production was fueled during this period by skyrocketing demand for consumer goods such as furniture cushioning, mattresses, bedding, and other items that use mostly urethane foams. Rigid foam found growing use in buildings, refrigerated transports, household refrigerators and freezers, dehumidifiers, dishwashers, packaging, and marine salvage.

CURRENT CONDITIONS

The main concern of industry leaders is, of course, market growth and expansion. Of particular interest are consumer durable goods, construction, and health care, which make up a large portion of demand for the industry's products. The early 1990s upturn in consumer spending, especially for durables such as appliances, (which use large quantities of rigid foam and adhesives) buoyed the market for plastic foams; construction, also rigid foam user, underwent similar growth.

The plastics industry faces challenges due to environmental damage caused by its use of certain processes and chemicals. The industry must comply with federal and worldwide environmental rules aimed at banning use of chlorofluorocarbons (CFCs), which are said to deplete the ozone layer. The rules have led to a competitive race to develop replacements for CFCs. In addition, political pressure is forcing companies to develop recycling processes; as of the early 1990s, only a small portion of plastic in general was recyclable.

The industry has devoted significant resources to developing alternatives to CFCs. They have been very successful in the flexible foam sector, but less progress has been made by rigid foam makers. For rigid foams, some firms are developing new formulations that use hydrochlorofluorocarbons (HCFCs), which have a lower ozone depletion potential than CFCs, while retaining some of CFCs' desirable properties. Flexible foams are also being reformulated. New machinery has been developed, tailored to the low boiling point agents that are gradually replacing CFCs.

Recycling efforts are also underway. For example, construction board has been made from rigid foam scrap and carpet pad has been produced from auto seating scrap. Though most of the focus in the recycling movement has been on bottles and foamed polystyrene containers, the push is on for polyurethane recycling. The plastics foam products industry and federal, state, and local governments are evaluating the merits of various recycling policies.

Finally, in addition to its recycling efforts, firms in the industry hope to improve the aesthetic of urethane foams, particularly in automobiles. For example, technology is being developed that would reduce foam scorching at high temperatures. And, in another effort, some are attempting to eliminate fogging that occurs on the insides of car windows when sunlight heats up plastics in passenger compartments.

Buoyed by continued growth and innovation, the plastics foam industry seems strong enough to meet the challenge of environmental regulation.

WORK FORCE

Over the period covering 1991 to 1994, total employment in the plastics products industry overall rose by 13 percent. Production worker employment followed roughly the same trend, rising from 47,800 to 55,800 in 1996. The increase is expected to maintain moderate growth until at least 1998.

In 1995, the major occupational categories for the plastics products industry (these data relate to the 3-digit Industry Group 308 for miscellaneous plastics products rather than the specific 4-digit SIC for plastics foam products) were: plastic molding machine operators, who made up 17.8 percent of total employment; assemblers and fabricators, who made up 8.6 percent; and packers and packagers, who comprised 4.8 percent. Approximately 20 percent of industry employees were engaged in some type of managerial or supervisory function or clerical, transportation, and accounting/financial tasks. The remaining employees were engaged in production activity.

The U.S. Bureau of Labor Statistics has forecast that all these occupational categories will grow by the year 2005, reflecting the growth in demand for this industry's products. The occupation making up the bulk of the industry's employment, plastic molding machine operators, should grow 29.5 percent to the year 2005, trailing 12 other industry categories in projected growth.

The industry job categories with the largest projected growth to 2005 were largely non-production jobs: sales and related workers, projected to grow by 69 percent; industrial production managers, 64.2 percent; industrial machinery mechanics, 50.9 percent; and tool & die makers, 44.9 percent. Categories uniformly forecast to grow by 35.8 percent were: blue collar worker supervisors; hand packers and packagers, inspectors, testers and graders; freight, stock, and material movers; and extruding and forming machine operators.

Concerning the industry's income distribution, while average hourly earnings of production workers in plastic products production rose from $3.27 in 1972 to $8.43 in 1987, the purchasing power of these wages actually declined by 10 percent. General payroll per employee, adjusted for inflation, fell from an average of $18,215 to $17,903. From 1987 to 1996, average hourly earnings rose by about 28 percent to $11.62. From 1972 to 1987, in terms of value added per production worker, wages per hour rose about two and one half times, while the value added per hour by these production workers rose by over three times, a shift in income distribution away from wages and toward profits.

FURTHER READING

Darnay, Arsen J. *Manufacturing USA.* 5th ed. Detroit: Gale Research, 1996.

Dubois, Harry. *Plastics History U.S.A.* Hanover, MA: Halliday Lithographic Company, 1972.

Graff, Gordon. "Improving Economics and Replacing CFCs Dominate Polyurethanes." *Modern Plastics,* December 1992.

Rosato, Dominick V., William K. Fallon, and Donald V. Rosado. *Markets for Plastics.* New York: Van Nostrand, Reinhold Co., 1969.

United Nations Centre on Transnational Corporations, United Nations. *Transnational Corporations in the Plastics Industry.* New York: United Nations, 1990.

U.S. Department of Commerce. *U.S. Industrial Outlook 1994.* Washington: GPO, 1994.

—John A. Sarich, updated by Arthur G. Sharp

SIC 3087

CUSTOM COMPOUNDING OF PURCHASED PLASTICS RESINS

This category covers establishments primarily engaged in custom compounding of purchased plastics resins. For more information related to this industry, see the **SIC 2821: Plastic Materials, Synthetic Resins, and Nonvulcanizable Elastomers.**

Custom compounding companies purchase plastic resins from plastic manufacturers. They alter and manipulate the resins to form new compounds, which they usually sell to companies making plastic products. They contribute to the plastic manufacturing process by upgrading the quality and performance of resins, improving the efficiency of the compounding process, and developing entirely new plastic substances. Custom compounding emerged as a separate industry during the 1980s and is credited with increasing the breadth of the U.S. plastics business during that decade. About one-third of all U.S. polymer production undergoes some sort of compounding.

INDUSTRY SNAPSHOT

There were 644 establishments in the industry in the mid-1990s, an increase of 69 percent since 1990. Industry shipments totaled $6.0 billion in 1995, an increase of 87 percent over 1990, when shipments totaled $3.2 billion. There were 25,531 employees in the industry in the mid-1990s, an increase of 41 percent since 1990.

ORGANIZATION AND STRUCTURE

Plastics are extremely long polymers, or long-chain molecules, which are shaped and molded under heat and pressure to form a resin. Resins typically take the form of pellets, flakes, powder, granules, or liquid. Although many resin manufacturers process their own resins and even make plastic products, they often sell resins to companies that make custom compounds. Custom compounders alter the physical properties of the resins they purchase by: mixing or melt-state blending several resins together; introducing additives, or adding fillers and reinforcements. An almost infinite number of compounds, each with varying grades and performance characteristics, can be created.

Several categories of additives are used to make compounds. Plasticizers, the most common additives, are chemicals that increase a resin's flexibility. Similarly, impact modifiers increase stress resistance. Plasticizers and impact modifiers are used, for example, to increase the resilience of plastic automobile body panels or to make polyvinyl chloride (PVC) resins used in construction materials. Various stabilizers and antioxidants are used to retard the oxidation and breakdown of resins that results from exposure to heat, light, air, and moisture. Heat stabilizers, for instance, help resins to retain their physical structure during processing. Flame retardants are added to reduce inflammability, and colorants are used to change a resin's hue.

Fillers and reinforcements are used to add texture, strength, and other characteristics to resins without changing their polymer structure. Examples of fillers are cotton and asbestos flocks, glass fibers, chopped monofilaments, carbon fibers, hollow glass spheres, metal powder, and carbon. Glass fiber, which is integrated as whole or chopped mat, and carbon fiber have traditionally accounted for the majority of filler and reinforcement material used in the plastics industry.

Plastic compounding companies work with and create four general grades of resins and compounds. Commodity resins, which receive little attention in this industry, are low-tech plastics made with standardized formulas. Intermediate resins are slightly more advanced. Engineering resins exhibit higher performance characteristics. Advanced resin compounds, the most expensive class, are those most able to withstand exposure to heat, weight, impact, acids, and other forces. They are typically used for applications in aerospace, microelectronics, and other high-tech industries.

BACKGROUND AND DEVELOPMENT

The first plastic, a natural material called Keratin, was developed in the early 1700s. Parkesine, the first synthetic plastic, was invented in 1862 by Englishmen Alexander Parkes; but, it was American John Wyatt who recognized the important plasticizing effect of the Parkesine production process. Wyatt renamed the substance Celluloid in 1870 and is recognized as the founder of modern day plastic making in the United States.

The use of plastics increased rapidly during the early 1900s as new processing techniques, such as molding, evolved. Compounding occurred, but in relatively simple ways. Resins were combined with paints and varnishes, for example, to increase their durability. Not until World War II were more advanced compounding processes used on a broad scale—to make items such as airplane gun turret covers and lightweight field equipment. Huge advances in the chemical additives industry during the 1950s through the 1970s created a strong demand for new compounds with specific characteristics. As compounders learned to make resins more flexible, durable, attractive, and flame retardant, the need for plastics compounds grew. By the early 1980s, the plastics industry was shipping $15 billion worth of resins, about 30 percent of which were compounded by resin manufacturers or plastic goods producers.

During the 1980s, the U.S. plastics industry began to shift its focus from commodity-like resins and compounds to higher grade products that could be used to replace steel, glass, and other natural, more expensive materials. The development of high-tech additives and alloys allowed U.S. producers to retain their global industry lead in spite of fierce foreign competition from low cost manufacturers. As the need for advanced, efficient compounding processes expanded, custom compounding firms proliferated.

By 1987, custom compounders were processing about 8.5 billion pounds of resins annually and grossing $2.5 billion. Despite a late 1980s recession, production volume jumped to 12.5 billion pounds by 1990, and industry revenues climbed to $5.080.1 billion by 1993, reflecting average annual sales growth of 8 percent between 1987 and 1993. As plastics consumers increasingly sought the expertise and efficiency of custom compounding companies, revenues swelled at a rate of approximately 7 to 10 percent annually during the early 1990s.

CURRENT CONDITIONS

Two dominant trends in the custom compounding industry in the early 1990s included increased competition and a growing demand for specialty and high-tech compounds. For example, fast growing product segments included electrically conductive plastic compounds, specialty color-concentrates, and liquid-crystal polymers. Although most custom compounding companies continued to realize revenue and profit gains in the early 1990s, greater competition was diminishing overall profit growth. Indeed, compounding firms in Taiwan, Singapore, Indonesia, and other low-cost manufacturing countries were vying for U.S. export market share.

Besides greater foreign competition, several major U.S. resin suppliers were entering the custom compounding arena by providing small orders of highly tailored materials. To combat new competition and to reduce costs associated with research, development, and environmental regulations, many custom compounders were acquiring or merging with their competitors. In addition, some commodity resin producers were acquiring custom compounding firms as a means of diversifying their operations.

Despite new competition, compounding revenues were forecast to grow at an annual rate of about 9 percent through the mid-1990s, and some niche market segments were expected to expand 20 percent or more annually. Continued growth in this market is expected to be driven by an ongoing trend toward highly differentiated resins and new plastic goods manufacturing methods. Importantly, new plastic assembly and molding techniques will continue to generate a market for compatible compounds. Likewise, a growing need for environmentally friendly production processes and biodegradable compounds will boost industry activity.

INDUSTRY LEADERS

Leading companies in the industry in 1996 include A. Schulman, Inc., Dexter Electronic Materials, and Goldmark Plastic Compounds, Inc. A. Schulman produces plastic compounds and resins and had sales of $1.03 billion; Dexter Electronic Materials, which manufactures epoxy and urethane compounds, had sales totalling $150 million; and Goldmark, which produces plastic resin compounds, had sales of $50 million.

RESEARCH AND TECHNOLOGY

A technological focal point in the mid-1990s was the development of techniques that allowed resin processors to create compounds and alloys while extruding plastic into molds. By melting and mixing compounds during the molding process, processors were able to eliminate problems caused by heating resins twice. Such compound/molding techniques were already resulting in higher performance and less expensive plastic products by the early 1990s. Specifically, new grades of materials created using these new compounding techniques were capable of making products with thinner walls, greater product uniformity, and more even molecular distribution—improvements that allowed for increased use of plastics in automobiles and packaging industries, for example.

Significant expenditures were also being directed toward the development of new environmentally safe compounds. Companies were striving to meet new chlorofluorocarbon (CFC) emission regulations by developing compounds that would not require hazardous manufacturing processes. Similarly, new additives and compounds were under development in the mid-1990s that would accelerate the natural breakdown of plastics products and reduce landfill waste. Although technologies like weak-link and bacterial polymers showed promise, extremely high production costs made them commercially impractical for most purposes in 1994.

FURTHER READING

Ainsworth, Susan J. "Plastics Additives." *Chemical & Engineering News,* 31 August 1992.

Byrne, Harlan S. "Spartech Corp." *Barron's,* 1 February 1993.

Coombes, Peter. "Compounders Change Shape." *Chemical Week,* 4 April 1990.

Darnay, Arsen J., ed. *Manufacturing USA.* 5th ed. Detroit: Gale Research, 1996.

Kreisher, Keith. "Compounding's Growth Fosters New Machines, Process Technology." *Modern Plastics,* July 1991.

Kreisher, Keith. "Compounding Goes On-Line with Big Payoff to Users." *Modern Plastics,* July 1990.

McCoy, Michael. "Compounds Credited for Plastics Growth." *Chemical Marketing Reporter,* 18 May 1992.

Miller, Bernie. "Molder-Friendly Resins Keep the Dream Alive." *Plastics World,* September 1993.

Modern Plastics Encyclopedia. New York: McGraw-Hill Inc., October 1987.

Smock, Doug. "Health Concerns Spur New Biocide Uses." *Plastics World,* March 1992.

Swain, Robert. "Ban on Cadmium: Is it Logical?" *Plastics World,* November 1993.

U.S. Bureau of the Census. *1994 County Business Patterns.* Washington: GPO, 1996.

———. *1995 Annual Survey of Manufactures.* Washington: GPO, 1997.

U.S. Department of Commerce. International Trade Administration. *U.S. Industrial Outlook 1993.* Washington: GPO, 1993.

Wood, Andrew. "Plastics Compounding: Restructuring Brings a Different Lineup." *Chemical Week,* 12 May 1993.

—Dave Mote, updated by Arthur G. Sharp.

SIC 3088

PLASTICS PLUMBING FIXTURES

This category includes establishments primarily engaged in manufacturing plastics plumbing fixtures. Establishments primarily engaged in assembling plastics plumbing fixture fittings are classified in **SIC 3432: Plumbing Fixture Fittings and Trim.** Establishments primarily engaged in manufacturing plastics plumbing fixture components are classified in **SIC 3089: Plastics Products, Not Elsewhere Classified.** As a result of the 1987 Standard Industrial Classification (SIC) reclassification, information is unavailable for the industry prior to 1987 at this level of aggregation.

INDUSTRY SNAPSHOT

In the 1990s, plastics plumbing products included among other items bathtubs, sinks, and lavatories. The value of industry shipments increased from $709 million in 1987 to an estimated $1.46 billion in 1996. There were about 420 establishments in the industry. Approximately one-third of these establishments had 20 or more employees. Average firm size as measured by the number of production workers per establishment was 15 percent lower than that for the manufacturing sector as a whole.

The industry employed an estimated 14,100 workers in 1996, 10,400 of which were production workers. The industry was relatively capital-intensive, although on average 58 percent lower than the manufacturing sector as a whole, by investment per production worker. Annual hours worked by production workers in the industry were slightly less than those worked in the manufacturing sector at large, and hourly wages were 25 percent lower.

ORGANIZATION AND STRUCTURE

Of the top 30 firms by sales in the plastics plumbing fixtures industry, two-thirds were private independents, the others being exclusively subsidiaries and divisions of larger firms. Only one of the top five firms was a private independent.

Production was concentrated in the relatively recently industrialized states of the south and southwest portions of the United States. The top-ranking states by number of establishments were, highest to lowest, California (with 43), Florida (with 31), Texas (with 29), Indiana (with 16), and Georgia (with 15). Together these 9 states accounted for 32 percent of all establishments and 35 percent of total employment for the industry, with California alone accounting for 15 percent of total employment. The average number of employees per establishment varied widely by state. Colorado, with the highest number of employees per plant, averaged nearly six times as many employees per plant as Florida and Ohio.

The industry is served by the Plumbing Manufacturers Institute, headquartered in Glen Ellyn, Illinois. It was founded in 1956 and had 50 members. The Institute, which organizes semiannual conventions, has committees on codes, government affairs, standards, intra-industry, and statistics.

BACKGROUND AND DEVELOPMENT

The development and use of plumbing fixtures increased rapidly after the introduction of pressurized water supply and sanitary drainage systems in the 1840s. Kitchen sinks and toilets were the first fixtures installed, followed by washtubs and bathtubs. The earliest sinks and tubs were made of wood lined with sheets of metal. Thereafter, cast iron and glazed pottery sinks came into broad use. One significant early improvement in sinks was the built-in overflow.

The 1870s saw the increased popularity of bathing and new techniques of bathtub production. These new tubs were made of enameled cast iron and were mass produced by a New York manufacturer.

The first modern toilet was designed by the Englishman Joseph Bramah in about 1790. Known as a valve closet, this design saw long use in the toilet compartment of railroad cars. The valve closet was followed by the less-expensive pan closet, which was in common use from the 1830s to the 1870s. Also developed in England, the pan closet had a lead bowl with a hole in the bottom sealed by a hinged copper pan. In the 1850s, glazed pottery toilets came into use, and in the 1880s the first all-earthenware toilets were developed in England.

The early plumbing fixtures were primarily of English design. This changed after the 1880s, when the United States became a center of fixture design. Louis Nielsen describes this change and possible causes for it in his book *Standard Plumbing Engineering Design*. After the 1880s, he writes, "developments in plumbing fixture design proceeded independently and at an accelerated pace in the United States. Much of this may be attributed to . . . [U.S. industrial expansion and] the continuous increase in population due to waves of immigration, and the tremendous demand for new homes and buildings to house the swelling numbers in industrial centers all over the country."

Many of the designs and materials developed in the United States around the turn of the century dominated the industry until very recently. Key among these was the development of the washdown toilet, similar in principle to today's toilet. One of the key advantages of this toilet was that it remained sanitary after extended use, thereby rendering earlier toilet designs obsolete. A number of improvements were made to this basic design in the twentieth century. These involved combining the components of the washdown toilet into a single integrated unit, using siphon jets to strengthen the flush, and reducing noise of operation.

With regard to materials, one of the key developments around the turn of the century was glazed vitreous chinaware. With its smooth impervious surface, vitreous chinaware was the dominant material for many plumbing fixtures, until the rapid growth in the use of plastic fixtures in recent years. Introduced by plumbing fixture manufacturers in 1952, plastics came to be widely used for toilets, bathtubs, whirlpool baths, shower stalls, utility and laundry sinks, and sink-washtray combinations in bathrooms.

The creation of industry-wide standards was important to the development of the industry. Nationwide standards first appeared just after World War I. Contemporary standards were established by the American National Standards Institute's Committee A112. These standards address both design and materials suitability. Regarding the general quality of fixtures, standards require that fixtures "shall have smooth impervious surfaces, shall be durable for the uses intended, and shall be free from defects and concealed fouling surfaces." The regulations also detailed standard dimensions and other specifications for fixtures.

CURRENT CONDITIONS

Industry conditions suggest future growth. The overall trend in shipments was strongly upward from 1987 to 1996, increasing by 49 percent in real terms over the period, with 1996 a peak year. Capital investments increased even more rapidly, with $15 million invested in 1987, $19 million in 1988, $69 million in 1989, $110 million in 1990, and $91 million in 1991. There was a sharp drop-off in 1992 to $31 million, after which investments started rising again to $31.2 million in 1993 and $57 million in 1994. The value of imports of plastics plumbing fixtures increased from $24 million in 1989 to an estimated $59 million in 1996, while the value of exports increased from $19 million to $40 million for these same years.

Employment of production workers declined overall from 1988 to 1993, increased in 1994, and declined again in 1995. The U.S. Bureau of Labor Statistics made employment forecasts at the general industry level for 30 occupational categories. For the period from 1990 to 2005, employment was projected to increase in all 30 occupations, with double-digit increases in 26 occupations. These projections were at odds with early 1990s employment patterns in the plastics plumbing fixtures industry, which however, made up only one percent of total employment at this general industry level in the 1990s.

Plumbing fixtures are primarily made of three materials and are classified into three different industries accordingly. In addition to the plastics plumbing fixtures industry are **SIC 3261: Vitreous Plumbing Fixtures** and **SIC 3431: Metal Plumbing Fixtures**. The primary demand for plumbing fixtures results from new construction. New construction slumped after the late 1980s and picked up again after 1992, and the fortunes of the plumbing fixtures industries followed accordingly. Recent increases in the number of bathrooms in new housing benefited the industry. From the early 1980s to the early 1990s, the number of newly built single occupancy homes with two and one-half or more baths doubled to 44 percent.

The use of plastic plumbing fixtures grew at the expense of the vitreous and metal plumbing fixtures industries. While from 1987 to 1994 the real value of shipments suffered overall declines of 8 percent for the metal plumbing fixtures industry and 15 percent for the vitreous plumbing fixtures industry the real value of shipments of plastic plumbing fixtures increased by 52 percent over these same years.

INDUSTRY LEADERS

The top five firms in the industry in the mid-1990s were Tomkins Industries Inc.-Lasco Products Group of Anaheim, California; Bristol Corporation of Bristol, Indiana; Aqua Glass Corporation of Adamsville, Tennessee; Hancor Company of Findlay, Ohio; and the Universal-Rundle Corporation Fiberglass Division of New Castle, Pennsylvania. Together these firms ac-

counted for about 50 percent of total sales and over 70 percent of total employment for the industry.

Tomkins Industries Inc.-Lasco Products Group was founded in 1947 and had $160 million in sales and 1,200 employees in the mid-1990s. The 13th largest producer in the industry, Lasco Bath Fixtures of Cordele, Georgia, was a division of the Lasco Products Group. The firm's immediate parent was Tomkins Industries Inc. of Dayton, Ohio, a diversified company with 16 manufacturing operations. Ultimate ownership of the firm was held by Tomkins PLC of the United Kingdom, which reported total sales of $5.4 billion in 1996.

The Aqua Glass Corporation was founded in 1969 and had $135 million in sales and 1,200 employees in 1995. The firm became a wholly owned subsidiary of the publicly held Masco Corporation in 1984. Aqua Glass manufactured acrylic bathtubs, showers, and whirlpools. The firm began marketing its products on the west coast in the early 1990s, and in 1993 announced the opening of its first west coast office in Klamath Falls, Oregon. The expanded facilities were to include manufacturing and warehousing operations and were expected to employ 300 persons by 1996.

The Bristol Corporation was founded in 1947 and had $110 million in sales and 500 employees in 1995. The firm was a subsidiary of the privately held Bristol Holding Corporation, also of Bristol, Indiana.

The Hancor Company was a private firm founded in 1902 with $54 million in sales and 600 employees in 1995. Hancor was originally a producer of clay drainage tiles. The firm had 14 plants in the early 1990s and announced plans to substantially expand its manufacturing facilities throughout the decade.

RESEARCH AND TECHNOLOGY

The key areas of industry development concerned water conservation and accommodation of the disabled and elderly. Conventional fixtures were wasteful of water, with waste rates of 70 percent for conventional toilets and 50 percent for conventional showers. The *U.S Industrial Outlook* for 1994 described the development of water-conserving fixtures as an emerging trend in the market because fixtures and fittings is the increasing popularity of products that use substantially less water. Industry standards mandating their use in new installations were scheduled throughout the 1990s. Among these regulations was the National Plumbing Products Efficiency Act of 1991.

Although water conservation fixtures typically cost up to 30 to 50 percent more than conventional fixtures, they sold well nationwide, but particularly in drought-afflicted California. In 1992 Toto Niki USA introduced a tankless computerized toilet that not only conserved water but flushed quietly. The industry standard for faucets was for flows of 2.5 to 2.7 gallons per minute in the early 1990s. New York state had the nation's strictest regulations regarding faucet flow in the 1990s, and 90 percent of bath faucets produced met these standards. Yet manufacturers expected to see new regulations that would lower this standard to as low as 2 gallons per minute.

Industry manufacturers, prompted by the Americans with Disabilities Act of 1990, accelerated the design and production of fixtures to accommodate the disabled. The Act defines disability broadly, such that some 43 million Americans fall within the definition, and the Act requires owners and tenants of buildings defined as 'public accommodations' to provide sinks, toilets, and drinking fountains that are accessible to those with disabilities.

FURTHER READING

"Accessibility Poses New Challenges to Plumbing Design." *Consulting Specifying Engineer,* February 1993.

Breger, Bill. "Pipe Maker Hancor a Long Way from its Clay Foundation," *Plastics News,* 2 March 1992.

———. "Hancor Inc. Building 15th HDPE Pipe Plant." *Plastic News,* 6 September 1993.

"Computerized Toilet Is Silent, Tankless." *Design News,* 21 December 1992.

Darnay, Arsen J., ed. *Manufacturing USA.* (5th ed.). Detroit: Gale Research, 1996.

"Elderly a Growing Category for Dealers." *National Home Center News,* 10 August 1992.

Encyclopedia of Associations. Detroit: Gale Research, 1996.

"Engineers at the Bar." *Consulting Specifying Engineer,* August 1992.

"Hancor Adds Lines at Four Facilities." *Plastic News,* 28 June 1993.

"Klamath Falls Attracts Aqua Glass Corporation." *Plants, Sites and Parks,* January 1993.

"Make Room for Water-Savers." *Hardware Age,* April 1992.

"Making it Easier to Soak the Elderly." *Wall Street Journal,* 17 January 1992.

Moody's Industrial Manual. New York: Moody's Investors Service Inc., 1993.

Moody's International Manual. New York: Moody's Investors Service Inc., 1993.

Nielsen, Louis S. *Standard Plumbing Engineering Design.* 2nd Edition. New York: McGraw-Hill Book Co., 1982.

Ruderman, Gary S. "Consumer Backlash to Flood Mandate for Low-Flow Faucets." *National Home Center News,* 12 October 1992.

Standard and Poor's Register of Corporations, Directors and Executives, Vol. I. New York: Standard and Poor's, 1994.

U.S. Census Bureau. *Annual Survey of Manufactures,* Washington: GPO, 1991.

U.S. Department of Commerce, *U.S. Industrial Outlook.* Washington: GPO, 1994.

Ward's Business Directory of U.S. Private and Public Companies. Detroit: Gale Research, 1996.

—David Kucera, updated by Arthur G. Sharp

SIC 3089

PLASTICS PRODUCTS, NOT ELSEWHERE CLASSIFIED

This category covers establishments primarily engaged in manufacturing plastics products not classified elsewhere. Establishments primarily engaged in manufacturing artificial leather are classified in **SIC 2295: Coated Fabrics, Not Rubberized.**

Companies in this industry manufacture a multitude of items, ranging from clothespins and air mattresses to shoe soles and septic tanks. This industry accounted for approximately 60 percent of all plastics products sales in the early 1990s. For more information about manufacturing processes and the history of plastics products, see other entries in industry group 3080. For information regarding resin manufacturing, see **SIC 2821: Plastics Materials, Synthetic Resins, and Nonvulcanizable Elastomers.**

There are at least 12 major processing techniques used to form plastics goods. A traditional and popular technique is extrusion, which entails melting and compressing plastic granules in a tube. A screw conveyor inside the tube forces the plastic through a nozzle at the end of the tube. The physical characteristics of the plastic can be altered by applying heat or cold to the barrel, adjusting the screw pressure, or by using different types and sizes of screws. Extrusion processes are used to make pipe, sheeting, films, and various forms.

Another popular processing technique is blow-molding, whereby extruded plastic is forced into a bottle-shaped mold. Compressed air inflates the hot plastic and pushes it against the cold sides of the mold, resulting in thin-walled plastic containers. Injection molding, one of the most popular processing operations, entails extruding plastic directly into a mold, where it hardens into a solid form. Sheets of plastic are created through calendaring or film and sheet extrusion. Foam is made in a process called foaming. Other popular plastic processing techniques include film casting, rotational molding, laminating, and casting.

The two main classes of plastics are thermosets and thermoplastics. Thermosets, which account for only 10 percent of the material used in this industry, harden by chemical reaction and cannot be melted and reshaped once they are created. Primary products created with thermoset plastics are epoxies and phenol formaldehyde (Bakelite). Epoxies are used to manufacture flooring, protective coatings, adhesives and cements, electrical hardware, and particle board. Bakelite is formed into electrical parts, pot handles, and various knobs.

Thermoplastics include acrylics, cellulose proportionate (Forticel), ABS (acrylonitrile-butadiene-styrene), polyphenylene oxide (Noryl), and polysulfone. Acrylics are utilized in the production of windows, signs, vehicle light covers, and textiles. Forticel is applied in the manufacture of items such as pens, typewriter keys, telephone housing, and other applications that require impact strength. ABS, which has very high impact resistance, is used to make drain pipes, automobile parts, and small appliances and tools. Noryl, which combines high impact strength with temperature stability, is used for products like machine parts and equipment housing. Lastly, polysulfone, which is heat resistant, is used in battery casings, smoke alarms, electronic connectors, and shower heads.

Although the markets for miscellaneous plastics products are extremely fragmented, a few major categories stand out. For instance, miscellaneous plastic packaging, such as caps, food trays, and bubble wrap, constituted a leading 12 percent of shipments in the 1990s. Fabricated plastics used for vehicles, such as turn indicator housings, also made up 12 percent of the market. Plastics used to make electrical devices accounted for about 8 percent of industry sales, and plastic siding contributed 2 percent of revenues. Other major product groups included doors and window frames, dinnerware and kitchenware, and plastic furniture parts.

BACKGROUND AND DEVELOPMENT

Keratin, a natural plastic, was used in the United States to make lantern windows and other simple items as early as 1740. Gutta Percha, or gum elastic, was first used during the middle 1850s to make billiard balls and ocean cable insulation. Manufacturers borrowed

forming and processing techniques from Malayan natives. Shellac plastics, developed by Samuel Speck, also emerged during the mid-1800s, and were used to create goods such as checkers, buttons, and insulators.

Following the invention of the first synthetic plastics in the late 1870s (see **SIC 2821: Plastics Materials, Synthetic Resins, and Nonvulcanizable Elastomers**), plastics products sales began to accelerate. American Dr. Baekland introduced the first moldable plastic, Bakelite, in 1909. Bakelite prompted a flurry of new molding techniques and resins during the early 1900s. Advances during World War II also bolstered the industry. The rampant proliferation of new synthetic chemicals and production processes during the 1950s, 1960s, and 1970s resulted in massive industry expansion. By the late 1970s, plastics products had become a staple of American life and were rapidly displacing conventional materials in a range of applications.

U.S. sales of miscellaneous plastics products expanded rapidly during the 1980s, but increased competition, both at home and abroad, contributed to lagging price growth. Total U.S. plastics products shipments were $105 billion by 1995. About 53 percent—or $55.3 billion—of that total was comprised of miscellaneous goods from this industry. Despite a late 1980s and early 1990s U.S. recession, shipment growth persisted as new additives and processing techniques were introduced.

CURRENT CONDITIONS

Stiff competition and weak prices continued to plague manufacturers in the early 1990s, but increased sales of plastic goods for automobiles, packaged goods, and construction materials boosted margins for many competitors. Output of all plastics products grew throughout the 1990s and prices in some important market segments rose an estimated three percent to five percent per year. Sales in some depressed sectors, such as high-tech engineering plastics, were rebounding. Industry receipts were expected to climb at a rate of three percent to six percent annually through the mid-1990s.

In the long term, the use of plastics products will proliferate. But successful manufacturers will be forced to develop and implement improved processing techniques that reduce costs and improve quality. As foreign competition mounts—particularly for commodity-like products—U.S. technological superiority in plastics will become paramount.

As in the early 1990s, many companies will respond to increased competition by acquiring or merging with competitors to reduce research and development costs, establish a global presence, and pool capital investment dollars for expensive new equipment. Some smaller firms with niche expertise will also find growth.

INDUSTRY LEADERS

Despite industry consolidation during the late 1980s and early 1990s, the miscellaneous plastics products industry remained relatively fragmented. About 8,330 companies competed going into the mid-1990s, up from only 8,045 in 1990. The number of companies is projected to drop slightly to about 8,200 by 1998. The average industry participant shipped about $6.6 million worth of goods, slightly less than 70 percent as much as the average U.S. manufacturer. The majority of producers are small and specialized.

One of the largest competitors in the mid-1990s was Premark International Inc. of Illinois. Premark, a diversified plastics manufacturer, had 1996 sales of $2.3 billion and employed 16,300 workers. Another industry leader was USG Corporation, also of Illinois, which had $2.6 billion in 1996 sales and employed about 12,500 workers. Other industry leaders included: Aeroquip-Vickers Corporation ($2.03 billion in 1996 sales), of Ohio; and Owens-Illinois, Inc. ($3.8 billion), of Ohio.

WORK FORCE

The industry's 470,000-member work force will benefit in the future from strong growth in demand for plastics products. However, productivity gains achieved through automation and the integration of more efficient processing techniques will contribute to a lag between shipment growth and new jobs. Opportunities for laborers will likely expand 30 percent to 40 percent between 1990 and 2005, according to the U.S. Bureau of Labor Statistics. For example, jobs for molding machine operators—which account for about 17 percent of the work force—will likely grow by 30 percent, as will positions for managers and executives. Better yet, jobs for sales professionals, industrial machine operators, and machinery mechanics will spiral 50 percent to 70 percent by 2005. Unfortunately, workers in this industry receive, on average, only 80 percent of the wages paid in other U.S. manufacturing industries.

AMERICA AND THE WORLD

Although exports and imports have traditionally played a minor role in the plastics products industry, imports (excluding bottles and plumbing) into the United States swelled six-fold during the 1980s to about $3.8 billion by 1991. By the early 1990s, the U.S. plastics products industry trade surplus had been whittled to only $200 million. While a weak dollar and increased industry productivity helped to buoy the trade surplus in 1992 and 1993, foreign competition was expected to increase in the long term.

One of the regions of greatest growth was China. Its plastics products shipments soared more than 200 percent during the 1980s, reaching approximately 4.1 billion tons by the early 1990s and reflecting average annual growth of about 12.5 percent. Chinese manufacturers suffered, however, from a lack of production equipment and access to processed raw materials. Although China's economic growth will stimulate increased imports, a low per capita plastic consumption will keep overall growth to 7 percent annually between 1997-2001. As capacity accelerates to meet demand during the 1990s, China will likely become a formidable competitor in export markets, particularly in fast growing East Asian countries. Asia, in general, is a strong growth area with predicted annual growth rates of 10 percent, especially in ethylene propylene, vinyl chloride, and acrylonitrile. Within the Asian market, the largest increases could occur among ASEAN (Association of Southeastern Asian Nations) members, as new complexes come online. The rapid increase of plastics consumption within the Asian market has stimulated U.S. producers to look at investing in local production plants.

Imports may also rise in the wake of the North American Free Trade Agreement, as U.S. manufacturers move production facilities south of the border to take advantage of inexpensive labor and reduced environmental restrictions. After Canada, Mexico was the second biggest importer of plastics goods into the United States during the mid-1990s. Mexican imports should rise rapidly over the next 5 to 10 years as Asian producers infiltrate the Mexican market to meet NAFTA requirements that 6 percent of a duty-free product's components be made in North America. The General Agreement on Tariffs and Trade (GATT) treaty has limited international import duties on resins to 6.5 percent by the year 2000, down from an average of 12.5 percent. The impact of the new tariffs on the market structure is still uncertain, although most predictions lean toward further increases in international trade.

RESEARCH AND TECHNOLOGY

Going into the mid-1990s, major technological trends in the plastics products industry included recyclability and faster concept-to-production cycles. Indeed, many companies were ardently seeking flexible processing, extrusion, and molding techniques that would allow them to design and quickly manufacture new products. One of the most important recycling tactics was ''design-for-recycling,'' whereby plastics products and devices are created in such a way that they can be efficiently ground, melted, and reused. For example, glue and adhesives that can contaminate reground materials were being eliminated from manufactured plastic goods.

FURTHER READING

Barlow, Rick Data. ''Plastics Prices Up 1%.'' *Hospitals Materials Management,* November 1992.

Darnay, Arsen J., ed. *Manufacturing USA.* 5th ed. Detroit: Gale Research 1996.

Dvorak, Paul. ''Putting the Brakes on Throwaway Designs.'' *Machine Design,* 12 February 1993.

Farris, Susan E. ''What's Ahead for Plastics?'' *Plastics World,* January 1993.

''First Annual Design Awards.'' *Modern Plastics,* June 1993.

Smock, Doug. ''Precise Plastics Targets Special Niches for Growth.'' December 1992.

U.S. Department of Commerce, *U.S. Industrial Outlook 1994.* Washington: GPO, 1993.

Wood, Andrew. ''Plastics '92—Engineered Plastics: Pinning Hopes on Renewed Growth.'' *Chemical Week,* 28 October 1992.

Zhengxing, Lu. ''Look at China's Plastics Market.'' *Plastics World,* November 1992.

—Dave Mote, updated by Arthur G. Sharp

LEATHER & LEATHER PRODUCTS

LEATHER TANNING AND FINISHING

This category includes establishments primarily engaged in tanning, currying, and finishing raw or cured hides and skins into leather. Converters and dealers who buy hides, skins, or leather for processing under contracts with tanners and/or finishers are also included in this category.

U.S. LEATHER TANNING AND FINISHING SHIPMENTS

Million dollars

Source: International Trade Administration   *estimate

INDUSTRY SNAPSHOT

Leather tanning and finishing in the United States is a multi-billion dollar industry. According to the International Trade Administration, the dollar value of U.S. leather industry shipments has been dropping in recent years, from $3.2 billion in 1993 to $3.1 billion in 1995. Similarly, production shipments have dropped from $3.3 billion in 1993 to nearly $3.2

billion in 1995. In the United States, automotive upholstery and casual footwear make up most of the leather market. The number of companies engaged in leather tanning and finishing has declined since the 1980s as larger firms acquired smaller ones. The number of U.S. tanning and finishing establishments shrank from 342 in 1982 to approximately 160 in 1996, also due in part to continued import competition. In 1996, about 70 plants directly processed raw hides and skins into tanned leather.

Leather tanning in the United States is primarily the work of privately held companies. Approximately 95 percent of the leather processed in the United States is cattlehide, while specialty leathers—including deer, calf, pig, goat, sheep, lamb, kangaroo, and various reptiles—represent the other 5 percent. The largest tanning establishments are in New York, Massachusetts, California, Wisconsin, Pennsylvania, New Jersey, Georgia, Michigan, and Texas.

ORGANIZATION AND STRUCTURE

Leather tanning is a process in which chemical agents and extracts are applied to various types of hides and skins in order to prevent rotting. Not all tanneries follow the same method of processing hides into leather. However, the process described here is used by the majority. First, the hides must be prepared for tanning at the packing house. This includes unhairing (a lime solution loosens the hair, making removal easier), fleshing (cleaning off the inner side of the hides), and bating (removing the lime from the hides). Next, the skins and hides are cured—salted or soaked in brine to preserve them until they reach the tannery. Once at the tannery, the hides are soaked to remove the salt. Two primary methods are used to then convert the raw material into leather: chrome tanning and vegetable tanning. The method used depends on the intended use of the leather. Chrome tanning, which involves the use of soluble chromium salts such as chromium sulfate, is used primarily to tan leather for the upper parts of shoes. Vegetable tanning, which uses tannic acid, is used to tan heavy leather for shoe soles, bags, straps, harnesses, and other products used in industrial equipment. Chrome tanning is the most widely used method in the United States.

Several basic stages are involved in the tanning process. First, the underlying layer of the hide is "split" off and shaved to uniform thickness. Tanning drums are then used to saturate the hides in the tanning solution, which preserves the hide and adds strength. The hides are tanned again, where dyes and oils are added to provide color, softness, and durability. Then the hide must be stretched and dried to remove all excess moisture. At this point, the leather is firm, flat, and ready to be trimmed. Finally, the hide is conditioned and finished. The finishing process involves softening the hide mechanically, spraying final colors onto the leather to meet customer requirements, and embossing to the required texture.

BACKGROUND AND DEVELOPMENT

Tanning—the process that turns raw animal hides into the soft, pliable, and enduring material called leather—is one of the world's oldest industries. Recovered specimens of leather tents and shoes date as far back as 6000 B.C., and ancient Egyptian carvings show tanners at work. Early Romans used leather not only for shoes, shields, and harnesses, but also as currency. As the centuries passed, tanning grew into a highly developed art. Twelfth-century England gave rise to tanners' guilds, and in America, early settlers learned that tanning was not new to the native Americans. Advances in the chemical and mechanical processes of tanning and the invention of the thermometer and hydrometer—for measuring density—opened up the industry worldwide and brought tanning from the realm of the arts to the sciences.

The Leather Industry in America. The first English leather worker to come to the New World was a shoemaker named Experience Miller. Miller arrived in Plymouth Colony in 1624 and soon found that the native Americans used bark tanning to preserve cattle and other hides. The abundance of deer hides and water resources in the colonies lead to the development of a flourishing tanning industry. By 1650, there were more than 50 tanneries in Massachusetts alone. Early colonial tanneries were small and often moved when the vegetable tanning materials or the source of hides in one area were exhausted. The first tanning machine used in the United States was a stone mill used to grind tree bark. It was invented by Peter Minuit, Governor of New Amsterdam. By 1800, there were 2,000 tanneries in the United States.

Technological innovations in the nineteenth century increased production. In 1805, Sir Humphry Davey, an Englishman, discovered that many trees other than oak could be used in the tanning process. The hemlock, mimosa, chestnut, and ash were also used, since all were abundant in the United States. An American, Samuel Parker, further advanced the tanning industry in 1809 by inventing a machine to split hides. Prior to this, it took one man a whole day to split four hides. With the aid of Parker's invention, one man could split 100 hides in one day. These developments made leather cheaper, opening the leather market to all classes. In 1884, August Schultz discovered that chromium salts could be used in the tanning process instead of vegetable material. This method, perfected ten years later by Martin Dennis, allowed more attractive and flexible leathers to be produced at a faster rate.

Other procedural changes and inventions, including a machine to remove hair and flesh from the skins, gave the U.S. leather industry an added boost by increasing the supply of leather. By the end of the nineteenth century, tanneries had begun to consolidate. The larger tanneries produced more goods than had the many smaller operations, since they could better maintain heavy, expensive machinery and a large work force. In 1899, 1,306 tanneries produced leather valued at $204 million, versus 6,664 tanneries producing only $40 million worth of leather in 1850. Integration and growth continued into the twentieth century. In 1919, 680 tanneries produced $900 million worth of leather. The number of tanneries continued to shrink with the slowdown of the Depression and the competition from synthetics after World War II. In the 1970s, the decline in meat consumption further decreased the availability of hides for tanning, which in turn began increasing the cost of leather worldwide.

CURRENT CONDITIONS

In 1996, U.S. leather imports totaled approximately $1 billion, down from $1.1 billion in 1995. Exports totaled $880 million in 1996, up from $870 million in 1995. Charles Myers, President of Leather Industries of America, Inc., an association of leather tanners and related industries, noted in 1997 that the tanning industry, which once produced primarily for U.S. markets, was now an aggressive exporter. He said, "We now export more raw material than finished product to countries that can finish more cheaply than we [can], and we have a very small domestic customer base.''

The future of the tanning industry was in contention in the 1980s but has stabilized during the past decade. Charles Myers predicted further consolidation of the industry to fewer players who will concentrate on the upper end leathers, selling some to domestic firms and exporting much of the rest. The International Trade Administration sees a similar future, predicting that industry shipments will reach $2.79 billion in 1996 and $2.90 billion in 1997. Production shipments should increase from an estimated $2.81 billion in 1996 to an estimated $2.93 billion in 1997. In addition, the Department of Commerce rated the long term outlook for the industry as ''good.'' Continued increases in the hide supply could mean lower prices and could encourage tanners to increase working capital and reduce debt. Primary growth opportunities for the tanning industry will continue to be automobile upholstery and footwear. According to Leather Industries of America's Charles Myers, the United States is the world's leader in leather tanning for the footwear industry.

INDUSTRY LEADERS

The top industry leaders were privately held companies and include two companies located in Milwaukee, Wisconsin: U.S. Leather, Inc. (sales in excess of $350 million annually) and Albert Trostel and Sons Co. (more than $300 million in sales annually). Another leader was Seton Co. of Norristown, Pennsylvania (sales in excess of $250 million annually).

WORK FORCE

The industry is unionized, but also highly mechanized. The U.S. Department of Labor reports employment of approximately 12,800 in the industry in 1996, about 4 percent below the 13,300 employees reported in 1995. According to the U.S. Department of Labor's Bureau of Labor Statistics, average hourly earnings for laborers in 1996 was $11.62, up from $11.21 in 1995. The leading states for employment in 1996 were Wisconsin and Pennsylvania.

Associated work for the tanning industry lay in the fields of chemistry and environmental management. The outlook for leather workers depends upon the continued demand for the leather product and the availability of hides.

AMERICA AND THE WORLD

The role of the United States in the export of leather should grow throughout the 1990s. Import and export in the leather tanning and finishing industry primarily involved the import and export of the raw and wet-blue hides and finished leather. Unlike many countries with abundant hide supplies, the United States did not restrict exports. Restriction of exports lowers the price of hides, making it cheaper to tan and produce leather products with one's own hides. Argentina, Brazil, and India restricted exports to support their national tanning industries.

Combined exports of raw and wet-blue cattlehides totaled 17 million hides in 1996, according to Leather Industries of America, Inc., and the same amount, or slightly more, should be exported in 1997. In 1995, the U.S. exported $151 million worth of leather to Mexico; $139 million to Canada; $111 million to Hong Kong; and $92 million to Japan. Both U.S. leather exports and imports increased in 1996, with upholstery being the major growth area in both cases.

According to Charles Myers: ''U.S. automobile upholstery leather tanners are expanding offshore and constructing cutting operations in Mexico, South Africa and Europe following the movement of their auto manufacturing customers into these areas. In addition, there is considerable potential for the U.S. in Asia, where a number of U.S. tanneries have located factories and warehouses. This strategy positions major American [footwear] leather tanners closer to where their U.S. and European customers are sourcing shoes.''

The weaker U.S. dollar stimulated export demand despite weak economies around the world. Mexico was the largest importer of U.S. hides in 1995, claiming approximately $151 million worth. In 1995, Argentina was the largest supplier to the United States, accounting for approximately $165 million in imported hides; Italy was a close second, supplying the United States with $163 million in hides. The United States imported a total of $1 billion in hides from 70 countries during 1995.

Both the United States and Europe continued to address the issue of Japan's tariff-rate quota on leather and leather footwear. During U.S.-Mexico negotiations on the North American Free Trade Agreement (NAFTA), Mexico refused to meet a U.S. request for immediate reciprocal reductions to zero for both U.S. and Mexican tariffs on leather. A compromise led to an agreement to reduce duties over a ten year period.

RESEARCH AND TECHNOLOGY

Innovations. The leather tanning industry began a series of technological innovations in the late 1970s and 1980s in response to the need to assess the effect of tanning chemicals used on the environment. The Leather Industries of America Research Laboratory, based in Cincinnati, Ohio, worked on changes relating to the chemical aspects of hide processing.

In 1995, Vista Leather Group's Irving Tanning Co. completed a $12 million investment in new facilities, including one of the most highly advanced coloring systems in the world. The system, regulated by a computer, has cut down employee workloads and has reduced employee exposure to chemicals.

Research support continues to make the industry more cost-effective and helps it respond to demands made by environmental protection laws passed in the 1980s and 1990s. The U.S. tanning industry spends millions of dollars each year in research and development, and continued low interest rates will encourage companies to invest even more in the development of state-of-the-art equipment, new technologies, and leathers. In addition to studies performed by individual firms, the Leather Industries of America Research Laboratory conducts ongoing industry research.

Environmental Issues. The leather tanning and finishing industry must meet Environmental Protection Agency (EPA) waste standards on three fronts: liquid, solid, and air. In 1985, the EPA established new standards to control pretreatment of the liquid wastes that tanners discharge indirectly to publicly owned waste treatment facilities. These standards applied to waste acidity and to wastes containing sulfides and chromium. All tanners discharging directly into waterways were required to operate with the EPA-approved National Discharge Elimination System (NDES) permits. The EPA standards for this group required control of conventional pollutants such as solids and biological oxygen as well as sulfides, chromium, and acidity. Further, the 1990 Clean Air Act and other strict federal standards curbing the emission of volatile organic compounds into the air have encouraged the industry to develop low-solvent or solvent-free finishing technologies.

In 1992, waste scrap leather and tannery sludge that contained chromium was exempt from hazardous waste regulation. Tanning systems that recycled chromium had been developed and were widely used throughout the industry to reduce the amount of chromium that appeared in the final waste. There had been talk of removing the exemption on waste from leather products, which would force the leather industry to come up with new techniques for the disposal of those products. However, in 1995, the EPA did a retrospective study on the industry's effluent guidelines and pollution prevention progress. The study found that the industry had taken major steps in modifying the chrome tanning process in order to get more of the chromium into the leather and less in the waste. Through these measures, chromium fixation was increased from 50 percent in 1982 to 90 percent in 1995. In addition, the industry's water use was reduced by 50 percent.

As an example of the high priority the industry assigns to environmental issues, Pfister and Vogel Leather Co., a division of U.S. Leather, Inc., began to recycle its cattlehide shavings and trimmings in 1994 to produce fertilizers rich in nitrogen. The Milwaukee based, state-of-the-art recycling plant converts approximately 12,000 tons of scraps annually. According to Pfister and Vogel, the industry produces approximately 50,000 tons of scrap each year, the majority of which is deposited in landfills.

FURTHER READING

Darnay, Arsen J., ed. *Manufacturing USA.* 5th ed. Detroit: Gale Research, 1996.

Interview with Charles Myers, President of Leather Industries of America, Inc., 1997.

Interview with James Byron, International Trade Specialist for the International Trade Administration, 1997.

Leather Facts. New England Tanners Club, 1994.

Rieger, Nancy. ''Tannery Converting Hide Scraps to Fertilizer.'' *Footwear News,* 8 August 1994.

Rieger, Nancy. ''Irving Tanning Expands Plant, Product Lines.'' *Footwear News,* 23 January 1995.

U.S. Census Bureau. *1996 Statistical Abstract of the United States.* 1996. Available from http://www.census.gov/prod/2/gen/96statab/96statab.html.

U.S. Department of Commerce. *U.S. Industrial Outlook 1994.* Washington: GPO, 1994.

U.S. Department of Labor. Bureau of Labor Statistics. *Employment and Earnings.* December 1996.

U.S. Environmental Protection Agency. *Effluent Guidelines, Leather Tanning, and Pollution Prevention: A Retrospective Study.* June 1995.

—Joan Leotta, updated by Kathy Kirn

SIC 3131

BOOT AND SHOE CUT STOCK AND FINDINGS

Establishments that fall under this category are primarily engaged in manufacturing leather soles, inner soles, and other boot and shoe cut stock and findings. The industry also includes finished wood heels.

Establishments primarily engaged in manufacturing heels, soiling strips, and soles made of rubber, composition, plastics, and fiber are classified in the major group for rubber and miscellaneous plastics products.

In 1996, the boot and shoe cut stock findings segment continued to suffer from the growing penetration of relatively low-cost imported footwear into the United States. According to footwear industry statistics, in 1966 the United States market for nonrubber footwear totaled 735 million pairs, and 641 million pairs were made in America. By 1996, the market had grown to 1,218 million pairs, but the U.S. produced only 143 million pairs. The import/export imbalance was even more telling—1,098 million pairs were imported in 1996, while only 24 million were exported.

In this environment, many footwear plants have been forced to close. Between 1966 and 1996, there was a net loss of 783 nonrubber footwear plants in the United States, and plant openings had slowed to a trickle. Pricing was also under intense pressure: the average factory price for nonrubber footwear increased about 2 percent to an estimated $21.16 a pair in 1993—the smallest advance in three years because of competition from imported shoes. In the labor intensive footwear industry, U.S. makers simply could not compete with manufacturers overseas whose wage rates were far below U.S. levels.

The drop in domestically produced footwear, of course, depressed the business of companies that supply shoe manufacturers. According to government statistics, shipments for the boot and shoe cut stock and findings segment in 1995 totaled $282 million, down from $319 million in 1994 and $425 million in 1981. Moreover, the number of workers totaled 3,100 in 1995—down from 3,400 in 1994 and 7,000 in 1981. Besides the dramatic increase in shoe imports, leather sole makers also had to contend with a shift by consumers to more casual footwear and the rising cost of leather. While there remained a market for the fine leather shoe, many Americans were no longer dressing up for work and did not require several pairs of dress shoes.

During the recession of the early 1990s, the repair trade picked up somewhat, as consumers have traditionally mended old shoes when they did not have the money to buy new ones. Some manufacturers thought sales were less robust than in previous recessions, however, because of the loss of white collar jobs. There was also concern about longer term trends in the repair market. During the Second World War, the number of repair shops totaled nearly 70,000; by 1996, there were fewer than 12,000. One estimate showed that only 8 to 10 percent of consumers made use of

shoe repair shops, and the average customer was 45 years old. The availability of inexpensive imported footwear may also encourage people to simply buy new shoes rather than repair old ones.

FURTHER READING

"A Recovery Is No Shoe-In." *The Wall Street Journal,* 28 May 1992.

"Statistics." *Footwear Industry Association,* 14 April 1997. Available from http://fia.org.

Kukolla, Steve. "Shoe Repair Suppliers See Business Slipping." *Knight Ridder/Tribune Business News,* 9 January 1996.

McNally, Pamela. "Vendors Taking Advantage of Manmades' Price and Texture." *Footwear News,* 25 January 1993.

Rieger, Nancy. "North American Exposure: Borders, Barriers and Free Trade." *Footwear News,* 11 October 1993.

Stebbins, John, et al. *Footwear Manual.* Washington: Footwear Industries of America, 1993.

—Bob Schneider

SIC 3142

HOUSE SLIPPERS

This classification includes establishments primarily engaged in manufacturing house slippers of leather or other materials.

The house slippers industry falls under the auspices of the nonrubber footwear industry, which produces all types of footwear except rubber protective and rubber-soled "sneakers." House slippers may be constructed with leather, vinyl, plastic, cloth, or textile uppers—or combinations of these materials for both genders of all ages.

The modern structure of house slipper manufacturing is characterized by several major brand names with primary distribution through department store venues. The leading brand names differentiate themselves by comfort and fashion levels. In the mid-1990s the leading brand names included Dearfoams by R.G. Barry Corporation and Isotoners by Aris. An article in the July 1993 edition of *Footwear News* indicated, however, that consumers' footwear buying habits had shifted to form, function, and comfort—and away from brand names. Many consumers were seeking lower-priced house slippers in strip shopping centers and outlet stores instead of in traditional higher-end shopping mall department stores.

A portion of the house slipper consumer market is represented by house-bound invalids and hospitalized patients. This sector of the market seeks products that are light-weight, comfortable, easy to put on and take off, and unlikely to fall off the feet. *American Salesman* magazine also listed house slippers among the items one should never fail to pack when traveling. Sales people and other frequent travelers opt for house slippers that are fashionable, light-weight, and easy to pack.

The house slippers industry is the smallest division within the nonrubber footwear industry. There were an estimated 19 establishments in 1996, the lowest in 15 years, down from 31 in 1992. In 1995 shipments of house slippers declined almost 50 percent from 1994 to a product value of $113 million. Of nonrubber footwear product shipments, house slippers accounted for about a quarter of the quantity but only 3 percent of the value, primarily because most slippers are produced from lower-cost vinyls and other textiles. Industry experts expect shipments of house slippers to continue to decline moderately throughout the end of the twentieth century. In 1995 2,000 employees worked for the industry, 1,800 of which were production workers who earned substantially less than the average manufacturing worker. House slipper manufacturers earned an average of $7.67 per hour compared to $12.37 per hour for all of manufacturing.

In order to maintain profitability in the face of declining demand, the house slipper industry considers new technology essential to increasing productivity and lowering costs of manufacturing. The increased use of computers has already integrated design, management, manufacturing, and marketing functions. Overall, the industry emphasizes such nonprice factors as quality and quick delivery in competition with imports. The industry has turned to computer-aided design (CAD) and computer-aided manufacturing (CAM). Through these methods, companies can link computer system data to autostitchers, milling, and turning machines. The industry has also increased its use of three-dimensional CAD, which produces more accurate slipper patterns and reduces the number of prototypes needed.

FURTHER READING

Darnay, Arsen J., ed. *Manufacturing USA.* 5th ed. Detroit: Gale Research, 1996.

''Shoe Manufacturing.'' *Moody's Industry Review,* Vol 13, 11 March 1994.

U.S. Department of Labor. Bureau of Labor Statistics. *Employment, Hours, and Earnings: United States, 1988-96,* Washington: GPO, August 1996.

SIC 3143

MEN'S FOOTWEAR, EXCEPT ATHLETIC

This category includes establishments primarily engaged in the production of men's footwear designed for dress, street, and work. Establishments primarily engaged in the production of such protective footwear as rubbers, rubber boots, storm shoes, galoshes, and other footwear with rubber soles vulcanized to the uppers are classified in **SIC 3021: Rubber and Plastics Footwear.** Establishments primarily engaged in the production of athletic shoes and youths' and boys' shoes are classified in **SIC 3149: Footwear Except Rubber, Not Elsewhere Classified,** and those manufacturing orthopedic extension shoes are classified in **SIC 3842: Orthopedic, Prosthetic, and Surgical Appliances and Supplies.**

INDUSTRY SNAPSHOT

The number of companies in the United States involved in the production of nonrubber men's dress, street, and work footwear remained constant in 1995 at around 200, but the impact of imports continued to increase. Footwear Industries of America (FIA) reported that imports captured over 75 percent of the domestic men's market that year, up from 73 percent in 1993, continuing a growth trend that began more than three decades ago.

BACKGROUND AND DEVELOPMENT

New England had become the center of a thriving footwear industry as early as 1800, and by 1850, the United States was exporting large quantities of high quality, inexpensive shoes to England and other European countries. Micajah Pratt, who began making and selling shoes in Lynn, Massachusetts in 1812, was considered an innovator in the industry. He was among the first to use standard patterns and sole cutting machines. Pratt eventually employed about 500 workers—many of whom lived in other towns and worked at home—and produced almost 250,000 pairs of shoes annually.

Shoemaking became industrialized in the early 1860s, prompted by the development of machinery for attaching the leather part of a shoe, known as the upper, to the sole. In 1858, Lyman R. Blake of Abington, Massachusetts invented a machine that attached the leather uppers with nails and wooden pegs. Soon after, Gordon McKay, also of Abington, improved on Blake's invention by substituting thread for the cumbersome nails and pegs. Recognizing the threat that McKay's sewing machine posed to their livelihood, shoemakers staged the first general strike in the foot-wear industry in 1859. Nevertheless, by 1864, the Blake sewer was used by most U.S. shoemakers.

The most important technological advance, how-ever, was probably the shoe-lasting machine, invented in 1882 by Jan Ernst Matzeliger, who also worked in a Lynn shoe factory. "Lasting" was the process of shap-ing the leather upper over a wooden form before attaching it to the sole. Matzeliger's shoe-lasting ma-chine, patented in 1883, allowed shoes to be mass produced for the first time.

Technology has remained relatively unchanged in recent years, but the U.S. industry has been dramati-cally altered nonetheless by the growing penetration of imports versus domestically produced shoes. And while the export of American-made men's footwear to other countries is still a significant factor at around 10 percent of the total, according to FIA statistics, pri-mary destinations have shifted from England and other European countries a century ago to Japan, Canada, and Mexico today.

CURRENT CONDITIONS

Nearly 56 million of the 159 million total pairs of nonrubber footwear produced by companies in the United States in 1995 were men's shoes, according to FIA. The overall total marks a continuing decrease in American production that has been measured every year since 642 million pairs were manufactured do-mestically in 1968. During that period, imports and domestics also swapped relative positions, with the latter accounting for more than 78 percent of the mar-ket three decades ago and less than 12 percent of it in 1995. More than 170 million out of the 1.08 billion total imports that year were men's shoes, up from the 133 million out of nearly 975 million imported in 1992. China increased its leading share of the U.S. market from around one half to two-thirds of the total imported during that time, with Brazil second at nearly 9 percent, Indonesia third at 6.5 percent, Italy fourth at 4 percent and Thailand fifth at 2 percent. Approxi-mately 20.5 million pairs of nonrubber footwear were exported by U.S. companies in 1995, of which 5.5 million were men's. Japan imported the most, with 12.5 percent of the total, followed by Canada with 11.6 percent; Mexico, the leading importer of American-made shoes in 1992 with 13.6 percent of the market, dropped to third place with 6 percent in 1995.

Fourteen U.S. shoe factories closed and two opened in 1995, according to FIA, leaving about 200 manufacturers operating 341 plants in 31 states, as production continued shifting overseas to take advan-tage of lower labor costs. One exception to the trend

was men's work shoes, where domestic production hit nearly 14.9 million in 1995—representing a 34 percent increase from 1993. Another submarket that remained strong was made up of the firms that produced top-quality leather dress shoes or filled unique export mar-kets, such as bootmaker Tony Lama, Inc. in El Paso, Texas. In 1989, Tony Lama, Jr., then the company's chairperson, told *Nation's Business,* "They don't make original cowboy boots everywhere in the world. [Foreign customers] don't mind spending money on a fine pair of cowboy boots, but its important that they be made in America." *Footwear +* reported in 1997 that exports of Western boots continued to grow, particu-larly to Germany, France, Norway, Sweden, and Den-mark.

INDUSTRY LEADERS

Timberland Company. A manufacturer of rugged, upscale hiking boots and walking shoes, The Timber-land Co. took over first place in the hierarchy of men's footwear producers in 1996—capturing more than one-third of the total market with $655 million in sales.

Russian immigrant Nathan Swartz founded Timberland when he purchased half interest in the Abington Shoe Company in 1951. His partner died four years later and he purchased the rest. His sons, Herman and Sidney, joined him in the business, and for the next 15 years they produced inexpensive, pri-vate-label men's shoes and work boots in a converted Boston warehouse. Their dress shoes were most often sold through discount stores, while their work boots became a staple in Army/Navy surplus stores.

Sales of Abington's leather work boots increased unexpectedly around 1970, as the company was one of the first to stumble upon a new fashion trend that combined styles and gear previously favored by out-doors enthusiasts. "When we visited the stores, we saw that a lot of young people, college students, were buying them. You don't have to be a genius to know that something's going on," Herman Swartz later told *INC.* magazine.

Abington had by then relocated to Newmarket, New Hampshire, and in 1973 selected the "Tim-berland" name from a list suggested by an advertising agency. The company created a subsidiary to manufac-ture its new line of insulated and waterproof leather boots, which were distinguished by their thick rubber soles. It produced just 2,500 pairs that first year, com-pared to 490,000 shoes and boots in the Abington line.

The company initially marketed Timberland and Abington boots by appealing to hunters and fishermen who shopped the Army/Navy surplus stores, and sales of the new line were unimpressive. However, in 1975 a marketing consultant suggested the company position Timberland as a fashion item sold through upscale department stores and retail outlets. A new advertising campaign was funded through a hefty price increase and launched with the slogan, "A whole line of fine leather boots that cost plenty, and should." In 1979, Abington officially changed its name to the Timberland Co. That year, it sold 500,000 pairs of Timberland boots as revenues topped $16 million. Revenues topped $100 million for the first time in 1987.

Florsheim Shoe Company. Chicago-based Florsheim Shoe Co., a subsidiary of Interco, Inc., was perhaps the best-known maker of men's dress shoes in the United States in the early 1990s when it accounted for about 20 percent of the market. By 1995, though, its share had dipped to 14.6 percent of total sales of $285 million.

The company was founded in 1892 by Milton S. Florsheim. He created one of the earliest brand names in the shoe industry by stamping the company name into the sole of every shoe it produced. In the early 1900s, Florsheim began advertising nationally in magazines such as *The Saturday Evening Post.* It was one of the first manufacturers to open its own retail stores, and was credited with introducing low-cut dress shoes for men.

A consumer survey in the early 1990s found the Florsheim brand name publicly associated with high prices, so the company reduced them on four of its most popular men's dress styles. It also introduced several new styles aimed at the increasingly popular casual market.

Other Leaders. By 1995, the outdoor look pioneered by Timberland spread throughout the industry, and several other companies were also achieving success with it. Wolverine Worldwide tallied $414 million in sales that year, at least partially because of its appeal. In addition, according to *Forbes* magazine, the rugged Rockport subsidiary of Reebok International Ltd. recorded sales of $447.6 million in 1996—a 21.6 percent increase from the year before and one of the few bright spots for the parent company.

WORK FORCE

The U.S. nonrubber footwear industry employed 53,800 in 1995, FIA reported, 43,900 of whom were production workers. The total represented a 7.1 percent decline from the year before and a 77 percent decrease since 1968, when employment was 233,400. The domestic industry's direct manufacturing payroll was $1.1 billion in 1995, with production employees earning an average of $7.67 per hour—up from $7.01 in 1992. A comparison of Indonesia's basic hourly wage of about 30 cents (in U.S. dollars), cited in a 1996 *Business Week* story, as well as the 50 cents per hour paid in China, graphically shows why production has largely shifted to those countries in recent years. Even the average salary in Taiwan, reportedly the highest among major foreign competitors, was less than half the U.S. figure.

AMERICA AND THE WORLD

Considered one of the most open footwear markets in the world because it was one of the few industrialized nations that did not impose high import tariffs, FIA said the United States accounted for 29 percent of all world imports in 1995. The trade association reported that U.S. imports of nonrubber footwear grew by 516 percent between 1968, when President Lyndon Johnson cut tariffs in half, and 1995, when import penetration reached 88.6 percent. More than 2,000 footwear plants operated in the United States at the start of 1968, but only 341 were open at the end of 1995—an average of nearly 60 factory closings every year.

After 1968, several attempts were made to impose higher import tariffs, most notable of which was the Textile, Apparel, and Footwear Act of 1990 vetoed by President George Bush. Similar bills had been rejected by Congress in 1985 and 1988. Also during this time, the industry filed complaints about unfair trade practices with the International Trade Commission (ITC), but in 1984 the ITC ruled that the U.S. footwear industry was not being harmed by imports. The Senate Finance Committee initiated a case with the ITC the following year, which resulted in a recommendation for five years of global quotas, but the plan was tabled in the early 1990s.

After the Textile, Apparel, and Footwear Act was vetoed in 1990, FIA—which had lobbied for import protection—effectively gave up the fight. Fawn Evenson, then executive director of the FIA, told *The Journal of Commerce and Commercial* in 1992, "We literally spent millions of dollars on trade cases. We almost went broke trying to protect jobs."

In 1990, FIA voted to expand its membership to include importers and tacitly supported the North American Free Trade Agreement (NAFTA) by focusing its efforts on ensuring that Mexico would not become a transit point for duty free shoes from other countries, most of which imposed tariffs of 25 percent or more on U.S. exports or locked out U.S. companies entirely. Evenson explained, "We are importers. We've stopped quota battles. We're going to spend a lot more time on market access and on exports. We're now going to devote our efforts to companies that are surviving."

One consequence of the increasing drive to manufacture U.S. footwear abroad was the widespread exposure in 1996 of the so-called "sweatshop" conditions under which many of these items were produced. Nike Inc., which made 70 million pairs of shoes in Indonesia alone that year, bore much of the criticism when publications like *Business Week* reported on the difficult conditions in many of its Asian factories. Under pressure from the public and U.S. labor groups, the Beaverton, Oregon-based firm vowed to correct the violations.

FURTHER READING

"Background on the Florsheim Shoe Company." Chicago: The Florsheim Company, 10 December 1992.

Bahls, Jane Easter. "U.S. Shoe Firms Thrive in High-Quality Market." *Nation's Business,* February 1989, 38.

Bentz, Kristen. "True West." *Footwear +,* March 1997, 24.

Clifford, Mark. "Pangs of Conscience." *Business Week,* 29 July 1996, 46-47.

"Current Highlights of the Nonrubber Footwear Industry." Washington: Footwear Industries of America, 25 July 1996. Available from http://www.fia.org/.

Flax, Steven. "Boot Camp." *INC.,* September 1987, 99.

"Florsheim . . . A Century of Quality and Fashion." Chicago: The Florsheim Company, 7 January 1993.

Marriott, Michel. "Out of the Woods." *New York Times,* 7 November 1993, V1.

McDowell, Colin. *Shoes: Fashion and Fantasy,* New York: Rizzoli International Publications, Inc., 1989.

Melamed, Dennis. "The Party's Over for US Manufacturers." *Journal of Commerce and Commercial,* 4 May 1992, 9A.

Pereira, Joseph. "Sneaker Makers, Hearing Clomp-Clomp of Competition, Launch 'Rugged' Lines." *Wall Street Journal,* 14 September 1993, B1.

Rhodes, Lucien. "Sole Success." *INC.,* February 1982, 44.

Waxler, Caroline. "Walking Wounded." *Forbes,* 20 May 1996, 280.

—Dean Boyer, updated by Howard Rothman

SIC 3144

WOMEN'S FOOTWEAR, EXCEPT ATHLETIC

This category covers establishments engaged in the production of women's footwear designed primarily for dress, street, and work. Establishments engaged

in the production of athletic shoes and misses', children's, infants', and babies' footwear are classified in **SIC 3149: Footwear, Except Rubber, Not Elsewhere Classified.** Establishments primarily engaged in the production of rubber or plastic footwear are classified in **SIC 3021: Rubber and Plastics Footwear,** and those manufacturing orthopedic extension shoes are classified in **SIC 3842: Orthopedic, Prosthetic, and Surgical Appliances and Supplies.**

INDUSTRY SNAPSHOT

The U.S. women's footwear industry is dominated by large companies that design and manufacture a wide variety of shoes each year. For many years now, it has been heavily influenced by the continuing popularity of rubber-soled athletic shoes and other outdoor-oriented casual models that do not fall directly into this category. A steady market of consumers eager for new styles, along with the short life span of a pair of shoes, have produced lucrative profits for the nation's well-established footwear manufacturers. According to Footwear Industries of America (FIA), U.S. companies produced and shipped nearly 49.5 million pairs of women's shoes in 1995 with a total value of more than $1.1 billion. In relation to the overall footwear industry, women's models accounted for about 31 percent of all shoes produced by manufacturers in the United States and 32 percent of the total value of these shoes. The import of foreign-made footwear has been the biggest problem for domestic shoe manufacturers as comparably stylish but lower priced models made outside the United States continue to dominate the market. Approximately 10 times as many imports as domestically made women's shoes were sold in the United States in 1995, arriving primarily from China, Brazil, and Indonesia. These imports carried lower price tags than similar American-made styles, primarily because of the lower labor and production costs.

ORGANIZATION AND STRUCTURE

Unveiling a wide assortment of new shoe styles each season is how industry leaders regularly improve their product lines and increase their market shares. A shoe company's in-house design staff, which closely monitors European and American fashion trends and then develops appropriate new versions of their firm's basic products, is a key aspect of these manufacturing operations—and one of the most expensive parts of the entire process. Consequently, more and more companies have attempted to reduce overall costs by relocating many preliminary manufacturing tasks to foreign factories where labor expenses are lower; however, shoes are returned often to the United States for a number of final production steps. The finished footwear is then distributed to stores around the nation by marketing teams that negotiate with retail outlets and department stores in an effort to place as much of their company's products on display shelves as possible. Competition is fierce and dramatic shifts within the industry based on the smallest stylistic or structural innovation are commonplace. To keep up with these changes, much of the industry's design, marketing, and management personnel meet at annual trade gatherings like the Fashion Footwear Association of New York show, the National Shoe Fair, and Shoes in New York.

CURRENT CONDITIONS

The domestic women's footwear industry has continued to undergo a slow but consistent decline as imports hold steady, per-capita consumption in the United States drops, and Americans find they can wear the same shoes for many different occasions. The total value of shipments for America's women's shoe manufacturers reached a peak of $1.4 billion in 1988, and began dropping from 2 to 9 percent in each subsequent year until reaching $1.17 billion in 1995. Over the same period, U.S. production fell nearly 35 percent. With U.S. per-capita shoe consumption falling from more than five pairs in the 1960s to 4.2 pairs in the 1990s, industry analysts have predicted the decline will continue. However, the growing popularity of casual shoes—boosted by the ongoing prominence of athletic styles and their increasing acceptance in the workplace and various social settings—has led to some optimism. Imported women's footwear, which reached nearly 497 million pairs in 1995, dwarfed the 49.4 million pairs manufactured domestically that year; at the same time, U.S. women's shoe exports increased slightly to total 3.7 million pairs.

INDUSTRY LEADERS

Nine West Group Inc. became the largest player in the U.S. women's shoe industry in 1995 when it purchased the footwear assets from its biggest competitor, United States Shoe Corp., for $600 million from a company called Luxottica. That year, Nine West employed 3,900 people and recorded $625 million in sales.

A relative newcomer to the field, this Stamford, Connecticut-based company was founded in 1977. The publicly held firm quickly attained a place of distinction by sourcing out much of its manufacturing tasks to factories in countries like Brazil, and then delivering fashionable products at competitive prices. Its shoes developed high brand recognition and were found in

department stores as well as the company's own retail outlets. This strategy proved successful, and by the early 1990s, its original Nine West stores—which accounted for 30 percent of all company sales at the time—tallied one of the industry's highest sales-per-square-foot ratios. Product lines in those years included the Nine West, Calico, and Enzo Angiolini brands, and by pricing them between $20-$55, the company appealed to younger working women who sought fashionable shoes at a reasonable price. In particular, its Enzo Angiolini division made great strides in the early 1990s against several major competitors also offering moderately-priced, European-styled dress and career shoes like the Bandolino line then produced by U.S. Shoe.

Such inroads ultimately proved fatal to the footwear efforts of U.S. Shoe, which was founded in 1931 and was once one of the largest American manufacturers of women's shoes. In 1995, that publicly held company—a large diversified manufacturing concern that also was a franchiser of retail shoe, apparel, and eyeglass stores—employed 40,000 and had annual sales of nearly $2.6 billion. Its shoe manufacturing divisions operated under a variety of corporate names including Bandolino, Selby, Easy Spirit, Vittorio Ricci, Capezio, Amalfi, Evan Picone, Pappagallo, Texas Boot, and Wrangler Boot. It also operated the August Max Woman, Caren Charles, Pappagallo, and Casual Corner nationwide retail apparel outlets, and LensCrafters optical-goods outlets.

U.S. Shoe began suffering major losses to Nine West in the early 1990s, especially as its once dominant Bandolino division—offering dress and career shoes priced from $55-$70 and targeted at fashion-conscious working women—fell victim to unfavorable exchange rates stemming from its manufacture in Italy, and the fresher styles in the same price range introduced by competitors such as Nine West. Retailers began discounting Bandolino and the brand's all-important image suffered among consumers; as demand decreased department stores ceded more shelf space to Nine West, and U.S. Shoe and Bandolino lost even more ground.

U.S. Shoe had made some strides through the early 1990s by emphasizing its Easy Spirit line of dress shoes, which it introduced in 1988. This label was a direct response to the growing needs of women in the workforce who were pairing business attire with athletic footwear for street travel, carrying their uncomfortable dress pumps in a bag, and then changing shoes after arriving at work. Pump sales had peaked in the mid-1980s but dropped off as they became less of a fashion staple and more of a basic wardrobe necessity.

Trying to capitalize on women's continuing need for a dressy shoe but increasing unwillingness to torture their feet in high heels, U.S. Shoe combined low- to medium-heeled pumps with flexible soles and padded linings. Advertising campaigns depicted women playing basketball in the shoes and trumpeted the slogan, "Looks like a pump, feels like a sneaker." Priced at around $100 a pair, the shoes cost more than average pumps, but nonetheless proved popular.

Ultimately, however, such efforts—along with a decision to begin manufacturing U.S. Shoe's more casual models in lower-cost Brazilian and Far Eastern production facilities—were insufficient to stem the negative tide and the company was sold to Luxottica in 1995. Luxottica ultimately kept LensCrafters, sold the women's apparel division to an Italian concern, and dealt all footwear businesses to Nine West.

Nine West immediately began incorporating various U.S. Shoe lines into its own operation, placing a number of shoe stores (such as Easy Spirit and Easy Spirit Outlet) under its management arm, and announcing in early 1997 that it would close three of its former rival's domestic manufacturing facilities and transfer the additional production overseas. This move reduced Nine West's U.S.-produced footwear from 8.5 million pairs in 1995 to about five million pairs—then representing less than 10 percent of its total production and continuing the strategy that helped it overtake U.S. Shoe in the first place. The move also eliminated about 1,000 of the company's 1,900 American manufacturing jobs.

Kenneth Cole Productions Inc., also a relative newcomer to the women's footwear industry, has garnered a lot of attention in recent years. Founded in 1982, this private New York City-based company employed about 500 people and reported sales of $114 million in 1995—up sharply from its nearly $85 million in revenues the previous year. Kenneth Cole markets trendy shoes carrying relatively high price tags to both men and women with an interest in current fashions and timely events, and is increasingly known for its controversial advertising campaigns that combine corporate imagery with politically oriented messages. (Several of its ads in the mid-1990s, for example, centered on AIDS.) The company, which also sells fashionable eyewear, practices what it preaches by making corporate financial donations to a variety of social causes and encouraging its employees to become involved in charitable projects.

The Stride Rite Corp. is another a key player in the industry whose women's division is only one part of its overall footwear operation. The Cambridge, Massachusetts, company profited in the 1980s by re-

marketing its lightweight canvas Keds sneaker, a standard product which it had made for more than 70 years. The renewed success of this casual shoe led to the reemergence of a similar product line, carrying the Grasshoppers label, which was aimed at older women. Models in this line included Keds-style canvas casuals, leather casuals, espadrilles, and leather sandals. Another major producer of both women's and men's sport-oriented casual footwear was the Maine-based Dexter Shoe Co., which employed 2,000 people and reported sales of $140 million in 1996. That year, additional large U.S. suppliers of footwear for women included G.H. Bass & Co., Brown Shoe Co., Bally Inc., and Cherokee Shoe Co.; together, these firms accounted for approximately $874 million in sales in 1996.

While many of these latter companies rely on dress-oriented models for the bulk of their sales, the continuing popularity of casual footwear based on athletic-shoe styling and comfort has led to a burgeoning new segment of the women's shoe industry. Footwear manufacturers, including many athletic shoe companies themselves, jumped into this niche in the early 1990s and began offering comfortable quasi-athletic shoes made with leather uppers and an emphasis on unique styling. This trend coincided with a general relaxation of office dress codes and created a new half-casual, half-workplace type of shoe.

One of the first companies to go after this segment was the Oregon-based athletic shoe giant Nike Inc.; its original "i.e. by Nike" line was introduced in 1988 to much success and spawned a rash of imitators, such as the Boks line made by Reebok and Converse's Athleisure models. Most utilized popular athletic-shoe materials and compressed air-cushioning pockets that were placed in the heel and the front of each sole, but were differentiated from their true sport-oriented cousins by a variety of bright colors and an array of street styles; they were intended primarily to complement casual apparel. By the mid-1990s, some of their cachet—particularly among younger consumers—had been transferred to a new group of upstart manufacturers that traced their roots to the skateboarding and beach cultures of Southern California. These companies such as Airwalk, Vans, Sketchers, and Simple, initially aimed their sneaker-like products at young men, but in 1995 began broadening their marketing approaches and design plans to include young women as well. "We've had a ton of people asking for cool but comfortable women's shoes," Simple president Eric Meyer told *Action Sports Retailer* magazine as one reason for the new emphasis.

WORK FORCE

Footwear manufacturers based in the United States have increasingly moved their production operations overseas to boost their profits and, according to Footwear Industries of America, shoe imports have accordingly risen by 516 percent between 1968 and 1995. About 89 percent of all non-rubber footwear designed for U.S. consumption is now produced in some 100 foreign countries primarily noted for having relatively few government rules on working conditions, health and safety matters, and the right to unionize. China, Brazil, and Indonesia alone accounted for nearly 84 percent of all non-rubber footwear imports in 1995, while several aggressive newcomers were attempting to move into the U.S. marketplace. Among them was Colombia, where hourly wages were just $3-$4 an hour. Only six million pairs of shoes were produced for export in the mid-1990s; local officials predicted, however, that this total would be increased to 15-20 million pairs by the turn of the century.

The continuing decline in domestically produced footwear in recent years resulted in the closure of 1,200 U.S. shoe factories between 1968 and 1995, and a loss of nearly 180,000 direct manufacturing jobs during that time. According to FIA, though, about 53,800 people remained employed domestically that year by nearly 200 manufacturers operating 341 plants in 31 states.

AMERICA AND THE WORLD

Manufacturers of women's footwear in the United States continue to face strong competition from cheaper imports. The amount of imported shoes on the American market has increased greatly in recent years, from 175 million pairs in 1968 to 374 million in 1978, and from 941 million pairs in 1986 to 1.08 billion in 1995. The majority of these shoes now come from the Far East, with imports from China growing by 39 percent each year since 1981 to top 716 million pairs in 1995. U.S. companies learned to reduce costs further by shipping cut footwear patterns to plants in Third World countries, where they were then either partially or completely assembled. The firms did this because it was cheaper for the footwear to be only partially assembled abroad, since American companies pay a lower duty (typically 5 percent) on unfinished goods being re-exported to the United States. The final, less labor-intensive manufacturing details—such as bottoming, finishing, and packing—are then completed at home.

On the other side of the international trade front, American companies shipped more than 20.5 million pairs of footwear abroad for sale in 1995—of which about 18 percent were women's models. The value of all U.S. shoe exports that year was $367 million, up more than 44 percent from the value in 1990. Japan received nearly 12.5 percent of this total, followed by Canada at 11.6 percent; Mexico, the biggest foreign market for American footwear only two years earlier, fell to just 6 percent. The United Kingdom, Hong Kong, France, Honduras, and Germany accounted for the rest of the exports.

Several consequences for the American women's footwear industry developed after the 1993 ratification of the North American Free Trade Agreement (NAFTA) by the United States, Canada, and Mexico. Under the agreement's guidelines, duties on shoes produced in Mexico were to be reduced over a 10-year period, which some thought could lead to an increase in imports. However, NAFTA's rules also addressed the origin of shoes produced in Mexico, setting limits on the amount of materials that could be produced in countries with burgeoning shoe industries in Central and South America. These content regulations should help insure that third-country manufacturers do not nominally assemble shoes in Mexico, then ship them to the United States and benefit from the reduced tariffs. These South and Central American countries, however, are also involved in negotiating similar trade agreements with the United States, which could result in lowered or nonexistent tariffs on U.S. imports in the late 1990s.

RESEARCH AND TECHNOLOGY

Like other industries, the production and sale of U.S. women's footwear has been greatly changed by computer technology. Companies have invested large sums of money to integrate the latest electronic equipment into all facets of their operations. In the research and development segment, the use of computer-aided design (CAD) is now common, and many firms have integrated it with computer-aided manufacturing (CAM) processes. The combination allows shoes to be produced in America more quickly and accurately, which dramatically lowered production costs but also eliminated jobs. The women's footwear industry has additionally brought robotics technology into the manufacturing process, utilizing robots to move shoes from one production module to the next. Computers are also used extensively in the industry's management sector, usually tracking production figures and coordinating them with distribution results and sales totals.

FURTHER READING

Agins, Teri. "Shoemakers Introduce Walking Pumps with Sneaker Comfort, High-Heel Style." *Wall Street Journal,* 27 March 1989.

"Boks by Reebok Get Independent Division Status." *Footwear News,* 9 December 1991.

Byrne, Harlan S. "United States Shoe." *Barron's,* 17 February 1992.

"Current Highlights of the Nonrubber Footwear Industry." Washington: Footwear Industries of America, 25 July 1996. Available from http://www.fia.org/.

Current Industrial Reports: Footwear, Fourth Quarter 1992. Washington: U.S. Department of Commerce, March 1993.

Foster, Caryl, and Rich Wilner. "Casuals Widen Athletics' Horizons." *Footwear News,* 16 November 1992.

"High Heeled Sneakers." *Time,* 14 May 1990.

Infantino, Vivian. "Fashion Viewpoints." *Footwear News,* 14 December 1992.

Lucas, Allison. "Heart and Sole." *Sales & Marketing Management,* May 1996, 30.

Marcial, Gene G. "U.S. Shoe May Be Hot to Trot." *Business Week,* 21 January 1991.

McAllister, Bob. "i.e.: In Other Words . . . Fashionable Technology." *Footwear News,* 5 August 1991.

McNally, Pamela, and Isabelle Sender. "Retail: Nine West Still Dynamic." *Footwear News,* 24 May 1993.

"Nine West Group." *Fortune,* 3 May 1993.

"Nine West to Open 146 Stores." *Footwear News,* 12 July 1993.

"NSRA Conference in Las Vegas." *Footwear News,* 27 February 1995.

Peale, Cliff. "Luxottica Settles Terms of U.S. Shoe Sale." *Cincinnati Post,* 30 May 1996.

Rooney, Ellen. "Marx & Newman Shuffles Management; Retailers Blame Styling, Prices." *Footwear News,* 15 March 1993.

Rooney. "Bandolino Will Pick up Enzo Angiolini Gauntlet." *Footwear News,* 6 December 1993.

Rossi, William. "Going Nowhere: Is Footwear Retailing Stuck In A No-Growth Rut?" *Footwear News,* 18 December 1995.

Rothman, Howard. "Rising to the Occasion." *Action Sports Retailer,* February 1995, 45.

Sohng, Laurie. "In Praise of Pumps: An Ode to Immortality." *Footwear News,* 22 November 1993.

Strassel, Kimberly. "Nine West Plans U.S. Plant Closings, Paring 1,000 Jobs." *The Wall Street Journal,* 13 February 1997, C16.

Tedeschi, Mark. "Colombia Out To Lure Shoe Business." *Footwear News,* 4 March 1996, 2.

Tedeschi, Mark. "Keds Wants Grasshoppers to Entice Women over 35." *Footwear News,* 22 July 1991.

U.S. Industrial Outlook 1994, Washington: U.S. Department of Commerce, January 1994.

—Carol Brennan, updated by Howard Rothman

SIC 3149

FOOTWEAR, EXCEPT RUBBER, NOT ELSEWHERE CLASSIFIED

This classification includes establishments primarily engaged in the production of shoes, not elsewhere classified, such as misses', youths', boys', children's, and infants' footwear and athletic footwear. Establishments primarily engaged in the manufacture of rubber or plastics footwear are classified in **SIC 3021: Rubber and Plastics Footwear,** and those manufacturing orthopedic extension shoes are classified in **SIC 3842: Orthopedic, Prosthetic, and Surgical Appliances and Supplies.**

INDUSTRY SNAPSHOT

The nonrubber footwear industry manufactured all types of footwear except rubber protective and rubber-soled fabric-upper (the traditional "sneaker"). Nonrubber footwear may be constructed with leather, vinyl, plastic, or textile uppers or combinations of these materials for all ages and both genders. Men's footwear producers, classified in **SIC 3143: Men's Footwear, Except Athletic**, and women's footwear producers, classified in **SIC 3144: Women's Footwear, Except Athletic**, composed their own independent industries.

As a group, the nonrubber footwear industry reported a 2.6 percent decline in shoe production in 1996 from 1995 figures, and recorded a 19.5 percent decline in profits. However, 94 percent of the group's total profits came from the two largest athletic footwear producers. Four companies, including the third largest athletic footwear producer, recorded losses in 1992.

In 1994, shipments of footwear began to steadily decline, dropping approximately 24 percent to 19 million pairs in 1995. The value of these shipments decreased 68 percent from 1994 to an estimated $139 million in 1996. Shipments of footwear in this group accounted for 15 percent by quantity and 7 percent by value of all categories of footwear sold. Production of all types of footwear within this industry fell in 1996, dropping by an annual rate of 3.2 percent over the last five years.

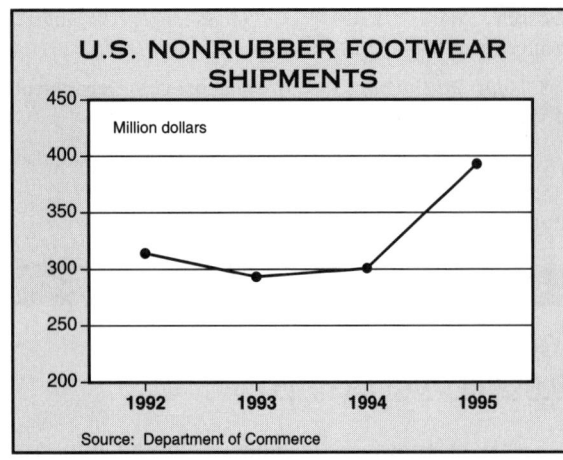

U.S. NONRUBBER FOOTWEAR SHIPMENTS

Million dollars

Source: Department of Commerce

ORGANIZATION AND STRUCTURE

In 1987, there were 120 companies operating in 129 establishments in this industry. In 1992, that number had gone down to just 84 companies operating 94 establishments. By 1996, establishments had dropped to an estimated 52, with 12 factories closing from 1995. Many of the plants closed in the early 1990s were owned by the largest manufacturing and retailing companies, which opted to source more footwear from less expensive producers overseas. In 1996, total employment declined about 11 percent to 46,100; production employment also declined by about the same amount.

More than half (56 percent) of the nonrubber footwear produced in the United States had leather uppers in 1996. This was up from 51 percent in 1991. Only 31 percent of juvenile types of shoes had leather uppers, while almost all athletic footwear had leather uppers.

Historically, consumers primarily have purchased their footwear at footwear specialty stores and department stores. In the past, customers were strongly brand-loyal and most often selected footwear purchases on the basis of brand recognition and style. During the 1980s, consumers took great interest in their appearance and became slightly extravagant at the sales counter. Personal consumption of footwear and other apparel nearly doubled in the 1980s, with an average annual growth rate of 7.3 percent. However, hurt by a recession, weak growth in disposable income, and high unemployment, consumers in the early 1990s became much more frugal.

Along with these economic changes came changes in consumer psychology. Designer names, high-priced shoes and apparel, and frequent shopping sprees became things of the past. Consumers became more value conscious and began purchasing less expensive products at lower-end retail establishments,

such as mass merchandisers. *Footwear News* indicated that consumers' footwear buying habits began to shift away from designer brands in 1993. The magazine also reported that many shoe buyers were seeking lower-priced goods in strip shopping centers and outlet stores instead of the higher-end shopping malls. According to *Women's Wear Daily,* department stores' share of all apparel expenditures fell to 24.3 percent in 1993, down from 33.6 percent in 1985. A survey by the *Wall Street Journal* confirmed that women were buying more of their families' shoes and other apparel at mass merchandisers, such as Kmart and Wal-Mart, and shopping less frequently at department and specialty stores.

In addition to opting for different types of retail establishments, shoppers also selected different types of merchandise by the early 1990s. Basic footwear and moderately priced brand name shoes were often the best selling items. This pattern reflected a more value-oriented consumer, as well as an aging population seeking comfort and less formality in footwear. In the late 1980s and early 1990s, many mass merchandisers added more recognizable national brand names to their in-store inventory. In the past, most brand names were distributed only through department stores.

By the 1990s, formal attire was less popular than it was in the 1980s, and footwear sales reflected this trend. A decrease in the size of the white collar work force and a trend toward more relaxed office attire contributed to a slide in the sale of formal footwear.

Throughout the late 1980s, the ten largest publicly traded apparel companies saw their market share increase by nearly 5 percent. Part of this growth was attributed to increased demand for these companies' products, but a series of acquisitions and consolidations also was beneficial. This consolidation of the footwear manufacturing industry paralleled developments in the retail industry as a whole. As large department store retailers merged in the late 1980s, they consolidated their buying functions. Larger apparel and footwear manufacturers benefited from this because it became more efficient for the fewer number of buyers to use one vendor rather than several. In response, growth-oriented apparel and footwear manufacturers increased their acquisition activity in search of new brands and broader product offerings.

In addition, the enormous growth of large mass merchandisers drove the industry to consolidate. From 1981 through 1991, Sears, the nation's largest retailer, saw its sales increase rapidly, as did Wal-Mart and Kmart. Savvy footwear manufacturers understood they could increase their sales and market share by offering these retail giants a broad array of brand-name merchandise. Historically, many brand-name manufacturers sold their goods only to department stores, but later sold nearly identical merchandise to mass merchandisers in order to participate in that sector's phenomenal growth. Not surprisingly, this affected manufacturers' relationships with department stores, which sought exclusivity in their products. To remedy the situation, many manufacturers began to produce several different categories of brand names, each of which was distributed through a different type of retailer.

Throughout history, retailers and footwear manufacturers have had an adversarial relationship because of issues centered around pricing. By the mid-1990s, pricing was still an important factor, but retailers still wanted more. Storage of inventory was one of the highest expenses a retailer faced. To reduce this expense, retailers increasingly were demanding that manufacturers carry the inventory instead, and make deliveries when the retailers' stock was low. In order for this type of relationship to work, especially when dealing with large quantities of merchandise required by stores such as Wal-Mart or Kmart, retailers and vendors found it necessary to form partnerships. Quick response is the most important aspect of this relationship. Orders must be replenished automatically via computer links called electronic data interchange (EDI).

Retailers also demanded a continual flow of new merchandise. Some footwear manufacturers responded to this need by creating "flow replenishment" programs, in which new products were introduced in a continual flow rather than in seasonal batches. In addition, retailers were demanding more marketing support and other services. Many manufacturers, as a result, were creating their own point-of-sale fixtures, and advertising their products nationally.

Experts attributed the growing appeal of outlet stores to the value-conscious shopper. Outlet stores' primary attraction was the price of their products. Customers generally purchased footwear and other apparel items at up to half the cost charged by conventional department and specialty stores. In many cases, the merchandise offered was no longer just the irregulars, overruns, or odd lots. Often, the merchandise was first-quality, coming from current inventory, although many footwear manufacturers used their own outlet stores to dispense extra or second-quality merchandise. Manufacturers preferred this form of distribution to off-price retailers because they could avoid tarnishing their brand names. This risk often occurred when too much merchandise was sold through discounters. In addition, outlet stores also tended to be located far from the selling areas of conventional department and specialty stores. This decreased the chance that the

manufacturer's regular retail store lost sales to the outlet store.

CURRENT CONDITIONS

Athletic Footwear. Athletic footwear was the largest-selling category in the footwear industry, and the only division within nonrubber footwear to post any gains. Production of athletic footwear reached a peak of about 6.5 million pairs in 1993, but declined to 5.5 million pairs in 1995. Consumption of athletic footwear, which includes imports, rose from a 1993 total of 382 million pairs to 408 million pairs in 1995. Imports continued to dominate representing 99 percent of consumption as U.S. production continued to decline. Imports rose by an average of 3.5 percent per year since 1990. However, even though the number of shoes purchased declined, the sales of athletic shoes actually increased, to $11.4 billion. Athletic footwear represented about 26 percent of combined nonrubber and rubber-fabric footwear consumption of approximately 1.6 billion pairs in 1995. Imports of juvenile footwear in 1996 were down from 1995, but still higher than any previous year; imports of athletic nonrubber footwear increased from 1995 but were still lower than any other year in the early 1990s.

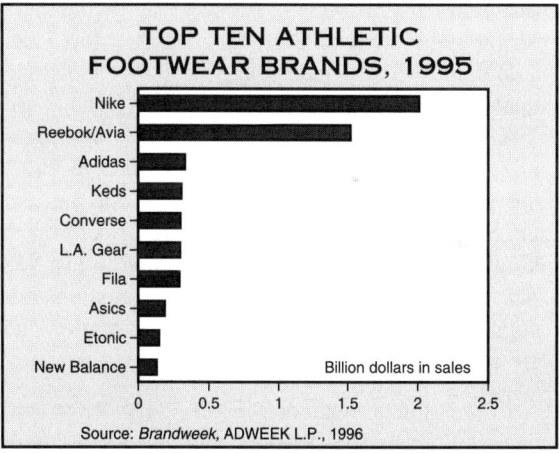

TOP TEN ATHLETIC FOOTWEAR BRANDS, 1995

Source: *Brandweek*, ADWEEK L.P., 1996

The largest selling and most consistently popular brand of athletic footwear was from NIKE, Inc.—in fact, men bought NIKE 70 percent of the time, and women, 61 percent of the time. Reebok was not far behind, and was in fact the only brand that gave stiff competition to NIKE. Reebok International Ltd.'s shoes represented 46 percent of purchases for men and 57 percent of purchases for women. Adidas, Converse, and Fila rounded out the top five brands, but none had more than 23 percent of purchases.

The Summer Olympics of 1996 gave the top athletic brands a chance to compete with each other for sponsorship and advertising rights. The general target audience was 18- to 34-year olds, and marketers reached them with a mix of sports, lifestyle television programming, and magazine titles. While NIKE, Converse, and Avia built strong followings in the performance shoe business, Reebok and L.A. Gear had more of a fashion than a performance-based image. Nike, though not an official sponsor of the Olympic games, led the way by spending more on advertising, and in fact, many people believed they were a sponsor. Reebok teamed with The Athlete's Foot in downtown Atlanta to show off "Planet Reebok," hoping to cash in on its proximity to the athletes and spectators. Most athletic shoe companies relied on high-priced, prime time television advertisements and major sporting event television advertisements for most of their media advertisements.

The nation's largest selling footwear company, Kinney Shoe Corporation, launched its own private label of athletic footwear in August 1993 through its Foot Locker sneaker and sports apparel retail chain. The new shoe brand, In the Zone or ITZ, had its own independent marketing budget and was set to compete with the volatile second tier of athletic shoe brands, such as L.A. Gear, Adidas, Converse, and Asics.

Outdoor Footwear. One of the fastest-growing categories in the footwear industry was outdoor footwear. Outdoor footwear included rugged hiking boots and casual outdoor sandals. Hiking boots sales had exploded, selling 27 million pairs in 1995, compared with just 22 million in 1994 and 11 million in 1992. Sales grew 14 percent to top $1 billion for the first time. Sales grew in spite of an average price drop in hiking boots, going from $42 dollars a pair to just $38 a pair. Many traditional athletic footwear companies recognized the potential profit in this category and were scrambling to participate.

In the athletic outdoor shoe category, Teva sandals, manufactured by Deckers Outdoor Corp., were one of the most popular styles of outdoor sports sandal in the 1990s. Sales for 1996 dropped by less than 1 percent to $102 million as the market was flooded with imitation Tevas and a wide array of sports sandals from all the major athletic shoe companies. After the initial excitement waned, however, consumers were going back to the original, and Deckers' first quarter sales for 1997 increased 20 percent over first quarter 1996, with sales of Tevas increasing by 30 percent.

One of the fastest-growing companies in the outwear shoe category was Timberland Company. In addition to streamlining its operations, Timberland cultivated the casual, outdoor fashion that began to

increase in popularity in the early 1990s. Sales increased by 125 percent since 1992, to $655 million in 1995. Many companies were attempting to imitate Timberland's style, but consumers still considered Timberland to be the "original." In *Adweek,* Don Maurer of Mullen Advertising stated that Timberland could become the next NIKE.

Safety footwear constituted yet another segment of the footwear industry. This type of footwear was worn mainly by workers with hazardous, physically demanding jobs. This segment included heavy leather work boots with steel toes for extra protection. According to *Occupational Hazards,* safety footwear was beginning to look much more like mainstream retail footwear in the mid-1990s. The article stated that workers cared as much about style and comfort as they did about protection, and that they were more inclined to wear shoes that are aesthetically pleasing. The most successful safety footwear manufacturers were designing shoes that provided a safe environment for the foot with an overall stylish appeal.

Juvenile Footwear. After many years of rapid growth due to the heavy sales demands of the post-war baby boom era, juvenile footwear sales slowed in the early 1990s. Despite reaching the peak of the baby boom, however, competition among this category's competitors was still tight. Production of juvenile's footwear had steadily declined through the 1990s, dropping below 10 million pairs (9,562) for the first time ever in 1996.

The undisputed leader in juvenile footwear was Stride Rite Corp. In 1993, after 27 consecutive quarters of increased earnings, company sales started dropping from $585 million in 1992 to $448 million in 1996. Stride Rite's primary competition in the juvenile footwear industry included Keds (a brand also owned by Stride Rite), Weebok (owned by Reebok), Sebago, Sam & Libby, and Toddler University. As in the case of adult footwear, the industry witnessed a trend away from shopping at higher-priced department stores and specialty shop retailers, toward lower-priced mass merchandisers and outlet stores.

With more two-career families, parents were finding less time to take children shopping. As a result, the industry also was witnessing a trend toward direct mail purchasing through catalogs. *Catalog Age* reported the founding of many new children's apparel catalogs with particularly aggressive marketing approaches. These merchandisers were careful not to dilute their efforts by focusing attention on their primary footwear merchandise.

AMERICA AND THE WORLD

With limited prospects for domestic growth, many footwear companies in the early 1990s were looking for growth opportunities abroad. For footwear merchandise, market penetration was limited since tastes in fashion apparel differ from one country to the next, yet every country in the world was looking to sell in America, the world's leader in footwear consumption. China's exports to the United States have grown 2,600 percent since 1986, at an average rate of 40 percent annually. In 1996 China exported 750 million pairs of shoes, with Brazil the second biggest exporter to the United States with 91 million pairs. The import penetration rate has ballooned over the last 20 years, going from around 40 percent in 1976 to topping 90 percent for the first time in 1996.

Overall exports in nonrubber footwear improved, shipping just under 25 million pairs in 1996. Athletic shoes improved slightly, while exports in slippers (which included the sports sandal) tripled from 1995, going from 607 million pairs to 1.8 billion pairs in just one year. Juvenile footwear also showed strong international sales in 1996, almost doubling its 1995 showing, increasing to 5 million pairs. Japan enjoyed its second year as main importer of U.S. footwear, taking the mantle from Canada in 1995. Exports to Japan totaled 3.6 million pairs in 1996, with Canada taking 2.4 million pairs. The U.K. market continued to grow, importing 1.6 million pairs, and Mexico imported 1.1 million pairs of U.S. footwear.

Many manufacturers believed that basic footwear, such as tennis shoes and children's shoes, had the potential for a large international market. Many brand-name products, such as NIKE, became major international franchises in the late 1990s. In 1996, international sales accounted for 36 percent of its total of $6.4 billion. Total worldwide orders for athletic footwear was $3.9 billion in 1996 compared to only $2.5 billion in 1995. Such rapidly rising worldwide sales were especially important to NIKE as it struggled to overcome slow growth in the United States. In China, NIKE found that its challenge was to get its shoes into stores and ensure that those stores knew how to display products that were extremely expensive by Chinese standards. In the Philippines, 20 percent of NIKE's shoe sales were made by door-to-door salesmen who sold the shoes on credit. Keeping control of its distribution operation and remaining flexible in the face of cultural differences were keys to boosting NIKE's sales in the region. According to the *Far Eastern Economic Review*, NIKE gained control of its distribution in Taiwan, Hong Kong, Malaysia, China, Singapore, Australia, and New Zealand within a three year period. NIKE executives spoke of creating an emotional tie with the consumer in these countries, and as a result, NIKE was one of the world's most recognized brand images in the 1990s and was the world's largest supplier of athletic footwear.

Timberland Company also was successful in exporting its footwear. In 1983, the company had no interest in foreign markets; in 1996, nearly 30 percent of its business came from overseas markets, and Timberland owned franchises and retail stores for its products in 50 countries. Timberland's executives developed an interest in the export business when they joined forces with an Italian consumer goods distributor to establish European operations. Once there, they learned that international marketing campaigns needed to be country-specific to succeed. According to the company's director of international business, Timberland became very sensitive to cultural differences and won many European customers by developing new flexible marketing techniques, which included "concept shops," "specialty shops," and filling retailers orders quickly.

RESEARCH AND TECHNOLOGY

Like most industries, manufacturers in the nonrubber footwear industry were under extreme pressure to limit the size of their work force, while boosting productivity and efficiency at the same time. For that reason, the industry considered new technology essential to increase growth and profitability. In the 1970s and 1980s, the use of computers integrated design, manufacturing, management, and marketing tasks. Computerized production allowed manufacturers to emphasize non-price factors such as quality and quick delivery to compete with imports.

Many footwear producers turned to computer-aided design (CAD) and computer-aided manufacturing (CAM) systems and software. As a result, these manufacturers produced tooling from CAD-generated data and linked it to auto-stitchers, milling, and turning machines. In the early 1990s, the industry witnessed a resurgence of interest in three-dimensional CAD, which produced more accurate shoe patterns and reduced the number of prototypes required to take a new shoe design to the retail level.

In the footwear industry, computers also enabled manufacturers to combine several operations or machines under fewer operators, thereby reducing handling time and the number of employees, while improving quality. The industry also developed computerized robots to handle and transfer operations within and between production modules.

In order to meet the demands of retailers' quick response requirements, more and more manufacturers were utilizing electronic data interchange (EDI). The goal of quick response was to maintain lean inventories and avoid overstocking, while insuring that retailers had the merchandise customers wanted to buy. EDI allowed retailers and manufacturers to link themselves together.

In the EDI system, inter-linked computer systems were placed at every point of the manufacturing and sales process. Through use of an electronic scanner and bar code tagged to the merchandise, retailers recorded which type of footwear was sold at the point of sale. All sales data on the individual products, including details of color and size, were transmitted immediately to the manufacturer. Through this method, the manufacturer kept track of every store's retail sales trends. This first-hand view of consumer purchasing trends allowed manufacturers to produce apparel based directly on customer demand. The information contained in the bar code set automatic re-ordering into motion. The industry also referred to this type of inventory replenishment as "flow" or "just in time." In addition to allowing automatic replenishment, EDI also ameliorated distribution and shipping processes. For example, once a shipment was ready to go, the manufacturer created a labeling document, and EDI sent an invoice automatically.

A great deal of this new technology was developed and used in Europe before coming to the United States. Most of it was easily transferred to Far Eastern footwear producers, depending on the availability of capital. For these Far Eastern manufacturers, however, the labor-saving benefits of this new technology were not as great as for producers with higher production costs. Industry experts predicted that the net effect of such technology would reduce the costs of U.S. production relative to Far Eastern production, although the latter would continue to maintain a competitive advantage for most categories of footwear.

FURTHER READING

Bednarski, Kate. "Convincing Male Managers to Target Women Customers." *Working Woman,* June 1993, 23.

"Switch Consumers Bought Fewer Athletic Shoes in 1995, But Spent More." *AFA News,* 26 March 1996. Available from http://www.sportsite.com.

"Statistics." Washington: Footwear Industries of America. 1997. Available from http://fia.org.

Gaffney, Andrew. "Footwear's Future." *Sporting Goods Business,* January 1994, 44.

Jensen, Jeff. "Sneaker Ads on the Wrong Track." *Advertising Age,* 29 November 1993, 3.

Jensen, Jeff. "Sneaker Giants Are Heeding the Call of the Great Outdoors." *Advertising Age,* 31 January 1994, 4.

Laabs, Jennifer. "Family Issues Are a Priority at Stride Rite." *Personnel Journal,* July 1993, 48.

Maremont, Mark. "Timberland Comes Out of the Woods." *Business Week,* 13 September 1993, 78.

Miller, Cyndee. "Pitch for Sneakers Is Also Campaign to End Violence." *Marketing News,* 6 December 1993, 13.

Sharkey, Betsy. "If the Shoe Fits." *Adweek,* 14 February 1994, 23.

Sloan, Pat. "Reebok, Nike Look Beyond Sneakers." *Advertising Age,* 28 June 1993, 8.

"Timberland Product Profile." Greensboro, NC: Kayser-Roth Corp., 1996. Available from http://www.pantimedia.com/itimber.html.

U.S. Department of Commerce. Bureau of the Census. *1995 Annual Survey of Manufactures,* Washington: GPO, 1997.

SIC 3151

LEATHER GLOVES AND MITTENS

This category includes establishments primarily engaged in the manufacture of dress, semi-dress, and work gloves, which are made exclusively of leather or leather with lining of other materials. Excluded are establishments primarily engaged in the manufacture of athletic gloves **SIC 3949: Sporting and Athletic Goods, Not Elsewhere Classified,** semi-dress and work gloves made primarily of cloth **SIC 2381: Dress and Work Gloves, Except Knit and All-Leather,** and safety gloves **SIC 3842: Orthopedic, Prosthetic, and Surgical Appliances and Supplies.**

Historical data shows that the industry has been shrinking in both output and the number of manufacturers over the latter part of the twentieth century due to competition from lower-priced imports. The U.S. glove industry began about 1760 when Sir William Johnson, founder of Johnstown and Gloversville, New York, brought in a group of glove makers from Perthsire, England, to make deerskin mittens and heavy gloves for nearby farmers. Native Americans had shown Johnson how to use the local barks for dying and tanning. The abundant supply of deer hides and the availability of streams and lakes for tanning the hides and transporting the finished gloves to nearby farm communities helped the industry flourish.

Nineteenth-century inventions that mechanized glove cutting and sewing increased productivity in the industry, but the industry still needed skilled workers. In the 1890s, many glove workers came from Italy.

Fulton County, where Johnstown and Gloversville are located, remained the U.S. glove-making center, and was home to the now-defunct industry association and union headquarters. Through the 1930s, the U.S. Department of Labor noted, men cut most of the materials for gloves in the area's many small factories, and most of the sewing was performed by women. Sewing of the heavier work gloves was done in the factories on heavy duty machines, while work on the dress and semi-dress gloves was often done on a piece-work basis in homes.

After World War II, competition from cheaper labor abroad began to cut into the American market. In 1997, the largest single segment of the U.S. glovemaking industry remained in the Johnstown-Gloversville area of upper New York State. One of those companies, Elmer Little and Sons, Incorporated, was ranked fifth in sales in the 1997 edition of *Ward's Business Directory of U.S. Private and Public Companies.* In fiscal year 1995, the company reported sales of $10 million and a workforce of 25.

Aris Isotoner, Incorporated, while not located in the Johnstown-Gloversville area, was ranked first in sales. A division of Sara Lee Corporation, Aris employed 200 people in fiscal year 1995 and had an estimated revenue of $250 million. In addition to manufacturing leather gloves, the company also made leather slippers, and knit mittens and hats.

FURTHER READING

Wards Business Directory of U.S. Private and Public Companies. Detroit: Gale Research, 1997.

World Book Encyclopedia. Chicago: World Book, Inc., 1986.

—Joan Leotta, updated by Rose Estioco

SIC 3161

LUGGAGE

This category covers establishments primarily engaged in manufacturing luggage of leather or other materials. The luggage industry produces a wide variety of products, including suitcases, briefcases, attache cases, hand luggage, tote bags, trunks, and occupational cases. Materials used in addition to leather include plastics, nylon, cotton, linen, and metals. Many products use a combination of these materials. Construction methods include sewing, molding, and laminating. About 25 percent of U.S.-made luggage products are made of leather, with leather use most common in attache cases and briefcases.

INDUSTRY SNAPSHOT

Luggage shipments increased about 17.1 percent between 1988-1989 reaching to almost $1.13 billion in 1996. Total industry employment declined 3.7 percent, to 13,000 employees, but employment in the area of production increased about 4 percent, to 10,200. This indicated that the industry was lowering overhead labor, while increasing production. There are more than two dozen types of occupations in the luggage/leather products industry, including sewing machine operators, plastic molding machine operators, leather workers, assemblers, inspectors, and packagers.

In 1996, the moderate economic recovery continued and resulted in slightly more travel and, hence, more demand for luggage. Luggage purchases amounted to $2.2 billion in the mid-1990s, up about 12 percent from earlier in the decade. Imports increased about 15 percent from 1.8 billion in 1994 to $2.1 billion in 1995.

BACKGROUND AND DEVELOPMENT

Luggage—defined as a product designed to carry items by hand from place to place—has been around in some form or another since the beginning of time. Cave men and women likely carried sticks, stones, bones, and furs in small leather sacks or large skins as they moved from cave to cave. Egyptians packed precious objects into casket-shaped trunks and buried them in tombs with their kings and queens. In those early days, separate trunks or chests were used to transport different types of items; there were, for example, jewelry, linen, and wardrobe cases. This practice endured for centuries and is still popular with those who have no need to travel lightly.

How one traveled dictated what type of "luggage" one used. When traveling by foot, for example, a simple sack was often sufficient. If beasts of burden were available, items were boxed or bagged and secured atop the animal. Travel by ship or barge made it possible to use large trunks and chests. Of course, the more money one had, the grander the style of travel and the type of luggage. "Heaven only knows how many people it took to get Cleopatra's barge up the Nile, Marco Polo to China, or Mrs. Vanderbilt across the Atlantic," wrote Diane Sustendal in *Showcase.* "It's only in recent years that hopping the Concorde with a single bag has become a status way to travel. Prior to that, three or more matched pieces of luggage lined up at a dock, train station, or airport said something about the status of the traveler."

Whole groups of people, she noted, have been identified by the types of luggage they carried. The

"Casket Girls of Louisiana," young women sent from France to the colonies (now the United States) to marry, carried their belongings in caskets. Carpetbaggers got their name from the bags in which they carried cash and clothing to the South following the Civil War. "Old Saddlebags" referred to the early Pony Express riders who carried mail in such pouches on the back of horses. Some types of luggage have gotten their names from modes of transportation: the coach bag, train case, flight kit, pullman case, and steamer trunk are all examples. The luggage lexicon has also been affected by war. British soldiers during World War I had their "kit bag." American G.I.s packed their belongings in a "duffle bag" or "furlough bag."

The luggage industry bubbled with new ideas after World War II. Many materials developed for the wartime effort were put to use in the industry: rip-stop nylon, fiberglass, plastics, simulated fabric, leather, and aluminum. Manufacturers learned to design products that were durable, yet light enough to meet plane travel requirements. Luggage became available in three categories:constructed, or molded luggage; semiconstructed, with such features as side zipper entry and compartments for easy packing; and soft luggage, which is lightweight and collapsible.

Color added a fashion statement previously missing from luggage. Fashionable women travelers could choose from such colors as bright red, pale blue, pink, and cream; men had gray, navy, forest green, and burgundy as alternatives to the more conservative black or brown. In the late 1960s, the colors of luggage mimicked the colors of fashion—hot pink, neon yellow and orange, and bright blue.

By the 1970s, with the idea of space travel no longer a distant reality, luggage resembling space suit fabrics first appeared. During that same time period, "designer luggage" became the vogue, and luggage sported designer logos. As plane travel became faster and more efficient, travelers began placing a higher priority on speed. Manufacturers recognized this and devoted more of their attention on carry-on luggage, which permitted passengers to save time by avoiding check-in lines and baggage claim areas. The Mac Pac by Casecraft Incorporated illustrated this trend. This European-styled set consisted of a three-suit garment bag, a four-zipper expandable boarding case, and a 10-inch grooming kit. "We are targeting those people who want three pieces in one package," reported Larry Wiviott, director of sales and marketing for Casecraft, in *Upscale Discounting.*

In the 1980s, an era known for conspicuous consumption, customers demanded that their luggage demonstrate their wealth, status, and personal taste.

They looked for classic styling, quality, and high-fashion touches. Leather, tweeds, and stripes were big sellers. For example, Henry Rosenfeld Travelware introduced several new tweeds and leather designs in 1988. One line of luggage featured interchangeable sets. Popular colors included earth tones, blue-black, burgundy, melon, pumpkin, olive green, and deep gold.

Responding to the consumers' increasing interest in quality, name-brand luggage, vendors introduced luggage with better fabrics and more features, such as zippers, pockets, and compartments to hold such items as shirts, hair dryers, running shoes, and tennis racquets. Peters Bag Corporation introduced a Sasson Executive Style Luggage set in 1989, which included a garment bag with full front zippered pocket, adjustable shoulder strap, boarding bag with dual zipper opening, front and side zipper pockets, and a utility kit with a fully-lined interior and two-way zipper.

Business cases. Attache cases or briefcases have been around as long as people have had to call on clients. Scribes and physicians may have been the first to use some form of business case. Blacksmiths, cobblers, carpenters, seamstresses, musicians, and artists used bags, boxes, and small cases to transport the tools of their trade. The attache, with its hard sides and box-like construction, is a direct descendant of an artist's paint box and the scribe's writing box. Early coverings designed to protect books, letters, sketches, and legal briefs were forerunners of today's portfolios or briefcases.

Throughout the twentieth century, the functions and appearance of the business case have changed frequently and sometimes dramatically. While leather business cases are still popular, there are now more choices than ever before—molded cases of plastic or metal, fashion cases, canvas cases, and cases made of exotic skins. In the late 1980s, R.F. Kilpatric and Associates even introduced a wooden briefcase from Sweden, available in natural wood and a mahogany color. Briefcases that doubled as luggage also made their appearance.

Like luggage, business cases eventually became available in a variety of colors. Gray, burgundy, tan, forest green, even red, white, and blue became acceptable options for business executives. Such features as contrasting trim, gleaming or burnished hardware, detachable shoulder straps, and retractable handles also became available. Compartments for holding pens, business cards, calculators, checkbooks, cellular phones, computers, and mini-televisions were added to many of the new designs, as were sleeves to accommodate portfolios, notepaper, computer readouts, legal pads, agendas, and reports.

Business cases and attache's were expected to retain their traditional flavor throughout the 1990s. Sales for business cases rose 4 percent in 1996.

INDUSTRY LEADERS

Samsonite Corp., headquartered in Denver, Colorado, is the world's leading manufacturer of luggage. In 1996, the company had an estimated $800 million in sales. Samsonite was founded in 1910 as the Shwayder Trunk Manufacturing Company. It was not until 1966 that the company operated under the name Samsonite. From a one-room business near downtown Denver with 10 employees, Samsonite has grown into a network of 30 manufacturing and distribution centers employing 10,000 individuals throughout the world.

Samsonite established its reputation by producing a product that was extremely durable. The company's original slogan—"Strong enough to stand on"—was first illustrated by a picture of founder Jess Shwayder, his father, and three of his brothers standing on a plank that rested on a Shwayder hardcase. Samsonite became famous in the 1980s with it's television commercial featuring a gorilla throwing around Samsonite luggage; the commercial emphasized the durability of the product. Today Samsonite makes both hardside and softside luggage. Hardside luggage is made by the molding and assembly of plastic components, utilizing either vacuum forming or injection molding techniques. Samsonite's softside luggage involves the manufacturing of hand-assembled luggage made of synthetic fiber materials and steel or plastic frames. The company's hardside luggage sales continued to grow dramatically in the early 1990s, particularly in the European market. Samsonite is the leading manufacturer of hardside luggage in the world. Samsonite holds 900 patents worldwide for it's luggage designs and is the parent company of the number two brand of luggage, American Tourister.

The second largest U.S. luggage manufacturer is Zero Corporation of Los Angeles, California, which had sales of $206.2 million in 1996 and employed over 1,800 workers. Zero Corp. is followed by American Trading & Production and Hartmann Luggage Company. Major foreign players in the luggage industry include Louis Vuitton, a manufacturer of high quality luggage based in Paris, France, and Delsey Luggage Incorporated, also based in Paris. Delsey entered the upscale U.S. market in 1985 after establishing itself as the leading manufacturer of hard-sided luggage in Europe. "Delsey is considered to be France's largest luggage manufacturer and among the top three world-

wide, although well behind industry leader Samsonite," wrote Kurt Kleiner in the *Baltimore Business Journal.*

AMERICA AND THE WORLD

The resurgence of pride in America and American-made products in the 1980s prompted many luggage manufacturers to focus on American-made goods and push the "Made in the U.S.A." logo. Promoting U.S.-made luggage was often challenging, however, since few luggage products are actually made in the United States. "Almost all nylon goods, whether it's Samsonite, American Tourister, Verdi, it's all imported," said Gallup. "It has the good old American name but basically it's an import." According to American Tourister manager Karl Czerny, however, approximately 25 percent of their merchandise is made in the United States. That percentage is made up primarily of their hardsided luggage, which is bulky and expensive to import.

Luggage imports continued to rise throughout the 1990s to an estimated $2.1 billion in 1995. Although almost 31 percent of all attache cases and briefcases are made of leather, only about 2 percent of all luggage imports are leather. Prime sources of luggage imports were China, with 59 percent of the total, followed by Taiwan (19 percent), and South Korea (7 percent). In 1995, U.S. luggage exports rose about 6 percent over 1994 to an estimated $175 million. Canada, Japan, and Mexico were the largest export markets.

FURTHER READING

Berman, Phyllis. "Is Traveling Well the Best Revenge?" *Forbes,* 8 August 1988.

Dickey, Christopher. "The New King of Luxury." *Newsweek,* 7 August 1989.

Gandee, Charles. "Gandee at Large." *HG,* February 1990.

Goodman, Wendy. "Living with Style." *HG,* March 1992.

Kleiner, Kurt. "Delsey Luggage Enjoys the Sweet Smell of Its Expansion." *Baltimore Business Journal,* 13 June 1988.

LeTellier, George. "Higher Fashion Key in Luggage." *Upscale Discounting,* March 1987.

Richards, Nora. "Putting a Tag on 'U.S. Made.'" *Upscale Discounting,* April 1988.

———. "Quality, Advertising Are Keys to Sales." *Upscale Discounting,* February 1988.

———. "Vendors Aim for Creativity in Merchandising." *Upscale Discounting,* March 1988.

———. "Vendors Quickly Fill Consumer Needs in Fashion. Function." *Upscale Discounting,* May 1988.

———. "Vendors Rely on Exotics & Basics." *Upscale Discounting,* January 1988.

Samsonite Corporation. *Samsonite Annual Report.* Denver, CO: Samsonite Corporation, 1992.

''Smart Sailing.'' *Forbes.* December 1, 1986.

Sustendal, Diane. ''Where We've Been:A History of Luggage, Business Cases, Personal Leather Goods and Components.'' *Showcase,* November-December 1988.

U.S. Bureau of the Census. *Statistical Abstract of the United States.* Washington: GPO.

U.S. Department of Commerce. International Trade Administration. *U.S. Industrial Outlook 1994.* Washington: GPO, 1994.

Walsh, John. ''Vendors Introducing Better Fabrics and Features in Luggage.'' *Upscale Discounting,* January 1989.

Zisser, Melinda. ''The Flyboy's Bag.'' *Florida Business Journal.* 24 September1990.

—Pamela Berry, updated by Jennifer L. Stong

SIC 3171

WOMEN'S HANDBAGS AND PURSES

This classification includes establishments primarily engaged in manufacturing women's handbags and purses of leather or other materials, except precious metals. Establishments primarily engaged in manufacturing precious metal handbags and purses are classified in **SIC 3911: Jewelry, Precious Metal.**

INDUSTRY SNAPSHOT

The women's handbag and purse industry produces all women's handbags and purses of leather and other materials, except precious metals. Approximately 64 percent of the domestic handbags shipped in the United States in 1996 were made of leather. Handbag production shipments declined about 4 percent in 1996 to an estimated $368 million. Total industry employment plunged 35 percent from the 1992 figure of 5,200 to just 3,000 in 1995. Production employment declined just above 30 percent to 2,700.

BACKGROUND AND DEVELOPMENT

Historically, women have made most of their handbag purchases at boutique specialty stores and department stores. Consumers in the purse and handbag industry most often selected handbag purchases on the basis of designer recognition and style. During the 1980s, consumers took great interest in their appearance and became slightly extravagant. Sales of high-priced and mid-range brands, such as Coach and Dooney & Bourke, proliferated. Personal consumption of handbags and other apparel accessories nearly doubled in the 1980s with an average annual growth rate of 7.3 percent. Then, hurt by the recession, weak growth in disposable income, and high unemployment, consumers became much more cost-conscious.

Along with these economic changes came changes in consumer psychology. Designer names, high-priced accessories, and frequent shopping sprees became much less frequent. Consumers became more value conscious and began purchasing less expensive products at lower-end retail establishments and mass merchandisers. A writer for *Footwear News* indicated that leather buying habits started shifting to form, function, and comfort, away from designer names.

Despite the recessionary economy, however, Coach and Dooney & Bourke lines, which ranged from just above $100 to more than $400 in 1996, remained consistently strong performers. But other high-priced segments of the handbag business have not fared as well. High-priced lines like Liz Claiborne stumbled badly at the retail counters. Many experts attribute the success of Coach and Dooney & Bourke to the lines' classic/casual styling versus Liz Claiborne's dressier appearance.

Shoppers changed their handbag-buying habits throughout the early 1990s. Consumer purchasing shifted toward the most basic, functional accessories. Rather than purchasing a handbag to match each outfit—the pattern during the first three-quarters of the twentieth century—shoppers began purchasing a single handbag versatile enough to match many outfits. This pattern reflected a more value-oriented consumer, as well as an aging population seeking comfort and casualness. In the past several years, many mass merchandisers have added more recognizable national brand names to their in-store inventory. In the past, most brand names were distributed only through department stores.

CURRENT CONDITIONS

In 1992 specialty and department store retailers were optimistic about the growth of the handbag category, according to *Stores Magazine.* At the time, retailers were predicting increases in handbag sales ranging from a low of 8 percent to a high of 20 percent. Through 1996, however, sales were continuing to drop by an average of 4 percent a year. The key for sales success was to have the right assortment of handbags, from the moderate-priced to the higher-priced brands. By 1992, the moderate-priced handbag business doubled its 1990 sales level. Brand names such as Perry Ellis America, Capezio, and Esprit led the pack in producing fashionable handbags at moderate prices and giving retailers new inventory options.

Shoppers began spending again in the late 1990s as the economy recovered and financial security was regular. In turn, the department store shares of sales began creeping up again, and shoppers who were seeking more basic handbags and lower-priced goods in strip malls and outlet stores were going back to the department stores. According to the National Retail Federation, department store share of all apparel expenditures began rising again to 48 percent in 1996, up from 39 percent in 1995, and 30 percent on 1994. Discount stores still held the largest share at 60 percent, down from 64 percent the year before, but had loosened its grip on retailing somewhat as the economy recovered and consumers were willing to shop at the specialty and department stores. For mass retail stores such as K-mart and Wal-mart, brand name recognition was still important, and such brands as Chic and Gitano have been particularly successful. Abe Chehebar, president of Gitano handbags, told *Discount Merchandiser* that functional, organizer-style bags have been solid performers for his company. As a result, shoulder bags and totes continue to be strong performers. Chehebar also considers designer signatures on handbags to be important features because they elevate the accessories as status items.

Storage of inventory was one of the highest expenses a retailer faces. To reduce this expense, retailers were increasingly demanding that a manufacturer carry the inventory instead and make deliveries when the retailers' stock was low. In order for this type of relationship to work, especially when dealing with large quantities of merchandise required by stores such as Wal-Mart or K-mart, retailers and vendors found it necessary to form partnerships. Quick response is the most important aspect of this relationship; orders must be replenished automatically via computer links called electronic data interchange (EDI).

Experts attribute the growing appeal of outlet stores to the value-conscious shopper. Outlet stores' primary draw is price. The merchandise is often top quality and comes from current inventory, although many manufacturers use their own outlet stores to move surplus and low-quality merchandise. Manufacturers prefer this form of distribution to off-price retailers because they avoid tarnishing their brand names, which can occur when too much merchandise is sold through discounters. In addition, outlet stores tend to be located away from the selling areas of conventional department and specialty stores. This decreases the chance that the manufacturer's regular retail customers will lose sales to the outlet stores.

INDUSTRY LEADERS

Throughout the late 1980s, the ten largest publicly traded apparel and accessory companies saw their market share increase by nearly 5 percent. Part of this growth can be attributed to increased demand for these companies' products. But the remaining growth was a result of acquisitions and consolidations. As large department store retailers merged in the late 1980s, they consolidated their buying functions. Larger manufacturers benefitted from this because it became more efficient for a fewer number of buyers to use one vendor rather than several. In response, growth-oriented handbag and purse manufacturers increased their acquisition activity in search of new brands and broader product offerings.

In addition, the enormous growth of large mass merchandisers was driving the industry to consolidate going into the mid-1990s. From 1981 through 1991, Sears—the nation's largest retailer—saw its sales increase rapidly, as did Wal-Mart and K-mart. Historically, many brand-name manufacturers sold their goods only to department stores, but they soon began selling nearly identical merchandise to mass merchandisers and catalogues in order to participate in the mass merchandisers' and catalogue's phenomenal growth. Not surprisingly, this affected the manufacturers' relationships with the department stores, who seek exclusivity in their products. To remedy the situation, many manufacturers began to produce several different categories of brand names, each of which was distributed through a different type of retailer. Each retailer had brand exclusivity within its own category.

Coach Leatherware Co. continued its domination of the industry, with mid-1990s sales of $460 million, and the only company within the industry to have over $100 million in sales. A division of Sara Lee, Coach was one of the few higher-priced brand names, along with Dooney & Bourke, to survive the recession of the early 1990s, and Coach Leatherware sales have increased steadily through the late 1990s.

Tandy Brands, a small manufacturer and marketer in the leather goods industry, was a spinoff from The Bombay Co. manufacturing a variety of brand names, and had sales of $27 million in 1991. After a flurry of brand name acquisitions—including Jones New York handbags—sales of purses, wallets, and belts almost tripled to 1996 sales of $86 million and was expected to top $100 million by the end of 1997. Over 34 percent of their profit came from women's accessories, and that figure was rising dramatically, especially as their new brands gained footing.

AMERICA AND THE WORLD

Because labor costs represent such a high proportion of total production costs, handbags and other personal leather goods industries encountered significant import competition in the 1980s and early 1990s. This competition came primarily from developing nations where wage rates are far below those in the United States. China, for example, has rapidly become the dominant supplier to the United States of all these products. Some of the world's leading brands of these goods are now produced in developing countries—a trend that is expected to continue because of the drastic differences in labor costs. Furthermore, because international demand for handbags and other leather goods was rising in the early 1990s, many more developing countries with appropriate supplies of leather and suitable production skills could possibly enter the trade. Most of these developing nations enter the trade by producing travel goods or small leather articles, which tend to stay in fashion longer than women's handbags. This way, the producers have opportunities to establish steady export businesses before turning to the production of the seasonal women's handbags.

U.S. exports of handbags, luggage, and personal leather goods increased about 16 percent to $97 million in 1995. Mexico was the largest market by quantity, accounting for 51 percent of all U.S. exports. However, most of these exports were cut parts for handbags that were assembled in Mexico and re-exported to the United States as finished goods. Japan was the leading market for finished U.S. handbags with about 15 percent, or nearly $30 million, of purchases in 1995.

The total value of U.S. imports of women's handbags or purses increased about 5 percent in 1994 to $949 million. The value of U.S. exports in this industry increased about 2 percent to $41.2 million. Imports of handbags, luggage and other personal goods totaled $1.49 billion, accounting for 62 percent of consumption in 1995. Foreign suppliers with the largest share, by sales, were Asia ($967 million) and Europe ($393 million).

RESEARCH AND TECHNOLOGY

More than many other industries, production of handbags and purses is labor intensive. Therefore, like most companies, large producers of women's handbags are under extreme pressure to limit their number of employees by boosting productivity and efficiency. The industry considers new technology to be the key to increasing growth and profitability and keeping more production jobs in the United States. In recent decades, increased use of computers has integrated design, manufacturing, management, and marketing functions. Computerized production allows manufacturers to emphasize such non-price factors as quality and quick delivery to compete with imports.

Many handbag producers have turned to computer-aided design (CAD) and computer-aided manufacturing (CAM) systems and software. As a result, these manufacturers can produce tooling from CAD data and link it to auto-stitchers, milling, and turning machines. Computers also enable manufacturers to combine several operations or machines under fewer operators—thereby reducing handling time and number of employees—and improve quality. The industry has also developed computerized robots to handle and transfer operations within and between production modules.

In order to meet the demands of retailers' quick response requirements, more manufacturers are utilizing electronic data interchange (EDI), which allows retailers and manufacturers to communicate data. The goal of quick response is to maintain lean inventories and avoid overstocking, while ensuring that retailers have the merchandise customers want to buy. In the EDI system, interlinked computer systems are placed at every point of the manufacturing and sales process. Through use of an electronic scanner and bar code that has been tagged to the merchandise, retailers record at the point of sale which merchandise has been sold. All sales data on the individual products, including details of color and size, are transmitted immediately to the manufacturer. Through this method, the manufacturer keeps track of every store's retail sales trends. This first-hand view of consumer purchasing trends allows manufacturers to produce handbags based directly on customer demand. The information contained in the bar code sets automatic reordering into motion. The industry also refers to this type of inventory replenishment as ''flow'' or ''just in time.'' The manufacturer can quickly restock a retailer's shelves, using no more than a computer for communication. In addition to allowing automatic replenishment, EDI also enhances distribution and shipping. For example, once a shipment is ready to go, the manufacturer creates a labeling document and EDI sends an invoice automatically. In the future, EDI is likely to include electronic funds transfer as well.

Much of this new technology was developed and used in Europe before coming to the United States. Most of it can be readily transferred to Far Eastern producers, depending on the availability of capital. For these manufacturers, however, the labor-saving benefits of this new technology will not be as great as for producers with higher costs of production. Industry experts predict that the net effect of such technology will reduce the costs of U.S. production relative to Far Eastern production, although the latter will continue to maintain a competitive advantage for most categories of handbags.

Handbag producers are also making environmental breakthroughs. In late 1993, a company by the name of Holiday Fair began producing handbags made of EEKO, a mainly water-based combination of natural and synthetic rubbers with the look, feel, and colorability of leather. Holiday Fair's management team hopes this new material will eventually replace leather and leather substitutes. To promote its product, the company is placing heavy emphasis on retail and consumer educational programs that include detailed point-of-purchase literature and a store video. The company also intends to assume responsibility for the safe disposal, recycling, and reuse of all its products by using tags that offer consumers a value coupon toward their next Holiday Fair purchase if they return used handbags to the company. In January 1994, Holiday Fair also began shipping a new line of handbags made of polypropylene EEKO2, a material that emulates cotton, for products ranging from tote bags to belts.

FURTHER READING

Abend, Jules, "Environmentalism Is In the Bag." *Bobbin,* December 1993, 46.

Corwin, Pat. "Branded Handbags Trending Well." *Discount Merchandiser,* July 1991, 28-30.

Darnay, Arsen, J., Ed. *Manufacturing USA.* 5th ed. Detroit: Gale Research, 1996.

Dunn's Business Rankings. New York: Dunn & Bradstreet, 1993.

Hensell, Lesley. "Tandy Brands Adds Fashion Names." *Dallas Business Journal,* 24 March 1997.

Reda, Susan. "Handbag Forecast." *Stores,* May 1992, 86-88.

Sauer, Ron. "Leather Goods: Attractive Exports for Developing Countries." *International Trade Forum,* 1993, 22-25.

Standard & Poor's Industry Surveys. New York: Standard & Poor's Corporation, 1994.

U.S. Department of Commerce. *U.S. Industrial Outlook 1993.* Washington: GPO, 1994.

U.S. Bureau of the Census. *1995 Annual Survey of Manufactures.* Washington: GPO, 1997.

SIC 3172

PERSONAL LEATHER GOODS, EXCEPT WOMEN'S HANDBAGS AND PURSES

This category covers establishments primarily engaged in manufacturing small articles normally carried on the person or in a handbag, such as billfolds, key cases, and coin purses of leather or other materials, except precious metal. Establishments primarily engaged in manufacturing similar personal goods or precious metals are classified in **SIC 3911: Jewelry, Precious Metal.**

The overall economic health of the personal leather goods industry is tied to the status of the domestic leather production industry as a whole. Both this small segment and its parent category are affected by many of the same problems in manufacturing, labor costs, and competition with foreign-made products. The products manufactured by this industry are sometimes referred to as flatgoods due to their small dimensions; they are generally designed to fit into pockets or handbags. Such items include wallets and billfolds, coin purses, and key and cigarette cases; these goods may be manufactured wholly or partially of leather, plastic, or fabric, or from a combination of these materials.

Wallets and billfolds have historically represented the largest production segment of this industry, accounting for almost a third of all goods produced in 1989 and over 75 percent of the total monetary value of shipments. Travel kits are the next largest portion of the flatgoods market, followed by jewelry boxes and small items such as key and eyeglass cases. Typically, manufacturers offer several product lines each season in a variety of colors and prices. Many of the products are interrelated; i.e., consumers of both sexes can purchase a wallet and accompanying accouterments in a single style at the department store counter, traditionally the largest retailer of such products. This industry category also includes such items as watchbands, compacts, and business-card cases, if made from leather.

According to U.S. Department of Commerce estimates, the value of shipments for this segment of the leather manufacturing industry totaled $437.3 million in 1995. This figure represented a nearly 20 percent increase since 1990. Total number of employees in this segment of the industry fell to 5,300 in 1995 from 6,400 in 1990. The number of production workers in the industry, a figure that has generally accounted for nearly 80 percent of all workers engaged in the industry, stood at 3,800 in the mid-1990s, down from 5,200 in 1990.

The number of firms engaged in the production of flatgoods has been in decline since the early 1970s. Approximately 244 firms were classified as manufacturers in this industry in 1972, but by 1987 that number declined 15 percent to 208. By 1995, there were approximately 166 establishments in the industry.

Since the early 1970s, the personal leather goods industry in the United States has been dramatically affected by foreign-made products. Due to the skilled nature of the work, labor costs for domestic manufacturers are relatively high. The estimated average hourly wage in the industry was $7.75 for a production worker in 1995. Foreign manufacturers, most notably in China, Korea, India, and Italy, can produce flatgoods at a much reduced cost due to significantly lower wages. Because of this, the American consumer market for these products has become saturated with imported wallets, key cases, and eyeglass cases that have lower retail prices than their domestically produced counterparts.

In 1995, the United States imported $475 million in flatgoods. However, while imports continue to increase, so do exports of domestically produced flatgoods. A strong dollar and increased trade with Japan and Canada have helped to double the amount of exports since 1989. Industry leaders include Tandycrafts, Inc. of Forth Worth, Texas and Aristocraft Leather Products of Northvale, New Jersey. These companies had sales of $256 and $60 million, respectively, in 1995.

FURTHER READING

U.S. Bureau of the Census. *County Business Patterns.* Washington: GPO, 1996

U.S. Bureau of the Census. *1992 Census of Manufactures.* Washington: GPO, 1995.

U.S. Bureau of the Census. *1995 Annual Survey of Manufactures.* Washington: GPO, 1997.

U.S. Department of Commerce. International Trade Administration. *U.S. Industrial Outlook 1994.* Washington: GPO, 1994. Available from http://sci.dixie.edu/BusinessInformation/IndustryOutlooks/Outlooks.html.

U.S. Department of Commerce. "Luggage and Personal Leather Goods 1989." *Current Industrial Reports.* Washington: GPO, 1990.

—Carol Brennan, updated by Paula Cohen

SIC 3199

LEATHER GOODS, NOT ELSEWHERE CLASSIFIED

This category covers establishments primarily engaged in manufacturing leather goods, not elsewhere classified, such as saddlery, harnesses, whips, embossed leather goods, leather desk sets, razor strops, and leather belting. Establishments primarily engaged in manufacturing gaskets and packing are classified in **SIC 3053: Gaskets, Packing, and Sealing Devices.** Establishments primarily engaged in manufacturing

leather and sheep-lined clothing are classified in **SIC 2386: Leather and Sheep-Lined Clothing.**

The industry category of manufacturers of miscellaneous leather goods encompasses a broad array of unusual products with somewhat archaic uses. For example, a significant number of items classified relate to antiquated equestrian pursuits and the reliance on the horse as a primary form of transportation, as it was during the eighteenth and nineteenth centuries in the United States. For this reason, the miscellaneous leather goods industry can trace its roots back to the first skilled leather craftspeople who arrived on the North American continent with early European settlers, and before that back to near prehistoric times when militia units roamed much of Eurasia on horseback. The demand for such items as saddles, feed bags, halters and harnesses, riding crops, helmets, and stirrups made from leather later declined with the advent of the industrial era.

More recently, the miscellaneous leather goods industry shifted to manufacturing products for use in factories and other mechanical establishments. Such items included textile machinery aprons, machinery belting, and sleeves and leggings for welders. Declines in the manufacturing segment of the economy led to another shift toward consumer products. This area, which dominated the industry in the 1990s, is involved in manufacturing small leather novelty items, such as leather collars and harnesses for household dogs and cats. A large portion of current earnings in this industry is derived from the manufacture and sale of leather desk accessories.

In the mid-1990s, there were 403 establishments in the industry, an increase of over 15 percent since 1987, when there were 349 establishments. The majority of establishments employed less than 20 people. Total value of shipments in 1995 was $507.9 million, an increase from $390.6 million in shipments in 1987. The number of workers in the industry was 7,900 in 1992, up 11 percent from 1987. By 1994, that figure was down to 6,600 and then rose slightly to 6,700 in 1995. Production workers in 1994 and 1995 accounted for 6,000 and 6,200 of the total employment, respectively. Payroll costs amounted to $107.1 million in 1995, with production workers earning $73.3 million of that figure.

While finished leather accounts for the majority of material utilized by the miscellaneous leather goods industry, broadwoven fabrics, coated plastics and fabrics, and other forms of plastics are also used in industry production. In 1977, the cost of materials used by the industry in manufacturing was $154 million; five years later, the figure had risen to just $165.3 million.

In 1987, the cost of materials totaled $181.4 million, a somewhat dramatic jump from the previous year's figure of $134.5 million. In 1995, the cost of materials was $149.4 million.

FURTHER READING

U.S. Bureau of the Census. *1987 Census of Manufactures.* Washington: GPO, 1992.

U.S. Bureau of the Census. *1995 Annual Survey of Manufactures.* Washington: GPO, 1997.

U.S. Bureau of the Census. *1994 County Business Patterns.* Washington: GPO, 1996.

U.S. Bureau of the Census. *1992 Census of Manufactures.* Washington: GPO, 1995.

—Carol Brennan, updated by Paula Cohen

Stone, Clay, Glass, & Concrete Products

FLAT GLASS

This group includes establishments primarily engaged in manufacturing flat glass. This industry also produces laminated glass, but establishments primarily engaged in manufacturing laminated glass from purchased flat glass are classified in **SIC 3231: Glass Products, Made of Purchased Glass.** Manufactured flat glass covered under this industry includes such types as building glass, cathedral glass, insulating glass, optical glass, picture glass, sheet glass, structural glass, and window glass.

INDUSTRY SNAPSHOT

The flat glass manufacturing market is dominated by products intended for use by the office and housing construction industry. In 1995, the construction market accounted for 56 percent of United States flat glass demand, the automotive industry accounted for 26 percent, and the specialty glass market (e.g., mirrors, solar panels, and signs) accounted for 18 percent.

The fate of the flat glass industry, like that of most manufacturing industries, is inextricably linked to the status of the nation's general economy. Thus the industry suffered during the recession of the late 1980s and early 1990s, which was accompanied by a decrease in housing and nonresidential construction starts. The value of U.S. flat glass product shipments fell from $3.5 billion dollars in 1987 to $2 billion dollars in 1992, at the height of the recession.

The flat glass industry began to recover in the mid-1990s. The value of U.S. flat glass shipments had risen to 2.5 billion dollars by 1994. However, it is still uncertain when, if ever, the industry will revisit the demand and sales levels it experienced in 1986 and 1987.

The flat glass industry of the mid-1990s faces many challenges, including more stringent expectations for environmental responsibility and the need, shared by many industries in an age characterized by sophisticated consumers and impatient stockholders, to produce better, more technologically advanced products more cheaply. But it is also reaping benefits from a number of new technologies and new uses of glass.

ORGANIZATION AND STRUCTURE

Flat glass producers can be divided into two major classes: (1) makers of raw float glass and (2) fabricators, or companies that treat raw glass with special coatings for finished products. Two popularly used types of treated glasses are tempered and laminated flat glass. Tempered glass is discussed in more detail below; information on laminated glass and other glass products can be found in **SIC 3231: Glass Products, Made of Purchased Glass.**

The U.S. flat glass industry is clearly dominated by one company, PPG Industries Inc. of Pittsburgh, Pennsylvania, whose total net sales were over $7 billion in 1995 ($2.7 billion of which came from the sale of glass). According to *Ward's Business Directory,* the second and third largest producers of flat glass, Apogee Enterprises Inc. and the Libbey-Owens-Ford Co., had sales in the $800 million range.

The distribution of flat glass once it has been manufactured and, when applicable, processed with special coatings, occurs along a multileveled chain, with sales possible at all levels. According to *Glass*

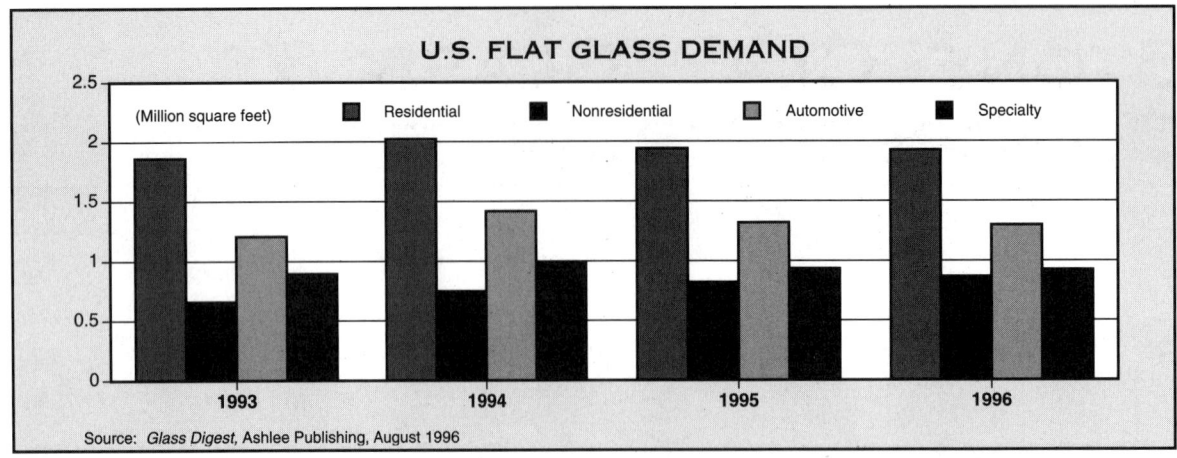

U.S. FLAT GLASS DEMAND

(Million square feet)   ■ Residential   ■ Nonresidential   ▨ Automotive   ■ Specialty

Source: *Glass Digest,* Ashlee Publishing, August 1996

Magazine, the normal distribution routes for domestic and imported flat glass are (1) directly from domestic or foreign producers to fabricators, glazing contractors, and retailers or (2) through independent glass distributors who, in turn, serve manufacturers, fabricators, glazing contractors, and retailers. However, many companies, which may have originated as either manufacturers or distributors, have found it profitable to expand from one segment of the market into another and have integrated manufacturing, fabrication, and sales into their operations.

The flat glass industry is subject to regulation by many government agencies and branches, including but not limited to the Consumer Product Safety Commission, the Environmental Protection Agency, the Occupational Safety and Health Administration, the National Bureau of Standards, and the Department of Commerce. Standards and recommendations for the glass industry are also set by such groups as the American National Standards Institute and the Building Officials and Code Administrators International, and more specialized groups such as the National Glass Association, the Chemical Manufacturers Association, the Glazing Industry Code Committee, and the American Architectural Manufacturers Association.

BACKGROUND AND DEVELOPMENT

Archeological remains indicate that glass was first made in the form of beads or small rods in the near East (possibly Mesopotamia), beginning about 2500 B.C. Ancient glass was made from the same basic raw materials as modern glass: sand, soda, and lime, with other materials like dolomite and salt cake added. Early glass was used to make beads, vases, and other largely aesthetic objects; its fragility and limited transparency and the difficulties inherent in its production precluded other uses.

From ancient times until the beginning of the nineteenth century, glass was made by laborious hand methods. But mechanization followed on the heels of the great advances made in science and technology in that century, and this led to decreased production costs. Flat glass also became more functional, and by 1925, 42 plants in the United States were producing 600 million square feet of sheet glass.

In 1959, the English firm of Pilkington Brothers perfected the revolutionary float glass manufacturing process, which enabled flawless clear or tinted glass to be produced without the cumbersome grinding and polishing steps that had previously been necessary. The transparency of the new float glass allowed 75-92 percent of visible light to be transmitted to the interior of a room. The float glass manufacturing process also brought about savings: capital investment costs decreased by 25-50 percent per ton of glass, and manufacturing outlays decreased by 15-30 percent.

The energy crisis of the 1970s forced glass manufacturers to develop energy efficient glasses, like tinted and coated glasses. However, since such glasses absorb and reflect heat, they reach higher temperatures than ordinary windows. Thus, manufacturers developed tempered glass, which is heat-treated to increase its strength and ability to resist thermal stress. Tempered glass is considered safer than ordinary glass because when broken, it shatters into cube-shaped particles without jagged edges. Tempered glass is thus ideal for high- and rough-usage areas and those that come into contact with high heat, for example, storefronts, shower doors, and fireplace screens. In addition, tempered glass cannot be cut, drilled, or edged, so it is used as a security glass in the construction and motor vehicle industries. However, use of tempered glass is limited in situations where building codes require fire-resistant glazing. In 1972, demand for tempered glass was at 317 million square feet; that number rose to 1 billion square feet in 1996.

In 1983, the glass industry took energy efficiency a step further by introducing "low-emissivity" glass. "Emissivity" refers to an object's power to radiate heat, light, etc.; in the flat glass industry, the term is used to measure the ability of window glass to control energy and minimize heat loss in cold weather. The lower a product's emissivity, the more energy efficient it is. The development of low-emissivity (low-E) glass is considered the industry's greatest advance in energy efficiency since the 1970s. Low-E glass is similar to aluminum foil in that it has an invisible, colorless, thin metallic coating that reflects radiant heat and maintains cool temperatures. It is believed that the use of low-E glass in commercial buildings decreased heating, cooling, and lighting needs by as much as 40 percent.

A trend that became apparent in the 1980s was an increased use of glass walls in new construction. Designers and building owners choose to incorporate them into building design for many reasons, including their dramatic aesthetic effect and the fact that glass is cheaper per square foot than most other, comparable, building materials.

The financial success of the flat glass industry waxed and waned over the years, usually in company with the health of the U.S. economy. The industry entered a healthy growth period in 1983, which peaked in 1987, when the value of product shipments reached $3.5 billion, the highest in 15 years. The value of flat glass shipments diminished in each subsequent year until 1992, however, when only $2 billion in flat glass products were shipped.

Concurrently, the industry experienced growing prices for raw materials. In 1992, *Glass Magazine* reported that "the cost of materials as a percentage of the value of industry shipments rose from 31.8 percent in 1970 to 38.9 percent in 1989."

The industry's labor force also suffered during this time. In 1990, the flat glass industry employed 17,000 people; in 1992, at the height of the U.S. recession, it employed only 14,700. In fact, the trend toward a smaller work force started much earlier than the recession. As early as the 1970s, manufacturers began actively seeking ways to further automate production processes, largely in an effort to reduce payroll costs. Their efforts resulted in a smaller glass work force.

The recession and its effects on demand and sales levels were not the only challenges the industry faced in the 1980s and 1990s. For example, the flat glass industry's pricing methods came under scrutiny. Since the eighteenth century, it had been standard practice

for glass manufacturers, distributors, and fabricators to calculate the price of total square footage by rounding up fractional amounts. However, after a glass retailer complained of unfair pricing due to this method, officials began to reexamine the flat glass industry's overall pricing methodology. Suggested alternatives included the adoption of either a unit price method or a fractional-inch computational method. Both methods require manufacturers, wholesalers, and the entire distribution chain to reprogram or recalculate glass costs to the actual fractional-inch square footage.

The industry was also rocked by a new standard proposed by the American Society of Heating, Refrigeration, and Air Conditioning Engineers (ASHRAE). ASHRAE 90.2, which was adopted in 1993, imposes limits on fenestration (the arrangement and design of windows and doors in a building) in the design of energy-efficient low-rise residential buildings. Fenestration area is normally 20 percent of conditioned floor area in a newly constructed single family detached home, but ASHRAE 90.2 limits that amount to 15 percent. It has been estimated that the new limitation could lead to a projected 2.75 million fewer windows sold for single-family detached homes and 750,000 fewer patio doors.

The industry also faced challenges in the 1980s and 1990s on environmental, energy, and safety fronts. Several landmark legislative actions were handed down by the Environmental Protection Agency (EPA), the Department of Energy, and various local regulatory agencies. The EPA's Clean Air Act Amendments of 1990 specifically address the hazardous rate of air pollutants emitted by specific facilities and processes. The flat glass industry has been forced to find ways to manufacture high-quality glass more cleanly; some of the technological developments in this area are discussed in the "Research and Technology" section below. The costs connected with the new law and standards, which are associated with the requirements of the law itself, the steps that a manufacturer must take to obtain an EPA permit, and the penalties that can be and are levied against the law's violators, represent one of the most serious and long-lasting legacies of this period. Other environmental concerns include water pollution and waste recycling.

CURRENT CONDITIONS

As the U.S. economy recovered from its recession, so did the flat glass industry. The value of shipments of flat glass rose from $2.0 billion in 1992 to $2.5 billion in 1994; the number of employees rose from 14,700 in 1992 to 15,400 in 1995. The industry began taking its lead from glass consumers in demanding higher-quality products at the lowest possible prices from its raw material suppliers: the cost of materials as a percentage of the value of industry shipments was down to 33 percent in 1994 from 38.9 percent in 1989.

Much promising research and product development has taken place in the mid-1990s, and much of it has focused on making glass windows more energy efficient. It has been found that adding gas between the sections of an insulating glass unit improves both thermal and sound control values. Heat loss by conduction occurs because of the tendency of heat to flow toward cooler temperatures. Argon gas filling in insulating glass slows the flow of building heat to the outside in winter and reduces the amount of outdoor heat entering the building.

Fire-resistant glass is another important and exciting segment of the glass market in the late 1990's. So-called "fire-rated glazing" is expected and required to both contain fire and allow visibility for building occupants and fire fighters during a fire. Various building codes and construction standards dictate the types of buildings, as well as which areas within buildings, must be fitted with fire-rated glass. Glass fire ratings are given in terms of time (e.g., 45 minutes). In the United States, a fire rating is achieved by first subjecting a particular glass to high-temperature flames. If a rating of more than 30 minutes is sought, the glass must also then be blasted with water from a fire hose. Thus, most fire-rated glass is expected to not only withstand heat but to remain intact (and thus continue to contain fire) even after being sprayed with water from a fire hose. A related concern is the ability of glass to resist heavy impact; glass that has been tested for impact resistance is called "safety-rated" glass. In many cases, builders are required to install glass that is both fire rated and safety rated.

Wired glass was the original fire-rated glass, and in 1996, wired glass continued to be the most popular type of fire-rated glass both because of its relatively low cost (at $7 to $12 per square foot, it is by far the cheapest fire-rated glass) and because it is the oldest and best-known fire-rated glass on the market. Most wired glass carries a fire rating of 45 minutes.

But wired glass has some limitations, such as its less than artful appearance and the fact that standards prohibit its use in sizes larger than 1,296 square feet. These have increasingly made wired glass an unattractive choice for building designers and owners seeking to use larger, clear glass windows and even walls in new construction. Two of the more promising alternatives that have gained acceptance in the 1990s are glass ceramic and transparent wall panels. Glass ceramic

looks like ordinary window glass and can be manipulated like glass, but its ceramic properties enable it to easily pass both portions of the fire test with ratings up to three hours. Safety-rated versions of glass ceramic are also manufactured. A transparent wall panel is, like wired glass, fire rated and safety rated, but since it has no wire mesh reinforcement, it looks better. Because it is able to act as a barrier to heat, it can be classified as a wall, not a window, and thus it is not restricted to a limited size. Transparent wall panels are made of several laminated sheets of float glass; the lamination enables them to carry the highest levels of glass safety ratings.

The issue of window labeling exploded in the 1990s. In 1995, the Canadian Window and Door Manufacturers Association (CWDMA) began a voluntary labeling program, which sets and uses a uniform "Energy Rating" (ER) standard for windows. This standard makes it easier for consumers to compare products and for building inspectors to confirm code compliance. The Canadian market is extremely important to U.S. glass manufacturers, so the Canadian initiative helped push the National Fenestration Rating Council (NFRC) of the United States to begin developing similar window and door energy performance standards. Those efforts were still underway in early 1997, but other, distinctly nonvoluntary, labeling programs have already begun in the United States. The 1996 Building Codes, e.g., include detailed and fairly complex rules on the labeling of wired and laminated glass. In some cases, the labels must be permanent; e.g., the code specifies that labels for tempered glass be either etched or ceramic fired. A February 1996 *Glass Magazine* article, "Building Codes Update," quoted an industry analyst saying that the new regulations were "one of the most onerous things that have happened to the glass industry."

INDUSTRY LEADERS

The three leading U.S. flat glass manufacturers, according to the 1997 *Ward's Business Directory of U.S. Private and Public Companies,* were PPG Industries Inc. of Pittsburgh, Pennsylvania, Apogee Enterprises Inc. of Minneapolis, Minnesota, and the Libbey-Owens-Ford Co. of Toledo, Ohio. (Note that many companies in the U.S. glass industry report higher sales than Apogee or Libbey-Owens-Ford, but these two rank second and third in the manufacture of *flat glass*).

PPG, a flat glass and fiberglass manufacturer, is by far the overall U.S. glass industry leader. PPG sales were reported at $7.1 billion dollars in 1995 (up from $6.3 billion in 1994), with total 1995 glass sales reported at $2.7 billion. According to "How the Industry Fared in 1995," in the July 1996 issue of *Glass Industry,* higher prices for worldwide flat glass and North American automotive replacement glass products accounted for much of the sales increase. Higher volume in automotive original glass products also contributed to the growth, though that was offset somewhat by lower volume in automotive glass replacement products.

Apogee Enterprises played a distant second to PPG, with $871 million in sales in 1996; the third largest flat glass manufacturer, Libbey-Owens-Ford, which is owned by the British glass firm Pilkington, reported sales of $850 million.

WORK FORCE

In 1979 the flat glass industry employed about 19,500 workers; by 1992 that number decreased to 14,700. The number of production workers experienced a parallel decline, from 15,200 in 1979 to 11,500 in 1992. Analysts attribute the work force reduction to manufacturing automation and production trimming, as well as to the oft-mentioned recession and its effects on the flat glass industry. In 1995, employment increased somewhat: the industry employed 15,400 workers, 12,200 of them in production.

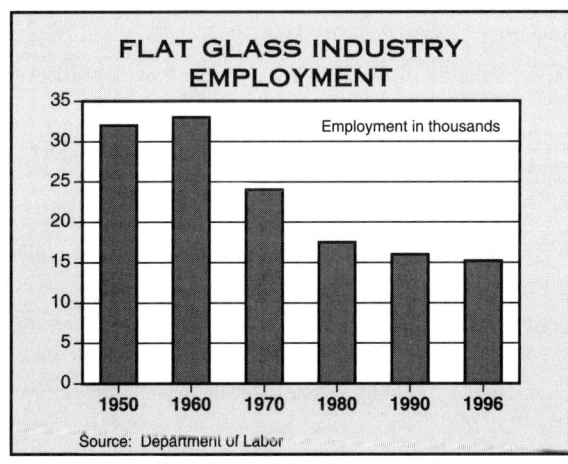

FLAT GLASS INDUSTRY EMPLOYMENT

Employment in thousands

Source: Department of Labor

A flat glass production worker earned, on average, $15.90 per hour in 1987, $16.49 in 1992, and $17.95 in 1995. Weekly overtime hours averaged 7.7 in 1988, 5.9 in 1992, and 7.1 in 1995.

Flat glass manufacturing can be difficult and dangerous work, though it is generally true that the rates of injury and work-related illness tend to be lower for companies with fewer than 50 employees and more than 100 employees than for mid-size establishments. In 1995, according to the U.S. Department of Labor's

Bureau of Labor Statistics, the flat glass industry ranked twenty-eighth among private industries for incidents of nonfatal injuries per 100 full-time workers. In the same year, the flat glass industry rated sixteenth among private industries for incidents of nonfatal disorders associated with repeated trauma per 10,000 workers. (An industry is considered "high rate" in either category if it ranks among the top 25).

AMERICA AND THE WORLD

Most U.S. flat glass manufacturers are engaged in some type of international commercial activity, either through joint ventures with foreign firms, licensing of technology to foreign producers, or acquisition of all or part of foreign flat glass manufacturers. The industry experienced a trend toward globalization in the 1980s. For example, in 1986, one of the major U.S. flat glass manufacturers, the Libbey-Owens-Ford Co., was bought by the British glassmaking giant, Pilkington, while U.S. firms like Guardian and PPG expanded by setting up factories overseas.

The value of flat glass exports from the United States rose each year from 1989 through 1994 (the last year for which such statistics are available). In 1989, the United States exported $497 million worth of flat glass products, while in 1994, it exported an estimated $895 million worth. The value of imports did not change as drastically during this period: in 1989, the United States imported $481 million worth of flat glass, while in 1994, it imported an estimated $488 million worth.

According to the January-February 1996 issue of *Chemical Industries Newsletter,* North America is the largest consumer of flat glass in the world, with 32 percent of total demand, followed by Asia/Oceania (29 percent), western Europe (26 percent), eastern Europe (6 percent), Africa and the Middle East (4 percent), and Central and South America (3 percent). It is expected that the majority of growth in flat glass demand through the year 2000 will come from the industrializing regions of South America and Asia.

Major foreign players in the international flat glass industry are Asahi Glass of Japan, Pilkington of England, and Saint-Gobain of France.

RESEARCH AND TECHNOLOGY

Computers and the Internet are causing major changes in the way that glass manufacturers, distributors, and retailers do business. Most obviously, information about glass products and manufacturing standards and specifications is increasingly available via the World Wide Web, so consumers can compare products and prices at many "stores" from home and manufacturers can access important information instantly. Plant management has also been revolutionized by new, increasingly advanced and user-friendly business computing tools.

Research continues in the area of energy efficiency. While great progress has already been made in improving the ability of window glass to keep heat and sound in or out of a room, some researchers have turned their attention to the window edge, where spacer design and construction can lead to significant heat loss, decreasing overall window energy efficiency by as much as 25 percent. "Warm edge technology" is helping manufacturers to better seal window perimeters by replacing the traditional frost-prone metal window spacers with high strength, thin stainless steel, molded-in thermal breaks, and split spacers or silicone foam. This not only helps to keep the temperature of the entire window higher, but reduces the incidence of condensation and frost. Though products using warm edge technology were available in 1997, it is fair to say that the technology is still developing. It is not yet known, e.g., how long existing products can be expected to last. And manufacturers are looking for a way around the facts that warm edge materials are often more expensive than standard ones and that many require an entirely new production system.

Improving low-E glass technology was considered a cutting-edge research problem in the late 1980s and early 1990s, and great strides were made in reducing emissivity. In the late 1990s, a better and more energy efficient window is still on many researchers' to-do lists, but now more demands have been added. In "Smart Windows," in the May 1996 issue of *Glass Digest*, Day Chahroudi noted that "it is becoming apparent that the glass industry expects its next major market expansion to come from . . . optical shutters, or smart windows." The technologies referred to here as "optical shutters" allow windows to perform some of the same functions as shutters or curtains—keeping sunlight out of a room, allowing it into a room, and even allowing daytime one-way viewing.

Another promising product under consideration is switchable glass, a liquid crystal glass that can be wired to any structure's electrical system and operated by flipping a switch. Liquid crystals make the glass cloudy but permit sufficient light without obstructing visibility. The electrical current changes the glass from opaque to clear. Its current use is in interior applications such as partitions and conference rooms, where privacy and optional visibility are desirable.

Tighter environmental regulations, specifically emissions standards, have brought about a significant manufacturing innovation—oxygen-fuel (oxy-fuel) combustion. According to Rich Deal, in *Glass Industry,* oxy-fuel offers many significant advantages over conventional combustion systems. Most crucial among these to the U.S. industry is significantly lower NOx and particulate emissions, but others include higher melt rates, reduced fuel consumption, improved workability of the resulting glass product, and the declining cost of producing on-site oxygen. Manufacturers in the late 1990s are still making the switch to oxy-fuel, and there are some real, if predictable, technological and efficiency issues still to solve.

FURTHER READING

Button, David A. "Glass for the Year 2000." *Glass Digest,* 15 January 1990.

"California Questions Glass Measurement Practices." *Glass Magazine,* April 1990.

"CEH Abstract: Glass Industry Overview." *Chemical Industries Newsletter,* January-February 1996.

Chahroudi, Day. "Smart Windows." *Glass Digest,* 15 May 1996.

Cunningham, R.C. "Industry Survey Finds Optimism in all Segments." *Glass Digest,* 15 June 1996.

Deal, Rich. "1997 Forecast Sees More Industry Change." *Glass Industry,* January 1997.

Destefano, James T. "How the Clean Air Act Impacts Glass Producers." *Glass Industry,* May 1992.

"The Evolution of the Industry over the Past Seven Decades." *Glass Digest,* 15 August 1996.

Francke, Hans-Christian. "Recommendations for Low-Emissivity Glasses." *Glass Digest,* 15 May 1996.

"A Glass Primer." *Glass Magazine,* April 1990.

"How the Industry Fared in 1996." *Glass Industry,* July 1996.

Joelson, Daniel. "It's Blue Skies in 1996, But There are Some Clouds, Too." *Glass Digest,* 15 January 1996.

Johns, Nicole. "Building Codes Update." *Glass Magazine,* February 1996.

"Looking at Economic Factors, Things Appear Bad." *Glass Digest,* 15 August 1996.

Miller, John. "Focus on Windows." *Buildings,* July 1987.

Penrod, Bret E. "Trends in Flat Glass Raw Materials." *Glass Digest,* 15 August 1996.

"Pilkington Research Forges Ahead." *Glass Digest,* February 15, 1990.

"A Preview of Fenestration in the Year 2000." *Fenestration.* New York: Ashlee Publishing Company, 1989.

"Proposed Residential Design Standard Could Hurt Fenestration Industry." *Fenestration.* New York: Ashlee Publishing Company, 1989.

Razwick, Jerry. "Fire-Rated Glazing Comes of Age." *Glass Magazine,* February 1996.

Sraeel, Holly. "Glass Building Facades: What's Hot, What's Not." *Buildings,* April 1989.

Sitrin, Todd W. "Glass on the Homefront." *Glass Magazine,* December 1989.

Tooley, Fay V., ed. *The Handbook of Glass Manufacture,* 3rd ed. New York: Ashlee Publishing Company.

U.S. Bureau of the Census. *1995 Annual Survey of Manufactures.* Washington: GPO, 1997.

U.S. Bureau of the Census. *Current Industrial Reports.* Washington: GPO, 1992.

U.S. Bureau of the Census. *Current Industrial Reports.* Washington: GPO, 1993.

U.S. Bureau of the Census. *Current Industrial Reports.* Washington: GPO, 1997.

U.S. Department of Commerce. *The Statistical Abstract of the United States, 1995,* 115th ed. Washington: GPO. Available from http://www.ita.doc.gov/industry/otesa/usio19551466.txt.

U.S. Bureau of Labor Statistics. *Employment, Hours, and Earnings. United States, 1988-96.* Washington: GPO, 1996.

U.S. Bureau of Labor Statistics. *Top 25 Rates, Injuries, Total Recordable Cases, 1995.* Available from http://stats.bls.gov/special.requests/ocwclusn/ostbo335.txt.

U.S. Bureau of Labor Statistics. *Repeated Trauma, Highest Rates with 1995 Numbers, 1995.* Available from http://stats.bls.gov/special.requests/ocec/osn/ostbo342.txt.

Ward's Business Directory of U.S. Private and Public Companies. Detroit: Gale Research, 1997.

Williams, Franklin E. "Flat Glass Industry Overview." *Glass Magazine,* September 1992.

———. "Flat Glass Technology." *Construction Review,* March/April 1990.

———. "Flat Glass Trends and Forecasts." *Glass Magazine,* January 1993.

—Attrices Dean Griffin, updated by Beth Gallagher

SIC 3221

GLASS CONTAINERS

This category includes establishments primarily engaged in manufacturing glass containers for commercial packing and bottling, and for home canning. Products include: ampoules; bottles, containers, jars, and jugs for packing, bottling, and canning; carboys; cosmetic jars; fruit jars; medicine bottles; packers' ware; vials; and water bottles.

INDUSTRY SNAPSHOT

In 1995, the industry shipped $4.3 billion worth of products, a 12 percent decrease since 1990, when product shipments totaled $4.9 billion. Imports of glass containers totaled $408 million; exports totaled $129 million. There were 78 establishments in the industry in the mid-1990s, a 27 percent decrease since 1990. The industry employed 29,987 in the mid-1990s, which is a 30 percent decrease since 1990.

A *Packaging* magazine survey in 1986 proved that promotion of glass containers had been successful. For several years, advertisers within the glass manufacturing industry have focused on the positive aspects of glass container use. At one point, glass container manufacturers sponsored advertising campaigns touting their product as a naturally pure, recyclable taste protector. Particularly innovative was the industry's Nickel Solution Trust, formed in 1983 by a coalition of labor organizations and glass container manufacturers. Employees of glass container companies pledged a nickel of each hourly pay, and the employers contributed matching funds to pay for glass promotions. Since its inception, the trust has expended more than $21 million for recycling program development and management. Despite aggressive promotions such as these, the glass container market remained sluggish. Consequently, the glass container industry has become smaller but also much smarter. Promotion, however, continues to target those areas where glass retains a winning edge as a premium product.

ORGANIZATION AND STRUCTURE

The glass container industry manufactures two basic types of containers: narrow neck and wide mouth containers. The industry further classifies containers by their end use, creating categories of glass designated for food, beverages, beer, liquor, wine; chemical, household, and industrial uses; toiletries and cosmetics; and other uses including medicinal and health supplies. Wide mouth and narrow neck bottles are used interchangeably, depending on the product, but tradition or utility occasionally dictates specific bottle types. For example, milk is normally packaged in wide mouth containers, both wide mouth and narrow neck bottles are used for cosmetics, while narrow neck bottles are more practical for perfumes.

Consumer preferences and marketing strategy often combine to determine whether a product is packaged in a wide mouth or narrow neck container. One company used feedback from consumer focus groups to determine the best container for mustard. Participants expressed preference for a wide-mouth jar that would allow the use of a large serving spoon or spatula. The company's selection of a wide mouth container originated from an entirely different perspective. A smaller jar, in the company's estimation, connoted saving the product for special occasions rather than using it as a special item for everyday meals. Thus the selection of wide-mouth jar satisfied consumer preferences and complemented the company's marketing strategy.

Shape is the most important feature of a bottle. To be practical, a bottle must be able to stand up, have a filling mouth, and withstand a variety of mechanical handling devices such as washing machines, filling tubes, labelers, and conveyors. According to experts, spherical-shaped containers present the most efficient use of glass container weight. After the sphere, the most efficient use of glass is a cylinder with similar dimensions of diameter and height. The container industry generally favors glass containers characterized by broad, rounded shoulders, edges, and corners. To ensure maximum strength, the industry avoids the use of square or rectangular shapes, flats or panels, or offsets. Glass containers are also designed to convey a brand image. Clear beveled-edge bottles offer high profile products an advantageous shelf presence and easy handling benefits for consumers.

Even more marketable are glass containers combining eye-catching designs with a functional after-life as decanters or collector items. A few decades ago, small, odd-sized and shaped bottles were replaced by standardized bottles, in part because manufacturers discovered that standardized bottles could be produced faster using the old machinery. While most odd-shaped bottles have disappeared, they are now prized and traded as antique collectibles. In the 1990s, Dr. Pepper issued a commemorative bottle saluting the involvement of U.S. troops in Operation Desert Storm. In contrast, plastic or aluminum containers rarely offer any collectible value. For the industry, bottle collecting could increase industry share of the beverage market by 3 percent and rise to account for 25 percent of all glass beverage bottles.

Manufacturers capitalize on designer appeal of glass containers by constantly adding innovative designs. Each year, the Glass Packaging Institute recognizes creative glass containers by granting awards in several categories, including food, beverage, package design, label, environmental awareness, and mature product repositioning. In 1989, Fireworks Popcorn captured first place as winner in the overall food category. The award winning package highlighted the product's vivid popcorn colors by using a clear, reusable 15-ounce jar shaped like a home canning jar. In the beverage category, first place honor went to Ocean

Spray's choice of a large, collector-type glass carafe packaging its premium fruit juice.

Changing the design of a glass container entails more than adding a new face. Most design changes create a ripple effect on the overall product manufacturing process, affecting cost and product positioning. Even the slightest modifications—such as availing a round food jar or adding a modest blown-in decorative effect—can increase the container's weight by 20 percent. Maintaining lighter weight without reducing container strength highlights one persistent industry concern. One solution to the weight problems is the use of the narrow neck press and blow technology capable of manufacturing more efficient containers at 15 to 20 percent lighter weights. Another possible solution to weight reduction of glass containers is the development of a process that uniformly maintains glass wall thickness and enhances the container strength through some type of coating. The results would be a 12-ounce capacity container made in the 3 to 4 ounce weight range. According to an industry spokesperson, once manufacturers improve control over the container production process, weight problems will be alleviated.

Many gloriously designed containers generate both consumer delights and production havoc. For example, Welch's redesign of a popular jelly jar featuring a new tear drop-shaped container proved popular with consumers but caused countless cost and handling problems. Because the tapered glass jar was smallest at the bottom, with jar-to-jar contact only at the shoulder, containers frequently toppled over on the conveyors. Case packing of the tear-drop jars necessitated manual rather than the usual mechanical handling, thereby adding three packers per shift. Because of the additional costs accompanying the new design, the company redesigned the container by making the container base the same diameter as the shoulders. The slightly heavier jar caused a modest increase in freight costs, but by eliminating the jar's tip-over tendency, case packing increased by 2,000 per shift, thereby eliminating the need for additional production shifts.

For many other products, the image qualities of glass containers combine with other features to convey a unique premium appeal. Glass packaged wine coolers, for example, were tremendously popular in the mid-1980s, with sales as high as three million bottles daily. Analysts attributed the boom in part to the popularity of the single-serving bottle, a concept that was virtually unknown a few years earlier. Successful demonstration of the concept with wine coolers led to single-serve juice beverages and later bottled water. Gatorade, for one, reported a 30 percent sales increase in one year following introduction of a 16-

ounce single-serve, wide mouth bottle, conveniently suitable for carrying "at the point of sweat." More than 100 companies later joined the promotion of the single-serve bottles' health advantages. The single-serve concept also motivated distilled spirits producers to carve their niche by introducing spirit coolers in single-serve glass bottles.

BACKGROUND AND DEVELOPMENT

For centuries, glass objects were made by artisans using hand blowing methods. Many products created by these highly trained craftsmen now adorn art museum collections. Mechanization came to the glass-making industry with the industrial revolution and subsequent introduction of pressing machines. This and other refinements promoted a range of new designs and uses of glass containers. Wide mouth Mason jars became popular in the United States in the early 1900s, while the popularity of narrow neck jars developed more slowly.

M.J. Owens and E.D. Libbey initiated a new process of bottle making by filling and dipping the first or blank mold into hot glass and evacuating the air from the mold. Several years of experimentation finally led to the development of an automated bottle machine. By 1920, 200 of these automatic machines accounted for approximately 45 percent of the total U.S. bottle production.

In 1975, the Environmental Protection Agency (EPA) issued standards and guidelines covering wastewater discharges from glass container manufacturing plants. The regulations targeted oil and grease pollution that originated from soluble oils used in glass shearing, machine lubrication, and condensation from compressed air systems. Oil and grease pollution stems from the biodegradable nature of emulsified oil that subjects cullet quench systems (broken or refuse glass added to new material to facilitate the glass-making procedure) to severe biological growth problems. According to *Glass Magazine,* biological growth within cullet quench systems degrades oil and grease removal efficiency, often resulting in discharge values exceeding regulatory standards. Additionally, the biologically fouled cullet quench system precipitates a potential health hazard in the form of Legionnaire's Disease, as well as contributes to unpleasant working conditions.

CURRENT CONDITIONS

In 1996, production of glass containers amounted to 253.8 million gross; shipments amounted to 257.3 million gross. In 1996, shipments of narrow neck containers totaled 179.7 million gross, while shipments of wide mouth containers totaled 77.5 million gross. Production and shipment of narrow neck containers consistently outrank those of wide mouth containers. Wide-mouth containers are most popular for food, including dairy products, and have held steady sales and production over the last few years. The lowest shipment and production levels are for narrow neck and wide mouth chemical, household, and industrial containers. At best, the glass container industry can be described as flat. Bottle shipments, according to analysts, will likely remain flat. Continued overcapacity and the threat of conversion to alternative packaging stands to keep price increases in the 3.0 to 3.5 percent range.

Several factors contribute to the flat conditions of the glass container industry. Since the 1980s, the glass container market has suffered a steady loss of market share to alternate plastic and can packaging. Analysts point to the beer industry as a major factor causing the decline of the glass container industry. More than 85 percent of the decline was due to brewers switching to aluminum cans, and the lingering residual of this change still poses an imminently significant threat, in the industry's opinion. Statistics may well support this threat. Although shipment and production of beer bottles remain high, at about 88 million, analysts feared a decline as higher price tags forced consumers to switch to lower-price canned beer.

One drawback to recycling cited by the Glass Packaging Institute relates to forced deposit laws requiring a consumer to pay a deposit and then return the containers to the store for a refund. The industry perceives such legislation as devastating to the market share of environmentally friendly glass containers and argues that it sways consumers to use plastic. GPI believes the most effective way to reduce solid waste is not forced deposit laws, but comprehensive curbside recycling. The practice of bottle refilling as an alternative to recycling may experience a comeback.

The Glass Packaging Institute noted that the 1990s began with five major bottling companies switching from plastic to glass containers, citing as reasons consumer preference, environmental climate, and packaging costs. According to investment analysts, however, falling resin prices could be an omen signaling a return to plastic. In 1989, a price differential of 20 percent between plastic and glass caused plastic to lose its market share to glass, primarily in the area of 16-ounce containers. When the differential was closer to 5 percent or less, plastic regained some of its share. Until the glass container industry develops a more cost-competitive, lighter weight, or break-resistant package, analysts foresee fewer gains derived from the anticipated growth of the soft drink market.

Another challenge facing the glass container industry involves raw materials leftover from the manufacturing process. According to an industry spokesperson, only 85 to 90 percent of the melted raw materials are converted to a marketable product. The remaining 10 to 15 percent of raw material becomes cullet or discarded waste, mostly broken glass. Industry leaders are attempting to devise satisfactory uses for this cullet.

INDUSTRY LEADERS

Major players in the industry include Owens-Illinois, Inc., Anchor Glass Container Corporation, and Ball Glass Container Corporation. In 1996, Owens-Illinois, had revenues of $3.76 billion and employed 30,100. Anchor Glass had sales of $957 million and had 5,700 employees, while Ball had revenues of $580 million and employed 13,000.

WORK FORCE

In 1995, the industry employed a total of 25,500, down 32 percent since 1990. Production workers' average weekly hours were 44.2 in 1995, up from 42.1 in 1990. Production workers' average hourly earnings were $14.51 in 1995, up from $13.16 in 1990.

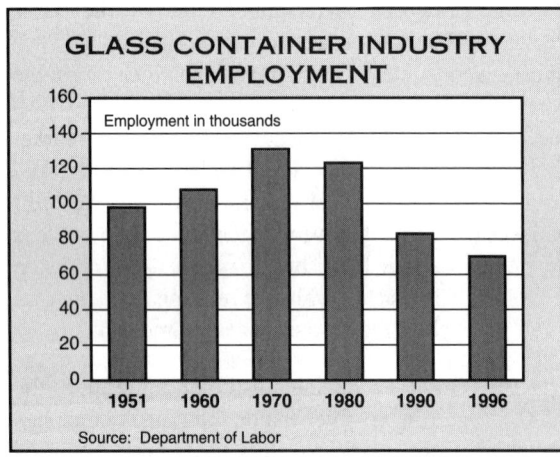

GLASS CONTAINER INDUSTRY EMPLOYMENT

Employment in thousands

Source: Department of Labor

Noting significant improvements in labor productivity per unit, an Owens-Illinois spokesperson commented that producing a quality product still requires an excessive amount of work. Labor constitutes 35 percent of the cost of glass, but only 9 percent and 13 percent for cans and plastic, respectively. Although use of sophisticated control systems in the future will require more operator interpretation rather than intervention, production workers must be better trained and more knowledgeable than most manufacturing employees.

RESEARCH AND TECHNOLOGY

Flexibility may determine the glass container's response to its environmental challenges. Glass is 100 percent recyclable. A used glass container can be melted and repeatedly made into a new glass container. Furthermore, glass recycling creates no additional waste or by-products. Yet glass recycling ranks lower than that of plastic. The Glass Packaging Institute (GPI), the glass container industry's trade group, questions the EPA's statistics quoting the recycling rate for glass at 10 to 12 percent, plastic at 20 percent, and aluminum cans at 55 percent. Still, glass retains a positive recyclability perception. In contrast, recyclability of plastic beverage containers is accepted by only 20.7 percent of consumers.

Recent testimony before a Congressional subcommittee by the Glass Packaging Institute cited three major problems for the glass industry's recycling program: (1) because plants are located primarily on the East and West coasts and the Southeast, transporting recycled glass from community collection facilities to these plants proves expensive; (2) recycling of increasing amounts of imported green containers exceeds the domestic demand for these containers; and (3) because of loose quality control at local collection sites, mixing recyclable and nonrecyclable glass damages the manufacturing process. The most viable recycling solution, according to some experts, comes from less packaging. In the last 10 years, 16-ounce glass bottles have been reduced by 30 percent, thus lowering the amounts of materials and waste.

To date, a few technologies have demonstrated capacity for breaking up oil and grease found in glass container plant wastewater. One technology consists of carbon absorption, a process in which wastewater passes through a bed of activated carbon that absorbs the oil and grease. This process is more applicable to small flows with relatively low oil and grease loadings. The process of chemical coagulation followed by dissolved air flotation (DAF) is another process where chemical emulsion breakers and other processes are added to wastewater to break emulsion. DAF has been successfully used and research studies continue to study various emulsion breaking chemistries.

Since 1975, compliance with national standards has enabled glass container manufacturers to make significant improvements in control of oil and grease in wastewater. In the 1990s, companies placed greater emphasis on research and development to upgrade wastewater treatment technologies to comply with stringent state and local effluent standards.

In the future, the recyclable features of glass products could play a major role in safe disposal of hazardous waste, according to the editor of *Glass Industry*. The Department of Energy opened a new $1.3-billion Defense Waste Processing Facility in South Carolina designed to test the feasibility of encasing radioactive materials in glass. This process, known as vitrification, entails encasing hazardous waste in "logs" of strong glass, wrapped in steel. Steel cylinders measuring 10 feet high and 2 feet around each hold 165 gallons of waste.

Parallelling this project was an experiment during the 1990s at the California-based Lawrence Livermore National Laboratory on radioactivity released from glass. A computer model was designed to predict the release of radioactivity, if any, from a nuclear waste repository incorporating glass. To ensure adequate leakage prevention of harmful radioactive material from glass, scientists performed a variety of laboratory experiments and computer simulations of potential environmental scenarios that might be affected by radioactive leaks.

Large and small glass container manufacturers have spent millions for high-tech equipment and computerized operations. Part of the $40 million Anchor Glass expended in the 1990s was for the installation of sophisticated quality control equipment on all the company's production lines. Wheaton Glass completed a $10 million investment in manufacturing operations of containers for the parenteral drug and the cosmetics industries. Over a period of three years, Kerr invested in excess of $22 million for improvements such as computerized furnace control systems, high-productivity forming machines, and quality control equipment.

Considerable industry attention now focuses on eliminating weak spots of containers by uniform redistribution of glass. The benefits would be strong, lightweight containers containing less glass produced faster and less expensively than at present. Several companies have achieved outstanding results by improving traditional machinery such as the latest press-and-blow molding. Owens-Illinois's "ten-quad machine" claims to be the fastest forming machine in the United States for glass containers. It operates at speeds well over 450 containers per minute.

Glass coatings remain a significant aspect of research and development. Through a program identified as the Advanced Glass Treatment Systems, various coatings for strength enhancement of glass containers are being studied. Manufacturers are also experimenting with sophisticated hot- and cold-end coatings to reduce breakage and scuffing. These coatings also increase container filling speeds. A New York-based company developed a coating procedure identified as the Brandt Color Coat process. The water-based acrylic coating expands colors and textures of glass beverage bottles. Glass can be tinted in a range of desired colors combined with transparent opaque, matte, or frost finishes. The process offers more cost-effectiveness and more scratch-resistance than conventional bottle-tinting methods, plus a resistance to ultraviolet light, normally harmful to beverages such as beer. It also allows bottle labels to be printed with UV-cured inks without fear of harm to the contents. Anchor Glass Container is only U.S. manufacturer to offer this new product.

FURTHER READING

Ashton, Robin. "Awards Highlight Glass Innovations." *Packaging*, April 1989.

"Ball Corporation to Close Santa Anna Factory." *Los Angeles Times*, 25 June 1992, D2.

Copperthite, Kimberly G. "Shipments to Rise Slightly in 1991." *Glass Industry*, January 1991.

"Glass Container Promotion Boosts Soft Drink Sales." *Glass Industry*, January 1992.

"Glass Provides a Class Image." *Packaging*, July 1987.

Heuer, Ross. "New Jar Is Key to Packaging Line Upgrading." *Packaging*, February 1987.

"How the Industry Fared in 1991." *Glass Industry*, June 1992.

Keister, Timothy. "How to Control Oil and Grease in the Effluent from Glass Container Plants." *Glass Industry*, May 1993.

Lang, Nancy A. "A Touch of Glass." *Beverage World*, June 1990.

———. "Hoisting the Glass." *Beverage World*, June 1989.

Larson, Melissa. "Glass Offers a Clear Alternative." *Packaging*, June 1992.

"Market Breakout of the U.S. Glass Manufacturing Industry: 1990 vs. 1987." *Glass Industry Fact Sheet*, June 1993.

Penberthy, Larry. "Why Glass Is a Good Host for Hazardous Waste." *Glass Industry*, May 1992.

Perrine, Lowell E., "Glass Could Play Major Role in the Safe Disposal of Hazardous Waste." *Glass Industry*, January 1991.

———. "Glass Problems Conference Features an Industry Status Report." *Glass Industry*, January 1991.

"Plants Modernize; Quality Improves." *Packaging*, July 1987.

Prince, Greg. "One for the Ages." *Beverage Worldline,* June 1991.

Russo, James R., "Hidden Strength for Glass Packages," *Packages,* August 1986.

Tooley, Fay V., ed. *The Handbook of Glass Manufacture.* Vol. 2. Ashlee Publishing Co., 1985.

U.S. Bureau of the Census. *1995 Annual Survey of Manufactures.* Washington: GPO, 1997.

U.S. Department of Commerce. "Glass Containers: Summary for 1996." *Current Industrial Reports.* Washington: GPO, 1996.

U.S. Department of Commerce. "Monthly Report on Glass Containers: April 1993." *Current Industrial Reports.* Washington. GPO, 1993.

Varshneya, A. K., and K. Frederes. "How Much Lead Leaches from Crystal Glassware?" *Glass Industry,* April 1993.

"Wide-mouth Glass Jar for R. T. French's Dip 'N Spread." *Packaging,* October 1987.

SIC 3229

PRESSED AND BLOWN GLASS AND GLASSWARE, NOT ELSEWHERE CLASSIFIED

This category includes establishments primarily engaged in manufacturing glass and glassware, not elsewhere classified, pressed, blown, or shaped from glass produced in the same establishment. Establishments primarily engaged in manufacturing textile glass fibers are also included in this industry, but establishments primarily engaged in manufacturing glass wool insulation products are classified in **SIC 3296: Mineral Wool.** Establishments primarily engaged in manufacturing fiber optic cables are classified in **SIC 3357: Drawing and Insulating of Nonferrous Wire;** and those manufacturing fiber optic medical devices are classified in the surgical, medical, and dental instruments and supplies industries. Establishments primarily engaged in the production of pressed lenses for vehicular lighting, beacons, and lanterns are also included in this industry, but establishments primarily engaged in the production of optical lenses are classified in **SIC 3827: Optical Instruments and Lenses.** Establishments primarily engaged in manufacturing glass containers are classified in **SIC 3221: Glass Containers,** and those manufacturing complete electric light bulbs are classified in **SIC 3641: Electric Lamp Bulbs and Tubes.**

INDUSTRY SNAPSHOT

The pressed and blown glassware industry manufactures products ranging from television tubes, ashtrays, candlesticks, stemware, tobacco jars, and optical lenses to Christmas tree ornaments. Throughout the 1980s, the industry maintained a steady level of employment at about 37,000 workers, while the value of shipments rose consistently to reach an estimated $5 billion by 1996. By 1998, the value of shipments was expected to be $5.23 billion. The total number of establishments engaged in the industry also grew during the 1980s and 1990s, from 331 in 1982 to approximately 500 in 1996.

ORGANIZATION AND STRUCTURE

The companies involved in the pressed and blown glass industry displayed much diversity in earnings and employment levels. Of the estimated 500 total industry establishments in 1996, only about 129 employed 20 or more people. However, the industry was dominated by large companies related in some way to Corning Incorporated, such as Owens-Corning, Owens-Illinois, and Owens-Corning Fiberglass. Anchor Hocking was another giant in the industry, although dwarfed by the Corning units. Steuben Glass (a Corning company) and Lenox Crystal were among those companies making handmade stemware, both of which shared the international market with Waterford Crystal of Ireland.

Due to the resurgence of interest in glass blowing in the United States, small craft shops could be found across the country where artisans sold their wares, displayed their techniques, and often taught classes. However, these shops were generally neither involved nor interested in producing the mass quantities of machine-made glassware supplied by such large corporations as the Corning conglomerate.

The product share within the industry was split between six types of goods. Textile glass fiber accounted for 30.82 percent of the overall market; machine-made table, kitchen, art, and novelty glassware claimed 19.13 percent; machine-made lighting and electronic glassware took another 28.27 percent; all other machine-made glassware accounted for 15.79 percent; handmade pressed and blown glassware claimed 2.89 percent; and pressed and blown glass not specified by kind comprised 3.10 percent. The materials consumed in the greatest amounts by the industry included plastic film and sheets, unsupported glass, all types of glass sand, and paperboard boxes.

BACKGROUND AND DEVELOPMENT

The Mesopotamians were credited by archaeologists with making the world's first glass, circa 2500 B.C. However, it was not until the Roman Empire that glass making evolved as a standard craft, much like baking and jewelry making. Venice eventually became known as the glass making capital of the world, and remained so through the 1600s. Glass making in the United States was very much a crude art form until the eighteenth century, and nearly died out several times. Glass items of any quality, such as windows or glassware, had to be purchased from England. However, several small shops where glass was blown provided wares for limited customer bases, and eventually larger manufacturers, such as Bakewell and Company of Pittsburgh, entered the marketplace. For the cosmetic enhancement of glass, etching was practiced during the seventeenth and eighteenth centuries. However, the ability to press glass in very large quantities did not develop until the nineteenth century.

The glass industry in the United States started to boom after the War of 1812. Between 1800 and 1825, America experienced strong demographic, economic, and political growth. Luxury items were in ever-increasing demand, creating a need for machine-made glass products. Glass pressing was already common in Europe by the late 1700s, although the pieces were small and made with waffle-iron-type presses. American inventors developed the first large, hand-operated pressing machine.

The introduction of glass pressing created a new challenge for glass makers. Only specific glass mixtures were adequate for pressing, which required experimentation. Also, experience was required to know how much molten glass could be placed in a press without scrapping the piece and how much time was required to produce the glass before it started to cool and crack. By the time these processes were perfected, glass makers started to produce molds exhibiting ornate designs, referred to as "lacy glass." Glass pressing continued to evolve during the colonial era, expanding to candlesticks and lamps. The Victorian era heavily influenced glass making, and by the 1880s, colored glass was the order of the day. Glass collecting became a pastime for many and an obsession for some, evidenced by collectors willing to pay heavily for early American, lacy, carnival, and depression glassware.

CURRENT CONDITIONS

The pressed and blown glass industry in the mid-1990s experienced low margins, high competition, and high technology. While glass tableware and cooking dishes did not share the high-tech image of fiber optic cables and devices, research and development continued for better materials for these purposes. Likewise, new marketing approaches, such as creative packaging and merchandizing, were constantly investigated.

INDUSTRY LEADERS

In the 1990s, many of the top-ranking companies in the entire glass industry are related to Corning Incorporated of Corning, New York—Owens/Corning Fiberglass of Toledo, Ohio; Owens-Illinois of Toledo; and Owens-Illinois of Vineland, New Jersey. The parent company had 1996 sales of $3.65 billion and employed approximately 20,000 people.

Corning Incorporated changed its name in 1989 from Corning Glass Works to better recognize its commitment to a number of diverse industries. The founder, Amory Houghton, moved his glass operation from Brooklyn to Corning, New York, in 1868. By 1875, Corning Glass Works was incorporated, and Houghton became president of the company—a position he retained until 1911.

The technical expertise of the company was recognized early, as Thomas Edison asked for its help in making electric light bulbs in 1880. In 1912, Corning invented borosilicate, which was used to produce Pyrex in 1915. Pyrex immediately became standard in the scientific community for laboratory equipment, although the consumer markets were not tapped until years later. Another significant milestone for Corning was the 1934 manufacture of a 200-inch diameter mirror for the Mount Palomar telescope. The company surpassed this accomplishment by creating the world's largest single-piece telescope mirror for the Japanese government in 1992. In the 1960s, Corning created the ceramic heat-resisting reentry shields and glass windshields for the Apollo moon program. The most significant research for Corning in past years was in the development of fiber optics. Corning realized the potential of the material in the 1960s and continued research and development even though market demand was low, and by 1984 invested $87 million in new fiber optic plant facilities.

Anchor Hocking Glassware of Lancaster, Ohio, was another leader in the glassware industry. The company's roots can be traced to 1905, when founder Ike Collins convinced a group of seven investors to contribute to the Hocking Glass Company's original capitalization of $25,000. By the end of its first year of manufacturing and marketing lamp chimneys and other glass items, the company had generated sales of $20,000. By 1919, Hocking boasted 300 employees (many of them highly skilled glass blowers) and $900,000 in annual sales, and had diversified from lamp chimneys (which were made obsolete by the invention of the incandescent light bulb) into glass tableware.

Acquisitions and mergers expanded the company's interests into glass containers, plastics, and hardware, increasing annual sales to a peak of more than $900 million in the early 1980s, but intense competition forced Anchor Hocking to sell out to the Newell Company in 1987. The sales of the Anchor Hocking Glassware unit were estimated at $150 million by the mid-1990s, and company employees totaled about 1,400.

Other mid-1990s industry leaders included Libbey Glass, of Toledo, Ohio, with sales of $281 million and 2,900 employees; Kimble Glass Inc., of Vineland New Jersey, with sales of $198 million and 1,000 employees; and Essilor of America, of St. Petersburg, Florida, with sales of $180 million and 1,700 employees.

WORK FORCE

In 1982, 37,600 people were employed in the pressed and blown glass industry, more than 78 percent of whom were production workers. Employment levels held steady through 1988, when the industry employed 36,600 people, 83 percent of whom were production workers. Average hourly wages increased by 23 percent over the same period, from $9.41 in 1982 to $12.23 in 1988. The 1988 hourly wage was $1.57 higher than the average for all manufacturing industries.

In 1996, industry employment was estimated at 33,200—with 27,600 working in production. The average hourly wage had increased to $15.18. By 1998, employment was expected to fall to 32,600, but hourly wages were expected to increase to $15.97.

Projections for occupations in the glass industry were not bright going into the twenty-first century. All but extruding and forming machine workers, which were expected to increase about 22 percent, were expected to decrease in numbers by 33 to 51 percent by the year 2005.

FURTHER READING

Darnay, Arsen J., ed. *Manufacturing USA.* 5th ed. Detroit: Gale Research, 1996.

Ellis, William S. "Glass: Capturing the Dance of Light." *National Geographic,* December 1993.

"Fiberglass Parts Made Faster than a Speeding Bullet." *Ward's Auto World,* February 1993.

Fink, Ronald. "Corning: Bad Breaks." *Financial World,* 6 July 1993.

Hammonds, Keith. "Corning's Class Act: How Jamie Houghton Reinvented the Company." *Business Week,* 13 May 1991.

Hast, Adele, ed. *International Directory of Company Histories.* Chicago: St. James Press, 1988.

Holusha, John. "A Huge Looking Glass for Japan." *New York Times,* 25 November 1992.

Lang, Sarah. "Corning's Blueprint for Training in the '90s." *Training,* July 1991.

Paul, Cynthia. "Corning Sets Complementary 'Lifestyle' for Mass." *HFD:The Weekly Home Furnishings Newspaper,* 17 May 1993.

Polak, Ada. *Glass: Its Tradition and Its Makers.* New York: Putnam's Sons, 1975.

"Process Produces Practically Perfect Preforms." *Machine Design,* 26 March 1993.

Roush, Gary B. "A Program for Sharing Corporate Intelligence." *Journal of Business Strategy,* January-February 1991.

U.S. Department of Commerce. Bureau of the Census. *1995 Annual Survey of Manufactures.* Washington: GPO, 1997.

SIC 3231

GLASS PRODUCTS, MADE OF PURCHASED GLASS

This category covers establishments primarily engaged in manufacturing glass products from purchased glass. Establishments primarily engaged in manufacturing optical lenses, except ophthalmic, are classified in **SIC 3827: Optical Instruments and Lenses,** and those manufacturing ophthalmic lenses are classified in **SIC 3851: Ophthalmic Goods.**

INDUSTRY SNAPSHOT

In the mid-1990s, there were 1,537 establishments in the industry, an increase of approximately 8 percent since 1989. In 1995, the industry shipped $7.9 billion worth of products, an increase of 29 percent since 1990. By 1998, the value of shipments was forecast to increase to nearly $9.5 billion. Employment has increased steadily, from 50,000 in the mid-1980s to an estimated 62,000 by 1996, 49,000 of which worked in production.

ORGANIZATION AND STRUCTURE

Firms in the purchased glass products industry are distinguished from other glass manufacturing firms—known as primary glass manufacturers—in that their products are not made directly from raw glass materials but from secondary glass purchased from other companies.

Companies within the industry manufacture everyday home glass products, such as mirrors, beverage glasses, shower doors, bathtub enclosures, picture glass, ash trays, lighting fixture glass, glass top tables, display shelving, window glass, automobile glass, clock glass, patio doors, oven door panels, novelty and souvenir glass items, appliance glass, and cosmetic and perfume containers. Industry products are also used in an extensive number of industrial, technical, and other non-household applications such as safety and bullet-proof glass, instrument dials, precision glass tubing, stained glass, industrial safety glasses and welding lenses, greenhouse glass, glass fiber used in optical components and for data and nondata transmission (faceplates, sensors, and glass-based optical coatings), chemical glassware, instrument panels, cathode ray tube screens, and high-tolerance specialty glass products such as elapsed-time indicators and gravity-sensing electrolytic transducers.

Important subgroups of industry products include beverage glasses such as tumblers and stemware, beer glasses, crystal glassware, and casual glassware, and glass fiber used in optical components and for data and non-data transmission (including faceplates, sensors, and glass-based optical coatings).

Product manufacture. Because industry firms do not manufacture glass from raw materials as do primary glass manufacturers, the methods for manufacturing glass products from purchased glass vary with the specific product. Firms within the industry purchase glass in the following forms: float glass (a type of flat glass manufactured by floating the glass in a bath of molten tin), sheet glass, plate glass, glass sand, and "cullet" or glass scrap.

Other materials and supplies used in the manufacture of purchased glass products include industrial inorganic chemicals, plastic film and sheets, ground or otherwise treated nonmetallic minerals, and sodium carbonate (soda ash) as well as paperboard containers, wood boxes and pallets, and lumber.

Some of the more common glass products, which illustrate different glass manufacturing methods, include laboratory glass, laminated glass, mirror glass, ornamental glass, safety glass, and stained glass.

Laboratory glassware. Laboratory glass products such as test tubes, beakers, vials, and glass for distilling liquids are often made of borosilicate glass (a combination of boric oxide, silica sand, and other chemicals) because it has a high natural resistance to temperature change and corrosion, making it ideal for scientific, pharmaceutical, and some household uses. A common manufacturing method for laboratory glassware is machine blowing, in which molten glass is fed into a blowing element where jets of air are blown into the liquefied glass, causing it, with the aid of molds, to expand and conform to predetermined dimensions. Another common glass making method is machine pressing, where molten glass, cut at regular intervals into individual dollops, is dropped into molds where it is then shifted beneath a plunging or pressing element that gives the glass, when cooled, its final shape.

Laminated glass. Laminated or compound glass is comprised of two or more sheets of glass and a layer of plastic fused together by heating in a pressurized tank or autoclave. When laminated glass products such as automobile windshields are broken, they crack rather than shatter because the fragments adhere to the plastic layer, maintaining the glass's transparency and preventing the scattering of shards.

Mirror glass. Mirrors are made by treating washed float glass with a tin-based mixture, then spraying the surface with a "silvering" solution made of silver nitrate and water followed by a "reducing" agent. The combination of the tin solution and the reducing agent creates a reflective silver film on the glass surface, which is then treated with a layer of copper and a protective lacquer and allowed to dry.

Ornamental glass. Ornamental glass products are manufactured by running sheets of glass through rollers that shape or emboss the glass surface according to the specific (and often trademarked) design of the individual firm. Some types of ornamental glass, each made using different techniques, include light scattering glass, "wave" glass, lined glass, curved or semicircular "roundel" glass, and glass with flower or other decorative impressions.

Safety glass. Safety or tempered glass is designed to break into small, rounded pieces of a predetermined size when shattered, thus reducing the creation of dangerous sharp fragments. Such glass is manufactured by heating sheets of flat glass, then subjecting them to bursts of cold air, which causes the interior of the glass to cool more slowly than the surface. The physical bond between the interior and external glass layers is such that when the pane is broken, the fragments are small, uniformly sized, and noninjurious.

Stained glass. Stained glass consists of segments of individually colored panes joined together to create an image or pattern. The three methods for staining glass are painting, fusion with metallic oxides, and enameling. Glass painting involves applying pigments to hardened glass, then permanently burning or baking the pigment on to the surface of the glass in an oven. Alternatively, metallic oxides of varying colors can be added to glass while it is still molten, changing the tint of the glass itself when it cools. Metallic oxides are also used in enameling methods but are applied to hardened rather than molten glass. The enamel coating is then bonded with the glass by firing or baking.

Industry specialization. Many industry firms manufacture more than one type of glass product. For example, Apogee Enterprises Inc. of Minnesota produces insulating, heat-tempered, laminated, non-glare, picture, automotive, and bullet-resistant glass. A few firms, however, such as American Mirror Company, Inc. (Virginia), Fisher Skylights, Inc. (New York), and Riordan Stained Glass Studio (Ohio), specialize in a single line of glass products. Industry specialization in glass product manufacturing is also reflected in the names of some industry firms, such as Artistic Shower Door & Mirror Company Inc., Pilkington Aerospace Inc., National Bullet Proof Inc., and Christmas by Krebs Corporation, among others.

End-users. The major users of glass products, including some nonindustry products but excluding containers such as bottles and jars, consist of individual consumers; manufacturers, such as motor vehicle and car body; exporters; restaurants, bars, and other eating and drinking establishments; automotive repair shops and service businesses; lighting fixture and equipment manufacturers; miscellaneous plastics products manufacturers; hotels and other hospitality businesses; and electric lamp manufacturers.

BACKGROUND AND DEVELOPMENT

Between 1972 and 1987, the purchased glass products industry experienced continuous solid growth, with the only declines in the value of shipments occurring in the mid-1970s. In that 16-year period, the value of industry shipments more than quadrupled from $1.3 billion to $5.4 billion, the number of industry firms increased 38 percent from 817 to 1,325, and employment grew 52 percent from 33,700 to 51,100. At the same time, the cost of materials and payroll as a percentage of total shipment value declined from 73 to 67 percent industry wide.

Faced with decreased demand for glass products, industry firms entered into joint ventures, introduced new products, and improved facilities in the early 1990s to stimulate sales. Between 1992 and 1994, glass container shipments averaged about 70,000 per quarter, with seasonal fluctuations.

INDUSTRY LEADERS

Three of the major companies in the industry are Guardian Industries Corporation, Donnelly Corporation, and Safelite Glass Corporation. Guardian, of Auburn Hills, Michigan, had 1996 sales of $2 billion and employed 8,100 people. Donnelly, of Holland, Michigan, had sales of $383 million and employed 2,500 people. Safelite, of Columbus, Ohio, had sales of $357 million and employed 3,600 people.

Several industry firms, including Dillmeier Enterprises Inc. of Arkansas and Glass Products Inc. of Pennsylvania, were exclusively engaged in the manufacture of purchased glass products in the 1990s. Other firms primarily engaged in purchased glass product manufacture were also active in such industries as local trucking, curtain and drapery manufacture, testing services laboratories, and wood household furniture manufacturing, among others.

WORK FORCE

In 1995, the industry employed 62,300, an increase of 15 percent since 1990. Production workers comprised 76 percent (47,800) of all employees in the industry, an increase of 5 percent since 1990. Production workers' average hourly earnings were $10.92 in 1995, up 12 percent since 1990.

The glass making occupations with the greatest number of workers were glass product assemblers and fabricators (12 percent of glass industry employment); general helpers, laborers, and material movers (8 percent); hand packers and packagers of manufactured products (6 percent); glass manufacturing machine feeders and offbearers—workers who deliver raw materials and carry them away from glass manufacturing machines (5 percent); and blue collar worker supervisors (5 percent). The remaining two-thirds of industry employees consisted of other production workers—such as glass product cutting and slicing machine setters, operators, and tenders; precision glass product inspectors, testers, and graders; glass hand cutters and trimmers; glass furnace, kiln, or kettle operators and tenders; and glass product coating, painting, and spraying machine operators—and nonproduction administrative positions such as sales staff, general managers and executives, support and clerical staff, and industrial production managers.

FURTHER READING

Berlye, Milton K. *Encyclopedia of Working with Glass.* Dobbs Ferry, NY: Oceana Publications, 1968.

Ceramic Industry. August, 1992; June, 1993.

Darnay, Arsen J. *Manufacturing USA*. 5th ed. Detroit: Gale Research, 1996.

''Hoover's Online.'' Austin, TX: Hoover's, Inc., 1997. Available from http:/www.hoovers.com.

Pfaender, Heinz G. *Schott Guide to Glass*. New York: Van Nostrand & Reinhold, 1983.

U.S. Bureau of the Census. *1995 Annual Survey of Manufactures*. Washington: GPO, 1997.

———. *1994 County Business Patterns*. Washington: GPO, 1996.

SIC 3241

CEMENT, HYDRAULIC

Establishments primarily engaged in manufacturing hydraulic cement, including portland, natural, masonry, and pozzolana cements.

Cement is manufactured by grinding minerals, typically a controlled mix of limestone and clay, in either a wet or a dry environment. The ground material is then heated in a kiln, chemically changing it into a substance called ''clinker'' that is cooled and reground with additional minerals such as gypsum. This leaves a finished powder—the cement itself—that reacts with water and can be mixed with gravel or sand to create concrete.

In 1995, the United States produced 75 million metric tons of portland cement, which accounted for 90 percent of this industry's output, and consumed 86 million metric tons. U.S. cement makers shipped a record $5.167 billion worth of all cement products in 1995, nearly a 10 percent increase over the previous year. Dry processing, which is more energy efficient, accounted for roughly 70 percent of this production. The U.S. cement industry ranked third largest in the world, following China and Japan. Growth in the industry was fueled by general strength in the economy, particularly the robust construction industry of the mid-1990s.

Cement is used in a variety of construction-related industries, particularly in building and roadway construction. In the mid-1990s, buildings commanded roughly 55 percent of U.S. cement consumption, followed by streets and highways at 29 percent, water systems at 9 percent, and miscellaneous construction and nonconstruction uses accounting for the remaining 7 percent.

The industry, which runs an annual trade deficit, has significantly reduced its reliance on imports as a proportion of consumption since the mid-1980s, when import volume was as much as 20 times greater than export volume. In the mid-1990s imports declined and exports increased, bringing the deficit down to less than a factor of ten.

Numbering 16,800 in 1995, industry employment dropped steadily since the 1970s due to automation and a decline of small producers. Approaching the twenty-first century, the industry was expected to increase employment levels by more than 10 percent, however, in three occupations: industrial machinery mechanics, sales workers, and industrial production managers. Most other occupations were expected to face reductions; those most significantly affected were hand packers, furnace operators, secretaries, and crushing and mixing machine operators. Positions for general managers and top executives will possibly decline by more than 5 percent as the hydraulic cement industry approached the year 2000.

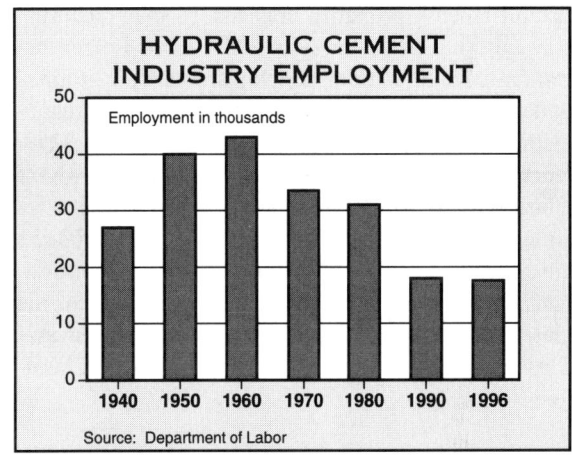

According to the Portland Cement Association (PCA), in 1996 there were approximately 50 companies manufacturing cement in 118 plants throughout the United States. Plants were typically located near the regional market they served to minimize transportation costs. During the mid-1990s construction boom, cement plants operated at just over 90 percent capacity. The PCA estimated that 65 percent of U.S. cement capacity was held by foreign companies.

Holding a 12.5 percent share of industry production, Holnam, Inc. of Dundee, Michigan, was the largest cement producer in the United States in 1996. It was followed by Lafarge Corporation, with a 1996 cement capacity of about 8 percent of the total U.S. active capacity. Other major producers included Southdown Inc., Ash Grove Cement Co., and Blue Circle, Inc.

FURTHER READING

Darnay, Arsen J., ed. *Manufacturing USA.* 5th ed. Detroit: Gale Research, 1996.

Portland Cement Association. *Portland Cement Association Homepage.* Skokie, IL, 1997. Available from http://www.portcement.org.

U.S. Bureau of the Census. *1995 Annual Survey of Manufactures.* Washington: GPO, 1997.

U.S. Department of Commerce. International Trade Administration. *U.S. Industrial Outlook 1994.* Washington: GPO, 1994.

SIC 3251

BRICK AND STRUCTURAL CLAY TILE

This category covers establishments primarily engaged in manufacturing brick and structural clay tile. Establishments primarily engaged in manufacturing clay firebrick fall under **SIC 3255: Clay Refractories;** those manufacturing nonclay firebrick are grouped under **SIC 3297: Nonclay Refractories;** those manufacturing sand lime brick are classified in **SIC 3299: Nonmetallic Mineral Products, Not Elsewhere Classified;** those manufacturing architectural terra cotta and other miscellaneous structural clay products are classified in **SIC 3259: Structural Clay Products, Not Elsewhere Classified;** and those manufacturing glass brick are classified in **SIC 3229: Pressed and Blown Glass and Glassware, Not Elsewhere Classified.**

ORGANIZATION AND STRUCTURE

In 1995, the largest product types were: building or common brick and face brick (98 percent of the value of the industry's total shipments), structural facing tile (including unglazed and salt glazed facing tile, ceramic glazed facing tile, and glazed brick; 1.5 percent of total shipment value); and structural clay tile (except facing; less than 1 percent). Other products manufactured by the industry in the mid-1990s were: clay book tile, clay ceramic glazed brick, corncrib tile, clay radial (rounded) chimney blocks, hollow and vitrified (heat-fused into glass or a glassy material) brick, clay building tile, clay floor arch tile, clay furring tile, clay fireproofing tile, clay flooring brick, clay paving brick, clay partition tile, silo tile, and slumped brick (brick with an expanded or "slumped" base).

The characteristics of brick and structural clay tile products vary depending on the type of clay or raw mineral material used, the manner in which they are manufactured, the temperature at which they are burned or baked, the relative absorptive and strength qualities, and the severity of the climates they will be used in. The standard dimensions of U.S. bricks range between 4 and 6 inches thick, 2 3/4 to 4 inches high, and 8 to 12 inches wide. Bricks come in roughly 10,000 different colors besides the traditional red, weigh about six pounds, and cost between 25 and 50 cents each. Typical uses for brick and clay structural tile have historically been in the construction of homes—66 to 76 percent of all industry brick sales—as well as office buildings and industrial and other structures.

In its most common form, brick is made from clay that has been mixed with water, formed or "tempered" into a rectangular block, dried, and burned in a kiln. "Common brick" refers to brick in its undifferentiated state as it comes from the kiln, and it is used as "backup" masonry for wall thickness and structural support behind face brick. Face brick is chosen based on its uniformity of appearance for use in the exterior or visible portions of walls and is divided into various grades of color, texture, and perfection. Glazed brick is brick that has been treated with a coating of melted ground glass to repel moisture, engender easy cleaning, and/or create a desired appearance.

Unlike the most common ceramic home floor tile, which is typically thin and flat, structural tile more resembles concrete construction blocks in that it is hollow or cored and is primarily used for structural support rather than for aesthetic, decorative purposes. Structural clay tile is derived from clay, ceramic, and refractory minerals including kaolin and ball clay, mixed with industrial chemicals, molded into specific dimensions by forcing the raw material through dies, and burned or baked in kilns or ovens. The basic types of structural clay tile are: load-bearing wall tile to bear the weight of floors, roofs, and facings; nonload-bearing tile used in the construction of partitions in buildings interiors and for backing up walls made of two or more materials; furring tile used to line the inside of walls and to provide an air space between the plaster and the wall; and fireproofing tile used to protect steel girders, beams, columns, and other structural elements from fire. Flooring tile—not to be confused with everyday decorative floor tile—is used in floor and roof construction, and structural clay facing tile is used in exposed or visible interior and exterior walls and partitions.

BACKGROUND AND DEVELOPMENT

The first bricks in North America appeared in the form of the ballast of English ships, but a native brickmaking industry soon emerged in which clay was pressed into wooden molds and baked in beehive-shaped kilns. This handmade method endured until the 1870s when early brick production machines began to transform the industry. Besides the handmade method, two basic brickmaking methods soon emerged. Machine-molded brick resembled the traditional method except that the moist clay was forced into the molds by machine. Extruded brick—the most common method today—uses a machine to press a continuous tube of moist clay through an aperture, after which a wire cuts the individual bricks at preset intervals.

The use of uniform or modular standards for brick and structural clay tile by the construction industry and the brick and structural clay tile manufacturing industry has a long history, and industry products are governed by precise specifications with respect to tile length, width, and thickness—as well as strength, endurance, and appearance. For example, in the early 1960s there were 12 distinct modular sizes or specifications for structural load-bearing wall tile. Sizes that become unpopular may be dropped, however, and new ones added as construction industry demand dictates. Traditionally, few manufacturers have produced all the tile sizes accepted as standard by the industry. Between 1985 and 1994, the U.S. brick industry languished with an annual growth rate well below 2.5 percent.

CURRENT CONDITIONS

In 1992, 117 U.S. companies operating 186 business establishments employed 14,200 workers and generated $1.12 billion in shipments of brick and structural clay tile products. Industry firms produced more than 6.6 billion bricks, over 24 million facing tiles, and almost 54,000 short tons of non-facing structural clay tile. Most production centered in Texas (10.5 percent of industry shipments in 1992) and Ohio (9.8 percent). The average industry establishment in 1994 had 59 employees, an average per-employee payroll of $23,524, and annual shipments valued at $5.47 million. The U.S. brick and structural clay industry was expected to enjoy a healthy 2.6 percent annual growth rate through the end of the century, largely as a result of continued growth in the new home construction industry. In 1997 alone, the U.S. home building industry was expected to construct 1.4 million new homes.

Issues confronting industry firms in the 1990s included conforming to environmental protection regulations, managing labor costs, coping with fluctuating construction demand, financing new facilities and expansion, and competing with imported products. Industry firms have increasingly benefited from improved brick making technologies, including better kiln designs, improved knowledge of brick and tile raw materials and their characteristics, greater use of modern manufacturing technology, and better control over the firing or baking process.

The explosive spread of computers in American industry has led to computer control of the brick manufacturing process and the adoption by some industry firms of the World Wide Web as a marketing tool. In the mid-1990s, brick makers continued to address the growing demand for the "human" feel (handmade bricks) by returning to historical handmade brick-by-brick manufacturing methods and by altering the look of machine-made bricks to give them a less uniform appearance. The use of recycled brick from demolished structures also continued to grow in the 1990s, as producers looked to cheaper raw material alternatives to clay.

INDUSTRY LEADERS

In 1995 the leading firms in brick and structural clay tile industry were Justin Industries Inc. of Texas ($483 million in sales and 5,000 employees), Boral Bricks Inc. of Georgia ($130 million in sales and 1,900 employees), and Mutual Materials Co. of Washington ($45 million in sales and 500 employees). In addition to its building materials operations, Justin Industries manufactures western boots and work and sport footwear and publishes books on western and southwestern Americana. Its building materials subsidiaries include Acme Brick, Featherlite Building Products, and American Tile Supply. Other leading industry firms in the mid-1990s included Bickerstaff Clay Products, Belden Brick, Georgia-Carolina Brick, Pine Hall Brick Company, and Richtex Corporation.

FURTHER READING

"The Brick Industry: Markets and Trends." *Ceramic Industry,* 1 October 1996, S13.

Brozda, Mike. "Building with Brick." *Home,* November 1995, 72.

Ceramic Industry. Troy, MI: Business News Publishing Co.

Masonry. Oak Brook, IL.: Mason Contractors Association of America.

U.S. Bureau of the Census. Department of Commerce. *1992 Census of Manufactures* Washington: GPO, 1995.

U.S. Department of Commerce. *1987 Census of Manufactures: Industry Series.* Washington: GPO.

—Paul Bodine

CERAMIC WALL AND FLOOR TILE

This industry covers establishments primarily engaged in manufacturing ceramic wall and floor tile. Establishments primarily engaged in manufacturing structural clay tile are classified in **SIC 3251: Brick and Structural Clay Tile,** and those manufacturing drain tile are classified in **SIC 3259: Structural Clay Products, Not Elsewhere Classified.**

INDUSTRY SNAPSHOT

Nearly 99 percent of this industry's product share is composed of glazed and unglazed floor tile and wall tile, including quarry tile and ceramic mosaic tile. Because this industry is so focused on decorative tiles, it is completely dependent on the economic health of the construction and remodeling industries.

Clay, ceramic, and refractory materials such as kaolin and ball clay are the raw materials consumed in the manufacture of ceramic tiles. Other industrial chemicals, some lead-based, are also used to produce ceramic tiles. Because of the industry's use and disposal of these lead-based chemicals, ceramic manufacturers are forced to comply with a wide array of Environmental Protection Agency regulations.

This industry has been experiencing steady growth through the 1990s in terms of establishments, shipments, and employment levels. In 1988, 112 establishments were present, 53 employing 20 or more people. By 1997, 142 establishments were engaged in the industry, 58 employing 20 or more people. Leading states involved in ceramic wall and floor tile manufacturing included California, Texas, and Ohio. The total work force in 1990 was 10,000, 83 percent of which were production workers. By the end of 1995, the total work force had grown to 12,000, with 84 percent of the employees working in a production capacity.

BACKGROUND AND DEVELOPMENT

The evolution of clay tiles began with the introduction of roofing tiles, followed by flooring tiles and wall tiles. The Roman historian Pliny wrote that tiles were invented in Greece on the isle of Cyprus by Cinyra, son of Agrippa. The earliest baked clay roof tiles were excavated near Argos, Greece, which date to around 1800 B.C. The technique for production of this architectural medium moved to southern Italy and Sicily and slowly spread throughout the rest of continental Europe. Until the industrial revolution when tile making was mechanized somewhat, only the very rich could afford tiled roofs and floors. This is evident in the 89 B.C. Charter of Tarentum, which stated that Senate membership and voting privileges were restricted to those men who owned housing within Tarentum, roofed with at least 1,500 tiles.

As with all industries, the Industrial Revolution forever changed the manufacture of clay tiles. By the 1850s, the British led the industry in machinery innovation and heavily influenced production methods in Germany, France, Belgium, Holland, Spain, and Portugal. The introduction of machines to aid in the manufacturing process resulted in dramatically higher production levels and far greater availability of tiles.

The ceramic tile industry in the United States entered its own period of enlightenment in the 1870s. The art form in ceramic tiles developed its own uniquely American twist during the Philadelphia International Centennial Exhibition of 1876; glazed tiles were produced in the United States approximately 30 years previously, though. This progress is documented by Charles Thomas Davis, writer of *Manufacture of Bricks, Tiles and Terra-Cotta,* published in 1884. He wrote, ''Nothing in the history of pottery is so remarkable as the progress which has been made in the manufacture of encaustic and decorative tiles, but especially in the latter, in this country since the Centennial Exposition of 1876 . . . .'' However, during 1870 and 1900, many American-produced tiles imitated the lifestyle in Victorian Britain, mainly because many of the artisans were trained either in Britain or directly by the British.

A new, distinctly different generation began to infuse the American ceramic tile industry in the early 1900s. These artisans were trained in American potteries and art schools and prided themselves on original, hand-made tiles. The leaders in innovation were the small companies that created a broad diversity in style and technique. This period was struck a deadly blow by the Great Depression of 1929, when the construction industry shuddered to a halt and many small tile firms were forced to close their doors.

The United States then entered World War II, and the Art Deco movement again changed the design of ceramic tiles. Screen printing became an important method of coloring tiles, and production methods were improved to lend great consistency to final tile products. The tile industry in the United States today is dominated by international conglomerates like Armstrong World Industries, which owns American Olean Tile. However, much of the artistry in the industry is still spurred by smaller tile companies.

CURRENT CONDITIONS

The ceramic tile industry is closely tied to the construction industry, both residential and nonresidential. In the first quarter of 1996, construction began an overall decline. Due to depressed sales, inventory accumulation stalled production of various ceramic products. Likewise, poor weather conditions throughout the United States slowed construction, directly affecting the sales and shipments of ceramic products. During the remainder of 1996, however, clay floor and wall tiles experienced strong growth in shipments because of economic recovery in other industries. Due to lower interest rates and general economic improvement, housing starts are projected to grow into the late 1990s, and residential remodeling is also forecast to grow. This growth will serve as a tremendous boon to establishments involved in ceramic wall and floor tile manufacturing.

INDUSTRY LEADERS

American Olean Tile Company of Lansdale, Pennsylvania, is owned by Armstrong World Industries. This acquisition, completed in 1988 in an effort to boost profitability, was the first of several restructuring moves for Armstrong, the largest outfit in this industry in terms of sales. Armstrong, a public company employing almost 20,000 workers in 1996, posted annual sales of almost $3 billion. Other key companies in this industry include Dal-Tile Corporation, American Biltrite Inc., United States Ceramic Tile Co., and Monarch Industries Inc.

WORK FORCE

In the late 1990s, the work force engaged in tile manufacture works in a highly mechanized, if not totally automated, setting or works in a small specialty studio setting, creating highly artistic and functional tiles.

The industries producing stone, clay, and mineral products are expected to engage in downsizing efforts across a variety of occupations by the year 2000. The number of hand packers and packagers is expected by some industry observers to be reduced by nearly 25 percent, largely as a result of increasing automation. Other occupations expected to experience work force reductions of about 15 percent include assemblers and fabricators; furnace, kiln, oven, and kettle operators; crushing and mixing machine operators; precision inspectors, graders, and testers; packaging and filling machine operators; machine feeders and offbearers; hand freight, stock, and material movers; secretaries; cutting and slicing machine operators; grinders and polishers; and metal and plastic machine forming oper-

ators. Occupations expecting growth in the industry include sales workers, industrial machinery mechanics, and industrial production managers.

RESEARCH AND TECHNOLOGY

Production methods for manufacturing ceramic tiles have greatly improved since the end of World War II. Machine decoration has increased overall output, while improved drying machines move tiles to shipping quicker. Additionally, new advances in airless and microwave drying techniques hold the promise of revolutionizing the drying process while cutting production time dramatically.

Increasing customer demand for greater variety in styles and uses of tiles has broadened the base of techniques used to produce final artistic effects. The most revolutionary of these procedures enables customers to choose designs from a computer's memory and see the finished product on a computer simulation of the customer's own bathroom. In the future, computers—combined with machine tile decoration—will allow customers to design their own tiles for the manufacturer to then produce. While clay tile making continues to resemble many of the practices used 1,000 years ago, better production methods and materials lend new levels of quality and consistency to the final product.

FURTHER READING

''An Overview of the Economy.'' *Ceramic Industry,* August 1996.

Belli, Anne. ''42 Residents Sue Tile Firm Over Waste.'' *Dallas Morning News,* 10 July 1992.

Berss, Marcia. ''Slippery Tile.'' *Forbes,* 6 December 1993.

''Blending Pottery Art With Computer Technology.'' *Ceramic Industry,* January 1996.

Brodribb, Gerald. *Roman Brick and Tile.* Wolfeboro, NH: Alan Sutton Publishing Inc., 1989.

Earl, David. ''The Feasibility of Microwave Drying Ceramic Tile.'' *Ceramic Industry,* October 1996.

''Florida Tile.'' *Custom Builder,* November-December 1992.

Jones, John. ''Advances in Tile Manufacturing Technology.'' *Ceramic Industry,* April 1996.

Lemmen, Hans van. *Tiles: 1,000 Years of Architectural Decoration.* New York: Harry N. Abrams, Inc., 1993.

Sheppard, Laurel. ''New and Better Additives Ensure Fabrication of Quality Ceramics.'' *Ceramic Industry,* March 1997.

Steele, Andrew. ''Inventory Glut Haunts Production Levels.'' *Ceramic Industry,* June 1993.

Stubbing, Thomas. "Airless Drying Improves Productivity and Reduces Energy." *Ceramic Industry,* March 1996.

—Valerie Wilson, updated by Michael Broyles

SIC 3255

CLAY REFRACTORIES

This category covers establishments primarily engaged in manufacturing clay firebrick and other heat-resisting clay products. Establishments primarily engaged in manufacturing nonclay refractories and all graphite refractories, whether of carbon bond or ceramic bond, are classified under **SIC 3297: Nonclay Refractories.**

INDUSTRY SNAPSHOT

In 1992, 95 companies employing 6,200 employees generated more than $887 million in shipments. Industry firms shipped 869,000 metric tons of refractory bricks and shapes, 600,000 metric tons of unshaped clay refractories, and 174,000 metric tons of refractory raw materials. Ohio, Pennsylvania, and Illinois accounted for 39 percent of the industry's shipments in 1992. In 1994, the average industry firm had 41 employees and $6.5 million worth of shipments. Leading industry firms in 1995 were North American Refractories of Ohio ($290 million in sales and 2,000 employees); Harbison-Walker of Pennsylvania ($243 million in sales, 1,800 employees); AP Green Industries Inc. of Missouri ($196 million, 1,700 employees); General Refractories of Pennsylvania ($160 million, 1,700 employees); and National Refractories of California ($120 million, 900 employees). Other leading firms in the mid-1990s were Martin Marietta Magnesia Specialties, General Shale Products Corporation, Plibrico Co., and CFB Industries Inc.

Refractories are mineral- and chemical-based materials with very high heat-resisting properties, which make them ideal for use in the construction of walls, ceilings, and associated elements of iron and steel industry blast furnaces, glass manufacturing tanks, cement kilns, hot stoves, ceramic kilns, open hearth furnaces, nonferrous metallurgical furnaces, and steam boilers. Most clay refractory products are manufactured in the form of bricks, but refractory clay may also be formed into special shapes, such as the T-sections of refractory pipes or the small stands that support ceramic products during firing in a kiln. Refractories have been an essential element in heat engineering plants since the 1960s, where they were successfully used to improve performance and energy efficiency.

ORGANIZATION AND STRUCTURE

In 1995, the clay refractory industry consisted of four general product groups: refractory bricks and shapes with 61 percent of the value of industry shipments, unshaped clay refractories with 34 percent, other lump or ground refractory materials with 2 percent, and unspecified refractories with 2 percent. Included in the refractory bricks and shapes category were fireclay bricks and shapes, pouring pit refractories, clay kiln furniture, and radiant heater elements—31 firms accounting for 38 percent of the shipment value of this product group; high alumina refractory brick and shapes including glass house pots, tank blocks, feeder parts, and upper structure shapes—32 firms, accounting for 52 percent; and insulating refractory bricks and shapes—15 firms; 10 percent. As many as 38 U.S. firms made unshaped clay refractories in 1995, which included everything from refractory bonding mortars and plastic refractories to ramming mixes, castable refractories, and fire clay gunning mixes. Fifteen industry firms made lump or ground refractory materials in 1995. These were generally sold directly to customers in raw form or as an export.

The refractory brick and shapes industry was a highly specialized supplier to such heat manufacturing industries as the iron and steel industry, the ceramics industry, and the glass-making industry. Its terminology and the specific products it sold to end-user industries were as specialized as the products they helped to make. For example, one industry product, known as refractory tank blocks, consisted of blocks of refractory clay used in the lower portions of glass-tank furnaces; and refractory feeder parts were devices for supplying refractory raw materials to a preparation machine prior to firing in a ceramic or glass oven. Many industry products were specific to the iron and steel making industries. Refractory "nozzles," for example, were used in ladles for extracting molten steel; "runners" were refractory-lined channels in which molten iron flowed from a blast furnace when tapped; and ladle gate parts included refractory pouring spouts for molten iron or steel. Other specialized products manufactured by industry firms included clay refractory cement, refractory tile made out of fire clay, and various refractory elements used in glass manufacturing, such as glasshouse floaters, melting pots, rings, saggers, and stoppers.

One of the most common methods for manufacturing clay refractories was extrusion, in which moist refractory clay was forced by pressure through a die of specific dimensions, creating a rectangular shaft of clay that could then be cut at regular intervals to form bricks. The extruded bricks could then be sent through tunnel driers or dried on hot floors. Another common manufacturing process for noncomplex refractory shapes was power pressing, in which brick presses weighing as much 3,600 tons produced bricks of up to 28 inches in length. Unlike brick extruding machines, brick presses did not require large amounts of water, and thus simplified the drying and handling of the bricks.

Other methods of refractory manufacture included slip casting, hydrostatic pressing, fusion casting, and hand molding. After initial forming, clay refractory bricks and shapes were often fired in tunnel-shaped kilns to strengthen the brick or shape and stabilize it at a temperature equal to or higher than it would experience in actual use—often 1800 degrees Fahrenheit or more.

Because of its low cost in comparison to other refractories, fire clay—a mixture of kaolinite clay and silica sand—was the preferred material for clay refractory brick, which was classified as "low," "intermediate," "high," and "superduty," according to the temperature at which softened when fired or baked. Typical specific uses of fire clay refractory bricks were boiler furnace linings, blast furnace linings, molten iron casting pit refractories, and other applications that did not entail extremely high temperatures.

Plastic fire clays were refractories that were moldable when mixed with water and were often used for furnace linings or as a binding agent in fire clay brick manufacture. Fire clay could be combined with other raw materials to increase its refractoriness and to reduce its shrinkage during firing. Because of improvements in the combustion properties of fuels used in industrial furnaces, performance requirements for refractory materials continued to be upgraded to extend operational life and conform to harsher furnace environments. This led to the development of "superrefractories" that consist of 50 to 80 percent alumina, a form of aluminum oxide found in minerals such as corundum and bauxite, and also used in the manufacture of aluminum.

In 1992, 51 percent of materials consumed by industry firms in the manufacture of clay refractories consisted of clay, ceramic, and refractory minerals, such as kaolin and ball clay, extracted and processed by mining firms (see **SIC 1455: Kaolin and Ball Clay,** and **SIC 1459: Clay, Ceramic, and Refractory Minerals, Not Elsewhere Classified**). More than 23 percent consisted of magnesia; clay or nonclay refractories; industrial chemicals; reprocessed clay and non-

clay refractories purchased from other industry firms; and other stone, clay, glass, and concrete products.

Between 1972 and 1987, the clay refractories industry grew from 86 to 111 firms, while industry employment fell from 11,200 to 6,400 workers (production and nonproduction). In the same period, the value of industry shipments more than doubled from $336 million to more than $788 million. Between 1987 and 1993, the number of companies in the industry began to fall along with the total work force, but shipments continued to rise, reaching $887 million by 1992 and projected to hit $945 million by 1998.

CURRENT CONDITIONS

Since about 1990, the industrialized world has experienced a significant drop-off in the amount of refractories produced and consumed. A number of factors contributed to this downward trend: a decrease in the production of steel around the world during this period; the use of higher-grade refractory materials; the use of new nonrefractory technologies in heat engineering industries; improvements in the durability of refractories already produced and sold; and the discontinuation of thermal pretreatment in the use of some raw materials.

Industry trends in the clay refractory industry in the 1990s included the emergence of new seamless refractory furnace linings that reduced air leakage into and out of industrial furnaces. Improvements in furnace operation and refractory materials resulted in increases in the number of tons of steel (up to 1 million) that could be produced before refractory linings needed replacing. Partnerships were also formed between refractory suppliers and steelmakers to develop new refractory materials and techniques. The industry continued to seek ways to find purer grades of refractory minerals that would increase the temperature-resisting limits of refractory products.

The long-term trend toward increased automation of refractory manufacturing processes (such as automatic brick batching) also continued in the 1990s. The development of robotic and remote control gunning machines enabled furnaces to be relined and refractory coatings applied without the expense of temporarily shutting down the furnace. The major issues facing refractories producers in the 1990s were environmental antipollution standards, increases in materials costs, and changing markets.

FURTHER READING

Ceramic Industry. Troy Michigan: Business News Publishing Co.

Dodd, A. E. *Dictionary of Ceramics.* London: George Newnes Ltd., 1967.

Norton, F. H. *Refractories.* New York: McGraw-Hill Book Co., 1968.

Refractory News, Pittsburgh: Refractories Institute.

''Refractories - Trends and New Developments.'' *Industrial Ceramics,* 1 September 1996, 181.

U.S. Bureau of the Census. *Census of Manufactures.* Available from http://www.census.gov.

—Paul Bodine

SIC 3259

STRUCTURAL CLAY PRODUCTS, NOT ELSEWHERE CLASSIFIED

This industry classification includes establishments engaged in the manufacture of clay sewer pipe and structural clay products, not elsewhere classified. Other products include adobe brick, clay chimney pipe, clay drain tile, and clay roofing.

Although this small industry's shipments increased regularly in current dollar value during the 1980s, by the mid-1990s both its shipments and employment were declining. The industry shipped $150.4 million worth of goods and employed 1,800 workers in 1995, which marked a 14 percent decline, not including inflation, since the industry's 1989 peak of $175 million in shipments. After inflation this reduction amounted to almost 30 percent. Production in the largest segment of this industry, vitrified clay sewage pipe and fittings, declined by nearly 40 percent between 1990 and 1995, from 255.6 million short tons of product in 1990 to only 152.3 million tons in 1995. Estimated 1996 production of clay sewage pipe was down to 112.9 million metric tons, representing about $40 million worth of product. Only seven companies manufactured clay sewer pipes in 1996, and an estimated total of 60 establishments comprised the whole industry.

Total employment was down by 18 percent since 1988, falling from 2,200 workers in 1988 to 1,800 workers in 1995; production workers totaled 1,400, or 78 percent, of total 1995 employment. Production workers' average wages in the industry, about $11 per hour in 1995, were lower than the U.S. average for manufacturing wages but were nearly equal to the average for all structural clay production combined. The industry was regionally concentrated in the 1990s,

with California and Ohio accounting for roughly two-thirds of the industry's employment.

Some industry observers expect significant downsizing to continue in this industry during the next decade. The only occupations expected to increase employment levels include extruding and forming machine operators, industrial machinery mechanics, sales workers, maintenance repairers, truck drivers, industrial production managers, and coating machine operators. Those occupations expected to face reductions are primarily in the realm of assembly/production and include assemblers, furnace operators, crushing and mixing machine operators, inspectors, hand packers, packaging machine operators, machine feeders, material movers, secretaries, cutting machine operators, general machine operators, grinders, and machine forming and machine tool cutting operators.

Firms in the industry tend to be small; no company primary to this industry had revenues of more than $100 million in the mid-1990s. Leading firms included A and M Products Inc. of Danbury, Connecticut; KMG Minerals of Kings Mountain, North Carolina; U.S. Tile Company of Corona, California; and Pacific Clay Products Inc. of Corona, California.

FURTHER READING

U.S. Census Bureau. *1995 Annual Survey of Manufactures.* Washington: GPO, 1997.

U.S. Census Bureau. *Current Industrial Reports.* Washington, 1997.

SIC 3261

VITREOUS CHINA PLUMBING FIXTURES AND CHINA AND EARTHENWARE FITTINGS AND BATHROOM ACCESSORIES

This industry consists of establishments primarily engaged in manufacturing vitreous china plumbing fixtures and china and earthenware fittings and bathroom accessories. Items manufactured in this industry include flush tanks, lavatories, bidets, urinals, toilet fixtures, closet bowls, drinking fountains, and sinks. Other items include vitreous china and earthenware bolt caps, bathroom accessories, faucet handles, soap dishes, and towel bar holders.

INDUSTRY SNAPSHOT

Manufacturers of vitreous china plumbing products function in the larger plumbing industry. The industry imposes strict standards that regulate everything from the width of pipe holes to the number of gallons used in each toilet flush. The manufacture of U.S. plumbing products suffered during the recession of the late 1980s. Of 156 manufacturing industries rated by the U.S. Department of Commerce's International Trade Administration, this industry was ranked 142 in its compound annual growth rate of -3.9 percent from 1988 to 1993.

Vitreous china is a ceramic product made primarily with specially treated clays and other chemicals including feldspar and silica, then glazed and fired at high temperatures in a kiln. The vitreous product lasts forever, and does not absorb water or other materials. It is a product that changed plumbing throughout the world.

Organization and Structure

The vitreous china plumbing industry is driven by trends in construction spending. Therefore, when the housing starts and remodeling trends plummeted in the 1980s, the industry suffered tremendously. Since vitreous china plumbing products are needed in both residential and commercial settings, both construction industries affect the industry. Foreign-trade conditions also affect the manufacturers, since imports still provide much of the plumbing ware in the United States.

Many manufacturers sell their wares only to distributors, who in turn sell the products to contractors and plumbers. Home centers, which have begun to change the way many Americans furnish or remodel their homes and businesses, have had an effect on the vitreous plumbing industry as well. For example, one large manufacturer, American Standard, sells to independent wholesalers who sell to the trade. The company allows their wholesalers to sell American Standard products to home centers and other retailers. Their new line is actually being manufactured in Thailand to be sold in the United States.

Conversely, another major U.S. manufacturer, Kohler Company, still insists on selling its products only through distributors. Even Kohler employees, who receive products at a discount, must go through the middleman. Many manufacturers have begun to sell their wares directly to the home centers in order to prevent competitors from gaining too much market share.

Background and Development

From the time civilization reached a point at which populations were centralized, plumbing has been an important concern. Typhoid fever and dysen-

tery spread during the Industrial Revolution when sewage systems were still combined with systems for drinking water. Once separate systems were designed, different plumbing fixtures were used to deliver drinking water and to remove waste materials from buildings.

Thomas Crapper invented the flush toilet, or water closet as it was known in England, in 1884. The mechanism he designed, with its float, valves, and arms that regulate the water in the flush tank, has remained virtually unchanged to the present. The early toilets as well as the earliest bathtubs, washbasins, and drinking fountains, were made from enameled cast iron. Vitreous china plumbing products were not introduced for several more decades.

By 1927, Walter Kohler was making vitreous china lavatories and toilets in his Wisconsin pottery operation, which emerged at that time as the third largest plumbing products company in the United States. As consumers began to customize their bathrooms, Kohler created vitreous china plumbing products in colors that matched the enameled cast iron bathtubs and accessories. In 1964, Kohler began manufacturing a self-rimming lavatory that eliminated the need for a metal frame or rim on the counter.

In the second half of the twentieth century, the American attitude toward the bathroom changed. People were spending more time there, and were using the bathroom not just for hygiene purposes, but also as a bastion of relaxation. Manufacturers also thrived as a result of the increasing numbers of bathrooms being placed in each residential setting.

Current Conditions

Coming out of the slump. Due to the drawn-out slump in housing starts and other new construction in the 1980s, the manufacturers of vitreous plumbing products suffered. The value of shipments of vitreous china plumbing fixtures reached nearly $1.02 billion in 1995, a substantial increase over the $790 million reported in 1992—but down $1 million from the high in 1994.

As housing starts picked up after the recession, plumbing experts believed their industry was heading toward a substantial recovery. Remodelers and do-it-yourselfers contributed to their optimism. Many manufacturers began to offer their goods for sale through home centers, and some consumers saw this as an opportunity to save money in their remodeling work. There has also been a trend away from intricate luxury items and flashy colors in favor of a back-to-basics look and an emphasis on quality and value. White plumbing fixtures are offered in great number and great variety, with white shades ranging from blue-white to dark beige.

Competition from abroad and from other materials. Imports of foreign vitreous plumbing fixtures have had a harmful impact on U.S.-made products. The U.S. Bureau of the Census measured the apparent consumption of vitreous plumbing fixtures by subtracting exports from the total amount of imports plus manufacturers' shipments. This apparent consumption dropped from $952.2 million to $901.9 million from 1994 to 1995. The percentage of imports to apparent consumption dropped from 9.1 percent to 7.8 percent. The weaker dollar made imports more difficult in the late 1980s—and made exports more affordable for foreign buyers.

In the early 1990s, the vitreous china plumbing fixtures industry experienced more competition than ever before from plastics. But by the mid-1990s, the threat from plastic plumbing fixtures had disappeared. The value of shipments of plastics plumbing fixtures in 1991 was $888.4 million, while the value of shipments of vitreous plumbing fixtures in 1991 was only $675.1 million. In 1995, the value of shipments of plastic plumbing fixtures was $337.2 million and vitreous plumbing shipments had a shipment value of $891.9 million. This trend was expected to continue as materials technology continued to improve the flexibility of style and design in ceramics.

Environmental consciousness. Water conservation became an important issue in the industry beginning in the 1970s. Most water closets used an average of 3.5 gallons per flush (gpf). A federal bill known as the National Plumbing Products Efficiency Act (NPPEA) was signed into law at the end of 1992 as part of the Comprehensive National Energy Policy Act. The bill regulated the amount of water required per flush of a toilet or urinal. It also regulated the flow rate of showerheads and faucets. The American Society of Plumbing Engineers Research Foundation conducted field studies in the early 1990s to explore the possibility of replacing 3.5 gpf toilets with 1.6 gpf fixtures. Despite the fact that they found more clogging in the low-flow fixtures, environmental concerns overrode their criticisms, and the new U.S. code was enacted.

Manufacturers of vitreous plumbing fixtures worked with other plumbing industry advisors to coordinate low-flow products, as well as other new products that were developed in response to consumer concerns. One group of these products featured so-called universal design. These plumbing fixtures were equally accessible by wheelchair-bound and elderly consumers. Another recent trend was the development

of lead-free plumbing. New requirements for plumbing systems came as a response to several lawsuits involving faucets. California's 1986 law, known as Proposition 65, specified toxic substances that were prohibited from being discharged into drinking water. These changes, which required implementation of lead-free plumbing, meant that entire plumbing systems had to be reworked.

INDUSTRY LEADERS

Most major industry players derive all or most of their sales from plumbing-related products. The most recognized names in the industry in the United States in the 1990s were Kohler Company, headquartered in Wisconsin; and American Standard in New York.

Kohler employed more than 15,000 people and generated total sales of $2 billion in 1996, a 9 percent increase over 1995. The company's vitreous china products were manufactured in Kohler, Wisconsin; Spartanburg, South Carolina; and Brownwood, Texas. Kohler purchased Jacob Delafon, a Paris-based manufacturer in 1986, with manufacturing facilities in France, Spain, Morocco, and Egypt. Kohler also opened a vitreous china pottery facility near Monterrey, Mexico, to produce a line of mid-priced plumbing products.

American Standard Companies Incorporated and its U.S. Plumbing Company division led the industry with 1996 sales of $5.8 billion. American Standard also had cultivated an overseas presence, with a holding company known as American Standard Sanitaryware in Thailand, which manufactured much of the vitreous china sold under the American Standard brand name. The company had an estimated market share of 35 to 40 percent in Thailand.

Other key manufacturers of vitreous china plumbing products in the United States included U.S. Plumbing Company of Piscataway, New Jersey; Eljer Industries of Dallas, Texas; Briggs Industries, Inc. of Tampa, Florida; and Universal-Rundle Corp. of Pennsylvania. During the economic downturn of the 1980s, several manufacturers in the industry were forced out. The industry saw many mergers and acquisitions until only the leanest and most successful companies remained.

Because of intense competition, both from in the United States and abroad, manufacturers have had to expand their product lines, innovate with new technology, cut production costs, and improve their relationships with distributors. Advertising costs had risen, and consumers exhibited a greater interest in the plumbing fixtures they purchased.

WORK FORCE

Average hourly earnings for workers in the vitreous plumbing fixtures industry, most of whom are involved in actual production, rose from $11.96 in 1990 to $12.75 in 1995. Wages were expected to increase slightly in the late 1990s. Many of the plants where vitreous china plumbing products are manufactured are unionized. Some belong to the Glass Molders, Pottery, Plastics and Allied Workers International Union (GPPAW), while some factories are part of the local United Auto Workers (UAW). The GPPAW publishes a health and safety manual that identifies potential workplace hazards for manufacturers of vitreous china products. Unions also negotiate wages, certain workplace standards, vacation time, and other benefits for their members.

Many workers in this industry spend their entire careers perfecting one job. Each job in production is unique, from the creation of the special clay mixture (called slip) to the packaging of the final products.

Some plants have a sliphouse, where there are machine operators, mixers, and others who must bring the raw materials to exactly the right consistency before it is cast. Casters pour the slip into plaster of Paris molds, where it dries for a specified length of time. The porous molds draw moisture out of the slip until a shell forms the outlines of the product. If it sits too long, when the rest of the slip is poured out, the shell will be too thick to be glazed and fired. Each manufacturer has its own recipe for the slip and its own methods for casting, but each step is carefully monitored. After pouring out excess slip, casters and finishers sponge the products to remove coarse edges and seams left from the mold.

The pottery where the fixtures are cast can be very dusty during the drying operations. During certain hours each day all workers are required to wear respirators. The plumbing fixtures, known at this point in the production process as greenware, must dry, usually overnight, before it is ready to be glazed and fired. Some glazing is still done manually by a glazer, who usually wears a protective mask. Other glazes are applied by glazing machines. In most factories, loaders place greenware onto tiered carts that can be moved from the casting room through the glazing department and directly through the kilns. Kiln operators and loaders become accustomed to the intense heat needed to vitrify the greenware. Glazes and ceramics become melded together, forming the impermeable vitreous china that is necessary for these plumbing fixtures. Kilns reach temperatures of up to 2,300 degrees Fahrenheit; the kilns are almost never shut down, as it would take close to two weeks to get them back up to firing temperature.

Once they emerge from the kiln, the fixtures are checked by inspectors and chosen by selectors. Pieces that are slightly defective are sent back for regrinding, reglazing, and refiring. Some vitreous china fixtures are then specially adorned by decorators. These must also be seen by inspectors before being sent to the packing department.

AMERICA AND THE WORLD

The manufacture of vitreous plumbing fixtures is a labor-intensive business. Costs for U.S. manufacturers have risen dramatically over the last decades, and foreign competition has increased, in part because of the low labor costs that foreign companies incur.

However, statistics charting the industry in the early 1990s show that the weaker dollar may have helped U.S. manufacturers in terms of international trade. The value of imports of vitreous plumbing fixtures in 1991 was $64.4 million, where it stayed fairly steadily until 1994. By 1995, it had gone up to $71.2 million, just shy of the high of $72.6 million in 1989. The value of exports in 1991 was $46.1 million, rising to $61.1 million in 1995.

RESEARCH AND TECHNOLOGY

Vitreous china materials and basic toilet designs have not changed significantly in the past half century. Much of the industry's research efforts have concentrated on perfecting current manufacturing methodologies. Quick-dry glazes, for instance, enable manufacturers to upgrade their rate of production. Many experiments in plumbing fixtures have gone by the wayside, while others are constantly being introduced. For example, Kohler recently introduced the Rosario Lite toilet, which flushes automatically when the user closes the lid.

Several foreign companies have proven adept in their aggressive efforts to improve their product line. Toto, one of Japan's largest plumbing products manufacturers, has introduced several new features, not yet available in the United States, for plumbing fixtures. The company's Washlet toilet features hot-water cleaning and hot-air drying. Toto's Sound Princess, developed in response to the practice of many Japanese women of flushing repeatedly during one sitting, plays a recording of flushing water so that the user does not feel compelled to flush in order to mask obtrusive noises. Japanese manufacturers also have produced toilets that send urine for medical tests. Another new product features an armrest that can simultaneously measure one's blood pressure, temperature, and pulse. As the population ages in the United States, these features might be requested more often, and local manufacturers may begin producing them.

FURTHER READING

"Bathroom Products Keep Pace with Consumer Trends." *Professional Builder & Remodeler,* March 1992: 61.

"Bold Craftsmen." Kohler, WI: Kohler Company, 1973.

Darnay, Arsen J., ed. *Manufacturing USA.* 5th ed. Detroit: Gale Research, 1996.

Ecenbarger, William. "Flushed with Success." *Chicago Tribune Magazine,* 4 April, 1993: 22-29.

Hardy, Quentin. "We Can Laugh, but Once Again Japan Has Forged Ahead of Us." *Wall Street Journal,* 10 November, 1992: B1.

Hooper, Larry R. "Clogs Cloud Use of Commercial '1.6' Closets." *Contractor,* June 1992: 1.

"Innovative plbg., 'Back to White'." *Contractor,* November 1990: 3.

Mahnke, Susan. "Kohler of Kohler of Kohler." *Wisconsin Trails,* Spring 1979.

Sefrin, Eliot. "Plumbing Suppliers Predict 'Comeback' in 1993." *Kitchen & Bath Design News,* February 1993: 20-22.

U.S. Department of Commerce. U.S. Bureau of the Census. *1995 Annual Survey of Manufactures.* Washington: GPO, 1997.

SIC 3262

VITREOUS CHINA TABLE AND KITCHEN ARTICLES

This industry consists of companies that manufacture vitreous china table and kitchen articles, such as bone china, vitreous china tableware, vitreous china dishes, and china cooking ware. Manufacturers of fine earthenware table and kitchen articles are in **SIC 3262: Fine Earthenware (Whiteware) Table and Kitchen Articles.**

Manufacture of vitreous china table and kitchen articles is an anomaly in twentieth-century America. It is a very labor-intensive industry, with skilled craftsmen perfecting work that has extremely high standards of quality. Modern technology has entered the industry, but in many ways, fine china and porcelain are made just as they were centuries ago.

Vitreous china is made of clays that are glazed and fired at extremely high temperatures. The temperatures cause the glaze to fuse with the clay and become non-

porous. This china is both delicate and extremely durable. For this reason, it is used in hotels and restaurants more often than the semi-vitreous earthenware manufactured in **SIC 3263.**

The industry is closely tied to economic conditions because many people consider china to be a luxury. Also, since the manufacturers sell to the hotel and restaurant trade, they suffer when there is a slump in new hotel and restaurant openings. The bridal market accounts for a large percentage of sales of bone china and other vitreous china table articles, and when the bridal market suffers, so does the industry. Competition from abroad is intense. Imports account for about half of U.S. market of home ware, kitchenware, and tableware. Some U.S. manufacturers have part of the work done overseas and finish their pieces in this country.

According to the 1995 *Annual Survey of Manufacturers,* 5,200 people were employed in this industry. Of these, 4,200 worked in production. The cost of materials used by the industry was $80.2 million dollars in 1995, a $1 million decline from 1994, but the value of industry shipments rose almost $7 million to $368 million.

Porcelain was being made in China as early as the ninth century. Many centuries later, the Ohio River valley became the first china manufacturing center in the United States. Here manufacturers had easy access to kaolin, the soft, white clay that is essential to the manufacture of china and porcelain.

As consumer confidence recovered following the economic downturn in the 1980s, the industry improved. Manufacturers began to respond to consumer concerns about lead content in chinaware. California's Proposition 65 required labeling on chinaware warning consumers if a product exposed them to more than 0.5 micrograms of lead per day.

Most industry leaders have been in the business for many years. Pfaltzgraff, founded in 1811 and headquartered in York, Pennsylvania, is said to be the oldest continuously operating pottery in the country. It is owned by the privately held company Susquehanna Broadcasting. Pfaltzgraff purchased another well-known chinaware manufacturer, Syracuse, in 1983. Lenox China, founded in 1889 in Trenton, New Jersey, was bought by Brown-Forman in 1983. Oneida, which bought Buffalo China in 1983, was founded in 1848 and was originally known for its quality flatware. Homer Laughlin was founded in 1871 in West Virginia.

Industry jobs include machine operators in the sliphouse; mold runners, casters, and jiggermen who shape and form the clay; cutters and finishers who dry and secondary shape; glaze grinders and decorators; kiln firemen and loaders; inspectors, selectors, and stampers; and packers. Average hourly wages for production workers in this industry were $10.81 in the mid-1990s. Kiln operators earned hourly wages of $6.06 to $9.26, while molders and casters earned $4.61 to $9.86 per hour.

The U.S. industry endures heavy worldwide competition, especially with Japan, Taiwan, China, and England. However, a weaker dollar has meant that exports from the United States have increased, especially to Taiwan, Canada, and Mexico, while foreign products have become more expensive, making domestic products more attractive at home.

In this industry, much of the technology is the same as it was ages ago. Many glaze recipes, clays, molds, casting, and firing processes have remained unchanged, but potters' wheels are electric and jiggerblades quickly shape the pieces. Some manufacturers were looking in new technological directions to beat foreign competitors.

Pfaltzgraff was the first in the industry to have a dry press system, which formed, finished, decorated, glazed, and fired china in one continuous process. It vastly increased productivity. The company also invested in a CAD/CAM system that provided 3-D images of finished china products.

FURTHER READING

Altman, Seymour, and Violet Altman. *The Book of Buffalo Pottery.* Atglen, PA: Schiffer, 1987, 19-20.

Belasco, Lisa. "How Safe Are Your Dishes, Glasses, Pots & Pans?" *Good Housekeeping,* June 1991, 199.

Bill, Andrew. "Dining with the Masters." *Town & Country,* April 1991, 169-71.

"Chinamakers Pressed to Label Wares." *Restaurant/Hotel Design International,* January 1992, 13.

Cotter, Wes. "Local China Factory May Get Second Life." *Pittsburgh Business Times,* 17 February, 1992, 1.

"CRA Warns about Lead in Service Wares." *Nation's Restaurant News,* 31 August, 1992, 21.

Darnay, Arsen J., ed. *Manufacturing USA.* 5th ed. Detroit: Gale Research, 1996.

Durocher, Joseph. "Fashion Plate." *Restaurant Business Manager,* 10 June, 1992, 188-90.

"The Fine China and Crystal Story." Lawrenceville, NJ: Lenox China, September 1990.

Foley, Denise. "Case of the 'Anemic' Diagnosis." *Prevention Magazine,* September 1991, 106-113.

"Glossary of Fine China and Crystal Terms." Lawrenceville, NJ: Lenox China, July 1991.

Hube, Karen. "Makers Try to Get the Lead Out." *HFD, The Weekly Home Furnishings Newspaper,* February 1993, 54.

Lewis, Herschell, and Margo Lewis. *Everybody's Guide to Plate Collecting.* Chicago: Bonus Books, 1988.

Manroe, Candace Ord. "Earth, Fire, Winds of Time." *Country Home,* June 1992, 44-46.

McCoy, Charles. "California Suits Say Faucet Makers Break Toxics Law." *Wall Street Journal,* 16 December, 1992, B8.

Nellett, Michelle. "Meet the Generations: Pfaltzgraff." *Gifts & Decorative Accessories,* April 1992, 68.

Oliver, Brian. "The China Syndrome." *Marketing,* 11 July, 1991, 26-27.

Pfaltzgraff: America's Potter. York, PA: Historical Society of York County, 1989.

"Tabletop Report 1991." *HFD, The Weekly Home Furnishings Newspaper,* 23 September, 1991.

U.S. Department of Commerce. Bureau of the Census. *1995 Annual Survey of Manufactures.* Washington: GPO, 1997.

SIC 3263

FINE EARTHENWARE (WHITEWARE) TABLE AND KITCHEN ARTICLES

This industry consists of companies manufacturing semivitreous earthenware table and kitchen articles. These include fine semivitreous whiteware, semivitreous earthenware used for cooking and serving food, and both commercial and household earthenware. Manufacturers of vitreous china table and kitchen articles are included in **SIC 3262: Vitreous China Table and Kitchen Articles.**

Fine earthenware table and kitchen articles have been made for centuries. Earthenware is porous, coarse, and opaque—unlike vitrified porcelain and bone china—which are non-porous and translucent. All are considered pottery and begin with clay and other raw materials, but earthenware is fired at lower temperatures and is more breakable.

The oldest form of pottery, earthenware, was made in China as early as the ninth century, where it was dried in the sun. Kilns have become the source of heat to fire pottery that becomes modern dinnerware, but in the industry as a whole, much of the technology is the same as it was centuries ago. Much has not changed—including the labor-intensive nature of the work and the skilled craftsmen who are employed to manufacture products with high standards of quality—

but pottery wheels are electric, and a jiggerblade can speedily shape a plate.

Many styles and types of earthenware have become popular as everyday dinnerware. Since earthenware is less expensive than bone china or other vitreous tableware, sales of it were less affected by the economic downturn of the 1980s. China and porcelain products have begun to draw more consumers, however, especially from high-income households headed by 45- to 54-year-olds. The bridal market also accounts for a large percentage of retail sales of semivitreous earthenware.

In the early 1990s, manufacturers were also beginning to respond to consumer concerns about lead content in chinaware. Some manufacturers changed the recipes of their glazes to reduce the lead content. Ceramic goods imported from other countries were more often to blame, since many countries did not have strict lead content rules. California's Proposition 65 required labeling on chinaware, warning consumers if a product exposed them to more than 0.5 micrograms of lead per day.

Although most of the same companies that manufacture earthenware also manufacture vitreous china, far fewer people work directly on these products. In 1996, approximately 600 people were employed in the industry, and this number was expected to decrease to 400 by 1998. Of the 600 workers in 1996, an estimated 500 worked in production. The value of industry shipments in 1994 was $57 million, but this was expected to decrease to $36.8 million by 1998.

The industry leaders in the mid-1990s were Bonny Products Inc., headquartered in Washington, North Carolina, with sales of $10 million and about 200 employees; Leeds Engineering Corporation, of Camarillo, California, with estimated sales of $7 million and 100 employees; and Vanguard Accents, of Hickory, North Carolina, with sales of approximately $2 million and fewer than 100 employees.

Industry jobs include machine operators in the sliphouse; mold runners, casters, and jiggermen who work to shape and form the clay; cutters and finishers who dry and again shape the product; glaze grinders and decorators; kiln firemen and loaders; inspectors, selectors, and stampers; and packers. The only occupation expecting growth through the year 2005 was painting, coating, and decorating workers—52.3 percent. Extruding and forming machine workers were expecting the most dramatic decrease—80.6 percent.

Average hourly wages for production workers in this industry were $11.27 in 1990. Kiln operators earned hourly wages of $6.06 to $9.26, while molders and casters earned hourly wages of $4.61 to $9.86. By 1995, the hourly wage remained at $10.07 and was expected to decline further to $8.62 by 1998.

Imports accounted for about one-half of the sales in earthenware and kitchenware in the mid-1990s. Most foreign competition came especially from Japan, Taiwan, China, and England. However, exports to Taiwan, Canada, and Mexico have increased as the dollar has weakened.

FURTHER READING

Altman, Seymour, and Violet Altman. *The Book of Buffalo Pottery.* Atglen, PA: Schiffer, 1987, 19-20.

Belasco, Lisa. ''How Safe Are Your Dishes, Glasses, Pots & Pans?'' *Good Housekeeping,* June 1991, 199.

''Chinamakers Pressed to Label Wares.'' *Restaurant/Hotel Design International,* January 1992, 13.

Darnay, Arsen J., ed. *Manufacturing USA.* 5th ed. Detroit: Gale Research, 1996.

Foley, Denise. ''Case of the 'Anemic' Diagnosis.'' *Prevention Magazine,* September 1991, 106-113.

Hube, Karen. ''Makers Try to Get the Lead Out.'' *HFD: The Weekly Home Furnishings Newspaper,* February 1993, 54.

Lewis, Herschell, and Margo Lewis. *Everybody's Guide to Plate Collecting.* Chicago: Bonus Books, 1988.

Manroe, Candace Ord. ''Earth, Fire, Winds of Time.'' *Country Home,* June 1992, 44-46.

McCoy, Charles. ''California Suits Say Faucet Makers Break Toxics Law.'' *Wall Street Journal,* 16 December 1992, B8.

Sullivan, Terry. ''Plates for Guys.'' *Gentleman's Quarterly,* September 1992, 106.

''Tabletop Report 1991.'' *HFD: The Weekly Home Furnishings Newspaper,* 23 September 1991.

U.S. Department of Commerce. Bureau of the Census. *1995 Annual Survey of Manufactures.* Washington: GPO, 1997.

SIC 3264

PORCELAIN ELECTRICAL SUPPLIES

This category consists of manufacturers of porcelain electronic insulators, molded porcelain parts for electrical devices, other electrical insulators, ceramic electronic and electrical supplies, and spark plug and steatitic porcelain.

Unlike other pottery product industries, the porcelain electrical supplies industry relies on high technology. Only the base material, clay, makes it similar to other pottery products. The products manufactured in this industry are ideal insulators for electrical currents because of the way they dissipate heat. The United States has the technological edge in most electronic ceramic components used in these high-performance markets.

The value of product shipments in this industry rose steadily in the late 1980s, from $759 million in 1987 to $936 million in 1990. Due in part to the decrease in U.S. military spending, the value of product shipments dropped in the early 1990s, to $927 million in 1991. However the industry experienced rapid growth in the mid-1990s, as the value of product shipments reached $1.4 billion in 1995. The world-wide advanced ceramics market was estimated to be worth between $2 and $3 billion in 1996, with U.S. companies dominating the industry overall. The structural and electronic ceramics segment of the market was estimated at nearly $1 billion. The U.S. Advanced Ceramics Association projected 9 percent annual growth in the advanced ceramics market through the end of the century.

In 1994, there were 11,400 people working in the porcelain electrical supplies industry, 73 percent of whom were production workers. In 1995, the work force grew to 14,000, with 78 percent working in production. The annual salary for production workers fell 2 percent in 1995, to $25,700, in line with the national average for production workers in manufacturing. Professional staff in the industry include inspectors, metrology and process workers, and application engineers.

Many of the companies working in this industry also make engineering supplies that are not porcelain-based. Some of the companies are small job shops making small quantities of a specific product and others are large international corporations. Brush Wellman Inc., for example, makes beryllia ceramics and beryllium alloys used as insulators for microelectronics. These products represent only about 10 percent of their business.

The Adolph Coors Company, whose primary business is malt beverages, was also making technical ceramics at a separate facility until late 1992, when the brewery became a separate company. Coors Ceramics Company, which was by far the largest U.S.-owned manufacturer of technical ceramics, became a part of the holding company called ACX Technologies. Although company outputs were primarily absorbed by Adolph Coors Company, sales for ACX fell more than 20 percent, from $910 million in 1995 to $712 million in 1996. Coors Ceramics represented about 30 percent of ACX net sales in 1995, with $271 million. The next largest competitor in the industry was Intermagnetics

General Corp. of Latham, Texas, with $88.5 million in sales.

Some of the latest technology employed by manufacturers in this industry includes dry press production equipment, automation such as computerized tool control systems and computer aided design, high volume tunnel kilns, and statistical process control that is integrated on a network. Precision operations include grinding, lapping, and polishing.

FURTHER READING

Abraham, Thomas. "U.S. Advanced Ceramic Market Surges Ahead." *Ceramic Industry,* December 1990, 32-35.

ACX Technologies, Inc. "The ACX Businesses." Golden, CO: Lighthouse Communications Group, Ltd, 1996. Available from http://www.acxt.com:80/ccc.html.

Darnay, Arsen J., ed. *Manufacturing USA.* 5th ed. Detroit: Gale Research, 1996.

"Pottery Deficit Revealed." *Washington Post,* 20 April 1991, B1.

Robertson, Jack. "Broken Ceramics." *Electronic News,* 11 January 1993, 8.

Stevens, Tim. "Structures Get Smart." *Materials Engineering,* October 1991, 18.

U.S. Bureau of the Census. *1995 Annual Survey of Manufactures.* Washington: GPO, 1997. Available from http://www.census.gov/prod/www/titles.html#mm.

—Fran Shonfeld Sherman

SIC 3269

POTTERY PRODUCTS, NOT ELSEWHERE CLASSIFIED

This industry consists of manufacturers of art and ornamental pottery, industrial and laboratory pottery, unglazed earthenware florists' articles, earthenware table and kitchen articles, as well as those establishments primarily engaged in firing and decorating white china and earthenware for the trade.

INDUSTRY SNAPSHOT

The manufacture of pottery products, like the manufacture of vitreous china table and kitchen articles (see **SIC 3262: Vitreous China Table and Kitchen Articles**) is an anomaly in twentieth-century American industry. It is labor-intensive, and to a large extent involves machinery and techniques that have changed little in the last half century.

Pottery is made of clays that are mixed with other chemicals. Some pottery products are made on modern versions of potter's wheels, and some are glazed and fired at extremely high temperatures to become vitreous china. Pottery that is glazed and fired in a kiln becomes vitrified, or nonporous and glass-like, when the high temperatures cause the glaze to fuse with the clay. This china is both delicate and extremely durable. For this reason, it is used for fine giftware such as bone china figurines and lamp bases.

Competition from abroad is intense. Pottery products are sold in the United States from Japanese, English, Chinese, and Spanish manufacturers, among others. Imports account for almost three quarters of the U.S. gift market. However, the weakened U.S. dollar has evened the tables somewhat in the last few years, enabling manufacturers from the United States to sell more of their wares in Canada, Taiwan, and Mexico.

The industry is also closely tied to economic conditions, as many consumers consider art and ornamental pottery to be a luxury. Although the U.S. economy was recovering in the early 1990s, the upturn in the giftware market was slower than in other industries. Even fine china, once considered a staple of the bridal market, was being rejected in the late 1990s by some young couples who preferred to put more money into electronic equipment or more expensive housing.

ORGANIZATION AND STRUCTURE

The pottery products industry is led by several manufacturers who also create tableware and kitchenware made of vitreous china and semivitreous earthenware. Much of the equipment used by these manufacturers is the same for all of these products. Glazes and kiln temperatures vary widely, however, and the manufacturers often keep their different lines separate. Some manufacturers, for example, create their unglazed red earthenware lines in a separate plant from their semivitreous tableware lines.

The giftware market is critical for these manufacturers. Some of the promotional or commemorative pottery items slid through the recession without suffering, as corporate buyers continued to purchase promotional ceramics at much the same rate.

BACKGROUND AND DEVELOPMENT

Porcelain was being made in China as early as the ninth century. By the seventeenth and eighteenth centuries fine porcelain art objects were being created in Europe as well. When immigrants came to the United States, they brought their crafting techniques with them. The Ohio River Valley, where manufacturers had easy access to kaolin, the soft, white clay that is essential to the manufacture of china and porcelain, became the first pottery manufacturing center. By the late 1990s, more of the companies working with pottery products were in California, but Ohio and Pennsylvania companies still accounted for $100 million in shipments, which was about 15 percent of the U.S. total.

The Industrial Revolution changed the manufacture of porcelain products just as it had changed other industries. Around the world, potters who had created hand-thrown ware and then painstakingly decorated their work one piece at a time, began to change the procedures they used. Mass copies of pottery objects became available at lower prices as the processes became more efficient. Some manufacturers objected to the new ways, however, and insisted on maintaining individuality and high quality in their wares.

Potters in the United States also had to adapt to the changing tastes and needs of their communities late in the nineteenth century. They had to compete with increasingly available glass and tin containers, and many of them expanded their product lines to include red earthenware pots, which became the only luxury many consumers allowed themselves through World War I and the Depression. For many U.S. potteries, these flowerpots were the company staple for decades.

CURRENT CONDITIONS

During the recession of the late 1980s the giftware market suffered. Even affluent consumers who purchased artware and other stoneware and earthenware items were becoming more price conscious. Manufacturers had to lower prices or develop newer lines to compensate for losses. However, while the retail market was sluggish, many manufacturers covered their losses by responding to increased demand for promotional giftware and tableware. In the dinnerware market (which is also covered in **SIC 3262: Vitreous China Table and Kitchen Articles** and **SIC 3263: Fine Earthenware (Whiteware) Table and Kitchen Articles**) more than half of sales were through mass merchants and department stores.

Giftware in the 1990s became increasingly diverse. New designs of ceramic and pottery items reflected interest in the environment and in multicultural themes. Both wholesalers and retailers displayed collections of pottery and stoneware that were reminiscent of specific cultures, or that were politically correct, environmentally friendly, or both. One popular cookie jar was designed to resemble the earth, complete with raised continents. Certain traditional items, such as elegant china and earthenware figures still sold well.

The increasing concern about lead content in earthenware, pottery, and other ceramics led to the establishment of the Coalition of Safe Ceramicware (CSC). In early 1992, the CSC pledged that its members complied with all of the FDA standards regarding safe levels of lead, with Proposition 65,which required labeling on chinaware warning consumers if a product exposed them to more than 0.5 micrograms of lead per day, and with the California Tableware Safety Program.

Good news in the housing industry in the late 1990s was another indication to the giftware industry that business would be improving steadily. As consumer confidence increased, small shops were again optimistic that their sales would increase accordingly.

According to the *1994 Annual Survey of Manufacturers,* the value of shipments in the industry was $720 million, up from $591.7 million in 1990, $519.7 million in 1987, and only $146.9 million in 1972. These figures included the shipments of products that were primary to the industry as well as those that were secondary to the industry. Most of the value of product shipments for this industry came from art and decorative ware made either of china and porcelain, or of earthenware and stoneware. Projections toward the year 2000 anticipated continued growth in the industry.

INDUSTRY LEADERS

In 1997, most of the recognized leaders in the manufacture of pottery products also manufactured fine earthenware and/or vitreous china table and kitchen products. Most industry leaders had been in the business for many years. Pfaltzgraff, founded in 1811 and headquartered in York, Pennsylvania, was recognized as the oldest continuously operating pottery in the country. It was owned by a privately held company called Susquehanna Broadcasting and operated by the fifth generation of the Pfaltzgraff family. Pfaltzgraff purchased another well-known manufacturer of pottery products, Syracuse, in 1983. In 1988, Pfaltzgraff bought Treasure Craft, a California company that was known for its giftware and household ceramic products.

Lenox China, founded in 1889 in Trenton, New Jersey, was purchased by Brown-Forman in 1983. Its founder, Walter Scott Lenox, formed the Ceramic Art Company, which made table items as well as gift and art pieces including parasol handles, vases, inkstands, and thimbles. Lenox opened a new facility in 1985 in

Oxford, North Carolina, expressly for the manufacture of Lenox China giftware. Other Lenox China plants were in Pomona, New Jersey, and Kinston, North Carolina.

A newer manufacturer was Beaver Falls China Company, which was formed when former employees of Mayer China Company reopened a local plant that had put about 100 skilled potters out of work when it closed in 1989. Besides making fine china for the hotel and restaurant industry (**SIC 3262: Vitreous China Table and Kitchen Articles**), the company planned to make pottery ashtrays, salt and pepper shakers, and other earthenware kitchen articles and accessories.

WORK FORCE

Many workers in this industry spend their entire careers perfecting one job. Each job in production is unique, from the creation of the special clay mixture, called slip, to the packaging of the final products. Training a potter takes many years, and most manufacturers in this industry hire production workers with the intention of investing the time required so that the workers learn the craft from top to bottom.

Some plants have a sliphouse, where there are machine operators, mixers, and others who must bring the raw materials to exactly the right consistency before it can be cast. Casters pour the slip into plaster-of-Paris molds where it dries for a specified length of time. The porous molds draw moisture out of the slip until enough of a shell forms the outlines of the product. If it sits too long, when the rest of the slip is poured out, the shell will be too thick to be glazed and fired. Each manufacturer has its own recipe for the slip and its own methods for casting, but each step is carefully monitored.

After pouring out excess slip, casters and finishers sponge the products, removing coarse edges and seams left over from the mold. In some plants, jiggermen work in shaping and forming the clay, and cutters and finishers in drying and secondary shaping. The pottery where the products are cast can be very dusty during the drying operations. During certain hours each day all workers are required to wear respirators. The pottery, then known as greenware, must dry, usually overnight, before it is ready to be glazed and fired.

Most glazing is done by a glazer, who usually wears a protective mask. Glazes are sprayed onto one piece at a time. Some glazes are applied by glazing machines. In most factories, loaders place greenware onto tiered carts that can be moved from the casting room through the glazing department and directly through the kilns. Kiln operators and loaders get used to the intense heat needed to vitrify the greenware. Glazes and ceramics become melded together, forming the impermeable vitreous china that is necessary for these plumbing fixtures. Kilns reach temperatures of up to 2,300 degrees Fahrenheit, and therefore are almost never shut down, since it would take close to two weeks to get them back up to firing temperature.

Once they emerge from the kiln, the products are checked by inspectors and chosen by selectors. Pieces that are slightly defective are sent back for regrinding, reglazing, and refiring. Many items, especially in giftware, are then specially adorned by decorators. These must also be seen by inspectors before being sent to the packing department.

The manufacturers also have support departments, including machine shops where machinery can be repaired or cleaned, mold departments, where plaster molds are made and repaired, and warehouses that handle shipping and receiving. They also have administrative departments covering human resources, public relations, corporate development, and other general business needs.

In the 1990s, many of the plants where pottery products were manufactured were unionized. Some of the organized workers belonged to the Glass Molders, Pottery, Plastics and Allied Workers International Union (GPPAW). The GPPAW published a health and safety manual that identified potential workplace hazards for manufacturers of dinnerware, chinaware, and other pottery products. The unions were also active in negotiating wages, certain workplace standards, vacation time, and other benefits for their members.

According to the *Annual Survey of Manufactures* published by the U.S. Bureau of the Census, 13,600 people worked in the pottery products industry in 1994. Of these, 10,900 worked in production. In 1985 there were only 7,100 people working in the industry. The average hourly wage for production workers in 1990 was $11.27. The wages rose from $7.06 in 1987, $5.96 in 1982, and $3.87 in 1977. In the late 1990s kiln operators earned hourly wages of $9.56 to $11.41, while molders and casters earned $5.82 to $15.97 per hour.

AMERICA AND THE WORLD

Nearing the year 2000, the U.S. pottery industry faced heavy world competition, especially with Japan, Taiwan, China, and England. However, the weaker dollar at this time also meant that exports from the United States increased, especially to Taiwan, Canada, and Mexico, while foreign products have become more expensive, and made domestic products more attractive at home.

U.S. potteries tried to capitalize on the desire of local consumers to buy products made in their country. They tried to keep close tabs on marketplace trends and to respond with items the American consumers would want. The new Beaver Falls China Company planned to stamp all of their wares "Made in Pennsylvania USA."

RESEARCH AND TECHNOLOGY

Much of the technology employed by the pottery industry in 1997 was the same as it was centuries ago. The factories in the early twentieth century used more machinery to produce more pottery, but the essential ingredients remained. For example, hand-throwing techniques were supplemented with hand-jigger machines. Today's potter's wheel is electric, and a jiggerblade is usually used to quickly shape a plate. Salt glazing was gradually replaced by dip-glazing, in which the ware was dipped before firing. In some plants, pottery is glazed automatically, while in others, glazers spray glaze onto only one item at a time. Only slight changes have been made in the recipes for clays, the shape and type of molds, casting methods, and firing techniques.

However, some manufacturers were looking in new technological directions to keep foreign competitors at bay. Pfaltzgraff was the first in the industry to have a dry press system, which formed, finished, decorated, glazed, and fired pottery products in one continuous process. It vastly increased productivity, especially for plates and small bowls. The company also invested in a CAD/CAM system that provided 3-D images of finished products so that problems could be anticipated and corrected before production began. In 1997, the company estimated that it saved 9 to 18 months in production and discarded one-quarter fewer pieces of china because of the CAD/CAM improvements.

The larger changes for the pottery products industry were in the general way business was conducted. In order to survive, these small, family-owned potteries had to become businesses that competed not only in the national but also the international market. It was no longer enough to make a quality product. Manufacturers also had to market and sell their wares, create new innovations, and pass on to a new generation of potters the desire to keep this age-old craft thriving.

FURTHER READING

American Ceramic Society Homepage. Available from http://www.acers.org.

Bill, Andrew. "Dining with the Masters." *Town and Country,* April 1991, 169-71.

"Ceramicware Group: Makers Meet Lead Norms." *HFD: The Weekly Home Furnishings Newspaper,* 16 March 1992, 97.

Cotter, Wes. "Local China Factory May Get Second Life." *Pittsburgh Business Times,* 17 February 1992, 1.

Deutsch, Claudia H. "Not Making Them Like They Used To," *New York Times,* 31 March 1997, C1.

The Fine China and Crystal Story. Lawrenceville, NJ: Lenox China, September 1990.

"Gifts, Tableware, Novelties." *Hardware Age,* December 1992, 53.

Glossary of Fine China and Crystal Terms. Lawrenceville, NJ: Lenox China, July 1991.

Manroe, Candace Ord. "Earth, Fire, Winds of Time." *Country Home,* June 1992, 44-46.

Nellett, Michelle. "Meet the Generations: Pfaltzgraff." *Gifts and Decorative Accessories,* April 1992, 68.

Oliver, Brian. "The China Syndrome." *Marketing,* 11 July 1991, 26-27.

Pfaltzgraff: America's Potter. York, PA: Historical Society of York County, 1989.

Rotenier, Nancy. "The Gifty Business," *Forbes,* 22 April 1996, 112-115.

"Tabletop Report 1991." *HFD: The Weekly Home Furnishings Newspaper,* 23 September 1991.

—Fran Shonfeld Sherman

SIC 3271

CONCRETE BLOCK AND BRICK

This category covers establishments engaged in manufacturing concrete building block and brick from a combination of cement and aggregate. Contractors engaged in concrete construction work are classified in the construction segment (see Vol. 2, Chapter 3: Construction Industries) while establishments primarily engaged in mixing and delivering ready-mixed concrete are classified in **SIC 3273: Ready-Mixed Concrete.**

In 1996 the concrete block and brick industry had approximately 17,900 employees, an increase of 12 percent above the 16,000 workers reported in the industry in 1993. Establishments in the industry shipped products with a total value of $2.6 billion in 1996. An estimated $1.5 million of those receipts were solely for concrete block and brick products. The 17,900 employees in the industry in 1996 earned a total of $519.7 million. Production workers made up 55 percent (10,000) of all employees.

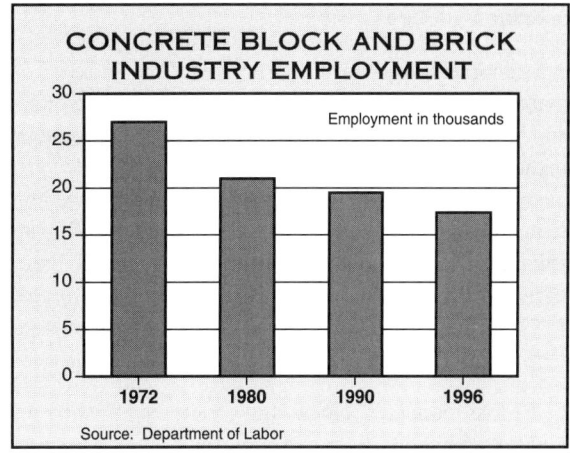

CONCRETE BLOCK AND BRICK INDUSTRY EMPLOYMENT

Source: Department of Labor

Although the industry has had slow and fluctuating growth in the 1980s and early 1990s, the part of the market that is expected to be strong in the latter 1990s is the public works segment, which should be helpful to the concrete block and brick industry. Dominant states in the industry included Pennsylvania, California, Texas, and Michigan.

The first solid concrete block patent was granted in 1832 and the first hollow concrete building block patent was in 1850, both in England. Harmon S. Palmer patented a concrete block machine in 1900 in the United States. Since then, the concrete block continued to increase in popularity because of the product's durability and economy. The industry also advanced in terms of product quality, production and distribution methods, and installation procedures. Concrete's fire safety compared to that of wood has been a major factor in its appeal. In the early days, small concrete manufacturing facilities sprouted up rapidly in most urban areas in the United States because they needed to be located near their users' destinations. A block machine could be bought for $100 in 1906, and the business opportunities appealed to entrepreneurial instincts.

The National Concrete Masonry Association (NCMA) was an affiliate of the Portland Cement Association in the 1930s. The NCMA became independent in 1942 and has since supported concrete block producers, machinery manufacturers, and related interests. Since its founding, the NCMA has conducted research and testing on concrete block products and structures.

Establishments in this industry tend to be relatively small, local operations, since it is generally not economical to ship concrete block and brick more than 50 miles because of its weight. For this reason, companies in the industry have grown by organizing or purchasing added concrete block and brick production operations in new areas.

Another factor in the structure of the industry is that most of the companies that produce concrete block and brick also produce other concrete related products, including ready-mixed concrete, concrete pipe, or various precast or prestressed products, such as building structural parts, which can be fabricated centrally and shipped to locations where they will be installed. Sales of these secondary products in 1992 were an estimated $127 million with an additional $451.6 million in earnings attributable to miscellany.

Most concrete block and brick establishments have one or more competitors in their areas of operation, and compete in matters such as price, location, service, quality, and reliability. They also compete with other building products such as lumber, clay brick, and steel.

Companies within this industry segment spent $1 million on materials services and fuels in 1992 with the products shipped valued at $2 million. Of the 1,071 establishments operating within this industry sector, these firms invested $57.3 million on new capital in 1992

None of the larger companies in the concrete industries has concrete block and brick as the primary product line. These larger companies produce concrete block as one part of a group of products in the concrete and other construction related fields. Leading corporations within this industry segment ranked by revenue as of early 1997, included: Texas Industries Inc. of Dallas, Texas, with $967.4 million in sales and 3,000 employees; Oldcastle Inc. of Atlanta, Georgia, with $600 million in sales and 9,000 employees; Blue Circle America Inc., also of Georgia and also reporting $600 million in sales; Rinker Materials Corp., a Florida company, reporting sales of $520 million; and Fort Worth-based Justin Industries Inc., with sales of $461.4 million.

Other leading concrete products manufacturers who have operations within this classification include Florida Rock Industries Inc. of Jacksonville, Florida; Pacific Coast Building Products Inc. of Sacramento, California; Blue Circle Cement of Marietta, Georgia; Tarmac Florida Inc.; and Marley (U.S.A.) Holding Corp.

Two of the leading concrete block and brick producers have been Zurn Constructors, Inc. and Concrete Pipe & Products Co., Inc. Zurn Constructors, Inc. had 500 employees and annual sales of approximately $160 million in the early 1990s. Its primary field was heavy construction, and concrete block and brick were its secondary product line with plastics pipe as its third area of business. It has been a subsidiary of Zurn Industries Inc., also headquartered in Erie, Pennsylvania, which has been involved in power plant construction, steam generators, and water and air purification systems. Concrete Pipe & Products Co., Inc.'s sales in the early 1990s were $90 million and its employees numbered 850. The company's primary product line is concrete products, except block and brick, and its secondary line is concrete block and brick. It also conducts a wholesale business in construction materials. Concrete Pipe was founded in 1925 and is based in Richmond, Virginia. The company has expanded by many acquisitions since its founding, and has acquired product and process patents, which helped further its growth.

Research has continued in the 1990s to improve the characteristics of concrete block as well as to make possible different features to fit varying users' needs and desires. New exterior appearance attributes have been developed such as ribbed, fluted, and split-faced surfaces, which have met the needs of innovative architects for the walls of buildings. Blocks of lighter weight have been created by mixing different raw material aggregates with the cement and water. And new uses have been found for concrete blocks, such as in a drainage system. Research has also been conducted in ways in which concrete block might be constructed automatically into building walls.

FURTHER READING

Nilson, Arthur H., and George Winter. *Design of Concrete Structures*. New York: McGraw-Hill, 1986.

U.S. Department of Commerce. *Census of Manufactures Concrete, Plaster, and Cut Stone Products*. Washington: GPO, 1987.

U.S. Department of Commerce. *Annual Survey of Manufactures Statistics for Industry Groups and Industries*. Washington: GPO, 1991.

—Douglas Hoyt, updated by Linda Paulson

CONCRETE PRODUCTS, EXCEPT BLOCK AND BRICK

This category covers establishments primarily engaged in manufacturing concrete products, except block and brick, from a combination of cement and aggregate. Contractors engaged in concrete construction work are classified in the Construction industries, and establishments primarily engaged in mixing and delivering ready-mixed concrete are classified in **SIC 3273: Ready-Mixed Concrete.**

INDUSTRY SNAPSHOT

The products included in this industry were made of concrete, formed and hardened at the cement facility, and shipped in finished form to customers or users. Many of the items were prefabricated parts to be assembled into buildings, bridges, or parking structures. Pipe was another major segment of the industry. Other products included a variety of utilitarian and decorative items, such as burial vaults, septic tanks, monuments, and bird baths.

In contrast to products that were poured on-site, the products of this industry were made in a controlled environment, away from a construction job site. Such controlled production conditions enabled concrete products to be made more structurally sound and in accordance with construction specifications.

In 1991 the concrete products industry employed 61,000 people and shipped products valued at $5.5 billion to its customers. In 1987 the states with the greatest employment in the industry were California, Florida, Pennsylvania, and Texas, which accounted for 35 percent of the total industry employment.

ORGANIZATION AND STRUCTURE

The great majority of customers for concrete products were building contractors and construction firms. This required industry firms to deal with architects and engineers as well as management. Many of the industry's sales comprised standard or off-the-shelf items that were produced, warehoused, and sold to multiple customers. Other items were tailor-made to the specific design of particular buildings, bridges, parking structures, or other facilities. Where products made of plastic or lumber were possible alternatives, precast concrete products were sometimes preferred and selected for environmental reasons.

Companies in the industry tended to grow by acquisitions and mergers. The greater size enabled the

companies to spread their marketing, research, and engineering costs over a larger number of activities. Industry firms also joined to form several trade groups, which generally conducted research into materials and methods to improve the products, performed promotion of the product specialty, and represented the industry in governmental matters. These associations included the American Concrete Institute, the American Concrete Pressure Pipe Association the Concrete Reinforcing Steel Institute, the Post-Tensioning Institute, the Portland Cement Association, the American Segmental Bridge Institute, and the Precast/Prestressed Concrete Institute.

Industry firms continually conducted research to improve the qualities of concrete products. Areas of focus included workability, strength, durability, weight, and insulating ability. Minimum quality standards for products were established by the American Society for Testing and Materials (ASTM), and were continuously modified as technology developed and changed.

BACKGROUND AND DEVELOPMENT

Concrete was made by mixing together cement, sand, gravel, possibly other aggregates, and water. The concrete then was molded and might be reinforced in a variety of ways to meet its different purposes. Molds were made of wood, fiberglass, concrete, or other materials. Precast concrete was poured into molds of the desired product shapes, in which it was hardened and cured. Reinforced concrete was strengthened by inserting steel rods or mixing in fibers. Prestressed concrete had steel wires or rods inserted and stretched so as to compress the concrete and make it resist tensile stresses. Other qualities of concrete were modified by use of different types of sand, gravel, crushed stone, and cement in differing proportions. All of these factors affected the properties relating to its strength, durability, workability, curing time, resistance to temperature and humidity changes, and appearance.

CURRENT CONDITIONS

In 1967 there were 2,687 companies in the concrete products industry, employing 70,000 workers and shipping products valued at $5.8 billion. By 1982 there were 2,749 companies, employing 20 percent fewer employees and shipping 39 percent less product value. In 1991 the industry purchased $2.7 billion worth of materials and made new capital expenditures amounting to $153 million.

The concrete products industry often experienced cyclical changes along with the construction industries on which it largely depended. The industry's business fluctuations were most apparent in the total number of employees. For example, the industry stood at 58,000 workers in 1975; 66,000 in 1979; 54,200 in 1983; 70,000 in 1987; and 61,000 in 1991.

Construction in public works projects in the United States—infrastructure construction ranging from construction of public buildings, highways, and conduits for utilities—was predicted to increase, then level off at about $120 billion through 1998. For example, a 1992 review found many of the 600,000 bridges in the Federal Highway Administration's jurisdiction as requiring either replacement or significant repairs. The water distribution system in New York City also broke and caused frequent flood conditions in the 1980s and early 1990s. In response to increased demand, the concrete products industry was expected to continue to enhance concrete's qualities and usefulness through engineering improvements.

United States total cement consumption grew by 19.2 percent between 1991 and 1994; March 1995 cement prices were 5.3 percent higher than the previous year. Also, production in 1995 was reported to be reaching capacity, save in New England and California, where the industry was feeling the impact of slower economic recovery.

INDUSTRY LEADERS

Ameron Inc.'s principal product lines were ready-mixed concrete, concrete products except block and brick, and concrete block and brick. Started in 1907, the company posted 1992 sales of $465 million with 3,000 workers. Ameron considered itself a leader in pipe technology and was a major pipe supplier in the western United States, with plants in California, Arizona, and Oregon. It also managed pipe manufacturing operations in Colombia and Saudi Arabia.

Based in Atlanta, Georgia, CSR Construction Materials USA Inc. had 2,000 employees and $202 million in sales in 1992, entirely from specialty concrete products. It was a subsidiary of CSR America Inc., also based in Atlanta, which in turn was owned by CSR Limited of Australia, which made and sold building materials and other products throughout Asia, the United Kingdom, Australia, and the United States.

Boral Concrete Products Inc., headquartered in San Bernardino, California, was a subsidiary of Boral Industries Inc. of Ontario. Boral Concrete had sales of $100 million and 500 employees in 1992. Its primary product category was concrete roofing tiles and slabs. Boral Limited was a global concern doing business in 23 countries, mostly in building materials and energy, with 1993 sales exceeding $4 billion.

North Star Concrete Inc., a subsidiary of Condux Corp., was headquartered in St. Paul, Minnesota. The company's 1992 sales were $70 million, and it had 500 employees. Founded in 1988, the company's facilities and marketing area were located in the midwest and eastern parts of the United States.

Spancrete Industries Inc. specialized in a precast, prestressed, hollow core plank or slab that was widely used for floors, roofs, and walls. These planks were made in a variety of shapes and sizes to fit the individual users' needs. The Spancrete process was based on a machine bought in Germany in 1953 by the company's founder. Subsequently, the machines were made and sold by a subsidiary of Spancrete Industries, and their use was supported by an association of companies that purchased the machines under a licensing agreement. Spancrete Industries was based in Milwaukee, Wisconsin, and had 1992 sales of $53 million with 420 employees.

WORK FORCE

The concrete products industry employed 61,000 people in 1991 and earned a total of $1.4 billion, for an average of $23,062 per employee. Almost 74 percent of the industry employees were hourly workers, who earned an average of $9.56 per hour. The industry's white collar jobs encompassed accounting, engineering, estimating, marketing, and management.

RESEARCH AND TECHNOLOGY

Industry firms conducted continuous research throughout the twentieth century to enhance the qualities of concrete products and construction operations and to improve the methods for producing and delivering concrete. Additional advancements were made by businessmen and managers, as with the adaptation of trucks for deliveries and mixing in the early part of the century.

Continual and sometimes dramatic changes in science and engineering produced positive changes in the industry. Industrialization of the precast concrete products industry began in earnest in the 1960s and 1970s as an increasing number of improvements in the strength and other qualities of concrete were made by scientific, engineering, and chemical research and analyses. Technicians in these specialties combined steel with concrete to enable its use in large bridge and skyscraper structural elements, as well as applied computers and automation to control and mix raw material ingredients accurately. Many studies and tests were conducted to determine the effects of different material ingredients, and varying proportions of those ingredients, in producing desired new concrete qualities.

These scientific activities were performed by both individual companies—each hoping to improve its own competitive position—and industry supported trade associations and institutes.

"Basically, most 'new' products in the precast concrete industry are an evolution of existing elements," according to one industry overview. "Nevertheless, the industry has developed (and is successfully marketing) valuable solutions in fields relative to, for instance, environmental problems such as sound barrier walls to protect residents living near highways or railways from noise hindrance."

In the mid-1990s, there was some controversy in the United States regarding the manufacture of concrete-related products using cement made in hazardous waste burning kilns. It was thought that perhaps the toxic chemicals not destroyed in the process could leach through the pipe or other products and into the environment; however, there has been little research which would either support or refute these claims. The concern spawned legislation at the local government level banning the use of or sale of "toxic cement," including the use of concrete pipe manufactured with cement made from hazardous waste fueled kilns in public water supplies.

The use of used tires as a kiln fuel was also challenged by environmental regulations. Proponents, however, as is the case with the use of hazardous waste as a kiln fuel, argued that using spent tires was an effective form of recycling. Both practices have met with numerous legal challenges.

FURTHER READING

Annual Survey of Manufactures Statistics for Industry Groups and Industries. Washington: U.S. Department of Commerce, 1991.

Census of Manufactures: Concrete, Plaster, and Cut Stone Products. Washington: U.S. Department of Commerce, 1987.

"Concrete Today—An ENR Special Advertising Section," *Engineering News-Record,* 3 May 1993.

The ENR Directory of Construction Information Services. New York: McGraw-Hill, 1993.

Nilson, Arthur H., and George Winter. *Design of Concrete Structures.* New York: McGraw- Hill, 1986.

Sawinski, Diane, and Wendy Mason, eds. *Encyclopedia of Global Industries.* Detroit: Gale Research, 1996.

"Set in Concrete: Trade." *The Economist,* 3 June 1995.

Waddell, J. J. *Concrete Construction Handbook.* New York: McGraw-Hill, 1968.

—Douglas Hoyt, updated by Linda Paulson

SIC 3273

READY-MIXED CONCRETE

This category covers establishments primarily engaged in manufacturing portland cement concrete manufactured and delivered to a purchaser in a plastic and unhardened state. This industry includes production and sale of central-mixed concrete, shrink-mixed concrete, and truck-mixed concrete.

INDUSTRY SNAPSHOT

A material similar to stone, concrete is made by mixing selected proportions and qualities of cement, sand, gravel, and sometimes other aggregates. Water is added and the soft mixture formed into desired shapes. Water and cement interact chemically to form a solid mass, binding the ingredient particles together, but the mixture remains soft so that it can be shaped before the cement hardens.

Concrete was a leading material resource for building construction and for various products because of its strength, ability to be molded into any shape, resistance to fire and weather, and because of the availability of materials from which it is made. Concrete's limited strength under tensile stress was substantially overcome by reinforcement with steel and other materials in various ways.

For all facets of the construction industry—particularly the cement and concrete industries—when spending on infrastructure and construction increases, there are corollary increases in product shipments.

In the mid-1990s, for example, increased public works projects, financed through increased sales of tax-exempt bonds in the United States, were expected to increase five to eight percent with a slight downturn expected in 1996. In addition to a healthy bond market, healthier state and local government budgets, which have been fraught with deficits since the 1980s, were expected to improve and stimulate public works spending.

Concrete businesses in the early 1990s furnished much of the basic resources for the construction industries, as well as for utilitarian and artistic products like railroad ties and birdbaths. A few of the larger construction contractors manufactured their own concrete materials and products, while others relied on concrete producers for their products.

The ready-mixed concrete industry included businesses that made concrete and delivered it to contractors or other customers for constructing buildings, bridges, roads, sidewalks, or other facilities. The concrete production process involved the use of large scale equipment and machinery located reasonably near to where the concrete was to be used, so that the concrete could be delivered while it was still soft enough to be shaped.

The concrete ready-mixed industry was heavily dependent on its primary customers, which were constructors of homes, industrial and office buildings, highways, and bridges. Consequently, the industry's market generally shadows the cyclical markets served by construction industries. For example, in the early 1990s the market for public works construction was strong while the other building markets were weak. Construction in public works projects in the United States alone—infrastructure construction ranging from construction of public buildings, highways, and conduits for utilities—was expected to continue through the decade, then predicted to level off at about $120 billion through 1998. Concrete industries were developing new technologies in the 1980s and 1990s to make concrete building parts stronger and more attractive, which helped the industry to reinforce its market in the construction industries.

In 1991 the ready-mixed concrete industry employed 86,100 people, and shipped products valued at $11.68 billion. The principal states in the industry in 1987 were California, Texas, Florida, and Arizona, which accounted for 31 percent of the industry's employment.

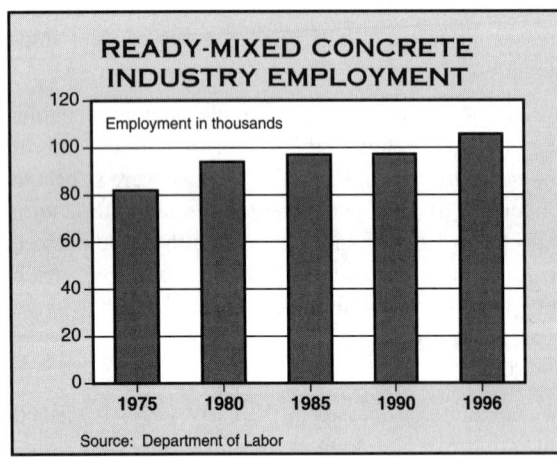

READY-MIXED CONCRETE INDUSTRY EMPLOYMENT

Employment in thousands

Source: Department of Labor

ORGANIZATION AND STRUCTURE

Many ready-mixed concrete companies were relatively small, having customers in one community or a limited region, primarily because soft concrete cannot be delivered beyond about 20 miles from where it is made. Yet to produce the concrete economically re-

quires considerable expenditures for plant and trucking facilities. Most concrete plants were fixed, but some were portable and could be moved close to major construction sites. Many larger companies have grown by expanding their territories as well as by purchasing smaller local firms. In 1987 there were 3,749 companies in the industry. Each employed an average of 25.8 workers and recorded $3.5 million in sales.

Most of the ready-mixed concrete producers also were involved in related concrete businesses, such as the mining of sand and gravel, the production of crushed stone, cement manufacture, or the manufacture of concrete blocks, pipe, building structural elements, and other concrete products.

Most industry establishments competed against several concrete businesses in a small market area. In addition, several non-concrete products substituted for concrete provided another arena of competition. These alternative resources included lumber, asphalt, brick, and steel.

The National Ready-Mixed Concrete Association (NRMCA) was the primary trade group supporting the industry. Headquartered near Washington, DC, the NRMCA helped its more than 1,000 members by fostering research, training, and product promotion programs, and by representing the industry before federal and professional groups. The NRMCA worked with many other trade associations in the ready-mixed concrete industry including the Portland Cement Association (PCA), the American Concrete Pavement Association (ACPA), the Concrete Reinforcing Steel Institute (CRSI), the Post-Tensioning Institute (PTI), and the American Concrete Institute (ACI).

The American Society for Testing and Materials began providing guidelines for the manufacture and testing of concrete products in 1933. Throughout its existence, the organization continued to revise its specifications as the ready-mixed concrete industry, and the technology it utilized, evolved. Additional organizations, including the American Concrete Institute (ACI) and the National Ready-Mixed Concrete Association (NRMCA), published other specifications.

BACKGROUND AND DEVELOPMENT

Though the first use of concrete dates back many centuries, widespread usage did not occur until the nineteenth century, when improvements in the materials combined to form the cement ingredient were made. In the twentieth century, reinforcement techniques were developed that made cement structural components for skyscrapers and large bridges over highways and rivers practical. The development of trucks equipped to mix concrete in transit in the 1920s made it possible for the ready-mixed approach to become the dominant process for concrete usage by the 1990s.

Portland cement was invented in 1824 by Joseph Aspdin, a British engineer, and had strength and water resistance qualities superior to those of previous cements. Limestone and clay were portland cement's principal ingredients. These raw materials were ground finely, combined, and heated in a kiln to form clinker, which was then pulverized. The name "portland" came from the Isle of Portland, where limestone was quarried. Portland cement was the primary type of cement used from its origination.

In 1909 concrete was first mixed in transit in a horse drawn wagon with gears from the wheels activating paddles in the mixing process. In 1913 concrete was taken to the work site in a dump truck. The first company to market a revolving horizontal drum mixer was the Paris Mixer Company in 1926. Between 1925 and 1930, the number of ready-mixed concrete plants in the United States increased from 25 to 100. The National Ready Mixed Concrete Association was formed in 1930 and helped foster industry growth.

Concrete, like stone, has very good compressive strength; it withstands considerable pressure from above without crumbling. However, concrete does not have great tensile strength. A concrete beam between two posts will crack if too much pressure is placed in the middle of the beam. To overcome tensile limitations, steel rods were placed in the concrete before it hardened, reinforcing its tensile strength. Reinforcing concrete techniques were begun in the first decade of the twentieth century. Prestressed concrete can withstand even greater tensile stresses. Rods or wires are stretched before the concrete hardens around them. The released wires or rods then compress the concrete, providing additional tensile strength. Prestressed technology enabled cement to be used in much greater spans as required in the construction of large scale buildings and bridges.

Between 1977 and 1987, the number of employees in the industry increased from 87,900 to 96,900, while the number of companies decreased from 4,317 to 3,749, reflecting a number of acquisitions and mergers.

CURRENT CONDITIONS

Many of the larger ready-mixed concrete companies benefitted from centralized purchasing, marketing, and engineering operations. Many were involved in manufacturing fields related to concrete production,

such as making concrete pipe, railroad ties, and construction structural elements. Because of the benefits of size, it was expected that the trend toward larger companies in the industry would continue.

There was steady improvement in the durability, appearance, and other qualities of ready-mixed concrete. Lower production costs and greater quality control also were achieved. These advancements were spurred by competition and aided by the many trade groups conducting research and providing training.

INDUSTRY LEADERS

Lafarge Corp. recorded $1.5 billion in sales in 1992. Headquartered in Reston, Virginia, the company had 7,600 employees in 1992. In 1993 the company operated 15 cement plants, 90 distribution terminals, and 450 construction materials facilities. It was one of the biggest producers of ready-mixed concrete and aggregates in the United States. The company underwent restructuring in 1993 and 1994, with headquarters in Canada. Lafarge's principal stockholder was Lafarge Coppee in Paris, France, one of the world's largest cement companies.

Founded in 1909 and headquartered in Birmingham, Alabama, Vulcan Materials Company had 6,400 employees and annual sales of $1.1 billion in 1992. It was engaged in the mining of construction sand and gravel, the production of crushed limestone, and in the manufacture of ready-mixed concrete, concrete pipe, and several chemical materials. The production of construction materials generated 64 percent of the company's sales. The company focused its marketing efforts in the southeastern United States. Its facilities included 129 stone quarries, 13 sand and gravel pits, 3 slag plants, 7 ready-mixed concrete plants, and 19 asphalt plants. The company increased its size through a variety of small acquisitions and a few larger mergers. It also became the country's largest producer of crushed stone. Ready-mixed concrete sales in 1992 were $12.4 million.

Texas Industries Inc. posted $614 million in sales in 1993 exclusively through the production of steel, cement, and concrete materials and products. Although about two-thirds of these sales were generated by steel products, the balance embraced the full range of concrete products, including sand and gravel, portland cement, ready-mixed concrete, concrete block and brick, pipe, prestressed concrete products, and architectural precast concrete panels. Headquartered in Dallas, the company employed 2,700 workers in 1993. It operated one steel mill, 29 ready-mixed concrete plants, and two cement plants in Texas, as well as 13 sand and gravel mine operations, most of which were located in Texas.

Ameron Inc., founded in 1906, was based in Monterey Park, California. The company employed 3,000 workers and reported $465 million in sales in 1992. Ameron's leading product was ready-mixed concrete, followed by other concrete products and concrete blocks. The company also manufactured paints and varnishes, noncement pipe products, and mined sand.

Florida Rock Industries Inc.'s largest business segment was ready-mixed concrete, but its other primary businesses included a wide range of mining, quarrying, and processing of raw materials for concrete, as well as the sale of various types of sand and stone for use in concrete manufacture. The company also produced concrete block, prestressed concrete, and other construction materials. Founded in 1931 and headquartered in Jacksonville, Florida, the company recorded $294 million in sales and employed 2,385 people. In 1993 the company operated 82 ready-mix concrete facilities, 12 concrete block plants, and owned 838 ready-mix and block delivery trucks. Most of its operations and customers were in the southeastern United States, especially Florida, Georgia, Virginia, Maryland, North Carolina, and Washington, D.C.

Lone Star Industries Inc. was formed in 1919. Its 1993 sales of $240 million was almost entirely produced through the sale of concrete-related products. Portland cement was its primary product, followed by ready-mixed concrete, then concrete blocks and other products such as pipe and prestressed concrete products. The company also mined for sand and gravel. Based in Stamford, Connecticut, the company employed about 1,600 people in 1993, of which some 1,000 were union members. The company operated facilities throughout the United States and in Canada and Brazil. With 15 cement plants, 17 aggregate plants and quarries, 36 ready-mixed and other concrete products plants, Lone Star generated $30.8 million in ready-mixed concrete sales in 1992. A leading producer of cement in the United States, the company had difficulties resulting from depressed prices for cement in the 1980s. In 1990, the company filed for protection from its creditors under Chapter 11 of the Federal Bankruptcy Code and in 1994 recovered from bankruptcy.

WORK FORCE

Most of the employees in the ready-mixed concrete industry were production workers. Larger companies and many smaller companies used computers not only for accounting but for controlling the processes of concrete mixing and other production operations. The larger companies in particular employed skilled engineers to help refine mixing and production processes.

The 86,100 employees in the industry in 1991 earned a total of $2.24 billion in wages, for an average of $26,052 per year per employee. The 62,800 production workers earned an average of $11.19 per hour that year.

AMERICA AND THE WORLD

The principal international relationships of the ready-mixed concrete industry have been that some of the raw materials have been received from overseas, growing operations in the United States have been foreign owned, and some American companies have had facilities that produced concrete in other countries.

Concrete transactions between countries were somewhat limited by the fact that ready-mixed concrete production and sales were local operations. Also, hardened concrete products, like pipe and concrete block, were prohibitively expensive to ship overseas because of their weight. However, there have been significant cases of international ownership of ready-mixed and other concrete operations.

In the 1980s, cement from foreign sources filled 15 percent of U.S. needs, but not without conflict. A battle between cement producers in the United States and Mexico started in the late 1980s and escalated through the next decade. Mexico's Cemex—the largest producer in that country as well as the globe's fourth largest firm in the industry—was accused of dumping product in the United States. The Department of Commerce started tacking on anti-dumping duties in 1990, which were raised again in May of 1995 from 43 percent to 62 percent. *The Economist* reported that 19 U.S. manufacturers grumbled because the duty was considered too low.

Reports were that U.S. cement companies prepared several proposals in order for the U.S. trade officials to address the issue, including the chairman of Lone Star Industries, Inc. Failing in his efforts to reduce import levels, Lone Star then became the largest importer of cement. By 1992, imported cement had dropped to 8 percent of consumption in the United States, but quickly increased because manufacturers were reaching plant capacity and sales had increased. The United States imported 11.3 million tons of concrete in 1994, 60 percent more than was imported in 1993 and the most since 1990, according to *The Economist.*

The ironic aspect of this dispute was that approximately two-thirds of all U.S. cement companies were foreign-owned. Subsidiaries of companies such as Lafarge, Mitsubishi Materials Corporation, and Blue Circle Industries PLC either fully owned or controlled significant financial interests in many cement and cement products plants throughout the United States.

Many U.S. cement companies had been acquired by foreign interests in the early 1990s because reduced profits had made them vulnerable to takeovers. More than 65 percent of U.S. cement production facilities were acquired by foreign interests. The two largest cement producing companies in the United States were foreign owned.

Lafarge Corporation, the largest cement producer in North America and a major manufacturer of ready-mixed concrete, was a subsidiary of a French construction company, Lafarge Coppee. Lafarge Coppee was a major building materials company operating in 35 countries and with sales of $5.8 billion in 1992.

RESEARCH AND TECHNOLOGY

With keen competition forcing ready-mixed concrete companies to improve service and cut costs, many of the larger companies looked toward research and technology to improve the quality of concrete products and reduce their production costs. Lafarge Corporation, for example, used scrap tires as a fuel as well as industrial by-products, such as spent refractory bricks and iron mill scale, as low cost raw materials for concrete. This practice was not without controversy, and soon the manufacture of concrete-related products using cement made in hazardous waste burning kilns in the United States was questioned. It is thought that perhaps the toxic chemicals not destroyed in the process leach through the pipe or other products and into the environment; however, there has been little research which would either support or refute these claims. The concern spawned legislation at the local government level in the mid-1990s that would ban the use of or sale of "toxic cement," including the use of concrete pipe manufactured with cement made from hazardous waste fueled kilns in public water supplies.

The use of used tires as a kiln fuel was also challenged by environmental regulations. Proponents, however, as is the case with the use of hazardous waste as a kiln fuel, argued that using spent tires was an effective form of recycling. Both practices have met with numerous legal challenges.

For years concrete producers and industry groups endeavored to improve concrete's strength, durability, uniformity, appearance, drying time, and weight. By the early 1990s, concrete's compression strength had been increased to withstand 20,000 pounds per square inch (psi), while in laboratory experiments strengths of 100,000 psi were reached. In the 1960s, 5,800 psi was considered high-strength concrete.

The American Society of Civil Engineers established the Civil Engineering Research Council (CERC) to spearhead a program of construction product improvements the society considered to be essential to meet infrastructure needs for the twenty-first century. The CERC developed plans to work with government, industry, and trade groups in designing and perfecting higher strength concrete.

Other research was conducted to create new types of concrete that would enable their use in products previously made from ceramics, plastic, or aluminum. Lone Star developed a new product named Pyrament that dried quickly enough to allow traffic on a road four hours after the concrete was laid. Greater strength to weight ratios and improved ability to absorb energy were achieved by incorporating reinforcing materials such as wood, glass, carbon, or steel into concrete.

Computer hardware and software were used by ready-mixed concrete manufacturers in a variety of ways, and also to prepare job estimates, control production processes, and schedule deliveries. In the late 1980s, the major ready-mixed concrete producer located in Seattle, Washington, Lakeside Sand and Gravel, instituted an efficiency and productivity improvement program that included many computer applications, such as computerized vehicle maintenance, computerized dispatching, and a computerized aggregate handling process.

In the late 1980s, Raia Industries Inc., based in Hackensack, New Jersey, applied Command Data software to help control the manufacturing and delivery of concrete. A 200 to 300 percent increase in productivity was reported from the computer system which delivered ingredients, monitored processing operations and moisture content, and also helped to load the trucks.

A faculty member of the Southern Illinois University designed an easy computer program for small concrete contractors to use in preparing estimates. With this program, the contractor entered the quantities of materials needed for a job, then the program applied the unit prices and produced a complete concrete estimate for the customer with all the costs and specifications clearly itemized.

Ready-mixed concrete companies as well as trade groups were continuously seeking more efficient manufacturing and processing approaches. Examples included enabling longer delivery span, reducing truck and equipment maintenance costs, facilitating filling of bags, and automated setting of concrete curbs.

In the late 1980s, Master Builders Inc. developed a technology that slowed the hardening process in the formation of concrete, thus enabling it to be transported over longer periods of time and distances. This technique was called the DELVO system, and was said not to be detrimental to strength or other concrete characteristics.

However, as Lionel W. Vincent of National Cement Company of California Inc. wrote in *Concrete Products,* "The zeal for putting all that information into the end product is for naught without imple menting the basics of concrete production. Over the years, our reliance on obtaining concrete durability has been unrealistically tied to a dependence on the increasing use of chemical admixtures, mineral additives, specialty cements, etc. . . . The cost of a cubic yard of basic concrete containing the three basic ingredients—cement, aggregates and water—can now be doubled by adding anywhere from three to five (or more) special additives. What is evident here is that after 40 years of innovative technology and 'allege' improved knowledge, the 'back to basics' theory is still very valid. . . . If you rely on additives or special cements and you disregard the basics of good concrete, you will most likely not attain durable concrete."

FURTHER READING

Annual Survey of Manufactures Statistics for Industry Groups and Industries. Washington: U.S. Department of Commerce, 1991.

Census of Manufactures Concrete, Plaster, and Cut Stone Products. Washington: U.S. Department of Commerce, 1987.

"Concrete Today—an ENR Special Advertising Section." *Engineering News-Record,* 3 May 1993.

Nilson, Arthur H., and George Winter. *Design of Concrete Structures.* New York: McGraw- Hill, 1986.

Sawinski, Diane, and Wendy Mason, eds. *Encyclopedia of Global Industries.* Detroit: Gale Research, 1996.

"Set in Concrete: Trade." *The Economist,* 3 June 1995.

Standard & Poor's Industry Surveys, New York: Standard & Poor's Corporation, 1993.

"U.S.-Mexico Trade Disputes Over Steel Products, Cement, and Tuna Gain Prominence in Late July and Early August." *SourceMex Economic News and Analysis on Mexico.* 10 August 1994.

Vincent, Lionel W. "Concrete: from A-Z and Back to A." *Concrete Products.* June 1993.

Waddell, J. J. *Concrete Construction Handbook.* New York: McGraw-Hill, 1968.

—Douglas Hoyt, updated by Linda Paulson

SIC 3274

LIME

The lime industry is comprised of establishments primarily engaged in manufacturing quick-lime, hydrated lime, and miscellaneous lime-related products. It is considered part of the larger concrete, gypsum, and plaster products industry.

Lime, or quick-lime, is calcium oxide derived from naturally occurring calcium carbonate. Its total production in the United States ranked fifth among all chemicals. Lime is produced at 109 plants in 33 states as well as in Puerto Rico, with the greatest number of plants operating in Colorado, Montana, and Wyoming. The total value of the product in 1994 was more than $1 million.

One of the oldest products of chemical reaction known to man, lime is a white or grayish-white solid with numerous applications. Its history dates to ancient Egypt, where it was used in mortar and plaster. Lime was traditionally used as a construction product until the Industrial Revolution, when its usage began expanding. The growth of the chemical industry at the start of the twentieth century gave lime production another boost, and of that produced, an estimated 90 percent is used in some sort of chemical process. Solid lime, for example, is used extensively as a fertilizer and building material. It is also commonly utilized as a chemical neutralizer to treat solid and gaseous wastes. Quick-lime accounted for approximately 72 percent of industry revenues in the early 1990s.

When mixed with water, lime turns into calcium hydroxide, or slaked lime, which is used to make mortars, plasters, and cement. Slaked lime represented about 19 percent of industry output in 1991. Lime is also used to make calcium carbide, which decomposes in water to form the flammable acetylene gas used in welding torches.

Blast furnace operators and steel manufacturers consume the largest amounts of lime products to melt and process steel. Steel production usage, the traditional driving force in this industry, consumed about 31 percent of industry output in 1994. Total use in chemical and industrial applications represented 64 percent of the lime market. Chemical firms, for example, use lime-related products in the production of plastic resins. Environmental uses, such as water, sewage, and smokestack emissions treatment, accounted for 26 percent of lime usage in 1994, and construction industries consumed about 8 percent, with refractory dolomite usage consuming 2 percent of United States total lime production.

Lime is considered a commodity, and industry profit margins are typically low. However, new applications for lime allowed the industry to realize steady demand growth throughout the mid-1900s and even through the 1980s. Between 1982 and 1988, for instance, sales of lime expanded 35 percent, from $543 million to about $830 million. Growth faltered in the late 1980s and early 1990s, and lime production dipped to about 17.5 million tons and $720 million in 1991. World production has been tapering off each year since 1990. U.S. lime producers were poised for recovery in 1993 and 1994; production in those years was 16.8 million metric tons at a value of $965 million, according to the Bureau of Mines, and 17.4 million metric tons worth just over $1 billion.

While some core lime markets remained stagnant into the mid-1990s, other segments were expected to buoy production volume and industry earnings throughout the next decades. Flue gas desulfurization in 1996 accounted for 15 percent of all lime sales and, as the market segment with the fastest growth, was poised to continue with utility deregulation. As environmental restrictions increase, so too will lime uses related to treating wastes. In 1995 alone, two midwestern utilities that invested in new lime scrubbers increased the market by a single-year record amount. By mid-1996, Dravo Lime Co., one of the nation's leading producers of lime, announced production increases and operations at full capacity expected, particularly with the introduction of a new product for the lime-based environmental technologies market.

A recovering economy and new lime applications will help boost industry employment between 1990 and 2005, according to the Bureau of Labor statistics. Lime manufacturers employed about 4,500 workers in the early 1990s, down from more than 5,500 in the early 1980s. Despite continued productivity gains, however, jobs in most occupations should rise by 5 to 20 percent by 2005. Truck drivers, which make up about 30 percent of the entire work force, will see their opportunities jump by 13 percent. Industrial production management jobs will grow approximately 23 percent. Sales and marketing positions will likely increase 27 percent.

Sixty-four U.S. companies produced lime in 1994; down from 70 in 1990. The largest U.S. lime producer was Chemical Lime Co., which underwent restructur-

ing in 1994. Dravo Lime Co., Mississippi Lime Co., Marblehead Lime Co., and Continental Lime Inc. were among the top 10 companies, which produced 64 percent of the nation's lime in 1994.

FURTHER READING

Chapman, Peter. "Lime Growth Doesn't Meet Expectations." *Chemical Marketing Reporter,* 1 January 1996, 5.

Darnay, Arsen J., ed. *Manufacturing USA; Industry Analyses, Statistics, and Leading Companies.* Detroit: Gale Research Inc., 1993.

Darnay, Arsen J., and Marlita A. Reddy, eds. *Market Share Reporter: An Annual Compilation of Reported Market Share Data on Companies, Products, and Services, 1993.* Detroit: Gale Research Inc., 1993.

Encyclopedia Britannica. Chicago: Encyclopedia Britannica, Inc., 1993.

"Lime Demand Eases, But Market Remains Strong." *Industrial Specialties News,* 6 May 1996.

"Lime is Special." *Chemical Marketing Reporter,* 31 August 1992.

Minerals Yearbook: Metals and Minerals, Volume I. Washington: U.S. Department of the Interior, Bureau of Mines, n.d.

Santos, William. "Lime Demand Strengthens With Squeeze on Waste." *Chemical Marketing Reporter,* 3 May 1993.

Standard & Poor's Industry Surveys. New York: Standard & Poor's Corporation, 5 August 1993.

U.S. Department of Commerce. *U.S. Industrial Outlook.* Washington: GPO, January 1993.

—Dave Mote, updated by Linda Paulson

SIC 3275

GYPSUM PRODUCTS

Companies predominately employed in manufacturing plaster, plasterboard, and other gypsum products constitute the gypsum products industry. The manufacturers in this industry produce products such as acoustical plaster, wallboard, cement, insulating plaster, orthopedic plaster (for casts), plaster of paris, and gypsum rock, lath, and tile.

Gypsum, or hydrated calcium sulfate, has been an important construction material for centuries. It is mined from hardened ocean and saline-lake brine deposits. Natural supplies of the material are abundant, particularly in the United States, Canada, France, Italy, and Britain. The largest U.S. lime producing states are Oklahoma, Iowa, Texas, Michigan, Nevada, California, and Indiana. These states contributed 75 percent of the total domestic production of lime, producing more than a million tons each in 1994.

Gypsum is used as a fertilizer, a filler in paper and textiles, and a retarding agent in cement. About 80 percent of total gypsum output, however, is used to make plaster that is formed into building products. When combined with water and additives, plaster becomes a white cementing material that sets and hardens by chemical reaction. It is an excellent construction material for interior walls because it is inexpensive, easy to install, fire retardant, and acts as a noise insulator.

The United States remains the largest consumer of wallboard, accounting for more than half of world sales in 1994. About 75 percent of the gypsum used in the United States is used in wallboard. About 40 percent of wallboard products are used in new residential construction. Another 35 percent of industry output is used for remodeling and repair, and 10 percent goes into new commercial construction. The remaining 15 percent of the market consists of numerous miscellaneous applications, such as mobile home walls.

Because the industry is dependent on new residential construction, sales are closely linked to U.S. housing starts. Strong housing markets during the post-World War II U.S. economic expansion pushed industry sales close to $2 billion in the late 1970s. But a housing slump in the early 1980s kept revenues to $2.3 billion in 1982.

A recovery in housing starts boosted gypsum industry sales to a peak of nearly $2.7 billion in 1987. A U.S. economic recession and depressed housing markets in the late 1980s and early 1990s, however, pummeled industry participants. Receipts plunged below $2 billion annually in the early 1990s, and wallboard prices crashed from $127 per thousand square feet in 1985 to $67 in 1992. In 1994, plant production was increased slightly; prices between December 1993 and 1994 rose 13 percent, with an average price of $149 per thousand square feet.

After being hammered by brutal markets, gypsum producers experienced a slight reprieve in 1993 as industry revenues rose a tepid 4 percent. Gypsum demand was forecast to rise about 3 percent per year through the mid-1990s. Prices were also expected to recover, albeit very slowly. New manufacturing technologies, mostly aimed at reducing energy consumption, were expected to raise productivity and boost profit margins. Demand increased in 1994 because of increased domestic construction. Sales increased 12 percent, while value rose 48 percent to $2.6 billion.

About 90 U.S. firms produced gypsum in the early 1990s. United States Gypsum Co. (USG), of Illinois, was the largest, with more than 30 percent of the U.S. wallboard market. The aftershocks of legal actions against the firm in the 1970s and 1980s, which ranged from anti-trust matters to various claims from asbestos contaminated products, meant the company had to retrench fiscally. The company had $1.5 billion in 1991 sales and about 10,000 employees in its diversified operations. USG was emerging from chapter 11 bankruptcy in 1993. Regardless of the restructuring and huge debt of the company, in the mid-1990s, it retained a third of the United States wallboard market.

National Gypsum Co., the second largest producer, was also emerging from bankruptcy in 1993. It had 1991 sales of $1.5 billion and about 6,500 workers. Other major gypsum producers in the early 1990s included Redco II, of California, and Republic Gypsum Co. and Aancor Holdings Inc., both of which are based in Texas.

The number of U.S. companies calcining gypsum for use in wallboard manufacturing in 1994 was 13. The activity was spread to 69 plants in 28 states, of which Iowa, California, Texas, Florida, Nevada, and New York had the greatest production—47 percent of national production. Six companies produced 79 percent of all gypsum in the United States in 1994. These included USG, National Gypsum, Georgia-Pacific Corporation, Domtar, Temple Inland Inc., and Celotex.

About 10,500 workers served the industry in the early 1990s. Most employees were blue-collar laborers. The average hourly wage for production workers was $12 in 1989, compared to $10.49 for the average U.S. manufacturing industry laborer. The average number of hours each laborer worked in 1989, however, was significantly higher than in other manufacturing sectors. Employment growth in the long-term will depend on housing starts. Because most mills are already highly automated, future productivity gains will result in negligible work force reductions.

FURTHER READING

Barron, Tom. "Recyclers Find New Uses for Newsprint." *Environment Today,* October 1992.

Darnay, Arsen J., ed. *Manufacturing USA; Industry Analyses, Statistics, and Leading Companies.* Detroit: Gale Research Inc., 1993.

Darnay, Arsen J., and Marlita A. Reddy, eds. *Market Share Reporter: An Annual Compilation of Reported Market Share Data on Companies, Products, and Services, 1993.* Detroit: Gale Research Inc., 1993.

Encyclopedia Britannica. Chicago: Encyclopedia Britannica, Inc., 1993.

Minerals Yearbook: Metals and Minerals. Volume I. United States Department of the Interior, Bureau of Mines, n.d.

Santos, William. "Lime Demand Strengthens With Squeeze on Waste." *Chemical Marketing Reporter,* 3 May 1993.

Sawinski, Diane, and Wendy Mason, eds. *Encyclopedia of Global Industry.* Detroit: Gale Research Inc., 1996.

Standard & Poor's Industry Surveys. New York: Standard & Poor's Corporation, 5 August 1993.

U.S. Department of Commerce. *U.S. Industrial Outlook 1993.* Washington: GPO, January 1993.

—Dave Mote, updated by Linda Paulson

SIC 3281

CUT STONE AND STONE PRODUCTS

This category covers establishments primarily engaged in cutting, shaping, and finishing granite, marble, limestone, slate, and other stone for building and miscellaneous uses. Establishments primarily engaged in buying or selling partly finished monuments and tombstones, but performing no work on the stones other than lettering, finishing, or shaping to custom order, are classified in either the wholesale or retail trade divisions. The cutting of grindstones, pulpstones, and whetstones at the quarry is classified in the mining division.

INDUSTRY SNAPSHOT

Dimension stone sales expanded steadily during the 1990s as construction markets grew. Sales jumped from almost $1 billion in 1990 to almost $1.5 billion in 1996. Despite a severe construction industry recession beginning in the late 1980s, a trend toward the use of stone in new buildings buoyed industry earnings, as did new technology that delivered productivity gains.

ORGANIZATION AND STRUCTURE

The three main materials utilized in this industry are granite, marble, and limestone. Granite products accounted for more than 50 percent of industry output in the 1990s. Granite is a light-colored rock—usually found in mountainous regions—that is comprised primarily of varying amounts of quartz and feldspar. About half of all cut granite is used in buildings, the remainder being consumed to create monuments and miscellaneous products.

Marble, which represented approximately 20 percent of production during the 1990s, is also used mostly in buildings. It is metamorphosed limestone, and is usually quarried from the core of young mountains in the Rockies or from the exposed roots of ancient mountains in the Appalachians. The presence of impurities and other minerals during metamorphosis is responsible for the many colors and streaks found in different types of marble. Its strength and appearance make it a popular stone for statuary and decorative applications.

Limestone, a sedimentary rock, is comprised primarily of calcite that resulted from the sedimentation of coral and dead organisms. Limestone varies greatly in texture and color. Although most limestone is crushed for use as agricultural lime or cement, cut limestone is often used as building stone. Limestone products, almost all of which is building stone, accounted for about 10 percent of industry shipments during the 1990s. Aside from the three major stone products groups, miscellaneous cut stone comprised the remaining almost 20 percent of sales. Slate, for example, is commonly used in construction and to make items such as billiard tables and chalkboards.

Dimension stone is usually removed from open pits in rectangular blocks, although some rock is mined from tunnel-type quarries. A channeling machine is used to cut softer rocks, such as limestone, marble, and sandstone, into blocks that are removed by cranes and hauled away. The rock may also be cut by wire sawing, which involves pulling a wire surrounded by an abrasive slurry back-and-forth along the stone.

From the quarry, the stone is hauled to a processing plant where it is cut, shaped, polished, and/or coated. Most dimension stone is finished into masonry veneer for use as fascia on buildings. The stone veneer is anchored to a structural frame or backing, often giving the impression that the structure is built with stone blocks. A significant portion of cut stone is shaped and finished into surfaces for floors, walls, tables, and counters.

BACKGROUND AND DEVELOPMENT

Dimension stone was quarried as early as Egyptian times. The Egyptian pyramids were built from quarried stone in about 2800 B.C.; the largest pyramid contains 2.3 million blocks with an average weight of 2.5 tons. The Babylonians used cut stone in 600 B.C. to build the renowned Hanging Gardens. The Greeks and the Romans also used cut and finished stone widely as construction, decorative, and statuary material. In fact, the Greeks quarried marble as early as 447 B.C.

Stone was quarried in America as a building and paving material before the Revolutionary War. But the U.S. cut stone industry lagged behind European production until the development of a railway system during the mid-1800s. Mechanized cutting and finishing tools and methods during the late 1800s and early 1900s significantly boosted industry activity, as did the building boom of the 1920s. Early U.S. stone structures include St. Patrick's Cathedral (1879) and The Cathedral of St. John the Divine, started in 1892 and completed in 1996.

Although stone remains an important building material, new construction materials and methods developed during the 20th century have limited its use almost entirely to a finishing element of mostly decorative value. Steel frames and concrete have particularly infringed on conventional uses of stone. Furthermore, new synthetic materials have replaced stone in many decorative and functional applications, such as counter tops, wall coverings, and architectural ornamentation. Many synthetic substitutes with the look and feel of marble or granite are less expensive, more durable, and easier to manufacture, ship, and install than real stone. Nevertheless, stone is still a popular and cost-effective building material for many indoor and outdoor construction projects and consumer products.

CURRENT CONDITIONS

Although synthetics and glass became popular building materials during the 1980s, an escalation in commercial construction spurred cut stone industry expansion. Sales climbed from about $900 million in 1988 to almost $1.3 billion in 1996. Despite a slow building activity during the 1990s, revenues continued to ascend to nearly $1.5 billion by 1996. Furthermore, increased interest in stone building materials, as opposed to concrete and glass, continued to buoy sales into the middle of the decade.

Many cut stone and stone product companies were crunched by the construction slowdown of the 1980s and early 1990s. As demand slowed, prices dropped and profit margins slipped as a result of overcapacity and increased competition. Most industry segments were stable, however. Granite producers, for example, were achieving greater demand at the expense of marble. Marble had been losing market share since the 1980s when it was determined that most varieties are affected by acid rain. Although granite producers were fighting stiff foreign competition, the use of granite for headstones and monuments remained strong, and a construction industry uptick in the mid 1990s bolstered the bottom line for many competitors.

Some companies were also benefitting from productivity gains implemented during the slowdown. The industry had succeeded at increasing its work force only 25 percent during the 1980s as its shipment value surged almost 80 percent. New automated cutting and finishing equipment, as well as advanced transportation and information systems, were credited with increasing efficiency. But while some producers had been able to boost profitability through automation, stone cutting remained a labor intensive industry susceptible to imports from low-cost emerging nations. India, for example, has made steady inroads into the U.S. granite industry throughout the 1990s.

The long term industry outlook was generally lackluster going into 1997. Limited opportunities for further productivity gains, coupled with greater foreign competition, were expected to hurt many industry sectors. And most traditional domestic markets, such as construction, will realize tepid growth at best. In addition, superior synthetic substitutes will continue to make gains. Because of stone's weight-to-value ratio, moreover, opportunities for U.S. export growth are slim with the exception of niche specialty stones. U.S. producers exported about two percent of production in 1996. The only potential bright spot on the horizon for the industry is the expected continued surge in historical restoration projects which require considerable amounts of stone to replace damaged pieces from the original construction. However, this represents only a faint glimmer against the overall gloom.

INDUSTRY LEADERS

Because of its logistical characteristics (i.e. transportation costs), the cut stone industry is highly fragmented into relatively small, local manufacturers. In 1996, just over 700 companies competed, and only the top 25 had sales higher than $10 million per year. The largest producer was General Crushed Stone Co., of Pennsylvania, which had 1996 sales of just over $200 million with a work force of about 1,500. Davidson Mineral Properties, of Georgia, had 1996 revenues of $130 million and about 800 employees. Other industry leaders included Pluess-Staufer Industries Inc., of Vermont, and Texas Granite Corp.

WORK FORCE

The employment outlook for the cut stone and stone products industry is dismal. In fact, most labor positions are expected to decline by about 20 percent by 2005, according to the U.S. Bureau of Labor Statistics. Jobs for helpers and material handlers, which account for eight percent of the work force, will likely diminish 22 percent by 2005; work for cutting machine operators, truck drivers, and finishers will fall 10 percent. Even management positions will decline 12 percent or more. Only opportunities for production managers are forecast to increase, though only slightly.

RESEARCH AND TECHNOLOGY

New cutting, finishing, and construction technologies in the mid-1990s were helping the cut stone and stone products industry remain competitive against new synthetics and low-cost imports. For example, advanced construction techniques were used in Washington D.C. in 1992 to create and erect massive 50-foot tall limestone columns for the Market Square Arena. 800,000 cubic feet of limestone was quarried to produce the 80,000 cubic feet of material actually contained in the columns. An advanced horizontal lathe rounded and fluted the huge structures, which were put into place as the concrete frame of the building was poured. The project was indicative of a trend toward greater use of natural stone in restorative building projects.

Cut stone producers were also benefitting from improved quarrying techniques, such as laser rockface profiling and robotic drilling and cutting machines. While much of this technology was being developed for extraction of crushed stone and other minerals, cut stone producers were finding applications for these and related innovations.

FURTHER READING

Barna, Ed. ''Vermont Mining Companies Stay Grounded.'' *Vermont Business Magazine,* January 1994.

Cook, Hugh. ''The Keys To Historic Masonry Restoration.'' *Building Design and Construction,* February 1997.

Garrett, Rodney. ''Technology Addresses Problems and Profits.'' *Pit and Quarry,* January 1994.

Gregerson, John. ''Old Reliable.'' *Building Design and Construction,* March 1997.

Hernan, Patrick. ''Southeast Report.'' *Pit and Quarry,* January 1997.

Tuunanen, Ari. ''Automation of Hard Rock Drilling Machines.'' *Pit and Quarry,* January 1994.

Paslawskyj, Michael. ''The Outlook is High.'' *Pit and Quarry,* July 1996.

''Construction Growth Tied to Population.'' *Pit and Quarry,* October 1996.

—Dave Mote, updated by Michael Broyles

SIC 3291

ABRASIVE PRODUCTS

This category covers companies that primarily make abrasive grinding wheels of natural or synthetic materials, abrasive-coated products, and other abrasive products. Companies cutting grindstones, pulpstones, and whetstones at the quarry are classified under mining industries.

INDUSTRY SNAPSHOT

The value of industry shipments in 1995 was $4.35 billion, up from $3.76 billion in 1991. In the early 1990s there were about 400 companies in the abrasive products industry, the same number there was during the early 1980s. Half of these 400 companies had 20 or more employees. Average firm size measured by number of production workers per establishment was 14 percent larger than for the entire manufacturing sector.

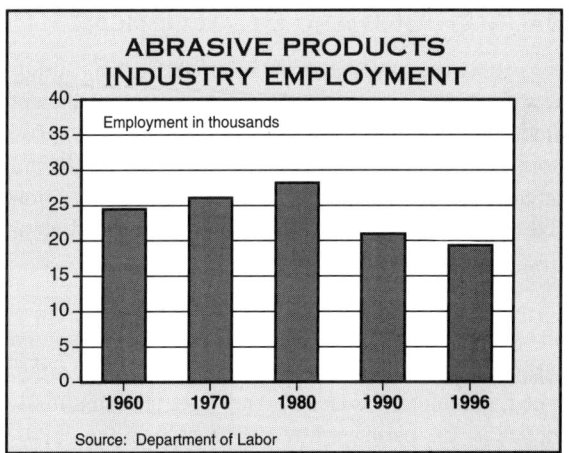

ABRASIVE PRODUCTS INDUSTRY EMPLOYMENT

Employment in thousands

Source: Department of Labor

This industry employed 15,600 production workers in 1995, down from 16,300 in 1991. The industry invested about the same money per production worker as other manufacturing sectors. Annual hours worked by production workers in the industry were about the same as those worked in the manufacturing sector at large, and hourly wages were 12 percent higher in the early 1990s.

ORGANIZATION AND STRUCTURE

Ranked by sales, two-thirds of the top 30 firms in the industry were subsidiaries and divisions of larger firms, while the others were private companies. Of the industry's 75 leading companies, 84 percent were private corporations. Each of the industry's top 30 companies generated more than $10 million and employed 100 or more workers.

The top four types of abrasive products by product share, prior to 1995, were nonmetallic coated abrasive products and buffing and polishing wheels (45 percent), nonmetallic sized abrasives (27 percent), other nonmetallic abrasives (23 percent), and metal abrasives (7 percent).

The largest organization serving the industry was the Abrasive Engineering Society, headquartered in Butler, Pennsylvania. The Society was founded in 1957 and has 400 members (its name changed from the American Society for Abrasive Methods in 1975). In addition to an annual technical conference and semi-annual educational seminars, the Society publishes the quarterly *AES Magazine,* circulation 3,000. The industry was also served by smaller organizations, such as the Abrasive Grain Association of Cleveland, the Coated Abrasives Manufacturers Institute of Cleveland, and the Industrial Diamond Manufacturers Association of New York City.

BACKGROUND AND DEVELOPMENT

Abrasives have been vital to making metal products since the earliest days of metallurgy in ancient times, but the modern abrasive products industry arose from the technical developments of the late nineteenth century. These developments involved not only abrasives, but also the binders used to create bonded abrasive products.

A key development for the industry was synthetic abrasives. In 1901, Dr. Acheson synthesized silicon carbide, the first synthetic abrasive grain to attain broad, commercial success. And fused aluminum oxide abrasives, pioneered by C.B. Jacobs in the 1890s, became a commercial product by 1904. Along with the naturally occurring corundum, garnet, and diamond, silicon carbide and fused aluminum oxide dominated the abrasive products market into the 1930s. In 1938, a new technique for producing aluminum oxide was developed, resulting in the most successful abrasive grain for precision grinding that existed to date. In the 1950s, aluminum oxides were produced by nonfusion methods. Fused mixtures of aluminum and zirconium oxides also became commercially viable.

Diamonds gained widespread use as abrasives in the 1930s. This resulted from the creation of the first bonded wheels, using industrial diamonds, and was accelerated by the need for a very hard abrasive to grind tungsten carbide, which became important in the 1930s. Synthetic diamonds were produced in 1960 by General Electric. Along with cubic boron nitride, dia-

monds made up the hardest class of abrasives, known as "superabrasives."

In 1987, aluminum oxide and silicon carbide, the oldest synthetic abrasives, led industry output, with $104 million and $51 million in value consumed, respectively. Ranking next in order of value of materials used were natural abrasive materials ($30 million), diamond ($27 million), aluminum-zirconium oxide ($23 million), and cubic boron nitride ($7 million).

The development of binders for bonded abrasive products, including grinding and buffing wheels and flexible abrasives such as sandpaper, were as important as the development of synthetic fibers. Rubber was used to bond abrasives for grinding wheels in the 1850s. Sand, corundum and diamond bonded by shellac were used to make grinding wheels in India in the early nineteenth century. The shellac process was utilized by the Waltham Emery Wheel Company. Rubber and shellac remained the only organic binders until synthetic resins came about in the 1920s.

Inorganic binders were developed in the late nineteenth century to simulate the properties of sandstone. Key among these were vitrified products commercialized by the Norton Co. of Massachusetts in the late 1800s. In addition to these binders, so-called "active" fillers were used to construct grinding wheels. Active fillers enabled cooler grinding, increased wheel porosity, and increased the uses for grinding wheels.

CURRENT CONDITIONS

Overall, the industry's value of shipments increased from 1982 to 1991, peaking in 1988. The value of shipments stagnated after 1988, declining by nearly $300 million in three years. Capital investments remained fairly strong however, totaling slightly less in 1990 than in peak years 1984 and 1985.

A 1990 study of the industry by the Business Communications Co. Inc. projected annual growth of 4 percent through 1995. Among those materials expected to show declining sales were fused aluminum oxides and metallic abrasives. The use of silicon carbides, aluminum-zirconium oxides, and superabrasives was expected to grow, with the most dramatic growth projected for superabrasives. The market share of superabrasives was projected to increase from 31 percent in 1990 to 36.5 percent in 1995. U.S. firms lagged behind competitors in Europe and the Far East in using high-technology superabrasives.

Theodore L. Giese, business manager of the Abrasive Engineering Society, argued in *AES Magazine* that the industry depended on developing formal education in abrasives technologies. Noting that only two

U.S. universities had recognized programs in these technologies, the University of Connecticut and the University of Massachusetts, Giese wrote, "We have learned that trial-and-error methods for solving problems are inefficient tools for product development and troubleshooting grinding operations. Measurement-oriented strategies such as SPC [statistical process control] are necessary. Control of a grinding operation now requires an understanding of the grinding system and the concepts behind the grinding process. That means . . . a better comprehension of ideas behind the technology we use. All this translates into the need for more education."

In the early 1990s, a cooperative venture between Japanese and American engineers began in an effort to improve industry production methods in both countries. This involved Japanese engineers using facilities at the University of Connecticut's Center for Grinding Research and Development and sharing that knowledge with university staff and students.

INDUSTRY LEADERS

The top firm in the abrasives industry in 1995 was the Norton Co. of Worcester, Massachusetts ($1.5 billion in sales, with 16,500 employees). Next was privately held G.S. Technologies, Inc. of Kansas City, Missouri ($415 million sales, 2400 employees), followed by S.K. Wellman of Solon, Ohio ($60 million sales, 600 employees).

The Norton Company was founded in 1885 and had $1.4 billion in sales in 1992, making it the largest abrasive products maker in the world. The firm had even greater sales and profits in the late 1980s. From one quarter in 1987 to the corresponding quarter in 1988, for example, income from operations rose 91 percent and operating profits rose 77 percent. The firm ran a number of divisions within the industry. Among these were Norton Co. Coated Abrasives of Troy, New York, founded in 1928; Norton Co. Advanced Ceramics of Worcester, Massachusetts; and Norton Co.'s Amplex Corp. of Bloomfield, Connecticut, founded in 1956. In July of 1990, the Compagnie de Saint-Gobain of France bought the majority of Norton's common shares. The French firm also owned Norton-affiliated makers of abrasives and ceramics in Australia, Bermuda, Japan, Germany, Belgium, Luxembourg, the Netherlands, Italy, Spain, Norway, the United Kingdom, Canada, and Brazil. Norton Co. restructured after the buy out by the Compagnie de Saint-Gobain, including $50 million in modernization investments over three years.

WORK FORCE

Employment of production workers declined from 1982 to 1991, and was lower in 1991 than in all of the 1980s except for 1987. Employment prospects for the industry appeared bleak. The Bureau of Labor Statistics made employment forecasts for 30 occupational categories included within the abrasive products industry. Based on projected changes from 1990 to 2005, employment was expected to decline by double-digit figures in 16 occupations and single-digit figures in 11 other occupations.

RESEARCH AND TECHNOLOGY

Much of the research and new technical developments in the industry were related to the increased importance of superabrasives. In *Superabrasive Grinding,* J.L. Metzger summarized future areas of superabrasives development, "Our experience indicates major developments are likely to continue— possibly even to accelerate—in the following areas: (1) New, custom-designed, 'hard-to-grind' materials for an ever widening spectrum of industrial applications; (2) Creep feed grinding, also known as plunge or deep feed grinding; (3) High performance, high-speed grinding of hardened steels with CBN-wheels [cubic boron nitride]; (4) Form or profile grinding, in part with electroplated, in part with crushable wheels, in high removal, high precision, high surface quality applications; (5) CNC-control [computer numerically controlled] of production grinding machines, with, possibly, partial adaptive control optimization." Other developments regarding superabrasives included the use of chemical vapor deposition for optimal bonding of diamond coatings. Flexible belt superabrasive products were advocated over bonded wheel superabrasives for grinding ceramics because flexible products were less likely to chip and crack ceramics.

Additional areas of technical development for the industry included improvements in coated (sandpaper-like) abrasives, such as new backings, adhesives, grains and joint designs (for belt abrasives), and the use of cushioned belts. These improvements made coated abrasives faster and more economical than traditional grinding and cutting techniques for many applications. Substantial research was also undertaken to improve liquid coolants and lubricants used in many grinding operations.

FURTHER READING

Anselment, George. "Guest Editorial." *AES Magazine,* Spring 1991, 30.

Coes, L. Jr. *Abrasives.* New York: Springer-Verlag, 1971.

"Cushioned Abrasives for Off-Hand Finishing." *Metal Finishing,* July 1993.

Daniels, Peggy Kneffel and Carol A. Schwartz, eds. *Encyclopedia of Associations.* 28th ed. Detroit: Gale Research, 1994.

Darnay, Arsen J., ed. *Manufacturing USA: Industry Analysis, Statistics, and Leading Companies* 3rd ed. Detroit: Gale Research, 1993.

"De Beers and GE are Sued." *New York Times,* 5 May 1992.

"Diamond/CBN Industry Shows Change, Growth." *Ceramics Industry,* January 1992.

"Diamonds and Dirt." *Business Week,* 10 August 1992.

Giese, Theodore L. "Editorial." *AES Magazine,* Spring 1992, 31.

"Japanese Scientists Help American Industry." *AES Magazine,* Winter 1991, 30.

Metzger, J.L. *Superabrasive Grinding.* London: Butterworth & Co., 1986.

Moody's Industrial Manual. New York: Moody's Investors Service Inc., 1993.

"Norton Reports Higher Sales and Income." *AES Magazine,* June-July 1988, 27.

"Saint-Gobain Bouscule Norton." *Usine Nouvelle,* 16 July 1992.

Standard and Poor's Register of Corporations, Directors and Executives, vol. 1, New York: Standard and Poor's, 1994.

Subramanian, K. "A Bright Future for Superabrasives." *AES Magazine,* Summer 1991, 30.

"Superabrasive Use to Increase." *AES Magazine,* Spring 1991, 30.

"Superabrasive for Ceramic Grinding, Finishing." *Ceramic Industry,* April 1992.

"Thin-Film Diamond at the Cutting Edge." *Tooling and Production,* July 1993.

U.S. Department of Commerce. *1995 Annual Survey of Manufactures: Statistics for Industry Groups and Industries.* Washington: GPO, 1997.

Visser, R.G. "Grinding with Flexible Superabrasive Products." *AES Magazine,* Summer 1992, 31.

Ward's Business Directory of U.S. Private and Public Companies. Detroit: Gale Research, 1993.

Wellborn, William. "Synthetic Mineral - The Foundation Stone of Modern Abrasive Tools." *AES Magazine,* Spring 1992, 31.

                                    —David Kucera, updated by Dave Fagan

SIC 3292

ASBESTOS PRODUCTS

This category includes companies that primarily make asbestos textiles, asbestos building materials (except asbestos paper), insulating materials for covering boilers and pipes, and other products composed wholly or chiefly of asbestos. Companies that primarily make asbestos paper are in **SIC 2621: Paper Mills.** Those making gaskets and packing materials are in **SIC 3053: Gaskets, Packing, and Sealing Devices.**

INDUSTRY SNAPSHOT

Asbestos use in manufactured products fell dramatically after early 1970s studies linked airborne asbestos fibers to asbestosis, a disease that scars the lungs and makes breathing difficult, and mesothelioma, a rare and deadly form of cancer. The Environmental Protection Agency (EPA) banned the use of spray-on asbestos insulation in 1973, and the U.S. tile and floor-covering industry, once a major consumer, voluntarily stopped asbestos use by 1986. According to the Census Bureau, the value of asbestos products made in the United States in 1990 was about $352 million. By 1995, sales fell so low that there were no figures available.

In 1989, the EPA ruled to eliminate all asbestos use in the United States by 1996. However, the ban was declared unreasonable by the federal courts, which permitted asbestos use in products imported or made in the United States as of July, 1989. The courts upheld an EPA ban on any new products with asbestos.

By 1994, fewer than 50 U.S. companies made products with asbestos. The majority made friction products for automobile brakes. The rest made roofing materials, heat-resistant gaskets, and safety clothing. Most of the asbestos used by U.S. manufacturers was chrysotile asbestos imported from Canada.

BACKGROUND AND DEVELOPMENT

Asbestos is a group of soft minerals composed of tiny fibers that is nearly impervious to acid, fire, and biological decay, and is a poor conductor of heat and electricity. During the late 1800s, when it was first widely used to insulate boilers, steam pipes, and other high-temperature industrial equipment, asbestos became known as "white gold," especially in Canada, which was the world's leading supplier.

Since 1900, asbestos was used in more than 3,000 products made in the United States, from safety clothing and automobile brake linings to textured paints and electrical insulation. The most extensive use of asbestos was as construction insulation. The United States used thousands of tons of asbestos insulation in ships built during World War II. Another surge in asbestos insulation use was in the 1960s when it was routinely sprayed on structural beams and roof decks. In the mid-1970s, the United States used an estimated 700,000 tons of asbestos per year, most of it in insulation products.

Health concerns. The ancient Greeks first noticed a link between asbestos and respiratory illness. However, the first medical studies were not done until the early 1900s when asbestos use became widespread. When asbestos's hook-shaped fibers are inhaled, they attach to the insides of the lungs. The body reacts by covering the fibers with proteins. As this scar tissue increases, the lungs clog and lose elasticity. The scarring and resulting respiratory problems are called asbestosis. Evidence also suggested prolonged exposure to asbestos increased the risk of cancer, including mesothelioma, which affects the visceral membranes. Asbestos exposure also greatly increased the risk of lung cancer for cigarette smokers.

In 1931, Great Britain became the first country to pass laws regulating exposure to asbestos. (The United States did not pass similar laws until the early 1970s.) In the 1960s, Dr. Irving Selikoff, an epidemiologist at Mount Sinai Hospital in New York, studied the incidence of respiratory diseases in men who had worked in the asbestos industry or in the shipyards during World War II. Selikoff also noted more respiratory problems in wives who shook asbestos dust out of their husbands' work clothes. Selikoff's controversial conclusion was that no level of exposure to asbestos was safe. However, later studies disputed Selikoff's conclusions. In the late 1980s, the United Kingdom Health and Safety Commission concluded the long-term risk to office workers in a building with asbestos insulation

was so low it was comparable to inhaling one puff of cigarette smoke every day for a lifetime.

Federal regulation. The United States began regulating industrial exposure to asbestos dust in the early 1970s. In 1986 the EPA declared, "no level of exposure to asbestos is without risk," and tried to ban asbestos use in consumer products. The EPA order would have phased out almost all use of asbestos by 1996. However, The Asbestos Institute, supported by the Canadian asbestos-mining industry, filed a petition for review of the ban with the U.S. Court of Appeals. In 1991 the court ruled the ban was unreasonable.

In its ruling, the court said the EPA overstepped its authority by trying to ban all asbestos use and failed to consider the financial costs and health risks posed by asbestos substitutes. The court said many proposed substitutes "actually may increase the risk of injury Americans face." For example, the court said there was "credible evidence that non-asbestos brakes could increase significantly the number of highway fatalities." The court found, based on the EPA's own studies, "a complete ban would save less than one statistical life [over] 13 years."

Under the court ruling, affirmed in 1993, U.S. companies could keep making asbestos products that were either imported or manufactured in the United States at the time the EPA announced the ban in 1989. The court let stand an EPA ban on new uses of asbestos or asbestos products.

Johns-Manville Corporation. The Johns-Manville Corporation was created in 1901 from the merger of two asbestos products companies. In 1969, Clarence Borel, a laborer who had spent more than 30 years installing asbestos insulation, sued Johns-Manville and other asbestos products makers alleging they knowingly manufactured a hazardous product *(Borel v. Fibreboard Paper Products Company, et al)*. Borel,

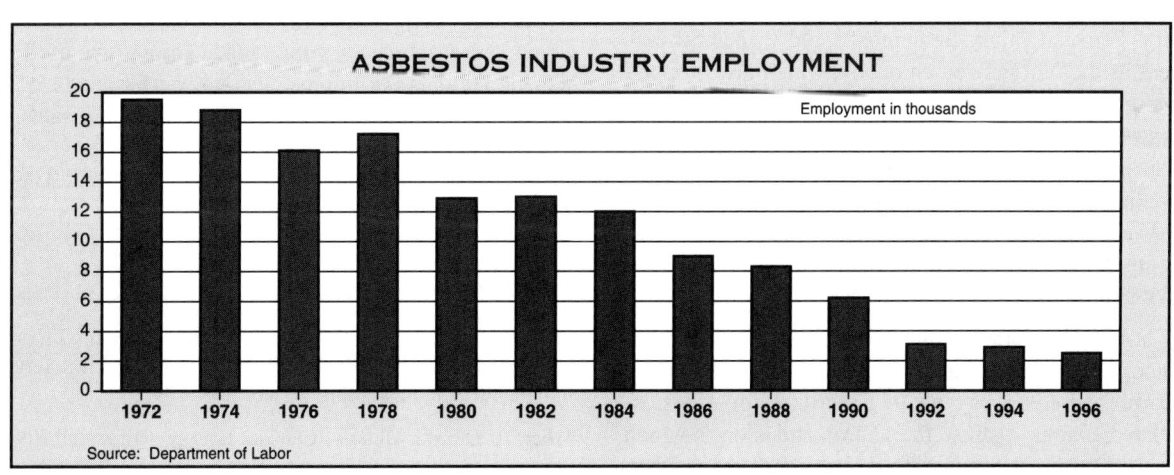

who suffered from asbestosis, testified that in all his years as an installer, no one had ever told him asbestos could make him ill.

In addition to Johns-Manville, the suit named the Pittsburgh Corning Corp., Owens-Corning Fiberglass Corp., Union Asbestos & Rubber Co., Combustion Engineering Inc., Eagle-Picher Industries Inc., the Philip Carey Corp., Armstrong Contracting & Supply Corp., Rubberoid Co., and the Standard Asbestos Manufacturing & Insulation Co. Those companies testified that most laborers knew the dangers but refused to wear breathing masks provided by insulation contractors. As the industry leader, Johns-Manville argued that it put warning labels on its products starting in 1964, as soon as it had sufficient evidence installation workers were at risk.

The jury found both Borel and the asbestos-products companies guilty of negligence. More importantly, Borel died in 1970 before the verdict was rendered, and the jury found the asbestos-products companies liable for his death. The jury awarded Borel's widow nearly $80,000. The U.S. Court of Appeals upheld the decision in 1973, and found Johns-Manville and the other defendants could have foreseen the dangers to Borel "at the time the products causing Borel's injuries were sold." That ruling opened the floodgates to litigation. By 1981, more than 16,000 lawsuits were filed against Johns-Manville. Most of the suits were filed by insulation workers and people who worked in the shipyards during World War II. Johns-Manville put the projected costs of the lawsuits at $2 billion—twice the company's assets at the time—and in 1982, the company filed for protection under Chapter 11 of the U.S. Bankruptcy Code. It was the largest U.S. corporation to ever file for bankruptcy.

Johns-Manville filed a plan for reorganization in 1983. As part of the plan, the company, which changed its name to the Manville Corporation, established a trust fund to pay for asbestos-related claims. The Manville Personal Injury Settlement Fund owned 80 percent of the reorganized company, which also stopped using asbestos. Initially, the trust fund held $1 billion. However, as the number of claims increased—to more than 200,000 by 1993—the fund was increased to almost $3 billion. Because asbestosis and other asbestos-related diseases develop over time, the Rand Corp. estimated claims against Manville and other asbestos companies could reach more than $50 billion.

After a decade of court battles, in 1993, two insurance companies, Chubb Corp. and CNA Financial Corp., agreed to pay up to $3 billion for asbestos-related claims against the Fibreboard Corp., which spun off from Louisiana-Pacific in 1988. More than 145,000 people claimed to have been harmed by Fibreboard products. The decision was expected to keep Fibreboard from declaring bankruptcy. However, at least a dozen other asbestos-products companies declared bankruptcy due to asbestos litigation along with Johns-Manville, including National Gypsum Co., Celotex Corp., and Eagle-Picher.

CURRENT CONDITIONS

In 1993, the EPA issued a report on what products were permitted under the court ruling. These included asbestos clothing, roofing materials, gaskets, and friction products for automotive use including brakes, brake linings, and clutch facings. Friction products accounted for about 70 percent of asbestos used by U.S. manufacturers. These products concerned the appeals court because automobile makers testified non-asbestos-lined brakes were less reliable, especially for trucks and heavier cars. The appeals court found there was "credible evidence that non-asbestos brakes could increase significantly the number of highway fatalities." After the court ruling, the EPA asked car makers to switch to non-asbestos brakes voluntarily by 1994, but no major manufacturers agreed to do so in 1993.

Asbestos in products allowed by the court order was considered "locked-in" or "encapsulated," and not considered a health risk. Asbestos fibers in friction products were mixed with various binders and only a small amount were released into the air during normal use. Auto repair shops used special equipment to sweep asbestos fibers from the air. The asbestos fibers in roofing materials and gaskets were surrounded by asphalt, latex, rubber, or other resilient material.

According to *Ward's Business Dictionary* at least two large companies still used some asbestos in their products as of 1995. The largest was Ray Tech Corp. of Shelton, Connecticut ($168 million annual sales, with 1,200 employees), which made automotive products including brake-linings. Second was Garland Co., Inc. of Cleveland, Ohio ($40 million in annual sales, 200 employees) which made a modified bitumen roofing material the company says has, "excellent UV resistance [and] fire retardance".

FURTHER READING

Anderson, Walter D. "Comments of the Resilient Floor Covering Institute." Washington, DC: Occupational Safety and Health Administration, 3 December 1990.

Asbestos, Ottawa, Ontario, Canada: Energy, Mines and Resources Canada, 1986.

"Asbestos: Manufacture, Importation, Processing, and Distribution in Commerce Prohibitions; Final Rule." *Federal Register,* 12 July 1989.

"Asbestos Production: The Chrysotile Crisis?" *Industrial Materials,* May 1992, 41.

Brodeur, Paul. *Outrageous Misconduct: The Asbestos Industry on Trial,* New York: Pantheon Books, 1985.

Chrysotile Asbestos: A Material for Today and Tomorrow. Ministry of Energy and Resources, Government of Quebec, 1986.

"Erecting a Firewall Against Asbestos." *U.S. News & World Report,* 17 July 1989, 10.

Galen, Michele. "The Man Who's Cutting Through the Asbestos Mess." *Business Week,* 28 January 1991, 71.

Garland Co., Inc. website. Available from http://www.garlandco.com.

Guidry, Lori L. "Asbestos: Tarnished 'White Gold.'" *Current Health,* February 1988, 28.

"Manville Corporation." *International Directory of Company Histories.* Vol. 7. Detroit: St. James Press, 1993, 291.

Mannin, Margaret. "The Asbestos Dilemma." *U.S. News & World Report,* 11 January 1991, 57.

Pigg, B. J. "The Uses of Chrysotile." Asbestos Information Association, November 1993.

Powell, Bill. "The Case for Asbestos" *Newsweek,* 29 September 1986, 40.

Richmond, Louis S. "Why Throw Money at Asbestos." *Fortune,* 6 June 1988, 57.

Sentes, Ray. "Poisonous Pits." *Canadian Dimension,* April/May 1990, 43.

Solomon, Stephen. "The Asbestos Fallout at Johns-Manville." *Fortune,* 7 May 1979, 196.

—Dean Boyer, updated by Dave Fagan

SIC 3295

MINERALS AND EARTHS, GROUND OR OTHERWISE TREATED

This category includes establishments operating without a mine or quarry and primarily engaged in crushing, grinding, pulverizing, or otherwise preparing clay, ceramic, and refractory minerals; barite; and miscellaneous nonmetallic minerals, excluding fuels. These minerals are the crude products mined by establishments of Industry Groups 145 (clay, ceramic, and refractory minerals) and 149 (miscellaneous nonmetallic minerals, except fuels), and by those mining barite in **SIC 1479: Chemical and Fertilizer Mineral Mining, Not Elsewhere Classified.** Also included in

this category are establishments primarily crushing slag and preparing roofing granules. The improvement or preparation of the minerals and metallic ores and the cleaning and grading of coal are classified in Mining, whether or not the operation is associated with a mine.

Products in this classification include barium, blast furnace slag, clay for petroleum refining, ground clay, activated clay desiccants, diatomaceous earth, filtering clays, Fuller's earth, kaolin, black lead, mica, pulverized earth, pumice roofing granules, talc, and vermiculite. The value of shipments in this industry tended to spike up and down throughout the 1980s and 1990s, dropping as low as $1.17 billion in 1985 and rising as high as $1.85 billion in 1993. In 1995 the value of shipments was $1.80 billion.

No single product dominated this industry, with no product taking more than 13 percent of the market. In 1996, lightweight aggregate held the largest share of the market, at 13.2 percent, followed closely by crushed slag at 8.8 percent, dead-burned magnesia at 5.8 percent, and natural graphite at 4.5 percent. A wide range of other materials and earths held the remaining 58.5 percent of the market. Kaolin was one of the biggest products within the industry in both intake and output, with kaolin being an ingredient in several products. Once the kaolin was processed it was sent to many different industries, with a wide range of products. The biggest consumer in 1995 was the fiberglass industry, taking 29.3 percent of the kaolin. Rubber and elastomeric industries took the next highest share at 25.6 percent. Sanitaryware and filler or extender each took about 13 percent, and refractories took 6 percent. Dinnerware accounted for 3 percent, ceramic tile took 2 percent, and electrical porcelain took 1 percent. The remaining 7 percent went to miscellaneous products.

The products produced by this industry tend to have a relatively low value compared to their weight. As a result of the weight of these products, truck transportation, warehousing, and rail transportation accounted for the highest percentage of the inputs used by the minerals and earths industry in the 1990s. The raw materials accounted for the next highest percentage of all inputs. The power required to process ground mineral and earth products were also important inputs, with gas and electric utilities accounting for another high percentage of all inputs.

The production of ground minerals and earths was concentrated in five states, with Pennsylvania, Ohio, Illinois, Louisiana, and California accounting for 30.2 percent of all product shipments. Pennsylvania was the largest single producing state, with 7.6 percent of the total and $134.5 million in shipments. The leading companies in the ground minerals and earths industry include Eagle-Picher Industries; Engelhard Corp.; Edward C. Levy Co.; ECC International; and Oil-Dri Corp. Of America. Many of these companies operate out of the southeastern and midwestern United States, where abundant supplies of clay (kaolin) are located. This industry employed an estimated 9,400 people in 1996—the same it's been since 1993. The total industry payroll in 1996 was $312.1 million, with an average hourly wage of $14.10.

FURTHER READING

Darnay, Arsen J., ed. *Manufacturing USA.* 5th ed. Detroit: Gale Research, 1996.

Lazich, Robert S., ed. *Market Share Reporter.* Detroit: Gale Research, 1997.

U.S. Department of Commerce. Bureau of the Census. *1995 Survey of Manufactures.* Washington: GPO, 1997.

SIC 3296

MINERAL WOOL

This category includes companies that make mineral wool and mineral wool insulation products made of such siliceous materials as rock, slag, glass, or combinations of these. Companies that primarily make asbestos insulation products are classified in **SIC 3292: Asbestos Products,** and those making textile glass fibers are classified in **SIC 3229: Pressed and Blown Glass and Glassware, Not Elsewhere Classified.**

This industry's products include mineral wool acoustical board and tile; fiberglass insulation; glass wool; mineral wool roofing mats; and insulation made of rock wool, slag, and silica minerals. The value of industry shipments grew relatively steadily throughout the 1980s, from $2.3 billion in 1982 to a peak of $3.4 billion in 1988. However, the mineral wool industry—like others in the United States—was hit hard by a major recession in 1989; and by 1991, the industry's value of shipments had fallen back to $3.1 billion. By 1995, the industry rebounded with total shipments of $3.96 billion.

This industry produced two major product categories: mineral wool for thermal and acoustical envelope insulation, which was 69.3 percent of the market in 1987; and mineral wool for industrial, equipment, and appliance insulation, which accounted for 25 percent.

Within the first category, batt, blanket, and roll insulation products had the largest market share at 35 percent of industry output in 1987. This area includes the familiar fiberglass insulation found in residential attics. Fiberglass insulation use in the upper stories and ceilings of homes varies by type. In 1991, batts accounted for 44 percent of all installations, while blown fiberglass was second at 43 percent. Other forms accounted for the remaining 13 percent. Acoustical mineral wool holds the next highest market share in the mineral wool industry at 19.1 percent.

Within the second major category—industrial, equipment, and appliance insulation—sales are spread among four categories: special purpose insulation pieces (9 percent), other (4.9 percent), flexible blankets (4.5 percent), and pipe insulation (3.73 percent).

Power requirements were the single biggest raw material purchased by this industry. In 1982, gas utilities accounted for 11.5 percent of all inputs, while electric utilities were another 9.7 percent. Other major inputs included: wholesale trade (7.7 percent); cyclic crudes and organics (6.5 percent); miscellaneous inorganic chemicals (5.2 percent); paper products, including kraft paper backing for fiberglass bats (4 percent); plastics (3.8 percent); and mineral wool (3.5 percent).

Because home insulation is a consumer product, advertising—such as the "Pink Panther" television spots for Owens-Corning Fiberglas Corp. products—made up 2.2 percent of inputs. New insulation for existing buildings was the largest use of mineral wool in 1982, accounting for 16.1 percent of production. New residential construction was the second largest user, consuming 11.5 percent, followed by insulation added later to homes (7.7 percent). Other major sectors buying mineral wool products were office buildings (7.6 percent of production), exports (5.8 percent), home remodeling (5.1 percent), and machinery, not elsewhere classified (4.1 percent). More than 30 other sectors—mostly manufacturing and construction—use mineral wool.

As of the early 1990s, mineral wool makers operated mostly in Georgia, California, Pennsylvania, Indiana, Texas, and New Jersey. Owens-Corning of Toledo, Ohio, was the leading manufacturer of mineral wool, with 1995 sales of $3.61 billion and approximately 17,300 employees. The company was also the leading U.S. maker of industrial asphalt and residential roof shingles. Owens-Corning had 83 manufacturing plants worldwide as of 1997, including 4 in China, and seemed well-positioned for expanding in a global economy.

The next leading company was Schuller Corp. of Denver, Colorado, with 1995 sales of $1.39 billion and approximately 7,500 employees. Schuller also made building insulation and roofing materials, plus mats for reinforcing flooring and roofing. The company's former name was Manville Corp. but changed its name due to decades worth of pending asbestos claims. Many older companies in this category made products with asbestos over the years and have ongoing problems with asbestos-related claims.

Employment for the industry remained stable throughout the 1980s, dropping from 19,700 in 1982 to 19,000 in 1990. In 1990, the mineral wool industry had a payroll of $582.5 million and an average hourly wage of $14.21. In 1995, approximately 20,000 people worked in the industry, with a total payroll of $718 million.

FURTHER READING

Darnay, Arsen J. *Manufacturing USA,* 5th ed. Detroit: Gale Research, 1996.

Darnay, Arsen J. and Marlita A. Reddy. *Market Share Reporter 1996,* Detroit: Gale Research, 1996.

Hoover's Company Capsules, Austin, TX: Hoover's, Inc., 1997. Available from http://www.hoovers.com.

U.S. Department of Commerce. *1995 Annual Survey of Manufactures: Statistics for Industry Groups and Industries.* Washington: GPO, 1997.

U.S. Industrial Outlook 1994. Washington: U.S. Department of Commerce, 1994.

—Alan Rooks, updated by Dave Fagan

SIC 3297

NONCLAY REFRACTORIES

This category includes establishments primarily engaged in manufacturing refractories and crucibles made of materials other than clay. This industry includes establishments primarily engaged in manufacturing all graphite refractories, whether of carbon bond or ceramic bond. Establishments primarily engaged in manufacturing clay refractories are classified in **SIC 3255: Clay Refractories.**

As defined in this industry's description, a refractory is a product such as brick that is resistant to intense heat. Some of the main uses of refractories are to create fire-resistant construction materials for industrial buildings and to create crucibles. Crucibles are vessels made of a substance that will withstand extreme heat and are used for melting metals or minerals. Another use of refractories is to create furnaces and other devices. While those are the biggest divisions within the industry, refractories are used for a wide variety of industries, from boiler combustion chambers

and incinerators to rotary kilns and mine ore dryers. Generally, refractory products are needed where commercial production processes exceed temperatures of 700 degrees Fahrenheit.

This industry includes establishments primarily engaged in manufacturing all graphite refractories, whether of carbon or ceramic bond. Products produced by the nonclay refractories industry include: alumina-fused refractories; bauxite brick; carbon brick; refractory brick; nonclay castable refractories; high temperature cement; magnesia cement; crucibles made of graphite, chrome, silica, or other nonclay materials; dolomite brick; nonclay gunning mixes; nonclay plastics refractories; nonclay refractory cement; and pyrolytic graphite.

The value of shipments in this industry grew dramatically through most of the 1980s, from $691 million in 1982 to $954.5 million in 1987 and $1.11 billion 1989. By 1996, the industry's value of shipments continued to grow to an estimated $1.41 billion, recovering from a U.S. recession in the early 1990s that hurt overall sales. The iron and steel industry accounted for about one-half of the U.S. refractory market, and steel and refractory production actually parallel each other.

Materials, ingredients, containers, and supplies were by far the largest category of materials consumed by the nonclay refractories industry in 1995, with an estimated delivered cost of $455.6 million. The next highest category—clay, ceramic, and refractory minerals—cost the industry $143.9 million, while dead-burned magnesia or magnesite had a delivered cost of $54.4 million. Clay or nonclay refractories accounted for another $60.4 million worth of materials. Miscellaneous products, components, ingredients, parts, containers, and supplies cost the industry a total of $177.5 million.

Monolithic refractories—those that do not have to be fired—account for about 50 percent of the market. Castables, plastics, and gunning mixes are the most popular of the nonfiring refractories, with new mixes, such as alumina-carbon and alumina-silica, creating stronger and longer lasting refractories. All refractories have to be replaced eventually, but, because of refractories improvements, the rate at which they are replaced is diminishing. Also, as the steel industry continues to change, refractory manufacturers need to constantly adapt.

The nonclay refractories industry is concentrated in two states—Ohio and Pennsylvania—which accounted for an estimated 41.6 percent of all U.S. production in 1996. The leading companies in this industry are relatively small niche manufacturers. In the mid-1990s, none had sales over $160 million, and all but two had sales under $70 million. Leading companies include: J.E. Baker Co. of York, Pennsylvania, with $160 million in revenues; MINTEQ International, Inc. of New York, with $140 million; and C-E Minerals, Inc., of King of Prussia, Pennsylvania, with $70 million.

Unlike many other American industries, the nonclay refractories industry increased employment during the 1980s, moving from 6,800 people in 1982 to 8,500 in 1989. By 1994, the work force began dropping to only 7,500 workers. The work force was also expected to decline through 2005. All types of occupations, from labor to top executives, were expected to decline by about 20 percent, with extruding and forming machine workers estimated to plunge by 80 percent. Only hand painting, coating, and decorating workers were expected to grow by about 50 percent. On average, workers in this industry made $14.49 an hour in 1994—slightly higher than an average of all manufacturing, which was $12.09.

FURTHER READING

Anderson, George. "An Introduction to Industrial Refractories." *George Anderson's Home Page.* 1 February 1997. Available from http://vanbc.wimsey.com/~gandersn/refrac.html.

Darnay, Arsen J., ed. *Manufacturing USA.* 5th ed. Detroit: Gale Research, 1996.

Heine, Hans J. "Refractories Revisited: A Review and Outlook." *Foundry.* March 1996, 44-52.

U.S. Department of Commerce. *U.S. Industrial Outlook 1993.* Washington: GPO, 1993.

SIC 3299

NONMETALLIC MINERAL PRODUCTS, NOT ELSEWHERE CLASSIFIED

This category is comprised of firms that manufacture goods made from plaster of paris, papier-maché, sand lime, and other miscellaneous nonmetallic mineral products. Examples of industry output include synthetic stones, clay and plaster plaques, architectural plaster work, plaster of paris sculptures, miniature gypsum images, plaster of paris flower boxes, and gypsum urns.

Markets for miscellaneous nonmetallic mineral products are extremely fragmented. The largest single industry product category is statuary and art goods,

which accounted for about 17 percent of industry output during the mid-1990s. The largest consumer of this industry's offerings is the nonferrous wire-drawing industry, which uses tubing made from quartz to produce electrical wire. Other major consumers include fabricated rubber product manufacturers and motor and generator makers, who also use quartz tubing. About 9 percent of production was exported in the mid-1990s.

The industry is relatively low-tech and manufactures many commodity-like products. The average amount of value contributed per production worker was about 65 percent lower than the U.S. manufacturing average in the early 1990s. Likewise, capital investment per employee represented 72 percent of the national manufacturing average. As a result, many producers of nonmetallic mineral products were highly susceptible to competition from low-cost foreign producers.

U.S. sales of miscellaneous nonmetallic mineral products topped $400 million in the early 1980s. During the mid-1980s, however, shipment growth slowed compared to the 1960s and 1970s. Although domestic demand for products such as electrical wiring and art supplies increased, foreign competition reduced profit opportunities in many sectors. Revenues increased at a tepid 5 percent annually between 1982 and 1990, slightly lagging behind inflation. Furthermore, a U.S. recession in the late 1980s and early 1990s stalled expansion—annual sales hovered around $650 million to $700 million. General economic improvement in the mid-1990s, as well as a boost in new commercial and residential construction, led to increased demand for electrical wire, which helped the industry resume average growth to over $900 million in sales in 1995.

About 500 companies competed in the industry in the mid-1990s. The majority of the top 25 firms generated revenues of less than $25 million per year. The industry leader was Carborundum Corp., of Niagara Falls, New York, with around $340 million in sales and about 3,200 employees. Ranking second was Hoechst CeramTec North, of Massachusetts, which had sales of about $170 million, and 1,800 employees. Other industry leaders included Carbo Ceramics Inc., of Irving, Texas, and Pabco, of Houston.

In the mid-1990s, there was significant development in the area of advanced materials such as ceramic fibers. Ceramic fibers are used primarily in composite materials, which are lighter, stronger, and more heat-resistant than pure ceramics or metals. In 1997, the market introduced "core-sheath" ceramic fibers, which are the result of a new process called biocomponent extrusion that increases strength, heat resistance, and efficiency in production. The new fibers provide advantages to end users such as auto and aircraft industries, which use composite materials in high-tech applications such as jet engines.

Miscellaneous nonmetallic mineral product manufacturers employed a work force of about 9,000 in the mid-1990s. The average annual salary for production workers was $19,400, about 75 percent of the national manufacturing average. Future prospects for employment in this industry are generally dismal, as positions for most laborers will likely decline by 15-20 percent between 1996 and 2005, according to the Bureau of Labor Statistics.

FURTHER READING

Darnay, Arsen J., ed. *Manufacturing USA*. 5th ed. Detroit: Gale Research, 1996.

"Spinning a Tough Yarn." *Financial Times*, 17 January 1997, 16.

U.S. Department of Commerce. Economics and Statistics Administration. Bureau of the Census. *1995 Annual Survey of Manufactures*. Washington: GPO, 1997. Available from http://www.census.gov/prod/www/titles.html#mm.

U.S. Department of Commerce. International Trade Administration. *U.S. Industrial Outlook 1994.*

PRIMARY METAL INDUSTRIES

STEEL WORKS, BLAST FURNACES (INCLUDING COKE OVENS), AND ROLLING MILLS

This classification includes establishments primarily engaged in manufacturing hot metal, pig iron, and silvery pig iron from iron ore and iron and steel scrap; converting pig iron, scrap iron, and scrap steel into steel; and in hot-rolling iron and steel into basic shapes, such as plates, sheets, strips, rods, bars, and tubing. Merchant blast furnaces and by-product or beehive coke ovens are also included in this industry. Establishments primarily engaged in manufacturing ferrous and nonferrous additive alloys by electrometallurgical processes are classified in **SIC 3313: Electrometallurgical Products, Except Steel.**

INDUSTRY SNAPSHOT

The first steel mill in North America was built in the 1600s, making the industry one of the oldest in the country. By 1996, 79 U.S. steel companies employed about 171,000 people, shipped about $65 billion worth of products, and produced more than 103 million tons of steel. With domestic shipments rising nearly 3 percent, U.S. steel mills ran flat out for the fourth consecutive year. Low-cost producers continued to grab big pieces of the rich domestic market for conventional steel. The automotive industry alone consumed in excess of 11.2 million tons of steel in 1995, and U.S. companies exported 7.1 million tons. In particular, exports of hot-rolled steel to the Far East reversed the usual trend of imports from that region.

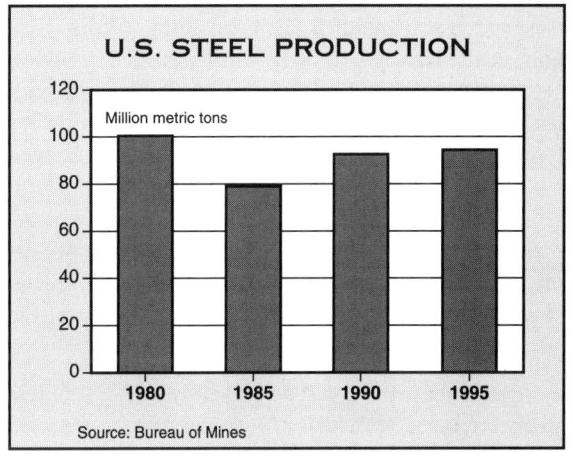

U.S. STEEL PRODUCTION

Source: Bureau of Mines

Despite its impressive size, the steel industry began declining in the mid-1970s and suffered a devastating depression between 1982 and 1986. After peaking in 1978 at over 137 million tons, U.S. steel production slipped to less than 90 million tons in 1991. Anemic market growth, expensive labor, increased production costs, and stagnant prices pummeled many manufacturers in the industry. In addition, the proliferation of foreign competition and the popularity of substitute materials, such as plastics and aluminum, gouged industry profits.

In response to a more competitive environment, the U.S. steel industry continued to restructure itself in the early 1990s. By 1993, new production techniques and facilities, as well as increased automation, had made U.S. steelmakers among the most productive in the world. Nevertheless, the economic slowdown in the late 1980s and early 1990s, coupled with the problems mentioned above, cast doubt on the future of most steelmakers. While more steel is being produced, the top seven companies reported a drop in the price per ton from \$43 in 1995 to \$25 in 1996. The likely glut in sheet steel, for instance, has forced companies to look for markets elsewhere, making each company a specialist in particular steel products.

ORGANIZATION AND STRUCTURE

Steel companies are involved in the manufacture of hot metal, pig iron, and silvery pig iron from iron ore, iron, and steel scrap. They are also involved in converting pig iron, scrap iron, and scrap steel into steel as well as hot-rolling iron and steel into plates, sheets, strips, and bars. These end products are purchased by companies in other industries, which usually shape and manipulate the steel to create finished products.

Products offered by steelmakers are classified into five categories according to the manner in which they were processed and their chemical compositions. Carbon steels are used mostly for flat rolled products because of their high malleability. Machines, auto bodies, ships, and building structures are made with this type of steel. In fact, carbon steels accounted for about 54 percent of all U.S. steel production in the 1990s. Alloy steels, which made up about 10 percent of the market, integrate elements into steel to enhance its physical properties. Corrosion resistance, greater strength, and increased conductivity are a few of the advantages offered by some alloys.

In comparison to carbon and alloy steels, stainless steels are highly resistant to rust and may be stronger or offer resistance to temperature changes. Accounting for 4.7 percent of the steel market volume, stainless steel is often used in pipes, tanks, and in the medical field. Tool steels and high-strength low alloy (HSLA) steels accounted for less than 1 percent of industry production, combined. They are used in applications in which strength and weight are critical.

Integrated Manufacturers vs. Minimills. Steel manufacturers can be divided into two camps—traditional integrated mills and non-integrated "minimills." Integrated steel mills undertake every step of the steel making process. These facilities typically begin by converting mixtures of iron ore, limestone, and coke (made from coal) into molten iron using a blast furnace. Basic oxygen furnaces (BOFs) are next used to convert the molten iron into steel, which is then cast into ingots. Ingots are then shaped into slabs, billets, or blooms of steel.

Increasing numbers of integrated mills in the early 1990s were using a process called continuous casting to bypass the production of ingots and cast billets, slabs, and blooms directly from molten iron. Com-

pared to the old ingot teeming process, continuous casting is less complicated and yields a superior product. In this process, molten steel from a furnace is quickly carried in a ladle directly to a refractory lined container, or tundish, at the top of the caster. The molten metal is then poured into the tundish, which feeds it continuously into the caster, the core of which is water-cooled mold open at both ends. When molten steel enters one end of the mold and cools, a "skin" of metal forms around a liquid core. The material leaves the other end of the machine and is further cooled by water sprays, solidifying the metal. Continuous casting cuts time, consume less energy, and increases yield. It has been estimated that it cuts operating costs by about \$30 a ton. Steelmakers next convert the finished, or semi-finished, steel into rolls, plates, bars, tubes, rails, or other more marketable products, especially for the auto industry, at a rolling mill. In 1995, every major U.S. manufacturer relied on continuous casting.

In the early 1990s, minimills, or non-integrated facilities, were using the same process as integrated mills with a few exceptions. Rather than process base materials—iron ore, coke, and limestone—minimills typically start with scrap iron or steel. The scrap, melted in an electric arc furnace (EAF), rather than a blast or basic oxygen furnace, is continuously cast into blooms and billets. Minimills typically produced fewer finished products than integrated mills. Although many manufacturers were broadening their offerings to include steel pipes, plates, and sheets, most minimills emphasized rods and bars used in light construction.

Minimills are capable of producing from 150,000 to 2 million tons of steel per year. In contrast, most integrated mills can generate 2 to 4 million tons per year. Minimills are also typically able to produce steel at a much lower cost than their larger cousins. Because minimills do not have to be located near supplies of raw ingredients, for instance, they are able to operate closer to their customers, thus reducing product transport costs. In addition, more minimills are located in the southern United States and benefit from less expensive, non-union labor. Integrated mills, on the other hand, employ union labor. Union contracts prevent integrated companies from reducing compensation costs when production declines due to downturns in demand. Furthermore, minimills are more likely to employ more advanced technology, such as continuous casting and EAFs, that reduce production costs and improve quality.

Competitive Structure. In 1992, integrated steelmakers accounted for approximately 75 percent of U.S. steel industry production. At that time, the industry was relatively concentrated and imposed formidable entry barriers, such as high start-up costs and intense competition. The top 75 competitors in the industry, for instance, dominated over 90 percent of the market in 1991, with about $55 billion in shipments. Furthermore, the top 6 firms in the industry accounted for about 40 percent of shipments, or $25 billion worth of product. In 1995, integrated steelmakers accounted for only 59.6 percent of U.S. steel production, with the top three accounting for 28.6 percent of the U.S. total.

On average, minimills realized about $500 in capital costs per ton of steel produced, while integrated mills incurred about $2,000 per ton. Likewise, during the mid-1980s and early 1990s, minimills generated about $32 in operating profit per ton of steel, compared to just $3 per ton for integrated mills. Minimills also shipped an average of 752 tons per employee during that period, compared with 381 tons per worker for integrated producers.

Service and distribution centers consumed 21 to 23 percent of U.S. steel production in 1995. The largest steel customer that built consumer products was the automobile industry, which used 13.5 million tons in 1995, or about 16 percent of total steel production. The construction industry purchased about 11.7 million tons of steel in 1995, and machinery manufacturers used about 2 million tons. Other large steel consumers included oil and gas companies with 2.7 million tons, container manufacturers with 3.8 million tons, and various commercial equipment producers with .7 million tons.

BACKGROUND AND DEVELOPMENT

The U.S. steel industry originated in 1645 in Massachusetts, when Saugus ironworks was established. By the beginning of the eighteenth century iron making was underway in almost every other colony. Despite English parliamentary acts that tried to restrict the burgeoning industry, manufacturers in North America continued to build new iron mills, and eventually finished steel mills, throughout the 1700s. Iron production in this early period entailed the use of charcoal fuel or water power, along with a small labor force, to melt iron ore in a blast furnace. Entrepreneurs could start a mill with several hundred dollars. By 1800, approximately 84,000 tons of iron were being produced in North America.

The production process changed very little throughout the 1800s, although advances in transportation freed the industry from many geographical constraints. Toward the end of the 1800s, however, the structure of the industry changed as it became more

concentrated and the number of firms dwindled. It was during this era that many of the great steel magnates and companies were born, such as Andrew Carnegie, Henry Clay Frick, Bethlehem Steel, and Illinois Steel Company. It was also during this time that the first steel import tariffs and trade associations were instigated. Many bitter and deadly labor disputes rocked the industry during the late 1800s and early 1900s.

In the early 1900s, the development of the open hearth furnace (OHF) made it possible for companies to produce higher quality steel and to use scrap metal in the production process. Improved steel quality was an important advantage for firms that were striving to serve the needs of the new automobile industry. Indeed, the massive growth in demand for new steel during the early 1900s, particularly in the 1920s, was a boon to the industry. After suffering setbacks during the Great Depression, when over 50 percent of U.S. steel production capacity stood idle, steel markets expanded significantly throughout World War II.

In the 30 years following the World War II, U.S. steelmakers dominated the global steel industry. In addition to the fact that many European and Japanese producers had been stifled by damage during the war, U.S. plants were technologically superior. Additionally, U.S. facilities were also an average of more than three times larger than those in other industrialized nations. In 1950 over 45 percent of the world's raw steel was produced in the United States. American firms produced about 90 million tons of steel, compared to about 30 million tons and less than 5 million tons produced by Europe and Japan, respectively.

Because U.S. firms enjoyed great economies of scale and technological supremacy, their steelworkers were by far the highest paid in the world. U.S. manufacturers enjoyed immediate access to the fastest growing economy in the industrialized world. These and other factors helped to push U.S. steel production from around 90 million tons in 1950 to nearly 140 million tons by the 1970s. Although the U.S. steel industry maintained a significant lead over the European Community (EC) and Japan from the 1950s through the 1970s, companies in those two regions gained quickly on their U.S. counterparts. By 1970, the EC and Japan were producing about 120 million and 90 million tons of steel per year, respectively.

Despite its size and its rapid growth, the U.S. steel industry began experiencing problems in the 1960s and 1970s. In addition to high labor costs, slowing growth in domestic markets, and a declining world market share, the industry was also beginning to pay the price for failing to invest the resources necessary to maintain its technological lead. Most companies, for example, had been slow to convert their operations to more productive basic oxygen furnaces (BOFs), which were replacing the old OHFs. Indeed, by the mid-1970s it was clear that U.S. companies had lost their leadership role in world steel markets—despite a flurry of capital investment by steelmakers in the late 1960s.

Since the Mid-1970s. The U.S. steel industry experienced its first significant reversal in the mid-1970s. A rise in energy prices was one of most significant factors that contributed to the industry's decline. In 1975, after oil prices had jumped from $3 to $12 per barrel in less than two years, U.S. steel production dropped by 20 percent. To make matters worse, U.S. companies had substantially increased their production capacity in the early 1970s in anticipation of strong market growth—a dreadful miscalculation. High labor costs continued to plague U.S. competitors as well, adding to their comparative inefficiency in the global market.

Other miscellaneous factors battered down industry profits. Environmental regulations, for example, forced the industry to spend a peak of nearly $400 million in 1981 to reduce pollutants. Also, government-subsidized imported steel was cutting into domestic market revenues. The dumping problem became so bad that the U.S. government enacted Voluntary Restraint Agreements (VRAs) in the early 1980s—which essentially amounted to anti-dumping legislation for 29 importing countries. Finally, steel substitutes were further reducing steel's market share. For instance, the average amount of steel and iron contained in an automobile fell from 2,535 pounds in 1977 to 1,757 pounds in 1992, but the average amount of plastic in an automobile rose from about 180 pounds to 245 pounds.

The proliferation of minimills also added to the woes of large steel producers. Although minimills had originated in the 1960s, by the late 1970s these facilities were beginning to compete directly with large producers in specific market niches. The more efficient and technologically superior minimills particularly benefitted from EAFs, which proved much more productive than even the BOFs in which large manufacturers continued to invest. As a result, the market share of the top six producers declined from 64 percent in 1980 to about 50 percent by 1990.

The end result of the problems affecting the industry was decreased production and profits beginning in the late 1970s and continuing throughout most of the 1980s. Total U.S. steel production declined from a peak of 136 million tons in 1979 to a low of about 81.5 million tons in 1986. U.S. manufacturers' share of

world steel production also plummeted from over 17 percent in 1976 to about 11 percent in 1990. Furthermore, industry employment plummeted from about 300,000 in 1982 to less than 190,000 by 1990. Industry profits fell through the floor, declining to a loss of over $1.8 billion in 1985, and a staggering loss of nearly $4.2 billion in 1986. Although industry net income jumped to over $1 billion in 1987, profits remained relatively stagnant throughout the decade.

Industry Restructuring. In response to the metamorphosis of steel markets, U.S. producers launched a major industry restructuring in the 1980s. Companies greatly increased investments in new production technologies. Integrated mills alone invested $23 billion in the 1980s to modernize their plants. The percentage of steel produced in older OHFs, for instance, fell from nearly 20 percent in 1977 to less than 5 percent by 1990. During the same period, steel produced using efficient EAFs increased from just over 20 percent to nearly 40 percent. Most importantly, manufacturers increased the amount of steel that was produced using continuous casting from just 15 percent in 1980 to over 75 percent by 1991—nearing the levels found in the EC and Japanese industries.

U.S. steelmakers made important gains in other areas, too. Investment in pollution controls declined to just over $100 million in 1990, although those costs began to rise again in the early 1990s. Manufacturers also succeeded in stabilizing their labor costs, although it was estimated that labor still represented 28 percent of the cost of production in as of 1994. Large investments in automation, however, had helped to bring labor expenses in line with overseas competitors. Also bolstering industry competitiveness was the success of highly efficient minimills that could produce steel nearly twice as fast as integrated facilities. By 1995, minimills represented 40.4 percent of industry production.

Domestic producers had also succeeded in reducing steel dumping by importers with such legislation as the VRAs. Furthermore, American companies had increased the quality of their products by investing in new production technology. They had developed new products, for instance, that allowed them to compete with many plastic substitutes. New steel products were being offered that had the corrosion resistance and weight advantages of many plastics, yet cost less to create.

CURRENT CONDITIONS

As a result of restructuring during the 1980s, U.S. steel companies in 1996 were the third most productive in the world. Manufacturers had dramatically reduced the average amount of labor required to produce one ton of steel from 11 man-hours in 1982 to 3 man-hours in 1994—less than both Japanese and European producers. At least one study estimated that pretax production costs in the United States were lower than costs in any other major steel producing nation, except Britain. Furthermore, exports, which have since slowed to 7 percent in 1995, had reached a peak of 8 percent of production in 1992, despite a more than 5 percent decline in foreign demand since the late 1980s. At the same time, an upturn in the U.S. economy in 1995 and early 1996 buoyed domestic demand.

The success of domestic steelmakers against foreign dumping in the U.S. market also aided the industry. There were 84 anti-dumping suits filed with the U.S. Department of Commerce and the International Trade Commission by 12 U.S. companies in 1992. In 1993, the Commerce Department agreed with the charges and imposed severe duties on those importing countries identified in the suits. This development was expected to help increase domestic sales and prices in through the 1990s.

Despite successful restructuring and positive legislation, industry problems persisted in 1995. U.S. companies still faced massive capital investments in the 1990s, which were necessary to upgrade outdated operations. For instance, about 40 percent of the industry's coke ovens will need to be replaced at a cost of around $250 million each before the year 2000. In addition to capital requirements, substitute materials, such as glass, ceramics, aluminum, and plastics, continued to threaten steelmakers. The share of the beverage can market held by the steel industry, for example, fell from 100 percent in 1960 to 5 percent by 1995. By 1995, the typical passenger car contained 1,781 pounds of steel and 389 pounds of iron. In addition, the use of plastics increased to 245 pounds per vehicle from 195 pounds, while that of aluminum rose to 195.5 pounds from 130 pounds.

Environmental expenditures were also expected to increase through the 1990s. Stringent new amendments to the Clean Air Act were passed in 1990 and were expected to raise production costs. Some industry participants predicted dire consequences for the industry as a result of the new standards. As reported by *American Metals Market,* The American Iron and Steel Institute estimated that the industry's capital expenditures for cleaning up facilities over the last 20 years totaled $7.2 billion. Also, an average of 15 percent of the industry's total capital investment was earmarked for environmental improvement during 1995. Minimills were expected to suffer from provisions affecting electric power plants. Steelmakers

hoped to offset some of these increases by boosting the use of recycled steel.

The new environmental regulations also made it easier to punish business executives for failing to have their companies comply with standards. For example, the maximum fine of $25,000 per day and one year in prison was increased to $250,000 per day for individuals, $500,000 per day for companies, and up to five years in prison for executives. The new amendments also allowed prosecutors to use circumstantial evidence, and increased the number of areas in which individuals could be held liable from 4 to 15.

The Future of Steel. Steel industry growth was expected to remain sluggish through 1997. The industry anticipated increased consumption by service centers, automobile manufacturers, and construction firms, at least in the short term. Oil and gas producers, on the other hand, while expected not to increase, did so by more than 100 percent in 1995. Demand from capital goods markets was also expected to increase slightly, and higher earnings for steelmakers were expected to result from long-awaited price increases, made possible by a recovering economy and anti-dumping legislation.

1995-1996 U.S. STEEL INDUSTRY SHIPMENT GROWTH BY MARKET

Source: American Iron and Steel Institute, 1997

Integrated steelmakers, which were under severe profit pressure during the 1980s, were expected to reap the most benefits from increased prices. Nevertheless, analysts expected that minimills would continue to gain market share and to significantly outperform integrated facilities throughout the 1990s. Minimills promised to pose a growing threat as they expanded their offerings to include flat-rolled sheet steel and large structural products—currently the domain of integrated producers. Furthermore, rapid advancements in minimill production technology were allowing this sector to compete with integrated manufacturers in a growing number of markets.

Direct steelmaking is the most likely long-term solution to problems caused by the capital-intensive nature of the integrated steelmaking process. Widespread implementation of the direct steelmaking process would also eliminate the need for coke ovens, many of which are badly in need of being rebuilt and have been the source for harmful emissions. One direct-process plant has been in operation since 1989. Located in Pittsburgh, this experimental facility is capable of producing five tons of steel an hour. It uses a coal-based, continuous in-bath melting process that substitutes a single vessel for coke ovens, blast furnaces, and basic oxygen furnaces. This technique's energy requirements are about 20 percent lower than those of conventional steelmaking, which uses three separate processes. A second, larger experimental facility was completed in 1995, and several foreign competitors have built similar plants.

The quality of domestic steel has also risen in the last five years. One of the most visible examples of enhanced U.S. steel quality since the early 1980s has occurred in the auto market. Ford Motor Company, for instance, realized a drop in its rejection rate of steel. More significantly, steelmakers were increasingly gaining access to Japanese auto manufacturing plants in the United States that have traditionally maintained the highest quality standards. Nissan in Tennessee, Honda in Ohio, and AutoAlliance in Michigan (a Mazda/Ford venture) were all receiving nearly 100 percent of their steel from U.S. producers in 1993.

INDUSTRY LEADERS

United States Steel, of Pittsburgh, a subsidiary of USX Corp., is the largest domestic steelmaker. USX's U.S. Steel Group had sales of over $6 billion and employed 21,310 workers in the mid-1990s. During that time period, the company showed a profit of $201 million, compared to a loss of $578 million in 1991. In 1973, this company produced a record 35 million net tons of raw steel. By 1990, however, its total steelmaking capacity had shrunk from 37 million to 19 million tons. The capacity reduction was the result of a restructuring effort in the 1980s that eliminated or modernized its facilities.

Another large U.S. steel producer, by revenues, was LTV Corporation, of Dallas. In the mid-1990s, this industry giant had sales of $4.2 billion and employed 15,300 people, down by 20,000 since 1991. LTV Steel, LTV Corporation's steelmaking subsidiary, was formed as a result of the merger of Jones & Laughlin and Republic Steel in 1984. Shortly thereafter, following a price collapse in 1985, LTV Steel filed for bankruptcy. Massive capital investments,

joint ventures, and automation efforts helped revive the company in the late 1980s. However, after rebounding with a profit in 1991, it again showed a loss in 1994 of $127 million. Other large integrated steel producers include: ARMCO, with sales of $1.4 billion and a profit of $77 million; Bethlehem Steel Corp., with sales of $4.8 billion and a profit of $80.5 million; Inland Steel, with sales of $4.5 billion and a loss of $107.4 million; and National Steel Corp., with sales of $2.7 billion and a profit of $168.5 million.

Nucor Corp. One of the most progressive and successful steel producers in 1995 was Nucor Corporation, of North Carolina. In contrast to the larger producers already mentioned, Nucor produces steel in minimills. With a net income of $226.6 million and sales of $2.9 billion in the mid-1990s, this company was the most profitable of the large producers. Established in 1967 with a single mill in South Carolina, Nucor had added five plants by 1991 with a production capacity of about 4 million tons per year. Using state-of-the-art technology, such as EAFs and continuous casting, Nucor was able to produce steel from scrap at a fraction of the cost incurred by its larger competitors.

Nucor has also been a leader in expanding the markets served by the minimill sector. In the early 1990s, the company broke into the flat-rolled steel market, which previously was controlled entirely by integrated producers and accounted for about 45 percent of their production. To produce this sheet steel, Nucor was utilizing a new technique called thin-slab casting. In this process, a machine employs a funnel-shaped mold to squeeze molten steel down to a thickness of 1.5 inches to 2.0 inches. This eliminates the need for primary stands that reduce the larger slabs, typically eight to ten inches thick, that conventional casters produce. This method has proved much less costly than conventional casting methods. Nucor's thin-slab casting operation became profitable in June 1990, only ten months after it started production, and was operating at its maximum capacity of 800,000 tons per year by 1992.

In July of 1992, Nucor opened a new $330-million, one-million-ton-per-year, thin-slab casting sheet plant in Arkansas. By 1996, both it and Nucor's Indiana plant were operating at full capacity. The company also announced plans to control 20 percent of the sheet steel market in 2000 by progressing to 8 million tons of capacity. In addition to its attack on the sheet steel market, Nucor also constructed a mill in partnership with Yamato of Japan to roll wide-flange beams—a product produced primarily by integrated mills in the early 1990s. As of mid-1996, five other steel companies had announced plans to build thin-slab plants.

WORK FORCE

U.S. steel productivity nearly doubled between 1980 and 1993. During the same period, the number of man-hours required to produce a unit of steel plummeted more than threefold. These factors, combined with a reduction in demand since the late 1980s, dealt a lethal blow to many jobs in the industry. The trend toward automation was expected to maintain a trend toward fewer workers. Furthermore, workers worried that passage of the North American Free Trade Agreement (NAFTA) would have potentially devastating effects on laborers. Workers in the industry were concerned that producers would be drawn to the low-cost labor and reduced environmental liability offered in Mexico and consequently close numerous U.S. plants.

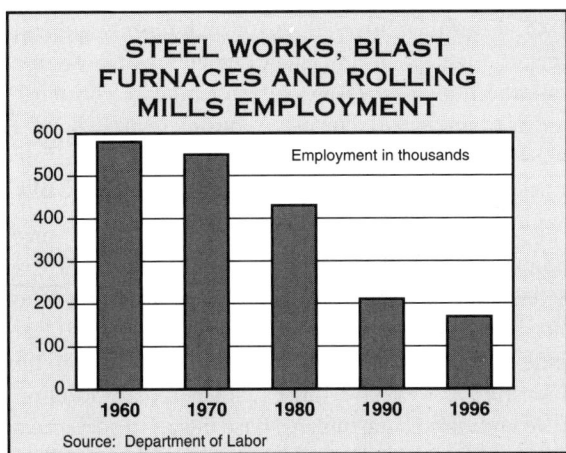

STEEL WORKS, BLAST FURNACES AND ROLLING MILLS EMPLOYMENT

Employment in thousands

Source: Department of Labor

While overall steel employment was likely to decline through the 1990s, new positions were expected in the emerging minimill sector. A wide gap existed in labor productivity between minimills and integrated producers. For example, in 1995 Nucor's 6,200 workers produced 7.9 million tons of raw steel, or 1,274 tons per employee. LTV, the nation's third largest integrated steelmaker, produced 8.5 million tons of raw steel with a work force of 14,400, or 590 tons per employee. In fact, employment growth at minimills rose by an average of 19 percent between 1986 and 1991, while employment at integrated companies fell by 30 percent. It's expected that over 4 million tons of new minimill capacity should come online in 1997.

AMERICA AND THE WORLD

U.S. exports of steel reached 7.1 million tons in 1995, or 7 percent of total shipments. Despite moderate export growth and the comparative productivity of U.S. steelmakers, however, the U.S. steel industry still faces huge trade deficits. Imports in 1995, for instance, exceeded $8.3 billion, versus just $3.8 billion in exports. The only region in which the United States held a surplus was North America, where Canada and Mexico purchased over $2 billion of U.S. steel, versus about $1.8 billion that the United States bought from those two countries. The EC, on the other hand, sold $2.4 billion worth of steel to the United States and purchased only $309 million from domestic steelmakers. Significant deficits also existed with Japan, Asia, and South America. Domestic producers hoped that new anti-dumping legislation would reduce the imbalance.

Total global steel production rose to 760 million metric tons in 1995 and the total value of the world industry hovered around $315 billion. The EC produced the largest portion of global output, at 160 million metric tons. Japan, the second largest producer, generated 105 million metric tons of steel in 1995. The United States was third with 104.9 million metric tons, followed by China with 90 and Russia with 50, a significant drop since 1991, when it was the top producer worldwide.

The International Iron and Steel Institute (ISI) estimates that world production will grow by about 32 million tons by the turn of the century. Most growth was expected to occur in developing nations. Asia, at least in the short term, offered the greatest likelihood of increased consumption.

RESEARCH AND TECHNOLOGY

Rather than expanding production capacity, producers in the late 1980s and 1990s were relying on new technology to help achieve greater efficiency and quality. Because the overall global steel market has matured, companies in the mid-1990s could grow only by increasing market share, raising profit margins, or by developing new steel products.

In addition to continuous casting, thin-slab casting, and EAFs, companies were experimenting with a variety of new production techniques. For example, an array of devices were being employed in the early 1990s to help companies spot, map, describe, and classify defects in sheet steel that were as small as .02 inches in diameter. Strobe lights, laser beams, and artificial intelligence systems were all at work ensuring higher quality output. Furthermore, continuing advancements in alloys and steel coatings were allowing manufacturers to create new steel products that could compete with advanced plastics and ceramics.

Nucor has also been experimenting with an electromagnetic braking system, designed to improve surface quality of the sheet by reducing turbulence in the mold. Less turbulence should result in fewer surface defects and allow for greater casting speed. In addition, AK Steel has pioneered an oxygen-blowing technique that shows some promise in the fight to become more competitive. AK uses a form of oxygen injection in its blast furnaces to increase output and to improve its ability to cope with the world steel market. It is believed that oxygen injection will allow a decrease in the break-even volume for making steel in a blast furnace.

Besides new production techniques, U.S. steelmakers were also realizing productivity gains in the mid-1990s through information technology. Bethlehem Steel, for instance, entered a 10-year contract with Electronic Data Systems, Inc. (EDS) to coordinate its operations. EDS will eventually provide Bethlehem with all necessary resources for data center management, applications development support, and process control activities. The goal of the effort was to fully integrate all aspects of Bethlehem's operations and to allow the company to concentrate on steelmaking, rather than information management.

FURTHER READING

Baker, Stephen. "Metals: Prognosis 1997." *Business Week,* 13 January 1997.

Barnett, Donald F., and Louis Schorsch. *Steel: Upheaval in a Basic Industry.* Cambridge: Ballinger Publishing Company, 1983.

Berry, Bryan. "Japanese Autos: Bodies in Red, White and Blue." *Iron Age,* July 1993.

Darnay, Arsen J., ed. *Manufacturing USA: Industry Analyses, Statistics, and Leading Companies.* Detroit: Gale Research, 1996.

"Green Wave Won't Capsize Steel." *Iron Age,* March 1993.

Hess, George W. "Providing Information Services for Big Steel." *Iron Age,* April 1993.

———. "The Eyes Have It." *Iron Age,* July 1993.

Hogan, William Thomas. *Global Steel in the 1990s.* Lexington, MA: Lexington Books, 1991.

Jacobson, John E. "Minimill Mentality Is Key to Survival." *Iron Age,* March 1993.

———. "Finding Success in the 1990s." *Iron Age,* January 1993.

McKenna, Maureen. "Steelmakers Focus on Survival Strategies." *Iron Age,* August 1993.

McManus, George J. "Integrateds Still Looking for Profits." *Iron Age,* March 1993.

———. "The Direct Approach to Making Iron." *Iron Age,* July 1993.

"Non-ferrous Metals." *New Steel,* June 1995.

Paskoff, Paul F. *Iron and Steel in the Nineteenth Century.* New York: Bruccoli Clark Layman, Inc., 1989.

Rudnitsky, Howard. "Annual Report on American Industry: Metals." *Forbes,* 13 January 1997.

Standard & Poor's Industry Surveys. New York: Standard & Poor's Corporation 21 November 1996.

—Dave Mote, updated by Bob Brooke

SIC 3313

ELECTROMETALLURGICAL PRODUCTS, EXCEPT STEEL

This category includes establishments that manufacture metal additive alloys for both ferrous and nonferrous metals using electrometallurgical or metallothermic processes. Establishments primarily engaged in manufacturing electrometallurgical steel are classified in **SIC 3312: Steel Works, Blast Furnaces (Including Coke Ovens), and Rolling Mills.**

The following alloying metals are those most commonly used to enhance iron and steel: nickel, molybdenum, manganese, silicon, aluminum, phosphorus, calcium, sulfur, lead, and selenium. Tungsten carbide powder and spiegeleisen also are produced in this industry. Alloys have three main purposes: to eliminate undesired elements in a base metal; to add special characteristics, such as strength, heat resistance, and corrosion resistance; and to neutralize unwanted properties of a metal.

Electrometallurgical products firms were shipping about $1.4 billion worth of products per year in the late 1990s. Nickel and molybdenum are the most common alloys produced in the industry. Nickel is used primarily to create stainless steel; molybdenum is used to strengthen steel for aerospace and other specialty steel applications.

North American metal workers have been strengthening and enhancing iron and steel with alloys since the 1600s. Only since World War II, however, has the mining and production of the alloying metals emerged as a significant industry. Since that time, the federal government has promoted the extraction and processing of various ferrous and nonferrous alloys as a means of insuring reserves for national defense and security.

Demand for alloy metals surged from the 1950s through the 1970s, as the U.S. economy expanded and new alloying technologies broadened the industry's market. The auto and capital equipment industries, particularly, became major consumers of ferroalloys during that period. By the end of the 1970s, the electrometallurgical industry employed about 6,000 workers and was shipping about $700 million worth of products each year.

As maturing markets, high production costs, and metal substitutes reduced U.S. steel production in the 1980s, growth of alloy demand slowed—despite the fact that the percentage of metals that used alloys continued to rise. The value of shipments ranged from $707 million in 1982 and $661 million in 1983 to $667 million in 1986. Employment in 1986 plummeted to 3,600.

As steel and other metal orders rose in the late 1980s, the alloy market rebounded, sending the value of shipments past $1.2 billion by 1988. Despite a huge increase in production tonnage, however, industry profitability sagged as the competitive and glutted market steadily eroded prices. The price of nickel, for instance, fell from $6.49 per pound in 1988 to about $3.55 by 1996. Similarly, molybdenum prices dropped to about $3.20 per pound in the late 1990s; it had traded at $7 to $8 per pound as recently as 1994.

Entering the 1990s, producers of ferrous and nonferrous alloys expected a mild reprieve from glutted markets and faltering prices. However, nickel prices were expected to rebound only slightly, perhaps to $4 per pound. Molybdenum was forecast to rise in price slightly by the end of the century, to $4.00 or $4.25; even that estimate was considered optimistic, however, where iron and steelmaking represented 75 percent of the molybdenum market. In addition, vanadium oversupply led to weakened prices for that alloy.

Producers expected little revenue growth going into the new century, as world steel production remained static. Weak demand globally, coupled with large inventories, were expected to keep prices low and even to lead them to decline over a ten-year period. Increased production of nickel-based superalloys in the late 1990s was expected to do little to bolster nickel's price due to the alloy's growing stockpile, up 6 percent from 1995 to 1996. Exports also were forecast to languish in the late 1990s.

The rising price of stainless steel in the late 1990s, however, was expected to aid the rise in nickel's price. As the profitability of stainless rose, it was predicted, more stainless steel companies would be established, boosting the demand for nickel.

Stagnant prices at the end of the century were viewed against a backdrop of price-fixing accusations levied against some of the largest electrometallurgical products companies. One federal civil antitrust complaint was filed in 1997 against five silicon firms, alleging a price-fixing conspiracy to boost sales prices. Defendants in the suit were: American Alloys Incorporated of New Haven, West Virginia; Applied Industrial Materials Corporation of Pittsburgh; Elkem Metals Company of Pittsburgh; Globe Metallurgical Incorporated of Cleveland, Ohio; and SKW Metals & Alloys of Niagara Falls, New York.

Also in 1997, Elkem Metals Co. and American Alloys Inc. pleaded guilty to price-fixing violations of the Sherman Act in a U.S. Justice Department criminal suit. Criminal charges against SKW Metals & Alloys also were filed. Other civil suits were filed in the late 1990s, as well. Allegheny Teledyne, for example, filed lawsuits alleging price-fixing, fraud, and violations of the Racketeer Influenced and Corrupt Organizations (RICO) Act against American Alloys Inc. and Globe Metallurgical Inc.

The largest producer in the industry in the late 1990s was Elkem Metals Company of Pittsburgh, Pennsylvania, with annual sales of $190 million. Founded in 1962, the company employed 2,000 workers in the mid-1990s, but that roster dropped to roughly 1,300 in the late 1990s as the steel industry increasingly looked to buy its ferroalloys overseas. Second-largest was Globe Metallurgical Inc. of Cleveland, Ohio, with other operations in Alabama and Oregon and a subsidiary in Ardingly, England. Globe's annual sales in 1995 were $160 million.

Other large electrometallurgical corporations in the late 1990s included: Steel of West Virginia of Huntington, West Virginia; Thompson Creek Metals Company of Englewood, Colorado; and American Alloys Inc. of New Haven, West Virginia.

In the late 1990s, the electrometallurgical products industry employed approximately 4,600 workers. The annual salary of those workers in 1994 was about 28 percent greater than the pay of workers in other manufacturing jobs. However, because income growth in the industry comes largely from increased productivity, employment was expected to decrease or hold steady toward the turn of the century. The number of workers employed in most sectors of the industry was expected to decline by 10 to 50 percent by 2005. Similarly, every occupation in the steel industry was forecast by the Bureau of Labor Statistics to decline between 1994 and 2005. New manufacturing and information technologies that increase automation will yield most of the productivity gains.

FURTHER READING

Adams, William. "New Stainless Startups to Boost Nickel Demand." *American Metal Market,* 7 January 1997.

"Armco Sues Silicon Firms." *Purchasing,* 16 January 1997.

Darnay, Arsen J., ed. *Manufacturing USA.* 5th ed. Detroit: Gale Research, 1996.

"Ferro-alloys: Let the Bears Take Stock." *Metal Bulletin,* 30 September 1996.

Fitzpatrick, Dan. "Elkem Puts Its Technology Center on the Block." *Pittsburgh Business Times and Journal,* 25 March 1996.

"Globe Metal Inc." *Foundry Management and Technology,* February 1994.

Phillips, E.H. "Memory Alloys Key to 'Smart' Wing." *Aviation Week & Space Technology,* 22 July 1996.

"Putting the V Back into Vanadium." *Metal Market,* 2 September 1996.

Rotondo, Michael. "Moly Market Continues to Fuel Wishful Thinking." *American Metal Market,* 7 January 1997.

Standard & Poor's Industry Surveys. New York: Standard & Poor's Corporation, 12 November 1992.

Stundza, Tom. "Alloying and Plating Metals: There's Plenty—And It's Cheap." *Purchasing,* 12 December 1996.

———. "Glut Smothers Pricing; Hikes Will Be Sluggish." *Purchasing,* 19 August 1993.

———. "High-Strength Alloys Pursue New Markets." *Purchasing,* 10 September 1992.

———. "Nonferrous 1992: Recovery, Yes; Bull Markets, No!" *Purchasing,* 5 March 1993.

———. "Slow-Growth Climate Supplants No-Growth." *Purchasing,* 1 April 1993.

———. "Soaring Demand Lifts Prices." *Purchasing,* 11 July 1996.

———. "Will Supply Keep Prices in Check?" *Purchasing,* 13 February 1997.

"Transaction Prices." *Purchasing,* 17 October 1996.

U.S. Department of Commerce. International Trade Administration. *U.S. Industrial Outlook 1994.* Washington: GPO, 1994.

—Dave Mote, updated by Tim Eigo

SIC 3315

STEEL WIREDRAWING AND STEEL NAILS AND SPIKES

This category covers establishments primarily engaged in drawing wire from purchased iron or steel rods, bars, or wire, as well as those which may be engaged in the further manufacture of products made from wire. Establishments primarily engaged in manufacturing steel nails and spikes from purchased materials are also included in this industry. Rolling mills engaged in the production of ferrous wire from wire rods or hot-rolled bars produced in the same establishment are classified under **SIC 3312: Blast Furnaces and Steel Mills.** Establishments primarily engaged in drawing nonferrous wire are classified in other industry categories.

INDUSTRY SNAPSHOT

The steadily expanding U.S. economy helped steel wiredrawing manufacturers to continue to expand their industry through 1995. Increased demand for product in the automotive and housing industries supported growth in this sector. Increasing supplies of steel bars indicated that prices should remain steady, if not lower, for the foreseeable future.

Steel wiredrawing represented approximately 1 percent of all American steel industry shipments in 1995. Wiredrawing plants manufactured a wide variety of products including barbed and twisted wire, steel baskets, brads, cable, chain link fencing, fence gates, posts and fittings, form ties, horseshoe nails, steel nails, paper clips, spikes, staples, wire cages, tacks, tie wires, wire fabric, wire carts, wire cloth, and wire garment hangers.

ORGANIZATION AND STRUCTURE

In 1995, approximately 370 companies produced steel wire and related products, and over 225 of these firms employed more than 20 employees. The largest concentration of firms by shipment value were in the Great Lakes region of the United States, with the southeast and New England regions ranking second and third, respectively. The largest producing states in descending order of shipments were Ohio, Pennsylvania, Missouri, California, Tennessee, Texas, and Georgia.

Seven major classes of steel wire and related products comprised the industry category. Noninsulated ferrous wire rope, cable, and strand manufactured in wiredrawing plants represented approximately 22.1 percent of the dollar value of the steel wire and related products industry shipments in 1995. Steel nails, staples, tacks, spikes, and brads made up 14.6 percent of this industry's total product shipments. Steel wire produced in mills not producing steel rods or hot-rolled bars accounted for 37.2 percent of total product shipments, while fencing and fence gates made in wiredrawing plants represented 8.08 percent. Ferrous wire cloth and other ferrous woven wire products made in wiredrawing plants comprised 2.38 percent of industry shipments. Other fabricated ferrous wire products, except springs, represented 13.3 percent of steel wire product shipments. Steel wire and related products not elsewhere classified made up approximately 2.29 percent of total industry shipments.

BACKGROUND AND DEVELOPMENT

The demand for steel wire evolved from the housing, construction, and automotive industries. To service these markets, steel wire makers bought steel rod from both domestic and foreign mills and drew it into wire and other related products. While steel wiredrawing companies shopped globally for the least expensive sources of steel bar, their ability to buy from foreign sources depended on the trade climate between the United States and its competitors. The rapid expansion of the Chinese, Russian, and South African steel industries saw steel supplies increase substantially in the 1990s. At the same time, steel consumption also increased as the demand for wiredrawing products, particularly in the housing industry and highway construction, aided growth.

During the 1980s, increases in imports of finished products during the recession coupled with high dollar valuations led many domestic steel wire producers to call for extended voluntary restraint arrangements and duties on imported steel wire and products. The high inflation rates, interest rates, and value of the dollar made offshore sources of steel wire attractive and affordable for domestic users. Industry shipments dropped 21.4 percent between 1981 to 1982.

From the mid-1980s to the early 1990s, American steel wire producers charged many countries with unfair trading practices, most notably with dumping product at prices less than the cost to make them. In February 1989, 30 Japanese producers were subject to duties as high as 29.8 percent. The Specialty Steel Industry of the United States, which represented virtually all U.S. producers of stainless and alloy tool steels and other high technology metals, found that import penetration grew to 20.2 percent of the U.S. market, up from 18.6 percent in 1990. Imports remain a problem for the industry. In the mid-1990s, the Specialty Steel Industry asked the Clinton administration to work quickly in establishing a Mutual Specialty Steel Agreement with the European Union and the rest of the world on stainless steel imports. Stainless steel buyers purchased 24 percent of their product from foreign mills, depressing domestic prices. More than 500,000 tons of stainless steel were imported in 1996, spurred by a 5 percent increase in consumption.

CURRENT CONDITIONS

Domestic steel producers increased prices four times in 1996, but faced increasing pressure from imports that may indicate lower prices in the future. In addition, world wide steel producing capacity, including domestic minimill production, kept future price increases for bars and rods uncertain. With greater demand for stainless steel and an increasing use of foreign mills for the product, domestic wiredrawing companies faced a changing price environment in the mid-1990s. The continued rise in housing construction, particularly the growth of steel-framed housing construction, and moderate interest rates fueled the demand for wiredrawing products.

INDUSTRY LEADERS

While the majority of steel wire producers were privately held firms, a relatively large number were subsidiaries or divisions of larger companies. Some of the largest producers by sales and number of employees in 1995 included BICC Cables Corp. ($735 million in sales and 3,100 employees); Bekaert Corp. ($350 million in sales and 1,400 employees); Duo-Fast Corp. ($240 million in sales and 1,500 employees); Keystone Steel and Wire ($190 million in sales and 1,600 employees); Sandvik Steel Co. ($125 million in sales and 500 employees); and Dickson Weatherproof Nail Co. ($110 million in sales and 100 employees).

Growth in the industry came mainly from a jump in residential housing construction and continued strength in the automotive industry and highway construction. Increasing consumer demand for manufactured products at home, coupled with increased steel supply and production capacity, looked to keep prices for steel wire products low through the end of the decade. Foreign demand remains sluggish, as economic conditions in Europe and Asia showed only slow improvement.

WORK FORCE

Employment in the industry peaked in 1979 at 33,800 and then reached an industry low in 1985, with a work force of 20,900. While sharp increases in hiring led to employment figures of 27,100 in 1989, employment fell through 1992 before rebounding in 1993. In 1995, the industry employed 26,900, an increase of 9.4 percent. Most workers were represented by the United Steel Workers of America.

Total compensation was $749.3 million in 1995, as average hourly wages increased from 1987's low of $10.16 to 1995's $12.62. Hours worked bottomed-out in 1992 at 39.9 million before increasing to 45.9 million in 1995, reflecting the resurgence of the construction industry.

Steel wire makers faced several employment issues in the 1990s, including spiraling health care costs and the need for fully funded company pension plans. During this time, many smaller companies had health care costs that exceeded company's earnings.

AMERICA AND THE WORLD

The North American Free Trade Agreement (NAFTA), ratified by Congress in 1993, was expected to reduce the level of steel wire duties among the United States, Mexico, and Canada. In the early 1990s, steel wire tariffs averaged between 10 to 15 percent in Mexico, 1.5 to 5.6 percent in the United States, and 5.7 to 6.8 percent in Canada. For stainless steel wire, tariffs averaged 10 percent in Mexico, between 3.3 to 10.6 percent in the United States, and up to 12.5 percent in Canada. Under NAFTA, all tariffs on steel wire products shipped within North America would fall to zero in the year 2004, while Mexican tariffs would slowly fall over a ten-year period. Many members of the American Wire Producers Association raised concerns over this discrepancy in phaseout periods.

RESEARCH AND TECHNOLOGY

Competition from companies offering specialty metals and new processes posed a continual challenge to the industry, as their traditional markets, such as the automotive and construction industries, looked to use lighter, stronger, and cheaper materials. Seeking to expand its market as well as its sources for raw materials, the industry regarded recycling as a potential important area.

FURTHER READING

Marcus, Peter F. "Metal Tags Encounter Fork in the Road." *Purchasing,* 16 January 1997. Available from http://www.manufacturing.net/magazine/purchasing/archives/1997/pur0101.97/011mnnews.htm#ME.

Stundza, Tom. "Supply Overwhelms a Weakening Market." *Purchasing,* 13 February 1997. Available from http://www.manufacturing.net/magazine/purchasing/archives/1997/pur0213.97/021bars.htm.

—William Bennett, updated by Norm Leahy

SIC 3316

COLD FINISHING OF STEEL SHAPES

This industry covers establishments primarily engaged in cold-rolling steel sheets and strip from purchased hot-rolled sheets; cold-drawing steel bars and steel shapes from purchased hot-rolled steel bars; and producing other cold finished steel. Establishments primarily engaged in the production of steel, including hot-rolled steel sheets that are then cold-rolled are classified in **SIC 3312: Blast Furnaces and Steel Mills.**

INDUSTRY SNAPSHOT

The demand for cold finished steel comes primarily from the automotive, aerospace, construction, housing, and home appliance industries.

As the industry entered the mid-1990s, its success hinged on its ability to meet the needs of domestic durable goods customers in a climate of rising competition, business costs, labor difficulties, and alternative uses of new metals and plastics. The industry was therefore called upon to improve quality, technology, and productivity while working in partnership with their customers to enhance their prospects for long-term survival.

ORGANIZATION AND STRUCTURE

Two hundred eight companies, divisions, and subsidiaries produced cold steel products in 1995, down from 219 in 1993. The largest concentration of firms by shipment value could be found in the Great Lakes region of the United States. The northeast and west coast were second and third, respectively. The largest producing states in descending order of shipments were Ohio, Pennsylvania, Illinois, Michigan, Indiana, Connecticut, and New York.

Cold-rolling is the process of rolling steel without first reheating it. This method produces a smooth steel surface that reduces thickness and enhances machinability. Cold-rolling gives steel the ability to be stretched and shaped without cracking and provides it with a bright finish. The three main product classes within the industry are steel sheet, steel strip, and steel bars.

Steel sheet and strip are both flat products that are generally less than 1/4 inch thick. Sheet is the wider of the two by 12 inches or more and is produced to less exact thickness than the strip. Steelmakers produce most sheet and strip in the form of large coils that the user can cut into pieces of any desired length. Much of the sheet and strip manufactured is used in automobile bodies, but thousands of other products also contain these forms of steel.

Steel companies make bars in many sizes and various shapes, including squares, circles, ovals, hexagons, and rectangles. Products made from steel bars include many precision-engineered components that power automobiles, trucks, tractors, hand tools, washing machines, and lawn mowers.

BACKGROUND AND DEVELOPMENT

The production of cold finished steel became industrialized early in the twentieth century, prompted by the mass marketing of automobiles, household appliances, and industrial machinery. New and more efficient steel production methods ensued at a rapid pace.

During World War II, the American steel industry boomed, while in other countries steel manufacturing facilities sustained considerable damage. Global steel markets were dominated by American firms during the post-war years, and by 1960, American shipments of cold finished steel shapes totaled 17 million tons, rising to 20 million tons by the middle of the decade. During this time, however, Japan and several European countries focused on rebuilding their steel industries, using the most modern facilities and equipment available, while American steelmakers continued to use older, less efficient equipment. Consequently, American shipments fell below 17 million tons in 1970.

Worldwide inflation and high interest rates in the early 1970s curtailed foreign steel production, particularly in developing nations, allowing U.S. shipments to realize significant gains. In 1973, U.S. shipments stood at 24.09 million tons, the highest level experienced by the industry in over two decades. However, economic recession in the United States eventually pushed shipments back down to 20.76 million tons in 1979.

The cold finished steel industry faced intense foreign competition during the 1980s. Due to the high value of the dollar, foreign steel became significantly less expensive than American steel. Furthermore, having rebuilt and improved their facilities, foreign producers were marketing a superior product, and this quality gap widened significantly during the decade. Consequently, American companies operating with outdated equipment and production methods were often priced out of the market. From 1979 to 1980, U.S. shipments of cold finished steel dropped 24 percent. The industry recovered slightly in 1981 with ship-

ments rising eight percent. However, the following year, shipments fell 25 percent to a 30-year low.

Hoping to become more competitive by realizing productivity gains, some American companies began installing completely automated, high-speed production equipment with computer controlled systems. In 1988, industry shipments were valued at $6.3 billion, representing a small increase over previous years. However, the Gulf War and early 1990s economic recession depressed the value of shipments to a low of $5.4 billion in 1991. By 1995, the industry increased production as world steel demand surged to levels higher than those before the Gulf War. In 1995, shipments of cold finished products stood at more than $7 billion.

CURRENT CONDITIONS

Many analysts doubted that cold finished steel makers would again reach the shipment levels enjoyed during the 1960s and 1970s. Steel sheet and bar shipments had apparently peaked in 1973 at 20.38 and 2.25 million tons each, while steel strip shipments peaked earlier, at 1.58 million tons in 1966.

Nevertheless, the industry regarded the 1990s with optimism. As the industry gradually shed its excess capacity, its ability to raise prices in the face of increasing demand was expected to help buoy profits. Steelmakers also relied on investments in new technologies and commitments to reducing costs to increase their chances for survival and long-term profitability.

While prices did rise somewhat through 1996, world wide steel capacity surged as foreign production, particularly from China and Russia, began to swell market reserves. The influx of foreign steel on the market diminished domestic producers' ability to pass on increasing cost to consumers. Some industry leaders, like Worthington Industries and LTV Corporation, sought to expand their operations to produce economies of scale and to diversify into more value-added steel products. The growth of nonunion steel mill competitors forced older members of the industry to seek additional cost-containment strategies to sustain profit margins.

The value of cold-finished steel shipments rose substantially in 1995 and was projected to make similar rises throughout the rest of the decade. As consumers pushed for cost reductions from all parts suppliers, however, some steel bar manufacturers were expected to have difficulty passing along their rising costs. Steel sheet price was five percent higher in 1996 than 1995, but remained well below 1994 levels. Imports were the major factor. Richard Aldrich, an analyst with Lehman Brothers, stated "Flat-rolled pricing is likely to come under more pressure soon from rising supply."

INDUSTRY LEADERS

LTV Steel Company of Cleveland, Ohio, was the country's largest cold-finisher of steel shapes, with 16,500 employees in 1995. The company emerged from protection under Chapter 11 of the Federal Bankruptcy Code in June 1993 after major losses in the 1980s, and its projected sales for 1995 were $3.5 billion. After substantial reorganization and the signing of several supply agreements, the company's orders stabilized and shipments increased.

Worthington Industries of Columbus, Ohio, was a diversified steel company employing 7,000 workers, with cold finishing operations serving the housing, auto, communications, and leisure industries. Sales for 1995 were expected to reach nearly $1.3 billion. Worthington diversified its production lines and added capacity throughout the mid 1990s. Sales were projected to rise to $2.1 billion by 1998. Other industry leaders included WHX Corp., and Sidtman Steel Products.

WORK FORCE

Approximately 16,200 employees served the industry in 1995, a substantial increase over the 15,100 in 1994. In the early 1990s, attrition and early retirement incentives were used more often than layoffs to cut back on labor costs. Flexible assignment of employees helped reduce the number of classes of skilled steel trades.

Average production wages per hour reached $18.16 in 1995. Payroll costs were $653 million. Nearly all non-management employees belong to the United Steelworkers of America (USWA), one of the largest labor unions in the United States. WHX Corp., the third largest company in the sector, experienced substantial labor problems in 1996. The USWA walked out of talks with the company over the issue of pensions. Work ceased at eight of the companies' facilities though both sides engaged a federal mediator to resolve the dispute.

AMERICA AND THE WORLD

In the early 1990s, the U.S. steel industry filed charges of unfair competition against several foreign firms. Upon review, the U.S. International Trade Commission (ITC) found that 25 of the claims were justified and assessed duties accordingly. Due to the increased potential for duties imposed by the ITC on

their steel, many foreign steelmakers reduced their exports to the United States in 1993.

Some domestic manufacturers filed complaints with the International Trade Commission protesting the imports of plate steel from China, Russia, South Africa, and Ukraine. Domestic imports from those countries increased four-fold between 1993 and 1995 and were expected to surpass 1 million tons in 1996.

The 1993 passage of the North American Free Trade Agreement (NAFTA) was expected to help eliminate tariffs placed on foreign steel entering America. Mexico, Canada, and the United States were scheduled to drop all tariffs on cold finished steel traded among the three countries before the year 2004. As of 1993, the tariff on steel sheet, strip, and bar exported by Mexico was ten percent. Canada's tariffs on sheet and strip were between 6.8 and 10.2 percent, and on bar between zero and 12.5 percent. The U.S. tariffs on sheet and strip were between 2.4 and 6 percent, and on bar between 3.3 and 10.6 percent.

RESEARCH AND TECHNOLOGY

In the early 1990s, the industry was concerned with improving the quality and reputation of steel in the face of aggressive marketing techniques by makers of alternative metals. Manufacturers that purchased steel bar typically looked to obtain straight components, tight tolerances, fast machining rates, and quality surfaces—characteristics that could be furnished by alternative materials such as plastics, aluminum, and brass. The low density of aluminum, for example, was found to lengthen tool life and productivity in machining operations as well as to produce a lighter weight, and thereby more fuel efficient, automobiles. Moreover, steep declines in brass and aluminum prices made those materials more attractive to manufacturers. Analysts estimated that by 1995, aluminum and plastic would displace more than 200,000 tons of steel in automotive panels alone.

In order to compete for market share, the steel industry sought a better understanding of the product's end use and to communicate to customers the advantages of steel. By becoming a part of their customers' product problem-solving and supplier development teams, steel firms hoped to win back lost markets and combat the substitution of alternative metals for their cold-finished steel.

FURTHER READING

Marcus, Peter F. "Metal Tags Encounter Fork in the Road." *Purchasing,* 16 January 1997. Available from http://www.manufacturing.net/magazine/purchasing/archives/1997/pur0101.97/011mnnews.htm#ME.

Stundza, Tom, "Supply Overwhelms a Weakening Market." *Purchasing,* 13 February 1997. Available from http://www.manufacturing.net/magazine/purchasing/archives/1997/pur0213.97/021bars.htm.

———. "On-Time Means a Lot to Steel Buyers." *Purchasing,* 3 April 1997. Available from http://www.manufacturing.net/magazine/purchasing/archives/1997/pur0403.97/041steel.htm.

"Schedule of Proposed Tariff Eliminations in the North American Free Trade Agreement." *American-Metal-Market,* 17 September 1992.

—William Bennett, updated by Norm Leahy

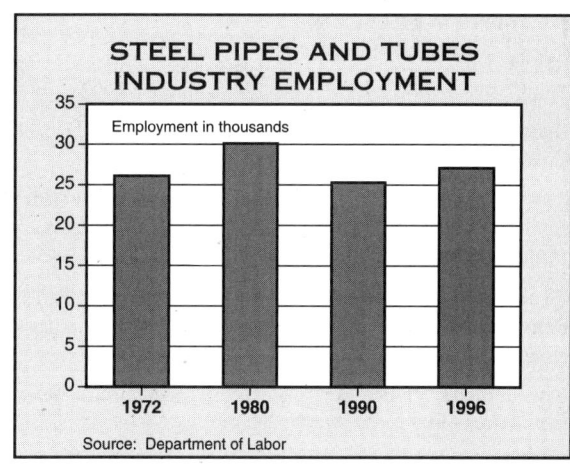

STEEL PIPES AND TUBES
INDUSTRY EMPLOYMENT

Employment in thousands

Source: Department of Labor

SIC 3317

STEEL PIPE AND TUBES

Included in this category are establishments primarily engaged in the production of welded or seamless steel pipe and tubes and heavy riveted steel pipe from purchased materials. Establishments primarily engaged in the production of steel, including steel skelp or steel blanks, tube rounds, or pierced billets, are classified under **SIC 3312: Blast Furnaces & Steel Mills.**

After some years of declining sales, the American steel pipe and tubes industry appeared to be entering a period of stronger economic growth in the mid-1990s. During the first seven months of 1993, shipments were running 22.1 percent ahead of 1992's first seven months. Total shipments were $6.792 billion in 1995, up just 1 percent from the 1994 level of $6.369 billion. Rising demand and increases in raw material and energy costs drove the prices of seamless carbon tubing up to $973 per ton, welded tubing up to $739 per ton, seamless carbon casing up to $701 per ton, and welded casing up to $560 per ton.

In the United States, the automotive, display fixture, juvenile furniture, and exercise and recreation equipment industries showed healthy increases in demand for steel pipes and tubes. Regionally, the Midwest, mountain, and southern states exhibited high demand, while sales in the northeast and on the West Coast remained stagnant. The U.S. market was expected to reach its peak in 1994-95, while strong global demand was expected as well.

In the steel pipe and tube industry, 243 establishments employed 25,300 workers, of which 19,800 were in production in 1995. That year total compensation reached an estimated $798.2 million. The largest producing states in descending order were Pennsylva-

nia, Ohio, Illinois, and California, which together shipped 55 percent of total U.S. shipments. New capital expenditures on plant and equipment totaled $181.5 million, an increase of over 50 percent from 1990 levels.

The American steel mill products industry, which includes steel tubes and pipes, exported $13.4 billion in 1995, a 44 percent increase over the 1994 level. Imports of foreign steel pipe and tubes totaled $3.2 billion, an increase of 7.3 percent from 1994.

In 1992, the U.S. International Trade Commission and U.S. Commerce Department ruled in favor of many American pipe and tube manufacturers, concluding that foreign countries were dumping their shipments into the U.S. market at less than the cost of production or values sold at home. The countries found guilty of dumping in 1992 (with corresponding duties assessed) were: Brazil (103.38 percent); South Korea (4.9-11.6 percent); Mexico (32.6 percent); Taiwan (19.5-27.7 percent); and Venezuela (52.5 percent).

Also during this time, the Committee on Pipe and Tube Imports was one of the few steel trade associations that supported the North American Free Trade Agreement (NAFTA). The industry believed NAFTA would increase demand for steel pipe and tubes among the United States, Canada, and Mexico. Phaseout of the 2 percent U.S. tariffs and 10 to 15 percent Mexican tariffs would occur under the pact.

The Quanex Corp. has long been at or near the top of this industry. With 1996 fiscal sales of $895.7 million and 4,016 employees, Quantex remained one of the muscles in the industry along with Aarque Cos. of Jamestown, New York, and Bundy International Corp. of Warren, Michigan. The TI Vari-Form operations of Bundy designed a tubular steel closure assembly for the Dodge Ram pickup trucks for the fall of 1993.

FURTHER READING

Beirne, Mike. "North Star Increases Tube Price $15 Per Ton." *American-Metal-Market*, 22 September 1993.

Darnay, Arsen J., ed. *Manufacturing USA*. 5th ed. Detroit: Gale Research, 1996.

Giobbe, Dorothy. "Pipe and Tubing Survey: Cautious Hope Again—On a Stronger Base." *Metal Center News*, February 1993.

"Tubular Steel Gets Chrysler Nod: It's for Radiator Part in Ram Pickup Truck." *American Metal Market*, 3 August 1993.

Vivani, Laura. "Pipemakers Allege Circumvention." *American Metal Market*, 26 April 1993.

Wrigley, Al. "Ford Nod To New Subframe Spurs Use of Steel Tubing." *American Metal Market*, 2 April 1993.

U.S. Department of Commerce. Bureau of the Census. *1995 Annual Survey of Manufactures*. Washington: GPO, 1997.

U.S. Department of Commerce. International Trade Administration. *U.S. Industrial Outlook 1995*. Washington: GPO, 1996.

SIC 3321

GRAY AND DUCTILE IRON FOUNDRIES

This classification covers establishments primarily engaged in manufacturing gray and ductile iron castings, including cast iron pressure and soil pipes and fittings.

INDUSTRY SNAPSHOT

As a whole, the foundry industry has been cut in half since 1955 when the number of establishments involved in ferrous and non-ferrous casting across the country was 6,000. Only 3,100 establishments remained in 1995, with approximately 700 engaged in casting gray and ductile iron. However, due to technological advancements and capacity gains through consolidations, output per remaining producer rose.

In 1995, total industry shipments were at only 33 percent of the tonnage shipped in 1978. Gray iron suffered a huge decline between 1978 and 1982—from approximately 18.5 million tons to 9.5 million tons. Throughout the remainder of the 1980's, gray iron shipments continued to decrease. In the mid-1990s, they finally leveled off at approximately 6 million tons per year. Ductile iron, however, has shown growth in shipments since 1982, continuing a trend started in 1966. In 1994, shipments of ductile iron had surpassed 4 million tons for the first time since its invention and is expected to surpass gray metal by the

turn of the century. The growth of ductile iron was largely due to its increasing recognition as more economical and structurally sound than gray and malleable irons, and in some cases, it can replace steel forgings and weldments.

The metal casting industry was wounded severely in the 1980s. During the 1970s, the industry was filled with back orders that exceeded annual capacity, providing a seller's market. The pricing strategies reflected this, as did profit margins. However, shipment volume—not quality—was the key issue during the 1970s. During the 1980s, foreign competitors who offered timely delivery of better quality castings at lower prices emerged. During the recession of the late 1980s and early 1990s, consumers turned to overseas suppliers, leaving the domestic producers behind. Consequently, U.S. foundries were operating at no more than 50 percent capacity by the mid-1980s.

ORGANIZATION AND STRUCTURE

This industry is heavily engaged in manufacturing pipes and pipe fittings. However, other segments of the industry are growing in response to changing market demands. For example, the automotive industry has switched most engine components to aluminum in response to consumer demands for lighter, more fuel efficient cars. While this move has hurt some gray and ductile iron foundries, it has forced them to find alternative markets. This is apparent since 52.6 percent of the product share is claimed by other gray iron castings, and 19.9 percent is claimed by other ductile iron castings. Only 3.9 percent of the product share is due to cast iron pressure, soil pipe, and fittings, whereas 14.0 percent is attributed to ductile iron pressure pipe and fittings.

Historically, the automotive and aerospace industries were the largest customers for gray and ductile iron foundries. When demand was at its highest, each of the Big Three automakers owned several foundries. Since the mid-1980s the poor financial performance of both the domestic automotive and aerospace industries forced closings of many self-contained foundries. Companies in these industries found that outsourcing the casting business was a cheaper alternative than under-utilizing plant and labor capacities.

In the 1980s and 1990s, the corporate average fuel economy (CAFE) standards mandated that automobile manufacturers produce lighter, more fuel efficient cars. As a result, the 650 pounds of iron casting found in a 1981 automobile was reduced to 350 pounds of gray iron per vehicle by 1995 and is expected to fall another 40 percent by 2005. Ductile iron, on the other hand, has experienced some growth in the automotive industry as the mechanical properties of the metal make it an attractive alternative to heavier cast components.

BACKGROUND AND DEVELOPMENT

Humans have been casting metals for at least 5,000 years. This is evidenced by early societies' progression from the Stone Age to the Bronze Age, when people started extracting ores and shaping them by melting or hammering methods. The Iron Age began in Europe circa 1100 B.C. Cast iron came into commercial use in the early 1700s when a mechanic named Abraham Darby and some Dutch workmen established a brass foundry in Bristol, England. It was there that Darby and his men started experimenting with iron as a replacement for brass. Because brass and iron are completely different pouring mediums in terms of their reaction with sand and solidification patterns, Darby faced many technical difficulties in his early experiments. With the help of John Thomas, a boy working in his shop, Darby succeeded in casting a complete iron pot. For proprietary reasons, Darby and Thomas entered into an agreement in which the boy was to remain his servant to keep the secret.

Ductile iron was not discovered until after World War II. Laboratory metallurgists at International Nickel Company noticed that the addition of a higher content of magnesium than is normally required for gray iron produced a structurally different material. When observing the material at a microscopic level, researchers noticed that the graphite particles had taken on a spheroidal shape, thus coining the name "nodular iron" in the United States, and "spheroidal graphite cast iron" in Great Britain. The recognition of nodular iron's mechanical strength—and its ability to provide more ductile than other metals in its class—provided it with its more commonly accepted name, ductile iron. Since its release to the marketplace in 1949, ductile iron has gained acceptance as an important engineering material and has replaced many of the previous applications formerly reserved for steels and other irons. The discovery of ductile iron was one of the greatest achievements in the engineering materials community in the twentieth century.

CURRENT CONDITIONS

Gray and ductile iron foundries rely on the health of the U.S. economy to spur growth with in their industries. With the increase in new housing during the late 1990s, there will also be a corresponding increase in demand for gray iron needed for boiler and radiator castings, valves and fittings, and pumps and compressors. This industry is also being aided by an increased volume in exports of heavy equipment—such as diesel engines, farm, and construction equipment. At the same time, gray iron is being replaced by plastics; this substitution is also being seen in the refrigerant and air conditioning markets.

The automobile market is expected to sustain ductile iron growth into the twentieth century as the preferred replacement for forged gears and shafts in power transmissions. Specialty industrial machinery—such as those used for paper, printing, and plastic manufacturing and for farm and construction equipment—will maintain the demand for ductile iron. The recent development of austempered ductile iron (ADI) allowed this metal to challenge forgings and cast steels in operations requiring strength and durability.

The foundry industry has also increased its world wide marketability by certification through the International Organization for Standardization. This series of certifications, referred to as ISO 9000, offered distinct competitive advantages for those who qualified and passed the certification audit. Although the audit was intensive, the result was the receipt of an internationally recognized benchmark standard, which signified the recipient was paying attention to details and distinguishing itself as a manufacturer of quality castings, engineered with integrity.

INDUSTRY LEADERS

The following companies were the top five gray and ductile foundries in 1997: Amsted Industries, Inc., with mid-1990s sales of $1.2 billion and 9,000 employees; Intermet Corporation, with sales of $542 million and 4,000 employees; Citation Corporation, with sales of $308 million and 3,900 employees; Sudbury Inc., with sales of $305 million and 2,500 employees; and United States Pipe and Foundry Company, with sales of $300 million and 2,700 employees. The 176 leading gray and ductile iron foundries reported total sales of $6.4 billion and employed 59,900 people.

Intermet Corporation recently launched a joint venture with Comalco Limited of Australia to extend its iron making expertise to aluminum. Intermet built a pilot plant in Lewisport, Kentucky banking on two prevalent trends in the automotive industry—outsourcing and aluminum auto components. The replacement of iron engine blocks with aluminum was expected to greatly exceed the nation's aluminum casting capacity by the year 2000. Without preparation to switch ductile and gray iron operations to incorporate aluminum into the product line, Intermet, along with all other limited foundries, stood to lose market share.

Waupaca Foundry Incorporated, located in Waupaca, Wisconsin, improved its efficiency and quality levels in its cleaning operations through the use of video camera data. The workers who ground excess iron from the castings were empowered with the responsibility to inspect the cleaned casting against a process control sheet, which contained a video image of the part and annotations. This innovative method of process control ensured that the grinder/inspector always used the most current work instructions. Waupaca Foundry reported sales of $180 million in 1996.

In 1993, the Gunite Corporation converted from steel to ductile iron for the manufacturer of truck spoke wheels. The 300 employee foundry needed to make the switch to remain competitive, so they developed a wire injection module that allows both gray and ductile iron to be produced from the same cupola. By 1996, the Gunite foundry had made over 13,000 treated casts and reduced scrap to 4 percent. The entire process has gradually improved overall foundry productivity with out requiring any new capital investments. Furthermore, a substantial savings in manpower costs has been realized since product quality has improved.

WORK FORCE

In general, most labor-intensive occupations in the gray and ductile iron foundries expected continued work force reductions through the 1990s. The occupations facing the most substantial reductions—30 percent and more—included worker supervisors, plastic and metal machine workers, plastic and metal grinding machine operators, maintenance, electricians, and machine tool cutting operators. Other occupations facing reductions—20 to 30 percent—included fabricators, assemblers, hand workers, general laborers, precision workers, molding machine operators, inspectors, welders, truck and tractor operators, and mechanists. The only occupations expecting to gain employment levels were hand grinders and polishers.

Hourly compensation in this industry was, on the average, substantially higher in comparison to other forms of manufacturing. In 1994, the industry's average hourly wage was $15.22, while the average hourly wage of all other manufacturing concerns was $12.09. In 1994 Ohio and Illinois, which offered the highest hourly compensation in the industry, were paying hourly wages of $19.19 and $18.20 respectively. Ohio and Pennsylvania have the highest concentration of gray and ductile iron foundries. Nearly 30 percent of the entire shipment activity in the United States is due to the combined efforts of the states of Ohio and Wisconsin.

The labor dilemma in the foundry industry started well before the late 1980s. In August 1895, *The Foundry,* a monthly journal, lamented the industry's lack of appeal to young talent. ''American foundries as a rule are not making any longer the high-grade mechanic needed to turn out the best work. . . .The smart, intelligent American boy can find more profitable, congenial employment than working in an iron foundry, where he will receive $2.50 a day, more or less—generally less—after he has served a several-year apprenticeship.''

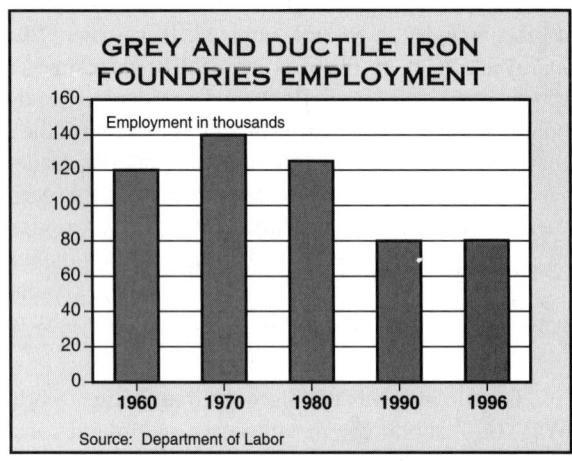

Women started making an impact on the work force at the turn of the twentieth century. According to the March 1899 edition of *The Foundry,* ''the introduction of women into the core room marks an interesting epoch in iron founding. Women are especially adept in the making of small cores, and to this branch of the industry they are always confined. After a six months apprenticeship the girls are able to earn from $7 to $9 per week.''

The effects of World War II dramatically changed the work place as women began fill the roles of men engaged in the War. According to the March 1943 edition of *The Foundry,* ''because the present critical manpower situation seriously threatens production of war goods, the war problems committee of the Wisconsin Chapter of the American Foundryman Association studied the possibility of women replacing men in making castings for ordnance, tanks, armament, navy parts, and other vital war materials. . . . The committee urged the same pay for women for equal jobs, which it felt would inspire better workmanship. . . . It was recommended that women be used as widely as possible.''

AMERICA AND THE WORLD

The foundry industry faced tremendous challenges in the global marketplace in the 1990s. During the five-year period from 1991 to 1995, there was a shift in metal cast production from the Pacific Rim to North America. The United States and Canada increased 63 and 56 percent respectively, while Japan dropped 12 percent. The 1995 ranking of the five largest gray and ductile iron producers was: the United States, 20 percent; China, 16 percent; the Commonwealth of Independent States (CIS), 15 percent; Japan, 10 percent; and Germany, 6 percent. With the demise of communism in the former U.S.S.R., much of their production capacity remains underutilized. For example, Ukraine produced 6 million tons of casting in 1985 and reported a little less than 1 million tons in 1995.

The financial impact of environmental and safety regulations continued to beleaguer foundries throughout the 1990s. For example, Mexico was being pressured by the United States to install air pollution control devices in the early 1990s. However, Mexican laws included a loophole which did not require the devices to operate. In Korea, foundry workers were not provided with safety equipment—such as eye protection, hard hats, respiratory devices, or ear plugs. Additionally, workman's compensation and minimum wage were much higher in the United States. The benefits that American workers enjoyed, and often took for granted, added significantly to the costs of U.S. companies. In financial terms, foreign competitors legally had an edge toward profit during the 1990s.

RESEARCH AND TECHNOLOGY

Conditions in the iron foundry industry and in particular, ductile iron production have improved during the 1990s. The U.S. Government was interested in replacing many forged steel components with cast ductile iron. Particularly, the U.S. Navy was researching the increased lethality of ductile iron projectiles over those made from steel. Other contractors were looking for less expensive alternatives to forged steel components in lower stress applications where the mechanical properties of ductile iron would suffice. However, more research and development was needed for this material because other lighter weight materials were replacing ductile iron in lower stress applications. Ductile iron's low production price tag was enticing to both manufacturers and consumers and served as one of the primary incentives for its use.

Cast thermal analysis—also called numerical modeling/simulation—was used to improve quality and productivity in the foundry through pattern design optimization. The benefits of using numerical model-ing were substantial, especially in relation to cost savings associated with time and material waste. Computer technology displaced the standard "pour and pray" method of metal casting and helped engineers optimize casting designs.

For the foundry industry as a whole, the advent of rapid prototyping technology was perhaps one of the most exciting advancements of the 1990s. Rapid prototyping is a computer integrated method of accelerating the step between design and manufacture of the part. Under normal circumstances, a foundry would take weeks to construct a pattern—and core boxes if necessary—from an original design. With rapid prototyping, this process took only days, in some cases only hours, to create a limited production pattern. The competitive edge this technology offered was substantial, especially considering the accuracy it lent to the price quoting process.

FURTHER READING

Considine, Douglas M., ed. *Van Nostrand's Scientific Encyclopedia.* New York: Van Nostrand Reinhold Company, 1976.

Darnay, Arsen J., ed. *Manufacturing USA.* 5th ed. Detroit: Gale Research, 1996.

Dudley, Jeffery A., et al. "Numerical Modeling of Castings in the Production Process." *Modern Casting,* December 1992.

Engels, Gerhard. "Foundries Challenges are Global in Scope." *Foundry Management & Technology,* June 1993.

"Foundry Industry History: The Gay Nineties." *Foundry Management & Technology,* September 1991.

"Foundry Industry History: World War II." *Foundry Management & Technology,* February 1992.

Gordon, Shelley. "ISO 9001 Certification: Was It Worth It?" *Modern Casting,* July 1993.

Krueger, L.S. "Castings: Commodity or Components?" *Modern Casting,* July 1993.

Moore, Alan. "Is the Future of Ductile Iron Precarious?" *Foundry Management & Technology,* June 1992.

Peters, Dean M., ed. "Internet's Big Push into Aluminum." *Foundry Management & Technology,* June 1993.

Rauch, A.H., ed. *Source Book on Ductile Iron.* Metals Park, OH.: American Society for Metals, 1977.

Rodgers, Robert C., ed. "Videos of Castings Simplify Cleaning Operations." *Foundry Management & Technology,* August 1991.

"The Foundry: Reminiscences from Foundry Management & Technology's Pages Past." *Foundry Management & Technology,* March 1993.

Uziel, Yehoram. "Functional Prototyping - Has the Future Arrived?" *Foundry Management & Technology,* March 1993.

Warden, T. Jerry. "Acquiring a Marketing Focus." *Modern Casting,* July 1993.

—Valerie Wilson, updated by Andrew J. Poss

SIC 3322

MALLEABLE IRON FOUNDRIES

This industry is made up of establishments primarily engaged in the manufacturing of malleable iron castings.

INDUSTRY SNAPSHOT

The 1996 shipments of malleable iron for the United States were estimated at 226,000 tons, down 13 percent from the production level of 260,000 tons in 1994. However, this is still better than the 1991 all-time low of 207,000 tons. Twenty-six companies employed over 37,100 people in the industry; together, these companies generated more than $3.5 million in sales.

The industry is in severe decline, and is not expected to return to its glory days of the 1960s. More than a third of the malleable foundries in the United States have been closed since the early 1980s, with further consolidation likely to continue. The factors that have contributed to this decline are strong foreign competition, the substitution of other metals and materials for malleable iron, rapid changes in technology, and unfavorable domestic economic conditions. Some analysts predict production values falling to record level lows of 150,000 metric tons if the automobile industry converts to ductile iron for their connecting rods.

ORGANIZATION AND STRUCTURE

Castings are used in 90 percent of all durable goods. In 1995, more than 3,100 U.S. metal foundries made over 100,000 distinct products and produced more than 14.4 billion metric tons of product. Malleable iron casting production represented approximately 1.7 percent of the total U.S. casting output. Capacity utilization in 1990 for malleable iron foundries was 78 percent, just slightly better than the 75 percent average for the entire foundry industry. This reflected the high rate of disinvestment in plants and equipment that occurred during the 1980s.

As an indication of the decline of this industry, government statisticians now classify malleable iron

foundries as job shops. These foundries generally operate on a job or on an order basis by manufacturing castings for sale to others or for interplant transfer. In the 1970s, half of all malleable iron foundry castings came from in-house or captive plants. But in the 1980s, a major shift occurred when large independent manufacturers of railroad cars, oil-drilling equipment, heavy machinery, automobile, trucks, and major appliances sold off, shut down, or consolidated their captive operations. Today, upwards of 75 percent of all malleable iron castings come from independent or custom casters.

Two types of malleable iron are produced by these foundries: standard malleable iron and pearlitic malleable iron. In the early 1990s, the value of shipments for each of these two product classes of malleable iron castings were 145,800 mt for standard malleable iron (62.1 percent of total) and 89,100 mt for pearlitic malleable iron (37.9 percent of total).

Most of the malleable iron foundries are found in the nation's midwestern and northeastern states. The largest malleable iron producing states, in descending order of shipments, are Wisconsin, Pennsylvania, Michigan, Connecticut, New York, Ohio, and Illinois.

BACKGROUND AND DEVELOPMENT

Malleable iron foundries are typically large plants in which workers make metal products called castings by pouring molten metal into molds that are left to harden. Malleable iron is made from white cast iron by annealing it at temperatures from 1500 to 1850 degrees Fahrenheit over several days. When annealed, the iron carbide breaks up, producing rosettes of graphite. The iron is known for its shock resistance, strength, machinability, and ductility. Products such as engine blocks, iron ornaments, and valves can be made from malleable iron castings. The automotive, railroad, construction, agricultural implement, and hardware industries have wide uses for malleable iron castings.

Casting molten metal is believed to be one of the most efficient and economical ways of shaping metal products. Cast iron was first made by the Chinese around the eighth century B.C. However, it wasn't until the invention of the blast furnace by the Europeans in the fourteenth century that large quantities of cast iron were produced. North America's first operational foundry was built in 1642 along the Saugus River, close to Boston. About eight tons per week of grey iron castings were produced at the site.

Malleable iron, which was also called American blackheart iron, replaced grey-iron as the standard cast-metal around 1820, when the commercialization of secondary heat treating of the metal was first used. In 1966 malleable iron castings production in the United States accounted for 50 percent of the total malleable iron cast in the world. However, the year 1967 saw ductile iron castings production surpass malleable iron castings production in the United States. U.S. malleable iron castings production accounted for roughly 12 percent of the world's total production in 1995.

During the 1960s, average yearly production of malleable iron castings reached its peak at around 983,300 metric tons. Production during the decade of the 1970s remained at respectable average yearly production levels of 854,900 metric tons. However, the 1980s reflected the difficult economic times for the industry, with average yearly production levels shrinking to 346,100 metric tons.

The foundry industry still ranks within the top ten manufacturing segments in the United States. However, it has been battered by technological and competitive forces throughout the last two decades. The high inflation rates, high interest rates, high value of the dollar, and deep recession during the early 1980s hurt this industry tremendously. The largest customers of malleable iron castings, the domestic heavy equipment manufacturers, realized that these economic conditions favored offshore sources of malleable iron castings. Foreign competitors not only had lower prices when compared to American malleable iron sources, but they also had high quality manufacturing capabilities. Consequently, the value of castings shipments in the United States dropped 55 percent from the 1977 level of $721.9 million to $323.2 million in 1982.

The high interest rates also raised the industry's cost of capital, which is the price to finance and replace existing operations. This practically shut off any new capital expenditures on plant and equipment in the United States. Capital reinvestment dropped 85 percent between the years 1978 and 1983. The high dollar, high interest rates, and high cost of capital made it very expensive to reinvest in the business of producing malleable iron castings. The lower rates of reinvestment by American malleable iron casters at a time when foreign competitors were raising their levels of casting quality put U.S. foundries at a technological disadvantage. In 1986, the Reagan Administration's decision to not sanction import restrictions further hurt the industry.

Even with the weakened dollar and improved quality of American malleable iron castings in the 1990s, imports are still likely to remain high. The offshore competitors that gained strong inroads to the American market are not likely to give up the market

share easily. To illustrate the damaging effects of adverse economic conditions and increased foreign competition, total shipments of 1.17 million mt of malleable iron castings in 1969 fell to production levels of 284,000 mt in 1982. A small recovery in the industry occurred in 1984 when production increased to 380,000 mt. However, production soon slid back to 299,000 mt in 1989 and declined to 249,000 mt in 1995. The number of establishments producing malleable iron castings decreased from 73 in 1972 to 26 in the late 1990s.

CURRENT CONDITIONS

Metal casting shipments remained relatively constant at 15 million tons of product per year from 1994 to 1996. This level is expected to be maintained into the twentieth century; however, the outlook for malleable iron casting production is expected to decline. In 1997, for instance, despite the moderate rate of continued growth of the U.S. economy (approximately 2.2 percent annually) and low level of inflation expected into the year 2000, malleable iron casting production is predicted to fall to 202,000 mt, down more than 20 percent from 258,000 mt in 1992. Current challenges facing the malleable iron foundry industry include:

Demand for Cheaper, Lighter, and Stronger Components. Many U.S. end use manufacturers are substituting plastics, ceramics, composites, lighter alloys, and nonferrous castings for malleable iron in appliances, aerospace equipment, builder's hardware, and automotive components to help them compete in a global economy and to meet government regulations. Total iron usage per passenger car and light weight truck was approximately 650 lbs. in 1981. By 1995, the usage had dropped to 350 lbs. and industrial analysts estimated that usage could drop to 215 pounds per vehicle by the year 2005. Similarly, only 25 percent of the intake manifolds produced for domestic vehicles in 1995 were made of iron. Many components that were once castings may now be weldments, forgings, or mechanical assemblies.

Changing Markets. The forecast for a continued expansion of the economy to the end of the century leads to an optimistic outlook for the casting industry. Steady demand for American made cars, trucks, farm equipment, machine tools, freight cars, and oil field machinery should maintain the need for malleable iron castings. On the down side, however, proposed changes in plumbing fittings and electrical standards could further erode an already dwindling demand.

Replacement by Ductile Iron Castings. Related to the need for lightweight and high-strength components and parts is the growth in the replacement rate of ductile iron castings for malleable iron castings. Malleable iron competes with ductile and grey iron in the traditional light and heavy industrial manufacturing markets, but ductile iron is lighter than malleable iron. Ductile iron actually doubled its share of the market in the last decade because of its unique compatibility with new casting techniques called "near-net-shapes." This new method of casting allows for thinner-walled castings with intricate and complex shapes and sizes. Secondary finishing like blasting and sanding are virtually eliminated through the use of this process. In the automotive industry, ductile iron engine blocks are increasingly replacing malleable iron engine blocks. In the housing industry, ductile iron valve castings are expected to continue to replace malleable iron valve castings because of their superior resistance to shock and impact. Ductile castings are also replacing malleable castings in the farm equipment, electrical fittings, and plumbing fittings markets.

Foreign Competition. In the 1980s, overseas competitors adapted more quickly to changes in the industry than did domestic producers. They also used the strong dollar of the early 1980s to gain a foothold in the U.S. market that they have yet to relinquish. Approximately 28 percent of all malleable plumbing fittings used in the United States in 1995 were imported. Thailand has been particularly responsible for the decline in American foundry's market shares in plumbing and electrical fitting castings. Recently, tariffs have been levied on these products in an effort to increase their sales price in the United States.

Increasing Customer Demands. Many malleable iron castings customers have shifted from placing large batch type orders of castings to lower castings order levels. Just-in-time technologies delivered high-quality parts and the increased technological support that must accompany such inventory practices put pressure on many small domestic malleable iron foundries to meet these changes in the marketplace. Those foundries that cannot make these transitions will not likely survive.

INDUSTRY LEADERS

The General Motors Corporation Central Foundry Division in Saginaw, Michigan, is the largest facility producing malleable iron castings. The plant primarily manufactures connecting rods for automobiles and light weight trucks. Industrial analysts expect automotive related malleable iron shipments to be 130,000 tons in 1997. Other leading companies include Texas Foundries of Lufkin, Texas, with $70 million in sales and 900 employees; Dunron Company Inc. Foundry Division of Dayton, Ohio, with 300 employees and an

estimated $26 million in sales; and Delcher Division of Easton, Massachusetts, with $10 million in sales and 300 employees.

WORK FORCE

Total employment in malleable iron foundries in the mid-1990s had fallen to 2,800, as compared with the 16,000 employed workers in 1980. Production workers numbered 2,400, accumulating 5 million production hours. Employment in the malleable foundry industry reached its peak in 1951 at 32,289, of which 28,388 workers were in production. Total payroll compensation in the mid-1990s was $112.3 million, with hourly wages at $18.90 as compared to $11.27 a decade earlier.

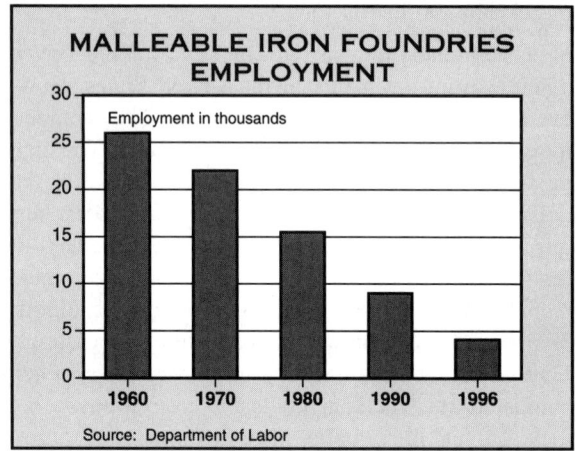

MALLEABLE IRON FOUNDRIES EMPLOYMENT

Employment in thousands

Source: Department of Labor

AMERICA AND THE WORLD

According to *Modern Castings'* "30th Census of World Casting Production," the world's production of malleable iron castings was approximately 2.1 million metric tons in 1995. This is roughly a drop of 38 percent from the record production levels of 3.4 million mt reached in 1973.

In 1995, the United States' share of total world production was roughly 12 percent (down from 50 percent in 1966). The largest producer of malleable iron castings was the Commonwealth of Independent States (CIS) with 40 percent of total world production. China's share of world production totaled 20 percent, Japan tallied 7 percent, and India and Germany contributed 4 percent each to global production of malleable iron castings.

RESEARCH AND TECHNOLOGY

Exotic materials and thin-walled castings are regarded by many industry observers as the wave of the future. Some of the rapid technological changes occurring around malleable iron casters are new mold designs; new metal casting techniques; new computerized casting, finishing, and monitoring; and new purchasing procedures by domestic consumer and industrial product manufacturers. The industry is under attack by new technology parts-making processes, and it has been slow to change to compete with these more efficient casting processes.

For future survival, American malleable iron foundries must keep up with the technological changes in the industry. New investments in operations to improve melting, alloying, metal flow, die and mold filling temperature control, and lubrication will all help in this regard. Today's global marketplace also demands stronger quality control, price restrictions, and tighter specifications. Casting has moved from an art to a science. The days of testing sand moisture by hand are over, for today computer controls are what drive the most exacting tolerances. Partnership arrangements between foundries and their customers and suppliers will help to promote future growth. Pricing, quality assurance, service, and the consolidation of suppliers using just-in-time production practices to keep costs low and response time to customers high will help protect domestic malleable iron casting operations from further market declines.

FURTHER READING

U.S. Bureau of the Census. *1987 Census of Manufactures.* Washington: GPO.

———. *1995 Annual Survey of Manufactures.* Washington: GPO, 1997.

"Cautious Optimism Prevails Among U.S. Metalcasters." Cleveland, OH: Penton Publishing.

Malleable Iron Castings. Ann Arbor Press, Inc., Malleable Founders Society, 1960.

"Modern Casting Census of World Casting Production." *Modern Casting,* December 1992.

Sanders, Clyde A. *History Cast in Metal.* Cast Metals Institute, American Foundrymen's Society.

Stundza, Tom. "Why Foundries Are Stalled in Neutral." *Purchasing,* October 1989.

—William A. Bennett, updated by Andrew J. Poss

SIC 3324

STEEL INVESTMENT FOUNDRIES

This classification covers establishments primarily engaged in manufacturing steel investment foundries.

INDUSTRY SNAPSHOT

The steel investment casting business was growing in the early 1990s. The industry was one of the few in which the growth of shipments matched growth in employment. After suffering a fairly small decline in business during 1982, the industry began a steady growth trend. In 1983, shipments were valued at $939.6 million, and the size of the total work force was 15,200. Five years later, shipments had grown to $1.47 billion, and total employment was at 20,800. By 1996, shipments had grown to $3.5 billion, and total employment increased to 37,100. The average hourly wage in the industry had grown from $10.09 in 1988 to $11.59 in 1994. The number of establishments dedicated to this type of steel casting remained somewhat constant during the 1980s. In 1982, approximately 131 establishments existed, and they remained through 1986. A sharp decrease in foundries—to 112—occurred in 1987. By 1994, that number had fallen to 100, with 95 of all industry firms employing more than 20 people.

In 1994, the product share was split between the following four product classes: high temperature metal castings, which claimed 47.4 percent of the market; stainless steel, which claimed 21.6 percent; carbon steel, which included low carbon alloy steel, claimed 15.8 percent; and alloy steel, including some stainless steel, claimed 9.2 percent. Non-specific steel investment foundries were contained in the remaining 6.0 percent of the industry.

Materials consumed were primarily those used to make steel. The delivered cost of pig iron was $3.8 million in 1994, and the delivered cost of iron and purchased steel scrap accounted for a collective delivered cost of $16.8 million. Other metals included: cobalt-based alloys, $24.4 million; nickel-based alloys, $88.0 million; and all other nonferrous shapes and forms, $25.3 million. Sand had a delivered cost of $10.6 million, and clay and nonclay refractories had delivered costs of $3.7 million and $4.3 million, respectively. Industrial dies, molds, jigs, and fixtures that were used to produce the wax patterns reported delivered costs of $10.0 million. Grinding wheels and other abrasives had delivered costs of $15.6 million. Industrial patterns carried a cost of $6.9 million and all

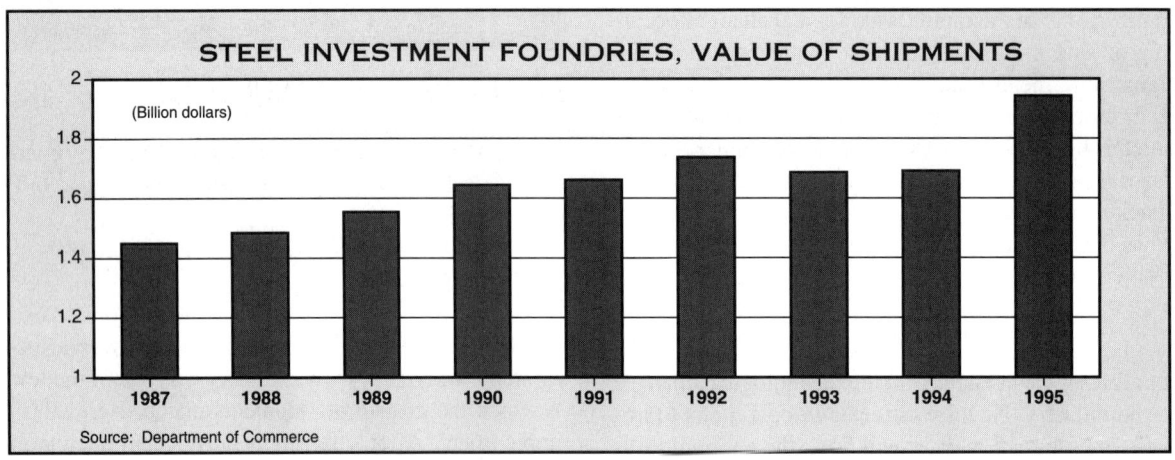

STEEL INVESTMENT FOUNDRIES, VALUE OF SHIPMENTS

(Billion dollars)

Source: Department of Commerce

other materials, components, parts, containers, and supplies reported delivered costs of $174.6 million.

ORGANIZATION AND STRUCTURE

Steel investment foundries are not necessarily in a class of their own. Many foundries practice investment casting regardless of the metal type, and many steel foundries may practice several casting processes beside investment. For example, the art industry used investment casting to create bronze sculptures, and the jewelry industry used investment casting to produce intricate designs. Relatively few steel foundries, with respect to the entire steel foundry industry, exclusively used the investment casting process.

This industry is at the mercy of the entire steel industry. The Environmental Protection Agency and the Occupational Safety and Health Administration also keep watchful eyes on the industry and continually impose regulations. One particular advantage of the investment casting process is that, compared to other casting processes, it is not harmful to the environment. The sand used can be further recycled; and since the process involves no chemical binders, there is no danger of producing hazardous fumes. With less waste and fewer pollutants produced, this process was not severely affected by increasing environmental legislation.

BACKGROUND AND DEVELOPMENT

According to Paul DeGarmo in his work *Materials and Processes in Manufacturing,* "investment casting actually is a very old process. It existed in China for centuries, and Cellini employed a form of it in Italy in the sixteenth century. Dentists have utilized the process since 1897, but it was not until World War II that it attained industrial importance for making jet turbine blades from metals that were not readily machinable. Currently millions of castings are produced

by the process each year, its unique characteristics permitting the designer almost unlimited freedom in the complexity and close tolerances he can utilize.''

Investment casting is also known as precision casting or the lost wax process. A pattern of wax or other expendable material is created and is attached, sometimes in clusters, to expendable down sprues. This conglomeration is then invested, or surrounded, by a refractory slurry, which then dries and hardens at room temperature. The mold is then heated to melt or burn out the wax or other expendable material. In the hollow cavity, molten metal is cast. This casting process is particularly adapted to the production of small, intricate parts using metals of higher melting points than are feasible for use in die casting. Steel is one of the primary metals used in the industry.

Investment casting is a high precision process, and is therefore expensive. The process allows highly complex shapes to be produced while maintaining good dimensional accuracy and surface finishes. The ability to produce thin wall sections are another advantage to using the investment casting process. Sections as thin as 0.015 inches, for example, have been cast.

The Investment Casting Institute (ICI) was founded in 1950, and it held its first meeting in 1953. At that time, the organization had 13 member companies. In the 1990s, 250 companies were affiliated with this organization. The ICI holds semi-annual meetings, a technical meeting in the fall, and a members-only meeting in the spring to discuss management issues. The ICI also provides training in several aspects of the industry.

CURRENT CONDITIONS

Investment casting has rebounded strongly from the recession of the early 1990s, and the demand throughout the last half of the decade is strong in the commercial investment casting applications. The United States had more than 300 members in the investment casting industry at the end of 1996. These foundries shipped 15.7 million tons of casting valued at $29.3 billion—40,000 tons of which were steel investment casting shipments. Investment casting, independent of the metal poured, totaled 143,000 tons in 1996, and analysts expect this number to increase steadily, reaching 195,000 tons by 2006. Approximately 49,000 tons of commercial valves are expected to be shipped in 1997; the total shipments for that year are forecast at 147,000 tons.

Steel investment castings require high quality steel due to the intricate nature of parts cast using this process. Because extreme precision is required in producing these castings, any inclusions in the metal will ruin a part. The primary quality issue facing the steel industry in the 1990s was the cleanliness of steel. Clean steel is important to the industry because steel that is free of tramp elements, slag, and dross creates better quality parts. According to John Svoboda, ''In the early 1980s a high level management task force representing the steel industry identified oxide macroinclusions as the major factor responsible for the lack of acceptance of steel castings by the design engineering community. This study augmented the already well-known requirements for cast steel to be free from tramp elements, gases, and microinclusions. In short, the mandate for 'clean steel' has been issued.'' By the 1990s, significant progress had been made in clean steel production. However, future studies were expected to establish a method of quantifying the cleanliness of steel and find the relationship between cleanliness, mechanical properties, and design performance.

INDUSTRY LEADERS

The 36 leading companies in this industry grossed total sales of $3.57 billion and employed 37,100 people. The Pechiney Corporation of Greenwich, Connecticut, reported mid-1990 sales of $2.78 billion and employed 28,000 people. Precision Castparts Corporation of Portland, Oregon, reported sales of $436 million and employed 5,200 people. Howmet Whitehall Casting of Whitehall, Michigan, ranked third with sales of $125 million and total employment of 1,100 people. Dolphin Inc. of Phoenix, Arizona, reported sales of $39 million and employed 500 people. Stainless Foundry and Engineering Inc. of Milwaukee, Wisconsin, reported sales of $30 million and employed 400 people.

The greatest concentration of steel investment foundries were located in the Great Lakes Region in

the 1990s. Wisconsin was the only state to disclose shipment figures. All other states withheld such financial data due to competitive reasons. Wisconsin's 10 establishments employed 1,100 people at an average hourly wage of $9.78 and had shipments of $74 million. This figure represented 5.1 percent of the industry's total shipments. California, with 19 establishments, contained the highest number of facilities dedicated to this industry. Michigan, Ohio, and Texas respectively had 13, 12, and 11 establishments in the industry.

WORK FORCE

The iron and steel foundry industry was facing major reductions in employment approaching the year 2000. In 1996, the foundry industry employed approximately 217,000, and 59 percent, or 128,000 employees, worked in the ferrous foundries. The number of workers in this industry is expected to decline steadily until it reaches the end of the slump in 1998. Industry analysts expect another 1 percent drop throughout 1997. The decline is primarily due to the shift by the automotive industry to nonferrous or aluminum components. By the end of the decade, employment in the foundry industry should reach 218,000 based on an increase in the number of new automated foundries.

Throughout the late 1990s, the foundry industry still employed 5,000 more workers than it did at the beginning of the decade. However, the ability to attract and retain good reliable production workers remained a significant dilemma. Production workers make up slightly more than 80 percent of the foundry workers and are expected to remain at this level throughout the turn of the century. Similarly, the foundry managerial and staff numbers are forecasted to stay around 40,000 employees. The trend in this industry is for labor productivity to increase from a yearly total of 130,800 tons of casting shipments per worker to 133,000 tons of shipments by the year 2000.

AMERICA AND THE WORLD

In 1994, the ratification of the North American Free Trade Agreement or NAFTA economically linked the United States, Canada, and Mexico. The agreement created one of the largest free trade zones in the world. International trade, especially the enforcement of export and import regulations, drastically changed. Many steel foundries have found that they must export their products in order to prosper and grow. At the same time questions arise as to how labor costs, environmental regulations, and product dumping issues across the steel industry would be resolved. The North American Steel Council (NASC) was founded to address NAFTA related disagreements. The council consists of approximately 12 CEO's from steel companies in Mexico, Canada, and the United States belonging to the American Iron and Steel Institute (AISI). The NASC is responsible for addressing trade issues associated with the steel industry and develop mutually acceptable solutions where possible. Despite these efforts, anti-dumping and countervailing laws were still in place in the member countries because NAFTA free-trade codes were worthless without unified support in the United States, Mexico, and Canada.

RESEARCH AND TECHNOLOGY

A major technological advancement in the foundry industry entered the market in the early 1990s. This advancement was known as either Rapid Prototyping or Functional Prototyping. Rapid prototyping is a computerized system that uses stereolithography and selective laser sintering to create a three-dimensional shape that has been drawn on a computer aided drafting station. A computer takes the three dimensional model and mathematically slices it into layers of specific thickness. Each layer is transmitted digitally from the design unit to the production unit where the material of choice is used to build the shape layer by layer. Using this new technology, a designer could take a customer's idea, design it, and, in several hours or days, depending on the size of the part, have a prototype available for the customer to evaluate. The new technology dramatically reduced both the time and expense of producing intricate designs.

The largest producer of rapid prototyping equipment in 1996 was 3D Systems of Valencia, California. They sell a system that uses ultraviolet light driven by a CAD program to slice through a photopolymer pool. The company is developing a process called QuickCast to improve the accuracy of the stereolithographic models used to produce the patterns for investment casting. The CAD program divides a part to be cast into a core and cavity then generates a negative of the part. The product is then molded with QuickCast and built in steel to produce a mold insert. In the December 1996 issue of *Modern Casting,* Mathew Duke of Precision Technology Inc. remarked that stereolithography allows a great reduction in lead time when used in the right applications, but for many parts the cost is still prohibitory.

FURTHER READING

Darnay, Arsen J., ed. *Manufacturing USA.* 5th ed. Detroit: Gale Research, 1996.

Delch, D. K. "Free Trade: Patient Needs Resuscitation." *American Metal Market,* 25 November 1996, 14.

Horton, Robert. "risk Demand Fuels Investment Casting Technology Innovations." *Modern Casting,* December 1996, 45.

Peters, Dean M., ed. "The Automation of Molding, Moldmaking, and Coremaking." *Foundry Management & Technology,* September 1992.

Rodgers, Robert C., ed. "Foundry Industry Organizations." *Foundry Management & Technology,* September 1992.

Schmitt, B. "Group Seeks Harmony in the Discord of Free Trade." *Am. Met. Mark,* 18 May 1995, 6A.

Svoboda, John M. "Clean Steel Technology." *Modern Casting,* October 1991.

"30th Census of World Casting Production - 1995." *Modern Casting,* December 1996.

Uziel, Yehoram. "Functional Prototyping—Has the Future Arrived?" *Foundry Management & Technology,* March 1993.

—Valerie Wilson, uptated by Andrew J. Poss

SIC 3325

STEEL FOUNDRIES, NOT ELSEWHERE CLASSIFIED

This classification provides coverage of establishments primarily engaged in manufacturing steel castings, not elsewhere classified.

Carbon steel castings held 44 percent of the market share in 1987, while high alloy and other alloy steel castings each held just over 22 percent of the market. Approximately 11 percent of the market was non-specific in 1987. On the whole, this industry steadily downsized employment levels between 1982 and 1986, with the highest level being 36,900 and the lowest level being 19,700. By the mid-1990s, however, the industry had begun a slow recovery. According to the *1995 Annual Survey of Manufactures,* employment levels in 1995 had risen to 25,700, an increase of 7.5 percent over 23,900 in 1994.

Republic Engineered Steels Inc. of Massillon, Ohio, was the industry leader in the mid-1990s, with $805 million in sales and 5,000 employees. Nucor-Yamato Steel Co. of Blytheville, Arkansas, was ranked second with $800 million in sales and 700 employees. American Steel Foundries of Chicago was ranked third, with an estimated $300 million in sales and 3,000 employees. Haynes International Inc. of Kokomo, Indiana, was ranked fourth, with $200 mil-

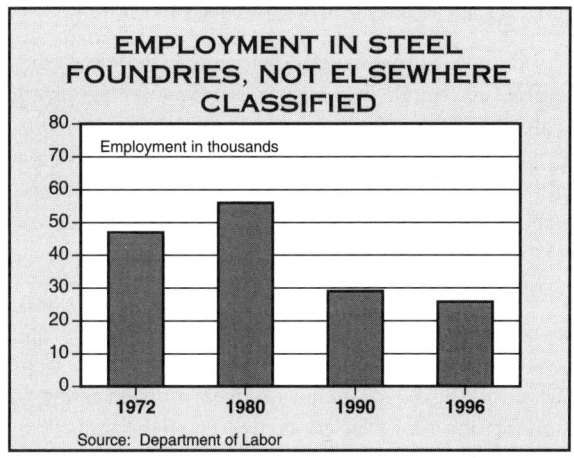

EMPLOYMENT IN STEEL FOUNDRIES, NOT ELSEWHERE CLASSIFIED

Employment in thousands

Source: Department of Labor

lion in sales and 900 employees. Hitchiner Manufacturing Co. Inc. of Milford, New Hampshire, was ranked fifth, with $125 million in sales and 2,300 employees. In terms of employment, Ohio, Wisconsin, Pennsylvania, and Texas ranked as industry leaders, making up 45 percent of the industry's employment.

The Bureau of Labor Statistics projected a bleak future for this industry's occupations. Except for industrial machinery mechanics, sales workers, millwrights, and industrial production managers, all other occupations are expected to face reductions in employment levels. The many steel foundry occupations expected to face over a 10 percent reduction going into the year 2000 include: general laborers, grinders, precision workers, blue collar worker supervisors, mold assembly and shakeout operators, inspectors, metal pourers, truck operators, grinding machine operators, furnace machine operators, welders, assemblers, hand workers, electricians, material handlers, and janitors.

The Great Lakes area has the heaviest concentration of steel foundries, and Ohio's 24 establishments ranked first in terms of shipments, which amounted to $285.1 million in the early 1990s. At the same time, Pennsylvania had more foundries than any other state; however, its 32 establishments were ranked third, with shipments of $190.8 million. Wisconsin ranked second with $233.4 million worth of shipments generated by 18 establishments. Hourly wages between these three states did not vary significantly during this period. Workers in Ohio were paid the highest hourly wage, compared to Pennsylvania and Wisconsin, at $13.86. On average, Wisconsin and Pennsylvania paid workers $11.42 and $10.41 per hour, respectively.

FURTHER READING

Darnay, Arsen J., ed. *Manufacturing USA*. 5th ed. Detroit: Gale Research, 1996.

U.S. Bureau of the Census *1995 Annual Survey of Manufactures*. Washington: GPO, 1997.

—Valerie Wilson, updated by Kenneth R. Shepherd

SIC 3331

PRIMARY SMELTING AND REFINING OF COPPER

This industry consists of companies that smelt copper from ore and refine copper by electrolytic or other processes. Those establishments engaged in rolling, drawing, or extruding copper are classified in **SIC 3351: Rolling, Drawing, and Extruding of Copper.**

INDUSTRY SNAPSHOT

Copper has excellent properties that made it useful to many industries. As a base metal, copper is used both alone and in alloyed combinations with other metals. The electrical, communications, and construction industries use copper in many of their products. Approximately 70 percent of U.S. copper consumption is for electrical and electronic uses, according to the U.S. Geological Survey. Copper faces increasing competition, however, from other materials such as plastics and other highly engineered materials in electronics and electrical applications.

The copper smelting business has been growing since the early 1980s. This industry, like many other metal industries, has had growth of shipments matched by a decline in employment. After suffering a fairly small decline in business during 1985 and 1986, the industry began a steady growth trend. In 1987, shipments were valued at $2.55 billion and the size of the total work force was 3,300. Five years later, shipments had grown to $5.58 billion with total employment at 5,600. By 1994, shipments had grown to $6.18 billion and total employment was at 6,400. The average hourly wage in the industry had grown from $14.34 in 1984 to $18.14 in 1994. The number of establishments dedicated to copper smelting reached a low during the 1980s when approximately 12 establishments existed in 1986. There were approximately 20 establishments in the mid-1990s.

In 1994, the product share was primarily refined primary copper representing 60.4 percent. Noncommercial grade copper smelter products which are produced for further refining made up 39.5 percent of the product share. Nonspecific primary copper products filled the remaining tenth of a percent of the industry. Nearing the end of the twentieth century, all of the players in the copper industry were involved in the recyclability of copper. Recycled copper is a highly valued, ''high-grade'' scrap which often has more than 90 percent of the value of newly mined copper.

ORGANIZATION AND STRUCTURE

Companies engaged in smelting and refining copper create products for a variety of national and international industries. End-use markets for copper and copper alloy can be categorized into five different functional uses. In 1994, 55 percent of copper products were used for electrical purposes and 25 percent of the products were used because they were corrosion resistant. Another 11 percent of copper products were used in heat transfer functions and 8 percent for structural purposes. The aesthetic use of copper products accounted for only 2 percent of its functional uses.

The end-use markets for copper were primarily building related or industrial machinery and equipment related. For 1994, the ten largest copper markets in the United States were: heating and plumbing with 16 percent of the market share, building wire had 14 percent, commercial refrigeration and air conditioning and power utilities each made up 8 percent of the total copper sold, automotive electrical, telecommunications and in-plant equipment each accounted for 7 percent of U.S. sales of copper, electronics made up 5 percent and industrial valves & fittings and automotive non-electrical were each 4 percent. The remaining 21 percent of the United States copper market was unspecified.

Copper in the United States went from the mines to the smelters. In some cases these were owned by the same company, and in some cases the mining and smelting were performed at nearby facilities. The mining and smelting companies are the producers of copper materials, while the wire rod mills and brass mills and foundries that work copper prepare the metal for delivery to manufacturers in various industries.

Mining companies process copper ores, most of which are retrieved from open-pit mines. These ores are refined and sometimes alloyed with other elements, such as zinc or beryllium. A primary smelting reactor such as a reverberatory furnace produces copper sulfide from concentrated ore. Some reverberatory furnaces were replaced by oxygen/flash smelting, which created less air pollution. The final step in smelting and refining works involves an electrolytic or other refining process. The resulting copper is often close to 100 percent pure.

BACKGROUND AND DEVELOPMENT

Copper mining had origins in the Middle East, but reached its zenith in America. In the mid-eighteenth century miners in the colonies discovered copper ores in what is now the northeastern United States. They mined these ores, but English law prohibited the establishment of smelting works in the colonies, so the ore was sent to England for smelting and refining.

After the American Revolution miners and smelters moved to the newly created United States and began working in American mines and refineries. Copper sheathing began to be used on wooden ships as early as the 1790s. The copper protected the ships from the pressure and corrosive effects of the ocean. Great demand from the shipping industry helped the budding copper industry, but the United States still depended on copper imports from England and South America. In 1806 U.S. importers of copper asked the Congress to exempt copper from customs duty. The protests lodged by copper industry pioneers succeeded in lowering tariffs applied to copper imports.

In the early 1800s U.S. companies began to use blast furnaces for smelting and refining copper. Later, with the rise of American industry, growing copper works created stripping, boiler plates, rivets and other copper-based items that were used in an increasingly diverse number of industries and products. Copper nails replaced cast iron nails in building and the boom in putting up towns and cities across the new nation resulted in a windfall for the copper industry.

The reserves of copper in the United States have not suffered appreciably during the twentieth century. Although copper has been in use for more than 10,000 years, about three-quarters of all copper consumed has been produced since World War II. New deposits have been found and better mining and extracting methods developed by copper companies.

U.S. smelter production of copper reached its peak in the early 1970s at 1.8 million metric tons annually. In the 1970s the trend in the copper smelting industry was toward the purchase of smelters, refining companies, and mines by oil companies. In the following decade, almost all of these oil companies sold off their copper companies, leaving them independent again, but this time with a renewed sense of the marketplace. Workers in some of these companies learned new technologies that would enable them to compete in the international copper arena. Instead of the pyrometallurgy of the reverberatory furnaces, many smelters introduced hydrometallurgical processing that produced copper whose purity and quality matched that of the electrolytically refined copper.

The 1980s were not boom years for many players in the various copper-related industries. The three largest U.S. producers of copper—Asarco, Phelps Dodge Corporation, and AMAX, Inc.—lost almost $2.5 billion from 1982 through 1985. These companies, however, remained leaders in the field despite their difficulties. Many other companies in the copper industry went out of business, though. Those that remained made drastic changes to cut operating costs and improve efficiency. These cost-cutting measures at times exacerbated difficulties with labor.

Copper consumption had fallen during the late 1980s and early 1990s. The compound growth rate for copper consumption from 1972 through 1991 was 1.3 percent. In 1991, the value of all shipments of primary copper hit a low of $3.8 billion.

CURRENT CONDITIONS

After the declines of the early 1990s, the industry posted modest growth during the mid-1990s. Its 1994 shipments valued at $5.2 billion; by 1995 shipments had climbed to $7.1 billion in current dollars, however production was actually lower than in 1994. Despite the growth of plastics as a substitute for copper pipe and fittings, industry analysts expect copper markets to grow at approximately 1 percent per year into the year 2000.

The United States maintained its world leadership in copper production during the 1990s. U.S. companies produced 1.8 million metric tons of copper ores and almost 2.7 million tons of refined copper products in 1995. Consumption of copper throughout the world was expected to increase into the twenty-first century. The supply levels of copper from mines in Peru has begun to solidify in the late 1990s due to the combined efforts of the World Bank, the International Monetary Fund, and various financial organizations which have taken important measures to restructure debt in Peru and thereby improve mining in that country.

The world smelter production of copper was 9.5 million short tons in 1993, this value was a decrease from the high of 9.7 million in 1989 according to the U.S. Geological Survey. International competition was a factor in the 1990s, as was an increased environmental consciousness in the United States. One copper company declined to build a new smelting facility in Texas after environmental groups protested.

Copper industry executives approached the turn of the century with guarded optimism. They saw successful applications of copper in many existing industries, and were working to expand the use of copper in other industries. One of the key roles of the Copper Devel-

opment Association (CDA), a leading representative body for the industry, is to work with manufacturers to develop new uses for copper. CDA created programs aimed at increasing the usage of copper in specific industries. In Europe, for instance, copper was used four times more than in the U.S. for architectural applications.

INDUSTRY LEADERS

In the 1990s, the primary smelters and refiners of copper that had survived the economic turmoil of the 1980s were expanding. Phelps Dodge Corporation, based in El Paso Texas, is the largest U.S. copper company. In 1996, they had sales of $92 million and employed 500 people. Phelps' domestic copper production was expected to rise in the late 1990s with the start-up of their Morenci SX-EW plant in Arizona.

The Colonial Metals Company of Columbia, Pennsylvania reported sales of $70 million and employed 200 people. GA Avril Company of Cincinnati, Ohio reported sales of $10 million and employed less than 100 people. Cox Creek Refining Company of Baltimore, Maryland also employs less than 100 workers and had an estimated sales of $6 million.

The largest concentration of primary copper foundries is located in the Arizona with 6 establishments responsible for 31 percent of the total employment in this industry. Texas has 3 establishments also responsible for 31 percent of the primary copper workers. The remainder of the primary copper establishments are in Michigan, New Mexico, and Utah with each state having two foundries.

AMERICA AND THE WORLD

According to the *Standard and Poor's Industry Surveys,* the United States was the world leader in smelter production of copper entering the 1990s. In 1994, 1.7 short tons of copper were smelted in the U.S. In comparison, 1.4 million short tons were smelted in Chile, which is the second-ranked country in copper smelter production. During that same year, 560,000 short tons were smelted in Canada, Germany smelted 296,000 shorts tons of copper, 1.1 million short tons were smelted in Japan, and 585,000 short tons were smelted in African nations. The Commonwealth of Independent States (CIS) smelted 900,000 short tons of copper in 1993.

The United States ranked second in mine production of copper at 1.8 million metric tons, while top-ranked Chile mined 2.2 million metric tons.

The copper industry was becoming increasingly global in its outlook in the 1990s. Smelters and refiners of copper were looking toward developing countries as markets for copper-based products. Those countries that were improving their infrastructures with telecommunications cables, power cables, and other basic building tools needed more copper. The Asian markets of China, Taiwan, and South Korea were expected to provide large new markets.

In 1993 a politically charged topic in the industry was the General Agreement on Tariffs and Trade (GATT). Copper industry leaders met with U.S. trade officials to request a reduction of Japanese and European tariffs under GATT. Their aim was to eliminate global tariffs on copper to gain better access to foreign markets and argued that the Japanese market was too heavily protected. The U.S. International Trade Commission (ITC) rejected high tariffs on imported metals.

The U.S. formed an International Copper Study Group in the 1990s in conjunction with 17 other countries involved in the copper industry. Their aim was to allow informational exchanges between producing and consuming countries as well as to increase copper production and consumption. The members of the group included Germany, China, Chile, Peru, and France.

RESEARCH AND TECHNOLOGY

A low-cost method of production being used in the 1990s in U.S. copper companies was known as SX-EW, or solvent extraction-electrowinning. Solutions of sulfuric acid were applied to dumps of copper-bearing ores, then the dissolved copper was recovered by depositing copper onto electrically charged cathodes. This process was known as electrowinning. SX-EW had fewer steps, and caused less pollution, at a lower cost than earlier production methods. But only some of the world's ore was able to be processed by this method. Primary sulfide ore, which is located deeper in mines and is usually found combined with other elements, was not eligible for SX-EW. SX-EW was effective for oxide ore and secondary sulfide ore, which are found closer to the mine's surface, where the ore has been oxidized. Unfortunately, the contents of U.S. mines often housed principally the primary sulfide ores rather than the oxide ores or the secondary sulfide ores. Another process for copper production is known as Escondida ammonia leach process. This process employs air combined with a solution of ammonia-ammonium sulphate which leaches cuprous salts from chalcocite solutions. Approximately half the copper is leached and the remainder can be recovered by a flotation recycle. This process was developed by and named for the Escondida mine in Chile and has been used successfully to produce cathode copper. An innovative leaching process, piloted at Chatwoods Austra-

lia is known as the Intec Process. This method of leaching has the added advantage that gold can be recovered on activated carbon, at the same time that copper is being separated as its halogen complex. The metal from the Intec process is used for copper briquettes and wire or strip.

The technical research and market development area of the copper industry has promoted new technologies that use copper materials in a wide array of applications. These new applications include the use of copper radiators in the automobile industry. The copper industry emphasizes copper's positive features such as its corrosion resistance and strength, and notes that the new radiators are also lighter and more durable than the current copper radiators.

Other proposed uses of copper include solar energy, nuclear waste disposal canisters, and superconductivity applications. Industrial applications, such as valves, fittings, and power utilities remain steady users of copper. Until 1982 another copper user was the U.S. mint, which coined pennies using a copper alloy. In 1982 the copper alloy used in the production of U.S. pennies was replaced by zinc. Another loss to the industry was the increasing use of fiber optics products, which began to replace some of the copper telecommunications equipment.

Recyclability became increasingly important as copper companies faced the next century. Because copper was more easily recycled than many other metals, more copper was recovered from recycled material than was obtained from newly mined ores. This combination of recycled copper materials and healthy U.S. deposits of copper made the country highly self-sufficient in copper. Aluminum, which competed with copper in many areas, was a more difficult metal for the United States to obtain.

FURTHER READING

Charlier, Marj. "Gold Companies Likely to Post Uneven Results; Copper Outlook is Grim." *Wall Street Journal,* 8 October 1993.

Copper Development Association Inc. "Annual Data: 1996: Copper Supply and Consumption, 1975-1995." New York, 1996.

———. "Copper in the USA: Bright Future—Colorful Past." New York, 1990.

Getler, Warren. "Copper Futures Rise, but Traders Warn Rally is Likely to be Short-Lived Amid Oversupply." *Wall Street Journal,* 12 October 1993, C18.

Gross, John E. "Copper Market Letter." *Copper Talk,* May 1993, 7.

Jolly, Janice L.W. "Copper Demand Could Exceed Supply in the Next Eight Years." *American Metal Market,* 17 February 1993, 6A.

Payne, Robert M. "Electrical Uses are Big Growth Area for Copper." *American Metal Market,* 23 November 1992, 10A.

Simon, Howard. "Traders Hope Copper Prices Will Blossom in the Spring." *Journal of Commerce and Commercial,* 16 February 1993, 8A.

Stundza, Tom. "Cheap Metal, and Plenty of It." *Purchasing,* 7 March 1991, 50.

Taylor, Jeffrey. "U.S. Copper Futures Fall as Available Stocks of the Metal Reach a 15-Year High in London." *Wall Street Journal,* 27 October 1993, C18.

Temes, Judy. "Polish and Tarnish." *Crain's New York Business,* 12 November 1990, 3.

Wrigley, Al. "Copper-Brass Comeback." *American Metal Market,* 20 September 1993, 4.

—Fran Shonfeld Sherman and Andrew J. Poss

SIC 3334

PRIMARY PRODUCTION OF ALUMINUM

This classification includes establishments primarily engaged in producing aluminum from alumina and in refining aluminum by any process. Excluded from this classification are establishments primarily engaged in rolling, drawing, or extruding aluminum, which are classified in the following product groups: **SIC 3351: Rolling, Drawing, and Extruding of Copper; SIC 3353: Aluminum Sheet, Plate, and Foil; SIC 3354: Aluminum Extruded Products; SIC 3355: Aluminum Rolling and Drawing, Not Elsewhere Classified; SIC 3356: Rolling, Drawing, and Extruding of Nonferrous Metals, Except Copper and Aluminum;** and **SIC 3357: Drawing and Insulating of Nonferrous Wire.**

INDUSTRY SNAPSHOT

Divided into product groups, the aluminum industry comprises three distinct segments: primary aluminum manufacturers, semi-fabricated aluminum manufacturers, and secondary, or scrap aluminum manufacturers. Of these three segments, the primary aluminum industry is the smallest when defined in terms of number of manufacturers. The primary aluminum industry generates revenues roughly equivalent to the sales recorded by secondary smelting manufacturers. The semi-fabricated aluminum industry accounts for the greatest amount of revenue within the broader, loosely structured aluminum industry.

To produce aluminum, primary aluminum manufacturers first process bauxite, an ore that is the basic raw material of aluminum, to create alumina. A powerful electric current is then passed through a solution containing alumina to produce aluminum in its most primary form. Aluminum in this form, either as a mass of metal in a bar or a block shape (referred to as an ingot), or as a smaller rectangular bar (referred to as a billet), serves as the raw material for manufacturers engaged in producing aluminum products. Primary aluminum manufacturers supply aluminum to semi-fabricated aluminum manufacturers and to a diverse array of manufacturers outside the aluminum industry who utilize aluminum to manufacture their products.

Throughout much of its existence, the primary aluminum industry comprised fewer than 10 manufacturers, but as of 1994 approximately 30 manufacturers were involved in producing primary aluminum. Much of the proliferation of manufacturers occurred during the 1980s—especially between 1982 and 1987—a period when the number of manufacturers climbed from 15 to 34. In 1994, these manufacturers generated $5.5 billion in sales, an aggregate value of shipments primarily derived from the production of aluminum ingot, which accounted for over 80 percent of the industry's total shipments. Billet primary aluminum, the only other type of aluminum produced by the industry that accounted for any appreciable revenue, represented 19.6 percent of the industry's shipments.

These shipments were purchased by the industry's primary markets: building and construction/infrastructure, packaging, transportation, equipment and machines, consumer durables, and electrical. In 1994, the bulk of the industry's aluminum was utilized by manufacturers involved in building and construction, container and packaging, and transportation industries, which together purchased approximately 60 percent of the industry's total shipments. Exports accounted for approximately 15 percent of aluminum shipments in 1994 and 20 percent was accountable to the industry's three major markets: electrical manufacturers, consumer durable manufacturers, and machinery and equipment manufacturers.

Throughout the 1990s, the growth of aluminum has been driven by the automotive industry. Car makers continue to produce lighter passenger vehicles and trucks in order to conform to the Corporate Average Fuel Economy (CAFE) regulations. By substituting one pound of aluminum for steel parts, the auto designers are able to remove 2.0 to 2.5 pounds of cast iron. This growth is expected to continue to the end of the twentieth century. Analysts expect the aluminum market to begin to level off by 2004 when automakers begin substituting aluminum components with plastic parts.

ORGANIZATION AND STRUCTURE

Although the industry consists of relatively few manufacturers, the size of a primary aluminum manufacturing facility, when defined in terms of the number of people employed per establishment, was comparatively large when measured against other manufacturing industries. Of the 44 establishments involved in producing primary aluminum in 1994, which includes all of the manufacturing facilities operated by the approximately 30 companies engaged in the industry during that year, only 17 employed less than 20 people. The average number of employees per facility, however, was more than seven times greater than the average of all other manufacturing industries in the United States. In 1994, the typical primary aluminum manufacturing establishment employed 349 people, while the average manufacturing facility in the United States employed only 49 people.

Geographically, a majority of the establishments involved in the primary aluminum industry were located in the Pacific Northwest, particularly in the state of Washington, which contained nine facilities that manufactured 26.7 percent of the industry's total shipments. California, Kentucky, and New York with three facilities each, ranked as the second largest concentrated area of primary aluminum manufacturing facilities.

The amount of money required to purchase raw materials for primary aluminum production was considerably higher than the expenditures incurred by the typical facility in all other manufacturing industries. This disparity was primarily due to the tremendous amount of electrical energy required to produce aluminum and because nearly all of the bauxite needed to produce alumina must be imported. Consequently, operating a primary aluminum manufacturing facility is very expensive with operating expenses sometimes 14 fold higher than an average manufacturing establishment. According to 1994 figures, the average cost per establishment in the primary aluminum industry, that is, the average amount of money paid for raw manufacturing materials, was $71 million, significantly more than the $5 million averaged by all other manufacturing establishments. The average investment per establishment, or the average expense earmarked for purchasing manufacturing machinery and paying for production retooling, was also significantly higher in the primary aluminum industry. In 1994, primary aluminum manufacturers paid an average of $2.3 million for such expenditures, versus the $321,011 value aver-

aged for all other manufacturing industries in the United States.

BACKGROUND AND DEVELOPMENT

In 1886, the concurrent development in the United States and France of an economical electrolytic process for refining aluminum immediately spawned widespread optimism. Many manufacturers regarded the discovery as the new metal of the future. Aluminum would continue to be regarded as the metal of the future throughout its first century of existence, indeed well past the point its future should have arrived, leading aluminum manufacturers and government officials to overestimate demand for the metal on occasion. But the creation of a process to economically produce aluminum did, in fact, warrant its fair share of hyperbole, even if the expectations associated with its production sometimes ran too high. The metal possessed desirable conductive and thermal properties, was lightweight, and could be used to form many hard, light, corrosion-resistant alloys. As American manufacturing industries slowly effected a move toward creating products that were lighter in weight, aluminum would prove to be an integral component in a wealth of manufacturing processes, eventually establishing a pervasive, global presence that would validate the hopeful projections held by aluminum's early proponents.

But in 1886, there was only the metal and no clear idea of how aluminum could become, in practical terms, the metal of the future. Discovery of the myriad applications for the new wonder metal fell entirely to the only aluminum manufacturing company of any consequence at the time, the Pittsburgh Reduction Company, later renamed the Aluminum Company of America, and more commonly known as Alcoa. Indeed, Alcoa would remain the only manufacturer of any consequence for the aluminum industry's first 60 years, establishing a monopoly over the U.S. aluminum market during the interim and, consequently, solely guiding the industry's direction for the first half of the twentieth century.

Under the partial stewardship of Charles Martin Hall, a young chemist who discovered the more economically feasible process of aluminum production while working in his woodshed, Alcoa faced, during its early years of operation, the daunting chore of creating first a need, then a demand for aluminum. Initially, the company utilized aluminum to manufacture a line of cooking utensils, which later, in 1901, were successful enough to merit the organization of a cookware subsidiary named American Cooking Utensil. The biggest market for aluminum, however, proved to be the automobile industry, a market that would fuel the industry's growth for its first five decades of operation. By 1915, 65 percent of all primary aluminum was utilized in automotive parts.

At this time, Alcoa still stood alone in the U.S. aluminum market, with the only competition coming from foreign manufacturers, whose penetration of the U.S. market was limited by high tariffs and comparatively higher energy costs. America's entrance into World War I quelled the negligible affect foreign manufacturers had on Alcoa and provided the opportunity for America's uncontested primary aluminum giant to begin exporting aluminum to Great Britain, France, and Italy. On the home front, Alcoa enjoyed commensurate success, supplying the federal government with aluminum for military applications.

By the conclusion of the war in 1918, Alcoa was producing 152 million pounds of aluminum annually and stood poised to further develop export markets it first penetrated during the war. The manufacturing of aluminum had become a lucrative business, thanks largely to escalating demand during the war and to the fervor with which the automobile industry embraced the still new metal. Alcoa, almost entirely responsible for creating this burgeoning demand, sought to capitalize on the boom wherever it could, spending the 1920s acquiring factories, bauxite mines, and power-generating facilities in Scandinavia, western Europe, and Canada. Toward the end of the decade, however, Alcoa's ubiquitous presence overseas made efficient management and production too difficult. In 1928, the company divested all of its foreign operations, excluding bauxite mines it owned in Dutch Guiana, which were spun off as Aluminum Limited and later renamed Alcan Aluminum Limited.

Reorganized and focused on domestic production, Alcoa struggled through the Great Depression, during which the company's sales plummeted from $34.4 million to $11.1 million and half of its work force was laid off. Once demand for aluminum returned in 1936, Alcoa quickly recovered from the earlier losses, still maintaining an omnipotent grip on the U.S. aluminum market. This enviable position, however, would not be enjoyed by the company for long, as the end of the 1930s signaled the end of Alcoa's overwhelming command over the production of U.S. aluminum and marked the beginning of a new era of competition in the U.S. primary aluminum industry, although it would be over a decade before competition in the industry would begin in earnest.

Anti-trust suits had been filed against Alcoa by the U.S. Justice Department dating back to 1911 without much success, but in 1937 a suit filed by U.S. Attorney General Homer Cummings, charging Alcoa with monopolization and restraint of trade, initiated proceedings that finally wrested control of the U.S. aluminum market away from Alcoa. The trial lasted from 1938 to 1940 and several appeals were made. Although a district court ruled in Alcoa's favor in 1942, the final decision, in 1945, sustained the government's appeal.

While lawyers for both parties scuttled among various courts, making a series of appeals that made the Alcoa anti-trust suit the largest proceeding in the history of U.S. law at that time, America entered another war, spurring demand for aluminum. The military applications for aluminum significantly increased during the 23-year span between World War I and World War II, creating a military appetite for aluminum that Alcoa, still the lone manufacturer in the United States of any consequence, found unable to satiate. Frustrated by Alcoa's inability to supply all the aluminum that was needed, the war department stepped in and financed new plants to provide additional production capacity.

These plants, built and operated by Alcoa, swelled the nation's output of aluminum and enabled the heightened demand to be met. As the war drew to a close and victory appeared assured, government officials were left with the responsibility of what to do with the additional capacity created during the war, which would be superfluous during peacetime. The answer to the problem was the solution of another exigency: How to effectuate an equitable conclusion to the anti-trust suit levied against Alcoa? The decision was made to offer the government-financed aluminum production plants at reduced prices to two fledgling aluminum manufacturers, Reynolds Metals Company and Permanente Metals Corporation, both of which were owned by industrialist Henry Kaiser. In 1950, a district court decree parceled out the U.S. aluminum market among the three manufacturers, giving Alcoa 50.9 percent of the nation's production capacity, Reynolds Metals 30.9 percent, and Permanente Metals, by this time renamed Kaiser Aluminum & Chemical Corporation, 18.2 percent of production capacity

Although the seven-year debate concerning the redistribution of the U.S. aluminum market did not necessarily spawn an industry comprised of numerous participants, but instead, left control of the market to a tightly knit cadre of manufacturers, competition was, nevertheless, quick in coming, particularly from Reynolds Metals. The company's aluminum production capacity doubled as a result of acquiring six of the government financed plants, which enhanced its ability to capitalize further on the introduction of its aluminum foil products several years earlier in 1947. Although much smaller in terms of sales volume and production capacity than Alcoa, Reynolds Metals established itself as the more aggressive marketer, expanding overseas at a rapid rate, while focusing on developing innovative applications for aluminum that would later help elevate the company's magnitude in relation to Alcoa's.

A postwar housing boom infused the industry with an increased demand for aluminum, but the problem of smelting over-capacity, unresolved by the government's actions following the war, remained as a potential impediment to the industry's continued success. Although the hazards posed by excess supply did not threaten primary aluminum manufacturers to any great extent during the 1950s, the danger still remained. To exacerbate matters, production capacity tripled during the decade, partly due to justifiable increases engendered by the rising demand for aluminum from the housing and construction and transportation industries, but also because of federal orders to augment aluminum production to meet the demand created by the nation's involvement in the Korean War. The industry was insulated from the negative affects of oversupply during the early 1950s thanks to an agreement with the federal authorities that guaranteed the purchase of excess aluminum at market prices by the government, referred to as a "put." But federal intervention merely masked the problem of over capacity, a problem that would plague manufacturers in the years to follow.

Despite their inherently precarious position, primary aluminum manufacturers entered the 1960s rightfully optimistic. The decade would bring with it the development of several new applications for aluminum that would enrich the industry considerably and fuel its growth for the next several decades. The utilization of aluminum to manufacture automobile engines, used in only one model in 1960, became more widespread during the early 1960s, as 1961 commenced with eight automobile models boasting aluminum engines. Further, aluminum bumpers and other new applications for automobiles were being developed, contributing to a rise in the amount of aluminum utilized per automobile to 62.1 pounds by 1961. A year earlier, Reynolds Metals introduced the first aluminum drill pipe, which was met with encouraging enthusiasm by other manufacturing industries, but Reynolds Metals' greatest gift to the future success of the primary aluminum industry came in 1963, with its fabrication of an aluminum beverage can. The utilization of aluminum in beverage cans would increase dramatically for the next 30 years, supporting the industry's growth throughout the 1960s and 1970s, and become a

linchpin to primary aluminum manufacturers' survival in the 1990s.

These developments, combined with a housing construction boom and the growing popularity of mobile homes, which contained a large amount of aluminum, drove demand from domestic customers upward, while the industry's export activity accelerated at a rapid rate. Foreign demand for U.S. aluminum tripled between 1959 and 1960, totaling over 500 million pounds in the first year of the decade, and enabling U.S. manufacturers to sidestep the pernicious affects of oversupply.

To foster the further development of overseas markets, U.S. manufacturers of primary aluminum also began striking affiliation agreements with foreign aluminum producers in the early 1960s. In addition to joint ventures already existing at that time in Guinea and elsewhere, primary production facilities were opened in Greece and Australia in 1960, concurrent with the development of a hydroelectric and aluminum project in Ghana.

By aggressively developing new markets for their product, instead of patiently waiting for demand to catch up to supply, which was the general practice in former years, primary aluminum manufacturers had ameliorated their position in the aluminum marketplace. However, as sales climbed for each manufacturer and production increased, industry participants found they were actually recording smaller profits, inducing one manufacturer to describe the industry's performance as characterized by "profitless prosperity." Indeed, profitless prosperity was an apt description, and one that would be equally applicable in the ensuing years. The price of aluminum deteriorated, shrinking profit margins, and an excessive amount of unused production capacity saddled manufacturers with a growing percentage of operating costs that did not generate revenue. To exacerbate matters, the importation of primary aluminum into the U.S. market saturated a market already sufficiently supplied with aluminum. Consequently, U.S. producers of aluminum were shipping more aluminum, but were reaping reduced earnings. The three largest manufacturers watched with dismay as their combined net profit margins slipped from 10.7 percent in 1956, to 5.2 percent by 1960. Alcoa, for example, which produced 36 percent of all the aluminum manufactured in the United States at this time, posted a sales total within 1 percent of its record high in 1960, yet lost $40 million, the company's worst profit performance in a decade. Thus, the paradoxical nature of the primary aluminum industry became readily apparent in the early 1960s— innovative applications for primary aluminum promised increased demand and production levels grew, but manufacturers garnered comparatively prosaic earnings.

By the mid-1960s, the primary aluminum industry was comprised of seven companies operating 23 separate plants. Conditions had improved considerably in the five years since earnings slipped from more lucrative levels, as the industry recorded its fourth consecutive, record year in shipments in 1965. Significant gains were realized in several markets that relied on primary aluminum for manufacturing purposes, most notably the burgeoning demand for aluminum to fabricate truck trailers, mobile homes, and related equipment. Aluminum usage in this segment of the transportation market soared 32 percent in 1964, complementing an increase in the usage of aluminum per automobile to nearly 70 pounds. The electrical market also provided additional business for aluminum manufacturers, as aluminum usage for underground residential distribution cable, building wire for industrial, commercial, and residential uses, and extra high voltage transmission lines increased 19 percent.

These surges in demand experienced by the primary aluminum industry's key end-use markets were imputable to the concerted search by aluminum manufacturers for new ways in which aluminum could be used. This, however, was nothing new; manufacturers had been exploring aluminum's potential applications for years, beginning with Alcoa's initial research and development efforts back in the 1890s. What was new, and what sparked a resurgence in optimism regarding the primary aluminum industry's future by manufacturers and industry observers alike, was a stabilization of aluminum prices, which previously had fluctuated wildly, glutting production capacity and squeezing profit margins. Also, the affiliations with foreign aluminum manufacturers that were initiated earlier in the decade began to buoy the industry's performance, as manufacturers benefitted from high-volume, global operations.

Providing further impetus to the industry's growth was a trend toward incorporating aluminum into many new large-scale construction projects during the mid-1960s, such as in skyscrapers and large ships. These emboldening developments led industry observers to note that, perhaps, the primary aluminum industry was emerging from its protracted adolescence, and had, indeed, become the metal of the future after nearly 80 years of commercial availability.

By the end of the decade, 9 manufacturers representing 13 companies were involved in producing primary aluminum. The building and construction market continued to be the largest consuming segment of pri-

mary aluminum, accounting for 23 percent of the industry's shipments. The transportation industry ranked second, purchasing 20 percent, followed by the electrical market, which accounted for 13 percent, and the rapidly growing packaging and containing market, enlarged by the increasing popularity of aluminum beverage cans, accounted for 10 percent. During the 1960s, aluminum shipments increased by an annual average rate of roughly 9 percent and the price of aluminum continued to remain stable. The estimated average price index for primary aluminum in 1969 reflected only a 4 percent increase from the 1960 level.

In the early and mid-1970s, an energy crisis touched off recessive economic conditions that sent many manufacturing industries' earnings spiraling downward. For primary aluminum manufacturers, the deleterious effects of the energy crises were particularly harsh, since their production facilities were the most energy-intensive of all manufacturing activities. Aluminum manufacturers consumed four percent of all the electric power generated in the United States, the purchase of which represented greater than a third of the total manufacturing cost of aluminum. Consequently, when the price of electricity soared, primary aluminum manufacturers suffered the brunt of the damage engendered by escalating energy costs. In 1975, the nadir of the recession, primary aluminum operating capacity dropped to 75 percent and the industry's total shipments plummeted 28 percent from the previous year's total.

Despite the decline in shipments, primary aluminum inventories swelled during the recession. It took two years to work off the aluminum ferreted away during the general economic decline once the economic scene improved, prolonging the industry's recovery. Not surprisingly, primary aluminum manufacturers intensified their efforts toward developing primary aluminum processes that reduced their dependence on electricity. Laudable achievements already had been achieved toward this objective; the energy consumption required to produce aluminum dropped from 12 kilowatt hours per pound of aluminum following World War II, to roughly eight kilowatt hours by this time. But after the recessive mid-1970s, manufacturers invested more time and money into developing alternative methods to produce aluminum. Additionally, a majority of primary aluminum manufacturers began concentrating more on the secondary smelting of aluminum, which required far less electric power.

Once the industry recovered from the negative affects of the energy crises in the late 1970s, manufacturers were unable to meet the rising demand for aluminum, as conditions within the industry quickly reversed. The transformation was only temporary, however, for demand just as quickly disappeared in the early 1980s, due, in part, to a significant decline in housing and construction activity. Compounding the situation, aluminum prices plummeted, causing the closure of a substantial percentage of production capacity. Despite the diminished production capacity, total operating smelter capacity in the United States fell to 72 percent, three percentage points below the low recorded in 1975. By the mid-1980s, key aluminum markets had become saturated, with foreign aluminum manufacturers carving a 21 percent share of the U.S. primary and fabricated aluminum market, up from the 9 percent market share they secured in 1980.

Sales in the U.S. aluminum market grew at twice the rate of the gross national product during the 1960s and 1970s, but in the 1980s the expansion into new, untapped markets was no longer possible. Buffeted by a rapidly growing scrap aluminum industry that benefitted from the trend toward recycling and an increasing use of plastic instead of aluminum for beverage containers, primary aluminum manufacturers faced unfavorable prospects as the industry faltered in its tenth decade of existence. The fabrication end of the aluminum industry, which generated 80 percent of the overall aluminum industry's revenues by the mid-1980s, began to attract more primary aluminum manufacturers as the decade drew to a close, while primary production facilities sprouted up overseas, signaling for some, the beginning of a new era in U.S. aluminum production.

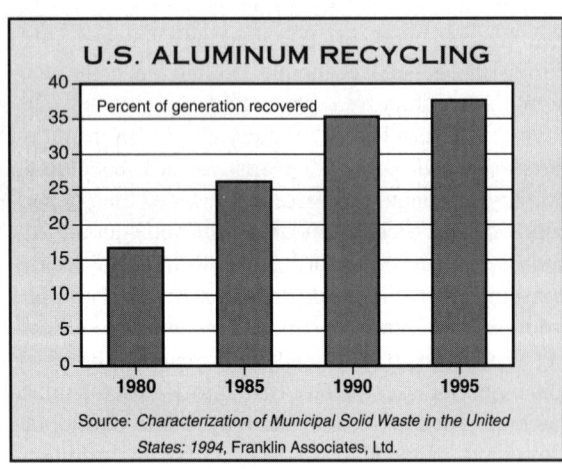

U.S. ALUMINUM RECYCLING

Source: *Characterization of Municipal Solid Waste in the United States: 1994*, Franklin Associates, Ltd.

CURRENT CONDITIONS

The price of electricity is a central component in the profitability equation for manufacturers of primary aluminum. The ability to purchase inexpensive electricity is crucial for this industry to remain profitable

and successfully compete internationally. Regulation of the electric utility industry has been maintained by the United States government, thereby squelching the competitiveness of electricity pricing. Some minor cost advantages have been gained by the manufacturers of primary aluminum by obtaining long term contracts with power authorities. These companies continue to push for deregulation of the power industry so that electricity prices will become more competitive and thereby lower.

The domestic construction of new smelting capacity was also limited by the amended Clean Air Act of 1990, which, in part, required electric utilities to reduce sulfur dioxide emissions. The costs incurred by electric utilities in making these emission reductions were, in turn, passed on to primary aluminum manufacturers. Alternatively, aluminum producers have had to invest large sums of capital into advanced scrubber systems in order to satisfy the Clean Air requirements. U.S. aluminum companies have begun to look for alternate suppliers of electricity and made efforts to start a futures market in electric power. Some aluminum producers purchased electricity generation stations or resorted to importing power from nearby Canadian hydroelectric plants.

To maintain demand for primary aluminum production, manufacturers continued their long tradition of searching for innovative uses of aluminum and augmenting the proportional use of aluminum for existing applications. For decades, manufacturers of primary aluminum have looked toward the automobile industry to boost the demand for aluminum, knowing that each incremental increase in the amount of aluminum utilized per automobile signaled an appreciable rise in aluminum demand. Looking forward from 1997, primary aluminum manufacturers were encouraged by the automobile industry's projections that the utilization of aluminum in passenger cars is expected to increase 5.7 percent in cars and 7.7 percent in light trucks. Analysts predict that the demand for aluminum in the automotive industry should peek near the end of the twentieth century, and then begin to decline since some automakers have already begun to substitute the even lighter weight plastics for aluminum components. Other traditional markets requiring aluminum components, such as computers, office machines, and small engines, continue to be future markets for long-term growth into the twenty-first century.

Aluminum beverage cans represent the largest end user for aluminum in the United States. The Can Manufacturers Institute (CMI) reported a 1 percent increase in the number of aluminum soft drink and beer cans produced from 1995 to 1996. This increase of approximately one billion cans brought the total number of cans in 1996 to 99.14 billion. The small gain was due to a 2.5 percent drop in beer cans offset by a 3.0 percent increase in soft drink can shipments. With consumption of beer in the United States slowing, and large plastic bottles emerging as an increasingly popular receptacle for pop producers, growth in this area is expected to remain modest to flat into the twenty-first century.

INDUSTRY LEADERS

In terms of sales volume, the two largest competitors in the primary aluminum industry in the late 1990s were Alcoa and Reynolds Metals; each was a major contributor to the advancement of the industry. Indeed, for the first 60 years of the industry, primary aluminum production meant Alcoa. Starting with a jump start on its competitors, Alcoa owned the patent for the electrolytic process that first made the production of aluminum commercially feasible. Reynolds Metals, joining the fray during World War II, established itself as a leading primary aluminum manufacturer from the outset, aggressively pursuing the development of innovative applications for aluminum and expanding into foreign markets.

Negatively affected by the overall slide of the primary aluminum industry during the 1980s, Alcoa and Reynolds Metals diversified their operations to mitigate their losses from the decline and placed a lesser emphasis on the production of primary aluminum. Instead, both companies concentrated more on the fabrication end of the aluminum industry and smelting secondary aluminum harvested from recycled aluminum. In 1995, Alcoa recorded sales of $12.5 billion and 72,000 employees. Reynolds Metals reported net sales of $1.8 billion and employed greater than 30,000 people. Alumax Inc. of Norcross, Georgia, had $2.9 billion in sales for 1995 with 15,500 workers and Norada Aluminum Inc., headquartered in Brentwood, Tennessee, reported 5,600 employees and $1.5 billion in sales

WORK FORCE

Total employment in the primary aluminum industry declined throughout much of the 1980s, then stabilized toward the latter end of the decade. By 1988, the industry's employment base was nearly 26,000, and during the period from 1990 to 1992 decreased to approximately 25,000 workers. Further reductions in the industry's production capacity and the trend toward relocating smelting facilities abroad eroded the industry's total employment level to 18,100 in 1995.

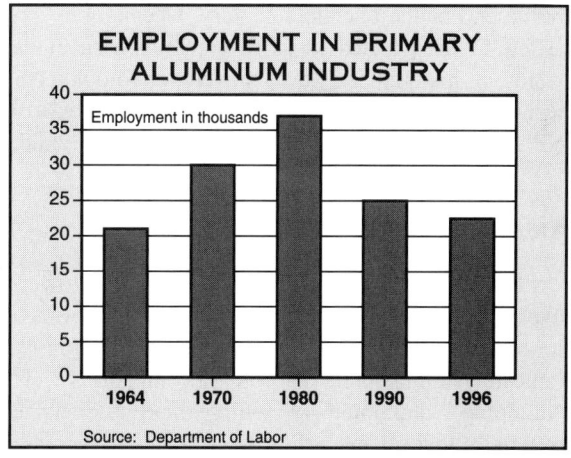

EMPLOYMENT IN PRIMARY ALUMINUM INDUSTRY

Employment in thousands

Source: Department of Labor

Of the 22,000 people employed in the primary aluminum industry in 1994, an overwhelming majority were employed as production workers. Salaried employees, or those performing managerial, administrative, or technical duties, composed the balance of the industry's work force. The typical primary aluminum manufacturing facility employed 263 production workers and 86 salaried employees.

Generally, production workers were employed by the industry on a full-time basis, averaging 6 percent less hours per year than the typical production worker employed by all other manufacturing industries. Average hourly wages in the primary aluminum industry were considerably higher than the average amount earned by production workers employed by all other manufacturing industries. In 1994, production workers in the industry were paid $19.20 per hour, 59 percent more than the $12.09 per hour paid to all other production workers.

As a consequence of the comparatively high hourly wage paid to production workers in the industry, the personnel costs per manufacturing facility, including both production workers' wages and salaries paid to managerial, administrative, and technical staff, were nearly 1.14 percent higher than the personnel costs incurred by the average of all other manufacturing industries. In 1994, the average payroll per establishment in the primary aluminum industry was $9,756,062, compared to $853,319 recorded by the average manufacturing facility.

Prognostications for the industry's work force in the year 2005 suggested a general decline for nearly every occupation employed by the primary metals industry, of which the primary aluminum industry is a subdivision. According to U.S. Bureau of Labor estimates, furnace operators and materials and ceramic engineers and metallurgists are expected to proportionately increase their representation in the industry by the end of the twentieth century. Occupations expected to be affected most severely were machine operators, material and stock movers, and bookkeeping and accounting clerks, each of which were expected to decline by 22 to 31 percent by the year 2005.

AMERICA AND THE WORLD

In 1993, aluminum prices plunged to their lowest level in history, as cheaper, foreign- produced metal flooded the U.S. market and led to the accusation by domestic manufacturers that foreign competitors were "dumping" aluminum, or selling their products at artificially low prices in the United States to increase their market share. This situation reversed by the mid-1990s with the privatization of Russia's aluminum smelters and the Commonwealth of Independent States' need for capital to modernize plants.

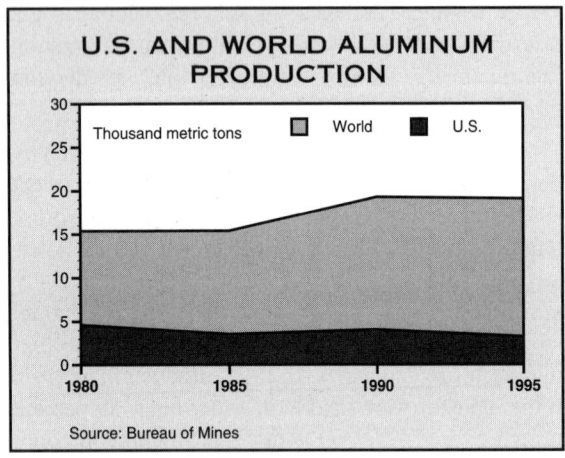

U.S. AND WORLD ALUMINUM PRODUCTION

Source: Bureau of Mines

The excess aluminum originated from several fronts, most notably from Japan and Taiwan, but the situation was exacerbated for U.S. manufacturers by the collapse of the Soviet Union in the early 1990s. Before the collapse, Soviet aluminum was almost entirely channeled to the Soviet defense industry, but when the country's military needs faded, its aluminum entered the U.S. market, saturating a market already filled with a surplus of aluminum. From 1989 to 1993, the amount of aluminum originating from the former Soviet Union and entering the United States ballooned from 250,000 metric tons to 1.6 million metric tons. *Business Week* commented in 1993 that, "Since the Russian avalanche began in late 1990, U.S. aluminum makers have cut production by 796,000 metric tons, or 20 percent of capacity, and laid off 1,300 employees. But prices continue to fall. Meanwhile, the European Community, after cutting production by 320,000 metric tons, is trying to limit shipments from Russia to

Europe—detouring more of the metal to North America."

The poor market situation corrected itself in 1995, when the 14 aluminum smelters in the Commonwealth of Independent States (CIS), that made up the former Soviet Union, were privatized. This resulted in no more subsidies from the government and the CIS manufacturers were liable for their own operating costs. They could no longer afford to sell aluminum below open market cost and remain operating. Many western companies also expanded into the Russian market and begun to modernized their inefficient factories. Reynolds Metals and Fata European Group of Italy formed a joint venture to build an aluminum foil plant in Sajanogordak, Siberia. The Russian Krasnoyarsk plant is expected to be modernized through the efforts of Alcoa and Pechiney, a French manufacturer. United States aluminum manufactures discovered that by expanding into Russia they can increase capacity for relatively little capital and at the same time avoid future dumping of products.

FURTHER READING

"Aluminum Fights Off a Double Whammy."- *Business Week,* 25 January 1982, 28.

"The Aluminum Glut: It Points Up the Pitfalls of Government Planning." *Barron's,* 16 October 1961, 1.

"Aluminum in the Seventies." *Wall Street Transcript,* 27 July 1970, 21, 291.

"Aluminum Industry Gears for Growth." *Steel,* 26 July 1965, 94-99.

Amos, J. "Reynolds Looks for the Low Power Rates." *American Metal Market,* 105, 1997, 14.

"Autopsy." *Forbes,* 1 April 1961, 15.

Baker, Stephen. "Suddenly, There's Aluminum Everywhere." *Business Week,* 25 October 1993, 46.

Boericke, William F. "Important Non-Ferrous Metals Picture for 1961." *The Magazine of Wall Street,* 28 January 1961, 506-526.

"Metal of the Future Is Getting There." *Business Week,* 24 June 1967, 116-123.

"Metals." *Forbes,* 1 January 1962, 37.

Nag, Amal. "Aluminum Makers Push Search for Ways to Slash Energy Use." *Wall Street Journal,* 26 December 1980, 9.

Osterland, Andrew. "Russian Overature." *Financial World* 164, no. 7, 14 March 1995, 24.

Regan, B. "Aluminum Can Shipments Inch Up." *American Metal Market,* 27 January 1997.

Regan, Bob. "Aluminum Smelters Make 72,938 Tons of Extra Metal in '91." *American Metal Market,* 14 January 1992.

"Reynolds Metals Posts Loss of $152.1 Million." *Wall Street Journal,* 19 January 1993, C21.

"Sales Boom Spurs New Wave of Aluminum Plant Projects." *Chemical Week,* 20 July 1963, 26-29.

"Smelter Electric Rate a Success, BPA Says." *American Metal Market,* 31 October 1996.

"US Aluminum Companies Fight for Competitive Power." *Platt's Metals Week,* 23 September 1996.

U.S. Department of Commerce. *U.S. Industrial Outlook.* Washington: GPO, 1993.

—Jeffrey L. Covell, updated by Andrew J. Poss

SIC 3339

PRIMARY SMELTING AND REFINING OF NONFERROUS METALS, EXCEPT COPPER AND ALUMINUM

This classification covers establishments primarily engaged in smelting and refining nonferrous metals, except copper and aluminum. Establishments primarily engaged in rolling, drawing, and extruding these nonferrous primary metals are classified in **SIC 3356: Rolling, Drawing, and Extruding of Nonferrous Metals, Except Copper and Aluminum,** and the production of bullion at the site of the mine is classified in various mining classifications.

This industry supplies nonferrous metals for further consumption to secondary smelting and refining establishments. The metals refined include antimony, babbitt, beryllium, bismuth, cadmium, chromium, cobalt, columbium, germanium, gold, iridium, lead, magnesium, nickel, platinum, rhenium, selenium, silicon, silver, tantalum, tellurium, tin, titanium, zinc, and zirconium. These metals are extracted from their ores and poured into basic shapes, such as slabs, pig molds, or ingots.

The industry shipped $4.1 billion worth of products in 1995, a decrease of 2 percent since 1990, when shipments totaled $4.2 billion. The number of establishments in the industry grew by 6 percent between 1990 and the mid-1900s, from 103 to 100. There were 9,400 employees in the industry in 1995, down from 10,900 employees in 1990.

Magnesium Refining. Due to the lower weight and comparable strength of magnesium components when compared to aluminum, magnesium is increasingly utilized as a manufacturing material. Because of this popularity, magnesium die casting has grown an average of 18 percent per year between 1983 and 1993.

However, the worldwide demand for magnesium has only grown at two percent per year. Moreover, domestic magnesium manufacturers have been hurt by increased imports, especially those from the Commonwealth of Independent States (CIS). The former Soviet Union was restricted from entering the free world magnesium markets due to trade barriers imposed, but by the second half of 1992 these barriers were lifted and the CIS was allowed to participate. The Commerce Department estimated that American imports of magnesium from the CIS would more than quadruple in 1993 compared to 1992.

Precious Metals Refining. The short-term outlook for precious metal smelting and refining is somewhat mixed. A recent *Barron's* feature discussed the prospects of these metals. According to Jeff Christian of CPM Group, gold prices are expected to increase, and the strengthening U.S. economy can support these prices. George Milling-Stanley of Lehman Brothers suggested the outlook for silver is not as strong, because a glut of silver is available on the market due to depressed demand. Also, silver is used primarily in industrial applications, and is dependent on growth rates in industrialized countries, and while the United States' economic picture appears solid entering the mid-1990s, other industrialized nations continue to struggle to extricate themselves from recessionary conditions.

Leading Companies. Significant companies in this industry in the early 1990s included Handy and Harman Co. and Horsehead Industries Inc., both in New York City; Johnson Matthey Inc., based in Wayne, Pennsylvania; Cookson America Inc. of Providence, Rhode Island; and Brush Wellman Inc., headquartered in Cleveland, Ohio.

Technological Advances. Late in October, 1993, researchers at the National Institute of Standards and Technology in Boulder, Colorado, announced they had developed a new alloy. The alloy is a combination of nickel, chromium, manganese, molybdenum, copper, nitrogen, and iron. It can withstand temperatures below -269 degrees Celsius (-516 degrees Fahrenheit), and is expected to find use in fusion energy studies, superconducting magnets, and physics experiments funded by the U.S. government. The importance of the alloy will lie in welding seams in superconducting magnets, which must resist fracture in such low temperatures.

FURTHER READING

Burgert, Philip. "China Tungsten Output Falling, Demand Rising." *American Metal Market,* 15 October 1996, 7.

————. "US Tungsten Market Expected to Rebound." *American Metal Market,* 3 October 1996, 4

Furukawa, Tsukasa. "China's Nonferrous Sector Lagging." *American Metal Market,* 25 September 1995, 5.

Gille, Gerhard. "Tungsten Applications Expand with Technology." *American Metal Market,* 22 August 1996, 7.

Kertes, Noella. "Silver's Use Seen Growing; Industrial, Decorative Applications Most Promising." *American Metal Market,* 8 January 1997, 1.

LaRue, Gloria T. "LME Proves Its Status as the Biggest Gold Forum." *American Metal Market,* 3 February 1997, 16.

Maby, Michael. "Tungsten Demand Increases, Prices Decline; Year-end Buying May Have Been Triggered by EU's New 5.8% Duty." *American Metal Market,* August 22, 1996, 5.

Ozols, Victor, and Furukawa, Tsukasa. "Gold loses luster; a deflated image?" *American Metal Market,* 5 February 1997, 8.

————. "Short Silver Supply Seen In 8th Consecutive Year." *American Metal Market,* 3 March 1997, 6.

Rudnitsky, Howard. "Metals: After a Tough Year Prices Are Climbing Back." *Forbes,* 13 January 1997, 174.

"Russia Tungsten Exports Fall." *American Metal Market,* 4 December 1996, 7.

Seddon, Mark. "Recovering CIS States Exporting." *American Metal Market,* 22 August 1996, 6.

—Valerie Wilson, updated by Lynne Cohn

SIC 3341

SECONDARY SMELTING AND REFINING OF NONFERROUS METALS

This classification comprises establishments primarily engaged in recovering nonferrous metals and alloys from new and used scrap and dross, or in producing alloys from purchased refined metals. This industry includes establishments engaged in both the recovery and alloying of precious metals. Also included in this industry are plants involved in the recovery of tin through secondary smelting and refining, as well as by chemical processes. Excluded from this classification are establishments primarily engaged in assembling, sorting, and breaking up scrap metal without smelting and refining the metal. These establishments are classified in **SIC 5093: Scrap and Waste Materials.**

INDUSTRY SNAPSHOT

Metal, utilized by nearly every manufacturing industry in the United States and abroad, is produced through two basic production methods: primary and secondary. Primary manufacturers produce metal by subjecting particular extracted ores to various metallurgical processes, creating metal in large block or bar form, while secondary manufacturers smelt, refine, and sometimes blend metal recovered from either the shaping and trimming of primary metal during production and fabrication, or from recycled metal. The secondary smelting and refining of nonferrous metals, as defined by **SIC 3341,** comprises the secondary production of metals that do not contain iron, such as aluminum, copper, gold, lead, nickel, silver, tin, and zinc. These metals are used in a wide variety of manufactured products, including ammunition, beverage cans, coins, automobiles, household appliances, and a wealth of other products that nearly encompass the breadth of U.S. manufacturing activity.

Copper, possessing superior electrical conductivity, is a strong, durable metal used in a variety of structural applications as well as for power, lighting, and communications transmissions. Domestically, the major markets for copper are construction, electrical and electronics, and industrial machinery and equipment.

Aluminum, the most widely used nonferrous metal, possesses several attributes, such as light weight, corrosion resistance, and high electrical and thermal conductivity that make the metal suitable for a variety of applications. Container and packaging manufacturers purchase a majority of the domestically produced aluminum, while other major end-use markets include the transportation sector, the buildings and construction sector, and the electrical sector.

Lead is primarily used for the manufacture of storage batteries, which in turn are incorporated into automobile ignition starters, uninterruptible power supplies for computer systems, and standby power supplies for emergency lighting systems and telephones. Other market sectors that purchase lead include paint and glass manufacturers and building products manufacturers.

Zinc is primarily used to galvanize products found in the automobile, steel, and construction industries, but a greater percentage of secondary zinc is used to produce brass and bronze, as well as assorted chemicals and dusts. Additional applications include the blending of zinc-based, die-cast alloys and brass alloys.

Approximately 350 companies in the United States were involved in the secondary smelting and refining industry in 1994. These manufacturers recorded $7.15 billion in sales for products included in the **SIC 3341** classification, an aggregate value of shipments primarily derived from the production of the industry's five key products: secondary aluminum, secondary precious metals (gold, silver, platinum), secondary copper, secondary lead, and secondary zinc. Although the secondary smelting and refining industry produces other metals, such as nickel and tin, these five metals accounted for the bulk of the industry's total shipments. Of all the metals produced by the industry, secondary aluminum represented the largest product category, accounting for 35.0 percent of the industry's aggregate shipments. Precious metals were the industry's second largest product category, representing 22.0 percent of total shipments, followed by secondary copper, which accounted for 14.2 percent. Secondary lead represented 9.8 percent and zinc was 6.3 percent.

ORGANIZATION AND STRUCTURE

In terms of the number of people employed per establishment, the secondary smelting and refining industry has been historically populated by relatively small manufacturing facilities. Of the 387 secondary smelting and refining establishments in operation in 1994, 225 employed less than 20 people, while the remaining 162 employed 20 people or more. These 387 establishments represented all of the individual production facilities operated by the approximately 347 companies engaged in smelting and refining secondary aluminum in 1994. When the secondary smelting and refining industry is compared against all other manufacturing industries in the United States, a clearer picture of the industry's size is provided. In 1994, the average number of employees per establishment for all U.S. manufacturing industries was 46, or 24 percent more than the average number of employees per establishment in the secondary smelting and refining industry.

Geographically, a majority of the secondary smelting and refining production facilities in the late 1980s were located in a four state area comprising Michigan, Illinois, Indiana, and Ohio. Together, these states contained 110 production facilities. The mid-Atlantic states of Pennsylvania, New York, and New Jersey formed the second largest regional concentration of facilities, with 74 establishments, followed by the Pacific region, which ranked as the third largest area of production solely by virtue of the 43 establishments located in California, the greatest number located in any one state and the only state within the

region that contained any secondary smelting and refining facilities. When ranked according to the number of establishments per state, California was followed by Ohio, with 36 production facilities, then Pennsylvania, which contained 32 establishments. The 11 manufacturing facilities in Alabama exceeded the production output of all other states, despite being dwarfed by the 43 facilities in California. The facilities in Alabama eclipsed the shipment volume of California by a tenth of a percentage point, accounting for 12.3 percent of the industry's total shipments and recording $543.6 million in sales, which is five million more than California's revenue total.

The expenses incurred from operating a secondary smelting and refining facility were substantially higher than the amount of money required to operate the average manufacturing facility in the United States. This disparity was most evident in the average cost per establishment, that is, the average amount of money paid for raw manufacturing materials. According to 1994 figures, the average cost per establishment in the secondary smelting and refining industry was $12.8 million, more than three times greater than the $4.2 million averaged by all other manufacturing industries. The average investment per establishment in the secondary smelting and refining industry for production machinery and other equipment necessary in the recovery of primary metal, however, was 43 percent higher than the average investment per establishment in all other manufacturing industries. The average investment per establishment in the secondary smelting and refining industry was $399,225, while the typical manufacturing establishment required an investment of $278,244.

BACKGROUND AND DEVELOPMENT

In the historiography of secondary smelting and refining, one chronicler traces the origins of recovering scrap metal to the seventh descendent of Adam, back to the founder of the iron and steel industry, and by implication, the founder of the scrap metal industry—Tubal-Cain. The writer then proceeds to chart the utilization of scrap metal throughout the span of civilization, making references along the way to documented accounts of scrap metal usage by such notable personages as Moses, Chaucer, Shakespeare, Paul Revere, Captain Kidd, and Thoreau. While this exploration into the depths of scrap metal's history may strike some as overindulgent, it does indicate the pervasiveness and integrality of secondary metal in the history of human existence. It also suggests that scrap metal has been used as long as metal has been used by mankind.

But, obviously, the processing of scrap in the days of Tubal-Cain bore no resemblance to the modern secondary metal industry. The smelting and refining of scrap metal as an organized and structured industry, the type of industry that operated in the 1990s, was a modern creation in the United States. It formed in the early 1900s, as secondary smelting and refining manufacturers began to shed their image as junk peddlers, and gradually became regarded as legitimate operators of an enterprise essential to the existence of modern manufacturing industries. This transition was hastened by the formation of the National Association of Waste Material Dealers, in 1913, which gave manufacturers, for the first time, formalized rules of operation, a code of ethics, and uniform specifications for scrap metal production. The creation of this governing body, renamed the National Association of Secondary Material Industries (NASMI) in 1960, lent cohesion to a loosely structured group of manufacturers struggling to attain order in a rapidly changing manufacturing environment.

Although the advent of NASMI helped define and shape the industry, the smelting and refining of secondary nonferrous metals had been occurring in an industrial setting for quite some time before NASMI came into existence. No statistical record of scrap consumption in the United States exists prior to 1900, but in 1900, the first year figures were recorded, U.S. manufacturers consumed 5.1 million gross tons of ferrous and nonferrous secondary metal. Indeed, the first American scrap metal company, Cline & Bernheim, based in Nashville, Tennessee, had begun operating nearly 40 years before industry-wide consumption figures were recorded in 1862. Following the records, the first market coverage of the scrap industry was published in 1865, when the *Commercial Bulletin of Boston* began providing scrap metal prices. And even further back in time, the first commercial use of scrap metal in the United States occurred at an iron works in Lynn, Massachusetts, in 1642.

Although some of these early uses of scrap metal were of the ferrous variety, the tradition of scrap metal usage had its roots stretching back to the founding of the United States. Accordingly, the scrap metal industry gathered more than a modicum of momentum by the time NASMI emerged. Once it did emerge, though, the modern version of the secondary nonferrous metal industry began and the recovery, smelting, and refining of such metals became distinguished from the production of primary metals, rather than lumped together under the more general and generic metal industry umbrella.

Following the founding of NASMI, secondary non-ferrous production occurred at a predictable, steady rate, devoid of any significant impulse from external market forces that, otherwise, would have proportionately boosted the industry's production volume. Military build-up during World War I, which had a positive effect on many manufacturing industries, provided less than its expected impact on secondary metal producers, largely due to the conspicuous absence of wartime scrap metal drives. A tremendous increase in secondary nonferrous metal production did occur, however, as a result of America's entrance into World War II. By early summer in 1942, the first summer after the Japanese bombed Pearl Harbor, the nation embarked on a virtually uninterrupted campaign to recover scrap metal, elevating the importance of secondary producers in the metal manufacturing industry.

During the immediate post-war years, a majority of American manufacturing industries flourished, and the secondary nonferrous metal industry, as a supplier of the raw material for much of the accelerated production, shared in the explosive growth of the American economy. By 1950, primary manufacturers of nonferrous metals held a commanding lead in the global market, producing nearly half of the world's supply of refined copper, aluminum, and zinc, and more than 25 percent of the world's supply of lead. Secondary producers of these metals, who literally benefitted from the crumbs of the prodigious production volume, were well positioned to profit from the increased demand for nonferrous metals, converting "old" scrap, or metal recovered from recycled products, and converting "new" scrap gleaned from the trimming and shaping of primary nonferrous ingot (referred to as "home" scrap).

This closely knit, interdependent relationship secondary producers maintained within the nonferrous metal industry, which matured and strengthened in the roughly four decades since the establishment of NASMI, invigorated production during robust economic conditions, but also made industry participants vulnerable to the vagaries of the overall metal industry. Although conditions were favorable in the 1950s, several portentous developments arose during this time that augured a somewhat bleaker future for all manufacturers of nonferrous metal.

The consumption of nonferrous metals increased exponentially since the turn of the century, fueled by a rapidly growing population and its needs for products manufactured with nonferrous metals. By the time the United States entered World War II, this increased demand depleted the country's metal ore reserves to the extent that the self-sufficient production of several key nonferrous metals, such as zinc and lead, was no longer possible, while the manufacturing of another key nonferrous metal, aluminum, required an ore more commonly found in countries other than the United States. During the 1950s, this development persuaded many primary manufacturers of nonferrous metals to affiliate with foreign metal manufacturers to meet existing U.S. demand, or to establish wholly owned operations overseas, where ore deposits were plentiful. While this expansion into foreign metal markets narrowed the gap between supply and demand and sparked the overall metal industry's growth, it also fostered the growth of the global nonferrous metal market, establishing, for the first time, manufacturing facilities in less-developed countries and encouraging output in more sophisticated, foreign markets. Repercussions from this shift overseas were not immediate, but in the years ahead, the evolution of a genuine global metal industry would engender a sharply contested nonferrous metal market.

Although the scarcity of particular ore deposits in the United States would affect primary manufacturers of nonferrous metals more severely than secondary producers, the fortunes of both sectors of the nonferrous metal industry were intertwined to the extent that neither entirely escaped the troubles of the other. But a technological innovation developed by primary manufacturers in the 1950s promised to impinge directly on the demand for secondary nonferrous metal, while reducing the manufacturing costs incurred by primary producers, which pitted these two, often complementary, industry segments against each other. The basic principle behind this innovation was relatively simple: introduce oxygen into the furnaces in which pig iron is converted to steel. The addition of oxygen quickened the conversion process, reducing the energy requirements of metal production, and most harmful to secondary producers, the new process needed far less scrap metal with which to manufacture ingot. Without oxygen, primary manufacturers needed a high percentage of scrap metal to efficiently produce metal, but with oxygen the proportion of scrap metal dropped to as low as 40 percent. Initially, steel manufacturers employed this new process, but by the mid- and late 1960s, the utilization of oxygen in the production of nonferrous metals had begun, as aluminum manufacturers adopted the process. Of course, the use of oxygen also reduced the conversion time in the production of secondary metals, but the losses suffered as a result of the diminished role scrap metal played in the manufacturing of primary metal were significant.

Fortunately for secondary metal producers, the popularity of this new production method was roughly concurrent with the birth of widespread recycling efforts, which bolstered the industry's production output and marked the beginning of a movement that would serve as a linchpin to the industry's existence and success into the 1990s. To varying degrees, the recycling of used products and materials had been occurring for many decades prior to the late 1960s and early 1970s—the existence of the secondary metal industry itself, comprised of former junk peddlers, was testament to the long tradition of recycling—but these efforts were intensified due to the growing outcry against pollution and waste, as landfills dotting the nation's landscape brimmed with refuse. Also, recycling had been generally limited to the recovery of industrial, or commercial by-products, not the recycling of consumer products, such as storage batteries and aluminum and tin cans.

Once recycling began in earnest, secondary producers of nonferrous metals began to play a more dominant role in the overall nonferrous metals industry, outpacing primary manufacturers in terms of production volume and capitalizing on governmental efforts aimed at reducing the amount of national waste. Federally led and financed attempts to reduce waste received an initial push from the creation of the Office of Solid Waste Management in 1965, which was strengthened in 1970 by the promulgation of the Resource Recovery Act. The Resource Recovery Act authorized a three-year budget of $461 million, but most important to secondary nonferrous metal producers, the Act changed the Office of Solid Waste Management's primary objective from the sanitary dumping of solid wastes to recycling those wastes. In a short time, the effect of this concerted push toward recovering solid wastes ameliorated the secondary nonferrous industry's position, driving scrap manufacturer's production output upwards. By 1971, the secondary production of lead accounted for roughly 50 percent of the total lead consumption in the United States and the proportional representation of other secondary nonferrous metals were no less impressive: secondary copper accounted for approximately 45 percent; secondary aluminum, 35 percent; secondary zinc, 23 percent.

By the mid-1970s, however, a recession and a worldwide energy crisis nearly crippled all sectors of the ferrous and nonferrous metal industry, as successive oil shocks quaked the foundations of an industry that relied on relatively large amounts of energy to exist. Indeed, the deleterious effects of the energy crises plagued metal manufacturers for the rest of the decade and stood as a turning point for the health of metal manufacturers worldwide. The annual growth rates in the consumption of nonferrous metals from 1979 to 1988 stood well below the pace recorded from 1950 to 1974: the annual consumption rate of aluminum, worldwide, from 1950 to 1974 was 9 percent, while from 1979 to 1988 the rate dropped to 2.3 percent; copper fell from 3.9 percent to 1.1 percent; lead from 2.7 percent to 0.5 percent; and zinc from 3.9 percent to 1.2 percent.

As the secondary smelting and refining industry entered the 1980s, a period of corporate restructuring began, as companies purchased, sold, and merged operations to enhance their competitiveness, while the key metals within the industry were each affected, either negatively or positively, by conditions peculiar to their markets. The production of secondary copper suffered a decline in total shipments in the early 1980s after effecting a rebound from the pernicious 1970s. By 1989, however, shipments eclipsed the one year surge experienced at the start of the decade, as manufacturers combated difficulties associated with aging production facilities and environmental regulations. Over the entire decade, secondary production accounted for 26 percent of the total U.S. copper production, a more encouraging representation than the 20 percent recorded from 1975 to 1979.

Secondary aluminum production fared comparatively better during the 1980s, increasing 40 percent over the decade. Hampered by decreasing primary production of aluminum in the United States and a nearly glutted beverage can market, secondary aluminum manufacturers also experienced capricious fluctuations in demand during much of the decade. Nevertheless, secondary aluminum producers concluded the 1980s with three solid years of production output, during which they recorded much of the production growth of the decade.

Primary lead manufacturers, struggling with the sharply decreased demand for tetraethyl lead (TEL), which is used to produce leaded gasoline, witnessed secondary manufacturers of lead increase their representation of total lead consumption during the 1980s. The reclamation of lead acid storage batteries, the largest market for lead and typically recyclable, elevated the importance of the secondary lead industry. In 1980, primary and secondary lead production was roughly equally split, with secondary producers supplying half of nation's total lead. By the end of the decade, secondary lead manufacturers supplied approximately 65 percent of the total lead consumed in the United States.

Secondary zinc manufacturers also figured more prominently within their nonferrous metal niche during the 1980s. The demand for zinc, both from primary and secondary suppliers, increased throughout much of the decade, excluding a temporary decline in 1982. Overall consumption rose 21 percent over the course of the decade, while secondary zinc producers increased their share of the total zinc production to 23 percent.

CURRENT CONDITIONS

As the secondary smelting and refining industry entered the late 1990s, there was an intensified interest in recycling by both the consumer and industrial sectors, which buoyed the production output of industry participants. From 1990 to 1997 shipments of nonferrous castings rose 9 percent, demonstrating that this sector of the market was experiencing a revitalization. Each of the metals within the industry were expected to demonstrate a positive but slow growth forecast by the expected increase in the reclamation of industrial and consumer solid waste. Additional success in this direction will continue to elevate the industry's importance within the overall nonferrous metal industry and fuel its future growth.

During the last three years of the twentieth century, aluminum is predicted to slowly grow at a rate of 4 percent annually. At the same time, copper is expected to remain steady or increase only about 1 percent per year. Zinc, on the other hand, is being constantly replaced by plastics and may experience no growth or limited growth into the end of the decade. Lead consumption is expected to experience a continual decline as this metal is removed from various metal formulations for toxicity reasons.

INDUSTRY LEADERS

Ranked according to sales volume, the largest manufacturer in the secondary smelting and refining industry in 1996 was Commercial Metals Company, located in Dallas, Texas, with 6,300 workers and $2.1 billion in sales.

Second is the Connell Limited Partnership, located in Boston, Massachusetts. Connell, a holding company with operations involved in fabricating special dies, plate work, and metal forming machine tools, as well as sheet metal production, is engaged in the secondary smelting and refining industry through its Wabash Alloys division, the leading producer of aluminum casting alloys in the United States. Deriving a majority of its business from the automobile industry, Wabash converts aluminum scrap into aluminum casting alloys, which are then sold to major automobile manufacturers or to die-casting companies that cater to the automobile industry. Approximately 70 percent of the scrap processed by the company is related to the automobile industry. With 2900 employees Connell recorded roughly $1.2 billion in sales in 1996.

U.S. Reduction Company, a more diversified producer of secondary nonferrous metals than Wabash, garnered approximately $300 million in sales in 1996 and employed 500 people. Other important companies in the secondary nonferrous metal market include: Tredegar Aluminum of Newnan, Georgia with $250 million in sales and 1000 employees and RSR Corporation headquartered in Dallas, Texas, with 700 workers and sales of approximately $140 million.

WORK FORCE

Total employment in the secondary smelting and refining industry dropped throughout much of the 1980s, effecting a slight rise in the late 1980s and into the 1990s. In 1982, the industry's total employment stood at 19,200, then slipped to 12,500 by 1987. The largest precipitous drops were from 1982 to 1983 and from 1986 to 1987. After 1987, the nadir of the industry's employment decline, total employment increased by an average of 800 per year. In 1994, the industry's employment base continued to rise, although at a less robust pace than during the late 1980s, reaching 14,400 by the end of the year.

Of the 14,400 people employed in the secondary smelting and refining industry in 1994, 3,800 were salaried employees, or those performing managerial, administrative, or technical duties, while the balance of the industry's work force comprised 10,600 production workers. A typical secondary smelting and refining facility in 1994 employed 26 production workers and 11 salaried employees.

Generally, production workers are employed on a full-time basis, averaging 12 percent more hours per year than the average number of hours worked by production workers in all other manufacturing industries. On an average, the production workers employed by the secondary smelting and refining industry earned slightly less than the typical production worker. In 1994, a typical production worker employed by a manufacturing industry earned $11.55 per hour, while production workers involved in the secondary smelting and refining industry earned $11.20 per hour.

Prognostications for the industry's work force in the year 2005 suggest a general decline for nearly every occupation employed by the primary metals industry, of which the secondary smelting and refining industry is a subdivision. According to the U.S. Bureau

of Labor estimates, only furnace operators, metallurgists, and ceramic and materials engineers are expected to proportionately increase their representation in the industry between the years 1994 and 2005. Occupations expected to be affected most severely are machine operators, material movers, bookkeepers, and accounting clerks, each of which are expected to decline by 22 to 31 percent by the year 2005.

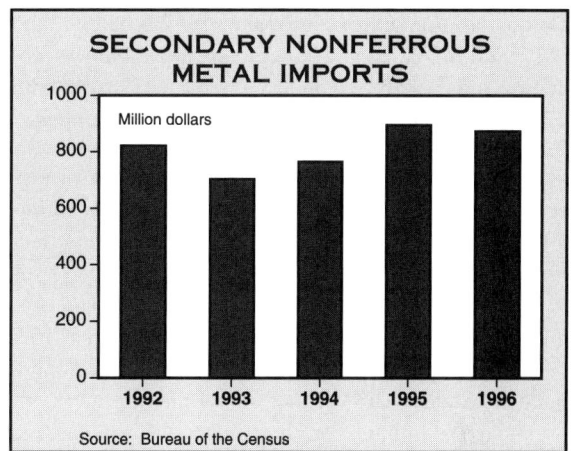

SECONDARY NONFERROUS METAL IMPORTS

Source: Bureau of the Census

AMERICA AND THE WORLD

The U.S. nonferrous metal industry, once the prominent, global leader in production volume, entered the 1990s harried by a combination of domestic exigencies, such as escalating production costs and mounting foreign competition. Consequently, foreign manufacturers of nonferrous metals, some of whom were located in less developed countries rich in metal ore deposits, were able to gain ground on domestic manufacturers during the 1980s, and with certain metals, supplant the United States as the leading metal manufacturer. This situation was further exacerbated for U.S. manufacturers because some of the foreign manufacturing companies, particularly in the less developed countries, were state-owned operations, financed and directed by local government, which muddled the global, nonferrous metal picture because these companies frequently pursued political goals, rather than economic objectives. These developments affected domestic manufacturers of primary nonferrous metals more severely than secondary producers, although any significant cutbacks in primary production eventually and inevitably affect secondary producers.

Despite the increasing competition and the flight of primary manufacturing facilities, secondary producers in the United States maintained a leading position in the international, nonferrous market well into the 1990s. With five secondary smelters, two electrolytic refineries and six fire refineries operating in 1992, the U.S. secondary copper industry ranked as the largest producer in the world, accounting for 35.3 percent of the 1.2 million metric tons of secondary copper produced by all countries with market economies. The Federal Republic of Germany ranked as the second largest producer, supplying an estimated 23 percent of the copper, followed by Japan, which accounted for 6 percent. Other prominent secondary copper-producing nations are the United Kingdom with 2.6 percent and Italy with 6.2 percent. The region responsible for producing most of the secondary copper is Europe with 47.5 percent and North America with 37.8 percent.

The United States' secondary aluminum producers held a larger lead in the global secondary aluminum market than their copper counterparts, manufacturing 44.6 percent of the 6.1 million metric tons produced in 1992. America's closest rival, Japan, produced 17.4 percent of the total, an estimated 13.7 percent was produced by the Commonwealth of Independent States (CIS). Other important producers of secondary aluminum are Italy with 5.7 percent and France with 3.6 percent. The production of this metal is regionally divided between North America with 47.3 percent, Asia with 32.4 percent, and Europe with 18.7 percent.

The production of secondary lead is regionally divided between Europe with 41.2 percent of the 1.7 metric tons produced world wide in 1992. Asia was responsible for 22.0 percent and North America for 32.8 percent. The United States was the leading producer of secondary lead with 26.7 percent and the Federal Republic of Germany produced approximately 15.9 percent. The United Kingdom was responsible for an estimated 11.0 percent of the world production of secondary lead and Italy produced 5.0 percent.

The international secondary zinc market was sharply contested in the late 1980s, as the former U.S.S.R. maintained a precarious lead over its two strongest competitors, the United States and the Federal Republic of Germany. Of the 349,602 metric tons of zinc produced globally in 1992, the United States controlled 36.5 percent of the market, followed closely by the Commonwealth of Independent States (CIS), which accounted for 35.4 percent of the total production. The Federal Republic of Germany supplied an estimated 10.0 percent of the international market. Japan accounted for 9.3 percent and France produced 4.0 percent. The production of secondary zinc divided in global regions showed that 44.7 percent of the metal was manufactured in Asia, 36.5 percent in North America, and 17.3 percent in Europe.

FURTHER READING

"Aluminum Gets Hot with Oxygen." *Business Week,* 10 August 1968, 80-81.

"Aluminum Plants Set Record." *American Metal Market,* 22 March 1991, 7.

Barringer, Edwin C. *The Story of Scrap,* Washington: Institute of Scrap Iron & Steel Inc., 1954.

Cardwell, Nancy. "Copper Processors Curtailing Operations, Doubtful Phase 4 Will Make Scrap Available." *The Wall Street Journal,* 23 July 1973, 4.

Codero, Harry G., and Leslie H. Tarring. *Babylon to Birmingham.* London: Quin Press Ltd., 1961.

"Copper-base Scrap Use in '87 at 1,576,620 Tons." *American Metal Market,* 17 March 1988, 9.

Darnay, Arsen J., ed. *Manufacturing Worldwide.* Detroit: Gale Research, 1995.

"Industry Looks Up to Copper Mine in the Sky." *Business Week,* 16 September 1967, 177-182.

Klein, Frederick C. "Russia Exports Scrap Aluminum to the U.S., Rousing Concern Here." *The Wall Street Journal,* 25 January 1966, 15.

"Metals Outlook." *Material Engineering,* January 1970, 29.

Miller, Herbert John. *Non-ferrous Metals Industry.* New York: United Nations, 1969.

"New Drive to Get Rid of Trash." *U.S. News & World Report,* 7 June 1971, 65-68.

Newman, Barry. "Recycling Backlash." *The Wall Street Journal,* 9 May 1973, 1.

O'Sullivan, Orla. "Zinc Recovery to Rise As '80s Autos Recycle." *American Metal Market,* 24 February 1993, 1.

"Process to Convert Scrap without Melting Disclosed." *The Wall Street Journal,* 26 June 1970, 18.

Rosenberg, Joseph. "Off the Scrap Heap." *Barron's,* 17 April 1972, 11.

Schroeder, Norman. "Small Secondary Lead Smelters Seen Cutting Environment Safeguard Cost." *American Metal Market,* 15 November 1988, 1.

Suisman, Michael, and Howard Wm. Rasher, eds. *Non-ferrous Scrap Metal Guidebook.* New York: National Association of Secondary Material Industries, 1960.

Tsukasa, Furukawa, and Gloria LaRue. "Foreign Nickel Buyers Shielded." *American Metal Market,* 17 March 1988, 1.

"Turning Junk and Trash into a Resource." *Business Week,* 10 October 1970, 66-75.

U.S. Congress, Office of Technology Assessment. *Non-ferrous Metals: Industry Structure—Background Paper.* Washington: GPO, 1990.

U.S. Department of Commerce. International Trade Administration. *U.S. Industrial Outlook 1994.* Washington: GPO, 1994.

Warden, Ed. "ARA: Specification Ingot Shipments Up." *American Metal Market,* 6 March 1989, 2.

—Jeffrey L. Covell, updated by Andrew J. Poss

SIC 3351

ROLLING, DRAWING, AND EXTRUDING OF COPPER

This industry consists of establishments that roll, draw, or extrude copper, brass, bronze, and other copper-based alloys. These establishments create basic shapes such as plate, sheet, strip, bar, and tubing.

INDUSTRY SNAPSHOT

The companies of this industry are known as copper fabricators, whose role in the larger copper industry is to create the strip, sheet, plate, rod, bar, and other copper products used in numerous products and industries. These companies receive smelted and refined copper from newly mined copper ore and copper scrap and turn them into products used in the building construction and electrical and electronic product manufacturing industries. Wire rod mills and brass mills comprised more than 85 percent of the fabricators in the United States. Copper foundries are discussed in **SIC 3366: Copper Foundries.**

During the economic downturn of the 1980s, there was a high degree of consolidation in the industry. This trend continued in the 1990s, as buy outs and mergers led to a leaner field of companies. Large, multi-product wire and cable mills used to be tied to mining companies, but in the mid-1990s, many of these mining companies spun off their fabricators in order to be more efficient. Some refining companies, however, added continuous cast wire rod mills to the end of their production process, thereby effectively opening their own millworks.

Most brass mills in the United States had three areas of production. One division produced rod, bar, and shapes; another division produced strip, sheet, and plate; and the third division produced commercial and plumbing tube. Brass rod and brass strip, two of the most popular copper alloys produced in the industry, had the kind of corrosion resistance, machinability, and electrical properties that enabled them to be used under adverse climatic conditions. Air-conditioning tube and plumbing tube were two examples of the unalloyed copper and high-copper alloys that comprised another major segment of the mill's output.

ORGANIZATION AND STRUCTURE

Copper that is rolled, drawn, and extruded is utilized by many different industries. End-use markets for copper and copper alloy were dominated by building construction and electrical and electronic products manufacturing. These two general industries accounted for more than 65 percent of all copper shipments in 1991. In 1995 the building construction industry used 3,049,000 short tons of wire mill products, which was an all-time high. Other end-use markets for copper were industrial machinery and equipment, transportation equipment, and consumer products.

Copper in the United States passes from the mines to the smelters. In some cases these facilities were owned by the same company, and in some cases the mining and smelting were performed at nearby locations. The mining and smelting companies were the producers of copper, and the wire rod mills, brass mills, and foundries were the consumers of copper who prepared the metal for delivery to manufacturers in various industries.

Mining companies processed copper ores, most of which were retrieved from open-pit mines. These ores were refined and sometimes alloyed with other elements, such as zinc or beryllium. The percentage of copper and copper alloys that went to wire rod mills was 49 percent, while 40 percent went to brass mills and 7 percent went to foundries. All of these fabricators created copper-based products used throughout U.S. industries. The total refined production of primary copper was 2,480,200 short tons in 1995, and net imports of refined copper were 232,000 short tons.

Several associations concerned with copper production have emerged over the years. One of the mainstays of the U.S. copper industry was the Copper and Brass Development Association (CDA). CDA tracked market statistics and published handbooks, reports, and bulletins. It also sought to broaden copper markets in this country and abroad. The Copper and Brass Servicenter Association served as a sales arm for brass mills and as a warehouse for manufacturers' inventory. The American Copper Council was another trade organization central to the copper industry. They reached more individuals and more companies in the 1990s by expanding their Internet presence.

BACKGROUND AND DEVELOPMENT

Copper mining had origins in the Middle East, but reached its zenith in the American West. Small mining operations allowed prosperous towns to grow up in Michigan and Arizona. In the mid-eighteenth century, miners in the colonies discovered copper ores in what is now the northeastern United States. They mined these ores, but English law prohibited the establishment of smelting works in the colonies, so the ore was sent to England for smelting and refining.

After the American Revolution, many copper workers moved to the newly-created United States. Copper sheathing began to be used on wooden ships as early as the 1790s. The copper protected the ships from the pressure and corrosive effects of the ocean. Great demand from the shipping industry helped the budding copper industry, but the United States still depended on copper imports from England and South America. In 1806 U.S. importers of copper asked Congress to exempt copper from customs duty. The protests lodged by copper industry pioneers succeeded in lowering tariffs applied to copper imports.

Steamships had copper parts by this time, as copper was better than pinewood boilers at containing steam. Later, with the rise of American industry, growing copper fabricators created stripping, boiler plates, rivets, and other copper-based items that were used in an increasingly diverse number of industries and products. Copper nails replaced cast iron nails in building, and the boom in putting up towns and cities across the new nation resulted in a windfall for the copper industry.

By the beginning of the twentieth century, due to "the development of efficient flotation processes around the turn of the century," according to the Copper and Brass Development Association, "open-pit mining techniques were developed . . . and the United States quickly became the world's largest producer of copper."

The brass mill industry began in the early days of colonial America, in Connecticut. Copper mills could be found from Waterbury south to Ansonia, where melting and rolling techniques were developed and tested. While little of this industry remains in Connecticut, it is centered in the eastern United States.

CURRENT CONDITIONS

The economic upheavals in the United States in the 1980s affected the copper industry only belatedly. Copper prices fell as a result of overstocks, and companies were forced to confront inventory problems. According to the American Bureau of Metal Statistics, copper shipments rose 7.6 percent in the summer of 1993 over the summer of 1992. In fact cathode and bar suppliers were selling out and trying to keep up with demand for their products. Brass mill executives were concerned that the downward trend in copper prices did not bode well for copper in the future, but five

years later prices were rising again. Competing materials, such as plastics, also caused industry leaders to focus on quality and cost effectiveness.

According to a 1993 article in the trade magazine *Copper Talk,* overall shipments of strip, sheet, and plate declined in the 1980s, but demand for copper products increased slightly. Shipments to the electrical and electronic products markets grew to represent 36 percent of shipments. This was an increase of 12 percent from just two years earlier, according to Copper and Brass Development Association statistics. The percentage of copper mill products that were consumed by the building construction industry was more than 40 percent in 1991. Electrical and electronic products industries received 24 percent, and the industrial machinery industry accounted for 13 percent.

In 1995, the consumption of copper by wire rod mills was 2,174,700 short tons. This was down from 2,295,000 short tons the previous year. The total copper consumed by wire rod mills, brass mills, foundries, and other industries also fell from a 1994 high of 4,029,400 short tons according to the American Bureau of Metal Statistics and the U.S. Geological Survey of the U.S. Department of the Interior.

The copper industry was shaken by the Sumitomo Corporation trading scandal in mid-1996. Yasuo Hamanaka, chief copper trader for the company, was exposed as a heavy speculator in copper futures. His unauthorized dealings cost his employer more than $1.8 billion and sent the price of copper plummeting. By mid-June, copper prices had fallen 64 percent to 79 cents per pound before rebounding to 91 cents per pound in the fall. The price for raw copper remained unsettled, as traders feared that Sumitomo possessed huge quantities of the metal that, if sold, would further depress prices. By 1997, copper prices stabilized and demand became steady.

In 1997, a strike at Chile's Escondida copper mine, the largest copper mine in the world, caused copper prices to rise as inventories fell. Stockpiles at the London Metal Exchange were low, falling in a year by more than 50 percent to 149,100 metric tons.

Demand for copper products remained steady in the housing industry as well as the consumer products market. However, copper products continued to face increased challenges from the aluminum and plastics industries and the outlook for growth in copper use was flat. Telecommunications companies looked to switch from copper wire to fiber optic cable, owing to the increased demand for on-line services. In construction, too, copper tubing, long a mainstay in the industry, faced pressure from plastics manufacturers. However, the general strength of the housing industry, including the remodeling of existing housing, pointed to new markets and potential growth.

Expanding power generation plants also represented a growth market for copper product manufacturers, though competition with aluminum represented a challenge to future growth.

INDUSTRY LEADERS

Major companies engaged in copper rolling, drawing, and extrusion processes included Marmon Group, Inc., with $3.9 billion in sales and 27,000 employees; Mueller Industries Inc., with $550 million in sales and 2,300 employees, and Mueller Brass, a subsidiary with $502 million in sales and 1,900 employees; Wolverine Tube Inc., with $526 million in sales and 2,300 employees; and Chase Brass and Copper, with $300 million in sales and 300 employees.

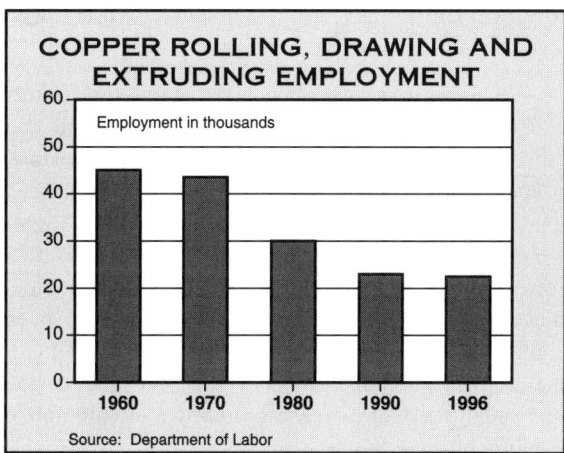

COPPER ROLLING, DRAWING AND EXTRUDING EMPLOYMENT

Source: Department of Labor

WORK FORCE

In 1995, the industry employed 22,500 workers, down from 22,900 in 1994. Compensation fell slightly to $711 million in 1995 from $721 million in 1994, though average hourly wages increased 3 percent to $14.56 in 1995. Worker production decreased around 8 percent to 105 million hours in 1995, reflecting the decrease in employment in the industry.

From 1990 through the year 2005, the expected percent change in the number of extruding and forming machine operators was a decrease of 1.1 percent. While there were better areas of the manufacturing sector in growth potential, this outlook was not nearly as bleak as that in other copper-related industries. The number of mining, quarrying, and tunneling occupations, for instance, was expected by some observers to fall by almost 20 percent, while the number of foundry

mold assembly and shakeout workers was expected to fall by more than 20 percent.

AMERICA AND THE WORLD

The Sumitomo trading scandal in 1996 caused wide fluctuations in copper prices, which dictate profit margins and end product prices to consumers. Worldwide copper prices were projected to increase through the end of the decade.

Copper was in demand for those countries that were improving their infrastructures with telecommunications cables, power cables, and other basic building tools, though domestic competition with aluminum cut into overall copper demand. The Asian markets of China, Taiwan, and South Korea were expected to provide large new markets. Copper has tended to be sensitive to supply constraints, however, and external factors such as political and financial troubles in copper-producing nations can affect the balance of supply and demand.

Exports from the brass mill industry were increasing through the 1990s while imports were decreasing. By 1996 the United States copper industry was exporting 21,853,588 kilograms of bars and rods to countries throughout the world. Exports went to Canada, Malaysia, Mexico, France, Hong Kong, and dozens of other countries. Many copper industry executives were expecting more Mexican consumption of brass mill items such as commercial and plumbing tube, strip, sheet, and plate, and rod, and bars after the passage of the North American Free Trade Agreement (NAFTA).

In the 1990s there were still legislative paths for concerned copper industry executives to take when faced with international competition that was viewed as unfair. Foreign manufacturers of brass sheet and strip, for instance, were watched carefully for charges of dumping products below market costs.

The United States formed an International Copper Study Group in the early 1990s, in conjunction with 17 other countries involved in the copper industry. Their aim was to allow informational exchanges between producing and consuming countries, as well as to increase copper production and consumption. Members included Germany, China, Chile, Peru, and France.

RESEARCH AND TECHNOLOGY

Patricia Foley, a copper executive writing in the trade magazine *Copper Talk,* said, "In the late 1980s, most strip and sheet producers invested to serve the growing electronic markets. They installed automatic gauge control and statistical process control capabilities to enable them to produce strip with consistent and close tolerances.'' The emphasis on these new precise technologies was apparent in most of the companies involved in the rolling, drawing, and extruding of copper. In order for them to remain competitive in the market, their products needed to meet a higher standard of excellence and precision. Existing companies improved their productivity and efficiency, which enabled the U.S. industry as a whole to increase production.

FURTHER READING

''Annual Data: 1993: Copper Supply and Consumption, 1972-1992.'' New York: Copper Development Association Inc., 1993.

''A.T.&T. in Copper Cable Venture in Venezuela.'' *New York Times,* 10 February 1994, C3.

Caney, Derek J. ''Servicenters Ship Less Copper.'' *American Metal Market,* 2 September 1993, 3.

———. ''Copper Rod Demand Strengthens.'' *American Metal Market,* 21 October 1993, 1.

''Copper in the USA: Bright Future—Colorful Past.'' New York: Copper Development Association Inc., 1990.

''Copper Prices Rise a 5th Day As Chile Strike Slows Output.'' *New York Times,* 24 April 1997, C12.

Einhorn, Cheryl Strauss. ''Red Metal Rising.'' *Barron's,* 6 January 1997, MW12.

Feldman, Amy. ''Tubes With Fins.'' *Forbes,* 31 January 1994, 46.

Gross, John E. ''Copper Market Letter.'' *Copper Talk,* May 1993, 7.

Hutheesing, Nikhil. ''Copper Highway?'' *Forbes,* 6 June 1994, 104.

Levinson, Marc. ''The Mighty Copper King.'' *Newsweek,* 24 June 1996, 48.

Stundza, Tom. ''Purchasing Deluge Will Ebb Slightly in '93.'' *Purchasing,* 4 March 1993, 34.

Taylor, Jeffrey. ''U.S. Copper Futures Fall as Available Stocks of the Metal Reach a 15-Year High in London.'' *Wall Street Journal,* 27 October 1993, C18.

Temes, Judy. ''Polish and Tarnish.'' *Crain's New York Business,* 12 November 1990, 3.

Whiteman, Maxwell. *Copper for America.* New Brunswick: Rutgers University Press, 1971.

U.S. Department of Commerce. ''U.S. Exports and Imports by 10-Digit Harmonized Code.'' Available from http://www.ita.doc.gov/industry/otea/Trade-Detail.

—Fran Shonfeld Sherman

SIC 3353

ALUMINUM SHEET, PLATE, AND FOIL

This classification covers establishments primarily engaged in flat rolling aluminum and aluminum-alloy basic shapes, such as sheet, plate, and foil, including establishments producing welded tube. Also included are establishments primarily producing similar products by continuous casting.

INDUSTRY SNAPSHOT

''The aluminum sheet market is like a box of chocolates: you never know what you're gonna get.'' With due credit to Forrest Gump, David Hamill of *American Metal Market* aptly described the volatility of this sector in the mid-1990s. In the 1993-96 period alone, the market bottomed out, peaked, and drew back once more. While the gyrations made life interesting for speculators, they were anathema to users who sought stable, predictable pricing.

Over the past several decades, aluminum makers have been successful in developing new products and taking market share from competitors like steel. Much of the industry's gains could be traced to the intrinsic qualities of the metal—aluminum is strong, lightweight, and eminently recyclable, all qualities that were still highly prized in the 1990s. Skilled management and smart marketing, however, had also been significant factors in the industry's advance. Thus it had come to dominate the beverage can market and had established an increasing presence in automobile manufacturing.

While the industry had done an excellent job in spurring demand, the volatility in aluminum markets was causing more than a few users to have second thoughts about the metal. In the important automotive market—and even in cans—some executives were taking another look at steel. Nevertheless, producers remained optimistic that aluminum's physical traits would make it the metal of choice in a growing variety of applications.

Aluminum sheet, plate, and foil represent the aluminum industry's major product group and account for the majority of shipments from aluminum producers. Aluminum is first produced in the form of sheet ingot. These ingots, which may weigh as much as 20 tons, are flat rolled and rerolled until the desired thickness, or gauge, is achieved. The gauge determines what product has been produced: plate is a quarter-inch thick or more; sheet is .006 inch to .249 inch; and foil is less than .006 inch. Sheet is by far the most widely used form of aluminum and is found in all of the industry's major markets, including containers and packaging (most notably beverage cans) and transportation (i.e. panels for automobile bodies). Plate is used for the skins of jetliners and to make storage tanks, among other heavy-duty applications. Foil is used, of course, to wrap the Thanksgiving turkey, but is also utilized in building insulation and electrical capacitors, as well as a wide variety of packaging applications.

ORGANIZATION AND STRUCTURE

Vertical integration in the aluminum industry is extensive—it goes well beyond the mining, refining, and smelting of primary aluminum (including sheet ingot, casting ingot, and extrusion billet) to the production of semifabricated and fabricated products downstream, including sheet, plate, and foil offerings. Four major producers—Alcoa, Reynolds Metals, and Alumax (which was spun off from AMAX in 1993)—dominate the North American aluminum industry and thus dominate the market for sheet, plate, and foil.

BACKGROUND AND DEVELOPMENT

The aluminum industry is relatively young. The first major application, cast cooking utensils, did not appear until the 1890s. Following the turn of the century, however, prices fell, production rose, and applications grew. World War I greatly expanded use of the metal, as armies searched for lightweight, durable materials for military equipment. In the 1920s, high-strength alloys were developed that were used in the development of the commercial airline industry in the 1930s. In World War II, aluminum output increased primarily due to demand from warplane production and soldiers' rations packaging. While consumption dropped briefly right after the war, consumer demand soon picked up the slack. The Korean War in the early 1950s produced another surge in aluminum shipments. As consumer demand grew in the postwar prosperity, the range of applications increased accordingly. Use of aluminum building products in commercial and residential construction expanded, and aluminum foil became a staple of the American kitchen.

The advent of a strong environmental movement gave new prominence to the industry, since aluminum was particularly suited to recycling. To produce aluminum from recycled scrap requires only 5 percent of the huge amount of energy that it takes to make it from scratch. Since the economics of recycling make so much sense, industry participants have supported the efforts of environmentalists in this area. Moreover, as governments pressure automakers to increase gas mileage of their vehicles and thus save energy, light-weight aluminum is gaining favor among manufacturers in a variety of applications.

CURRENT CONDITIONS

Aluminum is a notoriously cyclical business, and after a very strong performance at the end of the 1980s, a few lean years might have been expected. The extent of the downturn, however, was an alarming one for industry participants and well beyond expectations. In the early 1990s the aluminum industry became one of the unintended victims of the Cold War's aftermath. Russia no longer needed much aluminum for its defense sector, but it did hunger for export earnings. Before the fall of the Berlin Wall in 1989, Russia sent about 250,000 metric tons of aluminum overseas each year; by 1993, they were shipping aluminum at an annual rate of 1.2 million metric tons. As Clifford Gaddy, a Brookings Institution economist, told the *Wall Street Journal,* "We were used to a world in which one of the biggest commodity producers was the most stable and predictable—everything was planned five years ahead with the absolute minimum of surprise. Now it's switched to the exact opposite, where even their own government doesn't know what's happening."

In 1994, however, the industry staged a strong recovery on the back of an improved economy and tighter supply. Overall demand for aluminum sheet increased 11 percent; the transportation sector was particularly strong, with usage in passenger cars up 23 percent. Moreover, under the so-called Memorandum of Understanding, the aluminum-producing nations agreed to shut down 1.5 million to 2-million tons of overall capacity. Russia alone cut its production by 500,000 tons a year. As demand grew and supply was restricted, inventories fell, prices strengthened, and profits rose.

In late 1995 and 1996, however, market conditions again took a turn for the worse. Some industry observers traced the weakness to protracted "destocking" by aluminum consumers. Pricing for aluminum ingot on the London Metal Exchange—which has a strong effect on sheet and can stock prices—averaged 68 cents per pound in 1996 versus 82 cents per pound in 1995. According to statistics of the Aluminum Association, sheet, plate, and foil volume fell 4 percent in 1996 to 10.7 billion pounds. At that level, the three products accounted for 59 percent of the industry's total shipments. Demand for sheet fell 5 percent to 9.2 billion pounds; plate was down 16 percent to 0.3 billion pounds; and foil production rose 2 percent to 1.2 billion pounds. The lower level of shipments and weak pricing were reflected in the 1996 pretax profits of the six largest aluminum producers, which fell 36 percent.

The three major markets for aluminum in North America are packaging, building and construction, and transportation. Building and construction in the United States is a mature industry that is growing at a rate below that of the gross national product. And while shipments to the beverage industry had been the major factor driving new demand through the early 1990s, in mid-decade they had begun to stagnate. Thus the industry looked to the transportation sector for new markets and continued growth.

Automotive. In the 1990s, the aluminum industry invested substantial resources in both research and development and marketing to displace steel as the metal of choice in automobiles, and by mid-decade it had made significant progress toward that goal. According to the Aluminum Association, in 1994 aluminum shipments to North American carmakers increased 15 percent from the 1993 level. In total, automakers used 2.9 billion pounds of aluminum, up 386 million pounds from the year-earlier level. Sheet aluminum accounted for the greatest volume increase—usage rose by 67 million pounds. Overall, the amount of aluminum used by the automotive industry more than doubled in the 1985-94 period.

The potential for increased aluminum content is substantial. According to one estimate, only 5.8 percent of the typical family vehicle in 1995 consisted of aluminum, versus 67.5 percent for steel and 7.7 percent for plastic. In 1996, the average car had about 247 pounds of aluminum. Estimates of the proportion of aluminum content in passenger vehicles by the year 2000 vary, but some observers put the figure at 350 to 400 pounds. The large producers are optimistic that aluminum usage in cars will increase steadily.

In the automotive market, as in others, aluminum's advantages are its recyclability (at a time when governments and environmentalists are aiming for a totally recyclable car) and, especially, its light weight (which improves fuel economy). While aluminum is only 35 percent as dense as steel (its specific gravity is 2.7 versus 7.8 for steel), it can be nearly as strong, depending on car assembly methods. The development of higher strength alloys has increased the attractiveness of aluminum in recent years. Some observers believe that the Japanese auto industry has a particular interest in incorporating aluminum into vehicles because of the high price of gasoline in Japan and the high proportion of imported raw materials. Others believe that the electric car is the most promising market for aluminum, because such automobiles must

be light to compensate for the presence of heavy batteries.

One drawback of aluminum, however, is the relatively high cost, which has led some observers to believe that "all-aluminum" cars will continue to be restricted to luxury models. In 1996, there were only two such BIW (body-in-white) aluminum cars: the Honda Acura NSX and the Audi A8, and both were high-priced, low-volume sports cars. The Acura's aluminum BIW weighed 309 pounds, or 40 percent less than what a hypothetical steel model would have cost. But many observers believed that there would not be an affordable, all-aluminum, high-volume car for many years, owing to the more problematic assembly methods and the higher metalmaking cost. Aluminum requires more energy in spot welding and is less formable in stamping than steel.

Can Sheet Production. In 1963 almost none of the beverage cans were made from aluminum; 30 years later, 97 percent were constructed from the metal. Shipments of can sheet rose steadily throughout the 1980s and early 1990s, increasing from 2.9 billion bounds in 1982 to 4.3 billion pounds in 1992—24 percent of the aluminum industry's total shipments. Aluminum displaced both glass and bimetal cans partly because of its light weight and stackability. Moreover, in a period that saw rising ecological concern, aluminum's recyclability meant it was environmentally friendly.

But perhaps the main selling point for aluminum was its lower overall cost. In 1994, however, as supply contracted and prices rose, beverage makers had sticker shock. In December 1994, Coca-Cola announced that it would replace aluminum with steel in some of its European and Asian markets, and many beverage makers talked of switching to cheaper materials. By 1997, though, there were still no major changeovers. As Norm Nieder, Group director of packaging at Anheuser-Busch told *Beverage World* in 1995, "Outside the United States, steel cans may offer a nice alternative, but they produce higher coating emissions than aluminum cans do. There's no way you could run a steel can plant in California today, for instance, that's for sure."

Anticipating still-higher can sheet prices in 1995, beverage makers stockpiled inventories—soft drink can shipments rose 10.4 percent in 1994. The market overhang hurt 1995 sales, and beverage can shipments through the first nine months of the year were down by more than 2.6 billion cans, or 3.4 percent, to 75.367 billion.

Some of the longer-term trends in the beverage industry were not positive for aluminum producers. So-called New Age drinks have been increasing in popularity, and these have traditionally been sold in glass bottles. While the industry has tried to convert New Age bottlers to aluminum, in 1994 bottlers shied away from marketing their products in 24-ounce aluminum cans because of the high price. Meanwhile, in the beer segment, aluminum makers must contend with the growing popularity of products from microbreweries, which package their beer in bottles.

Moreover, for a variety of reasons, can makers are adopting smaller lid designs and are using thinner aluminum. As a consequence, manufacture of each can requires smaller amounts of aluminum than in past years. Thus, greater unit demand for cans does not necessarily translate into an equal rise in aluminum requirements. Additionally, there appears to be a trend toward the more economical large, plastic bottle as well. Producers had been hopeful that overseas beverage can markets, where aluminum's penetration has on average been much lower than in the United States, would pick up the slack. But with Coke and other producers shifting at least some of their packaging to steel, these expectations may be dashed.

Aerospace. The aluminum industry has aggressively penetrated the aerospace market; nearly all defense planes have an aluminum content of 70 to 90 percent. Demand for aluminum from the aerospace segment was strong during the 1980s, as both defense spending and commercial aircraft orders were buoyant. By the early 1990s, however, the aerospace segment was in decline. The airlines cancelled or delayed orders as their profits disappeared, and with the Cold War over the government cut outlays for the military. According to Aluminum Association statistics, annual shipments of both heat-treatable sheet and heat-treatable plate, which are primarily used in defense and aerospace applications, fell 23 percent and 19 percent, respectively, between 1989 and 1992.

In early 1994, some industry participants thought a bottoming out had been reached and that this industry niche would recover a bit. By 1996, the commercial jet aircraft market proved to be one of the few bright spots in an otherwise lackluster aluminum picture. Price hikes of 10 to 15 percent in some heat-treated and heat-plated products were announced at the end of the year by Alcoa, Reynolds, and Ravenswood Aluminum.

The aluminum producers continued to maintain a dominant role in the aircraft market despite the attempts of other materials makers to steal share. In the 1980s proponents of nonmetallic advanced composites claimed that by the second half of the 1990s they would account for up to 80 percent of commercial airframe weight. In 1994 those predictions appeared overblown. Aluminum in the newest commercial transport, the Boeing 777, accounted for about 65 percent of total weight, down from previous generations of airliners but nowhere near the 20-25 percent level that some pessimistic observers had forecast. The composites have made the most headway in the plane's tail, which in the 777 represents a loss of about 25,000 pounds of aluminum products.

Meanwhile, the industry continues to work on new alloys and new processes. Despite cutbacks in its budget, the Pentagon remains committed to maintaining its technological edge, which encourages aluminum companies to make new investments in research and development to service the military's needs.

INDUSTRY LEADERS

The largest aluminum producer in the world is Alcoa (Aluminum Co. of America). Indeed, in the early part of the century it was the only aluminum producer of consequence in North America. In 1928 it spun off its foreign operations into Alcan, the large Canadian producer, as it continued to dominate the U.S. market. In 1950, Alcoa's domestic monopoly—which had already been somewhat diluted by the federal government's efforts to create competitors during and following World War II—came to an end as the courts dismantled the company.

In the early 1960s the reconfigured company began to produce more semifabricated and fabricated products as it expanded output of can stock and products for the aerospace industry. In the late 1980s, after the acceptance of diversification earlier in the decade, the company refocused on its aluminum business. Alcoa stresses the importance of safety in its operations, and in the early 1990s had the best safety record of the major producers. In 1996, Alcoa's sales rose 5 percent to $13.1 billion; net profit fell 35% to $514 million, primarily due to lower prices for aluminum products.

Reynolds Metals Co. has been a leader in developing new aluminum products, from baseball bats to grain bins. It introduced the aluminum beverage can in 1963, when steelmakers had a lock on that market. Reynolds' two-piece can took about one-fifth the time to make and used 40 percent less metal than the three-piece can of its steel rivals, which it quickly displaced. In 1968 the company pioneered the huge can recycling program that gave makers a cheap source of aluminum and cheered environmentalists.

Reynolds had the wisdom to stick with its famous aluminum foil when it was a money-loser. It has built on the popularity of its foil by expanding into plastic and paper household packaging products. On the other hand, in the mid-1990s the company was criticized for investing in too many businesses and losing its strategic focus; it was also accused of having a high cost structure. Sales of $3.5 billion in 1996 yielded net income of $89 million, sharply below earnings of $389 million in 1995.

AMAX was a mining, metal, and energy company whose origins date from the late nineteenth century. The company began aluminum operations in 1962 when it purchased two Midwestern aluminum companies. At one point the company sold half its aluminum business to Mitsui & Co., but in the late 1980s rebought it. In 1993 AMAX merged with Cypress Metals while spinning off all of its aluminum operations to create Alumax, which is now the third-largest aluminum company in the United States. Alumax produces a wide range of sheet, plate, and foil products, a significant portion of which are marketed through distributors. In 1996 it acquired Cressona Aluminum, a leading, privately-held aluminum maker specializing in extruded products. In that year, Alumax recorded sales of $3.2 billion and earnings of $250 million, both slightly higher than year-earlier results. About 30 percent of its total sales were in building and construction markets.

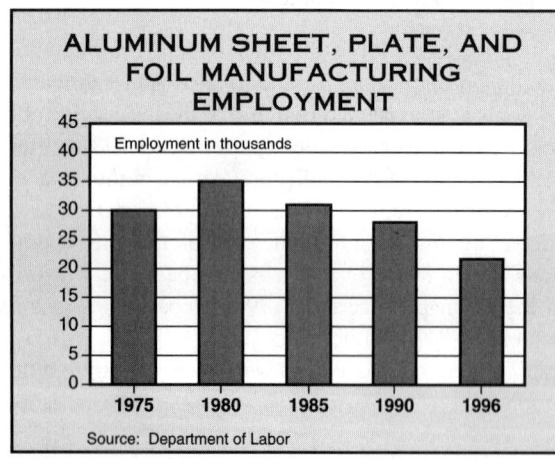

ALUMINUM SHEET, PLATE, AND FOIL MANUFACTURING EMPLOYMENT

Employment in thousands

Source: Department of Labor

WORK FORCE

The manufacturing work force of the major aluminum companies is heavily unionized. The industry's two major unions are the United Steelworkers and the Aluminum, Brick, and Glass Workers. New long-term labor agreements covering unionized workers were ratified in mid-1996. The agreements set broad, new goals for employee safety, job security, influence, control, and accountability for the work environment. Some observers, however, thought labor peace had come at a considerable price. Analyst John C. Tumazos, aluminum analyst at Donaldson, Lufkin & Jenrette, told *American Metal Market* that they were "more expensive than the national inflation rates and our own expectations."

AMERICA AND THE WORLD

Historically, the U.S. aluminum industry has been adept at expanding overseas and capitalizing on its foreign assets. Indeed, the aluminum industry has a greater presence abroad than many other U.S. industries. Some 50 percent of Alcoa's sales is derived from overseas sources; for Reynolds, the figure is 23 percent.

Alcan was formed in 1928 when Alcoa spun off its foreign operations to form the Canadian company. For more than 20 years thereafter, however, the same individuals controlled both firms. In 1950 the courts ordered investors to sell their shares of one company or the other, and the ownership ties between the two firms were severed. At that time Alcan's focus was on the primary aluminum market, but in the late 1950s it decided to expand significantly its fabricating operations. Alcan established semifabricating plants of its own in the United States that afforded stable outlets for its ingot. In 1971, for the first time, Alcan shipped more semifabricated and fabricated tonnage than ingot, and these products now account for about two-thirds of sales. In 1996, Alcan reported earnings of $410 million, down 24 percent from year-earlier net income of $543 million, owing to weak demand in Europe and soft pricing.

Russia. In the early 1990s, however, international developments were the source of the industry's major problems. While shipments in the U.S. in 1992 were healthy as the economy pulled out of recession, conditions in Europe and Japan remained depressed; meanwhile, Russia was rapidly increasing its aluminum exports. Since 1978, the price of aluminum ingot (which is eventually reflected in sheet, plate, and foil quotes) has been set on the London Metal Exchange (LME): it fell from above a peak of $1.65 in 1988 to $.50 in late 1993. With the international supply/demand equation unbalanced, producers worldwide were suffering. As Lloyd T. O'Connell, Reynolds Metals' chief economist, told the *Wall Street Journal:* "If the demand is weak abroad, it's almost as bad as if demand is weak domestically. The LME doesn't care where the metal is."

Thus, in 1994, the industry signed a two-year Memorandum of Understanding to limit worldwide supply; it reduced overall capacity by 1.5-million to 2-million tons, and Russian capacity alone by 500,000 tons. With the expiration of the agreement in 1996, some analysts predicted that Russian product would eventually be needed for rising demand from both industrialized and developing countries. Initially, however, Russian aluminum exports to the United States fell sharply, declining to 8,800 tons for the first ten months of 1996 compared with 112,500 tons for the same period in 1995. The sharp drop reflected the quality problems some users had encountered in even the most basic sheet alloys.

Japan. In recent years, U.S. producers have strengthened ties with Japanese aluminum and steel companies. In September 1990, Alcoa and Kobe Steel announced a strategic alliance to exploit worldwide opportunities in aluminum that has resulted in four joint ventures in the United States and Japan. The agreement was particularly noteworthy because the steelmaker has strong relationships with the automobile industry.

Mexico. With the passage of the North American Free Trade Agreement (NAFTA), trade between the United States and Mexico in aluminum has received increased attention. The role of Mexican aluminum manufacturers in the U.S. auto industry was expected to grow significantly between 1997 and the year 2000. Such companies as Nemak SA of the Alfa Industrial Group should be a major source for aluminum castings, particularly in powertrain applications. The increase in trade wasn't expected to be in just one direction: Mexico's imports of secondary aluminum rose to 20,000 tons in 1996, owing to increased auto production following the passage of NAFTA.

RESEARCH AND TECHNOLOGY

The enormous strides that aluminum has made in displacing steel and other materials in the container/packaging, automotive, aerospace, and construction markets demonstrates the substantial investment it has made in research and development. This effort has been instrumental in developing a wide range of new aluminum products including beverage cans, baseball bats, grain bins, roofing, windows, appliance parts, and semitrailers; it has also yielded stronger, lighter, cheaper alloys, and improved production processes. A comment of David Moison, a consultant at Resource Strategies, to the *Wall Street Journal* is telling: "People in aluminum don't have the belief somebody's going to use it just because they make it. They've had to fight like hell to convert people to aluminum."

Producers have also made remarkable strides in improving productivity, which has advanced from 15 man-hours per ton in the 1960s to six man-hours per ton in the early 1990s. Since aluminum by weight costs six times as much as steel and is so energy-intensive, the industry has had to strive constantly to reduce its costs to remain competitive. In 1994, Alcoa received grants totaling $33 million from the Department of Energy to develop more efficient methods for producing both alumina and aluminum sheet.

FURTHER READING

Alcoa 1996 10-K Pittsburgh: Alcoa, 1997.

Alumax 1996 10-K Atlanta: Alumax, 1997.

Ambrosia, John. "Aluminum Tries to Recycle its Past Success." *Iron Age,* June 1992.

Canby, Thomas. "Aluminum, The Magic Metal." *National Geographic,* August 1978.

Hamill, David. "U.S. Aluminum Sheet Market Is Like a Box of Chocolates." *American Metal Market,* 12 July 1995.

Petry, Corinna. "Aluminum Producers Optimistic About Future Markets." *American Metal Market,* 15 November 1996.

Pieters, Nancy. "Increasing Production and Mixed Signals." *New Steel,* May 1996.

Red, Brendan. "Steel vs. Aluminum in Detroit." *New Steel,* October 1995.

Regan, Bob. "Alcoa Lands Energy Research Pact." *American Metal Market,* 12 May 1994.

Regan, Bob. "Aluminum Softness Takes Financial Toll." *American Metal Market,* 17 February 1997.

Regan, Bob. "Aluminum Wage Pacts May Prove Expensive." *American Metal Market,* 5 June 1996.

Regan, Bob. "Demand Forecasts Give the MU Pact Whole New Sound." *American Metal Market,* 27 February 1996.

Regan, Bob. "Drier Days for Cans: Slower Sales Dent Aluminum Prices." *American Metal Market,* 20 October 1995.

Regan, Bob. "Off to a Disappointing Start." *American Metal Market,* 27 February 1996.

Regan, Bob. "Russia's Aluminum Products Seen Losing Popularity in US." *American Metal Market,* 9 May 1996.

Regan, Bob. "Subdued Aluminum Market Creeps Ahead Cautiously." *American Metal Market,* 25 February 1997.

Reynolds Metals 1995 10-K, Richmond, VA: Reynolds, 1996.

Sfiligoj, Eric. "At What Price?" *Beverage World,* June 1995.

Smosarski, Greg. "Steel Cans Rank as Tops in Europe Metals Race." *American Metal Market,* 25 March 1996.

"The Aluminum Situation." *Aluminum Association Monthly Report of Economics and Statistics,* February 1997.

Available from: http://aluminum.org/situ_ b25.htm#shipments

The Story and Uses of Aluminum, Washington: Aluminum Association, 1984.

Stuckey, John A. *Vertical Integration and Joint Ventures in the Aluminum Industry,* Cambridge, MA: Harvard University Press, 1983.

"Transportation Market Becomes Large Market for Aluminum Industry." *American Metal Market,* 20 October 1995.

Wrigley, Al. "Mexico's Aluminum Market Casting Bigger Net." *American Metal Market,* 25 February 1997.

—Bob Schneider

SIC 3354

ALUMINUM EXTRUDED PRODUCTS

This classification covers establishments primarily engaged in extruding aluminum and aluminum-base alloy basic shapes, such as rod and bar, pipe and tube, and tube blooms, including establishments producing tube by drawing.

INDUSTRY SNAPSHOT

The process of extruding aluminum has been compared to squeezing toothpaste from a tube, with the metal (initially in the form of extrusion billet) taking the shape of the die through which it has been pressed. While commercially pure aluminum is used in some extrusion applications, more often the aluminum is mixed with other metals—particularly magnesium and silicon—to form alloys. Aluminum extrusions are used to make windows, doors, and gates; as components in cars, trucks, and jet aircraft; in the manufacture of major appliances, furniture, and electrical equipment; and in a host of other applications, ranging from cranes to athletic goods.

The aluminum extrusion industry exhibited good growth over the 1993 to 1996 period, as annual shipments increased from 2.8 billion pounds to 3.6 billion pounds. Extruders did have to contend with substantial competition in many of their traditional markets from competing materials, like vinyl, wood, roll-formed steel, and aluminum and manganese die castings. But the transportation sector, especially automobiles, generated substantial incremental demand. The growing use of aluminum in automotive applications promised to spur additional extrusion demand in the future.

ORGANIZATION AND STRUCTURE

To some extent, the extrusion segment may be divided between the commodity-like output of large producers, which may be said to be sold by the pound, and specialty production of smaller makers, sold by the part. As in other industries, extruders have their areas of specialization. Some work primarily in certain alloy series, while others specialize in close tolerances, miniature shapes, or extremely large shapes.

Four of the major integrated North American producers—Alcoa, Alumax, Alcan of Canada, and Reynolds—have substantial extrusion operations. Between the mid-1980s and mid-1990s, about 40 aluminum extruders went out of business, and the industry continues to consolidate. The trend toward consolidation was furthered in 1996, when Alumax bought the largest privately owned extruder, Cressona Aluminum. And in early 1997, Reynolds Metals announced that it would sell its aluminum extrusion plant in El Campo, Texas, to Tredegar Industries, which had highly profitable extruding operations. The facility had 233 employees and produced standard and specialty extrusions for various markets.

BACKGROUND AND DEVELOPMENT

The first aluminum extrusion press in North America was opened by Alcoa in New Kensington, Pennsylvania, in 1904. During the 1930s large strides were made in the extrusion process, permitting the formation of virtually any type of aluminum cross section for a wide variety of applications. During World War II, the use of aluminum in aerospace applications grew rapidly, as the strength of Allied air forces was key to the war effort. In the postwar period, extruders continued to expand, benefiting from the growth in the residential housing sector.

CURRENT CONDITIONS

With a growing economy and increased shipments from the automotive sector, demand for aluminum extrusions in 1997 had recovered nicely from the recession in the early 1990s. Shipments of 2.4 billion pounds in 1992 rose to 2.8 billion in 1993 and 3.3 billion in 1994; in 1995 and 1996, growth was slower, but shipments still increased to 3.4 billion and 3.6 billion, respectively. The extrusion segment was not immune, however, to the price volatility shown by other sectors of the aluminum industry. Prices rose smartly in 1994 and early 1995, but weakened in late 1995 and 1996, thus following the pattern of the industry as a whole.

Automotive. The automobile sector presents the greatest opportunity for the aluminum extrusion industry. In 1991, the average American car had 182 pounds of aluminum, versus 247 pounds in 1996; some industry observers expected that number to rise to 350 pounds by the year 2000. At that level, each car would average about 45 pounds of aluminum extrusions, versus between 16 to 26 pounds in 1996. Since aluminum is lighter than steel, iron, and copper and easily recyclable, the metal fits well with a strategy of reducing energy consumption. Thus the prospects for extrusion applications—bumper beams, radiator tubing, evaporators, air-conditioning, compressor parts, among others—have steadily improved. In 1994 alone, shipments of extrusions for use in passenger cars, trucks, and buses rose from 189 million pounds to 314 million pounds. Shipments for trailers and semitrailers also expanded substantially, rising from 281 million pounds to 366 million pounds.

Symbolic of the hopes of the extrusion industry, in 1997, General Motors Corp. gave Alumax a contract to supply radiator enclosures for GM's Chevrolet C/K and GMC pickups, as well as its Suburban, Tahoe, and Yukon sports utilities vehicles. With Alumax supplying some 20 million pounds of extrusions over a 10-year period, the contract was the largest to date for an aluminum extrusion application in the domestic light-truck or passenger car industry.

Meanwhile, Hydro Aluminum of Holland, Michigan, has been supplying extrusions for several automotive applications, including seat-back frames for the Chevrolet Malibu and Oldsmobile Cutlass, third-row seat cushion frames for the Ford Expedition, and front and rear bumper beams and power seat tracks for the Buick Park Avenue. In aggregate, these applications were expected to total some 21.5 million pounds in 1997.

One application that particularly excites producers is the spaceframe, where aluminum extrusions are used to make the skeletal system of the car's structure. Rather than spot welding as many as 300 stamped steel components, less than 100 aluminum extrusions and interconnecting die-cast nodes are robotically welded to form the spaceframe. The spaceframe offers a weight saving of about 35 percent over steel bodies. In 1993, Alcoa began operating a plant in Soest, Germany, to supply aluminum spaceframes to Audi AG. In 1994, Audi began selling its A8 luxury sedan in Europe—the first car to utilize a complete aluminum spaceframe body structure.

Building and Construction. The extruders have been faced with stagnating demand in the key building and construction sector, reflecting substitution of competing materials and, in the early 1990s, a weak housing market. In the mid-1960s, this sector accounted for 60 percent of industry output; in the mid-1980s, 40 percent; and in 1995, about 32 percent. While the automotive market has recently picked up much of the slack, the loss of share in major products like windows and doors has had a major negative impact on the extrusion sector. The decline in the building and construction segment has resulted in considerable consolidation, with the number of extruders falling about 30 percent between the mid-1980s and mid-1990s. Small- and medium-sized firms that were thinly capitalized were the most vulnerable.

In an effort to boost demand, some extruders began providing customers with an increasing number of value-added services downstream. By offering a variety of machines for extra processing, extruders helped their customers get new products to market more quickly and saved them the costs of investing in the equipment themselves. This also reduced questions of accountability for poor quality, since the customer didn't have to send the parts on to a fabricator or finisher before using them. While some observers noted that providing additional services hasn't always resulted in increased profitability, they added that it has helped in developing customer loyalty.

Aircraft. The market for aircraft aluminum extrusions was depressed during the early 1990s because of the decline in U.S. military spending and a drop in orders for commercial airplanes. The segment underwent a shakeup in 1992 as one of the largest makers of small press aerospace alloy shapes, International Light Metals, went out of business; the company had at one time accounted for as much as 35 percent of aircraft extrusions of less than 5-inch circle size. The two major surviving producers were Alcoa, the largest maker, and Universal Alloy, owned by Swiss parent, AG Menziken. In a bid to find a niche between industry giant Alcoa and the distributors (who have traditionally accounted for most shipments to end users), Universal Alloy decided to sell the bulk of its shapes directly to end-users or their contractors. In early 1996, however, the aviation market appeared to have recovered. In 1995, Universal Alloy sold 10 million to 15 million pounds of light shapes, its largest market, compared with about half that in 1993. President John Ball told *American Metal Market,* "By 1998, I think it's going to be 20 million to 30 million pounds," citing growing production of both commercial airplanes and general aviation aircraft—and even military planes. He also announced plans to expand the physical size of Universal's plant by 40 percent.

Bridges. Extruders have been eyeing the infrastructure market for new demand, including the tens of thousands of bridges that need to be refurbished. While most of the work will probably go to producers of other materials, with each repair requiring perhaps 50,000 pounds of aluminum, even a small share of the market would generate significant sales. One factor weighing in favor of aluminum extrusions is that processes are now available to tailor parts to individual bridge design; they can then be quickly assembled and virtually snapped together, significantly reducing the time the bridge has to be closed for reconstruction.

INDUSTRY LEADERS

Alcoa has extensive extrusion facilities around the world. In the United States, Alcoa produces extrusions primarily at five U.S. locations: Chandler, Arizona; Lafayette, Indiana; Baltimore, Maryland; Tifton, Georgia; and Delhi, Louisiana.

In 1996, Alumax paid $437 million for privately held Cressona Aluminum, thereby more than doubling its extrusion capacity and sales volume. Alumax believed that, after merging Cressona with its existing extrusion operations, it had the world's largest soft-alloy extrusion manufacturing capacity. These facilities consisted of 12 plants with a total of 45 presses that ranged in size from 700 to 6,000 tons.

WORK FORCE

The manufacturing facilities of the major producers are heavily unionized; the two major unions are the Aluminum, Brick, and Glass Workers and the United Steelworkers. Contract talks between these unions and the major producers, which in 1996 were concluded without a strike, have a significant influence on pay rates throughout the industry. In general, wages at the major firms are about 10 to 20 percent above pay rates at smaller companies.

RESEARCH AND TECHNOLOGY

During 1993, a major research and development initiative was begun at the New York State Center for Advanced Technology in Automation & Robotics at Rensselaer Polytechnic Institute. The program grew out of a joint task force that included representatives of the university, the Aluminum Association, and the Aluminum Extruders Council. The research agenda includes basic metallurgical studies; die surface enhancement through plasma spraying and other processes; projections of metal flow and extrudability; and sensor utilization for inspection and process control. A long-term research goal of the program is to develop intelligent process-control techniques by combining process physics with artificial intelligence to improve process yield and quality. The emphasis will be on research that can assist companies in succeeding in the global economy. The program is funded by the New York State Science and Technology Foundation, federal agencies, and corporate donors.

FURTHER READING

"Alcoa to Build Spaceframe Plant in Germany." *Purchasing,* 16 January 1992.

Courter, Eileen. "Despite Gains, Extrusion Market's Still a Dogfight." *American Metal Market,* 4 September 1996.

———. "Extrusions on the Rise." *American Metal Market,* 27 September 1995.

———. "Extrusions Tackle the Technical Hurdles." *American Metal Market,* 9 September 1993.

Demmier, Al. "Aluminum Spaceframes." *Automotive Engineering,* January 1992.

Extrusion Spotlight: Competitive Materials. Wauconda, IL: Aluminum Extruders Council, 1989.

Grzelka, Constance. "Window Market Closing for Extruders." *American Metal Market,* 19 March 1993.

Haflich, Frederick. "Aluminum Extruder Sees Light; Firming Aircraft Market Prompts Expansion." *American Metal Market,* 8 February 1996.

Owen, Jim. "Flat '96 Not Necessarily Bad News for Extruders." *American Metal Market,* 12 January 1996.

Pinkham, Myra. "New Auto Applications Drive Extrusion Demand." *American Metal Market,* 25 February 1997.

Puffer, Raymond, "Aluminum Extrusion R&D Is Under Way." *American Metal Market,* 19 March 1993.

"Reynolds's Metals to Sell Aluminum Extrusion Plant to Tredegar Industrie." *PR Newswire,* 7 March 1997.

The Story and Use of Aluminum. Washington: Aluminum Association, 1984.

Schroeder, Manfred. "Extruders Press for Further Shipment Gains." *American Metal Market,* 12 July 1995.

—Bob Schneider

SIC 3355

ALUMINUM ROLLING AND DRAWING, NOT ELSEWHERE CLASSIFIED

This classification refers to establishments primarily engaged in rolling, drawing, and other operations resulting in the production of aluminum ingot, including extrusion ingot, and aluminum and aluminum-base alloy basic shapes, not elsewhere classified, such as rolled and continuous cast rod and bar. Establishments primarily engaged in producing aluminum powder, flake, and paste are classified in **SIC 3399: Primary Metal Products, Not Elsewhere Classified,** and those producing aluminum wire and cable from purchased wire bars, rods, or wire are classified in **SIC 3357: Drawing and Insulating of Nonferrous Wire.**

Aluminum rod, bar, and wire products are often grouped together in a single product category. Wire is made from rod or bar, and by definition is less than three-eighths inches in diameter, while rod and bar are larger. Electrical transmission lines represent the major end-use of rod/bar/wire products. Rod and bar are also used to make rivets, nails, screws, and bolts, and parts of machinery and equipment. According to the Aluminum Association, rod, bar, and wire shipments fell 0.7 percent during 1996 to 551 million pounds, representing 3 percent of total aluminum industry shipments.

Rod, bar, and wire production slumped during the late 1980s and early 1990s. Aluminum wire dominates the electrical transmission and distribution market, with copper a distant second. During the 1980s, demand for electrical transmission lines fell, as new construction was lackluster and electricity usage remained flat. Usage of aluminum wire in buildings also fell sharply in the 1980s. In the mid-1970s, aluminum had a 31 percent share of this market, but following publicity of aluminum wire hazards, its share dwindled to 8 percent in 1994. Several of the major aluminum companies thus elected to retreat from the electrical conductor market. In 1994-1995, however, there was a recovery in demand for rod, bar, and wire products. Stronger shipments to the transmission and distribution sector were driven by increased housing starts and the need to upgrade existing systems. Some producers have moved to expand their plants. In 1996, Alcoa Wire, Rod & Bar, located in Massena, New York, said that it expected to invest millions of dollars to improve its capacity and products. The company continues to invest in research and development for use in automobiles and other offerings.

FURTHER READING

Demmier, Al. ''Tech Briefs—Wear-Resistant Aluminum.'' *Automotive Engineering,* January 1992.

''Optimism for Electrical Wire, Cable.'' *American Metal Market,* 25 March 1994.

The Story and Uses of Aluminum. Washington: Aluminum Association, 1993.

Petry, Corinna. ''Aluminum Producers Optimistic About Future Markets.'' *American Metal Market,* 15 November 1996.

Worden, Edward. ''Copper is Facing Competition.'' 23 February 1994.

—Bob Schneider

ROLLING, DRAWING, AND EXTRUDING OF NONFERROUS METALS, EXCEPT COPPER AND ALUMINUM

This classification covers establishments primarily engaged in rolling, drawing, and extruding nonferrous metals other than copper and aluminum. The products of this industry are in the form of basic shapes, such as plate, sheet, strip, bar, and tubing. Excluded from this classification are establishments primarily engaged in recovering nonferrous metals and alloys from scrap or dross. Such establishments are classified in **SIC 3341: Secondary Smelting and Refining of Nonferrous Metals.** Those establishments primarily engaged in manufacturing gold, silver, tin, and other foils, except aluminum, are classified in **SIC 3497: Metal Foil and Leaf;** and those establishments manufacturing aluminum foil are classified in **SIC 3353: Aluminum Sheet, Plate, and Foil.**

INDUSTRY SNAPSHOT

Nonferrous metals are utilized by nearly every manufacturing industry in the United States and abroad, their existence critical to the production of a broad spectrum of products, from tin cans to semiconductors. The metals used by manufacturers to produce their products are purchased from three types of metal manufacturers, depending on the particular needs of the buyer: primary metal manufacturers, secondary metal manufacturers, and semi-fabricated metal manufacturers, each of which share an interdependent relationship with the other. Primary manufacturers produce metal by subjecting particular extracted ores to various metallurgical processes, thereby creating metal in its most basic form. Secondary manufacturers smelt, refine, and sometimes blend metal recovered from the shaping and trimming of primary metal during production and fabrication, or from recycled metal. The metal produced by these two types of manufacturers leaves the production site in either large bar or block form, a form known as ingot. As ingot, the metal exists in a convenient and efficient state for storage or shipping, ready for delivery to manufacturers requiring metal cast in this form, or ready to be shipped to a facility equipped to further shape or extrude the metal.

These latter facilities, the manufacturing establishments classified in this industry, take metal in its basic form, then roll, draw, or extrude the massive bar or block ingot into various shapes to make the metal suitable for a wide variety of applications. As semi-finished products, the metal is formed into plate, sheet, strip, bar, or tubing, then delivered to manufacturers involved in a multitude of industries.

Establishments in this sector are involved in shaping and forming precious metals, nickel, titanium, magnesium, lead, zinc, and other nonferrous metals (copper and aluminum are not included). The production of magnesium, lead, tungsten, molybdenum, and other nonferrous metal shapes accounts for 28.3 percent of production. Nickel and nickel-based alloys comprise 26.3 percent, while precious metals, titanium, and unclassified nonferrous rolling and drawing account for 20.5, 19.35, and 5.4 percent of production, respectively.

The industry shipped $2.9 billion worth of product in 1996, up marginally from its 1992 low of $2.7 billion in shipments and well below its recent high of $3.6 billion in 1989. Future shipment values were not expected to exceed the 1996 levels.

ORGANIZATION AND STRUCTURE

In 1996 approximately 159 companies derived the bulk of their revenue from the rolling, drawing, or extrusion of nonferrous metals other than aluminum and copper. These companies, some of which owned several manufacturing facilities, operated roughly 176 separate establishments.

More than half of the manufacturing establishments in operation in 1996 in this industrial sector employed 20 people or more, while the typical establishment employed 90 workers, slightly more than twice the size of the average manufacturing establishment involved in all other manufacturing industries.

Geographically, semi-fabricated metal manufacturing establishments were concentrated primarily in Pennsylvania, New Jersey, New York, and Michigan. The mid-Atlantic states, the Great Lakes region, and New England contained the greatest number of establishments, though production was also distributed throughout the South and West.

As with the other branches of the metal industry, the operating costs in the semi-fabricated metal industry are significantly higher than the costs incurred by the average manufacturing establishment. In 1994 the average cost per establishment in the semi-fabricated metal industry, that is, the average amount earmarked for raw materials, was $16.9 million, nearly double the average expense incurred by other manufacturing industries. However, the cost of materials for production continued to decline from highs established in the early 1980s. In 1996, material costs had fallen to $1.5 billion from a high of $2.2 billion in 1983.

BACKGROUND AND DEVELOPMENT

Historically, growth in the semi-fabricated metal industry depended on the metal market as a whole; if demand for particular metals experiences an increase, then semi-fabricators generally enjoy a commensurate upswing in business. The cyclical nature of the metals markets has resulted in similar behavior in the semi-fabricated metal industry. As a result, the industry's history mirrored the growth and decline of primary and secondary nonferrous metal producers, functioning as a dependent arm of the metal manufacturing industry and realizing earnings from the sundry markets that spur activity in the primary and secondary metal manufacturing industries.

Following World War II, however, a number of technological developments directly benefitted semi-fabricated, nonferrous metal manufacturers working with metals (other than aluminum and copper) took place. These stand as noteworthy achievements peculiar to the industry, developments that enabled manufacturers to play a more prominent role in the metal industry.

One of these technological advances made two of the less widely used metals more popular in the semi-fabricated metal industry. In 1964, after the conclusion of a seven-year research and development program financed by the U.S. Air Force and conducted by Republic Aviation Corp., a method was found by which titanium could be extruded more thinly than previously had been possible and at significantly lower costs, a capability that greatly enhanced titanium's applicability to the then burgeoning jet airplane and aerospace industries. In 1963, one year before the extrusion process was fully developed, 5,000 tons of titanium were consumed in the United States. Five years later, U.S. consumption had climbed to 25,000 tons and showed no signs of slowing down. During this five-year period, enormous technological strides were achieved in the production of titanium under the aegis of Reactive Metals Inc. and Titanium Metals Corporation of America in a joint venture to resolve the major problems associated with extracting the metal from its ores.

As the production of a supersonic transport aircraft neared completion in the late 1960s, domestic titanium consumption approached 80,000 tons annually, largely because supersonic transports and other high-speed aircraft required an appreciably greater percentage of titanium than slower aircraft because of temperature resistance qualities. Consequently, supersonic transports were 80 percent titanium, while slower aircraft such as Boeing Company's 727, were manufactured with less than 2 percent titanium. As the nation's space program intensified, the applications for titanium broadened, leading to widespread use of titanium in the aviation and aerospace industries in the 1990s.

Shortly after the titanium extrusion process was developed, another nonferrous metal began a similar rise in popularity, once again as result of an extensive research and development program. This time, however, the work was conducted outside U.S. borders by Canada's Cominco, Ltd., the world's largest producer of refined lead and zinc during the late 1960s. In 1964, concurrent with the conclusion of the U.S. Air Force's titanium research program, Cominco began exploring possible methods to improve the extrusion technology of zinc. Five years later, a suitable method was discovered that enabled zinc to be extruded without tearing, cracking, or sticking to the dies, problems that had restricted the use of zinc by the semi-fabricated metal industry. Prior to Cominco's discovery, zinc occasionally had been rolled or drawn, but it was more commonly known in the metal industry for its galvanizing and die casting properties. The capability to extrude the metal, however, greatly improved the metal's suitability for a host of component parts used in the production of automobiles and appliances. By using zinc, manufacturers could match colors more accurately, giving zinc an aesthetic advantage over aluminum and other metals. Consequently, the use of zinc by semi-fabricated metal manufacturers began in earnest during the 1970s, eventually becoming one of the key metals utilized by the industry in the early 1990s.

CURRENT CONDITIONS

Essentially affected by the same market factors that dictate the economic health of primary and secondary metal manufacturers, semi-fabricated metal manufacturers entered the mid-1990s bolstered by the strong performance of some metals and negatively affected by the static performance of others. Rarely is the industry's future easy to ascertain since its overall performance is dependent on the separate markets for individual metals, which frequently experience divergent bouts of growth and decline.

Emerging from the recessive early 1990s, however, the semi-fabricated metal industry's future was shaped by the encouraging strength of the lead market and the discovery of several new consumer markets for titanium. The zinc markets remained weak due to high levels of supply. Nickel prices remained unsettled due to strong supply and weak global demand for stainless steel, the principle end-use for nickel.

The worldwide demand for lead continued to expand through 1996 and record consumption and production was seen continuing through 1997. This increase was largely attributable to an increase in storage battery production and battery replacement, the primary end-uses of lead and a component of the semi-fabricated metal industry. Lead prices rose in 1996, but were tempered by continuing fallout from the Sumitomo commodities trading scandal, which depressed the market price for many nonferrous metals. Demand for lead was especially strong in the United States, but was weak in Europe and Japan due to sluggish economic growth. Lead consumption was expected to increase 1.2 percent in 1997.

Titanium producers entered the 1990s facing substantial cut backs in defense spending and in fluctuating demand for aircraft parts. However, the development of high-content titanium golf equipment saw a change in fortunes for the industry. Titanium golf club heads increasingly replaced traditional wood heads in the mid-1990s. The light metal offered golfers a larger and more favorable hitting surface. Titanium shipments increased from 34.4 million pounds in 1992 to 43.6 million in 1995. Moreover, titanium found its way into such diverse consumer products as eyeglass frames, cameras, bicycles, inline skates, cookware, and watches. Titanium product producers looked to increase this new segment of the industry not only as a substitute for falling defense needs, but to cushion the cyclical changes traditionally experienced in the commercial aviation industry, a large titanium consumer.

INDUSTRY LEADERS

Ranked according to sales volume, the three largest semi-fabricated metal manufacturers in 1996 were Teledyne Allvac/Vasco, a subsidiary of Allegheny Teledyne, Tremont Corp., and RMI Titanium Co., which generated more than $600 million in combined revenue. The bulk of the sector's companies earned less than $10 million.

The Teledyne Allvac/Vasco subsidiary of Allegheny Teledyne had revenues of $278 million on sales of more than $2 billion in 1996. Allvac/Vasco was engaged primarily in the production of nickel and nickel-alloy materials. Strong demand from the aerospace, biomedical and recreation markets, combined with internal cost-cutting measures, resulted in a strong earnings increase. On August 15, 1996, Allegheny Ludlum Corporation and Teledyne, Inc. merged to form Allegheny Teledyne Incorporated. The new company had sales in excess of $3.5 billion for 1996, with the bulk coming from the production of specialty metals for worldwide use.

Tremont Corp.'s subsidiary, Titanium Metals Corp. (TIMET), is the largest supplier of titanium to the aerospace and industrial industries. It also produced titanium sponge, an intermediate product from which titanium metal is derived, making the company one of the leading integrated titanium producers in the United States. TIMET experienced renewed growth due to resurgent demand for titanium products from the aerospace and recreational industries. The latter, particularly, represented a new area of growth due to the increasing use of titanium in the manufacture of golf club heads. The company posted revenues of $185 million in 1996.

RMI Titanium Co. became the largest nonintegrated producer of titanium mill products in the United States in 1993 when its 10,000 tons-per-year titanium sponge plant in Ashtabula, Ohio, was permanently closed in February of that year. Through the production of titanium metal products and titanium powder, a product classified in **SIC 3499: Fabricated Metal Products, Not Elsewhere Classified,** RMI generated $171 million in 1996, largely due to the expansion of the consumer titanium market for recreational equipment.

WORK FORCE

Total employment in the semi-fabricated metal industry fluctuated throughout the 1980s, effecting slight, sporadic gains, then suffering proportionate declines. In 1982 the industry employed 20,000, and by the mid-1990s, employment fell to 15,500, reflecting general consolidation and cost-cutting in the industry.

Production workers are generally employed on a full-time basis and earn more per hour than their counterparts in other manufacturing industries. The industry had nearly three times the average payroll per establishment in 1994 as did the rest of the manufacturing sector. Average payroll per employee in 1994 was $35,419 versus $30,620 for the wider manufacturing category.

FURTHER READING

Allegheny Teledyne Incorporated Report 10-K for the Year Ended 12-31-96. *Securities and Exchange Commission.* 27 March 1997.

"An Overlooked Metal Broadens Its Appeal." *Business Week,* 17 May 1969, 124.

Bierck, Richard. "How Golf Saved a Defense Supplier Hole in One." *U.S. News & World Report,* 2 December 1996, 56.

Stundza, Tom. "What the Trading Scandal Did!" *Purchasing,* 6 October 1996.

"Titanium Extrusion Knowhow Gets Big Boost." *Steel,* 21 December 1964.

Tremont Corporation Report 10-K for the Year Ended 12-31-96. *Securities and Exchange Commission.* 31 March 1997.

U.S. Bureau of the Census. *Statistical Abstract of the United States 1993.* 113th ed. Washington: GPO, 1993.

U.S. Department of Commerce. *Annual Survey of Manufactures.* Washington: GPO, 1996.

Walker, Robert. "Titanium Sales Poised for a Take-Off." *New York Times,* 14 January 1968, F1.

—Jeffrey L. Covell, updated by Norman Leahy

SIC 3357

DRAWING AND INSULATING OF NONFERROUS WIRE

This classification covers establishments primarily engaged in drawing, drawing and insulating, and insulating wire and cable of nonferrous metals from purchased wire bars, rods, or wire. Also included are establishments primarily engaged in manufacturing insulated fiber optic cable. Establishments primarily engaged in manufacturing glass fiber optic materials are included in **SIC 3229: Pressed and Blown Glass and Glassware, Not Elsewhere Classified,** while those manufacturing fabricated wire products from purchased wire are classified in **SIC 3496: Miscellaneous Fabricated Wire Products.**

INDUSTRY SNAPSHOT

Manufacturers involved in drawing and extruding nonferrous wire and cable supply five primary markets with various types of products manufactured from aluminum and copper, the two most widely utilized nonferrous metals, and other nonferrous metals. These products, ranging from fiber optic cable to insect wire screening, are drawn or extruded from wire bars or rods, a process that essentially winnows the larger bar and rod shapes into wire or cable. The wire and cable is then insulated with assorted materials such as paper or rubber or other materials, including polyethylene and polyvinyl chloride, for use in an assortment of applications, including wiring for residential and commercial buildings, communication networks, power distribution, automobiles, and appliances.

Historically, the five primary markets for the industry's products have been communication industries; electric utilities; automobile, truck, and boat manufacturers; the construction industry; and manufacturers of home appliances and industrial machinery. Since the conclusion of World War II, the composition of the industry's primary markets has remained unchanged, although the order of importance of each market to the industry has fluctuated.

By producing products for these and other markets, manufacturers shipped $15.7 billion worth of products in 1996, up from $15.2 billion in 1995. While shipment values increased, so has the cost of raw materials and capital investment.

ORGANIZATION AND STRUCTURE

As the nonferrous wire drawing and insulating industry entered the mid-1990s, approximately 380 companies in the United States were deriving the bulk of their revenue from the fabrication and insulation of wire and cable. These companies, many of which owned more than one manufacturing establishment, operated roughly 545 separate manufacturing facilities. Of these 545 establishments, 357, or nearly 65 percent, employed 20 or more workers, while the average size of a wire drawing and insulating establishment, in terms of the number of employees per establishment, was more than twice the size of the average manufacturing establishment.

Geographically, a majority of the industry's manufacturing establishments were located in the northeastern United States. By value of shipments, Indiana, Georgia, North Carolina, Illinois, and Texas lead the list. In terms of the greatest number of establishments located in one state, California led all other states with 60 manufacturing establishments.

Manufacturing establishments in this industry have historically been relatively costly to operate, more than three times the national average. This has been attributed primarily to the high price of raw materials needed to operate a wire drawing and insulation manufacturing establishment. The required production machinery to was also appreciably more expensive than the national standard posted by other manufacturing establishments.

BACKGROUND AND DEVELOPMENT

The wire and cable manufacturing industry changed enormously over the years because of technological progress, both in its own operations and in the systems and needs of its customers. The modern wire and cable manufacturing industry emerged in the late nineteenth and early twentieth century, a time during which the industrialization of the United States created a need for wire and cable products and provided a means for their production.

Once America became an industrialized nation, wire became a fundamental product underpinning the nation's growth, both industrially and commercially. For years, copper had been the preferred metal for a majority of the wire and cable manufacturing industry's products; its high conductivity elevated the metal above all others. Aluminum, which would eventually gain widespread acceptance in the industry, was first introduced as a cable conductor during the 1930s, but did not represent an appreciable portion of the market until the 1950s, when a tightened supply of copper, combined with its rising cost, forced manufacturers to search for an alternative.

Manufacturers' selection of aluminum to augment their copper supply came at an opportune time in the country's development: the population was rapidly expanding, creating a housing boom; televisions and radios were being manufactured at unprecedented levels; a community antennae television (CATV) market was burgeoning; more automobiles were being manufactured; and electric power generation in the country was about to begin two decades of exponential growth. Wire and cable manufacturers served each of these markets, experiencing enviable growth as the nation enjoyed an age of prosperity. By the beginning of the 1970s, the industry evolved into a $3 billion entity, primarily due to the growth of the national economy over the previous two decades.

The use of aluminum by the industry's products, however, particularly in the wiring of residential homes, caused considerable anxiety for some manufacturers when the U.S. Consumer Product Safety Commission (CPSC) filed a lawsuit against 26 manufacturers in 1977. Charging that 1.5 million homes wired with aluminum between 1965 and 1973 were in danger of catching fire, the CPSC sought to force manufacturers responsible for producing the wire to pay for the rewiring of each home, at an estimated cost of $300 per home.

The potential for fire stemmed from the poorer conductivity of aluminum when compared to copper. Since aluminum was less conductive than copper, more aluminum was required to form a wire, which created a thicker stock that wire installers were unable to fit tightly into wall outlets. This led to loose connections that, in turn, caused the wiring to overheat. The problem was corrected for all homes wired after 1973, but the scare sent aluminum's share of the wiring market cascading downward from 17.0 percent to 1.4 percent during the 1970s.

CPSC's revelation, however, did not dissuade manufacturers from eschewing aluminum as a key raw material in the production of wire and cable. By the late 1980s, manufacturers purchased more primary aluminum than any other nonferrous metal to produce wire and cable products.

CURRENT CONDITIONS

As the wire drawing and insulating industry entered the mid-1990s, manufacturing activity resumed its pre-recession levels, thanks largely to continuing strengths in the construction industry and increasing use of fiber optic cable by the telecommunications industry. Strong private residential housing starts augured well for manufacturers involved in producing building wire. Other wire and cable markets effected recoveries as well, enabling the industry to stanch its shrinking revenue volume. The brightest prospect for the industry's future lay in the growth of the fiber optics industry, for which the wire drawing and insulating industry supplies fiber optic cable.

From 1989 to 1993, U.S. shipments of fiber optic equipment—including optical fiber and cable as well as other products excluded from the wire drawing and insulating manufacturing industry—increased 13 percent annually, with prognostications calling for still greater growth later in the decade. In 1993 the world market for fiber optic equipment was estimated to be $5 billion, a market in which U.S. manufacturers maintained a lead over European and Japanese producers, although the gap separating the United States from other manufacturers was closing in early 1994. Some observers expect this market to double in value by the end of the decade, promising lucrative profit potential for manufacturers of fiber optic cable. As the conventional markets supporting cable and wire manufacturers' core business once again fueled the industry's growth, those manufacturers able to afford the costly nature of exploring ''next-generation'' technology began turning to the production of fiber optic cable in increasing numbers.

INDUSTRY LEADERS

Ranked according to sales volume, the two largest wire and cable manufacturers during the mid-1990s were Raychem Corp., based in Menlo Park, California, and privately-held Southwire Company Inc., based in Carrollton, Georgia.

Industry leader Raychem Corp., founded in 1957, manufactured electronic heat tracing systems and telephone cable splice closures in addition to its core manufacturing business—the production of wire and cable. Raychem continued to diversify its business through a number of overseas alliances and partnerships, including one with Essex Group, to produce high-temperature resistant wire and to increase overall demand for the companies' products. Raychem also

had a joint venture with Ericsson in the fiber optic producer Raynet. Raychem instituted a number of cost-cutting measures in an attempt to cushion the changing price and availability swings of its raw material inputs. The companies' electronics division sales increased owing to greater demand from commercial and defense clients. Its industrial and telecommunications divisions experienced mixed results, an indication of changes in the price of raw materials and depressed sales of its copper-related products. Copper accounts for 70 percent of Raychem's telecommunication's division products, and the instability of the copper markets in 1996 and 1997 indicated that this segment may face future earnings uncertainty. Raychem's extensive overseas operations—two thirds of its sales are to overseas clients—were also dependent on exchange rates and worldwide economic conditions. As the dollar strengthened in 1996 and 1997, Raychem's products faced increasing pressure from foreign competitors.

Southwire was initially founded by Roy Richards to manufacture wire for his primary business pursuit at the time, Roy Richards Construction Company. His wire business quickly dwarfed his construction interests, however, and Richards further buttressed his wire manufacturing business with several innovations, including a machine that could continuously cast aluminum rod. Southwire then sought to deliver a similar process for copper rod, a more difficult task given copper's troublesome metallurgical properties. After five years of research under a joint agreement with Western Electric Co., however, a process called the Southwire Continuous Rod (SCR) system was developed in 1963. Today, about half the world's copper rod is produced using this system and one third of all new buildings in the United States contain Southwire products. Most of the companies' manufacturing plants are in the United States, though it is actively seeking to expand through joint ventures overseas. By 1996, Southwire's diversification and cost-cutting resulted in sales of $1.5 billion.

Other leading companies involved in the drawing and insulating of nonferrous wire include privately held General Cable Corporation and GK Technologies, BICC Cables Corp., and Belden, Inc.

WORK FORCE

Total employment in the wire drawing and insulation industry declined throughout the 1980s and 1990s. A large percentage of this decline was attributable to the diminishing number of production jobs; in 1982 there were 50,000 production workers employed by the industry, but by 1996 their numbers had fallen to 44,100.

FURTHER READING

"Aluminum Gaining on Copper in Electric Transformer Race." *Industry Week,* 2 March 1970, 18.

Corwin, Phillip. "All Along the Line." *Barron's,* 4 April 1966, 11.

Donnelly, Richard A. "Hotter Lines." *Barron's,* 1 May 1972, 11.

"Electrical Cable Using Sodium as Conductor Appears to Pass Tests." *Wall Street Journal,* 2 February 1966, 4.

"Electrical Equipment Is Prime for Growth." *Industry Week,* 30 November 1970, 68.

Miller, Andy. "A Special Report: Georgia's Private Companies: No. 3: Southwire Cable Manufacturer Wired to International Market." *Atlanta Journal and Constitution,* 22 September 1996. Available from http://www.elibrary.com/s/cox/.

Miller, Gay Sands. "Electric Debate." *The Wall Street Journal,* 11 January 1978, 1.

"Most Defendants Plead No Contest in Wiring Case." *The Wall Street Journal,* 8 December 1977, 16.

"Nonferrous Metals: Try Living without Them." *Nation's Business,* August 1979, 65.

Raychem Corp Report 10-Q Quarterly Report for the Period Ended September 30, 1996. Securities and Exchange Commission, 8 November 1996. Available from http://www.sec.gov/cgi-bin/srch-edgar.

Torpy, Bill. "Southwire's Split Personality: Irony and Conflict: The West Georgia Company Is a Study in Contradiction: On Issues Ranging from Environmental Conscience to Politics." *Atlanta Journal and Constitution,* 12 February 1995. Available from http://www.elibrary.com/s/cox/.

U.S. Bureau of the Census. *Statistical Abstract of the United States: 1993.* 113th ed. Washington: GPO, 1993.

U.S. Department of Commerce. *Annual Survey of Manufactures,* Washington: GPO, 1995.

"Wire and Cable Business Up Despite Cutback in Home Building." *Electrical World,* 17 April 1967, 119,

—Jeffrey L. Covell, updated by Norman Leahy

SIC 3363

ALUMINUM DIE-CASTINGS

This classification is comprised of establishments primarily engaged in manufacturing die-castings of aluminum (including alloys).

Aluminum die-castings differ from other types of aluminum castings based on the type of mold used and the process by which the molten metal is delivered to the die. Whereas casting molds may be made of many different materials—including sand, plaster, iron, steel, and polystyrene—dies are made only of metal, most frequently steel. In die-casting, the die is filled with molten metal forced into it under pressure, unlike other casting processes where liquid metal is poured by gravity. Die-casting techniques are used to produce greater volumes of cast products than other types of casting.

In 1995, the value of U.S. shipments of aluminum die-castings totaled $4.213 billion. In that year the industry employed 28,000 people in 292 establishments, most of which were centered around the Great Lakes area for its proximity to the automotive industry. Wisconsin, Michigan, Ohio, and Illinois accounted for almost 50 percent of die-cast production. Establishments generally employed twice as many workers compared to all of manufacturing, yet paid them a smaller average wage at $11.79 an hour (compared to $12.09 per hour for all manufacturing). As automation became the standard, however, the work force was expected to substantially diminish throughout the rest of the decade.

The first commercially produced aluminum die-castings in the United States were manufactured in 1915. In 1946, the U.S. Department of Commerce reported that aluminum die-casting production totaled 73 million pounds, representing about 16 percent of the total die-casting production for all metals that year. Prior to the late 1960s, zinc was used in a majority of die-cast products, but in 1967, aluminum production surpassed that of zinc. Throughout the 1970s aluminum production continued to expand dramatically, and by 1988, aluminum die-casting production reached the 1.5 billion pound mark.

As the die-casting industry entered the 1990s, aluminum remained in the top position. Its chemical and physical properties offered many advantages to industrial users. For example, aluminum die-castings weighed about 60 percent less than identical iron products, they resisted corrosion, and they were stronger than permanent mold or sand castings. Automated production methods produced high quantities at low per-unit costs. By the late 1990s, the automotive industry had discovered the benefits of aluminum, and it became the largest market for aluminum castings, taking 25 percent of all aluminum produced and nearly one-half of aluminum die-castings produced.

One of the largest aluminum die-casters in the United States was Doehler-Jarvis. Doehler-Jarvis was founded by Herman Doehler, who developed the first die-casting machine around the turn of the century. During its long history, the company boasted many "firsts" in die-casting technology, including the first transmission case casing, the first die-cast oil pan, and the first automotive cylinder block. Doehler-Jarvis also was a pioneer in computer assisted design (CAD). In 1979, the company introduced CAD, a technology which permitted dies to be made with electronic information and eliminated the need to make blueprints. In 1980, Doehler-Jarvis introduced the "doehlercore system," a patented and proprietary process using expendable cores in high-pressure castings. This process enabled the company to cast parts with complex internal shapes.

Doehler-Jarvis decided to automate its production in 1997, with a full line of robots on the production line. With CAD and robotic production, Doehler-Jarvis remained on the leading edge of technological methods and product precision. Several robots, implemented in the summer of 1997, were to handle and produce all complex die castings, including products for Doehler-Jarvis' biggest consumer, the automotive industry.

By the early 1990s, Doehler-Jarvis operated three casting centers with combined manufacturing space totaling 2 million square feet. The company reported annual shipments of 75,000 tons valued at $300 million. In the mid-1990s, Doehler-Jarvis employed 1,500 workers and reported revenues of $200 million, more than twice the revenues of its nearest competitor.

FURTHER READING

The Aluminum Association. *Aluminum Statistical Review for 1991.* Washington: Aluminum Association, 1992.

"Aluminum Castings Shipments to Reach $6.5 Billion by 1994." *Foundry Management & Technology,* March 1991.

Darnay, Arsen J, ed. *Manufacturing USA.* 5th ed. Detroit: Gale Research, 1996.

"Die Casting Demand Seen Rising." *American Metal Market,* 18 May 1992.

Doehler-Jarvis. *Aluminum Casting Alloys Fact Book.* Toledo, OH: Doehler, 1991.

Doehler-Jarvis. *Diecaster to the World.* Toledo, OH: Doehler, 1992.

"Doehler-Jarvis Selects FANUC Robotics to Automate its Die Casting Operations." *PR Newswire,* 4 April 1997. Available from http://www.companylink.com/item.cfm/1718804.

Miske, Jack C. "A Progress Report on Diecasting." *Foundry Management & Technology,* August 1990.

SIC 3364

NONFERROUS DIE-CASTINGS EXCEPT ALUMINUM

This classification is comprised of establishments primarily involved in manufacturing die-castings from nonferrous metals and alloys other than aluminum. Establishments primarily engaged in manufacturing die-castings from aluminum and aluminum alloys are classified in **SIC 3363: Aluminum Die-Castings.**

According to figures released by the U.S. Bureau of the Census, zinc die-castings represented the largest category of die-castings other than aluminum. In 1996, domestic production totaled 140,000 tons. Industry analysts, however, expect that number to drop in 1997 as the automotive industry continues to move towards lighter metals and plastics. Casting shipments of magnesium, another important non-aluminum die-casting metal, were 29,000 tons in 1996 and expected to grow to about 31,000 tons in 1997, with sales of $171 million.

Die-casting techniques, which rely on injecting molten metal into steel molds under pressure, were developed around the turn of the twentieth century. Industrial development and needs spawned by both world wars brought increased use of die-castings.

In 1946, shipments of die-castings approximated 460 million pounds. Of this total, 376 million pounds represented die-castings fabricated with zinc. Zinc remained the top metal for die-casters until it was surpassed by aluminum in 1967. The 1970s and 1980s brought additional challenges to zinc die-casters when auto makers began replacing zinc components with plastic products, and domestic manufacturers faced increased challenges from imported products. Improvements in the ability to cast zinc parts using thin-wall technology were expected to help zinc recapture some of its lost market share.

As the die-casting industry prepared for the 1990s, the North American Die Casting Association (NADCA) predicted that technological improvements would increase demand for die-cast products. In addition to refinements in zinc production, the ability to work with magnesium held promise.

Innovations permitted fabricators to purify magnesium of contaminants associated with poor corrosion resistance. Refined magnesium possesses qualities making it competitive with aluminum, steel, plastics, and other traditional materials. These improvements resulted in dramatic increases in magnesium die-casting shipments. For example, in 1983, magnesium shipments totaled 4,700 tons. By 1990, the figure had increased to 15,500 tons. Although magnesium shipments dropped slightly in 1991 to 15,000 tons, industry analysts expected sales to rebound. Magnesium shipments fulfilled the industry expectations by doubling its shipments by 1996, and were expected to continue growing substantially throughout the rest of the decade.

The largest user of magnesium die-castings is the automotive industry. According to industry predictions, magnesium casting use in automobiles was expected to increase to 12,000 tons in 1997. Magnesium parts for cars include various housings, brackets, and steering column components. Other significant users of magnesium castings include manufacturers of chain saws, fishing rods, and power tools.

Another die-casting metal receiving increased interest during the early 1990s was titanium. Titanium possesses low weight, high strength, and good corrosion resistance. Although it had been used since the early 1950s in aerospace applications, widespread acceptance failed to develop because of the high costs associated with titanium production. Innovations developed during the 1980s, however, opened the door to expanded use.

FURTHER READING

"Diecastings Second Largest Consumer of Magnesium." *Foundry Management & Technology,* May 1991.

Heine, Hans J. "Casting Development Technology Opens Doors to New Titanium Applications." *Foundry Management & Technology,* March 1991.

Hilsdorf, Robert. "Technology Helps Zinc Regain Uses." *American Metal Market,* 19 October 1987.

Kirgin, Kenneth H. "1997 Metalcasting Forecast & Trends: Solid Casting Markets Fuel 1997 Expansion."

Modern Casting. Des Plaines: American Foundrymen's Society, 1997. Available from http://www.moderncasting.com.

"U.S. Zinc Diecasting Industry Hit by Indirect Imports." *Foundry Management & Technology,* January 1991.

SIC 3365

ALUMINUM FOUNDRIES

This category includes establishments primarily engaged in manufacturing aluminum (including alloys) castings, except die-castings, which are classified in **SIC 3363: Aluminum Die-Castings.**

INDUSTRY SNAPSHOT

Aluminum foundries create castings by pouring heated, liquified metal into hollowed-out molds. As the molten metal cools, it hardens and assumes the shape created by the mold's cavity. Aluminum foundries typically work with metal purchased in the form of ingots from primary producers or from secondary aluminum recyclers. Some foundries located in close proximity to primary smelters obtain aluminum in molten form.

There were 1.65 million metric tons of aluminum castings shipped during 1995. This total is nearly double the average yearly shipment of 650,000 tons during the 1960s and is four times that of shipments in the 1920s.

The largest user of aluminum castings was the automotive industry. Some analysts expect to see demand from the automotive sector expand as car designers use more aluminum products to help reduce vehicle weight and meet federally mandated fuel efficiency standards. The second largest market for aluminum is in containers and packaging such as food containers, beverage cans, and institutional and household foil. In 1994, packaging represented 24.4 percent of the market as compared to the 24.7 percent of aluminum castings used for transportation. Building and construction accounted for 15 percent of the total shipments of aluminum in that same year.

Overall, industry analysts predicted that shipments of aluminum castings would increase by 4.0 percent per year and reach 1.8 million tons by 1998. The two technologies expected to yield the highest production increases were die casting and permanent mold and sand casting.

BACKGROUND AND DEVELOPMENT

Aluminum is the most abundant metal in the earth's crust, but it never occurs naturally in isolation. It is a component of many gem stones such as rubies, turquoise, and jade, and it exists in the mineral bauxite. Clays with high aluminum content were used to make pottery in prehistoric times, and aluminum compounds were used by several ancient civilizations. The ability to break the chemical bonds between aluminum and other elements to produce the isolated metal was first discovered during the 1800s.

Bauxite, the source for virtually all modern aluminum, was first discovered in Lex Baux, France in 1821. Advances made during the nineteenth century in chemistry and electrolysis made practical the commercial production of aluminum metal from bauxite. In 1855, aluminum cost $115 per pound, but improvements in chemical production led to price reductions. By 1859, the price had dropped to $17 per pound.

Although falling prices permitted the introduction of some aluminum products such as surgical instruments and novelty items, they were still too high to permit widespread industrial use of aluminum. The most important breakthrough came later in the century when Charles Martin Hall of the United States and Paul L. T. Héroult of France independently developed commercial aluminum production methods based on electrolysis. As a result, by the turn of the twentieth century, aluminum prices had dropped to $0.33 per pound.

One of the most famous aluminum castings in the United States was placed on the tip of the Washington Monument in 1884. The first aluminum household utensils were created during the 1890s and gained popularity during the early 1900s. By the mid-1960s, more than half of the cookware on the U.S. market was aluminum.

In 1903, aluminum reached new heights when the Wilbur and Orville Wright launched their Kitty Hawk Flyer. Its converted engine contained 30 pounds of aluminum parts.

During World War I, items such as canteens, mess kits, ammunition cases, and tent pins were made from cast aluminum. The emerging automotive industry required engines, manifolds, crankcases, oil pans, and valve covers. World War II increased aluminum casting demands by the military, and brought growing needs within the aeronautic industry.

Modern Casting Techniques. During the mid-twentieth century, aluminum foundries relied on several different casting technologies to meet the diverse demands of their customers. The casting techniques are differentiated by the type of mold used and the process by which the molds are filled. One of the most common types of casting is called "sand casting." Sand castings are created using molds formed from precise blends of sands, clays, and moisture. After a mold is formed, molten aluminum is poured into it. When the aluminum hardens, the sand is removed. The advantages of sand casting are its versatility and low cost for producing small quantities. Its principle disadvantage is its slowness compared to other casting methods.

Shell mold casting is a type of sand casting that relies on a thin mold made of preformed, baked sand. Plaster mold casting is similar to sand casting but molds are fabricated from plaster instead of sand. Plaster mold casting produces products with an improved surface finish.

Permanent mold castings employ molds made of iron or steel into which aluminum is poured. Although aluminum die-casting also uses permanent steel molds, it differs from permanent mold casting by using pressure to force the molten aluminum into the dies, instead of relying on gravity. Permanent mold casting technology produces the strongest castings.

Investment casting is a complex type of casting in which two or more permanent molds are assembled with an intervening wax lining or in which a wax shape is formed and dipped into a special liquid ceramic. When dried, the ceramic creates a shell around the shape. In both cases, the wax is heated and drained to create a hollow for the liquid aluminum. Because the melted wax is drained out of the mold, investment casting is sometimes referred to as the "lost wax" method. After cooling, the mold is broken and an exact aluminum replica of the former wax image remains. One advantage of investment casting is its ability to duplicate intricate patterns.

One of the most recently developed casting processes is called expendable pattern casting, sometimes referred to as "lost foam casting" or "evaporative foam pattern casting." Expendable pattern casting employs a polystyrene pattern made from fused polystyrene beads surrounded by a special sand pack. When liquid aluminum is poured into the mold the polystyrene vaporizes. This procedure yields a casting of the same dimensions as the pattern. Thus, the process holds many advantages such as a reduction in finishing costs and an improved ability to make more complicated designs. According to one estimate, production cost savings associated with expendable pattern casting are as much as 50 percent over traditional casting techniques.

Why Aluminum? Many industrial users favor aluminum because of its physical and chemical properties. Aluminum reflects light, conducts heat and electricity, and weighs only one-third as much as an equal volume of steel. It is also nonmagnetic, nontoxic, and naturally resistant to corrosion. Cast aluminum products are made of pure aluminum or aluminum alloys. Pure industrial aluminum is defined as aluminum containing less than 1 percent impurities. Many of the alloys incorporated into aluminum are added to improve the mixture's hardness, tensile strength, or corrosion resistance. Binary aluminum alloys are made of aluminum and one other element, while complex alloys contain two or more other elements. The most frequently used metals in aluminum alloys include copper, magnesium, manganese, and zinc. Another element frequently alloyed with aluminum is silicon. Alloys of aluminum with silicon have a lower melting point which results in improved castability.

CURRENT CONDITIONS

The driving force for aluminum castings in the United States is the automobile industry's efforts to conform with the Corporate Average Fuel Economy (CAFE) governmental regulations. According to a study commissioned by the Aluminum Association, the average North American passenger car or light truck contained 183 pounds of aluminum parts in 1991. By 1996, the aluminum content per vehicle had increased more than 80 percent to 247 pounds. Approximately 58 percent of the total amount of aluminum in 1996 model cars was recycled metal.

The substitution of aluminum for steel in automobiles has provided a weight savings of approximately 55 percent. Typically, 1 pound of aluminum can replace 2.25 to 2.5 pounds of cast iron. In 1996, the Aluminum Association indicated that the lifetime fuel savings of the lighter 1996 model passenger cars and light trucks could amount to more than 600 gallons of gasoline in the United States. In addition to fuel savings, the Association cited other benefits of increasing reliance on aluminum, including better acceleration, improved stopping, enhanced handling, and less vibration.

Analysts predict that the demand for aluminum in the automotive industry should peek near the end of the twentieth century. Other traditional markets such as computers, office machines, and small engines, will continue to provide aluminum with opportunities for long-term growth. Recent advances in the refrigeration and air conditioning market sectors should also spur increased aluminum sales.

In an effort to save energy, natural resources, and landfills, more Americans are recycling. Approximately one-third of the aluminum supply in the United States comes from recycling. In 1995, all beverage cans produced were made from aluminum and approximately two-thirds of these were recycled. The change from 2.3 billion recycled cans in 1974 to 63.2 billion recycled cans in 1995 was made possible by the increase in recycling centers—there are now more than 10,000 throughout the nation. The aluminum industry continues to support and promote recycling.

The aluminum foundries are still experiencing difficulties in complying with the U.S. Environmental Protection Agency (EPA) policies on the treatment and disposal of used aluminum potliners. The agency classified the potliner contaminants (arsenic, cyanide, and fluoride) as hazardous waste in 1989 and revised the levels in 1996.

In response, the casting industry began investigating ways to reduce the amount of waste generated through programs such as sand reclamation and reuse. Some governmental jurisdictions instituted studies to evaluate potential applications for foundry waste. Proposed uses included: fill for highway embankments, sub-base materials for concrete slabs, and raw material for making construction products such as bricks.

INDUSTRY LEADERS

One of the largest aluminum foundries in the United States is CMI International, Inc. of Southfield, Michigan. CMI is a major producer of machine-cast and molded parts primarily for the automotive industry. Their products include intake manifolds, cylinder heads, engine blocks, suspension and chassis systems, and drivetrain components. The foundry also produces castings for trucking, mining, and construction equipment. In 1996, CMI International employed 4,900 workers and had sales of $561 million. Other industry leaders in 1996 were: Wabash Alloys of Wabash, Indiana, with sales of $300 million and 700 employees; Columbia Aluminum Corporation of Vancouver, Washington, with 1000 workers and estimated sales of $130 million; General Housewares Corporation headquartered in Terre Haute, Indiana, with sales of $119 million and 700 employees; and Consolidated Metco Inc. of Portland, Oregon, with 500 workers and $119 million in sales.

WORK FORCE

Aluminum foundries employed a wide variety of skilled and unskilled workers. Typical employees with specialized skills included technicians, engineers, and chemists. Other specialists included patternmakers (who produce the patterns necessary to create castings), molders (who make the sand molds), and coremakers (who make sand cores). Aluminum foundries also employed many workers with skills not specific to metalcasting. These included industrial hygienists, electricians, and millwrights.

According to the American Foundrymen's Society (AFS), 28 universities in the United States offered Cast Metals Studies programs. In addition, the Cast Metals Institute, established by the AFS in 1957, provided ongoing training to individuals within the industry.

Among employees in aluminum foundries, burns were one of the leading causes of work-related injuries. To help protect workers from the inherent dangers involved in handling hot, liquid metal, the Aluminum Association's recommended safety precautions including the use of shields and the establishment of areas in which personnel must wear protective equipment. Special protective clothing for workers directly exposed to molten aluminum is deemed essential because some types of fabrics are subject to igniting or melting upon contact with the liquid metal. As a result, industry standards require wrist to ankle coverage and mandate the use of special footwear, gloves, headgear, and safety glasses.

RESEARCH AND TECHNOLOGY

Ongoing research efforts within the cast aluminum industry were aimed at alleviating specific casting problems and producing castings of a better quality. Because aluminum shrinks as it cools, casting were sometimes prone to "hot tears," a type of fracture caused by the stresses created during solidification. Breaks in the finished product caused by insufficient metal flow during the casting process led to another problem. These types of deficiencies were termed "shrinkage cracks."

One of the biggest challenges, however, was the elimination of hydrogen-induced porosity in cast products. Under certain conditions, hydrogen, which was soluble in aluminum, could cause tiny pores within a casting's metal structure. According to Hans J. Heine, International Editor of *Foundry Management & Technology,* these tiny holes represented "a primary cause for rejection of an aluminum casting."

To help reduce hydrogen-induced porosity, a method was developed to pass nitrogen gas through the molten aluminum solution. The nitrogen was not soluble in aluminum and the action of its presence helped the mixture release trapped hydrogen prior to casting. Some researchers experimented with refinements using argon, freon, and chlorine. Although these methods were deemed effective, industry analysts judged them to be too expensive. Another promising method of reducing hydrogen-induced porosity involved degassing the molten aluminum under a partial vacuum. Pressurized conditions caused the gas to float to the surface of the molten mixture.

To produce castings with specific qualities, sometimes heat treatments were used. When a cast product was heated and cooled under precise conditions, it developed a uniform internal structure, removed stresses, and improved its strength, stability, and hardness. One type of heat treatment, called annealing, involved heating a casting to a temperature above the point where its metal crystals would melt and then cooling it to recrystallize the metal.

FURTHER READING

"Aluminum: Know the Facts." Washington: Aluminum Association. October 1992.

Ammen, C.W. *Casting Aluminum.* Blue Ridge Summit, PA: Tab Books, 1985.

"Compliance Date Extended." *American Metal Market,* 14 January 1997, 6.

East, William R. "Solid Waste—No Place to Go." *Foundry Management & Technology,* May 1991.

Heine, Hans J. "Reducing Porosity." *Foundry Management & Technology,* February 1992.

Kirgin, Kenneth H. "Nonferrous Foundries Vie for Continued Growth." *Modern Casting,* September 1996, 40.

Leitch, Robert R. "Making Aluminum Alloy Wheels in Permanent Molds." *Foundry Management & Technology,* February 1989.

Monks, Howard. "Ancient Casting Process Waxing in Modern Times." *American Metal Market,* 19 October 1987.

Rodgers, Robert C. "Quality Aluminum Casting Expands Its Capabilities." *Foundry Management & Technology,* September 1990.

Sasser, B.J. "Guidelines for Personal Protection with Molten Aluminum." *Foundry Management & Technology,* October 1990.

Tenaglia, Richard D. "Evaporative Casting Study Yields Solid Improvements." *American Metal Market,* 19 October 1987.

—Karen Bellenir, updated by Andrew J. Poss

SIC 3366

COPPER FOUNDRIES

This industry consists of companies primarily engaged in manufacturing copper and copper-alloy castings, except die-castings. Establishments that produce copper castings and also are engaged in fabricating operations for a specific product are classified in the industry of the specific product. Therefore, some of the companies considered to be a part of the copper foundry industry are not included in this classification, although some of the statistics covering the copper foundry industry do include these "captive" foundry departments of manufacturers.

According to the "30th Census of World Casting Production" compiled by the trade magazine *Modern Casting,* there were approximately 2,100 foundries of nonferrous metal in the United States operating in 1995. These foundries produced 311,000 metric tons of copper and copper-alloys. Foundries in the United

States produced more copper-based castings than foundries anywhere else in the world.

U.S. foundries consumed 17,200 short tons of refined copper in 1995, which was less than the high of 19,000 short tons in 1994. The foundries consumed far less refined copper than wire rod mills and than brass mills. They consumed more than ingot makers and powder plants, however. According to the U.S. Department of Commerce, the supply of copper content in wire mill products was 3,830,000 short tons in 1995—a new high—while the supply of foundry products fell from 425,000 short tons in 1994 to 395,000 short tons in 1995. Approximately 25 to 30 percent of the castings output in the U.S. came from captive foundry producers—those within a vertically integrated operation—in the 1990s.

Copper processing is divided among such activities as mining, smelting, and refining, and fabricating. Copper is mined and refined before alloys are added to it. Copper and copper alloys are sold to fabricators who create such products as forgings, rods, bars, and tubes that are used in the construction industry, telecommunications industry, and in various manufacturing industries.

Copper is renowned for its corrosion resistance, electrical and thermal conductivity, machinability, color, and ease of finishing. Foundries combined copper with several other elements to create alloys with a wide range of qualities. Copper-based castings are strong and corrosion-resistant, making them essential as a basic tool in the building, plumbing, and automobile industries.

Foundries cast copper in many different ways. The most common of these are sand casting, centrifugal casting, continuous casting, investment casting, permanent mold casting, and shell mold casting. Sand casting, in which molten metal is poured into a sand mold, is the most widely used method of producing large quantities of copper and copper alloy castings. One of its primary assets is that the cost of the sand mold patterns is usually reasonably low.

Centrifugal casting consists of pouring molten metal into a revolving or rotating mold. The molten metal is poured into a spinning mold cavity and the metal is held against the wall by centrifugal force. This method is often utilized for casting bearings, gears, or machinery pieces. In continuous casting system, molten copper alloy is fed through an open-ended mold to yield bar, tube, or other shape cables.

Investment casting, also called precision casting, was still used in the late twentieth century for decorative copper applications. The method was also used to make aircraft parts. Investment casting, also known as precision casting, has a long history that predates the Egyptian pyramids.

One of the mainstays of the U.S. copper industry is the Copper Development Association (CDA). Its members include the primary copper producers, miners and smelters, described in **SIC 3331: Primary Smelting and Refining of Copper;** manufacturers of mill products such as sheet, strip, rod, bar, tube, and pipe described in **SIC 3351: Rolling, Drawing, and Extruding of Copper;** as well as the copper foundries of this industry. CDA tracks market statistics and published handbooks, reports, and bulletins as part of its efforts to broaden copper markets in this country and abroad.

The American Foundrymen's Society (AFS) comprises the foundries of the United States, Canada, and Mexico. It is a professional, technical, and management association that works with government leadership to influence Congress on legislative issues, prepare educational programs, and perform research for its members and interested laypeople. With almost 13,000 members in more than 47 countries, it is the leading metalcasting association in North America.

Historical Use. Copper-based castings have a long history. Copper artifacts have been dated back to 8700 BC, and smelting was performed by 5000 BC. Casting, especially sand casting, is one of the oldest known methods of producing metal components. As agricultural equipment, shipping equipment, and plumbing developed, so did the need for advanced castings. Nonferrous castings, including copper-based castings, also became essential to the modern world with the proliferation of automobiles, televisions, airplanes, and telecommunications equipment.

In the 1950s and 1960s induction furnaces were used in most foundries to melt brass and other copper alloys. Core or channel furnaces and coreless or crucible furnaces were both induction furnaces in which current was induced into the metal before it was melted. The temperature of the metal to be poured was carefully monitored by a pyrometer, which measures the metal temperature. These pyrometers became increasingly accurate and easier to read as the technology improved during the 1960s.

There were tremendous advances in technology and environmental science from the 1960s through the 1980s. As foundry practices began to adapt to these advances, the improvements saved money, increased efficiency, and assisted U.S. foundries in maintaining world leadership in the field, which was becoming an increasingly difficult task with the emergence of casting producers in foreign countries. Many of these foreign foundries boasted state-of-the-art facilities, low labor costs, and subsidized work, whereas the U.S. foundries accused their foreign counterparts of dumping products below costs.

The metalcasting industry is a basic component of all industrial societies, but the economic upheavals in the 1970s and 1980s brought tremendous change to the industry. Many foundries had to close their doors, and many were merged into larger companies.

Copper foundries relied on the health of the U.S. economy and the success of their customers in the manufacturing industries in order to prosper. The business environment for copper-related industries has remained somewhat flat during the last decade of the twentieth century. They have experienced a continual fight between the eroding plumbing fitting market by plastic substitution and increased commercial growth in industrial valves and fittings. The latter market has been aided by reduced imports as U.S producers become more competitive. Some foundries have survived by investing in new plants and equipment to accommodate changes in technology. Many have cut their labor forces to become more cost effective. The surviving foundries have also worked with users of their end products to customize castings.

The largest U.S. independent copper foundry is the Brass Group Division of Olin Corporation with $654 million in reported sales and 3,300 employees. R. Lavin and Sons Inc. employed 400 people and estimated sales of $42 million. The Nippert Company of Delaware, Ohio ranked third in sales of $40 million and employed 300 people. Lee Brass Company of Anniston Alabama reported total sales of $36 million and total employment of 400 people. Ampco Metal Inc of Milwaukee Wisconsin employed 300 people and total sales of $36 million. Other large foundries in the United States include Babcock Thorn Ltd., Carbone of America, Phelps Dodge Corporation, and Chase Brass Industries Inc.

Most U.S. foundries are small by the relative standards of U.S. industry. Forty percent of the copper foundries employed fewer than 100 people. In 1994 there were 195 copper companies employing fewer than 20 people. The number of workers in the copper foundry industries remained relatively steady from 8,200 in 1987 to 8,100 in 1994. The number of hours worked per year per production worker in these foundries was 2,138 in 1994 as compared to the industry standard of 2,056. Hourly pay, that same year at $9.67 per hour was considerably less than all manufacturers at $12.09.

FURTHER READING

Copper Development Association Inc. "Annual Data: 1996: Copper Supply and Consumption, 1972-1995," New York, 1996.

————. "Copper in the USA: Bright Future—Colorful Past." New York, 1996.

Getler, Warren. "Copper Futures Rise, But Traders Warn Rally Is Likely to Be Short-Lived Amid Oversupply." *Wall Street Journal,* 12 October 1993, C18.

Kanicki, David P. "World Foundry Congress Highlights Computer Applications," *Modern Casting,* December 1993, 26.

Orogo, Constantine D., et al. "A Vision of Computer-Aided Casting in the Year 2000," *Modern Casting,* October 1993, 20.

Taylor, Jeffrey. "U.S. Copper Futures Fall as Available Stocks of the Metal Reach a 15-Year High in London." *Wall Street Journal,* 27 October 1993, C18.

—Fran Shonfeld Sherman and Andrew J. Poss

SIC 3369

NONFERROUS FOUNDRIES, EXCEPT ALUMINUM AND COPPER

This industry includes establishments primarily engaged in manufacturing nonferrous metal castings, including alloys, except aluminum and copper castings and all die-castings.

Metalcasters in this industry pour molten metals such as nickel, zinc, magnesium, beryllium, and titanium into molds made from sand, plaster, or other materials. When the metal cools, it forms a casting that can be used either as a part of a tool or machine to manufacture other products or as a component of a product being manufactured. Major casting products include parts for motor vehicles and other machine parts. Generally less costly than die-casting, these castings are also used to produce prototypes of machine parts for testing and evaluation prior to mass production.

The category is relatively new to the SIC system, as a reclassification took place in 1987 to narrow the scope of this industry. From a total of $339.9 million in 1987 shipments, the industry increased steadily to $617.1 million before inflation by 1995. Industry product share in the 1990s was distributed between nickel castings with 21.8 percent of the total share; zinc castings accounted for 7.9 percent; magnesium and magnesium-base alloy cast in sand mold claimed 7.1 percent; and the remaining 63.2 percent share of the industry was made up of titanium and miscellaneous nonferrous castings.

In 1995, the industry employed 4,600 laborers, of whom 3,200 were production workers. Production workers earned an average wage of $12.81 per hour, which was 3.6 percent higher than the average for all U.S. manufacturing.

Approximately 150 companies comprised the industry in 1997. Leading firms in the mid-1990s included Prime Alloy Castings Inc. of Port Hueneme, California; Ohio Decorative Products, Inc. of Spencerville, Ohio; Bunting Bearings Corporation of Holland, Ohio; and NGK Materials Corporation of Reading, Pennsylvania.

Approaching the twenty-first century, the occupational outlook for this industry was favorable compared to other manufacturing industries. Employment levels were expected to drop by less than 2 percent for grinders and polishers, inspectors, mold assembly and shakeout workers, metal pourers, assemblers, metal machine operators, machine forming operators, and secretaries. Those occupations expected to grow more than 20 percent include machinists, combination machine tool operators, tool and die makers, industrial machinery mechanics, maintenance repairers, sales workers, and industrial production managers.

In the late 1990s, manufacturing trends for the industry were similar to those for other metalcasting industries—producing castings with lower-cost materials and with greater efficiency. Research and development has focused on: developing new materials, particularly alloys, with similar or better physical characteristics and lower costs to produce than conventional metals; finding more energy-efficient processes since the energy needed to melt metals amounts to as much as 25 percent of production costs; implementing process improvements to make production less labor intensive and to reduce waste materials

FURTHER READING

Darnay, Arsen J., ed. *Manufacturing USA*. 5th ed. Detroit: Gale Research, 1996.

U.S. Census Bureau. *1995 Annual Survey of Manufactures*. Washington: GPO, 1997.

U.S. Department of Energy. Office of Industrial Technologies. *Industries of the Future: The Metalcasting Industry*. Washington, 1996. Available from http://oit.eh.doe.gov/pudesc/metal.htm.

METAL HEAT TREATING

This category covers establishments primarily engaged in heat treating of metal for the trade.

Industry shipments of heat-treated metals totaled $3.19 billion in 1995, which was roughly a 23 percent preinflation increase over the previous year. In the 1990s the value of this industry's output has grown by more than 50 percent before inflation.

The various forms of heat treating are used to make metals more durable and to improve their mechanical performance for manufacturing. Heat treating processes include brazing, annealing, hardening and tempering, normalizing, nitriding, and carburizing. In each of these processes, controlled heat is generated from an electrical or gas-based source and applied to metals, making heat treatment an energy-intensive industry. Heat treated metals are required in components produced for aerospace, industrial machinery, heavy equipment for construction and agriculture, motor vehicles, and general manufacturing.

An estimated 670 U.S. establishments performed metal heat treating in 1996. The total number of establishments declined slightly between the 1980s and 1990s. Mid-1990s leaders in the industry included Lindberg Corporation of Chicago, Illinois; Metal Improvement Company, Inc. of Paramus, New Jersey; Paulo Products Company of St. Louis, Missouri; Cooperheat Incorporated of Piscataway, New Jersey; and Hi Tecmetal Group, Inc. of Cleveland, Ohio.

Of the 19,500 workers in the industry in 1995, some 14,600 were engaged in production labor and earned an average of $12.77 per hour, which was about 3 percent higher than average for manufacturing employees in the United States.

As the twenty-first century approached, the employment levels of many occupations in the primary metal products industry, which includes heat treatment facilities, were expected to decrease. Those occupations expected to face reductions of more than 25 percent included miscellaneous hand workers, electricians, metal pourers, metal/plastic machine workers, furnace operators, and welders. Those occupations expected to face reductions between 10 and 25 percent included blue collar worker supervisors, general laborers, heat treating machine operators, furnace operators, truck and tractor operators, crushing and mixing machine operators, inspectors, crane operators, material movers, machine tool workers, secretaries, machine feeders, science and mathematics technicians, material moving equipment operators, and metal molding machine operators. Sales workers were expected to be in demand, as the employment level in this occupation was expected to increase by 12.5 percent by the year 2000.

FURTHER READING

Darnay, Arsen J., ed. *Manufacturing USA*. 5th ed. Detroit: Gale Research, 1996.

U.S. Bureau of the Census. *1995 Annual Survey of Manufactures*. Washington: GPO, 1997.

U.S. Department of Labor. Bureau of Labor Statistics. *Occupational Outlook Handbook, 1996-97*. Washington: GPO, 1996. Available from http://stats.bls.gov:80/ocohome.htm.

SIC 3399

PRIMARY METAL PRODUCTS, NOT ELSEWHERE CLASSIFIED

This category covers establishments primarily engaged in manufacturing primary metal products, not elsewhere classified, such as nonferrous nails, brads, and spikes, and metal powder, flakes, and paste. Steel nails, brads, spikes, and stables are classified under **SIC 3315: Steel Wiredrawing and Steel Nails and Spikes.**

Product share of the primary metal products industry is split into three major groups: metal powders, paste, and flakes claim 67.8 percent of the industry; primary metal products such as nonferrous nails, brads, tacks, and staples claim 22.9 percent of the industry; and other primary metal products, not specified by kind, claim the remaining 9.3 percent of the industry. The value of industry shipments was $3.13 billion in 1995. This represented a 32 percent increase over the previous year before inflation. Metal powder production for all of North America, however, was up only 1.8 percent from 1994, at 433,774 short tons in 1995, according to the Metal Powder Industries Federation. New capital expenditures for plant and equipment investment amounted to $137.9 million in 1995, up roughly 60 percent from 1994.

The vast majority of metal powders, more than 66 percent according to the Metal Powder Industries Federation, are used in the automotive industry. Other applications include office equipment, sporting goods, medical devices, industrial machinery and household appliances.

At $13.89 per hour, the average wages for production workers in this industry in 1995 was approximately 12 percent higher than average for manufacturing. Growing in the 1980s, the total number of establishments in the industry leveled during the mid-1990s to about 260.

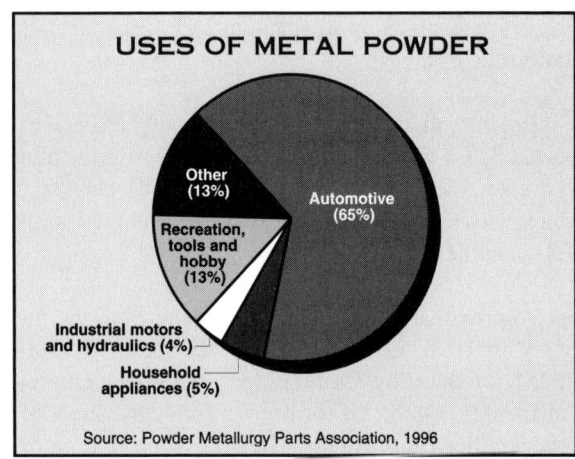

USES OF METAL POWDER

Automotive (65%)
Other (13%)
Recreation, tools and hobby (13%)
Industrial motors and hydraulics (4%)
Household appliances (5%)

Source: Powder Metallurgy Parts Association, 1996

The Hoeganaes Corporation of Riverton, New Jersey, was the leader in U.S. metal powder production with a sales volume of $173.2 million in 1996. This represented a 1 percent sales decline and a 3 percent production drop from fiscal 1995, largely due to increased competition and flat automobile production. Another leading auto and industrial supplier, SSI Technologies, Inc. of Janesville, Wisconsin, generated estimated sales of $110 million and employed 1,000 people.

As the twenty-first century approached, the employment levels of many occupations in the primary metal products industry, which includes nonferrous foundries and heat treatment facilities, were expected to decrease. Those occupations expected to face reductions of more than 25 percent included miscellaneous hand workers, electricians, metal pourers, metal/plastic machine workers, furnace operators, and welders. Those occupations expected to face reductions between 10 percent and 25 percent included blue collar worker supervisors, general laborers, heat treating machine operators, furnace operators, truck and tractor operators, crushing and mixing machine operators, inspectors, crane operators, material movers, machine tool workers, secretaries, machine feeders, science and mathematics technicians, material moving equipment operators, and metal molding machine operators. Sales positions were expected to increase, however, by as much as 12.5 percent during the 1990s.

FURTHER READING

Darnay, Arsen J., ed. *Manufacturing USA*. 5th ed. Detroit: Gale Research, 1996.

Metal Powder Industries Federation. *Metal Powder Industries Federation*. Princeton, NJ, 1996. Available from http://www.mpif.org.

U.S. Census Bureau. *1995 Annual Survey of Manufactures*. Washington: GPO, 1997.

Fabricated Metal Products, Except Machinery and Transportation Equipment

METAL CANS

The metal can and shipping container industry includes companies engaged in the manufacture of metal cans from purchased materials, primarily steel and aluminum. The majority of the cans and containers produced in this industry are used to package various foods and beverages. Foil containers are excluded from this classification.

INDUSTRY SNAPSHOT

In the early 1990s, can manufacturers experienced slow overall growth in a weak domestic economy, and while aluminum can shipments rose steadily, steel can production stagnated. In the mid-1990s the demand for beverage cans rose slightly but those gains were offset by a decrease in the use of cans by the country's brewers. As a result, many major manufacturers closed plants or cut back on production. The long term outlook for the maturing metal can industry depends on the industry's ability to exploit burgeoning foreign markets, new production technologies, and recycling opportunities. Employment in the industry was expected to decline as producers automated production and moved facilities to foreign countries in which labor was less expensive.

ORGANIZATION AND STRUCTURE

The metal can industry was divided along the lines of the raw material used in manufacturing: steel and aluminum. Of the two types of cans, steel proved less expensive to produce, easier to heat, and stronger, while aluminum offered a greater strength-to-weight ratio, making it less expensive to transport. Moreover, consumers generally preferred aluminum cans over steel for some products, particularly beverages. Technological advances in the recycling industry generally applied to aluminum rather than steel cans.

The manufacture of steel cans typically involved three pieces—a top, bottom, and body. The body of the can was rolled and then soldered, welded, or cemented at the seam, and the can's top and bottom were later mounted to the ends of the body. Tin-plated steel cans, on the other hand, were generally constructed from two pieces, including a body and bottom, which were stamped and drawn from one piece of metal, and a top that was later attached. Aluminum cans were also produced from two pieces of metal, but usually featured a slight "neck" at the top of the body, which reduced the amount of material needed.

Because of its packaging properties, steel was used to produce about 95 percent of all food cans and containers made from metal in the early 1990s. Steel also comprised about 50 percent of all non-food metal containers and about 4 percent of beverage cans. During this time, steel can manufacturers created about 30 to 35 billion cans from four million tons of steel per year. Eight billion vegetable cans, which accounted for 25 percent of the entire steel can market, were the largest single segment. The second largest market for steel cans was pet food, which required about 3.8 billion steel cans per year. Other market segments included: soft drinks; aerosol cans; fruit and fruit juices; seafoods; and baby food.

Aluminum cans were used primarily as beverage containers, largely because they were recyclable and held a greater appeal for consumers. In the early 1990s, aluminum can manufacturers annually produced about

95 billion containers weighing over 1.5 million tons. Aluminum can manufacturers used more aluminum than any other U.S. industry, providing 97 percent of all metal cans used in the beverage industry. Of containers used by soft drink manufacturers, 50 percent were made of aluminum, while about 45 percent of the beer industry's containers were aluminum. Less than three percent of the aluminum cans manufactured were used to contain food items, such as fruit juices, pet foods, and meat products.

Recycled cans provided an important source of production material for manufacturers. In the early 1990s, the equivalent of 68 percent of all aluminum cans and 50 percent of steel cans produced in the U.S. were recycled. While both steel and aluminum cans were nearly 100 percent recyclable, aluminum can manufacturers favored the process due to the high price of new aluminum, which was nearly double that of steel. Recycling saved 95 percent of the energy necessary to produce finished aluminum, and eliminated altogether the mining, shipping, refining, and reduction processes. While new steel production was a less expensive process, many steel can producers were also using recycled materials, given its cost-effectiveness and the country's increasing concern for environmental conservation.

BACKGROUND AND DEVELOPMENT

The canning industry traces its origins to 1809, when French confectioner Nicolas Appert developed a method for preserving food, using glass jars that had been boiled in water. The ability to keep raw food from spoiling over long periods of time proved an important discovery, of particular benefit to French troops at war during this time. The basic canning principles developed by Appert closely resembled canning processes still used in many applications in the 1990s; carefully prepared raw food was sealed in a container, heated to a predetermined temperature to destroy spoilage organisms, and then cooled.

The glass bottle was eventually replaced by the tin can in a procedure patented in England by Peter Durand. While canning technology reached the United States in 1820, the tin-coated steel container did not gain widespread use in America until 1939. In 1861, Isaac Solomon discovered that adding sodium chloride to the preserving and canning process allowed for a longer shelf life. Subsequent advancements in canning during the Civil War hastened industry growth.

The canning industry experienced rapid proliferation beginning in the early 1900s, when advancements in can and glass jar technology lowered costs and improved canning reliability. For instance, soldered

seams, which sometimes contaminated the food, were replaced by more reliable welding techniques during this time. Furthermore, the development of new machinery allowed producers to manufacture and fill mass quantities of cans.

Progress in can coatings and preservatives during the 1950s, among other technological breakthroughs, helped establish the United States as a world leader in the canning industry. By 1965, in fact, the United States was producing about 1.7 billion cans per year. The canning industry continued to enjoy high growth rates over the next two decades, as potential uses for the traditional steel can increased dramatically, most notably perhaps as a container for carbonated beverages. Although carbonated beverages constituted a negligible market for cans in the 1960s, by 1975 manufacturers were producing over 26 billion beverage cans per year, eclipsing the use of cans for food.

However, while the market for cans expanded, alternative packaging methods began offering stiff competition. Plastic and aluminum containers, which were developed into viable canning techniques during the early 1960s, began to enjoy widespread use in the 1970s. Because they offered price, weight, and convenience advantages important to beverage producers, aluminum cans quickly began to overtake that market segment. Furthermore, in 1974, Reynolds Metals Co. developed a pull tab for the aluminum can that remained attached to the can after opening. This innovation proved safer than the traditional steel pull-tab and also produced less litter, making the aluminum can especially attractive to the beverage market.

The market for metal beverage cans continued to escalate in the 1980s—from about 50 billion cans produced in 1980 to over 97 billion by 1995—and aluminum cans captured an increasing share of the market. Having entered the industry in 1961, aluminum's market share reached 79 percent by 1975, 82 percent by 1980, and accounted for 95 percent in the 1990s. Furthermore, the beverage can market had grown to dominate the entire can industry. By the early 1990s, nearly three times more aluminum cans than steel cans were being produced. Plastic containers, which accounted for more than 25 percent of all food container production, were also competing for can consumers.

During this time, the introduction of the aluminum can recycling industry augmented the popularity of the aluminum can. The amount of aluminum cans recycled annually leapt from about 300 million pounds in 1979 to nearly two billion pounds by 1991. In 1995, 62 percent of the 100 billion cans produced were recycled.

Although they had effectively been nudged out of the beverage can industry, steel can manufacturers continued to control the food and consumer products can market. Throughout the 1980s and early 1990s, steel cans represented approximately 95 percent of that market. By the mid-1990s, however, steel container revenues were in decline, due largely to increased competition from microwave and frozen food products that utilized plastic packaging. During this time, shipments of steel cans and containers remained between 4.1 and 4.5 billion tons.

CURRENT CONDITIONS

U.S. aluminum can manufacturers faced a slow economy and a mature domestic market in the mid-1990s. Growth in this segment of the industry slowed to 3.9 percent in 1990 and just over 3 percent in 1992. Beer sales showed a decline as new products and microbrewers turned to glass bottles. As a consequence, can shipments to the beer industry fell from 36.8 billion units in 1994 to 35.1 billion units in 1995. Furthermore, sales to the soft drink industry, normally an increasing segment, dropped from 66.3 billion units in 1994 to 62.6 billion units in 1995.

A rise in aluminum prices at the beginning of 1996 had can fillers pre-buying sizable shipments in late 1995 and early 1996 to beat the increase. This price-sensitive purchasing caused gains for those periods but overall aluminum can manufacturers are cutting back on production. In 1996, Reynolds Metals Co. closed a 1-billion-can-a-year plant in Fulton, New York, and in 1997, discontinued operations of a 14-million-can-a-year plant in Houston. Crown Cork & Seal Company, Inc. closed two can plants and shut operations on another plant that produced beverage can ends. While both companies are shrinking their U.S. can capacity, they are expanding their operations in other parts of the world.

In addition to the industry-wide maturation of markets, steel can manufacturers in particular were challenged by slight gains experienced by producers of aluminum and plastic containers. Shipments of steel containers posted disappointing declines of 4.4 percent in 1991 and 5.7 percent in 1992, following nearly a decade of stagnation. The most notable blow to the industry was delivered in 1993, when Bev-Pak Inc., one of the nation's largest remaining producers of steel beverage cans, announced plans to switch to aluminum cans. Weirton Steel Corporation also announced its decision to end marketing efforts of steel cans.

In addressing the effects of a mature domestic market for metal cans, manufacturers tried several tactics, including: increasing productivity through new

automation processes and information systems; exploiting international markets; diversifying existing product lines to appeal to niche market groups; and developing new product technologies that would broaden metal can markets. Diversification of existing product lines proliferated in the 1990s, as companies began offering new container designs—such as cans with fluted sides or smaller tops—that helped differentiate products on the market.

INDUSTRY LEADERS

The largest U.S. manufacturer of metal cans in the mid-1990s was Crown Cork & Seal Company, Inc. based in Philadelphia, with 20,400 employees and sales of $5.05 billion in 1995. American National Can Company, of Chicago was the second largest firm, with annual sales in excess of $4 billion and 14,000 workers. Ball Corporation, of Muncie, Indiana, which had sales of $2.9 billion in 1995, edged out the fourth place competitor, Reynolds Metals Co.-Can Division, of Richmond, Virginia. Reynolds garnered $1.2 billion in sales and employed 12,000 workers. Holding the fifth spot was U.S. Can Corporation, based in Oak Brook, Illinois, which had sales of $5.53 million and 3,400 employees.

Although these five companies were much larger than any of their competitors, their revenues represented a wide variety of operations outside of metal can manufacturing. The metal can industry as a whole remained relatively diversified, supporting several firms that generated revenues of less than $50 million and employed fewer than 500 employees. Like other maturing business sectors, however, the industry has become more consolidated in the 1990s. Between 1982 and 1992 the number of metal can manufacturing companies declined from 397 to 301.

WORK FORCE

Increased productivity in the industry prompted a reduced work force, and between 1982 and 1990, industry employment declined from about 50,000 to around 35,000. This trend continued in the 1990s with total employment in the industry falling to 30,900 in 1994. This reduction was fueled by increased automation and the movement of production facilities to less-regulated, low-wage paying countries, such as Mexico. Jobs for machinery mechanics, which accounted for 10 percent of the work force in 1993, were expected to decline by about 20 percent between 1990 and 2005. Positions for machine forming operators and tenders (7.4 percent of the work force) were expected to see declines in work force of over 45 percent during the same period. In fact, every occupation in the industry would likely plunge by 10 to 50 percent, with most job opportunities—including those for top executives and managers—decreasing by at least 30 percent.

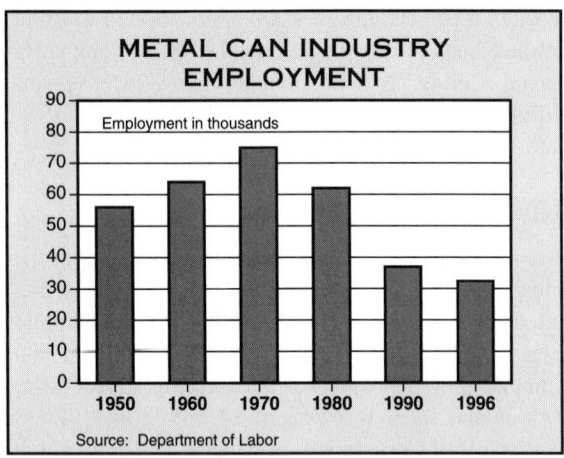

METAL CAN INDUSTRY EMPLOYMENT

Employment in thousands

Source: Department of Labor

Nevertheless, in the early 1990s, the metal can industry was more productive, paid higher wages, and invested more money in new products and facilities than most other U.S. manufacturing industries. Wages per hour, for instance, averaged over $18 in the 1994, compared to an average of just over $12 per hour average for all manufacturing industries. Moreover, investment per employee was $13,304 while all manufacturing industries averaged just $6,552. By 1998 workers were expected to earn $19.82 per hour.

AMERICA AND THE WORLD

Foreign food and beverage markets offered huge growth potential for U.S. canners, particularly aluminum can producers, who stood to benefit from the global shift away from steel cans. While 50 percent of all beverage cans produced outside the U.S. were steel in 1992, U.S. aluminum canners, operating the most technologically advanced and productive plants in the world, were poised to gain market share as other countries sought the environmental benefits associated with aluminum.

Foreign markets provided excellent opportunities for savvy U.S. exporters. Total U.S. food and beverage exports grew 23 percent between 1990 and 1992. During this time, soft drink and carbonated water exports shot up over 63 percent, overall beverage exports represented growth of 48 percent,and preserved fruit and vegetable exports increased by about 32 percent.

RESEARCH AND TECHNOLOGY

One of the most notable advances among metal can manufacturers in the early 1990s was the develop-

ment of thinner aluminum. By adjusting can shapes and production methods, manufacturers were successfully "lightweighting" and "downgauging" cans that were cheaper to produce and transport. The fluted can body was one example of an innovation in this area, as was the "202" beverage can, which sported a top that was one quarter of an inch smaller than most beverage cans used in 1993. Furthermore, Ball Corp. developed a spin-flow necking process that slimmed down both ends of its aluminum cans and thereby reduced the amount of aluminum required for manufacture as well as the amount of energy required in the production process.

Several steel beverage can developments also occurred in the early 1990s, as some producers tried to revive that market, including several Japanese firms. Despite these developments, most countries, including Japan, switched to aluminum in the 1990s. But steel cans had a slight resurgence in 1995 as six European can-makers changed from aluminum to steel. Additionally, Northern Can System, of Canton, Ohio, introduced a steel can made with a steel end (instead of the industry norm of aluminum) to be used with a variety of non-carbonated beverages. And in Germany, Coca-Cola debuted a contoured can that could only be made from steel because of the distortion limitations of aluminum.

FURTHER READING

"821 Billion Cans Can't Be Wrong." *Beverage World,* October 1993.

Boustead, I., and G. F. Hancock. *Energy and Packaging.* New York: John Wiley & Sons, 1981.

"Canmaking: Ball Puts a New Spin on Lightweighting Cans." *Packaging Digest,* September 1993.

Can Shipment Report 1988. Washington, D.C.: Can Manufacturers Institute, 1988.

Darnay, Arsen J., ed. *Manufacturing USA.* 5th ed. Detroit: Gale Research, 1996.

"Japan Brews Up New Packages." *Prepared Foods,* May 1993.

Larson, Melissa. "New Marketing Ideas Come in Cans." *Packaging,* April 1993.

Lenderman, Maxim. "On the Up and Up." *Beverage World,* June 1996.

Levandoski, Robert C. "Here Comes the Light-Weight 202 Narrow-Neck Soft Drink Can." *Beverage Industry,* April 1993.

———. "It's a Packaging War." *Beverage Industry,* July 1993.

"Light Metals Processing." *JOM,* March 1996.

Oman, Bruce. "Who Didn't Know That." *Beverage World,* May 1993.

"Packaging Outlook." *Purchasing World,* April 1990.

Regan, Bob. "Can Plant Shutdowns Announced by Crown." *American Metal Market,* 3 October 1995.

————. "Can Shipment Rate Declines." *American Metal Market,* 26 December 1996.

————. "Can Shipments Slowed in 1995 Aluminum Tally." *American Metal Market,* 24 January 1996.

————. "Cans Staying Under 1994's Record Pace." *American Metal Market,* 29 November 1995.

Sfiligoj, Eric. "Metal Cans: Supply-Side Economics." *BeverageWorld,* June 1992.

————. "The Shape of Cans to Come." *Beverage World,* June 1996.

"Steel and Aluminum Cans." *Packaging,* July 1990.

Stundza, Tom. "Metal Cans: Lusting for Market Share." *Purchasing,* 22 February 1990.

Suda, Rieko. "Japan Beverage Firms Tilt to Aluminum." *Journal of Commerce and Commercial,* 7 December 1992.

"Time to Sing the Requiem of the Can of Steel?" *Beverage World's Periscope,* 30 June 1993.

Walker, Tracey L. "Japanese Unveil 'Ultimate' Beverage Can at Bev-Pak." *Beverage Industry,* June 1992.

—Dave Mote, updated by Katherine Wagner

SIC 3412

METAL SHIPPING BARRELS, DRUMS, KEGS, AND PAILS

This category includes establishments primarily engaged in manufacturing metal shipping barrels, drums, kegs, and pails.

The metal shipping barrels, drums, kegs, and pails industry has changed little since 1982. The value of shipments has remained fairly flat, only rising from $1.21 billion in 1990 to an estimated $1.3 billion in 1996, while employment levels have dropped slightly. There were 146 establishments in the industry in 1996, employing 6,600 people, of which 4,600 were production workers. When compared to other forms of manufacturing, this industry paid lower-than-average hourly wages of $11.86 in 1994—the average was $12.09. Steel shipping barrels and drums accounted for over 67 percent of the industry's market share, with steel pails claiming 23.1 percent of the market. The remainder of the market was split between non-specific barrels, drums, and pails.

Two of the top three industry leaders in the mid-1990s were from California and represented one-half of the four companies that made above $100 million in revenues. Imacc Corp. of Emeryville, California reported sales of $170 million and employed 1,400 people, almost double the employment size of any other company within the industry. Hoover Group, Inc., of Alpharetta, Georgia employed 500 people and reported sales of $125 million. Myers Container Corp., also of Emeryville, California, reported $110 million in sales and employed 800 people, the closest in employment size to industry leader Imacc Corp. Russell-Stanley Corp. of Red Bank, New Jersey, with revenues of $110 million and 500 employees, was the only other company with more than $100 million in revenues.

Five states held well over one-half of the industry's establishments and accounted for 60 percent of U.S. sales. Illinois' 19 establishments shipped $180.5 million worth of metal barrels, drums, kegs, and pails in 1996 and accounted for 18 percent of U.S. sales. Ohio's 20 establishments shipped $148.9 million and cornered a 13.1 percent share. Texas's 11 establishments shipped $145.2 million, with a 12.8 percent share of sales. California's 17 establishments shipped $106.4 million, accounting for 9.4 percent, and Pennsylvania's 11 establishments shipped $101.4 million, with an 8.9 percent share. Illinois' workers averaged the highest wages in 1994, at $13.05 per hour. Texas hourly workers were paid the lowest wages, at $8.82 per hour.

Employment levels of most occupations in this industry were expected to decline approaching the year 2005. Those facing reductions of over 40 percent were machine feeders (expected to decline 40.4 percent), metal/plastic workers (a 41.3 percent decline), maintenance and repairers (40.5 percent), hand packers (43.3 percent), punching machine operators (47.0 percent), material handlers (47.1 percent), miscellaneous machine operators (41.6 percent), and welding machine setters (40.4 percent). All other types of employment were expected to decline by about 35 percent by 2005.

Modifications in the design of steel drums and higher quality steel has improved drum and pail performance considerably. The Department of Transportation (DOT) has also helped in improving the quality of the industry when their Performance-Oriented Packaging Standards went into effect in October of 1996. The new standards called for better formed individual drum parts, improved gasket and closing rings, and more secure joining of individual parts.

Both the improvement of technology and superior steel products have made incredible improvements to the drum and barrel industry. Computer controlled operations within the steel processing industry have improved thickness tolerances—creating stronger, yet thinner steel—and also eliminated pinholes. This meant that steel container manufacturers in the late 1990s had far better raw materials than they had just a few years before.

FURTHER READING

Darnay, Arsen J., ed. *Manufacturing USA.* 5th ed. Detroit: Gale Research, 1996.

Eckhouse, Kimberly. "Shaped-up Shippers More Space and Cost Efficient." *Food Processing,* May 1993.

Steel Shipping Container Institute. "Steel Container Performance Improved Under POP Standars." *Packaging Vision,* October 1996. Available from http://www.steel.org/markets/containers/oct96.htm.

SIC 3421

CUTLERY

This category includes establishments primarily engaged in the manufacture of items such as pocket knives, safety razors, razor blades, straight razors, table cutlery, scissors, shears, manicure tools, kitchen and butcher knives, and artisan's knives. Establishments primarily engaged in manufacturing precious metal cutlery and table cutlery with handles of metal are classified **SIC 3914: Sliverware, Plated Ware, and Stainless Steel Ware;** those manufacturing electric razors, knives, or scissors are classified in **SIC 3634: Electric Housewares and Fans;** those manufacturing hair clippers for human use are classified in **SIC 3999: Manufacturing Industries, Not Elsewhere Classified** and for animal use in **SIC 3523: Farm Machinery and Equipment;** and those manufacturing power hedge shears and trimmers are classified in **SIC 3524: Lawn and Garden Tractors and Home Lawn and Garden Equipment.**

INDUSTRY SNAPSHOT

Rated in 1872 by J.B. Hyde as one of America's "great industries," cutlery manufacturing has witnessed significant change during the twentieth century. Instead of small craft shops producing innovative but simple utensils, modern cutlery firms are more likely to be mass producers of one or two extremely simple products that can be sold anywhere in the world. However, sales of the various cutlery products showed steady growth throughout the century, increasing from $37,002 in 1921 to $1.1 billion in 1987. The value of shipments in the industry was $884.9 million in 1995,

up from $801.3 million in 1994 and $635.7 million in 1993.

ORGANIZATION AND STRUCTURE

The industry can be divided into two main components: kitchen and table cutlery, and nonelectric razors and razor blades. Shears and scissors comprise a third, but proportionately tiny segment of the industry. Of the $884.9 million in industry shipments, kitchen and table cutlery and shears and scissors accounted for $728.1 million; nonelectric razors and razor blades accounted for $128.8 million.

As of 1993, there were 104 establishments manufacturing cutlery, according to *Manufacturing USA.* This number was expected to decrease slightly over the next several years, to 95 by 1998.

Most cutlery products are sold by retail chain stores, warehouse clubs, specialty stores, or catalogue operations. Manufacturers supported retail sales with national advertising campaigns, promotional offers, and sales training programs.

Mass merchandisers like Wal-Mart, Kmart, Target and Bradlees accounted for 49 percent of all kitchen and table cutlery sales according to a 1993 *Weekly Home Furnishings Newspaper* article. Sales for that year were estimated at $350 million.

In 1993, disposable razors held 60 percent of the razor market, which hovered around $800 million. Scissors and shears manufacturing declined during the early 1990s. Half of the 12 companies operating in 1987 ceased operations by 1993. Their shipments totaled $51.8 million in 1987, but by 1993 two out of every three pairs of scissors or shears sold in the United States were imported.

BACKGROUND AND DEVELOPMENT

The production of quality cutting tools required skilled artisans, most of whom worked in the communities of Sheffield, England and Solingen, Germany. Because the cost to transport the finished product was small, early American efforts could not compete with the quality or price of imported products. The American industry was helped by a 20 percent ad valorem tax imposed in 1792 and an innovative machine-forged knife introduced in 1844. The U.S. industry continued to push for even higher tariffs in the 1890s with some success, but its greatest victory came during World War I.

Between 1914 and 1919, all German products disappeared from the Americas along with most British manufactures. Tariff increases in 1922 solidified the industry gain, ensuring prosperity for the industry and high consumer prices, although the 1930s saw a shift in demand to lower-priced products.

One of the biggest problems for the industry was the quality of steel available. Sheffield set the standard with its invention of crucible steel in 1740. That process took imported Swedish "blister" steel, known for its consistent quality, and melted it in clay crucibles along with precise amounts of manganese, carbon, and other materials. The result was a steel well-suited for knives and other blades. American firms imported this steel, thereby increasing production costs, until late in the nineteenth century. At the time, American crucible steel proved unreliable and experiments with cold and hot rolled carbon steel produced an inferior product. In 1910 stainless steel in the form of an alloy of cobalt, chromium, and steel made its debut as the "rustless steel," but the lack of accurate measuring instruments, like pyrometers and thermometers, along with the scarcity of skilled annealers to judge the preparation of the metal, often resulted in brittle knives or soft edges.

However, technology and demand continued to evolve, and by 1930 a consistent material became available and competition prompted its almost universal use in many product lines. Half of all cutlery produced during the early 1930s used the new stainless steel mixtures of steel, chromium, and cobalt, molybdenum, silicon, vanadium, or magnesium. Electric smelting furnaces provided the control necessary to produce high-quality steel consistently.

Meanwhile, the American mass production system made inroads into the cutlery plant, displacing expensive, hard-to-find craftsmen like grinders with automated machinery that required no special skills to operate. Generally firms specialized in a narrow range of products like butchers' knives or ax heads, but with excess manufacturing capacity available, especially just after World War I, many new firms entered the industry and produced cheaper knock-offs of the original products. The competition forced established firms to expand product lines and reduce inventory stock. At the same time, new product designs came and went as technology helped the product evolve.

The industry fought competition and falling prices with manufacturers' associations like the American Cutlers Association, which was founded in 1870 in Greenfield, Connecticut. It established uniform pricing, discount rates, and a method of absorbing freight costs into the price structure. The result was the continued dominance of East Coast firms as the market expanded westward. After fading for a few years, the association reappeared during World War II as a government lobbying group.

Trade unionism began to flourish in the early 1880s as a depression in the industry prompted manufacturers to attempt to reduce wages. In 1884, workers began to strike, although no official union backed the labor action at that time. Unofficially, the Knights of Labor Assembly was commonly accused of inflaming the workers. Despite intense labor organization and decades of strikes, the cutlery manufacturers associations managed to resist unionization and its demands by standardizing wage and hiring policies throughout the industry. The final blow to skilled labor came with industry-wide use of the grinding machine, which made the specialized artisans' skills obsolete.

The post-war period saw an influx of inexpensive Japanese and Chinese cutlery, along with a gradual reduction of import tariffs in the 1950s. The traditional centers of skilled trade for the industry gradually eroded as mass production techniques flooded the world markets. In the United States before tariff reductions, 50 domestic manufacturers supplied almost the entire country's demand for shears and scissors. By 1993, only six firms operated in the United States. Traditionally, cutlery manufacturers operated small plants in established rural communities, drawing on a base of family artisans.

In 1933, more than half of all cutlery produced in the United States came from cities of less than 500,000 people; most of those communities had fewer than 2,500 people. However, new industrial strategies gave the advantage to large cities with sizable pools of unskilled labor. Even so, some older firms like those in the Connecticut Valley retained a large portion of the market for certain specialty knives and other quality cutlery.

During the latter part of the twentieth century, small firms continued to join or be absorbed by large, diversified corporations. By 1987, only 61 establishments in the cutlery industry listed any form of cutlery as their primary product, according to the *Census of Manufactures*. The other 80 produced cutlery as a secondary or even tertiary product line.

The industry saw signs of an upturn during the 1980s, however, as a newly favored domestic lifestyle promised increased demand for products like cutlery, particularly high-tech innovative products that emphasized increased convenience. "Never-sharpen" knife sets with a $50 to $100 price range set the pace, but consumers quickly showed a predilection for midrange products. For instance, good-quality stainless steel flatware became the preferred alternative to silverware. At the same time, consumers insisted on brand-name products, but refused to pay high-end prices.

Industry reacted by consolidating production with universal products and reducing product lines to specialty, high-value, high-tech merchandise. In 1994, Gillette Company, the largest American razor manufacturer, announced it would reorganize its production arrangements by laying off 2,000 workers, or 6 percent of its work force, while hiring an equivalent number to increase production at other plants around the world. This strategy eliminated multi-product facilities, dedicating each plant to a specific product. Gillette's chairman and chief executive, Alfred Zeien, claimed the move was a continuation of his efforts to position the company as a global enterprise by producing universally accepted products that could be produced in large numbers and sold worldwide.

Other American cutlery firms became aware of the need to consider their global position with the introduction of ISO 9000 standards. Developed by the International Organization for Standardization, which was formed in Switzerland in 1946, the guidelines sought to reach across political boundaries and homogenize such industrial procedures as design, manufacturing, inspection, packaging, marketing, quality control, and measurement. European industry quickly moved to adopt ISO 9000 as the new international standard, but acceptance was slower in the United States.

CURRENT CONDITIONS

In 1996, there were about 73 operating companies in the U.S. cutlery industry. Cutlery sales continued to grow in the mid-to late 1990s due to the strength of the specialty segments. Strong performance in the swiss army knife, multi-tool, and lock back categories contributed to a very favorable outlook for this industry. Multi-tools in particular gained popularity since their introduction in 1983, cutting in on traditional knife sales.

Knives were also trying to make a comeback through the innovative lock back types. Continued popularity of the swiss army knives fuelled purchases. The industry followed the trend of many other successful industries to get more market driven.

Regent Sheffield was one of the companies that streamlined its organization in the second half of the 1990s to become more market driven rather than sales driven. The company's objective was to extend its market base beyond the mass market and into specialty stores and department stores.

Another trend of the mid- to late 1990s was the change in consumer purchasing. An increase in the purchase of well-known brands of cutlery, pushed cutlery sales to $355.7 million in 1995, an increase of over 7 percent since 1994. Consumers were more interested in the more expensive brands of cutlery rather than the private label.

INDUSTRY LEADERS

Most companies in this category were relatively small operations, with larger firms usually producing items in addition to cutlery. Some of the larger firms in the industry group include Gillette Company, BIC and American Safety Razor for the razor segment, Fiskars' Gerber Legendary Blades and Buck Knives for knife manufacturing, and Fiskars Inc. for scissors.

Gillette Company, the largest in the cutlery industry, commanded a 65 percent share of the razor market as of 1991. Based in Boston, the firm began operations in 1901. Gillette employed 33,500 workers for total sales of $6.7 billion in 1996.

The second largest company in the industry was Scott Fetzer Co. of Westlake, Ohio, with sales revenues of $860 million and 8,600 employees. Envirodyne Industries Inc. ranked third with sales revenues of $650.2 million. BIC Corp. ranked fourth with sales revenues of $439.3 million.

Ranking fifth, American Safety Razor of Verona, Virginia, was founded in 1989. It employed 1,250 people to produce sales revenues of $230.5 million in 1996. Bairnco Corp., ranked sixth, had 1996 sales revenues of $150.5 million. General Houseware Corp. with sales revenues of $119.3 million ranked seventh in the industry. Fiskars Inc. of Wassau, Wisconsin, ranked eighth in the industry. It was founded in 1978 and employed 1,000 people for sales revenues of $100 million in 1996.

WORK FORCE

Employment in the cutlery industry declined from 13,400 in 1972 to 11,200 in 1995. Meanwhile production increased from $428 million in 1972 to $921 million in 1995. The industry spent $202.3 million on wages that same year for 7,800 production workers. Total payroll for all employees was $329.1 million.

AMERICA AND THE WORLD

The nature of the typical cutlery firm changed dramatically by the 1990s. The small shop still existed, but was rare. Despite complaints of unfair competition and ''dumping'' from the traditional centers of the industry, accompanied by demands for ever-higher tariff protection, mass marketing firms in countries like

U.S. CUTLERY TRADE
(MILLION DOLLARS)

Source: Bureau of the Census

China, Japan, Brazil, and Korea made steady inroads and forced the old firms to reassess their operations.

Many failed; but some, like Westall Richardson of Britain, succeeded. Westall Richardson became Europe's largest producer of kitchen knives by 1987 and captured 33 percent of the British market. Most of its 400 employees were unskilled laborers; the company concentrated its expertise in engineering and marketing.

By the late 1980s the mecca of the industry, Sheffield, could only support a small number of specialized firms as well as an equally small collection of master cutlers, known as "little Mesters." In the late 1980s, one of the few remaining cutlery factories in Sheffield, the Globe Works, received a £1.5 million historic restoration grant. Because the center was built as an integrated factory in 1825, it included facilities for every part of the cutlery manufacturing process, from charcoal-burning furnaces to grinding and finishing workshops.

The grant was used to restore the workshops and manager's residence destroyed in a fire in 1970. The restored works provided a site where the vanishing skills of the little mesters could be passed on to later generations of crafters, Plans call for the complex to become a showplace for the industry and a training facility for the British Cutlery and Silverware Association.

Certainly the concept of specialization worked for the Swiss firm, Victorinox. The makers of the internationally renowned Swiss Army knife produced at least 4 million of their distinctive pocket knives annually as of 1984. Actual sales figures are a closely guarded secret. In addition to pocket knives, Victorinox makes kitchen and butcher's knives. Even Victorinox, however, felt threatened by foreign competition from mass-production factories.

Cheap knock-offs of the original Swiss pocket knife appeared routinely in Taiwan and Japan; the Far East, West Germany, Austria, and the United States were just as likely to have firms copying and marketing look-alike products. Even the Swiss Helvetia Cross appeared on the copies. Such copyright infringement invariably brought diplomatic protests, but the company found its only effective protection was to clearly brand "Victorinox, Switzerland, Stainless, and Rostfrie" on every knife it made.

Such careful branding, which also included date and place of manufacture, helped create the hobby of pocket knife collecting, which became one of the hottest new crazes in American antique collecting in the 1990s. With each knife clearly identified, value and collectibility could be determined and agreed upon easily.

In the mid-1990s, Melbourne, Australia-based McPhersons Ltd. figured prominently in the cutlery industry with 1996 sales revenues of $242.6 billion and 1,645 employees.

RESEARCH AND TECHNOLOGY

The twentieth century began with the introduction of stainless steel as the preferred metal in cutlery manufacturing. That led to mass production machinery and plant specialization as the old skills of the trade, geared to old metals, became increasingly obsolete. By the end of the century, stainless steel also faced the possibility of obsolescence as the industry sought high-tech replacement materials for increasingly rare and expensive natural resources like iron and aluminum. The new, computer-designed substances offered the advantages of being stronger, lighter, more durable, and easier to work with, which reduced the skill-level needed to form the finished product.

As Robert Newnham, professor of solid-state science at Pennsylvania State University, told *Time* magazine, "At one time, we had to settle for whatever Mother Nature gave us. Now if we're not satisfied we can go out and create our own materials." These materials were beginning to appear in 1990 in such products as ceramic scissors that never rusted and never got dull. The United States led the world in materials research for much of the century, but by the last decade the Japanese were forging ahead. The American preoccupation with military and aerospace applications restricted research for industrial and consumer applications, but the Japanese targeted those areas specifically.

FURTHER READING

"A New Edge for Cutlery." *Economist,* 4 April 1987, 48.

"Cutlery: Sicing It Up." *Weekly Home Furnishing Newspaper,* 19 April 1993, C1.

Darnay, Arsen J., ed. *Manufacturing USA.* 5th ed. Detroit: Gale Research, 1996.

"Disposable Razors Retain Their Broad Appeal." *Chain Drug Review,* 22 November 1993, 8.

General Business File. University of Michigan Kresge Library Online Database, February 1997.

"Gillette's Sensor Gets $175 Million Worldwide Launch." *Cosmetics International,* 10 November 1989.

Jacobson, Philip. "A Cutthroat Business." *Connoisseur,* December 1984, 56.

McCarrol, Thomas. "Solid as Steel, Light as a Cushion." *Time,* 26 November 1990, 94-95.

McEvoy, Christopher. "Sharper Image." *Sporting Goods Business,* November 1994, 38.

Pereira, Joseph. "Gillette to Realign Global Facilities; Change Is Slated." *Wall Street Journal,* 14 January 1994, C17.

Rifkin, Glen. "Gillette Will Cut 2,000 Jobs during Next 2 Years." *New York Times,* 11 January 1994, D4.

Taber, Martha Van Hoesen. *A History of the Cutlery Industry in the Connecticut Valley.* Northhampton, MA: Smith College Dept. of History, 1955.

Uchitelle, Louis. "Gillette's World New: One Blade Fits All." *New York Times,* 3 January 1994, C3.

U.S. Bureau of the Census. *Annual Survey of Manufactures.* Washington: GPO, 1995.

"U.S. Lags on Rigorous New Quality Standards." *American Cutlery Manufacturers Association Newsletter,* Winter/Spring, 1993.

Weisselberg, Tim. "'Little Mesters' Re-forged." *History Today,* December 1988, 3-4.

Werner, Holly M. "Cutlery Brands vs. Private Label." *HFN The Weekly Newspaper for the Home Furnishing Network,* 4 Nov 1996, 36.

———"Regent Sheffield Cutting Loose; Hones Campaign to Add Share, Widen Markets." *HFN The Weekly Newspaper for the Home Furnishing Network,* 22 July 1996, 37.

White, Richard. "Pocketknives: The Newest Collecting Craze." *Antiques & Collecting Hobbies,* October 1990.

—Al Cook, updated by Visi Tilak

SIC 3423

HAND AND EDGE TOOLS, EXCEPT MACHINE TOOLS AND HANDSAWS

Firms in this industry manufacture simple, edged hand-tools like files, axes, chisels, prying bars, rulers, soldering irons, tongs, rakes, and cutters for metal-working, woodworking, and general maintenance. Saws and saw blades are manufactured in **SIC 3425: Saw Blades and Handsaws,** while metal cutting dies and power driven hand tools, attachments, and accessories appear under the major group for industrial and commercial machinery and computer equipment.

The industry provides basic hand tools for domestic use and for professional mechanics. In 1995, industry shipments reached $4.6 billion, according to the 1995 *Annual Survey of Manufactures.* In the mid-1990s, there was a total of about 900 establishments employing about 40,700 people. While the number of establishments was projected to decline slightly to 890 by 1997, the number of employees was expected to rise slightly, to 41,200. Firms in this industry averaged 50 employees per establishment in the mid-1990s according to *Manufacturing USA.*

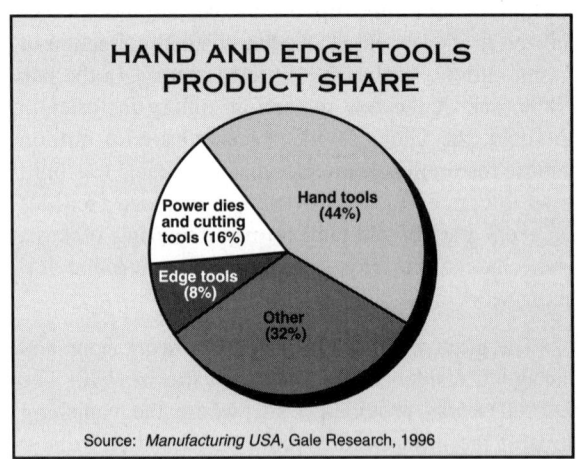

HAND AND EDGE TOOLS PRODUCT SHARE

Hand tools (44%)

Power dies and cutting tools (16%)

Edge tools (8%)

Other (32%)

Source: *Manufacturing USA,* Gale Research, 1996

Traditionally, production in this industry was centered in the New England area, paralleling the development of the cutlery industry. In the early 1900s, Massachusetts and Connecticut commanded 47 percent of the hand and edge tool and cutlery industries. However, the shift toward mass-production techniques and away from a reliance on skilled craftsmen resulted in the establishment of the hand and edge tool industry in heartland states. The industry tended to follow the source of cheap materials and markets, differentiating it from cutlery by its marked westward migration. In the early 1990s, the four main states producing hand

and edge tools were Ohio, Minnesota, Connecticut, and South Carolina.

INDUSTRY LEADERS

Three of the largest companies by sales volume in the hand and edge tool industry in the mid-1990s were Stanley Works of New Britain, Connecticut; Snap-on Tools Corporation of Kenosha, Wisconsin; and Stanley-Bostitch Incorporated, a subsidiary of Stanley Works, located in East Greenwich, Rhode Island. Stanley Works was founded in 1843 and manufactures a variety of hardware and electrical products in several industries. Stanley employed 19,000 workers for total sales of $2.6 billion. Hand and edge tools were produced by its Stanley Air Tools Division.

Snap-on Tools, established in 1920, also produces a variety of tools and furniture. Snap-on Tools employed 10,200 workers in the mid-1990s and grossed $1.29 billion. Stanley-Bostitch employed 2,500 people and generated total sales of about $400 million.

Employment figures for 1995 show that the industry had begun a slow growth by the mid-1990s. In 1995, 42,000 workers were employed in the industry, according to the *1995 Annual Survey of Manufactures,* an increase of 2.6 percent over the 40,900 employed in 1994. Payrolls also increased, up to $1.19 billion from $1.14 billion, an increase of 4.3 percent. The value of industry shipments increased 5.8 percent from $4.8 billion in 1994 to $5.08 billion in 1995.

FURTHER READING

Darnay, Arsen J., ed. *Manufacturing USA.* 5th ed. Detroit: Gale Research, 1996.

Taber, Martha Van Hoesen. *A History of the Cutlery Industry in the Connecticut Valley.* Northhampton, MA: Smith College, 1955.

U.S. Bureau of the Census. *1992 Census of Manufactures.* Washington: GPO, 1992.

U.S. Bureau of the Census *1995 Annual Survey of Manufactures.* Washington: GPO, 1997.

— Al Cook, updated by Kenneth R. Shepherd

SIC 3425

SAW BLADES AND HANDSAWS

This category covers establishments primarily engaged in manufacturing handsaws and saw blades for hand and power driven saws. Establishments primarily engaged in manufacturing power driven sawing machines are classified in the major group for industrial and commercial machinery and computer equipment.

Shipments for the saw blades and handsaws industry in 1994 totaled $1.35 billion. By 1995, that figure had risen to $1.38 billion, an increase of a little more than 2 percent. During the same period, employment had risen from 7800 workers to 11,000, a 41 percent increase, and payrolls advanced from $237.2 million to $334.8 million, also an increase of 41 percent.

Traditionally, production in the saw blades and handsaws industry was centered in the New England area of the United States, paralleling the development of **SIC 3421: Cutlery.** The shift towards mass-production techniques and away from a reliance on skilled craftsman resulted in the establishment of the industry in heartland states. The industry tended to follow the source of cheap materials and markets, differentiating it from cutlery by its marked westward migration.

Three of the largest companies by sales volume in the saw blades and handsaws industry in the mid-1990s were Blount Inc. of Montgomery, Alabama, with sales of $588 million and 4,400 employees; Vermont American Corp. of Louisville, Kentucky, with sales of $500 million and 4,300 employees; and Oregon Cutting Systems Div., a division of Blount Inc., located in Portland, Oregon, with sales of about $180 million and 1,000 employees.

The challenge to the industry towards the end of the twentieth century was to maintain a high level of precision for the cutting edges and to produce new metals and composites to cut the increasingly diverse range of hard-to-cut man-made materials. Modern blades must be able to last long periods of time, operating in unmanned, automatic feed industrial applications.

Sales in the saw industry were tied closely to the health of such industries as steel, housing, and lumbering, which used large quantities of saw blades and handsaws. Generally, in both America and Japan, the production of saws and blades increased steadily after World War II. Japanese exports went mainly to Asia, but North America took 27 percent of its production in 1990.

FURTHER READING

Darnay, Arsen J., ed. *Manufacturing USA.* 5th ed. Detroit: Gale Research., 1996.

Morikawa, Naohide. "Continued Steady Growth for Saw/Knife Industry." *Business Japan,* January 1991, 52-53.

———. ''Industrial Saw and Knife Industry Regains Smooth Growth Pattern.'' *Business Japan,* January 1990, 100.

Taber, Martha Van Hoesen. *A History of the Cutlery Industry in the Connecticut Valley.* Northhampton, MA: Smith College, Department of History, 1955.

U.S. Bureau of the Census. *1995 Annual Survey of Manufactures.* Washington: GPO, 1997.

—Al Cook, updated by Kenneth R. Shepherd

SIC 3429

HARDWARE, NOT ELSEWHERE CLASSIFIED

This category covers establishments primarily engaged in manufacturing miscellaneous metal products usually termed hardware, not elsewhere classified. Establishments primarily engaged in manufacturing nuts and bolts are classified in **SIC 3452: Bolts, Nuts, Screws, Rivets, and Washers;** those manufacturing nails and spikes are classified in the major group for primary metal industries; those manufacturing cutlery are classified in **SIC 3421: Cutlery;** those manufacturing hand tools are classified in **SIC 3423: Hand and Edge Tools, Except Machine Tools and Handsaws;** and those manufacturing pole line and transmission hardware are classified in industry group **SIC 3640: Electric Lighting and Wiring Equipment.**

This industry manufactures a diverse range of products, including brackets, clamps, couplings, door locks, fireplace equipment, handcuffs, nut crackers, and piano hardware. In 1995 industry shipments reached $10.6 billion, according to the *1995 Annual Survey of Manufactures*—an increase of 26 percent over the 1987 figures, but an increase of only about 1 percent over the 1994 figures. Employment in the industry decreased during the 1994-95 period, going down from 79,000 to 77,800 employees. Payrolls, however, increased during the same period, rising from $2.26 billion to $2.28 billion, an increase of 0.8 percent.

Traditionally, production in this industry was centered in the New England area. Many small blacksmith shops produced simple but useful household items, known as ''Yankee notions,'' of low grade iron and steel. The availability of rail and ship transport allowed for rapid distribution along the Eastern seaboard and the central United States. However, the shift toward mass production techniques and away from a reliance on skilled craftsman resulted in the migration of the industry to the Midwest. The industry tended to follow

the source of cheap materials and markets, differentiating it from cutlery by its marked westward migration. The industry adapted its production methods to the use of numerical control production (NC) with great success in both productivity and precision. In 1987, the four main states producing hardware in this industry were California, Michigan, Ohio, and Illinois.

Three of the largest companies by sales volume in this industry in the mid-1990s were Michigan Automotive Compressor Inc. of Parma, Michigan; Yale Security Inc. of Charlotte, North Carolina; and Master Lock Co. of Milwaukee, Wisconsin. Michigan Automotive Compressor Inc. manufactured $245 million worth of locks and lock sets and employed 500 workers. Master Lock Co., a subsidiary of Masterbrand Industries, was founded in 1976. It manufactured $200 million worth of padlocks, locks, lock-sets, door locks, bolts, and checks and employed 1,300 workers. Yale Security Inc. is a subsidiary of Yale & Valor Limited. Founded in 1987, it had sales of $200 million and employed 2,500 workers. It manufactured locks and lock sets as well as non-electric door opening and closing devices.

Both employment and sales in the industry increased steadily throughout the 1980s, but declined substantially with the general economic downturn near the end of the decade. The industry was particularly hurt by the soft housing market, since businesses in that sector use a substantial amount of hardware. By the early 1990s, the hardware industry showed signs of recovery. Unemployment figures also showed signs of improvement.

FURTHER READING

Darnay, Arsen J. ed. *Manufacturing USA.* 5th. Detroit: Gale Research, 1996.

Gallagher, Terrence V. ''Have We Turned the Corner?'' *Hardware Age,* January 1993, 11.

Taber, Martha Van Hoesen. *A History of the Cutlery Industry in the Connecticut Valley.* Northhampton, MA: Smith College Department of History, 1955.

U.S. Bureau of the Census. *1995 Annual Survey of Manufactures.* Washington: GPO, 1997.

—Al Cook, updated by Kenneth R. Shepherd

SIC 3431

ENAMELED IRON AND METAL SANITARY WARE

This category includes establishments primarily engaged in manufacturing enameled iron, cast iron, or pressed metal sanitary wares, such as bathtubs, sinks, toilets, and other bathroom and household plumbing fixtures. Nonmetallic plumbing products are listed in **SIC 3088: Plastic Plumbing Fixtures, SIC 3261: Vitreous Sanitary Ware,** and **SIC 3469: Porcelain Enameled Kitchen, Household, and Hospital Ware.**

INDUSTRY SNAPSHOT

Metal sanitary ware manufacturers compete in the household, commercial, and industrial plumbing product markets, producing products made of cast iron, enameled iron and steel, and stainless steel. Traditionally, these markets are directly influenced by the nation's construction markets and, therefore, are extremely cyclical. U.S. manufacturers' shipments of metal plumbing fixtures totaled approximately $757 million in 1995.

During the 1990s, increased usage of plastic and fiberglass plumbing products reduced the demand for iron and steel plumbing products. In response to this change, manufacturers have developed composite materials that combine the strength and durability of metal with the light weight and rust-proof features of plastic and fiberglass products. A steady demand for stainless steel products, especially kitchen sinks, has kept approximately 90 manufacturers in business in the 1990s, despite two severe slumps in the U.S. construction market.

ORGANIZATION AND STRUCTURE

Traditional wholesale distribution of plumbing products to building contractors is supplemented by retail distribution of plumbing products to the do-it-yourself market. Traditionally, metal sanitary ware manufacturers distributed products through independent wholesale distributors of building products. Any advertising was of a technical nature and was aimed at the knowledgeable plumbing professional. Recently, the growth of replacement/remodeling markets for building products has increased profitability of plumbing products marketed directly to the consumer. In response, manufacturers have expanded marketing efforts, focusing on a consumer more concerned with function and style than with the technical specifications of the product.

BACKGROUND AND DEVELOPMENT

The fate of the plumbing producer is most directly tied to the health of the nation's new construction markets. Economists label the demand for new construction a leading indicator because it provides insight into the future conditions of the overall economy. Hence, a decline in the demand for new construction usually precedes a slowdown in the nation's gross national product (GNP) growth. This held true in the recessions of 1982 and 1991, as construction activity began to decline a year before the rest of the economy slid into recession. Metal sanitary ware manufacturers felt the recessions early as well, as demand for metal sanitary wares fell with slowed construction activity.

During the 1980s, several trends in the construction industry impacted metal sanitary ware producers. Severe declines in construction activity in 1980 and 1982 caused many manufacturers to shut down. The number of metal sanitary ware manufacturing establishments dropped to 77 in 1982. However, after a severe decline, construction demand boomed in 1983 and 1984, as consumer optimism fueled demand for new houses. In addition, an unprecedented cut in the tax on capital gains implemented by the Reagan administration suddenly made business investment in commercial offices, stores, residential condominiums, and apartments extremely attractive. As a result, demand for both residential and commercial plumbing products boomed in the mid-1980s. By 1996, an estimated 92 metal sanitary ware manufacturing establishments were in operation.

By the end of 1990, however, the construction industry suffered a serious decline, as housing starts fell to near record lows. The cause of the decline was primarily attributed to an oversupply of commercial office space and residential housing caused by the building spree of the mid-1980s. Analysts suggested that this glut in the supply of newly constructed properties would take many years to clear, holding down construction growth well into the 1990s.

While metal sanitary ware manufacturers suffered through the latest downturn in construction, the decline was not as deep as was expected. This was attributed to plumbing ware manufacturers' success in the less cyclical home remodeling market.

In the late 1980s, remodeling projects and do-it-yourself repairs became popular hobbies for many homeowners. Disgust over the high cost of plumbing repairs and the urge to modernize bathrooms and kitchens led many people to undertake plumbing projects they would have avoided only a few years earlier.

As a result, manufacturers often market installation guides to consumers in the form of books or videos.

On the other hand, the move toward larger bathrooms with jacuzzis and whirlpools threatened metal sanitary ware manufacturers' bathtub market. Shower stall and wall-surround bathtubs with whirlpool technology are not feasibly made using cast iron and enameled steel. In response, several metal sanitary ware manufacturers developed composite materials that combine the features of steel and cast iron with the light weight and ease of transportation and installation of plastics and fiberglass products. Acceptance of these composite materials would allow metal sanitary ware manufacturers to take advantage of demand for more luxurious bathtub products. The industry was successful in shifting its focus from bathtubs to the kitchen and sink markets. In fact, sales for the industry doubled in the 1980s, despite a fall in bathtub market share from 62 percent to 38 percent during the decade.

Stainless steel kitchen sink demand offset the decline in cast iron and enameled steel bathtub demand. While sales nearly doubled during 1980s, profit margins for the industry declined steadily. As a percentage of total costs, material costs grew from 42 percent to 52 percent during the decade. The decline in profit margins was the direct result of a skyrocketing increase in the cost of materials for stainless steel production.

CURRENT CONDITIONS

Entering the 1990s, metal sanitary ware manufacturers faced a construction market in which slow growth was predicted for several years. This forced the industry to seek growth through other markets—mainly, the replacement and remodeling plumbing fixtures market. In addition, plumbing manufacturers faced a more environmentally-aware consumer who demanded efficient, water conserving plumbing products.

An influence on the growth in remodeling and replacement markets for plumbing products was attributed to the increasing desire for homeowners to entertain within the home. This phenomenon was expected to affect plumbing ware manufacturers for many years to come. Especially fruitful for metal sanitary ware manufacturers was the increased emphasis on the kitchen and the basement in the scheme of the house. Stainless steel was the most popular material for kitchen and bar sinks primarily because of low-price and ease of installation for the do-it-yourself homeowner.

In the mid- to late 1990s, however, new construction was again on the rise. The Turner Corp., the nation's leading builder, announced that first quarter results for 1997 were up 14 percent from 1996 to $1.2 million in net income. This, in combination with continued growth in the remodeling and replacement markets, forecasts favorable growth in the sanitary ware market as well.

Concern for the environment challenged metal sanitary ware manufacturers to use recycled metals and to provide more efficient products. Many states, for example, passed legislation requiring that all new toilets use only 1.6 gallons of water per flush as opposed to the traditional 3.5 gallons per flush.

INDUSTRY LEADERS

The two largest manufacturers in the industry—Kohler Company and Elkay Manufacturing Company—are both private. Both companies produce a full line of plumbing products in all types of materials. Kohler Company produces the majority of its metal sanitary ware products at its corporate headquarters in Wisconsin. In the mid-1990s, Kohler had sales totaling $992 million; Elkay, $264 million.

Other plumbing ware manufacturers include American Standard, Masco Corporation, and UNR Industries.

WORK FORCE

The industry employed approximately 6,000 workers in 1995, 5,000 of whom were involved in production. The decrease in profit margins has caused production workers' wages to remain stagnant. Despite yearly productivity gains, workers' wages have barely kept up with inflation. Production workers' hourly wages have hovered around $11.00 since 1985.

AMERICA AND THE WORLD

The U.S. market for plumbing ware fixtures does not include a large percentage of imported products. The added cost of shipping large cast iron and enameled steel products overseas usually makes imports too expensive for the U.S. market. This lack of import competition has given U.S. producers of plumbing ware products a luxury that many other industries do not enjoy. On the other hand, metal sanitary ware manufacturers are limited in exports for the same reasons. This makes U.S. producers highly vulnerable to the fluctuations of the domestic market for plumbing products.

The majority of U.S. trade in metal sanitary ware products occurs with Canada and Mexico. Transportation costs to these markets are minimal. Companies in the United States also compete in many overseas markets through foreign production in proximity to the particular market. Either through direct ownership of a plant on foreign soil, or through licensing agreements with foreign manufacturers, U.S. companies participate in foreign markets while eliminating expensive shipping costs.

The protection from foreign competition for U.S. metal sanitary ware producers has saved many domestic manufacturing jobs. Primarily, production job declines have been caused by productivity improvements. However, two significant occurrences threatened to change this in the 1990s. First, the stainless steel sink market was more open to foreign competition because these products are lightweight and, therefore, do not incur the high shipping costs of cast iron and enameled steel products. Secondly, the North American Free Trade Agreement (NAFTA) gave metal sanitary ware manufacturers access to low wage production workers without the large addition in shipping costs usually associated with foreign production.

FURTHER READING

"A New Use for Old Toilets." New York Times, 7 April 1991.

Darnay, Arsen J., ed. Manufacturing USA. 5th ed. Detroit: Gale Research, 1996.

Krause, Clifford. "Conference Committee Approves an Energy Bill." New York Times, 1 October 1992.

Lehman, H. Jane. "Proposals Seek to Set Plumbing Product Standards." Washington Post, 8 August 1992.

Stipp, David. "Cheap Retrofit Kits Save Toilet Water." Wall Street Journal, 21 February 1991.

U.S. Census Bureau. 1995 Annual Survey of Manufactures. Washington: GPO, 1997.

U.S. Department of Commerce. U.S. Industrial Outlook 1992. Washington: U.S. Department of Commerce, January 1992.

SIC 3432

PLUMBING FIXTURES AND FITTINGS

Companies that produce metal plumbing fixtures and parts make up the plumbing fixture and fittings industry. This classification also encompasses establishments engaged in the assembly of plastic components into fixtures and fittings. Companies that manufacture plastic, ceramic, earthenware, and other types of plumbing fixtures are classified in separate industries, as are firms that make steam or water line valves.

INDUSTRY SNAPSHOT

Although advanced plumbing systems have existed since 2000 B.C., metal pipes and fittings were not commonplace in the United States until the early 1900s, when they began playing an important role in the development of industrialized society. By 1996, sales of metal plumbing fittings approached nearly $3.51 billion, representing industry employment of about 18,700.

As fixture manufacturers approached the close of the twentieth century, they looked forward to sustained market growth and increased profits. The industry had enjoyed steady expansion since the 1970s, despite economic recessions. To maintain profitability in the mid-1990s, competitors were introducing new products, increasing productivity, and taking advantage of propitious demographic trends.

ORGANIZATION AND STRUCTURE

Plumbing refers to the system of pipes, fixtures, and other apparatus in a structure that supplies water and removes liquid and waterborne wastes. The foremost role of an integrated plumbing system is to safely deliver and remove water; therefore, fixtures and fittings must conform to strict codes, regulations, and trade standards. Manufacturers of fixtures are also concerned with producing styles that appeal to consumers by reflecting current trends in home decoration.

Most plumbing fixtures and fittings are built for residential use. Primary residential applications include kitchens, bathrooms, utility rooms and gardens. Fixtures also complement various commercial, industrial, and institutional plumbing systems. Most fixtures and fittings may be divided into one of four groups: traps, tubes, and drains; pipe fittings; faucets and toilets; and shower fixtures. Manufacturing metals used by the industry include copper, brass, bronze, and iron.

Basin drains usually incorporate traps or tubes. Traps are essentially drainage pipes with a bend, or trap, beneath the drain for holding water and preventing odors and gases from backing up out of the drain. P, J, and S shaped traps are commonly used for sinks, while drum and bottle-type traps, which are typically used for bathtub and kitchen drains, consist of a cylindrical metal box or settling basin attached to the waste pipe. Other types of traps include grease, laundry tray, and slop sink. Most traps incorporate a clean-out plug or screw to remove debris caught in the trap. Tubes are used to connect traps, garbage disposals, dishwasher drains, and other drains and devices. They come in a variety of shapes and materials to suit all applications and configurations.

Pipe fittings are used to connect pipes and tubes and come in a multitude of shapes and sizes; several categories of fittings exist. Nipples are used to extend a pipe and to provide proper threading for connection to other pipes. Couplings are used to join standard sizes of pipe. Similarly, floor flanges connect pipes to a wall, floor, or other flat surface. Elbow fittings make it possible to change the direction of a straight pipe. Reducers, when incorporated with couplings, provide a means of connecting different sized pipes. Three- and four-way tees allow a pipe to branch out into two or three other pipes, often of smaller size. Other common fitting types include return bends, flair and compression fittings, wye (Y) bends, slip joints, and ground joint unions.

Faucets are available in several different forms. Compression faucets, common in residential plumbing, use a washer to control water flow and are operated by turning a lever, moving a ball, or shifting a handle. Fuller ball faucets work similarly, but use a ball stopper instead of a washer mechanism. Ground-key faucets use a copper plunger to regulate water flow. Sill cocks, which are designed to resist freezing, are heavy duty exterior faucets.

Toilet fixtures and fittings include levers and other parts that control the flush and water inlet valves. The ballcock assembly is the primary mechanism that controls water supply in the tank and toilet.

Standard shower heads are typically made of chrome-plated brass or plastic, and they offer adjustable spray, swivel-ball joints, and self-cleaning rims. Massaging showerheads incorporate a diverting valve that allows for a pulsating action. Continental showers allow the shower head to be removed and used as a hand shower. Popular shower head enhancements include water-saving flow control mechanisms and anti-scald valves. Some regional building codes mandate inclusion of anti-scald valves in public facilities, as well as for showers in multi-family structures.

Sundry devices include water fountain heads, lawn hose nozzles and sprinklers, shower rods, various plumber's tools and supplies, water-saving devices, and anti-scald bath and shower valves. Special equipment of more durable material and incorporating a higher degree of technology is produced for hospitals, industrial plants, laboratories, and other niche markets.

Residential markets accounted for over 60 percent of the metal plumbing fixtures and fittings market in the 1980s. About 40 percent of that amount was attributable to maintenance, repair, additions, and alterations of single-family dwellings. Maintenance and repair of buildings represented about 12 percent of the market, while the remaining 27 percent of sales were divided among multiple commercial, industrial, and institutional sectors. Exports commanded around 4 percent of the market in the early 1990s. In the mid- to late 1990s, about 78 percent of the market was residential, and exports represented only about 2 percent of the market.

Single-lever sink and bathtub/shower controls represented 22 percent of industry production in the late 1980s. Two- and three-handle bath and shower fittings accounted for an additional nine percent of output. Miscellaneous lavatory fittings made up over 12 percent of the market, and sink faucets accounted for about 10 percent. Drains and overflow devices made up only one percent of sales. Miscellaneous fittings, trim, and fixtures accounted for about 45 percent of industry shipments. In the mid- to late 1990s, single-lever controls represented 31 percent of production, while two- and three-handle fittings were about 5 percent. Lavatory and sink fittings represented about 23 percent of output. The segment with the highest percentage (39) was miscellaneous fittings, trim, and fixtures.

BACKGROUND AND DEVELOPMENT

Latrine-like receptacles with crude drains are known to have existed as early as 8000 B.C., and advanced plumbing systems built of terra cotta and burned brick were used as early as 2500 B.C. The first latrine with a water flushing reservoir dates back to 2000 B.C. in the royal palace of the Minoans. Clay plumbing pipes were introduced by the Greeks in about 200 B.C., and, later, the Romans began developing complex plumbing infrastructure that incorporated the use of lead pipes. By 300 A.D., the Roman system was carrying over 50 million gallons of water per day to residents.

Advancements in plumbing technology languished after the fall of the Roman Empire until the seventeenth and eighteenth centuries. While cast iron pipes were introduced into plumbing in London in 1619, metal plumbing systems were not used on a significant scale in the United States until the nineteenth century. Between 1850 and 1900, the industry expanded rapidly, and by 1900, almost all U.S. towns with more than 2,000 residents had relatively advanced plumbing systems.

During the economic expansion that occurred in the United States after World War II, demand for metal fixtures and fittings escalated. Over the next three decades, massive increases in new single family homes, as well as growth in commercial and institutional structures, prompted a huge demand for all types of faucets, drains, fittings, and other fixtures. As the U.S. population skyrocketed, the percentage of families owning their own homes also increased from about 45 percent in 1940 to nearly 65 percent by the late 1970s. By 1980, metal plumbing fixture manufacturers were shipping about $1 billion worth of products each year.

Growth in the industry slowed in the late 1970s and 1980s, due to higher interest rates, demographic shifts, and other economic factors. Nevertheless, plumbing fitting and fixture manufacturers continued to report gains during the 1980s. Furthermore, the amount of plumbing fixtures used to build the average house during this time rose steadily. For instance, while most homes built prior to 1960 had only one bathroom, most homes built in the 1980s featured at least two baths. Moreover, kitchens became larger and utilized more elaborate fixtures than earlier homes, and new amenities, such as hot tubs and dual sink decks also helped the industry to sustain growth during this time. Importantly, the replacement market for existing home fixtures and fittings augmented the new home market.

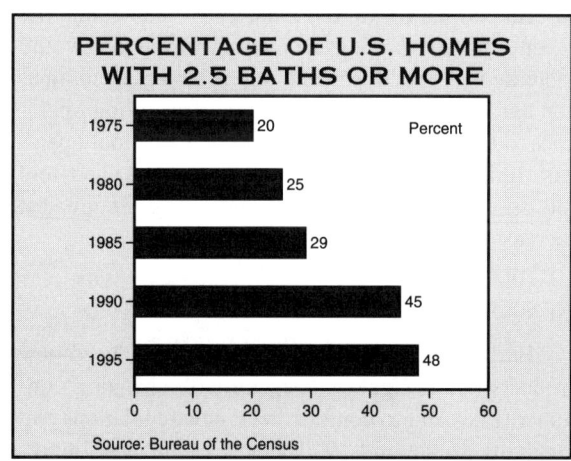

PERCENTAGE OF U.S. HOMES WITH 2.5 BATHS OR MORE

Year	Percent
1975	20
1980	25
1985	29
1990	45
1995	48

Source: Bureau of the Census

From $1.3 billion in shipments in 1982, industry sales steadily rose to about $3 billion by 1991, representing an average annual growth rate of more than seven percent. At the same time, productivity in the industry increased. While industry employment remained stable at about 15,000, dollar shipments per worker jumped over 230 percent. Many producers were able to supplement sales of traditional metal fittings and fixtures with new synthetic fixtures, including plastics, which are classified in other standard industry categories.

Faced with economic recession in 1989 and 1990, metal plumbing fixture and fitting manufacturers suffered temporary setbacks, and sales in 1990 grew only one percent over 1989 levels. Nevertheless, over the next two years, growth resumed a healthy eight percent per year. In the mid-1990s, manufacturers looked forward to several industry developments that promised to boost their earnings.

Renewed growth in housing starts was particularly encouraging for producers, as 1992 showed a 20 percent rise in new home construction—the first increase in five years. Furthermore, the trend toward larger and more luxurious bath and kitchen amenities appeared to be proliferating. The average new home in the early 1990s included 2.5 baths, while the master bath was generally 30 percent larger than those of 25 years ago. Moreover, a 1993 *Builder* magazine survey of new home buyers indicated that consumers were seeking more distinctive bath and kitchen fixtures.

Renewed growth in maintenance, alteration, and additions markets also contributed to growth in the industry. General home improvement expenditures by consumers rose 5.4 percent in 1992, and were expected to rise an average of 6.5 percent through 1997.

The National Energy Policy Act, passed by Congress in 1992, set maximum water-flow rates allowed for residential and commercial fixtures. Manufacturers hoped that this legislation would boost replacement market sales, as well as sales of new water-flow devices. Residential and commercial regulations, which were scheduled to take effect in the mid-1990s, allowed only 1.6 gallons-per-flush (gpf) for water closets, 1 gpf for urinals, and 2.5 gallons per minute for faucets and showerheads.

Fixture and fitting producers were also benefitting in the mid-1990s from new distribution channels. Discount hardware and home center warehouse stores were quickly becoming a primary outlet for consumer sales, as increasing numbers of consumers sought to install and repair plumbing themselves in order to avoid large mark-ups charged by plumbers and traditional hardware stores. HQ, Home Depot, Menards, and Builder's Square were a few of the massive warehouse chains that were bringing new buyers into the market.

Despite general optimism in the industry in the 1990s, some manufacturers faced potentially harmful publicity. Lawsuits filed in 1992 against 16 faucet manufacturers were brought to court the following year. Two environmental groups and the California attorney's office sued American Standard, B&K Industries, U.S. Brass, Kohler, and several other large fixture and fitting companies, charging that 19 brands of faucets leached lead into drinking water, violating California's drinking water laws.

CURRENT CONDITIONS

Metal plumbing fitting and fixture manufacturers were expected to sustain the moderate growth they achieved throughout the 1980s. Industry analysts suggested that continued low interest rates, combined with a mild economic recovery, would boost home construction and renovation activity, resulting in stronger sales. Nevertheless, the growing popularity of plastic fixtures demanded that metal fixture manufacturers diversify their product lines or risk losing valuable market share.

Foreign trade was also expected to play a slightly greater role in the industry. At the same time, manufacturers faced the possibility of increased competition from imported fixtures and fittings, particularly from Canada, Mexico, and the Pacific Rim.

By 1994, the value of shipments for the industry had reached $3.20 billion. Product shipments were valued at $3.37 billion in 1995. Miscellaneous plumbing fixtures represented the largest share of this value with $1.62 billion. This positive trend was expected to continue through the late 1990s with an estimated 1998 value of $3.80 billion.

INDUSTRY LEADERS

Masco Corp. and its Delta Faucet division, the largest company participating in the industry, generated over $3.24 billion in 1996 sales from its diversified operations, representing an increase of 11 percent over 1995. The Michigan-based company, which was founded in 1929, employed more than 22,800 workers. Approximately 23 percent of the company's sales were attributed to faucets; the remainder were attributed to kitchen and bath cabinets and other specialty products. More than 17 percent of sales come from its European operations.

Kohler Company, of Wisconsin, was also a leader in the plumbing fixtures industry. Company sales totalled $1.8 billion in 1995, a 14.4 percent increase from 1994. With approximately 18,000 employees, Kohler operated 33 manufacturing plants on 6 continents.

WORK FORCE

In the early 1990s, about 170 companies employed approximately 16,000 workers in the metal plumbing fixture and fitting industry. Several of the larger companies in the industry, however, were highly diversified and manufactured products in several industry classifications. In comparison to many other manufacturing sectors, the plumbing fixture and fitting industry was specialized and protected from new entrants by high start-up costs and established brand names.

Although total employment decreased between 1 and 5 percent per year between 1987 and 1991, the work force grew by nearly 8 percent in 1992 and 1993. In the mid-1990s, the industry had about twice the number of employees per establishment as the average of all manufacturers. In 1994, the number of employees was 17,400 and was expected to increase to 19,200 by 1998. The wages were relatively low in 1994 at $10.68 per hour, but this was estimated to increase to about $12.41 by 1998.

The number of establishments remained steady at about 177 throughout the mid- to late 1990s. California had the highest number of establishments with 47. They produced about 24 percent of U.S. shipments. Illinois' 13 establishments were responsible for almost 9 percent of the U.S. total, while Texas, with 11 establishments, produced about 6 percent. Together, these three states employed about 40 percent of the U.S. workforce in the industry.

The U.S. Bureau of Labor Statistics estimated that all occupations within the industry would decline between 1994 and 2005. Most manufacturing jobs would decrease by 15 to 30 percent, due to increased automation and the movement of some manufacturing operations to foreign countries. Jobs for machine tool operators, freight movers, bookkeepers, drafters, and tool and die makers were expected to realize the greatest decreases (more than 30 percent).

RESEARCH AND TECHNOLOGY

Fitting and fixture manufacturers introduced new products and designs to keep up with changing consumer tastes and to conform with new regulations and standards. In the mid-1990s, some of the most important developments included water-saving devices such as aerators and restrictors. One product, called ''Flush Wise,'' allowed a toilet to flush using only a preset fraction of the water actually held in the toilet tank. The easily installed device operated without reducing the pressure or scouring action of the water, according to the manufacturer.

New fixture packaging designs were also helping sales in the mid-1990s. Price Pfister Inc. was able to drastically reduce a 30 percent rejection rate for its packaged parts, caused by pieces that were scratched during shipping. The new boxes reduced damage and allowed consumers to fully view the parts before purchasing them. Moen, Inc. also developed a new packaging system.

Other products introduced in the mid-1990s included faucets with built-in soap dispensers, urinals with integrated electronic flushing devices, faucet systems with infrared sensors for water control, digital temperature readout showers, and new "push-on" fixtures.

FURTHER READING

Arnold, Don. "Record Crowds See Latest HVAC/Plbg Electronics." *Contractor,* June 1993.

"Buying Imports vs. Waving Old Glory." *Contractor,* May 1992.

Cory, Jim. "Big Chains Move into Small Markets." *Hardware Age,* July 1993.

Darnay, Arsen J., ed. *Manufacturing USA.* 5th ed. Detroit: Gale Research, 1996.

Fletcher, June. "Kitchens & Master Suites." *Builder,* November 1993.

Halverston, Richard. "Water-Saving Devices Offer Growth Potential." *Discount Store News,* 17 August 1993.

"Home Centers: Source or Scourge." *Contractor,* June 1993.

"Home Improvement Market Growth Projected at 6.5% Annually." *Contractor.* August 1993.

Hooper, Larry R. "Energy Bill Would Conserve Water, Even Cold Water." *Contractor,* July 1992.

Hoover, Jon. "Building Sales with the Basics." *Hardware Age,* April 1993.

Inlow, Alan R. "Plumbing Steps that Save Water." *Journal of Property Management,* September/October 1992.

"New Box, Cushioning Helps Faucets Arrive Safely." *Packaging,* October 1993.

"Plumbing Supplies." *Do-It-Yourself Retailing,* May 1992.

Smith, Roy. "Electronics Take Over Plumbing at ISH." *Contractor,* June 1993.

U.S. Department of Commerce. *Annual Survey of Manufactures.* Washington: GPO, 1997.

U.S. Department of Commerce. International Trade Administration. *U.S. Industrial Outlook 1994.* Washington: GPO, 1994.

HEATING EQUIPMENT, EXCEPT ELECTRIC AND WARM AIR FURNACES

This category covers establishments primarily engaged in manufacturing heating equipment, except electric and warm air furnaces, including gas, oil, and stoker coal-fired equipment for the automatic utilization of gaseous, liquid, and solid fuels. Establishments primarily engaged in manufacturing warm air furnaces are classified in **SIC 3585: Air-Conditioning and Warm Air Heating Equipment and Commercial and Industrial Refrigeration Equipment;** cooking stoves and ranges are classified in **SIC 3631: Household Cooking Equipment;** boiler shops primarily engaged in the production of industrial, power, and marine boilers are classified in **SIC 3443: Fabricated Plate Work (Boiler Shops);** and those manufacturing industrial process furnaces and ovens are classified in **SIC 3567: Industrial Process Furnaces and Ovens.**

INDUSTRY SNAPSHOT

The heating equipment industry is comprised of firms primarily engaged in manufacturing heating devices other than electric equipment and warm air furnaces. Residential and low-pressure boilers are included in this classification, as are steam and hot water furnaces, fireplaces, room heaters, heating stoves, and other mechanisms. Making fire and building devices to utilize the resultant heat were among the earliest and most noteworthy human achievements. Some stove, furnace, and other equipment designs implemented as early as 600 B.C. were still in use throughout the world in the twentieth century.

In the 1990s, the U.S. heating equipment industry was shipping about $2 billion worth of products each year—a figure that changed little in over 15 years. The industry was characterized by maturity, consolidation, and increasing foreign competition. In order to remain competitive, industry participants in the 1980s and 1990s reduced employment, increased productivity, and moved manufacturing facilities abroad.

ORGANIZATION AND STRUCTURE

The heating equipment industry generally encompasses all non-electric devices used to heat spaces in homes, buildings, and industrial structures. Such heaters are powered by coal, oil, gas, wood, or solar power. In addition to their different energy sources, industry offerings can be categorized as fireplaces and wood-burning stoves; supplemental heaters; or low-pressure steam and hot water boilers and furnaces. Warm-air furnaces and high-pressure steam and hot water systems, which are often used as central heating systems for larger structures, are included in **SIC 3585: Air-Conditioning and Warm Air Heating Equipment and Commercial and Industrial Refrigeration Equipment** and **SIC 3443: Fabricated Plate Work (Boiler Shops),** respectively.

Low-pressure boilers. Low-pressure steam and hot-water boilers differ from other industry offerings in that they are often used as central heating devices to warm several spaces within a structure. A hot-water system usually consists of a centrally located cast-iron boiler and a network of steel or copper pipes that are connected to satellite radiators. Water is heated in the boiler and transferred up through the pipes to the radiators. As the water travels through the metal radiator, it releases heat, becomes more dense, and falls back down to the boiler where it is reheated. Motor driven pumps are used to increase pressure and to allow rooms below the boiler to receive heat.

Steam heating systems work similarly to hot water systems. Because steam is a gas, however, it cannot hold heat as well as water and it is more susceptible to sharp temperature fluctuations. As a result, steam systems generally require more apparatus and are less efficient for many residential, as well as some commercial, applications.

Supplemental heaters. Non-electric supplemental heaters are used to heat spaces that are not connected to centralized heating systems, such as garages and warehouses. In addition, they are often used for ''zone'' heating, a complement to a central heating system that can reduce overall energy costs. Space heaters typically run on natural gas and oil.

Kerosene space heaters have traditionally been a popular residential device. Although they are cost-efficient and relatively easy to operate, safety concerns have reduced the desirability of these heaters in relation to competing products. Open flame kerosene heaters deplete oxygen and emit carbon monoxide. In addition, they can become a fire hazard if misused or poorly maintained. As a result, some local ordinances have banned kerosene heaters.

Gas and liquid propane (LP) supplemental heaters are of three types: infrared-radiant, which transfer most of their heat through direct infrared radiation from the heater to the objects in a room; convection, which heat and recirculate air, and; catalytic, which produce heat when gas is distributed and ignited over a platinum-plated grid. Gas and LP heaters are compara-

tively clean-burning and inexpensive to operate. They also require little or no ventilation.

Portable forced-air heaters are commonly used to heat work areas, such as outdoor construction sites. Although they are fueled by oil, kerosene, or gas, they may also use electric fans to disperse the heat. Industrial forced-air systems can supply as much as 600,000 British thermal units (BTUs) of heat. Other supplemental heating devices include baseboard units, duct fans, solar heaters, and various oil-filled heaters—many of which incorporate electrical devices.

Fireplaces and woodburning stoves. Because they use a relatively inexpensive and renewable energy source, fireplaces and woodburning stoves are a popular alternative to boiler and supplemental heating systems. Wood-fueled heat, however, is relatively inefficient and emits more pollution than oil, gas, or LP. A standard fireplace, for instance, is only 5 to 15 percent energy efficient when a fire is burning, and -5 to -10 percent inefficient when the fire is dying. Although many woodburning stoves are 40 to 65 percent energy efficient, most other heaters are much more efficient and pollution-free. Many furnaces, for example, offer greater than 70 percent efficiency.

The three principal types of woodburning stoves are: traditional box (radiant), airtight (circulating), and pellet-fed. Airtight stoves have a sealed firebox, a tight-fitting door, and a manually or thermostatically controlled air intake damper that controls burning. Pellet-fed stoves burn processed wood pellets that are fed into the stove's combustion chamber electronically, allowing greater heat control and efficiency.

Fireplace heating products offered by manufacturers in the industry include artificial gas fireplaces and various heat-saving accessories. Heat recovery systems, for instance, generate heat through convection and radiation using energy from an open fire. Tube grates pull cool air out of the room and blow hot air back out. Similarly, heat extractors, which are often installed in a chimney, heat and circulate air in a room using energy from the fireplace.

Market structure. In the early 1990s, cast-iron boilers, radiators, and convectors used in steam and hot water systems accounted for about 25 percent of industry sales—this represented the largest single industry segment. Floor and wall systems, unit heaters, infrared heaters, and stokers accounted for about 16 percent of production. Of that 16 percent, supplemental unit heaters made up about half. Domestic heating stoves of all fuel types represented about 13 percent of industry output. Various miscellaneous heating equipment accounted for about 45 percent of production.

Such devices included fireplace accessories, parts and attachments for boiler systems, and domestic stoves, forced-air devices, and specialty oil-burning heaters.

Residential and personal uses accounted for about 32 percent of heating equipment expenditures in the mid-1990s. Office buildings consumed about 10 percent of production, and miscellaneous farm, industrial, and commercial uses accounted for about 51 percent of the market. Exports consumed the remaining 7 percent of production.

BACKGROUND AND DEVELOPMENT

Woodburning stoves, believed to be the earliest heating devices, were first used by the Chinese in 600 B.C. Central heat was first used in 350 B.C., when the Greeks began building flues beneath building floors to heat rooms. The Romans developed more complex central heating systems called hypocausts in the early Christian era. These systems transferred heat from a furnace using conduction, convection, and radiation. Although the chimney was not developed until the fourteenth century, heating systems designed for European castles in the eleventh and twelfth centuries were important precursors to the flue and other space heating contraptions.

Woodburning and coalburning stove technology continued to advance before and during the Middle Ages. In fact, stoves similar in design to the earliest Chinese units were still in use throughout Russia and parts of Europe in the 1990s. The first manufactured cast-iron stove, which was essentially an iron box, was produced in Lynn, Massachusetts, in 1642. Benjamin Franklin improved this design in 1744 by joining the stove to a fireplace. The first round cast-iron stoves, which became popular in the nineteenth century, were built in Pennsylvania in 1800 by Isaac Orr.

Central heating system technology, in contrast to advances in stove systems, languished after the fall of the Roman Empire. The first central hot-water system that used pipes to heat a building, for instance, was created in 1792 to heat the Bank of England. Not until 1840, did similar technology reach the United States. Central steam heaters were also developed in the late 1700s and were implemented in the United States in the late 1800s. Not until the early twentieth century were hot air systems, similar to those used in the Roman hypocausts, revived for practical use.

In addition to new heat delivery methods, such as steam and hot water, central furnaces, and iron stoves, the burgeoning U.S. heating equipment industry also benefitted from the commercial application of new fuels in the nineteenth and twentieth centuries. In the early 1900s, particularly in the 1920s, heating devices which could efficiently utilize gas and oil increased the scope of the market served by traditional woodburning and coalburning device manufacturers. Likewise, the availability of liquified propane in the 1940s significantly boosted demand for gas-powered heaters.

Gas- and oil-powered heating equipment, as well as electrical equipment classified in other industries, proliferated during the 1940s through the 1970s. As a result, the share of the heating equipment market represented by coalburning and woodburning devices declined. Nevertheless, shipments of nearly all types of heating equipment ballooned in the postwar economic boom. As housing starts swelled in the 1950, 1960s, and 1970s, the demand for space heaters, stoves, and fireplace accessories blossomed. Booming commercial, industrial, and institutional markets hiked the production of boiler and radiator systems. The even faster proliferation of warm-air furnaces and electric heating equipment, however, cannibalized growth in some industry segments.

Despite solid market growth throughout much of the 1970s, manufacturers realized by the end of that decade that the heating equipment industry had entered maturity. Although fluctuations in energy prices caused temporary spurts in demand in various industry segments, the overall demand for heating equipment had stabilized. Throughout the 1980s the value of industry shipments stagnated at about $2.1 billion. Although energy-availability shortages in the late 1970s and early 1980s aroused interest in some alternative heating equipment, such as solar-powered systems, sales from these segments collapsed in the mid-1980s as energy costs stabilized and alternative-energy tax incentives faded.

Although some manufacturers were able to take advantage of budding foreign markets during the 1980s, domestic producers generally found themselves under increasing pressure from foreign rivals in their core U.S. market. Stagnant revenue growth and declining profit margins plagued many producers throughout the decade.

In response to idle markets and downward pressure on margins, heating equipment manufacturers in the early 1990s were continuing two trends which they started in the early 1980s—consolidation and increased productivity. Like companies in other mature businesses, heating equipment producers were consolidating the industry through merger and acquisition, or by exiting the market and abandoning market share. The primary benefits for competitors of mergers and acquisitions were related to multiple economies of scale and increased financial strength.

Increasing productivity, the second trend, was being achieved primarily through automation and work force reduction. Between 1980 and 1990, the total number of workers employed in the industry declined nearly 30 percent, from over 26,000 to about 18,500. Some producers also realized gains by exporting some production activities and by increasing use of foreign parts. By 1991, for instance, imported parts accounted for a full 35 percent of materials used by heating equipment producers.

CURRENT CONDITIONS

Going into the mid-1990s, manufacturers were facing a slight reprieve from the tepid growth that plagued them for more than a decade. This growth represented marked improvements over sales in the early 1990s. For instance, total unit sales of all types of heating equipment fell from $2.35 million in 1989 to $2.15 million in 1990. In 1992, conversely, sales of residential boilers jumped 8.7 percent to 321,942 units; this jump followed five successive years of decline.

In 1993, the residential heating business boomed. The result was a record shipment of 2.5 million gas furnaces. Thirteen of the 14 types of home heating equipment indexed by the Gas Appliance Manufacturers Association (GAMA) showed gains in 1993. Gas warm air furnaces had the warmest year in 1993, with shipments of 2.5 million units, up 21 percent from 1992. These furnaces accounted for more than half of all heating equipment shipments. Oil warm air furnaces showed a gain of 5.5 percent, with shipments of 148,803 units. Hydronic residential heating systems were also up. Gas boilers totaled 187,378 shipments, a growth of 4.7 percent. Oil-fired boilers totaled 118,119 units, a gain of 11.2 percent. The only negative statistic in the business was for gas floor furnaces, which were down 11 percent at 13,583 shipments.

Sales of residential baseboard and convector devices jumped in 1993, by an estimated 13.7 percent. Miscellaneous room heater sales were expected to rise by a less dramatic 9 percent in 1993. Increases in residential markets, caused by a surge in homebuilding activity, were partially offset by commercial and industrial sectors. Demand for nonresidential boilers, for instance, was projected to continue its steady 2 percent per year decline.

By the year 2000, potentially 2 million furnaces and 3000 boilers will need to be replaced; this will provide the majority of sales through the end of the 1990s. Replacement of central heating systems continues to lead the field, accounting for almost 70 percent of all central heating systems shipped, and virtually all homes that are built are built with central heating systems. This new construction accounts more than 1.3 million units a year, with about two-thirds of single family homes using a gas-heat furnace.

Despite the remarkable performance of 1993, on average, productivity gains declined in the 1990s. Producers were only able to increase margins by moving production to other countries, such as Mexico. Passage of the North American Free Trade Agreement in 1993 made this move easier.

The number of people employed in 1996 was 12,200; this number represents a steady drop since 1982, when there were 26,000 employed. Workers in the industry were paid less than the average for all U.S. manufacturing industries. In 1991 the average hourly production wage was $9.50—about $1 less than the national average. By 1996 it was $11.55, an increase of 28 percent for the ten years spanning 1987-1996. In the future, increased automation and movement of some production activities overseas will likely exert downward pressure on wage growth for traditional heating equipment manufacturing jobs.

The value of shipments has increased slowly, from $2.12 billion in 1987 to $2.28 billion in 1996, a mere 7 percent in 10 years.

Low energy prices will dilute opportunities for sales growth of high-tech, energy-efficient products. The energy intensive, comparatively low-tech nature of heating equipment, minimized opportunities for technological breakthroughs that might otherwise spur large numbers of replacement sales. However, producers in 1993 continued to make technological strides in several areas. The "zero-clearance" fireplace, which inserts into a traditional fireplace, promised up to 90 percent efficiency and reduced emissions of pollutants. Similarly, developers of "thermoformers," which use catalytic gas-fired infrared heaters, claimed their innovation could save up to 80 percent on electrical costs.

INDUSTRY LEADERS

Despite intensive consolidation efforts during the 1980s, the heating equipment industry remained highly fragmented going into the mid-1990s. The industry was comprised of a multitude of small companies, most of which produced a narrow line of products. Only the top five competitors generated more than $75 million in sales in 1991. The majority of the 50 largest firms employed fewer than 300 workers. In the early 1990s, fewer than 450 companies were competing in the industry—down from over 900 as recently as 1980.

The largest U.S. manufacturer of heating equipment in 1997 was Sterling Radiator Division of

Westfield, Massachusetts, with total sales of $112 million and 1,400 employees. The second largest was Weil-McLain Company of Michigan City, Indiana, with $100 million in sales and 700 employees. The next was Martin Industries Incorporated of Florence, Alabama, with sales of $97 million and 1,000 employees. The fourth largest was Gensco Incorporated of Tacoma, Washington, with about $85 million in sales and 400 employees. The fifth largest company in the industry was Majestic Products Company of Huntington, Indiana, with $70 million in sales and 600 employees.

WORK FORCE

Employment prospects in the heating equipment industry were bleak going into the mid-1990s. The U.S. Bureau of Labor Statistics estimates that employment in most heating equipment manufacturing positions will decline by 15 percent to 25 percent between 1990 and 2005. Positions for assemblers and fabricators, which account for a leading 15 percent of total jobs in the industry, were expected to decline by 23 percent. Jobs for grinders and polishers, machine tool workers, and lathe operators will also decline by over 20 percent. Manufacturing opportunities will arise, however, for some machinists, sheet metal workers, and tool and die makers. Furthermore, sales positions are expected to increase by over 22 percent.

FURTHER READING

Browne, Dan. *Alternative Home Heating.* New York: Holt, Rinehart and Winston, 1980.

"Comfort and Construction." *Air Conditioning, Heating & Refrigeration News,* 30 March 1992.

Darnay. Arsen J., ed. *Manufacturing USA.* 5th ed. Detroit: Gale Research, 1996.

"Heating." *Air Conditioning, Heating & Refrigeration News,* 29 March 1993.

"Heating and Cooling." *Do-It-Yourself Retailing,* May 1992.

Lindsay, Karen F. "Heaters Said to Cut Thermoforming Energy Costs By As Much as 80%." *Modern Plastics,* May 1993.

"Replacement Market." *Air Conditioning, Heating & Refrigeration News,* 29 March 1993.

Reynolds, Sharon M. "Business is Heating up for Sellers." *Lane Report,* March 1993.

Russ, Lynch. "Solar Company Sees Brighter Future." *Honolulu Star-Bulletin,* 3 December 1992.

Standard & Poor's Industry Surveys. New York: Standard & Poor's Corporation, 31 December 1993.

"Statistical Panorama." *Air Conditioning, Heating & Refrigeration News,* 29 March 1993.

U.S. Department of Commerce. International Trade Administration. *U.S. Industrial Outlook 1994.* Washington: GPO, 1994.

Ward's Business Directory of U.S. Private and Public Companies. Detroit: Gale Research, 1997.

Wasik, John F. "Fireplaces: Burning Better." *Popular Science,* February 1993.

—Dave Mote, Updated by Beaird Glover

SIC 3441

FABRICATED STRUCTURAL METAL

This classification includes establishments primarily engaged in fabricating iron and steel or other metal for structural purposes, such as bridges, buildings, and sections for ships, boats, and barges. Establishments primarily engaged in manufacturing metal doors, sash, frames, molding, and trim are classified in **SIC 3442: Metal Doors, Sash, Frames, Molding, and Trim;** and establishments doing fabrication work at the site of construction are classified in the Construction industries.

INDUSTRY SNAPSHOT

Industry shipment levels remained fairly constant between 1982 and 1994. In 1982 the value of shipments was $8.84 billion. By 1995 this value reached a high point of $10.82 billion. The lowest level during this period was in 1983 when the value of shipments was $7.95 billion. Employment levels showed a steady decrease since 1982 when 103,500 people were employed by this industry, 75,400 of whom were employed as production workers. In 1993 the total employment level dropped to a low of 70,700, then increased slightly to 71,300 in 1994. In 1995, this number increased again to 73,700. Production worker employment levels were at their lowest level of 50,800 in both 1992 and 1993.

The fabricated structural metal industry's products were divided into four categories: fabricated structural metal for buildings accounted for 52.9 percent of industry shipments; structural metal for bridges accounted for 6.2 percent; other fabricated structural metal accounted for 25.1 percent; and fabricated structural metal, not specified by kind, accounted for 15.8 percent.

Average hourly wages in this industry were slightly lower than the average recorded by all manufacturing industries. In 1982, average pay was $8.56 per hour; this steadily increased to $10.80 per hour by 1990. In early 1996, the average pay for this industry was $11.42 per hour, which again was slightly less than the national standard for all manufacturing industries.

ORGANIZATION AND STRUCTURE

Only Wyoming, Alaska, and Hawaii did not contain any fabricated structural metal manufacturing establishments. California's 251 establishments led the nation in value of shipments in 1987, reaching $809.5 million. This accounted for 9.3 percent of total U.S. shipments that year. By 1992, California shared that top spot with Texas, each state representing 8 percent of total U.S. shipments. Texas' 194 establishments made it the nation's top producing state with shipment value of $712.4 million. Following closely behind, California's 240 establishments made shipments valued at $710 million. The 6,300 employees in Texas earned an average of $9.08 an hour, while California's 5,500 workers were paid an average of $12.65 per hour. Employees in Connecticut earned the highest average pay in the industry at $14.17 per hour.

BACKGROUND AND DEVELOPMENT

At first, metals were hammered into shape, then when it was found that fire could alter the structure of the ores, furnaces were built to cast metals into useful shapes. The use of ferrous metals, however, did not begin until 7000 years after copper and bronze were first smelted. Once technology advanced and iron smelting began, iron rapidly replaced copper for tools and weapons. By 100 B.C. the use of iron as a semi-structural material was recognized.

By the 1990s the kiln, hammer, and anvil had been replaced with blast furnaces and multi-ton presses. Structural shapes were continuously cast and forged, later to be cut to standard lengths. Although greater understanding of the metallurgical properties of metals occurred over the course of the industry's development; and manufacturing processes evolved, which served to lend uniformity and structural integrity to the final product, working conditions in the industry changed little. Although steel and iron mills were much safer places to work in the early 1990s, thanks largely to the Occupational Safety and Health Act and the Environmental Protection Agency, the hazards remained, making mill work a fairly dangerous occupation in comparison to other manufacturing jobs.

CURRENT CONDITIONS

Foreign competition forced the fabricated structural metal industry to focus on quality and the reduction of costs. During the 1980s, fabricated iron and steel products became so expensive (because of labor and other overhead costs) that many purchasers began to buy products from foreign manufacturers. Increasing government regulations concerning environmental and safety issues also helped to increase production costs in the United States. Without similar government restrictions and regulations, developing countries stood as serious, competitive threats to U.S. manufacturers.

Although foreign competition adversely affected businesses in the 1980s, and a recession toward the end of the decade hindered capital investment, several signs indicated that the United States was effecting a turnaround. The productivity of American workers was increasing, and corporate reorganization of most companies helped to reduce costs. Capital investments in new equipment and advancing technology bolstered quality levels, while keeping costs in check. Leading companies, like Nucor Corporation, served as examples of the profitability possible in what were thought to be mature industries. Diversification was another strategy being employed by major structural metal producers, like Bethlehem Steel, which looked for new opportunities in related markets.

INDUSTRY LEADERS

In 1991, the leading 75 companies in this industry recorded $6.39 billion in sales and employed 47,400 people. In 1995, total sales for the leading 75 companies dropped to $4.42 billion and employment fell to 38,900. By 1996, the leader in terms of sales, FKI Industries, based in Fairfield, Connecticut, recorded $790 million in sales and employed 7,800 workers. Second to FKI was Valmont Industries, Inc., based in Valley, Nebraska. Valmont generated $545 million in sales and employed 3,800 workers. Ranking third was Acme Metals Inc., of Riverdale, Illinois, which reported $522 million in sales and employed 2,700 people. Interlock Industries Inc. based in Sellersburg, Indiana, ranked fourth, with $240 million in sales. Fabwell Inc., based in Elkhart, Indiana, ranked fifth, with $160 million in sales.

Nucor Corporation of Charlotte, North Carolina, made considerable capital investments in late 1993 and continued this trend through 1997. Its Jewett, Texas, mill received a continuous caster, online in June 1994. The company's Hickman, Arkansas, hot-rolled sheet mill received a $35 million thin-slab caster. These investments toward expansion helped Nucor record a

59 percent rise in profits in 1993 and gave the company the second-highest operating profit, $432.3 million, in 1995.

In December 1996, Nucor Corporation announced plans to spend $250 million for modernization and capital improvement projects. These items included $80 million for increased capacity and functioning of the Norfolk, Nebraska, mill; a galvanizing line at Berkeley, South Carolina, which would be capable of producing 10 million tons of steel a year at an estimated cost of $40 million; $30 million of improvements at the Crawfordsville, Indiana, facility; and a new steel-deck facility in Fort Payne, Alabama, at a cost of $10 million. These capital improvements are meant to reduce costs and increase Nucor's tonnage so that it can meet competition from other mini-mills such as Gallatin Steel Co., North Star BHP Steel Ltd., and Steel Dynamics Inc.

WORK FORCE

Several occupations were expected to increase their representation in the industry by the end of the 1990s. The number of combination machine tool operators was expected to grow by just more than 8 percent, cost estimators were expected to increase 12.6 percent, industrial production managers were expected to increase 15.5 percent, machinists were expected to increase 6.6 percent, light and heavy truck drivers were expected to increase 7.3 percent, and sales workers were expected to experience the highest hiring gain in the industry, increasing their numbers 18 percent.

FABRICATED STRUCTURAL
METAL INDUSTRY EMPLOYMENT

Employment in thousands

Source: Department of Labor

RESEARCH AND TECHNOLOGY

Innovations in casting technology boosted the productivity of structural metal manufacturers. One manufacturer of casting equipment and systems, Rokop Corporation, was experiencing growth as a result of two companies' capital investments. Nucor Corporation requested another continuous caster, making it the fourth piece of such equipment installed in its facilities. The other company making a capital investment with Rokop was TennesseeValley Steel Corporation. This project added a dual-stream ladle sequencing system, the fourth ladle system project for Rokop, two of which were sold to casters in China and Hungary. A fifth system similar to this was sold to Keystone Steel & Wire Company.

Rokop Corporation's projects were indicative of a trend in the structural metal industry to modernize facilities. Steel mills and iron casters have been around for centuries, while the principal technology has changed little. However, controlling processes to improve quality and reduce costs enabled great technological innovations. Bethlehem Steel participated in this strategy by investing $100 million in modernization of its new subsidiary, Bethlehem Structural Products, which was a leading supplier of structural steel and sheet-piling to the construction industry. The aim of this three-year project was to increase productivity, cut costs, and improve quality. However, in 1995, Bethlehem Structural Products Corp. underwent major overhauls that resulted in the discontinuation of its steel making operations.

FURTHER READING

Aeppel, Timothy. "Armco Inc. Posts Loss on a Charge; Nucor Net up 59%." *Wall Street Journal,* 22 October 1993.

Bethlehem Steel Corporation Website. Available at http://www.bethsteel.com/bspc-facilities.html.

Bierne, Mike. "Carolina Plan to Avail Bondholders." *American Metal Market,* 1 September 1993.

"Carolina Gains Financing." *American Metal Market,* 2 September 1993.

"Debt of Nucor, USX Placed Under Review by Rating Agencies." *Wall Street Journal,* 12 August 1993.

Fitch, John A. *The Steel Workers: From Conspiracy to Collective Bargaining.* New York: Arno & The New York Times, 1969.

Knauth, Percy. *The Metalsmiths.* New York: Time-Life Books, 1974.

Petry, Corinna. "Nucor's Cash Headed Into Modernization." *American Metal Market,* 30 December 1996.

Teaff, Rick. "Steel Chiefs Dash for Cash." *American Metal Market,* 30 May 1996.

—Valerie Wilson, updated by Katherine Wagner

SIC 3442

METAL DOORS, SASH, FRAMES, MOLDING, AND TRIM

Companies in this industry are engaged primarily in manufacturing ferrous and nonferrous metal doors, sash, window and door frames and screens, molding, and trim. Establishments primarily engaged in manufacturing metal covered wood doors, windows, sash, door frames, molding, and trim are classified in **SIC 2431: Millwork.**

INDUSTRY SNAPSHOT

The metal doors, sash, frames, molding, and trim industry is an extremely competitive, low profit margin industry. It has experienced moderate but steady growth in shipments since 1982, except for a slight dip in 1990 and 1991. Shipments were valued at $4.69 billion that year. By 1996, shipments had grown to $8.20 billion, with a projected estimate of $8.62 billion for 1998. Employment levels grew slightly in the early 1980s, but flattened between 1986 and 1988. In 1982, approximately 66,300 people were employed by this industry, 47,600 of those being production workers. These figures grew to 67,800 total employees and 49,300 production workers by 1996. It is projected that total employment numbers may decline to 67,400 in 1998, while production workers will remain the same.

Workers are paid poorly in this industry compared to average pay in all manufacturing industries combined. In 1982, the average hourly wage was $6.61; the figure had grown to $9.73 by the end of 1996. That same year, the average hourly wage for all manufacturing workers was $12.40. Other comparative ratios indicate this industry rates below the manufacturing average in terms of value added, cost, shipments, investment per establishment, employee, and production worker. In fact, in terms of investment this industry ranks more than two-thirds below the average manufacturing industry.

ORGANIZATION AND STRUCTURE

This industry is dominated by small independent companies with fewer than 20 employees. In 1982, of the 1,738 establishments engaged in this industry, only 673 employed more than 20 people. By 1996, the total number of establishments fell to an estimated 1,268, while those employing more than 20 people fell to 553.

The product share is divided into six areas. Metal doors and frames, except storm doors, held 47.54 percent of the total market share in the early 1990s. Metal window sash and frames, except storm sash, held 24.16 percent; metal molding and trim and store fronts held 4.86 percent; metal combination screen, storm sash, and storm doors held 6.09 percent; metal window and door screens and metal weather strip held 3.97 percent; and metal doors, sash, and trim, not specified by kind, held 13.39 percent of the market share in the early 1990s.

In the early 1990s, the leading states in employment were California, Texas, Pennsylvania, Ohio, and Florida. California led the industry in shipments with 192 establishments engaged in the manufacture of metal doors, sash, frames, molding, and trim. These establishments shipped 10.6 percent of the U.S. total in this industry, amounting to $756.8 million for that year. The total number of people employed in this industry in California was 7,700, averaging 40 people per establishment. These workers earned an average of $9.21 per hour. Ohio's 62 establishments shipped $601.2 million worth of product and employed 4,200. These employees earned an average $10.67 per hour. Texas's 105 firms engaged in this industry shipped $545.5 million worth of products and employed 5,600 workers who earned an average $7.51 per hour. Pennsylvania's 67 establishments had gross revenues of $460.5 million and employed 4,600 who earned an average $10.08 per hour. Tennessee's 42 companies had sales of $403.4 million and employed 3,600 earning $9.56 per hour. Florida's 116 companies had sales of $386.2 million and employed 4,200 who earned an average $7.80 per hour.

CURRENT CONDITIONS

According to a January 1997 article in *Forbes,* home builders enjoyed a boom year as housing starts rose about 8 percent to 1.5 million units, the highest level since 1987. The South led the pack, followed by the West, Midwest, and the Northeast, which had yet to recover jobs lost during the early 1990s.

According to *U.S. Glass Metal & Glazing,* the U.S. demand for windows and doors was expected to reach $26 billion by the year 2000. Older house maintenance was expected to help increase sales of windows and doors within the U.S. by 4.7 percent per year to $26 billion by the year 2000. More energy efficient products and regulations coupled with a lack of timber was expected to result in the highest demand increase for vinyl/plastic products, although wood windows and doors will still make up more than 56 percent of sales through 2000. Increase in metal doors and windows was expected to be slow because of the lack of insulation of metal products.

This industry is a natural fit for glass, aluminum, or building materials manufacturers wishing to diversify their operations. During 1993 the furnishings supplier LaSalle was acquired by the British building materials group Heywood Williams. The LaSalle purchase was considered a lucrative gain because operating profits for the company nearly doubled between 1991 and 1992, rising from $3.3 million to $6.4 million.

Phillips Products, a subsidiary of Tomkins PLC, was the largest U.S. supplier of windows, doors, and ventilation products to the manufactured housing and recreational vehicle industry. Benefitting from significant advances in manufacturing efficiency and the expansion of the market, Phillips enjoyed profit growth in the latter part of 1996. Phillips has also introduced a new line of vinyl ranges targeted to the residential and manufactured housing markets, which should contribute to improved performance.

Anything involved in the building industry, both commercial and residential, had an affect on this industry. A strong real estate market coupled with a strong economy was creating more growth and expansion, and causing small companies, like Hollow Metal Door of Witchita, Kansas, to expand and grow. When housing was up, sales were up. But even when housing was not up, people were remodeling, adding skylights, columns, and stairs; this created even more sales than housing.

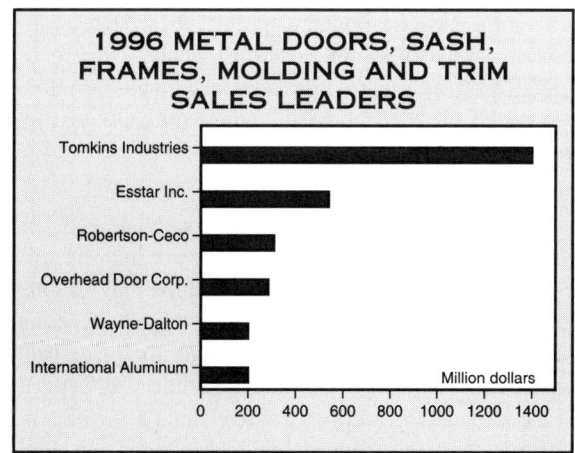

INDUSTRY LEADERS

The top 75 companies engaged in this industry grossed total sales of $5.79 billion and employed 59,900 people. The leading company was Tomkins Industries Inc., of Dayton, Ohio, which had sales of $1.4 billion and employed 14,000 in the mid-1990s. Following Tomkins was Esstar Holding Inc. and its

subsidiary Esstar, Inc., both of New Haven, Connecticut. They each had $540 million in sales and employed 5,800 people in 1996. Ranking next was Robertson-Ceco Corp. of Boston, Massachusetts, which grossed $309 million in sales and employed 1,600 people. Overhead Door Corp. of Dallas, Texas followed with sales of $285 million. International Aluminum Corporation, with estimated sales of $200 million, and Wayne-Dalton Corporation of Mount Hope, Ohio, with sales of $200 million, also were among the industry leaders.

WORK FORCE

As the industry looks toward the year 2005, a decrease in demand for workers overall is anticipated. Sheet metal workers and duct installers were expected to be reduced by 58.8 percent, followed by structural metal and precision fitters with a 50.6 percent decline; those were the sharpest declines estimated for this industry. Coating, painting, and spraying machine operators were expected to be reduced by more than 50 percent. Other occupations expected to be reduced between 30 and 50 percent included: metal and plastic machine forming operators; drafters; hand freight, stock and material movers; and bookkeeping, accounting, and auditing clerks.

RESEARCH AND TECHNOLOGY

A process developed that fuses glass and metal called UNI-SAN 6500, was made available in viewing windows from Jacoby-Tarbox. The process is reported to eliminate common causes of window breakage through its improved strength. Increased safety and durability are key to these single-unit windows.

In 1996, Wayne-Dalton Corporation of Mt. Hope, Ohio, premiered the Ironmax Classic Entry Door. The product was made of durable, 26-gauge steel panels; its core was filled with forced-in-place high-density polyurethane. The doors featured electrostatically applied prime coating and come with a warranty against warping or peeling.

FURTHER READING

Darnay, Arsen J., ed. *Manufacturing USA.* 5th ed. Detroit: Gale Research, 1996.

''Local Door Company to Expand.'' *Witchita Business Journal,* 23 August 1996.

Lubove, Seth. ''Construction.'' *Forbes,* 13 January 1997, 128-129.

''U.S. Demand for Windows and Doors to Reach $26 Billion by 2000.'' *U.S. Glass Metal & Glazing,* 1 December 1995, 100.

Ward's Business Directory of U.S. Private and Public Companies. Vol. 5. Detroit: Gale Research, 1997.

"Wayne-Dalton Releases Ironmax Door." *National Home Center News,* 5 August 1996, 230.

—Valerie Wilson, updated by Kaye Brinker

SIC 3443

FABRICATED PLATE WORK-BOILER SHOPS

This classification includes establishments primarily engaged in manufacturing power and marine boilers, pressure and nonpressure tanks, processing and storage vessels, heat exchangers, and weldments and similar products; these are made by cutting, forming, and joining metal plates, shapes, bars, sheets, pipe mill products, and tubing to custom or standard design for factory or field assembly. Excluded from this category are establishments primarily involved in manufacturing warm air heating furnaces, which are classified in **SIC 3585: Air-Conditioning and Warm Air Heating Equipment and Commercial and Industrial Refrigeration Equipment.** Those establishments primarily engaged in manufacturing nonelectric heating apparatus other than power boilers are classified in **SIC 3433: Heating Equipment, Except Electric and Warm Air Furnaces.** Also excluded from the fabricated plate work classification are manufacturers of household cooking apparatus and those manufacturing industrial process furnaces and ovens. The former are covered in **SIC 3631: Household Cooking Equipment,** and the latter are listed under **SIC 3567: Industrial Process Furnaces and Ovens.**

INDUSTRY SNAPSHOT

Plating—the application of a thin metal layer on a surface to enhance wearing quality, to prevent leakage, and to protect against corrosion—is used in the fabrication of many products. The manufacturing process is generally consigned to manufacturers involved in the fabricated plate work industry. Although the bulk of the industry's shipments comprises a multitude of products manufactured through plating processes, the core of the fabricated plate work industry essentially includes the manufacturing of power and marine boilers and various types of plate tanks and storage vessels.

Power boilers, as classified by the American Society of Mechanical Engineers, operate at greater than 15-psig steam pressure and are intended for stationary service, which excludes locomotive boilers from the scope of the fabricated plate work industry. Boilers operating at 15-psig steam pressure or lower, known as low-pressure heating boilers, are classified in **SIC 3433: Heating Equipment, Except Electric and Warm Air.** Power boilers, designed to operate at high pressures and temperatures, generate steam to provide power for utility companies and for various industrial processes. The boiler itself consists of two principal parts: the furnace, which provides heat, usually by burning fuel, and the boiler proper, in which water is converted to steam by the heat piped in from the furnace. A steam engine derives its power from steam generated under pressure in a boiler. Marine boilers are designed and fabricated for use aboard a wide range of vessels, including tugboats, oceanliners, oil drilling barges, freighters, and aircraft carriers.

ORGANIZATION AND STRUCTURE

The fabricated plate work industry is comprised of large and small manufacturing facilities. Of the 1,922 fabricated plate work establishments in existence in 1993, nearly one-half employed fewer than 20 people, while the industry average was 46 employees. Although the number of establishments was expected to drop 1,734 by 1998, about one-half of those would still employ fewer than 20 people.

Geographically, fabricated plate work manufacturing occurs throughout much of the United States, with 43 states containing five or more manufacturing facilities. The bulk of manufacturing activity in the mid-1990s took place in Texas, Pennsylvania, California, Ohio, and Oklahoma. Together, these states contained 712 manufacturing establishments, which generated $3.6 billion in sales and accounted for 38.9 percent of the total domestic shipments delivered by the industry. These states employed 37.2 percent of the industry's workforce.

Texas, with 210 establishments, contained the greatest number of fabricated plate work manufacturing facilities in any one state, and had the highest total revenue collected and shipment volume, posting $987.5 million in sales and accounting for 11 percent of the industry's total shipments. While California's 181 establishments topped Pennsylvania's 127, Pennsylvania came in second in terms of revenue and shipments with $864.3 million in sales and 9.5 percent of total U.S. shipments. California garnered third place with $576.7 million total sales, which was 6.3 percent of total U.S. shipments.

Operating a manufacturing establishment in the fabricated plate work industry is generally a less expensive venture than operating other typical manufacturing establishments, particularly in the area of average costs incurred. In 1989, the average cost incurred from purchasing the necessary raw materials for manufacturing fabricated plate work per establishment was $2.65 million, 41 percent lower than the average recorded by all other manufacturing industries. A greater difference is found in the area of average investment per establishment. In 1989, the average investment expenditure per establishment was $162,996, or approximately 50 percent below the $321,011 incurred by a typical manufacturing facility.

BACKGROUND AND DEVELOPMENT

The origins of the fabricated plate work industry may be traced to the early development of boilers, which began in the Middle Ages, when inventors experimented with the idea of harnessing the power of steam. For centuries, improvements were made in both the theory of deriving power from steam and in steam generators themselves. Seventeenth-century inventor Giovanni Battista della Porta was the first to discover that when steam condensed in a closed vessel it created a vacuum that could draw up water. Thomas Savery, an English engineer working in the late seventeenth century, created the first machine to provide mechanical power by utilizing steam. By 1800, vast improvements had been made in designing steam engines and boilers, but the expense involved in developing prototypes was prohibitive.

In 1800, a landmark development in the history of boiler development occurred when Richard Trevithick put together a steam engine and boiler, which, eventually, through the addition of tubes carrying gases from a fire, increased the heating surface and efficiency of the boiler. Several decades after Trevithick's achievements, John Stevens, an American engineer, developed one of the first boilers in which tubes carried water to be converted to steam, instead of gases from a fire. This "water-tube" boiler represented the culmination of roughly 50 years of work by Stevens in his efforts toward constructing an efficient steam system to power ships along the Hudson River. By the mid-nineteenth century, further improvements had been made in the water-tube design, which allowed the water to circulate more easily, provided more heating surface, and lowered the risk of boiler explosions.

During this time, boiler design was fostered by the industrialization of Great Britain. The shift from an agrarian and commercial society to an industrial society was prompting a similar transition in the United States, shaping that country into a modern manufacturing nation. Steam powered both of these industrialization movements; the power it provided proved intrinsic to the movement toward large and distinct manufacturing industries. In the United States, residences and local industries were the primary users of these steam generators until the latter half of the nineteenth century, when the applications for steam power broadened and spurred the emergence of a market segment for the fabricated plate work industry that would fuel its growth throughout the twentieth century.

The unveiling of this new use for steam took place at the 1876 U.S. Centennial Exhibition in Philadelphia, during which the practicality of generating electricity by steam power was demonstrated to the attending public. Five years later, four boilers were powering the Brush Electric Light and Power Company in Philadelphia, the nation's first commercial electric generating station, marking the beginning of a new era for both the United States in general and boiler manufacturers in particular. From this time forward, power boilers in mills and factories appeared with increasing frequency, particularly in sugar refining companies, as the industrialization of the United States neared its greatest intensity.

Similar advances had been made with marine boilers, another integral product that bolstered the U.S. fabricated plate work manufacturers, helping them to form a genuine, organized industry after the turn of the century. Beginning with the *Great Britain* in the early nineteenth century, marine engineers began exploring the possibilities of providing power to becalmed ships through steam. Eventually sails and masts were discarded and boilers became the sole source of power for ships of all classes and sizes, from the 1,154-ton *Britannica,* which "sailed" from Liverpool to Boston in 1840, to the *Monitor* and the *Virginia,* two iron-hulled steamboats pitted against each other during the American Civil War.

By the time boilers had become common in American industry, marine boilers were also fueling a majority of the U.S. vessels on water. Accordingly, by the end of the nineteenth century, fabricated plate work manufacturing, essentially comprising the fabrication of power and marine boilers, was being conducted in earnest. In 1889, the American Boiler Manufacturers' Association (ABMA) was chartered with elevating the standards of boiler design and manufacture and preventing the production and sale of boilers deemed unfit for safe operation. Moreover, the establishment of a national association for boiler manufacturers cohered a loosely organized group of manufacturers, marking the formal beginnings of the boiler shop, or fabricated plate work, industry in the United States.

Before the fledgling industry could emerge as an integrated and uniform group of manufacturers, national boiler manufacturing standards needed to be created and the alarming frequency of boiler explosions needed to be quelled, something the formation of the ABMA had failed to do. Another association with a vested interest in the production of boilers, the American Society of Mechanical Engineers (ASME), had also failed to curb the number of accidents related to boiler explosions, despite formulating a code entitled "Standard Method for Steam Boiler Trials" in 1884. In 1914, a committee under the purview of ASME published the "Boiler and PressureVessel Code," which provided manufacturers with standard specifications for the design, fabrication, installation, and inspection of boilers and pressure vessels. The adoption of nationwide standards helped curtail the number of boiler explosions, while providing manufacturers with a universal manufacturing language in which to communicate and enabling them to produce higher-quality boilers that conformed to the diverse needs of their customers.

Once ASME's Boiler Code gained widespread acceptance, many of the fabricated plate work industry's internal, organizational problems were resolved, or at least made more manageable, facilitating, and in some cases invigorating, the industry's growth. Technological improvements in the design of boilers followed at a rapid pace, as the onus of spearheading future design and production innovations fell to the companies involved in the industry, rather than to the independent engineers.

Several historic achievements followed the publication of the Boiler Code, the first of which involved the opening of the Edgar Steam Electric Station in Weymouth, Massachusetts. The electric station, operated under the aegis of the Boston Edison Company, opened in 1925 with a high-efficiency turbine and boiler system able to produce electricity at the rate of one kilowatt hour per one pound of coal. For its time, this ratio represented a considerable leap in efficiency—conventional power plants competing on the vanguard of technology were consuming 5 to 10 pounds per kilowatt hour—and the station remained a model of efficiency until it was dismantled and sold to a South American power company in the 1970s.

Thirty-three years after the Edgar Steam Electric Station demonstrated to the world the efficiency of steam generated electrical stations, President Dwight D. Eisenhower tripped a switch that activated the first North American commercial central electric-generating station to utilize nuclear energy. Located in Shippingport, a town northwest of Pittsburgh, the Shippingport Atomic Power Station was designed by the Westinghouse Electric Corporation, the Division of Naval Reactors of the Atomic Energy Commission for the Department of Energy and the Duquesne Light

Company. Generating 60,000 kilowatts of electricity, the Shippingport Station was small compared to the generating capacity of similar electric stations to follow, but it heralded the advent of a new method for generating electricity, a process that incorporated the use of boilers.

In 1960, the first commercial geothermal electric-generating station in North America began operating in Sonoma County, California, north of San Francisco. This geothermal field, from which generators received naturally produced steam, was first discovered in 1847 and then tapped in the early 1920s, but the steam and hot water billowing from the earth proved too corrosive for pipes and other equipment of the 1920s. By the late 1950s, however, significant advances in anti-corrosion technology enabled the Pacific Gas and Electric Company to successfully generate steam from the Sonoma field, which further broadened the applications for boilers in the production of energy.

These benchmark events in the development of additional uses for boilers, coupled with the increasing utilization of boilers by the industrial sector, accelerated the growth of the fabricated plate work industry. By the early 1960s, boiler shop manufacturers—producing power and marine boilers, pressure and non-pressure tanks, processing and storage vessels, heat exchangers, weldments, and sundry other plate products—represented a $1.5 billion a year industry. Consistent improvements in design and the increased requirements of U.S. industry led to the fabrication of massive boilers, some of which were able to generate 6.5 million pounds of steam per hour, heated by furnaces approximating the size of 40 medium-sized houses. In the electrical power field, the use of boilers in thermal power plants, which accounted for roughly 80 percent of all electrical power generated in the nation, was pervasive, as boiler manufacturers benefitted from their position as suppliers of equipment essential to a diverse customer base.

As the industry entered the 1970s, the demand for power boilers remained strong, stronger than manufacturers were able to satisfy. However, growing concern for the potentially harmful effects of additional electrical generating facilities on the environment began to make the selection of future power plant sites difficult. Consequently, an electrical production deficit existed during the late 1960s, which sparked a wave of concern by utility operators regarding the availability of the equipment necessary to construct additional facilities, as demand outpaced supply. During the1960s, this gap between production and consumption created a commensurate gap between new orders for power boilers and the production of power boilers. This gap narrowed by the beginning of the 1970s, when electric utility operators began ordering steam-generating equipment in advance as a hedge against an anticipated shortage of power boilers. For manufacturers in the fabricated plate work industry, particularly those focusing on the fabrication of power boilers, this panic boosted sales volume. The value of power boiler shipments increased 18 percent from 1969 to 1970, the culmination of a decade that saw industry-wide power boiler revenue climb from $341 million in 1963 to $631 million in 1970.

The 1970s, however, marked a turning point for the fabricated plate work industry. During the mid-1970s, utility companies became increasingly concerned about the availability of fuel, environmental exigencies, and future demand for energy, resulting in an energy crisis. Energy conservation efforts and soaring energy costs sharply reduced new orders for utility boilers. The fabricated plate industry also experienced slackening, reflecting the losses incurred by nearly every manufacturing industry in the United States during the energy crunch.

Revenue garnered from the production of power boilers fell from over $1 billion in 1974 to $860 million in 1978, while total boiler production fell from 90 million pounds of capacity to 36.5 million pounds, prompting manufacturers to plead for federal intervention. In response, the National Energy Act and the Industrial Fuel Use Act were passed in 1978. While the government hoped such measures would reduce the number of industrial boilers dependent on gas and oil for fuel, the fabricated plate work industry hoped they would invigorate the stagnant boiler market. Neither occurred, as both manufacturers and their customers became confused about which fuel was to be used.

As a result of the somewhat bleak prospects facing manufacturers in the industry, expected profit margins were reduced in the early 1980s, and competition intensified for the dwindling number of new orders. To mitigate their losses, some manufacturers exited the business entirely, while others began concentrating more on retrofitting and converting existing boilers. Although the latter were able to stave off the negative affects of the six-year downturn, their strategy did not preclude serious losses. Nationwide energy conservation by both of the industry's primary markets—industrial and utility—imposed, in effect, a limit on the extent to which boiler manufacturers could recover. In 1980, the Department of Energy estimated that the concerted movement toward conservation had reduced the growth in energy demand to half the growth rate of the gross national product, an unsettling

discovery considering that the two growth rates, historically, had been roughly equal.

Consequently, manufacturers entered the mid-1980s struggling to maintain their precarious presence in the boiler and fabricated plate work market. Electric utilities at this time were operating old electric generating equipment approaching the end of its economic life, but boiler manufacturers did not expect to realize any significant wave of new orders until the early 1990s, as electric utility operators forestalled the purchase of new equipment as long as possible. An increasing percentage of the industry's work continued to be the rebuilding and refurbishing of older units, but for a considerable number of manufacturers this type of work did not generate enough money to sustain operations, and the roster of fabricated plate work manufacturers shrank.

By the late 1980s, conditions had not improved greatly. Manufacturing operations were consolidated and some facilities were shut down due to decreased demand. As manufacturers looked toward the future, a reversal of the depressed state of the industry was largely predicated on the equipment purchasing decisions by electric utility companies and a return to more aggressive capital expansion programs by the industrial sector, both of which were stunted by the recessive economic conditions of the early 1990s.

CURRENT CONDITIONS

Approximately 1,735 companies in the United States were involved in producing fabricated plate work in 1997. This figure reflected the latest of a decade-long decline in the number of manufacturers engaged in the industry. The sharpest decline occurred from 1982 to 1987, when the number of participants dropped from 1,743 to 1,584. Total revenue garnered by the industry during the 1980s declined as well, dropping from $8.23 billion in 1982 to a low of $6.15 billion in 1986. In the late 1980s, however, the industry's performance improved, as revenue increased for three consecutive years to conclude what otherwise had been a decade of consistent decline. In 1987, the industry's revenue total increased to $6.79 billion, then leapt to $7.81 billion the following year.

Since 1990, there has been a steady growth in the number of fabricated plate work manufacturers with the largest increase from 1991 to 1992, when the number jumped from 1,694 to 1,942, leveling off in 1993 to 1,922. As the industry entered the 1990s, its sales volume eclipsed the total recorded in 1982, climbing to $8.65 billion in 1990. In 1993 revenue reached $9.11 billion, fell slightly to $8.94 in 1994, but rebounded to $10.08 billion in 1995.

Sales shipments are predominately derived from the industry's five primary product groups: heat exchangers and steam condensers; fabricated steel plate; steel power boilers, parts, and attachments; metal tanks and vessels (custom fabricated at the factory); and fabricated plate work not conforming to the parameters of standard fabricated plate work. This last product category, attesting to the wide range of products manufactured by the industry, was the most abundantly produced product by fabricated plate work manufacturers, accounting for 20.1 percent of the industry's total shipments. Standard fabricated plate work represented the industry's second largest product category, accounting for 16.7 percent of total shipments, followed by heat exchangers and steam condensers, which accounted for 14.4 percent. Steel power boilers and their parts and attachments represented 10.3 percent of the industry's shipments, and were closely trailed by metal tanks and vessels manufactured in a factory setting and according to customer specifications, which represented 10.2 percent. The remainder of the industry's products comprised storage tanks (5.3 percent), nuclear reactor steam supply systems (5.5 percent), and gas cylinders (3.7 percent).

INDUSTRY LEADERS

Ranked according to sales volume, the two largest companies involved in the fabricated plate work industry in the mid-1990s were McDermott Inc., based in New Orleans, Louisiana, and CBI Industries Inc., based in Oak Brook, Illinois.

McDermott Inc., controlled by McDermott International Inc., earned its position in the industry largely through a merger in 1978 with The Babcock & Wilcox Company, resulting in Babcock & Wilcox as a subsidiary in McDermott's Power Generation Systems and Equipment Division. Formed in 1867 as Babcock, Wilcox and Company, the company's roots actually stretched back to 1856, when a 26-year-old engineer from Rhode Island, Stephen Wilcox, applied his knowledge of water circulation theory to perfect a new boiler concept utilizing inclined water tubes. Later referred to by Thomas Edison as "the best boiler God has permitted man yet to make," the success of Wilcox's system persuaded him and his friend George Herman Babcock to form Babcock, Wilcox and Co.

Initially, the two partners sold a majority of their boilers to sugar refineries. Then, in 1881, the company began supplying the boilers for the country's first central electric power station at the Brush Electric Light and Power Company in Philadelphia. In subsequent years, Babcock & Wilcox boilers would continue to represent the vanguard of power generation technol-

ogy, pioneering significant advances in utility steam generation design and marine boiler development. Moreover, the company helped to shape the industry by playing an instrumental role in the development of the American Society of Mechanical Engineers' Boiler and Pressure Vessel Code in 1914.

Into the early 1990s, Babcock & Wilcox continued to set the pace for other companies involved in the industry, thriving as a major supplier of nuclear steam generating equipment, critical heat exchanges, and replacement recirculating steam generators. Employing approximately 20,000 workers, McDermott Inc. garnered $2.3 billion in sales for 1995. In April 1997, Babcock & Wilcox was awarded a $35 million contract to design and manufacture steam generator components for a nuclear plant in China that is expected to completed in 1999.

CBI Industries, Inc. was formed in 1979 to become the holding company of Chicago Bridge & Iron Company, founded in 1889, and other subsidiaries. Divided into three primary business segments, including contracting services, industrial gases, and investments, CBI was by the early 1990s involved in oil and refined product storage, and oil and gas production, as well as in providing engineering, design, and fabrication services. Chicago Bridge & Iron, the parent company of the contracting services segment, owned ten principal production plants in the United States, Canada, and Australia. This segment, the largest business segment within CB&I in terms of total sales collected, posted $793 million in revenue in 1992, nearly half of the $1.67 billion recorded by all the subsidiaries owned by the company. For 1996, CB&I reported $31.3 million in operating profits on revenues of $663.7 million for its worldwide engineering and construction company. In 1996, Praxair, a Danbury, Connecticut-based company bought CBI Industries Inc. In 1997, Praxair announced it would sell its stake in Chicago Bridge & Iron and the unit would become a separate corporation.

By the mid-1990s, McDermott Inc. was still the industry leader but Rosemont, Illinois based Alfa Laval Incorporated held the second spot with $350 million in revenue and 1,600 employees. In third place was Knolls Atomic Power Laboratory, of Schenectady, New York, which had $250 million in sales. DB Riley Consolidated Incorporated, and Aqua-Chem Incorporated rounded out the top five in fourth and fifth place respectively.

Foster Wheeler, a Clinton, New Jersey-based company posted record profits for 1996, despite several pending litigations. Foster Wheeler offered services such as design, engineering, construction, manufacturing, project development, plants operations, and environmental services on a global basis. The company reported net earnings of $82.2 million on revenues of $4 billion for 1996. In March of 1996, Foster Wheeler filed suit against the governor and state of Illinois, alleging that a repeal of a state retail rate law could, in the next 20 years, take away benefits of $300 to $500 million for a facility the company built in Robbins, Illinois. Additionally, in the fourth quarter of 1996, Foster Wheeler had to reflect a special charge of $24 million for possible future asbestos-related litigation.

WORK FORCE

Total employment in the fabricated plate work industry declined sharply during the 1980s, falling most precipitously, from 103,200 to 71,200, between 1982 and 1986, a period during which the industry's aggregate revenue experienced a commensurate decline. Toward the latter half of the decade, as sales recovered slightly, the industry's employment base grew. As the industry entered the 1990s, employment was buoyed but was still far below the employment total of the early 1980s.

Total employment in the industry fell from 81,500 in 1990 to 73,500 in 1991. By 1993, the number had begun to climb back with 76,200 total employees, and reached over 80,000 in 1994.

Of the people employed in the industry, an overwhelming majority were employed as production workers, while salaried employees—those performing managerial, administrative, or technical duties—composed the balance of the industry's work force. In 1994, the typical fabricated plate work manufacturing establishment employed 33 production workers and 13 salaried employees.

In general, production workers in the fabricated plate work industry are employed on a full-time basis, averaging, in 1994, three percent more hours per year than a production worker employed by a typical manufacturing industry. In 1990, production workers' hourly wage was $11.93, at which time salaried employees earned an average of $36,274 per year. By 1993, the average hourly wage rose to $12.64, only to fall slightly to $12.37 per hour in 1994. However, workers in this industry earned more per hour than their counterparts in manufacturing, where production workers averaged $12.09 per hour.

In terms of the total payroll per establishment, the fabricated plate work industry's work force expenditures were slightly less than the average payroll expenditures for all other manufacturing industries, largely because the fabricated plate work industry employed fewer workers per establishment than the average for manufacturing industries. In 1994, the average payroll per establishment in the industry was $1.4 million, 7 percent below payroll costs incurred by other types of manufacturing establishments. However, the typical fabricated plate work manufacturing establishment did employ approximately 6 percent fewer workers than the average manufacturing establishment, which accounted for, in part, the relatively lower payroll expenditures in the fabricated plate work industry.

RESEARCH AND TECHNOLOGY

During the 1980s, two technological developments in particular enabled manufacturers in the industry to increase production efficiency and improve the quality of their products. One of these advances, acoustic emissions technology (AET), had been available to manufacturers of metal-related products for centuries, but was not utilized in the production of fabricated plate work in a widespread fashion until much later. The other, computer-aided design, or CAD, technology, was developed in the 1980s, as an inevitable extension of the rapid technological advancements achieved by the computer industry as a whole during the decade.

The use of acoustic emissions technology emerged during the 1980s as a viable and effective means to gauge the quality of plate work, and its adoption by manufacturers quickly spread. Acoustic emission, the sound produced by various types of materials during production processes, was first used commercially by those involved in the production of pottery. Potters relied on the audible cracking sounds clay pots produced while cooling in a kiln. These sounds enabled the practiced listener to determine which pots would eventually crack. An application more closely related to the type employed by fabricated plate work manufacturers, however, was used by tin manufacturers, who listened to the sounds of smelted tin, known as "tin cry," to detect structural flaws in the manufactured metal. For manufacturers involved in the fabricated plate work industry, acoustic emissions provided similar information in identifying the inherent structural weaknesses of their products.

Perhaps the most valuable contribution that monitoring acoustic emissions provided was the ability of manufacturers to determine the rate of deterioration of their products, rather than merely the condition of the metal at the time of inspection. Moreover, the structural integrity of metal could be determined without cutting into it, which conventional methods required. By the late 1980s, acoustic emissions technology was embraced by manufacturers throughout the United States and regarded in the industry as the most reliable method of monitoring the structural defects of fabricated plate work during production.

Complementing the emergence of acoustic emissions technology, the fabricated plate work industry also benefitted from the increasing advancements in computer design and software applications during the 1980s, helping manufacturers to reduce the operating and production costs of their products and to improve their designs. The advent of computer aided design (CAD), in particular, provided manufacturers with an invaluable tool to determine the most economical and efficient design of power boilers and other products manufactured by the industry. Additional software applications—designed for use in industrial settings and able to perform tasks that previously had consumed a considerable portion of research and development expenditures—reinforced the industry's dependence on computers to effectively compete in a market that demanded the most sophisticated resources available.

FURTHER READING

Bennett, K. W. "Tank Industry: Lonely Bull Kicks Its Heels Up-High." *Iron Age,* 11 June 1970, 83.

"A Bureaucrat in Your Tank." *The Economist,* 23 March 1985, 31.

"Consent Decree to Tell Trade Groups to Certify Foreign-Made Boilers." *Wall Street Journal,* 14 June 1972, 38.

"Court Releases Pressure on Imported Equipment." *Chemical Week,* 27 September 1972, 28.

Cross, Wilbur. *The Code: An Authorized History of the ASME Boiler and Pressure Vessel Code.* New York: American Society of Mechanical Engineers, 1990.

"EPA Proposes New Standards for Hazardous-Waste Storage Tanks." *Chemical Engineering,* 8 July 1985, 20.

"Foster Wheeler Posts Record Profits for the Year." *The Star-Ledger,* 26 February 1997, O26.

"Foster Wheeler Sues Over Repeal of Retail State Law." *Waste Age,* May 1996.

"McDermott Gets Job in China." *Wall Street Journal Interactive Company Briefing Book,* 24 April, 1997.

"One Hundred Pounds of Plastic in Every 1990 Car?" *Iron Age,* 6 November 1978, 88.

"Regulatory Confusion Stymies Boiler Sales." *Industry Week,* 19 February 1979, 92.

"Two Engineers' Groups Face Antitrust Charges." *Wall Street Journal,* 23 July 1970, 3.

Young, David. "Chicago Bridge & Iron Set for Spinoff." *Chicago Tribune,* 6 March 1997, 3.

—Jeffrey L. Covell, updated by Katherine Wagner

SHEET METAL WORK

This industry encompasses companies primarily engaged in manufacturing sheet metal work for buildings (not including fabrication work done by construction contractors at the place of construction) as well as stovepipes, light tanks, and other products of sheet metal.

INDUSTRY SNAPSHOT

In 1992, 4,452 companies involved in the U.S. sheet metal work industry employed 104,300 workers and generated $11.5 billion in shipments. California, Ohio, Illinois, and Texas accounted for 35.6 percent of the industry's total shipments. The most common end uses for sheet metal that same year were electronic enclosures (such as personal computer housings or casings; 15.6 percent of end uses); roofing and roof drainage equipment (10.7 percent); air conditioning ducts and stove pipes (9.6 percent); sheet metal flooring and siding (7.9 percent); awnings, canopies, cornices, and soffits (4.6 percent); culverts, flumes, irrigation pipes (3 percent); bins and vats (2 percent); and other or unspecified uses (46.6 percent). Within these categories was a myriad of products used by every industry from aircraft manufacture (air cowls), building construction (siding, stove hoods, and gutters), heating, ventilation, and air conditioning (HVAC) applications (ducts, furnace flues), mineral processing (coal chutes), and highway construction (guardrails) to agriculture (irrigation pipes), business machines (computer casings, shipbuilding (ship ventilators), postal delivery (mail boxes), and food preparation (vats and bins).

ORGANIZATION AND STRUCTURE

Sheet metal forming was one of the most basic and pervasive manufacturing processes in U.S. industry. In general, sheet metal products manufactured by industry firms had thin walls, simple as well as complex designs, and greater surface area in relation to thickness. They were generally lighter in weight and more versatile than metal products formed and shaped through casting and forging processes. The manufacture of sheet metal products was generally characterized by low to moderate costs for labor, equipment, and dies.

Industry sheet metal products were manufactured with a wide range of metal-forming machine tools. Several different techniques could be used to produce the same sheet metal part. The factors determining which method was used included the cost of the die, the amount of labor available, the number of sheet metal parts to be made, and the speed of production. Deep-drawing methods, for example, involved more complicated machinery and cost more than other methods, but they were also faster and more cost effective for jobs involving the manufacture of many parts.

In 1994, the sheet metal industry consumed almost half the value of its total shipments on materials and supplies, primarily from blast furnaces and steel mills and aluminum rolling and drawing companies. Low-carbon steel was the most widely used metal for sheet metal processes because of its low cost and high strength and formability.

CURRENT CONDITIONS

From 1972 to 1993, the sheet metal industry experienced steady, uninterrupted growth. The number of firms grew from 2,960 to 4,600, and the value of shipments more than quadrupled, from $2.68 billion to $13.1 billion. In the same period, employment rose from 74,000 to 106,400. Between 1993 and 1998 the number of companies in the industry was projected to grow by 7 percent, employment by 13 percent, and shipment value by 21 percent.

In mid-1996, the entire steel sheet metal industry (which included many applications not included in this industry classification) enjoyed stronger demand than in last six months of 1995. Through the end of the decade the supply of steel sheet metal was expected to rise as a result of foreign imports and expanded U.S. production capacity from a new generation of new steel ''mini-mills.'' These low-cost producers were expected to control 21 percent of the U.S. steel sheet supply by the end of the 1990s, which suggested that prices of steel for sheet metal work industry firms would remain low. Because of the importance of HVAC systems and business/computer machines to the U.S. economy, these two largest buyers of the sheet metal work industry's products seemed to offer the greatest opportunity for future industry growth.

INDUSTRY LEADERS

The leading U.S. sheet metal work firms in 1995 were Consolidated Systems Inc. of South Carolina ($160 million in sales, with 400 workers), Alcan Building Products of Ohio ($120 million, 1,200 employees), Bouras Industries Inc. of New Jersey ($110 million, 500), Harrow Corporation of Michigan ($110 million, 1,200), and Hart and Cooley Inc. of Michigan ($100 million, 1,200). Other leading firms included Syro Steel, Symons Corporation, ASC Pacific Inc., and Coastline Distribution Inc.

In 1995 Consolidated Systems announced it was constructing a manufacturing plant and warehouse in Jackson, Mississippi, and the same year Alcan Building Products—a major manufacturer of canopies, awnings, and other exterior building products—was bought out by its management and renamed Alument Building Products. In 1996, Harsco Corporation announced that it had acquired Symons Corporation, a maker of prefabricated concrete forming equipment, and Watsco Inc. purchased Coastline Distribution, a maker of HVAC-related products.

WORK FORCE

In the 1990s, the vast majority of the nation's sheet metal workers worked for firms outside the sheet metal industry, as on-site construction contractors, for example, or in the plumbing and HVAC business. The sheet metal industry's 80,000 production workers, however, represented an important segment of the American sheet metal work force, which was represented in part by the Sheet Metal Workers' International Association (SMWIA). That union, formed in Toledo, Ohio, in 1888 claimed 134,000 members and 205 local unions in the mid-1990s. In 1996 in Milwaukee, the SMWIA Local 18 experimented with a novel way to ensure job security by offering consumers rebates if they bought furnaces or central air conditioning systems from union contractors. Sheet metal workers often learned the trade through apprenticeships involving four to five years of combined classroom and on-the-job training. The average production worker in the sheet metal work industry in 1994 earned $11.49 an hour and $23,828 per year.

RESEARCH AND TECHNOLOGY

Technological advances in the sheet metal work industry in 1990s were revolutionizing the efficiency and precision with which sheet metal products were fabricated. These advances centered in large part on improving tools, dies, and other equipment; relying more extensively on automated machinery; and embracing the benefits of the computer, new software, and—for marketing purposes—the World Wide Web.

A new turret punch press introduced in the 1990s allowed machine tool operators in the sheet metal industry to punch, cut, separate, and sort finished metal blanks in a single operation rather than the three-part operation previously required. The machine's 21 hole-punching tools could be adjusted to perform simple unsupervised operations or more complicated processes involving automatic retrieval and storage of parts. Similarly, electromechanically operated industrial robots were used extensively to accurately and tirelessly perform the continuous machining motions once performed by humans. Generally speaking, automating sheet metal manufacturing processes required resilient equipment and quick programming, startup, and retooling times to be effective.

Although in the early 1990s Japanese and European firms led U.S. manufacturers in the use of laser-cutting technology for cutting sheet metal to product specifications, as the decade progressed the United States gained ground on its foreign competitors in this crucial manufacturing technology. In the mid-1990s, an Ohio State engineering professor began experimenting with the use of lasers and light-emitting diodes (LEDs) to detect the wrinkles that develop when the pressure exerted by a die is inappropriately calibrated to the strength of the sheet metal being pushed into it. By instantaneously detecting wrinkles just as they begin to occur, the sensors enabled a computer to automatically readjust the pressure on the metal before the wrinkles marred the sheet. A laser application developed in the mid-1990s for sheet metal work in the aerospace industry combined the precision and automation of laser technology for finishing and trimming metal parts with the design and efficiency benefits of CAD/CAM (computer-aided design/computer-aided manufacture) software to reduce project lead time by two-thirds and costs by up to a quarter.

In response to the need to cut costs and increase equipment durability, in the 1990s some industry firms turned to plastics, epoxy, and polyurethane to replace traditionally metallic tools and dies. Software programs using finite element analysis (FEA) also enabled product designers to predict the effectiveness of sheet metal stamping dies for the manufacture of products with intricate surfaces and identified potential strains and stresses in the metal. FEA also enabled manufacturers to accurately predict potential problems in sheet metal bending operations before any metal was actually machined. Software packages such as ''PE/Sheet Advisor'' used a combination of ''expert system'' logic and three-dimensional modeling to enable sheet metal product manufacturers to incorporate data gathered from manufacturing operations into the design of new products.

Large sheet metal operations used central computers to direct all sheet metal-forming operations. This ''systems approach'' managed entire sheet metal processes using vast unified databases containing information on materials, tool and die parameters, and the mechanical properties of the variables of the sheet metal manufacturing process. The efficiency of such CAD/CAM programs as AutoCAD (the industry standard) was estimated to be four to five times greater than traditional methods. Small- to medium-sized firms that could not afford the costs of a truly integrated and centralized sheet metal CAM system could purchase simulation or modeling CAD software to eliminate the costly trial-and-error methods for developing and manufacturing new products. ''MetalMan,'' a Windows-based software program designing sheet metal parts, used a graphic user interface that simulated a machine shop, enabling designers to form three-dimensional solid models of the parts they wished to fabricate, exchange data with other CAD programs, and add to and evaluate new operations in the fabrication process. Such programs could also produce cost quotes and estimates, maintain manufacturing schedules, keep inventories, and generate specification reports for each part.

FURTHER READING

American Metal Market. Radnor, PA.

Babyak, Richard J. ''Designing with Metal.'' *Appliance Manufacturer,* November 1994, 40.

Census of Manufactures: Fabricated Structural Metal Products. Washington: Bureau of the Census, 1992.

''Combination Machining.'' *Mechanical Engineering,* October 1996, 34.

Connolly, Gary. ''Multiaxis Laser Cuts Manufacturing Time of Aerospace Parts.'' *Mechanical Engineering,* February 1994, 64.

''Getting the Wrinkles Out of New Cars.'' *USA Today Magazine,* June 1996, 8.

''Harsco Corp. Pursues Privately-held Symons.'' *Pit & Quarry,* February 1996, 35.

Holley, Paul. ''Union Hopes Rebates Spur Business.'' *Business Journal Serving Greater Milwaukee,* 15 June 1996, 5.

''Inter-City Products Sells Coastline Distribution to Watsco.'' *Air Conditioning Heating & Refrigeration News,* 2 December 1996, 1.

Kalpakjian, Serope. *Manufacturing Engineering and Technology,* Reading: Addison-Wesley Publishing Company, 1989.

Russell, Kelly. ''South Carolina's Consolidated Systems to Build Jackson Facility.'' *Mississippi Business Journal,* 16 October 1995, 7.

Strope, Leigh. ''Alcan Execs Join Forces for Buyout.'' *Dallas Business Journal,* 21 April 1995, 9.

Stundza, Tom. ''Suddenly, the Outlook Is Cloudy.'' *Purchasing,* 9 May 1996, 32B1.

—Paul Bodine

SIC 3446

ARCHITECTURAL AND ORNAMENTAL METAL WORK

This category includes establishments primarily engaged in manufacturing architectural and ornamental metal work, such as stairs and staircases, open steel flooring (grating), fire escapes, grilles, railings, and fences and gates, except those made from wire. Establishments primarily engaged in manufacturing fences and gates from purchased wire are classified in **SIC 3496: Miscellaneous Fabricated Wire Products;** those manufacturing prefabricated metal buildings and parts are classified in **SIC 3448: Prefabricated Metal Buildings and Components;** and those manufacturing miscellaneous metal work are classified in **SIC 3449: Miscellaneous Structural Metal Work.**

Manufacturers in the architectural and ornamental metal work industry provide construction contractors with building and finishing materials for all divisions of the development market. Product offerings include bank fixtures, guide rails for stairways and ramps, permanent ladders and stairways, lamp posts, flag poles, metal grates, fire escapes, decorative fences and posts, brass fixtures, and various metal adornments. Classified in other industries are firms that specialize in producing wire fences, prefabricated metal buildings and parts, and miscellaneous metal work.

Metal working is one of the world's oldest trades. It originated in about 2500 B.C. when bronze was discovered, although smiths prior to that time produced architectural ornaments using gold. Not until the discovery of iron in 1200 B.C., however, did the craft of structural metal work develop. The industry in the United States flourished when architectural styles progressed from the applied ornament period in the nineteenth century to the organic, or functional, ornament period in the 1900s. U.S. economic boom periods in the 1920s, 1950s, and 1960s all served to increase the size and scope of the industry.

Architectural and ornamental metal work firms realized market growth during most of the 1980s and early 1990's as a result of a fairly active construction market. Industry shipments climbed from less than $1.5 billion in 1982 to $2.9 billion by 1995. Industry employment rose from about 23,000 in 1982 to 30,000 in 1992, but declined to 27,000 by 1995.

A construction lull in the late 1980s stymied growth in the industry until 1990, but shipments were again increasing by 1991. While building markets still sagged in 1993, architecture and ornamental metal work firms were benefitting from a combination of increased public construction spending, renovation work mandated by the Americans with Disabilities Act, and an increase in the popularity of metal ornament in some building sectors. Products most in demand in 1995 were stairways, fences, railings, and gates, which accounted for a combined total of more than 24 percent of the market. Open flooring, grating, and studs made up about 16 percent of the market; and grilles, registers, and air diffusers represented another 12 percent of demand.

The industry is dominated by small private firms. In fact, in 1996 most of the top 80 firms employed 100 or fewer people; 79 percent of companies had 19 or fewer employees, and only 3 percent of companies employed more than 100. Furthermore, three-fourths of those companies generated revenues of less than $10 million. By far the largest producer in the industry, Harsco Corp. of Camp Hill, Pennsylvania, reported sales of $1.35 billion in 1996. The next largest player was Kawneer Company, Inc. of Norcross, Georgia, a subsidiary of Alumax, Inc., with sales of $306 million. Predominant locations for the greatest number of firms in the industry were California, New York, Florida, Pennsylvania, and Texas.

The architectural and ornamental metal work industry is served by several trade and/or professional associations. The National Ornamental and Miscellaneous Metals Association, headquartered in Forest Park, Georgia, has 675 member companies and publishes the bimonthly *NOMMA Newsletter.* The National Association of Architectural Metal Manufacturers, based in Chicago, Illinois, has 124 member companies. The largest organization, the International Association of Bridge, Structural, and Ornamental Iron Workers, headquartered in Washington, D.C., has 135,000 individual members and publishes *The Iron Worker.* Affiliated with this organization are Architectural and Ornamental Iron Workers local unions.

Growth in architectural metal work will likely remain average or below average compared to other U.S. industries through the early 2000s. Jobs in metal work are projected to lag behind the average for all occupations due to slow growth in construction in commercial and industrial areas. Most new employment is likely to result from experienced workers leaving the industry.

FURTHER READING

Braun-Feldweg. *Metal Design and Technique.* London: B.T. Batsford Ltd., 1975.

Darnay, Arson J., ed. *Manufacturing USA.* 5th ed. Detroit: Gale Research, 1996.

Directory of Corporate Affiliations: Who Owns Whom. New Providence, NJ: National Register Publishing, 1996.

Geerlings, Gerald K. *Metal Crafts in Architecture.* New York: Charles Scribner's Sons, 1929.

"Metals Products." *Architectural Record,* December 1992.

"On Their Metal." *Building,* 17 July 1992.

Standard & Poor's Industry Corporate Descriptions. New York: Standard & Poor's Corporation, 1993.

U.S. Bureau of the Census. *1995 Annual Survey of Manufactures.* Washington, GPO 1997. Available from http://www.census.gov/prod/www/abs/asm95as1.html and http://www.census.gov/prod/www/abs/msmfgo7c.html.

U.S. Department of Commerce. *County Business Patterns.* Washington, GPO. 1994. Available from http://www.census.gov/prod/2/bus/cbp94/cbp94.html.

U.S. Department of Commerce. International Trade Administration. *Occupational Outlook Handbook.* Washington GPO, 1997. Available from http://stats.bls.gov:80/ocohome.html.

—Dave Mote, updated by Patricia Moncada

SIC 3448

PREFABRICATED METAL BUILDINGS AND COMPONENTS

This category covers establishments primarily engaged in manufacturing portable and other prefabricated metal buildings and parts and prefabricated exterior metal panels.

Prefabricated metal buildings industry manufacturer's shipped $4.22 billion worth of such products as portable buildings and houses, silos, greenhouses, carports and garages, and other prefabricated metal buildings. The largest division within this industry was non-residential or farm prefabricated building systems, which included industrial and commercial, institutional, medical, and religious buildings. That section of the industry made up 60 percent of 1996 sales and accounted for $2.54 billion in shipments. Residential, farm, and portable dwellings and greenhouses made up 27 percent and $1.48 billion. The remaining 13 percent was accounted for by miscellaneous metal structures, which brought in $278 million.

Employment levels climbed steadily over the 1980s, growing from 23,500 people in 1982 to 30,000 in 1990. Through the early 1990s, however, the employment fluctuated from the high in 1990 to a low of only 21,000 in 1992. By 1996 the number evened off at 24,000 but was expected to decline by about 22 per-

cent through 2005. The total number of establishments declined from 569 in 1982, its all time high, to 517 in 1996. Establishments had been dwindling throughout the 1990s except for 1993, when 555 establishments, the most during the 1990s, were in operation. Wages for this industry climbed steadily from the early 1980s, but were still far below average for all of manufacturing in 1994. While the employees per establishment and production workers per establishment were the same, metal building workers made only $10.51 per hour compared to average manufacturers earnings of $12.09.

United Dominion Industries of Charlotte, North Carolina, employed 11,000 people and grossed sales of $1.89 billion in 1996. United Dominion had been a dominant force within the industry for the last decade, usually having more than double the sales of the nearest competitor. Dyson-Kissner-Moran Corp. was the nearest competitor to Dominion in years, with sales of $1.37 billion in 1996. These top two were running away with the industry, accounting for $3.17 billion (75 percent) of industry shipments. Varo-Pruden Buildings, a division of United Dominion, was third in terms of sales, with $340 million, but still was not close to matching the sales figures of the leaders.

Due to a decrease in construction of office buildings, commercial, and industrial sites in the early 1990s, the prefabricated metal building industry suffered a slight decline in sales. Nevertheless, the industry was expected to grow steadily through 2000 with new technologies and environmental concerns giving the industry a small boost. Steel was the most heavily recycled product in the world—more than plastic, paper, aluminum, and glass combined—turning construction firms onto steel to satisfy new environmental regulations. The steel industry also revolutionized new techniques in manufacturing to give those who process steel products the best raw materials the industry ever had. Also, as the residential construction industry continued to grow, an increase in demand for products relevant to that division of the industry was predicted to make up for the slack in commercial demand.

The Universal Prefab Metal Framing and Seismic Component System was seeking to revolutionize the industry with its computer automated system, introduced in 1997. The Universal system, though still fairly new and not widely used, claimed it could cut costs substantially by reducing production time, lowering insurance rates, and cutting workers compensation funds. The system was an automated cutting and design system that could be programmed to clients' demands and cut and shaped by the push of a button or by hydraulic controls. The worker was no longer required to cut the steel by hand—a dangerous, laborious, and time consuming task. The end product was stronger and more precise structures. Though the product was too new to be widely used, it tested superior by Sandia National Laboratories, a division of the U.S. Department of Energy, and the University of California State, Hayward.

FURTHER READING

Darnay, Arsen J., ed. *Manufacturing USA*. 5th ed. Detroit: Gale Research: 1996.

"OECA Prefabricated Metal Sector Notebook." *Envirosense,* 14 December 1995. Available from http://es.inel/gov/comply/sector/fab/fabintro.html.

"United Dominion Industries Limited." *Hoover's Online*. 1997. Available from http://www.hoovers.com/cgi-bin.

U.S. Census Bureau. U.S. Department of Commerce. *1995 Annual Survey of Manufactures*. Washington: GPO, 1997.

SIC 3449

MISCELLANEOUS STRUCTURAL METAL WORK

This category includes establishments primarily engaged in manufacturing miscellaneous structural metal work, such as metal plaster bases, fabricated bar joists, and concrete reinforcing bars. Also included in this industry are establishments primarily engaged in custom roll forming of metal.

Roughly 50 percent of U.S. structural metal work sales were derived from manufacturing custom roll-formed metals, which brought in $2.4 billion of the industry's $4.5 billion total revenues in 1996. Another 32 percent of industry sales came from fabricated bar joists and concrete reinforcing bars. The remaining 18 percent was split between manufacturing metal plaster bases, curtain walls, and other miscellaneous metal work.

Closely related to the construction and automobile industries, structural metal work manufacturers were heavily affected by the recession of the late 1980s and early 1990s, following a $1 billion boom in shipments between 1986 and 1988. Shipment values, after dropping sharply in the early 1990s, recovered and leveled out in 1993.

One reason for this stagnancy was the industry trade deficit between the United States and its foreign competitors. Customers of steel firms were adversely affected by the amount of complaints filed by U.S. firms against foreign steel manufacturers concerning this trade deficit. The deficit continued into the mid-1990s, as imports of steel drastically increased in 1996 to the second highest tonnage ever; 29 billion net tons of steel were imported, up an enormous 19.5 percent from 1995. The deficit, combined with U.S. steel producers' protests, diminished business at U.S. ports, increased prices for steel products, and left a shortage of specialty plate and sheet products previously supplied by foreign suppliers. As a result, some U.S. steel-using firms were contemplating relocation to Canada, Mexico, and other Pacific Rim countries.

Concentrated in the Great Lakes region, this industry employed an estimated 22,000 people in 694 establishments by 1996, paying average earnings of over $12.74 per hour. This industry typically employed fewer people per establishment and paid average wages compared to other forms of manufacturing in the 1990s.

With increased automation, the face of the industry was expected to change into the year 2000. Heavy reductions in employment of production workers were expected, while job prospects for sales personnel, industrial production managers, and cost estimators were expected to increase.

In the mid-1990s the industry focused on cost reduction through process improvement and materials research. In 1993, CF&I Corporation invented a new process which can produce rails continuously for a quarter of a mile, reducing the need for welding and reducing construction costs. Ford Motor Company, in partnership with Alcan Rolled Products Company, is experimenting with the effects of hybrid aluminum-steel sheet metal on an automobile's fuel economy, durability, service, and performance. A new rigid rod-polymer, developed in 1995, has the capability to replace structural metals, such as stainless steel and aluminum. The new polymer is four times stiffer than conventional plastics, and can be injection molded, extruded, or compressed. Though it was still in the experimental stage, its development could take business from the structural metal industry.

FURTHER READING

"1996 Steel Imports up 19.5 Percent." *American Iron and Steel Institute,* 19 February 1997. Available from http://www.steel.org/industry.impdec96.htm.

Buelte, Horst. "Trade Law Must Reflect Current Reality." *American Metal Market,* 7 May 1993.

Chamberlain, Gary. "Technology Bulletin: Late Developments That Shape Engineering." *Design News,* 8 May 1995.

Darnay, Arsen J., ed. *Manufacturing USA: Industry Analyses, Statistics, and Leading Companies,* 5th ed. Detroit: Gale Research, Inc., 1996.

Rizzuto, A. B., et al. Bear, Stearns, & Co. Inc. "Metals & Mining Industry—Industry Report." 17 March 1993.

Scolieri, Peter. "Continuous Rails Patented." *American Metal Market,* 16 April 1993.

Wrigley, Al. "Ford Tests Aluminum Friendly." *American Metal Market,* 15 February 1993.

SIC 3451

SCREW MACHINE PRODUCTS

This category includes establishments primarily engaged in manufacturing automatic or hand screw machine products from rod, bar, or tube stock of metal, fiber, plastics, or other material. The products of this industry consist of a wide variety of unassembled parts and are usually manufactured on a job or order basis. Establishments included in this industry may perform assembly of some parts manufactured in the same establishment, but establishments primarily engaged in producing assembled components are classified according to the nature of the components. Establishments primarily engaged in manufacturing standard bolts, nuts, rivets, screws, and other industrial fasteners on headers, threaders, and nut forming machines are classified in **SIC 3452: Bolts, Nuts, Screws, Rivets, and Washers.**

INDUSTRY SNAPSHOT

In 1996, there were approximately 1,500 establishments in the United States that manufactured screw machine products. Only 40 percent of these establishments employed more than 20 employees. Although the total number of establishments has been projected to decline by approximately 2 percent each year throughout the decade, the industry's value of shipments has been projected to increase from $4.4 billion in 1996 to $4.7 billion in 1998.

The screw machine products industry is defined more by the process of manufacture than by any specific product. Although screw machine products manufacturers produce a wide variety of products for many types of industries—ranging from ball holders for ball-point pens to precise components for medical equipment to gears and other parts for the automotive industry—they all use a variation on the screw machine, a large, usually cam-driven piece of machinery that allows roughly cylindrical material to be subjected to a variety of tooling and machining operations as the materials turned about its axis. Screw machines may have as many as eight spindles that act upon the part being machined, and are able to produce highly precise parts quickly. The screw machine, by ensuring the interchange ability of manufactured parts, was a major contributor to the development of modern manufacturing and assembly processes.

Screw machine products manufacturers are located primarily in the industrialized sectors of the Northeast and Midwest and near aerospace manufacturers in the West. The industry is dominated by smaller companies employing less than 50 workers, most of whom are highly-skilled machinists. Many of the shops are privately owned, and most are located close to the industries to which they supply parts. In addition, many larger companies that use screw machine products manufacture those products in-house. The automotive industry is the major purchaser of screw machine products and accounts for 30 percent of the industry's shipments.

ORGANIZATION AND STRUCTURE

The vast majority of screw machine products are manufactured on a job or order basis. The purchaser of a product provides the manufacturer with a precise description of the part desired, and the manufacturer then sets up its machines to produce that part. Part runs may call for the manufacture of as few as a hundred or as many as a million parts, requiring a single screw machine or a shop full of machines to produce the part on time. Because of the nature of their business, screw machine products manufacturers rely on the flexibility of their equipment and employees to accommodate the different needs of the various screw machine products purchasers.

Three types of screw machines are used by manufacturers: swiss, single-spindle, and multiple-spindle machines. Using these machines, a machinist may perform up to 32 different types of cutting and forming operations. Fred W. Lewis, discussing the screw machine products industry in the *Handbook of Product Design for Manufacturing,* stated, "The amount of work done is limited only by the number of tool positions available and the tool layout engineer's ingenuity." The tool layout engineer designs the cams that control the various machining operations and sets up the machine, which is then capable of producing millions of identical pieces. Many manufacturers are turning to computer-controlled rather than cam-controlled operations, because of the longer set-up time required for cam-driven machines and the level of expertise required to operate them. Computer-controlled screw machines, however, are not necessarily more productive than cam-driven machines.

The flexibility inherent in both machine and machinist allows screw machine products manufacturers to produce parts for many types of industries. While larger manufacturers have diversified their production, smaller companies have tended toward specialization, and may produce as much as 80 percent of their total output for one company. This degree of commitment means small manufacturers experience whatever economic downturns or upturns the industry they are captive to experiences. The actual screw machines account for the major capital expenditures of manufacturers in this industry. The screw machine is a remarkably durable piece of machinery, however; it can be rebuilt and overhauled, and computer controls can be added to enhance the machine's flexibility, thus spreading capital outlay out over a long period of time.

BACKGROUND AND DEVELOPMENT

Although the first machine-cut screws were produced in 1800, at the dawn of the first industrial age, the concept of a screw dates back as far the third century BC, when the Greek mathematician Archimedes designed a water-powered, screw-driven system to lift water. Much later, in the mid-1400s, Leonardo da Vinci drew plans for a screw-cutting lathe. But it was Henry Maudslay, an English mechanic, who in 1800 first cut a piece of lead on a lathe into the helical pattern we know as a screw. Early screw manufacturers were hampered by the lack of any standards for measuring their products or ensuring their uniformity. Thus, each producer made a different size and pitch of screw, making it very difficult to replace parts when needed.

The early manufacture of machined metal parts in the United States occurred primarily in the increasingly industrialized Northeast states, where small shops produced parts for the machines that would drive American economic growth. Such shops used belt-driven lathes that were powered by water or, occasionally, an ox tied to a treadmill outside the factory. It was not until the middle of the nineteenth century, however, that a small group of machinists centered around Windsor, Vermont, created the machine tools that preceded today's screw machines. Out of this innovative environment of skilled inventors and machinists, which included pioneers Francis A. Pratt, Richard Lawrence, and James Hartness came Christopher Spencer, who in 1873 created the Hartford Automatic Screw Machine.

According to Donald E. Wood, editor of *Automatic Machining* and author of *From Archimedes to*

Automation: The History of the Screw Machine, Spencer's automatic screw machine was "the prototype for all single-spindle machines in use today." This machine was manufactured by the Hartford Machine Screw Co., which is the oldest continuing screw product manufacturer in the country. Soon Pratt & Whitney Co. of Hartford, Connecticut, and Brown & Sharpe Manufacturing Co. of Providence, Rhode Island, began manufacturing screw machines that were famed for their precision and accuracy. The creation of precision screw machines contributed greatly to the development of modern manufacturing, as screw machines made products for the growing automotive industry and other developing industries. According to Wood, "The mass production of consumer goods, and its parallel problem, precise interchange ability of goods components, came only after machine tools had been devised which could make products alike in a rapid manner, and standardization of measurement had been established."

Although the screw machine was initially designed to produce threaded fasteners, users of the machine soon recognized that it was capable of producing a vast number of products. In fact, standardized screw thread manufacturers soon turned to a different process, called cold-heading, and this industry is now classified as **SIC 3452: Bolts, Nuts, Screws, Rivets, and Washers.** Because the screw machine could create any roughly cylindrical, symmetrical piece of stock, it soon was used to manufacture gears, pulleys, push rods, rollers, and other products. By 1960, more than 1,500 screw machine product manufacturers employed more than 30,000 workers and operated over 40,000 screw machines to produce nearly $1 billion in annual sales of special component parts.

CURRENT CONDITIONS

Alhough the screw machine product industry generally feels the effects of national economic downturns, it nevertheless fared relatively well in the overall economic downturn of the early 1990s. Between 1982 and 1996, there was growth in shipment levels. In 1982 the value of shipments was $2.17 billion, and by 1996 they reached $4.41 billion. The value of shipments for the industry was relatively stagnant in the late 1980s through 1991. However, shipment values grew from $2.97 billion in 1991 to $3.83 billion in 1992. This increase was tied to the strong recovery of the domestic automobile industry, which sought to cut costs even if this meant purchasing screw machine products from independent manufacturers rather than captive screw machine departments. Total employment for the industry remained fairly constant from 1984 to 1988. Employment levels reached 45,900 in 1989, but dropped to the lowest level of 40,600 in 1991. Following that, employment rebounded, and in 1996, the industry employed 47,700 people. Production workers' employment levels followed a nearly identical pattern to total employment levels, with a low of 32,300 in 1991 and a high of 41,900 workers in 1994. This number leveled off to 38,400 in 1996.

As American manufacturing concentrated in the midwestern states of Michigan, Illinois, and Ohio, so did the screw machine products industry. Michigan's 213 establishments led the nation in value of shipments in 1992, reaching 728.7 million. This accounted for 19 percent of total U.S. shipments. Ohio followed closely behind with 181 establishments and $534.2 million in shipments, and accounted for 13.9 percent of total U.S. shipments. Michigan's 7,000 employees earned an average of $11.97 per hour, ranking well below Massachusetts's $12.94 per hour average wage.

The screw machine products industry is characterized by a high degree of structural stability: the machinery it uses, the processes involved in manufacture, and the kinds of products it produces have remained essentially the same for nearly 100 years. Many manufacturers use screw machines that are decades old. Most employees learn their trade through hands-on training or a form of apprenticeship, though workers are increasingly receiving training in vocational education programs. Thus, the screw machine operator of two generations ago would recognize many of the operations being conducted in today's shop, though the veteran workers might be surprised to see young operators, who had not gone through an apprenticeship, programming computer-controlled screw machines to work on plastics and fibers as well as metals.

INDUSTRY LEADERS

Most manufacturers employ fewer than 50 workers and operate less than a dozen screw machines. A few large, diversified companies play major roles within the industry, however. In 1995, the 75 leading companies in the industry had total sales of $1.25 billion and employed approximately 12,900 people. By 1996, the leader in terms of sales was Duff-Norton Co. of Charlotte, North Carolina, with $100 million and 700 employees. Second was Horizon Enterprises Inc. based in Taylor, Michigan, with $66 million in sales and 500 employees. The third largest, Hi-Shear Corporation, of Torrance, California, employed 600 workers and sold $57 million. In early 1996, Hi-Shear Corp. was sold to GF Industries for $46 million. The fourth largest screw machine products company was Kelco Industries, based in Woodstock, Illinois, which

had sales of $55 million. Amtec Precision Products Inc. was fifth with $41 million in sales.

WORK FORCE

Manufacturers of screw machine products have traditionally employed a highly skilled work force, although the aging of highly trained employees and the availability of more accessible computer-controlled machines suggests that the work force of the future will be somewhat less skilled and younger. Because learning to set up a cam-controlled screw machine takes years of training, finding qualified employees has been one of the industry's biggest problems. Operators traditionally learned the intricacies of setting up a machine through an apprenticeship; but vocational training programs and on-the-job training have now supplanted formal apprenticeships. In addition, the National Screw Machine Products Association, located near Cleveland, Ohio, provides training manuals, videos, and seminars for its members. The industry's move to greater computerization is driven less by the inherent machining benefits of computer control than by the greater ease of training that computers allow.

Most employees in the screw machine products industry are machinists of some sort. Because manufacturers are provided with design specifications for their products, they employ no designers. Manufacturing engineers specify the machining operations and cams required to produce the job based on the design they are given, and machinists set up the machines and supervise their operation. In many smaller firms, the principal owner is also the head engineer.

The U.S. Bureau of Labor Statistics predicted that the industry would experience a 12.8 percent decline in employment opportunities for machinists of all sorts between the years 1986 and 2000. However, average wages for this industry have steadily increased from $7.72 per hour in 1982. The average pay of $11.25 per hour in 1994 was slightly lower than the national standard of $12.09 for all manufacturing industries.

FURTHER READING

Darnay, Arsen J., ed. *Manufacturing USA*. 5th ed. Detroit: Gale Research, 1996.

Lewis, Fred W. "Screw Machine Products." *Handbook of Product Design for Manufacturing: A Practical Guide to Low-Cost Production*. New York: McGraw-Hill, 1986.

U.S. Department of Commerce. *1987 Census of Manufactures*. Washington: GPO, 1987.

U.S. Department of Commerce. *U.S. Industrial Outlook 1994*. Washington: GPO, January 1993.

Ward's Business Directory of U.S. Private and Public Companies. Detroit: Gale Research, 1997.

Wood, Donald E. *From Archimedes to Automation: The History of theScrew Machine.* Brecksville, OH: National Screw Machine Products Association.

—Tom Pendergast, updated by Katherine Wagner

SIC 3452

BOLTS, NUTS, SCREWS, RIVETS, AND WASHERS

This category includes establishments primarily engaged in manufacturing metal bolts, nuts, screws, rivets, washers, formed and threaded wire goods, and special industrial fasteners. Rolling mills engaged in manufacturing similar products are classified in the major group for primary metal industries (33); establishments primarily engaged in manufacturing screw machine products are classified in **SIC 3451: Screw Machine Products;** and those manufacturing plastic fasteners are classified in **SIC 3089: Plastics Products, Not Elsewhere Classified.**

INDUSTRY SNAPSHOT

Manufacturers in **SIC 3452: Bolts, Nuts, Screws, Rivets, and Washers** produce the materials that hold American industry together: bolts, nuts, screws, rivets, and washers. Producing these items in lots as small as 1,000 and as large as 20 million, manufacturers make both custom-ordered and standard fasteners using processes quite different from that of the screw machine product industry, **SIC 3451: Screw Machine Products,** with which it otherwise shares many similarities. While screw machine product manufacturers produce their goods using some form of screw machine that cuts into a metal product to produce the needed tooling, fastener manufacturers use a variety of cold-forming and rolling processes to produce simpler parts with greater strength. Both industries trace their beginnings to the early stages of industrialization, which made possible innovations in the field of fastener engineering.

The fastener industry is remarkably decentralized, with hundreds of small shops producing the majority of fasteners. Manufacturers in the fastener industry tended to cluster around the industries that purchase its products, traditionally the automotive, defense, and aerospace industries. The industry is therefore concentrated in the auto-producing states of the upper Midwest and the defense and aerospace-oriented regions of

California. But such dependence has had its costs. Slumps in the auto industry in the 1980s posed severe challenges to fastener manufacturers, and defense downsizing in the 1990s posed an equally significant threat. Domestic fastener manufacturers were also seriously threatened by an influx of cheap, foreign-made fasteners in the 1970s and 1980s. The Fastener Quality Act of 1990, passed in response to complaints about poor quality and fraud on the part of foreign fastener manufacturers, promised some protection for the domestic industry.

ORGANIZATION AND STRUCTURE

Manufacturers within **SIC 3452: Bolts, Nuts, Screws, Rivets, and Washers** produce a wide and ever-changing variety of products that fall under the general name "industrial fasteners." According to the Industrial Fastener Institute, the trade association for the industry, a fastener is "a mechanical device for holding two or more bodies in definite position with respect to each other. A high percentage of fasteners have threads as part of their design, but unthreaded items such as rivets, clevis pins, machine pins, etc., are considered fasteners as well." The industry produces fasteners using the primary manufacturing operations of heading, upsetting, forming, forging, and extruding. Fasteners use primarily ferrous metals for their products, usually carbon and alloy steels. Most fasteners begin as wire, rod, or bar, which is cut to length, headed, and then threaded.

A typical hex-head bolt begins as a shaft of metal whose length is a number of times longer than its diameter. This shaft is placed in a die, a metal holder that maintains the shaft's position when it is struck by a punch, which is designed to impart the hexagonal shape of a bolt head to the shaft. Multiple punches are sometimes used to impart more intricate head shapes or to form harder metals. The headed shaft is then given an external thread in another cold-forming process called thread-rolling. In thread-rolling, the headed shaft is pressed between stationary and moving hardened-steel dies, which squeeze the material into the desired thread form. The nut that accompanies this bolt may also be cold-formed using a thread-forming tap that displaces rather than removes metal to form the interior thread. These and other processes like them constitute the major means by which industrial manufacturers produce their goods.

According to the *Manufacturers' Capability Guide,* published by the Industrial Fastener Institute, "Cold forming is a high-speed, high-volume production process, with economical production rates determined by part size, design complexity, and degree of forming required—all factors that determine the number of blows required to form the part and thus the complexity of the tooling and equipment required.'' Cold-forming has the advantage of allowing the manufacturer to produce many thousands of products an hour; according to John E. Neely and Richard R. Kibbe, authors of *Modern Materials and Manufacturing Processes,* ''Production rates on upsetting machines can be as high as 36,000/hr. for small unpierced rivets, and No. 8 size screw blanks can be made at 27,000/hr.'' Such economies of scale allow manufacturers to offset the very high costs of cold-forming equipment. Cold-forming also has the advantage of wasting no material, since the metal is pressed into shape rather than trimmed away by machining, and of allowing the metal grain to form in continuous unbroken lines, improving tensile and shear strengths and resistance to fatigue.

BACKGROUND AND DEVELOPMENT

According to *The Heritage of Mechanical Fasteners,* a publication produced by the Industrial Fastener Institute, ''Man's conquest of nature has depended upon his ability to fasten useful things together.'' Ever since an axle was bound to a wheel to provide the means of moving a cart, humans have been using fasteners to make their lives easier. People were fashioning nails as early as 2800 B.C., and the first screw appeared around 250 B.C., but it was not until the fifteenth century that what we now know as threaded fasteners began to appear in common usage. In this century, the first printing press was held together and run by a screw, tiny screws held Swiss-made watches together, and French mathematician Jacques Besson designed the first practical machine for cutting screws.

The Industrial Revolution, which swept the Western world in the late eighteenth century, brought about many of the technological innovations that gave birth to the modern fastener industry. In 1760, Job and William Wyatt became the first known manufacturers of threaded fasteners. The English brothers employed 59 people in their water-powered factory, producing 1,200 gross of wood-screws a week. Screw makers started up throughout England and America, but purchasers of their products were faced with a serious problem. Because fastener makers shared no common rules for size and thread pitch, a nut from one shop had little chance of fitting a bolt from another. Nuts and bolts had to be carefully paired, for once separated they were practically useless.

''The one man most responsible for starting threaded fasteners on their way to becoming the high-precision, freely interchangeable, taken-for-granted components we know today was the English inventor Henry Maudslay,'' according to *The Heritage of Mechanical Fasteners.* Maudslay invented a bar lathe capable of making highly accurate and duplicatable threads, and his ideas led others, including American inventor David Wilkinson, to design machines that would form the basis for the new machine tool industry. Most early threads were cut on a screw machine, but in 1836 William Keane of New York invented a process known as thread-rolling that formed threads without cutting away material. That process, which later became prevalent, differentiates the fastener industry (**SIC 3452: Bolts, Nuts, Screws, Rivets, and Washers**) from the screw machine products industry (**SIC 3451: Screw Machine Products**).

In 1834, the C. Read & Company of Providence, Rhode Island, became the first significant manufacturer of screws in the United States. Within ten years, the small firm had a number of competitors, including the A.P. Plant Company of Plantsville, Connecticut, which in 1842 became the first company to issue a price list and discount large orders. The 1840s saw an explosion of advances in the industry: in 1844, Julius B. Savage introduced machine-made nuts; and in 1847, William E. Ward patented the first automatic cold-heading machine.

Fastener manufacturers benefitted from the Civil War, when all of American industry was mobilized in the production of firearms, machinery, and railroad equipment to feed a war that devoured machinery as fast as it did men. Shortly after the war, the center of the American fastener industry shifted from the Northeast to the Midwest (then referred to as the West) in order to stay close to the expanding railroads and growing iron and steel production facilities. By the end of the nineteenth century, Cleveland, Ohio, was the capital of the American fastener industry, and most of the processes for creating its products had been established.

Beginning in 1864, U.S. fastener manufacturers adopted the Sellers Thread System over the Whitworth Screw-Thread used by the British. Having different thread systems posed no problem for the two countries, until it came time for them to cooperate during World War I. American manufacturers were not equipped to manufacture the British threads, and field repairs of machinery were disastrous. The fiasco was nearly repeated in World War II, but temporary adjustments helped avert disaster. In 1964, the International Organization for Standardization (ISO) announced two universal thread systems: ISO Inch and ISO Metric. Despite occasional efforts to convert manufacturers to the metric system, the United States remains the only country in the world still tied to the inch system. This practice leads to dual manufacturing facilities and inventories, but American manufacturers and the American public have resisted conversion to the metric system.

By 1969, the U.S. fastener industry had reached its peak of production. In that year, 450 companies operating 600 plants and employing over 50,000 employees manufactured more than two billion fasteners a year. By 1984, however, the industry decreased in size—to 250 manufacturers operating 350 plants and employing 35,000 people—because of severe challenges from foreign competition and dramatic changes in the requirements of original equipment manufacturers (OEMs). The biggest challenge came from foreign fastener producers, who took advantage of inexpensive Third-World labor and material costs to produce cheap "standards," or fasteners that met nationally-recognized product standards. The Industrial Fastener Institute reported that domestic manufacturers went from supplying 80 percent of American bolts, nuts, and large screws in 1969 to just 44 percent in 1984. During the same period, OEMs, especially automobile manufacturers, were pressing fastener manufacturers to develop specialized products at lower costs. The production of these items sustained many companies, but it drove the smaller, less technologically advanced companies out of the industry.

Beginning in the mid-1980s, the American fastener industry began to rebound. Many manufacturers allied themselves with companies in need of technically sophisticated products rather than simple standardized commodities, and the falling value of the U.S. dollar drove the prices of foreign products up. Then, in 1985, reports began surfacing in newspapers across the country of "bogus bolts," bolts that were graded to withstand high loads but were failing in service, leading to the destruction of property and, in one case, the loss of life. The Industrial Fastener Institute began an investigation, and in 1986, urged an investigation by the U.S. Customs Service.

In 1988, after an 18-month investigation, a U.S. House subcommittee published a report entitled *The Threat from Substandard Fasteners: Is America Losing Its Grip?* The report stated that "the failure of substandard and often counterfeit fasteners has killed people, reduced our defense readiness, and cost both the American taxpayer and the American industry untold millions in breakdowns, downtime, reconstruction, and other unnecessary inefficiencies." The subcommittee concluded that the substandard and counterfeit fasteners at fault were largely foreign made. The

"bogus bolts" controversy ended in the passage of Public Law 101c-92, the Fastener Quality Act, in 1990. This act provided for the "testing, certification, and distribution of certain fasteners used in commerce within the United States." Perhaps more important than the law, the investigation challenged the quality of the fasteners imported from abroad while affirming the quality of fasteners made in the United States.

CURRENT CONDITIONS

The industrial fastener industry experienced little or no growth through the late 1980s and into the early 1990s. Value of shipments rose from $5.08 billion in 1987 to $5.79 billion in 1994. From 1987 to 1994, employment within the industry dropped from 38,700 to 31,900 production workers. Hourly wages increased for this time period from $11.02 to $12.76, which made it higher than the $12.09 average hourly wage for all manufacturing industries in 1994. According to analyst Richard Reise, "Industrial fastener companies are feeling the effects of efforts by major equipment and machinery manufacturers, particularly the U.S. automobile manufacturers, to cut costs of components and supplies. This means lower prices and tighter profit margins for fastener suppliers." Such pressures may continue to drive small- and medium-sized fastener companies from the industry, since they have little choice but to comply with the requests of purchasers who may buy the vast majority of their products. Other challenges to the fastener industry in the 1990s came from decreases in defense spending and soft demand from domestic aircraft manufacturers.

The fastener industry is expected to benefit from increased export opportunities, especially to South America and western Europe. According to Reise, "U.S. fastener companies are becoming more aggressive in searching out export markets, rather than just responding to unsolicited export orders. U.S.-made fasteners that offer the best prospects for export are high-quality, high-price, low-weight products." The top five export destinations for U.S. companies in 1991 were Canada (53 percent), Mexico (13.6 percent), the United Kingdom (6.8 percent), France (3.1 percent), and Japan (3.0 percent). Passage of the North American Free Trade Agreement (NAFTA) promised further growth in exports.

The United States has been a major consumer of foreign-made fasteners for decades, especially of the cheaply made "standards" used in many areas of the automotive and residential construction industries. Taiwan was the major importer of fasteners for the first half of 1993, shipping 381 million pounds of fasteners worth over $245 million or 45.7 percent of total imports. Japan was the second largest importer (19.9 percent), followed by Canada (16.7 percent), China (4.3 percent), and numerous other importers. The adoption of regulations stemming from the Fastener Quality Act is expected to change the import market as manufacturers of low-quality products are forced to comply with more stringent fastener specifications and as U.S. Customs officials crack-down on price-fixing and product-dumping. The 1995 value of imports was $2.46 billion, an increase of $698 million from the previous year.

INDUSTRY LEADERS

Fastener manufacturers have long congregated near the industries that buy their products, and according to Industrial Fastener Institute sources, the major purchasers are automobile manufacturers, the federal government, and electronics, machinery, aerospace, and appliance manufacturers. For this reason, Illinois, Ohio, Michigan, and Pennsylvania, lead all states in fastener production. California, home to major players in the defense and aerospace industries, is also a major producer of fasteners. Illinois Tool Works (ITW), with headquarters in Glenview, Illinois, is by far the largest producer of industrial fasteners in the United States, with $4.15 billion in 1995 sales and over 22,000 employees. In 1996, ITW bought Milwaukee, Wisconsin-based Medalist Industries Inc., the sixth largest fastener producer in 1995. This purchase was part of a trend for ITW, which averages 15 to 20 acquisitions a year. As a result, in 1996, ITW reported $4.2 billion in sales from more than 300 business units with 21,000 employees working in 34 countries. SPS Technologies Inc. of Jenkintown, Pennsylvania came in second with $410 million in sales and 4,100 employees. In 1995, Textron Inc. purchased Elco Industries Inc. and formed Elco Textron Inc. based in Rockford, Illinois, and garnered the third spot with $249 million in sales revenue and 2,200 employees. Other major manufacturers include Camcar Textron Incorporated of Rockford, Illinois; and Huck International Incorporated based in Irvine, California. The majority of manufacturers listed in *Ward's Business Directory of U.S. Private and Public Companies 1997* employ just a few hundred workers and bring in less than $50 million in annual income.

RESEARCH AND TECHNOLOGY

In the 1990s, the fastener industry improved technology due to demands for stronger, lighter, and easier-to-use products. For example, although a rivet is a low cost item that is easily installed, it can be difficult to determine the correct rivet length for the job. In response to this problem, the fastener industry developed rivets that have a wider range and are capable of fastening several thicknesses of material at once. Recent product innovations have come in the area of electronics where fasteners play vital roles. Tiny screws hold together the circuitry, chips, and lasers in the typical computer disk drive while threaded fasteners secure control panels and ensure parts are not lost or dropped. While many developments in the fastener industry are made to meet the needs of a specific client, the resulting products and ideas are shared across companies and industries.

FURTHER READING

Beyerle, Richard A. ''Fasteners Keep Up with the Times.'' *Machine Design,* 21 March 1996, 70.

Bulkeley, William M. ''Textron Tops Illinois Tool's Bid.'' *Wall Street Journal,* 14 September 1995, B2.

''Cold Formed Parts Yield Impressive Benefits.'' *Manufacturing Engineering,* November 1984.

Darnay, Arsen J., ed. *Manufacturing USA.* 5th ed. Detroit: Gale Research, 1996.

Engineering Staff, Teledyne Landis Machine, James G. Bralla, ed. ''Screw Threads.'' *Handbook of Product Design for Manufacturing: A Practical Guide to Low-Cost Production.* New York: McGraw-Hill, 1986.

The Heritage of Mechanical Fasteners. Cleveland, OH: Industrial Fastener Institute, 1991.

Industrial Fastener Institute. ''Fastener Application Advisory.'' Cleveland, OH: Industrial Fastener Institute, May 1993.

Industrial Fastener Institute. ''Fastener Application Advisory: The Fastener Quality Act, Public Law 101-592.'' Cleveland, OH: Industrial Fastener Institute, May 1993.

''Industrial Fastener Shipments to Grow 6% Per Year as Markets Recover.'' *Fastener Industry News,* 22 April 1993.

Lanke, LuAnn. ''New Owner Plans Changes for Medalist Industries.'' *The Business Journal-Milwaukee,* 9 March 1996, 23.

''Manufacturers' Capability Guide. Division 2, Small Products: Fasteners & Accessories.'' Cleveland, OH: Industrial Fastener Institute, 1987.

Neely, John E., and Richard R. Kibbe. *Modern Materials and Manufacturing Processes.* New York: John Wiley & Sons, 1987.

U.S. Congress House Committee on Energy and Commerce, Subcommittee on Oversight and Investigations. *The Threat from Substandard Fasteners: Is America Losing Its Grip?* 100th Cong., 2d sess., 1988, Committee Print 100-Y.

U.S. Department of Commerce. *1987 Census of Manufactures.* Washington: GPO, 1987.

U.S. Department of Commerce. International Trade Administration. *U.S. Industrial Outlook 1994.* Washington: GPO 1994.

Ward's Business Directory of U.S. Private and Public Companies. Detroit: Gale Research, 1997.

Wick, Charles, and James G. Bralla, eds. ''Cold-Headed Parts.'' *Handbook of Product Design for Manufacturing: A Practical Guide to Low-Cost Production.* New York: McGraw-Hill, 1986.

Wood, Donald E. *From Archimedes to Automation: The History of the Screw Machine.* Brecksville, OH: National Screw Machine Products Association.

—Tom Pendergast, updated by Katherine Wagner

SIC 3462

IRON AND STEEL FORGINGS

This industry includes establishments primarily engaged in manufacturing iron and steel forgings, with or without the use of dies. These establishments generally operate on a job or order basis, manufacturing forgings for sale to others or for interplant transfer. Establishments that produce metal forgings for incorporation in end products produced in the same establishment are classified on the basis of the end product. Establishments further processing forgings are classified according to the particular product or process.

INDUSTRY SNAPSHOT

The forging processes of the iron and steel forging industry—not the industry's end products—characterize the industry. Forging reconfigures a substance by pressing, hammering, or constricting it with a great deal of pressure. Most substances are forged after they have been heated, but not melted. Liquefying metals to make parts is called casting.

There are three main processes for forging metal: closed die or impression die forging, which compresses a metal between two dies that contain an impression of the end product; open die forging, which hammers metal between two flat dies but moves the piece between blows to shape the end product; and seamless rolled ring forging, which punches a hole in the work piece and then rolls and squeezes it into a thin, seamless ring.

All forging processes make very strong parts known as forgings. Forgings are strong because forging processes create a grain flow in the parts of the finished product that require maximum strength. Forging processes also impart beneficial metallurgical

properties, such as ductility, resistance properties, dimensional stability, and absence of porosity. Although companies may forge many types of metal, the most commonly forged metals are carbon steel and alloy steel.

Establishments in the iron and steel forging industry are concentrated in the Midwest and Northeast, with the highest number of establishments in Ohio, Michigan, and Illinois. California and Texas also have a large number of forging establishments.

In addition to the U.S. establishments that concentrate their efforts on forging iron and steel, many companies produce their own forgings for manufacture of their primary products. The industry sold a record $4.4 billion worth of product in 1995, a 10 percent increase over 1994 and substantially greater than the most recent high of $3.8 billion in 1990.

Purchases of forgings came from industries concentrated in the same general regions as the forging companies, even though forging companies market their products nationally and internationally. The largest purchasers of forged products are the aerospace, national defense, and automotive industries, as well as agricultural, construction, mining, material handling, and general industrial equipment manufacturers.

BACKGROUND AND DEVELOPMENT

Humans first forged metals by hand-hammering them. The steam hammer automated the forging industry in 1843—the steam raised the hammer, but the weight of the hammer was the only pressure used to shape the metal. By 1888, a double-acting hammer used steam to supplement the pressure exerted by the falling hammer. Technology continued to advance the industry.

A census taken by *Forging* reported that two forging methods dominated the industry in 1992: closed die and open die methods. The closed die method was used by 248 companies, while the open die method was used by 109 companies, a margin of more than two-to-one. The ring rolling method was used as a primary method by 16 plants; 13 plants in the census cited other unnamed primary methods of forging. The *Forging* census included 32 Canadian companies and companies classified in **SIC 3463: Nonferrous Forgings.**

Forging developed as more of an art than a science, and even in the 1990s, when most forging was almost completely mechanized, forging processes could not be completely predicted with scientific methods. The unique problems posed by forging are the result of the many factors manufacturers must take into account. The most common factors to consider are the properties of the metal to be transformed, the strain or amount of pressure required to shape the metal, the rate at which the pressure can be applied to the metal for deformation, and the appropriate temperature for the deformation to occur without scaling or breaking the material. All the factors must be balanced to achieve consistently desired results from any of the forging processes.

Even with advances in technology, the complexity of some forging problems have not been solved. Determining the kind of die lubricant to use for forging operations is an example. Before the industrial revolution, animal oils, coal, soapstone, and crude oils were used because the products were "simple" and the processes requiring lubricants were "minimal," according to *Forging*. The advent of the steam-hammer demanded new lubricants, which were developed by the end of the nineteenth century. The new lubricants were steam-refined mineral oils, sawdust, salt water, fatty soap solutions, and oil and graphite flake combinations.

The oil and graphite mixtures proved to be effective as forging speeds increased with automation, but because those mixtures were explosive, other lubricants needed to be developed. Mixtures of water and graphite replaced the oil-based mixtures by 1970. In response to health related problems caused by graphite lubricants, research on synthetic lubricants began in the 1970s. In 1993, *Forging* reported that "water-based graphites make up about 60 percent of the forging industry sales, synthetics 15 percent, and oil-based graphites 15 percent."

The success of the forging process relies on the effectiveness of the lubricant, but no simple method for selecting a lubricant exists. Each lubricant has advantages as well as disadvantages. Oil and graphite applies easily and works well at many temperatures, but is explosive and expensive. Water and graphite costs less and helps cool dies, but requires careful application to work; in addition, graphite dust can collect in the work area and cause problems for workers. Synthetic lubricants are cost effective and less hazardous but must be applied through spraying, may impede metal flow, and are ineffective to use for forging complex shapes.

The industry has seen many changes in the cost of production. From a low of $1.2 billion in 1983, material costs rose dramatically to just over $2 billion in 1989, before falling to $1.8 billion in 1995. The cyclical nature of material costs is a key factor in the industries' overall financial health and growth. The average cost per establishment is lower than the manu-facturing sector as a whole, but so too are the capital investment and value added per employee. Conversely, wages and employment per establishment are slightly higher than the manufacturing average.

CURRENT CONDITIONS

There are three types of forging orders: custom forgings, which are made at the request of a customer; captive forgings, which are made for the company's own internal use; and catalog forgings, which are standard parts that are resold through various sources. Forged products range from precision aircraft parts to everyday hammer heads and wrenches.

Forgers faced a number of competition issues in the mid 1990s, as end-users looked for lighter, cheaper materials. Powdered metal, cast metal, plastics, and ceramics posed the greatest threat to the iron and steel forge industry. Industry analyst Joshua Billings told *Metals Watch* "the competitive pressure from plastics and new metal alloys will force forgers to reduce the weight of their components." Billings added, "Forgings may lose some market share for smaller parts to castings and powder metal parts, but will retain their preeminence for very large items or parts that are neither complex nor intricate."

Domestic forges developed computerized manufacturing, design, and testing, Strong growth in the aerospace industry benefited forgers, as did the overall health of the manufacturing sector. Of particular interest for forge operators was the anticipated demand from European-owned domestic auto manufacturers for new power train components. In the mid 1990s, these factories were importing $2.5 billion worth of forged components. Domestic forge operators expect to supplant these imports by the end of the decade as imports were expected to contract due to currency exchange rate fluctuations.

INDUSTRY LEADERS

The majority of the most successful forging companies are privately held. The top ten iron and steel forgings companies in 1996 were: Ladish Company ($175 million in sales and 1,600 employees); Scot Forge Co. ($126 million in sales and 400 employees); Letts Industries, Inc. ($115 million in sales and 400 employees); Griffin Wheel Division ($100 million in sales and 800 employees); publicly-held Defiance, Inc. ($93 million is sales and 900 employees); Interstate Forging Industries, Inc. ($80 million in sales and 500 employees); National Forge Co. ($74 million in sales and 700 employees); publicly traded SIFCO Industries, Inc. ($68 million in sales and 600 employees); Presrite Corp. ($65 million in sales and 300 employees); and Carlton Forge Works ($65 in estimated revenues and 200 employees).

WORK FORCE

Forging requires large amounts of capital investments to maintain the expensive equipment, but the industry sustains companies in a wide variety of sizes. Typical companies have an employee range of 50 to 250, but can have as few as 10 or as many as 1000. Machine forming operators make up the largest part of the work force in the industry. In 1996, the industry employed roughly 17,300 workers, reflecting a steady decline in almost every occupational category, and was down 45 percent from 1982.

RESEARCH AND TECHNOLOGY

New funding for research and technology will spur growth in the forging industry for 30 years past 1993. Federal funding of $80 billion was made available to American manufacturers by a mandate from the Clinton Administration. NIST expected a 1994 budget of $47.2 million, $6.6 million increase, to help expand American industry competitiveness through development of new technologies, according to *Forging*. Roger W. Werne, the associate director for engineering and technology transfer for Lawrence Livermore National Laboratory, noted in *Forging* that under the Clinton Administration's increased funding for national laboratories, the labs can act as an "'insurance policy' that can enhance the probability of success of a U.S. company or consortium of companies that decides to push the limit of their technology beyond existing boundaries." About the development of new technologies, the executive editor of *Forging*, John R. Wright, stated that "America is on the verge of wholesale new areas of technology development. We are close to breakthroughs—a technology blast that will carry this country for the next 30 years."

FURTHER READING

"Federal Spending to Highlight Research." *Forging*, Spring 1993, 8.

"Forging Industry Fact Sheet." Cleveland, OH: Forging Industry Association, August 1992.

"1992 Sales Shown in FIA Survey." *Forging*, Summer 1993, 8.

"Sowing the Seeds of Tomorrow's Technology." *Forging*, Spring 1993, 20-21.

Stundza, Tom. "Forging News," *Metals Watch: The Newsletter*, Vol. 2, April/May 1996. Available from http://www.steelforge.com/metals/issues.html.

Stundza, Tom. "Forging News." *Metals Watch: The Newsletter*, Vol. 2, December 1996. Available from http://www.steelforge.com/metals/issues.html.

"Taking a Tally of the U.S. Forging Industry." *Forging*, Summer 1993, 23-25.

U.S. Department of Commerce. *1987 Census of Manufactures*. Washington: GPO, 1987.

Werne, Roger W. "Grand Challenges for Industrial Competitiveness." *Forging*, Summer 1993, 34-36.

Wright, John R. "Tapping into Technology." *Forging*, Summer 1993, 5.

—Sara Pendergast, updated by Norm Leahy

SIC 3463

NONFERROUS FORGINGS

This category includes establishments primarily engaged in manufacturing nonferrous forgings, with or without the use of dies. These establishments generally operate on a job or order basis, manufacturing forgings for sale to others or for interplant transfer. Establishments that produce metal forgings for incorporation in end products produced in the same establishment are classified on the basis of the end product. Establishments that further process forgings are classified according to the particular product or process.

The forging industry as a whole, which includes **SIC 3462: Iron and Steel Forgings,** is characterized by its forging processes rather than its end products. Because many companies forge many types of metals, including both ferrous and nonferrous, industry information for this industry classification and **SIC 3462: Iron and Steel Forgings** are often reported together. The Forging Industry Association, for example, does not distinguish between the two SICs, presenting information on sales for the entire industry. Therefore, this entry will focus on the unique characteristics of the nonferrous forgings industry, and general information on forging can be found in the essay on **SIC 3462: Iron and Steel Forgings.**

Aluminum is the metal most often forged in this industry classification. It is "the most forgeable of all metals," according to *Forging*. Aluminum and its alloys can be forged into many different shapes and sizes. The metal is unique because it can be heated to the same temperature as the dies that will form it. The hardness of the dies is also lower than dies used for forging steel. The most common lubricant for forging aluminum is a graphite-water solution, with soap, to help the flow of the metal. Aluminum can also be forged into precision parts that need no further machining for use. Gravity or drop hammers are used for open die forgings, mechanical presses for closed die forgings, and hydraulic presses for complex pieces.

Other nonferrous forgings are made from magnesium and its alloys, whose coarse grains require that the metal be forged slowly in hydraulic presses; copper and its alloys, including brass and bronze; and titanium and its alloys, which are very sensitive to temperature changes but are extremely strong and resistant to corrosion.

The number of companies engaged in primarily manufacturing nonferrous forgings was only one-fifth the number of companies engaged in forging iron and steel. In 1986, 60 companies primarily used nonferrous metals to manufacture their forgings, a decrease of four companies since 1982. Capital investment within the industry slid in 1986 to 44 percent ($43.8 million) of that which was invested in 1982. Production in value of shipments also declined during that period by 1 percent, to $1,086 billion. As the value of shipments fell, however, the cost of materials and the value added by manufacture increased, by 3 and 8 percent to $586.1 million and $497.8 million, respectively.

In the 1990s, the nonferrous forging industry continued to be a small part of the total forging industry. In a 1993 census taken by *Forging,* 40 of 386 plants across the United States and Canada concentrated their efforts on forging aluminum, while 13 facilities concentrated on titanium and 12 on copper base alloys. The forging of nonferrous metals is not limited to these companies, however; the total number of plants that engage in nonferrous metal forging to some degree is significantly higher. When asked to provide all the types of metals a company forged, the number of plants that indicated at least a modicum of aluminum forging was 57 percent, while those engaged in titanium forging reached about 20 percent, and those forging copper base alloys fell to about 9 percent.

In 1994, the entire metal forgings and stampings industry employed 247,000, and the value of shipments was $36.75 billion. The nonferrous forgings segment had about 90 establishments in 1996. Capital investment was around $29 million, and the cost of materials was $664 million. The value of shipments was approximately $1.213 billion. In 1998, the industry was expected to have 94 establishments and shipment values of $1.230 billion. Capital investment was projected to fall to $24 million, but the cost of materials was expected to rise to $674 million.

Compared with other manufacturing establishments, the nonferrous forging industry is labor-inten-

sive. The industry employs almost twice as many employees per company than other manufacturers, with 80 workers per establishment on average as opposed to 49. The 1987 *Census of Manufactures* reported that the nonferrous forgings industry employed 7,300 employees, a drop of 8 percent since 1982. In 1994, the industry employed 6,900, and this number was expected to fall to 6,700 by 1998.

By 2005, a majority of the occupations employed by this industry are expected to decrease. Metal and plastic machine forming operators are expected to fall by almost 70 percent. Freight, stock, and material movers are expected to fall by 31 percent, along with janitors and cleaners. Combination machine tool operators are expected to rise about 28 percent, and punching machine operators are expected to increase by 15 percent. In the late 1990s, California's 20 establishments generated 19.4 percent of U.S. shipments. Illinois' and Connecticut's 9 establishments were producing about 12 percent of the U.S. total. Some of the most successful companies in this industry were Wyman-Gordon Company, Piper Impact Incorporated, EST Company, and Aluminum Precision Products Incorporated.

FURTHER READING

''Boeing Chooses Ti for 777 Designs.'' *Forging,* Summer 1993, 8-9.

Darnay, Arsen J., ed. *Manufacturing USA.* 5th ed. Detroit: Gale Research, 1996.

''Metals and Alloys.'' *Forging,* Spring 1993, 25-34.

U.S. Department of Commerce. *1987 Census of Manufactures.* Washington: GPO, 1987.

U.S. Department of Commerce. *Statistical Abstract of the United States.* Washington: GPO, October 1996.

''Taking a Tally of the U.S. Forging Industry.'' *Forging,* Summer 1993, 23-25.

SIC 3465

AUTOMOTIVE STAMPINGS

This category includes establishments that primarily manufacture metal auto parts, such as body panels, hubs and trim pieces, usually for sale to other manufacturers or for use in assembly facilities located offsite. Those firms which utilize the stamped products in the manufacture of end products in the same establishment are categorized by that end-product.

INDUSTRY SNAPSHOT

The automotive stamping industry remains closely dependent on the health of the domestic U.S. automobile market. With the decline of domestic car and truck production after 1988, the demand for stampings also decreased. The value of product shipments has barely kept up with inflation since the late 1980s. Worth $16 billion in 1987, the industry posted sales of $20.6 billion by 1995, a net decrease in value after inflation over the nine-year period. In 1995 the industry employed 116,400 workers at roughly 670 facilities in the United States. The technical expertise of industry production workers is increasing rapidly as the industry adapts to new production techniques and strategies, the challenges of new metal alloys, and the competition of plastic alternatives.

ORGANIZATION AND STRUCTURE

As with all manufacturers of automotive parts, stamping firms produce for two major market components: the original equipment manufacturer (OEM) and the after-market or replacement parts sector. Typical components include fenders, roofs, floor pans, exhaust systems, brake shoes and trim pieces. Such large pieces require a considerable investment in tooling and scale of operation. Consequently, businesses engaged in their manufacture are usually operated by the major automotive manufacturers or contracted by them. Small components, such as brackets, valves and hangers, do not require the same level of sophisticated engineering investment, which allows small, independent firms to specialize in such items. As a rule of thumb, automotive manufacturers contract out any stamped part needed in volumes below 200,000 pieces annually.

Stamping plants tend to be large operations employing many production workers. In 1982, 82 percent of all such establishments employed more than 100 workers. However, between 1972 and 1987 the number of production workers employed dropped 3 percent from 103,000 to 99,900, after dipping to 74,500 in 1982. At the same time the number of establishments rose by 57 percent, from 453 to 713. The average firm employed 135 workers in 1982, compared with 166 in 1988. Because the automotive stamping industry is a major supplier to automotive manufacturers, firms in the industry are concentrated in Michigan, Ohio, and Indiana, near the major U.S. automakers.

BACKGROUND AND DEVELOPMENT

The process or art of stamping metal to form hundreds or even thousands of identical parts evolved with the automotive industry. In 1912, Philadelphian

Edward Budd convinced the Hupp Motor Co., the Oakland Motor Co., and Garford Motors to begin incorporating metal into the design of their car bodies instead of the traditional wood. For the next few years, cars were made using a combination of both materials. In 1914, however, the Dodge brothers moved the automotive and the stamping industries into the modern era of industrial manufacturing with an order for 5,000 all-steel touring sedan bodies.

Stamping, or cold-forming, involves the use of power-operated clamping devices. A moving die, or forming-tool, presses into a sheet of metal and against a fixed die. The metal undergoes what is known as plastic deformation to take on the desired shape and thickness. Until the 1930s, the method was more art than science. Skilled artisans would produce relatively simple dies and use their collective experience to effectively produce parts mainly by trial and error. They often used an array of special tools and rituals to trick the sheet metal into shape.

As the industry needed to produce more sophisticated components, the unitized body which eventually replaced the frame entirely on domestic automobiles was developed. With the unitized body, once the die design, the metal material, and the blank sheet dimensions were chosen and found to be correct, the tool-system could create thousands of duplications under the supervision of relatively unskilled labor. That cost-saving attribute appealed to the needs of mass production manufacturers and overcame the disadvantage of the time-consuming process of die development. The new stamping process would require each individual component of the process to have a unique set of custom-designed dies.

A major advancement in press design came in the 1950s with the use of numerical controls. They made the new presses more accurate, faster, and easier to set up, allowing the industry to begin manufacturing a new range of products including mufflers, oil filler caps, some gears, engine mounts and brackets. By the 1970s, this technology gave way to computer numerical controls. The computer allowed the presses to run faster and operate more precisely, creating a need for automatic systems and robot loaders and unloaders.

The growing popularity of fuel-efficient Japanese-built cars challenged the mass-production philosophy of the American automotive manufacturers, particularly in the 1980s. The stamping industry felt the pressure directly. Its manufacturing philosophy prescribed large, regional facilities supplying several assembly plants in various geographic locations. However, the number of car models being produced, including foreign models, was steadily climbing. In

1986, there were 51 models sold in the United States; by 1990 there were 90. The capacity of press lines in operation had increased as older lines were replaced with more modern, efficient systems, which meant competition increased along with the number of required die changes.

Increased foreign competition also meant the domestic manufacturers had to improve the quality of their product. They needed new metals with better corrosion resistance. Instead of the standard 0.040-inch-thick carbon steel the industry had been using, manufacturers began specifying Zincrometal, one-sided and two-sided galvanized and coated alloy-steels. In addition, customers became far less tolerant of part variations which showed up as poor fit and finish. In 1981, many firms introduced Statistical Process Control and begin to implement Just-In-Time manufacturing systems in order to tighten the production belt. The resulting retrenching turned into downsizing and a massive reduction in production employment. Between 1972 and 1982, the number of production workers in the industry dropped from 103,000 to 74,500.

A major impediment to improved efficiencies in American stamping plants was the age of the equipment inventory. According to the 13th *American Machinist* inventory of metalworking machinery, almost one-half of all American metalforming equipment was at least 20 years old in 1983. Much of this equipment was cumbersome, designed for long production runs with long periods of shut down for maintenance and die replacement. During the 1980s, rebuilt and upgraded parts for these presses rose to 29 percent of all machine tool manufacturer's shipments. Even with the efforts to modernize, however, some machines could not be made competitive with the newer, more flexible Japanese technologies.

One of the most important battles for the American industry to win was the challenge of the rapid die change. Traditionally, American stampers took hours and sometimes days to change the dies in their machines. With the lines shut down for maintenance, one shift out of three working, and a warehouse full of finished product inventory in case of an unexpected breakdown, such long change-out times had not been a problem. However, with just-in-time production methods, inventories shrank to only hours of reserve parts and the number of die-changes increased to several per day. In contrast, in Japan during the early 1980s, die-changes took ten minutes, using small armies of workers. By 1991, Hirotec Corporation of Hiroshima could consistently change a die set in 80-to-90 seconds using just three men.

The difference between the United States and Japanese stamping processes was equipment design and planning. Older American machines required the complete removal of the old die before a new one could be installed. To do that, workers had to unfasten bolts and brackets. Having placed the new die, they would then set the piston stroke height and adjust the die position. Japanese presses use hydraulic clamps to hold standardized dies, and have openings on either side to allow the new die to be inserted as the old is withdrawn.

To remain competitive, in the early 1990s the Big Three U.S. automakers (Ford Motor Company, General Motors Corporation, and Chrysler Corporation) spent billions of dollars for new presses and new stamping plants tied to particular assembly facilities. The on-site stamping plant produces all the major parts required for the assembly of a specific car, cutting down on transportation costs and increasing the efficiency of shorter production runs. However, in 1991 the Big Three still had 22 major regional facilities which would be expensive to abandon and replace.

To increase the efficiency of those older plants, the industry began to standardize the die heights and improve the die designs and body panel designs so as to reduce the number of strokes needed to complete the forming process and reduce the amount of scrap steel produced. Formed parts almost always require multiple hits by the die or a series of dies to take the desired finished shape. Reducing the number of strokes required increases the rate of production and the life of the die. American molds typically average five and one-half hits per panel compared to less than three and one-half for Japanese systems.

During the early 1990s, the competitive need for higher efficiency through better quality control and increased flexibility drove the auto-makers to rethink their stamping arrangements and manufacturing philosophies. The traditional method of sourcing parts from several suppliers working from a manufacturer-supplied design gave way to a more cooperative and interactive approach. Copying the Japanese method, the manufacturers began to involve specific suppliers early on in the design stage and to require them to provide much of the engineering expertise, which reduced costs to the manufacturer and allowed the supplier to maintain an economy of scale in its actual production. It also meant fewer but larger suppliers. At the same time, manufacturers moved to on-site stamping plants equipped with sophisticated technology which effectively automated the process from start to finish. The increased efficiencies allowed the industry to compete effectively with foreign firms and to resist pressure from other materials like aluminum and plastics.

INDUSTRY LEADERS

The largest stamping firms in the OEM portion of the industry remain the automotive manufacturers themselves, but those firms outsource about 25 percent of their new car stamping requirements to independent firms. The largest of the independent stamping firms is The Budd Company of Troy, Michigan, a subsidiary of Thyssen AG of Germany. Budd employed 9,000 workers in 36 facilities to produce more than $1 billion in sales in 1996. Founded in 1912, the company pioneered the development of metal stampings throughout the early part of the century, racking up such firsts as the first four-door, all steel sedan body (Dodge), the first all-steel unitized body (Nash), stainless steel "streamliner" trains of the 1930s, the Navy's Conestoga RB-1 stainless steel cargo plane built during World War II, the prototype for the French Citroen, and the all-plastic-bodied 1954 Studebaker Coupe.

Metal stampings make up more than 50 percent of the company's sales, but it also manufactures fiberglass and plastic composite body panels, truck brake and wheel components, iron castings, and cold weather products like engine block heaters and interior car warmers. The German steel manufacturer and stamping firm, Thyssen AG, bought Budd Co. in 1978. The American firm had extended itself into many nonautomotive areas like aerospace and nuclear energy, reaching an employment high of 21,500, but it was loosing money. Thyssen propped up the company with influxes of capital, trimmed company operations, and limited operations to the automotive business to help it through the recession of the 1980s.

The second largest independent metal stamper, Magna Lomason Corporation, headquartered in Farmington Hills, Michigan, began operations in 1902 as Douglas and Lomason Co., a carriage rail maker. Acquired by Magna International Inc. of Canada in 1996, it produces seat systems and trim components for U.S. and Japanese automakers at 21 facilities using 5,300 employees. Most of its business comes from domestic car manufacturers. In 1995, Chrysler accounted for 25 percent of Magna Lomason's automotive sales. Ford made up 48 percent and General Motors, 12 percent.

WORK FORCE

Traditionally, the large stamping plants, using large quantities of relatively unskilled workers, have operated with union labor. The main unions are the United Auto Workers (UAW) in the United States and the Canadian Automobile Aerospace and Agricultural Implement Workers (CAW) in Canada. However, many transplant operations have tried to use non-union labor throughout their operations including the on-site stamping plants.

With the shift to advanced automation at the newer plants, the traditional union stance of clearly defined job descriptions and classifications is giving way to more flexible arrangements like Ford's Modern Operating Agreement at its Wayne, Michigan, on-site stamping facility. Under that agreement, only one category of production worker exists. Each worker receives training on the entire manufacturing process to produce a teamwork approach. Displaced by sophisticated automation, the number of unskilled operators continues to decline. In their place, skilled tradesmen and craft-workers design and maintain the complicated production machinery and its robot servers.

Manufacturers and a growing number of labor leaders see automation as the key to preventing manufacturing facilities from relocating in Mexico with the advent of the North American Free Trade Agreement (NAFTA). Without the competitive edge of tireless automation, the lower wages accepted by Mexican workers would force manufacturers to relocate to stay competitive.

AMERICA AND THE WORLD

The American stamping industry in the 1990s has been playing catch-up with their European and Japanese counterparts. American plants typically wasted twice as much material, used more press operations, and ran presses at half the speed of foreign plants with production runs five times as long. Body panel sets costing $300 in a Japanese plant could cost $700 in its American counterpart. By building newer, more flexible plants and up-grading old presses where possible, American manufacturers are slowly overcoming their impediments.

RESEARCH AND TECHNOLOGY

Modern stamping plants are using advanced technology to redefine themselves. Once the labor-intensive blacksmith shop of the auto industry, stamping now taps the skills and ingenuity of its workers to produce machines and computer monitoring systems to do repetitive work. At a fully automated plant like Ford's $600-million Wayne, Michigan, stamping plant, for example, human operators are used only to load raw steel into the plant and to remove the finished product at the end of the production line. Automatic guided vehicles follow roadways of wires embedded in the factory floor carrying bar-coded metal to the correct storage area or the next press that needs that particular type of material. Transfer presses pass the metal down lines of six or eight similar machines to form complicated components. The completed parts exit the production area, and enter the transfer area where operators manually check them and rack them on a conveyor. Their next stop is the assembly facility.

Transfer presses need less production floor room, but often achieve only 25-30 percent operating efficiency because of their complexity. Simpler, easier to repair robot systems may become the technology of choice where the need for flexibility dominates. Robot systems appeal to small-batch producers like Budd Company. A ''hard-tooled'' automation system like a transfer press line may need expensive retooling every few years, but a ''soft-tooled'' robotic system can be upgraded by reprogramming and minor physical relocations.

The computer has also improved new die design and raw material usage, reducing both the production costs due to wastage and the design time needed for the evolution of a new car. Such programs can reduce the skilled man-hours needed for die face design by 50 percent, die face manufacture by 30 percent, and die tryout and corrective modification by 30 percent. Such improvements went a long way in reducing the traditional domestic car manufacturers' five-year new car design period, putting it in line with Japanese design periods of two or three years.

FURTHER READING

Advances and Trends in Automotive Sheet Steel Stamping. Detroit: SAE International Congress & Exposition, 1988.

''Automakers Cut Steel Costs by Improving Stamping Operations.'' *Iron Age,* May 1988.

Berry, Bryan. ''Chrysler Drawn to Galvannealed.'' *Iron Age,* April 1990.

———. ''U.S. Automakers Overhaul Stamping.'' *Iron Age,* April 1987.

Brooke, Lindsay. ''At Arm's Length.'' *Chilton's Automotive Industries,* June 1993.

———. ''Japan's Stamping Master.'' *Chilton's Automotive Industries,* November 1991.

Davie, Michael. ''Stelco Quality 'Leadership' Gets Nod from Chrysler.'' *Hamilton Spectator,* 22 June 1993.

Fleming, Al. ''Budd Looks to Future after Weathering Bad Times.'' *Automotive News,* 2 February 1987.

———. ''Team Player.'' *Automotive News,* 9 July 1990.

Gould, Les, and Karen Auguston. ''GM's Oshawa Stamping Plant: Integrated Automation at Its Best.'' *Modern Materials Handling,* November 1989.

Harbour, Jim. ''How to Cut Stamping Costs.'' *Automotive Industries,* May 1989.

———. ''On-Site Stamping.'' *Automotive Industries,* September 1991.

Huber, Robert R. ''Technology Keeps Forming Competitive.'' *Production,* August 1990.

Iliescu, Constantin, ed. *Cold-Pressing Technology.* New York: Elsevier Science Publishing Company Inc., 1990.

Manjii, James F. ''GM Oshawa Meets Foreign Competition with Systems Integration.'' *Automation,* October 1991.

McElroy, John. ''Toyota's Stamping Break-Through.'' *Chilton's Automotive Industries,* May 1990.

Noaker, Paula M. ''Revamp Your Stamping Strategy—Not Just the Line.'' *Manufacturing Technologies,* March 1989.

U.S. Bureau of the Census. *1995 Annual Survey of Manufactures.* Washington: GPO, 1997.

U.S. Department of Labor. Bureau of Labor Statistics. *Employment, Hours, and Earnings, United States, 1988-96.* Washington: GPO, 1996.

Vasilash, Gary S. ''Competing.'' *Production,* December 1992.

———. ''Who Says Only the Young Are Innovatively Aggressive?'' *Production,* February 1989.

SIC 3466

CROWNS AND CLOSURES

This category covers establishments primarily engaged in manufacturing metal crowns and closures, including bottle caps and jar crowns and tops.

INDUSTRY SNAPSHOT

The crowns and closures industrial classification is a small portion of the stamped metals industry that is fading into a highly segmented industry. As bottlers seek lower production costs, more tamper-evident packaging, and better printability for product differentiation, many continue to move away from metal closures, preferring plastic ones instead. Despite this shift, shipments in the metal crowns and closures industry increased in the early and mid-1990s, moving from $720.2 million in 1990 to $770.9 million in 1995. Shipments reached a peak in 1993 at $837.1 million. Much of the increase was attributed to a shortage in plastic closures, forcing some bottlers to turn to metal. Employment in this industry, however, has steadily fallen. In 1983, this industry employed 7,100 people, 5,700 of whom were production workers. By 1995, this total was 4,300, with 3,500 production workers.

ORGANIZATION AND STRUCTURE

The product share of this industry is split into three sections. Metal commercial closures and metal home canning closures comprise 84.39 percent of the total market, and metal crowns for glass and metal containers represent 14.08 percent. The remaining 1.53 percent is represented by non-specific crowns and closures. Aluminum, in the form of sheet, plate, and foil, is proportionately the industry's largest input. Tin plate, tin free steel, terneplate, and blackplate represent the second most highly consumed materials. Carbon steel sheet and strips are also used.

Bottled and canned soft drink manufacturers use up 22.3 percent of the industry's outputs. Malt beverage makers use 10.6 percent; pickles, sauces, and salad dressings consume 10.5 percent; and canned fruits and vegetables take 7.7 percent of the industry's outputs. The industry's products are also used in the packaging of roasted coffee, wines, brandy, brandy spirits, toilet preparations, and confectionery products.

CURRENT CONDITIONS

Industry sales have picked up somewhat in the mid-1990s, since a high worldwide demand for polypropylene, a type of resin used to manufacture plastic closures, slowed the shift from metal to plastic closures. At the same time, some bottlers' market research has showed that in certain cases, consumers actually prefer metal closures over plastic. Alcoa, for example, found that consumers favor the popping sound aluminum closures make when a vacuum-packed glass bottle is opened. That technology doesn't yet exist in plastic closures, so some select segments of the beverage market are moving back to aluminum.

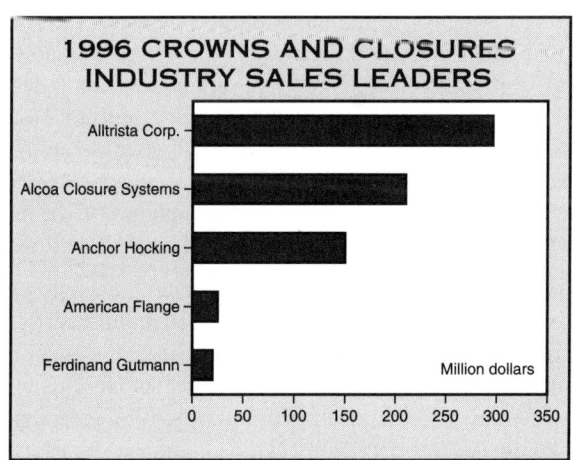

1996 CROWNS AND CLOSURES INDUSTRY SALES LEADERS

INDUSTRY LEADERS

Of the top six producers in the industry in 1996, the Alltrista Corporation ranked as the industry leader with sales of $296 million. Alcoa Closure Systems International was ranked second, with sales of $210 million. Third-ranked Anchor Hocking Packaging Company had sales of $150 million. Other industry leaders included American Flange and Manufacturing Company , Inc. with $25 million in sales; Ferdinand Gutmann and Co. with $20 million; and Allen Stevens Drum Accessories Co. with $6 million. These top six companies employed a total of 5,500 people in 1996.

Industry leader Alltrista Corporation is best known for its Ball home canning jars and closures; the Ball brand dates back to 1884. In addition to producing metal closures, the company's metal fabrication operations manufacture a wide range of zinc-based products, from battery cans to coin blanks to industrial components. In 1996 Alltrista acquired the Kerr Group, Inc., another maker of home canning products, and consolidated Kerr's manufacturing facility into Alltrista's existing operations. To complement its line of home canning products, Alltrista also makes a variety of food preservation products used in canning.

Alcoa is the world's largest integrated aluminum company, with operating and sales locations in 28 countries. Its products are used primarily by packaging, transportation, building, and industrial customers. In the metal crowns and closures industry, the company is best known for aluminum beverage container closures; it produces these closures in Richmond, Indiana; Worms, Germany; Nogi and Ichikawa, Japan; and near Barcelona, Spain. The company also makes equipment used for applying plastic or aluminum closures to beverage containers. Alcoa's 1995 annual report explains that the company "continues to examine all aspects of its operations and activities and redesign them where necessary to enhance effectiveness and achieve cost reductions. Alcoa believes that its competitive position is enhanced by its improved processes, extensive facilities and willingness and ability to commit capital where necessary to meet growth in important markets and by the capability of its employees."

Anchor Hocking Packaging Company is a subsidiary of Crown Cork & Seal, which makes numerous packaging products for consumer goods. Crown's products include not only metal closures, but also metal cans, plastic containers, and metal specialty and promotional packaging products. The company also manufactures filling and material handling machinery for the beverage and brewing industries, as well as machinery used in can manufacturing.

WORK FORCE

Machine operators in the fabricated metal products industry earned about $510 a week in 1994. This is somewhat less than many other metalworking and plastics-working machine operators; those in primary metals industries earned $640 weekly and those in industrial machinery and equipment earned $570.

Employment is expected to decline through the year 2005 for both metalworking and plastics-working machine operators. Those employed in metalworking are likely to be affected more than those in plastics; this is because in recent years, plastic products have increasingly been used in place of metal in consumer and manufacturing products. Another reason for the employment decline is the widespread use of computer-controlled production equipment.

AMERICA AND THE WORLD

According to Alltrista's 1996 annual Report, the home canning products segment of this industry was hampered by a poor U.S. growing season in both 1995 and 1996, resulting in lower earnings for establishments producing these products. Since the odds of having three poor growing seasons in a row are not high, Alltrista expects sales of home canning products to improve in 1997 and beyond.

RESEARCH AND TECHNOLOGY

A new development in aluminum can closures surfaced in 1996, building on the existing concept of the "eco-lid." The eco-lid is a tab that allows the consumer to open a beverage can by pushing the lid inside the body of the container. The lid stays attached to the can, reducing solid waste. Some hygienic concerns still exist over the eco-lid, since the beverage may come in contact with the exposed part of the package that gets pushed inside the can. An innovation called S.H.E.S (which stands for "Safe, Hygienic, Easy, Simple") addresses this concern with a fully recyclable dispenser inside the can. The dispenser is pulled out when the can is opened. S.H.E.S. represents about a 5 percent production cost increase over current can closure technologies. As of early 1997, this development has not been widely adopted by closure manufacturers.

FURTHER READING

Alltrista Corporation. *1996 Annual Report.* 1997.

"Alltrista Corporation Profile." Alltrista Corporation 1997. Available from http://www.alltrista.com.

Aluminum Company of America. *1995 Annual Report.* 1996.

Bureau of Labor Statistics. *Metalworking and Plastics-Working Machine Operators.* GPO, 1996. Available from http://www.stats.bls.gov.

Darnay, Arsen J., ed. *Manufacturing USA.* 5th ed. Detroit: Gale Research, 1996.

Sfiligoj, Eric. "Cap Squeeze." *Beverage World,* June 1995.

————. "S.H.E.S.' the One." *Beverage World,* September 1996.

U.S. Department of Commerce. *1995 Annual Survey of Manufactures.* Washington: GPO, 1996.

—Valerie Wilson, updated by Janette Maurene Brooks

SIC 3469

METAL STAMPINGS, NOT ELSEWHERE CLASSIFIED

This category includes establishments primarily engaged in manufacturing metal stampings and spun products, not elsewhere classified, including porcelain enameled products. Products of this industry include household appliance housings and parts, cooking and kitchen utensils, and other nonautomotive job stampings.

The largest portion of the industry stamps metal for motor homes, aviation, agricultural equipment, computers, electrical appliances, radios, televisions, kitchen appliances, and laundry equipment. Cooking and kitchen utensils, such as tea kettles, metal spoons, baking pans, and stainless steel mixing bowls, claim a distinct majority of the industry's product base. In 1995, aluminum made up 39.4 percent of cookware shipments, and bakeware accounted for 22.7 percent.

The stamping industry is currently entering into a new age of technology. Although computer aided drafting and manufacturing tools have been used to great advantage in the metal cutting industry, the related metal forming industries have not used available software tools. Specialized software is now being developed to add precision to the stamping process. Not only does computer software design better stamping dies, but it can also be interfaced with the machinery to tell the operator when the die is beginning to dull, or when the machine itself is beginning to malfunction.

The implementation of computer technology helps manufacturers reduce costs throughout machining operations. For larger production lines, the area of specialty tooling is gaining importance as more companies cut costs and competition grows. With specialty tooling, several operations can be combined by using unique punch dies. Louver, countersink, embossing, lettering, and lance-and-form tools are gaining popularity as more industry leaders seek to improve product quality and cost through process redesign.

Over 2,700 companies were engaged in the metal stamping industry in 1988. That year, the industry employed 97,000 people at an average hourly wage of $9.65. The value of shipments increased $2 billion between 1982 and 1988, while employment levels remained stable. A large reason for the increase in shipment values was the rising cost of materials. In 1995, the value of product shipments was $11.89 billion.

By 1998, the industry's employment rate was expected to fall to about 91,000; the number of establishments was also expected to decrease to about 2,677. The value of shipments was estimated to be over $12 billion.

Significant reductions in the labor pool are expected in several production line occupations by the year 2005. The largest segment of employment in the industry is occupied by metal and plastic forming machine operators. However, this segment is expected to be one of the hardest hit, with over 65 percent of the positions being eliminated. Other occupations facing reductions include welding machine setters and machine feeders (23 percent), assemblers and fabricators (18 percent), precision inspectors, truck and tractor operators, and sheet metal workers (15 percent), and cutting tool operators (13 percent). The only occupations expected to grow more than 10 percent include punching machine operators, combination machine tool operators, and machine tool cutting and forming.

In 1997, some of the industry's leaders were New Jersey-based US Industries Incorporated, with sales over $2 billion, Hexcel Corporation of California, with sales over $300 million, and Michigan-based JSJ Corporation with sales over $270 million. California had the most establishments with 352; Illinois had 316 and Ohio had 251. Together, these three states employed 31.5 percent of the U.S. total. Illinois had the highest percentage of U.S. shipments with 16.9 percent, Ohio generated 10.4 percent, and California contributed 7.2 percent.

FURTHER READING

Darnay, Arsen J., ed. *Manufacturing USA*. Detroit: Gale Research, 1996.

Gettelman, Ken. "Pressworking Joins the Computer Revolution." *Modern Machine Shop,* March 1992.

Lazich, Robert S., ed. *Market Share Reporter.* Detroit: Gale Research, 1997.

Sheridan, Gary. "Creative Tooling for Punch Presses." *Modern Machine Shop,* March 1992.

U.S. Bureau of the Census. *1995 Annual Survey of Manufactures.* Washington: GPO, January, 1997.

SIC 3471

ELECTROPLATING, PLATING, POLISHING, ANODIZING AND COLORING

This category includes establishments primarily engaged in all types of electroplating, plating, anodizing, coloring, and finishing of metals and formed products for the trade. Also included in this industry are establishments that perform these types of activities on their own account, on purchased metals or formed products. Establishments that both manufacture and finish products are classified according to the products.

INDUSTRY SNAPSHOT

The value of the industry's shipments in 1996 was an estimated $5.7 billion, up from $2.7 billion in 1982. There were just under 3,200 firms in the industry in 1996, 34 percent of which had 20 or more employees, up from 26 percent in 1982. In 1994, average firm size in the industry as measured by production workers per establishment was 50 percent lower than that of the typical manufacturing industry.

ORGANIZATION AND STRUCTURE

In the 1990s, there were two types of firms in the industry: small, private corporations and large, publicly held companies that were either subsidiaries or divisions of larger parent corporations. Of the top five firms in the industry in the late 1990s, one was a subsidiary and one a division; 88 percent of the leading 75 firms were private corporations.

While larger firms were often more diversified in the number of electroplating and finishing processes they utilized, smaller firms tended to specialize in one or two types of finishing processes. During the 1950s and 1960s, many companies established their own finishing operations, but with the onset of increased environmental regulation of the industry in the 1970s, many manufacturing firms opted to subcontract for finishing services, thus avoiding the added costs of waste treatment. In the 1990s, the trend once again was for manufacturing firms to own and operate their own finishing operations, often integrating production and finishing processes.

The states ranking in the top ten by value of shipments in the early 1990s were, in ranking order: California, Ohio, Illinois, Michigan, Indiana, Pennsylvania, Connecticut, New York, Tennessee, and Massachusetts. Together these states accounted for 70 percent of the industry's total shipments and 68 percent of its total employment.

BACKGROUND AND DEVELOPMENT

Historically, the most important activity in this industry was electroplating. Electroplating entailed adhering a thin metal coating to an object by immersing it into an electrically charged solvent containing the dissolved plating metal. Metals commonly used in plating included copper, nickel, chromium, zinc, lead, cadmium, tin, brass, and bronze, as well as precious metals such as gold, silver, and platinum. Electroplating served a number of functions, such as protecting from corrosion and wear, decoration, and electrical shielding.

Alessandro Volta's creation of the battery in 1800 first made electroplating possible. Commercial electroplating began around 1840. Before the development of commercial nickel plating in the 1910s, the metals most commonly used for plating were silver, gold, and brass. Nickel plating tarnished and developed green corrosion, but that problem was eradicated in the late 1920s with the development of commercially practical chromium plating. This was a key development in the history of the industry, especially in regard to plating applications for the automobile and appliance industries. Though nonmetallic materials had been electroplated since the mid-nineteenth century, they became increasingly important for the industry after the 1963 development of ABS plastic, which lent itself to electroplating.

Of increasing importance for the industry in the 1980s and early 1990s was plating utilized as electrical shielding, particularly for the plastic housings of computers. The Crown City Plating Company, based in El Monte, California, developed the electroless process used for such shielding around 1970.

The solvents used to dissolve plating metals often were highly toxic. Cyanide, for example, was a commonly used solvent. In addition to being one of the most toxic of commonly found pollutants, its toxicity was heightened when mixed with certain plating metals. Cyanide also interfered with water treatment processes and formed a toxic gas when converted to an acid. Of the plating metals, cadmium, chromium, and lead were the most problematic. The increasing regulation of the use of such solvents had a great impact on the industry's development.

Key statutes affecting the industry included the Federal Water Pollution Control Act Amendments of 1972, the Resource Conservation and Recovery Act of 1976, the Clean Water Act of 1977, and the Comprehensive Environmental Response, Compensation and Liability Act of 1980, better known as Superfund.

The number of enforcement actions by the Environmental Protection Agency (EPA) increased steadily from the late 1980s into the 1990s. In 1996, a record number of criminal enforcement actions were taken by the EPA. In that year, criminal fines amounted to more than double the previous record. A record 262 criminal cases were referred by the EPA to the Department of Justice in 1996, and $76.7 million in criminal fines were assessed. Total criminal, civil, and administrative fines and penalties in 1996 were the highest in EPA history, totaling $173 million, indicating that pollution abatement would continue to be a key issue for the industry.

The significant effect of environmental and safety regulations on the industry was suggested by the aims of one of the industry's trade organizations. Founded in 1955 and located in Chicago, the National Association of Metal Finishers (NAMF) had 850 members in the late 1990s who were managing executives of firms in the industry. Often committees of the NAMF were devoted to issues of regulation.

Difficulties facing the industry from the 1970s through the 1990s included increasing production costs, excessive competition, and a shortage of experienced employees. Excessive competition had a number of implications, one of which was the relatively slow rate of productivity growth in the industry. From 1958 to 1974, the value added per production worker hour more than quadrupled for computers and related machines and doubled for motor vehicles and parts and household laundry equipment. During the same period, the metal finishing industry experienced only a 17 percent increase. As of 1994, the value added per production worker in the plating industry was only half that of the average of the manufacturing sector as a whole.

CURRENT CONDITIONS

A 1992 study of the industry's future concluded that development of the industry lay in the nature of environmental regulations as well as future demand for more sophisticated finishes. As parts to be finished became larger and more complex, finishing processes also became more complex.

Demand for the industry's products was dependent on the demand for durable goods, and thus dependent on growth in the manufacturing sector at large. Growth and profitability also were dependent on the creation of environmentally safe manufacturing techniques. The pace of technical change was brisk entering the 1990s, which suggested that the industry could meet environmental and safety regulations in a cost-effective manner.

In the 1990s, capital investment in the industry was very low compared to the average capital expenditure in all other manufacturing industries. In 1994, the average investment per establishment in the metal finishing industry was 83 percent below the national average for manufacturing industries. This enabled relatively easy entry into the industry and accounted for the large number of small, often family-owned, private firms.

The ease of entry into the industry made for highly competitive conditions in which small, independent companies were positioned between large suppliers of finishing machinery and materials and the large corporations for which they provided services. This meant relatively low profits for small manufacturers.

Smaller firms' dilemma of keeping abreast of innovative techniques was exacerbated by their need to adhere to a host of environmental regulations. This problem was deepened by the less sophisticated control procedures many smaller companies were forced to utilize due to lower cost. For example, quality finishes could only be obtained through highly sophisticated processes often unavailable to smaller firms.

One bright spot for smaller companies arose from the EPA's own broad mandate to regulate industry with an overstretched budget. In 1995, the EPA proposed deferring Clean Air Act operating permit requirements for non-major sources in three industries, one being the decorative chromium electroplating and chromium anodizing segment. The EPA recognized the difficulty small businesses had in meeting the requirements and the massive assistance they would require from regulators. The deferral would last for five years; certain electroplating operations would be exempted permanently.

INDUSTRY LEADERS

In the late 1990s, the three largest firms in the industry were USS-Posco Industries, based in Pittsburgh, California; Siegel-Robert Inc. of St. Louis, Missouri; and Plastene Supply Company of Portageville, Missouri—a division of Siegel-Robert.

Together these three firms accounted for 54 percent of total sales for the industry. The rapid consolidation of the industry was evident in a striking statistic:

in the early 1990s, the three largest establishments in the industry accounted for only 16 percent of total sales.

With roughly $800 million in annual sales and 1,000 employees, USS-Posco was by far the largest firm in the industry in the late 1990s. A subsidiary of the USX Corporation, USS-Posco was created from a 1986 joint venture with the Korean Pohang Iron and Steel Corporation and was intended to rescue U.S. Steel's Pittsburgh plant.

Its success was evidenced by the subsidiary's 1996 study of a possible $100 million upgrade of its tinplate and tin-free facilities in Pittsburgh; if completed, the upgrade would allow the firm to make 48-inch-wide tinplate, the widest in the United States. In 1997, USS-Posco also planned to complete the $15 million expansion of a coating line facility to improve its galvanized steel capacity, which would be boosted by 7 percent. In 1996, the Pittsburgh facility also earned ISO 9002 certification. However, low steel prices in the late 1990s kept the firm's stock price low, and plunging profits for parent Pohang Iron clouded USS-Posco's future.

The second-largest firm in this industry in the late 1990s was Siegel-Robert Inc., a private company founded in 1947. Siegel-Robert had 1995 sales of $375 million and employed 3,500. Plastene Supply Company, a subsidiary of Siegel-Robert, was third-largest; the firm had 800 employees and $57 million in 1995 revenue.

WORK FORCE

The industry employed 79,700 workers in 1995, up from 62,000 in 1982. The industry was relatively labor-intensive, having an average of only 33 percent of the investment per production worker as that of the manufacturing sector as a whole. Annual hours worked by production workers in the industry were about the same as those averaged by production workers in a typical manufacturing industry, while hourly wages were 21 percent lower.

For workers in the industry, continued competition brought uncertainty, but increases in employment for most job positions were predicted through the year 2005 for the overall metal services industry. The U.S. Census Bureau projected fewer firms in the industry by 1998, but a higher percentage of them would be larger and employ more workers. Thus, a shakeout of smaller firms appeared inevitable.

RESEARCH AND TECHNOLOGY

Throughout the 1990s, many significant technical developments in the industry arose in response to environmental regulation. The Torrington Company of Connecticut demonstrated a method to recover cadmium and chromium from electroplating rinsewaters. In one study using the ion exchange method, both cadmium and cyanide were removed, sometimes to below detection levels, while the pH of the rinsewater remained constant. Following the exchange, cadmium was recovered and regenerated, while less cyanide was necessary for wastewater treatment.

In the 1990s, pollution prevention methods often took the path of reducing the need to coat or plate at all, sometimes by using coating-free materials such as titanium, reinforced plastics, weathering steel, and aluminum alloys. In addition, alternatives to traditional coating systems were found in emerging technologies. Studies found promise in nonelectroplating methods, including electron-beam cured coatings, super-critical carbon dioxide coating systems, and radiation-induced thermally cured coatings.

Some of the most promising technologies, such as the dry application of metal powders, were classified in **SIC 3479: Metal Coating & Allied Services.** The success of such techniques was expected to lead to a shift in production away from the plating industry.

Sandia National Laboratories in Albuquerque developed methods for gold-plating onto microelectronic devices that did not use cyanide. Metal-ceramic coatings were substituted for cadmium coatings for certain high-priced parts. Handy and Harman Electronic Metals Corporation, the seventh-largest firm in the industry, developed a formable silver-tin oxide as a replacement for silver-cadmium oxide for coating electrical contacts. Previously used silver-tin oxides were not formable, so the process of applying them was more labor-intensive and costly. In addition to their reduced environmental hazard, silver-tin oxides were also more highly conductive.

GE Research and Development devised a method for nickel-plating plastics to shield computer housings. This process did not use chromium—unlike Crown City Plating's process—and was applied with a water-based solution.

FURTHER READING

Abrahamson, Peggy. "EPA Sets Record for Case Actions." *American Metal Market,* 13 December 1991.

"Anodizing Protects Aircraft." *Defense-News,* 29 November 1992.

Arnett, Harold E., and Donald N. Smith. *The Metal Finishing Industry: A Framework for Success.* Ann Arbor, MI: University of Michigan, 1977.

Bassett, Susan M. "Title V Permitting Delayed for Some Non-Major Sources." *Pollution Engineering,* 1 March 1996.

Brenner, Abner. *Electrodeposition of Alloys: Principles and Practice.* New York: Academic Press, 1963.

Cherry, Kenneth F. *Plating Waste Treatment.* Ann Arbor, MI: Ann Arbor Science Publishers Inc., 1982.

Darnay, Arsen J., ed. *Manufacturing USA.* 5th ed. Detroit, Gale Research, 1996.

Dubpernell, George. *Electrodeposition of Chromium from Chromic Acid Solutions.* New York: Pergamon Press Inc., 1977.

Haflich, Frank. "USS-Posco Expansion Spurs Further Growth on West Coast." *American Metal Market,* 6 August 1996.

———. "USS-Posco Eyes Full Capacity Output, Profits." *American Metal Market,* 16 December 1991.

———. "USS-Posco Weighs $100M Tin Upgrade." *American Metal Market,* 6 December 1996.

"Impingement: The Key to Effective Aqueous Cleaning." *Metal-Finishing,* August 1992.

"Industry Activities: An Advanced Vapor Degreasing Technology." *Metal-Finishing,* July 1993.

Industry Norms and Key Business Ratios. New York: Dun and Bradstreet Information Services, 1982/83-1992/93.

Institute of Metal Finishing. *Nickel-Chromium Plating.* Teddington: Robert Draper Ltd., 1961.

Jaszczak, Sandra, ed. *Encyclopedia of Associations.* 32nd ed. Detroit: Gale Research, 1997.

"Mass Finishing in the '90s." *Metal-Finishing,* March 1992.

"Metal Finishing Not Bright." *Chemical Week,* 14 April 1993.

"Metallic-Ceramic Coating Replacing Plating with Cadmium for Expensive Parts." *Machine Design,* 23 July 1993.

Moody's Industrial Manual. New York: Moody's Investors Service Inc., 1992.

O'Sullivan, Orla. "New H&H Alloy Makes Gains." *American Metal Market,* 20 January 1993.

Park, Kyung Hee. "Analysts Warn Depressed Prices of Steel Will Keep Posco Down." *Asian Wall Street Journal Weekly,* 28 October 1996.

"Plating Polycarbonate." *Appliance Manufacturer,* August 1992.

"Plunge in Profits for Pohang Iron." *The New York Times,* 5 March 1997.

Quinn, Barbara. "EPA Does Pollution Prevention Research." *Pollution Engineering,* 1 September 1995.

———. "Looking at Technology We Already Own." *Pollution Engineering,* 1 January 1996.

———. "The Surface Coating Industries Try on New Coats." *Pollution Engineering,* 1 February 1995.

Raub, E., and K. Muller. *Fundamentals of Metal Deposition.* Amsterdam: Elsevier Publishing Company, 1967.

"RCRA Settlements Garner $6 Million More." *Chemical and Engineering News,* 24 May 1993.

Robertson, Scott. "Blending Cultures at Pittsburgh, California." *New Steel,* July 1994.

Ross, Robert B. *Handbook of Metal Treatments and Testing.* London: E. & F. N. Spon Ltd., 1977.

"Sandia Develops Safer Microelectronic Plating Process." *Mechanical-Engineering,* December 1991.

Sterner, Bob. "Electronic Shielding Process Uses Chromium." *American Metal Market,* 6 August 1992.

U.S. Environmental Protection Agency. *Enforcement Records Set for 1996,* 25 February 1997. Available from http://www.epa.gov/docs/PressReleases/1997/February/Day-26/pr-1009.html.

"US Steelmakers' Complaint Imperils Korean Venture." *Journal of Commerce,* 8 July 1992.

USS-Posco. *USS-Posco Corporate History.* Pittsburgh, California. Available from http://www.uss-posco.com/.

Viani, Laura. "Parties Squabble Over Posco Policy." *American Metal Market,* 2 July 1993.

—David Kucera, updated by Tim Eigo

SIC 3479

COATING, ENGRAVING, AND ALLIED SERVICES, NOT ELSEWHERE CLASSIFIED

This industry includes establishments primarily engaged in performing the following types of services on metals, for the trade: (1) enameling, lacquering, and varnishing metal products; (2) hot dip galvanizing of mill sheets, plates and bars, castings, and formed products fabricated of iron and steel; hot dip coating such items with aluminum, lead, or zinc; retinning cans and utensils; (3) engraving, chasing, and etching jewelry, silverware, notarial, and other seals, and other metal products for purposes other than printing; and (4) other metal services, not elsewhere classified. Also included in this industry are establishments that perform these types of activities on their own account on purchased metals or formed products. Establishments that both manufacture and finish products were classified according to the products.

INDUSTRY SNAPSHOT

The value of product shipments in 1995 was approximately $7.0 billion, up from $4.9 billion in 1990. The industry consisted of 2,008 establishments in the mid-1990s, the majority (22 percent) of which had between 20 and 49 employees.

Growth of output and employment stagnated entering the 1990s, but profit rates remained close to the average for the period 1982 to 1992. The industry stood to benefit from projected growth in the use of galvanized steel and in the use of alternatives to electroplating that it offered.

ORGANIZATION AND STRUCTURE

Of the top four firms in the industry, three were subsidiaries and one a public independent. Of the top 75 firms in the industry, 49 percent were private independents in the early 1990s. Whereas larger firms were often more diversified in their finishing activities, independents tended to specialize in one or two types of finishing. There was a tendency for manufacturing firms to set up their own finishing operations during the 1950s and 1960s. With the increased environmental regulation of the industry beginning in the 1970s, many manufacturing firms opted to subcontract for finishing services, thus getting around the added costs of waste treatment. Entering the 1990s, the tendency was once again for manufacturing firms to undertake finishing operations, often integrating production and finishing processes.

The capital requirements of the industry were low compared to the average for manufacturing. Average investment per establishment was only 27 percent for the manufacturing sector as a whole in 1989. This enabled relatively easy entry into the industry, and accounted for the large number of small private firms, often family proprietorships.

Parts to be finished were typically shipped to finishing firms by their customers, after which they were shipped back. Since the mid-1970s, about three-fourths of a finishing firm's business came from within a 50-to-75-mile radius of the firm. Since finishers needed to be near their customers, their operations were located in the same areas as producers of durable goods.

The states ranking in the top ten by value of shipments in the late 1980s were, in order of descending value: Ohio, California, Illinois, Pennsylvania, Texas, Indiana, New York, New Jersey, Massachusetts, and Connecticut. Together these states accounted for 74 percent of total shipments and 65 percent of total employment.

The outputs of the metal-coating industry were dispersed somewhat more widely across industry lines than the outputs of the metal-plating industry. The top ten industry segments buying the outputs of the metal-coating industry in 1982 made up 50 percent of the total output sold. Those segments were: prefabricated metal buildings (10.0 percent), sheet metal work (6.2 percent), crowns and closures (5.4 percent), electronic components, not elsewhere classified (5.1 percent), fabricated structural metal (4.9 percent), blast furnaces and steel mills (4.5 percent), metal cans (3.8 percent), x-ray apparatus and tubes (3.7 percent), motor vehicles and car bodies (3.3 percent), and metal coating and allied services (3.1 percent).

BACKGROUND AND DEVELOPMENT

Just over one-half of the output of this industry consisted of the application of organic coatings such as paints, varnishes, and lacquers. Although metals had been coated by like means since ancient times, their modern application was dependent on the development of phosphating as a surface preparation. Phosphating involved treating a metal, usually steel, with phosphoric acid. This greatly improved the adhesion and durability of coatings. Phosphating alone was also used as an anti-corrosive coating on steel in conditions where the potential for corrosion was not high. Although phosphating was developed in the 1860s, treatment times were exceedingly long until iron filings were added to the phosphoric acid bath after 1906 (following Thomas Watts Coslett's patent), shortening treatment time to about two-and-one-half hours. The treatment time was shortened to ten minutes by the addition of copper salts in 1929, after which the process became generally used as a surface preparation for organic coatings. More recent developments lowered treatment times to just five seconds.

Next to the application of organic coatings, galvanizing was the largest activity in the industry, making up 22 percent of output. Metal coating and allied services, not specified by kind, made up 21 percent of output; and the remaining 6 percent consisted of engraved and etched products.

Galvanizing is the process of dipping steel or iron into a bath of molten zinc. The zinc coating served as a corrosion prohibitor, and was applied to structural parts, sheeting, pipe, various containers, and hardware. During this process, the metal to be coated was immersed until it reached the same temperature as the bath (typically 1,562 degrees Fahrenheit). Thus, the process could not be used on springs or other objects in which desirable properties would be lost by such exposure to heat. Since uniformity of thickness was not

readily controllable in hot dip processes, galvanizing was limited to applications in which such uniformity was not required. Electroplating with zinc was sometimes also referred to as galvanizing or electrogalvanizing. This process was done cold, and could assure high uniformity of thickness, getting around the above-mentioned problems.

As with all metal-coating processes, it was vital that parts were thoroughly cleaned before being galvanized. This typically involved treating the parts to be galvanized in an acid bath, after which they were fluxed, a process that generally used hydrochloric acid. The wastes produced by such pre-treatment were toxic, as were the solvents used in the organic coatings processes. The minimization of such wastes continued to be central issues for the industry, as did the development of alternative solvents.

The industry is served by the National Association of Metal Finishers, located in Chicago, Illinois. Founded in 1955, the Association had 850 members in the mid-1990s, who typically are managing executives of firms in the industry. The American Galvanizers Association (AGA) also serves the industry. Founded in 1935, it has 150 members, who are galvanizers, material and equipment suppliers, and service companies in the industry.

CURRENT CONDITIONS

Growth prospects for firms involved in galvanizing appeared promising entering the mid-1990s. By 1996, the vast majority of automobiles with steel bodies were expected to feature two-sided galvanized steel. The Intermodal Surface Transportation Efficiency Act of 1991 required that all highways, bridges, and tunnels built with federal funds take into account the costs of materials over their life-cycles. This strongly favored the use of galvanized metals. The American Galvanizers Association estimated early in the decade that use of galvanized steel would double through the 1990s, largely as a result of increased use for highways, bridges, and wastewater treatment systems.

The most promising of the environmentally friendlier alternatives to electroplating were the application of metal powders and vacuum deposition, processes that were projected to become increasingly important. Thus, the effects of environmental regulation provided substantial benefits to the industry, and growth prospects appeared promising. From the perspective of the firms, the question remained whether plating or coating firms could more readily diversify into these technologies.

The relative ease of entry into the industry made for highly competitive conditions in which small independents were sandwiched between the large suppliers of finishing machinery and materials and the large firms for which they provided services. This meant relatively low profits for independents. Profit rates varied greatly among firms in the industry. Taking rates of return on equity, a firm ranking at the median had less than half the profitability of a firm ranking at the upper quartile.

Theoretical knowledge, as opposed to empirical knowledge rapidly increased in importance in the 1990s. Equipment and material suppliers developed many new techniques. Thus, smaller firms were able to obtain some of the same innovations as larger firms. Nonetheless, given the greater purchasing power of the captive and large independent firms, suppliers allocated a disproportionate amount of their research and technical support to such firms.

Another issue inhibiting investment by smaller firms in more capital-intensive techniques was that, unlike large captive firms, they were less able to absorb the losses resulting from excess capacity in the face of an economic downturn. Because the greater profitability of the more successful firms could be used to finance techniques that were more productive and sophisticated, the gap between large captive firms and smaller independents was likely to remain, if not widen.

INDUSTRY LEADERS

As of the mid-1990s, the three largest firms were: Engineered Materials of Iseline, New Jersey (with $1.2 billion in sales and approximately 1,500 employees); Material Sciences Corp. of Elk Grove Village, Illinois (with $228 million in sales and 900 employees); and Acheson Colloids Co. of Port Huron, Michigan (with $130 million in sales and 1,100 employees).

WORK FORCE

The number of industry employees increased from 44,100 in 1990 to an estimated 49,700 in 1996, 38,500 of which were production workers earning approximately $11.58 per hour. In 1998, the number of production workers is expected to increase to 39,800 workers earning $12.24 per hour.

AMERICA AND THE WORLD

Demand for paint and coatings is expected to rise through the year 2000, reaching a total of $18 billion, according to a report from the Freedonia Group, Inc. in Cleveland, Ohio. This should amount to an approximate 2-percent growth per year until 2000. Due to Environmental Protection Agency (EPA) regulations, the pressure will be felt most in the industrial coatings sector. The enforcement of these regulations made environmentally friendly powder solvents and high solids more popular. Because of this, the market for powder and radiation-curable coatings will see the greatest market gains, of approximately 9 percent, through the year 2000.

RESEARCH AND TECHNOLOGY

As with the metal-plating industry, a number of innovations in the metal-coating industry were motivated by increasingly pressing environmental regulations. For the process of stripping coatings from rejected parts, blasting with plastic particles was seen as a viable alternative to the more toxic methods of chemical stripping and incineration. In the early 1990s, Whirlpool Corp. installed a pre-treating line in its Evanston, Illinois, plant that made use of a safer alternative to traditional phosphating. The line used a chrome-free rinse and cleaners that lessened the production of heavy metal wastes. The new line also improved the quality of coatings and consumed less energy.

New developments in the deposition of metal coatings were expected to possibly cause a shift away from electroplating to alternative methods, such as new forms of vacuum deposition. This process involved reducing pressure in a closed container to produce a vacuum in which pure metals could be vaporized at low temperatures and then allowed to condense on a surface. Laboratory tests of new vacuum methods produced high-quality coatings with fast coating times. Vacuum coating also had the significant advantage that it did not generate the toxic sludges of electroplating processes. Another technology of increasing importance was the application of metal powders by spraying or through the use of centrifugal force. As with vacuum deposition, such applications of metal powders had the significant advantage that they did not produce toxic sludges.

While the initial costs of pollution abatement technologies may have been prohibitive to some firms, a number of these technologies could lower production costs. The BASE Corp. reported that pollution abatement measures at two of its coating plants saved it $1.3 million in the early 1990s, and that the payback period after initial investments ranged from 15 to 20 months. New technologies in the application of powder coatings made them not only an environmentally friendlier, but also a cost-effective alternative to electroplating.

FURTHER READING

Arnett, Harold E., and Donald N. Smith. *The Metal Finishing Industry: A Framework for Success.* Ann Arbor, MI: University of Michigan, 1977.

Cage, W.E., Jr. "Specialty Chemical Conference—Industry Report." *Wheat First Butcher & Singer, Inc.* 24 March 1992.

Darnay, Arsen J., ed. *Manufacturing USA.* 5th ed. Detroit: Gale Research, 1996.

Freeman, D.B. *Phosphating and Metal Pre-Treatment: A Guide to Modern Processes and practice.* New York: Industrial Press Inc., 1986.

Gannon, Virginia. "Highway Bill's Life-Cycle Clause May Boost Galvanizing." *American-Metal-Market,* 14 July 1992.

"Green Powder Coatings Come to the Forefront." *Performance Chemicals,* March 1992.

Industry Norms and Key Business Ratios. New York: Dun & Bradstreet Information Services, 1982/83-1992/93.

Izenberg, Jerry. "Paint, Coating Demand to Hit $18 Billion in U.S." *Rubber World,* December 1996.

"Mass Finishing in the '90s." *Metal-Finishing,* March 1992.

Murphy, H. Lee. "Material Eyes Stock Deal." *Crain's Chicago Business,* 12 July 1992.

"New Arc Method Could Spark Shift to Vacuum Coatings." *Research and-Development,* June 1992.

"The Road to Faultless Finishing." *Appliance-Manufacturer,* April 1993.

Ross, Robert B. *Handbook of Metal Treatments and Testing.* London: E. & F.N. Spon Ltd., 1977.

"A Safe and Cost-Efficient Method of Stripping Rejected Parts." *Metal-Finishing,* April 1992.

Scolieri, Peter. "Two Coating Lines Planned: 1994 Start-Up Set by Precoat Metals, Consolidated Systems." *American-Metal-Market,* 5 October 1992.

"U.S. Powder Coatings Industry Growing Strong." *Paint-and-Coatings Industry,* June 1993.

"Waste Minimization Pays Off at Base Coating Facilities." *Modern Paint and Coatings,* July 1992.

—David Kucera, updated Luann Brennan

SIC 3482

SMALL ARMS AMMUNITION

This industry includes establishments primarily engaged in manufacturing ammunition for small arms having a bore of 30 mm (1.18 inches) or less. Establishments primarily engaged in manufacturing ammunition, except for small arms, are classified in **SIC 3483: Ammunition, Except for Small Arms;** those manufacturing blasting and detonating caps and safety fuses are classified in **SIC 2892: Explosives;** and those manufacturing fireworks are classified in **SIC 2899: Chemicals and Chemical Preparations, Not Elsewhere Classified.**

INDUSTRY SNAPSHOT

The use of projectiles propelled by gunpowder played an important role in the settling, and subsequent defense, of the United States when Europeans first landed on American soil. By the 1990s, spurred by sport, defense, and construction markets, the U.S. small arms ammunition industry had grown into a $175 million business, employing about 2,000 workers. Although the ammunition industry approximated the size of the firearms industry, ammunition producers operated in relative obscurity.

Heading into the mid-1990s, ammo makers were engaged in fierce competition to maintain their share of a mature industry characterized by homogenous products. To boost sales and differentiate their products, manufacturers were offering specialized merchandise that appealed to niche market segments. They were also striving to increase productivity through automation.

ORGANIZATION AND STRUCTURE

Ammunition producers manufacture both cartridges and shells. The two types of cartridges used in rifles and pistols are rimfire and centerfire. Rimfire cartridges are comprised of a soft lead bullet, a case most often made of brass and the smokeless propellant (powder). The priming compound is spun into the rim of the case. When the firearm's firing pin strikes and indents the rim of the cartridge the priming mixture ignites and in turn ignites the propellant. Hence the name "rimfire." Centerfire cartridges differ in that a separate primer is seated in the base or head of the cartridge. When struck by the firing pin the primer ignites the propellant via the flash hole in the base of the cartridge, hence the name "centerfire." Cartridges developing relatively low pressure (such as the common .22 caliber cartridges for both rifles and pistols) lend themselves to the rimfire configuration because the brass head of the cartridge can be thin enough to allow ignition of the propellant.

Prior to the Civil War both large and small bore rifle and pistol cartridges were rimfire because they developed relatively low internal pressures when ignited. In the post-Civil War period however, more powerful cartridges began to be developed. These cartridges reached subsequently higher pressures and thus required case heads too thick to be indented by a firing pin. The centerfire ignition system solved this problem and is used in the same configuration in the 1990s for high pressure cartridges. Shotgun shells are also centerfire, but are made up of a paper or plastic cylinder with a brass base or head. The shell is filled with powder followed by a cupped plastic wad filled with birdshot or much larger buckshot. Birdshot may be lead or steel while buckshot is lead. Federal law mandates that all duck and goose hunting be done with steel shot. It has been found that wildfowl accidentally ingesting spent lead shot while feeding are subject to lead poisoning. Shotgun shells may also be loaded with a single heavy slug which in various configurations is made of lead or a lead alloy. Slugs are used in law enforcement and for hunting big game such as deer. In addition to cartridges and shells, the small arms ammunition industry also includes the manufacture of BBs and pellets, which are most commonly fired from spring- or pneumatic-powered pistols and rifles.

Rimfire cartridges were typically .22 caliber and used in rifles and pistols designated "small-bore" and accounted for about 8 percent of industry sales in 1992. Centerfire pistol cartridges, including those cartridges such as the .44 Magnum, which could be interchanged between pistols and rifles, represented about 14 percent of revenues. Centerfire rifle ammunition made up an additional 12 percent of sales, while shotgun shells accounted for about 22 percent of industry shipments. Primers and other ammunition components sold separately garnered about a 13 percent share of the market, and miscellaneous ammo products accounted for the remaining 30 percent of industry revenues. A significant portion of miscellaneous ammo was ramset shells, used in the construction industry to drive nails into concrete.

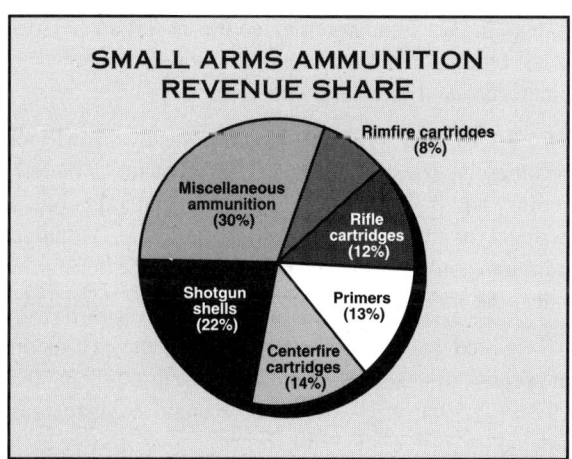

SMALL ARMS AMMUNITION REVENUE SHARE

Small arms ammunition is produced primarily for three types of firearms: handguns, including both semiautomatics and revolvers; shotguns; and rifles. In addition to these categories, smaller markets exist for fully automatic rifles as well as for BB and pellet guns. When using a single-action or double-action revolver the rounds of ammunition are loaded into the firearm's cylinder. The hammer of a single-action revolver (most "cowboy" pistols are single-action) must be pulled back or cocked by the shooter's thumb. This causes the cylinder to rotate aligning the cartridge with the barrel. When the trigger is pulled the hammer falls crushing the primer and igniting the cartridge. A double-action revolver (the modern police revolver is typical) may be fired single-action or by pulling on the trigger with the hammer in the down position. The latter move will cause the cylinder to rotate while simultaneously cocking the hammer. When the trigger reaches the end of its pull, the hammer falls causing the newly aligned cartridge to fire.

Semiautomatic pistols and some semiautomatic rifles hold rounds of ammunition in a spring-loaded clip. In early semiautomatics, the force of recoil ejected the fired case and loaded a fresh cartridge into the barrel. Semiautomatics in the 1990s, however, bleed off gas from a fired cartridge. This gas works against a piston which ejects the fired case and loads a fresh round in the barrel. Both methods also recock the weapon, but before it can fire again the trigger must be first disengaged and then pulled again. Fully automatic weapons, such as machine guns and military assault rifles, continue to fire and reload rounds as long as the shooter does not release the trigger. Federal law prohibits most citizens from owning or having in their possession fully automatic weapons.

Consumers and Trade Representatives. Ammunition sold to the general public represented about 40 percent of industry sales in the 1980s. Sales to the federal government for military and other uses accounted for about 20 percent of sales, a figure that fell to about 15 percent in the early 1990s. Exports, the third largest category, consumed approximately 10 percent of production. Cement and hydraulic industries made up about 6 percent of market share, while state and local governments and police accounted for about 5 percent. Various industrial and construction industries accounted for the remaining 20 percent of sales.

Hunters purchase 80 percent of the ammunition sold to the general public, or about 30 percent of total industry output. In addition to the use of rifles and shotguns for sport purposes, about 60 percent of hunters also own handguns, making people in that group significant consumers of pistol ammunition.

There are three industry and consumer groups that represent ammunition interests in the United States. Most ammunition industry executives are affiliated with the National Shooting Sports Federation (NSSF), which promotes hunting and target shooting. The NSSF's sister organization, the Sporting Arms and Ammunition Manufacturers Institute (SAAMI), sets voluntary national standards for ammunition and firearm design. These groups rarely participate in political lobbying efforts, although ammo producers have traditionally donated money to support game populations and preserve hunting areas. The third and best-known organization, the National Rifle Association (NRA), is heavily involved in lobbying efforts, most of which are of interest to ammo manufacturers and users. Only 12 percent of all hunters, however, belong to this organization.

An Obscure Industry. The ammunition industry is about 70 percent as large as the entire firearms industry that it complements. The comparably high-profile firearm industry receives large amounts of press and is often the target of state and federal regulatory initiatives. Ammunition makers, however, operate in relative obscurity, with little publicity, regulation, or outside analysis of the industry.

One reason that the industry has such a low profile is that most of its products are homogenous, resulting in a commodity-like business environment that is not dynamic. In addition, the largest producers in the industry are owned by massive conglomerates that view ammo operations as relatively small sideline businesses.

BACKGROUND AND DEVELOPMENT

The use of gunpowder to propel projectiles dates back to fourteenth century Europe. Iron darts with brass fittings were mounted on shafts, much like crossbow arrows of the time. The shaft held the gunpowder and was wrapped with leather to keep gases from the burning powder from leaking out of the sides of the shaft. During the fourteenth, fifteenth, and sixteenth centuries, armies experimented with a variety of projectiles. Gunpowder was used to fire rocks in the 1300s, though metal balls became the ammunition of choice by the 1400s. Hot shot, or heated metal balls, added a deadly twist to this technique.

The advent of rifled barrels following the American Revolution created a demand for new types of bullets. Although barrels were being rifled as early as the 1500s in Germany, it was not until the late 1700s

that this manufacturing technique became popular. Long spiral grooves or rifling cut into a barrel's inner surface causes a fired projectile to spin on its axis imparting ballistic stability and greatly increasing the firearm's accuracy and range. Because elongated projectiles benefited most from the rifling technique, this type of bullet grew in popularity throughout the nineteenth century gradually replacing the solid lead ball. All pistols and rifles manufactured in the 1990s have rifled barrels. Shotgun barrels are not rifled.

Muskets, which fire rounded lead balls and similar projectiles, were dominant in North American until the end of the Civil War. Westward expansion following the Civil War however created a market for heavier and more powerful firearms. Buffalo hunters needed long range rifles and settlers on lonely farms needed repeating firearms such as the Winchester lever action rifles. The cartridge technology used in the 1990s originated in this era and consisted of an elongated bullet enclosing powder and primer in a brass cartridge. The cartridge was powerful, virtually oblivious to weather, and could be used in repeating firearms. This technological breakthrough quickly spelled the end of the muzzle-loading Kentucky rifle of Daniel Boone fame.

Winchester rifles, Colt revolvers, and other famous weaponry created markets for a variety of new ammunition during the westward U.S. expansion. Widespread use of smokeless gunpowder, which was perfected in the late 1880s, hastened ammunition industry growth. Most importantly, advances in ammunition and firearms during both world wars broadened the scope of the industry to include specialized ammunition for automatic weapons and other new firearms.

In addition to a huge demand for ammunition by the military, ammunition producers in the United States enjoyed a large market for hunting products throughout the twentieth century. Except during times of war, in fact, hunters remained the largest consumers of all types of small arms ammunition throughout the nineteenth and twentieth centuries.

The 1970s and 1980s. Following steady growth in commercial sales during the first half of the twentieth century and throughout the 1960s, the general public's demand for ammo began to slip in the 1970s. Although military consumption provided sporadic boosts in sales, the industry's core market, hunters, stagnated.

Stalled growth in hunting impeded the expansion of profits for some manufacturers throughout the 1970s and early 1980s. After Ronald Reagan was elected to office in 1980, however, an increase in ammo sales to the military boosted revenues. Profits were further buoyed by an increase in target shooting.

By the mid-1980s the military consumed nearly 30 percent of industry production, and handgun and target shooters had become the primary growth market for manufacturers.

The value of ammo sales gradually edged upward from about $800 million in 1982 to approximately $920 million in 1985 and 1986. An increase in the cost of lead that caused inflated ammo prices was partially responsible for this rise, however. A decline in military consumption in the late 1980s reduced shipments to about $840 million by 1990, despite another jump in the cost of lead in 1989 and 1990. Depressed construction markets also quelled revenue growth, as the demand for ramset shells and other industrial products decreased.

The small arms ammunition business represented a mature industry throughout the 1980s and early 1990s. Stagnant growth, homogenous products, and low profit margins characterized the industry. As they entered the 1990s, producers sought means of increasing profits and maintaining market share.

CURRENT CONDITIONS

To boost profits in the 1990s, small ammo producers were slowly raising productivity, selling through new marketing channels, and offering new niche products. Manufacturers plowed an average of $25 million per year into production facilities in the 1980s, a very low investment compared to most other industries. Despite that low figure, industry employment fell from about 7.4 million to 6.3 million workers during the decade, at the same time that overall production increased.

Winchester, for instance, installed computer-controlled cartridge loading machines that allowed the company to produce 9 mm cartridges and other popular ammo at a rate of up to 450 units per minute. Despite industry efforts at low-cost, high-volume production in some areas, most manufacturers still used some very old production techniques. Even at Winchester many low-volume products in 1993 were still loaded at rates of 40 to 60 per minute using machines the company acquired in 1931. Lead shot, moreover, was produced using a two-century old process.

Besides moderate productivity gains, producers were benefitting in the early 1990s from new marketing channels. Sporting goods stores and gun shops continued to account for a declining share of total ammo sales, as they had since the 1980s. Instead, such discount stores as Wal-Mart and Kmart, accounted for 30 percent to 50 percent of commercial sales by 1992. In addition, mail order catalog sales were becoming an increasingly important channel of distribution. One of the largest ammunition catalogers, AcuSport Corp. of Ohio, increased mail order sales from $30 million in 1988 to over $75 million by 1992.

Many producers were also developing new bullet types to appeal to niche market segments. These unique items offered higher profit margins than popular commodity ammo. Police and handgun owners, for instance, had proved a viable market for sales of specialty bullets. The Black Talon, for example, was a bullet designed to enter a person's body, spread out, and extend tiny razors that stopped the bullet inside the body. Other ammo was designed to explode on impact and release tiny pellets into its target or pierce metal plate or protective gear.

As the mid-1990s approached, an area of potential growth for industry competitors was the export market. Productivity gains realized in the 1980s allowed U.S. producers to stem an influx of cheap import ammunition from Brazil and the Far East during that decade. As their production costs became more globally competitive, some manufacturers began eyeing burgeoning foreign ammo markets. Exports already accounted for more than 10 percent of total U.S. production in the early 1990s. Foreign producers had captured less than 20 percent of the U.S. ammo market by 1992, and import growth seemed to have stabilized.

Regulatory Efforts. Largely in reaction to soaring crime rates in major cities various federal and state initiatives sought to tether the industry in the early 1990s. By 1993 however the small arms ammunition industry remained loosely regulated. For example, New York City required ammo buyers to display to the seller a legal permit to use the gun that would the ammunition. That law was loosely enforced, however, and critics on both sides of the gun-control issue agreed that the information required by the law was of little help in criminal investigations. A similar federal proposal was defeated by Congress in 1986. Congress, with the support of the NRA, had succeeded in banning certain types of "cop-killer" bullets, designed to penetrate bullet-proof vests. That ban represented the only piece of legislation ever passed to directly limit the sale of small arms ammunition.

Senator Daniel Patrick Moynihan (New York) proposed legislation in the early 1990s to ban the sale of 9 mm, .25 caliber, and .32 caliber ammunition, which together accounted for 50 percent of the bullets fired at police officers. He also tried to pass legislation making many pistol cartridges prohibitively expensive. Moynihan was unsuccessful in both attempts. Critics argued that such laws could not be enforced and would have a negligible effect on crime. Nevertheless, the Clinton administration had indicated support for similar types of legislation.

The shooting and small arms ammunition industry remained at odds with the political climate promulgated by the Clinton administration in the early 1990s. Passage of the so-called Brady Bill and the Assault Weapons Ban put firearms and small arms ammunition manufacturers on the defensive.

In 1994, President Clinton signed the Brady Bill, which called for a waiting period for handgun purchases and required local police authorities to conduct an investigation before issuing a permit to purchase a handgun. However, because of a general fear of crime, and social and civil unrest, the sale of handguns and those military style assault rifles that were still legal skyrocketed along with ammunition for these arms. Many such firearms and ammunition were in short supply causing a booming business among gun stores, distributors, importers, and manufacturers. As a result, in 1995, the National Alliance of Stocking Gun Dealers predicted an annual growth rate of nearly 6 percent.

Industry observers also predicted strong sales in centerfire rifle ammunition throughout 1996 based on a growing demand for premium and thus more expensive lines of rifle ammunition. These ''boutique'' brands of cartridges have greater accuracy, flatter trajectories, and higher velocities. Representative of these enhanced performance cartridges are Federal's Premium Safari and Premium Self-Defense lines, Winchester's Fail-Safe Supreme cartridges and Remington's Extended Range speciality ammunition. Demand for these high quality and often exotic cartridges was expected to remain strong throughout the 1990s.

Spurred on by 1994 Republican majorities in the U.S. House and Senate the National Rifle Association, a multitude of progun grass roots organizations, and even such staid institutions as the Boy Scouts of America and the 4-H Clubs of America, began active campaigns to promote gun safety and shooting activities. In an attempt to increase its membership of young males the 4-H Clubs of America formed a Shooting Sport Committee which was charged with developing a shooting sports program in cooperation with various manufacturing interests. By mid-1996 the program had spread to chapters in 38 states. The Boy Scouts of America revived many of their shooting sports programs and began laying the groundwork for a Young Hunter Education Challenge, a nationwide competition which would test the shooting, firearms knowledge, and the firearms safety practices of its participants. The National Rifle Association continued its

''Eddie Eagle'' firearms safety program and played a major role in ''right to carry'' legislation at the state and local level. Such legislation allowed private citizens of good standing who have passed a handgun competency course to receive a permit to purchase and subsequently carry a concealed handgun. In 1996, South Carolina became the 31st state to pass such legislation.

INDUSTRY LEADERS

The largest producer of small arms ammunition in the United States in 1996 was the Federal Cartridge Co. of Anoka, Minnesota. This company employed approximately 1,000 people in the manufacture of 350 different rifle, pistol, and shotgun cartridges and shells with sales of $98 million. Federal accounted for over half of the annual $175 million in small arms ammunition sales in the United States. Other industry leaders were the Olin Corp. and Remington, which manufactured both firearms and ammunition.

The other approximately 80 companies that make up the industry were comparatively small. Most of them employed fewer than 100 workers and had sales of less than $1 million per year. Several companies specialized in producing specialty cartridges, construction industry products, and reused rounds.

WORK FORCE

Employment in the small arms ammunition industry was expected to decrease between 1990 and 2005, according to the U.S. Bureau of Labor Statistics. In 1992 there were 20,000 employed in the small arms and small arms ammunition industry. This figure was expected to decline to 14,000 to 15,000 by 2005. Productivity gains, movement of production facilities to countries with cheaper labor, and stagnant domestic market growth were expected to contribute to this trend. Jobs for assemblers and fabricators, which represented a leading 14 percent of industry positions, were forecast to fall by more than 50 percent. Other manufacturing positions, which accounted for the bulk of industry employment, were expected to decline by 25 percent to 50 percent. General management and executive positions also were expected to drop by more than 40 percent. Workers already employed in the industry, however, continued to enjoy higher wages than workers in most other U.S. manufacturing industries in the 1990s.

FURTHER READING

Darnay, Arsen J., ed. *Manufacturing USA*. 5th ed. Detroit: Gale Research, 1996.

Farnham, Alan. "A Bang That's Worth Ten Billion Bucks." *Fortune,* 19 March 1992.

Feder, Barnaby J. "Moynihan Wages Battle on 2d Front of Gun War." *New York Times,* 20 March 1992.

———. "As Gun Debate Rages, Ammunition Makers Are Quietly, and Busily, At Work." *New York Times,* 20 March 1992.

Gilbert, Nathaniel. "Careful Planning Keeps Olin Lucky." *Financier,* August 1991.

Jones, Maggie. "Gunmakers Target Women," *Working Woman,* July 1993.

Knox, Neal. "Knox's Notebook." *American Rifleman,* August 1996.

Lubove, Seth, "No More Adventures." *Forbes,* 7 December 1992.

Miller, Paul. "AcuSport Corp." *Catalog Age,* November 1992.

Robinson, Jerome B. "The Next Generation of Shooters." *Field & Stream,* May 1996.

Smart, Tim. "Ready, Aim. . . ." *Business Week,* 27 December 1993.

Sundra, Jon R. "1996 Will Be a Magnum Year for Centerfire Rifle Ammo." *Shooting Industry,* December 1995.

Sundra, Jon R. "Ammo Makers Offer More Choices." *Shooting Industry,* May 1996.

—Dave Mote, upated by Michael Knes

SIC 3483

AMMUNITION, EXCEPT FOR SMALL ARMS

This category covers establishments primarily engaged in manufacturing ammunition, not elsewhere classified, or in loading and assembling ammunition more than 30 mm (or more than 1.18 inches), including component parts. This industry also includes establishments primarily engaged in manufacturing bombs, mines, torpedoes, grenades, depth charges, chemical warfare projectiles, and their component parts. Establishments primarily engaged in manufacturing small arms are classified in **SIC 3482: Small Arms Ammunition;** those manufacturing explosives are classified in **SIC 2892: Explosives;** and those manufacturing military pyrotechnics are classified in **SIC 2899: Chemicals and Chemical Preparations, Not Elsewhere Classified.**

About 45 percent of U.S. large ammunition industry output in the early 1990s was bombs. An additional 40 percent of production included miscellaneous bullets and other projectiles, casings, and components.

Rockets made up the remaining 30 percent of shipments. Nearly 80 percent of all sales in 1991 were sold under U.S. government contract, mostly to the armed services. Another 15 percent of industry output was exported, and about 5 percent was consumed by various manufacturing sectors. Examples of manufacturing uses include demolition and mining.

The industry declined precipitously in the mid-1990s, in part because of the end of the Cold War and anticipation of military spending cuts. While the industry had employed 415,000 people in 1987, that number had dropped to 234,000 by 1992, and to only 12,000 in 1995—a decrease of almost 75 percent, according to the *1995 Census of Manufactures.* Those goods shipped in 1995 were valued at $2.034 billion, which was a slight increase over the 1994 figure of $2.008 billion, but well below the $3.1 billion reported in the 1992 Census of Manufactures.

Gunpowder was first employed to project missiles early in the fourteenth century, when large dart-like objects were propelled through the air during medieval battles. Darts were soon replaced by more reliable, rounded projectiles that were fired from canon-type devices. Napoleon III released one of the first written works about artillery that included large ammunition in 1338, entitled *Etudes Sur . . . l'artillerie.* Stone shot was replaced by iron shot in the mid-1300s, as iron allowed greater penetration of stone walls. Soon thereafter, shells were invented that could be filled with gunpowder, fired from canons, and made to explode. Rounded metal balls and shells remained the principal types of large ammunition from the fifteenth through the nineteenth century.

The large ammunition industry in the United States arose as a result of both internal and external military conflicts, particularly the Civil War and both world wars. Development of the rifled artillery barrel and smokeless gunpowder in the nineteenth century lead to the proliferation of elongated bullets and shells. This ammunition type dominated production throughout most of the twentieth century.

Although production of some large ammunition types peaked during World War II, the manufacture of other types of projectiles and explosives proliferated between 1950 and the late 1980s. Nuclear bombs and guided missiles, particularly, contributed to industry growth throughout the Cold War. By 1988, the industry employed about 26,000 workers and was producing a record $4.3 billion in shipments per year. During the Reagan presidency alone, the ammunition industry had grown from just $1.8 billion in shipments and about 16,000 workers.

The end of the Cold War in the late 1980s, punctuated by the demise of the Soviet Union, pummeled the large ammunition industry. As defense purchases plunged, sales dropped to $3.1 billion in 1990 and continued to plummet in 1991 and 1992. Likewise, industry employment crashed to about 14,500. Adding to employee woes were moderate increases in manufacturing productivity—the result of over $600 million in capital investments by producers in the early and mid-1980s.

Going into the mid-1990s, large ammunition manufacturers were expecting continued cuts in U.S. defense expenditures by the Clinton administration. Employment in every position in the industry was forecast to fall by 25 percent to 50 percent. For example, jobs for assemblers and fabricators, which accounted for a leading 14 percent of all workers, were expected to fall 51 percent between 1990 and 2005. Even white collar jobs were forecast to decline by over 40 percent during that period. Companies were counting on export growth to partially offset domestic declines.

The industry is highly concentrated and encompassed fewer than 70 firms in the early 1990s. Honeywell Inc. of Minnesota, the largest producer, earned over $1.5 billion in 1991 and employed more than 11,000 workers. The next largest competitor in 1991 was EG and G Rocky Flats Inc. of Golden Colorado. That enterprise generated $375 million in revenues and employed about 1,300. Other industry leaders in the early 1990s included Olin Corporation of Florida, Mason Company Inc., of Kentucky, and Grumman Corp. of New York.

FURTHER READING

Ambrosia, John. "Defense Cuts Won't Ground Lightweight Metals." *Iron Age,* April 1993.

Chakravarty, Subrata N. "Sink or Swim." *Forbes,* 14 October 1991.

Farnham, Alan. "A Bang That's Worth Ten Billion Bucks." *Fortune,* 19 March 1992.

Gilbert, Nathaniel. "Careful Planning Keeps Olin Lucky." *Financier,* August 1991.

Inglesby, Tom, and Elaine West. "Boom! On Time, All the Time." *Manufacturing Systems,* 12 February 1992.

1995 Census of Manufactures. Washington: Office of the Census, 1997.

Rapoport, Carla. "Japan's Rising Defense Industry." *Fortune,* 24 April 1989.

Standard & Poor's Industry Surveys. New York: Standard & Poor's Corporation, 31 December 1993.

—Dave Mote, updated by Kenneth R. Shepherd

SIC 3484

SMALL ARMS

This category includes establishments primarily engaged in manufacturing small firearms or parts for small firearms. Small firearms, defined as having a bore of 30 mm or less, include pistols, revolvers, rifles, shotguns, and submachine guns. This category also includes establishments that manufacture weapons with bores greater than 30 mm but which nevertheless are carried and employed by individuals, including grenade launchers and heavy field machine guns. Establishments primarily engaged in manufacturing artillery and mortars having bores greater than 30 mm are classified in **SIC 3489: Ordnance and Accessories, Not Elsewhere Classified.**

INDUSTRY SNAPSHOT

In 1996, there were 23 major companies engaged in manufacturing small arms in the United States. These companies employed approximately 6,500 people and shipped $1.338 billion worth of small arms. Most major manufacturers enjoyed steady growth and a strengthening market from 1987 into early to mid-1990s. The largest small arms manufacturer in the United States is Sturm, Ruger and Company Inc. of Southport, Connecticut, a relative newcomer to the industry. Starting with the manufacture of a small and relatively inexpensive .22 caliber semiautomatic pistol in the post-World War II years, Ruger had grown to a $193 million company by 1996.

Historically, the small arms industry was cyclical and subject to many external pressures, including the general state of the economy, worldwide military conflicts, and public and political vagaries concerning private ownership of firearms. By the mid-1990s, public debate concerning the "right" of citizens to own firearms, especially handguns and assault rifles reached new heights of acrimony. Gun control proponents pointed to high levels of firearm violence in the United States, while the National Rifle Association (NRA) and others argued that such gun-control efforts were misguided and flew in the face of rights guaranteed in the Constitution. Whether or not the second amendment protects the right of citizens to "keep and bear arms" is still a matter of contention as it has never been fully addressed by the United States Supreme Court. There is however a large and growing body of scholarly literature supporting both sides of the argument.

ORGANIZATION AND STRUCTURE

Many small-arms companies began in the late nineteenth century in the Connecticut River Valley between Hartford and Springfield, Massachusetts, known as Gun Valley because of its concentration of armories. Because of this long tradition, several small arms companies that no longer have manufacturing facilities in Gun Valley maintained headquarters there in the late twentieth century.

Following the Great Depression of the 1930s, many surviving small arms companies diversified or were purchased by large corporations. The trend towards amalgamation reversed itself in the 1980s when two of the largest corporations in the industry, Colt Industries and the Olin Corporation, divested themselves of poorly performing firearms divisions to form stand-alone companies. One of those new companies, the U.S. Repeating Arms Co., maker of Winchester rifles, was then sold to Belgian firearms conglomerate Fabrique Nationale Herstal, and then acquired by the French government-owned GIAT Industries. Fabrique Nationale and Italian firearms maker Pietro Beretta Fabbrica Amri also had large manufacturing facilities in the United States.

BACKGROUND AND DEVELOPMENT

The small arms industry played an important part in the historical development of the United States, and in the myths and ideals that accompanied that development. Early to mid-nineteenth century guns pioneered the use of interchangeable standardized parts, the technology that gave rise to modern manufacturing. Moreover, guns bearing the names Remington, Winchester, and Colt are associated with the settlement of the Old West, Manifest Destiny, and the development of the United States as a world power.

Although many prominent craftsmen produced firearms in colonial America, gunmaking as an industry really began in 1775 when the Continental Congress established the Committee of Safety, whose responsibilities included ensuring that the Continental Army had sufficient firearms. The Committee of Safety established specifications for manufacturing flintlock muskets and awarded contracts to various American gunmakers. In 1794, Congress established a national armory at Springfield, Massachusetts that stored and manufactured muskets for military use. A second armory was established at Harper's Ferry, Virginia in 1796. The armory at Harper's Ferry would eventually be burned in 1861 to keep it out of the hands of Confederate forces. The Springfield armory was in operation until 1975.

In 1808, as tensions mounted between the United States and England (which would eventually erupt into the War of 1812) the federal armories tooled up to manufacture 40,000 muskets a year. Private gunmakers were also awarded contracts to manufacture between 2,500 and 10,000 muskets each, with the goal of supplying nearly 100,000 militiamen. The federal armories provided "pattern" muskets for the private manufacturers to copy.

Early Innovators. One of the earliest gunmakers to receive a government contract was Eli Whitney, best known as the inventor of the cotton gin, who had established an armory in New Haven, Connecticut in 1798. Whitney was a Yale-educated engineer who realized that the most efficient and cost-effective way to make guns was to manufacture interchangeable parts that could then be assembled by unskilled workers. Although Whitney was far from being the most successful gunmaker of the day, he amazed government officials inspecting his plant by assembling muskets from parts chosen at random. Whitney was the first U.S. industrialist to manufacture interchangeable parts and was considered the father of mass production long before Henry Ford began building cars. By the 1850s, his "American System" of manufacturing was known throughout Europe. The Whitney Armory continued to manufacture guns until 1888.

Although rifles were invented in the early 1500s, and the famous Pennsylvania-made Kentucky rifles were used by some militiamen during the American Revolution, smooth-bore muskets remained common into the early nineteenth century. Despite their inaccuracy, they were easier to load and fire than a firearm with a rifled barrel. Then in 1810, an American gunsmith, John H. Hall, invented a breech-loading flintlock rifle that could be loaded quickly using a paper cartridge containing ball and powder. The U.S. Army ordered 200 rifles in 1818 for experimentation, and Hall supervised the construction at the federal armory at Harper's Ferry. The rifles performed well, but the military continued to rely on muskets up until the Civil War. The Springfield Armory did not begin manufacturing rifles until 1858, but had produced more than 840,000 by the end of 1865. On the other hand, hunters and frontiersmen who favored accuracy switched to breech-loading rifles much sooner. The 200 Hall rifles built in 1818 were also the first firearms manufactured in a government armory using interchangeable parts.

Samuel Colt. Samuel Colt was the first great American gunmaker. He was born in Hartford, Connecticut in 1814, and left school at the age of ten to work in his father's silk mill in Ware, Massachusetts. At the age of

16, he joined the crew of a ship bound for London and Calcutta. In London, Colt apparently saw a display of early attempts at designing repeating firearms. During the voyage home, and possibly inspired by the ship's clutch-controlled rotating capstan, he whittled a crude wooden model of a pistol with a revolving cylinder.

Between 1832 and 1835, Colt financed development of his revolving pistol as a lecturer and "practical chemist," billing himself as "the celebrated Dr. S. Colt of London and Calcutta" and giving demonstrations of laughing gas in the United States and Canada. He sent money and ideas for improvements in his design to John Pearson, a Baltimore gunsmith, who created a working model. Colt received patents on his design from England and France in 1835, and from the United States in 1836. The most radical feature of Colt's design was a ratchet that rotated and locked the cylinder in place when the gun was cocked.

Colt established the Patent Arms Manufacturing Company in Paterson, New Jersey in 1836 to produce revolving pistols and rifles. However, the head of U.S. Army Ordnance was not impressed with a demonstration and the company failed to receive a military contract. Although the Army eventually did order about 100 rifles and a few five-shot revolvers for fighting the Seminole Indians in Florida, Colt was forced to close down his company in 1842.

At the start of the Mexican War in 1846, General Zachary Taylor, who had used an early Paterson-model Colt revolver, asked Colt for 1,000 revolvers to be delivered within three months. Captain Samuel Walker of the Texas Rangers, which had used Colt revolvers to fight the Comanches, also asked for guns, only Walker wanted a larger caliber revolver that would fire six shots. Colt designed a gun to Walker's specifications, but without a factory of his own he subcontracted the manufacturing to Eli Whitney Jr., who was then running the armory his father had founded and was the Army's primary contractor for muskets. Colt personally supervised the manufacturing. The .44 caliber six-shooter became known as the Walker gun. Tragically, Walker was killed in action four days after he received a set of Walker-model revolvers from Colt.

In 1847, the Army ordered another 1,000 revolvers and Colt set up the renamed Colt's Patent Arms Manufacturing Co. in leased space in his hometown of Hartford. He also hired a talented machinist, Elisha K. Root, to manage the operation. Root, who received twice his former salary at a farm-implements company, was given a free hand in setting up the factory. He designed belt-driven machinery for turning gun stocks, boring rifling barrels, and making car-

tridges. Under Root's direction the Colt armory became a showplace for Eli Whitney's "American System."

In 1853, Colt became the first American manufacturer to establish a foreign branch when he opened a factory on the Thames River in London to supply guns to the British government. Colt became known as gunmaker to the world and successfully defended his patents against infringement until they expired in 1856. When he died six years later, a new factory he had built in Hartford in 1855 was the largest private armory in the world and Colt was one of the wealthiest men in America with an estate valued at $15 million.

Gatling, Maxim, and Browning. The Civil War was the proving ground for many advances in firearms and ordnance, including the famous Sharpes carbine, more than 80,000 of which were produced for Northern troops by the Sharpes Rifle Manufacturing Co. But no development was more dramatic than the introduction of the first practical machine gun, patented in 1862 by Richard J. Gatling.

Gatling was the son of a North Carolina planter who spent most of his career improving agricultural methods and inventing farm machinery. His hand-cranked machine gun actually performed erratically during the Civil War, but with some mechanical improvements the design was officially adopted by the U.S. Army in 1866. Gatling later sold his patent to the Colt's Patent Arms Manufacturing Co.

In 1884, another American inventor, Sir Hiram Stevens Maxim, developed the first semiautomatic rifle when he modified a Winchester rifle so the power of the recoil would eject the spent cartridge and load the next round. In 1889, Maxim also developed the first fully automatic machine gun. Maxim's designs were adopted by every major power in the world between 1900 and the World War I. English models of the Maxim machine gun, known as the Vickers, were used by both sides in World War II, and the North Koreans employed outdated Maxim machine guns in the Korean War.

Maxim also experimented with internal combustion engines, steam-powered flight, and electric lights, losing a critical patent lawsuit to Thomas Edison. A native of Maine, Maxim moved to England and became a British citizen in 1900. He was knighted in 1901. His son, Hiram Percy Maxim, invented the silencer, which mutes the report of a gunshot.

Jonathon M. Browning, the son of a Utah gunsmith, was the most prolific and successful American gun designer in history. He developed one of the earliest semiautomatic pistols and the first gas-operated machine gun. Browning sold or licensed most of his designs to the Colt Patent Arms Manufacturing Co., including several machine gun designs. He also licensed designs to the Winchester Repeating Arms Company, including the first lever-action rifle strong enough to use the high-power centerfire cartridges of the day. This rifle, named Model 1886, made Winchester the best-known name among American rifle makers.

In 1888, when no American companies expressed interest in his semiautomatic pistol, Browning licensed the design to the Belgian gunmaking firm of Fabrique Nationale Herstal. He also licensed the Browning name for use outside of North America. Browning and Nationale Fabrique later collaborated on some of the most famous firearms in history, including the Browning Automatic Rifle, or BAR, used during World War I and World War II. Fabrique Nationale purchased controlling interest in Browning Arms in 1977.

Browning also designed the first successful gas-operated machine gun. In 1890, he sold the design to Colt, which produced the Colt Machine Gun Model 1895, the first fully automatic machine gun used by U.S. military forces. In 1990, Colt also became the first U.S. company to produce an automatic pistol, also based on a Browning design.

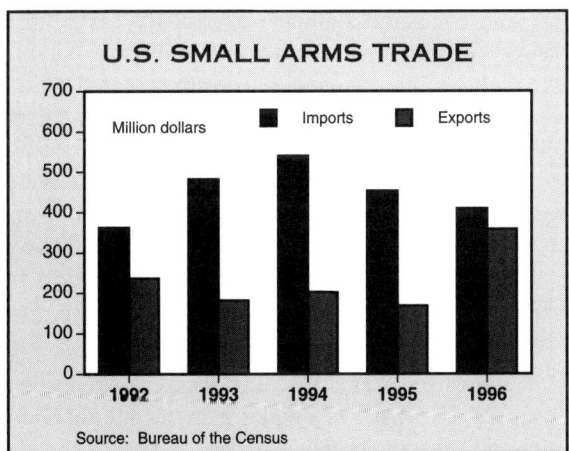

U.S. SMALL ARMS TRADE

Million dollars   ■ Imports   ■ Exports

Source: Bureau of the Census

CURRENT CONDITIONS

Sales of small arms in the United States rose sharply through the mid-1990s, in part because of federal gun control legislation. The Brady Bill, which calls for a five-day waiting period (and background check) before a customer can purchase a handgun, was passed in 1994 after bitter debate. A ban on 19 types of assault weapons was passed shortly thereafter in a dramatic 216-214 vote in the House of Representatives

(the measure passed the Senate by a comfortable margin). In analyzing the vote, *Time* noted that "the gun lobby has recently collided with . . . an increased fear of violent crime. Twenty-two cities had a record number of homicides last year. That has left many citizens feeling vulnerable and increasingly unsympathetic to those who interpret the Second Amendment as protecting the rights of Americans to own guns . . . Polls showed that people supported the [assault weapon] ban by ratios as lopsided as 4 to 1; a much quoted statistic by proponents of the measure held that though assault weapons may constitute only one percent of the firearms in the U.S., they are responsible for eight percent of the killings." Ironically, however, the measures actually spurred gun sales across the country as buyers sought to make their purchases before the new laws took effect. Anti-gun sentiment also caused several retail outlets to stop selling guns and convinced some large corporations to improve their public image by divesting gun-manufacturing divisions.

Less costly foreign imports also affected U.S. manufacturing, reducing the profit margin on the sale of guns. Foreign imports were less costly because of high U.S. wages and the fact that many gun factories were among the oldest industrial facilities in the United States. Also to blame was the high cost of product liability insurance in the United States, which some manufacturers considered a greater long-term threat to the industry than efforts to ban or restrict firearms. Nearly all major gun manufacturers were hit with multi-million dollar lawsuits in the 1980s.

Foreign gunmakers also established manufacturing facilities in the United States in the 1980s to avoid restrictions on imports, including Italy's Pietro Beretta Fabbrica Amri and Belgium's Fabrique Nationale. In 1985, Beretta USA signed a contract to provide 9 mm handguns to the U.S. military, ending Colt's 100-year dominance of military sidearms. Three years later, Fabrique Nationale wrested the Army contract for the M-16 automatic rifle away from Colt. The losses were a major reason that Colt Industries eventually sold its firearms division to a group of private investors. Two other famous names in American gunmaking, Winchester and Smith & Wesson, also were sold in the 1980s to avoid bankruptcy.

INDUSTRY LEADERS

Remington Arms Company, Inc. In 1993, Remington was a subsidiary of E.I. du Pont de Nemours and Company. Based in Wilmington, Delaware, Remington was the leading manufacturer of shotguns, producing more than 262,000 in 1991, or about one-third of all shotguns made in the United States. Remington,

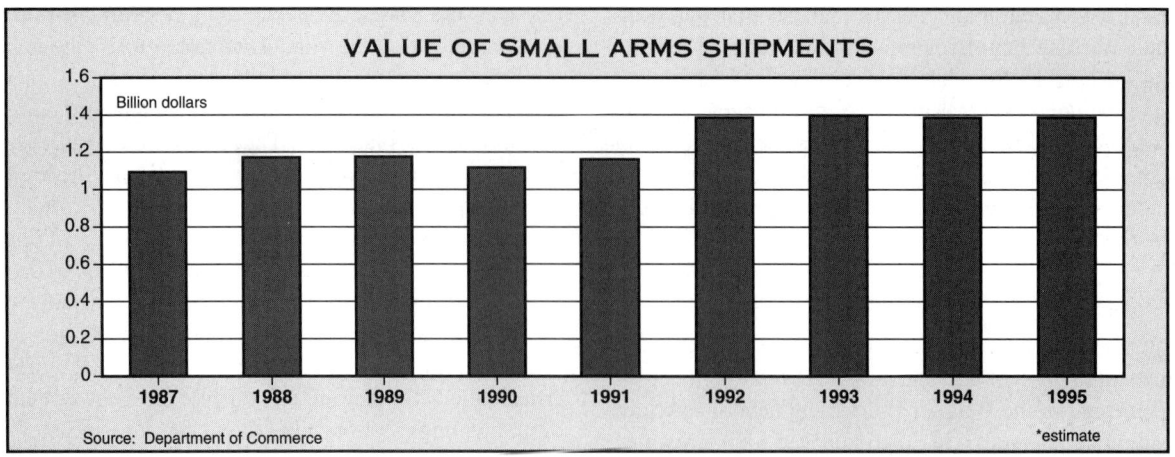

VALUE OF SMALL ARMS SHIPMENTS

Billion dollars

Source: Department of Commerce   *estimate

with revenues of $250 million, was also a leading manufacturer of rifles and ammunition and marketed a line of hunting apparel.

Remington traces its heritage to Eliphalet Remington, an early American gunsmith who produced his first flintlock rifle in 1816. Raised in Central New York, Remington purchased land along the Erie Canal in 1828 and established an armory. The town that developed around the armory became known as Remington's Corners until Eliphalet Remington insisted the town change the name to Ilion. Remington's manufacturing facilities were still in Ilion in 1993. The company was known as E. Remington & Sons during the Civil War. The Depression of 1884 forced the company into bankruptcy, and it was reorganized in 1888 as the Remington Arms Co. Du Pont purchased Remington in 1933 during the Great Depression.

Remington is considered a leader in introducing new technology and production techniques. After World War II, Remington began manufacturing parts that were interchangeable between models. The company also simplified the shape and design of many gun parts, which initially caused gun enthusiasts who were used to the elaborate showpieces of the past to treat newer Remington models with scorn. Some parts designed in the early 1950s were still being used on models introduced in the 1980s.

In the late 1980s, Remington became one of the first gunmakers to install computer-aided design/computer-aided manufacturing equipment (CAD/CAM) to reduce costs and increase its ability to respond to consumer trends. Paradoxically, the new manufacturing process produced parts by traditional machine tooling rather than stamping or casting, which most companies had turned to in the middle of the twentieth century to save money. The Remington plant in Ilion was considered one of the most advanced metal-work facilities in the United States.

O.F. Mossberg & Sons, Inc. O.F. Mossberg is the second leading maker of shotguns in the United States, manufacturing more than 209,000 in 1991. The New Haven, Connecticut-based company had revenues of $20 million in 1996. Oliver F. Mossberg was a Swedish immigrant who worked for several U.S. gunmakers before he began making .22 caliber "novelty guns" in his spare time to put his sons, Iver and Harold, through college. In 1919, the Mossbergs formed O.F. Mossberg & Sons. Between 1919 and 1932, they produced about 37,000 .22 caliber "Brownie" pistols. They began manufacturing .22 caliber rifles in 1922. Oliver Mossberg died in 1937.

The company continued to produce .22 caliber pistols and rifles after World War II, but also expanded into bolt-action shotguns. The first pump-action Mossberg shotguns were introduced in 1957. In 1986, Mossberg ended production of all rifles and pistols to concentrate solely on shotguns. Mossberg shotguns are widely used in law enforcement and the military. Mossberg claims to be the oldest family-owned and operated firearms manufacturer in the United States. In 1993, Alan I. Mossberg, grandson of the founder, was president and CEO.

U.S. Repeating Arms Co., Inc. The U.S. Repeating Arms Co. (USRAC) is a major manufacturer of shotguns and rifles under the legendary Winchester brand name. In 1991, USRAC produced more than 126,000 shotguns and 113,000 rifles, generating revenues of $74 million. The company was owned by GIAT Industries, a private company wholly owned by the French government.

The Winchester Repeating Arms Company was founded by Oliver F. Winchester in New Haven, Connecticut, in 1866. Winchester was a shirtmaker by trade, but became involved in gunmaking when he purchased the assets of the defunct Volcanic Repeating Arms Co. Volcanic had been founded in 1855 by

Horace Smith and Daniel B. Wesson, later of Smith & Wesson fame. Winchester was an early investor in the company, which went bankrupt in 1857. The Winchester Model 1866 was the first successful lever-action-repeating rifle. Later models made the Winchester name synonymous with American-made rifles.

When the market for guns collapsed during the Depression, the Olin Corporation purchased Winchester. In 1981, a group of Olin employees purchased Olin's Winchester gun division in a leveraged buyout, calling the new company the U.S. Repeating Arms Co., and licensing the Winchester name from Olin. Unfortunately, gun sales in the United States plummeted in the early 1980s, and USRAC filed for bankruptcy. USRAC was then purchased in 1987 by a group of investors led by Fabrique Nationale, a Belgium gunmaker and at one time the largest private arms company in the world. Fabrique Nationale became the sole owner in 1990, and was purchased by GIAT Industries in 1992.

Sturm, Ruger & Company, Inc. Sturm, Ruger & Co. is the largest maker of small arms in the United States, accounting for nearly 15 percent of the industry. It was the only U.S. gunmaker active in all four small arms categories of rifles, shotguns, revolvers and pistols. In 1991, Sturm, Ruger produced more than 240,000 rifles, more than any other U.S. gunmaker. The company also manufactured 170,000 pistols, 85,000 revolvers, and 8,000 shotguns. Based in Southport, Connecticut, Sturm, Ruger had sales of $193 million in 1996 and employed a work force of nearly 2,000.

Sturm, Ruger was founded in 1948 by William Batterman Ruger with a $50,000 stake from Alexander Sturm, a family friend and gun collector. Ruger had been a firearm designer for the U.S. government's Springfield Armory and the Auto Ordnance Corporation. Sturm, Ruger started by manufacturing a .22 caliber semiautomatic target pistol designed by Ruger, but gained special favor with gun enthusiasts in the early 1950s when it began producing Old West-style six-shooters that capitalized on the popularity of adult TV Westerns. Sturm, Ruger also utilized a manufacturing process known as investment casting. Rather than machine-tooling parts for its guns, Sturm, Ruger cast parts from molten steel using the "lost wax" process. The parts were not only cheaper to produce, they were stronger. Since perfecting this process Ruger has been casting parts for other manufacturers to the tune of $16 to $18 million annually or about 8 to 9 percent of sales. This figured jumped by nearly 70 percent in the first quarter of 1995, however, due to a large contract for titanium Big-Bertha golf club heads for Callaway Golf.

Between 1982 and 1992, when sales of small arms in the United States fell by almost 50 percent, Sturm, Ruger increased sales by nearly 75 percent. In 1986, Sturm, Ruger forced its distributors to choose between its guns and those made by Smith & Wesson. About half chose to stay with Sturm, Ruger.

In 1992, *Forbes* called Sturm, Ruger one of the 200 Best Small Companies in the United States. However, a discordant note was sounded by the *Wall Street Journal* in 1993 when the newspaper reported that more than 600 people had been injured and 40 killed in accidental shootings involving Sturm, Ruger's Old West-style revolvers. Between 1953 and 1972, Sturm, Ruger produced more than 1.5 million of the single-action revolvers patterned after the legendary 1873 Colt Peacemaker. Like the original Peacemaker, however, Sturm, Ruger six-shooters often discharged accidentally if the gun was dropped or the hammer struck. In 1994 for instance, 24 liability cases were tried, dismissed, or settled out of court. The average settlement was approximately $55,000.

Sturm, Ruger redesigned its single action revolvers in 1972 to make them safer. In 1982, Sturm, Ruger offered to retrofit older models with a safety device at no cost to their owners. However, fewer than 10 percent of the 1.2 million Old Model revolvers were modified. The company also ran a series of advertisements from 1981 to 1983 urging gun owners to load revolvers with only five bullets and leave the hammer resting on an empty chamber.

By 1995 Barron's reported that Sturm, Ruger could boast of a "squeaky-clean" balance sheet, superb profitability and 45 years in business without a negative balance sheet. Sturm, Ruger has continued to be profitable despite the anti-gun mood of much of America because most of its customers are hunters, law enforcement personnel, gun collectors, and sportsmen. Ruger has also survived the "assault weapons" legislation as its products have been exempted and named as "legitimate sporting firearms".

The Marlin Firearms Co. Marlin Firearms was the second leading manufacturer of rifles in the United States, and the largest maker of .22 caliber rifles. Privately owned Marlin Firearms had revenues of $50 million in 1996. Marlin was founded in New Haven, Connecticut in 1870 by John Mahlon Marlin, who had worked for the Colt Patent Firearms Co. during the Civil War. Trick shooter Annie Oakley used a specially made Marlin Model 1889 in Buffalo Bill Cody's Wild West show in the 1890s. Marlin was also known for its Colt-Browning machine guns and military rifles made during World War I, when it was known as the Marlin Rockwell Corporation. After the war, Rockwell had no interest in sporting guns and auctioned off the firearms division. Frank Kenna, whose family owned and operated Marlin Firearms into the 1990s, purchased the business for $100. In addition to firearms, Marlin produced razor blades from 1936 until the 1960s.

Smith & Wesson Corporation. Smith & Wesson is the leading manufacturer of revolvers and second leading producer of small arms in the United States, with sales of $140 million in 1996. Smith & Wesson's most popular revolver is the .38 Special, widely used by police officers. The company also manufactures the .44 Magnum revolver used by Clint Eastwood in the "Dirty Harry" movies. In the late 1980s, Smith & Wesson became a leader in the emerging market for handguns designed especially for women with the Lady Smith. The Lady Smith was a .357 Magnum with a grip and trigger mechanism designed for smaller hands. Many women's magazines refused to run ads for Lady Smith when it was introduced in 1988.

Horace Smith and Daniel B. Wesson formed their first partnership in 1851, creating the Volcanic Repeating Arms Co., which they later sold to Oliver F. Winchester. In 1856, when the Colt patents expired, Wesson developed a revolver that used a metallic rim-fire cartridge. He and Smith then formed Smith & Wesson in Springfield, Massachusetts in 1856. Smith retired from the business in 1873, but Wesson and his descendants continued to run the company until 1967, when it was purchased by the Bangor Punta Corporation. In 1984, the company became part of the Lear Siegler Holdings Corporation. Lear Siegler sold the company to F.H. Tompkins PLC, a British manufacturer of plumbing supplies and lawn mowers, in 1987. In 1996 the company had revenues of $140 million and a work force of 1,500.

Colt Manufacturing Company. At one time the largest and most important gunmaker in the United States, the Colt Manufacturing Co. was a relatively small maker of rifles and pistols in the early 1990s, producing 70,000 pistols and 38,000 rifles in 1991. Colt was owned by an investment group that included the United Auto Workers Union and the State of Connecticut. It had revenues of about $73 million in 1996.

Colt's Patent Arms Manufacturing Company, founded by inventor Samuel Colt in 1847, provided the Union Army with more than 107,000 revolvers during the Civil War. The famed Peacemaker, a six-shooter used in the Old West, was introduced in 1873 and manufactured continuously until 1941, and Colt produced commemorative Peacemakers after World War II.

The Colt family owned the company until 1901, when it was sold to a group of investors. The company suffered several setbacks in the 1920s and 1930s, beginning with its decision to stop manufacturing the Thompson submachine gun because it had become popular with gangsters. Nearly 2 million of the popular Tommy guns, as they were called, were produced during World War II by another contractor. Ironically, 60 years later Colt ended production of the AR-15, a popular semiautomatic civilian model of the military's M-16, in part because it was being used by drug dealers.

Like most other small arms manufacturers, Colt was hard hit by the Great Depression. Its difficulties were compounded by a violent strike in 1935, during which the home of its then-president Sam Stone was firebombed, and a hurricane in 1936, which destroyed most of what was left of the Colt Manufacturing Co. The company seemingly rebounded during World War II, but mismanagement later led to a financial crisis and manufacturing stopped altogether between 1945 and 1947.

In 1955, Colt was purchased by the Penn-Texas Corporation, a corporate raider who was expected to dismantle the company. In 1962, a stockholder's revolt forced out Penn-Texas and the company was reorganized as Colt Industries. In 1963, Colt became the sole contractor for the Army's new M-16 automatic assault rifle.

After nearly two decades of growth, during which Colt Industries became a diversified billion-dollar corporation, the Firearms Division suffered another series of market defeats in the 1980s. In 1985, the U.S. government dropped the Colt .45, standard military issue since 1911, and adopted a 9 mm semiautomatic pistol in its place. Colt lost the contract to the Beretta USA Corporation. Then in 1986, the United Auto Workers struck the Colt plant in Hartford. Replacement workers were hired, but the lingering strike and concerns about quality may have caused Colt to lose the M-16 contract in 1988. (An order for 500,000 rifles went to FN Manufacturing, the American manufacturing subsidiary of Fabrique Nationale.)

In 1990, a group of investors that included the State of Connecticut purchased the Firearms Division from Colt Industries. The UAW agreed to end the strike in exchange for rehiring striking workers and an 11 percent share of the company. The division was renamed the Colt Manufacturing Co. The new owners almost immediately found themselves embroiled in an old controversy when Colt announced plans in 1991 to market a rifle similar to the discontinued AR-15. At the time, Connecticut, with a 47 percent stake in the company and $25 million of its employee pension funds at risk, was considering a ban on all assault-style rifles.

In 1996, the U.S. Repeating Arms Co. opened its new $15 million, 225,000 square foot facility in New Haven, Connecticut. The plant, which contains state-of-the-art gun making equipment is staffed with 550 employees, produces shotguns and bolt action and lever action repeating rifles. The plant's production workers are grouped into "team cells" responsible for the production of a complete product instead of a single product component.

1994 was one of the best years in history for the U.S. firearms industry with total production exceeding 5 million units. A drop in handgun sales, however, was more than made up by a sales increase of shotguns and rifles over 1993. The top three manufacturers were Sturm, Ruger and Co., Remington Arms, and Smith and Wesson. Growth in 1995, however, was flat for the industry. Although there was an initial surge in sales due to the Brady Bill and the ban on selected assault weapons this situation proved to be temporary. The market appeared to be highly saturated by this time. While 50 percent of American households did not own a firearm, those that did averaged 4.5 guns each. Many manufacturers found a growing market for products among women and began marketing rifles, shotguns, and especially pistols suited to smaller frames. This led industry observers to predict renewed growth in 1996. The feeling was that many gun fanciers who purchased mostly handguns in 1994 and 1995 would turn their attention and wallets to shotguns and rifles in 1996.

FURTHER READING

Carmichel, Jim. "New Guns the Way They Used to Be." *Outdoor Life*, May 1988, 68.

Chant, Christopher. *New Encyclopedia of Handguns*. New York: Gallery Books, 1986.

"Fishing Flounders, But Firearms Is Still a Sure Shot: Women Shooters Give Manufacturers New Target." *Discount Store News*, 6 February 1995.

Gresham, Grits. "Winchester Rides Again." *Sports Afield*, November 1992.

"Guns, Clubs and Paint." *Barron's*, 10 July 1995.

Hausman, Robert M. "U.S. Repeating Arms Co." *Shooting Industry*, March 1996.

"The History of Marlin Firearms." North Haven, CT: Marlin Firearms Company.

Holusha, John. "Colt to Sell Unit that Won the West." *New York Times*, 29 April 1989, 33.

Isikoff, Michael. "New Colt Assault Rifle Revives Debate." *Washington Post*, 19 April 1990, A3.

Johnson, Kirk. "Gun Valley Tries to Adapt to the Winds of Change." *New York Times*, 21 March 1989, B1.

———. "Gun Import Ban Enriches Small U.S. Arms Makers." *New York Times*, 14 July 1989, A1.

———. "Emotions and History Tied to Colt Abandonment of Semiautomatics." *New York Times*, 17 March 1989, A18.

———. "Connecticut Debates Stake in Gun Maker It Saved." *New York Times*, 26 April 1990, A1.

King, Resa W. "United States Gunmakers: The Casualties Pile Up." *Business Week*, 19 May 1986, 77.

Larson, Erik. "Wild West Legacy: Ruger Gun Often Fires if Dropped, But Firm Sees No Need for Recall." *Wall Street Journal*, 24 June 1993, 1.

"Lethal Weapon 2." *Time*, 16 May 1994, 40-43.

Lockett, Bob. "Colt: What Went Wrong in Hartford?" *Shooting Industry*, July 1992, 34.

Maines, John. "Can Females Be Friends with Firearms?" *American Demographics*, June 1992, 22.

Matunas, Edward A. "U.S. Repeating Arms Company: On the Road to Glory." *Shooting Industry*, July 1988, 46.

Millman, Joel. "Steady Finger on the Trigger." *Forbes*, 9 November 1992, 188.

Moreton, Dave. "60 Years of History and Big Plans for the Future." *American Firearms Industry*, August 1979.

Sobel, Robert, and David B. Sicilia. *The Entrepreneurs: An American Adventure*. Boston: Houghton Mifflin, 1986.

Stevenson, Richard W. "Smith & Wesson Is Sold to Britons." *New York Times*, 23 May 1987, 33.

Thurman, Russ. "Firearms Business Analysis." *Shooting Industry*, June 1996.

Thurman, Russ. "Local Gun Sales Healthy." *Shooting Industry*, May 1996.

Tomkins, Richard. "The Four-Gun Family in Their Sights." *Financial Times*, 2 March 1996.

Walter, John. *The Rifle Book*, London: Arms & Armour Press, 1990.

"Why the Firearms Business Has Tired Blood." *Business Week*, 27 November 1978, 107.

Wilson, R. L. *The Colt Heritage*. New York: Simon and Schuster, 1979.

"Winchester Purchaser Sees Huge Potential." *New York Times*, 31 December 1987, D2.

Wyman, Stephen H. "Colt Loses Firepower in Weapons Industry." *Washington Post*, 17 March 1989, B12.

—Dean Boyer, updated by Michael Knes

SIC 3489

ORDNANCE AND ACCESSORIES, NOT ELSEWHERE CLASSIFIED

This category covers establishments primarily engaged in manufacturing ordnance and accessories, not elsewhere classified, such as naval, aircraft, anti-aircraft, tank, coast, and field artillery having a bore more than 30 mm. (or more than 1.18 inch), and components. Establishments primarily engaged in manufacturing small arms and parts 30 mm. or less are classified in **SIC 3484: Small Arms;** those manufacturing tanks are classified in **SIC 3795: Tanks and Tank Components;** and those manufacturing guided missiles are classified in Industry Group 376 (Guided Missiles and Space Vehicles and Parts).

The Ordnance and Accessories industry declined in the post Cold War era, along with other high-tech industries (aerospace and search and navigation equipment manufacturing). The decline in defense spending, along with the private sector recession of 1990-91, were the main causes of the employment losses and downturns experienced in this industry since 1987. The prospects are dismal towards the year 2000, unless companies are able to shift their products to commercial markets and adapt commercial practices.

The value of shipments in the ordnance and accessories industry was $1.31 billion in 1991. Shipments declined every year since 1989, and reached a five-year low in 1996. The peak year for the industry was 1984, with $1.93 billion in shipments. Annual capital investments were projected at $18.2 million in 1996, lower than every year since 1991. The peak year for capital investments was 1987, with $50 million invested.

The projected total number of workers in the industry in 1996 was 18,200, fewer than all years since 1982. The number of workers in this field has dropped slightly every year since 1984. As with the value of shipments, 1984 was a peak year, with 14,700 production workers employed.

The industry is highly labor intensive, having only 19 percent as much investment per production worker as that for the manufacturing sector as a whole. Annual hours worked by production workers in the industry are slightly lower on average than those worked in the manufacturing sector at large, and hourly wages are 49 percent higher. The average hourly wage in 1996 was about $20. This was expected to increase to $21.54 by 1998.

In 1996, there were approximately 60 establishments in the ordnance industry, just over half of which had 20 or more employees. The heaviest concentration of establishments was in California (with 8). Other states with a large number of establishments in the industry were Ohio (6), Florida, Texas, and Michigan (5 each). Together these five states account for about 64 percent of all industry establishments in the United States.

The top five industries and sectors buying the outputs of the ordnance and accessories industry are listed as follows: federal government purchase, national defense, with a 72.0 percent share; exports, with a 24.4 percent share; ordnance and accessories, not elsewhere classified, with a 2.4 percent share; change in business inventories, with a 1.0 percent share; and small arms ammunition, with a 0.2 percent share.

One of the largest companies in this industry in the late 1990s was Alliant Techsystems Inc., of Hopkins, Minnesota, with total sales of approximately $1.194 billion, and over 8,000 employees. It was founded in 1990 upon its acquisition of the Defense and Marine Systems Business of Honeywell Inc.

Other industry leaders included Litton Industries Incorporated Laser Systems Division of Apopka, Florida, with total sales of about $40 million; Loral Hycor Incorporated of Woburn, Massachusetts, with $30 million in sales; and Amron Corporation of Waukesha, Wisconsin, with about $25 million in sales.

FURTHER READING

"Alliant Announces Layoffs in Spring." *Defense News,* 2 March 1992.

"Alliant Techsystems Lowers Profit Forecast." *Interavia Air Letter,* 23 November 1992.

Hetrick, Ron L. "Employment in High-Tech Defense Industries in a Post Cold War Era." *Monthly Labor Review,* August 1996, 57-63.

Lashinsky, Adam. "FMC Girds for Waning of Defense Business." *Crain's Chicago Business,* 10 May 1992.

Moody's Industrial Manual. New York: Moody's Investors Service Inc., 1993.

U.S. Bureau of the Census. *1995 Annual Survey of Manufactures.* Washington, GPO, 1991

Ward's Business Directory of U.S. Private and Public Companies. Detroit, Michigan: Gale Research 1993.

—David Kucera, updated by Beaird Glover

SIC 3491

INDUSTRIAL VALVES

This category covers establishments primarily engaged in manufacturing industrial valves. Establishments primarily engaged in manufacturing fluid power valves are classified in **SIC 3492: Fluid Power Valves and Hose Fittings;** those manufacturing plumbing fixture fittings and trim are classified in **SIC 3432: Plumbing Fixture Fittings and Trim;** and those manufacturing plumbing and heating valves are classified in **SIC 3494: Valves and Pipe Fittings, Not Elsewhere Classified.**

INDUSTRY SNAPSHOT

Segments of the valve industry were reclassified in 1987; therefore, data prior to 1987 is unavailable. However, between 1987 and 1994 the industry's level of shipments increased from nearly $4.60 billion to $7.66 billion, while the level of employment increased slightly from 46,400 to 50,900, with 34,000 of these being production workers. Workers in the industry made an average hourly wage of $12.93 in 1994, compared to $12.09 for all manufacturing industries. In 1992 Texas was the clear leader in employment, with 6,300 employees—12.3 percent of the U.S. total. California, Ohio, Iowa, Pennsylvania, and Massachusetts each had between 5 to 10 percent of total U.S. employees.

Compared to other manufacturing industries, the industrial valves segment is labor intensive. Comparative ratios of employees, production workers, wages, and hours worked per establishment are much higher than in other manufacturing industries. Cost, shipments, and investment per establishment are also higher than the manufacturing average. In 1993, 331 of the 504 total establishments in this classification employed more than 20 people.

The valve industry accounts for a significant portion of the overall metal castings industry. Gray iron valve castings stood at 263,000 tons in 1996 with a projected rise to 268,000 tons in 1997. Ductile iron sales to the valve industry were around $229 million in 1996 and were expected to grow through 1999. Corrosion-resistant steels, of particular use in environmental cleanup work, are a growth field in the industry. Copper-based castings for valves and fittings were estimated to increase to 98,000 tons in 1997. Other materials consumed include mill shapes such as sheet, plate, and bars of carbon and stainless steel, copper, and aluminum. Fabricated rubber, plastics, and wire products; ball and roller bearings; screw machine products,

including bolts, nuts, screws, and rivets; and electric motors also contributed greatly to the list of products consumed.

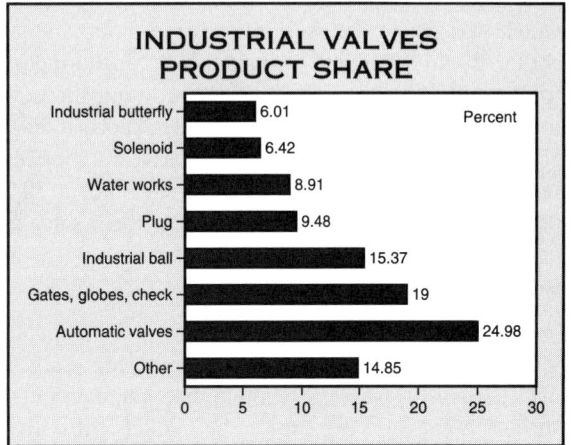

ORGANIZATION AND STRUCTURE

Industry market share is spread among ten product groups. The largest share, 24.98 percent, is automatic valves (regulating and control type) and parts. Other groups are: gates, globes, and check valves (19.0 percent); industrial ball valves (15.37 percent); industrial valves, not elsewhere classified (10.48 percent); industrial valves for water works (8.91 percent); solenoid valves (6.42 percent); industrial butterfly valves (6.01 percent); plug valves (5.00 percent); industrial plug valves (4.48 percent); nuclear valves (1.65 percent); and industrial valves, unspecified (2.71 percent).

Valve producers rely heavily on a number of economic sectors and industries for manufacturing input. The highest percentage of input is provided by blast furnaces and steel mills at 19.6 percent. Other inputs include imported materials (13.8 percent); wholesale trade (8.1); iron and steel foundries (7.5); and pipe, valves, and pipe fittings (3.2). The remaining almost 50 percent includes services such as advertising, banking, transportation, communication, and legal.

End use of valve shipments in 1996 was largely in five categories, which accounted for two-thirds of use: chemical (17.5 percent); water and sewage (17.1 percent); petroleum production (12.4 percent); petroleum refining (10.8 percent); and power generation (10.8 percent). The remaining one-third was divided among oil and gas transmission (5.4 percent), commercial construction (5.1 percent), gas distribution (2.3 percent), food and beverages (2.2 percent), iron and steel (1.9 percent), co-generation (1.8 percent), marine (1.5 percent) and miscellaneous uses (4.1 percent).

CURRENT CONDITIONS

The metal fabricating industry faced overall sluggish growth going into the mid-1990s as a result of heavy reliance on the industrial sector of the economy, which was recovering from a recession. International competition contributed to market loss for the industry; imports for the overall valve and fitting industry totaled over $2.6 billion in 1994, while exports totaled $2.2 billion. The industry in general saw weak prices in 1996, with a 3.7 percent rise in sales but a 30.1 percent drop in profits during the year. Steel sales in particular were poor, with a drop of 47.5 percent in earnings.

The industry expected to maintain a small annual increase in metal casting sales, which includes valves, of 1.6 percent from 1996 through 2006. Particular strong points were expected to be markets for corrosion-resistant metal valves, used by the petrochemical and chemical industries, plus cast stainless steel valves, used in environmental cleanup projects.

INDUSTRY LEADERS

Top companies in the industry fluctuate due to ongoing merger activity and sluggish profits due to economic downturns and foreign competition. Fisher-Rosemount Systems of Austin, Texas, through its Fisher Controls division—both owned by Emerson Electric Company—is considered the national leader by *Control* in the fields of sales, customer service, and product offerings. It also won a 1997 Microsoft Technical Innovations in Manufacturing award for designing a technologically sophisticated distributed control system for manufacturing plants.

Honeywell Inc., of Minneapolis, Minnesota, with overall sales of over $7.3 billion in 1996 and 53,000 employees, manufactures industrial control valves in addition to a host of other control products.

Tyco International now is the owner of several major companies within the industry and its 1996 sales grew to over $5.5 billion. In 1975 Tyco Laboratories purchased Grinell Corporation from International Telephone and Telegraph (ITT) with $14 million and the promise to pay 40 percent of Grinell's net earnings for the next ten years. This purchase, forced by federal courts on anti-trust grounds, was a boost for Tyco; in 1975 Tyco's sales were $58 million, compared to Grinell's $1.07 million. Subsequent acquisitions included Mueller Company in 1982, along with its water and natural gas flow control products, and the Henry Pratt Company (now a Mueller division). Tyco's major products include a full line of valves for industrial and process control—including butterfly, gate,

check, plug and ball valves, and sampling devices. Its major markets include heating, ventilation and air conditioning; gas and water distribution; commercial construction; automotive; hardware; petrochemical; oil and gas; food and beverage; and pharmaceutical markets.

Hunt Valve Company, of Salem, Ohio, manufactures specialty directional and control valves and complete valve systems for both commercial and military use. In 1996, it was sold by its parent company, Transtech Industries, to ValveCo, Inc.—a newly formed Delaware corporation in turn organized by an investment advisor company, Three Cities Research Inc.—for $18 million.

Like other successful competitors, Stockham Valves and Fittings of Birmingham, Alabama continued to expand operations. In 1991, it established cast products and flow control divisions. Later, in 1993, a joint venture was announced between Stockham and FlCOTECH, a manufacturer of fire safety equipment. The two will sell fire safety actuators which are designed to mount on Stockham valves, serving industries where fire or explosions are legitimate hazards. To expand overseas operations, Stockham acquired the Triangle Valve Company of England.

WORK FORCE

While the overall miscellaneous fabricated metal products industry faces significant downsizing in some occupations, other occupations are expected to grow through the year 2005. Combination machine tool operators, for example, are expected to boost their work force by 51 percent and machine tool cutting operators by 41.9 percent. Other occupations expected to grow significantly include industrial machinery mechanics (10.7 percent) and machine tool cutting and forming workers not elsewhere classified (20.8 percent).

The occupational group expected to face the most major reductions of over 25 percent is metal and plastic machine workers not elsewhere classified (28.7 percent). Groups with reductions between 10 to 25 percent include: bookkeeping and accounting clerks (24.5 percent); tool and die makers (18.7 percent); general office clerks (14.2 percent); hand packers and packagers (13.7 percent); and machine operators not elsewhere classified (11.3 percent). Other occupations expected to face reductions include: blue collar work supervisors; general managers and top executives; traffic, shipping and receiving clerks; machine feeders and offbearers; welding machine setters; lathe and turning machine tool operators; and general utility maintenance repairers.

AMERICA AND THE WORLD

The industry has faced tough competition from foreign companies along with drops in overall earnings. However, opportunities for valve manufacturers in overseas markets should increase as a result of increased concern over air and water quality and antiquated technologies in production and distribution, particularly in the oil industry. These factors, combined with worldwide reductions in trade barriers, should provide an important avenue for growth. By 1997, several companies had already made inroads into the Asian market, with General Signal opening a headquarters in Singapore and Crane Valves Group having entered into a joint venture agreement with the Hebei Ningjin Valve Plant in China, to market valves in China and the Pacific Rim countries.

RESEARCH AND TECHNOLOGY

Equipment leaks have become the focus of the U.S. Environmental Protection Agency (EPA), particularly in the area of air purification. With the implementation of the Clean Air Act Amendment of 1990, the National Emission Standard for Equipment Leaks became regulation. Emission concentration levels below 500 parts per million are now practical due to Fisher Controls' Enviro-Seal packing system for control valves. Similarly, Mark Controls patented a valve packing design that helps customers comply with the Clean Air Act. Honeywell developed an industrial control valve claimed to significantly reduce chemical pollution leakage.

Ten years of research resulted in a new aerodynamic prediction standard for control valves from the International Electronic Commission in 1995, allowing comparison of noise reduction claims made by manufacturers.

Several companies have introduced integrated process plant management control systems, of particular interest to refineries, petrochemical plants and gas processing facilities. The companies include Honeywell Inc., Foxboro Company, and Fisher-Rosemount. These systems are linked to other functions—such as billing, planning and scheduling, maintenance management and process simulation—and operate through a shared computer operating system.

FURTHER READING

Baumann, Hans. "Noise Regulated; Aerodynamic Noise Prediction Using Control Valves." *Process Engineering,* October 1996.

"Casting a Vote for Amcast." *Forbes,* 17 August 1992.

"Crane Co. Announces China Joint Venture." *PR Newswire,* 14 June 1995.

Darnay, Arsen J., ed. *Manufacturing USA.* 5th ed. Detroit: Gale Research Inc., 1996.

"Fisher Controls Ushers in Enviro-Seal Packing and Enviro-Service Maintenance to Meet Tough New Environmental Regulations." *Plant Engineering,* 19 November 1992.

International Directory of Company Histories. Chicago: St. James Press, 1991.

Kirgin, Kenneth H. "Solid Casting Markets Fuel 1997 Expansion: Industry Overview." *Modern Casting,* January 1997.

Lazich, Robert S., ed. *Market Share Reporter.* 7th ed. Detroit: Gale Research Inc., 1997.

Leach, Mark. "Higher Profit Is Seen by Amcast Industrial for Its Fiscal Year." *Wall Street Journal,* 23 July 1993.

"Monsanto to Sell Fisher Controls Subsidiary." *Chemical and Engineering News,* 10 August 1992.

"Monsanto Surprises with Fisher Sell-Off." *European Chemical News,* 10 August 1992.

Rhodes, Anne K. "Integrated Process Plant Management Systems Proliferating." *Oil & Gas Journal,* 7 October 1996.

Rudnitsky, Howard. "Metals." *Forbes,* 13 January 1997.

"Service/Suppliers: Stockham Valves & Fittings." *Oil & Gas Journal,* 9 August 1993.

"Service/Suppliers: Stockham Valves & Fittings." *Oil & Gas Journal,* 11 January 1993.

"Service/Suppliers: Stockham Valves & Fittings." *Oil & Gas Journal,* 9 September 1991.

Sherwood, Robert J. "Who's Where in the Industry Groups." *Forbes,* 13 January 1997.

Soloman, Caleb. "Forecast Spurs Dive in Cooper Industries Stock." *Wall Street Journal,* 26 January 1994.

"Taking Control of Industrial Processes." *Manufacturing Chemist,* February 1997.

"Transtech Industries Announces That It has Completed the Sale of Its Hunt Valve Subsidiary." *Business Wire,* 4 March 1996.

"Uniroyal Chemical and Fisher-Rosemount Systems Win Microsoft Technical Innovations in Manufacturing Awards." *PR Newswire,* 11 March 1997.

"US-based General Signal Opens Asia-Pacific Headquarters in Singapore." *Business Times (Singapore),* 21 February 1997.

"Wyman-Gordon Co.: Pact Is Reached to Acquire Cooper Industries Division." *Wall Street Journal,* 18 January 1994.

—Valerie Wilson, updated by Gerry Azzata

SIC 3492

FLUID POWER VALVES AND HOSE FITTINGS

This classification covers establishments primarily engaged in manufacturing hydraulic and pneumatic valves, hose and tube fittings, and hose assemblies for fluid power systems. Establishments primarily engaged in manufacturing fluid power cylinders are classified in **SIC 3593: Fluid Power Cylinders and Actuators;** those manufacturing fluid power pumps are classified in **SIC 3594: Fluid Power Pumps and Motors;** and those manufacturing hydraulic intake and exhaust motor vehicle valves are classified in **SIC 3592: Carburetors, Pistons, Piston Rings, and Valves.**

INDUSTRY SNAPSHOT

Industry data before 1987 is not available for this classification because it was not established as a separate category until that year. Between 1987 and 1994 the value of fluid power valves and hose fittings shipped by U.S. producers increased from $2.5 billion to $4.3 billion. Employment remained relatively flat, growing from 27,900 in 1987 to 30,100 in 1994, with about two-thirds being production workers throughout this time period. In the early 1990s, Ohio, California, Michigan, and Illinois accounted for 48 percent of the total employment. The wages of these workers were consistently higher than the average of all manufacturing industries; in 1994 they were $12.79 per hour, as opposed to manufacturing industries' overall $12.09 average.

The reduction of military spending, downward trends in the railroad industry, and negative publicity following the O-ring problem leading to the explosion of the Challenger space shuttle all contributed to the need for leaders in the industry to explore new markets in the 1990s.

ORGANIZATION AND STRUCTURE

Most of the establishments engaged in this industry employ more than 20 people. Therefore, this industry is characterized by larger businesses and labor intensive processes. In 1994 the amount of employees per establishment was higher than the average of all manufacturing, as were payroll, hours worked, and wage statistics and shipments per establishment. Shifting from earlier trends, shipments per establishment also were higher than average and investment per establishment was average.

Product share is split among 13 manufactured items. The largest segment of 12.45 percent was hydraulic and pneumatic hose or tube end fittings and assemblies. Other segments were: aerospace hydraulic and pneumatic fluid power hose or tube end fittings and assemblies, 10.94 percent; aerospace hydraulic fluid power valves, 10.89 percent; nonaerospace flareless fittings and couplings used in fluid power transfer systems, 10.35 percent; nonaerospace pneumatic directional control valves, 9.90 percent; nonaerospace hydraulic directional control valves, 9.72 percent; nonaerospace hydraulic valves, except directional control, 8.46 percent; nonaerospace hydraulic and pneumatic hose assemblies, 6.06 percent; nonaerospace flared metal fittings, couplings and tubing assemblies used in fluid power transfer systems, 5.83 percent; nonaerospace pneumatic valves, except directional control, 4.45 percent; parts for fluid power valves, 4.17 percent; fluid power valves not elsewhere classified, 3.48 percent; and aerospace pneumatic power control valves, 3.31 percent.

Fluid power valves rely heavily on a number of economic sectors and industries for the inputs to business. The highest percentage of input is provided by blast furnaces and steel mills, at 19.6 percent in the early 1990s. Imported materials claimed 13.8 percent of inputs, while wholesale trade claimed 8.1 percent. Iron and steel foundries contributed 7.5 percent, and pipe, valves, and pipe fittings made up 3.2 percent of the inputs required for manufacture. The remaining approximately 50 percent included contributors such as advertising and banking, transportation services, communication and legal services, and other heavy industrial suppliers.

The benefactors of the fluid power valves and hose fittings segment are similarly varied. Industrial buildings demanded the greatest amount of outputs from this industry in the early 1990s, at 12.2 percent—slightly more than gross private fixed investment at 11.7 percent. Approximately 8 percent of production was exported. Maintenance of nonfarm buildings consumed 5.5 percent of the output, while crude petroleum and natural gas required 4 percent. Other consumers of fluid power valves and pipe fittings include sewer system construction, household laundry equipment, paper mills, and oil field machinery.

CURRENT CONDITIONS

Although consumer confidence in the economy and earning potential was pessimistic going into the mid-1990s, lower financing terms made automobiles and housing more affordable and attractive, which was good for the support industries like fluid power valves.

Overseas, the outlook was much more grim. Europe's recession and turbulence over economic unification, added to Japan's slowed economy, caused forecasters to become cautious. Imported products in the general metal industry continued to be a great concern.

Industry leaders of the early 1990s were forced to re-examine their product lines and their key markets given the downsizing of the U.S. military, the decline of the railroad industry, and terrible publicity surrounding the defective O-rings that caused the Challenger space shuttle disaster. Companies needed to look to international markets, particularly Europe— where companies such as Manuli Rubber Industries Group of Italy are in turn seeking to enter the American market. Other emerging markets may be found in Central and Eastern Europe, China, South America, India, and South Africa. Product development began to focus on areas such as emission control and quick-assembly items for automotive hoses and similar uses.

INDUSTRY LEADERS

The top companies engaged in this industry include: ITT Fluid Technology Corporation of Midland Park, New Jersey; Fisher Controls of St. Louis, Missouri (a subsidiary of Fisher-Rosemount Systems of Austin, Texas); Keystone International of Houston, Texas; Applied Power Inc. of Butler, Wisconsin; and Duriron Company, Inc. of Dayton, Ohio.

ITT Fluid Technology Corporation—chiefly through its ITT Engineered Valves Unit—produces a range of pharmaceutical valve components and maintains four U.S. offices and facilities in Great Britain, Puerto Rico, and South America. The parent corporation has annual sales of over $1 billion.

Duriron focuses on fluid handling equipment for processing corrosive fluids used in manufacturing. Its products include: centrifugal process and chemical injection metering pumps; automatic control valves, rotary valves, and associated automation equipment; filtration equipment and complete waste water systems; laboratory drainage pipe and fittings; and high alloy castings. In 1996, Duriron reported sales of $605.5 million, an increase of 13.7 percent from the previous year, and had 3,900 employees.

Keystone International is genuinely an international company, with nearly 60 percent of 1995 sales coming from overseas. In 1996, Keystone consolidated its international sales and manufacturing into two groups, the Industrial Valves and Controls Group and the Engineered Products Group. It produces equipment for liquid and gas flow control, with application in wide settings such as the chemical, food and beverage, and petroleum industries. Its 1995 sales totaled $597.1 million—up 11.6 percent from the previous year—and it had 4,250 employees.

Applied Power Inc. defines itself as "a holding company managing a balanced portfolio of autonomous operating businesses primarily serving industrial markets. We seek to own and develop businesses with intrinsic competitive advantages that serve a variety of end-user markets in different geographic regions, with an emphasis on investment." The companies held are divided into two groups, the first being the Distributed Products Group which contains Enerpac and GB Electrical, and the second being the Engineered Solutions Group which contains Barry Controls and Power-Packer/APlTECH. In 1996, Applied Power had sales of $571.2 million—up 8.4 percent from the previous year—and 3,035 employees.

WORK FORCE

While the overall miscellaneous fabricated metal products industry faces significant downsizing in some occupations, other occupations are expected to grow through the year 2005. Combination machine tool operators, for example, are expected to boost their work force by 51 percent and machine tool cutting operators by 41.9 percent. Other occupations expected to grow significantly include industrial machinery mechanics (10.7 percent) and machine tool cutting and forming workers not elsewhere classified (20.8 percent).

The occupational group expected to face the most major reductions of over 25 percent incorporates metal and plastic machine workers not elsewhere classified (28.7 percent). Groups with reductions between 10 to 25 percent include: bookkeeping and accounting clerks (24.5 percent); tool and die makers (18.7 percent); general office clerks (14.2 percent); hand packers and packagers (13.7 percent); and machine operators not elsewhere classified (11.3 percent). Other occupations expected to face reductions include: blue collar work supervisors; general managers and top executives; traffic, shipping and receiving clerks; machine feeders and offbearers; welding machine setters; lathe and turning machine tool operators; and general utility maintenance repairers.

AMERICA AND THE WORLD

Through the latter part of the 1990s companies continued to look to international markets, particularly Europe where companies are in turn seeking to enter the American market. Other emerging markets may be found in Central and Eastern Europe, China, South America, India, and South Africa.

RESEARCH AND TECHNOLOGY

One of the biggest changes in valve technology lies in the micromachines markets. The Pentagon's Defense Advanced Research Projects Agency (DARPA), is currently working on the fabrication of a "tiny valve on a silicon chip that can replace bigger, costlier metal valves. One possible use: controlling the flow of samples into a small gas chromatograph that detects poisons in the environment." Fluid power valves and controls with electronic and microprocessor components have been under general development since the early 1990s.

Thermoplastic parts were a popular trend for a time, but metal parts are becoming the standard once again in engines. Thermoplastics proved to be less satisfactory for hoses and fittings because of rising temperatures near engines and the need for greater noise and vibration damping.

FURTHER READING

"Applied Power Inc." *Hoover's Company Capsules,* 1997. Available from http://www.hoovers.com/.

Applied Power, Inc. 1993 Annual Report. Milwaukee, WI: Applied Power Inc., 1994.

Autry, Ret. "Companies to Watch: Keystone International." *Fortune,* 6 May 1991.

Carey, John. "Meet the Champion of the Micro Age." *Business Week,* 26 April 1993.

Darnay, Arsen J., ed. *Manufacturing USA.* 5th ed. Detroit: Gale Research Inc., 1996.

"The Duriron Company, Inc." *Hoover's Company Capsules,* 1997. Available from http://www.hoovers.com/.

Duriron Company 1992 Annual Report. Dayton, OH: Duriron, 1993.

"Fluid Power Embraces Electronics." *Design News,* 4 November 1991.

International Directory of Company Histories. Detroit: St. James Press, 1991.

"Keystone International, Inc." *Hoover's Company Capsules,* 1997. Available from http://www.hoovers.com/.

"Keystone on Its Keister." *Forbes,* 30 August 1993.

Reimer, David M. "Machinery Industry." *The Value Line Investment Survey,* 11 February 1994.

"Services/Suppliers: Keystone International." *Oil & Gas Journal,* 18 May 1992.

"Valves Engineered to Pharmaceutical Process Standards." *Pharmaceutical Manufacturing Review,* December 1996.

White, Liz. "Activity Intensifies in Hose and Belting Industry." *European Rubber Journal,* December 1996.

Wisnia, Saul E. "Reaching New Heights With New Markets." *Industrial Distribution,* February 1997.

—Valerie Wilson, updated by Gerry Azzata

SIC 3493

STEEL SPRINGS, EXCEPT WIRE

This category includes establishments primarily engaged in manufacturing leaf springs, hot wound springs, and coiled flat springs. Establishments primarily engaged in manufacturing wire springs are classified in **SIC 3495: Wire Springs.**

The spring manufacturing industry does not differentiate between the standard industrial codes of steel springs, except wire and wire springs. Instead, the Spring Manufacturers Institute, Inc. (SMI) analyzes the industry as one unit. In 1992, SMI reported that the industry generated almost $1.9 billion in sales and employed 20,735 people. According to the *1995 Census of Manufactures,* the specific segment of the industry covered by **SIC 3493: Steel Springs, Except Wire** employed 4,000 people and had a payroll of $126.3 million. Industry shipments were valued at $570.9 million, a decline of about 4 percent from the 1994 level of $593.5 million. For more information on the spring manufacturing industry as a whole, consult the essay on **SIC 3495: Wire Springs.**

The automotive industry is the largest customer for steel springs. SMI reported that sales to automotive customers accounted for the largest portion, 41.3 percent of industry sales in 1992, followed by industrial equipment customers, which accounted for 8.8 percent of sales. Alloy, carbon, and stainless steels were the most commonly used spring materials because of their strength. Titanium was gaining popularity in the early 1990s because of its superior strength, light weight, and resistance to corrosion. Titanium's high cost was once prohibitive, but new titanium alloys expanded its use.

Advances in technology have boosted the production capabilities of some spring manufacturers, but this not a requirement for survival in the industry. Tecknow Education Services Inc. president, George Keremedjiev, noted in *Springs* that spring manufacturing companies were using anything from "state-of-the-art electronics in tooling to machinery and tooling that seemingly is frozen in time back in the 1950s." The technology employed can run the gamut from old machines fitted with electronic sensors that check spring positioning to the Spring Manufacturers Institute, Inc.'s (SMI) Spring Design software program, which enables the most novice engineer to successfully design springs. Hindering greater implementation of technology has been the lack of nationalized standards for spring making.

Because the capital investments required for advances in technology are high, companies must consider the competitive advantages of modernization. If a company is able to maintain or increase sales volume with old assets, it may not be beneficial to modernize its machinery because of the cost involved. SMI's *1992 Annual Market Summary* noted that modernization would be an inefficient use of assets unless it helped "to produce a higher profit percentage on net sales." Nevertheless, Keremedjiev predicted in *Springs* that modern methods of production are needed for a spring manufacturer "to achieve world class quality in the production process." Also, according to Scott Rankin of Vulcan Spring in *Springs,* there is "universal recognition" that technology will change the industry. Spring making, once known as the "Black Art" because of its difficulty, can now be mastered by a "spring maker with a month's knowledge and the ability to type numbers on a keyboard," noted Rankin.

As trade barriers are removed throughout the world, the American spring industry has had to compete for foreign manufacturing customers. Supplying American springs to foreign customers will keep the industry competitive because, according to SMI president Pete Peterson, "We don't worry too much about Japanese springs landing in America. But we must worry about the finished products coming here." To compete globally, some American spring makers counteract manufacturers' preferences for national suppliers by forming joint ventures with prominent foreign spring makers. One such joint venture allowed America's largest spring maker, Associated Spring of Bristol, Connecticut, to establish relationships with Japanese automakers through its association with NHK Spring Co., Ltd. of Japan, Japan's largest spring maker.

FURTHER READING

1995 Census of Manufactures, Washington: U.S. Department of Commerce, 1997.

Keremedjiev, George. "Sensors and Electronics in Spring Manufacture . . . the Key to Savings and Quality." *Springs,* May 1993, 27-28.

"Looking Ahead—Not Back—as SMI Celebrates its 60th Anniversary." *Springs,* October 1993, 54.

Peterson, Bud. "The Family Tree of Springmakers Withstands the Winds of Change." *Springs,* May 1993, 77-85.

"Petersons Stamp Success on Spring Industry." *Springs,* October 1993.

"Removing the Veil of the 'Black Art,° Newcomers Share Their Enthusiasm for the Springs Industry." *Springs,* October 1992.

"Spring Design Enters New Era." *Springs,* October 1992, 11-12.

U.S. Census Bureau. *Annual Survey of Manufactures,* Washington: U.S. Census Bureau, 1991.

Additional information provided by the Spring Manufacturers Institute, Inc.

—Sara Pendergast, updated by Ken Shepherd

SIC 3494

VALVES AND PIPE FITTINGS, NOT ELSEWHERE CLASSIFIED

This category includes establishments primarily engaged in manufacturing metal valves and pipe fittings, not elsewhere classified, such as plumbing and heating valves, and pipe fittings, flanges, and unions, except from purchased pipes. Establishments primarily engaged in manufacturing plastics pipe fittings are classified in **SIC 3089: Plastics Products, Not Elsewhere Classified;** those manufacturing plumbing fixture fittings and trim are classified in **SIC 3432: Plumbing Fixture Fittings and Trim;** and those manufacturing fittings and couplings for garden hoses are classified in **SIC 3429: Hardware, Not Elsewhere Classified.**

The valves and pipe fittings industry is heavily reliant on both the oil and construction industries. The domestic oil industry has been depressed since the mid-1980s, but the retrofitting of pipes in the housing market has served to maintain a level of stability in this industry.

Growth in the industry was assured because of changes in fire sprinkler laws. A fire in a Puerto Rico hotel in the early 1990s caused the federal government to review and change laws regarding automatic fire sprinkler systems in buildings exceeding six stories. Additionally, a low-rise hotel fire in Chicago, which killed 15 people in 1993, caused the federal automatic fire sprinkler laws to change regarding buildings lower than seven stories. As a result, many buildings started retrofitting to comply with new safety regulations.

In the late 1990s, approximately 69 percent of the metal valve and pipe fitting industry was engaged in producing metal fittings, flanges, and unions for piping systems. Nearly another 23 percent of the industry was engaged in producing plumbing and heating valves.

As of 1996, the industry employed nearly 12,000 people in the United States, whose earnings averaged $13 per hour. By 1998, overall employment was expected to decline to 8,500. The primary occupation of the industry was assemblers and fabricators. The occupations expected to increase are combination machine tool operators (51 percent) and machine tool cutting operators (42 percent). Those expected to decrease include metal/plastic machine workers (29 percent), bookkeeping personnel (25 percent), tool and die makers (19 percent), and machine forming operators and welding machine setters (9 percent).

In 1995, the value of shipments was $2.36 billion. By 1998, this was projected to decrease to $1.86 billion. The number of establishments was also expected to drop to around 130, down from about 200 in 1995.

Some of the industry leaders include Crane Company, of Connecticut; Automatic Switch Company, of New Jersey; Aeroquip Industrial Americas Group, of Ohio; and Keystone Valve USA Incorporated, of Texas. Texas had the highest number of establishments in the mid-1990s with 47, and they generated 9.6 percent of U.S. shipments. Pennsylvania produced 17.4 percent in its 21 establishments; and Ohio's 29 establishments produced 10.7 percent of U.S. shipments.

FURTHER READING

Darnay, Arsen J., ed. *Manufacturing USA*. 5th ed. Detroit: Gale Research, 1996.

U.S. Bureau of the Census. *1995 Annual Survey of Manufactures*. Washington: GPO, January 1997.

SIC 3495

WIRE SPRINGS

This industry consists of establishments primarily engaged in manufacturing wire springs from purchased wire. Establishments primarily engaged in assembling wire bedsprings or seats are classified in the Furniture and Fixtures industries.

INDUSTRY SNAPSHOT

The 1996 value of shipments in the wire springs industry—which includes the production of furniture, mechanical, clock, gun, instrument, sash balance, and hair springs—was approximately $2.23 billion, up

from $1.10 billion in 1982 (in current dollars). There were 392 establishments in the industry in 1993 (a sharp decline from the 432 establishments reported in 1982), with only 206 of these having 20 or more employees. Establishments were expected to decrease to 370 by 1998. The value of shipments rose from $1.1 billion in 1982 to $2.1 billion in 1994.

Employment through the 1980s and 1990s has been somewhat unsteady. The industry employed 17,900 production workers in 1982, rising to a high of 21,900 in 1985, then gradually falling to 19,400 by 1994. Employment in the late 1990s was expected to be about 19,500. Average wages for these workers, however, improved considerably, from $7.59 per hour in 1982 to $11.89 in 1994. Illinois, Ohio, and Michigan led in employment in the early 1990s.

ORGANIZATION AND STRUCTURE

A full 80 percent of the top 75 firms in the industry were private independents. The capital requirements for the industry were relatively low, with the average investment per establishment 41 percent of that for the manufacturing sector as a whole. Prior to the 1980s, it was rare for firms to cooperate in the production of springs, but this changed in more recent years. Firms learned to cooperate on a number of bases. For example, some firms developed expertise in grinding springs at high tolerances, while others developed high levels of efficiency in looping the wire on the ends of springs. Other spring-producing firms found it advantageous to hire these firms for such operations.

The smallest firms had fewer than 25 employees, and generally did not design the springs they produced, relying instead on specifications provided by their customers. They typically produced small batches of springs made from larger wires (up to about 3/8 inches in diameter), as well as batches both large and small from smaller diameter wires (up to about 0.08 inches in diameter). These versatile firms typically had one or two hand-operated spring coilers and several automatic spring coilers, in addition to a lathe or two for coiling heavier wires. Also, these small firms typically had a number of machines devoted to the other processes necessary for spring production, including grinders, spring testers, baking ovens, and various machine tools.

Medium-size plants had 25 to 100 employees, and these made up the largest share of firms in the industry. Three-fourths of the top 75 firms in the industry had 100 or fewer employees. These firms typically employed engineers to design and test springs. Medium-size firms either specialized in producing coil springs in large batches or were diversified in the production of a large number of spring types. These firms employed processes similar to those used in smaller firms, and the main distinctions regarding capital goods were the number and size of machines. These firms also typically had a greater variety of machines to supplement core production processes, such as electroplating equipment. Using computers in the design and production of springs after the 1980s led to greater qualitative distinctions in the production processes of smaller and larger firms.

Large firms had more than 100 employees. There were about 15 such firms in the United States in the early 1990s. These firms typically had a greater number of technical and scientific staff. In addition to engineers, such firms employed metallurgists and highly-trained inspectors. These firms also devoted substantial resources to specialized research equipment, such as fatigue testers and wire twisting machines. These large establishments were typically diversified in the production of all major spring types and were often diversified across industry lines.

In the years just after World War II, production of springs was tightly concentrated in the northeastern states of Connecticut, New York, Pennsylvania, Illinois, and Ohio. The states ranking in the top ten by value of shipments in the late 1980s were, in order of descending value: Illinois, Michigan, Indiana, California, Ohio, Pennsylvania, Kentucky, North Carolina, Tennessee, and Connecticut, indicating a proportional shift in regional production. Together these ten states accounted for 64 percent of total shipments and 65 percent of total employment. Some plants in the midwest produced principally for the automobile industry, while some in California and Pennsylvania produced principally for the aircraft and railroad industries, respectively.

The outputs of the wire springs industry were widely dispersed across industry and sector lines, reflecting the great extent to which the industry was dependent not only on the production of manufactures, but on the production of the economy at large. The top ten industries and sectors buying the outputs of the industry were: mattresses and bedsprings (5.8 percent); logging camps and logging contractors (5.1 percent); concrete products, not elsewhere classified (four percent); tires and inner tubes (3.2 percent); construction machinery and equipment (three percent); personal consumption expenditures (2.9 percent); exports (2.9 percent); office buildings (2.7 percent); retail trade, except eating and drinking (2.5 percent); and highway and street construction (2.4 percent). Precision mechanical wire springs comprised 42.6 percent of the product share. Other types of wire springs ac-

counted for the remainder of the product share— over half of these being wire spring units for box springs and mattresses, and seat and back wire springs for motor vehicles.

BACKGROUND AND DEVELOPMENT

The wire spring manufacturing industry grew rapidly in the post-World War II period. The number of plants producing precision springs increased by about six-fold from 1940 to 1980. Membership in the Spring Manufacturers Institute increased from 40 in 1940 to 350 in the 1990s.

The Spring Manufacturers Institute was founded in 1933 (its name changed from the Spring Manufactures Association in 1961). It had a staff of four in the mid-1990s, and was headquartered in Rolling Meadows, Illinois. The institute published two periodicals, the quarterly *Coiler's Gazette* (circulation 750) and the semi-annual *Springs: The Magazine of Spring Technology* (circulation 7,000), as well as the books, *Handbook of Spring Design, Spring Materials, Specification Cross Reference,* and *Mechanical Springs.* In addition, the institute produced the software program "Spring Design." The industry was also served by the American Society of Mechanical Engineers in New York, New York, the American Society for Testing and Material in Philadelphia, Pennsylvania, and the American Society for Metals in Metals Park, Ohio.

There are three primary types of wire springs: compression springs absorb energy as they are compressed, extension springs as they are extended, and torsion springs as they are twisted. The design and production of wire springs has been referred to as a "Black Art" because of the complexity of interactive variables that must be taken into account. The industry used about 100 types of metals in the production of springs. The choice of the optimal metal depends on such conditions as the potential for corrosion, conductivity, the loads to be borne by the spring, the temperature ranges to which the spring will be exposed, the desired working-life of the spring, and size constraints. The basic types of metals included high-carbon steels, steel alloys, stainless steels, and copper and nickel-based alloys. Since the cost of materials can vary from one to hundreds of dollars per pound and safety was often a factor (in production of vehicles, for instance), the optimal choice of materials was vital.

The production process begins with the operation of coiling metal wire. For smaller batches (several hundred or less), the manufacturer used a hand-operated coiler or a lathe. Larger batches used automatic coilers. Whereas in the mid-1970s, many coilers produced at the rate of 3,000 to 5,000 springs per hour, by the 1980s machines were sold that coiled up to 18,000 springs per hour. After being coiled, springs were baked to stabilize their shape. Thereafter, they were compressed to remove any set that would accumulate during usage. Lastly, the ends of the springs were shaped (in the case of extension and torsion springs) and ground. Precision grinding was among the most time-consuming and expensive operations in the production of springs. After they were thus formed, springs were typically finished by either oiling, painting, electroplating, or oxidizing.

In addition to the more common wire spring types are hairsprings. These are spiral springs made from very fine flattened wire (as thin as 0.0002 inches). These springs were used in clocks and watches, as well as specialized precision instruments. Hairsprings were produced by only a few firms.

The value of shipments continued to increase after 1985, though at a slower pace than in the early-1980s. There were $54 million in capital investments made in 1991, down from a peak of $71 million in 1984. Employment of production workers peaked in 1985 and declined thereafter. The Bureau of Labor Statistics made employment forecasts for 30 occupational categories in the miscellaneous fabricated metal products industries. Based on projected changes from years 1990 to 2005, employment was expected to decline by double-digit figures in nine occupations (occupations accounting for 30 percent total employment in 1990) and single-digit figures in ten other occupations. Only three occupations were projected to show double digit increases to 2005 (occupations accounting for only six percent of total employment in 1990). Thus, overall employment prospects for the industry did not appear promising. Projections made for the wire spring industry alone would have varied from these figures, but the trend toward automation of spring production suggested consistency with projections for miscellaneous fabricated metal products level.

Four top executives in the industry were interviewed in the October 1992 issue of *Springs: The Magazine of Spring Technology* regarding the current state and future of the industry. They regarded the industry as highly fragmented, with an excessive number of small firms. One executive stated, "Most companies are under five million dollars and a handful show ten million dollars in sales. It's ironic because I believe the critical size, at least five million dollars, is necessary to survive in the coming years." In the same light, another executive stated, "We'll need to investigate strategic alliances, the shrinking number of companies serving our industry plus more joint ventures." Executives described the industry as being excessively

price competitive. Two of them noted that firms' marketing and price strategies should emphasize the degree of engineering and the tight tolerances required for the production of springs. The impact of technological change and diffusion was expected to be of ever-increasing importance in coming years, and the possibility of the increased viability of plastic springs in the future was noted.

CURRENT CONDITIONS

The metal fabricating industry faced overall sluggish growth going into the later 1990s, as a result of increased competition, increased costs of raw materials, and declining demand. There also was potential competition for wire springs in a thermoplastic material being developed that would replace the need for springs and wires in automotive seat frames, a major segment of the industry.

The metal industry in general saw weak prices in 1996, with a 3.7 percent rise in sales but a 30.1 percent drop in profits during the year. Sales of steel (a prime component of many springs) were particularly poor, with a drop of 47.5 percent in earnings.

INDUSTRY LEADERS

Associated Spring, a division of the Barnes Group, Inc., is the industry leader. Incorporated in 1925, Associated Spring extended its operations widely across the United States and the world with facilities in ten states as well as in Mexico, the United Kingdom, Singapore, Canada, Brazil, and France.

The firm suffered declining sales and net losses entering the 1990s, and it announced in 1992 that it would close two of its plants as part of a broader consolidation strategy. William R. Fenoglio, president and CEO of the Barnes Group, stated that the concentration of manufacturing facilities in fewer locations would enable the firm to lower costs. In 1993, Associated Spring invested in new technologies using computer-aided design. An article in the July 23, 1993 issue of *Machine-Design* reported, "Associated Spring plans on taking an industry that has traditionally been low technology and bringing it into the twenty-first century, according to Andre Papillon, senior product design engineer for Associated Spring."

As the 1990s progressed, Associated Spring (and Bowman in general) initiated successful cost-cutting measures, many aimed at reducing losses in its European operations. In 1996 the Associated Spring plants in Milwaukee and Singapore were scheduled to be expanded, along with research and development facilities in Connecticut. Increased attention went to the growing electronics and residential products markets. Bowman reported record profits through the third quarter of 1996 (almost $450 million for the first nine months of 1996), including a 4 percent rise in profits at Associated Spring. The strongest segments of the spring operations were its automotive-related operations (boosted by the strong consumer market for sport-utility vehicles and light trucks), its die spring operations, and its Mexico City plant.

American Spring Wire, founded in 1968, was a private corporation and had about $80 million in sales and 300 employees in 1992. The firm purchased the equipment and inventory of J and S Metals, Inc. in 1991, thus expanding its operations by backwards integration. In late 1996, it also acquired Shinko Wire America's Houston facility, which produces high quality steel strand used in concrete construction, rather than wire springs. Its general sales manager, Timothy W. Selhorst, stated in *American Metal Market* on the general state of the industry in 1996: "Competition in the tempered wire business continues to be very, very tough. . . .We're holding our own, but there have been better times to be an American wire producer."

Peterson Spring was a division of Peterson American, a private corporation. Peterson Spring generated about $75 million in sales and had 600 employees in 1992. The firm was founded in 1929 and had 20 manufacturing plants, 14 U.S. offices, and seven foreign offices. A large portion of the firm's production was purchased by the automobile industry. The firm's plants were given several awards for quality production by its customers in the 1990s. Peterson Spring's Ontario plant received the Chrysler Quality Excellence Award in 1992, and its Windsor plant was awarded the General Motors Mark of Excellence Award in 1993.

RESEARCH AND TECHNOLOGY

The two key areas of development in the industry were the use of computers and electronics in the production and design of springs and the development of new materials. The Spring Manufacturers Institute developed a software program for the design of compression, extension, and torsion springs. The program was based on parameters drawn from the *SMI Handbook of Spring Design,* and enabled those with little experience to design springs that were optimal under various sets of constraints. The program was expected to be useful not only to spring manufacturers, but also to spring buyers. These buyers could better design their products with prior knowledge of the spring configurations.

The production process was substantially altered in recent years with the increased viability of Computer Numerically Controlled (CNC) spring-making equipment. The implementation of these technologies in spring-making lagged behind the machine tool industry both because of the relatively small size of the wire spring industry and because of the complex set of operations required for the production of springs. The newest CNC technologies made possible the increased speed of production, lesser setup and training times, greater precision, and lower costs. The increased use of electronic sensors was also advocated as a means of modernizing production.

Springs made from titanium alloys weighed one-half of those made from steel and were also highly resistant to corrosion. The cost of titanium alloys had been prohibitive for many applications, but new and less costly titanium alloys enabled their rapidly expanded use.

Neturen USA Inc. (a subsidiary of Neturen Company of Tokyo) and Laclede Steel Company have begun to manufacture cold-formed spring steel wire, which already is used by many European automobile manufacturers for suspension springs and is gaining a market among U.S. manufacturers. Cold-formed wire is less costly to produce and weighs less than conventional wire. American Spring has developed urethane compression springs that can be used where corrosion, vibration, and magnetism do not allow use of steel springs.

FURTHER READING

"American Spring Buying Shinko Facility." *American Metal Market,* 21 November 1996.

"Barnes Group Launches Worldwide Expansion Program to Meet Growth Needs in Its Manufacturing Operations." *Business Wire,* 18 March 1996.

"Barnes Group Reports All-time Record Earnings for Third Quarter of 1996." *Business Wire,* 10 October 1996.

"Barnes Group: Will Close Two Spring Production Plants and a Distribution Facility." *The Wall Street Journal,* 2 December 1992.

Carlson, Harold. *Spring Manufacturing Handbook.* New York, New York: Marcel Dekker, Inc., 1982.

Census of Manufactures. Washington: Bureau of the Census, 1992. Available from http://www.census.gov.

Daniels, Peggy Kneffel and Carol A. Schwartz, eds. *Encyclopedia of Associations.* 28th ed. Detroit: Gale Research Inc., 1994.

Darnay, Arsen J., ed. *Manufacturing USA: Industry Analysis, Statistics, and Leading Companies.* 5th ed. Detroit: Gale Research Inc., 1996.

Directory of Leading Private Companies. 7th ed. Wilmette, IL: National Register Reference Publishing, 1992.

"Firm Will Post Loss for Year After Charge of $40.7 Million." *The Wall Street Journal,* 27 January 1993.

Godfrey, Loren. "Justifying New Technologies; As CNC Machines Come of Age." *Springs: The Magazine of Spring Technology,* May 1993.

"Investing in the Future with Analysis." *Machine-Design,* 23 July 1993.

Keremedjiev, George. "Sensors and Electronics in Spring Manufacture . . . The Key to Savings and Quality." *Springs: The Magazine of Spring Technology,* May 1993.

"Laclede Steers for Spring Wire." *American Metal Market,* 26 May 1995.

Lanke, Ed. "Spring Design Enters New Era." *Springs: The Magazine of Spring Technology,* October 1992.

Moody's Industrial Manual. New York: Moody's Investors Service Inc., 1993.

"More Application Flexibility Afforded by New Associated Spring-Raymond Urethane Compression Springs." *News Release,* 24 July 1996.

"Neturen Sets Up Wire Deal in US." *American Metal Market,* 27 January 1997.

"Plant News." *Springs: The Magazine of Spring Technology,* October 1992.

"Plant News." *Springs: The Magazine of Spring Technology,* May 1993.

Pryweller, Joseph. "Thermoplastics Key to New Delphi Seats." *Plastics News,* 10 March 1997.

"Removing the Veil of the 'Black Art,' Newcomers Share Their Enthusiasm for Springs Industry." *Springs: The Magazine of Spring Technology,* October 1992.

Rudnitsky, Howard. "Metals." *Forbes,* 13 January 1997.

Sommer, Chris. "Titanium Offers Heavy-Weight Potential for Spring Makers." *Springs: The Magazine of Spring Technology,* October 1993.

"Steel Wire Makers Hit From Both Ends." *American Metal Market,* 1 October 1996.

Viani, Laura. "American Spring Wire Buys J&S Equipment, Inventory." *American Metal Market,* 5 June 1991.

—David Kucera, updated by Gerry Azzata

SIC 3496

MISCELLANEOUS FABRICATED WIRE PRODUCTS

This category includes establishments primarily engaged in manufacturing miscellaneous fabricated wire products from purchased wire, such as non-insulated wire rope and cable; fencing; screening, netting, paper machine wire cloth; hangers, paper clips, kitchenware, and wire carts. Rolling mills engaged in manufacturing wire products are classified in the Primary Metal Industries. Establishments primarily engaged in manufacturing steel nails and spikes from purchased wire or rod are classified in **SIC 3315: Steel Wiredrawing and Steel Nails and Spikes;** those manufacturing nonferrous wire nails and spikes from purchased wire or rod are classified in **SIC 3399: Primary Metal Products, Not Elsewhere Classified;** those drawing and insulating nonferrous wire are classified in **SIC 3357: Drawing and Insulating of Nonferrous Wire;** and those manufacturing wire springs are classified in **SIC 3495: Wire Springs.**

The miscellaneous fabricated wire products industry produces a wide variety of wire-based goods, from barbed wire to bird cages to conveyor belts to hog rings to paper clips. The largest single product produced by the industry is noninsulated ferrous wire rope and cable, representing 12.92 percent of the product share in the early 1990s. While ferrous and nonferrous wire cloth, ferrous woven wire products, fencing, and fence gates all claim significant shares of the market, the production of the majority of products produced by this industry is too limited to be represented statistically. The materials consumed by the industry include steel castings, plastics and bolts, stainless steel, and copper and aluminum wires. Steel wire is the most heavily consumed category of wire, with a delivered cost to the industry of $689.1 million in 1992.

The 1980s and 1990s saw the number of establishments involved in this industry drop then rise again almost to their 1982 level (1,171 establishments) by 1993. The value of shipments rose from $2.357 billion in 1982 to $4.063 billion in 1994. Shipment values were expected to reach $4.2 billion in 1998. The industry work force grew moderately, rising from 36,800 employees in 1982 to 41,100 by 1994. In 1994, the 31,600 production workers in this industry averaged $8.92 per hour. End users of these products vary widely, ranging from mattress and bedspring makers to tire makers, logging camps, and highway and building construction.

Barbed wire, the most famous of miscellaneous fabricated wire products, changed the course of American history. According to Henry D. and Frances T. McCallum, authors of *The Wire that Fenced the West,* "The introduction of barbed wire in the 1870s had remarkable social and economic consequences. Before the wire's invention, fences were intended to keep animals and trespassers out. Because barbed wire effectively kept animals in, the landholding concepts of cattlemen and small settlers changed radically with the new power that barbed wire gave them."

Before barbed wire, ranchers used plain wire, wooden fences, and natural hedges to mark their territory. However, these boundaries were generally impractical, labor intensive, and highly penetrable. When a rancher had only his family to tend the animals, maintaining a fence around the perimeter of hundreds or thousands of acres was out of the question. Having such a problem to deal with, the rancher kept his stock to a low, manageable number. Getting rich in the West off of cattle and horses required an investment in cow hands and a steady cash flow to keep them. The invention of barbed wire paved the way for large herds of cattle that needed little supervision. Credit for the invention is generally given to Isaac Ellwood and Joseph Glidden, who saw a sample of a wooden fence with sharp wire projections on display at the 1873 DeKalb (Illinois) County Fair, and quickly set about patenting and manufacturing barbed wire.

Barbed wire also influenced how the wars were fought. Barbed wire was first used as a war defense system during the Russo-Japanese War of 1904-1905. In 1914, the American Steel & Wire Division of United States Steel Corporation and many other U.S. manufacturers sent mile after mile of barbed wire to Europe, where it was tangled into barriers that were impenetrable by ground forces. In World War II, a new military occupation was created as a result of barbed wire's use. "Frogmen" were trained to cut clearings for submarines and ship propellers through the carloads of barbed wire dumped by the Japanese into the sea.

AXIA Incorporated of Oak Brook, Illinois, which manufactures diversified products including coated wire racks used in dishwashers, had total sales of $104 million and 996 employees in 1995, a 27.9 percent increase over the previous year. American Spring Wire, founded in 1968, was a private corporation, and had about $80 million in sales and 300 employees in 1992. The firm purchased the equipment and inventory of J and S Metals, Inc. in 1991, thus expanding its operations by backwards integration. In late 1996, it also acquired Shinko Wire America's Houston facility, which produces high quality steel strand used in concrete construction. Its general sales manager, Timothy W. Selhorst, was quoted in *American Metal Market* on the general state of the industry in 1996: "Competition in the tempered wire business continues to be very, very tough. . . .We're holding our own, but there have been better times to be an American wire producer."

The Great Lakes region traditionally led the nation in shipments of miscellaneous fabricated wire products, due to the area's access to raw materials. However, by 1992 the regional breakdown had shifted.

In the mid-1990s Pennsylvania's 71 establishments ranked first in shipments for an individual state. Its shipments of $331.2 million represented 9.3 percent of the value of all wire products in the United States. The state's 2,700 workers averaged $10.61 per hour. Illinois ranked second in shipments, with $321 million. Its 108 establishments employed 3,500 people at an average wage of $9.21 per hour. California's 125 establishments shipped $242.2 million and employed 2,500 people at an average hourly wage of $9.08. Missouri's 25 establishments shipped $229.9 million in goods. The 3,100 wire workers in Missouri averaged $7.41 per hour. Texas's 70 establishments shipped $198.0 million and employed a total of 2,500 people at an average hourly wage of $8.49.

FURTHER READING

"Axia Inc." *Hoover's Company Capsules.* Available from http://www.hoovers.com/.

"American Spring Buying Shinko Facility." *American Metal Market,* 21 November 1996.

Darnay, Arsen J., ed. *Manufacturing USA: Industry Analysis, Statistics, and Leading Companies.* 5th ed. Detroit: Gale Research Inc., 1996.

McCallum, Henry D., and Frances T. McCallum. *The Wire that Fenced the West.* Norman: University of Oklahoma Press, 1985.

"Steel Wire Makers Hit From Both Ends." *American Metal Market,* 1 October 1996.

Viani, Laura. "American Spring Wire Buys J&S Equipment, Inventory." *American Metal Market,* 5 June 1991.

—Valerie Wilson, updated by Gerry Azzata

SIC 3497

METAL FOIL AND LEAF

This category covers establishments primarily engaged in manufacturing gold, silver, tin, and other metal foil (including converted metal foil) and leaf. Also included are establishments primarily engaged in converting metal foil (including aluminum) into wrappers, cookware, dinnerware, and containers, except bags and liners. Establishments primarily engaged in manufacturing plain aluminum foil are classified in **SIC 3353: Aluminum Sheet, Plate, and Foil.**

INDUSTRY SNAPSHOT

The value of product shipments in 1995 was $3.26 billion in the metal foil and leaf industry, up from $3.04 billion in 1994. About 116 establishments operated in the industry, up from about 98 in 1987. Of these, 65 percent had more than 20 employees. In 1996, 11 of the top producing companies had 200 or more employees. The industry employed 9,300 production workers in 1995, down from 1994 figure of 9,400. States leading in employment in the industry were North Carolina, New Jersey, Illinois, and Ohio.

ORGANIZATION AND STRUCTURE

Aluminum foil, the bulk of which is converted into food containers and packaging for food and other products, is a major component for this industry. In 1995, a full 43 percent of the industry's output consisted of laminated aluminum foil rolls and sheets for flexible packaging uses, especially foil-paper laminate. Another 30 percent of the industry's output consisted of converted, unmounted aluminum foil packaging products. As a consequence, the fortunes of the industry were closely tied to the prosperity of the food packaging industry. The remaining 27 percent of the industry's output consisted of unconverted metal foil and leaf and converted foil for non-packaging applications.

Firms involved in the production of metal foil and leaf were not generally involved in the production of metals. As Hamilton Bowman wrote in his *Handbook of Precision Sheet, Strip and Foil,* a foil producer's ''operations are generally confined to the cold rolling, heat treating, flattening, slitting, and edge conditioning of coils of flat-rolled metal produced for him by a basic mill.'' The scope of operations in the industry has widened considerably in recent years as the use of foil for containers, packaging, electronics, and holograms has become increasingly important.

The industry is served by the Aluminum Foil Container Manufacturers Association, headquartered in Savannah, Georgia. The association, founded in 1955, has 14 member companies. Their journal, *Paper, Film and Foil Converter,* provides information to producers in the industry.

BACKGROUND AND DEVELOPMENT

Metalsmiths have produced flat metal sheets for many centuries. In its earliest forms, metal foil was produced by hammering malleable metals against a flat surface. As early as the seventeenth century, metal foils were produced by hand-operated rolling mills. These early mills made use of two parallel iron cylinders through which metals were passed in a number of successive stages, depending on the thickness of foil desired. Though hammering techniques are still used in the production of gold leaf and foil, the use of parallel cylinders remains the dominant method of foil

production. By the mid-nineteenth century, a great many powered rolling mills were in use in Europe and the United States. At that time, thinner products were referred to as sheet and thicker products as plate.

By the end of the nineteenth century, continuous-process roller mills came into use. These mills differed substantially from their predecessors. Instead of reducing the metal to desired thicknesses by making a series of passes, continuous-process mills operated on a longer piece of metal that was flattened to desired thickness by being passed once through a series of roller pairs set at ever-closer distances to each other. These mills substantially reduced the costs of production by optimizing the flow of materials and reducing set-up times.

Until the mid-1920s, continuous-process mills (also referred to as tandem or strip mills) were not able to produce widths of greater than 24 inches. More powerful mills were developed at that time that could accommodate greater widths, and subsequently, narrower widths were produced by slitting broader widths of material.

A wide variety of metal was converted to foils, among them copper, gold, lead, magnesium, nickel, platinum, silver, tin, and zinc. Foil is generally defined as being 0.005 inches or less in thickness. Foil producers also often produced precision sheet and strip, materials between 0.015 and 0.005 inches in thickness. Thicker products were generally produced at basic mills.

The cold rolling of foil and precision sheet and strip required much greater precision than the cold rolling of thicker sheets. Variations in thickness, temper, and finish needed to be much more controlled. Consequently, foil was produced at much slower speeds than thicker sheets, and complex systems were required to monitor variation. Key developments in the post-World War II period included the use of smaller diameter rollers, the more rigid mounting of rollers and more sophisticated drive mechanisms and systems of control.

Larger diameter rollers had the disadvantage of greater surface contact with the rolled metal. Greater force was required to overcome the greater frictional resistance of large rollers. Thus, for any given amount of energy used, large rollers could reduce sheet thicknesses by lesser amounts than smaller rollers. The greater flexibility of smaller rollers required that they be backed up by large adjacent rollers, called backup or support rolls. In four-high mills, each contact roller was backed up by a single support roll. In cluster mills, each contact roller was typically backed by nine support rolls. Steckel mills were four-high mills in which the rolls are not driven. Metal sheet was instead pulled through the rolls, permitting a great deal of thickness control, though somewhat less reduction per pass than a standard four-high mill. Large-diameter, two-high mills permitted reductions of only 10 percent per pass, whereas four-high mills permitted reductions of 50 to 60 percent, and cluster mills reductions of 75 percent per pass. Smaller contact rollers enabled not only greater reductions, but also lesser variations in foil thickness.

Cold rolling makes metal harder and more brittle. Depending on the thickness of foil desired, cold rolled metals needed to be heat treated, or annealed, in order to soften them for further reduction. Reductions obtained through cycles of annealing and cold rolling were constrained only by the mechanical limitations of the rolling machinery and by handling considerations.

Development of the metal foil and leaf industry was based on these basic technologies. In *Handbook of Precision Sheet, Strip, and Foil*, Hamilton Bowman wrote that the growth of the industry since the 1960s resulted ''as designers have come to appreciate the unique advantages of economy, weight saving, and dimensional precision inherent in these metals.''

CURRENT CONDITIONS

The overall value of product shipments from 1992 to 1995 increased. Total shipments rose from $2.91 billion in 1992 to $3.26 billion in 1995. Sales of unconverted unmounted aluminum foil dropped from $885.8 million in 1992 to $836.1 million in 1993, but rebounded to $966 million by 1995. Laminated foil shipments dropped from a high of $1.45 billion in 1993 to $1.35 in 1994, but resumed upward growth in 1995, reaching $1.43 billion. Converted foil and leaf shipments soared 28 percent, from $608.2 million in 1992 to $845.4 million in 1995. Non-specified metal foil and leaf shipments jumped 77 percent from 1992 to 1993, from $13.6 million to $59.4 million; however, in 1994 shipments dropped down to $17.9 million and reached $21.1 million in 1995.

Total employment in the industry grew from approximately 11,500 in 1993 to approximately 12,400 in 1995. Overall employment of metalworking machine operators is expected to decline through the year 2005 due to increasing use of computer-controlled equipment, which lowers production costs by eliminating lower-skilled positions. Thus, employment prospects for the industry do not appear promising.

The future of the industry is dependent in large part on technical developments within and outside of the industry. A number of viable substitutes for metal foil laminates have been developed in the 1990s, cutting into the market of the most important product of the industry. Among these materials are metallized polypropylene, metallized paper, polyethyene, and ethylene vinyl alcohol. On the other hand, new products such as extremely thin steel foils and improved foil baking products suggest the possibility of continued growth for the core products of the industry.

INDUSTRY LEADERS

The top seven firms in the industry in 1996 were Gould Electronics, Inc., of Eastlake, Ohio, a subsidiary of Japan Energy Corp., with sales of $280 million; Foilmark, Inc. of Newburyport, Massachusetts, with $36.8 million; Transfer Print Foils, Inc. of East Brunswick, New Jersey, with $35 million; Hampden Papers, Inc. of Holyoke, Massachusetts, with $32 million; Alumax Foils of St. Louis, Missouri, a subsidiary of Alumax Inc., with $31 million; Crown Roll Leaf, Inc. of Paterson, New Jersey, with $25.7 million; and Circuit Foil USA, Inc. of Bordentown, New Jersey, with $23 million.

FURTHER READING

Bowman, Hamilton B. *Handbook of Precision Sheet, Strip and Foil*. Metals Park, Ohio: American Society for Metals, 1980.

D & B Million Dollar Directory: America's Leading Public and Private Companies. Series 1997. Bethlehem, PA: Dun & Bradstreet, 1977.

Darnay, Arsen J., ed. *Manufacturing USA*. . 5th ed. Detroit: Gale Research, 1996.

Encyclopedia of Associations. 28th ed. Detroit: Gale Research, 1994.

''Handi-Foil Baking Lines Set.'' *HFD*, 16 December 1991.

''Holograms Making Inroads Into Converted Products.'' *Paper, Film and Foil Converter*, March 1993.

''Innovative Containers Give Foodservice a Boost.'' *Packaging US*, March 1993.

''New on the Menu.'' *Packaging US*, March 1993.

''Packaging - Industry Report.'' *The First Boston Corporation*, 7 June 1993.

Russell, John J., ed. *National Trade and Professional Associations of the United States*. 32nd ed. Washington, D.C.: Columbia Books, Inc., 1997.

U.S. Bureau of the Census. *Census of Manufactures* . Washington: GPO, 1992. Available at http://www.census.gov/mcd/mancen/download/mc92f344.sum and http://www.census.gov/mcd/mancen/download/mc92f349.sum.

———. *1994 Annual Survey of Manufactures*. Washington: GPO, 1994. Available at http://www.census.gov/prod/www/

abs/msmfg07b.html and http://www.census.gov/prod/www/abs/am94as1.html.

———. *1995 Annual Survey of Manufactures.* Washington: GPO, 1995. Available at http://www.census.gov/prod/www/abs/asm95as1.html and http://www.census.gov/prod/www/abs/msmfg07c.html.

———. *Occupational Outlook Handbook, 1996-97.* Washington: GPO, 1997. Available at http://stats.bls.gov:80/ocohome.html.

U.S. Department of Commerce. *County Business Patterns.* Washington: GPO, 1994. Available at http://www.census.gov/prod/2/bus/cbp94/cbp94.html.

U.S. Department of Commerce. International Trade Administration. *U.S. Industrial Outlook, 1994.* Washington: GPO, 1994.

—David Kucera, updated by Patricia Moncada

SIC 3498

FABRICATED PIPE AND PIPE FITTINGS

This industry covers establishments primarily engaged in fabricating pipe and pipe fittings from purchased metal pipe by processes such as cutting, threading, and bending. Establishments primarily engaged in manufacturing cast iron pipe and fittings, including cast and forged pipe fittings that have been machined and threaded, are classified in **SIC 3321: Gray and Ductile Iron Foundries;** those manufacturing welded and heavy riveted pipe and seamless steel pipe are classified in **SIC 3317: Steel Pipe and Tubes;** and those manufacturing products such as banisters, railings, and guards from pipe are classified in **SIC 3446: Architecture and Ornamental Metal Work.**

The U.S. fabricated pipe and pipe fitting industry is strongly dependent on the health of the domestic construction industry, which, after enduring rough economic conditions in the late 1980s and early 1990s, showed signs of rebounding in the mid-1990s; players in the fabricated pipe industry hoped to ride the coattails of that larger industry to increased prosperity throughout the remainder of the 1990s.

Improvements in the domestic as well as international economic climate, along with the replacement of old manufacturing processes, helped the industry rebound during the latter part of the 1980s and weather the downturn of the early 1990s. For pipe, valve, and fitting manufacturers, the last two years have seen marked gains in the industry's ability to meet the steady demand for fire protection flow control products. The industry's recent positive fortunes have also

been due in part to increased global competitiveness. Overseas producers have been chased away from the U.S. market by increased domestic quality, lower dollar valuations, and strong antidumping legislation.

Industry shipments for the approximately 780 establishments involved in this area of manufacturing fell to $2.27 billion in 1991, a 2.6 percent drop from the $2.33 billion level reached in 1990. In 1996, the estimated value of shipments reached $2.61 billion, and was only expected to increase slightly to about $2.63 billion by 1998. Texas's 96 establishments produced 15.1 percent of the U.S. shipment total. California had the second highest number of establishments with 90, producing 6.6 percent of U.S. shipments; and although Michigan had just 69 establishments, it produced 8.6 percent of U.S. shipments.

Industry leaders include Pennsylvania-based Victaulic Company of America, Davis Water and Waste Industries Incorporated of Georgia, Tyler Pipe Industry Incorporated of Texas, and Louisiana-based Shaw Group Incorporated.

The fabricated pipe and fittings industry employed roughly 21,500 in 1997, 15,300 of whom were production workers. Average hourly wages were about $11, which is about $1 less than the average hourly wage of all manufacturers. Employment highs in the industry were recorded in 1979, when 32,900 employees worked in the industry's manufacturing facilities.

Some industry occupations expected to decrease by 2005 were metal and plastic machine workers (29 percent); bookkeeping, accounting, and auditing clerks (25 percent); and tool and die makers (19 percent). The occupations with the largest expected increases were combination machine tool operators (51 percent) and metal and plastic machine tool cutting operators (42 percent).

FURTHER READING

Darnay, Arsen J., ed. *Manufacturing USA.* 5th ed. Detroit: Gale Research, 1996.

''UA Professor's Research Helps Birmingham Company.'' *Modern Casting,* June 1992.

U.S. Bureau of the Census. *1992 Census of Manufactures.* Washington: GPO, 1995.

U.S. Department of Commerce. ''Value of Product Shipments.'' *Annual Survey of Manufactures.* Washington: GPO, January 1997.

SIC 3499

FABRICATED METAL PRODUCTS, NOT ELSEWHERE CLASSIFIED

The fabricated metal products, not elsewhere classified industry encompasses establishments that manufacture miscellaneous metal goods for both commercial and residential applications. Examples of industry output include metal ladders, ironing boards, steel safes, toilet fixtures, trophies, lawnmower wheels, chairs, barricades, ammunition boxes, and automobile seat frames. For more information about miscellaneous fabricated metal products, see other entries in this industry group.

The background and development of the industry varies by product category. However, a general surge in demand characterized the overall industry during the post-World War II U.S. economic expansion. Approaching the 1980s, industry participants were churning out about $4.4 billion worth of goods per year and employing a work force of 65,000 people. Moreover, healthy economic growth during most of the 1980s boosted sales and profits. A surge in housing starts, for example, boosted shipments of metal furniture parts and ladders. Likewise, bank and vault manufacturers benefitted from growth in the savings and loan industry.

By 1989, industry sales had reached $6.95 billion, representing average annual revenue growth of 7 percent since 1983. Contrary to many other manufacturing sectors, both the number of employees and companies in the industry grew during the decade, to 80,000 and 900, respectively. Unfortunately, an economic recession in the early 1990s stalled expansion. Revenues actually declined about 1 percent in 1990 and remained flat throughout 1991 and 1992. Shipments of metal containers, for example, dropped about 6 percent in 1992, and purchases by the ailing savings and loan industry remained depressed. An upturn in housing and automobile markets in the mid-1990s, however, renewed optimism in some segments.

In 1996, the number of establishments had reached approximately 3,370. By 1998, this number was expected to rise to about 3,470. Some of the industry leaders were Steel Technologies Incorporated of Kentucky, California-based BW/IP International Incorporated Seal Division, and Werner Ladder Company of Pennsylvania.

In the late 1990s, California had the highest number of establishments with 380, but they only produced 8 percent of the U.S. shipment total. Pennsylvania's 211 establishments generated 11 percent of U.S. shipments. Overall, shipment values in the industry are expected to increase from about $8.44 billion in 1996 to $9 billion in 1998.

Because of its specialized nature, the industry is highly fragmented. The average industry participant grossed about 28 percent as much as the average U.S. manufacturer in the mid-1990s, and employed about half as many workers.

Although the industry is fragmented, a few product segments stood out in the late 1990s. Fabricated metal safes and vaults accounted for about 3 percent of production, and metal ladders were about 4 percent. Flat metal strapping accounted for about 5 percent; powder metallurgy parts were approximately 14 percent of production. The largest segment of production, 50 percent, was for all other fabricated metal products, not elsewhere classified, which illustrates the industry's fragmentation. In 1995, fabricated metal products', not elsewhere classified, shipment value was $5.3 billion, while powder metallurgy parts' value was $994 million.

Despite steady sales and employment growth throughout the 1980s, job prospects for the overall industry are dim. Automation and the movement of manufacturing facilities outside the United States will curtail job growth. In 1996, employment levels were fairly high for the industry at 77,400. This level is expected to rise to 78,800 by 1998. Openings for many positions will decline by 3 percent to 29 percent between 1994 and 2005. Jobs for assemblers and fabricators, which make up a leading 11 percent of the work force, will increase by about 1 percent. The occupations with the highest projected growth are combination machine tool operators (51 percent) and metal and plastic machine tool cutting operators (42 percent).

FURTHER READING

Darnay, Arsen J., ed. *Manufacturing USA*. Detroit: Gale Research, 1996.

Standard & Poor's Industry Surveys. New York: Standard & Poor's Corporation, 24 December 1992.

INDUSTRIAL & COMMERCIAL MACHINERY & COMPUTER EQUIPMENT

STEAM, GAS, AND HYDRAULIC TURBINES, AND TURBINE GENERATOR SET UNITS

This industry covers establishments primarily engaged in manufacturing steam turbines; hydraulic turbines; gas turbines, except aircraft; and complete steam, gas, and hydraulic turbine generator set units. Also included in this industry are manufacturers of wind and solar powered turbine generators and windmills for generating electric power. Establishments engaged in manufacturing nonautomotive type generators are classified in **SIC 3621: Motors and Generators;** those manufacturing aircraft turbines are classified in **SIC 3724: Aircraft Engines and Engine Parts;** and those manufacturing windmill heads and towers for pumping water for agricultural use are classified in **SIC 3523: Farm Machinery and Equipment.**

INDUSTRY SNAPSHOT

Turbine manufacturers faced challenging business conditions in the mid-1990s. Earlier in the decade, a new generation of gas turbines helped the industry recover from its prolonged slump in the 1980s. But by 1994, U.S. electric utilities were under renewed pressure to cut spending, and outlays for power plants was lackluster. Meanwhile, the industry's major manufacturers—General Electric, Westinghouse Electric, ABB Asea Brown Boveri, and Siemens AG—had all expanded their production facilities. By mid-decade, turbine capacity outstripped demand by as much as 30 percent. On the bright side, demand in Asia (particularly from China) was growing much faster than in the

United States or Europe. With all companies focusing on the same customers, however, price competition was severe. Still, by 1996 GE was reporting higher profits in this sector, and Westinghouse Electric's power operations were making a comeback.

In March 1995, the U.S. wind power industry received a huge blow: the Federal Energy Regulatory Commission (FERC) overturned a decision that had forced utilities in California—the key U.S. market—to buy wind-generated power. Overseas demand presented a much brighter picture, however. The European wind power industry was doing well because of the European Union's encouragement of renewable energy resources. China also was looking to wind power as a way of reducing the pollution generated by its utilities.

ORGANIZATION AND STRUCTURE

The manufacture of steam and gas turbines is concentrated among a few electrical giants. In the United States, the two historical competitors have been General Electric and Westinghouse. In 1996, General Electric (along with its worldwide partners) was estimated to have 50 percent of the gas turbine market, and a smaller, but still dominant, position in steam turbines. Other large international rivals include Siemens AG of Germany and ABB Asea Brown Boveri of Switzerland.

Nearly all of the companies that entered the wind turbine business in the early 1980s—when the industry was in its heyday—have simply disappeared. By 1987, only three manufacturers of the larger-scale turbines used by utilities were still in business, and only one was producing turbines in significant numbers. The number of companies making small wind turbines for stand-alone power has also contracted substantially.

BACKGROUND AND DEVELOPMENT

While early steam engines were reliable generators of electricity, they were big, heavy, inefficient devices. The modern steam turbine was developed in the late nineteenth century to replace them. By 1910 the largest steam turbine-generator unit could produce 30,000 kilowatts, compared with just 1,200 kilowatts ten years earlier. By 1940 single turbine units with a capacity of 100,000 kilowatts were in general use. During the 1950s and 1960s, steam turbines continued to dominate an expanding power-generation market, as fossil fuel prices remained low and ever-larger steam turbines were brought on line. In the 1980s, however, additions to the power capacity of utilities slowed because of erratic growth in consumption and the difficult political climate for utilities in many states.

Wind Power. Small wind turbines were set up in rural areas of the Midwest during the early twentieth century, but power from utilities largely displaced them during the 1930s. As oil prices surged in the 1970s, however, renewable energy resources became popular, and the wind industry was resuscitated. Tax relief was offered for wind farms, and research was greatly expanded. About 14,000 wind turbines were installed between 1980 and 1985, the vast majority of them in California. When oil prices dropped below $20 a barrel and tax incentives were eliminated, however, much of the domestic wind industry collapsed.

CURRENT CONDITIONS

After enjoying a recovery in the early 1990s, the turbine industry faced a tough market by mid-decade. U.S. utilities limited their outlays for new power-generating equipment, owing to competitive pressures and lackluster growth. Worldwide turbine capacity expanded, however, and by 1994 price-cutting had become severe. Moreover, even when winning sales overseas, producers have suffered long delays because of difficulties in project financing.

There were some bright spots, however. Westinghouse won a coveted partnership with Shanghai Electric Corp. of China, which is expected to be the largest market for power equipment over the next decade. Westinghouse Vice President Randy Zwirn told *The Wall Street Journal* in 1996 that, with an equity interest in Shanghai, ''we've got the crown jewel.'' Meanwhile, General Electric was reportedly shifting its focus from selling new equipment to rebuilding, upgrading, and supplying spare parts. Some analysts thought this strategy was wise, given GE's huge in-stalled base of turbines and the need for utilities to cap costs.

Domestic markets for wind turbines, however, had almost disappeared by the mid-1990s. A critical blow was the decision by the FERC in March 1995 to overturn California regulations that forced utilities to sign long-term contracts to buy wind-generated power. Wind power needed this regulatory support because it remained uneconomical, in part because of the short fatigue life (five years) of a wind turbine's major components and their costly replacement costs. At best, California-based Kenetech, the world's leading producer of wind-generated electricity, could produce power at five cents per hour, compared with three cents per hour for conventional natural gas plants.

Overseas markets, however, were healthier. The European Union (EU) set a target for renewable resources to account for 8 percent of Europe's primary energy by 2005. More specifically, the EU plan forecast that wind power would meet 2 percent of Europe's electricity demand by the same year. China, too, was encouraging the growth of wind power to satisfy its domestic energy needs.

INDUSTRY LEADERS

General Electric is the worldwide market leader in the turbine industry. In 1986, GE introduced a new series of advanced gas-fired turbines that turned around its faltering power systems segment. GE's relatively small and inexpensive gas turbines were ideal for utilities seeking to adjust to fluctuating demand by adding capacity selectively. In 1994, operating profits of its power division business reached a record $1.2 billion on $5.9 billion in sales.

Just one year later, however, profits had fallen about one-third, to $770 million, owing to several factors. Because of design flaws that could lead to cracks, GE had to make one of the biggest and most expensive recalls in the electric power business. In total, 22 GE turbines in the United States and overseas had to be shut down to be fixed; an additional 28 being shipped or installed required retrofitting with new components. GE has also lost some orders to competitors in Asia, including a key contract in China. Nevertheless, in 1996 GE still had a 50 percent share of the gas turbine segment, and a smaller—but still dominant—share of the steam turbine business. Moreover, the power division's sales and operating profits staged a comeback in 1996, climbing 11 percent and 39 percent, respectively, from 1995 levels.

Westinghouse is the second-largest United States producer. The company shipped its first steam turbine in 1897, actually beating GE by a few years. In the industry downturn of the 1980s, Westinghouse nearly exited the business, but by the mid-1990s it was doing better. Its turbine business was still much weaker than GE's, but it had scored several coups overseas. Most notably, it gained the right to a partnership with Shanghai Electric Corp., China's biggest power-equipment producer. In April 1996 it also won contracts valued at nearly $300 million to build power plants in South Korea and Pakistan.

Wind Power. In the wind power segment, the biggest U.S. company has been Kenetech of Livermore, California, founded in 1979 as U.S. Windpower. In early 1995, the company seemed to be poised for a turnaround. It made major sales to India and South Wales, as well as Palm Springs and Minnesota. However, a March 1995 decision by the FERC, freeing California utilities from buying wind power, cost the company contracts worth $945 million. Kenetech first laid off 115 employees, or about 12 percent of its workforce. By June 1996, the company had filed under Chapter 11 of the U.S. Bankruptcy Code.

AMERICA AND THE WORLD

During the 1990s, the turbine market increasingly became international in scope. Major American and European manufacturers strengthened their presence in each other's backyard. For example, the German industrial conglomerate Siemens AG took over a spinoff of Allis-Chalmers Co., known as A-C Equipment of Wisconsin, and invested $30 million in its Milwaukee plant.

More than 60 percent of Westinghouse's new orders in 1996 were coming from customers outside the United States. "Asia is the biggest power market in the world," Westinghouse's Mike Asquino told the *Orlando Business Journal* in 1996. "That's where we're seeing significant growth." Indeed, China was expected to be the world's fastest-growing market. In 1996, it had a total installed generating capacity of 200,000 megawatts, which was being expanded by 10,000 megawatts per year.

Wind Power. In overseas markets, Denmark, Germany, and Britain have been in the forefront of developing wind energy. Wind energy accounted for less than 0.1 percent of Europe's total power generation in 1992. However, under a European Community directive, that figure is slated to rise to 2 percent by 2005. In 1996, the European wind power market was the world's largest, with installed capacity of 2,420 megawatts. The wind industry in Europe enjoys government subsidies and is growing quickly; it has also been a pioneer in developing wind farms offshore.

China also offered excellent opportunities for the wind industry. It has a set a target of 1,000 megawatts of installed wind power by the year 2000, more than 20 times the 1996 level of 44 megawatts. While 1,000 megawatts would still only represent 0.3 percent of China's anticipated capacity at the next millennium, it would still require 2,000 to 3,000 large wind turbines. Chinese authorities were eager for a more environmentally friendly source of power, since three-quarters of its generating units were powered by coal.

RESEARCH AND TECHNOLOGY

Many of the advances in gas turbines over the past decade have their roots in jet engine technology, as manufacturers have adopted techniques perfected for the airlines and the Pentagon for power generation. Older gas turbines have a thermal efficiency of 25 percent—they capture and convert to electricity about one-quarter of the energy value of their fuel—versus a 33 percent thermal efficiency posted by steam turbines. Using the technologies developed for aircraft, however, some newer gas turbines have reached thermal efficiencies of 40 percent. Other recently developed gas turbines have achieved even higher efficiency levels through combined cycle generation, in which the turbines use the exhaust gases from the turbine to boil water into steam, which is then used in a steam turbine to generate additional electricity. A variation of this method is to boil water with the exhaust gases and inject some of the steam back into the gas turbine, so it is running on a combination of gases and steam. Some industry participants believe that gas-fired and combined-cycle power systems will be the leading technologies of the 1990s, representing about half of all new capacity additions worldwide. Fossil-fueled steam turbines, hydroelectric power, and nuclear plants will account for the balance.

The wind industry has made progress on several fronts that have historically hampered its growth. One major problem for the industry has been the variability and intermittent nature of wind. Traditional, fixed-speed wind turbines have had a relatively low capacity factor compared with other energy sources because they have not been able to take advantage of the full range of wind velocities. Improvements in wind turbine design and technologies, however, have allowed finer control of power output at both low and high wind speeds. Other advances—including more accurate weather forecasting, improved methods of picking the best sites for wind farms, and blades that can better cope with the destructive effects of dead insects—have contributed to more efficient wind energy production.

FURTHER READING

"California's Kenetech Windpower Inc. to Serve Customers During Chapter 11." *Knight-Ridder/Tribune Business News,* 5 June 1996, 6050327.

Cole, Benjamin Mark. "Generating Power Without Much Fuss (Capstone Turbine Corp.'s Small Turbine Power Plants)." *Los Angeles Business Journal,* 28 October 1996.

Collins, Steven. "Small Gas Turbines Post Gain in Performance." *Power,* October 1992.

Demoss, Timothy. "Modern Technology Breathes New Life Into Old Turbines." *Power Engineering,* August 1996.

Dillon, Paul. "Westinghouse Becomes Bigger in Asia." *Orlando Business Journal,* 26 April 1996.

Foroohar, Kambiz. "Blowing in the Wind." *Forbes,* 4 December 1995.

General Electric 10-K, 1996. Fairfield, CT: General Electric, 1997.

Hindley, Angus. "Thinking Long-Term in the Gulf." *MEED Middle East Economic Digest,* 31 January 1997.

Kirchen, Rick. "Siemens Transforms Former A-C Unit into a Powerhouse." *Business Journal-Milwaukee,* 3 October 1992.

Rickert, Lu. "Combined Cycle Power Plants." *Global Gas Turbine News,* May 1993.

Vogel, Shawna. "Wind Power." *Discover,* May 1989.

Wald, Matthew L. "Better Ways to Make Electricity." *New York Times,* 11 April 1990.

Zhang, Don. "China Sets 1000 MW Wind Power Goal." *Modern Power Systems,* June 1996.

Zink, John. "Steam Turbines Power an Industry: A Condensed History of Steam Turbines." *Power Engineering,* August 1996.

—Bob Schneider

SIC 3519

INTERNAL COMBUSTION ENGINES, NOT ELSEWHERE CLASSIFIED

This industry includes establishments primarily engaged in manufacturing diesel, semidiesel, or other internal combustion engines, not elsewhere classified, for stationary, marine, traction, and other uses. Establishments primarily engaged in manufacturing aircraft engines are classified in **SIC 3724: Aircraft Engines and Engine Parts,** and those manufacturing automotive engines, except diesel, are classified in **SIC 3714: Motor Vehicle Parts and Accessories.**

Diesel engines are used primarily in large trucks and buses, high-powered farm tractors, and in heavy construction machinery. Other markets include marine vessels and lawn & garden equipment. The industry dates from 1893, when Rudolph Diesel, a young German engineer, filed a patent application entitled "Theory for the construction of a rational thermal engine to replace the steam engine and other internal combustion engines currently in use." Four years later, Diesel built the first diesel engine.

The fortunes of U.S. diesel engine makers depend heavily on the market for heavy-duty trucks. The end-user has the option of choosing his own engine, so companies must impress both truck operators and truck makers, which may decide to make an engine standard on a specific line. In 1996, the heavy-duty truck market fell about 23 percent from the record level of 245,000 units in 1995, but it was still healthy by historical standards. Some industry observers thought the traditional boom-and-bust cycle of the industry had softened somewhat owing to modest inflation and a more stable economy.

The leading diesel engine makers are Cummins Engine Corporation, Detroit Diesel Corporation, and Caterpillar Inc. Detroit Diesel is a relative newcomer to the spotlight in the industry. In 1988 former auto racer Roger Penske bought control of the company from General Motors and proceeded to raise its share of the U.S. heavy-duty diesel truck engine market from three percent in 1987 to over 26 percent in 1995. That year, sales totaled over $2 billion, more than double what they were when Penske took over the company. Detroit Diesel's turnaround can be traced to its Series 60 engine, which provided far better fuel efficiency than previous models, as well as computerized features that could diagnose mechanical problems and monitor driver productivity.

As Detroit Diesel advanced, Cummins receded: it lost ten points of market share in two years and posted substantial losses in 1990 and 1991. The company had already suffered through tough times in the mid-1980s, when the firm cut both its prices and profitability to defend its markets against Japanese manufacturers. By the mid-1990s, however, Cummins had made a strong recovery: it reported earnings of $160 million on sales of $5.2 billion in 1996. That same year, it took about 35 percent of the heavy-duty diesel truck engine market, about the same level as in 1994 and 1995. The return to profitability reflected a strong upturn in demand for heavy-duty trucks, a more competitive product line, corporate downsizing, and an increased emphasis on establishing a presence in non-truck diesel engine markets, including that for recreational vehicles.

All of the Big Three, as the leading diesel-engine makers are known, are pursuing alliances with foreign manufacturers to enter Asian and European markets. In January 1995, Detroit Diesel bought VM Motori S.p.A., a major diesel-engine maker located in Cento, Italy. And in July 1996, Cummins announced the formation of a joint venture with Dongfeng Motor Corporation to produce 25,000 diesel engines annually in China within ten years; a previous joint venture of the two companies has resulted in production of 20,000 units annually since 1986.

FURTHER READING

"A Brief History of the Diesel Engine." *PSA Website,* 14 March 1997. Available from http://www.psa.fr/en_psaBB0026.html.

Koenig, Bill. "Cummins Engine Hope More Products, International Sales Will Boost Earnings. *Knight-Ridder/Tribune Business News,* 10 April 1996.

McElroy, John. "Miracles in the Heartland: How to Buy Part of GM and Make It Immediately Profitable." *Automotive Industries,* June 1995.

Osenga, Mike. "Cat Introduces Dual Truck Engines." *Diesel Progress Engines & Drives,* August 1996.

Zirnhelt, George. "Soft Landing, Soft Rebound Likely for Engine Markets in the Year Ahead." *Diesel Progress Engines & Drives,* December 1996.

—Bob Scheider

SIC 3523

FARM MACHINERY AND EQUIPMENT

This category covers establishments primarily manufacturing farm machinery and equipment, including wheel tractors, for use in the preparation and maintenance of the soil; planting and harvesting of the crop; preparing crops for market on the farm; or for use in performing other farm operations and processes. Included in this industry are establishments primarily engaged in manufacturing commercial mowing and other turf and grounds care equipment. Establishments primarily engaged in manufacturing farm handtools are classified as the Cutlery, Handtools, and General Hardware industries; and those manufacturing garden tractors, lawnmowers, and other lawn and garden equipment are classified in **SIC 3524: Lawn and Garden Tractors and Home Lawn and Garden Equipment.**

INDUSTRY SNAPSHOT

Beginning in the mid-nineteenth century, major advances in agricultural equipment technology allowed vast expanses of once intractable American land to be farmed. In the process, and as agricultural equipment grew in variety, complexity, and size, farming itself was transformed, until most of it was conducted on a vast scale with highly specialized machinery.

Although a lot of the scientific knowledge needed for high-yield agriculture existed in the 1930s, the Great Depression delayed its development. After this period of economic drought, however, technology production flourished, and farmers soon relied on a variety of machines to improve efficiency and to make work easier and more lucrative. In 1940, U.S. farmers produced 2.2 billion bushels of corn on about 76.5 million acres, with an average yield of only 28.9 bushels per acre, whereas in 1995, farmers produced about 7.3 billion bushels of corn on just 70.2 million acres, with an average yield of nearly 113 bushels per acre. The 1995 yield per acre average actually dropped from 1994's record yield of 138 bushels per acre.

Such a level of efficiency created chronic excess supply; the extent and fertility of the land available, in combination with sophisticated planting and cultivation techniques, caused American farmers to produce on a scale usually exceeding market demand. With surplus driving prices down, farmers could not make sufficient money to maintain or upgrade equipment, which meant that agricultural implement manufacturers were victims of their customers' efficiency.

The financial success of such manufacturers was also tied to farming profits in other ways. Unusually bad weather diminished farmers' yields, and unusually good weather merely underscored the tendency toward chronic excess supply. Equally unpredictable, political crises in various parts of the world often had an effect on market demand. All of these hazards affected the manufacturers of agricultural equipment at the same time they put the livelihood of many American farmers at risk.

ORGANIZATION AND STRUCTURE

Among other financial difficulties affecting many American farmers throughout the 1990s, was the major problem of surplus inventories created by unexpected reductions in demand; another was the increase in agricultural output efficiency that required fewer farmers to produce enough food for the country and for the international market. *Implement and Tractor* noted that farmers consider machinery costs in terms of bushels of corn, pounds of milk, or bushels of wheat.

Consequently, agricultural machinery sales plummeted in the 1980s, when farmers were struck by the crunch of the recession. Yet farmers still had to upgrade and replace their equipment, so they began purchasing new tractors every ten years, in contrast to every three to five years as in the past. The slumping sales of new machinery also impaired the sales of used machinery: when new equipment did not sell, the supply of quality used equipment decreased as well. However, sales of agricultural machinery have begun to increase. According to *Successful Farming* and U.S. Department of Agriculture (USDA) reports, domestic sales have risen, as have international sales, especially to developing countries. Actually, major farm equipment manufactures have posted record years in the mid-1990s.

As a result of reduced domestic customer spending, farm machinery companies had to reposition themselves in the market. They had to locate new customers and upgrade their products. Trade agreements such as the North American Free Trade Agreement (NAFTA) and the General Agreement on Tariffs and Trade (GATT) have given U.S. companies greater access to the agricultural economies of Mexico and the European Union. These trade pacts allowed the farm machinery companies greater tariff-free commerce with Mexico and lower-subsidy exportation to European countries. Furthermore, as incomes rose in developing countries such as India and China, U.S. companies began to market products there, and companies have targeted these countries as new growth areas for the future. Nonetheless, the industry's success also hinges on the success of domestic farmers, its domestic customers. When farmers experience financial trouble, the industry does as well. Hence, in addition to the expanded markets of farm machinery companies, the mid-to late 1990s prosperity of farmers also enhanced the industry's performance.

However, the American farm equipment manufacturing industry, like many other industries, has faced structural change in response to heightened ecological awareness and Environmental Protection Agency (EPA) rulings. The EPA standards concerning exhaust emissions were designed to take effect for engines of over 750 horsepower in the year 2000, for those of 50 to 100 horsepower in 1998, for those of 100 to 175 horsepower in 1997, and for those of 175 to 750 horsepower in 1996. According to *Implement & Tractor,* clean air legislation creating new diesel fuel standards was seen as making viable an otherwise too expensive diesel blend containing soy oil, and leading to a decline in carbon monoxide and hydrocarbon emissions. From the point of view of farmers, this cleaner fuel was not believed to have consequences for torque output, even if it did lead to small reductions in horsepower.

BACKGROUND AND DEVELOPMENT

The major expansion period for U.S. agriculture came during the late nineteenth century. A total of 408 million acres had been farmed prior to 1870, and in the next 30 years an additional 431 million acres were newly cultivated. As the scale of U.S. agriculture dramatically increased, so did its complexity, with locally-oriented farmers later engaged in an international system of storing, shipping, and selling engendered by increased mechanization, cash crops, and stock trading in commodities.

In the onset of these developments, the most significant role was played by the largest farming enterprises. Heralding increased mechanization, greater crop specialization, and a trend towards farming on a large scale, the 40,000-acre or more farms were run with military efficiency. The pace of mechanization was so rapid and extended into so many areas of farming technology that in 1860 alone, the U.S. Patent Office issued new patents for corn shellers, corn huskers, corn cultivators, corn-shock binders, cornstalk shocking machines, cornstalk cutters, corn cleaners, corn and cob crushers, seed drills, corn harvesters, rotary harrows, corn and cob mills, smut machines, and hundreds of corn planters.

The types of plows used since the earliest development of agriculture proved to be unsuitable in dense, heavy prairie, so new designs were essential. A first step came in the form of an adaptation of Jethro Wood's 1814 iron plow, a "prairie breaker" that was very heavy, clogged easily, and moved slowly, even when pulled by a team of oxen. In 1837, a blacksmith in Grand Detour, Illinois, developed the first "singing plow" by combining a wrought iron moldboard with a steel share scavenged from a broken band saw, enabling a far more thorough and clog-free scouring of the prairie. By the 1850s, this blacksmith was manufacturing approximately 10,000 examples of his invention annually at his mass-production plant in Moline, Illinois.

But better plows alone were not sufficient for all the needs of American farmers during the rapid escalation of agriculture in the late nineteenth century. Other key developments included design improvements for tractors, harrows, corn planters, and combine harvesters.

Though Hart and Parr Charles were responsible for pioneering the gasoline tractor in 1901, most

American farmers were unable to afford the new machine until the advent of Henry Ford's Fordson tractor in 1917, priced at $397. A critical new development came seven years later with International Harvester's Farmall tractor, its innovative addition of removable attachments making the machine highly versatile.

During the nineteenth century, harrows rapidly became stronger and more complex. Before the introduction of the tractor, these had to be dragged by animals. The first designs, hoes and brush harrows were outmoded in the 1840s by the Geddes, a hinged triangular construction of wood with teeth made of iron, which, in turn, was outmoded several decades later by an all iron and steel model. This design also was outmoded by a harrow called the Nishwitz rotary disk harrow, which through rollers or clod-crushers, sifted and tamped down the soil.

The planting of corn was both time consuming and inaccurate until technological advances permitted the mechanization of the planting and the measuring involved as well. In Galsburg, Illinois in the 1850s, George W. Brown pioneered a semi-mechanized method of corn planting with a horse-drawn vehicle that dropped seed by hand. Next, shoes or "furrow openers" were added to the front of the vehicle for better preparation of the soil, and the seed-dropping mechanism was refined, permitting vehicle operators to divide the tasks of driving and navigating. The latter improvement enabled operators to pay closer attention to where the corn was being dropped.

Developments in combine harvesting technology took a slower and more interrupted course than did those of the other forms of farming equipment. The steam-driven reaping and threshing machines introduced in the 1880s were replaced by the versatility of the Farmall tractor. The Second World War delayed the full implementation of the technological advances marked by Allis Chalmers' All-Crop Harvester of 1936, a gleaner equipped with a special corn-head attachment. With the resumption of peace, the versatile and efficient but expensive combines initially took a back seat to the much cheaper picker-sheller machinery. Only with the proliferation of silos and their efficient storage of vast quantities did the diesel-driven combines' capacity for mass-harvesting give them an unbeatable advantage.

CURRENT CONDITIONS

Though in the 1980s and early 1990s farm machinery and equipment manufactures took a beating, they prospered in the latter half of the 1990s due to

heightened domestic and international demand. Leading the turnaround, U.S. farmers started churning out record harvests of top cash grains such as corn and soybeans, giving farmers the capital to invest in new machinery. Whereas American customers bought only about 20,000 big tractors a year in the 1980s, they purchased substantially more in the mid- to late 1990s. As of July, 1995, for example, year-to-date tractor sales climbed to 70,217—an 11.4 percent increase from July, 1965 year-to-date postings, according to JoAnn Hays of *Successful Farming*. However, Hays reported that domestic combine harvester demand has tapered off. Only 3,697 were sold as of July, 1995 versus 4,400 in July, 1965, although international markets for U.S. combines have increased. Overall sales of agricultural equipment soared in 1994 to about $13.2 billion with a slight dip in 1995 to about $11 billion, climbing well above the dismal delivery reports of the mid-1980s when sales only totaled about $6.5 billion. Analysts predicted that sales would remain steady for the remainder of the 1990s, holding at about $11 billion in value.

Forecasting to 2005, the U.S. Department of Labor saw signs of health for the agricultural equipment industry, noting that farmers had generally recovered from the losses and excessive debts incurred during the 1980s. Farmers were expected to replace machinery that they had been unable to replace when times were hardest, and to invest in new machinery, taking advantage of improvements brought about by advanced technology. Indicative of this trend was 1997's 4 percent first quarter increase in nonreal estate loans. In addition, farm inputs, equipment, and machinery accounted for 50 percent of the increase in farm loan value in 1996, which rose to $2.3 billion up 3.2 percent from 1995.

The industry has made some technological breakthroughs that can substantially reduce producers' dependence on manual laborers. In 1995, Automated Harvesting Systems developed a pepper picker for harvesting delicate pepper varieties without damaging the vegetables. This diesel-powered harvester includes a liquid-cooled diesel engine and rated 86.9 horsepower at 2200 rpm, according to *Diesel Progress Engines and Drives*. The pepper picker has the potential of harvesting as much as 150 manual pickers, which would save farmers considerable labor costs. In addition, The Robotics Consortium is developing a robotic harvester that uses imaging sensors and intelligent motion control, according to *Design News*. The machine has been tested on alfalfa fields with success, and it marks a new frontier in farm machine design.

INDUSTRY LEADERS

In 1996, Deere and Co. of Moline, Illinois had sales of over $9 billion and 33,900 employees. Not only did Deere and Co. lead the farm machinery industry in the United States, but it also led worldwide. With factories in nine countries, Deere and Co. can distribute its products to about 120 countries around the world. Case Corp. of Racine, Wisconsin, ranked as the North America's second largest farm machinery operation and as the world's largest small and medium size construction equipment manufacturer. The company posted sales of $4.2 billion, with 16,900 employees. AGCO Corp. ranked third in 1996 with $2.3 billion in sales. AGCO marketed its diversified agricultural products worldwide and employed 7,800 people.

Deere & Co. has been the industry leader for years, but the company has faced some perilous challenges in the last decade. The recession of the 1980s helped erode the company's production apogee of 1987 when it employed 67,000 workers, according to *Implement and Tractor*. Today, the company employs only half as many people. Deere & Co. posted net losses of $902 million in 1993, but turned things around within a year to record its most profitable fiscal year ever. Global restructuring, lead by CEO Hans W. Becherer, brought the company back in the red and cut its employee base in half. The restructuring meant outsourcing to suppliers who could provide products at a lower cost. Deere, of course, held on to the production of unique and core Deere & Co. products. The result of these changes allowed the company to sell its 8000-series at about the same price as its older 60-series. In the future, the company plans to focus on international markets and on the continued evolution of its agricultural machinery, imbuing its products with the latest technology.

Case Corp., headed by Jean-Pierre Rosso, CEO, also reported record sales and earnings in 1994, after having slumping sales in 1980s, according to *Implement and Tractor*. Case took in $315 million in profits in 1994 compared to only $83 million in 1993. In fact, Case's 1994 fourth quarter profits of $67 million came pretty close to the previous year's total profits. Like other companies in this industry, Case had to implement changes in order to pull off the financial turnaround. The company's change of fortunes was also abetted by improved external conditions, (i.e., improved earnings of farmers). The company introduced new products as well as strategic tactics to improve efficiency. Coupled with the company's structuring efforts, Case's sales increased around the world: in North America, two-wheel and four-wheel drive tractor sales increased by double-digit percentages; in

Europe, the company's sales climbed 10 percent; and in Australia/New Zealand, sales of all tractors rose by 24 percent. Based on recent performance and industry projections, Case anticipates continued success in the coming millennium.

Of the companies in this industry, AGCO's performance and turnaround was the most remarkable. Under the guidance and leadership of CEO Robert J. Ratliff, AGCO became the Cinderella of the farm machinery industry. *Implement and Tractor* noted that Ratliff transformed a relatively small and unprofitable $200 million company into a $2 billion industry leader. Ratliff launched the changeover by expanding the company's narrow product line, thereby increasing its worldwide tractor market share to 20 percent. In fact, AGCO dominated the tractor market outside the United States in 1994, holding 58 percent of it, which made AGCO the world's leading supplier of tractors. Part of Ratliff's strategy included turning AGCO into a public company and establishing dealers with multiple brands, which gave the company access to several sectors of the market. To help build and reinforce the AGCO empire, Ratliff purchased the domestic and international operations of Massey-Ferguson in 1993 and 1994, respectively. With this move, the company wielded substantial power within the farm machinery industry. The company's sales have continued to climb each year; in 1994 they stood at $1.4 billion, whereas in 1996 they rose to $2.3 billion.

AMERICA AND THE WORLD

A *Census of Manufactures* report indicated that imports of farm tractors outweighed exports in 1995. The U.S. exported only 40,470 tractors valued at $823 million, but imported 100,246 tractors valued at $1.4 billion. However, the disparity swung in the other direction for international marketing of combines: the U.S. exported 4,232 with a value of $326 million and only imported 554 with a value of $27 million. The import/export difference was more equal for cultivators and weeders: the U.S. exported 35,020 valued at $19 million and imported 36,237 valued at $60 million.

According to the USDA members of the Commonwealth of Indepence States, such as Ukraine, could provide U.S. manufacturers with a new market for their farm machinery. The country's slow transition to a market economy and to privatization of agriculture has forced Ukrainians to seek farm equipment and other agricultural products elsewhere. In 1996, Ukraine purchased Deere and Co. combines for $187 million, the company's largest sale ever. Furthermore, Pakistan reported that it would increase its importation of U.S. tractors from 22,000 to 25,000 from 1995 to 1998. The Pakistani government goaded this increase by urging the cultivation of more of the country's 79 million acres of arable land to meet agricultural consumption requirements. Presently, Pakistan only cultivates 50 million acres of its arable land.

The Journal of Commerce and Commercial predicted that by 2005, 75 percent of farm machine manufacturers' sales to come from developing countries—Latin American, Asian, and Eastern European countries. As of 1997, sales to developing countries had already surpassed those of U.S. and Western European customers. Exports have been escalating for this industry since 1989, though U.S. imports of farm machinery have also been rising since this period. Up 7.7 percent from 1993, exports rose to $2.07 billion in 1994.

FURTHER READING

Banham, Russ. "Export Opportunities Sprout for U.S. Producers." *Journal of Commerce and Commercial,* 8 November 1996, 7A

Darnay, Arsen J., ed. *Manufacturing USA.* 5th ed. Detroit: Gale Research, 1996.

"Deere and AGCO Report Record '94 Sales." *Implement and Tractor,* January/February: 1995, 8 & 12.

Freiberg, Bill. "AGCO Corporation: A Living Example of the American Dream." *Implement and Tractor,* May/June: 1995, 4-6.

Hays, JoAnn. "From the Dealer's Seat." *Successful Farming,* November 1996, 32.

"Financial." *Implement and Tractor,* March/April 1995, 9.

"I&T 55th Annual Market Statistics." *Implement & Tractor,* January/February 1993, 18-21.

Little, Dale L. "Legacy of Science." *Farm Chemicals,* July 1993, 8.

McNeely, Mark. "Holy Peno, Now That's a Pepper Picker." *Diesel Progress Engines and Design,* December 1995, 38.

"Soyoil in Diesel Helps Cut Pollution." *Implement & Tractor,* August/September 1993, 6.

"U.S. Farm Wheel Tractor Retail Sales, 1987-1991." *Implement & Tractor,* January/February 1993, 22.

Yengst, Charles, "Trendlines." *Diesel Progress Engines & Drives,* December 1993, 4.

—Richard Hillyer, updated by Karl Heil

LAWN AND GARDEN TRACTORS AND HOME LAWN AND GARDEN EQUIPMENT

This entry discusses establishments primarily engaged in manufacturing lawn mowers, lawn and garden tractors, and other lawn and garden equipment used for home lawn and garden care. It also includes establishments primarily engaged in manufacturing snowblowers and throwers for residential use. Other equipment classified here includes: wagons and carts for lawn and garden use, lawn mover grass catchers, power hedge trimmers, power lawn edgers, loaders for garden tractors, mulchers, plow attachments for garden tractors, rototillers, seeders, and residential lawn vacuums.

Establishments primarily engaged in manufacturing farm equipment and machinery are classified in **SIC 3523: Farm Machinery and Equipment.** Those manufacturing hand lawn and garden shears and pruners are classified in **SIC 3421: Cutlery,** and those manufacturing other garden handtools are classified in **SIC 3424: Hand and Edge Tools, Except Machine Tools and Handsaws.**

According to figures from the Outdoor Power Equipment Institute—the trade organization representing 95 percent of the companies manufacturing lawn and garden equipment—lawn mowers, garden tractors, tillers, string trimmers, leaf blowers and other gas- and electric-powered consumer equipment represent a $4.5 billion industry and accounts for more than 30,000 jobs and $350 million in annual wages and benefits. Those figures jump dramatically when employees of industry suppliers and distributors are factored in (75,000 jobs and $875 million in wages and benefits).

In 1993, more than $4.2 billion in finished goods were produced by 70-plus domestic lawn and garden equipment manufacturers.

Many of the forces impacting the industry in the early 1990s—economic recession (which resulted in more people choosing to care for their own lawns rather than hiring professional landscaping companies) and environmental concerns about lawn and garden equipment engines—continue to have an effect. Companies manufacturing lawn and garden equipment, including Caterpillar, American Lawn Mower, Toro, Black & Decker, John Deere, Ariens, and a large number of smaller "private label" companies continue to respond to the 1994 U.S. Environmental Protection Agency (EPA) announcement of national emission standards for lawn mowers and other gas-powered gardening equipment.

Additionally, manufacturers are beginning to expand and upgrade their equipment offerings. Caterpillar, for example, has invested substantial money in research and development, which led to a wide array of new products being produced. As a result of this investment, Caterpillar saw a 12 percent increase in sales and a 19 percent profit surge, for a net increase in income of 18 percent. While gains for some of the other equipment manufacturers aren't quite as large, their numbers are also increasing. Caterpillar's chief financial officer, Douglas R. Oberhelman, predicted industry sales of power-generating engines alone will triple during the next 5 to 10 years.

The nation's enthusiastic interest in lawn maintenance is relatively new, although the lawn mower (developed in England) has been around since the 1830s. During the same time John Deere was promoting his sod-breaking plow as the most important piece of equipment frontier farmers of the prairie could own, the push lawn mower was familiar to children of antebellum America.

In the 1930s, U.S. lawn mower sales held at about 50,000 units annually. Following World War II and the American migration to suburbs, homeowners began to take a growing pride in tending their lawns, hedges, and gardens. During this same time, new grass seed varieties were also being developed, and the quest for the "perfect" lawn became a popular hobby and a point of pride.

Reel mowers were the standard home lawn grooming device until the 1950s, when gas-powered rotary motors developed into more than a rough cutting tool. By the end of that decade, power mowers outsold reel mowers by a margin of 9 to 1. The rise in the popularity of power garden equipment was accompanied by a corresponding surge in lawn mower accidents—wounds from flying debris and toe and finger amputations. In the mid-1990s, design changes combined with news stories about equipment safety that appear in the spring (as well as when the first mower-related accident is reported) have raised public awareness.

Some of the first safety measures included attaching decks to handles with bolt-on brackets instead of cotter pins and the positioning of the starter cord away from the discharge chute. Through the development of safety standards, injuries from walk-behind power mowers have decreased 40 percent since 1983.

An era of consumer activism began in 1969, with the publishing of *Unsafe at Any Speed* by Ralph Nader, a book focused on the automobile industry's "indifference" to safety concerns. In 1972, the federal Consumer Product Safety Act created a Consumer Product Safety Commission (CPSC); one of the initial concerns of that agency was power lawn mower accidents. At the time an estimated 77,000 people each year were injured by the whirling blades of this equipment. Following 10 years of CPSC data gathering and testimony from experts and consumers, the first safety requirements for power lawnmowers, the deadman control and blade housing and shield designs to prevent foot injuries, were adopted.

The deadman control prevents hand injuries that can occur when operators attempt to clear the chute of wet grass without shutting down the engine. It is now standard for lawn mower (as well as snowblower) blades to stop rotating once the operator releases a spring-loaded control on the handle. Less expensive mowers may feature a simple control that shuts down the entire engine when the operator releases the handle; more expensive models stop the blade action but allow the engine to keep running.

Blade housings and shields prevent an operator's foot from accidentally slipping under the deck of the mower and into the blade. Manufacturers are required to perform a standard "foot-probe test" to ensure their product designs meet this safety requirement.

Another design change initiated by the industry requires debris (nails, rocks, small branches) be deflected onto the ground rather than flying out the chute. All of these standards have added more than $25 to the cost of mowers—which generally range in price from $100 for lower-end mowers to $700-plus for riding tractors for home consumer use. These design changes, combined with an increase in liability insurance for power mower manufacturers, accounted for a near doubling in the price of garden equipment.

It is unclear what effect environmental concerns will have upon the lawn mower industry. A growing number of states and municipalities across the country are banning grass clippings and other organic wastes from local landfills; this has been seen as an incentive to produce a growing number of mulching mowers and composting equipment. With increasing government concern directed at the amount of particulate pollution generated by the smaller motors that power home lawn equipment, a resurgence in the sale of the classic push mower is also showing itself.

Between 1985 and 1995, sales of push mowers doubled, to about 250,000 units, according to American Lawn Mower, one of the industry leaders. Priced in the $100 range, push mowers offer other benefits such as an opportunity to get a higher level of exercise not available from powered mowers and an exchange of the louder engine sounds for the more peaceful clicking generated by push mowers. Nearly all of the safety concerns raised by power equipment are also diminished if not eliminated altogether, and push mowers distribute grass clippings evenly on a lawn, rather than leaving piles or clumps like power mowers. And while many garden experts now recommend leaving clippings on a lawn to feed the grass, mower manufacturers sell catchers in the $15-$25 range for homeowners who want a neater, more groomed look.

Industry experts estimate that there are over seven million riding mowers in operation today, with brand label sales accounting for 48 percent of equipment sold and private label retail sales making up the remainder.

While economic projections vary widely, the companies that manufacture lawn and garden equipment have experienced a steady increase in sales and revenues. The Toro Company of Bloomington, Minnesota reported its fourth consecutive year of growth at the end of 1996, posting record net earnings. Ariens, a family-owned company founded in Brillion, Wisconsin, has also seen increases in sales. But Toro, Ariens, Caterpillar, and other equipment manufacturers have all sought to expand their product offerings into non-garden-related products. Combined with active efforts to keep costs down—cutting workforces and consolidation among companies—it appears lawn equipment manufacturers will continue on a steady and profitable course. The battle for market share will also remain vigorous.

The Outdoor Power Equipment Institute (OPEI) identifies three factors that will continue to have a major impact on the lawn and garden equipment industry: aging baby boomers and their attitudes and behavior toward lawn and garden care; environmental considers and the related research and development needed to meet those concerns; and government legislation.

As a group, the baby boomer generation (persons born between 1947 and 1964) is now part of a key demographic for this industry. This age group is expected to do most of the purchasing of lawn and garden equipment, due to a strong interest in lawn care and gardening as hobbies. This age group also has respect for the environment and a desire "to do what is right." According to OPEI, boomers are people who recycle bottles and newspapers, mulch their lawns, and keep noise and pollution from their gardening equipment to a minimum. As federal, state, county, and municipal governments continue to address the problems of air and noise pollution and landfill citings, the garden equipment industry will continue to feel pressure to improve its products.

The Environmental Protection Agency continues to be a strong motivator when it comes to improving lawn and garden equipment. It has been the EPA's position for some time that lawn mowers are big polluters. A recent EPA-funded study compared gasoline mowers typically used across the country with cordless electric mowers. Gasoline-powered equipment emitted eight times more nitrogen oxides, 3,300 times more hydrocarbons, 5,000 times more carbon monoxide, and more than twice the carbon dioxide per hour of operation compared to the electric models.

The EPA study concluded that if just 20 percent of U.S. homeowners with gasoline mowers switched to cordless electric mowers, there would be annual emissions reductions of 10,800 tons of hydrocarbons, 340 tons of nitrogen oxides, 84,000 tons of carbon monoxide, and 70,000 tons of carbon dioxide. Gay MacGregor, a division director at the National Vehicle and Fuel Emissions Laboratory in Ann Arbor, Michigan, believes "People think that because these engines are so small, they must not pollute so much." Whereas automobiles have been regulated for 20 years, lawn mowers and other lawn and garden equipment have remained unregulated and now represent a significant source of pollution.

An important part of any manufacturing company's operation is its efforts to develop and improve its products; therefore, research and development is an important consideration for lawn and garden equipment manufacturers. When environmental considerations are factored in, research and development takes on even greater importance for this industry.

During 1996, Caterpillar was able to improve its balance sheets as a result of its vigorous financial support of research and development. This commitment was ultimately rewarded with the addition and/or improvement of 220 new and current products. Other manufacturers of lawn and garden equipment are pursuing similar courses of action.

While electric mowers are growing in popularity and sales, reviews of their performance are not totally positive. Participants in the EPA-funded study noted that electric mowers were not likely to have mulching features, lacked self-propulsion, and had difficulty cutting tall grass and weeds. Additionally, their one hour operating time limit was also considered to be a negative factor.

In a political climate again considering re-regulation and/or additional regulation of industry, legislation at all levels of government will also remain a concern of lawn and garden equipment manufacturers. All of these factors will continue to fuel a push toward safer and cleaner gardening equipment that will meet consumer needs in the United States and around the world.

FURTHER READING

Baker, Stephen. "Operation Push Mower." *Business Week,* 10 June 1996, 116.

Doyle Driedger, Sharon. "Ever Greener: Gardening is big business in Canada." *MacLean's,* 22 April 1996, 62-63.

Elstrom, Peter. "This Cat Keeps on Purring." *Business Week,* 20 January 1997, 82.

—Virginia M. Mayo Black

SIC 3531

CONSTRUCTION MACHINERY AND EQUIPMENT

This industry includes establishments primarily engaged in manufacturing heavy machinery and equipment used primarily by the construction industries, such as bulldozers; cranes, except industrial plant overhead and truck-type cranes; dredging machinery; pavers; self-propelled backfillers; backhoes; aggregate spreaders; construction plows; and power shovels. This industry also includes establishments primarily engaged in manufacturing forestry equipment and certain specialized equipment, not elsewhere classified, similar to that used by the construction industries, such as elevating platforms, ship cranes and capstans, aerial work platforms, and automobile wrecker hoists. Establishments primarily engaged in manufacturing mining equipment are included in **SIC 3532: Mining Machinery and Equipment, Except Oil and Gas Field Machinery and Equipment**; those manufacturing industrial plant overhead traveling cranes are classified under **SIC 3536: Overhead Traveling Cranes, Hoists, and Monorail Systems**; and those establishments manufacturing industrial truck-type cranes are classified under **SIC 3537: Industrial Trucks, Tractors, Trailers, and Stackers.**

INDUSTRY SNAPSHOT

In 1995, the industry shipped $18.2 billion worth of products, a 14 percent increase since 1990. The number of establishments grew from 863 in 1990 to 919 in 1995. Imports of construction machinery and equipment totaled $4.6 billion in 1995; exports totaled $5.4 billion.

Caterpillar's first-quarter net income of $394 in 1997 million may signal a healthy year for the industry as a whole. Construction company executives are optimistic about continued economic growth and low interest rates for the future of their trade, which has a direct link to the construction machinery and equipment industry.

ORGANIZATION AND STRUCTURE

This industry provides several major categories of equipment for use by the larger construction industry.

Earthmoving machinery is utilized by companies involved in residential and commercial construction, as well as those involved in highway construction and dambuilding. The passage of the Intermodal Surface Transportation Efficiency Act in 1991 provided state governments with more than $16 billion in federal funds for highway projects during 1992. This funding improved demand for highway construction equipment, as did state expenditures for roads, in many regions of the United States. Caterpillar Inc. is the industry leader in the production of earthmoving machinery, historically the cornerstone of its product line.

Excavators and cranes are used in a variety of construction areas. Excavators are used in most construction jobs and come in a wide variety of sizes and configurations, from small tractor-mounted backhoes to large power shovels. Cranes are used for bridge, highway, large commercial or industrial construction jobs, and in offshore oil drilling.

Other construction equipment includes underground mining machinery, asphalt and concrete pavers, air compressors and tools, pumps, hoists, and rock-crushing and screening equipment. Figgie International is a leading producer of concrete mixing trucks, while Ingersoll-Rand is a leader in the production of compactors and compressors.

BACKGROUND AND DEVELOPMENT

Weak American and overseas economies hurt the construction equipment industry in the early 1990s. Many analysts felt, however, that at least a modest turnaround in the industry's fortune was imminent. As *Standard & Poor's Industry Surveys* indicated, "In all likelihood, 1991 probably represented a trough; total construction spending peaked in 1986 at $421.4 billion and declined without interruption through 1991." *Industry Surveys* noted in 1992 that, thus far, "The recovery in construction spending . . . has been confined to private spending for residential buildings and government spending for public construction. Expenditures for nonresidential buildings continued to decline. Categories such as industrial, office, hotel, and motel reported double-digit declines through August.'' The U.S. Department of Commerce indicated, however, that ''because of recovery gains both in the United States and abroad in the 1990s, the construction machinery industry is expected to grow in constant dollars by about 3 percent. Assuming that highway and bridge reconstruction and repair will continue at a strong pace, as well as home building.

Sales of new equipment were down during the early 1990s, but sales of repair and replacement parts improved. Construction machinery manufacturing companies remained hopeful that mounting concern about the state of the nation's infrastructure would translate into increased sales over the course of the 1990s. Serious efforts to repair and resurface the nation's highways and bridges would stimulate sales. The U.S. Department of Commerce estimated that more than half the country's major highways and one-third of its bridges are in need of repair, and notes that such work will require highly automated bituminous and concrete paving equipment, milling machinery, and high-powered pavement breakers. Manufacturers also anticipate opportunity for growth through new construction projects as more communities build pollution control facilities, such as solid waste disposal and wastewater treatment facilities. In addition, the major earthquake that devastated vast portions of the Los Angeles transportation system will undoubtedly require major reconstruction efforts.

Recessions abroad also hurt the U.S. construction machinery industry well into the 1990s, as many construction projects and mining expansions were postponed until economies improved. In the early 1990s, for instance, U.S. exports in the area of construction machinery declined by approximately 14 percent. This situation did nothing to improve the fortunes of domestic producers, since about one-fourth of sales of U.S. construction equipment companies were generated by exports. Many U.S. manufacturers participated in joint ventures or sales agreements with foreign companies, especially companies in Europe and Japan. These partnerships allowed U.S. companies to shift production when costs of labor, raw materials, and currency values changed.

INDUSTRY LEADERS

The world's leading manufacturer of construction equipment is Caterpillar Inc., of Peoria, Illinois, with total sales and revenues in 1996 of more than $16.5 billion. Originally incorporated in 1925 as the Caterpillar Tractor Company, the company boasts more than two dozen major production facilities worldwide.

After suffering significant losses during the 1980s, the company embarked on a series of changes to regain their previous form. Although Caterpillar cut their work force from 90,000 to 60,000, closed 30 percent of their plants, introduced new machinery, and moved aggressively into foreign markets.'' The transformation was at times a painful one, particularly in the area of labor (a sector that continues to trouble the company), but analysis by industry observers such as *Standard & Poor's Industry Surveys* feel that Caterpillar has regained its footing, citing ''higher volume and firmer prices stemming from better end markets in the U.S., the absence of restructuring charges, and favorable adjustments to inventory. The company also reported that its operations had reached the point where the benefits of its factory modernization program exceeded its costs.''

Incorporated in 1868, Deere and Company was one of the largest agricultural and industrial equipment manufacturers in the United States. An industry innovator since founder John Deere introduced the first successful self-cleaning steel plow in 1837, the company has factories throughout the world and distributes its products through independent retail dealers. In the mid-1990s, Deere and Company employed 33,400 people and realized sales of nearly $10.3 billion.

Other industry leaders in 1996 include Komatsu America International Company, of Lincolnshire, Illinois, and Telex Corporation, of Westport, Connecticut. Komatsu had sales of $13.6 billion and employed 3,000, while Telex had sales of $1.03 billion and employed 3,749.

WORK FORCE

The industry employed 78,200 in 1995, an 11 percent decrease since 1990. The number of production employees in the industry also decreased, from 60,700 in 1990 to 53,300 in 1995. Average weekly hourly earnings for production workers decreased from $14.96 in 1990 to $13.43 in 1995.

For domestic construction equipment manufacturers, labor is a huge part of operating expenses for leading manufacturers such as Deere & Co. and Caterpillar. Labor at both companies is represented by the United Auto Workers, and both companies have had their share of labor disputes in the 1990s.

RESEARCH AND TECHNOLOGY

Construction equipment itself has often been considered relatively ''low-tech,'' but ''intelligent'' machinery is increasingly being developed for field work. Kraft TeleRobotics of Kansas, for instance is testing

Haz-Trak, an excavator and materials handler that can be operated by remote control from hundreds of yards away, allowing operators to handle dangerous materials such as radioactive waste from a safe distance. The excavator, it was hoped, can eventually be operated from even greater distances.

FURTHER READING

Bremner, Brian. "Can Caterpillar Inch Its Way Back to Heftier Profits?" *Business Week,* 25 September 1989, 75.

"Caterpillar Inc." *The Wall Sreet Journal,* 4 April 1997, C30.

"End Markets Begin to Recover in 1992." *Standard and Poor's Industry Surveys,* 24 December 1992, S36-8.

Flint, Jerry. "The Enemy of My Enemy." *Forbes,* 14 November 1988.

Kelly, Kevin. "Labor's Metamorphosis: The High Stakes at Caterpillar." *Commonweal,* 15 January 1993.

Langreth, Robert. "Smart Shovel." *Popular Science,* June 1992, 82-4, 108-109.

Moskowitz, Milton, Robert Levering and Michael Katz. *Everybody's Business, A Field Guide to the 400 Leading Companies in America.* New York: Doubleday, 1990.

Slutsker, Gary. "What's Good for Caterpillar . . . ." *Forbes,* 7 December 1992, 108-10.

U.S. Bureau of the Census. *1994 County Business Patterns.* Washington: GPO, 1996.

————. *1995 Annual Survey of Manufactures.* Washington: GPO, 1997.

SIC 3532

MINING MACHINERY

This category includes establishments primarily engaged in manufacturing heavy machinery and equipment used by the mining industries, such as coal breakers, mine cars, mineral cleaning machinery, concentration machinery, core drills, coal cutters, portable rock drills, and rock crushing machinery. Establishments primarily engaged in manufacturing construction machinery are classified in **SIC 3531: Construction Machinery and Equipment;** those manufacturing welldrilling machinery are classified in **SIC 3533: Oil and Gas Field Machinery and Equipment;** and those manufacturing coal and ore conveyors are classified in **SIC 3535: Conveyors and Conveying Equipment.**

INDUSTRY SNAPSHOT

The mining equipment industry suffered a substantial drop in shipments during 1982 and has not fully recovered. At the beginning of 1982, shipments were valued at $2.11 billion. By 1983 they dropped to $1.51 billion and only recovered to $1.64 billion by 1991. The industry continued a slow growth trend with total sales at approximately only $1.69 billion in 1996.

The employment level in this industry dropped sharply between 1984 and 1987 to 13,600. From 1989 to 1991, employment rose about 10 percent from the 1987 level, but then began to drop again in 1992. The projected level of employment for 1996 was 21 percent lower than that of 1987, with an estimated 10,400 people employed.

Diminishing demand for domestically produced minerals fueled the decline, decreasing mining activity substantially. To combat weakened demand, mining equipment companies relied on the export market for business opportunities, but this market has been far from stable. Foreign manufacturers gained ground against U.S. manufacturers in the 1980s, thanks to improved quality and lower prices. All of these factors pushed U.S. mining equipment companies to step up cost cutting measures and look to innovation as the key to success.

ORGANIZATION AND STRUCTURE

The mining equipment industry is highly dependent on mining activity in the United States and the world. When demand for mined materials is high, mine operators order new machinery; when demand is low, orders fall off. Mining machinery manufacturers are cushioned somewhat from demand cycles because different kinds of mines use similar machinery. Thus a decline in coal mining, for example, may be offset by a boom in salt mining.

The market share divisions within this industry was split between six categories. Underground mining machinery claimed 15.4 percent of the industry. Crushing, pulverizing, and screening machinery claimed 11 percent. Drills and other mining machinery, not elsewhere classified, claimed 9.4 percent. Mineral processing machinery claimed 4.9 percent. Parts and attachments for mining machinery and equipment claimed 50.1 percent of the industry. Mining machinery, not specified by kind, claimed the remaining 9.2 percent of the industry market.

The mining machinery industry draws its supplies from a variety of sources. Mill shapes and forms made from carbon alloy, stainless steel, copper, and aluminum are the most highly consumed materials. Castings from gray and malleable iron, steel, aluminum, and copper, and forgings from iron and steel are also heavily consumed. Fabricated structural metal products, speed changers, gears, industrial high-speed drives, and roller bearings constitute other significant materials consumed by the industry.

BACKGROUND AND DEVELOPMENT

Mining came late to the United States, for early surveyors assumed that there were no significant mineral resources to be found in the country. Politicians and statesmen arguing over currency shortly after the Revolutionary War ruled out gold and silver because the United States supposedly did not have the resources to produce this type of exchange. Benjamin Franklin said, "Gold and silver are not the produce of North America, which has no mines." Another eighteenth-century observer, Cornelius de Pauw of the Netherlands, remarked that "In all the extent of America there are found but few mines of iron, and these so inferior in quality to those of the old continent that it cannot even be used for nails." As history has shown, these remarks proved wildly presumptuous. Explorers moving westward across the country in the nineteenth century discovered rich reserves of gold, silver, lead, copper, iron, nickel, coal, and many other ores and minerals. The country proved far richer than any of the original settlers imagined.

The first mechanisms to dig and extract mineral resources from the earth were hammers, chisels, shovels, and buckets. More advanced operations used single cars on rail ways to convey materials to the surface of underground mines. The hammer and chisel were the first instruments to be replaced by pneumatically-powered cutting devices. British inventors were nearly one decade ahead of the Americans in the development of mechanical power to cut into the ground. In 1850, a Glasgow mine owner proved compressed air could be used to power underground machinery. By 1853, a cutting chain machine was developed, which matured into a machine called the Gartsherrie, patented in 1864. The Gartsherrie is considered the precursor of modern coal cutters.

A rock drill was invented and patented by Simon Ingersoll in 1870. After Ingersoll's patent changed hands several times and improvements to his invention had been made, Addison Rand was able to persuade mining companies to use his new technology instead of hammers and chisels. The two inventors came together in 1905 and advertised themselves as "the largest builder of air power machinery in the world." Ingersoll's side of the operation specialized in construction work, while Rand's specialized in under-

ground mining. Today, Ingersoll-Rand is a highly diversified company with many interests, most of which are related to its origins in mining.

Though the industrial revolution was dependent on abundant supplies of coal to generate power, the coal mining industry lagged far behind others in using machinery to ease the work of men. Men manually shoveled coal into coal cars well into the twentieth century. Keith Dix, author of *What's a Coal Miner to Do?*, wrote: "It is ironic that the advance in technology and management, which gave modern industry its momentum, bypassed the one industry on which most others depended." By 1948, roughly 33 percent of the country's underground coal continued to be loaded by hand.

Joseph Joy, who was responsible for the mechanization of coal loading, is considered the single most significant inventor in this industry; he was awarded 106 patents between 1904 and 1944. Joy developed the Joy Loader in response to two insistent demands: American industry's demand for an increasing supply of coal and newly-organized mineworkers' demand for improvements in working conditions that were frequently subhuman. Following the development of the Joy Loader, men would no longer need to shovel coal by hand, though many would lose their jobs as a result. The Joy Manufacturing Company, known today as Joy Technologies Incorporated, claimed that Joy Loaders accounted for 72 percent of all coal loaded mechanically by 1954.

During the 1970s, the U.S. Government pushed the development of new mining technologies through legislation on health and safety, air and water pollution, and environmental protection of the land mined. Such efforts changed the face of the mining industry, requiring skilled staff to operate and maintain mechanized production. Productivity in underground coal mines was hampered due to additional resources required to prevent accidents, black lung disease, and acid-runoff. In surface mining, additional resources were necessary to meet land restoration standards and to negotiate with those who claimed the land for agricultural purposes. Mining machinery manufacturers sought to capitalize on the changing industry by providing machines to do the required jobs.

CURRENT CONDITIONS

The growth rate of domestic orders for mining machinery slowed in 1996 after small growth in 1994 and 1995. Mining machinery industries were expected to improve in 1997 as the U.S. market expanded and international markets were in a state of recovery.

Stocks for this industry made profits in 1996 and were expected to be profitable in 1997 as well.

By the 1980s, U.S. Government interest in mining was concerned with addressing import-export imbalances. A 1986 report suggested that foreign penetration of the U.S. machinery market was primarily due to the strength of the dollar, high domestic material and capital costs, and generous financing and credit terms offered by some foreign governments to support export sales. The report projected that U.S. mining equipment manufacturers would face a steadily growing export market, shifting to Latin America, Asia, and Africa. Current world events, such as the North American Free Trade Agreement, the emergence of Korean and Taiwanese manufacturers, and the plea from South Africa, a major mining country, to lift trade sanctions, underscore the significance of these projections and the importance for U.S. manufacturers of developing the export market.

Due to the high price of new mining machinery, the used-machinery market was very healthy, especially outside the United States. This demand created an incentive for thieves to steal equipment, which is a relatively easy task. Machinery is usually left in unsecured areas, and is easy to start, difficult to trace, and easy to sell. The increase in equipment thefts in the early 1980s spurred Deere & Company to issue a Manufacturer's Certificate of Origin (MCO), which was adopted by the Construction Industry Manufacturers Association in 1983. Since then more than 20 manufacturers have used the MCO, which has reduced the thefts of certain machinery. As used-equipment buyers become more aware of the frequency of machinery theft, more MCOs have been requested upon the purchase of used-equipment.

U.S. manufacturers maintained a significant, though not a leading, share of the world mining machinery industry in the early 1990s. The strongest competitors in the world market were Japan, Germany, France, Canada, South Korea, Taiwan, and South Africa. While mining in the United States dropped sharply due to a worldwide surplus of metal and mineral supplies, mining abroad expanded quickly, opening new markets for U.S. manufacturers. The largest potential market was the former Soviet Union, which had vast amounts of natural resources. Although much of this marketplace was speculative in the early 1990s, analysts suggested that the way to jump-start the economy of Russia and the other nations was to enter the world marketplace through the sale of these resources. Many of the former Soviet Union's mines were in dire need of modernization and capital investment, pro-

viding a ready market for U.S. mining machinery equipment.

INDUSTRY LEADERS

The largest company in the mining machinery industry in 1997 was INDESCRO Inc. of Dallas, Texas. INDESCRO had a total sales figure of $597 million and employed 2,400 people. The second largest company was Boart Longyear Co. of Salt Lake City, Utah, with $340 million in sales and 2,500 employees. The next largest company was Hamischfeger Corporation of Milwaukee, Wisconsin, with sales of $295 million and 2,500 employees, followed by Svedala Industries Inc. of Waukesha, Wisconsin, with $250 million in sales and 1,110 employees. LeTourneau Inc. of Longview, Texas, with sales of $170 million and 1,200 employees, rounded out the top five.

WORK FORCE

U.S. Department of Labor projections for the year 2005 indicate that the workforce of the mining machinery industry will change significantly. Welders and cutters, who account for the largest segment in this industry, are expected to reduce their numbers by 11.1 percent. Others facing reductions of 10 percent or more include assemblers, welding machine setters, machine builders, secretaries, inspectors, truck and tractor operators, and material handlers. Machinists are expected to increase employment levels by 6.8 percent, sales workers by 18.2 percent, mechanical engineers by 9.5 percent, numerically controlled machine tool operators by 9.5 percent, industrial machinery mechanics by 18.3 percent, industrial production managers by 15.7 percent, engineering technicians by 6.0 percent, combination machine tool operators by 8.3 percent, and coating/painting/spraying machine operators by 7.5 percent.

West Virginia's 41 establishments, Pennsylvania's 22 establishments, and Virginia's 26 establishments employed and shipped significantly more than any other states in 1992. Virginia's mining machinery establishments accounted for 15.6 percent of U.S. shipments, which exceeded $243.5 million in 1982. Pennsylvania's establishments accounted for 14.7 percent of U.S. shipments, which topped $229 million in 1992. West Virginia and Wisconsin also contributed significantly to the industry, shipping 7.8 and 5.3 percent of total U.S. shipments, respectively.

The national hourly wage for mining machinery workers in 1995 was $13.96. This hourly wage was slightly higher than the national manufacturing average, and employees of this industry were working slightly more hours than the national average in all manufacturing industries. The number of people employed was consistently dropping from 24,600 in 1982, to 15,300 in 1993, but recovered slightly to 16,500 in 1995.

RESEARCH AND TECHNOLOGY

Mining equipment is considered mature in terms of design and innovation. Therefore, any improvements rely on research and development of new materials and advanced sensing, control, and computer techniques. Innovations in technology have typically sought to achieve gains in productivity or worker safety. The dangers of underground mining prompted underground machinery designers to develop remote controlled and automated mining systems. These systems reduce production costs, increase productivity, and increase worker safety.

Other technological devices are found in surface mining, where sensing and control systems are frequently installed. Blast hole drills employ automated systems that regulate the speed and feet rate of the drill bit. Mining shovels have on-board microprocessors, which relay information and record data. Because they can be added to existing equipment, these technologies have been developed by many manufacturers.

Another new machine is Caterpillar's autonomous truck control system, which is scheduled for introduction to the commercial market in 1998 in limited numbers. The benefits of the driverless robot mine truck include: it's less expensive than hiring human truck drivers; works continuously with no breaks; and it will operable in remote locations, such as northern Canada, where it is difficult to hire and get truck drivers to the machines at all. The Caterpillar truck was one of several robot mine trucks that was expected to be in general operation worldwide by the year 2000.

FURTHER READING

Brady, T. M., and T. W. Martin. "Metal Mining Equipment." *Mining Engineering,* May 1989.

"Caterpillar Opens New Conference and Training Facility in Arizona." *Mining Engineering,* August 1991.

Dagdelen, K. "Open Pit Mining." *Mining Engineering,* May 1991.

Darnay, Arsen J., ed. *Manufacturing U.S.A.* 5th ed. Detroit: Gale Research, 1996.

"Developments to Watch." *Coal Age,* April 1987.

Dix, Keith. *What's a Coal Miner to Do?* Pittsburgh: University of Pittsburgh Press, 1988.

"Exports Forecasted to Dominate Mining Equipment Market." *Mining Engineering,* October 1985.

Hast, Adele, ed. *International Directory of Company Histories.* Vol. 3. Detroit: St. James Press, 1988.

Huhta, Richard S. "Highlights of Hillhead." *Rock Products,* September 1987.

"Highlights of Hillhead '91." *Rock Products,* September 1991.

Kapp, William K. "Opportunities Improving for Machinery Exports." *American Mining Congress Journal,* 27 March 1985.

Leach, Mark, et. al. "Machinery (Construction and Mining)." *The Value Line Investment Survey (Part 3 - Ratings and Reports).* 8 November 1996.

"Metal Mining Equipment." *Mining Engineering,* May 1990.

"Metal Mining Equipment." *Mining Engineering,* May 1991.

O'Neil, Tim. "Finnish Mining and Technology." *Mining Engineering,* October 1988.

Peterson, Carl R. "Innovation in Mining Technology." *Mechanical Engineering,* August 1986.

"Protecting Equipment from Thieves." *Coal Age,* April 1987.

Rickard, Thomas A. *A History of American Mining.* New York: McGraw-Hill, 1932.

Tough, J. Brian, and Carl L. Livesay. "Innovation Key to Competitiveness in Equipment Market." *American Mining Congress Journal,* 27 March 1985.

U.S. Department of Commerce. International Trade Administration. *A Competitive Assessment of the U.S. Mining Machinery Industry.* Washington: GPO, 1986.

U.S. Department of Labor. Bureau of Labor Statistics. *Technological Change and Its Labor Impact in Five Energy Industries.* Washington: GPO, 1979.

von Lobenstein, J. G., Eduardo Julia, and Richard G. Hite. "Expanding and Mechanizing El Soldado." *Energy & Mining Journal,* March 1988.

Woof, Mike. "Look - No Hands!" *World Mining Equipment,* December 1996

—Valerie Wilson, updated by Beaird Glover

SIC 3533

OIL FIELD MACHINERY

This category covers establishments primarily engaged in manufacturing machinery and equipment for use in oil and gas fields or for drilling water wells, including portable drilling rigs. Establishments primarily engaged in manufacturing offshore oil and gas well drilling and production platforms are classified in **SIC 3731: Ship Building and Repairing.**

INDUSTRY SNAPSHOT

In the early and mid-1990s the condition of the oil and gas field machinery industry was dismal. As oil prices continued to remain depressed, the costs of drilling for oil did not reap satisfactory profits. Therefore, with little drilling activity, there was little need to produce the support machinery. Industry investment reports published by Merrill Lynch and Standard and Poor's shared the same opinion: oil and gas prices would remain relatively flat—compared to the early 1980s—throughout the remainder of the twentieth century. As a result, activity in other support industries would stagnate and possibly whither away, unless viable diversification strategies could be successfully implemented.

In 1993, there were 531 establishments in the industry, with projections that this figure would drop to only 245 by 1998. The value of shipments in 1994 was $3.75 billion, a far cry from more than $11 billion in 1982, and was projected to drop to less than $1 billion by 1998. Establishments were located primarily in the southern United States, with Texas being the industry hub.

Businesses involved in the industry were segmented as to the types of machinery produced. Manufacturers of production machinery and equipment controlled 39.9 percent of the market share, while manufacturers of rotary oil and gas field drilling machinery and equipment controlled 30.13 percent. Portable drilling rigs and parts claimed 11.35 percent, while oil and gas field derricks and well-surveying machinery claimed 2.21 percent. Another 10.25 percent of the market was classified as nonspecific oil support machinery and equipment.

ORGANIZATION AND STRUCTURE

The oil and gas field machinery industry includes field tools, oil derricks, drilling rigs and tools, well logging and surveying equipment, and general gas well and oil field machinery and equipment. Many companies exist in the United States that make specialty drilling equipment and other related machinery. Other companies, such as machine tool makers, produce smaller parts either for assembly at the more specialized companies or replacement needs while the rig is in service. The companies producing drilling rigs usually maintain a field service department; however, private consulting firms also specialize in field repair of all oil field related equipment.

By 1993, the entire oil industry was controlled, regulated, and lobbied for or against, to a certain degree, by organizations like the Organization of Pe-

troleum Exporting Countries (OPEC) and the American Petroleum Institute. Yet, domestically, the industry was ultimately controlled through regulations imposed by the U.S. government and the governments of international competitors. The Environmental Protection Agency had begun to place stringent restrictions on companies selling crude oil, which ultimately affected the cost of producing oil. This drove down profits, making oil drilling a losing proposition with standard low selling costs. Given these conditions, oil drilling was performed mostly by major oil-selling companies, like Exxon, Texaco, and Citgo. This was in sharp contrast to the early 1980s, when drilling rigs were common sights in the front yards of southern and midwestern private homes.

The decrease in drilling activity world-wide adversely affected the oil and gas field machinery industry. Smaller support machinery businesses that thrived in the early 1980s either went out of business or were bought out. By the 1990s, the organization and structure of this industry primarily consisted of very large, well-diversified companies. For example, the only remaining wholly owned domestic manufacturer of oil field pumping units was Lufkin Industries, which in the early 1990s was ranked twelfth in the industry (by dollar sales) by *Ward's Business Directory of U.S. Private and Public Companies.* Lufkin accomplished this through purchasing the inventory of its only domestic competitor, American Industries, when American closed its doors in the summer of 1992. Having cornered this market, Lufkin continued to realize low sales volumes and reduced capacity in this segment of its business. Throughout the 1990s, companies continued to vanish or to be absorbed by larger competitors.

BACKGROUND AND DEVELOPMENT

In the United States, oil drilling evolved as a result of seeking salt brine. Without refrigeration, one of the few means of preserving meat was through packing it with salt. Therefore, salt brine was a commodity in heavy demand. In 1806 two brothers, David and Joseph Ruffner, established a business supplying settlers near Charleston, West Virginia, with salt brine. Quickly, the demand for the salt became so great that the brothers devised a way to drill a hole to intercept the flow of the brine seepage. This well, responsible for developing the spring pole and drilling line, was the first well drilled in America with tools. From this point, other types of wells were drilled in the Ruffner fashion. In 1814, near Burkesville, Kentucky, the "American Well" was drilled, which was 475 feet deep and supposedly produced 1,000 barrels of oil per day.

The invention of the steam engine in tandem with cable tools changed the nature of oil and gas drilling from 1860 to 1930. During this time, crude oil was gaining favor as an illuminant, replacing whale oil used for lamps. Also, the use of machinery to aid man's endeavors was more widespread, and crude oil was known to be an excellent lubricant. Its use as a fuel was also gaining popularity. These three developments created a demand for oil drilling; thus the industry gained momentum. The first well drilled in America strictly for oil production to supply the machinery industry was the Drake well. Following the Drake well, patent applications were filed in abundance for a wide assortment of tools, rigs, and machines to support oil drilling activities. Among these patents were predecessors to common modern oil industry machinery, including rolling cutter rock bits, an offshore drilling rig, and rotary and percussion motion devices.

From this point, the oil boom was upon the world. An oil field in Corsicana, Texas, was the first well to catapult the blooming industry into the powerful economic prominence it holds today. In this oil field, the Lucas Spindletop well "blew" on January 10, 1901. Once it was contained, it produced approximately 75,000 to 80,000 barrels per day. Exploratory drilling in the Gulf Coastal Plain areas of Texas and Louisiana became commonplace and produced abundant supplies of oil. Likewise, oil fields in California and the midwestern plain states were cropping up.

It was not until the 1930s that oil drilling really became a science. Although the American Petroleum Institute organized its first equipment standardization committee in 1925, the industry did not really become specialized for another five to ten years. Before the 1930s, the parts of an oil drilling rig were made for other machines. While these makeshift rigs were practical and effective enough to achieve the purpose intended, vast improvements were necessary to efficiently produce oil with less waste. Mechanical engineers and petroleum engineers started designing oil field machinery and tools. From these efforts the following were created: better tooth and ball bearing designs of rock bits, roller bearing enclosed engines, automatic controls for steam generating plants, and gas engine electric generator sets with motors. Also, drilling rig personnel were becoming more educated about professional and safety practices.

Basically, the same principles are employed today as in the past. Aside from the demise of oil derricks, which have given way to pumping units, and the offshore drilling methods used along the coast lines, the industry has not radically changed since its inception. The oil drilling industry can be summarized as an evolution of improved techniques, which will continue as long as oil lies beneath the earth's surface.

Standard & Poor's March 1993 *Industry Survey* reported that crude oil prices were expected to maintain the downward trend throughout the rest of the 1990s at a rate of 2-4 percent. This was due to current production levels being higher than worldwide demand. Historical data showed U.S. light sweet crude oil prices fluctuated between $25 and $30 per barrel during 1983 and 1985. Suddenly, prices plummeted to record low levels in 1986, with a barrel of oil commanding between six and ten dollars. Prices crept back up, only to fall again in 1988. Once the Persian Gulf War started, U.S. light sweet crude prices jumped from about $13 per barrel to over $35 at the end of 1990, only to plummet again to the pre-war price range by the end of first quarter 1991. The first quarter of 1993 did not lend any comfort to oil investors, as oil prices continued the downward trend started in the second half of 1992.

As a result of low oil prices, the oil drilling industry was expected to continue its downward trend as long as oil prices remained lower than the cost of drilling. With no chance of profits on the horizon, the entire oil field machinery industry was depressed. This phenomenon might have been difficult for the average consumer to understand, as gasoline prices did not reflect the sharp decreases in price for a barrel of oil. The "pass the buck" policy was imposed at the gasoline pump, for any motorist who filled his or her tank was helping oil refineries pay for the costs of being a good environmentally-minded neighbor. Environmental regulations would continue to grow stiffer, as the Clinton administration embraced environmental policies. This added cost of doing business threatened many oil producers and transporters while barrel prices remained low. The profit margins would continue to diminish as long as added Environmental Protection Agency regulations were imposed. According to Standard & Poor's, "Oil companies are finding it cheaper to import refined products than to manufacture those same products in the United States. The major oil refiners, for example, are adding to their refining capacity in the Pacific Rim, where environmental regulations are more hospitable."

There was some improvement in the number of operating rigs at the end of 1992. Baker Hughes, an oil field machinery manufacturer, reported the domestic rig count at the end of 1992 was 935 working units, a 15 percent increase from the year before. Standard & Poor's attributed this to the warmer winter, but colder-than-normal spring temperatures, compounded with the off-shore drilling devastation caused by Hurricane

Andrew, all of which contributed to an extremely volatile oil price base. The second reason was that Congress passed laws ending special tax credits for those drilling in what are considered unconventional natural gas fields. These credits were created to encourage drilling through subsidizing the activity. Before the laws went into effect, the drillers stepped up production to take every last possible drop before taxes were imposed. This added to the volatility of oil prices in 1992.

Cleaner burning gasolines and policies such as the BTU (British thermal unit) tax were gaining support in the early 1990s in efforts to simultaneously purify the environment and eradicate the national debt. Gasoline producers were facing a reformulation of their product that included higher amounts of oxygenates in response to the Clean Air Act Amendments. This would help reduce smog, while increasing the efficiency of automobile engines. The effects of this reformulation would be seen by the consumer at the gasoline pump. Legislation imposing a BTU tax, or some similar energy tax that would tax consumers' usage of oil, oil products, natural gas, and coal, was proposed in Congress. An increase in utility bills could encourage consumers to practice conservation, decreasing the demand for those mentioned taxable products.

CURRENT CONDITIONS

Given the rapid decline of companies, revenues, rigs, and employees through the mid-1990s, the outlook for the oil and gas industry within the United States was not generally promising. The number of active oil and gas rigs around the world (including offshore equipment, not included in this category) fell from 5,600 to 1,700 in the decade between 1987 and 1997, and total U.S. employment in the oil and gas industry was cut in half. This occurred despite the fact that more oil was pumped worldwide every year (at prices greatly reduced from previous years). Some experts did predict that the prices of crude oil had reached a bottom and that the industry would begin to recover.

Despite the condition of the overall oil and gas industry, many oil and gas servicing companies were doing extremely well. Industry experts attributed this success to a number of factors, including drastic cost cutting at surviving companies, new technologies such as synthetic diamond drill bits that tripled the life of old bits, and the increase in markets outside of the United States. Great Britain, for instance, has eliminated its revenue tax on new oil fields in an attempt to lure new operations.

INDUSTRY LEADERS

In its 1997 annual report on the oil and gas industry, *Forbes* listed the top companies in terms of 1996 sales as follows: Schlumberger Ltd., $8.5 billion (16 percent increase over 1995); Halliburton Company, $6.7 billion (21 percent increase); Dresser Industries, $6.6 billion (17 percent increase); and Baker Hughes Inc., $3 billion (15 percent increase).

In 1996, Schlumberger (which produces electronic measurement equipment as well as oilfield services) and Baker Hughes (a leader in providing integrated services such as planning, engineering, and a full product line) formed an alliance to provide oilfield services, a move sure to increase future profits. Halliburton had become more of an industry leader as of 1993, when it purchased Smith International's directional drilling systems and servicing operations. Its chairman and CEO, Dick Cheney, drew on his experience as former Cabinet Secretary to focus on international markets and integrated services. Dresser shed some operations in order to focus on core operations such as drilling services and products. It also acquired several companies, including Baroid, whose business consisted of drilling services and products, including offshore operations. In 1997 Dresser announced creation of a new company, Dresser Kellogg Energy Services, designed to provide "one-stop shopping" for oil and natural gas companies. This would allow it to compete with similar services already being provided by Schlumberger and Halliburton.

Some much smaller companies, such as Lufkin Industries Inc., with 1996 sales of $226 million (an increase of over 9 percent from 1995), also continued to prosper. Founded in 1902, Lufkin radically altered the shape and function of the standard oil rig in 1923 by designing the first enclosed gear, crank-balanced oil well pumping unit. In 1991 the company began expansion into the international market, primarily Russia. Soon, over 66 percent of its pumping unit shipments were sent to locations outside the United States.

However, many other companies did not fare as well in the mid-1990s. For instance, in 1995 Cooper Industries of Houston, Texas, was forced to sell its poorly performing division, Cooper Cameron (a former leader in petroleum equipment manufacturing). It then invested the profits in an automotive lighting company.

WORK FORCE

Between 1982 and 1994, over half of the establishments in this industry either went out of business or were consumed by larger companies. In 1982, industry shipments were in excess of $11 billion, dropping to below $4 billion by 1994. Employment within the industry likewise plummeted, with the 25,400 workers in 1994 representing only a quarter of the 1982 work force and with projections of less than 1,000 workers by 1998. Wages nevertheless increased steadily from 1982 to 1994 to an average hourly rate of $15.59 in 1994, more than the overall manufacturing industry average of only $12.09 hour. Projected wages through 1998 were close to the 1994 level.

The industry was primarily composed of blue collar workers, such as welders, assemblers, machinists, and machine builders. The strongest employment opportunities in the industry in subsequent years would most likely be found in the fields of service and technical support rather than in the production of new units. While employment of machine assemblers in the general construction and related machinery industry was expected to increase by almost two-thirds by 2005, significant cuts were expected in almost all other areas, particularly machine builders and operators and clerical staff.

AMERICA AND THE WORLD

The influence of the OPEC nations cannot be ignored, as the cartel plays a huge role in the world economy. At no time was this more evident than during the Persian Gulf War of 1990-1991, when the absence of Iraqi and Kuwaiti oil sent the world economy reeling. These two countries accounted for 6.5 percent of the world supply of oil. Members of OPEC include Saudi Arabia, Iran, Kuwait, Iraq, and Venezuela.

Another world region in limbo was the Commonwealth of Independent Stores (former Soviet Union), the world's largest oil producer. It has been asserted that this area sits upon a large lake of oil, compared to the small pond beneath the Middle East. Chevron signed a deal to develop the Tenghiz field near the Caspian Sea in Kazakhstan. The field was first measured with inaccurate Soviet tools, which showed the field to contain 4.5 billion barrels of oil. Chevron intended to remeasure the field, and anticipated a value of possibly ten times the original estimate. Additionally, several tracts in the former Soviet Union had not been explored. The economic turmoil in this fragmenting giant was vitally linked to the production of oil; the doom of one would surely result in the doom of the other. In Russia, oil was the only commercial product. Russia's economic survival was dependent on its oil production, and a total collapse would be felt all over the world. Yet, Russia realized the health of their economy was totally dependent on the export of oil for

foreign currency. Beginning in 1995, Dresser Industries began to capitalize on the region's need for increased oil and gas exploration and entered into several joint ventures in Russia for the manufacture of field equipment.

The European Community (EC) was another area of concern, mainly because the monetary system was not standardized, and no definite time-frame for standardization was established. Europe both produced and consumed much of the world's oil, thereby making it a worldwide concern. While the EC was politically stable, compared to the Middle East and Russia, the monetary/commercial situation was not. As of January 1, 1993, commerce was united with regulations imposed on banking, airline, transportation, food, taxes, and certain utility industries. According to Standard & Poor's, ''The problem with the EC commercial union and its dealings with oil is that oil is bought in dollars and refined products are sold in each country's local currency. Thus, currency volatility exacerbates the erratic nature of crude oil prices.'' It was believed that once European currencies were unified, the oil industry and its price structure would stabilize. This, in turn, would increase capital investment.

The Pacific Rim was an economically expanding area, due to the growth of manufacturing related industry. Heavy manufacturing required oil-related products to run the machines used in the business, increasing the demand for oil. It was expected that Singapore's and Japan's refining and distribution centers would expand as industrialization efforts continued.

RESEARCH AND TECHNOLOGY

With limited resources for capital investment, research and development in oil related industries was limited. However, as competition increased the need to cut unnecessary costs and produce oil more efficiently would continue to be the top priority. Therefore, the major oil companies who produced the product would apply pressure to the machinery and equipment manufacturers to produce more efficiently operating products. Although the method of drawing oil from the ground had not changed significantly in theory or principle over time, the design of higher performance drilling rigs had. For example, Lufkin Industries bought a patent allowing it to produce a windmill pumping unit. The unit operated on the same principle as an ordinary windmill used to pump water from the ground. The advantage of this unit is that across the plains of Texas, Oklahoma, and Kansas, where the wind never seems to stop blowing, a constant source of power is available free of charge. By reducing the production costs, this type of innovation could encourage domestic drilling activity. Meanwhile, the search continued for alternative fuel sources. If significant breakthroughs were found, and allowed to be marketed by oil industry lobbyists, the demand for oil and its related products would continue to decrease. However, if the amount of oil in the former Soviet Union is as large as anticipated, the push for alternative fuels may subside until the resources have been completely exhausted.

FURTHER READING

"Baker Hughes Incorporated." *Hoover's Company Profile Database,* 1997.

Brantly, J.E. *History of Oil Well Drilling.* Houston: Gulf Publishing Company, 1971.

"Cooper Industries, Inc." *Hoover's Company Profile Database,* 1997.

"Dresser Industries, Inc." *Hoover's Company Profile Database,* 1997.

"Dresser Receives $130 Million of New Awards in Russian Federation." *PR Newswire,* 10 December 1996.

Graves, Edward. "Oil: Changes and Challenges for Clinton." *Standard & Poor's Industry Surveys,* 4 March 1993.

"Halliburton Company." *Oil & Gas Investor,* March 1996.

Hayes, Thomas C. "Cooper Industries is Looking for a New Conquest." *New York Times,* 9 June 1992.

Jones, Gregg. "Dresser Forms One-stop Energy Shop, Russian Gas Meter Firm." *Dallas Morning News,* 21 March 1997.

"Lufkin Industries, Inc." *Hoover's Company Capsules,* 1997. Available from http://www.hoovers.com/.

Manufacturing USA: Industry Analysis, Statistics, and Leading Companies. 5th ed., Detroit: Gale Research Inc., 1996.

McCann, J. "Global Capital Goods Group—Industry Report." *Merrill Lynch Capital Markets,* 4 March 1993.

McGinty, J. E. "Cooper Industries Inc. Company Report," *The First Boston Corporation,* 5 February 1993.

Palmeri, Christopher. "Energy [49th Annual Report on American Industry]." *Forbes,* 13 January 1997.

"Schlumberger Limited." *Hoover's Company Capsules,* 1997. Available from http://www.hoovers.com.

—Valerie Wilson, updated by Gerry Azzata

SIC 3534

ELEVATORS AND MOVING STAIRWAYS

This classification comprises establishments primarily engaged in manufacturing passenger or freight elevators, automobile lifts, dumbwaiters, and moving stairways. Establishments primarily involved in manu-

facturing commercial conveyor systems and equipment are classified in **SIC 3535: Conveyors and Conveying Equipment,** and those manufacturing farm elevators are classified in **SIC 3523: Farm Machinery and Equipment.**

INDUSTRY SNAPSHOT

The elevator and moving stairway industry manufactures a series of products designed for the vertical transportation of both materials and passengers. Machines manufactured for the exclusive purpose of moving materials, such as freight elevators and automobile lifts, comprise a small niche of the wide-ranging materials handling market. The majority of company revenues is from manufacturing passenger elevators and escalators—as well as from producing parts required for elevator renovation and modernization—and from servicing elevators.

The livelihood of this industry is based mostly on the well-being of the construction industry, since new buildings need new elevators. The demand for elevators in 1995 and 1996 was fairly low in the United States and Europe, but operations in Southeast Asia have increased with most of the large elevator firms selling products there.

The value of U.S. shipments rose each year from 1991 to 1996, with a value of $1.13 billion in 1996. The number of people employed in the business dropped consistently through the year, but hourly wages were slightly higher in this industry than the national manufacturing average.

ORGANIZATION AND STRUCTURE

In 1991, 175 establishments were engaged in manufacturing elevators and moving stairways, generating over $1.18 billion in shipments. Elevators and moving stairways accounted for roughly 75 percent of total shipments, while parts and attachments produced for separate sale was 18 percent of this figure. Electric and hydraulic passenger elevators—for roughly 45 percent of the industry's total shipments—were the largest product groups within the industry. Automobile lifts—10 percent of the total figure—were the next largest group, followed by freight elevators, other types of nonfarm elevators, and moving stairways and escalators—which each accounting for less than 6 percent of total shipments.

Establishments in the elevator and moving stairway industry employed an average of 57 people, approximately three less than the average for all manufacturing industries. Of the 175 establishments operating in 1991, 55 percent employed fewer than 20 workers. However, 69 percent of all employees in the industry were concentrated in establishments employing more than 100 people. While several of the industry's leading companies were subsidiaries of public companies, 31 of the 49 companies generating the highest revenues in the mid-1990s were privately owned.

Establishments engaged in the production of elevators and moving stairways could be found throughout the United States, with the greatest concentration of employees being located in the East. New York posted the greatest concentration of any state with 20 locations and 765 total employees. New York, combined with Pennsylvania and New Jersey, operated 24 percent of all establishments and employed 18 percent of the industry's total work force. Other strong contingencies of elevator and escalator producers could be found in Ohio, Illinois, Michigan, and California.

In 1991, this industry as a whole spent over $712 million on raw materials, which translated to about $4 million per establishment—roughly 12 percent below the average for all construction and related machinery establishments. New capital expenditures, at $28.5 million for the industry as a whole, or roughly $163,000 per establishment, also fell well below the larger industry group average of $230,000 per establishment. The projected cost of materials in 1996 was nearly $800 million, a figure steadily rising since 1987.

In an attempt to combat the unfavorable economic conditions of the early 1990s, the elevator industry attempted to fill the void in new elevator contracts by shifting its attention to the renovation and modernization of models installed 20 or more years ago. By replacing old control panels with new machinery and computer technology, the elevator industry hoped to survive the effects of the glutted real estate market. Elevator manufacturers also looked to take advantage of the new opportunities for renovation made available by legislation passed during the early 1990s requiring that elevators be updated to provide greater handicapped accessibility in public and private buildings.

The entrance of modern technology into the elevator industry also fostered greater competition between major contractors who were also engaged in manufacturing new elevators and smaller independent firms who derived their business exclusively from the service market. In an effort to guarantee future service and renovation contracts on the elevators they manufactured, many of the larger companies in the industry attempted to guard the technical data governing their elevators so that outside contractors lacking proper access codes would be unable to service their product. Although this form of proprietorship was frowned

upon by governing organizations such as the National Association of Elevator Contractors (NAEC), the profit margin on new elevators—about 5 percent—encouraged companies to protect their large capital investments in this manner.

BACKGROUND AND DEVELOPMENT

The genesis and evolution of the elevator industry closely paralleled the historical development of the Otis Elevator Company. The company was founded by Elisha Otis, the inventor of the first "safe" hoist—a technological development that generated public confidence in the elevator for the first time and laid the foundation for the elaborate vertical transportation systems of the twentieth century. An innovative advertiser as well as a skillful engineer, Otis brought his new invention to the Crystal Palace Exposition in New York City in 1854. During the middle of his demonstration, Otis stunned the crowd by cutting the rope that held up the hoist platform on which he stood, only to be kept securely in place by the release of the wagon spring safety mechanism he had invented. While Otis himself died before he was able to realize the financial rewards of his inventions, the company he founded reached the $1 million mark in sales in 1870 through the leadership of his sons, Charles and Norton.

As technology made the construction of taller buildings possible, the Otis-dominated elevator industry kept pace with developments of its own, introducing the hydraulic elevator in 1878, the electric elevator in 1889, and the gearless traction electric elevator in 1903. These innovations would later become the backbone of the industry, enabling passengers to be transported safely at greater speeds and to greater heights in buildings such as the 102-floor Empire State Building and the 110-floor World Trade Center.

As the volume of passengers and the number of taller buildings increased, the need arose for federal safety codes regulating the industry. In 1922, the American standard safety requirements for elevators were established, codifying the informal laws that had previously governed the industry. By keeping such concerns at the forefront, the industry was able to maintain an excellent safety record, strengthening consumer confidence and paving the way for the public acceptance of new technologies in future years.

As elevator speeds reached 700 feet per minute, the need for an automated control system became more evident. Consequently, in 1924 Otis developed the Signal Control System, which took the guesswork away from the operator by automatically slowing down the elevator as passengers on various floors pushed call buttons. The system was further refined with the invention of Peak Period Control, a control device which automated the job of the elevator starter, further increasing efficiency.

The widespread use of electronics in World War II ushered in a new era of technological advances in the elevator industry. In addition to providing improvements in safety devices, such as the development of a sensor that automatically returned the elevator doors to the open position when a person occupied the doorway, electronics technology finally eliminated the need for elevator operators and starters. With Otis's development and refinement of Autotronics, a system that electronically controlled when elevator doors should be opened and closed, most commercial elevators were fully automated by the mid-1950s.

The next two decades were marked by continued refinement of the automatic control systems developed in the 1950s. By 1970, for instance, solid state circuitry, which contained hundreds of printed circuit boards per system, was applied to the elevator industry. This innovation significantly reduced the size and weight of the control system, while improving its reliability and ease of maintenance in comparison to earlier models. New methods of production were introduced as well, such as the concept of the pre-engineered elevator, which brought forth the mass production of uniformly designed elevators. This manufacturing philosophy not only lowered production costs, but, by providing the architect with the exact hoistway dimensions and other elevator specifications, eliminated much of the arduous work required in designing elevators to fit individual construction projects. Such innovations enabled the industry to surpass the $1 billion mark in shipments by 1982, more than twice the total of a decade earlier.

As the 1980s progressed, however, the pattern of growth characteristic of earlier years was not sustained. An increased demand for escalators in shopping malls and other public building throughout the country was not enough to overcome the slowdown in the elevator market, a direct result of the severe decline in multi-story buildings. At the close of 1991, total shipments of $1.18 billion were recorded, reflecting only a 5 percent increase over the previous 10 years. In a similar fashion, new capital expenditures fell from $31.2 million to $16.3 million, nearly a 48 percent decline.

While the future of the industry largely depended on the condition of the real estate and construction markets, it would also be influenced by firms' abilities to sell clients on new technological developments, particularly those implementing the use of computerized control systems, which promised to revolutionize the industry in the 1990s. With the advent of various types of new computer technology, the future of the industry would largely be determined by the ability of elevator manufacturers to convince consumers that extensive modernization projects were indeed necessary. Without the support of a strong U.S. economy in the future, it appeared doubtful that such expenses would be justified by companies attempting to cut costs.

CURRENT CONDITIONS

In 1996, the elevator industry faced increased competition, and a slow construction industry made business difficult. Large European companies were in financial straits, such as the Swiss engineering firm Schindler. Their 1995 profits were one-half the preceding year's. Kone, a Finnish company, closed several of its factories. The American firm Otis, which controlled about one-fifth of the market, saw a 20 percent rise in operating profits in 1995; with $5.3 billion in sales, the company made $511 million in profits.

From 1990 to 1995, the demand for elevators and escalators fell from 90,000 units annually to 70,000 units. Large international firms and small local companies all suffered. They responded to the crunch by cutting costs, decreasing the number of employees, simplifying designs, and consolidating. In 1991 there were 175 companies operating in this industry; in 1997, there were 34—the top companies of which were subsidiaries of larger corporations.

Historically, the servicing of elevators has been the privilege of the manufacturer, but the servicing of elevators has become a fiercely competitive market of its own. Servicing contracts are of great importance because generally, in the first twenty years of its life, an elevator will cost its owner as much in repairs as the initial cost. To offset this, Otis started installing elevators equipped with electronics that allow engineers to remotely monitor elevators for faults and upcoming problems. The remote monitoring enables engineers to spot problems, and elevators can be serviced before breakdowns occur. This is a sour point among others trying to bid for the service contracts, as Otis is wary of giving up the secrets of this high-tech system.

INDUSTRY LEADERS

Otis Elevator Company has historically been the leader of elevator companies. In 1996 this continued to be the case, with total sales of $5.287 billion—almost twice as much as the entire Dover Corporation, which had a subsidiary company as the nearest competitor. Otis has been a wholly owned subsidiary of United Technologies Corporation since 1976, and employs more than 50,000 people in more than 1,700 worldwide locations. The company sold, manufactured, and installed more than 33,000 elevators and escalators per year, and maintained 700,000 elevators and escalators. Otis had more than 1.2 billion elevators in operation across the globe.

As of 1997, Otis was headquartered in Farmington, Connecticut, but over 80 percent of its employees were in countries other than the United States, and 80 percent of revenues were generated outside the United States. Otis claims to make one of every four elevators sold in the world.

The second largest company with shares in this industry in 1997 was Dover Corporation, which owned 60 companies but was most famous for its elevator division. This subsidiary Dover Elevator International Inc., was located in Memphis, Tennessee, and they had $823 million in sales and 7,000 employees.

The third largest company was Montgomery Elevator Co., of Moline, Illinois, with approximately $410 million in sales and 3,700 people employed. The next was Total Energy Services Inc., of Houston, Texas, with about $180 million in sales and 100 people employed. The fifth largest company was the United States Elevator Corporation of El Cajon, California, with over $130 million in sales and about 100 employees.

WORK FORCE

Total employment in the elevator and escalator industry encountered a period of gradual decline in the early and mid-1980s. After reaching a decade high of 13,000 total employees in 1982, employment figures declined to 10,200 in 1987 and to 8,400 in 1996.

Of the 8,900 employed by the industry in 1991, 5,800 were production workers, while the remaining 3,100 held technical, managerial, or administrative positions. Those in managerial and laboring positions all suffered from the general decline of the industry during the mid- and late 1980s. White-collar workers faced a greater rate of attrition, losing 41.5 percent of its work force between 1982 and 1991, while blue-collar positions were reduced by only 25 percent during the same period.

Employees in the elevator and moving stairway industry made a projected $14.27 per hour in 1996, about 11 percent higher than the national average for manufacturing jobs. White-collar workers, however, employed at an average annual salary of $36,968, acquired wages roughly 6 percent below the average for related industrial machinery fields.

As elevator and moving stairway establishments continued to downsize their work forces to accommo-

date the shift towards modernization and renovation and away from the manufacturing of new units, the education requirements for working in the industry promised to change as well. As evidenced by the NAEC's early campaign to improve the training of field personnel and recruit more people with computer experience, the industry's introduction of more sophisticated computerized technology demanded a larger percentage of workers with a strong college or trade school background in computers.

RESEARCH AND TECHNOLOGY

While the Japanese centered their efforts on the production of faster elevators during the 1990s, U.S. companies focused on making them run "smarter," or more efficiently, in relation to the needs of their patrons. One of the most promising developments in domestic elevator technology came in Otis's introduction of a new type of computer software that used "fuzzy logic" to decide upon the best way to accommodate the various traffic needs of a modern office building. This type of artificial intelligence software distinguished itself from the standard computer logic governing conventional modern elevators by its ability to process uncertainties of information more efficiently. Rather than simply sending the closest elevator when a patron signaled, fuzzy logic took into account the number of people waiting for elevators throughout the building, hoping to avoid the common problem of sending an elevator to service one individual at the expense of several left waiting somewhere else. This innovative system by Otis, first installed in Japan in 1993, encountered some problems, but it held great potential for the future of the industry.

In 1996, Otis began showing the Odyssey, a multidirectional system of transistor elevator cabs, which could take a person from parking lot to penthouse, even in structures more than 1,000 meters high.

As of 1996, the world's fastest moving elevator was located in the Landmark Tower, in Yokohama, Japan. It moved at about 41.6 feet per second.

FURTHER READING

Alborghetti, Marci. "UTC Divisions Rise to Occasion." *Connecticut Post,* 10 December 1993.

Anderson, Paul, ed. *Tell Me About Elevators.* Farmington, CT: Otis Elevator Company, 1978.

Chartrand, Sabra. "Computer Software from Otis Uses Fuzzy Logic to Make Elevators Smarter and More Efficient." *New York Times,* 13 September 1993.

Darnay, Arsen J., ed. *Manufacturing USA.* Detroit: Gale Research, 1996.

Hast, Adele, ed. *International Directory of Company Histories.* Chicago: St. James Press, 1994.

McManamy, Rob. "Contractors Rise on Modernizations." *Engineering News Record,* 26 July 1990.

"Otis Seizes the High Ground." *International Management,* November 1992.

Patton, Robert. "Mag Lift: Japan's Engineers Push the Envelope for Elevators." *Scientific American,* October 1993.

Philpot, Jerry. "Escalators into the Deep." *Mass Transit,* April 1992.

Pinder, Jeanne B. "Fuzzy Thinking Has Merits When It Comes to Elevators." *New York Times,* 22 September 1993.

Pollack, Andrew. "Fastest, Maybe Smoothest, Trip Up." *New York Times,* 22 September 1993.

Umlauf, Elyse. "Control Logic Makes Elevators 'Smarter.'" *Building Design and Construction,* May 1992.

Brown, Randy. "Need a Lift?" *Buildings,* December 1996.

"Schindler's Lift: Elevators." *The Economist,* 16 March 1996.

U.S. Bureau of the Census. *Annual Survey of Manufactures.* Washington: GPO, 1997.

U.S. Department of Commerce. *Census of Manufactures.* Washington: GPO, 1987.

U.S. Department of Commerce. *County Business Patterns.* Washington: GPO, 1991.

"World of Otis—Who Are We?" Available from http://www.nao.otis.com/whoweare.htm.

—Jason Gallman, updated by Beaird Glover

SIC 3535

CONVEYORS AND CONVEYING EQUIPMENT

This category covers establishments primarily engaged in manufacturing conveyors and conveying equipment for installation in factories, warehouses, mines, and other industrial and commercial establishments. Establishments primarily engaged in manufacturing farm elevators and conveyors are classified in **SIC 3523: Farm Machinery and Equipment;** those manufacturing passenger or freight elevators, dumbwaiters, and moving stairways are classified in **SIC 3534: Elevators and Moving Stairways;** and those manufacturing overhead traveling cranes and monorail systems are classified in **SIC 3536: Overhead Traveling Cranes, Hoists, and Monorail Systems.**

INDUSTRY SNAPSHOT

Conveying systems have been an integral part of mining operations for nearly a century, but manufacturing industries have also become dependent on them. Regulations mandated by the Occupational Safety and Hazard Administration (OSHA) limited human exposure to certain harmful materials, requiring more extensive machine automation. With increased automation, conveying systems became an absolutely necessary part of operating a manufacturing plant.

Global competition has forced business owners to look for ways to cut costs and improve productivity. In industrial firms, again, automating production processes are a way to help reach their goal. While ways to do this vary with the type of business and the degree to which production processes are repeatable, most manufacturing firms looked at material handling systems as a possible answer. It is for these reasons that material handling systems manufacturers experienced considerable growth during the profit-driven 1980s and the cost-cutting 1990s.

However, as with most mining and manufacturing support industries, builders of conveyors and conveying equipment were limited by industry-related economic cycles. Senior management officials, who were directly accountable to stockholders, heavily scrutinized the installation of non-value added equipment. Such investment was often viewed as an unnecessary expense, especially when the company's financial health was in question. Therefore, the conveying system industry was reliant on a company's willingness to invest in itself.

ORGANIZATION AND STRUCTURE

The conveying system industry is highly specialized, and therefore almost totally self-contained. While the industry relies heavily on suppliers for many of the materials consumed, the design and assembly of the systems is usually performed at one facility. Armed with design engineers and production facilities, the industry is capable of meeting individual material movement challenges in industries ranging from mining to heavy manufacturing to the airline industry. Standard equipment is produced in the pre-engineered sector of the industry.

According to *Manufacturing USA,* in 1993 there were 739 total U.S. establishments in this industry, with only 340 having 20 or more employees; this number was expected to remain relatively stable through 1998. The value of shipments in 1994 was $4.7 billion, the largest figure in the years measured since 1982. Growth was expected to rise steadily through 1998.

About 50 percent of the manufactured products in this industry were dedicated to unit handling conveyors and conveying systems, with an additional 4 percent dedicated to these systems' parts, attachments, and accessories. Another 27 percent of the product share was dedicated to bulk material handling conveyors and conveying systems, with about 10.5 additional percent dedicated to these systems' parts, attachments, and accessories. The remainder of the industry (approximately 8.5 percent) was allotted to miscellaneous conveyors and conveying equipment.

BACKGROUND AND DEVELOPMENT

The first conveying systems were developed to draw water from wells in the ground. This method was used in various applications over the centuries, but conveying systems really gained importance through the mining industry. In the beginning of the mining industry, mine cars were used as buckets to haul coal or other ores to the earth's surface. Mine cars have been replaced with continuous conveying systems such as belt conveyors, steel-apron conveyors, and chain-conveyors, which are used to haul as much as 5,000 tons per hour on lower grade slopes, and 1,300 tons per hour in high angle conditions. Since wages accounted for most of the production costs in the mining industry, mechanization was necessary. Likewise, as the government began to regulate worker safety and worker's compensation claims, the initial expense of installing a mechanized system seemed like a good investment, because the systems could minimize workers' contact with hazardous materials and reduce physical strain.

Although mining has long been the greatest force in the conveying system industry, the growing presence of production lines since Henry Ford's development of the assembly line has expanded the industry. The industry expansion brought new challenges. As machines were created to perform at higher capacities, the conveying systems delivering the materials to the machines have had to meet these capacities. For example, in some beverage industries today, conveying systems are required to maintain a flow of up to 1,600 units per minute.

The worldwide recession of the late 1980s and early 1990s affected the mining industry significantly. In countries where commodity prices fell, some mining operations ceased due to production costs exceeding the market value of the extracted raw materials. Capital expenditures in this area fell as well, with investment in conveying systems being an unjustifiable expenditure.

As one component of the greater material handling industry, conveyers found new importance in the flexible manufacturing systems (FMS) methodology during the 1980s. However, as this theoretical approach was moving in one direction, manufacturers were concentrating more on productivity in terms of cost reduction. The installation of FMS was often cost prohibitive and limiting to companies reliant on reacting quickly to changing market needs. Yet, in terms of lowering costs through increased quality and efficiency to increase profitability, the material handling improvements through FMS were justifiable costs. Companies with existing conveying systems that wished to increase productivity through improved material handling techniques provided a market for the retrofitting segment. Manufacturing industries, particularly where machining is a large portion of value-added production, employ palletization work-holding principles in everyday operations. These principles transfer materials from one machining center to another on the same work-holding device, eliminating setup time.

CURRENT CONDITIONS

Manufacturing USA projected that the number of establishments would remain basically level through 1998, with a steady increase in value of shipments to approximately $5.1 billion. It also predicted that employment would drop from the 1994 figure of 19,100 to 17,800 by 1998. Industry leaders in the latter part of the 1990s had increased earnings in some cases due to mergers, acquisitions, and sales of unprofitable divisions.

As of 1994, the conveyor industry was characterized by very low expenditures for plant investment, only about $89.4 million for the entire industry and $123,683 average expenditures per establishment (more than 60 percent below the total manufacturing industries average). Expenditures were expected to rise somewhat through 1998 (to approximately $101 million for the entire industry), but still reflecting minimal investments in plants. However, one industry expert, Dave Slager (marketing vice-president of Meyer Machinery Company), predicted in 1996 that new conveyors would be purchased with little concern about future capacity, being used for only a few years before being replaced. When introducing new products, he speculated, companies would also replace the equipment used to produce them.

INDUSTRY LEADERS

Industry leaders as of 1996 differed significantly from those of earlier years, due to mergers and divestitures. For instance, in 1995 Litton Industries, Inc., sold its industrial automation operations ("WAI"), which had operated at a loss of almost $200 million in 1994. Interlake Corporation, which had sales of over $709 million in 1996, bolstered its income by discontinuing some operations, including its packaging business.

Mid-West Conveyor Company Inc. ranked eighth in the industry in 1991 in sales, with $80 million and 400 employees. In March 1993, Mid-West announced it had developed a high capacity conveyor system, capable of transporting up to 5,000 tons of product per hour. The Matchappel Quick-set Folding Conveyor System is reportedly easy to install and extend, using belts ranging from 1,050 to 1,600 millimeters wide. It is used in many coal mining and quarrying operations in Australia, including Wambo Mining Corporation Proprietary Limited. In 1995, Mid-West merged with the Dearborn Fabricating & Engineering Company to form a new company called Dearborn Mid-West Conveyor Company. The reorganized operations are owned by a British holding company, Tomkins PLC. The intention was for the Mid-West plants to continue production of key products such as automotive plant conveyor systems.

Prab Inc., a relatively small designer and manufacturer of conveyors as well as other industrial equipment, reported record profits in 1996, based on sales of $15.4 million.

WORK FORCE

Employment levels in this industry were dropping as automation increased. In 1982, employment was 36,400 nationwide, falling to 30,600 by 1993. While this figure rose to 33,100 in 1994, employment was expected to remain under 31,000 through 1998.

With average earnings of $12.78 per hour in 1994, employees were paid 6 percent over the average reported by all other forms of manufacturing in the nation. However, workers were spending 4 percent more time on the job than most other manufacturing workers, which implies overtime compensation was granted.

The strongest employment opportunities in the industry in future years will most likely be found in the fields of service and technical support rather than in the production of new units. While employment of machine assemblers in the general construction and related machinery industry was expected to increase by almost two-thirds by 2005, significant cuts were expected in almost all other areas, particularly machine builders and operators and clerical staff.

AMERICA AND THE WORLD

The Commonwealth of Independent States (CIS) did not implement conveying systems in mining operations until the early 1990s. Rather, inefficient trucks remained the material handling equipment of choice at mining pits and quarries. Demand for conveying technology increased in response to increased demand for fuel efficiency. Various combinations of dead-end and lateral-field conveyors were being used for maximum fuel efficiency. The ex-Soviets also enjoyed productivity increases of between 11 and 25 percent, which were accomplished by implementing a material storage location midway through the conveying system. Other benefits enjoyed were increased worker safety by the automated equipment and decreased labor costs.

Conveying systems were used extensively by the Japanese, who invested heavily in automation. Japan's use of high-tech systems caught the attention of U.S. manufacturers, who by the mid- to late 1980s started experimenting with new approaches to material handling. One application that became a buzzword in manufacturing is "palletization." In automated systems, material is transported on a pallet through a conveying system. When pallets are designed as work-holding devices, personnel and machining resources are maximized and productivity increases. Leaving the machine operator free to set up machines, the material flow is refined because both horizontal and vertical machining centers can interface with palletized work-holding devices.

While the economy provides one set of influences on making business decisions, the U.S. government provides another. The Occupational Safety and Health Administration continues to impose regulations concerning worker safety. In applications where hazardous waste or dangerous fumes are employed, robotics and automated machining centers are the only solution for meeting government regulations. According to the Robotic Industries Association, 831 new installations of robots for assembly were reported in the United States in 1989, up from 701 in 1988. This figure represents approximately 21 percent of total robot installations.

While the Europeans and Asians do not regulate worker safety to the same degree as the United States, they do investigate ways to increase quality and productivity at minimal costs. The Japanese government provides programs for funding robot application development, education, tax credits, and loans to purchase the equipment.

RESEARCH AND TECHNOLOGY

The food and beverage industries employ conveying systems primarily as a function of labor savings. Speed, reliability, and performance are emphasized as being top priorities of beverage production lines. Production machines are continually being improved to perform at faster rates. However, the production rate of a machine is meaningless unless the conveyor system can deliver the containers on time. Because bottling companies are demanding higher production rates from machines, in some cases as much as 1,600 units per minute or more, material handling equipment manufacturers have had to redesign their products to meet the higher speeds. Computerized process flows have made the industry more sophisticated, allowing for variable speed control through "intelligent" software that accepts feedback from key points in the system.

Although conveyor manufacturers often specialize in designing and installing specialized conveying systems, some companies choose to build the system with internal engineering staff, using pre-engineered components. One such company is Richards-Wilcox Manufacturing Company, a builder of file and shelving products. In March 1993, Richards-Wilcox announced that it built a monorail conveyor system that was proving to be cost effective. The system, called the ZIG-ZAG, is used specifically for heavy components, sometimes weighing as much as a human is allowed to lift by law. The ZIG-ZAG is a continuous loop system that automatically loads and transports the file and shelving components through a final coating process at a rate of 22 feet per minute. At the end of the cycle, the system unloads the components. The system features an overhead transport and assembly system, which saves shop floor space.

Despite the tight world economy, some mining companies have chosen to invest in better conveying systems in light of the potential operational cost-savings. Due to many problems in the early 1970s, Neyveli Lignite Corporation, in India, tried this approach in 1974. As a result Neyveli was very successful through the 1980s. Again faced with problems common to the lignite mining industry, Neyveli announced in 1993 that it had installed a sophisticated system of belt conveyors that operate 24 hours a day. Through this system, Neyveli reported increased production capability, which improved its financial outlook.

Another mining advancement in recent years is Butterley Engineering's Moving Car Bunker system. The system keeps coal mine conveyor belts running at a constant rate through surge control technology. The surge control system is activated when the trunk belt becomes overloaded and coal starts to build up. This is an alternative to conventional design, in which trunk belts respond to peak tonnage. The bunker is designed with open-bottom storage units, coupled together. These units are capable of hauling as much as 3,000 tons of coal.

The Conveyor Equipment Manufacturers Association released a standard for unit-handling conveyors in 1996. Technological developments of particular significance in the later 1990s include: faster and quieter belt conveyors, such as the "European" or monofilament belt; self-powered conveyors, dividing the line into smaller zones, without the traditional belts, pulleys, and chains; "intelligent conveyors" being used by AT&T for computer assembly, which refill empty locations on the conveyor automatically; distributed logic control systems, which are used by NCR Corporation to allow assembly of specialized computer models; and more durable modular plastic and stainless steel designs that eliminate rubber belts.

FURTHER READING

"AT&T Relies Upon Intelligent Conveyors for PC Assembly." *Assembly,* April 1996.

Butkevich, G. R. "Conveyor Transport: A Viewpoint from Russia." *Pit & Quarry,* November 1992.

"Components Conveyed to Smooth Finish with Richards-Wilcox." *Industrial Engineering,* March 1993.

"Conveyor Maker Joins With Detroit Company." *Kansas City Star,* 18 August 1995.

"Game, Set, and Matchappel." *World Mining Equipment,* March 1993.

Geppert, Hans. "Palletization: The Best Lesson from the FMS Experiment." *Modern Machine Shop,* May 1992.

Gyorki, John. "Conveyor Controls Computer Manufacturing Mix." *Machine Design,* 12 September 1996.

Horton, Nick. "Conveyor Systems and Their Maintenance." *World Mining Equipment,* October 1992.

"Interlake Corp. Reports Earnings for Quarter to Dec. 31." *New York Times,* 28 January 1997.

Kasturi, T. S. "Progress through Perseverance: The Story of Neyveli Lignite's Conveyor System." *World Mining Equipment,* March 1993.

Knill, Bernie. "Less Noise and More Speed in Belt Conveyors." *Material Handling Engineering,* February 1996.

Leone, Paul. "Merrily They Roll Along." *Beverage World,* December 1992.

Litton Industries Home Page. Available from http://www.littoncorp.com/.

Mancini, Leticia. "Movin' on Down the Line; Conveying Equipment." *Chilton's Food Engineering,* 17 July 1996.

Manufacturing USA: Industry Analysis, Statistics, and Leading Companies, 5th ed. Detroit: Gale Research Inc., 1996.

"Prab Reports Record Profits in 1996." *Business Wire,* 23 January 1997.

Schreiber, Rita R. "Assembly Robots Build Quality." *Manufacturing Engineering,* June 1991.

"Self-powered Conveyors Get Smart." *Machine Design,* 18 April 1996.

Swenson, Peter W. "Automated Machining." *Manufacturing Engineering,* December 1990.

—Valerie Wilson, updated by Gerry Azzata

SIC 3536

OVERHEAD TRAVELING CRANES, HOISTS, AND MONORAIL SYSTEMS

This classification is comprised of establishments primarily engaged in manufacturing overhead traveling cranes, hoists, and monorail systems for installation in factories, warehouses, marinas, and other industrial and commercial establishments. Excluded from this classification are establishments primarily engaged in manufacturing cranes except industrial types, automobile wrecker hoists, and aerial work platforms, which are classified in **SIC 3531: Construction Machinery.** Also excluded from this industry are those manufacturing aircraft loading hoists, which are classified in **SIC 3537: Industrial Trucks, Tractors, Trailers, and Stackers.**

INDUSTRY SNAPSHOT

The overhead traveling crane, hoist, and monorail system industry includes a diverse assortment of products that fit within a narrowly defined segment of the materials handling equipment industry. Not to be confused with various types of mobile cranes used in construction projects, overhead cranes are variously structured machines that "travel" along a runway structure or pair of tracks located above the work floor of a plant or factory. They are further characterized by the presence of a fixed or trolley-mounted hoisting system that is connected to the tracks by a bridge structure, which consists of either a single or double girder.

The industry manufactures three basic kinds of overhead traveling cranes that accommodate the vast majority of materials handling needs. The first type is the overhead bridge crane, which is fixed to an overhead beam running the length of the building. Gener-

ally regarded as the most rugged of all overhead traveling cranes, this class of crane is noted for its ability to cover the entire width and length of a plant. The jib crane is the second variety of crane produced by the industry. It is usually mounted to a wall or pillar and is used to service a smaller area of a plant, usually the area of a single workstation. Gantry cranes, which are mounted overhead and are able to service a particular bay or workstation, comprise the third category.

While overhead traveling cranes are sometimes operated manually, they are usually powered by electricity and can be interfaced with automatic guided vehicles, stacker cranes, and monorails for increased efficiency. Accordingly, hoists and monorails, the other major segments of this industry classification, are often manufactured for use in conjunction with overhead traveling cranes. Employed mainly in an industrial capacity, products in this industry are also employed in stone and concrete pre-casting yards, steel fabricating shops, and storage facilities.

According to *Manufacturing USA,* 168 establishments, employing 7,900 people, were engaged in the manufacturing of hoists, overhead cranes, and monorail systems in 1994. These companies combined produced $1.07 billion in industry shipments that year, a drop from 1991's $1.21 billion, but a slight improvement over 1992 and 1993. The manufacturing of overhead traveling cranes and monorail systems accounted for about 47 percent of total shipments, as did the production of various types of hoists. Miscellaneous hoist, crane, and monorail products made up the remaining 6 percent.

ORGANIZATION AND STRUCTURE

In 1994, the average number of employees per establishment in the hoist, crane, and monorail industry was slightly lower than the average for all establishments engaged in the manufacturing of industrial machinery and equipment, according to *Manufacturing USA* statistics. The average establishment in this sector employed 47 people. The average hourly wage for production workers in 1994 was $12.83, down from a high of $13.45 in 1991.

Geographically, the greatest concentration of hoist, crane, and monorail manufacturing takes place in the five-state region of Ohio, Michigan, Pennsylvania, Illinois, and Wisconsin, where more than a third of all the industry's establishments are located and 3,300 of its 7,900 employees work. California, with only 300 employees, has the most establishments (19). Ohio, the state employing the most people in the industry (1,000), has 17 establishments, as does Michigan (with

600 employees). Texas (600 employees) and Pennsylvania (500 employees) each have 15 establishments.

As a whole, the industry spent over $500 million on raw materials in 1994, which translates to about $3 million per establishment, roughly 40 percent below the average for all construction and related machinery manufacturing establishments. New capital expenditures, just over $59,000 per establishment, also fell far below the larger industry group average of $321,000.

BACKGROUND AND DEVELOPMENT

While various types of jib cranes and other lifting devices were installed in foundries during the late eighteenth century, and the overhead traveling bridge crane existed as early as 1860, materials handling systems were not widely used in the United States until its entrance into World War II in 1941. During the 1940s, however, firms that had previously been hesitant to make the large capital investment necessary for implementing an extensive materials handling system were forced to do so in order to meet the production demands of war materials contracts. The fact that the implementation of materials handling systems actually lowered production costs in many cases was only a by-product of the more pressing concern of supplying the military with the necessary weaponry and machinery for winning the war.

New levels of production volume and efficiency demonstrated during the war through the use of materials handling systems led to a phenomenal increase in the use of various types of overhead traveling cranes, hoists, and monorails in the years immediately following the war. Having demonstrated its potential for lowering production costs during the war, materials handling emerged as the most effective tool for offsetting the rising costs of labor and materials. During this period, materials handling research and development efforts evolved into an integral segment of industrial management and engineering education programs as well, legitimizing the discipline of materials handling within both academic and industrial settings.

As technology—especially in the field of electronics—progressed during the 1950s and 1960s, gradual improvements were made in overhead traveling cranes, hoists, and monorail systems, enabling the industry to carve a profitable niche in the larger spectrum of materials handling equipment. As industries were being pressured to increase production while employing the same amount of floor space, equipment that could move materials overhead offered several advantages over its competitors in the broadly defined materials handling industry. While most types of conveyor systems, for instance, occupied a considerable

amount of floor space, overhead cranes kept this space free for other production activities. Offering this ergonomic advantage, the hoist, crane, and monorail industry grew into a $500 million a year business by the early 1970s, employing over 16,000 people, according to *Census of Manufactures* statistics.

As the 1970s progressed, the introduction of computer technology revolutionized the field. While the development of solid-state logic had signaled the end of many of the bulky relay-type controls of earlier years in storage-retrieval systems, the same technology could not be applied to complex one-of-a-kind systems without a relatively high capital investment. The widespread availability of microcomputers, however, solved this problem, enabling cranes to be regulated by programmable controllers. Rather than investing large amounts of capital to perform specialized tasks requiring automation, companies were often able to use existing hardware for a variety of tasks, changing only the computer software to accommodate the desired new function. Largely through the improvements in efficiency engendered by these technological advances, the overhead traveling crane, hoist, and monorail industry more than doubled the value of its annual shipments by the end of the decade, while increasing its production work force by only 7 percent.

Although the 1981 passage of the Economic Recovery Tax—which offered incentives to companies that invested in the modernization and expansion of production facilities—held promise for a strong decade for the materials handling business as a whole, such expectations did not hold true for most segments of the broad industry group. While the conveyor and conveying equipment industry enjoyed steady increases in revenues during the early and mid-1980s, the hoist, crane, and monorail industry lagged behind, suffering nearly a 50 percent decrease in revenue between 1981—the industry's best year of production with over $1.4 billion in shipping—and 1987, according to *Census of Manufactures* information. The increased use of robotics, the fastest growing segment of the materials handling industry in the 1980s, was partially responsible for this decline. Revenues for the hoist, crane, and monorail industry steadily improved during the late 1980s, however, as the nation's economy grew, enabling businesses to purchase materials handling equipment they had put off buying earlier in the decade.

The volume of materials handling equipment is generally thought to be closely correlated to the conditions of the U.S. economy as a whole. Accordingly, the recessive conditions of the early 1990s resulted in sluggish patterns of growth for all segments of the materials handling market during this period. Lacking the cash flow to justify new purchases of equipment, most companies relied on existing machinery to handle materials handling needs. The hoist, crane, and monorail industry, however, went against this general trend. While shipments for the industry's counterparts in the conveyor and conveying equipment and industrial truck and tractors industries fell 5 and nearly 12 percent, respectively, manufacturers of hoists, cranes, and monorails enjoyed a 20 percent increase in shipments between 1990 and 1991, according to the *Annual Survey of Manufactures*.

CURRENT CONDITIONS

Analysts have exhibited a guarded optimism for the future of both the hoist, crane, and monorail market and the larger materials handling industry. As segments of the U.S. economy crucial to the materials handling market, such as the construction industry, began to recover, sales of new equipment also were expected to increase. This expected pattern of growth would also be dependent on a continued reduction in the foreign trade deficit for materials handling equipment, which should benefit from the opening up of markets in Eastern Europe for retooling and rebuilding factories.

Many companies made heavy purchases of materials handling equipment in the late 1980s and so made minimal capital investments in the early 1990s, so that projections in *Manufacturing USA* presume significantly increased needs for capital investment through 1998 as equipment ages and the economy continues to improve. However, much of this investment may be in retrofitting of existing equipment, rather than new equipment purchases. These projections are bolstered by the increase in orders within the industry in early 1996, rising almost 6 percent in the first quarter over the last quarter of 1995. The renewed health of the U.S. automobile manufacturing industry should also translate into an improved financial outlook for the overhead crane, hoist, and monorail industry.

INDUSTRY LEADERS

Various companies have led the hoist, crane, and monorail industry in recent years, demonstrating the parity of this segment of the materials handling industry. AMDURA Corporation—formerly known as American Hoist and Derrick—was easily the industry leader in late 1980s, averaging $625 million in sales. However, faced with severe cash flow problems in the early 1990s, the company disappeared from the list of industry leaders, opening up its market share to a host of both new and experienced competitors.

Long-time producers of materials handling equipment, Columbus McKinnon Corporation (Amherst, New York) and JLG Industries Inc. (McConnellsburg, Pennsylvania) all raised their sales figures in AMDURA's absence. In 1996 Columbus McKinnon had sales of $210 million, an increase of almost 22 percent over 1995. JLG had sales of over $413 million in the same year, an astonishing 53.6 percent increase over 1995. Chatwins Group Inc. (Pittsburgh, Pennsylvania), a relative newcomer founded in 1988, continued to do well into the late 1990s. Its overall sales were over $153 million in 1996, with its Alliance Machine Company division having net sales of over $28 million.

WORK FORCE

Total employment in the hoist, crane, and monorail industry declined sharply in the early and mid-1980s, climbed to 8,400 in 1991, fell again in 1992 and 1993, and then rose back to 7,900 in 1994. Employment was expected to remain at this level through 1998.

Of the 7,900 employees of hoist, crane, and monorail establishments in 1994, 4,500 were classified as production workers, while the remaining 3,400 were engaged in technical, managerial, or administrative duties. The pattern of decline established in the 1980s proved to have lasting damage for the blue-collar work force, whose wages in 1994 (an average of $12.83 per hour) remained well below the 1991 level ($13.45), although they still were well above the total industry sector average of $12.09.

While the recovery of the U.S. economy may signal better times for the materials handling work force as a whole in the late 1990s, blue-collar employment prospects in the hoist, crane, and monorail industry may suffer from the very durability of the products they manufacture. With a life span of 30 years or more, cranes installed in the 1980s may not need to be replaced until well into the twenty-first century. As they face the need for new materials handling functions, companies in the future are expected to ''retrofit,'' or modernize, older model equipment to cut costs.

Consequently, the strongest employment opportunities in the industry in future years will be found, most likely, in the fields of service and technical support rather than in the production of new units. While employment of machine assemblers in the general construction and related machinery industry is expected to increase by almost two-thirds by 2005, significant cuts are expected in almost all other areas, particularly machine builders and operators and clerical staff.

RESEARCH AND TECHNOLOGY

For an industry whose fundamental hardware components originated more than a century ago, new developments in product technology have, for the most part, occurred gradually over a number of years as the country's material handling needs have changed. According to Clyde E. Witt, senior editor for *Material Handling Engineering,* "Crane technology has been stimulated through innovative thinking and creative efforts of manufacturers as well as users. Mechanical and technological advances have been a process of evolution, not revolution or major breakthroughs." This is not to say, however, that significant technological innovations have not been made in this segment of the materials handling industry.

The most significant of these changes in recent years has occurred, similarly to other manufacturing industries, as a result of the development and advancement of solid state logic and computer technology. Whereas overhead traveling cranes of the past were controlled by bulky relay-type systems, models developed since the 1970s were regulated by highly developed solid-state logic and computer regulated control systems. Although older control systems were sufficient for simple storage and retrieval tasks, they were less successful when applied to production functions, which often required the crane to perform a variety of precise movements by several different components. The development of these new forms of technology enabled overhead cranes to perform these complex production tasks more efficiently by reducing the size of control system hardware and improving its flexibility and durability.

In the 1980s and 1990s, control mechanisms for overhead traveling cranes and other types of equipment within this industrial classification were further refined and modernized to accommodate the changing needs of their users. The major developments in this period have involved the increased efficiency and wider range of applications for automated cranes regulated by programmable controllers or other computers. Such improvements have brought forth the introduction of automated cranes to a wide range of manufacturing environments, servicing locations as varied as an aerospace plant and a textile factory. The widespread acceptance of automated control systems has also facilitated a variety of interfacing applications, linking overhead cranes with other types of materials handling equipment, such as monorails, robots, and automated guided vehicles. Promising technological developments of special note in the late 1990s include more sophisticated radio programmable logic controllers, self-propelled floor cranes, cordless and infrared control technology, and retrofitting innovations.

FURTHER READING

Chatwins Group Inc. Annual Report. 1996. Available from http://www.sec.gov/.

"Columbus McKinnon Corporation." *Hoover's Company Capsules.* 1997. Available from http://www.hoovers.com/.

"Cranes, Hoists, Winches and Productivity." *Marine Log,* October 1993.

Darnay, Arsen J., ed. *Manufacturing USA.* 5th ed. Detroit: Gale Research, 1996.

Delano, Daryl. "Demand for Materials Handlings Systems, Equipment Strengthens." *Modern Materials Handling,* July 1996.

Holzhauer, Ron. "Bridge and Gantry Cranes: Masters of Overhead Handling." *Plant Engineering,* 13 April 1989.

"JLG Industries Inc." *Hoover's Company Capsules.* 1997. Available from http://www.hoovers.com/.

Laughlin, Tom. "What's New in Cranes, Remote Controls, and Magnets." *Metal Center News,* May 1995.

"Matching Cranes to Your Handling Needs." *Modern Materials Handling,* July 1987.

"New Reports Cite MH Market Trends." *Material Handling Engineering,* September 1983.

"Radio Contol System Handles Ten Hoists on Monorail." *Material Handling Engineering,* January 1997.

Semling, Harold V. "Commerce Predicts Good MH Sales Year." *Material Handling Engineering,* March 1982.

Shapiro, Howard I., Jay P. Shapiro, and Lawrence K. Shapiro. *Cranes and Derricks.* New York: McGraw-Hill, 1991.

Totu, A.R. "Guidelines for Overhead Crane Safety." *Plant Engineering,* 4 April 1991.

U.S. Department of Commerce. *Annual Survey of Manufactures.* Washington: GPO, 1991.

————. *Census of Manufactures.* Washington: GPO, 1987.

————. *County Business Patterns.* Washington: GPO, 1991.

————. *Trade and Employment.* Washington: GPO, 1993.

"U.S. Manufacturers' Sales of Material Handling Equipment to Top $12 Billion By Year 2000." *Manufacturing Automation,* June 1992.

"What Computers Can Do For Overhead Cranes." *Modern Materials Handling,* May 1977.

Witt, Clyde E. "Partnering Gets Lift from Crane Manufacturers." *Material Handling Engineering,* January 1992.

—Jason Gallman, updated Gerry Azzata

SIC 3537

INDUSTRIAL TRUCKS, TRACTORS, TRAILERS, AND STACKERS

This classification comprises establishments primarily engaged in manufacturing industrial trucks, tractors, trailers, stackers (truck type), and related equipment used for handling materials on floors and paved surfaces in and around industrial and commercial plants, depots, docks, airports, and terminals. Excluded from this classification are establishments primarily involved in manufacturing motor vehicles and motor vehicle type trailers, which are classified in **SIC 3710: Motor Vehicles and Motor Vehicle Equipment,** and those manufacturing farm type wheel tractors, which are classified in **SIC 3523: Farm Machinery & Equipment.** Also excluded from this industry are establishments primarily engaged in manufacturing tractor shovel loaders and track laying tractors, which are classified in **SIC 3531: Construction Machinery and Equipment,** and those manufacturing wood pallets and skids, which are classified in **SIC 2448: Wood Pallets and Skids.**

INDUSTRY SNAPSHOT

The industrial truck and tractor industry includes a narrowly defined yet diverse assortment of products that are part of a larger industrial classification commonly known as the material handling equipment industry. Equipment within the smaller industrial truck and tractor category is utilized to move, package, and store both finished products and raw materials used to manufacture finished products. Accordingly, industrial truck and tractor products are used in nearly every industrial setting, from supermarkets to missile manufacturing installations.

An estimated 447 companies in the United States were involved in manufacturing industrial trucks and tractors in 1996.These companies generated $3.7 billion in revenues for products included in this classification. This figure represents an aggregate value of shipments largely derived from the production of forklift trucks and other work trucks fitted with lifting or handling equipment machines—the largest product group within the industry. Industrial trucks, tractors, mobile straddle carriers and cranes, and automatic stacking machines accounted for 67.1 percent of the value of the industry's total shipments. Of these, self-propelled, electric-powered fork lift work trucks accounted for 27.2 percent, and liquid petroleum gas motor-powered accounted for 16.8 percent. Self-propelled nonriding forklift and other work trucks fitted

with lifting or handling equipment accounted for 10.4 percent. The other primary product group was comprised of parts and attachments for industrial trucks and tractors, which composed 21.7 percent of the industry's total shipments.

ORGANIZATION AND STRUCTURE

The average staff size of establishments in the truck and tractor industry was about 10 percent lower than that of all other manufacturing industries. The industry was predominately comprised of establishments employing less than 20 people. Of the 447 establishments in operation in 1996, only 161 employed 20 or more workers.

Geographically, the greatest concentration of industrial truck and tractor manufacturing establishments were in California, Michigan, Ohio, and Illinois, followed by New York and Pennsylvania. The 42 establishments in California represented the greatest number of industry establishments located in one state, followed by 31 in Michigan, 29 in Ohio, and 25 in Illinois. In the Northeast, New York had 29 establishments, followed by Pennsylvania with 23. Ohio led the industry in shipment value, totaling $399.8 billion, 15.4 percent of the U.S. total, and had 2,700 employees. Illinois followed, with shipments valued at $293.2 million, and 1,100 employees. While North Carolina had only 10 establishments, it employed 1,400 workers and accounted for $249.8 million in sales, the third highest after Ohio and Illinois.

In 1994, the average cost per establishment, that is, the average amount paid for raw manufacturing materials, was somewhat higher than the average recorded by all other manufacturing industries. A typical firm in the truck and tractor industry spent $5.9 million on these materials, while firms in all other manufacturing industries spent an average of $5.0 million. Likewise, the average amount spent on manufacturing machinery and production retooling for an industrial truck and tractor establishment was considerably lower than the average recorded by all other manufacturing industries. In 1994, the average investment per establishment in the industrial truck and tractor industry was $158,215, less than half the average of $321,011 spent by firms in all other manufacturing industries.

BACKGROUND AND DEVELOPMENT

America's entrance into World War II in 1941 signaled the beginning of a four-year surge in business activity that defined the future of many U.S. industries. The frenetic pace of production required to support the country's war efforts rejuvenated some industries, engendered the genesis of others, and launched many more toward exponentially higher production and sales volumes. For the industrial truck and tractor industry, the dramatically increased demand for manufactured goods created a commensurately heightened demand for material handling equipment; as the country manufactured more products, there was a growing need to move, stack, and store them quickly and efficiently. Consequently, the industrial truck and tractor industry was swept up into the expansion of U.S. industry as a whole, benefiting from the increased business activity enjoyed by the individual companies it served.

Augmenting this demand from the industry's traditional, industrial customers was a vast government market that opened up during the war, as industrial truck and tractor manufacturers answered the sundry material handling needs of the military itself. The combination of these two factors fostered a rapid growth rate for the industry, amplifying the importance of industrial truck and tractor products in the successful operation of any manufacturing plant or military installation. During this period, truck and tractor products enabled manufacturers to approach production and sales volumes proportionate to levels recorded 50 years later, in the 1990s. Though its foundation was established before the war, the industry's modern structure was not fully defined until the 1950s and 1960s, when industrial establishments nationwide were transformed by the trend toward automation.

The robust growth experienced as a result of the war and the increased applications for the industry's products prompted by the automation of U.S. industry following the war, created formative years for the industry, a period during which industrial truck and tractor manufacturing companies began to record production and sales levels that distinguished the industry from other segments within the material handling equipment industry.

In the early 1960s, the sale of industrial trucks and tractors and related products accounted for approximately $389 million of the nearly $1 billion generated by the material handling equipment industry. The leading manufacturers involved in the industry at this time were primarily publicly held companies engaged in the manufacture of other products included in the material handling industry, such as conveyor and monorail systems, but derived the majority of their revenue from the sale of industrial truck and tractor equipment, particularly from the sale of forklifts. The largest of these manufacturers, Clark Equipment Co. posted annual sales of approximately $200 million in the late 1950s and early 1960s, far exceeding the sales vol-

umes of its nearest competitors. These competitors, however, compensated for their more diminutive size by developing industrial truck and tractor equipment for more diverse applications, focusing on manufacturing equipment that increased efficiency in the industrial workplace.

Initially, the pace of the industry's growth was largely determined by the amount other businesses were spending on capital expansion, but by the early 1960s, U.S. industry as a whole began to focus on increasing the efficiency of manufacturing facilities. Manufacturers realized that industrial truck and tractor equipment could help them make great strides toward this goal. Decreasing the turning radius of a forklift, for example, allowed a manufacturer to reduce the distance between storage aisles and therefore increase inventory space without realizing any increase in land costs. Accordingly, many manufacturers, both large and small, were developing industrial truck and tractor products during the early 1960s that would eventually become integral components of modern manufacturing establishments.

Despite its relatively unimpressive revenue total of $49 million in 1960, Hyster Co. of Portland, Oregon, was, nevertheless, contributing to the industry's technological advancement by designing prototypes of forklifts that automatically weighed loads to be lifted and adjusted their operating speed accordingly. If a load was light, this sensing system enabled the forklift to operate at a higher speed than was normally achieved by earlier forklifts that operated at set speeds, regardless of load weight. Similar advancements were being made by other manufacturers. For instance, Barrett-Cravens Co.'s "Guide-o-matic" system controlled industrial tractors by a buried wire, enabling them to function without an operator.

The popularity of innovative products such as these fueled the industry's growth during the 1960s, as manufacturers increasingly began to look toward the industrial truck and tractor industry for solutions to problems associated with moving, stacking, and storing their manufactured products, and to aid in their transformation toward automated operation. This represented a significant shift in the nature of the needs that this industry's products filled. Instead of supplying equipment solely to manufacturers expanding the size of their plants, industrial truck and tractor manufacturing companies now could rely on business from companies that were streamlining their operations or automating their production processes.

Along with its move toward manufacturing more sophisticated products and designing complete material handling systems, the industry was enjoying increased demand for its newly developed large steel and aluminum containers. "Containerization," or the utilization of trailer-sized steel and aluminum containers for shipping purposes, was, in the early 1960s, one of the relatively recent innovations developed by the industry to help its customers cut costs. These containers, sometimes referred to as "ambulatory vaults," had been used by an increasing number of manufacturers in the 1950s because they reduced handling costs and allowed for quicker delivery.

Two developments in the early 1960s ensured that manufacturers could continue to rely on large containers to generate additional business. In early 1961, industry-wide standards were established for the production of containers, specifying that all containers in the future must be 8 feet in width and height and either 10, 20, or 40 feet in length. Following the establishment of these specifications, the Federal Maritime Board ordered that only ships built to accommodate these new, standardized containers would be eligible for government subsidies or government-insured mortgages.

By the mid-1960s the industry's annual value of shipments had eclipsed $500 million, making it the largest segment within the overall material handling industry. Growth continued to be spurred by the industry's development of innovative products, which persuaded some of its customers to apportion a larger percentage of their capital investment budget toward material handling needs, and others to scrap their existing machinery and invest in more sophisticated equipment. A considerable amount of the industry's growth, however, came through capital expansion programs initiated by its customers. While this presented no problem to industrial truck and tractor manufacturers when economic conditions were particularly favorable, this dependency on the health of the U.S. economy in general made the industry vulnerable to general economic downturns.

By the close of the decade, however, the overall U.S. economy had proven strong enough to support the continued growth of the industrial truck and tractor industry. Revenues exceeded $1 billion by 1970, representing an average annual growth rate of greater than 11 percent during the previous decade. While no single dramatic technological advancement launched the industry toward higher revenues, each year customer demands were stimulated by new products that incorporated innovative designs and functions.

Over the course of the next several years, as the nation's economy spiraled downward in reaction to a shortage of oil and petroleum products, the industrial truck and tractor industry's performance began to flag.

The industrial sector of the U.S. economy operated below capacity throughout the recession, causing the cancellation or postponement of many manufacturers' expansion plans. Because these investments represented a major source of industrial truck and tractor manufacturers' revenues, business faltered, demonstrating the volatility of the industry's market. With the industrial sector of the nation's economy operating at 70 percent of its capacity, the industrial truck and tractor industry's revenues dropped from $1.53 billion in 1974 to $1.30 billion in 1975.

The industry slowly recovered from the losses of the early and mid-1970s, generating revenues of $1.91 billion in 1977, and by the end of the decade, revenues skyrocketed to nearly $3 billion. This growth, however, masked the emergence of a pernicious force that threatened to derail the industry's leading companies from their meteoric recovery.

For years, industrial truck and tractor manufacturers' command of the U.S. market was virtually unassailable; foreign manufacturers relegated themselves to producing inexpensive equipment and left the manufacturing of higher-priced, more sophisticated equipment, which was by far the more lucrative segment of the global industrial truck and tractor market, to American companies. But by the late 1970s, domestic manufactures had become lulled into complacency by decades of dominance, and foreign manufacturers, particularly the Japanese, began to woo customers away from U.S. manufacturers. Ironically, the reason for this rise in demand for Japanese products was attributable largely to the success domestic manufacturers enjoyed for the past several decades. Each year new designs and features were incorporated into U.S.-produced equipment, creating, by the late 1970s, an assortment of highly-sophisticated equipment. The incremental advances in technology had, by this time, spawned equipment too advanced and too costly for the basic material handling needs of U.S. industries. Concurrently, an increasing number of industrial truck and tractor customers found the cheaper Japanese equipment suitable for their basic material handling tasks, a revelation that led to reduced operating costs for customers and to an erosion of U.S. industrial truck and tractor manufacturers' market share. American truck and trucking equipment had simply become too sophisticated for the needs of its average customers.

By the early 1980s, the price advantage afforded to purchasers of Japanese industrial truck and tractor equipment widened to as much as 30 percent. Still, in the face of this burgeoning trend toward more inexpensive, less sophisticated equipment, U.S. manufacturers were slow to responds. As conditions worsened, domestic manufacturers attempted to stave off mounting foreign competition by designing even more sophisticated products, which further aggravated their losses. Clark Equipment Co., for example, spent $25 million on the design of a high-technology lift truck equipped with oil-cooled brakes that failed miserably when it was introduced in 1982.

When the U.S. forklift market plummeted in 1982 and 1983, many domestic manufacturers were poorly positioned to sustain further losses. Caterpillar Inc., bereft of its once commanding lead over the industry, sought cheaper manufacturing sites for its production of industrial trucks and tractors, and, in 1983, the company moved the majority of its lift truck production to Korea under the aegis of a South Korean company, Daewoo Heavy Industries Ltd. Similarly, Clark Equipment relocated from Michigan to more inexpensive Kentucky, and, in 1986, Clark eventually followed Caterpillar's lead by signing a ten-year production accord with Samsung Group in Korea.

Among the industry's leaders, Hyster Co. was the one notable exception to domestic manufacturers' disregard toward the shifting market demands. Introducing an inexpensive "XL" line of forklifts in 1981, that matched the Japanese in terms of price and accounted for $44 million in sales in 18 months, Hyster avoided the debilitating losses suffered by its largest competitors. Moreover, Hyster revamped its design, engineering, and manufacturing methods to assimilate the cross-functional and more efficient style of Japanese production, enabling the company to manufacture as many industrial truck and tractor products by the end of the 1980s as it had ten years earlier, with half as many employees. Consequently, Hyster was the only U.S. industrial truck and tractor manufacture among the industry's three largest producers to remain profitable during the 1980s, further underscoring the imprudence of Clark Equipment's and Caterpillar's continued focus on producing technologically advanced equipment in the early 1980s.

The relocation of key manufacturing responsibilities to Korea by Clark Equipment Co. and Caterpillar failed to arrest the plunge of their integral fork lift operations. Korean wages tripled during the 1980s, erasing any benefits that would have been otherwise realized by relocating, and the dollar declined 24 percent against the Korean won between 1986 and 1989, further increasing the severity of their losses. By the early 1990s, the cumulative effect of the previous decade's failures forced Clark Equipment and Caterpillar Inc. to divest their core industrial truck and tractor businesses. In 1992, Clark Equipment sold its forklift operations to Terex Corp. for $95 million. Later that year, Caterpillar signed a joint venture agreement with Mitsubishi Heavy Industries Ltd. that ceded 80 percent of its fork lift business to the Japanese company.

CURRENT CONDITIONS

The industrial truck and tractor industry was slowly adjusting to the changing needs of its customers as it entered the mid-1990s. Sparked by the recessive economic conditions of the early 1990s, the U.S. industry as a whole was experiencing changes, and many businesses reduced their work force and streamlined their operations, leasing to greater operating efficiencies.

The concerted movement toward manufacturing a proportionately higher number of electric lift trucks, initiated by the Japanese in 1992, prompted a parallel response by U.S. manufacturers. These electrically powered lift trucks were more profitable for industrial truck and tractor manufacturers than gas-powered lift trucks and became the industry's most popular product in the mid-1990s.

Before softening in 1996, the worldwide lift truck market grew by approximately 30 percent, or 100,000 units, from 1992-93. Industry forecasts suggested that, on the whole, market levels will be sustained at higher levels going into the next century. The North American market declined by an estimated 13,000 units, 8 percent, during 1996.

Fork lift manufacturers also made changes. According to *Beverage World,* the forklift companies compete fiercely with each other. Consequently the electric forklift is in a constant state of flux, and each manufacturer regularly improves and updates its products, creating a "quality through competition" mentality for forklift manufacturers. This ensures better products and greater customer satisfaction.

INDUSTRY LEADERS

Shaken by the volatile economic conditions of the 1980s, the industrial truck and tractor industry's leading companies entered the 1990s searching for a way to return to their former preeminent positions within the industry. Both Caterpillar Inc., with $16.52 billion in revenues in 1992, and Clark Equipment Co., with $947 million in revenues in the mid-1990s, suffered disastrous losses during the 1980s, which left their presence in the industrial truck and tractor market considerably diminished. Hyster Co., which had been the industry's third largest company, demonstrated comparatively robust performance during the 1980s, which elevated the Portland, Oregon-based manufacturer to the fore of the industrial truck and tractor industry. Indeed, Hyster became the model of a successful industrial truck and tractor manufacturer for other companies in the industry to emulate, as it streamlined its operations and focused on producing low-cost, reliable equipment. Still, other manufacturers continued to concentrate on the high-end market and to operate with a surfeit of employees.

In the early 1990s, Clark Equipment Co. and Caterpillar Inc. turned their attention toward designing and manufacturing industrial truck and tractor products that could effectively compete with Japanese equipment. With the economic might of Caterpillar and Clark Equipment's long tradition of introducing innovative products, the two former powerhouses of the industrial truck and tractor industry possessed the necessary tools to strengthen their position within the industry.

In 1996, Caterpillar launched a new line of 24-volt narrow aisle reach trucks with 3,000-, 3,500-, and 4,000-pound capacity. The new line of trucks were ergonomically designed around an original ''CAT Command Center,'' which puts all controls within easy reach. The truck was controlled by Caterpillar's ''Micro Command,'' an advanced microprocessor control system. In 1995 Caterpillar introduced its E-series, a new line of articulated trucks, which offered operators added comfort and serviceability. The trucks were capable of any earthmoving function and were ideal to be used in distances between 0.5 km and 5.0 km.

In 1996, Clark announced plans to increase its U.S. production of industrial trucks and introduce new products to add to existing lines. Included were hydrostatic drive models in the Genesis line of IC counterbalanced trucks and two narrow-aisle models: a double reach truck and a straddle truck. Continued growth in narrow-aisle applications and the opportunity to provide domestic users with a lift truck technology (hydrostatic drive) uncommon in the United States were among factors behind the Clark actions.

Clark also brought production of its 3,000- to 3,500-pound GCX and GPX gas trucks back to Lexington from Samsung Heavy Industries in Korea. U.S. production will shorten lead times and enable Clark to be more responsive to customers.

In 1995, Navistar introduced new engine options for Navistar Cabovers: the Detroit Diesel and Cummins N14-E Celect series 60 engines with increased horsepower for its International 9800 Pro Sleeper cabover heavy duty trucks.

Statistics released in 1996 indicated that the top 88 companies engaged in this industry grossed total sales of $24 billion and employed 90,400 people. The leading company was Caterpillar Inc. of Peoria, Illinois, with sales of $16.07 billion and 54,400 employees. Second to Caterpillar was NACCO Industries Inc. of Mayfield Heights, Ohio with sales of $2.02 billion and 3,700 employees. NACCO sold its products under the Hyster and Yale brand names. At NACCO, development teams were utilizing three-dimensional computer-aided design techniques to build products that will strengthen the competitive positions of both Hyster and Yale. Following NACCO was Clark Equipment Co. of South Bend, Indiana, with $947 million in sales and 4,400 employees. AO Smith Automotive Products Division of Milwaukee, Wisconsin, with sales of $845 million and Crown Equipment Corp. of New Bremen, Ohio, with sales of $610 million, followed.

WORK FORCE

Total employment in the industrial trucks and tractors industry declined during the 1980s and 1990s, slipping from 24,000 in 1982 to a low of 17,300 in 1991, recovering to 19,800 in 1994. The number of employees in the industry is projected to decline again through 1998 with a projected low of 17,600.

Of the approximately 20,000 people employed by the industry, about 13,400 were production workers, while the remaining employees performed technical, managerial, or administrative duties. Although the number of production workers declined during the 1980s and early 1990s, falling from 14,100 in 1983 to 12,700 in 1996, executive or managerial positions suffered a greater rate of attrition, estimated to drop by over 13 percent from 1994.

Typically, production workers were employed on a full-time basis, averaging 2,060 hours annually in 1994, almost the same as the 2,056 hours averaged by production workers employed in all other manufacturing industries. Average hourly wages of workers in the industrial truck and tractor industry were slightly higher than those of workers in all other manufacturing industries. In 1994, production workers in the industrial truck and tractor industry earned an average hourly wage of $12.39, as opposed to the average hourly wage of $12.09 for all manufacturing industries..

Prospects in the industry's work force remain bleak, according to U.S. Bureau of Labor projections. Between 1994 and 2005, positions for general manufacturing assemblers and fabricators, welders, cutters, and machinists employed by the construction and related machinery industry, of which the industrial truck and tractor industry is a subdivision, were expected to decline 9.1 percent. Predicted to be even more hard hit were positions for drilling and boring machine tool workers, which were expected to drop 54.6 percent. Other job categories projected to decline by more than 20 percent were machine builders, drafters, and machine tool cutting operators. Non-production workers including bookkeepers, accountants, and general office clerks were also expected to experience declines of more than 20 percent.

AMERICA AND THE WORLD

As U.S. manufacturers of industrial trucks and tractors entered the mid-1990s, competition from foreign manufacturers posed the greatest threat to the industry's future. For years, U.S. manufacturers held the domestic market largely to themselves; businesses in need of industrial truck and tractor equipment generally shied away from purchasing products manufactured abroad, fearing a lack of spare parts and service. By 1970, imports accounted for a mere $13 million of the $1 billion U.S. industrial truck and tractor market. Moreover, the $13 million recorded by foreign manufacturers in 1970 reflected a 72 percent increase from the total posted two years earlier. Likewise, U.S. manufacturers explored profit potentials overseas. By 1970, the value of U.S. exports neared $100 million a year, with parts and complete trucks and tractors being shipped to Europe, South America, and Asia.

By the end of the 1970s, however, the commanding position that U.S. manufacturers held over foreign manufacturers was reversed, largely due to the gains achieved by Japanese manufacturers. By concentrating on supplying inexpensive, yet sturdy industrial truck and tractor products, the Japanese were able to secure a formidable presence in the U.S. market. Competition became fierce, leading one of the few large U.S. manufacturers of industrial truck and tractor products that fared well during the 1980s, Hyster Co., to petition the International Trade Commission in 1986, charging that Japan was selling equipment in the United States at prices below the cost of production. Two years later, the International Trade Commission ruled in Hyster's favor and applied import duties of up to 51.3 percent to Japanese products entering the U.S. market. Although these import duties provided a much needed respite from increasing Japanese competition, Japanese manufacturers began establishing assembly plants in the United States soon after the ruling to circumvent the tariff payments. Entering the 1990s, the Japanese continued to maintain a roughly 50 percent share of the U.S. market.

As stated in the *Caterpillar 1996 Annual report*, "In the next decade, global competitiveness will separate the leading companies from the rest." Areas like China, CIS, and the developing countries of the world were expected to grow by at least double the rate of other industrialized countries, and their needs will require industrial machines and engines in the years ahead.

FURTHER READING

"Caterpillar Is Offering Versatile Narrow Aisle Reach Trucks." *Vending Times,* 25 March 1996, 188.

Caterpillar 1996 Annual Report. 10.

"Clark Plant Gears Up for New Models." *Modern Materials Handling,* February 1996, 15.

Darnay, Arsen J., ed. *Manufacturing USA.* 5th ed. Detroit: Gale Research, 1996.

Drugan, Cheryl G. "Repairing." *Handling & Shipping Management,* March 1982, 36-40.

Guiles, Roger A. "Industry's Trucks: Will Next Stop Be Last Stop?" *Iron Age,* 1 February 1973, 40-41.

"Harnessing Air to Do Warehousing Chores." *Business Week,* 18 June 1966, 172.

Kelly, Kevin. "How U.S. Forklift Makers Dropped the Goods." *Business Week,* 15 June 1992.

Loehwing, David A. "Forklift Pick-Up." *Barron's,* 5 June 1961, 3, 15-17.

"Materials Handling Enjoying a Big Lift." *Business Week,* 29 May 1965, 60.

"Materials Handling Industry." *The Wall Street Transcript,* 19 March 1973, 32, 260.

"NACCO Materials Handling Group." *NACCO Industries, Inc. 1996 Annual Report.* 9-11.

"New Engine Options For Navistar Cabovers." *Diesel Progress Engines & Drives,* Oct. 1995, 8.

"Our Friend the Forklift." *Beverage World,* April 1995, 24.

Rohan, Thomas M. "Making 'Em Overseas." *Industry Week,* December 12, 1983, 28.

Rutter, Richard. "Automation Helps Material Handling." *The New York Times,* 3 May 1964, F1.

Schwind, Gene. "Clark Brings a Clear Sheet Approval to Narrow Aisles." *Material Handling Engineering,* April 1993, 20.

Thomas, Dana L. "Good for the Long Haul." *Barron's,* 9 September 1963, 3-12.

U.S. Department of Commerce. International Trade Administration. *U.S. Industrial Outlook.* Washington: GPO, 1960-1980.

"Wall Street Roundup." *The Wall Street Transcript,* 4 October 1976, 44, 857.

—Jeffrey L. Covell, updated by Kaye Brinker

SIC 3541

MACHINE TOOLS, METAL CUTTING TYPES

This industry details establishments primarily engaged in manufacturing metal cutting type machine tools, not supported in the hands of an operator when in use, that shape metal by cutting or use of electrical techniques; the rebuilding of such machine tools; and the manufacture of replacement parts for them. Also included in this industry are metalworking machine tools designed primarily for home workshops. Establishments primarily engaged in the manufacture of electrical and gas welding and soldering equipment are classified in **SIC 3548: Electric and Gas Welding and Soldering Equipment**; those establishments manufacturing portable power-driven handtools are classified in **SIC 3546: Power-Driven Handtools.**

INDUSTRY SNAPSHOT

The metal cutting industry is concerned with the removal of metal from a larger piece of metal to create a desired shape. Metal cutting, also referred to as machining, is performed on most manufactured items. The uses range from low-precision machining, such as grinding undesired protrusions from a rough casting, to high-precision machining, which involves working tolerances of less than half the thickness of a human hair (0.0001 inch). Classic metal cutting produces scrap pieces, called chips, that are relatively useless and generally cannot be reused through remelting or pressing. Both the environmental and economic consequences of such waste has created new processes referred to as chipless machining. General machining processes include turning, shaping, milling, drilling, sawing, abrasive machining, and broaching.

The machine tool industry as a whole is closely tied to national and world economic conditions. The total shipments of metal cutting machine tools dropped sharply between 1982 to 1983 from $4.5 billion to below $3 billion. From that point, shipments recovered somewhat, but remained greatly reduced. The worldwide recession of the late 1980s and early 1990s created a trough in machine tool-related sales. Shipments between 1990 and 1994 varied only slightly, hovering around $3.5 billion. It is unlikely that shipments will ever return to the 1982 level, an industry high point.

The prices for metal cutting machine tools ranged from under $100,000 to several million dollars, depending on the sophistication and purpose of the tool. Multiple machining centers, capable of performing several metal cutting processes, were becoming more popular with larger companies interested in decreasing the amount of time handling materials between machining stations.

As worldwide competition increases in areas of quality and precision, U.S. machine shops will be forced to update or totally replace machine tools with those that possess higher levels of technical innovation. However, a significant downward trend in employment levels continued through the 1990s as machine tool manufacturers cut direct labor costs. This trend, a disheartening one for those seeking employment in this industry, infers higher levels of automation throughout all related industries and will require the manufacture of more automated machine tools.

Half of the machine tool market is concentrated within the automotive industry, one-quarter within nonmechanical industries, and the remainder within aerospace, defense, and other industries.

ORGANIZATION AND STRUCTURE

Four major categories are represented in this industry: classic machine tools; automated machine tools; expendable tools; and machine tool repair. Classic metal cutting machine tools are characterized by manually operated, power driven (usually electric) stationary machines. These machines are operated by skilled machinists with relatively good trigonometry skills. The demand for these machines has dropped, giving way to the use of automated machine tools.

Automated machine tools are more commonly known as numerically controlled (NC) machine tools. NC machines use a generated program of coordinate values (numerics) to move machine parts quickly, with consistency and precision. Downtime between tool changes is minimized, compared to classic machining methods. The information is loaded into the machine by punched tape, punched cards, or magnetic tape that has been generated by a computer program written by an NC programmer. The NC machines have given way to computer numerically controlled (CNC) machines due to the affordability of microcomputers. The next wave of NC machines is expected to include downloadable numerically controlled (DNC) machines, which are network-based CNC machines. This technology reduces the steps between design engineering and manufacturing. All NC machines created a large market for manufacturers of machine controls, and increased microcomputer markets. Chipless machining processes implement some form of NC capabilities to the various machine configurations.

Expendable tools are the actual cutting pieces that wear as a result of use. Therefore, this segment of the industry is closely tied to client industry levels of activity. Although many of these tools can be re-sharpened and reused, many machine shops find it more economical to replace the tool once it is worn. When industry success is high, this segment of the industry experiences increased sales.

Machine tool repair has become a more specialized segment due to the increased popularity of NC machines. The nature of this business category requires that repair technicians have adequate computer hardware/software trouble-shooting skills. Machine tool repair in the late 1990s was thus closely related to computer electronics as well as mechanics.

BACKGROUND AND DEVELOPMENT

Various machine tools have been crafted through the centuries to address man's specific needs, but it was the invention of the clock in 1364 that created a need for higher precision machining methods. Clocks require accurately turned arbors, machine-cut gears, and screw threads. The concepts of precision and consistency in product quality thus pushed machine tool technology to the point that, by the seventeenth century, clock making was regarded as a particularly painstaking craft.

During the second half of the eighteenth century, the barriers between pure science and workshop technology were breaking down. Scientists began interacting more closely with mechanical engineers, spawning new ideas for improved machining techniques. The steam engine was born from this interaction, an invention that drastically increased the potential of the machine tool in the minds of the industrial leaders of the day. The industrial age was afoot. This period was greatly influenced by Henry Maudslay, who is known as the man responsible for the introduction of many of the early engineering machine tools.

Maudslay introduced the concept of precision to heavy machinery, which before that time had been only the concern of watch and scientific instrument makers. In the early 1800s he made the first screw-cutting lathe, a device that remains the standard even today. His second great contribution was the creation of a method of finishing a plane surface with a surface plate, marking compound, and hand scraper. Maudslay also constructed a micrometer in 1805 that enabled machinists to measure work to one ten-thousandths of an inch. Maudslay's successors furthered his craft and assisted in the evolution of machine tools, thus encouraging the industrial revolution.

Today, metal cutting tools remain very similar to those used in the nineteenth century. The implementation of computers has increased the precision and time efficiency of the metal cutting tools, but the basic processes have not changed significantly. However, new metal cutting advances are gaining acceptance and applicability in industry, whereby metal is eroded by chemical discharges, electric discharges, water jets, and laser beams. These advances could again bring significant changes to the methods employed to cut metal to achieve a desired shape.

CURRENT CONDITIONS

In the early 1990s, the industries placing the most orders with metal cutting machine tool manufacturers had limited orders due to large financial losses, as exhibited by the poor performance during that time of some American automakers. Decreases in spending by farming and construction industries in the late 1980s and early 1990s were offset by the aerospace industry. However, this industry too suffered due to the financial instability of various airline companies, as well as military spending cutbacks.

According to the 1996-1998 *Industrial Outlook for Machine Tools,* domestic purchases of metal cutting machine tools increased in 1995 to a total of $6.5 billion, but demand was expected to decline through 1998, to a projected total of about $5.2 billion in that year. The condition of the industry was attributed in that study to three factors: high sensitivity of the industry to the overall health of the economy; a lag time of a year between economic improvements and growth in machine tool shipments; and long-term decline in machine tool demand. The industry remains highly fragmented and competitive, with manufacturers seeing a decline in product prices and lowered profit margins.

High points within the industry in 1996 were the automobile industry and the potential need to replace rapidly aging equipment in many facilities (with an average equipment age of ten years). Another projected growth market is the nonelectrical machinery industry (e.g., food processing equipment). However, total investment in plant and equipment by the automotive and electrical machinery sectors were expected to decline by 1998.

INDUSTRY LEADERS

The top domestic manufacturers of metal cutting machine tools in the later 1990s included Cincinnati Milacron Inc. (Cincinnati, Ohio), Ingersoll Milling Machine Company (Rockford, Illinois; owned by Ingersoll International) and Giddings & Lewis, Inc. (Fond du Lac, Wisconsin). Cincinnati Milacron held a rare position in the early 1990s by reporting profits at a time when other metal cutting machine tool manufacturers were suffering losses. This was largely due to its diversified interests outside of the machine tool industry, including plastics machinery, computer controls, measurement and inspection equipment, and grinding wheels. In 1996 the company reported record sales of $1.73 billion, with machine tool sales remaining level with 1995 at about $372 million. In 1996 Giddings & Lewis, with operations in almost 70 countries, had foreign sales of 25 percent. Its largest customer, Ford Motor Co. accounted for another 16 percent of sales. Giddings & Lewis' total sales in 1996 were $763 million, a 4.4 percent increase over 1995. In the same year Ingersoll, hoping to increase its profits, introduced a new linear-motor machine. Twelve such machines would be capable of producing 100,000 automobile engine blocks a year.

The industry leaders in NC machine tools are General Electric and Allen-Bradley, both of which primarily manufacture control systems. Expendable tools, such as drills, taps, chucks, and reamers are produced by TRW Geometric Tools, Acme-Cleveland, and National Twist Drill, among others.

WORK FORCE

Roughly one-quarter of the entire metalworking industry employs machinists and tool and die makers. The rest of the industry is split between other jobs, such as managers and supervisors, machine tool operators, assemblers, drafters, accountants, and traffic clerks. Employment in almost all areas of the industry, particularly machine tool cutting and clerical staff, was expected to decline through the year 2005.

Most people employed by this industry reside in the Great Lakes region and the northeastern United States (Michigan, Ohio, Illinois, Wisconsin, and New York). One hundred metal cutting-related establishments call Michigan home, with 21 percent of all American machine tool shipments originating in that state. Hourly wages in the industry in 1994 were $16.31, well above the total industry average of $12.09.

AMERICA AND THE WORLD

Throughout the 1980s, the Japanese provided stiff competition for American manufacturers of metal cutting tools. In 1974, the United States enjoyed a machine tool trade surplus relative to the Japanese. In 1991 that surplus had been transformed into a $1 billion trade deficit. As a result, seven of the world's largest machine tool companies were based in Japan in the early 1990s. An increasing German presence also threatened the U.S. metal cutting industry, as German companies produced some of the leading specialty CNC machines.

In a survey conducted by *Ward's Auto World* in 1992, 52 percent of the responding automobile manufacturing executives stated that U.S. machine tools are the world's best. U.S. tools won accolades for their durability, flexibility, ease of repair, and leading-edge technology. Twenty-five percent of the respondents preferred Japanese machine tools, regarded as the best products for stamping and welding. Twenty percent preferred European machine tools, stating they were the best tools for painting and precision machining.

By 1995, import penetration of the metal cutting and metal forming market was estimated at 39 percent, and was expected to rise to over 46 percent by 1998. At the same time, manufacturers exported 27 percent of their products in 1994 and hoped to increase this amount to 32 percent by 1998. Companies such as Cincinnati Milacron made significant investments in operations in Asia.

RESEARCH AND TECHNOLOGY

Due to the limitations and adverse side-effects of traditional machining, chipless machining processes have been developed. These processes are primarily concerned with chemical, electrochemical, electrodischarge, water jet, and laser machining techniques. Intricate parts require non-traditional machining methods and the advent of the computer age have hastened the research and development of chipless machining processes. As NC controls become more sophisticated, environmental laws grow more stringent, and technology advances, the need for chipless machining processes is expected to increase. Promising technological developments in the later 1990s included robotized waterjet cutting systems (developed by Ingersoll-Rand Company of Woodcliff Lake, New Jersey, and a Swedish partner) and sophisticated laser cutting systems.

FURTHER READING

Brophy, Theresa. ''Machine Tool Industry.'' *The Value Line Investment Survey,* 12 February 1993.

DeGarmo, E. Paul. *Materials and Processes in Manufacturing.* New York: Macmillan, 1979.

''Giddings & Lewis, Inc.'' *Hoover's Company Capsules,* 1997. Available from http://www.hoovers.com/.

''Domestic Machine Tool Demand Should Moderate After Peaking in 1995.'' *Manufacturing Automation,* 1 March 1996.

''Industrial Laser Shipments Shine Through Third Quarter.'' *Manufacturing Automation,* 1 March 1997.

''Machine Tool Market by End Use.'' *Market Share Reporter.* 7th ed. Detroit: Gale Research Inc., 1997.

Manufacturing USA: Industry Analysis, Statistics, and Leading Companies. 5th ed. Detroit: Gale Research Inc., 1996.

"Milacron Reports Record Orders, Sales and Earnings in 1996." *PR Newswire.* 7 February 1997.

Plumb, Stephen E. "Machine Tool Trade Deficit Overlooked in US/Japan Dialogue." *Ward's Auto World,* May 1992.

Rolt, L.T.C. *A Short History of Machine Tools.* Cambridge, MA: M.I.T. Press, 1967.

Schiller, Zachary. "One Takes the High-end Road, the Other Takes the Low: Giddings: Bring on the Bells and Whistles." *Business Week,* 18 May 1992.

"Waterjet Cutting Now Available for Fully Automated Production Lines." *Manufacturing Automation,* 1 February 1997.

Winter, Drew. "US Machine Tools Are Still the Best." *Ward's Auto World,* July 1992.

Young, David. "Mammoth Machines Get Fitting Showcase." *Chicago Tribune,* 4 September 1996.

—Valerie Wilson, updated by Gerry Azzata

SIC 3542

MACHINE TOOLS, METAL FORMING TYPES

This industry covers establishments primarily engaged in manufacturing metal forming machine tools, not supported in the hands of an operator while in use, for pressing, hammering, extruding, shearing, die-casting, or otherwise forming metal into shape. This industry also includes the rebuilding of such machine tools and the manufacture of repair parts for them. Establishments primarily engaged in the manufacture of electric and gas welding equipment and soldering equipment are classified in **SIC 3548: Electric and Gas Welding and Soldering Equipment;** those manufacturing portable power-driven handtools are classified in **SIC 3546: Power-Driven Handtools;** those manufacturing rolling mill machinery and equipment are detailed in **SIC 3547: Rolling Mill Machinery and Equipment.**

The metal forming machine tool industry is closely related to the metal cutting industry. Many machine shops employ both types of machine tools. The primary difference between metal cutting and metal forming concerns the removal of metal. Metal forming is a process by which a piece of metal, generally flat sheet stock or a rod, is forced into another shape by means of pressing the material beyond its present yield strength condition. Because most metals can be formed in this way, the metal forming industry is significant to major industries throughout the United

States. According to Standard & Poor's *Industry Surveys,* "The automotive industry is the largest single market for metal-forming machinery."

Since the metal forming industry is linked so closely to the automotive industry, growth in the industry is closely linked to the health of domestic car manufacturers. It follows, then, that the metal forming machine tool industry did not enjoy extraordinary success in the 1970s and 1980s. However, public demand for American-made products has encouraged automakers, even those held by Japanese firms operating in the United States, to purchase American-made tooling whenever possible. Metal forming equipment manufacturers in the United States hope to benefit from this movement.

Most manufacturers of metal cutting tools also produce metal forming tools. In the mid-1990s, the three most notable manufacturers were: Ohio-based National Machinery Company, Minster Machine Company of Ohio, and Connecticut-based Trumpf Incorporated. The companies had a combined financial figure of approximately $247 million. In the 1996 U.S. market, punching, shearing, and bending machines held 25 percent of the total metal forming tool industry; presses held 24 percent; metal forming machine tools held 23 percent; and parts for metal forming machine tools held 27 percent.

The primary concentration of metal forming companies is around the Great Lakes region and some northeastern states. Another smaller concentration of metal forming interests lies along the West Coast and Alaska. Thirty-one establishments are located in Ohio that ship a total $345.8 million worth of metal forming equipment. Illinois is home to 32 such establishments, which ship $341 million domestically and internationally. Michigan also claims 27 establishments, shipping $173.3 million.

At the conclusion of the 1980s, the average worker in the metal forming tool industry was earning more than $13 per hour. At that time, approximately 14,600 people were employed in this industry. Machinists and tool and die makers accounted for 25 percent of the entire labor force. The industry expected a negative personnel growth rate into 2000 since restructuring, cost-cutting measures, and automation were expected to reduce the work force. In 1994, the industry had 13,100 employees making $16 per hour. Machinists and tool and die makers accounted for about 22 percent of the industry's work force. In 1998, the number of employees was estimated to be 10,500 people earning about $18 per hour.

The number of domestic shipments outweighed foreign shipments of complete metal forming tools. Foreign competitors have rallied for a share of the metal cutting tool market rather than the metal forming tool market. In 1994, U.S. machine tool production—cutting and forming—was valued at $3.7 billion, Japan's production was valued at $6.7 billion, and Germany's was $5.3 billion.

In 1995 the shipment of both metal cutting and metal forming machines was about $6.427 billion. The value of shipments of metal forming machine tools in 1995 was approximately $1.742 billion. By 1998, the shipment value was expected to be $1.840 billion.

FURTHER READING

Central Intelligence Agency. *Handbook of International Economic Statistics, 1996.*

Darnay, Arsen J., ed. *Manufacturing USA.* 5th ed. Detroit: Gale Research, 1996.

DeGarmo, E. Paul. *Materials and Processes in Manufacturing.* New York: Macmillan, 1979.

Nugent, Thomas M., ed. "Steel and Heavy Machinery: Basic Analysis." *Standard & Poor's Industry Surveys,* 24 December 1992.

U.S. Department of Commerce. "Value of Product Shipments." *1995 Annual Survey of Manufactures.* Washington: GPO, January 1997.

U.S. Department of Commerce. *Statistical Abstract of the United States.* Washington: GPO, October 1996.

SIC 3543

INDUSTRIAL PATTERNS

This category covers establishments primarily engaged in manufacturing industrial patterns.

Industrial patternmaking companies make patterns for forming and molding metal. These patterns are used by other companies to produce metal ornaments, tools, automobile parts, cutlery, and other goods. The largest consumer of industrial patterns was the architectural metalworking industry, which consumed more than 20 percent of industry output in the early 1990s. Producers of pipes, valves, and fittings represented roughly 12 percent of the market. Miscellaneous repair shops purchased 27 percent of output. Other specialized industries purchased patterns to make engineering and scientific apparatus, prefabricated structural metal, car parts, railroad equipment, and other metal products.

Industrial patterns are often used in foundries to create molds and dies for iron, steel, and other metals. Foundries typically melt scrap in an electric furnace; the liquid is then poured into a mold, which is usually formed from sand, metal, or ceramic material. The metal cools and solidifies into any number of complicated shapes, such as an engine block, a turbine blade, or surgical instrument.

Copper was the first material that metallurgists learned to melt and form. By 4000 B.C. smiths had developed sophisticated smelting (melting and molding) techniques. Iron ore was first smelted in 1500 B.C. to make utensils and weapons. The advancement of the blast furnace, which was invented in 1323, was hastened by the industrial revolution in eighteenth-century England. Advanced metallurgical and patternmaking techniques evolved during the 1800s and particularly during the 1900s, in the wake of both world wars.

U.S. industrial patternmaking emerged as a separate industry during the 1950s, 1960s, and 1970s. Patternmakers continued to enjoy relatively healthy growth during most of the 1980s as the demand for metal products, such as architectural metalwork and automotive parts, swelled. By 1988, the industry was generating revenues of about $719 million per year and employing a work force of 10,500. A real estate depression in the late 1980s that reduced demand for architectural metals, coupled with a general nationwide recession, hurt competitors in the late 1980s and early 1990s. Sales slipped to about $530 million in 1990 and employment plunged to 8,100.

In 1994, shipment values declined to $597 million, and employment fell to 7,600. The 1995 value of product shipments was about $552 million; the employment rate was approximately 7,200. It was estimated that 1998 shipments would be valued at $546 million, and the number of employees would be 6,300.

The average patternmaker employed 12 workers in the late 1980s and garnered revenues of about $750,000. In the mid-1990s, the average number of employees per establishment was 11. The industry consisted of approximately 625 companies, most of which were privately owned and located in the Midwest. Michigan and Ohio each had 94 establishments and Wisconsin had 59. The largest competitors in the mid-1990s were Michigan-based Progress Pattern Corporation, with sales of $25 million, and D And F Corporation, also of Michigan, with sales over $15 million. Other industry leaders included Anderson Pattern Incorporated, of Michigan, and Alabama-based Southern Precision Corporation.

Despite an economic boost going into the mid-1990s, the long term employment outlook for the overall metalworking industry is dismal. Jobs for most laborers are expected to decline 20-30 percent between 1990 and 2005, according to the Bureau of Labor Statistics. The demand for machine tool cutting operators, for example, was expected to plummet about 27 percent by 2005. Jobs for machine tool cutting and forming workers were expected to fall by about 19 percent. Positions for engineers and sales professionals, in contrast, should rise 10-20 percent. The average patternmaking industry employee earned about 14 percent more than the average U.S. manufacturing worker in the early 1990s. In the late 1990s, the average hourly wage for the industry was about $17 per hour.

FURTHER READING

Darnay, Arsen J., ed. *Manufacturing USA.* 5th ed. Detroit: Gale Research, 1996.

Grolier's Encyclopedia. Danbury, CT: Grolier's Inc., 1993.

U.S. Department of Labor. *Occupational Outlook Handbook.* Washington: GPO, 1992.

U.S. Department of Commerce. *U.S. Industrial Outlook 1993.* Washington: GPO, 1993.

U.S. Department of Commerce. "Value of Product Shipments." *1995 Annual Survey of Manufactures.* Washington: GPO, 1997.

Ward's Business Directory of U.S. Private and Public Companies. Detroit: Gale Research, 1997.

SIC 3544

SPECIAL DIES AND TOOLS, DIE SETS, JIGS AND FIXTURES, AND INDUSTRIAL MOLDS

This classification includes establishments commonly known as contract tool and die shops primarily engaged in manufacturing, on a job or order basis, special tools and fixtures for use with machine tools, hammers, die-casting machines, and presses. The products of establishments classified in this industry include a wide variety of special tooling, such as dies; punches; diesets and components, and sub-presses; jigs and fixtures; and special checking devices. Establishments primarily engaged in manufacturing molds for die-casting and foundry casting; metal molds for plaster working, rubber working, plastics working, and glass working and similar machinery are also included. Establishments primarily engaged in manufacturing molds for heavy steel ingots are classified in **SIC**

3321: Gray and Ductile Iron Foundries, and those manufacturing cutting dies, except metal cutting, are classified in **SIC 3423: Hand and Edge Tools, Except Machine Tools and Handsaws.**

INDUSTRY SNAPSHOT

The value of shipments in the tool and die industry in 1995 was over $13.5 billion, up from $10.2 billion in 1992. Over 50 percent of these shipments ($7.5 billion) consisted of special dies and tools, dies sets, jigs, and fixtures. Industrial molds and mold boxes comprised over 35 percent of all shipments ($4.7 billion); the remainder of shipments, over $1.1 billion, were not specified by kind. The number of establishments in the industry increased by over 3 percent since 1990, to approximately 7,280 in 1995.

The tool and die industry employed an estimated 161,000 employees in 1995, an increase of about 9 percent since 1990. There were about 123,000 production workers in 1995, up from 114,300 in 1990. Production workers accounted for about 77 percent of all employees in 1995, which was approximately the same percentage as in 1990. In 1995, production workers' average weekly hours were 44.1; hourly wages were $14.55. The 1995 averages for all production workers in manufacturing industries were 41.6 (weekly hours) and $12.37 (hourly wages).

ORGANIZATION AND STRUCTURE

In the mid-1990s, the states ranking in the industry top ten by value of shipments were, in order of descending value, Michigan, Ohio, Illinois, Pennsylvania, California, Indiana, Wisconsin, New York, New Jersey, and Minnesota. Together these ten states accounted for 81 percent of total shipments and 79 percent of total employment for the industry. Of the top 15 firms in the industry, five were located in Michigan. This reflected firms' proximity to centers of automotive design and production. The automobile industry has long provided tool and die producers with one of their most important markets.

The industry is served by the National Tooling and Machining Association of Fort Washington, Maryland, known as the National Tool and Die Manufacturers Association until 1960 and the National Tool, Die and Precision Machining Association until 1980. The Association was founded in 1943 and had 3,100 members and a staff of 40 in 1996, making it among the largest trade associations in the United States. Among the Association's publications were the annual *Buyers Guide of Special Tooling and Precision Machining Services, Basic Diemaking,* and *Advanced Diemaking.* The Association organizes an annual convention and semi-annual conferences. The industry was also served by the Tooling and Manufacturing Association of Chicago and the Michigan Tooling Association of Dearborn. The latter Association of 715 members was founded in 1933 and published the periodical *Tool Talk.* Other industry journals included *Tooling and Production, Modern Machine Shop, Precision Toolmaker,* and *American Machinist.*

Union Workers in this industry are represented by the International Union of Tool, Die and Mold Makers, based in Rahway, New Jersey, and founded in 1972. The Union absorbed the Tool, Die and Mold Makers Guild in 1975.

BACKGROUND AND DEVELOPMENT

There are essentially two types of dies, pressworking dies and molding dies. Pressworking dies (also called stamping dies) are used to cut and shape sheet metals with electrical or hydraulic presses ranging in size from bench presses to the three-story high giants used to stamp automotive body parts. A pressworking die set consists of two components, the upper part attached to the press ram, called a punch, and the lower part attached to the press bed, called a die (though die sets are often simply referred to as dies). Molding dies are used to form both metals and plastics. The most common type consists of two units that when closed form a cavity into which molten material is poured.

The development of the tool and die industry was central to the development of interchangeable parts and mass production technologies in manufacturing. As the *U.S. Industrial Outlook 1994* reported, "Nearly every manufacturer that mass produces a product relies to some degree on contract manufacturing support provided by the small business companies that make up the special tooling and machining industry in the United States." A key historical figure in the industry was Eli Whitney, who used jigs and fixtures to assure the uniformity and thus interchangeability of component parts of firearms used during the War of 1812.

The rapid growth of mass production technologies after the late nineteenth century led to the development of a great number of tool and die shops, most of them small independent contractors. The number of tool and die producing establishments increased from 5,209 in 1954 to 6,616 in 1972 and 6,983 in 1989. Of the total number of establishments in 1989, 1,665 had 20 or more employees. By 1996 the number of establishments increased to an estimated 7,924—1,740 these had 20 or more employees.

In their book *The Tool and Die Industry,* Harold E. Arnett and Donald N. Smith described the special characteristics of the tool and die industry. They wrote: "While mass production is made possible by tooling, the principal tools themselves cannot be mass produced. Tool making, and especially mold and diemaking, is one of the few activities connected with modern large-scale industry in which there has not been a general substitution of machinery for basic skills. These tools are custom-made, one-at-a-time by skilled artisans who patiently and precisely machine, finish, and construct the complicated devices. Only one die, or set of dies, is needed for the manufacture of many thousands, and sometimes millions, of automobile fenders or hoods of a given design."

There was substantial evidence that the characteristics of tool and die production as described by Arnett and Smith were undergoing significant change in the 1980s and 1990s. While the output of the industry increased by 14 percent in real terms from 1987 to 1993, the employment of production workers increased by only 1.25 percent. Such labor displacement was partially the result of computerized production technologies. The flexibility of these technologies also enabled tool and die producers to undertake a broader range of operations. A number of industry observers predicted the consolidation of tool and die firms, resulting in fewer and larger firms.

CURRENT CONDITIONS

Following the passage of the North American Free Trade Agreement (NAFTA), a number of U.S. tool and die producers were looking to export markets for growth. These producers hoped to serve both Mexican and Canadian manufacturers and also to benefit from the expanded export sales of U.S. manufacturers.

A number of large manufacturing firms were reducing or eliminating their in-house tool and die operations during the 1990s, creating new possibilities for independent producers. Among these was General Motors, which announced in 1993 that it expected to eliminate four of its 11 tool and die shops.

INDUSTRY LEADERS

The top firms in the tool and die industry were Great Lakes-Eglinton, D-M-E Company, and DT Industries, Inc. Founded in 1961 and located in Bridgeport, Michigan, Great Lakes-Eglinton is a division of Core Industries and had 2,462 employees and sales of $243 million in 1996. Located in Madison Heights, Michigan, D-M-E Co., is a division of Fairchild Corp. and had 700 employees and $126 million in sales in 1996. DT Industries, Inc., of Lebanon, Missouri, was founded in 1993 and had 1,300 employees and $107 million in sales in 1996.

RESEARCH AND TECHNOLOGY

The key area of research and technical change in the tool and die industry in the 1990s involved CAD/CAM technologies. The journal *Plastics Technology* surveyed 700 producers of industrial molds regarding their use of CAD. These producers used CAD for 10 percent of their tooling in 1992 and aimed to increase this to 40 to 50 percent. In 1993, Solingen Incorporated of Northridge, California, introduced a manufacturing process called direct shell production casting, which enabled the casting of metal parts directly from a three-dimensional image on a computer screen. Among the leading producers of software for the industry were the Roland Digital Group and Delcam International PLC.

FURTHER READING

Arnett, Harold, and Donald Smith. *The Tool and Die Industry: Problems and Prospects.* Ann Arbor, MI: University of Michigan School of Business Administration, 1975.

"Closing of Autodie Felt Throughout Local Economy." *Grand Rapids Press,* 9 August 1992.

"Commitment to Design Technology Market." *Precision Toolmaker,* January/February 1994.

Darnay, Arsen J., Ed. *Manufacturing USA.* 5th ed. Detroit: Gale Research, 1996.

Dickin, Peter. "Jack of All Trades or Master of None?" *Precision Toolmaker,* April/May, 1993.

Frame, Phil. "GM Expected to Shut 4 Tool and Die Shops." *Automotive News,* 1 March 1993.

Goldsberry, Clare. "New Metal Casting Process May Mean Faster Mold Making." *Plastic News,* 4 January 1993.

"JCI Buys Blow Molding Machinery Firm." *Plastic News,* 13 July 1992.

King, Angela. "New Offer for Autodie." *Crain's Detroit Business,* 6 December 1992.

"Mining Money in Mature Markets." *Fortune,* 22 March 1993.

Moody's Industrial Manual. New York: Moody's Investors Service, 1993.

Ostergaard, D. Eugene. *Basic Diemaking.* New York: McGraw-Hill, 1963.

————. *Advanced Diemaking.* New York: McGraw-Hill, 1967.

"Patience Pays." *Forbes,* 17 August 1992.

"700 Readers Say: Mold Analysis Makes the Grade." *Plastics Technology,* April 1992.

U.S. Department of Commerce. *1995 Annual Survey of Manufactures.* Washington: GPO, 1997.

SIC 3545

CUTTING TOOLS, MACHINE TOOL ACCESSORIES, AND MACHINIST'S PRECISION MEASURING DEVICES

This category covers establishments primarily engaged in manufacturing cutting tools, machinists' precision measuring tools, and attachments and accessories for machine tools and for other metalworking machinery, not elsewhere classified. Establishments primarily engaged in manufacturing handtools, except power-driven types, are classified in the Cutlery, Handtools, and General Hardware industries.

INDUSTRY SNAPSHOT

In the mid-1990s, there were about 1,900 establishments in the industry, an increase of about 9 percent over 1990. In 1995, the industry shipped $4.8 billion in products; over half ($2.6 billion) consisted of small cutting tools for machine tools and metalworking machinery; 22 percent ($1.05 billion) consisted of precision measuring tools.

BACKGROUND AND DEVELOPMENT

The background and development of cutting tools, accessories, and measuring devices is closely tied to the history of machine tool development. The first gear-cutting mechanism was designed by Leonardo da Vinci, however, no evidence indicates it was ever built. Through the clock making industry, the demand for precision gears and precision measuring devices grew. As time-keeping devices became more popular, production techniques were developed to meet the increasing demand. Metal removing devices were available with very small teeth, which served more as rotary files than chip-forming, cutting tools. Yet, it was not until the mid-1800s that the first cutting tool was developed.

The Phoenix Iron Works of Hartford, Connecticut, created the first tool to really form a metal chip, thereby cutting the metal. The tool had 56 teeth placed around its nearly three-inch diameter. The teeth were chipped by a hammer and chisel. While effective, the tool required too much labor when it needed sharpening. In 1864, the Brown & Sharpe Company, later the Brown & Sharpe Manufacturing Company, developed the first cutter that could be sharpened by grinding the face, without altering its shape. To date, the elements of this design are still in use.

CURRENT CONDITIONS

The cutting tools, machine tool accessories, and precision measuring devices industry is facing transition. Increased global competition in all aspects of manufacturing have created demand for better, longer lasting tools and accessories. Extensive development of tougher cutting tool materials and coatings has been the driving force of change in this industry, along with improved cutting tool design that lends extended performance. Increased emphasis on quality control is affecting the measuring device segment through demand for electronic gauges that link to statistical process control software packages. Modular tooling designs have affected the accessories segment.

Ironically, while this industry has paced itself to match industry demand for productivity improvements, it also has met with its own problems. The influx of foreign competitors to this market has been staggering, forcing cutting tool and measuring device manufacturers to look introspectively at their own operations. Process improvements and increased development became commonplace practices to remain profitable.

The current downturn in the machine tool industry does not necessarily correlate to the health of the cutting tool industry. Generally, cutting tool sales are viewed as an economic indicator of the nation's manufacturing productivity level. The difference is primarily a capital expense. A corporation may decide to purchase a used machine tool over a new one in recessionary times. However, if a company is cutting metal, the cutting tools wear or break and must be sharpened or replaced with new cutting tools. Therefore, the productivity of a metal cutting company is generally directly related to the purchasing levels of machine tools. However, longer lasting cutting tools are being manufactured with specialized coatings which extend the wear life of the tool—sometimes as much as four times the normal wear. With improved cutting tool materials and geometry, the volume of machine tool sales will inevitably drop because the tools are designed to reduce the frequency of replacement. Likewise, improved engineering design of metal castings intentionally reduce the amount of removable machine stock, requiring less cutting tool activity.

Improved tool coatings are also driving end mill innovation. Cubic boron nitride (CBN) coated tooling inserts are gaining ground on carbide and ceramic inserts in areas like high production milling of cast iron. Polycrystalline diamond (PCD) coated inserts are also expected to gain acceptance, largely due to research and development efforts in PCD film technology. PCD is especially suited for ultrahard cutting applications. Titanium Nitride (TiN) coatings can also provide significant benefits—including lower machining cost per part, longer tool life, higher feeds and speeds, improved finished part quality, and reduced tool deflection.

Another example of improved tool wear through coating is polycrystalline cubic boron nitride (PCBN). This innovation, when applied to turning inserts, threatens to replace many grinding operations. Used to machine hardened steel, PCBN turning inserts have no equal. Referred to as hard turning, the insert comes within or surpasses the accuracy and surface finish once reserved for grinding operations. The surface is improved because hard turning burnishes the surface, ending in a cleaner, rust- and crack-inhibitive surface.

End mill design is evolving into more specialized geometries for certain material applications. For example, when milling aluminum, a standard, two-flute, high speed, steel end mill was used. However, studies show that using a three-flute end mill on aluminum grants ample space for chip formation, while allowing a feed rate increase of up to 50 percent. The tool design change increases productivity by allowing aluminum to be machined faster, without increased tool breakage.

Quick change and modular tools are making inroads. Flexibility and adaptability have been emphasized by customers over the years, which these tooling configurations offer. Rapid precise tool changes save downtime and enable tailoring production schedules, thus using personnel and machine tools more efficiently. Modular tooling systems standardize spindle-to-tool interface connections, offering reduced hardware inventories. According to Charles R. Brown, Kennametal Incorporated's application engineering systems manager, "These systems move a process that for centuries has been manual into the age of automation. It's a quantum leap."

Statistical process control (SPC) is taking a new turn through increased use of electronic gauges on the shop floor. Wired to a computer, the gauges show digital readout of the measurement. This reading is input to the SPC software, which creates process control charts. The operator/inspector no longer shuffles through paperwork and calculations, and the readings are much more accurate. Such "real-time" information is beneficial in seeing trends, such as tool wear, before any parts are scrapped. The major trend in SPC today is moving measuring devices from the quality assurance department to the shop floor. Coordinate measuring machines and computer-linked electronic gauges are two examples of measurement equipment moving to the source to gain better control through improving response time, when a problem arises on the

SPC charts. The biggest drawback to implementing use of electronic gauges is the initial cost involved. Purchasing the computer equipment, special gauges, training employees in the use of the software and hardware, and specialized calibration require such an outlay of money that many machine shops are intimidated, while remaining skeptical of any additional cost savings. Mitutoyo/MTI Corporation studied the level of electronic gauge use in industry in 1989. They found 61 percent of the surveyed machine shops used both dial and electronic gauges, while 31 percent did not use electronic gauges at all. Only 1.5 percent of the machine shops surveyed were totally committed to electronic gauge use.

INDUSTRY LEADERS

In 1996, the top five companies, in terms of sales, were Harbour Group Ltd., with $1 billion; Kennametal Inc., with $984 million; Disston (a subsidiary of Greenfield Industries, Inc.), with over $500 million; L.S. Starrett Co., with $214 million; and Mettler-Toldeo, Inc., with sales over $200 million. Harbour Group has acquired over 80 manufacturing companies since its founding in 1976. It operates 45 plants in the United States and 8 overseas.

WORK FORCE

In 1995, there were over 50,000 employees in the machine tool accessories industry, a decrease of about 4 percent since 1990. Production workers in the industry earned an average of $12.31 per hour and worked 43.9 hours per week. The averages for all production workers in manufacturing based industries was $12.37 and 41.6 hours respectively.

Many occupations in this industry will be reduced as the country moves toward the next century. Those facing the most significant reductions, over 10 percent, include tool cutting operators, assemblers and fabricators, secretaries, machine builders, precision inspectors, and metal forming operators. Small increases in a few occupations are expected. These include industrial production managers, mechanical engineers, combination machine tool operators, numerically controlled machine operators, and machinists.

AMERICA AND THE WORLD

Competition and cost are the battle cries of the 1990s. Global competition is fierce, and only those who master cost savings measures will beat the competitors. Nowhere is this more evident than in the auto industry. Although the Americans have experienced difficulty in the marketplace where Japanese cars reign supreme, the Europeans face greater challenges. Nis-

san's plant in Sunderland, England lags one hour behind normal production time in Nissan's Japanese plants—18 man hours versus. 17 man hours per car. However, European plants, on the average, produce a car in 30 to 35 man-hours. German automakers generally require 40 man hours per car. In terms of cost cutting, it has been estimated that 150,000 jobs too many exist as a result of this inefficiency. Although work ethics differ between the cultures, so does the level of sophisticated machine tools and cutting tools. In order to bridge this gap, European manufacturers may order higher standard machine tools, cutting tools, and accessories and increase the order quantities.

The latest wave in quality improvement is a series of certifications known as ISO 9000. ISO stands for the International Organization for Standardization, which over 100 European countries have adopted as official. When business is viewed in a global perspective, the ISO certifications are becoming increasingly necessary to obtain. In the United States, many of the larger companies/organizations—such as Caterpillar, York International, and American Petroleum Institute—have developed their own quality standards. Once a company becomes a potential supplier for the larger company, a quality audit is performed at the potential supplier's facility. Depending on the customer-supplier base, it would be possible for a company to hold several quality certifications, each with their own unique requirements. The benefit to obtaining ISO certification is to achieve a quality level that is understood throughout the world. The ISO certification is reviewed and reaudited every six months. While this is relatively new and fairly controversial in the United States, over 15,000 certifications are held in Britain alone. The cost of compliance is one of the major obstacles to applying for certification—$15,000 to $20,000 for average sized companies. However, the cost of non-compliance in the future could mean fewer business opportunities, as ISO could become a general requirement for contract awards both domestically and internationally.

RESEARCH AND TECHNOLOGY

Cryogenic treatment, or deep freezing, of cutting tools is currently a relatively unexplored process. It has little technical data available to support the successes in increased tool life as a result of the process. For years, one small tooling and die company in Arcadia, Ohio, experimented with dropping several materials, like metals and nylon, to 320 degrees below zero Fahrenheit, or 77 degrees Kelvin. The results have been outstanding. Carbide inserts seem to last 2 to 8 times longer than untreated inserts. Blades for cutting abrasive rubber are lasting up to 37 times longer. Carbide dies stay in service for months, rather than weeks, before needing sharpened. Even nylon stockings seem better able to resist runners. The National Science Foundation has approved a research grant for the company to investigate the effect of cryogenic treatment on the wear life and microstructure of steel. If the research leads to significant findings, deep freezing may become another significant option for improvement of tool life.

FURTHER READING

Albert, Mark. "Cutting Tools in the Deep Freeze." *Modern Machine Shop,* January 1992.

Beard, Tom, ed. "Fast and Good." *Modern Machine Shop,* June 1993.

Darnay, Arsen J., ed. *Manufacturing USA.* 5th ed. Detroit: Gale Research, 1996.

Fruit, Robert. "Move SPC to the Shop Floor." *Modern Machine Shop,* April 1993.

"Hoover's Online." Austin, TX: Hoover's Inc, 1997. Available from http://www.hoovers.com.

Koepfer, Chris. "Getting Ready for ISO 9000." *Modern Machine Shop,* April 1993.

Miska, Kurt H. "Tools, Workholding & Machine Accessories." *Manufacturing Engineering,* August 1990.

Noaker, Paula M. "Hard Facts on Hard Turning." *Manufacturing Engineering,* February 1992.

Owen, Jean. "Gaging Quality." *Manufacturing Engineering,* April 1990.

Owen, Jean. "Inspection/Quality Assurance." *Manufacturing Engineering,* August 1990.

Owen, Jean. "Moving to Modular." *Manufacturing Engineering,* February 1992.

Peterson, Gary J. "Survival Training for the '90s." *Manufacturing Engineering,* August 1990.

"Steel & Heavy Machinery." *Standard & Poor's Industry Surveys,* 8 April 1993.

U.S. Department of Commerce. *1995 Annual Survey of Manufactures.* Washington: GPO, 1997.

Woodbury, Robert S. *Studies in the History of Machine Tools.* Cambridge, Massachusetts: The MIT Press, 1972.

SIC 3546

HANDTOOLS

This industry includes establishments primarily engaged in manufacturing power-driven hand-tools, such as drills and drilling tools, battery-powered (cord-less) handtools, pneumatic and snagging grinders, and electric hammers. Establishments primarily engaged in manufacturing metal cutting type and metal forming type machines (including home workshop tools), which are not supported in the hands of an operator are classified in **SIC 3541: Machine Tools, Metal Cutting Types** and **SIC 3542: Machine Tools, Metal Forming Types;** and those primarily manufacturing power-driven heavy construction or mining hand-tools are classified in a range of construction machinery and equipment industries.

INDUSTRY SNAPSHOT

The U.S. power-driven handtool industry includes professional and non-professional tools like electric drills, portable chain saws, portable electric sanders, and pneumatic hammers. The recession in the early 1990s hurt the industry seriously, but it is progressively bouncing back. For example, shipment values jumped from $2,872 billion in 1992 to $3,480 billion in 1993 and have risen steadily ever since. The industry's value of shipments was approximately $3.495 billion in 1994 and was projected to reach $3.886 billion by 1998. The United States is also a net importer of power-driven handtools. In 1992 exports accounted for 14 percent of total shipments, while imports represented 27 percent of those shipments.

Battery-powered (cordless) handtools, which include driver/drills and other tools, accounted for 12 percent of total shipments, while electric power-driven handtools represented approximately 45 percent of total shipments, according to *Manufacturing USA.* When combined, battery-powered and electric handtools represent 57 percent of the industry's total shipments; this emphasizes the success of the non-professional consumer handtool market, which represented 50 percent of the industry's shipments in the early 1990s. Pneumatic, hydraulic, and powder-actuated hand tools, which are produced for industrial and professional customers, represented 26 percent of total shipments in 1992, while internal combustion power-driven handtools and unspecified handtools represented the remaining 17 percent of total shipments.

ORGANIZATION AND STRUCTURE

Success for the power-driven handtool industry depends on a variety of economic factors influencing industrial and consumer spending. Capital spending by business and industry directly affects power-driven handtool manufacturers, particularly in their manufacture of pneumatic power tools.

Pneumatic handtools operate by forcing compressed air through rotor blades. They are lightweight, durable, high performance tools used in demanding industrial situations. Pneumatic handtools comprised 26 percent of the industry's total shipments in 1992, up two percent from the shipment percentage of pneumatic handtools in the late 1980s. Examples of pneumatic products include: drills, grinders (metalworking machinery), pneumatic chip removal guns, hammers, ratchet wrenches, and sanders.

According to the 1996 edition of *Manufacturing USA,* retail sales to the do-it-yourself consumer sector accounted for 57 percent of the industry's total shipments in 1992 and have become a major influence on the success of the industry. Industry leader Black & Decker, for example, received $1.826 million, or 39 percent, of its revenues from its power tool division by the end of 1995—largely a result of do-it-yourself retail sales at home improvement stores such as The Home Depot. Because of this success, Black & Decker planned to introduce an assortment of new products for do-it-yourself customers in 1996. This sales strategy emphasizes the industry's sensitivity to spending trends for home improvement, maintenance, and repair. Electric power handtools dominated these sectors because they were generally less expensive than pneumatic tools. They accounted for 45 percent of the industry's total shipments. The cordless battery-powered handtool market also gave the industry a boost in the early 1990s and continued its success through 1994, when battery-powered handtools accounted for 12 percent of the industry's total shipments. Industry sales in this sector were expected to increase throughout the mid- to late 1990s due to technology improvements in battery power and charge duration. Examples of electric power handtools include: buffing machines, chipping hammers, drills, grinders, hammers, polishers, sanders, saws, shears, screwdrivers, and wrenches.

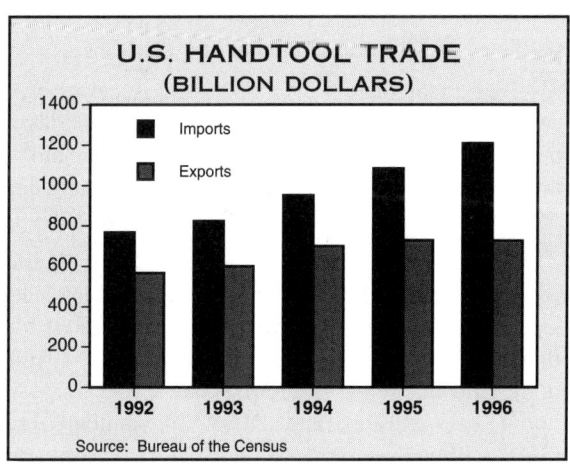

U.S. HANDTOOL TRADE
(BILLION DOLLARS)

Source: Bureau of the Census

The power-driven handtool industry also includes gasoline-powered chain saws. This product class is directly tied to the success of the timber industry. Lower timber harvests, due in part to environmental concerns, became a serious problem for chain saw manufacturers in the early 1990s and continued to effect sales in the mid-1990s. Moreover, lower consumer purchases—due to a declining use of firewood for home heating—contributed to a decade of flat sales. Gasoline powered chain saws comprised an estimated 11 percent of the industry's total shipments in 1992.

BACKGROUND AND DEVELOPMENT

The power-driven handtool industry developed in conjunction with the rest of the United States' industrial growth. U.S. manufacturers often started as small operations producing specific power tools for local markets. As the United States grew into a world economic leader, the power-driven handtool industry likewise expanded internationally.

The Black & Decker Corporation, for example, founded in 1910 by S. Duncan Black and Alonzo G. Decker in Baltimore, first began manufacturing milk bottle-cap machines and candy dippers. By 1917 Black & Decker patented the first pistol grip, trigger switch electric drill. The company's success enabled it to begin international operations by 1918. According to *Hoover's Handbook of American Business,* Black & Decker developed products that defined the power tool industry. For example, the company introduced the first portable screwdriver in 1923, the first electric hammer in 1936, and the first portable electric drill for the consumer in 1946. In 1993 Black & Decker was the world's leading power-driven handtool manufacturer.

Another contemporary industry leader, Danaher Corporation, was organized in 1969 originally as a Massachusetts real estate investment trust known as DMG, Inc. In 1989, the corporation entered the handtool market by merging with Easco Hand Tools, Inc., and now handtools make up approximately half of Danaher's total sales. By opening its doors to this market, Danaher Corp.'s 1992 sales rose to $897 million, the best year in the company's history for per share earnings. A year later, the company's international sales rose to more than 10 percent of total sales.

CURRENT CONDITIONS

According to *U.S. Industrial Outlook,* the recession seriously hurt the handtool industry in 1990 and 1991 when overall shipments dropped by $163 million (6.9 percent). The industry recovered by 1994 when the value of shipments reached $3.495 billion; this success was expected to continue through 1998.

During the early to mid-1990s, automation played a major role in reducing the number of workers employed by the industry. The falling employment rate had not affected the industry's continued status as a net importer by 1992, however, when imports comprised 27 percent of total shipments, and exports represented 14 percent of those shipments.

The proliferation of large home centers, such as The Home Depot and Lowe's, gave manufacturers additional markets in which to sell their products. Technology also boosted the power-driven handtool industry by opening new markets for cordless tools, which accounted for 12 percent of the industry's total shipments in 1992.

Near-term Conditions. The industry's value of shipments was expected to rise from $3.495 billion in 1994 to $3.886 billion in 1998, and the industry's capital investments were also expected to rise from $104 million to $111 million during that period. Employment was expected to drop slightly from 15,600 total employees in 1994 to 14,200 in 1998, but these decreases were expected to boost average hourly wages from $11.19 to $11.98 in 1998. In 1993 the home improvement sector was expected to rise by 5 percent, while sales in the home repair and maintenance sector were expected to increase 4 percent. These sectors, as well as flooding and other natural disasters, helped increase the industry's value of shipments by 21 percent between 1993 and 1994 to $3.495 billion.

Long-term Conditions. The U.S. power-driven handtool industry was expected to experience annual growth of 2.25 percent from 1994 to 1998. Industry growth depends upon increased expenditures in the home improvement, home repair and maintenance, and residential and commercial construction sectors. In addition, new battery technology is helping the industry expand the market for advanced cordless tools.

INDUSTRY LEADERS

Black & Decker continued its domination through 1996 as the world's largest power-driven handtool manufacturer in the world. The Towson, Maryland-based company employed 35,800 people in 1996 and produced $4.766 billion in sales. By the end of 1995, the company's best-selling sector, its power tool division, brought in $1.826 billion in sales, accounting for 39 percent of the company's overall sales. According to *Hoover's Handbook of American Business,* Black & Decker eventually set the pace for the industry by

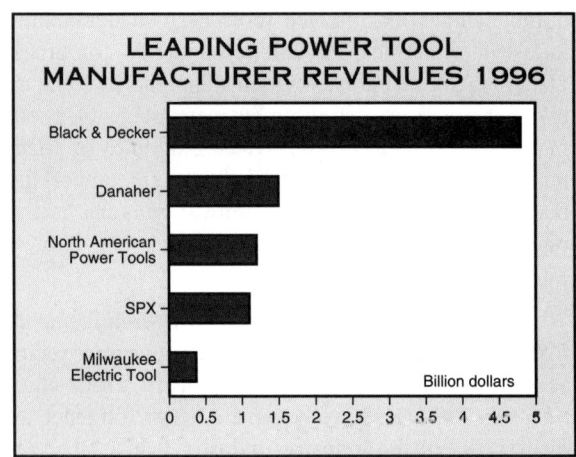

LEADING POWER TOOL MANUFACTURER REVENUES 1996

introducing innovative power tools like the first portable screwdriver in 1922 and portable electric drills in 1946. By the early 1990s, Black & Decker was an international company that carried the seventh most recognized brand name in the United States. Its brand recognition was also among the top-20 in Europe. In 1995, the company expanded this international presence by beginning joint operations in India and China and introducing DeWALT power tools to Europe and Latin America. DeWALT power tools continue to lift Black & Decker's global sales.

The second largest U.S. power-driven handtool manufacturer in 1996 was Washington, D.C.-based Danaher Corporation. Danaher Corp. was founded in 1984 as a holding company, and in December 1986 bought New York-based Chicago Pneumatic Tool Company, a leading U.S. manufacturer of pneumatic handtools for industrial purposes in the 1980s. According to *International Directory of Company Histories,* in 1994 Danaher Corporation was recognized as the world's largest producer of drill chucks, the country's largest producer and marketer of Swiss screw machine components, and the leading automotive tools supplier to the National Automotive Parts Association (NAPA) and Sears. In 1996, the company employed 9,960 and produced $1.487 billion annually in sales.

North American Power Tools and Accessories, a subsidiary of Black and Decker, was the United States' third largest manufacturer of power-driven handtools in 1996. The Towson, Maryland-based company employed 3,300 and produced $1.2 billion in sales in 1996.

Other major U.S. power-driven handtool sales leaders in 1996 included: SPX Corporation ($1.1 billion), Milwaukee Electric Tool Corporation ($370 million), Hilti Inc. ($347 million), Porter-Cable Corporation ($150 million), and DESA International Inc. ($150 million).

WORK FORCE

The U.S. power-driven handtool industry employed 15,600 people in 1994, a 10 percent drop from the 17,100 workers employed by the industry in 1990. Employment was expected to fall to 14,200 by 1998, a reflection of the industry's increasing reliance on automation. In 1994 production workers represented 10,900 of the 15,600 employees and earned an average weekly salary of $449. Some of the occupations in the power-driven handtool industry include: tool and die makers, machinists, mechanical engineers, drafters, blue collar worker supervisors, inspectors, industrial production managers, and stock clerks.

AMERICA AND THE WORLD

The United States is a world leader in the manufacture of power-driven handtools, and most U.S. manufacturers were significant exporters in the mid- to late-1990s. Black & Decker, for example, had total export sales (for all products) of $1.956 billion in 1996, or 37 percent of its total sales revenues. In 1994, the U.S. trade deficit was $108.1 billion compared with $75.7 billion in 1993, and was expected to widen slightly to $113 billion in 1995. Also during that year, world economic conditions and stronger foreign economic growth were expected to favor U.S. exports of goods and services, spurring increases in exports of 10 to 11 percent. These favorable conditions were expected to contribute to faster U.S. export growth in the range of 8.5 to 10.0 percent annually in current dollars, compared to 6.7 percent since 1990. A strong domestic U.S. economy also increased consumption of imports by 12 percent in the mid-1990s. The U.S. trade deficit was expected to improve in the late 1990s if strong foreign economic growth, a reduction in the U.S. budget deficit, and/or an increase in other domestic savings were present.

Major U.S. competitors include Germany, Japan, and Great Britain. The Robert Bosch Company, with its headquarters in Stuttgart, Germany, had total sales of $33.6 billion in 1991 and employed 181,498. Another large German power tool manufacturer is the Stihl Andreas Co. They manufacture chain saws, hand saws, and replacement parts. The company had total sales of $1.15 billion in 1991 and employed 5,666.

Sumitomo Electric Industries LTD of Osaka, Japan exported $126.113 million in 1992. The company had total 1992 sales of $1.157 billion and 14,833 employees.

In Great Britain, Dobson Park Industries exported $73,600 to the United States in 1992. Its power tool sales were $19,849, totaling 9 percent of the company's 1992 revenues.

Other large power-driven handtool manufacturers include: the Hitachi Koki Co. (Japan), the Makita Corp. (Japan), the Shibaura Engineering Works Co. (Japan), the Hilti Ag Co. (Switzerland), Johnson Electric Holdings Ltd. (Hong Kong), and the Kanematsu-Nnk Corp. (Japan).

RESEARCH AND TECHNOLOGY

Most research in the power-driven handtool industry in the 1990s was directed toward ergonomics and portability. Ergonomic designs create tools that are more comfortable and efficient for the user. Long term use of poorly designed power-driven handtools can have serious consequences to workers' health and safety. According to John Bonnanzio in *Industrial Distribution,* injuries caused by constant exposure to noise and vibrations can cause such injuries as hearing loss, carpal tunnel syndrome, and hand-arm vibration syndrome (HAVS). Injuries of this type cost companies an estimated $100 billion annually. For example, according to the Manufacturing Information Resource Center (MIRC) home page on the Internet, Pratt & Whitney reported 1,500 claims in 1994 averaging approximately $5,000 each, costing the company over $5 million in claims that year. As a result, Pratt & Whitney made plans to reduce its cumulative trauma disorder (CTD) claims related to the use of power hand tools by 10 to 15 percent, which would save the company $500,000 to $750,000 a year.

Improved ergonomic designs can significantly reduce injuries caused by long term use of power-driven hand tools. Stanley Tools recently presented a new line of ergonomically designed tools that help the user maximize job performance, enhance work quality, and minimize physical stress and fatigue. All the tools in this new line were tested by BCAM International, Inc., an internationally recognized software technology company specializing in ergonomic solutions. Stanley Contractor Grade tools, for example, feature cushioned, dual-durometer grips that improve user comfort and reduce the likelihood of the tool slipping in the user's hand. The tools more efficiently lower the number of repetitive motions needed to execute a given task and reduce the occurrence of CTDs.

The power-driven handtool industry has also changed due to the development of cordless battery operated tools. According to *Business Week,* the key advantages of cordless tools are indoor safety and outdoor convenience. Cordless tools were an expanding area for power-driven handtool manufacturers in the early 1990s, and in 1992 accounted for 12 percent of the industry's total shipments.

FURTHER READING

Avery, Susan. "Power Tools Take a Pounding." *Purchasing,* 22 October 1992, 57-58.

Bonnanzio, John. "Designs That Sell." *Industrial Distribution,* June 1990, 27-28.

Darnay, Arsen J., ed. *Manufacturing USA.* 5th ed. Detroit: Gale Research, 1996.

"The 'Do It Yourself' Stocks." *Financial World* 144, (23 July 1975) 15.

"Dun's Marketing Services." *Dun's Business Rankings, 1996.* Dun & Bradstreet, Inc., 1996.

Eastman, Martin. "Vibration Shakes Workers: Nerves and Blood Vessels Can Suffer Irreversible Damage from Prolonged or Repeated Motion." *Safety & Health,* May 1991, 32-35.

Industry Surveys. New York: Standard & Poor's Corporation, 1997.

International Directory of Company Histories. Vol. 7. Detroit: St. James Press, 1994.

International Trade Administration. *Executive Summary.* Washington: U.S. Department of Commerce, 1997. Available from http://www.ita.doc.gov.

International Trade Administration. *1996 Report on U.S. Trade Deficit and World Economic Conditions.* Washington: U.S. Department of Commerce, 1996.

Manufacturing Information Resource Center (MIRC). 1997. Available from http://www.ncms.org/mirc/index.html.

Notable Corporate Chronologies. Vol. 1. Detroit: Gale Research, 1995.

Spain, Patrick J., and James R. Talbot, eds. *Hoover's Handbook of American Business 1997.* Austin, TX: Hoover's, Inc., 1996.

U.S. Department of Commerce. "Distribution of Sales by Class of Customer." *1987 Census of Manufactures.* Washington: GPO, 1987.

U.S. Department of Commerce. "General Summary." *1987 Census of Manufactures.* Washington: GPO, 1987.

U.S. Department of Commerce. "Metalworking Machinery and Equipment." *1987 Census of Manufactures.* Washington: GPO, 1987.

U.S. Department of Labor. *Employment, Hours, and Earnings, United States, 1909-90.* Washington: GPO, 1991.

Warner, Joan. "Charged-up Cordless Tools." *Business Week,* 29 March 1993, 100.

—Scott Plamondon, updated by Elizabeth Shugg

SIC 3547

ROLLING MILL MACHINERY

This category covers establishments primarily engaged in manufacturing rolling mill machinery and processing equipment for metal production, such as cold forming mills, structural mills, and finishing equipment.

The U.S. government divides rolling mill machinery into four classifications: hot rolling mill machinery (except tube rolling), cold rolling mill machinery, other roll milling machinery (including tube mill machinery), and rolling mill machinery that is not classified elsewhere. In 1995, the value of shipments for these four classifications was $621 million. The most valuable classification was "other rolling mill machinery" with a product shipment value of $244.5 million.

The total value of shipments in the rolling mill machinery industry in 1997 was an estimated $610 million, up from $521 million in 1994. There were about 105 establishments in the industry that same year. Forty percent of these establishments had 20 or more employees in 1994. Average firm size as measured by the number of production workers per establishment was 19 percent smaller than that for the manufacturing sector as a whole. Annual capital investments were $9.9 million in 1994, and approximately $9.8 million was invested in 1997.

The rolling mill machinery industry employed about 4,200 production workers in 1997, down from a peak of 5,400 in 1992. The industry was relatively labor-intensive, having 30 percent as much investment per production worker as that for the manufacturing sector as a whole. Annual hours worked by production workers in the industry were 9 percent higher on average than those worked in the manufacturing sector at large, and hourly wages, at approximately $15 per hour, were 18 percent higher. By 2005, machinist jobs are expected to decrease 17.4 percent. Tool and die makers jobs are expected to decrease 15.3 percent. A 37.7 percent increase is expected for combination machine tool operators.

The capital requirements for the industry are relatively low, with average investment per establishment at 25 percent of that for the manufacturing sector as a whole. In 1997, capital investment for the industry was about $9.8 million.

The top three firms in the rolling mill machinery industry are Tippins Incorporated of Pittsburgh, Pennsylvania; Bliss-Salem Inc. of Salem, Ohio; and BCO

Industries Incorporated of Moundridge, Kansas. Together these firms accounted for nearly two-thirds of total sales for the industry in the mid-1990s.

The top rolling mill machinery products by share are hot rolling mill machinery (47 percent), rolling mill machinery, not elsewhere classified, including tube mill machinery, processing lines, and machined rolls for rolling mills (37 percent), and cold rolling mill machinery (12 percent). The states ranking in the top five by number of establishments in the industry are Ohio (with 16), Pennsylvania (with 10), Illinois (with 8), Michigan (with 7), and Massachusetts (with 6). Together these five states account for 79 percent of total employment for the industry in the United States. Ohio by itself accounts for about 31 percent of total employment in the industry.

The top five industries and sectors buying the outputs of the industry are: gross fixed private investment, with a 75.4 percent share; exports, with a 17.8 percent share; change in business inventories, with a 3.7 percent share; rolling mill machinery, with a 2.6 percent share; and federal government purchases, for national defense, with a 0.1 percent share.

FURTHER READING

Darnay, Arsen J., ed. *Manufacturing USA.* 5th ed. Detroit: Gale Research, 1996.

U.S. Department of Commerce. "Value of Product Shipments." *Annual Survey of Manufactures.* Washington: GPO, 1997.

U.S. Department of Commerce. *U.S. Industrial Outlook.* Washington: GPO, 1994.

Ward's Business Directory of U.S. Private and Public Companies. Detroit: Gale Research, 1997.

SIC 3548

ELECTRIC AND GAS WELDING AND SOLDERING EQUIPMENT

This industry includes establishments primarily engaged in manufacturing electric and gas welding and soldering equipment and accessories. Also included are establishments primarily engaged in coating welding wire from purchased wire or from wire drawn in the same establishment. Establishments primarily engaged in manufacturing hand held soldering irons are classified in **SIC 3423: Hand and Edge Tools, Except Machine Tools and Handsaws,** and those manufacturing electron beam, ultrasonic, and laser welding equipment are classified in **SIC 3699: Electrical Ma-**

chinery, Equipment, and Supplies, Not Elsewhere Classified.

Welding and soldering equipment manufacturers, as a whole, experienced a more than $2 billion increase in shipments between 1987 and 1996. In that year, the industry employed an estimated 19,000 people and paid significantly higher wages than other forms of manufacturing. The average compensation for an hourly worker in 1994 was $15.28, compared to a total manufacturing average of $12.09 per hour. There were 246 establishments in 1996, with most concentrated in the Great Lakes region, supporting the automotive industry. Michigan claimed the most establishments, followed by Ohio.

Although industry employment levels were relatively stable toward the end of the 1980s, certain occupations were expected to face reductions going into the year 2000. These included secretaries, metal and plastic machine forming operators, precision inspectors, machine builders, assemblers and fabricators, and metal and plastic machine tool cutting operators. The only occupations expected to increase by over nine percent into the year 2000 are sales workers and industrial production managers.

Approximately 31 percent of the industry's manufacturers produced arc welding machines and their components and accessories, while another 27 percent made arc welding electrodes. The rest of the industry was split between manufacturing resistance welders, gas welding and cutting equipment, welding apparatus, and miscellaneous welding equipment.

Lincoln Electric Company, the industry leader in terms of sales volume, is located in Cleveland, Ohio. Employing approximately 5,700 people in 1995, the company brought in over $1 billion in sales, including $320 million in overseas sales. Lincoln's pay structure and bonus-incentive plans have created a source of study for management researchers and motivational theorists. Lincoln has an open-door policy to encourage communication between various employee levels. Rather than resorting to layoffs as the only course of down-sizing, Lincoln practices hiring freezes and voluntary layoffs. Lincoln credits its outstanding production volumes to this type of management-worker relationship. While Lincoln had the highest sales figures, it did not control the highest share of the welder manufacturing market. Although it controlled 41 percent, 51 percent was owned by The Miller Electric Manufacturing Co.

Miller Electric Manufacturing Company, located in Appleton, Wisconsin, generated sales of an estimated $180 million in 1996. Although it controlled the highest share of the welder manufacturing market, its lack of diversity put its ranking in terms of sales at only fourth. The company was able to increase product quality and worker productivity through the installation of a thermal storage air conditioning system. The thermal storage system has also reduced the company's electricity bills because the system produces ice at night when utility rates are low.

Second in sales was Thermadyne Holdings Corp. based in St. Louis, Missouri. That fact that it was second is quite an achievement considering Thermadyne is still under financial duress. In 1994 the company filed for bankruptcy reorganization. Its long-term debt in 1996 was $458 million and $63 million in shareholders equity. Yet its sales were recovering, and its losses were dwindling. Sales rose 30 percent between 1995 and 1996 to $414 million, and losses dropped 13 percent for the first three quarters of 1996.

Other industry leaders included Progressive Tool and Industries Co. ($190 million in revenues), ESAB Welding and Cutting Products ($120 million), and Deloro Stellite Inc., Weldmation Inc., and Alloy Rods Corp., each with $100 million in revenues.

FURTHER READING

"Big Three Saves $23,000 a Month." *Communication News,* September 1990.

Carey, Christopher. "Color Them Red LBOs, Losses Leave Firms Deep in Debt." *St. Louis Post Dispatch.* 13 May 1996.

Castronovo-Fusco, Mary Ann. "Dealing with Recession: Twenty-five Ways HR Executives are Leading Their Companies." *Employment Relations Today,* Spring, 1991.

Darnay, Arsen J., ed. *Manufacturing USA: Industry Analyses, Statistics, and Leading Companies.* Detroit: Gale Research, Inc., 1996.

Lazich, Robert S., ed. *Market Share Reporter.* Detroit: Gale Research, 1997.

"Lincoln Electric." *The Lincoln Electric Co.,* 1997. Available from http://www.lincolnelectric.com.

Porteus, Evan L., et al. "On Manufacturing / Marketing Incentives." *Management Science,* September 1991.

Schwed, Robert L. "Plant Cooling Increases Quality, Productivity." *Air Conditioning, Heating & Refrigeration News,* 12 October 1992.

"Thermodyne Holdings Corp." *Market Guide: Company Snapshot,* 1997. Available from http://www.marketguide.com/MGI/SNAP/A0EA0-CS.ohtml.

METALWORKING MACHINERY, NOT ELSEWHERE CLASSIFIED

This classification covers establishments primarily engaged in manufacturing metalworking machinery, not elsewhere classified. Establishments primarily engaged in manufacturing automotive maintenance equipment are classified in **SIC 3559: Special Industry Machinery, Not Elsewhere Classified.**

This industry includes special purpose machinery such as robotics machinery, which alone encompasses a growing trend in manufacturing. As the industry continues to automate repetitive and often dangerous tasks, the use of assembly machines is expected to increase. The growth in this industrial classification during the early to mid-1980s was a testament to this trend, and it is still growing in the late 1990s.

Due to reclassification of industry classification content in 1987, the level of employment and shipments dropped significantly. Both of these segments have since recovered. In 1994, employment was at 15,100 people and was estimated to be 15,900 in 1998. The value of shipments in 1994 was $2.144 billion, and in 1998, shipments were expected to be valued at $2.613 billion.

Ingersoll-Rand Company Automated Production Systems Division of Farmington Hills, Michigan was the largest business in the industry; the company sold an estimated $85 million worth of machinery. The closest competitor, Giddings and Lewis-Assembly Automation of Janesville, Wisconsin had about $70 million in sales. The third highest selling machinery company was Ristance Corporation of Mishawaka, Indiana, with sales of more than $65 million. Cummings Mid-America Incorporated of Kansas City, Missouri, reported about $47 million in sales.

The product share of this classification is split between assembly machinery with 55 percent; coiling, cut-to-length, and slitting line metalworking machinery with 31 percent; and miscellaneous metalworking machinery with 12 percent. In 1995, total sales in this industry were $2.67 billion.

Although the industry is showing growth in sales, certain employment levels are expected to decline by the year 2005. Those occupations expected to downsize by 15 to 20 percent include machinists, tool and die makers, secretaries, and blue collar worker supervisors. Staffing in the following occupations is expected to be reduced by less than 10 percent: machine tool cutting operators, assemblers, fabricators and hand workers not elsewhere classified, and industrial production managers. Janitors are expected to decrease about 27 percent, and drafters are expected to decrease about 29 percent. Combination machine tool operators are expected to increase by 38 percent, though.

In the mid-1990s, Michigan had the highest number of establishments involved in this industry. In 1996, Michigan's 65 establishments sold $456 million worth of machinery, which accounted for 28.2 percent of the industry's total shipments. Approximately 2,900 people in Michigan were employed in this industry, receiving average hourly wages of $16.10. Ohio was ranked second in terms of shipments, reporting over $222 million in 1996. Approximately 1,900 Ohio residents were employed by this industry at an average wage of $13.74 per hour. Connecticut was the highest paying state in this industry in 1996. Reporting about $60 million in sales and employing 500 people, Connecticut's establishments paid workers an average hourly wage of $17.14.

FURTHER READING

Darnay, Arsen J., ed. *Manufacturing USA.* 5th Ed. Detroit: Gale Research, 1996.

U.S. Department of Commerce. ''Value of Product Shipments.'' *Annual Survey of Manufactures.* Washington: GPO, 1997.

Ward's Business Directory of U.S. Private and Public Companies. Detroit: Gale Research, 1997.

SIC 3552

TEXTILE MACHINERY

This industry deals with establishments primarily engaged in manufacturing machinery for the textile industries, including parts, attachments, and accessories. Establishments primarily engaged in manufacturing industrial sewing machines are classified in **SIC 3559: Special Industry Machinery, Not Elsewhere Classified,** and those manufacturing household sewing machines are classified in **SIC 3639: Household Appliances, Not Elsewhere Classified.**

INDUSTRY SNAPSHOT

Between 1990 and 1994, the textile machinery industry experienced an increase in its shipment value from $1.505 billion to $1.908 billion. However, the number of employees and establishments engaged in

the industry dropped slightly from 17,400 to 16,700 during that period. Between 1987 and 1990, textile manufacturers' capacity utilization dropped sharply from approximately 92 percent to below 82 percent, directly depressing the machinery industry. However, a strong resurgence was seen between 1990 and 1992, as capacity utilization increased from below 82 percent to nearly 90 percent. Inventories also grew significantly between 1985 and 1993, rising from a value of nearly $4.5 billion to $6 billion. During the mid-1990s, most companies in the machinery industry became much more competitive in the global marketplace by achieving significant cost reductions. These reductions were made by upgrading plants and equipment, reducing employment, increasing inventory turnover, and selling marginal businesses. Many of the companies have also made recent acquisitions that consolidated operations to further reduce costs.

These figures indicate that textile manufacturers of the early- to mid-1990s were secure in a potentially growing market. The development of machinery to support this industry mirrors the outlook of the entire retail industry. Likewise, technological developments in machinery that offer textile manufacturers a competitive edge in terms of cost savings, increased productivity, and better quality, also serve to stimulate the machinery side of the textile industry.

ORGANIZATION AND STRUCTURE

The textile machinery industry encompasses all machinery used from the start of the yarn-making process through weaving the cloth, final treatments, and dyeing. Most fabrics produced by weaving or knitting must undergo a number of further processing treatments before they are ready for sale. In the finishing operations, the fabric is subjected to mechanical and chemical treatment, whereby its appearance and quality are improved and its commercial value is enhanced. Each of these processes requires different machinery, thus the scope of textile machinery is very broad.

The industry is comprised of every machine needed in all stages of the development of textiles, from yarn spinning to final dressing. The term ''finishing'' or ''dressing'' is collectively applied to the various finishing treatments required for each type of fabric. For example, textiles produced from vegetable fibers require different treatment—raising, singeing, dyeing, printing—than those produced from animal or synthetic fibers. These procedures require mechanical treatment and processing by chemicals to improve the glaze, shape-retaining properties, crease resistance, smoothness, and drape of the material. Additionally, depending on the kind of material and the purpose for which it is to be used, a textile can be made shrinkproof, water-repellent, supple, soft, or heavy. Mechanical finishing treatments may consist of mangling, pressing, rolling, milling, shearing, calendering, raising, and singeing. Before undergoing these treatments, the material is passed through liquid baths or steam baths in which various substances, such as starch, vegetable gums, glues, gelatins, and mucilages are added to the fabric.

Of the 500 U.S. textile machinery establishments, less than 200 make complete machines. Although a number of textile machinery manufacturers produce a variety of different products, original-equipment manufacturers tend to concentrate production on one or two types of machines.

Revenues derived from the sale of parts and accessories account for approximately 36 percent of yearly industry sales. Fiber-to-fabric textile machinery holds 9 percent of the product share. Fabric machinery for weaving, knitting, embroidering, braiding, tufting, and lace making comprises 6 percent of the industry. Finishing machinery claims a 5 percent product share. Machines used for bleaching, mercerizing, and dyeing claim 5.5 percent product share. Machinery for drying stocks, yarns, cloth, carpet, and other non-woven materials represents 4.2 percent of the product share. Non-specific machinery and machinery not-elsewhere classified represents the remaining 34.3 percent of the products manufactured by the industry.

BACKGROUND AND DEVELOPMENT

The first hand weaving looms are thought to date back to 4000 B.C. Although the East is credited with the first horizontally arranged weaving plane, its date of origin is unknown. A shedding mechanism, which originated in China, was not introduced in Europe until the third or fourth century A.D. Only minor advances were made with the hand loom over the next millennium. The first major development occurred in 1733, when the flying shuttle was introduced. Designed by an Englishman, the shuttle came equipped with wheels, which reduced resistance as the shuttle passed through the fibers. This considerably decreased the time constraints of producing woven fabrics and expanded the capabilities of the hand loom.

Several blueprints for power looms were submitted during the sixteenth, seventeenth, and eighteenth centuries. Circa 1500, Leonardo da Vinci sketched a hydraulic-driven power loom. This idea was repeated in 1678 and later in 1745; however, none of these were built. It was not until 1784 that an English parson designed the first manufacturable and

functional power loom, which was able to produce a limited number of fabrics. In 1796 an automatic loom stopping system, called the "shuttle stop motion," was developed. In 1822, an English engineer made further improvements to the power loom, which prompted the manufacture of the first large series of power looms.

The oldest known patterning device is drawn in a Chinese book dating back to the twelfth century A.D. In 1725, a punched cardboard card served as the first dobby, a device used for creating unusual weaves. The first patterning machine was created by J. M. Jacquard in 1805, and variations of this machine still bear his name. Another significant advance occurred in 1835, when a shuttle was developed that enabled different thread colors to be inserted into the fabric weave.

CURRENT CONDITIONS

Shipments reached $1.9 billion in 1994 and are expected to climb to $2.1 billion by 1998. Due to higher sales volumes and increased efficiencies from capital investment in machinery, profits in the textiles industry exploded in the early 1990s. Record profits of $1.9 billion were reported in 1992, rising from $882 million in 1991 and $433 million in 1990. However, industry profits had dropped to $832 million by the end of 1996, despite predictions that the industry's explosive growth would continue.

Continued investment in textile machinery climbed from $6.9 million in 1993 to $71.4 million in 1994, reflecting textile manufacturers' optimism toward the industry's future. However, capital investments were expected to plunge to $51.8 million in 1995. Investments should have risen to about $57.3 million by 1998, leveling off the downward trend of previous years. Buyer demands for higher quality apparel and home furnishings at lower prices encourage capital investment. Manufacturers have also shifted to automated processes in lieu of labor intensive operations that can increase costs.

INDUSTRY LEADERS

The following companies led the industry in 1996: Hirsch International Corporation, with $88 million in sales and 146 employees; Day International Inc., with $80 million in sales and 525 employees; and Speizman Industries, Inc., with $62 million in sales and 72 employees. Other industry leaders were Hollingsworth Saco Lowell Corporation with $42 million in sales, Vanguard Supreme with $40 million in sales, and Setco Sales Company with $36 million in sales. In 1994, the textile machinery industry consisted of approximately 500 companies that employed 16,700 people and earned $832 million in sales.

WORK FORCE

The employment level in the textile machinery industry fluctuated from 17,500 employees in 1983 to 15,600 in 1987 and back up to 17,400 in 1990. The number of industry employees declined to 16,700 employees in 1994 and was expected to decrease by 10 percent to 15,000 employees in 1998. Since there are now fewer employees than there were in the late 1980s, wages have increased. In 1994, the average hourly wage of industry employees was $11.92, up from 1988's average of $9.86 per hour, which was slightly below the average wage of $10.66 earned by employees of all other manufacturing industries. Wages are expected to reach $13.29 by 1998 as the employment level continues to decrease.

The industry is expected to make significant reductions in several occupations by 2005. The occupations anticipating cuts in excess of 10 percent include secretaries; drafters; engineering, mathematical, and science managers; bookkeeping, accounting, and auditing clerks; welding machine setters and operators; machine tool cutting operators (excluding those in North Carolina); general office clerks; and stock clerks. However, job opportunities for machine builders and North Carolina machine tool operators are expected to increase by at least 10 percent. Industrial machinery mechanics positions should increase by about 8 percent.

Although textile machinery manufacturing facilities are located in 22 states, they are concentrated primarily in South Carolina, North Carolina and Georgia. The industry is made up of small- to medium-sized companies.

AMERICA AND THE WORLD

The textile machinery industry is ultimately driven by the retail buying habits of American shoppers. In 1992, sales profits hit a record high of $1.9 billion, but by 1994, those profits had plunged 55 percent to $832 million. Lagging consumer confidence has been cited as the main reason for this trend. However, such factors as decreasing leisure time and increased bargain shopping have also contributed to the decline in retail sales. Consequently, the industry suffered from decreasing domestic demand through the mid-1990s.

Ratification of the North American Free Trade Agreement (NAFTA) has opened new markets, expanded sales, and increased production for the textile industry. Canada and Mexico are the two largest export markets for U.S. textile and apparel products. These markets, which currently support more than 80,000 export-related jobs in the United States, are growing rapidly. U.S. exports to Canada have grown an average of 19 percent per year since 1986, reaching $2.5 billion in 1994 and resulting in a trade surplus in the sector of $892 million. U.S. exports to Mexico have increased by 25 percent on average each year since 1986, reaching $2.3 billion in 1994. U.S. imports from Mexico exceeded sector exports by $7 million in 1994, largely reflecting the increased use of offshore production, where cut fabric parts are exported to Mexico for assembly into apparel, and then re-exported to the United States. NAFTA contains a "rule of origin" clause that will gradually enable Canada, Mexico, and the United States to waive duties and quotas on products made from raw materials that were produced in one of the three nations. Tariffs will be phased out in a maximum of ten years for products manufactured in North America that meet NAFTA rules of origin. In time, this will give U.S., Mexican, and Canadian manufacturers a competitive advantage over textile producers in other countries.

The dramatic political and economic changes in Europe and the former Soviet Union have also created new markets for textile machinery. However, while many machinery suppliers exist within Europe, their technology is inferior to that of the West and Japan. Consequently, textile producers in these European countries may look to U.S. manufacturers for assistance in modernizing their facilities.

With nearly half of its production exported, the U.S. textile machinery industry markets its equipment aggressively in many foreign markets. The major markets are China, Canada, Japan, Mexico, Germany, Thailand, and Italy. Shipments by the U.S. textile machinery industry are expected to grow at an annual real rate of about 3 percent through 1998. Growth will be spurred by the industry's ability to market its products competitively in expanding foreign markets.

RESEARCH AND TECHNOLOGY

Several companies are leading the industry in technical innovation. Muratech Textile Machinery, for example, has developed an automatic transportation system for synthetic fibers. This system is capable of fully automating every aspect of a synthetic textile plant, from package transportation to package inspection, reducing the need for extensive employment in those areas. By automating the inspection process, consistency in quality is assured and human error is eliminated. The company also developed an automatic transportation system for spun yarn, a full system which does everything from transporting bobbins to inspecting packages. These automation systems enhance quality and production control, improve working environments, and save labor.

Hollingsworth Saco Lowell Corporation has developed an automatic, state-of-the-art bale opening system. The Rotomix automatic bale opening system employs counter-rotating heads that blend the top, middle, and bottom of the bales to achieve a superior blend over other bale mixing equipment. The Rotomix can open three different bale sizes and boasts a maximum production speed of 1,500 kilograms per hour.

Another innovative company is Marshall & Williams (M&W), which reported sales of $33 million in 1996. In the early 1990s, M&W developed a better dye pen that operates in a vertical orientation. The pen offers the control and accuracy normally reserved for horizontally orientated pens, while achieving efficiency characteristic of vertically oriented pens. Heat-treated, powdered steel alloy components give the pen equipment durability and stability, and enable it to achieve a superior pen line. Additionally, the pen's close-return design features an offset for the return track and reduces nozzle-to-cloth distance. Another innovation developed by M&W is an internal incineration system. The system consists of small incinerators which are placed in several oven zones. Oven exhaust air is drawn into the incinerators, where it is heated to between 1,000 and 1,500 degrees Fahrenheit. That temperature is maintained until all volatile organic compounds in the exhaust have been destroyed; and finally, clean exhaust is passed through a heat exchanger before it is released from the oven. Demand for this system is expected to grow dramatically as manufacturers strive to meet increasingly strict regulations imposed by the Environmental Protection Agency.

FURTHER READING

Darnay, Arsen J., ed. *Manufacturing USA.* 5th ed. Detroit: Gale Research, 1996.

Dun's Business Rankings, 1996. Bethlehem, PA: Dun & Brandstreet, Inc., 1996.

Fallon, James. "Creditors Give Platt-Saco-Lowell Until May to Find a Buyer." *Daily News Record,* 22 April 1993.

"The Industry." American Textile Machinery Association, 1997. Available from http://www.webmasters.net/atma/.

International Trade Administration. *Executive Summary.* U.S. Department of Commerce, 1997. Available from http://www.ita.doc.gov.

"Marshall & Williams: Vertical Tinter System." *Textile World,* April 1993.

McAllister, Isaacs, III. "Combing Resurgence Rides New Technology Fast Track." *Textile World,* February 1992.

Pinto, Akiva. "Hollingsworth: Rotomix Automated Bale Opening System." *Textile World,* April 1993.

Standard & Poor's Industry Surveys. New York: Standard & Poor's Corporation, 1997.

"Steel Heddle: Carbon Fiber Harness Frames." *Textile World,* April 1992.

"Steel Heddle Uses High-Tech Motion Analysis." *Industrial Engineering,* June 1992.

Talavçsek, Oldrich, and Vladim'r Svaty. *Shuttleless Weaving Machines.* Amsterdam: Elsevier Scientific Publishing Company, 1981.

Witkin, Philip M. "Marshall & Williams: Internal Incineration for Finishing Ovens." *Textile World,* April 1992.

—Valerie Wilson, updated by Elizabeth Shugg

SIC 3553

WOODWORKING MACHINERY

This category includes establishments primarily engaged in manufacturing machinery for sawmills, for making particleboard and similar products, and for otherwise working or producing wood products. Establishments primarily engaged in manufacturing hand tools are classified in cutlery, handtools, and general hardware manufacturing industries, while those engaged in manufacturing portable power-driven hand tools are classified in **SIC 3546: Power-Driven Handtools.**

In 1995, according to the *1995 Annual Census of Manufactures,* this industry employed 9,800 workers, an increase of about 36 percent over the 7,200 workers reported in 1992. The figure was also about 10 percent above the 8,900 workers reported in the previous census of 1987. In 1995 the industry shipped goods to the value of about $1.48 billion, an increase of about 23 percent over the $1.2 billion reported in 1994. In 1992, Oregon, Tennessee, Mississippi and Indiana accounted for 39 percent of all workers employed in the industry. In 1987 North Carolina, Ohio, Oregon, and Tennessee were the leading states. Equipment made by the industry included machinery used in cutting, shaping, sanding, gluing, laminating and finishing wood products.

In the 1980s, the woodworking machinery industry was affected by a slowdown in the housing industry and a general recession in the U.S. economy. In the early 1990s, the industry was further affected by cutting limits imposed on the logging industry in the

Pacific Northwest. However, in 1992, George Delaney, then president of the Wood Machinery Manufacturers of America (WMMA), which represented more than 100 companies in the industry, said the number one issue facing the organization's membership was product-liability reform legislation. Woodworking machinery manufacturers often paid as much as 10 percent of their annual sales for liability insurance, a cost that foreign competitors did not face.

In the early 1990s, the woodworking machinery industry benefited from legislation that required woodworking companies to reduce the amount of dust in the air of their factories. Several companies in the industry increased their revenues by manufacturing dust-reduction equipment. Environmental concerns over logging also prompted production of new machinery. With stricter limits on logging, the forest products industry was buying updated equipment that reduced the amount of waste in manufacturing wood products.

The Coe Manufacturing Co., founded in 1852, was one of the first companies to manufacture computerized woodworking machinery, introducing a computer-controlled veneer lathe in 1977. The company operates manufacturing facilities in Tigard, Oregon, and Painesville, Ohio, where its headquarters are located. In 1992, Coe, a privately held company, employed approximately 760 workers and had revenues of $80 million. Most of Coe's woodworking machinery is sold to plywood manufacturers.

Founded in 1919, Delta International Machinery Corp. was the largest manufacturer of general purpose woodworking machinery and accessories in the United States. The company operates manufacturing facilities in Tupelo, Mississippi, and Limeira, Brazil, and has headquarters in Pittsburgh, Pennsylvania. In 1992, the company, a subsidiary of Pentair, Inc., employed approximately 1,000 workers and had revenues of $100 million.

U.S. Natural Resources, Inc., formed in 1928, has expanded its business by acquiring woodworking machinery manufacturers. By 1993 several companies had come under the company's aegis. The oldest company was Irvington Forest Industries, a saw manufacturer founded in 1907 and acquired by U.S. Natural Resources in 1969. Other companies included the Moore Dry Kiln Co., founded in 1910 and acquired in 1968; Schurman Machine Works, founded in 1934 and acquired in 1975; and Applied Theory Associates, a consulting firm founded in 1969 and acquired in 1982. Based in Vancouver, Washington, U.S. Natural Resources employed approximately 800 workers and had sales of $84 million in 1992.

FURTHER READING

1993 Buyer's Guide and Directory. Philadelphia: Wood Machinery Manufacturers of America, 1993.

"American Technology in Action." *Furniture Design & Manufacturing,* June 1992.

Anderson, Michael A. "Coe Helping the Wood Industry to Computerize." *Portland Business Journal,* 24 March 1986, 23.

"IWF '90 Packs 'em in: 32,000 People, 903 Exhibits." *Forest Industries,* October 1990, 7.

U.S. Bureau of the Census. *1995 Annual Survey of Manufactures.* Washington: GPO, 1997.

—Dean Moyer, updated by Kenneth R. Shepherd

SIC 3554

PAPER INDUSTRIES MACHINERY

This category covers establishments primarily engaged in manufacturing machinery used in the pulp, paper, and paper products industries. Establishments primarily engaged in manufacturing printing trades machinery are classified in **SIC 3555: Printing Trades Machinery and Equipment.**

INDUSTRY SNAPSHOT

The United States is the world's leading producer of paper-making machinery. In 1994, the industry had a shipment value of $2.8 billion and consisted of more than 300 companies with 17,400 employees. The U.S. Department of Commerce estimated that shipments peaked at $2.8 billion in 1990, after five years of steady growth, but subsequently declined by 7 percent during the global recession of the early 1990s. Shipments had returned to $2.8 billion by 1994, and were expected to reach $3.4 billion by 1998. Supply and demand drove paper costs up dramatically in mid-1994. This occurred because of the recession of the early 1990s, which resulted in the paper industry's worst financial slump since the Great Depression. One of the most capital-intensive manufacturing industries in the nation, the paper industry wasn't able to invest in new mills or upgrade existing mills during the demand shortage. But in 1994, paper demand shot up in the United States, Japan, and Europe as economies improved, and the industry did not have the capacity to match the demand. At this time, many mills were running at 98 percent capacity, so they were unable to slow production down enough to even oil their machinery.

Growth during the 1980s was the result of several factors, including a demand for de-inking systems and other equipment used in recycling newspapers, magazines, and corrugated containers. Despite lower shipments in 1992, strong demand for machinery capable of meeting environmental standards continued. In addition, economic reform in Eastern Europe and the former Soviet Union was expected to create an expanded overseas market for U.S. manufacturers of paper industries machinery. In fact, exports accounted for about 45 percent of all shipments of paper industries machinery in 1992. Ratification of the North American Free Trade Agreement (NAFTA) in 1993 has opened new markets, expanded sales, and increased production for the paper industry. NAFTA contains a ''rule of origin'' clause that will gradually enable Canada, Mexico, and the United States to waive duties and quotas on products made from raw materials that were produced in one of the three nations. Tariffs will be phased out in a maximum of ten years for products manufactured in North America that meet NAFTA rules of origin. In time, this will give U.S., Mexican, and Canadian manufacturers a competitive advantage over producers in other countries.

The growing free market in Eastern Europe also resulted in a 25 percent increase in the export of U.S. paper products in 1991, further increasing demand for new or rebuilt paper industry machinery at home. According to industry figures, parts for rebuilt machines accounted for as much as 70 percent of the paper-making machinery market. There also was a growing market for used machinery, particularly in the specialties paper industry.

BACKGROUND AND DEVELOPMENT

The first machines used for making paper were invented in France in the late eighteenth century. In 1799, Frenchman Nicholas Louis Robert received a patent on a machine that could produce a continuous roll of paper. Several years later, London stationers Henry and Sealy Fourdrinier financed improvements for Robert's paper-making machine, which eventually came to bear their name. Manufacturers began using the Fourdrinier machine for the commercial production of paper in England in 1812. Eventually, the Fourdrinier machine became the foundation of the paper-making industry.

The first Fourdrinier machine used in the United States was imported from England in 1827 and put into operation at a paper mill in Saugerties, New York. However, by 1829, an American company, Phelps & Spafford, began manufacturing Fourdrinier machines,

the first of which was installed at Norwich, Connecticut. Phelps & Spafford reorganized after the recession of 1837 as Smith and Winchester, and continued to operate into the twentieth century. Several other U.S. manufacturers of paper machinery were also founded prior to the Civil War, including the Merrill Machine Company and the Bakers Falls Iron Machine Works, both of which were still leading companies in 1993, although under different names.

Pulping. Until the mid-1800s, paper was made principally from rags rather than wood. Between 1840 and 1860, several mechanical processes were developed that produced wood pulp suitable for making rough-grained paper. One of these pulp grinders was known as the Jordan refiner. Invented in 1858 by two Americans, Joseph Jordan and Thomas Eustace, the Jordan refiner was the principal pulping machine until it was replaced in the early twentieth century by disk refiners. In 1867, American chemist Benjamin Tilghman found that pulp could also be produced by dissolving wood in a solution of sulfuric acid. A German chemist, Carl Dahl, perfected chemical pulping in the late 1880s. Mechanical pulping was extremely efficient, converting as much as 90 percent of the basic raw material into usable pulp. Although chemical pulping was considerably less efficient, the pulp generated by this process could be used to produce a higher grade of paper. Newsprint was generally a blend of about 25 percent mechanical pulp and 75 percent chemical pulp. Top quality stationery was still made from rag pulp. Many of the machines manufactured by the paper machinery industry during this period, such as barkers, chippers, and refiners, were used for the pulping processes.

INDUSTRY LEADERS

Harnischfeger Industries Inc. of Milwaukee, Wisconsin, lead the industry with $2.15 billion in sales and 14,300 employees in 1996. Founded in 1884, Harnischfeger Industries is an international holding company with business segments involved in the manufacture and distribution of equipment for papermaking (Beloit Corporation), surface mining (P&H Mining Equipment), underground mining (Joy Mining Machinery), and material handling (P&H Material Handling).

Wisconsin-based Beloit Corporation, acquired by Harnischfeger Industries in 1986, was the second-largest U.S. producer of machinery for the paper industry, with sales of $713 million in 1996. Founded in 1858 as the Merrill Machine Company, the company's name was changed in 1885 to the Beloit Iron Works. The

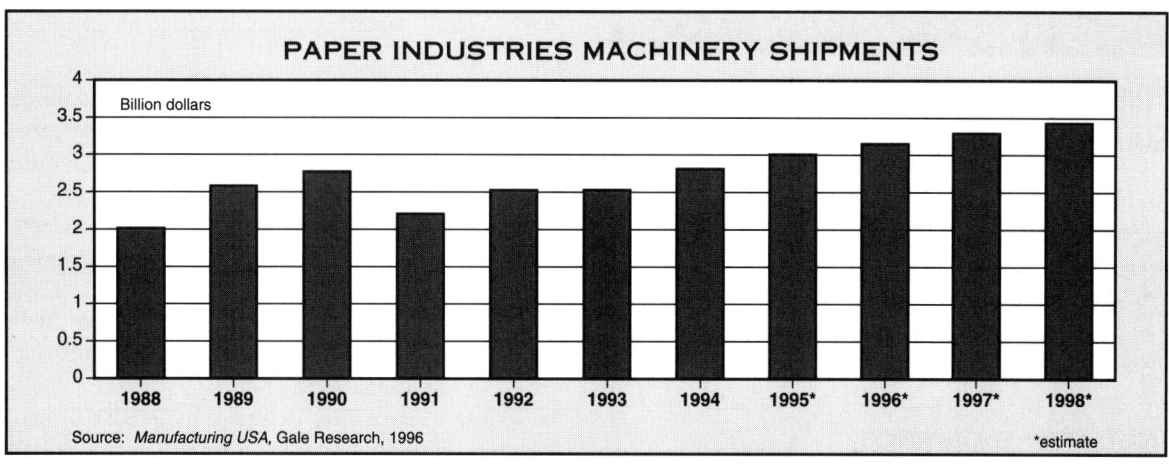

PAPER INDUSTRIES MACHINERY SHIPMENTS

Billion dollars

Source: *Manufacturing USA*, Gale Research, 1996   *estimate

company achieved some fame in 1893 when it built a paper-making machine that was displayed at the Chicago World's Fair. The name Beloit Corp. was adopted in 1961. In addition to its U.S. facilities, the company has manufacturing operations in the United Kingdom, Canada, Italy, and Brazil.

The third-largest producer of paper industry machinery in 1996 was Voith Sulzer Paper Technology North America Inc., founded in 1900. The Appleton, Wisconsin-based company produced $200 million in sales in 1996 and concentrates solely on producing paper industry machinery.

Other industry leaders in 1996 were EIMCO Process Equipment, with $200 million in sales; Black Clawson Company, with $190 million in sales; Paper Converting Machine Company, also with $190 million; and Enterprises International Inc., with $120 million in sales.

AMERICA AND THE WORLD

Historically, the United States has been a net exporter of paper industries machinery, with Canada, the United Kingdom, Mexico and Australia being its most important foreign markets. However, imports began growing in relation to exports during the 1970s, and in 1979 the balance tipped in favor of imports. Before the rise of imports, nearly 90 percent of all new paper-making machines installed in the United States came from U.S.-based manufacturers. By the early 1980s, however, 50 percent of the new machines came from foreign manufacturers.

Much of the imported machinery came from Germany, the leading exporter of paper industries machinery in the world. Finland, Sweden, Switzerland, and Japan have also sold significant amounts of paper-

making machinery in the U.S. market. There was a brief recovery in 1982, when exports exceeded imports by about $110 million. However, the downward trend returned in 1983, and by 1987 the industry's trade deficit had grown to almost $300 million. Exports began to improve in the late 1980s and early 1990s, with imports accounting for 25.8 percent of total shipments and exports comprising 19.7 percent. The Department of Commerce estimated that the U.S. industry would again be a net exporter by 1993.

FURTHER READING

Abrahams, Edward D. *A Competitive Assessment of the U.S. Paper Machinery Industry.* Washington: U.S. Department of Commerce, 1989.

Darnay, Arsen J., ed. *Manufacturing USA. 5th Ed. 1996.* Detroit: Gale Research, 1996.

Dun's Business Rankings, 1996. Bethlehem, PA: Dun & Brandstreet, Inc., 1996.

International Trade Administration. *Executive Summary,* U.S. Department of Commerce, 1997. Available from http://www.ita.doc.gov.

Pagano, Elizabeth "Paper Prices Pinch Printers, Publishers." *Nashville (Tennessee) Banner,* 29 January 1996.

Press. Falls Church, VA: American Paper Machinery Association, May 1993.

Special Industry Machinery, 1987 Census of Manufacturers. Washington: U.S. Department of Commerce, 1990.

Standard & Poor's Industry Surveys. New York: Standard & Poor's Corporation, 1997.

U.S. Industrial Outlook 1994. Washington: U.S. Department of Commerce, 1993.

—Dean Boyer, updated by Elizabeth Shugg

SIC 3555

PRINTING TRADES MACHINERY AND EQUIPMENT

This category covers establishments primarily engaged in manufacturing machinery and equipment used by the printing and bookbinding trades, including printing presses, bookbinding machines, typesetting and photoengraving equipment, and a variety of specialized tools for the printing trades.

INDUSTRY SNAPSHOT

There were approximately 450 companies involved in making machinery for the printing trades industry in the mid-1990s. In 1995, these manufacturers shipped slightly more than $3 billion worth of equipment, an increase of 36 percent since 1992. The number of establishments increased from 430 in 1990 to approximately 525 in the mid-1990s.

BACKGROUND AND DEVELOPMENT

Letterpress printing, using raised images to print on paper, was an ancient art developed by the Babylonians as early as 2000 B.C. for producing playing cards. However, the first printing presses were derived from machines used to press grapes and cheese and were not invented until the early fifteenth century, more than 3,000 years later. The modern printing industry was generally considered to date from the mid-fifteenth century with the invention of moveable type by a German printer, Johannes Gutenberg. The Gutenberg press used a flat wooden plate, or platen, to press a single sheet of soft paper against a form containing letters cast in metal from clay molds.

The printing press changed very little over the next 400 years. When Stephen Daye established the first publishing house in the American Colonies in 1639, his English-made press was not significantly different from Gutenberg's. Christopher Sauer, Jr. of Cambridge, Massachusetts, also followed the Gutenberg model when he manufactured the first press built in the American Colonies in 1750. However, printing machinery technology began to change radically in the early 1800s, with many of the advancements developed by American manufacturers. Among the most important U.S. contributions to printing machinery were the development of the Columbian press, the rotary press, the Linotype machine, and the offset press. The United States was the leading manufacturer of printing presses from the mid-1800s until after World War II, when Germany began to challenge the U.S. dominance.

Columbian Press. In 1813, George Clymer, a printer in Philadelphia, replaced the cumbersome screw mechanism of the Gutenberg press with a much faster system of levers that allowed press operators to achieve sufficient pressure for printing. The elaborate system had a long handle known in the printing trades as "the devil's tail." Clymer's Columbian Press was cast from iron and was noted for its intricate metal work that included dolphins, flowers, and an intimidating American eagle perched on top. However, due to the Western expansion of the United States, many American printers preferred lighter wooden presses that could be transported more easily. Clymer moved to England in 1817 where Clymer & Company manufactured presses until 1851.

Rotary Press. The rotary press was an American adaptation of the cylinder press. Friedrich Koenig, a German clockmaker who emigrated to England, developed the first practical cylinder press about 1811. Koenig replaced the flat platen with a cylinder that allowed press operators to maintain a uniform pressure as the type bed was moved horizontally. The first Koenig press, which could print about 1,100 sheets per hour, was installed at *The Times of London* in 1816. Koenig later returned to Germany where he established the first printing press factory. The Koenig press, however, cost about 10 times as much as other presses and never became popular.

Richard March Hoe, a New York City manufacturer, built the first cylinder press in the United States in 1830. Hoe also realized that the greatest limitation to Koenig's press was the time it took to move the massive type bed back and forth. In 1846, R. Hoe & Company developed the first rotary press. Instead of using a flat type bed, Hoe mounted type around the outside of a huge cylinder. This cylinder was surrounded by four smaller platen cylinders. Instead of the back and forth motion of the Koenig press, the Hoe type cylinder revolved in a continuous motion. Each of the four hand-fed platen cylinders could print about 2,000 sheets per hour. This gave the Hoe rotary press a capacity of 8,000 copies per hour. The speed was later increased to 20,000 sheets. The first Hoe rotary press was installed at *The Philadelphia Public Ledger*. Hoe & Co. continued to manufacture presses and other printing machinery until 1968, when it declared bankruptcy.

William Bullock, a Philadelphia printer, perfected the first rotary press able to print on both sides of the paper. In 1880, he also developed the first high-speed press to print from a continuous roll of paper. The Goss

Printing Company, founded in Chicago in 1885, was the first company to combine multiple high-speed rotary presses into a single machine that could print entire newspapers in one press run. In 1889, Goss installed a set of six presses for *The New York Herald* that could print 72,000 newspapers per hour.

Typesetting. For 400 years after Gutenberg invented moveable type, printers composed lines of type by hand, one letter at a time. When the printing was completed, the letters were returned to a type case. It was a tedious process, and one that resisted all attempts at mechanization. *American History Illustrated* once called it "the century's most perplexing invention problem." By one account, more than 200 inventors attempted to solve the enormous engineering problem posed by typesetting. Most ended up frustrated, and many went bankrupt. Mark Twain lost most of his fortune backing the Paige Compositor, which turned out to be an impractical failure. An examiner in the U.S. Patent Office reportedly went insane trying to cope with the technical complexity of the many patents filed on mechanical typesetters in the late 1880s.

In 1884, Ottmar Mergenthaler, an immigrant German clockmaker working for a scientific instruments company in Baltimore, invented a machine he named the Linotype. The Linotype allowed an operator sitting at a keyboard to compose lines of type from brass molds, or matrices. Separate lines of type were then cast in metal and slid into galleys for printing. The brass matrices returned to their original position until they were needed again. After printing, the type was melted down and the metal could be reused.

The Linotype, which Thomas Edison called "the eighth wonder of the world," solved several critical problems. First, because the brass matrices were immediately reusable, there was no need for a large precast supply of type. Since every line of type was newly cast from an alloy of lead, tin and antimony, printers always received a quality impression. The Linotype also justified each line of type automatically by sliding wedge-shaped pieces of metal between each word. The first 12 Linotypes were installed at *The New York Tribune* in 1886. Within ten years, there were Linotypes in use throughout the United States and Europe.

The Monotype, a machine similar to the Linotype, was invented in 1887 by an American, Tolbert Lanston. The Monotype cast individual letters from brass matrices and was especially popular with book publishers because it could cast special symbols or non-Latin alphabets. Additionally, corrections could be made by changing a single letter rather than an entire line of type.

The first photo typesetting machines were patented about 1880, but did not become practical until after World War II when the graphic arts industry began to grow. Linotype and Monotype typesetters were used almost universally by commercial printers until photo typesetting machines began to replace them in the 1970s. By the mid-1980s, most major newspapers had switched from "hot lead" to "cold type."

In 1992, *The New York Times* printed a story about "The Last Yiddish Linotype in America." Linotype machine No. 23,211 was one of nine made for the *Jewish Daily Forward* in New York in 1918. Outfitted with Hebrew letters and converted to compose type right to left, this machine was in operation until 1991, when the 3,000 pound machine, and a host of other equipment, was replaced by a single desktop computer.

Other American developments in printing machinery included offset printing. This process is often attributed to an American printer named Ira Rubel. Offset lithography had been used since the 1880s to print labels directly on tin containers. In 1905, Rubel was operating a rotary press when he unintentionally transferred an image onto the rubber impression cylinders. When he then fed paper through the press he noticed that the images left by the rubber cylinders were much sharper than the direct image left by the raised type. For many years, offset printing was used for high-quality work. In the 1970s, offset presses also began to replace letter presses for such high-speed printing needs such as for newspapers.

Leading members of the printing equipment industry banded together in 1910 to form the Printing Press Manufacturers Association (PPMA), whose stated purpose was to convince Congress to pass laws protecting the industry from foreign imports. President Franklin Roosevelt's National Recovery Administration was created by the National Industrial Recovery Act of 1933 to help pull the country out of the Great Depression by enforcing codes of fair competition for business and industry, including minimum wages and standard work weeks. The printing equipment industry estimated that manufacturers sold more than $100 million worth of printing equipment in 1928, a year before the stock market crash that plunged the economy into depression. By 1933, sales had dropped to about $18 million and employment had been cut in half, from 18,000 to 9,000. In addition to establishing a code of fair competition for the industry, the manufacturers also hoped to control the market for used equipment. More than 100 commercial printing plants failed between 1929 and 1933, flooding the market with used equipment.

In 1933, the National Printing Equipment Association was founded. An industry code proposed by the NPEA was accepted by the National Recovery Administration in 1934, but in 1935, a unanimous U.S. Supreme Court ruled that the National Industrial Recovery Act was unconstitutional. Although the NPEA code of fair competition was invalidated, the organization voted to continue as a source of information and education for the printing equipment industry.

The name of NPEA was changed to the National Printing Equipment and Supply Association in 1978, and changed again in 1991 to the Association for Suppliers of Printing and Publishing Technologies (NPES). In 1996, NPES had more than 300 members, which included computer manufacturers and software companies, as well as traditional printing machinery manufacturers. NPES conducts market research and promotes international trade on behalf of its members.

New York World Fair. In 1939, more than 100,000 people visited a display of printing machinery technology at the New York World Fair, including the original Stephen Daye Press, then owned by the Vermont Historical Society. More than 200 companies participated in the exhibition, which covered 50,000 square feet in the Grand Central Palace. Mayor Fiorello LaGuardia declared the last week in September to be "Printing Industry Week," and the U.S. Post Office issued a 3-cent stamp commemorating the 300th anniversary of printing in the United States.

World War II. Rationing of critical supplies such as steel and rubber nearly shut down the printing machinery industry during World War II. However, many manufacturers compensated by accepting government contracts to build weapons. As early as 1939, even before the United States entered the war, the Goss Printing Company turned down a major contract with the *St. Louis Post Dispatch* because the newspaper was unwilling to accept a clause that would excuse Goss if the war prevented it from fulfilling the contract. However, Goss did negotiate a contract with the U.S. Navy to build gun mounts, sighting mechanisms, and other weapons machinery.

After the United States entered the war, the War Production Board (WPB) halted the manufacture of all printing equipment for civilian use. By July 1942, nearly the entire industry had been converted to the production of war material. Industry leaders, including Goss, R. Hoe & Company, and the ATF-Webendorfer Company, were building recoil mechanisms for anti-aircraft guns. Mergenthaler Linotype Company was making fire control instruments, F.P. Rosback Company was making parts for anti-aircraft guns and wing tips for P-38 airplanes, and the Miehle Printing Press & Manufacturing Company was making shell casing and naval ordnance.

Eventually, the WPB allocated some material to manufacture spare parts for printing equipment, but between 1943 and 1945 the printing machinery industry nearly quadrupled its pre-war output—and more than 80 percent was for the war effort. The WPB later reported, "No other segment of the metal-working industry showed a higher degree of conversion to war work." According to the Board, 22 printing machinery manufacturers were awarded the Army-Navy "E" for production excellence, including every manufacturer of printing presses.

Xerography. After World War II, the printing machinery industry began to face increased competition from foreign manufacturers, especially German companies that received favorable trade agreements as part of the European rebuilding effort. The industry also began to change with the rapid development of photo typesetting and photocomposition. However, a process of transferring images invented in the 1938 by Chester F. Carlson may ultimately prove to have an even greater impact on the printing machinery industry. Carlson, a patent attorney in New York with a degree in physics, called his process "electrophotography." The Battelle Memorial Institute, a nonprofit research organization, and the Haloid Co., a producer of photo supplies founded in 1906, later renamed the process "xerography." In 1961, Haloid became the Xerox Corporation. Xerography began replacing job presses for many printing functions in the 1970s.

The printing machinery industry began undergoing tremendous change in the 1970s as computer technology replaced or significantly changed the type of machinery used by the printing trades. This included developments in photo typesetting and photocomposition, and greater automation of traditional printing press operations.

With the development of photo typesetting, photocomposition, and non-impact printing, the printing trades were evolving from a craft to a high-technology industry. Consequently, the printing machinery industry evolved as well. In the early 1990s, there was still a need for the massive presses that dominated the industry and the equipment necessary to run them. However, just as Linotypes gave way to computer typesetters, industry leaders were predicting that non-impact printing would someday replace the huge presses. In 1992, AM International Inc., a Chicago-based manufacturer of printing machinery, unveiled the Electrobook Press, a non-impact press based on electrostatic imaging. The Electrobook Press was developed jointly by AM International, publisher McGraw-Hill,

Inc., and commercial printer R.R. Donnelly & Sons. McGraw-Hill expected to use the new press to publish customized textbooks for university professors.

INDUSTRY LEADERS

Leading companies in the printing trades machinery industry include Rockwell International, Volt Information Sciences Inc., and A.B. Dick. Rockwell's revenues in 1995 were $11 billion, Volt's 1996 sales were over $1 billion, and A.B. Dick's 1995 revenues were over $380 million. Other major players in the industry include Baldwin Technology Company, MAN Roland Inc., and Bobst Group Inc.

WORK FORCE

Employment in the printing machinery industry remained at about 22,000 in 1995, which was about the same as in 1990. Within that time period, there were significant fluctuations, the greatest between 1990 and 1991, when the figure decreased by 23 percent from 24,000 to about 19,000. In 1995, slightly more than 50 percent of all employees in the industry were production workers, about the same as in 1990. Production workers' average hourly earnings have increased from about $14 in 1990 to $15 in 1995.

FURTHER READING

"An Idea Looking for a Company." *Appliance Manufacturer,* November 1988.

Angrist, Stanley W. "The Last Yiddish Linotype." *The Wall Street Journal,* 5 March 1992, A12.

Arnold, Edmund. *Ink on Paper.* New York: Harper & Row, 1963.

Gustaitis, Joseph. "Ottmar Mergenthaler's Wonderful Machine." *American History Illustrated,* June 1986, 28.

Marketing Handbook for Printing & Publishing Technologies. Reston, VA: NPES: The Association for Suppliers of Printing and Publishing Technologies, 1993.

Moran, James. *Printing Presses: History and Development from the Fifteenth Century to Modern Times.* Berkeley: University of California Press, 1973.

Oswald, John Clyde. *Printing in the Americas.* Port Washington, NY: Kennikat Press, Inc., 1937.

Reilly, Patrick M. "Digital Press Is Introduced By Three Firms." *The Wall Street Journal,* 14 April 1992, B6.

U.S. Census Bureau. *1995 Annual Survey of Manufactures.* Washington: GPO, 1997.

U.S. Department of Labor. Bureau of Labor Statistics. *Employment, Hours, and Earnings, United States, 1988-96.* Washington: GPO, 1996.

SIC 3556

FOOD PRODUCTS MACHINERY

This industry covers establishments primarily engaged in manufacturing machinery for use by the food products and beverage manufacturing industries and similar machinery for use in manufacturing animal foods. Establishments primarily engaged in manufacturing food packaging machinery are classified in **SIC 3565: Packaging Machinery;** those manufacturing industrial refrigeration machinery are classified in **SIC 3585: Air-Conditioning and Warm Air Heating Equipment and Commercial and Industrial Refrigeration Equipment.**

INDUSTRY SNAPSHOT

In 1993, 516 establishments were engaged in the U.S. food processing machinery industry, employing nearly 18,000 people and shipping nearly $2.2 billion of equipment that year. Approximately $741 million of manufactured machinery was exported to over 150 foreign markets in 1993. Domestically, nearly 20,000 food processing plants shipped $321 billion of processed food in 1988 and $345 billion in 1989. In 1996, the food industry marked sales of over $165 billion and employed over 1.6 million workers. U.S. citizens spent 16.7 percent of their disposable personal income on food in 1995, up from 9.1 percent in 1980. The machinery industry as a whole is stable and growing in certain segments. The presence of foreign made machinery, however, has been increasing since the early 1990s.

The food products machinery industry and the processed food industry enjoy a very strong relationship. This is illustrated by the presence of engineering departments within large food processing corporations. For their own specialized applications, many of which may be considered proprietary, patents may be obtained. Often, the level of this cooperation depends on the sophistication of the processing operations and the equipment required to carry out those steps.

ORGANIZATION AND STRUCTURE

Food products machinery and packaging equipment were included in the same industrial code until 1987, and much of the literature and data from the 1970s and 1980s combines the two industries into one category. The 1987 classification split the two types of businesses into separate categories, recognizing that the industries were serving divergent business niches.

According to a United Nations report, the industrial production of food processing machinery in North America was characterized by the following features: (1) a still large, but declining, part of manufacturing takes place in small and medium sized independent firms; (2) production is usually based on orders received; (3) the markets for many types of machines are restricted; (4) equipment production is heterogeneous; (5) production series are relatively small; (6) concentration similar to that in food industries is taking place; and (7) internationalization is accelerating. In the United States, over 500 establishments shipped processing equipment, which had an estimated total value of $2.8 billion in 1996. The smaller, specialized equipment manufacturers produced nearly 80 percent of all food processing equipment in the United States, while the 12 largest companies in the industry supplied the remaining 20 percent.

CURRENT CONDITIONS

The trend for Americans to eat healthier has had a direct impact on this industry. For example, demand for lower fat meats such as poultry and seafood increased, while annual per capita beef consumption dropped significantly. Likewise, changing demographics radically changed the entire food industry. The most significant demographic change that affected the food industry in the early 1980s was the increasing number of women in the work force. Double income families have driven consumer demand for foods that can be prepared quickly and easily. However, U.S. Department of Commerce studies show that the number of women joining the work force showed a moderate decline in the early 1990s. As a result, sales of at-home food products improved.

Indications of an improving economy in the 1990s provided optimistic news for the food and beverage industry in general. Even during the recession of the late 1980s and early 1990s, the food industries did not suffer heavy losses. Price stability—a direct impact of the recession on the cost side of the industry—provided constant prices for consumers and steady wages for employees. The wage increases across the food industry were comparable to inflation, at about 5 percent. As long as food stocks such as agricultural commodities and meat production remain strong, the entire food industry is expected to remain healthy.

In developed countries, demographic trends determine the focus of the food industry. According to a UN report, longer lives, earlier marriages, more divorces, and fewer children are giving rise to new population patterns, where more one- and two-person households are establishing new consumer patterns, such as eating out more often. A new structure in age distribution—more people in the over 60 group—leads to new demand patterns, as the requirements from aged people differ from those of the younger. For example elderly people eat smaller portions but need a higher concentration of essential proteins and vitamins in those portions. Market forecasters are keenly aware of this trend as Baby Boomers reach middle age and have altered consumption patterns.

The increasing number of women in the work force is perhaps the most important of the demographic trends affecting the industry, as women have been the traditional food preparers in the family unit. Working women have less time to fix meals for their families and consequently purchase food that requires little preparation. The effects of this trend can be seen especially in meat processing, where secondary operations are employed in response to consumer eating habits. Both the processing and packaging industries have been influenced by the trend because meats in the fresh chilled form, already marinated, skinned, and sectioned, are growing in availability. There is also an increasing variety of frozen foods available.

Technological home innovations, such as microwave ovens, have also led to new consumption patterns. These differences were directly influencing the development and design of food processing equipment, especially where secondary operations may be employed.

INDUSTRY LEADERS

The top 75 companies in the industry reported combined sales of $5.4 billion and employed 53,900 people. In 1996, the highest concentration of shipments originated from Illinois' 47 food processing machinery establishments. Illinois' shipments, valued at $290.5 million, represented 12.1 percent of the nation's total shipments. Ohio's 31 establishments shipped $253.8 million worth of equipment, claiming 10.5 percent of the nation's total shipments. California, which has 77 establishments engaged in this industry, claimed an 8 percent share of the market with $191.5 million in shipments.

In 1995, Premark International Inc., located in Deerfield, Illinois, was an industry leader with estimated sales of $1.2 billion and a work force approximately 9,000. PMI Food Equipment Group, located in Troy, Ohio, ranked second with sales of $990 million and a work force of 9,200 in the mid-1990s. One of the top companies in the nation was APV Consolidated Incorporated, located in Chicago, Illinois, with estimated sales of $330 million in food products machinery and a work force of 3,100 in the mid-1990s.

Another industry leader was FMC Corporation, located in Chicago. In 1996, sales totaled about $5 billion, with machinery contributing about one-quarter of the year's total revenue. FMC employs approximately 22,000 throughout all of its divisions.

Premark International, Inc. is a relatively new company; it was created in 1986 after the failed Dart & Kraft merger. Kraft, feeling its earnings were stifled by the Dart interests, returned alone to its primary concern, food products. The Dart companies formed Premark, which consisted of Tupperware products, Ralph Wilson Plastics, and West Bend. Premark also obtained Hobart, which was acquired by the Dart & Kraft group. The Tupperware operation lost $57.9 million for Premark in its first year and continued to lose money until 1994, when demand for Tupperware in Europe and Latin America increased. In 1992, Premark announced it would close the Tennessee factory that makes Tupperware products, and in 1996, as part of an extensive reengineering plan, Premark sold its Tupperware division.

The Hobart line was the core of Premark's food equipment group. Hobart was acquired by Dart & Kraft in 1981 after a hostile takeover attempt by Canadian Pacific Enterprises failed. Canadian Pacific offered a reported $300 million for Hobart's operations, but Hobart, preferring independence, declined. Congressmen supported Hobart and appealed to U.S. Treasury Secretary Donald Regan to prohibit the takeover on grounds of breaching national security. Hobart finally sold out to Dart & Kraft for $460 million, having realized it probably did not have the strength to battle future takeover attempts alone. In 1996, the Hobart line of products generated $960 million in sales, accounting for 80 percent of Premark's total sales.

Americans' changing lifestyles and eating habits boosted Premark's food equipment sales. Fast food menus began changing in the mid-1980s and required new equipment—such as catalytic chicken fryers and grooved griddles for fajitas. Take-home foods, such as bakery products from grocery stores, were more readily available for consumers as 2,500 in-store bakeries were built in 1987. These bakeries generally cost $130,000 to equip with the necessary machinery, although some cost as much as $300,000. International lifestyles and eating habits were changing too, as the English started eating more pizza, and the Japanese started eating more hamburgers. Improved sales of these foods helped the food equipment group to contribute $57.8 million to Premark's profits.

Since 1985, the United Kingdom branches of APV have been involved in joint venture agreements with Bulgaria and Hungary. In Bulgaria, industry ef-

forts include engineering and consulting in biotechnology, refrigeration, air conditioning, and food processing. In Hungary, the manufacture of food processing machinery and equipment is of primary concern to the venture. Food production equipment is a main priority in the former U.S.S.R., as much of the present equipment is old and in need of replacement. Equipment used where sanitation is critical—such as dairy and meat processing machinery—is receiving the greatest emphasis.

WORK FORCE

Productivity in the food products machinery industry, as measured by output per production worker, increased somewhat between 1989 and 1994. The average value added per production worker rose from $112,901 in 1989 to $131,725 in 1994. Productivity has grown annually since 1981, largely owing to the increased automation of plants and equipment. The industry has been quick to adopt new technology, especially computer technology, to improve efficiency and create new product lines, and the capital to labor ratio has risen significantly since 1989.

While the industry's stock of machinery and equipment has grown in the late 1980s and early 1990s, the number of production worker man-hours has decreased steadily. Increased competition from imports has been a motivating force, as has consumer demand for a broader range of food products. Industry shipments increased by about 18 percent—from $2.63 million in 1992 to $2.84 million in 1996. The average hourly wage for an employee in this industry was $13.39 in 1995.

As previously mentioned, the employment outlook for the industry is expected to decrease going into the twenty-first century. Significant staff reductions of greater than 17 percent are expected in occupations such as machine builders, assemblers, secretaries, precision inspectors, welding machine setters, and machine assemblers. Increases of greater than 10 percent are expected for sales workers, production managers, machinery mechanics, engineering and science managers, and electrical and electronics engineers.

AMERICA AND THE WORLD

According to a UN report, the relatively low U.S. dollar value spurred competitiveness in this industry during the 1980s and helped many U.S. manufacturers increase market share. Throughout the world, the U.S. share of food product machinery peaked in 1981 and 1982 at about 19.7 percent, declining steadily through 1986. Germany has lost market share since 1978, when it claimed the largest share of the world market at 28.9 percent. Many food product machinery companies have begun to focus on international markets, and some have established production facilities abroad. While Austria, Italy, Japan, and the Netherlands have reported great increases in their market shares, they now face increasing competition from some of the newly industrialized countries—notably Mexico, Brazil, and Taiwan.

In 1995, 34 percent of the food product machinery manufactured in the United States was exported, with a value of $7.91 million. Maintenance parts for machinery constituted nearly 20 percent of exports. The greatest U.S. export customers for food processing machinery in 1993 were Canada and Mexico, which grossed sales at approximately $253 million. Other major export markets were the United Kingdom, Central America, Chile, and Colombia.

In contrast, U.S. importing activity has grown steadily. The U.S. was the largest importer of food products machinery, spending $481 million. The Germans and Italians had been dominant suppliers throughout the 1990s, while additional machinery was imported from the Netherlands, Canada, Switzerland, Denmark, and France. Food product machinery imported in 1995 amounted to $612 million—a 23 percent increase over the 1994 figure.

The U.N. report also stated the largest food processing machinery import categories in value terms for 1988 were: wrapping and packaging machinery ($213 million), bakery machinery ($56 million), chocolate and confectionery machinery ($41 million), and meat processing equipment ($28 million). All these import categories registered strong growth between 1980 and 1986. In 1993, the categories changed slightly as bakery and pasta machinery, confectionary machinery, and meat and poultry processing equipment were among the largest imports.

As many more countries started establishing industrialized economies, the subsequent standard of living advancements are expected to create a demand for more nutritional, sterile, and convenient foods. The United Nations' Economic Commission for Europe reports that the world's most populous countries—China, Russia, and India—are starting to improve their processing, preserving, and distribution systems to produce better quality foods. The recent reforms in Russia will dramatically increase the level of funding for new food processing technology and equipment. Russia's government and food industry will look increasingly to the West for much needed new technology. In the early 1990s, the United States was in an excellent position to exert its influence in this industry,

as the standards placed on domestically produced machinery were attractive to foreign purchasers.

FURTHER READING

Bohman, Jim. "Hobart Corp: Oakwood Resident to Head U.S. Group." *Dayton Daily News,* 20 August 1996.

"Capital Investment After the Squeeze." *Prepared Foods,* November, 1994.

Darnay, Arsen J., ed. *Manufacturing USA.* 5th ed. Detroit: Gale Research, 1996.

Dempsey, Dale. "Business: PMI to Cut 301 Workers at Troy Plant." *Dayton Daily News,* 12 June 1996.

"Do Your Homework on Mexico." *Food Engineering,* November 1993.

Hast, Adele, ed. *International Directory of Company Histories.* Volume III. Chicago: St. James Press, 1988.

"Premark International Inc." *Chicago Tribune,* 2 June 1996.

"Premark Will Take Charge to Shut Plant for Tupperware Line." *Wall Street Journal,* 12 October 1992.

Shea, Kenneth. *Industry Surveys.* New York: Standard & Poor's Corporation, 6 August 1992.

United Nations. Economic Commission for Europe. *Food-Processing Machinery.* New York: United Nations, 1991.

U.S. Department of Congress. *U.S. Industrial Outlook 1994.* Washington: GPO, 1994.

—Valerie Wilson, updated by Kris Barnett

SIC 3559

SPECIAL INDUSTRY MACHINERY, NOT ELSEWHERE CLASSIFIED

This classification covers establishments primarily engaged in manufacturing special industry machinery, not elsewhere classified, such as equipment for smelting and refining, cement making, clay working, cotton ginning, glass making, incandescent lamp making, leather working, paint making, printed circuit boards, semiconductors, rubber working, cigar and cigarette making, tobacco working, shoe making, stone working machinery, industrial sewing machines, and automotive maintenance machinery and equipment.

INDUSTRY SNAPSHOT

As of the mid-1990s, the special industry machinery, not elsewhere classified industry was comprised of companies that manufactured a wide variety of miscellaneous machines used to produce goods in other industries. Numerous product offerings ranged from broom making contraptions to zipper makers, although semiconductor manufacturing equipment accounted for the largest portion of the classification's output.

In 1992, this industry had employment of 81,900, 2 percent below the 1987 level. The total value of shipments for establishments classified in this industry was $10.5 billion in 1992, up from $7.9 billion in 1987. Industry shipments were expected to reach $14.8 billion by 1995 and $17.3 billion by 1998, though those figures could be much higher. The leading states in industry employment in 1992 were California, Ohio, Michigan and Massachusetts, accounting for about 39 percent of total employment. The total cost of materials, services, fuels and energy used by establishments classified in SIC 3559 was $5.1 billion in 1992.

The number and production volume of machines classified in this industry increased substantially during the industrial revolution, and particularly after World War II. By the early 1980s, about $5 billion in annual U.S. machinery sales were attributed to SIC 3559. Although overall U.S. industrial machinery sales growth slowed during the 1980s, a surging demand for high-tech semiconductor manufacturing equipment doubled industry revenues to about $10 billion in 1989.

While a U.S. recession in the late 1980s and early 1990s depressed many industrial machinery segments, semiconductor machine sales continued to grow. Renewed U.S. competitiveness in high-tech equipment manufacturing allowed domestic competitors to thwart their Japanese rivals. In addition, increased semiconductor demand from industries such as telecommunications augmented growth. Output was expected to expand throughout the mid- to late 1990s, though the cyclical nature of the industry was expected to drive output down in 1997.

Despite being affected by business cycles in the chip making industry, the long-term prospects for semiconductor equipment manufacturing appeared strong. In the mid-to late 1990s, there were several powerful trends behind the growing demand for silicon wafer fabrication systems. A global increase in PC sales drove increased demand for semiconductors of all kinds, plus new chips being produced required more memory. For example, Intel's Pentium chip required at least 16 megabytes of memory, almost double that of 486-based PCs. Also, the rapid growth of telecommunications and the use of electronics in automobiles increased semiconductor sales.

ORGANIZATION AND STRUCTURE

The special industry machinery industry encompassed a plethora of devices as of the mid-1990s, including: tire retreading machinery, stone tumblers, tile making equipment, automotive frame straighteners, lumber drying kilns, cork cutters, brick makers, shoe repair equipment, leather-working devices, and plastic molding machines.

Semiconductor manufacturing equipment was the leading segment in this industry, and saw spectacular growth in the 1990s. For example, in 1987, shipments from this segment were valued at just $1.01 billion, but by 1992 had more than doubled to $2.27 billion, or 21.6 percent of the total industry's output, according to the *Census of Manufactures* by the U.S. Department of Commerce. By 1995, that total had ballooned even more, reaching $6.8 billion, or 38 percent of the industry's output.

The next largest industry category in 1995 was plastics working machinery and equipment, at $2.3 billion (13 percent), followed by chemical manufacturing machinery and equipment, at $1.06 billion (5.9 percent); printed circuit board manufacturing machinery, at $856 million (4.8 percent); automotive maintenance equipment, at $630 million (3.5 percent); foundry machinery and equipment, at $531 million (3 percent) and rubber working machinery and equipment, at $371 million (2.1 percent). Over 28 percent of this industry shipments in 1995, valued at $5.1 billion, were classified in an "all other" category. This category included petroleum refining machinery, glass making machinery and footwear manufacturing machinery, among many other categories.

Semiconductor equipment was expected to remain the largest and fastest growing sector of the industry throughout mid to late 1990s. As of the mid-1990s, semiconductor production involved a sequence of more than 200 steps using numerous machines. Although the manufacturing process varied depending on the type of chip produced, four basic functions were typically performed to complete a semiconductor wafer, or circuit: 1) deposition of thin film on the (usually silicon) wafer; 2) impurity doping, when selected impurities were introduced that controlled conductivity; 3) lithographic patterning, which determined the geometric features and layout of the circuit; and 4) etching, which removed coating material to reveal the structure patterned in the lithographic process. These steps were repeated sequentially until the semiconductor wafer was complete. After the semiconductor was created using "front-end" fabrication equipment, "back-end" machines were used to test and assemble the chips. Back-end devices included three categories of machines: material handling, process diagnostics and testing, and assembly.

Semiconductor Equipment Markets. According the *1992 Census of Manufactures,* the equipment market for semiconductor manufacturing equipments was divided into four categories: wafer processing equipment; assembly and packaging equipment; parts for semiconductor manufacturing equipment; and all other equipment.

In the wafer manufacturing category, the leading product categories included thin layer deposition equipment, which accounted for $601 million in product shipments in 1992; etch and strip equipment ($306 million); microlithography (figures not available); ion implantation (figures not available); and other wafer processing equipment ($309 million).

The second-largest segment, plastics working machinery and equipment, was divided into several categories, including compression molding machinery; extrusion machines; injection molding machines; blow molding machines; granulators and pelletizers; thermoforming machines; calendaring or other rolling machines; machinery for cold working plastics; and parts for all of the above.

In 1994, injection molding accounted for 62 percent of the value of shipments in plastics working machinery, followed by blow molding at 12.5 percent; extrusion at 11.5 percent; and thermoforming at 4.1 percent, according to *Plastics News.* Other machinery accounted for the remaining 10.3 percent.

The third-largest segment, chemical manufacturing equipment, was divided into several categories, including distilling, rectifying or fractionating equipment; heat exchange units; dryers; gas or air liquefying units; mixing machines; and parts for all the above.

BACKGROUND AND DEVELOPMENT

The history of miscellaneous special industry machinery varied by product group. One of the earliest and most renowned machines in this industry was the cotton gin, which Eli Whitney invented in 1793. The gin removed seed from cotton by pulling the fiber through a set of wire teeth mounted on a revolving cylinder. Because the device could be powered by man, animal, or water, it received immediate and widespread acceptance and made cotton a staple of nineteenth century southern life.

The development and widespread dissemination of electric power during the late nineteenth and early twentieth centuries resulted in the introduction of a multitude of machinery for miscellaneous industries. Likewise, postwar U.S. economic expansion propelled

product introductions and sales throughout the mid-1900s. A pivotal breakthrough was Bell Laboratories' introduction in 1947 of the solid-state transistor, which utilized semiconductors. By the 1960s a market for semiconductor manufacturing equipment began to emerge.

Spurred by important chip advances such as Intel Corporation's 1971 introduction of the memory integrated circuit, U.S. producers took the early lead in producing semiconductor manufacturing equipment. The mass production of chips allowed by these high-tech machines resulted in dramatic semiconductor price reductions. As a result, the demand for chips surged as semiconductors were integrated into all types of electronic consumer and business devices. Importantly, the use of semiconductors in personal computers caused chip manufacturing equipment sales to balloon during much of the 1980s.

The 1980s. Although domestic manufacturers took the early lead, Japanese semiconductor machinery makers successfully captured much of the global market during the 1980s. The Japanese particularly excelled at delivering equipment for high-volume commodity chips. To combat Japanese strengths, U.S. semiconductor producers restructured, increased their manufacturing efficiency, and concentrated on developing new technologies during the mid-1980s. As the U.S. chip industry made a transition from commodity to proprietary chip production, it ceded a 45 percent share of the global semiconductor equipment market to Japanese producers.

Despite a loss of market share, chip machinery makers increased sales substantially during the 1980s. However, most other special industry machinery producers suffered. Capital spending on new equipment by other industries declined or grew at a slow pace in comparison to pre-1980 expenditures. Spending on new equipment by the transportation industry stagnated, for example, as did equipment purchases by the important petroleum and coal sector. Nevertheless, growth of semiconductor equipment demand helped double industry revenues to more than $10 billion by 1990.

CURRENT CONDITIONS

Strategies adopted by U.S. semiconductor manufacturers in the 1980s began to pay off in the early 1990s. Aided by a weak dollar and a recession in Japan, U.S. producers boosted revenues to $5.8 billion in 1991. Although sales dropped 3 percent in 1992, shipments climbed an impressive 18 percent in 1993 to about $6 billion. Assisted by a technological lead in growing product segments and newfound productivity,

U.S. manufacturers were able to recover a 4 percent share of the global market from Japan. In 1993 they held 51 percent, compared to 41 percent controlled by Japan.

Also boosting U.S. semiconductor equipment competitiveness was the development of Sematech, a joint private sector/government funded research and development consortium. Sematech was formed in 1987 to combat increasingly competitive Japanese semiconductor producers. In addition, industry participants on both sides of the Pacific benefitted from technology exchanges and partnerships with foreign and domestic competitors. Indeed, U.S. firms learned from the Japanese that traditional methods of developing and producing manufacturing technology in isolation from competitors were no longer feasible. While government funding for Sematech was reduced sharply in the mid-1990s, the organization restructured, increased dues, and remained a viable organization.

Front-end equipment sales led industry growth going into the mid-1990s. Most importantly, shipments of deposition equipment rose 17 percent in 1993. U.S. producers held the lead in deposition technology, and benefitted from a proliferating trend toward smaller, more integrated chips that required more complex deposition. A shift toward the production of high-profit, application-specific, integrated circuits (ASIC) also boosted sales of U.S. front-end manufacturing devices. In contrast, sales of lithographic machinery, of which the U.S. supplied only a 16 percent global share in 1993, plummeted in the early 1990s.

Back-end equipment sales also rose at a steady clip. Global shipments of test equipment gained 14 percent in 1993, and sales of material handling and diagnostic machines increased about 13 percent. Production of assembly devices, of which the U.S. made 30 percent globally, jumped 15 percent.

The market for semiconductors has traditionally been very cyclical, and as a result the market for semiconductor equipment is cyclical as well. For example, in 1994 and 1995, semiconductor equipment firms enjoyed a booming market. A study conducted by VLSI Research on the ten largest global semiconductor equipment suppliers showed that they sold $14.2 billion of equipment in 1995, a 74.4 increase over their net sales for 1994. Applied Materials was the largest supplier, with $3 billion in sales, followed by Tokyo Electron, the largest Japanese supplier, with just under $3 billion. Nikon, another Japanese company, was third, with $1.8 billion in sales. Six other companies topped the $1 billion annual sales mark.

However, in 1996 this strong growth rate slowed to 12 percent and semiconductor manufacturing equipment suppliers such as Applied Materials Inc., Lam Research Corp. and Varian Associates Inc. cut back on production and laid off workers. Conditions were expected to worsen in 1997. Elizabeth Schumann, senior market analyst for Semiconductor Equipment and Materials International in Mountain View, California, predicted that the industry's revenue would decrease 15 to 20 percent in 1997. However, growth rates of 15 percent or more were expected to return in 1998 and 1999.

Despite these predictions, other industry observers were predicting a quick upturn in semiconductor manufacturing machinery orders in 1997. The expectation was that chipmakers would have to re-tool so their manufacturing lines could make chips with a 0.25 micron line width, compared to the existing standard of 0.5 to 0.35 microns. However, according to a January 1997 industry report by PaineWebber, many semiconductor manufacturers were able to bypass expensive new equipment by adapting their processes to the 0.25 micron standard through "adding deep-UV steppers, high-density CVD and CMP equipment to existing lines to do the critical layers." Intel, the world's leading chip manufacturer, expected to have a higher equipment re-use rate during this conversion, compared to past technology shifts.

Some industry observers were also predicting an upsurge in sales of semiconductor manufacturing equipment during 1997 due to a major change in the manufacturing process for dynamic random access memory (DRAM) chips. As manufacturers moved to produce higher memory chips (for example, from 16MB DRAM to 64 MB DRAM), it was expected that they would change from using 200 mm wafers to 300 mm wafers. This would create the need for a major retooling of manufacturing capacity. However, the PaineWebber report cautioned that complete 300 mm production lines would not likely be available until well into 1998, which would not help the semiconductor manufacturing equipment industry's performance in 1997.

Markets for other kinds of equipment in this industry were down in 1996. For example, total shipments of domestically produced plastic injection molding machinery decreased by about 15 percent in 1996 after strong growth in 1995. Capital investment in equipment was expected to decline throughout all of 1996 due to the decline in injection molding resin sales.

INDUSTRY LEADERS

Over 2,000 companies participated in the special industry machinery industry in the early 1990s. Semiconductor equipment manufacturers dominated the top spots. Applied Materials was the clear leader in the semiconductor equipment manufacturing industry and has been called ''the Microsoft of the semiconductor chip industry.'' Applied Materials' sales grew from $567 million in 1990 to $1.7 billion in 1994. Its 1995 revenues reached $3 billion, nearly double that of 1994. The firm's success was said to be due to the surging demand for semiconductor chips in the international marketplace, and to its ability to exploit this global market expansion through the introduction of new product lines and entry into new foreign markets.

Other than Applied Materials, leading semiconductor equipment manufacturing firms in the mid-1990s included Lam Research Corp.; Advantest Corp.; Teradyne Inc.; and Varian Associates Inc. Their leading Japanese competitors included Tokyo Electron Ltd.; Nikon Inc.; Canon Inc. Hitachi Ltd.; and Dainippon Screen Manufacturing Company Ltd.

In addition to the major semiconductor equipment manufacturing companies, several major firms participated in this industry as of 1996, though they sold many products outside of this industry as well. These firms included: Cooper Industries Inc., Houston,, with revenues of $4.8 billion; Air Products and Chemicals Inc., Allentown, Pa., ($4 billion); Dover Corp., New York ($3.7 billion); Western Atlas Inc., Beverly Hills, California ($2.2 billion); BTR Inc., Stamford, Conn. ($1.7 billion); and Cincinnati Milacron Inc., Cincinnati, Ohio ($1.6 billion).

WORK FORCE

Despite expectations of healthy growth in production, employment in the special industry machinery business was expected to remain relatively static in the 1990s. This continued an earlier trend. When this industry's production more than doubled in the 1980s, the work force grew by only about 10 percent, and in the 1990s the work force grew hardly at all while the value of shipments continued to rise. Continued restructuring and the movement of some manufacturing activities to low-cost countries were expected to prevent increases in U.S. employment.

Total employment was expected to remain stable throughout the 1990s. For example total employment was 85,400 in 1990, and was expected to be 85,800 in 1998. Industry wages were about 20 percent above the U.S. manufacturing industry average as of the mid-1990s.

AMERICA AND THE WORLD

In 1995, about a third of all special industry machinery shipments were exported. These shipments were valued at $5.3 billion, a 57 percent increase over 1994. At the same time, imports were valued at $3.4 billion, a 30 percent increase over 1994.

U.S. semiconductor machinery producers were very active in the export market in the 1990s and increased their share of the global market from 35 percent in 1991 to 42 percent in 1992 and 51 percent in 1993. Japan supplied 41 percent of worldwide equipment demand in 1993, while Europe controlled about 8 percent of the market. Those percentages remained essentially the same in the mid-1990s. According to the Semiconductor Equipment & Materials Institute (SEMI), the trade association for equipment makers, U.S. equipment makers held a 50 percent share of total world sales in 1995, followed by Japanese suppliers with a 44 percent share, and European companies with 6 percent.

The United States, which purchased 37 percent of global production in 1993, was also the biggest consumer of chip making machinery. Japan consumed 33 percent of worldwide output, down from 43 percent in 1990. European and Southeast Asian countries comprised most of the remainder of the market.

U.S. producers exported 40 percent of their chip machinery in 1993. They shipped $756 million, or about 33 percent, of their exports to Japan, a 15 percent increase over 1992. South Korea and Taiwan, the second- and third-largest importers of U.S. chip machinery, bought about $295 million worth of goods. Total exports to Asia (excluding Japan) climbed 13 percent in 1993, and exports to Europe swelled in response to decreasingly competitive producers on that continent. The U.S. imported only 20 percent of its semiconductor equipment, most of which came from Japan.

With the exception of lithography equipment, U.S. producers held a technological and market lead in front-end machinery. They also led in the production of testing equipment, though Japan was stronger in assembly and material handling markets. Going into the mid-1990s, the United States was positioned to take advantage of the fastest growing and most technologically advanced equipment segments. However, Japan was expected to again emerge as the world's largest semiconductor equipment consumer following its recession.

In the long run, partnerships between Japanese and U.S. equipment firms were expected to blur national distinctions. Demand for semiconductor manufacturing equipment in emerging markets should provide strong growth for producers in both countries. Purchases of equipment in China, for example, swelled 140 percent in 1993.

There are significant overseas markets in this category outside semiconductor equipment manufacturing as well. For example, Brazil's plastics machinery industry was said to be growing in 1997 with new joint ventures forming to serve the 6,000 Brazilian processing companies. As of 1997, injection molding was the major plastics processing technique used in Brazil.

RESEARCH AND TECHNOLOGY

Semiconductor equipment manufacturers were heavily dependent upon research and technology to sustain competitiveness. Applied Materials, for example, injected about 10 percent of its total revenues into capital investments in the early 1990s. For comparison, the average capital investment for all U.S. manufacturers was closer to 4 percent of gross sales. In contrast, capital spending by other firms in the special industry machinery industry were much lower than even the national average.

U.S. semiconductor machinery makers invested heavily in productivity, quality, customer service programs, and new plants and equipment during the 1980s and early to mid-1990s. Most importantly, though, research and development outlays allowed them to sharpen their competitive edge in the development of high-tech, value-added machinery. They especially advanced in the fast-growing market for chemical and physical vapor deposition equipment, which was expected to lead industry growth throughout the mid-1990s. They also stretched their lead in automatic test equipment technology.

In the latter half of the 1990s, development efforts were expected to emphasize, among other technologies, machinery for advanced multichip modules, which mounted multiple integrated circuits on one unit. The Advanced Research Projects Agency (ARPA), a high-tech consortium, already provided funding for this research in the early 1990s. Equipment for manufacturing liquid crystal displays (LCDs) should also be a priority. LCDs were used for flat-panel displays on portable computers, and were manufactured using a process similar to that used to make chips. The U.S. Display Consortium, which included ARPA and several equipment and display providers, was formed in 1993 to further LCD manufacturing technology.

While its government funding was reduced dramatically in the mid-1990s, Sematach continued to be an important force for research and development in the semiconductor equipment manufacturing industry in the late 1990s. In response to the cuts in government funding, Sematach members raised their dues and cut back on staffing to keep the group viable. Dues at Sematech were expected to go up by 30 percent for the 10 members in the semiconductor trade organization. The increase was expected to take effect in January 1998 and would bring the group's total revenue to $120 million per year from $92 million in 1996.

William Spencer, the chairman of Sematech as of January 1997, said that the members of the consortium had a 400 percent return on investment in 1995. Sematech continued to be involved in key chipmaking standards in the mid- to late-1990s. In 1996, it awarded a contract to a consortium to complete an electronic design automation (EDA) standard. This EDA standard, if widely accepted, would help solve sub-0.25-micron fabrication difficulties for semiconductor manufacturers.

While American semiconductor manufacturing equipment companies were planning to continue investing in vital R&D projects, so were their Japanese rivals. Japan's government and semiconductor manufacturers planned to spend between $500 million and $1 billion from 1996 to 2001 on consortiums and cooperative research programs. This investment was seen as an attempt to counter the influence of Sematech, develop advanced technology and improve the competitiveness of Japan's semiconductor industry in the growing South Korean and American markets.

FURTHER READING

Banks, Howard. "Made in the U.S.A." *Forbes,* 11 September 1995, 37.

Barrett, Larry. "Reversal of Fortunes Not Likely Anytime Soon for Chip Makers." *The Business Journal,* 30 December 1996, 16.

Darnay, Arsen J., ed. *Manufacturing USA.* 5th ed. Detroit: Gale Research, 1996.

"Equipment Makers Chase Mercosur Outlets." *Chemical Week,* 12 March 1997, S14.

Morris, Kathleen. "The Alpha Principle: No Guts, No Glory. That's How Applied Materials Plays the Game. Take Notes." *Financial World,* 21 November 1995, 30.

Jareaux, Robin. "Winning through cooperation: An Interview with William Spencer." *Technology Review,* January 1997, 22.

Pollack, Andrew. "Japan Aims to Regain Semiconductor Leadership." *New York Times,* 18 November 1996, C1.

Semiconductor Capital Equipment Industry Report. New York: PaineWebber Inc., 21 January 1997.

''Sematech Dues Will Grow 30%.'' *Electronic News,* 29 July 1996, 1.

''Vlsi Research's Top 10 at Peak Level.'' *Electronic News,* 4 March 1996, 24.

Wood, Bill. ''Machinery Demand Will Shrink in 1996.'' *Plastics World,* December 1995, 73.

                                        —Dave Mote, updated by Alan K. Rooks

SIC 3561

PUMPS AND PUMPING EQUIPMENT

This category covers firms primarily engaged in manufacturing pumps and related equipment for general industrial, commercial or household use, including domestic water and sump pump manufacturers. It does not cover manufacturers of fluid power pumps or motors (**SIC 3594: Fluid Power Pumps & Motors**); manufacturers of measuring and dispensing pumps for gasoline service stations (**SIC 3586: Measuring and Dispensing Pumps**); non-laboratory-use vacuum pumps (**SIC 3563: Air and Gas Compressors**); laboratory vacuum pumps (**SIC 3821: Laboratory Apparatus and Furniture**); or motor vehicle pumps (**SIC 3714: Motor Vehicle Parts and Accessories**).

INDUSTRY SNAPSHOT

Pumps are one of the most common machines used by industry, second only to electric motors. As such the health of the pump manufacturing industry depends to a great extent on the general health of industrial America. Particularly important are the petrochemical and the pulp and paper industries, but steel making, electric power generation, oil and gas wells, fields and pipelines, sewage system construction, and general housing and commercial construction also depend on a variety of special purpose pumps.

Such pumps, which can be abrasive by nature themselves, often wear quickly because they frequently move materials contaminated with abrasives in challenging climatic and environmental conditions. This requires frequent replacement or repair, making the replacement parts segment of the industry particularly important. The U.S. pump industry is considered mature, with the bulk of growth tied to replacement purchases in the late 1990s and beyond.

ORGANIZATION AND STRUCTURE

Some 613 establishments manufactured pumps and pump equipment in 1977, an increase of 10 percent over the 1972 census figures. However, this number dropped to 528 by 1987 and an administrative redistribution of SIC codes left the industry with only 405 establishments at the end of 1987. The other 123 establishments were reclassified into **SIC 3594: Fluid Power Pumps and Motors.** An estimated 470 establishments existed by 1996, however, employing approximately 36,600 workers.

At nearly 50 percent of output, industrial pumps constituted the largest product class in the business. Replacement parts and accessories generated the next-largest share of sales, at about 25 percent, followed by domestic water systems and sump pump (12 percent) and oil and oil-field pumps (3 percent). Other miscellaneous pumps made up the remaining 10 percent.

Historically, manufacturing in this industry has been heavily concentrated; in 1977 more than half the industry's employees worked in the four largest facilities, and 79 percent of all facilities employed fewer than 100 workers. By 1987 this had changed slightly with 75 percent of all facilities employing fewer than 100, but diffusion was more evident in the larger firms. The 1987 Census showed the largest 41 firms employing 52.6 percent of all workers.

BACKGROUND AND DEVELOPMENT

The world's first pump was probably the force or air pump built by Ktesibios of Alexandria about 270 B.C. He used a cylinder and plunger arrangement to pump air through pipes of various lengths, creating the first water organ. The water was used to maintain a steady air pressure in the system. Simple pumps became common fairly quickly for domestic use and as fire extinguishers. Roman ruins yield examples of pumps used for fire control and for lifting water in wells. The famed Roman aqueducts were probably not fed with pumps, but rather used water wheels to lift water from reservoirs directly to the piping system.

A major advancement in pumping technology came in 1698 with the issuing of a British patent to Thomas Savery for a steam powered pump for use in coal mines. The device was later adapted to provide water to some country houses. This pump was effectively replaced by the Newcomen engine, patented in 1712, which placed the steam boilers and piston assembly at the top of the mine shaft instead of at the bottom. The concept introduced the now familiar working or balance beam to transfer power to the pump mechanism in the mine.

The industrial revolution found many uses for the now-powered pump, including industrial processing and domestic distribution of water. However, the twentieth century introduced a new refinement, electrification. The first American factory to replace its central steam plant and its maze-like system of pulleys and belts with electric motors was a cotton mill in 1894. All new factories used the new technology.

Economic and technological expansion in the 1960s stimulated pump production and encouraged the adoption of new manufacturing techniques. The industry adopted specially designed milling machines and combination machines that could perform milling, radial drilling and facing (smoothing) in one operation. Automatic tool changing devices, operated by numerical control tape programs, increased production efficiency.

In general the pump industry manufactures large specialty items to meet a client's specific needs. To accommodate such a need for flexibility, the industry quickly adopted numerically controlled machine tools and computer numerical controls. This shifted the center of production control to the firm's engineering department and away from the craftsmen on the shop floor. Computer assisted drafting and modeling programs have further increased design efficiency.

The general industrial slowdown of the 1980s hit the pump industry hard. Major clients like the nuclear power industry, the oil well and pipeline industry, and the construction industry, cut back on orders for new equipment and idled existing components. A strong U.S. dollar made American products uncompetitive in foreign markets.

By 1988, this began to change. A weakening dollar increased exports and a general pickup in the manufacturing climate sparked new domestic orders in almost all sectors. The industry continued to modernize production by consolidating facilities and adopting sophisticated CAD/CAM systems and metalworking and casting technologies. New materials and designs were explored to extend the life of components in corrosive environments and to increase reliability.

The most important markets served by the pump industry have been the steel, oil, construction, and chemical industries.

Steel mills and blast furnaces used industrial pumps to move liquid fuels and water for coolant. The move in the steel industry away from open-hearth furnaces to oxygen and electric furnaces and to continuous casting instead of slabbing mills necessitated larger, more powerful pumps to provide higher volumes of coolant water. This meant the development of higher-output centrifugal pumps.

The oil-well and pipeline industries took another big chunk of output. Demand in this sector dropped off dramatically in the 1960s but recovered after that. This industry bought reciprocal pumps for mud circulation, submersible centrifugal units for lifting crude oil and standard centrifugal pumps to maintain pressure with water-flooding. Pipelines require high-horsepower centrifugal pumps. In the 1960s the average pipeline diameter was enlarged by 33 percent, requiring much larger pumps to move the higher volumes of petroleum products.

The construction industry used centrifugal pumps and trash pumps, which could accommodate up to 25 percent small solids in the pumped liquid. New sewage plant construction to accommodate increasingly stringent environmental regulations was expected to increase the demand for pumps. In the 1990s, infrastructure replacement and upgrading was expected to do the same.

Another important user of pumps was the chemical industry. Pumps for this market used special materials like fiberglass, plastics, and stainless steel to accommodate salt solutions, acids, and chlorine.

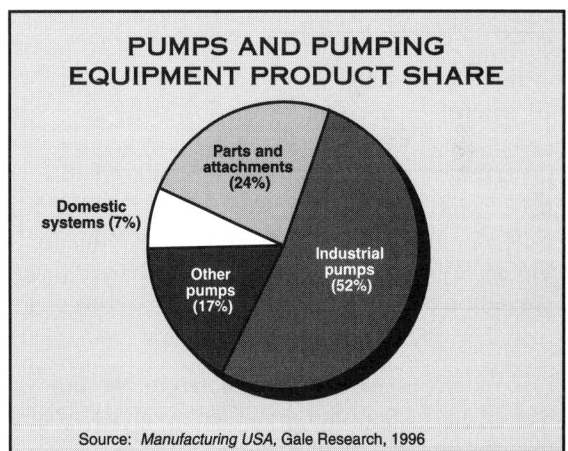

PUMPS AND PUMPING EQUIPMENT PRODUCT SHARE

Parts and attachments (24%)
Domestic systems (7%)
Other pumps (17%)
Industrial pumps (52%)

Source: *Manufacturing USA*, Gale Research, 1996

CURRENT CONDITIONS

The U.S. Census Bureau's *Current Industrial Reports* reported 1996 industry revenues at $7.2 billion on unit sales of 20.2 million. Some analysts projected growth of more than 5 percent per year for the U.S. pump industry in the last five years of the twentieth century.

INDUSTRY LEADERS

Dallas-based Dresser Industries Inc. led the pump industry in the mid-1990s with over $1 billion in sales of pumps and compressors. Founded in Pennsylvania during that state's late nineteenth century oil boom, Dresser has long catered to the oil and gas industries. This diversified company's revenues totaled $6.6 billion in 1996, and its multinational workforce neared 20,000.

Having celebrated its 150th anniversary in 1994, Goulds Pumps Inc. of Seneca Falls, New York was almost exclusively concerned with pump manufacture. In 1995, its 4,900 employees manufactured $718.8 million worth of pumps and accessories for the industrial, agricultural, and consumer markets.

Other leading firms included BWIP International Inc. of Long Beach, California, with $451.2 million in overall sales in 1995; Commercial Intertech Corp. of Youngstown, Ohio, with an estimated $294.3 million in pump sales ($465.2 million overall); and the highly-diversified General Signal Corp., with about $666.5 million in pump revenues ($1.9 billion total).

WORK FORCE

The *Monthly Labor Review* noted that the general industrial machinery group generally used a high proportion of skilled trades, about 30 percent of all production workers compared to the 26 percent proportion in all manufacturing. Pump production made up about 29 percent of all labor in the industrial machinery group. Metal working craftsmen and machinists were three times more common in this industry than in manufacturing as a whole while laborers were half as common. Average hourly wages were estimated at $15.34 in 1996. The industry also employed a high proportion of non-production workers, perhaps indicative of its reliance on mechanical engineers.

The *Industry-Occupation Matrix,* of the U.S. Bureau of Labor Statistics, projected decreases of more than 20 percent in several occupational categories through the year 2005. These included: machine operators, machine forming operators, and inspectors. Sales representatives, assemblers, secretaries, and machine tool cutters, among others, were projected to experience double digit decreases. The report forecast 20-plus percent increases for machine builders, mechanical engineers, combination machine tool operators, and engineering, mathematical, and science managers. Total employment in the industry grew approximately 16 percent from 35,200 in 1987 to an estimated 40,900 in 1996.

AMERICA AND THE WORLD

Pumps and pumping equipment were manufactured to international standards allowing American manufacturers to compete effectively in the international market. These same standards, however, also made the United States vulnerable to foreign competition, particularly on price and quality. During the early half of the 1980s, the strong American dollar made such competition particularly difficult, undermining an already weak industrial climate in American manufacturing. As a result, the U.S. merchandise trade deficit quadrupled between 1982 and 1984, reaching $145 billion. This effect showed up in the pump manufacturing industry, but was delayed. In 1985 the industry showed a trade surplus, but by 1987 it had become a $1.9 billion deficit. The drop of the value of the U.S. dollar, which began in March of 1985, provided new impetus for the pump industry. By 1987, the average export price expressed in foreign currency of pumps and other machinery had fallen 23.1 percent. By 1990, even though domestic prices increased an average of 5 percent each year, the foreign currency price of pumps and components had dropped more than 11 percent. This made American operations more profitable, increased export volumes, and discouraged imports. It also encouraged foreign firms to establish manufacturing and assembly facilities in the United States.

By 1990, exports approached $1.1 billion while imports exceeded $.7 billion. By mid-decade, *Purchasing* magazine estimated foreign purchases at 45 percent of overall demand. This share was expected to decline as companies set up overseas manufacturing operations. Major markets for American products included Canada, Mexico, the United Kingdom, Saudi Arabia, West Germany, Venezuela, and Japan. The top importers included Japan, West Germany, Canada, and the United Kingdom. Emerging markets included Latin America, Africa, the Mideast, and Asia, especially China.

Goulds Pumps was particularly focused on international sales. By 1995, 45 percent of its revenues were generated overseas, with 29 percent of its total sales coming from Europe. The company expected most of its future growth to be concentrated in the Asia-Pacific region.

China appeared an especially appealing target. In 1985, Portland, Oregon-based Bingham-Willamette sold the country six pumps valued at $600,000 and expected to increase that to 200 pumps per year, but the business dwindled within two years. Goulds, in 1988, signed a joint-venture agreement with Nanjing Deep Well Company to produce 600 pump units for four petrochemical plants, a deal worth several million dollars at each plant.

The industrialization of developing nations around the world was expected to fuel global pump industry growth of 8 percent per year in the late 1990s.

RESEARCH AND TECHNOLOGY

The majority of pumps manufactured are custom made to a client's specific requirements for use in complex applications where the failure of the pump could be disastrous. Consequently, manufacturing innovation has stressed flexibility and reliability. Major innovations included the adoption of numerical and computer control manufacturing systems and the reliance on engineering expertise, assisted by computer modeling software, to custom design components for short run production. New corrosion resistant materials have been developed and refinements to old processes adopted. Specially designed metal-forming machines were created for the industry, including combination milling, radial drilling and facing machines, variable setting grinders which automatically form tapered shafts, and automatic tool changing devices controlled by NC tapes or computer software. Foundry operations for production of pump casings and core-making have advanced with rapid-cycle machinery, synchronous fabricating machinery, and a no-bake molding process using a resin binder and catalyst. Closer tolerances were achieved in components by replacing wooden molds and cores with ceramic.

Demands for higher-efficiency pumps meant an industry shift from fixed displacement pumps to variable displacement because they do not waste energy by venting excess pumped material through a relief valve. A variable displacement pump adjusts its own flow rate to match demand.

Ongoing research concerns include: noise and leakage reduction, increased efficiency, corrosion-resistance, and development of oil-free and self-lubricating models.

FURTHER READING

1987 Census of Manufacturers. Washington: U.S. Department of Commerce, 1987.

Darnay, Arsen J., ed. *Manufacturing USA: Industry Analyses, Statistics, and Leading Companies,* Detroit: Gale Research, 1996.

"Dollar's Fall Boosts U.S. Machinery Exports, 1985-90." *Monthly Labor Review,* July 1991.

"Easy Maintenance Pumps Up Demand." *Purchasing,* 8 September 1994, 34A27.

"Expert System Lets Users Configure Pumps on a PC." *Machine Design,* 12 October 1989.

"Goulds Sees Opportunity Abroad." *Democrat and Chronicle Rochester,* 2 May 1996, B8.

Margus, Edward. "Nonmetallic Pumps for Corrosive/Erosive Services." *Plant Engineering,* 22 October 1992.

"Productivity in the Pump and Compressor Industry." *Monthly Labor Review,* December, 1982.

"Recovery, New Projects Spur Pump Growth." *Purchasing,* 1 June 1995, S28.

Renner, Kevin. "Bingham Shifts Tactics; Will Close Plant." *Business Journal,* 24 March 1986.

Segelken, Jane Baker. "Seeing Red Puts This Company in the Black." *Central New York Business Journal,* February 1988.

U.S. Industrial Outlook 1990. Washington: U.S. Department of Commerce, 1990.

Villaume, John M. "Sale of Six Pumps to China Buoys Bingham-Willamette." *Business Journal,* 24 June 1988.

Ward's Business Directory. Detroit: Gale Research, 1997.

—Al Cook, updated by April Dougal Gasbarre

SIC 3562

BALL AND ROLLER BEARINGS

This industry covers establishments primarily engaged in manufacturing ball and roller bearings (including ball or roller bearing pillow block, flange, takeup cartridge, and hangar units) and parts. Establishments primarily engaged in manufacturing plain bearings are classified in **SIC 3568: Mechanical Power Transmission Equipment, Not Elsewhere Classified.**

INDUSTRY SNAPSHOT

The ball and roller bearing industry is very large, but mature. It touches everything from space shuttles to household appliances, automobiles, dentist drills, roller skates, and computer disk drives. In the mid-1990s this industry was worth about $6 billion and employed more than 36,000 workers.

Issues facing the bearing industry are complex. As a secondary steel product manufacturing industry, it is in the middle of the production chain. However, policies favoring the steel industry may not be in the best interest of the bearing industry, and vice versa. Because bearings are essential components of military and civilian machinery and equipment, the federal government has historically been a major customer of the industry. However, high labor and production costs have caused the bearing industry to lose business to foreign competitors who have been able to sell bearings of equal quality at lower prices.

ORGANIZATION AND STRUCTURE

The ball and roller bearing business is unusual because it is strictly a component manufacturing industry. The industry accommodates its markets by selling loose or packaged bearings; packaged bearings are installed in races that allow manufacturers to interchange complete bearing components. The industry has continued to evolve by developing new materials and lubricants and researching alternative uses for bearings. Bearings have been found to have almost limitless applications and are expected to be in demand as long as machines are manufactured.

Ball bearings are spherical in shape, while roller bearings are cylindrical and may be tapered on one end or flattened to resemble needles. Generally, a ball bearing is used when speed is important; a roller bearing is used more often when load is most important. The manufacture of antifriction bearings starts from rod or wire. In a typical production process, pieces of wire are cut off in a press, placed between dies, and pressed into the shape of a ball or roller. Large rollers are produced by machining turning processes. The fin of surplus material that forms in the pressing process is removed between rotating file discs, and the diameter of the bearings is reduced through grinding and tumbling processes. Roundness specifications and surface finish improvements are also attained during grinding and tumbling. The bearings are then hardened, tempered, and given a high polish by further tumbling with a polishing agent. Finally, the elements are graded according to diameter.

Ball and roller bearings are used in anything that slides, glides, or rolls and in some cases are as large as 15 meters in diameter. Two general classes of bearings exist: commodity and precision. Commodity bearings are used in rotating elements that have relatively low revolutions per minute and do not face extreme stresses. Precision bearings, on the other hand, are highly accurate in terms of material quality, consistency of finish and diameter, and repeatability of tolerance levels. These bearings go through rigorous tests that check internal structure for failure tendencies and measure diameters to within one-millionth of an inch. Because the bearing industry has achieved such high product standards, it is widely respected for its ability to ensure an extraordinarily high level of quality control.

Product share within the industry is split into six categories. In 1992, unmounted ball bearings accounted for 38 percent of the product share, while unmounted tapered roller bearings accounted for 23 percent. Roller bearings that were neither mounted nor tapered accounted for 19 percent of the product share. Mounted bearings held 9 percent and parts for ball and roller bearings held 10 percent of the product share. Nonspecific ball and roller bearings accounted for the remaining 1 percent.

The materials consumed by the industry primarily include alloy steel mill shapes. However, cold steel and iron forgings are also widely used in the bearing industry. Other materials and devices used by the industry include raw and composite ceramics, electric motors, machine cutting tools, grinding wheels, powdered metals, copper wire, stainless steel sheets, carbon steel bars, and iron, steel, and copper scrap.

Manufacturers of motor vehicle and related parts consume approximately 31 percent of the roller bearings and 38 percent of the ball bearings produced by the industry. General industry and machinery consume nearly 10 percent of the industry's roller bearings and just over 9 percent of its ball bearings. Construction and farm machinery together consume 17.2 percent of the industry's roller bearings and 16.1 percent of its ball bearings. The mining, oil drilling, and metalworking industries are also heavy consumers of antifriction bearings. Additionally, bearings of various types and sizes are widely used in refrigeration and heating equipment, motors and generators, aircraft and related parts, and railroad equipment.

Antifriction bearings offer several advantages to machine designers. The friction placed on the bearings due to loads exerted is much lower than for other types of bearings. It is the lack of bearing friction that prevents excessive wear and abrasions on machines that start and stop while loads are applied. Automobile parts are examples of elements that benefit from less friction and wear. Roller bearings, in particular, are easily lubricated, can carry heavy loads relative to their size, and remain accurately aligned over extended periods of use. For these reasons, the huge market for antifriction bearings is stable and nearly recession proof.

BACKGROUND AND DEVELOPMENT

Since the invention of the wheel, the theory of bearing movement has been understood as a powerful phenomenon. The transfer of power to a rolling element has allowed societies to develop increasingly sophisticated structures and innovative machinery. As engines became more advanced and technology and production techniques improved, bearing manufacturing itself became a high-precision trade. Because virtually anything that rolls or spins uses bearings, the performance of the moving part is directly related to the bearing component. As such sophisticated machinery as military and commercial aircraft and nuclear-powered submarines have demanded increasingly high levels of precision and performance, bearing technology has evolved as a science and industry of its own.

In the mid-1980s, bearing manufacturers were subjected to a marketing tactic known as dumping. Dumping is a strategy that involves selling products in foreign countries at prices lower than the cost of manufacture in the parent country. The strategy is designed to allow a manufacturer to gain market share in a foreign country by providing a product at a price that is too low for competitors to match. Eventually competitors will be forced out of business, and the foreign competitor can command much higher prices because the competition has died.

Between 1968 and 1986, market share of imported bearings in the United States rose from 30 percent to 64 percent. After experiencing significant market share losses, Timken Company and the Anti-Friction Bearing Manufacturers Association (AFBMA, now known as the American Bearing Manufacturers Association) petitioned the Department of Commerce to conduct an investigation of import practices in 1987. The Trade Expansion Act of 1962 makes provisions for such investigations if the industry has been eroded to the point that it cannot compete internationally and if the nation's security is at risk. Until this appeal in 1987, only two other appeals had met with any success. The first case was related to the oil industry during the Kennedy administration and the second involved negotiating voluntary restraint concessions for the U.S. machine tools industry in 1986.

Because bearings are used in missile guidance systems, aircraft engines, tanks, and machine guns, dependence on foreign suppliers could leave this military equipment vulnerable to sabotage. Moreover, because U.S. equipment manufacturers do not have control over foreign companies' schedules they could be limited in their response to a surge in production and mobilization demands during wartime.

While many accused the bearing industry of being bad sports, the Department of Commerce was motivated to listen to Timken and the AFBMA when additional evidence of dumping was presented. Although the yen had gained value against the dollar, Japanese companies were unwilling to raise prices to compensate for this rise. The Japanese preferred to sell bearings at a loss by absorbing costs, rather than losing market share. Timken and the AFBMA won the petition and the Department of Commerce instructed U.S. Customs to collect duties on shipments from Great Britain, Sweden, Italy, France, West Germany, Japan, Romania, Singapore, and Thailand. However, because SKF of Sweden, FAG of Germany, and Koyo Seiko and Nippon Seiko of Japan already owned plants in the United States at the time of this decision, they were free from import duties. The Defense Department, however, supported domestic manufacturers by issuing a buy-American policy for antifriction bearing purchases.

The purchasers' side of the issue is quite different from that of the manufacturers. As prices began to climb, purchasers were incensed. Although the decision to impose duties only affected imported antifriction bearings, distributors took this as an opportunity to implement across-the-board increases. By 1989, a coalition of original equipment manufacturers called the American Manufacturers for Trade in Bearings (AMTB) took a stand against the duties levied. The AMTB, which included Black & Decker, 3M, AT&T, IBM, Briggs & Stratton, Emerson Electric, GE, Hewlett-Packard, Westinghouse, and Xerox, represented manufacturers that collectively purchased over 200 million ball bearings annually. This amounted to two-thirds the consumption of commodity ball bearings and double the amount produced by U.S. bearing manufacturers. The AMTB claimed that domestic bearing manufacturers had been unable to meet U.S. demand for commodity ball bearings since the early 1980s and argued that the imports made up for this shortfall.

The specific bearings the AMTB was fighting for were commodity ball bearings, which have specific applications. The five most popular models in this line collectively account for more than 50 percent of the commodity bearings sold in the United States. Their primary applications are in power tools, appliances, automobiles, office equipment, and computer components. According to the director of commodities purchasing at Black & Decker, only three companies in the United States were capable of producing commodity ball bearings at the time of this decision.

CURRENT CONDITIONS

Because bearings are vital components of machinery, the market shows no signs of vanishing. While employment levels may drop as a reaction to increased automation of manufacturing processes, the shipment levels are not expected to drop. However, domestic manufacturers in the early 1990s were not investing the capital necessary to keep up with technical advances. New nondestructive quality control methods, such as using eddy currents to measure surface variance, monitoring interior surface integrity with x-rays, and verifying chemical composition through gas, are innovations that have improved the quality of bearings. As production and testing techniques improve, domestic manufacturers will be expected to implement this technology in order to compete. However, the buy-American push implemented by the Defense Department and other manufacturers should allow bearing manufacturers to enjoy stability, and even expansion, through the year 2000.

In 1995, the industry shipped more than 15 billion units valued at $5.8 billion, representing a 25 percent increase in current dollars since the early 1990s. Unit production was down, however, from 1994. Unmounted roller and ball bearings made up more than half of industry revenues. Growth has been relatively even across the different product segments of the industry.

INDUSTRY LEADERS

The highest regional concentration of bearings manufacturers was in the Great Lakes area. In terms of shipments, however, South Carolina ranked first. Its 14 bearing establishments shipped $627.4 million worth of bearings in 1992, which accounted for 14.6 percent of the total bearings shipments in the United States. In 1992, South Carolina employed 5,000 bearings workers who received an average hourly wage of $11.22 per hour. Other leading states included Pennsylvania, Connecticut, Indiana, and Illinois. Together these states accounted for approximately 40 percent of all U.S. bearings shipments in the 1990s.

In 1996, Ingersoll-Rand Company led the industry in sales. Based in Woodcliff Lake, New Jersey, Ingersoll boasted sales of $6.7 billion and employed 40,000 people. The Timken Company of Canton Ohio ranked second, with 19,000 employees and sales of $2.4 billion in 1996. The Torrington Company of Torrington, Connecticut ranked third with estimated sales of $1.3 billion and a work force of 12,000. SKF U.S.A. Incorporated, located in King of Prussia, Pennsylvania, ranked fourth with estimated sales of $800 million and 6,000 employees.

Since its beginning in 1905, Ingersoll-Rand was primarily an engineering products firm that specialized in coal mining equipment and air compressors. However, by the 1960s the company was searching for diversified product lines that would complement existing products. In 1968 Ingersoll-Rand entered the bearing industry through the acquisition of The Torrington

Company. This placed Ingersoll-Rand in the business of making needle and roller bearings as well as knitting needles, metal-forming machines, universal joints, and roller clutches. This investment turned out to be extremely beneficial to Ingersoll-Rand, as it protected the company from the cyclical downturns of the mining equipment market.

Timken has been perfecting its tapered roller bearings since 1898, and by the early 1990s the company offered 26,000 different bearing combinations. Boasting that it is the world's largest tapered roller bearing producer, Timken attributes part of this success to international trade. After establishing a sales office in Japan in 1974 in an effort to serve Asian distributors, Timken finally made inroads with Japanese automobile manufacturers in 1987. The currency exchange rate and political climates contributed to the company's success in 1987, but the company received an important image boost primarily by maintaining a good reputation for quality when other U.S. goods were perceived as being inferior to Japanese products. While price competitiveness was not possible, technical expertise from Timken's side won praise from Japanese design engineers who started specifying tapered roller bearings for their products. With patience and expertise, Timken started supplying Nissan Motor Company and Mazda Motor Corporation with wheel bearings.

Due to the recession, however, Timken was forced to temporarily cut salaries and reduce work weeks for production workers in many plants in August 1991. The company's financial status worsened, and by December Timken was forced to lay-off approximately 300 workers at six plants in Canton, Ohio. During these difficult times, Timken was able to arrange temporary price cuts from vendors. Reportedly, over 95 percent of the company's suppliers agreed to negotiate temporary price cuts to allow Timken to remain strong through the recession.

Sweden-based SKF, which was incorporated in 1907, is the acknowledged leader of the world's roller bearing industry. In 1988, SKF controlled 20 percent of the world market in bearings, which was more than twice the market share held by its closest competitors. The company's entrance into the bearings market was motivated by its frustration with the poor quality and high cost of other bearings. The parent company, Gamlestadens Fabriker, a textile manufacturer, granted funds for research into producing bearings. Subsequently, the founder of SKF, Sven Wingquist, went on to develop the double row, self-aligning ball bearing that introduced SKF as a leader and innovator in the industry. From the onset, SKF aligned itself with the automotive industry and pushed its operations into France and the United Kingdom in order to compete directly with German manufacturers. In 1916, SKF expanded by acquiring another Swedish ball bearing producer as well as a steel works company to increase its steel supply for bearings. During the 1920s, SKF furthered its reputation for innovation when it introduced spherical and taper roller bearings.

By the 1970s, SKF faced serious competitive threats in its European market due to the influx of Japanese bearing makers like NTN, NSK, and Koyo Seiko. In response, SKF began to place more emphasis on bearing quality in an effort to retain customer loyalty. The company introduced a global forecasting and supply system that allowed all of its European plants to be aware of demand. Additionally, the company was able to expand product lines by increasing its funding of product research and development. In 1986 SKF formed a 50-50 joint venture with Koyo Seiko, making it the first foreign bearings manufacturer to participate in the Japanese market. While Koyo Seiko was interested in SKF's technology, SKF was interested in the Japanese company's 20-percent stake in Toyota and the booming market in Southeast Asia.

WORK FORCE

Although shipments have climbed steadily since 1983, employment levels have been declining since 1984. The total employment level in the industry dropped 15.5 percent between 1982 and 1987, from 43,700 to 36,900. Production workers, who have traditionally made up between two-thirds and three-quarters of the industry's entire work force, suffered fewer layoffs than other industry workers in the 1980s and made larger gains when manufacturers began rehiring in the early 1990s. By 1995, the industry employed approximately 36,000 workers, according to the U.S. Bureau of Labor Statistics. Average hourly earnings of production workers in 1995 was at $14.12, well above the manufacturing average of $12.37 for the same year. Annual industry payroll amounted to more than $1.2 billion for all workers.

As a reflection of global competition, the work force was expected to change significantly in the late 1990s. While certain occupations are expected to decline in numbers, others are expected to grow. Those facing reductions include assemblers, inspectors, secretaries, machine tool cutting operators, machine builders, welders, sheet metal workers, machine assemblers, machine forming operators, and welding machine setters. Those occupations expected to increase by 20 percent or more include sales workers, industrial machinery mechanics, industrial production

managers, and engineering and science managers. Those occupations expected to increase by 12 percent to 15 percent include machinists, mechanical engineers, numerically controlled machine tool operators, and combination machine tool operators. Occupations expected to increase at levels between 5 percent and 11 percent include precision woodworkers, production and inventory control clerks, traffic clerks, general office clerks, and engineering technicians.

One company that is highly respected in the industry is Industrial Tectonics. At Industrial Tectonics, employees are empowered to be responsible for bearing quality by three basic ethics. The first ethic is that the employees must be able to measure everything produced. The second ethic is an assurance that verifiable quality control systems are in place. The third is related to employees improving themselves and participating in these quality control efforts. Industrial Tectonics confers responsibility and accountability to all employees, forcing them to understand quality-related issues. Machinists gauge the parts they produce and correct problems when statistical control trends show correction is necessary. Employees are expected to engage in practical and theoretical application classes both on company time and on their own time. The company takes comprehensive skills inventories to decide what types of job-related training would benefit employees. For this type of involvement, Industrial Tectonics rewards employees with promotions and other incentive programs. Due to such emphasis on quality and investment in human resources, Industrial Tectonics is the only bearing manufacturer to supply master balls to the National Bureau of Standards. The U.S. Navy has selected Industrial Tectonics as a supplier of precision ball bearings for nuclear use. The company has also shipped millions of flow control parts to General Motors for over two years without one reject.

AMERICA AND THE WORLD

In 1987, the U.S. Air Force and Army launched the Engine Bearing Technology Modernization Program in an effort to support U.S. bearing manufacturers. This program came as a response to the U.S. Department of Commerce's findings that foreign manufacturers were dumping bearings in the U.S. market and potentially jeopardizing national security.

While the Japanese may appear to pose the most significant threat to U.S. bearing manufacturers, Singapore and Korea are mounting strong competitive campaigns against the Japanese. Also contending for world market share are the Europeans and some countries from the former Soviet Union. The North American Free Trade Agreement is expected to hurt the bearing industry as new plants are built in Mexico and lower manufacturing costs are realized.

U.S. exports of bearings were valued at more than $900 million in 1995, while imports totaled more than $1.2 billion in the same year.

RESEARCH AND TECHNOLOGY

The production of precision bearings is changing quickly, as technology allows greater and more accurate measurements to be taken. In 1989 it was announced that The Timken Company developed production equipment, gauges, and methods of manufacture to produce bearings called Precision Plus. The Precision Plus bearings boast a radial run-out of less than 40 millionths of an inch. Radial run-out is a measure of how closely the bearings will run in a perfect circle in a given bearing-ring path. Timken was able to create this new class of bearings through assessing grinding wheel variables such as type, speed of the wheel, feed rate into the wheel, coolant type, coolant temperature, and wheel dressing techniques. When bearings are produced to precision units of a millionth of an inch, shelf life becomes a factor. If bearings sit on a shelf for less than six months, the diameter can change several millionths of an inch. In high precision applications, this is unsatisfactory. Therefore, Timken developed a proprietary heat treatment process that prevents dimensional changes from occurring over time. The Precision Plus bearings are available in standard sizes ranging from 3/8 inch to 12 inches in diameter.

Silicon Nitride that has been through a process called Hot Isostatic Pressing (HIPing) is one of the best-suited materials for producing high-quality bearings. Standard bearings are typically made of steel, and are consequently subject to wear. In the early 1990s, however, researchers were experimenting with hybrid steel/ceramic bearings and all-ceramic bearings. The Japanese were leading the way in this investigation, having found methods for producing ceramic components with consistency and accuracy. Ceramic bearings are attractive to manufacturers for several reasons: they exert less centrifugal force on the outer race; they can operate at higher temperatures and speeds; and they provide better control and more accuracy in given applications. Japanese manufacturers have tested ceramic bearings in aircraft engines with no appreciable wear observed.

The Japanese are also aggressively researching alternative processing techniques and methods for improving corrosion resistance in aircraft quality bearings. New forms of failure analysis are also lending insights to the behavior of bearings under specific conditions. In both the United States and Japan, x-ray and gas chromatography are becoming more common nondestructive testing methods. High-temperature applications are also under aggressive study abroad at Japanese Universities and bearing manufacturers. Solid lubrication is an area where the United States leads the way in research, and the Japanese have shown keen interest in those findings.

Although the bearing industry generally implements very precise test sequences, some purchasers of bearings are finding that acceptance testing is necessary before shipping a product that uses ball or roller bearings. The reason for this is that each bearing is individually produced, and therefore unique. The U.S. Army, for example, had an embarrassing and expensive mishap with a tank's firing mechanism due to problems with its bearing components. Therefore, acceptance testing by original equipment manufacturers is a growing trend in manufacturing.

One of the most innovative applications for bearings is in anti-lock braking (ABS) and traction control systems. ABS operates through electronically controlled bearings, which act as sensors. The sensors are able to relay information about wheel speeds to the car control system. In a January 9, 1992 *Machine Design* article Michael Courtright commented, ''Wheel-bearing hubs are an optimum location for monitoring wheel speed for two reasons: bearings and hubs are mechanically precise and close to the wheel.'' The ABS computer receives information about the wheel speeds and decides if the regulation of brake fluid to one wheel will be necessary to prevent lock-up. General Motors' Delco Chassis Division innovated this approach, and currently Timken and SKF Bearings supply instrumented bearing packages to automakers. However, the product is not standardized across the auto industry and presently lacks the support of some executives who feel the life of the sensors is much more volatile than the life of the hub. Consequently, when a sensor fails the entire hub must be replaced, making the system potentially expensive in maintenance terms. More standardization is needed to ensure ABS is successful. However, government regulations could force the issue of instrumented bearings and ABS in all cars.

FURTHER READING

Avery, Susan. ''Bearing Makers: First the Good News.'' *Purchasing,* 11 February 1988.

Courtright, Michael L. ''Instrumented Bearings Get Rolling with ABS.'' *Machine Design,* 9 January 1992.

Darnay, Arsen J., ed. *Manufacturing USA.* 5th ed. Detroit: Gale Research, 1996.

"Dumping Case Trips Bearing Price Hikes." *Purchasing,* 15 December 1988.

Imberman, Woodruff. "Improve: Upgrade: Innovate." *Modern Machine Shop,* February 1988.

"Industry Group Seeks Quotas on Bearing Imports." *Industrial Distribution,* September 1987.

Mason, Fred. "6-Spindle Automatics Get CNC." *American Machinist & Automated Manufacturing,* March 1987.

Purchase, Michael. "Acceptance Testing for Bearings." *Machine Design,* 23 March 1989.

Raia, Ernie. "Buyers Fight Ball Bearings Dumping Claim." *Purchasing,* 4 May 1989.

"Tapered Roller Bearings Made to Highest Precision Ever." *Machine Design,* 23 March 1989.

U.S. Bureau of the Census. *1992 Census of Manufactures.* Washington: GPO, 1995.

U.S. Bureau of the Census. *1995 Annual Survey of Manufactures.* Washington: GPO, 1997.

U.S. Department of Commerce. International Trade Administration. *A Competitive Assessment of the U.S. Ball and Roller Bearings Industry.* Washington: GPO, February 1988.

West, Bartlett. "Three Quality Ethics Spell Success." *Modern Machine Shop,* May 1988.

Zimmerman, Susan. "Competition Changes the Buying Landscape." *Purchasing,* 6 February 1992.

SIC 3563

AIR AND GAS COMPRESSORS

This category covers firms primarily engaged in manufacturing air and gas compressors for general industrial use, and non-agricultural spraying and dusting equipment. It does not include manufacturers of refrigeration and air-conditioning compressors, which are classified in **SIC 3585: Air-Conditioning and Warm Air Heating Equipment and Commercial and Industrial Refrigeration Equipment**; pneumatic pumps and motors for fluid power transmission, classified in **SIC 3594: Fluid Power Pumps and Motor**; agricultural spraying and dusting equipment, classified in **SIC 3523: Farm Machinery and Equipment**; or laboratory vacuum pumps, classified in **SIC 3821: Laboratory Apparatus and Furniture.**

INDUSTRY SNAPSHOT

Compressors provide one of the most versatile forms of energy used in industry today. Compressed air as a power source ranks as the most commonly used, behind only electricity, gas, and water. In addition, compressors provide the motive force needed to economically transport gas and other materials in pipelines. Since compressors are required to operate in difficult environments and conditions, they wear quickly. As a result, the replacement parts portion of the industry composes a significant portion of shipments. In 1995, for example, the Bureau of the Census's *Annual Survey of Manufactures* gave the value of air and gas compressor shipments at $2.7 billion, while additional parts and attachments shipments were valued at $663.1 million. Major markets for such products included the chemical industry, steel mills and blast furnaces, energy-related extraction industries, pipelines and well-drilling, and general construction.

ORGANIZATION AND STRUCTURE

Some 258 establishments manufactured air and gas compressors in 1992, essentially holding steady from the 1987 figure of 259. Historically, manufacturing in this industry has been heavily concentrated; in 1977 more than half the industry's employees worked in the four largest facilities, and 79 percent of all facilities employed fewer than 100 workers. By 1992 this had changed somewhat—while 79 percent of all facilities still employed fewer than 100 workers, diffusion was more evident in the larger firms. The 54 firms that had over 100 employees accounted for 81 percent of all workers.

The use of compressed air and gas can be divided into three major categories, according to the *Compressed Air and Gas Handbook:* compressed air and gas for process services, compressed air for power, and compressed air for general industrial applications.

Process services include chemical alterations like combustion, nitrogen fixation, polymerization, hydrogenation and alkylation, and change of state operations like quenching, drying, and atomization. Products that result from these types of procedures include liquid fuels, plastics, synthetic rubber, ammonia, and fertilizers.

Power uses utilize the potential energy of stored compressed air to directly perform work. The tools and devices powered by compressed air are termed pneumatic. They generally perform more slowly than electric tools, but are faster than hydraulic and provide smooth power application. The energy potential can be translated into rotation and torque with the use of rotary air motors, vanes, or air turbines. Reciprocating motion and direct force provide easily controllable presses, clamps, and feeding devices. Air pressure can be used to accelerate a mass such as a pile driver or pavement breaker. Blowguns use the air pressure stream directly to move materials such as chips, debris, and paint. Air can displace fluids, semi-fluids, and solids to drive materials through pipelines. When air and liquid are mixed, the resulting bubbling action provides agitation, mixing, and aeration.

Industry uses of compressed air include plant maintenance and the powering of pneumatic tools for production line work. This has been especially important for automation of thread-tightening, pressing, hammering, feeding, positioning, and safety-control sensors.

BACKGROUND AND DEVELOPMENT

The world's first pump was probably the force or air pump built by Ktesibios of Alexandria about 270 B.C. He used a cylinder and plunger arrangement to pump air through pipes of various lengths, creating the first water organ. The water was used to maintain a steady air pressure in the system. Simple air pumps and bellows provided low-pressure compressed air for such devices as organs and blacksmith furnaces, but major advancements in compressor technology had to wait until the arrival of the Industrial Revolution.

Generally the term compressor was applied to any blower that produced compressed air in excess of 40 psi. Below that pressure, the device is simply called a blower or industrial fan. With new industrial processes came new demands for flexibility of power sources. Coupling the air pump to a steam engine showed the potential of air power. By 1900, the stationary air compressor was a common tool for industry, albeit a massive one requiring bulky, space-consuming foundations. In 1900, the portable compressor made its debut by the simple expedient of placing wheels under some of the smaller stationary engines. Until 1910, the most common power for such compressors was the steam engine or an oil engine. The main application for the devices was for rock drilling. The invention of a lightweight air drill spurred development of the portable compressor.

Major advances came in the 1930s, when the two-stage, air-cooled compressor appeared, followed by multi-speed regulation by the end of the decade. The 1950s saw the introduction of the rotary-screw compressor in the United States, which allowed for considerably higher operating speeds in smaller, lighter units. Continued improvements made possible the now common truck-mounted diesel-powered units used by utilities and construction companies as a completely portable and flexible power source.

One industry that especially benefited from the new technology was oil exploration and drilling. In 1938 some oil companies began experimenting with air-powered drills. The technique used a rotating bit and pumped either mud or air through holes in the bit to clear the cutting face. New booster compressors producing 1,500-psi were developed specifically for the industry. By the end of World War II, portable drilling rigs were quickly and efficiently boring shallow wells.

The construction industry borrowed the technology for its blast-hole drillers in 1946. In 1954 it developed its own bottom-hole tool, which used 100-psi compressed air to rotate a carbide-tipped tool. Water-well drills used 250-psi air to clear water from the hole while drilling.

The two most common types of compressors are the positive-displacement and the velocity or dynamic. Positive-displacement machines trap air in a confined space and then reduce the volume of that space to increase the pressure. The bicycle pump is a familiar example of this type of compressor. It need not use a piston assembly, a rotating gear, or a screw mechanism. Such compressors can be powered by electric motors, oil or gas engines, and steam engines or turbines. The most common applications for these compressors are off-shore oil drilling, construction applications, locomotives, ships, mining, and smaller units in machine shops, bakeries, dry cleaning plants, food processing plants, furniture factories, printing plants, textile mills, automotive service shops, and other industrial and commercial applications using compressed air.

The dynamic system uses a fan or turbine mechanism to force the air or gas against the casing by centrifugal force. Such systems often use several stages or series of compression to achieve high pressures. The systems can be either axial, expelling gas along the line of its impeller axis, or radial, expelling gas against the casing by centrifugal force. The most common applications for these devices are in refineries, petrochemical plants, steel mills, ammonia plants, sewage aeration, pipeline boosters, wind tunnels and supercharging diesel engines.

By the early 1980s, the chemical industry had become one of the largest users of compressors. According to the *Monthly Labor Review,* in 1982, the chemical industry was using about 10 percent of the compressor industry's output. In comparison, steel mills and blast furnaces took about 7 percent of output. The oil well and pipeline industries took 18 percent of output. Demand in this sector dropped off dramatically in the 1960s but steadily recovered. Compressors are used in both oil drilling and oil field maintenance operations, particularly for secondary recovery efforts. Construction took 18 percent of output. Particularly important in this market category were the sales of portable compressors used to drive pneumatic tools on the construction site where other sources of energy might be restricted.

CURRENT CONDITIONS

The general industrial slowdown of the 1980s hit the compressor industry hard. Major clients like the nuclear power industry, oil well and pipeline industry, and the construction industry cut back on orders for new equipment and left existing components idle. A strong U.S. dollar made American products noncompetitive in foreign markets.

By 1988, this started to change. A weakening dollar spurred exports and a general pickup in the manufacturing climate sparked new domestic orders in almost all sectors. The industry continued to modernize production by consolidating facilities and adopting sophisticated CAD/CAM systems and metalworking and casting technologies. New materials and designs were explored to extend the life of components in corrosive environments and to increase reliability. The steady growth experienced by the industry in the early 1990s was expected to continue. *Manufacturing USA* predicted that the value of air and gas compressor shipments would grow from the actual 1994 figure of $4.170 billion to $5.267 billion in 1998. At the same time it estimated that the number of production hours would increase from 27.4 million hours to 29 million hours, while the total number of establishments was expected to decrease from the 1993 count of 283 to 239 in 1998.

INDUSTRY LEADERS

Three of the top firms by sales in the air and gas compressor industry in 1993 were Thomas Industries of Louisville, Kentucky; Cooper Industries Inc. Energy Services Group of Mt. Vernon, Ohio; and Calmar Spraying Systems Inc. of City of Industry, California. Their listings in *Dun & Bradstreet* show that Thomas Industries was established in 1928 and employs 3,530 workers to produce $408 million in annual sales. It has one subsidiary, the Power Air Division. Cooper Industries Energy Services Group is one of several divisions of Cooper Industries producing pumps and compressors for various applications. It was established in 1833 and 3,300 workers produce $330 million in annual sales. Calmar Spraying Systems Inc. was a subsidiary of CSS Holding Inc. It was established in 1983

and employs 3,020 workers to produce annual sales of $290 million. It has one subsidiary, Calmar Inc.

WORK FORCE

The *Monthly Labor Review,* 1982, noted that the general industrial machinery group generally used a high proportion of skilled trades, about 30 percent of all production workers compared to the 26 percent proportion in all manufacturing. Compressor and pump production made up about 29 percent of all labor in the industrial machinery group. Metal working craftsmen and machinists were three times more common in this industry than in manufacturing as a whole, while laborers were half as common. Average wages were 10 percent higher in this industry indicating a higher degree of necessary skill. This disparity continued as late as 1988 when the compressor industry paid an average hourly wage of $12.68 compared to the manufacturing average of $10.66. The industry also employed a high proportion of nonproduction workers, indicating a reliance on mechanical engineers. This employment group was three times more common in the compressor industry than in general manufacturing.

The Bureau of Labor Statistics projected a continuation of this trend with its estimate of employment changes until the year 2000. It expected double digit increases for industrial machinery mechanics, sales workers, engineering and science managers, industrial production managers, NC tool operators for both plastics and metals, mechanical engineers, combination machine tool operators, machinists, and engineering technicians. According to the Census Bureau's *1992 Census of Manufactures,* total employment was 23,400, a 2 percent drop from the 23,400 employed in 1987 and a 10 percent drop from 1991. More than half of these employees worked in New York, Pennsylvania, Illinois, and Ohio.

AMERICA AND THE WORLD

Air and gas compressors were manufactured to international standards allowing American manufacturers to compete effectively in the international market. These same standards also made the United States vulnerable to foreign competition, particularly on price and quality. During the early half of the 1980s, the strong American dollar made such competition particularly difficult, undermining an already weak industrial climate in American manufacturing. As a result, the U.S. merchandise trade deficit quadrupled between 1982 and 1984, reaching $145 billion. This effect showed up in the compressor manufacturing industry, but was delayed. In 1985 this industry showed a trade surplus, but by 1987 it had become a $1.9 billion deficit. The drop of the value of the U.S. dollar that began in March of 1985 provided new impetus for the compressor industry. By 1987, the average export price expressed in foreign currency of compressors and other machinery had fallen 23.1 percent. By 1990, even though domestic prices increased an average of 5 percent each year, the foreign currency price of compressors and replacement parts had dropped more than 11 percent. That made American operations more profitable, increased export volumes, and discouraged imports. It also encouraged foreign firms to establish manufacturing and assembly facilities in the United States.

In 1994, exports passed $810 million while imports exceeded $300 million. Major markets for American products included Canada, Mexico, the United Kingdom, Saudi Arabia, West Germany, Venezuela, and Japan. The top importers included Japan, West Germany, Canada, and the United Kingdom.

RESEARCH AND TECHNOLOGY

The majority of compressors manufactured are custom made to a client's specific requirements for use in complex applications where the failure of the compressor could be disastrous. Consequently, manufacturing innovation has stressed flexibility and reliability. Major innovations included the adoption of numerical and computer control manufacturing systems and the reliance on engineering expertise assisted by computer modeling software to custom design components for short run production. New corrosion resistant materials were developed and refinements to old processes adopted. Specially designed metal-forming machines were created for the industry, including combination milling, radial drilling and facing machines, variable setting grinders that automatically form tapered shafts, and automatic tool changing devices controlled by NC tapes or computer software. Foundry operations for production of compressor casings and core making advanced with rapid-cycle machinery, synchronous fabricating machinery, and a no-bake molding process using a resin binder and catalyst. Closer tolerances were achieved in components by replacing wooden molds and cores with ceramic. Increasing concern over energy efficiency dictated more advanced compressor designs with larger displacements.

FURTHER READING

"Build Your Working Knowledge of Process Compressors." *Chemical Engineering Progress,* February 1993.

Compressed Air and Gas Handbook. New York: Compressed Air and Gas Institute, 1973.

"Compressor Diagnostics Software Being Developed." *Oil & Gas Journal,* 28 September 1992.

"Dollar's Fall Boosts U.S. Machinery Exports, 1985-90." *Monthly Labor Review,* July 1991.

Hanlon, Paul. "Plastics Fight Friction in Reciprocating Compressors." *Machine Design,* 9 April 1992.

Kirsch, F. William. *Waste Minimization Assessment for a Manufacturer of Compressed Air Equipment Components.* Cincinnati, Ohio: U.S. Environmental Protection Agency, 1991.

Kranzberg, Melvin, and Carroll W. Pursel, Jr., eds. *Technology in Western Civilization.* Vol. 1, New York: Oxford University Press, 1967.

Manufacturing USA. 5th ed., Detroit: Gale Research, 1996.

1982 Census of Manufactures. Washington, D.C.: Department of Commerce, 1987.

1992 Census of Manufactures. Washington, D.C.: U.S. Department of Commerce, 1995.

1995 Annual Survey of Manufactures: Statistics for Industry Groups and Industries. Washington, D.C.: U.S. Department of Commerce, 1997.

1995 Annual Survey of Manufactures: Value of Product Shipments. Washington, D.C.: U.S. Department of Commerce, 1997.

"Productivity in the Pump and Compressor Industry." *Monthly Labor Review,* December 1982.

Scheel, Lyman F. *Gas and Air Compression Machinery.* New York: McGraw-Hill, 1961.

Usher, Abbot Payson. *A History of Mechanical Inventions.* Boston: Beacon Press, 1929.

—Al Cook, updated by Paula Pyzik Scott

SIC 3564

INDUSTRIAL AND COMMERCIAL FANS AND BLOWERS AND AIR PURIFICATION EQUIPMENT

This category covers firms primarily engaged in manufacturing blowers for general industrial and commercial use, and commercial exhaust fans, ventilating fans and attic fans. Also included are manufacturers of duct collection equipment and other air purification equipment for heating and air conditioning systems and equipment for industrial gas cleaning systems. It does not include manufacturers of refrigeration and air-conditioning components, which are covered under **SIC 3585: Refrigeration and Heating Equipment.**

Small household fans, kitchen and bath ventilation fans, or other domestic fan components are included in **SIC 3634: Electric Housewares and Fans.**

INDUSTRY SNAPSHOT

U.S. industry depends on the low-pressure, high-volume movement of air. Without it, much industrial and commercial activity would quickly suffocate. Consequently, the fan can be found in applications as diverse as huge blowers used to bubble air through sewage water and industrial waste, to street cleaners and industrial leaf blowers. In modern shopping centers and commercial/industrial strip malls, unnoticed roof ventilators silently exchange contaminated air for fresh; the attic fan performs the same function for residential buildings. Heating and air conditioning systems depend on fans to move heat away from coils and heat exchangers and into the structure, and to feed the fossil fuel combustion processes with large quantities of oxygen-bearing air. Exhaust systems push the products of this combustion outside the structure or extract grease and heat from commercial cooking appliances and industrial ovens.

The fan's ability to move large quantities of air makes it the base component of the rapidly expanding air pollution control industry. Starting with the plant, the device has been harnessed to help trap and remove pollutants like dust and metal particles, carbon monoxide, nitrous oxides, sulphur dioxide, sulfuric acid, and hydrocarbon solvents in a variety of filters and traps. Estimated 1995 U.S. shipments of such pollution abatement equipment were valued at $753 million.

ORGANIZATION AND STRUCTURE

More than 500 companies manufactured fans and blowers at roughly 600 locations in the mid-1990s. This figure grew gradually since the 1970s, as did total employment in the industry, which rose from 23,500 in 1977 to an estimated 26,500 in 1995. Ohio, California, Illinois, New York, and Pennsylvania were the leading states in this industry in the 1990s, accounting for nearly 40 percent of its establishments, 39 percent of its revenues, and 38 percent of its labor force.

Fans and blowers belong to the same family of devices as compressors and pumps. A pump moves liquids, while the others move gases. A compressor will provide a means of increasing the pressure of the gas to more than 40 pounds per square inch (psi). That gas can then either be delivered directly to the application or stored for metered use. A blower can also increase the pressure of the gas to as much as 40 psi, but delivers it directly to the application through an area of high resistance such as a pipeline. Fans provide

large volumes of uncompressed gas and operate in low-resistance environments that could also include ducting systems. Technically, an increase in gas density of less than 7 percent between inlet and outlet defines the gas as uncompressed.

The two most common types of fans and blowers are the axial and the centrifugal, which together account for about 45 percent of the industry's output. Axial fans are used in applications that produce low resistance to airflow. The gas is moved in the same direction as the fan's axis of rotation, much as a water wheel on a classic mill or paddle steamer. In the centrifugal fan, the gas moves perpendicular to the fan's axis of rotation. Most domestic fans use angled and curved blades to produce the centrifugal effect at low pressure. Centrifugal blowers and fans are used in relatively high resistance applications and usually provide quieter operation than axial units.

The main uses of fans and blowers, according to the *Compressed Air and Gas Handbook,* are for process services (including chemical alterations like combustion, nitrogen fixation, polymerization, hydrogenation, and alkylation), and for change-of-state operations (including quenching, drying, and atomization). Products that result from these types of procedures include liquid fuels, plastics, synthetic rubber, ammonia, and fertilizers.

BACKGROUND AND DEVELOPMENT

The world's first pump was probably the force or air pump built by Ktesibios of Alexandria about 270 B.C. He used a cylinder and plunger arrangement to pump air through pipes of various lengths, creating the first water organ. The water was used to maintain a steady air pressure in the system. Simple air pumps and bellows provided low-pressure "compressed" air for such devices as organs and blacksmith furnaces, but major advancements in fan technology had to wait until the arrival of the Industrial Revolution.

As large-scale manufacturing emerged in the late nineteenth and early twentieth centuries, fans became an integral part of factory and commercial building infrastructure in the United States. The fan and blower industry's successes have been largely tied to the health of commercial and industrial construction and renovation.

The general industrial slowdown of the 1980s hit the fan and blower industry hard. Major clients like the petrochemical industry; heating, ventilation and air conditioning industry; and the construction industry cut back on orders for new equipment and left existing components idle. A strong U.S. dollar made American products uncompetitive in foreign markets.

By 1988, this started to change. A weakening dollar stimulated exports and a general pickup in the manufacturing climate sparked new domestic orders in almost all sectors. The industry continued to modernize production by consolidating facilities and adopting sophisticated CAD/CAM systems and metalworking and casting technologies. New materials and designs were explored to extend the life of components in corrosive environments and to increase reliability.

New environmental regulations like the Clean Air Act Amendments of 1990 and their counterparts in other countries spurred the development and sale of air pollution abatement equipment. Two major products in this category were particle emission collectors, with shipments of $513 million in 1990, and gaseous emission control units, with sales of $220 million that year. In 1990, the major clients for such products were steam electric power generators; industrial steam plants; pulp and paper mills; chemical and fertilizer producers; and petroleum refiners.

CURRENT CONDITIONS

In 1995 the industry generated more than $3.8 billion in sales, which represented a 22 percent preinflation increase over 1992. By product, centrifugal fans accounted for more than $1 billion alone, or nearly 28 percent of industry shipments; propeller and axial fans made up 20 percent of revenues; filtration equipment for incoming air made up 25 percent; filtration equipment for outgoing air made up 21 percent; and the remaining 6 percent was filled out by miscellaneous industrial and commercial fans and parts. The two smallest categories by sales also exhibited the highest growth in the 1990s, while sales of filtration equipment for incoming air have actually declined since the early 1990s. Other segments have shown average growth compared to the industry average.

The industry was expected to benefit in the mid- and late 1990s from the Clean Air Act Amendments of 1990, because they imposed time limits on the reduction of specified hazardous industrial air pollutants. Compliance was expected to generate significant capital investment into this industry's products.

WORK FORCE

The industry's estimated 19,000 production workers earned an average of $10.73 per hour in 1995 compared to the manufacturing average of $12.37. Annual payroll for the industry was more than $800 million in 1995.

The Bureau of Labor Statistics projected declines for most occupations within this industry through 2005. Significant growth was expected, however, for machine builders, machine tool operators, and welders and cutters.

AMERICA AND THE WORLD

Blowers and fans and the increasingly important air pollution abatement equipment are manufactured to international standards, allowing American manufacturers to compete effectively on the international market. These same standards, however, also make the United States vulnerable to foreign competition, particularly on price and quality.

Globalization is particularly important in the air pollution abatement equipment (APC) sector. U.S. and European multinationals use direct investment, cross-border mergers, acquisitions, joint ventures, and foreign collaboration to gain entry to each other's markets and to other markets around the world. The main target markets for such equipment have been Asia, Eastern Europe, and Latin America, since the industry already faces significant competition from domestic producers in major trading partners like Japan, Germany, and France. Mexico is also a potentially significant market for U.S. fan and blower products. Many firms prefer to license to foreign manufacturers instead of competing directly, creating a brisk trade in environmental technology. Unlike the industry in general, this segment posted a trade surplus in the 1990s.

RESEARCH AND TECHNOLOGY

New and more stringent environmental regulations in the United States and around the world encouraged research into new air pollution abatement technology. This was especially true since some regulations called for pollution limitations in excess of what was technically possible at the time.

However, the industry also found ways of applying old technologies in new ways. Some major areas of research included electrostatic precipitators with the addition of high-voltage direct-current pulses to capture fly-ash; filter bags treated with microporous films or membranes to keep dust cake out of the filter material; conditioning flue gas streams with sulfur trioxide or ammonia before filtering to improve the life of the filter; the development of sulfur trioxide generators to convert flue gases without the need of adding chemicals; new plastic materials to extend the concept of flue gas cooling with water beyond the wood products industry; and sorbent injection of such materials as carbon, char, and sodium sulfide to capture heavy metals like mercury.

FURTHER READING

Bouley, Jeffrey. "Fans & Blowers." *Pollution Engineering,* 15 April 1993.

Compressed Air and Gas Handbook. New York: Compressed Air and Gas Institute, 1973.

Kranzberg, Melvin, and Carroll W. Pursel, Jr., eds. *Technology in Western Civilization.* Vol. 1. New York: Oxford University Press, 1967.

Nudo, Lori. "Capturing Heavy Metals." *Pollution Engineering,* September 1993.

"Productivity in the Pump and Compressor Industry." *Monthly Labor Review,* December 1982.

U.S. Bureau of the Census. *1992 Census of Manufactures.* Washington: GPO, 1995.

————. *1995 Annual Survey of Manufactures.* Washington: GPO, 1997.

U.S. Department of Commerce. International Trade Administration. *U.S. Industrial Outlook 1994.* Washington: GPO, 1994.

"U.S. Utilities Will Commit $6 Billion More for Flue Gas Desulfurization (FGD) Systems." *Environmental Science Technology,* January 1992.

SIC 3565

PACKAGING MACHINERY

Firms in this industry manufacture machinery used in packaging, wrapping and bottling. In 1987 the classification code was changed to combine two 1972 categories, SIC 35514: Food Packaging and Bottling Machinery and SIC 35691: Non-food Packaging and Bottling, along with parts of the two general categories: **SIC 3551: Food Products Machinery** and **SIC 3569: General Industry Machinery.** The 1972 category numbered **SIC 3565: Industrial Patterns** was renumbered as **SIC 3543.**

In 1995 the industry shipped $3.63 billion worth of products, a 31 percent increase since 1990. Employment in the industry increased 7 percent since 1992, to 28 thousand employees.

The industry found itself challenged to change and innovate in the late 1980s and early 1990s, as industry shifted to leaner production methods requiring just-in-time (JIT) inventory management and as consumers rebelled against excessive and expensive product packaging. This meant new technology to manufacture smaller, more flexible machinery and more packaging options for manufacturers.

To meet the demand, the industry introduced programmable logic controllers, robotics, self-diagnostic systems, microprocessor controls, automated testing, vision inspection systems, and built-in fault correction devices. Hydraulic and pneumatic actuators reduced clamping time and sped line changeover rates. Modern lines could shift from producing one part to an entirely different component in minutes instead of the previously common hours.

Illinois, Ohio, California, and Wisconsin led the country in employment in the production of packaging equipment in 1992. These states accounted for 43 percent of the nation's total employment in the industry. The 1995 survey did not cover single-establishment companies with less than ten employees, but such firms accounted for only thirteen percent of the total value of shipments in the industry.

Three of the largest companies in the industry in 1996 in terms of sales were Bemis Company, Inc., of Minneapolis, MN; Signode Industries, of Glenview, IL; and Thermo Power Corporation, of Waltham, MA. Bemis was founded in 1858, employed 7,950, and had sales of $1.5 billion. Signode was founded in 1989, employed 1,500, and generated $355 million in sales. Thermo Power was founded in 1987, employed 100, and had $103 million in sales.

Exports formed an important part of the industry's market with 24 percent of its 1992 production shipped to about 140 foreign countries. This represented $647 million in sales, a six percent increase over 1991 figures, and the seventh consecutive yearly rise in exports. The largest purchaser of American equipment was Canada followed by Europe, the Asia-Pacific region, and Central and South America. *U.S. Industrial Outlook 1993* identified five exceptional growth markets: Japan, South Korea, Taiwan, Germany, and France.

The industry faced major challenges by environmental and energy concerns both in the United States and in foreign countries, especially Europe. The demands for recyclable and reusable materials and containers prompted more than 500 legislative proposals in fifty states to control solid waste. Other countries instituted their own measures. Concerns over conflicting regulations prompted interest in such measures as the ISO 9000 international machinery standard which would define the rules of manufacture and prevent such national or state standards from becoming nontariff barriers to trade.

At the same time, industry was demanding lighter materials both in the actual packaging and the machinery, to reduce energy costs in transportation. Responding to JIT philosophies, packaging equipment companies were beginning to use air freight to speed delivery time.

FURTHER READING

"Exporting Pays Off." *Business America,* 7 October 1991.

"Fluid Power in Action: Packaging Equipment." *Hydraulics & Pneumatics,* September 1991.

"Simple Is Better for Packaging Machine Manufacturer." *Modern Machine Shop,* May 1992.

U.S. Bureau of the Census. *1995 Annual Survey of Manufactures.* Washington: GPO, 1997.

U.S. Department of Commerce. International Trade Administration. *U.S. Industrial Outlook 1993,* Washington: GPO, 1993.

—Al Cook, updated by Kenneth R. Shepherd

SIC 3566

SPEED CHANGERS, INDUSTRIAL HIGH-SPEED DRIVES, AND GEARS

Firms in this industry manufacture speed changers, industrial high-speed drives and gears. Hydrostatic drives are classified under **SIC 3594: Fluid Power Pumps and Motors**; automatic transmissions are in **SIC 3714: Motor Vehicle Parts and Accessories**; and aircraft power-transmission devices are found in **SIC 3728: Aircraft Parts and Auxiliary Equipment, Not Elsewhere Classified.**

INDUSTRY SNAPSHOT

The industry provides basic mechanical power transmission components used in most industrial machinery. In 1995, industry shipments reached $2.13 million, according to the U.S. Department of Commerce's *Annual Survey of Manufactures.* This is up from the 1992 value of $1.82 million. In 1992 there were 256 companies in this industry, with the largest four companies accounting for 28 percent of the total value of shipments. In 1995, firms in this industry averaged 142 employees per establishment, although the largest four establishments (by sales) each had 900 employees or more.

BACKGROUND AND DEVELOPMENT

Typical manufacturing includes metal grinding, cutting, degreasing, and surface finishing (including hardening). Such metal-working includes basic metal shaping, heat treatment, and metallurgic modifications using chemicals during processing.

The origin of the gear concept remains uncertain. It was not one of the basic five "simple machines" defined by Hero of Alexandria (the wheel and axle, the lever, the pulley, the wedge, and the screw), but it probably evolved from the screw. Until the Industrial Revolution, craftsmen used the gear primarily in small mechanisms like clocks, or to guide and locate machinery components. The idea of using it to transmit power in larger machines did not gain prevalence until nineteenth-century England.

In America, the technology and the expertise of local artisans to produce quality gears lagged behind Europe until near the end of that century. According to Robert S. Woodbury, this changed when G.B. Grant developed the first machine to cut teeth in a rotating gear blank with a rotating hob. In 1896, F.W. Fellows patented a gear-shaping machine that could turn out a wide variety of gears quickly and cheaply. The rise of the "American system" of mass manufacturing on an assembly line made such tools quickly popular, displacing the traditional hand-chiseled and filed gears of Europe. These two machine concepts became the dominant technology used in the manufacture of almost all gears in the United States and elsewhere.

By the 1990s, however, the advantages of mass production faded in the face of demands for more flexibility in the design and delivery of individual part orders. Gear manufacturers shifted to heavily automated production systems using Statistical Process Control (SPC), Computerized Numerical Control (CNC) and Just-In-Time (JIT) philosophies. These systems allowed greater precision and faster production shifts. Three-dimensional, computer-digitized master components maintain closer tolerances than can be achieved even with a skilled craftsman, and allow the same master to be used as a benchmark at production facilities around the globe.

CURRENT CONDITIONS

Since the industrial process of making large quantities of gears produces large amounts of waste by-products, the Environmental Protection Agency (EPA) targeted the industry as a waste minimization opportunity in 1992. In particular, it noted that the use of trichloroethane as a degreasing agent would eventually need to be replaced with other chemical solvents or a more advanced technology like ultrasonics. Trichloroethane is one of 17 chemicals listed by the EPA as an industrial toxin. International agencies have identified trichloroethane as an ozone-depleting substance contributing to global warming. For this reason, production of trichloroethane for emissive uses was banned in 1995 under amendments to the Clean Air Act of 1992. Chemical manufacturers have attempted to preserve sales by offering alternative chlorinated solvents as replacements to trichloroethane.

INDUSTRY LEADERS

In 1996, the four largest companies by sales volume in the speed changers, industrial high-speed drives, and gears industry were Falk Corporation of Milwaukee, Wisconsin; the Standard Drives Division of Allen-Bradley Company in Mequon, Wisconsin; Fairfield Manufacturing Co. in Lafayette, Indiana; and Twin Disc, Inc., located in Racine, Wisconsin.

Falk, a subsidiary of Sundstrand Corporation, was acquired in 1968. Sundstrand's entire industrial division, of which Falk is a part, had $736 million in sales in 1996; Falk accounted for $220 million of this number. That same year, the company employed 1,400 people. The Standard Drives Division of Allen Bradley, which is part of Rockwell Automation, had 1996 sales of $200 million. Third-ranked Fairfield Manufacturing Co., a subsidiary of Lancer Industries, Inc., employed 1,100 workers to produce $150 million. Twin Disc, which was established in 1918, also employed 1,100 workers in 1996 and reported sales of $164 million.

WORK FORCE

Employment in this industry peaked in 1974 at 27,000, then dropped to 17,400 in 1986 before recovering to 19,300 by 1988. Employment has steadily fallen since that time, however, and is expected to continue declining through the year 2000. By 1995, the industry employed 16,900 people, with 12,100 production workers. The average hourly wage in this industry in 1991 was $12.84. The *1992 Census of Manufactures* found that the leading states in employment were Illinois, Indiana, New York, and Wisconsin, compared to 1987, when Wisconsin, Illinois, Indiana, and Pennsylvania were the leaders in employment.

FURTHER READING

1995 Annual Survey of Manufactures. Washington: U.S. Department of Commerce, 1996.

Cavanugh, Tim. "Planning for 1,1,1's Demise." *Chemical Marketing Reporter,* 29 November 1993.

Darnay, Arsen J., ed. *Manufacturing USA.* 5th ed. Detroit: Gale Research, 1996.

Hoffman, John. "Chlorinated Solvents on a Phaseout Course." *Chemical Marketing Reporter,* 25 September 1995.

Humer, Caroline. "1,1,1 Demand Chips Into Rationed Supply." *Chemical Marketing Reporter,* 26 April 1993.

Moody's Industrial Manual, New York: Investors Service, Inc., 1996.

Owen, Jean. "Gearing Up." *Manufacturing Engineering,* September 1993.

Sundstrand Corporation. *1996 Annual Report.* Racine, WI, 1997.

Standard & Poor's Register of Corporations, Directors and Executives. New York: McGraw-Hill, 1996.

Twin Disc, Inc. *1996 Annual Report.* 1997.

Ulbrecht, Alan. *Waste Reduction Activities and Options for a Manufacturer of Hardened Steel Gears.* Cincinnati: U.S. Environmental Protection Agency, Risk Reduction Engineering Laboratory, 1992.

—Al Cook, updated by Jeanette Maurene Brooks

SIC 3567

INDUSTRIAL PROCESS FURNACES AND OVENS

Firms in this industry are primarily engaged in manufacturing industrial process furnaces, ovens, induction and dielectric heating equipment and related devices. Products not included in the classification include bakery ovens (**SIC 3556: Food Products Machinery**); cement, wood and chemical kilns (**SIC 3559: Special Industry Machinery, Not Elsewhere Classified**); cremating ovens (**SIC 3569: General Industrial Machinery and Equipment, Not Elsewhere Classified**); and laboratory furnaces and ovens (**SIC 3821: Laboratory Apparatus and Furniture**).

Between 1992 and 1995, the industry showed steady growth in both production and employment with shipments rising from $1.8 billion to $2.65 billion—an increase of 47 percent—and employment increasing from 17,000 to 18,700, an increase of ten percent. The 1995 figures also represent a four percent increase over the 18,000 workers listed in the 1994 census, and an increase of about 20 percent over the $2.2 billion in shipments listed the same year.

The concept of using heat to modify a material in some desirable manner originated very early in human history. Its application gave us names for eras like the Bronze Age and the Iron Age, as scientific advancement combined furnace design and fuels to achieve higher and more controllable temperatures and chemical reactions within the combustion or heating chambers. The Industrial Revolution brought the biggest advancements and launched the Steel Age as industry abandoned charcoal as the most common fuel and adopted coal and coke. By the end of the 20th century natural gas and electricity were displacing much solid fuel use.

Near the end of the century, though, many of the industry's prime customers did not utilize the new technologies. For instance, the steel industry used the Bessemer process which involved blowing large volumes of heated air through molten iron in a furnace. The American steel industry began using the process in the 1860s. The open hearth method, developed in the same decade, produced larger volumes of steel over longer periods of time, allowing for better quality control. By 1907, the open hearth method was more popular than the Bessemer. In the 1950s, however, furnace designers found they could improve the performance of the Bessemer furnace by using oxygen instead of air and the Bessemer furnace once again took the lead. By 1990, U.S. steel producers were using the Bessemer oxygen furnace for 59.7 percent of production, the open hearth method for 3.5 percent and electric furnaces had grabbed 36.8 percent of the market, according to *Market Share Reporter*.

This was only after more efficient foreign competition forced U.S. steel manufacturers to close outdated smelters and blast furnaces across the country. The area around Pittsburgh once supported 80,000 steel manufacturing jobs, but by 1990 fewer than 4,000 remained as the industry shut down and shifted production to newer mini-mill facilities.

Robert J. Pasquarelli, president of New Jersey Steel Corp., summarized the trend to electric in *Iron Age:* "I think what's going on in the flat-rolled [steel] business is tantamount to what happened with Bessemer in the last century. I think the whole industry's going to be reconfigured in the next ten years." In the 1990s, concern over air quality prompted passage of the Clean Air Act which mandated reductions of nitrous oxide emissions from such facilities as smelters and blast furnaces and designated such facilities as prime areas of concern. The legislation required special operating permits and monitoring provisions.

Three of the largest firms by sales volume in the industry in 1996 were Emerson Electric Company, General Signal Corporation, and Rheem Manufacturing Company. Emerson, founded in 1890 and located in St. Louis, MO, generated $10 billion in sales and employed 78,900. General Signal, located in Stamford, CT, had sales of $1.86 billion and 12,200 employees. Rheem, of New York, NY, had sales of $1 billion and employed 5,500.

FURTHER READING

Darnay, Arsen J., ed. *Manufacturing USA.* 5th ed. Detroit: Gale Research, 1996.

''Industrial Archeology: Monument to a Blast-Furnace.'' *Economist,* 3 February 1990.

Kranzberg, Melvin, and Carroll W. Pursel, Jr., eds. *Technology in Western Civilization.* New York: Oxford University Press, 1967.

McManus, George. ''High-Voltage Spending by the Electric Steelmakers.'' *Iron Age,* September 1993.

''Modelling and Optimization of the NO Formation in an Industrial Glass Furnace.'' *Journal of Engineering for Industry,* November 1992.

U.S. Bureau of the Census. *1995 Annual Survey of Manufactures.* Washington: GPO, 1997.

—Al Cook, updated by Kenneth R. Shepherd

SIC 3568

MECHANICAL POWER TRANSMISSION EQUIPMENT, NOT ELSEWHERE CLASSIFIED

The Mechanical Power Transmission Equipment, Not Elsewhere Classified, Industry is comprised of companies that manufacture mechanical power transmission equipment and parts for industrial machinery. Products include ball joints, pulleys, bearings, drive chains, sprockets, shafts, couplings, and other parts. Companies that make transmission devices for vehicles and aircraft are classified in **SIC 3714: Motor Vehicle Parts and Accessories** and **SIC 3728: Aircraft Parts and Auxiliary Equipment, Not Elsewhere Classified,** respectively.

The market for miscellaneous transmission equipment is fragmented. Motor vehicle manufacturers were the largest buying sector, accounting for ten percent of industry revenues in the early 1990s. The construction and farm machinery industries consumed six percent and four percent, respectively, of output. Motorcycle and bicycle makers purchased about four percent of production. Other significant markets for transmission equipment included shipbuilders, steel makers, the missile industry, and logging companies. About eight percent of production is exported.

Power transmission refers to the transfer of power through mechanical devices. The invention of the steam engine by James Watt in 1765 and the development of the internal combustion engine during the mid-1800s greatly expanded applications for power transmission equipment and played an important role in the industrial revolution. The industry realized its greatest growth during the U.S. economic expansion of the post-World War II era. Indeed, by the early 1980s, makers of miscellaneous transmission equipment were shipping about $2 billion worth of goods annually.

The effects of global competition seriously cut into the profits of U.S. manufacturers during the 1980s. In an effort to sustain profitability, miscellaneous transmission manufacturers increased productivity through automation and restructuring. As real output rose, the industry work force shrank more than 13 percent during the decade, from over 27,000 to about 24,000. Employment continued to drop, reaching a low of 21,800 in 1992. With the recovery of the economy in the mid-1990s, however, employment figures began to rise. By 1995, employment in the industry had climbed back to 22,700—a four percent increase over the 1992 figures, although still almost six percent below the employment figures at the end of the previous decade.

Despite efficiency gains, a recession in the late 1980s and early 1990s reduced profits for many competitors. Sales dropped about 2.5 percent in 1992. In that year, the industry shipped goods worth $2.4 billion. By 1994, the total value of goods shipped reached $2.79 billion—an increase of 16.4 percent—and in 1995, that total had risen to $2.89 billion, a further increase of 3.5 percent.

The largest competitor in the early 1990s by far was Ifint USA, of New York, which had 1991 sales of $915 million. U.S. Tsubaki Inc., of Illinois, placed second with about $100 million in sales. Third-place Funk Manufacturing Co., of Kansas, boasted revenues of $70 million. About 300 companies competed in the industry in the early 1990s, but only the top ten reached sales of over $30 million.

Future employment prospects are dim. Productivity gains and the movement of some production facilities across U.S. borders has resulted in continued work force reductions. Most labor opportunities have declined and will continue declining by about 20 percent to 30 percent by the year 2005, according to the Bureau of Labor Statistics—although the *1995 Annual Survey of Manufactures* reports that the number of jobs remained constant from 1994 to 1995. Even jobs for managers will decline significantly. Sales and marketing positions, however, will likely increase slightly.

FURTHER READING

Avery, Susan. "Power Transmission Recovers; Manufacturers Hike Prices." *Purchasing* , 17 June 1993.

Darnay, Arsen J., ed. *Manufacturing USA*. 3rd ed. Detroit: Gale Research, 1993.

U.S. Bureau of the Census. *1995 Annual Survey of Manufactures*. Washington: GPO 1997.

U.S. Department of Commerce. International Trade Administration. *U.S. Industrial Outlook 1994*. Washington: GPO, 1994.

—Dave Mote, updated by Kenneth R. Shepherd

SIC 3569

GENERAL INDUSTRIAL MACHINERY AND EQUIPMENT, NOT ELSEWHERE CLASSIFIED

This category covers establishments primarily engaged in manufacturing machinery, equipment, and components for general industrial use, and for which no special classification is provided. Machine shops primarily engaged in producing machine and equipment parts, usually on a job or order basis, are classified in **SIC 3599: Industrial and Commercial Machinery and Equipment, Not Elsewhere Classified.**

Companies in this industry produce miscellaneous manufacturing equipment. The plethora of industry offerings includes items such as altitude testing chambers, hydraulic bridge machinery, industrial centrifuges, cremating ovens, industrial fluid filters, swimming pool heaters, fire hoses, hydraulic jacks, and fire sprinkler systems.

The general industrial machinery and equipment industry is heavily dependent upon sales to other manufacturing businesses and to construction industries. In addition, about 30 percent of revenues are derived from exports. Intense capital investments during the U.S. industrial boom of the mid-1900s resulted in steady growth in demand for all types of industrial machinery. By the early 1980s, in fact, domestic producers of miscellaneous industrial machines were shipping about $4.5 billion worth of products each year and employing a work force of about 65,000.

Rampant growth in U.S. capital spending slowed in the 1980s, as foreign-manufactured goods reduced U.S. producers' share of capital goods markets. Machinery purchases by transportation industries were particularly slow. As a result, sales of miscellaneous machinery stagnated. Industry revenues lagged as a result of inflation and climbed at an average rate of about 2 percent per year during the 1980s to about $5.36 billion. Recessed commercial and residential construction markets added to industry woes in the late 1980s and early 1990s. Ailing manufacturers scrambled to sustain profitability by raising productivity, cutting their work force, and merging with or acquiring competitors.

Going into the mid-1990s, producers of miscellaneous machinery hoped to benefit from increased capital spending by the Clinton administration, an uptick in capital equipment replacements, and a devalued dollar, which was boosting exports. In addition, sales of machinery to some sectors showed signs of increasing. Construction equipment sales, for example, rose about 3 percent. However, spending on new manufacturing facilities and infrastructure was expected to remain flat at least through the mid-1990s.

The industry began a slow recovery after the recession ended in the mid-1990s. In 1995, according to the *1995 Annual Survey of Manufactures,* the industry employed 46,200 workers, a decrease of about 46 percent. However, this figure was 11.3 percent above the 41,500 workers in the industry reported in the 1992 census, and 13.8 percent above the 40,600 workers in the 1987 census. Industry productivity continued to rise as well, with $7.03 billion in value of goods reportedly shipped in 1995. This was 13.75 percent above the $6.18 billion worth of goods shipped in 1994 and 27.8 percent above the $5.5 billion shipped in 1992.

The industry is primarily run by numerous specialty manufacturers. Despite industry consolidation, over 1,000 companies competed going into the 1990s. Of the top 75 competitors, over half had sales of less than $40 million and employed fewer than 300 workers. The top producer was Tyco Laboratories of New Hampshire, which had 1996 sales of $5.089 billion from its diversified operations and employed move than 32,000 people. Grinnell Corp., which is also based in New Hampshire, had 1995 revenues of $3.26 billion and 24,000 employees. Other major manufacturers of miscellaneous industrial machinery included Figgie International, Inc. of Ohio, with 1995 revenues of $359 million and 2,582 employees; and Pall Corp. of New York with $822.8 million in 1995 revenue and 6,500 employees.

As companies continue to automate production facilities and move manufacturing operations across U.S. borders, the Bureau of Labor Statistics suggests that general industrial machinery industry employment will continue to decline. Jobs for assemblers and fabricators, which make up over 10 percent of the work force, will likely decline 32 percent by 2005, as will positions for machinists. Management opportunities will also deteriorate significantly. Sales and marketing positions, on the other hand, may increase slightly.

FURTHER READING

1995 Annual Survey of Manufactures. Washington: Bureau of the Census, 1997.

Darnay, Arsen J., ed. *Manufacturing USA; Industry Analyses, Statistics, and Leading Companies,* Detroit: Gale Research, 1993.

Heil, Scott F., ed. *Ward's Business Directory of U.S. Private and Public Companies,* Detroit: Gales Reasearch, 1997.

Standard & Poor's Industry Surveys. New York: Standard & Poor's Corporation, 24 December 1992.

U.S. Industrial Outlook 1993. Washington: U.S. Department of Commerce, January 1993.

—Dave Mote, updated by Kenneth R. Shepherd

SIC 3571

ELECTRONIC COMPUTERS

The industry encompasses companies primarily engaged in manufacturing electronic computers. By definition, this includes machines that:

- Store the processing program or programs and the data immediately necessary for execution of the program;

- Can be freely programmed in accordance with the requirements of the user;

- Perform arithmetical computations specified by the user; and

- Execute, without human intervention, a processing program which requires them to modify their execution by logical decision during the processing run.

Included in this industry are digital computers, analog computers, and hybrid digital/analog computers. Establishments primarily engaged in manufacturing machinery or equipment which incorporate computers or a central processing unit for the purpose of performing functions such as measuring, displaying, or controlling process variables are classified based on the manufactured end product.

INDUSTRY SNAPSHOT

Computer manufacturing is one of the most dynamic industries in the United States and the world. Despite its large size, the industry is still growing and changing at a fast pace. As certain sectors of the industry have begun to decline, other product categories have experienced enormous growth.

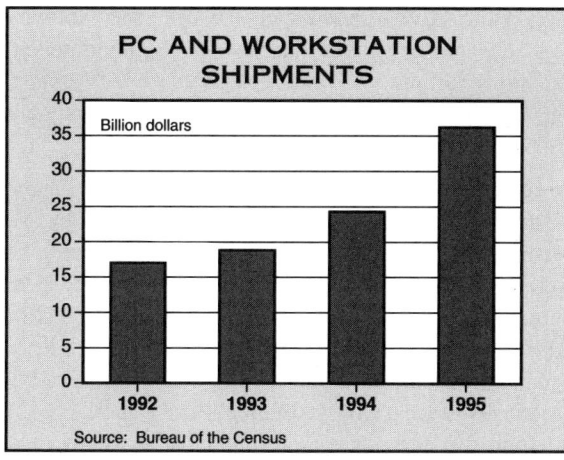

PC AND WORKSTATION SHIPMENTS

Billion dollars

Source: Bureau of the Census

Following a period of rampant expansion in the 1970s and 1980s, the industry's growth slowed down in the in early 1990s but then picked up pace again by the mid-1990s. Total U.S. manufacturers' shipments for computers in 1995 were valued at $52 billion, an increase of 36 percent over the previous year's total of $38.26 billion. The number of computer units shipped in 1995 totaled 20.5 million, up 22.9 percent from 16.7 million in 1994. There were 205 manufacturers of electronic computers in the United States in 1995. The general outlook for the industry remained very positive heading into the late 1990s.

ORGANIZATION AND STRUCTURE

The computer industry is segmented by product category. Different kinds of computers contain differing components, varying performance and price levels, and, to a certain extent, service different functions and markets.

At the most fundamental level, electronic computers can be categorized as either analog or digital. Analog computers are electromechanical devices whose operation is based on continuously variable quantities such as lengths, weights, or voltages. Digital computers, by contrast, operate by processing discrete quantities of digits or characters. Digital computers offer greater flexibility in programming. Thus, almost all computers today are digital. Analog computers are designed only for very specific functions. Digital computers, on the other hand, usually serve general functions. It is the configuration of added software and peripheral hardware devices, however, that make a digital computer suited for specific functions. In 1995, general purpose digital computer shipments accounted for $49.52 billion out of the computer industry total of $50.3 billion, and 20.38 units shipped out of a total of 20.52 million units.

General purpose digital computers are traditionally categorized by computer size and processing power. These main categories are supercomputers, mainframes, midrange systems, and microcomputers.

Supercomputers are high-speed number crunchers that allow scientists, engineers, and government researchers to process and manipulate massive amounts of data very quickly. Their performance is typically measured in terms of billions of floating point operations per second, or gigaflops, as opposed to millions of instructions per second (MIPS) assigned to most other types of computers. The fastest supercomputer, delivered in December 1996, reached a processing speeds of 1.06 teraflops, or trillions of floating point operations-per-second. These technological taskmasters are used to complete complex feats, such as forecasting weather, designing ships and automobiles, conducting nuclear research, and carrying out advanced simulations.

An important distinction exists between traditional high-powered "vector," and low-powered "parallel" supercomputers. The newer parallel devices join as many as tens of thousands of cheap microprocessors to accomplish what vector systems achieve with a handful of more expensive processors. Though usually less expensive, systems that use Massively Parallel Processing (MPP) technology can perform many tasks faster than traditional vector systems.

Mainframe computers generally offer less raw computational power than supercomputers, and are most often used to handle large volumes of general purpose business or institutional applications. Users access the mainframe through satellite terminals that are connected to the system. Some mainframes also offer add-on features that make them competitive with low-end supercomputers. Systems range between $500,000 and $30 million. In 1996, mainframe processing speeds ranged from approximately 50 MIPS to over 360 MIPS.

Midrange computers, also called minicomputers serve anywhere from a few to several hundred users, either locally or at remote locations. Small to medium-sized businesses, company departments, and manufacturing facilities commonly use midrange systems for communications processing, automation, reporting, and networking. Midrange systems often employ vendor-developed proprietary applications which are tailored to the organization's needs. Newer "open systems," though, allow the use of standardized operating systems and applications. Midrange computers can range in price from $10,000 to approximately $1 million.

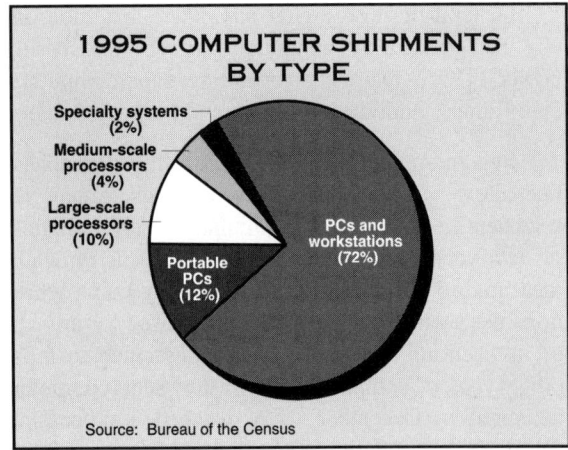

1995 COMPUTER SHIPMENTS BY TYPE

Specialty systems (2%)
Medium-scale processors (4%)
Large-scale processors (10%)
Portable PCs (12%)
PCs and workstations (72%)

Source: Bureau of the Census

Microcomputers, or personal computers (PCs), unlike the systems mentioned above that serve users at satellite terminals, are single-user self-contained units. They offer the least raw computing power of any segment of the industry, but provide the greatest amount of flexibility, diversity, and portability. Although PCs are well-suited for home and personal use, about two-thirds of all units sold in the early 1990s were used for business and professional purposes. Prices ranged from $250 for low-powered clones to more than $25,000 for fully configured systems with advanced graphic and communications capabilities. This segment includes laptop and notebook computers.

Workstations are a special class of high-powered microcomputers. Because of technological advances in the 1980s, many workstations are capable of performing intensive research, engineering, and graphics tasks that allow them to compete with low-end supercomputers and mainframes. High-performance microprocessors allow many workstations to employ high-resolution or 3-D graphic interfaces, sophisticated multi-task software, and advanced communication capabilities. Workstation prices can range from $3,000 to over $100,000. The traditional definition of workstations are microcomputers based on RISC (reduced instruction set computing) microprocessor design, but the distinction between workstations and other personal computers is becoming increasingly blurred.

A new category of computers that has emerged is based on function, rather than structure. These are Local Area Network (LAN) servers, which are the newest, fastest growing category of computers. Servers are similar to midrange or mainframe computers in function, by serving multiple users with shared data, yet are similar to personal computers in structure, by being based on microprocessors. In fact, the lowest-end servers are merely high-end personal computers or

workstations configured with the necessary software and telecommunications hardware. High-end servers contain multiple microprocessors, and have begun to cut into the market traditionally served by midrange or mainframe computers.

Personal computers (PCs) make up the largest segment of the computer industry. Total PC and workstation shipments in 1995 were $36.23 billion in value and 15,685,620 units. Despite the disappointments, the notebook market, which has been fueling the PC industry's overall unit sales growth, still grew 21.3 percent to 8.9 million units shipped worldwide in 1995 over 1994, according to International Data Corp. Although PC sales were greater than sales in any other industry segment, low producer concentration and a commodity-like environment in 1993 resulted in the lowest profit margins in the computer industry. For instance, while margins on PCs were typically between 5 percent and 30 percent, mainframe producers often earned a mark-up of 50 percent to 70 percent.

BACKGROUND AND DEVELOPMENT

The first mechanical calculating devices were built in Europe in the seventeenth-century. The English mathematician Charles Babbage carried that concept a step further in the nineteenth century with the design of the Analytical Engine, the first digital computer. The Engine design showed how programs could be stored on punched cards similar to those used by French looms. Although the Analytical Engine was never built, it influenced the first digital mechanical computers and helped pave the way of the computer revolution that changed the world.

The few computers in existence in the 1940s were primarily used to grind out tables of complex mathematical functions. Researchers that understood the potential of more advanced devices, however, were successful in securing sizable U.S. government and military grants to fund further development. The first general-purpose electronic computer, ENIAC, was completed in 1946. ENIAC, which stands for electronic numerical integrator and calculator, required partial rewiring in order to program it for different tasks. The first operational stored-program electronic digital computer, similar in function to computers of today, was completed in 1949 at the University of Cambridge. Although various analog devices were also developed and tested in the 1930s and 1940s, analog computers played a relatively minor role in the development of the industry.

The electromechanical computers of the mid-1940s had already been replaced by the early 1950s with more powerful and flexible electronic versions.

The UNIVAC system, developed for the U.S. Bureau of the Census, and a similar system used by the General Electric Company were two of the first commercially viable electronic computers put into use. By the end of the 1950s, business, government, and scientific communities began to view the computer as a dependable and potentially effective tool for an enormous variety of tasks.

Timesharing systems, pioneered at the Massachusetts Institute of Technology, allowed public and private entities to gain extensive access to large, expensive mainframe computer systems in the 1960s. Timesharing allowed several users at remote locations to simultaneously use a single machine. Users were charged for the amount of time that they were actually connected to the computer by cables or telephone lines. Although timeshare technology was first used primarily for scientific and technical endeavors, business and industry participants soon learned that they, too, could benefit from access to centralized processors.

By the end of the 1960s the computer industry was poised for rapid growth. Computers in the 1960s were already up to 100 times faster than their counterparts of the 1950s—and computer memory and speed continued to rise at an increasing rate. Furthermore, the first minicomputer was installed in 1965, breaking ground for an entirely new segment of the industry. The number of digital computers had increased from less than 15 in 1950 to over 40,000 by the late 1960s. Going into the 1970s, though, all sectors of society were beginning to seek the computational power offered by supercomputers and mainframes to handle labor-intensive tasks. In addition, industry leaders were continually striving to expand their market by increasing computer access to end-users, rather than only trained computer professionals.

Development of the microprocessor in 1971 allowed the entire central processor of a computer to be placed on a single silicon chip. It was this development that led to subsequent rapid expansion and transformation of the industry. In addition to the proliferation of supercomputers, mainframes, and midrange systems that took advantage of new chip technology, workstations and PC devices began to emerge. By the early 1980s, over 500,000 general-purpose computers had been installed in North America. Furthermore, the market was growing at an annual rate of about 20 percent.

In the early 1980s, the computer industry consisted of several niches, each dominated by one or two manufacturers that had been the first to successfully exploit an opening in the market. International Business Machines (IBM), Sperry, Wang, Unisys, and Digital Equipment Corporation (DEC) were among the many companies that generated immense revenues during the decade. For the most part, these companies succeeded by developing proprietary hardware and operating systems that effectively prohibited customers from switching to a competitor's product.

Manufacturers often enjoyed profit margins of 70 percent to 90 percent on sales of various mainframe and minicomputer installations. Demand ballooned throughout the decade as business, industry, and the public sector invested billions of dollars to computerize and automate information management, manufacturing, computationally-intensive research, and other activities. As many mainframe companies settled into their respective niches, however, the rapid advancement of microprocessor technology caused a market shift that took many industry leaders by surprise.

Many industry participants failed to foresee the dominance of PCs, workstations, and some midrange systems. Within a period of a few years, in fact, technological innovations turned the slow and limited microcomputer of the early 1980s into a relatively low-cost, powerful, and speedy contender. Furthermore, by networking these smaller devices, users were able to develop cost-effective systems that could handle tasks that were previously performed only by mainframes and powerful minicomputers.

Although the demand for mainframe and supercomputer sales advanced throughout most of the decade, manufacturers that focused solely on those products and failed to respond to the inevitable dominance of workstations and PCs found themselves in serious financial trouble in the mid-1980s. The number of PCs purchased by Americans rose from fewer than 500,000 PCs in 1980 to approximately 7 million in 1984. By 1989, annual PC sales approached 10 million. Sales of RISC workstations grew at a rate of over 110 percent annually between 1986 and 1988. As PCs increased their share of the entire computer-related market revenues from 10.6 percent in 1987 to 15.2 percent in 1991, the share of the market held by large-scale systems fell from 12.6 percent to 9.5 percent.

Many companies which led the computer industry in the 1980s suffered massive financial losses in the early 1990s, as they either retrenched or shifted their focus. Wang Laboratories, for instance, declared bankruptcy after posting an $11 million loss on $1.2 billion in sales and has since restructured itself as a software-only company. IBM accrued more losses in 1992 than most industry leaders generated in sales revenue.

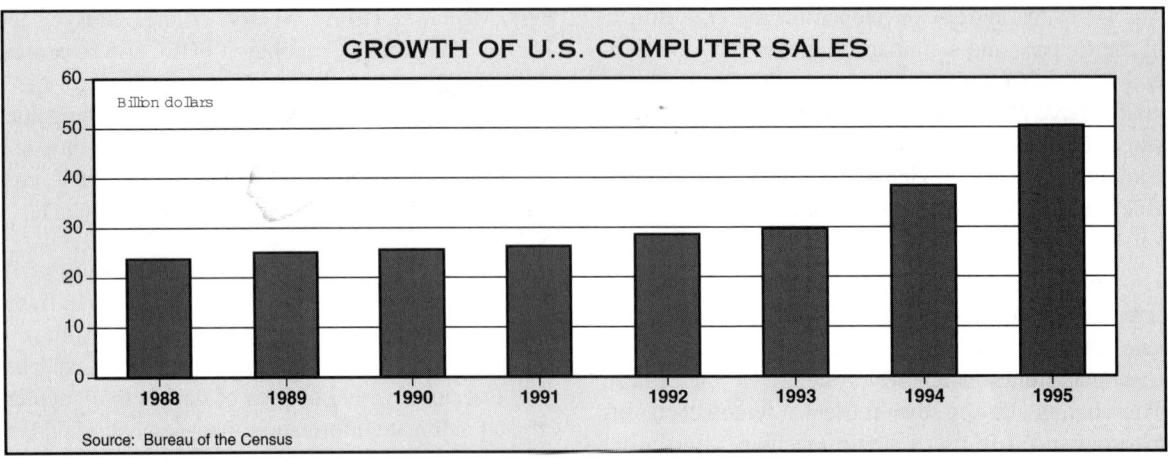

GROWTH OF U.S. COMPUTER SALES

Billion dollars

Source: Bureau of the Census

Strong growth and solid profits enjoyed by most computer manufacturers during the 1980s faded in the early 1990s, as the industry realized a serious reduction in the overall growth of domestic demand. Several factors contributed to the downturn. In addition to the global recession of the early 1990s, manufacturers were beginning to confront the fact that the U.S. computer market was becoming saturated. In addition, the shift from high-profit, large-scale proprietary systems to low-margin, open architecture, desktop computers was reducing profit opportunities.

Indeed, inexpensive personal systems that offered computing power similar to that offered by the mainframes of the early 1980s were now viewed as a commodity by many consumers. Rather than purchasing a PC system from a retail outlet at a price of $4,000 or $5,000, many customers in the early 1990s began purchasing more advanced systems through the mail or at discount warehouses for approximately $1,000 to $2,000.

In response the new environment of the 1990s almost all companies, and especially older competitors, were: slashing prices in an effort to boost sales volume; emphasizing smaller, cheaper systems; increasing sales of services and software; forming alliances; and downsizing their work force.

CURRENT CONDITIONS

Despite the slowing growth of the industry in the early 1990s and an apparent saturation of the market, other developments led the computer industry to rebound and return to fast-paced growth in the mid-1990s.

The biggest trend in the computer market since the end of the 1980s has been the adoption of networks of PCs, particularly in the client-server configuration. At the high end, such networks have come to replace midrange systems, and at the low end, such as in small offices, they offer sharing of data between previously unlinked PCs. Where in the past, an organization would have a single midrange computer shared by many simultaneous users through terminals, now each user had his own full-featured computer at his desktop, the client computer, while still being able to share central data located on a server computer. As more businesses found it advantageous to migrate to client-server systems, sales for new PCs and LAN servers grew enormously.

The continued growth in sales of PCs to expand and upgrade LAN users is no longer assured, however. In the mid-1990s an entirely new computer category emerged, called the network computer. The network computer (or NC, as opposed to PC), is an inexpensive, low-powered unit that utilizes the processing power and memory of the server computer to which it is connected over a network. Network computers may or may not have a hard drive to run software applications locally. Those that do not, execute software that is on a server accessed through the Internet or a local network. Dubbed NC-S (network computer-server), models available in early 1997 included HDS Network Systems Inc.'s @workStation, Wyse Technology Inc.'s Winterm, and Network Computers Devices Inc.'s Explora. By contrast, NC-C (network computer-client) computers execute computers on the local desktop, and available models include IBM's Network Station, Sun Microsystems Inc.'s JavaStation, and devices from Acorn Computer Group Ltd. with technology licensed from Oracle Corp.'s Network Computing subsidiary. Whether they would succeed in competing with full-featured PCs was still uncertain.

Another major development contributing to the acceleration in computer sales in the mid-1990s was the incredible growth in popularity of the Internet and online services. On the one hand, the presence of the

Internet and commercial online services spurred on further growth of the home computer market, as people who did not yet have computers finally decided to buy them for the purpose for getting on-line. At the same time, more and more businesses and organizations wanted to put their information on the Internet, and this trend fueled the sales of servers, which could be used as Internet host computers. The popularity of the Internet among companies led to the emergence of internal corporate intranets, which was yet another use for more, new LAN servers. The Internet was also the impetus for development of the network computer. The idea was that there were potential users of the Internet who did not want to spend the higher price of a full-featured computer. For the home user, the NC does not even have its own monitor, but uses a television screen instead.

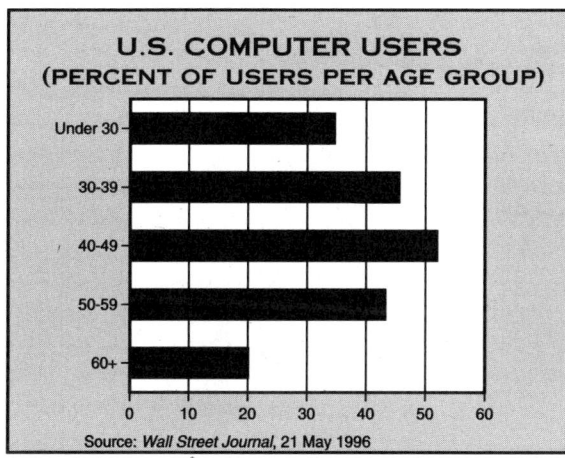

U.S. COMPUTER USERS
(PERCENT OF USERS PER AGE GROUP)

Source: *Wall Street Journal*, 21 May 1996

Also encouraging the growth in computer sales is the advancement in multimedia technology. Multimedia refers to the incorporation of detailed graphics, sound, animation, or video into a computer program. In order to fully support such complex software, computers with ever faster processing speeds are required. The processing demands for multimedia have encouraged purchases of faster, more powerful computers by existing computer owners wanting to "upgrade." It is predicted that 44.1 percent of PCs sold to home users in 1997 will be to homes that already own PCs.

Finally, the ever-present trend of lower costs in computer components and the resulting lower prices that can be asked for the end products, continues to fuel sales. Consumers and businesses are not hesitant to replace only slightly outdated computers, since newer models offer greater capabilities at the same or even lower prices than the older models.

Industry Segment Status. After a period of stagnation in the early 1990s, the mainframe market

picked up again by 1994. Client/server architecture, which at first seemed to compete with mainframes, actually began to be implemented along with mainframes, by networking PCs to mainframe computers. In 1993 less than 3 million networked PCs were connected to mainframe or midrange computers, but this was expected to increase to 29 million PCs by 1997, according to WorkGroup Technologies. Costs for mainframes have also been falling with the adoption of a new kind of chip called CMOS (complementary metal-oxide semiconductor). It costs \$18,000/MIPS (millions of instructions per second) as opposed to the \$23,000/MIPS cost of the bipolar chips that it is replacing. Furthermore, CMOS-based computers do not need to be water-cooled as the bipolar-based computers are. According to a 1995 survey of leading companies by Softlab, the mainframe computer is expected to be in mainstream use past the year 2000. For many applications that require large volumes of data processing, the mainframe remains the best solution.

Midrange computers have also withstood the challenge from networked PCs and workstations, as the server function that both midrange and PCs can offer has blurred the distinction between the categories. Positioning midrange computers as servers to which PCs could be networked has involved migrating to "open systems" of standardized connectivity architectures and operating systems, such as Unix. One of the top two midrange manufacturers, DEC, has migrated from proprietary operating system software to Unix and the "open-systems" that it offers. At the end of 1994, Unix owned a 44 percent share of the market share in the enterprise resource planning arena, while IBM's proprietary AS/400 dropped down to 40 percent, from 46 percent in 1993. Nevertheless, IBM has stayed on top by moving to superior computing technology. In 1995 IBM migrated its AS/400 midrange series from 48-bit CISC architecture to 64-bit RISC architecture, and had enormous sales of 70,000 units in 1996. By 1997 HP still had not migrated its HP 3000 to 64-bit processing.

The distinction between high-end PCs and workstations has become blurred, and thus the status of the workstation market segment depends on how it is defined. Sales of traditional workstations, which are based on RISC processors and run the Unix operating system slowed toward the second half of the 1990s. Meanwhile, Intel processor-based personal workstations running Windows NT were poised for enormous growth. International Data Corp. predicted that the traditional workstation market would grow at only about five percent per year during the second half of the 1990s, while the personal workstation market would sustain the 40 percent-range growth it experienced in 1996.

The PC segment of the industry is the largest and most closely watched, but after more than a decade of shifting technologies, competitors, and marketing strategies, the industry segment had achieved relative maturity and stability by the mid-1990s. After a period of price reductions, the marketing strategy had shifted to keep prices around $2,000 for a fully configured system, but to add more and more features. PC shipments in the United States were expected, according to research firm Dataquest, to reach 26.9 million in 1996, up 13 percent over the previous year. In 1995 the U.S. PC market grew 21 percent.

In the mid-1990s notebook computer sales picked up. One reason for the notebooks' popularity is that their screens, whose images were previously of poor quality, increased in size and clarity due to the drop in price in technology that allowed manufacturers to use higher-end, 12.1-inch TFT (thin film transistor) displays.

INDUSTRY LEADERS

The leading company of the computer industry in revenues has always been and still is International Business Machines Corporation (IBM). Its 1996 revenues earned from computer hardware sales, which includes peripheral devices, were $36.3 billion. (Total 1996 revenues were $75.9 billion.) The next leading company, Hewlett-Packard Co. (HP), had total revenues of $31.52 billion. The remaining top ten of the U.S. computer industry according to 1995 revenues were Compaq Computer Corp., with $14.76 billion, Digital Equipment Corp. (DEC), with $13.81 billion, Apple Computer Inc., with $11.06 billion, NCR Corp. with $8.0 billion, Unisys Corp., with $6.20 billion, Sun Microsystems Inc., with $5.90 billion, Dell Computer Corp., with $5.30 billion, and Packard Bell NEC, with $4.5 billion. These are total revenue figures, and most of these companies earn part of their revenues, in some cases up to half, from sources other than computers, such as software sales, computer systems maintenance service, or systems integration services. Hewlett-Packard also manufacturers computer printers and medical test and measurement equipment.

Market share. The diverse and segmented electronic computing industry contains several major players that dominate particular niches. The mainframe segment has always been dominated by IBM, which holds about two-thirds of the market. The second leading company in the U.S. sales is Hitachi Data Systems Ltd., with 22 percent of the market share in 1996, which was predicted by the Meta Group to reach 25

percent in 2000. Amdahl Corp. is third with 10 percent of the market in 1996. The midrange segment is also led by IBM, but by a much slimmer margin. DEC is third and HP is third in midrange market share. The workstation segment has been dominated by Sun Microsystems since 1987. In 1995 Sun Microsystems had 39 percent share of the worldwide market, followed by HP with 22 percent. In that year Silicon Graphics over took DEC and IBM to obtain a third-ranking market shared of 11 percent.

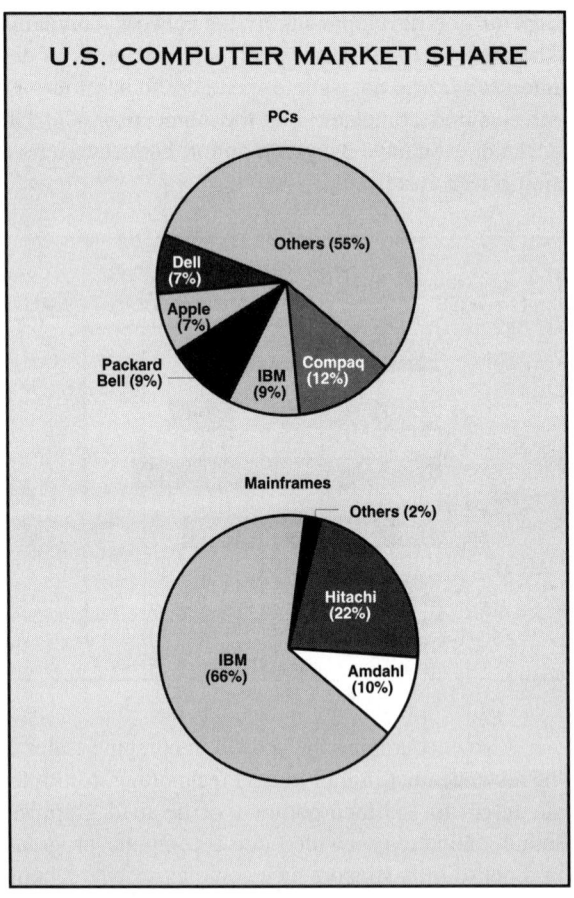

The PC market in the 1980s and early 1990s had been dominated by IBM, with Apple Computer in second place. In 1985, for example, IBM's market share was a solid 27 percent. By the mid-1990s, however, the PC market had become extremely competitive. In 1994 IBM and Apple Computer were both overtaken in both U.S. and world market share by Compaq Computer. In second quarter 1996 Compaq held 12.4 percent of PC shipments in the United States, followed by IBM with 9.0 percent, Packard Bell with 8.7 percent, Apple Computer with 7.4 percent, and Dell with 7.2 percent. Packard Bell dominated the consumer sector within the PC market. Up-and-coming competitors in the PC market in the early 1990s included Gateway 2000, AST, and Everex. Compaq similarly dominated the world market, obtaining 9.7 percent of worldwide shipments of PCs in second quarter 1996, followed by IBM with 8.8 percent of world market share.

The LAN server market, which includes both PC and Unix servers, is dominated by Hewlett-Packard. In 1995 it gained more than $8 billion in revenue for its combined Unix and PC server sales. IBM was second with $4.05 billion in combined revenue for its Unix and PC servers. IBM had refocused on industry-standard PC servers in 1995, transitioning from its proprietary MCA communications architecture to Peripheral Component Interface. Compaq was third with $3 billion in revenue from server sales. Sun Microsystems was fourth with $1.3 billion in server revenue. Meanwhile, Compaq dominates the fast-growing PC server segment of the market. In 1995 it held a 34 percent of the worldwide market of 850,000 units shipped. It was followed by HP with 12 percent, and IBM with 14 percent.

Companies. IBM, based in Armonk, New York, remains the unmitigated mammoth of the global electronic computing industry. The company, founded in 1910 under the name of Calculating-Tabulating-Recording (CTR), got its start by producing punch-card tabulating machines. IBM grew quickly by stressing large-scale, custom-built systems, and by leasing, rather than selling, its products to most of its customers. Government contracts were largely responsible for the company's rapid growth during the 1940s. It was during this period that IBM developed the Mark I, the first computer capable of retaining a set of rules that could be applied to information that was input at a later time. By the mid-1960s, IBM owned 65 percent of the U.S. computer market. IBM's mainframe models, the 360 and 370, generated massive profits for the company during the 1970s. Although IBM continued to grow through the mid-1980s, the company began to lose focus, and its hesitation in taking the PC market seriously was only belatedly realized as a miscalculation. Between 1985 and 1992, IBM dismissed 100,000 employees and restructured its operations several times. After a period of losses in the early 1990s, IBM was profitable and better focused by 1996. It dominated the mainframe market with its System/390 model and still had hopes for growth in this sector, its AS/400 midrange computer was very popular as an efficient server, its Aptiva-S desktop PC was receiving good reviews, and its Thinkpad 560 notebook computer was one of the most popular on the market.

Hewlett-Packard (HP), founded in 1938 and based in Palo Alto, California, is a leading company in PCs,

workstations, servers, notebooks and handheld computers, in addition to being the leading U.S. manufacturer of computer printers. The company also produces scientific and medical instrumentation, but computers and peripherals account for 80 percent of its revenues. HP is a leader in Unix operating system-based workstations and computers in general, for which it has designed its own microprocessor chips and developed a version of the Unix software. HP's Unix server sales alone grew by 60 percent in 1995, primarily through its HP 9000 and HP 3000 series servers. Its latest lines of PCs are the HP Vectra for business users and the HP Pavilion for consumers. HP has always been a financially successful company, and in 1995 was chosen by *Forbes* magazine as the outstanding corporate performer of the year.

Compaq Computer, which introduced its first product, an IBM-compatible PC, along with many other new PC clone manufacturers in 1982, managed to pull ahead of the competition through a strong capital base and superior marketing. In time, Compaq, based in Houston, Texas, became the fastest-growing publicly held company ever. Compaq has traditionally focused sales through dealers and distributors, but in face of rising competition from Dell, in 1997 Compaq began expanding its direct sales efforts for the first time. Compaq produces microcomputers in the desktop, laptop, and server categories. Its sales for 1996 were $18.1 billion, up 23 percent from the previous year.

Digital Equipment Corp. (DEC), located in Maynard, Massachusetts, made its name and fortune in the 1960s and 1970s by pioneering the midrange computer category. It introduced the world's first minicomputer in 1959, two years after the company was founded. Its flagship minicomputer was the VAX. The decline of the midrange category and in particular computers running proprietary operating system software, as does the VAX, led DEC to refocus its computer products on PCs, workstations, and servers. In 1995 only 10 percent of DEC's product revenues were derived from VAX systems, down drastically from 34 percent in 1993. Meanwhile, sales of microprocessor-based PCs, whether desktops or servers, reached 26 percent of product sales in 1995, up from only 9 percent in 1993. Sales of computers based on DEC's own Alpha chip, most of which are workstations, had reached 22 percent of total product sales in 1995, up from only 3 percent in 1993. The remaining 42 percent of DEC's product sales in 1995 came from software and computer peripherals and subsystems. All these product sales accounted for $7.6 billion, or only 55 percent of DEC's total operating revenues of $13.81 billion, with computer-related services accounting for the remaining revenue dollars.

Apple Computer, despite its relatively high market share in the PC market, has stood apart from other PC manufacturers by its use of a proprietary operating system for its computers, MacOS. Apple, based in Cupertino, California, was a pioneer in PC technology when it was founded in 1977 and, after several short-lived models, introduced its immensely successful Macintosh line of computers in 1984. From the beginning, Apple's marketing efforts were aimed at the school, college, and home markets. It was never as successful in the business market. By the 1990s, the position of the rival PCs based on Intel microprocessors and DOS/Windows operating systems had become solidly entrenched, and Apple's market share began to decline. Apple finally decided to license its MacOS operating system in 1995 to spurn the development of Macintosh clones, but the move came too late to have a significant impact on the overall PC market. Management crises and lack of a strategic direction plagued the company in the mid-1990s. In fiscal 1996 Apple posted a significant loss of $816 million on top of revenues that had declined 11 percent to $9.83 billion. Although the long-term survival of the company has been called into question, Apple maintains a strong position in the market of publishing and graphic arts businesses.

Sun Microsystems Inc., based in Mountain View, California, became the leader of the workstation industry segment only five years after the company was founded in 1982 and only six years after the first workstations appeared on the market. Sun pioneered the "open system," Unix-based workstation, as opposed to those which ran only proprietary software, which enables the sharing of software and hardware components among competing workstation manufacturers. Sun has also been a leader in developing computers based on the RISC microprocessor chip architecture. It developed its own improved version of RISC called SPARC (scalable performance architecture) and it licenses the technology to silicon chip manufacturers. Sun's SPARCstation workstation computer, introduced first in 1989 and based on the SPARC technology, became the most popular workstation model. As growth in the workstation market began to slow in the early 1990s, Sun began to focus more on developing Unix-based servers and has been doing quite well in this market segment.

WORK FORCE

The computer industry employs large numbers of electrical engineers, programmers, assemblers, and technicians. In fact, these occupations represent about 30 percent of the industry total. Companies also hire large numbers of people for miscellaneous management, sales, and clerical positions. In 1993, total employment in the entire computer industry, of which electronic computer manufacturers represented about 50 percent, totaled about 220,000. Employment was significantly down from the industry peak in the mid-1980s, when electronic computer manufacturers employed over 150,000 workers.

Despite the continued growth in industry sales, employment in the industry has been declining since its peak in 1984. Between 1984 and 1995, the computer manufacturing industry lost 32 percent of its workforce, an average annual rate of 3 percent. The computer industry is one of the more highly automated manufacturing industries, and many manual assembly jobs have been eliminated. By 1996 only 35 percent of all jobs in the industry were directly involved in production, compared with 65 percent in 1960 and compared with 70 percent in the manufacturing sector as a whole in 1996. Companies that had traditionally been computer manufacturers shifted part of their activities to software and service, as these areas became more profitable. Many computer manufacturers transferred some of their production facilitates overseas to take advantage of lower labor costs. In addition, more foreign-owned computer companies are supplying the U.S. market with either computers or parts through imports. Companies are expected to continue to introduce labor-saving automation and to outsource manufacturing activities to low-cost foreign producers. Furthermore, corporate alliances should moderate the demand for research and development professionals.

While the demand for programmers in the industry was expected to rise slightly, the demand for other occupations will likely fall, according to the Bureau of Labor Statistics. The demand for engineers, for instance, will slip about 3.5 percent by 2005. Likewise, technician and engineering management jobs will fall by 2 percent to 5 percent. Manufacturing jobs, especially, will disappear. The demand for electrical and electronic assemblers, for example, will likely plummet 55 percent by 2005. Analysts project that assemblers and fabricator positions will decline by about 37 percent, while the demand for production planning professionals will fall over 20 percent.

Management executive positions are expected to decrease as well—by an estimated 22 percent. Even the number of lower level management jobs is expected to fall by about 20 percent by 2005. The one bright spot in the job picture is an expected 47 percent increase in the demand for systems analysts and computer scientists. This group currently accounts for only about 2.4 percent of employment in the computer and office equipment industries.

Professionals with bachelor's degrees in computer engineering (BSCE) were in high demand in the mid-1990s. Computer and business-equipment manufacturers planned to hire almost 66 percent more graduates in 1997 than in 1996. Graduates with BSCE degrees could expect starting salaries on average of $37,301 in 1997, up 5.9 percent over 1996. Many of these new employees were not be directly involved in computer manufacturing, however, rather in services. Most of the biggest computing companies—IBM, Unisys, DEC—have extensive and growing service and consulting divisions that hire hundreds of new graduates every year.

AMERICA AND THE WORLD

U.S. computer companies continued to dominate the world equipment industry in the 1990s, though they have been gradually losing market share since the mid-1980s. In 1996 exports were estimated to have accounted for 45 percent of all U.S. computer equipment shipments, which also included peripherals and parts. This rate of exports has remained constant throughout the first half of the 1990s. The United States maintains a positive trade balance in computers, although the trade gap is narrowing. In computer parts and peripherals, however, the United States has had a growing trade deficit since 1991.

U.S. exports of computers were increasing only gradually in the 1990s and not as quickly as the industry was growing overall. According to U.S. Department of Commerce statistics, exports of computer systems increased from $8.1 billion in 1990 to $9.48 billion in 1996, an increase of less than 3 percent annually. Exports actually declined by 8.2 percent in 1996 from $10.33 billion in 1995. Exports of peripherals and parts, meanwhile, have been increasing more rapidly.

Europe continued to be the largest foreign market for the U.S. computer industry in the late 1990s. Europe accounted for $14.4 billion or 38 percent of all U.S. computer, computer peripheral, and computer part exports in 1996. Asia is second, with $11.7 billion or 31 percent of U.S. computer equipment exports that year. Latin America is the fastest growing market, with computer equipment exports to the region increasing 32 percent from 1995 to 1996. Canada, Japan, and the United Kingdom are the top three export destinations for U.S. computer equipment.

Imports of computers to the United States, according to the Department of Commerce, increased from $2.7 billion in 1990 to $6.37 billion in 1996, an average rate of 15 percent per year. Imports jumped 26 percent in 1996 from the previous year. Imports of peripherals and computer parts have been increasing at an even faster rate. Asia is the largest importer of computer equipment to the United States, accounting for $48.4 billion or 81 percent of all computer, computer peripheral, and computer part imports in 1996. The leading importers are Japan and Singapore.

In terms of overall market growth for PCs, the Western European PC market grew by 7.1 percent in 1996 to 15.9 million units, according to preliminary results from International Data Corp. PC shipments in Latin America grew by over 30 percent in 1996 to reach 3.1 million units, due to the strong PC growth in Mexico, Colombia, Argentina, and Brazil according to Dataquest. Brazil is the leading Latin American market with 1.3 million units shipped in 1996. Mexico, on the other hand, is the fastest-growing country with a 73 percent increase of shipments over 1995. In both Western European and Latin American markets, U.S. manufacturers account for the majority of the shipments.

The U.S. computer industry faces its most serious competition abroad from Japanese computer makers. Although the United States still maintained a technological advantage in large-scale systems and workstations, some Japanese competitors had made significant strides in those segments. Although Japanese companies were trying to infiltrate the supercomputer market, over 90 percent of which was controlled by U.S. companies, their systems offered limited performance and lagged in MPP technology. Acquisition of U.S. and European firms, in addition to their own research and development, will likely make Japanese manufacturers contenders for supercomputer market share in the future. The Japanese domestic market for all computer categories, meanwhile, is the only one not dominated by the United States, partly due to Japanese protectionism. A U.S.-Japanese trade agreement that went into effect in 1993 belatedly helped open the Japanese public sector to U.S. firms.

The global market for U.S. computers is expected to offer even more opportunities as emerging economies demand more high-tech equipment and tariffs on the imports of computers are reduced. The International Trade Agreement approved in December 1996 by 28 countries was expected to eventually free U.S. computer manufacturers of having to pay customs tariffs in stages by January 1, 2000.

RESEARCH AND TECHNOLOGY

The computer industry has historically benefited from considerable government funds in research and development. This was especially the case during the Cold War. More recently government funding of research in high technology industries has declined, and, according to a study by the Institute for the Future, the industry's own investments in research have not been as great to make up the difference. Furthermore, in the early and mid-1990s computer companies have even been decreasing the percentage of their revenues that they invest in R&D. Computer companies still invest considerable resources in new product research and development, but this is mostly for the short term. Long-term basic research in entirely new technologies is not funded as well as it was in the past. Shorter product life cycles and a commoditization of the computer industry have contributed to this trend.

Nevertheless, the computer industry remains very technology-driven. Many of the technological innovations that impact the computer industry are being developed in other, related industries, however. These include faster and more powerful microprocessors developed by the semiconductor industry, the capacity for more memory storage developed by the computer storage device industry, the support of more detailed graphic and video developed by manufacturers of computer monitors and displays, faster communications capabilities between computers developed by the telecommunications equipment industry, and more robust operating systems and sophisticated applications developed by the computer software industry. A trend toward smaller, faster, cheaper machines with greater memory will continue.

One continuing trend that is common among all these aspects of computers and related devices is miniaturization. Beginning with the invention of the microprocessor chip in 1971, and followed by the ability to store more data on smaller data storage media, the development of flat-panel displays, and computer system designs that better conserve space, computers have been getting smaller while retaining or increasing their processing power. *PC Magazine* predicts that the majority of computers by 2000 will be laptop-size.

Which standards to support for the new computer peripheral technologies is a major issue in the area of new technologies. For example, in the area of 56K bit/sec modems, AST Computer, Inc., Compaq Computer Corp., Hewlett-Packard Co. and Toshiba Corp. said they would support K56Flex, the protocol proposed in November 1996 by Rockwell and Lucent. Whereas, Hitachi Ltd. and Dell Computer Corp. announced support for the competing U.S. Robotics x2 technology standard.

Another trend in computers is the integration of communications and processing equipment technologies that allow computers to act as telephones, answering machines, video-conferencing devices, and, television sets. Still cameras, video cameras, and video players may also be attached. Eventually the distinction between television sets and computers will be blurred. Not only is broadcast receiver hardware available as an add-on component for computers, but also the NC and the adoption of high-definition television sets in the late 1990s, whose screens can display the same high resolution of computers, will turn television sets into computers.

FURTHER READING

Anthes, Gary H. "Supercomputer Tops 1 Teraflop." *Computerworld,* 23 December 1996.

Bellinger, Robert. "More Jobs, Better Offers for '97 Computer Grads." *Electronic Engineering Times,* 25 November 1996.

Bliss, Jeff. "Notebooks." *Computer Reseller News,* 3 June 1996.

Buckler, Grant. "Personal Workstations Drive Market Growth - IDC." *Newsbytes,* 14 January 1997.

Churbuck, David, and Gary Samuels. "Can IBM Keep It Up?" *Forbes,* 3 June 1996.

"Compaq Results Rise In 4Q, Year." *Electronic News (1991)* , 27 January 1997.

"Computer Equipment: U.S. Trade Summary 1996." U.S. Department of Commerce, Office of Computers and Business Equipment. 7 March 1996. Available from: http://www.ita.doc.gov/industry/computers/data6.html

"Computer Industry Trends and Trade Data." U.S. Department of Commerce, Office of Computers and Business Equipment. 21 January 1996. Available from: http://www.ita.doc.gov/industry/computers/data4.txt

"Computers - Major." *Moody's Industry Review,* 4 October 1996.

Damore, Kelley, and Deborah Gage. "Servers." *Computer Reseller News,* 3 June 1996.

Darnay, Arsen J., ed. *Manufacturing USA.* 5th ed. Detroit: Gale Research, 1996.

Dataquest. "New Era Emerges in the Advanced Desktop Market." San Jose, California; 23 December 1996.

DePompa, Barbara. "Hitachi's Big Win." *InformationWeek,* 24 February 1997.

Doyle, T.C. "What Makes HP Tick." *VARbusiness,* 1 May 1996.

Gross, Neil, Emily Smith, and John Carey. "Windows on the World of Atoms." *Business Week,* 30 August 1993.

Guterl, Fred. "The Sleeper of Supercomputers." *Business Week,* 9 August 1993.

Hast, Adele, ed. *International Directory of Company Histories, Volume III,* Chicago: St. James Press, 1991.

Howard, Bill. "Looking Forward: Technology on the Way." *PC Magazine,* 25 March 1997.

Johnston, Stuart J. "The PC is Alive and Well." *InformationWeek,* 3 June 1996.

Kirkpatrick, David. "Why Compaq Envies Dell: The Leading Maker Alters Course." *Fortune,* 17 February 1997.

Korzeniowski, Paul. "Manufacturers Debate Platform Futures." *Software Magazine,* August 1995.

Lagnado, Ike. "Is the PC Party Really Over?" *HFN The Weekly Newspaper for the Home Furnishing Network,* 20 January 1997.

"Latin American PC Market Grew 30 Percent in 1996, According to Dataquest; Compaq is the No. 1 Vendor in the Region." *Business Wire,* 25 February 1997.

Linden, Dana Wechsler, and Bruce Upjohn. "Top Corporate Performance of 1995: Boy Scouts on a Rampage." *Forbes,* 1 January 1996.

Moltzen, Edward F. "High-tech Firms Cut Back on R&D Pie." *Computer Reseller News,* 11 September 1995.

"NCs Move Beyond Hype." *PC Magazine,* 7 January 1997.

Niccolai, James. "Allies Line Up For 56K Bit Modem Standards." *Computerworld,* 16 December 1996.

Ouellette, Tim. "Amdahl Rates a Buy." *Computerworld,* 24 February 1997.

Ramo, Joshua Cooper. "Act Two for Big Blue." *Time,* 4 November 1996.

Schlosberg, Jeremy. "Independence Day." *PC Week,* 24 June 24 1996.

"Strong Industry Demand Fuels Transpacific Flow of Computer Parts, Finished Goods to Pacific Rim." *Traffic World,* 3 June 1996.

"Survey: Mainframe to Remain in Mainstream Beyond the Year 2000." *EDGE: Work-Group Computing Report,* 2 October 1995.

Thibodeau, Patrick. "Trade Pact Could Boost Computer Sales." *Computerworld,* 16 December 1996.

Verity, John. "The Parallel Universe Grows." *Business Week,* 16 August 1993.

Ward, Judy. "How Bright is Sun's Future? Sun Microsystems is Stronger Than Ever, But so is the Competition." *Financial World,* 5 December 1995.

"Western European PC Market Grows 7.1 Percent Year on Year, According to IDC." *PR Newswire,* 4 February 1997.

—Dave Mote, updated by Heather Behn Hedden

SIC 3572

COMPUTER STORAGE DEVICES

This classification covers establishments primarily engaged in manufacturing computer storage devices.

INDUSTRY SNAPSHOT

The computer memory storage device industry is comprised of firms that manufacture tape, magnetic, and optical memory components that are used with computers. CD-ROM drives, floppy disk drives, and hard disk drives are a few of the products represented by industry participants.

Memory storage devices played a critical role in the development of the computer industry during the twentieth century. By the early 1990s, memory storage manufacturers represented 15 percent of the entire U.S. computer products and services industry, with over $6.2 billion in domestic shipments. In 1995, the value of computer storage devices and equipment shipments had increased to $8.1 billion, an increase of 38.8 percent over 1994. In 1995, U.S. firms generated over $1 billion in worldwide hard disk drive sales, which accounted for over 75 percent of global demand in that sector. The top 267 companies in the industry employed over 138,500 workers in 1996.

Going into the mid-1990s, memory storage companies were focusing on new product development in a dynamic industry characterized by short product life cycles and intense price competition. Most makers of magnetic disk drives, for instance, were struggling to overcome the effects of severe price reductions in a commodity-like environment that had developed in the early 1990s. The most profitable companies were those that were successfully developing and delivering cutting edge technologies, such as CD-ROM, RAID, and flash cards.

ORGANIZATION AND STRUCTURE

Most computer memory storage devices can be classified as either optical or magnetic. In 1997, about 135 million magnetic devices were sold by U.S. manufacturers, up from 107 million in 1996. Optical components and other storage devices were being shipped at a rate of about 6.3 billion units per year. In addition to optical and magnetic storage, semiconductor memory chips that store data and programs in the form of digital impulses had gained recognition as a viable new technology by the early 1990s.

Magnetic Storage. Magnetic devices record information in the form of magnetized spots that represent a binary code—a series of digits represented by either 1 or 0. A magnetized head suspended slightly above the surface of a medium reads and writes information on the disk. To record information, electrical charges that register a pattern on the surface of the magnetically sensitive medium are delivered through the head. To read data, the same head detects and converts spots into electrical impulses. The data can be retained indefinitely, or erased and replaced with new magnetic spots.

The three primary classes of magnetic storage devices are hard disk drives, floppy disk drives, and magnetic tape machines. Magnetic tapes, which were once the most widely used method of computer memory storage, store data on ½-inch-wide or 8 millimeter tape coated with a magnetically sensitive compound. Tape units typically read and write at a rate of 183 to 722 kilobytes per second, and can store more than 270 gigabytes. Some units, called autoloaders, combine several tape cartridges to maximize speed and capacity.

The advantage of magnetic tape storage is that massive quantities of information can be stored in a relatively compact space. Furthermore, tape devices have historically been the fastest method of reading and writing large amounts of data. The drawback of tape systems, however, is that the tape must be read from one end to the other in order to retrieve and store information. For this reason, magnetic tape is most often used to copy, or backup, large amounts of data stored on a network or mainframe system (or for other purposes in which stored data can be sequentially accessed). In 1995, about 3.5 million magnetic tape storage components were sold by U.S. manufacturers.

A hard disk magnetic storage device resembles a stack of small metal plates that rotate at a constant speed. Between each plate, a magnetic head is positioned on an arm that sweeps across the disk's surface. Each plate is coated on both sides with a magnetically sensitive compound on which a head can read or write information. Every bit of information stored on the disks is accessible by the heads each time the stack rotates.

The advantage of hard drives is that they can quickly retrieve information nonsequentially. Furthermore, because they are compact they make excellent storage devices for micro computers. Of the over 1 billion hard drives sold in 1995, most held a gigabyte or more of information. According to Disk/Trend Inc., a California market research firm, leading-edge disk drives in 1997 had a density of 1.36 billion bits per square inch. Disk drives with greater capacities were commonly used in workstations, minicomputers, local area networks (LANs), and mainframes.

Hard drives for larger computer systems are generally 14-inch, 10-inch, or 8-inch drives. Microcomputers typically have 5.25-inch, 3.5-inch, 2.5-inch, or 1.8-inch drives. Smaller disks usually hold one to two megabytes of information. In 1994, hard disk drives sold 33 percent more units—67.2 million—than in 1993, with revenues totaling $16.9 billion. In 1995, 2.8 million 3.5-inch drives were sold by U.S. firms. Sales of older 5.25-inch drives lagged at about 91,000 units. Sales of 2.5-inch drives had sales of about 5.7 million in 1992, and approximately 300,000 1.8-inch drives were sold in 1992.

Computers communicate, or interface, with disk drives through a controller. Most drives comply with high-performance interface standards such as the Enhanced Small Drive Interface (ESDI), or the Small Computer Systems Interface (SCSI). SCSI drives are more easily integrated into other manufacturers' products; consequently, they are the most common type of drive.

Floppy diskette drives read and write information to a single rotating disk that can be removed from the drive. They are used to transfer and temporarily store information on 3.5-inch or 5.25-inch diskettes. Floppy drive technology is essentially the same as that used in hard disk drives, but floppy disks are made of coated synthetic material rather than metal. Although some U.S. manufacturers produce floppy drives, the domestic magnetic drive industry emphasizes hard drive production.

Optical Storage. Compact Disc - Read Only Memory (CD-ROM) drives use laser beams to read information on a rotating synthetic disk. Most consumer disks are composed of three layers: an overcoat that protects the information on the disk; the dye layer, where the information is recorded as digital bits of information; and a mirrored base that reflects the laser back to its source.

CD-Write Once Read Many (CD-WORM) drives and discs also allow users to store their own information on a disc, though that data cannot be erased and replaced with new information. CD-Recordable (CD-R) is a write-once technology like the CD-WORM that has become one of the first of such devices to be priced within the consumer/small business market. In 1996 the cost of the technology ranged from $800 to $1,000 for the drives and $6 to $8 per disc. CD-R drive prices were expected to drop to about $300 within a few years, with disc prices dropping to $3. Another optical storage option available in the late 1990s was the "erasable CD-ROM," which had the capability to rewrite or replace existing data. Finally, another optical storage device gaining popularity in the late-1990s was the DVD, or high-density compact disc. The drives and discs have more capacity to handle video with storage levels of 4.7 to 17 gigabytes. Conventional CD-ROMs used in most PCS have a capacity of roughly 650 megabytes.

The advantage of optical storage is that comparatively massive amounts of information can be inexpensively stored on a small, portable medium. Because a single CD can store up to 300,000 pages of information, CD-ROM is often used for storing such memory intensive applications as information databases or programs with elaborate graphics. The name and phone number of every household in the United States, for instance, was available on three CDS in 1997 for less than $100.

The disadvantage of CD-ROM is that information retrieval is significantly slower than that of magnetic devices. Also, optical storage is relatively inflexible because it does not allow users to easily write and erase information. In 1995, U.S. firms shipped 38.7 million CD-ROM drives, a 130 percent increase over 1994. About 250,000 CD-WORM drives were shipped in 1992.

Semiconductor Memory. Manufacturers in the early 1990s were also delivering computer storage on innovative new semiconductor memory chips called flash cards. Flash memory stores programs and data in the form of digital impulses. Data can be easily read, written, and erased on cards that hold two to four megabytes of data. The cards can be inserted and removed from a flash card slot just like a floppy diskette. Flash cards perform much faster than magnetic devices and require much less power to operate.

Because flash memory is nonvolatile and requires no moving parts, a user can turn off his computer, turn it back on later, and find himself at the same place he was when he powered down. Because of its advantages, flash memory technology is popular with manufacturers of notebook, pen-based, and hand-held computers. The Personal Computer Memory Card International Association (PCMCIA) represents the interests of this industry segment and strives to maintain manufacturing standards.

Competitive Structure. A multitude of different organizational structures are represented in the computer memory storage industry. The industry is highly fragmented and is characterized by technological volatility. Firms that do not develop and produce breakthrough products are often forced to compete in a high-

volume, low-margin, commodity-like market environment. Leading firms, in contrast, can reap huge short-term profits as a result of innovation. These firms, though, must often risk large research and development expenditures to generate new technology for rapidly shifting, unpredictable markets.

Original equipment manufacturers, such as IBM, Digital, and Hewlett-Packard, produce or purchase devices that are integrated into their own computers. Other large vendors, such as Seagate Technologies and Conner Peripherals, produce devices that are installed in, or used with, other computer manufacturers' products. These companies tend to purchase few of their components from other companies. In contrast to the more vertically integrated companies just described, several companies utilize foreign manufacturers to produce their drives or to manufacture many of the components that go into their storage devices.

BACKGROUND AND DEVELOPMENT

The punch card, the first storage mechanism used with a mechanical computer, was introduced by Herman Hollerith in 1886 to help the U.S. Bureau of the Census calculate demographic data. The punch card concept was actually developed by Charles Babbage and was demonstrated in his 1833 design of the Analytical Engine. Although Babbage's engine was never built, it provided a model for Hollerith and others. Punch cards allowed computer operators to automatically repeat arithmetic operations on numbers that were represented by holes punched into successive cards.

In 1944, International Business Machines (IBM) developed the first large-scale automatic digital computer, which was conceived by Howard H. Aiken of Harvard University. The Automatic Sequence Controlled Calculator (nicknamed the Mark I) utilized over 750,000 parts and relied on punched cards and punched tape to store data. The device was used to compute ballistic data for defense purposes and could calculate three additions per second. In 1946, Bell Telephone Laboratories developed a similar computer that stored and read sequences of instructions on loops of paper tape.

The Electronic Numerical Integrator and Calculator (ENIAC), which was completed in 1945, stored numbers and computing instructions entirely by electronic circuits containing over 18,000 vacuum tubes. Although ENIAC still used punched cards for input and output data, the computer could electronically store 20 numbers. The computer had to be programmed by tedious rewiring in order to accomplish different tasks. Despite its limitations, the computer was used until 1956.

During the mid-1940s researchers realized that a major hurdle in the advancement of computer technology was a lack of adequate resident memory storage capacity. During the 1940s and 1950s, four storage techniques were developed: acoustic delay lines, magnetic drums, electrostatic devices, and magnetic cores. Mathematician John von Neumann was one of the most influential developers of storage technology during this era.

The first magnetic core computer, the Whirlwind, was developed at the Massachusetts Institute of Technology in 1953. By the mid-1950s magnetic core memory had become the principal storage system. At this point, many companies realized that computer production and design had the potential to be a viable industry. IBM, Sperry, Rand, Burroughs, RCA, General Electric, and other companies quickly began introducing computers for a variety of commercial and institutional applications. By 1960, in fact, approximately 5,000 stored-program computers were operating in the United States. Throughout the 1960s this number doubled every two to three years.

As the computer industry expanded during 1960s and 1970s, the need for mass memory storage devices that could hold programs and backup data drove the development of a variety of mechanisms. Some of the most successful storage devices used magnetic ''Winchester'' technology. These devices, which were developed by IBM in 1956, evolved into what is now the magnetic hard disk drive.

The 1980s. During the 1980s the use of Winchester drives began to dominate the memory storage industry. Prior to disk storage, magnetic tape was the industry's primary information storage medium. Advancements in disk technology, though, quickly outpaced the speed and efficiency of tape systems—resulting in the obsolescence of tape for most applications.

Augmenting growth of both hard disk and floppy disk drives in the 1980s was the proliferation of the microcomputer. Throughout the 1980s these personal computers (PCs) relied solely on magnetic disk technology for memory storage. Sales of PCs skyrocketed from less than 500,000 per year in 1980 to 10 million in 1990; the demand for disk storage devices soared. Growth in workstations, microcomputers, and mainframes also spurred demand. By 1990, manufacturers were shipping over 26 million Winchester hard drives and about 40 million floppy drives per year.

Despite the decline of market share attributable to magnetic tape drives, this segment experienced steady growth during the 1980s and early 1990s. By 1989, manufacturers were shipping about 1.6 million tape drives per year, most of which were being used to backup hard disks and network systems. Furthermore, tape drive sales were expected to grow at an annual rate of approximately 8 percent in the early 1990s.

As computer memory storage device manufacturers entered the 1990s, new storage technology was beginning to gain widespread attention by the industry and consumers. Optical memory, which had been viewed essentially as an experimental or specialty technology during the late 1980s, was beginning to establish itself in mainstream business and consumer markets. There was also an increasing interest in semiconductor memory.

The Early 1990s. Magnetic disk drives continued to dominate industry offerings in the early 1990s. The number of hard drives sold, for instance, climbed steadily to 31 million in 1991 and to 37 million by 1992. Floppy drive sales volume also climbed, much as it had during the 1980s, to about 45 million per year by 1993. Despite a massive shakeout in the PC market, which was placing severe downward price pressure on PC manufacturers, many storage device producers enjoyed solid profit growth in 1991 and 1992. This was partly a result of PC industry price wars that were boosting PC unit shipments.

As is often the case with high-tech products, the price of most individual drives continued to decline in the early 1990s. In fact, the price of the average magnetic disk drive typically fell 3 percent to 5 percent every three months. This phenomenon occurred as a specific drive technology became obsolete when a new product was introduced.

Only in unique instances will producers realize gains rather than losses in profit margins on individual components. This situation occurred in the PC hard drive market during 1992 for several reasons. Most importantly, a jump in the use of new memory-consuming PC operating systems caused a surge in demand for larger PC hard drives. As a result, producers were able to realize significant price gains after several years of deteriorating margins. The average price of 3.5-inch 40 megabyte drives, for instance, vaulted to $165—18 percent higher than the average 1991 price.

CURRENT CONDITIONS

Magnetic Disk Drives. The size of the magnetic disk drive industry continued to grow in 1993. The market for hard drives, for instance, grew from $24.2 billion 1991 to $26.2 billion in 1992, and to approximately $27 billion in 1993. The value of hard drive shipments increased from $2.1 billion in 1994 to $2.9 billion in 1995. Nevertheless, increasing competition was depressing profits in the magnetic drive segment of the storage industry. Though PC price wars buoyed drove manufacturers' earnings in 1992, plummeting prices decreased profits in 1993. Between February and June of 1993, for example, disk drive prices dropped 25 percent.

Following impressive gains in 1992, the stock price of larger producers tumbled in 1993 and forecasted earnings also fell. Conner Peripherals' stock, for instance, fell 52 percent in price, and Wall Street analysts projected a 22 percent decline in 1993 earnings. The price of Western Digital's stock plunged 49 percent, and the company's expected earnings were 26 percent below those of 1992. Even Seagate Technology, which some analysts believed was best prepared to compete in the mid-1990s environment, expected its earnings to fall by 14 percent. Most memory storage device manufacturers were accustomed to volatile markets, however, and were only mildly phased by the temporary setbacks.

To counter the commodity-like environment that characterized most segments of the magnetic storage industry in the mid-1990s, many companies were trying to expand their development and production of technologically superior products that offered higher profit margins. Some firms were banking on 2.5-inch and 1.8-inch hard disk drives that could be used in notebook computers to stimulate sales. Although the market for 2.5-inch drives leapt from about 2 million in 1991 to 3 million in 1992, demand for that sector was not growing at the rate that many manufacturers had expected. The number of shipments of newer 1.8-inch drives rose from about 300,000 in 1992 to an estimated 850,000 in 1993, and was expected to reach 9 million by 1995.

Casting doubt on analysts' predictions for 1.8-inch and 2.5-inch hard drive shipments was the unveiling of an even smaller drive in 1992. Hewlett-Packard disclosed its 1.3-inch, 20 megabyte, matchbox-sized hard disk drive. The company expects to direct the product toward the burgeoning hand-held and sub-notebook computer market. Similarly, Areal Technology Inc. announced its development of a 2.5-inch drive platter that could store 91.5 megabytes—more than any other drive plate on the market. Another breakthrough included a 3.5-inch hard drive with a memory capacity of 1.47 gigabytes, which was developed by Conner Peripherals. Seagate, IBM, and DEC, among others, were striving to develop competing 3.5-inch drives with capacities of 1.6 to 2 gigabytes.

By 1995, several companies had expanded the marketing and manufacturing of removable media, both tapes and disks, into the home computer market. Companies such as Iomega and SyQuest developed affordable tape drives and removable disks available for $150 to $200, with cartridges and disks costing between $20 and $25 each. These removable units could hold between 100 megabytes and 800 megabytes of information to backup or enhance hard drive capacity.

Magneto-Optical Drives. Magneto-optical (MO) drives gained popularity in the mid- to late 1990s. These storage devices combined the ease and transportability of a floppy disk with the capacity and speed of a hard disk. The systems use both magnetic and optical technology. The drive reads and writes the disk with a read/write head assisted with a pulse-modulated laser beam. In 1996, MO drives came in two sizes, just like floppy disks, 5.25-inch and 3.5-inch. At the time, MO disks could store between 128 megabytes and 1.3 gigabytes of data.

RAID Technology. A major advance boosting magnetic memory device manufacturers in the mid-1990s

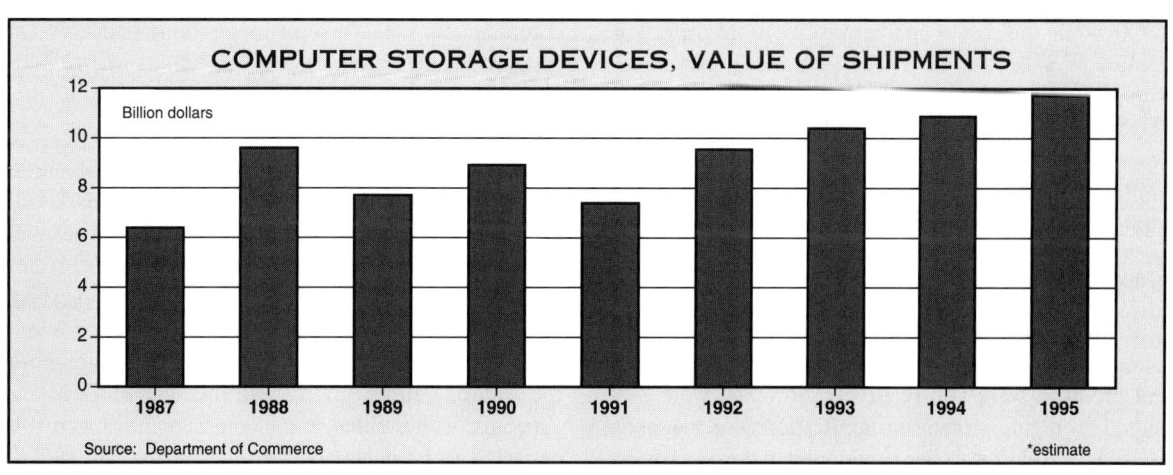

COMPUTER STORAGE DEVICES, VALUE OF SHIPMENTS

Source: Department of Commerce   *estimate

involved Redundant Arrays of Inexpensive Disks (RAIDs), which were first introduced in 1987. RAIDs allow several hard drives to work in concert as a single, high capacity, relatively inexpensive, and dependable memory backup device. Applications include backup storage for mainframes, networks, and other high-end systems. In 1993, RAID systems offered storage capacity of as much as 183 gigabytes.

Worldwide shipments of RAIDs grew from 16,000 units in 1991 to 30,000 in 1992, worth an estimated $1.2 billion. Moreover, the market for RAIDs was expected to boom to $2.4 billion in 1993, $4.1 billion in 1994, and to more than $5 billion by 1995. RAIDs will likely dominate the high-end storage device market by the late 1990s. Although IBM held the largest share of the RAID market in 1993, at 17.4 percent, a vast number of companies were racing to capture market share in the mid-1990s—reflecting the viability of this highly profitable and competitive segment.

CD-ROM. As the demand for magnetic drives grew in the early and mid-1990s, CD-ROM and CD-WORM optical devices were expanding the scope of the memory storage industry and augmenting producer revenues. During the late 1980s and early 1990s, manufacturers worked to establish the new technology in commercial markets. Primary users included libraries, law and accounting firms, and other entities that could afford the relatively expensive technology. By 1993, though, CD-ROM was also making its way into the mass consumer market.

Small businesses, game players, and home computer users were embracing CD-ROM, and a plethora of new disk titles were prompting consumers to buy the devices. Many computer manufacturers were beginning to build CD drives into their PCs; furthermore, optical drive prices were falling. In 1992, for instance, peripheral CD-ROM drives typically sold for $300. By 1993, though, the price had fallen to between $200 and $300, while the cost of an internal CD-ROM drive was as low as $100. As CD-ROM technology gained acceptance, sales soared. Worldwide shipments of CD-ROM drives rose to about 1.4 million in 1991, according to Disk Trend, Inc. Shipments jumped to about 2.3 million in 1992, and they reached an estimated 4.8 million in 1993. Analysts predicted annual shipments to approach 6.5 million in 1994, over 8 million in 1995, and over 13 million by 1997.

Optical memory products posed little immediate threat to magnetic device manufacturers in 1993. Optical products were still relatively slow and were best suited for memory intensive applications that magnetic devices couldn't handle. Developers were improving

optical technology, however, and were racing to create fast CD drives that could read, write, and erase information with the same speed and ease of magnetic drives—a goal that, if reached, could quash magnetic technology. Some companies were already offering "double-speed" CD-ROM drives in 1993 at an average price of $700 per unit, and much faster drives were under development.

Disk Trend estimated that 34 percent of CD-ROM drives were used for games in 1994, while educational and entertainment uses represented about 30 percent of demand. Although CD-ROM use by commercial and institutional sectors will continue to balloon, their 36 percent share of the market will likely decrease in the late 1990s as drive prices fall.

Some analysts were reluctant to project the long-term popularity of CD memory technology—likening it to beta-format videotape technology that floundered in the 1980s. Nevertheless, developers had poured over $3 billion into research and development of the technology by 1992. Although total revenues from this segment were still lower than the $3 billion investment, IBM, Apple Computers, Sony, and other large producers were working to promote optical memory devices. IBM, for instance, was busy developing a magneto-optical rewriting technology that would allow drives to erase and store information. Likewise, Apple was preparing to promote a line of computers that provided CD-ROM drives as a standard feature.

Flashcards. Technologically superior semiconductor flash memory technology, which was still in its commercial infancy, offered one of the greatest opportunities for growth in the computer memory storage industry. The compact, energy efficient, high-capacity devices proved to be weighty contenders in the bid to serve the rapidly expanding notebook and pen-based computer markets. Several major semiconductor and disk producers were investing large sums in the development of the new technology.

Intel, which served 85 percent of the world market for flash memory cards in 1993, had been marketing the technology since 1990. Intel teamed up with disk giant Conner Peripherals in 1992 to advance flash card technology and unveiled a line of 20 cards. Analysts expected flash memory to become a dominant force in computer and telecommunications memory storage in the future. Falling prices, enforcement of PCMCIA standards, faster chips, and increased card capacity are expected to propel market growth in the late 1990s.

INDUSTRY LEADERS

The largest company engaged primarily in the manufacture of computer storage devices in 1997 was Seagate Technologies Inc., of Scotts Valley, California. The company earned revenues of $8.59 billion in fiscal year 1996 and employed approximately 50,000 workers. In 1995, Seagate had total earnings of $7.26 billion. During 1996, Seagate bought out Conner Peripherals, its closest competitor. Conner Peripherals had led the market in 3.5-inch hard drive capacity technology. Seagate is one of the most vertically integrated firms in the industry; Seagate manufactures most of the parts that go into its drives.

Quantum Corp. of California took second in the industry in 1996, with its takeover of Digital Equipment Corporation's storage device business. The company's 1996 revenue totaled $2.13 billion, with growth to $1.2 billion in revenues in just the first quarter of 1997. In 1996, Quantum Corp. had 3,000 employees.

Other industry leaders in 1996 included: Western Digital Corp. of California, with $1.5 billion; Storage Technology Corp. of Colorado, with $1.4 billion; IBM Corp. Storage Systems Division of California, with $1.2 billion; and Maxtor Corp. of California, with $1.15 billion. In addition to storage industry participants, computer vendors like Compaq and DEC were major suppliers of storage devices. In the 1996 RAID drive market, for instance, IBM, DEC, Compaq, and Hewlett-Packard owned over 75 percent of the market.

WORK FORCE

The computer storage industry work force includes a higher proportion of electrical and electronics engineers than most other U.S. industries. The industry also hires large numbers of trained precision assemblers, as well as a significant number of parts assemblers and fabricators.

As with most segments of the computer and computer services industry, analysts expect little or no employment growth with storage device manufacturers throughout the end of the 1990s and during the early 2000s. In fact, demand for almost every occupation in the industry will decline significantly. Between 1990 and 1993 alone, total computer industry employment plummeted by 50,000 to about 214,500. Massive productivity gains were largely to blame.

The number of both precision and parts assemblers employed by manufacturers was expected to decline between 40 and 55 percent from 1990 to 2005. Automation, as well as outsourcing of labor tasks to foreign countries, will account for much of this loss. Clerical positions will also decline drastically, by about 30 percent. Even the demand for engineers will fall by 1 percent or 2 percent by 2005, as companies form corporate alliances that allow them to reduce overlapping research and development expenditures.

On the bright side, the demand for systems analysts and computer scientists is expected to increase by about 40 percent between 1990 and 2005. Furthermore, opportunities will become available to professionals who can help develop cutting edge technologies, particularly for optical and semiconductor products.

AMERICA AND THE WORLD

U.S. computer storage device firms led the world market in the mid-1990s. U.S. firms served 75 percent of the $24 billion global hard drive market in 1993, while Japan only held about 15 percent. Japanese firms, though, played an important role in the hard drive sector by supplying most of the spindle motors, bearings, and other parts that U.S. firms incorporate into the drives that they build.

Japanese firms dominated the world floppy drive market, though U.S. companies manufactured about 44 percent of the floppy diskettes used worldwide. Japanese firms have invested heavily in American companies that produce drives and diskettes. Japan also maintains a technological lead in the burgeoning CD-ROM market, with Sony, Hitachi, and Toshiba leading industry advancements. Philips NV, a Netherlands competitor, was also a major force in this segment. Intel, however, garnered the dominant share of the semiconductor market for America in the mid-1990s.

One factor thwarting global progress for American exporters was the inaccessibility of one of the largest computer storage device markets in the world—Japan. Despite relatively open U.S. markets, shrewd Japanese trading tactics were succeeding in leaving U.S. producers out of many segments of that market. Japan accounted for about 20 percent of the global demand for all computer equipment and services in 1993.

Europe participated in the growth of optical storage devices by 1997. Sales of CD-ROM drives in Europe were expected to climb 12 percent annually to sales of about 16 million drives in the year 2001. In 1996, consumer sales accounted for 79 percent of total sales, but sales were expected to shift to European business and education. Consumer sales were forecasted to drop to 72 percent of the total CD-ROM drive sales by 2001.

RESEARCH AND TECHNOLOGY

Industry research and development will increasingly result both from strategic alliances and from government initiatives. For example, General Electric, AT&T, Honeywell, and IBM established the Optoelectronic Technology Consortium (OTC) in July 1992 to advance domestic optical technology. Consortium members will share research already completed on their own, and will release their combined findings to other U.S. computer and semiconductor firms. The OTC was scheduled to continue for 30 months and was backed by $8 million in initial funding. Half of the funding for the OTC was supplied by the Federal Defense Advanced Research Projects Agency (DARPA).

In addition to the OTC, the Microelectronics and Computer Technology Corp. (MCC), also an industry consortium, began a five-year research project on holographic mass-storage subsystems. This effort was backed by $10.3 million in federal grants and $12.7 million from consortium members. A similar government/private enterprise effort was underway in California that involved the National Institute of Standards and Technology and several universities. Its purpose was to integrate optical technology into a prototype computer that might eventually lead to a desktop supercomputer.

The High Performance Computing and Communications Initiative (HPCCI), which was the major federal computing research project underway in the early 1990s, was expected to result in residual advancements in storage technology. The HPCCI received $657 million in federal funds in 1992.

In 1995, the U.S. Department of Commerce's National Institute of Standards and Technology sponsored research projects at 3M Co. of Minnesota, Seagate Tape Technology of California, and Advanced Research Corp. of Minnesota. The goal of the projects was to develop a high-performance, variable-data-rate, multimedia magnetic tape recorder that would have the ability to accommodate the high-data capacity, transmission, and acquisition rates needed for applications such as teleconferencing and satellite-based television.

Another project at LOTS Technology Inc. of California was targeted to develop an optical tape storage device that could read and write 180 tracks simultaneously. The multiple laser beams with independent control could result in data systems that would have the ability to store, retrieve, and transfer one trillion bytes of data. In 1997, IBM announced the development of components that could read and write data on a computer hard disk at 5 million bits, the data equivalent of the text on 312,500 double-spaced, typewritten pages. The newly developed technology would increase hard-disk density by nearly five times.

The Future. Memory storage devices will continue to play a leading role in the advancement of computer technology, as they have since the birth of the computer industry. The role of the memory storage device industry will become increasingly blurred, however, as the computer, telecommunications, consumer electronics, information, and entertainment industries converge into a massive multimedia industry that interconnects various technologies and services. Multimedia, by its most basic definition, will combine data, audio, and video signals into one digital stream.

The dominant technologies that will drive this metamorphosis are data processing, storage, interface, fiber optics, wireless, compression, and digital broadband switching. As a result, companies from many industries will find themselves competing and cooperating with firms in completely separate industries. Firms that once delivered memory storage solely for the computer industry will be selling their technology to a wide range of markets. The advancement of flash memory technology provides evidence of this trend. In 1993, semiconductor and disk storage companies were already cooperating to develop flash memory storage products not only for computers, but also for telephones, automobiles, and other industries.

Optical memory will likely play an integral role in the future of multimedia because of its capacity to store text, images, animation, and video. Virtual reality products represent another area in which optical technology can be applied. CD drives were already in production in 1993 that could read and write to laser discs that held twice as much memory as disks sold in 1992. These disks also delivered information at twice the speed of the earlier disks. As it did with flash cards, the implementation of industry standards will likely propel this technology to center stage.

FURTHER READING

Aragon, Lawrence. ''Driving Out of a Rut.'' *PC Week,* 26 August 1996.

Booker, Ellis. ''When Storage Is State of the Art.'' *Computerworld,* 17 May 1993.

Byers, T.J. ''All About Removable Media Drives.'' *Electronics Now,* September 1996.

''CD-ROM Hardware Sales in Europe Are Expected to Climb 12% Annually in Next 5 Years to 16 Million Drives in 2001.'' *Television Digest,* 24 February 1997.

''CD-ROM Sales Soar.'' *HFN The Weekly Newspaper for the Home Furnishing Network,* 19 February 1996.

"CD-ROM Ships Top 400 Million." *HFN The Weekly Newspaper for the Home Furnishing Network,* 10 June 1996.

Crawford, Walt. "Stowing Your Stuff; Mass Storage Options." *Online,* November-December 1996.

Current Industrial Reports Computer and Office and Accounting Machines - 1995, Washington, D.C.: U.S. Census Bureau, 1996. Available from http://www.census.gov/industry/ma35r95.txt.

Darnay, Arsen J., ed. *Manufacturing USA.* 5th ed. Detroit: Gale Research, 1996.

Deck, Stewart. "Extreme Density." *Computerworld,* 20 January 1997.

"Disk Sales on Rise." *Computerworld,* 10 March 1997.

"Eking Out More Space for Data on PC Disks." *Electronic Business,* May 1993.

Ferelli, Mark. "Do-It-Yourself CD-R Impacts Bottom Line." *Computer Technology Review,* August 1993.

Ferelli, Mark. "Don't Wait For A Disaster Before Autoloading Backup." *Computer Technology Review,* August 1993.

Ferelli, Mark. "CD-ROMs Board and Storm The LAN." *Computer Technology Review,* August 1993.

Jorgensen, Barbara. "CD-ROM Leaps into the Consumer Market." *Electronic Business,* July 1993.

Lee, Yvonne. "PCMCIA Spec Debated." *InfoWorld,* 31 May 1993.

Lesser, Roger. "Commerce Department Pursues Data Storage." *Defense & Security Electronics,* October 1995.

Mannes, George. "Tale of the Tape: Tape Drives Move from a Backup Role for Hard Drives to a Starting Position as Portable Data Carriers." *Popular Mechanics,* December 1995.

McCloughan, Alexa and Crawford Del Prete. "Winchester Disk Drive Industry in 1994: An Up Cycle with Resilience." *Computer Industry Report,* 13 January 1995.

Quickel, Stephen W. "The Worst is Yet to Come." *Electronic Business,* June 1993.

"Quantum Warns of Slow Quarter." *Electronic News,* 17 June 1996.

Rose, John. "New Competitors Will Scramble the Opportunities." *Electronic Business,* July 1993.

"Seagate Revs, Net Slips; Charges Cited." *Electronic News,* 12 August 1996.

"Socket and Card Services." *Machine Design,* 11 June 1993.

"Where Have All the High-Tech Jobs Gone?" *Electronic Business,* August 1993.

—Dave Mote, updated by Sonya Shelton

COMPUTER TERMINALS

Companies primarily engaged in manufacturing computer terminals, teleprinters, and multistation cathode ray tubes (CRTs) make up the computer terminal industry. Personal computers, workstations, minicomputers, and other systems that contain central processing units (CPUs) are classified in the electronic computer industry. Establishments primarily engaged in manufacturing point-of-sale, funds transfer, and automatic teller machines are classified in **SIC 3578: Calculating and Accounting Machines, Except Electronic Computers.**

A computer terminal acts as an interface between a user and a system server that has a CPU and storage capacity. Typically, a network of terminals are attached to the server. While some network systems allow terminals to have unimpeded access to the server, most systems require users to share the processor. As a result, such "timeshare" servers operate more slowly as more users access the processor.

Terminals were first used to access large mainframe systems that became popular in the 1970s. As the speed and memory capacity of computers increased and prices of desktop computers fell during the 1980s, the popularity of systems that used terminals declined.

Despite some limitations, systems that use network terminals offer several advantages over computers. For instance, microcomputers and workstations run applications locally, and therefore require more memory and an operating system. Many terminals, on the other hand, run only the display part of a computer application locally, and rely on the server to handle data processing and storage. As a result, terminals offer advantages in costs, centralized control, and security.

Although sales of network servers and systems remained strong in the late 1980s and early 1990s, terminal sales lagged. According to a 1997 report by Forrester Research, Inc., corporations began looking to network computers and servers to replace existing dumb terminals. Unlike other sectors of the computer hardware industry, terminal manufacturers' shipments fell from $2.3 billion in 1988 to about $1.9 billion in the early 1990s. Furthermore, industry employment had fallen from about 18,000 in 1988 to 12,000 by 1991. Terminal manufacturer shipments were expected to decrease only slightly until 1998. However, employment was expected to drop to nearly 1,300 by 1998.

Much of the industry's decline was a result of increased competition from personal computers (PCs). As PC prices plummeted, consumers increasingly networked low-cost PCs with servers to achieve the advantages of both desktop and terminal systems. In contrast to the declining sales of terminals, sales of PCs approached $30 billion in 1992. In 1996, PC manufacturers sold 10 million more machines than they did in 1995, for a total of 71 million units worldwide.

During the mid-1990s, terminal manufacturers increased revenues with new products, such as X-terminals and Windows terminals. X-terminals contain internal software, and therefore allow the interaction of concurrent applications running in the popular "Windows" environment. In addition, X-terminals cost nearly 50 percent less than PCs in 1996. X-terminals also offered higher resolution, larger screens, and greater networking capabilities than many desktop and workstation computers. However, the disadvantages of X-terminals included slower running application and slower Internet access than that of PCs.

Sales of X-terminals grew in the early 1990s due to concerns about system and information security in companies, as well as budget and staff cutbacks in system support departments. X-terminals also reduced the need for hardware upgrades with the introduction of new software, such as Microsoft's Windows 95. However, shipments of X-terminals decreased slightly from about 178,000 in 1994 to approximately 158,000 in 1995.

Wyse Technology Inc. led the introduction of Windows terminals in 1995. These terminals give users the ability to access Windows-, mainframe-, or Unix-based applications and carry e-mail, word processing, spreadsheet, and scheduling application data and information to the network server.

Another innovation in resurrecting the computer terminal industry came with the development of the network computer (NC) in 1997. Although not all of the first NCs fulfilled these requirements, the NC has the ability to support text input, audio output, at least VGA monitor resolution, IP network connections, Java software applications, network communications, a Web browser, and basic file formats.

Anacomp Inc. of Georgia was a major player in the computer terminals industry in the 1990s, with early decade sales of $652 million and about 5,000 employees. However, the company filed Chapter 11 financial restructuring in 1996, reducing revenues to $486 million in fiscal year 1996. Wyse Technology of California, a major producer of X-terminals, was another large competitor in the mid-1990s, with approximately $300 million in sales and 2,000 workers. Wyse also became the largest manufacturer of Windows terminals in 1997. By this time, Hewlett-Packard Company of California was the leading X-terminal manufacturer, with more than $150 million annual business in X-terminals alone.

The majority of the top 50 companies in the industry employed fewer than 100 workers and generated less than $20 million in annual revenues in the early. Employment prospects in the computer terminal manufacturing industry are bleak, according to the U.S. Bureau of Labor Statistics. Employment for most occupations in the industry is expected to fall by 10 to 40 percent between 1993 and 2005.

FURTHER READING

"Anacomp Announces Improved Fourth Quarter and Year-End Financial Results." *Newswire,* 20 November 1996. Available from http://www.anacomp.com/press/11209601.html.

"Current Industrial Reports: Computer and Office Machines, 1995." U.S. Census Bureau Statistics, 1996. Available from http://www.census.gov/industry/ma35r95.txt.

"Forrester Sees NCs as Terminal Replacement." *PC Week,* 10 March 1997.

Francis, Bob. "A Smart Look for Dumb Terminals." *Datamation,* 1 September 1992.

Kinnucan, Paul. "Jury Still Out on X-Terminals." *Systems Integration,* October 1990.

Kirchner, Jake. "When No News Is Good News." *PC Magazine,* 25 March 1997.

Pinella, Paul. "WYSE Technology." *Datamation,* 15 June 1992.

Shaffer, Richard A. "The Story of X." *Forbes,* 3 August 1992.

Valigra, Lori. "X Terminals: Cheap and Easy." *Datamation,* 15 April 1996.

Yager, Tom. "X Terminals for Workstation Power at PC Price." *Byte,* May 1991.

—Dave Mote, updated by Sonya Shelton

SIC 3577

COMPUTER PERIPHERAL EQUIPMENT, NOT ELSEWHERE CLASSIFIED

The computer peripheral equipment, not elsewhere classified, industry includes establishments that manufacture miscellaneous computer accessories supporting the activities of a computer's central processing unit (CPU). Companies in this industry manufacture a variety of products, including printers, input devices, plotters, graphic displays (monitors), and optical scanners. Not included in this industry segment are computer terminals, storage devices, modems and other communications devices, or computer-driven office machines. For information on computer peripheral equipment classified elsewhere, see **SIC 3571: Electronic Computers, SIC 3572: Computer Storage Devices, SIC 3575: Computer Terminals, and SIC 3579: Office Machines, Not Elsewhere Classified.**

INDUSTRY SNAPSHOT

Peripheral equipment accounted for a major share of U.S. computer industry revenues. In the early 1990s, for instance, computer peripherals from all industries represented about $65 billion, or 20 percent, of the global computer equipment and services market. U.S. sales of printers alone exceeded $11 billion that year. According to the market research firm International Data Corp. (IDC), the industry's unit sales will rise from 250,000 in 1996 to over 1.6 million units by the year 2000.

By the mid-1990s, the number of establishments in the industry totaled 800—by the year 1998, this number was expected to reach 937. *Manufacturing USA* reported that an estimated 46,700 people were employed by these establishments in 1997.

Peripheral manufacturers benefited from new markets created by technological advancements in the computer industry. Faster, less-expensive personal computers with greater memory capacity boosted peripheral sales, as did the increasing interest in multimedia equipment, which incorporated the capabilities of computers, telephones, video display terminals, and fax machines. In addition, as the popularity of the Internet grew rapidly in the mid- to late 1990s, companies that manufactured routers, switches, and other networking equipment reaped the benefits. Throughout the 1990s, industry competitors hastened to bring out new technology that could take advantage of computer advancements and could broaden the scope of the peripheral market.

ORGANIZATION AND STRUCTURE

Facilitating communication with a computer's processor, peripheral equipment is used with supercomputers, mainframes, minicomputers, workstations, and personal computers. The three largest categories of peripherals are graphic displays, printers, and scanners. In addition to the major peripheral categories, numerous miscellaneous products include: computer input devices, computer sound systems, magnetic ink recognition devices, graphic and technical plotters, graphics production equipment, and various multimedia devices.

Graphic Displays. The most popular types of graphic displays are traditional cathode ray tube (CRT) monitors and flat panel liquid crystal displays (LCDs). Although some displays are built into computer terminals, most are offered as peripheral devices that may be added to a personal computer or network terminal. A video card interfaces between the monitor and the CPU, allowing compatibility for specific monitors and computer systems.

CRTs provide either monochrome or color graphics and deliver varying degrees of flexibility, performance, resolution quality, and size. Low resolution monitors, for instance, contained 640 x 480 pixels per inch, while higher resolution CRTs could deliver 1,280 x 1,024; 1,600 x 1,200; or more pixels per inch. Most CRTs measured between 10 and 17 inches diagonally. In 1995, over 2 million CRTs were shipped by U.S. manufacturers. CRT prices ranged from $50 for monochrome displays to several thousand dollars for large, high-definition color monitors.

Among the fastest growing and most dynamic segments of the graphic display market was the LCD. Because LCDs were flat, they were the display of choice for the rapidly growing notebook computer industry. Although far fewer LCDs than CRTs were purchased in the early 1990s, LCDs provided manufacturers with much larger profit margins than older, commodity-like CRTs. Global LCD sales grew to over $3.1 billion in 1992. In 1995, manufacturers shipped more than 140,000 units, an almost 20,000-unit increase over 1994. Monochrome displays accounted for more than 70 percent of LCD revenues in the early 1990s. The remaining 30 percent of sales represented a variety of color LCDs. However, as technology improved the color LCD market rapidly surpassed monochrome as consumers demanded color displays into the late 1990s. About 75 percent of all color LCDs sold were passive-matrix displays, also called super-twisted nematic (STN). Active-matrix displays, also called thin-film transistors (TFTs), made up the remaining 25 percent of color LCDs. TFTs provided the highest graphic quality in this segment, and mimicked large semiconductors in which many transistors functioned as a cohesive unit. High-tech TFTs sold for an average price of $1,200 in 1992—about twice as much as passive-matrix LCDs. Most LCD screen sizes ranged from 8.5 to 10.4 inches.

Input Devices. Before the introduction and rapid growth of multimedia computer systems, the input device segment faced near extinction. Input devices include computer keyboards, mice, joysticks, and virtual reality headsets. In 1993, the market had revenues of $600 million and grew to over $1 billion in 1995. Manufacturers of keyboards alone shipped over 80 million units in 1995. The nearly universal adoption in the early 1990s of graphical operating systems such as Microsoft Windows in the consumer software market pushed sales of mice up rapidly. By 1997, most new consumer computer systems sold also included a mouse.

Printers. The three principal printer types are dot-matrix, ink-jet, and laser. Dot-matrix printers were one of the first responses to demands by computer users for an output device that offered more flexibility than impact character printers. Dot-matrix devices dominated the printer market and continued to account for over 50 percent of unit sales in the early 1990s but offered relatively poor resolution. By the mid-1990s, the dot-matrix printer was largely being replaced since it offered smaller profit margins and appealed to consumers less than newer technology. Dot-matrix prices typically ranged from $75 to $200.

Ink-jet printers, which averaged between $200 and $700 in price, featured much higher resolution and flexibility than dot-matrix technology. Ink-jets commonly offered resolution of 300 to 600 dots per inch (dpi) and provided several fonts and graphic capabilities. According to the market research firm International Data Corp., color ink-jet printers were expected to continue to grow to 97 percent of the ink-jet market by 1998. Ink-jets were expected to grow to 30 percent of the U.S. printer market by 1998. More than 4.3 million ink-jet printers valued at more than $960 million were shipped by U.S. firms in 1995.

Laser printers ranged in price from about $700 for low-end personal devices to between $1,500 and $3,000 for heavy-duty business printers in 1993. Laser printers typically offered 300 to 1,200 dpi resolution in 1997. However, laser printers were typically faster and more flexible than ink-jets and usually had a greater paper handling capacity. In 1995, manufacturers shipped over 3.5 million laser printers worth $3.5 billion. Laser printers were forecast to achieve 50 percent of the printer market by 1998.

Scanners. Peripheral scanners are used to translate optical images to electronic signals. Able to recognize characters, line art, gray-scale, and color images, scanners use photosensitive arrays that reflect light to digitize printed information. The three types of scanners common in the 1990s were handheld, desktop, and drum. Drum scanners are not considered peripheral equipment, however, because they were a high-end tool used primarily in the printing industry.

Desktop, or flatbed, scanners were the most common device. Using optical character recognition (OCR) technology, these scanners were most often used to translate printed pages into a document that could be viewed, searched, and manipulated using a word processor. As the technology grew, desktop scanners were also frequently used to input and manipulate photographs and other graphic images. Typical flatbed scanners had a resolution of 300 to 1,200 dpi. In 1995 manufacturers shipped approximately 540,000 flatbed scanners worth $350 million. Handheld scanners were priced much lower than flatbeds and were regarded as more useful for scanning small graphics. They also delivered lower resolution and limited OCR compatibility. In 1992, approximately $1 billion worth of scanners were sold worldwide. As the storage devices increased in type and capacity, scanners became more prevalent for storing images and text by the late 1990s.

BACKGROUND AND DEVELOPMENT

The miscellaneous peripherals industry emerged from the commercial computer industry in the 1970s. Not until the creation and subsequent widespread acceptance of desktop and personal computers (PCs) in the 1980s, however, did the industry capture a significant share of all computer-related expenditures. PCs extended the market for peripherals to the mass consumer market and generated a demand for numerous computer add-on products.

Some of the early peripherals included card punching and sorting machines, microfilm output units, plotter controls, tabulators, tape cleaners, and tape print units. During the 1980s, however, scanners, printers, and displays that complemented PCs, workstations, and network systems grew to dominate the market. As the speed and memory storage capacity of desktop computers increased, so did the capabilities of peripherals. By the mid-1980s, peripherals accounted for 20 percent of all computer industry revenues.

Global computer equipment and services sales escalated from $243 billion in 1988 to about $280 billion in 1990. Despite an overall slowdown in computer industry growth in the early 1990s, revenues from peripherals continued their spiral to $290 billion in 1991, reaching nearly $320 billion in 1992. Throughout this period the market for peripherals, including storage devices as well as some other peripherals classified in other industries, maintained about a 20 percent share of the total market—peaking at about $65 billion by 1992. Peripherals not elsewhere classified captured an estimated $18 billion of that amount. However, with the popularity of the Internet and multimedia technology, the peripherals industry had a slight increase in the mid-1990s and forecasts predicted growth would stay level through 1998.

CURRENT CONDITIONS

In the early 1990s, the peripherals industry exceeded growth in other computer equipment industry segments, largely due to the severe price slashing by PC vendors effected during this time. As PC manufacturers' revenues fell in the early 1990s, the number of units shipped increased substantially, prompting a greater demand for all types of add-on peripherals. As demand for computers increased through the mid-1990s, the computer peripheral industry was expected to grow at a good pace throughout the end of the decade.

Annual sales of scanners and other electronic imaging peripherals multiplied at a rate of nearly 20 percent in 1992 to about $2 billion. Furthermore, this segment of the peripherals industry enjoyed relatively high profit margins, and analysts predicted that annual scanner sales would increase 100 percent by the end of 1997. Falling prices, more powerful and simple imaging software and technology, the proliferation of color scanners, and advances in computer memory storage techniques were the dominant factors driving market growth in this segment, while flatbed scanners would continue to account for the majority of product sales.

Printer shipments were expected to jump from over 10 million units in 1995 to about 24 million by 1998, worth nearly $19 billion. By 1998, laser printers would likely hold a 50 percent share of the printer market, while ink-jets would represent over 30 percent.

CRT displays utilized technology that had been changed only slightly during the 1990s—resulting in a price-intensive commodity environment for CRT vendors. LCDs, in contrast, still offered solid growth and profit opportunities. Sales and prices of color LCDs were particularly competitive. From $917 million in 1992, color LCD sales reached nearly $3 billion in 1996. Advances in LCD technology were expected to keep profit margins relatively high through the rest of the decade.

Sales of multimedia peripherals, such as computer sound-systems, were expected to post strong gains throughout the 1990s. Creative Technology Ltd., which led the industry with two-thirds of the market in 1993 sales of add-on sound boards and chips that could digitally recreate human speech, offered evidence of this sector's viability. It was also quick to develop computer add-ons called circuit cards that could give PCs the ability to show full-motion video.

With the increasing popularity of the Internet and World Wide Web, the need for multimedia video and sound systems became more and more in demand through 1990s. By 1994, three out of four consumer PCs included audio capability.

INDUSTRY LEADERS

One of the largest producers of peripheral computer equipment in the world in the 1990s was International Business Machines Corporation (IBM), of New York. IBM held a 12.6 percent share of the global peripheral market in the 1990s. Although the company generated $64.5 billion in revenues in 1992, it lost $6.87 billion. IBM's share of the world peripheral market declined in 1992, as revenues from that division fell nearly 23 percent. By 1996, company sales bounced back to nearly $76 billion, a 5.6 percent increase from 1995, but its market share was still down. Peripheral equipment accounted for about $2.3 billion, or 9 percent, of IBM's 1996 sales. IBM employed 240,615 people in 1996.

Another large supplier of peripherals was Hewlett-Packard Company (H-P) of California, which accounted for 7.3 percent of global peripheral revenues in the early 1990s. The largest U.S. supplier of printers, H-P was an important market innovator in the 1990s. Its Ink-jet and laser technology during this time helped the company reap huge profits from printer sales and thrust the company to a 50 to 60 percent share of the entire printer market by the mid-1990s. The company also held a 51 percent share of the multifunctional peripheral market in the mid-1990s. By 1996, company sales totaled $38.4 billion, a 22 percent increase from the previous year, and the total number of employees reached 112,000.

Other leaders included NEC America Inc., which held a $745 million share of computer monitor sales for 1995. Its parent company, NEC Corporation of Japan, saw total 1996 sales of $41.4 billion and employed approximately 152,700 people. Samsung Electronics held the lead in the computer monitor market, however, with sales of $2.7 billion in the mid-1990s. Headquartered in Korea, the parent company, Samsung Group, had sales of $87 billion in 1995, and employed 233,000 people. Canon Inc., Hitachi, Ltd., Fujitsu Limited, Digital Equipment Corporation, Xerox Corporation, AT&T Corporation, Quantum Corporation, and Apple Computer, Inc. are likewise major forces in the peripherals industry.

WORK FORCE

Like most other computer-related segments, the peripheral industry was expected to realize a significant reduction in its work force during the 1990s. This downsizing was expected to occur even among the industry's more successful companies, due to increased productivity gains and mergers effected to benefit from economies of scale. Nearly 20,000 jobs were expected to be eliminated between 1994 and 1998. For more information about jobs and opportunities in the computer hardware industry, see **SIC 3571: Electronic Computers.**

RESEARCH AND TECHNOLOGY

U.S. firms were on the leading edge of almost every peripheral technology in the industry in the mid-1990s. At least two efforts were underway during this time to advance the role of U.S. firms in the production of the rapidly growing color LCD market. One was a joint venture between Motorola Inc. and In Focus Systems, called Motif. Motif sought to develop high-quality LCDs that could be manufactured inexpensively. The other effort was initiated by the Defense Advanced Research Projects Agency (DARPA). DARPA planned to provide $15 million in seed money for a consortium of large and small companies that would assemble the framework necessary to effectively compete in the color LCD market.

Scanner and printer manufacturers were striving toward similar technological and productivity goals. The demand for higher resolution, faster input and output, lower production costs, and greater flexibility were driving investment and development in both printer categories. In 1997, manufacturers were already delivering low-end laser printers capable of printing 600 DPI or greater.

Advances in the input devices market focused on ease and multifunctions. In 1995, Other 90% Technologies of California was working on a mouse that controls action by reading the electromagnetic signals within the user's skin. Arizona-based SC&T had keyboards with built-in radios and telephones in development.

In the future, the computer peripheral industry will likely become increasingly integrated with complementary industries, as data processing, interface, storage, fiber optics, wireless, and digital broadband switching technologies converged into a massive multimedia industry. Scanners, printers, and displays would also likely be used in conjunction with other communications and information equipment.

FURTHER READING

Arnold, Bill. "Color LCDs: From Famine to Feast." *Electronic Business,* April 1993.

"Boomin' World of PC Audio." *PC Week,* 31 October 1994.

Brandt, Richard. "Sound Blaster Hears the Blare of Competition." *Business Week,* 12 April 1992.

Braun, Ellen. "Computer Printers: More Power, Less Cost." *Office Systems,* March 1992.

———. "Scanners Give PCs New Eyes." *Office Systems,* August 1993.

"Electronic Imaging Collides with Health Care Cost Control." *Electronic Business,* July 1993.

Howard, Bill. "A Scanner on Every Desk." *PC Magazine,* 9 April 1996.

"The Internet's Golden Switch Makers: Computer Networking." *The Economist,* 2 December 1995.

Lazich, Robert S., ed. *Market Share Reporter.* Detroit: Gale Research, 1997.

McCracken, Ted. "Video Amplifier Keying Performance." *Computer Technology Review,* August 1993.

McNamara, George. "Will Scanners Ride Image Management's Breaking Wave?" *Computer Technology Review,* August 1993.

Niemond, George A. "Computer and Peripherals Industry." *The Value Line Investment Survey,* 24 January 1997.

Ransdell, Eric. "The Mouse that Really Roared." *U.S. News & World Report,* 20 May 1996.

Rose, John. "New Competitors Will Scramble the Opportunities." *Electronic Business,* July 1993.

Ryan, Ken. "Printer Power." *HFN, The Weekly Newspaper for the Home Furnishing Network,* 29 April 1996.

Ryan, Kimberly. "Peripherals: Powerful, Plentiful and Colorful." *Datamation,* 15 January 1993.

Schlak, Mark. "The New IT Industry Takes Shape." *Datamation,* 15 June 1993.

Siatt, Wayne. "Lasers, Ink-Jets Pack Practical Printing Power." *Office Products Development,* July 1993.

Silverthorne, Sean. "It's Input Ooh La La." *PC Week,* 7 August 1995.

Thomas, Mike. "Electronic Imaging Posts Impressive Gains." *The Office,* January 1993.

———. "Multifunctional Peripherals Will Overcome." *Computer Technology Review,* December 1990.

Trowbridge, Dave. "OmniScan Aims to Reverse Slump in Fortunes of Handheld Scanners." *Computer Technology Review,* August 1993.

U.S. Bureau of the Census. "Computer and Office Accounting Machines." *Current Industrial Reports.* Washington, 1996. Available from http://www.census.gov/industry/ma35r95.txt.

"Where Have All the High-Tech Jobs Gone?" *Electronic Business,* August 1993.

—Dave Mote, updated by Sonya Shelton

SIC 3578

CALCULATING AND ACCOUNTING MACHINES, EXCEPT ELECTRONIC COMPUTERS

This industry covers establishments primarily engaged in manufacturing point-of-sale devices, fund transfer devices, and other calculating and accounting machines, except electronic computers. Included are electronic calculating and accounting machines which must be paced by operator intervention, even when augmented by attachments. These machines may include program control or have input/output capabilities.

Charles Xavier Thomas, of France, is credited with starting the calculating and accounting machines industry when he introduced the arithmometer in the 1870s. Frank Baldwin and William S. Burroughs were also major innovators in early calculating machine technology. During the industrial revolution and until the mid-1900s, mechanical and electrical adding machines dominated industry offerings. The invention of the hand-held calculator in 1948 and the integrated circuit in the late 1960s, however, initiated the demise of traditional adding machines.

Producers of desk-top and hand-held calculators shipped goods worth a total of $1.4 billion in 1995. Both products had essentially become commodity items by that time. Electronic cash registers, an offshoot of calculating machines, offered higher profit margins for manufacturers. Scanning technology and the demand for related inventory tracking systems in the 1980s and early 1990s spurred the development of new "high-tech" cash registers that buoyed profits for some prior producers of traditional calculating machines. Other competitors exited the market or shifted to production of other equipment.

ATMs and POS devices, which were added to industry offerings in the 1980s, quickly escalated sales of cash registers and adding machines. Sales of ATMs, which store cash and are used primarily by bank customers to conduct account transactions, skyrocketed past a total of 90,000 units by 1993. Less expensive POS devices, which allow consumers to conduct electronic account transactions from a purchase point such as a gas station or supermarket, numbered about 300,000 in 1993.

By the early 1990s, the market for ATMs was becoming saturated in comparison to the 1980s. Manufacturers' earnings were expected to rise as industry analysts projected a growing demand for replacement machines and a 20 percent rise in the number of ATM installations between 1993 and 1997. The number of POS devices sold, on the other hand, is expected to increase to more than 1.1 million by 1997 as a growing number of retailers adopt this method of accepting payment.

In 1992, the top 25 companies in the industry generated about $1.6 billion in sales from all adding and calculating machines. Diebold Inc., which produced over half of all ATMs sold in 1992, was the largest producer—with $476 million in sales and about 3,800 employees. The Minnesota-based National Computer Systems was the second largest company in the industry with $300 million in sales and about 3,000 employees. Most companies in the industry, however, are small. Only the top ten competitors, for example, employed more than 100 people or generated over $15 million in revenues.

Manufacturers hoped to increase ATM sales in the mid-1990s by integrating video-conferencing and imaging capabilities into their products. Some banks were also experimenting with selling mutual fund shares through ATMs. Cash register manufacturers were striving to jump-start lagging sales by integrating advanced inventory tracking and information systems technology into new product offerings.

Despite the popularity of ATMs and POS devices in the United States, the technology has been slow to catch on overseas. Only about 40,000 ATMs, for example, have been installed outside the United States. Spain and the United Kingdom combined have approximately 10,000 ATMs, while Austria, Denmark, Germany, Ireland, Norway, and Sweden have none. ATMs in Japan are available for use only in the daytime.

FURTHER READING

Angel, Abcede. "Marketers Total ECR Costs, Benefits." *National Petroleum News,* March 1993.

Barthel, Matt. "Point of Sale Devices Seen Outpacing ATMs." *American Banker,* 19 July 1993.

Cody, Angela. "Calculators + PCs = Performance." *Today's Office,* August 1990.

Cope, Debra. "Equity Funds by ATM Seen as Wave of Future." *American Banker,* 17August 1993.

Darnay, Arsen J., ed. *Manufacturing USA; Industry Analyses, Statistics, and Leading Companies,* Detroit: Gale Research, 1993.

Darnay, Arsen J., and Marlita A. Reddy, eds. *Market Share Reporter: An Annual Compilation of Reported Market Share Data on Companies, Products, and Services, 1993,* Detroit: Gale Research, 1993.

"Don't Bank on ATMs Abroad." *Money,* April 1993.

Encyclopaedia Britannica. Chicago: Encyclopaedia Britannica, Inc., 1989.

Mitchell, Richard. "ATM Sales Rise with Bank Profits." *Bank Management,* May 1993.

1995 Annual Survey of Manufactures. Washington, DC: Bureau of the Census, 1997.

Rehr, Darryl C. "Calculators: You Can Count on Them." *Office,* July 1991.

—Dave Mote, updated by Kenneth R. Shepherd

SIC 3579

OFFICE MACHINES, NOT ELSEWHERE CLASSIFIED

Companies principally engaged in manufacturing miscellaneous office machines and devices comprise this industry classification. Such devices include typewriting, mailroom, dictation, and facsimile machines. In addition, a multitude of companies in the industry produce specialty products, such as paper shredders, envelope stuffing machines, ticket counters, and coin wrapping machines. Establishments primarily engaged in manufacturing modems and other communications interface equipment are classified in **SIC 3661: Telephone and Telegraph Apparatus.**

INDUSTRY SNAPSHOT

In the early 1990s, sales of miscellaneous office machines declined due to increased use of computers, foreign competition, lackluster economic growth, increased productivity, reduced corporate spending, and U.S. demographic changes. The value of shipments for the industry reached approximately $3.65 billion in 1994, but reportedly dropped every year since. In 1996 industry shipments were estimated to reach $3.16 billion; by 1998, they were expected to drop to $2.95 billion. The number of establishments in the office machines industry has also continuously decreased throughout the 1990s. The 202 establishments in existence in 1990 had dropped to 152 in 1994; this number was projected to reach 150 in 1997.

Manufacturers responded to the more competitive environment of the 1990s by integrating the latest technology into new product offerings, infiltrating new channels of distribution and targeting home offices. During this time, new businesses were being started at a record pace. From 1984 to 1995, the U.S. Small Business Administration reported that the number of small businesses doubled to almost 22 million. In 1995, the number of business start-ups hit a 12-year high of 810,000. All of these new businesses require office equipment and supplies.

ORGANIZATION AND STRUCTURE

Typewriters. Typewriters and word processing machines accounted for the largest segment of the miscellaneous business machines industry in the 1990s, representing move than 40 percent of total shipments. While most of the units sold were electronic typewriters, some companies were still marketing electromechanical typewriters, which resemble traditional manual typewriters, but use electricity to reduce the effort required by the typist and to increase the quality of type.

Electronic typewriters take the electromechanical concept a step further by reducing the number of moving parts and featuring advanced capabilities. For instance, many electronic typewriters can recall a series of pressed keys and then delete those characters from a sheet of paper on command. Some units also allow the typist to store a word or phrase in the machine's memory, which automatically recalls and prints on command.

A third model of typewriter is the personal word processor (PWP). PWPs allow the typist to view text on a screen before it is actually transferred to paper, much like a personal computer (PC). Most PWPs are simply an electronic typewriter with a liquid crystal display and a central processing unit attached. Unlike PCs, PWPs usually offer access only to internally stored proprietary software programs. Many PWPs are also equipped with spreadsheet software, and some advanced units offered disk drives, DOS compatibility, and hand-held scanners.

Typewriters and PWPs are less expensive and typically regarded as easier to use than most PCs. Compact electronic typewriters typically sold for $250 to $700 in the mid-1990s, while the most advanced PWP models sold for $2,000 to $6,000.

Other Products. Making up the remaining 50 to 60 percent of the miscellaneous office machines industry were a variety of specialty devices. Dictation machines, for instance, have been used by professionals and executives, for whom certain jobs require the recording of their voices for later transcription. Depending on the features offered, dictaphones ranged in price from $150 to $2,500 in the mid-1990s.

Shredders, used to destroy internal printed documents, also accounted for a slim segment of the market. In the mid-1990s, personal shredders used by small companies and professional practices ranged widely in options and prices. Inexpensive shredders could be purchased for as little as $500, while larger shredders usually started at about $5,000, and industrial, full-featured shredders were available for as much as $100,000. The more-expensive models featured conveyer belts and were capable of shredding boxes, metal binders, and entire wastebaskets.

The facsimile (fax) machine was also an important and popular product in the industry. The fax scanned a document and produced electrical signals that were sent to another fax machine, which converted the signals into a copy of the original document. In the mid-1990s, the average large company sent 260 faxes per day, while mid-sized firms sent about 40 faxes per day.

A fifth major segment of the industry consisted of mailroom equipment. In fact, various mail machines accounted for about 25 percent of industry sales in the 1990s. Designed to meter, sort, and track mail, such machines were used by the postal service, as well as private organizations. While sorting machines could mean an initial cost of anywhere from $5,000 to $500,000, they greatly reduced the cost of sorting mail manually from $35 per thousand to less than $3 per thousand pieces of mail. The most advanced sorters utilized optical character recognition (OCR) to read addresses and U.S. Postal Service bar codes.

BACKGROUND AND DEVELOPMENT

The business machine industry emerged from the industrial revolution in the latter part of the nineteenth century. As the need to record and manage business information grew, several products, including the typewriter, were developed to meet demands. Although the typewriter was invented in 1714 by London engineer Henry Mill, the most famous devices were developed in the late 1800s. The Remington typewriter, first offered to the public in 1874, was one of the more popular early machines.

The first electromechanical typewriter was invented by Thomas Edison in 1872, although practical application of this device did not occur until the twentieth century. One of the first electric models, the Electromatic, was purchased by International Business Machines in 1933; after World War II, several other companies introduced electric typewriters. During the post-war era, the business machine industry flourished. A booming economy and new technology soon prompted the development of a plethora of labor-saving devices.

Although an early version of the facsimile machine was introduced in 1843 by Scottish inventor Alexander Bain, this device did not have any practical application in the United States until 1925. That year, the American Telephone & Telegraph Company introduced a wirephoto service. The following year, RCA opened the first trans-Atlantic radiophoto circuit for commercial use, which used fax technology. Advances in production technology, which drastically reduced the price of fax machines, made the machine available to the general public during the late 1970s and 1980s.

While dictation machines also gained widespread public acceptance during the mid-1900s, the invention of the integrated circuit in the 1960s brought hand-held recording devices into the professional mainstream. Dictaphones remained the primary means of recording information for doctors, lawyers, and business executives throughout the 1970s and much of the 1980s. The advent of personal computers, notebook computers, and cellular telephone technology adversely affected sales of dictation equipment in the 1980s, and by the early 1990s, dictation machines were largely being replaced with machines featuring alternative technologies.

As increasingly inexpensive computer and cellular technology was rendering dictaphones and typewriters obsolete, many business machine companies struggled to adapt to evolving market demands. Nevertheless, technological advances were opening new markets for other miscellaneous business machines—particularly postal equipment—in demand due to increased postal volume and new postal requirements for addresses.

CURRENT CONDITIONS

Shipments of miscellaneous business machines peaked in 1985 at over $5 billion. After that time, however, several factors combined to deflate revenues and profit margins for manufacturers. Most importantly, the popularity of superior computer technology was affecting revenues from industry staples such as typewriters and dictation equipment. Although business machine manufacturers countered with PWPs and other low-cost, higher technology products, computers threatened to eventually deplete the market for even those items.

At the same time that computers and cellular phones were making industry waves, the U.S. business machine market experienced an economic recession in the late 1980s. Revenues from miscellaneous business machines fell to about $3.2 billion in 1987. Although sales picked up in 1988 and 1989, shipments only reached $3.5 to $4 billion per year before slumping again in the early 1990s. By 1996, this number was estimated to drop to $3.16 billion. Reduced expenditures by large businesses were a primary cause for the decrease.

In addition to alternative technologies and the economic recession, manufacturers were also facing a more competitive market in the 1980s and early 1990s. Many products, such as typewriters and facsimile machines, had become low-cost commodity items that offered slim profit margins. In response to price competition from both domestic and foreign manufacturers, many U.S. companies moved their production operations overseas or increased automation in domestic facilities. The number of establishments in the industry dropped 23 percent from 1990 to 1996. As a result, industry employment in the United States plummeted from about 45,000 in 1982 to about 30,000 in the early 1990s, down to an estimated 20,000 going into the latter part of the decade.

Industry Response. In response to inclement market conditions, manufacturers scrambled to buoy profits and remain competitive. Besides diverting investments into competing industries, such as computer-related office products, producers tailored product offerings to appeal to the growth market of the 1990s—small businesses.

In 1989, industry analysts predicted that 25 million home offices would exist by the mid-1990s. Instead, about 40 million home offices emerged, representing an increase in 1992 of 2.2 million. Because the average home office spent $40 to $50 per week on business supplies, manufacturers increasingly cater to this segment.

In an effort to reach small businesses and home office buyers, manufacturers were also adjusting their marketing and distribution strategies in the mid-1990s.

While producers once sold products primarily through dedicated office device resellers, many companies were using 50 or more different types of retailers to move their equipment in the 1990s.

One of the fastest growing distribution channels during this time was the discount superstore and business center, such as Wal-Mart, Office Depot, and K-Mart. In the mid-1990s, manufacturers distributed an estimated 7 to 10 percent of their shipments through these retail chains, and some industry participants suggested that this figure would eventually exceed 20 or 30 percent. By 1997, there were more than 1,600 superstores in the North American market, with a potential for more than 3,000 stores according to some industry analysts.

Manufacturers were also boosting sales by emphasizing distribution through equipment leasing companies. Many businesses favored the lease agreement in order to take advantage of changing technology and certain tax benefits. In addition, leasing allowed companies to reduce their capital equipment investment— an important point in the capital-starved environment of the 1990s.

Some manufacturers looked forward to increased sales in Mexico as a result of the North American Free Trade Agreement (NAFTA), which was expected to increase capital spending in that nation. Furthermore, some competitors hoped to shore up their bottom line by moving manufacturing facilities south, where they could take advantage of inexpensive labor and a loosely regulated manufacturing environment.

INDUSTRY LEADERS

The largest supplier of miscellaneous business machines in the United States in the mid-1990s was the Xerox Corp., headquartered in Stamford, Connecticut. The company had total revenues of about $17.4 billion in 1996, an 8 percent increase over 1995, most of which was derived from business equipment classified in other industries, such as photocopiers. Pitney Bowes, also headquartered in Stamford, Connecticut, placed second with sales of $3.8 billion in 1996. The company operates within the industry segments of business equipment (including mailing systems such as postage meters and letter scales, copying systems and supplies, facsimile systems and supplies, and related financing); business services (such as facilities management and mortgage servicing); and commercial and industrial financing (including large-ticket financing programs of such products as aircraft, locomotives, and high-technology equipment).

Employment by miscellaneous business equipment manufacturers, like employment in most other business equipment and computer-related industries, was expected to drastically decline during the 1990s and into the next century. Contributing to this decline will be advances in productivity and automation, outsourcing of manufacturing activities to foreign firms, and stagnation in demand for traditional equipment such as typewriters.

Analysts predicted an employment decline of 20 to 50 percent among most manufacturers between 1993 and 2005. Electric and electronic assemblage positions, which accounted for 10 percent of industry jobs in 1992, were expected to fall by about 55 percent. Similarly, positions for general assemblers and fabricators were projected to decline by nearly 40 percent.

Moreover, positions on the higher end of the pay scale, including those of engineer, technician, and management support, were expected to fall by 4 to 15 percent by the year 2005, and executive and managerial positions would likely decline by about 20 percent. On the other hand, experts speculated that sales jobs and computer programming positions would increase by about 1 percent; and information systems jobs, which accounted for 2.5 percent of total industry employment in 1993, would experience growth of about 44 percent by the year 2005.

RESEARCH AND TECHNOLOGY

Manufacturers sought to retain market share and revenues by delivering new products and technology in the early 1990s. PWPs represented efforts by typewriter companies to combat the dominance of PCs. New typewriters by Lexmark International Inc., a division of IBM, sought to combine the best features of typewriters and computers. Eight models introduced in late 1993 offered advanced text editing, long-term storage, and word processing features—functions that helped make typewriters the tool of choice for such activities as individual envelope typing, invoicing, and labeling.

Competitors were also improving fax machines, often combining the functions of copiers, electronic mail, scanners, and computers into a single unit. In 1993, Sharp Electronics introduced the first two-sided, or duplex, fax machine, which could scan, collate, and fax a set of two-sided documents. Major advances were also occurring in the large postal machine market. Datatech, for instance, offered a new machine in 1993 designed to address business envelopes with Delivery Point Barcodes—a feature that helped reduce postal rates.

FURTHER READING

"Buyers Find Savings by Leasing Equipment." *Purchasing,* 19 August 1993.

Carbonara, Joseph. "Home Office Market: Has It Delivered?" *Office Products Distribution,* May 1993.

Cosgrove, Nancy Dunn. "The Paperless Office: Still a Myth in the Nineties." *The Office,* April 1993.

———. "Typewriters Adapt: They're Here to Stay." *The Office,* January 1993.

Darnay, Arsen, ed. *Manufacturing USA.* 5th ed. Detroit: Gale Research, 1996.

Gragg, Ellen. "Shredders Give Protection from Espionage and Gossip." *Office Systems,* July 1993.

Johnson, Leone. "Dictation Machines Seek to Specialize." *The Office,* January 1993.

LeGallee, Julie. "Typewriters: Are Computers Driving Them to Pasture." *The Office,* August 1993.

"Low Cost Printer Does #10 Envelopes." *Purchasing,* 15 July 1993.

"New Typewriter Complements PC Office Environment." *Purchasing,* 23 September 1993.

"Range of Equipment to Meet USPS Rules." *Purchasing,* 23 September 1993.

Sopko, Sandra. "The Well-Connected, Efficient & High-Tech." *The Office,* September 1993.

Thomas, Howard, and David Stockwell. "Office Products Marketing: The Next Generation." *Office Products Distribution,* May 1993.

"Use of Plain Paper Faxes Rise." *Purchasing,* 15 July 1993.

—Dave Mote, updated by Gertrude Mandeville

SIC 3581

AUTOMATIC VENDING MACHINES

This industry consists of establishments primarily engaged in manufacturing automatic vending machines and coin-operated mechanisms for such machines.

INDUSTRY SNAPSHOT

In 1995, manufacturers' shipments of coin-operated vending machines totaled $767.0 million, an increase of 10 percent from the 1994 figure of $698.2 million. Shipments of beverage vending machines increased 20 percent, while confections and foods decreased 11 percent, from $239.0 million to $211.6 million. Approximately 4,700,000 vending machines are on location throughout the 50 states, providing a 24-hour point of sale. Two of the most common places that vending machines are found are in schools and in the workplace. Industry sales of food and refreshments alone are estimated to exceed $25 billion annually. Non-food sales, including cigarettes, are estimated to approximate another $4 billion.

The industry segments itself by the kind of service provided by the vending operator. Some of the major categories include: the 4 C's, which include coffee, club soda, candy, and cigarettes; full-line vending, which includes hot food, canned soda, and diary and frozen food; specialty vending, which encompasses such special products as pizza or french fries; OCS, or office coffee service; bulk vending, focusing on such un-packaged items as gum or nuts; and street vending, which includes music machines, video games, and other vending machines used in public places.

ORGANIZATION AND STRUCTURE

Vending is essentially a three-step process involving three separate industries: manufacturing companies, distributors, and vending machine operators. This industry group (SIC 3581) primarily covers the manufacturing step in this multi-state industrial sequence.

About 90 U.S. companies produced automatic vending machines or parts for them in the 1990s. Although a vast majority of vending machines were manufactured by large companies, the industry did sustain quite a few smaller firms. The merchandise vending industry is essentially part of the small business community.

The U.S. Department of Commerce reported that 47 companies were engaged in manufacturing coin-operated vending machines in 1994. Of these, 14 produced beverage machines, 18 manufactured machines that sold food and confections, and 32 manufactured other types of vending machines, including those selling cigarettes, water, and postage stamps. Canned and bottled soft drink machines made up by far the largest share of beverage machines manufactured in 1995, totaling 298,491 units. Among confection and food vending machines, those that sold bulk confections and charms predominated, totaling 128,097 (shipped in 1995) while bagged snacks and confections made up another significant share at 86,539.

The National Automatic Merchandising Association (NAMA) has been the most important trade organization in the vending industry in the 1990s. NAMA represents companies involved in every facet of vending, from machine manufacturers to suppliers of vended products. Founded in 1936, NAMA compiles a broad range of statistics and produces several periodicals, including a regular industry newsletter, a review

of pertinent state legislation, and a labor issues bulletin. Headquartered in Chicago, the organization had 2,400 members, 35 state groups, and an annual budget of about $2.5 million in 1996.

The National Bulk Vendors Association (NBVA) concentrates specifically on the manufacture and operation of bulk vending equipment. The NBVA was founded in 1949 and is based in Chicago.

BACKGROUND AND DEVELOPMENT

The earliest recorded ''vending machine'' was in 215 B.C. when the mathematician Hero described and illustrated a number of inventions conceived by himself and his teacher, Tesibius, in a book called Pneumatika. Included in the book was the plan for a completely automatic, coin-operated machine that dispensed a small amount of sacrificial water when a five-drachma coin was deposited. It is unlikely that the machine was used on a large scale, and there is no evidence to suggest that anything was sold automatically again for centuries.

Coin-operated machines that sold snuff and tobacco appeared in English taverns around 1615. These machines were actually cruder than Hero's device and required the proprietor to shut the lid after each use. Usually made of brass, the machines were portable and were carried from customer to customer.

In the nineteenth century, vending machines began to appear in much greater variety and quantity. An early incarnation of the newspaper machine appeared in England in 1822. The device was the brainchild of Richard Carlile, a bookseller trying to avoid arrest for peddling copies of banned works such as Thomas Paine's *The Age of Reason*. While his machine worked, his plan to avoid arrest didn't.

The first known patent for a vending machine was issued in 1857 to Simeon Denham for a penny postage stamp device. Over the next couple of decades, inventors began showing up at patent offices all over the world with coin-operated machines that sold candy, cigarettes, handkerchiefs, and other small items. In 1884, the first U.S. vending machine patent was issued to W.H. Fruen for a contraption remarkably similar to Hero's holy water machine.

The American vending machine industry was truly born in 1888, when Thomas Adams of the Adams Gum Company began selling his Tutti-Frutti gum out of machines on the platforms of New York's elevated rail system. These machines were an immediate success, and toward the end of the century, postage stamp machines also became more common. The Automatic Machine Company of Buffalo, New York, was the first company to sell stamps automatically on a large scale, beginning in 1891. Bulk vending machines began to appear around the turn of the century. The Mills Novelty Company introduced the first of these, which sold a pre-set amount of peanuts for a penny, at the Pan American Exposition in 1901. The following year, the Horn & Hardart Baking Company revolutionized vending in the United States by opening is first Automat restaurant in Philadelphia.

Prior to 1908, beverage vending machines dispensed only the beverages themselves, which the customer then drank out of a common cup. That year, with public awareness of sanitation growing, the Public Cup Vendor Company of New York (later to become the Dixie Cup Company) unveiled a machine that dispensed water in individual paper cups.

By the 1920s, the vending industry had been divided into manufacturers and operators. The Doehler Die Casting Company, for example, developed machines for vending a diverse range of products that included Life Savers, lighter fluid, and sanitary napkins. Another industry revolution took place in 1925, when three new machines were developed, all of which sold cigarettes. Candy machines offering customers a choice of products began to spread in the 1930s. Nathaniel Leverone, the founder of the Canteen Company, was a pioneer in the development of this type of machine.

The manufacture of vending machines was suspended during World War II, but at the war's conclusion the industry regained its momentum. Among the machines that appeared during this time were the first hot coffee vendors and a hot dog machine. In the first decade after World War II, hundreds of small manufacturing companies entered the vending machine arena, and vast improvements were made in design—especially in the area of coin mechanisms. In 1960, paper money changers came into widespread use. When machines for vending canned soft drinks were introduced in 1961, vending sales soared.

Since that time the vending machine industry has been consolidating to a great degree. Manufacturing has become increasingly dominated by large companies. At the same time, advances in electronic components, which first appeared in vending machines in 1980, have made machines "smarter," enabling them to keep records and diagnose glitches. The variety of products vended automatically has continued to grow explosively, as items specifically created for machine vending, such as microwave popcorn, have made their appearances.

In the early 1990s, vending machine manufacturing appeared to be entering a new era. The emergence of "smart" machines was certain to affect every part of the industry. The availability of full-service machines that could handle a variety of products and perform their own record keeping was enabling bottling companies to take over many of the chores that were previously handed over to third-party operators. This represented the reversal of a trend that began in the 1950s, when bottlers began to remove themselves from the day-to-day servicing of machines. In addition, the replacement of moving parts by electronic components was expected to contribute to a further concentration of manufacturing companies, since the demand for spare parts was sure to decline sharply.

The new generation of smart vending machines was also expected to give manufacturers a healthy boost. Since the beginning of the 1990s, the slumping U.S. economy had led operators to seek ways to hold their costs in check. Frequently, this meant refurbishing old machines rather than purchasing new ones. Dixie-Narco Inc., for example, saw its sales drop by about 18 percent in 1990, while its parts business was actually more active than usual. The improved security and record keeping capabilities offered by newer machines, and their potential to save operators money in the long run, might provide operators an incentive to invest in the latest equipment.

Inflation in the 1990s affected the vending industry adversely as well. The convenience of dropping coins into a machine in exchange for merchandise disappeared when the price of an item exceeded the amount of change reasonably accommodated in a pocket. Manufacturers reacted to this problem in two ways. One involved the introduction of debit cards, first introduced in 1985. Debit cards eliminated the need to carry change, enabling regular users of a vending area to pre-pay for several dollars worth of merchandise at a time. Mechanized dollar bill acceptors, notoriously fussy and uncooperative, had also improved somewhat by the mid-1990s. The other angle from which the industry attacked the inflation problem was by lobbying for the reintroduction of a dollar coin. The issue of such a coin would benefit the vending industry immensely, especially given the growing presence of upscale items, like cappuccino, in vending machines.

CURRENT CONDITIONS

Several significant changes were taking place in the vending industry in the 1990s. Some resulted from new technology, while others stemmed more directly from general societal changes. New machines developed during this time were capable of vending food of much higher quality than was previously possible. This ability was having a particularly noticeable effect in the work place, as corporate downsizing necessitated the replacement of many company cafeterias with vending areas. With a new emphasis on hot, nutritious foods, the major manufacturers began producing machines that sold items such as french fries, fresh pizza, and a much broader line of microwaveable frozen foods.

Tom Goodwin, owner of Vending and Food Service, speculates that the nation's increasing knowledge of health issues has caused an increased demand for more healthful foods. Items such as fat-free pretzels, baked potato chips, and bottled water are now popular vending machine items. "Ten years ago, if you offered a person a bottle of water for sale in a vending machine, he'd probably laugh at you," Goodwin stated.

With coffee shops springing up all over the United States, flavored and specialty coffee sales soared. This was also true for vending machines that sold flavored coffee and even ground their own beans. The price for a cup of cappuccino or other hot beverages was about 35 to 50 cents in the 1990s.

The sharp decline in cigarette smoking the United States throughout the 1990s has had a dramatic impact on the vending industry. Once a huge seller as one the four C's of vending, cigarettes only generated a small portion of the vending operator's revenue compared to the considerable percentage of revenue cigarettes generated in the 1960s (at 45.5 percent). Dick Bakala, owner of Dick's Vending Service notes that while cigarettes used to make up 20 percent of his business, they now make up only 2 percent.

Employment in the vending manufacturing industry declined from 1984 to 1994. In 1995 approximately 7,000 workers were employed in the industry. The total payroll for its workforce during that year was about $198 million.

INDUSTRY LEADERS

Dixie-Narco, Inc., a division of Maytag Corporation, was the nation's leading manufacturer of automatic vending machines in the mid-1990s. Headquartered in Williston, South Carolina, Dixie Narco employed 1,500 workers, and reported annual sales of about $150 million in the mid-1990s. Rowe International, Inc. of Whippany, New Jersey, was a privately held company with annual sales of $100 million and about 550 employees in 1996. Other major companies

in the industry included Booth, Inc., Multiplex Co., Inc., and Leer Manufacturing.

AMERICA AND THE WORLD

The United States was not alone in its obsession with the convenience offered by vending machines. Industry leader Dixie-Narco, for example, was selling a complete line of models in over 30 countries by 1990. The company began to emphasize exports, tailoring machines for the specific needs of its foreign markets rather than merely making small adjustments in existing models.

The popularity of the vending machine proved even stronger in Japan. Half of Japan's retail soft drink sales in the early 1990s came through vending machines, and this market share is expected to increase. In Japan, the machines lined the sidewalks, playing music and offering a wide variety of merchandise, including beer, sushi, and panty hose. One advantage that vending operators in Japan had over their American counterparts was that vandalism was almost unheard of in that country in the 1990s.

The enthusiasm for vended goods was not global, however. Although American manufacturers sold machines successfully in Europe for years, the machines were not always welcome. Cafe proprietors in Bordeaux, France, for example, refused to serve Coca Cola for a period in 1990 in protest of the placement of Coke machines on public sidewalks in their city, an offense to both their sense of good taste and fair competition.

RESEARCH AND TECHNOLOGY

Flexibility and security are two areas in which engineers in the vending industry were making great strides in the 1990s. The Merlin 2000 series developed by a company called InterBev in 1989 provided a good example of the flexibility built into the new generation of vending machines. The Merlin 2000 machines could sell both sodas and juice from a single machine, with an improved mechanism for adjusting prices from one selection to the next.

Furthermore, electronic bill and coin changing mechanisms made fraud more difficult. A common form of vandalism, injecting salt water into the coin mechanisms, and putting the machine in "jackpot" mode by shorting out the electronic parts was circumvented by improved shielding of electronic components. Programmable security code devices were also installed on many new machines to prevent unauthorized individuals from tampering with pricing and removing money or merchandise.

The Automatic Merchandiser Vending Manufacturers Conference was first held in 1995 as a forum to educate vending product and equipment manufacturers about the industry and customers needs. The first of its kind, the two-day program consisted of seminars in which industry experts, vending operators, and consumers addressed various critical topics facing the vending industry. The most exciting new vending technology has been the computerized capabilities of the machines to record their own vending statistics.

FURTHER READING

"About Vending." Chicago: National Automatic Merchandising Association, 1996. Available from http://www.vending.org/about.htm.

"Automatic Merchandiser." Fort Atkinson, WI: Johnson Jill Press, 1997. Available from http://www.amonline.com-Automatic Merchandiser.

Batdorf, Tracey L. "Vending Money Making Machines Keep Improving." *Beverage Industry,* May 1990.

Brotman, Barbara. "Demand for Quality Exacts Change from Vending Industry." *Chicago Tribune,* 8 October 1993.

Colmer, Michael. *The Great Vending Machine Book.* Chicago: Contemporary Books, 1977.

Current Industrial Reports: Vending Machines, Coin-Operated. Washington: GPO, 1993.

Fitzell, Phil. "Opening the Floodgates." *Beverage World,* January, 1990.

———. "Whistlin' Dixie." *Beverage World,* October, 1991.

Hall, Trish. "Vending Machines: The Next Generation in Dining." *New York Times,* 9 September 1992.

Henry, Ann. "High-Tech Vending," *Appliance,* December, 1991.

Remich, Norman C., Jr. "Coin to Replace $1 Bill?" *Appliance Manufacturer,* July, 1992.

Schreiber, G.R. *A Concise History of Vending in the U.S.A.* Chicago: National Automatic Merchandising Association, 1990.

Sfiligoj, Eric, and Laurie MacDonald. "Splendor in the Vendor." *Beverage World,* February, 1992.

Tanzer, Andrew. "War of the Sales Robots." *Forbes,* 7 January 1991.

"Vending Machines Offering Healthier Choices." *Beloit Daily News,* 11 September 1996.

Walker, Tracey L. "Defending Your Vendors." *Beverage Industry,* January, 1991.

Woutat, Donald. "Sizzlers in the Vending Machine. " *Los Angeles Times,* 22 November 1990.

—Robert R. Jacobson, updated by Diane M. Hornbeck

SIC 3582

COMMERCIAL LAUNDRY EQUIPMENT

The commercial laundry, dry cleaning, and pressing machine industry encompasses companies primarily engaged in manufacturing nonresidential laundry equipment. Coin-operated machines are classified in **SIC 3633: Household Laundry Equipment.**

The largest product group in this industry is washers and extractors, which account for almost 40 percent of sales. Commercial dryers and presses make up about 16 and 11 percent of output, respectively. Dry cleaning equipment accounts for an additional 11 percent of production, while parts, attachments, and miscellaneous equipment represent the remainder of sales.

Hotels, hospitals, and contract laundry services that serve commercial and institutional customers were the biggest consumers of commercial laundry equipment in the early 1990s. Dry cleaners represented about 17 percent of the market. Government institutions, including the armed services, prisons, schools, and hospitals, bought about 11 percent of industry output; and 12 percent of production was exported.

Maytag Corporation introduced the first electric washing machine in 1907. Not until the 1950s, however, did commercial laundry equipment producers achieve widespread market penetration. The proliferation of hotels, hospitals, and government institutions during the post-World War II economic boom pushed industry revenues to almost $300 million per year by the end of the 1970s. Continued growth in demand during the 1980s, particularly in hotel and hospital markets, increased sales to $587 million by 1988.

The commercial laundry industry faltered in the late 1980s and early 1990s as recession gripped the U.S. economy. Sales plummeted to $480 million during 1989 and bobbed up to only $526 million in 1990. Although commercial construction markets remained sluggish in the early and mid-1990s, increased sales to institutional consumers helped some manufacturers stabilize their earnings. An increase in new construction in 1993 and 1994, moreover, partially renewed industry optimism.

Manufacturers in the mid-1990s were striving to boost profits by building machines that were more energy efficient, conserved water, and offered more features. Pellerin Milnor Corp., for example, introduced a valve that allowed commercial washing machines to reuse water. Speed Queen designed a line of commercial laundry machines that took more time, effort, and noise to steal. The machines also increased dryer airflow and allowed easier loading and servicing.

The largest U.S. company primarily engaged in the production of commercial laundry equipment in the mid-1990s was Unimac Company, Inc. of Marianna, Florida. Unimac had sales of $40 million in the mid-1990s and employed 700 workers. Cissell Manufacturing Company of Louisville, Kentucky, was the second largest competitor. It boasted revenues of about $40 million and had 400 employees. Other major players included Hotsy Corporation of Colorado and American Dryer Corporation of Massachusetts. Approximately 70 companies were included in the industry in the mid-1990s.

Although sales and unit shipments grew by more than 50 percent during the 1980s, industry employment rose less than 10 percent, to about 5,200. Industry consolidation, company restructuring, manufacturing productivity gains, and the movement of production facilities to Mexico all contributed to stagnant job growth. By the mid-1990s, however, jobs continued to increase slowly but steadily. The 1992 Census of Manufactures reported 4,700 workers employed in the industry, only 2 percent over the figure of 4,600 reported in the 1987 census. By 1994, however, that figure had risen to 4,800; and in 1995, it increased to 4,900. Although the growth level was still only 2 percent, the growth was happening over a much shorter period of time. The growth of jobs in the industry in 1995 was the same as that in the period 1992-94, and was the same as the period 1987-92.

FURTHER READING

Colliers Encyclopedia. New York: P.F. Collier, Inc., 1988.

Darnay, Arsen J., ed. *Manufacturing USA.* 5th ed. Detroit: Gale Research, 1996.

"Laundry Suppliers Move to Improve Savings, Efficiency." *Hotel & Motel Management,* 22 November 1993.

Remich, Norman C., Jr. "Maytag at 100." *Appliance Manufacturer,* November 1993.

———. "Security One Key to Commercial Line." *Appliance Manufacturer,* May 1993.

———. "Shipments Show Strength." *Appliance Manufacturer,* November 1993.

U.S. Bureau of the Census. *1995 Annual Survey of Manufactures.* Washington: GPO, 1997.

—Dave Mote, updated by Kenneth R. Shepherd

REFRIGERATION AND HEATING EQUIPMENT

This category includes establishments primarily engaged in the manufacture of commercial or industrial refrigeration equipment or domestic, commercial, or industrial air conditioning units. Other equipment manufactured under this classification includes warm air furnaces, humidifiers and dehumidifiers, soda fountains, and beer dispensing machines. Some equipment not covered by this category include household refrigerators and freezers, and electric space heaters and portable humidifiers and dehumidifiers.

INDUSTRY SNAPSHOT

A trip to the local supermarket provides graphic evidence of the importance of the heating, refrigeration, and air conditioning industry (HVAC) to modern American society. Many of the products found in the air-conditioned aisles, like fresh fruits or live fish, could never have been transported without cooling technology. The Air Conditioning and Refrigeration Institute (ARI) estimates that more than three-fourths of all foods consumed by Americans have been produced, packaged, shipped, stored, or preserved by refrigeration. Temperature control systems have also become common in shopping malls, commercial office buildings, and hospitals. In 1992, 77 percent of all new houses in the United States were built with central air conditioning.

However, high interest rates and a sluggish economy slowed new construction in the late 1980s and early 1990s. This slowdown in construction softened the demand for new heating, refrigeration, and air conditioning equipment, but spurred the repair and upgrade replacement segment of the industry. Much of the housing built in the 1950s, 1960s, and 1970s needed replacement equipment since the average domestic furnace or air conditioner had a useful life of only twenty years. Many American power utilities promoted energy conservation and higher efficiency upgrades. However, U.S. manufacturers shipped 5.7 million air conditioners in 1996, up 11 percent from 1995.

The Clean Air Act of 1990, which introduced extensive air-quality standards and the incremental reduction and eventual banning of chlorofluorocarbons (CFCs) by the year 2000, challenged the industry to improve its technology. This challenge caused uncertainty in the industry as new systems were developed, using chemicals which were not compatible with the old refrigerants. In the early 1990s, the fear of products becoming obsolete caused the industry to stagnate, while alternative refrigerants were researched.

The number of firms in the industry rose slowly from 730 companies operating 865 establishments in 1982 to 769 companies operating 891 establishments in 1994. The State of Ohio with 44 establishments produced 11.3 percent of the total U.S. shipments and 10.1 percent of the total number of workers employed in the heating and air conditioning industry. The largest number of establishments, 118, was located in Texas and accounted for 8.9 percent of the shipments in the United States and 9.7 percent of the total work force.

BACKGROUND AND DEVELOPMENT

Until the industrial revolution, refrigeration depended on the natural mediums of ice, snow, and water. The early Chinese harvested winter ice and packed it in dried straw for use in the summer. The Egyptians used porous earthenware jugs placed on their rooftops at night to cool their liquid contents by the natural process of evaporation. Since changing a liquid to a gas requires a considerable amount of heat energy, the liquid remaining in the containers became much cooler by morning. During colonial times, the ice hut was a familiar part of the landscape. It used the Chinese concept of harvesting ice to preserve food during the summer. Well into the 1800s, Americans sold ice to foreign countries as a natural refrigerant. The periodic home deliveries of ice were a commonplace experience for most Americans during the early part of the twentieth century.

The first attempts to find an industrial method to duplicate and improve on nature came in 1748 from Dr. William Cullen of Scotland. In 1851, Dr. John Gorrie, director of the U.S. Marine Hospital at Apalachicola, Florida, built the first commercial machine, receiving U.S. Patent 8080 for it. By 1880, the fledgling industry had developed reciprocating compressors which made possible such things as commercial ice making, brewing, meat packing and fish processing. In 1904, 70 of the industry pioneers formed the American Society of Refrigeration Engineers , officially creating a new profession.

In 1911, Willis H. Carrier presented the mathematical bases for the now-standard psychometric charts, which define the theoretical properties of heat transfer through air. His work earned Carrier the title of "the father of air-conditioning." In 1922, he invented the centrifugal refrigeration compressor. During World War II, he contributed to the building of a 10 million cubic foot wind tunnel that could be cooled to -67 degrees Fahrenheit. The most notable use of the

new air-conditioning technology was in the motion picture theaters of the 1920s. New York City theaters, including the Rivoli, Paramount, Roxy, and Lowe's in Times Square, lead the innovation. By the end of the decade hundreds of theaters across the country offered a controlled climate along with their feature film.

The heating industry refined the early concept of the open fire by enclosing the fire with brick or stone structures equipped with chimneys. These dirty and inefficient first efforts generally heated only the room they occupied, but could also be used for cooking and provided a central focus to the household. Throughout the nineteenth century, developments in metallurgy and forging promoted the use of remote water boilers attached to radiators by metal piping. These sturdy contrivances often used layers of asbestos to retain the heat in the water.

The warm-air furnace reduced the cost of heating, making the concept of central heating more available. Early systems were usually coal-fired, cast-iron machines that filled whole basements. They distributed the heat by means of "gravity" through large metal ducts attached to ornate grills in floors and walls. Like any other material when heated, air becomes lighter and tends to be pushed upwards by the cooler air surrounding it. The gravity is actually "working" on the cooler air, pushing it down to displace the lighter warm air. Later, electric fans attached to the heaters created the first forced-air systems. Cast-iron heaters have been replaced by compact sheet-metal cabinets, which contain burner, blower, and filter.

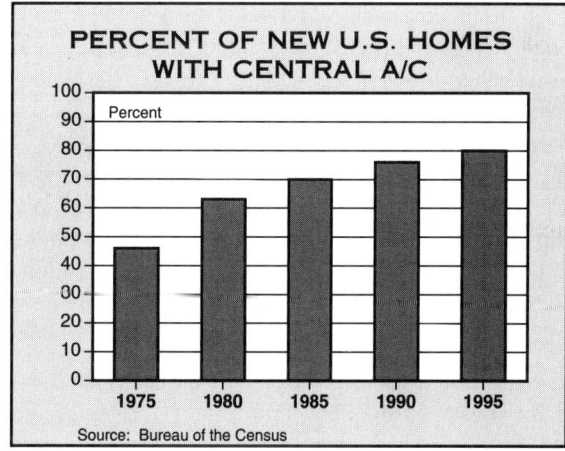

PERCENT OF NEW U.S. HOMES WITH CENTRAL A/C

Source: Bureau of the Census

Burning Alternatives. A more integral change occurred in the fuel being burned. The early machines used coal or even wood or charcoal. Such material required large storage areas and considerable labor in feeding the furnace and cleaning out the burnt residue of cinders and ash. The fire produced great amounts of air pollution in the form of sooty smoke and smog. London's famous pea-soup fogs of Victorian days disappeared when the British parliament banned the burning of coal within the city limits.

The first technological revolution in modern heating fuel technology came with the use of fuel oil as a replacement for coal. The Gilbert and Barker company claims to have produced the first industrial oil burner in North America in 1889, but patents for several burners were not issued until 1892. These early machines were often called range burners because they were primarily used for the kitchen stove. New heat resistant metals made the use of fuel oil as a furnace fuel both practical and desirable by the late 1920s. That began a shift in consumer fuel preference which virtually eliminated coal as a domestic fuel by the late 1950s. A second fuel revolution came with the OPEC oil embargoes of the 1970s. Once cheap and plentiful, fuel oil quickly rose in price and scientists began predicting a world-wide oil shortage and depletion of reserves by the year 2000. To compensate, the industry shifted to domestically-available natural gas and, to some extent, electricity. By 1992, with the cost of generating electricity escalating, natural gas became the clear preference of most American consumers, reaching a market penetration of 65 percent, according to the *Detroit Free Press.*

Modern refrigeration and air conditioning work on essentially the same principle. Both collect heat from one area and transfer it to another where it dissipates into some medium. The basic system consists of a compressor driven by an electric motor and two coils. In the first coil, called the condenser, the refrigerant gas is compressed into a liquid, discharging heat as it changes state. In the second coil, called the evaporator, the refrigerant becomes a gas again, absorbing heat from outside the coil. The essential ingredient is the refrigerant gas. Early refrigerant materials included air, water, butane, propane, ether, ammonia, sulphur dioxide and methyl chloride. Some, like ammonia, continue to be used in large commercial applications like skating rinks and ice factories. Many of these materials were highly toxic, corrosive, and flammable.

In 1930, Thomas Midgely of the DuPont Company developed the first fluorocarbon refrigerant and demonstrated his faith in its safety at a company press conference by inhaling a stream of the gas and blowing out a candle with it. In 1956, the industry adopted DuPont's numbering system for all fluorocarbon refrigerants. The most common used in the 1990s were the chlorofluorocarbons R-12 for automotive and appliance applications and R-502 for commercial and industrial applications. A second generation of refrigerant compound displaced CFCs in many applications. The hydrochlorofluorocarbon (HCFC) R-22 dominated the domestic central air conditioning market and was gaining popularity for some commercial applications.

Until 1953, water remained the most common cooling medium for air conditioning and refrigeration. Systems of that day used municipal water supplies or cooling towers, making the technology difficult for most domestic applications. The introduction of air-cooled systems in 1953, followed by the now-familiar split-system, launched the concept of controlled cooling into national acceptance. By 1973, 75 percent of industry sales were residential units. The development of electrically activated refrigerant reversing valves allowed cooling systems to be used for heating as well. The heat pump concept pioneered in the 1960s exchanged the functions of the two coils, as the evaporator became the condenser and the condenser acted as an evaporator. The systems scavenged usable heat out of the fall and winter air and pumped it into the building. Early models operated inefficiently in unsuitable climates, earning the technology a bad reputation with consumers. In 1960, only 28 percent of new homes were installed with central air conditioning, but by 1992, the technology was included in 77 percent of new homes.

The technology sparked development of the commercial rooftop combination heating and cooling unit. Placing the heating and cooling equipment in a single box on the roof freed up valuable commercial space and simplified servicing and installation. In addition, improvements in compressor design, particularly the hermetic or sealed compressor, allowed the size and capacity of industrial refrigeration machines to increase and spurred the advancement of the chiller systems that dominated the large building and industrial markets.

CURRENT CONDITIONS

The 1990s marked a decade of revolutionary change for the HVAC industry. The Centers for Disease Control and Prevention reported 1,604 cases of Legionnaires' disease in the United States for 1994, but epidemiologist believed the total to range between 10,000 and 100,000 cases. Office building operators across the country were reporting cases of ''sick-building syndrome,'' in which workers developed debilitating symptoms from a build-up of pollution levels in sealed, air conditioned buildings. In 1993, Congress passed a new energy bill that mandated higher efficiency standards for heating and air conditioning appliances and promised to make the requirements stricter in 1998. But the most devastating event to the HVAC industry was the discovery of a 7 million square kilometer hole in the ozone layer above the South Pole, and the scientific evidence which linked that phenomenon to the release of chlorofluorocarbons (CFCs) into the atmosphere. That revelation threatened the basic component of the HVAC industry. Midgley's supposedly safe refrigerant, around which the industry was designed, had become an unacceptable pollutant.

Global Warming and Ozone Depletion. The first rumblings of environmental damage were initiated by the British scientist, James Lovelock. In 1973, Lovelock wrote that carbon dioxide and CFCs in the atmosphere created a "greenhouse" effect by trapping heat in the lower atmosphere. Although few scientists argued the physics, the expected warming did not materialize as predicted. Other factors intervened, making it clear that the atmosphere and its energy transmission characteristics were too complicated to be fully understood as of yet. In 1995, the Nobel Prize in Chemistry was awarded to Paul Crutzen, who identified the chemical reactions that destroy the ozone layer, and F. Sherwood Rowland and Mario Molina who determined that chlorofluorocarbons, CFC's were responsible for triggering ozone depletion. The essential problem is the chlorine component of the CFC. The chlorine atom destroys ozone molecules in the high atmosphere through a complicated series of chemical reactions. Each chlorine atom destroys one ozone molecule every minute for about one year.

In 1973, the industrial world was dumping almost one megaton of CFCs into the atmosphere every year. CFC production was a $2 billion a year business. Its leaders resisted the scientific theories, calling for extensive studies and time to develop replacement materials. Eventually Sweden, Norway, and Canada banned CFCs used in aerosol cans, but nothing further happened until the British Antarctic Survey discovered a hole in the ozone layer half the size of Antarctica. In 1987, 24 industrialized countries signed the Montreal Protocol, calling for a 50-percent reduction in CFC production by the year 2000.

In June 1990, the protocol timetable was amended. CFC production in developed nations was banned by the year 2000 but developing nations could continue to produce them until 2010. As a temporary replacement refrigerant, hydrochlorofluorocarbons (HCFC) were scheduled for phase-out in 2030. This answered a concern by developing nations that the ban would work to the advantage of European and American firms who had the money to invest in alternative refrigerant technology. Manufacturers in those two

regions produced two-thirds of the world's CFCs at that time.

Also in 1990, the refrigeration industry petitioned the Environmental Protection Agency to develop and issue uniform national recycling standards and requirements in anticipation of the large quantities of old refrigerant which would need to be removed from refurbished machinery. In 1992, ARI estimated the existing stock of refrigeration and air conditioning equipment in the United States exceeded $135 billion. In February 1992, President George Bush reset the Montreal Protocol timetable, moving its requirements ahead by four years and calling for other nations to follow suit. On January 1, 1996, the production of chlorofluorocarbons was banned in the United States and other developed countries. Hydrofluorocarbon blends were already being used as refrigerants since they were legal until 2010 and these could be used to service old HCFC equipment until 2020.

The problem for the industry revolved around finding a suitable replacement refrigerant which could be produced quickly enough to meet the phase-out schedule. To make the ban effective, that technology would have to be shared with developing nations in order to persuade them not to continue building their own CFC industry. Refrigerant engineers looked for chemical combinations which were not flammable, corrosive, or toxic and which would operate reasonably well in existing equipment. The lubricants in the old systems had to be compatible with the new gases and in some cases new lubricants had to be found. In addition, the new designs had to meet the higher energy efficiency standards of 1993. Most of the new chemicals worked reasonably well but not as efficiently as CFCs, therefore, equipment redesigns were necessary to meet the efficiency ratings. The research and new technology added to the cost of the machinery at a time when sales of refrigeration equipment were at best stagnant. Another round of higher energy requirements was slated to go into effect in 1998, but the industry could not build towards that higher target because the standard was still being developed.

The process of replacing CFCs required a shift to HCFC-22, which was the only proven substitute for CFC refrigerants in 1993. In 1996, AlliedSignal Inc. introduced Genetron AZ-20 (R-410a) as a new alternate refrigerant. This non-ozone depleting replacement for HCFC-22 was quickly adopted by Carrier Corporation for use in their air conditioning units. Genetron AZ-20 is a patented azetropic blend of HFC-125 and HFC-32 and demonstrated a 7.5 percent higher energy efficiency rating (EER) over HCFC-22. At the same time, equipment manufacturers were redesigning compressors to match the characteristics of the new gases.

In the 1990s, modern HVAC systems were designed to isolate the indoor environment from an increasingly polluted urban world. With the rising cost of energy after the OPEC oil shocks, consumers sought to minimize consumption through energy conservation. The first and most obvious method was to tighten homes and buildings to prevent heat loss through the use of insulation and thermal window glass. In some cases, overzealous efforts had deadly consequences when the structures became too tight and the heating equipment burned up all the available oxygen. Instead of air, the occupants found they were breathing high concentrations of carbon dioxide or, even more deadly, carbon monoxide. In 1986, the Consumer Products Safety Commission reported that more than 200 Americans died each year from carbon monoxide poisoning in their homes. To combat this problem the industry promoted sealed combustion appliances, high-efficiency, chimney-less furnaces and outside-air-intake devices called make-up-air units.

In large buildings the problem surfaced as the "sick-building syndrome," first noted in the 1970s. Workers complained of fatigue, headaches, eye and respiratory-tract irritations, excessive colds, and dry, itchy skin. Investigators discovered air-borne asbestos particles, bacteria, chemicals, carcinogenic tobacco residues in the forced air systems. The EPA reported the presence of asbestos in 733,000 public and commercial buildings in 1988. Legionnaires disease developed from bacteria carried by aerosols in ventilation systems. As with the atmospheric environment, the building micro-environment was a complicated system requiring careful scientific evaluation and monitoring to keep it safe for human occupation.

The American HVAC market of the 1990s was saturated. New construction had slowed, and older housing, commercial, and industrial buildings were already retrofitted with HVAC systems. Much of this equipment was aging and needed replacing by the mid-1990s. In the housing sector, replacement work reached 60 percent of the domestic market in 1991. For the commercial segment, that share was over 45 percent. The effect on the industry was a shift away from dependence on the cyclical construction industry to a more stable and long-cycled replacement industry.

INDUSTRY LEADERS

At the close of World War II, America's clear leader in the HVAC industry was Carrier Corporation, which controlled 90 percent of the market. By the 1990s, Carrier Corp., by then a subsidiary of United Technologies Corp., no longer held a stable lead in the industry. Decades of under-investment in research and development, poor quality control, and inconsistent dealer relations coupled with a decision to terminate its marketing agreement with the department store giant Sears Roebuck and Co., cut Carrier's market share to 37 percent in 1991. The company began to fight back by selling off unrelated business ventures, trimming white collar workers and concentrating on new product development. It targeted 75 percent of its product line for replacement with high-tech innovations. Carrier spent $90 million on research and development in 1990, but other major firms like Lennox and York were beating Carrier to the marketplace, forcing it to play catch-up. Cutting energy costs, noise levels, and developing CFC-free equipment in automated factories became the market strategy of the 1990s.

Carrier maintained an 11 percent worldwide market-share, with its primary success in Europe. It was the only U.S. firm to break into Japan, where it had a 1 percent foothold. To expand its sales in Japan and protect its 17 percent share of the Asian market, Carrier invested $30 million into specialized research and development in Japan and doubled its research staff there to 40 in 1989. Headquartered in Farmington, Connecticut, the company employed 27,000 with production sales of $5.4 billion in the mid-1990s.

American Standard Companies Inc., formally ASI Holding Corp., was the second largest firm in this industry in 1994. It controlled American Standard Inc., which in turn operated Trane Commercial Systems Group. American Standard, the leading U.S. bathroom fixture firm, and Trane, the largest U.S. producer of air conditioners, joined forces in 1983. The companies then restructured in 1988 to form ASI Holding Corp. Trane specialized in custom-built heavy refrigeration and cooling equipment for large buildings, but expanded into the domestic air conditioning market with the purchase of General Electric's air conditioning division. The move was intended to stave off an unfriendly take-over bid by IC Industries, but it also made Trane attractive to American Standard. Standard had tried to enter the air conditioning business in the 1960s but found the competition too stiff. American Standard Companies Inc. employed 38,000 workers to produce 1996 sales of $5.8 billion.

Another major competitor in the industry in the mid-1990s was York International Corp., formed in 1986 when its parent company, Borg-Warner, experienced three years of constant losses. In 1988, an investor group took over the new company in a leveraged buy-out. York started its air-conditioning business in 1981 when it purchased Westinghouse Electric's air conditioning division. Following was the development of a distinctive, technically sophisticated product which was sold through exclusive dealerships. By 1992, the company was doing well even with the slump in new housing starts and the declining economy. Much of its success came from its export business, which made up 40 percent of total sales, and its concentration on commercial refrigeration, which accounted for 70 percent of sales. Future marketing strategies targeted Pacific Rim and Latin American countries as prime growth areas. In the mid-1990s, it operated its head office at York, Pennsylvania, employing 19,000 to produce total sales of $2.9 billion.

WORK FORCE

Traditionally, the heating, refrigeration and air-conditioning manufacturing industry has been highly labor intensive. In 1994, the average number of production workers at an establishment in the industry was 107, compared to the average number of 34 workers in all other manufacturing. Much of the assembly work was done by hand fitting many small parts and cutting metal shapes with the use of templates. By the mid-1980s, the industry was shifting towards more automated production with the use of numerical control machining tools and welding robots. Eventually computerized control led to fully automated plants such as Rheem's Texarcana air conditioning facility. Consequently, even though shipments increased between 1982 and 1995 from $12.39 billion to $26.2 billion, production worker employment experienced changes depending on market conditions. In 1982, 85,000 workers were employed in this industry, rising to 103,200 in 1995.

The Bureau of Labor Statistics predicted that employment in occupations like drafters, stock clerks, machine tool cutting operators, freight and material movers would decline between 17 and 22 percent by the year 2005. On the other hand, machine builders, combination machine tool operators, industrial machinery mechanics, and mechanical engineers showed moderate gains. Machine assemblers were the group that was expected to be in the highest demand in the industry.

AMERICA AND THE WORLD

The refrigeration and air conditioning industry has clearly become global; U.S. firms have been applying flexible manufacturing philosophies and taking advantage of foreign currency exchange fluctuations. New American manufacturing facilities in Asia, Europe, Latin America, and the Middle East, have resulted in an increase in U.S. production offshore. Japanese man-

ufacturers, America's primary foreign competitor built two compressor plants in the United States in 1990. Generally, the industry has seen a positive balance of trade which increased in 1994 when imports increased almost 8 percent. The industry exported $4.13 billion in 1994 compared to imports of $1.86 billion. The top export markets were Canada (26 percent), Mexico (8.8 percent), Japan (5.9 percent), South Korea (5.5 percent) and Saudi Arabia (6.9 percent), according to *U.S. Industrial Outlook.*

The market competition was much tighter on a global scale. In 1993, American manufacturers controlled 28 percent of the world market-share compared to the 29 percent held by Japanese manufacturers. The largest portion of the world market was retained by Southeast Asia which controlled 34 percent. This was a significant increase from the 18 percent value of three years earlier. North American manufactures produced 75 percent of the 5.9 million packaged units but only 13 percent of the 18.1 million room units.

The Japanese market demanded a different technology than what was common in the United States. Ironically, Japanese firms produced primarily what is known as a ductless-split, which was first developed and abandoned in the United States during the 1960s. The system looks much like a window air conditioner, but the compressor is housed in a separate condenser box placed outside the structure. Refrigerant tubing connects the two coils and their independent fan assemblies. The Japanese saw the concept as ideal for their relatively compact homes and perfected the technology.

In the 1990s, Japanese manufacturers used the system to earn a 55 percent market-share in Asia, the world's fastest growing market, compared to the United States' 22 percent share. They also began an assault on the European and U.S. markets. In Europe, the Japanese models made air conditioning available to many older buildings equipped with boiler heating systems where installing a duct system would be impractical. The Japanese models also worked well in small computer-room applications. American manufacturers responded to the threat of foreign competition and a softening domestic market with massive influxes of capital into their own research and development and co-operative ventures with Japanese and other foreign competitors to take advantage of specialized expertise.

The 1994 worldwide air conditioning and refrigeration industry enjoyed a $40-45 billion market. The United States and Japan supplied the majority of this market. In 1995, the U.S. exports were valued at $4.4 billion, an increase of 9 percent from 1994 levels. Mexico and Canada are the top two markets for export, and Asia is expected to offer the greatest opportunities for future growth. The United States represented 88.7 percent of the imports into Canada and 75 percent of the Mexican air conditioning equipment market. In 1992, France imported 52 percent of their refrigeration equipment from the United States, whereas Japan dominated the import markets in Spain with 44 percent, Italy with 30 percent, and Singapore with 44 percent. China, with its 350 factories, is expected to have market growth of 30 percent annually.

The challenges of the 1990s caused the industry to begin considering alternative technologies. Concerns over indoor air quality made it clear that heating, ventilation, humidification, and air cleaning could not be considered as separate fields of endeavor, but instead all must be integrated into the design of new buildings to become part of the essential operational architecture of an organic system. The Munich, Germany, Airport Center provided an excellent example of the incorporation of all these systems. The structure was designed with its energy and ventilation needs in mind as part of the original concept. Using glass and fabric panels in the roof structure, the architects avoided the need for heating or air conditioning equipment and reduced the amount of artificial lighting required. Design of the building relied heavily on computer modeling to predict how the system would work under extreme conditions.

The efficiency of the Munich Airport Center illustrates how the use of microelectronics for computer modeling and for control systems revolutionized the HVAC industry, by allowing more sophisticated designs and more accurate control to deliver energy savings and increased health and comfort levels. In 1993, 20,000 French families lived in fully automated houses, a concept catching on in America. The system controls lighting, heating, security and entertainment devices. New HVAC systems were making the home more independent and self-sufficient. The new technology, called cogeneration devices, used basic refrigeration technology to cool or heat the structure, produce hot water, and generate sufficient electricity to run the house. Simpler systems sacrificed the cooling function by eliminating the refrigerant circuit. In both cases, a natural gas engine drives the generator to produce the electricity. The heat from the exhaust gas is reclaimed by water in the system's heating circuit. The full heat-pump system, which also gathers heat from outside the house, uses only half the gas needed by a conventional furnace, or two-thirds used in a high-efficiency condensing furnace.

Space has always been a problem in the commercial world, and finding room and the right location for a noisy air conditioning system was often difficult for builders and for architects. One answer promoted in the 1990s was computer generated "antinoise." By analyzing and matching the sound waves created by the HVAC equipment, the computer could order up an exact counter-wave. The result was actual silence, not just a deadening of noise behind bulky sound barriers.

In addition to "antinoise", the industry also considered some older technologies abandoned in earlier, more wasteful days. Solar heating, particularly for domestic hot water, made a comeback in the 1990s after losing favor in the 1970s. About 1.5 million homes in America used solar-powered hot water heaters to displace up to one-quarter of their domestic energy needs. Solar pool heaters also gained popularity. Another surprising but effective old technology involved using heat from burning natural gas to cool a structure. This concept uses an absorbent, usually lithium bromide, and water to produce the refrigeration effect. Earlier models were bulky and not easily understood, but advancements in Japan made this an environmentally friendly system and a prime alternative to traditional CFC systems.

Another modern reworking of an old concept which gained popularity in the 1990s was thermal storage. The effectiveness of this strategy relied on the use of off-peak electricity rates or alternative, cheaper fuel sources to power industrial air-conditioning chillers or ice-making machines during evening or weekend hours. Instead of using the machines to directly cool the structure, the designers channeled the refrigerant output to large tanks of water to make ice. During normal operating hours, the ice absorbed heat from the building, providing effective cooling. This allowed the designers to select smaller equipment than would be needed to cool the structure on demand. They could also use naturally-occurring ammonia as a refrigerant rather than CFC. Ammonia lost favor with the introduction of CFC because of its toxicity and flammability.

FURTHER READING

Alper, Joe. "Antinoise Creates the Sounds of Silence." *Science,* 252, 2 April 1991.

Barlas, Stephen. "Congress/Bush Approve Energy Bill." *Appliance,* November 1992.

Beddows, Norman A. "Concerns About Indoor Air Quality Warrant Review of HVAC Systems." *Occupational Health & Safety,* 59, May 1990.

Brand, Horst, and Clyde Huffstutler. "Productivity in Making Air Conditioners, Refrigeration Equipment, and Furnaces." *Monthly Labor Review,* 107, December 1984.

Carey, John. "Is the World Heating Up? Well, Just Listen." *Business Week,* 4 February 1991.

Chege, James M., ed. *Refrigeration and Air-Conditioning,* Englewood Cliffs, NJ: Prentice-Hall Inc., 1979.

Clifford, Mark. "Back to Basics." *Forbes,* 30 June 1986.

Cox, J.E., and Charles R. Miro. "Worsening Ozone Layer Outlook Points to Quicker CFC Ban." *ASHRAE Journal,* 34, February 1992.

Darnay, Arsen J. ed. *Manufacturing Worldwide.* Detroit: Gale Research, 1995.

Dickson, David, and Eliot Marshall. "Europe Recognizes the Ozone Threat." *Science,* 243, 10 March 1989.

Edelson, Edward. "The Man Who Knew Too Much." *Popular Science,* 234 January 1989.

Eklund, Christopher S. "Stan Hiller Is Old-Fashioned: He Fixes Broken Companies." *Business Week,* 31 March 1986.

Geake, Elisabeth. "Dial C for Central Heating, D for Dishwasher . . . " *New Scientist,* 132, 14 December 1991.

James, C. S. *Information Bulletin TC72-24: Fuel Oils and Burning Equipment,* Toronto, Ontario: Imperial Oil Limited, 1973.

Konrad, Wally. "Solar Energy's New Place in the Sun." *Business Week,* 7 October 1991.

Lemonick, Michael D. "Deadly Danger in a Spray Can." *Time,* 2 January 1989.

Lueders, David. "Cooling a Modern Plant for a Week at a Time with Ice." *Control Engineering,* 39, Mid-March 1992.

Marcial, Gene G. "A Cooling Play That's Heating Up." *Business Week,* 2 March 1992.

"1993 HVAC&R Technology Review." *ASHRAE Journal,* 35, January 1993.

Norberg-Bohm, Vicki. "From the Inside Out: Reducing CO2 Emissions in the Buildings Sector." *Environment,* 33, April 1991.

Perry, Chris, and Todd Vogel. "How Japan is Beating the Others Cold." *Business Week,* 3 September 1990.

Remich, Norman C. "Industry Backs Bush on CFC-ban Speedup." *Appliance Manufacturer,* April 1992.

Russell, James S. "A Model of Efficiency." *Architectural Record,* 180, April 1992.

Samuel, Peter. "Will Your Next Refrigerator Explode?" *Consumers' Research,* 75, July 1992.

Stepanek, Steven. "Air Apparents: Emerging HVAC Technologies May Rule Replacement Decisions." *Buildings,* 85, November 1991.

Szerlag, Hanz. "By the Numbers: Houses Get Cooler." *Detroit Free Press,* 27 June 1993.

———. "By the Numbers: Gassing Up." *Detroit Free Press,* 4 July 1993.

"Total CFC Ban Needed to Halt Global Warming." *New Scientist,* 127, 8 September 1990.

"Trane Has Finally Found a Refuge." *Business Week,* 19 December 1983.

U.S. Department of Commerce. *U.S. Industrial Outlook 1994,.* Washington: GPO, 1994.

Vogel, Todd. "Can Carrier Corp. Turn up the Juice?" *Business Week,* 3 September 1990.

"What's Next in Home Energy." *Popular Science,* 237, November 1990.

Wison, Alex. "Combustion Gases, an Indoor Threat." *Home Mechanix,* October 1991.

Wurm, Jaroslav, and Richard Biederman. "Status of the HVAC Industry." *ASHRAE Journal,* 34, January 1992.

—Al Cook, updated by Andrew J. Poss

SIC 3586

MEASURING AND DISPENSING PUMPS

The Measuring and Dispensing Pumps Industry is comprised of establishments primarily engaged in manufacturing pumps used in service stations for dispensing gas, oil, and grease. This category also includes grease guns. Industrial pumps are classified in **SIC 3561: Pumps and Pumping Equipment.**

In the early 1990s, multi-pump units, which offer several grades of gasoline from the same pump, accounted for about 22 percent of industry sales. More traditional single-pump units still held a 19 percent share of the market. Lubricating oil pumps represented about 4 percent of output, and grease guns made up 3 percent of sales. Approximately 30 percent of industry revenues were made from the sale of parts and attachments, such as vapor recovery systems and replacement hoses.

Non-industrial gas, oil, and grease pumps were a corollary of the proliferation of cars and trucks during the early and mid-1900s. As American society became increasingly mobile, markets for service station pumps expanded rapidly. Indeed, by the late 1970s the service station pump industry was shipping more than $600 million worth of products per year and employing about 8,000 workers.

Despite an oil shortage in the United States in the late 1970s and a recession in the early 1980s, industry revenues climbed sporadically to $1.14 billion by 1988. Although growth of demand for new gas, oil, and grease pumps waned in comparison to growth in previous decades, other product segments prospered. Importantly, environmental regulations forced service stations in many states to equip their pumps with costly new vapor recovery systems and safety devices.

A U.S. economic recession in the late 1980s and early 1990s suppressed pump sales to about $1.03 billion per year in the early 1990s. As sales faltered, industry employment plummeted from a high of 9,400 in 1987 to about 8,000 by 1990. Figures for 1992 showed that employment levels were at 6,500 workers, 31 percent below 1987 levels, while the value of goods shipped slipped to $896.3 million. In 1993, however, the economy began to improve, and the industry responded. In 1995, according to the *1995 Annual Census of Manufactures*, the industry reported 7,300 employees and shipment of goods worth $1.48 billion—an increase of 12.3 percent and 6.0 percent respectively.

Going into the mid-1990s, pump manufacturers scrambled to revive profits by introducing new gas pump systems, focusing on the multi-pump market, and incorporating computer technology into their machines. New pumps with point-of-sale credit card devices, for example, allowed customers to fill a vehicle with gas and pay without leaving their car, thus reducing labor costs. Likewise, to help service stations comply with Federal "Stage II" vapor recovery guidelines, producers of vapor recovery pumps and attachments were introducing a variety of new systems and designs.

The largest U.S. company primarily engaged in the production of service station pumps and equipment in the mid-1990s was Graco Inc. of Minneapolis, Minnesota. Graco boasted sales of $386 million and had 2,100 employees. Gilbarco Inc of Greensboro, North Carolina, placed second, with $300 million in sales and 1,200 employees. Other major players included Dresser Industries, Wayne Division, of Maryland, and Tokheim Corp., of Indiana. In all, about 80 companies were classified in the industry in the mid-1990s.

Industry participants were able to increase production yet keep a lid on employment growth during the 1980s primarily through productivity gains. The movement of some manufacturing activities overseas also reduced work force gains. The future of employment in this industry was uncertain going into the mid-1990s. However, the outlook for job growth in the overall service machinery sector was generally positive through 2005, according to the U.S. Bureau of Labor Statistics.

FURTHER READING

Darnay, Arsen J., ed. *Manufacturing USA*. 5th ed. Detroit: Gale Research, 1996.

Shook, Phil. "Stage II Equipment: Meeting the Challenge." *National Petroleum News,* July 1993.

Upton, Howard. "When the Feds Controlled Pump Prices." *National Petroleum News,* July 1993.

U.S. Bureau of the Census. *1995 Annual Survey of Manufactures.* Washington: GPO, 1997.

U.S. Department of Commerce. *U.S. Industrial Outlook 1993.* Washington: GPO, 1994.

—Dave Mote, updated by Kenneth R. Shepherd

SIC 3589

SERVICE INDUSTRY MACHINERY, NOT ELSEWHERE CLASSIFIED

Companies in this classification are principally engaged in manufacturing miscellaneous equipment for use in service businesses. Examples of industry products are floor sanding machines, cafeteria food warmers, commercial fryers, sludge processors, sewage treatment equipment, mop wringers, and commercial corn poppers. Household appliances and machinery are classified in **3630: Household Appliances.** For more information on the history and structure of U.S. machinery industries, see **SIC 3552: Textile Machinery** through **SIC 3559: Special Industry Machinery, Not Elsewhere Classified.**

The largest segment of the miscellaneous service machine industry is food service equipment, which accounted for about 26 percent of industry revenues in the mid-1990s. Commercial ranges, stoves, and broilers made up the bulk of that group. Industrial floor and carpet cleaning equipment represented 12 percent of the market, as did miscellaneous sewage treatment products. Parts for water heaters and softeners accounted for 8 percent of sales. Other major categories include commercial car and bus washing equipment, commercial dishwashers, sand blasting machines, and industrial vacuum systems. In 1995, imports were valued at $122.4 million, while exports were valued at $228.6 million.

General industry expansion between 1950 and 1980 resulted in aggregate shipments of more than $2.5 billion by the early 1980s. Steady growth of service industries during the 1980s, particularly food services, resulted in rapid growth. Sales went from about $2.6 billion in 1983 to $3.4 billion by 1986, and to $4.9 billion by 1990. As revenues grew at an average annual pace of almost 9 percent per year, industry employment jumped from 31,000 in the early 1980s to about 39,000 by the early 1990s. Employment levels reached 40,900 by 1994 and were expected to increase further to an estimated 44,200 by 1998.

Despite U.S. economic malaise in the early 1990s, most service machinery manufacturers sustained moderate growth. Sales of food service products, for example, grew at a rate of 5 to 6 percent per year in 1992 and 1993, and overall U.S. production machinery shipments increased 4 to 6 percent per year between 1991 and 1993. In addition, manufacturing productivity gains and industry consolidation boosted profit margins for many competitors.

The miscellaneous service machinery industry is extremely fragmented and is dominated by relatively small, specialty manufacturers. The average industry participant employed only 38 workers in 1994, compared to an average of 49 for all other U.S. manufacturers. Furthermore, of the approximately 1,000 competitors in the early 1990s, only six had more than $100 million in sales. Most of the top 100 companies had less than $30 million in revenues and fewer than 200 workers. The largest company in the industry was Welbilt Corp. of Connecticut. The company had mid-1990s sales of about $400 million and employed about 2,100 workers. Hoover North America, of Ohio, employed about 2,700 workers and generated sales of $350 million. Other leaders included Ionics Inc., of Michigan, and Tennant Co., of Minnesota.

Despite continued productivity increases and the movement of some manufacturing facilities to foreign countries, employment prospects for the overall service machinery industry were positive. Opportunities for most occupations were expected to swell by 10 to 20 percent between 1990 and 2005, according to the U.S. Bureau of Labor Statistics. Jobs for assemblers and fabricators, which account for about 25 percent of the work force, will likely decline slightly. However, the number of labor positions should grow. Openings for some workers, such as sales and marketing professionals, will likely increase by as much as 50 percent.

FURTHER READING

Darnay, Arsen J., ed. *Manufacturing USA.* 5th ed. Detroit: Gale Research, 1996.

Standard & Poor's Industry Surveys. New York: Standard & Poor's Corporation, 1992.

U.S. Department of Commerce. *U.S. Industrial Outlook 1993.* Washington: GPO, 1993.

—Dave Mote, updated by Kenneth R. Shepherd

SIC 3592

CARBURETORS, PISTONS, RINGS, AND VALVES

This category includes establishments primarily engaged in manufacturing carburetors, pistons, piston rings, and engine intake and exhaust valves. Establishments primarily engaged in manufacturing metallic packing are classified in **SIC 3053: Gaskets, Packing, and Sealing Devices,** and those primarily engaged in manufacturing machine repair and equipment parts (except electric), on a job or order basis for others, are classified in **SIC 3599: Industrial and Commercial Machinery and Equipment, Not Elsewhere Classified.**

INDUSTRY SNAPSHOT

Carburetors, pistons, valves, and rings account for a relatively small and declining portion of the broader automotive and machine engine parts industries, which are valued at more than $150 billion. The industry's fortunes have declined significantly since the 1980s, when shipments peaked at $3.096 billion in 1984. Since then, sales have gradually edged downward—at just $2.3 billion in current dollars in 1995. Employment in the industry has declined by nearly 50 percent since the mid-1980s; in 1995 this figure was at 20,200, according to the U.S. Census Bureau. The greatest factors contributing to this long decline were technological changes and greater reliance on imported parts. Despite this decline, workers in this industry averaged $14.22 per hour in 1995, well above the average of $12.37 recorded by all manufacturing industries.

ORGANIZATION AND STRUCTURE

The industry supplies engine parts as original equipment and as aftermarket replacement parts. Dominated by mid-sized and large companies, the industry employed an average of 137 workers per establishment in 1994. The materials consumed by the industry cover most of the materials used in manufacturing: ferrous and nonferrous stock, ceramics, rubber, and plastic. The industry supplies carburetors, pistons, rings, and valves either as original equipment for manufacturers of new products or as replacement parts for older products. The industry's product share is broken into three major categories, each with several subcategories. In the mid-1990s, carburetors and pistons each claimed roughly 40 percent of the total industry sales, while valves claimed 18 percent, and miscellaneous related products made up the final 2 percent. In each segment, the largest share of parts was manufactured for use in motor vehicle engines, and roughly 50 percent of industry output overall was used in motor vehicle manufacturing. Miscellaneous non-motor vehicle internal combustion engines and farm machinery made up the second and third largest uses of this industry's products.

CURRENT CONDITIONS

The industry continues to change in response to foreign competition and to technological change that has resulted in some of its products needing to be replaced less frequently or not needing to be used at all. In the automotive market, the traditional carburetor has largely been supplanted by fuel injection, which is more precise and fuel-efficient. After-factory rebuilding and replacement of existing carburetors constitutes the extent of this declining market. Motorcycles and heavy trucks typically still use carburetors, as do other types of nonautomotive engines. Among all industry products, demand for more reliable components has led to longer lasting parts that require servicing and replacement less often than in the past. The industry's pistons, rings, and valves are still viable components for the automotive market.

Because half of its revenues come from motor vehicle applications, the industry is highly reliant on the sales of motor vehicles in general, and automobiles in particular, which are considered saturated markets within the United States. While U.S. automakers posted a modest recovery in the mid-1990s from their 1980s and early 1990s slump, growth has been tempered by slim margins and has been uneven across different segments.

While the aftermarket looks good for the automotive parts industry, original equipment suppliers will continue to fight for survival. One strategy has been to become heavily involved in the early design of automobiles, forming alliances with auto manufacturers. The Japanese in particular support this trend and have chosen specific suppliers that are involved in the initial design to exclusively supply parts. To the extent this industry is made up of major affiliated and unaffiliated manufacturers, it should reap benefits from the U.S. auto industry's emphasis in the mid- and late 1990s on further outsourcing its parts production while keeping its supplier count down.

AMERICA AND THE WORLD

U.S. auto parts companies continue to pursue overseas markets largely through expansion of existing overseas operations. Foreign markets are considered this industry's best prospects for growth. Supplier families have been formed, which are joint operations between parts manufacturers. Although parts exports represent a growing share of industry shipments, overall trade performance since the late 1970s has diminished greatly. While Canada, Europe, and Mexico contain subsidiaries of many U.S. auto parts firms, U.S. firms have lost domestic market share to Japanese competitors and have had difficulty penetrating the Japanese market.

The globalization of the industry is predicted to continue, especially as the Japanese continue to engage in joint ventures with U.S. firms. Japanese manufacturers are becoming more willing to share the risk of business, as many have encountered losses or have not become profitable in a timely manner. Therefore, foreign mergers and acquisitions will continue in an attempt to distribute more thinly the costs of product research and development. The trade imbalance may be counteracted by growing exports to Canada, Europe, and Mexico. While short-term benefits of the North American Free Trade Agreement (NAFTA) have been negligible to this industry, longer-term trade with Mexico is expected to grow substantially, as the vehicular market in that country is projected to increase significantly and as the Mexican economy showed emerging strength entering the late 1990s.

RESEARCH AND TECHNOLOGY

While many of the advancements in this industry are driven by the automotive industry, concern for public safety and the liabilities involved also pushes contributions to research and technology. One example of this is the field testing conducted in Iowa,which helped analyze the failure of piston skirts in diesel engines that drive emergency generators for nuclear power plants. Two similar failures occurred within one month at a Pennsylvania plant run by the municipal electric utility company. The failure was analyzed using state-of-the-art computer modeling systems, which were then supported by field tests with a similar diesel generator in Iowa. The detrimental design feature of the piston skirt was changed and new data from the field tests was input to the databases accessed by the computer modeling systems.

Current developments in the automotive industry concerning valves and pistons are aimed at pollution control, reliability, performance, and fuel efficiency. The 1993 "Excellence in Design" award, granted by *Design News* magazine, went to an engineer who developed an exhaust-gas recirculation and idle-air control valve which simplifies the implementation of smog-control equipment. Due to the development of airflow analysis, the combustion rate for different engines with different cylinder heads can be analyzed, thereby helping engineers to improve engine performance.

The challenge in the automotive parts industries is to deliver performance and fuel economy to the consumer, while protecting the environment. With increasing government regulations such as the Clean Air Act and fuel efficiency standards, automotive engineers are kept busy in laboratories and racing pits. Additionally, the media is skeptical of automobile makers since fuel efficiency claims were inflated in the early 1980s. With current technologies, fuel efficiency becomes a trade-off against low cost, good driveability, low noise, low emissions, and 100,000-mile durability. More research into these factors is being performed globally.

FURTHER READING

"Combustion Effects of Asymmetric Valve Strategies." *Automotive Engineering,* December 1993.

Darnay, Arsen J., ed. *Manufacturing USA.* 5th ed. Detroit: Gale Research, 1996.

Graddage, M. J. "Field Testing to Validate Models Used in Explaining a Piston Problem in a Large Diesel Engine." *Journal of Engineering for Gas Turbines and Power,* October 1993.

Keebler, Jack. "Those New 'Miracle' Engines Must Pass Five Stiff Tests. *Automotive News,* 26 August 1991.

Lynch, Terrence. "Integrated Valve Meters EGR and Idle Air." *Design News,* 22 February 1993.

O'Conner, Leo. "A New Turn for Rotary-Valve Engines." *Mechanical Engineering,* January 1993.

U.S. Bureau of the Census. *1992 Census of Manufactures.* Washington: GPO, 1995.

———. *1995 Annual Survey of Manufactures.* Washington: GPO, 1997.

U.S. Department of Commerce. International Trade Administration. *U.S. Industrial Outlook 1994.* Washington: GPO, 1994.

SIC 3593

FLUID POWER CYLINDERS AND ACTUATORS

This classification covers establishments primarily engaged in manufacturing hydraulic and pneumatic cylinders and actuators for use in fluid power systems.

Companies in the fluid power cylinders and actuators industry manufacture hydraulic and pneumatic cylinders used in various devices, such as jacks, lifters, and machine tools. These devices are used to exert massive amounts of force in a controlled manner. One of the simplest machines that uses a fluid power cylinder is the hydraulic press, which is used, for example, to press plastics into forms.

The three primary types of modern hydraulic cylinders are single-acting, double-acting, and differential. Single-acting devices consist of a large plunger, or piston, into which oil (or air in a pneumatic cylinder) is pumped. A valve keeps the oil from backing up into the pump and allows a controlled release of the pressure. Double-acting cylinders work similarly, but oil is pushed against one side of the cylinder, thus allowing a push or pull motion; these cylinders are used in construction machinery such as cranes and earth-moving machines. A differential cylinder has a large piston that requires a greater amount of oil to displace the cylinder, thus allowing greater uniformity of force than a typical single-acting cylinder.

Although hydraulic pumps for powering hydraulic cylinders were developed in the nineteenth century, it was not until the twentieth century that fluid power devices became a widespread means of energy transmission. By 1987, the first year in which this industry was classified separately by the federal government, fluid power cylinder manufacturers were generating sales of about $1.9 billion. Although receipts rose to more than $2.2 billion by 1989, a recession in the late 1980s and early 1990s reduced demand from industrial sectors such that sales slipped below $2 billion annually during the early 1990s.

Industry participants in the mid-1990s have benefitted from a gradual U.S. economic recovery, as the total value of product shipments in the industry was $2.56 billion in 1995, up 42 percent from 1992. Although growth was flat in the aerospace industry in the early 1990s, steady recovery was projected for this market through the end of the decade. However, continued slack demand from the defense industry and a slumping commercial airline industry boded poorly for overall industry growth. As domestic market growth was uncertain, manufacturers were looking to exports and advanced technology to boost sales.

About 360 companies competed in this industry in the late-1990s. The largest competitor in 1996 was AlliedSignal Aerospace, a division of AlliedSignal Inc., which logged $5.7 billion in total sales. Ranking second was Parker Hannifin Corp., of Ohio, with 1996 sales of $3.59 billion, and a work force of over 30,000. Other industry leaders included Rexroth Corp., with $270 million in sales, and Berendsen Fluid Power Inc., with $200 million in sales. The majority of the top 20 companies had less than $50 million in sales and fewer than 500 employees.

Although industry sales were expected to remain stable or increase slightly through 2000, substantial gains in manufacturing productivity and the movement of some production activities overseas will significantly reduce employment opportunities, according to the Department of Labor Statistics. Labor positions in miscellaneous industrial machinery industries in general will fall by 10 to 20 percent for most occupations between 1996 and 2005. Even the demand for engineers and managers will likely decline or increase only marginally.

FURTHER READING

Banks, Howard, Jason Zweig, Alyssa A. Lappen, Philip Glouchevitch, and Julie Pitta. "Annual Report on American Industry." *Forbes,* 8 January 1990.

Darnay, Arsen J., ed. *Manufacturing USA,* 5th ed. Detroit: Gale Research, 1996.

Green, Larry. "Hydrostatics: Back to Basics." *Equipment Management,* May 1990.

Smith, A. C. "Control System Basic." *Equipment Management,* October 1990.

U.S. Department of Commerce. Economics and Statistics Administration. Bureau of the Census. *1995 Annual Survey of Manufactures.* Washington: GPO, 1997. Available from http://www.census.gov/prod/www/titles.html#mm.

U.S. Department of Commerce. International Trade Administration. *U.S. Industrial Outlook 1994.* Washington: GPO, 1994.

SIC 3594

FLUID POWER PUMPS AND MOTORS

This classification covers establishments primarily engaged in manufacturing hydraulic and pneumatic fluid power pumps and motors, including hydrostatic transmissions. Establishments primarily engaged in manufacturing pumps for motor vehicles are classified in **SIC 3714: Motor Vehicle Parts and Accessories.**

Manufacturers in this industry produce pumps and drives for hydraulic and pneumatic power mechanisms, primarily for use in industrial and aerospace applications. Because fluid power devices can exert massive mounts of controlled pressure, they are commonly utilized to power aircraft landing gear, industrial presses and lifts, heavy earth-moving equipment, and other heavy-duty equipment. They are also often integrated into smaller machines that require precise power transfer.

Fluid power systems combine cylinders, couplings, valves, and pumps and motors. A positive displacement hydraulic pump, such as a piston pump, is the part of the system that delivers the oil required to drive or control hydraulic machinery. It creates pressure in a series of short bursts. In contrast, impulse pumps, such as the centrifugal pump, deliver steady, continuous oil pressure with less vibration. Hydraulic motors typically operate in conjunction with pumps and are often used to precisely vary the rotational speed of various machines.

Pascal's law, which states that pressure exerted upon a liquid is evenly transmitted in all directions, was posited in the mid-1600s. However, pumps that could efficiently deliver high and controlled pressure were not introduced until the 1800s. Not until the mid-1900s, in fact, did hydraulic pumps and motors become a common means of power transfer. By 1987, the first year in which this industry was separately classified by the U.S. Government, sales of fluid power pumps and motors approached $1.5 billion. Although industry revenues increased to nearly $1.8 billion by 1990, a U.S. recession halted sales and earnings growth for most competitors throughout the early 1990s.

Industry participants in the mid-1990s benefitted from a moderate upturn in the U.S. and global economy that boosted pump and motor demand in the industrial sector. Unfortunately, vital aerospace and defense markets remained depressed and offered little hope for gains in the near future. The most successful competitors countered market malaise with productivity gains and the introduction of cutting edge, high-performance equipment. Many also looked to increased demand in overseas markets for high-tech U.S. pumps and motors. The industry experienced rapid growth in 1995, as the value of all product shipments increased 14 percent from 1994 figures, to $2 billion, and up 36 percent from $1.4 billion in 1992.

About 150 companies served this industry going into the 1990s, the largest of which was Aeroquip-Vickers Corp., of Ohio, with 1996 revenues of $2.03 billion and 15,000 employees. Mannesmann Capital Corp., of New York, was also a large competitor with $2 billion in sales and 7,000 employees. ITT Fluid Technology Corp., a subsidiary of ITT Industries, Inc., logged $1.3 billion in net sales, comprising 15 percent of ITT total sales revenue. The company employed about 8,000 workers in 1996. The majority of the top 50 companies, however, generated sales of less than $15 million and employed fewer than 50 workers.

The average salary for production workers in the industry was $31,300, which is considerably higher than the average for all manufacturing. Although in the mid-1990s the industry employed about 11,500 Americans, long-term employment prospects were bleak, according to the U.S. Bureau of Labor Statistics. Increased foreign competition and continued productivity gains, through automation and restructuring, were projected to be factors in work force reduction, for labor and white-collar workers alike.

FURTHER READING

Avery, Susan. "Fluid Power Takes Off." *Purchasing,* 17 June 1993.

Darnay, Arsen J., ed. *Manufacturing USA.* 5th ed. Detroit: Gale Research, 1996.

Nuck, Frank, and John Plout. "Composite Cylinder Tubes Cut Weight, Costs." *Machine Design,* 12 November 1993.

Smith, A. C. "Control System Basics." *Equipment Management,* October 1990.

U.S. Bureau of the Census. *1995 Annual Survey of Manufactures.* Washington: GPO, 1997. Available from http://www.census.gov/prod/www/titles.html#mm.

U.S. Department of Commerce. International Trade Administration. *U.S. Industrial Outlook 1994.* Washington: GPO, 1994.

SIC 3596

SCALES AND BALANCES, EXCEPT LABORATORY

This industry is made up of establishments primarily engaged in manufacturing weighing and force-measuring machines and devices, except those regarded as scientific apparatus for laboratory work which are classified under **SIC 3821: Laboratory Apparatus and Furniture.** Prior to 1987 nonscientific scales and balances were classified as SIC 3576, which this category replaced.

Vehicle and industrial scales, which are used primarily in factories and truck weighing stations to measure amounts of goods to be packaged or delivered, comprise the largest segment of the industry, accounting for roughly 42 percent of U.S. shipments. Retail, commercial, and milling scales form the second largest category at approximately 31 percent and include household scales, scales in grocery stores and delicatessens, and postal scales. Parts and accessories total 22 percent of shipments, and miscellaneous balance and scale equipment make up the remaining 5 percent.

In 1995, manufacturers in this category shipped $642.8 million in products, a 3.8 percent increase over

1994 before inflation. Scales and balances alone, however, sold $590.3 million in 1995, which was less than half of 1 percent greater than in 1994. The industry spent $12.4 million in new capital expenditures in 1995. Real growth in the industry has been largely flat to negative since the 1980s, when the industry posted record sales. New business for the industry is often dependent upon external factors, such as postal rate changes and other government regulation, that require its customers to upgrade weighing systems.

The estimated 110 establishments in the scale and balance industry are geographically concentrated, with California and the Midwest employing roughly half of the industry's work force. The industry's production labor force of 3,400 in 1995 earned an average of $11.78 per hour, roughly 4.7 percent lower than average for manufacturing industries. Total employment was at 5,600 in 1995, a slight increase from 1994. Annual compensation for all workers in 1995, including management, averaged $31,130. Major occupations within the industry include machinists, machine tool operators, assemblers, and product inspectors. The outlook for many of this industry's occupations, however, is limited, as the U.S. Bureau of Labor Statistics forecast declines of 5 to 15 percent for most of the industry's job titles.

Mettler-Toledo, Inc., a New Jersey-based subsidiary of Mettler-Toledo Albstadt GmbH of Germany, was one of the top manufacturers of industrial scales in the mid-1990s. Mettler's U.S. operations generated approximately $190 million in sales and employed 1,400 workers. Health O Meter Products, Inc., an Ohio-based manufacturer of household scales and medical and commercial scales, had sales of approximately $283 million in 1996, about one-third of which came from its scale business. Chronos Richardson Inc. of New Jersey, another industrial scale maker, posted mid-1990s sales of approximately $90 million and employed about 100. Fairbanks, Inc. of Kansas City, Missouri, posted sales of $81 million and employed 775.

FURTHER READING

Darnay, Arsen J., ed. *Manufacturing USA.* 5th ed. Detroit: Gale Research, 1996.

Drake, Bob. "Controlling Truck Loads One Bucket at a Time." *Pit & Quarry,* September 1992.

"In-Motion Checkweigher Pays for Itself in 1 Month." *Modern Materials Handling,* September 1993.

Spaulding, Mark. "New Weigh Systems Raise Overall Productivity: Latest Units Offer Higher Accuracy, Faster Speeds and Less Giveaway for a Better Bottom Line." *Packaging,* June 1993.

U.S. Bureau of the Census. *1995 Annual Survey of Manufactures.* Washington: GPO, 1997. Available from http:// www.census.gov/prod/www/titles.html.

SIC 3599

INDUSTRIAL AND COMMERCIAL MACHINERY AND EQUIPMENT, NOT ELSEWHERE CLASSIFIED

This industry is made up of firms that manufacture miscellaneous machinery and equipment not elsewhere classified. It also encompasses establishments primarily engaged in producing or repairing machinery and equipment on a job or order basis for other companies. Examples of industry output include carnival amusement rides, catapults, sludge tables, flexible tubes and hoses, weather vanes, and non-vehicle engine filters. Motor vehicle engine filter manufacturers are classified separately in **SIC 3714: Motor Vehicle Parts and Accessories** and those manufacturing coin-operated amusement machines are classified in **SIC 3999: Manufacturing Industries, Not Elsewhere Classified.**

The industry is highly fragmented. Of the approximately 23,000 firms participating in this industry, none had revenues of more than $100 million. Typically, small to mid-sized machine shop receipts account for as much as 70 percent of industry revenues.

Capital investment by domestic industry accounted for approximately 55 percent of miscellaneous industrial machinery purchases. About 30 percent of the industry's mid-1990s sales were exports, and the remaining 15 percent of production was consumed by numerous market niches. The armed forces,

for example, purchased about 2.4 percent of output, and communication service industries made up slightly less than 1 percent of the market.

A slowdown in capital spending by durable goods manufacturers during the 1980s dampened sales and profit growth in comparison to the 1960s and 1970s. Revenue growth averaged only 4 percent annually between 1982 and 1990, mirroring capital spending increases. New capital expenditures for all manufacturing were up roughly 14 percent in 1995, contributing to the relative health of this industry. In 1995, the value of products in this category totaled $26.87 billion; this was a 19 percent increase from 1994. Strong U.S. economic performance in the mid- to late 1990s and recovering foreign markets, notably in Europe and east Asia, were expected to produce continued prosperity for the industry.

The industry's labor force numbered 319,000 in 1995, 77 percent of whom were engaged in production work. The average hourly production wage of $12.33 was slightly below average for manufacturing in general. Opportunities for most workers were expected to decline significantly between 1990 and 2005, according to the U.S. Bureau of Labor Statistics, with drops in total employment in many of the industry's primary occupations such as machinists and assemblers.

FURTHER READING

Darnay, Arsen J., ed. *Manufacturing USA.* 5th ed. Detroit: Gale Research, 1996.

Reimer, David M. "Machinery Industry." *Value Line Investment Survey.* 9th ed. New York: Value Line Publishing, Inc., 1997.

U.S. Bureau of the Census. *1995 Annual Survey of Manufactures.* Washington: GPO, 1997. Available from http:// www.census.gov/prod/www/titles.html.

Electronic & Other Electrical Equipment & Components, Except Computers

SIC 3612

POWER, DISTRIBUTION, AND SPECIALTY TRANSFORMERS

This category covers establishments primarily engaged in manufacturing power, distribution, instrument, and specialty transformers. Radio frequency or voice frequency electronic transformers, coils, and chokes are classified in **SIC 3677: Electronic Coils, Transformers, and Other Inductors**, and resistance welder transformers are part of **SIC 3548: Electric and Gas Welding and Soldering Equipment.**

A transformer is used to reduce or increase the voltage, or electromotive force, of electricity traveling through a wire. It accomplishes this by transferring electric energy from one coil or winding to another coil through electromagnetic induction. Electric-generating plants use generator transformers to "step-up," or increase, voltage that is transferred through power lines. When the high voltage electricity reaches a community, a "step-down" transformer reduces its power. A distribution transformer makes a final step-down in voltage by diminishing the force of the electricity to a level usable in homes and businesses. Some electrical devices, such as doorbells and small appliances, use additional step-down transformers to decrease voltage.

A typical transformer has two windings, or coils of wire, that are insulated from each other. The two coils are wound on a common magnetic circuit of laminated sheet metal, called the core. Each end of the primary coil is connected to the incoming alternating current (AC) power source. Each end of the secondary coil, which receives the energy, is connected to the outgoing power line. The ratio between the number of windings in each coil determines whether the voltage will be boosted or diminished.

There are two types of transformers: core and shell type. In core-type equipment the windings surround the laminated metal core. In shell-type transformers the metal core surrounds the windings. Distribution transformers are usually core-type, while more advanced high-voltage devices are often shell-type. Transformers can also be classified according to the type of cooling system they use; smaller transformers are usually cooled by air and larger equipment is liquid-cooled. Finally, transformers are either single-phase or polyphase. Polyphase devices typically have a three-legged core that can produce at least three different voltages.

The majority of apparatus manufactured in this industry are power and distribution transformers purchased by electric utilities. These devices accounted for about 49 percent of industry shipments in 1995. Because most transformers are simple and rugged, they often last as long as 40 years. Therefore, producers are largely dependent on purchases by utilities that are expanding service. Shipments of distribution transformers, for instance, are closely linked to new housing starts. But demand is also influenced by conversion to more efficient or aesthetically pleasing transformers.

The other 51 percent of the transformer market was primarily comprised of step-down equipment integrated into individual electrical devices. Fluorescent lamp ballasts, for instance, represented approximately 19 percent of production in 1995. Various specialty transformers, such as machine tool and high-intensity light transformers, accounted for 10 percent of sales. Other popular industry offerings include transformers for electric furnaces, rectifiers, ignition systems, consumer electronics, and toys.

BACKGROUND AND DEVELOPMENT

Transformer operation is based on a principle discovered in 1830 by Joseph Henry that electrical energy can be moved efficiently from one coil to another through electromagnetic induction. Michael Faraday and Henry independently observed in 1831 that a magnet moved through a closed coil of wire induces a current. When Faraday replaced the magnet with a charged electromagnet, he had built the first transformer. The value of the transformer was not fully understood until later in the nineteenth century, when devices that used alternating current became popular.

As the demand for electricity swelled during the late 1800s and early twentieth century, the need for electrical transforming devices emerged. As the United States built its massive electrical distribution infrastructure during the early part of the century, transformer sales ballooned. During the post-World War II economic expansion, moreover, the industry benefitted from aggressive government attempts to bring electricity to every American home. The Rural Electrification Administration was established in 1935, and was charged with distributing power to even the most remote regions and communities of the nation. In addition, electricity demand swelled during the mid-1900s as new applications for electricity, such as air-conditioning, became popular.

By the early 1980s, the transformer industry was shipping about $3 billion worth of equipment annually and employing a work force of 40,000. Growth slowed throughout the 1980s as the demand for new infrastructure equipment leveled. Total U.S. electric utility capacity rose roughly 20 percent between 1978 and 1991—tepid growth in comparison to the increases of the 1950s and 1960s. However, manufacturers were aided by healthy housing starts during the mid-1980s and the development of more efficient transformers that boosted replacement demand. Industry revenues climbed at an average annual rate of six percent between 1983 and 1990, to about $4.2 billion.

Low housing starts and a general U.S. recession stalled transformer demand in the early 1990s, as sales slipped to about $4.1 billion in 1991. The total value of shipments continued to recede about 4 percent from 1992-93, to around $3.9 billion, however there was significant growth from 1993-94, as the value of shipments increased nearly 50 percent, to about $4.5 billion. While demand for the very largest transformers increased, shipments of most industry offerings declined. Utility construction activity declined, and the

number of new generation and transmission projects built by utilities was expected to recede during the late 1990s.

CURRENT CONDITIONS

The demand for transformers in the mid-1990s remained relatively stable. Of the high-voltage and distribution transformers already in service, many were scheduled for replacement during the 1990s and early 2000s. In addition, many utilities were replacing good units with newer, more efficient designs. Almost all transformer manufacturers in the mid-1990s focused on products that integrated advanced silicon low-loss steel or amorphous metal cores, and offered greater serviceability. Likewise, the market for overhead transformers, which are typically mounted on poles, was being displaced by newer ground units.

While replacements were expected to bolster sales, transformer industry growth is forecast to diminish through the end of the decade, dropping as low as 1.5 percent by the year 2000. The North American Electric Reliability Council estimated that existing transmission systems will be generally adequate to meet demand throughout the 1990s. The need for smaller units from the private sector was expected to grow slowly.

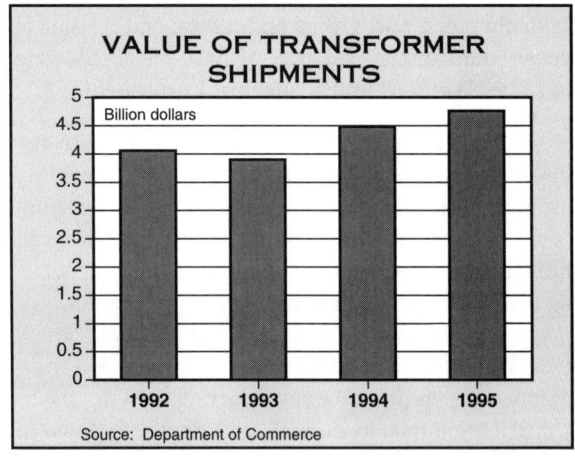

VALUE OF TRANSFORMER SHIPMENTS

Source: Department of Commerce

U.S. producers were also expecting to suffer from an influx of transformer imports from Mexico. International competition traditionally had made a minimal impact on this industry because of the high weight-to-value ratio of larger transformers and the propensity of some utilities to purchase American products. However, in the mid-1990s the North American Free Trade Agreement (NAFTA) boosted imports from nearby Mexico, which was already the largest industry importer. $325 million worth of transformers were imported from Mexico in 1994, and domestic producers exported $384 million worth of industry goods in 1995, mostly to Mexico and Canada.

Deregulation. As a result of the 1992 Federal Energy Policy Act (FEP), electric utilities, which have traditionally been regulated at the state and national level, began a conversion to open market competition. Market-based pricing began to replace regulatory rate structures, as electrical energy continued to become a marketable commodity. Transmission lines started to become "open access," and companies that owned high-voltage lines had to make them available to distribution companies wanting to rent their capacity to "wheel" energy over them. As a result, it has been predicted that the industry will undergo massive restructuring, and is likely to be affected at many levels, including the manufacturing sector. In the mid-1990s, electric utility deregulation was still only beginning to take effect, but as of 1996, legislation in four states required deregulation by 1997-98. Similar legislation is being drafted in 43 states, and industry analysts predicted nationwide deregulation of the electric utilities over the next ten years. It is not yet clear how deregulation will affect the transformer industry, but the initial results of competition among electric utilities are widespread mergers and a downsized work force, which may impact the demand for replacement transformers. Opponents of deregulation claim mergers will create monopolies in many regions, and that the consistency and quality of electric service will suffer. Proponents claim deregulation will lower rates for consumers and increase quality through competition.

INDUSTRY LEADERS

Only 286 companies participated in this consolidated industry in the mid-1990s, and only a few dominated. Eaton Corp., of Pennsylvania, had 1996 sales of nearly $8 billion and employed a work force of 116,000. Eaton is a manufacturer of electric power and protection equipment for industrial and commercial uses. In 1994 Eaton acquired the distribution and control business unit of Westinghouse Corp., which increased their revenues by 37.5 percent. Cooper Industries, of Texas, was the second largest manufacturer with revenues of $4.8 billion, and about 40,800 workers. Siemens Energy, the third largest player, shipped $1.2 billion worth of goods and employed 10,500. In the fluorescent lamp ballast market, leaders included Advance Transformer Co. of Illinois with $250 million in sales and MagneTek Electric Inc. of Wisconsin with $90 million in sales.

WORK FORCE

The long-term employment outlook for manufacturers of transformers and related equipment is poor. The work force had already shriveled 25 percent during the 1980s, to about 30,000 by 1992, and cutbacks were expected to continue. Increased productivity, through automation and management restructuring, were responsible for work force reductions. The U.S. Bureau of Labor Statistics estimated that jobs in this sector for assemblers and fabricators, which accounted for roughly 20 percent of the electric distribution equipment work force, would plummet by nearly 50 percent between 1990 and 2005. Other labor positions were expected to decline similarly. However, opportunities for sales professionals, engineers, and industrial production managers were anticipated to expand about 15 percent by the year 2005.

RESEARCH AND TECHNOLOGY

Industry-related technical innovations in the early 1990s included new transformer test equipment that allows operators to select and apply test voltage to any leg of a transformer winding, thereby eliminating the need to disconnect the leads. Also, new insulating materials were allowing companies to refurbish old transformers and boost their efficiency, a development that was anticipated to reduce demand for new, more efficient replacement units. Another threat to industry growth is the advent of new technologies such as semiconductors and microprocessors, which can increase the capacity of existing transmission lines, reducing demand for new distribution equipment.

In the mid-1990s, the consequence of controversial electromagnetic fields (EMFs) was still undetermined. The EPA's 1990 finding that EMFs are a "probable" cause of cancer has not yet had a tangible impact on the transformer industry. However, as an environmental protection measure, the EPA has restricted the use of polychlorinated biphenyls (PCBs) as a cooling medium for liquid-filled transformers, due to the toxicity of the fluid, as well as its flammability. Environmentally viable replacements such as polydimethyl siloxane and fire-resistant hydrocarbon fluids are less flammable, and are phasing out use of PCBs.

FURTHER READING

Darnay, Arsen J., ed. *Manufacturing USA.* 5th ed. Detroit: Gale Research, 1996.

"Executive Summary, U.S. Transformers." *MarketLine U.S. Snapshots OnDisc.* London: MarketLine International, 1996.

Hillesiand, Glen. "Effects of Electric Utility Deregulation on Manufacturers." *CIRAS News* vol. 30, no. 2 (winter 1996).

Reason, John. "How Electric Utilities Buy Quality When They Buy Transformers." *Electric World,* May 1992.

Reason, John. "Transformer Rebuild Increases Load Capacity." *Electric World,* February 1994.

Standard & Poor's Industry Surveys. New York: Standard & Poor's Corporation. 31 December 1993.

U.S. Department of Commerce. Economics and Statistics Administration. Bureau of the Census. *1995 Annual Survey of Manufactures.* Washington: GPO, 1997. Available from http://www.census.gov/prod/www/titles.html#mm.

U.S. Department of Commerce. International Trade Administration. *U.S. Industrial Outlook 1994.* Washington: GPO, 1994.

Whitlow, Alan W. "Portable Test Box Saves Time on Transformer Checks." *Transmission & Distribution,* January 1993.

SIC 3613

SWITCHGEAR AND SWITCHBOARD APPARATUS

This category covers establishments primarily engaged in manufacturing switchgear and switchboard apparatus. Important products of this industry include power switches, circuit breakers, power switching equipment, and similar switchgear for general industrial application; also, switchboards and cubicles, control and metering panels, fuses and fuse mountings, and similar switchboard apparatus and supplies. Relays and switches in electronic devices and industrial controls are classified elsewhere. This industry was reclassified in 1987 thus figures from prior years include additional product categories.

A switchgear is used to interrupt or reestablish the flow of electricity in a circuit. It is generally used in combination with metering, protective, and regulating equipment to protect and control motors, generators, transformers, and transmission and distribution lines. A switchboard is comprised of one or more panels with various switches and indicators that are used to route electricity and operate circuits.

Switchgears are typically concentrated at points where electrical systems make significant changes in power, current, or routing, such as electrical supply substations and control centers. Switchgear assemblies range in size from smaller, ground-mounted units to large walk-in installations and can be classified as

outdoor or indoor units. Commercial and industrial assemblies are usually indoors, while utilities and co-generation facilities are more likely to have outdoor gear. Manufactured for a variety of functions and power levels, all switchgear conforms to standards set by the Institute of Electrical and Electronic Engineers (IEEE), the American National Standards Institute (ANSI), or the National Electrical Manufacturers Association (NEMA).

Metal-clad switchgear assemblies are the most common devices used in electricity distribution. They usually contain: circuit breakers, which can be deactivated; primary circuits, such as transformers; insulating materials; interlocks, which ensure that circuit breakers can be safely inserted into and removed from the assembly; and, instrument panels that control the assembly. Metal-clad power center switchgear is used to regulate and route power in high-voltage applications. Similarly, medium-voltage vac-clad switchgear is used in circuits involving transmission and distribution lines and motors. Other common types of assemblies used in electrical distribution include metal-clad interrupter, low voltage, and station-type cubicle switchgear.

Low voltage panelboards and distribution boards represented about 30 percent of industry revenues in 1995, and circuit breakers made up about 26 percent of sales. Switchgear units and fuses accounted for about 26 percent and 8 percent of shipments, respectively. Miscellaneous parts and apparatus comprised the remainder of output.

The market for switchgear and related apparatus is highly fragmented. Approximately 21 percent of purchases in the mid-1990s were classified as fixed capital investments, mostly by utilities and power generation companies. Six percent of industry output was used in office buildings, and industrial building applications consumed approximately five percent of production. Other significant market segments included refrigeration and heating equipment manufacturers, residential home builders, and communications industries. About 7 percent of production was exported.

BACKGROUND AND DEVELOPMENT

Power transformation technology was conceived as early as 1830 by Michael Faraday and Joseph Henry, who discovered the theory of electromagnetic induction. But the first commercially practical manual switching systems emerged during the late 1800s to service the flourishing telephone industry. By the late 1880s, shortly after Alexander Graham Bell's invention of the telephone in 1876, the telephone switchboard had evolved to a state where thousands of calls could be switched and connected at the same time. The first automatic switching system was introduced at the 1881 Paris Electrical Exposition, and a workable system had been patented by 1889. A similar device was installed in New Jersey in 1914. Using electrical impulses, it raised and rotated a shaft in a series of movements to make a contact.

The need for gear that would protect and control high-power electric circuits, which constitutes most of the equipment in this industry, resulted from advances in electricity during the early 1900s. Lee De Forest's 1906 invention of the electron tube and a plethora of subsequent breakthroughs spawned a huge demand for electricity in the United States. As the country built its massive electrical power infrastructure, sales of fuses, control panels, and all types of switchgear soared. Notably, the Rural Electrification Administration, which was established in 1935, and other government initiatives expended massive funds to try to bring electricity into every American home.

Electricity demand swelled during the mid-1900s as new applications for electric power, such as air-conditioning and television, became popular. In addition, post-World War II U.S. economic growth resulted in a great demand from industry for circuit control and protection apparatus. Equipment also improved as manufacturers developed means of reducing arcing (damaging sparks that occur when switches are activated), and integrated circuits were applied to switchboards and control devices. By the late 1970s, manufacturers of switchgear and switchboard equipment were shipping about $5 billion worth of goods annually and employing a work force of more than 66,000.

Industry sales effectively stagnated during the 1980s, continuing a trend started in the 1970s. Indeed, the rampant expansion of the U.S. electric power infrastructure had subsided. Total U.S. electric utility capacity increased a modest 20 percent between 1978 and 1990—pitiful in comparison to growth during the 1950s and 1960s. Industry revenue growth was well below inflation rates during the early 1980s, rising to only $5.5 billion by 1986. Official industry content was changed in 1987, reducing sales volume to about $4.9 billion. Sales continued to slightly increase at an annual rate of less than 2 percent during the late 1980s, to about $5.5 billion by 1990.

Slack demand for new electric power infrastructure, recessed construction sectors, weak industrial demand, and a generally despondent U.S. economy hindered many industry participants in the early 1990s. Sales slipped in 1991 and fell again in 1992—by one percent in inflation-adjusted terms. Likewise, in 1993

shipments rose only 4.5 percent before inflation, despite an overall U.S. economic recovery and a surge in new construction. Furthermore, the long term industry outlook was lamentable going into the mid-1990s. Domestic demand for new switchgear was expected to likely decline further, or stagnate, and because most switchgear was rugged and durable, replacement activity offered limited profit opportunities.

CURRENT CONDITIONS

Product shipments showed mixed returns entering the late 1990s. In 1995 shipments grew 12.5 percent in current dollars to $6.6 billion. That year represented the highest growth the industry had enjoyed since the 1980s. Modest growth was expected to continue at 3 to 4 percent annually through 2000.

Despite lackluster performance overall, opportunities for savvy U.S. exporters remained strong in the early and mid-1990s, particularly in Mexico and East Asia. Export activity was 18 percent in early 1992, bolstered by a weak dollar and a growing demand for reputable U.S. equipment by developing countries. Sales were especially swift to Mexico, which accounted for approximately 30 percent, or $454 million, of all cross-border sales in 1991. Also, exports to Mexico were expected to jump in the wake the North American Free Trade Agreement (NAFTA). Other major importers of U.S. switchgear were Canada ($224 million), the United Kingdom ($95 million), and Japan ($81 million). The United States imported about $1.7 billion worth of switchgear in the early 1990s, most of which came from Mexico, Japan, and Canada.

INDUSTRY LEADERS

There were roughly 530 establishments manufacturing switchgear in the late 1990s. This figure remained fairly constant since the early 1990s. Despite this growth there has been steady corporate consolidation in the industry as companies merged with and acquired rivals in an effort to boost capital and take advantage of other economies of scale.

The biggest manufacturers of switchgear and switchboard equipment were large, diversified communications and power equipment conglomerates. Leading companies include Allen-Bradley Company, Inc., a subsidiary of Rockwell International Corporation; General Electric Company; Siemens Corporation; and Square D Company, a subsidiary of Groupe Schneider of France. Among these only Square D derives more than half of its revenues from switchgear and related products. Together these firms represented an estimated 45 percent share of industry sales. Other major manufacturers include Schlumberger Industries

Inc., of Georgia, Liebert Corp., of Ohio, and C and K Components Inc., of Massachusetts.

WORK FORCE

Approximately 41,000 workers served this industry in 1995, down from 44,000 in 1987. In addition to slack demand, productivity gains contributed to work force reductions during the 1980s and early 1990s. Specifically, factory automation and advanced information systems allowed many manufacturers to boost international competitiveness and retain profits in spite of stagnant markets. Likewise, the long term employment outlook for makers of switchgear was generally poor. The number of jobs for assemblers and fabricators, which make up almost 30 percent of the work force, was expected to decline by more than 40 percent between 1990 and 2005, according to the Bureau of Labor Statistics. Most labor positions were expected to fall 10 to 30 percent. Opportunities for engineers and sales professionals, on the other hand, were expanding and an increase by approximately 15 percent by 2005 was expected.

RESEARCH AND TECHNOLOGY

The switchgear and switchboard industry invests relatively little in research and development. In the early 1990s, for example, companies invested an average of $2,720 per employee back into their business, compared to about $5,520 spent by the average U.S. manufacturer. One of the most important areas of technological advancement in the early 1990s was switchgear that integrated sulfur hexafloride gas (SF6). SF6 has insulation and arc-quenching properties that could be used to reduce damage caused by arcing. The newer switches are safer, more reliable and require less maintenance than conventional switchgear.

FURTHER READING

Darnay, Arsen J., ed. *Manufacturing USA.* 5th ed. Detroit: Gale Research, 1996.

Lazar, Irwin. "Understanding Switchgear and Its Specifications." *Consulting-Specifying Engineer,* February 1992.

Lazar, Irwin. "Specifying Switchgear for Maximum Reliability." *Consulting-Specifying Engineer,* August 1989.

Palko, Ed. "Taking Advantage of Fused Interrupter Switchgear." *Plant Engineering,* 2 May 1991.

Reason, John. "SF6: Revolution in Switchgear." *Electrical World,* December 1989.

U.S. Bureau of the Census. *1995 Annual Survey of Manufactures.* Washington: GPO, 1997.

SIC 3621

MOTORS AND GENERATORS

This classification comprises establishments primarily engaged in manufacturing power generators, motor generator sets, and electric motors, excluding engine-starting motors. Also covered in this classification are establishments primarily involved in manufacturing railway motors and control equipment, as well as motors, generators, and control equipment for gasoline, electric, and oil-electric buses and trucks.

Establishments primarily engaged in manufacturing turbo generators are classified in **SIC 3511: Steam, Gas, and Hydraulic Turbines, and Turbine Generator Set Units** and those manufacturing starting motors and battery-charging generators for internal combustion engines are grouped in **SIC 3694: Electric Equipment for Internal Combustion Engines.** Establishments primarily engaged in manufacturing generators for welding equipment are classified in **SIC 3548: Electric and Gas Welding and Soldering Equipment.**

INDUSTRY SNAPSHOT

Approximately 250 companies in the United States were involved in manufacturing motors and generators in 1995. These companies recorded more than $10.4 billion in sales for the industry's products which consisted of four primary product groups—fractional horsepower motors, integral horsepower motors and generators, prime mover generator sets, and parts and supplies for motors and generators. Other products manufactured by the industry included land transportation motors and fractional and integral motor generator sets. Of these products, fractional horsepower motors represented nearly 50 percent of the industry's shipments, followed by integral horsepower motors and generators, which accounted for 18.5 percent. Prime mover generator sets accounted for another 11.2 percent of the industry's shipments, while parts and supplies for motors and generators represented nearly 8 percent.

Motor and generator manufacturers are heavily dependent on the health of several industrial markets to sustain their growth. Fractional horsepower motors are used in various household appliances—including refrigerators, freezers, air conditioners, automatic dishwashers, and microwave ovens—as well as other products requiring a small horsepower motor, such as computer disk drives. Consequently, fluctuations in the residential construction market and changes in consumer spending are mirrored by the fractional motor market.

Integral horsepower motors are best suited for industrial uses, where greater horsepower is required. Integral motors power vehicles used in large construction projects and provide the necessary power for many different types of manufacturing facilities. Any significant changes in nonresidential construction activity or capital expenditures in the industrial sector generally have parallel affects on integral motor production.

In addition to these market dependencies, motor and generator sales are affected by the vacillating costs of raw materials. Steel—an essential element in the production of motors, generators, and their related parts and supplies—is subject to pernicious price swings that could impinge on the industry's profit margin. Other materials, such as wire and brushes used in the manufacturing of motors and generators, also demonstrate a propensity for erratic jumps in price and have an appreciable affect on the motor and generator industry.

ORGANIZATION AND STRUCTURE

The motor and generator industry is predominantly populated by medium and large sized companies, or those employing more than 20 people. The 75 largest establishments employ an average of 6,742 people. While this figure includes employees engaged in manufacturing or managing the production of some other types of goods, it is indicative of the relatively large size of facilities involved in the industry. On average, a motor and generator establishment employs 163 people—more than three times the number of people employed in a typical manufacturing facility for all other U.S. industries.

Geographically, motor and generator production occurred throughout much of the nation, according to 1992 *Census of Manufacturers* studies, but was particularly concentrated in Wisconsin, Missouri, Arkansas, and Ohio.

The costs involved in establishing and operating a motor and generator manufacturing facility are substantially higher than the average manufacturing facility. In 1989, the average cost per establishment for raw manufacturing materials was $8.14 million in the motor and generator industry, compared to $4.54 million for the average of all manufacturing industries. The average investment for purchasing manufacturing machinery and paying for production retooling was $461,456 in the motor and generator industry—55 percent higher than the average for other industries.

The relatively expensive nature of conducting business in the motor and generator industry tends to discourage the entry of small manufacturing companies. Since manufacturers frequently encounter expensive retooling costs—when a particular product becomes obsolete and is replaced by a new product, for example, or when a significant technological advancement dictates the implementation of a new production process—many companies manufacture a diverse line of products, some of which are excluded from the boundaries of the SIC 3621 classification. This diversity helps to insulate companies from potentially deleterious financial conditions affecting the motor and generator industry.

BACKGROUND AND DEVELOPMENT

The principle of the electric motor was first developed by Michael Faraday in 1821, but a diverse group of scientists and lay innovators quickly followed Faraday's lead and began experimenting with amended designs. Improvements on Faraday's design followed in quick succession, as inventors of the nineteenth century were swept up by the inspiring and momentous technological advancements that characterized the era. This work helped pave the way toward developing the type of electric motor that became an integral component in twentieth century factories, stores, and homes.

Sixteen years after Faraday first announced his discovery, Thomas Davenport, a blacksmith from Vermont, developed a motor that successfully powered a printing press. This invention marked one of the earliest uses of the electric motor for commercial purposes, and Davenport was granted Patent No. 132 for it. Not to be outdone, Moses Farmer, another Yankee pioneer in the development of the electric motor, created a miniature electric railway as an exhibit for country fairs. Charles G. Page used this application of the electric motor on a larger scale in 1857 when he made an experimental run with a full sized locomotive from Washington to Baltimore.

While these developments were encouraging and marked significant technological advancements, the design of these early motors limited the ways in which they could be used. Since they derived energy from large, expensive batteries, these early versions were essentially suitable only for demonstration purposes—to utilize them in a commercial or industrial setting on a daily basis was still impractical. But this shortcoming disappeared with the advent of practical dynamos, or direct-current generators. No longer fettered by cumbersome batteries, early models of these smaller, cheaper to operate motors appeared at the Electrical

Exhibition and National Conference of Electricians in Philadelphia in 1884. These were electrically driven rather than battery powered motors, and their development greatly increased the potential applications for the electric motor. By 1887, there were already 15 well known manufacturers of small electric motors in the United States, and more than 10,000 electric motors of 15 horsepower or less had been produced.

The development of direct current generators greatly enhanced the economic feasibility of electric motors in the workplace and the home. But, while the technology was in place, the fledgling industry's growth suffered from the shortsightedness of some business leaders. The individuals spearheading the movement towards electrification focused their efforts on employing electricity to generate light rather than on the vast industrial and commercial applications for the electric motor. In fact, the majority of early electric utilities were established as lighting businesses. As a result, other uses for electric motors were lost in the rush. But the incorporation of the first practical dynamo into the operation of the electric motor slowly drew the attention of more than a few enterprising individuals, and the industry formally began to experience a substantial demand for its products.

As the nation entered a new century, two companies became established as pioneers in the industrial and commercial development of electric motors. General Electric Company (GE), created to market and manufacture the innovations developed by Thomas Edison, entered into the electric motor field through mergers and acquisitions. Emerson Electric Manufacturing Company, formed to explore applications for the newly developed alternating current electric motor, entered the market with manufacturing processes it had developed specifically to use electrically driven motors. Both of these companies figured prominently throughout the course of the industry's history and helped catapult the use of electric motors and generators toward the pervasive levels of the 1990s.

The nation slowly became electrified during the first half of the twentieth century. It took until the 1950s for certain segments of the country to install the necessary electrical wire to enable the transmission of electricity. GE manufactured a broad assortment of electric motors and generators to run cement, paper, and steel manufacturing facilities and also spent considerable effort on developing electric powered locomotive engines. Emerson, meanwhile, concentrated on producing electric motors for use in home appliances such as sewing machines, water pumps, and fans and also carved a niche in the growing market for electric motors within products intended for business offices.

Emerson and GE were joined by many other manufacturers of motors and generators during these pre-World War II decades, as the relatively new technology beckoned entrepreneurs into the market and expanded the size of the industry. Rural Electrification Administration crews were constantly stringing transmission wire, convincing observers that electrification of the entire nation was inevitable. For those contemplating a foray into the electric motor and generator industry, this development translated into encouraging prospects for the future. Manufacturing facilities mechanized their processes to be powered by electricity, if they had not already done so, and appliances used in the home increasingly depended on electricity for power.

When the postwar economic boom of the 1950s exponentially increased consumer spending and invigorated both residential and nonresidential construction, the motor and generator industry gained a solid foundation. Every American home aspired to own at least two modern appliances, which marked the dawn of a new era and infused motor and generator manufacturers with increased business. Manufacturing activity in general increased as well, with electrically driven production lines becoming the norm.

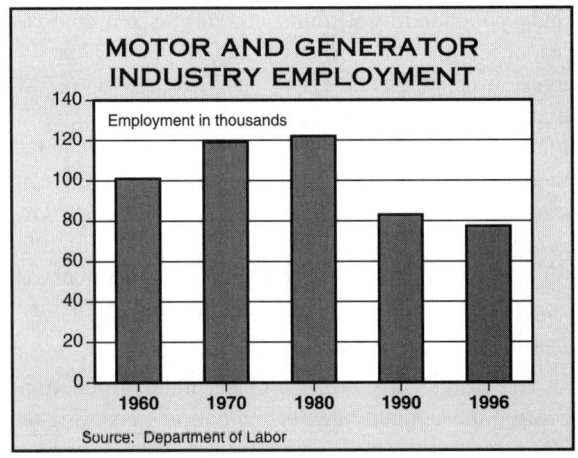

The lucrative conditions characterizing the market attracted more and more manufacturers, and by the end of the decade competition became intense within the industry. In addition, the nature of the competition changed during this period, as the smattering of smaller companies that had proliferated before World War II began consolidating into large conglomerates.

In the 1960s, Emerson and GE competed for market share against such manufacturers as Reliance Electric & Engineering Co., Wagner Electric Co., and Westinghouse Electric Corp. This competition resulted in a significant decline in the price of fractional horsepower motors, the primary product within the motor and generator industry. Exacerbating the effect of the shrinking profit margins was the increasing cost of raw materials used in the production of fractional motors, particularly of magnetic wire. By the middle of the decade, a majority of the leading companies raised their prices for fractional motors in an attempt to stave off the debilitating effects of rising raw material expenditures.

At this time, there were approximately 325 companies competing in the industry, operating more than 400 establishments and employing slightly more than 100,000 workers. Despite the shrinking profit margins and other problems associated with the rapid pace at which the industry was maturing, the demand for electric motors continued to increase, attracting more and more competitors. Growth of the industry primarily stemmed from demand for fractional motors, which far outpaced other motor and generator products in terms of proportional representation of industry shipments. Fractional motors accounted for over 36 percent of total industry shipments by the mid-1960s—up from less than 30 percent in the 1950s—and this percentage would increase in the coming years. The reasons for this growth were as numerous as the different types of household items and appliances that were sold to consumers. Fractional motors were used in such diverse items as electric lawn mowers and hedge trimmers, electric toothbrushes, refrigerators, and washing machines.

Other products classified in the motor and generator industry recorded respectable sales figures, but their growth was less dramatic than the increasing demand for fractional motors. Products such as small generating sets powered by diesel and other internal-combustion engines benefitted from stable demand from the farming and transportation industries, while shipments of integral horsepower motors spiraled downward during the late 1950s and early 1960s. Integral motors could be reconditioned, whereas fractional motors were rarely rebuilt. This, in part, accounted for an increasing disparity between fractional and integral motor shipments. In 1958, the value of shipments for fractional and integral motors was approximately even, at $430 million. Six years later, the value of shipments of fractional motors had soared to nearly $600 million, while integral motor shipments had fallen to roughly $375 million.

This period in the history of the motor and generator industry also witnessed the increasing encroachment of foreign manufacturers into the U.S. market. In 1963, 5 million units of motor and generator products were imported into the United States, but this figure

nearly quintupled four years later when more than 23 million imported units were sold. This growth in total imports was occasioned by significant increases in the value of shipments recorded by two countries—the United Kingdom and Japan. The United Kingdom increased motor and generator product shipments to the United States from $1.5 million in 1963 to $18.4 million by 1967. But this was a one-time surge for U.K. producers: five years later shipments dropped to $12.6 million, and by the end of the 1970s U.K. imports slipped below $10 million. Japan, on the other hand, went from negligible shipments in 1963 to over $15 million worth four years later, and this continued to increase to $27.8 million by 1972 and $67 million by the end of the decade.

High inflation in the early 1970s negatively affected manufacturers of motors and generators, as residential and nonresidential construction declined and many consumers delayed purchasing appliances. The total value of industry shipments declined by five percent between 1974 and 1975 to $3.12 billion, while production worker employment within the industry decreased from 77,700 to 60,600. Hoping to escape the rising costs of materials and supplies occurring at this time, many manufacturers overstocked their inventories. This led to a later downward adjustment in production, further eroding the industry's profit margins. Once consumer appliance purchases returned to normal levels and construction picked up in the late 1970s, however, the industry again exhibited robust growth. Shipment values increased by 12 percent between 1977 and 1978 to $5 billion and approached $6 billion by the beginning of the 1980s.

Entering the 1980s, however, high inflation continued to inflict damage on the motor and generator industry, particularly due to reduced capital expenditure programs initiated by other industries. In the absence of vigorous, nationwide plant expansion and the consequent orders for motors and generators, the industry was forced to look elsewhere for money. Since major retooling of production machinery was prohibitively expensive, many manufacturers streamlined their operations, relying on more efficient production procedures to help them withstand the decline in business. Part of this effort to economize resulted in a reduction of the industry's labor force. From 1981 to 1982, employment of production workers dropped from 93,400 to 84,100—the latest of a series of significant declines from the 107,000 high recorded in 1979.

In the meantime, the value of import shipments entering the United States continued to increase dramatically during the 1970s, and by the early 1980s foreign competition stood as a formidable force. The value of all import shipments classified in the motor and generator industry in 1972 was $181 million, but this figure ballooned to $801 million ten years later. U.S. manufacturers, however, had simultaneously intensified their efforts to increase exports in order to combat escalating material costs and declining business. Consequently, domestic exports, a majority of which were shipped to Canada and Mexico, also grew substantially. Between 1979 and 1981, the value of export shipments increased from $887 million to nearly $1.4 billion, maintaining a favorable trade balance for U.S. manufacturers.

CURRENT CONDITIONS

The motor and generator industry was expected to expand at a compound annual rate of 2 percent from 1993 to 1997, suggesting the beginning of a recovery from the effects of a recession in the early 1990s. During the recession, flagging consumer spending and a decline in housing and industrial construction compounded the existing difficulties associated with foreign competition, excess industry capacity, and cascading prices. The restoration of these integral markets was anticipated to improve the industry's condition as it moved into the twenty-first century, but additional challenges loomed on the horizon.

Escalating energy costs, coupled with federal regulations requiring new energy efficiency standards, made the development of new technology and manufacturing processes intrinsic to any manufacturer's future profitability. The motor and generator industry made progress in this direction during the 1980s, including the development of a highly efficient fractional motor in 1985 that enabled appliances to operate more quietly and at lower cost. However, the industry needed further advances in the 1990s to ensure its viability. In 1992, GE unveiled a variable speed motor for air conditioning and heating equipment that operated 20 percent more efficiently than other motors used at the time. Manufacturers able to produce equally innovative and energy efficient products would most likely figure prominently in the industry's future.

INDUSTRY LEADERS

Ranked according to sales volume, the two largest companies engaged in the motor and generator industry in 1996 were General Electric Company and Emerson Electric Company. These companies began competing for market share before the turn of the century and have managed to lead the motor and generator industry through much of its history.

Emerson Electric, with about 79,000 employees, recorded roughly $11.1 million in sales in 1996—a

considerable gain in magnitude from its origin as a small, regional manufacturer of fans and electric motors. Founded in 1890 in St. Louis, Missouri, by judge John Wesley Emerson, Emerson Electric at first engaged in the production of alternating current electric motors. The company enjoyed considerable success well into the twentieth century incorporating electric motors into sundry household appliances. By the 1920s, electric fans became the company's primary product, accounting for 40 percent of total sales.

Following the Great Depression in the 1930s—when sales plummeted, stock dividend payments were halted, and hotly contested labor disputes threatened to bankrupt the company—Emerson Electric's financial condition was buoyed by military contracts obtained during World War II. The company manufactured a variety of war-related products, including gun turrets installed in Air Force bombers such as the B-17, B-25, and B-26. Combined with its other contributions toward the war effort, these products infused the company with $100 million annually.

Defense-related work continued to support Emerson Electric following the war, although during the immediate postwar years military contracts dropped to as low as $1.5 million. But defense-related work picked up again in the 1950s, when the Air Force modernized its bomber fleet, elevating sales from military contracts to 30 percent of the company's total. To supplement its armament production, company management also decided to branch out into the engineering and development of electronics and avionics.

By the end of the 1950s, however, Emerson Electric's management grew fearful of the company's dependence on the military for such a considerable portion of its revenues. To address this, they began an aggressive acquisition program in the 1960s, averaging one acquisition per year throughout the decade. These additional companies enabled Emerson Electric to increase its presence in consumer markets and diversify the company's product mix to include such items as lighting fixtures, door chimes, and intercom units, thus providing for a more stable future. Acquisitions and diversification continued into the 1970s and 1980s, as Emerson Electric became a leader in both consumer and industrial markets. By the 1990s, Emerson Electric's products were sold to commercial and industrial businesses involved in a wide assortment of factory automation and process control enterprises.

General Electric posted $78 million in sales in 1996, with enough employees—222,000—to populate many cities in the nation. Growing from a storied past, it became one of the handful of behemoth corporations dictating the health of the national economy. In fact, GE's history charted some of the most significant technological discoveries and advancements of the twentieth century. From Thomas Edison's development of the light bulb to advances in turbine engines, to the refinement of nuclear power production processes, GE has stood as a pioneer in the engineering and manufacturing world for over 100 years.

While this impressive past elevated the company into the upper echelon of international businesses, GE's more recent achievements, especially in the motor and generator industry, have been comparatively dismal. During the 1970s and 1980s, the company suffered increasing losses from foreign competition, labor disputes, and "indirect imports" (finished products that were assembled with electric motors already included). These mounting difficulties forced GE to close several motor and generator manufacturing plants in the late 1980s and to lay off a considerable percentage of its work force. In 1987, for example, GE discontinued production of large horsepower integral motors, ranging in size from 800 to 8,000 horsepower, which left 825 workers without employment. GE judged the heavy duty industrial market for these motors to be oversaturated, unattractive due to low prices, and unlikely to recover in the foreseeable future. Harder hit by these market-wide developments than rival Emerson Electric, GE began to slip from its almost unassailable position atop the motor and generator industry in the late 1980s and early 1990s.

WORK FORCE

Total employment in the motor and generator industry decreased through much of the 1980s. This trend continued into the 1990s, as a nationwide recession weakened the motor and generator market. Beyond the negative effects of market fluctuations, manufacturing industries as a whole continued to streamline their operations by eliminating layers of managerial staff and altering production processes to reduce the number of workers required to perform certain tasks. This general movement toward fewer employees per manufacturing facility made future reductions of the motor and generator industry employment base likely.

Of the 77,300 total people employed in the motor and generator industry, 61,800 were production workers. Managerial, administrative, and technical employees composed the remainder of the industry's work force. Generally, production workers were employed on a full time basis, worked the same average number of hours per year as workers in other manufacturing industries, and averaged $11.69 per hour.

AMERICA AND THE WORLD

The international market for motors and generators is intensely competitive with Japan, Mexico, Canada, Germany, and the United Kingdom shipping just over $2 billion worth of products to the United States in 1991. Canada and Mexico combined for a 30.1 percent share of the U.S. import market, followed by the European Community with a 24 percent share, and Japan with a 22.4 percent share.

Exports from the United States totalled $2.016 billion in 1991, $15 million greater than the import total. The primary markets for motors and generators manufactured in the United States were Canada, Mexico, Nigeria, South Korea, and the Netherlands. Canada and Mexico accounted for the greatest share of U.S. exports at 31.4 percent, followed by East Asia at 19.9 percent, the European Community at 15.4 percent, and South America at 5.8 percent. The largest disparity between U.S. import and export totals in 1991 existed with Japan. For the year, Japan shipped $449 million worth of motor and generator products to the United States, compared to the $48 million worth of products the United States shipped to Japan.

FURTHER READING

Bureau of the Census. *Annual Survey of Manufacturers.* Washington: GPO, 1995.

Bureau of the Census. *Census of Manufacturers.* Washington: GPO, 1992.

Bureau of the Census. *Current Industrial Report.* Washington: GPO, 1996.

Darnay, Arsen J., ed. *Manufacturing USA.* 5th ed. Detroit: Gale Research, 1993.

"Electric Motor Price Rises Set by Some Makers." *Wall Street Journal,* 20 January 1966, 4.

"Engineering the Electric Century: Motor Development Creates New Loads for Utilities, Changes Industrial Practice." *Electrical World,* 15 August 1973, 38-40.

Gates, Ward. "Electronics Industry Finally Entering Growth Stage." *Magazine of Wall Street,* 23 March 1963, 26-29.

"GE Electric Motors Will Feature the Use of Superconductors." *Wall Street Journal,* 9 July 1976, 3.

"GE Introduces a Motor that Is More Efficient." *Wall Street Journal,* 1 July 1992, B6.

Glaberson, William. "An Uneasy Alliance in Smokestack U.S.A." *New York Times,* 13 March 1988, F1.

"Going on the Straight and Narrow." *Business Week,* 20 January 1968, 134-138.

"Putting Customer Demands First." *Business Week,* 28 November 1970, 62-63.

Rifkin, Glenn. "Using Spin to Power Electric Cars." *New York Times,* 11 November 1992, D5.

Stipp, David. "Big Advance in Power Making Works Wonderfully in Theory." *Wall Street Journal,* 17 January 1986, 21.

Weimer, George A. "Power Transmission: A Drive for Efficiency." *Iron Age,* 26 May 1980, 32-37.

—Jeffrey L. Covell, updated by Susan King

SIC 3624

CARBON AND GRAPHITE PRODUCTS

This category covers establishments primarily engaged in manufacturing carbon, graphite, and metal-graphite brushes and brush stock; carbon or graphite electrodes for thermal and electrolytic uses; carbon and graphite fibers; and other carbon, graphite, and metal-graphite products.

INDUSTRY SNAPSHOT

Carbon and graphite products manufacturing establishments were responsible for shipments worth approximately $1.53 billion in 1994. Total value of shipments during the 1980s reached a peak of $1.30 billion in 1988 before declining by 11 percent to $1.16 billion in 1990.

Although the industry demonstrated signs of renewed life in the 1990s, carbon and graphite products output slowly declined in the early 1980s. The lackluster performance of the industry was attributed to the effect of several economic forces that created product oversupply and excess capacity in the industry. One of the main causes cited for the decade-long stagnation of the industry was the decline of the steel industry, a prime market for the industry's products. In addition, world demand for carbon and graphite electrodes plummeted, due to the development of more efficient electrode performance in steel production. This decline in demand for carbon and graphite electrodes for use in steel production, coupled with the strength of the dollar in the mid-1980s, allowed rival foreign producers to increase their profitability in the U.S. market, which adversely affected the industry's output and profitability.

On the positive side, structural changes in the industry led to a rebound in the 1990s, including a slight growth in some export markets. Although the industry was a perennial net importer of carbon and graphite products, the volume of carbon and graphite exports increased 27 percent from 1990 to 1991.

ORGANIZATION AND STRUCTURE

In 1994, approximately 96 establishments were engaged in the production of carbon and graphite products. These establishments employed approximately 95 workers each, 69 of which were employed as production workers. For the same year, the average value added per production worker was $84,440. This figure was small compared to the national standard of $93,930.

In 1994, the product share was split between two product classes—electrodes, which claimed 42.3 percent of the market and all other graphite and carbon products, which claimed the remaining 57.7 percent. Graphite electrodes for use in electrolytic cells and electric furnaces represented the largest portion of the electrode product share.

Geographically, the greatest number of establishments producing carbon and graphite products in 1994 were located in the Northeast and Southern United States. Ranked by the number of establishments per state, Ohio ranked first with 14, followed by Pennsylvania with 12, California with 11, New York with 7, and Michigan and South Carolina with 5 each.

The bulk of the industry's revenue was garnered by a limited number of manufacturers. It was estimated that UCAR International Inc., with sales of $901 million, accounted for over 50 percent of industry sales in 1996. Moreover, the leading three companies accounted for almost 90 percent of the total industry's output in 1996. The other two dominant companies in the carbon and graphite products industry were: Keystone Consolidated Industries Inc. of Dallas Texas, with a 22 percent share; and Carbide/Graphite Group Inc. of Pittsburgh, Pennsylvania, with a 15 percent share. The remaining 10 percent of the market was controlled by about 20 companies. All of the top companies in the industry are private concerns.

BACKGROUND AND DEVELOPMENT

The products composing the carbon and graphite products industry were mostly carbon products of a very high carbon content, including graphites, both natural and synthetic. Carbon's hardest form is known as diamond; graphite is its softest form. Graphite appears naturally in three forms: amorphous, which is the last stage of the coalification process; crystalline flake, which is used in brake linings and pencils; and lump, used mostly in batteries and found primarily in Sri Lanka.

Synthetic carbon and graphite comes in three basic product categories. Electrodes composed the industry's largest product category. Making up over half of the industry's products, electrodes were used in all types of electric furnaces. Graphite fibers were the second largest category of graphite products. Synthetic powder, made from scraps that are pulverized into a powder, make up the bulk of the remainder of synthetic products.

Industrial uses of graphite and carbon began in the early 1800s. In 1800, Sir Humphrey utilized carbon in the electric arc, which used an electrode made out of charcoal. By 1857, after seven years of experiments with new electrodes yielding a purer carbon, De Grasses B. Fowler patented the process of making carbon plates by mixing ground coke with tar and shaping the mixture under pressure in molds. Soon after, in 1877, Charles F. Brush and Washington H. Laurence of Cleveland began to experiment with carbon electrodes, and by 1878, Brush was manufacturing electrodes.

In 1896, E.G. Atcheson patented a process that transformed amorphous carbon to synthetic graphite by heat treatment, which laid the foundation for the modern graphite industry. A succession of inventions followed in the electrothermal field, all of which required electrodes of carbon or graphite for their applications. For example, in 1896, H.Y. Castner patented a process that involved the heating of carbon electrodes by means of electricity so that a graphite-like form of carbon was produced. By 1899, the Atcheson Graphite Company was formed in Niagara Falls, New York, producing electrodes for Castner's electrochemical processes, with most of the production being exported to Europe, which was the center of the industry at the time.

In 1906, the first steel made with electric power was manufactured in the United States by the Holcomb Steel Company in Syracuse, New York, using German electrodes. As the industry progressed, larger and larger electrodes were needed. By 1914 there was a vast expansion in electric furnace capacity and in the electrochemical industry, leading to a rise in the demand for electrodes of all varieties. The 30-inch carbon electrode was produced in 1927 and the 40-inch carbon electrode followed a year later. Graphite electrodes progressed similarly, but at a slightly slower pace, with the 14-inch electrode introduced between 1914 and 1918. By 1937, the size of graphite electrodes reached 20 inches. At that time, Germany, England, France, Italy, and Sweden made graphite and amorphous electrodes. Carbon products were made in most countries including Europe and Japan.

By 1959 many new products followed. Filamentary carbon was made into graphite cloth and eventually carbon and graphite cloth, felt, yarn, tape, and fibers were to follow. These products had the desirable properties of not melting at high temperatures and under high pressures. Such applications for carbon and graphite increased exponentially, with many new firms capitalizing on the thermal stability, electrical conductivity, thermal conductivity, and corrosion resistance of carbon and graphite fibers.

By the early 1980s, however, world demand began to collapse because of the decline in consumption of graphite electrodes, particularly by the steel industry. This decline was attributed to improved electrode performance as well as lower priced electrode imports. By 1985, leading producer Union Carbide suspended production at its Clarksville, Tennessee, plant. A lower cost of production at their facilities in Yabucoa, Puerto Rico, and Columbia Tennessee, attributed to this closure. Later, they reopened the Clarksville facility in 1987.

At that time costs were rising, and carbon products firms were experiencing poor profitability. Union Carbide was not the only firm experiencing poor profitability and excess capacity. Fierce domestic and foreign competition was making it hard to meet rising costs in new carbon electrode plants. Declining demand led to over-capacity in electrodes due mostly to low operating rates in steel mills. Coupled with this was the decline in the U.S. steel industry caused by heightened competition from foreign producers. Another key factor was the increased costs of fuels, such as natural gas used to carbonize coal to make carbon and graphite. Foreign competition was strengthened further by the strength of the U.S. dollar at the time, which increased prices of U.S. goods in proportion to foreign goods, and enabled consumers to purchase lower priced products from rival producers, predominantly the Italian and Japanese companies. Lastly, alternative products (titanium diboride electrodes were substituted for carbon or graphite) provided a 25-percent savings on electrical energy, which is a major expense in aluminum smelting. Accordingly, key aluminum producers, such as Kaiser Aluminum, Alcoa, and Alcan began using titanium diboride instead of carbon or graphite.

CURRENT CONDITIONS

In the late 1980s and early 1990s, mergers and acquisitions consolidated the industry, which shed some of its excess capacity. Towards the end of the 1990s, UCAR International, Inc., the largest manufacturer of carbon and graphite electrodes, remains positive for future growth in this market. In 1996, UCAR chairman and CEO, Robert Krass, indicated that over 78 million metric tons of new capacity in the electric steel making industry had been planned for installation between 1996 to 1999. This should maintain a constant demand of 1 to 2 percent per year for the carbon and graphite electrodes consumed in this manufacturing process. Furthermore, electrode pricing has remained favorable and there is no expected change in their global market. UCAR also announced the purchase of the graphite electrode business of Elektrokohle Lichtenberg AG in Berlin, Germany, in 1996 and in 1997, which completes the acquisition of Graphite PLC, the maker of graphite electrodes in Viazma, Russia.

WORK FORCE

From 1987 to 1991, total employment in carbon and graphite production fell from 9,800 to 8,400 people and by 1996, employment stabilized around 10,000 workers. Production worker employment fell from 8,500 in 1982, to 6,600 in 1986, before rising to 7,400 in 1988 and declining to 6,000 in 1991. In the mid-1990s, production worker employment was approximately 7,300 people.

Average hourly earnings of production workers in carbon and graphite production rose steadily from $4.25 in 1972 to $11.21 in 1987. In 1994, production worker wages reached $13.87 per hour, which was 15 percent higher than the $12.09 average of all manufacturing.

FURTHER READING

"Carbide Plans Major Expansion Program." *The Journal of Commerce,* 15 March 1977.

Darnay, Arsen J., ed. *Manufacturing USA,* 5th ed. Detroit: Gale Research, 1996.

Duffy, Hazel. "BOC Subsidiary Expands U.S. Graphite Production." *Financial Times,* 15 September 1979.

Glynn, Don, and Jones, Susan R. "At the Brink in Niagara Falls." *Chemical Week,* 5 June 1985.

"Great Lakes Carbon, Sigri Merge Operations." *Ceramic Industry,* March 1992.

Henry, David K., and Richard Oliver. "The Defense Buildup, 1977-85: Effects on Production and Employment." *Monthly Labor Review,* August 1987.

Mantell, Charles L. *Carbon and Graphite Handbook.* Huntington, New York: Robert E. Krieger Publishing Company, 1979.

Taylor, Harold A., Jr., "Graphite." *Mineral Facts and Problems 1985 Edition.* Washington: GPO, 1985.

Taylor, Harold A., Jr. "Graphite." *Minerals Yearbook.* Washington: GPO, 1991.

U.S. Bureau of the Census. *Census of Manufactures.* Washington: GPO, May 1990.

U.S. Department of Commerce. *U.S. Industrial Outlook 1994.* Washington: GPO, January 1994.

—John A. Sarich, updated by Andrew J. Poss

SIC 3625

RELAYS AND INDUSTRIAL CONTROLS

This category covers establishments primarily engaged in manufacturing electronic relays and industrial controls used for starting, regulating, stopping, and protecting circuits and electric motors. Mechanical switches and relays are classified elsewhere.

The industry encompasses two major categories: electronic relays and industrial controls. Electronic relays are used in circuitry for computers, communications equipment, and a multitude of other electronic devices. A relay is basically a switch that is used to open or close a circuit. It controls the flow of electricity to create a desired result. Most industrial controls are essentially switches, but of a more complex nature; They are usually associated with the control of electric motors and systems. Industrial controls include devices such as motor starters, contactors, control centers, and programmable logic controllers.

A conventional electronic relay contains a solenoid, which is a coil of wire with an enclosed, fixed iron core. When electricity passes through the wire a magnetic field is created that energizes the core. An armature connected to the core allows it to move and activate, or trip, the relay. Smaller relays used in transistorized equipment work similarly, but are much smaller and require a fraction of the power consumed by electromechanical relays. The tiny reed relay, for example, is made with two flat magnetic strips. The separated strips are sealed in a capsule filled with an inert gas (to prevent corrosion), which sits inside a coil. When electricity is applied to the coil the two magnetic strips are drawn to each other, thus completing a circuit. Finally, miniaturized solid-state relays are not magnetically activated, but are instead triggered by electrical pulses.

Relays made up only about 8 percent of product shipments in 1995. A wide range of industrial controls, many of which incorporate electromechanical and solid-state relays, constituted more than 80 percent of shipments. Two standards for industrial controls are administered by the International Electrotechnical Commission (IEC) and the National Electrical Manufacturers Association (NEMA). IEC-approved controls conform to standards which have brought them a reputation for compactness and affordability. Controls rated by NEMA, while considered less streamlined, are generally perceived by users to be more reliable and serviceable for heavy industrial uses. Parts, accessories, and miscellaneous related items made up the remaining share of industry products.

The largest consumer of relays and industrial controls in the 1990s was the computer equipment industry, which purchased 14 percent of production. Most of the remaining output was consumed by various manufacturing industries, particularly those producing electrical and electronic equipment. Machine tool producers, for example, made up about three percent of the market, and manufacturers of heating and air-conditioning equipment represented two percent of industry revenues. Other consumers of industrial controls included producers of mining machinery, automobiles, railroad equipment, aircraft, and construction equipment.

BACKGROUND AND DEVELOPMENT

One of the first practical applications of electrical relay technology was the telegraph, which was patented by Samuel F.B. Morse in 1844. Relays that were used to operate electronic devices were not developed on a significant scale until late in the nineteenth century, following Thomas Edison's work with the electronic vacuum tube. As the demand for lighting, phonograph, and other electrical devices flourished during the early 1900s, the need for relays surged. Importantly, U.S. investments in electronics research during World War II, which topped $1.5 per year, spawned significant advancements in all types of electronic components.

When integrated circuits were introduced in 1958, many manufacturers of relays and other electromechanical devices feared that the new solid-state components would make some conventional products obsolete. But the development of miniaturized relays served to expand the breadth of the industry and culminated in demand growth for both traditional and new devices during the 1960s and 1970s. Demand for relays boomed as a result of expanding consumer electronics, business machine, computer, and communications markets. Likewise, industrial controls evolved from relatively simple relay and switch devices used to start and control motors into complex, high-tech mechanisms used to regulate speed, pressure, timing, and other mechanical characteristics.

Overall demand for electronic components grew during the 1980s, bolstered by the proliferation of personal computers and peripherals, telecommunications equipment, and the integration of electronics into industrial and consumer products. Worldwide sales of integrated circuits, for example, jumped 464 percent during the decade. Shipments of many conventional relay products stagnated or declined, largely as a result of foreign competition. But the demand for new high-tech industrial controls, as well as some types of relays, thrived. By 1987, the peak of the 1980s economic expansion, industry sales reached $6.1 billion and employment topped 66,000.

CURRENT CONDITIONS

While the United States slumped into a recession during the late 1980s and early 1990s, sales of relays and industrial controls continued to climb at a healthy pace until 1991, when sales dipped by about 6 percent. Entering the mid-1990s, sales in 1995 climbed to more than $9.5 billion. In addition to strong demand, manufacturers benefitted from industry consolidation and increased efficiency which had characterized electrical component manufacturers during the 1980s. Indeed, as shipments grew producers continued to reduce employment through automation and restructuring.

The relays and industrial controls industry began to feel the pinch of recession in the early 1990s. Conventional relay shipments, which had already dropped 2.7 percent in 1991, were hit hardest. Nevertheless, overall sales climbed about three percent in both 1992 and 1993, and growth in some segments remained strong.

Three factors contributed to the success of relay and industrial control makers in the mid-1990s:

- The recovery of industries that purchased their products.

- Increased global competitiveness, which was the result of productivity gains and a devalued U.S. dollar.

- Technological advances that broadened the market for industrial controls.

Long term industry gains will partially depend on U.S. export growth. While exports accounted for only about 6 percent of sales in the early 1990s, they made up the fastest growing market segment and offered lucrative long term potential for sales of high-tech industrial controls. Canada and Mexico were the largest foreign consumers of U.S. exports and represented about 30 percent of cross-border revenues. European nations also consumed 30 percent of U.S. exports. But East Asian markets, which purchased 14 percent of exports in the early 1990s, showed the fastest growth. The United States imported a total of $650 billion worth of relays and controls annually in the early

1990s, more than 40 percent of which came from Japan.

INDUSTRY LEADERS

Despite steady consolidation in electronics components industries during the 1980s and early 1990s, the relay and industrial controls industry remained relatively fragmented in the mid-1990s with about 1,200 competitors. Most companies built industrial controls and specialized in a specific industry niche. With about 17 percent of the market share, the largest competitor was Allen-Bradley Company Inc., a producer of diverse electromechanical goods. This subsidiary of Rockwell International Corporation implemented a major restructuring effort in the early 1990s based on its benchmarking, or comparison, of other companies. It built a 27,000-square-foot, high-tech production facility that emphasized efficiency and the ability to quickly bring new products to market. The effort had successfully lowered development and manufacturing costs by 1993. Allen-Bradley had mid-1990s sales of more than $2 billion for all product lines.

Other significant forces in the industry include Siemens Corporation, a subsidiary of Siemens AG of Germany, and Square D Company, a subsidiary of Groupe Schneider of France.

WORK FORCE

The industry employed 63,400 workers in 1995. Despite a generally positive outlook for most companies in this industry, long term job prospects are less pleasant. Productivity gains and imports of some commodity-like relays and controls will continue to diminish opportunities, particularly for laborers. Jobs for assemblers and fabricators, which account for about 25 percent of the U.S. electrical apparatus work force, were predicted to decline by 30 to 50 percent between 1990 and 2005, according to the Bureau of Labor Statistics. Even positions for white collar managers and top executives expected to see cuts by about ten percent. Only jobs for sales professionals and engineers will increase, though slightly.

RESEARCH AND TECHNOLOGY

Advanced industrial controls represented roughly 20 percent of industry shipments going into the mid-1990s and is expected to continue to provide the greatest profit opportunities for U.S. firms throughout the decade. Electronic and computer-based controls were seen as eventually displacing conventional equipment, and devices based on the IEC standard were expected to replace NEMA-rated products in an increasing number of applications. Regardless of high-tech trends, U.S. producers in this industry lagged behind most other industrial sectors in capital investments, research, and development expenditures during the late 1980s and early 1990s.

One of the most prolific industry trends in the mid-1990s was the integration of fuzzy-logic into control systems. Fuzzy-logic employs the chaos theory, which holds that there are identifiable tendencies of movement amid apparently random patterns. Fuzzy-logic industrial controls are particularly well-suited for complex systems that are heavily dependent on human supervision. In addition to U.S. initiatives, Siemens and several Japanese firms were investing heavily in this new technology.

FURTHER READING

Avery, Susan. "What Buyers Need to Know About Industrial Controls." *Purchasing,* 20 June 1991.

Bergstrom, Robin P. "Where Fuzzy Thinking Isn't Wrongheaded." *Production,* August 1991.

Burrows, Peter. "Back to Basics Strategy Revives Control Maker Oak Industries." *Electronic Business,* March 1993.

Darnay, Arsen J., ed. *Manufacturing USA.* 5th ed. Detroit: Gale Research, 1996.

"Fuzzy Coprocessor Sharpens Industrial Controls." *Machine Design,* 23 July 1993.

U.S. Bureau of the Census. *1995 Annual Survey of Manufactures.* Washington: GPO, 1997.

Vasilash, Gary S. "A Singular Device." *Production,* June 1993.

Wexler, Joanie. "Users Grapple With New Option for Switched Data." *Network World,* 14 February 1994.

Yost, Larry. "The Allen-Bradley Story." *Journal of Business Strategy,* May/June 1993.

SIC 3629

ELECTRICAL INDUSTRIAL APPARATUS, NOT ELSEWHERE CLASSIFIED

This category covers companies that primarily make industrial and commercial electric apparatus, such as fixed and variable capacitors and rectifiers for industrial applications.

Product examples in the miscellaneous electrical industrial apparatus industry include battery chargers, non-electronic condensers, non-electric rectifiers, surge suppressors, and thermoelectric generators.

Companies that make capacitors and rectifiers are classified elsewhere.

Nonelectric rectifying apparatus used to convert alternating current to direct current accounted for about 50 percent of industry output in the early 1990s. Non-electric capacitor equipment made up about 12 percent of revenues. Other major product groups included coil windings (3.65 percent of sales), solenoids (2.53 percent), and cathodic protection equipment (1.7 percent). About 50 percent of output was sold to other manufacturing industries, and 30 percent was made for the U.S. military. Federal non-defense purchases contributed 10 percent of revenues. The remaining output went to other sectors, such as the automotive repair and communications industries.

American Lee DeForest patented an electrical vacuum tube in 1906, based on a design by Thomas Edison. This marked the beginning of practical electronics applications. Technological breakthroughs during both world wars also broadened the scope of the electronics industry. As electrical apparatus sales surged during the U.S. economic boom after World War II, miscellaneous electrical industrial apparatus shipments swelled. By the beginning of the 1980s, the industry was generating revenues of about $1.1 billion per year and employing a work force of more than 16,000.

Industry growth lagged during the 1980s, partly due to foreign goods coming into the United States containing parts made overseas. Also, more popular solid state components reduced demand for traditional electromechanical equipment produced in this industry. Even greater U.S. defense spending did not bring much growth. Sales increased to just $1.5 billion by 1990, reflecting a decline in inflation-adjusted revenues since 1980.

The industry emerged from a U.S. recession in the mid-1990s, with a healthier-looking future. Industry shipments for 1995 totaled $2.68 billion, up from $2.37 billion in 1994. Employment totaled 17,500 in 1995, 12,200 of which were in production. The total payroll for 1995 was $514.6 million, with $252.6 million of that devoted to production workers.

More than 1,700 companies competed in the miscellaneous electrical industrial apparatus industry in the mid-1990s. This was an increase from 450 companies competing in the late 1980s. The largest player was Exide Electronics Group Inc. of Raleigh, North Carolina. This public company had 1996 sales of $459 million and about 2,500 workers. Exide Electronics Group designs and makes UPS's, an Uninterruptible Power System. These devices, along with Exide's re-

lated software, protect information technology systems (e.g., PC's, mainframes, LANs, and WANs) from power surges, spikes, or interruptions.

Next in this category was Zexel USA Corp. of Decatur, Illinois, the U.S. subsidiary of a private Japanese company. Specializing in electronics and air-conditioning, Zexel's 1995 sales were estimated at $170 million, and the company employed approximately 800 people. Their most well-known product, as of 1997, was the Navistar electronic navigational system installed in Oldsmobiles.

Job prospects for this industry, at least for production workers, is projected to decline. Automation, restructuring, and foreign labor could reduce positions for U.S. production workers such as electrical assemblers, machine operators, and coil winders. There may be, however, more industry jobs for engineers, sales people, and technical support staff.

FURTHER READING

Darnay, Arsen J., ed. *Manufacturing USA*. 5th ed. Detroit: Gale Research, 1996.

Exide Electronics Group, Inc. company website. Available at http://www.exide.com/exide.

Hoover's Company Capsules. Austin, Texas: Hoover's, Inc., 1997. Available from http://www.hoovers.com.

U.S. Department of Commerce. *1995 Annual Survey of Manufactures*. Washington: GPO, 1997.

U.S. Industrial Outlook 1993. Washington: U.S. Department of Commerce, January 1994.

—Dave Mote, updated by Dave Fagan

SIC 3631

HOUSEHOLD COOKING EQUIPMENT

This category covers establishments primarily engaged in manufacturing household electric and non-electric cooking equipment, such as stoves, ranges, and ovens, except portable electric appliances. This industry includes establishments primarily engaged in manufacturing microwave and convection ovens, including portable. Establishments primarily engaged in manufacturing other electric household cooking appliances, such as portable ovens, hot plates, grills, percolators, and toasters, are classified in **SIC 3634: Electric Housewares and Fans.** Establishments primarily engaged in manufacturing commercial cooking equipment are classified in **SIC 3589: Service Industry Machinery, Not Elsewhere Classified.**

INDUSTRY SNAPSHOT

Household cooking equipment is part of the estimated $17 billion appliance market that includes white goods—washing machines, refrigerators, and other long-term appliances—in the United States. Like white goods, household cooking equipment is dependent on the housing economy and previous housing slumps have impacted the industry rather severely. This category also is described as a "mature" industry, with much consolidation occurring among the major appliance manufacturers. Demand for replacement of old and worn-out appliances drives the market, since most major appliances last 10-15 years.

White goods sales peaked in 1987 with 38 million units sold, but the industry endured a slowdown during the early 1990s. Overall product shipments of appliances grew 3 percent in 1993 to $17.7 billion, while housing starts only increased about 4 percent during the same period of time, according to the *1994 U.S. Industrial Outlook.* Household cooking equipment represented an estimated $3.3 million worth of shipments or about 20 million units in 1993.

Five major corporations dominate the household appliance industry and imports make up more than 50 percent of the domestic market in many categories of small appliances like coffeemakers. An objective of many of the main appliance manufacturers is to expand their markets globally. Many firms accomplished this by opening factories in Europe and Asia.

Appliance shipments were expected to increase 4 percent in the mid-1990s, reported the *U.S. Industrial Outlook.* The North American Free Trade Agreement may also help expand U.S. exports of home appliances to Mexico. In terms of five-year growth, shipments were projected to increase about 2 percent every year due in part to the fact that appliances are a mature industry. Most appliances are purchased for new housing, replacement, or remodeling. Private housing starts were predicted to increase 4 percent in the mid-1990s, as well, and the number of occupied housing units was expected to grow about 1 percent annually.

ORGANIZATION AND STRUCTURE

The top industry leaders of household cooking equipment were: Whirlpool Corp., General Electric Company (GE), White Consolidated Industries Inc., Sony Electronics, Inc., Maytag Corp., Sharp Electronics Corp., Washington Energy Co., and Sunbeam-Oster Company, Inc. Whirlpool is the largest major appliance manufacturer in the world, and dominates the industry. For example, Whirlpool has been the

major supplier of Sears, Roebuck & Co.'s Kenmore household cooking range line.

These main manufacturers produce the following brand name household cooking appliances: Whirlpool Corp. produces Kenmore, KitchenAid, and Whirlpool ranges; Maytag Corp. produces Magic Chef, Maytag, Admiral, Hardwick, and Jenn-Air ranges; General Electric produces GE, Hotpoint, and RCA electric ranges; White Consolidated Industries produces Frigidaire, Tappan, White-Westinghouse, and Gibson ranges.

About 98 percent of all major appliances, except microwave ovens, are American-made. Smaller appliances like coffee makers, food processors, and toasters, however, are imported from Europe. Some cooking equipment, like the GE cooktop range, sold in the United States is also manufactured overseas.

BACKGROUND AND DEVELOPMENT

A roaring fire in the chimney or pot bellied stove was the only way to cook food until Benjamin Franklin tried to tame the unpredictable flame with the Franklin stove. But his stove was only an iron box with flues and not a "range" as we know it—his invention only slightly improved open hearth cooking.

The development of cast iron ranges that burned coal or wood was the next improvement during the nineteenth century, but the heat source was also unpredictable and food had to be monitored constantly to prevent cooking disasters. While this type of device enabled a variety of foods to be cooked at once, these stoves were still dirty and often a fire hazard.

To the rescue came the gas burning stoves, developed in the mid-nineteenth century. The first use of gas to cook food in the home was demonstrated by James Sharp in Northhampton, England, between 1830 and 1832, states Lawrence Wright in his book *Home Fires Burning, the History of Domestic Heating and Cooking.* Gas burners concentrated heat at the cooking source and ensured that food was cooked more evenly and all the way through. The transition to gas cooking, however, required a major plumbing overhaul as pipes had to be hooked up to a stove. Middle- and upper-class housewives used the first gas stoves. Thermostatically controlled gas ovens began appearing in 1915, and essentially, freed cooks from the kitchen. Cooks could finally leave food unattended for brief periods of time without major incident.

The 1893 Columbian Exhibition at Chicago featured a "Model Electric Kitchen." Attempts to use electricity in home cooking occurred as early as the late nineteenth century. In 1905, the "General Electric

Range,'' equipped with its own switchboard, sat on metal legs with the oven well above the cooking surface. But until 1912, most electric ranges were converted gas cookers made of cast-iron and some insulation. In this type of range, all the heating elements were sealed in airtight containers to keep from burning out. Electric cookers relied on the "Bastian heater," or a wire spiral contained inside a quartz tube. Other improvements on this theme consisted of the Dowsing Electric Fire (with sausage lamps), resistance wires of nickel and chromium that heated without oxidization. But early electric cooking overloaded circuits, and was not made efficient until power companies were able to supply more electricity to homes.

Eventually, tabletops, cabinets, and drawers were added to gas burning stoves, which transformed the devices into "kitchen furniture." Because of the gas stove, cooking utensils evolved from wood to heavy cast iron and tin, to lightweight aluminum, tempered glass, and ceramic. Shirley Abbott and Bonnie Slotnick in *American Heritage Magazine* wrote that by the 1920s, gas ranges were made of white porcelain enamel, and within a decade, were produced in decorative colors to match other kitchen appliances and cabinetry. "The look of the American kitchen was thus set for the rest of the century," they wrote, " . . . light, spotless, efficient." Gas ranges revolutionized cooking, making it more sanitary and time saving, even considering the advances made in electric ranges. Gas ranges were still a preferred method of cooking in the latter twentieth century.

Consumers favor gas ranges over electric ovens because food can be cooked faster on a gas range, and gas ovens do not interfere with other electrical appliances. A gas range also does not leave residual heat. On the other hand, an electric range does not need to be lit. According to Wright, " . . . most have more useful cooking space in their ovens; some will simmer when the lid of the pan is on; all have or can have, automatic oven timers and more have spits . . . . Electric ranges did not compete with gas or solid fuel ranges until the 1930s.

"So if you are particularly keen on instant control of the heat, you will choose gas, if on cleanliness, and a wide choice of extras, electricity." However, improvements made on both types of ranges make them competitive in the market place. The choice between the two, in the 1990s, is one of preference and price.

In 1945, Percy L. Spencer, a researcher at Raytheon Co., invented the microwave oven. Spencer looked for a way to cook by radio waves. But it wasn't until he was working around a magnetron that he discovered that a candy bar melted in his pocket even though he had not felt any heat. He placed Indian corn in front of the magnetron and witnessed kernels popping.

Spencer later added a cabinet with trays to the machine and created the first "radar range." Microwave ovens were first used commercially before entering the home cooking market. Raytheon and Litton Industries Inc., both defense contractors, tried to sell microwave ovens in the United States, but did not meet with much success. Most consumers thought it was unnecessary to use a microwave in addition to a gas or electric range.

The Japanese entered the market, and became one of the first big manufacturers of microwave ovens, in part because the appliances fit the Japanese lifestyle perfectly. Japanese cooking requires reheating. And with Japanese houses and kitchens being smaller, microwave ovens were the perfect space savers. Japan exported microwaves to the United States in the 1970s, and five years later, the market had swelled to 2.2 million microwaves. American appliance manufacturers didn't try to reenter the market until the late 1970s. However, by this time, the Japanese already controlled 25 percent of the market.

Korean manufacturers like Samsung began entering the American market in the early 1980s, by supplying merchandisers like J.C. Penney Company, Inc. with inexpensive microwave ovens. Eventually U.S. manufacturers began producing microwave ovens that would compete directly with other imported models. Americans soon began to perceive microwave ovens as an adjunct to the kitchen. Microwave ovens can reheat leftover food and frozen items quickly, cleanly, and conveniently making meal preparation less of an ordeal. The development of such models like General Electric's Spacesaver oven helped make microwave ovens a valuable asset to the kitchen. However, conventional convection ovens (gas or electric) have not been completely replaced. Studies conducted in the late 1980s show that convection ovens are used to prepare the main meal or to cook meals from scratch. By 1994, statistics showed that 92 percent of all American households had a microwave. During 1995, 8.596 million microwave ovens were shipped and Sharp held 23.6 percent of the market share.

CURRENT CONDITIONS

Industry reports projected 14.3 million units of household cooking equipment were expected to be shipped in the first quarter of 1994. And according to *Appliance Magazine,* " . . . cooking appliance trends continue to emphasize cleanability, convenience, and sophisticated design, with a growing concern for energy efficiency.'' Major manufacturers focused on improving the overall product with new engineering. Consumers, the magazine stated, are becoming more interested in convection cooking appliances like wall ovens. And gas ranges may be gaining in more popularity as improvements in technology catch up with electric range and microwave ovens. Also, the glass ''cook tops'' that cover burners and electric coil eyelets became popular, as well as combined microwave/oven arrangements that save space and are more energy efficient.

INDUSTRY LEADERS

The top leading manufacturers of household cooking equipment are in order of ranking: Whirlpool Corp., $8.6 billion; General Electric Company (GE Appliances), $6.4 billion; Sony Electronics, Inc., $5.5 billion; White Consolidated Industries, Inc., $4.82 billion; Maytag Corp., $3 billion; Sharp Electronics Corp., $2.2 billion; Sunbeam-Oster Company, Inc., $984.2 million; Washington Energy Co., $967.2 million; and Whirlpool Corp. Findlay Division, $400 million.

Market share differs among the industry leaders depending on the household equipment category, although Whirlpool has been cited as the world leader in overall market share in core appliances including gas and electric ranges. Whirlpool's marketing strategy has been to produce specific appliances to serve a widening global consumer base. For example, it sells a 42-inch oven to African markets large enough to cook a whole sheep or goat.

General Electric held 24.5 percent of the electric range market and 16.7 percent of the gas range market in 1995. Maytag improved its share in electric ranges and dishwashers.

In terms of gas ranges, of which 2.853 million units were shipped in 1995, General Electric held the most market share of this category with about 16.7 percent, followed by Kenmore at 16.5 percent, and Tappan with 13.3 percent each. Maytag's share has been steadily slipping according to a Lehman Brother's 1993 industry report. It stated the company endured problems with a gas valve problem in its Magic Chef ranges in 1992. In 1995, Magic Chef still held the number four spot for market share according to brand name. GE acquired Roper's manufacturing facilities in 1991. GE also made gas ranges in Mexico, and had the capacity to produce more than its 1 million unit per year rate.

Market share in electric ranges, of which 4.048 million units were shipped in 1995, experienced more

shifts in share. Fifty-five percent of all units manufactured were white in color. GE leads here with 24.5 percent in 1995—the first time in ten years the company has fallen below 40 percent market share, according to a 1993 Lehman Brothers industry report. Sears/Tappan commanded 17.5 percent of the market share coming in second place, while Whirlpool came in third with 15.25 percent. Maytag dramatically slipped from 14 percent in 1992 to 4 percent in 1995.

WORK FORCE

Total employment for the household appliance industry was 106,000 in 1993, down from 117,000 in 1987. Production workers, however, numbered about 85,700 compared to 92,500 in 1987. Government sources also projected that workers in this industry would earn hourly wages averaging $11.29 in 1993, compared with $10.75 an hour in 1987. Employees in this category represented a total payroll of about $442.2 million in 1989.

AMERICA AND THE WORLD

Many appliances are American-made; however, other countries like Japan and South Korea became leading suppliers of white goods to the United States. The supplying other countries are Mexico, China, and Taiwan.

Imports and exports of appliances increased at nearly the same rate, according to the *1994 U.S. Industrial Outlook*—about 7 percent to $4.1 billion for imports and 6 percent to $2.5 billion for exports. American appliance manufacturers like General Electric formed joint partnerships with foreign companies to make stoves and microwave ovens overseas for the American market. Many of these foreign-made appliances then come under an American label. The *U.S. Industrial Outlook* stated that ''Mexico is expected to increase its lead regardless of the fate of the North American Free Trade Agreement, because of the growing integration of its appliance industry with that of the United States.'' Countries with traditionally lower wages, like South Korea and China, will continue to be major suppliers of small appliances. Microwave ovens still represent the majority of imported appliances, but in recent years, demand for microwaves has tapered off.

American manufacturers expanded their markets to be global leaders in the industry. Whirlpool led the way by owning a 70 percent stake in Inglis of Canada and in an Italian company. Whirlpool also has developed joint ventures with Indian and Mexican companies. In 1988, the company formed a joint venture with N.V. Philips of the Netherlands to make appliance for international markets. The leading markets for American appliances are Canada, Mexico, Japan, Germany, and Saudi Arabia, respectively. The lowering of tariffs between countries resulted in the doubling of exports to Canada since 1990. American exports to Mexico also doubled in the early 1990s because of such tariff reductions.

RESEARCH AND TECHNOLOGY

As mentioned earlier, household cooking equipment has undergone a gradual evolution since man discovered fire. But what is startling is that recent leaps and bounds in technology occurred within the last decade. Gas ranges used a basic grate and burner as the basic heating element needed to cook food. And although the microwave oven had been invented in the mid-1940s, it did not become widely used until the mid-1980s. Consumers only used gas or electric ranges (electric heating coils and or disks) for cooking.

In 1987, the National Appliance Energy Conversation Act established national efficiency standards for major household appliances including kitchen ranges and ovens. The law authorized the U.S. Department of Energy to propose standards in 1994. After a comment period, final standards were published in late 1994 to become effective by the end of 1997.

This national mandate comes in the wake of such improvements in technology that offer new options such as convection, induction, halogen, sealed burners, solid black glass and ceramic cooktops, and downdraft and radiant heating techniques—an array of options never available before. The new technologies have made ovens "self-cleaning," more fuel and energy efficient, safer, and even streamlined for decorative purposes. A consumer can reheat, thaw, barbecue, broil, grill, griddle, bake, boil, and poach food at the same time, on the same appliance, and in less time.

FURTHER READING

Abbott, Shirley, and Slotnick, Bonnie. "The Gas Range." *American Heritage,* May/June 1991, 30.

Cornell, R.T., et al. "Monthly Appliance Shipment Forecast-Industry Report." *Lehman Brothers, Inc.,* 29 October, 1993.

Darnay, Arsen, ed. *Service Industries USA.* Detroit: Gale Research, 1992.

Flint, Jerry. "Consumer Durables." *Forbes,* 8 January, 1994, 142.

"Global Growth Strategies." *Appliance Manufacturer,* January 1992, 13.

"Gas Ranges Cooking; Hot in Sept., 9 Months." *HFD-Weekly Home Furnishings,* 5 November, 1990, 144.

Harris, John M. "Household Appliances." *U.S. Industrial Outlook, 1994,* 36-11.

"In Praise of Mighty Microwave Oven, FF Leaders Call for Standardization." *Quick Frozen Foods International,* January 1988, 108.

Lazich, Robert S. *Market Share Reporter 1996.* Detroit: Gale Research, 1996.

Lazich, Robert S. *Market Share Reporter 1997.* Detroit: Gale Research, 1997.

Magaziner, Ira C., and Patinkin, Mark. "Fast Heat: How Korea Won the Microwave War." *Harvard Business Review,* January-February 1989, 83.

"Microwave Ovens Are Making Macro Advances." *Nation's Restaurant Business News,* 18 October, 1993, 58.

Predicasts Forecasts, 1993. Foster City, CA: Information Access Co., Annual Issue No. 32, 4th Quarter.

Predicasts Forecasts, 1994. Foster City, CA: Information Access Co., Annual Issue No. 134, Jan. 18, 1994, 2nd Quarter.

"Three New England Inventions that Changed Parties Everywhere." *Yankee,* January 1993, 30.

Underwood, Elaine. "Manufacturers Look for New Frontiers," *AdWeek's Marketing Week, Superbrands* 1990 supplement, September 1990.

Wright, Lawrence. *Home Fires Burning, the History of Domestic Heating and Cooking,* London: Routledge & Kegan Paul, 1964.

—Evelyn Dorman, updated by Jennifer L. Stong

SIC 3632

HOUSEHOLD REFRIGERATORS AND HOME AND FARM FREEZERS

This category covers establishments primarily engaged in manufacturing household refrigerators and home and farm freezers. Establishments primarily engaged in manufacturing commercial and industrial refrigeration equipment, packaged room coolers, and all refrigeration compression and condenser units are classified in **SIC 3585: Air-Conditioning and Warm Air Heating Equipment and Commercial and Industrial Refrigeration Equipment**, and those manufacturing portable room dehumidifiers are classified in **SIC 3634: Electric Housewares and Fans.**

INDUSTRY SNAPSHOT

As the household refrigerator and freezer industry, and the appliance industry in general, entered the 1990s, it was dominated by five companies in the United States. In order of dominance, these companies included: Whirlpool, General Electric, Electrolux (brand name Frigidaire), Maytag, and Raytheon (brand names Amana, Caloric, Speed Queen, Unimac, and Heubsch). In 1996 freezer sales totaled $1.69 billion, and sales of refrigerators totaled $8.67 billion. Most of these companies sold appliances under many brand names, which have been around since home refrigeration became feasible in the late 1920s. The top refrigerator in the mid-1990s was Whirlpool's Kenmore, sold by Sears, Roebuck and Co. with 20.1 percent of the market, and closely followed by GE's Profile line with 19.6 percent, Whirlpool's own brand with 11.5 percent, and Amana with 8.5 percent. Other brands with small fractional ratings included Hotpoint, Roper, Maytag, Admiral, and White-Westinghouse. Among leading freezer brands, according to the May 1996 edition of *Dealerscope,* Tappan held the lead in a very fragmented market with 5.25 percent in 1995; Amana followed with 4.2 percent. That year, a combined total of 4.87 million refrigerators and freezers were sold, according to *Appliance* magazine.

By the beginning of the 1990s, decades of consolidation had left an industry with little room for growth domestically. There were no smaller companies left for the large corporations to buy. According to *Appliance* magazine, the industry was mature with 99.9 percent of American households possessing refrigerators; about 40 percent of homes contained a freezer.

Shipment of refrigerators represented the largest share of the appliance industry, with General Electric the leader, and Whirlpool following. According to *Standard and Poor's* industry survey, brand loyalty was strong in the replacement appliance market, and although percentages shifted from year to year, it was unlikely that any manufacturer would take a serious bite out of another manufacturers' market shares.

The five big companies of this industry all instituted programs to improve productivity. The industry was considered one of the most efficient in the country—leaving little room for foreign products to take any significant market share as they had in the car and electronics industries. In addition, prices of American refrigerators and freezers remained reasonable. Several stylish European appliances found a small market in the United States, but they were unlikely to take any significant market share because of their expense. The mid-1990s also saw domestic appliance manufacturers increasing their focus on a stylish product.

The manufacturers' best opportunities for growth in a low-growth industry were to expand their profit margin, either by raising prices or cutting production costs and operating expenses, and by increased sales

abroad. The refrigerator industry enjoyed a steady market for replacements and units for new homes.

U.S. manufacturers were under serious environmental pressure in the 1990s to increase recyclability of refrigerators, reduce energy consumption, and eliminate chlorofluorocarbons as the refrigerant in refrigerators and freezers.

ORGANIZATION AND STRUCTURE

Both the manufacturers and appliance distributors were busy consolidating in the 1970s and 1980s. As the distributors became larger, they wanted more pricing and service concessions. This put pressure on manufacturers as they had to accept smaller profit margins. The manufacturers were better able to provide concessions through their own consolidation, which streamlined operations. This consolidation enabled them to produce more efficiently and maintain tight profit margins despite large volume discounts to giant distributors and mega-retailers. The suppliers of the manufacturers—especially the steel industry—rose to the challenge in the early to mid-1990s improving processes and the ability to deliver more finished and more flexible products and processes. Gains in such procedures as powder painting and custom steel cutting made for faster turn-around and further cuts in the cost of manufacture.

Home Furnishings Daily wrote that 10 retailers handled more than 44 percent of the appliance market in 1992. The largest was Sears with a 29 percent share of the market. The large retailers deal directly with the manufacturers rather than with a middleperson, the distributor. In a slow economy, manufacturers try to streamline marketing and distribution and one way to do this is to cut out the distributor.

This trend towards selling directly to mass merchandisers hurt many distributors who had exclusive contracts with particular manufacturers. Many smaller distributors were driven out of business because they heavily depended upon a particular manufacturer for most of their inventory, or they depended upon a few large retailers, who suddenly decided to deal directly with the manufacturer for most of their sales. Meanwhile, small retailers were concerned that they were too small to have much clout dealing directly with the manufacturer and needed distributors to represent them.

But some manufacturers were also becoming disenchanted with marketing directly to large retailers, finding that brand loyalty and profits were declining, and loyal distributors and dealers were going out of business. GE's network of small dealers was down from 50 percent of sales in 1981 to only 35 percent 10 years later. In response, GE let its dealers electronically tap into the company's production schedules and place direct orders with a guarantee of two-day delivery.

Traditionally, dealers maintained large inventories of products; however, this trend was changing, and there was some speculation that retailer outlets would become showrooms, and products would be shipped directly from the manufacturer to the customer. In response, manufacturers would have to be able to guarantee delivery of appliances within a two- or three-day period. Appliance companies were also restructuring their sales departments to offer greater exposure of their entire product lines to more distributors or retailers. In the mid-1990s, all of the top manufactures had friendly "showrooms" on the Internet—homepages designed to speak directly to the consumer, and packed not only with a catalog of merchandise, but also with tips on how to set your refrigerator, how to choose the size of fridge you need, the proper way to move a fridge, and other practical facts.

BACKGROUND AND DEVELOPMENT

The history of electric refrigerators is relatively short. In the 1920s, few American households had refrigerators. Ice and ice boxes, an insulated box or cabinet in which a block of ice was set to keep items cool inside were the norm for keeping items cold.The ice could keep for several days if the box was well insulated and well sealed. Every few days, the ice had to be replaced.

During the mid-nineteenth century, many inventors patented their own versions of mechanical refrigerating machines that could make ice, and others that could keep things cool in a large compartment. In the Northeast, natural ice was available during the winter months; however, selling manufactured ice became a big business in the southeastern United States by the 1890s, and a few years later in the North as well. Breweries all over the country adopted refrigeration. Cold storage buildings became common in cities, meat packers were using refrigeration units, and even railroad cars and ships provided refrigerated transportation. But home refrigeration would wait several decades; the refrigeration required a bulky cooling system that was not practical for home use.

The quest for an effective mechanical refrigeration system for the home was widespread. Large companies as well as individual inventors could see how popular home refrigerators would be. People working to develop a refrigerator were often backed by large manufacturers who knew that if their inventors were

successful, the invention would be worth millions of dollars since the market was so vast. Cities in the United States and abroad were expanding and people lived farther and farther from the places where food was produced. They needed to keep more supplies on hand, but they needed a place to preserve them. Use of ice boxes was widespread, but a refrigerator would be more convenient.

Building and marketing a home refrigerator had many restrictions that the commercial units did not. The home unit had to be small enough to fit easily into the house; it had to be automatic and not require an operator as the commercial units did. It also had to use safer chemicals than the highly toxic or flammable ones used in commercial units. And even if those requirements were met, the unit had to be affordable, which meant mass production had to be possible.

During the beginning of the twentieth century, two avenues of development were being pursued—compression technology and absorption technology. Compression required electricity to power a pump called a compressor. Absorption required gas power and did not even need a motor. The first functional household refrigerator, the Domelre, was produced in Chicago in 1912. Six years later, American Nathaniel Wales designed a unit called the Kelvinator, which employed compression technology. The Kelvinator became the first mass-produced home refrigerator. In 1919, General Motors bought a small refrigerator company called Frigidaire, which also made compression refrigerators. By 1920, about 75,000 homes had refrigerators.

Since gas was the most widely used energy source, the absorption refrigerator would have seemed a better choice than compression. Yet dozens of companies were involved in refrigerator development, the few that had substantial corporate backing were working on compression machines.

General Electric had been working on commercial and household refrigerator development for many years, but it wasn't until 1923 that it put substantial resources into development of the home version. Officials at the company realized that refrigerators already on the market had certainly not been perfected and whoever solved some of the early problems could dominate the market. Refrigerators were expensive. They had dropped in price but still cost $450 for the most inexpensive model, a lot of money in a time when most people had annual incomes of less than $2,000. These early compression models used refrigerants ammonia, sulfur dioxide, or methyl chloride, which carried danger of explosion or poisonous leaks. The refrigerators also had a short life since these refrigerants were corrosive.

The first home refrigerators were also noisy and needed servicing every few months. Fortunately, the noisy motor was separate from the cooling box. The motor could be put in the basement or elsewhere. But the separation of the two parts also forced the compressor to work harder to pump the refrigerant to the cooling box in the kitchen.

Considering government requirements in the 1990s calling for refrigerators that would run on less electricity, it is ironic that in the 1920s a compelling reason to pursue compression technology was that it required electricity 24 hours a day and therefore, would use a lot of power. It was clear that most homes would soon have either gas or electric power. Electricity was in its infancy, but GE was betting that electricity would win out over gas. General Electric was also watching out for the interests of the electric utility companies, their main customers.

In 1927 General Electric began marketing the first refrigerator with a hermetically sealed motor and an attached cooling box. It was called the ''Monitor Top,'' because the motor was in a circular box on top of the cooling compartment. By 1929 the company had sold an astonishing 50,000 Monitor Tops. That same year, GE replaced the wood cabinet with steel and brought out its first all-steel refrigerators. In 1931, GE produced its one millionth Monitor Top refrigerator.

In the 1930s, General Motors' Frigidaire company developed the first use of chlorofluorocarbons as a refrigerant, technology that became the standard for decades and essentially eliminated the danger of fire and poisoning. In 1939, GE produced the first refrigerator with a freezer compartment as well as a cooling compartment.

The absorption unit was not completely out of the picture, however. Inventors were still working on improved versions, and once perfected they would have offered many advantages over the compression machines: they were not as noisy, they had few movable parts, and in many places gas was cheaper than electricity. But slowly the companies developing these machines went out of business; they received very little development or promotional capital from the gas companies or other corporations. Between 1926 and 1957 only one large company, Servel, manufactured and marketed absorption refrigerators. By 1940 there were four major manufacturers of compression refrigerators, and each was associated with a large corporation: General Electric, Westinghouse, American Motors' Kelvinator, and General Motors' Frigidaire.

Ice boxes remained common well into the 1930s and even into the 1940s, but refrigerators were becoming a large industry by the 1930s, despite the Depression. Prices came down with improved mass production, and consumers were also offered the opportunity to buy the appliance on an installment plan. The industry grew as refrigerator motors and refrigerant systems were made smaller and safer for home use. The refrigerator was constantly being improved, with features such as automatic defrost, ice makers, and redesigned interior shelving.

The freezer has not been nearly as successful as the refrigerator. The process for quick-freezing food started to take off in 1925, and families bought frozen food to keep in their new freezers. In the 1940s and 1950s freezers and the convenience of frozen food were in their heyday; families saved money by purchasing meat, frozen vegetables, and other items in large quantities. However, the freezer never quite caught on. They were expensive to run, which offset any savings from bulk purchases of food.

Until the early 1980s, there were 15 to 30 domestic appliance manufacturers. Consolidation whittled them down to the five major companies. Some of the most familiar names in refrigerators and freezers were actually owned by Electrolux of Sweden: Frigidaire, Kelvinator, White-Westinghouse, Gibson, and Tappan. Raytheon, primarily a defense contractor, acquired Amana in 1965 and produced refrigerators and other appliances under that established brand name.

CURRENT CONDITIONS

Market factors. Sales of refrigerators and freezers depend upon many factors. About 75 percent of appliance sales were for replacements due to serious repairs, redecorating, or moving. Market saturation for refrigerators was estimated at 99.9 percent in 1996, which meant only new development and replacement markets were left to develop. For freezers, saturation was at 41 percent in 1996. Compression refrigerators built in the previous few decades had an average life span of about 16 years, and refrigerators and freezers built in the 1990s had an average life expectancy of 15 and 12 years, respectively. In 1997 it was projected by *Appliance* magazine that 4.3 million refrigerators and 1.5 million freezers would need replacement. That year, only about a third of American homes contained freezers, however, although the replacement market was smaller, there was also room for expansion.

Refrigerator sales were also dependent upon housing starts. About 25 percent of appliance sales were linked to new construction of houses and apartment buildings. However, because of its steady replacement market, refrigerators were less dependent than other appliances upon housing starts.

The state of the economy also had a direct effect on refrigerator-freezer sales. Consumers were less likely to make purchases of replacement appliances during difficult economic periods, unless absolutely necessary. Prognosticators for 1997 projected very slow growth, -0.7 percent for standard refrigerators, 3.7 percent for compact refrigerators, and 1.0 percent for freezers. This stable, predictable market was expected to remain essentially unchanged through the turn of the millennium.

Environmental impact. Refrigerator and freezer makers faced strict new guidelines from the Department of Energy for 1993. The guidelines required higher efficiency standards, and manufacturers were making small changes to meet the energy-use goals, such as improving insulation, compressors, motors, and door gaskets. Interior dimensions on some machines were to be smaller to allow for thicker walls and doors. Another set of guidelines calling for even stricter energy efficiency was likely with a possible target date of 1998 for full implementation. Manufacturers were concerned that they would not be able to meet those requirements.

For the typical home of the early 1990s, a frost-free refrigerator or freezer was the second most expensive home appliance to operate besides the water heater. Appliance makers were required to include labels listing an estimate of the cost per year of running each appliance so that consumers could compare costs and energy usage.

In 1996, standards for a typical refrigerator limited total energy consumption to 690 kilowatt hours per year. Energy consumption for refrigeration declined 4 percent annually between 1987 and 1996, and is anticipated to decline another 2 percent per year through the year 2015.

The refrigerator and freezer industry was also under pressure to find an alternative coolant to chlorofluorocarbons (CFCs), which were believed to cause depletion of the ozone layer that protects the planet from dangerous cancer-causing ultraviolet rays. An agreement called the Montreal Protocol called for complete elimination of the use of CFCs by the year 2000; however, officials and environmentalists from many countries were pushing for elimination of CFCs sooner because of evidence that the level of CFCs in the stratosphere over North America was even worse than originally reported. (See the Research and Technology section for more on the redesign of refrigerators and freezers.)

Congressional bills called for manufacturers to recycle both packaging and the products themselves. The bills stipulated that new products had to be easier to disassemble for recycling and that some packaging had to be reusable.

INDUSTRY LEADERS

Whirlpool was the leading refrigerator maker in 1996, with GE a close second. Whirlpool, including its Kenmore for Sears, Roebuck and Co. was also the top freezer maker, with GE a tight second. Whirlpool had sales of $8.69 billion in 1996.

In 1997, *Good Housekeeping* gave a "#1 in Customer Satisfaction" award to Whirlpool for its appliance line. The company, which started out making washing machines only, became a full-line appliance manufacturer in the 1950s and 1960s. At that time, it also became the principal supplier of the Sears Kenmore brand. Sears accounted for about 19 percent of Whirlpool's revenues in 1991. Between 1981 and 1991, Whirlpool's revenues shot up from $2.4 billion to $6.8 billion. Refrigeration equipment accounted for $2.3 billion in 1991.

In 1986 Whirlpool acquired KitchenAid, a high-end producer of appliances, including refrigerators. In 1991 Whirlpool completed its acquisition of Philips, the second largest appliance company in Europe. It also had partners in Eastern Europe, Brazil, Argentina, Mexico, Italy, and India. The Philips acquisition boosted Whirlpool's global presence and made Whirlpool one of the top two appliance makers in the world, along with Electrolux.

General Electric was a huge American conglomerate with revenues of more than $79 billion in 1996. Sales of major appliances accounted for about $7 billion. GE spent $120 million to build a new automated plant in Columbia, Tennessee, to make rotary compressors for refrigerators and establish a center at which employees would learn the skills to operate the high tech plant. GE bought a 50 percent share in a British appliance company in order to increase its European presence, and in 1996 made a landmark agreement with Japan's Kojima to distribute products directly through the 160-store Japanese retailer. In 1996 GE also invested $70 million in upgrading the top-mount refrigeration plant in Louisville, Kentucky.

At the beginning of the 1980s, Maytag was a small company making top-of-the-line washers and dryers in Newton, Iowa. But with the decade of consolidation beginning, Maytag saw that it either had to expand its product line or risk being taken over. When the decade ended, Maytag was making refrigerators, freezers, stoves, washers, dryers, microwaves, and even soft-drink vending machines and dollar-bill changers. It had plants in eight states and eight foreign countries. Sales of major appliances accounted for $2.8 billion in 1991 and $3.0 billion in 1996.

Maytag's acquisition of Hoover gave the company an instant presence overseas. In the United States, Hoover was known as a vacuum cleaner company, but overseas it also made refrigerators, as well as washers, dryers, and dishwashers. Of Hoover's sales of $1.4 billion, 60 percent was generated abroad.

Between 1970 and 1985, Electrolux, a Swedish company, bought more than 300 companies in 40 countries. Through its 1987 acquisition of White Consolidated Industries in the United States, it acquired rights to sell refrigerators and other appliances under the familiar American brand names.

Raytheon, an aerospace company, joined the appliance business through its acquisition of Amana in 1965. Amana was a cooperatively owned company run by the Amana Society, a German religious sect that had emigrated to Iowa. The society began making refrigerators in 1934. Raytheon also acquired two other appliance makers, Caloric and Speed Queen. In the early 1990s, there was speculation about the fates of Raytheon's Amana division and General Electric's appliance divisions. Because appliances made up a very small share of either company's business, industry observers wondered if the appliance divisions of these two corporate giants would be sold to foreign companies.

WORK FORCE

General Electric employed about 30,000 people at 12 domestic appliance plants in the early 1990s. The company was at the forefront of innovative workplace programs. With its "Work-Out" program, teams of 50 to 60 people, including suppliers, customers, production workers, engineers, and marketing and sales people, met to brainstorm and come up with recommendations to the business staff.

Whirlpool was involving workers in a different way. It was trying a special incentive program at one of its appliance plants in order to improve production. Improved productivity translated into an extra $2,700 in annual pay, raising average annual wages for production workers to $26,400 in 1991. The more productive the plant, the larger the pool of money for the workers to share. The improvements in productivity reduced costs for the company and boosted profits; quality also improved at the plant, with fewer mistakes or bad parts. The plant also opened a new training

center. As part of its program to involve production workers more in the total process, the company offered workers the opportunity to see how the components made were used in the finished appliance. Other Whirlpool plants were also achieving higher productivity and lower costs.

Maytag established "focus groups" to improve its manufacturing productivity. All products in a category were to be produced at one plant; therefore, all refrigerators in all price ranges would be developed in one plant to improve design and efficiency.

AMERICA AND THE WORLD

Domestic appliance makers became more active in the European market as another avenue for growth. GE especially looked overseas in the mid-1990s to increase profits and invest for long-term growth. In 1991, Europe accounted for about a third of Whirlpool's sales and 15 percent of Maytag's sales. In 1996, Whirlpool was disappointed by dropping European profits, but the company was looking forward to slightly better overseas performance in 1997. Because of stronger markets in North and Latin America, they posted record earnings—a rise of 21 percent for the first quarter of 1997 compared against first quarter 1996. In 1996, GE's profits from its entire European operations, including non-appliance related, resulted in $1 billion, or almost 15 percent of its net profit worldwide.

European demands differed from American demands in appliances; European appliances tended to be smaller and more stylish. In 1996 GE redesigned the distinctive Profile line of appliances to appeal to the European eye.

Southeast Asia was a tough market that U.S. makers for the most part had left alone since it was dominated by three Japanese businesses: Matsushita, Hitachi, and Toshiba. In 1996, GE struck a deal with Japan, allowing GE products to be retailed directly to Japanese consumers.

The leading export markets for U.S. appliances were Canada, Mexico, Taiwan, Germany, and Saudi Arabia. The complete lifting of any tariff on appliances between the United States and Canada was scheduled for 1998, and the gradual reduction in tariffs in the meantime brought increased sales there.

RESEARCH AND TECHNOLOGY

A typical 15-year old refrigerator consumed about 1,700 kilowatts of electricity, for an average cost of $136 based on a cost of eight cents a kilowatt-hour. That meant a consumer would pay 5 or 6 times the price of the refrigerator in energy costs over the refrigerator's lifetime.

More recent models consumed less than half that many kilowatts, generally about 700 kilowatts annually. According to industry demands, a responsible, state-of-the-art refrigerator would consume between 350 and 525 kilowatts a year. According to the Environmental Protection Agency (EPA), that represented an annual savings for American consumers of half a billion dollars or more in electrical bills. This reduction in energy costs would translate into a reduction in use of the fuels that generate electricity—coal, oil, and nuclear materials. The EPA estimated that widespread adoption of the new refrigerators would save the country 3 to 6 billion kilowatt-hours a year, which would require from 5 to 10 million barrels of oil to generate. According to utility companies, refrigerators and freezers consume 20 percent of the electricity used in a home. Development of more efficient refrigerators would reduce demand for electricity and even curtail the need for new power plants.

A compression refrigerator works when the refrigerant, a liquid chemical, is pumped through the tubes in the cooling cabinet. It evaporates there and pulls heat from the air. The gas is pumped out of the cabinet and into the compressor and condenser where the heat is expelled into the room. The evaporator chemical becomes liquid again and is pumped back into the food area.

Chemical companies, such as DuPont, as well as refrigerator makers and environmentalists were involved in development of alternative refrigerants. One of the alternative refrigerants being suggested was a hydrofluorocarbon (HFC). Use of an alternate substance such as this would allow refrigerator makers to retain the current technology of the vapor-compressor refrigerator. One of the other proposed refrigerants was said to be dangerous because it posed a risk of fire or toxic fumes, while environmentalists claimed that another posed an environmental threat because, although it was not harmful to the ozone, it might contribute to the greenhouse effect. Furthermore, because chlorofluorocarbons (CFCs) were also used in refrigerator insulation, several possible replacements would require new liner materials.

Another approach was represented by the work of U.S. physicist, Steven L. Garrett, who was developing a thermo-acoustic refrigerator that used sound instead of CFCs to transfer heat. This technology, which was first designed for military satellites, would be less harmful to the environment than any substance in a vapor-compressor refrigerator. Even so, thermo-acoustics would require big changes by manufacturers

to retool their facilities or send their production workers back to school to learn a new technology. Alternative refrigerants would not require these changes.

Researchers financed in part by the EPA built demonstration CFC-free refrigerators that were 8 to 16 percent more energy-efficient than existing refrigerators cooled by CFCs. These test refrigerators also cooled freezer and refrigerator sections separately instead of using the same air to cool both sections, as traditional models did.

German scientists were working on a refrigerator that used a mixture of propane and butane in place of CFCs. The unit they were working on, however, had no freezer compartment and used more electricity than that used by a typical refrigerator cooled by CFC vapor compression. Italian scientists used the same vapor-compression technology that is found in CFC-refrigerators, but substituted a hydrofluorocarbon—HFC-134a. The refrigerator had two modules for refrigeration and one for freezing; the modules were made from polystyrene and made recycling and manufacture easier. The power pack was easily removable for recycling or repairs.

FURTHER READING

1995 Annual Report. General Electric. Available from http://www.ge.com/annual95/ibb6a18.htm.

Bergstrom, Robin. "It's Not by Magic." Production, February 1991,36-9.

Business Rankings Annual 1997. Detroit: Gale Research, 1997.

Cohen, Daniel. The Last Hundred Years: Household Technology. New York: M. Evans, 1982.

Conley, Thomas P. "Combating the Slow Growth Scenario for Housewares." Appliance. January 1997,68.

Cowan, Ruth Schwartz. More Work for Mother. New York: Basic Books, 1983.

Enders, John. "The Race for a Safer Fridge Heats Up." Syracuse Herald-American, 13 June 1993.

"Energy Demand by End Use." Available from www.eia.doe.gov/oiaf/aeo97/res_com.html.

Koenig, Peter. "If Europe's Dead, Why Is GE Investing Billions There?" Fortune. 9 September 1996.

Lazich, Robert S., ed. Market Share Reporter. Detroit: Gale Research, 1997.

Le Blanc, Jenny. "1997: Slow Growth Ahead." Appliance, January 1997, 38.

McCoy, Charles. "Two Big Firms to Vie to Build a Better Fridge." Wall Street Journal, 8 December 1992, B1.

Moskowitz, Milton, Robert Levering, and Michael Katz. Everybody's Business: A Field Guide to the 400 Leading Companies in America. New York: Doubleday, 1990.

"Portrait of the U.S Appliance Industry." *Appliance,* September 1996.

"Process and Product Design." *Appliance,* September 1996.

Samuel, Peter. "Will Your Next Refrigerator Explode?" *Consumers' Research,* July 1992, 16.

Tannenbaum, Jeffrey A. "Enterprise: Amana Refrigeration Fights Tiny Distributor." *Wall Street Journal,* 26 February 1992, B2.

———. "Enterprise: Distributors' Links to Producers Grow More Fragile." *Wall Street Journal,* 28 October 1992, B2.

Wartzman, Rick. "Sharing Gains: A Whirlpool Factory Raises Productivity." *Wall Street Journal,* 4 May 1992, A1.

"Whirlpool Earnings Rise 21 Percent." *Reuters,* 16 April 1997.

—Wendy Stein, updated by Lisa Calhoun

SIC 3633

HOUSEHOLD LAUNDRY EQUIPMENT

This classification covers establishments primarily engaged in manufacturing laundry equipment, such as washing machines, dryers, and ironers, for household use, including coin-operated equipment. Establishments primarily engaged in manufacturing commercial laundry equipment are classified in **SIC 3582: Commercial Laundry, Drycleaning, and Pressing Machines,** while those manufacturing portable electric irons are classified in **SIC 3634: Electric Housewares and Fans.**

INDUSTRY SNAPSHOT

Although mechanical washing contraptions existed before the start of the twentieth century, only since the 1950s has gas and electric-powered laundry equipment achieved widespread use. By the early 1990s, over 70 percent of all U.S. homes had both a washer and a dryer. In 1997, Whirlpool Corporation held the lion's share of the market. With its own Whirlpool brand, combined with the Kenmore brand it manufacturers for Sears, it held 53 percent of the market. General Electric Company and Maytag Corporation were tied at 17 percent, and Frigidaire Company and Raytheon Company brought up the rear in a market essentially dominated by these five appliance companies.

In 1996, 6.921 million washers and 5.240 million dryers (both electric and gas) were shipped. Laundry equipment was the second largest home appliance market, following refrigeration. With commercial laundry appliances, the total number of shipments in the industry was 12.165 million units in 1996.

ORGANIZATION AND STRUCTURE

Household laundry equipment represented about 17 percent of the overall U.S. household appliance industry in the 1990s. Although ironers and mangles, or pressing machines, account for a small portion of industry sales, washers and dryers made up the lion's share of production.

Nearly 80 percent of all household laundry equipment is purchased by individuals for home use. An additional 6 percent of industry output is consumed by laundromats, dry cleaners, and other services that use domestic laundry equipment. The remainder of the U.S. market is comprised of state, local, and federal government institutions, such as the armed forces and prisons. Over 7 percent of U.S. production in the early 1990s was exported.

The market for first-time purchasers of washers and dryers is relatively saturated. As a result, the industry is highly dependent upon sales of replacement appliances. Most laundry equipment has a life span of 10 to 12 years. However, several factors may influence the replacement rate of washers and dryers. An increase in sales of existing homes, for example, boosts replacements because new occupants are more likely to buy new appliances. Likewise, heightened remodeling activity also spurs replacements.

Changes in home trends may also spawn premature replacements. For instance, as laundry equipment was increasingly moved out of basements and closer to living areas in the 1980s, the need for quieter and more attractive washers and dryers caused an influx of consumers to upgrade. Increases in repair costs in relation to price of new units can also shorten replacement cycles. Finally, because appliances are discretionary purchases that can be postponed, industry revenues are closely tied to the health of the overall economy.

Types of Products. The three major household laundry product categories were electric washing machines, electric dryers, and gas dryers. Washers are of two types: top-load and front-load. Top-load washers have an agitator in the center of the wash tub that thrashes the water and the fabric. Front-load, or tumble-type, washers lift and drop the laundry into the wash water as the tub spins. Both washer types wring out excess water by spinning.

Although many top-loading machines are easier to access, tumble-type washers require less water and detergent to clean a load of laundry. Both types of washers are differentiated primarily by their features, which include washing actions, capacity, water temperature combinations, water levels, and noise levels. Most top-load washers range in price from $400 to $550, while front-load machines usually cost an additional $100.

Dryers are basically revolving drums which tumble clothes through heated air. Different features and product quality result in a price range of $400 to $800. More expensive dryers offer as many as three different heating cycles, extended tumble cycles, wrinkle-remove features, and sturdier construction, such as porcelain coated drums and tops. Although gas dryers are typically more expensive to purchase initially, they are often significantly cheaper to operate. In 1996, manufactures sold 1.2 million gas dryers, compared with 4 million electric dryers.

BACKGROUND AND DEVELOPMENT

Numerous washer and dryer devices, ranging from washboards to hand-cranked wringers, were used to clean laundry prior to the twentieth century. The first electric washing machine was introduced in 1907 by the Maytag Company. But not until after World War II, during the post-war U.S. economic expansion, did electric washing machines, and later dryers, realize mainstream acceptance. As the demand for all types of appliances proliferated during the 1950s, 1960s, and 1970s, the laundry equipment industry grew rapidly. The introduction of fully automatic washers and dryers in the mid-1960s rocketed the industry to prominence during the following decade, as washers and dryers became standard household amenities.

By the early 1980s, the laundry equipment industry was shipping over $2 billion worth of goods annually and employing over 16,000 workers. Well over 50 percent of U.S. households had both a washer and a dryer. Strong home construction and appliance replacement markets, moreover, allowed producers to enjoy solid gains throughout the 1980s. Indeed, industry revenues grew at an average annual rate of over five percent between 1982 and 1990, despite an economic slowdown in the late 1980s. Sales surged past $3.2 billion in 1990, stagnated in 1991, and grew about 3 percent in 1992.

An important dynamic which characterized the laundry equipment industry during the 1980s was consolidation. As the vigorous growth of the late 1960s, 1970s, and early 1980s waned, producers tried to achieve economies of scale though merger and acquisition. By the end of the 1980s only 16 competitors remained, compared to over 25 at the start of the decade. In fact, the top two companies controlled nearly 70 percent of the market, and the top four

manufacturers accounted for about 80 percent of sales. Antitrust laws enacted during the 1980s succeeded in slowing the rate of consolidation by the early 1990s.

Positive demographic trends and healthy housing starts helped boost household laundry equipment sales by more than 50 percent between 1980 and 1990. Although industry participants suffered the effects of recessed construction markets and economic malaise in the early 1990s, sales were rebounding going into the mid-1990s and analysts predicted that shipments would continue to grow at a rate of 1 percent to 3 percent through the end of the decade.

To boost sales and profits in 1994, washer and dryer manufacturers were striving to develop new and better appliances which would spur replacement sales, while also scrambling to comply with new federal environmental regulations. In addition, most were seeking growth overseas, in regions such as Asia and Mexico.

Manufacturers were able to boost unit shipments faster than revenues and retain profit growth through productivity gains. Indeed, hefty capital investments in automation and information systems during the 1980s helped the appliance industry become one of the most efficient businesses in the United States. As the value of washer and dryer shipments grew 50 percent during the 1980s, unit prices remained stable in real dollars and unit volume soared. Despite a huge surge in real output, industry employment actually declined slightly during the decade. Efficiency gains contributed to the industry's dominance of the domestic market, of which it controlled a whopping 85 percent.

In addition to short term economic factors and production efficiencies, laundry equipment manufacturers in the mid-1990s also benefited from long-term demographic factors and buying patterns. Importantly, the baby boom generation, aged 35 to 54 years, was becoming wealthier and was investing a greater share of its income in home-related goods. Because this important market segment was also spending an increasing amount of time working and having children, analysts expected boomers to begin spending a greater proportion of their income on conveniences, such as washers and dryers.

Augmenting renewed sales were new distribution and customer service programs, which manufacturers were initiating. Many producers, for example, were strengthening their support for retailers with training and service programs. Likewise, customer relationship initiatives were helping manufacturers cultivate consumer loyalty. Whirlpool, for example, announced early in 1994 that it was going to replace its system of independent distributors with factory-direct distribution.

CURRENT CONDITIONS

Laundry industry sales grew about 2 percent per year from 1990-1997. Unit volume grew annually at a steady 2-3 percent. Increased sales were largely the result of an uptick in housing starts and escalating consumer expenditures following the recession. The replacement market for washers and dryers was a constant; for example, in 1996, 3.396 million washing machines were replaced.

Federal Regulation. New U.S. Department of Energy Standards (DOE) initiatives, which took affect in May of 1994, required machine makers to lower rinse-water temperatures, reduce water consumption, and install energy-efficient motors and insulation. In a 1996 study conducted by a Maytag R&D team, it was discovered that a high-efficiency washer can save from 3,500-6,000 gallons of water per household per year. In the mid-1990s, manufacturers strove to rise to the challenge. They started using solid concrete weights in washers to steady the machine during the spin cycle. Previously, energy-intensive iron casts weighted laundry machines. New washers also offered wash programming, to allow the user to program the washing machine to start the wash during nonpeak electric hours. New methods also included recycling the dirty wash water into clean rinse water, increasing the use of enzymatic detergents and reducing foaming detergents, and spray rinse cycles instead of deep rinse.

Manufacturers were also under pressure to increase the recyclability of their machines. Two Congressional bills that failed to pass in 1992 would have mandated product material content, recycling rates, and packaging. In anticipation of new laws, some producers were striving to improve the recyclability of their machines by making them out of components that could be recovered, restored, and reused.

Future Growth. Besides baby-boom patterns, overall U.S. household formations were expected to rise during the 1990s, from 93.1 million in 1990 to 106 million in 2000. This should result in steady growth of first-time appliance buyers. Furthermore, because a large percentage of existing washers and dryers were purchased in the early 1980s, some observers expect replacement sales to increase in the latter part of the 1990s as old machines wear. The industry was also expected to benefit from low interest rates, a reduction in inventories in 1994, more strategic inventory management in the future, and export growth. Greater demand for compact washers and dryers that suit smaller living spaces will offer a small, high-growth

niche. In 1996 *Appliance* magazine cited five technologies that will help define the laundry manufacturer's path to the millennium: increasing water extraction to improve clothes care; using low-sudsing detergents and creating technologies that use those kinds of detergents effectively; faster spin cycles; and electronic sensing and process of the wash.

INDUSTRY LEADERS

The laundry equipment industry was highly consolidated. The top four companies accounted for about 80 percent of all shipments. Whirlpool Corporation, the industry behemoth, captured over 50 percent of the U.S. washer and dryer market in 1996. General Electric Company and Maytag Corporation each garnered about 17 percent of overall sales. Electrolux, of Sweden, met approximately 13 percent of U.S. demand.

Maytag is credited with giving birth to the industry, and has a proven reputation for supplying high quality washers and dryers. Maytag began by selling farm equipment, but invented electric laundry machines in the early 1900s. In 1966 Maytag introduced fully automatic washers, and in 1976 brought out a complimentary line of dryers. It maintained a focused product line until the 1980s, when it acquired Hardwick Stove in 1981, Jenn-Air in 1982, and Magic Chef in 1986. In an effort to expand its overseas operations, Maytag formed a strategic alliance with Germany's Bosch-Siemens in 1993. Maytag and Siemens shared design and process technologies. Maytag's total sales in 1996 were $3 billion, a touch below its 1995 figures of $3.039 billion.

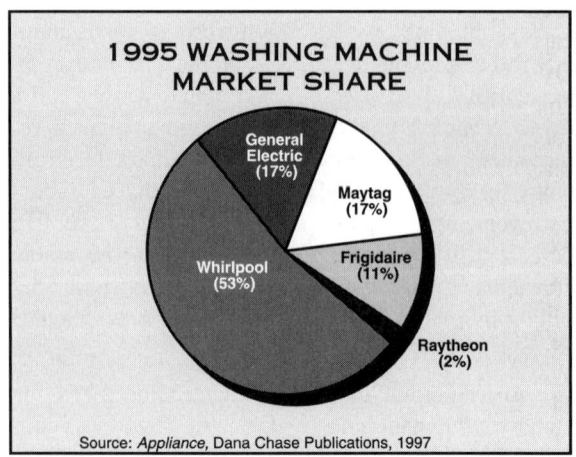

1995 WASHING MACHINE MARKET SHARE

General Electric (17%)
Maytag (17%)
Frigidaire (11%)
Whirlpool (53%)
Raytheon (2%)

Source: *Appliance*, Dana Chase Publications, 1997

Whirlpool overtook General Electric in 1993 to become the world's largest appliance manufacturer, with 1996 revenues of $8.69 billion. Leading edge production techniques and improved product quality helped Whirlpool achieve a record $205 million profit in 1992 from $6.3 billion in sales. After realizing growth of 14 percent annually during the 1980s, Whirlpool was concentrating on global expansion in the 1990s, and was investing heavily in Asian and European markets.

WORK FORCE

Although the top four laundry equipment producers expected to increase production throughout the 1990s, many analysts expected industry employment in the United States to decline. Heightened campaigns for greater productivity, the likely movement of some manufacturing activities to Mexico, and continued management restructuring may diminish opportunities for workers in the industry.

Assemblers and fabricator positions, which accounted for about 40 percent of the entire workforce, will plummet by as much as 37 percent between 1990 and 2005, according to the Bureau of Labor Statistics. Other blue-collar jobs in this industry will drop by 15 percent to 50 percent. Management and support opportunities are expected to decline as well. In fact, only jobs for sales and marketing workers were expected to increase. Despite workforce reductions, in the early 1990s laborers in this industry earned wages approximately 25 percent greater than the average of all other U.S. manufacturing industries.

AMERICA AND THE WORLD

U.S. washer and dryer makers supplied about 30 percent of global demand going into the mid-1990s. Although they exported less than 10 percent of total production, domestic producers were avidly seeking to capture a greater share of the world export market. Overall appliance exports grew 16 percent in 1992, continuing a trend started in the 1980s. The leading foreign markets were Canada, Mexico, Taiwan, Germany, and Saudi Arabia.

In the early 1990s a weak U.S. dollar boosted exports, particularly to Europe and Japan. In addition, exports to Mexico grew a healthy 18 percent, though imports from that country soared an estimated 40 percent as U.S.-Mexican joint ventures proliferated. While U.S. producers were benefitting from cheap Mexican labor, low-cost appliance manufacturers in other emerging regions, especially in Asia, posed a threat to future U.S. export growth.

Whirlpool, which derived about one-third of its revenues from overseas sales, had been the most successful U.S. exporter. It maintained substantial interests in South American countries, such as Brazil and Argentina, and was working hard at penetrating the European market. Maytag was also advancing in Europe in the 1990s, and was garnering about 15 percent of its revenues from foreign operations. U.S. manufacturers have enjoyed less success in the Asian arena, which was dominated by three major Japanese appliance conglomerates.

Although U.S. washer and dryer makers held a stranglehold on domestic markets, their dominance was expected to wane in the wake of increased imports from Mexico. Passage of the North American Free Trade Agreement (NAFTA) in 1994 was expected to accelerate the movement of production facilities across U.S. borders—a trend which analysts predict should increase corporate earnings and reduce domestic employment and payrolls.

RESEARCH AND TECHNOLOGY

Capital investments during the mid-1990s were being used to develop more efficient production and distribution methods and to achieve compliance with environmental regulations and pressures. They were also being used to create better and less-expensive products. For example, control software that was being incorporated into machines optimized wash and dry cycles for different types of laundry, adjusted temperature and water levels during a cycle, and allowed machines to talk to users. These microprocessors were also making possible many advanced features, such as self-diagnostic systems, delayed-start timers, and touch controls with cycle programming. New features were also being designed to maximize energy efficiency—an improvement which could expedite replacement sales.

One of the most advanced innovations under development in the mid-1990s involves the study of washing machines that can use "fuzzy-logic." In 1993 South Korea's Goldstar Co. claimed to have invented the first consumer product that exploited the chaos theory, which holds that there are identifiable tendencies of movement amid the apparent randomness of patterns. Goldstar analyzed the movements of water in a standard washing machine, identified those that produced cleaner and less-tangled clothes, and then designed a washing machine that mimicked the movements. Whirlpool was integrating similar technology into some of its models. In the mid-1990s, machines appeared that could use Dialogic, a new term coined by Merloni Elttrodomestici, an Italian manufacturer. The machine only needs to be loaded, and told what is the most delicate garment in the wash. It then evaluates other wash factors to create the "perfect" wash—lowest possible noise, cleanest rinse, appropriate detergent, and appropriate water usage. "Smart" dryers sense the clothes' dampness, exactly when to shut off, and what kinds of temperatures at which to dry.

FURTHER READING

Babyak, Richard. "Team Effort." *Appliance Manufacturer,* April 1993.

Berardinis, Lawrence A. "It Washes! It Rinses! It Talks!" *Machine Design,* 12 September 1991.

"Clothes Dryers." *Consumer Reports,* July 1993.

Conley, Thomas P. "Combating the Slow Growth Scenario for Housewares." *Appliance.* January 1997, 68.

Crystal, Charlotte. "How Not to Move to Mexico." *International Business,* September 1993.

Koselka, Rita. "Red Faces in Michigan," *Forbes,* 2 August 1993.

Darnay, Arsen J., ed. *Manufacturing USA.* Detroit: Gale Research, 1996.

"Factory Unit Shipments." *Appliance,* February 1994.

General Electric Company. *1995 Annual Report.* Fairfield, CT, 1996. Available from http://www.ge.com/annual95/ibb6a18.htm.

Holding, Robert L. "Anticipating 1994 for Home Appliances." *Appliances,* January 1994.

Kindel, Stephen. "World Washer: Why Whirlpool Leads in Appliances, Not Some Japanese Outfit." *Financial World,* 20 March 1990.

LaPat, Kimberly L. "Clothes Encounters." *Appliance.* September 1996.

Le Blanc, Jenny. "1997: Slow Growth Ahead." *Appliance.* January 1997, 38.

Market Share Reporter. Detroit: Gale Research, 1997.

Nevin, Frederick. "Demand Building for Feature-Laden Laundry Appliances." *HFD-The Weekly Home Furnishings Newspaper,* 16 March 1992.

"Portrait of the U.S. Appliance Industry." *Appliance.* September, 1996.

Remich, Norman C., Jr. "Maytag at 100." *Appliance Manufacturer,* November 1993.

———. "Shipments Show Strength." *Appliance Manufacturer,* November 1993.

Somheil, Timothy. "1994: The Key Word is Improvement." *Appliance,* January 1994.

Stewart, Thomas A. "A Heartland Industry Takes On the World." *Fortune,* 12 March 1990.

"Whirlpool Earnings Rise 21 Percent." *Reuters,* 16 April 1997.

—Dave Mote, updated by Lisa Calhoun

ELECTRIC HOUSEWARES AND FANS

This category includes establishments primarily engaged in manufacturing electric housewares for heating, cooking, and other purposes; and electric household fans, except attic fans. Important products of this industry include household-type ventilation and exhaust fans; portable household cooking appliances, except convection and microwave ovens; electric space heaters; electrically heated bedcoverings, electric scissors; and portable humidifiers and dehumidifiers. Establishments primarily engaged in manufacturing attic fans and industrial and commercial exhaust and ventilation fans are classified in **SIC 3564: Industrial and Commercial Fans and Blowers and Air Purification Equipment;** and those manufacturing room air-conditioners and humidifying and dehumidifying equipment, except portable, are classified in **SIC 3585: Air-Conditioning and Warm Air Heating Equipment and Commercial and Industrial Refrigeration Equipment.**

INDUSTRY SNAPSHOT

Electric housewares and fans comprise a major portion of the widely diverse products of the general housewares category, ranking third in shipments—refrigeration is first and laundry equipment second. In 1997, the industry shipped an estimated 16 billion units, totalling $3 billion worth of product and employing 20,000 workers. Like the other sectors of the housewares industry, the economic success of this industry is tied to the health of the housing industry and to general consumer confidence levels.

ORGANIZATION AND STRUCTURE

By the 1990s, little product was sold directly to the consumer. Instead, manufacturers sold to major mass distribution networks wholesale, using account representatives who not only knew the company's product line, but also the best way to market and promote sales. These account representatives replaced the earlier door-to-door salesmen of the industry's infancy. At first, sales representatives were company employees working directly for the manufacturing firm, but in the early 1990s some firms started to contract out the sales function to independent marketing firms who specialized in product promotion.

To support new marketing activities, manufacturers engaged in national advertising and promotion campaigns, headlining the product and directing customers to major retail chains. One very successful medium for the industry was the infomercial. Manufacturers discovered that by packaging advertising material as a television talk show and featuring celebrity guest appearances, they could capture consumer attention and raise awareness of new products dramatically. Consumers seemed to like the option of gaining detailed information on a product without the pressure of dealing directly with a salesperson. Infomercials were used to target specific television audiences as a direct sales pitch or to supplement national advertising campaigns. They also appeared in the stores as part of point-of-purchase displays.

BACKGROUND AND DEVELOPMENT

Housewares evolved with the changing needs of the modernizing kitchen and the growing demand for more efficient, less labor-intensive work spaces and appliances. In *The Housewares Story,* Earl Lifshey describes the transition from wasteful disorder to luxurious convenience. An important part of this progress was the advent of the first electric houseware, the electric iron. The first iron patent was issued on June 6, 1882, but the power needed to run it was not available till 1890. Generating companies had to first be convinced to keep generators on during the day. A more successful iron followed in 1905 when Earl Richardson, an electric company plant supervisor and meter reader, developed the first iron with the heating elements concentrated at the point. He marketed the new concept, developed with input from homemakers, under the trademark "Hotpoint," according to Lifshey.

Many of the early housewares designs met with manufacturer resistance. The inventors needed a marketing network, and the most logical one was the power generating and distributing companies themselves. Often, to gain a foothold, inventors would offer free samples to homeowners and then take these field test results to the utilities as proof of the existence of a market as proof of the product's quality. Eventually, utilities realized the market potential of electric housewares and bought into the concept of load building as a way to increase profitability. They began offering appliances directly to homeowners, allowing them to finance their purchases through utility billings.

Some major electric appliance contributions were Landers, Frary & Clark's 1908 introduction of the "universal" coffee percolator, General Electric and Westinghouse's 1909 marketing of the first electric toaster, Westinghouse's first electric frying pan introduction in 1911, Landers, Frary & Clark's 1918 introduction of an electric waffle iron that plugged into a light socket, and A. F. Dormeyer's 1927 introduction

of an electric household beater that featured a detachable motor for cleaning.

The proliferation of products in the industry prompted retailers to consider the future of electric appliances. The first to adopt a marketing strategy to promote them was Wanamaker's in New York. In October 1906, it opened its "Electro-Domestic Science" exposition. Continuing a decades-long tradition, the department store placed the display in its basement, the poorly-lit, badly-ventilated, unevenly-heated space that had become associated with housewares. However, it was not long before the department found itself displaced upwards by the "bargain basement" concept and into the mainstream of department store marketing. Other marketers, such as hardware and drug stores and discount and wholesale outlets, quickly entered the arena, but with the poor transportation facilities of the day, they provided essentially local and somewhat isolated markets. To grow into a mass-production industry, electric housewares needed a mass-distribution system. The "drummer" or traveling salesman, so named because of the huge drums of product he carried around, could only begin to tap the potential of this market.

The mail order catalogue was already a success by the turn of the century. Mail order companies provided an excellent alternative to traveling salesmen because they bought large volumes of goods cheaply and distributed them by means of the mail system. By 1972, mail order comprised $261 million worth of retail sales in general housewares.

During the mid- to late 1980s, many long-time industry giants were beginning to falter or fail. In 1985, the biggest name in the industry, General Electric Company, sold its housewares division to The Black & Decker Corporation, but that was only one of many deals that rearranged the list of major players in the industry throughout the 1980s. Much of the activity was driven by a shift from traditional mass-production and inventory systems to more time-sensitive "just-in-time" production. Some poorly capitalized corporations could not handle the erratic production schedules of the latter method and provide reliable product delivery. The result was a concentration of production in fewer larger companies using modern production techniques. Between 1972 and 1987, the number of establishments dropped from 299 to 230. At the same time, automation and more efficient production techniques reduced the number of production workers from 41,000 to 19,300.

In 1988, the leading firm in the electric housewares industry, Allegheny International (AI), filed for Chapter 11 bankruptcy and began a long series of maneuvers to recapitalize. At one point, AI accepted an offer from Black and Decker that would have given that company 63 percent of the iron market, 59 percent of hand-held mixers, and almost 40 percent of food processors. That seemed to be too much concentration for the industry and a campaign of determined opposition scuttled the deal. AI eventually emerged from Chapter 11 as Sunbeam-Oster Corp. in 1990 and in 1996 achieved stature as the most profitable public appliance manufacturer—ahead of even such behemoths as Whirlpool and Black & Decker.

As the economy began to pick up in the early 1990s, consumer confidence buoyed industry production, but the consolidation trend continued. By 1992, three of the largest firms, the revitalized Sunbeam-Oster Inc., Rival Co., and Toastmaster Inc., had each successfully floated large initial public offerings and intended to spend at least some of that capital on corporate acquisitions. They targeted firms with less than $10 million in sales, since those companies would be having difficulty meeting the increasingly demanding shipment requirements of the major retailing chains. Some of the $299 million raised was to be used to erase debt incurred during the 1980s and some was earmarked for new product development.

New product may have been the real driving force of the early 1990s for the electric housewares industry as baby-boomers began to cocoon, retreating into their homes and looking for ways to optimize comfort and style. Sunbeam estimated that 24 percent of its 1992 sales came from products introduced for the first time within the preceding four years.

One area that came of age in the 1990s was the fan portion of the electric housewares industry. The Vornado fan, with its modernistic styling and quiet but high-volume air moving capabilities, revitalized the domestic circulation fan business for many retailers. At the same time, the ceiling fan, most popular in the southern United States, changed from the functional, low-priced favorite of the mass-merchandiser to an upscale designer product. Style and color as well as quiet, efficient and variable operation became important selling features.

The Freedonia Group estimated sales of fans would increase an average of 2.2 percent per year from 1980 to 1995, boosting production from $741 million to $1.2 billion. Sixty percent of the 17 million fans sold in 1996 included some type of light fixture, and many of those were of the chandelier style, incorporating French glass, lead cut crystal, and solid Italian brass.

CURRENT CONDITIONS

In 1996, *Appliance* magazine analyzed manufacturers of blenders, can openers, coffee makers, food processors, hand mixers, irons, toaster ovens, and toasters to decide rankings of household small appliance marketshare. The results determined that Hamilton Beach/Proctor-Silex held 27.9 percent, Black and Decker 18.5 percent, Oster/Sunbeam 9.2 percent, and the rest of the shares divided between Toastmaster, Rival, HPA/Betty Crocker, Braun, and others.

Color and shape became important criteria as consumers demanded innovation in form as well as function. Products included the "Robochef," which used microprocessor technology to computerize food preparation from raw ingredients to finished meal, West Bend's "Chip Factory," which automatically prepared and dispensed customized potato chips for the home consumer, and completely automatic bread makers that also prepared dough for cookies, pies, and pasta.

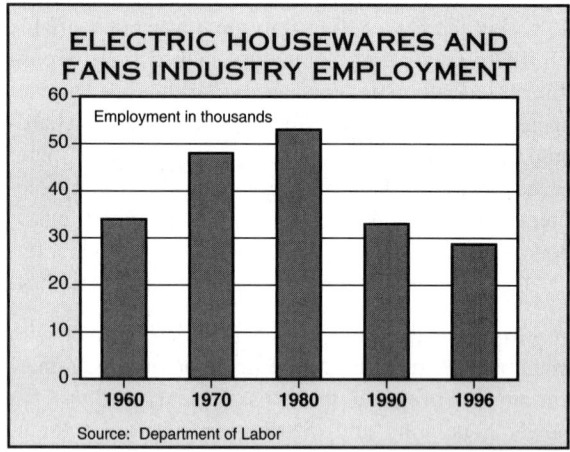

ELECTRIC HOUSEWARES AND FANS INDUSTRY EMPLOYMENT

Employment in thousands

Source: Department of Labor

Current directions in the appliance market include consolidating functions (like a handheld mixer with kneading, whisking, and drink-blending attachments), taking a smaller "footprint" (counter space), creating stylish and color-coordinated appearances, and completing functions more quickly.

Manufacturers in the mid-1990s developed extensive home pages on the World Wide Web primarily to market to a Generation-X audience. Sites like Sunbeam's offered a virtual home that the cyberconsumer could tour, "touching" and eliciting information about a variety of products. The InterCenter Company opened an Internet shopping center that allowed consumers to cybershop for everything from skillets to blenders and gourmet coffee supplies.

INDUSTRY LEADERS

In 1991, Sunbeam-Oster, the number one electric housewares manufacturer, reported $886 million in sales and employed 10,000 people. By 1996, the company reported $984.2 million in sales with only 6,000 employees. Sunbeam-Oster operated under the name Allegheny International Inc. until 1990, when it emerged from bankruptcy, reorganized, and with a new name. In 1992, Sunbeam-Oster offered its stock on the public market for the first time. According to Japonica Partners, "Public investors realized a 50 percent value appreciation in a matter of months . . . creating over $500 million in shareholder value."

By 1993, Black & Decker U.S. Inc. of Baltimore, Maryland, was no longer the largest electric housewares manufacturer, relinquishing its title to Sunbeam-Oster. The company concentrates on its hardware products. In 1996 B&D reported annual sales of $4 billion and a work force of 29,200. Founded in 1910 by Duncan Black and Alonzo Decker, B&D now markets products in over 100 countries. One-third of the company's revenues comes from overseas. Some of its small appliance brand names are Brew 'N Go, Dustbuster, HandyChopper, Spacemaker, Sure Steam, and Toast-R-Oven.

WORK FORCE

In 1972, the average production worker in the electric housewares industry earned $3.03 per hour and added $11.58 worth of value to the product for each production hour. By 1996, that wage had jumped to $8.14 per hour. According to the 1987 *Census of Manufactures,* workers in this industry earned 71 percent of the average industrial hourly wage. In 1996 there were nearly 30,000 people employed in this industry, a number expected to slowly but steadily decline through the turn of the century.

AMERICA AND THE WORLD

The industry slowdown of the 1980s prompted some firms to look beyond the United States for future markets. As the U.S. dollar weakened compared to European and Japanese currencies, American exports cut into the market share of European products by pushing their relative costs up by as much as 25 percent. Much product already flowed freely into Canada by the early 1990s because of the Canada-U.S. Free Trade Agreement and the similar cultural and living standards found in each country.

Sunbeam-Oster already operated and marketed its products in more than 60 countries by 1992. In 1997, the company signed a licensing agreement with South Africa. In Latin America, the Oster brand often claims more than 75 percent market share. Sunbeam operates offices and some manufacturing facilities in Peru, Venezuela, Ecuador, Colombia, and Mexico.

Sunbeam named Europe as the prime target for expansion throughout the remaining part of the decade. To help in broaden its markets, it opened marketing offices in Germany, France, and the United Kingdom. Generally, American products have more features than the equivalent European design, although the Europeans traditionally excel on styling and environmental friendliness.

RESEARCH AND TECHNOLOGY

The kitchen of tomorrow will be smarter looking, with stylish innovative shapes that belie function, and will work smarter, drawing on microprocessor technology to automate food preparation. Those machines will even be able to learn. Once shown a task, or recipe, they will memorize it and be ready to perform it flawlessly whenever needed. They will be easier on the environment, using less electricity than earlier models and featuring replaceable components made of recyclable materials.

One dilemma for the industry remains the effect of electromagnetic fields from power lines and electric appliances. Suggested links between those fields and cancer prompted some manufacturers to abandon the electric blanket market in 1988. However, Sunbeam opted instead to reduce the devices electromagnetic field by 97 percent and rename the product "automatic warming blankets."

FURTHER READING

Darnay, Arsen J., ed. *Manufacturing USA.* 5th Edition. Detroit: Gale Research, 1997.

"Effecting Efficiency: Hamilton Beach/Proctor-Silex Stages a Turnaround with Cost Controls and Price Positioning." *HFD: The Weekly Home Furnishings Newspaper,* 1 February 1993.

Farnsworth, Steve. "Sunbeam-Oster Sets Expansion; Company Plots Strategy to Bolster Sales in International Markets." *HFD: The Weekly Home Furnishings Newspaper,* 6 July 1992.

"Healthy Home Relations." *Appliance,* 1997. Available from http://www.appliance.com/app/cover.story.

Japonica Partners. "Sunbeam-Oster Investment Summary." Available from http://www.japonica.com/japonica/socsummary.html.

Jiambalvo, John R. "The Skinny On Small Appliances." *Appliance,* January 1997.

"Life After Chapter 11 for Six Big Survivors." *Fortune,* 11 February 1991.

Lifshey, Earl. *The Housewares Story: A History of the American Housewares Industry.* Chicago: National Housewares Manufacturers Association, 1973.

Magid, Lawrence J. "Home, Sweet, Automated Home." *Los Angeles Times Syndicate,* MNSBC, 1997. Available from http://www.msnbc.com/news/6966.asp.

Maras, Elio. "Changes Needed to Build Electrics Trade." *Housewares,* 21 November 1990.

Market Share Reporter. Detroit: Gale Research, 1997.

"A Portrait of the US Appliance Industry." *Appliance,* September, 1996.

Purpura, Linda. "The Future Is Now as Food Cookers Go High Tech." *HFD: The Weekly Home Furnishings Newspaper,* 27 January 1992.

Ratliff, Duke. "Electrics Vendors See Infomercials Continuing to Drive the Category." *HFD: The Weekly Home Furnishings Newspaper,* 17 May 1993.

Rees, Clifford, Jr. "Good Year to Follow Great Leap Forward." *Appliance,* January, 1997.

Santorelli, Dina. "Fan-tastic: Ceiling Fans Come of Age through Style and Innovation." *HFD: The Weekly Home Furnishings Newspaper,* 22 March 1993.

Schroeder, Michael. "Allegheny's Battle to Come Back from the Abyss." *Business Week,* 26 June 1989.

"Small-appliance Makers Hot." *HFD: The Weekly Home Furnishings Newspaper,* 14 September 1992.

"Small Electric Appliances." 1997. InterCenter Company Website. Available from http://www.intercenter.com/cgi-local/webSession/store = home_store/department.

U.S. Department of Labor. *Employment, Hours, and Earnings—United States, 1981-93.* Washington: GPO, 1993.

—Al Cook, updated by Lisa Calhoun

SIC 3635

HOUSEHOLD VACUUM CLEANERS

This classification covers establishments primarily engaged in manufacturing vacuum cleaners for household use. Establishments primarily engaged in manufacturing vacuum cleaners for industrial use are classified in **SIC 3589: Service Industry Machinery, Not Elsewhere Classified.** Establishments primarily engaged in installation of central vacuum cleaner systems are classified in **SIC 1796: Installation or Erection of Building Equipment, Not Elsewhere Classified.**

Vacuums remove 80 percent of soil from carpet, making them essential for carpet care. Vacuums are more desirable if they have a rotating brush, beater bar, and powerful suction capabilities. Even with these features, they must be adjusted to carpet height, bags must be changed when full, and belts and brushes must be maintained.

The four primary categories of household vacuums are upright, canister, stick, and handheld models. The upright vacuum cleaner, which was the first vacuum to gain widespread acceptance in the United States, descended from the manual carpet sweeper. Uprights come in two styles, those with a vertically-mounted soft collector bag and those with an exterior plastic shell that contains the bag. Because they have a rotating brush, uprights are usually better at cleaning carpets. Their limited suction makes them less efficient at cleaning upholstery and bare surfaces, however. U.S. manufacturers sold nearly 9 million upright cleaners in 1993, according to *Appliance* magazine in 1994, up from about 7.8 million in 1992.

Canister vacuums have more suction and are easier to use on stairs. But they are generally difficult to store, have a small collector bag, and require the user to pull the canister along the floor behind the nozzle. About 1.8 million canister vacuums were shipped in 1993, down from more than 2 million in 1992. *Appliance* predicted this downward trend would continue.

Stick vacuums are similar to upright cleaners, but they usually lack a rotating brush and are less adept at cleaning than either canister or uprights. Stick vacuums, though, are usually light-weight, easy to store, and inexpensive. About 1.6 million stick vacuums were sold by U.S. producers in 1993, up from 1.5 million in 1992.

The two types of handheld vacuums are electric and rechargeable. About 3.3 million and 2.2 million electric and rechargeable units, respectively, were shipped in 1993 according to *Appliance*. These figures mark a slippage in shipments from 1992, when 3.6 million electric and 2.7 million rechargeable units were sold.

Following solid industry growth during the 1960s and 1970s, the household vacuum cleaner industry realized steady expansion during the 1980s. Prodded by new product introductions and positive demographic trends, vacuum cleaner sales rocketed from $775 million in 1982 to $1.87 billion in 1990, reflecting an average annual growth rate of more than ten percent. Stick and handheld vacuums were the fastest growing product segments during this period.

Economic recess sent industry revenues tumbling below $1.7 billion in the early 1990s. A recovery entering the mid-1990s, however, buoyed earnings and promised to revive struggling manufacturers. Overall unit shipments were forecast by some observers to rise as much as four percent in 1994, with stick and upright vacuums leading industry growth.

Appliance manufacturers in general found that 1995 sales were not as spectacular as they had speculated, but 1996 was estimated to be healthy. The 1997 economy was expected to be relatively stable, so sales were expected to be stable also; that year, the value of shipments was over $2.3 billion. The number of establishments was also increasing from 40 in 1993 to about 45 in 1997.

In the mid-1990s, the largest vacuum manufacturer was the subsidiary Hoover Co., of Ohio, generating sales of an estimated $1.5 billion and employing over 10,000 workers. Other industry leaders included Eureka Company, of Illinois and Kirby Company, of Ohio. Ohio had the greatest number of establishments in the United States.

In the mid-1990s, vacuum makers were trying to boost sales with new high-tech products. Vacuum manufacturers wanted consumers to be alerted to the damage caused by fine dusts so filtration systems would be more desirable. Eureka, for example, introduced a line of environmentally-friendly vacuums that were designed to filter out 99 percent of the dust and dirt that enters the vacuum. Philips Home Products Corp. brought out Blue Magic, a high-tech vacuum with a turbo-compressor that operates by fuzzy logic. Blue Magic also has a silencing mechanism and can be operated with a remote control. Another technological highlight included new polymers, which allowed vacuum manufacturers to reduce unit costs and weight and improve quality.

FURTHER READING

Darnay, Arsen J., ed. *Manufacturing USA*. 5th Ed. Detroit: Gale Research, 1996.

"Effective Filtration for Domestic and Industrial Cleaners." Hepworth Air Filtration. Available from http://www.hepair.com/nf_ap_v.html.

Holding, Robert L. "Anticipating 1994 for Home Appliances." *Appliances*, January 1994.

Leaversuch, Robert D. "Vacuum-Cleaner Upgrades: A Fertile Polymer Market." *Modern Plastics*, May 1993.

Remich, Norman C., Jr. "Clean Comfort." *Appliance Manufacturer*, June 1993.

———. "Industry Outlook." *Appliance Manufacturer*, January 1994.

———. "World Vac More Than Floor Care." *Appliance Manufacture*, June 1993.

Somheil, Timothy. "1994: The Key Word is Improvement." *Appliance*, January 1994.

U.S. Department of Commerce. International Trade Administration. *U.S. Industrial Outlook 1994*. Washington: GPO, 1994.

SIC 3639

HOUSEHOLD APPLIANCES, NOT ELSEWHERE CLASSIFIED

This industry includes establishments primarily engaged in manufacturing household appliances, not elsewhere classified, such as water heaters, dishwashers, food waste disposal units, and household sewing machines. Major product groups include water heaters, dishwashers, food disposers, trash compactors, floor waxers, and sewing machines. Laundry equipment, refrigerators, and other major household goods are classified separately, as are commercial appliances.

INDUSTRY SNAPSHOT

A uniquely American innovation, electric and gas household appliances became commonplace in U.S. homes during the post-war economic expansion of the 1950s, 1960s, and 1970s. By the early 1980s, miscellaneous appliance makers in the United States were shipping about $1.5 billion worth of goods each year and employing a work force of more than 14,000. Continued rapid growth in the 1980s, moreover, pushed industry sales past $3.2 billion by the early 1990s.

Although manufacturers suffered during an economic recession in the early 1990s, sales began to pick up entering the mid-1990s. Export growth was augmenting the domestic recovery and promised to provide an avenue for long-term expansion. Furthermore, positive demographic trends and U.S. replacement markets were expected to buoy domestic revenues throughout the decade. Challenges faced by competitors in the early 1990s included federal regulations designed to address environmental concerns and a lack of major new product lines.

In the mid-1990s, renovations of homes reached a record $69.5 billion, reflecting the increasing trend for home-improvement and bolstering the U.S. replacement market.

ORGANIZATION AND STRUCTURE

Miscellaneous appliances represent about 8 percent of the overall U.S. appliance manufacturing industry, which generated 1991 revenues of about $18.5 billion. The largest segment of this business category is water heater manufacturing, which accounts for roughly 40 percent of industry sales. Dishwashers, the second largest product category, are trailed by sewing machines, trash compactors, disposers, floor waxers, and related supplies and attachments.

About 26 percent of industry revenues in the early 1990s was garnered from individual consumer purchases. Residential builders consumed about 20 percent of aggregate output, while commercial and institutional developers made up approximately 24 percent of the market. Roughly 5 percent of production was exported. The remaining 25 percent of sales were made to the armed forces, state and local governments, mobile home builders, and other sectors.

Appliance sales are driven primarily by three factors: replacement sales; product market penetration, particularly in the case of completely new appliances; and new construction, which generates demand by builders that perform first-time installations. Because most product categories have achieved almost full market penetration, miscellaneous appliance sales are highly dependent upon replacement sales and new construction, and are closely linked to housing starts and economic growth.

The appliance industry can be differentiated from other manufacturing sectors by its production characteristics. Appliance manufacturing is essentially an assembly-line process whereby ready-made components are assembled. Because it has low fixed costs and is labor intensive, appliance production offers abundant opportunities for manufacturing efficiency gains. This characteristic contributes to a high weight-to-value ratio that limits overseas appliance imports into the United States, and has caused prices to remain effectively fixed during the 1980s and early 1990s.

Products. The two main types of water heaters are electric- and gas-powered. Gas heaters made up nearly 60 percent of all water heater sales in the early 1990s. Although electric heaters are often priced lower, gas heaters usually operate less expensively. Most water heaters consist of a tank that is made of galvanized iron or aluminum alloys and holds between 20 and 140 gallons. A glass or plastic liner is used to reduce corrosion inside the tank. Water temperature can be adjusted between 100 and 200 degrees Fahrenheit. In 1993 U.S. producers sold about 7.3 million water heaters.

The two main categories of household dishwashers are portable and built-in. Of 3.5 million dishwashers shipped in 1993, only 180,500 were portable units. Most dishwashers use pumps and impellers to throw the same water against dishes over and over to clean them. Fresh rinse water is then used. The cycle is typically completed by heat-drying the dishes. About 50 percent of all U.S. homes had a dishwasher in the early 1990s, up from 45 percent in 1980.

Garbage disposal units are motor-operated grinders that are installed in kitchen sinks. These devices allow food to be washed down the drain. Approximately 50 percent of all U.S. homes were equipped with a disposal unit in the early 1990s, and nearly 4 million units were sold in 1993. Only 114,000 trash compactors were shipped in 1993, representing a negligible share of the appliance market. Sewing machines also accounted for a meager share of U.S. miscellaneous appliance output (70 percent of these machines are manufactured in Japan).

BACKGROUND AND DEVELOPMENT

Many of the appliances classified in this industry have existed for centuries. Not until the twentieth century, however, did self-contained electric- and gas-powered household appliances appear. A primary impetus for the development of such tools was the almost total disappearance of full-time domestic servants.

Appliances available in the early 1900s included electric clothes washers, water heaters, refrigerators, and sewing machines. In the second half of the century, during rapid post-war U.S. economic growth, a demand emerged for dishwashers, clothes dryers, food disposers, floor polishers, and similar devices of convenience. A rise in discretionary income, growth in the number of U.S. households, and a desire for more recreational time were major factors contributing to the rise of the miscellaneous appliance industry from the 1950s to the 1970s.

By the early 1980s, miscellaneous appliance manufacturers were shipping about $1.5 billion worth of goods each year, and employing over 14,000 workers. Strong industry growth continued during the 1980s as housing starts surged and growing home renovation markets spurred replacement sales. In addition, an increase in the number of working women boosted market penetration by some products.

Although industry revenues shot up over 100 percent between 1982 and 1990, to about $3.3 billion, unit shipments grew at an even faster rate and industry profits climbed. Manufacturers were able to achieve such growth through economies-of-scale and productivity gains. Indeed, as revenues and shipments more than doubled during the 1980s, industry employment remained steady. Hefty investments in automation and information systems permitted these efficiency gains.

Economies of scale were attained primarily through mergers and acquisitions, which characterized almost all appliance sectors throughout the 1980s and early 1990s. As manufacturers joined forces to increase investment capital and reduce research and production expenditures, the number of competitors in the miscellaneous appliances industry lessened. Anti-trust legislation enacted during the 1980s slowed the rate of consolidation by the early 1990s.

CURRENT CONDITIONS

Sluggish economic conditions, which suppressed housing starts and replacement sales, battered manufacturers of miscellaneous appliances in 1990. Home building and consumer expenditures picked up in 1992, though, prodded by low interest rates and pent-up demand. After plunging to $3.1 billion in 1990, industry revenues climbed to $3.3 billion in 1991 and grew about four percent annually during 1992 and 1993. Unit sales volume climbed even faster. Dishwasher shipments, for example, jumped almost eight percent in 1993, and water heater orders increased by about six percent.

Although appliance makers lacked major new product offerings that could broaden their industry, they were having some success enticing new buyers to the market by adding new features to established products. Manufacturers were also benefitting from generally positive demographic trends. For instance, aging baby-boomers were investing an increasing proportion of their income into their homes reflecting a desire for products that make the lives of two income families more convenient and more comfortable. In addition, large numbers of appliances sold in the early 1980s were rapidly approaching replacement age.

Although the strong growth that miscellaneous appliance makers enjoyed during the 1980s was unlikely to occur in the 1990s, observers expect steady modest growth for the next several years. In addition, some industry niches, such as portable dishwashers, may realize periods of faster growth. Furthermore, continued gains in manufacturing productivity should boost bottom-line profits throughout the decade.

In an effort to exceed forecasts, producers in the mid-1990s were striving to accelerate replacement sales by developing more energy-efficient, convenient, and versatile machines. They were also hoping to expand export sales. Encouraging industry participants were the likelihood of continued low interest rates, diminishing inventories, steady annual growth in consumer spending, and the potential of completely new product introductions.

New government environmental regulations were one of the greatest hurdles facing appliance makers in the mid-1990s. The Department of Energy's (DOE's) National Appliance Energy Conservation Act of 1987, for example, set new standards that limit energy consumption by new appliances. The act requires manufacturers to cut energy consumption by their products by 25 percent every five years. DOE mandates that became effective in May 1994 also required dishwasher manufacturers to build machines that use less water and make more efficient use of electric energy. Likewise, new regulations that may be implemented by the DOE in 1997 encompass water heaters. Other regulatory initiatives were aimed at making appliances more recyclable.

Most industry participants expected to achieve compliance with all regulations on schedule, and some manufacturers even hoped to boost sales with environmentally-friendly products. Nevertheless, some appliance makers resented the new regulations, citing the capital investments required to meet the stipulations of such legislation.

INDUSTRY LEADERS

The appliance industry is highly consolidated; five major firms supply over 90 percent of all U.S. appliances. The biggest players in the miscellaneous appliance market are General Electric (GE) and Whirlpool. GE produced over 40 percent of all dishwashers sold in America in 1993, for example, while Whirlpool products accounted for another 30 percent of that total. Some smaller product segments, however, are dominated by niche firms. In-Sink-Erator, for example, controlled 60 percent of the U.S. disposal market in 1993.

The largest company primarily engaged in the production of miscellaneous appliances in the early 1990s was Nortek Inc., of Rhode Island. Nortek generated sales of $1.04 billion in 1991 and employed over 8,500 workers. SSMC Inc., of New Jersey, another major company that primarily produced appliances in this industry, had 1991 sales of $992 million. State Industries Inc., of Tennessee, garnered $280 million in sales during 1991 and employed 2,600 workers. Other major miscellaneous appliance producers included Mor-Flo Industries, Inc. ($213 million in 1991 sales), Emerson Electric Co. ($190 million), and A.O. Smith Corp. ($165 million).

WORK FORCE

Although productivity gains allowed manufacturers to boost shipments, revenues, and earnings during the 1980s, the workforce suffered cutbacks as a result of those gains. Continued advances in efficiency combined with the movement of manufacturing facilities overseas during the 1990s could significantly curtail industry job prospects in the future. In fact, most blue-collar workers will realize cutbacks of 20 to 40 percent between 1990 and 2005, according to the Bureau of Labor Statistics.

AMERICA AND THE WORLD

The United States is the largest consumer and producer of appliances in the world. It produces and consumes more than 30 percent of global output of most product segments and maintains the highest level of market saturation in virtually every major line of appliances. While 50 percent of U.S. households had a dishwasher in 1993, for example, only 35 percent of French homes were so equipped, and just 15 percent of households in the United Kingdom had dishwashers. Generally low penetration of major appliances in comparison to the United States reflects higher energy costs, less space, and lower living standards characteristic of other countries.

Exports. Because manufacturers have achieved close to maximum market penetration with most miscellaneous appliances in the United States, they have increasingly focused their expansion efforts in the 1990s on foreign markets that offered a greater potential for growth. Europe proffered the greatest prospects for profits. Appliance industries on that continent were still fragmented, leaving the market open for massive U.S. conglomerates. Sweden's Electrolux, the largest European competitor, controlled only 20 percent of the market in 1993, and Germany's Bosch-Siemens held just 12 percent. Whirlpool had already captured more than ten percent of the European market by 1994 and was rapidly expanding its presence. Like Whirlpool, GE was advancing in Europe and was positioning itself to take advantage of burgeoning Eastern European economies.

While opportunities prevailed in rapidly unfurling Asian markets, U.S. producers were largely avoiding that region. Three successful Japanese conglomerates—Hitachi, Toshiba, and Matsushita—had established a strong grip on much of the Asian market and posed formidable entry barriers to even the most savvy American competitors. Likewise, Japanese producers were avoiding North American markets for fear of their U.S. counterparts, which maintained a lead in production efficiency, distribution, and marketing know-how—U.S. producers supplied over 75 percent of domestic demand for all types of appliances in 1993. Japanese companies had succeeded in penetrating the sewing machine market, though, and were supplying over 70 percent of global demand for that appliance going into 1994.

U.S. appliance exports jumped 16 percent in 1992. Canada and Mexico consumed about 46 percent of those shipments, while the European Community purchased about 15 percent. East Asian and South American consumers accounted for 12 percent and six percent of U.S. exports, respectively. In the short term, Canada and Mexico will continue to offer strong growth opportunities, particularly in the wake of the North American Free Trade Agreement (NAFTA) that Congress passed in 1994. Exports to Mexico leapt 18 percent in 1993, while shipments to Canada ballooned 20 percent following a 1992 reduction in tariffs.

Imports. As domestic appliance makers continued to boost exports, imports into the United States surged. Imports increased by an uncharacteristically high 28 percent in 1992, despite a weak U.S. dollar, and imports were forecast to rise steadily during the 1990s and early 2000s. The main reason for import growth was the proliferation of U.S.-owned manufacturing plants in foreign countries. U.S. producers were shifting production to low-cost countries, such as Mexico and China, that offered cheap labor and materials. Imports from Mexico, for example, grew by 40 percent in 1993 and were expected to expand further with the passage of NAFTA.

RESEARCH AND TECHNOLOGY

Technological advancements in the mid-1990s centered around compliance with environmental regulations and the development of more efficient appliances. Producers were striving to retain the cleansing power of dishwashers, for example, while reducing water usage. Meanwhile, water heater manufacturers continued to search for more efficient heating, insulation, and distribution technology.

European manufacturers were involved in production of a noise-free dishwasher in the early 1990s. Although the cleansing power of such machines was not yet acceptable to U.S. consumers, manufacturers from all continents were trying to develop a soundless machine. Frigidaire, for example, was offering three sound-blanketing packages with its dishwashers which incorporated vinyl-backed fiberglass, quilted foil-backed fiberglass, and asphaltic sound-damping materials. Manufacturers were also experimenting with quieter motors and noise-cancellation frequency generators.

Advancements related to all types of appliances were being achieved through the increased use of plastics. New thermoplastics, for example, were being used to reduce heat loss that occurs in appliances encased in metal. Other plastics were helping manufacturers reduce shipping weight and increase the strength and durability of their products. Waste King Inc., for instance, switched from a stainless steel housing on a garbage disposal to one made of an engineered polymer compound. It reduced the unit's weight by five ounces, made it smaller, and decreased its noise level by five decibels.

FURTHER READING

Bendall, Daniel. "Waste Handling." *Restaurant Hospitality,* March 1990.

Darnay, Arsen J., ed. *Manufacturing USA.* Detroit: Gale Research, 1993.

Dzierwa, Richard. "The Energy & Intensity." *Appliance,* February 1994.

"Factory Unit Shipments." *Appliance,* February 1994.

Heil, Timothy W. "A Variety of Design Factors Govern Water Heater Choices." *Consulting-Specifying Engineer,* January 1991.

Holding, Robert L. "Anticipating 1994 for Home Appliances." *Appliances,* January 1994.

Jaccoma, Richard. "Talking Dishwashers." *Dealerscope Merchandising,* August 1992.

Jancsurak, Joe. "Plastics Take the Heat." *Appliance Manufacturer,* May 1991.

———. *Marketing Power Supplement,* November 1996

Nagahama, Yuji. "Trends of the Domestic & Industrial Sewing Machine Industry." *Japan 21st,* December 1992.

Remich, Norman C., Jr. "Next Dishwasher Generation: Noise-Free?" *Appliance Manufacturer,* February 1992.

———. "Industry Outlook." *Appliance Manufacturer,* January 1994.

———. "Shipments Show Strength." *Appliance Manufacturer,* November 1993.

Somheil, Timothy. "1994: The Key Word is Improvement." *Appliance,* January 1994.

Stewart, Thomas A. "A Heartland Industry Takes On the World." *Fortune,* 12 March 1990.

U.S. Department of Commerce. *U.S. Industrial Outlook 1993.* Washington: 1993.

Yasui, Nobuyuki, and Motoi Sekiguchi. "Sewing Machine Industry to Form New Organization; Japan's Industrial Sewing Machine Industry Dominates World Market." *Business Japan,* December 1991.

—Dave Mote, updated by Gertrude Mandeville

SIC 3641

ELECTRIC LAMP BULBS AND TUBES

This industry classification covers establishments primarily engaged in manufacturing electric bulbs, tubes, and related light sources. Important products of this industry include incandescent filament lamps, vapor and fluorescent lamps, photoflash and photoflood lamps, and electrotherapeutic lamp units for ultraviolet and infrared radiation. Establishments primarily engaged in manufacturing glass blanks for bulbs are classified in **SIC 3229: Pressed and Blown Glass and Glassware, Not Elsewhere Classified.**

INDUSTRY SNAPSHOT

The first practical light bulbs were invented in 1878. A bulb industry emerged early in the twentieth century as an infrastructure capable of carrying electricity to the general population evolved. By the early 1980s, about 70 U.S. firms were selling over $2 billion worth of bulbs and tubes each year. Erratic market growth during the 1980s pushed industry sales to approximately $2.8 billion per year by 1992. By 1995, sales had increased to $2.9 billion, with 26,200 individuals employed in the industry. Industry experts forecast sales of $3.6 billion for 1997.

Going into the mid-1990s, U.S. bulb producers were battling a sluggish domestic economy. Sales were down, and many market segments had matured. Some manufacturers, however, were boosting profits with high-tech lamps and bulbs that could burn longer, brighter, and more efficiently. The implementation of laws prohibiting the continued manufacture of more than 45 electric lamps that didn't meet newly established energy standards will certainly create additional changes in the market in the years to come.

ORGANIZATION AND STRUCTURE

The light bulb and electric lamp industry provides a practical means of converting electric energy into usable light. In the mid-1990s about 25 percent of all the electricity sold in the United States was used for lighting. Besides illuminating businesses, schools, and homes, light bulbs are used in a plethora of applications and products—including automobiles, flashlights, sports fields, medical equipment, airport runways, and emergency exit signs.

The industry produces thousands of different bulbs, tubes, strobes, and flashes. But the three primary products sold by U.S. electric lamp manufacturers are incandescent, fluorescent, and electric-discharge lights and bulbs.

Incandescent bulbs produce light by heating a filament to a high temperature. The filament, which is usually composed of tungsten, emits a yellowish glow as electricity flows through it. The bulb is filled with an inert gas, such as argon, to keep the filament from melting and evaporating. Most incandescent bulbs are designed to operate at between 30 and 150 watts of power and at 120 volts of electricity. They typically produce between 750 and 2,500 lumens of light (a lumen is the amount of light that falls on each square foot of a 1-foot radius sphere when a candle is placed at the center).

One reason incandescent bulbs are popular is because they are inexpensive to purchase. A standard bulb usually costs less than $1 and provides about 750 hours of light. Incandescent bulbs are also relatively compact, operate well at low temperatures, and offer a high degree of optical control. The primary disadvantage of this type of lamp, however, is low efficiency. A typical 100 watt bulb, for example, dissipates about 95 percent of its electric current as heat. Less than 5 percent is actually converted to light, resulting in high operating temperatures and superfluous energy consumption.

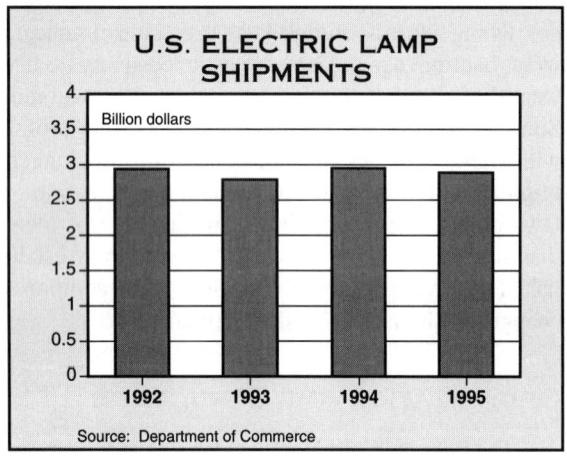

U.S. ELECTRIC LAMP SHIPMENTS

Billion dollars

Source: Department of Commerce

A second type of incandescent bulb is the halogen lamp, which became popular during the 1980s. Halogen bulbs are filled with iodine or bromine gas, which prolongs the filament's life by reducing tungsten evaporation. A standard halogen bulb lasts about 3,000 hours. Some halogen lamps also consume less energy. Because these bulbs emit ultraviolet radiation and can get extremely hot, however, they are often encased in a heat resistant material, like quartz, within the outer bulb. For this and other reasons, halogen lamps cost as

much as five or even ten times more than traditional tungsten bulbs.

The second major category of electric bulbs is the fluorescent bulb and tube sector, which serves as the primary electric light source in the United States. Most fluorescent lamps are tube shaped, have a tungsten filament or tungsten coils, and are filled with mercury vapor and argon gas. When electricity is applied to the lamp, an electrode at one end emits electrons that travel through the bulb, react with the mercury, and emit ultraviolet radiation. The radiation reacts with a phosphor coating on the inside of the bulb to produce visible light. Fluorescent lamps are usually tubular, but also come in compact rod, ring, and globe shapes.

Although they are larger than incandescent bulbs and cost more to produce, fluorescent lamps are more energy efficient and have a longer life. Compact florescent lamps that can be substituted for standard incandescent bulbs, for example, produce between 35 and 70 lumens-per-watt. Incandescent bulbs, in contrast, deliver only 14 to 18 lumens-per-watt. While compact fluorescent bulbs typically cost between $15 and $30 each, their overall cost is lower. By January 1997, the cost for many compact fluorescent replacement bulbs had dropped from a high of $20 to less than $5 each. The only drawback of compact fluorescent bulbs is that retailers currently have limited supplies available, and there is not as much variety as with conventional incandescent fixtures.

Electric-discharge lamps, the third major industry category, produce light through a gas or a metallic vapor. The color and intensity of the light can be altered by using different types of gas and varying the pressure in the bulb. Gases such as neon, argon, krypton, mercury, and xenon allow electric-discharge lamps to be used in a variety of applications. Mercury lamps, which deliver an efficient 65 lumens-per-watt, are widely used to light industrial spaces and roadways. Although electric-discharge lamps are expensive, slow-starting, and usually produce an unappealing bluish-greenish glow, they are long lasting, energy efficient, and compact. Recent developments have brought neon lamps into the home sector with the development of microelectronic transformers—necessary for the operation of neon lamps—which are now smaller than a pack of cigarettes.

Markets. Approximately 35 percent of light bulb industry revenues in the mid-1990s were derived from sales to individual consumers. State and local governments, including schools, hotels, and hospitals account for small percentages of revenues. The remainder of the market was highly fragmented. Motor vehicle manufacturers and electric utilities consume small portions of total production units.

BACKGROUND AND DEVELOPMENT

Oil lamps were used for illumination in the earliest known civilizations and were a common artificial light source for over 6,000 years. Gas lamps became popular early in the nineteenth century, particularly in Europe. Neither gas nor oil lamps, however, were sufficient to light entire rooms or mimic daylight.

The first incandescent electric lamp was produced in 1802 by Humphrey Davy, an English chemist. Davy heated strips of platinum in the open air using an electric current. The strips soon burned up, and the lack of a satisfactory source of electric power made the concept impracticable. Similar efforts during the succeeding 70 years caused some scientists to declare the development of a long burning electric lamp impossible.

Good vacuum pumps that removed air from glass bulbs made the creation of the first commercially viable incandescent lamps possible. Joseph Wilson Swan, of England, and Thomas Edison, of the United States, separately invented the first successful light bulbs in 1878. Both lamps used carbon filaments in evacuated glass bulbs. Edison received most of the credit for the invention, however, because he subsequently invented much of the equipment needed to implement his lamp in a practical lighting system.

Edison's first lamp provided the same amount of light as 16 candles and produced about 1.4 lumens-per-watt. But technological advancements soon improved Edison's original bulb. Notably, in 1911 tungsten was introduced as a filament. In 1913 filaments were coiled for the first time, and bulbs were filled with inert gas. Beginning in 1925, bulbs were frosted on the inside to emit a diffused glow instead of a glaring brightness. Improvements in energy flow and bulb pressure helped boost standard 40 watt bulbs to 1,000 hours of life and 14 lumens-per-watt by the early 1960s. Incandescent lamps with more power had developed by the 1960s as well.

The first electric arc lamp was patented in 1845 by Thomas Wright. Wright's carbon-arc lamp led to the development in the late 1800s of electric-discharge bulbs that could produce ten times the light emitted by carbon-filament incandescent lamps. These early bulbs were largely limited to use as heavy-duty street lights, however, because they had to be continuously fed with carbon rods. The mercury-arc lamp, developed in 1901, eliminated many drawbacks of early electric-discharge bulbs. Likewise, the introduction of neon

tubes in 1920 led to the popularization of electric-discharge lamps for advertising signs. Sodium lamps developed during the 1930s became popular for various outdoor and industrial applications.

The fluorescent lamp was invented by Frenchman Alexandre Edmond Becquerel in 1859, but it was not introduced commercially in the United States until 1938. By the early 1950s, though, fluorescent lamps had overtaken incandescent bulbs as the primary source of artificial light in the United States. Superior efficiency, long life, and greater light output drove the growth of this important industry segment. By the 1960s, in fact, manufacturers were offering more than 50 shapes and sizes of fluorescent lamps ranging from four to 240 watts in power.

Booms in residential, commercial, and institutional construction from the 1950s to the 1970s vastly expanded U.S. light bulb markets. By the early 1980s, in fact, about 60 U.S. producers were shipping $2 billion worth of various electric lamps and were employing more than 22,000 workers. Following a development lull in the late 1970s and early 1980s, renewed demand pressed industry sales past an impressive $2.8 billion per year by 1986. This figure reflected average annual growth of nearly 10 percent between 1982 and 1986. Although sales increased at a more tepid pace through 1988—to about $3.2 billion—a U.S. recession in the late 1980s and early 1990s depressed industry revenues back below $3 billion. Sales of $2.9 billion in 1995 reflected a continuance of this trend; however, the workforce of 26,200 shows a modest increase from previous years. Projected sales of $3.6 billion for 1997 may mark a period of upswing for the industry.

CURRENT CONDITIONS

Going into the late 1990s, U.S. electric lamp manufacturers were hoping to benefit from slowly strengthening commercial and residential construction industries. Nevertheless, demand from builders was expected to remain suppressed indefinitely. Instead, bulb makers were focusing on increasing profits through sales of advanced lamps that could reduce energy consumption, improve lighting, boost longevity, and minimize adverse environmental impacts. Compact fluorescent and halogen bulbs, particularly, offered solid growth potential. Sources estimate that for 1997, sales of fluorescent lamps will account for 37.8 percent of total industry sales, followed by large incandescents (34.9 percent), miniature incandescents (14.5 percent), electrical discharges (11.9 percent), and photo incandescents (1 percent).

The National Energy Security Act of 1992 effectively mandated the use of such advanced bulbs. The act sought to prevent the sale of inefficient fluorescent light bulbs beginning in 1994, and other energy-inefficient bulbs by 1995. It banned most standard four-and eight-foot fluorescent light tubes, some incandescent reflector lamps, and many types of flood lamps. Likewise, the Environmental Protection Agency's (EPA's) "Green Lights" voluntary conservation program was designed to encourage corporations to install new lighting. Full national participation, according to the EPA, could reduce total U.S. electric consumption by 10 percent and slash lighting electricity requirements by 50 percent, resulting in an annual $18.6 billion savings. By January 1, 1996, consumers were having to pay approximately 4 to 6 percent more for their bulbs due to the implementation of the Act.

Sales of advanced high-margin lamps were already ballooning in the 1990s. Consumers were increasingly switching to long lasting halogen bulbs costing as much as $20. In addition, energy-efficient compact fluorescent bulbs that could be screwed into standard bulb sockets were realizing widespread appeal. But recent evidence of halogen bulbs being responsible for more than 100 fires since 1992, coupled with the fact that the power now consumed by the over 40 million halogen bulbs in use exceeds the savings that compact fluorescents have achieved in replacing incandescent bulbs nationwide, points to a possible decline in the popularity of halogens. In the long run, low-energy fluorescents are much cheaper to operate than halogens.

INDUSTRY LEADERS

Forty-four companies participated in the U.S. electric lamp manufacturing industry as of 1996. Slightly more than one-half of companies had less than $10 million in sales and fewer than 100 employees. With the exception of the top three, every company posted total sales of less than $100 million and had fewer than 600 employees.

The three largest industry participants are General Electric Lighting; MagneTek, Inc.; and Philips Lighting Company. General Electric, the recognized light bulb industry leader, does not release financial information on its subsidiaries to the public. MagneTek had 1996 sales of $860 million and employed about 6,000. Philips Lighting Co. was the third largest company in the business, with $490 million in revenues and about 6,000 U.S. workers. Other major competitors included Fusion Systems Corp. ($99 million in 1996 and 600 employees) and Chicago Miniature Lamp, Inc. ($57 million in 1996 and about 800 employees).

WORK FORCE

Although sales and production volume increased for most industry participants during the 1980s, aggregate employment actually dropped about 12 percent to less than 25,000 in the early 1990s. Manufacturing productivity gains and management restructuring were the primary culprits of recessed employment figures. For 1995, the work force actually rose to 26,000—an increase of 23 percent over the early 1990s. This increase may be due in part to the implementation of the National Energy Policy Act of 1992 (EPACT), which called for compliance by 1995. Manufacturers had to cease production of certain energy-inefficient lamps and replace them with new products which met the new standards. Additionally, the increase in housing construction in the mid-1990s called for greater lamp production.

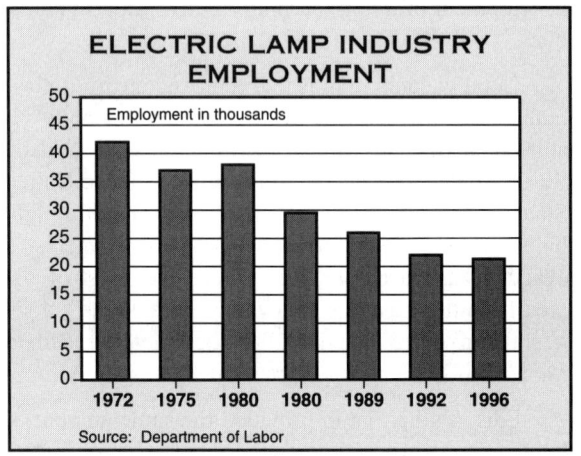

Jobs for production workers, which accounted for a leading 53 percent of this industry's work force in 1995, will likely decline by 2005, according to the Bureau of Labor Statistics. The average payroll per worker in the industry is roughly equivalent to the mean for all U.S. manufacturing sectors.

AMERICA AND THE WORLD

Besides domestic sales, many manufacturers were also striving to take advantage of growth opportunities overseas. Global electric lamp sales were estimated at about $9 billion in the mid-1990s and were expected to increase to about $11.5 billion by the turn of the century. U.S. producers met nearly 30 percent of worldwide demand in the mid-1990s and hoped to further boost their global market share. Although low-cost foreign manufacturers posed significant obstacles to exporters of traditional, commodity-like incandescent bulbs, U.S. manufacturers maintained a decided advantage in markets for high-tech lamps.

General Electric Company took the lead in foreign expansion in 1990 when it purchased Hungarian light bulb maker Tungsram Co. Tungsram lost money in the early 1990s, but GE invested $90 million in the operation between 1990 and 1993 to increase productivity and cut costs. GE planned to build Tungsram into the cornerstone of its European lighting business.

RESEARCH AND TECHNOLOGY

As light bulb producers labored to develop new, high-tech lamps that could increase their market share and boost profit margins, a steady stream of technological advancements greeted consumers in the mid-1990s. Most bulbs offered superior lighting characteristics, greater efficiency, and improved longevity. Other advances were making bulbs more environmentally safe for disposal; this is a particularly relevant development in the case of fluorescent bulbs, which contain mercury.

One notable breakthrough was the Intersource bulb, developed by Intersource Technologies Inc. in 1993 and scheduled for sale in 1994. The Intersource light bulb, or E-lamp, uses radio wave technology to produce light, and does not use a tungsten filament. It emits much less heat and consumes up to 75 percent less energy than conventional incandescent bulbs. The 20,000 hour E-lamp was priced at $15 to $20, fit normal bulb sockets, and was designed to provide 20 years of normal service.

Panasonic Lighting of Japan's new electronic light capsule lamp is expected to have a great impact on the industry in the United States. The lamp operates at 25 watts and can be used as a replacement for a 90 watt incandescent lamp and offers superior color rendering capability.

FURTHER READING

"Bright Ideas in Light Bulbs." *Consumer Reports,* October 1992.

Brooks, Andree. "Fire Hazards Seen in Some Torchere-Style Halogen Lamps." *The New York Times,* 16 January 1997, C2.

"Bulbs in Bulk." *Supermarket News,* 19 July 1993.

Burgert, Philip. "This Bright Idea May Dim Lighting Filament Market." *American Metal Market,* 31 August 1993.

Cross, Michael. "Eternal Life for Light Bulbs." *New Scientist,* 20 February 1993.

Dinley, Brigg. "The What, Where and Why of Bulbs." *HFD-The Weekly Home Furnishings Newspaper,* 17 August 1992.

Elson, Joel. "Halogens in the Spotlight." *Supermarket News,* 17 May 1993.

"Energy Act Sets New Light Bulb Standards." *Hardware Age,* December 1992.

Frickel, Fred. "Energy and Cost Savings with Compact Fluorescent." *Journal of Property Management,* January/February 1992.

"How the New Energy Law Affects the Lighting Buy." *Purchasing,* 1 April 1993.

Lazich, Robert S., ed. *Market Share Reporter.* Detroit: Gale Research, 1997.

"Light Bulbs: Is Bigger Better?" *Progressive Grocer,* December 1995, 82-83.

Miller, William H. "The 20-Year Light Bulb Clicks On." *Industry Week,* 16 November 1993.

Murphy, Elena Epatko. "Efficient Lamps Stretch Buyer Dollars." *Purchasing,* 7 March 1996, 70-71.

Ramstad, Evan. "Prospects Dim for Hot, Costly Halogens." *Wall Street Journal,* 10 March 1997, B1+.

"Retailers Light the Way Through New Bulb Mandates." *Stores,* May 1996, 83-84.

Schares, Gail E. "GE Gropes For the On-Switch in Hungary." *Business Week,* 26 April 1993.

Snyder, Glenn. "Shedding Light on Bulb Sales." *Progressive Grocer,* June 1993.

Sun, Marjorie. "Bright Sparks with Bulbs." *Far Eastern Economic Review,* 24 January 1991.

U.S. Bureau of the Census. *1995 Annual Survey of Manufacturers.* Washington: GPO, 1997.

U.S. Department of Commerce. International Trade Administration. *U.S. Industrial Outlook 1994.* Washington: GPO, 1994.

U.S. Department of Labor. Bureau of Labor Statistics. *Employment, Hours, and Earnings, United States, 1988-96.* Washington: GPO, 1997.

Verespej, Michael A. "The $20 Light Bulb: A Start-up Challenges GE with Technology GE Rejected." *Industry Week,* 15 February 1993.

Woods, Wilton. "Neon Comes Home." *Fortune,* 20 March 1995, 22.

—Dave Mote, updated by Matt Peck

SIC 3643

CURRENT-CARRYING WIRING DEVICES

The current-carrying wiring devices industry is comprised of establishments principally engaged in manufacturing current-carrying wiring devices; primarily interior electrical components used to connect equipment to a power source.

In the mid-1990s the industry was divided into six major categories: switches, wire connectors, convenience and power outlets, lampholders, metal contacts, and other devices such as plug caps and connector bodies. Miscellaneous products encompass items such as trolley line materials, lightning protectors, and fluorescent starters. The value of all industry shipments in 1995 was about $4.8 billion.

In 1729 Stephen Gray, an English physicist, was one of the first to discover that some substances could carry electricity from one location to another. These substances were called conductors. In 1820, Danish physicist Hans Christian Oersted found that a metal wire carrying a current of electricity would cause a compass needle to change direction. Georg Simon Ohm was credited with developing the theory of electric circuits in 1825. Subsequent advances gave birth to manufactured current-carrying wiring devices.

Rapid development of residential, commercial, and institutional structures in the United States between 1945 and 1980 propelled industry revenues past $2.5 billion per year. Strong development during most of the 1980s, moreover, resulted in average annual growth of about 8 percent. By 1989, sales of current-carrying devices had surged to about $4.4 billion. Economic recess in 1990 stalled industry growth, as sales dropped nearly 2 percent. Stagnant construction markets repressed growth throughout the early 1990s, although an increase in housing starts and general economic improvement in 1993 boosted shipments 2 percent, to about $4.5 billion.

In the mid-1990s, wiring device manufacturers benefitted from steady residential construction markets, and an upsurge in home renovations. In addition, new government building regulations mandated the use of certain wiring products. The National Electrical Code (NEC) that was implemented in 1993, for example, required the installation of special ground-fault circuit interrupters (GFCIs) that detect ground faults and shut off power to protected circuits. The revised 1996 NEC code augmented GFCI requirements. The sale of these and other devices are expected to bolster industry growth, as total shipments are projected to reach nearly $6 billion by the end of the decade.

To compensate for slow domestic sales, some industry participants capitalized on expanding export demand, which rose as a result of a weak U.S. dollar. Exports gained 14 percent in 1991, reaching a record $1.4 billion, or nearly 30 percent of total shipments, but growth of exports was flat through 1995. In combination with slow export growth, imports increased significantly in the mid-1990s, adding to the deficit trend that began in the early 1990s. Major importers

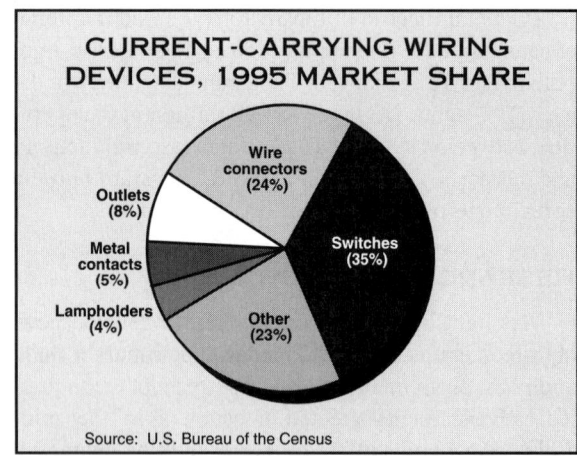

CURRENT-CARRYING WIRING DEVICES, 1995 MARKET SHARE

Wire connectors (24%)
Outlets (8%)
Switches (35%)
Metal contacts (5%)
Lampholders (4%)
Other (23%)

Source: U.S. Bureau of the Census

into the United States were Japan, Mexico, Taiwan, and Germany. Imports from Mexico were expected to continue growing in the mid-1990s, particularly in light of the North American Free Trade Agreement (NAFTA), which was initiated in 1994.

The industry is extremely fragmented, with over 420 companies vying for market share in the mid-1990s. The largest competitor was Thomas and Betts Corp., of Memphis, Tennessee. Thomas and Betts is a manufacturer of electrical and electronic connectors and components, and boasted almost $2 billion in sales and 8,700 employees in 1996. Hubbell Inc., of Orange, Connecticut, ranked second in sales with revenues of $1 billion and about 7,400 employees. Leviton Manufacturing Inc., of New York, was the third largest producer with $790 million in sales and about 8,000 workers. Other industry leaders included Cherry Corp., of Illinois, and Group Dekko International of Indiana.

Prospects for most occupations in this industry are weak throughout 2005, according to the U.S. Bureau of Labor Statistics. Aggregate industry employment fell slightly during the 1980s, despite output growth. Continued productivity gains will contribute to a decline of 15 to 35 percent for many labor positions between 1995 and 2005. Some positions, such as those for sales and marketing professionals, are forecast to grow as much as 38 percent.

FURTHER READING

Darnay, Arsen J., ed. *Manufacturing USA*. 5th ed. Detroit: Gale Research, 1996.

U.S. Bureau of the Census. *1995 Annual Survey of Manufactures; Value of Product Shipments*. Washington: GPO, 1997. Available from http://www.census.gov/prod/www/titles.html#mm.

U.S. Department of Commerce. Bureau of the Census. *Current Industrial Reports, Wiring Devices and Supplies, 1995*.

Washington, 1996. Available from http://www.census.gov/industry/ma36k95.txt.

U.S. Department of Commerce. International Trade Administration. *U.S. Industrial Outlook 1994.* Washington: GPO, 1994.

SIC 3644

NONCURRENT-CARRYING WIRING DEVICES

The noncurrent-carrying wiring devices industry is made up of companies that primarily manufacture hardware used to support electrical systems. Popular products include electrical conduits and fittings, boxes for outlets, switches, and fuses, and pole and transmission line devices. Insulators are also included in this industry, with the exception of those made from glass or ceramics. For information about the history of electrical systems, see **SIC 3641: Electric Lamp Bulbs and Tubes** and **SIC 3643: Current-Carrying Wiring Devices.**

Most noncurrent-carrying wiring products are consumed by the nonresidential construction sector. A leading 51 percent of industry output in the mid-1990s was attributed to electrical conduit and fittings, which includes conduit, connectors, junction boxes and related products. Pole and transmission line hardware, which was purchased by cable television and utility companies, comprised about 17 percent of production. The remainder of the market was highly fragmented. Store and restaurant construction, for example, accounted for about 1 percent of sales, as did construction related to mobile homes. Other industry outputs included highway and street construction, sewer system development, industrial controls, and lawn and garden equipment. The total value of shipments in 1995 reached $4 billion, and the total value of exported shipments was about $1 billion.

Rampant infrastructure growth and commercial development during the post-World War II U.S. economic boom helped the industry reach $2 billion by the late 1970s. Steady market growth during the 1980s, moreover, generated average annual revenue growth of about 4.5 percent. By 1989, industry participants were shipping about $3.4 billion worth of goods per year.

A severe depression in commercial development and stagnant institutional construction markets contributed to industry decline in the early 1990s. Sales slipped by about 2.5 percent in 1990 and continued to fade approximately 1.5 percent per year through 1993.

Although sales reached nearly $4 billion in 1994, growth in 1995 was nearly flat, with revenues increasing only 2 percent. From the mid-1990s through the end of the decade, analysts expected only a slight reprieve from these lackluster markets, as sales were forecast to grow slowly at 2 to 3 percent through 1998.

About 200 companies competed in the noncurrent-carrying wiring device industry in the mid-1990s, with about 17,000 employees. The majority of the top 50 producers had sales of less than $20 million and employed fewer than 200 workers, and there were only seven establishments with more than 500 employees in 1994. The average annual salary for production workers was $24,654 in 1996.

The largest competitor in the mid-1990s was Lamson and Sessions Co. of Ohio with $289 million in sales and 1,000 employees. Lamson and Sessions is a leading producer of thermoplastic electrical enclosures, fittings, conduit and pipe, and wiring devices for the construction, consumer, power, communications and waste-water markets. The second largest competitor was Panduit Corp., of Illinois, with $260 million in sales and 2,000 employees. Appleton Electric, of Chicago, which is a division of Emerson Electric Co., had sales of $200 million and about 1,400 workers. Other leaders included Allied Tube and Conduit Co., and O-Z Gedney Co. Inc.

Prospects for employment in this industry are relatively poor. Although output increased during the 1980s, employment declined from about 26,000 in the early 1980s to around 22,000 a decade later. There were 16,700 employees in the industry in 1996; 75 percent of which were classified as production workers. Productivity gains, management restructuring, and the movement of some manufacturing activities to foreign countries were the primary reasons for work force reductions. Although many labor positions will be eliminated between 1996 and 2005, according to the Bureau of Labor Statistics, some jobs, such as those for sales and marketing professionals, are likely to increase.

FURTHER READING

Darnay, Arsen J., ed. *Manufacturing USA.* 5th ed. Detroit: Gale Research, 1996.

U.S. Department of Commerce. Bureau of the Census. "Wiring Devices and Supplies, 1995." *Current Industrial Reports.* Washington, 1996. Available from http://www.census.gov/industry/ma36k95.txt.

U.S. Department of Commerce. Economics and Statistics Administration. Bureau of the Census. *1995 Annual Survey of Manufactures; Value of Product Shipments.* Washington:

GPO, 1997. Available from http://www.census.gov/prod/www/titles.html#mm.

U.S. Department of Commerce. International Trade Administration. *U.S. Industrial Outlook 1994.* Washington: GPO, 1994.

SIC 3645

RESIDENTIAL ELECTRIC LIGHTING FIXTURES

The residential electric lighting fixtures industry encompasses manufacturers that produce a variety of equipment and components for home use. Popular offerings include chandeliers, desk and floor lamps, glass and metal lamp shades, yard lights, and wall-mounted lighting fixtures. Light bulbs, cloth and plastic lamp shades, flashlights, and lanterns are classified in other industries.

About 50 percent of industry revenues in the mid-1990s were derived from stationary, or mounted, fixtures, such as ceiling and wall lamps. Portable lamps, like movable desk and floor lamps, accounted for about 36 percent of shipments. The remainder of revenues were garnered from the sale of lamp shades and various types of parts and accessories. The total value of shipments in 1995 was $2 billion, and about 4 percent of production was exported.

The first lighting apparatus pre-dates the light bulb—in 1650, German, Otto von Guericke produced a luminous glow from a spinning globe of sulfur. However, the evolution of modern day lamps and fixtures parallels the popularization of the electric light bulb, which Thomas Edison invented in 1879. Rapid demand for all types of lighting devices helped the residential lighting fixture industry grow to a $1.4 billion business by the early 1980s.

Industry revenues grew sluggishly during the 1980s, despite healthy residential construction markets. Increased foreign competition was a primary reason for stagnant sales. Although revenues reached about $1.8 billion by 1988, the industry suffered a severe commercial development depression and stalled housing starts in the late 1980s and early 1990s. Sales plummeted about 16 percent between 1988 and 1990, to $1.56 billion.

New home construction buoyed sales to about $1.6 billion in 1992 and to $1.8 billion by 1993. In the mid-1990s, the industry benefitted from the passage of nationwide energy initiatives and legislation. The National Energy Security Act of 1992 mandated the use of new energy-saving bulbs, and the EPA's "Green Lights" program encouraged companies to install new energy-efficient lighting fixtures and related products. Many U.S. residential lighting fixture producers rejuvenated lagging margins with sales of the new energy-saving lighting equipment, while others sought profit growth through mergers and acquisitions. The number of companies dwindled from about 650 in the early 1980s to 498 in 1994, as companies combined forces to survive withering demand.

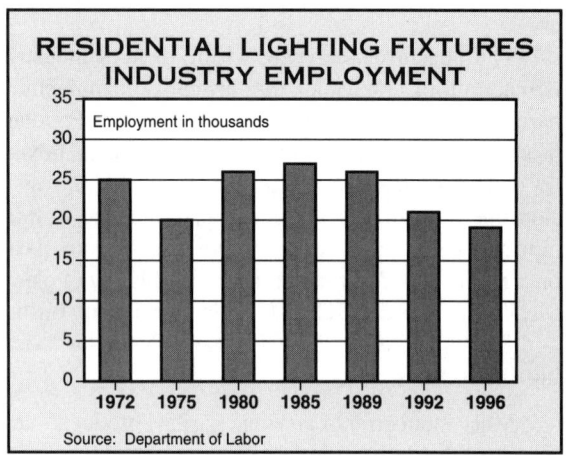

Despite consolidation, the residential lighting fixture industry remained fragmented in the mid-1990s. The majority of the top 50 competitors had sales of less than $25 million in the mid-1990s and employed fewer than 400 workers. The largest producer was Genlyte Group Inc. of New Jersey, which had sales of $456 million from its diversified operations and employed about 2,600 workers. Genlyte and its subsidiaries produce a variety of lighting products for commercial, industrial, and residential applications. Lightolier Inc., a division of Genlyte, produces track, decorative, and flourescent lighting fixtures, and represented $198 million in 1996 sales. Metalux Lighting Co. of Georgia was the second largest competitor, with $272 million in sales and about 1,300 employees. The third largest competitor was Catalina Lighting Inc. of Miami, Florida, with $184 million in sales and 300 employees.

Industry trends show that job growth for most occupations will remain stagnant through the year 2000. Aggregate employment fell from about 22,000 in the early 1980s to about 19,000 in 1995—the result of work force reductions and manufacturing productivity gains. The number of production workers was expected to decrease by almost 20 percent from 1995 to 1998, according to the Bureau of Labor Statistics, but selected positions such as those for sales professionals and machinists were expected to increase in number.

FURTHER READING

Darnay, Arsen J., ed. *Manufacturing USA*. 5th ed. Detroit: Gale Research, 1996.

U.S. Bureau of the Census. *1995 Annual Survey of Manufactures*. Washington: GPO, 1997. Available from http://www.census.gov/prod/www/titles.html#mm.

SIC 3646

COMMERCIAL, INDUSTRIAL, AND INSTITUTIONAL ELECTRIC LIGHTING FIXTURES

The commercial lighting fixture industry is comprised of establishments primarily engaged in manufacturing electric lighting fixtures for commercial, industrial, and institutional customers. Popular industry offerings include hotel and restaurant chandeliers, desk and floor lamps for offices, luminous ceiling panels, and industrial fluorescent lighting fixtures.

INDUSTRY SNAPSHOT

About 80 percent of industry output in the mid-1990s was used for commercial and institutional purposes, and 15 percent was utilized in industrial applications. Approximately 4 percent of production was exported. The largest single market for commercial lighting devices was office buildings, which purchased about 9 percent of all fixtures produced by both residential and commercial fixture manufacturers. Hospitals and parking garages both consumed about 1 percent of production. The remainder of the market was highly fragmented.

BACKGROUND AND DEVELOPMENT

The use of lighting fixtures in commercial applications followed Thomas Edison's invention of the light bulb in 1879. During the industrial revolution in the late 1880s and early 1900s, electric light fixtures became common in factories, hospitals, hotels, and other commercial structures. Fixtures for fluorescent bulbs, which were introduced in 1938 and were more energy-efficient than previous bulbs, became the industry emphasis by the 1950s. Steady market growth during the post-World War II U.S. economic expansion pushed sales of commercial fixtures past $1.5 billion by the early 1980s.

Healthy commercial development throughout most of the 1980s resulted in average annual revenue growth of nearly eight percent for the commercial fixture industry. By 1990, sales topped $3 billion per year. Despite a severe downturn in commercial development in 1989 and the early 1990s, sales dipped only 1 percent in 1991 before increasing an encouraging 4 percent in 1992. Healthy institutional demand and sales of fixtures for new energy-saving bulbs continued to buoy earnings in 1994-95, as industry revenues climbed to around $3.5 billion, up more than 16 percent from 1992. Industry projections show revenues surpassing $4 billion by 1998.

In the mid-1990s U.S. commercial lighting fixture producers benefitted from government initiatives that encouraged businesses to replace existing lamps and fixtures with new energy-saving devices, gradually phasing out the old equipment. The new devices and lamps produce more light per watt, so that less electricity is needed to power the fixture. Companies also boosted profits through cost-cutting programs and productivity gains, which has traditionally meant reductions in the work force. In light of increasing foreign competition, as well as the introduction of the North American Free Trade Agreement (NAFTA), many manufacturers were forming joint ventures with overseas producers and moving production facilities outside the United States. Shipments by both residential and commercial fixture producers were expected to grow at a rate of between three and five percent annually through the end of the decade.

INDUSTRY LEADERS

About 250 U.S. companies competed in the commercial lighting fixture industry in the mid-1990s, however the leading two competitors garnered almost twice the amount of sales of all the top 50 competitors combined, the majority of which had less than $50 million in sales and fewer than 200 employees. The largest industry participant was National Service Industries Inc., of Georgia, which had sales of about $2 billion, and 2,100 employees throughout its diversified operations. Osram Sylvania, Inc., of Danvers, Massachusetts, had sales of $1.8 billion and employed 1,300 workers. Other industry leaders included Lithonia Lighting Co. with $764 million in sales, and CPM Lighting with $300 million in sales.

WORK FORCE

Although industry employment rose from 19,000 in the early 1980s to 23,000 by the early 1990s, future employment prospects in this industry are not encouraging. Many manufacturing positions were expected to decline significantly between 1990 and 2005, according to the Bureau of Labor Statistics, in the wake of productivity gains and the movement of production facilities overseas. However, sales positions and some specialized machinist occupations, which account for a relatively small share of this industry's work force, will probably increase.

FURTHER READING

Darnay, Arsen J., ed. *Manufacturing USA.* 5th ed. Detroit: Gale Research, 1996.

U.S. Department of Commerce. International Trade Administration. *U.S. Industrial Outlook 1994.* Washington: GPO, 1994.

U.S. Bureau of the Census. Economics and Statistics Administration. *1995 Annual Survey of Manufactures; Value of Product Shipments.* Washington: GPO, 1997. Available from http://www.census.gov/prod/www/titles.html#mm.

SIC 3647

VEHICULAR LIGHTING EQUIPMENT

This category includes establishments primarily engaged in manufacturing vehicular lighting equipment. Establishments primarily engaged in manufacturing sealed-beam lamps are classified in **SIC 3641: Electric Light Bulbs and Tubes.**

The world has come a long way since the first driver of a horseless carriage attached two kerosene lamps to his vehicle to light his way at night. Aftermarket electric lighting systems were available for vehicles as early as the turn of the century, and acetylene headlamps started appearing on cars around 1905, but it was not until 1912 that Cadillac featured electric lights as standard equipment on its cars. Lights for airplanes were also an afterthought, first appearing some years after the Wright Brothers flew their aircraft at Kitty Hawk. Vehicular lighting is now standard equipment on aircraft, automobiles, boats, bikes, motorcycles, and locomotives, and is even used on roller skates and baby buggies. Vehicular lights flash, flicker, and give signals; their messages have become an integral part of our daily lives.

Companies that manufacture vehicular lighting equipment generally do so for a wide range of vehicles, including automobiles, airplanes, trains, boats, bicycles, motorcycles, and amusement rides. Also, companies frequently work together on the same lighting project, often on a contractor-subcontractor basis. According to the *1995 Annual Survey of Manufactures*

the vehicular lighting equipment industry shipped goods to the value of approximately $3.0 billion and employed approximately 17,400 people. This was an increase from the previous year's figure of $2.7 billion and 15,600 employees.

In the mid-1990s, the leading companies in the vehicular lighting equipment industry were North American Lighting Inc., Peterson Manufacturing Company, Truck-Lite Co., Inc., and Federal-Mogul Corp. Lighting and Electrical Division. North American Lighting's sales were $250 million in the mid-1990s, with 1,600 employees. Peterson, a leading manufacturer of vehicle lights, reflectors, and mirrors for the automotive and trucking industry, had sales of about $107 million and employed 1,200 people. Truck-Lite's sales were $93 million, and the company employed 1,200 people.

The United States was expected to import more automotive parts and accessories, including vehicular lighting equipment, than it exports through the middle of the 1990s. This trade imbalance is due chiefly to increased shipments from Japan. Overall, however, *U.S. Industrial Outlook* projects that U.S. parts exports should increase slowly. Other opportunities exist for U.S. manufacturers, however. Some U.S. companies are looking to Mexico for increased export business, mainly because of the North American Free Trade Agreement. Others, including Allied-Signal and Federal-Mogul Corp., are exploring joint ventures with foreign manufacturers and acquiring overseas manufacturing facilities. Foreign investment in the U.S. parts industry is also expected to grow slowly.

FURTHER READING

"Allied-Signal, Chrysler Contract." *The Wall Street Journal,* 2 February 1993.

"Buck Rogers Lights: Tess." *Bicycling,* November 1992, 31.

Darnay, Arsen J., ed. *Manufacturing USA.* 5th ed. Detroit: Gale Research, 1996.

Henderson, Breck W. "FAA: Aircraft Strobe Lights May Fall Short of Standard. *Aviation Week and Space Technology,* 14 September 1992, 42.

Lynch, Terrence P. "Aircraft Beacon Design Eliminates Fresnel Lens." *Design News,* 18 November 1991, 99-100.

"Portable Lights." *Bicycling,* January 1992, 26-28.

Scott, David. "Safety Headlights." *Popular Science,* March 1993, 49.

Scott, William B. "Companies Pursue Conformal Electronics for Civil and Military Applications." *Aviation Week and Space Technology,* 29 January 1990, 56-58.

Siuru, Bill. "Lighting Up the Road of Tomorrow." *Mechanical Engineering,* August 1991, 64-67.

U.S. Bureau of the Census. *1995 Annual Survey of Manufactures.* Washington: GPO, 1997.

"Taillight Change?" *Motor Trend,* January 1993, 32.

U.S. Department of Commerce. *U.S. Industrial Outlook 1993.* Washington: GPO January 1993.

—Ron Schultz, updated by Kenneth R. Shepherd

SIC 3648

LIGHTING EQUIPMENT, NOT ELSEWHERE CLASSIFIED

This classification covers establishments primarily engaged in manufacturing miscellaneous lighting fixtures and equipment, electric and nonelectric, not elsewhere classified. Examples of such products include flashlights and similar portable lamps, searchlights, ultraviolet lamp fixtures, and infrared lamp fixtures. Establishments primarily engaged in manufacturing electric light bulbs, tubes, and related light sources are classified in **SIC 3641: Electric Lamp Bulbs and Tubes.** Those establishments producing glassware for lighting fixtures are classified in various glass manufacturing industries. Those establishments manufacturing traffic signals are classified in **SIC 3669: Communications Equipment, Not Elsewhere Classified.**

INDUSTRY SNAPSHOT

The two major groupings in the industry were outdoor lighting equipment, which constituted 57 percent of industry output in the mid-1990s, and electric and nonelectric equipment not elsewhere classified, which represented 37 percent of industry production. The majority of products in this category were hand portable lighting equipment, such as flashlights and lanterns. The remainder of the market was highly fragmented among various electric and nonelectric devices. Personal consumption expenditures represented about 16 percent of consumption, and 4 percent of the industry's output was exported. Institutional and commercial sectors accounted for the majority of sales.

BACKGROUND AND DEVELOPMENT

Late 1980s revenues of over $1.8 billion per year for the miscellaneous lighting equipment industry (approximately 20 to 25 percent of total lighting equipment industry total) represented an average annual growth rate of more than 8 percent between 1982 and 1988, when sales were about $1 billion. Strong commercial and residential construction markets boosted shipments through the late 1980s, but growth faltered in the early 1990s as economic malaise and depressed construction sectors pinched profits. Recovering residential building and remodeling markets boosted demand in 1992 and 1993, however, and these markets continued to improve through the mid-1990s.

Miscellaneous lighting equipment manufacturers were hoping to overcome analysts' predictions of slow 1990s growth by introducing new and better fixtures. Much of the emphasis was on devices that could reduce energy consumption and accommodate new high-tech bulbs. The National Energy Security Act of 1992 even mandated the use of more efficient bulbs and equipment. In addition, the Environmental Protection Agency's voluntary "Green Light" conservation program was encouraging corporations to install new energy-efficient equipment and fixtures. Growth through the mid-1990s was stable, as the total value of shipments increased 22 percent from 1992 to $2.4 billion in 1994. Despite this trend, there was no increase in the value of shipments in 1995. The industry exported about $540 million in goods.

INDUSTRY LEADERS

The largest company in this industry in the mid-1990s was Coleman Company Inc. This Colorado-based outfit generated 1996 sales of $934 million from its operations, and had about 3,200 employees. AM-SCO Healthcare Division ranked second according to sales, with $216 million. The third-biggest competitor was Juno-Lighting, based in Illinois, with $131 million in sales, and 900 employees. Other leaders included Stabler Company, Mag Instrument Inc. and Publicker Industries Inc.

WORK FORCE

Although industry employment grew from about 8,500 to more than 9,500 during the 1980s, the outlook for employment growth was poor from the mid-1990s through the end of the decade. Productivity gains and the transfer of some manufacturing activities to low-cost producers in other countries are expected to contribute to job losses for several occupations. Positions for assemblers and fabricators, which account for over 16 percent of the work force, were expected to decline by seven percent between 1994 and 2005, and positions for machine operators were projected to drop as much as 35 percent, according to the Bureau of Labor Statistics. While most blue-collar opportunities will wane, jobs for specialized groups such as industrial machinery mechanics were projected to rise significantly. Prospects were also good for sales and marketing positions through 2005.

FURTHER READING

Darnay, Arsen J., ed. *Manufacturing USA.* 5th ed. Detroit: Gale Research, 1996.

''Energy Act Sets New Lightbulb Standards.'' *Hardware Age,* December 1992.

''How the New Energy Law Affects the Lighting Buy.'' *Purchasing,* 1 April 1993.

U.S. Department of Commerce. International Trade Administration. *U.S. Industrial Outlook 1994.* Washington: GPO, 1994.

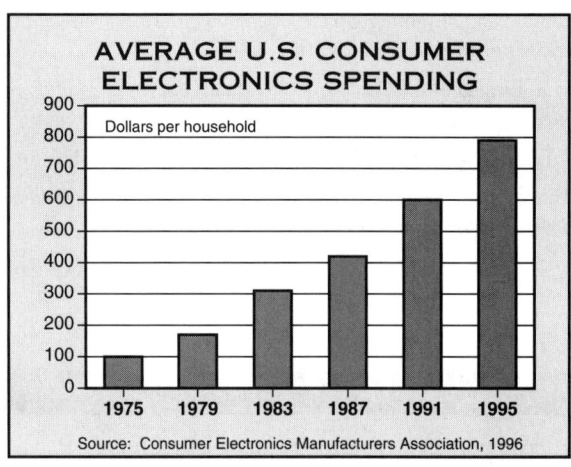

AVERAGE U.S. CONSUMER ELECTRONICS SPENDING

Dollars per household

Source: Consumer Electronics Manufacturers Association, 1996

SIC 3651

HOUSEHOLD AUDIO AND VIDEO EQUIPMENT

This category includes establishments primarily engaged in manufacturing electronic audio and video equipment for use at home or in automobiles, such as televisions, video recorders and players, radio receivers and amplifiers, phonographs, cassette tape players, and compact disc (CD) players. This industry also includes companies that manufacture microphones, speakers, and public address systems.

INDUSTRY SNAPSHOT

In 1996, U.S. manufacturers of household audio and video equipment reported sales of $10.8 billion. The industry employed 56,000 workers—including approximately 34,000 production workers. U.S. manufacturers are focusing almost exclusively on producing audio speakers and advanced technology televisions. Virtually all other consumer electronic components sold in the United States were manufactured abroad or manufactured in the United States by foreign-owned companies.

Video equipment—televisions, videocassette recorders, and camcorders—accounted for more than 65 percent of 1995 sales in this industry, while audio equipment—radios, cd players, tape recorders and players, and car audio units—accounted for nearly 35 percent of 1995 sales. More than 146 million audio units were shipped for purchase in the United States in 1996, with 66 million video units shipped during the same period.

Approximately 210 companies manufactured household audio and video equipment in the United States in 1996, down from a peak of more than 350 companies in the early 1990s—a decrease of 40 per-

cent. The decline was due in large part to intense foreign competition, primarily from Japan and South Korea, which forced many U.S. manufacturers to abandon consumer electronics altogether.

ORGANIZATION AND STRUCTURE

The U.S. household audio and video manufacturing industry was dominated in the early 1990s by American subsidiaries of Japanese companies who used technologies developed by American companies. These subsidiaries assembled color televisions and high fidelity audio equipment from components imported from Japan or from Japanese-owned manufacturing facilities in other countries. The exception was speaker systems, where U.S.-owned companies were recognized as market leaders worldwide. The Zenith Electronics Corporation in Glenview, Illinois was the only major U.S.-owned company still manufacturing color televisions in 1993. Zenith controlled about 10 percent of the U.S. market. Bose Corporation of the United States supplies 22 percent of the speakers purchased in the country—more than twice the amount as the next leading competitor.

BACKGROUND AND DEVELOPMENT

American manufacturers dominated the household audio and video industry from the first experimental radio and television broadcasts until the 1980s, when many U.S.-owned companies were forced out of manufacturing by foreign competition. The first radios to be mass manufactured were developed by RCA in the 1920s, which also pioneered television manufacturing in the 1930s. For years, American manufacturers like RCA, Westinghouse, General Electric, Motorola, Philco, and Zenith dominated the industry.

Television Manufacturing. Although the nature of television manufacturing in the United States began to change in the late 1960s, the stage was set more than a decade earlier when several major Japanese manufacturers formed the Home Electronic Appliance Market Stabilization Council. Despite opposition from the Japanese Fair Trade Commission, this cartel successfully lobbied the Japanese government to establish tariffs and other trade barriers that protected the manufacturers from foreign competition. This allowed the cartel to establish minimum prices and control their domestic market. In addition, U.S. companies locked out of the Japanese market began to license advanced technology to the Japanese. In 1962, RCA Corporation became the first company to license color technology to the Japanese manufacturers.

In 1963, the Japanese manufacturers began to export televisions to the United States—using the profits from their protected domestic market to subsidized below cost sales in the United States, in violation of U.S. trade laws. In addition, a Department of Justice investigation later revealed that the Japanese gave American importers, including Sears, Roebuck & Co., illegal rebates on every Japanese television they sold in the United States. Sales of Japanese-made televisions soared while U.S. companies suffered.

The United States Electronic Industry Association filed a complaint about the illegal "dumping" in 1968. However, Japanese manufacturers stonewalled the investigation for more than three years. In addition, the U.S. government was not eager to upset trade negotiations with Japan and proceeded with the investigation reluctantly. In 1971, the Treasury Department ruled that the Japanese companies had violated U.S. law and owed millions of dollars in antidumping levies. Nine years passed before a settlement was reached, however, and the Japanese paid about one-tenth of what they owed. The damage to U.S. television manufacturers was irreversible.

In 1968, there were 28 U.S.-owned companies manufacturing televisions in this country. By 1976, there were only six. More than 20,000 jobs were eliminated. Several financially strapped U.S. companies were purchased by Japanese or European competitors, while others simply went out of business. Matsushita Electric Industrial Company, the largest consumer electronics company in the world, purchased Motorola's Consumer Products Division. Magnavox was purchased by N.V. Philips, S.A., a Dutch manufacturer. Among the brand names to disappear were Admiral and Dumont. In addition, dozens of smaller manufacturers making parts for U.S.-made televisions also failed.

In 1977, the Japanese manufacturers signed an Orderly Marketing Agreement limiting exports to the United States to 1.5 million sets annually. However, the agreement allowed the Japanese to manufacture televisions in the United States in excess of the quotas. Three of the five largest Japanese companies—Matsushita, the Sony Corporation, and Sanyo Electric Company—had already established manufacturing facilities in the United States, and Hitachi and Tokyo Shibaura Electric soon followed suit. The Japanese also established manufacturing facilities in other countries with abundant, low cost labor such as Mexico and Argentina to circumvent the limits on imports from Japan. In addition, Taiwan and South Korea began exporting televisions to the United States. Taiwanese imports more than doubled in 1977, increasing that country's share of the U.S. market from 7 to 14 percent.

An investigation later revealed that Robert Strauss, the former Democratic Party chairman who had been appointed by President Carter as special trade representative to Japan, signed a secret agreement in which he promised that the United States would settle financial claims against the Japanese manufacturers "expeditiously" and would limit an International Trade Commission investigation into further allegations of illegal dumping. Strauss also promised that the Carter Administration would appeal a ruling court decision in favor of Zenith, who had won a $400 million predatory pricing suit against Matsushita. The award would have been trebled under U.S. antitrust law to $1.2 billion. Finally, Strauss agreed to ignore official Japanese government policies that prevented U.S. companies from competing in the protected Japanese home electronics market.

Congress did not learn of the secret agreement until 1979, but nevertheless agreed to honor the commitment. Under the Strauss agreement, the Japanese eventually paid about $66 million of the $500 million the Treasury Department said they owed for illegal dumping; the antitrust suit filed by Zenith was eventually dismissed by the Supreme Court. Meanwhile, the Japanese solidified their hold on the U.S. television market.

At least one U.S. company, however, blamed irrational cost cutting by U.S. market leaders as much as the Japanese for the decline of U.S. manufacturing. Robert J. O'Neil, then president of GTE Consumer Electronics Co., told *Business Week* in 1978 that "RCA and Zenith are the biggest problem in the industry." At the time, RCA and Zenith were battling each other for the number one position in U.S. sales of color televisions. According to O'Neil, cost cutting by RCA and Zenith forced other U.S. companies to lower their prices to unprofitable levels. In dismissing the antitrust suit against Matsushita, the Supreme Court noted that

Zenith and RCA were still the leading television makers in the United States, with more than 40 percent of the market between them, despite 20 years of Japanese competition. GTE eventually sold its consumer electronics company, including the Sylvania and Philco brand names, to the Dutch company that purchased Magnavox, N.V. Philips.

Among the last major U.S.-owned companies to manufacture televisions were the General Electric Corporation and the RCA Corporation, which together accounted for about 45 percent of all color television sets sold in the United States in 1980. General Electric quit manufacturing televisions in 1984 and began importing sets made by Matsushita with the GE brand name. In 1985, General Electric temporarily re-entered the market when it purchased RCA. However, despite a 23 percent share of the market for color televisions in the United States and 17 percent of the market for VCRs, the RCA consumer electronics division was losing money. In 1986, General Electric sold the RCA consumer products division to Thomson, S.A., a French electronics corporation second only to Matsushita in size. The sale left the United States without a single American-owned firm manufacturing VCRs.

Audio Equipment. The experience of the audio equipment manufacturing industry in the United States was similar to that of television manufacturers. Until the mid-1960s, most of the leading manufacturers in the world were U.S. owned companies with such well known brand names as Fisher, Bose, Sherwood, and Marantz. The first Japanese brand to appear in the annual *Stereo/Hi-Fi Directory and Buyers Guide* was Kenwood, in 1965. However, over the next five years, the number of Japanese brands sold in the United States increased dramatically. Sony, Pioneer, and Sansui were introduced in 1968; JVC was introduced in 1970.

By 1980, most U.S. owned companies had either moved their manufacturing facilities offshore to take advantage of cheap labor, or they had licensed their brand names to Japanese companies and become distributors for foreign manufacturers. Many Japanese companies eventually built manufacturing facilities in the United States. It soon became difficult to distinguish U.S.-made from foreign-made products. Or, as William Livingstone, then editor-in-chief of *Stereo Review Magazine,* wrote in 1986, ''Do you give more support to the labor force and overall economy of the United States by buying a component manufactured in Hong Kong for an American company or by buying one made by American hands in a Japanese-owned factory in California or Tennessee?''

VCRs, Camcorders, and CD Players. With the exception of RCA, major American manufacturers disdained entering the market for VCRs, camcorders, and CD players as those technologies were developed in the 1980s. In many cases, U.S. companies apparently underestimated the tremendous markets that developed. But economist Pat Choate, writing in the *Washington Post,* pointed out that the loss of U.S. television manufacturing also hamstrung U.S. manufacturers' ability to enter these new fields by undermining the companies that produced high technology components. U.S. companies were relegated to a marketing role, rather than manufacturing, which helped create a huge trade deficit in consumer electronics in the 1980s.

CURRENT CONDITIONS

In 1989, the New York attorney general charged Matsushita, whose products sold in the United States under the Panasonic and Technics brand names, with price fixing. Although the company denied any wrongdoing, it agreed to pay an $18 million fine. This indicated to some industry analysts that Japanese manufacturers, having virtually eliminated American competition through predatory pricing policies, now intended to squeeze larger profit margins from the U.S. market.

However, a lingering recession was also affecting the industry. Ironically, many of the same Japanese companies that established U.S. manufacturing facilities in the 1970s to avoid restrictions on imports were beginning to move their operations to Mexico, where labor costs were considerably lower. Televisions made in Mexico by foreign companies went almost exclusively into the U.S. market. The North American Free Trade Agreement (NAFTA), endorsed by President Clinton in 1993, was expected to hasten this movement to Mexico.

Increased competition from Korean and Taiwanese manufacturers also continued to affect the U.S. consumer electronics manufacturing in the mid-1980s. Reminiscent of Japan's entry into the U.S. market, Goldstar Electronics, a leading Korean television manufacturer, was found guilty in 1984 of selling its televisions in the United States for 20 percent less than those same sets were sold for in Korea. To avoid paying a 20 percent antidumping tariff, Goldstar began beefing up production at a plant it opened in Alabama in 1981.

In 1993, several major corporations, including Zenith and General Instruments, were waiting for the Federal Communications Commission to set technological protocols for High Definition Television (HDTV) in the United States. These companies—and a third partnership led by Thomson, Philips, and

NBC—were hopeful that HDTV would help revitalize the U.S. electronics manufacturing industry. However, after considerable activity in the late 1980s, interest in HDTV appeared to be waning. Meanwhile, to maximize profits, U.S.-based manufacturers were beginning to concentrate on large-screen televisions and home-theater units, leaving low-margin color televisions to be manufactured elsewhere. There also were persistent rumors in the early 1990s that Zenith was looking to sell its television division. In November 1995, LG Electronics Inc., of South Korea, formerly known as industry giant Lucky Goldstar, invested $351 million in Zenith, which had lost money on operations every year since 1984. For 1995, Zenith lost $92.4 million on sales of $1.27 billion and losses continued through the first half of 1996. More recently, Zenith's stock tripled when news of Zenith s venture into the Internet television market would likely a produce a Internet ready television for less than $1,000 in the late 1990s.

INDUSTRY LEADERS

The leading makers of household audio and video equipment in the United States were subsidiaries of foreign-owned companies, including Mitsubishi Electronics America Incorporated, with 1996 sales of $2.2 billion, and Philips Consumer Electronics Company, with 1996 sales of $1.8 billion. Zenith Electronics Corporation was next in sales with $1.27 billion, followed by Harman International Industries Incorporated with $1.17 billion and Bose Corporation with sales of $700 million. It is difficult to ascertain exactly who the industry leaders are in this classification, since some of the sales figures include electronics products not covered by this classification. Bose is the industry leader in sales of audio speakers, while Zenith is the second largest supplier of televisions in the country.

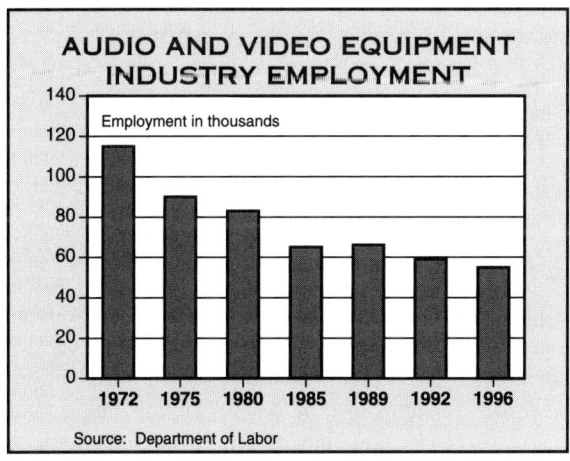

AUDIO AND VIDEO EQUIPMENT INDUSTRY EMPLOYMENT

Employment in thousands

Source: Department of Labor

WORK FORCE

The work force in this classification continues to decline, due mostly to the fact that American companies are increasingly getting out of the business due to foreign companies' domination. The industry has lost more than 9,000 employees since 1989. This trend may slow or possibly reverse depending upon the success of Internet TVs in the United States.

RESEARCH AND TECHNOLOGY

In early 1994, the HG Digital Conference—a committee representing 50 electronics companies in Europe, Asia, and the United States—agreed on a proposed standard for VCRs that will use digital technology. The agreement was reached in part to avoid future format battles such as the one that took place in the 1980s between Beta and VHS systems. This new technology, which is expected to provide manufacturers with the ability to increase image quality, involves storing tape images with ones and zeroes of binary computer codes rather than the current wave-like form. These new VCRs are expected to use video tapes that are one-quarter inch wide—one-half the width of existing VHS tapes. As noted in the *New York Times,* "some industry experts think it will take a few years for costs to come down enough for such machines to become popular. Initial estimates range up to $3,000, which is up to 10 times the cost of some current VCR models."

Arguably the greatest innovation in the industry revolves around the production of Internet TV equipment, which began in late 1996. Industry sources believe that sales of software/Internet TV equipment will increase from $2.3 billion in 1995 to more than $25 billion by 2002, when an estimated 33 percent of all American households will own such devices. Internet TVs and set top units will allow television users to access the Internet without having to use a personal computer. Among the potential drawbacks of Internet TV is that the average American views television from 8-12 feet away, making script on the screen difficult to see. Increasing the size of the text would mean less information would be available on each screen, meaning more scrolling up and down.

Zenith is marketing an Internet TV that is ready for operation right out of the box, while other companies, such as Sony and Philips, are manufacturing set top devices that convert ordinary televisions to Internet accessible ones. The market potential for this technology appears to be tremendous, since 85-90 percent of American homes are not currently connected to the Internet. Zenith's unit will sell for about $1,000, while the set tops devices will sell for $200 - $300. Available television-PC hybrids retail for between $3,500 and $4,500—out of reach for many households.

FURTHER READING

Blair, Roger D., et. al. "An Economic Analysis of Matsushita." *Antitrust Bulletin,* Summer 1991, 355.

Choate, Pat. "Japan and the Big Squeeze." *Washington Post,* 30 September 1990, D1.

Dreyfack, Kenneth. "Japan Can't Make a Quick Yen in the U.S. Anymore." *Business Week,* 23 February 1987, 120.

Dumaine, Brian. "Goldstar's U.S. Debut." *Fortune,* 15 October 1984, 141.

Elstrom, Peter. "The Angry Angels at Zenith." *Business Week,* 12 August 1996, 32.

Fantel, Hans. "American Speakers—Loud and Clear." *New York Times,* 2 June 1991, H36.

Gall, Norman. "Close the Door, They Come in the Window." *Forbes,* 15 February 1982, 80.

Greene, Richard. "One to Watch." *Forbes,* 13 February 1984, 114.

Hirsch, Julian. "Is American Audio Technology Dead?" *Stereo Review,* June 1987, 24.

"Hot Duel over Dumping." *Time,* 26 March 1979, 64.

"Imports Fuzz the Future of Color TV Makers." *Business Week,* 26 May 1980, 51.

Kallen, Barbara. "Down the Tube?" *Forbes,* 3 June 1985, 186.

"Kickbacks in Living Color." *Time,* 13 June 1977, 63.

Krantz, Michael. "The Biggest Thing Since Color." *Time,* 12 August 1996.

Lazich, Robert S., ed. *Market Share Reporter.* Detroit: Gale Research, 1997.

Livingstone, William. "Audio in America." *Stereo Review,* June 1986, 8.

Markoff, John. "Zenith Plans TV Set That Can Access Internet Without PC." *The New York Times CyberTimes,* 10 May 1996. Available from http://www.nytimes.com/web/docsroot/library/cyber/week/051zenith.html.

Morri, Aldo. "ITV Hardware and Software Market Showing Signs of Maturity." *News & Views,* March 1996. Available from http://165.247.175.190/mmp/mmp_mar96/dep_news.html.

"No Happy Ending." *Forbes,* 11 December 1978, 35.

Pearlman, Jerry K. "Save the Lectures, Give Us Some Help." *New York Times,* 14 December 1986.

Petre, Peter. "GE's Gamble on American-Made TVs." *Fortune,* 6 July 1987, 50.

Pollack, Andrew. "Technology Pact Prepares for Digital VCR Production." *Detroit Free Press,* 16 April 1994.

"Tactics to Outwit U.S. Protectionists." *Business Week,* 28 March 1977, 36.

Therrien, Lois. "Zenith Is Sticking Its Neck Out in a Cutthroat Market." *Business Week,* 17 August 1987.

"The TV-Set Competition That Won't Go Away." *Business Week,* 8 May 1978, 86.

Verespej, Michael A. "Un-American Activities." *Industry Week,* 7 September 1987, 32.

—Dean Boyer, updated by Matt Peck

SIC 3652

PHONOGRAPH RECORDS AND PRERECORDED AUDIO TAPES AND DISKS

This category includes establishments primarily engaged in manufacturing phonograph records and prerecorded audio tapes and disks. Establishments primarily engaged in the design, development, and production of prepackaged computer software are classified in Computer Programming, Data Processing, and Other Computer Related Services; and those reproducing prerecorded video tape cassettes and disks are classified in the Motion Picture industries.

INDUSTRY SNAPSHOT

"When Thomas Edison invented practical phonograph recording in 1877 he could hardly have anticipated the powerful mass entertainment medium it would become," wrote Michael Fink in *Inside the Music Business.* After a rocky start in the first decades of the twentieth century, the business of recording and selling music has grown into an international industry worth billions of dollars. Analysts from the International Federation of the Phonographic Industry (IFPF) estimated that in 1990 international record sales, a category that includes audiotapes and disks, grossed $24.1 billion. Though five major companies dominate the industry, the nature of the music business has always guaranteed a place for the small record company attuned to new forms of popular music.

ORGANIZATION AND STRUCTURE

The business of producing recorded music is like digging for gold—a record company has to pan many streams before it hits the jackpot. The principal work of each recording company consists of locating promising musical acts, producing them in the most commercial way, promoting them to fit into a rapidly changing market, and providing efficient distribution. Record companies lose money on albums that do not sell as well as anticipated, but those that become "hits" provide such immense profits that they make up for the failures.

Industry Organization. Although the Recording Industry Association of America (RIAA) claims 220 members, five of those corporations account for over 90 percent of the market. In November of 1992, *Music and Media* reported that PolyGram held 27 percent of the market, Sony Music Entertainment Inc. held 17.8 percent, Time Warner and Thorn/EMI both held 16.7 percent, and the Bertelsmann Music Group (BMG) held 15.3 percent. The smaller companies, called independent labels, together accounted for only 6.5 percent of the market.

Recording companies are often referred to as "labels," though that term became less accurate when large companies began marketing music under several different labels, or brands. Originally, the label was synonymous with the company, for each recording company had one label that identified its records. During the years, however, big companies have bought little companies, and single firms have acquired several smaller companies and their labels. When CBS bought the American Record Corporation in 1938, for example, they acquired both the Brunswick and Vocalion labels. After the very large corporate mergers and buyouts of the late 1980s and early 1990s, each one of the five companies that dominated the market owned many labels: PolyGram had 27 and Sony had 25. These companies are known as the major labels, or simply "the majors." Many of the individual labels owned by a large corporation retain their own staff, which enables the large companies to maintain better and more personal relations with the artists, who record on only one label. Independent record companies are usually still identified with a single label and are referred to as "the independents" or "the indies."

Single labels often produce only one kind of music. For example, Deutche Grammophone is a classical music label, Mercury carries country-western music, and Motown is a rhythm and blues (R&B) label; all are owned by PolyGram. Occasionally, a major label will create, rather than buy, a new label to produce one specific genre, as when Warner launched Warner Western in 1992. On the other hand, not all labels are thus limited. Koch International, an independent label, produces classical, country, pop, and jazz.

Company Organization. The first job of any recording company is to sign up musicians. This job is handled by the Artists and Repertoire (A&R) department, which scouts for and signs contracts with new talents, finds them songs if they do not write their own, and finds the right producer to oversee their records. In the first few decades of the industry, the A&R department

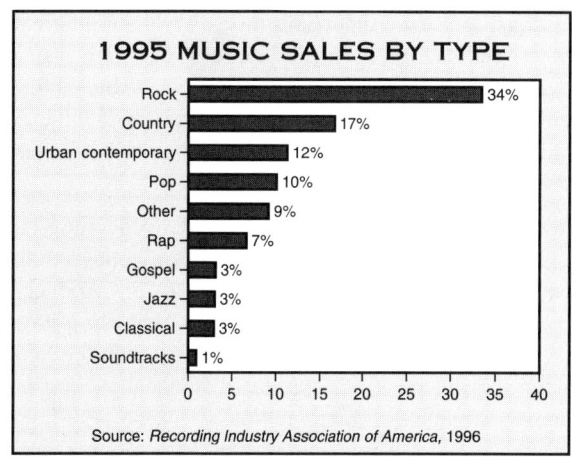

1995 MUSIC SALES BY TYPE

Type	Percent
Rock	34%
Country	17%
Urban contemporary	12%
Pop	10%
Other	9%
Rap	7%
Gospel	3%
Jazz	3%
Classical	3%
Soundtracks	1%

Source: *Recording Industry Association of America, 1996*

hired singers, found new songs for these singers to perform, and produced the record. These functions made the A&R department one of the largest and most powerful in any recording company.

Rock and roll music changed much of the music industry and affected A&R departments more than any other type of music. Rock musicians often wrote their own songs and found their own producers. As Steve Chapple and Reebee Garofalo explain in *Rock 'n' Roll Is Here to Pay: The History and Politics of the Music Industry,* "In the fifties the bulk of music was produced with staff producers who were assigned by the all-powerful A&R heads to record several of a company's acts. But these men often did not understand the new music. What's more, since many new groups wrote their own material, an A&R person was not needed to bring publisher and performer together. As conflicts between staff producers and groups increased, and as company A&R men proved for the most part unable to recognize underground talent, record companies turned to independent producers." Today the role of the A&R department is much more limited than what it was, and relies heavily on the independent producer for the sound of the final product.

The producer of a record, as the name implies, oversees the production of the master recording. The producer serves as the artistic director and business manager for the recording. The record company, through the A&R department, contracts with the artist and producer and provides the advance money for both. The producer then handles the main business aspects of recording the album. This includes budgeting for the project, arranging the copyright licenses when necessary, booking the recording studio, and hiring any extra musicians and equipment as needed. While recording companies frequently own studios, independent studios are also used for a variety of reasons, including the local musical styles of an area. Most records are still made in one of the three major musical cities—Los Angeles, New York, and Nashville—but the studios of smaller cities with unique musical roots are often hired for their unique sounds.

The producer also oversees the rehearsing, recording, and mixing of the musical tracks. Depending on the musicians involved, the producer sometimes has an enormous artistic role in the recording. The producer may hire out or write an arrangement, choosing how the accompaniment will sound. Working with the musicians in rehearsal, the producer frequently contributes to the musical interpretation. "My job is to help writers," Chris Thomas, rock star Elton John's producer, told *Billboard* in 1993. "That's the reason you're there: to help them get their song realized in recorded form." Thomas defines producing as "filling in the colors of a picture." No matter the size of the group, each instrument and voice is recorded separately on its own track. The producer oversees the mixdown of the tracks, combining the individual instruments into the final ensemble sound. "Recording basic tracks is a game. It's fun. It's easy," said Thomas. "Mixing is much harder because you can't always fix it tomorrow. . . . You've got to balance it very carefully." The final balance of instruments and voices, as well as the use of different electronic effects such as tone-quality filters, reverberation, delay, and echo, are determined by the producer. Today, musicians who want complete control over their own artistic productions will sometimes produce their own work, but many recordings are still governed by producers who are trained in sound engineering.

After the master recording is made and delivered to the record company, the production and promotion departments take over. The production department makes the physical items that the consumers will buy, both the recording and, just as importantly, the packaging. Both the producer and the promotion department may have roles in the artwork for the packaging. Music videos, a major form of promotion on MTV and other music television networks, may have the same producer as the album.

Since the ultimate goal of record companies is to sell a record, the marketing department is frequently the largest and most important. In this intensely competitive industry, promotion and marketing play a large part in the final success of any recording. Marketing departments use two primary avenues of publicity: radio promotion and media advertising.

Airplay is the most effective form of promotion for any popular recording, whether it be on radio or television, and having a new record programmed onto the playlist is the goal of all promoters. While there are several thousand music-format radio stations across the United States, only several hundred are important. Record promoters may send promotional copies to all stations, but they concentrate their personal efforts on the important few—the stations that determine the poll lists in the trade publications, such as Billboard's Top Ten. Most radio stations, however, usually play less than 40 songs in rotation in a week. Since the recording industry produces several hundred new albums each week, the competition for these spots is fierce. Since the early 1960s, "payola," or money paid to radio stations to play music, has been outlawed, but legal giveaways to radio station program directors and other personnel include albums, T-shirts, concert tickets, and invitations to press parties. Music television works much the same way. To become a hit, a song now must not only be played on the radio, but also be shown in video format on television.

Since 1957, when Dick Clark introduced hit after hit on his dance show, American Bandstand, television has been an effective promotional tool to supplement radio. In 1981, Warner Amex Cable Communications, which has since become Time Warner, introduced rock music programming to cable television in the form of MTV, and music videos revolutionized the industry. During the first few years, when not every pop musician made videos, MTV provided an avenue for new artists to reach audiences. By the middle of the 1980s, however, MTV became as play-list oriented as radio, and competition to have a video shown became as fierce as on any top-40 radio station. Other channels have also shown music videos, including VH-1, the adult-oriented MTV spin-off; Video Music Channel; Country Music TV; the Nashville Network; and NBC's Friday Night Videos. Videos have become essential to music promotion, and, as Michael Fink wrote in his 1989 book on the music industry, "[any] new record/tape release with aspirations to be a hit must have a music video clip to accompany it."

Publicity and advertising departments also cultivate the popular music press when releasing albums. Press kits for new artists include carefully prepared biographies presenting the most profitable image for the artist. Established and beginning artists alike go on publicity tours, although the rising costs of concert tours have kept record companies from providing full financial support for this element of publicity. In the late 1980s, retail outlets started sponsoring in-house concerts of relatively unknown artists as part of the promotional package. National and local radio and television interviews, help to publicize new releases; music critics receive advance copies of the new albums with the hopes that favorable reviews will sell disks. Music trade publications carry much advertising for artists and their recent releases.

Large companies distribute their records through branch distributors, independent distributors, and mail-order record clubs. In major musical cities, branch offices of the recording company distribute their recordings locally in conjunction with local promoters and advertising specialists. In smaller areas not covered by branch offices, record companies use the services of independent distributors, one-stops, and rack jobbers, who deal with many different record companies and distribute to record stores, department stores, and other record outlets (see **SIC 5735: Record and Prerecorded Tape Stores**). While retailing is considered a different industry altogether, some of the major labels own retail outlets; they do not limit their distribution to these stores, of course.

The first company foray into record-company-owned retail was the formation of record clubs, pioneered by Columbia Records when they formed Columbia House in the mid 1950s. RCA soon followed, and both have remained the biggest sponsors of direct-mail distribution. Since direct mail avoids middle-man costs, the companies can make more profit while still giving consumers a discounted price. From their inception, record clubs have proved profitable for the majors. Shortly after Sony bought CBS Records in the late 1980s, they entered into an agreement with Time Warner, owners of Warner Records, to jointly operate Columbia House Records. In 1993, the two conglomerates announced a new joint ownership and operation of two other direct-mail operations, Warner's Music Sound Exchange for the U.S. market, and Sony's Music $More in Germany.

Corporate Structure of Independents. Independent labels, while varying greatly in size and complexity, generally have few of the administrative capabilities of the major labels. Their strong point is signing and producing new music, and they often contract out other elements of their business. The small companies, like the rap-music label Flavor Unit Records, which released its first recording in December of 1992, have a skeletal administrative and production staff. Major label Epic Records agreed to promote and distribute Flavor Units' records. The small company's benefit from such an arrangement is access to the publicity power of a major label; the larger company reaps the benefits of an expanding market without much company investment. "Epic hasn't ventured that deep into rap," Epic executive vice-president Richard Griffith told *Billboard*. "We've been looking for people to be our partners as experts." Small labels that do not

connect with major labels often hire out for such services, contracting with independent public relations firms, distributors, studios, and disk factories.

BACKGROUND AND DEVELOPMENT

A few years after Thomas Edison invented phonograph recording using wax cylinders in 1877, Emile Berliner developed the disk format of recording. These two formats competed in popularity for a few years, but by the beginning of the twentieth century, the disk format had won. The earliest music recorded was classical opera and popular tin-pan alley and Broadway songs. In 1917, the first jazz recordings were made, and in 1920, the first blues were recorded. These recordings signalled the industry's discovery of music performed by and for African-Americans, which influenced the industry and American popular music greatly throughout the century. By the 1940s, the genre was universally known as "rhythm and blues."

From the outset, the industry has been dominated by a few large companies. The two earliest recording companies have remained among the majors throughout the century. The Victor Talking Machine Company, formed as an offshoot of the English Gramophone and Typewriter Company in 1901, eventually became RCA records; the Columbia Gramophone Company became Columbia Records in the late 1930s. Together, RCA and Columbia have shared the majority of the market for decades and, although by the early 1990s they were owned by different corporations, they still belong to the majors. The industry grew rapidly after 1900, peaking in 1921 with sales of $106 million. By 1922, however, radio had destroyed the market with the free music it offered over the airwaves. Sales fell throughout the entire decade, and when the stock market crashed in 1929, most of the smaller companies either went out of business or were bought by the two larger companies.

Although radio almost destroyed the industry in the 1920s, it saved the industry in the 1930s. The two rival radio networks, Radio Corporation of America and Columbia Broadcasting System, bought the rival record firms, Victor and Columbia Gramophone, respectively. The large profits from the radio industry financed recorded music. New technologies developed for radio, such as the electronic microphone, enhanced music recording as well. Record stars became radio stars and radio became the main promotional tool for selling records. In the mid-1930s when Jack Kapp—of the newly-formed independent label Decca—reduced the price of records from 75 cents to 35 cents, people could afford to buy them again, and the demand for recordings began to pick up. Music popular in the late thirties and early forties included big-band jazz and popular Broadway and movie songs, and in limited but growing regional markets, country music, and rhythm and blues. The record format during these early years was shellac disks playing at 78 rotations per minute (rpm) with only one song on each side (singles).

The social and economic changes accompanying World War II created changes in the music world that would impact the industry forever. Because of the war-induced shortages of shellac, RCA and CBS limited their record production to mainstream popular music, leaving a hole in the R&B and country market. Small independent labels grew to fill the gap left by the majors.

Radio also filled this gap between supply and demand: some stations began programming R&B between the pop music programs, some began to program country music, and new stations formed to play only R&B or country. While both R&B and country records had previously sold only in small and isolated areas of the country, both could now be heard everywhere on radio. A few companies, like Capitol Records, continued to produce both R&B and country, and succeeded in spreading this music into the pop market. Young people, mostly teenagers, began buying all three: R&B, country, and pop. Thus, the market was diversifying. Record formats changed from the 78 rpm single to the 45 rpm single with better sound, and the 33 1/3 rpm Long Playing album started gaining popularity as well, especially for classical music.

The kids who listened to a variety of popular music in the 1940s became the musicians of the 1950s who played a new kind of music that synthesized all three: rock and roll. Elvis Presley's "Heart Break Hotel," an early rock and roll hit, topped pop, R&B, and country charts. This new music drew even bigger teenage audiences, who were, in the affluence of the 1950s, able to spend more on luxuries like records than their predecessors. Sales soared. The new music, with its stronger rhythms and stronger lyrics than Broadway pop tunes, scandalized conservative critics and frightened the major labels. Independent labels, growing more numerous and larger than ever before, cashed in on the new music while the majors tried to control the market by making records of their contracted popular crooners singing the new hits. By the end of the decade the frenzy for the new music had subsided, and the majors were moving back onto the charts with their watered-down versions of the rock songs, thanks in part to Dick Clark and his dance show, American Bandstand, which captivated thousands of teenagers by bringing the recording stars into their homes through the medium of television.

The arrival of The Beatles in the early 1960s injected a new fever of activity into the industry, benefiting both the independents and majors. Independent producers, who seemed to understand the new music better than the staff producers of the major companies, became the "wizards" of the industry, discovering and recording the new talents that fed the business. Sales patterns began to change as well. Albums started replacing singles as the dominant format. A wide spectrum of popular musical styles flourished, and FM radio grew in popularity as it played and promoted the different types of rock and pop.

Even with the economic recession of the 1970s, which slowed record sales and bankrupted many of the smallest independents, the market has continued to grow since the advent of rock and roll. In an effort to produce something for everyone at great profits, record companies have expanded the types of popular music available. As Michael Fink wrote in *Inside the Music Business,* "American taste and the U.S. market for records and tapes has splintered and broadened to an extreme degree in the 1980s. A 1984 report issued by the Recording Industry Association of America (RIAA), covering the years 1979-1983, identified no fewer than ten distinct 'music types': rock, country, pop/easy listening, dance, gospel, classical, show/soundtracks, jazz, children's, and other (ethnic, nostalgia, folk, Latin, and so forth)." As the decade progressed, some of these categories splintered further; dance includes rap and hiphop, while rock includes acid, punk, techno, and fusion, just to name a few.

The introduction of the compact disc (CD), with its greater durability and much higher fidelity, brought new profits to the industries. Sales jumped as consumers began to replace their vinyl collections with the better sounding product, and new markets for older records opened up as companies began reissuing older albums in the new format. By the end of the 1980s, sales of vinyl records had almost completely died out, and most companies stopped producing the older format completely in the early 1990s.

The late 1980s and early 1990s saw the absorption of the biggest independent companies into huge conglomerates, as large electronics firms bought up record labels. Sony Corporation started the trend in 1987 when it bought CBS Records for $2 billion, an unheard of figure. Two years later, EMI, Philips, and Bertelsmann Music Group led bidding wars for the largest independent labels like A&M and Motown, which eventually went to Philips' PolyGram division. By 1996, six conglomerates controlled all the major labels—Time Warner Inc., Sony Corporation, Philips

N.V., Thorn/EMI, Bertelsmann A.G., and Seagram (MCA).

CURRENT CONDITIONS

After several years of sluggish sales due to economic recession, 1992 record industry sales figures began to recover. While unit sales were down 7.5 percent in 1991, they bounced back up 6.7 percent in 1992, with total gross income up 11 percent—the strongest gain since 1987. Strong growth continued through 1993 and 1994, with sales in 1994 leaping by more than 17 percent over 1993 figures. Industry euphoria was short-lived, however. 1995 U.S. music sales totaled an estimated $11 billion, up slightly from 1994 sales. Time Warner's labels (including Warner Brothers, Electra, and Atlantic) grabbed the lion's share of the market, taking 21.6 percent, followed by Sony Music with 13.9 percent, and PolyGram with 13.5 percent. German-based Bertelsmann A.G.'s Columbia Records came fourth with 12.4 percent, followed by Thorn/EMI with 9.8 percent and MCA's UNI with 9.7 percent.

Overall, music sales growth was expected to slow between 1995 and 2000. The anticipated slowdown was predicated on two factors: overexpansion of the retail sector and the maturing of the CD format. Much of the growth of the previous decade had come as the result of consumers replacing their libraries of vinyl and cassette albums with high-priced CD versions. Though CDs were the dominant recorded medium in 1995 and 1996, accounting for an estimated 70 percent of total industry revenues—the number of CDs sold in 1995 was up 11 percent over 1994, while the volume of prerecorded cassettes dropped by about 16 percent—some analysts feared the high retail cost of CDs was limiting sales to younger consumers. As the CD market became more dependent on sales of current releases in the latter part of the decade, this price factor was expected to start hurting the industry.

Another threat to new CD sales came from the fast-growing used CD market. Because of the CD's durability and high price tag in relation to previous records and cassette, several of the largest music retail chains in the United States began selling used CDs. Previously, only small locally owned stores sold used products. Rather than lowering the prices on CDs, which retailers had been requesting for years, the industry leaders fought back by withholding cooperative advertising dollar. They thought this would be effective since distributors and retailers share some publicity costs at the local level. Artists began to get involved in the fray. For example, country music superstar Garth Brooks declared that he would refuse to distrib-

ute his albums, the best-selling country albums at the time, to any store selling used CDs. Such tactics had little effect. Independent record retailers responded by filing lawsuits against the four major distributors that instituted the punitive policies; this occurred at roughly the same time the Federal Trade Commission announced it was launching an investigation into the policies. The distributors quickly retreated from their hard line stance, putting an end to the confrontation.

Growth for both CD singles and music videos was expected to accelerate. The price of a CD single dropped to just over $5 in 1995, putting them well within the budget of younger consumers and sales increased by more than 84 percent. A decline in the price of music videos also prompted a surge in sales.

INDUSTRY LEADERS

Today the industry is dominated by six huge conglomerates, called the majors. Each owns many different record labels, and each produces hundreds of new potential "hit" records each month.

Technically, Warner Communications Inc. is the only American-owned conglomerate in the majors, though the purchase of MCA by Canada's Seagram Company put another major label in the hands of a North American company. The Warner brothers—Jack, Albert, Harry, and Sam—established a successful film production and distribution company in the 1910s. The company remained strong well into the 1950s, when television began to change consumer entertainment patterns and cut into the film market. In 1966, the last Warner brother sold the company to Seven Arts Productions, which was more interested in selling television rights to old movies than making new movies, and the company continued to decline.

Warner Brothers-Seven Arts first got into the record business in 1969, when they bought the large independent Atlantic Records. In 1971, after being purchased by Stephen Ross, the company was renamed Warner Communications. Under the new director, the company once again flourished, and began buying up smaller record labels and launching new ones. They acquired contracts for many of the hottest musical acts in the business and became a prominent force in the industry.

In 1989, Warner was purchased by Time Inc., and became Time Warner Inc., one of the largest media conglomerates in the world. By 1992, when record sales for Time Warner reached the $3 billion mark, the company owned some of the most profitable labels, including Atlantic, Elektra, Warner Bros., and Giant/Reprise. The company has continued to grow by creat-

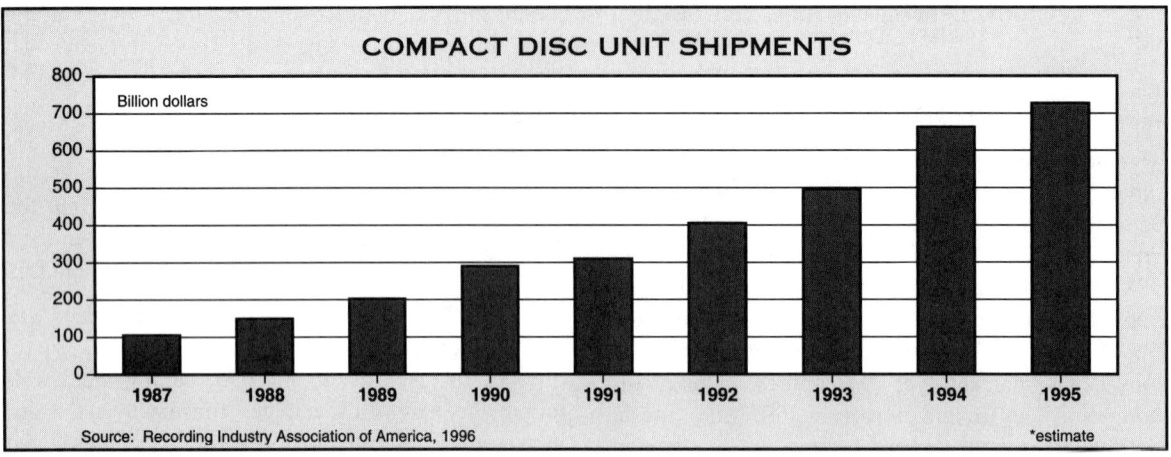

COMPACT DISC UNIT SHIPMENTS

Billion dollars

Source: Recording Industry Association of America, 1996   *estimate

ing new labels for new markets, such as Warner Western. By 1995, with a market share of 21.6 percent, the company had taken over the top spot in the record business from Sony Music.

Sony Corp., one of the best known names in consumer electronics, was established shortly after World War II. Their early products, tape recorders and transistor radios, sold well. In the 1960s they led the international electronics industry with their miniaturized products based on the transistor. After faltering sales growth in the mid 1970s due to increasing competition, Sony once again came to dominate the market in 1978 with their introduction of the portable stereo system, the Walkman. Within another three years, they broke new ground again when they developed and introduced the CD in conjunction with the Dutch electronics firm, Philips.

Sony established itself as the largest record producer when it formed its subsidiary, Sony Music Entertainment International, and bought CBS Records in 1987. Sony wanted to gain better control over the sales of new formats by producing both the hardware (equipment) and the software (recordings). The Columbia Broadcasting System, which had been formed in the late 1920s as a separate entity from Columbia Phonograph, entered the record business in 1938 when it purchased the American Record Corporation; their new record division then became Columbia Recording Corporation, or Columbia Records. The record group remained a profitable arm of CBS, and a major presence in the industry for decades. In the 1980s, when CBS began faltering in the television ratings and losing revenues, they sacrificed their record group to Sony Corporation, despite the fact they were the best selling U.S. record company.

The third largest distributor in 1995 was PolyGram N.V. Owned by Dutch electronics giant, Philips N.V., PolyGram's labels included A&M,

Island, Mercury, Motown, and Polydor. PolyGram was also the leading supplier of classical music through labels such as Deutche Grammaphone, as well as being one of the largest music publishers.

AMERICA AND THE WORLD

While American music enjoys wide-spread popularity even in non-English speaking countries, America no longer dominated the industry after the large electronic conglomerates bought out the major and independent labels. While most of the labels were still American, the biggest of the majors were European and Japanese. Sony, the firm that bought CBS records and owns over 20 labels, is a Japanese electronics conglomerate. Philips N.V., a Dutch electronics firm, owns 80 percent of PolyGram, which carries the American labels Motown and A&M, and also owns European labels like Deutche Grammophone. Thorn/EMI of England owns Capitol, an American label. The German Bertelsmann Music Group bought RCA and Arista in 1986, and the Japanese company Matsushita, bought MCA in 1991, then sold it a few years later to beverage giant Seagram. All companies, of course, have international distribution. Time Warner, once the only North American company among the majors (until Seagram took over MCA), continues to increase international distribution to remain competitive. In 1992, they signed a deal with Starstream Communications Group Inc. to begin distributing their records in Eastern Europe.

RESEARCH AND TECHNOLOGY

Because the industry is highly reliant on electronics technology, research and technological development in the electronics industry has a large impact on the recording industry. The developments with the greatest impact have been newer electronic formats with greater sound fidelity.

In the 1940s, a better sound resulted from the development of the Long Play records (LPs); as sound quality improved, customers seemed willing to spend more on the product. In the 1960s, Philips introduced the cassette format, which was more durable and portable than the LP; when Sony introduced the Walkman personal stereo in the 1980s, which used cassettes and allowed consumers to carry music everywhere, the cassette market really took off. In the 1980s, the new format of the CD again presented a quantum leap in sound quality, so much so that many audiophiles replaced their entire collection of vinyl recordings with the new format. As record companies issued older recordings in the new format, previously out-of-print recordings, especially old jazz favorites, became available to new generations of listeners, and the market expanded again.

In the early 1990s, two new formats were introduced, the mini disc and the digital compact cassette (DCC). Both of these formats brought CD quality fidelity to home recording. Industry analysts in 1992 claimed the new formats would benefit long term growth prospects, encouraging customers once again to replace their older recordings in the new format. The new formats worried many in the industry, however, and artists and companies alike feared the loss of copyright revenues from home recordings; piracy has always been the major form of income loss. In 1992, however, the consumer electronics industry worked out compromise legislation with government and industry leaders which provides compensation for prospective copies done on the digital machines by imposing royalty fees on the equipment sales. By early 1993, both formats had been released. Due to high initial equipment costs, sales started slowly, but analysts agreed that once prices come down, both formats would do well. While many agreed that one format would eventually dominate over the other, none could predict which format would win.

As it turned out, such speculation turned out to be moot. Consumers once again confounded the experts by failing to show any interest in the new formats. As with the earlier digital audio tape format (DAT), sales languished and consumer enthusiasm was lukewarm at best. The failure of DCC in particular came as a surprise, since this format at least offered backward compatibility with conventional analog cassettes, allowing users to play their old tapes on their new digital decks. Nevertheless, consumers seemed far more interested in convenience and affordability than in improved quality, staying away from the new formats in droves. The failure of these formats was puzzling to many in the industry, given the success of CDs. The success of the CD, however, probably had more to do with its convenient small size and durability than its improved sound quality. In fact, many audiophiles still insisted that analog sound (as represented by vinyl records) was superior to digital sound.

FURTHER READING

Bakker, Machgiel. "PolyGram Continues EHR Top 40 Reign." *Music and Media,* 7 November 1992.

Chapple, Steve, and Reebee Garofalo. *Rock 'n' Roll Is Here to Pay: The History and Politics of the Music Industry,* Chicago: Nelson-Hall, 1977.

Christman, Ed. "Majors Lash Out at Used-CD Biz." *Billboard,* 20 March 1993, 1.

Christman, Ed. "Black and Red are the Colors in this Year-End Report Card." *Billboard,* 23 December 1995.

Clark-Meade, Jeff. "CD Still Drives 14% Globa Sales Growth." *Billboard,* 28 October 1995.

Clark-Meade, Jeff, and Catherine Applefeld. "Courting the Classical Consumer." *Billboard,* 31 October 1992, 75.

Cromer, Ben. "Chris Thomas: The One Helping Guide Elton's Sound." *Billboard,* 9 January 1993, 50.

Denisoff, R. Serge. *Tarnished Gold: The Record Industry Revisited.* New Brunswick, NJ: Transaction Books, 1986.

Fink, Michael. *Inside the Music Business: Music in Contemporary Life.* New York: Schirmer Books, 1989.

Gubernick, Lisa, and Kate Bohne. "Garth's Barbecue." *Forbes,* 2 August 1993, 120.

International Directory of Company Histories. Chicago: St. James Press, 1988-1991.

Jeffrey, Don. "Music Sales Growth Seen Slowing From 1995-2000." *Billboard,* 31 August 1996.

Knoedelseder, William K., Jr. "Back in the Groove." *Los Angeles Times,* 17 April 1989.

McGuire, Stryker. "Why Garth Brooks Feels Used." *Newsweek,* 26 July 1993, 41.

Nelson, Havelock. "Latifa Label Brings Rap Flavor to Epic." *Billboard,* 19 December 1992, 12.

Newcomb, Peter. "I Heard It at the Record Store." *Forbes,* 8 July 1991, 88.

Standard & Poors Industry Surveys. New York: Standard & Poors Corporation, 1993.

"Pre-Recorded Music." *Standard and Poor's Industry Surveys.* New York: McGraw Hill, January, 1997.

U.S. Department of Commerce. *U.S. Industrial Outlook 1993.* Washington: GPO, 1993.

"With FTC Inquiry Under Way, Suits Mount in Used-CD Fray." *Billboard,* 14 August 1993.

—Robin Armstrong, updated by Christopher Hunt

SIC 3661

TELEPHONE AND TELEGRAPH APPARATUS

This industry covers establishments primarily engaged in manufacturing wire telephone and telegraph equipment. Included are establishments manufacturing modems and other telephone and telegraph interface equipment. Establishments primarily engaged in manufacturing cellular radio telephones are classified in **SIC 3663: Radio and Television Broadcasting and Communications Equipment.**

INDUSTRY SNAPSHOT

The industry shipped $24.6 billion worth of products in 1995, which was a 43 percent increase since 1990. The number of establishments in the industry stood at 528 in the mid-1990s, which was a 21 percent increase since 1990. In 1995, the United States imported $6.9 billion worth of telephone and telegraph apparatuses; exports totaled $5.7 billion.

ORGANIZATION AND STRUCTURE

The organization and structure of the telephone and telegraph equipment market is broken down into two broad categories: network equipment manufacturers, who sell telephone switching and switchboard equipment primarily to local and long distance phone companies; and end-user or terminal equipment manufacturers, who sell data and voice communications equipment, facsimile equipment, call/voice processing equipment, consumer communications electronics, private branch exchanges (PBX), and videoconferencing equipment to both large and small businesses and residential users. The breakdown of equipment sales in these market segments for 1993 and their respective market shares based on 1993 sales were: network equipment, with $12.6 billion and 39.3 percent; datacom equipment, with $8.2 billion and 25.6 percent; facsimile equipment, with $3.3 billion and 10.4 percent; call/voice processing, with $3.2 billion and 10.1 percent; consumer electronics, with $2.3 billion and 7.3 percent; private branch exchanges, with $2.1 billion and 6.7 percent; and videoconferencing, with $223 million and 0.7 percent.

BACKGROUND AND DEVELOPMENT

In the wake of the deregulation of telecommunications in the United States and worldwide, the business user faced a bewildering choice of services and equipment. The growing importance of voice, data, and text communication links for conducting everyday business demanded that information about telecommunica-

tions networks and equipment and the costs involved find its way out of the specialist departments and into the hands of business managers and residential users. Access to information and reliable communication links are vital.

In the past, business telecommunications were more or less a straightforward matter. Services were provided by AT&T with its undisputed monopoly as the carrier of voice, data, and text communications. Large business users had private branch exchanges, or PBXs, for internal and external voice traffic, telex machines for instantaneous transmission of text, and dedicated data lines for communications with mainframe computers. Small businesses used key telephone systems and facsimile machines.

Progress in microelectronics and the deregulation of the telecommunications structure in the United States have changed all that. The boundaries between computing and telecommunications have become blurred. With the advent of the Integrated Service Digital Network, or ISDN, the telecommunications network would no longer distinguish between voice, text, data, and image traffic. Everything went over the wire or fiber optic cable in bits. There would be a uniform ISDN plug for telephones, computers, and fax machines. Personal computers not only become immensely powerful, they also double as telex and data communications terminals, as fax machines, and as telephones and telephone answering machines. Electronic data interchange (EDI) would eventually do away with forms completed in duplicate and triplicates. Videophones would bring the person at the other end of the line right into the office. In short, the management of the flow of, and access to, communication takes an ever more important place in the organization and the running of a modern business, independent of its size.

Telecommunications equipment and services swamped the market, which became ever more complicated for the ordinary business person. Manufacturers announced new products and services almost daily. The talk moved towards digital networks and equipment linked by fiber optics; ISDN and electronic mail, fax, videotext, and mobile communications; and networking, voice data integration, and compatibility.

Knowing what these terms mean, how they relate to the plethora of products available on the market and how to use them for business, will become as indispensable to the manager of a small business as familiarity with the personal computer. Because it is not the telecommunications equipment itself, but its judicious use that will be instrumental in a company's success.

Changes in telecommunications regulations since the early 1980s transformed the way telecommunications can be used. Competition in network provision has improved the quality of traditional services. Waiting lists for business and residential voice and data lines have fallen dramatically. Telecommunication and equipment prices have also declined. New telecommunication based services have sprung up, bringing revenue not only to telecommunication operators and the information providers, but also generally enhancing the value of business operations. Even domestic users with touch tone telephones are beginning to avail themselves of network-based facilities that ten years ago only users with sophisticated communications equipment could afford.

The proliferation of the equipment market not only means greater choice at lower prices for the user, it also opens up more possibilities of creative use of telecommunications in the way business is conducted. A private branch exchange (PBX) offering direct dial-in could route facsimile as well as telephone traffic. Therefore, businesses would find it unnecessary to install a separate fax line. The availability of electronic mail services opened up the world of telex and text-based fax to the users of personal computers without the need for expensive terminal equipment.

CURRENT CONDITIONS

Central Office Switching Systems. The real value of the United States' telecommunications system lies in its ability to access a wide range of users wherever they are located (Universal Service). This is the role of telephone switching systems.

When large scale integrated circuits were perfected in the 1970s, it became technically feasible to develop a digital-switching network to replace the electronic network in central offices. Current state-of-the-art of central office technology has a digital switching network controlled by a programmable central processor. Most modern switching equipment, ranging from small PBXs to large toll tandem switches that can handle thousands of trunks, used this technology. Further research was underway to develop even less costly switching systems capable of switching light streams rather than electrical pulses.

Switching systems route calls between themselves and selected terminating stations by addressing. Station addresses in the United States consist of a three-digit area code and a seven-digit telephone number. From overseas locations, a country code is added.

Centrex. Before the arrival of microelectronics and stored program control private branch exchanges, large companies were reluctant to place switching systems on the premises to provide private branch exchange service. Centrex is a PBX-like service furnished by the local telephone company through equipment located in the central office. Centrex features allow direct inward dialing (DID) to a telephone number and direct outward dialing (DOD) from a number without operator intervention. For calls into the Centrex, the service is equivalent to individual line service. Outgoing calls differ from individual line service only in the requirement that the caller dials an individual access code (usually 9). Calls between stations in the Centrex group require four or five digits instead of the seven digits required for ordinary calls. An attendant position located on the customer's premises is linked to the central office over a separate circuit. Centrex service provides PBX features without locating a switching system on the user's premises.

The demand for Centrex service provided by the Regional Bell Operating Companies was expected to grow by 4 to 5 percent annually. Small business Centrex service (less than 100 lines) experienced 5 to 10 percent growth rates, while the intermediate to large line size segments experienced flat or negative growth rates. The distribution of the current 8 million-line Centrex installed base is as follows: less than 100 company lines, 1.4 million total lines; 100 to 399 company lines, 1 million total lines; 400 to 1,000 company lines, 1.55 million total lines; 1,000 or more company lines, 4.05 million total lines.

Customer Premise Equipment. It was forecasted that sales of telephone products would grow by 7.3 percent annually from $3.1 billion in 1992 to almost $4.1 billion in 1996. This category includes telephone sets, cordless telephones, and answering machines. The projected increase in this group was due primarily to a jump in marketshare for cordless phones from 41.9 percent in 1992 to 49.4 percent in 1996, and an expected growth in telephone answering systems from 31.9 percent in 1992 to 36.7 percent in 1996. The market share for one and two-line phones was forecasted to decline from 21 percent to 10.9 percent for single line units and 4.4 percent to 3 percent for two-line phones between 1992 and 1996.

In recent years, cordless telephones have gained wide consumer acceptance with an estimated 40 percent household penetration in the United States. These instruments use a low-powered radio link between a base unit and the portable telephone. In 1992, sales of cordless phones reached $1.34 billion, a 6.6 percent growth rate from 1991 levels. Manufacturer sales approached the 20 million unit level in 1992 with the average unit price dropping from $85 to $76 dollars during this timeframe. Leading manufacturers AT&T, General Electric Company, and Sony Corporation expected continued price declines in this category.

The latest generation of cordless telephones were multibutton units that could be assigned to outside lines, intercom paths, or system features such as speed dial. The handset and base could talk on any of the channels, and the user could accept the channel with the best reception. Standard key features such as transfer and hold were activated from the cordless unit.

The sale of telephone answering equipment experienced significant growth in 1992, reaching the $1 billion dollar sales level on an 8-percent growth rate. Answering apparatus once provided exclusively by the LECs, were widely available from leading suppliers AT&T, Panasonic Co., and Sharp Corporation. Unit sales for this product reached the $14.5 million mark with manufacturers distributing stock primarily through mass merchants and electronic and appliance stores.

The telephone answering machine market will continue to grow, but technological innovation was replacing the traditional stand-alone telephone answering machine connected to a telephone with integrated telephone answering devices. These units will include telephone answering devices incorporated into every piece of communications equipment from basic telephones to cordless integrated answering telephone devices to personal computer systems.

The market offers two categories of telephone sets: general purpose sets or corded phones and special purpose telephones, such as coin operated telephones. The sale of corded phones grew 9.2 percent in 1992 to achieve $654 million in dollar sales. Unit sales were up 5 million to reach 26.1 million units in 1992. Leading suppliers AT&T, General Electric, and Conair Corp. distributed products primarily through electronics/appliance stores and mass merchant outlets.

The price of general purpose sets is often a clue to quality. Many inexpensive instruments provide poor transmission quality and fail when dropped. At the high end of the scale, price usually is a function of features or looks. Two-line phone sets are expected to show only modest unit growth (3.9 percent) over the next several years with an overall decline in total dollar sales due to average price declines in manufacturer prices. Single-line phone sets will be replaced by feature phones with many more characteristics and capabilities than existing models.

Coin Telephones. The advent of the customer-owned coin operated telephone (COCOT) is another by-product of divestiture that is confusing to many users. In the

first few years following the dissolution of the Bell System, many private companies saw COCOTs as a potentially lucrative business. The companies that ventured into this market with less than adequate equipment, however, quickly discovered what the local exchange companies or LECs have long understood: the risks and administrative costs of coin telephones are high, and the companies that enter this market without understanding the hazards can lose large amounts. The two major risks are fraud and vandalism. These can be combatted with durable instruments and by building defenses into the telephone.

The North American Telecommunication Association estimated that there were 265,000 COCOTs in service competing against 1.88 million telephone company-owned pay phones. This number was expected to reach 340,000 by 1996. The average gross revenue per unit is forecast at $1,004 annually. Equipment manufacturers for this category sell close to $210 million a year in pay phone instruments to telephone and COCOT companies, and increased growth was forecasted due to an expanding market.

Key Telephone Systems. Key Telephone Systems (KTS) are not high-technology products compared to radio, satellite, and fiber optics, and they don't have the technical appeal of a PBX, but they are the workhorses of American business. Like other customer premise products, KTSs have evolved from wired logic and electromechanical operation to stored program or firmware control. In the process, they adopted many features that were once the exclusive province of PBX. The difference between the PBX and the key system was indistinct enough that the industry used the term, "hybrid," to describe one class of system that has elements of both.

The Electronic Key Telephone System offers most of the features of a PBX, especially the hybrid version, which is a cross between a PBX and a Key System. The distinction between the KTSs and PBXs is becoming more blurred as technology brings more intelligence to the KTS. Further blurring the trend between Key Systems and PBXs is the propensity of some manufacturers to make Key Telephone instrument lines compatible with PBX lines, allowing a company to grow out of its KTS and into a larger more sophisticated PBX.

Private Branch Exchanges. Many organizations operate private telecommunications systems. These systems range in size from the federal telephone system, which is larger than the telecommunications systems in many countries, to small private branch exchanges (PBXs). As of December 1992, an installed base of 28.5 million PBX stations were in operation with

AT&T responsible for 30 percent of this market, Northern Telecom, 20 percent, and Siemens/Rolm, 18 percent.

Nearly every business with more than 30 to 100 stations is in the market for a PBX, or its central office counterpart, Centrex (a service by the local phone companies where the guts of the system are located on the local phone company premise). PBXs are economical for some very small businesses that need features that most key systems do not provide such as restriction and least cost routing. They are also economical for very large businesses that have PBXs using central office switching systems of a size that rivals many metropolitan public networks. Most PBXs can be mounted in a cabinet on the business user's premises and can operate without air conditioning in an ordinary office environment.

The office PBX increasingly controls private voice networks. As the network evolves into all-digital, so does the PBX in all but the low end systems of 100 stations or fewer, which remain analog. The advent of the T-1 carrier as the preferred transmission medium is the principle force driving the evolution of the PBX. The long distance carriers make it increasingly attractive for business users to bypass the local central office with T-1 trunks directly to the long distance carrier's central office. The cost of T-1 service for PBX lines is particularly advantageous when data transmission facilities parallel the route of voice. The integration of voice and data reduces the cost of access lines to the outside world.

Call/Voice Processing Equipment. Several converging forces have increased the importance of incoming call management systems. First, there is the increasing use of telemarketing. A telemarketing center typically has banks of 800-numbers with different numbers associated with different product lines or promotions, and different agents with access to various databases to handle callers' questions. A caller distribution system is needed in this case to direct incoming calls to the appropriate agent. Secondly, most incoming 800-calls are delivered via T-1 technology. With this technology, calls need to be routed to the appropriate party when they reach the customer premise. Finally, call distribution technology has advanced to the point where it is basically a merger of telephone and computer operations. Any organization with more than a few answering positions finds that the cost of some machine-controlled call distribution pays for itself quickly.

Call/voice processing systems accounted for 10.1 percent or $3.2 billion of all telecommunication and data equipment sales in the mid-1990s. This figure was up $329 million or 11.33 percent from 1992. Sales of U.S. call processing equipment were forecasted to grow at an annual compound rate of 21 percent between 1992 and 1998 to $8.2 billion. This category consists of uniform call distribution systems, call sequencers, automatic call distributors, and voice processing systems.

A uniform call distribution system (UCD), a standard feature of many PBXs, often significantly improves call handling. The stand-alone counterpart of a UCD is the call sequencer. This device may work with a PBX or key telephone system, or it may be connected directly to incoming lines. Unlike the UCD, a call sequencer does not direct calls, but alerts agents to the presence of incoming calls. The most sophisticated device is an automatic call distributor (ACD), which can either stand alone or integrate with a PBX. An ACD routes calls to the least busy agent to equalize the work load. The ACD administrator typically has a video display terminal that presents call statistics in real time, and has many management tools that monitor and improve service and measure the agent's effectiveness. Any organization that has a large number of incoming calls targeted for service positions is a potential ACD user. This includes departments that handle mail orders, literary delivery, inquiries, field service, credit, and collections.

The marriage of computer and telecommunications technologies brought a family of equipment collectively known as voice processing systems to the market. Three classes of equipment comprise voice processing: voice mail, automated attendant, and voice response or audiotex equipment. Octel Communications controls 17 percent of the voice messaging market with Northern Telecom registering 14 percent and AT&T with 13 percent of overall market sales. Five other companies—VMX, Rolm, Centigram, Active Voice, and Boston Technology—make up the remainder with less than 10 percent of the market each.

Facsimile Equipment. Over the last decade facsimile equipment (FAX) has become an indispensable business machine essential to the every day transactions of most businesses. The FAX machine works by scanning the printed page, encoding it, and transmitting a facsimile of the images in shades of black and white without identifying individual characters. Facsimile can convey both text and graphic information, source documents can be retransmitted without rekeying, and facsimile transmission is affected less by transmission errors than other types of data communication. Facsimile is also fast. Some facsimile machines also double as printers and copiers.

The sale of home facsimile equipment grew 12.3 percent to $247 million in 1992. Although unit sales grew an estimated 30 percent from 1991 levels, overall dollar sales volume declined due to a drop in the average unit sales price from $550 in 1991 to $475 in 1992. Leading suppliers Canon USA, Muratec, and Sharp accounted for 89 percent of 1992 sales volume in this category.

Data Communications Equipment. Like other types of telecommunications equipment, modems have become faster, cheaper, and smarter. The ready availability of inexpensive personal computers has expanded the demand for modems, and basically two types of modems exist in the market: dial-up modems and private line modems. Dial-up modems either plug into a personal computer slot, or are self contained devices that plug into the computers serial port. Many of the modem's features are designed to emulate a telephone. These features include: dial tone recognition, automatic tone and dial pulse dialing, monitoring call progress tones such as busy and reorder, automatic answer, and call termination. These items are priced on a commodity type basis and use the public network for the transmission of information. Private line modems work exclusively with voice and data private lines, and although it has the same functions as a dial-up modem, they are not as popular as their sister model the dial-up modem.

Many data applications, by nature, are incapable of fully using a data circuit. Rather than flowing in a steady stream, data usually flows in steady, short bursts with long, idle periods intervening. To make use of this idle capacity, data multiplexers are employed to collect data from multiple stations and combine it into a single, high-speed bit stream.

Data multiplexers come in two types: time division multiplexers (TDM) and statistical multiplexers (statmux). In a TDM, each station is assigned a time slot, and the multiplexer collects data from each station in turn. If a station has no data to send, its time slot goes unused. A statmux makes use of the idle time periods in a data circuit by assigning time slots to pairs of stations according to the amount of traffic they have to send. The multiplexer collects data from the terminal and sends it to the distant end, with the address of the receiving terminal minimizing idle times between transactions.

Analog or frequency division multiplexers are also available to divide a voice channel into multiple segments for data transmission. Their primary use is to connect multiple, slow-speed data terminals over voice channels. A concentrator is similar to a multiplexer except that it is usually a single-ended device which connects directly to a host computer. The primary application for multiplexers is in data networks that use asynchronous terminals. Since many of these items cannot be addressed and have no error correction capability, they are of limited use by themselves in remote locations. The multiplexer provides end-to-end error checking and correction and circuit sharing to support multiple terminals.

INDUSTRY LEADERS

Industry leaders in 1996 included 3Com Corporation, DSC Communications Corporation, GTE Government Systems Corporation, NEC America, Inc., and GTE Communication Systems Corporation. The largest in terms of sales was 3Com, of Santa Clara, CA, and had sales of $2.8 billion and employed 6,000. DSC, of Plano, TX, had sales of $1.4 billion and employed 5,860. GTE Government, of Needham Heights, MA, sold $1.3 billion worth of products and had 7,600 employees. NEC's sales totaled $991 million, while its employee count was 2,450. GTE Communication, of Stamford, CT, had sales of $924.9 million and employed 2,044.

WORK FORCE

There were 111,800 employed in the industry in 1995, an increase of 18 percent since 1990. Production workers in the industry totaled 59,600 in 1995, a 28 percent increase since 1990. Production workers' average hourly wages have decreased since 1990, from $14.48 to $13.30 in 1995.

Technological advances eliminated many of the traditional positions associated with the manufacture of telephone equipment and apparatus. A study by the U.S. Bureau of Labor anticipated a 51 percent decline in electrical and electronic assemblers between the years 1990 and 2005. This group accounted for 16.5 percent of the employees of manufacturers of telephone equipment and apparatus. A related group of electrical and electronic engineers, who accounted for 8.2 percent of the work force, was expected to grow by 5.7 percent over this timeframe.

On the whole, there will be a substantial reengineering of the workflow in this industry, with many traditional jobs becoming automated and a downsizing in administrative and support staff. An increase of 17 percent was expected for computer programmers, and sales/marketing personnel would be needed to sell the products in a market driven by price/features.

Due to a substantial reengineering of the workflow in this industry, many traditional jobs were predicted to become automated and downsizing would occur across the various employment classifications. Positions unaffected by this downsizing were computer programmers and sales/marketing personnel. This group was expected to grow by 17 percent during this timeframe.

AMERICA AND THE WORLD

Historically, the United States has been the leader in telecommunications equipment technology and innovation. This factor was due primarily to the monopoly that AT&T (the Bell System) had on the nations' telephone system for the first 100 years of its existence. The breakup of the Bell System in 1984 created a new playing field for telecommunication equipment manufacturers worldwide. Since telephone technology is not drastically different from computer technology, and in fact, many of the same components and techniques are used in both, the race to compete in this market became a global endeavor. This factor coupled with the regulatory barriers harnessing the former Bell Operating Companies resulted in the United States losing this 100 year advantage almost overnight.

Between the years 1983 to 1989, the United States export of telecommunication equipment increased at a compound annual rate of 15 percent. During this same timeframe, imports of telecommunication equipment grew by 30 percent. In 1989, the U.S. telecommunication equipment industry had a trade deficit of $2.7 billion, which improved 15 percent in 1990 to $2.4 billion. Low technology, terminal equipment (i.e., telephones) accounted for the largest component of foreign imports. Foreign producers in the Far East were able to capture this market through lower manufacturing costs. China, Malaysia, and Thailand contributed the most to this market. Japan accounted for almost 34 percent of the U.S. imports of telecom equipment in 1992, down from 47 percent in 1982. This trend is due primarily to the United States' shift to Canada and Western Europe for high technology switching equipment. The U.S. Senate, in response to these developments, passed the Telecommunications Equipment Research and Manufacturing Act of 1991 in an attempt make the market more competitive.

Although the United States is no longer the dominant manufacturer in the telecommunications equipment market, it is currently reestablishing itself as an international force. Despite an enormous trade deficit with Japan and other Far Eastern suppliers, the United States is the largest manufacturer of foreign-produced equipment in Japan. From 1987 to 1990, the United States had a trade surplus with Europe exceeding $700 million.

Only two out of the top 15 telecommunications equipment manufacturers worldwide are U.S. companies based upon 1991 revenues. Alcatel Corporation of France led this list with 15.5 percent of the market followed by AT&T (United States) with 10.3 percent, Siemens (Germany) with 9.9 percent, Northern Telecom (Canada) with 8.2 percent, NEC Corporation (Japan) and L.M. Ericsson (Sweden) with 6.7 percent each, and Motorola, Inc. (United States) with 6.6 percent.

RESEARCH AND TECHNOLOGY

All of the trends involving computers and communications ultimately converge at the desktop. Higher-speed processors, more powerful and higher capacity networks, and more flexible software and management systems are redefining the way we utilize communication products at our work space. While voice, video, and data communications have each evolved independently, they were starting to come together into a "multimedia" environment to make future communications more efficient, effective, and user-friendly.

While the personal computer revolution has been thoroughly documented over the past decade, the familiar telephone instrument found virtually everywhere has undergone a transformation of its own. This piece of communications equipment has been dramatically rethought, redesigned, and reequipped to accomplish a new role in the communications revolution. The standard telephone is becoming a voice terminal in a market where voice, video, and data applications are being formed into integrated communication systems.

The 1990s saw the emergence of Integrated Service Digital Network, or ISDN, as mode of interfacing in this new communications environment. This interface is an important step toward achieving universal compatibility among different manufacturers.

In addition to the deployment of ISDN technology, an entirely new level of integration between telephones and computing is being developed on hardware and software systems called application programming interfaces, or APIs. APIs will enable the user to integrate his personal computer and voice terminal into one instrument. The personal computer's processing and memory-storage capabilities offer the potential for a new dimension of multimedia communications capabilities at the desktop. As this technology evolves, the basic telephone will be transformed from a stand-alone voice terminal to a device that integrates voice, data, text, fax, and video services. Eventually, push-button dial pads and handsets will be replaced by voice-activated terminals with integrated speaker and microphone capabilities.

The revolution in communications technology occurring at the desktop has also been taking place in the switched networks. Electromechanical switching will all but disappear by the year 2000. Around the mid-1990s, the country reached the crossover point between analog and digital switching with more than half the lines in the United States being served by digital central offices. The local exchange companies or LECs are basing their networks on ISDN technology, which uses circuit switched technology and it was estimated that most PBX manufacturers will retain circuit switching as well. The technology with the most intriguing future is photonic switching, estimated to be 1,000 times faster than present switching products. As fiber-optic cable extends to the desktops with a photonic switch in the network, users can link high-bandwidth facilities around the world presenting businesses with a myriad of communication opportunities for the future.

FURTHER READING

''American Telephone and Telegraph Corporation.'' *Hoover's Handbook of American Business,* 1 January 1994.

Beyda, William J. *Basic Data Communications-A Comprehensive Overview.* Englewood Cliffs, NJ: Prentice-Hall, 1989.

Brewster, R.L. *Communication Systems and Computer Networks.* New York: John Wiley & Sons, 1989.

Connelly, Joanne. ''U.S. Computer Hardware up Four Percent '92 Forecast.'' *Electronic News,* 6 January 1992.

''Consumer Electronics Sales for '92 up 7.9 Percent; Electronics '92 Statistical Report.'' *HFD - The Weekly Home Furnishings Newspaper,* 15 March 1993.

''Cordless, TADS top $4 Billion Phone Market; Cordless Telephones; Telephone Answering Devices; Computers, Business Systems & Office Products.'' *Purchasing,* 16 December 1993.

Darnay, Arsen J. and Redding, Marlita A. *Market Share Reporter: An Annual Compilation of Reported Market Share Data on Companies, Products, and Services 1994.* Detroit: Gale Research, 1994.

Darney, Arsen J. *Manufacturing USA. Industry Analysis, Statistics and Leading Companies.* 3rd ed., Vol. 2. Detroit: Gale Research, 1994.

''Digital Equipment Corporation.'' *Hoover's Handbook of American Business,* 1 January 1994.

Dordick, H.S. *Understanding Modern Telecommunications.* New York: McGraw-Hill, 1986.

''GTE Corporation.'' *Hoover's Handbook of American Business,* 1 January 1994.

''International Business Machines.'' *Hoover's Handbook of American Business,* 1 January 1994.

Labate, John. ''Companies to Watch.'' *Fortune,* 21 March 1994.

Leibowitz, Ed. ''The Great Dumb Switch Debate-Part One: Dumb Switches and Intelligent Switches; An OAI Focus.'' *Teleconnect,* July 1992.

McKay, Deborah. ''Technology Explosion Brings Flood of New Equipment.'' *The Financial Post,* 13 November 1993.

''Motorola, Inc.'' *Hoover's Handbook of American Business.* 1 January 1994.

Noll, A. Michael. *Introduction to Telephones and Telephone Systems.* Norwood, MA: Artech House, 1988.

Robinson, Brian. ''Telephone Services Make Their Way Into LAN.'' *Network World,* 4 October 1993.

''Rockwell International Corporation.'' *Hoover's Handbook of American Business,* 1 January 1994.

Sulkin, Allan. ''Centrex Providers Discover that Small Can Be Beautiful.'' *Business Communications Review,* April 1992.

''TADS, Cordless to Drive Phones; Cordless Telephones and Telephone Answering Devices to be Major Factors in Consumer Telephone Market; BIS Strategic Decisions Report.'' *HFD - The Weekly Home Furnishings Newspaper,* 29 November 1993.

Tissot, Anthony F. ''The Changing Role of The PBX in Today's Office Environment.'' *Telecommunications,* November 1993.

''Toshiba Launches Small Digital Key Telephone System.'' *RBOC Update,* April 1993.

''U.S. Call Processing Markets to Triple and Top $8 Billion.'' *Telephone IP News,* March 1994.

''U.S. Telecommunications Equipment Market To Reach $58.2 billion by 1996.'' *RBOC Update,* July 1992.

''Vanguard's Voice Processing Industry Temperature Check.'' *Voice Technology News,* 6 April 1993.

Waite, Andrew, J. *The Inbound Telephone Call Center.* New York: Telecom Library, 1989.

—Andrew Burke, updated by Christopher Hunt

SIC 3663

RADIO AND TELEVISION BROADCASTING AND COMMUNICATIONS EQUIPMENT

This industry manufactures radio and television broadcasting and communications equipment. Important products of this industry are closed-circuit and cable television equipment; studio audio and video equipment; light communications equipment; transmitters, transceivers, and receivers (except household and automotive); cellular radio telephones; fiber optics equipment; communication antennas; receivers; RF power amplifiers; satellite communications systems (space and ground segments); and fixed and mobile radio systems. Establishments primarily engaged in manufacturing household audio and communications equipment are classified in **SIC 3651: Household Audio and Video Equipment;** those manufacturing intercommunications equipment are classified in **SIC 3669: Communications Equipment, Not Elsewhere Classified;** and those manufacturing consumer radio and television receiving antennas are classified in **SIC 3679: Electronic Components, Not Elsewhere Classified.**

INDUSTRY SNAPSHOT

This industry covers a range of interrelated and sometimes competing communications systems. The industry continues to reinvent itself as individual segments grow. The emerging structure is being shaped by consumer trends, regulations, technological advances, and corporate decisions. The electromagnetic spectrum, through which the wireless communications companies of this industry transmit signals, is controlled by the federal government, which has exerted profound influence over this industry in recent years with new regulations and legislation.

Because communications systems are rapidly being transformed by the demand for customized, interconnected, and wireless services, products leading growth in this industry include wireless communication systems (pagers, cellular phones, personal communications systems) mobile communications equipment, and satellite communications devices.

ORGANIZATION AND STRUCTURE

This category contains several different types of communications technologies. Connectivity between these technologies is increasing, resulting in hybridized products and systems. This is reflected in the fact that the players in this industry include cable television, cellular, electronics, telephone, computer, and satellite communications companies. Wireless communications services include cellular, paging, and specialized mobile radio. Cellular and paging, the largest segments of this market, generated more than $19 billion in service fees alone in 1995.

Typically, high-technology consumer electronics equipment becomes less expensive in the years after introduction. This has been true in the case of many products offered by this industry, and it has helped drive growth by attracting new consumer markets. The

average wholesale price of cellular phones, for example, decreased to about $280 in 1993, when about 5 million cellular telephones were sold in the United States, up 13 percent over 1992.

Pagers. Significant growth in the paging industry has been attributed to increasingly sophisticated and lower-priced products and services. The number of paging subscribers in the United States reached approximately 17 million at the beginning of 1994, up from 14 million at the beginning of 1993. In 1992 revenues were $2.3 billion. Some of this growth can be attributed to a trend toward non-business use. Whereas a decade ago pagers were most commonly found on doctors and other busy professionals "on call," they are now likely to be found on parents trying to contact their children, or waiters who need to know when orders are ready.

Consumers have taken to pagers because a new generation of models with new services, such as phone numbers, text messages, customized stock prices, news flashes, and sports scores. There is also a developing consumer trend toward integrating and customizing communications services that contributes to growth and reduces competition among different communication services. For example, about 20 percent of cellular subscribers use paging in conjunction with cellular service to mediate costs, because being paged is less expensive than receiving an incoming call on a cellular phone.

Cellular telephones. Cellular telephones get their name from the small regions (cells) into which service areas are divided. Each cell contains a base station with a low-power transmitter/receiver. Base stations are connected to mobile telephone switching offices (MTSOs) either by telephone wire or microwave transmission. A computer at the switching office coordinates calls for the service area, and monitors a call's signal strength. When the signal loses strength because the caller is exiting the cell, the MTSO switches the call to the next cell. Cells sometimes overlap one another or have gaps between them because of topographical obstructions.

Cellular subscribers numbered 33.8 billion in 1995, drawn by enhancements such as improved capacity, seamless networking, and personal 800 service. Cumulative capital investment and revenues from cellular services were both expected to continue increasing through the 1990s. Equipment sales should continue to rise, to the benefit of companies in this category, as operators add to their analog capacity and some begin the transition to digital technology. This transition is critical to the cellular industry's competitiveness. A digital cellular system transmits a caller's voice by converting the sound waves into a numerical code, rather than a wave pattern, as in analog systems. Calling capacity is expected to increase by a factor of three or more with digital cell sites. In addition to increased capacity, the conversion to digital offers other advantages: lower unit costs; better quality and increased privacy; and the promise of advanced services and data transmission. Several domestic suppliers, including Ericsson, Hughes, and Motorola, offer dual-mode digital/analog cellular telephones.

Business users still account for the majority of cellular users, but much of the growth in cellular, as with paging, has come from the consumer market since the equipment has become more affordable. A decrease in prices may drive down average revenues per consumer but should not hamper overall growth, because of increased volume and product innovations. Technological innovations in electronic circuitry and in the intelligence built into the cellular network have resulted in new features that make cellular more attractive. Short messaging can be displayed on an alphanumeric display, for example. Some companies have introduced cellular phones that can also handle regular wired calls, faxes, or modems.

Another development affecting the structure of the cellular industry is the creation by Independent Telecommunications Network, Inc. (ITN) of a nationwide Signaling System 7 backbone network to transport cellular calls between cell sites. Signaling System 7 is an advanced network protocol that manages traffic flow through a telephone network. This is significant because it will eliminate charges related to "roaming" agreements between operators and special access codes that now complicate the use of a cellular phones outside of home service regions. Cellular carriers are trying to capitalize on the increasing mobility of business people by moving into data transmission. In 1992, nine major cellular carriers teamed up with IBM to provide a data network called CelluPlan II over existing analog cellular networks. Their competition comes primarily from two major providers of mobile data services: Ardis, a joint venture between IBM and Motorola, and RAM Mobile Data, a creation of Bell-South and RAM Broadcasting. These networks are independent of the cellular network and serve businesses only via radio waves.

The involvement of BellSouth, a long-distance wireline telephone company, in a cellular venture is not unusual. Several major long-distance wireline telephone companies have staked a claim in the cellular market by buying cellular companies—Sprint acquired Centel Corporation in 1993, and AT&T acquired McCaw Cellular. In addition to giving the wireline companies the chance to join rather than compete with wireless services, this gives the cellular companies access to the huge marketing resources of the parent companies.

Personal Communications Services. Personal communications networks, or services, (PCS) describes low-powered microcellular technology that operates in the 900 MHZ band. Although available to consumers in Europe and tested in the United States, PCS systems are not widely available in the United States. PCS are expected to make a person carrying a pocket-sized phone available at the same number no matter where the person goes. They transmit calls via radio waves to base stations clustered in many service areas. The system is digital and is expected to be cheaper than existing cellular once widely available to consumers. Some analysts believe that it would be ideally suited for telecommuters because digital technology allows PCS to provide data and video services as well as voice, and will give employees the ability to hook up to office computers or fax machines while traveling.

On September 23, 1993 the Federal Communications Commission (FCC) authorized 160 MHZ of spectrum for PCS. Starting in 1994, the FCC began auctioning PCS licenses, which generated billions for the federal government and stimulated the creation of a new generation of wireless services and products. Hundreds of companies applied to the FCC to operate PCS systems. Carriers invested in new transceivers, and consumers purchased feature-rich new phones and wireless portable devices.

The FCC enforces anticollusion rules upon business contracts between broadband licensees, auction winners, and eligible participants in ongoing broadband block auctions. These rules "place significant limitations on an auction participant's ability to pursue business opportunities involving services in the geographic area in which it has applied for a license," according to the FCC. The anticollusion rules were intended to ensure competitiveness in the auction process and in the post-auction market structure, according to a public notice issued by the FCC on August 28, 1996.

Microwave and Satellite Systems. This is a more mature technology than others in this category. Microwave transmission can be achieved via terrestrial or satellite systems. Terrestrial, or ground, systems work by sending very high frequency signals from transmitters to repeater stations and back to receivers. For these systems to work, there must be no obstructions, such as mountains, between stations. Satellite transmission works similarly but the repeater station is placed in orbit, usually with the region it serves. Because satellites lack the geographic constraints of terrestrial systems, they are better suited for long-distance, point-to-multipoint transmissions such as television broadcasts. Microwave and satellite systems can also be used to transmit audio, video, and data.

Microwave systems can be categorized as long-haul (transmission distances greater than five miles) or short-haul applications. Long-haul microwave equipment is used by common carriers, oil companies, electric utilities, broadcast and cable television operators, pipeline industries, and government agencies. Almost 90 percent of public and private television stations transmit signals via satellite. Short haul customers include universities, institutions, corporations, hotel chains, hospitals, local area networks, cellular phone networks, and local governments. According to the FCC, the majority of users of the 36,538 existing private microwave networks are industrial. Public services hold about 22 percent of private microwave network licenses.

Shipments of land-based microwave systems increased to about $1 billion in 1993, while component sales increased moderately to almost $1.3 billion. The growth is mostly in short-haul applications, such as computer LANs and video conferencing.

In recent years, the United States has seen an explosion in Global Positioning System (GPS) units. The GPS marks the beginning a technological revolution in navigational aids. Originally developed by the U.S. Department of Defense as an alternative to traditional radio navigation, the GPS uses a system of 24 satellites to triangulate the position of a receiver. The signals can identify a receiver's position within a range of about 100 meters. New products that use the GPS for military, aviation, marine, survey and mapping purposes, and tracking and car navigation, come onto the market about every 18 months.

The United States is the global leader in sales of GPS equipment and technology, producing more than twice as many units per month as Japan, the next largest producer. From 1993 to 1995, sales of GPS systems for car navigation alone tripled, bringing in $310 million in 1995. As GPS technology becomes more affordable, the technology will come within reach of millions of consumers. According to James Brandon in *Industry, Trade, and Technology Review,* by 2000 GPS systems are projected to net $8 billion in sales, with U.S. products accounting for about $4 billion. In addition, Brandon states, the number of new jobs arising from GPS technology should reach 100,000 by 2000.

BACKGROUND AND DEVELOPMENT

This industry has developed by continually shedding its old identity as new technologies come along. For example, Motorola, one of the giants in the industry, began in the car radio business. The company sold Handie-Talkies to the Army in World War II and later installed radios in police cars. Many of the companies in this category have been defense contractors.

In the early 1980s, when cellular phones were introduced, AT&T predicted that by 2000 about 900,000 mobile phones would be in use in the United States. By 1993, that prediction had already been exceeded a dozen times. In the early 1990s, cordless phones began to outsell corded phones. Much of this activity would have been inconceivable before the U.S. Justice Department filed suit against AT&T and the Bell monopoly was broken up in the early 1980s. Until 1957, when the courts ruled that telephone customers had the right to use non-AT&T telephone equipment as long as it didn't interfere with the public network, everyone used AT&T equipment and service. AT&T's dominant position as the primary U.S. carrier was finally challenged in 1969 by a company using newly developed microwave technology. That company would become MCI Communications Corporation. The industry did not undergo complete restructuring, however, until the Justice Department officially broke the monopoly in 1984, making way for new communications technologies, equipment, and services.

Some industry observers believe the shift from wireline to wireless communications could be as profound as the shift from gaslight to electric light bulbs. After first underestimating the market for wireless communications, major communications, computers, electronics, and data companies have begun investing heavily in it. AT&T's deal to pay $12.6 billion for McCaw Cellular is one of many examples. A highly publicized health scare in 1993, in which a Florida widower claimed that cellular phone use caused his wife's brain cancer, has spurred research into a possible cellular/cancer link. Long-term impact on the growth of the market will be negligible unless a link is found. The FCC decision to reallocate 200 MHZ of spectrum to make way for emerging PCS technologies is vital to the development of the industry and will likely be considered a landmark decision in the future.

CURRENT CONDITIONS

The current status of this industry is healthy and dynamic. Because of excitement surrounding the idea of a national "information superhighway" and growth in new communications technologies, companies in this industry are keenly watched by Wall Street. The Clinton administration's technology friendly position should foster industry growth. Clinton has proposed a broad ten-year plan to force the Pentagon and other federal agencies to cede control of a big block of the nation's airwaves and make them available for new commercial technologies. This comes in addition to the FCC's 1993 decision to reallocate the public airwaves. Even the older, less cutting-edge areas of this industry are profitable. While the biggest revenues are anticipated in wireless communications services, rather than in equipment, some analysts predict a $1.6 billion hardware market by 2000.

The value of shipments of radio and television broadcasting and communications equipment increased to $29.36 billion in 1995 from $17.8 billion in 1992. The accelerating development of wireless personal communications services will continue to fuel the demand for radio base station equipment, antennas, low earth orbit satellite systems, and wireless equipment. An important development in the cellular segment is the gradual replacement of analog cellular technology with digital cellular technology. Because there has been no decision on which of two rival digital standards—time division multiple access (TDMA) and code division multiple access (CDMA) will be the industry standard—there is currently a market for products that support multiple interfaces. Generic base station transceivers that handle calls using all modulation standards, including U.S. and foreign, analog and digital, voice and data, may also be available for use with a variety of wireless networks, including paging and PCS.

Technological advances like cellular digital packet data (CPCD) for cellular service were introduced to help analog cellular systems compete with new digital systems. CPCD has been adopted by companies with analog systems to make them more competitive with digital systems. The FCC decision regarding the reallocation of spectrum is a powerful one for this industry because it means companies have a chance at gaining more transmission access. Ultimately, it will translate into money. As a result of the FCC decision green-lighting PCS, the formulation of strategic alliances, the valuation of desired PCN territories, and the sale and purchase of cellular holdings will occur furiously as companies try to maneuver into the emerging PCS market.

The FCC decision to reallocate 220 MHZ of spectrum previously occupied by fixed microwave users will boost microwave equipment sales by allowing fixed microwave users to relocate to higher frequen-

cies, and by freeing 200 MHZ of formerly government-occupied spectrum for private sector use. Rather than take business from the existing cellular market, some analysts believe PCS may enhance it. Innovations in digital and microcellular technologies, as well as market stimulation from PCS, are likely to push new equipment purchases by cellular carriers and customers until the end of the decade. Other industry observers predict that PCS will threaten to supersede both cellular and wired service.

New business applications for wireless data technologies are currently being explored in many areas. Executives were the first to adopt cellular phones, but repair and service people have also found that they can increase productivity with wireless devices. Copier repair technicians from Pitney-Bowes now carry $2,500 wireless data terminals connected to the wireless Ardis network, a creation of Motorola and IBM, which tells them everything they need to know about their assignments and even allows them to order parts. Motorola predicts that by 2000 the market for such two-way wireless systems could reach $5 billion.

The Telecommunications Competition and Deregulation Act of 1996 has also had a strong impact on the radio and electronics field. It eliminated monopolies in cable television and telephone companies, opening fields traditionally regulated as public utilities to competition. Perhaps the most controversial part of the law, however, was the introduction of the so-called "v-chip"—a programmable microchip that interprets an encoded program rating transmitted as part of the television signal. The v-chip is intended to allow parents to block programs whose content ratings are deemed unacceptable. It has been perceived by some as a veiled form of censorship. Its impact on the radio and television industry, however, has so far not been determined.

INDUSTRY LEADERS

The massive capital requirements of building unique telecommunications systems guarantees that the companies involved will be large and powerful ones. The biggest players in the computer, communications, and information industries are all maneuvering for the anticipated wireless revolution. Motorola is the leader in this industry with $13 billion in sales and more than 100,000 employees. Motorola has a broad product line compatible with most standards and long-standing experience in radio electronics. It is the world's leading supplier of pagers, two-way radios, and dispatch systems for commercial fleets. Motorola has the largest segment of the global cellular telephone market, according to U.S. International Trade Commission (ITC) reports. In addition to its strong position on the equipment side, it is buying radio frequencies around the world. Motorola is also developing the Iridium project, a proposed $3.8 billion system which will use 66 small satellites in low earth orbit to connect calls around the world. By 2001, companies were expected "to spend up to $50 billion to build and launch new satellites—and twice that for antennas, phones, switches, and other gear to support their birds aloft," according to William J. Cook in *U.S. News & World Report.*

One of Motorola's biggest competitors is AT&T, the long-distance giant which invested heavily in the cellular business through its purchase of McCaw Cellular Communications, the nation's largest cellular telephone carrier. AT&T also plans to be heavily involved with PCS. Other major companies in this industry include General Electric Co., General Signal Corporation, GTE Government Systems Corporation, Scientific-Atlanta Inc., McDonnell Douglas Corporation, and General Instrument Corporation, Harris Corporation, and Ericsson. None of the top ten companies in this category have sales of less than $380 million or fewer than 3,600 employees.

WORK FORCE

Employment in this industry has remained steady at approximately 123,000 since 1991. Mergers and consolidations among manufacturers, as well as improved productivity and technology, may mean employment declines in the future. However, this effect may be countered by the growing demand in certain segments of the industry.

Average hourly earnings are estimated at $12.75. Electrical and electronic assemblers, engineers, and technicians accounted for 30 percent of the employment in this industry as of 1990. By 2005, it is estimated that the need for electrical and electronic assemblers will decrease by about half.

AMERICA AND THE WORLD

This industry is positioned to take advantage of demand from developing markets abroad, such as Eastern Europe, Central and South America, and China. American companies are increasingly linking up with overseas competitors to create global partnerships. For example, in the personal communicator market (which includes wireless communication devices such as Apple Computer's Newton and Motorola's digital personal communicator), AT&T has joined Matsushita and Olivetti. Intel has joined Ericsson, the Swedish phone-equipment maker, in a similar venture.

In 1995, the largest export markets for U.S. telecommunications products in general, including products outside of this industry, were Japan and Canada, followed by the United Kingdom and Mexico. Together these markets accounted for nearly $5.5 billion in U.S. exports—more than one-third of total exports in this category. East Asia, especially Japan, China, and Malaysia, is the source of about 66 percent of total imports to the United States. Radio transceivers are the leading export category, followed by parts for radio equipment.

The U.S. cellular industry is highly competitive in cellular licenses awarded to foreign operators. About 70 percent of the total licenses to operate cellular systems abroad have been awarded to U.S. firms. American companies will continue to dominate international cellular operations, however, the lack of a common digital standard has hindered sales of U.S. cellular network equipment abroad.

RESEARCH AND TECHNOLOGY

Because of the technological orientation of this industry, research and technology are a continual, high priority concern. Much of the research and technology being carried out is intended to achieve one of several goals: to maximize an existing technology, such as CDPD; to combine existing technologies for enhanced competitiveness across technologies, such as PCS; and to improve technology in existing products to attract consumers with next-generation models, like a new generation of pagers.

FURTHER READING

Brandon, James. "The Global Positioning System Advances Toward Universal Acceptance." *Industry, Trade, and Technology Review,* July, 1996, 13-18.

Burrows, Peter. "The 1993 Up & Comers." *Electronic Business,* March 1993.

Cook, William J. "1997: A New Space Odyssey." *U.S. News & World Report,* 3 March 1997.

Cringely, Robert X. "Who, What, and Wireless." *Forbes ASAP,* 1993.

"Dimensions of U.S.-based TV Industry." *Television Digest,* 16 August 1993.

Federal Communications Commission. *Wireless Telecommunications Bureau Provides Guidance on the Anti-Collusion Rule for D, E and F Block Bidders.* Washington, 1996. Available from http://www.fcc.gov/wtb/auctions/def/da961460.txt.

Gilder, George. "George Gilder's Telecosm." *Forbes ASAP,* 29 March 1993.

O'Malley, Chris. "Blueprint for a Revolution." *Popular Science,* July, 1996, 69-72.

Therrien, Lois. "Pagers Start to Deliver More Than Phone Numbers." *Business Week,* 15 November 1993.

Ziegler, Bart, et al. "Building a Wireless Future." *Business Week,* 5 April 1993.

— Leslee York, updated by Kenneth R. Shepherd

SIC 3669

COMMUNICATIONS EQUIPMENT, NOT ELSEWHERE CLASSIFIED

This classification covers companies primarily engaged in manufacturing communications and related equipment, not elsewhere classified. Important products of this industry include intercommunication equipment, traffic signaling equipment, and fire and burglar alarm apparatus. Establishments that provide security systems monitoring and maintenance are discussed in **SIC 7382: Security Systems Services.**

While this miscellaneous communications equipment industry includes a number of visible and important products, such as railroad signaling devices and various traffic control equipment, the revenue accrued in this industry is traceable largely to security and smoke/fire alarm systems.

Alarm Systems. The United States has long dominated the alarm manufacturing and alarm monitoring industries worldwide. Myriad alarm manufacturers have been able to establish themselves over the years; in the early 1990s the National Burglar and Fire Alarm Association estimated that more than 13,000 local installation companies were operating in America. The popularity of the product enabled both manufacturers and monitoring services to thrive. STAT Resources Inc. estimated in 1992 that 1 in 11 households in the country is equipped with a monitoring system, while other statistics indicate that more than 18.5 million burglar alarm systems are in use in the United States. Expensive alarm systems were especially popular entering the mid-1990s, a result, most observers say, of increased public concern about safety. *Security Distributing & Marketing* reported that sales of residential security systems grew at a rate of 37 percent in 1993. The industrial and commercial security market, worth $1.6 billion by the end of 1994, was also expected to perform well throughout the decade with a compound annual growth rate of 13.8 percent predicted. By 2001, according to a study conducted by Frost & Sullivan Inc., this market should be worth close to $4 billion.

Three major trends drove the growth of the security systems market in the mid-1990s: growing public concern about crime, reluctance on the part of the U.S. Government to increase public safety expenditures, and a combination of technological advances and intensified price competition that made home security systems more affordable. By the middle of the decade, a basic home security system could be had for $200 or $300—down from about $1500 only a few years earlier.

Increasing penetration of personal computers into American homes also opened a new market niche for manufacturers of security systems to exploit. For example, security systems manufacturers are developing software that integrates equipment from various providers or allows for future upgrades.

Manufacturers of alarm systems typically produce two kinds of component systems—perimeter and interior alarms. Perimeter systems may include contacts that detect the opening of doors and windows, detectors that pick up the cutting and breaking of glass, and alarm screens that allow windows to be opened for fresh air, but activate an alarm if the screen is tampered with. Interior systems usually include infrared motion detectors located in strategic areas, fire alarms, panic buttons that can be operated manually to alert the monitoring station, and a key pad to operate the system. In recent years, manufacturers created new alarm systems capable of operating in concert with other home automation features so that homeowners can manipulate their surveillance system as well as their entertainment systems and heating and cooling systems. The factors that determine price are the size of the area being defended, the number of apertures that need to be protected, and the quantity and nature of the devices installed. The average family home can be protected for between $800 and $1500. Over the last several years prices for such goods have fallen significantly and basic systems could be purchased in the early 1990s for as little as $200.

Fire Systems. There are two smoke-sensing technologies commonly used in residential smoke detectors—photoelectric and ionization. Both are available in 9-volt battery and 110-volt house current models. Photoelectric detectors are more sensitive to slow, smoldering fires, while ionization detectors respond to fast burning fires such as stove grease or burning newspapers.

With gross revenues of $1.53 billion in 1996, ADT Limited of Boca Raton, Florida, is the nation's largest provider of electronic security alarm systems, providing electronic security monitoring services to more than 615,000 residential customers and over 400,000 business customers in North America and Europe. ADT's 18,000 employees provide specialized security systems to residential and business customers in retail, financial services, manufacturing, and the public sector.

Pittway Corporation of Chicago, Illinois, has long reigned as a leader in the smoke alarm manufacturing arena via its Ademco Security Group. Swayed by the high-growth security alarm sector, however, Pittway has increasingly concentrated on security system manufacturing opportunities, though Pittway's System Technology Group is the leading manufacturer of automatic fire alarm control systems. Its AlarmNet wireless cellular-like communication network transmits security alarm signals by radio. Pittway's Notifier Engineered Systems Company (NESCO) subsidiary provides systems design, training, and marketing services to distributors of its fire alarm systems. Pittway had 1995 sales of $945.7 million and a work force of 6000 employees.

FURTHER READING

Hoover's Company Capsules. Online edition. Austin, TX: Hoover's Inc., 1997.

Bowman, Eric J. "Security Tools Up For the Future." *Security Management,* January 1996.

Nix, Shann. "Homeowners Focus on Security Systems." *Orlando Sentinel,* 5 June 1993.

Rossi, Douglas. "A Bell Goes Off, and a Business Blooms." *Newsday,* 28 February 1994.

Schulman, Robert. "All About Home Alarm Systems: Burglar, Fire, Flood—Name It, You Can Guard Against It." *New York Times,* 10 January 1993.

Shiver, Jube, Jr. "Alarmed Industry Reacts to a Threat." *Los Angeles Times,* 6 May 1994.

U.S. Department of Commerce. International Trade Administration. *U.S. Industrial Outlook 1994.* GPO, 1994.

—Andrew Burke, updated by Christopher Hunt.

SIC 3671

ELECTRON TUBES

This category covers establishments primarily engaged in manufacturing electron tubes and tube parts. Establishments primarily engaged in manufacturing X-ray tubes and parts are classified in **SIC 3844: X-Ray Apparatus and Tubes and Related Irradiation Apparatus;** those manufacturing liquid crystal displays (LCDs) are classified in **SIC 3679: Electronic Components, Not Elsewhere Classified;** those manufacturing computer terminals are classified in **SIC 3575: Computer Terminals.**

INDUSTRY SNAPSHOT

In 1992, 189 industry establishments generated $3.1 billion in shipments, a 13 percent increase over 1987. The industry employed 22,200 workers—a 22 percent decline from 1987—with nearly three-quarters of all workers employed in production activities. Sixty-one percent of the value of industry revenues in 1992 was derived from the production of new and rebuilt receiving-type electron tubes such as TV and cathode-ray tubes, up from only 43 percent in 1987. The second major product group, accounting for 32 percent of the value of total 1992 shipments, consisted of transmittal, industrial, and special-purpose electron tubes (except X-ray tubes).

ORGANIZATION AND STRUCTURE

The two most recognizable types of electron tubes were the ordinary television and computer tube and the once common vacuum tube traditionally used in radios and other electronic equipment. Generally speaking, electron tubes were sealed glass, enamel, or metallic tubes of varying sizes into which electrons were fired for the purpose of displaying images or conducting, transmitting, or multiplying light for nondisplay purposes. Although television tubes and computer displays were the most common products, industry firms also manufactured camera tubes, microwave tubes, Geiger counters, radar screens, and such specialized devices as electron beam (beta ray) generator tubes, klystron tubes, magnetron tubes, planar triode tubes, and tubes for operating above the X-ray spectrum.

Electron tubes varied according to the extent to which they were "evacuated," or emptied, of gases and vapors; by the capability and type of the electron source; and by the number and configuration of electrodes they contained. The amount of power used in electron tubes ranged from milliwatts to hundreds of megawatts, and the frequency of operation ranged between zero and ten-to-the-eleventh-power Hertz depending on the type of tube. In general, CRTs operated by playing a beam of electrons of varying intensities over a display surface such as a phosphor screen, which formed patterns of light that took the form of characters or images. The three basic components of a CRT were the envelope, the electron gun, and the phosphor screen. The envelope, which was usually made of glass, was a funnel-shaped element through which the electrons were fired toward the faceplate on the broad end of the envelope. The electron gun was the source of the electrons, which, when heated and formed into a beam, were directed to differing parts of the screen by magnetic fields surrounding the envelope. The phosphor screen itself consisted of a layer of phosphor dots that coated the inner surface of the CRT's faceplate. Color CRTs used a screen made up of red, green, and blue phosphors, with an electron gun for each color; monochrome CRT screens employed one electron gun.

In the everyday family "direct view" TV, the face of the picture tube on which the electrons are projected is the same as the screen the viewer sees. In rear-projection TV sets, which became increasingly common in the 1980s, a translucent screen was used against which images were projected indirectly from three small CRTS (one each for the colors red, green, and blue) through a series of mirrors. In the mid-1990s projection TV tube manufacturers were using compact CRTs and lenses with shorter focal lengths to reduce the amount of space taken up by the television box, reducing the size of the once bulky rear projection sets by a third. In contrast to the 4:3 aspect ratio of the standard television tube, wide screen TVs employed a 16:9 ratio that resembled the wide ratio of movie theater screens and were therefore marketed as the precursor to the so-called high-definition television (HDTV) technology that Japanese TV makers trumpeted throughout the 1990s.

Despite its continued popularity in the 1990s, the CRT was by no means a perfect piece of technology. In a world increasingly permeated by digital solid state electronics technology, the CRT remained the last holdover of the old analog glass vacuum tube, which in fact it essentially was. The CRT was bulky, hot, and heavy, used large amounts of power, and was prone to the disruptions of glare and magnetic and electrical fields. By the mid-1990s, in fact, few experts doubted that for mainstream computer and TV uses the CRT's days were numbered.

The second largest industry product group, transmittal, industrial, and special-purpose electron tubes, included electrooptical tubes, microwave tubes, gas and vapor tubes, high vacuum tubes, and miscellaneous special-purpose tubes. The electrooptical tube segment included everything from camera tubes and photo cells to other photo-conductive and photo-emissive tubes, most notably the airport bomb detector picture tube, the largest market of the electrooptical tube segment.

Microwave tubes were primarily used in high and ultrahigh frequency applications such as radars, telecommunications equipment, military communication and control systems, high-frequency microwave ovens, scientific research equipment, FM radio transmitters, and industrial heating equipment. Traveling wave tubes, which were divided into forward and backward wave electron tubes, accounted for about

two-thirds of the microwave electron tubes produced in 1992. Microwave tubes as a whole comprised roughly 40 percent of the power and special-purpose tube market. Gas tubes were used primarily in industrial applications because of their efficiency and ability to handle high levels of power or current at generally low frequency levels. Product types included diodes, rectifiers, control-type industrial triodes, hydrogen and nonhydrogen thyratons, and other gas and vapor tubes. High-power tubes were also used in broadcasting transmitters. Vacuum tubes, once the primary element in electrical circuits, were primarily used in applications where low noise and high frequency were involved.

BACKGROUND AND DEVELOPMENT

Electron tubes were the principal components of almost all electronic circuits and equipment until semiconductors were developed and began to replace them in the late 1940s and 1950s. The first application of CRT technology was for an oscilloscope in 1897, and the first television using a CRT was developed in the late 1920s. Commercial production of monochrome television picture tubes began in the late 1940s. After World War II, U.S. electron tube manufacturers found a diverse and lucrative market in defense applications, ranging from radar to communication and control equipment.

By the mid-1990s, the fastest-growing segment of the TV picture tube market was big-screen TVs, those providing from 31 to 58 inches of viewable screen image. Despite the fact that by the mid-1990s nearly every U.S. home had at least one TV, in 1994 alone over 26 million color TVs were sold in the United States. Spurred on by a demand estimated to reach $20 billion by the turn of the century, industry firms were making significant strides in improving CRT's resolution, brilliance, size, energy usage, and cost. Television tubes and computer monitors were becoming flatter and bigger (the standard 14-inch PC monitor, for example, was giving way to 17- and even 20-inch models), digital circuits were being used to enhance picture quality, and advances in non-electron tube technology were coming on so quickly that the CRT itself seemed destined for only niche uses in specialized applications.

CURRENT CONDITIONS

In the 1990s the CRT sector of the electron tube industry continued to establish itself as the sector's primary revenue machine, accounting for 61 percent of the value of the industry's total shipments in 1992. Despite a drop-off in government spending for military-related CRT display technologies, the consumer computer CRT and television tube markets were promising to provide more than enough demand to fuel the industry's continuing growth.

In the mid-1990s the battle between the computer CRT and the flat panel display (FPD) intensified. Developed in America but later co-opted by Japanese firms, the FPD encompassed several display technologies, from active- and passive-matrix liquid-crystal displays (LCDs) to field-emission, micromirror, diamond emission, and neon- or xenon-based gas plasma displays. Between 1989 and 1995, demand for LCD FPDs alone grew from $1 billion to $10 billion, and it appeared to be only a matter of time before FPD manufacturers broke out of the laptop and avionics display markets into the television tube and PC monitor markets, the electron tube's home turf.

In the mid-1990s, however, FPD manufacturers still had to overcome hurdles in FPD design complexity and subsequent high cost and the technology's high power requirements. For the time being the CRT remained about the one-tenth the cost of a comparably sized FPD, and the only CRT markets immediately threatened by FPDs were point-of-sale terminals, medical imaging applications, and displays for instrumentation and factory automation.

Throughout the 1990s high-resolution HDTV was marketed as the next great advance in television technology. Because its superiority was only noticeable in 40-inch screens, the resulting increases in TV tube size spelled more trouble for the electron CRT's future. As the resolution of television screens increased, the brightness of the traditional CRT fell and the FPD became no more expensive than a comparably sized CRT, but 75 percent thinner. Indeed, in the mid-1990s, one producer, Photonic Imaging, had already tested a thirty-inch plasma FPD television that was only a few inches thick but whose image was virtually indistinguishable from a standard thirty-inch CRT television. Finally, in the mid-1990s the distinction between the television tube and the computer monitor itself threatened to vanish. So-called "Web TV" technologies like Zenith's "NetVision" allowed consumers to watch TV or surf the World Wide Web from the same screen by using a combined remote-control channel switcher/keyboard and a set-top modem box to link the TV to the Internet.

INDUSTRY LEADERS

Among the leading firms in the electron tube industry in the mid-1990s were Zenith Electronics Corporation, Philips Display Components Company, Hitachi Electronic Devices, and Toshiba Westing-

house Electronic. Other major industry players included GM Hughes Electronics Corporation, Hewlett-Packard Co., ITT Corporation, Litton Industries Inc., Electron Devices Division, Philips Electronics North America, and Raytheon Electronic Components. The pace of change in the electron tube industry was frenetic in the mid-1990s. In 1994, Display Technologies Inc., a joint venture of International Business Machines Corporation (IBM Corp.) and Japan's Toshiba Corporation, continued to develop IBM's flat-screen CRT product line. The same year, Fluke Corporation sold off its CRT operation, and in 1995, Advanced Technology Materials Inc. and Silicon Video Corporation agreed to market a new generation of thin CRT flat panel displays. Varian Associates Inc., once an industry leader, sold its electron devices operations to Leonard Green & Partners L.P. for $200 million in 1995; in 1996, Thomson Consumer Electronics pursued plans to modernize its picture tube plant in Indiana, and in December Zenith Electronics announced it would be eliminating about 1,200 jobs, or one quarter of its workforce. Finally, in 1996 Japan's Sony Corp. and the U.S. firm Tektronix Inc. unveiled a big-screen "Plasmatron" television line that offered consumers a 25-inch flat-screen television (about four inches thick), with 40- and 50-inch flat TVs to follow.

RESEARCH AND TECHNOLOGY

The growing demand for computer monitors for use in homes and offices starting in the 1980s forced industry firms to develop more user-friendly monitor designs, such as the "flat square CRT," in which the curvature of the CRT's screen was greatly reduced. CRT display technology also continued to evolve in the areas of unit price and color display capabilities.

The application of multifunctional CRT displays in the instrument panels of military and to a lesser degree commercial aircraft also continued in the 1990s. However, the inherent disadvantages of CRTs—limited screen size, unwieldy shape, high power requirements, and fragility—led manufacturers to investigate alternatives to CRT technology, such as light-emitting diodes, FPDs, and LCDs. Improvements in LCDs, which were thinner and lighter than CRTs, enabled them to compete in price with CRT-based, large-screen, video-data projectors while offering roughly 2 to 4 times their brightness. In aircraft cockpit applications in particular—where limited space and high levels of glare diminished the usefulness of CRTs—flat panel displays increasingly emerged as the favored display technology. Another emergent technology, the field emission display, was structurally less complex than LCDs and even thinner in size and further threatened to unseat the electron CRT. In general terms, field emission displays were based on vacuum microelectronics and combined the advantages of the old vacuum tube technology with the benefits of digital computer chips. Advances in research and technology also continued in non-CRT product categories in the 1990s. So-called direct broadcast satellites for noncable, HDTV transmissions (among other uses) were developed that used electron tubes, such as traveling wave tubes, for satellite tubes and uplink stations with tube lifetimes of up to fifteen years.

FURTHER READING

"ATMI, SVC Expand CRT Partnership." *Electronic News* 41, no. 2062 (24 April 1995): 4.

Barry, James. "Big Screen Bonanza." *Stereo Review* 60, no. 4 (April 1995): 53 + .

Cataldo, Anthony. "CRTs Are Solid Fixtures but FPDs Keep Pressing On." *Electronic News* 41, no. 2070 (19 June 1995): 68.

Churbuck, David C. "The Last Picture Tube." *Forbes* 155, no. 10 (8 May 1995): 136 + .

Dawson, Fred. "The State of the Display." *Digital Media* 3, nos. 9-10 (February/March 1994): 10 + .

"Information Impact." *Fortune* (technology guide supplement), Winter 1997, 93 + .

Normile, Dennis. "Reinventing the Cathode-ray Tube." *Popular Science* 244, no. 2 (February 1994): 34.

"Preparing for Prime Time," *Economist* 340, no. 7980 (24 August 1996): 49.

U.S. Bureau of the Census. *1992 Census of Manufactures.* Washington: GPO, 1992. Available from http://www.census.gov.

"Varian Sells Off Electron Devices." *Electronic News* 41, no. 2081 (4 September 1995): 40.

—Paul Bodine

SIC 3672

PRINTED CIRCUIT BOARDS

This category includes establishments primarily engaged in the manufacture of printed circuit boards, sometimes referred to as printed wiring boards.

A printed circuit board (PCB) is a thin piece of insulating material onto which tiny electrical wiring pathways or "traces" have been printed, usually by a photoengraving process. PCBs provide the physical structure for mounting electronic components, such as semiconductors; the printed traces then serve to inter-connect the components, forming an electronic system. PCBs are used in a wide range of electronic products, including computers, telecommunications equipment, electronic instruments, and automobiles.

INDUSTRY SNAPSHOT

In the mid-1990s, there were more than 650 U.S. facilities that manufactured about 238 million printed circuit boards each year. More than 10 million pounds of trim and rejected boards were generated each year. This was one of the reasons for the increasing popularity of recycling in the printed circuit boards industry.

Through 1997, contract manufacturers continued to invest heavily in conventional surface mount technology (SMT) equipment rather than in new technologies such as chip on board (COB) and ball grid arrays (BGA). The manufacturers were slow in adopting the new technologies; about 25 percent of them, however, focused on BGA as their next generation packing technology. By mid-1996, copper-clad printed circuit board materials were increasingly being used in the electronics industry because of its excellent electrical and thermal properties.

ORGANIZATION AND STRUCTURE

According to the Institute of Interconnecting and Packaging Electronic Circuits (IPC), approximately 750 to 800 independent companies produced PCBs in the United States in 1992. Yet independent manufacturers accounted for only 66 percent of the entire market. So-called "captive" PCB-makers, primarily large original equipment manufacturers (OEMs) who make their own boards, comprised the remaining 34 percent. Though the largest market for OEM boards was in computer applications, captive board makers also served a large number of communications and government/military users as well.

U.S. PCB production reached $5.3 billion in 1991, according to IPC, while worldwide sales of PCBs reached $20.2 billion in 1992, according to the Electronic Outlook Corporation. Total value of the industry, including bare boards, components, and various activities involved in the assembly of boards, was estimated at $60 billion in the early 1990s.

Computer makers were the major consumers of independently produced PCBs in 1991, when over 43 percent of overall independent board production went to computer companies. Communications constituted the second major market for independently produced PCBs with more than 17 percent. The role of independent PCB manufacturers has increased steadily over the years. Though more than 90 percent of independent

PCB-makers reported annual sales of less than $10 million in 1991, OEMs were increasingly relying on them to supply boards for their products, and industry observers expected this trend to continue.

Printed circuit board assembly companies (PCBAs) comprised a growing, specialized segment of the PCB industry. More than just contract assemblers, PCBAs provided design, global procurement, and cost reduction services and access to advanced technology. The early 1990s saw a dramatic growth in the use of PCBAs, and industry observers expected that trend to continue because of the cost savings these companies provided. There were nearly 800 PCBAs in operation in the United States in 1992 with an estimated total value of $5.9 billion. PCBAs employed approximately 80,000 workers in 1991, while independent board makers employed about 70,000.

At the start of the 1990s, PCB makers were adapting to two important industry trends: increasing use of smaller circuitry products and greater demand for surface mount technology. The drive among electronics firms toward smaller components had been cited as part of the cause of a decline in PCB usage from 1988 to 1991. Smaller components required less space on the PCB and smaller or fewer boards.

Spurred by the demand for smaller, higher-performance PCBs, the industry moved quickly toward surface mount technology. Surface mounting involves the soldering of components directly onto the surface of a board. The process allows components to be mounted closer together and even on both sides of a board. In 1989, less than 12 percent of boards included surface mounted components; by 1992 more than half of all PCBs were assembled with one or more surface-mounted components.

Though the domestic PCB industry continued to remain globally competitive in utilizing advanced manufacturing technologies, increasing overseas production resulted in a significant decrease in the U.S. share of the world PCB market from 40 percent in 1980 to 29 percent in 1990. In 1991, Japan ranked first in worldwide production of rigid PCBs with 33.8 percent of the market; the U.S. ranked second with 26.9 percent. Germany, Taiwan, the United Kingdom, and Hong Kong ranked third through sixth, respectively.

CURRENT CONDITIONS

Shipment values were about $8.5 billion in 1996 and were expected to increase to an estimated $9 billion by 1998. In the mid- to late 1990s one of the most popular trends in the printed circuit boards industry was to reuse the vast amounts of waste generated each year. Proler International Corporation launched a new circuit board recycling operation, Proler Recycling, in Coolidge, Arizona, where they started processing recycled boards in the summer of 1995. According to *American Metal Market,* in 1995, Proler Recycling was the only company in the United States that recovered all three metal components—tin, copper, and lead—from circuit boards and converted them to high purity metals. At the time, the other companies were typically recovering only one of the metals from the circuit boards.

In 1996, Daimler Benz was using a four stage process for recycling the circuit boards. The technology, which was in the pilot plant stage in Germany, involved Benz's customized version of first shredding the electronic scrap and then using various techniques to separate out and clean the various elements of the shredded scrap. According to Benz, the recycling technique cost them about $198.48 to $338.80 per metric ton of circuit board scrap and gave them a return of $529.28 to $1,984.80 per ton depending on gold content.

Another popular trend of the mid- to late 1990s was the increased use of signal analysis tools to design printed circuit boards capable of operating at high frequency levels. These tools were used to accurately analyze the signal integrity of printed circuit board designs with respect to several circuit parameters, such as crosstalk, ground bounce, resonance, and dispersion.

New via technologies capable of addressing complex capability requirements were becoming the trend of the mid-1990s. The 1996 IPC Printed Circuits Expo showcased several of these new technologies. According to *Electronic Design* magazine, DuPont Advanced Fiber Systems demonstrated a new method of producing high speed micro-vias in dimensionally stable, non-woven Aramid reinforced laminates using laser-ablation technology. Mommers Print Service B.V. demonstrated a cheaper but more complex technique that also involves laser formation of micro-vias. As circuit board makers scramble to stay ahead of the curve on inner layer via density, increased IC integration and the need for greater interconnect density on printed circuit boards seems to be the next step for circuit board manufacturers.

INDUSTRY LEADERS

In the mid-1990s, Micron Technology, Inc. of Boise, Idaho, was the industry leader with $3.7 billion in sales and 9,900 employees. Second place was held by Solectron Corporation, with $2.0 billion in sales and 11,049 employees. Diamond Multimedia Systems

Incorporated, came in third with $467.6 milion in sales and 747 employees. Avex Electronics Incorporated held fourth place with $430 million in sales and 3,750 employees.

Other leaders were Solectron Technology Incorporated with sales of $300 million and 1,100 employees, Hadco Corporation with sales of $265.2 milion and 2,346 employees, Photocircuits Corporation with sales of $265 million and 2,400 employees, QMS Incorporated with sales of $259.7 million and 1,194 employees, Reptron Electronics Incorporated with $237.8 million in sales and 1,300 employees, and Starks Building with $200 million in sales and 1,600 employees.

California had the most establishments—417. Texas had 83, and Illinois had 72.New York's 60 establishments produced 26.9 percent of U.S. Shipments, while California's produced 22.8 percent.

FURTHER READING

Bylinsky, Gene. *High Tech: Window to the Future.* Hong Kong:Intercontinental Publishing Corporation Ltd., 1985.

Haystead, John.''Look Before You Leap.'' *Electronic Business Today,* January 1997, 67.

LaRue, Gloria T. ''Daimler-Benz Develops Circuit Board Process.'' *American Metal Market,* 13 November 1996, 6.

Maliniak, David. ''Solving Inner-layer Via Problems.'' *Electronic Design,* 1 May 1996, 20.

Maliniak, Lisa. ''Signal Analysis: A Must For PCB Design Success.'' *Electronic Design,* 18 Sept 1995, 69.

Pease, Robert A. ''What's All This Copper Clad Stuff, Anyhow?'' *Electronic Design,* 19 August 1996, S62.

''Proler Set to Start Circuit Boar Unit.'' *American Metal Market,* 25 May 1995, 7.

Standard & Poor's Industry Surveys. New York: Standard & Poor's Corporation, 1993.

U.S. Department of Commerce. International Trade Administration. *U.S. Inudustrial Outlook 1994.* Washington: GPO, 1994.

—John K. Waters, updated by Visi Tilak

SIC 3674

SEMICONDUCTORS AND RELATED DEVICES

This category covers establishments primarily engaged in manufacturing semiconductors and related solid-state devices. Important products of this industry are semiconductor diodes and stacks, including rectifiers, integrated microcircuits (semiconductor networks), transistors, solar cells, and light sensing and emitting semiconductor (solid-state) devices.

INDUSTRY SNAPSHOT

No longer wholly dependent on personal computer sales, the U.S. semiconductor industry provides components for a wide range of consumer and industrial electronics. Computers still account for a significant portion of the industry's sales, however. After growing 40 percent in 1995, the semiconductor industry was poised for ten years of extremely rapid growth, according to industry analysts.

Entering the twenty-first century, the information technology sector accounted for 11 percent of the U.S. gross domestic product and one-fourth of the U.S. manufacturing output. U.S. semiconductor manufacturers supplied some 40 percent of the world's output of microchips. In the aggregate, U.S. chipmakers derived more than half of their sales from international markets. The semiconductor industry was one of the fastest growing sectors in the U.S. economy. With the rapid pace of technological advance in the semiconductor industry, a facility that commenced production in 1997 would be a mature factory by the year 2000, according to the Semiconductor Industry Association.

The overall chip market for 1996, however declined 10.5 percent, reversing the previous three-year trend, according to World Semiconductor Trade Statistics. The fall of computer DRAM (the most common memory unit) prices was the cause. Memory chip prices went down 33 percent but microprocessors grew by 17.5 percent, according to *Electronic Business Today.* However, due to decreased inventory levels caused by consumer spending, the global chip industry was expected to grow 13 percent into 1997. By the year 2000, with the semiconductor content of electrical equipment reaching 28 percent and with the emergence of new markets, industry analysts were optimistic that the semiconductor industry would double its sales.

ORGANIZATION AND STRUCTURE

Sometimes referred to as ''the crude oil of the information age,'' semiconductors are a pervasive but generally unseen aspect of everyday life. The tiny electronic circuits etched on chips of silicon are critical to the operation of virtually all electronics, from automatic coffee makers and antilock braking systems to cellular phones and supercomputers.

The computer industry is by far the largest market for semiconductors. In the early 1990s, sales to computer manufacturers and related enterprises accounted for 41 percent of overall sales of semiconductors in this country. Consumer electronics and the automotive industry are also important users of semiconductors and related products. Sales to these two industries combined accounted for 25 percent of total sales in that same period.

Semiconductor chips are manufactured in "clean rooms," free of contaminating dust. In those facilities, thin, round silicon wafers are processed in batches. Chipmakers buy polished blank wafers from companies that specialize in growing silicon crystals, from which the wafers are cut. Each wafer is about half a millimeter thick. Microelectronics circuits are built up on the wafer layer by layer.

Circuit patterns—the collection of transistors, capacitors, and associated components and their interconnections—are inscribed on large glass plates called photomasks. The photomasks are later reduced and photolithographically projected onto the silicon wafers. Each mask comprises a total integrated circuit design.

Semiconductor companies design and manufacture primarily two types of products: integrated circuits (ICs) and discrete devices. A discrete semiconductor is an individual circuit that performs a single function affecting the flow of electrical current. For example, a transistor, one of the most common types of discrete devices, amplifies electrical signals; rectifiers and diodes generally convert alternating current into direct current; capacitors block the flow of alternating current at controlled levels; and resistors limit current flow and divide or drop current.

Integrated Circuits. Also called chips, integrated circuits are a collection of microminiaturized electronic components, such as transistors and capacitors, placed on a tiny rectangle of silicon. A single integrated circuit can perform the functions of thousands of discrete transistors, diodes, capacitors, and resistors. There are three basic types of integrated circuits currently produced by American semiconductor manufacturers: memory components, which are used to store data or computer programs; logic devices, which perform such operations as mathematical calculations; and components that combine the two. This latter category of integrated circuit is the most sophisticated and includes microprocessors, the computer "brain" that manipulates a wide range of data, and microcontrollers, which perform repetitive tasks.

The two largest selling types of memory integrated circuits are DRAMs and SRAMs. A DRAM (dynamic random access memories; pronounced DEE-ram) stores digital information and provides high-speed storage and retrieval of data. It is called a "dynamic" circuit because the data is stored in a temporary medium that allows it to fade, and so must be constantly refreshed electronically.

SRAMs (static random access memories; pronounced ESS-rams) perform many of the same functions as DRAMs, but at higher speeds. Unlike DRAMs, they do not require constant electronic refreshing, hence the term "static." They also contain more electronic circuitry and are more expensive to produce than DRAMs.

Both of these integrated circuit products are manufactured in large quantities, and so are considered to be "process drivers." That is, the manufacturing processes used to produce them are constantly being refined, and those refinements often affect manufacturing processes of other products.

Two other important semiconductor memory products are EPROMs (erasable programmable read-only memories) and EEPROMs (electrically erasable read-only memories). EPROMs are used to store computer programs. Unlike older read-only memories (ROMs), which carried fixed programs, EPROMs are programmed by the customer. EEPROMs are easier and faster to update than EPROMs because they are programmed using electricity. While EPROMs are usually programmed only once, EEPROMs can be reprogrammed without removing them from their applications, so they can be updated virtually anytime.

ASICS. Most logic semiconductors are now customized products tailored to the specific needs of each customer. In fact, ASICS (application-specific integrated circuits) have become the most commonly manufactured non-microcomponent logic semiconductors.

There are four basic classes of ASICs; each class has a different degree of customization of the chip. Full-custom ASICs are designed from scratch; standard cells are designed by combining modular cells from a cell library; semi-custom chips are customized in only one or two areas; and programmable logic devices are programmed by blowing fuses in a device to alter the logic function. Because of high design costs and the often limited quantities produced, ASICs tend to be more expensive than integrated circuits built from off-the-shelf components. But because they combine several specialized functions on a single chip, they offer some important advantages: they are smaller, simpler, and fewer of them are needed; they allow for a greater degree of integration, which leads to more efficient use of circuitry; and, since they contain less circuitry, fewer interconnections are needed and overall performance is enhanced.

Microprocessors and Controllers. Microprocessors (MPUs) are the central processing units in all microcomputer-based systems. These products perform a variety of tasks by manipulating data within a system and controlling input, output, peripherals, and memory devices.

The two major types of MPUs are CISCs (complex instruction set computing) and RISCs (reduced instruction set computing). Though CISCs used to be the basis for all MPU operations, RISCs became increasingly popular in the 1990s because of their faster operating speeds, their ability to run more sophisticated software, and their ability to deliver better graphics. MPUs are used in local area networks (linked personal computers and workstations; called LANs) and satellites. The latest generation of these circuits operate at speeds of from 40 to 50 million cycles per second.

Microcontrollers (MCUs), which combine a microprocessor, memory circuits, and input/output circuitry, are used as embedded controllers in virtually every electronic product. They perform such repetitive tasks as controlling the antilock brake systems in automobiles.

BACKGROUND AND DEVELOPMENT

Semiconductors were invented in the United States in the late 1950s, but the invention that truly began the electronics revolution appeared nearly 50 years earlier. The three-element vacuum tube was invented by Lee de Forest in Palo Alto, California, in 1906. Called the audion, the tube was used as a sound amplifier and generator of electromagnetic waves; its invention laid the foundation for the development of radio, television, radar, computers and many other ground-breaking electronic devices. These early tubes, however, were bulky and fragile. For example, ENIAC (Electronic Numerical Integrator and Computer), the world's first large electronic computer, ran on 18,000 vacuum tubes and was the size of a house.

The tubes also played a vital role in the development of early telephone communications networks. But as those networks expanded across the United States, the unreliability of the tubes became intolerable. Consequently, the main push for a replacement for the vacuum tube came from researchers at AT&T Bell Laboratories in New Jersey.

For a number of years, the company had been studying potential uses of solid materials that were poor conductors of electricity, primarily silicon and germanium. Silicon, one of the world's most plentiful elements, is found in the earth's crust as silica and silicate and is the principal component of sand, quartz, and glass. In its pure form, silicon is a very poor conductor, but Bell Lab researchers found that it could be treated, or "doped," with other materials to act as a conductor under some conditions and an insulator under others.

These new "semiconductors" allowed for the development in 1947 of the transistor, which marked the beginning of the age of solid-state electronics. In 1956, William Shockley, John Bardeen, and Walter H. Brattain—the Bell Labs research team responsible for the development and refinement of the transistor—received the Nobel Prize for their invention. The same year he was awarded the Nobel Prize, Shockley returned to his boyhood home of Palo Alto, California, and established his own semiconductor manufacturing operation. To staff his new company, Shockley recruited many of the country's brightest young scientists and engineers.

Disagreements eventually led seven of Shockley's recruits to set out on their own. The company they founded, Fairchild Semiconductor, would become "the mother of semiconductor companies." According to the Semiconductor Industry Association, more than 23 semiconductor and related enterprises can trace their origins back to Fairchild. Among them were such important and well-known companies as Intel, Advanced Micro Devices, and National Semiconductor.

Probably the most important technological development to come out of Fairchild was the integrated circuit or "chip." Both the head of Fairchild, MIT graduate Robert N. Noyce, and Texas Instruments researcher Jack Kilby are credited with inventing the integrated circuit almost simultaneously in 1958. The original Texas Instruments version of the chip required the soldering of tiny gold wires on the outside to connect the components. The Fairchild version, on the other hand, relied on a thin layer of metal conducting film, which was sprayed onto the chip like paint. Roadways were then cut by lithography into this metallic layer to create the desired pattern of connections between elements of the circuit. This version of the chip was more readily manufacturable, and Fairchild soon emerged as the early leader of the semiconductor industry.

Noyce left Fairchild in 1968, along with Gordon E. Moore, a respected physical chemist. Together, they formed Intel Corporation and set out to manufacture a computer memory chip. Intel eventually came to dominate the industry as the undisputed leader in semiconductor technology. In addition to the first memory chips, Intel was responsible for pioneering the development of the microprocessor, the so-called "computer-on-a-chip."

U.S. manufacturers continued to dominate the semiconductor industry until the 1980s, when foreign industrial targeting and illegal dumping practices combined to erode U.S. worldwide market share. This "blood bath," as it was referred to in industry publications at the time, drove Intel, Motorola, National Semiconductor, Advanced Micro Devices, and Mostek out of the dynamic random access memory (DRAM) market altogether. Japanese manufacturers, however, who utilized investment cost advantages to conquer the DRAM market, saw that market plunge at the onset of the 1990s. As *Forbes* noted in 1991, DRAM sales in 1990 "contracted instead of growing, plunging 24%— or roughly $2 billion in annual revenues."

Consequently, U.S. semiconductor manufacturers began to refocus their efforts on proprietary products during the early 1990s, capitalizing on their well-known strengths in design and innovation, and moving away from commodity products. According to industry observers, two Congressional actions were instrumental in paving the way for this development.

The first was the establishment in 1982 of the U.S. Court of Appeals for the Federal Circuit in Washington, D.C., a court specifically formed to hear patent cases. Previously, patent cases had been tried in federal district courts, where an estimated 70 percent of patents were successfully challenged. With the new court, however, that statistic was reversed, with about two-thirds of patents upheld.

The second was the Semiconductor Chip Protection Act, passed by Congress in 1984. The new law specifically protected semiconductor design, or "mask work," for up to 10 years. As electronics firms began to exercise their rights, the courts continued to provide stronger legal protection for proprietary chip designs. In 1991, Congress extended the Act through 1995.

The U.S. semiconductor industry experienced generally sluggish conditions during the mid 1980s, but seemed to be entering a period of renewed growth in the early 1990s. Worldwide sales of semiconductors and semiconductor products exceeded $21 billion in 1991; by 1992, the U.S. Department of Commerce was predicting a strong recovery for the industry, with the overall value of shipments reaching nearly $30 billion.

The health of the semiconductor industry remains closely tied to three other economically sensitive and cyclical industries: computers, automobiles, and consumer electronics. Consequently, the industry has a history of erratic earnings.

Industry observers predicted an especially profitable rebound for semiconductors in the mid-1990s due to several factors. Inventories were at historically low levels in 1992, while the U.S. economy surged upward in 1993, signaling improved financial outlooks for key industry customers such as the automotive manufacturers. New generations of semiconductors were proving popular as well, selling at higher average prices and wider margins. Finally, sales of electronic equipment in general were accelerating worldwide, with the semiconductor content of that equipment increasing.

The early 1990s also saw the continuation of the trend toward strategic alliances and corporate partnering among semiconductor companies. This trend was fast becoming an important competitive tool, allowing individual firms to share the ever-increasing costs of production. Entering the mid-1990s, U.S. semiconductor manufacturers were shifting their attention from commodity products to the development of innovative proprietary products, which they have begun vigorously protecting with the help of new patent legislation.

In late 1992, industry observers began to note signs of an economic rebound for U.S. semiconductor manufacturers. In June of that year, a price war in the personal computer market gave the industry a much-needed boost. By November, orders were outpacing shipments and the industry was clearly expanding. By 1993, the U.S. semiconductor industry was experiencing a strong upturn. Worldwide semiconductor sales had increased 9 percent in 1992.

The strategic shift among U.S. chipmakers away from commodity products in favor of the higher priced proprietary products was expected to yield increased profits and fuel a continuation of the 1992 rebound, although a temporary reduction in revenues was expected as older facilities and products were phased out. In fact, the industry saw itself on the path of solid growth through 1997. The increasingly robust recovery of the U.S. economy, as well as improvements in Japanese consumer electronics markets, were also expected to positively influence the industry's growth.

Two additional factors were expected to contribute to the continued growth of the semiconductor industry: overall increases in worldwide sales of electronic equipment, and the increasing semiconductor content of electronic products. Integrated Circuit Engineering Corp. (ICE), a market research firm based in Scottsdale, Arizona, estimated an increase in worldwide electronics sales from $595 billion in 1992 to $900 billion by 1997. ICE also estimated an increase in the semiconductor content of electronic equipment—

from 12.5 percent in 1992 to 15.3 percent in 1997. This growth was driven by the increasingly sophisticated nature of consumer electronics. Manufacturers of fax machines, notebook computers, and camcorders, for example, used semiconductors in these products to perform increasingly complex operations.

Despite the industry's anticipated overall rebound, evidence suggested that growth would vary considerably among market segments. For example, while sales of memory products experienced a deep recession, microprocessors grew rapidly; while some companies reported serious losses, others reported record earnings.

Military demand for semiconductors was weak in the 1990s because of cutbacks in U.S. defense spending. Semiconductor sales to the military, which accounted for 5 percent of sales in 1988, accounted for only 3 percent of sales by 1992. Also, sales of consumer electronics worldwide grew only 5 percent in 1992, partly due to the global recession that hit Western Europe and Japan especially hard.

The continuing development of Integrated Services Digital Network (ISDN) technology was expected to provide an important new market for chipmakers in the future. The ISDN is a high-speed digital communications network capable of carrying voice, data, and video signals simultaneously over existing telephone lines. The network, which was first commercially introduced in the early 1990s, requires large numbers of semiconductors.

Another factor in the industry is the shrinking number of production options available to players in the field. Many companies that have emerged in recent years in this realm have farmed out production to other facilities with spare capacity in their wafer fabrication plants. As *Business Week* noted, by using these facilities, "U.S. entrepreneurs avoided the main hurdle for a chip start-up: the tens or hundreds of millions in wafer-fabrication costs. A new venture could thus devote its resources to innovative designs . . . By pioneering these cutting-edge products, fabless companies grew faster and earned higher returns than established chipmakers—giving them clout way beyond their 5 percent share of the $77 billion world chip market.'' In the mid-1990s, however, that capacity glut had disappeared and companies without their own production facilities faced possibly substantial investment to secure guaranteed access to production facilities.

CURRENT CONDITIONS

By the mid-1990s the semiconductor industry had become one of the most explosive segments of the economy. The history of the semiconductor industry was cyclical, with semiconductor products having short life cycles caused primarily by rapid technological innovations and resulting in pricing pressures. The semiconductor industry—a $100 billion industry in 1995—was expected to become a $200 billion industry in 1997, and by 2000 grow into a $350 billion industry.

The demand for chips was driven not only by the increasing sales of PCs but also by the use of chips in consumer electronics, telecommunications, and networking. As inventory exceeded demand, in late 1995, DRAM prices started plummeting creating an overall impact on the global chip market. After experiencing a growth rate of 45 percent in 1995, the cyclical trends caused the growth rate to decrease to 26 percent in 1996.

In spite of the fluctuation in the growth rate, the semiconductor industry continued to grow rapidly. The use of semiconductors as components in almost all industries continued to accelerate. Microchips were being made to do all types of things faster. Intel, which had a 90 percent share of the microprocessors market, was partnering with Rambus, a semiconductor maker, to develop what would be the fastest ever semiconductor.

INDUSTRY LEADERS

The five largest corporations in this industry in terms of overall sales revenue were International Business Machines Corporation (Armonk, New York) with $71.90 billion in sales revenues and 225,347 employees; Motorola, Inc. (Schaumburg, Illinois) with $27.04 billion in sales and 142,000 employees; Intel Corporation (Santa Clara, California) with $20.80 billion in sales and 48,500 employees; Texas Instruments (Dallas, Texas) with sales of $13.13 billion and 59,574 employees; and Siemens Corporation (New York, New York) with $7.30 billion in sales revenues and 46,300 employees.

Intel Corporation was ranked the leader in the electronics and electrical equipment industry by *Fortune*. Also ranked as one of the 10 most admired companies in the United States by *Fortune*, Intel Corporation held a more than 90 percent share of the microprocessors market because of the success of its Pentium chip. Intel was founded in what would become California's Silicon Valley in 1968 by industry pioneers Robert N. Noyce, Gordon E. Moore, and Andrew S. Grove. Starting with 12 employees, Intel pursued research that led to the development of the first computer chip. The company also played an instrumental role in the development of metal oxide semiconductor (MOS) technology.

Originally a supplier of semiconductor memory for mainframe computers and mini-computers, Intel eventually became a leading supplier of microcomputers. The company sells its microcomputer components, modules, and systems directly to companies that incorporate them into their products. These are primarily computer systems manufacturers, but also include makers of automobiles and a wide range of industrial and telecommunications equipment. The company also sells personal computer enhancements and networking products through distributors, resellers, and retail stores worldwide. The company sells supercomputers directly to end users. Intel has design, development, production, and administration facilities throughout the Western United States, Europe, and Asia.

Motorola Corporation was ranked the third leader in the electronics and electrical equipment industry by *Fortune*. Motorola was also among the 40 largest industrial companies in the United States ranked by total sales.

Motorola was founded in 1928 in Chicago, Illinois, by Paul V. Galvin. As the Galvin Manufacturing Corp., the company's first product was a "battery eliminator" that allowed consumers to operate radios directly from household current instead of the batteries supplied with early models. In the 1930s the company successfully commercialized car radios under the brand name "Motorola." The company's name was changed to Motorola, Inc., in 1947, the same year it began research into solid-state electronics.

The company's semiconductor division designs and produces a broad line of discrete semiconductors and integrated circuits, including microprocessors, microcomputers, and memory products. These products are sold to computer, consumer, automotive, industrial, federal government/military and telecommunications markets. In addition to being one of the world's leading providers of semiconductor technology, Motorola also provides wireless communication and advanced electronics equipment and services to worldwide markets. The company maintains sales and service offices around the world.

Texas Instruments was ranked the fifth leader in the electronics and electrical equipment industry by *Fortune*. Headquartered in Dallas, Texas, the company has manufacturing facilities in 18 countries and marketing or engineering services in more than 30 countries.

The company was founded in 1930 as the "Geophysical Service" by J. Clarence "Doc" Karcher and Eugene McDermott. It was the first independent contractor to specialize in reflection seismograph methods of exploration. The firm's name was changed to Texas Instruments, better known as TI, in 1951. The company entered the semiconductor business in 1952 with the purchase of a license from Western Electric Company to manufacture transistors.

In addition to semiconductors, TI products and services include defense electronics systems, software productivity tools, computer and peripheral products, custom engineering and manufacturing services, electrical controls, metallurgical materials, and consumer electronics products.

WORK FORCE

Semiconductor jobs more than doubled from 115,200 workers in 1972 to 258,500 workers in 1996. According to the U.S. Department of Labor, the all-time high of almost 300,000 semiconductor workers in 1985 was reached amidst a robust economy. However, from 1985 to 1993 employment levels declined, in spite of a brief upsurge in 1988. U.S. firms employed about half of their work force in facilities abroad, according to the Semiconductor Industry Association.

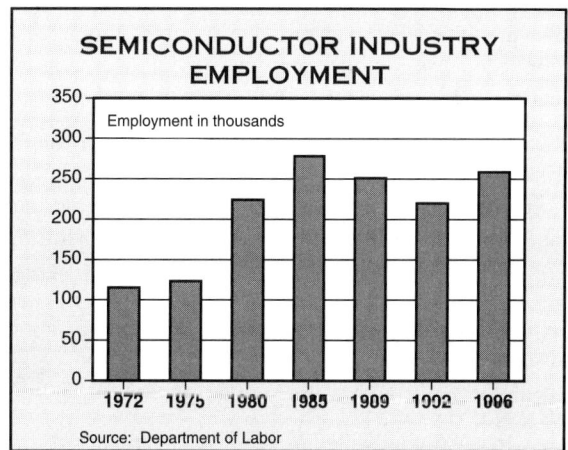

Within the United States, average hourly earnings for production workers in the semiconductor industry were $14.59 in 1995, 18 percent above the average for all manufacturing. According the U.S. Department of Labor, this reflected in part, the higher skill and value added associated with the capital intensive processing steps and research and development activities performed by U.S. semiconductor workers.

AMERICA AND THE WORLD

The United States has produced a trade deficit in semiconductors throughout the 1990s—in 1995, this deficit amounted to some $16 billion. Total U.S. imports were valued at $38 billion that year, compared with exports of $22 billion.

Japan is the world's largest producer of memory chips, but in the early 1990s, its industry was in a severe slump and the country's overall economy was growing at only 1.5 percent. Consequently, there was a 6.3 percent drop in Japanese semiconductor sales.

In 1992, the market for North American chipmakers' products outgrew Japan's for the first time since 1985. The European market also grew, boosted by the weaker dollar. In fact, these factors led to an overall shift in worldwide market share for the semiconductor industry. North American companies' share increased to 30 percent in 1992, up from 28 percent the previous year. European firms held on to a steady 19 percent market share. Meanwhile, Japanese market share fell from 38 percent in 1991 to 33 percent in 1992. Many observers expect this trend to continue in the mid-1990s, as companies in the United States and smaller countries grow rapidly and Japan struggles to regain its momentum.

The early 1990s domestic industry rebound resulted in increased capital spending on the part of U.S. semiconductor manufacturers. By contrast, capital spending among Japanese companies dropped from the previous year's levels, due to the difficult economic condition and overcapacity for DRAMs, a product niche the Japanese largely control.

In an effort to reduce costs and lower financial risks, Japanese chipmakers entered into alliances with foreign companies. Since 1989 Japan has entered into about 88 such alliances, ranging from manufacturing joint ventures to joint product development agreements. These alliances have focused primarily on HDTV chip development, microprocessor development, ASIC development, and computer-aided design projects.

In 1986, the United States and Japan entered into an agreement called the U.S.-Japan Semiconductor Arrangement, which was designed to eliminate dumping of Japanese products in world markets and to increase market access for foreign semiconductor manufacturers in the Japanese market. In 1991 the follow-on agreement to the 1986 agreement went into effect. The new agreement reflected U.S. expectations that more than 20 percent share of the Japanese market could be captured by foreign suppliers by 1992 through the efforts of government and industry.

While U.S. semiconductor companies were consolidating in the early 1990s, companies in the so-called dynamic Asian economies (DAEs) were expanding. DAE countries include South Korea, Taiwan, Hong Kong, China, Singapore, and Malaysia. DAE countries dominated U.S. semiconductor imports in 1992. Southeastern Asian markets present extensive opportunities for U.S. chip exporters as well, since most of the world's major electronics companies have established operations there, and more electronic products means more need for semiconductors. The re-establishment of trade relations with Vietnam in 1994 also presents U.S. companies with still another market to explore.

According to data compiled by the World Semiconductor Statistics organization, the European market for semiconductors was expected to grow by 7.7 percent in 1992, making Europe approximately 19 percent of the world market. The European market was considered a battleground for competition among the global electronics giants. Both South Korean and Japanese semiconductor companies increased their presence in Europe, but American companies still held 44 percent of market share in 1991.

In the late 1990s, America's market (including North and South America) remained as the world largest market for the semiconductor industry, representing one-third of all sales. Chip sales were expected to grow by 7.8 percent in 1996 to $50.6 billion, 9.2 percent in 1997, 15.7 percent in 1998, and 19.1 percent in 1999 as sales hit $76.1 billion, according to the Semiconductor Industry Association.

With nearly 26 percent of the chip market, Japan remained the second largest market for semiconductors. The Japanese market was expected to grow 10 percent in 1997, and by 1999 show a 15.8 percent growth as sales reached $57 billion. The fastest growing chip market, the Asia-Pacific, grew by 54.1 percent in 1995. By 1999 this market was expected to grow 23.3 percent to $53.4 billion. The Asia Pacific sector represented 20.9 percent of the world chip market, according to the Semiconductor Industry Association. The European market, which represented 20.5 percent of the world market, was expected to grow 18.7 percent in 1999 to $47.8 billion in sales.

RESEARCH AND TECHNOLOGY

According to Dataquest, about one-third of U.S. semiconductor industry revenues is spent on technology development and capital; 14 percent of revenues is spent on research and development alone. Costs for new semiconductor fabrication facilities, a major capital consideration for many companies, range from $600 million to $900 million.

High Definition Television. One emerging technology that could trigger a boom in semiconductor sales is high definition television (HDTV). HDTV produces pictures that are four to five times clearer than the standard television picture. In addition to commercial broadcast television, the first of which were expected by the mid-1990s, HDTV technology could also find applications in areas such as medical imaging and computer graphics. Since the sets require a huge number of semiconductors, they are expected to be a major new market for chipmakers.

Fuzzy Logic. Another emerging semiconductor technology expected to create important future markets was called "fuzzy logic." As *Standard & Poor's Industry Surveys* noted, "Currently led by Japanese manufacturers, fuzzy logic allows microcontrollers to create gray areas between the yes/no, on/off choices of the binary world. The result is that engineers can design microprocessors that allow machinery to operate with gradual refinements."

With the unprecedented growth in the mid- to late 1990s, some believe the industry faces a slowdown due to the eventual breakdown of Moore's Law, according to *The Wall Street Journal*. Moore's Law named after Intel's co-founder Gordon Moore, referred to the accumulation of transistors on microchip, doubling the computing capabilities on a single chip the same size every 18 months. Moore's Law was seen to reach its limits due to barriers imposed by quantum physics. According to *The Wall Street Journal,* the end of continued progress within the semiconductor industry was slated for the year 2010 by the U.S. Semiconductor Industry Association. This prompted American companies to initiate new research projects.

FURTHER READING

Business Rankings Annual. Detroit: Gale Research, 1996.

Dylinksky, Gene. "Halcyon Days for Chipmakers, But How Long Will They Last?" *Fortune,* 16 October 1995.

Cohen, Warren. "Why the Chip Is Still the Economy's Champ." *U.S. News and World Report,* 25 March 1996.

Hamilton, David P., and Takahashi, Dean. "Scientists Are Battling to Surmount Barriers in Microchip Advances." *The Wall Street Journal,* 10 December 1996.

Hof, Robert D. and Port, Otis. "Silicon Goes from Peak to Peak." *Business Week,* 8 January 1996.

Moris, Francisco A. "Semiconductors: The Building Blocks of the Information Revolution." *U.S. Department of Labor,* 1996.

"Rambo Rambus." *The Economist,* 8 February 1997.

Ristelhueber, Robert. "Semiconductor Makers See Brighter '97." *Electronic Business Today,* January 1997.

Robinson, Edward A. "America's Most Admired Companies." *Fortune,* 3 March 1997.

Rosch, Winn L. "The Evolution of the PC Microprocessor." *PC Magazine,* 31 January 1989.

"Semiconductor Industry Report." *The American Stock Report,* February 1996.

"Semiconductor Industry Report." *The American Stock Report,* October 1995.

Sexton, Jean Deitz. *Silicon Valley: Inventing the Future.* Chatsworth, CA: Windsor Publications, Inc., 1992.

"Squeeze, Gently: Intel and Microchips." *The Economist,* 30 November 1996.

Standard & Poor's Industry Surveys. New York: Standard & Poor's Corporation, 1993.

U.S. Industrial Outlook 1994. Washington, DC: U.S. Department of Commerce, 1993.

Weber, Samuel. "For Chip Maker, 'Another Year of Blah Growth'." *Electronics,* January 1992.

"Where Companies Rank in Their Own Industries." *Fortune,* 3 March 1997.

—John K. Waters, updated by Visi Tilak

SIC 3675

ELECTRONIC CAPACITORS

This category covers establishments primarily engaged in manufacturing electronic capacitors. Establishments primarily engaged in manufacturing electrical capacitors are classified in **SIC 3629: Electrical Industrial Apparatus, Not Elsewhere Classified.**

INDUSTRY SNAPSHOT

The value of shipments in the electronic capacitors industry in 1995 was an estimated $1.8 billion, up from $1.2 billion in 1982. There were about 386 establishments in the industry in 1996, three-fourths of which had 20 or more employees. Average firm size as measured by the number of production workers per establishment was over three times as large as that for the manufacturing sector as a whole.

Employment of production workers in the industry declined from 21,600 in 1982 to 13,500 in 1991, but had increased to 21,200 by 1995. The industry was relatively labor intensive, having 44 percent as much investment per production worker as that for the manufacturing sector as a whole. Annual hours worked by production workers in the industry were slightly lower on average than those worked in the manufacturing sector at large, and hourly wages were 23 percent lower.

ORGANIZATION AND STRUCTURE

The *U.S. Industrial Outlook 1994* described organizational changes in the industry: "The U.S. capacitor market is dominated by foreign-owned subsidiaries, reflecting major consolidation and numerous buyouts over the past 5 years. There are fewer, but bigger, companies." Of the top five firms in the industry, two of them, the AVX Corp. and the Murata Erie North America Inc. State College Division, were owned by Japanese firms.

The states ranking in the top nine by employment in the electronic capacitor industry were, in order of descent, South Carolina, New York, Maine, Massachusetts, Connecticut, Pennsylvania, and California. Together these nine states accounted for 79 percent of total employment, over 75 percent of total shipments, and about 73 percent of all establishments for the industry in the United States. The top two firms by sales in the industry, the AVX Corp. and the Kemet Electronics Corp., were both based in South Carolina.

The top four types of capacitors by product share in 1992 were those made from ceramic, at 48 percent; tantalum, at 26 percent; paper and film, at 16 percent; and aluminum, at 9 percent. The share of ceramic capacitors increased from 39 percent in 1983 whereas the share of paper and film and aluminum capacitors declined from 19 and 13 percent, respectively. The share of tantalum capacitors held steadily during the 1990s.

Among the largest of the several trade organizations serving the industry are the Electronic Industries Association of Washington, D.C., and the American Electronics Association of Santa Clara, California. The Electronic Industries Association was founded in 1924 and has 1,200 members, a staff of 150, and an annual budget of $26 million. The association produces a number of publications, catalogued in its semiannual *EAI Publications Index.* The American Electronics Association was founded in 1943 and has 3,500 members and a staff of 140. In addition to organizing an annual convention, the Association publishes the monthly *American Electronics Association Update,* with a circulation of 35,000, as well as a number of handbooks, among them *Government Affairs Bulletin, Benchmark Wage and Salary Survey,* and *Operating Ratios Survey.*

BACKGROUND AND DEVELOPMENT

In his *Basic Electricity and Electronics,* Delton T. Horn defined capacitors and capacitance: "A capacitor is a device capable of storing charge in a circuit, and typically consists of two metal plates separated by an insulator, called a *dielectric.* Capacitance is directly proportional to the area of the plates and the dielectric constant of the insulator and is inversely proportional to the distance between the plates." Capacitors can store charges from voltage sources for a wide range of time, to be released as needed. The classification of capacitor types by material such as paper, ceramic, or tantalum refer to the insulating dielectric. Electronic capacitors are part of a class of electronic components called passive components. They differ from active components, such as vacuum tubes and transistors, in that they can neither distinguish voltage polarity nor amplify a signal.

The first capacitor was the Leyden Jar, invented independently in the mid-1740s by Germans Dean von Kleist and Peter von Muschenbrock. A glass jar acted as the insulating material. The mica capacitor was developed in Germany in 1874 by M. Bauer. Mica had advantages over glass in that it better withstood shocks and that the same capacitance could be produced with a smaller capacitor. The paper capacitor was patented by D. G. Fitzgerald in the United Kingdom in 1876. Ceramic capacitors were first produced in 1900 by L. Lombardi in Italy. Ceramic capacitors can withstand extreme temperatures and are highly stable. The tubular glass capacitor was produced in 1904 by I. Moscicki in the United Kingdom. It was this capacitor that Marconi used in his early experiments with radio communication.

World War I provided an important catalyst for technical change in electronic communications, during which new radio tubes and circuits were developed. The interwar years saw the rapid growth of radio, and millions of radios were in use worldwide on the eve of World War II. Paper dielectric capacitors enclosed in cardboard tubes and bakelite-enclosed stacked mica capacitors were the types in most common use in the interwar period.

During the World War II years, substantial developments were made in communications electronics, radio astronomy, xerography, and radar and computer technology as well as in miniaturization and improving the energy efficiency of components. The harsh conditions and importance of reliability imposed by the war led to the development of metal-cased and metalized paper dielectric capacitors as well improvements in ceramic capacitors. The tantalum capacitor was produced in 1956 by D. McLean and F. Power of the

United States, after which it became among the most widely used capacitor types.

Among the most significant developments in electronic components in the postwar period were the transistor and integrated circuit. Transistors are based on solid-state technology, serving as substitutes for the older triode vacuum tube active components, developed by de Forest in 1906. The transistor (whose name derives from transferred resistor) was developed by the Bell Laboratories in 1948 and enabled electronic equipment to be produced in increasingly smaller sizes. The first integrated circuit was produced by Texas Instruments in 1959. This device made use of transistors and other components mounted on a semiconductor chip to form an entire electronic circuit. Prior to the development of integrated circuits, electronic circuits were made exclusively of discreet and separable components—combinations of vacuum tubes or transistors and passive components. Since capacitors with high capacitance values were relatively large, they were generally not produced within an integrated circuit but rather added externally.

Chip capacitors are surface-mounted to circuit boards, in contrast to traditional capacitors with wire leads. Although chip capacitors are generally higher-priced than those with leads, the price gap decreased in recent years. Chip capacitors came into increasing use during the 1990s, especially in equipment such as portable phones, video cameras, and electronic notebooks, items for which space constraints were a prime consideration. The *U.S. Industrial Outlook 1994* described these developments: "Trends in the capacitor industry are toward surface mounting and the miniaturization of multilayer capacitor chips. Capacitors were one of the first components to become available as surface-mount or chip components and have led the miniaturization drive in passive components. . . . Ceramic and tantalum chip capacitors are two of the largest passive component products in the North American market. . . . More than 80 percent of tantalum electrolytic capacitors produced are surface-mount devices, which is above average for the capacitor industry." The sales of multilayer ceramic chip capacitors increased by 20 percent in real terms in 1991.

CURRENT CONDITIONS

The value of shipments in the electronic capacitor industry declined from $1.7 billion in 1988 to $1.5 billion in 1990. This pattern reversed itself in the 1990s, with $1.6 billion in shipments in 1992 and nearly $1.8 billion in 1995. Annual capital investments

were $95 million in 1988, $52 million in 1990, and $57 million in 1995.

Employment of production workers declined from 18,100 in 1988 to 14,200 in 1991. The peak year for employment of production workers was 1984, with 25,100 employed. The Bureau of Labor Statistics made employment forecasts at the SIC 367 level for 20 occupational categories. Based on projected changes from 1990 to 2005, employment was expected to decline by double-digit figures in five occupations, which accounted for 27 percent of total employment in 1990. Nine occupations were projected to show double-digit increases by 2005, occupations accounting for 23 percent of total employment in 1990. The occupations with projected declines were those directly associated with production processes, while those with projected increases included managerial, technical, and sales personnel. Projections made for the electronic capacitors industry alone would have varied from these figures, but past employment trends in the industry suggested consistency with projections made at the SIC 367 level.

The *U.S. Industrial Outlook 1994* summarized recent developments in the electronic capacitor industry: "Due to the prospect of continuing moderate sales, defense-spending cutbacks, economic slowdown in several key markets, and vendor reduction, capacitor makers are striving to differentiate themselves within a small but highly competitive group of manufacturers. This requires increased service and a continual search for the right product mix. Vendors report growing demand from telecommunications and surface-mount product lines. The successful companies in 1993 have reduced cycle times, and have employed just-in-time (JIT), dock-to-stock delivery, with supplier-managed inventories."

INDUSTRY LEADERS

The top five firms in the electronic capacitor industry in 1995 were the AVX Corp. of Myrtle Beach, South Carolina; the Kemet Electronics Corp. of Greenville, South Carolina; the Sprague Electric Co. of Stamford, Connecticut; the General Electric Co. Capacitor and Power Protection Operation of Fort Edward, New York; and the Aerovox, Inc. of N. Dartmouth, Massachusetts.

AVX Corp. was founded in 1972 and had $1.2 billion in sales and 12,000 employees in 1996. The firm produces ceramic and tantalum capacitors. The firm became a subsidiary of Kyocera America Inc. of San Diego as a result of a 1990 merger, with ultimate ownership held by the Kyocera Corp. of Japan (previously the Kyoto Ceramic Co.). Their customers include leading original equipment manufacturers (OEMs) in the telecommunications, computer, medical device, aerospace, and consumer electronics industries.

The Kemet Electronics Corp., a privately held firm, was founded in 1954 and had $555.3 million in sales and 8,400 employees in 1996. Kemet was a key supplier to the Zeus/Semicap Division formed by Zeus Components Inc. in 1992, thus enabling Zeus Components to provide its OEMs with a full line of Kemet's tantalum and ceramic capacitors.

The Sprague Electric Co. had $140 million in sales and 1,400 employees in 1996. The firm produced electronic resistors (classified in **SIC 3676: Electronic Resistors**) as well as electronic capacitors. Sprague is a subsidiary of the publicly held STI Group Inc. of Stamford, Connecticut. Sprague's tantalum capacitor division was bought out by publicly held Vishnay Intertechnology Inc. of Malvern, Pennsylvania, in 1992. Sprague represented part of Vishnay's strategy of acquiring electronic components producers around the world and selling components under their original brand names.

The General Electric Co. Capacitor and Power Protection Operation was founded in 1903 and had $225 million in sales and 2,000 employees in 1996. The firm is a division of the publicly held General Electric Co. of Fairfield, Connecticut.

Aerovox, Inc. manufactures AeroMet and AeroMax brand film, paper, and aluminum electrolytic capacitors for worldwide markets. The company's products are used in air conditioners, fluorescent and high-intensity discharge (HID) lighting, microwave ovens, defribrillators, lasers, phone switching systems, heat pumps, ventilator fans, garbage disposals, washing machines, dimmer controls, motors, power supplies, photocopiers, telecommunications equipment, computers, medical instrumentation, industrial electrical systems, and other appliances and electrical equipment. Aerovox sells primarily to original equipment manufacturers, or OEMs, of electrical and electronic products. They employed 1,400 people and posted sales of $128 million in 1996.

AMERICA AND THE WORLD

In the early 1990s, the United States experienced a trade surplus in capacitors. Mexico is the largest export market for U.S. capacitors, accounting for 33 percent of total 1992 exports. The United States had a trade surplus of about $40 million with Mexico in 1992. Exports to Mexico were 21 percent higher in the first

two quarters of 1993 compared to the same 1992 period.

Singapore is the second-largest export market for U.S. capacitors. A dramatic 66 percent increase was recorded for exports to Singapore in the first two quarters of 1993 over the same period in 1992. Exports to Hong Kong, the third largest capacitor export market, dropped 12 percent during the first two quarters of 1993.

Germany and the United Kingdom are the next largest export markets. All component markets, including capacitors, in Germany seem to be tapering off, while the U.K. market experienced some recovery.

Imports continued to challenge U.S. manufacturers. Import penetration was particularly strong from Japan. Japanese capacitors made up 41 percent of total U.S. imports in 1992, and continued to increase throughout 1993. Levels of production and sales of paper capacitors are higher in Asian markets because of the production of consumer electronic products there.

U.S. imports also are high from Mexico. Most Mexican capacitor shipments come from plants run in east Asian export-processing zones. Mexican capacitor exports to the United States decreased 6 percent in the first half of 1993, compared with the same period the year before. Imports from Mexico accounted for 29 percent of total capacitor imports in the United States in 1992.

Imports from Taiwan, Germany, and the United Kingdom have also had extreme growth rates. Imports from Taiwan increased 64 percent in the first half of 1993 over that of 1992. Imports from Germany rose 31 percent in the same period, with those from the United Kingdom being up 29 percent.

Japan, South Korea, and Taiwan are the primary Asian markets to monitor capacitor developments. The economic recession hit Japan's capacitor industry hard in 1992. Small and medium-sized companies took the greatest losses. Japanese markets experienced production declines of up to 20 percent in paper-film capacitors in 1992. Since the chip or surface-mounted models are used in newer, higher-growth product lines, they have weathered the challenge better than the older models with wire leads. Japan is expected to continue to dominate the world chip capacitor market, even though U.S. and other Asian producers are beginning to ramp up production.

According to Electronic Components, Taiwanese capacitor makers have resorted to cut-throat tactics, reducing prices by as much as 50 percent since 1992 because of strong competition from Japan. Taiwan's competitive advantage is in the niche product areas, where its chip makers are able to fill small orders of larger varieties with shorter lead times. Taiwan also has advantages in labor costs over Japanese, European, and U.S. producers. However, competition in 1993 was stronger than previously from the French-based firm, SGS Thomson, and from Philips in the Netherlands.

Surface-mount devices are the major trend in Taiwan; this is complemented by the emphasis on automation in production. Taiwanese vendors are employing cost-savings measures similar to those employed in Japan, as they emphasize in-house materials development. Ceramic chip capacitors dominate the market, while plastic-film and tantalum also have a strong presence.

Only three South Korean companies now produce and export chip capacitors. However, these companies emphasize capital investment in automated facilities and predict that capacity tripled by the end of 1993. South Korean capacitor makers are experiencing strong demand from other electronic product segments in southeast Asia, such as monitors, camcorders, and personal computers.

RESEARCH AND TECHNOLOGY

Among the key technical developments in the electronic capacitor industry in the 1990s was the use of new insulating, or dielectric, materials. Voltronic received a patent in 1993 for a capacitor with a Teflon dielectric. This device achieved capacitance to size ratios 4 to 10 times greater than previously existing capacitors. Electrocube announced in 1993 the development of a capacitor with a polyester and metal-foil dielectric that was available in smaller sizes than other capacitor types. Both Voltronic's and Electrocube's capacitors are representative of the strong trend toward miniaturization of electronic components. The Toshiba Marcon Electronics America Corp. developed a capacitor with an organic dielectric that it hoped would be a viable alternative to tantalum capacitors.

FURTHER READING

Burrill, G. Steven, and Stephen E. Almassy. *Electronics 90: The New Competitive Priorities.* San Francisco:Ernst & Young, 1990.

Darnay, Arsen J., ed. *Manufacturing USA.* Detroit: Gale Research, 1996.

Dummer, G. W. A. *Electronic Inventions and Discoveries: Electronics from its Earliest Beginnings to the Present Day.* Headington Hill Hall, England: Pergamon Press Ltd., 1983.

Dunn, Darrell. "Murata Erie Adds Another National to Its Roster." *Electronic Buyers' News,* 9 March 1992.

EIA Marketing Services Department. *1993 Edition Electronic Market Data Book.* Washington: Electronic Industries Association, 1993.

Encyclopedia of Associations. Detroit: Gale Research, 1994.

Horn, Delton T. *Basic Electricity and Electronics.* Westerville, OH: Glencoe Division, 1993.

Jorgensen, Barbara. "Vishnay Opens Direct Sales Office." *Electronic Buyers' News,* 18 October 1993.

Kozicki, Michael N. *Modern Electronics Guidebook: An Overview.* New York: Van Nostrand Reinhold, 1991.

Levine, Sy. *Basic Concepts and Passive Components.* Plainview, NY: Electro-Horizons Publications, 1986.

McKeefry, Hailey. "Toshiba Gives Traditional Capacitor Technology an Organic Twist." *Electronic Buyers' News,* 27 September 1993.

Moody's Industrial Manual. New York: Moody's Investors Service Inc., 1993.

Moody's International Manual. New York: Moody's Investors Service Inc., 1992.

"Polyester Capacitors Conserve Real Estate." *Electronic Engineering Times,* 5 July 1993.

"Progress Continues in Capacitor Technology." *American Ceramic Society Bulletin,* March 1993.

U.S. Bureau of the Census. *Annual Survey of Manufactures.* Washington: GPO, 1991.

———. *Annual Survey of Manufactures.* Washington: GPO, 1996.

U.S. Department of Commerce. *U.S. Industrial Outlook 1994.* Washington: GPO, 1994.

"Vishnay Gets Bigger, Concentrates on Big Customers." *Electronic Business Buyer,* September 1993.

"Voltronics Wins Trimmer Patent." *Microwave and RF,* November 1993.

Votapka, Timothy. "Zeus Eyes More Passives." *Electronic Buyers' News,* 6 April 1992.

———. "AVX to Build R&D Center." *Electronic Buyers News,* 12 April 1993.

—David Kucera, updated by Susan Wood King

SIC 3676

ELECTRONIC RESISTORS

This category covers establishments primarily engaged in manufacturing electronic resistors. Establishments primarily engaged in manufacturing resistors for telephone and telegraph apparatus are classified in **SIC 3661: Telephone and Telegraph Apparatus.**

INDUSTRY SNAPSHOT

The value of shipments in the electronic resistors industry in 1995 was an approximately $1 billion, up substantially from $869 million in 1994. There are just over 100 establishments in the industry, 85 percent of which have 20 or more employees. The number of establishments and the percentage of these with more than 20 employees was stable throughout the 1980s. Average firm size as measured by the number of production workers per establishment is over three times as large as for the manufacturing sector as a whole.

Employment of production workers in the industry declined from 12,400 in 1982 to 6,900 in 1995. The industry is relatively labor intensive, having 60 percent as much investment per production worker as that for the manufacturing sector as a whole. Annual hours worked by production workers in the industry are 10 percent lower on average than those worked in the manufacturing sector at large, and hourly wages are 31 percent lower.

ORGANIZATION AND STRUCTURE

Of the top ten firms by sales in the electronic resistors industry in 1996, two were private independents, one was public, and the remaining seven were either subsidiaries or divisions of larger firms. Though average investment per production worker is relatively low for the industry, capital requirements are relatively high, with average investment per establishment 88 percent greater than that for the manufacturing sector as a whole.

The states ranking in the top ten by employment in the electronic resistors industry are California (with 2,500 employees), Indiana (with 1,900), Texas, North Carolina, and Nebraska (with 1,700 employees each), New Hampshire (with 1,000), Illinois, Massachusetts, and New York (with 700 employees each), and Florida (with 600). Together these ten states account for 84 percent of total employment and about 73 percent of all establishments for the industry in the United States. The average number of employees per establishment varies widely across these states. The average establishment in Nebraska and North Carolina, with the highest number of employees per establishment, has between 6 and 14 times as many employees per establishment as does the average establishment in New Jersey and Connecticut.

The top ten industries and sectors buying the outputs of the electronic components and accessories industries are: radio and TV communication equipment, which purchases a 13.5 percent share of the industry; exports, with a 9.8 percent share; telephone

and telegraph apparatus, with a 9.6 percent share; electronic computing equipment, with a 9.4 percent share; electronic components, not elsewhere classified, with a 9.1 percent share; radio and TV receiving sets, with a 5.8 percent share; guided missiles and space vehicles, with a 3.2 percent share; personal consumption expenditures, with a 2.9 percent share; X-ray apparatus and tubes, with a 2.6 percent share; and aircraft, with a 2.2 percent share.

There are three basic classes of resistors: fixed resistors, variable resistors, and resistor networks. The most important of these classes by product share in 1991 were fixed resistors, with a 34 percent share, followed by variable resistors, with a 27 percent share, and resistor networks, with a 21 percent share. Fixed resistors grew by product share from 1990 to 1991 at the expense of variable resistors, while the share of resistor networks remained stable.

Within the class of fixed resistors, the four types by product share were metal and other film, at 39 percent; wirewound, at 33 percent; chip, at 16 percent; and carbon composition and carbon film, at 12 percent. Metal and other film and chip fixed resistors grew by product share from 1990 to 1991 at the expense of wirewound and carbon composition and carbon film fixed resistors. Within the class of variable resistors, the share of non-wirewound and wirewound devices remained stable at 71 and 29 percent, respectively. Within the class of resistor networks, the top three types by product share were SIP (single in-line package), at 41 percent; surface mount, at 29 percent; and DIP (dual in-line package), at 16 percent. The product share of surface mount resistor networks grew by fully 38 percent from 1990 to 1991, a dramatic increase in product share at the expense of other resistor network types. The product share of surface mount resistor networks in relation to all electronic resistors increased by 33 percent from 1990 to 1991.

Among the largest of the several trade organizations serving the industry is the Electronic Industries Association of Washington, D.C., founded in 1924; it has 1,200 members, a staff of 150, and an annual budget of $26 million. Another large trade organization serving the industry is the American Electronics Association of Santa Clara, California, founded in 1943; it has 3,500 members and a staff of 140.

BACKGROUND AND DEVELOPMENT

In his *Basic Electricity and Electronics,* Delton T. Horn defined resistors and resistance: "A resistor is a device which opposes current in a dc (direct current) circuit; a measure of this opposition is called *resistance,* measured in ohms. . . . Ohms's Law, the relationship between voltage, current, and resistance, states that current is directly proportional to voltage and inversely proportional to resistance in a circuit." Resistance is one of the three variables of Ohm's Law, and is thus a necessary pre-condition for any functioning circuit. Resistors are either fixed, with a designated ohm value, or variable, with a designated range of ohm values. Variable resistors are either potentiometers, which control voltage, or rheostats, which directly control resistance. Electronic transistors are part of a class of electronic components called passive components. They differ from active components, such as vacuum tubes and transistors, in that they can neither distinguish voltage polarity nor amplify a signal.

The first electronic resistor was patented in the United Kingdom by C.S. Bradley in 1885. This was a molded carbon composition resistor made of a carbon-rubber mixture. The earliest carbon film resistor was produced in the United Kingdom by T.E. Gambrell and A.F. Harris in 1897. As with the carbon composition resistor, this device preceded the development of broadcasting by a number of years. The first thin metal film resistor was developed in the United Kingdom by W.F. Swann in 1913. The first high-resistance metal film resistor was produced in Germany by F. Kruger in 1919.

The first cracked carbon resistor was produced by Germans Siemens and Halske in 1925. Siemens produced so many of these resistors that they became commonly referred to as "Siemens resistors." The first sprayed metal film resistor was developed in Germany by S. Loewe in 1926. This was produced by spraying an atomized solution of platinum impregnated with resin, after which the sprayed form was heated. In his *Electronic Inventions and Discoveries,* G.W.A. Dummer described developments in the industry around this time: "It might be considered that this period (the early 1920s) saw the birth of the components industry. Resistors were produced in large quantities and used as grid leaks, anode loads, etc., and consisted of carbon compositions of many kinds compressed into tubular containers and fitted with end caps. . . . Cracked-carbon film-type resistors were introduced from Germany . . . and by 1934 were being manufactured in quantity in the United Kingdom." An ever-growing market for resistors and other electronic components in the period between the World Wars was provided by the rapidly expanding use of radio and other forms of electronic communication.

During the early 1950s, electronic engineers realized that the working portion of a resistor was only a small fraction of the total volume. For plastic-molded carbon film resistors, for example, only 3.6 percent of the total volume was actually used. This realization led to the development of early thick film and thin film circuits. One of the most important of these was the nickel-chromium (or nichrome) thin film resistor, produced in the United Kingdom by R.H. Alderton and F. Ashworth in 1957. This became the most widely used type of thin film resistor in recent years. It was also in the 1950s that automation techniques were developed for attaching traditional electronic components with wire leads to circuit boards. These processes could produce up to 10,000 finished circuit boards per day. A key development in the production of thick film resistors was the use of lasers for trimming in the late 1960s.

The first integrated circuit was produced by Texas Instruments in 1959. This device made use of components mounted on a semiconductor chip to form an entire electronic circuit. Prior to the development of integrated circuits, electronic circuits were made exclusively of discreet and separable components—combinations of vacuum or transistors and passive components. In *Electronic Inventions and Discoveries,* Dummer wrote, "The present explosion of integrated circuits in the form of VLSI (very large-scale integration) and VHSIC (very high-speed integrated circuit) has been the most important development in the history of electronics."

The mass production and widespread commercial viability of integrated circuits was made possible by the planar process of production, developed in the United States in 1959 by Jean Hoerni, a Swiss physicist, and Robert Noyce, an American physicist. Chip resistors are surface-mounted to circuit boards, in contrast to traditional resistors with wire leads running through circuit boards. Surface mount resistor types became of ever-increasing importance in the 1990s.

CURRENT CONDITIONS

Though technical change remained dynamic in the electronic resistors industry, growth prospects did not appear promising until 1994. The value of shipments in the electronic capacitor industry increased from $716 million in 1993 to $869 million in 1994 and to $1.05 billion in 1995. Employment of production workers declined from 11,700 in 1989 to 9,700 in 1995. The peak year for employment of production workers was 1984, with 13,000 employed.

The *U.S. Industrial Outlook 1994* noted, "Overall, the U.S. resistor industry is mature, and profit margins are slim." The 1990s saw substantial consolidation of electronic components distributors **SIC 5065: Electronic Parts and Equipment, Not Elsewhere Classified.** The December 12, 1991, issue of

Electronic News noted the possible effects of this consolidation on suppliers of electronic components: "So much consolidation could expectedly be accompanied by a feverish degree of franchise shuffling as suppliers attempted to shore up their distributor networks against a persistent recessionary climate."

INDUSTRY LEADERS

The top five firms by sales in the electronic resistors industry in 1996 were Bourns Inc. of Riverside, California; Dale Electronic Inc. of Columbus, Nebraska; Murata Erie North America Inc. of Smyrna, Georgia; CTS Resistor Network of Berne, Indiana; and IRC Inc. of Boone, North Carolina. Bourns Inc. is a privately held firm founded in 1946 with $250 million in sales and 4,500 employees in 1996. The firm's products are distributed across North America and in 12 European countries by the ITT Corporation's Electronic Components Distribution unit. Bourns underwent a streamlining operation in 1991, which resulted in the elimination of a number of managerial positions. The firm entered into a cooperative agreement with number four producer IRC Inc. in early 1992. By mid-1992, between 50,000 and 100,000 thin-film precision resistor networks were being produced each month under the agreement. Bourns announced in 1992 that it was diversifying into the production of miniature electronic switches **SIC 3679: Electronic Components, Not Elsewhere Classified.**

Dale Electronics Inc. was founded in 1951 and had $110 million in sales and 2,100 employees in 1996. In addition to electronic resistors, the firm also produces electronic capacitors **SIC 3675: Electronic Capacitors** and non-electronic power transformers **SIC 3612: Power, Distribution, and Specialty Transformers.** Dale Electronics is a subsidiary of Dale Holdings Inc., itself a subsidiary of Vishay Intertechnology Inc. of Malvern, Pennsylvania. Vishay Intertechnology is a manufacturer of resistor-based stress measurement sensors **SIC 3829: Measuring and Controlling Devices, Not Elsewhere Classified,** inductors **SIC 3677: Electronic Coils, Transformers, and Other Inductors,** and specialized connectors **SIC 3678: Electronic Connectors.** Dale Electronics represented part of Vishay's strategy of acquiring electronic components producers around the world and selling components under their original brand names.

Murata Erie North America Inc. was founded in 1981 and had $100 million in sales and 1,200 employees in 1996. The firm is a subsidiary of the Murata Manufacturing Co. Ltd. of Japan, and in addition to producing electronic resistors produces electronic ca-

pacitors. CTS Resistor Network held the number five position in 1996 with 500 employees and $30 million in sales. The firm is a subsidiary of the publicly held Emerson Electric Co. of St. Louis, which produces electric motors **SIC 3621: Motors and Generators** and electric relays **SIC 3625: Relays and Industrial Controls.** Beckman sold its $30 million per year Instrumentation Products Division to Wavetek in 1992. IRC Inc. (also International Resistive Co. Inc.) was founded in 1973 and had $50 million in sales and 1,000 employees in 1992. In 1990 the firm became a subsidiary of Crystalate Electronics Inc., a subsidiary of the TT Group PLC.

AMERICA AND THE WORLD

The United States had a trade deficit in electronic resistors of $170 million in 1992. Exports of electronic resistors produced in the United States increased by an estimated 5 percent in 1993, to $254 million. Chip resistors were expected to experience the most rapid export growth in coming years. The three largest export markets for resistors produced in the United States are, in order of descent, Mexico, Canada, and Japan. Mexico and Canada by themselves account for 34 percent of all U.S. resistor exports in 1992. Among the most rapidly growing export markets for U.S. resistors are Malaysia, Singapore, and Mexico, with growth rates in the first half of 1993 at 65, 57, and 24 percent, respectively.

Imports of electronic resistors into the United States increased by 15 percent in 1992, to $411 million. Imports from Japan accounted for 37 percent of this total. In the first half of 1993, imports of electronic resistors into the United States increased by 40 percent for Japan and 19 percent for Mexico.

In early 1997, the Components Group of the Electronic Industries Association (EIA) described to officials of the United States Trade Representative, the catastrophic effects upon the U.S. capacitor and resistor industry, if the Information Technology Agreement (ITA) was implemented and no follow-up action taken to remove non-tariff trade barriers in existence in markets outside of North America.

The Information Technology Agreement would eliminate all tariffs on information technology products by the year 2000. Negotiations on the ITA among the quad countries of the United States, Japan, Canada, and the European Union were completed at the inaugural ministerial meeting of the World Trade Organization (WTO) held in December 1996. Products to be covered by this agreement include semiconductors, computer hardware, and telecommunications equipment. Also included in the coverage are electronic components such as resistors and capacitors.

RESEARCH AND TECHNOLOGY

The Electronic Industries Association's *1993 Edition Electronic Market Data Book* described technical developments in the electronic resistors industry: "The move to surface mount resistor chips is the dominant technology trend in the resistor industry. A strong link is developing between the expansion of the automotive industry's use of printed circuit boards (PCBs) and the increased use of surface mounted resistor chips. Product developments trends in resistors are primarily toward thin- and thick-film resistor networks." Resistor networks combine a set of electronic components, such as integrated circuits and resistors, to carry out coordinated functions. These networks have come to replace individual resistors, a trend that was expected to continue.

As of 1992, approximately 10 percent of trimming potentiometers, variable resistors used in high-volume PCB applications, were surface mounted types. A marketing manager at Bourns Inc., the industry's largest producer, expected this share to reach 25 to 30 percent by the late 1990s. Trimming potentiometers were the most important class of potentiometers. In 1992, Ohmtek Inc., a division of Vishay Intertechnology Inc., announced the development of its Quick-Net program, which reduced lead times for the production and delivery of resistor network prototypes to two weeks. Previously, it typically took 10 to 12 weeks for a firm to complete this process.

FURTHER READING

Burrill, G. Steven, and Stephen E. Almassy. *Electronics 90: The New Competitive Priorities.* San Francisco: Ernst & Young, 1990.

"Coming: Speed, 'Catchy Name.'" *Electronic Buyers' News,* 20 July 1992.

"Consolidation Breeding Competition." *Electronic Buyers' News,* 25 October 1993.

Darnay, Arsen J., ed. *Manufacturing USA.* Detroit: Gale Research, 1993.

"Distribution Trends 1992: The Year in Review." *Electronic News,* 12 December 1991.

Dummer, G. W. A. *Electronic Inventions and Discoveries: Electronics from Its Earliest Beginnings to the Present Day.* Headington Hill Hall, England: Pergamon Press Ltd., 1983.

Dunn, Darrell. "Pact Payoff Expected." *Electronic Buyers' News,* 1 June 1992.

EIA Marketing Services Department. *1993 Edition Electronic Market Data Book.* Washington: Electronic Industries Association, 1993.

Encyclopedia of Associations. Detroit: Gale Research, 1994.

Horn, Delton T. *Basic Electricity and Electronics.* Westerville, OH: Glencoe Division, 1993.

Kozicki, Michael N. *Modern Electronics Guidebook: An Overview.* New York: Van Nostrand Reinhold, 1991.

Levine, Sy. *Basic Concepts and Passive Components.* Plainview, New York: Electro-Horizons Publications, 1986.

McKeefry, Haily. "Pots Are Surfacing Everywhere." *Electronic Buyers' News,* 15 June 1992.

Million Dollar Directory. Parsippany, NJ: Dun & Bradstreet, Inc., 1993.

Moody's Industrial Manual. New York: Moody's Investors Service Inc., 1993.

Norman, Diane. "Bourns in Strategy Switch." *Electronic Buyers' News,* 23 November 1992.

Thryft, Ann. "More Changes at Bourns: Streamlining Continues, New Markets Are Tried." *Electronic Buyers' News,* 27 April 1992.

U.S. Bureau of the Census. *Annual Survey of Manufactures.* Washington:GPO, 1991.

———. *Annual Survey of Manufactures.* Washington: GPO, 1996.

———. *Current Industrial Report.* Washington: GPO, 1996.

U.S. Department of Commerce. *U.S. Industrial Outlook 1994.* Washington: GPO, 1994.

"Vishnay Gets Bigger, Concentrates on Big Customers." *Electronic Business Buyer,* September 1993.

"Wavetek Acquires Division." *Microwaves and RF,* November 1992.

—David Kucera, updated by Susan Wood King

SIC 3677

ELECTRONIC COILS, TRANSFORMERS, AND OTHER INDUCTORS

This industry classification includes establishments primarily engaged in manufacturing electronic coils, transformers, and inductors. Establishments primarily engaged in manufacturing electrical transformers are classified in **SIC 3612: Power, Distribution, and Specialty Transformers;** those manufacturing transformers and inductors for telephone and telegraph apparatus are classified in **SIC 3661: Telephone and Telegraph Apparatus;** and those manufacturing semiconductors and related devices are classified in **SIC 3674: Semiconductors and Related Devices.**

INDUSTRY SNAPSHOT

The value of shipments in the electronic coils and transformers industry was an estimated $1.56 billion in 1995, up from $1.38 billion in 1994 and continuing to reverse a decline in the late 1980s. There were just under 400 establishments in the industry, 61 percent of which had 20 or more employees. Average firm size as measured by the number of production workers per establishment was 15 percent larger than for the manufacturing sector as a whole.

Employment of production workers in the industry was 17,000 in 1995, continuing a declining trend from a peak of 21,200 in 1983. Employment of production workers was lower in 1994 than in all years of the prior decade. The industry was highly labor-intensive, having only 20 percent as much investment per production worker as that for the manufacturing sector as a whole. Annual hours worked by production workers in the industry were 7 percent lower on average than those worked in the manufacturing sector at large, and hourly wages were 34 percent lower.

ORGANIZATION AND STRUCTURE

Of the top ten firms by sales in the electronic coils and transformers industry in 1995, five were private independents, three were subsidiaries or divisions, and two were publicly held. Of the remaining 67 firms ranking by sales in the industry, 45 (67 percent) were private independents. Capital requirements were relatively low for the industry, with average investment per establishment 25 percent that for the manufacturing sector as a whole.

The states ranking in the top ten by employment in the industry were Illinois (with 3,200 employees), New York (with more than 2,500), California (with 2,500), Indiana (with 2,300), Massachusetts and Virginia (with 1,700 employees each), New Jersey (with 1,300), Minnesota (with 900), and Florida and Connecticut (with 800 employees each). Together these ten states accounted for more than 75 percent of total employment and more than 69 percent of all establishments for the industry in the United States. The average number of employees per establishment varied widely across these states. Virginia, with the highest number of employees per establishment, had an average of 9 times as many employees per establishment as Florida and 13 times as many as California. Of the top six firms by sales in the industry in 1992, five were from either Illinois or New York.

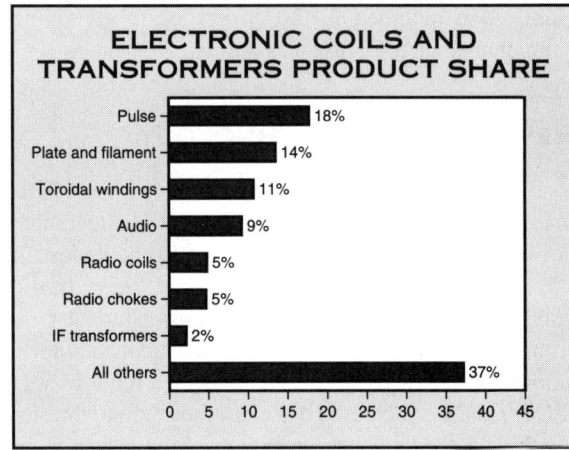

The top nine types of coils and transformers by product share were, in descending order, pulse transformers, computer and other (at 15.5 percent); plate and filament transformers (at 13.5 percent); toroidal windings(at 10.7 percent); audio transformers (at 9.2 percent); radio frequency coils (at 4.8 percent); radio frequency chokes (at 4.7 percent); low frequency chokes (at 3.9 percent);IF transformers (at 2.2 percent); and television transformers and reactors (at 2.2 percent). (The "other" category accounted for 33.2 percent of product share in 1991, up from 22.9 percent in 1982.)

Among the largest of the several trade organizations serving the industry were the Electronic Industries Association of Washington, D.C., and the American Electronics Association of Santa Clara, California. The Electronic Industries Association was founded in 1924. In 1997 it had 1,350 member organizations, a staff of 185, and an annual budget of $43 million. The Association produced a number of publications, catalogued in its semiannual *EAI Publications Index.* The American Electronics Association was founded in 1943 and had 3,500 members and a staff of 140. In addition to organizing an annual convention, the Association published the monthly *American Electronics Association-Update,* with a circulation of 35,000 well as a number of handbooks, among them *Government Affairs Bulletin, Benchmark Wage and Salary Survey,* and *Operating Ratios Survey.*

BACKGROUND AND DEVELOPMENT

"Inductor" is a generic term for an electronic coil, sometimes also referred to as an electronic choke. Inductors function to either filter or select certain frequencies within AC or pulsating DC circuits. In his *Basic Electricity and Electronics,* Delton T. Horn defines inductors and inductance as follows: "An inductor is a device capable of storing magnetic energy in a circuit. Typically it consists of a coil of wire around some type of core, which may be magnetic or nonmagnetic. Inductance is directly proportional to the square of the number of turns (of wire). An inductor opposes changes in current. It also opposes current, and this opposition increases as the frequency of the signal increases.'' Coil wire must be coated with an insulating material, usually varnish, lacquer, or enamel, to prevent turns of wire from coming into electrical contact. The greater the ferrous content of the core, the greater the coil's inductance. Coils with non-ferrous cores are referred to as ''air core'' inductors.

In his *Basic Concepts and Passive Components,* Sy Levine defines transformers as follows: ''A *transformer* is a component consisting of a group of separate and unconnected lengths of wire wound around a common core. Its purpose is to provide an efficient transfer of electrical power between circuits connected to its various sections while maintaining electrical isolation between them. This transfer of power is accomplished magnetically.'' Transformers serve a number of functions, and transformer types are defined by function. Among the most important of these types are power transformers, output transformers, radio frequency (RF) transformers, and pulse transformers. Power transformers convert distribution voltages (typically 110-220 volts AC) to other levels required by electrical and electronic devices. Output transformers function to transfer signals from an audio amplifier to a loudspeaker. RF transformers function to transfer signals between stages of radio frequency amplification circuits. Pulse transformers function to transfer signals between stages of digital electronic systems.

Electronic coils and transformers are part of a class of electronic components called passive components. They differ from active components, such as vacuum tubes and transistors, in that they can neither distinguish voltage polarity nor amplify a signal.

The pioneering figure in the industry was Michael Faraday, the English chemist and physicist (1791-1867). Faraday is credited with discovering the phenomenon of electromagnetic induction in 1831 and was the first to use a magnetic circuit to connect two electric circuits. In his experiments with induction, Faraday developed an early version of the transformer. The earliest patent for a power transformer was granted to C. Zipernowski, O. Blathy, and M. Deri of Budapest in 1885. Deri also received the first patent for a distribution transformer in 1885.

The *U.S. Industrial Outlook 1994* reported that, ''The chief end uses of coils and transformers are in stereos and other home entertainment equipment, computers, telecommunications equipment, and industrial and control instruments.'' As with other electronic components, the growth of the coil and transformer industry was tied up with the growth of radio broadcasting after World War I. Stringent demands were made on all electronic components during World War II. This led to a large number of technological improvements, among them standardization, energy efficiency, miniaturization, ease of maintenance, and reliability— especially in the face of mechanical shocks, vibration, temperature extremes, humidity, and high altitude. During these years, resin-encased transformers were developed, as were oil-filled transformers sealed in metal housings.

The most important recent trends in coil and transformer production were continued miniaturization and weight reduction as well as surface mounting. Surface mounted components (or SMD for surface mounted device) offered a number of advantages over traditional components with wire leads inserted through holes in printed circuit boards. Since SMDs could be placed on both sides of a circuit board, they optimized space and thus reduced cost. SMDs were lighter than components with wire leads and enabled automated assembly techniques. SMDs made possible shorter distances between components, which reduced circuit capacitance and resistance and minimized interference.

As a result of size constraints, coils with high levels of inductance were very difficult to produce in integrated circuits. Nonetheless, the pace of technical change in the industry was brisk, suggesting that such integration problems might be overcome. Integrated coils were generally produced by forming flat spirals of metal on the face of a circuit.

CURRENT CONDITIONS

The value of shipments in the electronic coils and transformers industry declined every year from 1988 to 1991. This pattern appears to have been broken in more recent years, however, with the estimated value of shipments growing to $1.47 billion in 1995. The *U.S. Industrial Outlook 1994* noted that export growth may play an important role for the industry. It reported as follows: ''Since the primary end market for coils and transformers are consumer electronic products, such as television sets, U.S. exports will grow in conjunction with increased production in the major consumer electronics (industries) in Mexico, Japan, Singapore, Hong Kong, and Taiwan. China is expected to be a strong long-term growth market for U.S. exports.'' Annual capital investments showed consecutive declines from 1989 to 1991. Annual capital investments exceeded $30 million in 1982 and 1983 but in no year thereafter up to 1991 (all values in current dollars).

Employment of production workers declined from 19,100 in 1988 to 16,600 in 1991, but grew to 21,300 by 1995. The U.S. Bureau of Labor Statistics made employment forecasts at the SIC 367 level for 20 occupational categories. Based on projected changes from 1990 to 2005, employment was expected to level off in five occupations. Nine occupations were projected to show double-digit increases to 2005— occupations accounting for 23 percent of total employment in 1990. The occupations with projected declines were those directly associated with production processes, while those with projected increases included managerial, technical, and sales personnel. Projections made for the electronic capacitors industry alone would have varied from these figures, but past employment trends in the industry suggested consistency with projections made at the SIC 367 level.

In their *1993 Edition Electronic Market Data Book,* the Electronic Industries Association published their forecast for sales of defense-related electronics for years 1993 to 2002. The Association summarized their forecast as follows: ''Despite the forecast of a flat budget for defense procurement, there will be increasing purchases of electronic equipment, with contractors the winners. Production will be limited to the most advanced weapon systems and high technology will be inserted into existing equipment through modifications and upgrades. In addition, a majority of the research and development investment will be in electronics. Suppliers of state-of-the-art electronic systems can therefore expect modest growth in their defense market.''

INDUSTRY LEADERS

The top five firms by sales in the electronic coils and transformers industry in 1995 were, in order of descent; Valor Electronics Inc. of San Diego, California; American Precision Industries Inc. of Buffalo, New York; Products Unlimited Corp. of Stirling, Illinois; Midcom Inc. of Watertown, South Dakota; and the Delevan Division of American Precision Industries Inc. of East Aurora, New York.

Valor Electronics Inc., a division of GTI Corp. of San Diego, had estimated 1995 sales of $123 million. The company employed 7,600 people.

American Precision Industries Inc. was founded in 1946 and had $83 million in sales and 1,000 employees in 1995. The publicly held firm's secondary activities included the manufacture of heat transfer

products, electromagnetic clutches, and brakes used in rotary control applications.

The Products Unlimited Corp. was a privately held firm founded in 1978, with $57 million in sales and 700 employees in 1992. The firm purchased a line of electrical contactors from Cooper Industries in 1992.

Midcom was a privately held firm operating in Watertown, South Dakota, since 1968. It had 1995 sales of $50 million and total employment of 2,210 in 1997. It built additional factories in Huron, South Dakota, in 1992; Aberdeen, South Dakota, in 1994; Waverly, Iowa, in 1995; and Nogales, Mexico, in 1996.

AMERICA AND THE WORLD

The United States had a trade surplus in electronic coils and transformers of $101 million in 1992, compared to a deficit of $3.11 billion for all passive components for that year. Exports of electronic resistors produced in the United States increased by 8 percent in 1992, to $501 million. Mexico was by far the largest export market for electronic coils and transformers produced in the United States, accounting for 67 percent of U.S. exports in 1992. The United States ran a $140 million surplus with Mexico in electronic coils and transformers in that year. Other important export markets included Canada, Singapore, Taiwan, Hong Kong, and Japan.

Imports of electronic coils and transformers into the United States increased by 23 percent in the first half of 1993. The three largest importers of electronic coils and transformers into the United States were, in order of descent: Mexico, Japan, and Taiwan. In the first half of 1993, imports from Japan increased by 39 percent, whereas imports from Taiwan decreased by 18 percent.

RESEARCH AND TECHNOLOGY

There was a considerable amount of new product development in the electronic coil and transformer industry in the 1990s. Beta Transformer Technology introduced a series of surface mount transformers that were only 0.13 inch thick. The J.R. Miller Division of Bell Industries began the production of four new series of surface-mount inductors. Schaffer EMC announced the development of a new series of toroidal inductors. Ohmite Manufacturing, primarily a producer of electronic resistors, began production of miniature high-current radio-frequency inductors. The Signal Transformer Co. announced its development of a high-power transformer that was the first in its class to meet international certification standards.

Significant developments were made in the production of thermoplastic encapsulated coils, which the May 1993 issue of *Appliance* describes as follows: "Recent developments include the first successful encapsulation of integrated circuit chips in an electrical device; further increases in the production of thermoplastic-encapsulated solenoids, sensors, transformers, motor components and other coil devices; new wire-friendly nylon resins that minimize magnet wire corrosion; and direct encapsulation of components with crimped connections as a low-cost alternative to the potting of complex circuits." Thermoplastic encapsulated coils were one of the more promising products the industry had to offer, and demand for these devices was rising.

The U.S. Department of Energy's Argonne National Laboratory and the Intermagnetics General Corp. announced the development in 1993 of a superconducting coil with a magnetic field 50 thousand times as strong as that produced by the Earth. The American Superconductor Co. received a $1.9 million, three-year contract from the Department of Commerce in 1992 to manufacture superconducting magnetic coils.

FURTHER READING

"AC Power Line EMI Suppression Chokes." *Electronic Buyers' News,* 29 March 1993.

"Appliance Coil Winding: Advances in Thermoplastic Encapsulation of Transformers and Small Wound Coils." *Appliance,* May 1993.

U.S. Bureau of the Census. *Annual Survey of Manufactures.* Washington: GPO, 1995.

Burrill, G. Steven, and Stephen E. Almassy. *Electronics 90: The New Competitive Priorities.* San Francisco: Ernst & Young, 1990.

Darnay, Arsen J., ed. *Manufacturing USA,* 5th ed. Detroit: Gale Research, 1993.

"Dry Transformers Aren't All Wet." *PIMA,* August 1992.

Dummer, G.W.A. *Electronic Inventions and Discoveries: Electronics from its Earliest Beginnings to the Present Day.* 3rd ed. Headington Hill Hall, England: Pergamon Press Ltd., 1983.

1993 Edition Electronic Market Data Book. Washington, DC: Electronic Industries Association, 1993.

Horn, Delton T. *Basic Electricity and Electronics.* Westerville, Ohio: Glencoe Division, 1993.

Kozicki, Michael N. *Modern Electronics Guidebook: An Overview.* New York: Van Nostrand Reinhold, 1991.

Levine, Sy. *Basic Concepts and Passive Components.* Plainview, New York: Electro-Horizons Publications, 1986.

Moody's Industrial Manual. New York: Moody's Investors Service Inc., 1993.

Norman, Diane. "Ohmite Adds Components." *Electronic Buyers' News,* 13 January 1992.

"Products Unlimited Buys Arrow Line." *Appliance Manufacturer,* March 1992.

"Public-Private Collaboration Produces Strongest Field by High-Tc Coil." *JOM,* October, 1993.

"Superconducting Coils to be Developed for Electric Motor." *Power Engineering,* July 1992.

"Surface-Mount Inductors Have Ratings to 2.6 A." *Electronic Buyers' News,* 27 September 1993.

U.S. Department of Commerce. International Trade Administration. *U.S. Industrial Outlook 1994.* Washington: GPO, 1994.

Votapka, Timothy. "Approval Pending: Signal's Transformers Await International OK." *Electronic Buyers' News,* 21 June 1993.

———. "Low-Profile Transformer." *Electronic Buyers' News,* 11 April 1993

— David Kucera, updated by Jim Casey

SIC 3678

ELECTRONIC CONNECTORS

This industry is comprised of manufacturers of electronic connectors, e.g. coaxial, cylindrical, rack and panel, and printed circuit connectors. Establishments primarily engaged in manufacturing electrical connectors are classified in **SIC 3643: Current-Carrying Wiring Devices;** those manufacturing electronic capacitors are classified in **SIC 3675: Electronic Capacitors;** and those manufacturing electronic coils, transformers, and other inductors are classified in **SIC 3677: Electronic Coils, Transformers, and Other Inductors.**

INDUSTRY SNAPSHOT

The health of the electronic connectors industry is tied to that of electronic equipment and other finished-product (e.g. automobile) manufacturers. A cutback in military spending and a depression in the prices of personal computers (PCs) has reduced the number of connector manufacturers through closures and mergers. The most successful companies, such as AMP Inc. and Molex, have traditionally invested heavily in research and development, effectively differentiating their products in a competitive environment.

ORGANIZATION AND STRUCTURE

Makers of electronic connectors and other passive electronic components must rely on manufacturers of finished products to maintain favorable prices and provide a market for their goods. As is the case in most components industries, military markets generally require the most advanced products, which are usually the most expensive. When an industry such as the PC industry slows or is forced to reduce its prices, as was the case worldwide in the late 1980s and early 1990s, connector manufacturers have difficulty maintaining profits.

Throughout the 1980s and 1990s, the connector industry was overcrowded, with approximately 800 manufacturers worldwide. Consolidations and mergers reduced the number of players in the United States considerably by the mid-1990s.

BACKGROUND AND DEVELOPMENT

The beginnings of the electronic connectors industry can be traced to products such as the solderless electrical connectors AMP Inc. manufactured for use in aircraft and boats in the 1940s, and the introduction of the printed wiring board in 1936 by Dr. Paul Eisner. The increased use of electronic components, particularly in military applications in the 1980s, was ironically foreshadowed by growth in demand for electrical components in military ships and aircraft during World War II. At the end of the War, contract terminations eliminated many shops. However, the postwar explosion of the semiconductor-related industries eventually made the connectors field more attractive, so that by the 1990s, the number of connector manufacturers had risen to approximately 800.

CURRENT CONDITIONS

In 1996 the industry was estimated to be worth $30 billion. The United States produced an estimated $4.6 billion worth of connectors in 1996, up from $4.0 billion in 1994. The market was expected to grow between 5 and 8 percent until the end of the century.

A promising long-term trend was the proliferation of electronics in such varied industries as automobiles and telecommunications. Automotive electronics, desktop units, network, and miscellaneous wiring were expected to spur demand for newer connector technologies. Surface-mount connectors were expected to show the strongest growth as the new technology gained acceptance.

INDUSTRY LEADERS

The worldwide connector industry has been dominated by AMP Inc. of Harrisburg, Pa., with Thomas and Betts Corp. a distant second. Notable competitors include Molex Inc., Amphenol Corp., and Berg Electronics Corp. AMP had sales of $5.2 billion in the mid-1990s, and a market-share of about 18 percent. The company employed 40,000 workers in 43 countries.

AMP, originally known as Aircraft Marine Products, was founded by Uncas A. Whitaker in 1941. Whitaker, trained as a mechanical and electrical engineer, started the company after working for Westinghouse Electric, the Hoover Company, and American Machine & Foundry, now known as AMF Inc. The company's chief products were solderless electrical connectors used in aircraft and boat production. These allowed electrical connections to be made quickly with only a crimping tool, rather than a soldering iron. The company thrived on war production orders as electrical components became increasingly important in aircraft and boat design.

The roots of AMP's international success can be traced to 1957, when it began operations with Japanese companies. It obtained a monopoly in the Japanese automotive market for electrical connectors that has kept it the largest passive components manufacturer in Japan into the 1990s. Thirty foreign subsidiaries, most with engineering and production capability, helped AMP remain responsive to the needs of overseas clients. The company achieved over half of its sales and revenues outside of North America.

AMP experienced its greatest growth, about 15 percent per year, between going public in 1956 and a slowdown in the electronics industry in 1989. After this slowdown, the number of AMP Inc. manufacturing facilities fell from about 140 in the mid-1980s to approximately 100 in 1990. During the same period, the company cut back its work force by 4,000. An emphasis on developing new products helped AMP maintain its position as the top-ranked connector manufacturer. The company spent 12 percent of sales in research, development, and engineering. AMP moved its strategies from marketing connectors to marketing complete harnesses, sensing customers' desires to do as little assembly as possible, and reducing labor costs. It has also provided software for customers to see how AMP products fit with their own via CAD programs. AMP closed several facilities in the United States and abroad in the mid-1990s. In response to slow growth, AMP diversified into other electronics-related enterprises, including eMerce Internet Solutions, which started in 1996 to help business conduct electronic commerce over the Internet.

Thomas and Betts acquired Augat in December, 1996. With the acquisition, Thomas and Betts employed 13,500 employees worldwide and posted sales of $1.2 billion. Another industry leader with strong international connections was Molex Inc. of Lisle, Ill. Approximately 70 percent of this company's sales and profits were garnered outside the United States. The fact that Molex maintained factories in many overseas countries, 21 in 1996, seemed to contribute to its continuing success abroad. The company's annual revenues were approximately $11.2 billion, with about 5.4 percent of the world connector market. Like AMP, Molex invested heavily in research and development. It employed 10,100 people in 1996.

AMERICA AND THE WORLD

Imports of electronic connectors were valued at $271.9 million; exports were valued at $337.4 million. Canada, Japan, Singapore, Mexico, and Germany were the top markets for the U.S. connectors. Mexico, Germany, and Singapore showed promise to grow as export markets. A strong U.S. dollar hurt manufacturers; however, sales to Latin American countries were up.

RESEARCH AND TECHNOLOGY

About one-third of electronic connectors sold in the United States are printed circuit boards. Cylindrical, rack and panel, planar hermetic sealed, and fiber optic connectors divide the rest of the electronic connector market, with fiber optic connectors showing a strong potential for growth. The demand for increasing miniaturization will drive technological advances in the future. Specialized military and commercial applications will also fuel research.

Citing the failure of solder joints under fatigue as a causative factor in avionics failures, Westinghouse introduced Solder Free Interconnects, secured by cantilever spring clips, and Lockheed Sanders introduced folding printed circuit boards with flexible printed wiring. Although some aspects of the emerging technology made manufacturing less labor-intensive, others, particularly the small size of the components, required heavy investments in specialized machines able to handle the process.

The drive for miniaturization was also fueled by the laptop computer industry, which required in 1994 high density interconnections for such next-generation components as miniaturized memory cards and 1.8-inch disk drives, and connectors for linking the laptops with networks and desk-based PCs. Specialty Electronics marketed two-millimeter and one-millimeter

connectors for use in the smallest of computers and electronic devices, such as pagers.

Connectors designed to operate in high-current applications were offered by Panduit Electronics Group of Tinely Park, Il., for use in computers, appliances, and other heavy-duty applications. Panduit utilized "hertz stress" theory to determine the optimum arrangement of dimples used to make the contact in the connector.

Apple planned to introduce a new high-speed serial standard called "Firewire" in 1995 to replace the existing connectors on Macintosh computers. The new system was planned to enhance the speed of transmission of data. The technology featured other advances, too, such as greatly simplified use and an improved capacity for handling real-time video. IBM and other computer manufacturers endorsed the standard as of 1994, helping to insure its success.

Challenging operational environments of industry and the military continued to provide a demand for specialized connectors. In 1991, Ocean Design Inc. introduced an oil-filled, pressurized connector for military and petroleum industry use undersea and in damp conditions. This connector could be mated underwater without shutting off power. The design relied on a thin layer of a specially engineered thermoplastic to strengthen its protective epoxy layer. Another specialized connector with military applications was the BetaFlex circuit board connector. This connector was developed to meet a need for very fast data transmission in the high vibration environment of avionics. At the core of this design was a nickel-titanium memory alloy. Pave Technology Co. introduced a radiation-resistant "push-through" connector, allowing workers to replace its connection without entering a sealed chamber.

Not content with the connector's status as the weak link in the signal chain, W.L. Gore & Associates of Newark, De. introduced a coaxial connector-and-cable assembly in which the connectors as well as the cable were shielded, preventing signal loss of as much as 30 percent. In addition, the connector assembly featured a four-beam contact, providing more surface area than the standard two-beam contact. In 1992 AMP Inc. introduced a hybrid called the Active Eurocard Connector. This high speed connector featured a small printed circuit board on which microchips could be placed, freeing motherboard space. The design was said to allow space to be utilized more efficiently and to dramatically increase bus speed. Highly controlled impedance was a feature of all these high-density connectors.

Providing standards for the vast number of new technologies remained a problem going into the mid-1990s, although some manufacturers preferred proprietary standards, forcing customers to purchase many different components from one source. A trend of working closely with suppliers to develop customized connectors developed in the 1990s, which was expected to provide somewhat higher profit margins.

FURTHER READING

"AMP." *Machine Design,* 26 November 1993.

"AMP Inc.: Fourth-Quarter Net Rose Despite International Woes." *Wall Street Journal,* 27 January 1994.

Avery, Susan. "Interconnects May Get Rise Out of Buyers." *Purchasing,* 2 April 1992.

Barrett, Amy. "Intimations of Mortality." *FW,* 18 September 1990.

Brothers, J.T. "Historical Development of Component Parts Field." *Proceedings of the I.R.E.,* May 1968.

Byrne, Harlan S. "Molex: Global Connection Protects Its Business." *Barron's,* 25 October 1993.

Byrne, Harlan S. "Augat Inc.: A Confident Bet on Autos." *Barron's,* 25 May 1992.

Coombs, Clyde F., ed. *Printed Circuits Handbook.* New York: McGraw Hill, 1988.

Electronic Components: Gaps in Technology. Paris: Organisation for Economic Cooperation and Development, 1968.

Erdman, Andrew. "Staying Ahead of 800 Competitors." *Fortune,* 1 June 1992.

"Hicks Muse to Acquire Unit of Du Pont for $400 Million Cash, Preferred Stock." *Wall Street Journal,* 10 November 1992.

"Interconnections." *Machine Design,* June 1993.

International Directory of Company Histories. Vol. 2. Detroit: St. James Press, 1990.

Leventon, William. "Connectors Close the Reliability Gap." *Design News,* 21 December 1992.

Levine, Bernard. "Passive Components Outlook: U.S. on Course; Offshore Adrift." *Electronic News,* 4 January 1993.

Lineback, J. Robert. "Connector Makers Fight a Price Plunge." *Electronic Business Buyer,* January 1994.

McClenahen, John S. "Samtec's European Connection." *Industry Week,* 4 October 1993.

Murray, Charles J. "Hermetic Connector Improves Glovebox Safety. *Design News,* 16 December 1991.

Nordwall, Bruce D. "Companies Reduce Solder to Increase Reliability." *Aviation Week & Space Technology,* 6 December 1993.

Norr, Henry. "SCSI Gets Burned: Apple's New Firewire Technology Promises Faster Connections." *MacUser,* March 1994.

Peppler, Michael. "When 'Less' Is More: Epoxyless Fiber-Optic Connectors Can Reduce Premises Cabling Costs Significantly." *Telephone Engineer & Management,* 1 February 1994.

Shames, Germaine W. "Master Every Peak." *Success,* March 1996, 30-31.

"Shape-Memory Alloys Aid Mil-Spec Connector." *Design News,* 21 January 1991.

"Thermosets Strengthen Undersea Connectors." *Design News,* 21 January 1991.

"Vendors Find Size Challenge in Notebook CPUs." *Electronic News,* 7 October 1991.

—Frederick C. Ingram

SIC 3679

ELECTRONICS COMPONENTS, NOT ELSEWHERE CLASSIFIED

The Electronic Components, Not Elsewhere Classified industry segment is comprised of firms primarily engaged in manufacturing a multitude of miscellaneous electronic devices. Examples of more popular industry offerings include automobile antennas, oscillators, mechanical rectifiers, solenoids, quartz crystals, and electronic switches. For information on semiconductors, resistors, capacitors, connectors, and coils, see related electronic component industries.

INDUSTRY SNAPSHOT

Since its inception in 1883, the electronics industry has emerged as one of the most encompassing and significant industries of the modern era—worldwide equipment sales approached a staggering $791 billion in 1995. Although U.S. electronic component shipments rose rapidly during the 1980s and early 1990s, miscellaneous equipment classified in this industry, which includes many low-tech commodity devices, experienced tepid growth. Industry revenues climbed at a meager pace of less than 2 percent per year during the 1980s to about $17 billion, not even keeping up with inflation.

Going into the mid-1990s, U.S. miscellaneous electronic component manufacturers were struggling to overcome intense competition from low-cost foreign producers. Makers of many traditional products were also striving to retain market share in the face of increasingly popular solid state components. Nevertheless, rising exports and gains in selected product lines were predicted to allow participants in this industry to maintain growth of 2 percent per year throughout the decade.

ORGANIZATION AND STRUCTURE

Miscellaneous electronic component manufacturers supply products for five broad areas: communications, such as radios, televisions, and satellite systems; computers and calculators; scientific instruments; military applications, particularly missile and radar systems; and power control and manufacturing equipment, such as machine controllers and industrial robots.

The single largest market for electronic components, in the early 1990s was radio and television transmission equipment producers, which consumed about 14 percent of industry output. Telephone and telegraph communications equipment makers purchased about 10 percent of shipments, and computer manufacturers represented 9 percent of the market.

Other major market segments included: radio and television receiving equipment (which made up 6 percent of sales); guided missiles, space, and aircraft components (7 percent); X-ray apparatus (3 percent); and individual consumers (5 percent). Ten percent of production was exported, and the remainder of output was used in numerous niche markets, such as musical instruments, surgical equipment, children's toys, and surveillance devices.

Products. Most miscellaneous electronic components are used to accomplish or support the primary electronic functions of rectification, amplification, oscillation, and switching and timing. In addition, this industry encompasses several peripheral products, such as headphones and phonograph needles. Finally, some unrelated odds and ends are lumped into this industry, such as hermetic seals for equipment, record cutting styli, and video triggers (except those on remote control devices).

In comparison to the leading edge semiconductors and circuits manufactured in other electronic sectors, the majority of components classified in this industry are low-tech, commodity-like products. The major product groups listed below, for example, were developed during the birth of the electronics industry and remain similar in function to their earliest predecessors. For example rectifiers, which are used to convert alternating current (AC) to direct current (DC), were one of the first electronic components developed.

Piezoelectric devices, like oscillators, are used in clocks, pressure gauges, communications equipment, and other contraptions. They utilize materials, such as slivers of quartz, that can convert high-frequency AC into ultrasonic waves of the same frequency. They can also change a mechanical vibration into an electrical signal. Properly cut quartz crystals, for instance, are used as frequency controls in radios and televisions.

Switches and relays are devices that open and close electronic and electrical circuits. Common switches, which are manually operated, include pushbutton, rotary, slide, and toggle mechanisms. Types of relays, which are triggered electronically, are timing, electromechanical, and reed. Solid state relays are excluded from this industry. Relays are often activated by a solenoid, which is a uniformly wound coil of wire in the form of a cylinder. Passage of DC through the wire creates a magnetic field that moves a metal (usually iron) core that actuates the relay.

Liquid crystal displays (LCDs) represent one of the few, new, high-growth segments of this industry. LCDs combine fluidity characteristic of light oils with the orientation properties of crystals to absorb or transmit incident light. Inexpensive monochrome (gray) LCDs, are used in calculators, watches, and similar applications. The most significant growth and technical progress is in color LCDs that are used in flat-panel displays for lap-top computers and other computer display apparatus, such as projectors. In 1994 and 1995, active-matrix color LCD displays for portable personal computers (PCs) largely displaced monochrome and passive-matrix displays. LCD display sizes exceeded 10 inches diagonally in PCs and achieved 20 inches in demonstration flat-panel displays. Because the technology used to produce LCDs is more like integrated-circuit fabrication than the mechanical processes familiar to traditional component manufacturers, it is likely that new companies will dominate this area.

BACKGROUND AND DEVELOPMENT

Thomas Edison gave birth to the electronics industry in 1883, ten years after he invented the light bulb, when he induced electrons to jump from a carbon filament to a metal plate inside a vacuum tube. Edison did not exploit this discovery. Lee De Forest, another American, patented a tube based on Edison's concept in 1906. De Forest's discovery marked the beginning of practical applications in electronics.

Many of the products in the miscellaneous components industry, such as piezoelectric devices, relays, and rectifiers, were developed during the initial stages of the electronics revolution. Wireless communication systems, for example, were pioneered by the British Marconi Company. The National Electric Signaling Company of the U.S. General Electric Company, which was formed by Edison interests, led the development of lighting, phonograph, and other electrical equipment. Later, Westinghouse and the Radio Corporation of America made significant contributions to component advancements.

Intense development efforts during World War I spurred electronic component improvements. Piezoelectricity, for example, had been discovered in 1880. Not until World War I, however, was it applied—piezoelectric devices were used to produce underwater acoustic waves in an early form of submarine-detecting sonar, and later as control devices in radios.

The popularization of the radio after World War I, combined with the proliferation of commercial broadcasting, generated a huge demand by the general public for radio components during the 1920s and 1930s. Although television was invented during the late 1920s and 1930s, World War II delayed the expansion of television broadcasting. But World War II did spawn huge advancements in new electronic components, such as radar, as electronic research expenditures reached $1.5 billion per year.

Integrated circuits that were introduced in 1958, as well as other advanced semiconductors that were popularized during the 1960s and 1970s, threatened to displace some components that were electromechanical or moved electrons by heat. Instead, these devices served to expand the breadth of the electronics industry, resulting in demand growth for most traditional electronic components.

The proliferation of military electronics, particularly during the Korean War, and of consumer electronics during the 1950s resulted in massive industry expansion. Likewise, the introduction of microwave communications, computers, electronic scientific apparatus, and aerospace equipment during the 1960s and 1970s resulted in huge new markets for all types of switches, rectifiers, piezoelectric devices, and other miscellaneous components. Indeed, as new applications for electronic components mushroomed, industry revenues surged to about $13 billion by the late 1970s.

The 1980s. Demand for all electronic components mushroomed during the 1980s, ramroded by the global explosion of personal computers and peripherals, telecommunications equipment, and the introduction of electronics into a broad range of industrial and consumer products. Worldwide sales of integrated circuits, for example, swelled 464 percent during the decade. U.S. shipment growth of the miscellaneous electronic components in this classification, however, stagnated.

As high-tech semiconductors encroached upon their market share, manufacturers of miscellaneous components realized aggregate expansion of only two percent per year throughout the 1980s, not even keeping up with inflation or increases in materials costs. The industry fared better than many analysts had predicted it would, though, in the face of falling prices and fierce foreign competition from low-cost producers. Industry revenues surged as high as $19 billion in 1984, but then waffled between $15 and $17 billion throughout the remainder of the decade and into the early 1990s.

Realizing that profit opportunities from traditional miscellaneous components were dwindling, many U.S. manufacturers simply abandoned the industry or switched their emphasis to related growing segments of the electronics industry. Other producers maintained profitability through vast manufacturing productivity gains. Importantly, many makers of traditional components maintained a resilient market presence by developing and introducing miniaturized products with greater reliability.

The dominant feature of this industry during the 1980s, which reflected the three trends above, was consolidation. In an effort to maximize efficiency, take advantage of new manufacturing processes, and increase capital, companies rapidly merged with or acquired their competitors. In fact, the number of industry participants plummeted from over 3,700 in the early 1980s to less than 2,500 by the late 1980s.

CURRENT CONDITIONS

Miscellaneous electronic component producers enjoyed encouraging revenue gains of between 3 and 5 percent per year between 1988 and 1990. Economic recess caught up with the industry in 1991, however, when sales rose a tepid 2.2 percent. Shipments of filter devices, for example, increased 2.2 percent, as did piezoelectric components. Sales of piezoelectric mechanisms, though, had fallen dramatically from a peak of $295 million in 1987 to about $238 million in 1991. Bucking analysts predictions, relay sales declined only 2.7 percent in 1991, to $495 million, as solid state devices encroached on their market dominance.

As domestic sales of miscellaneous devices continued to sputter in the early 1990s, manufacturers increasingly looked to exports to buoy thinning profit margins. Export growth had been consistently strong since 1989, and cross-border sales had grown to more than $2 billion by the early 1990s. The strongest export markets were Canada, Mexico, Japan, and the United Kingdom. The largest importers to the United States, which were increasingly grasping domestic market share, were Japan, Taiwan, Singapore, Mexico, and

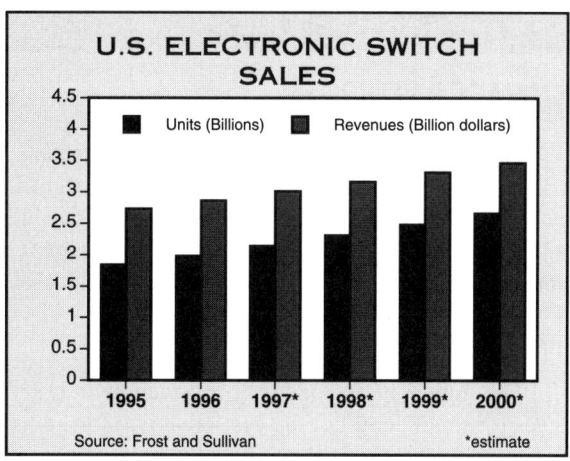

U.S. ELECTRONIC SWITCH SALES

Units (Billions)   Revenues (Billion dollars)

1995 1996 1997* 1998* 1999* 2000*

Source: Frost and Sullivan   *estimate

Canada. Japan dominated U.S. miscellaneous component imports with a staggering 53 percent share.

Going into the mid-1990s, economic recovery in the United States and abroad was expected to boost worldwide demand for passive components, which also includes some items outside of this industry. In 1995, the value of industry shipments totalled $31.07 billion, and the number of employees grew to 20,300. Although integrated circuits and other advanced devices will continue to cannibalize miscellaneous component market share, slow expansion through the mid-1990s will be fueled by strengthening computer, telecommunications, and automotive industries.

Exports will offer growth opportunities, as well, boosted by the weak dollar and the passage of the North American Free Trade Agreement (NAFTA) in 1994. Imports, though, may rise significantly as U.S. manufacturers move production to low-cost production regions, particularly Mexico and the Pacific Rim.

One company's response. In 1989, Oak Industries, Inc. of Massachusetts, implemented a major restructuring in an effort to shore up shrinking profits and growth. Oak divested its cable box business, dumped entertainment investments, and focused its resources on its core businesses of controls, solenoids, and switches. It slashed its work force by 25 percent (to 1,500) and cut its corporate staff from 47 to 22. Oak also acquired components-maker Gilbert Engineering Co. to help it attain an advantage over smaller industrial controls producers. In 1991, Oak Industries was ranked 24th by revenues. By 1993, the company had more than doubled its sales per employee and had boosted annual revenues to over $200 million.

INDUSTRY LEADERS

Because of the breadth and diversity of its offerings, the miscellaneous electronic component in-

dustry is still fragmented, despite consolidation. Over 2,000 firms participated going into the mid-1990s. Even most of the top 75 firms in the industry had less than $100 million in sales in the early 1990s, and fewer than 1,000 workers. Some companies, such as FEI Microwave, Inc. and Electro-Scan, Inc., specialize in producing a few niche proprietary products. Companies like Texas Instruments and Motorola, which are primarily engaged in producing products in other electronics segments, manufacture miscellaneous components to support other product lines. Other companies produce high-volume commodity components for sale to other manufacturers, like auto makers and appliance manufacturers.

The largest U.S. manufacturer of electronic components, in the 1990s was the Harris Corporation of Melbourne, Florida. Harris generated 1995 revenues of more than $3.65 billion from its diversified operations, and employed 26,600 workers. Four other companies had revenues in excess of $1 billion in 1996: SCI Systems Inc. of Huntsville, Alabama, with $2.67 billion and 13,200 employees; General Instrument Corp., based in Chicago, with $2.43 billion and 12,300 employees; ITT Defense and Electronics Inc., with $1.71 billion and 15,000 employees; and Read-Rite Corp. of Austin, Texas, with $1 billion and 23,100 employees. All these companies were highly diversified, with only General Instrument listing SIC 3679 among its five principal lines of business.

WORK FORCE

Industry employment peaked in 1984 at 243,000. Productivity gains, company consolidation, and the movement of some manufacturing activities outside the United States contributed to significant work force reductions after that year, though. Employment plummeted to about 160,000 by the late 1980s, a decline of about 35 percent, and was stable going into the early 1990s.

Despite shipment growth, production jobs in the overall electronic components industry was forecast to fall considerably between 1990 and 2005, according to the U.S. Bureau of Labor Statistics. Past trends indicated that sales of miscellaneous components would decline at a much faster rate, however. Jobs for electrical assemblers, which comprise a leading 20 percent of the overall electronic component work force, will likely decline by about 40 percent by 2005. However, employment prospects for management and sales professionals and engineers were less discouraging.

RESEARCH AND TECHNOLOGY

The most rapid technological advancements in the electronic components industry were occurring in integrated circuit and advanced semiconductor sectors. However, some producers of traditional miscellaneous components were striving to combat high-tech components with improved devices of their own. Smaller and more dependable relays, for example, had allowed electromechanical relay manufacturers to maintain a 96 percent share of that market, despite jumps in solid state relay sales in the early 1990s.

Some segments of the miscellaneous component industry were experiencing pivotal breakthroughs. For example, U.S. manufacturers were racing to establish a presence in the swelling global LCD industry, of which Japan controlled an impressive 95 percent. In 1994, new U.S., European, and Israeli joint ventures planned to begin shipping LCDs that could compete with advanced Japanese flat-panel products. Despite their domination of LCD markets, however, Japanese LCD manufacturers continued to improve their products and cut production costs, and planned to introduce several lines of improved LCDs. In contrast to most other miscellaneous electronic components, worldwide LCD sales were forecast to jump 25 percent per year throughout the mid-1990s.

FURTHER READING

Burrows, Peter. "Back to Basics Strategy Revives Control Maker Oak Industries." *Electronic Business,* March 1993.

Darnay, Arsen J., ed. *Manufacturing USA.* Detroit: Gale Research, 1996.

Darnay, Arsen J., ed. *Market Share Reporter.* Detroit: Gale Research, 1993.

Gross, Neil. "Japan's Liquid-Crystal Gold Rush." *Business Week,* 17 January 1994.

Lineback, J. Robert. "LCD Glut Doesn't Scare New Players." *Electronic Business Buyer,* December 1993.

Morita, Tatsuo. "An Overview of Active Matrix LCDs in Business and Technology." *Proceedings of the Second International Workshop on Active-Matrix Liquid Crystal Displays,* Sept. 25-26, 1996.

Standard & Poor's Industry Surveys. New York: Standard & Poor's Corporation. 31 December 1993.

Tessler, Franklin N. "Input Alternatives." *Macworld,* June 1992.

U.S. Department of Commerce. *U.S. Industrial Outlook 1994.* Washington: GPO, 1994.

—Dave Mote, updated by Jim Casey

STORAGE BATTERIES

This category is comprised of establishments primarily engaged in manufacturing storage batteries, including alkaline cell storage batteries, rechargeable batteries, lead acid storage batteries, nickel cadmium storage batteries, and other types of storage batteries.

INDUSTRY SNAPSHOT

The storage battery industry is driven by industry needs for small, long-lasting, cost-effective storage, or rechargeable, batteries. Batteries have been named as the limiting factor in the design of products ranging from laptop computers to electric automobiles. They are important in supplying starting and lighting power for conventionally fueled vehicles; supplying emergency power for various applications; for load-leveling or supplying additional power during peak demand as part of electrical utility systems; and as a supplement to solar, wave, or wind power. Uninterruptable power supply systems, usually designed to combat drops in power for personal computers (PCs), have created a new market for storage batteries. In all of these applications, the main feature of the storage battery is that it can retain energy supplied from an external electrical charge, whereas the electrochemical reaction within primary batteries cannot be reversed.

ORGANIZATION AND STRUCTURE

Approximately 133 major U.S. establishments competed in the $4.0 billion storage battery industry in 1996, with 84 having more than 20 employees. According to one accounting, regional producers accounted for about 13 percent of sales of automotive and specialized storage batteries. The overall market was dominated by large manufacturers such as Duracell International and Rayovac Corp., and by companies specializing in SLI (starting, lighting, and ignition) and industrial storage batteries, such as Exide Corp. and Gates Energy Products. These latter companies gained market share through acquisitions of related manufacturers since the earliest days of the industry.

BACKGROUND AND DEVELOPMENT

Credit for the invention of the first true storage battery has been given to Gaston Planté for a lead-acid battery he developed in 1859. It was made of two coiled lead strips separated by a cloth. However, his storage battery required charging by primary cells, a process taking months to years. The introduction of the French "Faure Electric Accumulator" two decades later generated excitement in continental Europe, Great Britain, and the United States. It was conceived that the devices would be delivered to homes and businesses daily, like milk deliveries. Demand for electric, rather than gas, streetlights was strong from the beginning, and electrical lighting in the home gradually became a status symbol. However, similar designs of batteries patented by Faure, a Frenchman, and Charles Brush, an American, resulted in patent litigation, which paralyzed American storage battery manufacturers for four years.

Electricity was not readily available on a large scale until the 1880s. This gave impetus to the development of storage batteries, used for over 35 years while alternating current systems were being developed and perfected. The batteries used were large enough to power over two million homes for an hour. Although AC power began to carry more of the load, storage batteries continued to be used in the operation of electrical switches in the power networks. The appearance of "horseless carriages" in the 1890s also fueled demand for storage batteries.

In the early days of the automobile, storage batteries were seriously considered as an alternative to horses and internal combustion engines. Storage batteries powered racing horseless carriages and electric cabs. However, the batteries could not compete in long distance travel and use declined with an increase in better roads. However, they continued to be well-suited for town travel; gasoline vehicles of the day had to be hand-cranked, a risky prospect. Storage batteries helped provide a solution for this difficulty, thereby relegating the electric passenger car to obsolescence. The first automobile to use an electric starter as standard equipment was the 1912 Cadillac.

The use of electric street trucks continued into the 1930s. By this time, storage batteries powered household appliances, boats, and the first submarines. In World War II they also powered torpedoes, aircraft radios, and commercial broadcast stations. In addition, they were also used to power local telephone exchanges and intercontinental repeater stations. Storage batteries excelled in other industrial uses, such as powering electric shuttles in mines and battery-powered trains, which became quite popular in Germany. Golf carts provided an important market for the batteries as well.

CURRENT CONDITIONS

The market for automotive, commercial, and industrial storage batteries had long been considered ma-

ture and highly competitive by the 1990s. This competition drove many smaller manufacturers out of business as prices fell because of excess capacity. Successful producers of these types of batteries sought to maximize economies of scale; new technologies were often quite expensive to introduce. Replacement batteries made up over 80 percent of the automotive battery market. An emphasis on technological improvement was most evident with suppliers for military and space programs, electric vehicles, laptop computers and cellular phones, and power management accessories.

Environmental legislation has driven carmakers to develop electric vehicles. Laws were introduced in various states requiring carmakers to sell a certain amount of emissionless vehicles. The limiting factor in efforts to create such vehicles was the creation of storage batteries that were light and powerful, yet cost effective. Recycling efforts were another important theme in the storage battery industry, as many metals (e.g. cadmium) used, posed health and environmental risks. The recycled metals also form an important part of commodity supplies, particularly recovered lead.

INDUSTRY LEADERS

Notable storage battery companies include Duracell International Inc. (bought in 1996 by Gillette Co. for over $7 billion), the largest U.S. storage battery company, with $2.3 billion in sales in 1996 and more than 9,000 employees worldwide. Exide Corporation, which after several large acquisitions saw gross sales double to $2.3 billion in 1996, was ranked second. Eveready Battery Co. (owned by Ralston-Purina) was the third largest manufacturer in America.

WORK FORCE

The top 500 industry competitors employed about 26,300 workers in 1995. In the mid-1990s, Exide employed 1,501 salaried employees and 3,791 hourly employees. It reported that 40 percent of its salaried employees were engaged in sales, service, and marketing, and 30 percent were engaged in engineering and manufacturing. Of its hourly employees, 32 percent were represented by unions, with whom the company claimed good relations.

AMERICA AND THE WORLD

In the mid-1990s, Duracell controlled 40 percent of the lucrative alkaline battery market worldwide, whereas Eveready claimed a sales advantage in lower performance zinc-carbide batteries more widespread in developing countries.

In the mid-1990s, Japan's storage battery industry pulled out of a slump caused by imbalanced trade with the United States. New technologies, such as lithium-ion and nickel-hydrogen batteries, and marketing geared toward the consumer electronics market appeared responsible for the turnaround.

Japan has been slow to embrace the electric car, perhaps because its environmental lobbies have lacked the clout of those in the United States and Europe. Great Britain and Germany have generally embraced battery-powered vehicles, where postal services were likely users.

RESEARCH AND TECHNOLOGY

Most SLI batteries have been of the lead-acid variety developed in the late nineteenth century. They are an excellent potential power supply for other applications because of their low cost and availability. They are also easy to recycle. Specialized military and aviation-related applications have called for nickel-cadmium cells, which were popularized through portable radios and other consumer devices. Their cost remained prohibitive for automotive use, however, due to the high cost of cadmium. As used in vehicles, they offer somewhat higher performance than lead-acid batteries but are equally as heavy and much more difficult to recycle.

A similar type of battery to the nickel-cadmium, the iron-nickel oxide alkaline battery, was invented by Thomas Edison and patented in the United States in 1901—the same year as Jungner's nickel-cadmium battery. Due to poor performance, the iron-nickel oxide batteries did not meet with the same success as the nicads.

Nickel hydrogen batteries have been introduced as an alternative to nicads. They possess a greater capacity and boast environmental benefits since they do not contain cadmium. Sanyo Electric has been the leader in developing and producing these cells, used in portable telephones, laptop computers, and camcorders, in the early 1990s. Other types of secondary cells invented at the end of the nineteenth century included those utilizing zinc as an electrode. These have been used in satellites, military aircraft, submarines, and assorted military equipment. On satellites, they have generally been used in conjunction with solar power.

Sony introduced a lithium ion secondary storage battery for use in portable telephones and camcorders. It featured twice the capacity of a hydrogen storage cell and one-third the weight. An innovation among consumer battery manufacturers was announced by Rayovac in 1993: reusable alkaline batteries, a concept traditionally thought unworkable. The company claimed its batteries could hold a charge for up to five years, compared to three months for nicads. In 1993, toy manufacturer SLM International introduced a controversial recharger for ordinary alkaline batteries. In 1994, Duracell Inc. announced its Advanced Battery-Pack Interconnect for nickel-metal-hydride connections, which featured an automatic battery contact cleaner and other refinements. The number of competing designs among manufacturers, in addition to the higher initial cost for rechargeables, seemed to slow this segment's growth.

Nickel-metal-hydride (NiMH) batteries showed great promise in the 1990s for applications involving laptop computers. However, both nickel-cadmium and nickel-metal-hydride (NiMH) batteries deteriorate if they are overcharged. A strategy to combat this has been to install integrated circuits capable of monitoring battery voltage, charge/discharge current, and cell case temperature. The goal in the mid-1990s was to recharge a typical laptop battery in 15 minutes. Several automobile manufacturers, including General Motors, Honda, and Toyota, gambled that NiMH would become the next generation fuel source for electric vehicles. Other research tested nicad, sodium sulfur, zinc-air, and lithum technologies as possible alternatives to lead-acid batteries.

Consumer demand, environmental legislation, and other factors made electric car research a high priority in the last quarter of the twentieth century. Electric utility companies supported research in electric cars, partially to encourage the more consistent electricity use that would occur from the vehicles being charged at night, during off-peak hours. Vehicle traction batteries, the kind used to drive vehicles, have been produced in various configurations. Lead-acid batteries were found not to be powerful enough or light enough for the task.

Other more complex electric vehicle options included hybrid systems involving a battery in addition to an internal combustion engine.It was hoped that a practical vehicle of this type, not immediately foreseeable by the mid-1990s, would also allow increased efficiency by means such as regenerative braking. Hybrid battery types were also considered, such as a lead-acid battery for acceleration and a zinc-oxide one for cruising.

Other technological innovations included gauges to indicate the remaining life on individual alkaline batteries. Both Duracell and Eveready used these to market their batteries in the mid-1990s. In addition, at least one company was investigating insulation as a means of maintaining the performance of lead-acid batteries in cold weather.

FURTHER READING

Bottoms, David. "Rechargeable Batteries: The Quest for More Power." *Industry Week,* 3 June, 1996.

Bulkeley, William M. "Duracell Pact Gives Gillette an Added Source of Power." *The Wall Street Journal,* 13 September, 1996.

Ferelli, Mark. "Power Protection Plays Its UPS Card." *Computer Technology Review,* June 1992.

Frankel, Doris. "Lead-Acid Batteries Seen as Wave of the Future in Electric Vehicles." *Journal of Commerce and Commercial,* 13 December 1993.

Hooper, Laurence. "A Movable Feast: Power to the People." *Wall Street Journal,* 16 November 1992.

Horwitt, Elisabeth. "Software Checks UPS Pulse." *Computerworld,* 14 June 1993.

Jacobs, Karen J. "Rayovac Corp. Unveils Reusable Alkaline Batteries." *Wall Street Journal,* 16 June 1993.

Johnstone, Bob. "More Power to Electric Cars." *Far Eastern Economic Review,* 7 November 1991.

Kerridge, Brian. "Battery-Management ICs." *EDN,* 13 May 1993.

Levingston, Stephen E. "SLM Seeks Added Spark with Recharger." *Wall Street Journal,* 8 February 1993.

Lowentstein, Roger. "Intrinsic Value: Blades, Batteries, and a Fifth of Gillette." *The Wall Street Journal,* 19 September, 1996, C1.

Malinak, David. "NiMH Battery-Pack Interconnect Advances Standardization." *Electronic Design,* 2 December 1993.

Naj, Amal Kumar. "Latest Version of Zinc-Air Batteries Promises to Show Long-Lasting Results." *The Wall Street Journal,* 10 November, 1995.

———. "You Can Buy Yourself an Electric Car, But It Isn't Going to Take You Very Far." *The Wall Street Journal,* 15 May 1996.

Negishi, Shigeru. "Another Difficult Year for Japan's Storage Battery Industry." *Japan 21st,* October 1994.

"New Type of Secondary Storage Battery Draws Attention—a Key Device Following Semiconductors and Panel Displays." *Japan 21st,* October 1993.

Reda, Susan. "Cost, Standardization Issues Plague Rechargeable Market." *Stores,* June 1996.

Rolph, S. Wyman. *Exide: The Development of an Engineering Idea.* New York: The Newcomen Society in North America, 1951.

Schimpf, Mark. "Portable Power for the 1990s." *Telephony,* 30 August 1993.

Shipman, Alan. "Power Struggle." *International Management,* April 1993.

Sullivan, Kristina B. "Environmental Concerns Linger for Battery Safety." *PC Week,* 28 June 1993.

Vincent, Colin A., Bruno Scrosati, Mario Lazzari, and Franco Bonino. *Modern Batteries: An Introduction to Electrochemical Power Sources,* London: Edward Arnold, 1984.

Wrigley, Al. "Nickel Batteries Seen for Electric Cars, Vans." *American Metal Market,* 16 December 1991.

Wyatt, Edward A. "Batteries Not Included." *Barron's,* 14 March 1994.

Yuasa,Teruhisa. "Storage Battery Industry Sees Revival." *Japan 21st,* October 1996, 41.

—Frederick C. Ingram

SIC 3692

PRIMARY BATTERIES, DRY AND WET

This industry covers establishments primarily engaged in manufacturing primary batteries, dry or wet.

INDUSTRY SNAPSHOT

In the mid-1990s, demand for primary (disposable, nonrechargeable) batteries remained healthy owing to the expanding use of portable electronic products. Longer-lasting alkaline batteries, introduced in the 1980s, continued to expand their share of the U.S. retail (household) market, which was growing at a rate of six to eight percent per year. The industry had also met the challenge of producing a mercury-free battery that satisfied environmental concerns. The two major primary battery manufacturers, Duracell and Eveready, were faced with some competition from the rechargeable sector, where significant strides in research and development had been made. Given their relative convenience and low initial cost, however, disposable batteries were expected to remain dominant in the household sector at least to the year 2000.

ORGANIZATION AND STRUCTURE

Duracell (which became a division of Gillette in 1996), Eveready Battery (a division of Ralston-Purina), and Rayovac are considered the "Big Three" of disposable batteries, representing about 90 percent of U.S. sales. One estimate of market share for 1996 showed Duracell with 44 percent; Eveready, 37 percent; and Rayovac, less than 10 percent. Both Duracell and Eveready are powerful players in the European and other international markets.

Other companies have tried to wedge into the battery business, but they've generally been unsuccessful. In 1986, for example, Kodak entered the alkaline market. But even with its powerful brand name, gold-tipped batteries, and flashy commercials featuring Stevie Wonder, Kodak was unable to become a strong contender. In 1995, Kodak had less than 1 percent of the U.S. alkaline market.

BACKGROUND AND DEVELOPMENT

The first battery was constructed by Alessandro Volta in about 1800. The Leclanché cell, developed by the French engineer Georges Leclanché in 1866, immediately became a commercial success in large sizes because its component materials were easily available. Until fairly recently, however, the major use for primary batteries in the home was in flashlights. The strong growth in primary battery sales began to accelerate in the 1950s, with expanding demand for transistor radios. The continuing introduction of new electronic products— including pagers, hand-held video games, cellular phones, and portable CD players—and the increasing desire for portability has fueled the growth in sales for primary batteries. Zinc chloride batteries, which are similar to Leclanché cells, but produce more energy, were dominant in the U.S. market in the 1970s and the early 1980s, when longer-lasting alkalines began to overtake them. Alkalines now represent the dominant share of the U.S. consumer battery market.

Other important primary batteries include silver oxide-zinc cells, which are used in watches, hearing aids, and cameras. Lithium cells have attracted the most research in recent years; they are particularly suited for such applications as personal paging systems, heart pacers, and automated cameras.

CURRENT CONDITIONS

In 1995, battery sales at U.S. retailers totaled about $1.8 billion. Sales at mass merchandisers rose 11 percent year over year to $835 million; at grocery stores they were up 4 percent, to $480 million; but at drug stores, they dipped 1 percent to $536 million. According to one estimate, portable/audio applications accounted for 22 percent of all purchases; toys/games, 20 percent; lighting products, 16 percent; remote controls, 9 percent; photo, 8 percent; and all other, 25 percent.

In 1993, Rayovac introduced a rechargeable alkaline battery, named Renewal, in the standard AAA, AA, C, and D sizes, putting it in direct competition with disposable alkaline products. As of early 1995, no other firm produced a rechargeable primary cell. According to *Machine Design,* "the basic chemistry is alkaline, but the anode construction (which differs from primary cells) allows recharging the battery with

a special power supply." Rechargeable batteries made of nickel metal hydride and lithium ion also represented possible alternatives to primary cells in certain applications.

Nevertheless, most observers did not believe that throwaways would soon be obsolete, or even lose their dominant position in many consumer markets. Despite heavy spending by Rayovac on an advertising campaign featuring Michael Jordan, reusable alkalines had only a 1 percent share of the battery market as of early 1996. Most consumers still preferred the convenience of throwaways, even if they could ultimately save a few dollars by consistently using rechargeables.

Some of the supposed environmental benefits of rechargeables were also open to question, since primary batteries, while numerous, represented less than one percent of all municipal solid waste. Battery makers have been making additional efforts to cut their waste products: Panasonic, for example, designed new packaging for its batteries that was made of high-density polyethylene and was therefore recyclable through 6,000 service centers nationwide.

Another argument for rechargeables had been that the throwaways contained relatively high levels of mercury, which is said to damage the nervous system and increase the risk of cancer when ingested in even small quantities. The Mercury-Containing and Rechargeable Battery Management Act of 1996 banned the practice of adding mercury to almost all alkaline and zinc carbon batteries. But the aspects of this law pertaining to mercury usage, as well as similar legislation passed by many states, were actually moot— battery makers had already solved the problem. According to the U.S. Bureau of the Mines, the battery industry reduced the use of mercury by 99.4 percent between 1984 and 1994.

The top three battery companies battle fiercely for the consumer's dollar, especially at Christmas time, when batteries are needed for toys, games, and other electronic gifts. Indeed, some 35 to 40 percent of all household battery sales are made in the final quarter of the year, while under 20 percent take place in the first quarter. To distinguish their brands and maintain or expand share, the major firms spend huge sums on advertising—some 22 percent of sales for both Duracell and Eveready in 1995. Such heavy expenditures create a significant barrier to entry for new companies. It also makes characters like Eveready's Energizer Bunny, familiar to almost every American who owns a TV.

Besides advertising, the big firms continue to find innovations to gain the consumer's attention. In the spring of 1996, both Duracell and Eveready introduced on-cell battery testers. Both batteries use similar technology that measures the power based on the amount of heat generated in the tester. The Duracell battery gives a graduated reading; the Eveready Energizer, in contrast, reads "Good" at full power, but remains black when less than 25 percent power remains.

The two companies have spent millions on research for these products, and their market research indicated that up to 90 percent of consumers liked the testers after they had tried them. Nevertheless, according to retailers, neither product has sparked much consumer interest or affected sales. As Nelson Rodenmayer, a marketing director for Winn-Dixie Stores, told *Supermarket News,* "While a new technological innovation may be a nice novelty for consumers, I don't know if they're going to make a difference in terms of sales. In my experience, it's been a nonissue."

Besides struggling to gain the consumer's interest, the companies also jockey for shelf space in consumer outlets—particularly near the checkout counter, where last-minute purchases are made. Indeed, Duracell has attributed much of its growth to increased distribution at mass merchandisers and warehouse clubs. The manufacturers walk a fine line as they try to gain new distributors without offending old ones.

INDUSTRY LEADERS

In 1988, a leveraged buyout (LBO) led by Kohlberg Kravis Roberts (KKR) took Duracell private. While some leveraged buyouts have come under attack for weakening strong companies by saddling them with debt, Duracell's LBO was generally judged a success. The company completed an initial public offering in 1991 that reduced its $1.6-billion of debt by one-third, and it once again became profitable in fiscal 1992.

In 1996, Duracell once again changed hands when Gillette bought the company for $7.1 billion in stock. Most analysts were pleased with the combination, since they believed Gillette's international marketing muscle would help Duracell overseas. The company already held a solid lead in the global alkaline market, with a 42 percent share compared with 24 percent for Eveready. Since only 20 percent of Duracell sales came from outside North America and Western Europe, Gillette management believed the company offered excellent opportunities for international expansion.

Worldwide, batteries made by Duracell have been marketed under the Duracell trademark. That gave it an advantage in Europe over Eveready, which initially marketed its alkalines under local brand names in Europe. Duracell was also the first company to include a tester in its packaging. Some analysts believed that the tester, introduced in 1990, helped Duracell pick up a few points of market share against Eveready in the first half of the decade. Duracell is also a leading producer of lithium batteries for consumer applications and zinc air batteries, most of which are so-called button cells, which are used in hearing aids and medical equipment.

Eveready is one of the oldest battery companies, with origins in the nineteenth century. Eveready was sold by Union Carbide in 1986 to Ralston-Purina, which also markets pet foods and other consumer and agricultural products. While Eveready is a leading manufacturer of alkaline batteries (according to one estimate, its U.S. market share in 1996 was 37 percent, versus 44 percent for Duracell), it also continues to make zinc carbon brands in huge numbers. While zinc carbon usage is declining worldwide, these batteries remain good moneymakers: margins are generally higher than on alkalines because they are cheaper to produce.

Overall, however, Eveready's margins have been below those of Duracell. As noted earlier, Eveready initially elected to keep the many brand names of the companies it bought in Europe, rather than consolidating them under the Eveready name. The strategy proved unworkable, and in the mid-1990s Eveready has been busy trying to consolidate all of its alkaline brands under the Energizer name.

In 1996, Boston financier Thomas Lee bought an 80 percent interest in Rayovac Corp., number three in the battery business. While the company has had some success selling low-cost alkalines, its overall share in dollar volume remains less than 10 percent. As noted earlier, despite a $20 million advertising campaign featuring Michael Jordan, in 1996 its Renewal alklaline rechargeable line had yet to catch on with American consumers.

AMERICA AND THE WORLD

Overall, the worldwide disposable battery market totals about 20 billion units annually. The widespread diffusion of portable electronic products in Europe and Asia has, as in the U.S., been accompanied by strong sales of batteries to operate them. And again as in the U.S., there has been a move toward more-powerful alkaline batteries from zinc-chloride cells; but nonalkaline batteries still predominate. According to one estimate, in 1996 only one-third of all batteries sold worldwide were alkalines.

In 1996, the overseas market that had battery manufacturers most excited was China. Duracell was selling alkalines in all but one of China's provinces. It was also finishing construction of a $60 million alkaline plant. The plant was expected to give Duracell a huge cost advantage, since the heavy tariffs ordinarily imposed on imported batteries would be eliminated by producing locally. Also, the first two years of Duracell's profits in China will be tax-exempt. Duracell expected that China would be its third largest market, after the U.S. and Italy, by the year 2000. Its takeover by Gillette, which in 1996 had already been doing business in China for more than a decade, only improved Duracell's prospects for better penetration of the Chinese market.

RESEARCH AND TECHNOLOGY

One major focus of research and development in the early 1990s was the effort to produce mercury-free alkaline batteries. By 1994, researchers had been able to reduce mercury levels that had one time been as high as six to eight percent to merely trace elements. With the goal of mercury-free batteries largely accomplished, manufacturers have been able to concentrate on producing lighter, more powerful and longer-lasting batteries. As electronics makers produced ever-smaller and smarter products, traditional batteries account for an increasing proportion of total weight. Thus, the development of lithium batteries has been emphasized, since these cells have the advantages of extremely high-energy density and long shelf life. In addition to their widespread use in consumer products, by 1996 lithium primary batteries had become the power source of choice for a range of medical implants.

FURTHER READING

"A Call for More Action." *Supermarket Business,* May 1996.

Bailey, Steve, and Steven Syre. "Battery Market Sparks Bostonians' Interests." *The Boston Globe,* 13 September 1996.

Capell, Kerry. "How Gillette Wowed Wall Street." *Business Week,* 30 September 1996.

Dan, Pnina. "Recent Advances in Rechargeable Batteries." *Electronic Design,* 3 February 1997.

Elson, Joel. "Charging Batteries." *Supermarket News,* 1 April 1996.

Gillette Annual Report and 10-K, 1996. Boston: Gillette, 1996.

Lamonica, Paul R. "Battling Batteries: Why Duracell and Eveready Are Neck and Neck in Market Share, But Not Brand Value." *Financial World,* 30 January 1996.

Murphy, Elena Epatko. "New Markets Charge Ups Sales and Recycling Efforts." *Purchasing,* 15 August 1996.

Radice, Carol. "Batteries: Specialty Batteries Recharge Category." *Progressive Grocer,* March 1996.

Ralston-Purina Annual Report and 10-K, 1996. St. Louis: Ralston-Purina, 1996.

"Reviving Primary Cells." *Machine Design,* 9 March 1995.

Siskin, Jonathan. "Testing the Charge: Shoppers Appear to be Attracted to Competitive Price Points in Batteries Rather than to a Built-In Added Value." *Supermarket News,* 10 February 1997.

Toor, Mat. "Energizer: The Birth of a Brand." *Marketing,* 4 March 1993.

Vincent, Colin. "Recent Developments in Battery Technology." *Chemistry and Industry,* 16 September 1996.

—Bob Schneider

SIC 3694

ELECTRICAL EQUIPMENT FOR INTERNAL COMBUSTION ENGINES

This classification covers establishments primarily engaged in manufacturing electrical equipment for internal combustion engines. Important products of this industry include armatures, starting motors, alternators, and generators for automobiles and aircraft; and ignition apparatus for internal combustion engines, including spark plugs, magnetos, coils, and distributors.

INDUSTRY SNAPSHOT

The automotive electrical parts sector did well in the mid-1990s, as annual U.S. sales of new vehicles reached and exceeded the 15-million-unit level. Besides higher unit volume, the sector was buoyed by increasing demand for the safety, environmental, and convenience features that electronic parts and components could offer. As electronic engine management became increasingly sophisticated, the dollar-value content of these systems in new vehicles continued to rise.

Nevertheless, the segment was not insulated from the competitive pressures that faced the entire automotive industry. Electrical-equipment makers were trying to adapt to the restructuring of the auto sector. The Big Three, Ford, Chrysler, and GM, were cutting the number of suppliers they dealt with and concentrating their business on a select group of component manufacturers. The Big Three were also shedding their non-core parts operations in favor of buying more parts from outside vendors, thereby avoiding the overhead costs for plant and material necessary for in-house manufacture. Furthermore, there was also a movement toward standardization of parts across model lines.

The aftermarket segment of the electrical autoparts business devoted to repair and maintenance of existing automobiles presented a mixed picture. The tendency of car owners to keep their vehicles longer— the average age of cars on the road was 8.9 years in 1997, compared with 7.4 years in 1986—was expected to boost sales for replacement parts. The push for increasingly tough auto-emission standards also augured well for the future.

But longer-lasting and better-made parts also decreased the need for replacements. The significant percentage of imported vehicles also hurt U.S. suppliers in the aftermarket, since their share of the business for these cars was relatively small. The do-it-yourself (DIY) segment was also expected to be hurt by the consumer's wariness of doing any work on the increasingly sophisticated electrical systems in new vehicles. Still, in the face of these negatives, sales of items like spark plugs held up remarkably well throughout the mid-1990s.

ORGANIZATION AND STRUCTURE

The automotive electronics industry can essentially be divided into two parts: original equipment manufacturing (OEM) and the automotive aftermarket. OEM manufacturing is for new autos; the aftermarket is for used ones. In both segments, the manufacturers comprise the components groups or affiliates of the large automakers, and independent parts makers, which themselves may be divisions of much larger industrial entities. As Japanese companies took an increasing share of the U.S. market, Japanese-affiliated suppliers began to open local branches; by 1993, almost 300 such companies were located in the United States.

BACKGROUND AND DEVELOPMENT

The application of electronics in automobiles has become increasingly sophisticated since commercial production of the automobile began in the early twentieth century. The first electric starter appeared on a 1912 model and, by the 1930s, six-volt electrical systems were standard. Electrical requirements grew as engines became larger and additional features—for example, radios and multispeed windshield wipers— were added. By the late 1950s, 12-volt systems had replaced six-volt systems as a requirement. In the 1970s, electrical, or transistorized, ignition systems,

which required less maintenance and were more reliable than mechanical breaker-point systems, were introduced. In the 1990s, distributorless ignition systems (DIS) were gaining popularity; rather than distributors, they use a small ignition coil for each spark plug. The ignition computer triggers the coils individually, using engine sensors to time the pulses correctly.

CURRENT CONDITIONS

Estimates of the dollar volume of automotive electronic systems are difficult to evaluate, since they can be calculated in several different ways. According to one survey performed by *Ward's Auto World,* the automotive electronics market in 1994 totaled about $15 billion. Of that amount, perhaps 40 percent to 50 percent went for engine and drivetrain applications, or about $6 billion to $7.5 billion.

The OEM parts industry, which had been depressed since 1989, began to pick up in 1992 and continued to be strong in the mid-1990s. In 1996, U.S. car and truck sales totaled some 15.4 million units. Stable and healthy demand for vehicles translated into buoyant conditions for automotive electronics makers. Moreover, the electronics content in each vehicle was rising steadily as safety, environmental, security, and comfort needs were increasingly performed by electronic systems and parts. According to one forecast, the growth rate in electronics content per vehicle would be six percent per year from 1994 to the year 2000, reaching $1,800 per vehicle by the new millennium. Electronic modules were expected to become more sophisticated and efficient in carrying out functions like engine control. As Derrick Kuzak, Ford Motor's director of electric/electronics systems engineering, told *Purchasing* in 1995, ''Rather than having a number of stand-alone modules—like processors— that are controlling individual features of a car, there is a trend toward functional integration with more control in fewer, larger modules.''

The growth in demand for engine and drivetrain electronics was also driven by the mandates of the Clean Air Act. By 1996, all new vehicles had to meet On-Board Diagnostics Series II emission rules (OBD II). Two more steps of emissions regulations were expected to be introduced in 1998 and 2003.

The OEM segment was also benefiting from a steady shift of production from Japan to the United States. For many years, U.S. parts makers struggled without success to sell their products to Japanese automakers producing in the United States. Because of trade friction, many Japanese companies promised to increase their buys of U.S. parts substantially. Whether they had actually done so remained a topic of heated debate in the mid-1990s. The U.S. trade deficit with Japan in the overall auto sector was more than $60 billion in 1995, and auto parts accounted for perhaps $10 billion or more of the total. Nevertheless, there were signs that American manufacturers could expect increasing sales to North American assembly sites (although a more powerful dollar in 1997 made domestic sourcing less attractive). Increasing export sales to plants in Japan, however, was still expected to be a step-by-step battle.

The tremendous financial pressure that The Big Three came under during the early 1990s made them rethink the way they were doing business. They gave their top suppliers greater responsibility for design and engineering. In return for taking on these greater burdens, the supplier received a longer contract—often for the life of the model rather than one to three years. The automakers, wishing to reduce the number of suppliers they dealt with, began awarding contracts for entire components or subassemblies to so-called Tier 1 suppliers. For example, in its North American operations, Ford reduced the number of suppliers it dealt with from 2,400 in 1980 to 1,400 in 1993, and planned to deal with only 1,000 suppliers by the year 2000 or earlier. The Tier 1 companies gained the added responsibility of dealing with smaller sub-contractors that had previously provided goods and services directly with the automakers themselves.

Automakers also moved towards the standardization of more parts and components across model lines. Rather than customizing each component for a specific car or truck, the manufacturers planned to use common designs for a variety of models. Electrical components, as examples of parts that consumer don't perceive as distinguishing one model from another, were likely candidates for standardization. Suppliers would be able to amortize research and development costs and expenses connected to tooling over larger volumes. They would also be able to reduce the wide variety of low-volume parts in held inventory to satisfy infrequent orders.

For smaller suppliers, however, these trends were more portents of the increasing consolidation in the industry. According to one estimate, the number of auto parts makers in the United States fell from 3,000 to 2,000 during the years 1983 to 1992.

The Big Three also sought to reduce the proportion of auto parts that they manufactured themselves. In 1994, General Motors spun off Delco Remy, its automotive engine parts subsidiary, to a group of investors headed by a former auto executive. Also in 1994, Chrysler sold a large portion of its Acustar parts-making subsidiary to Yamazaki of Japan, including eight plants in Mexico that made electrical wiring systems for cars and trucks.

In the aftermarket segment of the industry, business trends were mixed. On the positive side, the number of cars on the road was increasing. According to one estimate, in 1996 there were 101 million vehicles on American roads that were three to seven years old. Those were the cars on which most repairs were performed. And because fuel prices generally remained low, the number of miles driven dramatically increased.

The legislative environment has also favored replacement part companies, since tougher emission standards related to the Clean Air Act of 1990 and other environmental legislation acted together to add to consumer demand. Efforts by several states to enhance their emission inspection programs were expected to contribute to improved vehicle-maintenance practices. The Environmental Protection Agency estimates that the 20 percent of all vehicles that fail emission tests are responsible for some 60 percent of all toxic emissions. The cost of bringing them up to required standards was estimated to run into billions of dollars, much of which would flow to parts companies.

But there were also negative trends for the industry. Manufacturers utilized technological advances that allowed them to build parts and components with extended life-expectancies—most electronically driven systems proved to be very reliable and consequently needed less maintenance. Moreover, parts were made of better, longer-lasting materials, a fact which also lengthened the time periods necessary between maintenance or replacement. For some engine parts, quality had so improved that, barring an automobile accident, they would never be replaced during the auto's lifetime. New technologies had superannuated much traditional auto maintenance: few cars needed such items as breaker points, and the annual tune-up had become a relic of the past. As the number of service stations declined, there were fewer outlets performing preventive maintenance.

Moreover, the nature of the aftermarket business was changing: the increasing sophistication of the engine's electrical system had made some consumers skeptical of doing work themselves rather than taking their car to a trained mechanic. As systems became more complex, strong technical training became an important factor for professionals and DIYers alike. Some observers also commented that, as in other consumer products, brand loyalty was declining among many auto owners who were more concerned with buying quality parts at a competitive price.

Parts counterfeiting was another challenge for the aftermarket industry. In 1993, the Federal Trade Commission estimated that auto-parts counterfeiting was a $3-billion-a-year business in the United States. General Motors contended that it and its suppliers were losing $1.2 billion annually to counterfeits; among the parts most copied were electronic ignition modules. Although Congress attempted to deal with the problem in 1984 by passing the Trademark Counterfeiting Act, the counterfeiting business continued to thrive.

The incursion of foreign cars into the U.S. auto market also had a negative impact on U.S. parts makers in the aftermarket. Some professional installers and do-it-yourselfers working on import vehicles continued to feel that, at least in certain applications, it was better to use original equipment version (OEV) products than the aftermarket offerings of U.S. parts manufacturers. In addition, some potential DIYers were reluctant to work on their imported vehicles, and thus were more likely to bring their cars to dealer service departments that used OEV parts. Despite this hesitancy, however, since the early 1980s—when sales for imported vehicles accounted for only one percent of revenue—domestic parts-makers have made important strides in supplying the import aftermarket.

Just as the introduction of electronic ignition systems erased demand for points and condensers, the advent of the distributorless ignition system (DIS) has resulted in a shrinking market for distributor caps and rotors. The introduction of the emission-reducing catalytic converter has also tended to prolong the life of spark plugs because of its requirement of unleaded fuel. By 1997, spark plugs that could last 100,000 miles were becoming commonplace. In addition, smaller, four-cylinder engines, which require fewer plugs than their six- and eight-cylinder counterparts, became more prevalent. And the compact engine departments of many newer vehicles tended to discourage plug-changing, which some contend now require the abilities of a contortionist.

Despite the negatives the aftermarket sector faced, the positive trends of increased number of cars and miles driven were powerful antidotes. Aftermarket sales of electronic parts did not collapse in the mid-1990s. Indeed, sales in the key spark plugs segment rose to $806 million in 1995, which was $66 million higher than in 1994 and a $105 million jump in two years.

INDUSTRY LEADERS

In the 1990s, the major U.S. carmakers were restructuring their operations to remain cost-competi-tive and meet the challenges of the increasingly global auto industry. Reflecting this trend, the automotive electronics operations of General Motors, the leading U.S. maker, underwent substantial reorganization. In 1994, the company sold its Delco Remy subsidiary to a group of investors led by former Chrysler and Ford Motor executive Harold Sperlich. Delco Remy, which had about $600 million in sales in 1996, made starter motors, alternators, and generators. In 1997, GM proposed the breakup of its multibillion-dollar Hughes Electronics subsidiary, which included its Delco Electronics unit. GM was contemplating merging Delco Electronics with its Delphi Automotive Systems division, and eventually selling off a 20 percent interest to the public.

Bosch, one of the largest overseas electrical components companies in the world, was founded in 1886 by Robert Bosch, a German engineer. Sales to the automobile industry during the first six months of 1996 totaled some $7.3 billion, or 60 percent of the company's revenues. Bosch has been credited with developing the first electronic fuel-injection system, used on the 1967 Volkswagen. The company, among Germany's largest, spent $1.6 billion on research and development in 1996 and had thousands of employees working on automotive electronic applications.

One of the largest companies making products almost exclusively for the automotive aftermarket was Echlin. A little less than a third of its $3.1 billion sales in fiscal 1996 came from engine-system parts, which included distributor coils, ignition coils, electronic voltage regulators, electronic fuel-injection systems, and other such offerings. The company's products were primarily sold as replacement products for use by professional mechanics. The company sold its products under names like NAPA-Echlin, Raybestos, and Borg-Warner.

In 1996, there were three major U.S. manufacturers of spark plugs. AlliedSignal Filters & Spark Plugs (Autolite) sold most of its OEM output to Ford. The Champion Ignition Products division of Cooper Automotive supplied Chrysler and many foreign OEMs. The majority of General Motors's plugs were obtained from Delphi Energy and Energy Management Systems. Other important manufacturers included NGK and Nippondenso of Japan, Robert Bosch of Germany, and Eyquem from France.

WORK FORCE

Overall, the industry employed an estimated 71,000 workers in 1996. Pay levels in auto-parts manufacturing can vary widely for basically the same type of work, depending on whether they are unionized or

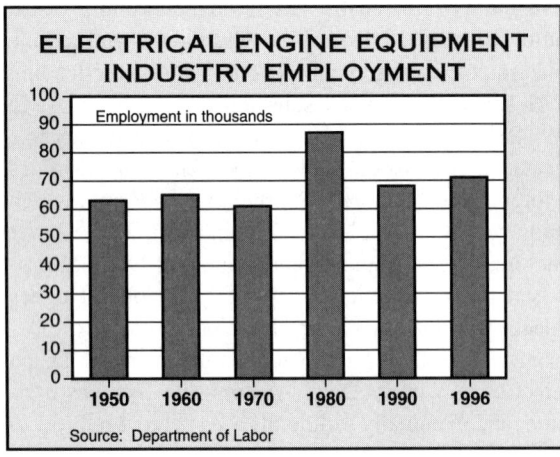

ELECTRICAL ENGINE EQUIPMENT INDUSTRY EMPLOYMENT

Employment in thousands

1950 1960 1970 1980 1990 1996

Source: Department of Labor

not. Where the company had been owned until recently by a Big Three maker, union leaders often argued that these workers should get the same wages paid at the Big Three. In March 1997, United Auto Workers locals at Delco Remy set a strike deadline in support of their demand that its workers be paid under provisions of the Big Three contract negotiated in the fall of 1996. The UAW may have reasoned that, if it allowed parts-making businesses like Delco Remy to cut wages so soon after being set loose by GM, it could embolden GM and Ford to spin off more operations.

AMERICA AND THE WORLD

In the late 1980s, Japanese makers agreed to purchase more American-made parts for their U.S. built vehicles. Originally, the Japanese had anticipated filling less than 50 percent of their needs from domestic suppliers, but they subsequently increased this commitment to as much as 80 percent. Whether the Japanese were living up to their word was a source of continuing controversy in the mid-1990s. Nevertheless, as production of so-called transplants continued to grow, Japanese makers were increasing their orders of U.S. made parts.

U.S. parts makers were also looking to increase sales for cars produced in Japan. A 1995 trade accord between the two countries made provision for U.S. suppliers to have increased access to the automotive aftermarket. In addition, cars produced by the Big Three were achieving some success in Japan, although they still represented a small part of the overall market.

RESEARCH AND TECHNOLOGY

The drive to control automotive emissions and reduce air pollution remained a primary challenge for the auto industry as a whole and electronic parts makers in particular. The three government-regulated auto pollutants are hydrocarbon, carbon monoxide, and ox-

ides of nitrogen exhaust emissions. The catalysts that break them down in the exhaust stream must have a carefully balanced chemistry to work properly. Essential to this process is electronically controlled fuel injection and ignition systems with feedback from various sensors. Some makers have tried to provide additional controls through electronic valve-timing, individual cylinder control, and combustion-quality sensors.

Other factors being equal, older cars—especially those with more than 100,000 miles—pollute more than new vehicles because exhaust gases become dirtier as spark timing and other factors begin to vary. The environmental regulations that require ignition designers to build more efficient combustion systems have led them to scrap the traditional rotor-based distributor and use a distributorless, all-electronic ignition system (DIS). General Motors introduced the first DIS in 1984.

DIS systems do away with the small variations in spark timing that develop as the mechanical distributors wear. Misfirings are sensed by the DIS, which compensates by signaling corrections in the fuel/air mixture and in timing, which is controlled by a microprocessor. While DIS eliminates the distributor, it does add one coil for each pair of cylinders. But in cost/benefit terms, improvements in gas mileage and reduced emissions offset the expense of additional coils and semiconductors. In 1992, about 25 percent of the ignition systems in new cars operated without distributors. Many industry observers expected that number to rise to 100 percent within a few years.

In March 1997, Toyota Motor introduced a hybrid electric-and-gasoline power system that it intended to offer on several models. The system combines a gasoline engine, an electric motor, and a nickel-metal-hydride battery on a single power train. All the power from idling to 22 miles per hour comes from the electric motor; but at faster speeds, power comes from primarily the gasoline engine, assisted by the electric motor. Toyota said the new system doubles fuel efficiency and cuts emissions 90 percent.

FURTHER READING

Adler, Alan. "General Motors Announces Breakup of Hughes Electronics Subsidiary." *Knight Ridder/Tribune Business News,* 17 January 1997.

Adler, Alan. "General Motors Faces Labor Strike at Another Supplier." *Knight Ridder/Tribune Business News,* 22 March 1997.

"Delphi Focuses on Emerging Markets." *Ward's Automotive Reports,* 3 March 1997.

Echlin Inc. 10-K, Branford, CT: Echlin, 1996.

"Electronics Content in Autos Increasing 6%/Yr." *Purchasing,* 19 October 1995.

Geer, John F. Jr. "Parting Company: Why Echlin's Top Management Needed Fixing." *Financial World,* 15 April 1997.

"Growth on Track for Automotive Electronics." *Ward's Auto World,* October 1994.

Jost, Kevin. "The Continuing Evolution of the Spark Plug." *Automotive Engineering,* February 1996.

Keebler, Jack. "Emissions Balancing Act Gets Electronic Boost." *Automotive News Insight,* 23 November 1992.

Keenan, Tim. "Bosch Raises the Bar: Microelectronics Advances Keep Company on Cutting Edge." *Ward's Auto World,* November 1996.

Lowell, Jon. "Is the Party Over (Automotive Electronics Growth)." *Automotive Industries,* August 1995.

Koenig, Bill. "Delco Electronics Looks Hopefully Upon GM Spin-Off Fever." *Knight Ridder/Tribune Business News,* 23 June 1996.

"Potential for Growth in the Market." *Ward's Auto World,* October 1994.

Reitman, Valerie. "Toyota to Sell Hybrid Gas-Electric Car." *Wall Street Journal,* 26 March 1997.

Robinson, Gail. "Integrated Ignition IGBT Takes Up Less Space." *Design News,* 4 October 1993.

"The Wide World of Auto Parts." *S&P Industry Surveys,* 13 June 1996.

1996 Ward's Automotive Yearbook. Southfield, MI: Ward's Communications, 1996, 37-39, 55-57.

"Whoever Said Plugs Lost Their Spark Was Wrong." *Aftermarket Business,* 1 April 1996.

—Bob Schneider

SIC 3695

MAGNETIC AND OPTICAL RECORDING MEDIA

This classification comprises establishments primarily engaged in manufacturing blank tape, disk, or cassette magnetic or optical recording media for use in recording audio, video, or other signals. Excluded from this classification are establishments primarily engaged in manufacturing blank or recorded records and prerecorded audio tapes, which are included within the scope of **SIC 3652: Prerecorded Records & Tapes.** Also excluded are establishments primarily engaged in manufacturing prepackaged computer software and those establishments manufacturing

prerecorded video tape cassettes and disks. The former are classified in **SIC 7372: Prepackaged Software** and the latter are classified in **Industry Group 78: Motion Pictures.**

INDUSTRY SNAPSHOT

The magnetic and optical recording media industry manufactures blank audio and video recording tape, computer tape, and both rigid and floppy computer disks, utilizing either magnetic or optical recording technology. To an extent, the magnetic and optical methods of recording data, images, and sound are competing technologies: the magnetic method offers the user quick retrieval of recorded material, while the optical method benefits those with large storage requirements. Consumers and businesses must choose between the two according to their needs.

Before 1987, the U.S. Census Bureau did not recognize manufacturers of blank audio and video tapes, and floppy and rigid computer disk manufacturers, as composing a distinct industry; instead, these manufacturers were grouped together with manufacturers of such products as phonograph needles, radio headphones, and microwave components. In 1987 the U.S. Census Bureau began separately tracking the recording industry, which had emerged as a significant force, generating $3.5 billion in revenue and comprising 181 manufacturing companies scattered throughout the United States. That figure had increased to $5.4 billion in 1995.

The industry's growth from 1987 to the mid-1990s was remarkable, not in terms of its sales volume—only modest gains were recorded from 1987 to the mid-1990s—but rather, remarkable growth in the form of technological progress. With announcements of improvements in both the production of data storage products and the production of audio and video tape occurring almost monthly during the late 1980s and early 1990s, the industry underwent repeated periods of flux. Predictions for the industry called either for its collapse due to the discovery of a competing technology that would render magnetic and optical recording technology obsolete, or industry forecasts promised a meteoric rise in sales. Rarely did industry observers or participants predict modest gains in revenue or a continuation of the status quo. But in fact, despite the leaps manufacturers achieved in the technological sophistication of their products, industry-wide sales figures did not enjoy a proportionate increase. The bulk of the industry's products experienced between 11 and 13 percent annual growth rates during the early 1990s—an enviable rate of growth for any industry. However, when the industry's actual revenue growth was measured against its predicted growth, reality fell short of expectations.

Nevertheless, manufacturers of magnetic and optical recording media were involved in a robust industry in the mid-1990s, poised to garner an appreciable share of the revenue realized from the enormous popularity of home audio and video entertainment and the increasing necessity of computers for both professional and personal needs. Financial success in the industry is predicated on the manufacturer remaining at the forefront of technology, consistently developing new products to stimulate public interest and to meet the increasingly sophisticated demands of audio, video, and computer equipment. It is an industry characterized by frenetically evolving technologies that, some have argued, are still in their nascence. Thus, manufacturers in the industry during the early 1990s were challenged by, not only an undetermined future, but also often by an undecided present.

ORGANIZATION AND STRUCTURE

Approximately 194 companies in the United States were involved in manufacturing magnetic and optical recording media in 1995. These companies recorded $5.4 billion in revenue that year. This sales volume represented an increase of $1.4 billion from the total of $4.03 billion generated in 1990.

The top seven companies, ranked according to sales volume, earned $100 million or more each in annual revenue, while the majority of the industry's manufacturers, approximately 170 of the 180 total companies, garnered under $50 million each in annual sales.

Of the approximately 215 manufacturing establishments in operation during the early 1990s, less than half employed 20 or more workers. Although this suggests an industry populated by relatively small manufacturing establishments, a true picture emerges when the average size of all magnetic and optical recording media manufacturing establishments is considered against the average size of manufacturing establishments in all other industries. In the early 1990s, the average manufacturing establishment in the United States employed 54 workers, less than one-half the total averaged by the magnetic and optical recording media industry, which employed an average of 118 workers.

In the early 1990s, the greatest geographic concentration of magnetic and optical recording media manufacturing establishments was in California. California, with 76 manufacturing establishments, produced 35 percent of the industry's total shipments,

employed 38 percent of the industry's total work force, and generated $1.22 billion in revenue. The next greatest concentrations of manufacturing establishments were found in Massachusetts, Maine, and New Hampshire. Together, these states contained 17 manufacturing establishments. Despite the predominance of manufacturing establishments in the Western and Northeastern United States, industry activity was fairly widespread throughout the country, with manufacturing establishments located in 21 states.

BACKGROUND AND DEVELOPMENT

The magnetic and optical recording media industry is a modern phenomenon, its emergence stemming from technological advancements that began following World War II. First, came dictating and audio recording machines, which required blank audio tapes. Next, computers and video tape recorders created a need for tape recording information. As equipment relying on magnetic media became more advanced, magnetic media evolved as well, with improvements in both sound, image, and data recording capabilities occurring alongside advances in the way the tape itself was housed: first on reels, then inside cassettes and cartridges. Eventually, during the 1970s, magnetic recording technology advanced to disks, a response to the advent of personal computers.

Just as the pursuit of better ways to manufacture magnetic media created entirely new forms of magnetic media, the push for progress also led to the discovery of an entirely new method of recording and storing data, images, and sounds: optical recording. Emerging during the 1970s, but experiencing its most appreciable growth during the 1980s, optical recording technology promised to greatly increase recording and storage possibilities for the industry and enrich manufacturers along the way.

The origin of magnetic recording technology dates back more than 50 years before magnetic media became a commercially viable product in the 1950s. The principle of magnetic recording was first developed in 1893 by a Danish inventor named Valdemar Poulsen. Poulsen's encouraging discovery led to the formation of a U.S. company twelve years later called the American Telegraphon Co., organized especially to manufacture Poulsen's recording machines. This initial attempt to employ magnetic recording technology failed, largely because the wire Poulsen's design used had a tendency to become twisted, which produced unsatisfactory and irregular results.

For the next fifty years, magnetic recording development remained at a relative standstill, at least in the United States. In Germany, however, experiments continued, particularly during the two decades bridging World War I and World War II, when Karl Bauer and A. Nasavischwily designed a machine called the "Magnetophone," a recording machine that used magnetized plastic tape.

Toward the end of World War II, U.S. soldiers discovered the German Magnetophones and brought them back to the United States, recognizing that the German recording machines were capable of much higher fidelity than the wire recorders used in the United States. Once the German tape recorders became the property of the U.S. Government, they were given to the Brush Development Co. to begin production of the far superior tape recorders. Brush Development began marketing tape recorders in 1946, which, obviously, created a need for magnetic tape, a need first filled by Minnesota Mining & Manufacturing (3M) one year later, when the company introduced its Scotch brand magnetic recording tape.

Once 3M began producing magnetic recording tape, formally launching the magnetic media industry in the United States, other manufacturers soon joined the fray. By the end of the decade, three years after 3M began manufacturing magnetic tape, the industry's ranks included four manufacturers: four companies that would lead the industry for roughly the next decade and produce virtually all magnetic tape sold in the United States. These four manufacturers were Reeves Soundcraft Corp., which started producing magnetic tape in 1950; Audio Devices, Inc.; Reeves Soundcraft, of Orradio Industries, whose president, Herbert Orr, was one of the military officers who discovered the Magnetophones in Germany; and, finally, the industry's pioneer, 3M.

As these manufacturers entered the 1950s, a decade of exponential growth, the magnetic tape market represented a $500,000 a year business. Although a recent innovation, magnetic tape already had many applications. Initially, its use as instrumentation tape outstripped its sound recording applications, as manufacturers of enormous room-size computers, missiles, satellites, and aircraft purchased magnetic tape to monitor production and performance of their products. The petroleum industry used magnetic tape in geophysical exploration equipment, telephone companies used tape to record toll calls, and a host of diverse industries used magnetic tape in automation equipment. In addition to these instrumentation uses, magnetic tape was also used to record radio programs and was purchased by consumers to use with their audio equipment.

By the mid-1950s, the magnetic tape industry had grown considerably, however, not in terms of the number of manufacturers producing magnetic tape. Audio Devices, Reeves Soundcraft, 3M, and Orradio Industries still produced nearly all the tape in the country. In terms of its sales volume, the industry had increased nearly thirtyfold. From $500,000 in 1950, the industry's annual revenue soared to nearly $15 million by the middle of the decade, largely due to the increasing number of applications for magnetic tape in industrial settings, and also to the growing popularity of home stereo systems and recorders. More than three million home audio units existed at this time and unit sales were increasing by more than 500,000 annually, providing blank audio tape manufacturers with a burgeoning customer base. Music connoisseurs had discovered that magnetic tape offered better sound quality than phonograph records. But perhaps the most significant development during the 1950s occurred in 1957, when Ampex Corporation, a manufacturer of recorders and instrumentation machines and 25 percent owner of Orradio Industries, developed the first practical video tape recorder.

Ampex' discovery would soon ignite demand for blank video tape, an entirely new market for tape manufacturers. While television producers explored the possibilities of taping television programs, the industry demonstrated a robust vitality throughout the late 1950s and early 1960s, growing 35 percent to 40 percent annually in revenue volume. By the mid-1960s, the magnetic tape industry represented a $100 million business, which now included blank video tape as one of its primary products, in addition to audio and instrumentation tape. Television had switched from live to taped broadcasts, creating a nearly insatiable demand for blank video tape, while automobiles outfitted with cassette decks spurred the sales of blank audio tapes. Competition for this lucrative market had intensified since the 1950s: approximately 30 manufacturers now vied for market share, a competition in which 3M still held a commanding lead. Controlling roughly 50 percent of the market during the 1950s, 3M continued to account for one-half of the industry's sales during the 1960s, thanks in part to its early lead in both the blank video and audio tape production markets.

Despite the greater number of manufacturers in the industry, its leading companies, with a few exceptions, were the same companies that led the industry in the early 1950s. Reeves Soundcraft still ranked among the industry's top five manufacturers, as did Audio Devices, and, of course, 3M. Ampex Corp., by virtue of its partial ownership of Orradio Industries, and its development of the video recorder, now ranked as the second largest manufacturer, while a relatively new player, Memorex Corporation, had quickly ascended to the industry's upper echelon. Founded in 1961, Memorex was formed by a group of former 3M and Ampex employees, and owed its rise to concentrating on computer tape production, which by now accounted for the largest segment of the magnetic tape market. The lucrative magnetic tape market also attracted much larger manufacturers, such as Radio Corporation of America, and Eastman Kodak, but these companies did not derive enough revenue directly from the manufacture of magnetic tape to rank as industry leaders.

As these manufacturers entered the 1970s, they kept pace with the growing sophistication of audio and video equipment by producing higher quality tape and offering consumers various types of blank tape. In addition to choices in tape length, consumers could now opt for low noise or high noise tape, high energy or low energy tape, or ferri-chrome tape—a selection process many found confusing. This problem would continue to plague manufacturers into the 1990s, but the industry's sales volume swelled nevertheless, climbing to approximately $350 million by the early 1970s.

In 1975, North American Philips Corp., through its subsidiary Magnavox Co., unveiled, in a joint venture with MCA and its subsidiary MCA Disco-Vision Inc., an optical video-disk system for the home. This system employed a light beam rather than a needle or stylus to transmit images and sound from a disk to a television screen. Although it would be several years before optical disk production represented an appreciable portion of industry shipments, the advent of optical media broadened the industry's scope and provided a new breed of competition.

As the industry entered the 1980s, the prospects for further growth were encouraging. Personal desktop computers began to emerge as a popular product, creating a need for magnetic media disks, and the blank video tape market exploded. Blank audio tape, now almost entirely sold in cassette form, also realized exponential growth fueled primarily by the popularity of automobile stereo systems. Consumers continued to be confused by the array of audio tapes from which to choose, a problem now shared by blank video tape manufacturers, who produced tapes for either Beta or VHS video equipment in addition to low-bias and high-bias tape. To combat the confusion, manufacturers began color-coding their products, but assisting consumers in their selection was not of paramount importance during the early 1980s, particularly for blank video tape manufacturers, as the most pressing problem facing consumers was simply locating tape. Blank video tape sales to duplicators, who then sold cassettes of prerecorded programs, were growing as

fast as sales to consumers during the early 1980s, creating a shortage of blank tape at the retail level. Capital expansion programs initiated by several large manufacturers aggravated the problem. As manufacturers added production capacity, some facilities had to reduce their output due to the construction, leaving few blank tapes for neighborhood stores. This problem, however, was only temporary and underscored the vitality of the video market. The market continued to expand at an accelerated rate throughout the decade as the sales of video cassette recorders increased.

The strong steady growth of the blank audio and video tape markets, however, did not overshadow equally encouraging developments in another segment of the magnetic and optical recording media industry, a segment that promised to greatly increase financial rewards. Several years earlier, in 1973, IBM developed the Winchester computer drive, a magnetic disk housed in an air-tight container. Earlier computer drives were housed in containers that could open and shut to allow the removal of a disk, but the Winchester was permanently sealed in its container, free from dust particles. The air pressure inside the container kept the lightweight recording and writing head a fraction of a millimeter above the spinning disk, enabling the drive that held the head in place to manipulate the magnetic field on the disk's surface with unprecedented precision. The development of the Winchester was a historic event, allowing computer users to store far more data than had been possible with data tape; manufacturers now stood to benefit enormously from the fledgling personal computer market.

As recording media manufacturers charted their course through the remainder of the 1980s, the computer market came to the fore, making the production of computer disks a fiercely contested and lucrative segment of the industry. The increasing number of personal computers spurred the sale of 5.25-inch floppy disks, at first one-sided, then double-sided and high density, and had a matching effect on the sale of 3.5-inch rigid disks, developed after the introduction of 5.25-inch disks. Improvements in optical disk storage by the middle of the decade gave optical systems a decided advantage over magnetic systems for particular tasks, such as searching databases of fingerprints to solve criminal cases. However, optical disk storage was unsuitable for many other chores and needed further refinement before gaining widespread usage. In the latter part of the decade, 3.5-inch disks eclipsed 5.25-inch disks as the industry's biggest seller, while the price of personal computers continued a decade-long price decline, causing more and more consumers to become disk consumers.

CURRENT CONDITIONS

The late 1980s and early 1990s witnessed the emergence of several new forms of magnetic and optical recording media. Manufacturers, put in the position of predicting which products would fuel the industry's growth five or ten years into the future, gambled to a certain extent on the development of particular technologies and products, hoping to gain an early lead. Each year new products utilizing innovative technology led some observers to state that advances in optical recording technology would make magnetic media obsolete, while others announced that optical recording technology would never match magnetic media's importance in the industry. Finally, others foresaw a confluence of the two technologies into hybrid products utilizing both magnetic and optical recording technologies.

Against this backdrop, the industry demonstrated vitality, recording enviable growth in the early 1990s despite recessive economic conditions. The trend in video tape production during the early 1990s aped the audio tape trend during the 1980s, as manufacturers sought to increase their market share by producing tapes of greater length. BASF, the industry's leading company in the early 1990s, marketed the first nine-hour video cassette in 1991, then introduced a 10-hour cassette the following year, paving the way for other manufacturers to follow. Although long-length tapes represented a relatively small portion of the video tape market, sales grew steadily in 1994 and 1995, these tapes increased their proportional representation in the video tape market.

Although blank video tape sales rose to 13.8 million units in 1995, this growth did not necessarily translate into increased profits. The retail price of video cassettes plunged during the 1980s, dropping from nearly $25 per cassette in the late 1970s, to below $2 per cassette by the beginning of the 1990s. Larger manufacturers with financial interests in businesses unrelated to blank video tape production could offset this decline in profit margin with their larger cash reserves and, thus, gain market share from smaller manufacturers wholly dependent on blank video tape production for revenue. Yet as these larger manufacturers entered the mid-1990s, the decline of video tape prices at the retail level formed a formidable obstacle to future profit growth in the video tape market.

Three new audio recording formats developed in the late 1980s and early 1990s provided a glimpse of the market's future, as the drive for higher quality recording technology spawned Digital Audio Tape (DAT), Digital Compact Cassette (DCC), and Mini-Disc (MD). Each of these products were still in their infancy during the early 1990s, both in terms of consumer product awareness and the manufacturers' marketing efforts, and, consequently, represented only a small part of the blank audio tape market. However, each was predicted to play a more significant role as the decade progressed. DAT was developed to provide sound quality equal to the high quality of compact disks, but on a medium that could record as well as play back. DAT was also adapted for use with computers, proving to be an ideal medium to back up large capacity hard disk drives.

In November 1996, Sanyo-Verbatim CD Company announced the availability of DVD production in the first quarter of 1997. The Digital Versatile Disc offers many benefits to the user, including the ability to store seven times the capacity of a CD-ROM. The DVD features 4.7 GB capacity, (single side, single layer) or the 8.5 GB capacity, (single side, dual layer) disc. A dramatic illustration of the storage capacity of the DVD is that full-length feature movie videos can be stored onto a DVD. Sanyo-Verbatim CD Company, is a joint venture company that was formed in 1995 as a partnership between Sanyo Laser Products and Verbatim Corporation. Verbatim has over 25 years experience in the data storage markets and Sanyo Laser Products has been producing CDs since the early 1980's. A threat to the new DVD technology in early 1997 was Terastor's developmental 4.75 inch disk capable of storing 20 gigabytes on one side. That's enough to store four feature-length movies. IBM was also working at that time on holographic storage devices. Known as volumetric holographic storage, this technology uses light and three-dimensional space to store digital information.

By 1993, nearly every manufacturer participating in the blank audio tape market had plans to market DCC or MD products, roughly a year and a half after BASF became the first independent blank media company to engage in large-scale DCC tape production. MD products entered the market in early 1993 through Sony's Recording Media division, which, later in the year, adapted the 2.5 inch audio disk for use as computer data storage, much like the adaptation of DAT technology. As the industry entered the mid-1990s, Sony, with its audio MD, and Philips, with its DCC, were pitted against each other in a battle that could likely determine the future success of each product, according to the International Association of Magnetic and Optical Media Manufacturers and Related Industries, the industry's trade organization.

Sales of floppy disks reached a record high in 1992, with more than 1.6 billion units sold. Continuing the trend established during the late 1980s, sales of

5.25-inch disks declined, while sales of 3.5-inch disks increased, accounting for over 64 percent of units sold. DATs, initially developed for audio play back and recording, emerged as the fastest growing data recording product in the magnetic media market segment, sales projected to quadruple by 1996 from the five million units sold in 1992. The advent of CD-ROM technology created additional optimism for manufacturers in the industry, intensifying the debate between proponents of magnetic media and those predicting the future domination of optical media.

Mounting foreign competition in the global computer disk market, particularly from China, dampened what otherwise were encouraging developments in the early 1990s. With more than 60 factories manufacturing computer disks, China's growing prominence threatened to wrest market share from U.S. manufacturers in an industry already dominated by foreign manufacturers. Although disks made in China were inferior those made in the United States during the mid-1990s, their effect on domestic disk prices was an unpleasant development for U.S. manufacturers.

INDUSTRY LEADERS

Ranked according to sales volume, the three largest manufacturers of magnetic and optical recording media in 1996 were BASF Corporation, Komag, Inc. and Verbatim Corporation. Together, these companies generated approximately $1.9 billion dollars in revenue, led by the $997 million recorded by BASF Corporation.

Formed as a U.S. subsidiary of BASF Group, an enormous German conglomerate based in Ludwigshaafen with interests in pharmaceuticals, chemicals, cosmetics, and electronics, BASF Corporation gained prominence in the magnetic and optical recording media industry by pioneering long-length audio and video tapes. Backed by the massive financial resources of its parent corporation, which posted nearly $997 million dollars in sales in 1996, BASF Corporation was able to withstand the dramatic decline in retail prices of blank video tapes during the 1980s, while smaller manufacturers ceded market share. Another U.S. subsidiary of BASF Group, BASF Information Systems, which operated as a subsidiary of BASF Corporation, ranked as the industry's fourth largest manufacturer, recording $300 million in sales in 1993.

Positioned in between these two subsidiary companies of BASF Group were Komag Inc. and Verbatim Corporation. Komag, the lone U.S. representative in the industry's top four, posted $578 million in 1996 primarily through the production of thin magnetic films for disk drives. Based in Milpitas, California,

Komag unseated Sony Recording Media of America, as the industry's second largest manufacturer in 1993. Verbatim Corporation, based in Charlotte, North Carolina, recorded sales of $290 million in 1996.

WORK FORCE

In 1995, 24,700 people were employed by the magnetic and optical recording media industry in the United States, representing an increase of 1,000 from the previous year's total. Of the 24,700 people employed in 1995, a majority were employed as production workers, a segment of the work force that increased its proportional representation in the industry during the decline in total employment. In 1995, there were 15,500 production workers employed by the industry, while the balance of the industry's work force was composed of 9,200 salaried employees, or those performing managerial, technical, or administrative duties.

Typically, production workers are employed on a full-time basis, but average 3 percent fewer hours per year than production workers employed by other manufacturing industries. Production workers in the magnetic and optical recording media industry averaged $14.18 per hour in 1995. In 1990, the hourly wage for production workers employed by the magnetic and optical recording media industry increased to $11.29, at which time salaried employees averaged $37,644 per year.

Predictions in the early 1990s by the U.S. Bureau of Labor for the future of the industry's work force were generally optimistic, although several occupations were expected to suffer severe declines in their proportional representation. From 1990 to 2005, the number of electronic assemblers and precision electronic equipment assemblers were expected to decline by 40 percent and 41 percent, respectively. Those occupations projected to experience the greatest proportional growth were electronic engineers, salespeople, and electronic technicians, each of which were expected to increase in number by more than 29 percent.

FURTHER READING

"BASF Video Promotions Lead the Industry." *Dealerscope Merchandising,* February 1990, 48.

"Better-Than-Expected Sales Raise Threat of Blank Videotape Shortages." *Merchandising,* July 1980, 87.

"Blank Audio, Videotape Suppliers Set Promos, Debut New Packaging." *Merchandising,* March 1981, 52.

Cornell, Christopher. "Kicking Off the New Season." *Dealerscope Merchandising,* January 1993, 142.

———. "A Tough Room." *Dealerscope Merchandising,* May 1992, 22.

———. "Turn, Turn, Turn." *Dealerscope Merchandising,* November 1992, 28.

———. "Twelve DCC Issues Raised at ITA." *Dealerscope Merchandising,* May 1991, 32.

———. "A Wake-Up Call." *Dealerscope Merchandising,* April 1993, 16.

———. "The Way They See It." *Dealerscope Merchandising,* April 1993, 32.

Darney, Arsen J., ed. *Manufacturing USA.* Detroit: Gale Research, 1993.

Dunn, Ashley. "The Quest for Surplus Memory." *The New York Times,* New York: 9 October 1996.

Endrijonas, Janet. "Magnetic Media Changed Our World in 11 Years." *The Office,* February 1992, 20.

Finaly, Douglas. "Optical Disk: Good but Not Dominating." *The Office,* October 1992, 18.

Fisher, Lawrence R. "3M Chases Dream of Building Better Disk." *The New York Times,* 11 March 1996.

Gelfand, Michael. "Blank Tapes: Untangling the Market." *Dealerscope Merchandising,* April 1992, 66.

———. "Blank Videotape Update." *Dealerscope Merchandising,* March 1993, 70.

Goldston, Terry. "Nowhere to Go but Up." *Dealerscope Merchandising,* November 1990, 34.

———. "Unraveling Magnetic Media." *Dealerscope Merchandising,* March 1991, 50.

"A Groovy Way of Stretching Computer Memories." *The Economist,* 25 April 1981, 99.

Harvey, David A. "State of the Media." *Byte,* November 1990, 275.

Kalow, Samuel Jay. "Magnetic Media Still Continues to Innovate." *The Office,* April 1990, 79.

Lion, Karina. "DAT's a Solution." *Byte,* November 1990, 323.

"The Little Floppies That Could." *Dealerscope Merchandising,* March 1991, 44.

"A Maturing Market Takes Hold." *Dealerscope Merchandising,* April 1990, 39.

Nee, Eric. "Trillions of Bytes." *Forbes,* 24 March 1997.

Roth, Cliff. "A Day for Crystal Gazing." *Dealerscope Merchandising,* January 1993, 118.

Ryan, Bob. "Entering a New Phase." *Byte,* November 1990, 289.

———. "The Once and Future King." *Byte,* November 1990, 301.

Shidaker, Geoff. "Demise of Low-End Cassette Boosts Premium Tape Sales." *Merchandising Week,* 19 August 1974, 3.

Tazelbar, Jane Morill. "Magnetic vs. Optical." *Byte,* November 1990, 272.

U.S. Bureau of the Census. *Statistical Abstract of the United States: 1993.* Washington: GPO, 1993.

U.S. Bureau of the Census. *Statistical Abstract of the United States: 1993.* Washington: GPO, 1996.

U.S. Department of Commerce. *U.S. Industrial Outlook,* Washington: GPO, 1994.

Ward's Business Directory. Detroit: Gale Research, 1997.

—Jeffrey L. Covell, updated by Susan Wood King

SIC 3699

ELECTRICAL MACHINERY, EQUIPMENT, AND SUPPLIES, NOT ELSEWHERE CLASSIFIED

This classification is comprised of establishments primarily engaged in manufacturing electrical machinery, equipment, and supplies, not elsewhere classified, including high energy particle acceleration systems and equipment, electronic simulators, appliance and extension cords, bells and chimes, and insect traps.

INDUSTRY SNAPSHOT

Industries classified in the *Standard Industrial Classification Manual* as including products "not elsewhere classified" essentially are comprised of a collection of miscellaneous products that share a broadly defined similarity, but rarely are produced by the same type of manufacturers. These "not elsewhere classified" industries (usually abbreviated as NEC) are created as such to retain the integrity or homogeneity of other industries, which otherwise would become muddled by the inclusion of products that are instead consigned to NEC industries. Consequently, NEC industries frequently include distinctly separate types of manufacturers, competing in entirely different markets, and manufacturing a diverse assortment of products.

SIC 3699: Electrical Machinery, Equipment, and Supplies, Not Elsewhere Classified includes various types of amplifiers, such as magnetic and pulse amplifiers, maser amplifiers, DC amplifiers, and differential and facsimile amplifiers, but excludes audio or video amplifiers. This category also includes various types of particle accelerators (also known as atom smashers), automatic garage door openers, scientific electronic equipment, electronic kits to be assembled by purchaser, and consumer electronic equipment. In the mid-1990s, this segment accounted for roughly 24 percent of the industry's shipments.

The products within the electronic teaching machines, teaching aids, trainers, and simulators category represented approximately 26 percent of the industry's shipments, primarily through the manufacture of electronic trainers and simulators. According to 1992 U.S. Census Bureau figures, electronic trainers and simulators accounted for $1.28 billion of the $4.93 billion generated by the entire product category, or 26 percent, a total largely derived from the manufacture of flight simulators. That figure was predicted to drop by the late 1990s, however, as electronic systems and equipment, NEC and laser systems and equipment were to move into primary market share position.

The laser systems and equipment, except communication, product category includes laser designator/ranging equipment, laser instrumentation equipment such as laboratory alignment devices and surveying equipment, industrial laser equipment, and medical laser equipment. In the mid-1990s, this category accounted for roughly 16 percent of the industry's shipments.

The electrical products, NEC category includes a host of diverse products such as electric gongs, bells, and chimes; electric Christmas tree lighting sets; electric insect killers; electric fence chargers; and electric outboard motors for boats. The category represented approximately 11 percent of the industry's shipments.

The apparatus wire and cordage product category includes appliance cords manufactured primarily from purchased insulated wire for various household appliances, including electric irons, grills, and waffle irons. This category accounted for approximately 6 percent of the industry's shipments.

The smallest product category within the industry, ultrasonic equipment, except for medical and dental use, includes ultrasonic equipment manufactured for industrial applications, such as ultrasonic cleaners, drills, welders, and solderers. This category accounted for roughly 3 percent of the industry's shipments in the mid-1990s.

Although this classification includes a multitude of diverse products, the industry's core businesses—those products that generate the greatest amount of revenue for manufacturers—are the primary products from the three largest product categories. Accordingly, the miscellaneous electrical machinery, equipment, and supplies industry essentially includes manufacturers of consumer electronic products, particle accelerators, flight simulators, and laser equipment.

The majority of the products that constitute the industry's core businesses were added to its classification in 1987, when **SIC 3699: Electrical Machinery, Equipment, and Supplies, Not Elsewhere Classified** was reclassified. Added to the industry's classification were particle accelerators, flight simulators, laser equipment, and ultrasonic equipment, as well as other, less significant products. The effect of this reclassification on the industry's revenue total was enormous; in 1986, the miscellaneous electrical equipment and supplies industry represented a $1.76 billion business; the following year, after reclassification, it represented a $5.05 billion business.

ORGANIZATION AND STRUCTURE

The miscellaneous electrical equipment and supplies industry became a much more densely populated industry following its reclassification in 1987. Prior to that year, approximately 700 companies in the United States were involved in manufacturing products ascribed to the industry. Once reclassified, the industry's roster nearly doubled to include 1,324 manufacturers and 1,379 individual manufacturing establishments, more than twice as many individual, separate manufacturing establishments as were in operation the previous year. From 1987 into the 1990s, however, the number of manufacturers in the industry declined, falling to 1,185 in 1990 and 912 by 1993. The downward trend was predicted to continue, with fewer than 500 companies forecast to exist by the late 1990s.

During the 1980s, the industry's sales volume rose steadily before and after the reclassification, but realized a greater rate of growth before being reclassified. From 1982 to 1986, aggregate revenue increased nearly 30 percent, more than twice as much as the percentage increase from 1987 to 1990. In 1990, the industry's sales volume reached $5.84 billion, an increase of $792 million from the total recorded in 1987. By 1994, however, the value of industry shipments had fallen to $5.1 billion.

In the mid-1990s, individual manufacturing establishments in the industry averaged $6.2 million in annual revenue, about 65 percent of the sales volume generated by the typical manufacturing establishment in industries overall. Although generating less revenue than the average facility industry wide, however, electrical equipment and supply manufacturing plants had an investment per establishment in 1994 that was only 48 percent of that found in other industries. This highlighted the labor-intensive nature of the work and the relative ease of entry into the market for potential manufacturers. Despite this, however, the number of establishments in the industry dropped from over

1,300 in 1987 to about 800 in 1994; that number was predicted to drop again by half by the turn of the century.

Geographically, the bulk of the industry's manufacturing activity took place in California, which employed 19 percent of the industry's work force and accounted for 22 percent of the industry's sales volume. With 158 manufacturing establishments, California contained the most manufacturing establishments of any one state, distantly followed by Florida, which contained 62 facilities. The third-greatest concentration of manufacturing establishments in the mid-1990s was in New York, with 59 facilities. Production facilities were located throughout the United States in the 1990s, with 36 states containing manufacturing establishments.

BACKGROUND AND DEVELOPMENT

Each product segment composing the miscellaneous electrical machinery and equipment industry possesses a history distinct from the other products grouped into this classification. For the most part, the manufacturers of these disparate product categories have little in common with each other and rarely compete in the same market. Manufacturers of flight simulators, for example, have little in common with manufacturers of automatic garage door openers and compete for market share in entirely different markets. Essentially then, the miscellaneous electrical machinery and equipment industry includes six smaller, subsidiary industries—three of lessor importance and three of greater importance—each of which has experienced different paths of development.

These subsidiary industries, however, do share one common thread; their products depend on electricity and a branch of science and engineering closely related to the science of electricity, electronics. Some of the products within the industry rely solely on electricity to operate, but generally these products are of lesser importance to the growth of the industry as a whole. Rather, many of the more important products that contribute significantly to the industry's growth rely on electronic technology, particularly those products added to the industry after the 1987 reclassification. Accordingly, without electrical power and, perhaps more important, without the emergence of electronics, the miscellaneous electrical equipment and supplies industry would not exist.

Before the electrical machinery industry could emerge as representing an appreciable portion of all manufacturing activity in the United States, sufficient electrical power had to be developed. By the beginning of the twentieth century enough electrical power was being generated in the United States—2.2 billion kilowatt hours in 1902—to engender the electrical machinery industry as a viable sector of U.S. manufacturing. At that time, the electrical machinery industry accounted for roughly 1 percent of the total manufacturing activity in the country, a proportion that would increase to 4.5 percent by 1929 and reach 6.6 percent by the beginning of the 1960s. During those six decades of growth, the electrical machinery industry expanded more than six times as rapidly as did American industry as a whole, and the level of technological sophistication in the country increased sufficiently to encourage the production of electronic products in earnest.

In 1907, American inventor Lee DeForest ushered in the electronic age with his development of a three-electrode vacuum tube, which he called an audion, making it possible to amplify weak radio signals and transmit them over long distances, a capability earlier vacuum tubes failed to provide. From this discovery, the world was introduced to the radio, creating a small but lucrative market for a new breed of manufacturer—radio makers. These manufacturers flourished during the 1920s and 1930s, but their numbers began to dwindle as the United States neared involvement in World War II. Infused with orders from the U.S. government for electronic equipment to aid in the war effort, the electronic industry was buoyed for several years during the war, but at its conclusion the small group of electronics manufacturers still represented only slightly more than a fledgling industry, employing relatively few people, contributing a comparatively small amount to the national economy, and amounting to little more than $500 million at the factory level.

The industry's growth during its first 40 years of existence only appeared lackluster in retrospect, however, for in the 10 years following the war the industry expanded at a tremendous pace, becoming the fifth largest industrial segment of the national economy by the late 1950s, employing more than one million people, and comprising more than 2,500 large and small manufacturers. By 1957, the industry's annual sales volume at the manufacturer level had increased 14 times in the previous 10 years, reaching $7 billion, considered at the time to be the most prolific growth rate in the shortest time span of any industry in U.S. history. This prodigious growth witnessed the development of many innovative electronic applications, which inspired a host of sophisticated products for commercial, industrial, and consumer use, including the primary products in the miscellaneous electrical machinery and equipment industry. During this decade, flight simulators, an assortment of consumer electronic products, particle accelerators, and lasers each emerged as substantial, revenue-generating products.

Two U.S. physicists, Arthur L. Schawlow and Charles H. Townes, first propounded the theory of the laser (an acronym for light amplification by stimulated emission of radiation) in 1958, which was based on Townes' development of the maser (microwave amplification by stimulated emission of radiation) roughly eight years earlier, when the electronics industry was beginning to expand exponentially. Two years after the idea was born, the first laser, a ruby laser, was constructed by Theodore H. Maiman in 1960. Particle accelerators, first developed by John D. Cockcroft and Ernest T.S. Walton in 1932, did not become commercially viable products until the 1950s, their evolution largely attributable to the work of Robert J. Van de Graaff and the company he helped found in 1946, High Voltage Engineering Corporation. During the 1950s, a decade of enormous growth in the electronics industry, flight simulators also appeared as a commercially viable product, although they had been in existence for a number of years. Receiving a significant boost from their military applications during World War II, flight simulators gained the attention of the burgeoning commercial airline industry, creating an incentive for electronics manufacturers to convert their facilities to the production of simulators.

From the 1950s forward, the major product categories of the miscellaneous electrical machinery industry were generating appreciable amounts of revenue, albeit from different markets. By the late 1950s, there were eight manufacturers worldwide producing particle accelerators. The largest of these, Van de Graaff's High Voltage Engineering Corporation, controlled 40 percent of the $20 million global market. Although it was still a comparatively small market, industry pundits foresaw the market for particle accelerators increasing to nearly $80 million dollars by the mid-1960s. Their optimism stemmed from the various and remarkable industrial applications for particle accelerators, which were then beginning to overshadow their scientific contributions, or at least command more of the limelight.

Functioning as a machine that synthetically produced radiation energy, particle accelerators were used in various production processes, from sterilizing surgical sutures after they had been packaged, to irradiating wire and cable insulation used in missiles and jet aircraft as well as other electronic gear exposed to high temperatures. Particle accelerators also could perform other feats, such as converting sawdust into digestible feed for livestock, transforming sugar into acid, and waterproofing shoe leather.

The main obstacle facing particle accelerator manufacturers as they entered the 1960s was the expensive nature of their business and the high price of their products. Some units sold for up to $150 million each, limiting the manufacturers' clientele to those businesses for which the high price tag and operating costs of accelerators were offset by their ability to perform a task that otherwise could not be completed. Consequently, there were only 250 particle accelerators in the world by the beginning of the 1960s, but prices were coming down rapidly as manufacturers augmented the world supply by producing 40 to 45 units per year.

As the push toward reducing the manufacturing cost and operating cost of particle accelerators progressed—the cost per kilowatt hour, for example, was cut in third in just two years—scientists also sought to construct bigger and bigger units. The bigger the accelerator, the greater the speed at which particles could be slammed against each other, providing scientists with more information about the basic laws of matter with each incremental increase in size and power. Particle accelerator power, measured by the number of electron volts produced by the accelerated particles, increased throughout the 1960s and 1970s, standing at 30 billion electron volts at the beginning of the 1960s, then increasing to 500 billion electron volts by the beginning of the 1970s. These and further advances in power and research broadened the particle accelerator's applicability for industrial and medical use, particularly in the form of powerful x-ray machines used to detect hidden flaws in metal castings, in the production of semiconductors, and to diagnose and treat cancer.

From the first primitive trainers manufactured in the 1940s by Singer-Link to the early 1990s, the market for flight simulators, marine simulators, and other electronic training devices remained a vital component of the miscellaneous electrical machinery and equipment industry, despite being heavily dependent on military spending, which has fluctuated dramatically since the emergence of simulators. Military sales, both to the U.S. government and to other countries, essentially created the industry during World War II and fueled its growth into the 1950s. The growth of the civilian aircraft industry and the airline industry during the 1950s added to this business. Yet another market segment for flight simulator manufacturers emerged during that decade, when the Soviet Union launched the world's first space satellite in 1957 and formally christened the Space Age. Thus, in quick succession three primary markets for the flight simulator industry were created, inducing a growing number of simulator manufacturers to replicate as best they could the rapid technological advancements taking place in the burgeoning aerospace industry.

The bulk of flight simulator manufacturers' space simulation business came soon after the Soviets launched their satellite, when the frenetic race to reach the moon began. In the early 1960s, the U.S. government earmarked $65 billion to be spent over a seven-year period to win the race, $300 million of which simulator manufacturers could expect to garner. Initially, more 200 space simulators were ordered, as NASA sought to simulate each stage of a moon voyage.

While space simulators were intended to provide training for hypothetical equipment traveling in a hypothetical environment, flight simulators for military and civilian aircraft replicated existing aircraft and would prove to be the linchpin of simulator manufacturers' financial stability in the years to come. As the costs of operating aircraft increased dramatically, simulating the flight without having to pay for fuel and ground support—or the possibility that the plane could be destroyed—became a desirable alternative. Consequently, any significant decline in military spending usually had an insignificant effect on simulator manufacturers, since their products could be construed as cost-saving purchases. For the industry's commercial clientele, the same rationale held true, particularly during the energy crises in the early and mid-1970s. With the rising cost of fuel, many airlines opted for simulators to augment their traditional pilot and crew training. To be sure, simulator manufacturers were negatively affected by the usual economic exigencies, and their market was comparatively small, but their business was not affected as severely when economic conditions soured as were other manufacturers dependent on the aerospace industry.

Simulator manufacturers' role in the civilian aircraft industry received a tremendous boost in 1981, when the Federal Aviation Administration authorized the training of pilots by Braniff Airlines without its pilots recording any actual flight time. Instead, pilots trained in a 747 simulator manufactured by U.K.-based Rediffusion. With this edict, the simulator industry reached "total realism," spurring the industry's growth for the decade.

CURRENT CONDITIONS

As the 1990s neared its close, one product category that had been a traditional leader in the industry overall was predicted to fall behind in product shipments. Electronic teaching machines and trainers, which comprised 27 percent of the industry as recently

as 1992, was expected to fall behind electronic systems and equipment, NEC (including automatic garage door openers), and laser systems and equipment. The U.S. Census Bureau predicted that by the late 1990s, electronic systems and equipment, NEC would comprise 28 percent of the industry, laser systems would comprise 20 percent, and teaching machines and trainers would account for only about 17 percent of the industry overall.

Particle acceleration scientists and its allied industry got a boost in the late 1990s as the Large Hadron Collider appeared on track to be fully operational by the year 2005, three years ahead of schedule. The collider, which cost an estimated $2 billion, was predicted to be the most powerful accelerator ever built. Constructed at Cern, the European particle physics center near Geneva, the collider was to be funded by 19 member nations, including the United States, which pledged $530 million to the effort, both to aid in erection of the collider and for detectors at which U.S. scientists would do research.

The development of the Large Hadron Collider was some consolation to U.S. industry participants disappointed in the abandonment of the 54-mile-long particle accelerator known as the Superconducting Super Collider. Due to ballooning cost estimates, Congress voted to cancel the project in 1993—after more than $2 billion dollars had been spent to finish roughly 20 percent of the accelerator—and allotted $615 million to formally terminate construction.

Prognostications for flight simulator manufacturers generally were encouraging, as the industry emerged from the economically recessive early 1990s. Increases were predicted in the size of the world's aircraft transport fleet through the year 2005, which led industry observers to project a nearly 150-percent increase in the demand for full-flight simulators. In Asia and the Pacific region, aircraft operators during this period were expected to require 200 percent more simulators than they possessed in 1992, while western European aircraft operators were predicted to require 155 percent more simulators; similar percentage increases were predicted by North American and Latin American operators. Driving this increased demand, which promised to expand the size of the simulator industry greatly, was a projected growth in demand for very-long-range aircraft, or those aircraft designed to fly distances greater than 5,500 nautical miles.

That scenario was not embraced wholly by the U.S. Census Bureau, however. It tracked an erosion of the market share of trainers and simulators as the 1990s progressed. That erosion was due at least partly to the growing strength of two other industry segments, electronic systems and equipment, NEC, and laser systems and equipment. Even discounting the gains of those segments, however, the trainer and simulator segment exhibited real declines in the 1990s. Its 1992 value of product shipments was $1.2 billion, about 27 percent of the entire industry's shipments. The segment's shipments dropped to $932 million in 1993, and to $840 million in 1994, about 18 percent of the total. The segment's $874 million value of 1995 shipments represented a resurgence, however, driven by new aircraft technologies requiring new simulators.

INDUSTRY LEADERS

In the late 1990s, five companies in the industry recorded more than $100 million in annual sales. These manufacturers reflected the eclectic and changing nature of this industry. Two of the leading five companies were involved in manufacturing electrical equipment, one manufactured electronic products, one company produced lasers, and another manufactured shop lighting, extension cords, and appliance cords for household electrical equipment. None of the top five establishments were involved in the flight simulator category.

Together, the five largest companies generated $910 million in revenue in 1997. In ranking order these manufacturers were Coherent Inc., Zero Corporation, Core Industries Inc., Manufacturers' Services Limited, and Woods Industries Inc.

The leader of the industry in the late 1990s was Coherent Inc., a designer and manufacturer of scientific, medical, and industrial lasers. Based in Santa Clara, California, Coherent recorded $286 million in sales in 1997. Employing about 1,500 people, Coherent served both scientific and commercial customers as well as the medical market. In addition to its laser manufacturing, the company produced thin film coatings for high-performance laser optics, electro-optical components, and laser accessories. The firm also manufactured laser measurement instruments.

Besides leading the industry in sales in 1997, Coherent Inc. also led its own industry segment by a wide margin. In 1995, its revenue was almost two times that of its nearest competitor in the laser market.

The industry's second position was occupied by Zero Corporation of Los Angeles, a maker of enclosures used to transport and cool electronic equipment. The company also manufactured containers and systems used in air transport. In 1997, the company reported $206 million in revenue. Incorporated in 1988, Zero Corporation employed 1,800 and utilized manufacturing plants and office buildings containing approximately 1.5 million square feet of floor space as of 1995. Its operations were spread over six states; it also had facilities in Mexico and the United Kingdom.

The industry's third-largest manufacturer, Core Industries Inc., manufactured fluid control equipment; test, measurement, and control equipment; and farm equipment. The company generated $188 million in sales in 1997. A primary segment of the company served the electrical market and the heating, ventilation, and air conditioning (HVAC) market. In 1995, Core Industries acquired Promax Industries Inc., a manufacturer of products for the HVAC industry; the purchase was intended to strengthen that market segment for Core.

The fourth and fifth positions in the industry were held by private companies. Manufacturers' Services Limited, based in Concord, Massachusetts, was a subsidiary of Donaldson, Lufkin & Jenrette Inc. that manufactured inspection and gauging equipment. It recorded 1997 sales of $120 million. Fifth-largest was Woods Industries Inc. of Carmel, Indiana. A manufacturer of trouble lights, portable extension cords, and heavy-duty industrial extension cords, the employer of 800 reported $110 million in sales in 1997.

WORK FORCE

Of the approximately 800 manufacturing establishments operating in the industry during the mid-1990s, nearly 400 employed fewer than 20 workers. In 1994, the typical manufacturing establishment employed 49 workers, divided evenly between those who performed managerial, technical, or administrative duties and those who were production workers. In contrast, the typical manufacturing establishment in the United States employed 69 percent of its work force as production workers.

In 1986, 24,700 people were employed by the industry, the majority of whom were employed as production workers. One year later, after the reclassification, the industry's payroll swelled to include 60,300 employees and comprised nearly as many salaried employees as production workers. Before the reclassification, approximately 75 percent of the industry's work force were employed as production workers, while the remaining 25 percent were employed as salaried workers performing administrative, technical, or managerial duties. After the inclusion of manufacturers involved in producing sophisticated, high-technology products the following year, the composition of the industry's work force was nearly evenly divided between the two types of employees, with 47 percent working as salaried employees and 53 percent employed in production.

Following the reclassification, which more than doubled the size of the industry's work force, total employment declined, dropping to almost 40,000 in the mid-1980s. Production workers bore the brunt of the decline, as more than 12,000 lost their jobs by 1994.

Generally, production workers are employed on a full-time basis, working, in the mid-1990s, 6 percent fewer hours per year than the typical production worker, while earning slightly more per hour than the typical production worker. In 1989, production workers employed by all other manufacturing industries averaged $10.49 per hour, compared to the $10.50 per hour averaged by production workers employed by the miscellaneous electrical equipment and supplies industry. This hourly wage fell to $10.37 in 1994, compared to $12.09 industrywide. Salaried employees in 1994 earned an average of $33,273 per year, slightly more than their counterparts worldwide.

RESEARCH AND TECHNOLOGY

Some of the most striking research being done in the industry was in the area of particle physics. As the abandonment of the Superconducting Super Collider and the costs of the Large Hadron Collider made clear, advancements in atom smashing in the 1990s were stymied by the astronomical funding and expansive open spaces required to hurl atomic particles quickly enough through a tunnel. Eliminating the need for huge tunnels and their attendant cost occupied a number of researchers, who sought to create what essentially was a tabletop atom smasher. Researchers at the University of Michigan Center for Ultrafast Optical Science were able to generate and manipulate short, powerful laser pulses, which strip electrons from atoms to create a plasma of charged particles. The electric fields created focused the electrons into a tight beam. Using different methods, researchers at the University of California, Los Angeles, the University of Texas, and Argonne National Laboratory worked to achieve similar results.

Such focused beams that could be manipulated by users were predicted to make possible compact, relatively inexpensive devices, to replace or at least supplement their elephantine counterparts. However, the energy generated by the smaller prototypes in the late 1990s was far short of that generated by large supercolliders. At that time, smaller, less expensive accelerators found their abilities best suited to medical uses rather than to studying the nature of matter itself.

FURTHER READING

"Biggest Atom Smasher Rises on Illinois Prairie." *Engineering News-Record,* 6 August 1970, 60.

Byrne, Harlan S. "Broadening Its Niche: Core Industries." *Barron's,* 6 May 1996, 22.

Crawford, Wilby. "New Technology Keeps Costs Down." *Interavia Aerospace Review,* August 1991, 15.

Darnay, Arsen J., ed. *Manufacturing USA* 5th ed. Detroit: Gale Research, 1996.

Dornheim, Michael A. "Low-Cost Simulation Likely to Reshape Market." *Aviation Week & Space Technology,* 2 September 1991, 38.

Electronics Manufacturers Directory. Twinsburg, OH: Harris Publishing, 1994.

"Extra Zip for Atom Smashers." *Business Week,* 27 March 1981, 78.

"First Industrial Laser Retired to Smithsonian." *Iron Age,* 24 September 1979, 9.

Gutman, Walter K. "Atomic Alchemy." *Barron's,* 19 October 1959, 5.

Hellemans, Alexander. "CERN Sets Sights on an Early LHC." *Science,* 3 January 1997, 19.

"House Backs Funding of 'Big Science' Projects." *Chemical & Engineering News,* 17 June 1991, 6.

"Hurrah for Second Thoughts." *The Economist,* 27 June 1970, 73.

Kolcum, Edward H. "Gulf War Training Deficiencies to Dictate Future of Simulation." *Aviation Week & Space Technology,* 16-23 December 1991, 51.

Lazich, Robert S., ed. *Market Share Reporter.* Detroit: Gale Research, 1997.

"Link Flight Simulation Consolidating Military Programs to Cut Costs." *Aviation Week & Space Technology,* 12 November 1990, 71.

Macilwain, Colin. "Laboratories Collide Over Rival Tritium Scheme." *Nature,* 13 June 1996, 543.

McKenna, James T. "Very-Long-Range Aircraft Seen Driving 150% Rise in Simulator Demand." *Aviation Week & Space Technology,* 20 July 1992, 36.

Moody's Investors Service. *Moody's Industrial Manual.* New York: Moody's Investors Service, 1996.

Moorman, Robert W. "From the Beginning." *Air Transport World,* August 1992, 62.

Nelms, Douglas W. "Changing Times." *Air Transport World,* April 1991, 92.

"The New Business of Space Simulation." *Steel,* 9 July 1962, 59.

Nordwall, Bruce D. "Airline Demand for Flight Simulators to Outstrip Growth in Transport Fleets." *Aviation Week & Space Technology,* 3 August 1992, 55.

Peterson, Ivars. "Surfing a Laser Wave: Toward a Tabletop Particle Accelerator." *Science News,* 10 February 1996, 95.

"Push for Biggest Atom Smasher." *Business Week,* 8 April 1961, 29.

"Radiation for Industry." *Chemical Week,* 5 May 1962, 51.

———. "Simulator Market to Stay Strong Despite Budget Cuts." *Aviation Week & Space Technology,* 12 November 1990, 24.

Standard & Poor' s Corporate Descriptions. New York: Standard & Poor' s Corporation, 1997.

Stein, Kenneth J. "New Technology Spurs Simulator Gains." *Aviation Week & Space Technology,* 30 November 1981, 129.

"Tunnel Visions: Particle Physics." *The Economist,* 16 March 1996, 82.

"Wanted: Bigger Atom Smashers." *Business Week,* 10 September 1960, 75.

Whitehead, Ross. "Rapid Growth Ahead for Industrial Lasers." *Industry Week,* 28 April 1980, 95.

—Jeffrey L. Covell, updated by Tim Eigo

TRANSPORTATION EQUIPMENT

SIC 3711

MOTOR VEHICLES AND PASSENGER CAR BODIES

This industry classification is comprised of establishments primarily engaged in manufacturing or assembling complete automobiles, trucks, commercial vehicles, and buses, as well as specialty motor vehicles intended for highway use such as ambulances, armored cars, hearses, fire department vehicles, snow plows, and tow trucks. This classification also includes establishments involved in manufacturing passenger car bodies and all types of vehicle chassis. Although some establishments within the industry also manufacture motor vehicle parts, establishments primarily involved in manufacturing motor vehicle parts (other than chassis and passenger car bodies) are classified in **SIC 3714: Motor Vehicle Parts and Accessories.**

Establishments primarily engaged in the manufacture of truck and bus bodies, or in the assembly of completed trucks and buses on purchased chassis, are classified in **SIC 3713: Truck and Bus Bodies.** Establishments primarily engaged in the manufacture of truck trailers are classified in **SIC 3715: Truck Trailers.** Other motor vehicle classifications include motor homes assembled on purchased chassis (**SIC 3716: Motor Homes**), motorcycles (**SIC 3751: Motorcycles, Bicycles, and Parts**), off-highway tractors (**SIC 3523: Farm Machinery and Equipment**), industrial tractors (**SIC 3537: Industrial Trucks, Tractors, Trailers, and Stackers**), combat tanks (**SIC 3795: Tanks and Tank Components**), and stamped passenger car body parts (**SIC 3465: Automotive Stampings**).

INDUSTRY SNAPSHOT

The motor vehicle industry represents one of the largest segments within the U.S. economy and forms the core of the nation's industrial strength. In the mid-1990s, an estimated 121 million vehicles were on U.S. roads. The U.S. motor vehicle manufacturing industry consisted of three American, two German affiliated, and seven Japanese affiliated manufacturers of light vehicles (LV) plus five large and approximately 100 medium and smaller assemblers of commercial vehicles. Collectively, the industry produced nearly 12 million vehicles in 1995.

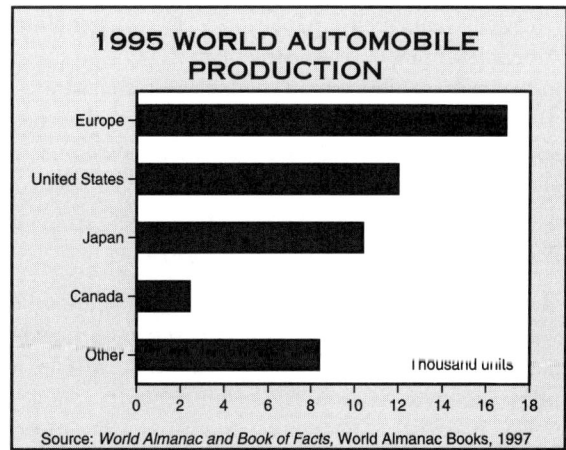

1995 WORLD AUTOMOBILE PRODUCTION

Source: *World Almanac and Book of Facts,* World Almanac Books, 1997

On an average, the industry generated one-sixth of all U.S. manufacturers' shipments of durable goods and consumed 30 percent of all iron, 15 percent of all steel, 25 percent of all aluminum, and 75 percent of all natural rubber purchased by U.S. industries. According to the U.S. Department of Commerce, on average, every dollar of manufacturing input in the United

States allocated to producing motor vehicles added two and one-half dollars to the economy.

At the retail level in 1995, sales of motor vehicles exceeded $259 billion, or 3.6 percent of the nation's gross domestic product—the broadest measure of the nation's economic output. In 1992, sales totaled $205 billion, or 3.3 percent of the total gross domestic product. In the second quarter of 1996, sales gained 3.5 percent over the same period in 1995, reaching an annualized total of $263 billion. The American Automobile Manufacturers Association (AAMA) estimated that in 1992, there were 589,000 establishments in the United States representing the motor vehicles industry and all related industries.

ORGANIZATION AND STRUCTURE

In the United States, auto production is dominated by three manufacturers—General Motors, Ford, and Chrysler. Together, these establishments are referred to as the "Big Three." In 1993, they were the only remaining members of the AAMA. The AAMA, formerly the Motor Vehicle Manufacturers Association (MVMA), was originally founded as the National Automobile Chamber of Commerce in 1915. Its purpose was to administer the cross licensing of patents, and during the 1930s, the organization established a code of fair competition.

The MVMA changed its name to the AAMA and moved its offices from Detroit to Washington following the ouster of its foreign members— Honda of America Manufacturing, Inc. and Volvo Cars of North America—in 1992. The restructured AAMA promised to better serve the common interests of domestic car makers, to serve as a lobbying agent, and to oversee cooperative research ventures undertaken by domestic auto makers.

BACKGROUND AND DEVELOPMENT

History of the Automobile. The modern automobile was not invented by one person. Many people in many nations contributed the ideas, inventions, and innovations required to assemble useful motor vehicles. Roger Bacon, the thirteenth-century English philosopher and scientist, prophesied its development. Leonardo da Vinci envisioned plans for its construction. Nicholas Joseph Cugnot constructed the first functioning self-propelled unit; Cugnot's vehicle, built in 1769, had three wheels and was powered with a steam engine. The first U.S. patent for a self-propelled vehicle was awarded to Oliver Evans by the state of Maryland in 1787. The newly organized Federal Patent Office awarded its first patent for a self-propelled landcar-

riage to Nathan Read in 1791. By 1891 the country had seen more than 100 renderings of motorized vehicles.

The first internal combustion engine was developed by the Belgian inventor, Etienne Lenoir. He used it to power a car during a demonstration in Paris in 1862. Nicholas Otto, a German inventor, developed a quieter four stroke, coal-gas engine in 1878. The first gasoline vehicles were developed in 1885 by two Germans working independently—Karl Benz and Gottlieb Daimler. The world's first motor vehicles built for commercial sale were offered in France by Armand Peugeot in 1889 and Panhard and Levassor in 1890. The French are also credited with coining the term "automobile," formed from two Latin words meaning self-moving.

During the early 1890s many people in the United States were working separately on producing better "horseless carriages." According to some accounts two brothers—Charles and Frank Duryea of Springfield, Massachusetts—developed the first successful American gasoline automobile. The Duryea model was based on Benz's work as reported in *Scientific American.* Other contenders for the honor of producing the first American motor-car included Gottfried Schloemer of Milwaukee, Wisconsin; Henry Nadig of Allentown, Pennsylvania; Charles H. Black of Indianapolis, Indiana; and John W. Lambert of Ohio City, Ohio.

The 1890s brought commercial automobile production to the United States. Elwood Haynes and Edgar and Elmer Apperson were among the first entrepreneurs of the new technology. They built Haynes-Apperson vehicles in a machine shop located in Kokomo, Indiana. By 1899, 30 motor vehicle producers were offering electric, steam, and gasoline powered vehicles. The 1900 U.S. Census listed motor vehicle manufacturers under "Miscellaneous Manufactures."

Among the long list of early automotive pioneers, the best remembered is undoubtedly Henry Ford. Henry Ford built his first car, called a "quadricycle," in 1896. He established the Detroit Automobile Company in 1899—the venture failed. Ford's second company, the Henry Ford Company, founded in 1901, also failed. He finally achieved success with his third organization, the Ford Motor Company, officially founded on June 10, 1903.

Many other popularly known names in automotive history entered the industry during the last decade of the nineteenth century and the first decades of the twentieth century. Studebaker, originally a manufacturer of wagons, carriages, and horse-drawn vehicles, entered the automotive industry in 1897. Packard Motor Company was founded in 1899 and produced its first car in 1900. Ransom Eli Olds established the Olds Motor Vehicle Company in 1897. The company was later reorganized to form the Olds Motor Works, and by 1904 Olds was producing 5,000 "Olds-mobiles" annually. Cadillac Motor Car was established in 1902 with the help of financial backers who abandoned Henry Ford's earlier efforts. Buick Motor Car Company was founded by David D. Buick in 1903 and later sold to William Durant, the founder of General Motors. Louis Chevrolet, born in Switzerland, came to the United States in 1905 and began his automotive career as a race car driver for Buick. Walter P. Chrysler purchased his first car in 1908. Following a career at Buick Motor Car Company, he assumed the presidency of the Chrysler Corporation, formed from the remnants of the Maxwell Motor Car Company on June 6, 1925.

Industry growth. Throughout the early decades of the twentieth century, Ford dominated the industry. He achieved nearly legendary status by introducing the automotive industry to the benefits of automated production and by providing an automobile at a price that most people could afford. In 1908, Ford decided to focus his company's efforts on the construction of only one model—the Model T. To help lower costs and speed production, he began moving toward assembly line production.

In 1913 a moving belt was installed in Ford's magneto department. (A magneto was a part that provided the electric current required for ignition.) After its installation, the moving belt enabled each worker to perform a single task rather than assemble a completed magneto. Production experienced a four-fold increase, and Ford transferred moving assembly lines to other parts of the plant. In its first complete year of assembly line production, the company built 248,000 cars—compared with 78,000 the previous year. In 1915, Ford's annual production reached 500,000 and prices fell. The 1912 Model T sold for $600, the 1914 Model T cost $490, a 1915 touring car cost $440, and the price of the 1925 model dropped to $290. By 1920, an estimated three-fifths of U.S. cars and 50 percent of all the cars in the world were Model Ts. Although its sales diminished as consumers turned to more modern offerings, the Model T earned its place in history. When Model T production was halted in 1927, an estimated 11 of every 20 cars on American roads were Model Ts. Fifteen million units had been sold. No other single model surpassed Model T sales until the 1960s, when the record went to the Volkswagen Beetle.

During the mid-1920s, the automobile market became saturated. To bolster sales, auto manufactures aimed their marketing efforts at creating two-car families. To help families make purchases more quickly, they offered financing, and an estimated 75 percent of all new cars were purchased on installment in 1925. By 1929 motor vehicles had been driven a total of 198 billion miles, and the average motorist logged 7,500 miles per year.

Auto sales dropped in 1929—an indication of the coming depression. As the 1930s opened, auto output was down 37 percent. Production in 1931 tumbled 30 percent. The auto industry fell from first place, as measured according to the value of products sold, to fourth in the national economy, and its decline created a ripple effect throughout the nation's entire economic infrastructure. Auto makers, however, were among the first to emerge from the depression years. By 1936, for example, General Motors was close to its pre-Depression profits.

The late 1930s brought technical innovations to the automotive industry. Automatic transmissions became common, increased precision enabled manufacturers to produce better cars, and attention to styling and aerodynamics improved stability and fuel efficiency. Post-depression era work projects also improved the nation's highway system, and the mileage of paved roads more than doubled between 1933 and 1941. The Pennsylvania Turnpike opened in 1940, and although initial estimates projected the toll road would carry 715 vehicles per day, within two weeks 26,000 vehicles were using the new roadway each day.

Post World War II Period. When World War II arrived, the nation refocused its attention on producing items for the war effort; civilian car production stopped in 1942. One of the most popular cars developed for military use was the "Jeep." Although not all historians agree, some contend that the name "Jeep" was coined from the initials GP—taken from the military lexicon where the "General Purpose Vehicle" had become a "GP." After the war's end, the Jeep was redesigned for civilian use and designated a "Civilian Jeep" or "CJ" model.

American auto makers found an eager market in the post-war years. One-half of the nation's 25.8 million registered cars were ten or more years old, and people were ready to purchase new cars. Between 1946 and 1950, 21.4 million new cars were sold. Production in 1949 topped the five million mark for the first time since the pre-Depression era. The dominance of car and truck transportation was further assured in 1958, when the National Highway Act was passed. This legislation provided funds for significant construction to improve the nation's highway system.

During the 1950s the car's appearance assumed greater importance. Car buyers preferred big and powerful vehicles, which resulted in advertising that emphasized engine horsepower. Ornamental tail fins, inspired by aircraft fuselages, were first incorporated into a Cadillac design and came to symbolize cars of the era. Technical developments included power steering, power brakes, and improvements in automatic transmissions—all necessary to help control large cars.

Modernization of the Motor Vehicle Industry. By the 1960s the new car market was saturated. Manufacturers relied on promotions and annual model changes to boost sales. The market was dominated by the "Big Three" and American Motors Corporation, which had been formed following the merger of two independent producers—Hudson and Nash—in the post-war years. Imported cars, led by the Volkswagen Beetle, began to make an impact on the American market during this period. In 1968 10 percent of all auto sales were captured by foreign manufacturers. The two largest Japanese manufacturers, Toyota and Nissan (Datsun), had entered the U.S. market during the late 1950s and saw rapid growth during the 1960s. By 1970 Toyota was the nation's number two import; Datsun was number three. That year imports accounted for 15 percent of the U.S. passenger car market.

In addition to increased competition, the 1960s brought rising criticism to the auto industry. Ralph Nadar's *Unsafe at Any Speed: The Designed-in Dangers of the American Automobile* was published in 1965 and inaugurated a crusade for safer cars. In 1966 Congress passed the National Traffic and Motor Vehicle Safety Act which mandated improvements in passenger safety, driver visibility, and braking. The Act also required public announcement of recalls to correct safety defects. During the first ten years of regulation, 52 million cars and trucks were recalled. Safety was not the only arena for critics; cars were also identified as a source of air pollution. In 1965 Congress passed the Vehicle Air Pollution and Control Act setting mandatory pollution standards. The 1970s opened with another anti-pollution effort—Congress passed the Clean Air Act which mandated a 90 percent reduction in auto emissions within six years.

Concerns about fuel efficiency dominated the 1970s. In 1973, General Motor's cars averaged less than 12 miles per gallon and other domestic car makers offerings were only slightly better. Two oil crises during the decade brought the nation increased gas prices, local shortages, a 55 miles per hour speed limit, and federally mandated fuel efficiency. The Energy Policy and Conservation Act, passed in 1975, specified that car manufacturers must meet a sales weighted "Corporate Average Fuel Economy" (CAFE) standard of 20 miles per gallon by the 1980 model year and 27.5 miles per gallon by the 1985 model year.

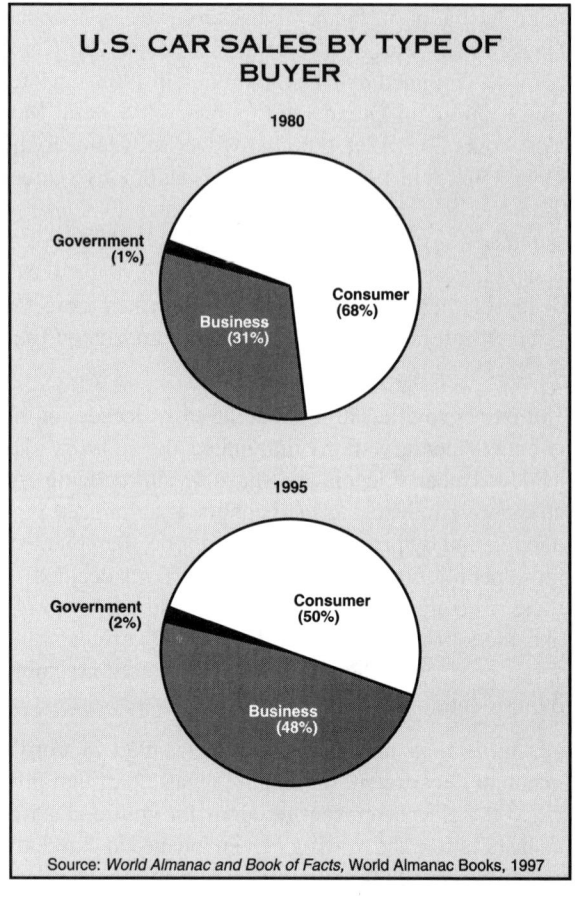

U.S. CAR SALES BY TYPE OF BUYER

1980

Government (1%)

Business (31%)

Consumer (68%)

1995

Government (2%)

Consumer (50%)

Business (48%)

Source: *World Almanac and Book of Facts*, World Almanac Books, 1997

During the early 1980s, domestic auto makers found themselves unprepared for the sudden surge in the small car market, and as a result they lost substantial ground to imports. A growing sense that the products coming out of Detroit were inferior to those of imports further exacerbated the slide of the domestic automotive manufacturers. Chrysler Corporation wavered on the brink of bankruptcy and secured a federal loan guarantee of $1.5 billion to survive. A resurgence during the middle of the decade failed to provide long term stability. The auto industry achieved record sales of 16.3 million units in 1986, but new light vehicle sales fell in four out of the five years between 1986 and 1991. In 1990 the Big Three reported combined losses of $1.1 billion, and General Motors was in particularly bad shape. During 1991 U.S. production facilities operated at only 60 to 65 percent of their capacity. In 1991, sales of cars and trucks totaled $189 billion, representing 3.3 percent of the nation's GDP.

U.S. auto makers' profitability suffered during the economic slowdown of the late 1980s and early 1990s, but vehicle sales during 1992 and 1993 indicated that the industry was rebounding. In the fall of 1993, *Fortune* reported that domestic production was up 6 percent. Lower costs and improved productivity helped bolster the industry's profit picture. Cars were manufactured more efficiently, and manufacturing processes had less environmental impact.

Environmental concerns, however, continued to influence the industry. California introduced stringent clean air standards in 1990. The legislation required auto makers to begin offering Zero Emission Vehicles (ZEV) in 1998. The regulations also called for incremental increases in the percentage of ZEV cars sold— beginning with 2 percent in 1998, moving to 5 percent in 2001, and expanding to 10 percent by 2003. Other states were considering adopting California style legislation. Moreover, the federal government continued to insist on compliance with the CAFE standards previously established by the Energy Policy and Conservation Act.

New passenger cars were required to average 27.5 miles per gallon, and light trucks needed to average 20.2 miles per gallon. Non-compliance by a manufacturer brought penalties of as much as $7,700 per vehicle. According to EPA statistics, the U.S. passenger car fleet averaged 26.9 miles per gallon in 1992; U.S. light trucks averaged 20.4 miles per gallon. Imported passenger cars averaged 29 miles per gallon, and imported light trucks averaged 22.4 miles per gallon.

Some critics in the industry charged that fuel efficiency standards were contradictory to safety requirements. The Coalition for Vehicle Choice (CVC) was formed to counter legislative attempts to increase CAFE requirements to 40 miles per gallon. The CVC argued that high CAFE standards reduced the availability of family sized vehicles and impeded efforts aimed at enhancing auto safety. To speed efforts at increasing vehicle safety, Congress passed the Intermodal Surface Transportation Efficiency Act in 1992. Its requirements included the installation of driver and front seat air bags in passenger cars by 1998 and in trucks, minivans, and sport/utility vehicles by 1999. The legislation also established rules concerning rollovers, brakes, child booster seats, head injury protection, and side impact protection.

Another issue facing domestic auto makers during the early 1990s was the continued impact of foreign competition. Entering the mid-1990s, however, the Japanese manufacturers were on the defensive. "Why are the Big Three suddenly so hot?," asked *Business Week* in 1993. "'One reason is that the yen has risen sky-high,' notes Chrysler Corp. President Robert A. Lutz, 'and exchange rates are really working against [Japanese companies] big time.' Quality [of the domestic fleet] is also way up, Buy American sentiment is strong, and slumping profits are forcing the Japanese to raise prices to boost margins." The magazine also noted that, contrary to past recoveries, the Big Three are showing restraint in their pricing strategies. Another factor is that "major new product launches should keep customer interest high. In 1994, *Fortune* noted that GM, Ford, and Chrysler all introduced new small and intermediate size cars.

Still another reason for the success enjoyed by GM, Ford, and Chrysler was in the realm of truck sales. As *Automotive Industries* observed in May 1994, "trucks are the single biggest reason the Big Three are re-capturing market share. The numbers tell the story. While car sales increased 312,000 units in 1993, truck sales shot up by 725,000 units—more than twice as much. And the Japanese automakers collectively sell less than 10 percent of the trucks sold in America." While the quality of the American products is one reason for their success, America's 25 percent tariff on imported trucks is another important factor.

In 1993 General Motors, Ford, and Chrysler sold 14.2 million cars and trucks—the most since 1989 and a figure indicative of the turnaround the three Detroit based automakers have enjoyed in the early 1990s. By the first quarter of 1994, Chrysler was posting a profit per vehicle sold in North America of $1,203, while Ford tallied $656 of profit for every vehicle sold, and General Motors posted $355 of profit for every car sold.

During the late 1980s and early 1990s many consumers postponed auto purchases. As a result, the average age of passenger cars on U.S. roads increased to 7.9 years, and an estimated 35 percent of the nation's passenger car fleet was nine or more years old. Declining interest rates and debt restructuring made more money available for vehicle purchases.

Minivan sales represented one of the fastest growing market segments in the United States and Europe. *Business Week* estimated U.S. minivan sales at 1.1 million units in 1993 and forecasted annual sales of 1.3 million by 1995. According to one report, European minivan sales held the potential to grow by as much as 230 percent by 1996. Manufacturers favored minivans because their price range of $14,000 to $28,000 brought profits of about $4,000 per vehicle.

Although analysts forecasted short term growth within the automotive industry, long term projections offered less promise. The U.S. Department of Com-

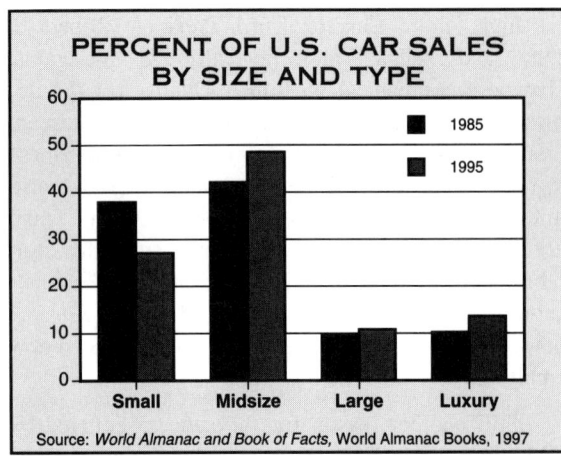

PERCENT OF U.S. CAR SALES BY SIZE AND TYPE

Source: *World Almanac and Book of Facts*, World Almanac Books, 1997

duction strategies, the auto industry increased its use of recycled materials.

Exports of U.S. Motor Vehicles. The U.S. motor vehicle market reached maturity over the course of the mid-1970s through the mid-1990s, resulting in an annualized long term sales growth rate of just 1 to 2 percent per year. On the other hand, many foreign markets were expanding very rapidly. This simple supply and demand formula led the Clinton administration to make opening closed markets a high priority. Establishing the nation's first National Export Strategy to take advantage of the market opening initiatives enabled total U.S. motor vehicle exports to the world to grow impressively—rising from $18.8 billion in 1992 to $22.9 billion by the end of 1995, a 22 percent increase.

The Clinton administration's efforts to pry open the Japanese market produced a surge in exports to Japan, which increased by 250 percent between 1992 and 1995, reaching a total of $3.1 billion. Detroit auto makers were very pleased with the Clinton administration's deal with Japan. According to the *New York Times,* Chrysler's Chairman and CEO, Robert J. Eaton, said the Big Three would be able to compete in Japan and the Japanese would not be able to continue using high prices in Japan to subsidize lower car prices elsewhere.

At the end of 1994, U.S. motor vehicle exports to Mexico jumped 250 percent over the previous year, reaching $683 million—a direct result of the industry's renewed effort to export and the increased access to the Mexican market afforded by the 1994 implementation of the North American Free Trade Agreement (NAFTA). Mexico experienced a severe economic slump in 1995, and U.S. motor vehicle exports declined to $394 million for the year. However, they remained at a level 100 percent greater than in 1993—the year before the agreement became effective. Although additional efforts were necessary, initial efforts to open the Korean market were beginning to be successful. U.S. shipments to Korea rose from 1992's $62 million to $88 million by the end of 1995, a 42 percent boost.

In the first half of 1996, total U.S. motor vehicle exports advanced by 3 percent over the same period in 1995, to a total of $12.7 billion. Exports to Japan jumped 23 percent, reaching $1.6 billion, while shipments to Mexico rose to $547 million, 175 percent greater than in the first half of 1995. Exports to Korea also increased, rising by 130 percent to a total of $106 million.

merce concluded that the domestic market and other major markets around the world were saturated, holding little prospect for long term annual growth rates of more than 1 or 2 percent. In addition, analysts noted growing price resistance among consumers. As new vehicles became more reliable and more expensive, replacement cycles lengthened. Purchases were viewed as discretionary rather than necessary. Increasingly, the automakers have countered such market realities through restrained pricing strategies and other steps. Coupled with an economic outlook in 1994 wherein interest rates were low, players in the industry hope the strides made in recent years could be sustained.

CURRENT CONDITIONS

In 1994, for the first time since 1979, motor vehicle assembly in the United States exceeded that of Japan by 16 percent—a feat that was repeated in 1995 by 18 percent. The optimistic car and truck sales expected for 1995 however did not occur; the industry could not even beat the 15.2 million units sold in 1994. In the first half of 1996, vehicle exports increased by 3 percent, compared with the first half of 1995, reaching a total of almost $34 billion. In the first seven months of 1996, vehicle production was off a slight 2 percent. In 1994 the Big Three reported record earnings of $13.9 billion, followed by an additional $13 billion in 1995. Their profits in the second quarter of 1996, $4.8 billion, were 21 percent higher than in the second quarter of 1995.

Young buyers accounted for nearly 25 percent of car sales, and that figure was also declining. Auto manufacturers reexamined their marketing strategies and automobile designs to offer less expensive vehicles to the generation of buyers who were born in the 1960s and early 1970s. In keeping with the growing awareness of industrial recycling and economical pro-

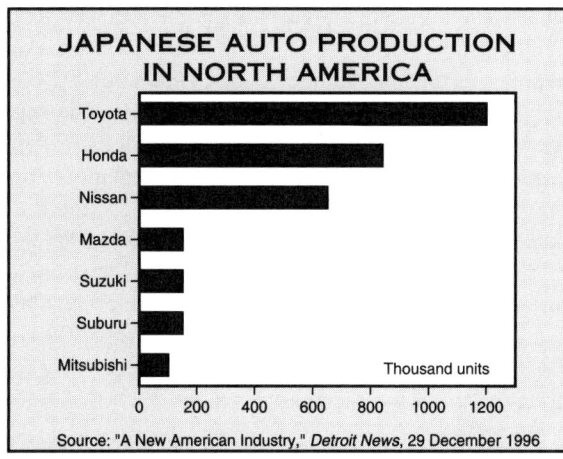

JAPANESE AUTO PRODUCTION IN NORTH AMERICA

Thousand units

Source: "A New American Industry," *Detroit News*, 29 December 1996

According to the *U.S. Global Trade Outlook: 1995-2000,* East Asia and Latin America were likely to account for more than one-half of all the growth in the world motor vehicle market during the late 1990s. U.S. producers were expected to obtain export orders worth $5.4 billion from these fast growing countries in 1995—an increase of six percent— rising to $6.5 billion annually in 2000.

INDUSTRY LEADERS

General Motors. In 1997, the world's largest full line vehicle manufacturer was General Motors Corporation. GM offered domestic automobiles under the nameplates Chevrolet, Pontiac, Oldsmobile, Buick, Cadillac, GMC Truck, and Saturn. International products included Opel, Vauxhall, Saab, Lotus, and Isuzu.

General Motors was incorporated in 1908 by William C. Durant. Its first components were Oldsmobile and Buick. The company acquired two more manufacturers in 1909—Oakland and Cadillac—and between 1910 and 1920, Durant obtained more than 30 companies. The unit that would go on to become GM's largest division, Chevrolet, was acquired in 1918 and accounted for 49 percent of GM's sales in 1992. Although it remained the largest auto manufacturer, GM saw its market share drop during the 1980s and early 1990s.

In 1992 GM reported sales of 7,146,000 units valued in excess of $118.5 billion. Worldwide GM employment stood at 571,000. When workers at the company's subsidiaries were included, the company's employment totaled 750,000—a figure that has steadily dropped in the last couple of years as GM fights to control production costs. In 1993 General Motors posted higher sales than any company in America— $138 billion. The company parlayed that into $1.176 billion in earnings. While still struggling in some areas, GM entered the mid-1990s in better financial

condition than it had seen in several years. General Motors had a sales revenue of $168.828 billion in 1995.

Ford. The second largest auto manufacturer in the United States and in the world in the mid-1990s was the Ford Motor Company. In 1992 Ford sold 3.17 million units under its domestic nameplates—Ford, Lincoln, and Mercury—and the company's Taurus was the best-selling car in the United States. Ford represented the corporation's largest division, accounting for 81.8 percent of sales. In addition to its own units, the company owned 25 percent of Mazda (Japan), 10 percent of Kia Motors (South Korea), 100 percent of Jaguar (United Kingdom), and 75 percent of Aston Martin (United Kingdom). In 1992 Ford's worldwide factory sales totaled 5.76 million units. In 1993 the company reported earnings of $2.5 billion on $108.5 billion in total sales—a $3 billion turnaround from the year before—and attributed the good numbers to dramatically improved car and truck sales in the United States, worldwide cost-cutting, and the performance of its financial subsidiaries. Ford had a 1995 sales revenue of $137.137 billion.

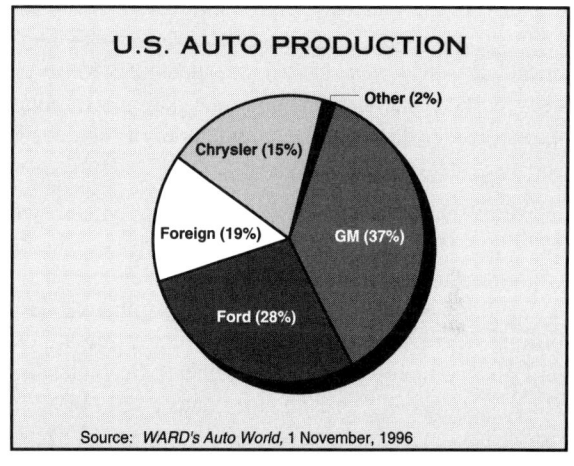

U.S. AUTO PRODUCTION

Other (2%)
Chrysler (15%)
Foreign (19%)
GM (37%)
Ford (28%)

Source: *WARD's Auto World,* 1 November, 1996

The Ford Motor Company was established in 1903 by Henry Ford, whose early models bore alphabetic designations. His first offering, the Model A, was introduced in 1903, and the company introduced the Model C the following year. Looking for a car with mass appeal that could be produced at a low cost, Ford continued making innovations. The Model N was introduced for the 1906 and 1907 season and boasted speeds up to 45 miles per hour and a fuel economy of 20 miles per gallon. It sold for $600. The Model N was followed by an upgraded Model R and a refined Model S. Arguably the most famous car in automotive history, Ford's Model T was introduced for the 1908 and 1909 season. Ford's ninth model in six years, the

Model T achieved nearly legendary status and dominated the industry for 18 years.

Chrysler. The third company of the U.S. Big Three is the Chrysler Corporation. Chrysler was formed out of remnants of the Maxwell Motor Car Co. in 1925 by Walter P. Chrysler. Its first line of cars, the ''Chrysler Six,'' were aimed at the medium priced market. A year later Chrysler rose from 57th in industry sales to fifth and expanded its operations into Canada. By 1929, the company was counted as one of the Big Three.

Chrysler experienced high sales during the early 1970s, but events later in the decade pushed the company to the brink of bankruptcy. The challenge of rebuilding the company was taken on by Lee A. Iacocca, who became Chrysler's President in 1978 and Chairman in 1979. To help ensure Chrysler's survival, Congress passed the Chrysler Corporation Loan Guarantee Act, which provided the company with $1.5 billion in federal loan guarantees. Chrysler's new line of K-cars helped create the momentum necessary for a return to profitability, enabling the company to pay off its federal loan guarantees seven years early.

Chrysler's pioneering efforts in the minivan market also helped the company achieve success. The Dodge Caravan and the Plymouth Voyager, both introduced in 1983, gave Chrysler leadership within the new market. Chrysler remained the nation's minivan market leader throughout the remainder of the decade and into the 1990s.

By 1991 Chrysler's worldwide employment was 123,000. The company's products were sold in 80 countries through a network of 8,000 dealers, and sales of 2,175,447 cars and trucks in 1992 totaled $36.9 billion. The Dodge nameplate accounted for almost half the company's sales and other nameplates included Chrysler, Plymouth, Jeep, and Eagle. In addition, Chrysler owned a 15.6 percent interest in Maserati. In 1993 Chrysler continued its sharp recent performance, pulling in $3.8 billion in pretax operating profits—more than four times more than in 1992—and $2.41 billion in after tax profits. Chrysler's total sales for 1993 reached $43.6 billion. Chrysler had a 1995 sales revenue of $53.195 billion.

WORK FORCE

During the early 1990s approximately one of every seven jobs in the U.S. domestic economy related to the production, sale, operation, or maintenance of motor vehicles. As the *Detroit Free Press* noted in 1993, ''the U.S. auto industry was a major force in the creation of new jobs for many years, with employment peaking in 1978 at more than one million workers. But

since then employment has slid and the industry is no longer a source of new jobs.'' The *Free Press* went on to point out that auto industry employment in 1992 was 812,200 jobs, of which a little over 413,000 were hourly positions. This was in part a result of increasing productivity per worker at the Big Three manufacturing plants—one of the primary reasons for the dramatic upswing in fortunes for GM, Ford, and Chrysler in the early 1990s. According to the U.S. Department of Commerce and the Federal Reserve Bank of Chicago, GM, Ford, and Chrysler have all, from 1980 to 1991, cut by at least one-third the number of worker hours required to assemble a vehicle.

According to the U.S. Department of Labor's Bureau of Labor Statistics, employment by producers of complete cars and trucks increased 4 percent in 1995, reaching a total of 355,000 workers. Auto workers were among the most productive and highest paid production workers in the country. In May 1996, their average weekly earnings totaled $980—85 percent greater than the $529 average earned by all U.S. manufacturing production workers.

GM, Ford, and Chrysler provided three-fourths of the industry's total direct employment. Their payrolls listed a total of 721,000 employees in the United States in 1995, compared with 632,000 in 1992. By the year 2003, a University of Michigan study estimated that the Big Three would need to hire at least 168,000 employees for their U.S. operations.

The U.S. Bureau of Labor Statistics also reveled that at the end of 1995, the seven Japanese affiliates' total payroll was 40,700—an increase of 22 percent over 1992's level of 33,200. Expansion within their existing facilities, plus the addition of new factories, was expected to add several thousand more workers over the next several years to the employment roles of the Japanese affiliates. In 1998, for example, Toyota was expected to assemble a light truck in a $700 million plant in Indiana. The facility would have an annual capacity of 100,000 vehicles and was expected to hire 1,300 Americans. Other foreign car makers who were establishing new plants in the United States, like Benz's massive facility in Alabama, were expected to hire many Americans by the turn of the century.

Unions in the Automotive Industry. The United Auto Workers (UAW) union represents many employees within the automotive industry. UAW membership peaked in 1979 with 1.5 million members and fell to 900,000 members in 1993. The largest employer of UAW members was General Motors. Organization of auto workers began in the post-Depression era. During the Depression, growing labor unrest resulted as companies cut workers' pay, shortened work weeks, fired people irrespective of their seniority, and rehired only younger workers. Workers also expressed job dissatisfaction as companies increased the pressure to speed productivity. In 1933 Congress passed the National Industrial Recovery Act, which gave labor the right to organize and bargain collectively. Although the act was declared unconstitutional in 1935, the rights to bargain collectively and insure union elections were again secured when Congress passed the Wagner-Connery Act (Wagner Act), establishing the National Labor Relations Board.

In 1936, the American Federation of Labor (AFL) granted the United Automobile Workers of America its charter. The union later became the United Automobile, Aerospace and Agricultural Implement Workers (UAW) and was affiliated with the Committee for Industrial Organizations (CIO). Ford was the last of the major auto producers to bargain with the UAW. Elections were held at the Ford Rouge plant in 1941 following years of conflict, sometimes violent, between union organizers and anti-union forces. Union activity increased following World War II as auto production resumed. Workers joined together to maintain pay levels achieved during the war. Walter Reuther, the UAW's leader, fought for wage packages with a cost of living index and pension plans.

Current Contracts. The *Monthly Labor Review* observed in 1994 that "after picking Ford Motor Co. as its settlement target for the 1993 round of auto negotiations, the United Automobile Workers appeared about to sign a 6-year contract with the automaker that would guarantee fully paid health care coverage and job and income security to current employees in return for more flexible work rules and a lower starting rate for new hires. . . .but the agreement unraveled, apparently because the union believed that it would be too costly in terms of plant closings and consolidations." The ensuing settlement broke little new ground, basically preserving existing contract terms.

In the eyes of some observers, the parties lost an opportunity to restructure labor costs in the industry and become more competitive with Japanese automakers and their American transplants. Instead, Ford and the UAW reached agreement on a three year deal that "preserved employees' health care coverage and job and income security arrangements, improved employees' pension benefits, strengthened the union's position on subcontracting work, and gave the company more advantageous provisions regarding new hires." Subsequent settlements with Chrysler and General Motors followed the same basic pattern as the one consummated with Ford.

AMERICA AND THE WORLD

In 1991 the U.S. Department of Commerce estimated that 48.5 million motor vehicles were produced worldwide, an indication of its long time presence in all corners of the world. Indeed, the automobile industry, almost from its inception, has been international in scope. Ford began assembly in Britain in 1911 and by 1914 was the largest British producer. General Motors established an export company in 1911 to sell the company's products overseas. Following World War I, Ford built assembly plants in Denmark, France, Germany, Italy, Spain, and Sweden. General Motors purchased existing corporations such as Vauxhall in Britain and Opel in Germany. Ford and General Motors entered the Japanese market in 1925 and 1927 respectively. And Chrysler established Chrysler de Mexico in 1938 to import and distribute Chrysler products.

The first foreign companies to sell products in the United States offered luxury and sport models such as Rolls-Royce, Mercedes, Jaguar, and Porsche. In 1950, import sales totaled less than half percent of total car sales. The first foreign car to penetrate the mainstream market with a small family car was the Volkswagen Beetle. By 1968, Volkswagen accounted for 62 percent of all imports, but the German manufacturer began losing ground to Japanese producers.

At the same time, Japanese manufacturers were battling difficult exchange rates in their efforts to sell cars and trucks in America. The result was a decreased U.S. market share for Japanese companies in the early 1990s. "In 1993, for the second straight year, their share of the U.S. market for cars and light trucks fell—this time to 23.2 percent, off 2.6 points since 1991," noted *Business Week*. "Beleaguered by the strong yen and deep slumps in the Japanese and European auto markets, Japan's car companies are sounding ever more content to back off the market-share race." Japanese manufacturers have nonetheless attempted to address the mid-1990s environment, cut into overhead costs, introduce new models in areas of traditional weakness such as minivans, and shift production increasingly to facilities in America, where production costs are lower.

Many Japanese firms established production facilities in the United States. Honda, Toyota, Nissan, Mazda, Mitsubishi, and Subaru-Isuzu all built plants in the United States during the 1980s. By 1992, these "transplant" facilities were producing 1.6 million units annually—about 17 percent of the total light vehicle output. Approximately 200,000 units were produced under contract for the Big Three manufacturers. According to one estimate, by 1993 one-half of the sales of Japanese vehicles in the United States would

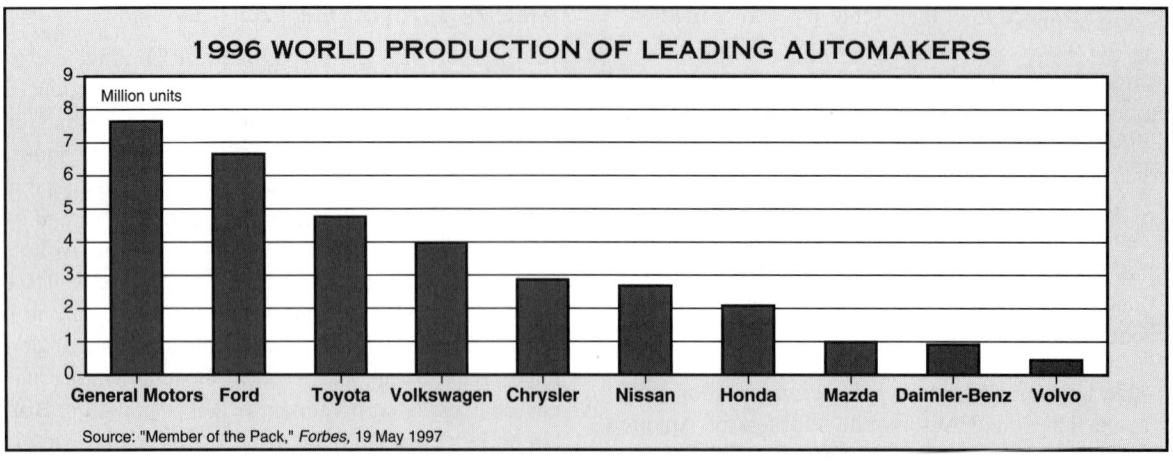

1996 WORLD PRODUCTION OF LEADING AUTOMAKERS

Million units

General Motors Ford Toyota Volkswagen Chrysler Nissan Honda Mazda Daimler-Benz Volvo

Source: "Member of the Pack," *Forbes,* 19 May 1997

be units assembled in the United States. Forecasters predicted that foreign capacity on U.S. soil would increase to 2.4 million cars and light trucks before the decade's end. Additional investments were expected to be made by Honda, Nissan, Toyota, Suzuki, and the South Korean manufacturer, Hyundai. In addition, BMW announced its intention to establish a plant in South Carolina with the ability to produce 75,000 units per year beginning in 1995. Other companies expected to add production in either the United States or Mexico were Volkswagen and Mercedes-Benz.

The proliferation of foreign car manufacturing on U.S. soil led to increased concern regarding distinctions between domestic and foreign built automobiles. In response, the U.S. Congress passed the American Automobile Labeling Law. The legislation, scheduled to go into effect on October 1, 1994, required new vehicle stickers to contain information relating to the automobile's domestic content.

In early 1993 Japan was the world's top producer of automobiles, accounting for 34.7 percent of the units sold worldwide. The United States was second in the world with 33.6 percent, followed by Western Europe with 25.4 percent.

United States-Japan Automotive Framework Agreement. In August 1995 the United States-Japan Automotive Framework Agreement came into being. This agreement, which culminated two years of intensive negotiations, was crafted to increase U.S. and other foreign access to the Japanese motor vehicle and parts market. According to the U.S. Department of Commerce, the three main goals of the Agreement were: improved access to Japan's motor vehicle distribution system; increased purchases of U.S. parts by Japanese auto-makers; and deregulation of Japan's $60 billion replacement parts market.

As a result of this agreement, sales of Big Three vehicles in Japan were up 40 percent in the first half of 1996, according to the U.S. Department of Commerce. In August 1996, *The Detroit News* reported that one year after the Agreement was signed, Big Three vehicle sales in Japan were still short of the goal. Besides political reasons, this was attributed to the stagnant Japanese auto market and a yen that had slid 18 percent during 1996.

NAFTA. Within the U.S. market, analysts expected increased exports for the revitalized domestic producers, in part because of the passage of the North American Free Trade Agreement (NAFTA), which in its first few months pushed a dramatic surge in U.S. car sales to Mexico. In keeping with the Clinton Administration's policy to open foreign markets for the U.S. automotive industry, NAFTA was signed in 1993 and implemented on January 1, 1994. Increased market access for U.S. automotive products in Mexico was imperative, especially since trade in motor vehicles was essentially one way—from Mexico into the United States. In the years since the implementation of NAFTA, the U.S. automotive industry already experienced significant benefits. In 1994, U.S. passenger car and light truck exports tripled pre-NAFTA levels. In 1995, U.S. exports of motor vehicles were over twice their pre-NAFTA levels, despite the severe economic crisis in Mexico.

Korea's Memorandum of Understanding. In 1993, the U.S. automotive industry requested assistance from the Clinton Administration to open the Korean auto market to U.S. automobiles. In September 1995, the Korean government signed a Memorandum of Understanding (MOU) with the United States, under which it explicitly committed to increase access for U.S. and other foreign passenger vehicles. Total foreign auto sales were expected to reach 13,000 in 1996—1 percent of the Korean market, compared with

.10 percent previously. Sales of U.S. automobiles were expected to account for approximately 40 percent of the foreign total.

According to *The Detroit News,* Korean car manufacturers were in turn increasing their presence in the U.S. market. Following Hyundai's entrance, Kia was the other car company to lead a wave of Korean car makers including Daewoo Motor, which had plans to enter the U. S. market in the fall of 1997, Samsung Group which was just entering the auto manufacturing arena and had plans to enter the U.S. market by the turn of the century, and Ssang Yong Business Group, parent of Ssang Yong Motor which had plans to enter the U.S. market in 1998 with a sports utility vehicle.

GATT. In 1994, the Clinton Administration passed the Uruguay Round of the General Agreement on Tariffs and Trade (GATT). According to the U.S. Department of Commerce, the Agreement greatly enhanced the export potential of the U.S. automotive industry by improving access to both major and developing markets by achieving a 27 percent reduction in the motor vehicle tariffs of major markets, a 58 percent reduction in the automotive parts tariffs of major markets, and the ''binding'' of automotive tariffs in many developing countries—including Brazil, Argentina, India, and Indonesia. The U.S. automotive industry experienced positive export results since the January 1995 implementation of the Uruguay Round, especially with developing markets. According to the U.S. Department of Commerce, motor vehicle exports to Malaysia grew 52 percent to $6.5 million, and shipments to Brazil jumped by 50 percent to $429 million. U.S. automotive parts exports to these countries grew by 61 and 40 percent, respectively.

TransAtlantic Business Dialogue (TABD). In December 1995, the Clinton Administration and the EU announced the formation of a New Transatlantic Agenda. The auto industry was one of the priority sectors for this effort because U.S. automotive exports were expected to grow significantly through harmonization of standards. In the first Transatlantic Automotive Industry Conference on International Regulatory Harmonization— the first time that harmonization was addressed by the U.S. and EU at such a high political and industry level. The two industries jointly proposed actions the U.S. Government and the EU Commission should take to remove global trade barriers in the automotive industry including: international harmonization of motor vehicle safety and environmental regulations; the intergovernmental regulatory process necessary to achieve such harmonization; and coordination of vehicle safety and environmental research.

RESEARCH AND TECHNOLOGY

In the fierce competitive environment of the international automotive industry, any edge in design, engineering, or technology assumes tremendous importance and can result in shifts of market share worth millions of dollars. Timely research and swift technological adaptation are vital in a wide array of automotive niche markets. A typical example of this dynamic can be seen through an examination of the diesel pickup truck market. Until recently, Ford enjoyed a huge edge in market share in diesel pickups— approximately 12 percent of the total sales of pickups in the United States. Ford's position, however, has fallen from a commanding 75 percent stake to around 40 percent by the beginning of 1994. As the *Detroit Free Press* noted, ''Ford owned the market for most of the '80s. General Motors had developed a lousy reputation for diesel engines when it tried to convert gasoline engines into diesels for passenger cars during the late '70s. And Chrysler only became a player in the diesel market in 1987 when it began buying diesel engines from Cummins. With the much-revered Cummins engine under the hood, Dodge quickly began taking diesel market share from Ford. Its penetration peaked at 36 percent in 1991, just as GM came back with a new turbocharged 6.5-liter engine for its diesel trucks. . . . Now Ford, having stood by while its lead all but evaporated, is out with the latest advancement, a massive 7.3-liter turbocharged, direct-injection diesel from Navistar that gives it a competitive edge in horsepower, hauling and fuel economy.'' Thus the search for the competitive advantage in technology and design remains a central bulwark of the industry mentality.

As the automotive industry entered the 1990s, private industrial research and government funded research focused on improving fuel efficiency, developing alternative fuels, reducing vehicle emissions, developing environmentally friendly manufacturing processes, and recycling junked vehicles. Alternative fuels, such as ethanol and methanol mixtures, liquid natural gas (LNG), and liquid petroleum gas (LPG) were under investigation as clean burning energy sources. Researchers were also working on developing a viable electric car.

The U.S. Advanced Battery Consortium (USABC) was developed by the Big Three and the U.S. Department of Energy to work on new battery technology. Battery types other than conventional lead acid batteries included nickel cadmium, sodium sulfur, zinc air, nickel hydride, lithium polymer, and hydrogen fuel cells. Nickel cadmium batteries were preferred by Japanese manufacturers, although some critics claimed they were unsuited for mass production because cadmium was a scarce mineral and highly toxic.

Solar Car Corporation in Melbourne, Florida was one of the country's pioneering organizations in the construction of hybrid solar/electric vehicles. Hybrid vehicles contained a small auxiliary engine powered by gasoline or other alternative fuel to assist in recharging batteries or extending a vehicle's range. Solar panels helped supplement the battery and extend its life from two to three years to five to six years. According to company statements, its electric vehicles were capable of attaining top speeds of 75 miles per hour and able to travel 50 to 80 miles before recharging.

Another type of alternate vehicle under development by the automotive industry was fueled by natural gas. According to the American Gas Association, an estimated 30,000 natural gas vehicles (NGVs) were operating in the United States in 1993. Some projections anticipated as many as 500,000 NGVs in the United States by the year 2000. In 1993 an estimated 700,000 were in use worldwide. Natural gas proponents cite several advantages the fuel holds over conventional gasoline—it costs 25 to 30 percent less than gasoline, produces 90 percent less carbon monoxide and 50 percent less hydrocarbons, and spurs increased engine efficiency. In addition, because of deep domestic reserves, natural gas holds the potential to help the United States reduce its dependance on imported oil.

Researchers within the automotive industry were also working on creating safer ways to manage traffic. To help further the advancement of traffic management, reduce traffic congestion, and lessen the number of accidents in congested urban regions, Congress appropriated $660 million to be spent during fiscal years 1992 through 1997 on a study of Intelligent Vehicle Highway Systems (IVHS). Potential IVHS technologies included radar, microwave, ultrasonics, and video. Its aim was to assist with driver tasks such as visibility and navigational assistance. Necessary ingredients included anti-lock brakes, better traction control, improved steering responses, refined suspension systems, and the ability to monitor tire pressure.

The other alternate means of energy being researched was electricity. Besides the Big Three researching the electric car, many small private companies were also involved in the development of these cars. According to *Forbes* magazine, 10 percent of all new cars sold in California by the year 2003 must be zero emmission vehicles, which means electric. Thus, in seven years Californians alone were supposed to be buying at least 200,000 cars annually.

PNGV. Partnership for a New Generation of Vehicles (PNGV) was established in September 1993 to develop technologies for a new generation of affordable, mid-size passenger vehicles that would travel the equivalent of 80 miles per gallon—three times greater than the average achieved in 1994— while at the same time producing much lower emissions. PNGV was coordinated by the Commerce Department, from the government side, and on the industry side, it was coordinated by USCAR, the pre-competitive research venture established by Chrysler, Ford, and General Motors. In addition, PNGV included research from over 350 automotive suppliers and universities. Research to develop new power plant, drive train, and chassis technologies were being studied, along with more economically efficient and environmentally safe ways of employing the manufacturing processes. According to the U.S. Department of Commerce, by the year 2000 each car company would have a PNGV concept car, followed by PNGV production prototypes in 2003.

FURTHER READING

"'95: Flat, But Never Dull." *Automotive Industries,* October 1995.

"The Big Three Are Learning to Hold a Lead." *Business Week,* 26 April 1993.

"The Big Three: Hearty Cheers In Detroit As Japan Renews Earlier Goals." *New York Times,* 29 June 1995.

1992 Chrysler Corporation Report to Shareholders. Highland Park, MI: Chrysler Corporation, 1993.

Adler, Alan L. "Competitive Torque." *Detroit Free Press,* 4 April 1994.

Armstrong, Larry, Kathleen Kerwin, and Bill Spindle. "Trying to Rev Up." *Business Week,* 24 January 1994.

Bolan, Nelson. *How Detroit Changed History.* Lawrenceville, VA: Brunswick, 1987.

Brady, Howard. "Company Profile: Solar Car Corporation." *Brevard Technical Journal,* March 1993.

"Chrysler Corporation Fact Sheet." Highland Park: Chrysler Corporation, 9 February 1993.

"Chrysler Sees Record U.S. Auto Sales by 1996." *New York Times,* 16 July 1993.

Cimini, Michael H., Susan L. Behrmann, and Eric M. Johnson. "Labor-Management Bargaining in 1993." *Monthly Labor Review,* January 1994.

Dammann, George H. *Seventy Years of Chrysler.* Sarasota, FL: Crestline Publishing, 1974.

Elridge, Earl. "Korean Automakers Ready Bigger Plans for U.S. Sales." *The Detroit News,* 24 July 1996.

Gates, Max. "Labeling Law Comes at a Cost." *Automotive News,* 21 December 1992.

Gates, Max, and Lindsay Chappell. "MVMA Kicks Out Honda's U.S. Arm." *Automotive News,* 30 November 1992.

General Motors Annual Report 1992. Detroit: General Motors Corporation, 1993.

General Motors Annual Report Form 10K for Year Ended December 31, 1992. Detroit: General Motors, 1993.

General Motors: The First 75 Years of Transportation Products. Princeton, NJ: General Motors Corporation, 1983.

Hill, Steve. "Reincarnation: Recycling in the Automotive Industry." *Materials World,* October 1996.

"How Federal Officials Ignored Auto Safety." *Consumer's Research,* April 1992.

Langworth, Richard M. *The Complete History of Ford Motor Company.* New York: Beekman House, 1987.

Lienert, Anita. "Mobility Changed Cities, Lifestyles; It Could Soon Alter World of Work." *The Detroit News,* 12 June 1996.

Lubove, Seth. "A car that Runs on Gravy." *Forbes,* 15 July 1996.

Ludel, Moses. "The Jeep Legend Lives!" *Off-Road,* August 1992.

Matthews, Harry W., Jr. "100 Year Dash." *Automotive News,* 3 May 1992.

McCann, Hugh, and David C. Smith. "NGV's: Natural Gas Nears Lead in Alternate Fuel Race." *WARD's Auto World,* June 1993.

McElroy, John. "The Lesson of '78." *Automotive Industries,* May 1994.

Muller, Joann. "Ford Makes $3-Billion Turnaround." *Detroit Free Press,* 10 February 1994.

"The New Car Market's Lost Generation: Auto Industry Struggles to Satisfy the Tastes of First-Time Buyers on a Budget." *New York Times,* 15 August 1996.

"One Year after Agreement, Big Three Vehicle Sales in Japan Still Short of Goal." *The Detroit News,* 6 August 1996.

Rae, John B. *The American Automobile Industry.* Boston: Twayne Publishers, 1984.

Sears, Stephen W. *The Automobile in America.* New York: American Heritage Publishing, 1977.

Sherman, Don. "Blink of an Eye." *Motor Trend,* May 1993.

Simanaitis, Dennis. "Electric Vehicles." *Road & Track,* May 1992.

Sorge, Marjorie. "UAW Walks a Tightrope between Old and New Jobs." *WARD's Auto World,* June 1993.

Swan, Tony. "Jeep Thrills." *Popular Mechanics,* January 1991.

Taylor, Alex. "Why Electric Cars Make No Sense." *Fortune,* 26 July 1993.

———, "U.S. Automakers Go Flat Out." *Fortune,* 21 February 1994.

U.S. Census Bureau. *1987 Census of Manufactures.* Washington: GPO, 1990.

U.S. Department of Commerce. "Motor Vehicles." *U.S. Global Trade Outlook: 1995-2000.* Washington: GPO, 1995.

U.S. Department of Commerce. "The Road Ahead." Office of Automotive Affairs. Washington: GPO, February 1997.

U.S. Department of Commerce. "U.S. Automotive Industry Sector Report." Office of Automotive Affairs. Washington: GPO, 17 September 1996.

U.S. Department of Commerce *U.S. Industrial Outlook 1993.* Washington: GPO, 1993.

Ward's Automotive Yearbook. Detroit: Ward's Communications, 1993.

Woodruff, David. "The Minivan Free-For-All." *Business Week,* 26 July 1993.

Woods, Wilto. "The World's Top Automakers Change Lanes." *Fortune,* 4 October 1993.

Wysner, John. *Rays of Hope . . . A Critical (and Hopeful) Cultural History of the American Automotive Business.* Los Angeles: Authors Unlimited, 1991.

—Karen Bellenir, updated by Visi Tilak

SIC 3713

TRUCK AND BUS BODIES

This industry is comprised of establishments primarily involved in the manufacture of truck and bus bodies. Some establishments also provide complete vehicles by assembling the bodies they make onto purchased chassis. Establishments engaged in the manufacture of vehicle chassis are classified in **SIC 3711: Motor Vehicles and Passenger Car Bodies.** Establishments primarily engaged in the manufacture of truck trailers and demountable cargo containers are classified in **SIC 3715: Truck Trailers.**

Other related motor vehicle classifications include establishments primarily engaged in the assembly of motor homes on purchased chassis **SIC 3716: Motor Homes,** stamped body parts for trucks and buses **SIC 3465: Automotive Stampings,** cabs for agricultural tractors **SIC 3523: Farm Machinery and Equipment,** cabs for industrial tractors **SIC 3537: Industrial Trucks, Tractors, Trailers, and Stackers,** and cabs for off-highway construction tractors **SIC 3531: Construction Machinery and Equipment.**

INDUSTRY SNAPSHOT

The truck and bus bodies industry had a boom in 1994 driven by the growing U.S. economy and an aging fleet. However, in 1996 the industry had a slump. Truck sales tended to be volatile because they were subject to cyclical changes in the overall economy. The nation's industrial sector created the largest portion of freight tonnage, and changes in the volume of industrial freight shipments led to parallel shifts in total truck sales. Interest rates and fuel costs also impacted the industry.

Government forecasters and industry watchers predicted continued expansion during the mid-1990s. Although initial orders showed faster growth within the heavy duty truck segment, some analysts expected long term demand for medium duty trucks to outpace the heavier vehicles. Reasons cited included a growing number of service industries and ''just-in-time'' inventory practices. Service industries typically required smaller vehicles than manufacturing industries, and ''just-in-time'' inventory practices required smaller, more frequent deliveries, making the lighter trucks more economical.

BACKGROUND AND DEVELOPMENT

Established guidelines in the United States categorized on-road trucks and buses into one of eight classes according to their gross vehicle weight. As a group, Classes 1 through 3 were referred to as light duty trucks; Classes 4 through 7 were referred to as medium duty trucks; and Class 8 vehicles were referred to as heavy duty trucks. Light duty trucks included personal pickups, minivans, and sport/utility vehicles. Class 1 vehicles were those weighing up to 6,000 pounds; Class 2 vehicles weighed between 6,001 and 10,000 pounds; and Class 3 vehicles weighed between 10,001 and 14,000 pounds. Medium duty trucks included service or local delivery vehicles, some types of construction vehicles, school buses, and refuse collection vehicles. Class 4 vehicles weighed between 14,001 and 16,000 pounds; Class 5 vehicles weighed between 16,001 and 19,500 pounds; Class 6 vehicles weighed between 19,501 and 26,000 pounds; and Class 7 vehicles weighed between 26,001 and 33,000 pounds.

Purchasers of medium duty trucks tended to be small to medium sized businesses. Heavy duty trucks, listed as Class 8, were the largest type of on-road vehicle sold in the United States. Class 8 vehicles weighed more than 33,000 pounds and were primarily purchased by large industrial manufacturers and interstate fleet operators.

Trucks and buses were made up of three primary parts—the chassis, the body, and the engine. The chassis contained the wheels, axles, and fuel tank, as well as all the structural elements necessary to provide sup-

port to the body and engine. Manufacturers often used one single chassis style with many different body types.

Truck and bus body makers provided a variety of body styles to meet different hauling requirements. Van bodies were used to transport enclosed cargo, and types of vans varied. For example, refrigerated vans were air tight, while livestock vans featured vents to allow for air flow. Tank bodies were used to transport liquids. Hoppers were a special type of tank used to carry chemicals, salt, wheat, and cement. Flat bed truck bodies were designed to carry large, heavy loads such as machinery, steel beams, and telephone poles.

Other factors also distinguished different types of trucks. ''Straight'' or ''rigid'' trucks were mounted on a single chassis, with their cab and load areas forming one unit. ''Semi'' or ''tractor trailer'' trucks were mounted on two chassis, with their cab and load areas forming two separate units. The units were attached with a device located behind the cab on the tractor called a ''fifth wheel.''

Straight trucks, semi-trucks, and buses were available in two basic configurations termed ''conventional'' and ''cab-over.'' In conventional designs, the vehicle's engine was located under a traditional hood in front of the driver cab. In cab-over designs, the driver cab was mounted directly over the engine. The cab-over design permitted manufacturers to make shorter cabs. In areas where total vehicle length was limited by law, cab-over tractors permitted drivers to pull longer cargo trailers.

Another type of truck designation, based on numerical references, was used to describe how many wheels a vehicle possessed and how many of its wheels were powered by the engine. For example, a 4 x 2 truck was one with four wheels, two of which were drive wheels. A 4 x 4 vehicle had four wheels and all four were drive wheels. A 6 x 4 truck had a total of six wheels and four of them were drive wheels.

In the United States, many truck engines differed from automobile engines because they ran on diesel fuel rather than gasoline. Diesel engines, invented by Rudolf Diesel in 1897, were a type of internal combustion engine powered by the controlled explosion of fuel sprayed into a cylinder under pressure. Diesel engine design was simpler than gasoline engine design and required no spark plug. Diesel fuel also cost less than gasoline and did not burn as readily if spilled. Diesel engines, however, were more expensive to construct because they required heavier gears to accommodate a more powerful stroke. Because diesel engines were especially suited for heavy duty hauling and long distance running, they gained popularity in cartage vehicles in the United States.

Trucks developed in response to the need to transport goods. John B. Rae, automotive historian and author of *The American Automobile Industry,* wrote, "At the beginning of the nineteenth century the cost of moving goods thirty miles inland by road in the United States was as great as the cost of carrying the same goods across the Atlantic." Although steam locomotives helped provide alternatives to animal power during the mid- and late 1800s, railroads could not offer "door-to-door" service.

As the emerging automotive industry began to supply people with self propelled vehicles for personal transportation, enterprising innovators began to apply the technology toward the development of commercial vehicles. The popular Model T chassis, introduced in 1908, found itself used in a variety of applications. Ford Motor Company offered it as an Ice Cream truck, an urban delivery truck, and a farm vehicle.

One of the first types of specialty trucks was the twin boom wrecker, designed by Ernest Holmes in 1914. The truck's twin booms featured cables powered by the vehicle's engine. One cable could be deployed to rescue or lift a disabled vehicle; the other cable could be hooked to a tree to provide additional support. Other truck innovations made during the early decades of the twentieth century included four wheel drive, four wheel steering, and an improved clutch system.

With the coming of World War I, unfavorable front line driving conditions compelled truck designers to make other improvements and refinements. One popular truck developed during the war era was the Mack AC. The Mack AC earned itself the nickname "Bulldog" because of its blunt nose and reputation for toughness. To help it perform in mud, the Bulldog's engine was connected to the vehicle's rear wheels with a drive train, and the truck's solid rubber tires were puncture proof. The Mack Truck Company honored the Bulldog by incorporating the image of a bulldog in the organization's official logo.

During the period between World War I and World War II, truck makers turned increasingly to pneumatic tires. Pneumatic tires were filled with air and provided a smoother ride. Truck designers made larger vehicles capable of carrying heavier loads, making additional wheels necessary to distribute their weight more evenly and avoid damaging tires and road surfaces.

During the 1920s, semi-truck designs were introduced. Semi-trucks featured a tractor front end, which was used to pull a trailer section behind. Semi-trucks were better able to turn tight corners, and they replaced large, rigid, single section trucks. In addition to the improved maneuverability, semi construction provided for more efficient tractor use. Because the trailer could be detached for cargo loading and unloading, the tractor was freed for other tasks. The 1920s also saw the introduction of modern motor buses. In 1923, two brothers, Frank P. and William B. Fageol, organized the Twin Coach Company. Twin Motor Coach buses were the first to offer underneath engines.

By 1930, the number of trucks on American roads had grown to 3.6 million, up from 1.1 million in 1920. An estimated 1 in 4 were farm owned and the era saw vast improvements in farm to market roadways. Although many pioneering truck manufacturers were also involved in making automobiles, the different economies of scale involved in producing the two types of vehicles resulted in a different mix of major manufacturers. Passenger car makers relied on capital intensive mass production technology. This led to industry consolidation and the emergence of the Big Three automobile companies—Ford, Chrysler, and General Motors. Truck makers, however, built a variety of vehicles, each type customized to perform a special task. As a result, a greater number of smaller companies were able to compete. During the 1930s the nation's principle truck manufacturers were the White Motor Company, Mack International, Autocar Company, and International Harvester.

During World War II, auto makers and truck makers focused their energies on providing military vehicles. Special task trucks, missile carriers, troop transports, and cargo haulers were all necessary to the war effort. Manufacturers, working under government contract, intensified research and development projects aimed at building better, more reliable trucks. Following the war, the knowledge gained was transferred to civilian undertakings, and the 1950s saw tremendous expansion in the trucking industry.

Improvements in the nation's highway system also played a role. In 1956, Congress passed the Interstate Highway Act, which authorized the construction of 41,000 miles of interstate highways and offered to fund 90 percent of the project with money from the Highway Trust Fund. As the nation's infrastructure improved, long distance trucking became more feasible. Prior to the 1950s most of the nation's long distance freight shipments were made by rail, and trucks were used primarily to provide local delivery to and from rail stations. Unloading and reloading cargo for rail to truck transfers increased the cost of moving goods and provided an economic incentive for shippers to switch to long distance, over the road transport.

The percentage of freight deliveries made by truck increased from about 17 percent of all deliveries in 1950 to almost 25 percent by the end of the decade.

Another national phenomenon, suburban growth, increased the importance of trucks to American life. Decentralized, suburban lifestyles required the kind of flexible freight transport trucks provided. Trucks made suburban development possible, and suburban development increased the demand for trucks. Trucks served the construction industry as it built suburbs; trucks carried household possessions as families moved into the suburbs. Trucks also served the businesses that moved from the central city to outlying areas.

During the 1960s and 1970s the increased presence of large trucks on American roads led to increased concern about their safety. Semi-trucks were notorious for their tendency to jackknife under adverse braking conditions. When the trailer's wheels locked during breaking, it pushed the trailer forward causing the vehicle's two parts to bend into a jackknife position and skid. To help prevent jackknifing, anti-lock brake systems were investigated. The Federal Motor Vehicle Safety Standard 121, enacted in 1975, set performance standards for vehicles with air brakes and mandated the use of anti-lock braking systems through its stipulation of minimum stopping distances. Unfortunately, available technology was not able to meet the standard.

Anti-lock brakes worked by modulating the amount of air applied to the brakes. When a sensor indicated that a wheel was in danger of locking, it applied air pressure in a pulsing manner. The pulsing pressure enabled the wheel to keep rolling and prevented it from skidding. During the 1970s, however, available computer technology was too slow to immediately interpret sensor input. The resulting time lag caused brake failure. In April 1978, the 9th U.S. Circuit Court of Appeals struck down the "no-lock" and minimum stopping distance requirements.

The 1980s brought renewed efforts at making trucks safer. A study done by AAA of Michigan found that in car-truck accidents, motorists sustained a higher percentage of fatalities because trucks were becoming longer, wider, and heavier, while cars were getting smaller and lighter. Researchers investigated ways of preventing small vehicles from underriding trucks during crashes. Congress mandated a study of truck brake systems and legislators enacted regulations establishing national standards for licensing truck drivers and sharing driver information among the 50 states.

According to figures reported by the U.S. Department of Commerce, **SIC 3713: Truck and Bus Bod-**ies shipped products valued at $4.6 billion in 1987. Of this total, $4.2 billion represented products considered primary to the industry. Secondary products were valued at $184.7 million, and $222.9 million represented miscellaneous transactions. These figures yielded a specialization ratio of 96 percent, an increase from the 93 percent reported in 1982.

Medium and heavy duty truck makers marked their most productive year in 1988 when the industry sold 334,000 units. Sales tumbled in subsequent years, however. In 1991, heavy duty truck makers recorded their worst year since 1983. An improving national economy helped sales begin to rebound in 1992. During that year, combined heavy duty and medium duty truck sales rose 11 percent over 1991, reaching 246,000 units.

During the late 1980s and early 1990s, truck manufacturers suffered the effects of a nationwide economic slow down. In 1992, however, sales and orders began to show improvement. According to the *1993 Ward's Automotive Yearbook,* overall truck sales in 1992 were 12.8 percent higher than those for 1991. Medium duty trucks in Classes 4 through 7 posted a 6.5 percent gain, and heavy-duty Class 8 truck sales increased 20.6 percent.

The recovery extended into 1993. In January 1993, Class 8 sales were 44.7 percent higher than those for January 1992. Production continued to be high during the early months of the year, and industry watchers estimated that Class 8 factory sales would hit 160,000 by the year's end. Although increases in medium duty truck sales lagged behind heavy duty sales in the early months of 1993, the medium duty segment began to catch up during the middle of the year.

According to a report in *Automotive News,* the truck market was expected to continue improving through 1994. The rebound was attributed to a better economic climate and the effect of an aging national truck fleet. Another factor bolstering expectations among truck makers was a government announcement of plans to spend $15 billion to upgrade the nation's infrastructure. Planners predicted an increased demand for vehicles such as dumpers, haulers, and mixers needed to construct and repair road surfaces.

Within the motor coach segment of the industry, manufacturers placed an ever increasing emphasis on luxury. Motor coaches offered amenities such as VCR systems, kitchens, and larger bathroom facilities. Buses were also available in a wide variety of vehicle sizes—ranging from small 20 seat mini buses to large vehicles capable of seating 76 passengers.

One segment of the industry unique to Canada and the United States was the manufacture of school buses for student transport. School bus models, however, because they were simpler and less expensive than other types of buses, were a common export item. In developing countries such as Costa Rica, Nicaragua, Columbia, Venezuela, and Bolivia, they were used to provide community transportation.

Safety issues continued to be a primary concern within the industry. The 1990s brought a newly designed anti-lock braking system based on digital computer technology. Advanced computer capabilities helped anti-lock brakes overcome some of the problems associated with earlier systems. The National Highway Traffic Safety Administration (NHTSA) began studying the new anti-lock brake systems and was expected to complete its tests by June of 1994. New regulations were expected to go into effect during 1996.

Underride regulations were also forthcoming. In an effort to reduce traffic fatalities resulting from cars striking the rear ends of trucks and truck trailers, NHTSA was considering mandating design modifications. One possible future alteration was a change in bumper heights. Some researchers argued that if collisions occurred at the car's frame elevation, occupants would be better protected by the controlled crush design features of the automobile.

In environmental matters, truck makers were preparing to meet newer, more stringent emission standards. Many medium and heavy duty trucks burned diesel fuel. Diesel exhaust contained pollutants such as nitrogen oxides, hydrocarbons, carbon monoxide, and particulate matter visible as black smoke. Between 1988 and 1991, emissions of nitrogen oxides had been cut by more than one-half. New emission standards were scheduled to begin in 1994 and 1998. The 1994 standards required that levels of particulates be cut by more than 50 percent; the 1998 standards required a further 25 percent cut in emissions of nitrogen oxide.

CURRENT CONDITIONS

According to the American Automobile Manufacturers Association in Detroit, all U.S. heavy truck makers set a monthly production record in June 1994—17,247 vehicles. According to the *Puget Sound Business Journal,* the key factor driving the industry upswing was the growing U.S. economy, which directly affected the need for transportation equipment to move parts and finished products. The other factors for the demand were the age of the truck fleets, which were about eight years old in 1993, relatively low interest

rates, and competition for trucking firms among customers.

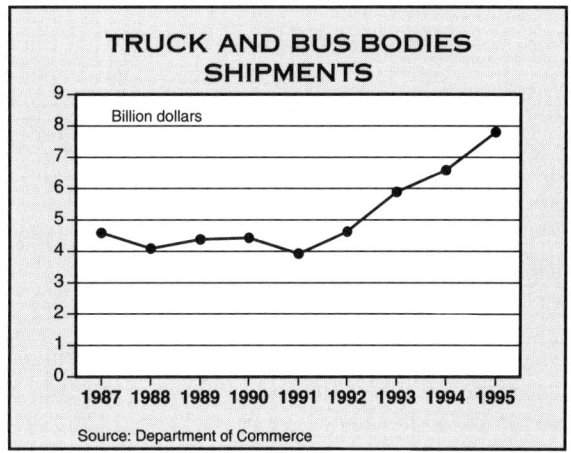

Another reason for the high demand was stated to be the federal government's deregulation of the trucking industry during the 1980's which heightened competition and forced weaker carriers out of business and caused most of the rest of the carriers to economize and delay truck purchases, says the *Oregonian.*

Analysts predicted that the Class 8 truck demand was expected to be robust through 1997. This proved to be wrong when the 1996 truck sales slumped 25 percent from 1995. According to *Forbes,* the business was in a serious recession; one of the key reasons was that freight sales were off, hence there was no rush to buy additional or even replace equipment. The other reason was that the average age of trucks—which was eight years—had been reduced to five because of the increased buying in the last few years, which meant that the truck fleet was fairly modern.

The truck makers were also under enormous pressure to improve productivity and efficiency and to become suppliers of high quality, low cost service. While trucking firms and carriers were struggling to attract drivers by providing creature comforts offered by new generation trucks, the truck manufacturers were also under pressure to provide amenities for drivers in their newer models to increase sales.

INDUSTRY LEADERS

Perhaps one of the best known names within the truck-making industry was Mack Trucks, Inc., which was the industry leader with a sales revenue of $22 billion. Headquartered in Allentown, Pennsylvania, Mack achieved popularity during World War I when its ''Bulldog'' truck was acclaimed for toughness, and the phrase ''built like a Mack Truck'' entered the

American lexicon. Mack built trucks in Classes 6, 7, and 8, but most of the company's total 1992 production of 13,375 units fell into the heavy duty segment where Mack held 10.1 percent of the market. In the worldwide market, Mack's heavy duty and medium duty diesel products were sold in more than 65 countries. Although Mack Trucks had a long history of truck making in the United States, the company was not U.S. owned. In 1979, the French Renault Vehicules Industriels SA began purchasing an interest in Mack. Renault's ownership totaled 46 percent in 1985, and in 1990 the French firm purchased the remainder, acquiring complete ownership.

Mack encountered serious financial difficulties during the late 1980s and early 1990s. In 1992, Mack posted its fourth consecutive year of losses. Cost cutting measures, employee reductions, and an emphasis on improved productivity were aimed at helping the company return to profitability. Between 1990 and 1993, the company reduced its work force by more than 25 percent, down to 4,800 employees. In May 1993, Mack announced plans to permanently close its assembly plant in Oakville, Ontario, idling an additional 250 workers. The Oakville plant made Mack's RD model, which was used for construction, ready mix, logging, and refuse applications. Mack planned to transfer its Oakville assembly to the company's plant in Macungie, Pennsylvania.

Navistar, located in Chicago, Illinois, was the ranked second in this industry with sales of $6.3 billion. Navistar's products encompassed many types of trucks in Classes 5 through 8. The company's diesel powered products were marketed under the "International" brand.

Navistar was also the nation's leading supplier of school bus chassis—a position it had held for more than two decades. Navistar sold bus chassis to body manufacturers who completed the buses and delivered them to end consumers. In addition, the company manufactured chassis for small capacity buses such as those operated to provide service to disabled students. American Transportation Corporation, maker of Ward brand school bus bodies, was partly owned by Navistar.

Navistar's roots can be traced back to the first decade of the twentieth century. The company, headquartered in Chicago, Illinois, was built on a foundation laid by International Harvester. International Harvester was founded in 1907 and played a leading role in the development of the industry through the early decades of the 1900s.

In the early 1990s, Navistar operated seven manufacturing and assembly plants in the United States and one in Canada. The eight plants provided the company with eight million square feet of assembly floor space. Navistar products were sold through 949 dealer and distribution outlets, and the company's customers included common carriers, private carriers, government and service organizations, the construction industry, the energy and petroleum industries, and student transportation services.

In 1992, according to figures published by *Ward's Automotive Yearbook,* Navistar produced 38,559 medium duty and 25,283 heavy duty trucks. Although its combined sales of medium duty and heavy duty trucks gave the company a total market share of 25.6 percent—the highest in the industry—Navistar held neither individual number one position. In the medium duty segment it placed second behind Ford Motor Company. In the heavy duty segment, Navistar occupied the number one position for 28 years, but in 1992 the company dropped to the number two position, and Freightliner climbed to number one.

Navistar faced serious financial difficulties during 1992. The company posted its third consecutive year of losses and found itself entangled in a legal challenge by the UAW over retiree health care costs. The company claimed that without an agreement to restructure the costs it would need to file for bankruptcy. In order to provide the cash necessary to fund post-retirement health care benefits and to provide money for working capital, Navistar filed a registration statement with the Securities and Exchange Commission on September 20, 1993, to offer 22 million shares of common stock. Through the stock offering the company planned to raise $500 million.

Nissan Motor Manufacturing Corporation, headquartered in Smyrna, Tennessee, was ranked third with sales of $2.9 billion. Other major participants in the industry included Grumman Aerospace with sales of $1.9 billion, and Kenworth Truck Co. with $1.0 billion in sales.

Kenworth was one of the nameplates of another major participant in the truck manufacturing industry, PACCAR, Inc. PACCAR, a domestic corporation with headquarters in Bellevue, Washington, offered two truck nameplates—Kenworth and Peterbilt. Combined, Kenworth and Peterbilt captured 20.6 percent of the Class 8 market in 1992. Their market share, however, represented a decrease from 21.4 percent in 1991 and 22 percent in 1990.

Another company with a long history in the American truck making industry was Oshkosh Truck Corporation. Oshkosh Truck focused on providing specialized trucks and transport equipment for specific market niches. The company's product line included heavy duty commercial trucks, military vehicles, buses, and walk-in delivery vans, as well as equipment for heavy snow removal and specialized refuse pickup.

Oshkosh Truck traced its beginnings back to two inventors, William R. Besserdich and Bernhard A. Mosling. Besserdich and Mosling held patents for innovations necessary to produce four wheel drive vehicles. One patent was for a method of transferring the engine's power to all four vehicle wheels using an automatic locking differential. A differential enabled the wheels on the axle to go around corners at different speeds. The other patent improved the front axle's steering and drive abilities. In 1915, Besserdich and Mosling approached several major car manufacturers but were turned away. They incorporated their own company, Wisconsin Duplex Auto Company, in 1917. Wisconsin Duplex later moved to Oshkosh and became Oshkosh Truck. The company's first vehicle, nicknamed "Old Betsy," had a three speed transmission, one ton hauling capacity, and weighed 3,280 pounds.

The Big Three. The Big Three U.S. car manufacturers also had subsidiaries manufacturing heavy trucks. One of the largest truck makers was Ford Truck Operations, a division of Ford Motor Company. Ford Truck, with headquarters in Dearborn, Michigan, was the number one producer of medium duty trucks and the number two producer in combined medium duty and heavy duty units. In 1992, Ford reported sales of 44,996 units in Classes 4 through 7 and sales of 13,798 units in Class 8 vehicles.

Another truck maker affiliated with one of the Big Three auto makers was GM Truck and Bus, a division of General Motors. GM's North American Truck Platforms subsidiary was ranked fourth in the industry with sales of $2.13 billion. GM participated in only the medium duty truck market, primarily within Classes 6 and 7. The company offered vehicles under the GMC and Chevrolet nameplates. GM's market share fell from 25 percent in 1990 to 23.5 percent in 1991. In 1992, GMC held 15.6 percent of the medium duty market, and Chevrolet held 8.5 percent, giving GM a combined market share of 24 percent.

GM's involvement in Class 8 trucks changed in 1988 with the establishment of Volvo GM Heavy Truck Corporation. Volvo GM was formed as a joint venture between GM and the heavy truck divisions of the Swedish firm Volvo—White Motor Trucks and Autocar. Although GM initially retained a 27 percent interest in Volvo GM, it later sold some of its interest

to Volvo, giving Volvo a total of 83 percent of the venture.

In 1992, Volvo GM held 6.2 percent of the total medium and heavy duty truck market. Within the medium duty segment, however, the company participated only in Class 7 vehicles. Its primary focus was in the Class 8 market, where it sold 14,641 units. Volvo GM sales within the United States accounted for approximately 33 percent of Volvo's medium and heavy duty truck deliveries worldwide.

WORK FORCE

According to government statistics, the truck and bus body industry employed 37,800 workers in 1987. This total represented a 35 percent increase over the employment of 28,100 reported in 1982 and an increase of 14 percent over 1986. Top states in employment were Pennsylvania, Indiana, Ohio, and California. Single establishment companies with 20 or fewer employees accounted for 14 percent of shipments as measured by value.

AMERICA AND THE WORLD

During the early 1990s, North America was the world's largest combined medium and heavy duty truck market. As a result, the region attracted interest from overseas establishments, and the U.S. market experienced an increasing presence of foreign owned participants. Three large foreign owned companies with domestic manufacturing facilities—Freightliner, Volvo GM, and Mack Trucks—increased their combined market share from about 20 percent in 1990 to about 22 percent in 1991. Japanese manufacturers—Isuzu Truck of America, Hino Diesel Trucks USA, Nissan Truck of America, and Mitsubishi Fuso Truck of America—boosted their U.S. sales by 31 percent between 1991 and 1992.

Imported vehicles represented 11 percent of vehicles sold in the medium duty classes during 1991, up from 3.1 percent in 1986. Within the Class 8 segment, however, imports captured less than 1 percent of 1991's total sales. According to a Hino representative, differences between the heavy duty truck markets in the United States and Japan made the shipment of Class 8 trucks from Japanese manufacturers into the United States impractical. The U.S. market was unique because trucks were custom manufactured using a combination of in-house and outsourced components in accordance with a particular customer's specifications.

American exports of medium and heavy duty trucks totaled $1.1 billion in 1991—an increase over the $951 million recorded in 1990. The ability of U.S. companies to compete overseas was bolstered by a drop in the value of the dollar in relationship to the yen and European currencies. U.S. opportunities in the European Community, however, were limited by import duties ranging from 17 to 22 percent of the vehicles' landed value. Talks were underway to negotiate a more favorable tariff situation.

The biggest U.S. trading partner in heavy and medium duty trucks was Canada. Canada received 43 percent of U.S. exports and supplied 73 percent of U.S. imports. Some analysts expected Mexico to be the fastest growing market for U.S. medium and heavy duty trucks. Other growing overseas markets included South and Central America, eastern Europe, and nations formed following the break up of the former Soviet Union.

U.S. exports to Mexico were expected to grow steadily over the turn of the century. The signing of the North American Free Trade Agreement (NAFTA) provided for Mexico's adoption of U.S. safety standards for trucking, and elimination of all restrictions on U.S. exports of medium and heavy duty trucks, buses, and special purpose motor vehicles to Mexico by January 1, 1999, among other provisions. In addition, analysts foresaw growing demand for U.S. built medium and heavy duty trucks, buses, and special purpose vehicles during the mid- to late 1990s as Mexico replaced its aging trucking fleet. New production of some of these vehicles in Mexico were also expected to utilize U.S. parts and components—another bonus for exports of U.S. OE and after-market parts.

RESEARCH AND TECHNOLOGY

During the early 1990s, truck and bus makers were facing many challenges to improve their environmental and safety records. Research toward improving the industry's environmental impact focused on reducing vehicle emissions, improving fuel economy, and developing alternative fuels.

The Clean Air Act Amendments of 1990 imposed increasing reductions in vehicle emissions creating a need for expanded research in clean-burning diesel technology. Efforts were also underway to make vehicles with increased fuel economy. Designers worked toward making lighter trucks with smaller dimensions, better aerodynamic styling, and improved engine performance. In a similar vein, some groups were advocating the development of alternate fuels. One of the most promising alternate fuels was natural gas. Many environmental groups favored natural gas over gasoline and diesel fuels because it emitted 90 percent less carbon monoxide and 50 percent less hydrocarbons.

Safety issues under investigation included searches for innovative designs offering improved driver visibility, better braking systems, and the development of collision avoidance technologies. Greyhound Lines, Inc. planned to provide radar collision avoidance on buses by the middle of the 1990s. The system under development used a light and buzzer to alert drivers when other vehicles got too close.

Other changes were also being studied. Manufacturers investigated possible alterations to improve driving and sleeping accommodations for truck operators. They were also developing advanced drive trains to permit the construction of trailers capable of carrying more cargo.

FURTHER READING

Berg, Tom. "What's This? Fleets Now Asking for ABS?" *Modern Tire Dealer,* June 1993.

Bohn, Joseph. "Alarm Sounded on Truck Fatalities: New Laws on Books; More Analysis of Problems Proposed." *Automotive News,* 29 December 1986.

———. "Big Trucks Make Strong Start in '93." *Automotive News,* 22 February 1993.

———. "Class 8 Sales Fire Spreads to Medium-Duties." *Automotive News,* 26 April 1993.

Bolan, Nelson. *How Detroit Changed History.* Lawrenceville, VA: Brunswick, 1987.

Bradley, Peter. "Medium Trucks: Safe, Lean, Clean Machines." *Purchasing,* 18 February 1993.

Colby, Richard N. "Freightliner Enjoys Successful Run." *Oregonian,* 2 August 1994.

"DRI Predicts 6% Drop in West Europe Sales." *WARD's Auto World,* July 1992.

Field, Mike. "Building a Better Bus; Inspired by European Designs, the Industry Is Upgrading Its Vehicles and Its Image." *Travel Weekly,* 29 March 1990.

Flint, Jerry. "In Good Times, Prepare For Bad." *Forbes,* 1 July 1996.

"From Four-Wheel Drive to Ten-Wheel Drive." *Communication,* December 1992.

Jefferis, David. *Giants of the Road: The History of Land Transportation.* New York: Franklin Watts, 1991.

Kahn, Helen. "Dual Trucker Licenses Banned." *Automotive News,* 8 June 1987.

———. "NHTSA Urges Better Brakes to Cut Heavy-Truck Accidents." *Automotive News,* 8 June 1987.

Keaton, Joanne. "Back to School." *Indiana Business Magazine,* September 1992.

Langworth, Richard M. *The Complete History of Ford Motor Company.* New York: Beekman House, 1987.

"Mack Closing Ontario Plant." *Automotive News,* 17 May 1993.

"Mack Ready for Rebound in Heavy-Duty Truck Market." Allentown, PA: Mack Trucks Inc., January 1993.

McCann, Hugh, and David C. Smith. "NGV's: Natural Gas Nears Lead in Alternate Fuel Race." *WARD's Auto World,* June 1993.

Moore, Walt. "A Second Chance for Anti-Lock Brakes." *Construction Equipment,* October 1990.

"Navistar Files Registration with SEC, Offering 22 Million Shares of Common Stock." News Release, 20 September 1993.

"Navistar International Corporation." *Prospectus,* Chicago: Navistar, 1993.

"Oshkosh Truck Corporation." *Annual Report for the Year Ended September 30, 1992,* Oshkosh, WI: Oshkosh Truck, 1992.

Paccar Annual Report 1992. Bellevue, WA: Paccar Inc., 1993.

"Paccar Reports Earnings." *Automotive News,* 1 February 1993.

Plumb, Stephen E. "EC '92 Creates Opportunity and Consolidation." *WARD's Auto World,* July 1992.

Rae, John B. *The American Automobile Industry.* Boston: Twayne Publishers, 1984.

Schine, Eric, Mark Maremont, and Christina Del Valle. "Here Comes the Thinking Car." *Business Week,* 25 May 1992.

Sears, Stephen W. *History of the Automobile in America.* New York: American Heritage Publishing, 1977.

U.S. Bureau of the Census. *1987 Census of Manufactures.* Washington: GPO, 1990.

U.S. Department of Commerce. "The Road Ahead." Office of Automotive Affairs. Washington: GPO, February 1997.

U.S. Department of Commerce. "U.S. Automotive Industry Sector Report." Office of Automotive Affairs. Washington: GPO, 17 September 1996

U.S. Department of Commerce. *U.S. Industrial Outlook 1993.* Washington: GPO, 1993.

Ward's Automotive Yearbook, Detroit: Ward's Communications, 1993.

Wilhelm, Steve. "Record Year at Paccar Likely as Truck Purchases Roll Along." *Puget Sound Business Journal,* 14 October 1994.

Zim, Herbert S., and James R. Skelly. *Trucks.* New York: Morrow, 1970.

—Karen Bellenir, updated by Visi Tilak

SIC 3714

MOTOR VEHICLE PARTS AND ACCESSORIES

This industry includes establishments primarily engaged in manufacturing motor vehicle parts and accessories but not engaged in manufacturing complete motor vehicles or passenger car bodies. Establishments primarily engaged in manufacturing or assembling complete automobiles and trucks are classified in **SIC 3711: Motor Vehicles and Passenger Car Bodies;** those manufacturing tires and inner tubes are classified in **SIC 3011: Tires and Inner Tubes;** those manufacturing automobile stampings are classified in **SIC 3465: Automotive Stampings;** those manufacturing vehicular lighting equipment are classified in **SIC 3647: Vehicular Lighting Equipment;** those manufacturing ignition systems are classified in **SIC 3694;** those manufacturing storage batteries are classified in **SIC 3691;** and those manufacturing carburetors, pistons, piston rings, and engine intake and exhaust valves are classified in **SIC 2592: Carburetors, Pistons, Piston Rings, and Valves.**

INDUSTRY SNAPSHOT

An estimated 15,000 parts and accessories are used in the production of motor vehicles. These parts represent the principle products of about 5,000 companies and a portion of the output of thousands of others. The annual U.S. production of motor vehicle parts and accessories is valued at over $90 billion. The Motor Equipment Manufacturers Association (MEMA) is the leading industry trade organization and compiles industry statistics.

ORGANIZATION AND STRUCTURE

The auto parts industry is divided into two principle segments: original equipment (OE) suppliers and aftermarket suppliers.

Original Equipment Suppliers. Original equipment suppliers sell parts and components directly to automobile manufacturers for the production of new vehicles. Consequently, sales in the OE market depend on the number, size, and complexity of new vehicles produced. Primary products include wheels, frames, axles, transmissions, transaxles, bearings, springs, bumpers, brake systems, fuel injectors, seats, seat belts, airbags, cushioning, and safety padding materials. For many large suppliers, OE parts provide the majority of sales, although most suppliers also produce parts for aftermarket sales. Companies that supply both OE and aftermarket parts can generally cover development and tooling costs on the OE sales volume and supply the aftermarket at higher volumes than pure aftermarket suppliers.

Furthermore, spreading research, development, and tool and die outlays over several contracts with different manufacturers provides OE suppliers a cost advantage over the in-house parts divisions of vehicle manufacturers. OE suppliers typically concentrate on a few components and systems requiring a high degree of technological skill and manufacturing efficiency. By supplying parts for new vehicles, OE manufacturers are generally on the leading edge of technology, and vehicle manufactures have begun to turn to suppliers for increased engineering and development responsibilities. Auto makers also look to leading suppliers for financing and services related to inventory management, logistics, and tooling.

Aftermarket Suppliers. Aftermarket parts suppliers manufacture and sell replacement products for used vehicles. Primary products include spark plugs, shock absorbers, struts, springs, brakes pads, rotors, filters, wiper blades, and exhaust systems. Aftermarket parts are distributed through a few major parts distributors and thousands of small jobbers and local firms, and they are for sale by auto dealers, service stations, repair shops, auto parts stores, tire stores, department stores, discount stores, and home and do-it-yourself stores. Aftermarket sales tend to be more stable than OE sales, particularly during recessionary times. As owners put off the purchase of new autos, they tend to extend the life of their current vehicles through increased maintenance and parts replacement.

With industry restructuring and realignment, the auto industry's supplier and original equipment manufacturer (OEM) roles were expected to change dramatically. Automakers and suppliers were expected to forge long-term agreements that focused on quality rather than price. Three layers of suppliers were expected—the system integrator, the direct supplier, and the indirect supplier. The ratios of these types of suppliers were also expected to change with system integrators growing to include 35 percent of suppliers—a 13-percent increase—and the indirect suppliers decreasing to 40 percent from 70 percent.

BACKGROUND AND DEVELOPMENT

The automotive parts industry began with the development of the automobile at the turn of the century, and the growth in the parts industry followed that of the automotive industry. By 1970, automobiles were manufactured in long production runs of few vehicle models. The vehicle population consisted of a fairly homogenous group of cars—known to be not particularly well made. Automobiles of the era were easy to

repair, and, with nearly all of the 225,000 service stations in operation providing repair services, mechanics were abundant. Parts suppliers found it easy to predict the demand for a relatively narrow range of parts and profited from their manufacture.

Beginning in the 1970s, several trends in the U.S. automobile industry started to affect domestic parts producers. The number of vehicle models produced began to expand, buoyed mostly by the increased sales of Japanese automobiles in the U.S. market. The continued proliferation of models and the shortening of model lives increased the number of parts required for vehicle manufacture and repair while lowering the volume of individual part production. Lowered economies of scale began to dampen the profits of parts suppliers while growing product lines increased the number of niche suppliers.

During the 1980s, small trucks began to sell more rapidly than passenger cars—requiring an increased production of parts for the truck population. During this time, the increasing market share gained by foreign vehicle manufacturers—whose OE and replacement parts were principally supplied by foreign parts producers—resulted in a decrease in the overall market for domestic parts.

Responding to this global competition, U.S. vehicle manufacturers placed a stronger emphasis on quality and reliability. However, more reliable new cars led to fewer repairs, slowing growth in aftermarket parts sales. In addition, the increased technical complexity of newer vehicles made performing repairs more difficult. Of the roughly 130,000 service stations in existence in 1990, only about 50 percent still performed repair services; dealers and independent service facilities were gaining a share of repair services.

The increased cost of repairing more complex systems, the inability of do-it-yourselfers to perform their own repairs, and the decreased number of service stations performing routine checks led to an underperformance of maintenance and repair. To a limited extent, these effects were counteracted by the aging automobile population. While the number of cars under three years old remained relatively constant between 1970 and 1991, the number of cars greater than three years old increased significantly, and the aging vehicle population provided a growing market for vehicle repair and parts replacement.

In the late 1980s and early 1990s, parts manufacturers were forced to respond to major changes in technological advances, relationships with vehicle manufacturers, and the impact of Japanese auto makers.

Technology. Parts makers worked to meet the increased technological sophistication of new automobiles. Protective airbags were installed in 51 percent of 1992 model year cars compared to almost none in 1989. With regulations requiring the use of passive restraints, airbags were expected to be standard equipment on almost all cars and light trucks by 1998. Antilock braking systems were installed on 32 percent of new automobiles in the 1992 model year, and traction control systems and innovative suspensions gained popularity.

Additional developments were underway to increase the use of lighter weight materials throughout new vehicles. While increasing research and development costs, the use of complex and expensive components and systems improved opportunities for revenue and profit increases for parts suppliers. Further opportunities were provided by new clean air regulations. More stringent regulations increased the complexity of engine control and emissions systems, and a required increase in inspection programs led to more repair and parts replacement opportunities for aftermarket suppliers.

Relationship with the Auto Makers. With an influx of auto makers, the United States evolved into the most competitive automotive market in the world. To meet the demands of increased competition, the Big Three U.S. auto makers— General Motors, Ford, and Chrysler—focused efforts on quality improvement, cost reduction, and strategic sourcing—reducing the number of primary suppliers while increasing their responsibilities. These efforts had tremendous impact on parts manufacturers. Although in the past OE parts were sold largely on annual contracts covering the model year, in a move to improve supplier relationships, vehicle manufacturers began to award contracts for the life of a vehicle model.

In addition, auto makers reduced the number of suppliers they dealt with directly, awarding primary suppliers more responsibility for the design and development of entire systems and sub-assemblies. Primary suppliers were expected to integrate and coordinate the purchase of parts from smaller secondary and tertiary suppliers, and suppliers of all levels were urged to raise their quality standards while reducing costs. In response, many parts suppliers reduced the number of vendors they dealt with. Large parts suppliers who were able to increase the services they offered to vehicle manufacturers benefited most from these trends.

Each of the Big Three auto makers initiated programs for supplier management. Between 1980 and 1991, Ford reduced its worldwide supplier base by one-half, and in 1991, it began a restructuring plan that included increased supplier reductions. The company also asked suppliers to cut costs by 1 percent annually until 1997 and opened up its bidding system so that outside suppliers competed evenly against Ford Automotive Components Group—which supplied about 50 percent of the company's parts in the early 1990s.

Chrysler implemented its Supplier Cost-Reduction Effort (SCORE) program, urging suppliers to come up with ideas for improvements and cost savings in manufacturing, scheduling, inventory, and shipping. Chrysler attempted to establish long-term relationships with suppliers by naming suppliers for specific commodities. The company had fewer than 2,500 suppliers in 1992—down from more than 3,000 in the late 1980s—and it had a goal of eventually reducing the number of suppliers to 750. The company's 1993 LH model used 170 suppliers, compared to 600 to 800 suppliers for cars of earlier model years.

General Motors initiated the industry's most controversial supplier management plan with its Purchased Input Concept Optimization with Suppliers (PICOS) program, which demanded significant price reductions from suppliers given long-term contracts. Under the program, GM sent teams of engineers, designers, and purchasing cost accountants to meet with parts suppliers at their plants to investigate production inefficiencies and propose solutions leading to cost reductions. The program also allowed GM to accept unsolicited bids from worldwide suppliers for contracts it had already negotiated for future models, and it stripped away advantages to GM's Automotive Components Group. In addition, the company offered suppliers the opportunity to lease factory space in GM plants and a supply of labor from idled workers.

In 1992, the Big Three announced plans to develop a standardized quality assessment program for suppliers. Such a move, which would reduce the time and paperwork required in undergoing several quality audits by different auto makers, was expected to eventually save suppliers $160 million annually. A first step toward a common standard was taken by eliminating a major source of redundancy in quality auditing.

Previously, first-tier suppliers were required to audit second- and third-tier suppliers from whom they purchased parts. However, because many companies acting as second- and third-tier suppliers also sold parts directly to one of the Big Three, they were already required to be audited under either the Ford Q101, Chrysler Supplier Quality Assessment, or GM Target for Excellence quality program. With the new arrangement, suppliers that were already qualified through one of the Big Three were no longer required to be audited by a primary supplier. The agreement was expected to save the supplier industry $500,000 a year.

The Impact of Japanese Auto Makers. Increased sales of Japanese automobiles affected the operations of both OE and aftermarket parts manufacturers. Because most Japanese aftermarket parts were furnished by Japanese OE suppliers, the volumes of replacement parts for domestic parts suppliers dropped as Japanese vehicles increased their market share in the United States. Domestic parts suppliers started increasing their offerings of replacement parts for Japanese vehicles, but at the same time, Japanese suppliers started seeking higher profit margins through the supply of aftermarket parts for U.S. vehicles.

While Japanese manufacturers increased their production of cars within the United States, the move had not significantly improved the opportunities for domestic parts manufacturers. Foreign vehicles manufactured in the United States had significantly fewer domestic suppliers than Big Three cars. Domestic OE suppliers argued that the Japanese plants in the United States continued to purchase parts from suppliers based in Japan and the growing number of Japanese suppliers operating in the United States. Furthermore, with the increased capacity of many American factories manufacturing Japanese cars, Japanese suppliers started competing for OE contracts with the Big Three. Some suppliers believed that their industry could be permanently suppressed by these developments.

Some domestic parts suppliers claimed they were hampered by the Japanese *keiretsu* system—the close relationship between auto makers and their suppliers—arguing that the system impinged on their ability to supply parts to Japanese vehicle manufacturers in North America and Japan. At the request of U.S. suppliers, the Federal Trade Commission (FTC) began an investigation of alleged antitrust violations by Japanese auto producers in the United States.

Japanese producers argued that they purchased from suppliers meeting their needs, and so far the FTC had concluded that there was no clear evidence of collusion among Japanese companies. During President Bush's 1992 trade mission to Japan, Japanese auto makers pledged to purchase $19 billion worth of U.S. auto parts annually by 1995. During 1992 and 1993, Japanese purchases of U.S. auto parts began to increase. The rising value of the yen relative to the dollar made shipments of parts from Japan more expensive, encouraging Japanese transplant manufacturers to purchase more U.S. parts.

CURRENT CONDITIONS

The automobile industry continued to buy an increasing number of automotive parts from outside suppliers through the 1990s because it reduced costs, provided more flexibility, and allowed for a greater specialization of technology according to an article in *Fortune* magazine. During the mid-1990s, the U.S. automotive parts industry comprised some 5,000 firms—including about 500 Japanese, European, and Canadian manufacturers—that supplied either the original equipment (OE) market, the replacement parts market, or both. According to the U.S. Department of Commerce, industry production hit an all-time high in 1994, reaching $134 billion. The following year, output fell slightly to $131 billion, mirroring the slight decline in motor vehicle production. However, the motor vehicle parts industry represented a 25 percent growth since 1992.

The U.S. industry was dominated by 50 large manufacturers that accounted for the large majority of sales. From 1992 to 1995, North American sales by these top 50 suppliers increased by almost 50 percent, growing from $68 billion to $101 billion according to U.S. Department of Commerce reports. The United States was home to the world's sales leader, Delphi Automotive Systems, with 1995 global sales of over $26 billion,$10 billion more than its nearest foreign competitor.

In the mid-1990s, the fight was on among automotive parts manufacturers to dominate the growing *Smart Car* parts market. With the establishment of the Partnership for a New Generation of Vehicles (PNGV) by President Clinton in 1993, auto manufacturers were competing to produce new generation concept cars. The ripple effect of this affected the automotive parts industry. High-tech console gadgetry was being produced by most large auto manufacturers.

"Competition for space on your dashboard is looming, as TRW, Texas Instruments, and Eaton among others, race to recast their batttlefield products for the U.S. car market," reported a *Fortune* article. Competition for this market was global. Smart car products already available and in the works included satellite navigation and mayday systems, radar intelligent cruise control, and night vision.

With the restructuring of the automotive parts industry, the U.S. automotive industry was expected to be challenged by foreign competition and customer demands for continued cost cuts and quality improvements. The global automotive parts market was expected to total about $519 billion by the year 2000. According to the *U.S. Global Trade Outlook,* growth in major markets was expected to average less than 2 percent annually, hence the biggest opportunities for U.S. exporters were expected to be in the fast growing Asian and Latin American markets.

INDUSTRY LEADERS

For many leading automotive parts suppliers—including Allied-Signal, Eaton, ITT, Rockwell, and TRW—motor vehicle supply provides only a portion of the sales of a much larger organization. These diverse manufacturers often supply components and systems to other transportation industries such as aerospace and defense. For other large suppliers, including Dana and Federal-Mogul, automotive supply is the primary business. The Big Three auto manufacturers produce many parts through their own subsidiaries.

General Motors, Ford, and Chrysler were the highest ranked companies in terms of sales revenue with $168.83 billion, $137.147 billion, and $53.20 billion, respectively. Other industry leaders ranked by sales revenue were: Hughes Electronics Corporation of Los Angeles, California, with $14.77; AlliedSignal Inc. of Morristown, New Jersey, with $14.35 billion; Rockwell International Corp. of Seal Beach, California, with $12.98 billion; TRW Inc. of Cleveland, Ohio, with $10.17 billion; Textron Inc. of Providence, Rhode Island, with $9.97 billion; ITT Industries of White Plains, New York, with $8.88 billion; Dana Corp. of Toledo, Ohio, with $7.60 billion; Eaton Corp. of Cleveland, Ohio, with $6.82 billion; and Cummins Engine Company Inc. with $5.25 billion.

WORK FORCE

Vehicle manufacturers generally have higher labor costs than parts suppliers, who are able to employ more non-union workers. The percentage of workers at aftermarket supply businesses represented by the United Auto Workers (UAW) declined from 50 percent in 1978 to 25 percent in 1990. In 1995, U.S. automotive parts industry employment reached 711,000—its highest level since 1979. Employment had grown at an average of 5 percent annually since 1992, when it totaled 610,000.

AMERICA AND THE WORLD

U.S. parts manufacturers have been forced to match the growth in global operations of domestic auto makers to maintain their primary supply relationships. Additionally, international growth has been spurred by the desire to gain supply contracts with overseas vehicle manufacturers. Most leading domestic producers have established manufacturing facilities in the principle auto producing regions of the world—including Canada, Europe, and Mexico. In Europe alone, seven leading U.S. parts manufacturers have combined annual sales exceeding $1 billion. The global integration of the auto industry has led many suppliers to develop joint ventures with foreign parts producers. As the industry continues to globalize, increased U.S. supplier investments are expected in Mexico, Asia, and Europe.

The United States has posted a trade deficit in automotive parts since 1983, primarily due to a large deficit with Japan. Between 1989 and 1992, the parts trade deficit with Japan remained between $9 billion and $10 billion, accounting for one-fifth of the overall trade deficit with Japan. Canada is the only major nation with which the United States has maintained a trade surplus, and Canada remains the leading trading partner of U.S. firms. Between 1985 and 1991, Canada received over 60 percent of total U.S. parts exports and supplied one third of total imports.

The number of foreign firms producing parts in the United States increased dramatically throughout the 1980s and early 1990s. In the early 1990s, approximately 350 wholly owned foreign part plants, and over 120 joint ventures, operated in the United States. Japanese suppliers owned 167 U.S. parts plants and were part of 123 joint ventures. European firms, led by German manufacturers, owned 168 plants in the United States, and Canadian firms owned 17, with one joint venture. While fairly well established in Europe and Canada, U.S. penetration of the Japanese domestic market remained weak. In 1992, one wholly owned U.S. parts plant—and a few joint ventures—were operating in Japan.

Continued consolidation and increasing global competition are forecast for the automotive parts industry. The future prospects for large domestic producers are likely to depend on their ability to obtain contracts with Japanese transplant manufacturers as well as to retain contracts with the Big Three against competition from Japanese suppliers. For smaller second- and third-tier suppliers, the key is likely to be establishing strong relationships with primary suppliers.

U.S. Automotive Parts Exports. During the late 1980s and early 1990s, exports had become more vital to the U.S. automotive parts industry, growing from 15 percent of production in 1986 to 30 percent of output in 1995. The Clinton Administration's trade policy efforts to open closed markets made the U.S. automotive parts industry one of the leading exporters. From 1992 to 1995, U.S. exports of automotive parts grew at an average annual rate of 12 percent, rising from $28 billion to $40 billion according to the Office of Automotive Affairs, U.S. Department of Commerce.

Expanded efforts by the industry, backed by the Clinton Administration's work to increase U.S. access to the Japanese automotive parts market, resulted in a 58 percent increase in exports to Japan—growing from $1 billion in 1992 to $1.6 billion in 1995. Japanese car manufacturers purchased $19.9 billion worth of U.S. made automotive parts and materials in the 1994 fiscal year. Approximately 75 percent was spent to transplant Japanese manufacturing operations in the United States, while the remaining 25 percent was spent on exports to Japan. Exports to Mexico and Canada benefited from the passage of the North American Free Trade Agreement (NAFTA)—growing from $26 billion in 1993 to $29 billion in 1995.

During the first half of 1996, U.S. automotive parts exports to the world grew to $20.8 billion, up 3 percent from the previous period. Exports to Japan advanced 11 percent to $901 million. Exports to Canada and Mexico increased 6 percent to $15.1 billion as Mexico began to rebound from its 1995 slump.

FURTHER READING

Hoffman, Gary. "Suppliers Seek Bigger Chunk of Inside Jobs." *The Detroit News,* 19 July 1996.

"Japanese Increase Auto Purchases." *Ward's Automotive Reports,* 17 July 1995.

Office of Automotive Affairs. U.S. Department of Commerce. "Automotive Parts." *U.S. Global Trade Outloook: 1995-2000.* Washington: GPO, March 1995.

Office of Automotive Affairs. U.S. Department of Commerce. "The Road Ahead." Washington: GPO, February 1997.

Office of Automotive Affairs. "U.S. Automotive Industry Sector Report." Washington: GPO, 17 September 1996.

Robinson, Edward A., and Hillary Margolis. "Soon Your Dashboard Will Do Everything (Except Steer)." *Fortune,* 22 July 1996.

Standard and Poor's Industry Surveys. New York: Standard & Poor's, 1993.

Taylor III, Alex. "The Auto Industry Meets the New Economy." *Fortune,* 5 September 1994.

Templin, Neal. "Japan Auto Makers Buy More U.S. Parts." *The Wall Street Journal,* 24 August 1993.

"The Next Supplier Evolution." *Automotive Industries,* 1 January 1996.

U.S. Department of Commerce. *U.S. Industrial Outlook 1993.* Washington: GPO, 1993.

—Paolo Motta, updated by Visi Tilak

SIC 3715

TRUCK TRAILERS

This industry covers establishments primarily engaged in manufacturing truck trailers, truck trailer chassis for sale separately, detachable trailer bodies (cargo containers) for sale separately, and detachable trailer (cargo container) chassis for sale separately.

ORGANIZATION AND STRUCTURE

Like heavy trucks, truck trailers are purchased for specific applications and are therefore manufactured in a variety of styles and types. Van, container chassis, and flatbed trailers comprise the majority of trailer shipments, while the remainder consists of a small number of more specialized trailer types. Both the number of axles and length of trailers vary, with the most popular trailers having two axles, followed by single axle designs and trailers with three or more axles. Popular trailer lengths are 48 feet and 28 feet.

Trailers are used single or in combinations of three, as in triple "pups." Pups are 28 foot trailers that have limited use in 16 states. Sometimes three of these trailers are attached to a truck tractor to form triple pups, which together span about 104 feet. Trucking firms continue to urge Congress to expand the use of triples. Even though the triple pups save trucking firms millions of dollars, The Citizens for Reliable and Safe Highways, a not-for-profit organization, is fighting to keep larger trucks off the roads.

BACKGROUND AND DEVELOPMENT

In the early 1980s, in response to an increase in intermodal shipments of goods—a system using two or more methods of transport, including trucks, trains, and ships—container chassis trailer shipments increased. The demand for a variety of trailer types, including custom designs, prompted the establishment of several original equipment manufacturers (OEMs) in the trailer industry. Furthermore, increased competition arose from deregulation of the industry in 1980, making manufacturers leaner and more efficient. Many trailer manufacturers were small businesses serving local areas, often employing 50 or fewer workers.

In 1984 approximately 400 truck trailer manufacturers were operating in the United States, employing almost 28,000 workers. Approximately 214,000 trailers were shipped that year for total sales of $3.31 billion. In 1995, an improvement in the economy brought the industry work force up to 38,700 workers, of which 31,700 were production workers. Trailer shipments totaled 187,000 units in 1992, and total industry sales were estimated at $3.47 billion. The industry was operating below capacity during the early 1990s.

The market for exporting truck trailers was expected to expand throughout the 1990s. The United States maintains a trade surplus in truck trailers, and in 1991 the value of exports for the truck trailer industry was $175 million, while the value of imports was only $23.9 million. These figures were expected to reach $250 million and $45 million, respectively, by the mid-1990s.

Truck trailers are manufactured in most of the 50 states. Texas, California, and Pennsylvania led the nation in the number of manufacturing establishments per state. In 1992 Great Dane Trailers, Wabash National, and Fruehauf Trailer were the leading manufacturers of truck trailers of truck trailers.

CURRENT CONDITIONS

In mid-1990 the demand for truck trailer reached an all time high. Projections for 1994 put the total order for truck trailers at approximately 211,500 units, just short of the record 214,000 truck trailers set in 1984. Stronger U.S. economic growth was seen as the cause for this demand. The sharp rise freight shipments was seen as the reason for higher spending by truckers.

The record highs for the demand for truck trailers continued to rise through 1995. The demand for truck trailers was expected to increase to 221,000 units by 1995 because of economic and industry factors. The increase in trailer shipments was expected to parallel that of tractor production as a result of record improvement in the truck tractor industry.

1996 saw the launch of a host of new truck trailer models. The emphasis was on ease, safety, lightness, and stable frame designs capable of hauling heavier payloads. The trailers were easier to attach, had lower load angles, and were made of lighter but stronger steel to make heavier loads possible.

One of the safety related additions to new truck models was the implementation of anti-lock brakes in truck trailers. The new anti-lock braking system (ABS), designed especially for truck trailers, was expected to result in substantial savings for motor carriers by providing controlled braking, enhanced vehicle stability, increased driver control, and stable stopping during emergency brake situations. Rockwell WABCO Vehicle Control Systems' Easy-Stop (TM) was one of the first innovators of ABS for truck trailers.

INDUSTRY LEADERS

Out of about 134 operating companies in this industry, Great Dane Holdings Inc. was the industry leader with a 1996 sales revenue of $1.293 billion. Based in Kalamazoo, MI, Great Dane had about 5,750 employees. Terex Corp. of Connecticut ranked second with 1996 sales revenue of $1.03 billion and 6,071 employees. Great Dane Trailers Inc., of Savannah, Georgia, ranked third with $1 billion in 1996 sales revenues. Wabash National Corp. of Indiana and Utility trailer Manufacturing Co. of California ranked fourth and fifth with respective sales revenues of $734.3 million and $450 million.

Other leading companies among the top ten industry leaders were Fruehauf Trailer Corp. of Indiana with $418.8 million in sales revenue, Trailmobile Inc. of Illinois with sales revenue of $400 million, Monon Corp. of Indiana with $300 million in sales revenue, Fontane Industries Inc. of Alabama with $280 million in sales revenue, and Stoughton Trailers Inc. of Wisconsin with sales revenue of $270 million.

FURTHER READING

Gruebnau, Pam. ''Today's Trailers Work to Make Hauling Easier.'' *Construction Equipment,* October 1996, 45.

Isidore, Chris. ''Triple 'Pups' Not Everyone's Best Friends.'' *Journal of Commerce and Commercial,* 26 November 1996, 1B.

Landberg, Lynn. ''New Trailers For 1996. *Construction Equipment,* October 1995, 44.

Pennington, Mike D. ''Rockwell WABCO Introduces New ABS for Trailers.'' *Business Wire,* 29 September 1994.

U.S. Department of Commerce. *U.S. Industrial Outlook 1993.* Washington: GPO, 1993.

Watson, Rip. ''Record Highs for Trailer Demand Likely to Continue throughout 1995.'' *Journal of Commerce and Commercial,* 16 December 1994, 7A.

Watson, Rip. ''Truck Trailer Building May Rival 1984's Record.'' *Journal of Commerce and Commercial,* 27 September 1994, 2B.

—Paula Motta, updated by Visi Tilak

SIC 3716

MOTOR HOMES

This category covers establishments primarily engaged in manufacturing self-contained motor homes on purchased chassis. Establishments engaged in manufacturing self-contained motor homes on chassis manufactured in the same establishment are classified in **SIC 3711: Motor Vehicles and Passenger Car Bodies.** Establishments primarily engaged in manufacturing mobile homes are classified in **SIC 2451: Mobile Homes;** and those manufacturing travel trailers and pickup campers are classified in **SIC 3792: Travel Trailers and Campers.** Establishments primarily engaged in van conversion on a custom basis are classified in Services, **SIC 7532: Top, Body, and Upholstery Repair Shops and Paint Shops.**

INDUSTRY SNAPSHOT

In the recession years of the early 1990s, the motor home industry faced contracting markets and recorded weak results. Sales began to recover in 1993 and rose further in 1994; while results in 1995 and 1996 were sluggish, they were still above 1993 levels. Overall, growth prospects remained good, as demographic, economic, and cultural factors were weighted heavily in the industry's favor. The U.S. population is aging, and it is older, more affluent Americans who are the industry's best customers. Many urbanites of all ages seem eager to spend their free time out in the country, and they are showing a strong preference for vehicles that also provide lodging. In the mid-1990s, interest rates remained at low levels, making financing of new motor homes relatively easy. And gasoline shortages, which had hurt the business badly in the late 1970s, were nowhere in sight, while fuel prices were relatively low.

ORGANIZATION AND STRUCTURE

The recreational vehicle (RV) industry can be divided into two groups—towables, which include conventional and fifth-wheel travel trailers, folding camping trailers, and truck campers; and motorized vehicles, which include motor homes and van conversions. The overwhelming majority of motor homes sold in the United States are built on chassis that have been purchased from an outside manufacturer. The two key manufacturers of gasoline-powered chassis for motor homes are General Motors Corp. and Ford Motor Co.

Motor homes are classified as either Class A, B, or C models. A Class A vehicle is probably what most people think of when they hear the term "motor home": it is a living unit entirely constructed on a bare, specially designed motor vehicle chassis, and the driver sits within the vehicle itself. Class A models have been the most popular: in 1995 they represented about 62 percent of all motor homes shipped (and more in terms of dollar value). Class C models are smaller vehicles wherein the driver usually sits inside a sepa-

rate cab; they accounted for about 31 percent of unit shipments. A Class B motor home, also called a van camper, is defined by the Recreational Vehicle Industry Association (RVIA) as "a panel-type truck to which the RV manufacturer adds any two of the following conveniences: sleeping, kitchen, and toilet facilities." Class B vehicles represented about 7 percent of 1995 shipments.

The two largest manufacturers in the industry, Fleetwood Enterprises and Winnebago Industries Inc., held about 44 percent of the motor home market in 1995. Together, the 10 largest makers accounted for over 85 percent of all sales.

The RVIA defines a van conversion as "a completed or incomplete automotive van chassis modified decoratively or aesthetically in appearance by the RV manufacturer for transportation and recreational purposes. These changes may include windows, paneling, seats, sofas, and accessories." One of the largest van converters in 1997 was privately owned Mark III.

BACKGROUND AND DEVELOPMENT

According to one source, the first motor home in the United States was built to take tourists out West for the San Francisco Exposition of 1915. Although its promoters claimed that it had all the advantages of an ocean cruiser—with hot running water and electric lights—testimony confirming the comfort of the journey does not appear in any historical record. Wealthy industrialists, notably Henry Ford and Thomas Edison, were among the pioneers of the motor home industry; they built relatively luxurious caravans with amenities like leather swivel chairs and refrigerators. The well-to-do were imitated by the middle class, who bolted boxes to the backs of Model T's and fastened a bed and dresser inside to create what was then called a "house car." American individualism soon made itself felt, and by the late 1920s house cars that looked like log cabins, miniature mansions, and even airplanes could be seen on the highways.

The early motor home riders stayed overnight at farms and ranches, but eventually large campgrounds were built that could hold over 1,000 vehicles. The sites were often overcrowded and unsanitary, and a far cry from the outdoor life these early RV users sought. Driving the first professionally built motor homes was not much fun either. They were made with heavy materials that overtaxed the chassis and gave poor weight distribution; insulation was poor, and the vehicles were not suited to the existing roads. Thus, until the 1960s the towable trailer was the more popular form of RV.

In the mid-1950s some small companies began to build what might be called motorized trailers. While they represented a significant improvement, they were still overweight and underpowered. A few years later, however, Winnebago began to introduce its innovative products, which became popular in the late 1960s and early 1970s. The company developed a special wall construction called Thermo-Panel that had the required structural strength and offered good insulation; at the same time, it was light enough to raise gas mileage and engine performance. Moreover, once Winnebago introduced assembly line production, it was able to make its motor homes a lot cheaper than the competition could.

CURRENT CONDITIONS

According to a survey performed by the RVIA in 1993, about 69 percent of motor home purchasers have a gross income of between $50,000 and $100,000 a year, while 59 percent have been in the same job or the same industry for ten years or more. Nevertheless, because buying a motor home represented a major commitment—in 1994 the average price of a Class A motor home was more than $62,000—customers must feel financially secure before they will purchase. When the market for large motor homes took a dip in 1995, some observers attributed it to the uncertainty about the future financing of Medicare and other programs that serve older consumers, the industry's key customers.

According to *RV Business,* unit shipments of all motor homes in 1995 were down 8.3 percent from 1994 levels to 53,460 units. Notably, shipments in the important Class A category were down 17 percent to 33,280 units; Class C vehicles registered an 8 percent drop to 16,410, while Class B models rose 18 percent from a relatively low base to 4,170. While shipments in 1995 were below 1994 levels, the motor home industry had undoubtedly recovered from the slowdown in the early 1990s. For the first eleven months of 1996, Class A shipments rose 7.2 percent to 32,800 units; but Class C units performed less well, which some observers linked to high prices. Total van conversions in 1995 were down 12 percent to 231,000.

Overall, however, industry participants in 1997 were optimistic about the industry's long-term prospects. The essential economic ingredients appeared to be in place—expanding economy, low interest rates, and low unemployment—while demographic trends were on the industry's side. The prime buyers of motor homes were people 50 years of age or older, a cohort that was expanding with the aging of the U.S. population. At the same time, those between the age of 30 and 49 were entering the RV market in significant numbers. While they tended to buy inexpensive towables, their purchases signaled that they liked the RV lifestyle and would be ready to trade up to a motor home when they had more leisure time and more money. Some also believed that the growing preference of consumers for "car substitutes" like light trucks would make the prospect of tooling around in a 40-foot Class A motor home less formidable.

Indeed, there has been a notable trend toward larger vehicles and more equipment. A corollary has been the increasing importance of slideouts, i.e., rollout room extensions that allow manufacturers to increase existing floor plans. Slideouts have become extremely popular, even though they pose problems for campground and resort operators. Even industry leaders who dislike slideouts—like Chairman Kay Toolson of Monaco Coach Corp., a maker of large Class A vehicles—have had to provide them. "I said I would go down screaming and fighting," he told *RV Business* in 1996, "but slideouts have become about 30% of the market."

INDUSTRY LEADERS

Fleetwood Enterprises is the largest motor home manufacturer with about 28 percent of the market. Total revenues in fiscal 1996 were $2.8 billion, about 26 percent of which came from motor homes; the company also has a large manufactured-housing operation, which accounted for about 50 percent of its sales. Most of the remaining revenue was derived from sales of other RVs. Earnings in 1996 were $80 million, down somewhat from the $85 million recorded in 1995, but still well above the 1993 total of $57 million.

Fleetwood has a reputation for innovation that is embodied in its Bounder model. Introduced in the late 1980s, the Bounder offered a basement-like storage compartment that gave owners a place for storing items like golf bags and suitcases, while raising the level of the living quarters to that of the driver. The company has also built customer loyalty from its excellent after-sales support: every buyer of a Fleetwood product is called to get feedback and suggestions for improvement.

Winnebago, the industry's second-largest company, is almost a generic term for motor home. Some 89 percent of its fiscal 1996 revenues of $484 million came from sales of motor homes. While net income fell to $12 million from $28 million in 1995, all of the decline reflects a different effective tax rate. Founded in 1958 by John K. Hanson—who died in 1996 at the age of 83—the firm posted increasingly strong sales and profits in the late 1960s and early 1970s. Afterward, however, recessions, gas shortages, and, some say, poor management cost the company market share and hurt profitability. Between 1989 to 1992 the company lost money each year. In fiscal 1993, however, Winnebago benefited from a new line of motor homes that was well received, as well as reduced costs and greater automation of production. These factors, coupled with the improved economy and low interest rates, continued to support the company's profitable performance in 1995 and 1996.

AMERICA AND THE WORLD

European motor home markets tend to differ substantially from those in the United States. While European RVs can be as sophisticated as American models, their campgrounds lag notably behind: they often lack the amenities of U.S. sites, including dumping stations and full hookups. European RVs tend to be smaller because of higher gasoline prices—as much as $4 per gallon in Germany—and licensing rules that limit motor homes to about 6,000 pounds. Certainly Europe offered attractive demographics, with an affluent workforce that gets four to six weeks of vacation each year. Thus far, however, the experience of U.S. makers on the Continent has been less than overwhelming. Indeed, the industry's participation in European markets took a step back in 1996 when Fleetwood sold its German subsidiary, Niesmann and Bischoff. Fleetwood had sustained significant losses since acquiring a majority interest in the company in 1992.

U.S. makers have made some inroads into the Japanese market. The focus has been on Class B models, because Japanese motorists can operate them with regular driver licenses. Since Japanese roads tend to be narrower, compact motorhomes that can also be used for everyday driving are popular. American makers need to modify their designs for the special needs of the Japanese market—e.g., kitchen sinks are made one-foot deep so they can accommodate a rice cooker.

RESEARCH AND TECHNOLOGY

As with many industries, the growth of the Internet is having an impact on the motor home industry. By 1997, significant numbers of manufacturers and dealers had created websites to advertise their product lines and supply customers with information. The Internet is particularly useful for motor home rentals—RVers from all over the world can now conveniently reserve vehicles online at a low cost to the dealer. But future websites may also allow consumers to learn the dealer invoice price for any motor home, which would obviously have repercussions for the industry.

While the Net is affecting marketing, new technology is changing manufacturing. Motor home producers are seeking to incorporate lightweight materials that are nonetheless strong and resilient. In some instances, aluminum is replacing rubber in roofs and fiberglass in sidewall paneling. Winnebago is using a combination of aluminum and steel to eliminate wood framework.

Moreover, manufacturers are investing more capital in the production process and becoming less labor intensive. For example, Winnebago has moved to a flexible manufacturing system in its metal-stamping operations. As Ron Buckmeier, director of engineering, told *RV Business,* "There's some labor savings, but the real advantage is quality improvement and the variability to do mixed-model manufacturing."

FURTHER READING

"'95 Adjusted Shipments Show Decline Over '94," *RV Business,* March 1996.

Byrne, Harlan. "Winnebago Industries." *Barron's,* 17 January 1994.

Cummings, Tim. "History also Rides an RV in Excursion through Time." *Sheridan Press,* 30 August 1989.

Estes, Bill. "Euroscene." *RV Business,* November 1995.

Fleetwood Enterprises. *Annual Report.* Riverside, CA, 1996.

Goldenburg, Sherman. "Appealing to Boomer Tastes. *RV Business,* October 1996.

"Industry Posts Best Retail Sales Since 1986." *RV Business,* April 1996.

Keech, Mike. "Dealer Numbers Drop by Over 20% Since '90." *RV Business,* March 1993.

Kovell, Hank. "Seeing America by RV." *Los Angeles Times,* 13 February 1994.

Kurowski, Jeff. "Tokyo Show Targets New RVers with U.S., International Imports." *RV Business,* May 1996.

"Motorhomes Offer Independence on the Open Road." *Columbia Record,* 2 February 1988.

Norland, Jim and Elaine Norland. "RV Construction Trends: Turning Toward Lighter, Stronger, Affordable." *RV Business,* October 1994.

Norland, Jim, and Elaine Norland. "Construction Refinements Continue to Make RVs Better." *RV Business,* July 1995.

"November Shipments Impacted by Lagging Conversion Market." *RV Business,* February 1997.

Recreation Vehicle Industry Association "RV Types & Terms," Reston, VA

"RVIA's Annual Survey Profiles RV Buyers." *RV Business,* September 1993.

"Shipment Trends." *RV Business,* March 1994.

Sullaway, John. "Creating Coaches for the Physically Challenged." *RV Business,* June 1996.

Thompson, John. "Selling in Cyberspace." *RV Business,* February 1997.

Williams, Rolla. "Going Camping on Wheels." *San Diego Union,* 2 July 1988.

Winnebago Industries. *Annual Report,* Forest City, IA, 1996.

—Bob Schneider

SIC 3721

AIRCRAFT

This category includes establishments primarily engaged in manufacturing or assembling complete aircraft. This industry also includes establishments owned by aircraft manufacturers and primarily engaged in research and development on aircraft, whether from enterprise funds or on a contract or fee basis. Also included are establishments engaged in repairing and rebuilding aircraft on a factory basis. Establishments primarily engaged in manufacturing engines and other aircraft parts and auxiliary equipment are classified in **SIC 3724: Aircraft Engines and Engine Parts** and **SIC 3728: Aircraft Parts and Auxiliary Equipment, Not Elsewhere Classified.** Establishments primarily engaged in the repair of aircraft, except on a factory basis, are classified in **SIC 4581: Airports, Flying Fields, and Airport Terminal Services;** and research and development on aircraft by establishments not owned by aircraft manufacturers are classified in **SIC 8731: Commercial Physical and Biological Research.**

INDUSTRY SNAPSHOT

The aerospace industry consists of space vehicles, space propulsion parts, guided missiles, aircraft, aircraft engines, and aircraft parts. The total value of all products and services for the aerospace industry was $101.5 billion in 1995, estimated to be $112 billion in 1996, and projected to become $125 billion in 1997. The value of all products and services of the aircraft industry alone is nearly one-half that of the aerospace industry total. The production and sale of aircraft further constitutes about 50 percent of the total aircraft industry's value.

According to the International Trade Administration (ITA), the total value of all products and services in the aircraft industry was estimated to be $48.5 billion in 1995, down slightly from the previous year, representing 49 percent of shipments for the total aerospace industry.

The Aerospace Industries Association of America (AIAA), states that there were 1,677 shipments of civilian (transports, general aviation, and rotocraft) aircraft valued at $22.19 billion in 1996. There were a total of 431 aircraft accepted by U.S. military agencies in 1995 (down from 775 in 1994) at a flyaway value of $11.76 billion. The number of shipments of complete U.S. aircraft in 1995, according to ITA, was estimated to be 2,275 with a predicted value of $28.39 billion. This number dropped from a peak of 19,381 in 1978, when the total value of shipments was $10.1 billion. The greatest drop in production occurred in general aviation (primarily due to product liability) from peaks of 17,800 units in 1978 to an estimated 1,077 in 1995. The Teal Group predicts 25,537 aircraft valued at $655.5 billion will be built throughout the world during the decade 1997-2006.

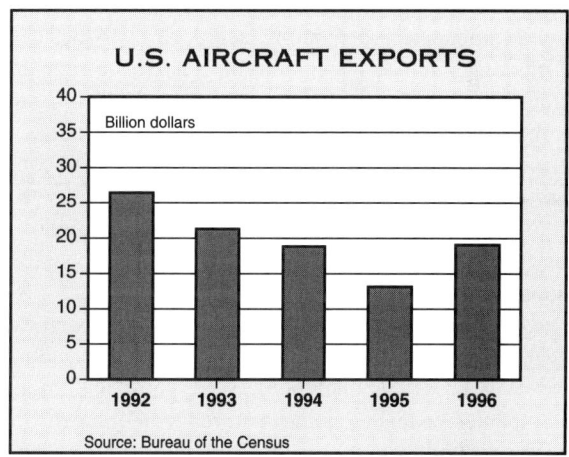

U.S. AIRCRAFT EXPORTS

Source: Bureau of the Census

Commercial aircraft deliveries are expected to rise from 400 in 1996 to over 700 by the year 2000. The commercial jet fleet was estimated to be 11,500 by the end of 1996 and 23,600 by the year 2016, 7,000 of which were expected to be Boeing aircraft. The industry entered 1997 with $96 billion in orders. Boeing alone had $7.5 billion in new orders in September 1996, was hiring 1,000 new workers a month for its wide body and jumbo jet production, and entered 1997 with a backlog of orders for 1,239 aircraft. Business jet deliveries rose from 307 in 1995 to 330 in 1996 and are estimated to reach 400 by 1998. Business jet sales are expected to be $14-28 billion over the next 15 years. Aircraft deliveries are expected to crest in the year 2000.

Industry earnings rose to $7.6 billion in 1996, the highest in three decades, as a result of downsizing and increased productivity that boosted stock market interest. Military sales were predicted to decline from 1996 to 1997 by 6 percent. The military market is still active in some parts of Europe and the Far East. Central European nations could buy more than 200 planes worth $8 billion in the next five years according to a 1996 issue of *Business Week.*

The growth of the commercial market over the military market, increased foreign competition, and continuing mergers and acquisitions are some of the major factors that will drive the industry during the next few years.

Aircraft manufacturing has historically been one of the most consistently profitable and successful of American industries, and by all indications this trend is likely to continue. Led by companies such as the recently merged Boeing-McDonnell Douglas, and Lockheed, the aerospace industry collects a higher amount of export earnings than any other American industry. Until recently, no foreign manufacturer has been able to keep up with the pace of technological achievement or brute output achieved by American firms. The industry maintains a positive balance of trade with exports exceeding imports by $10.5 billion, although this balance has dropped by nearly 28 percent from 1994 to 1995. Airbus Industries, a European consortium, and Montreal based Bombardier have moved into competition with the American giants, however, and growing companies in the Far East, especially Japan, threaten to encroach further on the once distinctly American industry. Industry analysts suggest that future growth in the aircraft manufacturing industry will cross national borders as more and more companies engage in joint ventures with competitors from around the world, taking advantage of the strengths of the individual companies to provide the most competitive product available.

ORGANIZATION AND STRUCTURE

American aircraft companies provide airplanes for three distinct markets: the military, commercial aviation, and general aviation, which includes business aviation. From the end of World War II until the collapse of the Soviet threat in 1989, the American military services had a voracious appetite for sophisticated aircraft, which American firms sought to satisfy. This 49-year boom in military spending not only guaranteed the health of many manufacturers, but it also allowed those manufacturers to devote resources to research and development, ensuring that American aircraft would be the most technologically advanced in the world. The end of the Cold War, which has reduced military spending in the United States and around the world, has provided the greatest challenge for Ameri-

can aircraft manufacturers, who had grown accustomed to lucrative Department of Defense contracts. As a result, the military aircraft industry appears to be shrinking. Although the U.S. government has sought to guarantee its technological dominance through continued funding of research and development, funds are declining.

The development of commercial aircraft poses far greater risks than that of military aircraft. The development process for a passenger airliner capable of carrying several hundred people is both lengthy and costly, requiring manufacturers to anticipate the needs of airlines far in advance and to gamble vast amounts of money on the product's success. This is the main reason why Boeing canceled its development of the super jumbo aircraft. Manufacturers have usually designed new or modified aircraft in response to the demands of carriers, who have typically asked for more fuel efficiency and more seating rather than major redesigns. The *Economist* estimated that a new medium-sized airliner costs over $2 billion to develop, with engines costing another $1.5 billion, and noted that "aerospace companies bet their futures on each product."

As a result of the risks involved, commercial aircraft manufacturers have been rather conservative, pursuing modifications on existing airframes rather than reinventing complete aircraft, and most existing commercial airliners have changed little in recent history. However, some exciting new aircraft developments are taking place in the areas of speed, range, capacity and efficiency. Given the tremendous financial risks associated with developing new aircraft, many manufacturers today work cooperatively, jointly developing a design and dividing work among partners if the design is successful. The development of a new aircraft might involve many dozens of companies, each contributing some portion of a plane that they have perfected. The merger of the two dominate aircraft companies, The Boeing Company of Seattle, Washington, and the McDonnell Douglas Company of St. Louis, Missouri, will result in economies of operation that could allow more funds for development. In a calculated risk, Boeing canceled its plans to develop a super jumbo jet and concentrated instead on long range, fuel efficient planes with a modestly higher passenger capacity, citing the ratio of development costs to demand as justification. Airbus was still pursuing the super jumbo concept.

Though military and commercial aircraft manufacturers dominate the industry, American companies also produce a number of aircraft for the general aviation and the helicopter market segments, which include fixed wing aircraft and rotorcraft for business transportation, regional airline service, recreation, specialized uses such as ambulance service and agricultural spraying, and training. American manufacturers have historically produced about 60 percent of the world's general aviation aircraft and 30 percent of the helicopters. Major U.S. manufacturers of general aviation aircraft include the Beech Aircraft Corp., the Fairchild Aircraft Corp., the Cessna Aircraft Co., Gulfstream Aerospace, and the Learjet Corp.

Most aircraft manufacturers derive a significant proportion of their profits from the production of replacement and upgrade parts for their airplanes. Since large commercial jets represent such a large investment—a new twin-engine passenger jet may cost several hundred million dollars—airlines try to keep them in the air for many years. Moreover, the Federal Aviation Administration (FAA) sets stringent guidelines on repair and replacement procedures for passenger aircraft. Manufacturers provide parts through a network of suppliers and subcontractors, which comprise **SIC 3728: Aircraft Parts, Not Elsewhere Classified.**

BACKGROUND AND DEVELOPMENT

The American aircraft manufacturing industry traces its origin to one of the seminal events of the twentieth century: the Wright brothers' first powered flight in 1903. While many others had flown with gliders, balloons and dirigibles, Wilbur and Orville Wright marked a tremendous breakthrough with powered flight, because they proved the dynamics of flying a wing. In cross section, a wing is flat on the bottom but curved on top. As a wing moves through the air, air passing over the wing is forced to travel a greater distance than air passing under the wing. This causes a pocket of low pressure that literally sucks the wing up into the air. In order to work, the wing must be driven forward, or powered. These principles were described years before the Wrights' flight by Samuel P. Langley, a luckless professor whose aviation experiments were either ignored or a failure.

The Wrights originally hoped to sell airplanes to the United States Army as battlefield reconnaissance devices. The idea of employing aircraft to attack or drop bombs had not yet occurred to anyone. One of those on hand to witness the Wright brothers' first demonstration for the Army was a young conscript named Donald Douglas. Despite several impressive flights, Army officials were unmoved. The Wrights took their show to Europe, where they flew for the German, French and British armies. In the process, they prompted interest with such European aviation pioneers as Louis Blériot, Willy Messerschmidt, Anthony Fokker and Marcel Dassault.

Aviation was immediately embraced in Europe as a powerful new force in warfare, but it also made for good entertainment. Blériot and others such as Louis Paulhan built their own airplanes and began touring flying circuses. During 1910 and 1911, these European aviators toured the United States, flying before garage tinkerers like Glenn Martin, Clyde Cessna, Glenn Curtiss and Bill Boeing. Curtiss, a motorcycle repairman, was immediately drawn to flight, and he had access to the lightweight engines needed to power aircraft. Curtiss was one of the first to mount a propeller on the front of the aircraft in a "tractor" design. Until that time, propellers had been rear-mounted "pusher" models which are still found on some aircraft today, particularly amphibians.

After several of the Army's Wright planes crashed, killing the pilots, the Army found a new supplier in Curtiss, who escaped the enforcement of the Wrights' patents by incorporating the first ailerons. Curtiss thus emerged as the nation's leading aircraft manufacturer and the new supplier of choice to the Army.

Wilbur Wright died in 1912, leaving his brother in charge of their company. A poor manager, Orville Wright naively sold the company and its patents to a group of financiers led by William Boyce Thompson.

With the outbreak of war in Europe in 1914, Germany and France were quick to apply aviation to the battlefield, producing the world's first aces, Roland Garros and Manfred von Richtofen. The United States Army embraced air power in 1914 by creating an aviation group within the Signal Corps. One of its first members was Donald Douglas. Douglas, an engineering graduate of the Massachusetts Institute of Technology, was briefly employed by Glenn Martin, who had experimented with gliders since 1905. He built his first powered aircraft near Los Angeles about 1909, having been bankrolled by another aviation enthusiast, inventor Alexander Graham Bell. Douglas helped Martin develop his first production aircraft, the TT trainer, before he was dispatched to Washington to oversee the government's aviation program. Thompson's group later purchased Martin's company to form an aircraft combine called the Wright-Martin Company.

By 1918, the government had shown its interest in aviation through expansion of an air squadron and active intervention in the industry. Having seen the effect of air power in Europe during World War I, it was determined not to see American air power stunted by legal wrangling or patent hoarders. What emerged was a loosely policed competition for government contracts, primarily military and later air mail business. Hundreds of airplane builders emerged from garages and warehouses.

Automobile executives were chosen to head the government's ambitious 22,000-plane military aeronautics program. Favored for their ability to turn out huge quantities of a standardized product, these executives openly conspired to keep aircraft builders out of the industry. But Douglas, a member of the government board, fed information on the aeronautics program to other aircraft designers. Finally, upset with the performance of the Army's air squadron, and disgusted with government bureaucracy, Douglas resigned in 1919 and moved to Los Angeles to start his own company.

In 1919, automotive interests led by Delco persuaded Orville Wright to lend his name to another venture called Dayton-Wright. Wright was retained only for his venerable name and its ability to draw investment dollars. As an automotive venture, Dayton-Wright built only aircraft engines, and later fell under the control of General Motors. At the close of World War I, the government canceled 90 percent of the aircraft it had ordered, forcing many airplane builders to close. An investigation later revealed criminal collusion and widespread scandal among those who were empowered to grant contracts. However, virtually all involved escaped without prosecution.

Having briefly regained the services of Donald Douglas, Glenn Martin abandoned Thompson's company and struck up an important relationship with General Billy Mitchell, the Army's most powerful advocate of air power. With Mitchell's backing, Martin won a contract to build twenty MB-2 bombers, which Mitchell subsequently used in a spectacular demonstration off the Virginia Capes, sinking the supposedly unsinkable captured German battleship *Ostfriesland.*

A separate aircraft concern was established in 1914 by Allan and Malcolm Loughead. The brothers built their first aircraft in a small garage in San Francisco with financial backing from Max Mamlock and his Alco Cab company. After crashing it and scaring away Mamlock and his money, the brothers began flying exhibitions and sold Curtiss airplanes to raise money. The Lougheads, intent on military applications for aircraft, embarked on the construction of a large bomber at a site near Santa Barbara. There they met a young builder with an understanding of mathematics named Jack Northrop, whom they asked to join the company as chief engineer.

President Coolidge appointed Dwight Morrow to devise a government program for measured development of the industry in 1925. The resulting Air Commerce Act of 1926 set annual procurement levels for 2,600 military aircraft. Loughead and Northrop, who had drifted for six years, suddenly regained their market and managed to secure financial backing from a Los Angeles venture capitalist named Fred Keeler. As a condition, however, Keeler demanded that Loughead change the spelling of his Scotch-Irish name to accurately match its proper pronunciation. Apparently tired of being addressed as "Mr. Lug Head," Allan relented, and the new company was called Lockheed. The company later completed an all-metal, single-skin model called the Vega. This model, based on a design by Holland's Anthony Fokker, was developed by Northrop, who then left the company to work for Donald Douglas.

Douglas, whose business was growing on the strength of government sales, had been approached by David R. Davis, who offered to invest $40,000 for a transcontinental airliner. With Northrop's help, Douglas produced the Cloudster, of which the government ordered several hundred for military use. Davis, fearing the risk, bailed out immediately. The Cloudster, however, led Douglas to a series of successful designs, including the DT series torpedo planes and Douglas World Cruiser. Between 1921 and 1928, Douglas' annual production grew from six aircraft to more than 300.

The growing aircraft industry received a tremendous boost in 1927 when Charles Lindbergh completed the first successful trans-Atlantic flight using a modified Ryan Aeronautical tri-motor. Lindbergh's daring and nearly suicidal stunt so strongly revived interest in aviation that investors began pumping millions of dollars into aircraft companies. The following year, Martin relocated to Baltimore to be closer to his customers in Washington. Building bombers, he purchased the engine business of Louis Chevrolet, whose automobile business had been acquired by General Motors.

United Aircraft was the creation of Bill Boeing, a rich Seattle forester who purchased his first plane in 1910 from Glenn Martin and took flying lessons from the builder himself. Boeing and his partner Conrad Westerveldt built a number of early floatplane models for maritime postal delivery. After producing aircraft for the military during World War I, Boeing was persuaded by a customer named Ed Hubbard to form an airline service. In 1920, Boeing won a contract to haul mail between Chicago and Seattle. For the job, he developed a new design, the Model 40, fitted with a

Pratt & Whitney engine. Boeing's association with Pratt & Whitney brought him the acquaintance of that company's president, Frederick Rentschler.

The Kelly Airmail Act of 1925 returned airmail service to private bidders after a series of bloody crashes by the government's own air service. Postmaster William Folger Brown actively encouraged the formation of large airline companies by carefully awarding profitable air mail contracts. Boeing acquired numerous private airmail companies and their lucrative contract rights, and in 1928 banded them together to form the National Air Transport Company. The following year, Boeing and Rentschler merged their airframe and engine businesses to form the United Aircraft & Transportation Company. By the end of 1929 the company had taken over two propeller makers as well as Northrop's Avion company, and laid out an air transportation network that later became United Air Lines.

In August of 1929, Allan Loughead (who retained his own name) and Fred Keeler sold the Lockheed company to a group of automotive investors organized as the Detroit Aircraft company. The company drew tremendous investor interest after aviatrix Amelia Earhart crossed the Atlantic with one of the company's Vegas. Only one month later, world financial markets were buffeted by a stock market crash that plunged the nation into the Great Depression. Aviation company stocks, valued at more than $1 billion on total earnings of more than $9 billion, were decimated.

Detroit Aircraft, whose share price had tumbled from $15 to 12.5 cents, failed in 1932. The Lockheed operation was purchased out of receivership for $40,000 by Robert and Courtlandt Gross. The acquisition included an important new design, the Orion. Meanwhile, Allan Loughead had returned to his original real estate business. Jack Northrop, however, returned to Douglas, where he established yet another company as a subsidiary of the Douglas enterprise.

Douglas was associated with an aviation combine similar to Boeing's, called North American Aviation, which controlled Eastern Airlines and TWA. As a result of this relationship, Douglas, who had grown rich on military contracts, was now called upon to develop commercial airliners for his parent company. The first of these, the Douglas Commercial One, or DC-1, emerged during the worst years of the Depression. In February of 1934, the government reduced its subsidy to airmail carriers, creating a sudden demand for faster, more efficient aircraft. Douglas refined his DC design to meet this demand, and in 1935 produced the DC-3, an extremely versatile craft that nearly rendered competitors such as Boeing's 247 obsolete. The

Gross Brothers and their Lockheed company likewise improved upon earlier designs and emerged with the Electra.

Even Glenn Martin, spurned by the War Department, was brought into the commercial market. The devout Republican was forced to mortgage his plant under a Democratic New Deal program. Desperate for business, Martin built a luxurious flying boat, called the China Clipper, for Pan American's trans-Pacific routes. But when Martin only managed to sell three Clippers, the government was forced to support his business by purchasing the company's newly developed B-10 bomber.

The Depression would have destroyed the aircraft industry were it not for government support. It became official policy to award contracts to an increasingly privileged club of manufacturers, so that their expertise could be preserved and developed for military purposes. This policy hardened the cycle of concentration promoted by Brown. American aviation was controlled by three huge vertical monopolies, each maintaining huge airframe and engine manufacturing facilities and airline services.

In 1934, Senator Hugo Black completed an investigation of improprieties in these aviation investment trusts, which included United Aircraft, North American Aviation, and a third group called the Aviation Corporation of the Americas, or Avco. Several magnates were called to testify at hearings, including Bill Boeing, Donald Douglas and Glenn Martin. All admitted huge profiteering from aviation activities but, due to the absence of laws against these practices, no prosecution could result. Boeing, however, was so incensed by the nature of the investigation that he sold all his aviation interests and retired.

The combines were eventually dissolved on antitrust grounds, creating an enduring line of business restriction in American aviation. Airframe, engine and airline companies could not now be associated in any way. Boeing's conglomerate was divided into The Boeing Company in Seattle, United Aircraft in Connecticut, and United Air Lines, headquartered in Chicago. Likewise, North American Aviation lost its association with TWA and Eastern Airlines, and Avco lost American Airlines and Pan Am. Martin and Lockheed remained intact, as did Consolidated Aircraft, a company whose growth sprung from its acquisition of the defunct Dayton-Wright's designs.

By 1937, the emergence of the DC-3 and Electra enabled airlines to make money from passenger services alone, ending the reliance on airmail. The efficiency of these aircraft was recognized by belligerents

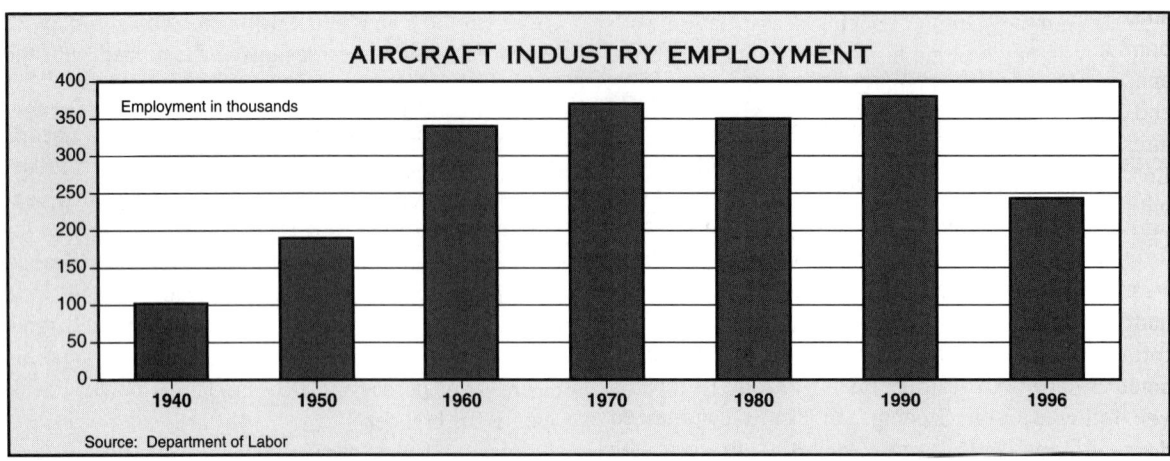

AIRCRAFT INDUSTRY EMPLOYMENT

Employment in thousands

Source: Department of Labor

in the small wars being fought in Europe and Asia. Unbeknownst to them, Lockheed, Douglas and Martin frequently sold aircraft to fictional airline companies and other front organizations for the Japanese and German armed forces. The discovery of this led to neutrality laws, which prescribed an aircraft embargo to any belligerent. But the demand for aircraft, particularly from Britain and France, was so great that the Roosevelt Administration created loopholes designed to allow the export of aircraft to American allies. This enabled the industry to fund development of new designs from large, lucrative export orders.

Much of this development was highly experimental. Northrop, whose subsidiary had been consolidated by Douglas in 1937, formed another company in 1939 with backing from LaMotte Cohu. After raiding Douglas of dozens of engineers, he resumed work on his radical flying wing project. Lockheed produced an equally strange design, a triple-hull fighter called the P-38 Lightning, while Boeing began work on its large B-17 bomber.

Several other smaller manufacturers gained admission to the defense industry club during this time. Grumman, a company established in 1929 to build naval aircraft, grew quickly after winning a contract to supply folding-wing F4F Wildcats to the Navy. By 1941 the company, established by Leroy Grumman and Leon Swirbul, had become the primary supplier to the Navy, overtaking even Martin. McDonnell Aircraft began building aircraft on a large scale in 1939, producing fighters for the Army Air Force. Meanwhile, Consolidated merged with the Vultee Company, forming a huge manufacturing operation in Texas called Convair.

While military preparations were stepped up in 1940 and 1941, the event that sparked tremendous growth in the aircraft industry was the Japanese attack on Pearl Harbor. Huge amounts of government money

were poured into engineering and production facilities. President Roosevelt ordered 60,000 aircraft in 1942, and 125,000 the year after. Douglas converted its DC-3 into military cargo planes and bombers, more than 10,000 of which were built. Other manufacturers were suddenly able to complete new designs. Convair produced the B-24 Liberator, and Martin the B-26 and A-30 Baltimore bombers and 70-ton Mars freighter. North American turned out the B-25 Mitchell bomber and the P-51 Mustang, while Douglas added the A-20 Havoc and SBD Dauntless dive bomber. The newly reconstituted Curtiss company returned with its C-46 cargo craft. Grumman provided the Navy with its Widgeon, TBF Avenger and F6F Hellcat.

Boeing, which at one point turned out 16 bombers every day, went into production on its B-29 Super Fortress. Even Ford, which exited the aircraft business during the Depression, was pressed into service, building B-24s. Northrop got his flying wing, the B-49, to fly. With every surface of the craft devoted to creating lift, it was capable of tremendous payloads. The Army, however, refused to develop the boomerang-shaped bomber, fearing possible instability in flight and the use of electronic, rather than cable, controls.

Small airplane builders, such as Beech Aircraft, Cessna and Piper, also participated in the war effort. But due to their limited manufacturing facilities and lack of advanced engineering talent, they were relegated to building support aircraft and parts for other manufacturers. Employment in the industry peaked at 1.3 million people in 1943, as every manufacturer participated in some way in the war effort.

The war completely changed the aircraft industry. In addition to demonstrating the power and strategic importance of aerial combat, it established the parallel relationship between investment and technological development. The war allowed the perfection of strategic bombing tactics, carpet bombing, dogfighting, naval attack bombing and, in the last days of the war, atomic bombing. Wars that were previously fought with tanks and battleships were now waged from above. By the end of the war, work had begun on a new generation of aircraft: jets. Larry Bell's Bell Aircraft Company, Lockheed and McDonnell were the first to experiment with jet power, having gained volumes of captured German jet airframe research.

While the military threat from Germany and Japan had been vanquished, a new adversary emerged in the form of the Soviet Union and became the focus of continued government investment in aviation. The development that began during World War II was scaled down, but concentrated in promising new technologies. Development centered on long-range strategic bombers for delivering nuclear bombs to targets in the Soviet Union and speedy fighters to intercept a similar threat from Soviet bombers.

Transition to a peacetime economy was considerably better managed than after World War I, due to the Contract Settlement Act of 1944. Still, the entire industry was forced to choose between commercial and military manufacturing. North American, Grumman, McDonnell, Northrop and Vought chose to develop only military craft, while Douglas pursued commercial designs. Boeing, Martin, Lockheed and Convair elected to develop commercial as well as military designs.

The most important postwar commercial entries were the four-engine Douglas DC-4, the Boeing 377 Stratocruiser and the triple-finned Lockheed Constellation, designed by Howard Hughes for TWA. Having emerged from the war with tremendous manufacturing capacity and engineering talent, these three companies dominated the commercial aircraft industry. Competitors, including Curtiss, Martin and Convair, were forced to exit the market in rapid succession, taking refuge in the more secure military businesses. Hughes Aircraft, famed for its massive Spruce Goose amphibian freighter, failed to break into the production market. After building a few experimental designs, it became the plaything of its owner, the difficult millionaire Howard Hughes. Hughes Aircraft later retreated into the missile and aviation controls business.

Boeing and Lockheed also became leading defense suppliers after the war. Lockheed extended its lead in jet fighter designs during the Korean War with its F-94 interceptor and, later, F-104 Starfighter. Boeing developed a family of huge intercontinental bombers, including the B-57, B-50 and B-52. Meanwhile, Convair introduced its B-36, with six pusher propellers, and supersonic B-58 Hustler.

On the recommendations of the Finletter Air Policy Commission, the government made air power the crux of its military establishment. While tremendous competition existed for seemingly open-ended military contracts, manufacturers found new ways to commercialize military designs. Boeing was the first to develop an entirely new passenger aircraft with technologies gained from a jet bomber. Boeing requested permission to use government-funded technologies from its successful eight-engine B-52 to develop a new four-engine jetliner called the 707. Eager to prevent a European monopoly in passenger jets—DeHavilland had just introduced its sleek Comet—the government agreed.

Soon after the 707 flew in 1954, American Airlines, a good Douglas customer, announced plans to buy 30 of Boeing's new jets. Douglas, which had put off introduction of a jet in favor of its DC-6s and DC-7s, was forced to rush a similar design into production or risk following Curtiss and Martin into oblivion. Douglas emerged the following year with highly similar jet design called the DC-8. Ironically, United Air Lines, historically associated with Boeing, placed the first order for the DC-8. Boeing, however, had eclipsed Douglas as the premier American aircraft builder.

Two new jet designs emerged from Europe during the early 1960s, the Sud Aviation Caravelle and Hawker Siddeley Trident. These jetliners featured engines tucked onto the rear of the fuselage, rather than under the wings. At the request of Eastern Airlines, Boeing pursued a three-engine 727, delivered in 1964, while Douglas built a more economical two-engine DC-9, delivered in 1965. Boeing introduced a smaller twin-engine jetliner, the 737, in 1967.

Tremendous consolidation occurred in the aircraft industry during this period. Convair was acquired by General Dynamics in 1952. Martin, which had abandoned aircraft production during the 1950s to concentrate on missiles and aircraft parts, was acquired by the American Marietta Corporation in 1961. North American, a builder of Air Force fighters, was thrown into deep disarray in 1967 after a fire destroyed one of its Apollo space capsules, killing three astronauts. The company was taken over that year by the machinery manufacturer Rockwell Standard. Also that year, financial difficulties resulting from the DC-8 and DC-9 finally caught up with Douglas. Unable to keep up with the demand for its aircraft, Douglas neared bankruptcy. Eventually, McDonnell Aircraft, a manufacturer of fighter jets and space capsules, prevailed in its bid to acquire Douglas.

The 1960s were a period of feverish development in military aviation, due to continued investments by the Defense Department in new technologies and academic programs, and the creation of the National Aeronautics and Space Administration (NASA). Some of the major accomplishments of this period were in the development of supersonic and rocket-powered aircraft. North American built a six-engine, triple sonic delta wing bomber called the B-70. Obsolete before its first flight, this aircraft evolved into the B-1 Bomber a dozen years later. Lockheed marked two great achievements, with its ultra high-altitude U-2 and triplesonic SR-71 spy planes. Developed in 1964 at Lockheed's super-secret "skunk works," this aircraft remains the fastest jet ever to fly in the American arsenal.

After abandoning research on a revolutionary nuclear-powered bomber, General Dynamics' Convair group became involved in the development of a multiuse fighter/bomber called the F-111 and the F-16 fighter. During the 1960s, McDonnell, Douglas, Martin, Boeing, Grumman and Convair became major participants in the space program. Other manufacturers were reduced to production of single-mission aircraft, such as Vought, with its A-7 Corsair, and Fairchild, with its A-10 Warthog. Northrop began work mainly as a subcontractor to McDonnell Douglas, building the F-18.

A postwar boom in private aviation greatly expanded the fortunes of small aircraft manufacturers such as Cessna, Beech and Piper. General aviation accounted for 17,811 or 90 percent of all U.S. aircraft by 1978. A wave of personal injury law suits precipitated by one pilot's suit against Piper Aircraft brought general aviation aircraft manufacturers to their knees. Manufacture of the most popular single-engine propeller plane in the world was halted in 1986.

In 1969 aviation engineer Bill Lear introduced the first private jet, which Cessna and Beech later imitated. Fairchild and Beech Aircraft became active in the small airliner market, defined as nineteen seats or less. Fairchild, which built the Fokker 27 under contract, developed the Metro airliner. Beech introduced its King Air, followed some years later by its Model 1900. These craft were operated on small airline "feeder" routes.

In commercial circles, a new market was emerging for larger 300 to 400 passenger jumbo jets. Boeing and McDonnell Douglas, eager to maintain their passenger jet franchises, began the extremely costly development of their 747 and DC-10, respectively. Surprisingly, Lockheed re-entered the market after 20 years, building a three-engine jumbo called the L-1011 Tristar. Boeing was nearly ruined by its four-engine behemoth, and at one point was forced to lay off two-

thirds of its work force. McDonnell Douglas fared little better, and Lockheed, mired in huge cost overruns from its massive C-5 Galaxy military cargo plane, required a federal loan guarantee to remain solvent.

The 747 and Tristar hit the market in 1970, and the DC-10 followed in 1971. These aircraft revolutionized air travel by offering airlines the capability to move as many as 400 passengers over distances of up to 5,000 miles. While sales of the DC-10 gained slowly, the 747 soon dominated the skies.

The Airline Deregulation Act, meanwhile, was signed in 1978. This legislation had a tremendous impact on airlines across the country, and plane manufacturers soon felt its repercussions as well. Major national carriers were unprepared for the newly competitive environment created by the Act and found themselves with fleets of Boeing 707s and McDonnell Douglas DC-8s that, because of fuel costs, become prohibitively expensive. In the meantime, new regional carriers utilized fuel-efficient aircraft that fit their needs. The national trunks were forced to examine their fleet configurations and make significant new purchases. Even then, however, analysts charge that the carriers were sluggish in responding. In many cases orders for new aircraft were not made to Boeing or McDonnell Douglas or any other manufacturers until well into the 1980s. The backlog of orders subsequently reached all-time high levels, with waiting periods for delivery of new aircraft ranging as long as seven years by 1986.

Efforts to build a supersonic transport, or SST, were abandoned by Lockheed and Boeing in 1970 after the market evaporated and the government refused to cover skyrocketing development costs. A European consortium succeeded in building a jet capable of breaking the speed of sound, but the plane proved so costly to build and operate, and its sonic boom so disruptive, that flights were severely curtailed and the planes operated at a loss.

On the success of its F-4 Phantom in Vietnam, McDonnell Douglas developed a family of new military aircraft during the 1970s, including the F-15 Eagle and A-4 Skyhawk. Boeing developed its venerable 707 into tankers and powerful AWACs airborne radar platforms, while Lockheed built large new military cargo craft, such as the C-130 and the Galaxy. Northrop remained a strong player in the military market with aging entries such as its F-5, and failed designs such as the export-intended F-20 Tigershark. Grumman did extremely well in the 1970s with its F-14 Tomcat and a smaller version of the AWACs, the E-2C Hawkeye.

The American military aircraft arsenal gained a huge boost in 1980. The industry, starved for investment since Vietnam, was the primary beneficiary of a massive armament program started by President Carter and trebled by President Reagan. Reagan resurrected Rockwell's $200 million B-1 bomber, canceled by Carter in 1977, and ordered development of a range of new radar-evading aircraft. Pentagon funding poured into these super secret "black projects." One of the beneficiaries was Lockheed, whose success with the SR-71 won it the right to develop the tiny diamond-shaped F-117 Stealth Fighter. Another was not revealed until 1988, when Northrop unveiled its sinister-looking B-2 Stealth Bomber. A flying wing, the B-2 represented the culmination of the late Jack Northrop's life-long dream. It also emerged, along with the B-1, as the replacement for the elderly but still devastating B-52 and the versatile F-111.

The flood of investment into military aircraft resulted in a series of scandals unrivaled since World War I. Several companies were investigated for vastly overcharging the Pentagon and misappropriating funds. In response, the government began shifting contracts away from offenders and forcing them to compete for business they had earlier taken for granted. In one of the few signs of growth, a consortium of Lockheed, Boeing and General Dynamics was chosen to develop the Advanced Tactical Fighter. In a period of decline for the defense industry, the ATF was one of the few large military projects remaining.

Significant activity also occurred in the commercial airliner market during the 1980s. Boeing introduced several upgraded versions of its hugely profitable 747, and a new series of economical, large twin-engine aircraft, the 757 and widebody 767. These aircraft finished off Lockheed's otherwise excellent L-1011 which, with three engines and a larger crew, was discontinued in 1981. Unable to design entirely new aircraft, McDonnell Douglas upgraded its DC-9 into the MD-80 series, and offered a similarly improved DC-10, called the MD-11.

The late 1980s and early 1990s saw manufacturers seeking partnerships to develop commercial aircraft. McDonnell Douglas failed to establish a limited merger with Taiwan Aerospace in 1990, and was seeking a partner to share development costs of a new four-engine MD-12 jetliner. Boeing, meanwhile, investigated a partnership with Deutsche Airbus, the disaffected German member of Boeing's arch rival, Airbus. Similarly, Boeing was seeking a partner for a planned 1000-passenger super jumbo craft. Boeing eventually dropped this project due to the billions of dollars necessary to develop a new jet. Airbus remained committed to this questionable project.

The combination of the long-term impact of the hub concept, the increasing concerns of passengers, greater concern for reduced operating costs on the part of the airlines, and rapid technological developments especially in the area of GPS (Global Position Satellite) are affecting the industry. GPS navigational devices will allow more direct flights from airport to airport. Historically, pilots have relied on VOR (VHF Omnidirectional Range) transmitters which emitted a distinct radio signal for each degree of the 360 degrees from magnetic North. For tracking purposes pilots routinely fly from one VOR at a fixed location to another via established routes, which at lower altitudes is not necessarily a straight line. Pilots using GPS navigational systems can now fly in a straight line from airport to airport and even fly an instrument approach using GPS navigational systems (precise within 50 feet), thus reducing actual mileage necessitated by the fixed location of VORs. This could reduce both travel time and fuel costs, especially for regional airlines. The growing number of regional jets has the potential for allowing for the return of more direct flights. Newer, more fuel efficient planes with longer ranges, such as the Boeing 777, will also impact the airlines.

CURRENT CONDITIONS

Aircraft industry analysts expect that the 1990s will see a period of great change in aircraft manufacturing. For years the industry had been propelled by ever-increasing military budgets and ever-increasing numbers of commercial airline passengers, but both of those stimuli changed in the 1990s. Government military expenditures peaked in 1987, when aircraft manufacturers supplied over 1,200 planes. In 1994, U.S. manufacturers shipped only 755 military aircraft or $7.9 billion in sales, approximately two-thirds the number shipped in 1987. By 1995 the number of military aircraft had dropped to 410 although the value had risen to $11 billion, generally reflecting budget cuts with corresponding reductions in employment by military aircraft manufacturers. During 1992, McDonnell Douglas, General Dynamics, Northrop, Lockheed, Rockwell, and Grumman cut over 29,000 jobs and were expected to cut another 20,000 jobs during the following two years. The increased competition for scarce military dollars is expected to reduce the number of military aircraft providers or possibly force industry consolidation. Deputy Defense Secretary William Perry told *Interavia* that the "DOD budget will not come back . . . The companies that succeed are those that will plan accordingly in accepting the new reality despite the hardships it will cost to downsize.''

"While procurement of aircraft has declined significantly,'' noted *U.S. Industrial Outlook 1993,* "research, development, testing, and evaluation funding has remained somewhat stable, providing some haven for U.S. providers of advanced military aircraft technologies.'' In 1993, the Clinton Administration took steps to protect the U.S. aerospace industry's long-held technological superiority, increasing NASA's research and development budget, maintaining the DOD's research and development budget, and creating the National Commission to Ensure a Strong, Competitive Airline Industry, which has attempted to challenge the subsidies provided by European Community countries to their aircraft manufacturers. Such efforts are expected to maintain the technological superiority of the American aircraft manufacturing base even while the number of manufacturers shrinks.

Much of the ordering activity for new planes was from leasing companies. British Aerospace Asset Management's jet and turboprop divisions manage and lease more than 500 planes with $700 million in revenues. Another leader is GE Capital Aviation Services, which ordered 45 Airbus jet transports with options on another 45, with delivery beginning in 1997 and continuing at the rate of 15 to 20 per year until the order is complete. Leasing is the primary means by which the global air industry will acquire new aircraft in 1997-99 and beyond.

While military aircraft manufacturers struggled to adjust to changing military budgets, commercial aircraft manufacturers had to adjust to declining demand for aircraft by major carriers, production overcapacity, and government-supported foreign competition in the first half of the 1990s. These challenges were made all the more pressing in 1991, when for the first time in history, the number of passengers riding on commercial airlines declined. This drop in air travel prompted many airlines to cancel or postpone orders for aircraft, leaving manufacturers with an excess of inventory. U.S. manufacturers shipped 408 large transport aircraft valued at $26 billion in 1993, down from their peak of 610 aircraft valued at $30 billion in 1992. Both Boeing and McDonnell Douglas had to reduce production and lay off nearly 10,000 employees each. Fortunately, by 1996 the industry had begun to recover.

According to *Interavia* contributor John Crampton, "Aerospace manufacturers are learning to live with a whole new set of rules brought about by the industry-wide recession and the peace dividend.'' Manufacturers were adjusting to this changed marketplace in a number of ways. Most notable was been a

trend toward industry consolidation and cooperation. Many of the smaller manufacturers in the industry were eliminated by the recession, and those that have survived have increasingly banded together to share the risk of developing new products. For both Boeing and McDonnell Douglas, this has meant teaming with Asian manufacturers in order to better penetrate the rapidly expanding Asian market. Industry analysts believe that those manufacturers best able to form working partnerships will be the ones to succeed in the 1990s. In 1996 there were many mergers, primarily precipitated by the effects of deregulation and the decline in military contracts. In order to remain competitive, aircraft manufacturers must also reduce costs by as much as 30 percent, concluded Crampton. Technological advances will pave the way for some cost reduction, as manufacturers increasingly turn to computer-assisted design mock-ups and paperless workplaces as ways of reducing costly experimentation and excess paperwork exemplified by Boeing's 777.

In an effort to lock-in its customers, Boeing has recently established an "exclusive supplier'' relationship with several airline companies. Its twenty-year agreement with American Airlines gives the airline more flexibility in aircraft selection types and delivery dates than previous arrangements did.

In April 1997, the new F-22 Raptor single seat fighter—a joint effort of Lockheed, Boeing, and Pratt Whitney (United Technology Corp.)—was unveiled and scheduled to make its debut flight in May 1997. At $70 million per unit, this fighter was designed to secure dominance over any adversary aircraft. Original plans for the U.S. military to purchase 438 of these planes at more than $71 billion, however, may not survive the budget cuts of 1997.

U.S. manufacturers Boeing and McDonnell Douglas are two of the top three aircraft manufacturing companies, along with the European Community's Airbus Industries. Airbus Industries is actually a consortium of the France's Aerospatiale, Germany's Daimler-Benz Aerospace, British Aerospace, and Spain's CASA. Since Boeing was founded in 1916, it has sold over 6,500 jet airliners, more than all other manufacturers in the western world combined, according to the *Economist.* Currently employing nearly 108,000 people around the world, Boeing controls approximately 50 percent of total world airline sales. Airbus Industries, founded in 1971 as an experiment in European collaboration, accounts for 30 percent of world airline sales with its range of Airbus planes. Airbus's American competitors complain that the consortium survives only because of hefty subsidies paid by European governments, but efforts at ending those subsidies in the mid-1990s should prove whether Airbus is capable of surviving on its profits alone. McDonnell Douglas accounts for 17 percent of world airline sales and employs close to 100,000 workers. Though the company has had to tolerate a declining share of the market, potential cooperation with Airbus on the construction of a jumbo jet might allow the venerable firm to recapture some of Boeing's market share.

Boeing had gross revenues of $19.5 billion in 1995 and $22.7 billion in 1996, reversing a decreasing trend from the previous three years. Lockheed Martin had gross sales of $26.9 billion in 1996, up 18 percent over 1995.

Montreal-based Bombardier, Inc. originally a snowmobile manufacturing company, had gross revenues of $5.1 billion in 1996, up 23 percent over 1995, making it the fourth largest manufacturer of commercial aircraft in the world. Concentrating on the regional airline market with its 50-seat Canadair Regional Jet, it has grabbed 42 percent of the world market for 20-90 seat jets in 1996. It received nearly $1 billion in orders in January 1997. Its advanced Global Express business jet can carry 19 passengers from New York City to Tokyo at a speed of .8 Mach. The company won an order from Atlantic Southeast Airlines, a Delta connection, to supply carriers with 50 seats.

The U.S. general aviation market has seen years of decline, as shipments of its aircraft have fallen from 17,817 in 1978 to just 780 in 1992. The decline has been blamed primarily on tough American product-liability laws, which have required manufacturers to purchase costly insurance in case their products are implicated in accidents. Rising fuel costs and the decreasing cost of flying on commercial airlines also contributed to the decline of this segment of the industry. This market segment decline drove Piper, one of the largest manufacturers of light aircraft, from the industry in 1991, and forced Cessna, long the industry leader, to reduce the size of its work force from 16,000 employees in 1979 to just 3,600 in 1988. Cessna has built nearly half of the aircraft flying in the free world, according to the *Economist.* Other manufacturers of general aviation aircraft include Beechcraft, Fairchild, Gulfstream, and Learjet. The military market is dominated by Lockheed, General Dynamics, Northrop, Rockwell, and Grumman, as well as Boeing and McDonnell Douglas.

Another impact of general aviation litigation was to escalate the market for used aircraft. The value of the remaining used aircraft increased phenomenally over the past several years in part due to the scarcity of new planes and the export demand for old planes.

According to Gene Unterman, President, Heartland Aircraft Group, Ltd., " . . . over 1,000 aircraft a month" are "leaving our shores for Europe, Australia, and even the Asian continent."

The General Aviation Revitalization Act of 1994 forbade any civil actions against manufacturers for death or injury from an incident in a less than 20-passenger aircraft more than 18 years old. The 18 year limitation is superseded by states having lesser periods. Thirteen states have absolution from liability after six to twelve years. This Act eliminated the devastating impact that product liability suits had upon the industry and revitalized single engine propeller aircraft manufacturing. Cessna resumed production of the world's most popular four single engine land plane, the Cessna 172, along with its 182 and 206 models, which was halted in 1986. Cessna was expected to employ 2,000 additional people in 1996. The first new production model 172, which sells for between $124,000 and $140,000, was delivered in November 1996. Piper Aircraft hoped to emerge from bankruptcy in 1995. With 74 percent of the general aviation fleet more than 18 years old, the market ought to be good. U.S. light aircraft manufacturers delivered 1,130 new aircraft in 1996. With the resumption of production by Cessna this figure could rise dramatically. General aviation resolves some of the longstanding scheduling problems by flying direct to a destination instead of going through a hub.

General Aviation accounted for 57 percent of the total aviation hours flown, 33 percent of the miles, 75 percent of the departures and 87.3 million, or 14 percent, of the passengers. The demand for corporate business jets was on the rise in 1996, with sales up 23 percent from 1995 to $2.06 billion and expected to increase by 10 percent in the next year. Gulfstream Aerospace Corporation expects to double revenues by 1998 with the popularity of its new $37.5 million, 6,500 nautical mile range new corporate luxury jet. Over 70 Gulfstreams have been sold, and a backlog of orders totaling nearly $3 billion has accumulated to the year 2000.

Although General Aviation is the largest volume producer in terms of the number of aircraft, the leading money makers in this industry are in the military and commercial sectors. Boeing posted sales in 1993 of more than $25 billion on the strength of commercial sales and contracts for the F-22 fighter plane and the RAH-66 Commanche helicopter. United Technologies posted total sales of $20 billion in 1993, partly on the strength of helicopter and aircraft sales. But according to *Fortune* in 1993, the "severely depressed airline market will force [United Technologies'] Pratt &

Whitney division to cut 11,000 jobs by end of '94.'' This recession in the industry began to turn around in 1995-1996.

Eurocopter sold 228 new helicopters valued at $2.26 billion in 1996. The world market for helicopters is recovering from a four year downturn and is expected to grow modestly. Strong, stable worldwide economies and a resurgence of off-shore drilling are setting the stage for the helicopter industry in 1997. Membership in Helicopter Association International has grown by 25 percent in the past four years, indicating a growing interest. Japan conducted its first flight of a tandem seat light helicopter in 1996. Sikorsky developed a helicopter with better performance and a reduced crew load, the S-76C.

Lockheed garnered sales of $13 billion that same year, in part because of its F-22 and F-16 military aircraft. Martin Marietta posted 1993 sales of $9.4 billion, but lost out on its bid to merge with Grumman Corp. in 1994 because of Northrop Corp.'s late bid. Northrop, which had sales of more than $5 billion in 1993, topped Marietta's bid for Grumman with its own $2.11 billion offer. Northrop's $62-per-share bid overmatched Marietta's bid of $55-per-share. The combined company, with total annual revenues of more than $13 billion, is called Northrop Grumman Corp. The battle for control of Grumman reflected the merger/acquisition trend prevalent in the industry in response to the shrinking military market. Boeing is expected to reduce annual operating costs by $1 billion due to its merger with McDonnell Douglas Corp. and heighten its advantage over Europe's Airbus Industrie. Aircraft deliveries are expected to climb 52 percent in 1997 and helicopter deliveries to jump 31 percent. Consolidations are anticipated to continue especially among defense related companies. Lockheed Martin wound up with $30 billion in revenues in 1996 as the result of its acquisitions, including Loral Corp.

WORK FORCE

The total aircraft industry employment was 259, 600 in December 1996, with 103,900 employed as production workers at an average wage of close to $20.00 per hour. The aerospace industry employed 465,000 total. With the backlog of orders at several manufacturers, the potential for employment should remain good until the year 2000.

Although there have been reductions in defense spending, cuts in aircraft purchases by troubled commercial airline carriers, and the elimination of thousands of jobs in the industry prior to 1996, the industry seems to be improving with commercial orders making up for the deficit from the military sector.

AMERICA AND THE WORLD

The value of aircraft exports has declined slightly during the five year period from 1990-1995 (from a high of $26.4 billion to $13.6 billion). There was a corresponding decline in aircraft imports from $3.9 to $3.5 billion during the same time period. Japan, the United Kingdom, South Korea, Canada and the Netherlands were the top export markets in 1995. France, the number one market in 1991 and number two or three until 1994 was not among the most recent top five, but has consistently remained the number one importer to the U.S. for the same period.

While the worldwide market for military aircraft was a tepid one in the early 1990s because of overcapacity and diminished demand, the market for commercial aircraft rebounded somewhat in 1996. As *U.S. Industrial Outlook 1994* notes, ''demand in world commercial markets, particularly the expanding economies of Asia and the Pacific Rim, is expected to show increases over the next 10 to 15 years.'' In fact, the larger share of the commercial transport market is now overseas. The U.S. share, as a percentage of the world market, will shrink. Airline traffic, especially international traffic, is expected to show strong growth throughout the rest of the decade requiring more aircraft over the next 20 years.

In January 1997, the French government announced the merger of Aerospatiale and Dassault Aviation. France's state-owned Aerospatiale is expected to be sold to Dassault Aviation and privatization is planned for Thomson, its defense-electronics giant. Marriages between Britain's General Electric Co. and Aerospace LP were foreseeable in response to U.S. mergers.

USAir has placed orders for nearly 400 aircraft with Airbus, possibly making it the largest Airbus carrier. Aviation Industries of China is developing a 90-140 seat twin-jet. In a joint Russian-Ukranian effort the AN-70 transport was scheduled for flight tests in March 1997. Brazil's Embraer delivered two EMB-145 50-seat regional jets to Continental Express in December of 1996. Continental Airlines ordered twenty-five 50-seat EMB-145s from Embraer in 1996. Chinese enterprises are expected to buy 1,200 aircraft costing $90 billion in the next two decades. The Korean Aircraft Industry saw plans for a 100 seat jet collapse. However, Daewoo Heavy Industries has developed fuselages and panels for F-16 fighters.

Boeing has proposed a production facility in Turkey after an earlier statement from Prime Minister Erkaban to buy 50 civilian aircraft worth a total of $4 billion with an offset agreement whereby Turkey would manufacture some of the parts. Turkey also received proposals from McDonnell Douglas, Airbus Industrie and Lockheed Martin. Aeroflot agreed to buy ten 737s from Boeing on to be delivered in 1998-1999. Most of China's 32 airlines are expected to remain loyal to Boeing.

There is an Indo-Russian project to develop a twin turbo transport. Taneja Aerospace and Aviation of India produced its first trainer, the Hansa 3 in 1996 which was made of composite materials. Israel Aircraft Industries is building a new business jet in cooperation with French and U.S. companies that is expected to be certified in 1998.

The Canadian Aerospace industry—6th largest in the world selling $10 billion annually in 1996—is expected to move to 4th place by the year 2000.

RESEARCH AND TECHNOLOGY

Augmented reality, a variation of virtual reality, lets the user see the world as an overlay of information so that it appears attached to a work piece, and has been installed in Boeing's wire shop. It assists workers by highlighting drilling locations. Airbus Industrie was experimenting with a thin-film skin of nearly imperceptible ridges developed by 3M. By reducing surface turbulence, this skin could cut fuel burn by one percent. Northrup Grumman used advanced laser-based technology to reduce manufacturing and scheduling costs in its efforts to establish a digital airframe factory using a laser tracking system.

FURTHER READING

Aboulafia, Richard. "Flat Market for Business Aircraft." *Aviation & Space Week Technology,* 13 January 1997.

———. "Helo Makers: Decisions Pending." *Aviation & Space Week Technology,* 13 January 1997.

———. "Uncertain Upturn Challenges Commercial Transport Makers." *Aviation & Space Week Technology,* 13 January 1997.

"Aeroflot [AEF.CN], Boeing (Boeing Co) Sign Plane Deal." Available from http://biz.yahoo.com/finance/97/04/15/ba_1.html.

Aerospace Industries Association. "Military Aircraft Accepted by U.S. Military Agencies: Number and Flyaway Value: Calendar Years 1981-1995." *Aerospace Facts and Figures 1996/1997.*

"Air China Orders Five Boeing 777s." Available from http://biz.yahoo.com/finance/97/03/24/ba_seattl_1.html.

"Airbus See Exclusive Pacts as Bad for Business." Available from http://biz.yahoo.com/finance/97/04/14/amr_ba_ca_1.html.

"An-70 Set to Fly." *Aviation Week & Space Technology,* 13 January 1997.

Ashley, Steven. "Precision Metrology with Laser Trackers." *Mechanical Engineering,* October 1996.

"BAE Australia Wins Exports." *Aviation Week & Space Technology,* 3 March 1997.

Barrett, Patrick. "Airbus Ads to Woo Passengers." *Marketing,* 5 September 1996.

Baum, Geoff. "The Essential Capitalist Tool." *Forbes,* 24 February 1996.

Bickers, Charles. "Will it Fly?" *Far Eastern Economic Review,* 21 November 1996.

Biddle, Wayne. *Barons of the Sky,* New York: Simon & Schuster, 1991.

Bilstein, Roger E. *Flight in America 1900-1983: From the Wrights to the Astronauts.* Baltimore, MD: Johns Hopkins University Press, 1984.

Blay, Roy, ed. *Lockheed Horizons.* Burbank, CA: Lockheed Corporation, 1983.

"Boeing Buying Rockwell Units." Available from http://cnnfn.com/hotstories/companies/9608/01/boeing_rockwell.

"Boeing Co. to Discuss Production in Turkey." Available from http://biz.yahoo.com/finance/97/04/14/ba_2.html.

Boeing Company. "1996 Annual Report." Available from http://www.reportgallery.com/Boeing/comlair.html.

"Boeing Creates Enterprise Unit." *Aviation Week & Space Technology,* 3 February 1997.

"Boeing Projects Healthy Airplane Demand Over Next 20 Years." Available from http://biz.yahoo.com/prnews/97/03/04/ba_y0002_1.html.

"Boeing Reports First Quarter Deliveries." Available from http://biz.yahoo.com/prnews/97/04/07/ba_y0001_1.html.

"Boeing 777 Breaks Speed and Distance Records." Available from http://biz.yahoo.com/finance/97/04/02/ba_y0002_1.html.

"Boeing to Acquire McDonnell Douglas for Under 1 Time Annual Revenue." *Corporate Growth Report (Weekly),* 23 December 1996.

Byrne, Harlan S. "Borne Winners." *Barron's 1997,* 17 February 1997.

"Civil Aerospace." *Economist,* 3 September 1988, S1-S28.

Crampton, John. "Going Back to Basics." *Interavia,* November 1993, 18-20.

Crock, Stan. "Aviation & Defense." *Business Week,* 13 January 1997.

Dahl, Robert V. "Air Freight Market is Expanding." *Aviation & Space Week Technology,* 13 January 1997.

Darlin, Darmin. "Aerospace & Defense." *Forbes,* 13 January 1997.

"Decision Expected Shortly on Indo-Russian Turboprop." *Aviation & Space Week Technology,* 2 December 1996.

''Deflating the Jumbo.'' *Economist,* 25 January 1997.

Donoghue, J.A . ''AE-100 at Center Stage.'' *Air Transport World,* January 1997.

———. ''Boeing's Afternoon Delight.'' *Air Transport World,* February 1997.

Donohue, Nancy, and Pankaj Ghemawat. ''The U.S. Airline Industry, 1987-1988.'' Boston, Harvard Business School, 1989.

Egan, Mark. ''Gulfstream Looking for Revenues to Soar.'' Available from http://biz.yahoo.com/finance/97/04/08/ba_gac_ge_1.html.

Edmundson, Gail. ''Europe Can't Delay any Longer.'' *Business Week,* 13 January 1997.

Engardio, Pete. ''The Relentless Giant of Guanxi.'' *Business Week,* 30 September 1996.

''Equipment.'' *Air Transport World,* 1 September 1996.

''Financing China: Are Aeroplanes Leading the Way?'' *Crossborder Monitor,* 23 October 1996.

Flint, Perry. ''Business as Usual.'' *Air Transport World,* February 1997.

Franklin, Roger. *The Defender: The Story of General Dynamics.* New York: Harper, 1986.

Friedman, Matthew. ''How Bombardier Created Sleek Global Express.'' *Computing Canada,* 3 February 1997.

Fulghum, David A. ''Chile Agrees to First Foreign T-6A JPATS Sale.'' *Aviation Week & Space Technology,* 13 January 1997.

''GAMA Reports Record Billings.'' *Aviation Week & Space Technology,* 17 February 1997.

Haines, Thomas B. ''A Tradition Continues: The Skyhawk is Back.'' *AOPA Pilot* December 1996.

''Hansa Trainer to Be Privately Produced.'' *Aviation & Space Week Technology,* 2 December 1996.

''How the Top Defense Contractors Stack Up.'' *Fortune,* 22 February 1993.

Industry & Trade Summary: Aircraft, Spacecraft, and Related Equipment. Washington: Office of Industries, November 1991.

''Industry Awaits Impact of Boeing Merger.'' *Industrial Distribution,* February 1997.

Kaplan, Ellen, ed. *In the Company of Eagles.* Stamford, CT: Pratt & Whitney, 1990.

Katz, Jan. ''Embraer's Little Jet Could Circle the Globe.'' *Business Week,* 4 November 1996.

Kim, S. C. ''Cleared for Take Off.'' *Business Korea,* October 1996.

Krumenaker, Larry. ''Virtual Assembly.'' *Technology Review,* February/March 1997.

Langfield, Martin. ''U.S. Military Unveils New 'Raptor' Stealth Fighter.'' Available from http://biz.yahoo.com/finance/97/04/09/ba_lmt_utx_2.html.

''Lockheed Martin Corp Boeing Co. Get Hellfire Work.'' Available from http://biz.yahoo.com/finance/97/04/07/ba_lmt_1.html.

''Lockheed Settles Out of Court.'' *ENR,* 19 August 1996.

Mattera, Philip. *Inside U.S. Business: A Concise Encyclopedia of Leading Industries.* Homewood, IL: Dow Jones-Irwin, 1987.

Lubov, Seth. ''Destroying the Old Heirarchies.'' *Forbes,* 3 June 1996.

Mecham, Michael. ''3M Thin Skin Tested by Airbus.'' *Aviation & Space Week Technology,* 2 December 1996.

Mooreman, Robert W. ''Hidden Assets.'' *Air Transport World,* December 1996.

North, David M. ''IAI's Galaxy Back on Track: Certification Planned in 1998.'' *Aviation & Space Week Technology,* 2 December 1996.

O'Lone, Richard G. ''U.S. Airframe Outlook Bright Despite Gloomy 1991 Results.'' *Aviation Week & Space Technology,* 16 March 1992, 53-55.

''On a Wing and a Prayer.'' *Economist,* 5 October 1996.

''Paying for Planes.'' *Business China,* 14 October 1996.

Proctor, Paul. ''Boeing Balks, Airbus Talks——Big.'' *Aviation Week & Space Technology,* 27 January 1997.

———. ''First Flight of Updated 737 Rejuvenates Narrow-Body Line.'' *Aviation Week & Space Technology,* 17 February 1997.

———. ''Helicopter Sales Bouyed by Strong Economics.'' *Aviation Week & Space Technology,* 3 February 1997.

Reinhardt, Andy. ''Booming Boeing.'' *Business Week,* 30 September 1996.

Ropelewski, Robert, and Bill Sweetman. ''US Government, Industry Seek Competitive Solutions.'' *Interavia,* August 1993.

Shapiro, Stacy. ''Liability Bill Offers Hope.'' *Business Insurance,* 23 May 1994.

———. ''Product Liability Reform Revitalizes General Aviation.'' *Business Insurance,* 15 May 1995.

Shifrin, Carole A. ''A Big Win for Airbus in North America.'' *Aviation & Space Week Technology,* 13 January 1997.

———. ''American Commits to All-Boeing Jet Fleet.'' *Aviation & Space Week Technology,* 11 November 1996.

———. ''Atlantic Southeast Plans Order of CJRs.'' *Aviation Week & Space Technology,* 13 January 1997.

———. ''Derivatives of 777 and 767 Take Shape at Boeing.'' *Aviation Week & Space Technology,* 17 February 1997.

———. ''Regional Aircraft Market Comes Alive.'' *Aviation & Space Week Technology,* 9 September 1996.

Smart, Tim. ''Finally, We Have Ignition.'' *Business Week,* 16 September 1996.

Solberg, Carl. *Conquest of the Skies,* Boston: Little, Brown, 1979.

Sparaco, Pierre. "Airbus Plows Ahead with A3XX Plans." *Aviation Week & Space Technology,* 27 January 1997.

———. "Eurocopter Forecasts Modest Market Upturn." *Aviation Week & Space Technology,* 3 February 1997.

———. "Eurocopter Seeks Recovery in a Weak Market." *Aviation & Space Week Technology,* 23 September 1996.

———. "French Merger Makes Progress." *Aviation & Space Week Technology,* 13 January 1997.

Symonds, Willam C. "Bombardier Is Doing Barrel Rolls." *Business Week,* 3 March 1997.

"Teal Group Predicts 25,537 Aircraft Valued at $655.5 Billion Will be Built Throughout the World in the 1997-2006 Decade." Available from http://biz.yahoo.com/prnews/97/02/14/ba_md_y00_1.html.

Thruelsen, Richard. *The Grumman Story.* New York: Praeger, 1976.

Unterman, Gene. *How to Buy a Used Aircraft.* Batavia, Illinois: Heartland Aircraft Group, Ltd., 1990.

U.S. Department of Commerce. Economics and Statisistics Administration. Bureau of the Census. *Statistical Abstract of the United States 1996.* 116th ed. Washington: GPO, 1996.

U.S. Department of Commerce. International Trade Administration. *U.S. Industrial Outlook 1993.* Washington: GPO, 1993.

———. *U.S. Industrial Outlook 1994.* Washington: GPO, 1994.

U.S. Department of Labor. Bureau of Labor Statistics. *Employment, Hours, and Earnings, United States, 1988-96.* Washington: GPO, 1996.

———. *Occupational Outlook Handbook: 1996-97.* Washington: GPO, 1996.

Velocci, Jr., Anthony L. "Global Express vs G percent: The Contest Heats Up." *Aviation & Space Week Technology,* 2 September 1996.

———. "Fewer Players to See Late-Decade Upturn." *Aviation Week & Space Technology,* 15 March 1993.

———. "GECAS Study Reveals Leasing Paramount to Aircraft Acquisition." *Aviation & Space Week Technology,* 25 November 1996.

———. "Jumbo Market Too Slim for Two Manufacturers." *Aviation & Space Week Technology,* 27 January 1997.

Ward's Business Directory of U.S. Private and Public Companies. Detroit: Gale Research, 1996.

Wasny, Garrett. "A Canadian Flyover." *World Trade,* October 1996.

Whitehouse, Arthur. *The Sky's the Limit.* London: Macmillan, 1979.

Whitford, David . "Sale of the Century." *Fortune,* 17 February 1997.

Wolk, Martin. "Boeing Considers Move into Airline Maintenance." Available from http://biz.yahoo.com/finance/97/04/11/ba_brka_md_1.html.

—John Simley, updated by David C. Genaway

SIC 3724

AIRCRAFT ENGINES AND ENGINE PARTS

This industry includes establishments primarily engaged in manufacturing aircraft engines and engine parts. This industry also includes establishments owned by aircraft engine manufacturers and primarily engaged in research and development on aircraft engines and engine parts, whether from enterprise funds or on a contract or fee basis. Also included are establishments engaged in repairing and rebuilding aircraft engines on a factory basis. Establishments primarily engaged in manufacturing guided missile and space vehicle propulsion units and parts are classified in **SIC 3764: Guided Missile and Space Vehicle Propulsion Units and Propulsion Unit Parts;** those manufacturing aircraft intake and exhaust valves and pistons are classified in **SIC 3592: Carburetors, Pistons, Piston Rings, and Valves;** and those manufacturing aircraft internal combustion engine filters are classified in **SIC 3714: Motor Vehicle Parts and Accessories.** Establishments primarily engaged in the repair of aircraft engines, except on a factory basis, are classified in **SIC 4581: Airports, Flying Fields, and Airport Terminal Services;** and research and development on aircraft engines on a contract or fee basis by establishments not owned by aircraft engine manufacturers are classified in **SIC 8731: Commercial Physical and Biological Research.**

INDUSTRY SNAPSHOT

The total value of aircraft engines and engine parts was $16.5 billion in 1995 according to the U.S. International Trade Administration. While the overall value of shipments has decreased from a high of $25.3 billion in 1990, the positive balance of trade (exports over imports) has continued to improve from 1992 to 1995. The consumption of aircraft engines is obviously a function of aircraft production and usually a multiple function due to the fact that many aircraft have several engines. The current health of the aircraft industry is well-documented under SIC 3721, and projected growth on aircraft orders should bode well for the future of engine manufacturers as long as the aircraft industry continues to improve.

The world aircraft engine industry is dominated by three companies: General Electric (GE), Pratt & Whitney, which is a division of United Technologies Corporation, and Rolls-Royce. Each of these companies achieved their leading role through the successful development of jet engine models for commercial aircraft, though GE and Pratt & Whitney maintain significant interest in the development of engines for military aircraft. The big three offer jet engines in nearly every thrust range and compete with each other for use on commercial aircraft produced by Boeing, McDonnell Douglas, and Airbus Industries. Several other engine manufacturers, including Allison, Garrett and Lycoming, are involved primarily with small jet turbines and piston engines, which power propeller-driven aircraft.

Aircraft engine manufacturers enjoyed a long period of industry growth from the end of World War II until the first years of the 1990s, when changes in military spending and changing commercial air travel patterns caused dramatic shifts in industry planning and expectations. Industry analysts predict that engine manufacturers will struggle to adjust to an industry-wide recession throughout the mid-1990s when a revitalized commercial air travel market will increase orders for aircraft engines. The future of the aircraft engine market seems likely to depend on the development of big engines with a thrust of 60,000 pounds or more, according to *Interavia*. Each of the leading engine manufacturers is expected to take steps to develop engines to compete in this market category, which is expected to generate $210 billion in sales of engines and parts between 1992 and 2012. There were 14,925 new and used piston and turbine engines (including parts) exported in 1995 at a total value of $6.16 billion new and used. New total engine delivery rates were expected to be about 1,700 in 1996, turning short-range pessimism into long-range optimism.

ORGANIZATION AND STRUCTURE

The manufacture of aircraft engines was once controlled by the same companies assembling aircraft and operating airlines, but industry regulation initiated in 1934 forced aircraft engine manufacturers to work independently of aircraft manufacturers. This antitrust legislation is partly responsible for the intense competition that characterizes the aircraft engine industry in which each of the leading engine makers seeks to provide engines to fit the requirements of a wide range of aircraft. Engine companies are typically chosen to design an engine at the concept stage of a new aircraft. Once the engine is developed, the engine builder may try to adapt the design for other aircraft. In fact, it is common to find the same engine on a variety of competing aircraft. Engine manufacturers rarely develop an engine that is not capable of multiple applications.

For decades following the end of World War II, military funding supplied much of the research and development money that allowed U.S. manufacturers to continually upgrade their engines. Technical breakthroughs achieved on military projects found their way into commercial engine applications, thus allowing engine manufacturers to achieve substantial profits from commercial engine sales. This arrangement has changed significantly since the end of the Cold War when the U.S. military budget decreased dramatically. Though the Clinton administration has promised to continue providing research and development funding to the aerospace industry, engine manufacturers are increasingly faced with incorporating the cost of research and development spending into the price of their engines. Bob Leduc, director of strategic planning at Pratt & Whitney, told *Interavia* that his company will need to spend close to $6 billion in development to compete for the large engine market—costs that will require the manufacturer to recover $1.3 million per engine just to cover engineering and development costs. Such prohibitive costs may force manufacturers to remove themselves from competition in some market segments.

All of the American aircraft engine manufacturers are divisions of larger corporations. Pratt & Whitney is a division of United Technologies; GE Aircraft Engines is a unit of General Electric; Allison is owned by General Motors, Garrett is a part of AlliedSignal; Lycoming is part of Textron. Pratt & Whitney and GE are thought to possess an advantage over their British competitor, Rolls-Royce, because of their corporate support which allows them to better weather industry cycles. While the Pratt & Whitney Power Group contributes approximately 32 percent of United Technologies revenue and GE Aircraft Engines supplies 12 percent of GE's revenue, the aircraft engine portion of Rolls-Royce totals 60 percent of that companies turnover.

BACKGROUND AND DEVELOPMENT

The development of powered aviation, which began with the Wright Brothers in 1903, fell mainly to those who understood engines, rather than those who understood flight. In fact, aeronautical scientists—such as Samuel P. Langley, who was perhaps the first to describe the dynamics of lift over a wing—had very little to do with powered aircraft. Instead, a pair of bicycle mechanics, Wilbur and Orville Wright, and a motorcycle mechanic named Glenn Curtiss were the first to demonstrate propeller-driven aircraft. In fact, Curtiss gained an early lead over the Wrights and a third aviator, Glenn Martin, precisely because he knew how to build lighter, more powerful motors. The first ten years of motorized flight was pioneered by eccentric inventors working out of their garages by night and flying in air shows by day. These barnstormers relied on show earnings to fund their building efforts, and many died in the process.

Industrial support for aviation did not materialize until European aviators demonstrated the strategic use of aircraft in World War I. Major industrial involvement in the United States occurred only after the U.S. Army requested funding for aviation projects. Financiers and industrial magnates were drawn to the industry not by their love of aviation, but by the opportunity to enrich themselves with government contracts. Some of the earliest investors in aircraft ventures were automobile manufacturers and automobile fleet owners. They sponsored specific aircraft builders and later pulled dishonest financial stunts to take control of aircraft builders' fledgling companies.

Edward Deeds, founder of Delco and the first to commercialize an electric starter, formed a one-sided partnership with the well-known Orville Wright called the Dayton-Wright Company. The company built engines, but no aircraft. The company was later acquired by William Boyce Thompson, who established the first American aircraft combine. Thompson acquired the patents owned by Wright and later Martin; he purchased the rights to a light, European-designed engine called the Hispano-Suiza, and he acquired the facilities of the Simplex Automobile Company to build his engines. Shut out from the management of the company by Thompson and unhappy at only building engines, Wright retired and Martin simply started another company.

Unwilling to allow any single group of financiers to corner the aviation industry, U.S. government officials created the Aircraft Production Board to oversee the development of the American aviation industry. This Board was soon dominated by the automobile industry, which assembled an industrial federation called the Manufacturers Aircraft Association. Auto manufacturers, led by the Packard and Hall-Scott Motor Car companies, convinced the Aircraft Production Board to support the mass production of a single type of aircraft motor—a 400-horsepower, 8-cylinder model called the "Liberty." As evidence of the industry's widespread complicity, this huge water-cooled engine featured an unnecessary electronic ignition system supplied by Delco. Completely inappropriate for

use on existing aircraft designs, the monstrosity was better suited for a truck or a boat than an aircraft.

Under pressure from auto manufacturers, the government ordered the production of 11,000 Libertys. This so infuriated Donald Douglas, the leading aircraft designer on the board, that he resigned his position and returned to making airplanes for Glenn Martin. Confident of the program's failure, he, like many other aircraft manufacturers, simply ignored the Liberty. Despite problems with Delco's starter and with the reconfiguration of the Liberty into an even larger 12-cylinder engine, the government remained perfectly comfortable entrusting the future of aviation to such experienced transportation pioneers as Packard, Hudson, Nash, and Ford.

An Indianapolis, Indiana engine builder named Jim Allison recognized the futility of placing the huge Liberty motor in the light aircraft of the day and decided to build a light engine of his own. As he pursued the development of lighter engines, he stumbled across a variety of high-quality manufacturing techniques. Engines, he discovered, ran most efficiently at about 30,000 rotations per minute while propellers generated the greatest amount of thrust at about 2,000 rotations. What was required was a precisely-machined reduction gear. Allison was the first major manufacturer to perfect an engine and clutch mechanism with acceptable tolerances. His lead in this area greatly advanced the Allison reputation and provided the company with hundreds of profitable orders.

Another engine builder of the day was Frederick Rentschler, one of the original founders of Wright Aeronautical. Rentschler grew increasingly weary of managerial interference from automobile magnates, whom he thought were interested only in short-term profit. The development of engines required years of expensive and often fruitless experimentation. Rentschler resigned from Wright in 1924 and began searching for a factory and financial backing to develop better engines. Like Douglas and Allison, Rentschler knew the Liberty design was a failure. He learned from a naval officer that the service would soon announce a competition for a powerful, lightweight, air-cooled design.

In 1925, Rentschler acquired the Pratt & Whitney company, a small machine tool manufacturer located in Hartford, Connecticut. Rentschler raided the Wright company of its best engineering talent and enlisted the help of Chance Vought, an aircraft builder. By Christmas of that year, Pratt & Whitney completed its first air-cooled radial engine, the 425-horsepower Wasp. The radial design meant that the cylinders were arranged in a circular fashion around the prop shaft, rather than being lined up along the shaft as in an automobile. This allowed the cylinders to be directly exposed to the thrust of air generated by the propeller. As a result, there was no need for a bulky radiator or heavy liquid coolant, as in the Liberty. Barely one year old, the new Pratt & Whitney company secured an order from the Navy for 200 Wasps. This provided the capital needed to develop an even larger, 525-horsepower engine, the Hornet.

In 1929, automotive interests organized yet another company, Curtiss-Wright, bearing the name of aviation's first pioneers. While neither Glenn Curtiss nor Orville Wright were active in the company, it did manage to turn out a successful product, the Cyclone radial engine. General Motors made the switch to air-cooled engines when its Dutch designer, Anthony Fokker, chose Pratt & Whitney's Wasp engine for his aircraft. Ford, meanwhile, dropped out of the aircraft business to concentrate on automobiles. The Lycoming Foundry and Machine Shop, established in Williamsport, Pennsylvania in 1908, began building aircraft engines during the late 1920s. Its position in the industry was secured by the success of its nine-cylinder R-680 radial engine, which was standard on many aircraft.

Pratt & Whitney gained dominance in the industry when it gained the attention of Bill Boeing, an aircraft builder based in Seattle, Washington. Boeing, too, was looking for a replacement for the Liberty and considered the Wasp to be the perfect engine for his fighters and mailplanes. When Boeing married the Wasp to his Model 40 mailplane, he discovered the craft could carry an additional 500 pounds of mail, or even passengers, making it extremely profitable. Boeing, Rentschler and Vought later merged their companies into what became America's most powerful aeronautical combine. The new company, called United Aircraft & Transportation, acquired the amphibious airplane builder Sikorsky, the light aircraft manufacturer Stearman, Jack Northrop's Avion experimental aircraft company, propeller makers Hamilton and Standard Steel, and a combination of small airline companies.

United Aircraft grew at an extremely fast pace. While the Great Depression virtually destroyed the industry, United Aircraft continued to expand, taking over the routes of defunct airline companies and providing a stream of exclusive Pratt & Whitney-driven aircraft for the military. In 1934, Senator Hugo Black led an investigation of the industry that resulted in legislation that broke up the aircraft combines. The Boeing Company was separated from United Aircraft, as were the airline services, which were reincorporated

as United Airlines in Chicago. Pratt & Whitney, however, remained a division of United Aircraft.

The importance of efficient, powerful engines was well understood by manufacturers in Germany and Japan, who embraced aviation as an instrument of warfare during the mid-1930s. Companies such as Daimler-Benz and Mitsubishi closely studied the advancements in American engine designs and were heavily sponsored by their governments. As a result, during the years leading up to World War II, Japanese and German aircraft advanced beyond the capabilities of American designs. By 1940, however, with the war raging in Europe, the U.S. government began a massive mobilization of its war industries.

Pratt & Whitney, which had developed a new 2,000-horsepower Double Wasp engine, was required to vastly expand its production capacity. Still unable to meet the demand for nearly 8,000 of these engines, Pratt & Whitney licensed production of its designs to Ford, Buick, Chevrolet, and Nash-Kelvinator. By the end of the war, Pratt & Whitney and its licensees produced a staggering 363,619 aircraft engines, representing half of all the horsepower used by the U.S. military during the war.

Meanwhile, Curtiss-Wright's R1820 Cyclone was used to power the Boeing B-17 bomber, the Douglas Dauntless dive bomber, and a number of DC-3s. A second design, the R3350, powered Boeing's B-29 bomber and, later, Lockheed's Constellation airliner. Curtiss-Wright provided 35 percent of American wartime horsepower. Allison occupied a special position during the war, producing 70,000 of its V1710 engines for aircraft such as the Lockheed P-38 and Curtiss P-40 Tomahawk. Lycoming, now a division of Avco, built only smaller engines—one of which powered Sikorsky's first helicopter in 1939.

Another manufacturer, the Garrett Corporation, was drawn into engine manufacture during the war. Garrett entered the market first by building intercoolers and turbochargers, devices that heated and concentrated the mix of oxygen and fuel in the combustion chamber for higher engine performance. Garrett turbochargers were fitted to existing engines on American aircraft, vastly improving their performance. Garrett also was active in the production of air conditioning systems and flight controls. Established in 1935 by Cliff Garrett, the company emerged from the war with an excellent reputation among airframe builders and later launched an aggressive diversification that included the development of engines. Garrett's first engine design was the 575-horsepower Model 331 gas turbine, intended for use on helicopters and light aircraft. This engine was later used to power the Beechcraft 18, Aero Commander, and Mitsubishi models.

Curtiss-Wright emerged from the war as the number two engine builder in the industry—a position it did not hold for long. Rather than plow its substantial earnings back into product development, Curtiss-Wright chose to invest its profits in other businesses, thus ceding its position to more enlightened competitors such as Pratt & Whitney and General Electric.

During the war, government war procurement officials had designated Pratt & Whitney, Curtiss-Wright, and Allison to produce only piston-driven engines. Meanwhile, the development of jet engines was given to Allis Chalmers, General Electric, and Westinghouse, which were experienced with steam turbines. The introduction of the jet engine was the most significant development in aviation since the Wright Brothers' first flight. Existing engines used fuel to drive pistons down, turning a shaft while driving other pistons up for another firing. Jet engines used an entirely different principle: air was scooped into a chamber and compressed by a series of turbine blades. Behind these blades, a highly refined fuel was sprayed into the compressed air and ignited. The resulting blast was channeled out the rear of the engine, where it drove a second turbine that powered the intake compressors. With their enormous thrust, jet engines could propel an aircraft at much greater speeds than conventional propellers.

The first jet engines were successfully built in Germany and England. Britain's Rolls-Royce held a strong lead in jet engine technology, due to the work of the inventor Frank Whittle. It was several years before American companies assumed leadership in jet technology, using Whittle's designs. General Electric, whose experience in turbine technology originated with steam-driven electrical generators, was given a government contract to develop Whittle's engine for a new jet, the Bell Aircraft XP-59A, which first flew in 1942. A practical jet engine emerged only after the war, however, with the J33 and J35, which were used to power the Boeing B-47 and Northrop B-49 flying wing. GE turned over its licenses for these designs to Allison in 1946.

Westinghouse scored an early coup in jet technology by building the first axial flow engine; earlier models used less efficient centrifugal compression. But Westinghouse lost its early lead in jet technology when the Navy changed its weight specifications for the engines and canceled millions of dollars worth of orders for Westinghouse engines. Unable to adapt quickly, Westinghouse simply abandoned the jet engine market.

Pratt & Whitney was first introduced to jet engines as a subcontractor to Westinghouse. Later, because American law required that foreign designs for military craft be manufactured domestically, Pratt & Whitney built versions of Rolls-Royce's Nene and Tay jet engines, which saw action during the Korean War. Pratt & Whitney's future was secured when it achieved a major engineering breakthrough. General Electric had been planning engines with up to 7,000 pounds of thrust, but Pratt & Whitney decided to leapfrog other competitors by building an engine that would produce 10,000 pounds of thrust. The result, the J57/JT3, was used to power the F-100, F-101, and F-102 fighters while eight of the engines were used on Boeing's massive new B-52 bomber. Thus the continuing battle for ever-increasing amounts of jet thrust was born.

General Motors' Allison division, initially paralyzed by postwar labor action, pursued jet engine development with GE's J33 design. Allison manufactured 15,525 of these engines for a variety of fighter aircraft, and secured its position in the postwar engine market. Lycoming capitalized on its involvement with helicopters after the war. Under the direction of Dr. Anselm Franz, the company built the T53, the first jet engine designed specifically for helicopters. Nearly 20,000 were produced.

Following World War II, government-led industry coordination ended and free market competition, fueled by Cold War military budgets, began. As a result GE terminated its technological partnership with Allison and began work on the J47, which drove the North American F-86 in combat over Korea. A later model, the high-performance J79, powered Convair's B-58, the Lockheed F-104 and McDonnell F-4 Phantom. As in the airframe industry, many of the advancements earned from wartime engine development were applied to commercial markets. Thousands of airliners were retrofitted with more efficient turbo-powered engines.

The advent of jet-powered bombers gave aircraft builders the experience necessary to create jet airliners. After Britain's DeHavilland built the first commercial jet, the Comet, Boeing, Douglas and Convair scrambled to develop their own jetliners. When Boeing's 707 was introduced in 1954, it was powered by four Pratt & Whitney JT3s. Douglas' DC-8, which took to the air in 1955, used the same engine. A commercial version of GE's J79 powered Convair's short-lived 880 and 990 jetliners.

While jet engine companies had successfully converted military engines to civilian uses, the Defense Department continued to press for even greater advancements in propulsion technology. The leading manufacturers began testing ramjets, engines that were designed for such high-speed flight that they required no compressor fans. General Electric was given a contract to build a nuclear-powered jet engine, and Pratt & Whitney was asked to develop liquid hydrogen-fueled rocket motors. Allison built a counter-rotating propeller engine for Convair's vertical takeoff and landing "Pogo Stick" airplane. All the projects were successful, though only the rocket technology was developed.

Within the conventional jet engine arena, General Electric built a massive new J93 engine in 1963. This boron-fueled engine, rated at 30,000 pounds thrust, was developed for North American's brilliant but obsolete Mach-3 B-70 bomber. Pratt & Whitney had better luck in triplesonic flight, developing the J58 engine for Lockheed's SR-71. Capable of crossing the United States in only 68 minutes, the SR-71 established numerous performance records. Pratt & Whitney also built the J75 for Lockheed's high altitude U-2 spy plane. The J52, however, was the company's military mainstay. In production for 30 years, the J52 powered a long line of naval aircraft.

Among the smaller manufacturers, Curtiss-Wright's sales were declining rapidly by 1960. In 1963, as part of a scheme to bolster its position in the market and acquire a staff of talented engineers, Curtiss-Wright launched a hostile takeover bid for Garrett. Garrett's management remained deeply suspicious of its suitor, however, and enlisted the support of Signal Oil & Gas, a company with the financial resources to thwart Curtiss-Wright's bid. Signal acquired Garrett in 1964, permitting the company to operate autonomously. Garrett was firmly established as a manufacturer of auxiliary power units, small engines that are used to provide power to start main engines. Garrett built this business into a series of successful small propulsion engines, principally the TFE731, which powered the Learjet 25, Cessna Citation, and Hawker Siddeley 125 business jets.

Lycoming regained its position in the fixed wing market in the mid-1960s, after developing its own small turbofan. This design evolved into the ALF502 which, like Garrett's design, was popular with a variety of business jets. The engine was chosen to power the Hawker Siddeley 146, which eventually emerged as the popular British Aerospace BAe 146 commuter jet.

In the airliner market, Allison briefly extended the life of turboprops by developing a T56 powerplant for a family of Convair airliners, the 440, 540, and 580. Meanwhile Boeing was developing a new medium-range trijet called the 727 and asked for an engine similar to Rolls-Royce's Spey. Allison formed a part-

nership with Rolls-Royce, but lost the 727 business to Pratt & Whitney, whose JT8D became a best-seller in the industry. In addition to the 727, the versatile engine was used on four twinjets: the Boeing 737, Douglas DC-9, Sud Aviation Caravelle, and Dassault Mercure.

While Pratt & Whitney and its JT8D dominated the commercial market, General Electric's J79 derivative declined with the increasingly unpopular Convair jetliners. But General Electric expanded its market for jet engines well beyond the aircraft industry. Variations on the company's engines powered missiles, helicopters, hovercraft, speedboats, and even electrical power generators. GE's J85 series became a favorite among the growing ranks of private jet manufacturers. The company scored a major coup in 1965 when it was chosen to develop the engines for Lockheed's super transport, the C-5 Galaxy. To lift the massive freighter into the sky, GE had to develop a more efficient high-bypass "turbofan" engine.

With early turbofans, about half the air taken into an engine passed concentrically around its combustion chamber, providing additional thrust and allowing the engine to operate more efficiently. GE's high-bypass design, the TF39, increased the bypass ratio to eight to one. Four of the engines, which generated 41,100 pounds of thrust, would enable the C-5 to carry 132 tons of cargo. Airline companies immediately embraced the quieter, more fuel-efficient turbofan, which was perfectly suited for subsonic passenger aircraft. But because the engines were considerably fatter, it was impossible to retrofit the thousands of existing aircraft that were designed for the long, skinny JT8D turbojet. Instead, turbofans were reserved for the new line of jumbo jets. The TF39 gave GE the lead in engines for large passenger aircraft such as Boeing's 747, McDonnell Douglas' DC-10 and Lockheed's L-1011. A commercial version of the high-bypass turbofan, the CF6, was developed for the DC-10 in 1971 and Airbus' A300 in 1974.

Pratt & Whitney began development of its own high-bypass engine in 1960. The company's TF30 was used aboard General Dynamics' F-111 and Grumman F-14, and led to a civilian version, the JT9D, which could generate more than 43,000 pounds of thrust. The JT9D entered service with the 747 in 1969 and was the only 747 powerplant until 1975, when GE developed a CF6 for the jumbo jet.

Meanwhile, Lockheed's L-1011 Tristar, a competitor to the DC-10 and 747, was powered by RB211 engines from Rolls-Royce. Allison, Rolls-Royce's American partner, wisely elected to steer clear of the RB211, sure that its pricing was flawed. When problems later arose with the engine, Allison avoided the brush with bankruptcy that nearly ruined Rolls-Royce and Lockheed. Allison did, however, convert its production of Rolls-Royce's Spey into its own TF41, which went on to power Vought's A-7 Corsair. In addition, Allison's T56 turboprop was chosen for the Lockheed C-130 transport, Grumman E-2C, and Lockheed Orion.

During the late 1960s, GE was asked to apply its experience with the J93 toward the development of an engine for Boeing's supersonic transport. The resulting design, the GE4, generated nearly 70,000 pounds of thrust. Four of these engines would enable the SST to reach 1,800 miles per hour. However, Boeing canceled the program after airlines lost interest in the SST.

General Electric was awarded a contract to develop a new engine for Rockwell's B-1 bomber in 1970. Unlike the B-52, which the bomber would replace, the B-1 was fitted with afterburners. A common feature of fighter jets, the afterburner was a mechanism that detonated a second spray of fuel into an engine's exhaust thrust. The resulting blast could add as much as 50 percent more power to an engine. The B-1, and the F101 engine GE developed for it, were canceled in 1977. But the engine went back into production when the B-1 program was revived in 1981.

Engine manufacturers benefitted greatly from drastically increased defense spending under the Reagan administration. But the heavy investment in defense industries during those years led to several scandal-ridden cases of overcharging and non-performance. While few of these cases involved engine manufacturers, the laws put in place to correct the abuses still applied to them. These laws were meant to extract more economical and responsible development by mandating strict competitions for government business, particularly between General Electric and Pratt & Whitney.

General Electric's F404 engine, developed for McDonnell Douglas' F-18 fighter, was fitted to Grumman's X-29, an experimental high-maneuverability aircraft with forward swept wings. The engine was later used for Lockheed's F-117 Stealth fighter—which flew secretly as early as 1981—and SAAB's Gripen fighter.

Pratt & Whitney developed the F100 in 1970 for McDonnell Douglas' F-15. The engine, which could send an F-15 to 98,000 feet in only three minutes, was later fitted to General Dynamics' F-16. However, turbine wear on the F100 took years to correct, enabling General Electric to step in with an alternative. GE combined the finest elements of the F101 and F404 to produce the versatile F110. This engine powered all of America's leading fighter jets, including the F-15, F-16 and F-14. Eventually, GE's F110 gained 75 percent of the F100's market.

The loss convinced Pratt & Whitney to pay closer attention to the Pentagon's needs. The company developed variants with special new capabilities and by 1990 had won back a quarter of the government's Fighter Engine Competition business. Meanwhile, Pratt & Whitney developed a second derivative of its F101, the F118, which was chosen to power Northrop's B-2 Stealth bomber.

Strong growth in airline traffic during the 1970s led aircraft manufacturers to create a new family of airliners to replace the aging DC-8, DC-9, and 727. Boeing designed two large twin-jets, the 757 and 767. The European Airbus consortium introduced a new line of A310, A320, and A330 aircraft. McDonnell Douglas, however, elected to update its existing models. The DC-9 became the MD-80, and the DC-10 became the MD-11. Development centered on improved avionics and control functions, but the greatest advancement occurred with engines, which were now quieter and far more fuel-efficient.

Pratt & Whitney's position in the commercial markets started to wane in the 1980s. The company was reviled for its growing arrogance and lack of customer focus, and had rested too long on the laurels of its successful JT8D. General Electric's deliveries surpassed Pratt & Whitney's in 1986. General Electric captured a large portion of the new market through its CF6 series and a partnership with the French engine manufacturer SNECMA called CFM International. The company's CFM56 was used to re-engine the old fuel-guzzling DC-8 and military versions of the 707, and was the standard engine on Airbus' A320. In 1987, GE formed a second partnership with Garrett called the CFE Company. This company developed the CFE738, a 6,000 pounds thrust turbofan for the small jet market, specifically the Dassault Falcon 2000 business jet.

Eager to remain in the game, Pratt & Whitney established its own international partnership with the German Motoren und Turbinen Union and Italy's Fiat Avianzione. The company developed the PW2037 for Boeing's 757, and the PW4000—designed specifically to compete with the CF6—for the 747. The PW2037 caused General Electric to abandon its entry for the 757, but Pratt & Whitney still faced competition from a modified version of Rolls-Royce's RB211. Pratt & Whitney later formed a second consortium, called International Aero Engines, with MTU, Fiat, Rolls-Royce, and Japanese Aero Engines. The company's V2500 engine was used to power Airbus' A320. The partnerships helped preserve Pratt & Whitney's position in the industry until it could mend its relations with airline companies and aircraft manufacturers.

While manufacturers were often able to convert military engines into commercial versions, the two markets held fundamentally different requirements. Airline companies wanted highly reliable, fuel-efficient engines that were quiet and did not pollute. The military, on the other hand, wanted powerful light-weight engines that remained cool enough to avoid detection by enemy tracking. During the mid-1980s, demand grew for a new type of commercial engine with little or no use for the military. Conventional high-bypass jet engines burned too much fuel for the increasingly cost-conscious airline industry, which requested development of a new hybrid propjet.

General Electric and Pratt & Whitney immediately began work on elaborate jet engines whose turbines drove two rear-mounted counter-rotating propellers with crescent-shaped blades. This "propfan," while slightly slower than conventional engines, was twice as fuel efficient as turbofans. The propfan was an unducted pusher propeller design, intended for installation on the rear fuselage of aircraft. Accordingly, Boeing and McDonnell Douglas tested propfans on a 727 and MD-80, and began development of two new twin-propfan designs, the 7J7 and MD-91. In England, Rolls-Royce began work on a ducted propfan, with its blades enclosed within a large shell, called the contrafan. Such a propfan would be suitable for the thousands of aircraft whose engines were wing-mounted.

During the late 1980s, a vicious cycle of competition drove airlines into near bankruptcy while fuel prices dropped. Airline companies canceled orders for hundreds of new aircraft, choosing instead to squeeze a few more years of service out of their existing fleets. As a result, airframe and engine manufacturers were forced to shelve the propfan indefinitely. Despite this, Boeing began planning a larger super twinjet, the 777, intended to compete with the MD-11. Pratt & Whitney's PW4000 was chosen as the launch customer for the 777.

CURRENT CONDITIONS

After the worst recession in over a decade, the turbine engine was slowly rebounding in 1996. Airframes manufacturers and engine producing counterparts had a successful year in 1996 and expect a substantial increase in 1997. Intense competition threatened profitability in the recent past but also led to the development of new products. General Electric and

Pratt & Whitney teamed to help reduce the threat of competitiveness to earnings.

Fundamental forces have reshaped the jet engine market. Solutions to the challenges posed by developing near perfect engines and competition have resulted in alliances between competitors, new pricing mechanisms, increase participation in aftermarket, and a reduction in the number of engine types per platform.

Cooperative ventures are being forced because of competition. Two rival—GE Aircraft Engines and Pratt & Whitney—had joined together to develop a new power plant for the Boeing 747-500X primarily in reaction to GEAE, Rolls-Royce, and Pratt's price competition for the Boeing 777. Boeing subsequently decided to cancel the 747X program. Airbus remains committed to the super jumbo, however. Several joint ventures such as GE Aircraft and Pratt & Whitney, Rolls Royce and Pratt & Whitney, and GEAE and Snecma have had varying degrees of success. In the past several have fallen apart over strategies or details.

The early 1990s saw one of the biggest shakeups in aerospace industry history, as military budgets shrank and fewer people chose to fly. Commercial airlines canceled or postponed their orders for airplanes, and aircraft manufacturers in turn canceled their orders for aircraft engines. The industry recession proved particularly challenging for the aircraft engine industry, which was in the process of developing a number of engines for the expected orders of large jet-powered aircraft. General Electric, which had been pouring money into the development of its GE90 engine for the Boeing 777 aircraft, was the most severely affected of the big three engine manufacturers, but all three companies faced dismal short-term prospects.

Industry analysts wondered if the intense competition that had characterized the aircraft engine industry through the 1980s could continue through the 1990s. *Air Transport World* contributor J.A. Donoghue noted that "all three major manufacturers say they are committed to a battle across a broad front; the trend is for competitive offerings to increase as the defense market continues its decline. Airlines undoubtedly are the beneficiaries of these aggressive competitive matchups virtually across the board. The key question is whether this level of competitiveness is sustainable." The biggest drain on the competitors is likely to be research and development costs, which following the end of the Cold War are no longer boosted by Department of Defense dollars.

One difficulty, according to *Interavia* is that "engine manufacturers live in a world where the time unit is not the year, but the decade." Dozens of years are needed to develop an engine and expand it across a wide range of aircraft, and dozens more to realize that engine's impact on the market. Luckily, engine manufacturers are rewarded for successful development by a lucrative spare parts and upgrade market. Since aircraft engines represent such a large investment for airlines, those airlines seek to extend engine life up to 25 years through frequent maintenance and upgrading. According to *Interavia,* ''Pratt & Whitney derives about 40 percent of its pre-tax earnings from commercial engine spares sales,'' a figure characteristic of the industry.

The leasing of engines is becoming increasingly popular as airlines seek to obtain totally predictable engine costs and to avoid stocking inventories of back-up engines and spare parts. Leasing is packaged with fixed maintenance service costs. However, Steve Forbes argued against recent IRS decisions not to allow regional carriers to expense the cost of inspecting aircraft engines and a proposed technical change regarding leasing rules that could cost the industry millions of dollars. Willis Lease Finance Corporation was leasing 35 engines in October of 1996 and expected to increase this number to 40 by the end of 1996 with additional increases in 1997.

Industry forecasts are much more optimistic when they are extended into the twenty-first century. ''Forecasters estimate that between 1992 and 2012, about $330 billion in engines and spare parts will be sold to commercial carriers outside of the former Soviet Union, with $200 billion of the quantity directly attributable to engine sales,'' according to *Aviation Week & Space Technology.* According to estimates, 54 percent of this money will be spent on engines with thrust greater than 45,000 pounds, 32 percent on engines with thrust less than 30,000 pounds, and the remainder on mid-range engines. The anticipated boom in engine sales is expected to begin after 1995 and continue for at least a decade as airlines retire their older aircraft and trade up to larger aircraft capable of carrying over 200 passengers.

Meanwhile, in the military arena, the Pentagon is sponsoring a competition for a new Advanced Tactical Fighter, or ATF, between Northrop and Lockheed. Similarly, General Electric and Pratt & Whitney were asked to compete for the engine to drive the ATF. In this test, Pratt & Whitney's F119 will challenge GE's F120. The successful model could be worth more than one billion dollars to the winner.

INDUSTRY LEADERS

Though there are more than a dozen companies with significant aircraft engine businesses, only

General Electric, Pratt & Whitney, and Rolls-Royce have access to the global market. GE is in the forefront with 1996 engine and spare parts sales of $6.58 billion, Pratt & Whitney's sales of $5.9 billion, and Rolls-Royce's sales of $93 million. Though Rolls-Royce's sales were significantly smaller, early 1992 orders put the British firm in close competition with the American giants. Garrett, Allison , and Lycoming continue to operate on the fringes of the industry, supplying smaller turbine engines and piston-driven engines for commuter and private aircraft.

Each of the leading engine makers responded to the early-1990s recession with significant cuts in employment and reductions in production. GE Aircraft Engines cut employment from 41,000 people in 1987 to just 26,000 in 1993 while substantially shifting its focus from military to commercial applications. GE was expected to produce between 500 and 600 large commercial engines in 1993. Pratt & Whitney's employment dropped from 46,000 in 1990 to 33,000 in 1993 according to *Interavia,* and 1993 production stood at 400 engines. The smallest of the leading companies, Rolls-Royce, expected the smallest drops in employment, from 29,500 to 24,500 employees by 1994. Rolls-Royce produced just 200 large engines in 1993.

General Electric's F414, despite minor problems, has met or exceeded performance requirements in the Navy's F/A-18E/F which is in the second year of a three year test flight. GE tested an improved GE90 engine designed to have better combustion with reduced emissions and a decrease in weight of 60 pounds per engine for production in 1997.

Pratt & Whitney PW4090 engines which received FAA certification are being used to power the Boeing 777-200 IGW (Increased Gross Weight) airplane. The PW4090 allows the plane to carry and additional 14,220 gallons of fuel increasing its range from 5,925 miles to 8,225 miles. Deliveries of the 777- 200 IGW powered by this engine was scheduled for March 1997 to United Airlines and Korean Airlines. Boeing's shelving of a stretched 747 caused GE and Pratt & Whitney to scrub plans for developing and certifying their GP7000 powerplant by the year 2000. Pratt & Whitney F119 engines were planned to power the 4 Joint Strike Fighter concept aircraft.

A radical improvement team replaced 10 computer controlled, 12 axis, blade grinding machines that shape cast blades with 8 simple 3-axis automated grinding machines in 1994 halving the total manufacturing costs.

The FAA was urged to mandate more frequent inspections in high pressure compressor disks in Pratt & Whitney JT8D, -209, -217C and -219 series engines for cracks and to prevent failure due to pitting.

WORK FORCE

In November 1996 there were 98,200 employees in the aircraft engine industry, 50,800 of which were specifically engaged in production. These employees were averaging eight hours in overtime per week and earned an average of $18.56 per hour. If the aircraft industry is able to replace losses in military orders with civilian orders, employment in the industry should be steady.

AMERICA AND THE WORLD

Singapore Airlines named the Boeing 777 as its choice over the Airbus A330 in late 1995; however, the $12.7 billion deal selected the Rolls Royce's Trent 800 engine for its planes over the PW4084 or GE90. The decision was driven by engine pricing competition. Airbus plans to power its A340-600 line with 50,000 to 60,000 pound thrust engines. According to Airbus forecasts, major carriers are expected to order 3,600 planes in the 250-400 seat category during the next 20 years. BMW Rolls-Royce BR710, the first of a family of engines that will power commercial and corporate aircraft, has been certified. This 14,750 pound thrust engine powers the long-range Gulfstream V and the Bombardier Glopel Express corporate jets. Singapore Aircraft Lease Enterprise used International Aero Engines to power the twelve Airbus A320s it ordered in October 1996.

RESEARCH AND TECHNOLOGY

Duke University has discovered a new way of detecting aircraft engine wear that is safer and more accurate than conventional diagnostic techniques by creating bubbles in the engine's oil through ultrasound. General Electric conducted durability tests of a low-observable-axisymmetric nozzle. A GE facility tested a sub-scale turbofan developed by a consortium headed by the Japanese at flight conditions simulating Mach 2.5 at 66,000 feet. This propulsion technology is needed for commercial high-speed transport planes.

A new artificial intelligence system was developed to diagnose AN-24 aircraft engines, based on four models—phenomena, inference, learning and interpretation—to diagnose engine problems through comparison of the experiences of mechanics and engine experts was developed.

FURTHER READING

Aboulafia, Richard. "Turbine Market Slowly Rebounds." *Aviation Week & Space Technology,* 13 January 1997.

Biddle, Wayne. *Barons of the Sky.* New York: Simon & Schuster, 1991.

"Boeing 777, Powered by Pratt & Whitney Engines, Receives Certification." Available from http://biz.yahoo.com/prnews/97/02/28/ba_y0002_2.html.

"BR710 is Certified." *Air Transport World,* October 1996.

"Civil Aerospace." *Economist,* 3 September 1988, S1-S28.

Condom, Pierre. "Engine Manufacturers Slug It Out." *Interavia,* November 1993.

Donoghue, J. A. "A Broad Battle on Many Fronts." *Air Transport World,* November 1992.

———. "Buy 10, Lease 2." *Air Transport World,* December 1996.

"Engine Makers Persevere in Face of Boeing Challenge." *Aviation Week & Space Technology,* 27 January 1997.

Flint, Perry. "Big Engine, Big Risk. Big Payoff?" *Air Transport World.* August 1993.

———. "No More 'Three on a Wing.'" *Air Transport World,* 26 August 1996.

Forbes, Steve. "Ground These Changes." *Forbes,* 2 December 1996.

General Electric. *Propulsion.* Cincinnati, OH: GE Aircraft Engines, 1991.

Green, William. *Modern Commercial Aircraft.* New York: Portland House, 1987.

Hui, Yang. "A Artificial Intelligence System of Trouble Diagnosis for Aircraft Engines." *Computers & Industrial Engineering,* December 1996.

Kandebo, Stanley W. "Engine Makers Predict Improved Industry Health over Long Term." *Aviation Week & Space Technology,* 16 March 1992, 59-60.

———. "F119 Versatility Challenged by JSF Requirements." *Aviation Week & Space Technology,* 25 November 1996.

———. "General Electric Tests Improved GE90 System." *Aviation Week & Space Technology,* 21 October 1996.

———. "GE Tests Japanese Engine Aimed at Future SSTs." *Aviation Week & Space Technology,* 20 January 1997.

———. "Manufacturers Predict $50-Billion Engine Market During Next Decade." *Aviation Week & Space Technology,* 20 March 1989.

———. "Reduced-Signature Nozzle Tested by GE." *Aviation Week & Space Technology,* 17 February 1997.

———. "Stable Engine Sales Seen in Late 1994." *Aviation Week & Space Technology,* 15 March 1993.

Kaplan, Ellen, ed. *In the Company of Eagles.* Stamford, CT: Pratt & Whitney, 1990.

Mattera, Philip. *Inside U.S. Business: A Concise Encyclopedia of Leading Industries.* Homewood, IL: Dow Jones-Irwin, 1987.

Mecham, Micahael. "Two Chinese Carriers Named to A320 List." *Aviation Week & Space Technology,* 11 November 1996.

————. "Year's Biggest Order Goes to Boeing 777." *Aviation Week & Space Technology,* 20 November 1995.

"Mixed Results on Alliances." *Air Transport World,* August 1996.

Phillips, Edward H. "Cracks Focus of FAA Airworthiness Directives." *Aviation Week & Space Technology,* 14 October 1996.

————. "F/A/-18E/F Meets Flight Test Goals." *Aviation Week & Space Technology,* 20 January 1997.

————. "NTSB Targets JT8D Cracks." *Aviation Week & Space Technology,* 3 February 1997.

"Recent Trends: Aircraft Engines and Engine Parts (SIC 3724)." Available from http://www.ita.doc.gov/industry/tai/green/trnds372.txt.

Solberg, Carl. *Conquest of the Skies.* Boston: Little, Brown, 1979.

Sonnenberg, Paul. *Allison: Power of Excellence.* Malibu, CA: Coastline Publishers, 1990.

Sparaco, Pierre. "Airbus Plows Ahead with A3XX Plans." *Aviation Week & Space Technology,* 27 January 1997.

————. "Airbus Seeks to Enter Boeing's 747 Market." *Aviation Week & Space Technology,* 14 October 1996.

Textron Corporation. *Company Profile.* Stratford, CT: Textron Lycoming, 1993.

"Toppling the Monuments at Pratt & Whitney." *Harvard Business Review,* September/October 1996.

U.S. Department of Labor. Bureau of Labor Statistics. "B-12. Employees on Nonfarm Payrolls by Detailed Industry." *E&E: Employment and Earnings,* December 1996.

Valenti, Michael. "Airplane-Engine Wear Bubbles Up." *Mechanical Engineering,* July 1996.

Whitehouse, Arthur. *The Sky's the Limit.* London: Macmillan, 1979.

Woolsey, James P. "Riding the '96 Buying Surge." *Air Transport World,* January 1997.

—John Simley, updated by David C. Genaway

SIC 3728

AIRCRAFT PARTS AND AUXILIARY EQUIPMENT, NOT ELSEWHERE CLASSIFIED

This category includes establishments primarily engaged in manufacturing aircraft parts and auxiliary equipment, not elsewhere classified. This industry also includes establishments owned by manufacturers of aircraft parts and auxiliary equipment and primarily engaged in research and development on aircraft parts, whether from enterprise funds or on a contract or fee basis. Establishments primarily engaged in manufacturing or assembling complete aircraft are classified in **SIC 3721: Aircraft;**those manufacturing aircraft engines and parts are classified in **SIC 3724: Aircraft Engines and Engine Parts;**those manufacturing aeronautical instruments are classified in **SIC 3812: Search, Detection, Navigation, Guidance, Aeronautical, and Nautical Systems and Instruments;**those manufacturing aircraft engine electrical equipment are classified in **SIC 3694: Electrical Equipment for Internal Combustion Engines;**and those manufacturing guided missile and space vehicle parts and auxiliary equipment are classified in **SIC 3769: Guided Missile and Space Vehicle Parts and Auxiliary Equipment, Not Elsewhere Classified.** Establishments not owned by manufacturers of aircraft parts but primarily engaged in research and development on aircraft parts on a contract or fee basis are classified in **SIC 8731: Commercial and Biological Research.**

INDUSTRY SNAPSHOT

The total value of shipments of aircraft parts and equipment (products and services) for SIC 3728 was $16 billion in 1995. Exports of $10.7 billion exceeded imports by $7.5 billion and has trended upward over the past several years.

The American aircraft industry may be divided into four segments. In one segment, manufacturers such as Boeing-McDonnell Douglas and Lockheed build the wings and fuselages that comprise the airframe. Meanwhile, companies such as General Electric and Pratt & Whitney manufacture the engines that propel aircraft. The third segment covers flight instrumentation, an area where the most profound advances in aviation have taken place. But the fourth segment, broadly defined by industrial classification as "aircraft parts not otherwise classified," includes manufacturers of surface control and cabin pressurization systems, landing gear, lighting, galley equipment, and general use products such as nuts and bolts. This highly diversified industry generated shipments in 1992 of $20.2 million and regularly was running a $6 million trade surplus at that time, contributing significantly to the greater aerospace industry, which ranked sixth in the United States in overall value of shipments and first in exports.

ORGANIZATION AND STRUCTURE

Aircraft manufacturers rely on a broad base of suppliers to provide the thousands of subsystems and parts that make up their products. There are more than 4,000 suppliers contributing parts to the aerospace industry, including rubber companies, refrigerator makers, appliance manufacturers, and general electronics enterprises. This diversity is necessary because in most cases it is simply uneconomical for an aircraft manufacturer to establish, for example, its own landing light operation. The internal demand for such a specialized product is insufficient to justify the creation of an independent manufacturing division.

Aircraft manufacturers have found it cheaper and more efficient to purchase secondary products from other manufacturers, who may sell similar products to other aircraft companies, as well as automotive manufacturers, railroad signal makers, locomotive and ship builders, and a variety of other customers. For example, an airplane builder such as Boeing, Grumman, or Beech is likely to purchase landing lights from a light bulb maker such as General Electric. Such subcontractors supply a surprisingly large portion of the entire aircraft. On the typical commercial aircraft, a lead manufacturer such as McDonnell Douglas may actually manufacture less than half of the aircraft, though it is responsible for the design and assembly of the final product.

When a major manufacturer discontinues an aircraft design, as Lockheed did with its L-1011 Tristar, a ripple effect is caused that affects every manufacturer that supplied parts for that aircraft. Therefore, parts suppliers strive to diversify their customer base to ensure that the decline of one manufacturer will be tempered by continued sales to others. Given the unstable nature of the industry, parts manufacturers also attempt to find customers outside of the aircraft business as well.

BACKGROUND AND DEVELOPMENT

Aircraft parts manufacturing may be said to predate the invention of powered aircraft. The Wright Brothers' first airplane, little more than a propeller-driven kite, was equipped with cables, chains, and an engine that were built by others. In the purest sense, Orville and Wilbur Wright merely designed and assembled their aircraft from existing parts. The same was true of innovator Glenn Curtiss, a motorcycle repairman from upstate New York. While Curtiss had access to the lightweight engines required for flight, he began to experiment with flight controls and invented the aileron, a movable surface on the trailing edge of a wing that revolutionized handling characteristics. The

Wrights had clearly invented the airplane, but Curtiss had undoubtedly developed a key control mechanism that made flight practical.

American aviation remained the province of tinkerers from the Wrights' first flight in 1903 until 1916, when European combatants in World War I demonstrated the utility of aircraft as strategic battlefield weapons. The government hastily created an aviation program within the Army Signal Corps and held a competition for the right to supply more than 20,000 aircraft. Hundreds of amateur flyers, including Glenn Martin, Bill Boeing, Donald Douglas, and Allan and Malcolm Loughead, rushed into the business. Limited in their resources and working out of garages, these pioneers were forced to incorporate whatever parts they could find into their aircraft. The designs of these aircraft were simple, often consisting of fabric stretched over a wooden frame and manipulated with cables and hinges. But the most important part of these aircraft was the engine.

At the time, automobile manufacturers held a virtual monopoly on advanced engine designs. They also had the manufacturing capacity to mass produce the thousands of aircraft the government wanted. As a result, automobile executives easily muscled their way into control of the nation's aviation industry. While this arrangement bred only bad designs and corruption, it established an enduring organizational structure in the aviation industry. General Motors, Ford, Nash, and Packard had long subcontracted manufacturing of parts for its automobiles to independent manufacturers. Unwilling to build manufacturing facilities for something as speculative as aircraft, these manufacturers simply turned to the established automotive supply network for items such as glass, wheels, instrumentation, and seats.

As quickly as they had entered, automobile companies abandoned aviation after the government canceled its 20,000-plane order at the end of World War I. Aircraft designers were once again in charge of their destinies as manufacturers. But they continued to be supplied by the very same parts network that served the automobile industry. Aviation enterprises floundered until 1927, when Charles Lindbergh's daring cross-Atlantic flight inspired tremendous investment in the industry. This growth was choked off after 1929, however, as the nation sunk into the depths of the Great Depression. Traumatized by changes in the industry, aviation companies continued to make small advances on the strength of military sales and a growing air mail business. Eventually this led to the formation of three enormous aviation combines, the largest of which, United Aircraft, might one day have rivaled General Motors in size.

United Aircraft consisted of four airframe builders, Boeing, Vought, Northrop, and Stearman, the engine maker Pratt & Whitney, and a series of airline companies that later became United Air Lines. This powerful organization took over two propeller makers and numerous other manufacturers and began manufacturing a greater proportion of its own parts. The other two monopolies, North American Aviation and the Aviation Corporation of the Americas, were in the process of building similar organizations when, in 1934, the government stepped in with antitrust investigation that broke up the combines and decentralized aircraft manufacturing.

This breakup provided new growth opportunities for a wide variety of potential suppliers. Companies that had previously never even considered the aircraft parts business suddenly discovered the viability of extending their product line into aviation. The driving force behind this expansion was technology. Where aviators were once limited to day flight, lighting and instruments enabled them to fly in darkness. Where navigation had once required visual landmarks, such as railroad tracks, now there were radio and gyroscopes. And where flying was once limited to lower elevations, now there were cabin pressurization systems and oxygen supplements.

The greatest advances in aviation took place during World War II, when heavy government investment in the industry enabled new technologies to be developed that enabled aircraft to fly higher, faster, and with more agility than ever before. This placed new stresses on conventional parts and encouraged the development of specialized engineering. Jet aircraft, first tested in 1942, provide the best example of this. While airframes had to be fundamentally redesigned to handle the rigors of jet flight, so too did items such as terminal wiring, indicator lamps, pumps, and fluid systems. Repeated exposure to vibration and powerful G-forces caused many conventional parts to break apart. As a result, the development of high-performance aircraft was hampered as much by weak light bulb filaments and rivets as by weak airframes.

The specialized engineering required for postwar aviation necessitated tremendous research funding and elevated manufacturing occupations to fine sciences. Companies that were ill-prepared for this new type of work were forced out of the market or into consolidation with other, stronger manufacturers. Aircraft contractors necessarily became fewer, and the prices of their products grew higher.

Generally, navigation and communications systems were handled by companies that specialized in instrumentation, such as Sperry, Lear, and Motorola. Meanwhile, with a few notable exceptions, heating, hydraulics, and pressurization systems were handled by engine manufacturers such as Pratt & Whitney, Curtiss-Wright, Allison and General Electric. Manufacturers such as Garrett, Teledyne, Litton, and Dowty manufactured adjunct systems that provided compressed air, temperature regulation, cabin pressurization, and hydraulic pressure. Other companies historically associated with the automotive industry, such as BF Goodrich, Bendix, and Cleveland Pneumatic, provided products such as wheel assemblies, pumps, hoses, gaskets, and even window seals.

A large constituent in the industry consisted of companies that were already associated with aviation, including United Aircraft, Boeing, Lockheed, and McDonnell Douglas. Other smaller manufacturers, such as Cessna and Beech, also found a place in the market as suppliers of specialized parts. As a result of bad management, Curtiss-Wright was slowly forced out of engine manufacturing during the 1950s. But the company managed to maintain a leading position in the parts industry, particularly with propellers and a series of wing actuator systems.

Heavy government investment in aviation, primarily through military programs and a budding space agency, continued to result in ever more advanced aircraft. North American Aviation's B-70 bomber and Lockheed's SR-71 reconnaissance jet established new triplesonic speed records, while a variety of other craft managed to climb to more than 100,000 feet. Such planes required paint that exhibited special heat deflection properties. Even landing tires required coating with aluminum paints and inflation with lithium. Windshields were required to withstand tremendous impacts, such as collision with a bird at 2,200 miles per hour. In each case, aircraft parts suppliers never led development of new aircraft. Instead, lead manufacturers conceived of new designs and issued required specifications, and parts manufacturers filled their requirements.

While the Cold War confrontation with the Soviet Union provided the justification for new weapons, American involvement in Vietnam often provided the testing ground. New military designs enabled aircraft manufacturers to develop a further variety of new aircraft, including a supersonic passenger transport, jumbo jets, and huge freighters. Advances funded by military dollars helped lower the costs of commercial flight and allowed airline companies to offer passengers more sophisticated in-flight services, including radio headphone entertainment and movies. In addition, galley service became more efficient, incorporating microwave as well as convection heat sources and complex food storage conveyors and dumbwaiters. As aircraft became ever more complex, the aircraft parts industry grew proportionally, until it numbered almost 11,000 suppliers.

CURRENT CONDITIONS

The entire aerospace industry had enjoyed nearly fifty years of growth following the end of World War II, but an industry recession beginning in the late 1980s and early 1990s caused major shifts in the industry. Military spending peaked in 1987 and dropped precipitously following the end of Cold War tensions in 1989, forcing many military-oriented parts suppliers to leave the market. According to *U.S. Industrial Outlook 1993,* about 15,000 suppliers left the aerospace defense market between 1982 and 1987, a decrease that continued into the 1990s, though at a slower rate. A similar decrease occurred in the commercial aircraft parts industry, as the supplier base dropped from 11,000 to 4,000, driven by aircraft manufacturer's demands for greater efficiency. "For parts suppliers, this streamlining has meant that only the most efficient and highest quality manufacturers have been able to stay in this market," noted *U.S. Industrial Outlook 1993.*

Exacerbating the effects of industry streamlining has been the increasing competition from foreign parts suppliers. In order to penetrate international markets, U.S. aircraft and aircraft engine makers have entered into international teaming agreements that specify that a certain proportion of parts are purchased from overseas suppliers. Such agreements have helped foster advances in the aerospace industries of many countries, particularly in the Far East, but have contributed to the shrinkage of the U.S. aircraft parts industry. Employment fell 13 percent between 1990 and 1992, and an additional 6 percent decline was expected in 1993. Total employment numbered 166,000 people in 1993. According to *U.S. Industrial Outlook 1993,* "long-term prospects are for continued declines on the military side, and stabilizing employment on the commercial side."

The problem of bogus parts continues to plague the industry. The cause of a ValuJet engine explosion on the ground at Atlanta in June 1996 was determined to be an engine that had been overhauled by a repair station in Turkey that lacked Federal Aviation Administration (FAA) approval. The engine contained a crackled and corroded compressor disk. The National Transportation Safety Board (NTSB) uses the term "unapproved parts" in its official accident reports. A three-month investigation by *Business Week* revealed that bogus parts, including fakes, used parts sold as new, and new parts sold for unapproved purposes have found their way into the inventory of every major airline in the country. In 1996 some fire extinguishers intended for Air Force One were found to be falsely certified by a repair station. While bogus parts are not routinely causing accidents, the problem of substandard parts has grown substantially in the past five years. One supplier mislabeled spacers with fake Pratt & Whitney labels, but was caught by an astute airline mechanic. Clearly, parts are not labeled as bogus by the suppliers, but are laundered from used, stolen or substandard parts, or are incorrectly specified as meeting standards via a number of means. Parts brokers adding false paperwork sell to unsuspecting brokers which sell to an unwitting FAA approved facility or airline. The FAA regulates manufacturers, repair facilities, and aircraft operators, but it is more difficult to regulate parts brokers. Although there have been 164 indictments and 130 convictions in the past decade, the airlines rely primarily on sharp-eyed mechanics to spot counterfeit parts.

The late 1980s saw a rash of problems associated with the manufacture of faulty and inadequate parts. The Federal Aviation Administration sets guidelines for the quality and precision of airline parts and certifies the acceptability of manufacturers, but prior to the appearance of bogus parts in the late 1980s it had no measures in place to enforce conformity with these standards. When aircraft mechanics discovered that parts of inferior quality had infiltrated the spare parts marketplace, several task forces set about to establish more stringent means of identifying and monitoring parts. Such guidelines are expected to be in place by 1994. According to *Aviation Week & Space Technology,* most of the manufacturers of defective parts are "small companies, in the $3-10 million range. The companies have been immediately suspended from doing business with the government, and could be debarred for three to five years."

INDUSTRY LEADERS

The major manufacturers are Sunstrand Corp., Coltec Industries and Coltec Holdings, Lucas Aerospace, BF Goodrich, Fairchild, Boeing, and Textron Aerostructures.

The largest supplier of aircraft parts is Sundstrand, a Rockford, Illinois-based defense electronics company that broke into the aviation market during World War II. The company established a leading position in hydraulics and generators that paved the way for its involvement in jet aircraft technologies during the 1960s. Sundstrand's aviation supply operations expanded rapidly after 1967, due to an aggressive acquisition campaign that gave it the ability to manufacture instrumentation, entertainment systems, temperature controls, and gear drives.

The company's earnings from aircraft parts grew rapidly during the 1980s as a result of generous defense budgets. Sundstrand acquired several more aviation supply companies that broadened its position as a military contractor and provided new opportunities in civilian aviation. Accused of fraud in 1988, Sundstrand was fined and temporarily suspended from bidding on government contracts. The company later endured reverses from a rapid decline in defense spending. However, Sundstrand managed to realign its operations toward more stable civilian work, supplying products to Boeing, Airbus, McDonnell Douglas, and other customers. Sundstrand is the largest parts manufacturer, comprising nine percent of the segment's total sales.

The second largest manufacturer in this category is Coltec Industries, a former coal and coke supplier in Pennsylvania. The company entered the aviation products industry during a diversification campaign in the 1950s, when it purchased a fuel control systems manufacturer and the Colt firearms business. Known as Colt Industries after 1964, the company's rapid rise in the aircraft parts market occurred only after 1977, when it took over a landing gear manufacturer and a flight control systems company. In 1983, well into the defense build-up that so benefitted Sundstrand, Colt branched into fuel nozzles and other jet engine components, and later turbine engine parts and cockpit indicators and sensors. The company divested much of its non-aerospace operations, including Colt firearms, in 1990. It changed its name to Coltec, and presently accounts for about seven percent of sales in the industry.

The steel conglomerate LTV is also a major manufacturer of aircraft parts, accounting for about five percent of the segment's output. This company was founded by Jim Ling, whose circuitry business merged with Temco Electronics in 1960 to form a leading defense company. The following year, the company acquired Chance Vought Aviation from United Aircraft, giving the company the third letter in its name and enabling it to become deeply involved in the development of aircraft electronics and missile systems. LTV invested heavily in declining steel businesses during the 1980s. The company's only bright spot was its aerospace division. Still, LTV was forced into an eight-year bankruptcy that ended only in 1993.

During this time the company sold Vought, but retained much of its parts manufacturing operations, which are concentrated in naval aircraft systems.

In fourth place, with virtually the same market share as LTV, is Lucas Aerospace, an American subsidiary of the British company Lucas Industries. This company gained its expertise in aviation products early, adapting its core automotive parts line for British aircraft manufacturers during World War I. Lucas was introduced to American aviation in the 1930s through a partnership with Bendix called Rotax. Rotax was closely involved with jet engine technologies, and manufactured a variety of electronic and fuel control systems in the post-World War II period. Rotax became Lucas Aerospace in 1971, and prospered from its parent company's involvement with British Aerospace and the Airbus consortium. Due to the fact that Lucas is foreign-controlled, its sales are mainly confined to the civilian aircraft market. Lucas has moved away from the traditional job shop mode into a just-in-time production and integrated disparate manufacturing and business systems using CONTROL, an enterprise resources planning software system from Cincom Systems.

BF Goodrich, with 4 percent of total parts sales, began as a supplier in 1909, providing the wheels for Glenn Curtiss' early designs. The company subsequently branched into de-icing systems, flight suits, self-sealing fuel tanks, and later inflatable aircraft evacuation slides. BF Goodrich sold its tire operations to Michelin in 1986 specifically to concentrate on the aircraft supply market. Through a series of acquisitions, the company expanded into engine and fuel systems, test equipment, and flight instruments. In 1993 BF Goodrich took over Cleveland Pneumatic, a supplier of landing gear for the 747, 767, MD-11, and B-2 bomber. Fairchild remains active in the market through its association with the now defunct Republic Aircraft company. Allied-Signal also plays a major role, stemming from its acquisition of Garrett, as does Boeing, by virtue of its leading role in the airframe industry.

Boeing Commercial Airplane Group and Concentra Corporation were developing a strategic electrical-configuration application that would reduce the cycle time for routing aircraft wire harnesses. Boeing also was charged with integrating avionics, sensors, and vehicle management system with cockpit controls and displays for the F-22 scheduled to become airborne in mid-1997.

Commercial aerospace vendors have developed a new generation of cabin equipment that reduces operating costs, enhances passenger comfort, are lighter and more reliable, and require less maintenance. Envirovac introduced a new glide rinse valve for toilets that ended the failure connected with wet solenoid rinse valves. Boeing enhanced this product with a device that allows the flush cycle to be independently adjusted in the front and the rear of the aircraft to reduce unnecessary noise.

By the end of 1997, 300 planes will be retrofitted with EmPower, a standard interface for in- flight power mounted in the armrest of the seat. This device will free portable computers from dependence on batteries during long flights.

A new in-flight financial services terminal to accommodate the need for foreign exchange, cstimated to be $20 billion in currencies a year, is needed by passengers who travel on long-range wide-body planes. The developer, Aero-Design Technology, has also sold more than 1,000 galley trash compactors to over 40 airlines.

The new National Route Program and ensuing transition to Free Flight is posing a cockpit challenge that is being met with new electronics equipment. In the Fall of 1997 the Boeing 737- 700 will carry this new crystal display cockpit. Such equipment will replace aging analog electromechanical instrumentation.

In August 1996 Motorola announced a two-way messaging device that lets users send and receive e-mail unobtrusively and access the Internet. Transmission is via Sky Tel's network of ground transmitters.

Using FANS-I, the Future Air Navigation System's suite of the Global Positioning System (GPS), and satellite data link communication, United Air Lines was permitted to fly from Chicago to Hong Kong through Chinese and Siberian airspace. Clearance through this airspace was made available only to planes with this equipment and clearance was on a flight by flight basis. By the end of 1997 certified FANS packages will be available for new installation or retrofitting on most of the major aircraft types. Rockwell Collins Air Transport Division expects use will continue to grow, especially in India, as more Required Navigation Performance routes are established. The sole in-service FANS equipment as of September 1996 was on 747-400s which used the Honeywell equipment. The Boeing 777 includes FANS as standard equipment with its Increased weight aircraft. It is optional on 757/767 planes. Over 650 HT9100 units were sold in 1996. Airbus is also constructing its own FANS package.

By the year 2000, the GPS market is expected to reach $8.4 billion compared to $1.9 billion in 1996.

Prices have been dropping at the rate of 20 percent a year. Applications are endless.

WORK FORCE

A total of 120,800 persons were employed in the aircraft parts and equipment industry in December 1996 (an increase of 9,100 or nearly 9 percent over December 1995) with 75,800 in production alone. Average hourly earnings were $16.68 in December 1996.

AMERICA AND THE WORLD

British Aerospace has contracted to supply two South African firms with supply components for its Hawk jet trainers. The Russian Glonass satellite navigation system could remove reliance on a satellite system controlled only by the United States. A joint GPS/Glonass use was envisioned via the European Geostationary Navigational Ovrlay Service which would provide greater accuracy. Ashtec, a major U.S. manufacturer, has entered the GPS/Glonass market.

RESEARCH AND TECHNOLOGY

A team of aerospace and material manufacturers participating in the Affordable Composites for Propulsion (ACP) program are focused on cost-effective, lightweight, durable composite parts for future ultrahigh bypass engines which should yield fuel savings, increased payloads, reduced noise, and lower cost airframes. Team members are: Pratt & Whitney, Northrop Grumman, Alliant TechSystems, Dupont, and Dow-United Technologies Composite Products, Inc. NASA recently completed tests of a low-altitude collision avoidance system for the military aircraft which also has applications for certain civilian applications.

Rockwell Collins is developing a new Pro Line 21 avionics system that will cut purchase costs and match with future air traffic management requirements. Its flat AMLCD panel weighs half as much as a cathode ray tube, requires less volume, can operate with passive cooling without fans, and consumes less power.

Ciba Aersospace Products has developed a new Accustick epoxy synthetic that simplifies repairs and reduces production time. Technicians can cut the dough like resin into needed amounts, knead it briefly, and install it in the seam between pieces of honeycomb. It is a rapid cure for damaged aircraft composite parts and allows a quick turnaround.

Quantum Manufacturing Technologies is commercializing a new surface treatment method composed of light-weight ions that improves microstructures by healing microcracks and smoothing or hardening surface. This is particularly useful in airplane fuselages. As the result of a program funded by the Defense Advanced Research Projects to find new technology suitable for both military and civilian applications, an integrated opto-electronics module for fiber optic gyros was developed. This will greatly reduce the cost of medium performance fiber optic gyros. Fiber optic gyros are expected to replace ring laser gyros in 5 to 10 years.

Honeywell developed a portable computer like option that automates many administrative tasks of a flight deck as part of its Primus Epic suite of avionics. This will cause a major shift in the way pilots interact with aircraft avionics and on-board utility systems.

FURTHER READING

"Aerospace." *Business Africa,* August 1996.

"Aircraft Repair Station Speeds Turnaround." *Adhesives Age,* May 1996.

BF Goodrich. *Company Profile.* Akron, OH: BF Goodrich, 1993.

Biddle, Wayne. *Barons of the Sky.* New York: Simon & Schuster, 1991.

Coltec Holdings, Inc. *Annual Report.* New York: Coltec Holdings, Inc., 1993.

Donoghue, J. A. "Equipping for FANS." *Air Transport World,* September 1996.

Flint, Perry. "I Want Pilots, Not Monitors." *Air Transport World,* October 1996.

"Flying High." *Manufacturing Systems. Supplement for Makers of Highly Engineered Products Supplement,* May 1996.

"Foreign Exchange Goes Airborne." *Air Transport World,* November 1996.

Henderson, Breck W. "Aircraft Parts Firms Facing U.S. Charges." *Aviation Week & Space Technology,* 21 September 1992.

"Ion-Based Treatment Fills Microcracks." *Manufacturing Equipment,* July 1996.

Klass, Philip J. "New Device Cuts Cost of Fiber-Optic Gyros." *Aviation Week & Space Technology,* 11 November 1996.

LTV Corporation. *Looking Ahead.* Dallas: LTV Corporation, 1980.

McKenna, James T. "A Team of Engineers from Boeing." *Aviation Week & Space Technology,* 12 August 1996.

Nordwall, Bruce D. "Chicago-Hong Kong: First Direct FANS-1 Flight." *Aviation Week & Space Technology,* 12 August 1996.

———. "Collins Pro Line 21 Features Adaptive Flight Displays." *Aviation Week & Space Technology,* 18 November 1996.

———. "Optimism Grows for GPS/Glonass." *Aviation Week & Space Technology,* 14 October 1996.

Ott, James. "Crackdown on 'Bogus' Aircraft Parts Irks Maintenance Industry Officials." *Aviation Week & Space Technology,* 16-23 December 1991.

———. "Faulty, Bogus Part Evades Safety Net and Sparks Probe." *Aviation Week & Space Technology,* 20 January 1992.

———. "Twin Task Forces to Battle Bogus Parts." *Aviation Week & Space Technology,* 15 March 1993.

Patterson, Lee. "A Mode Less Traveled." *Forbes,* ASAP Supplement, 24 February 1997.

Proctor, Paul. "F-22 Components Underway at Boeing." *Aviation Week & Space Technology,* 10 June 1996.

———. "Low-Level Collision Avoidance Tested." *Aviation Week & Space Technology,* 3 February 1997.

Scott, William B. "Composite Parts Will Pay Dividends in Future Engines." *Aviation Week & Space Technology,* 26 August 1996.

———. "Pentium Powers Epic' Integrated Avionics." *Aviation Week & Space Technology,* 18 November 1996.

———. "Shortage of Replacement Parts May Delay Aging Aircraft Repairs." *Aviation Week & Space Technology,* 2 July 1990.

Schwartz, Ephriam. "In-Flight Power on the Way." *InfoWorld,* 10 March 1997.

Solberg, Carl. *Conquest of the Skies.* Boston: Little Brown, 1979.

Stern, Willy. "Warning! Bogus Parts Have Turned Up in Commercial Jets." *Business Week,* June 1996.

Sundstrand Corporation. *A History of the Company.* Rockford, IL: Sundstrand Corporation, 1992.

Sykes, Rebecca. "Motorola's Tango Offers Wireless E-mail. *InfoWorld,* 26 August 1996.

U.S. International Trade Administration. "No. 11495. Recent Trends in Aircraft and Aircraft Engines & Engine Parts." Available from http://www.ita.doc.gov/industry/otea/usio/95s1495.txt.

U.S. Department of Commerce. *U.S. Industrial Outlook 1993.* Washington, DC: January 1993.

Velocci, Anthony L. "Operating Costs Drive Cabin Product Design." *Aviation Week & Space Technology,* 5 September 1996.

———. "Raytheon Pursues Double Acquisition." *Aviation Week & Space Technology,* 13 January 1997.

Whitehouse, Arthur. *The Sky's the Limit.* London: Macmillan, 1979.

—John Simley, updated by David C. Genaway

SIC 3731

SHIP BUILDING AND REPAIRING

This category covers establishments primarily engaged in building and repairing ships, barges, and lighters, whether self-propelled or towed by other craft. This industry also includes the conversion and alteration of ships and the manufacture of offshore oil and gas well drilling and production platforms (whether or not self-propelled). Establishments primarily engaged in fabricating structural assemblies or components for ships, or subcontractors engaged in ship painting, joinery, carpentry work, and electrical wiring installation are classified in other industries. Boat building and repairing are excluded as they are in a separate category, **SIC 3732: Boat Building and Repairing.**

INDUSTRY SNAPSHOT

The U.S. commercial shipbuilding and repair industry entered the last half of the 1990s with the brightest prospects it has had in decades. The dramatic turnaround, according to former Maritime Administrator Adm. Albert Herberger, is due in large part to President Clinton's five-point national shipbuilding initiative.

Speaking in the spring of 1996 at the first American International Shipping Exposition (AISE) in New Orleans, Admiral Herberger credited the recovery to determination by shipbuilders and the president's support of the industry. Clinton's five-point plan calls for his administration to negotiate for the elimination of foreign shipbuilding subsidies, improve competitiveness, deregulate existing programs, enhance private sector financing of shipbuilding with federal loan guarantees, and expand international marketing activities. As of April 1996, Admiral Herberger said, 15 oceangoing ships were under construction in American shipyards, the largest number in more than a decade. Even more encouraging were the first U.S. exports of commercial vessels in 30 years.

Until this startling turnaround during the mid-1990s, virtually all merchant tonnage built in American shipyards was destined for domestic customers under a subsidy program or under the protection of the Merchant Marine Act of 1920, the Jones Act, which specifies that all intercoastal traffic must move in U.S.-built vessels. The U.S. Navy in recent years has been the largest customer of the industry. As a result, American yards have a greater capability to build one-of-a-kind sophisticated ships than to mass-produce less complex large merchant vessels.

U.S. shipyards build about 1.1 percent of world commercial deadweight tonnage annually (deadweight tons is a measure of ship carrying capacity), which is well below that produced by Japan, Korea, China, and several other countries. An illustration of the decline of the United States in the world shipping market can be measured as a percentage of world vessel tonnage under order.

With the end of the Cold War, the U.S. military industrial base began shrinking dramatically, as did the nation's shipbuilding industry, dependent as it was on defense orders. This made it all the more imperative that a means was found to get the U.S. industry moving in another direction. In January of 1990, an American shipbuilding concern received the first order for a commercial oceangoing vessel since 1984. Shipowners, including American companies, favored foreign shipyards because of cheaper prices and faster order turnaround time. Government subsidies in Japan, Korea, and Germany ranged from 20 percent to 30 percent of the cost of the ship, enabling these builders to capture almost all of the commercial shipbuilding business.

It became very clear that unless foreign shipbuilding and repair subsidies were eliminated, it would be difficult for U.S. shipbuilders to fully participate in the forecasted replacement of the world's aging merchant fleet during the 1990s. With the downsizing of the U.S. Naval fleet and the lockout of U.S. shipbuilders from the commercial market in the face of government-subsidized competition, the future of the U.S. shipbuilding and repair industry was looking bleak. The industry was facing massive layoffs and yard closures in this noncompetitive market.

One of the biggest obstacles to U.S. shipbuilding competitiveness was high state-sponsored shipbuilding subsidies, which were enjoyed by shipyards in a number of other countries. In early 1997, an international agreement to end such subsidies, thus leveling the playing field for U.S. shipyards, was pending before Congress. A continuing recovery for the U.S. shipbuilding industry depended heavily on the successful passage of such measures.

ORGANIZATION AND STRUCTURE

The United States has four shipbuilding regions: the Atlantic Coast, Gulf Coast, Pacific Coast, and Great Lakes. All four have capabilities to construct commercial and military ships. The Great Lakes yards, however, can only export ships that fit within the constraints of the Welland Canal and the St. Lawrence Seaway. For this reason, Great Lakes shipbuilding employment is only a small percentage of the industry total in the United States. Peterson Builders Inc. was the last major shipbuilder in the area with less than 5 percent of the shipbuilding industry's work force. The Atlantic Coast has the largest percentage of total employment, followed by the Gulf Coast, with the Pacific Coast third.

In the United States, most major shipbuilding yards are owned by conglomerates or large corporations. The Bethlehem Steel Corporation is an example of this type of entity—BethShip is its shipbuilding unit and is located in Port Arthur, Texas, and Sparrows Point, Maryland. One of the problems with this type of alignment is that it places the shipbuilding division in competition with other divisions of the corporation for investment dollars for expansion, modernization, or other purposes. With an average return on equity of 6 percent in the shipbuilding industry, shipbuilding divisions have been losing the fight for corporate resources. An argument in behalf of this structure is that the parent corporation may have more success in obtaining favorable financing than a relatively small subdivision would have if it operated independently.

The shipbuilding and repair industry is a capital-intensive business requiring extensive initial capital to enter the industry and meet subsequent outfitting and technological requirements. These factors provide substantial barriers to entry, especially since the industry is not very profitable. The protection of the Shipping Act of 1916 is important to the survival of industry members because it helps them consistently attract sufficient cargo to cover initial outlays and fixed costs. The conference system was created to help protect this Act. Through agreements enforced among the member groups, the conference system stabilized freight rates and the production of new commercial vessels. The stability of this system is necessary for individual shipbuilders to establish a cost structure and pricing policy.

As compared with the shipbuilding industry overseas, there has been relatively little cooperation among the yards in the United States. In Norway and Sweden for example, research is sponsored jointly by the major shipyards. Other shipbuilding and shipping organizations abroad jointly sponsor computer programming and economic studies for the common benefit. U.S. shipyards operate independently as they seek contracts competitively. Limited though these exchanges may be, they have stimulated programs of research, ship computer programming, and ship construction techniques.

Despite the strong government ties to the industry of the Maritime Administration and Navy-supported programs, until very recently there was little government intervention in industry-wide planning, quotas,

and other programs. This restraint reflects policies of antitrust legislation as well as the traditions of free, competitive enterprise. Unfortunately, U.S. shipyards have been denied many benefits they could acquire from cooperation, such as the use of standard parts and components (as employed profitably by Japanese shipbuilders). Benefits could also be gained from exchanges of engineering and other technical information. Hopefully, President Clinton's MARITECH program will go a long way toward addressing some of these problems in the U.S. shipbuilding and repair industry.

MARITECH is a key component of the Clinton administration's program to strengthen U.S. shipyards by assisting efforts to make the transition from the military to the commercial market. This program will keep the industrial defense base healthy by helping U.S. shipyards become commercially competitive in the international market.

The MARITECH program is an industry-led five-year campaign funded and managed by the Department of Defense's Advanced Research Projects Agency in consultation with the Maritime Administration. In addition, MARITECH is being executed in full partnership with the Navy through the Office of Naval Research. Total government funding for the 1994-1999 MARITECH program is $220 million. The MARITECH program will award matching federal funds to develop and implement technologies and advances processes for the competitive design, marketing, production, and support of commercial ships.

The basic production facilities of the industry are the shipbuilding positions, either shipways or docks, along with work areas, essential supporting shops, and engineering and design capability. Heavy-duty equipment is used for bending, rolling, forming, cutting, and welding plates and shapes; for forming pipe and sheet metal; and for performing a wide range of machining operations. In addition, shipyards require storage facilities—open areas for steel, piping, subassemblies, and other items requiring minimal protection; and shelters for machinery, equipment, stores, outfits, and other items requiring protection from rain, sun, or pilferage. Facilities for the assembly of heavy steel include large cranes and handling and conveying equipment. The shipyard must also have piers where the ships can be outfitted after launching. These piers are equipped completely with service facilities such as fire mains, electrical power supply, compressed air, and fresh water.

Ship Repair. Ship repair is a sustaining element in the maritime industry. It has enabled many shipbuilders to ride the storm in a capital-intensive and cyclical industry. Selection of a repair facility depends upon the magnitude and type of work, the preference of the ship or boat owners, and the proximity of the repair facility to the ship or boat. Periodic and emergency maintenance and repair work is essential to keep vessels operable. A report by the Ocean Shipping Consultants, an industry trade group, predicts a positive outlook for the repair industry throughout the 1990s. This trend can be attributed to the aging fleet of operational ships and the decision by shipowners to extend their useful life.

Repair crews are also called into action when it becomes necessary to break out mothballed merchant and naval ships from the reserve fleets located strategically on Atlantic, Gulf, and Pacific coasts. All vessels must also undergo special surveys every five years in addition to regular repairs to remain seaworthy. The rapid growth in tank deliveries between 1973 and 1975 should result in a 17 percent increase in mandatory repair work in 1994. Economically, many shipowners have found it more profitable to increase the life of their existing fleet due to the high building costs of a new vessel. The results are increased surveys and repair work for the yards. Finally, environmental issues arising as a result of accidents and oil spills have put pressure on shipowners to improve maintenance standards.

A critical requirement for a successful repair yard is its ability to meet schedules and complete work rapidly and satisfactorily. Many shipbuilding facilities have repair yards capable of dry-docking vessels of 400 feet or more. These firms handle a majority of the repair dollar volume, with the rest going to smaller docks or pier facilities. The balance are shops that do special or limited repairs, transporting labor or material to the work site. Repair firms without dry docking facilities do not work on such underwater parts as the hull and the propeller. An integrated repair yard uses extensive waterfront acreage with facilities capable of dry-docking and berthing large ships. These integrated yards, as well as smaller repair facilities, cluster around active ports.

Repair yards also require a heavy financial investment. Dry docks are expensive, and most integrated yards have two or more piers, about 1,000 feet long and 40 feet wide. These features are in addition to the cranes, electrical, and mechanical facilities. All such yards have warehouses to stock and shops to process raw materials. In addition, each must have a wider variety of tools than shipbuilders require, since each repair job can be unique. Ship repair yards do not need to invest as heavily in capital as shipbuilding yards. Most of the investments are directly connected with the prospect of using these facilities for ship construction. This long-range planning will help the shipbuilder manage the business when shipbuilding demands have abated.

The Shipbuilders Council of America, the one industry body that functions for private yards as a group, is the basic source of industry planning. This organization's membership covers most but not all of the major shipbuilding and repair yards and major segments of allied industries that supply materials and equipment. As a trade association, the council informs and appropriately presents the views of its members concerning pertinent legislative, executive, and judicial government actions and worldwide industrial and economic trends as they affect the private shipbuilding industry.

BACKGROUND AND DEVELOPMENT

The colonists came to North America with strong maritime backgrounds. Shipping and shipbuilding, since colonial days, have exerted a powerful influence on the development of the United States. The transport of people and commodities until late in the nineteenth century was accomplished most easily and expeditiously by water, and with few exceptions, populations clustered at seaports or river ports. During its early history, moreover, the country imported many of its finished goods and industrial products from Europe and exported raw materials and agricultural products. The coastal forests provided an apparently inexhaustible supply of inexpensive virgin timber for the construction of the many ships the colonists needed.

Legislation by the first Congress of the United States was similar in intent to modern maritime subsidies. The first tariff, enacted in 1789, stipulated a 10 percent reduction in custom duties for goods imported in American vessels and a tonnage tax in favor of American shipping. The first literal subsidy by the government was paid in 1845, when Congress authorized the Postmaster General to award mail subsidies, with preference to steamships that could be converted into vessels of war. These subsidies were discontinued in 1858 as an unnecessary drain on the Treasury.

Infant maritime industries continued to flourish. By 1850, American clipper ships were showing the flag in most ports of the world and were widely considered to be the world's best sailing vessels at that time. The American merchant marine was second in size only to England's. Although coastwise shipping was protected from foreign flag competition by the Navigation Act of 1817, the American merchant fleet received little more in the way of government assistance before 1845 than discriminatory duties or taxes and periodic contracts for mail. Essentially, throughout this successful era, the maritime industries of the United States were strictly private enterprises.

The Civil War began the decline of the American foreign-trade merchant fleet. As vessels were lost as prizes, American vessels shifted to foreign registry to lessen the risk of capture and to avoid exorbitant insurance rates. Vessels so transferred were not permitted to return to the U.S. registry. Even more far-reaching in its effects than the war itself was the development of steel-hull, steam-propelled ships. The advanced technology of England and of other European countries gave foreign builders a considerable advantage in the cost of building iron vessels. Since it was prohibited by law to register foreign-built ships under U.S. documentation, the high cost of domestically built ships demanded a heavier capital investment for American-flag ships than for ships built abroad. The capital costs reduced potential earnings in foreign trade to a point where investment in American transoceanic shipping was unattractive. Under these conditions, private capital was not attracted to the highly competitive field of shipping. The American merchant marine declined from its once prominent position to a level in 1914 where only 9 percent of the value of foreign commerce, imports and exports, was carried in American bottoms.

Awareness of the inadequacy of the U.S. merchant fleet led to attempts to reduce shipbuilding costs by removing tariffs from imported materials, but these measures were ineffective. Between 1900 and 1914 Congress made several attempts to expand and strengthen the U.S. merchant marine fleet by enacting various subsidy programs and establishing a Merchant Marine Commission in 1904. All of these efforts failed as U.S. merchant tonnage fell to an historic low as a percentage of foreign-flag tonnage.

The outbreak of war in Europe in 1914 finally aroused the country to correct this imbalance in its merchant fleet as American ports were glutted with cargo for export with nowhere to go. That year emergency legislation permitted foreign-built vessels of any age to be documented by the United States for use in foreign trade. The Shipping Act of 1916 was enacted, which established a Shipping Board of Commissioners to oversee the acquisition of vessels by purchase, to regulate the use of these vessels through liner and conference agreements, and to provide general instructions for the sale or disposal of vessels to U.S. citizens. The Act was modified in 1918 to prohibit the sale or lease of ships, shipyards, or dry docks to a foreigner in time of national emergency. It provided further that no U.S. shipyard could build for a foreign

account. This was the first piece of comprehensive maritime legislation of the twentieth century and it remains current law in the U.S. shipping industry.

Under the Act, the United States embarked upon its largest shipbuilding program up to that time to yield 2,300 vessels. The American merchant fleet grew from 6.8 percent of the world total in gross tons in 1914 to 22.2 percent in 1920. The Merchant Marine Act of 1920 was established after the Shipping Act to facilitate the disposal of surplus government owned vessels, to settle claims among carriers, to provide assistance to the U.S. merchant marine, and to regulate foreign commerce. The goal of the United States was to establish a merchant marine fleet that could meet all of the country's commerce and military needs. Congress ultimately wanted this fleet to be owned and operated privately by U.S. citizens and enacted provisions such as tax savings and subsidy assistance to stimulate the transfer of the government-owned fleet to private firms. Disposal of the ships to private citizens under the Act of 1916 and later under the Act of 1920 progressed slowly, and most of the fleet operated under the direction of the Shipping Board.

The disposal of ships to the private sector fluctuated from year to year, with most of the surplus ships sold at prices below cost. At the same time, the opening of the Panama Canal expanded the development of intercoastal shipping. Availability of ships at low prices, fluctuations in the volume of foreign commerce, and the inability of the U.S. ships built under wartime conditions to compete with swift, modern foreign-flag tonnage resulted in a decline in foreign trade for the United States. This backdrop, combined with congressional dissatisfaction with mail-contract payments to the industry, resulted in the passage of the Merchant Marine Act of 1936. This Act set the congressional foundation on which modern-day maritime policy rests and was the first attempt to set down a comprehensive maritime policy in the post-1916 Act period.

The Merchant Marine Act of 1936 provided subsidies to private U.S. shipowners on essential foreign trade routes. It also provided for the payment of subsidies to cover differentials in construction costs of foreign and domestic builders of vessels ordered for private operators for use on these routes. In addition, the Act authorized the government to build and charter vessels for operation on trade routes when private enterprise was unwilling to fill this role. Other provisions of the Act required subsidized lines to establish special funds to replace older vessels and to provide for loans and mortgage insurance, established citizen requirement for crews, required the establishment of manning scales and conditions for living and working on subsidized vessels, and authorized the establishment of a training program.

Under this Act, a building program of 50 ships a year over a ten-year period was planned to rehabilitate the dry-cargo tonnage of the merchant marine. This program turned out to be of inestimable value. At the outbreak of World War II, a substantial number of ships under construction provided an impetus to the required expansion of the shipbuilding industry with high-quality ships of proven design and performance for wartime service. The U.S. shipbuilding industry reached a peak of ship production by the end of World War II, having built 5,700 vessels during the war. Fifty-seven major private shipyards were in operation—23 on the Atlantic Coast, 22 on the Pacific Coast, and 12 on the Gulf Coast. In addition to achieving high production levels, these yards were innovative and brought new concepts to the industry, including multiple production of standardized designs, a switch from riveted to welded shipbuilding, and techniques for fabricating large subassemblies.

When it became apparent that World War II was drawing to a close in March of 1946, the Ship Sales Act was passed. The objective of the Ship Sales Act was to dispose of surplus tonnage of ocean vessels while promoting the national policy of maintaining a merchant marine owned and operated by private citizens of the United States and to avoid some of the mistakes of the past. It provided for the sale, over a limited period of time, of war-built vessels to citizens and foreigners alike on a fixed-price basis. Charter of war-built vessels to foreigners was not permitted, but U.S. citizens could charter vessels on a short-term basis.

The postwar period began the decline of the U.S. shipbuilding industry. The downturn was interrupted by four spurts of orders. The first program began in the late 1940s and carried into 1950. It grew primarily out of the need for replacement tonnage that could not be met sufficiently by foreign yards, in part because the German and Japanese yards and component manufacturers could not operate on or near capacity. The second program was sparked by the Korean conflict and continued into 1954. The third program began in 1956 with the Suez crisis, and the fourth began in 1961 with the beginning of deliveries under the Maritime Administration cargo vessel replacement program. Wide fluctuation in demand over the postwar period, coupled with ambitious spending plans by U.S. shipyards to increase automation and an increasingly competitive environment, resulted in the decline of the U.S. shipbuilding industry.

In an effort to maintain the operation of a certain number of shipyards, the U.S. Government parceled out orders among several yards, rather then giving a single yard the run of a specific ship. In effect, this put shipbuilders in the position of contractors, building small numbers of ships to individual specifications, rather than that of manufacturers producing large quantities of identical items. Shipbuilders were unable to profit from learning curve benefits that accrue with long runs, and although the government's intentions were good, its actions killed the incentive of shipbuilders to diversify, and they lost their competitive edge. Government subsidies that supported the industry and paid for a small number of expensive vessels discouraged capital investment among the shipbuilders and expansion of their yards. The resulting shipyards had a high ratio of labor to capital, making the industry labor-intensive and cost prohibitive. The industry became dependent on government subsidies and Naval construction for its survival.

The industry has been hurt by overcapacity since the 1970s, which was driven by the lack of linkage between supply and demand. Shipping companies, which were not forced to suspend operations, moved to U.S. trades to attract high-value cargo. As a result of the influx of carriers, U.S.-flag shipping was hit especially hard. A more recent threat posed by open conferences is the entry of state-controlled carriers in world trade. These carriers do not operate in pursuit of profit. Rather, they exist to promote their country's national shipping policies and to earn foreign exchange. The subsidies provided in many of these countries created an artificially high supply of ships that were later sold at low prices. In addition, the rates charged by these carriers were substantially lower than conference rates and resulted in foreign carriers siphoning off high-rated freight. The U.S. shipbuilding industry had not made the conversion from the military to civilian markets and was effectively shut out of this area because of the foreign subsidies. Even if there were a curb on foreign subsidies, it is still uncertain whether U.S. shipyards could make the transition to the civilian markets. The industry structured shipyards around the complexity of the Navy projects, and they were not prepared for the simplicity of design, speed of delivery, and low-cost requirements of the commercial sector.

In the early 1980s, the Reagan administration eliminated the direct federal subsidies of about $200 million each year that made U.S. shipyards competitive with foreign manufacturers. Almost all commercial shipbuilding moved overseas. At the same time, however, the president called for a 25 percent expansion in the Navy to increase the fleet to 600 ships. The defense buildup was enough to insulate the shipbuilding industry for the time being, but the industry was working from a much smaller base. In 1979, U.S. shipyards employed 150,000 workers and had 166 oceangoing vessels under construction, 67 of which were commercial ships. In the last ten years, employment has dropped to 72,000 workers and 45 yards have closed, leaving only 17 yards capable of building oceangoing vessels. In 1990, 96 Navy ships and one commercial vessel were under construction at American shipyards. The shipbuilders that survived relied on the Naval building program; which increased its fleet from roughly 450 ships in 1980 to more than 580. In 1990, 95 percent of the business in the shipbuilding industry was Navy construction, overhaul, and repair, with ship repairs accounting for the remaining 5 percent.

After the Cold War, the U.S. military-industrial base began shrinking dramatically, as did the nation's shipbuilding industry. In January of 1990, an American shipbuilding concern received the first order for a commercial oceangoing vessel since 1984. This was despite the fact that cabotage laws remain in effect that require that containerships serving only U.S. ports must be manufactured in a domestic yard. Shippers, including American companies, have favored foreign shipyards because of cheaper prices and faster order turnaround time. Government subsidies in Japan, Korea, and Germany range from 20 to 30 percent of the cost of the ship, enabling those builders to capture almost all of the business. In 1989 the Bush administration failed in a year-long effort to persuade foreigners to end their subsidies. As of early 1997, an international accord to phase out shipbuilding subsidies worldwide was pending before Congress. Giving additional hope for the U.S. shipbuilding industry was the Clinton administration's plan to help shipyards become competitive in the international market. However, its success remains to be seen.

CURRENT CONDITIONS

The shipbuilding down cycle of the 1980s was unusually severe because it was preceded by a period of massive speculative overbuilding. During the early part of that decade, governments of most shipbuilding countries made decisions to pour money into commercial shipyards. The lone exception was the United States, which terminated its shipbuilding subsidies instead. This decision by the Reagan administration, coupled with the "Section 615" waivers that encouraged American shipbuilders to buy overseas, devastated commercial shipbuilding in the United States.

These yards then became dependent on the U.S. defense budget for survival. Because of cuts in the defense budget and reduced requirements for Navy ships for the remainder of the 1990s, the Shipbuilders Council of America estimated that most of the private shipyards in the United States would have to close. The transition to competitive commercial shipbuilding by U.S. shipbuilders was the goal of the Clinton administration's five-point national shipbuilding initiative. The fate of the U.S. shipbuilding industry rested in large measure upon the success of this and similar programs that could follow, as well as on the elimination of shipbuilding subsidies worldwide.

Although the world shipbuilding market began to turn around in 1988, foreign yards continued to depend on government support to capture contracts and build ships. They received government payments to modernize facilities through restructuring and investment aid, indirectly benefited from government-supported ship financing provided to and domestic customers from export and home credits, and realized special tax benefits. In addition, many of these foreign yards were awarded government grants to capture shipbuilding and repair contracts, and benefited from government-aided research and development of advanced manufacturing technology. During this same period, U.S. shipyards received none of these advantages.

Throughout most of the 1980s, the justification for foreign shipbuilding subsidies was low demand. In the 1990s, however, the reluctance of many foreign shipbuilders to let go of government subsidies was caused by the desire to capture as many contracts as possible while demand was high, and while denying market access to U.S. shipyards. The U.S. shipyards have been losing the battle with the international commercial shipbuilding market during the last ten years as measured in the number of new merchant vessels under construction or on order at U.S. private shipyards.

INDUSTRY LEADERS

The four leading U.S. shipbuilders as measured by shipyard capabilities and employment level are: Newport News Shipbuilding & Drydock Co. located in Newport News, Virginia; Ingalls Shipbuilding Corp., headquartered in Pascagoula, Mississippi; Bath Iron Works Corporation in Bath, Maine; and Avondale Industries Inc., based in New Orleans, Louisiana. The remaining major U.S. shipyards are clustered on the Atlantic, Pacific, and Gulf coasts. Peterson Builders, Inc. is the last major shipbuilder serving the Midwest region.

Newport News Shipbuilding is the largest, most diversified shipyard in the United States. It is strategically located in Newport News, Virginia, with deepwater access to major shipping lines served by all major airlines and rail transportation. It has the resources to accommodate major overhaul and repair work, new construction, conversion, and routine maintenance work. In addition, its Sperry Marine subsidiary develops, designs, and markets marine instrumentation and communication systems.

Ingalls Shipbuilding, the second largest American shipbuilder, is a division of Litton Industries and is headquartered in Pascagoula on the Gulf Coast of Mississippi. Ingalls is one of the nation's leading systems companies for the design, engineering, construction, life cycle and fleet support, and repair and modernization of advanced surface combatant ships for the U.S. Navy and international navies, as well as for commercial marine structures of all types. In continuous operation since 1938, Ingalls is Mississippi's largest private employer with 10,000 employees.

The shipyard of Bath Iron Works Corporation, located in Bath, Maine, is on the Kennebec River 15 miles from the Gulf of Maine, and its fabrication facility is located eight miles west in Brunswick. Bath Iron works is renowned for its design and construction of the Arleigh Burke Class guided missile destroyer but is also capable of building high technology commercial vessels.

Avondale Shipyards, a division of Avondale Industries, Inc., is located on the Gulf Coast in Avondale, Louisiana. The shipyard uses computer-aided design and modern series and modular construction methods to build a variety of military and complex commercial vessels.

WORK FORCE

The shipbuilding and repair industry employed 118,300 workers in 1992, down about 2 percent from 120,200 in 1987. Many of these workers have special skills such as welding, cutting, assembling and fabricating, blue collar supervising, shipfitting, and a host of other important trades necessary for the completion of shipbuilding tasks. Most of the major yards are also active in repair and conversion. The balance of the industry is engaged in the construction or repair of small ships, drill rigs, and small, specialized commercial craft.

Basic skill requirements for the repair industry are generally higher than those required for shipbuilding. In yards that do both construction and repair, it is common practice to assign the same workers either to building or repair as the workload shifts. These floating assignments help maintain the continuity of em-

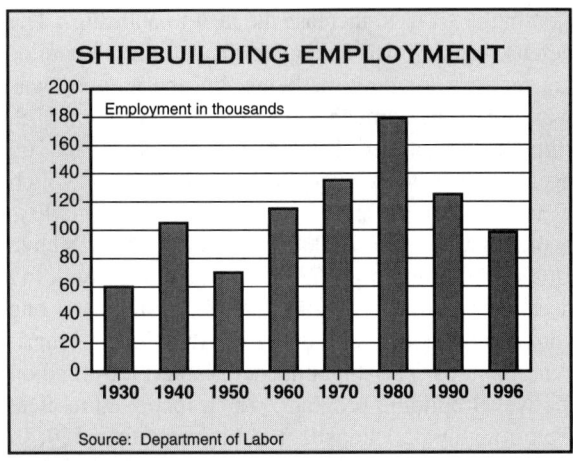

SHIPBUILDING EMPLOYMENT

Source: Department of Labor

ployment at a stable level. Other workers may migrate between shipbuilding yards and repair yards. Although supervisory and planning skills for repair and construction differ distinctly, both sets of skills may be learned and used by the same person.

Industry Problems. The first and foremost problem of a shipbuilder is that of utilizing the resources at his command to produce a reasonable return on investment. Within this context, as with any commercial enterprise, the shipbuilder has the problem of maintaining an adequate orderbook, obtaining necessary financing, obtaining and retaining competent personnel, establishing and maintaining suitable facilities, obtaining and utilizing the proper materials, and maintaining an organization that will use these resources properly and efficiently.

One of the most difficult and important problems is the maintenance of a stable orderbook. All of the foregoing considerations, from finance through organization, are strongly supported by stability in the orderbook and suffer severely from instability. The beneficial effects and the efficiency of the enterprise are materially enhanced if the orders are repetitive, to permit series production. The need for an assured market, of course, is implicit throughout all considerations.

In the United States, the problem of obtaining series production has been more difficult than in countries where the government, consortia, and individual yards by mutual agreement can allocate particular types of construction to specific yards. Antitrust provisions prevent this type of rationalization in the United States. U.S. yards therefore have to compete with each other for series production and attempt to obtain series production and develop special capabilities for the types of vessels they prefer to build. The industry's reliance on Naval orders has put them at a competitive disadvantage because they are building smaller numbers of ships to individual specifications, rather then producing large quantities of identical items.

Finance for needed expansion has not been difficult to obtain in the past. However, massive demands on the capital markets for other needs of the industry during the mid-1990s may pose future restrictive problems. This factor, coupled with past overbuilding trends in the industry and the current competitive climate facing U.S. shipbuilders, has resulted in a lack of capital available to shipbuilders.

The matter of obtaining and retaining competent personnel has also been a difficult problem for most shipyards. This problem is chiefly due to the cyclic nature of the orderbooks and the workflow. Compounding the problem is the work availability in the construction industry at higher levels of pay. A workload with a reasonable promise of continuing stability is the most significant factor in the attraction and retention of competent personnel.

The establishment and the upgrading of facilities to improve operating efficiency are always under consideration by a shipbuilder. Again, such commitments are only practical with reasonable assurance or high expectation of a market sufficient to produce an adequate return on investment. The cost and availability of material similarly is always important to a shipbuilder, since material constitutes about half the cost of the usual commercial vessel. The small demand for material and equipment from the shipbuilding industry leaves the shipbuilder with little bargaining power to improve prices and delivery.

AMERICA AND THE WORLD

The building of oceangoing ships is practiced throughout the world. All nations engaged in major shipbuilding participate heavily in world trade. Many build ships as a significant export commodity and their economies are closely tied to the success of this industry. The areas responsible for most of ship production are grouped broadly into three sectors: the United States, the Far East, and Europe. European membership is represented by the Association of Western European Shipbuilders and includes Belgium, Denmark, Finland, France, Germany, Italy, the Netherlands, Norway, Spain, Sweden, and the United Kingdom. The industry has been dominated by the Far East sector with Japan and South Korea controlling over 50 percent of the orders of commercial vessel tonnage. Although American shipyards were once again beginning to build for foreign customers, U.S. yards were not a significant factor in international competition with only 1.1 percent of the commercial tonnage under construction at U.S. shipyards in 1992. This was due

primarily to foreign subsidized shipbuilding practices, which could change dramatically if a global accord to phase out such subsidies was approved by major shipbuilding countries.

FURTHER READING

All about Shipbuilders Council of America. Fairfax, VA: Shipbuilders Council of America, 1983.

"All about Shipbuilding; After a Long Slump, World Shipping Is Embarking on a Modest Recovery." *New York Times,* 6 May 1990.

"All Ashore That's Goin' Ashore—The Era of Bargain Prices for Ocean Shipping Services Is Slowly Coming to an End." *Purchasing,* 9 November 1989, 66-69.

"American Ship: Can It Survive?" *St. Petersburg Times,* 12 July 1992, Section 1, 1.

Beazer, Cox, and Harvey Watkins. *U.S. Shipbuilding in the 1970's.* Lexington, MA: Lexington Books, D.C. Heath and Company, 1972.

Bringing Back America's Shipyards—A Major Step toward Bringing Back America's Independence. Fairfax: Shipbuilders Council of America, 1988.

"Corporate Profiles '93: NASSCO." *San Diego Daily Transcript,* 11 January 1993.

"Cycle Set to Bottom Out." *Straits Times,* 20 June 1993.

"Department of Transportation: Federal Highway Administration." *Environmental Law Reporter,* 1992.

International Shipbuilding Aid June 1993. Fairfax: Shipbuilders Council of America, June 1993.

Lazich, Robert S., ed. *Market Share Reporter 1996.* Detroit: Gale Research, 1996.

Litton Industries. "Ingalls Shipbuilding . . . America's Shipyard." Available from http://www.ingalls.com/company.htm.

Mack-Forlist, Newman. *The Conversion of Shipbuilding from Military to Civilian Markets.* New York: Praeger Publishers, 1970.

McCoy, Cynthia Y. "The Sinking Ship Industry." *Journal of International Law and Business 99,* Evanston, IL: Northwestern School of Law, 1983.

1989-1990 in Review Ship Construction Report, July 1991. Fairfax: Shipbuilders Council of America, 1990.

Shertz, A. "The Shipping Act of 1984: A Return to Antitrust Immunity." *14 Transportation Law Journal 153.* Denver, CO: University of Denver, 1985.

"Ship Maker Can't Get Under Way." *Houston Chronicle,* 18 July 1993.

Shipbuilders Council of America Annual Report 1981. Fairfax: Shipbuilders Council of America, 1982.

"Shipbuilding: Talks on Phasing Out Aids at a Standstill." *European Report,* 21 March 1990.

"Shipping; Pushed in at the Deep End." *Economist,* 5 June 1982, 32.

"The Shipping Revival Has Not Extended to the Shipbuilding Industry." *Lloyds List,* 31 January 1989.

"Shiprepair Sector Ready to Pick Up." *Lloyds List,* 6 October 1992.

U.S. Census Bureau. "Description of Industries and Summaries of Findings: Industry 3731, Ship Building and Repair." Available from http://www.census.gov/mcd/mancen.

U.S. Department of Transportation. "Maritime Administrator Lauds Reemerging U.S. Shipbuilding Industry." Available from http://www.dot.gov/affairs/mar0496.htm.

"Waiting for Better Times at America's Shipyards." *New York Times,* Section 3, 11.

White House Office of the Press Secretary. "President Clinton Announces Selection of 20 MARITECH Projects." Available from http://www.gwjapan.org/ftp/pub/policy/whouse/1994/may/wc052694.txt.

"World Annual Report on Shipbuilding." *Lloyds List,* 22 March 1989.

—Andrew Burke, updated by Don Amerman

SIC 3732

BOAT BUILDING AND REPAIRING

This industry consists of establishments primarily engaged in building and repairing boats. Establishments primarily engaged in operating marinas and that perform incidental boat repair are classified in **SIC 4493: Marinas.** Membership yacht clubs are classified under **SIC 7997: Membership Sports and Recreation Clubs;** and outboard motor repair is classified under **SIC 7699: Repair Shops and Related Services, Not Elsewhere Classified.**

INDUSTRY SNAPSHOT

In the second half of the 1990s, the recreational boating industry in the United States was continuing to recover from a devastating industry-wide slump that began in the late 1980s and continued into the early 1990s. During the industry recession, stretching from 1988 through 1992, constant-dollar product shipments declined at a compound annual rate of approximately 15 percent. The turnaround began in 1993, when the industry cut its decline in shipments to less than 1 percent. In 1996, an unseasonably cool, damp summer in much of the United States cast something of a chill over the domestic market for pleasure boats. But market observers and U.S. boat builders were optimistic

that many of these sales would occur during a bulge in 1997 sales of recreational boats.

Total retail spending on recreational boating in 1995 hit $17.23 billion, up more than 22 percent from 1994 expenditures of $14.07 billion, according to the National Marine Manufacturers Association (NMMA), a trade association based in Chicago. This spending total includes not just boats, both new and used, but motors, engines, accessories, safety equipment, fuel, insurance, docking, maintenance, launching, storage, repairs, and club memberships.

According to the NMMA, total U.S. boat registrations at the beginning of 1995 were 11.43 million, an increase of 1.3 percent from registrations of 11.28 million at the beginning of 1994.

The outlook for the recreational boating industry in 1997 was reasonably bright, according to the marine equipment economist of the Commerce Department's International Trade Administration. Among the factors cited for this cautious optimism were the Environmental Protection Agency's new emissions standards. The standards don't take full force until 2005, but they are being phased in gradually. ITA's economist said many consumers might have postponed purchases because they want to see what this new technology is and how it will affect them. In 1994, the government projected real annual growth of 3 percent for the period through the end of the decade.

ORGANIZATION AND STRUCTURE

Repairs account for only about a 4 percent share of the boat building and repairing industry's revenue. In 1987, in the thick of the industry's boom period, 151 of the 2,176 establishments in this classification were engaged primarily in repairing boats. These establishments employed 3,500 workers and generated $223 million in shipment value. There was some evidence that slow sales of new boats in recent years have provided a bit of a spark to the repair business. In the early 1990s, boat yards specializing in refurbishing older boats charged in the range of $50 to $60 an hour for semiskilled labor on repairs.

Types of Boats Manufactured. Outboard boats make up the largest category of boats built in the United States, accounting for approximately 47 percent of all pleasure boats owned. In 1992, about 192,000 outboard boats were sold, a slight drop from the previous year and a 40-year low. Nearly 150 companies specialized in the manufacture of outboard boats in 1987. The value of outboard boats shipped that year was $1.173 million. About 8 million of these boats were currently owned in the United States in the mid-1990s. Boats in this category include runabouts, bass boats, utility boats, offshore fishboats, and pontoons. Aluminum and fiberglass are the most common materials used in the construction of these boats.

Inboard/outdrive (I/O) boats, also known as sterndrive boats, account for nearly 11 percent of U.S. pleasure boats. More than 90 companies specialized in I/O boats in 1987. Larger, higher-priced sterndrive boats were among those that suffered particularly harsh sales declines since the late 1980s. As a result of this decline, manufacturers attempted to attract buyers with significantly lower prices. This resulted in a 2,000-unit increase in sales of sterndrive boats in 1992.

Inboard boats include mainly cabin cruisers and sportboats. The inboard cruiser business was hit hard by the recession and the 10 percent excise tax on luxury boats that took effect in 1991 (but was repealed by the Clinton administration in 1993). Largely due to the tax, inboard cruiser sales were cut in half in 1991, and had yet to recover in 1997. Ski boats accounted for 88 percent of the inboard sportboats manufactured. Other inboard sportboats include runabouts, which represent about 9 percent of the market, and inboard fishing boats (under 25 feet).

Of the boats owned in the United States (about 1.37 million units), 8 percent are sailboats. This includes both nonpowered sailboats (1.3 million) and auxiliary-powered craft (70,000). Altogether, sailboats represent about 4 percent of boats manufactured. The vast majority of sailboats built were in the 12- to 19-foot range. From 1991 through 1993, sales of larger sailboats plummeted, largely attributable to the excise tax on luxury boats. In 1994, even after the repeal of the excise tax on luxury boats, large sailing craft's percentage of total sailboat production continued to be quite small. Of the 13,000 sailboats produced that year, about two-thirds were in the 12- to 19-foot class. Another 20 percent were sailboats ranging from 20 feet to 29 feet in length. Sailboats of 41 feet or more in length accounted for a mere 2.9 percent of total production.

One of the fastest-growing segments of the U.S. recreational boating market in 1997 was personal watercraft, sales of which have almost doubled, from 1993's 107,000 units with a retail value of $618 million to sales in 1995 of 200,000 units with a value of $1.14 billion. Personal watercraft are small in-board engine boats powered by a jet propulsion unit and operated by a person or persons sitting, standing, or kneeling on it.

Until fairly recently this segment of the market was supplied very heavily by imports, with the three leading producers being Canada's Bombardier and Japan's Kawasaki and Yamaha. The Japanese companies have since established extensive U.S. manufacturing facilities, and in 1993, traditional U.S. boat manufacturers Sea Ray Boats and Boston Whaler Inc. began producing personal watercraft.

Other types of boats include unregistered small craft (canoes, rowboats, dinghies, etc.), open-deck boats (deck-style monohull runabouts and aluminum pontoons), and houseboats.

Markets. In 1994, sales of boats, motors, trailers, and marine accessories were highest in Florida, which took more than 21 percent of total sales, followed by Michigan and Texas, each accounting for slightly more than 12.5 percent of total sales. Californians bought the next highest share of boating equipment, accounting for 10.8 percent of total U.S. sales. Minnesota and New York followed, with shares of 8.7 and 8.6 percent, respectively.

Establishment Distribution and Size. Boats are built primarily where there is a lot of water. Geographically, Florida and California dominate the boat building and repairing industry. More than $1 billion in product shipments, about 21 percent of the U.S. total, originate in Florida, where over 400 establishments are located. California is home to about 250 establishments in this industry. Washington and Tennessee, the latter of which has extensive recreational boating waters (though it is landlocked), round out the top four states in the manufacture of pleasure boats.

Boat building and repairing concerns can vary dramatically in size. About half of the more than 2,000 establishments in the industry employ only one to four people. The largest share of revenue, however, is generated by more sizable operations, especially the approximately 100 companies with between 100 and 500 employees. This group accounts for about half of the dollar value of the industry's shipments.

BACKGROUND AND DEVELOPMENT

Prior to the mid-nineteenth century, boats in the United States were built primarily by the people who used them. Most were workboats designed for specific uses. These included whaling boats for the Arctic seas, dories for the Grand Banks, log canoes used by oystermen, and a huge variety of skiffs and other small craft. Eventually boats became more versatile. The Whitehall was a pulling boat first used in New York harbor as sort of a water taxi. A classic rowing boat, the Whitehall was found to be well suited as a sailing vessel as well, and it began to appear in other harbors on both coasts, both with and without sails, and was sometimes used for fishing.

Around 1850, recreational boating began to grow significantly in the United States. Boat builders throughout the Northeast, previously makers of workboats, were in demand for the production of leisure boats for weekend amateurs. This led to a proliferation of Whitehalls, guide boats, and Saint Lawrence skiffs on lakes from New England to the Midwest. The popularity of row boats dropped when the gasoline engine appeared in the United States in 1878. Fishermen, both professional and recreational, began using boats with motors instead.

Some of the companies that entered the early motorboat industry were automobile manufacturers. One such company was the Lozier Motor Company, which began building boats around the turn of the century. Another important company in the early 1900s was the Electric Boat Company of Bayonne, New Jersey, which manufactured a wide variety of boats, including tiny launches and huge luxury cruisers by the time of the company's demise around 1950. Chris-Craft Boats was another important powerboat manufacturer by 1930. By the middle of the twentieth century, there was a renaissance of classic boat designs. New boats modeled on the vessels of the past were constructed using fiberglass and other modern materials. To an extent, this trend has continued.

In the 1950s, the number of recreational boats owned in the United States more than doubled, reaching over 7 million by 1961. This number has climbed slowly and steadily for the most part since then. In the mid-1980s, the pleasure boat industry boomed, with product shipments growing at an average rate of 13 percent a year. In 1989, however, the economy soured, sending boat manufacturing into a tailspin from which it has yet to emerge. The industry's problems were compounded in 1991 when a 10 percent federal tax on boats retailing for over $100,000 was enacted. Largely as a result of the tax, the share of the pleasure boat market by dollar value accounted for by boats in that high-price bracket slipped from 33 percent to 25 percent in one year.

CURRENT CONDITIONS

Three factors contributed to the major drop in the demand for boats in the United States between 1989 and 1991. One was the reluctance on the part of consumers to take on additional debt on top of that incurred during the industry's boom years of 1982 through 1988. Another factor was the overall decline in the economy during this period. As disposable personal income declines, pleasure boats, being large and

unnecessary (or "luxury") purchases, are among the first items deleted from shopping lists during economic downturns. A third factor was the 10 percent federal luxury tax on pleasure boats with price tags over $100,000. The tax, which was repealed in 1993, has generally taken the blame for the departure of several luxury boat builders from the market, and the loss of thousands of industry jobs.

Signs of Recovery. The earliest signs of a recovery emerged in 1992. The 1993 repeal of the luxury tax appears to be helping complete the recovery. Part of the increase in orders that took place was to rebuild dealers' inventories, which had reached the lowest levels in history by the beginning of 1992. Nevertheless, most manufacturers reported improving conditions, and some began rehiring laid-off workers. Viking Yacht Co. (a maker of high-end vessels), for example, began rehiring after seeing its work force plunge to 65 employees from its 1990 level of 1,500. Industry analysts expect the recovery to continue at a modest pace through the end of the 1990s. In order to affect the expected recovery, the boating industry must meet the challenge of restoring consumer demand. Manufacturers are hopeful that the rapidly growing 35- to 54-year-old age group will live up to its demographic billing as big spenders on leisure activities such as boating.

INDUSTRY LEADERS

The world's leading manufacturer of pleasure boats and motors in the mid-1990s was Brunswick Corporation, based in Lake Forest, Illinois. Brunswick's total 1996 revenues topped $3.16 billion, up nearly 4 percent from 1995 revenues of $3.04 billion, and a whopping 53.5 percent higher than 1992 revenues of $2.06 billion, at the depth of the recreational boating slump. In addition to its boat and boating motor product lines, Brunswick is a leading manufacturer of bowling and bicycling equipment. Among the boat brands Brunswick builds are Sea Ray, Bayliner, Maxum, Baja, and Boston Whaler. Brunswick also manufactures Mercury, Mariner, and Force outboard engines.

Brunswick was founded in 1845, and for much of its history was principally a maker of billiards and bowling equipment. In the early 1960s, the popularity of bowling declined, and the company diversified. By the following decade, Brunswick was building boats on a large scale. In 1986, Brunswick bought two important boat companies, Bayliner and Ray Industries. Between 1982 and 1991, the share of company sales contributed by boating rose from 42 to 66 percent. Since 1989, however, Brunswick has cut 40 percent of its work force and closed 18 of its 49 boat building plants.

Another major player in the boat building industry is Genmar Industries Inc., which is headquartered in Minneapolis but builds recreational powerboats in Florida, Minnesota, Wisconsin, North Carolina, Louisiana, and Arkansas. Genmar's boat brands include Hatteras, Trojan, Crestliner, Glastron, Aquasport, Cajun, and Wellcraft. In addition to its U.S. facilities, Genmar builds boats at a plant in the Canadian province of Manitoba. Genmar's worldwide employees total approximately 5,000.

WORK FORCE

About 44,500 people in the United States were employed in boat building and repairing in the mid-1990s, about 22 percent less than the 57,200 employees reported in 1987, but 9 percent more than the number of employees in 1991. Production workers, who made up 82 percent of the total industry employment, earned an average of $8.13 an hour in 1987. Welders and cutters made up the largest occupation class, accounting for 7.4 percent of the industry's employment in 1990. Blue collar worker supervisors and shipfitters each accounted for 5.4 percent of the industry's workers. A variety of skilled and semiskilled occupations each contributed between 2 and 4 percent of the work force. Workers in these jobs included carpenters, machinists, electricians, riggers, and sheet metal workers. The rest of the industry's workers were primarily engineers, painters, clerks, managers, mechanics, and helpers.

AMERICA AND THE WORLD

The boat industry in the United States exported $658 million in products in 1995, an increase of 29.8 percent over exports of $507 million recorded in 1994. Through the first half of 1996, U.S. exports of all products and services sold by the boat building and repair industry were down 6.83 percent from the comparable period 1995.

From 1990 through 1994, the United States enjoyed a surplus in the marine equipment trade. But when the U.S. domestic market began to rebound in 1994, the balance of trade turned unfavorably for the United States. Marine equipment imports of $279 million in 1990 compared with exports of $793 million. The following year, exports still outpaced imports by $774 to $207 million. In 1992, this trend continued with exports at $714 million and imports at $257 million. In 1993, however, there was a distinct narrowing of the trade balance, with exports of $534 million and imports of $425 million. And by 1994, imports topped exports, totaling $564 million against exports of $507 million.

The largest foreign markets for the U.S. boat industry were Canada and Japan. Exports to Canada were valued at $131 million in 1991, and grew an estimated 22 percent the following year. Two factors contributed to this increase: the U.S.-Canada Free Trade Agreement; and, ironically, an industry-wide recession, which put several Canadian manufacturers out of business and opened the market for U.S. firms.

Canada is also the largest supplier of foreign-made pleasure boats to the United States. In 1992, shipments from Canada totaled about $150 million, an 84 percent increase over the previous year. Taiwan and Japan also ship significant numbers of boats to the United States.

Exports to Japan have been on the decline, dropping 41 percent to $71 million in 1992, following a period of dramatic growth in that country's pleasure boat market in 1989 and 1990. Other major markets for U.S.-made boats were Germany, Italy, France, and Spain. Spain was the only country other than Canada in the top ten to increase its imports of U.S. boats in 1992.

Two international developments may help to sustain the growth of U.S. pleasure boat exports in the coming years. First, the European Union has embraced the same safety standards that were adopted in the United States. Second, the approval of the North American Free Trade Agreement (NAFTA) by Congress has removed Mexico's 20 percent tariff on pleasure boats, opening that market for potential exports.

RESEARCH AND TECHNOLOGY

Boat builders look to both the past and the future when it comes to designing their products. Many innovations involve incorporating new materials into classic designs. One example is the use of fiberglass on tin hulls. Since 1990, manufacturers have also sought ways to combine the features of different types of boats into one model. This was illustrated by the 1991 introduction by OMC and other companies of deck-style boats that are roomy, like pontoons, while performing more like runabouts.

Some of the most impressive innovations in the boat industry in recent years have been in electronics. VHF (very high frequency) radios, among the most common pieces of boating equipment, have evolved from heavy, permanently installed instruments to hand held, portable devices. Advances have also been made in atmosphere sensor technology, including equipment for detecting carbon monoxide. Another major technological development in boating was the Global Positioning System (GPS), a satellite-based navigational system. GPS was originally developed by the Defense Department for use in deploying weapons. The system, which is available to the public in a semi-crippled form, can be used for navigating on land and in the air as well as at sea.

The boat repair industry has also benefited from technological advances of recent years. Computer-based inventory systems have enabled companies to keep their inventories smaller, while at the same time improving the efficiency of parts delivery.

FURTHER READING

Amerman, Don. "Cool Summer Dampens Pleasure Boat Sales." *The Journal of Commerce,* 23 September 1996.

Banse, Tim. "The Parts Game: Is There a Computer in Your Future?" *Boating Industry,* May 1993.

Boating 1992. Chicago: National Marine Manufacturers Association, 1992.

"The Boating Business." *Boating Industry,* January 1993.

Bongiorno, Lori. "Profits Ahoy!" *Business Week,* 30 August 1993.

The Classic Boat. Alexandria, VA: Time-Life Books, 1977.

Harper, Doug. "Electronic Systems Run Aground." *Journal of Commerce,* 1 October 1992.

Henick, Arthur R. "Tampering with Tradition: Builders Float New Models." *Boating Industry,* August 1991.

Lawrence, Richard. "Politics, Boat Sales Make Strange Bedfellows." *Journal of Commerce,* 1 October 1992.

Lazich, Robert S., ed. *Market Share Reporter 1996.* Detroit: Gale Research, 1996.

Palmer, Jay. "Rough Seas." *Barron's,* 14 October 1991.

Platt, Gordon. "Used-Boat Market Riding Tidal Wave." *Journal of Commerce,* 1 October 1992.

U.S. Bureau of the Census. "Description of Industries and Summary of Findings: Industry 3732, Boat Building and Repair. Available from http://www.census.gov/mcd/mancen.

—Robert R. Jacobson, updated by Don Amerman

SIC 3743

RAILROAD EQUIPMENT

This classification covers establishments primarily engaged in building and rebuilding locomotives (including frames and parts not elsewhere classified) of any type or gauge; and railroad, street, and rapid transit cars and car equipment for operations on rails for freight and passenger service. Establishments primarily engaged in manufacturing mining cars are classified in **SIC 3532: Mining Machinery and Equipment, Except Oil and Gas Field Machinery and Equipment.** Repair shops owned and operated by railroads or local transit companies that repair locomotives or cars for their own use are classified in various transportation industries. Establishments primarily engaged in repairing railroad cars on a contract or fee basis are classified in **SIC 4789: Transportation Services, Not Elsewhere Classified;** and those repairing locomotive engines on a contract or fee basis are classified in **SIC 7699: Repair Shops and Related Services, Not Elsewhere Classified.**

INDUSTRY SNAPSHOT

In 1995, the railroad equipment industry reported total shipments of approximately $4.6 billion to the nation's rail systems. In 1996, the industry employed 45,300 persons. Leading states in railroad equipment industry employment were Illinois, New York, Pennsylvania, and Texas in 1992. This represented a change from five years earlier when Illinois, New York, Ohio, and Pennsylvania were the leading states.

The railroad equipment industry was becoming increasingly focused on the production of primary products for the railroad industry. In 1992, the industry reported a 95 percent specialization ratio (the ratio of primary products to the total of both primary and secondary products), compared with a specialization ratio of only 88 percent in 1987. The total cost of materials, services, and energy used by companies in the railroad equipment industry amounted to $2.7 billion in 1992.

The railroad equipment manufacturers that supply the nation's railroads with cars and track are slowly recovering from several extremely difficult decades. Despite new light-rail projects being developed across the nation and an increase in federal money targeted toward mass transit projects, domestic demand was not regarded as a strong enough motive to attract new American manufacturers to the business until the mid-1990s. As part of an effort to shore up the industry, the U.S. Department of Transportation promulgated a "Buy America" program that required rail passenger vehicles purchased with federal funds from foreign companies to have a "domestic content" of 60 percent. Also of great import to the manufacturers of rail equipment was the improved financial performance of several major rail carriers in the early 1990s.

Forbes discussed the "railcar glut that had developed in the late 1970s and early 1980s. In normal years maybe 60,000 railcars were built. But then railcars were marketed as tax shelters; in 1980, 85,000 were built, and industry capacity had exploded to 150,000 . . . . When the shelters were curbed in 1981, some 400,000 cars—a six- or seven-year supply—were sitting on sidings unused.'' By the end of the 1980s, however, as *Forbes* notes, ''the number of freight cars in use had declined from 1.8 million to 1.2 million, and industry capacity had dropped to 50,000 cars a year.'' The stage was set for an upsurge in the industry's fortunes. A major indicator of the railroad equipment industry's health is the number of new freight cars delivered. In 1993 approximately 35,000 railcars were delivered, a significant increase over the 25,000 freight cars delivered in 1992. Moreover, industry observers expect this trend to continue through the second half of the 1990s. This forecast was based primarily on equipment shortages and the age of the current fleet (railways and private owners were currently retiring 60,000 to 80,000 cars a year that had been in service for over 20 years), as well as improved performance by major railroad lines.

The nation's domestic rail passenger car industry, however, has not rebounded in the manner enjoyed by freight car manufacturers. Whereas half a dozen manufacturers were engaged in such production 25 years ago, only one U.S.-owned manufacturer, Morrison Knudsen Corporation makes rail passenger cars today.

ORGANIZATION AND STRUCTURE

The nation's freight railroads carry more than one-third of all intercity ton-miles of freight. Their rails are used for all commuter rail traffic and for Amtrak's long-distance passenger traffic, except for the Northeast corridor, which Amtrak owns. The railroads rely upon suppliers to provide equipment, supplies, many services, and the research and development required to help them improve productivity.

Railroad equipment manufacturers sell products not only to the railroads, but also to leasing companies, manufacturing concerns, farmers, and other entities that use the rails for the transportation of their commodities.

Unlike flatcars and boxcars, which are purchased or leased by the railroads, rail tankcars are owned primarily by chemical manufacturers and other manufacturers, such as food and fabricated metal products/ machinery companies, who use the rails to transport goods on a regular basis. Recent proposals by the U.S. Department of Transportation (DOT) requiring more expensive better protected cars for the transportation of hazardous waste have caused concern among the nation's railroad carriers, who worry that forcing shippers to pay for these more expensive, cars will force them to use trucks as the first choice of transport. Rail

market share has already suffered attrition at the hands of the trucking industry and other transportation sectors. Since 1945, the railroads' share of the freight business has fallen almost in half to 37 percent, while the truckers' share has climbed from 5 percent to more than 25 percent.

The rail industry is the transport method of choice for commodities that are not ''time-sensitive,'' such as perishable products, and for goods that need to be transported over distances greater than 500 miles. For short-haul food shipments, trucks have captured most of the traffic in the freight market. Recently, there has been an increase in intermodal transportation where manufacturers use the railways to transport their goods for a leg of the journey via trailers and containers and then switch to another form of transport such as trucks or ships. Intermodal loading has almost doubled in capacity since 1980.

Industry Representation. The Railway Progress Institute (RPI), originally founded as the Railway Business Association in 1908, is the international trade association of suppliers to the nation's freight railroads and rail passenger systems. Headquartered in Alexandria, Virginia, it has more than 100 members. The association's objectives are threefold: to support and promote a strong nationwide free enterprise system of railroads for the United States; to support and promote rail rapid transit and light rail systems in major metropolitan areas; and to represent and further RPI members' interests.

In 1992 the Rail Supply and Service Coalition (RSSC) was formed to act as a lobbying group to Washington and state governments. The group consists of the National Railroad Construction and Maintenance Association, the Railway Engineering-Maintenance Suppliers Association, the Railway Supply Association, and Railway Systems Suppliers, Inc. The coalition actively represents the interests of its member groups to further their bargaining position on federal and state issues affecting the industry.

BACKGROUND AND DEVELOPMENT

The railroads were one of the nation's first big businesses. With their intricate network of lines, these companies gave inland points access to navigable waters and joined these waters to the seaboard, linked farms and villages to the rising industrial cities, opened millions of acres of land to cultivation, provided the means to ship raw materials and finished goods quickly and cheaply, and created billions of dollars in capital for reinvestment in the nation's economy.

At the outset of the 1830s the steam locomotive made its arrival. On Christmas Day, 1830 the *Best Friend of Charleston,* the first locomotive built for sale in the United States, made its maiden run. The nation's rail system grew rapidly during the next several decades. The lines largely served cities along the Atlantic coast; New England and the mid-Atlantic states had over 50 percent of the total track mileage in the United States. American railroads, however, did not have a uniform track gauge (distance between the rails). This confusion of gauges necessitated expensive and inefficient transshipment of goods where lines of different gauges intersected.

Early Advances. Throughout this time period, the companies constantly improved tracking and rolling equipment. The first railroads were built on tracks of iron straps or bars fastened to wooden rails that were attached to blocks of stone embedded in the earth. The iron straps often broke loose under the weight of the passing trains and damaged the bottom of the cars. In response to this, the iron T-rail was developed and wooden ties replaced the stone underneath the rails. A roadbed surface covered with crushed stone or gravel supported the track. Originally most of the engines were imported from England, but Philadelphia jewelry manufacturer Matthias Baldwin entered the business in the 1830s, and soon thereafter other locomotive builders emerged in the Northeast. Passenger cars that were once nothing more than stagecoaches with railroad wheels quickly evolved into more spacious, comfortable accommodations. Diminutive four-wheeled freight cars were replaced by longer and heavier eight-wheeled cars with greater carrying capacity. Thus the railways spawned auxiliary enterprises in T-rail manufacturing, locomotive works, and car and wheel shops, and gave impetus to the lumber industry that furnished the wooden ties.

During the 1840s and 1850s there was a proliferation of railroad construction. By 1860 many of the shorter railway lines were consolidated through the merger of regional railroad companies. The federal government supported this expansion through land grants and other forms of financial incentives to railroad companies. Land grants became the major form of financial assistance offered to railroad companies to encourage the development of railroads to the West in advance of settlement. Revelations of corruption and bribery caused public opinion to demand that such assistance be ended. By the 1870s, most direct federal aid to the railroads had terminated, and most state and local support was stopped within the next decade. But government aid, in any case, was relatively small in comparison to investment by private capital in the

form of stocks and bonds in rail companies. With the continued growth of the railway industry, companies that provided needed equipment to that industry remained prosperous.

By 1880 carriers had standardized their gauge to 4 feet 8 1/2 inches as the railroads established transcontinental operations. To further facilitate the interchange of railroad traffic, railroad companies required standardized coupling devices, car trucks, bills of lading, and classification of products. Larger locomotives and freight cars with increased carrying capacities required that steel rails be implemented in place of the iron rails. The steel rails provided a smoother, safer, and faster track and lasted much longer than wrought iron, saving the railroads significant maintenance costs. The link-and-pin couplers, long utilized to engage railcars together, had over the years cost thousands of men their fingers; these were replaced by more effective automatic safety couplers. Similarly, the hand brake system that required men to run along the top of cars to set the devices was replaced by an air brake system mandated by federal law in 1893.

The railroad industry continued as the primary transportation mode throughout the first half of the twentieth century in America. Throughout the 1920s and 1930s, the railroads generally improved and modernized their operations. New steam locomotive designs were introduced by the major builders—Baldwin, Lima, and the American Locomotive Company. These designs increased efficiency, raised average speeds for passenger and freight trains, and reduced the need for double-headed trains and pusher locomotives in mountainous terrain. Capital improvement programs were begun that increased freight car capacities, length of freight trains, and the net tonnage capable of being carried by the average train. Many of the infrastructure systems installed at this time remained for many years as well. The rise of the automobile and air transportation, however, dramatically impacted on the fortunes of rail lines and affiliated industries.

By 1940, the heyday for railroads was over and many of the railroads were in receivership. Industries that had long had the railroad companies as their primary clients suffered accordingly. The Railroad Credit Corporation was created to aid the carriers, but the problems surpassed this emergency type of legislation. The entry of the United States into World War II temporarily alleviated this problem and brought much needed liquidity to the railroads. During this time frame, the Offices of Defense Transportation coordinated the operations of the railroads. Between 1942 and 1945, the railroads moved more freight each year than they had since 1918, although they did so with fewer freight and passenger cars, locomotives, and employees. The vast increase in traffic produced record profits for the railroads and allowed them to reduce their debts and establish financial health.

Rise of the Diesel. By 1945 many of the carriers had dieselized locomotive fleets. The Electro-Motive Division of General Motors developed separate locomotive units for freight service that was adopted by several railroads. Diesel locomotives cost far more than steam power locomotives to acquire, but operational savings came quickly. The diesels did not need the vast amounts of water that steam locomotives required, a significant factor in parts of the West where water was scarce. Diesels also required far less maintenance, had a high level of availability, were fuel efficient, and could operate for many miles without servicing. The diesel also was less harmful to railroad tracks than the steam engine and when placed in reverse could act as a dynamic braking system. This saved the railroad millions of dollars in freight car brake shoes. By 1955 carriers had spent $3.3 billion for 21,000 diesel locomotives from Electro-Motive, American Locomotive Company, Fairbanks-Morse, and Baldwin Locomotive Works. These manufacturers provided the carriers with a wide range of diesel products to choose from for passenger and freight service.

The revolution in transportation opportunities available to the general public, however, made these railroad advancements seem insignificant. The internal-combustion engine placed the automobile in the hands of virtually every family. As a result, the long-distance passenger train almost died. The diverse railroad-reliant industries also suffered from the emergence of airlines, which provided speedy service between major cities. Pipelines, barges, trucks, and intercoastal shipping companies carried a large percentage of commodity products as well.

By the 1960s the rail industry as a whole was in a state of decline. In 1971 Congress created the National Railroad Passenger Corporation , known as Amtrak, to operate virtually all of the nation's remaining rail passenger services. In 1976 the federal government created the Consolidated Rail Corporation (Conrail) to salvage Penn Central and other bankrupt lines in the Northeast. Several carriers prospered by focusing on long-haul freight lines and piggyback trailer traffic.

The railroads survived by scrambling for market share, often establishing services for special product niches. Carriers introduced unit trains dedicated to one cargo—coal, wheat, sulfur, or chemicals that moved in continuous runs from the production site to docks, generators, or factories. The unit trains often utilized specially designed equipment to accommodate the transport of different commodities such as grain or liquid chemicals, resulting in reduced freight rates. Railroads also established "run through trains" that stopped only for crew changes and retained the locomotives of the original carriers. To succeed, the carriers acquired pipelines, barge lines, and trucking companies and invested in airfreight forwarding to obtain a total intermodal position.

Dieselization, the utilization of new technologies, the introduction of new services, the renewed emphasis on marketing, and the end of money losing passenger business failed to prevent a massive restructuring of the nation's railroads. The Staggers Act of 1980 provided significant relief for the railroads in rate development as the federal government moved into an era of deregulation. This brought giant mergers, massive line abandonments, and shrinking locomotive and equipment fleets. Railway managers in an era of deregulation continued line rationalization, sought new technologies, and placed a major emphasis on marketing transportation.

CURRENT CONDITIONS

The railroad equipment manufacturers that supply the nations' railroads with cars and track and other equipment are slowly recovering from the lean decade of the 1980s. Capital expenditures by the railroads for equipment contracted went from $2.3 billion in 1980 to $995 million in 1990 for a total decline of 58 percent. Moreover, carriers were not purchasing new locomotives; 70 percent of locomotives in operation in 1990 were more than 15 years old, with another 15 percent constructed prior to 1984. The number of freight cars in service dropped as well, falling almost 30 percent between 1980 and 1990, from 1.7 million to 1.2 million.

Looking ahead as 1997 began, James J. Unger, chairman of the Railway Progress Institute, assured his membership that RPI had on its agenda several legislative issues crucial to the railway supply industry. "You can be sure that the Railway Progress Institute and its staff will diligently work at 'tracking the issues' on behalf of you and your company," Mr. Unger wrote in his annual letter to members. "RPI activities undertaken in 1997 will be handled by a staff with almost one hundred years of cumulative experience working with Congress, the Department of Transportation, and the railroad and railway supply industries."

RPI's chairman said the organization marked 1996 as a successful year for the rail supply industry. "We knew back in 1995 when Congress began calling for fiscal responsibility and budget cuts that it would mean cuts in transportation, so we were prepared. We are fortunate to have fared as well as we have.''

In 1996, RPI worked with Transportation Secretary Frederico Peña to recognize the supply industry's issues as DOT began working on legislation reauthorizing the Intermodal Surface Transportation Efficiency Act (ISTEA). During the year RPI monitored several congressional hearings on this subject.

Mr. Unger noted that the 1996 national elections had brought changes to the Clinton Administration and Congress, where there are many new members and new staff who will need to be introduced to the rail supply industry's issues. He wrote that 1997 was likely to be an extremely busy year for the railway supply industry with the reauthorization of ISTEA being on top of the agenda.

The railways' steady return to health has helped equipment manufacturers supporting the industry climb out of a prolonged slump, although it will be difficult for the industry to reach 1980 levels of production, when more than 93,000 railcars were built. Carbuilders' deliveries, considered a benchmark of the industry's health, climbed to 35,000 new freight cars in 1993, up from 25,000 in 1992.

The upturn in equipment manufacturing is more reflected in subtle design changes to existing technology, as well as car types that provide the shipper with rapid loading and unloading capabilities, sanitary cleanout, and a large carrying capacity. The three major types of cars in demand are covered hopper cars, intermodal cars, and tankcars. Most of the design changes in the last several years have occurred in the tankcar-manufacturing arena, and were brought about by concerns about environmental safety and product liability. Changes in the tankcar design include sloping bottoms, improved heater systems, better gates and hatches, new kinds of insulation, and better interior coating. These changes help to protect the product from contamination while also serving to insulate the tanker from corrosion.

INDUSTRY LEADERS

Only three American companies currently engage in locomotive manufacturing. Morrison Knudsen Corp., long a major producer of other rail equipment, announced in 1993 that it would produce a prototype engine powered by liquefied natural gas. Morrison Knudsen thus joins General Electric and General Motors, the only other domestic locomotive manufacturers, in the locomotive market.

The number one company in the production of railroad equipment in 1996 was Trinity Industries, based in Dallas, Texas. Trinity produces a wide range of railcars, including railroad tankcars, gondola cars, intermodal cars, and hopper cars. Trinity, with a total of 16,300 employees, is involved in a wide variety of other metal product manufacturing, including marine products, such as tugboats, ferries, barges, and construction products, including airport conveyor systems and highway guardrails.

The second largest railroad equipment manufacturer in 1996 was Morrison Knudsen Corp., which is headquartered in Boise, Idaho, but has manufacturing operations scattered around the country. Like Trinity, Morrison Knudsen is not involved exclusively with the production of railroad equipment but manufactures a broad range of other products as well.

The third largest U.S. manufacturer of railroad equipment in 1996 was Johnstown America Industries Inc., which is headquartered in Chicago.

The next largest U.S. producers of railroad equipment were the Electro-Motive Division of General Motors Corporation, headquartered in La Grange, Illinois; Westinghouse Air Brake Company, based in Wilmerding, Pennsylvania; and Greenbrier Companies Inc. of Lake Oswego, Oregon.

ABB Traction, Inc., an Elmira Heights, New York, privately held company, manufactures light rail vehicles, commuter railcars, and high-speed trains. ABB Traction also produces subsystem components including advanced AC propulsion, railcar shells, and trucks.

Thrall Car Manufacturing Company of Chicago Heights, Illinois, is the leading manufacturer of freight cars including intermodal equipment, auto racks, aluminum coal cars, centerbeams, coiled steel, pressured differential, plastics, and woodchip cars. The company is privately owned and operates five plants in Illinois and Georgia.

AMERICA AND THE WORLD

Overseas, European and Japanese manufacturers have developed extensive rail lines using high-speed rail technology. This thriving domestic market has provided these countries with an industrial base that they have used to expand internationally. This manufacturing base has enabled these countries to capture a large percentage of the U.S. freight and passenger car market. In North America, for instance, the Canadian Bombardier Corporation has had a virtual monopoly on the U.S. passenger railcar business. Morrison Knudsen, based in Boise, Idaho, recently reentered the passenger railcar business, however, and has secured several domestic contracts. Included in those was a contract from Amtrak for 50 sleeping cars that was valued at $100 million. As *The Washington Post* noted in December 1992, Morrison Knudsen's coup was "a blow to Bombardier . . . which has plants in the United States [and] bought the rights to the last U.S. passenger car designs from Pullman Standard Co. and Budd Co. when they went out of business."

RAILROAD EQUIPMENT TRADE
(BILLION DOLLARS)

Source: Bureau of the Census

The U.S. government, mindful of the systems in place in Europe, is exploring high-speed rail initiatives for America's railways. Proposals are aimed at creating an industrial base for high-speed train equipment utilizing traditional railroad equipment suppliers and the defense and aerospace industries.

Regarding to international legislation, the railroad industry as a whole supported passage of the North American Free Trade Agreement (NAFTA). The agreement was expected to dramatically increase railroad traffic into Mexico in the coming years, a plus both to carriers and railroad equipment manufacturers.

RESEARCH AND TECHNOLOGY

The U.S. intermodal rail system was undergoing significant change through the use of information technology. Carriers were going high-tech with innovative electronics equipment and computers designed to improve tracking of shipments and make the railroads increasingly user friendly for commodity transfer. Information technology changes were proposed for nearly every aspect of the railroad industry, including

Automated Equipment Identification. This program mandates that all railroad equipment be outfitted with electronic identification tags that allow each freight container to be identified by a trackside laser scanner. This system will track freight container shipments among multiple carriers and eliminate the need for railroad staff to visually identify containers and manually type in shipment information.

Interline Service Management. The U.S. rail network is divided into various regional carriers. When a customer books a coast-to-coast shipment, he or she must deal with several carriers who will bill that customer separately and track the freight only within their individual rail systems. Interline service management is designed to link the communication systems of the different carriers and provide an apparently "seamless" service to the customer.

Computer Systems. Railroads are working together to create a single computer hardware package that allows customers to communicate with all their carriers. In addition, railroad locomotives are being outfitted with computers that communicate via wireless technology with the railroad's mainframe or central computer. It's hoped that data radio technology will improve shipment information and increase operational efficiency and productivity.

On-Board Locomotive Diagnostics. This technology will help to identify potential mechanical/electronic problems and to correct them before the locomotive breaks down. This system will reduce shipment delays and increase reliability.

In addition to innovations in information technology, changes in the industry's traditional hardware such as locomotives, freight cars, air brakes, and couplers have taken place or are undergoing redesign. For example, locomotives once powered by diesel fuel are being powered by liquid methane. Natural gas is less expensive, less polluting, and easier on engine parts than diesel fuel. A new rack-and-loader system is being used to load autos, truck, and shipping containers onto intermodal cars for easier transport via flatcars. Modern lightweight aluminum grain and coal hoppers are being employed in freight transport.

Advances in Tankcar Safety. The nation's rail system is today used to transport a wide range of hazardous materials. The Railway Progress Institute noted that in 1991, "U.S. railroads delivered more than 1.9 million carloads of hazardous materials, an 80 percent increase since 1979." As *Chemical Week* noted as far back as 1978, however, "concern about carrier safety has been mounting in chemical traffic circles for several years. Nearly half of the total 100 billion ton-miles registered annually by chemical movements are carried by rail." Efforts were increased to buttress the safety of rail transport of chemicals. In 1989 *The New York Times* noted that the "Association of American Railroads says that from 1980 to 1987, the number of rail accidents in which there was a release of hazardous materials dropped by 61 percent.'' The *Times* went on, however, to note that, according to the Illinois Public Action Council, a nonprofit advocacy group, ''although the number of railroad accidents involving hazardous materials has been declining, the severity of the accidents has been worsening. In 1987, the number of accidents involving evacuations was twice as high as five years earlier. The number of cars that released hazardous materials increased, as did the percentage of all accidents involving toxic chemicals.''

In response to these continuing environmental concerns, many older tankcars have been retrofitted and new tankcars have been outfitted with safety devices to prevent accidents in the transportation of these materials. New technology and research into tankcar safety has helped to identify safety issues to address in tankcar design. Shelf couplers that prevent car couplers from overriding one another and puncturing the ends of tankcars in a derailment or sudden stop are currently in use. Head shields, constructed with half-inch steel, are attached to the ends of tankcars to protect against head punctures. Shields are currently required for cars carrying liquefied flammable gases, anhydrous ammonia, or ethylene oxide. Tankcars are also being designed with thermal protection to help keep the tank's lading cool enough to avoid or delay explosions in fires. General-service tankcars have added bottom outlet protection devices that protect the outlets from being sheared off during an accident. All these advances have contributed to progress in the industry's safety record. The Railway Progress Institute, an association of industry suppliers, noted that, according to the Federal Railroad Administration, more than 99.99 percent of hazardous material carloads in 1991 reached their destination safely.

FURTHER READING

Ainsworth, Don, Asaph Hall, Richard Briggs, et al. *Railroad Research Study Background Papers*. Federal Railroad Administration, U.S. Department of Transportation, 1975.

Allen, Leslie J. ''Rail-Supply Industry Gets Back On Track.'' *St. Louis Post Dispatch*, 5 March 1989.

Boselovic, Len. ''Aging Rail Cars Should Help This Company Pick Up Steam.'' *Pittsburgh Post-Gazette*, 19 September 1993.

Challenges Accepted-The Story of Railroading. Association of American Railroads, n.d.

Cushman, John Jr. ''Chemicals on Rails: A Growing Peril.'' *The New York Times*, 2 August 1989.

An Integrated Transportation Policy For An Era Of Rising Expectations. Association of American Railroads, 1989.

Flint, Jerry, ''A Market Cleared.'' *Forbes*, 6 June 1994.

Jouzaitis, Carol. ''Rail Suppliers Back On Track After Slump.'' *Chicago Tribune*, 26 September 1988.

Parrish, Michael. ''Hazardous Spill Rate Rises For Thin-Skin Tankcars;Freight: Railroads Say Safety Is Improving But Accidents Have Potential For Large Catastrophe.'' *Los Angeles Times*, 22 September 1992.

Pena, Federico. ''The Ice-Train Cometh; Technology Could Fit Industries Changing From Defense To Civilian Production.'' *St. Louis Post-Dispatch*, 21 September 1993.

Phillips, Don. ''Morrison Knudsen Receives $100 Million Amtrak Order.'' *The Washington Post*, 4 December 1992.

Phillips, Don. ''Getting U.S. Back On Track; Transit Agency Uses Economic Muscle To Revive Pullman Rail Car Legacy.'' *The Washington Post*, 24 May 1992.

Railroad Facts. Association of American Railroads, September 1991.

Railway Progress Institute. ''Chairman's Message.'' Available from http://www.idsonline.com/business/rpi/chairmn.htm.

Sanchez, Jesus. ''Domestic Rail Car Industry Has Virtually Disappeared.'' *Los Angeles Times*, 24 January 1992.

Suppliers and Railroads-On the Same Track, 1992 Annual Report and Membership Directory. The Railway Progress Institute, 1992.

U.S. Bureau of the Census.''Description of Industries and Summary of Findings: Industry 3743, Railroad Equipment.'' Available from http://www.census.gov/mcd/mancen.

Wald, Matthew L. ''Railroads Are A Growth Industry, For A Change.'' *New York Times*, 20 June 1993.

Ziemba, Stanley. ''Rail-Car Firm Doesn't Trail In Importance.'' *Chicago Tribune*, 23 March 1992.

———. ''Hardware and Software Innovations On Track-Natural Gas Powers Locomotives; Computers Can Follow Every Train.'' *Chicago Tribune*, 1 November 1992.

—Andrew Burke, updated by Don Amerman

SIC 3751

MOTORCYCLES, BICYCLES, AND PARTS

This category includes establishments primarily engaged in manufacturing motorcycles, bicycles, and similar equipment, and parts. Establishments primarily engaged in manufacturing children's vehicles, except bicycles, are classified in **SIC 3944: Games, Toys, and Children's Vehicles, Except Dolls and Bicycles.** Establishments primarily engaged in manufacturing golf carts and other similar personnel carriers are classified in **SIC 3799: Transportation Equipment, Not Elsewhere Classified.**

INDUSTRY SNAPSHOT

In one form or another, the two-wheeled personal vehicle has played an important role in U.S. transportation systems. Establishments in the bicycle industry had revenues of about $2.5 billion in 1995, largely bolstered by the phenomenal sales of mountain bikes. In that same year, 100 million Americans reported riding a bicycle at least once, according to the Bicycle Federation of America; 6.3 million rode more than 100 times, according to a study by American Sports Data; and 1 in 10 Americans owned a mountain bike. Bicycling was ranked as America's third most popular sporting activity, according to the National Sporting Goods Association.

Sales of small commuter motorcycles fell in the late 1980s. Motorcycle registrations dropped from 5.6 million in 1980 to 4.2 million in 1989. Reported commuter-miles ridden plummeted 32 percent during the same period, from a total of 3.1 to 2.1 million miles. In the 1990s, the "heavyweight" motorcycle, with engines larger than 700 cubic centimeters (cc) displacement, sparked renewed interest among potential buyers. Harley-Davidson Inc., America's only remaining major motorcycle manufacturer, rose from the brink of bankruptcy and claimed a 55 percent share of the total U.S. market in 1995. It did so primarily by catering to baby boomers' nostalgia with safe, reliable replicas of older models that evoked the image of a "wilder" lifestyle. Known in the industry as "RUBs" (Rich Urban Bikers), these consumers are targeted as the prime consumers of larger motorcycles for well into the next century. Annual sales of heavyweight cycles reached more than $1.3 billion by 1996 and sales of smaller, faster "sportbikes" were about $500 million.

ORGANIZATION AND STRUCTURE

Harley-Davidson Inc. of Milwaukee, Wisconsin, knows it is selling more than "bikes." The image of the Harley as America's motorcycle has become integral to its marketing success. Its extensive national dealer network sells motorcycles, parts, and service, and also promotes Harley-Davidson's own line of "Motorclothes" in "designer stores." The company sponsors a motorcycle enthusiast club, the Harley Owners Group (H.O.G.), and organizes rallies and product demonstrations.

Japanese motorcycle makers Honda and Kawasaki built manufacturing facilities in Ohio and Nebraska, respectively, in the early 1980s. Like other Japanese and European motorcycle manufacturers, they maintain their own dealer networks and generally enjoy a price advantage over comparable Harley models. Even so, the effectiveness of the Harley-Davidson lifestyle marketing campaign has made the "Hog," as the Harley-Davidson is affectionately known, a desirable status symbol in the biking world. In the mid-1990s, used Harleys routinely sold for more than their original price.

The bicycle segment of the industry also sells much of its product through specialized dealer networks. These dealer networks generally carry the sophisticated, higher-priced models for the cycling enthusiast. Bikes in this category, like Schwinn's Paramount line, can sell for more than $5,000. Cut-throat competition and rapid innovation in the bicycle segment of the industry forced many firms out of the market. Chicago, once the world's bike manufacturing capital with more than 90 manufacturers, only has Schwinn left, and that in name only. Schwinn, established in 1895, sold 25 percent of America's bikes during the 1960s, earning it the reputation as America's bicycle manufacturer although it was never the largest. A 1981 labor dispute prompted Schwinn to phase out its U.S. manufacturing operations in favor of overseas facilities. That move created a new competitor, Giant Bicycles of Taiwan, which eventually drove Schwinn out of the market after supplying 70 percent of Schwinn's product in 1984. In 1991, Schwinn filed for bankruptcy. Scott USA of Ketchum, Idaho, bought its remaining assets, including the Schwinn trademark, for $41 million in 1993.

BACKGROUND AND DEVELOPMENT

Bicycles. The bicycle originated in France when Paris carriage maker Pierre Michaux fitted cranks to the front wheel of the German designed draisienne, or hobby horse. By 1867, a bicycle craze was sweeping Europe. According to David A. Hounshell, author of *From the American System to Mass Production: 1800-1932,* the Boston merchant Albert A. Pope deserves credit for introducing the device to America. Pope began importing the British High-Wheel, also known as the "Penny-Farthing," in 1876. By 1878, he was producing his own version at the Weed Sewing Machine plant in Hartford, Connecticut.

The new product tapped a growing demand in America for increased mobility and provided work for the idling American arms industry. Much of the industrial expertise developed for the weapons industry during the Civil War found useful employment in the production of bicycle components. In 1890, 27 bicycle manufacturers produced 40,000 "safety" bicycles, featuring two equal sized wheels.

By 1897, bicycle production increased to 1.2 million annually. Then demand evaporated as the horseless carriage began to make its impact felt. Auto manufacturer Hiram Percy Maxim noted that the bicycle revealed the advantage of quicker personal transportation but failed to answer the challenge. According to Maxim, the bicycle created the demand for the automobile and provided the technology needed to mass produce it.

Bicycles retained a steady but small popularity through the first half of the twentieth century; it was the baby boomer generation that fueled the resurgence of the bicycle starting in the 1950s. The single-speed child's bike gave way to multiple speed versions and, eventually, the popular light-weight 10-speed. Throughout the 1970s, the 10-speed dominated the market with a market share of 56 percent. However, an American innovation, the mountain bike, changed everything. Initially designed for climbing the scrubby hills north of San Francisco, mountain bikes and all-terrain bikes sported fat tires, heavy frames, and multiple gears. By 1991, they boomed in popularity even in areas miles from any mountain and commandeered a 50 percent market share.

Many traditional companies like Schwinn and Murray failed to react quickly enough to the popularity of the mountain bike, leaving the door open for small innovators to carve out a niche, and for large foreign firms like Taiwan's Giant and China's CBC to gain control of trademarks. The showroom models still sport familiar brand names, but many are foreign-made while others use components no longer made in America. Those firms that did react, like Trek and Cannondale, are enjoying great success in the export market, especially in Europe and Japan

Motorcycles. The motorcycle represented a first step from the bicycle to the automobile. The simple expedient of attaching a gasoline-powered engine to a bicycle frame produced a device, which was at once exotic and affordable. During the early 1900s, more than 100 companies began manufacturing motorcycles, including Harley-Davidson, Indian, Orient, Excelsior, Cyclone, Henderson, and Marsh. By 1915, they produced models that could exceed 100 mph. The 1915 Cyclone, designed specifically for racing, had one speed, which reached speeds of 124 mph, but had no throttle and no brakes. Harley-Davidson began production of its first model, the Silent Grey Fellow, in 1903, the same year Henry Ford unveiled the Model A. When Ford introduced his mass-produced Model T in 1913 and sold it for $500, most motorcycle manufacturers could not compete. After World War I, only Harley-Davidson, Indian, and Excelsior remained. By 1953, only Harley-Davidson remained.

With the OPEC oil embargo of the early 1970s, motorcycles became popular for commuting—but not the Harley. Consumers wanted cheap, reliable, peppy bikes, and those came from Japan. In 1973, sales of motorcycles reached an all-time high of 1.5 million. In 1983, Harley-Davidson sought and received tariff protection from the Reagan administration to help it battle Japanese competition. Even with the 45 percent tariff protection, the company was almost bankrupt by 1985 due to poor quality and inefficient production. By applying Japanese management techniques, Harley-Davidson finally reversed its situation and asked for the tariff to be removed one year before it was due to expire. Meanwhile, Honda miscalculated the heavy-weight motorcycle market, concentrating instead on small bikes and high-priced, high-tech super-bikes. Honda's market share dropped from 44 percent in 1985 to 32 percent in 1989.

CURRENT CONDITIONS

The average motorcycle rider of the mid-1990s looks little like the stereotypical biker depicted in popular movies like *Easy Rider*. A biker is more likely to be an aging baby boomer who bought an expensive, heavy-duty "cruising bike," most commonly a Harley-Davidson. While the median age of a Harley rider was 34 in the mid-1980s, by 1995 that age had risen to 42. Many Harley buyers are professionals who spend weekends and vacations on their bikes. First-time motorcycle buyers and long-absent return buyers more than tripled between 1987 and 1994. Between 1988 and 1996, Harley-Davidson's sales rose an average of 13 percent per year. Sales of similar bikes from Japanese makers fell 39 percent between 1988 and 1991, but then began to increase again. The market for smaller and faster "sportbikes," which appeal largely to younger riders, was stagnant due to high prices. In the late 1990s, such bikes were being marketed to the ever popular baby boomers, with their greater disposable income.

According to the Motorcycle Safety Foundation, rider education programs helped reduce the accident rate. Its figures indicate that motorcycle accidents dropped 42.1 percent between 1973 and 1992, and fatalities dropped 29.5 percent. This improvement in safety enhanced the appeal of motorcycles for many potential riders.

The motorcycle sector of the industry will be competing with the bicycle sector as it targets much of the same audience, playing on that group's high level of physical activity. Increased pressure to use bicycles for environmentally friendly commuting in congested cities may also continue to push the domestic market. Strong demand in foreign countries will push exports up, especially if the North American Free Trade

Agreement (NAFTA) succeeds in reducing tariff barriers to the sizeable Mexican market. At the same time, since bicycle manufacturing is labor intensive; NAFTA may encourage firms to relocate to Mexico to take advantage of cheap labor.

The phenomenon of the mountain bike may be dwindling in importance, as the sales of these bikes decreased in 1996 for the first time in ten years (from $1.6 billion in 1995 to $1.5 billion in 1996). Once again, the baby boomer market may be fertile, as shown by the introduction of expensive "nostalgia" bicycles by companies such as Schwinn. Some automobile manufacturers have begun to produce bicycles under their own logos, hoping to appeal to customers who want to lead an active lifestyle (or at least to project that image). These companies include Mercedes-Benz, Volkswagen, BMW, and Jeep. Bicycles also are being used more frequently by non-recreational riders such as commuters, couriers, and police officers.

INDUSTRY LEADERS

The undisputed leader in the U.S. motorcycle industry is Harley-Davidson of Milwaukee, Wisconsin, which maintained a market share of about 55 percent of the domestic motorcycle market in 1995-96. The company's sales rose 113 percent between 1988 and 1996. Sales of heavy "cruiser" bikes topped 125,000 in 1996, with Harley-Davidson producing 25 to 40 percent fewer bikes than the estimated demand for its products. Harley-Davidson now exports 30 percent of its bikes, and plans to produce smaller bikes tailored for riders in Europe, Asia, and Latin America, in cooperation with Buell Motorcycle of East Troy, Wisconsin. Sales of sportbikes within the United States have not fared so well, only holding on to 24 percent of the total motorcycle market in 1996. Companies that focus primarily on production of sportbikes, such as Honda, Kawasaki, Suzuki, and Yamaha, together maintained 45 percent of the total motorcycle market in 1995.

The unforeseen popularity of the mountain bike has totally upset the traditional list of leaders within the bicycle manufacturing industry. Old industry leaders such as Schwinn did not enter this market soon enough and so were overtaken by producers of the new product. Trek USA, founded in Waterloo, Wisconsin, in 1976, became the industry leader in 1995 with a 24 percent share of the total bicycle market. Other companies selling mountain bikes and high-performance bicycles also swooped into market leadership, such as Cannondale Corporation (12 percent share in 1995) and GT Bicycles (producer of the popular BMX model), which held 6 percent of the total market in

1995 and reported record profits in 1996. Traditional leaders Huffy Corporation and Schwinn Cycling & Fitness Inc. (the name taken after bankruptcy filing in 1992) have had to refocus and to address the mountain bike craze in order to survive. Huffy and Schwinn recovered somewhat in 1995 and 1996, although not enough to overtake the new leaders. Schwinn sold about 480,000 bicycles worldwide in 1995, as opposed to Trek USA's 950,000.

AMERICA AND THE WORLD

The expansion of exports in both bicycles and motorcycles throughout the late 1980s and 1990s has been steadily growing. Between 1990 and 1994, the value of motorcycle and parts exports rose 13.7 percent, to $511 million in 1994. Harley-Davidson now exports 30 percent of its bikes. By contrast, sales of street bikes from Japanese manufacturers in the United States fell 39 percent between 1988 and 1991 before finally beginning to rise again. Harley-Davidson maintains 55 percent of the total U.S. market, far more than all Japanese manufacturers combined.

Since 1990, the value of bicycle and parts exports rose 15.1 percent, to $200 million in 1994. Much of the bicycle's success resulted from the introduction of the mountain bike to Europe and other countries, and was bolstered by the introduction of mountain biking as an Olympic event in 1996. A prime example is Trek USA, a Wisconsin company that exported none of its products in 1986. Trek USA has international sales that represent 32 percent of its total sales volume (which amounted to 950,000 bicycles in 1995). It maintains subsidiaries in Austria, the Netherlands, Germany, Japan, Switzerland, and the United Kingdom, with 65 international distributors.

American companies are seizing on new opportunities in countries such as China, which traditionally had been markets locked up by domestic manufacturers. In early 1997, ZAP Power Systems of Sebastopol, CA, received a grant from the U.S. Environmental Protection Agency to promote sales of its electric-powered bicycles in China. This grant came on the heels of Shanghai's ban on the licensing of new gas mopeds and bicycles, and its plans to replace 80 percent of the 470,000 gas vehicles in the city with cleaner vehicles.

RESEARCH AND TECHNOLOGY

The manufacturing expertise of Harley-Davidson has grown steadily since its first 1903 model, which used a tomato can for a carburetor. Faced with sophisticated competition from Japanese manufactures in the 1980s, the company adopted modern Just-In-Time inventory management and computerized information systems. It retrained its production workers to use statistical monitoring methods, and re-educated managers to work as team leaders instead of bosses. New production line techniques included a state-of-the-art robot assembly system and a $23-million paint center at York, Pennsylvania. The result was the vastly improved quality and productivity needed to overcome Harley-Davidson's reputation as unreliable and expensive.

The mountain bike continued the technological revolution begun with the 10-speed bicycle by reducing cost and increasing comfort levels. Innovators in bicycle design use new materials and electronic gadgets to bring the century-old "safety" bicycle into the computer age. The molded carbon fiber metals that made stronger, lighter frames possible, for example, come from missile technology, while Special Bicycle Components' new three-spoke wheel, which combines carbon fiber, epoxy resin, Kevlar, and aluminum, was designed on the Cray Supercomputer. In addition, hydraulic brakes are replacing the familiar cable systems, and electronic shifters make changing gears a snap. Some manufacturers are investigating a new enclosed automatic transmission system, which could banish "gear fear" forever. The most visible innovation in bicycling may be a completely new design. The new recumbent bicycle places the rider in a sitting position with the pedals in front, providing a low center of gravity, which improves cornering and pedaling efficiency.

Foreign manufacturers are changing the way they do things, as well. National Bicycle Industrial Co., a subsidiary of Matsushita, builds its bikes one at a time. Using robots and computer tracking, its 20 employees custom manufacture the product from the individual customer's order. From a base of 18 models of racing, road, and mountain bikes, they can build 11,231,862 variations in 199 color patterns.

FURTHER READING

"About the Motorcycle Safety Foundation." Irvine, CA: Motorcycle Safety Foundation, 1997. Available from http://www.tiac.net/users/emax/MSFaboutMSF.html.

Bahniuk, Douglas E. "Bicycles Become Featherweights." *Machine Design,* 10 November 1988.

Beals, Vaughn L. "Operation Recovery: How Customers Helped Us Turn Around Harley-Davidson." *Success,* January/February 1989.

"Bicycle Transmission Eliminates Shifters, Levers." *Design News,* 6 April 1992.

Brown, Christie. "Then and the Art of Motorcycle Maintenance." *Forbes,* 4 March 1991.

Brown, Don J. "Systemic Change: 1986-1996; Motorcycle Industry." *Dealernews,* January 1997.

Castro, Janice. "Rock and Roll." *Time,* 19 August 1991.

Celente, Gerald. "Americans Finding Happiness Outdoors." *Trends in the News,* 19 June 1995.

Clapp, Wallace L., Jr. "Insuring the New Breed of RV." *Rough Notes,* September 1992.

Collingwood, Harris. "For Schwinn, Fewer Bumps Ahead." *Business Week,* 1 February 1993.

Doyle, Rob. "No Saddlebags on This Screamer." *Business Week,* 21 October 1996.

Drake, Geoff. "Toy Story: Workaday Role of the Bicycle." *Bicycling,* January 1997.

"Electric Bike Firm Receives EPA Grant to Expand Market in China." *Business Wire,* 18 March 1997.

Fauber, John. "Bike Helmets Found to Cut Risk of Head Injury by 69%." *Milwaukee Journal Sentinel,* 6 January 1997.

Feder, Barnaby. "Schwinn Ready to Sell Most Assets." *New York Times,* 2 January 1993.

Friedman, Dorian, and Sara Collins. "Pedaling for Profits." *U.S. News & World Report,* 26 August 1991.

"GT Bicycles Reports Record Fourth Quarter and Full-Year 1996 Results." *Business Wire,* 19 February 1997.

Hannon, Kerry. "Lots of Eggs, Several Baskets." *Forbes,* 20 April 1987.

"Harley-Davidson Net Doubled in 4th Period as Sales Climbed 31 Percent." *Wall Street Journal,* 22 February 1993.

"Harley-Davidson: Ready to Ride on Its Own." *Newsweek,* 30 March 1987.

"Harmony in Hog Heaven." *Time,* 25 February 1991.

Hounshell, David A. *From the American System to Mass Production: 1800-1932.* Baltimore: John Hopkins University Press, 1984.

"How Harley Beat Back the Japanese." *Fortune,* 25 September 1989.

"Japanese Motorcycles: Mean Machines?" *Nation's Business,* January 1983.

Jesitus, John. "On the Road Again; New Top Management Uses a Teamwork Approach to Put Schwinn Back Into the Bicycle-Industry Race." *Industry Week,* 4 November 1996.

Kim, Irene. "Racer, Rough Riders, and Recumbents." *Mechanical Engineering,* May 1990.

King, Julia. "Harley-Davidson Revs Up IS Teamwork." *Computerworld,* 3 February 1992.

Kinsler, Christen. "Two-wheeling-and-dealing; Automakers Beginning to Make, Sell Bicycles." *Ward's Auto World,* September 1996.

Lafee, Scott. "Relive Your Childhood—For $3,000." *Business Week,* 18 March 1996.

La Franco, Robert. "The Battle of the Bikes." *Forbes,* 26 August 1996.

Larson, Jan. "The Bicycle Market." *American Demographics,* March 1995.

Lazich, Robert S., ed. *Market Share Reporter.* Detroit: Gale Research, 1997.

Lowe, Marcia. "Reinventing the Wheel." *Technology Review,* May/June 1990.

Marvel, Mark. "The Gentrified Hog." *Esquire,* July 1989.

Melcher, Richard A. "Tune-up for Harley." *Business Week,* 8 April 1996.

Moffat, Susan. "Japan's New Personalized Production." *Fortune,* 22 October 1990.

"Mountain Bikes' Demographics Are Broader Than Gen X." *The Public Pulse,* July 1995.

"Mounting the Drive for Quality." *Manufacturing Engineering,* January 1992.

Okubo, Toshihiko. "Motorcycle Production Recovers from Slump." *Business Japan,* July 1989.

Phillips, Stephen. "That Vroom You Hear Is Honda Motorcycles." *Business Week,* 3 September 1990.

Pruzzin, Daniel R. "Born to Verruckt." *World Trade,* May 1992.

Schonfeld, Erick. "Betting on the Boomers." *Fortune,* 25 December 1995.

Shao, Maria. "Mountain Bikes Just Keep on Climbing." *Business Week,* 7 January 1991.

Stern, Richard, L. "The Graying Wild Ones." *Forbes,* 6 January 1992.

Stodghill, Ron, II. "Joe Montgomery's Wild Ride." *Business Week,* 19 April 1993.

Tanzer, Andrew. "Bury Thy Teacher." *Forbes,* 21 December 1992.

U.S. Department of Commerce. Bureau of the Census. International Trade Administration "Recent Trends in Motorcycles, Bicycles, and Parts." Washington: GPO, 1995.

Waldrup, Judith. "The Pace Setters." *American Demographics,* May 1991.

"Welcome to Trek Bikes Online." Waterloo, WI: Trek Bicycle Corp., 1997. Available from http://www.trekbikes.com.

Williams, Linda. "Reinventing the Wheel." *Time,* 7 May 1990.

Wilson, David Gordon. "A Short History of Human-Powered Vehicles." *American Scientist,* July/August 1986.

—Al Cook, updated by Gerry Azzata

SIC 3761

MANUFACTURERS OF GUIDED MISSILES AND SPACE VEHICLES

This category covers establishments primarily engaged in manufacturing guided missiles and space vehicles. This industry also includes establishments owned by guided missile and space vehicle manufacturers and primarily engaged in research and development on these products, whether from enterprise funds or on a contract or fee basis. Establishments primarily engaged in manufacturing guided missile and space vehicle propulsion units and propulsion unit parts are classified in **SIC 3764: Guided Missile and Space Vehicle Propulsion Units and Propulsion Unit Parts;** those manufacturing space satellites are classified in **SIC 3669: Communications Equipment, Not Elsewhere Classified;** those manufacturing guided missile and space vehicle airborne and ground guidance, checkout, and launch electronic systems and components are classified in **SIC 3812: Search, Detection, Navigation, Guidance, Aeronautical, and Nautical Systems and Instruments;** and those manufacturing guided missile and space vehicle airframes, nose cones, and space capsules are classified in **SIC 3769: Guided Missile and Space Vehicle Parts and Auxiliary Equipment, Not Elsewhere Classified.** Research and development on guided missiles and space vehicles, on a contract or fee basis, by establishments not owned by guided missile or space vehicle manufacturers are classified in **SIC 8731: Commercial Physical and Biological Research.**

INDUSTRY SNAPSHOT

In the mid-1990s, the United States had approximately 50 establishments in this industry, with total gross sales of just over $15 billion, down $4 billion from 1992. Of the total value of net new orders, about 16 percent of this industry's production was for complete guided missiles and space vehicles; 12 percent was for other aircraft, space vehicle, and missile activities; 8 percent for research and development of guided missiles and space vehicles; and 16 percent went toward services on these products. The military accounted for 61 percent of net sales, with the U.S. government purchasing 52 percent and other governments purchasing 9 percent. Of the 39 percent of nonmilitary sales, the U.S. Government accounted for 6 percent and other customers 33 percent.

This industry's history and growth have depended on world political affairs (which define America's military needs) and technological developments (which define the country's military and space exploration capabilities and international competitiveness).

This industry's largest customer has long been the U.S. government. However, the government's market share started to decrease in the late 1980s with the end of the Cold War, reducing defense needs and a rapidly growing commercial market dominated by foreign-owned companies. Military spending dropped to $36.1 billion in 1997, down about 6 percent from 1996 levels. In constant dollars, that figure represented less than half of the 1987 spending peak.

ORGANIZATION AND STRUCTURE

This industry is a large part of the aerospace industry, which is made up of roughly 4,000 companies. The production of missiles accounted for 5 percent of sales in the aerospace industry, and space vehicles (along with related equipment) accounted for 25 percent of sales.

Of the companies in the aerospace industry, only 60 were primary contractors, mostly in the guided missile and space vehicle sectors. These establishments regularly hired subcontractors in other sectors of the aerospace industry. Due to the size and technical scope of aerospace programs, many primary contractors also were subcontractors in cases where they were not the primary contractor.

This industry is also categorized by the type of manufacturing workload an establishment undertakes. Basically, three types of manufacturing establishments exist in this industry: manufacturers of conventional, battlefield, and short- to medium-range guided missiles; producers of strategic (including ballistic missiles), antiballistic, and long-range missiles; and manufacturers of space vehicles (subdivided into launch vehicles and spacecraft).

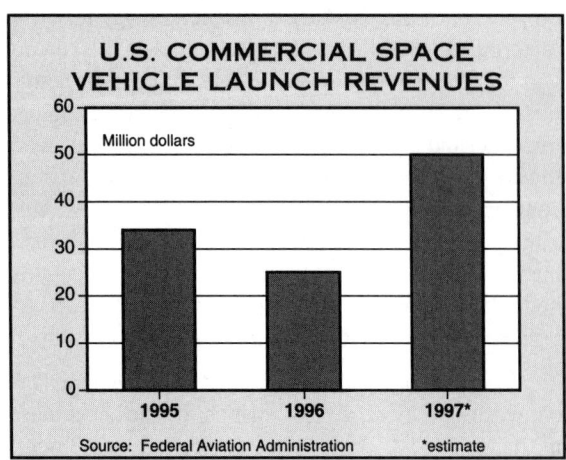

U.S. COMMERCIAL SPACE VEHICLE LAUNCH REVENUES

Million dollars

Source: Federal Aviation Administration   *estimate

Establishments rely on state-of-the-art systems management, in which a subcontractor, often the major computer hardware supplier, supervises hundreds of companies at one time. (The development of systems management in the United States has been credited to this industry.)

BACKGROUND AND DEVELOPMENT

The history of this industry is characterized by the world political climate and technological developments. Wars and American foreign policy directly affected the production of guided missiles, while the space race with the Soviet Union advanced America's production of space vehicles. Technological advances have shaped the growth of this industry with two major advances: the gas turbine engine developed in the late 1940s, for supersonic speed, and the ballistic missile first developed in the late 1950s, for long-range capabilities in war and space exploration.

The aerospace industry emerged from the aftermath of World War II, which introduced jet rockets and atomic weaponry. These developments added to the already growing aviation industry. Aviation properly started in the late 1920s with the success of Charles Lindbergh's flight across the Atlantic; many companies that entered the aviation business later made the transition into aerospace technology, manufacturing missiles for the U.S. military during the war.

Space vehicles entered this industry during the mid-1950s, with the Cold War placing America into the space race against the Soviet Union. Initially, most manufacturing of space vehicles was for exploration of the earth's upper atmosphere and the moon. Man's first trip to the moon sparked new interest in space technology, which peaked in the late 1960s.

The 1960s also marked tremendous growth in the development of guided missiles. Missiles manufactured in the United States were being sold to parties in conflicts in the Middle East and to other troubled areas of the world at that time.

Both the production of missiles and space vehicles decreased during the mid- to late 1970s because of the end of the Vietnam War and the economic recession. The number of satellites used for military surveillance decreased, and those used for communications increased substantially. However, during this period, major projects involving stealth sea vessels and aircraft were initiated.

During the 1980s, the guided missile portion of this industry hit its all-time peak as a result of renewed defense spending. Under the Reagan administration, fears of an escalating Cold War increased missile sales from just over $10 billion in 1983 to nearly $14 billion in 1988 (according to the Electronic Industries Association). President Reagan proposed the development of antiballistic strategic defenses, commonly known as Star Wars initiatives, to counter possible Soviet attack.

However, by the end of the 1980s, yet another dramatic shift occurred in this industry. With the dissolution of the Soviet Union and the end of the Reagan Administration, America's defense spending was greatly reduced. From 1987 to 1994, U.S. Defense Department outlays for aircraft dropped from over $30 billion to just over $19 billion. Similarly, the government budget for research and development in defense and space technology dropped significantly. This was also due to the explosion of the *Challenger* space shuttle, in which seven astronauts perished.

Products. Among the types of guided missiles this industry manufactures are antitank and assault, antiship, air-to-surface, air-to-air, and surface-to-air. Antitank and assault missiles were developed in the United States after World War II (though some accounts have Germany developing these missiles near the end of the war). These missiles were first installed on light trucks and helicopters and equipped with warheads to penetrate armor. In early models, tracking was visual, with commands controlled by a hand-operated system transmitted by wire. Later, antitank missiles transmitted commands by radio and laser and infrared homing techniques. By the 1980s, optical fibers became the standard guidance device for these missiles.

Antiship missiles were designed to fight against the heavy armor of warships. These types of guided missiles received little attention by U.S. manufacturers after World War II, because the Americans and British had used torpedoes, bombs, and unguided rockets to attack naval targets. However, in response to Soviet development of antiship missiles, the United States countered with turbojet-powered missiles, such as the Harpoon, which weighed about 1,200 pounds and carried a warhead weighing 420 pounds. Later, the U.S. Navy Tomahawk introduced a new type of antiship missile, a long-range cruise missile intended for strategic nuclear defense. Its antiship version carried a modified Harpoon guidance system. By the 1980s, antiship missiles were developed for stealth aircraft with visual, infrared, and radar tracking.

Air-to-surface missiles became standard in U.S. combat by the late 1950s with the AGM-12 Bullpup, a rocket-powered tracking missile with visual tracking and radio transmitted commands. After several variations of the AGM-type missiles were employed during the Vietnam War, the Bullpup was replaced by the AGM-64/65 Maverick group of rocket-powered missiles, which first used television tracking, and later, infrared devices.

Air-to-air missiles were first developed in the United States in the late 1940s with the subsonic Firebird, a radar-guided missile. However, this particular missile became obsolete within a few years, being replaced by supersonic missiles, such as the Falcon, the Sidewinder, and the Sparrow. The Sidewinder became the most used of these missile types; later versions of this missile had highly sensitive emission seekers. Tactical demands saw significant improvements in air-to-air technology, which resulted in long-range air-interception missiles and missiles with higher maneuverability.

Surface-to-air missiles were first introduced by the Germans during World War II, but were not widely used until the 1950s and 1960s. The most important American-produced, surface-to-air missile was the Hawk; this missile was extremely effective in targeting low-flying aircraft. In the mid-1980s, the Hawk was replaced by the Patriot, which gained popularity as a result of the Persian Gulf War.

The missiles described above are also classified as conventional or strategic. Strategic missiles refer to long-range missiles, especially those with nuclear warheads, and include ballistic and cruise missiles. Ballistic missiles are rocket-propelled systems that are launched either from land or sea and move by the launch rocket momentum. Cruise missiles are powered continuously by air-breathing jet engines. These types of missiles are aided by guidance systems and early warning devices on satellites.

Three basic types of space vehicles exist in this industry: space capsules with rocket boosters, reentry vehicles, and satellites. These space vehicles are made of two basic components—the launch vehicle and the spacecraft, also referred to as the payload. The launch vehicle provides the propulsion to send the space craft into space. While the spacecraft itself is basically unpowered, it relies on the initial velocity provided by the launch vehicle, and either enters an orbit around the earth or continues to a further destination.

Space capsules with rocket boosters were first designed and tested in the United States in the mid-1950s with the intent of sending a man into outer space. These capsules are environmentally controlled containers for living organisms. After a few flights in the early 1960s, animals were preferred over humans. The rockets attached to the space capsule are used for launching the space vehicle and later separate from the capsule.

Reentry vehicles, such as space shuttles, were first launched by the United States in 1981. These space vehicles were designed to go into the Earth's orbit, drop off a payload, such as a satellite, and return to earth by making a gliding landing. Shuttles are made of three basic components: a winged orbiter that houses crew and cargo, an external tank containing fuel and liquid oxygen, and booster rockets, which separate from the space craft and return to earth. By 1990, the United States had used four shuttles, many on repeated missions, but also with much difficulty. Technical and design problems frequently delayed launches, and the worst of the problems caused the explosion of the *Challenger* space shuttle in 1986.

Satellites are spacecraft that revolve around planets and are used for communications, weather forecasting, scientific research, and military reconnaissance. The first satellite was launched in 1957 by the Soviet Union. By the end of the 1980s, there were hundreds of satellites orbiting the Earth and nearby planets. In the early 1990s, an estimated $3 billion annually went into the manufacturing of communications satellites in America alone. The estimated figure for 1995 was almost $8 billion, more than double the figures from the early 1990s.

CURRENT CONDITIONS

By the 1990s, the end of the Cold War initiated cuts in defense spending, drastically affecting the manufacturing of guided missiles and military-employed space vehicles. However, with the view that the United States needed to retain its technological base in defense, an increase in funding for research and development occurred. This trend was expected to continue with 57 percent of procurement going toward research and development in 1997, compared with 30 percent in 1985. New products have been manufactured only as a limited number of prototypes, which are taken to a full-scale production on the basis of need and available funding.

This industry was further affected by the signing of the Strategic Arms Reduction Treaty (START) in July 1991. According to the treaty, guided missiles with nuclear warheads would no longer be produced while 30 percent of existing ones would be destroyed.

The end of the twentieth century also started a new phase in the production of space vehicles, whereby space exploration would be trimmed while a new commercial industry would open up. As a result of the *Challenger* disaster and other highly publicized space failures costing millions of dollars, Congress reduced NASA's budget. NASA has flown fewer flights annually, but with larger and more expensive

payloads, subsequently producing greater financial risks. Such problems as the *Challenger* incident were a factor in space vehicle manufacturers' move away from government projects and into the commercial market. According to Otis Port of *Business Week,* ''Thanks mainly to advances in technology, aerospace companies and some in Washington think they see a chance to make space travel an airline-type business.'' Port added that the goal has become ''to stimulate private enterprise in space.'' The high cost of producing space vehicles since the beginning of the space program was to see a turnaround as commercial business saw a potential market and foreign competition meant NASA no longer monopolized space travel. Radical changes are sculpting the defense industry with an emphasis on acquisition reform, commercial off-the-shelf (COTS) technology, and other commercial aspects. The trend has now been to fund space projects with greater relevance to living on Earth than early space explorations; the orbiting of communication satellites and the construction of the *Freedom* space station are new priorities for the continued presence of America's space program.

Throughout this industry, establishments responded to these developments by diversifying and consolidating. Some companies manufacturing satellites diversified into producing spacecraft electronic components, thereby expanding their roles in the telecommunications industry. Other companies in aerospace developed new areas of scientific and technological research, such as designing medical laboratory equipment usable in specialized environments and software for growing industries in the communications field.

Recent trends in aerospace saw decreases in total employment, imports, and exports. In order to meet the challenges proposed by military downsizing, major companies merged in 1996 and shifted their emphasis toward non-military commercial enterprises.

INDUSTRY LEADERS

In 1996, the major industry leaders in the production of guided missiles and space vehicles were: Lockheed Martin Corporation with $27 billion in gross sales, McDonnell Douglas Corporation with $13.8 billion, Raytheon Company with $11.7 billion, and Rockwell International Corporation with $10.3 billion. Other key companies in the manufacture of guided missile systems and space vehicles included GM, Hughes Electronics Corporation, Tracor, Inc., Loral Space & Communications, Ltd., ITT Defense and Electronics, and Boeing.

Lockheed Corporation began as the Loughead Aircraft Manufacturing Company in 1916 (but the company soon changed its name to Lockheed to reflect the correct pronunciation). This company started with the development of their twin-engine, F-1 flying boats. By 1927, Lockheed became widely known for its planes, including the Lockheed Vega, flown by Amelia Earhart.

Lockheed entered the defense industry in 1938, when commissioned to build reconnaissance bombers for the British. Lockheed went on to produce a wide range of military planes and early cruise missiles during World War II, including the Harpoon. By the end of the war, the company had produced over nine percent of America's military aircraft.

After the war, Lockheed established its missile and space division, starting with submarine launched missiles. During the Cold War, Lockheed developed guided missiles for the Pentagon, including its U-2 spy plane, which had notable success during the Cuban missile crisis in 1962. In addition to military contracts, Lockheed stayed in the commercial aircraft business, manufacturing jetliners; however, this division nearly placed the company into bankruptcy by the early 1970s. The company finally gained some success in jetliners in the foreign market, but at the expense of being involved in an international scandal. Lockheed was implicated in accepting bribes from several countries, including Iran and Japan.

During the 1980s, Lockheed led the industry in government defense contracts, primarily in building F-19 stealth bombers and the Trident II missiles, and in servicing NASA's space shuttles. During the early 1990s, the company remained successful in defense technology, with its stealth fighters being used in the Persian Gulf War. After an unsuccessful expansion of its commercial divisions, Lockheed reversed course to attempt to become the nation's largest defense contractor. In the mid-1990s, the company employed 81,300 workers, and predicted a 10 percent annual increase in its earnings.

In March 1995, Lockheed merged with Martin Marietta Corporation, which, like other industry leaders, had its origins in airplane production in the early days of aviation. Martin Marietta remained closely aligned with U.S. Military projects from bomber production in World War II, rockets and missiles in the 1960s, to space vehicles from the 1970s to the present. In April, 1996, Lockheed Martin bought Loral Corporation, emerging as the largest defense contractor in the United States with gross sales of $27 billion and over 190,000 employees worldwide.

McDonnell Douglas Corporation (MD) was the world's leading military aircraft producer. MD was the second-largest defense contractor (after Lockheed Martin) in the United States and the third-largest commercial aircraft manufacturer in the world (behind The Boeing Company and G.I.E. Airbus Industrie of France), led by its MD-80 and MD-90 commercial jets. The company was also involved in manufacturing components for the space station, the Delta Launch Vehicle, Tomahawk missiles, and targeting systems. In 1996, MD accepted a bid from Boeing to merge the companies. While it faced strong objections from European competitors, the merger was expected to be completed in 1997. Figures for MD in 1996 showed $13.8 billion in sales, down 3.47 percent since 1995.

Raytheon Company has four segments to its company: electronics, aircraft, engineering and construction, and appliances. Its electronics segment ranked Raytheon number six nationwide. Listed among its products are the Patriot missiles. In 1997, the company was in the process of buying the defense electronic businesses of Texas Instruments and Hughes Electronics. Raytheon had $12 billion in sales for 1995, up 4.65 percent from the previous year.

Rockwell International had its origins in 1919 as Rockwell-Standard, a manufacturer of truck axles. By the late 1960s, the company had evolved into producing industrial machinery and vehicle parts. In 1967, Rockwell merged with North American Aviation, a company that had been in the aviation business since the late 1920s and later played a major role in producing rockets and spacecraft for the U.S. space program. Prior to its merger with Rockwell, North American Aviation was nearly bankrupt as a result of an electrical fire in an Apollo space capsule, in which three astronauts were killed. This incident cost North American a large legal settlement and a bruised reputation.

After the merger, the company was renamed North American Rockwell. With its new name and Rockwell's established history, the company regained its reputation in the aerospace industry. The new company extended beyond government contracts into the private sector, manufacturing a wide range of automotive parts, household appliances, and electric instruments for aviation. In aerospace, the company developed the Saturn V rocket engines used for later Apollo missions. By the early 1970s, the company, again renamed Rockwell International, was the largest NASA contractor and NASA's primary contractor of space shuttles.

In the late 1970s, Rockwell experienced severe financial setbacks due in part to management problems, but also as a result of the government shifting away from the development of bombers, which Rockwell was in the middle of producing. But the company retained its defense contracts, including the production of the MX "Peacekeeper" missiles and five space shuttles.

With a reduction in space shuttle contracts and defense systems in general, Rockwell International entered the 1990s starting commercial ventures with foreign-owned companies. In the mid-1990s the company employed over 105,000 workers and retained its principle subsidiaries in Canada and Great Britain. By 1996, Rockwell had sold its space and military operations to Boeing and made the switch to commercial ventures complete.

Tracor, Inc., one of Americas fastest growing defense electronics and information technology companies, announced that first quarter sales for 1997 showed a 30 percent increase over first quarter 1996. Based in Austin, Texas, Tracor was listed as one of the 15 largest defense electronic firms in the United States with 1996 sales topping $1 billion. The company provided sophisticated electronic and information technology products, systems, and services to its customers in the U.S. Department of Defense as well as to nondefense U.S. government agencies, other governments, and the commercial marketplace. In 1997, Lockheed Martin, Tracor, and TRW planned to form a joint venture to bid for all work related to national missile defense.

ITT Defense and Electronics (ITTD&E), a unit of ITT Industries, Inc., has been selected by NASA as its sole supplier of meteorological instruments for the newest members of the NOAA's Geostationary Operational Environmental Satellite (GOES). The company has been a leading supplier of high technology commercial and defense electronic systems and services.

Loral Space & Communications Ltd. has as its primary operations the manufacture of satellites and satellite-based telecommunications systems. The company was formed by the remains of Loral Corporation, the bulk of which was acquired by Lockheed Martin.

Boeing completely assimilated Rockwell International's defense and space unit. Prior to the merger, defense and space work made up 25 percent of Boeing's business. Not including the anticipated $13 billion merger with McDonnell Douglas, Boeing's earnings were estimated at $1.17 billion for 1996 and $1.77 billion in 1997.

WORK FORCE

In the mid-1990s, this industry employed more than 76,000 workers. Of these, nearly 25,000 worked

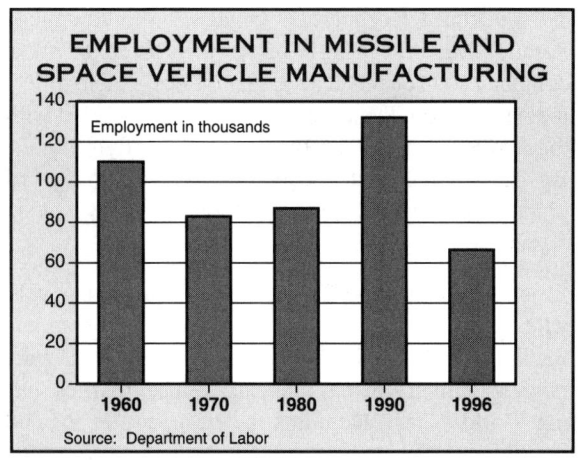

EMPLOYMENT IN MISSILE AND SPACE VEHICLE MANUFACTURING

Employment in thousands

Source: Department of Labor

in production, with the remaining workers mostly in research and development. For both production and research and development, the main occupations needed for this industry are engineers, scientists, and technicians. Engineers have usually specialized as either aeronautical engineers, working with aircraft; or astronautical engineers, working with space vehicles. In 1992, engineers in the aerospace industry started with an average annual salary of $30,000 if they possessed a bachelor's degree, $35,000 with a master's, and $47,000 with a Ph.D. Scientists in this industry included astronomers, mathematicians, physicists, metallurgists, and chemists—all of these occupations required Ph.D.s, and offered salaries between $45,000 to $70,000, depending on the specialty. Technicians working in this industry include laboratory technicians, electrical technicians, and draftsmen, with an annual starting salary of $50,000. Other occupations required by this industry include technical writers, machinists, assembly workers, system managers, worker supervisors, computer programmers, and various clerical workers.

AMERICA AND THE WORLD

America's production of guided missiles and space vehicles and the political environment after World War II have made the United States the world's leading exporter of these products. In the early 1990s, U.S. exports of missile systems totaled over $600 million in sales, with air-to-air missiles representing the largest portion of sales. However, this strength in the air-to-air sector of the market has been challenged since 1992, when the European Advanced Short Range Air-to-Air Missile program began. Exports in 1994 dropped to $3.6 million.

The countries of the former Soviet Union, which had invested more money and resources in air defense systems than any other nation in the world, have been

America's greatest competitor for arms sales to other countries. Upon entering the 1990s, France and Great Britain rapidly became two other leading competitors in the production of missiles.

The production of strategic missiles, given their nuclear capabilities, were originally restricted to the United States and the Soviet Union. However, since the end of the Cold War, there has been worldwide concern that the superpowers would sell their stockpile of weapons—and possibly new weapons—to third world countries. Other countries that developed missile technology became somewhat successful in ballistic missiles, but less so with cruise missiles. Ballistic missiles do not require the sophisticated guidance system of cruise missiles and adapt to chemical weaponry more easily.

The end of the Cold War, coupled with worldwide economic recession, gave rise to change in the international market for space programs in the 1990s. An industry first monopolized by the United States and the former Soviet Union entered into competition with the European Space Agency, the People's Republic of China, and Japan. The new political and economic climate allowed for more cooperative efforts in space. NASA considered Russian contributions to America's *Freedom* space station and other ventures. In the commercial market, plans were made for the International Maritime Satellite Organization, an international consortium, to use a Russian-made rocket to launch its satellites.

Since the late 1980s, foreign competition remained strong for selling space satellites. Arianespace, a European joint venture, dominated the commercial satellite business, and Russia's space agency began shifting its investment to the commercial marketplace. Launch executives have predicted continued growth over the next decade with an emphasis on customer service, especially reliability, as new competitors enter the market. Europe's Ariane 5 booster, McDonnell Douglas' Delta 3, Boeing's Sea Launch, and Lockheed Martin's Atlas 2AR (with the Russian derivative engine RD-180) are all expected to enter the commercial market by 1998 while Japan's H-2A commercial booster and the U.S. Air Force's Evolved Expendable Launch (EELV) are expected early in the next decade.

The United States also imports guided missiles and space vehicles, but only on a small scale and mostly for research and development. In the mid-1990s, U.S. imports in this industry totaled approximately $1.6 million.

RESEARCH AND TECHNOLOGY

Manufacturers of guided missiles and space vehicles depend on research and development of new technologies, most of which are produced within the industry itself. The three main forces shaping the future of this industry were the development of ballistic missiles, low-cost space vehicles, and the construction and operation of the *Freedom* space station.

Ballistic and anti-ballistic missiles have been continuously developed in order to compete with defense technology of foreign countries. Since the late 1980s, the market for these types of missiles at low prices developed from economic crises in the former Soviet Union and other countries, who sold conventional and nuclear weapons to third world countries no longer wanting to rely on superpowers to protect them. This market was met by research and development in low-cost manufacturing of relatively small ballistic and antiballistic missiles, a variety of surface-to-air ballistic missiles, and medium-range ballistic missiles that can be adapted for many uses. Since the Persian Gulf War, researchers of these types of missiles directed their interests toward weapons like those used in the war, but with improved high-precision strike capabilities.

Of low-cost space vehicles, expendable launch vehicles (ELV) were expected to replace the failed space shuttle programs. Research for these vehicles focused on unmanned operations to launch mostly commercial payloads. Given the cost factor, the aim was to launch larger and heavier payloads on each trip. NASA and the U.S. Defense Department are developing an Advanced Launch System to be in operation early in the twentieth century. In the early 1990s, launch capacity exceeded demand, and the industry became concerned that improved technology would increase the life of satellites—both factors would reduce the need for new space vehicle launches. However, space launch executives told a National Space Symposium audience that new applications for satellites should create a demand that would more than offset any cyclical launch market downturns.

Another technological development aimed at reducing costs has been work on a reentry vehicle that takes off and lands vertically. In 1993, McDonnell Douglas Corporation began experimental launches of their Delta Clipper, which was the first rocket to launch and land vertically on earth. This launch vehicle cost $10 million to build, with an estimated cost of $1,000 per kg to launch into a low-Earth orbit, compared with NASA's space shuttles, which cost $500 million to produce and $21,000 per kg to launch.

Other innovations in launch vehicles include new airplanes designed to carry spacecraft into orbit. In the United States, Boeing Defense and Space Group proposed the use of a supersonic carrier the size of a 747 airplane. Similar designs are being developed by the British and Germans. Like other new developments in space technology, these aim to reduce costs. Boeing's proposed system would cost roughly $600 per pound to place a spacecraft into orbit.

To compete with the commercial satellite market, research into a new rocket to carry satellites and other types of spacecraft was proposed in 1993. Lockheed's X-33, a futuristic wedge-shaped spacecraft, was slated to replace the Space Shuttle around the turn of the century. Its design to operate without an onboard crew, using only guidance from onboard computers and satellite navigation systems would reduce the cost of lifting payloads into orbit, thus enabling the United States to recapture much of the commercial market it lost to European and Asian launch systems. Other space launch vehicles include the Titan IVB rocket for the Air Force, which can lift 25 percent more weight than Titan IVA; Trident II, a submarine launched ballistic missile with external fuel tanks for the Space shuttle; and the Atlas 2AR, using the RD-180 Russian derivative engine. The Atlas 2AR's increased reliability over the Atlas 2AS was due to the elimination of 15,000 parts and the reduction of staging events from five to none. This would allow more launches per year, smaller crews, and greater performance reliability.

The Russian Space Station Mir has offered Shuttle-Mir participants answers to vital questions about the future of human life in space. Mir has been operating as a test site for three main areas of experience and investigation: the opportunity for participants from many nations to work together and learn from each other; the opportunity for long-duration data gathering; and the experience of working under complicated logistical situations. Mir has hosted a series of NASA astronauts as crewmembers since March 1995.

FURTHER READING

Anselmo, Joseph C. "Launchers See Nothing But Blue Skies Ahead." *Aviation Week & Space Technology,* 7 April 1997.

———. "NASA Begins Shuttle Handover." *Aviation Week & Space Technology,* 7 October 1996.

Asker, James R. "NASA Struggles with Station Redesign." *Aviation Week and Space Technology,* 12 April 1993.

Banks, Howard. "McDonnell Douglas' Last Flight?" *Forbes,* 16 December 1996. Available from http://www.forbes.com/forbes/121696/581.

———. "Preparing for Even More Draconian Cuts in Defense Spending, Suppliers Are Cutting Jobs and Costs." *Forbes,* 6 January 1992.

"Booming Boeing." *Business Week,* 30 September 1996.

Bright, Charles D. *The Jet Makers: The Aerospace Industry from 1945-1972.* Lawrence, KS: Regents Press, 1978.

Corcoran, Elizabeth and Tim Beardsley. "The New Space Race." *Scientific American,* July 1990.

Covault, Craig. "Ambitious Decade Ahead for Europe's Space Effort." *Aviation Week and Space Technology,* 15 March 1993.

Crock, Stan. "Does Firepower = Earning Power?" *Business Week,* 6 May 1996.

Curry, Malcolm R. "Expert Opinion: Peace Is Transforming Aerospace and Military Industries." *IEEE Spectrum,* January 1993.

Darlin, Damon. "Aerospace & Defense." *Forbes,* 13 January 1997. Available from http://www.forbes.com/forbes/97/0113/590.

"Defense Firms Switch, Go For a Makeover." CMP Media Inc., 22 November 1996.

Dornheim, Michael A. "U.S. Navy Unveils Sea Shadow Stealth Vessel." *Aviation Week and Space Technology,* 26 April 1993.

"First Quarter Earnings Per Share Climb 10 Percent for Lockheed Martin." 22 April 1997. Available from http://www.infoseek.com.

"F-16, EA-6B to Fire Missiles Cued by Intelligence Satellites." *Aviation Week and Space Technology,* 19 April 1993.

"Frost & Sullivan—Defense Industry Faced with a Reality Check: Adapting and Surviving in This Critical Period of Rapid Change." 22 April 1997. Available from http://www.infoseek.com.

"Global State of the Industry." *Aerospace.* 1996. Available from http://www.oregonbusiness.com/ae-global.html.

Lavitt, Michael O. "Market Forces." *Aviation Week and Space Technology,* 5 April 1993.

Lenorovitz, Jeffery M. "Steady Growth Seen for Commercial Space." *Aviation Week and Space Technology,* 15 March 1993.

"Lockheed Develops Low-End Launch Vehicle." *Aviation Week and Space Technology,* 10 May 1993.

"Lockheed Martin to Link Headquarters Operating Budgets Worldwide Using Comshare's Commander Budget Plus." 23 April 1997.

"Lockheed Martin Corporation." *Infoseek Company Capsule.* 1996. Available from http://www.infoseek.com.

"Loral Space & Communications Ltd." Infoseek Company Capsule. 1996. Available from http://www.infoseek.com.

"MA37D—Aerospace Industry, 1994." Available from gopher://una.hh.lib.umich.edu/ . . . /ma37d94.cen.

"NASA Shuttle-MIR Web." Available from http://shuttle-mir.nasa.gov.

"Next Generation Space Shuttle, the X-33 Will Exploit Veda Systems Technology." News Center Article, 23 April 1997. Available from http://www.infoseek.com.

Payne, Seth. "Can't Afford NASA? Call Rent-A-Rocket." *Business Week,* 12 March 1990.

Port, Otis. "Is Buck Rogers' Ship Coming In?" *Business Week,* 21 June 1993.

"Raytheon Company." *Infoseek Company Capsule.* Available from http://www.infoseek.com.

"Recent Trends: Guided Missiles and Space Vehicles (SIC 3761)." Available from http://www.ita.doc.gov/ . . . /tai/green/trnds376.txt.

"Reusable Rocket Flies Again." *USA Today Nation.* 8 June 1996. Available from http:www.usatoday.com/news/nds1.htm.

Ricks, Thomas E. "Unit of LTV Pleads Guilty in 'Ill Wind' Case." *Wall Street Journal,* 19 May 1993.

Rosewicz, Barbara. "Aerospace Firms Seek Alliance on New Rocket." *Wall Street Journal,* 6 May 1993.

"Rockwell International Corporation." *Infoseek Company Capsule.* Available from http://www.infoseek.com.

"Russian Proton Booster Offered in Indonesian Launch Competition." *Aviation Week and Space Technology,* 12 April 1993.

"Russian Proton to Launch Inmarsat-3 Satellite in 1995." *Aviation Week and Space Technology,* 19 April 1993.

Rybak, Boris. "Feeble Russian Economy Hinders Space Efforts." *Aviation Week and Space Technology,* 15 March 1993.

Sawyer, Kathy. "Silence at Red Planet Reverberates on Earth." *Washington Post,* 13 November 1993.

Schine, Eric. "Lockheed Sticks to Its Guns." *Business Week,* 26 April 1993.

Scott, William B. "Lockheed Martin, Energomash Development of RD-180 on Track." *Aviation Week & Space Technology,* 7 April 1997.

Scovell, Dawn. "Solid Rockets." *Aerospace America,* December 1992.

Smith, Bruce A. "U.S. Firms Face Long Adjustment." *Aviation Week and Space Technology,* 15 March 1993.

"Space Shuttle: The Next Generation Winner Announced Tuesday." *Detroit News.* 1996. Available from http://www.detnews.com/menu/stories/54302.htm.

Spiegel, Peter. "Free Launch." *Forbes,* 24 February 1997. Available from http://www.forbes.com/forbes/97/0224/590.

"Tracor Reports Strong Growth and Record Backlog in First Quarter." Infoseek News Center Article, 21 April 1997. Available from http://www.infoseek.com.

U.S. Bureau of the Census. *Statistical Abstract of the United States: 1996.* 116th ed. Washington: GPO, 1996.

"U.S. Entrepreneurs Seek Russian SLBMs." *Aviation Week and Space Technology,* 19 April 1993.

Velocci, Anthony L., Jr. "Fewer Players to See Late-Decade Upturn." *Aviation Week and Space Technology,* 15 March 1993.

—Paola Trimarco, updated by Susan Harrison

SIC 3764

GUIDED MISSILE AND SPACE VEHICLE PROPULSION UNITS AND PROPULSION UNIT PARTS

This industry consists of establishments primarily engaged in manufacturing guided missile propulsion units and propulsion unit parts. This industry also includes establishments owned by manufacturers of guided missile and space vehicle propulsion units and parts and primarily engaged in research and development on such products, whether from enterprise funds or on a contract or fee basis. Research and development on guided missile and space propulsion units, on a contract or fee basis by establishments not owned by manufacturers of guided missile and space vehicle propulsion units and parts are classified in **SIC 8731: Commercial Physical and Biological Research.**

INDUSTRY SNAPSHOT

In 1995, American manufacturers of propulsion units, jet engines, and propulsion unit parts for guided missiles and space vehicles recorded $2.4 billion in gross sales. The number was roughly split 50-50 between military and non-military markets; $1.1 billion accounted for military markets, $1.3 billion accounted for civilian markets. The end of year backlog was $6.1 billion; with $792 million for the military, and $5.3 billion for non-military.

In the 1990s, there were two basic types of propulsion systems used for guided missiles and space vehicles, solid-fueled and liquid-fueled engines. Solid-fueled engines were the more commonly used of the two because liquid fuels needed to be stored at very low temperatures. Other rockets produced by this industry included hybrid rockets, which use a combination of solid and liquid fuel systems, small propellant rockets for adjusting the altitude of space vehicles, and rockets for track-borne research sheds.

ORGANIZATION AND STRUCTURE

Establishments in this industry were generally subcontractors for producers of complete guided missiles and space vehicles. Primary contractors and subcontractors were hired by a single customer. In 1995 net sales for the entire industry (complete aircraft, space vehicles, missiles, and selected parts) was $101 billion, with $52 billion military related, and $49 billion non-military. Of the non-military sales, $7 billion was to the U.S. Government. The industry's shipments manufactured under government contracts were primarily for the U.S. Department of Defense and NASA. The balance of the industry's shipments manufactured for companies in the private sector were involved primarily in producing propulsion and engine systems to launch commercial satellites.

BACKGROUND AND DEVELOPMENT

Propulsion units and engines were often referred to as "rockets." Rockets were believed to have originated in China during the thirteenth century, soon after the invention of gunpowder. Rockets appeared in Europe in the early fourteenth century, but did not see regular military use until the War of 1812 and the Napoleonic Wars. Rockets during this period still used some form of gunpowder for propulsion. It was not until the late nineteenth and early twentieth century that modern rocketry, using stored fuels, was first developed.

World War II witnessed the first guided missiles and military aircraft that were powered by propulsion systems. During the war, only the Germans used propulsion guided missiles, though other countries possessed the technological capabilities. It was not until after the war that other countries, including the United States, developed these systems.

The development of the propulsion units used in ballistic missiles led to the development of systems that enabled the launching of the first space vehicles into orbit by the end of the 1950s. Another significant development in propulsion systems came in the 1970s, concurrent with the first designs for space shuttles. These engines were built with propulsion units that jettisoned off the spacecraft, as well as with permanently fixed units that were reusable.

Rockets using nuclear and solar fuel sources also were tested for space missions. Nuclear propulsion was first developed in the 1960s, and was considered 20 years later for missions to Mars, but concerns about space debris kept this system in the experimental stages. Solar propulsion was investigated for its ability to run an engine at tremendous cost savings.

CURRENT CONDITIONS

Entering the 1990s, the guided missile and space vehicle propulsion industry, like other aerospace industries, was downsizing its operations, but trying to retain a strong base in research and development. With the end of the Cold War, new propulsion systems for military and space exploration programs were limited to prototypes, which were then taken to full-scale production on the basis of need and available funding.

With federal cut-backs, a number of fixed-price contracts created losses for companies in the late 1980s and early 1990s. In the late 1980s, the U.S. Air Force proposed the "SRMU stabilization program," a development of the Titan 4 Launcher, but did not fund the implementation of the program. Both the contractor, Martin Marietta Corp., and the subcontractor, Hercules, Inc., invested substantially in the program, and both ended up suing each other over contract terms as a result. In 1993 the U.S. Government agreed to appropriate funds for some of the losses.

The end of the twentieth century also began a new phase in the production of space vehicles as a new commercial industry emerged. For the guided missile and space vehicle propulsion industry, this meant producing more lower-cost propulsion systems instead of more expensive systems. U.S. exports of guided missiles and space vehicle parts increased to $2.31 billion in 1995 as compared to $1.58 billion in 1994. Imports from foreign countries slightly decreased to $3.77 billion in 1995 as compared to $4.00 billion in 1994. The largest foreign supplier to the U.S. aerospace market in 1994 was France. The largest overseas market in 1995 was Japan, followed by the United Kingdom, South Korea, Canada, and the Netherlands.

Like other industries in aerospace, the guided missile and space vehicle propulsion industry was expected to undergo restructuring as a result of federal defense budget cuts. According to industry leaders, by the end of the century, the industry was expected to be smaller, with many individual companies having a larger market share than they did in the mid-1980s. While the aerospace industry is smaller than it was a decade ago, conditions may be on the upswing. In the first quarter of 1997, Gulfstream Aerospace Corp. reported revenues 75 percent higher than for the same period in 1996. Raytheon Electronic Systems showed an increase in both sales and operating profits for the first time in 15 quarters. McDonnell Douglas reported solid results for this period, with total revenues slightly above what they were during the same period in 1996. Northrup Grumman Corp. reported first quarter earnings for 1997 that were up 23 percent from the same period in 1996.

INDUSTRY LEADERS

In 1996, the three leaders of the guided missile and space vehicle propulsion industry were GenCorp, Inc. who recorded $1.52 billion in sales; Thiokol Corp., which recorded $889.5 million in sales; and Alliant Techsystems, with net sales of $1.19 billion. Alliant is a newcomer to the industry, having purchased the Aerospace component for $300 million in March 1995 from Hercules, Inc., a Delaware-based company and diversified worldwide producer of chemicals and related products. One of the leaders in the industry before selling the division, holds 30 percent ownership and 2 out of 8 non-employee seats on Alliant's Board of Directors. Hercules, Inc. reported $2 billion in sales in fiscal year 1995, with aerospace sales accounting for $693 million. Alliant Techsystems, Inc. became a business entity of its own following a spinoff from Honeywell, Inc. in October 1990. Previously it had been a wholly owned subsidiary in the defense and marine systems business. Its marine systems were involved in a number of key U.S. Navy programs, but it sold that component to Hughes Electronics. With the acquisition of Hercules Aerospace Company, it became a major aerospace and defense company, and is a leader in solid rocket propulsion, munitions, and smart weapons. With 7,700 employees, the Minnesota-based company hopes to build on its world leadership position in low-cost, high-quality solid propulsion systems, and expand its role as a systems integrator. Despite the general downsizing of the aerospace industry in recent years, Alliant plans to focus on its financial and management resources in order to expand its presence in aerospace and defense systems, according to Richard Schwartz, President and CEO.

GenCorp, Inc. was established in 1915 as General Rubber Manufacturing Co. In 1996 GenCorp had 8,950 employees and Aerojet, the company's aerospace and defense division, accounted for nearly one third of GenCorp's total sales. In addition to producing solid and liquid propulsion systems and their related parts, Aerojet manufactured sensors, warheads, and munitions used in the aerospace industry. Aerojet was most widely known for its Titan IV engines and its second stage Delta engines, which allowed spacecraft to maneuver in orbit. The U.S. Army recently awarded Aerojet with a $43.8 million product improvement contract for the Sense and Destroy Armor Program. Currently scheduled to extend through December 1998, the contract's value may increase to over $150 million by October 1999 if all options are exercised.

Thiokol Corp. was established in 1969 as Morton-Norwich Products, Inc., and changed its name later that year to Morton Thiokol, Inc. Thiokol, the nation's leading supplier of solid rocket propulsion systems for space launch vehicles since the inception of manned space flight was engaged in research and development, and production of solid-fueled propulsion systems. In 1992, 96 percent of the company's sales came from government contracts, including providing propulsion units for NASA's space shuttle programs and the military's Trident and Patriot missiles. During 1996 space systems remained Thiokol's largest and most profitable business, with 46 percent of fiscal 1996 sales. Approximately 95 percent of space systems sales came from Thiokol's support of NASA as the exclusive builder and refurbisher of Reusable Solid Rocket Motors used in the Space Shuttle program. In 1992 Thiokol employed over 11,000 workers. In 1996 they downsized to 5,900 employees, restructured their defense and non-shuttle space activities, and closed their Huntsville, Alabama, plant.

WORK FORCE

In 1995 the guided missile and space vehicle propulsion industry employed roughly 20,500 workers in the United States. Of these, an estimated 25 percent were engineers, mainly aeronautical, astronautical, electronic, and industrial engineers. Other occupations needed in the manufacturing of guided missile and space vehicle propulsion systems included systems analysts, computer scientists, specialized technicians, production managers, and machinists.

Overall employment in this industry was expected to drop considerably by the year 2005. The largest decline was expected to be in jobs related to the inspection and testing of products. Computer scientists, however, were expected to increase their representation in this industry to facilitate the development of computerized prototypes to replace full-scale testing of new products. Overall employment in the aerospace industry has declined; direct employment related to aircraft, missiles, and space vehicle manufacture declined more than 35 percent from 905,100 in 1989 to 586,800 in 1994. The Aerospace Research Center predicts that some employment growth in the defense sector may occur by the end of the decade, but any significant upturn in aerospace jobs will come from the commercial sector.

AMERICA AND THE WORLD

Manufacturers of guided missile and space vehicle propulsion and engine systems were affected by developments in foreign countries. Entering the 1990s, France and Great Britain were leading competitors with America in the production of missiles. In 1995 American aerospace companies exported $3.3 billion worth of products overseas, down from $3.73 billion in 1994. In the mid-1990s, the superpowers no longer competed solely between themselves for the defense- and space-related business of smaller nations. Other nations, such as France, Great Britain, Australia, Canada, China, Germany, and Japan entered this market. The European conglomerate, Arianespace, was the world leader in the production of commercial satellites. In 1995, Japan was the biggest market for U.S. aerospace products.

The change in America's relationship with the former Soviet Union also helped to create a highly competitive international market for commercially operated communication satellites and low-budget commercial satellites. Another factor in creating this market was an economic recession in the early 1990s, which forced smaller nations to invest in joint ventures in science and industry.

RESEARCH AND TECHNOLOGY

With a growing interest in the commercial space market, manufacturers of guided missile and space vehicle propulsion systems were focusing on low-cost technology. Engines that could be manufactured for less money and carry heavier payloads for fewer trips were the goals of the industry's research efforts.

In the early 1990s industry leaders were developing Advanced Launch Systems using cryogenic fuels, as opposed to stored fuels. These systems were also capable of carrying extremely heavy payloads. Another development that met the demand for sending heavy payloads into space was the use of highly successful ballistic missile propulsion units on launch vehicles. In 1993, Lockheed Corp. proposed developing engines for space vehicles similar to its solid- fueled sea-launched missiles.

From the 1970s to the early 1990s, there was strong interest in electronic propulsion systems, but given the cost of this research and the success of solid- fuel systems, research efforts were limited until the 1990s, when cost-cutting objectives renewed interest in this area. According to *Aviation Week and Space Technology,* ''to put payloads into their proper orbits, chemical rockets require more fuel than EP (electronic propulsion) systems to do the same job.'' These systems required burning fuels, but 2 to 3 times less than solid-fueled propulsion systems.

FURTHER READING

The Aerospace Research Center. ''Aerospace Employment Trends, 1962-1995.'' May 1995. Available from http://www.access.digex.net/%7Eaia/emptrd00.htm.

''At a Glance.'' Thiokol Corp. Available from http://www.thiokol.com/AtaGlance/Glance.htm.

Bright, Charles D. *The Jet Makers: The Aerospace Industry 1945-1972.* Lawrence, KS: Regents Press, 1978.

Corcoran, Elizabeth, and Tim Beardsley. ''The New Space Race.'' *Scientific American,* July 1990.

Covault, Craig. ''Ambitious Decade Ahead for Europe's Space Effort.'' *Aviation Week and Space Technolog,* 15 March, 1993.

Dornheim, Michael A. ''USAF May Pay Hercules For SRMU Losses.'' *Aviation Week and Space Technology,* 1 March, 1993.

''Gencorp Aerojet Receives $43.8 Million Product Improvement Contract for SADARM.'' *PR Newswire.* Available from http://www.prnewswire.com/cgi-bin/stories.pl?ACC.

''GenCorp Announces Improved Fourth Quarter Results.'' *PR Newswire.* Available from http://www.prnewswire.com/cgi-bin/stories.pl?ACC.

Hoover's Online. ''Company Capsule.'' Available from http://www.hoovers.com.

Kandebo, Stanley W. ''France Records Advances in Scramjet Program.'' *Aviation Week and Space Technology,* 4 January 1993.

Lavitt, Michael O. ''Market Forces.'' *Aviation Week and Space Technology,* 5 April 1993.

Lenorovitz, Jeffery M. ''Task Force Urges SSME Safety Improvements.'' *Aviation Week and Space Technology,* 8 March 1993.

''Lockheed Develops Low-End Launch Vehicle.'' *Aviation Week and Space Technology,* 10 May 1993.

''McDonnell Douglas Posts Record First-Quarter Earnings.'' *Aviation Week and Space Technology,* 26 April 1993.

Payne, Seth. ''Can't Afford NASA? Call Rent-A-Rocket.'' *Business Week,* 12 March 1990.

''Potential Launch Cost Reduction Spurs Electrical Propulsion Tests.'' *Aviation Week and Space Technology,* 14/21 December 1992.

''Russian Proton Booster Offered in Indonesian Launch Competition.'' *Aviation Week and Space Technology,* 12 April 1993.

Schine, Eric. ''Lockheed Sticks to Its Guns.'' *Business Week,* 26 April 1993.

Scovell, Dawn. ''Solid Rockets.'' *Aerospace America,* December 1992.

''Steady Growth Seen For Commercial Space.'' *Aviation Week and Space Technology,* 15 March 1993.

U.S. Securities and Exchange Commission. ''Annual and Quarterly Reports.'' Available from http://www.sec.gov/cgi-bin/srch-edgar.

—Paola Trimarco, updated by Roxanne Nelson

SIC 3769

SPACE VEHICLE EQUIPMENT, NOT ELSEWHERE CLASSIFIED

This category covers establishments primarily engaged in manufacturing guided missile and space vehicle parts and auxiliary equipment, not elsewhere classified. This industry also includes establishments owned by manufacturers of guided missile and space vehicle parts and auxiliary equipment, not elsewhere classified, and primarily engaged in research and development on such products, whether from enterprise funds or on a contract or fee basis. Establishments primarily engaged in manufacturing navigational and guidance systems are classified in **SIC 3812: Search, Detection, Navigation, Guidance, Aeronautical, and Nautical Systems and Instruments.** Research and development on guided missile and space vehicle parts, on a contract or fee basis by establishments not owned by manufacturers of such products, are classified in **SIC 8731: Commercial Physical and Biological Research.**

Products manufactured by this industry are mostly airframe assemblies for guided missiles, castings for missiles and missile components, nose cones for guided missiles, and space capsules for space vehicles. In the early 1990s, roughly 70 percent of this industry's production went towards manufacturing these types of products and the remaining 30 percent went towards research and development. By 1995, research and development only made up 15 percent of industry production, and manufacturing made up 85 percent.

In 1992, this industry's sales were valued at $1.6 billion, a considerable drop from $1.8 billion in sales in 1988 at the height of the larger aerospace industry's production, and continued to drop through the late 1990s. Sales had dipped to $861 million in 1996, and were projected to keep sliding throughout the rest of the decade. The U.S. government was the industry's largest customer, with over 65 percent of the market

The number of workers in this industry also dropped from 19,400 in 1988 to 17,200 in 1992 to only an estimated 7,800 in 1996. Total employment was projected to continue dropping rapidly over the rest of the decade to only 5,200 in 1998. Production workers made up a majority of workers in 1992, but by 1994 their percentage of total employment had dropped by 66 percent in the case of precision assemblers, and 15 percent in the case of planning and production. The number of computer programmers fell by 31 percent; engineering technicians by 24 percent, and clerical

workers and stock clerks each by about 32 percent. One of the few areas of employment to show growth was nonaeronautical or electrical engineers, which grew by 1.6 percent to lead with 14 percent of all jobs. Systems analyst showed the highest growth, 36 percent, but only controlled a 2 percent share. Other major occupations found in this industry include aeronautical and electrical technicians and astronomical scientists.

The growth and stability of this industry is dependent on manufacturers of complete guided missiles and space vehicles **SIC 3761: Manufacturers of Guided Missiles and Space Vehicles,** who act as primary contractors in the manufacturing of these products. Both industries rely largely on the world political situation that dictates military needs, and since the late 1980s, on the competitiveness of the world market for space exploration and commercial space ventures, mainly in launching communications satellites.

Like other sectors of the aerospace industry, U. S. space vehicle equipment exports far exceed imports. In 1994, this industry exported over $669 million in equipment to overseas markets, a 2 percent decline from the previous year. In the same year, this industry only imported $86 million, up 2.1 percent from the previous year.

In 1996, the industry was led by Intercontinental Manufacturing, with $58 million in sales, followed by Engineering Group Inc. with $54 million in sales, and Alpha Q Inc. with $20 million in sales. Sales for individual companies continued to plummet through the late 1990s as government contracts continued to shrink, with constant dismantling of missiles and reduced spending on space missions.

Research and development for guided missile and space vehicle equipment and auxiliary parts followed the trend of the aerospace industry as a whole in focusing on reduced-cost reusable products. In the early 1990s, new developments to emerge from this industry included pressurized lockers for space research on space shuttles, external vehicle tanks for manned missions, and equipment for materials processing by commercial industries.

FURTHER READING

Asker, James R. "NASA Leases Spacehab for $184 Million for Commercial Experiments on Shuttle." *Aviation Week and Space Technology,* 10 December 1990.

Darnay, Arsen J., ed. *Manufacturing USA.* 5th ed. Detroit: Gale Research, 1996.

Kolcum, Edward H. "Martin Marietta Poised to Adapt External Tank for NLS Core Vehicles." *Aviation Week and Space Technology,* 26 August 1991.

Lavitt, Michael O. "Market Focus." *Aviation Week and Space Technology,* 5 April 1993.

SIC 3792

TRAVEL TRAILERS AND CAMPERS

This industry consists of establishments primarily engaged in the manufacture of travel trailers and chassis and campers for attachment to motor vehicles, pick-up coaches and caps, covers and canopies for mounting on pick-up trucks, and tent camping trailers. This classification includes travel trailers of up to 35 feet long and 8 feet wide (with storage facilities for waste and water), but excludes mobile home manufacturers. Mobile home manufacturers are classified in **SIC 3716: Motor Homes.**

INDUSTRY SNAPSHOT

There are approximately 70 U.S. establishments in this industry. Most are private subsidiaries of companies that manufacture a range of recreational vehicles. Manufacturers of trailers and campers often assemble chassis made elsewhere on to their products; these chassis are produced by large auto makers such as Ford Motor Co. and General Motors.

BACKGROUND AND DEVELOPMENT

Travel trailers and pick-up cabs were introduced in the early 1930s, with camper attachments entering the market in the late 1940s. The emergence of mobile homes, also in the late 1940s, shifted manufacturers' emphasis away from travel trailers and camper attachments. However, while mobile homes dominated the recreational vehicle market in the 1950s and 1960s, the market for travel trailers and camper attachments continued to grow.

The economic recessions of the 1970s and 1980s dramatically reduced sales and manufacturing in this industry. Also, during that time some travel trailer and chassis producers were negatively effected by recalls of their products; over 10,000 units of small mobile homes attached to Toyota pick-up truck chassis were recalled.

The future for the industry was an uncertain one. The recreational vehicle field is an increasingly competitive and crowded one. Some analysts felt that the continued development of other types of recreational vehicles bode ill for this segment of the transportation manufacturing industry. Richard Rescigno of *Barron's,* however, predicted that sales of small campers

and travel trailers might actually improve in the 1990s since such products were at the inexpensive end of the recreational vehicle market. Rescigno reasoned that such products would appeal to the growing number of retirees on limited incomes.

Upon entering the 1990s, this industry's tow-trailer leaders included Fleetwood Enterprises Inc., with approximately 20 percent of the market, followed by a pack of other companies jockeying for position in the 5 to 8 percent market share range. These establishments include Jayco Inc., Skyline Corp., Coachmen Industries Inc., Starcraft Corporation, and Mallard Coach Company, Inc.

Just as Rescigno had predicted, motor home sales rose sharply as retail figures went up by 19.4 percent from September 1992. Recreational vehicle (RV) trailers also posted a 15 percent gain in overall sales for September 1993. The growth trend continued into the mid-1990s with sales of RV trailers and motor homes growing by 18.8 and 16 percent to 13,962 units and 3,423 units,respectively, for the first half of 1994.

Sales for RV trailers and motor homes accounted for 3,575 units and 541 units in 1994. The continued growth trend was attributed to strong sales in the east north central region and west north central region of the United States. RV shipments increased by 2.7 percent in May 1994 as compared to May 1993.

CURRENT CONDITIONS

America's increasing demand for travel trailers and motor homes continued into the mid-1990s. This growth was attributed to the nation's growing population of aging baby boomers. People between the ages of 55 and 65 accounted for much the industry sales. Sales were expected to grow over the next ten years.

In June 1995, the Recreational Vehicle Industry Association (RVIA) gave its final approval to an RV weight labelling requirement. Motorhomes, travel trailers, fifth-wheels and folding camping trailers would be required to comply. Truck campers and conversion vehicles were exempted from this requirement.

By the mid-1990s the state of Indiana had the distinction of being the RV capital of the world, producing 49.8 percent of all RVs in the country. During the mid-1990s, according to the *Tribune Business Weekly,* the total retail value of the industry nationwide was $9.5 billion, with $4.5 billion being generated from the production in Indiana.

INDUSTRY LEADERS

Fleetwood Enterprises Inc. of Riverside, California, was the industry leader with 1996 sales revenues of $2.8 billion. Fleetwod employed about 18,000 people and was ahead of the second lead by approximately $2.1 billion in sales revenue. Known as the "Big Guy" in the industry, Fleetwood was the only Fortune 500 company in Riverside and rolled out about 50 RVs out of its California plants alone.

Skyline Corp. of Indiana was the second when ranked by its sales revenue, which was $645.9 million, and employed about 3,600 people. Thor Industries of Ohio was a close third with 1996 sales of $602.1 million and 2,670 employees. Coachmen Industries Inc. of Indiana had sales of $515.9 million, while Gillig Corp. of Hayward, California, posted 1996 sales of $225 million.

FURTHER READING

Callahan, Joseph M. "Winnebago's Hanson: Building Up, Up, Up." *Automotive Industries,* November 1984.

Crider, Jeff. "National RV Reports 96% Income Jump." *Press Enterprise,* 23 September 1994.

Longsdorf Jr., Robert. "RVIA Board OK's Labelling, Market Expansion Plan." *RV Business,* August 1995, 7.

McLane, Alice. "RV Production Just Keeps Rolling Along." *Tribune Business Weekly,* 30 November 1994.

Rescigno, Richard. "Revved Up For Recovery: Recreational-Vehicle Makers Seem Ready To Roll Again." *Barron's* 17 June 1991.

"RV Market Travels Steady Road in May." *RV Business,* August 1994, 42.

Smith, Rosalind. "Stepping Out of the Big Guy's Shadow." *Press Enterprise,* 23 May 1994, sD 1.

———. "Strong Growth Marks Industry Sales for the First Half of 1994." *RV Business,* October 1994, 42.

Walworth, Thomas. "Industry Strength builds in September." *RV Business,* January 1994, 36.

—Paola Trimarco, updated by Visi Tilak

SIC 3795

TANKS AND TANK COMPONENTS

This category covers establishments primarily engaged in manufacturing complete tanks, specialized components for tanks, and self-propelled weapons. Establishments primarily engaged in manufacturing military vehicles, except tanks and self propelled weapons, are classified in **SIC 3710: Motor Vehicles and Motor Vehicle Equipment,** and those manufacturing tank engines are classified in **SIC 3510: International Combustion Engines, Not Elsewhere Classified.**

INDUSTRY SNAPSHOT

The end of the Cold War has reduced U.S. tank production to almost nothing. From a peak of about 900 new tanks produced each year in 1987-88, no new tanks were being built in the United States in 1996-97. The only work being done was upgrading of older tanks with new equipment at the rate of about 120 tanks per year. Nor were foreign countries picking up the slack. Although orders were anticipated in the post-2000 era from Denmark, Turkey, and Greece, no tank production was underway in the mid- to late 1990s for any of America's allies. This drop in production has resulted in the consolidation and closure of many defense-related manufacturers and subcontractors with further structural adjustments needed to accommodate the proposed cutbacks.

The two largest U.S. tank manufacturers, General Dynamics Corporation of Virginia and FMC Corporation of Illinois, have adopted different corporate strategies to survive in this uncertain environment. General Dynamics has continued to focus its business on defense contracting, filling such key niches as nuclear submarines for the Navy and a new amphibious vehicle for the Marine Corps. FMC Corporation, on the other hand, has pursued a diversification strategy into performance chemicals and machine and equipment.

ORGANIZATION AND STRUCTURE

The tank manufacturing and component industry has relied mostly on government procurement trends to fund both the development and production of military armor. With few exceptions, defense manufacturers are privately held. Most of the contracts issued by the U.S. Department of Defense are fixed-price contracts that cover both the research/development and production of armored vehicles. These contracts have been problematic for manufacturers because they require considerable investment during the development stage. Traditionally, even though many of these contracts are multi-year and provide compensation if cancelled, such payments usually do not cover the price of new machinery and plants. As a result, there has been a consolidation of players in the defense industry, with many manufacturers having to shed facilities and workers to remain competitive in an uncertain defense-spending environment.

Plants that manufacture tanks and tank components vary between those that are contractor owned and others that are government owned and contractor operated. In the latter case, a plant may close but the facilities remain for possible future mobilization. It is extremely expensive, however, to mothball such facilities and then reopen them.

The only tank production plant still active in the United States during the mid-1990s was the General Dynamics facility in Lima, Ohio, operated by the company's Land Systems Division. General Dynamics closed its other tank facility, in Sterling Heights, Michigan, in December 1996. By the time the Detroit facility closed, manufacturing employment there had shrunk to fewer than 100 workers, from a high of about 2,500 a decade earlier. The Lima plant was capable of assembling completed tanks as well as producing tank components. While the Lima plant was responsible for the assembly of the M1A1 and M1A2 tanks, it relied on countless subcontractors across the United States to supply it with key components in the tank assembly process. By 1997, the plant in Lima was upgrading about 120 older tanks a year for the U.S. Army, the sole tank production work being done at that time. Long-range plans to develop the next-generation Block III tank were scrapped for budgetary reasons in the early '90s. Some long-range planning was underway but no completely new tanks were expected to be produced until after the year 2010 at the earliest.

BACKGROUND AND DEVELOPMENT

The tank, a British invention from World War I, had the mission of advancing on the static German defense lines in northern France. It was developed to flatten thick coils of barbed wire, fend off machine-gun fire, and to rumble over previously inviolable trenches. In short, the tank was to do what great waves of infantry men had failed to do—break the stalemate of trench warfare.

The tank performed as required during World War I, but was viewed by most strategists as merely a precursor to infantry attack. That sentiment was ultimately put to rest by the German *blitzkrieg* into Poland in September of 1939, when a Polish brigade of cavalry vainly attacked an onrushing wedge of German tanks.

In June of 1920, the U.S. National Defense Act was passed into law. This act disbanded the army's tank corps, a unit created three years previously, and placed all tanks under the command of the infantry branch. Further, the act stipulated that no new branch of the army, such as a revived tank corps, could be created without congressional approval. This decision was based on the army's conclusion that the tank corps had failed to provide either a doctrine or a justification for itself as an independent arm of the American war effort.

The early perception was that the tank-based armies of the twentieth century were slower then the foot soldier's marching rate of a century before. This spec-

ulation concerning tank warfare inhibited its role as a support weapon for the infantry for years.

Following World War I, the most plausible threat to U.S. security was a naval war in the Pacific against Japan. In the following decade, Congress reduced the military budget. Senior officers cut costs by halting production and maintenance of equipment. Inevitably, tanks suffered from this policy, and the U.S. Army had no large tank formations during this inter-war period.

The beginning of the mechanization of the U.S. Army began in 1928 after Secretary of War Dwight D. Davies observed the British Army's Experimental Mechanical Armed Force. In response, the United States developed the Christie, complete with a modern suspension system and capable of speeds approaching 40 miles per hour. It was during this period that the war department recognized that the development of future armies depended on the proliferation of a mechanized force. The tank was, for the first time, perceived as an offensive power in its own right.

In the spring of 1939, America's main battle tanks were still the M1917 and the Mark VIII of World War I vintage. In the previous several years the army had produced several hundred tanks, the majority being experimental models of light tanks armored with only machine guns. Although some effort had been made to keep the United States abreast of mechanized warfare, until the outbreak of World War II the American experience of armor hardly existed.

Following the collapse of France in June of 1940, Congress passed a munitions program to provide material for an army of 1.2 million. Supplemental defense appropriations acts authorized $5 billion for armed forces expenditure. By the end of 1940, the country had produced only 331 tanks. By the end of 1941, it had outproduced Germany with 4,052 tanks, while tank production for the next two years was 24,997 and 29,497 tanks respectively. By the end of the war in Europe, American industry had produced 88,410 tanks, of which 57,027 were medium tanks. More than 8,000 subcontractors working in some 850 different towns and cities throughout the United States had a hand in the production of these tanks.

By 1943, the U.S. Army had created 16 armored divisions and 65 independent tank battalions. Each of these armored divisions consisted of 10,937 men and 2,650 vehicles, of which 248 were tanks. Tanks were used as a highly mobile force for pursuit, exploitation, and disruption of unarmored forces, rather than as an arm of attack against other armored formations. This doctrine had important consequences for American tank design and development. The first of the wartime tanks, the M3 Stuart light tank and M3 Grant/Lee medium tank, were developed from pre-war designs. The main American battle tank of the war, the M4 Sherman, was first planned in March of 1941 and produced a year later. Weighing approximately 33 tons and equipped with a 75mm dual-purpose gun, it was highly maneuverable and reliable and boasted a road speed of just under 30 miles per hour (mph).

The U.S. responded to Germany's Panther and Tiger tanks by producing the M26 Pershing. This tank held a 90mm gun, weighed 42.5 tons, and had a top speed of 25 mph. This tank, however, played a relatively small role in the war because it had less speed and maneuverability than the M4 Sherman and because tactical air power was generally used to halt the German armored thrust. By 1947, due to the success of air power and the invention of atomic weapons, the role of the tank had again come into question.

During the Korean War, American tanks proved less than perfect. The M26 Pershing was underpowered for Korea's mountainous terrain, and the army at first was compelled to rely upon its Shermans. The army eventually added the more powerful M46 and M47 Patton tanks to its lineup. In fact, the Korean War confirmed the tank's role as an essential part of the U.S. fighting forces. The heavier armor developed during this conflict changed the tank's principal role to fighting and destroying other tanks.

Throughout the 1950s and early 1960s, the U.S. Army continued to regard its armored forces as central to its fighting doctrine. When U.S. forces were committed to Vietnam in 1965, however, armor had a reduced role. Still, the M48 tanks' firepower and mobility were valuable assets in creating quick reaction teams for preventing infiltration by enemy units. But to work well, the teams had to be part of an all-arms formation; without helicopters, air and artillery support, and infantry, the armored units could be unwieldy, noisy, and less then effective. Tank battalions successfully carried out roles such as route security, convoy escort, and border protection.

There were no major developments in the tanks industry during the 1970s. The anti-war movement of the late 1960s and early 1970s—coupled with the perception that the United States had fought a losing battle—resulted in the redeployment of government resources into domestic endeavors. In 1980, however, President Reagan vowed to rearm America with an unprecedented $1.6 trillion defense spending program over the next six years. The Defense Department's renewed interest in planning and multi-year funding of contracts boosted the sagging defense industry. The tanks and tank component sector of the defense industry was expected to grow by 12.6 percent over this period with nondefense growth hovering at 4.5 percent.

The army's M-1 tank benefited greatly from the increased defense expenditures. A heavy tank with a combat load of 54.5 tons, the M-1 was able to carry a crew of four and had a maximum speed of 45 mph on the road and 30 mph cross country. The tank's road range stood at 275 miles and it main armament was a 105mm gun. The M-1 tank was criticized for transmission malfunctions and the need for frequent maintenance of other components during the test process. In addition, the M-1 was found to be incapable of digging itself into a hull-down battle position without the assistance of bulldozers. Nonetheless, the Defense Department budgeted for 7,058 M-1s at a cost of roughly $19 billion.

By 1986, defense budget outlays had grown to $200 million annually. These high levels of defense spending stimulated many U.S. industries. In 1986, 75 sectors of the economy produced at least 5 percent of output for defense purposes and 13 sectors produced at least 30 percent of output for delivery to the U.S. Department of Defense. The passage of the Gramm-Rudman deficit reduction bill, as well as reduced government research and development budgets, however, resulted in declines in defense production throughout the remainder of the 1980s.

CURRENT CONDITIONS

The multi-year structure of rearmature programs from the 1980s temporarily insulated the defense industry from budget cuts. In the wake of reduced defense expenditures, many manufacturers began to look to foreign markets to maintain and expand their production base

The trend toward private venture projects and cooperative agreements with foreign countries is necessary for the survival of U.S. defense manufacturers. General Dynamics, for example, expects to build between 500 and 1,000 tanks for Turkey between 2000 and 2010. This joint venture operation will see the tanks designed here but both components and final assembly taking place jointly in both countries. General Dynamics also expects to produce between 200 and 500 tanks for Greece in the period after 1999.

Significant events in the 1990s that had a major impact on defense forces and their supporting industries included: the departure of Soviet forces from Eastern Europe; the dismantling of the Warsaw Pact; the reunification of East and West Germany; the successful eviction of Iraq from Kuwait by the Allied coalition forces; and various United Nations peace-keeping efforts. The very success of Operation Desert Storm prompted questioning in the U.S. legislature about the rationale behind developing new, costly weapons systems. (The ground war lasted just 100 hours with little loss of life or equipment on the Allied Coalition side while Iraqi forces suffered massive losses in both men and equipment.)

INDUSTRY LEADERS

General Dynamics Corporation, the Falls Church, Virginia-based company is among the nation's largest defense contractors and produces a wide range of major weapons systems for all branches of the armed forces. In 1992 the company had approximately $3 billion in military sales. In 1996, this figure was up to $5 billion. Of this total, the vast majority was to the U.S. government with the remainder to foreign countries. By the mid-1990s, the company had concentrated its defense work in a few key areas: nuclear submarines, surface ships, radios, and armored vehicles. The company's Land Systems division produced the upgraded M1A2 battle tank, radios for the army, and was working on the Advanced Amphibious Assault Vehicle for the Marine Corps.

Chicago-based FMC Corporation produces the Bradley armored tank. FMC recently merged with Harsco Corporation in a 60-40 venture that combined their defense businesses. The new company's products include armored tanks, artillery systems, and naval guns.

Subcontractors make up the remainder of the industry players in the tank and tank components industry. This group includes not only many of the top ten defense manufacturers, but also hundreds of smaller entities that produce more specialized and highly sophisticated subsystem equipment.

WORK FORCE

In the tank and tank components industry, approximately 25 percent of the plant labor force is directly engaged in production, while the remaining 75 percent is engaged in management and support functions.

AMERICA AND THE WORLD

The United States' tank and tank components industry is the largest and most technically advanced in the world. The health of the industry is closely tied to its ability to forge international cooperative agreements with larger arms-producing countries such as Russia, Germany, Britain, France, and China and to increase foreign military sales of tanks and tank con-

version kits. The reduction in the U.S. military budget has had a direct impact on the ability of defense manufacturers to compete in foreign markets. Foreign sales of tank and tank components are an essential element in the survival of U.S. tank production facilities. In order to achieve this goal, the industry requires a sound and profitable production base to invest in the future and to maintain current cost/pricing levels. By protecting the industrial base, the United States will be able to honor pricing levels in completed foreign tank sales contracts and to assure foreigners of the U.S. manufacturers' ability to meet future demand at competitive pricing levels.

RESEARCH AND TECHNOLOGY

Research and development funding in the tank industry has suffered along with production as defense spending dwindled. That which continues focuses on upgrades of systems dealing with targeting and night vision. Much of the production in the defense industries is inherently inefficient because high volume, mass production techniques are not applicable. Except for the turret and hull components of a tank, most of the production involves small batch processing of relatively complex items with frequent modifications or changes in design. In this type of low volume manufacturing, specialized equipment is under utilized and inventories are relatively high.

Although computer-aided automation has moved slowly into the tank production process, computer-controlled machine tools are standard fixtures in machining operations. Examples of these processes include automated spray systems used for coating metals; automated inspection and optical measuring systems; and computer-aided manufacturing applications used for forging and electron beam welding in tank production. Other areas of the production process which have been computerized consist of process modelling, performance measurement, and on-line production information systems.

Many of the technological changes that have taken place in tank manufacturing involve metalworking. Automated metal cutting systems are in place that use computer-controlled laser machining techniques. Computer-integrated welding systems are in place that make use of sensory process controls. The technology is available to transform the manufacturing system of tank production facilities into a totally computer-integrated process, but the economies of scale associated with expensive outlays in plant and equipment have deterred the manufacturers from pursuing this option.

In the mid-1990s, main battle tanks possessed nuclear, biological, and chemical (NBC) systems that regulate the environment within the tank in case of this type of warfare. The Department of Defense has made land navigational systems a priority for improvement and installation in all tank subsystems. In the wake of Operation Desert Storm, more emphasis was placed in the development of friend or foe devices to reduce friendly fire causalities. Such technology would become a part of the tank's vehicle protection system, which already includes threat displays, sensors, and decoy launchers.

Other areas of research include ways to construct smaller and lighter main battle tanks, armored turrets to protect the vulnerable top of the tank, development of more powerful cannons, experimentation into a common chassis for futuristic combat vehicles, guns that will utilize electromagnetic and electrothermal cannons. Electromagnetic guns use electric currents as their power source and can power a round farther and faster than a conventional cannon. Electrothermal guns use hot gases and a high-energy charge to propel artillery with comparable results.

FURTHER READING

Baker, Caleb. "Army Weapon Budget Shortfall Hits Armor Modernization Plan Budget." *Defense News,* 1990.

———. "Revised ASM Plan Emphasizes Support Vehicles Over Tanks." *Defense News,* 1991.

Belloc, Hilaire. *The Elements of the Great War.* Hearts International Library Company, 1970.

Egyptian Defense Minister on Arms Production and Purchases. The British Broadcasting Corporation, 1987.

"Employment, More Than 334,000 Jobs Were Lost In Defense-Related Industries Since 1986." *Daily Report For Executives,* 1993.

"General Dynamic Gets First Egyptian M1A1 Coproduction Contract." *Aerospace Daily,* 1989.

Graham, George, and Martin Dickson. "U.S. Rethinks Arms Procurement Philosophy." *Financial Times,* 1992.

Humble, Richard. *Tanks.* Weidenfeld & Nicolson, 1977.

"Industrial Base, Pentagon Report Projects Defense Spending by Industry, State." *Federal Contracts Report,* 1991.

"Is Industry Ready For Defense Buildup?" *Business Week,* 1982.

Jane's Armour and Artillery. London: Janes Info Group, 1987.

Kelly, Orr. *King of the Killing Zone.* New York: W.W. Norton, 1989.

"Levin Says Warren Tank Plant Threatened." United Press International, 1988.

Mackay, Robert. "Saudi Arabia to Buy 315 Next-generation Tanks." United Press International, 1990.

Middleton, Drew. "British Expert Says M-1 Tank May Be Hailed As Innovation." *New York Times,* 1982.

Morrison, David. "Base Concerns-As the Services Scale Back Their Weapon Buys, The Health of the Defense Industrial Base Is Bound to Suffer." *Government Executive,* 1992.

Munro, Neil. "U.S. Army Hurries Tank Upgrade Plans." *Defense News,* 1992.

"Pentagon Issues Report Projecting Defense Spending Industry-By-Industry." *Daily Report For Executives,* 1991.

Silverberg, David. "U.S. Army Tank Cuts Put Foreign Sales in Doubt." *Defense News,* 1990.

Simpkin, Richard. *Tank Warfare: An Analysis of Soviet and Nato Tank Philosophy.* New York: Crane Russak, 1979.

"Take Time For Take Research." *Defense News,* 1990.

"Turkey: U.S. Tank." *Defense and Foreign Affairs,* 1986.

"U.N. Lists Big Tank Imports By Greece and Turkey." Reuters, Limited, 1993.

—Andrew Burke, updated by John Gallagher

SIC 3799

TRANSPORTATION EQUIPMENT, NOT ELSEWHERE CLASSIFIED

This industry consists of establishments primarily engaged in manufacturing transportation equipment, not elsewhere classified. The transportation equipment classified under this industry includes specialty vehicles and all-terrain vehicles for military, industrial and agricultural purposes; towing bars and systems and trailers for transporting animals; recreational vehicles, such as snowmobiles, water jet-skis, golf carts and recreational all-terrain vehicles; boat trailers; and wheelbarrows. Associated establishments involved in manufacturing industrial vehicles are discussed in **SIC 3537: Industrial Trucks, Tractors, Trailers, and Stackers.**

In 1996, the leading establishments in this industry all had interests in different divisions within the industry. Polaris Industries, L.P., a snowmobile and recreational all-terrain vehicle manufacturer, led the entire industry with $11.4 billion in sales, more than twice the sales of its nearest competitor. TriMas Corp., a manufacturer of industrial trailer system products, ranked second in sales within the industry bringing in $536 million. Club Car Inc., a manufacturer of golf carts and recreational vehicles, had $186 million in sales.

All-terrain vehicles, built with wide tires for driving over difficult terrain and road conditions, are produced primarily for military purposes. For this reason, the prosperity and growth of this segment of the industry is dependent on government defense spending. With the decreases in defense spending for the 1990s, manufacturers of all-terrain vehicles began to diversify. Oshkosh Truck Corp., which had 1991 sales of over $600 million (due mainly to the Persian Gulf War), responded to a reduction in military orders and defense spending proposals by diversifying into hauling trucks and cement mixers. Its revenues, after a brief slowdown, went up again to $437 million in 1996 due to its diversification efforts.

All-terrain vehicles, including military and recreational, accounted for more than 50 percent of the industry market share. Automobile and light truck trailers accounted for 23 percent. People-movers—items such as golf carts, electric or gas powered carts, or industrial personnel carriers—held 14 percent of the division, with miscellaneous items such as wheelbarrows, trailer hitches, and parts holding the final 12 percent.

All-terrain recreational vehicles carried only a small portion of the recreational vehicle market, and snowmobiles dominated that particular section of the market. In 1954, Polaris Industries, L.P. became the first American manufacturer to produce snowmobiles. In the United States, snowmobile sales reached their peak in 1971, having over 500,000 sold. In the late 1970s and early 1980s, snowmobile sales decreased dramatically, the "victims of higher energy costs, recessions, a few snowless winters, and a serious rash of overbuilding by manufacturers," said *Forbes*. By 1983 only 87,000 snowmobiles were sold in the United States. At the beginning of the 1990s, sales figures and profits began to increase again, with Polaris' revenues almost doubling between 1994 and 1996.

FURTHER READING

Byrne, Harlan S. "Oshkosh Truck Corp.: A Bright Outlook Despite Pentagon Cutbacks." *Barron's,* 20 January 1992.

Darnay, Arsen J., ed. *Manufacturing USA.* 5th ed. Detroit: Gale Research, 1996.

Dubashi, Jagannath. "Designer Trucks." *Financial World,* 18 May 1987.

Harris, John. "Noisemakers." *Forbes,* 29 October 1990.

"Kawasaki's Newest Addition is Stubborn as a Mule 4X4." *Purchasing,* 14 September 1989.

Winter, Don. "Air Cushion Vehicle Looks for a Federally Funded Niche." *Traffic World,* 18 September 1989.

MEASURING, ANALYZING, & CONTROLLING INSTRUMENTS

SEARCH, DETECTION, NAVIGATION, GUIDANCE, AERONAUTICAL, AND NAUTICAL SYSTEMS AND INSTRUMENTS

This category includes establishments primarily engaged in manufacturing search, detection, navigation, guidance, aeronautical, and nautical systems and instruments. Important products of this industry are radar systems and equipment; sonar systems and equipment; navigation systems and equipment; countermeasures equipment; aircraft and missile control systems and equipment; flight and navigation sensors, transmitters, and displays; gyroscopes; airframe equipment instruments; and speed, pitch, and roll navigational instruments and systems. Establishments primarily engaged in manufacturing aircraft engine instruments or meteorological systems and equipment, including weather tracking equipment, are classified in **SIC 3829: Measuring and Controlling Devices, Not Elsewhere Classified.**

INDUSTRY SNAPSHOT

In 1996, more than 220 companies in the United States were involved in the manufacture of search and navigation systems and instruments. Together these companies generated $76.73 billion in sales and employed 501,700.

The search and navigation industry experienced declines in shipments in the early 1990s due to decreased defense budgets, the end of the Cold War, diminished commercial aircraft industry purchases, and a recessionary economy. Sharp reductions in the military-related expenditures that formed the back-

bone of industry profits hastened restructuring and globalization trends and continued to negatively impact the industry. Nevertheless, the United States was expected to continue leading the world in new technology in this market throughout the 1990s. The market will, however, be buoyed by increasing demand for these products from the civilian sector. Especially important will be those instruments relating to Global Positioning Systems (GPS) and innovative automobile navigation and safety systems. The decrease in overall demand is expected to spur competitiveness as companies fight for market share and market niches. The export market is expected to be driven by orders from Russia, Singapore, China, South Korea, Canada, Turkey, and India as these countries upgrade existing aircraft radar and navigation systems rather than investing in new hardware.

ORGANIZATION AND STRUCTURE

With few exceptions, the principle suppliers of search and navigation equipment are the same contractors who comprise the larger U.S. aerospace industry. The search and navigation equipment industry accounted for about one-quarter of aerospace industry shipments ($129 billion) in the early 1990s, which in turn represented about two-thirds of the worldwide aerospace industry. Many of the largest and most recognizable corporations in the United States—including AT&T, Boeing, Chrysler, General Electric, General Motors, and IBM—manufacture search and navigation industry products for the domestic and international defense and commercial markets.

Along with such aerospace sectors as the business and commercial jet, helicopter, aircraft maintenance, and spare parts industries, the search and navigation industry comprises a so-called "niche segment" of the larger aerospace manufacturing group. A substantial majority of the industry's product types fall into the avionics (aviation electronics) product classification, which includes aeronautic radar systems, air traffic control systems, weaponry sighting and fire control systems, and autopilots. Product groups traditionally associated with the avionics industry but excluded from the search and navigation industry include flight trainers and simulators, which are included in **SIC 3699: Electrical Machinery, Equipment, and Supplies, Not Elsewhere Classified;** and radio communications equipment and telemetry systems and equipment, which is classified under **SIC 3663: Radio and Television Broadcasting and Communications Equipment.** Conversely, product groups classified as search and navigation industry products but excluded from the avionics industry's product mix include such nautical instruments as fathometers, hydrophones, sonabuoys, marine sextants, sonar fish finders and other sonar systems, and taffrail logs (i.e., torpedo-shaped instruments dragged behind ships to determine distance traveled or speed).

Historically, the primary customer for industry products has been the U.S. government and in particular the Department of Defense, Federal Aviation Authority, and National Aeronautics and Space Administration. Industry sales to commercial establishments adhere to the traditional terms and conditions of the business marketplace, and products are evaluated in terms of competitive value for technical superiority, reputation, price, delivery schedule, financing, and reliability. Sales to the federal government, however, tend to follow a highly specialized and structured set of procedures.

Government procurement. Funds for government search and navigation equipment contracts are authorized by Congress based on budget requests submitted by the executive branch for the agency or department requiring the equipment. Congress appropriates specific funding for programs on an annual basis, which often means that programs originally approved for development over several years are subject to adjustments or outright cancellation on a yearly basis. Contractors submit bids to government officials at bidding conferences attended by "prime" contractors—firms or consortia who submit the final integrated system directly to the end-user agency—and subcontractors who attend the conferences to seek out prime contractors with whom to team.

Contracts may be awarded to a single contractor in a "winner-take-all" competition or divided among several contractors or consortia as a percentage of the total awarded contract. Contracts may cover specific phases of the product development process: the concept/design or project definition stage, the prototype or demonstration/validation stage, or the execution or large-scale production stage. Government contracts are also awarded according to the method by which the contractor is paid. In cost reimbursement contracts, the contractor is paid for allowable or "allocable" costs such as engineering and manufacturing expenses, special tooling and test equipment costs, marketing and administrative expenditures, and the cost of the bid proposal itself. Cost plus fixed fee contracts involve payments to the contractor by the government of a preestablished fee regardless of the firm's actual final costs. Such contracts award contractors who deliver systems below the contracted price and penalize contractors who experience cost overruns. In cost plus incentive fee contracts, the government reimburses the contractor based on the firm's ability to meet certain targets such as cost guidelines, "mission success" parameters, and delivery time constraints. The average industry "win rate"—the ratio of contracts awarded to total contracts bid on—is about 25 percent in the aerospace and thus the search and navigation industry as a whole. Some firms, however, achieve win rates nearly twice as high.

Contractors are generally paid through periodic "progress payments" for work performed, with a final payment for remaining costs paid upon delivery of the product. Contracts may be extended through "replenishment" and "follow on" orders by the government customer and may be terminated without cause at the sole discretion of the government. Disputes regarding unpaid or overpaid amounts are handled by a Defense Contract Management District Termination Contracting Officer to whom settlement proposals are submitted by the contractor for claimed expenses and "termination costs." The Contracting Officer may award the contractor funds for work performed prior to the contract's termination or may require that the contractor reimburse funds paid out for canceled work.

The "monopsonic"—or single customer—nature of the government procurement market has led to a unique division of operations in the search and navigation industry: one set of rules and procedures for commercial clients and a second, completely segregated set of rules and procedures for government contracts. The purpose of the complex government procurement apparatus is to protect the government's interest in fair and reasonable prices, to eliminate contractor fraud, to ensure equal access by all bidders, and to guarantee that federal funds appropriated for government contracts reflect the economic and social priorities of the government. As a result, the process of bidding on federal contracts entails separate data collection and accounting procedures, conformance to supplier network requirements, adherence to hiring and personnel guidelines, and the disclosure of the contractor's corporate financial information to government auditors. These and other requirements regarding contractor certification and auditing and oversight conformance have resulted in historical labor costs for the industry three times higher for federal contracts (as a percentage of sales) than for equivalent commercial contracts.

Procurement agencies. Several government agencies perform oversight and other procurement-related functions that directly affect search and navigation industry activities. The Defense Contract Audit Agency oversees expense, scheduling, and product performance reviews of industry contractors and specifies guidelines for planning and implementing federal contracts. The Government Accounting Office (GAO) and Office of Federal Procurement Policy of the Office of Management and Budget perform watchdog reviews of government contracts. "First tier" contractors—firms whose products are delivered directly to a prime contractor—may experience as many as 100 government audits in a single year for pricing, quality, and safety reviews. Similarly, an "operational readiness review" administered by a defense department branch can involve as many as 50 auditors assigned to a single contractor plant at one time.

Contractors may be temporarily suspended or permanently debarred from bidding on government contracts if they are found to be in violation of employment practice laws, standard accounting procedures, or product pricing guidelines. A contractor, for example, who falsely claims that a delivered product has passed more tests than it actually has may be given a "not a responsible contractor" designation and debarred from government bids. In 1989, the GAO guaranteed Litton Industries, a producer of guidance and control systems, a percentage of a production contract for a radar warning receiver when it determined that Loral Corporation had improperly obtained a Litton briefing book outlining Litton's estimated costs. Four years later, the GAO was asked to reconsider a contract awarded to Westinghouse Electric for an anti-submarine warfare sonar system because the contract had been awarded based on a bid that was almost 50 percent lower than the actual cost that the contract's other bidder had incurred for the same work the previous year. Improper enhancement of a product's capabilities in order to inflate the contractor's bill is termed "goldplating" and represents another significant area

of potential abuse that government procurement oversight agencies are charged to monitor.

Other agencies, such as the Navy's Operational Test and Evaluation Force and the Department of Defense's Operational Test and Evaluation Office, perform the tests that gauge the delivered system's adherence to contracted performance specifications. Federal projects like the Army's Contractor Performance Certification Program recognize contractors who consistently deliver quality products, and the NASA-funded National Technology Transfer Center serves as a medium for sharing federal research project advances with firms in the industry.

Prime contractors vs. subcontractors. In 1984, in response to concerns that government contracts were inadequately available to all potential contractors, Congress passed the Competition in Contracting Act, which liberalized the eligibility qualifications of firms submitting bids on federal contracts. Despite such legislation, a senior official of a flight controls subcontractor testified before Congress in 1989 that government procurement policies were freezing subcontractors out of the federal defense market. He cited "decreased progress payment rates, unreasonable profit ceilings . . . the criminalization of honest mistakes . . . overzealous audits and increased oversight procedures" as factors preventing subcontractors from competing profitably for government contracts.

Establishments in the search and navigation industry can be classified in terms of their place in the product delivery hierarchy for government procurement contracts. The major prime contractors dominate the industry and are themselves the greatest source of competition for the subcontractors. The influence prime contractors have on subcontractors' profits is reflected in the announcement in the early 1990s by a major prime contractor, Allied Signal, that it planned to reduce its pool of 9,500 suppliers by 79 percent in just two years. Historically, about half of the worth of government contracts to prime contractors is channeled through subcontracts with firms supplying the "primes," and of this amount roughly 50 percent is divided between divisions of other prime contractors and the smaller subcontractors. Government procurement trends fluctuate between an emphasis on "single sourcing"—awarding whole contracts to a major prime contractor—and "multiple sourcing"— distributing procurement funds more evenly through the industry structure.

Business environment. The unique nature of the government procurement environment entails business trends uncommon in other U.S. industries. Although industry profit rates as a percentage of sales have historically been less than for other industries, profits measured in terms of rate of return on investment are comparable to rates enjoyed by other manufacturing sectors. Search and navigation firms, like other defense sector businesses, may invest in plants and equipment at half the rate of firms in other industries because government contracts often reimburse firms for aging or obsolescent equipment, make available government-owned plants and equipment to the contractor, and offer no guarantee that the plant or equipment utilized for the procured product will ever be contracted for again. Moreover, government progress payments generally cover only "certified costs" and make few allowances for contractor investment in new facilities. Like members of other defense industries, search and navigation contractors require less working capital because they can rely on regular government progress payments instead of depending on unpredictable commercial revenues.

The search and navigation industry is subject to business risks not shared by other American industries. These include unusually high costs for obtaining skilled employees, intense domestic and international competition, continual need to retrain employees and retool facilities, inevitable cost overruns resulting from untried technologies and advanced designs, and instability in the price of raw materials and supplies. Because defense-related products are driven by the requirement of continuing technological improvement and superiority, the rate of obsolescence for industry products is much higher and much more unpredictable than in other American industries.

Product Groups. Search and navigation products can be divided into two broad divisions and several subcategories. Search and detection systems and navigation and guidance systems and equipment ($31.76 billion in early 1990s shipments) constitute about 90 percent of the total search and navigation market and include the following product groups: light reconnaissance and surveillance systems; identification-friend-or-foe equipment; proximity fuses; radar systems and equipment; sonar search, detection, tracking, and communications equipment; specialized command and control data processing and display equipment; electronic warfare systems and equipment; and navigation systems and equipment, including navigational aids for aircraft, ships, and navigation applications.

The remaining 10 percent of the industry's market ($2.66 billion in the early 1990s) consists of aeronautical, nautical, and navigational instruments (excluding aircraft engine instruments) and includes the following product groups: flight and navigation sensors, transmitters, and displays; gyroscopes; airframe equipment instruments; thermocouple and thermocouple lead wire; nautical instruments; other aerospace flight instruments; and parts and components.

Light reconnaissance and surveillance systems. This product group includes infrared, ultraviolet, and visible light reconnaissance systems excluding radar systems such as bomber-defense equipment, weapon fire control equipment, infrared fuses, infrared detection and warning systems, and such night vision equipment as sniperscopes, snooperscopes, and night driving equipment.

Radar systems and equipment. This category includes airborne, ship-based, and ground-based radar systems such as early warning radar, air defense and fighter control radar, harbor control radar, meteorological radar, highway speed control radar, bomber navigational radar, space satellite tracking radar, precision approach radar, and other forms of tracking radar technology.

Sonar systems. This product group consists of airborne-, surface ship-, and submarine-based sonar systems including depth-finding equipment, guidance hydrophones, sonabuoys, sonar fish finders, navigation and mapping sonar, and anti-submarine sonar equipment.

Electronic warfare equipment. Electronic warfare systems include such missile-borne and non-missile-borne "countermeasures" equipment as radar jamming devices, underwater countermeasures technology, beam-riders, infrared homing systems, specialized signal processing and intelligence equipment, and other "active" countermeasures equipment (excluding such passive systems as chaff and windows).

Navigation systems and equipment. Included in this category are such navigational aids as beacons, transponders, collision warning systems, inertial navigation systems, radio compasses and direction-finders, autopilots, data systems/flight recorders, distance measuring equipment, pilots' "head-up" instrument displays (HUD), aircraft proximity warning systems, flight directors/situation displays, and ship and submarine navigational systems.

Flight and navigation sensors, transmitters, and displays. This product group includes altimeters, compasses, artificial horizon instruments, and airspeed, acceleration, rate-of-climb, angle-of-attack, and bank and turn indicators.

Airframe equipment instruments. This category includes position indicators for landing gear and cowl flaps, hydraulic systems for liquid level and temperature indicators, and cabin environmental instruments such as air conditioning, cabin pressure, oxygen, and heating.

BACKGROUND AND DEVELOPMENT

Before the invention of the floating gimball gyroscope in the first years of the twentieth century, sea navigators had relied on celestial azimuths, star tables, the sextant, timekeeping instruments, and dead reckoning (a type of inferential estimation) with a magnetic compass.

Rudimentary radio direction-finders consisting of large manually-rotated loop antennas for receiving the homing signals of coastal radio beacons came into wide use in the years before World War I. With the discovery that radio waves striking seagoing vessels produced measurable echoes, radar technology became possible, and by the 1930s, the first on-board VHF radars were installed on ocean liners and naval vessels. By the close of World War II, every capital ship in the U.S. fleet was equipped with a radar unit.

The invention of radar, however, had its greatest impact in air operations and immediately began to play a critical role in the European and Pacific theaters. Prior to its invention, pilots navigated using magnetic compasses, airspeed instruments, and direction-finding gyros. Radio beacons that enabled pilots to plot their position relative to intercepted radio signals came into use in the late 1920s. These early developments were followed by advances in flight control technology, including General Electric's first flight control system in 1931 and Honeywell Inc.'s first electric autopilot in 1941.

During World War II, radar proved most effective as a fighter-interceptor tool, a strategic early warning device, an anti-submarine weapon, and as a navigation resource for bombardiers approaching enemy targets. Raytheon Company emerged as the leading producer of radar tubes and systems during the war, and General Electric Company produced more than 50 different types of radar for the U.S. armed services. A precursor of Texas Instruments developed the first anti-submarine detection system in 1941.

Sonar, which was based on the principal that transmitted sound waves deflecting against underwater objects could be used for detection and identification purposes, had been invented by the U.S. Navy in 1922, and by World War II became a strategic weapon for airborne, surface ship, and underwater surveillance. Electronic warfare and countermeasures technology grew out of the discovery that radars could be "spoofed" or "jammed" into misinterpreting returning signals. Strips of aluminum foil called "chaff" or "windows" proved to be effective anti-radar measures and led scientists to modify radar technology to overcome such obstacles. Most major radar technology breakthroughs since World War II, such as pulse and phased array, have been attempts to overcome existing or anticipated jamming or countermeasure technologies.

The development of search and navigation systems in the post-War years was driven by revolutionary advances in jet aircraft, missile technology, satellite systems, digital computers, miniaturization of electronic components, and the specialized needs of the space program. The 1950s witnessed the emergence of the first inertial guidance systems for missiles and submarines. By 1958, the submarine Nautilus was able to successfully navigate underwater to the North Pole using inertial guidance systems modified from Air Force cruise missiles. In 1955, a tactical air navigation system (TACAN) had been introduced, and a year later the first efforts at developing an air collision avoidance system began.

In 1960, Litton Industries introduced an inertial navigation system using a central integrated digital computer for attack aircraft. Four years later, the Navy's Navigational Satellite System became operational with the launching of the Transit satellite. In the 1960s, sonar technology evolved beyond surface ship and submarine applications to networks of fixed sonar systems capable of identifying and tracking vessels from the ocean floor. The decade also saw the emergence of the modern automatic flight control system for aircraft. General Electric's systems for the F-105, F-111, and F-4 used sensors and computerized components that issued automatic commands to the aircraft's flight control surfaces for stabilization and control. In 1967, the first automatic landing using guidance systems designed for low visibility landing approaches was made at JFK Airport, and Texas Instruments developed the first solid state radar using semiconducting materials and components. Two years later, Texas Instruments delivered its first laser-guided missile systems to the United States Air Force.

During the 1970s, the Global Positioning System satellite network, which is expected eventually to become the dominant source of navigational coordinates, first came under development. Inertial navigators using digital computers also became common on civil and military aircraft. In the early part of the decade, Sundstrand Corporation developed a multimode radar for mapping terrain and seeking airborne targets. The late 1970s and early 1980s saw the emergence of radical new "stealth" or radar-evading "low observable" technologies in the form of the B-1, F-117, and

B-2 aircraft. Using radar absorbing materials, innovative airframe shapes, and a variety of other design techniques, the radar "signature" of the B-2 bomber on enemy radar screens was estimated to be the equivalent of a large insect. The emergence of stealth technology—and the likelihood that eventually it would become available to potentially hostile nations—compelled search and navigation manufacturers to investigate alternative technologies to radar detection—such as infrared, ultraviolet, and electro-optical detection—and to search for new, more sensitive radar technologies capable of counteracting stealth "invisibility."

Space programs begun by NASA in the 1960s generated new navigation technologies for satellites, interplanetary probes, lunar landing and "roving" vehicles, and, in the 1980s, the space shuttle. In 1985, Texas Instruments developed a new phased array radar technology that offered greater sensitivity and versatility over previous radar systems, and in the latter part of the decade, land navigation systems for automobiles, emergency vehicles, and rental cars began to be developed for complex urban environments. In 1989, the first five Global Positioning System satellites were launched, offering unprecedented accuracies up to a few yards to system users.

The Gulf War between Iraq and a coalition of international forces demonstrated the degree to which search and navigation industry products could influence the outcome of military conflicts. The so-called "Microchip War" was the first conflict fought directly with real-time support from satellite surveillance and communications systems, and Raytheon's Patriot missile—a ground-to-air defensive missile system employing advanced seeking technology—proved itself as a reliable and effective weapon system.

CURRENT CONDITIONS

The search and navigation industry produced more than $76.7 billion in shipments in 1996 and employed over 500,000 people. As a result of the reductions in defense spending of the late 1980s and early 1990s, several establishments in the search and navigation industry committed themselves to reducing the percentage of contracts dependent on government funds.

INDUSTRY LEADERS

Many of the largest search and navigation industry firms are prominent Fortune 500 multinational corporations whose highly diversified corporate activities cover a wide range of industry groups including heavy construction equipment, engineering services, elec-

tronic components, business credit services, office furniture, ship construction, oil and gas services, semiconductors, computers, and radio and television equipment.

Broad product diversification, aggressive market share protection and expansion strategies, and innovative managerial techniques are among the characteristics of the industry's largest and most dynamic firms. Many of the industry's most recognizable establishments stand at the forefront of American industry's attempts to adopt novel methods for increasing productivity, streamlining corporate decision-making processes, and reshaping rigid organizational structures.

Sundstrand Corporation, a leading producer of commercial and military avionics equipment, adapted to decreased revenues from government military purchases by implementing lower business overhead strategies, cutting back on excess manufacturing capacity, and enhancing employee performance through self-directed work teams and "continuous improvement" programs. In 1996, Sundstrand total sales reached $411 million.

Westinghouse Electric Company, which manufactures airborne fire control radar, electro-optical and infrared detection systems, anti-submarine combat systems; and command, control, and communications equipment (in addition to its broadcasting and refrigeration operations), is the only U.S. company to have implemented "Total Quality Management" techniques in all manufacturing and design phases of product development. Partly as a result of these efforts to make the traditionally separate operations of engineering and manufacturing part of a single unified process, Westinghouse posted total sales and operating revenues of $8.45 billion and employed approximately 59,300 in 1996.

General Electric Company, a producer of technologies in virtually every product group of the search and navigation industry, implemented a number of strategies in the late 1980s and early 1990s aimed at "empowering" employees and increasing productivity. The company employed 239,000 workers and posted sales of $78 billion in 1996, making it the fifth largest company overall in the United States.

Texas Instruments, a leading manufacturer of anti-radar weapons and seekers, electronic warfare systems, and anti-submarine systems, was the first defense contractor to receive the Malcolm Baldridge Quality Award for Manufacturing in 1992. Self-directed and cross-functional work teams represent one of Texas Instruments' attempts to implement a "flatter," more quality-driven organizational structure and helped the company achieve 1996 sales of $9.44 billion—an increase of 24.3 percent over 1995. The company employed approximately 60,000 people.

Lockheed Martin Corporation is one of the largest defense contractors for the U.S. government, manufacturing missiles, fuel tanks, and products for Motorola's satellite communication network. The company posted sales of $26.9 billion and employed approximately 190,000 in 1996.

WORK FORCE

Employment by search and navigation industry firms declined steadily in the late 1980s and early 1990s. From 369,400 employees in 1987, industry employment fell to 314,000 in 1990 and to 220,400 in early 1993. Cutbacks in government defense contracts were the primary reason for these declines although companies with large "backlogs" of awarded but still uncompleted projects continued to hire even despite diminished prospects for new contracts. By 1998, employment was expected to fall to about 100,000.

In 1996, approximately 34 percent of the industry's employees were classified as production workers. Establishments in four states—California, New York, Texas, and Florida—employed about 54 percent of the industry's workforce in the mid-1990s.

Average pay across all occupational categories was $38,491 in early 1993 and average hourly earnings were $15.95. IN 1996, hourly wages were estimated at $19.76 for the industry. The industry product groups with the highest concentration of employers were missile-borne and space vehicle systems and equipment with 45 establishments, specialized electronic and communication equipment with 44 employers, and light reconnaissance and surveillance systems and equipment with 39 establishments in 1991.

Occupational categories employed in the industry included production workers such as machinists and assemblers, administrative support staff, administrators and executives, and engineers and other technical personnel. The industry employed a wide variety of engineering professionals—from aeronautical, civil, electrical, mechanical, quality assurance, and manufacturing engineers to computer and digital systems, hardware, software, logistical, and algorithm systems engineers. Salaries for degreed engineers ranged between $18,000 and $78,000 per year depending on experience, professional specialization, job responsibilities, and other variables.

Because the search and navigation industry historically has been dependent on multi-million dollar, large-scale, limited duration government contracts,

fluctuations in employment can be severe. In the early 1990s, for example, Hughes Aircraft Company released 60,000 workers in a single layoff. Layoffs of 8,000 workers or less, however, are more common.

AMERICA AND THE WORLD

The United States continues to lead the world in developing and manufacturing search and navigation instruments and systems. This global dominance is reflected in U.S. export and import superiority relative to other leading nations. In 1992, the search and navigation industry exported about $2.1 billion in shipments. By contrast, Japan, the next leading exporting nation, shipped $301 million in shipments, followed by Canada ($213 million in shipments), the United Kingdom ($212 million), and France ($168 million). Similarly, while U.S. imports of search and navigation instruments and systems rose to $990 million in 1992, America's closest foreign competitors imported $196 million (Canada), $111 million (the United Kingdom), and $107 million (Japan) in the early 1990s.

Historically, the U.S. search and navigation industry has experienced trade surpluses reflecting its advantage in developing advanced technology. In 1991, however, the U.S. trade surplus in search and navigation equipment declined for the first time—by more than 14 percent over 1990. This unprecedented decline reflected the weakness of the dollar overseas and the increasingly aggressive and competitive global search and navigation market.

Foreign markets. Prior to an industry-wide slump in the early 1990s, the avionics product groups, which comprise the broad majority of the industry's products, experienced increased demand from democratizing Eastern European nations, growing industrial states in Southeast Asia, and Middle Eastern allies of the United States seeking military avionics upgrades. In the straitened climate of the early 1990s, demand for U.S. search and navigation equipment centered on radar equipment and parts (25 percent of U.S. industry exports) and avionics equipment for civil aircraft and space navigation applications (20 percent of industry exports). Potential export markets for U.S. search and navigation instruments include NATO bases in Europe, which were being evaluated for possible conversion into dual-use civil/military facilities; South and Central American nations considering purchases of surveillance equipment for drug interdiction; and Middle Eastern allies reassessing their defense and avionics needs in the post-Gulf War environment.

Air traffic control systems represented the product group with the largest export growth potential for U.S. search and navigation firms. Although the U.S. domestic market was the largest air traffic control market in the world in the early 1990s, contracts for most of its systems and technology upgrades had already been awarded in 1992. U.S. search and navigation firms looked to anticipated upgrades of aging overseas air facilities and new airports planned in such nations as China, Mexico, Iran, Turkey, India, and the republics of the Commonwealth of Independent States (CIS), the former Soviet Union. Global air traffic control business, which was expected to center on radars, transponders, and integrated control systems, was estimated to total $6.3 billion in 1991 and grow to $14.4 billion by 2002. Air traffic control needs for the CIS was estimated at $12.5 billion alone in 1992.

Joint ventures. The globalization of the search and navigation market offered the potential for enhanced efficiency, improved market access, and increased worldwide competition. Rationalization, standardization, and interoperability of technology and the growing number of international business arrangements resulted from an increasingly interlinked global marketplace for search and navigation equipment. Joint ventures, in which a technologically superior U.S. manufacturer typically teams up with a less advanced foreign partner firm, are the most common industry business arrangement and often hinge on the U.S. firm's willingness to surrender technology to the foreign producer in exchange for cheaper labor costs, larger markets, or some other ''sweetener.'' In offset agreements, an exporter agrees to obtain domestic markets for the products of the purchaser, and in some cases the exporter is obliged to buy products within the purchasing nation equal to a certain percentage of the contract's value. Offset agreements may also require the production of the product in the purchasing country or some form of co-production under a licensing arrangement. Although some degree of joint venture or co-production between U.S. firms and other nations in the larger defense industry began in the early 1950s, the number, variety, and geographic breadth of such arrangements continues to grow.

Government intervention. Some domestic aerospace and defense contractors have claimed that the historical unwillingness of the U.S. government to imitate foreign governments by actively intervening to aid exporting companies has weakened U.S. competitiveness. Competitive financing of exports by government bodies (such as the United States Export Import Bank), federal funding of ''blended'' commercial/military foreign sales, or government guarantees of commercial financing for military products are among the remedies advocated by some industry leaders to increase the

U.S. position internationally in search and navigation and other defense sectors.

In 1993, the Clinton Administration signed into law a National Cooperative Production Amendments Act that modifies U.S. antitrust law so that penalties imposed on U.S. firms for engaging in joint ventures are reduced. The legislation also includes provisions allowing industry firms to share technology, pool resources, and share the burden of risks associated with equipment and research and development costs. The Act also enables foreign firms to engage in joint ventures with U.S. firms if equal treatment to U.S. firms is extended by their home country.

International activity. The extent of foreign activity by U.S. search and navigation firms is reflected in the international projects of the Raytheon Company, one of the industry's largest producers. In the early 1990s, Raytheon teamed with Litton Industries to win a radar jamming contract for the government of Greece, entered into a co-production agreement with a Japanese company for development of a version of the Patriot missile, initiated a similar program with Taiwan, gained a contract with the Egyptian navy for mine-hunting sonar systems, formed a joint venture with Deutsche Aerospace AG to pursue international missile projects, and through its International Air Traffic Control division landed contracts for airports in India, the Netherlands, Germany, and Norway. Raytheon's contract with Saudi Arabia for a Patriot missile defense system in 1992 represented the largest single foreign sale ($327 million) in the company's history.

RESEARCH AND TECHNOLOGY

Research and development (R&D) costs for new technology in the search and navigation industry are assumed by both the federal government and industry contractors. As the amount of R&D subsidized by the U.S. government decreased in the 1990s, industry firms either began to replace that support with company funds or simply reduced R&D investment.

Long-term R&D contracts made by industry firms with the federal government are often undertaken with no expectation of immediate profit. These so-called ''loss contracts'' sometimes involve the granting of exclusive data or technical rights to the contractor, which enable the firm to become the sole producer of the technology should it eventually reach a production phase.

The search and navigation industry is one of the most technologically sophisticated sectors of American industry. Major advances in virtually every product group continue to occur at a rapid rate because unlike many other industries, search and navigation and other defense sectors are driven not only by intrinsic market competition but by a government-sponsored national security mandate to produce technologies superior to future projected threats as well as existing ones.

New technologies. Overall trends in search and navigation systems include increased reliability, "fault-tolerance" (i.e., ability to operate through system failures), and reduced size, cost, weight, and power consumption of system components. Specific innovations now operational or under development in the area of flight control and guidance include night-vision helmets for pilots in which flight instrument data are displayed on a visor; "three-dimensional" synthesized cockpit voices that help pilots visualize threats surrounding the aircraft; aircraft optical sensors that can imitate the processes of the human optic nerve for increased sensitivity and responsiveness to external threats; and windshear warning systems that can give pilots up to 90 seconds advance notice of dangerous conditions. Other advances include moving map displays projected onto the cockpit windscreen for navigation, voice-controlled avionics that respond to pilots' verbal commands, and on-board "Stormscope" systems that can detect lightning threatening commercial aircraft.

The major technological development in the field of search and navigation instruments is the growth of Global Positioning Systems (GPS) for the commercial and especially for the consumer market. GPS originated with the U.S. Air Force and was used by all branches of the military as guidance systems for troops, vehicles, and weapons. The system is dependent on 24 U.S.-government supported satellites in six separate orbits around the earth. A GPS receiver measures the time interval between a satellite's high-frequency radio signal and its reception by the receiver on the ground. With this data the user can instantly acquire the latitude, longitude, and altitude of the receiver via electronic triangulation. Depending on a number of factors accuracy can range from 100 meters to less than a centimeter. By 1989 the civilian market for GPS instruments was $40 million but it quickly leaped to $1.2 billion by 1995 and is expected to top $8 billion by the end of the century. Although GPS systems are used by marine and air vehicles the greatest growth is predicted for the automobile market.

By late 1996, American automobile makers were offering GPS systems as an option on select vehicles. Like other GPS systems, automobile navigators rely on satellite signals to plot the car's position and direction on an electronic road map stored in a computer memory. Industry observers predict that by the year 2000 automobile navigation systems will be a $1 billion industry and by 2005, 30 percent of all new cars will be equipped with this instrumentation. In 1995, 700,000 GPS devices were operating in Japanese cars, 20,000 in Europe, and 2,000 in the U.S.

Costs for automobile navigation systems in 1996 began at around $900 for a basic no-frills unit from Delco Electronics to $3,000 for a state of the art system from Rockwell International. Designed for delivery fleets the Rockwell system offers real time vehicle location on an electronic road map as well as route and destination location. In the U.S. Hertz and Avis are beginning to offer navigation systems in select areas on their rental units.

Other electronic systems being tested for automobile applications are radar, intelligent cruise control, and night vision. Intelligent cruise control automatically decreases and automobile's speed as it approaches a slower moving vehicle. This system is expected to available in 1999 and was expected to sell for around $500. Also being developed are radar systems that will monitor a vehicle's blind spots for approaching automobiles and provide an visual warning signal in the side and rear view mirrors. An introductory date for these crash protection radar systems has not been announced but the price for the consumer is expected to be under $1000. Texas Instruments is testing a thermal imaging camera, which will be mounted in an automobile's grill. Reacting to temperature rather than light the camera will project a brick sized image of what it "sees" on the lower part of an automobile's windshield. The introductory date for the system, which developers claim can image a deer standing in back of a bush at 500 yards, was set for the year 2000 with a target price of around $1,500.

The National Highway and Traffic Safety Administration however was leery of many of these devices. The concern is that a plethora of electronic devices may prove distracting to a driver and cause more accidents than they are intended to prevent. One electronics engineer in the Office of Crash Avoidance stated that drivers can't be expected to become fighter plane pilots. Other industry insiders fear that the high cost of these systems will scare away the consumer. An executive for Onstar, which is working on electronic systems for Cadillac, told a reporter that it is difficult to generate consumer enthusiasm for systems that cost more than $1,000. "If you want to get broad acceptance, you have to get (the option) below $500.00."

The second largest market for GPS devices after the automobile market is the consumer/cellular or hand held GPS receivers. These instruments are about the same size as TV remote controls and are used by outdoor enthusiasts intent on not getting lost. Sold by major retailers such as Wal-Mart and L.L. Bean these devices sold for around $3,000 in 1989 but the mid-1990s saw the price drop to a few hundred dollars. Growth of this market segment is expected to be ten-fold between 1995 and 2000 with sales approaching $2 billion annually. Similar devices are currently being used for everything from keeping track of rare tortoises to locating oil wells in New Guinea. In early 1996, the U.S. Office of Science and Technology recommended continued support via the defense budget for the GPS satellite system and world wide availability of free C/A-code (commercial use) satellite signals.

Advances in nautical and marine search and detection technology include new mine-hunting sonar systems, vessel alert systems for oil tanker navigation in dangerous seas, sonar fish finders that project live-action sonar images onto display screens, and digital sonar systems that can see through large ocean-bottom objects to detect severed cables or an aircraft's submerged ''black box.'' The U.S. National Oceanic and Atmospheric Administration, which is part of the Department of Commerce, is also using search and navigation instrumentation to make America's waterways safer for commercial ships and recreational boaters. Automated nautical charts, a Differential Global Positioning System, and a Real-Time Tide and Current System are part of this agencies innovative approach to maritime safety.

FURTHER READING

Aerospace Industries Association. *AIA Member Company Product Directory, 1993-94.* Washington: AIA, 1993.

Ball, Nicole, and Milton Leitenberg, eds. *The Structure of the Defense Industry.* New York: St. Martin's Press, 1983.

Current Industrial Reports: Selected Instruments and Related Products. Washington: U.S. Department of Commerce, 1992.

Howes, Daniel. ''High-Tech Cars Stall in the U.S.'' *Detroit News,* 25 February 1997.

''Internationalization of the Aerospace Industry.'' *Hearing Before the Subcommittee on Economic Stabilization, United States Congress.* Washington: GPO, 1989.

Kayton, Myron, ed. *Navigation: Land, Sea, Air and Space.* New York: IEEE Press, 1989.

Nordwall, Bruce. ''Broadening Base for Avionics.'' *Aviation Week & Space Technology.* 15 March 1993.

Robinson, Edward A. ''Soon Your Dashboard Will Do Everything Except Steer.'' *Fortune,* 22 July 1996.

Safe Passage into the 21st Century: Modernizing NOAA's Navigational Services. Washington: U.S. Department of

Commerce, National Oceanic and Atmospheric Administration, 1995.

Sedgwick, David. ''Navigators Try to Locate Serious Market Niche.'' *Automotive News,* 29 January 1996.

Stevens, Tim. ''GPS Comes Down to Earth.'' *Industry Week,* 20 May 1996.

''Swedish-Developed Radar to Penetrate Foliage, Ground.'' *Aviation Week & Space Technology.* 18 January 1993.

U.S. Department of Commerce. *U.S. Industrial Outlook 1994.* Washington: GPO, 1993.

Velocci, Anthony L., Jr. ''Fewer Players to See Late-Decade Upturn.'' *Aviation Week & Space Technology,* 15 March 1993.

—Paul Bodine, updated by Michael Knes

SIC 3821

LABORATORY APPARATUS AND FURNITURE

Establishments in this industry are primarily engaged in manufacturing laboratory apparatus and furniture. The main products of this industry include baths and melting point apparatus, laboratory furniture such as furnaces and ovens, component parts and accessories for instruments, and centrifuges.

The laboratory apparatus and furniture industry in the United States is stable domestically, with a small, but growing market for international trade. In 1996 this industry was valued at $2.3 billion, an 8 percent increase over its value in 1991, and a 3 percent increase over its 1995 value. This increase has been attributed to growth in exports, which totaled $243 million in 1994, and to an increase in medical and scientific research.

In the United States an estimated 358 establishments, employing roughly 16,700 workers, provided laboratory furniture and apparatus manufacturing services in 1996. Establishments were generally smaller in both size and sales volume when compared to the entire manufacturing industry. Of the top 20 companies within the industry, only five had more than 500 employees, and only three had revenues of more than $100 million. Of the 358 establishments, less than half (140) employed more than 20 people. Manufacturing as a whole employed 34 production workers per establishment, whereas laboratory apparatus manufacturers employed just 26. That number is projected to go down by 2005, with the industry employment rate projected to shrink by 1.2 percent.

The 1996 industry leader was Edwards High Vacuum International, with $130 million in sales. With 1,000 employees and the highest sales figures, Edwards was a relative giant within the field. Other leaders included Fisher Hamilton, with $120 million in sales; Newport Corp., $102 million, Helena Laboratories Corp., $88 million, and Corning Costar Corp., with $75 million.

Some of the smaller companies in this industry, such as Labconco, Inc., with sales of $31 million in 1996, and I-STAT Corp., with sales of approximately $20 million in 1996, have experienced rapid growth since the mid-1980s by developing their export markets. These companies found the largest markets for their products in Canada, Europe, and Japan. Indeed, exports are widely regarded as a vital element in spurring expected industry growth in the near future. The export market for this industry has not been dominated by any one customer, though NAFTA and Japan remained the strongest trading partners. Japan and NAFTA were almost even in the amount they imported in 1995, each accounting for roughly 25 percent of export dollars. Europe and Asia accounted for another 25 percent, and the rest of the world divided up the remaining 25 percent. Imports in this industry, meanwhile, were estimated at $148 million in 1995, which was a hefty 17 percent increase over the 1993 figure.

Technological Advances. New apparatus needs, along with and the need to make laboratory costs more efficient have increased several product lines in this industry. Autosamplers, which separate chemicals within a liquid sample, have been in high demand as environmental, pharmaceutical, and biological applications have increased. According to *Research and Development,* most manufacturers of autosamplers developed these apparatus for use with their own analytical instruments and are making the apparatus more useable to laboratory personnel without formal training. For medical labs, I-STAT developed a hand-held blood analyzer that could perform many common blood tests with just a few drops of blood in under two minutes, keeping the labs efficient and reducing the number of resources used to conduct the tests.

The effort to control laboratory costs has resulted in numerous product developments, which are also better for the environment. Heto Lab Equipment of Denmark designed several new lines of equipment for laboratory use, including a vacuum pump that recirculates water, saving up to five tons of water daily.

FURTHER READING

Darnay, Arsen J. *Manufacturing USA.* 5th ed. Detroit: Gale Research, 1996

"Exporting Pays Off." *Business America,* 13 February 1989.

Hyatt, Joshua. "The G Factor" *Inc.,* January 1992.

"i-STAT Company Information." Princeton, NJ: i-STAT Corp, 1997. Available from http://www.i-stat.com/testver/coinfo.htm.

Jones, Robert R. "Electrical and Electronic Instrument Markets Strong." *Research and Development,* February 1990.

"Making Your Lab Greener." *Research and Development,* April 1992.

Mosbacher, C. J. "Use of Electrical and Electronic Instruments." *Research and Development,* April 1988.

Studt, Tim. "Autosamplers Do Much More Than Take Samples." *Research and Development,* February 1992.

U.S. Department of Commerce. *U.S. Foreign Trade Highlights 1995.* Washington: GPO, 1995. Available from http://www.ita.doc.gov/industry/otea/usfth/tabcon.html.

U.S. Department of Commerce. *U.S. Industrial Outlook 1994.* Washington: GPO, 1994.

SIC 3822

AUTOMATIC CONTROLS FOR REGULATING RESIDENTIAL AND COMMERCIAL ENVIRONMENTS AND APPLIANCES

Establishments in this industry are primarily engaged in manufacturing temperature and related controls for heating and air-conditioning installations and refrigeration applications, which are electrically, electronically, or pneumatically actuated, and which measure and control variables such as temperature and humidity; and automatic regulators used as components of household appliances. Automatic controls for regulating residential and commercial environments include heating, ventilating, air-conditioning (HVAC) unit controls and building monitoring controls for temperature and humidity modulation. Automatic controls for appliances include oven temperature controls, dryness controls for clothes dryers, controls for gas burners, and refrigeration thermostats and pressure controls. Establishments primarily engaged in manufacturing industrial process controls are classified in **SIC 3823: Industrial Instruments for Measurement, Display, and Control of Process Variables; and Related Products**; those manufacturing motor control switches are classified in **SIC 3625: Relays** and **Industrial Controls**; those manufacturing switches for household appliances are classified in **SIC 3643: Current-Carrying Wiring Devices**; and those manufacturing appliance timers are classified in **SIC 3873: Watches, Clocks, Clockwork Operated Devices, and Parts.**

INDUSTRY SNAPSHOT

The total value of shipments in this industry sank slightly in the early 1990s, but it has been gradually rising since then. The projected total for 1996 was about $3.03 billion and was expected to reach $3.23 billion in 1998.

Customers for these products are primarily equipment and appliance manufacturers, electrical contractors, and large industrial users. The market for environmental controls is principally affected by activity in residential and commercial construction. In addition, the market for American manufacturers is greatly affected by foreign competition, which has been rising since the 1980s.

ORGANIZATION AND STRUCTURE

This industry is composed of two groups: manufacturers of automatic controls used in residential and commercial HVAC units and manufacturers of automatic controls used in household appliances and industrial equipment. Manufacturers of automatic controls for HVAC units primarily distribute their products to suppliers for building construction and contracting firms. For industrial upgrades of HVAC systems, the controls are also sold directly to end users. Manufacturers of automatic controls for household appliances and industrial equipment are typically subsidiaries or divisions of large establishments, where other subsidiaries or divisions of the same establishment use the controls to assemble appliances and equipment.

BACKGROUND AND DEVELOPMENT

Major Products. HVAC unit controls are the industry's major product. These controls are produced for residential and commercial buildings and in a variety of styles to meet industrial needs. Factories using temperature and humidity-sensitive chemicals and materials require highly sophisticated environmental controlling systems. Computerized HVAC monitoring and controlling have made some printing plants more efficient; the systems provide information for facility operators to electrically monitor HVAC operations from a central location and independently provide cooling and heating of water pumps in ways that save energy.

Another major product line for this industry is automatic igniters and thermostats for appliances and equipment. These controls include gas-fired igniters used for water-heaters and gas stoves in the food-service industry; thermostats used in office equipment, such as photocopiers; and custom-designed thermostats for medical equipment, such as blood analyzers and respiratory humidifiers, and kitchen appliances for the home.

As environmental control equipment has grown in size and sophistication, basic designs of automatic controls have undergone considerable changes. Heavy wiring and cables have been replaced by hydraulic systems and low-voltage ignition starters. Electrical controls have also been used increasingly for their high sensitivity and fast response capabilities. In laboratories and factories, pneumatic controls used in exhaust and ventilating systems have been replaced by digital controls, which are basically electronic versions of the original pneumatic devices.

Environmental and Energy Concerns. Concerns about the environment and the resulting legislation have helped this industry. Environmental issues created an increased demand for controlling systems that control air quality and conserve energy. In the early to mid-1990s, companies in the United States have invested significant capital on devices to lower air, water, and solid waste pollution. Factories from a variety of industries are continuing to monitor and control pollution through the purchase and implementation of highly sensitive control systems.

Along with energy conservation, energy management systems (EMS) have also kept this industry active in redesigning and improving their products; energy management systems are computerized control systems implemented mostly by the utility industry, but also by large manufacturers with their own power stations. Automatic controls have been altered and redesigned for energy efficiency to work within these systems and for the HVAC units in the buildings in which they are stored. Computerized energy management systems, on a smaller scale, are also being installed in commercial buildings as a result of the Comprehensive National Energy Policy Act of 1993. These systems combine monitoring and controlling of HVAC units with security, lighting, and fire safety systems.

Hotels, department stores, and grocery stores, all large users of energy, began implementing energy management systems in the 1980s. In hotels, automatic controls on heating and air-conditioning units are regulated by sensors in individual rooms that detect whether the rooms are occupied; the controls are also linked up with the hotel's front desk in order to respond to check-ins and check-outs. For hotel owners, these systems cost an average of $120,000 in 1991, but their energy-cost savings were estimated at $30,000 annually. Similarly, energy management systems have saved energy and money for department and grocery stores. In these cases, computerized systems are monitored for a chain of stores by a centralized network. According to Steve Thompson of McRae's department stores, ''(the) automated system has not only maintained the chain's standards for temperature and humidity, but has also strengthened them.''

CURRENT CONDITIONS

This industry entered the 1990s experiencing small growth following the decline in construction of residential and commercial buildings. This modest growth, along with small sales margins, has limited research and development in new technologies and investment in new facilities. In addition, as a result of the weak economy, many companies have chosen to upgrade their existing HVAC systems. Upgrading increased commercial repair and maintenance, while sales of new HVAC systems dropped by three percent in 1991 and 1992.

Although the number of establishments dropped slightly in 1994—from the high of 329 in 1993 to 309—it was expected to return to 1993 levels by 1998. During 1998 the industry is also expected to see an industry-high shipment value of $3.231 billion.

INDUSTRY LEADERS

The industry's largest establishment, Honeywell Inc. of Minneapolis, Minnesota, reported $6.3 billion in sales in 1992 and nearly $7 billion in 1996, employing more than 50,000 people. Honeywell is a global company operating in more than 95 countries and generating 40 percent of revenues outside the United States. Honeywell manufactures products for three segments within this industry: homes and buildings, industry, and space and aviation. For homes and buildings, Honeywell makes thermostats, gas valves, and other residential heating and cooling controls. For industry, the company provides HVAC controls and digital control systems for use with computerized energy management systems. The company's space and aviation segment manufactures environmental controls and guidance system controls.

One of the keys to Honeywell's success in the 1990s was in China. The company's sales target of $10 billion by the year 2000 called for 8 percent sales growth through the 1990s, and as North America and Europe were expanding at 2 percent and China at 8

percent, China was the most likely place to do business. Honeywell expected to double its revenues in China from $250 million in 1996 to $500 million by the year 2000.

The second largest company in this industry, operating at 10 percent the capacity of Honeywell in 1996, was Landis and Gyr Inc. of Buffalo Grove, Illinois. This company had total sales of approximately $530 million and 5,000 employees.

Other industry leaders included Robertshaw Controls Company of Richmond, Virginia, with about $500 million in sales and over 5,500 employees. Watsco Inc. of Coconut Grove, Florida, reported sales over $330 million and about 1,200 employees. Therm-O-Disc, Inc. of Mansfield, Ohio, had over $300 million in sales and over 1,000 employees.

WORK FORCE

In the early 1990s, over 49,000 workers were employed in this industry. Nearly 60 percent of these were production workers, including electricians and assembly line workers; their wages were $9.50 per hour. The remaining 40 percent were employed in administration and management and sales capacities; their salaries varied greatly.

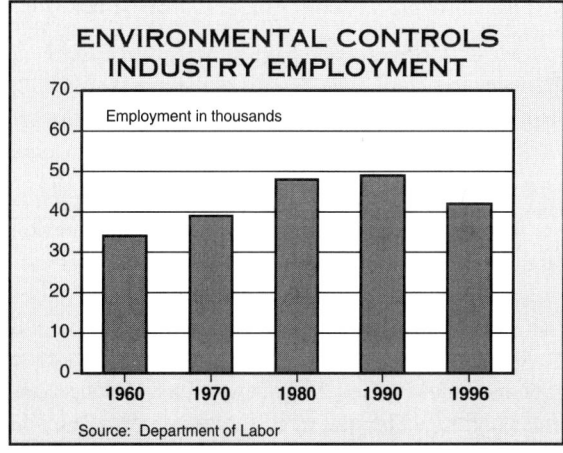

ENVIRONMENTAL CONTROLS INDUSTRY EMPLOYMENT

Employment in thousands

Source: Department of Labor

For establishments that sell products directly to end users, additional personnel are sometimes needed in heating and air-conditioning service and maintenance. In 1993 salaries for these service and maintenance technicians averaged between $400 to $600 per week, with their apprentices starting at 50 percent of those salaries.

The 1996 level of employment was estimated at 42,400 people with hourly wages of about $12. The number of people employed in this industry dropped steadily since 1987, with 24 percent fewer people employed in 1996 than in 1987.

AMERICA AND THE WORLD

This industry is competitive in international trade in both exporting and importing capacities and boasts a trade surplus that has continued to grow into the 1990s. In 1992 imports increased by 13 percent to $2.4 billion, and exports increased by 8 percent to $4.4 billion. In 1995, U.S. total imports for both measuring and controlling instruments experienced a 17.1 percent increase to $8.8 billion; exports increased 13.5 percent to $13.6 billion.

Over 20 percent of imports come from European Community members; Mexico accounts for nearly 19 percent of all imported automatic controls. Roughly 16 percent are imported from Japan, while another 16 percent are from Canada.

Canada is the largest market for exports of automatic controls made in the United States, making up nearly 59 percent of this industry's exports. Exports of these products to Canada increased five times from 1989 to 1993, mostly as a result of the U.S.-Canada Free Trade Agreement, enacted in 1989. This market is expected to continue to grow as Canadian manufacturers address environmental concerns, such as energy savings, through modernized and improved controls.

Mexico is the second largest market for exports in this industry, holding 21 percent of the market in 1992. Exports to Mexico were expected to increase further with the implementation of the North American Free Trade Agreement (NAFTA) in the mid-1990s.

East Asian countries make up a substantial portion of this industry's export market. In 1992 Japan accounted for over six percent of the exports of American automatic controls and China, Singapore, and South Korea combined for more than ten percent of the overseas market. Combined, these East Asian countries purchased $65 million in automatic controls made in the United States in 1992.

China has been especially important to this industry in the 1990s. In the 1980s China resembled the United States of the 1950s by building new cities, electric power systems, immense factories, and a much improved highway system. Consumerism was also growing and being fueled by democratic capitalism. In the 1990s, China appeared more like the United States of the 1960s, 1970s, and even the 1980s, as it has narrowed the gap between itself and global competitors. High-tech companies have been incredibly important to the economic emergence of this nation and

will continue to be necessary into the twenty-first century.

RESEARCH AND TECHNOLOGY

With the downturn in the real estate market in the late 1980s and early 1990s, building owners and developers have become interested in automated building systems as a way of cutting overhead costs and as a marketing device to showcase cost savings and modernization. Upon entering the 1990s, technology in these systems included management-regulated HVAC controls to lower energy costs.

Automated building systems are also being developed for in-home use, combining heating and air-conditioning control with security and fire and smoke detector systems. Honeywell's TotalHome, an automated home control system, uses a remote control to program room temperature, appliances, lights and locks. More research is expected in this area as consumer interests in these systems increases.

Continued research is also predicted for automatic controls within energy management systems. Some of these projects involve the use of artificial intelligence and complex information systems.

FURTHER READING

Babyak, Richard J. "Multi-Function Ignition Controls." *Appliance Manufacturer,* July 1991.

———. "Mini-Igniter Speeds Gas-Fired Hot Water Booster." *Appliance Manufacturer,* July 1991.

Bonsignore, Michael. "Balancing Risk and Reward in China." *Chief Executive (U.S.).* December 1996, 34.

"Custom Temperature Sensors Simplify Assembly." *Appliance Manufacturer,* December 1991.

Darnay, Arsen, J., ed. *Manufacturing USA: Industry Analyses, Statistics, and Leading Companies.* 5th ed. Detroit: Gale Research, 1996.

Hauprich, Jerry. "How to Save Energy the Easy Way." *Lodging Hospitality,* February 1992.

Horenovsky, Mirek. "Facility Custom-Designed for Energy Control Center." *Electrical World,* April 1991.

"Hot-Surface Ignition Without Warmup." *Appliance Manufacturer,* May 1991.

International Trade Administration. "U.S. Aggregate Foreign Trade Data." *U.S. Foreign Trade Highlights.* Available from http://www.ita.doc.gov/tradestats/.

Jaben, Jan. "Owners, Tenants More Concerned With Automated Building Systems." *National Real Estate Investor,* June 1991.

Jancsurak, Joe. "Thermostats Rise to Meet Market Demands." *Appliance Manufacturer,* May 1991.

Jesitus, John. "Energy Savings Beckon." *Hotel and Motel Management,* 16 December 1991.

"Learning Curve: The Evolution of System Control." *Electrical World,* September 1990.

Maczka, John R. "EMS Designed for Future Expansion." *Electrical World,* March 1992.

Paoli, A. Delli, Jr., and G. Thomas Saunders. "Design Your Exhaust System to Meet Your Lab's Real Needs." *Research and Development,* August 1987.

Reinbach, Andrew. "The Buzz About Energy Controls." *Buildings,* October 1992.

Selwitz, Robert. "Managing Energy." *Hotel and Motel Management,* 16 December 1991.

"Staying in Control." *American Printer,* June 1992.

"System Exchanges for EMS." *Electrical World,* February 1992.

"System Reduces Energy Costs at McRae's." *Chain Store Age Executive,* January 1992.

Tichy, Noel, and Stratford Sherman. *Control Your Destiny or Someone Else Will.* New York: Doubleday, 1993.

Ward's Business Directory of U.S. Private and Public Companies. Detroit: Gale Research, 1997.

Zelenko, Laura. "Empty Homes Get Cozy by Computer." *American Demographics,* October 1992.

—Paola Trimarco, updated by Beaird Glover

SIC 3823

INDUSTRIAL INSTRUMENTS FOR MEASUREMENT, DISPLAY, AND CONTROL OF PROCESS VARIABLES, AND RELATED PRODUCTS

This category includes establishments primarily engaged in manufacturing industrial instruments and related products for measuring, displaying (indicating and/or recording), transmitting, and controlling process variables in manufacturing, energy conversion, and public service utilities. These instruments operate mechanically, pneumatically, electronically, or electrically to measure process variables such as temperature, humidity, pressure, vacuum, combustion, flow, level, viscosity, density, acidity, alkalinity, specific gravity, gas and liquid concentration, sequence, time interval, mechanical motion, and rotation.

Establishments primarily engaged in manufacturing electrical integrating meters are classified in **SIC 3825: Instruments for Measuring and Testing of Electricity and Electrical Signals;** those manufactur-

ing residential and commercial comfort controls are classified in **SIC 3822: Automatic Controls for Regulating Residential and Commercial Environments and Appliances;** those manufacturing all liquid-in-glass and bimetal thermometers and glass hydrometers are classified in **SIC 3829: Measuring and Controlling Devices, Not Elsewhere Classified;** those manufacturing recorder charts are classified in the Commercial Printing industries; and those manufacturing analytical and optical instruments are classified in **SIC 3826: Laboratory Analytical Instruments** and **SIC 3827: Optical Instruments and Lenses.**

INDUSTRY SNAPSHOT

More than 900 U.S. companies manufactured process control instruments (PCIs) in 1997, and the value of all industry shipments in 1994 was more than $7 billion. Because of the industry's technology-intensive products, variety of product types, and the tendency of end-user industries to continue to invest in process improvements even during recessions, PCI manufacturers were expected to experience solid growth through the turn of the century. The global sensor industry as a whole (of which the PCI industry was only one segment) was dominated by small ($10 million in sales or less) firms in the mid-1990s. The U.S. PCI industry was expected to generate over $7.8 billion in shipments in 1998. As computerized advanced process control techniques continued to become the norm in American industry, PCI end-users increasingly demanded more accurate sensing devices and process control computers (or "controllers") capable of providing real-time direction of a sophisticated range of manufacturing process operations.

Shipments of general industrial process display/control instruments and temperature measuring instruments—the two fastest-growing product groups—grew at an estimated annual rate of 13.6 and 10.8 percent, respectively, between 1987 and 1995. Intense competition from foreign PCI manufacturers challenged U.S. producers at home while growing markets in Asia, Eastern Europe, and the former Soviet Union offered U.S. producers opportunities to expand their leading role in the international PCI marketplace.

ORGANIZATION AND STRUCTURE

At the heart of industrial process control is the measurement of the variables, such as temperature and pressure, used in manufacturing processes to transform raw materials into finished products. Measurements made by sensors, meters, or other measuring instruments on the manufacturing process line are sent by a transmitting device to an indicator or recorder for display and/or to a controller (by the 1990s a computer) where the data is compared to a preestablished set of parameters. The controller calculates the difference between the measured data and the programmed ''setpoint'' values and, if necessary, adjusts the process variables to conform to the desired parameters. This feedback-and-response cycle is called a loop, and continuous, repeating loops are performed during the industrial process to ensure product quality, efficient use of raw materials, and process safety. Processes typically involving control include reacting, heating and cooling, distilling, petroleum refining, and pulp and paper manufacturing.

PCI end-users. The PCI industry is tightly linked to its end-user industries and to the process or so-called wet industries in particular. Capital expenditures by these industries on plant and process improvements has a direct effect on the profits of PCI manufacturers. The process industries use raw materials in fluid or bulk solid form for product manufacture and include the chemical, petroleum, petrochemical, pharmaceutical, pulp and paper, food processing, plastics, and municipal water and waste treatment industries.

Historically, the process industries have accounted for almost two-thirds of all PCI purchases. The chemical industry alone traditionally purchases 25 percent of all PCI shipments, followed by the petroleum (19 percent), pulp and paper (10.5 percent), and food processing industries (6.5 percent). Other important purchasers include non-process or discrete-piece manufacturing industries, which manufacture iron, steel, and nonferrous metals (such as aluminum and copper), glass and ceramic products, textiles, and machine tools; mining industries; and electric and gas utilities.

Competitive structure. In spite of historically strong growth performance and high technology product groups, the PCI industry has traditionally been undervalued by the financial community. This sometimes prevented PCI companies from attracting the capital necessary to maintain growth and made firms in the industry ideal targets for acquisition by foreign and domestic companies. Although changes in the PCI industry's structure challenged the traditional hold of the largest companies in the 1990s, such major producers as Thermo Electron Corporation, EG&G Inc., Rosemount Inc., and Foxboro Co. dominated the industry and were the leaders in sales and employment in the mid-1990s. Due to advances in digital technology, however, PCI system integratibility and product compatibility increased considerably in recent years. As a result, manufacturers who formerly dominated the industry now face competition from firms whose prod-

ucts can be tied into larger manufacturers' systems, thereby allowing these smaller firms to penetrate closed markets.

An increasing number of end-user manufacturers sought out PCI vendors who could provide them with complete integrated systems for their process control applications. Instrument manufacturers who formerly produced only components were thus forced to broaden their product lines. Despite increasing system compatibility, PCI vendors still competed in the areas of price, quality, added features, delivery, reputation, reliability, and service.

Legislation. Antipollution regulations by the Environmental Protection Agency (EPA)—the largest single regulatory influence on the PCI industry—required manufacturers to purchase instruments to monitor and control their industrial waste levels. Mandated spending to comply with Occupational Safety and Health Administration (OSHA) plant safety regulations was the next largest regulatory action affecting PCI purchases in the 1990s. PCI producers were also affected by Food and Drug Administration (FDA) policies regulating the manufacture of pharmaceuticals. While government regulation stimulated the sale of antipollution-related PCI products, it also reduced the capital available for new projects that would increase sales of PCIs.

Product groups. The products of the PCI industry can be divided into several broad groups: general-purpose control system instruments (1991 shipments, $1.5 billion); flow and level instruments ($871.5 million); pressure instruments ($411.3 million); temperature and primary temperature instruments ($547.8 million); gas and liquid analyzers ($362.3 million); humidity instruments ($21.2 million); instruments for process variables such as speed, weight, density, and specific gravity ($105.2 million); and other PCI instruments and spare parts, supplies, accessories, and related products ($950.9 million).

General purpose control system instruments. The largest-selling type of PCIs, general purpose control system instruments included multifunction computer control systems as well as general instruments for measuring, displaying, transmitting, and controlling process variables. General-purpose measuring instruments operate electronically or pneumatically to register and quantify process variable conditions in the manufacturing process. In the mid-1990s sensor products were available for measuring more than 40 different physical properties, from wind to acceleration, and roughly 75 different sensing technologies (for example, acoustic or zirconium oxide) were in use worldwide. The sensor's measurement or reading is transformed into a signal that is displayed or sent to the controller for comparison with process variable setpoints.

Indicators receive the data gathered by the measuring sensor and present it to the operator in digital or analog form. Digital indicators represent process variable data in discrete numerical or alphanumerical form on a liquid-crystal or light-emitting diode display or through a computer screen. Recorders are used for graphing or permanently storing process variable measurements. Early recorders used pen-and-ink mechanisms to mark rolled strips of paper or circular charts. Computer technology has enabled measurements to be recorded digitally in computer memory for later display in printed form or on computer graphics programs. Controllers receive data signals remotely or directly from measuring or transmitting instruments and send instructions or error signals to actuating valves or other components on the process line if the signals indicate that the process variables are diverging from desired conditions.

Flow and level instruments. Flowmeters have historically constituted one of the largest sources of industry revenue. Although there are over 100 meter types, the most common are differential-pressure, turbine, mass-flow, variable-area, magnetic, and positive-displacement meters. Flowmeters are used to measure the rates of flow of fluid chemicals, gases, liquids containing particulate matter (slurries), water, sewage, and gas, among other applications. Level instruments can be used to determine the amount of raw materials available for production purposes or the number of items manufactured by the process. They are typically installed in tanks, bins, hoppers, or other storage devices to monitor levels of materials such as gasoline, milk, solvents, plastic granules, coal, or oil.

Pressure instruments. The vast majority of products manufactured by industry firms are the result of processes that use pressure to perform work. Punch presses and boilers are typical pressure-based industrial process machines. Pressure-measuring instruments such as gauges and pressure transmitters operate hydraulically, pneumatically, or electronically to measure pressure, absolute pressure, vacuum pressure, or draft pressure. The two most common types of pressure gauges are liquid-filled columns or tubes (similar to household barometers) and elastic pressure elements, which operate on spring-action, diaphragm, or bellows principles.

Temperature and primary temperature instruments. More than half of all measured process variables undergo some form of temperature measurement during the manufacturing process. Accurate tempera-

ture measurements are important in many industrial processes but are critical in processes like rubber curing, food processing, and medical sterilization, where slight temperature variances can destroy final product quality. The four basic temperature-measuring instrument types are thermocouples, resistance thermometers, thermal radiation meters, and non-glass filled systems, such as industrial mercury-filled thermometers. Primary temperature instruments are the sensors that receive and measure the initial temperature data in the process control loop.

Gas and liquid analyzers. Analyzers of gas and liquid in continuous on-stream industrial processes are often classified according to the nature of the interaction between the gas and liquid to be measured and an external source of energy. Analyzers allow molecular-level measurement of process materials without interruption of the process for sample extraction. Analyzers are used to measure industrial effluents and waste products, viscosity of liquids used in mixing processes and food processing, the acidity or alkalinity of process materials, and the octane number in petroleum refining, among other applications. In addition to gas and liquid analyzers, the most common instrument types are oxygen, chromatographic, infrared, and pH analyzers.

Humidity instruments. Instruments such as hygrometers and psychrometers measure the water vapor content of air in such industrial applications as test chambers, pharmaceutical and food packaging, heat treating, and industrial drying. Wet-bulb/dry-bulb humidity, relative humidity, vapor pressure, and dew point are the most common types of measurements performed by industrial humidity instruments.

Other process control instruments. This category includes instruments for measuring such process variables as specific gravity, density, viscosity, weight, or force. Instruments in this category are used in such specialized applications as determining the "freeness" of pulp and paper products, the size of particulate solids in slurries, or the boiling point in petroleum refining

BACKGROUND AND DEVELOPMENT

The modern process controls industry grew out of three historical developments: the emergence of mass production technology, the evolution of instruments for measuring and analyzing process variables, and the development of computer technology in process control applications.

Eli Whitney's invention of the interchangeable part in 1800 represented an important early milestone in the evolution of mass production manufacturing techniques. In the early 1800s, Oliver Evans developed the principle of the automatic manufacturing sequence, which was followed later in the century by advances in machine tooling and the gradual transition from rudimentary assembly-line manufacturing methods to true industrial mechanization.

The nineteenth century also saw fundamental progress in the measurement of properties like temperature, pressure, and fluid flow. In 1822, Thomas J. Seebeck's development of the principle of continuous electrical current flow across metals of differing temperatures laid the foundation for the modern industrial thermocouple. Contemporary thermistor technology grew out of Michael Faraday's discovery of the principles of temperature resistance in the 1830s. E. Bourdon's invention in 1852 of a method for measuring pressure based on the effect of internal pressure variations on the closed end of a curved tube remains a common pressure instrument technology, and the production of the first commercial venturi tube flowmeter in 1887 marked a major advance in fluid meter technology that was still in wide use in the 1990s.

The first commercial industrial controller using newly developed computational procedures, or algorithms, for regulating processes was marketed in 1936. The earliest form of process control was performed solely by the operator who read data from a measuring gauge on the process line, determined whether the measurement varied from some desired setpoint value, and turned a valve if the process variable required adjusting. Later controllers were pneumatically or electrically powered devices designed to maintain constant, hard-wired setpoints and sometimes contained both the component for measuring process variables and the component for actuating the regulating valves.

The earliest computer-based control systems appeared in the mid-1950s. Computer technology allowed controllers to communicate with other PCIs (such as measuring sensors) as well as a central control room computer. These controllers contained a computer-driven version of a control algorithm for indicating, controlling, and actuating control components. In addition to allowing process setpoints to be altered remotely and automatically through a computer terminal, computerized controllers offered lower cost, greater control speed, and increased reliability in comparison to earlier analog systems.

The first automated industrial process plants were constructed in the 1950s, and by 1965 over 1,000 industrial plants worldwide were computer controlled to some extent. The evolution of computer operation—from vacuum tubes to transistors, then from integrated circuits to microchips—led to the introduction of faster and smaller microprocessing computers in the 1970s and 1980s. Identical microprocessor-based controllers located at different points on the process line—so-called distributed control systems—quickly began to replace centralized stand-alone control computers. This generation of high-powered, reprogrammable controllers gave operators direct control over more process loops and also enabled them to reconfigure control programs for new processes or applications.

INDUSTRY LEADERS

The largest firms in the U.S. PCI industry in 1995 were Thermo Electron Corporation ($1.59 billion in sales, 10,200 employees), EG&G Inc. ($1.3 billion, 14,000), Rosemount Inc. ($1.1 billion, 10,000), Elsag Bailey Process Automation ($680 million, 6,000), and Foxboro Company ($540 million, 5,000). Thermo Electron was founded in 1956 in Massachusetts by a professor of mechanical engineering with a vision of creating a "technology-driven" company that produced new technologies to meet emerging social needs. Since its inception, Thermo Electron has spun off no fewer than 18 publicly traded companies. Among its PCI-related operations, its Thermo Instrument Controls division manufactured PCIs and systems, from gas analysis to flow automation, for the chemical, petrochemical, refining, oil and gas, and mining industries. Incorporated in 1947, EG&G provides engineering and scientific services to customers such as the National Aeronautics and Space Administration (NASA) and the U.S. auto industry and manufactures mechanical aerospace components; optoelectronic sensors and imaging systems; and process control sensing and analysis hardware and software (amounting to 21 percent of its sales) for such applications as oil refining, petrochemical and food processing, and wood, cement, and coal production.

Like Thermo Electron, Rosemount was founded in 1956 and initially built up its business through government aerospace contracts until it diversified into PCIs in the mid-1960s. After gaining a reputation for manufacturing reliable pressure and temperature transmitters, Rosemount merged with Emerson Electric in 1976 and in 1993 acquired Fisher Controls International to form Fisher-Rosemount, one of the world's largest manufacturers of PCI equipment. Other leading industry firms in the mid-1990s included IDEA Inc., Simpson Industries Inc., Modicon Inc., Barber-Colman Co., and Analogic Corporation. The industry was also represented by the PCI divisions of several well-known major instrument and/or computer giants, including Texas Instruments Inc., Rockwell International Corp., Honeywell Inc., and Hewlett-Packard Co.

WORK FORCE

Although the number of establishments in the U.S. PCI industry has been growing steadily since 1972 (more than 900 establishments in 1996 compared to 175 in 1972), the size of the industry's work force declined since its peak in 1989. In 1996 the PCI industry employed approximately 63,000 people, with a further decrease projected by 1998. Companies in four states—Pennsylvania, California, Massachusetts, and Illinois—accounted for 47 percent of the industry's employment and shipments in 1992.

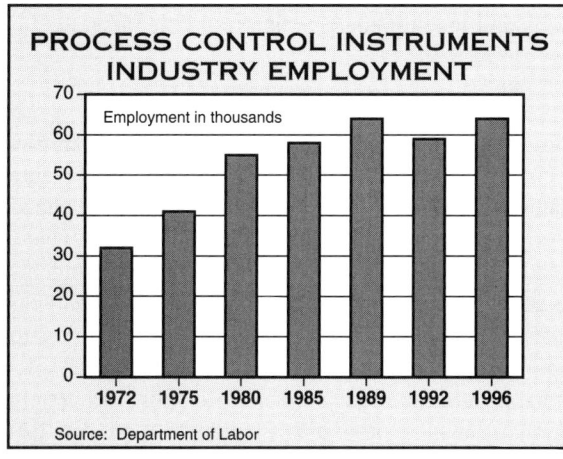

PROCESS CONTROL INSTRUMENTS INDUSTRY EMPLOYMENT

Employment in thousands

Source: Department of Labor

Production positions accounted for more than half of the industry's employment in 1992. The production positions most representative of the industry included machinists, precision electrical and electronic assemblers, and instrument makers. Workers in these categories built and integrated the components that constituted the industry's product groups and in some applications fabricated instruments requiring accuracies of one ten-millionth of an inch. Engineers—from electrical and electronics engineers to mechanical and computer engineers—comprised another significant segment of the industry's employment. Only electrical and electronics engineers were expected to see significant employment growth to 2005.

AMERICA AND THE WORLD

U.S. companies have played a leading role in the worldwide PCI marketplace. However, foreign PCI industries—led by Germany, Japan, and the United Kingdom—have made significant inroads into the U.S. domestic and overseas markets. For example,

between 1989 and 1993 alone, PCI imports rose 65 percent, fueled by comparatively lower foreign labor costs, foreign government subsidies of overseas PCI manufacturers, and the ability of some foreign manufacturers to bring research breakthroughs to commercial use sooner than U.S. firms. Moreover, some foreign PCI manufacturers responded to the focus placed by many U.S. companies on quarter-to-quarter profits by adopting long-term market penetration strategies, which allowed them to absorb short-term losses.

Although the United States continued to lead the world in new PCI technology in the mid-1990s, American engineers tended to focus on revolutionary breakthroughs in technology while foreign research tended to concentrate on gradual, evolutionary innovation. At the same time, foreign manufacturers' readiness to embrace new technologies enabled them to market PCI innovations sooner than more cautious U.S. producers. While U.S. funding of industrial research and development, for example, has favored product development two to one over improvements in industrial processes, the emphasis of Japanese funding has been the reverse, thus contributing in part to Japan's competitiveness in new PCI technology. Foreign firms looking for acquisition targets have been drawn to PCI industry firms because of the industry's history of continual growth, its high technology base, and its generally undervalued stocks and book value.

Exports and free trade. Despite the success of foreign companies in penetrating the U.S. market, the United States continued to show a trade surplus in PCIs, aided by continuing U.S. advances in new technology and the weakness of the dollar overseas. Historically, one-fifth to one-quarter of U.S. PCI shipments have gone to the export market, with the highest concentrations in high technology products like computer controllers and process analyzers. Because of its high labor costs, European firms (especially those in France, Germany, and Switzerland) turned increasingly to PCI technology to streamline their manufacturing processes in the mid-1990s. Moreover, improved European process data acquisition products which allowed process engineers to monitor and control process machines, security and access, and process variables remotely—also fueled the growth of Europe's PCI industry.

In 1994, the market for sensors (which included many products not produced in the PCI industry) in the United States, western Europe, and Japan combined was estimated at roughly $24.3 billion, with western Europe accounting for about 40 percent of the demand. The annual growth rate for the European PCI industry was expected to be roughly 3.9 percent between 1994 and 2001. Process sensors, transmitters, and converters were expected to account for 45 to 46 percent of the total European PCI market between 1997 and 2001, followed by distributed control systems (23 to 24 percent), programmable logic controllers (9.5 percent); stand-alone controllers (4.5 percent); and indicators, recorders, and displays (about 3.5 percent).

Efforts to ease international trade barriers and open foreign markets—such as the General Agreement on Tariffs and Trade (GATT)—promised to offer U.S. PCI producers potential new opportunities overseas in the 1990s. The North American Free Trade Agreement (NAFTA) in particular was projected to increase substantially the markets for U.S. PCIs in Mexico and Canada, which ranked first and third, respectively, in imports of U.S. PCIs in 1992. Other leading foreign markets for U.S. PCIs included the European Community nations, eastern Europe (especially Poland), Asia (especially China), and South America. In the mid-1990s, for example, U.S. PCI firms Westinghouse Electric Corp. and Honeywell Inc. sold process control systems to the Czech Republic and Kazakhstan, respectively.

RESEARCH AND TECHNOLOGY

The major developments in PCI technology involve advances in the power and usefulness of the computers used in process control applications, the continued evolution of artificial intelligence software applications for process control, and the development of an international standard for communicating between components in process control systems. In the mid-1990s, the rapid emergence of the World Wide Web as a source of industry information and a medium for commercial marketing also allowed small PCI firms to overcome their limited marketing budgets and ply their wares globally.

PCI computer hardware. The PCI industry is the most computer-automated segment of the combined measuring and control industry. As throughout U.S. industry, the computers used in industrial process control continued to fall in price and increase in power, speed, and memory in the mid-1990s. Advances in microchip technology allowed PCI producers to offer a wider range of functions in smaller, lighter, and cheaper instrument packages. Personal computers were increasingly used as process monitors, as workstations for configuring control systems, and as a means for gathering process data and coordinating controllers. Microchip technology also resulted in microprocessor-based "smart" instruments with self-learning and self-tuning capabilities.

PCI computer software. Many of the research advances benefiting the PCI industry involve artificial intelligence software used in experimentation, analysis, design, and prototyping of process control systems. Computer graphics modeling or simulation software programs allowed designers of process control systems to simulate complex manufacturing processes before they were actually created. Because they could also predict the final properties of raw material mixtures, these systems could also be used in the formulation of new products. Some programs also permitted simulated process system models to be tested through online interaction with the sensors and actuators that measure and control the variables in the manufacturing process. Self-diagnosing systems are capable of analyzing their own operation, anticipating future conditions and making changes before problems arise.

Knowledge-based or expert systems used alogical, inductive reasoning and pattern recognition techniques to simulate the imprecise and unpredictable nature of manufacturing processes. These and related "fuzzy logic" programs learn from process events, make qualitative instead of purely logical adjustments to process conditions, and can evaluate and compensate for faults in the process design. In addition to optimizing efficient use of process variables, such software programs allow end-users to more accurately predict the final properties of process mixtures. Because expert systems are programmed to learn and "think" independently, they are able to make instantaneous changes in the quantity and quality of the raw materials introduced into the process without the intervention of human operators.

Communication standards. Although long delayed, so-called fieldbus communications, an international protocol for linking all data communications between process control components regardless of design or manufacturer, was expected to eventually have a profound effect on the structure of the process controls industry. Fieldbus would allow the immediate conversion of data from traditionally analog-operating process sensors into digital signals, thus greatly expanding the integratibility or interoperability of PCIs. It represented a trend toward open or "transparent" system architectures that would allow end-users to mix and match system components, resulting in less expensive system expansion, improved performance, and enhanced reliability. Because of protracted debate over which fieldbus standard should be the international norm, full implementation of fieldbus communications was not expected until the turn of the century.

FURTHER READING

Adrian, Peter. "From the Editor: U.S. Sensor Companies Benefit from Strategically Exploiting European Markets." *Sensor Business Digest,* 1 April 1997.

Caro, Robert H. "The Fifth Generation Process Control Architecture." *ISA Transactions* 28 no. 4 (1989): 23-28.

Considine, Douglas, and Glenn D. Considine, eds. *Process Instruments and Controls Handbook.* 3d ed. New York: McGraw-Hill, 1985.

Fardo, Stephen W., and Dale R. Patrick. *Industrial Process Control Systems.* Englewood Cliffs, NJ: Prentice-Hall, 1985.

Frost & Sullivan. *The Process Control Equipment Market (1978-89).* New York: Frost & Sullivan, 1990.

Industrial Computing. Instrument Society of America, 919/549-8411. Available from http://www.isa.org.

Instrument Society of America, 919/549-8411. Available from http://www.isa.org.

InTech: The International Journal of Measurement and Control. Instrument Society of America, 919/549-8411. Available from http://www.isa.org.

Migliorini, Ron. "The Future of Instrumentation." *Process Engineering,* January 1991, 75.

Motion Control. Instrument Society of America, 919/549-8411. Available from http://www.isa.org.

U.S. Bureau of the Census. *1992 Census of Manufactures.* Washington: GPO, 1992. Available from http://www.census.gov.

—Paul Bodine

SIC 3824

TOTALIZING FLUID METERS AND COUNTING DEVICES

This category includes establishments primarily engaged in manufacturing meters for registering or tallying quantities of fluids, motor vehicle measuring instruments, and instruments for counting the frequency of items or events. This category includes establishments that manufacture domestic, commercial, and industrial gas and water meters; meters for measuring speed, distance traveled, and other variables for the motor vehicle industry; and counters and timers for quantifying production rates in industrial processes. Establishments primarily engaged in manufacturing electricity integrating meters and electronic frequency counters are classified in **SIC 3825: Instruments for Measuring and Testing of Electricity and Electrical Signals.** Establishments primarily engaged in manufacturing flowmeters for industrial process control and

other industrial process instruments are classified in **SIC 3823: Industrial Instruments for Measurement, Display, and Control of Process Variables; and Related Products.**

Approximately 190 U.S. companies manufactured totalizing fluid meters and counting devices in 1995. These establishments employed over 16,200 people (1992) and generated over $3.48 billion in sales (1995). In 1995, about 26 percent of the value of the industry's shipments, or $917 million, was generated by integrating and totalizing fluid meters for gas, water, and other liquids; liquid fuel dispensing meters (excluding service station pumps); and related parts and components. Totalizing fluid meters measure fluids in quantity terms (such as gallons or cubic feet) and indicate total fluid volume rather than the rates of flow indicated by flow meters used in industrial process control. The most common type of totalizing fluid meter is the positive-displacement meter, which operates by allowing the fluid to enter a chamber where the force of fluid motion causes a diaphragm, disk, vane, or other element to move or rotate. Each cycle of the rotating or moving element generates a signal that is sent to the registering component of the meter, which tallies or indicates the total fluid quantity.

Small positive-displacement meters used for registering consumption of water in households or businesses have traditionally been the largest product type in the integrating and totalizing fluid meter segment, followed by meters for registering residential gas consumption. Other significant product groups in this segment include registering or totalizing gas meters for commercial or industrial use, impeller meters and consumption-registering rotary and turbine gas meters, gauges for computing pressure and temperature corrections in industrial processes, and liquid meters used in industrial bulk plants and pipelines.

Fuelled by the needs of the process control industry beginning in the 1980s, fluid meter technology began to evolve at a dramatic pace, offering enormous improvements in reliability, accuracy, and range of measurable flow rates. Among the most important new flow measurement technologies likely to influence the totalizing fluid meter industry were the use of "nonintrusive" measuring devices that do not change the characteristics of the fluids they measure; improved meter maintenance performance through advanced diagnostic techniques; a trend toward solid-state meters with no moving parts; and perhaps even the eventual replacement of the traditional meter itself by pipes that contain their own measuring sensors.

In 1995, about 63 percent of the value of the industry's shipments, or $2.2 billion, were derived from the motor vehicle instrument sector, which produced speedometers, tachometers, odometers, fuel level gauges, water temperature gauges, ammeters, oil pressure gauges, and other motor vehicle instruments. Counters and timers are used in a wide variety of manufacturing applications and typically indicate how many items have been fed into a machine, how fast a machine is operating, how many items have been produced, how long it will take to perform a process, or what time a specific event will occur. In 1995, these nonautomotive counters and timers accounted for almost 11 percent ($370 million) of the value of the industry's shipments.

Firms in four states—California, Ohio, Illinois, and Pennsylvania—accounted for 23 percent of the value of all industry shipments in 1992. Schlumberger Industrial Water ($250 million in 1995 sales), Moorco International Inc. ($211 million), Daniel Industries Inc. ($204 million), Milton Roy Co. ($140 million), and American Meter Co. ($100 million) were among the largest companies in the industry in 1996.

FURTHER READING

Blickley, George J. "Flowmeter Selection Isn't Easy, But Tools Are Here." *Control Engineering,* 1 November 1996.

Considine, Douglas M., ed. *Process/Industrial Instruments and Controls Handbook.* 4th ed. New York: McGraw-Hill, 1993.

Control Engineering. (trade magazine) Des Plaines, IL: Cahners Publishing, 847/635-8800.

Furness, Richard. "Future Flow Measurement Has Digital Influence." *Control Engineering,* 1 October 1996.

Instrument Business Outlook. Los Angeles, CA: Strategic Directions International, Inc., 310/641-4982.

U.S. Bureau of the Census. *Current Industrial Reports: Selected Instruments and Related Products - 1995* MA38B(95)-1, November 1996.

U.S. Department of Commerce. *Census of Manufactures, 1992. Industry Series—Instruments and Related Products.* Washington: GPO, 1992.

—Paul Bodine

SIC 3825

INSTRUMENTS FOR MEASURING AND TESTING OF ELECTRICITY AND ELECTRICAL SIGNALS

This industry is made up of companies that manufacture a multitude of analytical devices. Examples of industry output include voltmeters, ammeters, wattmeters, watt-hour meters, semiconductor test equipment, and circuit testers. Establishments that produce monitoring and testing equipment for navigational, radar, and sonar systems are described in **SIC 3812: Search, Detection, Navigation, Guidance, Aeronautical, and Nautical Systems and Instruments.**

INDUSTRY SNAPSHOT

The industry for instruments to measure electricity has seen the value of shipments increase every year from 1991 to 1997. This industry did not suffer as badly as many did in the recession of the early 1990s. Many establishments came into operation in the 1980s and employment for this industry was highest in 1984. In the late 1980s, U.S. companies were shipping over $7 billion worth of goods per year, employing around 90,000 workers, and exporting equipment valued at about $2 billion annually. While shipments were projected to be 27 percent greater in 1996 than in 1987, the projected number of people employed was 44 percent less than the record high of 95,800 employed in 1984.

Growth in the mid-1990s was due to demand for Automatic Test Equipment (ATE), a devalued U.S. dollar, and shipments of high-tech devices to telecommunications industries. Despite increased foreign competition, the United States widened its $2 billion trade surplus in 1993 and poised itself for steady global expansion into the twenty-first century.

ORGANIZATION AND STRUCTURE

The electrical T&M (Testing and Measuring) instruments industry encompasses eight major product groups. ATE, the largest industry segment, represented about 25 percent of sales going into the early 1990s. ATE includes T&M instruments for semiconductors, circuit boards, and computer disk drives. Communications test equipment, the second-ranked product group, constituted approximately 7 percent of revenues. This group includes T&M devices for landline, wireless, and fiber-optic communications gear.

Other major industry categories include: signal generators (6 percent of sales in the early 1990s), electrical integrating instruments (5 percent), multimeters (2 percent), oscilloscopes (1 percent), and spectrum analyzers (.7 percent). Each of these product groups is comprised of a plethora of different devices. In addition, the remaining 60 percent of industry revenues are garnered from a wide range of miscellaneous T&M instruments, such as: tube testers, impedance measurers, frequency meters, battery testers, stroboscopes, tachometers, oscilloscopes, reflectometers, ammeters, and ohmmeters.

Ohmmeters, a common and traditional product of the industry, are used to measure the amount of electrical resistance in a circuit. Likewise, watt-hour meters are most often used to measure the amount of power that is used by a utility customer, and are mounted on an outside wall of most homes and buildings. Potentiometers are used to precisely measure direct current or voltage, as are voltmeters and ammeters. The galvanometer, another indicating instrument, indicates extremely small currents. Reflectometers measure the amount of light or energy reflected from a surface. An oscilloscope converts electron motion into a visual display on a cathode-ray tube.

More than 50 percent of electrical T&M device industry output in the early 1990s was purchased by private industry for use in manufacturing. The U.S. Government consumed about 8 percent of production, mostly for defense-related endeavors. Companies within the electrical measuring instrument industry accounted for 6 percent of sales, and radio and television businesses consumed approximately 2 percent of production. Miscellaneous markets that each accounted for less than 1 percent of consumption included utilities, natural gas and petroleum companies, and state and local governments. Exports represented almost 30 percent of sales.

About 850 U.S. companies produced electrical T&M equipment in the 1990s, up from 750 in the early 1980s. The top ten industry participants generated revenues of more than $150 million. The top 25 companies had sales of $50 million; the top 75 had sales of $13 million, but many of them employed only 100 or 200 people. Most companies were niche-oriented and specialized in a single product or category.

T&M manufacturers traditionally invest more money in their companies than most other U.S. manufacturers. In the early 1990s, the average T&M producer made about $330,000 in capital investments, compared to less than $290,000 for the average U.S. manufacturer. The industry invests heavily in manufacturing productivity.

Nearly one-third of the companies in the industry, representing almost 25 percent total sales, were located in California in the early 1990s due to the large defense, semiconductor, and telecommunications industries in that state.

BACKGROUND AND DEVELOPMENT

In 1833, Englishman Carl Friedrich Gauss was the first to show that magnetic quantities could be mea-

sured in terms of mechanical units. Wilhelm Weber, also of England, defined a system of electrical units in 1851 that foreshadowed the development of the ohm (1864), a measure of electrical resistance. The ampere, a unit used to measure electrical current, soon followed. The United States made the ohm and ampere legal units of electrical measurement in 1894.

Early measuring devices were functional, though generally unreliable for precise readings. The earliest device that would deliver a standard for voltage (electromotive force) for measuring instruments, which was built in 1836, was reproducible only to about 1 percent accuracy. The Clark Cell of 1872, which was used to establish a standard voltage measurement, also proved unreliable. The Weston Cell, introduced in 1892, became the first device to successfully provide a standard for electrical measuring devices.

Following the development of electrical units and credible standards, numerous electricity measuring devices emerged during the early 1900s. Among the first devices were instruments used to measure electrical resistance, such as ohmmeters. In addition, power meters, or wattmeters, became industry mainstays. One of the largest classes of early devices was indicating instruments, such as voltmeters and ammeters.

Many of the first indicating instruments were iron-vane devices, which utilized a plate of steel, a spring pointer, and a damper to form the vane, or moving elements of the meter. As electricity passed through a magnetic coil, the vane tipped to provide a reading. These rugged instruments remained the primary indicating devices for much of the twentieth century, despite the development of more advanced meters. Electrodynamic instruments, which were much more precise than iron-vane mechanisms, were also developed in the early part of the twentieth century. These indicating instruments utilized two sets of coils and became popular for laboratory applications.

The development of the transistor in 1947 by Bell Telephone laboratories lead to a profusion of extremely accurate electrical T&M equipment during the latter half of the century. Tube-type and electromechanical instruments were soon replaced by devices accurate to within one-millionth of a unit. As the number of applications for solid-state electronics ballooned, the demand for various T&M equipment flourished throughout the 1950s, 1960s, and 1970s.

By the end of the 1970s, electrical T&M equipment manufacturers were shipping about $6 billion worth of goods per year. Although industry growth decelerated during the previous decade, shipments continued to increase and U.S. manufacturers maintained a significant technological lead over their global counterparts. In 1982 the industry had sales of $6.1 billion and a work force of 90,000 employees.

As the T&M industry recovered from a major recession in the late 1970s and early 1980s, revenues jumped to $6.5 billion in 1983 and then to $7.8 billion in 1984. Increased defense spending, growth in telecommunications, and a general proliferation in computers and other electronic devices also contributed to growth. In 1986, total sales fell 10 percent from the previous year, from $7.7 billion to $6.9 billion. Then in 1987, the industry was on its feet again with sales of $7.7 billion. Foreign competition was making itself known, taking some of the profits from U.S. firms, as other countries began to produce electrical devices.

In an effort to maintain profitability, U.S. T&M instrument companies initiated aggressive productivity programs during the 1980s, and focused on research and development efforts in high-tech fields. As a result, industry employment dropped to 81,000 by 1989, but the United States retained its significant technological lead in high-profit T&M devices, such as ATE and telecommunications testing equipment.

A low U.S. dollar and a resurgence in domestic semiconductor manufacturing spurred electrical T&M device receipts up 6 percent in 1990, to $8.4 billion. Although a global recession pushed sales down 1 percent in 1991, revenues lurched upward 6 percent in 1992 and up to $9.17 billion in 1993. Continued improvements in the value of shipments saw $9.50 billion in 1994, and $9.55 billion in 1995.

In addition to healthy demand, producers enjoyed the benefits of massive productivity gains achieved during the 1980s and early 1990s. Despite shipment growth, industry employment continued to decline between 1990 and 1992, by 12 percent. Improved efficiency was allowing some domestic producers to compete in markets for low-priced, traditional equipment. At the same time, however, many companies were striving to move their low-tech production facilities overseas.

Exports also raised the profit margin, as foreign demand for price-competitive, high-tech equipment rose. Overseas shipments were up 10 percent in 1991, 7 percent in 1992, and 4 percent in 1993. At the same time, import growth stagnated as U.S. firms pelted their competition with efficiency gains and advanced product introductions. U.S. exports rose about 4 percent in 1993, to $2.8 billion, resulted in a healthy industry trade surplus of more than $2 billion.

CURRENT CONDITIONS

The projected value of shipments for 1996 was $9.78 billion, up from $9.55 billion in 1995. Capital investment in the industry was on the decline, to $228 million in 1996, dropping each year from 1992, or becoming 27 percent lower than it was in 1987.

Many analysts were surprised at the impressive performance of this industry in the early 1990s, particularly because of drastically reduced spending in the defense sector and the recession. But sales of advanced T&M devices were rising fast enough to make up for slower traditional markets. Shipments of digital oscilloscopes and multimeters that were priced to compete with their analog cousins, for instance, offered significant profit opportunities. Likewise, new products related to wireless communications displayed excellent growth.

The fastest growth sector of the electrical T&M device industry in the 1990s was ATE. After ceding market share to Japanese semiconductor manufacturers in the previous decade, U.S. chip producers were turning the tables by dominating the market for a new generation of high-speed semiconductors (called application specific integrated circuits). T&M device makers benefitted as U.S. semiconductor shipments rose from $14 billion in 1990 to about $28 billion in 1994.

Sales of these high-tech, high-profit ATE instruments had grown at a rate of 11 percent per year between 1987 and 1992, and were forecast to increase at an annual pace of 12 to 13 percent between 1992 and 1997. U.S. producers controlled nearly 65 percent of the global ATE market in 1993, compared to 35 percent held by Japan.

INDUSTRY LEADERS

The giant of the electrical T&M industry is Hewlett-Packard Company, of California. It was founded in 1938 by William Hewlett and David Packard, graduates of Stanford University's electrical engineering program. With $538 in start-up funds, the two entrepreneurs developed an audio-testing oscillator that was used by one of their first customers, Walt Disney, for the classic movie *Fantasia*.

Hewlett-Packard realized steady growth during World War II and the 1940s by developing and selling various electrical T&M equipment. Their first major breakthrough was the HP-524A. Introduced in 1951, this device reduced the time required to measure radio frequencies from ten minutes to about two seconds.

The specific leader in the industry of instruments to measure electricity in 1997 was Tektronix Incorporated of Wilsonville, Oregon. Tektronix had total sales of $1.472 billion and employed 7,600 people. In order to stay at the top of this industry, and to retain its 10 percent market growth in the electricity testing field, Tektronix released two new digital real-time (DRT) oscilloscopes in 1996. The $995 TDS 210, and the $1,625 TDS 220 were aimed at educational, manufacturing and service sectors. They were priced at about half the normal cost of digital scopes and had many features of analog oscilloscopes, and menus available in 10 languages.

The second largest company was Teradyne Incorporated of Boston, Massachusetts, with sales of $1.191 billion and 5,200 employees. Teradyne introduced several new electronic test devices at the Semicon/ Korea show in 1997 that were priced between $1.0 million and $2.5 million.

The third largest was KLA Instruments Corporation of San Jose, California, with $442 million in sales and 1,700 employees. The next largest company was Fluke Corporation of Everett, Washington, with $358 million in sales and 2,500 people employed. The fifth largest company was Alen Group Incorporated of Beachwood, Ohio, with sales of $315 million and 2,700 employees.

WORK FORCE

Despite sales continuing to go up, employment prospects in the electrical T&M device business were bleak going into the mid-1990s. Continued productivity gains and the movement of manufacturing facilities overseas resulted in diminished opportunities for virtually every occupation in the industry. In 1982 there were about 90,000 workers employed, in 1984 the number jumped to 95,800, but a certain and steady decreased followed. The total workforce was down to 85,200 in 1987, to 77,100 in 1990, to 59,600 in 1993, to an estimated 55,400 for 1996.

Overall, jobs for most production workers were expected to decline from 20 to 50 percent between 1990 and 2005, according to the Bureau of Labor Statistics. Jobs for general managers and executives are expected to drop 20 percent. Even positions for research engineers and technicians will decrease by 1 to 3 percent by 2005.

AMERICA AND THE WORLD

U.S. electrical T&M device manufacturers are the most technologically advanced in the world, as evidenced by their strong trade surplus. Their primary competitive advantage is the ability to develop and manufacture high-tech, high-profit devices, such as

ATE and telecommunications instruments. U.S. exports of telecommunications devices, for example, went up an impressive 21 percent in 1992 and about 13 percent in 1993. In contrast, many firms have licensed their low-end technology to regions such as China and India, where production costs are lower than in the United States.

Japan was by far the leading importer of U.S. T&M instruments, accounting for more than 16 percent, or about $430 million, of U.S. overseas sales in 1993. Canada and the United Kingdom each represented 8 percent of the U.S. export market. Germany and Mexico purchased 7.0 and 5.5 percent, respectively, of U.S. exports. The European Community took 36 percent of overseas shipments, and East Asia (not including China) purchased 22 percent. Japan was also the largest exporter of T&M to the United States, exporting about $175 million worth of equipment to this country in 1993.In 1995 the total value of imports was $2 billion, and the total value of exports was $4.2 billion.

Although competition was increasing in the mid-1990s, particularly from Europe and Japan, U.S. manufacturers in this industry expected to maintain their technological lead into the twenty-first century. Sales to the viable domestic semiconductor industry will be augmented by strong growth in demand from new wireless telecommunications industries, in which the United States also maintained a technological edge.

RESEARCH AND TECHNOLOGY

U.S. electrical T&M producers were ardently pursuing technological advances in the mid-1990s that would allow them to sharpen their competitive edge at home and abroad. Several emerging industry segments, such as wireless data communications and digital transmission, offered solid growth opportunities for companies on the cutting edge. One of the fastest growing fields that required new types of T&M instruments was thin film transistor liquid crystal displays (LCDs), which are commonly used on portable computers. Although Japan dominated LCD markets, several U.S. producers were developing T&M devices and were communicating with Japanese LCD manufacturers.

Another emerging industry technology was virtual instruments. These are T&M instruments that combine computer software and instrumentation hardware. The instrument appears on a personal computer screen and provides readings as would a T&M device. In fact, an exact replica of the device is displayed on the computer screen, complete with tuning knobs, meters, and digital readout. Instrumentation hardware is used to take readings that are fed into the computer, analyzed by the software, and displayed on the screen. An important advantage of virtual instruments is that they are easily upgraded with new software, as opposed to T&M devices that become obsolete and must be scrapped.

A multitude of other advances in the mid-1990s included miniature, battery-powered, hand-held oscilloscopes. These devices were being used by automotive technicians, for example, to easily monitor electronic modules in cars and trucks. Similarly, Sentech Systems Incorporated of Pennsylvania introduced a device in 1993 that employs laser-based optics to measure the distortion of a turbine shaft. The technology held promise for like applications in the power generation industry. Also in 1993, Motorola, Inc., of Illinois, introduced a sensor that monitors a vehicle's intake manifold to compute the amount of fuel required for each cylinder.

In 1997, digital multimeters (DMMs) were greatly improved over earlier years, to provide users with improved accuracy with better display resolution, true root mean squared AC measurements, and upgraded capabilities, including graphical waveform displays, time-stamping of minimum/maximum values, dual-measurement displays, and trend plotting.

FURTHER READING

1993 Britannica Book of the Year. Chicago: Encyclopedia Britannica, Inc., 1994.

Andrews, Walter. "U.S. to Lead ATE's in Boom." *Electronic News,* 3 January 1994.

Bradley, Gale. "Teradyne Shows Muscle at Semicon/Korea Show." *Electronic News (1991).* 10 February 1997.

Britannica Encyclopaedia. Chicago: Encyclopedia Britannica, Inc., 1968.

Darnay, Arsen J., ed. *Manufacturing USA.* 5th ed. Detroit: Gale Research, 1996.

Dehne, Tim. "Virtual Instruments—What They Are, Where They're At." *Electronic Products,* July 1993.

"Electronic Business 200." *Electronic Business,* July 1993.

Hast, Adele, ed. *International Directory of Company Histories, Volume III.* Detroit: St. James Press, 1991.

Holden, Daniel. "Test Equipment: Back on Track." *Electronic News,* 4 January 1993.

Hunt, Jim. "You May Not Recognize Today's DMMs." *Quality,* February 1997.

Martin, Thomas W. "SCSI Test Systems Are Changing." *Electronic Products,* July 1993.

Mockry, Scott. "No Code Diagnostics: Using a Handheld Digitizing Oscilloscope for Automotive Diagnostics." *Motor Age,* October 1993.

Schneck, Marcus. "High-Tech Firm Introduces Next Generation of Optical Sensing." *Central Penn Business Journal,* January 13, 1993.

"Sensors and Transducers." *Electronic Products,* June 1993.

Strassberg, Dan. "Analog/Digital Scopes Offer the Best of Two Worlds." *EDN,* 18 March 1993.

"Tek Pins Growth Rate on New Scopes." *Electronic News (1991).* 2 September 1996.

—Susan King, updated by Beaird Glover

SIC 3826

LABORATORY ANALYTICAL INSTRUMENTS

This group covers establishments primarily engaged in manufacturing laboratory instruments and instrumentation systems for chemical or physical analysis of the composition or concentration of samples of solid, fluid, gaseous, or composite material. Establishments primarily engaged in manufacturing instruments for monitoring and analyzing continuous samples from medical patients are classified in **SIC 3845: Electromedical and Electrotherapeutic Apparatus;** and from industrial process streams are classified in **SIC 3823: Industrial Instruments for Measurement, Display, and Control of Process Variables; and Related Products.**

INDUSTRY SNAPSHOT

Laboratory analytical instruments manufactured by this industry were used to conduct physical and chemical analyses. Major product groups included clinical laboratory, chromatographic, and spectrophotometric instruments, and mass spectrometers. Industry shipments were worth over $6 billion in 1995, and the industry's work force numbered almost 39,000. This high-technology sector exported 30 percent of its output in the early 1990s, resulting in a $1 billion trade surplus.

Devices used to measure the purity of gold date back to the fourth century B.C. The term "analysis," in the chemical sense, was first posited in the 1660s. A series of breakthroughs in chemical measuring methods occurred during the 1800s that preceded the development of more advanced analytic instruments later in the nineteenth century. But not until the twentieth century did the industry begin to resemble the state it achieved in the 1990s.

Laboratory analytical instrument sales swelled to about $3.5 billion in 1987, the first year in which this industry was recognized as a separate industrial classification. Revenues are expected to continue expanding through the end of the 1990s. U.S. technological superiority and increasing demand for analytical instruments make this an important growth industry.

One of the two largest product segments in this industry is chromatographic equipment used to separate chemical substances to determine their content, or to prepare them for further testing. Chromatography instruments are used in oil refineries and on space vehicles to analyze atmospheres on other planets. Chromatograph equipment accounted for 16 percent of industry sales in 1992.

Spectrophotometric equipment, which also represented 16 percent of the industry's shipments in 1992, is used to view, meter, and record spectrums of light or forms of radiated energy. Spectrochemical analysis usually involves the examination of the emission of radiation by molecules that have been heated or excited by some other form of energy, or the absorption of radiation of particular wavelengths by certain molecules.

Mass spectrometry equipment composed about 5 percent of industry shipments in the early 1990s. This type of equipment analyzes chemicals by sorting gaseous ions in electric and magnetic fields. The two major types of mass spectroscopes are spectrographs, which use non-electric means to detect the sorted ions, and spectrometers, which measure ions electrically.

In addition to the three major product segments, 60 percent of industry sales were derived from many other devices. A wide range of instruments made for clinical laboratories, for instance, accounted for about 23 percent of production, while parts and accessories represented 17 percent of output. Specialized instruments represented about 18 percent of the industry's sales. Examples of other specialized devices included: titrimeters, which measure the concentration of a substance in a solution; densitometers, which gauge the optical density of a material; coulometric analyzers, which detect the amount of a substance released during electrolysis; and turbidimeters, which are used to measure the scattering of a light beam through a solution that contains suspended particulate matter.

ORGANIZATION AND STRUCTURE

The laboratory analytical instruments industry is an international business dominated by large, innovative companies. In addition, numerous small firms compete by forming alliances or operating in niche markets. The industry is characterized by high-profits, an emphasis on advanced technology, and sporadic growth. Companies typically sell their products directly to research laboratories in pharmaceutical firms, food companies, hospitals, and other establishments that work with chemicals or analyze substances.

Roughly 40 percent of industry sales in the early 1990s were classified as private sector fixed investments, mostly by laboratories of U.S. companies. About 30 percent of production was exported. The federal government purchased 8 percent of output, while engineering and scientific instrument manufacturers consumed 5 percent of production. Other significant markets were aerospace and communications industries, and state and local governments.

BACKGROUND AND DEVELOPMENT

Rudimentary analytical instruments and measuring devices predate the birth of Christ. Naturalist Robert Boyle of England was credited with introducing the term "analysis," in the chemical sense, in his book *The Sceptical Chymist,* published in 1661. In 1669, Isaac Newton conducted light spectrum experiments that eventually lead to the development of the spectroscope. Also in the seventeenth century, the first precise gravimetric analysis equipment (used to measure specific gravity) was believed to have been created by Friedreich Hoffman, a German physician and chemist. Numerous key inventions and discoveries during the eighteenth century included the flame test for alkali metals, qualitative analysis techniques, and titrimetric analysis.

Most instruments and methods before the eighteenth century yielded qualitative analyses. But in the nineteenth century, French chemist Antoine-Laurent Lavoisier ushered in quantitative analysis, or the determination of the amounts and proportions of chemicals or elements in a substance or gas. Major breakthroughs in analytical instruments and methods during the 1800s included electrochemical analysis methods and gas analysis. In addition, German chemists Gustav Robert Kirchoff and Robert Bunsen introduced the first practical spectroscope in 1859. This important development lead to the discovery of new elements. Spectrographic equipment improved greatly during the late 1800s and early 1900s with the introduction of mass spectrography, in 1920, flame photometry, in 1928, and radiochemical methods developed after World War II.

Perhaps the greatest innovations in the history of this industry related to the development of chromatography. Although first conceived in 1903, workable chromatography equipment was not built until the early 1940s. Gas chromatography and other advanced techniques that emerged during the 1950s significantly expanded the breadth of the analytical instrument industry. These pivotal innovations, combined with steady market growth during the post-World War II economic expansion, resulted in healthy revenue gains for instrument manufacturers. The U.S. assumed a global technological lead it enjoyed throughout the 1960s and 1970s.

Although shipments of all types of U.S. laboratory equipment surged during the 1980s, not until 1987 did the U.S. Government classify analytical instruments as a separate industry. By that time, sales of goods in this sector had grown to about $3.5 billion and were rising rapidly compared to most laboratory equipment industries. Indeed, sales jumped 11.5 percent in both 1988 and 1989, and in 1990, as the U.S. economy slumped into a recession, shipments bulged 14 percent to almost $5 billion. In addition to steady growth in domestic demand, U.S. producers benefitted from a global interest in their high-technology products. While imports hovered at about $700 million between 1989 and 1992, U.S. exports ballooned from $1.3 billion to $1.7 billion.

CURRENT CONDITIONS

The laboratory analytical instruments industry continued to benefit during the early 1990s from four key factors: 1) the increased concern over the spread of viruses, such as acquired immune deficiency syndrome (AIDS); 2) an intensified quest for new drugs by pharmaceutical companies; 3) a proliferation of environmental concerns and regulations, and; 4) strong demand overseas for high-technology, high-profit instruments. As a result, industry shipments rose approximately 22 percent between 1990 and 1995 to over $6 billion. Furthermore, exports, bolstered by a weak U.S. dollar, bulged about 6 percent in 1993 to an estimated $1.8 billion.

At the same time that manufacturers in this industry were boosting sales and profit margins on high-technology items, many were also increasing their profits through gains in productivity. Increased automation, advanced information systems, and management restructuring allowed many competitors to cut costs. Thus, as the amount of value added during the manufacturing process increased over 30 percent between 1987 and 1995 to $3.6 billion, for the average industry participant, the size of the work force grew less than 20 percent, to approximately 39,000. Gains in productivity were partly offset by higher research and development costs.

Entering the mid-1990s, manufacturers focused on product quality and customer service to help them regain the rampant growth they enjoyed during the late 1980s. They also emphasized new product introductions. Environmental and pharmaceutical markets offered the strongest growth domestically. But demand from food processing, biotechnology, and chemical industries remained relatively healthy.

In the long term, makers of laboratory analytical instruments were predicted to become increasingly dependent on sales of advanced technology products utilized by highly industrialized nations. Gas chromatography and mass spectrometry equipment were anticipated to be major growth segments, as were several newer niche product groups, such as capillary electrophoresis devices. Markets for low-technology products were expected to be controlled by low-cost producers in emerging regions, such as Mexico and East Asia.

INDUSTRY LEADERS

Market share in the laboratory analytical instruments industry was concentrated, with a few industry leaders controlling the market. High start-up costs and rigid technological requirements discouraged new entrants. Perkin-Elmer Corp., the largest manufacturer, generated roughly $1.06 billion in sales in 1996 and employed 5,900 workers. The company reorganized three times between 1988 and 1993, and formed alliances with corporate giants such as Dow Chemical and Hoffmann-La Roche. Despite a drop in earnings in 1993 caused by an accounting change, Perkin-Elmer was positioned for growth during the mid-1990s. In 1993, for example, the company introduced a breakthrough system of medical testing. The testing system integrated an advanced method of replicating DNA, which was more accurate and less expensive than competing systems.

Beckman Instruments Inc. of California was the second largest company with 1996 sales of $930 million and about 5,700 workers. Beckman developed an instrument in the early 1990s that analyzed extremely small amounts of rare genetic and other biochemical materials. Other industry leaders in the early 1990s include: Thermo Instrument Systems, Inc., with $678 million in 1996 sales; Millipore Corporation, with $595 million in sales; and Sequoia Turner Export Company, with $126 million in sales. The majority of the leading 75 firms had annual sales of less than $25 million and employed fewer than 100 workers in the early 1990s.

WORK FORCE

Despite expectations for market growth, future employment opportunities in this industry are questionable. The overall outlook for U.S. measuring and controlling device industries was bleak, with most labor positions expected to decline 15 to 50 percent between 1990 and 2005, according to the U.S. Bureau of Labor.

Positions for managers, engineers, and sales professionals are forecast to diminish about 10 percent. Although workers in the laboratory analytical instruments business are expected to fare better than their counterparts in related industries, continued productivity gains, consolidation, and the movement of some manufacturing activities overseas would likely thwart long term job growth.

AMERICA AND THE WORLD

The U.S. laboratory analytical industry is the most advanced and productive in the world. Despite lower sales to Canada and western Europe, total exports, which constitute 11 percent of product shipments, grew 5 percent, to $178 million in current dollars. Much of this growth came from healthy sales in east Asia. In Japan, U.S. producers achieved an impressive $170 million annual surplus by 1991. Foreign demand for advanced proprietary gear remain strong going into the mid-1990s. Japan, with significant research and development in process, replaced Canada as the major U.S. export market. U.S. exports to Europe dropped in 1993, because of competition and Europe's economic problems. U.S. imports grew nearly 3 percent and the trade surplus increased 9 percent.

The export market for U.S. goods is extremely fragmented, suggesting solid long term growth potential. Product categories realizing the greatest overseas demand in the early 1990s included chromatographs and electrophoresis instruments, general chemical instruments, and viscosity measuring devices.

Demand is expected to increase with the growing biotechnology field, more stringent requirements for environmental testing, and increased capital spending by the pollution control, semiconductor, paper, automotive, and food industries. Development of new foods and flavors has increased purchases of laboratory equipment for assessing moisture content, quality, and shelf lives. U.S. sales to Europe were not expected to increase noticeably, because of a slow economic recovery there. However, exports to east Asia and Mexico are expected to grow. Imports are expected to remain flat.

While global markets are expected to offer opportunities, many competitors in the mid-1990s felt that a global industry presence was a necessity in light of rising development costs and maturing domestic markets.

RESEARCH AND TECHNOLOGY

Major technological trends in the mid-1990s include the proliferation of combined equipment, such as single units that integrated both chromatograph and spectrometer functions; smaller instruments, particularly portable environmental field equipment, increased quality and precision, and growth in information systems and robotics. The growth in information systems and robotics was evidenced by rising installations of laboratory information management systems (LIMS), as well as a growing demand for automated sample preparation systems for bio-pharmaceutical applications. A new system introduced in 1993, for example, handled multiple sample preparation tasks and was operated by Windows-based personal computer software for easy use. Several other automation and robotics systems, offered by companies such as CRS Plus Inc. and Zymark Inc., were aimed at relatively inexperienced users that wanted to conduct complex sample preparations and analyses.

Similarly, manufacturers were also introducing easier-to-use chromatography and mass spectrometry devices. Advanced systems automatically optimized and tuned themselves during operation, thereby eliminating much of the practice and guess-work associated with conventional instruments. In addition, many newer instruments combined as many as three major functions into one unit. While these high-technology workhorses were regularly priced at more than $200,000, they were typically easier to operate and less expensive than two or more side-by-side units with commensurate capabilities.

In early 1997, MEMS, also known as micro-electro-mechanical systems, began to make their appearance with the promise of an impact as profound as the microchip. Many small American companies are bringing new MEMS applications to the market. Biomedical testing micro-instruments are being developed using MEMS applications and are expected to reach the market by early 1998.

FURTHER READING

"$3 Billion From Underseas in Decade," *American Metal Market,* 12 January 1994.

Darnay, Arsen J., ed. *Manufacturing USA.* 5th ed. Detroit: Gale Research, 1993.

DeYoung, H. Garrett. "Managing Technology at Warp Speed." *Electronic Business,* 21 January 1991.

"DOC Forecasts Modest Increase in Instruments." *R & D,* February 1992.

"Dow, Perkin-Elmer Sign Process Technology Pact." *Chemical & Engineering News,* 10 May 1993.

Harlans S., Byrne. "Perkin-Elmer: Fine Tuning Product Line Leads To Improved Performance." *Barron's,* 21 June 1993.

"Instrumentation '94." *Chemical & Engineering News,* 14 March 1994.

Markoff, John. "New Wave in High-Tech: Deus Ex(Tiny) Machina." *The New York Times,* 27 January 1997.

"P-E Turns $13.8M Profit in Q3." *Electronic News,* 25 May 1992.

Resa, King. "A Gene Machine Starts Cloning Cash; Roche and Perkin-Elmer Are Ready To Reap Big Rewards From PCR." *Business Week,* 22 November 1993.

U.S. Bureau of the Census. *Annual Survey of Manufactures.* Washington: GPO, 1996.

———. *Current Industrial Report.* Washington: GPO, 1996.

U.S. Department of Commerce. *U.S. Industrial Outlook 1993.* Washington: GPO, 1993.

———. *U.S. Industrial Outlook 1994.* Washington: GPO, 1996.

Wolf, Kenneth. "France is Major Market for American Scientific Gear." *Journal of Commerce and Commercial,* October 15, 1992.

—Dave Mote, updated by Susan Wood King

SIC 3827

OPTICAL INSTRUMENTS AND LENSES

This category covers establishments primarily engaged in manufacturing instruments and apparatus that measure an optical property and optically project, measure, or magnify an image, such as binoculars, microscopes, prisms, and lenses. Included are establishments primarily engaged in manufacturing optical sighting and fire control equipment.

INDUSTRY SNAPSHOT

There were 425 establishments in the industry in the mid-1990s, an increase of 63 percent since 1990. Shipments of optical instruments and lenses increased 22 percent between 1992 and 1995, from $2.2 billion to $2.69 billion. The industry employed 20,700 in 1995, up 11 percent since 1990.

ORGANIZATION AND STRUCTURE

Companies in this industry manufacture a plethora of devices, including: weapon firing control mechanisms, optical laser sighting systems, binoculars, borescopes, camera lenses, contour projection apparatus,

gun sights, opera glasses, interferometers, microscopes, telescopes, periscopes, and spyglasses. Most devices in this industry use lenses. But some products that don't utilize lenses, such as rifle aiming circles and some types of surveying equipment, simply help users to align or measure objects. Electronic optical devices that don't use glass or plastic lenses, like the electron microscope, are classified elsewhere.

The largest segment of this industry is sighting, tracking, and fire control equipment, much of which is used in missile systems, combat aircraft, and other defense applications. These advanced products accounted for about 30 percent of industry revenues in the early 1990s. Optical test and inspection equipment, which made up about seven percent of sales, included a variety of mechanisms. Much of it was used by other industries, like automobiles and steel, for quality control and other purposes. Four percent of industry output was in the form of binoculars and astronomical instruments, and about three percent consisted of microscopes. The remaining 50 percent of sales was garnered from miscellaneous devices.

Most products in the industry use compound (more than one) lens systems. A series of several convex and/or concave lenses is often used to magnify light reflected from an image. Although a single convex lens will theoretically focus incoming light, such a system typically suffers from defects which cause blurring and distortion. Therefore, many lens systems, such as those in cameras, use eight or more lenses in series or cemented together to reduce aberration, coma (blurring), and distortion.

Lenses are typically manufactured from glass in a process called grinding. First, the glass is cast in blocks, strips, panes, and rods, or may be molded into a rough lens form. Then it is cut and rough-ground using a diamond abrasive on a grinding wheel. Fine grinding is accomplished using a silicon carbide or emery abrasive. For fine optical instruments, final polishing may take several hours using a precise lapping tool. Finally, the edge of the lens is ground so that its axis is precisely centered. Sometimes the lens is coated with a substance that reduces distortion. In addition to glass, transparent plastics are also used for lenses. They are simply molded, rather than ground.

BACKGROUND AND DEVELOPMENT

Modification of simple glass lenses has been practiced since ancient times, but the development of compound lens devices did not occur until 1600. Dutch lensmaker Hans Jannsen and his son, Zacharias, mounted sliding lenses in a tube in 1600 to form the first simple microscope. In 1611, a compound lens system which used a convex lens in the microscope's eyepiece was built by Johannes Kepler.

Historians often credit Hans Lippershey of Holland with inventing the telescope in 1608, as he accidentally aligned two lenses of opposite curvature and different focal length. However, the concept may have been understood earlier in the thirteenth century, by Roger Bacon. Galileo Galilei developed the first lens, or refracting, astronomical telescope in 1609. Christian Huygens improved his design soon afterward with a telescope that reduced aberration. While these simple devices suffered a variety of defects, they achieved useful results.

During the remainder of the seventeenth century, compound optical instruments were vastly improved to increase magnifying power and reduce distortion. Important developments included Isaac Newton's design in 1668 of a reflecting telescope that used mirrors to reduce aberration. Innovations during the eighteenth century largely reduced aberration and distortion in both telescopes and microscopes, resulting in apparatus which closely resemble the instruments commonly used during most of the twentieth century.

Early during the twentieth century, optical apparatus manufacturers focused on increasing power, or magnification. New lens manufacturing and mounting techniques allowed significant gains. Telescopes, for example, with refracting lenses of 36 and 40 inches and reflectors of 150 inches, were eventually built in the largest observatories. But conventional glass lens magnifying technology was approaching its limit. Large refracting lenses suffered from distortion caused by sagging under their own weight. After World War II, scientists began searching for optical instruments that used alternatives to glass lenses, such as radio waves and magnetic lenses, to improve microscope and telescope devices.

In addition to the development of optical devices that don't use glass lenses, new types of optical devices emerged during the mid-1900s. Optical apparatus that could be used to control laser beams, for example, became an important industry offering. And the creation of new electro-optical devices opened up entirely new markets in other industries. By the 1980s, electro-optical equipment was being used to analyze and control manufacturing processes, guide missiles, operate audio-visual systems, and to perform many other functions. Optical interferometers, for example, were developed to measure wavelengths , and optical metallographs were created to study the structure of metals and their compounds.

CURRENT CONDITIONS

Although U.S. export growth had slowed some in the early 1990s, optical industry imports had grown at a rate of about one percent per year during the 1980s, to about $900 million. U.S. producers were poised to compete in the burgeoning high-tech market with new innovations such as advanced laser-optics and new liquid crystal devices, which accounted for a combined 35 percent of U.S. exports. Sales in the next few years did not continue to decline, as previously expected, but instead continued a gradual inclined pattern. By 1996, sighting, tracking, and fire-control equipment (optical-type) made up 34.38 percent of total shares in the optical industry. Optical instruments and lenses made up 62.02 percent. And finally, binoculars and astronomical instruments made up 4.79 percent of the total shares.

INDUSTRY LEADERS

Leading companies in the industry in 1996 included Hughes Electronics Corporation, Bausch & Lomb Incorporated, and Tracor, Inc. Headquartered in Los Angeles, CA, Hughes had sales of $14 billion and employed 84,000. Bausch & Lomb, headquartered in Rochester, NY, had revenue of $1.93 billion and employed 14,400, and Tracor, of Austin, TX, had $886.9 million in sales and 9,700 employees.

RESEARCH AND TECHNOLOGY

Long term growth will depend on the ability of U.S. companies to continue to introduce new, high-profit optical technologies, and also to improve on existing ones. Scanning equipment, used for business, home, security, and banking purposes, has been one of the most promising areas for the optical industry. Once the size of copier machines, scanners can now fit on a desktop quite easily. They perform similar functions as a fax or copy machine, some with the added capability of copying an image onto a computer screen. Approximately 1.6 million scanners were shipped in 1995, 25 percent of which Infotrends Research Group Inc. estimates were for home use. This group also predicts that eight million of these scanners will be sold by the year 2000.

In the hopes of increasing efficiency and decreasing labor costs, Star Market Company of Cambridge installed four scanner stations in one of its stores. In this system, consumers scan, bag and pay for their merchandise, while filmed on a nearby security monitor. Similar types of scanners are also being used for tagging items in retail stores to aid in loss prevention. Another use for them is in banking institutions. A check-scanning system has already been employed at

Wachovia Corp. Officials claim improved accuracy and speed of transactions.

Down-sizing has increased sales of a new type of lightweight binoculars. One model, created by BNOX Inc. of New York, weighs a mere four ounces and measures 2 x 2 x 4 inches. Other companies have picked up on this trend, apparently anticipating the predicted increase demand for birding-specific and compact binoculars. 1996 sales figures showed a 11.4 percent sales increase in binoculars. The *Sporting Goods Business* 1997 Vendor Optics Survey found that manufacturers predict a 14.9 percent sales growth in binocular sales.

Researchers hope to reach into distant galaxies with the help of new innovations in telescope technology. Scientists from the John Baldwin School in Cambridge have immensely improved upon existing telescopes by developing a telescope called the Cambridge Optical Aperture Synthesis Telescope which has a fifty times greater magnification than current models. Another telescope, called the Very Large Telescope, is currently being developed in Chile atop Mt. Paranal by the European Southern Observatory. This telescope will measure 8.2 meters in diameter, with capabilities for detecting extra-solar planets and also conducting spectroscopic studies of distant galaxies.

A depth-sensitive lens, created by entrepreneur Chris Mayhew, enables a wider, sharper field to be captured on film. Mayhew acquired $4.5 million from investors to launch what he calls Vision III. The lens operates in conjunction with a computer- programmed controller, and is compatible with both TV cameras and standard motion picture.

FURTHER READING

Bureau, William H. "Properties in Perspective." *Graphic Arts Monthly,* March 1991.

Darnay, Arsen J., ed. *Manufacturing USA.* 5th ed. Detroit: Gale Research, 1996.

Dorminey, Bruce. "Into Infinity." *The Financial Times,* 10 September 1996.

Dykeman, John. "A Scanner at Your Desk?" *Managing Office Technology,* March 1996.

Farhi, Paul, "Vision III's Depth-Defining Feat." *Washington Post,* 4 March 1996, WB15.

Grolier's Encyclopedia. Danbury, CT: Grolier's Inc., 1993.

Holve, Donald J. "Sizing Particles With a Laser." *R&D,* March 1991.

McEvoy, Christopher. "SGB Survey: Optics '97.' *Sporting Goods Business,* Dec 1996.

Owen, Jean V. "Seeing the Unseen." *Manufacturing Engineering,* April 1993.

Polidor, Edward T. "Noncontact: Faster Measurement Data." *Quality,* August 1991.

Port, Otis and Neil Gross, "Japan: Scientists." *Business Week,* 15 June 1990.

Stout, Gail. "Machine Visions Systems." *Quality,* January 1993.

Tejada, Carlos. "Scanners Finally Find a Place in Homes." *The Wall Street Journal,* 20 May 1996.

Tracy, Brian. "Wachovia Moves Into Check Imaging Elite." *American Banker,* 3 April 1995.

U.S. Department of Commerce. International Trade Adminstration. *U.S. Industrial Outlook 1993.* Washington: GPO, 1993.

Ward's Business Directory of U.S. Private and Public Companies. Detroit: Gale Research, 1996.

Zimmerman, Denise. "Star Market to Install Self-Scanning Stations in One Unit." *Supermarket News,* 12 February 1996.

—Dave Mote, updated by Jill Stanley

SIC 3829

MEASURING AND CONTROLLING DEVICES, NOT ELSEWHERE CLASSIFIED

This industry is comprised of companies primarily engaged in manufacturing a multitude of miscellaneous monitoring instruments. Major industry product segments include aircraft engine instruments (14 percent of industry sales in the late 1990s), nuclear radiation detection devices (13 percent), geophysical and meteorological equipment (32 percent), and physical properties testing and inspection equipment (27 percent). This industry also encompasses companies that produce selected surveying and drafting supplies (6 percent), such as transits, slide rules, and T-squares. For more information on the history of measuring devices, see other entries in SIC group 382.

After 1950, rising demand for measuring and controlling devices by aerospace, nuclear, and petroleum industries pushed industry revenues to about $2 billion by the end of the 1970s. Likewise, increased defense spending and general U.S. economic growth, combined with steady export gains, almost doubled revenues during the 1980s. Indeed, as aerospace and nuclear device sales proliferated, overall industry sales grew at an average rate of 7 percent between 1982 and 1990, to more than $4 billion. Exports represented 40 percent of shipments.

Sharp cutbacks in defense spending and the virtual cessation of new nuclear facility construction in the United States rattled industry participants in the early 1990s. Despite some domestic setbacks, the demand for meteorological measuring devices continued to grow, and exports surged. Sales in physical properties testing took up the rest of the slack in the industry, passing up meteorological measuring in 1995 as the biggest division within the industry in terms of sales dollars. Total value of shipments in 1995 was $4.6 billion, with physical properties accounting for $1.5 billion of that total, and meteorological measuring devices accounting for $1.4 billion. Exports still had a commanding portion of sales, at 40 percent, though imports increased, bringing the trade surplus down to $1.1 billion.

In the long term, the miscellaneous measuring and controlling devices industry will likely realize tepid growth. Low interest in domestic nuclear facility development and reduced defense expenditures will severely curtail industry expansion. Japan, South Korea, and Taiwan, which will offer major export markets for radiation testing devices, should partially offset a slowdown in major domestic segments.

The industry was fragmented in comparison to other U.S. manufacturing sectors, with an estimated 908 companies competing in the late 1990s. The average industry participant employed only 38 workers in 1994, compared to 49 for all other U.S. manufacturing firms. Most firms were specialized, and only two of the top 20 companies even made above $500 million. A large number of the firms were small, though the larger ones continued to grow. In the early 1990s, most top firms employed less than 400 people. Through 1996, each of the top 20 companies employed more than 700 people.

The largest producer was Vishay Intertechnology, Inc, boasting 1996 sales of $1.1 billion. Although sales were down slightly from their $1.2 billion figure of 1995, Vishay remained dominant. Vishay's nearest competitor in 1996 was AMETEK, Inc., with sales of $808 million. Imo Industries Inc., of New Jersey, which had 1991 sales of $1 billion, came in third with $464 million in sales, a virtual plummet from their dominant position in the early 1990s. Other leaders included MTS Systems Corp. ($234 million in 1996 sales), Computer Products, Inc. ($191 million), and Electroglas, Inc. ($170 million).

Although industry employment remained steady during the 1980s—at about 37,000 workers—increased automation and the movement of some manufacturing activities overseas will likely result in work force cutbacks during the 1990s. Most labor jobs, such as those for assemblers and material handlers, will decline by 30 percent to 50 percent between 1990 and 2005, according to the Bureau of Labor Statistics. In fact, by 1996 the work force as a whole had dropped 17 percent from 1990, and production workers fell 11 percent since 1992. Likewise, executive and managerial support positions were projected to fall 10 percent to 20 percent. Only openings for sales and marketing professionals were forecast to rise—by a slim 2.5 percent by 2005.

FURTHER READING

Darnay, Arsen J., ed. *Manufacturing USA; Industry Analyses, Statistics, and Leading Companies.* Detroit: Gale Research Inc., 1996.

''Financial News.'' *Vishay Intertechnology, Inc.,* 4 April 1997. Available from http://vishay.com/vishay/news/freleases/FourthQ.html.

Standard & Poor's Industry Surveys. New York: Standard & Poor's Corporation, 24 December 1992.

U.S. Department of Commerce. *U.S. Industrial Outlook 1994.* Washington: GPO, January 1995.

SIC 3841

SURGICAL AND MEDICAL INSTRUMENTS AND APPARATUS

This category covers establishments primarily engaged in manufacturing medical, surgical, ophthalmic, and veterinary instruments and apparatus. Establishments primarily engaged in manufacturing surgical and orthopedic appliances are classified in **SIC 3842: Orthopedic, Prosthetic, and Surgical Appliances and Supplies;** those manufacturing electrotherapeutic and electromedical apparatus are classified in **SIC 3845: Electromedical and Electrotherapeutic Apparatus;** and those manufacturing X-ray apparatus are classified in **SIC 3844: X-ray Apparatus and Tubes and Related Irradiation Apparatus.**

INDUSTRY SNAPSHOT

The first medical instruments of precision were used in the seventeenth century. Not until the eighteenth century was surgery recognized as a definite branch of science. Rapid advances that took place in the twentieth century resulted in the evolution of a $28 billion U.S. surgical instrument industry by 1996. Without question, the U.S. maintains the most advanced surgical device industry in the world. Besides serving a critical role in the care of Americans' health, the medical and surgical instrument industry presently employs 102,000 individuals.

In the early 1990s, manufacturers continued to enjoy the fruits of their success. Revenues increased at an average rate of over 9 percent in 1990, 1991, and 1992, and they were expected to rise similarly in 1993. Profit growth mimicked this trend. International demand for U.S. surgical and medical instruments continued to set new industry standards as 1996 revenues exceeded $10 billion. And, notwithstanding productivity gains, industry employment had grown at approximately 5 percent per year in the early 1990s. Substantial growth is anticipated for employment abroad in 1997 as a result of a recent effort by Congress to reform U.S. Food and Drug Administration (FDA) regulations.

Despite an overall positive industry environment, medical instrument producers faced several hurdles going into the mid-1990s. Reduced availability of capital for research and development (R&D), a frustrating slowdown in FDA new product approvals, and the promise of a nationalized health care system under the Clinton administration were the major issues concerning competitors. Several segments of the industry appeared to be reaching maturity, indicating that overall profit growth might begin slowing in the future.

ORGANIZATION AND STRUCTURE

Major consumers of industry output in the early 1990s, in order of market size, included foreign consumers, the federal government, medical and health services, doctors and dentists, hospitals, individuals consumers, and drug companies.

Over 20,000 medical device manufacturers were registered in the United States in 1996. Fewer than 1,500 of these firms, however, were engaged primarily in this industry.

The industry is relatively unconcentrated, partly because it is in a stage of growth and has not matured. However, unlike many other high-growth businesses, barriers to entry are significant. Companies often must incur huge start-up costs to cover research and product development costs. Furthermore, acute technical expertise is typically needed to develop proprietary knowledge necessary to differentiate products from others in the marketplace and to obtain approvals and patents. Companies that overcome these hurdles, however, often reap large profits if their products succeed.

Products. The industry encompasses a plethora of non-electric diagnostic and therapeutic surgical devices. ''Diagnostic'' refers to equipment used to identify physical problems based on signs and symp-

toms. Therapeutic devices are used to actually treat ailments and illnesses. Some of the largest general categories of equipment are hand instruments, monitoring equipment, intravenous apparatus, syringes, and catheters.

Examples of hand instruments include forceps, knives, saws, retractors, clamps, bone drills, and other products. Forceps are used to grasp, pull, and hold objects during delicate operations. Several monitoring devices also exist. Gastroscopes, for instance, are used to view the interior of the stomach. Cystoscopes provide a view of the interior of the bladder. Likewise, a laryngoscope is used to study the larynx and vocal cords. Ophthalmoscopes permit inspection of the retina, and stethoscopes are used to listen to internal organs, particularly the heart and lungs. Intravenous equipment basically consists of IV transfusion apparatus, which transfer blood or other fluids into the body.

Other devices produced in the industry include tonometers, speculums, skin grafting equipment, sphygmomanometers, silt lamps, hypodermic rifles, surgical probes, operating tables, needle holders, inhalators, and bone plates and screws.

Catheters, an important industry segment, are tubes that are inserted into various body cavities to drain liquids or remove material. In 1996, 6.3 million catheterizations were performed by cardiologists and radiologists. Cardiac catheterization involves introducing a small catheter into a vein and then passing it into the heart. This procedure allows doctors to get accurate diagnostic measurements or to clear blocked arteries. A more advanced procedure, angioplasty, incorporates a tiny balloon into the procedure. As an ultra-thin catheter is slipped into an artery, the balloon is inflated, thereby widening clogged arteries. Catheters are also used to drain urine and other bodily fluids.

Federal Regulation. An important dynamic influencing the industry's production and profitability is FDA regulation. The FDA is responsible for insuring that all products sold in the industry comply with federal safety standards. The FDA possesses the authority to recall products, temporarily suspend devices it deems high-risk, and impose monetary penalties for violations. Much of the FDA's export approval power over American medical devices was taken away by Congress in a 1996 amendment.

The 1990 Safe Medical Devices Act (SMDA), which defined procedures for bringing medical products to the market, is one of the most significant pieces of legislation governing producers. Among other stipulations, the SMDA requires certain manufacturers to track patients that should be notified in the case of product failure; submit follow-up reviews for certain implants and devices; and, when applying for pre-market clearance, provide a summary of safety and effectiveness data for each device.

The FDA reviews medical devices under one of two procedures. Firms introducing completely new devices are required to submit a Product Marketing Application (PMA). The PMA must demonstrate the device's safety, as well as its diagnostic or therapeutic benefit. Detailed documentation of extensive animal and human tests must be provided to the FDA to support manufacturer claims. New devices resembling products already on the market are reviewed under a less stringent procedure called "501(k) pre-market notification." In 1992 about 2,500 new products were approved under the 501(k) procedure. Conversely, only 12 PMAs were approved in that year.

BACKGROUND AND DEVELOPMENT

In the early 1600s, Sanctorious, an Italian professor, was the first physician to employ diagnostic instruments of precision in the practice of medicine. Using a pendulum made from a cord and a weight, he was able to measure a pulse rate by adjusting the weight until it swung at an even tempo with the patient's pulse. Sanctorious later implemented a type of thermometer that could measure a patient's weight and temperature. Both inventions were influenced by his friend Galileo.

Although crude forms of surgery had been practiced prior to that time, the seventeenth and eighteenth centuries produced several advancements in surgical and anatomical knowledge. Noted physicians—such as Englishmen William Harvey, John Monro, Robert Sibbald, and Archibald Pitcairne—contributed to the science and helped to establish some of the first formal educational institutions for doctors. Microscopes, injection needles, and instruments of dissection were a few of the tools that allowed researchers of that period to gain a comprehensive understanding of the internal human structure, as well as of physiological processes.

An important American contribution to the advancement of surgery was anesthetic devices, which were introduced in the mid-1800s. Crawford Long, Gardner Colton, and Horace Wells shared credit for breakthroughs in ether and nitrous oxide anesthetics. The nineteenth century also brought important inventions such as the ophthalmoscope, the sphygmomanometer (for measuring blood pressure), and the stethoscope. The first stethoscope, which was invented in 1816, consisted of a perforated wooden cylinder that transmitted sounds from the patient's chest to the doctor's ear. Perhaps more important than new instruments, though, was a gradual understanding of germs

during the 1800s. This evolution led to the use of antiseptics, as well as surgical caps, masks, and rubber gloves in the 1890s.

While surgical tools and techniques advanced throughout the eighteenth and nineteenth centuries, surgery remained a relatively crude science up until the early 1900s. Even by the turn of the century, surgery more closely resembled a craft than a science. Forceful, hearty surgeons of the time viewed themselves as omniscient pioneers heralding in a new age. Armed with antiseptics, they were prepared to tackle any challenge.

Despite their knowledge of germs, most surgeons before 1910 continued to operate without gloves, masks, or caps. They commonly wore the same smock until it was caked with blood from several surgeries and would continue using instruments that had been dropped on a bloody floor. Surgery was usually performed in a theater-type setting before an audience as the patient lay on a narrow wooden table. Instruments were usually forged steel, without plating, and had wooden or ivory handles. Because amputation was one of the most common procedures, the saw was a favored tool.

The twentieth century, particularly the first 40 years, ushered in an entirely new era of medicine. Better anesthetics, more highly educated and specialized surgeons, and X-ray machines prompted a transition to more scientific surgery and the demand for new types of instruments. New materials, such as stainless steel and plastics, broadened the scope of the device and apparatus industry. Catheters, suction devices, intravenous infusion apparatus, and various mechanical and electrical diagnostic devices were a few of the important inventions that occurred prior to 1930. This new equipment opened up entirely new surgical specialties, such as neurosurgery and cardiac and urinary tract surgery.

Instruments and apparatus introduced in the postwar period were numerous. Inactive metals, such as vitalium and tantalum, were used to create wire and mesh devices that could be left inside the body. Likewise, nylon thread and special plastics, orlon tubing used in place of arteries, plastic sponges that patched heart defects, and other indwelling devices were introduced. In addition, the vast array of diagnostic and therapeutic equipment that comprised industry offerings by the 1980s was gradually developed in the 1950s, 1960s, and 1970s to complement ever-increasing medical knowledge.

By 1980, the medical instrument and apparatus industry was shipping nearly $4 billion worth of products each year. Stellar sales growth since the 1960s was attributable to several factors. Employer-sponsored health care systems developed after World War II offered few incentives for providers to control costs. As a result, expenditures on instruments and apparatus, as well as other health care products and services, ballooned. In fact, throughout the 1970s and 1980s, U.S. health care expenditures rose at a rate of more than 10 percent per year.

Other factors that contributed to growth in expenditures—particularly during the 1970s and 1980s—included a burgeoning elderly population and a general increase in demand for health care. General demand growth was largely a result of the development of new, more advanced procedures and equipment designed to deliver more comprehensive and higher quality care. Indeed, between 1965 and 1990, the percentage of the gross domestic product (GDP) Americans spent on health care jumped from 6 percent to over 15 percent. Some of the fastest growing segments included instruments for angioplasty, cardiac catheterization, and orthopedic operations.

As expenditures leapt during the 1980s, development and sales of instruments and apparatus blossomed. While manufacturers made massive investments in new product research and development, expenditures on industry products averaged jumps of more than 10 percent annually between 1980 and 1990. Furthermore, exports continued to grow as foreign markets looked to the United States as a source of state-of-the-art surgical instruments and apparatus. Throughout the 1980s, in fact, U.S. firms dominated over 50 percent of the world market for surgical supplies.

By 1990, industry participants were generating over $10.2 billion in revenues per year, employing nearly 90,000 workers, and exporting over $1.8 billion in shipments. Besides providing a trade surplus of more than $1 billion annually, the industry was a comparatively non-polluting member of the manufacturing community and was a source of many high wage jobs.

Surgical and medical instrument and apparatus manufacturers continued to post solid gains in the early 1990s, in light of a generally sluggish U.S. and global economy. Revenues ascended about 10 percent in both 1991 and 1992 and were projected to grow by over 8 percent in 1993. Exports, moreover, jumped an average of 14 percent per year between 1989 and 1993.

CURRENT CONDITIONS

As the industry's sales volume clambered past an impressive $28 billion, employment surged to over 102,000 in 1996. Success was partially attributable to massive industry investments, which amounted to about 6.5 percent of revenues in the early 1990s. The average investment for other U.S. industries was about 3.6 percent of sales. Medical device firms in the European Community and Japan, moreover, reinvested only 5 percent and 6 percent, respectively.

Leading growth in the 1990s was a promising new sphere of "minimally invasive" surgical instruments. These devices allowed surgeons to conduct complex operations without the pain, time, and expense associated with conventional procedures. Laparoscopic and endoscopic devices, for instance, involved the insertion of narrow tubes, called trocars, into a patient's abdomen. A laparoscope inserted into the tube is used to take pictures of the patient's inner organs, and miniature devices sent through the tube are used to perform complex surgical procedures. The market for minimally invasive devices was expected to explode in the 1990s and 2000s.

Another leading growth segment in the early 1990s was angioplasty catheters. In 1992 about 400,000 angioplasty procedures were performed at a cost of $550 million—compared with 184,000 such operations in 1987 and only 82,000 in 1982. The procedure provided an important alternative to heart bypass surgery in many cases.

Indeed, because of the changing dynamics of the health care market, cost-containment pressures were driving the growth of new money-saving procedures like angioplasty and laparoscopy. As purchasing decisions in the 1980s and 1990s shifted from physicians to hospitals and managed care facilities, producers were being forced to demonstrate the cost effectiveness of their products. Devices that could reduce hospital stays, increase labor productivity, and facilitate patient care in less expensive settings had become the dominant growth market by the mid-1990s.

Industry executives maintained an expectedly rosy outlook going into the mid-1990s, according to a 1993 survey of 242 company presidents and CEOs in *Medical Device & Diagnostic Industry (MDDI)*. The survey indicated that 80 percent of respondents predicted that their business would improve in 1993, while only 2 percent expected a decline. Eighty percent of the respondents believed that new product introduction and overall increased unit sales would spur growth, while 21 percent were relying on price growth to boost profits. About 66 percent of the respondents planned to increase research and development expenditures, while less than 1 percent planned a reduction.

Challenges. Despite strong growth and optimism, competitors were facing significant obstacles to continued profitability as they entered the mid-1990s. Growing regulatory costs and barriers, decreased access to investment capital, and increased competition in the health care industry all posed formidable challenges. Furthermore, some large segments, such as catheters, appeared to be entering a stage of maturity—meaning slower growth and reduced profit margins.

Inadequate funding for growth and research and development was the primary concern of industry executives in 1993, according to the *MDDI* survey. A decline in venture capital, traditionally a significant source of medical device research and development funding, was a major reason for the shortfall. As FDA regulations increased, venture capitalists viewed new projects as riskier. Furthermore, the promise of nationalized health care by the Clinton administration had created a perception of industry instability in the minds of many lenders.

The impact of reduced funding was made most apparent by the reduction in the growth of new start-up companies. After increasing 12 percent in 1991, the number of new start-up firms grew only 7 percent in 1992. "Companies looking for venture capital to fund research and development for a breakthrough product that has yet to see its first dollar of sales should look for something else to do," said Brent Rider, a venture capitalist, in *MDDI.*

Besides decreasing research and development capital, President Clinton's national health care proposal in 1993 boded poorly for manufacturers. Clinton backed a system during his campaign which emphasized comprehensive national care—a plan which would add 35 million people to the U.S. medical device market. The proposal that the Clinton administration delivered to Congress in 1994, however, incorporated sweeping government controls that implied some negatives for manufacturers. Specifically, the use of high-priced exotic devices would decline, and less expensive drug therapy would increase in proportion to procedures requiring surgical implements.

Most important, though, analysts feared that the "health care review board" and price controls proposed by the plan would debilitate new product development, crush capital investment in the industry, curb the demand for high-tech products, and reduce foreign demand for advanced U.S. exports. The review board, rather than the market, would have been authorized to decide on the cost effectiveness of new technology. It would also determine the eligibility of products for insurance reimbursement. Industry representatives were rigorously opposed to the plan.

FDA Stymies New Products. Besides a capital shortage and the threat of nationalized health care, the most prolific problem facing manufacturers in the early 1990s was a slowdown in FDA product approvals. In 1993 producers were still scrambling to learn how to comply with stringent new product standards imposed by the SMDA of 1990. And, the FDA seemed unable to efficiently process applications for approvals. Device executives labeled this dilemma the number two concern facing the industry in 1993.

After the FDA's initiation of the SMDA, approvals for new products fell dramatically. Although the FDA received 5,000 501(k) applications in 1991 and 1992, the number of approved products slipped from 3,000 in 1991 to just 2,500 in 1992. Furthermore, in mid-1993 the FDA had a backlog of 1,400 applications that had been pending for over three months—the historical norm is closer to 20. PMAs showed even greater declines. Usually submitted at a rate of 60 to 70 per year, PMA approvals fell from 47 in 1990 to 27 in 1991, and to only 12 in 1992. The FDA was also under Congressional order to review 130 products that went on sale prior to 1976. FDA approval for new medical devices in 1996 takes an average of 2.2 years, which is twice the amount of time the same process took in 1992.

In an effort to speed the process, the medical device industry began supporting proposed user fees. Under the proposal, firms would be required to pay a fee for each application processed by the FDA. A similar fee system implemented in 1993 for pharmaceutical firms was costing that industry approximately $36 million per year. However, the FDA had reason for caution. It came under fire in the 1980s and 1990s for approving a heart valve connected with 300 deaths and for permitting the sale of silicon breast implants.

In response to FDA initiatives, the Medical Device Manufacturers Association (MDMA) was formed in November of 1992. It succeeded the Small Manufacturers Medical Device Association that was established in 1980. The organization's focus was to ensure that FDA regulations did not adversely affect the industry, particularly smaller manufacturers.

The Future. Congress loosened the collar on the FDA's regulations of the surgical and medical instruments industry in 1996. U.S. companies will no longer need FDA approval for products intended solely for the export market. This provision will undoubtedly ensure that Europe will become the industry testing ground for U.S. companies. Historically significant industry segments, such as catheters and syringes, will offer less profit potential as markets for those products mature and become more competitive. Market growth for leading-edge minimally invasive surgical tools and devices, however, will supplant profits from declining segments.

Although growth attained in the 1970s and 1980s will likely wane, shipments are expected to grow at a healthy 6 percent per year (above inflation) through 1997. The market for endoscopic instruments, for example, was expected to grow from $550 million in 1992 to over $3 billion by 1996. Laparoscopic surgery, moreover, will likely account for 80 percent of all abdominal surgery performed by the turn of the century.

An aging population requiring more health care will augment overall growth. In addition, U.S. firms were well positioned to take advantage of emerging foreign markets going into the mid-1990s. Increased efficiency of the new FDA approval process should eventually diminish that industry hurdle, though possibly at a significant cost to competitors.

INDUSTRY LEADERS

The largest manufacturer of surgical and medical instruments and apparatus in the mid-1990s was Baxter International Inc. and its subsidiary, Baxter Healthcare Corp. Based in Deerfield, Illinois, this industry giant racked up over $5.4 billion in 1996 sales while employing 37,000 workers. For more information about Baxter, see **SIC 3842: Orthopedic, Prosthetic, and Surgical Appliances and Supplies.**

Siemens Medical Systems, Inc., of New Jersey, was the second largest producer of surgical and medical instruments in 1996 generating $4.6 billion in sales. The industry's runner-up, whose parent company is based in Germany, provided employment for 18,000 individuals.

Other companies with significant international sales in 1996 were Becton, Dickinson & Co. of Franklin Lakes, New Jersey ($2.7 billion); Minneapolis, Minnesota based Medtronic ($2.2 billion); Boston Scientific Corp. ($1.1 billion); and United States Surgical Corp. ($1.02 billion). The industry also saw five additional member companies enjoy sales in excess of $700 million while each also provided employment opportunities for at least 4,000 individuals.

Despite the dominance of a few massive competitors, such as Baxter and Siemens, the industry remained relatively unconcentrated in the mid-1990s. Like most growth industries, revenues are spread among a multitude of niche firms that have developed proprietary products or production techniques, or excel at marketing or distribution. The majority of the top 75 firms competing in the industry through 1996 each produced sales of less than $100 million and employed fewer than 1,000 workers.

WORK FORCE

The ongoing FDA approval barrier has caused U.S. companies in this industry to focus their attention overseas when introducing new products. A 1996 study conducted by the Wilkerson Group for the Health Industry Manufacturers Association showed that roughly 10,000 industry jobs with average salaries of $50,000 are being exported yearly. Industry analysts cite that while both corporate and industry growth stand to benefit from Congress' export-approval provision, U.S. operations will continue to dwindle.

SURGICAL INSTRUMENTS INDUSTRY EMPLOYMENT

Employment in thousands

Source: Department of Labor

Although a total of more than 21,000 companies were licensed to produce medical devices in 1993, only about 1,200 of those firms were primarily engaged in producing surgical and medical instruments and apparatus. Those firms employed over 100,000 in 1993. An undetermined number of workers were engaged in making products that fit this industry classification but were produced by companies primarily engaged in other industries.

Assemblers and fabricators comprised 14 percent of this industry's work force in the early 1990s. Inspectors, testers, and graders accounted for 3.4 percent of employment, and manufacturing supervisors made up 3.3 percent. Other blue collar manufacturing positions represented an additional 60 percent of the work force. Salespersons accounted for 6 percent of nonlabor workers, while secretaries and clerical staff accounted for about 5 percent. Relatively high-paying engineering positions accounted for over 6 percent of the work force, while white collar managers and executives represented about 3.3 percent.

Fifteen percent of industry executives indicated a desire to move manufacturing facilities to foreign countries in 1993, and many competitors were seeking increased productivity through automation. Despite these facts, employment prospects were positive going into the 1990s. The Bureau of Labor Statistics estimated that most occupations in the industry would grow significantly through 2000. Jobs for engineers, for instance, were expected to grow by 60 to 70 percent between 1990 and 2005. Sales and marketing positions, moreover, were forecast to rise by more than 70 percent. Most management jobs will increase by around 40 percent by 2005.

Although blue collar production jobs will generally rise, the jump will be less substantial. Inspection, supervision, packaging, and shipping positions will rise by 30 to 50 percent by 2005. However, the number of jobs related to parts assembly, which account for about 18 percent the industry's work force, will stagnate or decline.

AMERICA AND THE WORLD

With roughly one-half ($2.7 billion) of Baxter International's 1996 sales coming from outside the United States, this industry giant more than doubled the 1993 surgical and medical instruments export figures of all U.S. companies ($2.6 billion). Although the U.S. share of the entire global medical device market fell from 60 percent in 1980 to about 50 percent in 1993, rapid expansion of global markets allowed domestic producers to sustain record export growth throughout that period. America's share of the world market was expected to decline to 40 percent by 2000, though export sales volume should rise steadily, even outpacing domestic growth.

The United States remained the world leader in medical device technology and maintained an especially dominant role in medical and dental instruments and supplies. This role was threatened, however, by an increasingly competitive global industry. Japanese and German producers had made significant strides in some market segments, such as high-tech electromedical equipment and some diagnostic machines. Furthermore, Japan plans to increase its investment in medical device research and development in an effort to catch up with capital expenditures made by their U.S. and German counterparts during the early 1990s.

Although Japan maintained the second largest market for medical devices in the world, the United States held a meager 12 percent share of that market in

the early 1990s. Japan, in contrast, enjoyed relatively free access to American markets and accounted for over 20 percent of U.S. imports. Surgical and medical instrument imports into the United States in 1993, though, captured less than 9 percent of that market. The European Community delivered about 29 percent of U.S. imports in the early 1990s, Mexico and Canada sold 16 percent, and East Asian firms garnered about 14 percent of import revenues. Miscellaneous countries captured the remaining 20 percent. The largest buyer of U.S. goods was Canada, followed closely by Japan and Germany. Those three countries, combined with France and Mexico, consumed 50 percent of all industry exports.

Improving U.S. manufacturer prospects in the global instruments and apparatus market were two important international agreements that were hammered out in 1993. In July, seven major industrialized nations agreed to remove all inter-country tariffs on drugs and medical equipment, contingent on passage of the larger General Agreement on Trade and Tariffs (GATT). This development was expected to save U.S. medical industries $400 million per year. If the European Community agreed on a similar proposal, U.S. firms would benefit by only having to file for one permit to sell each product, rather than one for each of the 12 nations.

The second major agreement expected to boost sales was the North American Free Trade Agreement (NAFTA), which Congress passed in November of 1993. NAFTA was expected to save companies in the industry $100 million annually from eliminated tariffs. In addition, investment restrictions on companies seeking to do business in Mexico were eliminated. The agreement also insured that the Mexican government, which made 70 percent of all national health care purchases, would open procurement processes to U.S. bidders.

In the *MDDI* survey, industry executives identified their most promising export growth markets in order of importance as Canada, Europe, Japan, the Pacific Rim, Mexico, and Latin America.

RESEARCH AND TECHNOLOGY

The medical and surgical device and apparatus industry is heavily driven by technological advances. In fact, much of the growth in U.S. health care expenditures which occurred during the 1960s, 1970s, and 1980s is attributable to the introduction of costly, high-tech equipment. For manufacturers that have devised new and better devices to help remedy ailments and illnesses, care providers have afforded an enthusiastic market. Life-saving procedures that were unheard of before 1970, such as angioplasty and coronary by-pass, were commonplace in the early 1990s. Industry profits were booming partially as a result of the increased demand for these new procedures.

Although U.S. producers already invested nearly 7 percent of their revenues into research and development in the early 1990s, industry executives indicated their intent to boost this figure in the mid-1990s. Furthermore, additional money for research was expected to flow from government sources. The Clinton administration's "Defense Reinvestment and Conversion Initiative," which was developed in 1993, made available half a billion dollars for business partnerships designed to integrate America's high-tech defense industries into the civilian marketplace.

Although some industry analysts believed that medical device companies could be major benefactors of the program, similar efforts in the past had yielded mixed results. Efforts to use NASA technology in the industry, for example, were credited with development of only 100 devices between 1976 and 1990. The Defense Technology Conversion Council (DTCC), a consortium of five federal agencies that was formed in 1993, planned to improve the transfer of technology to the private sector with its Technology Reinvestment Project. The DTCC selected health care as one of its 11 focus areas and Clinton had proposed a $20 billion DTCC package.

Besides new product development, manufacturers were also concentrating on increased productivity going into the mid-1990s. A number of new flexible computer-integrated manufacturing techniques were being implemented. These techniques promised to synthesize manufacturing operations and promote international production standards. New information software had been developed, for instance, that helped device manufacturers integrate and manage software development, design changes, and testing data. The primary goal of such techniques was to reduce labor costs and increase productivity. Other companies were experimenting with cost-saving approaches like cellular manufacturing. By assigning a cell, or team, of workers responsibility for production of each product, some companies had increased productivity by 25 percent and improved product quality.

New and improved products in the early 1990s were numerous. Shape-memory polymers, for instance, are polyurethane-based polymers that can undergo and retain dramatic changes in hardness, flexibility, elasticity, and vapor permeability when exposed to heat. Among other uses, the resins were being used to form catheters that would remain stiff until inserted into the body. Similarly, new plastic springs offered an alternative to metal components in operations requiring resistance to corrosion and static charges.

The vast number of yearly catheterizations has left a hole in a market which has several companies willing to capitalize upon. Kensey-Nash, Datascope, and Perclose have all recently introduced sealing devices which make it plausible for catheterization holes to fill in as little as two minutes. Previously, small holes incurred as a result of a catheterization could take up to 30 minutes of pressure to seal while recovery could take up to 24 hours, or longer, if anticlotting drugs were used. The products from Kensey-Nash, of Exton, Pennsylvania and Datascope, of Montvale, New Jersey have both received FDA approval. Perclose expects to receive their approval in 1997.

Silicone balloon cuffs that could be manufactured through extrusion, rather than molding, were offering producers of laparoscopic and other devices the advantage of reduced production costs. Likewise, new injection-molded components were offering more efficient prototyping of new instruments and devices. Other new or improved products included miniature cables, high-tensile wire, heat-shrinking tubing, and a variety of minimally invasive instruments. Major product innovations were also occurring in the area of disposable devices, which were dominating many market segments in 1993 because of their convenience.

FURTHER READING

Baxter Financial Higlights. *1996 Annual Report.* Available from http://www.baxter.com/www/financialhighlights/ annualreport/1996/ financialhighlights.html.

"Beating Swords into Medical Devices." *Medical Device & Diagnostic Industry,* May 1993.

"Capital Slump Hits Device Start-Ups." *Medical Device & Diagnostic Industry,* August 1993.

Darnay, Arsen J., ed. *Manufacturing USA.* 5th ed. Detroit: Gale Research Inc., 1993.

Gianturco, Michael. "A Play on Catheterization." *Forbes,* 30 December 1996, 146.

Henke, Cliff. "1993 Business Outlook: Growing at Home and Abroad." *Medical Device & Diagnostic Industry,* March 1993.

"Industrial Outlook Positive Again." *Medical Device & Diagnostic Industry,* February 1993.

"Industry Weighs Long-Term Promise of NAFTA." *Medical Device & Diagnostic Industry,* January 1993.

Jereski, Laura. "Block That Innovation!" *Forbes,* 18 January 1993.

Lane, Randall. "It's a Start." *Forbes,* 3 June 1996, 97-98.

McGlynn, J. Casey. "Preparing for Health Care's New World Order." *Medical Device & Diagnostic Industry*, October 1993.

McVay, Patrick W., and Benjamin L. Hochman. "Federal Consortium Offers New Opportunities for Developing Medical Technologies." *Medical Device & Diagnostic Industry*, June 1993.

Moukheiber, Zina. "Dopey Duck's Revenge." *Forbes*, 27 September 1993.

Perle, Richard, and Martin Cannon. "Turning Swords into Market Shares." *Chief Executive*, May 1993.

"Putting the Lock on Medical Device Costs." *Industrial Engineering*. April 1993.

"Readers' Choice: The Year's Top 20 Products & Services." *Medical Device & Diagnostic Industry*, July 1993.

Rogers, Gregg. "Sites in the Sum: Device Start-Ups Find Warmth in California and Florida." *Medical Device & Diagnostic Industry*, May 1993.

Schooleman, Susan. "Industry Forecast Is That FDA Regulations Will Slow U.S. Market Growth During This Decade." *Health Industry Today*, December 1992.

Schooleman, Susan. "OR Industry Split on Merits of Disposable/Reusable Instruments." *Health Industry Today*, May 1993.

Standard & Poor's Industry Surveys. New York: Standard & Poor's Corporation, 31 December 1993.

Standard & Poor's Register CD. New York: McGraw-Hill Companies, Inc., 1997.

U.S. Department of Commerce. International Trade Administration. *U.S. Industrial Outlook 1993*. Washington: GPO, January 1993.

"U.S. Leader in Key International Standard, New Study Says." *Medical Device & Diagnostic Industry*, February 1993.

—Dave Mote, updated by Matthew C. Peck

SIC 3842

ORTHOPEDIC, PROSTHETIC, AND SURGICAL APPLIANCES AND SUPPLIES

This classification covers establishments primarily engaged in manufacturing orthopedic, prosthetic, and surgical appliances and supplies, arch supports, and other foot appliances; fracture appliances, elastic hosiery, abdominal supporters, braces, and trusses; bandages; surgical gauze and dressings; sutures; adhesive tapes and medicated plasters; and personal safety appliances and equipment. Establishments primarily engaged in manufacturing surgical and medical instruments are classified in **SIC 3841: Surgical and Medi-**

cal Instruments and Apparatus. Establishments primarily engaged in manufacturing orthopedic or prosthetic appliances and in the personal fitting to the individual prescription by a physician are classified in **SIC 5999: Miscellaneous Retail Stores, Not Elsewhere Classified.**

INDUSTRY SNAPSHOT

During the twentieth century, rapid medical advances spawned a huge market for all types of surgical and medical appliances and supplies. By the early 1990s, makers of devices classified in this industry were generating over $13 billion in annual sales and employing over 90,000 workers. Furthermore, they maintained a nearly $1 billion trade surplus.

In the mid-1990s, surgical appliance and supplies manufacturers hoped to benefit from solid market growth that had characterized the industry for over two decades. However, several issues clouded the industry's future. Slow product approvals from the Food and Drug Administration, the potential overhaul of the U.S. health care industry, and reduced availability of outside investment capital curtailed growth of the industry. In addition, several major players in the industry agreed to pay a total of $4.7 billion to as many as two million women who have experienced breast implant-related illnesses. Demographic factors and export opportunities, however, are regarded as sources of optimism for the industry.

ORGANIZATION AND STRUCTURE

The entire medical device industry, which is divided into six sub-industries, shipped about $42 billion worth of products in 1993. The surgical appliances industry described in this entry is the largest of those divisions, accounting for about 33 percent, or approximately $14 billion, of total medical product sales in 1995.

The industry experienced overall growth, large capital investment, and high profit margins in the early 1990s—indicators that an industry has usually not yet reached maturity. While high-tech devices accounted for most revenue and profit, other segments offered limited opportunities. For example, personal safety equipment and some appliances, such as wheelchairs and crutches, represented sectors of modest growth.

Personal consumption expenditures accounted for about 22 percent of industry sales in the 1980s. Government purchases, including purchases through health care facilities and hospitals, consumed about 15 percent of industry output. Hospitals represented an additional 14 percent of the market, and doctors and dentists purchased about 4 percent of manufacturers goods. Approximately 14 percent of sales were attributable to exports, and 12 percent of industry revenues were classified as gross private-fixed investment in the early 1990s. Miscellaneous consumers, which accounted for the remaining 19 percent of sales, included child care services, construction industries, correctional and educational institutions, the U.S. Department of Defense, and police departments.

Products. Surgical, orthopedic, and therapeutic appliances and supplies accounted for over 88 percent of industry output in the late 1980s, with orthopedic and prosthetic appliances comprising the largest share. (Orthopedic equipment refers to devices used in the preservation, restoration, and development of the form and function of the extremities and spine. The term prosthetic appliances in this industry refers to devices related to artificial limbs and joints. Popular hip and knee replacement devices, for instance, reduce pain and allow patients to regain mobility.)

Prosthetic and orthopedic appliances represented approximately 20 percent of industry sales in the late 1980s. Artificial joints, the largest single segment, accounted for about 6.5 percent of total sales, while artificial limbs made up less than 0.5 percent of shipments. Electronic hearing aids represented over 3 percent of revenues, and elastic braces and supports represented about 1.2 percent of shipments. Additionally, arch supports accounted for 1.5 percent of sales, and replacement and add-on parts for orthopedic and prosthetic devices accounted for 12 percent of industry shipments. This industry segment also includes the following products: bone plates, screws, and nails; mechanical braces; elastic stockings; surgical corsets; splints and trusses, and; intraocular lenses, or lens implants.

Therapeutic appliances and related supplies include a wide array of surgical dressings and devices. Surgical dressings, which include elastic bandages, plaster, gauze, and cotton swabs, represented nearly 13 percent of total industry sales in the late 1980s. Bed pads, adult diapers, and incontinent pads constituted an additional 6 percent share, and wheelchairs and other patient transport appliances accounted for about 2.5 percent of shipments. Examples of other products in this category are surgical kits, tongue depressors, breathing devices, and therapeutic whirlpool baths.

In addition to the 88 percent of the market represented by the products described above, this industry also encompasses a variety of personal and industrial safety equipment, which includes protective clothing, welders hoods, motorcycle and racing helmets, fire fighting suits and breathing apparatus, safety gloves,

bullet-proof vests, ear and nose plugs, safety goggles, and space suits.

Expected to show profit are high-ticket and technology items. The growth was comparatively less than the gains of the 1990s because of the flux of managed care spread among the industry at all levels.

BACKGROUND AND DEVELOPMENT

Prosthetics date back to 600 B.C. during the Roman Empire, when artificial legs were used to help amputees regain mobility. It was not until the sixteenth century, through the efforts of French surgeon Ambroise Pare, that prosthetics became a science. His work lead to the development, during the sixteenth and seventeenth centuries, of replacements for upper extremities. Metal hands, some of which contained moving parts and springs, became popular prosthetics in Europe during the 1600s. They were replaced in the 1700s by two innovations—a single hook, or a leather-covered, nonfunctioning hand attached to the forearm by a leather or wooden shell.

Public acceptance of prostheses, as well as improvements in design, paralleled major wars during the eighteenth, nineteenth, and twentieth centuries. In particular, World War I and World War II boosted the use of prosthetics, which benefited from the integration of new light-weight metals and better mechanical joints. Advances in materials and mechanical design were rampant during the post-World War II era, when the development of indwelling materials, such as coated steel, inactive metals, and durable synthetics, gave specialists new ways to replace or mend body joints and parts. New materials and mechanisms also made possible the creation of artificial limbs that more closely mimicked the natural body.

The term orthopedics was given to that specialty in 1741 by Nicholas Andre, a Frenchman. Orthopedic surgery originally applied only to the prevention and care of deformities in children. However, the branch soon grew to encompass treatment of extremities, the spine, and associated structures of all humans. The first institute dedicated to the treatment of skeletal deformities was established in Switzerland in the eighteenth century. One of the first notable devices introduced by the industry was the Thomas Splint, which was used for leg fractures. An important U.S. leader in the development of therapeutic orthopedic devices was F.H. Albee (1876-1945), who developed the motor bone saw in 1909.

Rapid advances in medical technology caused a shift in orthopedic treatment during the twentieth century from the use of braces, splints, and other mechanical devices, to surgical procedures. Such procedures incorporated implants and devices which helped surgeons perform advanced operations, like spinal reconstruction, skin grafts, tendon transplants, limb lengthening, restoration of shattered bones and joints, and bone grafts.

Surgical advances in the twentieth century, which paralleled both orthopedic and prosthetic breakthroughs, greatly increased the demand for procedures and treatments that required apparatus developed and manufactured by the surgical appliance industry. In addition, generous employer-sponsored health care plans made large sums of insurance money available for such equipment. Indeed, as a result of overall increased U.S. expenditures on health care during the 1950s, 1960s, and 1970s, sales of orthopedic and prosthetic appliances skyrocketed. Sellers of surgical dressings and other supplies realized similar gains.

The 1980s. By 1980, the surgical appliance and supply business had grown into a $5 billion industry that employed over 40,000 workers. This growth epitomized the immense proliferation of U.S. health care expenditures, which rose at an annual rate of more than 15 percent throughout most of the 1960s and 1970s. By the early 1980s, in fact, Americans were spending more than 10 percent of their gross domestic product on health care. The demand for surgical appliances and supplies continued to balloon throughout the 1980s, as money spent on health care soared. Between 1982 and 1990, industry revenues grew an average of 8.6 percent annually. Moreover, despite manufacturing productivity gains, industry employment increased more than 25 percent during the same period to exceed 85,000.

Driving revenue and profit growth during the decade was the development of high-tech, high-cost prosthetic and orthopedic devices. Better and stronger artificial joints, limbs, and associated devices allowed specialists to deliver treatments unheard of just a few years earlier. As surgical procedures in general increased, the demand for surgical dressings, drapes, and other supplies grew as well. Exports, too, provided significant profit opportunities.

CURRENT CONDITIONS

Notwithstanding a U.S. economic downturn, surgical appliance and supply manufacturers continued to post solid gains in the early 1990s, although growth appeared to be slowing in comparison to the 1980s. Employment grew by roughly 3 percent between 1990 and 1995, to around 94,000.

Despite strong markets, medical device manufacturers faced several hurdles to continued success. Concerns about a lack of outside investment capital necessary to fund research and development of new products emerged, as analysts pointed to the uncertainties associated with various health care reform initiatives. Industry participants were also suffering from cost-containment pressures, which particularly affected low-tech items such as surgical dressings, drapes, and sutures. Increasingly cost-conscious hospitals were working to ensure that prices of conventional supplies remained near the overall inflation rate. At the same time, domestic sales of personal and industrial safety equipment were down—a result of recessed construction and manufacturing activity in the early 1990s.

Cost-containment pressures also hindered makers of orthopedic and prosthetic supplies. The average orthopedic implant, for instance, cost more than $2,400 in 1993. Many manufacturers of such high-tech products, however, were even more concerned with a slowdown in FDA new product approvals. New stringent approval requirements were keeping some new products out of the market and diminishing outside investment in new product development.

The Future. A rise in services and procedures provided in outpatient settings will stimulate demand, as will an aging U.S. and world population. The home health care market, which includes kidney dialysis items that can be used in outpatient settings, implantable infusion pumps, and nutritional therapy products, was expected to realize significant profits as a result of the U.S. Congress's passage of the North American Free Trade Agreement (NAFTA).

Silicone Implant Settlement. In 1994 eight companies that manufactured silicone breast implants agreed to contribute nearly $4.7 billion to a fund for two million women worldwide who have had breast implants. The agreement marked the single largest product liability settlement in U.S. history. The fund is expected to cover routine testing, medical care, and surgery (including implant removal), for the next 30 years. As the *Detroit Free Press* noted, "the settlement attempts to resolve two and a half years of bitter controversy and one of the stormiest chapters in U.S. medical history." Companies making the largest contributions to the settlement were Bristol-Myers Squibb Co., Baxter Healthcare Corp., and Dow Corning Corp., once the country's foremost producer of implants.

Healthcare Recoveries, Baxter Healthcare, Bristol-Myers Squibb, McGhan Medical, 3M and Union Carbide all participated in the $50 million silicon breast implant settlement, which originated in

1992. This was one of the first instances in which health care payers received medical expenses on a large scale involving a personal injury class-act suit. Dow Corning declined their original contribution and filed for bankruptcy protection in Michigan.

The top five states by number of manufacturers for 1996 were: California, with 1,947 manufacturers and 4,583 establishments; New York, with 807 manufacturers and 2,631 establishments; Illinois, with 628 manufacturers and 1,500 establishments; Massachusetts with 578 manufacturers and 997 establishments; and Texas with 507 manufacturers and 1,117 establishments.

INDUSTRY LEADERS

Kendall International, Incorporated of Massachusetts, was the number one surgical appliance and supply company in 1997, with $816 million in sales and 8,500 employees. In second place was St. Jude Medical Inc. of Minnesota, with $724 million in sales and 2,300 employees. Third, with $699 million in sales and 6,600 employees, was the Chemed Corporation of Ohio.

After the early 1990s, buyouts increased within the medical equipment supply industry because of increased demand for cost reduction and quality medical care, combined with a decrease in inpatient hospital usage and increase in outpatient care (outpatient surgery, home health care, and rehabilitation).

Merger and acquisition activity was also on the increase. In 1995, for example, Johnson & Johnson acquired Cordis, a top manufacturer of angioplasty and angiographic equipment, for $1.8 billion in stock. The largest infection control company, Steris Corporation, purchased Amsco International in 1996. These two companies had combined earnings of $45 million on $545 million in revenues for 1995 and combined assets worth approximately $450 million. St. Jude Medical Incorporated acquired Cyberonics Incorporated (maker of implantable devices for epileptic seizure prevention) for $72 million.

FDA restrictions, which held back operations of the medical companies were expected to improve because of congressional pressures to quicken the FDA's new medical product review process. As a result of product use-related deaths and injuries—discussed at the AAMI/FDA's Human Factors in Medical Devices Conference in 1995—the FDA was to begin reviewing how medical devices are designed to prevent human error.

WORK FORCE

The 1,400 companies primarily engaged in the industry employed about 91,000 workers in 1992, representing a jump from less than 70,000 in the early 1980s. About 66 percent of the work force held production jobs in 1992, up 3.8 percent from 1991. Assemblers and fabricators comprised about 15 percent of production positions. Positions in sales and marketing accounted for 7 percent of industry employment, and white collar administration jobs accounted for less than 3 percent.

The industry's work force was expected to grow throughout the 1990s. Manufacturing positions, for example, were expected to rise by 10 percent to 50 percent between 1990 and 2005, according to the Bureau of Labor Statistics. A few positions, however, such as electrical and electronic assemblers, were expected to fall by over 25 percent. Jobs in sales and marketing were likely to rise by more than 70 percent, and positions related to engineering, math, and science were expected to increase by 50 percent to 65 percent.

SURGICAL SUPPLIES INDUSTRY EMPLOYMENT

Employment in thousands

Source: Department of Labor

In 1997, San Diego, California, had the largest medical equipment and services work force, which included surgical appliances and supplies employees, with 4,682 jobs. Bethesda, Maryland, had 3,339 employees, and Minneapolis, Minnesota, had 3,155 employees.

A 1996 court ruling addressed insufficient warnings on device labels, which, as a result, are now illegal. The California Supreme Court ruled in *Carlin v. The Superior Court of Sutter Court,* citing the 1996 U.S. Supreme Court case, *Lohr v. Medtronic.* Medical product makers now have to furnish adequate warnings of any possible risks that were known or "reasonably scientifically knowable." The Health Insurance Portability & Accountability Act of 1996 included additional clauses to prevent fraud that could affect device and drug manufacturers.

AMERICA AND THE WORLD

As domestic prices and market growth declined in the early 1990s, manufacturers were increasingly looking overseas to boost profits. Because U.S. medical equipment producers offered the most advanced products in the world, they controlled approximately 50 percent of the world export market in 1990. Although they lost were losing ground to foreign competitors, particularly the Germans and Japanese, the rapid growth of foreign markets allowed U.S. firms to expand their overseas activities. The demand for high-tech implantable devices led the export surge. In 1997, other factors favoring U.S. sales were the absence of customs duties levied on medical surgical devices and no other major trade restrictions.

In 1989, surgical appliance and supplies producers exported less than 10 percent of their output. Between 1990 and 1993, though, the industry increased exports by an average of 18.3 percent annually. By 1993, the industry shipped nearly 14 percent, or $1.87 billion, of its total production overseas, with Canada, Mexico, and Germany having purchased about 50 percent of all U.S. exports. In contrast, importers served less than 7 percent of the U.S. market in 1993. Of the six medical supply segments, surgical appliance manufacturers maintained the greatest trade surplus in the early 1990s. The surplus increased 8.4 percent in 1992, to about $855 million.

Rapid export growth is expected to continue through the 1990s and early 2000s. Standardization of European Community (EC) medical device regulations will cause producers to emphasize sales in that region, which already consumed 36 percent of U.S. exports in 1992. Popular export items to the EC include respiratory products, orthopedic equipment and supplies, and artificial joints.

Infection control device sales are expected to increase in the mid- to late 1990s in China and India. Steris Corp., a manufacturer of such items, expanded international operations to accommodate the demand.

Japan entered the nursing care product market because of the government's drug price reductions and decreased medical supply profits from other markets. Imports are expected to grow at an approximate 5 to 8 percent annual increase into the late 1990s, with the imports of U.S. industry products growing at an estimated 5 to 10 percent.

The medical device market for 1996 ranked by country in (U.S. dollars) included: Brazil-$980 million, China-$1 billion, India-$680 million, Korea-$920 million, Mexico-$615 million, and Taiwan-$630 million. The medical device market for Asia and Latin America grew two to four times more than Japan, Europe, and the United States, according to a Health Industry Manufacturers Association (HIMA) study released in 1996.

The European market for orthopedic products increased from $1.44 billion in 1995 to a projected $1.89 billion in 2001. Hip implants dominated the European market, with increased demand also for renal supplies and peritoneal dialysis, which both facilitate at-home care.

RESEARCH AND TECHNOLOGY

Many surgical appliance and supply manufacturers relied heavily on development of new technology to create high-profit products and to increase market share—particularly for orthopedic and prosthetic devices. An example of an innovation in the early 1990s were porous hips and knee replacements that allowed bone to grow directly into the metal implant. Similarly, the Variable Geometry Orthosis, an invention of the early 1990s, was an all-plastic, light-weight orthopedic brace that offered a better fit and greater mobility.

In the late 1990s and 2000s, research was expected to emphasize development of better metals and plastics, new non-metallic plastic and ceramic products, and new synthetics that can be used to create implants. Although outside investment capital for new product development waned in the early 1990s, various government partnering programs promised to boost research and development funding. For instance, the Clinton administration backed programs, such as the Defense Technology Conversion Council, to transfer military and other public technology to the private sector.

Ethicon, a division of Johnson & Johnson, joined efforts with Lifecore Biomedical on the development of this product, impending approval as of 1996. The FDA approved Genzyme's post-surgical adhesion membrane, which became available in 1996, which is a product targeted for 3.1 million surgical procedures performed in the U.S. annually. Sales of this product are expected to reach $100 million in 1997, $200 million in 1998, and $300 million after that.

Medex Inc. was bought by Furon Co., California, for $160 million in 1996. Medex, a leader in plastic components had sales of over $99 million in 1996. Its new company, Furon makes silicones, thermoplastics elastomers, and thermoplastic polyurethanes to help Medex expand its product line.

In 1995, besides the One Touch Profil System, an advanced home blood glucose monitoring system, J & J introduced Endopath Optiview Optical Surgical Obturator, which grants physicians the ability to see multilevels of tissue while operating; Fibracol Collagen-Alginate Dressing, an advanced surgical dressing; EZ45 Thoracic Linear Cutter, which allows a videoscopic approach to surgery; and Ortho Summit Processor, which automates blood virus testing.

The first HIV-Aids over-the-counter test was made available in 1996 and nationally available in 1997. The introduction of this product may have an effect on laboratory equipment sales.

FURTHER READING

"'96 Mantra: Let's Make a Deal." *Crain's Cleveland Business,* 6 January 1997, 18.

Anstett, Patricia. "3 Breast Implant Firms Settle." *Detroit Free Press,* 24 March 1994.

"Beating Swords into Medical Devices." *Medical Device & Diagnostic Industry,* May 1993.

"Breast Implant Manufacturers Settle Medical Subrogation Suit." *Business Insurance,* 2 December 1996, 30.

"Business Briefs: U.S. Court Trims Judgement in Patent-Infringement." *The Wall Street Journal,* 8 August 1996.

"California Has Twice as Many Medical Mfgrs as Any Other State." *Biomedical Market Newsletter,* August 1996, 6.

"Capital Slump Hits Device Start-Ups." *Medical Device & Diagnostic Industry,* August 1993.

"European Rehabilitation Products Market to Reach $1.5 Billion." *Medical Devices Business News,* October 1996, 8.

"FDA Clears Steris Corp. Acquisition." *Plain Dealer,* 8 January 1997.

"5 More Implant Makers Join Settlement." *Detroit Free Press,* 25 March 1994.

"Healthdyne Recommends Rejection of Invacare Offer." *New York Times,* 1 February 1997.

Henke, Cliff. "1993 Business Outlook: Growing at Home and Abroad." *Medical Device & Diagnostic Industry,* March 1993.

"Hip Implants Dominate European Orthopaedic Market." *Medical Device Business News,* July 1996, 5.

"Industrial Outlook Positive Again." *Medical Device & Diagnostic Industry,* February 1993.

"Industry Weighs Long-Term Promise of NAFTA." *Medical Device & Diagnostic Industry,* January 1993.

"Insufficient Warnings on Device Labels Are Now Against the Law." *Biomedical Market Newsletter,* 30 September 1996, 6.

"Invacare Is Acquiring Frohock-Stewart." *Chain Drug Review,* 26 February 1996, 18.

"Invacare Broadens Its Base." *Plain Dealer,* 21 April 1996.

"Invacare Offers to Buy Healthdyne Technologies." *New York Times,* 11 January 1997.

"Japanese Domestic Market for Nursing Care Products, Inc." *Medical Device Business News,* November 1996, 9.

"Johnson & Johnson Band-Aid Brand Adhesive Bandages with Antibacterial Ointment." *Product Alert,* 8 April 1996, 26.

"Johnson & Johnson's Acquisition of Florida's Cordis." *Miami Herald,* 23 January 1996.

"Johnson & Johnson's Pharmaceutical Pipeline: 1995 Research and Development Expenditure: $1.63 Billion." *PharmaBusiness,* November 1996, 12.

"LifeCell Raising $12.4M." *Private Equity Week,* 25 November 1996, 3.

McVay, Patrick W., and Benjamin L. Hochman. "Federal Consortium Offers New Opportunities for Developing Medical Technologies." *Medical Device & Diagnostic Industry,* June 1993.

"Medical Disposables Market in Mexico Is Growing Rapidly." *Biomedical Market Newsletter,* March 1996.

"New Business For Old." *Chemist and Druggist,* 5 October 1996.

"Pacific Dunlop Is to Sell Telectronics to St. Jude Medical for $135 Million." *Medical Device Business News,* November 1996, 9.

Perle, Richard, and Martin Cannon. "Turning Swords into Market Shares." *Chief Executive,* May 1993.

"Protein Polymer Technologies Raises $4.8M with Private Placement." *Private Equity Week,* 20 January 1997, 4.

"Purchase Boosts Furon's Presence." *Rubber & Plastics News,* 2 December 1996, 9.

Schooleman, Susan. "Industry Forecast Is That FDA Regulations Will Slow U.S. Market Growth During This Decade." *Health Industry Today,* December 1992.

"St. Jude Medical's Acquisition," *The Wall Street Journal,* 24 July 1996.

"Seprafilm Wins FDA Approval." *Boston Globe,* 14 August 1996.

"Steris Adds to Growing Stable of Infection-Control Businesses." *Plain Dealer,* 28 November 1996.

"Topsy-Turvy Industry Posts Merger Record." *Modern Healthcare,* 23 December 1996, 26.

—Dave Mote, updated by Beth Yocca

SIC 3843

DENTAL EQUIPMENT AND SUPPLIES

This classification comprises establishments primarily engaged in manufacturing artificial teeth, dental metals, alloys, and amalgams, as well as a wide variety of equipment, instruments, and supplies used by dentists, dental laboratories, and dental colleges. Excluded from this classification are dental laboratories that construct artificial dentures, bridges, inlays, and other dental restorations on specifications from dentists; these are classified in **SIC 8072: Dental Laboratories.**

INDUSTRY SNAPSHOT

Essential to the practice of dentistry, the dental equipment and supply industry represents a modestly sized market and is considered to be one of the smallest industries in terms of sales than the other medical supply and equipment industries. It is also an industry of expected growth due to increases in the cost of dental care, Baby Boomers taking better care of both their teeth and their children's teeth and technological advances in dental equipment such as advanced root canal procedure machines, oral cameras available in the United States at a more reasonable cost to dentists, and the Food and Drug Administration (FDA) approval of Perioglass, a surface active bone-grafting material.

Dental equipment and dental supplies are regarded as separate markets, with some companies manufacturing only supplies, others manufacturing only equipment, and others, generally the larger companies (with a diverse mix of medical products) in the industry, manufacturing both equipment and supplies. These products are then sold to dentists, dental laboratories, and dental colleges.

Products manufactured by industry participants include dental chairs, dental hand instruments, and drills, which are considered equipment; and plaster, amalgams (alloyed metals used for filling cavities), and cements, which are considered supplies. Other products, more than 25,000 of them, include abrasive points, wheels, and disks; dental cabinets; denture materials; orthodontic appliances; and artificial teeth, which are not made in dental laboratories. Dental accessories, which include dental picks, dental floss, dental stimulators, mouth mirrors, and other items, accounted for $35 million in sales in 1995 and were expected to grow at a 5 to 10 percent increase per year, according to Eric Happell, director of retail marketing, at John O. Butler Company. Niche products have been developed and are expected to become increasingly popular. Examples include: premixed temporary fillings (DenTek's Tempenol), reusable toothpicks, and plastic dental cleaning equipment for those who are ''metal sensitive.'' These products are mostly sold through drug stores. In 1995, 41 percent of all dental floss sales were at drug stores.

By manufacturing these and other products, dental equipment and supply manufacturers recorded $2.39 billion in revenue in 1995. The production of equipment and supplies for dentists, particularly dental chairs, instrument delivery systems, dental hand instruments, and dental cements and metals, contributed most heavily to the industry's total revenue, accounting for 51 percent of total shipments. Shipments of dental laboratory equipment and supplies to dental laboratories ranked as the industry's second largest market, accounting for 31 percent of total shipments.

In this technology oriented industry, out of 17 companies ranked for manufacturing job growth, medical came in sixth place with an expected growth rate of 5.1 percent. Northern California was ranked highest for technology company job growth and also for the most projected growth, which was 12.1 percent. (These figures cover industries in Industry Group 384, which includes **SIC 3843: Dental Equipment and Supplies, SIC 3841: Surgical and Medical Instruments and Apparatus** and **SIC 3842: Orthopedic, Prosthetic, and Surgical Appliances and Supplies,** diagnostic, therapeutic, rehabilitation, and veterinary areas).

ORGANIZATION AND STRUCTURE

In the early 1990s, approximately 500 companies in the United States were manufacturing dental equipment and supplies as their primary business. The majority of these manufacturers were small and medium size companies, with only 25 percent of the total employing 20 or more employees. The typical dental equipment and supply manufacturing establishment was half the size of the typical establishment in all other U.S. manufacturing industries, employing 26 people compared to the national standard of 54 employees per establishment.

By the mid- to late nineties, larger medical supply companies also started to include dental products in their portfolios and changed the market from exclusive type manufacturers (small to medium size companies) to multi-manufacturers (larger companies). Mergers and acquisitions became more common among medical companies to enhance the current product line of companies because it is financially lucrative, and to share research and development costs of new dental products and supplies.

The bulk of the industry's manufacturing establishments were located in California, which contained 124 facilities in the early 1990s, by far leading all other states in dental equipment and supply production. New York ranked second with 48 manufacturing establishments, followed by Illinois with 39 facilities. Aside from the concentration of facilities on the West Coast, in the Northeast, and in the Great Lakes region, dental equipment and supply production was scattered throughout the country, with 25 states containing manufacturing establishments.

BACKGROUND AND DEVELOPMENT

Manufacturers of dental equipment and dental supplies first emerged as an appreciable component of American industry in the 1890s, although the first manufacturers of such products undoubtedly originated much earlier, appearing during the genesis of the nation itself, when the practice of dentistry first began in the United States. In fact, the earliest progenitors of the dental equipment and supply industry were the dentists themselves, who made their own equipment in workshops adjoining their public offices. Over the ensuing decades, as the nation's population grew and the magnitude of the country's commerce increased, the production of dental equipment and supplies became distinct from the practice of dentistry, leading to the emergence of small, independent dental manufacturing companies by the latter half of the nineteenth century.

Once the manufacture of dental equipment and supplies became a distinct segment of the dental industry, characterized by small, frequently family owned businesses, many of which appeared in the decade leading up to the turn of the twentieth century, the formal beginning of the dental equipment and supply industry can be said to have begun. But for roughly the next half century, the industry remained small, comprised of companies that generated a negligible amount of revenue, at least in contrast to the larger manufacturing industries in the country and to other manufacturers in the broadly defined medical industry. The modern version of the dental equipment and supply industry, which began to assume the characteristics of the industry in existence during the 1990s, would not emerge until after World War II, specifically during the 1960s, when a combination of developments engendered a new breed of dental equipment and supply manufacturers.

During the earliest days of the nation's history, dentists manufactured dental equipment and supplies. Small manufacturing establishments appeared as a natural response to the country's growth. However, during both phases of the dental industry's development, whether a dentist or a manufacturer was producing the equipment, the list of products manufactured was short. This was primarily attributable to the nature of dentistry at the time—a branch of medicine that was essentially consigned to extracting teeth or affixing bridge work. Years before biannual visits to a dentist were recommended, indeed years before dental hygiene was even a common concern, preventive measures to forestall tooth loss or decay were seldom employed, and dentists merely responded to emergency or near emergency situations. Once dentistry became a preventive science following World War II—engendered in large part by the growing affluence of the American populace and the emergence of federally subsidized dental insurance—the nature of dentistry changed dramatically, transforming the dental equipment and supply industry into a much more sophisticated business.

By the 1960s, the scope of the dental equipment and supply industry widened considerably and its market matured significantly, drawing the attention of would-be manufacturers and investors. The shift toward preventive dentistry altered the complexion of the dental equipment and supply industry, but it had not significantly changed the composition of the industry, at least not yet. Still primarily comprised of small, independent manufacturing companies, roughly 500 of them in the early 1960s, the industry continued in many ways to resemble itself 50 years earlier. Its sales volume still represented a modest sum, amounting to roughly $150 million per year as the movement toward preventive dentistry gained momentum, and it had not yet attracted large manufacturing concerns; its largest manufacturer, S.S. White Dental Manufacturing Co., generated $40 million in sales in 1961. The optimism pervading the industry, therefore, was not so much attributable to a dramatic transformation of the industry, but rather stemmed from the expectation of a future transformation.

Essentially, these prognostications called for a dental equipment and supply industry of much larger magnitude, predictions that, when sketched out on paper, appeared highly plausible. During the early 1960s, American families on average were spending twice as much per year on dental care as they had ten years earlier—the natural extension of a society growing increasingly more affluent—while the number of prepaid dental plans multiplied during the same period, covering approximately 700,000 Americans. These prepaid plans, coming from either private insurance plans or union-employer agreements, would grow exponentially throughout the decade and into the

1970s, fueling much of the optimism articulated by manufacturers and industry pundits during this 20 year period. Union-sponsored dental care plans proliferated after the landmark agreement reached between the International Longshoremen's & Warehousemen's Union and the Washington State Dental Association in 1954, when the first such program was initiated.

By the mid-1960s, thanks in large part to the growth of union dental care plans, the number of Americans provided with an opportunity for dental care increased to three million from the 700,000 covered roughly five years earlier. Also, Medicare, a U.S. government health insurance program for those over 65 years of age, and Medicaid, a program that provided medical care to those who could not pay for it, both came into existence in 1965, and promised to extend dental coverage throughout the country in a sweeping fashion. By the end of the decade, the number of Americans covered by dental care plans doubled again in a five year period and included more than six million people, the result of a growing awareness of preventive dental care and a surge in the number of dental care coverage plans.

The increase in the number of potential dental care customers that was sparking much of the interest in the dental equipment and supply industry during the 1960s, persuaded larger, conglomerate manufacturing companies with no previous vested interest in the dental field to begin dental equipment production. Many of the smaller, independent manufacturing concerns were absorbed by the incursion of these larger companies, altering the composition of the industry. Meanwhile, those manufacturers already in the industry were diversifying, applying the same technology used in the production of dental equipment to the manufacture of non-dental products. Consequently, as this period of mergers and diversification occurred into the late 1960s, the typical manufacturer in the industry changed from a small, independent company, almost entirely devoted to the production of dental-related products, to a larger, more diversified manufacturer.

This transformation did not, however, have an equally significant effect on the industry's sales volume. From the $150 million generated by U.S. manufacturers at the beginning of the decade, the industry's sales volume only increased to roughly $280 million by the beginning of the 1970s, a total that seemed to belie the industry's growth in other areas over the course of the decade. Dental equipment manufacturers supplied two revolutionary pieces of equipment during the dental industry's emergence as a more visible sector of the health care field: the air-driven, high-speed drill and the reclining dentist's chair, both of

which proved to be linchpins in the dental industry's climb to the fore, yet revenue totals had not responded in kind.

The reasons for this rather stagnant revenue growth became apparent shortly. By the mid-1970s, approximately 30 million Americans were covered under some sort of dental care plan, reflecting a tremendous increase during the previous 15 years, but when this figure was analyzed to reflect the number of those who actually visited dentists, rather than the number who were provided the opportunity to visit a dentist, the reason for the industry's laggard growth in sales volume became readily apparent. Of all the people receiving dental care in the United States, only 15 percent were covered by dental insurance, compared to more than 90 percent for health care. Since a large proportion of the people covered by dental insurance opted not to receive dental care, the number of people insured in the country, which over the past 20 years had inspired much of the optimism within the dental equipment and supply industry, proved to be a misleading figure, at least to the extent that the more people covered would directly translate into an increase in the industry's sales volume.

Once this misleading measure of the industry's potential growth was removed, a clearer estimation of its true position within the larger health care field showed a relatively small industry—generating roughly $670 million in revenue in 1975—that nevertheless played an essential role in the dental arena. To be sure, the nearly $700 million posted in 1975 by all manufacturers in the United States represented robust growth from a decade earlier, more than tripling in volume during that time. The percentage of people covered by dental insurance who actually visited dentists would increase as public awareness of dental hygiene grew, but the dental equipment industry had not expanded to the degree that prognosticators had earlier envisaged, and neither did a realistic assessment of its future call for a dramatically different type of industry to emerge. Instead, the dental equipment and supply industry was destined to record more modest growth, from roughly 5 to 10 percent annually in aggregate sales, a rate of growth not prodigious enough to spawn the optimism of the 1960s, but a rate of growth that nonetheless supported the existence of manufacturers into the future.

As the industry progressed past the mid-1970s, when it was mired for several years in a global recession, its growth during the 1980s continued at a moderate rate. By 1982, the industry's sales volume increased to $1.11 billion, having eclipsed the $1.0 billion mark three years earlier. In the face of a sharp decline in the number of labor contract agreements that included dental care coverage, the industry's sales volume increased only marginally by the end of the decade, reaching $1.27 billion.

The average expenditure of $14 thousand for dental care in 1988, increased to $16 thousand in 1995 and was expected to increase to $17 thousand in the year 2000. These figures are based on household projections from the Census Bureau.

CURRENT CONDITIONS

Ambiguity about U.S. health care reform and its effect on dentistry coupled with deleterious economic conditions during the early 1990s stunted the dental equipment and supply industry's growth in 1995, causing the value of its shipments to increase by only 2 percent to $2.39 billion, compared to the 14 percent growth recorded between 1993 and 1994. Projections for the industry's growth called for a 3 percent increase in aggregate revenue from 1995 to 1998, fueled in part by the growth of certain fledgling areas of dentistry, such as periodontal surgery, treatment with lasers, and cosmetic dentistry.

Dental products and accessories have become more specialized (niche-like), targeted to end users: adults, children, and infants. Dental floss and dental picks, products for healthier gums, and pre-mixed fillings are all examples of these niche products. The biggest introduction in products has been to accommodate the special dental needs of children. Various manufacturers added specialty-type products for children, including brighter colors, different packaging, timers to help children know when to brush, and smaller sizes.

Manufacturers' focus in the 1990s is on gum care. Dental supply and equipment manufacturers are building relationships within the community of 140,000 dentists by conducting research on dental care and publishing the results in various studies. For example, Bausch & Lomb was conducting one of the largest ongoing studies on plaque removal by using different brushes on implant wearers to remove plaque.

From 1995 to 1997, the dental care industry offered advanced toothbrushes that enabled users to decrease the plaque formation around the gumline (for adults and children), and dental floss with fluoride, mint-taste, whitening abilities, and a special feature called non-shredding, which prevents breakage of the floss. Also, new ways to floss were introduced that allowed users greater precision and control to reach plaque in between teeth by using specially designed prongs.

Other introductions in the dental equipment industry that are expected to increase sales to dentists are oral cancer tests, digital radiography (which decreases radiation exposure to the patient by 90 percent), "Save-A-Tooth" program developed by 3M, oral cameras that allow dentists an easier option for root canals, and more consumer-related dental products to increase patients' awareness of the importance of self-care.

INDUSTRY LEADERS

Ranked according to sales volume, the three largest manufacturers of dental equipment and supplies in the United States during the early 1990s were Block Drug Company, Inc., based in Jersey City, New Jersey; Sybron Corporation, based in Milwaukee, Wisconsin; and Dentsply International Inc., based in Rockford, Illinois.

In 1997, out of the 53 dental equipment and supply companies with $2.7 million in sales, the top three companies are Block Drug Company, Dentsply International Inc., and Sybron International Corp., respectively.

Block Drug, perhaps better known as the marketer of Polident, a widely popular brand name most closely tied to denture care products, recorded $563 million in sales in 1993 and $693 million in sales in 1996. The industry's highest-ranking privately owned manufacturer, Dentsply International, the former Dentists' Supply Co. and long-time competitor of Sybron, posted an estimated $260 million in sales in 1993 and $572 million in 1996. Sybron Corp., a perennial industry leader in existence since the emergence of the modern dental equipment and supply industry during the 1960s, generated $383 million in 1993, $519 million in 1996 and like Block Drug, was a publicly held company.

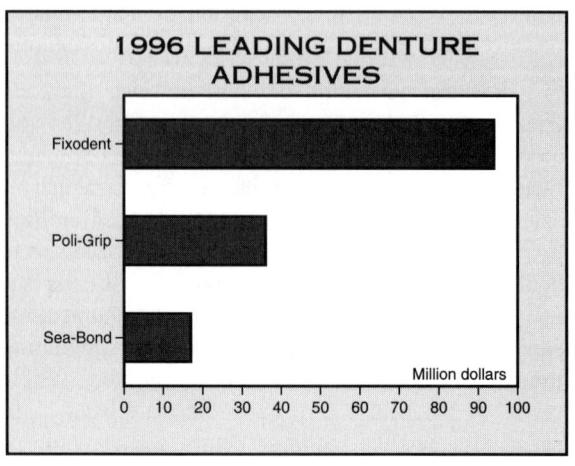

1996 LEADING DENTURE ADHESIVES

Braun, Sonicare, and Interplak, which were recently purchased by Conair, were the major players in the dental accessory market, which raked in $143 million in sales in 1996. These three companies all introduced rotary type toothbrushes that cleaned in between teeth.

Rowenta, a company that led the industry in iron sales (home appliances) introduced two new interdental brushes, Dentacontrol for adults ($80 retail) and Dentiphant for children ($25) retail. This market was expected to grow at a 5 percent rate in 1997. The number one selling floss for 1996 was Glide, considered a premium product at $4. Denture adhesives represented $211 million in sales for June 1995 to June 1996. Procter & Gamble had the number one seller, Fixodent, with sales of $94 million. Block's Poli-Grip sales increased 14 percent to $36 million, and product line grew to include Poli Grip Free, Super Poli-Grip, and Ultimate Hold Poli-Grip. With more Baby Boomers entering the denture market, another product, Sea-Bond, gained a 15 percent increase in sales to $17 million.

WORK FORCE

In 1991, with a total of 100 companies with 20 or more employees, employment was around 91,000. The number of companies remained fairly stable, and the number of employees increased to 103,000 in 1994 and declined to 101,000 in 1996. Only slight increases were expected through 1998 to around 102,000 total employees in the dental equipment and supply industry. Payroll for 1994 was around $103 million and increased to $111 million in 1996 and was expected to increase to $114 million by 1998. The average number of employees per company was 49 in 1994 with an average wage per hour of $13.09 in 1994.

Production workers in the dental equipment and supply industry generally earned slightly less than the national standard for production workers employed by manufacturing industries. In 1989, this difference amounted to 18 cents per hour, with the typical production worker earning $10.49 per hour compared to the $10.31 per hour averaged by production workers in the dental equipment and supply industry. In 1994, the hourly wage for production workers in the dental equipment and supply industry climbed to $11.43, at which time salaried employees in the industry earned an average of $43,441 per year.

There was a total of around 103,000 production workers in the industry in 1994, a figure expected to decrease to 99,000 by the year 1998. Wages per hour went from $103 to $114 million in 1996 and were expected to increase to $121 million by the 1998.

AMERICA AND THE WORLD

The international market for dental equipment and supplies in 1993 totaled $5.5 billion, of which U.S. manufacturers enjoyed a commanding share, controlling roughly 50 percent of the market. This lead in the global dental equipment and supply market, largely predicated on the ability of U.S. manufacturers to incorporate high technology into the production of their merchandise, garnered the country a $258 million trade surplus in 1993, with 35 percent of the industry's shipments going overseas. The dental equipment and supply markets in Canada, Germany, Japan, Italy, and France proved to be the strongest export destinations for U.S. manufacturers, while manufacturers in Germany, Japan, Switzerland, Italy, and France posed the greatest threat to the overwhelming lead of U.S. manufacturers in the global market.

Fluctuations in foreign exchange rates tend to work for the U.S. import market. In 1994 the United States had 62.3 percent of the import market, and further growth was expected. No customs duty was levied on medical, surgical, and dental instruments and supplies, which also had a favorable effect on U.S. dental supply and accessory sales.

China imported $737,000 or 30,910 kg of dental cements, dental fillings, and bone reconstruction cements in the first three quarters of 1996. Japan's imports of medical and dental equipment were expected to rise steadily from $3.33 billion in 1994. Imports from the United States accounted for 62.3 percent of the import market, totaling $3.51 billion in 1995 and $3.86 billion in 1996. Japan's expected introduction of social insurance for long-term care, improvement of government relations during the past decade, and U.S.-Japan agreement on government procurement, all provided more opportunities for U.S. suppliers of health care products.

FURTHER READING

"Bausch & Lomb Selling its Dental Implant Business." *New York Times,* 24 July 1996.

"Best-selling Denture Adhesives." *Chain Drug Review,* 6 January 1997, 19.

"Braun Shifts Marketing." *HFN,* 30 September 1996, 70.

"Colgate Oral." *Drug Store News,* 4 November 1996, 18.

CorpTech Technology Industry Growth Forecaster. January 1997.

Darnay, Arsen J., ed. *Manufacturing USA.* 5th ed. Detroit: Gale Research, 1996.

"Dental Accessories Yield Chewy Profits." *Drug Store News,* 23 September 1996, 18.

"Dental Equipment Firms Are Still in Recession." *Industry Week,* 6 September 1976, 92.

"Dental Equipment Picks up Pace." *Business Week,* 15 November 1969, 142.

"Dental Suppliers: Expanded Markets." *Financial World,* 24 June 1970, 40.

"Dentsply to Buy New Image." *Wall Street Journal,* 26 December 1996, 125.

"Dental Tech Firm Bites Into Sales." *Crain's Small Business-New York,* May 1996, 3.

"Inside Industry: USBiomaterials." *Genetic Engineering News,* 1 November 1996, 16.

"Japan Medical and Dental Equipment & Supplies Markets Are Steadily Increasing." *Biomedical Market Newsletter,* 30 September 1996, 6.

"Johnson & Johnson." *Drug Topics,* 4 March 1996, 140.

Jones, Stacy. "Metal Bonded Directly to Teeth." *New York Times,* 8 October 1966, 37.

"Mergers and Acquisitions." *Med Ad News,* February 1996, 15.

"Natural White Whitening Floss-Fresh Mint." *Product Alert,* 8 April 1996, 26.

"New Flosses from Colgate." *News Brief Journal,* 2 December 1996, 46.

"A Next Step for Rowenta." *HFN,* 30 September 1996, 70

"Phoenix Shannon PLC." *New York Times,* 20 April 1996.

"Picking the Right Floss." *Non-foods Merchandising,* August 1996, 38.

Prial, Frank J. "The Denture Venture: Bootleg False Teeth Cutting into Market." *Wall Street Journal,* 4 May 1966, 1.

"Putting Teeth In Relationships." *HFN,* 8 April 1996, 70.

"Quik Floss." *Product Alert,* 12 February 1996, 26.

Rutter, Richard, "Dentists to View Newest Supplies." *New York Times,* 3 December 1961, F1.

"Save-A-Tooth is Unveiled at Retail by 3M." *Chain Drug Review,* 20 May 1996, 18.

"Shiseki-Ya Kun Teeth Cleaner and Mirror." *International Product Alert,* 19 February 1996, 13.

"Statistics: China Chemical Import & Export Data From January to October 1996, Part 80." *China Chemical Reporter,* 26 December 1996.

"Sullivan Deal." *Barron's,* 10 February 1992, 13.

Sullivan, Michael B., "Painless Extraction." *Barron's,* 16 November 1964, 11.

"Super Poli-Grip Denture Adhesive Cream." *Product Alert,* 9 September 1996, 26.

"Sybron in '82 to Close Ritter Dental Plant; 250 Will Face Layoffs." *Wall Street Journal,* 5 November 1981, 20.

"Tooth-Whitening Business Has Utah's Ion Laser Technology Smiling." *Salt Lake Tribune,* 8 June 1996.

U.S. Department of Commerce. International Trade Administration. *U.S. Industrial Outlook.* Washington: GPO, 1960-1993.

Wheeler, George. "Nor Poor Mouth." *Barron's,* 23 August 1969, 11.

Willatt, Norris. "That Certain Smile." *Barron's,* 21 March 1966, 11.

"Zila Inc. to Absorb Bio-Dental Technologies Corp." *Denver Post,* 4 June 1996.

—Jeffrey L. Covell, updated by Beth Yocca

SIC 3844

X-RAY APPARATUS AND X-RAY TUBES

Firms in this industry engage primarily in the manufacture of radiographic X-ray, fluoroscopic X-ray, and therapeutic X-ray equipment and tubes for use in medical, industrial and research applications. They also produce irradiation equipment using gamma-ray and beta-ray technology.

INDUSTRY SNAPSHOT

Four consecutive years of double-digit growth made X-Ray Apparatus and Tubes one of America's fastest growing industries in the early 1990s. Its 1992 shipments grew 11.2 percent over the previous year to reach $3.1 billion. Much of its success came from the growing sophistication and portability of its products. The massive machines of hospital X-ray departments still had their place, but now miniaturized versions found every-day use in doctors' and dentists' offices nationwide. In addition, the industry discovered new uses for the non-destructive technology that both increased efficiency and quality of manufacturing processes. With the fall of communism and the relaxation of U.S. technology bans, the industry found vast new and expanding markets in Eastern Europe and other portions of the former Soviet Union.

The U.S. sales volume for 1996 was estimated to be $369.8 million for conventional x-ray and fluoroscopy equipment and $36 million for radiation detection equipment. The U.S. sales volume for 1997 was estimated to be $550 million for X-ray apparatus and tubes.

Among medical services, lab tests and X-rays ranked as the fifth category in terms of consumer usage behind physician's services, dental services, eye care services and service by other than physician. For 1995 (in 1988 dollars), the average expenditure on X-rays for 100,308 households (in thousands) was $2,685 million out of a total of $135,134 million aggregate health care expenditure. The largest volume of consumer monies were spent on X-rays for individuals between the ages of 35-74. The projected figure for the year 2000 is $2,856 million based on 105,933 households (in thousands) with aggregate expenditures of $141,524 million. The highest consumer expenditure for 2000 is expected to be between the ages of 35-74.

X-ray Corp., Georgia and Chesapeake X-ray Corp. were acquired by Physician Sales & Service, Inc., Florida for $18 million in stock and another $6.8 million of debt in 1996.

A 1996 cooperative alliance was formed between Siemens Medical System's Inc. Oncology Care Systems Group and Intraop Medical Inc. to deliver Intraop's cancer treatment, the first of its kind, a mobile and self-shielded electron beam system that treats cancer using intraoperative radiotherapy.

A buyout of Diagnostic Imaging (which had 1995 sales of $58 million), for $19.2 million of stock and debt took place in 1996 by Physician Sales and Service, a medical supply, equipment and pharmaceutical distributor that reported $236.2 million in sales.

ORGANIZATION AND STRUCTURE

Approximately one-half of all sales in this industry went to hospital end-users, with the medical profession in general making up the majority of all shipments. Other demands for X-ray equipment have evolved with the need for increased security measures at airports in the late nineties. Research facilities provided another avenue for sales of major pieces of often experimental equipment. However, the industry was growing increasingly interested in the non-destructive and non-intrusive nature of the imaging technologies.

According to the 1987 Census, 69 firms operating 75 establishments produced $1.5 billion in sales. Sales of primary products, those directly covered by the industry classification, reached $1.3 billion. Secondary products accounted for $74.3 million, and miscellaneous contract work and resales totaled $138.8 million yielding a product specialization ratio for the industry of 95 percent. The coverage ratio, the amount of products sold by those firms classified in the industry, reached only 86 percent.

The medical industry, which also includes dental, electromedical, surgical, and ophthalmic goods, ranked sixth out of 17 major technological manufacturers of various equipment. Out of 282 firms surveyed, a 5.1 percent growth rate is expected for 1997. Overall firms surveyed project that northern California expected 12.1 percent growth in the medical equip-

ment and services industry, which included X-ray apparatus and X-ray tubes. Mid-Atlantic states came in second with a nine percent projected growth rate and the southeast U.S. came in third with 7.2 percent projected growth.

BACKGROUND AND DEVELOPMENT

The discovery of the X-ray was an accident. In 1895, Wilhelm Conrad Roentgen, experimenting with electrical discharges in an evacuated tube called a Crookes' tube, discovered that the invisible rays given off from his experiment could penetrate a human hand and project a skeletal image onto a florescent screen. Later, he substituted photographic film to make a permanent record. Since then, scientists have discovered that X-rays are a type of electromagnetic radiation. An x-ray's wavelength of 0.01 to 300 angstroms is shorter than visible light, lying between and partially over the ultraviolet and gamma-ray segments of the electromagnetic spectrum. They are produced by the collision of high-energy particles with other charged particles.

American scientist, William D. Coolidge, developed the first efficient X-ray tube, called a Coolidge tube, in 1913. Modern tubes fire electrons from a tungsten filament cathode at a target anode, usually made of tungsten, molybdenum or copper and coated with a thin film of gold.

The speed of passage of the x-radiation through a body depends on density. Relatively dense material, like bone, yielded white images, while less-dense material like lungs appeared black. Doctors found the phenomenon invaluable for accurately diagnosing such things as tuberculosis, miners' black lung, and broken bones. However, it only provided a two-dimensional image of the problem area, superimposing layers of body components one on top of another without any indication of depth. One solution to that problem was to use a contrast medium like liquid barium to high light the esophagus, stomach, and intestine. By using a fluoroscope, which produces real-time images on a video screen, the physician tracked the medium through the digestive system, pinpointing any problem areas.

The late-1960s saw a major advancement in the effective use of X-rays for medical diagnosis. By linking the computer to a moving X-ray emitter inside a doughnut-shaped machine, Geoffrey Hounsfield of EMI produced a three-dimensional image of an entire object. Instead of a few X-ray photographs, the computer-aided-tomograph (CAT) took hundreds of thousands of carefully directed, slice-like images which the computer reassembled. Tomograph comes from the Greek word for slice. The results, startlingly clear, could be manipulated to highlight specific areas. CAT scans could locate bleeding inside a brain, find and measure tumors, or help to evaluate injuries anywhere in the body.

Concerns over the amount of radiation a patient would be exposed to and over the cost and sheer physical immensity of the equipment led to the development of ultrasound tomograph which did not use X-rays. By the mid-1980s, the ultrasound systems were beginning to gain popularity. Ultrasound systems are classified under **SIC 3845: Electromedical Apparatus.**

Magnetic Resonance Imaging (MRI) uses a powerful magnet to align the hydrogen atoms in a patient's body. When the magnetic field is released, the atoms return to their original orientation, but different tissues realign at different rates. By using a computer to clock the relative rates of change, physicians can map joints, tumors, post-surgical changes in the chest, abdomen, pelvis, brain and spinal cord.

The safety and effectiveness of all medical devices became the responsibility of the Food and Drug Administration in 1938. Radiation emitting devices were specifically targeted in 1968 by the Radiation Control for Health and Safety Act and, in 1976, by the Medical Device Amendments to the Food, Drug and Cosmetic Act.

In the late nineties, the continued concern for radiation exposure to patients lead to further advances in X-ray equipment development and technological advances. One of the technological advances in 1997, called a ''soft'' X-ray, is a new technology that uses long wavelengths to decrease radiation.

CURRENT CONDITIONS

Even though other, safer technologies were displacing X-rays by the 1990s in their traditional medical applications, radiation proved useful in unique ways. The fluoroscope could show movement within the body like the operation of the heart and the intestines. It facilitated angioplasty, providing the physician with a real-time way of guiding a balloon-tipped catheter down a blood vessel to the point where the balloon insert could be expanded with the greatest effect. Radiation oncology used X-rays or gamma-rays to attack cancerous tumors without damaging surrounding tissue. With this technique a linear accelerator, betatron or cobalt machine is used to direct a beam of radiation from outside the patient's body at the pinpointed tumor.

Initial investigations of the radiation in the research laboratory led to many useful applications for the non-visible light energy. X-ray crystallography led to X-ray microscopes. Crystal structures direct and control X-rays much as lenses do with normal light energy. Using this principle, researchers were able to delve ever-deeper into the structure of crystals. The fact that X-rays are absorbed by material led to absorption spectroscopy, which studies metals in living systems. The industry began using lithography to produce densely packed computer chips. Holography made it possible to glimpse the world within a living cell.

Scientists also used the radiation to look beyond this world. By launching satellites equipped with X-ray detectors, they were able to observe and theorize about the structure of the universe. The first such satellite, UHURU, was launched from a site near Kenya in 1970 and was followed by an international series of successors. Gamma-ray astronomy extended the reach of X-ray astronomy, making visible the processes of the destruction and creation of chemical elements throughout the universe.

Archeology and paleontology also benefitted from the use of X-ray technology. Previously, the study of such ancient artifacts as mummies and fossilized bones required the systematic destruction or at least the disassembly of the scientific treasures. Using a CAT scan, often tied to a supercomputer, researchers in the late 1980s could get clear three-dimensional images without reducing the artifact to dust. Such scans often revealed surprising facts about the subject giving a glimpse of what life, society, disease, nutrition and intrigue was like in historically distant times.

X-rays also proved invaluable in probing modern-day intrigues. In the 1980s and 1990s, plane hijackings and bombings brought terror to the skies, and advances in weapons technology threatened to make conventional X-ray scanners ineffective in preventing them. Although all metals show up clearly on an X-ray scan, lighter materials like plastics do not. Plastic explosives and the mostly-plastic handgun, the Glock 17, could be smuggled through security inspections undetected. Specially designed innovations like American Science & Engineering Inc.'s Model Z scanner sought ways to tighten security. The Z-scanner concentrates a high intensity beam of X-rays onto the carry-on luggage to compensate for the low absorption rate of softer materials. It then displays both the normal X-ray image which would pick up metals and the Z-image which catches plastics. In 1991, France extended that technology for use in its massive cargo inspection facility at Paris' Charles de Gaulle airport. Their building-size X-ray machine examines entire pallet loads of luggage or entire vehicles at once, producing a sophisticated, easily read image.

By increasing the power and size of the X-ray equipment, industry businesses were able to probe though several feet of metal to map interior details. Defense sub-contractors used CAT scans to inspect MX missiles and Saturn rockets looking for cracks, poor material bonds, migration of fuel or coolants, integrity of castings, and gaps in insulation. In traditional CAT scans, the object to be probed sits within the doughnut shaped emitter ring, but in the late 1980s industry leaders developed a new innovation on the technology, backscatter imaging tomography (BIT). By capturing only the portion of the beams which are reflected back, BIT machinery allowed operators to probe objects even if they could only access one side.

The process provided an efficient method for checking quality of manufactured parts and allowed inspectors to certify and document such critical items as pipe welds in nuclear reactors. X-rays have also been used to examine the nation's highways by detecting early signs of failure and allowing preventative maintenance in place of major periodic rebuilding.

Because the industry still sold most of its output in the medical community, changes in Medicare allowances scheduled for 1993 caused some concern. *U.S. Industrial Outlook - 1993* suggested that tightening Medicare reimbursements would tend to limit the expansion of new X-ray technology in larger hospitals.

Mergers and acquisitions of X-ray apparatus and tubes companies became popular in the mid 1990s to match the trend in hospitals downsizing, physician's offices combining, changes in managed care and decreases in insurance availability for medical services.

Notable X-ray industry ventures in 1996: a home healthcare provider, Option Care acquired Continental X-Ray Corp. for $19.3 million. FluroScan Imaging Systems was bought by Hologic Inc. for $57.8 million in stock in 1996. Varian Associates Inc., California signed a $90 million supply deal with Toshiba, Tokyo, to provide them with several thousand X-ray tubes for CT scanning systems and other medical equipment.

The estimated 1996 U.S. sales volume for conventional fluoroscopy was $369.8 million and $36 million for radiation detection equipment, according to the March 1996, Biomedical Marker Newsletter. Bone density scanning tests were more popular among research centers, hospitals and physicians. Until the mid 1990's to 1996, osteoporosis was usually detected by breaking bones. In 1996, normal X-rays are no longer considered acceptable to detect bone loss. The bone density scan tests costs around $220 per patient and the demand for this testing equipment is expected to increase as patients use Fosamax and wish to have their results and condition monitored.

According to a 1996 Department of Defense news release, 19 companies were awarded $50 million in indefinite quantity contracts for systems, sub-systems or components of X-ray systems, with work expected to be completed in 1997. The companies awarded were: Fisher Imaging Corp., Toshiba America Medical System, Gendex, Siemens Medical Systems, Eastman Kodak Co., Xi Tec Inc, Dynarad, Phillips, General Electric, Lievel-Flarsheim, OEC Medical Systems, Picker International, Bennett X-ray, Dornier Medical Systems, Flucroscan, Lorad, Fuji Medical Systems, Polaroid, 3M,

INDUSTRY LEADERS

Siemens Medical/Nuclear Group, Illinois, with a total of 925 employees, was ranked number one out of 10 companies that in 1997 were considered to be the largest emerging operating units.

In 1997, *Ward's Business Directory of U.S. Private and Public Companies* ranked Siemens Medical Systems Inc. Nuclear Medicine Group, Illinois, as the largest X-ray apparatus equipment company with and estimated $110 million in sales. OEC Medical Systems-Inc.,Utah, had $102 million in revenues and Fischer Imaging Corporation, Ohio, had $77 million in sales.

The German conglomerate Siemens Aktiengesellschaft wanted to buy a company, Diasonics in 1980, but early market conquests by that company put it beyond reach. In 1990, Siemens formed Siemens-Gammasonics as a subsidiary of Siemens Medical Systems Inc. In 1992, the subsidiary had sales of $175 million and employed 900.

Sony Corp. (Japan) and the National Institute of Radiological Sciences developed a computerized sectional radiograph that has the ability to take 3-dimensional images of human anatomy parts. This device, introduced in 1996, can take up to 360 photographs in 12 seconds. A drug which became popular during the discovery of treatment for osteoporosis (a bone thinning disease), Fosamax, increased the demand for Hologic's Acclaim series, a line of X-ray machines, by 50 percent. Hologic shipped around 700 to 750 units per year with sales of $43.5 million in 1995. This figure was expected to double in 1997. Digital radiography machines, which became available in 1995 by Schick Technologies predicts that the $7 million sales figure will be a $50 million business by 1998. Intraoral cameras were also expected to become more popular to help dentists examine and diagnose their patients more accurately.

WORK FORCE

X-ray equipment manufacturing facilities tend to be large, high-tech facilities. In 1988, the average establishment employed 117 compared to the manufacturing average of 57. Wages accordingly ran about 20 percent higher than average reaching $12.49 per hour in 1988 compared to the average hourly wage in all manufacturing firms of $10.66, according to *Manufacturing USA, 2nd Edition.* Total employment in the industry incrcascd throughout the late 1980s and early 1990s reaching 13,740 in 1992 according to *U.S. Industrial Outlook.* Production workers made up 51.7 percent of the industry's work force. The users of X-ray equipment are radiologists. In the United States, they must take four-to-seven years of specialized training after graduating from medical school.

The number of companies continued to grow throughout the nineties with a total of 103 for 1993, up to 120 in 1996. Out of the 103 companies, 92 of them or 90 percent had over 20 employees in them. Correspondingly, in 1996, 105 of the 120 companies had over 20 employees. Employment steadily increased until 1993, decreasing to 99,000 total and then increasing up to 117,000 people in 1996. The total payroll increased from $102 million in 1992 to $132 million in 1996, with wages per hour at $104 million and $113 million respectively.

Employment went from a total of 14,300 in 1992 to 16,700 in 1996 with production workers equaling 50 percent in 1992 and 45 percent in 1996, with wages averaging $14.79 and $16.69 respectively. Hourly pay increases were expected for 1997 and 1998 up to $17.70 per person.

The medical equipment and services 1997 workforce which includes X-ray and apparatus, ranked San Diego, California as number one with 4,682 jobs, Bethesda, Maryland (2) with 3,339 employees and Minneapolis, Minnesota with 3,155 employees.

AMERICA AND THE WORLD

Foreign imports of X-ray equipment accounted for 42 percent of industry sales in 1992 according to *U.S. Industrial Outlook,* higher than any other segment of the medical industry group. America's largest competitors were Japan and Germany, contributing 60 percent. Overall, the American X-ray industry ran a trade deficit with 1992 imports of $1.1 billion compared to exports of $783 million.

However, imports declined 2.7 percent that year, the first decline in five years. The main export markets for American products were Japan, Germany, and Canada but exports to Eastern Europe tripled their 1991 level reaching $8 million and making that region a prime future growth area.

In 1996, the diagnostic imaging equipment (3844) accounted for $331 million of the $443 million Italian electromedical market (3845). For 1997, projected growth of two percent was expected. Hong Kong's Chek Lap Kok Airport and Kuala Lumpur International Airport in Malaysia were supplied by at $19 million contract with Vivid Technologies to supply explosive screenings equipment. A European hospital was the first in 1996 to integrate their clinical and administrative systems with a digital medical imaging system. The system allows physicians to have access to patient's X-ray images anywhere on the hospital network. Electronic imaging has benefitted the medical industry by providing greater diagnostic accuracy, better resource utilization and increased productivity. A Japanese device, Compact X 3720A was developed and can detect up to 10 chemical elements using wavelength-distribution optics. This device, which became available in 1996, can show 20 times better resolution than traditional type energy-distribution optics. The manufacturer, Rigaku Industrial Co. Ltd., was expected to sell 25 units in 1997. Siemens Medical Systems assisted Kazanskij Optiko-Mekhanicheckij Zavod, a former defense industry, in producing X-ray medical complexes. Annually, up to 250 units were expected to be produced starting in 1997. Primary Health Technology (PHT) was set up to be launched in 1996 in India by a joint venture between Wipro GE Medical Systems. PHT consisted of six components: X-ray, ultrasound, whole body CT scanners, and three service oriented components.

RESEARCH AND TECHNOLOGY

The uses of X-ray technology and its spin-offs continued to grow in the early 1990s. Medical advancements included such procedures as mammograms, which allowed physicians to detect cancerous tumors in women's breasts, before they became apparent by traditional methods. Even so, the technology had its limitations. In 1993, a Canadian study revealed that mammograms were ineffective in predicting breast cancer for women younger than 50. The relatively dense tissue in younger women's breasts hid developing tumors resulting in no difference in diagnosis rates for women who received mammograms and those who did not. In 1997 there still remains a strong amount of controversy as to when women should be tested for breast cancer and how often they should be checked with a mammogram.

Tomography has also found its way into agriculture to observe harvesting techniques for fruits and vegetables and find out when and why crop damage occurred. The rays showed distribution patterns of pesticides and rates of water absorption by different types of roots and different soil-seed combinations.

Micro-tomography opened the miniature world of ceramics and plastics to the researcher and quality control inspector. By using high-energy sources like synchrotron radiation, industry researchers could analyze the internal structures of rocks and minerals like coal and oil-bearing shales, aiding companies like EXXON in their search for new oil and coal fields. Synchrotron radiation is produced by accelerating particles like electrons to nearly the speed of light within a magnetic field. The result is an intense white light. By channeling that light, researchers can create pencil-thick concentrated beams of x-radiation, ultraviolet, and infrared radiation.

This tunable radiation source could map chemical elements within an object. Exxon has used the technology to map elements within copper, nickel, and iron. Biomedical researchers have used the technology to study calcium to gain more knowledge of the makeup of human bones. Intense X-rays could look within the walls of living cells to study their structure and watch the movements of elements like calcium within a body; however, the individual cells targeted by the X-rays would be killed.

A gamma-ray version of the CAT scan—Positron-emission-topography (PET)—measured brain activity. Areas of the brain engaged in thought processes absorbed glucose tagged with positron radiation. Decaying positrons gave off gamma-rays which receptors picked up and translated into a light-and-dark image of the brain. Brains which showed higher IQ levels in standard tests showed less activity than those which scored lower. Researchers theorized that the more intelligent brain was "wired" more efficiently and so used less of its capacity to solve a problem. PET was also used for diagnosing cancer and Alzheimer's disease and in evaluating epileptic patients. In the mid-to-late nineties, scientists have also been able to test the areas of the brain for depression, aggression, gender differences and memory loss using the PET scan.

Another recent advance also used gamma-rays. The single photon emission computed tomograph (SPECT) also tracked radioactive isotopes through the body and used a computer to build an image of a metabolic function. It was particularly useful for monitoring heart functions.

Researchers used the technology to examine the internal structure of the earth and to test the "Global Warming" hypothesis. Using seismic waves, rather than X-rays, they mapped the boundary between the earth's core and its mantle. In 1991, researchers began sending a series of sound waves from Heard Island in Antarctica through the naturally stable environment of deep ocean water. Scientists will need to continue this research for several years in order to obtain accurate and meaningful information. American Science & Engineering Inc, MA was interested in using its screen equipment technology for airports to screen cargo and mail. Because of the expense of the equipment—ballet scanners cost around $1.2-$1.5 million—and level of skill needed to operate the machinery, the company president doubts airlines will purchase the equipment anytime soon.

The 60-year-old gamma camera that uses vacuum tube technology, was replaced by a gamma camera called Notebook Imager that uses a cadmium-zinc-telluride, solid-state detector array. It was a 1996 leading product of Digirad Corporation.

A 1996 study done on rats examined the ability of X-rays to help restore paralyzed limbs to partial use, if applied at the right moment with the right dosage.

Universal Plastics Corp., and Eastman Kodak Scientific Imaging Division worked cooperatively in 1996 to develop a sequencing device to identify strands of DNA. Kodak also indicated they would replace X-ray film used to capture the images of the strands with a digital imaging capability.

Shimadzu developed a X-ray machine that measures X-rays as digital input. The data can be sent to physicians all over the world as a image because it is stored on optical and magnetic disks. The Japanese manufacturer expected to make it available in 1997 and will retail for 60 million yen.

FURTHER READING

Ambry, Margaret, K., Consumer Power, How Americans Spend Their Money, *New Strategist Publications*, 1991, Chapter 7.

"Airline Baggage Inspection Systems Developer Eyes IPO Market," *The IPO Reporter*, 28 October 1996, 20.

"AS&E's Cargo Scanners," *Traffic World*, 16 December 1996, 248.

Begley, Sharon. "How to Tell If You're Smart." *Newsweek* (February 29, 1988): 64.

Carey, John. "Is the World Heating Up? Well, Just Listen." *Business Week* (February 4, 1991): 82.

"CAT Scratches into 3-D." *High Technology Business* (September-October, 1989): 5.

"Coming to an X-ray Room Near You: 3-D Anatomy," *Nikkei Weekly,* 22 April 1996, 34.

"Core Questions." *Scientific American,* 1 February 1987.

"Demand for Drug Lifts Hologic X-ray Product," *Boston Globe,* 3 April 1996.

"Dental Tech Firm Develops an Alternative to X-rays," *Crain's New York Business,* 1 April 1996.

Devaney, Anthony J. "Ultrasound Tomography." *Physics Today* 37 (January 8, 1984): S-37-8.

"Diagnosing Ailing Highways." *USA Today,* Dec. 12, 1989.

Dorminey, Bruce. "Technology: A Source of High Energy: 'Soft' X-ray Advances Have a Variety of Medical and Dental Applications." *Financial Times London Edition,* 28 January 1997.

Drew, Glen. "Medical devices: A Primer on Medical Device Regulation." *FDA Consumer* (May, 1986): 24-7.

"Eastman, Universal Device Charts DNA," *Plastics News,* 10 June 1996, 8.

"Fischer Imaging Corp.," Department of Defense News Release, 12 September 1996. (DDNR 96)

"Fluroscan Imaging Systems Inc.," *Crain's Chicago Business,* 29 July 1996, 19.

Fox, Jeffrey L. "PET Scan Controversy Aired." *Science* 224 (April 13, 1984): 143-44.

"Gamma Camera Developer Raises $6M," *Private Equity Week,* 28 October 1996, 3.

Gregory, William. "Medical X-ray Measuring Device Finds Use in Explosive Detection." *Aviation Week & Space Technology* 124 (April 28, 1986): 31.

Hall, Nina. "X-rays Slice into the Heart of Matter." *New Scientist* 116 (October 15, 1987): 54-6.

Henderson, Breck W. "USAF Seeks Aerospace Applications for Innovative X-ray Tomography." *Aviation Week & Space Technology* 131 (July 31, 1989): 93, 97, 99.

"Hologic Agrees to Merge With Fluorscan," *New York Times,* National Edition, 20 July 1996.

"Industry News (Joint Venture) Alliance Formed to Distribute Products to Treat Cancer," *Cancer Weekly Plus,* 7 October 1996.

"Italy Diagnostic Industry Shows Modest Growth in 1995," *Medical Device Business News,* July 1996.

"Italy: Medical Diagnostic Imaging Equipment," *Journal of Commerce,* 18 December 1996, 410.

Leitch, Andrew. "Leave Them Bones Alone." *Discover* (March, 1992).

Lenorovitz, Jeffrey M. "France Nears Service Introduction of X-ray-Based Cargo Inspection System." *Aviation Week & Space Technology* 134 (March 25, 1991): 64.

Magnet, Myron. "Diasonics' Winning Ways to Look Inside You." *Fortune* (May 16, 1983): 170-72, 174, 176.

Marcial, Gene G. "Why the Buybacks at Diasonics?" *Business Week* (February 4, 1991): 80.

Merrifield, John T. "USAF Considers Using Computed Tomography Inspection for MX." *Aviation Week & Space Technology* 124 (March 3, 1986): 81, 83.

Monastersky, Richard. "Climate Test: Hum Heard 'round the World." *Science News* 139 (January 26, 1991): 53.

Moss, Carol. "Scanning Ancient Egypt." *Science* 85 (January/February, 1985): 82-4.

"New Questions about Mammograms." *Newsweek* (March 8, 1993).

"Physician Sales and Service," *Modern Healthcare,* 23 September 1996, 26.

"Physician Sales and Service," *New York Times,* National Edition, 20 November 1996.

Pomerantz, Martin A. "Gamma-Ray Astronomy." *Grolier's Academic American Encyclopedia.* Compuserve AAE.

"Rigaku Industrial Develops X-Ray Device that Analyzes Magnetic Disks Thickness and Chemical Composition of Magnetic Disks," *Nikkei Sangyo Shimbun,* 22 August 1996.

"Shimadzu Develops Digital X-Ray Machine," *Nihon Keizi Shimbun,* 12 January 1996.

"SMS Clinical Imaging System," *Medical Device Business News,* October 1996

Stein, Harry and Keri J. Sperry. "X-rays." *Grolier's Academic American Encyclopedia.* Compuserve AAE.

Stern, Richard L. "Solid as a Rock?" *Forbes* (February 27, 1984): 89-90.

Thomsen, Dietrick E. "A Most Powerful X-ray Machine." *Science News* 132 (October 31, 1987).

Tracy, Eleanor Johnson. "A New X-ray Scanner to Hinder Hijackers." *Fortune* (April 28, 1986): 146.

"Varian Signs Supply Deal with Toshiba for X-ray Tubes." *Biomedical Market Newsletter,* April 1996.

"Vivid Technologies Inc." *New York Times,* 8 January 1997

Weiss, Rick. "You Say Tomato, They Say Tomography." *Science News* 132 (Sept 12, 1987).

"X-Rays May Help to Repair Spine Damage, Study Suggests," *New York Times,* National Edition, 1 October 1996.

—Al Cook, updated by Beth Yocca

SIC 3845

ELECTROMEDICAL AND ELECTROTHERAPEUTIC APPARATUS

This classification comprises establishments primarily engaged in manufacturing electromedical and electrotherapeutic apparatus. Establishments primarily engaged in manufacturing electrotherapeutic lamp units for ultraviolet and infrared radiation are classified in **SIC 3641: Electric Lamp Bulbs and Tubes.**

INDUSTRY SNAPSHOT

In the half century following World War II, the electromedical industry recorded greater growth than the four other industries composing the medical and dental industrial category, outpacing the revenue growth of the surgical and medical instruments industry, the surgical appliances and supplies industry, the dental equipment and supplies industry, and the x-ray apparatus and tubes industry. The rise of the electromedical industry to a position of prominence within the medical and dental category was attributable primarily to the revolutionary nature of the products manufactured under its purview, a diverse selection of technologically sophisticated medical devices that greatly ameliorated the art of medicine not only in the United States, but throughout the world.

Born from the rapid technological advances that occurred in the electronics field following the war, specifically from the technological achievements that spawned the semiconductor and computer industries, the list of products manufactured by companies within the electromedical industry comprises a host of medical devices regarded in the 1990s as indispensable to the practice of medicine. These products include pacemakers, heart defibrillators, magnetic resonance imaging (MRI) devices, ultrasonic scanning devices, computerized axial tomography (CAT) scanners, and cardiographs, as well as a number of other medical devices equally essential to the diagnosis and treatment of diseases.

Although classified as a distinct industry by the U.S. Government's *Standard Industrial Classification Manual* in the early 1990s, the electromedical industry was not always regarded as such, functioning for roughly the first 25 years of its existence in an ancillary position to the then-larger X-ray apparatus and tubes industry. From the early 1960s to 1987, electromedical industry statistics were combined with those of the X-ray apparatus and tubes industry. During that time, the electromedical industry evolved from a group of manufacturers representing a modestly sized market into a genuine industry of it own. The classification "X-Ray Apparatus and Tubes; Electromedical and Electrotherapeutic Apparatus," initially was a logical combination of what became two separate industries, primarily because the X-ray apparatus segment overshadowed the smaller electromedical segment, generating the bulk of the industry's revenue and representing a more formidable economic force.

In 1987, when many industries were reclassified to more accurately reflect the true nature of American industry, the X-ray apparatus and tubes segment of the classification "X-Ray Apparatus and Tubes; Electromedical and Electrotherapeutic Apparatus," became **SIC 3844: X-ray Apparatus and Tubes and Related Irradiation Apparatus,** while the electromedical segment, by then a larger industry than the X-ray apparatus industry, became **SIC 3845: Electromedical and Electrotherapeutic Apparatus.** This reclassification by the *Standard Industrial Classification Manual,* however, came more than a decade after the electromedical industry had eclipsed the X-ray apparatus industry in magnitude, serving as a somewhat belated recognition of the electromedical industry's force. Consequently, during the electromedical industry's prolific rise to the fore in the 1970s, all of the statistics that tell the story of its growth are somewhat inflated due to the inclusion of the statistical information generated by X-ray apparatus manufacturers.

Growth, which came quickly during the 1970s, slowed during the 1980s. Circumstances within the medical industry, specifically the reduced capital expenditures of more budget-conscious hospitals and the maturation of the electromedical market itself, brought annual revenue growth down to approximately 8 percent, half of the annual percentage increase realized during the 1970s. Despite the slower pace, the electromedical industry continued to enjoy enviable revenue growth during the late 1980s and early 1990s, increasing its value of shipments from $3.57 billion in 1987 to $5.90 billion in 1992 and recording positive growth in each of these years except 1991. The estimated growth of 1996 U.S. sales volume was $118.1 million for electrosurgery equipment and $186.9 million for respiratory care, resuscitors, and ventilators.

ORGANIZATION AND STRUCTURE

Approximately 200 companies in the United States manufactured electromedical or electrotherapeutic devices as their primary business in the early 1990s. Of the approximately 230 manufacturing establishments operated by the industry's manufacturers, roughly 150 employed 20 or more workers. Compared to the typical size of a manufacturing facility in the United States, the electromedical industry exceeded the national standard by 155 percent, employing 137 workers per establishment compared to the 54 employed on average by all other manufacturing industries.

California led all other states in electromedical device production, manufacturing 24 percent of the industry's total shipments and employing 21 percent of the industry's total work force. With its 39 manufacturing facilities, California contained more than twice as many facilities as the second and third ranking states, Massachusetts and New York, which both contained 15 manufacturing facilities. Other states with a significant number of manufacturing facilities were Texas and Illinois with 13 each, Pennsylvania with 11, and Wisconsin, Florida, and Minnesota with 10 manufacturing establishments each. All totaled, 23 states contained electromedical device manufacturing establishments.

BACKGROUND AND DEVELOPMENT

Truly a product of a technologically modern society, the electromedical industry owes its emergence largely to research and development conducted in the 1950s by scientists and manufacturers in the then-nascent semiconductor and computer industries. From these two technological staging grounds, combined with advancements in the electronic field resulting from the enormous effort put forth by the nation's space program, the process by which electronic technology developed was greatly accelerated. The knowledge gained from these three components of American industry, each heavily dependent on electronic technology, proved to be a boon to other industries as well, strengthening some, while enabling the outright creation of others. Such was the case with the electromedical industry, which emerged during the 1960s.

To be sure, there were precursors to electromedical devices before the 1960s. Electrical pulsing as means to treat a variety of ailments had been employed since before the turn of the twentieth century, but these early devices were more curiosities than representative of a genuine industry. Instead, perhaps the first piece of equipment that could justify prognostications for the emergence of a future electromedical industry appeared in the late 1950s, when Earl Bakken, chairman of a bio-medical company named Medtronic, and cardiologists from the University of Minnesota developed one of the first workable cardiac pacemakers.

Nothing more than an automobile battery resting on a dolly and attached to the patient's chest through wire cables, this first pacemaker was rather primitive, but led to further ameliorations and the emergence of much smaller versions that soon were regarded as viable medical devices suitable for implantation. As improvements were made in pacemakers, additional products that would later compose the electromedical industry, such as ultrasonic medical equipment and cardiographs, were developed as well. Their development would take time, but the developmental challenges, though formidable, were not the major obstacles barring the appearance of the electromedical industry. Instead, marketing these new products posed the greatest challenge to the fledgling electromedical manufacturers, as industry participants found it difficult to convince the medical community that electromedical devices provided in many cases a preferable alternative to extant medical equipment. This took time as well, but eventually doctors and hospital administrators embraced the new electronic equipment, and by the end of the 1960s, the industry began to emerge as a recognizable economic force.

For electromedical manufacturers, the rewards were worth the wait. The industry quickly flourished, its growth fueled by the widespread acceptance of all kinds of electromedical equipment throughout U.S. health care institutions. Sales amounted to a modest $233 million in 1967, particularly small considering electromedical manufacturers were responsible for generating only a fraction of the total, overshadowed by their larger cousins, x-ray apparatus manufacturers. But the electromedical industry would not be cast in this supportive role for long, and indeed from this point forward, growth of the electromedical industry would outpace that of the X-ray apparatus industry and thereby fuel the growth of the industry as whole. When, five years later, total sales climbed to $429 million, the leap was even more pronounced for electromedical manufacturers, having started from much below the $233 million figure in 1967, yet accounting for a large part of the nearly $200 million increase.

By 1974, the electromedical industry had closed the gap separating its revenue production with that of the X-ray apparatus industry and drew even, with each segment accounting for half of the $650 million in sales recorded that year. With slightly less than 100 X-ray apparatus and electromedical device manufacturers in the country at that time, the number of manufacturers would swell to nearly 240 in two years, a dramatic increase once again reflective mainly of the electromedical industry's rapid rate of growth. From 1974 to the end of the decade, the electromedical industry's revenue volume skyrocketed at a compound annual rate of 31 percent, an increase that dropped to a less prolific 16.4 percent when adjusted for inflation, yet still represented robust vitality.

Still benefiting from further improvements and from the continued acceptance of their products, which by the mid-1970s had firmly established the electromedical industry as a major player in the broadly defined medical industry, electromedical manufacturers had gained great strides since the first awkward and rudimentary pacemaker appeared in the late 1950s. No longer attached via cable or measuring as large as a hat box, pacemakers were now roughly the size of a fingertip and enjoyed widespread demand. In 1970, 53,000 pacemakers were implanted, and by 1976 the yearly implants had increased to 175,000, representing a quarter of a billion dollars in sales. At this time, the prospects for further sales appeared almost guaranteed, as a development of great significance augured a dramatic increase in the number of pacemakers installed each year. Powered by mercury-zinc batteries, pacemakers typically needed to be replaced at least three times during a patient's life span, but the use of lithium-powered batteries, a development that promised to reshape the market for pacemakers, reduced the average replacement expectation of pacemakers to one per patient. Although the switch to lithium-powered batteries would sharply reduce the industry's replacement sales, the prospect of undergoing fewer surgical procedures induced more patients to opt for pacemaker implants, which drove sales upward.

By 1976, the electromedical and X-ray apparatus industry's aggregate revenue neared the $1 billion mark, then shot past it the following year, increasing 86 percent to reach $1.88 billion. Underpinned by strong pacemaker sales and even stronger ultrasonic equipment sales, which were increasing 18 percent annually, the electromedical industry approached the end of its decade of prodigious growth nearing $2.5 billion in sales. Success came slower in the early 1980s, but only in contrast to the dramatic growth of the 1970s. Sales eclipsed $5 billion in 1984, then began to suffer in the ensuing years, falling 2.7 percent in 1985 and increasing only marginally thereafter, as flat demand, a buildup of inventories, and strong competition from imports combined to arrest the industry's expansion.

In 1987, the electromedical industry was separated at last from the X-ray apparatus industry, their respective statistics no longer pooled together. In the last year of their combination, total sales were estimated to be $5 billion; their separation gave, for the first time, a clear indication of their individual magni-

tude. The electromedical industry emerged as a $3.57 billion industry, employing 29,200 workers, while the X-ray apparatus industry's value of shipments amounted to $1.55 billion and its work force totaled 8,700.

As the electromedical industry entered the late 1980s, manufacturers attempted to effect a recovery from the mid-1980s, a downturn that was exacerbated by the increasingly cost-conscious health care industry. By 1989, price increases at the manufacturer level averaged only 3 percent in the previous four years, as increased competition and production overcapacity limited the manufacturers' ability to raise prices. Profits suffered as a result, but revenue continued to grow, sending many manufacturers overseas to forge joint ventures with other companies to lessen the financial constraints of a capital-intensive business.

CURRENT CONDITIONS

After recording double-digit growth between 1987 and 1990, the electromedical industry entered the early 1990s watching its inspiring growth shudder to a stop, particularly in 1993, when sales were flat. In 1994, the industry's revenue total was an estimated $6.23 billion. The industry-wide stagnation of the early 1990s was attributable largely to a sharp decline in MRI shipments, which plummeted nearly 20 percent compared to shipment increases of pacemakers and ultrasonic scanning devices of 3 and 5 percent, respectively. The decline in MRI shipments, more capital-intensive than pacemakers or ultrasonic scanning devices, was attributed primarily to recessive economic conditions during the early 1990s, coupled with uncertainty regarding the future of health care as a result of President Bill Clinton's health care reforms. As the industry entered the mid-1990s, these uncertainties and their eventual resolution promised to have great import on the future of the industry.

Looking forward from the mid-1990s, prognostications for the electromedical industry were predicated on the further technological development of MRIs, and generally on advancements emanating from the diagnostic side of the electromedical industry. With improved imaging systems, operating at significantly higher speeds, this type of electromedical equipment provided the industry's best answer to the health care industry's need for cost-cutting, more efficient equipment in the 1990s.

Tattoo removal was also becoming a larger market for the electromedical industry. A dermatological laser distributed only by Laser Photonics, Florida, signed a 1996, three-year deal for $5.4 million to provide medical lasers for removing tattoos, pigmented skin, and unwanted hair to American Laser Corp.

As of 1996, medical device manufacturers can be subject to product-liability claims in state court. The U.S. Supreme Court found Medtronic Inc., the world's largest pacemaker manufacturer, liable for design defects, a ruling that could influence the 11 million people in the United States with such implanted medical devices as pacemakers, silicone breast implants, hearing aids, penile implants, hip replacements, and knee replacements.

INDUSTRY LEADERS

The largest manufacturer in the electromedical industry during the mid-1990s, General Electric's Medical Systems Group based in Milwaukee, Wisconsin, stood as a classic example of the electromedical industry's efforts to further penetrate the international electromedical market and reduce the production costs of its products. With joint ventures scattered across Asia, General Electric's Medical Systems Group entered into a joint venture with a personal computer manufacturer, Wipro Ltd., in India in 1990 to produce and sell a wide variety of ultrasound devices. By forging such ties, the Medical Systems Group became one of General Electric's most profitable divisions in the mid-1990s, recording more than $5 billion in sales in 1993.

In ranking order behind General Electric's Medical Systems Group were IMCERA Group Inc., based in Northbrook, Illinois, with $1.70 billion in sales, and Picker International Inc., based in Highland Heights, Ohio, with $1.18 billion in sales.

St. Jude Medical, Inc., a heart valve manufacturer, acquired Ventritex, a leading heart defibrillator company, for $501 million. The heart defibrillator market reached $800 million in sales for 1996 and is expected to increase 25 percent per year. The market potential for external defibrillators was $3 billion in 1996.

WORK FORCE

Total employment during the electromedical industry's history generally paralleled its pattern of revenue growth, climbing while sales increased and leveling off when revenue growth became less prolific. In 1974, when the industry already was experiencing a phenomenal surge of growth and its total employment included employees involved in the production of X-ray apparatus, there were 13,000 employees composing its work force. Two years later, total employment vaulted to 30,900, largely due to the growth of the electromedical segment of the industry. This figure continued to increase, reaching 41,500 by 1981, then

climbing to 48,800 by 1984, at which time total employment in the industry began to record successive annual declines as manufacturers streamlined their operations. By 1988, total employment had fallen to 31,400, then began to increase once again, rising to 34,400 by 1991.

Of the 34,400 people employed by the electromedical industry in 1991, less than half were production workers, an atypical ratio of production workers to salaried employees in American manufacturing industry. The greater proportional representation of salaried employees, those performing managerial, administrative, or technical duties, was primarily due to the technological sophistication of the products manufactured by the industry, which, as the level of sophistication increased over the course of the industry's existence, winnowed the ranks of production workers in the industry.

Generally, production workers were employed on a full-time basis during the early 1990s, averaging 4 percent more hours per year than the typical production worker employed by other manufacturing industries. Production workers in the electromedical industry generally earned more per hour than their counterparts as well, averaging $10.91 per hour in 1989, compared to the national average of $10.49 per hour. In 1996, this average hourly wage increased to $12.90.

AMERICA AND THE WORLD

Historically, the electromedical industry's international presence has been a major source of its strength, providing manufacturers with ample room to market their highly sophisticated products in markets bereft of similar equipment. In 1993, this presence continued to support the industry at a time when domestic conditions had soured. In that year, U.S. exports of electromedical equipment increased 8 percent to $2.4 billion, giving U.S. manufacturers a $1.1 billion trade surplus. Much of this business was attributable to the strong sales performance of electrodiagnostic devices, ultrasonic scanners, and patient monitoring systems. These products were sold chiefly to European Community countries, Japan, and Canada.

RESEARCH AND DEVELOPMENT

Recent technological advances have led to the improvement of current instruments. One such device, a smaller, lighter, defilbrillator, restores the heartbeat of cardiac arrest victims more quickly than the older version. Since it improves the survival rate of these patients, sales of the instrument are expected to reach $150 million per year by 2000.

New diagnostic tools and surgical devices are expected to benefit the industry and patients alike. In-body blood and tissue surveillance systems sales approximated $360 million in 1996, and the industry anticipates sales of $630 million by the year 2000. A non-evasive, 15-minute cancer test, approved in 1997, was expected to reduce the number of biopsies and increase early detection of the disease.

FURTHER READING

"Ambry, Margaret K. *Consumer Power, How Americans Spend Their Money.* New Strategist Publications, 1991.

American Journal of Emergency Medicine, January 1995, 13.

"Americas: FDA Tightens Manufacturing Quality Standards." *Medical Device Business News,* October 1996.

"Asahi Glass Engineering: Electrolysis Water Generator Approved by Ministry of Health and Welfare." *Nikkan Kogyo Shimbun,* 8 January 1997.

"Automation, Resolution & Speed Mark Capillary Electrophoresis Trends." *Genetic Engineering News,* 15 January 1997, 17.

"Breast Disease (Screening) Adjunctive Screening Device Enhances Early Detection." *Cancer Weekly Plus,* 11 November 1996.

"Brit, Dr. Reddy's Lab in Technical Collaboration." *Business Line,* 10 July 1996.

Chiu, Yvonne. "California Couple Markets Reusable Fertility Test Device." *Sacramento Bee,* 12 April 1996.

"Circon Expected To Seek White Knight." *Mergers & Acquisitions Report,* 19 August 1996, 9.

"Court Allows State Litigation in Medical Device Lawsuits." *Plastics News,* 1 July 1996, 8.

Darnay, Arsen J., ed. *Manufacturing USA.* 5th edition, Detroit: Gale Reearch, 1996.

"Diagnosis by Videophone-Teledoc From NEC." *Newsbytes News Network,* 23 February 1996.

"Electronic Age of Medicine." *Financial World,* 9 September 1964, 10.

Engardio, Pete. "An Ultrasound Foothold in Asia." *Business Week,* 8 November1993, 68.

"Expanding the Pie." *HFN,* 8 April 1996, 70.

"FDA OKs Device to Remove Lesions." *Household & Personal Products Industry.* August 1996, 33.

"FDA Panel Backs Pacemaker Device." *Chicago Tribune,* 16 July 1996.

"Financing Business." *Wall Street Journal,* 7 October 1996.

"Florida's Laser Photronics Signs Deal with Utah's American Laser Corp." *Orlando Sentinel,* 19 July 1996.

Greene, Joan. "Ya Gotta Have Heart." *Barron's,* 27 December 1976, 11.

"Heartsteram, Physio-Control Vie to Arrest Cardiac Arrest." *Seattle Times,* 26 September 1996.

"Hitachi Setting Up R&D Group." *Plain Dealer,* 26 May 1996.

"Hologic Announces $59M Plan to Merge with Fluroscan." *Boston Globe,* 20 July 1996.

"ISG Technologies." *Globe & Mail,* 23 July 1996.

"Italy: Medical Diagnostic Imaging and Equipment." *Journal of Commerce,* 18 December 1996, 410.

"LG Industrial Systems Launches R&D Centers Worldwide." *Korea Economic Daily,* 14 August 1996.

Loehwing, David A. "Best of Health: Biomedical Technology—All Systems Are Go." *Barron's,* 5 November 1973, 3.

———. "'Ya Gotta Have Heart': Bio-Medicine Abounds in Risks as Well as Rewards." *Barron's,* 12 November 1973, 5.

"Medical Device Makers Face State Court Suits." *Chicago Tribune,* 27 June 1996.

"Medical Market Turns to Non-Invasive Products." *Business Marketing,* October 1983, 18.

"Medtronic." *Modern Healthcare,* 29 April 1996, 26.

"Now Surgeons Can Nip and Tuck in 3-D." *Business Week,* 3 February 1997.

"Outlook Brightens for Ultrasound Firm Advanced Technology Labs." *Seattle Times,* 9 May 1996.

"Quorum Sells ISG Stake." *Globe & Mail,* 19 December 1996.

"Roche Bioscience Deal with Affymetrix." *Marketletter,* 20 January 1997.

"St. Jude Medical Agrees to Acquire Ventritex." *Wall Street Journal,* 24 October 1996.

"Ultrasound Market in Emerging Countries." *Biomedical Market Newsletter,* 31 October 1996, 6.

U.S. Department of Commerce. International Trade Administration. *U.S. Industrial Outlook.* Washington: GPO, 1993.

"U.S. Sales of Electronics up 11%." *Newsbytes News Network,* 2 August 1996.

—Jeffrey L. Covell, updated by Beth Yocca

SIC 3851

OPHTHALMIC GOODS

This classification includes establishments primarily engaged in manufacturing ophthalmic frames, lenses, contact lenses, and sunglass lenses. Establishments involved in manufacturing molded glass blanks are included in **SIC 3229: Pressed and blown glass and glassware, Not Elsewhere Classified;** and businesses engaged in grinding lenses and fitting glasses to prescriptions are classified in **SIC 5995: Optical Goods Stores.**

INDUSTRY SNAPSHOT

Over 500 companies in the United States were involved in manufacturing ophthalmic goods in the mid-1990s. These companies expected about $3.39 billion in 1997 shipment values for products covered in this industry classification. This figure represented an aggregate value of shipments largely derived from the production of the four primary products in the ophthalmic goods industry: ophthalmic lenses and frames, sunglasses, industrial eyewear, and contact lenses. Contact lenses, by far the dominant ophthalmic goods product in the mid-1990s, accounted for over 31 percent of the total shipments delivered by the industry, with soft contact lenses representing 22 percent of the contact lens product share. Plastic ophthalmic focus lenses accounted for approximately 15 percent of the industry's shipments while ophthalmic frames and industrial eyewear each accounted for six percent of the product share. Non-prescription sunglasses represented four percent of the total shipments delivered by the industry. Other products within the ophthalmic goods industry include underwater goggles, reading and simple magnifiers, and a ophthalmic lens coating.

The ophthalmic goods industry entered the 1990s with a decade of solid growth behind them, except for a temporary downturn in the mid-1980s. The value of shipments manufactured by the industry rose from $1.28 billion in 1982 to $2.27 billion in 1990, an increase partly attributable to the increasing popularity of sunglasses and to technological innovations in the development of contact lenses.

ORGANIZATION AND STRUCTURE

The ophthalmic goods industry was predominantly populated by relatively small manufacturing operations. Of the 517 establishments involved in producing ophthalmic goods in 1989, nearly 360, or 68 percent of all the facilities engaged in the industry, employed less than 20 people. Together, these 517 establishments represented all of the facilities operating in the industry that were operated by the approximately 500 companies engaged in manufacturing ophthalmic goods. Typically, the larger companies do not solely manufacture ophthalmic goods, but rely on manufacturing a diverse line of products to generate sales. For example, the leading company in the industry, Bausch & Lomb Inc., garnered over 60 percent of its sales in 1991 from healthcare products.

A majority of the facilities engaged in manufacturing ophthalmic goods are located in the eastern United States, although California has the greatest number of establishments located in any one state. In terms of regional concentration, New York, New Jersey, and Pennsylvania, contain the most ophthalmic goods facilities, with 101 establishments. The Pacific region, including Alaska and Hawaii, ranked as the second most populated area of ophthalmic goods manufacturing facilities, solely by virtue of the 80 establishments located in California, the only state within the region to contain manufacturing facilities. Michigan, Illinois, and Ohio, home to 65 establishments, represent the nation's third largest regional concentration of ophthalmic facilities.

During the 1980s, the cost of conducting business in the ophthalmic goods industry rose sharply, far outpacing the increase in sales during the decade. In 1982, the industry recorded $1.28 billion in sales and spent $41 million on capital investment. By 1990, sales had climbed to $2.27 billion, but capital investment had more than tripled to $137 million. In 1998, capital investment was expected to reach $2.56 billion. Despite this exponential increase in capital outlays, the average investment of ophthalmic goods facilities was comparatively less expensive than the average investment of facilities in all other manufacturing industries. The average investment required to operate an ophthalmic facility in 1989 was $282,398, which was five percent below the average investment per establishment of $296,864 for all other manufacturing industries. A more dramatic difference is shown in the cost per establishment. In 1989, $1,284,526 was the average cost for facilities operating in the ophthalmic goods industry, 72 percent below the $4,542,893 averaged by establishments in all other manufacturing industries. In 1992, the operating cost for the industry was $1,314,587 while the average for all manufacturers was $4,239,462.

BACKGROUND AND DEVELOPMENT

Until the 1960s, growth in the ophthalmic goods industry had occurred at a steady, predictable rate, largely dictated by the rate of population growth in the United States. During the 1960s, however, an increased demand for ophthalmic products elevated the production and sales levels of manufacturers to an unprecedented high. A combination of several factors prompted this remarkable surge in growth, including a dramatic rise in the nation's population and an increase in the availability of eye examinations. The advent of contact lenses in the 1950s as a genuine alternative to conventional corrective eyewear, however, contributed most significantly to the growth of the ophthalmic goods industry.

Although extraordinary gains were achieved by contact lens manufacturers and retailers during the first years of quantifiable production in the 1950s, certain difficulties associated with the early development of contact lenses slowed the public's acceptance of the new product. On average, a pair of contact lenses sold for $200, an exceedingly high price to pay for many consumers, and the discomfort caused by wearing the hard, hydrophobic lenses, which initially covered most of the exposed eyeball, dissuaded a considerable percentage of consumers from making a long-term conversion to contact lenses. According to industry estimates, roughly half of the people who began fittings for contact lenses reverted back to conventional corrective eyewear, a rate of attrition that would continue to plague contact lens manufacturers into the 1970s.

Despite the high cost of these lenses and the discomfort they often caused, consumers purchased enough contact lenses to push annual sales from $2 million in 1950 to $60 million by 1959. The number of contact lens manufacturers, the majority of which were small, privately-owned companies, also increased at a commensurate rate during the decade, climbing from 20 in 1950 to more than 400 by 1960. This proliferation of contact lens manufacturers led to a rash of deceptive advertising complaints issued by the Federal Trade Commission (FTC) and sparked several fiercely contested patent disputes, as the excitement generated by the creation of a new, potentially lucrative market within the ophthalmic goods industry attracted increased competition. Complaints filed by the FTC, 15 of which were recorded in 1961 compared to only four prior to 1960, patent disputes, along with issues such as whether only ophthalmologists and oculists should be allowed to prescribe and fit contact lenses, caused the sales of contact lenses to stagnate at the close of the decade. But these were problems generally associated with the nascence of the market and, as such, inflicted only a temporary setback on the burgeoning industry.

By the mid-1960s, improvements had been made in contact lenses, although their cost still hovered around $200 a pair. The thickness of the plastic used to manufacture the lenses had been reduced, alleviating some of the irritation experienced when a contact lens wearer's eyelid passed over the lens, and the diameter of the lenses had also been reduced so that they only covered the iris and the pupil, rather than the entire exposed eyeball. Shortly before these improvements were made, however, a discovery of lasting importance for the future of the contact lens market overshadowed the technological strides made by the industry in hard contact lens design—although it would be years before its impact would be felt by manufacturers

and retailers. In 1965, two Czechoslovakian scientists, Otto Wichterle and Drahoslav Lim, were awarded a patent for their invention, five years earlier, of a soft plastic suitable for body implants that could also be used to produce contact lenses. Marking the beginning of soft contact lenses, which would eventually account for an overwhelming percentage of contact lens sales, the pliable, hydrophilic material absorbed tears rather than shedding them, as did hard contact lenses, and virtually eliminated any sensation of the eyelid passing over the lens.

Concurrent with the encouraging development of soft contact lenses, the rest of the ophthalmic goods industry was expanding at a robust rate, exceeding the rate of growth in the nation's population. From 1955 to 1965, the population over the age of five increased 18.4 percent, while the number of corrective eyewear users rose by 30 percent. This growth was primarily attributable to a greater portion of the population undergoing complete eye examinations, a trend facilitated by Medicare and Medicaid health programs, increased screening for vision acuity in public school systems, and states requiring mandatory eye examinations for people applying for driving licenses. The increasing number of union optical plans, coupled with a greater number of corrective lens wearers purchasing more than one pair of ophthalmic lenses and frames, also fueled the expansion of the ophthalmic market in the 1960s.

New product developments in the conventional corrective eyewear field also contributed to the gains achieved by the ophthalmic industry in the 1960s. One of the four leading publicly-held companies engaged in the ophthalmic goods industry at the time, American Optical Corporation, introduced a new single vision lens that provided increased visual sharpness and less distortion from peripheral angles of view. Another leader in the industry, Univis, developed bifocal lenses in 1964 without a visible line separating each half of the lens. Plastic, shatterproof, and lightweight lenses also made their debut in the 1960s. Accounting for only 5 percent of the total corrective lens sales by the mid-1960s, plastic lens sales, nevertheless, had been growing faster than the industry itself during the decade.

Sunglasses also experienced a surge in sales during the 1960s, further accelerating the rapid pace at which the ophthalmic goods industry was expanding. During the 1960s, sunglasses became fashionable accessories worn throughout the year and were no longer considered seasonal products. As the product in the ophthalmic goods industry most sensitive to fashion trends, sunglasses quickly became a lucrative product to manufacture and sell, as unit sales rose from 60 million pairs in 1960 to 175 million pairs in 1966. By the end of the decade, the sunglass market had leapt 70 percent from the sales volume recorded in 1965, to approximately $200 million.

Conspicuously absent from the contact lens market during the 1960s were the leading manufacturers in the ophthalmic goods industry. American Optical Company and Bausch & Lomb Inc., which together controlled over 90 percent of the conventional eyeglass market, had eschewed entrance into the contact lens market primarily because the directors of the companies perceived the competition to be too intense. Moreover, neither company felt it had developed a technological innovation in the product encouraging enough to warrant a foray into the market. In 1966, however, Bausch & Lomb acquired the exclusive rights to manufacture and sell the soft, hydrophilic lenses developed by the two Czechoslovakian scientists, and by 1972 had begun distributing soft contact lenses nationwide.

In the 1970s, the ophthalmic goods industry continued to benefit from the population growth, as the prodigious sales increases of the 1960s continued. Wholesale billings for the optical industry as a whole increased from $400 million in 1959 to $900 million by 1969, then doubled to nearly $2 billion by the end of the 1970s. The success of the industry attracted the attention of the FTC once again, in 1974, when it began investigating restraints on price advertising in the optical industry. In the course of its investigation, the FTC found a significant discrepancy in the price of eyewear throughout the nation, with the average price of eyewear running 25 percent higher in states where advertising was illegal and varying by as much as 300 percent within the same state. In 1978, the same year in which eyeglass coverage became mandatory under Medicaid, the FTC lifted the restrictions on advertising with the hope of saving consumers as much as $400 million annually. Consequently, competition within the ophthalmic goods industry intensified as pricing strategies became of paramount importance.

Along with this transformation of the retail side of the optical industry, ophthalmic goods manufacturers continued to experience growth, engendered in part by the expansion of the sunglass market. In the early 1980s, sunglass sales dropped, with unit demand slipping 15 percent in 1981 and 1982, but sales began rising as the decade progressed. Indicative of the product's dependency on fashion trends, the increase in sales was partly attributable to the popularity of several films during the early 1980s that featured well-known actors wearing sunglasses. For example, per-

haps the greatest boost from the motion picture industry came when a pair of Bausch & Lomb's Ray-Ban Wayfarer sunglasses were prominently featured in *Risky Business*. In 1981, 18,000 pairs of the Wayfarer sunglasses were sold; however, after the film was released in 1983, unit sales ballooned to 330,000 pairs. Retail sales in the sunglass market rose from $361 million in 1985 to $1.5 billion by the end of the decade, reflecting a 100 percent increase from 1980.

CURRENT CONDITIONS

Although the number of contact lens wearers in the United States tapered off at approximately 24 million in the four or five years prior to 1992, the dynamics within this segment of the ophthalmic goods industry were rapidly changing in the early 1990s. Disposable soft contact lenses, first marketed by Johnson & Johnson in 1988, grabbed the attention of consumers during the product's first years of availability and were expected to woo many contact lens wearers away from conventional contact lenses in the future. Projected to represent half of the contact lens market by 1995, disposable lenses appear to be the product of the future in the ophthalmic goods industry. Consequently, the ability of contact lens manufacturers to respond to this development could determine their success in the future.

Severely affected by the global recession in the early 1990s, the sunglass market plummeted 36 percent from $1.76 billion in sales in 1991 to $961 million in 1992. Especially sensitive to the health of the national economy, the sunglass market also suffered from its robust growth during the 1980s, as the proliferation of sunglass manufacturers exacerbated the effect of the stagnant economy and saturated the market. The surfeit of manufacturers entering the U. S. market from both the domestic and international fronts does not bode well for the immediate future of sunglass sales, but the growing trend of purchasing sunglasses for protection from ultra-violet rays could expand the market somewhat.

Additionally, pending legislation regarding the restructuring of the nation's healthcare system will undoubtedly affect individuals' ophthalmology coverage, and will in turn have a significant impact on ophthalmic goods manufacturers. Doubts concerning what provisions will be included for the optical industry, which ranks below the medical and dental industries in terms of size and strength, characterized the industry's anxiety the last time national health care legislation was seriously considered in the early and mid-1970s. These same concerns were revisited as the industry entered the mid-1990s.

SUNGLASS RETAIL SALES BY TYPE OF OUTLET

Source: Sunglass Association of America

Another factor in the eye-care industry was the emerging struggle featuring optometrists and manufacturers who joined together against mail-order outlets and, to a lesser degree, other discount outlets, who have sought to gain a share of the market in recent years. Many manufacturers, including the giants of the industry, refuse to sell lenses to mail-order companies or discount outlets that don't have eye-care professionals on-site.

The Contact Lens Council reported that more than half of all Americans need vision correction of some sort in 1997; this number continues to grow with the aging Baby Boomers. Around 26 million Americans are contact lens wearers. The products that became available in 1995 were daily disposable lenses, and the introduction of additional colored contact lenses (either for cosmetic or prescriptive purposes), which became increasingly popular among lens wearers. Also available, RGP lenses that have low content silicone/high decay flourosilicone acrylates.

The eyeglass market began to shift in 1994 towards larger chains like Wal-Mart and LensCrafters. An example of a company jumping on the bandwagon was an Italian eyeglass manufacturer, Luxottica. LensCrafters was purchased for $900 million by Luxottica. And in turn, the Italian eyeglass manufacturer restocked the big lens retailer's shelves with Luxottica frames like Armani, Valentino, and Calvin Klein along with midrange lines. These frames sold in 1997 for around $150 a pair.

A trend introduced in sunglasses for 1997 was "cosmetic lensing," where there can be one to three colors in the frame. Gucci, for example did a darker plastic frame at the top in green or orange and went to a cream color at the bottom. Just about every designer followed this trend. The idea in mind for the sunglass wearer: variety of color and fashion in sunglass wardrobe.

At the large retail level like Wal-Mart, the Kathie Lee (Gifford) Collection is coming out in spring 1997. Kmart has the Jaclyn Smith line and Target offers 'glarewear.'

The sunglass industry was estimated to be $2.5 billion, of which discount department stores were expected to be $183.3 million, although this was hard to estimate because of high theft rates. In addition to fashion being a reason for increased sunglasses sales, consumers were also more concerned about the protection of their eyes from ultraviolet rays on a year-round basis.

It seemed that almost everyone from clothing stores and manufacturers, to top designers, drug stores, and discount stores are offering sunglasses and eyewear: Timberland licensed their name to Gargoyles to produce Timberland eyewear for March 1997 with costs per pair averaging $150. ActiveEyes were introduced by Penmar Inc. in 1996 for the fitness and sport oriented consumer. Nike Inc. entered the market, with prices of $145-$160. Bausch & Lomb entered the midrange market to sell to drugstores with i's brand. They were designed for boating, bicycling, in-line skating, skiing, and motorcycle riding and are sold at sporting goods stores. Serengeti eyewear developed new sunglasses for skiing and snowboarding that have photochromic wrap-around glass lenses. Retail sales of sunglasses in 1995 were $2.3 million.

Counterfeit goods thrusted a lawsuit involving activewear, sportswear, and luxury goods manufacturers to file against landlords selling imposters of their sunglasses. Ralph Lauren, Nautica, Donna Karan, Tommy Hilfiger, Guess, and Oakley all filed in 1996.

INDUSTRY LEADERS

With over 13,000 employees and manufacturing or marketing operations in 26 countries, Bausch & Lomb is the dominant company operating in the ophthalmic goods industry. A leader in the industry since its inception in 1853, Bausch & Lomb secured a lasting foothold in the optical field by developing the first rubber eyeglass frames, contributing significantly to the advancement of microscope and telescope technology, and through the creation of Aviator-style Ray-Ban sunglasses. The acquisition of the rights to manufacture and sell soft contact lenses in 1966 and the subsequent Federal Drug Administration (FDA) approval to market the lenses in 1971, coupled with the company's diversification in the early 1980s into health care and biomedical business lines, have contributed most appreciably to the company's success in the 1980s and 1990s. With optical products accounting for less than half of the company's sales, Bausch &

Lomb posted $1.70 billion in sales in 1992, compared to the $510 million recorded ten years earlier. Rated number one company again in 1997 was Bausch and Lomb Inc., New York, with $1.933 billion in sales and 14.4 thousand employees.

The second largest company in the ophthalmic goods industry was Allergan Inc., a manufacturer and marketer of contact lenses and a broad assortment of other ophthalmic products not included in this industry classification. Allergan employed approximately 5,100 people and garnered $897 million in sales in 1992 and came in second for 1997 with $947 million in sales and 4.9 thousand employees.

Other leading companies in 1997 were Sola International with $346 million in sales; American Optical Corp. with $210 million in sales; Cabot Safety Corp. with $200 million in sales and Oakley Inc. with $173 million in sales.

A top sunglass store operation was Sunglass Hut International Inc. Opened in the early 1970s by optometrist Dr. Sanford Ziff, the company had 2,000 stores worldwide with net earnings of $20.9 million for 1995.

WORK FORCE

The ophthalmic goods industry employed 28,200 people in 1994, 18,800 of whom were production workers, with the remaining workers performing administrative, technical, or managerial duties. By 1998, the employment rate was expected to reach 31,000. Employment within the industry shrank during the mid-1980s to a low of 21,700 but rebounded by the end of the decade to surpass levels established during the early 1980s.

Typically, production workers in the ophthalmic goods industry are employed on a full-time basis, averaging 2 percent more hours per year than the average of production workers employed by other U.S. industries. However, they earn on average 20 percent less than other production workers. In 1989, the average hourly wage for production workers in the ophthalmic goods industry was $8.36, while the average wage in all other manufacturing industries was $10.49. The average annual salary of employees holding administrative, technical, or managerial positions in the industry was $31,416 in 1989. By 1994, the average wage was $10.09 per hour, and by 1998 this was expected to increase to $11.63.

FURTHER READING

Ambry, Margaret K. *Consumer Power, How Americans Spend Their Money.* New Strategist Publications, 1991.

"AAi Shines with Foster Grant Acquisition." *Discount Store News,* 9 December 1996.

"All Eyes AGOG During Manufacturing Week." *Chicago Tribune,* 19 March 1996.

"Accessories Advance: Seeing the Forest for the Trees." *DNR Accessories for Men Supplement,* 3 January 1997.

"Bausch and Lomb to Let I's Have It." *Drug Store News,* 21 October 1996, 18.

"Business is Bubbling." *Women's Wear Daily,* 20 May 1996, 171.

"Color Evolution." *Women's Wear Daily Accessories Supplement,* January 1997.

"Cytomegalovirus (Treatment) FDA Approves Eye Implant." *AIDS Weekly Plus,* 18 March 1996.

"Double Vision." *Women's Wear Daily,* 26 December 1996, 172.

"Future May Not Be so Bright for Restructured Bausch & Lomb." *Wall Street Journal,* 9 August 1996.

"Goggles for In-Your-Face Video Footage." *Nikkei Weekly,* 24 June 1996, 34.

"Hut One, Hut Two..Hut Two Thousand!" *DNR,* 2 December 1996, 26.

"Luxottica Inks Deal to Make Eyewear for Bulgari." *Women's Wear Daily,* 6 September 1996, 172.

"Makers Sue Landlords in Bogus Goods Case." *Women's Wear Daily,* 14 November 1996, 172.

"Nike Entering Premium Sunglasses Market." *Orange County Register,* 10 October 1996.

"Private Eyes Work for Discounters." *Discount Store News,* 6 January 1997.

"Retailers Look on Bright Side with Sunglasses." *Drug Store News,* 18 November 1996, 18.

"Shades of Things to Come." *DNR,* 31 May 1996, 26.

"Sport Optics." *Sportstyle,* May 1996, 18.

"Total Women's Accessories." *Accessories,* January 1997, 98.

"Vision Correction and Contact Lenses." *Contact Lens Council,* 1 July 1996. Available from http://www.iglobal.com/CLC/clc-01.html.

—Jeffrey L. Covell, updated by Beth Yocca

SIC 3861

PHOTOGRAPHIC EQUIPMENT AND SUPPLIES

This classification includes establishments primarily engaged in manufacturing photographic apparatus, equipment, parts, attachments, and accessories utilized in both still and motion photography. Also covered in this classification are establishments primarily involved in manufacturing photocopy and microfilm equipment, blueprinting and diazotype (white printing) apparatus and equipment, sensitized film, paper, cloth, and plates, and prepared photographic chemicals.

Those establishments involved in manufacturing products that are related to the photographic industry, but are not grouped in the photographic equipment and supplies classification, include manufacturers of unsensitized photographic paper stock, and paper mats, mounts, easels, and folders utilized for photographic purposes. These establishments are classified within the paper and allied products industry. Photographic lens manufacturers are classified in **SIC 3827: Optical Instruments and Lenses,** and manufacturers of photographic glass are delineated in the stone, clay, glass, and concrete products industry. Also excluded are manufacturers of chemicals produced for technical purposes that are not specifically prepared and packaged for use in photography and those manufacturing photographic flash, flood, enlarger, and projection lamp bulbs. The former are classified within chemicals and allied products, and the latter are classified in **SIC 3641: Electric Lamp Bulbs and Tubes.**

INDUSTRY SNAPSHOT

Approximately 800 companies were involved in manufacturing photographic equipment and supplies in the United States in the mid-1990s. These companies together recorded an estimated $24.4 billion in shipments for products included in the classification. The aggregate value of shipments predominantly derived from the industry's six primary product groups: sensitized photographic film, paper, and plates; photocopy equipment; prepared photographic chemicals; still picture equipment; microfilming equipment; and motion picture equipment. Of the various products, still picture equipment had the highest share of the market in 1995 with 43.9 percent of sales, and sensitized photographic film accounted for 24.3 percent of sales, giving still photography equipment a commanding lead over other products within the industry. Photocopy equipment accounted for 23.2 percent of industry sales, and prepared photographic chemicals, microfilming equipment, and motion picture equipment together totaled 8.6 percent of industry sales.

Growth in the photographic equipment and supplies industry was usually fueled by the introduction of new products utilizing innovative technology. Historically, the emergence of a new product into the market invigorated sales, which, in the case of still and motion camera equipment, also increased sales of film and related supplies. Since a majority of the products manufactured in the photographic equipment and supplies industry were considered leisure or non-essential goods, they were particularly sensitive to economic conditions and tended to suffer as a consequence of reduced consumer spending. However, its broad range of products insulated the industry from the effects of vacillating demand to some extent. For example, still picture film and photocopying equipment typically sold consistently despite economic downturns.

ORGANIZATION AND STRUCTURE

The photographic equipment and supplies industry is comprised mostly of small manufacturing operations. There were 832 facilities operating in the industry in 1992, with California, Illinois, Massachusetts, and New York holding the most facilities. In 1987 most of the facilities were concentrated in the mid-Atlantic states, while in 1992 it was beginning to spread out across the country.

The operating costs associated with a photographic equipment and supplies facility, at $7.1 million per year, were much higher than the average manufacturing facility in 1992, with an average of only $1.7 billion. This gap was likely to widen as electronic imaging products, which required more expensive equipment to manufacture than conventional photographic products, gained popularity and caused more manufacturers to convert their facilities.

BACKGROUND AND DEVELOPMENT

Although photographic equipment and supplies first became available to consumers in the 1880s, it was not until the 1950s that the industry's sales grew rapidly toward modern proportions. The confluence of several developments occasioned this defining decade for the photographic industry: a significant increase in consumers' disposable income; the emergence of photocopying and microfilming products as lucrative components within the industry; and the development of still cameras that were very easy to operate.

Several remarkable technological achievements that occurred much earlier enabled the industry to experience this formative surge in growth during the 1950s. These innovations took place primarily under the aegis of the industry's leader—the Eastman Kodak Company. Perhaps the most significant contribution to the industry's evolution came from Kodak's founder, George Eastman. In the late 1870s, Eastman adapted a photographic process then being used in Britain that replaced wet-plate developing chemicals and equipment with a dry-plate process. Less cumbersome, cleaner to operate, and generally easier to use than wet-plate cameras, Eastman's dry-plate system represented the industry's first step toward making photographic equipment available to all consumers. In Eastman's words, he intended to make the camera "as convenient as the pencil"—affordable and operable for every stratum of society. Eastman followed this innovation with the introduction of roll-film in the 1890s—a product first developed by film and camera manufacturer Rev. Hannibal Goodwin, but initially marketed by Kodak.

In a bid to capture the nation's interest in photography, manufacturers of this era labored to improve the performance of cameras and the quality of film. A giant leap toward this goal was taken in 1900 when Kodak introduced the first model of its popular, inexpensive, and easy-to-operate Brownie line of cameras. Retailing for $1, the first Brownie signaled the beginning of affordable cameras with mass-market appeal. Having achieved its first appreciable market penetration with the Brownie, Kodak later began to develop products aimed at diversifying the applications of photographic equipment. The first 8 mm motion picture system designed for the amateur photographer entered the market in 1932, followed by the advent of color film three years later.

Additional products intended to spark interest in amateur photography emerged before the onset of World War II; but in the immediate postwar years, a discovery by the founder of Polaroid Corporation, Dr. Edwin H. Land, overshadowed the recent product innovations and forever changed the dynamics of the photographic industry. In 1947, Dr. Land announced the development of a process to instantly develop film, thereby giving birth to the first instant camera and film. When it became available later that year, the product would pique the buying public's interest and catapult Polaroid toward a multi-billion dollar sales volume.

By this time, manufacturers had ameliorated the performance of their products, and consumers had grown accustomed to using photographic equipment. As these two market conditions dove-tailed following the war, the economic and population boom of the 1950s ignited photographic sales. According to industry estimates, purchases of photographic products more than doubled during the decade, jumping from less than $500 million in 1950 to $1.2 billion by 1960. This prodigious growth of the industry was partly attributable to the robust national economy following the war, which translated into an increase in the amount of disposable income possessed by many of the nation's consumers. The high birth rate also persuaded a considerable segment of the population to purchase cameras and film in order to photograph newborn babies and young children—the object of approximately 55 percent of the 2.2 billion photographs taken in 1960.

Kodak held a virtual monopoly of the photographic industry from the turn of the century through this period, perennially controlling roughly 90 percent of the film market and an equally overwhelming share of the camera market. By the early 1950s, the federal government began to intervene, filing an antitrust suit against Kodak that eventually resulted in a consent decree in 1954. Part of Kodak's dominance before the decree was attributable to a film processing fee that was automatically included with every Kodak film purchase. By including a built-in processing fee, Kodak in effect cornered the processing end of the industry and consequently discouraged any competition for its film manufacturing business—the dearth of alternative processing facilities inhibited film sales by manufacturers other than Kodak. This practice, however, ended in 1954 when Kodak agreed to sell film without a processing charge and to license other processing companies to develop Kodak film and prints. Although the 1954 consent decree did not appreciably lessen Kodak's grip on the industry, it did enable interested parties to enter a market that previously was essentially closed to outside competition. It also provided those few film manufacturers engaged in the industry before 1954 with a much needed respite from Kodak's stranglehold.

As competition intensified in the film manufacturing market, competitors scurried to secure a foothold in the fledgling photocopying market, which also promised to be a lucrative enterprise. Although total photocopying sales did not exceed $100 million until 1958, this figure increased rapidly when a product was developed for office use. Photocopiers were primarily targeted toward industrial users during the 1950s, but manufacturers developed new technology to enable the production of smaller machines—grabbing the business community's attention. Each of the market leaders manufactured photocopiers that utilized a different photocopying process. Controlling roughly one-third of the market, Minnesota Mining and Manufacturing and Kodak used Thermofax and Verifax processes, respectively, while American Photocopy Equipment Company, the third-largest manufacturer, used a diffusion transfer process. In the end, however, these types proved inferior to the process marketed by Xerox Corporation. Xerography featured electrostatic dry copying that replaced the chemicals required by the other photocopying machines with a cleaner process requiring no specially manufactured paper.

Photocopiers utilizing xerography grew from 1 percent of Xerox's total sales in 1950 to more than 60 percent in 1960, infusing not only Xerox but the industry as a whole with exponential growth. Other companies that followed Xerox's lead into electrostatic copying included American Photocopy, Charles Bruning, BBM Photocopy, and Smith Corona Corporation, launching the market toward an eventual multi-billion dollar sales volume. The pace of this growth quickened with the introduction of the Xerox 914 office copier in 1960, which enabled rapid duplication of small quantities of original source documents for business offices—a task that previously had to be completed manually. Three years after the introduction of the 914, Xerox's sales more than tripled, and the industry as a whole soared to $500 million per year. By this time the market was heavily contested among more than 100 competitors, many of whom were still not convinced of xerography's merits and continued to manufacture wet-type machines. But this issue was soon settled by the response of the industry's business customers, and photocopiers rapidly became an indispensable accessory for nearly every office in the United States.

Equally dramatic events simultaneously took place in the photographic market, as the momentum generated in the 1950s carried over into the 1960s. Once again an innovative product emerged to invigorate the market—the Instamatic camera. First marketed by Kodak in 1963, the Instamatic camera and film formed a completely integrated system that afforded several attractive features to make photography simpler for a mass market. The system used a film cartridge that popped into the camera's back, so the task of threading film into the camera was no longer required. The camera was also notable for a rapid-action lever that advanced the film and automatically positioned it for each exposure, eliminating the inaccurate and awkward winding knob found on earlier camera models. Some of the key innovations of the camera and film had been developed as far back as the 1940s, but never before had so many convenient features been combined into a single product.

Mysteriously named Project 13, the development of Kodak's Instamatic was shrouded in secrecy, catching all of its competitors by surprise and heightening the camera's popularity. Within the camera's first two years of availability, approximately 7.5 million units were sold, and the effect on Kodak's film sales was similarly positive. According to estimates by Kodak, the average camera owner purchased four rolls of film a year, but with the easy-to-use Instamatic, camera owners increased their purchases to eight rolls a year.

Buoyed by the additional sales generated by Kodak's Instamatic, the photographic industry also experienced a considerable boost from industrial and government purchases. As photographic technology advanced, the useful applications of photographic equipment in factories and for high technology purposes broadened, making the development of more sophisticated products almost as lucrative as the development of simplistic products. High-speed photographic equipment, taking as many as 5,000 photographs per second, was used to identify product inconsistencies occurring along production lines and to improve the design of industrial products. Cameras were also used inside missiles to photograph foreign countries for military purposes, inside layer cakes to improve leavening agents manufactured by chemical companies, and aboard rockets to record details of the moon's surface. Such diverse applications combined to increase sales to the industrial and government sectors from $360 million in 1959 to $630 million in 1964, which represented nearly half of the $1.4 billion photographic industry for that year.

As the photographic equipment and supplies industry entered the 1970s, each component continued to generate a larger sales volume. The photocopying market had become a $1 billion a year business, with Xerox sitting atop the field ever since its introduction of the 914 photocopier. In 1963 Xerox followed the 914 with a smaller version, the 813, and subsequent models entered the market throughout the rest of the decade. Photocopying technology advanced rapidly during these years—increasing the production output of the machines and reducing their size—which heightened the popularity of photocopiers in business and government offices.

Xerox began marketing the Model 4000 photocopier in May 1970, which turned out to be a timely response to IBM's announcement a month earlier that it intended to enter the photocopying market. The Model 4000 churned out 45 copies a minute, or 2,700 an hour, compared to the approximately 1,000 copies the 914 could produce in a day. It contained two paper trays capable of holding different sizes and types of paper, and was the first photocopier able to automatically copy both sides of a single sheet of paper. Xerox was not the only pioneer in the photocopying equipment market, however, and consumer demand increased as other manufacturers developed attractive features for their machines. This, in turn, meant both more revenue for industry participants and more competition from companies involved in related businesses. Competition intensified for the remainder of the decade, and Xerox began to cede a large portion of its commanding lead to domestic and foreign competitors.

The microfilm market also expanded during the early 1970s, fueled by the growing utilization of computer systems in the business and government sectors. Computers became capable of storing massive amounts of data—one reel of magnetic computer tape stored enough information to fill 3,500 pages of paper, a task that took impact printers nearly four hours to complete. However, this new technology proved a perfect match for micrographic technology's ability to reduce documents to a fraction of their original size, since the same amount of information could be placed on microfilm in 12 minutes. This process, a fusion of micrographics and computer technology known as computer-output microfilm (COM), promised to provide a considerable boost to the microfilm market. Sales were sluggish until Minnesota Mining and Manufacturing and Kodak, two of the leading companies involved in the microfilm market, opened a network of regional COM centers in 1971 that met with positive response.

Micropublishing was another area in which microfilming equipment performed well in the 1970s. Although micropublishing represented only a $50 million a year business in 1970, a myriad of possibilities for micrographics existed in a nation that produced and stored documents at an ever-accelerating rate. Bank checks were microfilmed, newspapers and periodicals were microfilmed for storage in libraries, and many businesses needed to consolidate the plethora of documents they produced each year—all of which combined to invigorate sales of microfilming equipment. In the early 1970s, the microfilm market grew at a rate of 18 percent annually and evolved into a $500 million a year business. This decade established the foundation for future growth as computer usage became more pervasive and the nation moved into the information age. By early 1997 most companies involved in microfilm were moving into CD-ROM. Instead of putting information onto microfilm, they would scan it into digital format to be placed onto a CD-ROM. This allowed more information to be stored on a disk and the information to be accessed and printed faster using a personal computer.

Entering the 1980s, manufacturers of conventional film, paper, and cameras began to suffer the effects of a saturated market and foreign competition. Nearly every leading company involved in the industry initiated a major reorganization, as corporate strategies shifted in an attempt to capitalize on the trend toward electronic imaging products. Several early versions of products utilizing the new technology emerged in the

mid-1980s—including Sony Corporation's electronic still camera called the Mavica, Canon Incorporated's Xapshot, and Fuji Photo Film Company's Fujix—but sales were disappointing. One product that did sell well, however, was the camcorder, which was introduced in 1983 and quickly offered encouragement to proponents of electronic imaging. In its first two years of availability, 500,000 units were sold, a remarkable success considering each unit sold for an average of $1,000. The popularity of camcorders continued to increase through the end of the decade, laying the foundation for the buying public's acceptance of electronic imaging products. By 1990, unit sales exceeded 3 million.

CURRENT CONDITIONS

As the photographic equipment and supplies industry moved into the mid-1990s, it entered a period of technological transformation that was expected to have significant effects in both the manufacturing and retail segments. The advent of electronic imaging—a technology that utilized semiconductor sensors instead of film to record images and then displayed the images on television screens or computer monitors rather than paper—threatened to radically affect the sales of photographic equipment and supplies. Industry observers' and participants' reactions ranged from worry that the new format would entirely supplant conventional photographic equipment and supplies, to less severe predictions that electronic imaging would merely augment the existing market. Initially, much of this debate was academic; electronic imaging products were prohibitively expensive and the quality of images were far inferior to those generated via film. However, as the technology improved and attracted the attention of an increasing number of consumers, concern increased as to which direction the photographic industry would follow. The digital field began to explode in the late 1990s. Digital point-and-shoot cameras were being developed with price tags ranging as low as $300 to $500. Only professional style cameras had previously been available, and those came with price tags in the $20,000 range that kept everyone but commercial photographers and large studios out of the market. Even though the new hand-held digital cameras had relatively poor resolution, they were gaining popularity quickly, with sales of digital equipment doubling annually. In 1995, 500,000 digital cameras were sold. That number jumped to 1.2 million in 1996 and was expected to continue doubling annually all the way through 2001, when sales were predicted to top one billion units.

The digital wave affected much more than just the photographic industry. With new digital imaging printers, copiers, cameras, software, and film, other industries were making the move into digital. Throughout much of 1996 and 1997, the photocopier industry was also beginning to move heavily into digital. Whether fully digitized, or using digital scanners with conventional toners, copiers were heading full force into the digital age. Most companies had brought digital lenses and optics into standard copiers, making them more efficient and higher quality, using less toner and appearing, sometimes, even sharper than the original document. Xerox developed a high-end copier for sale in April 1997, mixing digital sensors with standard printing, that could print up to 135 copies per minute. The digital transition set up the photocopying industry for record sales figures in 1996. Canon, Inc. reported a record year for 1996 with a boost of 31 percent in their copier sales. Oce-Van der Grinten also reported record sales with a 57 percent jump. Xerox, after sitting on a second or third place ranking in sales, suddenly leapt to the top ranking of all companies within the field and predicted a $200-million digital print boom in 1997.

Advanced Photo Systems. On April 22, 1996, five companies who had been working together on a new film format finally released the Advanced Photo System (APS). Kodak, Fuji, Canon, Nikon, and Minolta spent billions of dollars in research—$500 million by Kodak alone—in developing the new format. Working directly with consumers, these companies interviewed more than 22,000 people in 11 countries to develop a new format that would be easier to operate, create better pictures, and use some of the new digital technology alongside standard film formats. During the research, customers were given a camera size wooden block, and told to place features where they thought they would be easiest and most efficient to operate, with fewer mistakes. Looking to make the new format augment rather than compete with the existing format, all five companies shared their research and development to avoid a conflict like the Beta-VHS competition in the 1980s that ended up hurting the video industry.

The new format was to be a link between digital and standard film techniques. Silver-based emulsion technology was married with digital input and output devices to create the APS film and cameras. A new, highly durable, and higher resolution emulsion was developed with a magnetic covering for information storage. With this magnetic strip, in addition to technology being placed into the APS cameras, the film and camera can actually "speak" to each other. Standard cameras could previously only read film type and

ISO off the film, and the film couldn't read anything from the camera. APS film and camera keep up a constant dialogue, sharing and storing information back and forth.

The new emulsion was developed due to the design of storing developed film in its original container. The new film had to have a stronger emulsion that could take the tight winding and unwinding of going in and out of the canister. APS film was slightly smaller, 24mm, but yielded a higher resolution print due to the new emulsion, which produced one half to one third the grain size of standard 35mm film. The emulsion, even with the added magnetic strip, was flatter, allowing for a greater length of film stored in a smaller area. It was also more durable, making it less susceptible to regular damage that comes over time.

Three formats were available to an APS camera user. With a switch of a button on the camera, a photographer could take 4x6 (standard 35mm dimensions), 4x7 (APS film dimension), or panoramic 4x10, previously available only on specific panoramic cameras. Once taken, the film stored information such as camera settings, format, time, date, exposure number, and even personal information provided by the photographer such as a title or names to be printed on the back of the print. Photofinishers, with new APS lab equipment, used the information to make the best possible print. For example, if the subject was washed out and the background was too dark, which happens in many night flash pictures, the printer could automatically read directly from the film the camera settings used in that particular picture, and adjust printing to bring down the subject and brighten the background. The photographer could also input that the settings chosen were intentional; the processor would read that information and print the picture as taken. The printer could also read the format chosen for the print and process it accordingly. The image taken was always uniform, with only the print being affected by the format choice, which allowed for different sized reprints to be made.

In a follow-up survey of APS customers, 90 percent felt the new system was better, and 70 percent believed they would take better pictures. The new system has been viewed as revolutionary by professional and amateur photographers alike, and Mitchell Gladstone, president of 30 Minute Photos, proclaimed the new format, "The industry's good luck charm." Companies saw amazing growth in 1996 as the new system began to take hold. During December, when 30 percent of camera buying occurs, APS cameras were as high as 60 percent of non SLR cameras sold and 30 percent of all cameras sold. More than 5 percent of the more than two billion rolls sold in 1996 were APS, and it was still only eight months old. Kodak's goal was for APS to account for 20 percent of all film sales and 80 percent of all camera sales by the year 2000—APS was nearly there by 1997.

Although brand new, APS was greatly affecting manufacturer's sales, especially through the last quarter of 1996. Kodak saw its overall sales jump 5 percent despite the loss of Office Imaging, a division that manufactured and marketed photocopiers, which was sold during 1996. Not figuring the loss of revenue from that division into the overall sales, figures showed a 10 percent improvement. The company's quarter alone jumped from $275 million in 1995 to $395 million in 1996, including the loss from the Office Imaging division, which was 13 percent of sales. Fujifilm's sales also got a huge boost, jumping from $5.4 billion in 1995 to $10.2 billion in 1996. Their fourth quarter more than doubled between 1995 and 1996. Photofinishers, retailers, and manufacturers alike were expected to make vast improvements in sales through 1997 with the new format.

INDUSTRY LEADERS

Ranked according to sales volume, the two largest companies engaged in the photographic equipment and supplies industry were Eastman Kodak Company and Polaroid Corporation. Kodak, the long standing leader in the industry, posted a net income of $1.3 billion in 1996, a significant increase from the $17 million it earned in 1991. The low profit figure for 1991, however, was primarily the result of an $873 million patent infringement payment to Polaroid. The increase of 1996 still came in spite of a substantial loss of revenue due to Kodak's sale of its Office Imaging division.

Incorporated in 1889, Kodak enjoyed enviable success throughout much of the century. However, the industry giant struggled with the growing popularity of electronic imaging, restructuring its organization on four separate occasions in the 1980s and early 1990s. In a bid to enter the race for share in the electronic imaging market, Kodak unveiled its Photo CD system in 1992, which enabled purchasers to transfer images captured on conventional film to a digital disk for display on a television screen or computer. Following the introduction of its Photo CD system, Kodak offered 20 new products in early 1993, the largest number introduced at one time in the company's storied history. The products were designed and marketed primarily for children and elderly people, with the hope of expanding what Kodak perceived as a saturated market in the 25- to 40-year-old age group.

Photocopiers were consistent losers for Kodak in the late 1980s and early 1990s, a situation that was exacerbated as the company fell behind its competition technologically. A pressing concern for Kodak was the successful development of a digital color copier that would enable the company to respond to the significant trend in that direction. But during the last quarter of 1996, Kodak sold its Office Imaging division, due to the fact that it was constantly trailing in the photocopying industry. Despite these problems and the concerns revolving around the impact of electronic imaging—on which the company had spent over $1 billion in research throughout the early 1990s—Kodak still maintained a considerable lead over its competitors as it planned for the twenty-first century. The company controlled 70 percent of the market for film and photographic paper in both the United States and worldwide in 1995.

Polaroid Corporation, the world's leading manufacturer of instant cameras and film, recorded $2.24 billion in sales in 1996. The company was established in 1923 by Edwin H. Land, who left college after beginning the research that eventually led to the development of the first synthetic light polarizing material. Polaroid experienced its first considerable growth spurt during World War II, when sales skyrocketed from $1 million in 1941 to $15 million in 1945. Since this exponential leap in sales was primarily attributable to the company's work for the military, which utilized Land's discovery for a variety of purposes, sales returned to their prewar levels afterward, falling to $1.5 million in 1947. In that same year, Land introduced his first instant picture camera and sales ballooned once again.

After enjoying considerable success with subsequent instant developing film and camera models, Polaroid's revenues declined in the early 1970s due to unexpectedly low demand for its SX-70 camera. But the company's sales were revived in 1975 with the introduction of its inexpensive Pronto camera—six million units were sold in the first year. Kodak introduced an array of instant cameras in that same year, touching off a hotly contested and long drawn out patent infringement lawsuit filed by Polaroid.

Polaroid's sales plummeted once again during the 1980s, while the company streamlined its operations to invigorate profits and forestall a hostile takeover attempt by Shamrock Holdings. The company's Spectra camera and film, introduced in 1986, provided a much-needed boost to revenues and brightened what was generally a disappointing decade of performance. The company began manufacturing conventional film for the first time in 1989, and two years later it finally received $873 million from the patent infringement lawsuit it filed against Kodak 16 years earlier.

WORK FORCE

Total employment in the photographic equipment and supplies industry declined during the 1980s, as corporate restructuring, consolidations, and layoffs established a decade long trend of employment instability. From over 130,000 employees in 1980, employment dropped to 100,000 by 1990 and to 90,000 by 1992. Of the more than 70,500 people employed in the photographic equipment and supplies industry in 1994, there was a fairly even split between production workers and salaried employees—or those performing managerial, administrative, or technical duties. A proportionately larger number of production jobs were lost during the decade of employment decline, which narrowed the discrepancy between production and salaried positions in the industry to nearly equal representation.

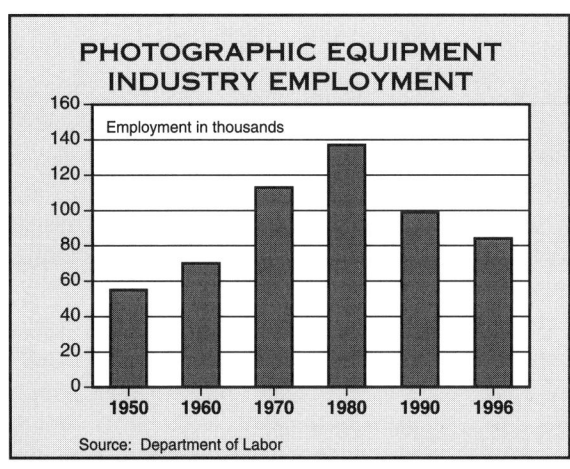

PHOTOGRAPHIC EQUIPMENT INDUSTRY EMPLOYMENT

Employment in thousands

Source: Department of Labor

Generally, production workers were employed on a full time basis, with regular overtime. Production workers in the photographic equipment and supplies industry earned an average of $14.70 per hour in 1992. This hourly wage increased in 1994 to $15.11, about $.35 higher than the average hourly wage of the highest paid worker in the entire manufacturing field, which was $14.75.

AMERICA AND THE WORLD

Historically, foreign manufacturers of photographic equipment and supplies have enjoyed considerable success competing in the U.S. market. This tradition continued in the early 1990s, as a global recession exacerbated the competition for flagging consumer spending and retarded the sales of U.S. products overseas. Exports of domestic photographic products were flat in 1992 at an estimated $3.8 billion, after a 10 percent increase in 1991. In 1993, after slumping for so long, exports began to rise again to $4.6 billion in 1995, a 12.2 percent growth between 1994 and 1995. The rise was partially attributable to Japan's own economic slump, which decreased the competition. During the first six months of 1996, exports increased 10 percent over the same period of 1995 to $2.3 billion. Sensitized film, paper, and plates accounted for 47 percent of the export total and had the fastest growth rate at 17 percent. Photocopying equipment and photographic chemicals both increased about 8 percent. Still picture equipment increased by 2 percent. Motion picture equipment continued to decline, down 14 percent from 1995.

The European Union accounted for $1.4 billion of all domestic photographic sales overseas—the largest export market for U.S. manufacturers in 1995. Sales to Eastern Europe declined in 1992 after demonstrating encouraging results the previous year, especially in photocopying equipment sales. Exports to eastern and western Europe combined fell 2 percent in 1992, following a 6 percent increase in 1991. North America, mainly Canada and Mexico, was second at $1.2 billion, followed by the rest of the Americas with $715 million. Exports to Japan were rising again, back up to $522 million for 1995 and were getting nearer to the high of $533 million of 1991.

Imports of photographic equipment and supplies to the United States increased in 1995 to $8.84 billion—the highest it had been in years. Through the first six months of 1996, however, it dipped again, dropping to an estimated $8.1 billion by the end of 1996. Imported motion picture equipment and copying equipment rose while everything else was decreasing. Motion picture equipment went up by over 33 percent, and copying equipment rose 2.6 percent. Imports of still picture equipment dropped 6.9 percent, sensitized film dropped 1.6 percent, and photo chemicals went down by 8.5 percent through the first half of 1996. Despite motion picture equipment's rise, the overall change in imports had decreased by a little more than 1 percent.

The majority of U.S. imports were manufactured in Japan, which continually increased its international presence since supplanting West Germany in 1962 as the world's second largest exporter. Japanese manufacturers attained their commanding position in the international photographic industry by producing inexpensive, reliable photographic equipment that employed the latest technological advancements. Japan used these two marketing and manufacturing strategies to increase its share of the international photographic market since the early 1960s and gained a solid position as the United States major competitor. In 1995, Japan accounted for $5.1 billion of the import total of $8.8 billion in the United States. The European Union followed with $1.5 billion, and North America accounted for $581 million.

As exports continued to grow and imports continued to shrink, the trade balance had been narrowing. The expected economic recovery of international markets, particularly in Europe, could ameliorate overseas sales, especially considering the low saturation level of photographic equipment in Eastern Europe and the European Community. However, the economic slump in Japan through the mid-1990s, the worst since the late 1970s, continued to affect the trade balance as exports to Japan were steadily dropping through 1994. Moreover, any reduction of the tariff and trade barriers among European Community countries could have a positive effect on U.S. export performance as well. Within North America, the North American Free Trade Agreement (NAFTA) had eased the traffic of photographic products among Mexico, Canada, and the United States—an arrangement that promised to benefit photographic equipment and supplies manufacturers in the United States. Photographic trade balance between the United States and NAFTA was $555 million in 1995, with imports totaling $581 million and exports bringing in $1.14 billion. The trade balance had been improving overall as consumers in the United States purchased fewer foreign made still picture products. In 1993 the trade deficit had gone to $3.3 billion, increased to $4.0 billion in 1994, and by 1995 there was a trade deficit of $4.3 billion. Through the first six months of 1996 the deficit was narrowing. For the first half of 1995, the trade deficit was $1.9 billion, but it declined to $1.7 billion for the same period of 1996.

FURTHER READING

Bart, Peter. "Spectrum Widens in Film Field." *New York Times,* 9 July 1961.

Bernstein, Peter W. "Polaroid Struggles to Get Back in Focus." *Fortune,* 7 April 1980.

"Infotrends Study Shows Digital Camera Market Is Doubling Annually." *Business Wire.* 10 February 1997. Available from http://www.businesswire.com.

"Cameras Focus on U.S. Buffs." *Business Week,* 23 March 1963.

Chakravarty, Subrata, N. "Xerox—Back on the Road to Success." *Forbes,* 7 July 1980.

Darnay, Arsen J. ed. *Manufacturing USA.* 5th ed. Detroit: Gale Research, 1996.

"Disposable Cameras?" *Forbes,* 1 March 1970.

Driscoll, Lisa. "The New, New Thinking at Xerox." *Business Week,* 22 June 1992.

"Honeywell Discloses Electronic Focus Device." *Wall Street Journal,* 23 September 1975.

"Janofsky, Michael. "Kodak Adds 20 Products in Big Shift." *New York Times,* 11 February 1993.

Lazich, Robert S., ed. *Market Share Reporter.* Detroit: Gale Research, 1997.

Maremont, Mark. "Getting the Picture." *Business Week,* 1 February 1993.

"Microfilm Looks for a Booming Market." *Business Week,* 29 May 1971.

"New Life for Photocopiers." *Financial World,* 29 January 1964.

"The New Look of Photography." *Forbes,* 1 July 1991.

"Office Copier Industry Rumbles with Reports That IBM Is Coming." *Wall Street Journal,* 14 April 1970.

Palmer, Jay. "The Picture Brightens: At Eastman Kodak, Things Are Looking Up at All Divisions." *Barron's,* 25 June 1990.

"Photo Industry Changes Its Image." *Discount Store News,* 3 February 1992.

"Polaroid Profit Fell 10 Percent in Third Quarter, But Sales Climbed 4 Percent." *Wall Street Journal,* 20 October 1993.

Sheehan, Robert. "Picture—Sunshine and Shadow." *Fortune,* May 1965.

"Rich Market in Copying." *Moody's Stock Survey,* 18 September 1961.

"Shooting the Works." *Time,* 17 January 1964.

"Small Copiers/Big Advantage." *PRNewswire.* 24 February 1997. Available from http://www.prnewswire.com.

U.S. Department of Commerce. *U.S. Industrial Outlook 1994.* Washington: GPO, 1994.

U.S. Department of Commerce. *U.S. Trade Summary.* Washington: GPO, 1996.

White, Larry. "APS . . . It's Finally Here! The Advanced Photo System: Will It Change Photography Forever?" *Hyperzine.* 10 February 1997. Available from http://www.hyperzine.com.

"Xerox Introduces the Most Advanced Unit Company Has Produced Yet." *Wall Street Journal,* 20 May 1970.

SIC 3873

WATCHES, CLOCKS, CLOCKWORK OPERATED DEVICES, AND PARTS

This segment covers establishments primarily engaged in manufacturing clocks, watches, watchcases, mechanisms for clockwork operated devices, and clock and watch parts. This industry includes establishments primarily engaged in assembling clocks and watches from purchased movements and cases. Establishments primarily engaged in manufacturing time clocks are classified in **SIC 3579: Office Machines, Not Elsewhere Classified;** those manufacturing glass crystals are classified in **SIC 3231: Glass Products, Made of Purchased Glass;** and those manufacturing plastic crystals are classified in **SIC 3089: Plastics Products, Not Elsewhere Classified.**

INDUSTRY SNAPSHOT

The watch and clock industry has always been small compared to other industries, and since the late 1980s and early 1990s, the number of manufacturers has declined. This is due in large part to the movement—begun in the 1970s—of watch parts manufacture from the continental United States to offshore facilities. The popularity of quartz watches, which are produced primarily in Asia as well as Japan, have prompted the shift to offshore facilities. In 1996 there were about 88 operating U.S. companies in this industry.

BACKGROUND AND DEVELOPMENT

The clock industry has existed in the United States since pre-revolutionary days, but did not begin to flourish until the early 1800s when such companies as Ingraham Clock Co. and Chelsea Clock Co. were established. The first clocks manufactured for home use were pendulum clocks that, despite their excellent timekeeping, were rather cumbersome. Whether a huge mantle clock or a floor clock, the instrument had to be set perfectly plumb to keep time accurately. Such clocks were hand-made, and the cost was prohibitive. A clock was considered an investment and bought with the understanding that it would be passed from generation to generation. With the advent of the Industrial Revolution, new technologies were developed, clocks became less cumbersome and expensive, and watch manufacturing began.

Prior to the 1920s almost all watches were carried in the pocket or purse. Some women's watches were designed as pieces of jewelry in the form of brooches or integrated into necklaces. The first watches were analog—the time was displayed via hands pointing at markers or numerals. In addition, the watches were mechanical, powered by a coiled mainspring that required manual winding.

The industry grew as further technological advances were made. In the 1950s the first battery powered watch was introduced, ushering in the electronic age in personal timekeepers. The spring mechanism

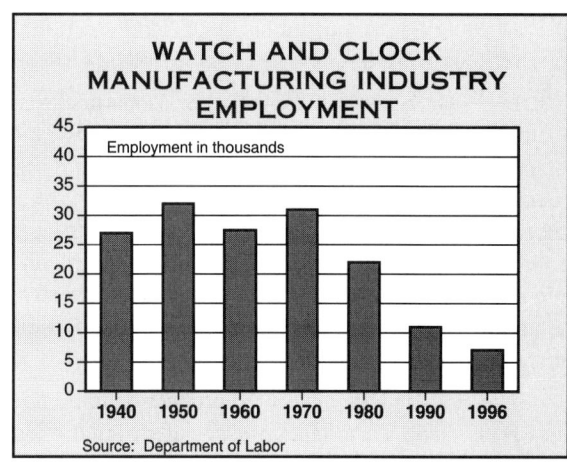

WATCH AND CLOCK MANUFACTURING INDUSTRY EMPLOYMENT

Employment in thousands

Source: Department of Labor

was replaced by vibrating quartz crystals that contained a battery powered silicon chip, and the use of integrated circuits led to the development of the digital watch.

The first digital watch, the Pulsar by Hamilton, was launched in the 1970s. Two types of digital watches were introduced—the LCD (Liquid Crystal Display), which required light to read the numerals and the LED (Light Emitting Diode), which required the wearer to push a button to light it and read the time. Neither gained true acceptance because the LCD was not practical at night, and the LED battery was short lived. The main reason digital watches did not become popular, however, was the reluctance of consumers to accept it. People felt more comfortable with a watch that gave a visual indication of the time remaining until a meeting or appointment.

The digital clock fared much better than the digital watch. The clock companies solved the problems with LCD and LED displays by designing a digital clock run by an electronic chip that called for a light to plug directly into the line cord, stay lit, and give a constant display. The result is that approximately 40 percent of all bedside alarm clocks have digital readouts.

While the digital watch was not a success, the quartz watch was. In the 1980s the production of the mechanical watch fell, and watches with quartz chip movements became popular. The vanguard of the industry was the analog quartz watch—more than half are sold in North America, western Europe, and Japan.

Although the components of the watches are mainly manufactured overseas, assembly takes place in plants in the United States. While the number of people employed in the U.S. watch and clock industry has been steadily declining since 1970, wages have been growing. Production workers were earning $8.69

per hour in 1990, compared to figures from the previous year showing hourly wages at $8.06.

In 1991, according to the U.S. Department of Commerce, watchcases; watch straps; bands and bracelets; and movements were imported from Switzerland, Japan, Hong Kong, Thailand, and several other countries. However, the trend in the industry was toward having both the manufacture of the parts and the assembly of the watches done overseas. Most of the major clock companies still produce their parts domestically.

The clock industry expected production to remain steady. Bedside alarm clocks, especially digital ones, continued to be strong items, and sales of fine clocks were rising. One explanation for the increase was growing consumer interest in home fashion and decorating. More and more clocks are being considered accessories for the home.

CURRENT CONDITIONS

Watch companies registered impressive sales in 1994 and repeated their robust performance in 1995. The biggest factor behind the surge in sales was the revival of interest in fashion watches. Another factor partly responsible was the strong marketing campaigns for both the newer brands as well as the established brands. The moderately priced watches recorded the highest sales during this period.

Swatch USA launched a new line of metal watches in 1995, known as the Irony Line. The line, which was the company's first venture in traditional design, featured 12 new varieties with leather wristbands. In 1996 the major growth areas for clock manufacturers were consolidation and licensing.

1996 sales were driven by massive print and television advertising campaigns. Fashion trends, fostering growing interest in watches that complement clothing, also continued to boost watch sales.

INDUSTRY LEADERS

Timex Corp. of Connecticut was the industry leader, followed by SMH (US) Inc. Timex Enterprises Inc., with estimated 1996 sales of $850 million, employed about 7500 people; SMH (US) Inc., a subsidiary of the Swiss company that makes Swatch watches, followed at a distance with $200 million in sales and 400 employees.

The Movado Group Inc. of New Jersey ranked a close third, with $185.9 million in sales revenue and employing about 600 people. Fossil Inc. of Texas came fourth with $181.1 million in sales revenue, followed by Intermatic Inc. of Illinois with $170 million

in sales revenue. Jostens Inc., General Time Corp., and Spartacus Corp. were some other prominent players in the industry.

AMERICA AND THE WORLD

The 1980s saw a profound change take place in the watch industry. The Swiss industry had hit hard times—production was down and the industry was in trouble. A turnaround occurred in 1983, however, when Nicolas G. Hayek, chairman of SMH Group, introduced the Swatch watch. This inexpensive, trendy watch in a plastic case was a deviation from the traditional high-priced luxury watch usually associated with the Swiss industry. The Swatch was an immediate success and sparked a continuing interest in inexpensive fashion watches.

The analog quartz watch, once the industry weakling, had become its mainstay—more than 500 million were produced in 1992. Despite its impact, the Swatch did not re-establish Switzerland as the leading watch producer. For the past decade Japan has led the field in production with Hong Kong second and Switzerland third. Figures from 1992 indicated Japan's production accounted for roughly 44 percent of total global output, Hong Kong was responsible for about 20 percent, and Switzerland contributed approximately 17 percent. U.S. production had little impact on total global figures.

The United States, the biggest single market, has a large trade deficit in watches—1991 exports totaled $73.4 million compared to an import total of $1.84 billion. Japan led in the import of quartz watches, accounting for 32 percent of that category. Switzerland, however, was responsible for by far the largest number of imported of mechanical watches. While production of mechanical timepieces had been steadily declining, small gains were made in the early 1990s in conjunction with rising value that was attributed to increased demand for the high-end models.

In the area of watch and clock parts, 1990 statistics showed imports of clock movements valued at $22.1 billion; watch movement imports totaled $13.2 billion; imports of watch straps, bands, and bracelets reached $43.2 billion; and $26.7 billion of watch cases were imported. Overall growth in the watch market has slowed from double-digit to single-digit figures. Nonetheless, production is expected to reach the one billion mark by the end of the 1990s, aided by the entrance of such nations as China, India, and Thailand into the field.

With the advent of the 1990s the global watch industry began to assess its ecological impact, and in

1992 watchmakers pledged to support and aid environmental efforts. Among the steps taken were the development of watch batteries with life spans of 10 to 20 years and the use of recycled biodegradable materials for packaging, catalogs, press material and publications.

Sports sponsorship continued to boost watch sales worldwide. Watches have been linked to many high profile sports and sports stars. Citizen's sponsorship of the US Open Tennis Tournaments, and Seiko's deal with figure skater Nancy Kerrigan were some of the more prominent efforts of watch makers.

Luxury watches was another sector of this industry which was growing worldwide. The UK market for luxury watches alone was forecast to grow 22 percent in value between 1996 and the year 2000. The 1995 market for luxury watches in the UK was valued at 250 million pounds sterling.

One of the biggest problems faced by watch manufacturers in the mid 1990s was counterfeiters, who were becoming increasingly ambitious and producing high quality products. The 1995 sales of counterfeit watches accounted for about 10 percent of the value of world wristwatch trade. Ties, fragrances, and other consumer goods were also branded with names of prominent world watch manufacturers. The 1994 Uruguay Round Agreement confirmed the role of intellectual property rights was expected to reduce counterfeiting.

FURTHER READING

Balfour, Michael. "Fakers' Time is Running Out." *The Financial Times,* 18 April 1996.

Fuhrman, Peter. "Jewelry for the Wrist." *Forbes,* 23 November 1992, 173-78.

"Luxury Watches." *Market Intelligence,* July 1996, 1B.

Shuster, William George. "Watches: Global Recession Beaters." *Jewelers' Circular-Keystone,* August 1993, 95-99.

"Sports Events Help Promote Watches." *Jewelers Circular Keystone,* Vol. 166, no. 1, January 1995, 183.

"Swatch's New Irony Aimed at Jewelers." *Jewelers Circular Keystone,* Vol. 166, no. 1, January 1995, 107.

Thompson, Joe. "The Watch World in Figures." *Modern Jeweler,* August 1992, 65-67.

Thompson, Michael. "Fashion and Marketing to Boost Watch Sales." *Jewelers Circular Keystone,* Vol. 166, no.1, January 1995, 90.

———. "Time On Your Side." *Jewelers Circular Keystone,* Vol. 167, no. 1 January 1996, 77.

"Watches & Clocks." *Jewelers' Circular-Keystone,* July 1993, 649-51.

Werner, Holly M. "Keeping Clocks Ticking." *HFN The Weekly Newspaper for the Home Furnishings Network,* Vol. 71, no. 3, 20 January 1997, 38.

—Annabelle McIlnay, updated by Visi Tilak

MISCELLANEOUS MANUFACTURING INDUSTRIES

JEWELRY, PRECIOUS METAL

This category encompasses those establishments primarily engaged in manufacturing jewelry and other articles worn on or carried about the person, made of precious metals such as platinum, gold, and silver (including base metals clad or rolled with precious metals), with or without stones. In addition to personal jewelry, products of this industry include cigarette cases and lighters, vanity cases and compacts; trimmings for umbrellas and canes; and jewel settings and mountings. Establishments primarily engaged in manufacturing costume jewelry from nonprecious metals and other materials are classified in **SIC 3961: Costume Jewelry and Costume Novelties, Except Precious Metal.**

In 1990, the U.S. Department of Commerce identified 2,147 manufacturers of precious metal in the United States. The industry employed approximately 38,000 people in 1990. By 1996 the employment rate was about 36,000. Four states—California, New York, Rhode Island, and Massachusetts—accounted for about 56 percent of all employment in the industry, and firms shipped 63 percent of goods.

Despite the lingering recessionary conditions of the early 1990s and fierce international competition, the industry managed to grow slightly. The estimated value of precious metal jewelry shipments in 1992 was $3.7 million, an increase of 0.9 percent from the 1991 figures. Nonetheless, some retailers experienced sales decreases because of lowered consumer confidence and decreased discretionary income. Expectations of an improved economy, and the hope that customers

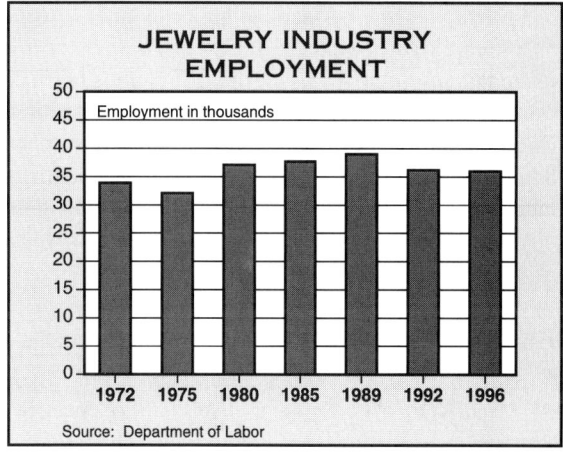

JEWELRY INDUSTRY EMPLOYMENT

Employment in thousands

Source: Department of Labor

would begin indulging in long-deferred purchases, led to an optimistic view of the industry's future. By 1998 shipment values were expected to reach $4.9 million.

The precious metal jewelry industry encompasses retailers, wholesalers, manufacturers, and suppliers, including lapidaries, refiners, stone dealers, findings manufacturers (manufacturers of the small parts used in making jewelry, such as clasps and other items), and subcontractors who provide services such as polishing and electroplating. Manufacturing firms in the precious metal jewelry industry tend to be small establishments and are concentrated in the New York City area. The industry's major expenses are the costs of raw materials and highly skilled workers.

Two major issues of concern to the precious metal jewelry industry are the 10 percent luxury tax imposed on jewelry sales exceeding $10,000 and environmental regulations related to manufacturing processes. Regulations concerning the removal of toxic levels of metals used in electroplating have added financial burdens to many manufacturers and subcontractors. Beginning in May 1993, products that were made with ozone-depleting chemicals were required to carry identifying labels.

Despite the falling value of the U.S. dollar abroad, the United States maintained an unfavorable trade balance in 1992. Italy, one of the United States' major competitors, supplied 40 percent of all precious metal jewelry imports in 1992. Thailand, Israel, and Hong Kong were also key suppliers. Thailand and Israel both benefitted from the Generalized System of Preferences (GSP), a program that permits developing countries to export some products to the United States duty-free.

The main markets for U.S. exports of precious metal jewelry were Switzerland, Japan, and Thailand. Exports to Mexico were expected to increase after ratification of the North American Free Trade Agreement, which enables American goods to enter Mexico duty-free. Most Mexican goods already enter the United States duty-free under the GSP; tariffs between Canada and the United States were already being eliminated under the U.S.-Canada Free Trade Agreement. Some industry experts also hoped that the establishment of product standards for the European Community would benefit the United States. In 1995 the value of exports was $402.9 million.

FURTHER READING

Frankovich, George R. *The Jewelry Industry,* Providence, RI: Manufacturing Jewelers and Silversmiths of America.

Jewelers' Circular-Keystone. *1993-94 Jewelers' Almanac.* July 1993, 602, 605, 613, 646.

U.S. Bureau of the Census. *1995 Annual Survey of Manufactures,* Washington: GPO, 1997.

U.S. Department of Commerce. *U.S. Industrial Outlook 1993,* Washington GPO, 1993.

U.S. Department of Labor. *Occupational Outlook Handbook.* 1992-93 edition, Washington: GPO, 1992.

—Patricia G. Huerster, updated by Kenneth R. Shepherd

SIC 3914

SILVERWARE, PLATED WARE, AND STAINLESS STEEL WARE

This category includes businesses whose primary activities consist of manufacturing flatware (including knives, forks, and spoons), hollowware, ecclesiastical ware, trophies, trays, and related products made of sterling silver; metal plated with silver, gold, or other

metal; nickel silver; pewter; or stainless steel. The category also includes establishments primarily engaged in manufacturing table flatware with blades and handles of metal. Establishments primarily engaged in manufacturing other metal cutlery are classified in **SIC 3421: Cutlery**, and those manufacturing metal trophies, trays, and toilet ware made of metals other than silver, nickel silver, pewter, stainless steel, and plated, are classified in **SIC 3499: Fabricated Metal Products, Not Elsewhere Classified.**

INDUSTRY SNAPSHOT

The flatware industry was dominated by stainless steel in the mid-1990s. The dominance was expected to continue as a result of consumers seeking to bridge the gap between low-end flatware and silverware. Stainless steel flatware's affordability, attractiveness, and durability has made it the most popular. Although the principal manufacturers of flatware also produce silver or silver-plated jewelry or decorative products such as bowls and goblets, flatware is typically the mainstay of the business.

In 1997 the value of shipments was an estimated $818 million. Hollowware had 42 percent of the product share—pewter hollowware accounted for 35 percent, while electrosilver plated was about 22 percent. Flatware was about 52 percent of the product share.

BACKGROUND AND DEVELOPMENT

Sterling silver is a term used by the U.S. Government to describe a silver alloy consisting of 92.5 percent silver and 7.5 percent of another metal, such as copper. The baser metal is used to add strength to silver, which in its pure state is too soft to be practical. Silverplate, which also includes hollowware or hotelware, refers to products made from silver bonded onto a baser metal, such as brass or copper. Silverplating creates a material which is far cheaper to produce than sterling silver and yet gives a similar appearance. It is not, however, as durable as sterling silver, since the plating will eventually wear off. Stainless steel consists of steel alloyed to another metal such as chromium to produce a strong, rust-resistant, and easy-care metal.

The total value of shipments for the tabletop market in 1992, according to *HFD,* reached $3.5 billion. Of this, dinnerware accounted for $1.5 billion and flatware accounted for $628 million (the remaining total went to crystal and glassware, with $1.4 billion). The 1990 preliminary estimates by the U.S. Department of Commerce indicated that manufacturers of silverware and plated ware employed 7,300 workers.

The early 1990s found the industry still struggling to counter the effects of a lingering recession and changes in consumer preferences, which particularly affected the sterling silver segment of the industry. While manufacturers and retailers hoped to improve sales of sterling silver through aggressive advertising campaigns, many producers of sterling were also introducing new stainless steel lines to augment their business.

In the early 1990s, American manufacturers were producing approximately 20 percent of the world's silverware. Other major producers included Japan, Korea, France, and Italy.

Department stores were the most common points of sale for products in this industry, accounting for 28 percent of flatware sales and 30 percent of dinnerware sales in 1991.

CURRENT CONDITIONS

The trend towards casual dinnerware and flatware was becoming apparent in the mid-1990s. Increasingly casual lifestyles were changing the face of the industry. Alternative metal products contributed to the industry's growth in 1994. The key trends in 1995 were widespread acquisitions, changes in management, and tough competition from companies entering the housewares market.

1996 was an extreme year for importers of tabletop and giftware products. While some reported record-breaking profits, others barely made it. Many unsuccessful firms had left the industry, thereby increasing the overall profit of the industry. Tableware makers continued to exploit the growing popularity of collectibles and giftware by manufacturing holiday specific items.

INDUSTRY LEADERS

All the leading suppliers of flatware in the United States offered flatware patterns in both sterling silver and flatware, although Gorham and Wallace were better known for their sterling. Oneida is best known for its silver plate products and for its stainless steel flatware.

Oneida Ltd. and Oneida Silversmiths Division led the industry with overall sales revenues of $514 million and $250 million, respectively, and 5,400 and 2,850 employees, respectively. Located in Oneida, New York, the company has used its brand image to move into additional tabletop categories. Having introduced cutlery in January 1996, Oneida was planning an extensive array of tabletop products for 1997 and

1998. Oneida reported tableware sales of $365 million in 1995.

Other well-known American manufacturers in the industry include Syratech Corp. ($169.5 million in overall sales revenue), Clear Shield National Inc. ($80 million in overall sales revenue), Wallace Siversmiths Inc. ($75 million in overall sales revenue), Towle Manufacturing Co. ($56 million in overall sales revenue), Gorham Inc. ($50 million in overall sales revenue), WorldCrisa Corp. ($50 million in overall sales revenue), and American Silver Co. ($47 million in overall sales revenue).

FURTHER READING

Andreoli, Teresa. "Holiday Tableware Presents Whole Packages." *Discount Store News,* 19 February 1996.

"Housewares: '92 Statistical Report—Dinnerware." *Home Furnishings Daily,* 15 March 1993, 60.

Hube, Karen. "Steel Cuts into Silver Flatware." *Home Furnishings Daily,* 21 December 1992, 71, 76.

Jewelers' Circular-Keystone. *1993-1994 Jewelers' Almanac,* July 1993, 646, 652-53.

Kehoe, Ann Margret. "Alternative Metals' Tabletop Sales Glow." *HFN The Weekly Newspaper for the Home Furnishing Network,* 20 February 1995.

———. "1995 a Tumultous Year." *HFN The Weekly Newspaper for the Home Furnishing Network,* 15 January 1996.

———. "Oneida Gets Set for the Next Step." *HFN The Weekly Newspaper for the Home Furnishing Network,* 15 July 1996.

———. "Stainless Cashes in on Casual." *HFN The Weekly Newspaper for the Home Furnishing Network,* 5 June 1995.

Neiss, Doug. "Economy's Woes Temper Small Industry Gains." *Home Furnishings Daily,* September 1992, 4-7, 10, 13.

———. "Star Segment: Housewares; Casual Lifestyles Change Face of Industry." *HFN The Weekly Newspaper for the Home Furnishing Network,* 18 September 1995.

"Spotlighting Silver as a Sterling Investment." *Home Furnishings Daily,* 15 February 1993, 62-3.

—Patricia G. Huerster, updated by Visi Tilak

SIC 3915

JEWELERS' FINDINGS AND MATERIALS, AND LAPIDARY WORK

This category covers establishments primarily engaged in manufacturing unassembled jewelry parts and stock jewelers' materials such as wire, tubing, and sheeting; and establishments of lapidaries primarily engaged in cutting, slabbing, tumbling, carving, engraving, polishing, or faceting stones from natural or manmade precious or semiprecious gem raw materials, either for sale or on a contract basis for the trade; in recutting repolishing, and setting gem stones; or in drilling, cutting, or otherwise preparing jewels for instruments, dies, watches, chronometers, and other industrial uses. This industry includes the drilling, sawing, and peeling of real or cultured pearls. Establishments primarily engaged in manufacturing synthetic stones for gem stones and industrial uses are classified **SIC 3299: Nonmetallic Mineral Products, Not Elsewhere Classified,** and those manufacturing artificial pearls are classified in **SIC 3961: Costume Jewelry and Costume Novelties, Except Precious Metal.**

The approximately 400 establishments in this industry produced roughly $900 million worth of products in 1995. More than half of these revenues came from precious metal findings.

Production in this industry is centered in the New England area. The six main states producing jewelers' findings and lapidary work were Rhode Island, Massachusetts, New Jersey, California, New York, and Florida. Together these states accounted for roughly 50 percent of total U.S. output in this industry.

Diamond cutting takes careful planning and entails a certain amount of risk. Marvin Samuels of Premier Gem Corp. of New York spent four years planning the cutting of what could have been the largest finished diamond in the world. At that time, that title belonged to Cullinan I, one of the British Crown jewels, with a weight of 530.2 carats. Shape and surface problems meant choosing between the largest cut diamond with flaws or the second largest but perfectly finished diamond. Samuels chose the latter, finishing the cutting in early 1988 with a stone weighing 407.43 carats.

The jewelry industry in general suffered with the economic downturn of the late 1980s. One-carat diamonds once valued at $60,000 sold for $12,000. Many large chain dealers entered Chapter 11 reorganization and shut down stores across the country. These included Zale Corporation, the country's largest jeweler, and Barry's Jewelers Inc., the third largest. These bankruptcies, closings, and reorganizations sent shock waves through the industry. Many unsecured manufacturers and suppliers in the findings and lapidary segment toppled. That trend was aggravated by a 10 percent luxury tax on jewelry over $10,000, though the tax affected only a small portion of the industry.

The worldwide downturn depressed prices on many gems along with gold and silver, but the DeBeers' Central Selling Organization restricted the supply of diamonds along with sapphires, emeralds, and rubies to keep prices up. By 1986, it was supporting diamond sales in the United States with a $35 million advertising campaign. Even so, worldwide downsizing continued. In Antwerp, where diamonds make up 6 percent of Belgium's imports and exports, the number of diamond workers dropped from more than 19,000 in the 1970s to around 7,500 by 1986. Much of the polishing and grinding business traditionally commanded by that city went to lower cost shops in Bombay, India.

FURTHER READING

Darnay, Arsen J., ed. *Manufacturing USA.* 5th ed. Detroit: Gale Research, 1996.

Koselka, Rita. "Brand Name Diamonds?" *Forbes,* 28 April 1986, 64.

U.S. Bureau of the Census. *1992 Census of Manufactures.* Washington: GPO, 1995.

———. *1995 Annual Survey of Manufactures.* Washington: GPO, 1997.

SIC 3931

MUSICAL INSTRUMENTS

This category covers establishments primarily engaged in manufacturing musical instruments and parts and accessories for musical instruments. The primary products in this category are pianos, with or without player attachments, and organs. This industry also includes string, fretted, wind, percussion, and electronic instruments.

INDUSTRY SNAPSHOT

At one time, the ability to play a musical instrument was considered an essential part of a person's basic education. During the later half of the twentieth century, however, electronic advances like video games and music-playback machines combined with increasingly hectic lifestyles to make the effort of mastering a musical instrument somewhat less appealing. Nevertheless, in 1994 there were more than 62 million musicians in the United States. According to *Manufacturing USA,* musical instrument manufacturers shipped less than $1 billion worth of product in 1996.

As part of the personal consumer durables category, musical instrument purchases depend greatly on consumer confidence. Such purchases are made with disposable personal income. In addition, in times of recession discretionary spending for school bands and orchestras, personal music lessons, and high-end instruments become the first casualties of austere budgets.

ORGANIZATION AND STRUCTURE

While dominated by a few large manufacturers, the musical instruments industry of the 1990s remained rather fragmented. In 1996, the top five companies commanded more than 50 percent of total industry sales, but there remained hundreds of small shops with annual revenues in the single-digit millions. Traditionally, the musical instruments industry has been dominated by the production of pianos, player pianos, organs (including electronic), and parts for those products. Keyboard instruments were estimated to account for over one-third of the industry's sales in the mid-1990s. Wind instruments generated about 17 percent of shipments, nonelectric stringed instruments added 14 percent, electronic instruments (including synthesizers) accounted for about 9 percent, and percussion instruments were another 9 percent.

While some automation has been introduced to the manufacture of musical instruments, the processes generally remained labor and materials intensive. The cost of building quality pianos soared during the later half of the twentieth century. A good piano used more than 8,000 moving parts, many of which required rare super-quality materials like ten-grain-per-inch spruce and highest-grade wool. Foreign competitors pushed into the market with innovative man-made materials and mass-production techniques that dramatically lowered the cost and increased the flexibility of the instruments.

A convergence of demographic and competitive factors that had shrunk the musical instruments industry in the 1980s continued in the 1990s. Business failures and consolidation were expected to reduce the number of industry firms from the 1987 level of 400. Similarly, across-the-board employment levels were forecast to continue their multi-decade decline.

BACKGROUND AND DEVELOPMENT

The Victorian era (1830-1880) saw the enthroning of music, especially piano music, as an essential stabilizing element of society and particularly the family. In 1881, the *Chambers' Journal* reported: "In every house there is an altar devoted to Saint Cecilia, and all are taught to serve her to the best of their ability. The altar is the pianoforte."

The expected devotees of music were mainly women. In 1922, the Music Teachers National Conference noted that 75 percent of all concert audiences were women and 85 percent of music students were female. In 1978, 57 percent of all music students were female and 79 percent of all piano students were as well. As early as 1840, the American "piano girl" was a recognizable stereotype; at the time, musical ability was thought to enhance a woman's social prestige.

The piano brought families together to play and listen, becoming the centerpiece of the Victorian family and an avidly sought after item in the growing industrialization of hectic post-World War I America. The musical instruments industry sought to capitalize on that interest and place a piano in every parlor in the nation.

Before 1800, all pianos were grand pianos that required a lot of space, but that year saw the development of the John Hawkins' Portable Grand Piano, the precursor of the now-familiar upright piano. That innovation allowed the piano into the parlors of the middle class, a development paralleled by the refinement of the music box, particularly after 1815. This device provided good quality music without the needed effort of the piano or other instruments. These two trends in musical instruments continued throughout the century, with the appeal of passive listening becoming more important in twentieth century America. The first electromechanical piano, the Telharmonium by Thaddeus Cahill, appeared around 1896.

Playing a piano well required effort and practice. Few could develop the talent to any great degree, a fact that prompted piano manufacturers to look seriously at self-playing pianos. These devices held the promise of combining the social values associated with piano ownership with the pleasures of passive listening. The French led the way in 1863 with a patent on music rolls, but like the German versions they never worked well. The American Angelus player-piano of 1897 achieved the first commercial success, followed by the Pianola in 1898 and the Apollo in 1900. By 1918 it was estimated that more than 800,000 player pianos were in operation in America east of the Mississippi alone and that 75,000 piano rolls were sold every month in Philadelphia. Most played popular ragtime pieces but many delivered concert-quality renditions of classics "recorded" on cylinder by famous concert pianists from America and Europe. More than 100,000 coin-operated electric pianos produced by Wurlitzer and the J.P Seeburg Piano Company were distributed throughout the country and automatic self-playing pianos became common in many movie houses.

Despite manufacturer claims that anyone could play a player-piano, even a child, proper operation required careful and consistent operation of the foot pedals. By 1923, player-piano sales peaked at 56 percent of all pianos sold. The automated devices could not compete with the growing popularity of radios and phonographs, however, which provided simple, reliable listening and took up far less room in the family parlor.

Faced with the evaporation of its market, the industry reversed itself, promoting active piano playing with National Music Week, which encouraged awareness of music in general and music lessons in public schools. In 1928, 358 schools provided piano lessons; that figure jumped to 2,004 by 1930. The National Piano Manufacturers Association, founded in 1901, stressed the joys of active piano playing and encouraged group instruction.

The industry also had to fight an image problem, as mass production techniques led to marketing abuses. The American industrial system of mass production and standardized parts, coupled with the expansion of the railroad transportation system near the end of the nineteenth century, sparked a realignment of the traditional piano craft shop. The corporation became the common business structure and manufacturers often bought components to assemble a finished product without the need of a manufacturing facility at all. This was a similar development to what was happening in the automotive industry, with small firms becoming adept at supplying specific component elements to an assembly and marketing firm. The result, according to Frank L. Wing of Wing & Sons Piano Company, was the manufacture of the world's best pianos as well as the world's worst. Wing & Sons produced three distinct grades of pianos: professional instruments bought by wealthy middle class clients for about $600 in 1916, commercial pianos which provided reasonable sound quality and durability for $400, and the low-grade "assembled" piano which sold for about $200. Many of the last category were "stencil" pianos that did not carry the name of the manufacturer or assembler anywhere on the instrument. Dealers usually stenciled their own names onto the casings after delivery and often used names similar to those found on top quality instruments, such as "Baldin" for "Baldwin."

A major innovation in the production of the American piano was the introduction of the console piano in 1935. This smaller, more streamlined instrument fit better with modern American architecture, blending with the living room decor instead of dominating it. The console piano and the new electronic organ formed a major part of the rising postwar demand of the mid-1940s.

In 1969 Baldwin Piano executive Morley Thompson predicted piano sales would double by 1980, but instead they dropped by 30 percent. *Forbes'* Aura Saunders cited demographics as a primary element of the piano and musical instrument industry's problems, noting that the birth rate declined by nearly one-third from 1965 to 1975. The resulting decline in school-age children decimated the industry's core market. At the same time, high interest rates and rising raw materials costs accelerated the decline of the market. Competition, both from other leisure and entertainment categories and from foreign manufacturers, whittled away at domestic producers' share of the market. By 1986, imports had captured 43 percent of the U.S. acoustic piano market.

The industry once again faced the problem of lack of interest in pianos in the home and a decline of music instruction in the schools. Other, less expensive instruments, like acoustic guitars and electronic instruments, gobbled up market share while many consumers opted for computer synthesizers or video games.

CURRENT CONDITIONS

Demographics held out some promise for the musical instrument industry of the 1990s. The baby-boomer generation entered the 35-to-54 age group during the decade, bringing with it a pent-up demand from recent recessions and considerable purchasing power. The instruments of choice for this generation were the acoustic guitar and similar instruments. Other factors, however, weren't as positive. Austerity budgets at schools trimmed music classes, bands, and orchestras before making any other cuts. Meanwhile, music dealers continued to push instruments with price-cuts and "blow-out sales" rather than promote music production with education and innovation.

The industry was expected to pick up slightly during the 1990s, with growth of about two percent annually. Shipments increased from $814.7 million in 1987 to $872.9 million in 1990, peaking at $945 million in 1993. Sales were estimated by *Manufacturing USA* to have declined to $895.4 million by 1996.

Future gains in the industry have been keyed to continued increases in consumer confidence, an increased number of children attending school, increased educational music budgets, and the ability of American industry to fend off foreign competition.

INDUSTRY LEADERS

At the beginning of the twentieth century, the American musical instruments industry was dominated by a few big names like Baldwin, Steinway, Aeolian, American, Kimball, Wurlitzer, Steger, and Kohler. By the mid-1990s, after a century of reorganization, merger, takeover, and bankruptcies, many of these once-famous names had disappeared. And while Baldwin continued to dominate the piano segment, its hegemony over the musical instruments category was usurped by Selmer in 1995.

Baldwin Piano and Organ Co. of Loveland, Ohio, survived dropping sales and rising interest rates by getting into the finance business: it bought and sold loan agreements on its pianos and organs. The company was established in 1862 by Dwight Hamilton Baldwin, a retail dealer of pianos and organs in Cincinnati. Its later success resulted from the takeover of many small piano manufacturers and the development of a consignment-based dealership contract arrangement. The system, actually begun by the W.W. Kimball Co. of Chicago, put pianos in showrooms across the country without major investments from the dealer and made pianos available to consumers on monthly payment terms. By the late 1930s, innovative marketing and quality products had established Baldwin as the industry leader. Hoping to capitalize on its decades of experience in consumer financing, the company diversified into financial services in the 1970s. By the early 1980s, the piano business was a mere three percent of the holding company's $3 billion operations. When parent company Baldwin-United went bankrupt in 1983, it spun off its piano interests in a management-led leveraged buyout. Faced with intense foreign competition, heavy debt and a shrinking customer base, the company struggled to achieve consistent profitability in the 1990s. Sales rose from $110.1 million in 1992 to $122.6 million in 1995. Net income slid from a high of $5.9 million in 1992 to just $345,000 in 1994, rebounding to just under $4 million in 1995. A new CEO, 48-year-old Karen Hendricks, hoped to guide the company's 1,500 employees to profitable growth in the late 1990s.

Founded before the turn of the twentieth century, for most of its history Selmer Co. concentrated primarily on wind instruments—clarinets, trumpet, and saxophones—as well as violins. Leveraged buyouts in 1988 and 1993 put the company in private hands. In 1994, the company acquired Steinway Musical Properties, Inc. for $101.5 million. Steinway had also built a reputation as a maker of quality instruments. Established in 1853 in New York, the firm eschewed price competition, instead cultivating a top-quality image

via international endorsements by concert pianists, sponsorship of national concert tours, and with award-winning national advertising campaigns. In 1983, it became Steinway Musical Properties Inc. and in 1985 it spun off the subsidiary, Steinway Inc. of New York. Steinway enjoyed a resurgence in the 1990s, with revenues increasing from $90 million in 1993 to $125 million in 1995, when the company earned record profits. While saddled with over $150 million in long-term debt, the privately-held Selmer's 1995 sales of $189.3 million earned it the top spot among musical instrument manufacturers.

Leaders of the guitar segment of the industry included Fender Musical Instruments Corp. and Gibson Guitar Corp. Headquartered in Scottsdale, Arizona, privately-held Fender was acquired by CBS Inc. in 1981 and taken private in 1985. New management reinvigorated the company such that by 1995, the company boasted almost 50 percent of the guitar market. *Forbes* estimated its sales at $160 million, surpassing even pianomaker Baldwin's revenues.

Nashville-based Gibson can be traced to the 1870s, when company namesake Orville Gibson opened a mandolin shop in Kalamazoo, Michigan. By the mid-1990s, this privately-held company's revenues were estimated at about $80 million.

WORK FORCE

The musical instrument industry has consistently downsized its work force since the 1970s. From 1975 to 1985, industry-wide employment fell from 24,500 to 12,200. By 1990, the industry retained only 11,000 workers. However, the average hourly wage for production employees—who constituted over two-thirds of the work force—increased from about $3.25 to nearly $10 during the 20-year period. Much of the loss of employment resulted from automation, a switch to materials that were easier to work with, and overseas production. This trend was expected to continue at least until 2005, with double-digit losses projected for most production positions.

AMERICA AND THE WORLD

In the early 1990s, exports of American musical instruments were a bright spot for the industry, with six straight years of increased shipments. Sales increased seven percent in 1992 to reach $330 million worth of acoustic guitars, acoustic pianos, brasswinds, and woodwinds, and $360 million in sales were expected for 1993. More than half those exports went to Japan, Germany, the United Kingdom, Canada, and Mexico, supported by a favorable currency exchange.

Many of the instruments imported into the United States come from Japan, who supplies 47 percent of the imported electronic instruments, synthesizers, portable keyboards, acoustic guitars, and band instruments. Along with Korea and Taiwan, Japan provided 72 percent of the 1991 imports to the United States. Germany contributed 7 percent while imports from Mexico doubled between 1989 and 1992 as American companies established manufacturing facilities in that country to take advantage of lower wages.

RESEARCH AND TECHNOLOGY

The electronic revolution had a great effect on the musical instrument industry. Between 1981 and 1986 the price of an acoustic piano doubled because of increasing labor and material costs, while unit sales dropped from 282,172 in 1978 to 166,555 in 1986. Compare that with a 40 percent increase in the sales of electronic keyboard instruments between 1985 and 1986. In fact, Americans bought twice as many keyboards in 1986 (206 million) than in 1985 and more than four times as many as in 1984. Sales of synthesizers jumped from 220,000 in 1985 to 350,000 in 1986. All that was driven by the increased power and flexibility of computer-assisted music production and a drop in the price of such electronic equipment.

Robert Moog introduced the synthesizer concept in 1964, but his company folded in 1977 and Moog moved to Kurzweil Music Systems Incorporated. The company's Kurzweil 250 used computer memory to reproduce the sounds of any musical instrument. The real breakthrough, however, came in 1983 with the musical instrument digital interface (MIDI), which allowed musicians and composers to connect synthesizers, instruments, and even computers together and have electronic signals successfully pass between them. Computer hardware and accompanying MIDI software sales jumped to $500 million in 1987. The computerized equipment allows composers and musicians to master new instruments quickly and to develop new music faster and more efficiently. They can also incorporate other, non-musical sounds into their compositions and performances. The system breaks down the barriers between composer, performer, music printer, and instrument builder, allowing the musician full control of the creative process.

The technology, however, brings a new set of problems. It allows a musician to "sample" sounds from anywhere and anyone and then modify the sound to fit the need. Entire orchestras can be synthesized by one person, and other performers can be used to computer-produce totally new performances. This has led to copyright battles and fears of lack of work for live-performance musicians. In addition, the old fear that plagued the piano industry during the heyday of player-pianos—that the technology will displace the art—has returned.

Introduced in the U.S. in 1989, acoustic/digital pianos offered the best of both worlds—for a price. The equivalent of a digital age "player piano," these instruments combined the traditional, full sound of a grand or upright piano with computer-driven options like automatic playback of famous performances, self-recording, and headphones for silent practice.

Another advancement in musical technology is the use of virtual reality. Peter Williams of Virtual S of London experimented with a virtual-reality keyboard in the shape of a checkerboard and bouncing ball. Each square could be a specific instrument or effect controlled by filters and other electronic controllers. The effect is a random music piece accompanied by the visual representation of the bouncing ball on the checkerboard. "This is one class of music programming that you couldn't do in the real world," said Williams in *New Scientist.* "We're not trying to replace violins and other instruments; this is a different way of doing it."

Other developments in the industry include a new process for making a plastic clarinet, which was developed by an English clarinetist and teacher along with an industrial designer. By fusing two molded halves instead of injection-molding a single piece, they eliminated the traditional tone problems of earlier plastic clarinets. Traditionally clarinets are made from African hardwoods usually found in endangered rainforests. Consequently the price of such wooden instruments was skyrocketing. The inventors hoped to begin using the same molding technique in the production of saxophones.

FURTHER READING

Bloch, Georges. "Will the 'Piano' of the Year 2000 Be Intelligent?" *Impact of Science on Society,* no. 147 (1987), 269-76.

Bode, Harald. "History of Electronic Sound Modification." *Journal of the Audio Engineering Society,* October 1984, 730-39.

Census of Manufacturers, 1987. Washington, DC: U.S. Department of Commerce, 1990.

Darnay, Arsen J., ed. *Manufacturing USA.* 5th ed. Detroit: Gale Research, 1996.

Feibelman, Adam. "The Good Wizard: He Saved Gibson Guitars From Being a Firm That Sold Seconds." *Memphis Business Journal,* 14 October 1996, 1-2.

Geake, Elisabeth. "And Hello to Playing Music without Keys." *New Scientist,* 14 August 1993, 17.

Gill, Chris. "Gibson's Century of Excellence." *Guitar Player,* September 1994, 32-35.

Hirokazu, Sayama. "Efforts to Promote Sales Pay off for Musical Instrument Business."

Lim, Paul. "How You Can Get a High-Tech Piano That's Truly Grand." *Money,* February 1997, 168.

Matzer, Marla. "Play It Again." *Forbes,* 27 February 1995, 138-139.

Matzer, Marla. "Playing Solo." *Forbes,* 25 March 1996, 80-81.

Parcel, Ronald. "Music by Proxy: The Invention and Evolution of Mechanical Music." *Impact of Science on Society,* no. 147 (1987), 261-67.

Roell, Craig H. *The Piano in America, 1890-1940.* Chapel Hill, NC: University of North Carolina Press, 1989.

Saunders, Laura. "Mood Indigo." *Forbes,* 29 August 1983, 50-52.

Sauttaur, Omar. "Plastic Molds the Clarinet to Children's Needs." *New Scientist,* 28 December 1991, 14.

"Steinway & Sons is Sold for $100 Million." *New York Times,* 19 April 1995, C5.

Stern, Richard, and Paul Bornstein. "What Happens When the Music Stops?" *Forbes,* 20 December 1982, 31-33.

Thompson, Terri. "Music Is Alive with the Sound of High Tech." *Business Week,* 26 October 1987, 114-16.

U.S. Department of Commerce. International Trade Administration. *U.S. Industrial Outlook 1994.* Washington: GPO, 1994.

Upbin, Bruce. "The Sweet Sound of Leverage." *Forbes,* 20 November 1995, 47-48.

Watson, Bruce. "How to Take on an Ailing Company and Make It Hum." *Smithsonian,* July 1996, 52-58.

Winzeler, Megan. "Steinway Strikes a Chord." *Sales & Marketing Management,* August 1995, 16.

—Al Cook, updated by April Dougal Gasbarre

SIC 3942

DOLLS AND STUFFED TOYS

This category covers establishments primarily engaged in manufacturing dolls, doll parts, and doll clothing, except doll wigs. Establishments primarily engaged in manufacturing stuffed toys are also included in this industry. Doll wigs are classified under **SIC 3999: Manufacturing Industries, Not Elsewhere Classified.**

In 1995 industry shipments in the dolls and stuffed toys industry reached an estimated $2.8 billion, according to the New York-based trade group Toy Manufacturers of America. That represented a 12 percent increase over 1994 production and marked continued confidence in the market.

Most of the American demand for dolls and stuffed animals was supplied by Japan, China, Taiwan, and South Korea; in 1991 $1.9 billion worth were imported. Imports from China alone grew 170 percent between 1987 and 1990 after that country gained "Most Favored Nation" status in 1980. That country supplied 21.8 percent of the world's $21.97 billion toy market in 1989, according to Market Share Reporter. The ratio of imported dolls to apparent consumption was 88 percent in 1991 and was expected to grow into the 1990s. The U.S. export market took 24 percent of U.S. production in 1991, but much of that was shipment of partially completed products to Mexico for finishing and eventual reimport into the American market.

The biggest name in doll manufacturing is Mattel, Inc., maker of the ever-famous Barbie doll. That one product alone was responsible for almost 40 percent of Mattel's 1995 sales of $3.6 billion. In its first year of distribution in 1992, the "Totally Hair" version of Barbie sold more than $100 million. On the average, young females in the United States own up to eight Barbie dolls, and 95 percent of all young females have at least one. Mattel hoped to achieve similar market penetration overseas; Mattel chairman John Amerman stated in Forbes: "Children's wants and desires, their play patterns, are the same around the world."

In America, however, the traditional caucasian, blonde, fashion-model Barbie attracted some serious competition from a growing collection of ethnic dolls. Mattel introduced an African-American Barbie in 1980, but only the coloring—not the doll's features—was modified. In 1991 the company introduced a line of dolls designed to "reflect the natural beauty of the African-American woman." The "Shani" line represented a reaction to demographic reality in the United States, where in 1990 15 percent of children under the age of 10 were African-American, 14 percent were Hispanic, and 3 percent were Asian or Pacific Islander. The ethnic dolls produced by the major toy manufacturer only imitated products already being marketed by minority entrepreneurs.

Mattel, Inc., of El Segundo, California, was founded in 1945. In 1996, Mattel had offices and facilities in 37 countries and sold its toys and products in more than 140 countries. Mattel employed 25,000 workers to produce sales of $3.6 billion in 1995. In addition to Barbie, Mattel sells Cabbage Patch Kids and in 1996 reached a three-year exclusive licensing agreement with Walt Disney to sell toys from Disney's television and film productions.

A growing number of retailers came under scrutiny in the mid-1990s for how the goods they make and sell are produced. Mattel was not immune. Tens of millions of Mattel's Barbies were reportedly made in China each year where young Chinese workers were alleged to earn less than China's minimum wage of $1.99 a day.

Mattel's closest competitor in the doll industry is Hasbro, Inc., of Pawtucket, Rhode Island, which sells a doll perhaps equally as famous as Barbie—G.I. Joe. Hasbro started business as Hassenfeld Brothers in 1923, when brothers Henry and Hillel started a business to distribute fabric remnants. During the 1940s the company began introducing toy nurse and doctor kits. G.I. Joe was introduced in the mid-1960s and quickly became Hasbro's primary toy line; Hasbro reported total 1995 sales of $2.86 billion for such products as dolls and stuffed toys, games, clothing, and baby pacifiers.

In 1997, Mattel agreed to purchase the third largest toy maker in the U.S., Tyco Industries Inc. of Mount Laurel, New Jersey, for $755 million. Tyco made news in 1996 for the introduction of the holiday blockbuster toy—Tickle Me Elmo. Tyco reported sales of $709 million in 1995 for such products as toy automobiles and trucks, games and toys, and dolls and stuffed animals. It employed 2,200 workers.

The social effect of dolls cannot be ignored. In 1983 Matthew Mansfield in *Advertising Age* noted that "the first Barbie children are, or are about to be mothers." The plastic figurine has been the role model for a significant portion of a generation currently it its 20s and 30s. That fact concerned researchers at the University of Nevada, Reno. They studied Barbie's form mathematically and discovered that a 5-foot-6-inch woman with Barbie's form would have a waist as little as 17 inches in circumference. Elaine Pedersen and Nancy Markee in Perceptual and Motor Skills concluded: "The fashion dolls' proportions, including those of Barbie, did not represent either the Greek ideal or the fashion model's body proportions. They do not represent a healthy individual's body proportions. . . . While Mattel, the makers of Barbie, have said they visualize the doll as being an inspirational role model, the question should be asked—do girls playing with fashion dolls perceive these dolls' bodies as the ideal to be achieved?" Also not comfortable with Barbie's influence on young girls were mathematicians, scientists, and women's groups, who in 1992 protested when Mattel released a talking Barbie who lamented that "Math class is tough."

The doll itself underwent a transformation as the twentieth century proceeded. The "play doll" intended for girls four to ten years old has given way to doll sets. To keep entry-point pricing below $10, manufacturers sold dolls and accessories separately and introduced new-model releases periodically. That led to accessories like specialty clothing and toys based on the doll's created lifestyle. It also encouraged collecting. As prices of antique dolls soared, modern dolls, especially Barbie dolls, became more appealing as "modern collectibles." By 1983, that segment of the market was estimated at $30 million retail. Out of that grew dolls designed specifically for adult collectors with price tags as high as $1,000. The average collector in 1983 owned 200 to 400 dolls and spent $600 annually.

FURTHER READING

Bryant, June Smith. "More Dolls of Color." *Black Enterprise,* December 1991, 18.

Darnay, Arsen, J., ed. *Manufacturing USA.* Detroit: Gale Research, 1989.

Darnay, Arsen, J., ed. *Market Share Reporter.* Detroit: Gale Research, 1992.

Dunn, Don. "See Those Mouse Ears? They're Worth a Mint." *Business Week,* 30 December 1991, 157.

Dunn, William. "The Move Toward Ethnic Marketing." *Nation's Business,* July 1992, 39-41.

Fitzgerald, Kate. "Barbie Grows Up." *Advertising Age,* 1 June 1992, 30.

Holstein, William J. "Santa's Sweatshop." *U.S. News & World Report,* 16 December 1996. Hoover's Online, 1997.

Mansfield, Matthew R. "Dolls Aren't Merely Child's Play." *Advertising Age,* 20 June 1983, M4-5.

"Mathematicians Talk Tough to New Barbie." *Science,* 16 October 1992, 396.

Miller, Cyndee. "Toy Companies Release 'Ethnically Correct' Dolls." *Marketing News,* 30 September 1991, 1-2.

Morgenson, Gretchen. "Barbie Does Budapest." *Forbes,* 7 June 1991, 66-69.

1987 Census of Manufactures—Industry Series. Washington: U.S. Department of Commerce.

Pedersen, Elaine L. and Nancy I. Markee. "Fashion Dolls: Representations of Ideals of Beauty." *Perceptual and Motor Skills,* August 1991, 93-94.

Stark, Ellen. "Barbie Looks Like a Million Bucks." *Money,* May 1993, 982.

U.S. Department of Commerce *U.S. Industrial Outlook 1992,* Washington: GPO, 1992.

—Al Cook, updated by Lin Grenging-Pophal

SIC 3944

GAMES, TOYS, AND CHILDREN'S VEHICLES

This entry consists of establishments primarily engaged in manufacturing games and game sets for adults and children and mechanical and non-mechanical toys. Important industry products include games; toy furniture; doll carriages and carts; construction sets; mechanical trains; toy guns and rifles; baby carriages and strollers; children's tricycles, coaster wagons, play cars, sleds and other children's outdoor wheel goods and vehicles, except bicycles. Also included are establishments primarily engaged in manufacturing electronic board games; electronic toys; and electronic game machines, except coin-operated. Establishments primarily involved in manufacturing dolls and stuffed toys are included in **SIC 3942: Dolls and Stuffed Toys.**

INDUSTRY SNAPSHOT

The U.S. toy industry is a fast-paced industry. Product-driven, it rides the crest of a fad until the next fad happens through a combination of product merit, marketing, and luck. Although the classics such as Monopoly, Scrabble, and Slinky have demonstrated strong, long-term sales performance, few toys or games stay on the shelves for more than a year or two. The early 1990s were healthy years for the toy industry, although the fortunes of various companies have swung wildly. Several factors make the toy industry a risky business, including boom-or-bust sales patterns, short product life, and only one major selling season, Christmas, which historically has accounted for 50 to 60 percent of annual sales. In 1992, total annual sales were $15.3 billion, up 19 percent from the year before.

Game makers think of themselves as publishers more than toy makers because many games have a longer sales life than most toys and sell at a fairly predictable level. But game publishers are subject to the same instability of the market, with some games failing and others, such as Trivial Pursuit and Pictionary, experiencing unpredictable success. The game segment used to be a relatively staid component within the toy industry until Trivial Pursuit's sudden success tipped the market upside down and showed that games were not just products for children. Soon,

other companies were also looking for the key to success in the adult game market.

ORGANIZATION AND STRUCTURE

Because the industry is heavily dependent on capricious trends, miscalculation or misjudgment at times can result in enormous losses. The life span of even the most successful toys is often brief, with sales dropping as quickly as they rise. Typically, companies count themselves among the fortunate if they have one product that sells well for a year. Even if a product remains popular after its debut year, it is likely to be copied, since toy manufacturers often attempt to replicate each other's successful products.

The Toy Manufacturers of America (TMA), the industry's trade organization, was founded shortly after the United States entered World War I, when toy makers faced severe shortages of materials, and Congress was considering an embargo on the buying and selling of Christmas presents to conserve materials needed for the war. TMA was formed and successfully lobbied Congress to continue producing toys for America's children despite the war. A few years later, TMA convinced representatives to impose large tariffs on toy imports to protect the American toy industry. TMA continued to lobby and compile information and statistics for the toy industry in the early 1990s.

Ideas for games and toys may originate in-house, but the industry also relies heavily on the ideas of freelance inventors. A company may pour thousands, even hundreds of thousands of dollars into market testing before committing to production. Toy development is risky and speculative. During the course of its development, a concept may change drastically. Most toy manufacturers also subscribe to *Toy Retail Sales Tracing Service* for quantitative market research that reveals trends, product performance, and competition. Qualitative market research involves product testing, usually with small focus groups of children. Until it is officially previewed at the annual American International Toy Fair, a project can be aborted at any stage if it does not meet expectations or if buyers do not express much interest.

Historically, distributors and wholesalers were the toy manufacturers' biggest customers, but in the early 1990s large retail chains ordered directly from the toy makers. Smaller toy stores looked to regional distributors, but for the most part distributors were a dying breed.

According to some industry sources, Toys 'R' Us accounted for as much as 20 percent of the toy market in the United States during the early 1990s. The rest of

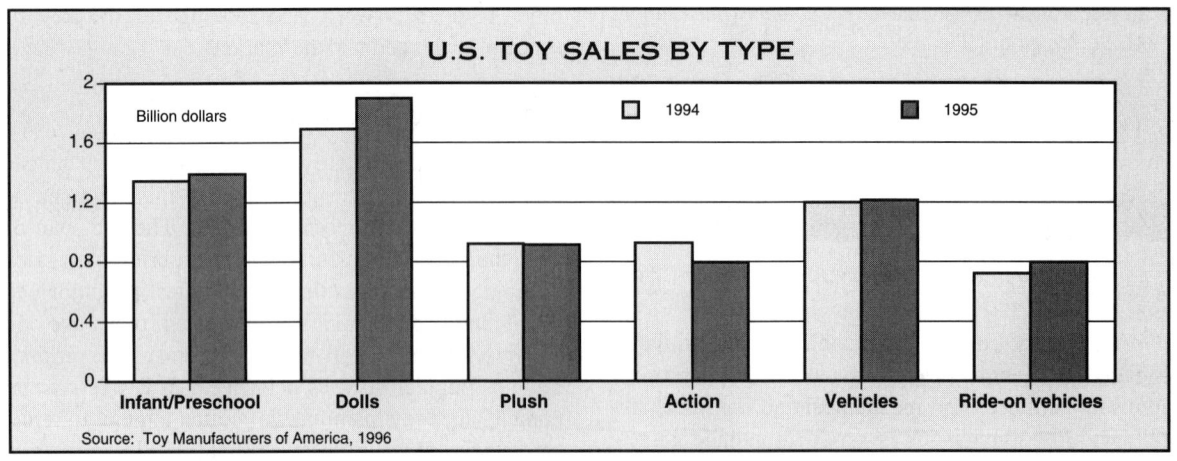

U.S. TOY SALES BY TYPE

Billion dollars   □ 1994   ■ 1995

Infant/Preschool   Dolls   Plush   Action   Vehicles   Ride-on vehicles

Source: Toy Manufacturers of America, 1996

the toy market comprised national and regional toy store chains, mass merchandisers, wholesalers, catalog showrooms, variety stores, discount stores, department stores, drugstores, local chains, and independent toy stores. There were also "jobbers" who bought close-out merchandise from toy makers to sell to retailers. Mass merchandisers, such as Kmart Corp. and Wal-Mart Stores Inc., did not carry as wide a range of merchandise as the large toy stores, but these retailers had tremendous clout with toy makers. The national distribution and volume buying that these stores and others, such as Sears, Roebuck & Co. and Service Merchandise Company Inc., offered helped them negotiate beneficial deals with toy makers.

Although the law prohibits manufacturers from selling merchandise to different customers at different prices, in reality, the larger the customer, the larger the volume discount. The purchasing power of the customer also affects many other negotiable terms, including credit against future sales and extra merchandise from the manufacturer. These discounts and special terms result in widely varying retail prices. Powerful customers also are able to receive markdown money from manufacturers of products that failed so badly retailers were forced to sell them below cost.

BACKGROUND AND DEVELOPMENT

The first U.S. toy manufacturer was established in the 1830s. Tower Toy Company produced doll furniture, toy tools, and toy boats. In 1860, Milton Bradley Co. established a publishing and lithography business, but as financial problems plagued the company, Bradley diversified by inventing and publishing The Checkered Game of Life, the precursor of The Game of Life, still popular in the mid-1990s. The Civil War slowed the toy industry somewhat, although toy guns were

popular, as were Milton Bradley's portable editions of chess, checkers, and dominoes.

In 1883, 16 year-old George S. Parker started his own game company. When his brothers joined him, the company became Parker Brothers & Company Inc. It became the publisher of many games popular in the mid-1990s, including the perennial number one-selling board game, Monopoly, as well as Sorry!, Risk, and Clue.

Around the turn of the century, the "Golden Age of Toys" brought walking and talking dolls, toy pianos, friction motorized vehicles, steam-powered toys, the Erector Set, the Flexible Flyer sled, Lionel toy trains, and Crayola crayons. In 1906, the Teddy bear craze began with the stuffed animals named for Teddy Roosevelt because he refused to shoot a trapped bear cub during a hunting trip. Between 1900 and 1910, American toy production doubled. During the next decade, it grew 500 percent, largely because World War I had halted the import of European toys. In 1923, Hasbro Inc. brought out its classic real estate game, Monopoly, and Milton Bradley introduced Easy Money—games that allowed players to imagine being rich by making deals with play dollars. In 1930, Herman G. Fisher and Irving R. Price established the very successful Fisher-Price, Inc. which in the early 1990s was the biggest name in infant and preschool toys and merchandise.

World War II slowed the toy industry's growth because of labor and material shortages, but the post-war years brought prosperity to the entire country, and the toy industry reaped the benefits as well. Following World War II, the toy world was revolutionized with the introduction of plastic.

Television Advertising. In 1955, an advertising move by Mattel, Inc. changed the way toys and games were marketed and also launched the promotional toy business. The nascent American Broadcasting Company (ABC) television network approached Mattel about weekly national advertising on its new show, Walt Disney Co.'s "The Mickey Mouse Club," beginning in November, just as the Christmas shopping season opened. To the surprise of many, Mattel took a big financial risk and paid half a million dollars to become a sponsor. Before this bold move, most advertising money was spent on catalogs and trade ads during the Christmas season and an occasional local TV ad to promote the most promising items. With this advertising agreement between Mattel and ABC, Mattel's famous slogan was born—"You can tell it's Mattel, it's swell"—and the power of weekly advertising to kids was launched. The product Mattel had advertised, the Burp Gun, was sold out, and the promotional toy business was on its way too.

Promotional toys were products advertised on television directly to the consumers—the kids. Television became the number one advertising force in the toy industry. With the line between advertising and entertainment blurred in the late 1980s and early 1990s, entire shows became based on the exploits of a line of characters invented or promoted by a toy company. In 1969, Mattel underwrote a program based on its very successful Hot Wheels line. When a competitor complained, the Federal Communications Commission (FCC) banned it, calling it a "program-length commercial." In 1983, the FCC ruled that the marketplace should determine programming. This change of policy cleared the way for toy-based programming. By the 1986-1987 season, more than 40 toy-based programs were on the air.

According to Sydney Stern and Ted Schoenhaus in *Toyland, The High Stakes Game of the Toy Industry,* television changed the very nature of toys by allowing the toy industry to sell toys that they could never sell before because they could now demonstrate the features of the product. Products that could do something—walk, talk, move, crash—had existed for a long time, but now they came to life on television and soon dominated the market. Advertising even began to dictate product development. Products were developed on the basis of how well they would lend themselves to television commercials. Television also allowed the toy makers to create a fantasy around the product, so that children were not only demanding a toy, they were buying into the fantasy which made that particular toy unique. By the 1980s, the commercial became more important than the product itself because it was the commercial that created the concept, while the product actually did little on its own. Retailers, trying to anticipate what toys kids would want, paid close attention to the manufacturers' ads and ad budgets in making their purchasing decisions during the early 1990s. At toy fairs for buyers, toy manufacturers previewed the commercials as well as the toys.

The Advent of Video Games. A second "revolution" in toy making began with the first video games. In 1972, Nolan Bushnell and a friend invested $250 each to found Atari Corp. and produce Pong, a simple video table tennis game. It became a coin-operated hit in bars and arcades, and in 1975 Bushnell began marketing a home version to compete with Odyssey, a video game system being produced by Magnavox Co. Atari was sold to Warner Communications Inc. in 1976. Mattel followed with Intellivision in late 1979 and Coleco Industries Inc. brought out ColecoVision in 1983.

Soon, the industry was licensing the most popular arcade games for home video systems. Video games were bringing in hundreds of millions of dollars. Many new companies formed just to manufacture and sell cartridges for Atari and other game systems, thus taking valuable profits from the systems' developers. Large and small toy companies rushed to produce their own video systems. In a few short years, however, the video game and cartridge fad ran out of steam. Warner lost $539 million on its consumer electronics segment in 1983, and it ended up burying truckloads of game cartridges. Warner, Mattel, and Coleco sold their video game businesses during the next two years.

Nintendo Co., Ltd., a Japanese electronics company, learned from the mistakes of its predecessors. In the late 1980s, Nintendo was generating sales of more than $1 billion in the United States alone. It was making this money at the expense of other traditional toys and games, taking market share from industry leaders Hasbro Inc. and Mattel. Nintendo controlled licensing and sales of all game cartridges so that it would not meet the same fate as Atari.

Sega Enterprises Co., Ltd., another Japanese company, challenged Nintendo in the United States during the early 1990s. In 1991, Sega introduced its Genesis system, and Nintendo responded with Super Nintendo. The battle continued throughout the 1990s with Sega launching a major market offensive with its high-performance, CD-based Saturn game system. During this period, a number of other companies entered the fray—most notably a U.S. company, 3D Co., and the Japanese electronic giant Sony Corp. While Sony's PlayStation managed to establish itself in the market, 3D's game player eventually fell by the wayside, largely as a result of being priced too high for the average consumer. In late 1996, Nintendo struck back with the 64-bit Nintendo 64. Boasting high-resolution 3D graphics, Nintendo 64 delivered processing power exceeding that of many personal computers, and its eagerly awaited introduction led to long waiting lists, high-priced black marketing, and even theft.

CURRENT CONDITIONS

Because toy manufacturers sell to children, their ads are designed to appeal to children, thus generating much controversy about ethics in children's advertising. Children are easily exploited, children's advocates contend; they lack the experience to discern poorly-made products or recognize that a commercial has presented a fantasy world rather than the reality of a particular toy. Action for Children's Television unsuccessfully tried to convince the FCC that toy-based shows were 30-minute commercials and should be purchased as advertising time. Critics of children's television and its ads also continued to protest the promotion of violence through toy-based shows and the weaponry toys advertised, as well as gender stereotyping reflected in many shows and advertised toys.

In the 1980s, television networks ABC, the National Broadcasting Company Inc. (NBC), and CBS Inc. required the last five seconds of a toy commercial to show the product all alone so that children could see what they are really getting. The networks also limited animation within the ad to one-third of the total ad time. Independent stations, however, had no such restrictions, and with the growth of cable, the independents became important advertising channels for toy makers during the early 1990s.

Video games continued to present a threat to the traditional toy market in the 1990s. Nintendo and Sega were the video leaders, and unlike other toy trends, which soared briefly and then saw sales drop dramatically, this generation of electronic games remained popular, with sales expected to keep rising. During the early 1990s, traditional toy makers were considering whether to compete for market share with traditional, non-video toys, or to enter the video market themselves.

By the mid-1990s, another threat challenged both traditional toy makers and the electronic game giants. This threat came in the form of computer games. Long the poor cousin of the video game, computer games increased their market share rapidly with the advent of the CD-ROM and continued reductions in the cost of personal computers. Market penetration of computers was moving quickly towards 50 percent by 1997, and most new computers came with multimedia capabilities built in, making it easy for users to take advantage of their gaming capabilities.

The toy industry turned to more intensive brand management during the early 1990s, focusing on either extending existing lines of products, or spending more money marketing the "classics." For example, Hasbro added new products to the Nerf line of foam sports toys, including Nerf Turbo Football and Nerf Bow 'n' Arrow. The company augmented its Monopoly line of products with the introduction of Monopoly Junior.

American companies were seeking to expand sales and profits in 1992 by aggressively marketing abroad. Tyco Toys Inc. opened four European subsidiaries. Hasbro expanded its operations in a number of Asian countries, including acquiring a small Japanese game and toy company in order to enter the Japanese toy market, which, in the 1990s, was the second largest in the world behind the United States. Mattel began selling its merchandise directly rather than dealing with distributors in foreign countries.

Although the industry was dominated by several giants, small companies also had opportunities for success. Some smaller companies acquired rights to products that the big companies had retired, such as Erector Sets and Creepy Crawlers, or launched their own new products. The toy and game industry was attractive to small businesses because start-up costs remained low when manufacturing was subcontracted. Smaller companies could be more innovative, since they did not have the layers of bureaucracy associated with the larger companies, and they did not have to generate as much income. Consolidation also reduced the likelihood that a large company would take a chance on an item able to generate only $1 or $2 million. By the early 1990s, large manufacturers needed $10 million in product sales to justify spending their advertising dollars.

1995 proved a tough year for U.S. toy makers. A difficult retail environment resulted in slower sales, product failures, and rising costs. While scrambling to come up with an innovative new product that would catch on and propel sales, toy makers also became increasingly cautious, relying more and more on TV tie-ins to stimulate sales. Although the total U.S. market for toys was forecast to grow 6 percent in 1996, much of this growth was expected to come from increasing demand for electronic games—an area in which none of the leading U.S. toy manufacturers played a significant role. U.S.-based manufacturers also faced a growing threat from imports, which were forecast to capture an 82.3 percent share of the market by the year 2000. On the plus side, exports were rising at a rate of 8.4 percent a year, accounting for nearly 37 percent of domestic shipments.

INDUSTRY LEADERS

The toy industry underwent extensive consolidation after the video game era began. Some of the most familiar brands lost their independence and became part of large toy corporations such as Hasbro.

Thanks to its acquistion of Fisher-Price, Mattel Inc. had risen to the top spot among toy manufacturers in the United States by 1996, with sales of close to $3.8 billion. Mattel built a strong alliance with Walt Disney Co., and Mattel's president called its Disney-related products "the second cornerstone of our company"— its primary "cornerstone" was Barbie and Barbie-related products. Mattel also made an exclusive licensing agreement to produce toys based on Hanna-Barbera characters, such as Flintstones, Scooby Doo, Jetsons, and Yogi Bear. Other principal Mattel brands included Fisher-Price, Hot Wheels and Cabbage Patch Kids. Convinced that children everywhere like the same toys, the company made no effort to modify its products for different markets. Instead, it designed products with universal appeal and marketed them globally. That the company sold its toys in more than 35 countries, with about half of its revenues coming from outside the United States, attests to the success of this policy.

Hasbro Inc., a small company in the early 1980s, became the largest U.S. toy manufacturer in 1985 by eschewing the video market and benefitting from widely popular products such as G.I. Joe, Transformers, and My Little Pony. In 1984, Hasbro bought the Milton Bradley company, the fourth largest company in the toy industry. With Milton Bradley came the rights to The Game of Life, Twister, and other solid-selling games. By 1988, Milton Bradley accounted for 20 percent of Hasbro's sales. Hasbro also acquired Coleco and then Tonka just as each was headed for bankruptcy. Tonka had owned Kenner Products and Parker Brothers, so the acquisition of Tonka also brought a second most-famous game company into the Hasbro empire. Hasbro decided to leave the two separate divisions with their own identities. In the 1990s, Hasbro's position as the leading U.S. toymaker was eclipsed by Mattel. Nevertheless, Hasbro finished a strong second with 1996 sales of more than $3 billion. In an effort to regain its number one position, Hasbro embarked on another wave of acquistions (Western Publishing Group Inc.'s puzzle and board game line) and began introducing new toys based on movies, comics, and TV shows such as "Batman Forever" and "The Mask."

Tyco Toys, Inc. remained the third largest U.S. toy manufacturer behind Hasbro and Mattel through 1996. Despite such acquisitions as Universal Match-box Group Ltd. and ViewMaster-Ideal Group Ltd., the company experienced little year-to-year growth in the 1990s with 1996 sales of $721 million, down from $768 million in 1992. Some of the company's leading products included Matchbox (die-cast vehicles); Incredible Crash Test Dummies; Disney's "The Little Mermaid," "Blossom," Secret Talk Betsy, Maggie Doodle and MagnaDoodle Dan dolls; and Doctor Dreadful. Tyco was also the market leader in children's radio controlled, battery-operated, and electric racing cars.

FURTHER READING

Annicelli, Cliff. "Tackling a New Year." *Playthings,* January 1995.

Darrow, Barbara. "Engineering in Toyland." *Design News,* 12 December 1987, 66.

"Disney, Mattel to Strengthen Ties in Toyland." *Wall Street Journal,* 12 November 1991, B1.

Hoover's Company Capsules. Austin, TX: Hoover's Inc., 1997.

"Hot Products Give Toy Industry Strong Year." *Standard and Poor's Industry Surveys.* 11 March 1993.

Leccesse, Donna. "Searching for Innovation." *Playthings,* January 1996.

Levy, Richard, and Ronald O. Weingartner. *Inside Santa's Workshop.* New York: Henry Holt and Company, 1990.

Reysen, Frank Jr. "U.S. Toy Market Expected to Grow 6 Percent in 1996." *Playthings,* April 1996.

Rudnitsky, Howard. "Bang, Mom, You're Dead." *Forbes,* 16 June 1986, 86-7.

Sheff, David. *Game Over: How Nintendo Zapped an American Industry, Captured Your Dollars, and Enslaved Your Children.* New York: Random House, 1993.

Stern, Sydney Ladensohn and Ted Schoenhaus. *Toyland, The High-Stakes Game of the Toy Industry.* Chicago: Contemporary Books, 1990.

"Warfare in Toyland." *Maclean's,* 15 December 1986, 38.

Yoshihashi, Pauline. "Hanna-Barbera Reaches Toy Pact with Mattel Inc." *Wall Street Journal,* 22 November 1991.

—Wendy Stein, updated by Chris Hunt

SIC 3949

SPORTING AND ATHLETIC GOODS, NOT ELSEWHERE CLASSIFIED

This industry covers establishments primarily engaged in manufacturing sporting and athletic goods not elsewhere classified, such as fishing tackle; golf and tennis goods; baseball, football, basketball, and boxing equipment; roller skates and ice skates; gymnasium and playground equipment; billiard and pool tables; and bowling alleys and equipment. Establishments primarily engaged in manufacturing athletic apparel are classified in major group for apparel and other finished products made from fabrics and similar materials; those manufacturing athletic footwear are classified in **SIC 3021: Rubber and Plastics Footwear** and **SIC 3149: Footwear, Except Rubber, Not Elsewhere Classified;** those manufacturing small arms ammunition are classified in **SIC 3482: Small Arms Ammunition;** and those manufacturing small arms are classified in **SIC 3484: Small Arms.**

INDUSTRY SNAPSHOT

Like other sectors of the U.S. economy, the sporting goods industry was undergoing substantial change in the mid-1990s. Computer technology was linking sports equipment manufacturers more closely to retailers. The trends of globalization and restructuring were transforming the organization of sporting good companies. Sports equipment makers pondered how to exploit the stunning growth of the Internet. And changing demographics and lifestyles affected the popularity of individual sports and past-times.

Overall, the industry shared in the general prosperity of the U.S. economy. The 3 percent increase in U.S. wholesale sales of sports equipment recorded in 1996 was somewhat disappointing, but the outlook for the industry remained generally positive. While the American population was aging, much of the postwar baby-boom generation remained committed to staying fit. Growing numbers of women were becoming sports enthusiasts, and manufacturers were designing offerings specifically for their needs (rather than simply painting existing products in pastels). In general, companies were creating new demand by appealing to specific market segments (e.g. basketballs and backboards especially designed for children). Overseas markets were also a source of new demand because of expanding economies and liberalized trade regulations.

Performance among the industry's numerous segments continued to vary significantly in the mid-1990s, as a sport's popularity waxed or waned depending on demographics, economics, marketing skill, and fads. The golf and fitness segments were doing well because of technologically improved products and new adherents among an older population. After several years of spectacular growth, the in-line skating segment contracted significantly in 1996. Meanwhile, tennis sales were showing some improvement, al-

though they were still below the levels of the mid-1980s.

ORGANIZATION AND STRUCTURE

The sporting goods industry encompasses a wide variety of businesses and products, and there are hundreds of participants. Within a specific segment, however, a few large companies may dominate. In the mid-1990s, ownership of many sporting goods companies changed hands. Most notably, in 1996 Kohlberg Kravis Roberts & Co. acquired Spalding Sports Worldwide in a deal estimated at $1 billion—the largest deal ever made in the sporting goods industry. Other companies, like Wilson Sporting Goods, consolidated and restructured their operations.

The sporting goods sector offers stunning success stories, as a new or substantially improved product, or even an entirely new sport, can capture the public's fancy and produce spectacular returns for the originator. But for every Rollerblade, Inc., a company that rode the in-line skate boom, there are dozens of failures. As John Riddle, president of the Sporting Goods Manufacturers Association told *Nation's Business,* "Having a good idea is 10 percent of the trick, albeit no easy feat. The other 90 percent is in getting enough capital behind your product and marketing it correctly. A little luck never hurts either."

BACKGROUND AND DEVELOPMENT

Albert G. Spalding, the man often misidentified as the inventor of baseball, was actually one of the pioneers of the sporting goods industry. After pitching his team, the Boston Red Stockings, to victory in three consecutive National Professional Association pennant races in the early 1870s, Spalding helped found the National League in 1876. In 1878 he opened a sporting goods store with his brother in Chicago. The company expanded from 2 to 14 stores within two years, and soon afterwards began selling products it manufactured directly to other retail dealers. Spalding is given much of the credit for introducing gloves to baseball; after developing a sore arm from pitching, he switched to first base in 1877 and started wearing highly visible black gloves. (Cynics have suggested, however, that Spalding's interest in wearing gloves was not unrelated to his desire to sell them.)

Spalding also figures prominently in the history of basketball. James Naismith, the inventor of the game, commissioned him to create the world's first basketball in 1892. In 1994, Spalding balls were still the official ball of the National Basketball Association (NBA).

Another important sporting goods company with a colorful history is Wilson. The firm was originally known as the Ashland Manufacturing Company and was a subsidiary of a meat-packing firm. It sold violin strings, surgical sutures, and strings for tennis products, all by-products of animal gut. In 1914 the company was forced into receivership and taken over by New York bankers. They picked Thomas Wilson to manage the company, partly because of his name—President Woodrow Wilson was then at the height of his popularity, and the owners hoped to capitalize on the association in the consumer's mind. The new firm became Wilson & Company. The firm soon expanded into tennis rackets, hunting and camping equipment, and fishing tackle. It continued to be one of the top manufacturers in the 1990s, with a full line of sports equipment.

A more modern, but already legendary, figure in the history of sports equipment is Scott Olson. Olson was a 19-year-old goaltender with a minor-league hockey team in 1980 when he found a pair of roller skates on which the wheels were arranged in a single row. While the skates felt slow and clumsy, they gave him the sense of skating on ice that traditional roller skates did not. Olson contacted the manufacturer, who had stopped making the line, and bought up the back stock. He put the blades on good skate boots and began selling them out of his house. In 1983 he quit pro hockey, bought up the existing patents, and started the company that would eventually become Rollerblade. While Olson was forced out of the business in 1985, he continued to design and develop new products, including a lightweight golf bag with wheels and a built-in pull handle.

CURRENT CONDITIONS

According to the annual survey of the Sporting Goods Manufacturers Association (SGMA), domestic shipments of sporting goods at the wholesale level were $15.2 billion in 1996, about 2.6 percent higher than the 1995 total. The increase compared with a 5.4 percent advance for 1995/1994, and an 11.6 percent jump in 1994/1993. The relatively slow advance in 1996 reflected a downturn in the in-line skating segment after several years of strong growth. Sports equipment makers generally remained upbeat about the industry's business prospects. The economy was doing well, demographic trends and healthy lifestyles were boosting demand in the over-40 age group, more women were playing sports, and enactment of the North American Free Trade Agreement and other pacts liberalizing trade augured well for overseas business.

The industry did face several challenges, however. Short-term, consumer installment debt was rising, which, coupled with a general sense of job uncertainty, could lead to tighter consumer spending. Longer term, there was concern that lack of time and lack of motivation may hurt participation levels in some sports. Many sports were not attracting significant numbers of new enthusiasts, but were rather competing for participants against each other.

Another challenge for equipment manufacturers was product liability costs. These expenses ran so high that manufacturers were discontinuing production of certain products. The number of football helmet manufacturers, for example, fell from 18 in 1970 to 2 in 1993.

For individual companies, however, the positives and negatives of the industry as a whole are often overshadowed by the environment in its particular segment. The following paragraphs discuss business conditions in important sports.

Golf. According to the SGMA survey, in 1996 shipments of golfing equipment rose 5 percent to an estimated $2.3 billion. Sales of clubs and balls have done best in the 1990s, rising at compound annual growth rates, respectively, of 13 and 10 percent during the 1991 to 1996 period. Golfing continued to attract older, more affluent players. In 1992, in fact, 30 percent of all golfers had incomes of $50,000 to $74,000, the highest proportion for any sport. They had the means to buy the technologically improved products that were introduced in the late 1980s and 1990s, such as clubs with graphite shafts, oversized heads, and beryllium copper facings. At Callaway, demand for Big Bertha metal oversized woods produced truly astonishing growth, as sales rose from $132 million in 1992 to $678 million in 1996.

Whether better clubs have actually helped the golfer's game is questioned by some observers, but there was little doubt they've done wonders for investors in golf club stocks. In January 1996, conglomerate American Brands bought Cobra Golf, makers of the King Cobra Titanium club that duels with Callaway's Big Bertha for the golfer's dollar. American paid $715 million for a company that had just $152 million in sales for the nine months ended September 30, 1995.

Despite Wall Street's enthusiasm, in 1996 some industry observers thought the industry's long drive was about to hit the rough. According to the National Golf Foundation, the number of golfers in the United States fell to 25 million in 1995 from 27.8 million in 1990; total rounds played dropped to 490 million from 505 million in 1992. According to the foundation's research, time for work and for family competed strongly for the golfer's loyalty. Industry optimists argued, however, that spending will continue to increase to make the most of the available time. The optimists also thought that the miraculous play of Tiger Woods would attract new fans to the game.

Tennis. Tennis made a small comeback in 1996. According to the SGMA survey, sales for the segment rose to an estimated $245 million from $235 million a year before; sales of racquets and balls increased for the first time in four years. Nevertheless, overall sales were still down from the $300 million level of 1993. According to one study, the number of players fell by half-a-million between 1989 and 1992 to 13.7 million. While the sluggish economy and bad weather were partly responsible for the decline, it also appears that people are choosing other sports, like in-line skating or fitness training, rather than tennis.

In-Line Skating. The growth of in-line skating has been truly astonishing. According to one estimate, in-line skating participation grew 634 percent from 1987 to 1995. By that time, 22.5 million Americans went skating at least once a year; some 9.4 million Americans skated 25 days a year or more. Naturally, the surge in popularity catapulted sales, which rose from nearly nothing to $725-million in 1995, according to the SGMA survey. Demand has been spurred by the interest in roller hockey, which has become one of the fastest growing sports in the country.

In 1996, however, the industry had a bad fall, as sales declined 14 percent to $625 million. Some of the reasons offered for the industry's decline were overloaded inventories at the retail level, poor weather conditions, and a lack of exciting new products. The industry was also worried about the number of skaters injured and legislation limiting access to streets for in-line skating. Nevertheless, many in the industry were predicting a pick-up in sales for 1997, partly because of new product introductions, including hybrid soft-boot skates.

Fitness Equipment. The desire of an aging American population to keep fit conveniently has supported sales of the fitness equipment segment. According to the SGMA survey, sales of fitness products totaled an estimated $2.07 billion in 1996, up from $1.93 billion in 1995 and compared with just $680 million in 1986. The most popular exercise in 1995 was using free weights, which replaced stationary bicycling for the number-one spot. Fitness walking, including treadmill use, was the most popular activity among women and seniors.

So-called "infomercials" and television shopping networks have also given a big boost to sales of fitness equipment. Sales of the abdominal exerciser reached over $200 million in 1996, although some observers think that the popularity of these machines has crested. The aero rider/glider was another product whose sales were propelled by the infomercial.

Basketball. Basketball has benefited from increasing participation by women, spurred by the formation of professional women's leagues and the success of the women's team at the 1996 Olympics. Moreover, Title IX and other gender equity programs have encouraged more women to take up the game. Meanwhile, men aged 35 to 44 are playing the game in growing numbers. According to the SGMA, sales grew about 3 percent in 1996.

Baseball and Softball. Sales in the baseball and softball segment have been lackluster, as participation rates stay flat or decline. Few adults played baseball, and some youngsters found soccer and in-line skating more entertaining. The Major League Baseball strike of 1994-95 and the cancellation of the World Series for the first time in 90 years certainly didn't help the game's appeal. Softball had also seen better days; participation dropped 16 percent between 1987 and 1996. One bright spot was women's fast pitch, whose image was enhanced by the excellent performance by the U.S. team in the 1996 Olympics.

Bowling. More than 53 million people aged six or older bowled at least once in 1995, making it one of the largest participant sports. But league play, the traditional segment of the business, has been falling since the 1970s. Indeed, the decline in league play gained notoriety in 1995 when Harvard professor Robert Putnam linked it to a general drop in participation of all kinds of neighborhood- and community-level groups. Calling the syndrome "Bowling Alone," Putnam blamed it for the collapse of the democratic process. According to the SGMA survey, sales of bowling products declined 5 percent in 1995 to $215 million.

INDUSTRY LEADERS

Brunswick Corporation is among the largest sporting goods companies. The company is a leading name in bowling, and the products of its Zebco division are well known to fishermen. The firm also makes billiard tables. In total, the company's so-called recreation segment accounted for about 26 percent of the firm's sales of $2.9 billion in 1995. The balance of the company's revenues mostly came from sales of boats and outboard motors.

The sporting goods division of Amer Group Ltd. of Finland encompasses both Wilson Sporting Goods, a leading producer of golf, racquet, and team sports equipment, and the Atomic Group, which makes skiing equipment and in-line skates (under the Oxygen brand). In February 1997, Amer completed the sale of its MacGregor Golf division. Amer's Wilson, based in Chicago, was founded in 1914 and is one of the oldest names in American sporting goods. In 1996 it had over 3,000 employees worldwide.

Spalding, one of the most famous names in sporting equipment, makes a complete line of golf and team sports equipment. Founded in the 1870s by Boston Red Stockings pitcher Albert Goodwill Spalding, the company grew from a small sporting goods store to a global manufacturer of sporting goods. The company claims a long list of firsts, including first Major League baseball (1876); first American-made football (1887); first official basketball (1894); and first American-made golf club (1894), among many others. In 1996 it was acquired by Kohlberg Kravis Roberts & Co. for an estimated $1 billion.

Callaway's Big Bertha line has made it the largest maker of metal golf woods in the world. During the early 1990s the company grew astonishingly fast, with revenues doubling and net income tripling every year. Of its $678 million in sales in 1996 (up 23 percent from the 1995 level), 71 percent came from metal woods, 25 percent from irons, and 4 percent from putters and other accessories. While some believe that state-of-the-art stainless steel clubs will ultimately prove to be just one more in a long line of golf fads, others are convinced that worldwide demand will remain strong for the company's clubs.

AMERICA AND THE WORLD

In recent years, U.S. sporting goods companies have done well in overseas markets. According to the SGMA, total export sales for the entire sporting goods industry, which includes items like footwear outside of this classification, grew at an average rate of 25 percent per year in the 1995-96 period. The top export markets are Japan, Germany, and the rest of Europe. Growth in traditional Asian markets like Japan, however, has been lackluster. In 1997, much interest centered on China, where entire industries can spring up almost overnight. For example, bowling has surged in popularity and new lanes were being built at extraordinary rates. Some experts believed China could be the world's top bowling market by the year 2010.

The broad penetration of U.S. culture overseas has been a boon to the sporting goods industry. Often there is a dynamic interplay between the popularity of the

American lifestyle, the star-quality of American athletes, and the marketing savvy of American industry. For example, the growing popularity of basketball among kids in Europe has been linked to the NBA's Shaquille O'Neal, whom they know solely through watching Pepsi commercials. U.S. sporting goods products are thus valued in some countries simply because they are made in the United States. Consumers believe they are participating in the American lifestyle by purchasing them. The perception that U.S. sporting goods are of unusually high quality in certain product categories has also spurred sales.

U.S. manufacturers were also eyeing South American markets. The restoration of democracy to many Latin American governments was accompanied by better economic conditions, giving consumers more spending power. Moreover, the trend toward freer trade has been marked, as Argentina and Brazil have sharply reduced trade barriers to overseas goods. While Latin Americans have always been passionate about soccer, they have started to take up typically American sports like basketball and in-line skating, where U.S. companies hold an edge.

The manufacture of many sporting goods is labor-intensive, so U.S. companies have shifted much of their production to east Asia, where wage rates are generally lower. High-tech computer systems enable companies to institute global manufacturing programs that maximize efficiency. The move toward more open markets and reduced tariffs also accelerates the trend toward globalization. Thus companies can produce wherever efficiencies are greatest: the SGMA estimated in 1997 that 25 percent of all sporting goods emanate from China.

RESEARCH AND TECHNOLOGY

New technology plays a vital role in the sports market. Consumers are often driven to buy new equipment because of the real or perceived advantages of product introductions. On the other hand, tradition also has a hallowed place in sports, and participants have to feel comfortable that their equipment is in the historical spirit of the game. Additionally, innovative manufacturers can create substantially new sports through their products.

In some sports there have been revolutionary changes in equipment over the past 20 or 30 years. The traditional wooden tennis racket had pretty much stayed the same until the 1960s, when manufacturers began to redesign it in an effort to improve performance and ease of play. The introduction of durable metal and fiber-reinforced-composite rackets was followed by oversized and wide body models. More recently, finely balanced rackets that have shock- and vibration-damping handles and new string bed patterns for greater accuracy have been introduced. Compared with the classic wooden model that weighed 14 ounces and had a hitting area of 68 square inches, rackets sold in the early 1990s were 35 to 40 percent lighter, with the weight redistributed for better performance, and had a hitting area of 120 square inches.

In 1997, softball bats also received an upgrade. A division of Spalding was set to introduce the Fusion bat; a composite of aluminum and graphite, it was supposed to provide a lighter, faster swing. The SZ1-C from Easton Sports, on the other hand, is made from a rare material used in Soviet MiG fighter jets. Meanwhile, Worth Inc. was expected to offer a new line of cryogenic bats, which are first heated, then chilled to temperatures as low as -310 degrees.

Intriguingly, engineers have also had stunning successes in overhauling the humble bowling ball. Several new urethane and reactive resin bowling ball shells and complex inner core configurations—designed to vary the ball's rotation as it goes down the lane—have substantially altered the ball's hook as it approaches the pocket. According to some observers, the sharp rise in the number of perfect games—17,654 during the 1992-93 season versus 14,889 during the prior year—is closely related to the improvements in ball designs.

Smart entrepreneurs have also developed innovative products for niche markets. Passengers on cruise ships used to drive thousands of regulation golf balls into the sea. But in 1990 the International Maritime Organization banned the practice as part of its effort to protect sea life. Responding to opportunity, Patrick Kane of Bonita, California, developed a golf ball that flies almost as well as a traditional ball but is made of materials that decompose quickly and can be consumed safely by fish and other marine life. He told the *New York Times* that "It's basically fish food . . . you can market it on the basis of sympathy for the environmentalists."

The sporting goods industry is also improving its technology in the more mundane, but nonetheless important, areas of inventory and delivery systems. Better information systems allow manufacturers to keep retailers stocked in goods that are selling well and reduce their own inventories of slow-moving items. Manufacturers can also alert stores to overall sales patterns so that retailers can better react to market trends. Sporting goods companies have also worked to develop packaging that is more environmentally friendly.

FURTHER READING

Ashley, Steven. "High-Tech Rackets Hold Court." *Mechanical Engineering,* August 1993.

Barry, Scott. "Blades and Bikes Blasting Off." *MEDIAWEEK,* 17 October 1994.

Bergstrom, Robin. "All This So You Can Have Fun." *Production,* July 1991.

Broida, Rebecca. "In-Line Market Going Soft." *STN,* March 1997.

Castle, Ken. "South America: A Slam Dunk for Sports." *Sporting Goods Business,* September 1993.

Dolbow, Sandra. "Holding Court (Tennis Equipment Industry)." *Sporting Goods Business,* February 1996.

Falcioni, John. "Striking at the Core of Bowling Balls." *Mechanical Engineering,* August 1993.

"Football Caps Reduce Impact." *Machine Design,* 8 January 1993.

Geer, Carolyn. "Gold Mine or Sand Trap: If Golf is Such a Great Business, How Come the Number of Players and Rounds Has Been Dropping?" *Forbes,* 12 August 1996.

"Growing Stars: Major League Soccer." *The Economist,* 13 April 1996.

Hyman, Mark. "The New Bats of Summer." *Business Week,* 21 April 1997.

Leivenberg, Richard. "Tennis, Anyone?" *Sporting Goods Business,* February 1995.

Marks, Peter. "Perfect Pitch: Tony Little's Infomercials Keep the Fitness Gear Moving." *New York Times,* 9 May 1994.

Murphy, Ian. "Bowling Industry Rolls Out Unified Marketing Plan." *Marketing News,* 20 January 1997.

Pesky, Greg. "Labor Pains (Impact of the Professional Baseball Strike on the Sporting Goods Industry." *Sporting Goods Business,* November 1994.

Riddle, John. "State of the Industry Report."

Shafran, Michael. "Inventory Bah-Humbugs Holdiay Sales." *Sporting Goods Business,* January 1997.

"Slower Sales Seen in Next Millenium." *Sporting Goods Business,* March 1992.

"Super Show Exercises Options; Flood of Innovations Try to Appeal to the Time Pressed." *Discount Store News,* 3 March 1997.

Young, Kevin. "Splitting Arrows (Archery Equipment Industry)." *Sporting Goods Business,* December 1994.

—Bob Schneider

SIC 3951

PENS, MECHANICAL PENCILS AND PARTS

This industry contains establishments primarily engaged in manufacturing pens (including ball point pens), refill cartridges, mechanical pencils, fine and broad tipped markers, and parts.

INDUSTRY SNAPSHOT

Sales of all writing instruments hit an all-time high in 1990 at $3.4 billion. This record can be attributed to the increasing diversity of products, the growing popularity of highlighting markers, and the newfound interest in high-end fountain pens.

Nearly 50 companies manufacture writing instruments that are sold in the United States and throughout the world. The ball point pen, introduced to the U.S. market in 1945, continues to dominate writing instrument sales. Newly created roller ball pens and highlighters also have been selling well.

ORGANIZATION AND STRUCTURE

Manufacturers and suppliers of pens and other writing instruments generally have been large public companies, such as BIC Corporation, the largest supplier of ball point pens in the United States. Some are conglomerates like the Gillette Company, which sells writing instruments and other non-writing related products.

Writing instruments are sold to wholesalers and retailers and then are resold to consumers through fine jewelry stores, stationery and office supply stores, department stores, discounters, mass merchandisers, catalogue showrooms, and specialty stores. Pen manufacturers not only produce writing instruments but also are responsible for selling and marketing these products to retailers and consumers.

BACKGROUND AND DEVELOPMENT

The Pen. The earliest writing instruments were developed during the ancient civilizations of China, Greece, Egypt, and Mesopotamia nearly 5,000 years ago. Mesopotamians used wooden styluses to impress their characters on wet clay tablets. The Egyptians used hollow reeds to apply ink on sheets of papyrus, while the Chinese drew ideograms with brushes made from animal hair.

The Europeans began to use goose quills as ink pens in the sixth century, and this practice grew rapidly during the Middle Ages. Flocks of geese were specifically bred for their feathers as quill production became an important industry throughout Europe. For nearly 1,000 years the quill pen remained the most popular writing instrument.

In the nineteenth century, however, the steel pen replaced the quill. The steel pen point (or nib) first appeared in England sometime between 1790 and 1803, but this product was not manufactured efficiently or economically until the 1830s. In another 50 years American inventor Lewis Edmon Waterman created the fountain pen with its own self-contained ink supply. Waterman's product ushered in a new generation of writing instruments that dominated the first half of the twentieth century. His basic design, which includes a metal nib, a built-in ink supply and an outer shell, are still the main components of fountain pens today.

Ball Point Pens. The ball point pen also dates back to the late nineteenth century. This type of pen consists of a metal ball housed in a socket that rotates freely. The ball, constantly covered in ink from a reservoir, rolls across a writing surface.

Commercial models of ball point pens appeared in 1895 and the first satisfactory model was patented in Argentina by Hungarian Lazlo Biro. His ball point pen, commonly called the "biro," soon became popular in Great Britain during the late 1930s and 1940s. The ball point pen was introduced to the U.S. market in 1945. U.S. manufacturers quickly adopted the new design and soon dominated production in the ball point industry. Today more than three billion ball point pens are manufactured each year in a variety of styles, point sizes, colors, with prices ranging from no-frills disposables selling for $1.00 a dozen to state-of-the-art, solid gold retractables costing hundreds of dollars.

The Felt-Tip Pen. In 1964 the porous-point or "felt-tip" pen was developed in Japan. Papermate's Flair was among the first felt-tip pens to hit the U.S. market in the 1960s, and it has been the leader ever since. Following their initial success with felt-tips, manufacturers branched out with a variety of fiber-tipped instruments, including newly popular highlighters.

Roller Ball Pens. The most recent large-scale innovation in the writing instrument industry has been the introduction of the roller ball pen in the early 1980s. Unlike the thick ink used in a conventional ball point, roller ball pens employ a mobile ball and liquid ink to produce a smoother line. Technological advances achieved during the late 1980s and early 1990s have greatly improved the roller ball's overall performance.

CURRENT CONDITIONS

Sales of writing instruments soared to an all-time high of $3.4 billion in 1990, according to statistics available as of July 1993. Product diversification has been one explanation for the rise in sales. Besides the various categories of pens and pencils, the writing instruments market includes highlighters, markers, and any other device used to mark a document. Product mix projected by the Department of Commerce for 1997 is 47.8 percent pens, 28.3 percent pencils, 21.1 percent markers, and 2.7 percent desk sets, according to *The Office.*

The Fountain Pen Market. Although totaling less than 5 percent of all writing instrument sales, fountain pens have shown a tremendous resurgence in popularity and usage. By 1990 fountain pen sales had reached 25.5 million units, a dramatic rise from the all-time low of 6.4 million units in 1978. By 1991 sales at the wholesale level rose 16 percent to $79 million, nearly double the wholesale figures in 1986.

According to retailers, the most popular fountain pens have been bought by individuals and corporations for use as business gifts and promotional items. Two reasons for the pen's popularity have been its association as a status symbol and its improved technology, especially with the creation of replacement ink cartridges.

''The fountain pen market is hot, and promises to get hotter,'' reported Joshua Levine in a 1992 issue of *Forbes.* ''Like wearing a prestige watch, carrying and publicly wielding a prestige fountain pen has become an 'in' thing,'' added Levine.

Nearly two dozen firms have attempted to gain a piece of the growing fountain pen market, especially the high-end sector. For example, A. T. Cross, known for its prestigious ball point pens, has been pushing its newly created Townsend line of larger, thicker pens. However, the upper-end fountain pen leader continues to be the German Montblanc, selling half of all pens costing more than $100. Second place Parker Pen has a 25 percent market share. Other important producers of fountain pens include Filofax, based in Great Britain, Italian Aurora, French Recife, and Italian Omas. Some of their pens, produced in limited editions, command prices of nearly $2,000.

Fountain pens and other luxury writing instruments continue to hold a significant place in the market during the mid-1990s. ''Just as consumers have created wardrobes of fashion watches and eyeglasses,'' writes Wendy Hessen in *WWD*, ''manufacturers say it became clear about five years ago that the buying public was interested in more frequent product changes and increased design variety from the writing instrument market.'' Marketers revived elements of classic pen styles, updating them to suit modern tastes and requirements. Limited editions and collectible pens have brought in prices of up to $40,000 and can, according to some sources, double or triple in price over a period of two to three years.

The Ball Point Market. Despite the recent surge in popularity of the fountain pen, the ball point pen continues to be the leader of the writing instrument market. Known for its low price and reliability, the ball point pen has accounted for nearly one-third of industry sales. Three billion ball point pens are manufactured annually. The BIC Corporation alone has sold more than seven billion pens in the United States since 1983.

The Roller Ball Pen. Roller ball pens brought in sales totaling $201 million in 1989, a 51 percent increase over sales figures just two years earlier. This segment makes up nearly 14 percent of the writing instruments market and has been growing at 10 percent since 1990.

The Highlighter Market. The marker and the highlighter market has been considered a separate entity from the porous-point pen industry and posted sales of $232 million in 1989. Felt-tip highlighters have been one of the fastest growing products in the writing instruments business with sales of 260 million units in 1990, up from 70 million units in 1985.

The Pencil Market. Another 25 percent of overall writing instrument sales has come from the pencil market, both woodcased, represented in **SIC 3952: Lead Pencils, Crayons, and Artists' Materials,** and mechanical (included in this classification). The overall pencil market was a $215.9 million industry in the early 1990s.

INDUSTRY LEADERS

BIC Corporation. The Connecticut-based BIC Corporation has been the largest manufacturer and distributor of ball point pens in North America. BIC pens have made up approximately 40 percent of the office products market in the United States and 60 percent of the over-the-counter market. BIC ball point pens are available in non-retractable, non-refillable models and retractable, refillable models, and in various ink and barrel colors and point sizes. BIC also manufactures highlighting markers and roller pens and distributes mechanical pencils.

In 1992 BIC Corp. posted its highest sales and earnings in company history. Total sales increased to nearly $417.4 million from approximately $369.2 in 1991. Its growth included revenues, profits, and profit margins in all of its core businesses, including the Stationery Products division (formerly known as Writing Instruments).

During 1992 BIC began marketing Soft Feel, a retractable pen with a rubberized barrel. BIC also introduced Body Heat pens, which have heat-sensitive barrels that change colors when held. Body Heat pens are part of BIC Wavelengths, a line of fashionable ball pens and mechanical pencils. The company also has extended its holiday line of Halloween and Christmas pens to include Valentine's Day.

During 1993 the company expanded its production capacity and now operates three facilities in South Carolina. BIC also moved both its research and development divisions to a suburb of Greenville, South Carolina, its market production to Gaffney, SC, and expanded its Wavelengths production in Spartanburg, SC.

BIC's international operations have consisted of subsidiaries located in Canada, Mexico, Puerto Rico, and Guatemala. Sales by foreign subsidiaries were approximately 16 percent of consolidated net sales in 1992 and 1991, and 15 percent in 1990.

Gillette Company. More commonly associated with men's shaving products, Boston-based Gillette has become a leader in the writing instruments industry. With the low-price Paper Mate, mid-price Parker, and high-end Waterman franchises, Gillette has established a strong position in the industry at all price levels, distribution channels, and geographic areas.

Gillette built its leadership position in the writing instruments market through the acquisition of Waterman in 1987 and Parker Pen Holdings Ltd. in 1993. After its purchase, Gillette soon began to sell Waterman fountain pens at discount outlets in the United States. Francine Gomez, then chief executive of Waterman S.A. and a third-generation family operator, was displeased with this decision. Although sales increased by 40 percent since the Gillette takeover, Gomez argued that the company's marketing strategy in the United States devalued the luxury image of Waterman in France. Gomez resigned from the company in 1988.

Meanwhile, the Parker Pen acquisition should increase Gillette's share of the $5 billion international writing instruments market to approximately 15 percent from 8 percent. Gillette may face possible antitrust problems in some European countries since its market share of refillable pens may be as high as 60 percent. Nonetheless, market analysts have applauded the Parker Pen acquisition as a strategically sound move to foster global expansion for the company.

Gillette's manufacturing operations for all of its products have been conducted at 62 facilities in 28 countries.

A. T. Cross. Based in Lincoln, Rhode Island, A. T. Cross Company has been a major international manufacturer of fine writing instruments sold to the consumer gift market through stores worldwide, and to the business market via a network of companies specializing in recognition and awards programs. Cross products include ball point pens, mechanical pencils, rolling ball/porous-point pens, and fountain pens.

A. T. Cross has been long known for its slim gold-filled and sterling silver pens and mechanical pencils, which once dominated the high end of the U.S. luxury pen market. Led by these products, the company earned $36 million in 1989.

Consumer tastes changed in late 1980s as increasing numbers of high-end customers starting buying larger pens like Montblanc. A failure to keep up with this trend was reflected in Cross' drop in earnings to $8 million in 1993. Stock prices followed from a high of $41 per share in 1989 to $15.5 in mid-1994.

In 1990 Cross attempted to reenter the high-end market with its pricy Signature line, but the recession of the early 1990s defeated this product. By 1992, under the direction of new company president Russell Boss, the company tried again to regain market share with the introduction of its Townsend line. This product line offers larger, heavier pens, including ball point and fountain models, selling for $50 to $150 each. The line sold well and two more pen lines were introduced by Cross in late 1995. The Townsend success, however, was not enough to offset company losses. Lower-priced pens, including the Solo and Metropolis lines, did not sell as well, and Cross reported a drop of 50% in earnings for fiscal 1996. Sales, according to a report by Nora Lockwood Tooher in *Knight-Ridder/Tribune Business News,* were down 6% from the 1995 level of $191.1 million.

A. T. Cross manufacturing plants are located in Lincoln, Rhode Island and Ballinasloe, Republic of Ireland. The company's primary foreign markets have been Europe and the Far East, bringing in 34 percent of total sales.

WORK FORCE

According to *Manufacturing USA,* 46 companies produce writing instruments in the United States, employing 19,300 workers. A large percentage of these establishments have been located in California, New Jersey and New York. The largest number of employees at pen manufacturing companies have been assembly workers and fabricators, comprising 15.6 percent of total employment in 1990. Second were sales staff and related workers at 4.3 percent and plant supervisors at 4.2 percent. The most significant projection for employment in this industry has been the 18.7 percent decline in assembly workers and the 30.1 percent increase in sales personnel by the year 2005.

RESEARCH AND TECHNOLOGY

Research and technology has affected both company operations and product development in the writing instruments industry. Retailers have begun to expect more from pen manufacturers, and companies such as BIC have turned to Electronic Data Exchange (EDI) to keep up with retailers' demands. EDI, which now accounts for 40 percent of BIC's core U.S. business, has allowed company representatives to communicate directly with their customers' computers. BIC also has assisted retailers' with their inventory management, providing a computer-controlled automatic inventory replenishment system.

Technological advances have also affected the design and manufacture of writing instruments. Research at Gillette has produced the Dynagrip refillable ball point pen. The key feature of this pen has been its patented grip, which is formed by molding a soft, flexible material called elastomer. Pockets of air are trapped within the grip, creating tiny air cushions. Manual pressure on the walls surrounding the air pockets causes the wall to change shape, the air pockets to deflate, and the elastomer material to compress. This creates a comfortable writing grip with sufficient resiliency for control. When the grip is released, the elastomer returns to its original shape.

Less high-tech but equally revolutionary has been the creation of environmentally friendly writing instruments. Paris-based Recife has produced a line of pens encased in ebonite, a vulcanized rubber "tapped harmlessly" from trees found in the rain forest. "Unlike plastic pens, whose shells scratch and dull, ebonite pens become more beautiful with age, as their natural sheen richens from contact with skin oils," reported Lesley Alderman in *Money.* These fountain, roller ball, and ball point pens sell for $78 to $200 each, with five percent of Recife's annual sales donated to a rainforest conservation group.

FURTHER READING

Alderman, Lesley. "Green Pens." *Money,* May, 1992.

Curry, Gloria M. "Versatile Is the World for Today's Writing Instruments." *The Office,* November 1989.

Darnay, Arsen J., ed. *Manufacturing USA.* 3rd edition, Detroit: Gale Research, Inc., 1993.

Elsberry, Richard B. "Returning to Writing Basics." *Office Systems,* April 1993.

"Gillette Agrees to Buy Parker Pen Holdings for $562.3 Million." *Corporate Growth Report,* 21 September 1992.

Glennon, Anthony J. "A. T. Cross." *Value Line Investment Survey,* 19 February 1993.

Hessen, Wendy. "The Signature of a Fine Pen." *WWD,* 8 May 1995.

LeGallee, Julie. "Writing Instruments Are Key Business Communication Tools." *The Office,* July 1993.

Levine, Joshua. "Pen Wars." *Forbes,* 6 January 1992.

Mancini, Richard. "Writing Instruments: Tried, True and New." *The Office,* August 1991.

Maremont, Mark, and Paula Dwyer. "How Gillette Is Honing Its Edge." *Business Week,* 28 September 1992.

Schuman, Michael. "Thin Is out, Fat Is In." *Forbes,* 9 May 1994.

Tooher, Nora Lockwood. "A. T. Cross Expects to Report 50 Percent Earnings Drop for 1996." *Knight-Ridder/Tribune Business News,* 11 December 1996.

Wise, Deborah. "Waterman Rift: A Tearful Farewell." *New York Times,* 16 December 1988.

—Catherine Quagliana, updated by Ken Shepherd

SIC 3952

LEAD PENCILS, CRAYONS AND ARTISTS' MATERIALS

This category includes establishments primarily engaged in manufacturing lead pencils, pencil leads, and crayons; and materials and equipment for artwork, such as airbrushes, drawing tables and boards, palettes, sketch boxes, pantographs, artists' colors and waxes, pyrography goods, drawing inks, and drafting materials. Establishments primarily engaged in manufacturing mechanical pencils are classified in **SIC 3951: Pens, Mechanical Pencils, and Parts,** and those manufacturing drafting instruments are classified in **SIC 3829: Measuring and Controlling Devices, Not Elsewhere Classified.**

INDUSTRY SNAPSHOT

According to the U.S. Census Bureau, there were less than 200 establishments primarily producing pencils and art supplies in the mid-1990s. A work force of roughly 7,000 generated the industry's $1.1 billion in shipments in 1995. General-use pencils, in particular, serve a mature and possibly declining market as computers and other electronic devices continue to serve such traditional school and office functions as test taking and mathematical calculation.

The majority of the industry's sales, about 54 percent in the early 1990s, come from pencils, crayons, and chalk. Art goods make up an additional 42 percent, and the remaining 4 percent of sales come from miscellaneous related goods.

BACKGROUND AND DEVELOPMENT

The Smithsonian Institution estimated that America's 100 billionth pencil was produced in 1976, and by the early 1990s, U.S. companies produced the seven-inch-long, two-for-a-quarter writing utensils at the rate of 2.5 billion per year.

The image of pencils was tarnished in 1971 when a child who chewed pencils was found to have lead poisoning, and the media blamed the pencil "lead." Even though pencils were made with graphite, not lead, the story pushed the industry to start a product certification program open to any pencil manufacturer.

In 1988, Congress passed the Labeling of Hazardous Art Materials Act, which required that all art materials be reviewed to determine the potential for causing a chronic hazard and that appropriate warning labels be placed on those materials. The artists' materials law was finalized in 1992 with the U.S. Consumer Product Safety Commission's issuance of definitions of chronic toxicity and the codification of ASTM D-4238 as a mandatory regulation.

When the lead in crayons became an issue in the industry in 1994, the problem was easily solved. Hazardous amounts of lead were found in the yellow and orange color crayons imported from China by Concord Enterprises. In 1994 when the U.S. Consumer Product Safety Commission and Concord Enterprises announced the recall of the crayons because of a lead poisoning hazard, parents were instructed to buy only crayons and children's art materials labeled with "Conforms to ASTM D-4236," indicating that the materials had been approved by a toxicologist and labeled appropriately.

A recall of a different sort occurred in August 1991, when two importers, the Brandy Trading Corp. and Mirage Imports, announced they would no longer sell novelty pencils that resembled hypodermic syringes. The Taiwan-made "Gold Doctor" pencils were sending the wrong message to schoolchildren, parents and teachers complained.

INDUSTRY LEADERS

The largest U.S. concern in this industry is Newell Co., a diversified manufacturer of home and office products. In the early and mid-1990s, Newell acquired three top U.S. pencil and art goods companies: Sanford Corporation, Faber-Castell Corporation, and Empire-Berol Corporation. All three were integrated into Newell's Sanford division, which also includes the art materials brand M. Grumbacher. In 1996 Newell's combined office products sales, which include products outside of this industry, reached $742 million. The other leading firm in the late 1990s was Binney & Smith, Inc., of Easton, Pennsylvania, the maker of Crayola crayons and a subsidiary of Hallmark Cards, Inc., with estimated sales of $300 million.

The industry trade association, formerly known as the Pencil Makers Association (PMA), is the Writing Instruments Manufacturers Association (WIMA), which merged with the PMA in 1994. WIMA represents pencil manufacturers and makers of markers, mechanical pencils, and pens. In 1996, WIMA had 100 member companies, including 30 in the pen and pencil industry, and its membership represented the majority of U.S. pencil shipments.

AMERICA AND THE WORLD

The United States imported $156 million in pencils and artists' supplies in 1995, compared to exports of only $62 million in that year. Major trading partners include Thailand and China, which are both sources of low-priced imports in this category. Imports of pencils from these two nations have grown substantially since the 1980s. The U.S. industry has not competed well against the imports, which has led to the shutdown of several domestic manufacturers.

RESEARCH AND TECHNOLOGY

Responding to rising environmental consciousness on the part of the pencil consumer, Faber-Castell Corporation introduced a pencil made of recycled materials in 1992. Instead of the traditional wood casing, Faber-Castell said its American EcoWriter would offer a pencil shaft made from reprocessed newspapers and cardboard boxes. The project involved developing a material that could be sharpened as easily as a wood pencil. Faber developed the material with Lydall Inc., the company that reprocesses the paper into slats used by Faber in manufacturing. The EcoWriter was Faber-Castell's second environmental contribution, following the American Natural, which was introduced in 1991 to highlight Faber's use of "sustained yield" cedar supplies—meaning no more wood would be harvested than could be replaced by new planting.

FURTHER READING

"Amid Furor, Importers Drop Syringe Pencil." *New York Times,* 11 August 1991.

Newell Co. *Annual Report.* Freeport, IL, 1997.

Trumball, Mark. "'Eco' Pencils: A Tree-Sparing Option." *Christian Science Monitor,* 13 May 1992, 12.

U.S. Bureau of the Census. *1995 Annual Survey of Manufactures.* Washington: GPO, 1997.

"U.S. Pencil Makers Point to Thai, Chinese Imports." *Wall Street Journal,* 24 November 1993, C11.

Winerip, Michael. "No. 2 Pencil Fades as Graduate Exam Moves to Computer." *New York Times,* 15 November 1993, A1.

SIC 3953

MARKING DEVICES

This category covers establishments primarily engaged in manufacturing stencils for use in painting or marking, steel letters and figures, and rubber and metal hand-stamps, dies, and seals. Establishments primarily engaged in manufacturing felt tip markers are covered in **SIC 3951: Pens, Mechanical Pencils, and Parts.**

As of 1993, leaders in this category were: Weber Marking Systems Inc. of Arlington Heights, Illinois; Diagraph Corp. of Earth City, Missouri; Cosco Industries Inc.; Consolidated Stamp of Chicago of Harwood Heights, Illinois; GM Nameplate Inc. of Seattle, Washington; and Pannier Corp. of Pittsburgh, Pennsylvania.

Several of the devices in this category date from antiquity and have changed very little over the centuries, but technological innovations have also made a key difference in some cases. The introduction of the mass-production automobile assembly line, for instance, led to notable advances in die-casting technology and to the very precise formation of even the tiniest metal parts.

The introduction of stenciling has been dated to eighth century China, and this technique of reproducing designs has long been deemed well-suited for metal or cardboard cut to simple shapes. Only with the introduction of silk-screen printing, however, was it possible to overcome the inherent limitations of stencils' great simplicity. The stencil does not permit the reproduction of one design enclosing another (as in the case of a figure eight), unless it is halved to prevent the necessarily unattached central sections from dropping out. The fine meshes used in silk screen printing were substantial enough to support the unattached elements of a stencil, without posing a barrier to the passage of the dye or paint being forced through a water-soluble glue into the desired design. A variant to this blockout-stencil or glue-cut-out-stencil method was the film-stencil method, whereby designs were cut into a colored lacquer laminated to a sheet of glassine paper, so the whole assemblage could be mounted on a screen before the removal of the uncut paper backing and subsequent printing.

The advances made possible by computer technology were transforming many features of office life in the United States near the end of the twentieth century, including the use of certain numbering and lettering devices. However, such age-old implements as hand presses, stamps, and seals remained widely used as a means of officially marking paperwork of various sorts. Indeed, the increasing automation of offices had given a new lease on life to such marking devices. Highly sophisticated photocopying machines, for instance, could reproduce documents with such great fidelity as to make forgeries easy in the absence of a physical impression left by the impact of a notary public's or government official's seal, for example.

FURTHER READING

Rothman, Raymond C. *Notary Public Practices & Glossary.* Woodland Hills, CA: National Notary Association, 1978.

Seals and Other Devices in Use at the Government Printing Office. Washington, D.C.: U.S. Government Printing Office, n.d.

—Richard Hillyer, updated by Elaine Winters

SIC 3955

CARBON PAPER AND INKED RIBBONS

This industry contains establishments primarily engaged in manufacturing carbon paper, spirit or gelatin process and other stencil paper, and inked or carbon ribbons for business machines.

The value of 1996 industry shipments were an estimated $922 million. There were approximately 137 establishments in the industry in 1996—about 64 of these establishments had 20 or more employees. Average firm size, as measured by the number of production workers per establishment, was 20 percent larger than that for the manufacturing sector as a whole. Annual capital investments were $13 million in 1991—down from a peak of $23 million invested in

1982. The cost of purchased fuels and electric energy for the industry in 1995 was $9.3 million.

According to *Manufacturing USA,* the carbon paper and inked ribbons industry employed approximately 7,600 production workers in 1996. Their annual hours worked were about 12.2 million, and their average hourly wage was about $8.23.

Of the top 30 firms by sales in the industry, 77 percent were private independents. The capital requirements for the industry were relatively low, with average investment per establishment 59 percent of that for the manufacturing sector as a whole.

In the mid-1990s, the top three firms in the carbon paper and inked ribbons industry were Nu-Kote Holding Inc., of Dallas, Texas; Bobbie Brooks Inc., of Cleveland, Ohio; and the Pubco Corp., of Cleveland, Ohio. Nu-Kote Holding had $151 million in sales and about 1,100 employees. Bobbie Brooks Inc. had $96 million in sales and about 1,000 employees. Pubco also had $96 million in sales and about 1,000 employees.

The states with the highest number of establishments in the industry in 1992 were California with 19, New York with 12, New Jersey and Texas with 10, Colorado with 9, Pennsylvania with 8, and Ohio and Illinois with 7. Together these eight states accounted for 66.5 percent of total employment in the industry.

The top industries and sectors buying the outputs of the carbon paper and inked ribbons industry included businesses buying manifold business forms, state and local government purchases for education and hospitals, exports, banking, and the retail trade.

FURTHER READING

U.S. Census Bureau. *Annual Survey of Manufactures.* Washington: GPO, 1991.

Darnay, Arsen J., ed. *Manufacturing USA.* 5th ed. Detroit: Gale Research, 1996.

U.S. Department of Commerce. *U.S. Industrial Outlook 1994.* Washington: GPO, January 1994.

—David Kucera, updated by Charlotte Weisman

SIC 3961

COSTUME JEWELRY AND COSTUME NOVELTIES, EXCEPT PRECIOUS METALS

This category encompasses businesses primarily engaged in manufacturing costume jewelry, costume novelties, and ornaments made of all materials, except precious metal, precious or semiprecious stones, and rolled gold paste and gold-filled materials. The products manufactured within this category include such items as necklaces, rings, artificial pearls, compacts, cuff links, and rosaries. Businesses primarily engaged in manufacturing jewelry of precious and semiprecious material are classified in **SIC 3911: Jewelry, Precious Metal;** those manufacturing leather compacts and vanity cases are classified in **SIC 3172: Personal Leather Goods, Except Women's Handbags and Purses;** and those manufacturing synthetic stones for gem stone and industrial use are classified in **SIC 3299: Nonmetallic Mineral Products, Not Elsewhere Classified.**

INDUSTRY SNAPSHOT

There were almost 900 firms actively manufacturing costume jewelry in the United States in the late 1990s. Many of the older companies were still based in Rhode Island. The combined value of all goods produced by these companies totaled $1.604 billion in 1996. Nearly 10 percent of the industry's total production was exported to other countries, including Canada and Mexico. Some of the firms were only involved in the manufacture of pieces using purchased components. The items were then sold to costume jewelry retailers, especially department stores. Other firms, however, both fabricate and market their own product lines.

The government was beginning to play an increasingly significant role in the industry. Costume jewelry manufacturers found it necessary to upgrade facilities in order to comply with environmental legislation. While such measures meant increased costs, the industry remained healthy and expected to benefit from free trade arrangements that were recently signed by the government.

ORGANIZATION AND STRUCTURE

American costume jewelry companies manufacture products using various methods, primarily using base metals, including tin and lead, to fashion such findings as clasps and pin-backs, the basic components of a finished piece. One manufacturing process used is stamping, a labor-intensive method that produces a finer, more polished piece of metal. The more typical method in the shaping of metal for costume jewelry however, is casting, which involves pouring molten metal into a mold. This process lends itself more readily to mass-production of the jewelry. Manufacturers also utilize relatively recent methods of centrifugal casting and injection molding of plastic. The findings produced from these processes are then used to fabricate finished pieces or sold to individual costume jewelry houses. Another integral function is electroplating, the electrolytic process of coating base metals with a small amount of a precious metal to give the jewelry its gold or silver appearance.

Most large costume jewelry companies sell their wares through department stores, an innovative marketing strategy that evolved in the 1950s. Earrings are one of the biggest sellers, followed in volume by necklaces and pins. One-third of all costume jewelry purchased in the United States is purchased as a gift— Christmas, Mother's Day, and Valentine's Day are the peak selling seasons. Two-thirds are purchased for individual use. Costume jewelry is also a popular product on the novel home-shopping networks found on cable channels, with celebrities such as Kenneth Jay Lane and Joan Rivers appearing on-camera to sell their wares.

BACKGROUND AND DEVELOPMENT

The industry is centered today in the city of Providence, Rhode Island, which originally attracted fine jewelry artisans in the eighteenth century. A craftsperson by the name of Nehemiah Dodge introduced gold-plating technology to the area in the late 1700s. The costume jewelry industry benefited from the nineteenth century's great advances in industrial technology, including the development of new machinery that allowed inexpensive jewelry to be mass-produced, and by 1900 the items had found a significant domestic market. Portuguese immigrants skilled in the necessary handiwork accounted for a large part of the labor pool and proved influential in the rise of Rhode Island as a base for costume jewelry manufacturers.

The term "costume jewelry" was first used in a 1933 article in the *New Yorker*. The development of the modern industry was directly influenced by such European fashion designers as Elsa Schiaparelli and Coco Chanel. These designers commissioned original pieces that were clearly not real and whose sole purpose was to complement the sartorial ensemble. Many of the early examples of costume jewelry were larger-than-life imitations of fine jewelry, but the burgeoning industry soon spawned innovative artisans who experimented with a variety of shapes, materials, and color palettes. Designers of costume jewelry then, as now, were often freed by the disposable nature of the product to experiment wildly and inject a good dose of imagination into their work, an attitude not often encouraged within the realm of more traditional fine jewelry.

In the early decades of the twentieth century, costume jewelry manufacturers primarily used cut-glass stones, imitation pearls, and enamel. Costume jewelry became overwhelmingly popular during the social upheavals of the 1920s, and the materials of choice for fashionable flappers were the glass materials of jet and crystal. The Great Depression that choked the American economy during the 1930s brought many new customers to the costume jewelry market, as those who lost fortunes could no longer afford fine jewelry. White metal became the most common material in inexpensive metal jewelry, but World War II restrictions on the use of metals was manifested in the proliferation of gold- and silver-plated pieces. In addition, the war caused American manufacturers to be cut off from their Czechoslovakian and Japanese suppliers of cut glass and pearls.

The 1950s saw the rise in popularity of ornate gilt pieces and the continued use of crystal, jet, and inexpensive stones. An important court decision at that time was instrumental in solidifying the respectability of the creators and manufacturers of costume jewelry. When First Lady Mamie Eisenhower wore Trifari pieces to both presidential inaugural balls in 1952 and 1956, the much-publicized act spawned legions of copycat pieces. Trifari successfully filed suit to protect the copyright of their designs.

Innovative uses of materials and forms were the hallmark of costume jewelry styles in the 1960s. After the profitable synthetics industry burgeoned in the aftermath of World War II, molded plastics such as Perspex became commonplace as a material for inexpensive jewelry that could be easily transformed into daring shapes and colors complementing the outrageous fashions of the decade. In 1971 the U.S. gold market was deregulated, and this set off waves of sizable price increases over the next decade that raised the cost of fine jewelry. This had a beneficial effect upon costume jewelry manufacturers, as more consumers turned to higher-end costume pieces from upscale designers, including Kenneth Jay Lane and Robert Lee Morris, rather than purchasing the genuine article from fine jewelers. Sterling silver also became a popular material during the late 1960s and early 1970s.

The British punk movement of the late 1970s even exerted its influence on costume jewelry trends of the 1980s as the "creative salvage" look, utilizing leather and rubber, became popular. The legions of women that began entering the work force in the 1970s were also influential in the development of costume jewelry styles. The working woman's choice of clothing was often restricted to conservative styles that fit into a business environment, and thus costume jewelry became a way of personalizing a wardrobe. In the 1990s, an interest in multiculturalism was evident in the use of motifs and materials inspired by indigenous cultures and natural elements, a prime example of which was the popularity of faux-ivory materials. By the mid-1990s, one of the most popular new looks in costume jewelry was the cubic zirconia, a simulated diamond. It can be made clear to resemble a diamond, or colored to simulate precious stones, and is used primarily in rings, earrings, bracelets, and necklaces.

CURRENT CONDITIONS

Costume jewelry sales in the early 1990s were noteworthy, as consumers hit hard by the recession of the late 1980s became less likely to purchase fine jewelry. Indeed, some of the largest U.S. fine jewelry firms suffered severe financial setbacks in the early 1990s, a fate that did not befall costume jewelry companies at that time. A newly popular niche in the market was the "fakes" category that marketed relatively inexpensive pieces that look amazingly similar to the genuine article. Industry analysts noted that the economic downturn of the mid- to late 1990s, while affecting overall consumer spending, had relatively little effect on the overall health of the industry.

Legislation regarding environmental issues had an adverse effect on the industry, however. Clean air and water laws enacted in the 1990s presented challenges to manufacturers, particularly those firms involved in electroplating, causing the cost of the process to increase significantly. Such establishments were generally required to have wastewater treatment facilities that removed harmful chemicals and metals from discharge water, and some manufacturers were also required to install air scrubbers to clean exhaust.

Although the projected forecast for the future of the industry was positive, this prediction proved to be false. The industry took a downturn after 1993, and costume jewelry sales continued to languish into 1995. One sign of recovery was seen when the Jewelry Manufacturers Association reported increased attendance at their 1995 exhibition by overseas companies, including buyers from South America, Japan, Ireland, the Czech Republic, and Romania.

Beginning in 1995, the costume jewelry industry began to pick up again. According to Amanda Meadus and Wendy Hessen of *WWD,* "designer-manufacturers" were in the best position for a comeback. The largest of those companies were Carolee Designs and Erwin Pearl, each of whose sales volumes was estimated to be $50 million.

As of August of 1995, retailers and vendors were reporting a definite upturn in costume jewelry sales. According to Wendy Hessen of *WWD,* "manufacturers were reporting relatively steady reorders, and stores reported stronger-then-anticipated sales."

INDUSTRY LEADERS

The top company involved in the costume jewelry industry in 1995 in the United States was Illinois-based Artra Group, a publicly held conglomerate founded in 1933. Artra held many subsidiaries, including the number-two firm, Lori Corp. Lori Corp's 1995 sales totaled approximately $160 million. Third in line was the Napa Company, whose origins can be traced back to 1875, making it the oldest costume jewelry manufacturer in the United States. Their 1995 sales totaled approximately $70 million. The New York City-based firm of Trifari Krussman and Fischel, Inc. was fourth in production and sales, with origins that date back to the early 1920s and sales totaling around $63 million. Industry leaders in the Rhode Island area included Victoria Creations, Inc. ($43 million), Swarovski Jewelry U.S. Ltd. ($50 million), and Monet Jewelers ($7 million).

WORK FORCE

Employment figures for the costume jewelry industry rose from a five-year low of 166,000 by the close of 1992 to 180,00 by 1996. However, average hourly wages for production workers in the field increased to a high of $8.00 per hour. In addition, the increase in public awareness of such repetitive-injury afflictions as carpal-tunnel syndrome resulted in improved working conditions for costume jewelry industry employees.

FURTHER READING

Gonzalez, Crissy. "Costume Jewelers' Sales Sparkle While Results at Fine Gem Retailers Lag." *Los Angeles Times,* 5 February 1992.

Hessen, Wendy. "Providence: Where's the New Stuff?" *WWD,* 19 June 1995.

———. "Fashion Jewelry: Outlook Positive." *WWD,* 28 August 1995. Available from http://sbweb2.med.iacnet.com.

Meadus, Amanda and Wendy Hessen. "Designer-makers in Driver's Seat." *WWD,* 21 February 1995. Available from http://sbweb2.med.iacnet.com.

Mulvagh, Jane. *Costume Jewelry in Vogue,* New York: Thames & Hudson, 1988.

Nemy, Enid. "Self-Proclaimed King of Junque Brings His Jewelry to the Masses." *New York Times,* 27 June 1993.

Shields, Jody. *All That Glitters: The Glory of Costume Jewelry.* New York: Rizzoli, 1987.

Sloane, Leonard. "Costume Jewelry: A Buyer's Guide." *New York Times,* 3 February 1990.

—Carol Brennan, updated by Sharyn Kolberg

SIC 3965

FASTENERS, BUTTONS, NEEDLES, AND PINS

This industry includes companies that make notions, such as slide and snap fasteners and zippers, machine and hand needles, pins, hooks and eyes, buckles, buttons, button parts, and button blanks. Companies that make these items from precious metals or from precious or semiprecious stones are classed in **SIC 3911: Jewelry, Precious Metals.**

Needles and pins and fasteners—made from metals and both natural and manmade fibers—had the largest share of industry output. Zippers, slide fasteners, buttons, and button parts made from plastics and metals, were less dominant but notable types of industry products. Close to 90 percent of industry output re-entered as components for other manufacturing industries. Of these, apparel, shoes, knitting mills, and household furniture makers were most prominent. Items sold directly to consumers made up the remainder.

In 1982 this industry had 356 companies. By 1990 their number fell to 237, a 33.7 percent decline. Over the same period total employment fell from 16,100 in 1982 (with 12,700 production jobs), to 9,000 in 1990 (with 7,100 production jobs). Two economic trends may have brought these declines. First, the average productivity per production worker rose, from $35,200 in 1982 to $66,400 by 1990. Companies that could not keep pace with the industry's rising productivity rates did not maintain a competitive cost per unit and went out of business. Surviving companies had to do more with less, which often meant cutting jobs. In an effort to reduce high cost materials, some of the industry's leading companies were experimenting with fasteners made from ceramic processes. Also, the 1980s and early 1990s brought more foreign competition which further reduced the U.S. apparel sector. Being the principal purchasing source of the industry's output, the fall-off in apparel demand burdened the industry with high levels of unused capacity.

The industry employed 8,600 people in 1995, with 6,000 of those in production. The total payroll for 1995 was $199.5 million, with $120.0 million of that paying production workers. According to the last Bureau of Labor Statistics (BLS) data available, assemblers and fabricators were the industry's largest job category, holding 15.6 percent of all jobs. Another 4 percent were jobs such as supervisors, hand packers and packagers, and sales and sales-related workers. A 1992 BLS survey predicted jobs for assemblers and fabricators may decline 18.7 percent by 2005. Jobs for machine operators, tenders and setters, and hand workers not elsewhere classified could also decline. The BLS also predicted electrical and electrical assemblers jobs could fall 41.7 percent.

In 1995, the total value of goods shipped was $856.9 million. During the 1990s, manufacturers of fasteners, buttons, needles, and pins were primarily on the east coast of the United States. New York, with 82 establishments, and Connecticut, with 25, lead the nation in the number of establishment per state. The industry leader in 1995 was Coats Crafts North America of Greenville, South Carolina, with $200 million in annual sales and 2,000 employees. Number two was MacLean-Fogg Co. of Mundelein, Illinois, with sales of $110 million and 1,300 employees. The third highest for the category was Scovill Fasteners, Inc. of Clarkesville, Georgia, with $65 million in annual sales and 600 employees.

FURTHER READING

Darnay, Arsen J., ed. *Manufacturing USA.* 5th ed. Detroit: Gale Research, 1996.

Textile Highlights. Washington: American Textile Manufacturers Institute, March 1997.

U.S. Department of Commerce. *1995 Annual Survey of Manufactures.* Washington: GPO, 1997.

—Daniel King, updated by Dave Fagan

SIC 3991

BROOMS AND BRUSHES

This category covers establishments primarily engaged in manufacturing household, industrial, and street sweeping brooms; and brushes, such as paintbrushes, toothbrushes, toilet brushes, and household and industrial brushes.

U.S. manufacturers generated approximately $1.3 billion in broom and brush shipments in 1995. Brooms accounted for roughly 13 percent of total sales, with paint and varnish brushes accounting for 29 percent and the remaining 58 percent divided between personal brushes (such as toothbrushes and hairbrushes), maintenance brushes, and artists brushes. The industry employed some 16,000 people in 1995, three-quarters of whom were engaged in production labor. At approximately $8.90 per hour, the average hourly production wage for the industry was considerably lower than that for U.S. manufacturing positions in general.

Manufacturers range from small, family-owned businesses to large corporations for whom broom or brush manufacture is one of many interests. The 1980s and early 1990s were characterized by a series of acquisitions of smaller firms by larger corporations. Empire Brush Company of Greenville, North Carolina, acquired six companies in that period and reported a 100 percent increase in sales. Two of the largest makers of "stick goods," O-Cedar and Vining Industries, merged in 1993.

The vast majority of companies are privately owned. The industry is most heavily concentrated in the Midwest and Mid-Atlantic states, with Ohio, New York, and Wisconsin responsible for over 30 percent of shipments. Illinois is considered the center of the broom industry in the United States.

Until the mid-twentieth century, brushes were made of natural materials such as hog bristles, horsehairs, and Tampico fibers. Brooms were made of birch and willow twigs until replaced in the early 1800s by broomcorn straw (actually a type of sorghum). In 1906, the entire brush industry generated $19 million in sales. The innovative sales techniques of the Fuller Brush Company helped revitalize the industry, so when founder Alfred Fuller turned operations over to his son Howard in 1946, Fuller Brush alone earned $41 million. Fuller Brush, a division of the Sara Lee Corporation, saw its importance as an industry leader diminish from 1968 through 1989.

The replacement of original materials with longer-lasting synthetic fibers and metal alloys caused a major change in the industry. This, combined with advances in mass production techniques following World War II, decreased production costs and allowed for greater profit margins. Broom making was also affected by mass production. Plastic brooms became more common, although over half of all brooms are still made of broomcorn.

Industry growth in the 1980s continued slightly but steady. Profit margins in the early 1990s were above average compared to other manufacturing industries. This was due largely to increased sales caused by new designs. Oral-B Laboratories of Redwood City, California, led the nation in the development of new toothbrush designs.

Broom manufacturers in particular became concerned with the potential threat caused by the North American Free Trade Agreement (NAFTA). Before NAFTA, the American industry was protected by a 32 percent tariff on imports, due to phase out over an 11-year period. Mexico, already the largest supplier of brooms, was expected to benefit from the elimination of tariffs.

FURTHER READING

Barmash, Isadore. "Fuller Industries Picks Executive from Avon." *New York Times,* 13 February 1991.

Feder, Barnaby. "Tiny Industry Fears NAFTA's Reach." *New York Times,* 24 September 1993.

Fischman, Carol. "Better Brushes Expanding Oral Care Sales." *Supermarket News,* 5 June 1989.

"How Many Broom-Makers Does It Take to Kill a Trade Pact?" *Business Week,* 20 July 1992.

Huyser-Honig, Joan. "A Bounteous Crop of Broom." *Americana,* October 1991.

Muirhead, Greg. "Brush Strokes: New Toothbrushes Designed to Promote Better Hygiene Are Creating Opportunities for Growth." *Supermarket News,* 16 November 1992.

"Oral-B Plans Upgrades, New Products." *ADWEEK Eastern Edition,* 12 October 1992.

"Sweeping Sales: Brushes Produce Better than Average Margins." *Industrial Distribution,* February 1993.

Underwood, Elaine. "The Modern Trials of the Fuller Brush Man." *Adweek's Marketing Week,* 9 September 1993.

SIC 3993

SIGNS AND ADVERTISING SPECIALTIES

This category covers establishments primarily engaged in manufacturing electrical, mechanical, cutout, or plate signs and advertising displays, including neon signs, and advertising specialties. Sign painting shops doing business on a custom basis are classified in **SIC 7389: Business Services, Not Elsewhere Classified.** Establishments primarily engaged in manufacturing electric signal equipment are classified in **SIC 3669: Communications Equipment, Not Elsewhere Classified;** and those manufacturing commercial lighting fixtures are classified in **SIC 3646: Commercial, Industrial, and Institutional Electric Lighting Fixtures.**

INDUSTRY SNAPSHOT

Over 3,500 establishments were engaged in the manufacture of signs and advertising displays in 1992, producing industry sales of $3.12 billion. The industry grew at a healthy pace throughout the 1980s, spurred largely by developments in computer technology. In 1990 and 1991, it followed the national economic downturn with consecutive 8 percent decreases in sales volume, but rebounded with a 4 percent increase in 1992.

Throughout its history, and especially in recent years, the industry has fought against perceptions of signs as visual pollutants, which must be controlled or even banned except when conveying "vital information." These perceptions were often countered with new stylistic designs and aggressive government lobbying.

In 1996, electric signs made up 24 percent of all specified types of signs and advertising displays. Of those, 34 percent used fluorescent lamps, 28 percent used luminous tubing (neon, argon, hydrogen, etc.), and 5 percent used incandescent bulbs. The most common materials in nonelectric signs (34 percent of the total product output) were polymers and plastics (including vinyl), followed by metal and wood. Advertising specialties accounted for less than 15 percent of the total output.

ORGANIZATION AND STRUCTURE

A sign shop is an establishment where signs and advertising specialties are manufactured. Sign shops are located throughout the country, with the greatest number of establishments (about 539) in the state of California. In general, though, the largest amount of shipments and the greatest number of employees were in the Midwest and eastern seaboard states. In 1996, Illinois' 224 establishments accounted for $580 million in shipments, 10.7 percent of the U.S. total. Shipments from New York, Illinois, Ohio, California, and Wisconsin made up 42.4 percent of the 1996 U.S. total, and 37.1 percent of all U.S. employees worked in those states. A 1992 state-of-the-industry survey reported a significant increase in the percentage of shops doing business in the central, Midwest, southern and eastern regions. Also, many sign shops expanded operations to serve a wider geographic base. This expansion may be the result of a trend toward larger shops, whose greater output quantities and increased sales forces allow them to serve larger areas.

The largest buyer of signs and advertising specialties was the gross private fixed investment industry (68.5 percent of total buying outputs in 1996). The next largest were highway and street construction, eating and drinking places, and wholesale trade.

Size of establishments in 1996 ranged from single-person sign shops to industry leaders such as Everbrite, Inc., and Signmark, each with sales estimated at over $100 million. An estimated 75 percent of sales volume in 1992 was generated by less than 10 percent of all sign shops. This top-heaviness may continue due to the increased volume of signs and the prevalence of quantity orders over custom or finely-crafted work. The development of computer technology decreases the need for specialized skills and gives rise to rapid-sign franchises, which facilitate same-day construction of signs. According to the 1992 survey, large sign shops (those generating more than $5 million in sales) employed an average of 36.7 employees.

A 1996 *Signs of the Times* state-of-the-industry survey reported the electric sign industry experienced great expansion and had an all-time high of $4.1 billion in sales in 1995, up from 3.7 billion in 1994. This represents an 11 percent increase. Unfortunately for the industry, the average profit margin decreased from 1994's 8.4 percent to 6.9 percent in 1995. Also, the average sales per employee dropped from $89,548 to $86,302. More optimistically, as reported in the 1996 survey, the average sign shop enjoyed a sales-volume boost of nearly 20 percent in 1995. On balance, the state-of-the-industry report implies the overall picture is better for product manufacturers and suppliers than for the small sign shops.

The 1996 survey also showed that about 64 percent of respondents outsourced under 10 percent of sales in 1995, up from 62 percent in 1994. A total of 23.1 percent outsourced between 10 percent and 24 percent of their sales, and 12.9 percent outsourced more than 25 percent of sales. Generally, as indicated in the survey, companies that outsourced more than 10 percent of their business showed higher sales-per-employee figures.

BACKGROUND AND DEVELOPMENT

In the nineteenth century, signs and advertising displays were a common sight in residential neighborhoods as well as commercial areas. Since electronic media was not yet developed, outdoor advertisements played a more crucial role in name recognition than they do today. Advertisements were often painted on empty brick walls, storefronts, or barns. The growth of cities reduced the amount and visibility of available space and necessitated free-hanging signs made of wood or metal. The advent of the automobile also increased the amount of road and traffic signs.

The public perception of advertising signs as eyesores was slow to develop. If it existed at all in the first half of the twentieth century, it was not evidenced by the popularity of such cultural icons as the Burma Shave signs. With the ascendancy of television, the use of signs as part of nationwide advertising campaigns diminished.

Regulation and zoning have been recurring trends throughout the latter part of the century. Long considered the province of local governments, limitation of signs became a federal issue during the Johnson administration, with the passage of the 1965 Highway Beautification Act. Again in 1990, the introduction of the Visual Pollution Control Act by Republican Senator John H. Chafee of Rhode Island reflected a national concern for removing many highway signs by making it easier for governments to compensate owners. Funds earmarked for highway construction and maintenance were to be used for sign removal. Up to $428 million was allocated to the Federal Highway Administration to compensate sign owners who had erected signs before laws were passed making them illegal. Federal regulation of sign display has been opposed by active lobbying, as well as by publications such as the *Wall Street Journal.* For the most part, control of sign proliferation has remained on the community level. The potential negative impact to the industry caused by the reduction of advertising signs has been offset by an increased demand for signs of other types.

Electric Signs and Luminous Tubing. At the end of the nineteenth century, luminous signs were a new phenomenon. The hazardous and expensive gaslit method of lighting quickly gave way to electricity. In 1898, Sir William Ramsay and Morris William Travers discovered neon. In 1910, French physicist Georges Claude experimented with sending an electric discharge through a neon-filled tube. The charge produced a bright red light whose color and luminosity could be modified by altering the current. The subsequent development of luminous tubing using inert gases provided a relatively safe method of lighting. Though too expensive for general purposes, its brightness made it ideal for advertising and other special uses. Increased production of hydroelectric power under the Roosevelt administration lowered the cost involved in electric sign manufacture and use and expanded the use of neon as an advertising tool—and as an art form. Two of the best-known neon-using locales, Las Vegas and the Times Square area of New York, were developed during this neon heyday of the 1930s and 1940s. Artkraft Strauss Company, the original manufacturer of virtually all of Broadway's electric signs, continues to be the major supplier for the area and to redevelop and renovate signs that are now considered historic landmarks (such as Times Square's famous Coca-Cola sign).

Neon reached the peak of its popularity in the 1950s. In the 1960s, regarded as an example of the opulent decadence of the previous generation, it gave way to inexpensive plastics as the advertising medium of choice. Electric signs in general continued to thrive. Electric advertising displays with moving mechanical parts proved to be attention-getting, point-of-purchase devices. Computer software also allowed for the programming of changeable messages on road signs, advertisements, and architectural signs.

The industry has also been spurred by changes in signs on roadways and other public places. As travel becomes easier and tourism from non-English-speaking countries grows, a trend toward universal symbols to replace or augment public signs has increased demand. The National Park Service was at the forefront of a movement to make recreational signs easier to read.

CURRENT CONDITIONS

The most important development in the industry since the early 1980s has been the introduction of computer technology in the manufacture of signs and displays. The ability to program sign design and manufacture through software greatly reduces turnaround time, often to less than a day. It also increases quantitative capabilities and reduces the amount of craftsmanship necessary in production.

At the same time, however, there has been a resurgence of hand craftsmanship in sign making (perhaps in response to the stylistic standardization caused by computer technology). Major consumers such as Disney and MGM have ordered signs made of ornately hand carved gold leaf. In addition, neon has regained much of its former popularity.

According to *Entrepreneur,* Sign Biz Inc., a computer-aided sign network, has attained a measure of distinction by providing its franchisees with good support without charging royalties. Store owners are given turnkey equipment and training material for $72,500.

Another important industry development is the response to the Americans With Disabilities Act (ADA). Its enactment in 1992 required that all public buildings display architectural signs (including exit signs, emergency instructions, elevator signs, etc.) that are readable by disabled persons, including the blind and visually impaired. In practice, this entails creating signs with raised characters at least three inches high that are accessible by touch. Since many architectural signs were originally engraved, replacing them with raised-letter signs would necessitate complete retooling.

The expected increase in sales caused by the ADA had not occurred by the end of 1993. Consumers were slow to enact the required changes, and the federal government was slow to enforce them. In the absence of a test case, the government was unwilling to provide its own interpretation of the act, so businesses, building managers, and architectural firms were uncertain as to exactly what changes were required.

For the first time in the history of the sign industry, over $1 billion was spent on materials in 1992, a year in which the industry posted total sales of $3.12 billion and profits of $209 million. The ratio of payroll costs to sales increased by 6.4 percent from 1990 to 1992. During the same period, the profit margin dropped from 7.4 percent to 6.7 percent. The median sales volume per sign shop in 1992 was $652,000, an increase over previous years that reflects the increase in size of the average shop.

According to *Forbes,* Whiteco Industries (Merrillville, Indiana) was the largest private business in the billboard industry, as of October 1996, occupying a 7-percent share. Averaging $850 per month for highway signs and $3,500 monthly in large markets, they have a yearly cash flow of about $60 million.

In the mid-1990s, television broadcasters and cable networks started to show electronic sponsorship signs on the playing fields during the broadcasting of sports events. The effect that virtual signs would have on sports enthusiasts had not really been discerned by 1997.

One continuing trend was electric and/or architectural sign companies diversifying or merging their operations. A total of 91 percent of surveyed companies in *The State of the Industry Report* made at least some custom electric signs (as compared to 86 percent in the previous year) and about 82 percent (as compared to 76 percent in the previous year) maintained and repaired electric signs and/or lighting. In July, 1996, Outdoor Systems of Phoenix contracted to purchase Gannett Outdoor for $690 million to merge their industry strengths.

The Internet greatly influenced the signs and advertising in the mid-1990s. In particular, the vinyl type of signshop demonstrated much enthusiasm for the Web. One popular vinyl site in the United Kingdom was at http://ourworld.compuserve.com/homepages/Extratext. According to *Signs of the Times,* the most useful website for the industry in the mid-1990s was at http://www.sign.web.com. Originally planned as a ''mall'' for the sign industry, by 1997, it typically received as many as 10,000 hits on some days.

In the mid-1990s, fiber optics (FO) turned up as an option to neon and other lighting. In a *Signs of the Times,* corporate sales director Fritz Mayne Jr. of SuperVision (Orlando, Florida) enumerated some of FO's advantages over neon, including: FO does not require electrical permits, and as a material poses no fire threats; with FO, users can alter the cable's color at any time, with a dichroic color wheel; FO requires very little maintenance, just lamp replacement and illuminator cleaning.

Despite the changing conditions of the sign industry, vinyl is still of paramount importance to the business; in fact, in a 1996 survey, it was revealed that over 75 percent of all signs manufactured by responding shops employed at least some vinyl in their products. Of the electric shops that took part in the survey, only 31 percent used vinyl at all. However, about 80 percent of respondents said they used more vinyl on individual signs in 1996 than in 1994.

WORK FORCE

The industry as a whole experienced reductions in total number of employees, payroll, and production workers in the early 1990s. On the other hand, sales per employee reached an all-time high of $97,700 in 1991, which indicated that many companies were involved in streamlining the work force. In 1996, signs and advertising specialties manufacturers employed about 74,800 workers, of which about 47,400 were production workers. This was up from 72,000 workers (46,200 production workers) in 1994. Total 1996 payroll of roughly $1.9 million was up from $1.8 million in 1994. The 1992 state-of-the-industry survey showed that the average number of full-time employees per firm jumped from 23.5 in 1991 to 36.7 in 1992. Of this average, 25.8 were production workers, 4.9 were sales staff, and 6.0 were administrative and clerical staff. The 1996 survey indicated the average number of employees per firm had decreased to 32.3 for 1995. Of this number, 22.9 represented full-time production workers, 5.0 were full-time administrative/clerical, and 4.4 were full-time sales/sales management.

By far the largest production group employed by the industry consisted of assemblers and fabricators. These workers made up 17 percent of the entire work force in 1994. The next largest groups were sales workers at 4.3 percent, production supervisors at 4.0 percent, and general managers and top executives at 3.8 percent. The Bureau of Labor Statistics estimates that by the year 2005, the number of assemblers, fabricators, machine operators, and hand workers as a percentage of the total work force will be reduced by 18.7 percent. Automation may be chiefly responsible for this decline. During the same time span, the sales force was expected to increase by 30.1. This may be explained by the expanded size and geographical client base of the average sign shop. Precision workers, sheet metal workers, and duct installers were predicted to increase by 16.2 percent.

RESEARCH AND TECHNOLOGY

American industry started the revolution in computer-aided sign making in 1983. The most important innovation gave an operator the ability to key instructions to a CAD-based knife plotter, an instrument that cuts a pressure-sensitive design (such as a logo or lettering) from a sheet of perforated vinyl. This vinyl substrate (the material on which the actual sign information is contained) can then be attached to a signboard or directly to another surface, such as a store window or truck door.

Most large and mid-sized sign companies now have computerized systems, and it has been estimated that up to 90 percent of hand lettering jobs have been taken over by computers. Startup costs for computer systems range from $6,000 to $35,000, but the increased speed of production reduces turnaround time and employee hours. Orders that previously took six weeks to complete are now done in a single day. The demand for quickly made signs has spawned a number of rapid-sign franchises. Fastsigns, a national vinyl-graphics chain, had 165 stores nationwide by mid-1992.

Another computer-based innovation is the electronic message sign programmable through software. Traffic signs benefit from this innovation, as do supermarkets and retail stores. In 1989, Videocart introduced a video screen mounted on the handle of a shopping cart. As the cart passes electronic sensors placed in the store, a message appears on screen relating to a specific item or promotion. At the checkout counter the screen displays news and entertainment features. The Videocart and other electronic merchandising, such as electronic coupon machines, were slow to gain acceptance in the marketplace in the early 1990s, however. *Progressive Grocer* reported that only 12 percent of chain groceries used electronic media in 1990 and 1991.

Though Norway, Germany, and Japan added important contributions to computer-aided sign making, America was still the leader in the field at the end of 1993. Calcomp, Xerox, and Hewlett Packard Corporations pioneered in four-color imaging, a process which produces a color image directly onto the substrate by a method similar to that of a laser printer. This technique will bring more color and versatility to computerized sign design.

Advances in the area of luminous sign manufacture have served primarily to increase safety. A solid-state transformer has been developed to replace the core-and-coil construction previously used in neon lighting.

In response to a growing public concern over the rights of disabled people, a "talking sign" has been developed which may satisfy the requirements of the Americans with Disabilities Act. This small, hand-held device, when pointed in the direction of a sign, would activate a sensor that converts the sign's information to a voiced message. The talking sign's limitation is that it only works with signs equipped with the sensors; however, it has applications in public arenas, government offices, rapid rail systems, and other large venues.

FURTHER READING

Bureau of Labor Statistics, Trade & Employment. 1994-95.

Chafee, John H. and John Lewis. "Signs of the Billboard Lobby." *The Washington Post,* 11 June 1991.

Colford, Steven W. "Feds Set Fund to Ax Outdoor Boards." *Advertising Age,* 16 March 1992.

Darnay, Arsen J., ed. *Manufacturing USA.* 5th ed. Detroit: Gale Research, 1996.

Dundas, Bill. "Fiber Optics on the Fast Track." *Signs of the Times,* March 1997.

Fensholt, Carol. "Electronic In-store Media: A Sign of the Times?" *Supermarket Business Magazine,* October 1991.

Graebner, Lynn. "Rapid-sign Franchises, Armed with Artful Computers, Popping Up Fast." *The Business Journal Serving Greater Sacramento,* 5 February 1990.

Hildebrand, Carol. "Sign Maker Glitters with IS Gear." *Computerworld,* 11 March 1991.

Hudis, Mark. "All the Signs Point Up." *Mediaweek,* 15 July 1996.

"Interview with Terry Wike, ed." *Sign Business Magazine.*

Korman, Richard. "Next Generation of Stars in the 'New' Times Square." *ENR,* 7 June 1990.

Kueny, Barbara. "Everbrite's Future Shines in Flashing Neon, Despite Signs of Dull '91." *The Business Journal-Milwaukee,* 27 May 1991.

Lefton, Terry. "The New Sign Age." *Brandweek,* 27 January 1997.

O'Dwyer, Jessica. "When Neon Signs Were Art." *Americana,* May-June 1989.

O'Harrow, Robert, Jr. "Guerilla War Waged to Save Rural Aesthetics." *The Washington Post,* 8 May 1993.

Pierson, John. "Disabilities Act Stymies Many Sign Designers." *The Wall Street Journal,* 31 August 1992.

Pierson, John. "Sign Rules May Not Foster Communication." *The Wall Street Journal,* 26 April 1991.

Riggs, Carol R. "They Light Up Broadway." *D & B Reports,* May-June 1990.

Samuelson, James. "You Can't Zap It." *Forbes,* 21 October 1996.

Souhrada, Paul. "Sign of the Times: Neon Maker Rides Revived Popularity." *Cincinnati Business Courier,* 30 January 1989.

Stage, Wm. *Ghost Signs: Brick Wall Signs in America.* Cincinnati: ST Publications, Inc.

Swormstedt, Wade, ed. "The 1992 State-of-the-Industry Report." *Signs of the Times,* July 1993.

———. "The 1996 State-of-the-Industry Report." *Signs of the Times,* July 1996.

———. "Vinyl Usage; The Signshops Speak." *Signs of the Times,* January 1996.

"A Sure Sign." *Entrepreneur,* January 1997.

"Tech Tips: Showing Energy Wasters the Exit." *Black Enterprise,* August 1989.

Tymoski, John. "Sign Making on the Internet Goes Mainstream." *Signs of the Times,* June 1996.

United States Congress Senate Committee on Public Works. *Visual Pollution Control Act of 1990: Report Together With Minority Views.* Washington: U.S. Government Printing Office, 1990.

—Michael Maschinot, updated by David Levine

SIC 3995

BURIAL CASKETS

This industry includes companies primarily engaged in manufacturing burial caskets, vaults, and cases, including shipping cases, of wood, metal, fiberglass, or other material except concrete.

INDUSTRY SNAPSHOT

High overhead and limited market potential have limited the number of participants in this industry. A complete set of dies necessary to manufacture a metal casket shell is estimated to cost as much as $1 million, not including the cost of the stamping machines in which the dies are used. The Casket & Funeral Supply Association (C&FSA) estimated in 1997 that there were fewer than 325 companies involved in the various aspects of casket manufacturing in the United States. According to the U.S. Census Bureau, in 1995

the burial casket industry employed 7,900 with a total payroll of $205 million. Of these employees, 6,300 were production workers, working 12.9 million production hours resulting in $146.8 million in wages.

The 1995 value of industry shipments totaled $1.2 billion. Shipped metal caskets comprised 64.3 percent of the total dollar value of caskets shipped, with wood comprising 23.7 percent and alternative materials such as fiberglass, cardboard, and composite materials making up the final 12 percent. By comparison, in 1992 metals comprised 66.2 percent, wood 21.8 percent, and alternative materials 12 percent of industry shipments.

ORGANIZATION AND STRUCTURE

Caskets are generally made of two types of material, wood and metal. Wooden caskets are available in both soft and hardwood. Because they do not generally have a sealing mechanism, wooden caskets are known as nonprotective caskets. Nonprotective caskets are not designed to prevent the entrance of air or moisture. Metal caskets are available in carbon steel, copper, bronze and stainless steel. Carbon steel caskets are available in different gauges, ranging from 20 gauge (the thinnest) up to 16 gauge (the thickest). Bronze and copper caskets are available in 32 and 48 ounces of material per square foot. The majority of metal caskets are protective caskets, meaning that they use some type of sealing mechanism, usually a natural rubber gasket, to prevent the entrance of air or moisture into the casket. There are lower end metal caskets that are nonprotective. Alternative materials such as fiberglass or plastics are also used in casket manufacturing, but none of the major U.S. casket manufacturers employ these materials in their shell production.

Casket costs vary according to the type of material the casket is made of, the quality of the construction and the type of interior used. Also the most expensive material used to make a casket, bronze is considered by the industry to be the material most suitable for casket construction due to its strength and natural ability to resist rust. Copper is comparable to bronze, but is a less expensive material. Stainless steel has a higher tensile strength than either bronze or copper and is also a naturally rust resistant material, but is not used as a primary material for shell construction by any major manufacturer other than the Aurora Casket Company of Aurora, Illinois.

Consumer selection of wooden caskets over metal caskets has in the past been governed by regional preferences, with rural areas being more likely to purchase wooden caskets, a material with which the consumer is more familiar. Urban areas have traditionally had higher sales of metal caskets. Marketing wood as a natural and renewable material has contributed to a steady increase in wooden casket sales.

Materials consumed by the casket manufacturing industry include steel and nonferrous metals in various shapes and forms and rough and dressed lumber for outer shell construction.

The outer shells are typically finished in paints, stains, lacquers and applied fabric coverings made of wool or felt. Hardware consists of cast and forged metals and formed plastics. Interior materials are usually cotton, satin, velvet, and other manmade fabrics.

BACKGROUND AND DEVELOPMENT

The U.S. casket industry has its origins in the 1800s. Merchants operating furniture stores were called upon by the community to supply a casket at the time of a death. As time passed, casket manufacturing developed into an industry separate from furniture manufacturing and the sell moved from the furniture store to the newly emerging funeral parlor.

By the early 1950s, there were over 700 casket manufacturing companies in the United States, with more than half of the units sold being cloth-covered caskets. Cloth-covered caskets are generally softwood, composite wood or high strength cardboard covered in felt. Availability of sheet steel grew after the end of the Korean War allowing casket manufacturers to increase production of steel units. As a result of this, by the mid to late 1970s almost two-thirds of all caskets were made of metal, with cloth-covered caskets being relegated to the role of inexpensive alternatives.

CURRENT CONDITIONS

The casket manufacturing industry is faced with a unique obstacle to growth that other industries rarely, if ever, face. Annual casket sales are dependent on several variables, the most obvious being the number of deaths for that year. The low U.S. death rate—projected to grow at 1 percent annually through 2010—and an increasing number of noncasketed cremations have created a stable to declining market for the last 15 years.

With the rate of cremations projected to increase over the coming years, the major casket manufacturers have had to position themselves for further changes in the industry. Looking to offset a market with little or no growth, the casket manufacturers have begun to enter market areas formerly left to other vendors. Cremation urns and specialized cremation caskets are being both manufactured and aggressively marketed by companies who had traditionally limited themselves to casket manufacturing and sales.

Traditionally, funeral homes have been the only source of caskets for the retail consumer. But due to the 1994 Federal Trade Commission ruling prohibiting funeral homes from charging casket handling fees for caskets purchased from a source other than the funeral home, retail casket stores have started appearing across the United States. These retailers sell their caskets from display rooms, catalogs, and over the Internet. While claiming to offer caskets at 40 percent to 60 percent less than funeral homes, these casket stores have become a source of competition for the funeral home industry. While not directly having an adverse effect on the casket manufacturing industry, there is potential for loss of funeral home showroom space of manufacturers that sell to casket stores because funeral homes have been reluctant to carry stock available on the retail market. Batesville Casket Company, the largest firm in the industry, is so aware of this potential that it does not sell its products to anyone other than a licensed funeral director.

Increasing manufacturing cost and stagnant market growth seem to indicate that consolidation of the smaller companies is necessary for the continued survival in an industry dominated by Batesville, Aurora, and the York companies. Inventive marketing techniques and product support will be essential to the growth of the casket manufacturing industry.

INDUSTRY LEADERS

In 1996 there were only seven companies producing all of the necessary components for metal caskets. According to the C&FSA that of the more than 30 companies that assemble metal caskets, 90 percent are produced by around a dozen companies. Hardwood casket manufacturing is believed to be limited to another dozen companies, with the manufacturing of both metal and hardwood caskets being limited to a very small number of companies.

Hillenbrand Industries, located in Batesville, Indiana and parent company of Batesville Casket Company, reported sales of $524 million for their funeral service division for 1996. Batesville Casket Company is the largest manufacturer of caskets in the United States. The York Group, Inc. of Houston, Texas, was second largest, commanding approximately a 15 percent share of the market. The publicly held York had sales of $138.2 million in 1996. The third largest manufacturer was privately held Aurora Casket Company of Aurora, Indiana.

FURTHER READING

Darnay, Arsen J., ed. *Manufacturing USA*. 5th ed. Detroit: Gale Research, 1996.

"Has a Casket Store Opened in Your Neighborhood Yet?"
Batesville Source, March 1997.

U.S. Bureau of the Census. *1995 Annual Survey of Manufactures.* Washington: GPO, 1997.

—Scott Rhodes

SIC 3996

LINOLEUM, ASPHALTED-FELT-BASE, AND OTHER HARD SURFACE FLOOR COVERINGS, NOT ELSEWHERE CLASSIFIED

This category covers establishments primarily engaged in manufacturing linoleum, asphalted-felt-base, and other hard surface floor coverings, not elsewhere classified. Establishments primarily engaged in manufacturing rubber floor coverings are classified in **SIC 3069: Fabricated Rubber Products, Not Elsewhere Classified,** and those manufacturing cork floor and wall tile are classified in **SIC 2499: Wood Products, Not Elsewhere Classified.**

Companies in the $1.67 billion hard surface floor coverings industry supply flooring primarily for residential homes, which accounted for almost 60 percent of the market in the early 1990s. Coverings used in apartment buildings represented 10 percent of industry sales. Other major consumers of hard surface flooring, in order of industry purchases, include office buildings, mobile homes, hospitals, industrial facilities, hotels and motels, stores, and restaurants.

Linoleum, a traditionally popular industry offering, is made in sheets by pressing a mixture of heated linseed oil, rosin, powdered cork, and pigments onto a textile backing, such as burlap or canvas. Synthetic coverings similar to linoleum are created with mixtures of resins, elastomers, and plasticizers. These newer types of flooring are often more moisture resistant, durable, and workable than linoleum.

The linoleum production process was invented in 1860 by Frederick Walton of England. The use of linoleum and similar floor coverings expanded greatly during the 1920s. Asphalt tiles were developed in 1930, and vinyl floor was invented in 1945. But it was not until the 1960s, when flat concrete subsurfaces became standard in U.S. homes, that hard surface coverings exploded in popularity. A profusion of synthetic flooring products during the 1960s and 1970s sharply increased industry sales. By the early 1980s, manufacturers were shipping about $600 million

worth of flooring each year and employing about 3,000 workers.

Steady market growth and the development of new and better floor coverings more than doubled industry revenues during the 1980s. Advanced polymer technology and new plasticizers allowed the introduction of less expensive materials with higher performance. By 1989, industry participants were enjoying sales of $1.4 billion. The industry showed mixed performance in the early and mid-1990s. Showing only modest gains in the early 1990s, industry sales peaked in 1994 at $1.73 billion but then drew back to $1.67 billion in 1995, when manufacturers reported sluggish retail sales. Continued strength in new housing starts in 1997, as well as general U.S. economic growth, were expected to contribute to modest growth in hard surface flooring into the late 1990s.

The hard surface flooring industry is extremely consolidated—only about 20 companies made up the industry in the 1990s, according to the U.S. Census Bureau. The largest producer was Armstrong World Industries, Inc., of Pennsylvania, which had 1996 sales of approximately $1.1 billion from its floor covering operations and employed 10,500 workers in all operations worldwide. Mannington Mills Inc., of New Jersey, was the second largest industry participant, with sales of about $600 million and 3,000 employees.

Increased manufacturing efficiency, achieved through automation and restructuring, will inhibit employment growth in this industry in the long term. However, increased demand for new synthetic coverings will create opportunities for some occupations. The number of sales positions, for example, was expected to rise 30 percent for the miscellaneous manufacturing sector between 1990 and 2005, according to the Bureau of Labor Statistics. About 6,300 workers made up the industry in 1995. The average production wage was about $18.36 per hour, which was well above the $12.37 hourly average for all U.S. manufacturing industries.

FURTHER READING

Armstrong World Industries, Inc. *Annual Report.* Lancaster, PA, 1997.

Darnay, Arsen J., ed. *Manufacturing USA.* 5th ed. Detroit: Gale Research, 1996.

U.S. Census Bureau. *1995 Annual Survey of Manufactures.* Washington: GPO, 1997.

U.S. Census Bureau. Manufacturing and Construction Division. *Construction Reports, Series C20, Housing Starts.* Washington: GPO, 1997.

MANUFACTURING INDUSTRIES, NOT ELSEWHERE CLASSIFIED

This category covers establishments primarily engaged in manufacturing miscellaneous fabricated products, including beauty shop and barber shop equipment; hair work; tobacco pipes and cigarette holders; coin-operated amusement machines; matches; candles; lamp shades; feathers; artificial trees and flowers made from all materials, except glass; dressed and dyed furs; umbrellas, parasols, and canes; and other articles, not elsewhere classified.

This fragmented category accounts for all U.S. manufacturing activities not included under other headings. In 1995 products shipped in this category, including those made by firms primarily involved in other industries, totaled $6.04 billion. Despite its obscurity and fragmentation, the miscellaneous manufacturing industry produces a few well-known items. By product group, coin-operated amusement devices, such as arcade games, accounted for the largest share, 13.7 percent, at $825.8 million in 1995 sales. Candles were a distant second at $494.6 million, or about 8.2 percent; chemical fire extinguishers were a close third with $470.9 million in sales and a 7.8 percent share of industry shipments. All other products made up less than 3 percent each—although 70 percent collectively—of the industry total. These small segments include such diverse items as wigs and barber and beauty shop equipment; artificial Christmas trees and nonglass, nonelectric Christmas ornaments; artificial flowers and plants; matches; umbrellas; potpourri; and lamp shades.

The profile of miscellaneous manufactured goods consumers mimicked that of the manufacturing sector at large in the early 1990s. About 45 percent of industry consumption was classified as private fixed investment (for use in other for-profit businesses). Personal consumption expenditures made up about 15 percent of sales. Four percent of output was exported, and state and local governments received about 3.5 percent of shipments. The remainder of the market was highly fragmented.

The industry's approximately 3,000 establishments are predominately small and mid-sized companies, but there are several larger corporations as well. The largest company primarily manufacturing for this industry was International Game Technology of Nevada, with 1996 game machine sales of $417 million out of total revenues of $733 million. Another high performer was candle and potpourri maker Blythe Industries, Inc. of Connecticut, with $495 million in 1996 revenues and an estimated 25 percent share of the U.S. candle market. Gaming giant WMS Industries, Inc. of Illinois posted 1996 sales of $338 million, just under half of which were from coin-operated games. WMS was also a strong presence in the consumer market through its 1996 acquisition of Atari Games Inc. Other leading firms included game machine manufacturer and casino operator Bally's Grand, Inc., which had 1996 total revenues of $313 million; hair care manufacturer Windmere Corporation of Florida, with 1996 revenues of $197 million; and contract manufacturer Mid-South Industries, Inc. of Alabama, with estimated revenues of $190 million.

The industry employed 68,600 workers in 1995. Production workers made up 69 percent of the labor force and earned an average of $9.11 per hour, which was about 25 percent below average for manufacturing positions in general. Job growth was expected to remain flat or decrease for many of this industry's occupations.

FURTHER READING

Darnay, Arsen J., ed. *Manufacturing USA*. 5th ed. Detroit: Gale Research, 1996.

U.S. Census Bureau. *1995 Annual Survey of Manufactures*. Washington: GPO, 1997.

U.S. Department of Labor. Bureau of Labor Statistics. *Occupational Outlook Handbook, 1996-97 Edition*. Washington: GPO, 1996.

SIC TO NAICS
CONVERSION GUIDE

The following listing cross-references four-digit 1987 Standard Industrial Classification (SIC) codes with 1997 North American Industry Classification System (NAICS) codes. Because the systems differ in specificity, some SIC categories correspond to more than one NAICS category. Please refer to the introduction under "About Industry Classification" for more information.

AGRICULTURE, FORESTRY, & FISHING

0111   Wheat *see* NAICS 11114: Wheat Farming

0112   Rice *see* NAICS 11116: Rice Farming

0115   Corn *see* NAICS 11115: Corn Farming

0116   Soybeans *see* NAICS 11111: Soybean Farming

0119   Cash Grains, NEC *see* NAICS 11113: Dry Pea & Bean Farming; NAICS 11112: Oilseed Farming; NAICS 11115: Corn Farming; NAICS 111191: Oilseed & Grain Combination Farming; NAICS 111199: All Other Grain Farming

0131   Cotton *see* NAICS 11192: Cotton Farming

0132   Tobacco *see* NAICS 11191: Tobacco Farming

0133   Sugarcane & Sugar Beets *see* NAICS 111991: Sugar Beet Farming; NAICS 11193: Sugarcane Farming

0134   Irish Potatoes *see* NAICS 111211: Potato Farming

0139   Field Crops, Except Cash Grains, NEC *see* NAICS 11194: Hay Farming; NAICS 111992: Peanut Farming; NAICS 111219: Other Vegetable & Melon Farming; NAICS 111998: All Other Miscellaneous Crop Farming

0161   Vegetables & Melons *see* NAICS 111219: Other Vegetable & Melon Farming

0171   Berry Crops *see* NAICS 111333: Strawberry Farming; NAICS 111334: Berry Farming

0172   Grapes *see* NAICS 111332: Grape Vineyards

0173   Tree Nuts *see* NAICS 111335: Tree Nut Farming

0174   Citrus Fruits *see* NAICS 11131: Orange Groves; NAICS 11132: Citrus Groves

0175   Deciduous Tree Fruits *see* NAICS 111331: Apple Orchards; NAICS 111339: Other Noncitrus Fruit Farming

0179   Fruits & Tree Nuts, NEC *see* NAICS 111336: Fruit & Tree Nut Combination Farming; NAICS 111339: Other Noncitrus Fruit Farming

0181   Ornamental Floriculture & Nursery Products *see* NAICS 111422: Floriculture Production; NAICS 111421: Nursery & Tree Production

0182   Food Crops Grown under Cover *see* NAICS 111411: Mushroom Production; NAICS 111419: Other Food Crops Grown under Cover

0191   General Farms, Primarily Crop *see* NAICS 111998: All Other Miscellaneous Crop Farming

0211   Beef Cattle Feedlots *see* NAICS 112112: Cattle Feedlots

0212   Beef Cattle, Except Feedlots *see* NAICS 112111: Beef Cattle Ranching & Farming

0213   Hogs *see* NAICS 11221: Hog & Pig Farming

0214   Sheep & Goats *see* NAICS 11241: Sheep Farming; NAICS 11242: Goat Farming

0219   General Livestock, Except Dairy & Poultry *see* NAICS 11299: All Other Animal Production

0241   Dairy Farms *see* NAICS 112111: Beef Cattle Ranching & Farming; NAICS 11212: Dairy Cattle & Milk Production

0251   Broiler, Fryers, & Roaster Chickens *see* NAICS 11232: Broilers & Other Meat-type Chicken Production

0252   Chicken Eggs *see* NAICS 11231: Chicken Egg Production

0253   Turkey & Turkey Eggs *see* NAICS 11233: Turkey Production

0254   Poultry Hatcheries *see* NAICS 11234: Poultry Hatcheries

0259   Poultry & Eggs, NEC *see* NAICS 11239: Other Poultry Production

0271   Fur-Bearing Animals & Rabbits *see* NAICS 11293: Fur-bearing Animal & Rabbit Production

0272   Horses & Other Equines *see* NAICS 11292: Horse & Other Equine Production

0273   Animal Aquaculture *see* NAICS 112511: Finfish Farming & Fish Hatcheries; NAICS 112512: Shellfish Farming; NAICS 112519: Other Animal Aquaculture

0279   Animal Specialities, NEC *see* NAICS 11291: Apiculture; NAICS 11299: All Other Animal Production

0291   General Farms, Primarily Livestock & Animal Specialties *see* NAICS 11299: All Other Animal Production

0711   Soil Preparation Services *see* NAICS 115112: Soil Preparation, Planting & Cultivating

0721   Crop Planting, Cultivating & Protecting *see* NAICS
       481219: Other Nonscheduled Air Transportation;
       NAICS 115112: Soil Preparation, Planting & Cultivating

0722   Crop Harvesting, Primarily by Machine *see* NAICS
       115113: Crop Harvesting, Primarily by Machine

0723   Crop Preparation Services for Market, Except Cotton
       Ginning *see* NAICS 115114: Postharvest Crop Activi-
       ties

0724   Cotton Ginning *see* NAICS 115111: Cotton Ginning

0741   Veterinary Service for Livestock *see* NAICS 54194:
       Veterinary Services

0742   Veterinary Services for Animal Specialties *see* NAICS
       54194: Veterinary Services

0751   Livestock Services, Except Veterinary *see* NAICS
       311611: Animal Slaughtering; NAICS 11521: Support
       Activities for Animal Production

0752   Animal Specialty Services, Except Veterinary *see*
       NAICS 11521: Support Activities for Animal Produc-
       tion; NAICS 81291: Pet Care Services

0761   Farm Labor Contractors & Crew Leaders *see* NAICS
       115115: Farm Labor Contractors & Crew Leaders

0762   Farm Management Services *see* NAICS 115116: Farm
       Management Services

0781   Landscape Counseling & Planning *see* NAICS 54169:
       Other Scientific & Technical Consulting Services;
       NAICS 54132: Landscape Architectural Services

0782   Lawn & Garden Services *see* NAICS 56173: Landscap-
       ing Services

0783   Ornamental Shrub & Tree Services *see* NAICS 56173:
       Landscaping Services

0811   Timber Tracts *see* NAICS 111421: Nursery & Tree Pro-
       duction; NAICS 11311: Timber Tract Operations

0831   Forest Nurseries & Gathering of Forest Products *see*
       NAICS 111998: All Other Miscellaneous Crop;
       NAICS 11321: Forest Nurseries & Gathering of Forest
       Products

0851   Forestry Services *see* NAICS 11531: Support Activities
       for Forestry

0912   Finfish *see* NAICS 114111: Finfish Fishing

0913   Shellfish *see* NAICS 114112: Shellfish Fishing

0919   Miscellaneous Marine Products *see* NAICS 114119:
       Other Marine Fishing; NAICS 111998: All Other Mis-
       cellaneous Crop Farming

0921   Fish Hatcheries & Preserves *see* NAICS 112511: Finfish
       Farming & Fish Hatcheries; NAICS 112512: Shellfish
       Farming

0971   Hunting, Trapping, & Game Propagation *see* NAICS
       11421: Hunting & Trapping

MINING INDUSTRIES

1011   Iron Ores *see* NAICS 21221: Iron Ore Mining

1021   Copper Ores *see* NAICS 212234: Copper Ore & Nickel
       Ore Mining

1031   Lead & Zinc Ores *see* NAICS 212231: Lead Ore &
       Zinc Ore Mining

1041   Gold Ores *see* NAICS 212221: Gold Ore Mining

1044   Silver Ores *see* NAICS 212222: Silver Ore Mining

1061   Ferroalloy Ores, Except Vanadium *see* NAICS 212234:
       Copper Ore & Nickel Ore Mining; NAICS 212299:
       Other Metal Ore Mining

1081   Metal Mining Services *see* NAICS 213114: Support Ac-
       tivities for Metal Mining; NAICS 54136: Geophysical
       Surveying & Mapping Services

1094   Uranium-radium-vanadium Ores *see* NAICS 212291:
       Uranium-radium-vanadium Ore Mining

1099   Miscellaneous Metal Ores, NEC *see* NAICS 212299:
       Other Metal Ore Mining

1221   Bituminous Coal & Lignite Surface Mining *see* NAICS
       212111: Bituminous Coal & Lignite Surface Mining

1222   Bituminous Coal Underground Mining *see* NAICS
       212112: Bituminous Coal Underground Mining

1231   Anthracite Mining *see* NAICS 212113: Anthracite Mining

1241   Coal Mining Services *see* NAICS 213113: Support Ac-
       tivities for Coal Mining

1311   Crude Petroleum & Natural Gas *see* NAICS 211111:
       Crude Petroleum & Natural Gas Extraction

1321   Natural Gas Liquids *see* NAICS 211112: Natural Gas
       Liquid Extraction

1381   Drilling Oil & Gas Wells *see* NAICS 213111: Drilling
       Oil & Gas Wells

1382   Oil & Gas Field Exploration Services *see* NAICS
       54136: Geophysical Surveying & Mapping Services;
       NAICS 213112: Support Activities for Oil & Gas
       Field Operations

1389   Oil & Gas Field Services, NEC *see* NAICS 213112:
       Support Activities for Oil & Gas Field Operations

1411   Dimension Stone *see* NAICS 212311: Dimension Stone
       Mining & Quarry

1422   Crushed & Broken Limestone *see* NAICS 212312:
       Crushed & Broken Limestone Mining & Quarrying

1423   Crushed & Broken Granite *see* NAICS 212313: Crushed
       & Broken Granite Mining & Quarrying

1429   Crushed & Broken Stone, NEC *see* NAICS 212319:
       Other Crushed & Broken Stone Mining & Quarrying

1442   Construction Sand & Gravel *see* NAICS 212321: Con-
       struction Sand & Gravel Mining

1446   Industrial Sand *see* NAICS 212322: Industrial Sand
       Mining

1455   Kaolin & Ball Clay *see* NAICS 212324: Kaolin & Ball
       Clay Mining

1459   Clay, Ceramic, & Refractory Minerals, NEC *see* NAICS
       212325: Clay & Ceramic & Refractory Minerals Min-
       ing

1474   Potash, Soda, & Borate Minerals *see* NAICS 212391:
       Potash, Soda, & Borate Mineral Mining

1475   Phosphate Rock *see* NAICS 212392: Phosphate Rock
       Mining

1479   Chemical & Fertilizer Mineral Mining, NEC *see* NAICS
       212393: Other Chemical & Fertilizer Mineral Mining

1481   Nonmetallic Minerals Services Except Fuels *see* NAICS
       213115: Support Activities for Non-metallic Minerals,;
       NAICS 54136: Geophysical Surveying & Mapping
       Services

1499   Miscellaneous Nonmetallic Minerals, Except Fuels *see*
       NAICS 212319: Other Crushed & Broken Stone Min-
       ing or Quarrying; NAICS 212399: All Other Non-
       metallic Mineral Mining

CONSTRUCTION INDUSTRIES

1521   General Contractors-single-family Houses *see* NAICS
       23321: Single Family Housing Construction

1522   General Contractors-residential Buildings, Other than
       Single-family *see* NAICS 23332: Commercial & Insti-
       tutional Building Construction; NAICS 23322: Multi-
       family Housing Construction

1531   Operative Builders *see* NAICS 23321: Single Family
       Housing Construction; NAICS 23322: Multifamily
       Housing Construction; NAICS 23331: Manufacturing
       & Industrial Building Construction; NAICS 23332:
       Commercial & Institutional Building Construction

1541   General Contractors-industrial Buildings & Warehouses *see* NAICS 23332: Commercial & Institutional Building Construction; NAICS 23331: Manufacturing & Industrial Building Construction

1542   General Contractors-nonresidential Buildings, Other than Industrial Buildings & Warehouses *see* NAICS 23332: Commercial & Institutional Building Construction

1611   Highway & Street Construction, Except Elevated Highways *see* NAICS 23411: Highway & Street Construction

1622   Bridge, Tunnel, & Elevated Highway Construction *see* NAICS 23412: Bridge & Tunnel Construction

1623   Water, Sewer, Pipeline, & Communications & Power Line Construction *see* NAICS 23491: Water, Sewer & Pipeline Construction; NAICS 23492: Power & Communication Transmission Line Construction

1629   Heavy Construction, NEC *see* NAICS 23493: Industrial Nonbuilding Structure Construction; NAICS 23499: All Other Heavy Construction

1711   Plumbing, Heating, & Air-conditioning *see* NAICS 23511: Plumbing, Heating & Air-conditioning Contractors

1721   Painting & Paper Hanging *see* NAICS 23521: Painting & Wall Covering Contractors

1731   Electrical Work *see* NAICS 561621: Security Systems Services; NAICS 23531: Electrical Contractors

1741   Masonry, Stone Setting & Other Stone Work *see* NAICS 23541: Masonry & Stone Contractors

1742   Plastering, Drywall, Acoustical & Insulation Work *see* NAICS 23542: Drywall, Plastering, Acoustical & Insulation Contractors

1743   Terrazzo, Tile, Marble, & Mosaic Work *see* NAICS 23542: Drywall, Plastering, Acoustical & Insulation Contractors; NAICS 23543: Tile, Marble, Terrazzo & Mosaic Contractors

1751   Carpentry Work *see* NAICS 23551: Carpentry Contractors

1752   Floor Laying & Other Floor Work, NEC *see* NAICS 23552: Floor Laying & Other Floor Contractors

1761   Roofing, Siding, & Sheet Metal Work *see* NAICS 23561: Roofing, Siding, & Sheet Metal Contractors

1771   Concrete Work *see* NAICS 23542: Drywall, Plastering, Acoustical & Insulation Contractors; NAICS 23571: Concrete Contractors

1781   Water Well Drilling *see* NAICS 23581: Water Well Drilling Contractors

1791   Structural Steel Erection *see* NAICS 23591: Structural Steel Erection Contractors

1793   Glass & Glazing Work *see* NAICS 23592: Glass & Glazing Contractors

1794   Excavation Work *see* NAICS 23593: Excavation Contractors

1795   Wrecking & Demolition Work *see* NAICS 23594: Wrecking & Demolition Contractors

1796   Installation or Erection of Building Equipment, NEC *see* NAICS 23595: Building Equipment & Other Machinery Installation Contractors

1799   Special Trade Contractors, NEC *see* NAICS 23521: Painting & Wall Covering Contractors; NAICS 23592: Glass & Glazing Contractors; NAICS 56291: Remediation Services; NAICS 23599: All Other Special Trade Contractors

FOOD & KINDRED PRODUCTS

2011   Meat Packing Plants *see* NAICS 311611: Animal Slaughtering

2013   Sausages & Other Prepared Meats *see* NAICS 311612: Meat Processed from Carcasses

2015   Poultry Slaughtering & Processing *see* NAICS 311615: Poultry Processing; NAICS 311999: All Other Miscellaneous Food Manufacturing

2021   Creamery Butter *see* NAICS 311512: Creamery Butter Manufacturing

2022   Natural, Processed, & Imitation Cheese *see* NAICS 311513: Cheese Manufacturing

2023   Dry, Condensed, & Evaporated Dairy Products *see* NAICS 311514: Dry, Condensed, & Evaporated Dairy Product Manufacturing

2024   Ice Cream & Frozen Desserts *see* NAICS 31152: Ice Cream & Frozen Dessert Manufacturing

2026   Fluid Milk *see* NAICS 311511: Fluid Milk Manufacturing

2032   Canned Specialties *see* NAICS 311422: Specialty Canning; NAICS 311999: All Other Miscellaneous Food Manufacturing

2033   Canned Fruits, Vegetables, Preserves, Jams, & Jellies *see* NAICS 311421: Fruit & Vegetable Canning

2034   Dried & Dehydrated Fruits, Vegetables, & Soup Mixes *see* NAICS 311423: Dried & Dehydrated Food Manufacturing; NAICS 311211: Flour Milling

2035   Pickled Fruits & Vegetables, Vegetables Sauces & Seasonings, & Salad Dressings *see* NAICS 311421: Fruit & Vegetable Canning; NAICS 311941: Mayonnaise, Dressing, & Other Prepared Sauce Manufacturing

2037   Frozen Fruits, Fruit Juices, & Vegetables *see* NAICS 311411: Frozen Fruit, Juice, & Vegetable Processing

2038   Frozen Specialties, NEC *see* NAICS 311412: Frozen Specialty Food Manufacturing

2041   Flour & Other Grain Mill Products *see* NAICS 311211: Flour Milling

2043   Cereal Breakfast Foods *see* NAICS 31192: Coffee & Tea Manufacturing; NAICS 31123: Breakfast Cereal Manufacturing

2044   Rice Milling *see* NAICS 311212: Rice Milling

2045   Prepared Flour Mixes & Doughs *see* NAICS 311822: Flour Mixes & Dough Manufacturing from Purchased Flour

2046   Wet Corn Milling *see* NAICS 311221: Wet Corn Milling

2047   Dog & Cat Food *see* NAICS 311111: Dog & Cat Food Manufacturing

2048   Prepared Feed & Feed Ingredients for Animals & Fowls, Except Dogs & Cats *see* NAICS 311611: Animal Slaughtering; NAICS 311119: Other Animal Food Manufacturing

2051   Bread & Other Bakery Products, Except Cookies & Crackers *see* NAICS 311812: Commercial Bakeries

2052   Cookies & Crackers *see* NAICS 311821: Cookie & Cracker Manufacturing; NAICS 311919: Other Snack Food Manufacturing; NAICS 311812: Commercial Bakeries

2053   Frozen Bakery Products, Except Bread *see* NAICS 311813: Frozen Bakery Product Manufacturing

2061   Cane Sugar, Except Refining *see* NAICS 311311: Sugarcane Mills

2062   Cane Sugar Refining *see* NAICS 311312: Cane Sugar Refining

2063   Beet Sugar *see* NAICS 311313: Beet Sugar Manufacturing

2064   Candy & Other Confectionery Products *see* NAICS 31133: Confectionery Manufacturing from Purchased Chocolate; NAICS 31134: Non-chocolate Confectionery Manufacturing

2066   Chocolate & Cocoa Products *see* NAICS 31132: Chocolate & Confectionery Manufacturing from Cacao Beans

2067   Chewing Gum *see* NAICS 31134: Non-chocolate Confectionery Manufacturing

2068   Salted & Roasted Nuts & Seeds *see* NAICS 311911:
        Roasted Nuts & Peanut Butter Manufacturing

2074   Cottonseed Oil Mills *see* NAICS 311223: Other Oilseed
        Processing; NAICS 311225: Fats & Oils Refining &
        Blending

2075   Soybean Oil Mills *see* NAICS 311222: Soybean Pro-
        cessing; NAICS 311225: Fats & Oils Refining &
        Blending

2076   Vegetable Oil Mills, Except Corn, Cottonseed, & Soy-
        beans *see* NAICS 311223: Other Oilseed Processing;
        NAICS 311225: Fats & Oils Refining & Blending

2077   Animal & Marine Fats & Oils *see* NAICS 311613: Ren-
        dering & Meat By-product Processing; NAICS
        311711: Seafood Canning; NAICS 311712: Fresh &
        Frozen Seafood Processing; NAICS 311225: Fats &
        Oils Refining & Blending

2079   Shortening, Table Oils, Margarine, & Other Edible Fats
        & Oils, NEC *see* NAICS 311225: Fats & Oils Refin-
        ing & Blending; NAICS 311222: Soybean Processing;
        NAICS 311223: Other Oilseed Processing

2082   Malt Beverages *see* NAICS 31212: Breweries

2083   Malt *see* NAICS 311213: Malt Manufacturing

2084   Wines, Brandy, & Brandy Spirits *see* NAICS 31213:
        Wineries

2085   Distilled & Blended Liquors *see* NAICS 31214: Distil-
        leries

2086   Bottled & Canned Soft Drinks & Carbonated Waters *see*
        NAICS 312111: Soft Drink Manufacturing; NAICS
        312112: Bottled Water Manufacturing

2087   Flavoring Extracts & Flavoring Syrups NEC *see* NAICS
        31193: Flavoring Syrup & Concentrate Manufacturing;
        NAICS 311942: Spice & Extract Manufacturing;
        NAICS 311999: All Other Miscellaneous Food Manu-
        facturing

2091   Canned & Cured Fish & Seafood *see* NAICS 311711:
        Seafood Canning

2092   Prepared Fresh or Frozen Fish & Seafoods *see* NAICS
        311712: Fresh & Frozen Seafood Processing

2095   Roasted Coffee *see* NAICS 31192: Coffee & Tea Manu-
        facturing; NAICS 311942: Spice & Extract Manufac-
        turing

2096   Potato Chips, Corn Chips, & Similar Snacks *see* NAICS
        311919: Other Snack Food Manufacturing

2097   Manufactured Ice *see* NAICS 312113: Ice Manufacturing

2098   Macaroni, Spaghetti, Vermicelli, & Noodles *see* NAICS
        311823: Pasta Manufacturing

2099   Food Preparations, NEC *see* NAICS 311423: Dried &
        Dehydrated Food Manufacturing; NAICS 111998: All
        Other Miscellaneous Crop Farming; NAICS 31134:
        Non-chocolate Confectionery Manufacturing; NAICS
        311911: Roasted Nuts & Peanut Butter Manufacturing;
        NAICS 311991: Perishable Prepared Food Manufac-
        turing; NAICS 31183: Tortilla Manufacturing; NAICS
        31192: Coffee & Tea Manufacturing; NAICS 311941:
        Mayonnaise, Dressing, & Other Prepared Sauce Manu-
        facturing; NAICS 311942: Spice & Extract Manufac-
        turing; NAICS 311999: All Other Miscellaneous Food
        Manufacturing

TOBACCO PRODUCTS

2111   Cigarettes *see* NAICS 312221: Cigarette Manufacturing

2121   Cigars *see* NAICS 312229: Other Tobacco Product
        Manufacturing

2131   Chewing & Smoking Tobacco & Snuff *see* NAICS
        312229: Other Tobacco Product Manufacturing

2141   Tobacco Stemming & Redrying *see* NAICS 312229:
        Other Tobacco Product Manufacturing; NAICS 31221:
        Tobacco Stemming & Redrying

TEXTILE MILL PRODUCTS

2211   Broadwoven Fabric Mills, Cotton *see* NAICS 31321:
        Broadwoven Fabric Mills

2221   Broadwoven Fabric Mills, Manmade Fiber & Silk *see*
        NAICS 31321: Broadwoven Fabric Mills

2231   Broadwoven Fabric Mills, Wool *see* NAICS 31321:
        Broadwoven Fabric Mills; NAICS 313311: Broadwo-
        ven Fabric Finishing Mills; NAICS 313312: Textile &
        Fabric Finishing Mills

2241   Narrow Fabric & Other Smallware Mills: Cotton, Wool,
        Silk, & Manmade Fiber *see* NAICS 313221: Narrow
        Fabric Mills

2251   Women's Full-length & Knee-length Hosiery, Except
        Socks *see* NAICS 315111: Sheer Hosiery Mills

2252   Hosiery, NEC *see* NAICS 315111: Sheer Hosiery Mills;
        NAICS 315119: Other Hosiery & Sock Mills

2253   Knit Outerwear Mills *see* NAICS 315191: Outerwear
        Knitting Mills

2254   Knit Underwear & Nightwear Mills *see* NAICS 315192:
        Underwear & Nightwear Knitting Mills

2257   Weft Knit Fabric Mills *see* NAICS 313241: Weft Knit
        Fabric Mills; NAICS 313312: Textile & Fabric Finish-
        ing Mills

2258   Lace & Warp Knit Fabric Mills *see* NAICS 313249:
        Other Knit Fabric & Lace Mills; NAICS 313312: Tex-
        tile & Fabric Finishing Mills

2259   Knitting Mills, NEC *see* NAICS 315191: Outerwear
        Knitting Mills; NAICS 315192: Underwear & Night-
        wear Knitting Mills; NAICS 313241: Weft Knit Fabric
        Mills; NAICS 313249: Other Knit Fabric & Lace Mills

2261   Finishers of Broadwoven Fabrics of Cotton *see* NAICS
        313311: Broadwoven Fabric Finishing Mills

2262   Finishers of Broadwoven Fabrics of Manmade Fiber &
        Silk *see* NAICS 313311: Broadwoven Fabric Finishing
        Mills

2269   Finishers of Textiles, NEC *see* NAICS 313311: Broad-
        woven Fabric Finishing Mills; NAICS 313312: Textile
        & Fabric Finishing Mills

2273   Carpets & Rugs *see* NAICS 31411: Carpet & Rug Mills

2281   Yarn Spinning Mills *see* NAICS 313111: Yarn Spinning
        Mills

2282   Yarn Texturizing, Throwing, Twisting, & Winding Mills
        see NAICS 313112: Yarn Texturing, Throwing &
        Twisting Mills; NAICS 313312: Textile & Fabric Fin-
        ishing Mills

2284   Thread Mills *see* NAICS 313113: Thread Mills; NAICS
        313312: Textile & Fabric Finishing Mills

2295   Coated Fabrics, Not Rubberized *see* NAICS 31332: Fab-
        ric Coating Mills

2296   Tire Cord & Fabrics *see* NAICS 314992: Tire Cord &
        Tire Fabric Mills

2297   Nonwoven Fabrics *see* NAICS 31323: Nonwoven Fabric
        Mills

2298   Cordage & Twine *see* NAICS 314991: Rope, Cordage
        & Twine Mills

2299   Textile Goods, NEC *see* NAICS 31321: Broadwoven
        Fabric Mills; NAICS 31323: Nonwoven Fabric Mills;
        NAICS 313312: Textile & Fabric Finishing Mills;
        NAICS 313221: Narrow Fabric Mills; NAICS 313113:
        Thread Mills; NAICS 313111: Yarn Spinning Mills;
        NAICS 314999: All Other Miscellaneous Textile
        Product Mills

APPAREL & OTHER FINISHED PRODUCTS MADE FROM FABRICS & SIMILAR MATERIALS

2311 Men's & Boys' Suits, Coats & Overcoats *see* NAICS 315211: Men's & Boys' Cut & Sew Apparel Contractors; NAICS 315222: Men's & Boys' Cut & Sew Suit, Coat, & Overcoat Manufacturing

2321 Men's & Boys' Shirts, Except Work Shirts *see* NAICS 315211: Men's & Boys' Cut & Sew Apparel Contractors; NAICS 315223: Men's & Boys' Cut & Sew Shirt, Manufacturing

2322 Men's & Boys' Underwear & Nightwear *see* NAICS 315211: Men's & Boys' Cut & Sew Apparel Contractors; NAICS 315221: Men's & Boys' Cut & Sew Underwear & Nightwear Manufacturing

2323 Men's & Boys' Neckwear *see* NAICS 315993: Men's & Boys' Neckwear Manufacturing

2325 Men's & Boys' Trousers & Slacks *see* NAICS 315211: Men's & Boys' Cut & Sew Apparel Contractors; NAICS 315224: Men's & Boys' Cut & Sew Trouser, Slack, & Jean Manufacturing

2326 Men's & Boys' Work Clothing *see* NAICS 315211: Men's & Boys' Cut & Sew Apparel Contractors; NAICS 315225: Men's & Boys' Cut & Sew Work Clothing Manufacturing

2329 Men's & Boys' Clothing, NEC *see* NAICS 315211: Men's & Boys' Cut & Sew Apparel Contractors; NAICS 315228: Men's & Boys' Cut & Sew Other Outerwear Manufacturing; NAICS 315299: All Other Cut & Sew Apparel Manufacturing

2331 Women's, Misses', & Juniors' Blouses & Shirts *see* NAICS 315212: Women's & Girls' Cut & Sew Apparel Contractors; NAICS 315232: Women's & Girls' Cut & Sew Blouse & Shirt Manufacturing

2335 Women's, Misses' & Junior's Dresses *see* NAICS 315212: Women's & Girls' Cut & Sew Apparel Contractors; NAICS 315233: Women's & Girls' Cut & Sew Dress Manufacturing

2337 Women's, Misses' & Juniors' Suits, Skirts & Coats; NAICS 315212: Women's & Girls' Cut & Sew Apparel Contractors; NAICS 315234: Women's & Girls' Cut & Sew Suit, Coat, Tailored Jacket, & Skirt Manufacturing

2339 Women's, Misses' & Juniors' Outerwear, NEC *see* NAICS 315999: Other Apparel Accessories & Other Apparel Manufacturing; NAICS 315212: Women's & Girls' Cut & Sew Apparel Contractors; NAICS 315299: All Other Cut & Sew Apparel Manufacturing; NAICS 315238: Women's & Girls' Cut & Sew Other Outerwear Manufacturing

2341 Women's, Misses, Children's, & Infants' Underwear & Nightwear *see* NAICS 315212: Women's & Girls' Cut & Sew Apparel Contractors; NAICS 315211: Men's & Boys' Cut & Sew Apparel Contractors; NAICS 315231: Women's & Girls' Cut & Sew Lingerie, Loungewear, & Nightwear Manufacturing; NAICS 315221: Men's & Boys' Cut & Sew Underwear & Nightwear Manufacturing; NAICS 315291: Infants' Cut & Sew Apparel Manufacturing

2342 Brassieres, Girdles, & Allied Garments *see* NAICS 315212: Women's & Girls' Cut & Sew Apparel Contractors; NAICS 315231: Women's & Girls' Cut & Sew Lingerie, Loungewear, & Nightwear Manufacturing

2353 Hats, Caps, & Millinery *see* NAICS 315991: Hat, Cap, & Millinery Manufacturing

2361 Girls', Children's & Infants' Dresses, Blouses & Shirts *see* NAICS 315291: Infants' Cut & Sew Apparel Manufacturing; NAICS 315223: Men's & Boys' Cut & Sew Shirt, Manufacturing; NAICS 315211: Men's & Boys' Cut & Sew Apparel Contractors; NAICS 315232: Women's & Girls' Cut & Sew Blouse & Shirt Manufacturing; NAICS 315233: Women's & Girls' Cut & Sew Dress Manufacturing; NAICS 315212: Women's & Girls' Cut & Sew Apparel Contractors

2369 Girls', Children's & Infants' Outerwear, NEC *see* NAICS 315291: Infants' Cut & Sew Apparel Manufacturing; NAICS 315222: Men's & Boys' Cut & Sew Suit, Coat, & Overcoat Manufacturing; NAICS 315224: Men's & Boys' Cut & Sew Trouser, Slack, & Jean Manufacturing; NAICS 315228: Men's & Boys' Cut & Sew Other Outerwear Manufacturing; NAICS 315221: Men's & Boys' Cut & Sew Underwear & Nightwear Manufacturing; NAICS 315211: Men's & Boys' Cut & Sew Apparel Contractors; NAICS 315234: Women's & Girls' Cut & Sew Suit, Coat, Tailored Jacket, & Skirt Manufacturing; NAICS 315238: Women's & Girls' Cut & Sew Other Outerwear Manufacturing; NAICS 315231: Women's & Girls' Cut & Sew Lingerie, Loungewear, & Nightwear Manufacturing; NAICS 315212: Women's & Girls' Cut & Sew Apparel Contractors

2371 Fur Goods *see* NAICS 315292: Fur & Leather Apparel Manufacturing

2381 Dress & Work Gloves, Except Knit & All-leather *see* NAICS 315992: Glove & Mitten Manufacturing

2384 Robes & Dressing Gowns *see* NAICS 315231: Women's & Girls' Cut & Sew Lingerie, Loungewear, & Nightwear Manufacturing; NAICS 315221: Men's & Boys' Cut & Sew Underwear & Nightwear Manufacturing; NAICS 315211: Men's & Boys' Cut & Sew Apparel Contractors; NAICS 315212: Women's & Girls' Cut & Sew Apparel Contractors

2385 Waterproof Outerwear *see* NAICS 315222: Men's & Boys' Cut & Sew Suit, Coat, & Overcoat Manufacturing; NAICS 315234: Women's & Girls' Cut & Sew Suit, Coat, Tailored Jacket, & Skirt Manufacturing; NAICS 315228: Men's & Boys' Cut & Sew Other Outerwear Manufacturing; NAICS 315238: Women's & Girls' Cut & Sew Other Outerwear Manufacturing; NAICS 315291: Infants' Cut & Sew Apparel Manufacturing; NAICS 315999: Other Apparel Accessories & Other Apparel Manufacturing; NAICS 315211: Men's & Boys' Cut & Sew Apparel Contractors; NAICS 315212: Women's & Girls' Cut & Sew Apparel Contractors

2386 Leather & Sheep-lined Clothing *see* NAICS 315292: Fur & Leather Apparel Manufacturing

2387 Apparel Belts *see* NAICS 315999: Other Apparel Accessories & Other Apparel Manufacturing

2389 Apparel & Accessories, NEC *see* NAICS 315999: Other Apparel Accessories & Other Apparel Manufacturing; NAICS 315299: All Other Cut & Sew Apparel Manufacturing; NAICS 315231: Women's & Girls' Cut & Sew Lingerie, Loungewear, & Nightwear Manufacturing; NAICS 315212: Women's & Girls' Cut & Sew Apparel Contractors; NAICS 315211: Mens' & Boys' Cut & Sew Apparel Contractors

2391 Curtains & Draperies *see* NAICS 314121: Curtain & Drapery Mills

2392 Housefurnishings, Except Curtains & Draperies *see* NAICS 314911: Textile Bag Mills; NAICS 339994: Broom, Brush & Mop Manufacturing; NAICS 314129: Other Household Textile Product Mills

2393   Textile Bags *see* NAICS 314911: Textile Bag Mills

2394   Canvas & Related Products *see* NAICS 314912: Canvas & Related Product Mills

2395   Pleating, Decorative & Novelty Stitching, & Tucking for the Trade *see* NAICS 314999: All Other Miscellaneous Textile Product Mills; NAICS 315211: Mens' & Boys' Cut & Sew Apparel Contractors; NAICS 315212: Women's & Girls' Cut & Sew Apparel Contractors

2396   Automotive Trimmings, Apparel Findings, & Related Products *see* NAICS 33636: Motor Vehicle Fabric Accessories & Seat Manufacturing; NAICS 315999: Other Apparel Accessories, & Other Apparel Manufacturing; NAICS 323113: Commercial Screen Printing; NAICS 314999: All Other Miscellaneous Textile Product Mills

2397   Schiffli Machine Embroideries *see* NAICS 313222: Schiffli Machine Embroidery

2399   Fabricated Textile Products, NEC *see* NAICS 33636: Motor Vehicle Fabric Accessories & Seat Manufacturing; NAICS 315999: Other Apparel Accessories & Other Apparel Manufacturing; NAICS 314999: All Other Miscellaneous Textile Product Mills

LUMBER & WOOD PRODUCTS, EXCEPT FURNITURE

2411   Logging *see* NAICS 11331: Logging

2421   Sawmills & Planing Mills, General *see* NAICS 321912: Cut Stock, Resawing Lumber, & Planing; NAICS 321113: Sawmills; NAICS 321918: Other Millwork; NAICS 321999: All Other Miscellaneous Wood Product Manufacturing

2426   Hardwood Dimension & Flooring Mills *see* NAICS 321918: Other Millwork; NAICS 321999: All Other Miscellaneous Wood Product Manufacturing; NAICS 337215: Showcase, Partition, Shelving, & Locker Manufacturing; NAICS 321912: Cut Stock, Resawing Lumber, & Planing

2429   Special Product Sawmills, NEC *see* NAICS 321113: Sawmills; NAICS 321912: Cut Stock, Resawing Lumber, & Planing; NAICS 321999: All Other Miscellaneous Wood Product Manufacturing

2431   Millwork *see* NAICS 321911: Wood Window & Door Manufacturing; NAICS 321918: Other Millwork

2434   Wood Kitchen Cabinets *see* NAICS 33711: Wood Kitchen Cabinet & Counter Top Manufacturing

2435   Hardwood Veneer & Plywood *see* NAICS 321211: Hardwood Veneer & Plywood Manufacturing

2436   Softwood Veneer & Plywood *see* NAICS 321212: Softwood Veneer & Plywood Manufacturing

2439   Structural Wood Members, NEC *see* NAICS 321912: Cut Stock, Resawing Lumber, & Planing; NAICS 321214: Truss Manufacturing; NAICS 321213: Engineered Wood Member Manufacturing

2441   Nailed & Lock Corner Wood Boxes & Shook *see* NAICS 32192: Wood Container & Pallet Manufacturing

2448   Wood Pallets & Skids *see* NAICS 32192: Wood Container & Pallet Manufacturing

2449   Wood Containers, NEC *see* NAICS 32192: Wood Container & Pallet Manufacturing

2451   Mobile Homes *see* NAICS 321991: Manufactured Home Manufacturing

2452   Prefabricated Wood Buildings & Components *see* NAICS 321992: Prefabricated Wood Building Manufacturing

2491   Wood Preserving *see* NAICS 321114: Wood Preservation

2493   Reconstituted Wood Products *see* NAICS 321219: Reconstituted Wood Product Manufacturing

2499   Wood Products, NEC *see* NAICS 339999: All Other Miscellaneous Manufacturing; NAICS 32192: Wood Container & Pallet Manufacturing; NAICS 321999: All Other Miscellaneous Wood Product Manufacturing

FURNITURE & FIXTURES

2511   Wood Household Furniture, Except Upholstered *see* NAICS 337122: Wood Household Furniture Manufacturing

2512   Wood Household Furniture, Upholstered *see* NAICS 337121: Upholstered Household Furniture Manufacturing

2514   Metal Household Furniture *see* NAICS 337124: Metal Household Furniture Manufacturing

2515   Mattresses, Foundations, & Convertible Beds *see* NAICS 33791: Mattress Manufacturing; NAICS 337121: Upholstered Household Furniture Manufacturing

2517   Wood Television, Radio, Phonograph & Sewing Machine Cabinets *see* NAICS 337129: Wood Television, Radio, & Sewing Machine Cabinet Manufacturing

2519   Household Furniture, NEC *see* NAICS 337125: Household Furniture Manufacturing

2521   Wood Office Furniture *see* NAICS 337211: Wood Office Furniture Manufacturing

2522   Office Furniture, Except Wood *see* NAICS 337214: Nonwood Office Furniture Manufacturing

2531   Public Building & Related Furniture *see* NAICS 33636: Motor Vehicle Fabric Accessories & Seat Manufacturing; NAICS 337127: Institutional Furniture Manufacturing; NAICS 339942: Lead Pencil & Art Good Manufacturing

2541   Wood Office & Store Fixtures, Partitions, Shelving, & Lockers *see* NAICS 33711: Wood Kitchen Cabinet & Counter Top Manufacturing; NAICS 337212: Custom Architectural Woodwork, & Millwork Manufacturing; NAICS 337215: Showcase, Partition, Shelving, & Locker Manufacturing

2542   Office & Store Fixtures, Partitions Shelving, & Lockers, Except Wood *see* NAICS 337215: Showcase, Partition, Shelving, & Locker Manufacturing

2591   Drapery Hardware & Window Blinds & Shades *see* NAICS 33792: Blind & Shade Manufacturing

2599   Furniture & Fixtures, NEC *see* NAICS 339113: Surgical Appliance & Supplies Manufacturing; NAICS 337127: Institutional Furniture Manufacturing

PAPER & ALLIED PRODUCTS

2611   Pulp Mills *see* NAICS 32211: Pulp Mills; NAICS 322121: Paper Mills; NAICS 32213: Paperboard Mills

2621   Paper Mills *see* NAICS 322121: Paper Mills; NAICS 322122: Newsprint Mills

2631   Paperboard Mills *see* NAICS 32213: Paperboard Mills

2652   Setup Paperboard Boxes *see* NAICS 322213: Setup Paperboard Box Manufacturing

2653   Corrugated & Solid Fiber Boxes *see* NAICS 322211: Corrugated & Solid Fiber Box Manufacturing

2655   Fiber Cans, Tubes, Drums, & Similar Products *see* NAICS 322214: Fiber Can, Tube, Drum, & Similar Products Manufacturing

2656   Sanitary Food Containers, Except Folding *see* NAICS 322215: Non-folding Sanitary Food Container Manufacturing

2657   Folding Paperboard Boxes, Including Sanitary *see* NAICS 322212: Folding Paperboard Box Manufacturing

2671   Packaging Paper & Plastics Film, Coated & Laminated *see* NAICS 322221: Coated & Laminated Packaging Paper & Plastics Film Manufacturing; NAICS 326112: Unsupported Plastics Packaging Film & Sheet Manufacturing

2672   Coated & Laminated Paper, NEC *see* NAICS 322222: Coated & Laminated Paper Manufacturing

2673   Plastics, Foil, & Coated Paper Bags *see* NAICS 322223: Plastics, Foil, & Coated Paper Bag Manufacturing; NAICS 326111: Unsupported Plastics Bag Manufacturing

2674   Uncoated Paper & Multiwall Bags *see* NAICS 322224: Uncoated Paper & Multiwall Bag Manufacturing

2675   Die-cut Paper & Paperboard & Cardboard *see* NAICS 322231: Die-cut Paper & Paperboard Office Supplies Manufacturing; NAICS 322292: Surface-coated Paperboard Manufacturing; NAICS 322298: All Other Converted Paper Product Manufacturing

2676   Sanitary Paper Products *see* NAICS 322291: Sanitary Paper Product Manufacturing

2677   Envelopes *see* NAICS 322232: Envelope Manufacturing

2678   Stationery, Tablets, & Related Products *see* NAICS 322233: Stationery, Tablet, & Related Product Manufacturing

2679   Converted Paper & Paperboard Products, NEC *see* NAICS 322215: Non-folding Sanitary Food Container Manufacturing; NAICS 322222: Coated & Laminated Paper Manufacturing; NAICS 322231: Die-cut Paper & Paperboard Office Supplies Manufacturing; NAICS 322298: All Other Converted Paper Product Manufacturing

PRINTING, PUBLISHING, & ALLIED INDUSTRIES

2711   Newspapers: Publishing, or Publishing & Printing *see* NAICS 51111: Newspaper Publishers

2721   Periodicals: Publishing, or Publishing & Printing *see* NAICS 51112: Periodical Publishers

2731   Books: Publishing, or Publishing & Printing *see* NAICS 51223: Music Publishers; NAICS 51113: Book Publishers

2732   Book Printing *see* NAICS 323117: Book Printing

2741   Miscellaneous Publishing *see* NAICS 51114: Database & Directory Publishers; NAICS 51223: Music Publishers; NAICS 511199: All Other Publishers

2752   Commercial Printing, Lithographic *see* NAICS 323114: Quick Printing; NAICS 323110: Commercial Lithographic Printing

2754   Commercial Printing, Gravure *see* NAICS 323111: Commercial Gravure Printing

2759   Commercial Printing, NEC *see* NAICS 323113: Commercial Screen Printing; NAICS 323112: Commercial Flexographic Printing; NAICS 323114: Quick Printing; NAICS 323115: Digital Printing; NAICS 323119: Other Commercial Printing

2761   Manifold Business Forms *see* NAICS 323116: Manifold Business Form Printing

2771   Greeting Cards *see* NAICS 323110: Commercial Lithographic Printing; NAICS 323111: Commercial Gravure Printing; NAICS 323112: Commercial Flexographic Printing; NAICS 323113: Commercial Screen Printing; NAICS 323119: Other Commercial Printing; NAICS 511191: Greeting Card Publishers

2782   Blankbooks, Loose-leaf Binders & Devices *see* NAICS 323110: Commercial Lithographic Printing; NAICS 323111: Commercial Gravure Printing; NAICS 323112: Commercial Flexographic Printing; NAICS 323113: Commercial Screen Printing; NAICS 323119: Other Commercial Printing; NAICS 323118: Blankbook, Loose-leaf Binder & Device Manufacturing

2789   Bookbinding & Related Work *see* NAICS 323121: Tradebinding & Related Work

2791   Typesetting *see* NAICS 323122: Prepress Services

2796   Platemaking & Related Services *see* NAICS 323122: Prepress Services

CHEMICALS & ALLIED PRODUCTS

2812   Alkalies & Chlorine *see* NAICS 325181: Alkalies & Chlorine Manufacturing

2813   Industrial Gases *see* NAICS 32512: Industrial Gas Manufacturing

2816   Inorganic Pigments *see* NAICS 325131: Inorganic Dye & Pigment Manufacturing; NAICS 325182: Carbon Black Manufacturing

2819   Industrial Inorganic Chemicals, NEC *see* NAICS 325998: All Other Miscellaneous Chemical Product Manufacturing; NAICS 331311: Alumina Refining; NAICS 325131: Inorganic Dye & Pigment Manufacturing; NAICS 325188: All Other Basic Inorganic Chemical Manufacturing

2821   Plastics Material Synthetic Resins, & Nonvulcanizable Elastomers *see* NAICS 325211: Plastics Material & Resin Manufacturing

2822   Synthetic Rubber *see* NAICS 325212: Synthetic Rubber Manufacturing

2823   Cellulosic Manmade Fibers *see* NAICS 325221: Cellulosic Organic Fiber Manufacturing

2824   Manmade Organic Fibers, Except Cellulosic *see* NAICS 325222: Noncellulosic Organic Fiber Manufacturing

2833   Medicinal Chemicals & Botanical Products *see* NAICS 325411: Medicinal & Botanical Manufacturing

2834   Pharmaceutical Preparations *see* NAICS 325412: Pharmaceutical Preparation Manufacturing

2835   In Vitro & in Vivo Diagnostic Substances *see* NAICS 325412: Pharmaceutical Preparation Manufacturing; NAICS 325413: In-vitro Diagnostic Substance Manufacturing

2836   Biological Products, Except Diagnostic Substances *see* NAICS 325414: Biological Product Manufacturing

2841   Soaps & Other Detergents, Except Speciality Cleaners *see* NAICS 325611: Soap & Other Detergent Manufacturing

2842   Speciality Cleaning, Polishing, & Sanitary Preparations *see* NAICS 325612: Polish & Other Sanitation Good Manufacturing

2843   Surface Active Agents, Finishing Agents, Sulfonated Oils, & Assistants *see* NAICS 325613: Surface Active Agent Manufacturing

2844   Perfumes, Cosmetics, & Other Toilet Preparations *see* NAICS 32562: Toilet Preparation Manufacturing; NAICS 325611: Soap & Other Detergent Manufacturing

2851   Paints, Varnishes, Lacquers, Enamels, & Allied Products *see* NAICS 32551: Paint & Coating Manufacturing

2861   Gum & Wood Chemicals *see* NAICS 325191: Gum & Wood Chemical Manufacturing

2865   Cyclic Organic Crudes & Intermediates, & Organic Dyes & Pigments *see* NAICS 32511: Petrochemical Manufacturing; NAICS 325132: Organic Dye & Pigment Manufacturing; NAICS 325192: Cyclic Crude & Intermediate Manufacturing

2869   Industrial Organic Chemicals, NEC *see* NAICS 32511:
        Petrochemical Manufacturing; NAICS 325188: All
        Other Inorganic Chemical Manufacturing; NAICS
        325193: Ethyl Alcohol Manufacturing; NAICS 32512:
        Industrial Gas Manufacturing; NAICS 325199: All
        Other Basic Organic Chemical Manufacturing

2873   Nitrogenous Fertilizers *see* NAICS 325311: Nitrogenous
        Fertilizer Manufacturing

2874   Phosphatic Fertilizers *see* NAICS 325312: Phosphatic
        Fertilizer Manufacturing

2875   Fertilizers, Mixing Only *see* NAICS 325314: Fertilizer
        Manufacturing

2879   Pesticides & Agricultural Chemicals, NEC *see* NAICS
        32532: Pesticide & Other Agricultural Chemical Man-
        ufacturing

2891   Adhesives & Sealants *see* NAICS 32552: Adhesive
        Manufacturing

2892   Explosives *see* NAICS 32592: Explosives Manufacturing

2893   Printing Ink *see* NAICS 32591: Printing Ink Manufac-
        turing

2895   Carbon Black *see* NAICS 325182: Carbon Black Manu-
        facturing

2899   Chemicals & Chemical Preparations, NEC *see* NAICS
        32551: Paint & Coating Manufacturing; NAICS
        311942: Spice & Extract Manufacturing; NAICS
        325199: All Other Basic Organic Chemical Manufac-
        turing; NAICS 325998: All Other Miscellaneous
        Chemical Product Manufacturing

PETROLEUM REFINING & RELATED INDUSTRIES

2911   Petroleum Refining *see* NAICS 32411: Petroleum Re-
        fineries

2951   Asphalt Paving Mixtures & Blocks *see* NAICS 324121:
        Asphalt Paving Mixture & Block Manufacturing

2952   Asphalt Felts & Coatings *see* NAICS 324122: Asphalt
        Shingle & Coating Materials Manufacturing

2992   Lubricating Oils & Greases *see* NAICS 324191: Petro-
        leum Lubricating Oil & Grease Manufacturing 2999

RUBBER & MISCELLANEOUS PLASTICS PRODUCTS

3011   Tires & Inner Tubes *see* NAICS 326211: Tire Manufac-
        turing

3021   Rubber & Plastics Footwear *see* NAICS 316211: Rubber
        & Plastics Footwear Manufacturing

3052   Rubber & Plastics Hose & Belting *see* NAICS 32622:
        Rubber & Plastics Hoses & Belting Manufacturing

3053   Gaskets, Packing, & Sealing Devices *see* NAICS 339991:
        Gasket, Packing, & Sealing Device Manufacturing

3061   Molded, Extruded, & Lathe-cut Mechanical Rubber
        Products *see* NAICS 326291: Rubber Product Manu-
        facturing for Mechanical Use

3069   Fabricated Rubber Products, NEC *see* NAICS 31332:
        Fabric Coating Mills; NAICS 326192: Resilient Floor
        Covering Manufacturing; NAICS 326299: All Other
        Rubber Product Manufacturing

3081   Unsupported Plastics Film & Sheet *see* NAICS 326113:
        Unsupported Plastics Film & Sheet Manufacturing

3082   Unsupported Plastics Profile Shapes *see* NAICS 326121:
        Unsupported Plastics Profile Shape Manufacturing

3083   Laminated Plastics Plate, Sheet, & Profile Shapes *see*
        NAICS 32613: Laminated Plastics Plate, Sheet, &
        Shape Manufacturing

3084   Plastic Pipe *see* NAICS 326122: Plastic Pipe & Pipe
        Fitting Manufacturing

3085   Plastics Bottles *see* NAICS 32616: Plastics Bottle Man-
        ufacturing

3086   Plastics Foam Products *see* NAICS 32615: Urethane &
        Other Foam Product Manufacturing; NAICS 32614:
        Polystyrene Foam Product Manufacturing

3087   Custom Compounding of Purchased Plastics Resins *see*
        NAICS 325991: Custom Compounding of Purchased
        Resin

3088   Plastics Plumbing Fixtures *see* NAICS 326191: Plastics
        Plumbing Fixtures Manufacturing

3089   Plastics Products, NEC *see* NAICS 326122: Plastics
        Pipe & Pipe Fitting Manufacturing; NAICS 326121:
        Unsupported Plastics Profile Shape Manufacturing;
        NAICS 326199: All Other Plastics Product Manufac-
        turing

LEATHER & LEATHER PRODUCTS

3111   Leather Tanning & Finishing *see* NAICS 31611: Leather
        & Hide Tanning & Finishing

3131   Boot & Shoe Cut Stock & Findings *see* NAICS 321999:
        All Other Miscellaneous Wood Product Manufactur-
        ing; NAICS 339993: Fastener, Button, Needle, & Pin
        Manufacturing; NAICS 316999: All Other Leather
        Good Manufacturing

3142   House Slippers *see* NAICS 316212: House Slipper Man-
        ufacturing

3143   Men's Footwear, Except Athletic *see* NAICS 316213:
        Men's Footwear Manufacturing

3144   Women's Footwear, Except Athletic *see* NAICS
        316214: Women's Footwear Manufacturing

3149   Footwear, Except Rubber, NEC *see* NAICS 316219:
        Other Footwear Manufacturing

3151   Leather Gloves & Mittens *see* NAICS 315992: Glove &
        Mitten Manufacturing

3161   Luggage *see* NAICS 316991: Luggage Manufacturing

3171   Women's Handbags & Purses *see* NAICS 316992:
        Women's Handbag & Purse Manufacturing

3172   Personal Leather Goods, Except Women's Handbags &
        Purses *see* NAICS 316993: Personal Leather Good
        Manufacturing

3199   Leather Goods, NEC *see* NAICS 316999: All Other
        Leather Good Manufacturing

STONE, CLAY, GLASS, & CONCRETE PRODUCTS

3211   Flat Glass *see* NAICS 327211: Flat Glass Manufacturing

3221   Glass Containers *see* NAICS 327213: Glass Container
        Manufacturing

3229   Pressed & Blown Glass & Glassware, NEC *see* NAICS
        327212: Other Pressed & Blown Glass & Glassware
        Manufacturing

3231   Glass Products, Made of Purchased Glass *see* NAICS
        327215: Glass Product Manufacturing Made of Pur-
        chased Glass

3241   Cement, Hydraulic *see* NAICS 32731: Cement Manu-
        facturing

3251   Brick & Structural Clay Tile *see* NAICS 327121: Brick
        & Structural Clay Tile Manufacturing

3253   Ceramic Wall & Floor Tile *see* NAICS 327122: Ce-
        ramic Wall & Floor Tile Manufacturing

3255   Clay Refractories *see* NAICS 327124: Clay Refractory
        Manufacturing

3259 Structural Clay Products, NEC *see* NAICS 327123: Other Structural Clay Product Manufacturing

3261 Vitreous China Plumbing Fixtures & China & Earthenware Fittings & Bathroom Accessories *see* NAICS 327111: Vitreous China Plumbing Fixture & China & Earthenware Fittings & Bathroom Accessories Manufacturing

3262 Vitreous China Table & Kitchen Articles *see* NAICS 327112: Vitreous China, Fine Earthenware & Other Pottery Product Manufacturing

3263 Fine Earthenware Table & Kitchen Articles *see* NAICS 327112: Vitreous China, Fine Earthenware & Other Pottery Product Manufacturing

3264 Porcelain Electrical Supplies *see* NAICS 327113: Porcelain Electrical Supply Manufacturing

3269 Pottery Products, NEC *see* NAICS 327112: Vitreous China, Fine Earthenware, & Other Pottery Product Manufacturing

3271 Concrete Block & Brick *see* NAICS 327331: Concrete Block & Brick Manufacturing

3272 Concrete Products, Except Block & Brick *see* NAICS 327999: All Other Miscellaneous Nonmetallic Mineral Product Manufacturing; NAICS 327332: Concrete Pipe Manufacturing; NAICS 32739: Other Concrete Product Manufacturing

3273 Ready-mixed Concrete *see* NAICS 32732: Ready-mix Concrete Manufacturing

3274 Lime *see* NAICS 32741: Lime Manufacturing

3275 Gypsum Products *see* NAICS 32742: Gypsum & Gypsum Product Manufacturing

3281 Cut Stone & Stone Products *see* NAICS 327991: Cut Stone & Stone Product Manufacturing

3291 Abrasive Products *see* NAICS 332999: All Other Miscellaneous Fabricated Metal Product Manufacturing; NAICS 32791: Abrasive Product Manufacturing

3292 Asbestos Products *see* NAICS 33634: Motor Vehicle Brake System Manufacturing; NAICS 327999: All Other Miscellaneous Nonmetallic Mineral Product Manufacturing

3295 Minerals & Earths, Ground or Otherwise Treated *see* NAICS 327992: Ground or Treated Mineral & Earth Manufacturing

3296 Mineral Wool *see* NAICS 327993: Mineral Wool Manufacturing

3297 Nonclay Refractories *see* NAICS 327125: Nonclay Refractory Manufacturing

3299 Nonmetallic Mineral Products, NEC *see* NAICS 32742: Gypsum & Gypsum Product Manufacturing; NAICS 327999: All Other Miscellaneous Nonmetallic Mineral Product Manufacturing

PRIMARY METALS INDUSTRIES

3312 Steel Works, Blast Furnaces , & Rolling Mills *see* NAICS 324199: All Other Petroleum & Coal Products Manufacturing; NAICS 331111: Iron & Steel Mills

3313 Electrometallurgical Products, Except Steel *see* NAICS 331112: Electrometallurgical Ferroalloy Product Manufacturing; NAICS 331492: Secondary Smelting, Refining, & Alloying of Nonferrous Metals

3315 Steel Wiredrawing & Steel Nails & Spikes *see* NAICS 331222: Steel Wire Drawing; NAICS 332618: Other Fabricated Wire Product Manufacturing

3316 Cold-rolled Steel Sheet, Strip, & Bars *see* NAICS 331221: Cold-rolled Steel Shape Manufacturing

3317 Steel Pipe & Tubes *see* NAICS 33121: Iron & Steel Pipes & Tubes Manufacturing from Purchased Steel

3321 Gray & Ductile Iron Foundries *see* NAICS 331511: Iron Foundries

3322 Malleable Iron Foundries *see* NAICS 331511: Iron Foundries

3324 Steel Investment Foundries *see* NAICS 331512: Steel Investment Foundries

3325 Steel Foundries, NEC *see* NAICS 331513: Steel Foundries

3331 Primary Smelting & Refining of Copper *see* NAICS 331411: Primary Smelting & Refining of Copper

3334 Primary Production of Aluminum *see* NAICS 331312: Primary Aluminum Production

3339 Primary Smelting & Refining of Nonferrous Metals, Except Copper & Aluminum *see* NAICS 331419: Primary Smelting & Refining of Nonferrous Metals

3341 Secondary Smelting & Refining of Nonferrous Metals *see* NAICS 331314: Secondary Smelting & Alloying of Aluminum; NAICS 331423: Secondary Smelting, Refining, & Alloying of Copper; NAICS 331492: Secondary Smelting, Refining, & Alloying of Nonferrous Metals

3351 Rolling, Drawing, & Extruding of Copper *see* NAICS 331421: Copper Rolling, Drawing, & Extruding

3353 Aluminum Sheet, Plate, & Foil *see* NAICS 331315: Aluminum Sheet, Plate, & Foil Manufacturing

3354 Aluminum Extruded Products *see* NAICS 331316: Aluminum Extruded Product Manufacturing

3355 Aluminum Rolling & Drawing, NEC *see* NAICS 331319: Other Aluminum Rolling & Drawing,

3356 Rolling, Drawing, & Extruding of Nonferrous Metals, Except Copper & Aluminum *see* NAICS 331491: Nonferrous Metal Rolling. Drawing, & Extruding

3357 Drawing & Insulating of Nonferrous Wire *see* NAICS 331319: Other Aluminum Rolling & Drawing; NAICS 331422: Copper Wire Drawing; NAICS 331491: Nonferrous Metal Rolling, Drawing, & Extruding; NAICS 335921: Fiber Optic Cable Manufacturing; NAICS 335929: Other Communication & Energy Wire Manufacturing

3363 Aluminum Die-castings *see* NAICS 331521: Aluminum Die-castings

3364 Nonferrous Die-castings, Except Aluminum *see* NAICS 331522: Nonferrous Die-castings

3365 Aluminum Foundries *see* NAICS 331524: Aluminum Foundries

3366 Copper Foundries *see* NAICS 331525: Copper Foundries

3369 Nonferrous Foundries, Except Aluminum & Copper *see* NAICS 331528: Other Nonferrous Foundries

3398 Metal Heat Treating *see* NAICS 332811: Metal Heat Treating

3399 Primary Metal Products, NEC *see* NAICS 331111: Iron & Steel Mills; NAICS 331314: Secondary Smelting & Alloying of Aluminum; NAICS 331423: Secondary Smelting, Refining & Alloying of Copper; NAICS 331492: Secondary Smelting, Refining, & Alloying of Nonferrous Metals; NAICS 332618: Other Fabricated Wire Product Manufacturing; NAICS 332813: Electroplating, Plating, Polishing, Anodizing, & Coloring

FABRICATED METAL PRODUCTS, EXCEPT MACHINERY & TRANSPORTATION EQUIPMENT

3411 Metal Cans *see* NAICS 332431: Metal Can Manufacturing

3412 Metal Shipping Barrels, Drums, Kegs & Pails *see* NAICS 332439: Other Metal Container Manufacturing

3421   Cutlery *see* NAICS 332211: Cutlery & Flatware Manufacturing

3423   Hand & Edge Tools, Except Machine Tools & Handsaws *see* NAICS 332212: Hand & Edge Tool Manufacturing

3425   Saw Blades & Handsaws *see* NAICS 332213: Saw Blade & Handsaw Manufacturing

3429   Hardware, NEC *see* NAICS 332439: Other Metal Container Manufacturing; NAICS 332919: Other Metal Valve & Pipe Fitting Manufacturing; NAICS 33251: Hardware Manufacturing

3431   Enameled Iron & Metal Sanitary Ware *see* NAICS 332998: Enameled Iron & Metal Sanitary Ware Manufacturing

3432   Plumbing Fixture Fittings & Trim *see* NAICS 332913: Plumbing Fixture Fitting & Trim Manufacturing; NAICS 332999: All Other Miscellaneous Fabricated Metal Product Manufacturing

3433   Heating Equipment, Except Electric & Warm Air Furnaces *see* NAICS 333414: Heating Equipment Manufacturing

3441   Fabricated Structural Metal *see* NAICS 332312: Fabricated Structural Metal Manufacturing

3442   Metal Doors, Sash, Frames, Molding, & Trim Manufacturing *see* NAICS 332321: Metal Window & Door Manufacturing

3443   Fabricated Plate Work *see* NAICS 332313: Plate Work Manufacturing; NAICS 33241: Power Boiler & Heat Exchanger Manufacturing; NAICS 33242: Metal Tank Manufacturing; NAICS 333415: Air-conditioning & Warm Air Heating Equipment & Commercial & Industrial Refrigeration Equipment Manufacturing

3444   Sheet Metal Work *see* NAICS 332322: Sheet Metal Work Manufacturing; NAICS 332439: Other Metal Container Manufacturing

3446   Architectural & Ornamental Metal Work *see* NAICS 332323: Ornamental & Architectural Metal Work Manufacturing

3448   Prefabricated Metal Buildings & Components *see* NAICS 332311: Prefabricated Metal Building & Component Manufacturing

3449   Miscellaneous Structural Metal Work *see* NAICS 332114: Custom Roll Forming; NAICS 332312: Fabricated Structural Metal Manufacturing; NAICS 332321: Metal Window & Door Manufacturing; NAICS 332323: Ornamental & Architectural Metal Work Manufacturing

3451   Screw Machine Products *see* NAICS 332721: Precision Turned Product Manufacturing

3452   Bolts, Nuts, Screws, Rivets, & Washers *see* NAICS 332722: Bolt, Nut, Screw, Rivet, & Washer Manufacturing

3462   Iron & Steel Forgings *see* NAICS 332111: Iron & Steel Forging

3463   Nonferrous Forgings *see* NAICS 332112: Nonferrous Forging

3465   Automotive Stamping *see* NAICS 33637: Motor Vehicle Metal Stamping

3466   Crowns & Closures *see* NAICS 332115: Crown & Closure Manufacturing

3469   Metal Stamping, NEC *see* NAICS 339911: Jewelry Manufacturing,; NAICS 332116: Metal Stamping; NAICS 332214: Kitchen Utensil, Pot & Pan Manufacturing

3471   Electroplating, Plating, Polishing, Anodizing, & Coloring *see* NAICS 332813: Electroplating, Plating, Polishing, Anodizing, & Coloring

3479   Coating, Engraving, & Allied Services, NEC *see* NAICS 339914: Costume Jewelry & Novelty Manufacturing; NAICS 339911: Jewelry Manufacturing; NAICS 339912: Silverware & Plated Ware Manufacturing; NAICS 332812: Metal Coating, Engraving , & Allied Services to Manufacturers

3482   Small Arms Ammunition *see* NAICS 332992: Small Arms Ammunition Manufacturing

3483   Ammunition, Except for Small Arms *see* NAICS 332993: Ammunition Manufacturing

3484   Small Arms *see* NAICS 332994: Small Arms Manufacturing

3489   Ordnance & Accessories, NEC *see* NAICS 332995: Other Ordnance & Accessories Manufacturing 3491

3492   Fluid Power Valves & Hose Fittings *see* NAICS 332912: Fluid Power Valve & Hose Fitting Manufacturing

3493   Steel Springs, Except Wire *see* NAICS 332611: Steel Spring Manufacturing

3494   Valves & Pipe Fittings, NEC *see* NAICS 332919: Other Metal Valve & Pipe Fitting Manufacturing; NAICS 332999: All Other Miscellaneous Fabricated Metal Product Manufacturing

3495   Wire Springs *see* NAICS 332612: Wire Spring Manufacturing; NAICS 334518: Watch, Clock, & Part Manufacturing

3496   Miscellaneous Fabricated Wire Products *see* NAICS 332618: Other Fabricated Wire Product Manufacturing

3497   Metal Foil & Leaf *see* NAICS 322225: Laminated Aluminum Foil Manufacturing for Flexible Packaging Uses; NAICS 332999: All Other Miscellaneous Fabricated Metal Product Manufacturing

3498   Fabricated Pipe & Pipe Fittings *see* NAICS 332996: Fabricated Pipe & Pipe Fitting Manufacturing

3499   Fabricated Metal Products, NEC *see* NAICS 337215: Showcase, Partition, Shelving, & Locker Manufacturing; NAICS 332117: Powder Metallurgy Part Manufacturing; NAICS 332439: Other Metal Container Manufacturing; NAICS 33251: Hardware Manufacturing; NAICS 332919: Other Metal Valve & Pipe Fitting Manufacturing; NAICS 339914: Costume Jewelry & Novelty Manufacturing; NAICS 332999: All Other Miscellaneous Fabricated Metal Product Manufacturing

INDUSTRIAL & COMMERCIAL MACHINERY & COMPUTER EQUIPMENT

3511   Steam, Gas, & Hydraulic Turbines, & Turbine Generator Set Units *see* NAICS 333611: Turbine & Turbine Generator Set Unit Manufacturing

3519   Internal Combustion Engines, NEC *see* NAICS 336399: All Other Motor Vehicle Parts Manufacturing; NAICS 333618: Other Engine Equipment Manufacturing

3523   Farm Machinery & Equipment *see* NAICS 333111: Farm Machinery & Equipment Manufacturing; NAICS 332323: Ornamental & Architectural Metal Work Manufacturing; NAICS 332212: Hand & Edge Tool Manufacturing; NAICS 333922: Conveyor & Conveying Equipment Manufacturing

3524   Lawn & Garden Tractors & Home Lawn & Garden Equipment *see* NAICS 333112: Lawn & Garden Tractor & Home Lawn & Garden Equipment Manufacturing; NAICS 332212: Hand & Edge Tool Manufacturing

3531   Construction Machinery & Equipment *see* NAICS 33651: Railroad Rolling Stock Manufacturing; NAICS

333923: Overhead Traveling Crane, Hoist, & Monorail System Manufacturing; NAICS 33312: Construction Machinery Manufacturing

3532   Mining Machinery & Equipment, Except Oil & Gas Field Machinery & Equipment *see* NAICS 333131: Mining Machinery & Equipment Manufacturing

3533   Oil & Gas Field Machinery & Equipment *see* NAICS 333132: Oil & Gas Field Machinery & Equipment Manufacturing

3534   Elevators & Moving Stairways *see* NAICS 333921: Elevator & Moving Stairway Manufacturing

3535   Conveyors & Conveying Equipment *see* NAICS 333922: Conveyor & Conveying Equipment Manufacturing

3536   Overhead Traveling Cranes, Hoists & Monorail Systems *see* NAICS 333923: Overhead Traveling Crane, Hoist & Monorail System Manufacturing

3537   Industrial Trucks, Tractors, Trailers, & Stackers *see* NAICS 333924: Industrial Truck, Tractor, Trailer, & Stacker Machinery Manufacturing; NAICS 332999: All Other Miscellaneous Fabricated Metal Product Manufacturing; NAICS 332439: Other Metal Container Manufacturing

3541   Machine Tools, Metal Cutting Type *see* NAICS 333512: Machine Tool Manufacturing

3542   Machine Tools, Metal Forming Type *see* NAICS 333513: Machine Tool Manufacturing

3543   Industrial Patterns *see* NAICS 332997: Industrial Pattern Manufacturing

3544   Special Dies & Tools, Die Sets, Jigs & Fixtures, & Industrial Molds *see* NAICS 333514: Special Die & Tool, Die Set, Jig, & Fixture Manufacturing; NAICS 333511: Industrial Mold Manufacturing

3545   Cutting Tools, Machine Tool Accessories, & Machinists' Precision Measuring Devices *see* NAICS 333515: Cutting Tool & Machine Tool Accessory Manufacturing; NAICS 332212: Hand & Edge Tool Manufacturing

3546   Power-driven Handtools *see* NAICS 333991: Power-driven Hand Tool Manufacturing

3547   Rolling Mill Machinery & Equipment *see* NAICS 333516: Rolling Mill Machinery & Equipment Manufacturing

3548   Electric & Gas Welding & Soldering Equipment *see* NAICS 333992: Welding & Soldering Equipment Manufacturing; NAICS 335311: Power, Distribution, & Specialty Transformer Manufacturing

3549   Metalworking Machinery, NEC *see* NAICS 333518: Other Metalworking Machinery Manufacturing 3552

3553   Woodworking Machinery *see* NAICS 33321: Sawmill & Woodworking Machinery Manufacturing

3554   Paper Industries Machinery *see* NAICS 333291: Paper Industry Machinery Manufacturing

3555   Printing Trades Machinery & Equipment *see* NAICS 333293: Printing Machinery & Equipment Manufacturing

3556   Food Products Machinery *see* NAICS 333294: Food Product Machinery Manufacturing

3559   Special Industry Machinery, NEC *see* NAICS 33322: Rubber & Plastics Industry Machinery Manufacturing; NAICS 333319: Other Commercial & Service Industry Machinery Manufacturing; NAICS 333295: Semiconductor Manufacturing Machinery; NAICS 333298: All Other Industrial Machinery Manufacturing

3561   Pumps & Pumping Equipment *see* NAICS 333911: Pump & Pumping Equipment Manufacturing

3562   Ball & Roller Bearings *see* NAICS 332991: Ball & Roller Bearing Manufacturing

3563   Air & Gas Compressors *see* NAICS 333912: Air & Gas Compressor Manufacturing

3564   Industrial & Commercial Fans & Blowers & Air Purification Equipment *see* NAICS 333411: Air Purification Equipment Manufacturing; NAICS 333412: Industrial & Commercial Fan & Blower Manufacturing

3565   Packaging Machinery *see* NAICS 333993: Packaging Machinery Manufacturing

3566   Speed Changers, Industrial High-speed Drives, & Gears *see* NAICS 333612: Speed Changer, Industrial High-speed Drive, & Gear Manufacturing

3567   Industrial Process Furnaces & Ovens *see* NAICS 333994: Industrial Process Furnace & Oven Manufacturing

3568   Mechanical Power Transmission Equipment, NEC *see* NAICS 333613: Mechanical Power Transmission Equipment Manufacturing

3569   General Industrial Machinery & Equipment, NEC *see* NAICS 333999: All Other General Purpose Machinery Manufacturing

3571   Electronic Computers *see* NAICS 334111: Electronic Computer Manufacturing

3572   Computer Storage Devices *see* NAICS 334112: Computer Storage Device Manufacturing

3575   Computer Terminals *see* NAICS 334113: Computer Terminal Manufacturing

3577   Computer Peripheral Equipment, NEC *see* NAICS 334119: Other Computer Peripheral Equipment Manufacturing

3578   Calculating & Accounting Machines, Except Electronic Computers *see* NAICS 334119: Other Computer Peripheral Equipment Manufacturing; NAICS 333313: Office Machinery Manufacturing

3579   Office Machines, NEC *see* NAICS 339942: Lead Pencil & Art Good Manufacturing; NAICS 334518: Watch, Clock, & Part Manufacturing; NAICS 333313: Office Machinery Manufacturing

3581   Automatic Vending Machines *see* NAICS 333311: Automatic Vending Machine Manufacturing

3582   Commercial Laundry, Drycleaning, & Pressing Machines *see* NAICS 333312: Commercial Laundry, Drycleaning, & Pressing Machine Manufacturing

3585   Air-conditioning & Warm Air Heating Equipment & Commercial & Industrial Refrigeration Equipment *see* NAICS 336391: Motor Vehicle Air Conditioning Manufacturing; NAICS 333415: Air Conditioning & Warm Air Heating Equipment & Commercial & Industrial Refrigeration Equipment Manufacturing

3586   Measuring & Dispensing Pumps *see* NAICS 333913: Measuring & Dispensing Pump Manufacturing 3589

3592   Carburetors, Pistons, Piston Rings & Valves *see* NAICS 336311: Carburetor, Piston, Piston Ring & Valve Manufacturing

3593   Fluid Power Cylinders & Actuators *see* NAICS 333995: Fluid Power Cylinder & Actuator Manufacturing

3594   Fluid Power Pumps & Motors *see* NAICS 333996: Fluid Power Pump & Motor Manufacturing

3596   Scales & Balances, Except Laboratory *see* NAICS 333997: Scale & Balance Manufacturing

3599   Industrial & Commercial Machinery & Equipment, NEC *see* NAICS 336399: All Other Motor Vehicle Part Manufacturing; NAICS 332999: All Other Miscellaneous Fabricated Metal Product Manufacturing; NAICS 333319: Other Commercial & Service Industry Machinery Manufacturing; NAICS 33271: Machine Shops; NAICS 333999: All Other General Purpose Machinery Manufacturing

ELECTRONIC & OTHER ELECTRICAL EQUIPMENT & COMPONENTS, EXCEPT COMPUTER EQUIPMENT

3612   Power, Distribution, & Specialty Transformers *see* NAICS 335311: Power, Distribution, & Specialty Transformer Manufacturing

3613   Switchgear & Switchboard Apparatus *see* NAICS 335313: Switchgear & Switchboard Apparatus Manufacturing

3621   Motors & Generators *see* NAICS 335312: Motor & Generator Manufacturing

3624   Carbon & Graphite Products *see* NAICS 335991: Carbon & Graphite Product Manufacturing

3625   Relays & Industrial Controls *see* NAICS 335314: Relay & Industrial Control Manufacturing

3629   Electrical Industrial Apparatus, NEC *see* NAICS 335999: All Other Miscellaneous Electrical Equipment & Component Manufacturing

3631   Household Cooking Equipment *see* NAICS 335221: Household Cooking Appliance Manufacturing

3632   Household Refrigerators & Home & Farm Freezers *see* NAICS 335222: Household Refrigerator & Home Freezer Manufacturing

3633   Household Laundry Equipment *see* NAICS 335224: Household Laundry Equipment Manufacturing

3634   Electric Housewares & Fans *see* NAICS 335211: Electric Housewares & Household Fan Manufacturing

3635   Household Vacuum Cleaners *see* NAICS 335212: Household Vacuum Cleaner Manufacturing

3639   Household Appliances, NEC *see* NAICS 335212: Household Vacuum Cleaner Manufacturing; NAICS 333298: All Other Industrial Machinery Manufacturing; NAICS 335228: Other Major Household Appliance Manufacturing

3641   Electric Lamp Bulbs & Tubes *see* NAICS 33511: Electric Lamp Bulb & Part Manufacturing

3643   Current-carrying Wiring Devices *see* NAICS 335931: Current-carrying Wiring Device Manufacturing

3644   Noncurrent-carrying Wiring Devices *see* NAICS 335932: Noncurrent-carrying Wiring Device Manufacturing

3645   Residential Electric Lighting Fixtures *see* NAICS 335121: Residential Electric Lighting Fixture Manufacturing

3646   Commercial, Industrial, & Institutional Electric Lighting Fixtures *see* NAICS 335122: Commercial, Industrial, & Institutional Electric Lighting Fixture Manufacturing

3647   Vehicular Lighting Equipment *see* NAICS 336321: Vehicular Lighting Equipment Manufacturing

3648   Lighting Equipment, NEC *see* NAICS 335129: Other Lighting Equipment Manufacturing

3651   Household Audio & Video Equipment *see* NAICS 33431: Audio & Video Equipment Manufacturing 3652; NAICS 51222: Integrated Record Production/distribution

3661   Telephone & Telegraph Apparatus *see* NAICS 33421: Telephone Apparatus Manufacturing; NAICS 334416: Electronic Coil, Transformer, & Other Inductor Manufacturing; NAICS 334418: Printed Circuit/electronics Assembly Manufacturing

3663   Radio & Television Broadcasting & Communication Equipment *see* NAICS 33422: Radio & Television Broadcasting & Wireless Communications Equipment Manufacturing

3669   Communications Equipment, NEC *see* NAICS 33429: Other Communication Equipment Manufacturing

3671   Electron Tubes *see* NAICS 334411: Electron Tube Manufacturing

3672   Printed Circuit Boards *see* NAICS 334412: Printed Circuit Board Manufacturing

3674   Semiconductors & Related Devices *see* NAICS 334413: Semiconductor & Related Device Manufacturing

3675   Electronic Capacitors *see* NAICS 334414: Electronic Capacitor Manufacturing

3676   Electronic Resistors *see* NAICS 334415: Electronic Resistor Manufacturing

3677   Electronic Coils, Transformers, & Other Inductors *see* NAICS 334416: Electronic Coil, Transformer, & Other Inductor Manufacturing

3678   Electronic ConNECtors *see* NAICS 334417: Electronic ConNECtor Manufacturing

3679   Electronic Components, NEC *see* NAICS 33422: Radio & Television Broadcasting & Wireless Communications Equipment Manufacturing; NAICS 334418: Printed Circuit/electronics Assembly Manufacturing; NAICS 336322: Other Motor Vehicle Electrical & Electronic Equipment Manufacturing; NAICS 334419: Other Electronic Component Manufacturing

3691   Storage Batteries *see* NAICS 335911: Storage Battery Manufacturing

3692   Primary Batteries, Dry & Wet *see* NAICS 335912: Dry & Wet Primary Battery Manufacturing

3694   Electrical Equipment for Internal Combustion Engines *see* NAICS 336322: Other Motor Vehicle Electrical & Electronic Equipment Manufacturing

3695   Magnetic & Optical Recording Media *see* NAICS 334613: Magnetic & Optical Recording Media Manufacturing

3699   Electrical Machinery, Equipment, & Supplies, NEC *see* NAICS 333319: Other Commercial & Service Industry Machinery Manufacturing; NAICS 333618: Other Engine Equipment Manufacturing; NAICS 334119: Other Computer Peripheral Equipment Manufacturing; Classify According to Function; NAICS 335129: Other Lighting Equipment Manufacturing; NAICS 335999: All Other Miscellaneous Electrical Equipment & Component Manufacturing

TRANSPORTATION EQUIPMENT

3711   Motor Vehicles & Passenger Car Bodies *see* NAICS 336111: Automobile Manufacturing; NAICS 336112: Light Truck & Utility Vehicle Manufacturing; NAICS 33612: Heavy Duty Truck Manufacturing; NAICS 336211: Motor Vehicle Body Manufacturing; NAICS 336992: Military Armored Vehicle, Tank, & Tank Component Manufacturing

3713   Truck & Bus Bodies *see* NAICS 336211: Motor Vehicle Body Manufacturing

3714   Motor Vehicle Parts & Accessories *see* NAICS 336211: Motor Vehicle Body Manufacturing; NAICS 336312: Gasoline Engine & Engine Parts Manufacturing; NAICS 336322: Other Motor Vehicle Electrical & Electronic Equipment Manufacturing; NAICS 33633: Motor Vehicle Steering & Suspension Components Manufacturing; NAICS 33634: Motor Vehicle Brake System Manufacturing; NAICS 33635: Motor Vehicle Transmission & Power Train Parts Manufacturing; NAICS 336399: All Other Motor Vehicle Parts Manufacturing

3715   Truck Trailers *see* NAICS 336212: Truck Trailer Manufacturing

3716   Motor Homes *see* NAICS 336213: Motor Home Manufacturing

3721   Aircraft *see* NAICS 336411: Aircraft Manufacturing

3724   Aircraft Engines & Engine Parts *see* NAICS 336412: Aircraft Engine & Engine Parts Manufacturing 3728; NAICS 336413: Other Aircraft Part & Auxiliary Equipment Manufacturing

3731   Ship Building & Repairing *see* NAICS 336611: Ship Building & Repairing

3732   Boat Building & Repairing *see* NAICS 81149: Other Personal & Household Goods Repair & Maintenance; NAICS 336612: Boat Building

3743   Railroad Equipment *see* NAICS 333911: Pump & Pumping Equipment Manufacturing; NAICS 33651: Railroad Rolling Stock Manufacturing

3751   Motorcycles, Bicycles, & Parts *see* NAICS 336991: Motorcycle, Bicycle, & Parts Manufacturing

3761   Guided Missiles & Space Vehicles *see* NAICS 336414: Guided Missile & Space Vehicle Manufacturing 3764

3769   Guided Missile Space Vehicle Parts & Auxiliary Equipment, NEC *see* NAICS 336419: Other Guided Missile & Space Vehicle Parts & Auxiliary Equipment Manufacturing

3792   Travel Trailers & Campers *see* NAICS 336214: Travel Trailer & Camper Manufacturing

3795   Tanks & Tank Components *see* NAICS 336992: Military Armored Vehicle, Tank, & Tank Component Manufacturing

3799   Transportation Equipment, NEC *see* NAICS 336214: Travel Trailer & Camper Manufacturing; NAICS 332212: Hand & Edge Tool Manufacturing; NAICS 336999: All Other Transportation Equipment Manufacturing

MEASURING, ANALYZING, & CONTROLLING INSTRUMENTS

3812   Search, Detection, Navigation, Guidance, Aeronautical, & Nautical Systems & Instruments *see* NAICS 334511: Search, Detection, Navigation, Guidance, Aeronautical, & Nautical System & Instrument Manufacturing

3821   Laboratory Apparatus & Furniture *see* NAICS 339111: Laboratory Apparatus & Furniture Manufacturing

3822   Automatic Controls for Regulating Residential & Commercial Environments & Appliances *see* NAICS 334512: Automatic Environmental Control Manufacturing for Regulating Residential, Commercial, & Appliance Use

3823   Industrial Instruments for Measurement, Display, & Control of Process Variables; & Related Products *see* NAICS 334513: Instruments & Related Product Manufacturing for Measuring Displaying, & Controlling Industrial Process Variables

3824   Totalizing Fluid Meters & Counting Devices *see* NAICS 334514: Totalizing Fluid Meter & Counting Device Manufacturing

3825   Instruments for Measuring & Testing of Electricity & Electrical Signals *see* NAICS 334416: Electronic Coil, Transformer, & Other Inductor Manufacturing; NAICS 334515: Instrument Manufacturing for Measuring & Testing Electricity & Electrical Signals

3826   Laboratory Analytical Instruments *see* NAICS 334516: Analytical Laboratory Instrument Manufacturing

3827   Optical Instruments & Lenses *see* NAICS 333314: Optical Instrument & Lens Manufacturing

3829   Measuring & Controlling Devices, NEC *see* NAICS 339112: Surgical & Medical Instrument Manufacturing; NAICS 334519: Other Measuring & Controlling Device Manufacturing

3841   Surgical & Medical Instruments & Apparatus *see* NAICS 339112: Surgical & Medical Instrument Manufacturing

3842   Orthopedic, Prosthetic, & Surgical Appliances & Supplies *see* NAICS 339113: Surgical Appliance & Supplies Manufacturing; NAICS 334510: Electromedical & Electrotherapeutic Apparatus Manufacturing

3843   Dental Equipment & Supplies *see* NAICS 339114: Dental Equipment & Supplies Manufacturing

3844   X-ray Apparatus & Tubes & Related Irradiation Apparatus *see* NAICS 334517: Irradiation Apparatus Manufacturing

3845   Electromedical & Electrotherapeutic Apparatus *see* NAICS 334517: Irradiation Apparatus Manufacturing; NAICS 334510: Electromedical & Electrotherapeutic Apparatus Manufacturing

3851   Ophthalmic Goods *see* NAICS 339115: Ophthalmic Goods Manufacturing

3861   Photographic Equipment & Supplies *see* NAICS 333315: Photographic & Photocopying Equipment Manufacturing; NAICS 325992: Photographic Film, Paper, Plate & Chemical Manufacturing

3873   Watches, Clocks, Clockwork Operated Devices & Parts *see* NAICS 334518: Watch, Clock, & Part Manufacturing

MISCELLANEOUS MANUFACTURING INDUSTRIES

3911   Jewelry, Precious Metal *see* NAICS 339911: Jewelry Manufacturing

3914   Silverware, Plated Ware, & Stainless Steel Ware *see* NAICS 332211: Cutlery & Flatware Manufacturing; NAICS 339912: Silverware & Plated Ware Manufacturing

3915   Jewelers' Findings & Materials, & Lapidary Work *see* NAICS 339913: Jewelers' Material & Lapidary Work Manufacturing

3931   Musical Instruments *see* NAICS 339992: Musical Instrument Manufacturing

3942   Dolls & Stuffed Toys *see* NAICS 339931: Doll & Stuffed Toy Manufacturing

3944   Games, Toys, & Children's Vehicles, Except Dolls & Bicycles *see* NAICS 336991: Motorcycle, Bicycle & Parts Manufacturing; NAICS 339932: Game, Toy, & Children's Vehicle Manufacturing

3949   Sporting & Athletic Goods, NEC *see* NAICS 33992: Sporting & Athletic Good Manufacturing

3951   Pens, Mechanical Pencils & Parts *see* NAICS 339941: Pen & Mechanical Pencil Manufacturing

3952   Lead Pencils, Crayons, & Artist's Materials *see* NAICS 337127: Institutional Furniture Manufacturing; NAICS 325998: All Other Miscellaneous Chemical Manufacturing; NAICS 339942: Lead Pencil & Art Good Manufacturing

3953   Marking Devices *see* NAICS 339943: Marking Device Manufacturing

3955   Carbon Paper & Inked Ribbons *see* NAICS 339944: Carbon Paper & Inked Ribbon Manufacturing

3961   Costume Jewelry & Costume Novelties, Except Precious Metals *see* NAICS 339914: Costume Jewelry & Novelty Manufacturing

3965   Fasteners, Buttons, Needles, & Pins *see* NAICS 339993:
        Fastener, Button, Needle & Pin Manufacturing

3991   Brooms & Brushes *see* NAICS 339994: Broom, Brush
        & Mop Manufacturing

3993   Signs & Advertising Specialties *see* NAICS 33995: Sign
        Manufacturing

3995   Burial Caskets *see* NAICS 339995: Burial Casket Manu-
        facturing

3996   Linoleum, Asphalted-felt-base, & Other Hard Surface
        Floor Coverings, NEC *see* NAICS 326192: Resilient
        Floor Covering Manufacturing

3999   Manufacturing Industries, NEC *see* NAICS 337127: In-
        stitutional Furniture Manufacturing; NAICS 321999:
        All Other Miscellaneous Wood Product Manufactur-
        ing; NAICS 31611: Leather & Hide Tanning & Fin-
        ishing; NAICS 335121: Residential Electric Lighting
        Fixture Manufacturing; NAICS 325998: All Other
        Miscellaneous Chemical Product Manufacturing;
        NAICS 332999: All Other Miscellaneous Fabricated
        Metal Product Manufacturing; NAICS 326199: All
        Other Plastics Product Manufacturing; NAICS
        323112: Commercial Flexographic Printing; NAICS
        323111: Commercial Gravure Printing; NAICS
        323110: Commercial Lithographic Printing; NAICS
        323113: Commercial Screen Printing; NAICS 323119:
        Other Commercial Printing; NAICS 332212: Hand &
        Edge Tool Manufacturing; NAICS 339999: All Other
        Miscellaneous Manufacturing

TRANSPORTATION, COMMUNICATIONS, ELECTRIC, GAS, & SANITARY SERVICES

4011   Railroads, Line-haul Operating *see* NAICS 482111:
        Line-haul Railroads

4013   Railroad Switching & Terminal Establishments *see*
        NAICS 482112: Short Line Railroads; NAICS 48821:
        Support Activities for Rail Transportation

4111   Local & Suburban Transit *see* NAICS 485111: Mixed
        Mode Transit Systems; NAICS 485112: Commuter
        Rail Systems; NAICS 485113: Bus & Motor Vehicle
        Transit Systems; NAICS 485119: Other Urban Transit
        Systems; NAICS 485999: All Other Transit & Ground
        Passenger Transportation

4119   Local Passenger Transportation, NEC *see* NAICS
        62191: Ambulance Service; NAICS 48541: School &
        Employee Bus Transportation; NAICS 48711: Scenic
        & Sightseeing Transportation , Land; NAICS 485991:
        Special Needs Transportation; NAICS 485999: All
        Other Transit & Ground Passenger Transportation;
        NAICS 48532: Limousine Service

4121   Taxicabs *see* NAICS 48531: Taxi Service

4131   Intercity & Rural Bus Transportation *see* NAICS 48521:
        Interurban & Rural Bus Transportation

4141   Local Bus Charter Service *see* NAICS 48551: Charter
        Bus Industry

4142   Bus Charter Service, Except Local *see* NAICS 48551:
        Charter Bus Industry

4151   School Buses *see* NAICS 48541: School & Employee
        Bus Transportation

4173   Terminal & Service Facilities for Motor Vehicle Passen-
        ger Transportation *see* NAICS 48849: Other Support
        Activities for Road Transportation

4212   Local Trucking Without Storage *see* NAICS 562111:
        Solid Waste Collection; NAICS 562112: Hazardous
        Waste Collection; NAICS 562119: Other Waste Collec-

        tion; NAICS 48411: General Freight Trucking, Local;
        NAICS 48421: Used Household & Office Goods Mov-
        ing; NAICS 48422: Specialized Freight Trucking, Local

4213   Trucking, Except Local *see* NAICS 484121: General
        Freight Trucking, Long-distance, Truckload; NAICS
        484122: General Freight Trucking, Long-distance, less
        than Truckload; NAICS 48421: Used Household &
        Office Goods Moving; NAICS 48423: Specialized
        Freight Trucking, Long-distance

4214   Local Trucking with Storage *see* NAICS 48411: General
        Freight Trucking, Local; NAICS 48421: Used House-
        hold & Office Goods Moving; NAICS 48422: Special-
        ized Freight Trucking, Local

4215   Couriers Services Except by Air *see* NAICS 49211:
        Couriers; NAICS 49221: Local Messengers & Local
        Delivery

4221   Farm Product Warehousing & Storage *see* NAICS 49313:
        Farm Product Warehousing & Storage Facilities

4222   Refrigerated Warehousing & Storage *see* NAICS 49312:
        Refrigerated Warehousing & Storage Facilities

4225   General Warehousing & Storage *see* NAICS 49311: Gen-
        eral Warehousing & Storage Facilities; NAICS 53113:
        Lessors of Miniwarehouses & Self Storage Units

4226   Special Warehousing & Storage, NEC *see* NAICS
        49312: Refrigerated Warehousing & Storage Facilities;
        NAICS 49311: General Warehousing & Storage Facil-
        ities; NAICS 49319: Other Warehousing & Storage
        Facilities

4231   Terminal & Joint Terminal Maintenance Facilities for
        Motor Freight Transportation *see* NAICS 48849: Other
        Support Activities for Road Transportation

4311   United States Postal Service *see* NAICS 49111: Postal
        Service

4412   Deep Sea Foreign Transportation of Freight *see* NAICS
        483111: Deep Sea Freight Transportation

4424   Deep Sea Domestic Transportation of Freight *see* NAICS
        483113: Coastal & Great Lakes Freight Transportation

4432   Freight Transportation on the Great Lakes - St.
        Lawrence Seaway *see* NAICS 483113: Coastal &
        Great Lakes Freight Transportation

4449   Water Transportation of Freight, NEC *see* NAICS
        483211: Inland Water Freight Transportation

4481   Deep Sea Transportation of Passengers, Except by Ferry
        see NAICS 483112: Deep Sea Passenger Transporta-
        tion; NAICS 483114: Coastal & Great Lakes Passen-
        ger Transportation

4482   Ferries *see* NAICS 483114: Coastal & Great Lakes Pas-
        senger Transportation; NAICS 483212: Inland Water
        Passenger Transportation

4489   Water Transportation of Passengers, NEC *see* NAICS
        483212: Inland Water Passenger Transportation;
        NAICS 48721: Scenic & Sightseeing Transportation,
        Water

4491   Marine Cargo Handling *see* NAICS 48831: Port & Har-
        bor Operations; NAICS 48832: Marine Cargo Handling

4492   Towing & Tugboat Services *see* NAICS 483113:
        Coastal & Great Lakes Freight Transportation; NAICS
        483211: Inland Water Freight Transportation; NAICS
        48833: Navigational Services to Shipping

4493   Marinas *see* NAICS 71393: Marinas

4499   Water Transportation Services, NEC *see* NAICS
        532411: Commercial Air, Rail, & Water Transporta-
        tion Equipment Rental & Leasing; NAICS 48831: Port
        & Harbor Operations; NAICS 48833: Navigational
        Services to Shipping; NAICS 48839: Other Support
        Activities for Water Transportation

4512   Air Transportation, Scheduled *see* NAICS 481111: Scheduled Passenger Air Transportation; NAICS 481112: Scheduled Freight Air Transportation
4513   Air Courier Services *see* NAICS 49211: Couriers
4522   Air Transportation, Nonscheduled *see* NAICS 62191: Ambulance Services; NAICS 481212: Nonscheduled Chartered Freight Air Transportation; NAICS 481211: Nonscheduled Chartered Passenger Air Transportation; NAICS 48799: Scenic & Sightseeing Transportation , Other
4581   Airports, Flying Fields, & Airport Terminal Services *see* NAICS 488111: Air Traffic Control; NAICS 488119: Other Airport Operations; NAICS 56172: Janitorial Services; NAICS 48819: Other Support Activities for Air Transportation
4612   Crude Petroleum Pipelines *see* NAICS 48611: Pipeline Transportation of Crude Oil
4613   Refined Petroleum Pipelines *see* NAICS 48691: Pipeline Transportation of Refined Petroleum Products
4619   Pipelines, NEC *see* NAICS 48699: All Other Pipeline Transportation
4724   Travel Agencies *see* NAICS 56151: Travel Agencies
4725   Tour Operators *see* NAICS 56152: Tour Operators
4729   Arrangement of Passenger Transportation, NEC *see* NAICS 488999: All Other Support Activities for Transportation; NAICS 561599: All Other Travel Arrangement & Reservation Services
4731   Arrangement of Transportation of Freight & Cargo *see* NAICS 541618: Other Management Consulting Services; NAICS 48851: Freight Transportation Arrangement
4741   Rental of Railroad Cars *see* NAICS 532411: Commercial Air, Rail, & Water Transportation Equipment Rental & Leasing; NAICS 48821: Support Activities for Rail Transportation
4783   Packing & Crating *see* NAICS 488991: Packing & Crating
4785   Fixed Facilities & Inspection & Weighing Services for Motor Vehicle Transportation *see* NAICS 48839: Other Support Activities for Water Transportation; NAICS 48849: Other Support Activities for Road Transportation
4789   Transportation Services, NEC *see* NAICS 488999: All Other Support Activities for Transportation; NAICS 48711: Scenic & Sightseeing Transportation, Land; NAICS 48821: Support Activities for Rail Transportation
4812   Radiotelephone Communications *see* NAICS 513321: Paging; NAICS 513322: Cellular & Other Wireless Telecommunications; NAICS 51333: Telecommunications Resellers
4813   Telephone Communications, Except Radiotelephone *see* NAICS 51331: Wired Telecommunications Carriers; NAICS 51333: Telecommunications Resellers
4822   Telegraph & Other Message Communications *see* NAICS 51331: Wired Telecommunications Carriers
4832   Radio Broadcasting Stations *see* NAICS 513111: Radio Networks; NAICS 513112: Radio Stations
4833   Television Broadcasting Stations *see* NAICS 51312: Television Broadcasting
4841   Cable & Other Pay Television Services *see* NAICS 51321: Cable Networks; NAICS 51322: Cable & Other Program Distribution
4899   Communications Services, NEC *see* NAICS 513322: Cellular & Other Wireless Telecommunications; NAICS 51334: Satellite Telecommunications; NAICS 51339: Other Telecommunications

4911   Electric Services *see* NAICS 221111: Hydroelectric Power Generation; NAICS 221112: Fossil Fuel Electric Power Generation; NAICS 221113: Nuclear Electric Power Generation; NAICS 221119: Other Electric Power Generation; NAICS 221121: Electric Bulk Power Transmission & Control; NAICS 221122: Electric Power Distribution
4922   Natural Gas Transmission *see* NAICS 48621: Pipeline Transportation of Natural Gas
4923   Natural Gas Transmission & Distribution *see* NAICS 22121: Natural Gas Distribution; NAICS 48621: Pipeline Transportation of Natural Gas
4924   Natural Gas Distribution *see* NAICS 22121: Natural Gas Distribution
4925   Mixed, Manufactured, or Liquefied Petroleum Gas Production And/or Distribution *see* NAICS 22121: Natural Gas Distribution
4931   Electric & Other Services Combined *see* NAICS 221111: Hydroelectric Power Generation; NAICS 221112: Fossil Fuel Electric Power Generation; NAICS 221113: Nuclear Electric Power Generation; NAICS 221119: Other Electric Power Generation; NAICS 221121: Electric Bulk Power Transmission & Control; NAICS 221122: Electric Power Distribution; NAICS 22121: Natural Gas Distribution
4932   Gas & Other Services Combined *see* NAICS 22121: Natural Gas Distribution
4939   Combination Utilities, NEC *see* NAICS 221111: Hydroelectric Power Generation; NAICS 221112: Fossil Fuel Electric Power Generation; NAICS 221113: Nuclear Electric Power Generation; NAICS 221119: Other Electric Power Generation; NAICS 221121: Electric Bulk Power Transmission & Control; NAICS 221122: Electric Power Distribution; NAICS 22121: Natural Gas Distribution
4941   Water Supply *see* NAICS 22131: Water Supply & Irrigation Systems
4952   Sewerage Systems *see* NAICS 22132: Sewage Treatment Facilities
4953   Refuse Systems *see* NAICS 562111: Solid Waste Collection; NAICS 562112: Hazardous Waste Collection; NAICS 56292: Materials Recovery Facilities; NAICS 562119: Other Waste Collection; NAICS 562211: Hazardous Waste Treatment & Disposal; NAICS 562212: Solid Waste Landfills; NAICS 562213: Solid Waste Combustors & Incinerators; NAICS 562219: Other Nonhazardous Waste Treatment & Disposal
4959   Sanitary Services, NEC *see* NAICS 488119: Other Airport Operations; NAICS 56291: Remediation Services; NAICS 56171: Exterminating & Pest Control Services; NAICS 562998: All Other Miscellaneous Waste Management Services
4961   Steam & Air-conditioning Supply *see* NAICS 22133: Steam & Air-conditioning Supply
4971   Irrigation Systems *see* NAICS 22131: Water Supply & Irrigation Systems

WHOLESALE TRADE

5012   Automobiles & Other Motor Vehicles *see* NAICS 42111: Automobile & Other Motor Vehicle Wholesalers
5013   Motor Vehicle Supplies & New Parts *see* NAICS 44131: Automotive Parts & Accessories Stores - Retail; NAICS 42112: Motor Vehicle Supplies & New Part Wholesalers

5014   Tires & Tubes *see* NAICS 44132: Tire Dealers - Retail; NAICS 42113: Tire & Tube Wholesalers

5015   Motor Vehicle Parts, Used *see* NAICS 42114: Motor Vehicle Part Wholesalers

5021   Furniture *see* NAICS 44211: Furniture Stores; NAICS 42121: Furniture Wholesalers

5023   Home Furnishings *see* NAICS 44221: Floor Covering Stores; NAICS 42122: Home Furnishing Wholesalers

5031   Lumber, Plywood, Millwork, & Wood Panels *see* NAICS 44419: Other Building Material Dealers; NAICS 42131: Lumber, Plywood, Millwork, & Wood Panel Wholesalers

5032   Brick, Stone & Related Construction Materials *see* NAICS 44419: Other Building Material Dealers; NAICS 42132: Brick, Stone & Related Construction Material Wholesalers

5033   Roofing, Siding, & Insulation Materials *see* NAICS 42133: Roofing, Siding, & Insulation Material Wholesalers

5039   Construction Materials, NEC *see* NAICS 44419: Other Building Material Dealers; NAICS 42139: Other Construction Material Wholesalers

5043   Photographic Equipment & Supplies *see* NAICS 42141: Photographic Equipment & Supplies Wholesalers

5044   Office Equipment *see* NAICS 42142: Office Equipment Wholesalers

5045   Computers & Computer Peripheral Equipment & Software *see* NAICS 42143: Computer & Computer Peripheral Equipment & Software Wholesalers; NAICS 44312: Computer & Software Stores - Retail

5046   Commercial Equipment, NEC *see* NAICS 42144: Other Commercial Equipment Wholesalers

5047   Medical, Dental, & Hospital Equipment & Supplies *see* NAICS 42145: Medical, Dental & Hospital Equipment & Supplies Wholesalers; NAICS 446199: All Other Health & Personal Care Stores - Retail

5048   Ophthalmic Goods *see* NAICS 42146: Ophthalmic Goods Wholesalers

5049   Professional Equipment & Supplies, NEC *see* NAICS 42149: Other Professional Equipment & Supplies Wholesalers; NAICS 45321: Office Supplies & Stationery Stores - Retail

5051   Metals Service Centers & Offices *see* NAICS 42151: Metals Service Centers & Offices

5052   Coal & Other Minerals & Ores *see* NAICS 42152: Coal & Other Mineral & Ore Wholesalers

5063   Electrical Apparatus & Equipment Wiring Supplies, & Construction Materials *see* NAICS 44419: Other Building Material Dealers; NAICS 42161: Electrical Apparatus & Equipment, Wiring Supplies & Construction Material Wholesalers

5064   Electrical Appliances, Television & Radio Sets *see* NAICS 42162: Electrical Appliance, Television & Radio Set Wholesalers

5065   Electronic Parts & Equipment, Not Elsewhere Classified *see* NAICS 42169: Other Electronic Parts & Equipment Wholesalers

5072   Hardware *see* NAICS 42171: Hardware Wholesalers

5074   Plumbing & Heating Equipment & Supplies *see* NAICS 44419: Other Building Material Dealers; NAICS 42172: Plumbing & Heating Equipment & Supplies Wholesalers

5075   Warm Air Heating & Air-conditioning Equipment & Supplies *see* NAICS 42173: Warm Air Heating & Air-conditioning Equipment & Supplies Wholesalers

5078   Refrigeration Equipment & Supplies *see* NAICS 42174: Refrigeration Equipment & Supplies Wholesalers

5082   Construction & Mining Machinery & Equipment *see* NAICS 42181: Construction & Mining Machinery & Equipment Wholesalers

5083   Farm & Garden Machinery & Equipment *see* NAICS 42182: Farm & Garden Machinery & Equipment Wholesalers; NAICS 44421: Outdoor Power Equipment Stores - Retail

5084   Industrial Machinery & Equipment *see* NAICS 42183: Industrial Machinery & Equipment Wholesalers

5085   Industrial Supplies *see* NAICS 42183: Industrial Machinery & Equipment Wholesalers; NAICS 42184: Industrial Supplies Wholesalers

5087   Service Establishment Equipment & Supplies *see* NAICS 42185: Service Establishment Equipment & Supplies Wholesalers; NAICS 44612: Cosmetics, Beauty Supplies, & Perfume Stores

5088   Transportation Equipment & Supplies, Except Motor Vehicles *see* NAICS 42186: Transportation Equipment & Supplies Wholesalers

5091   Sporting & Recreational Goods & Supplies *see* NAICS 42191: Sporting & Recreational Goods & Supplies Wholesalers

5092   Toys & Hobby Goods & Supplies *see* NAICS 42192: Toy & Hobby Goods & Supplies Wholesalers

5093   Scrap & Waste Materials *see* NAICS 42193: Recyclable Material Wholesalers

5094   Jewelry, Watches, Precious Stones, & Precious Metals *see* NAICS 42194: Jewelry, Watch , Precious Stone, & Precious Metal Wholesalers

5099   Durable Goods, NEC *see* NAICS 42199: Other Miscellaneous Durable Goods Wholesalers

5111   Printing & Writing Paper *see* NAICS 42211: Printing & Writing Paper Wholesalers

5112   Stationery & Office Supplies *see* NAICS 45321: Office Supplies & Stationery Stores; NAICS 42212: Stationery & Office Supplies Wholesalers

5113   Industrial & Personal Service Paper *see* NAICS 42213: Industrial & Personal Service Paper Wholesalers

5122   Drugs, Drug Proprietaries, & Druggists' Sundries *see* NAICS 42221: Drugs, Drug Proprietaries, & Druggists' Sundries Wholesalers

5131   Piece Goods, Notions, & Other Dry Goods *see* NAICS 313311: Broadwoven Fabric Finishing Mills; NAICS 313312: Textile & Fabric Finishing Mills; NAICS 42231: Piece Goods, Notions, & Other Dry Goods Wholesalers

5136   Men's & Boys' Clothing & Furnishings *see* NAICS 42232: Men's & Boys' Clothing & Furnishings Wholesalers

5137   Women's Children's & Infants' Clothing & Accessories *see* NAICS 42233: Women's, Children's, & Infants' Clothing & Accessories Wholesalers

5139   Footwear *see* NAICS 42234: Footwear Wholesalers

5141   Groceries, General Line *see* NAICS 42241: General Line Grocery Wholesalers

5142   Packaged Frozen Foods *see* NAICS 42242: Packaged Frozen Food Wholesalers

5143   Dairy Products, Except Dried or Canned *see* NAICS 42243: Dairy Products Wholesalers

5144   Poultry & Poultry Products *see* NAICS 42244: Poultry & Poultry Product Wholesalers

5145   Confectionery *see* NAICS 42245: Confectionery Wholesalers

5146 Fish & Seafoods *see* NAICS 42246: Fish & Seafood Wholesalers

5147 Meats & Meat Products *see* NAICS 311612: Meat Processed from Carcasses; NAICS 42247: Meat & Meat Product Wholesalers

5148 Fresh Fruits & Vegetables *see* NAICS 42248: Fresh Fruit & Vegetable Wholesalers

5149 Groceries & Related Products, NEC *see* NAICS 42249: Other Grocery & Related Product Wholesalers

5153 Grain & Field Beans *see* NAICS 42251: Grain & Field Bean Wholesalers

5154 Livestock *see* NAICS 42252: Livestock Wholesalers

5159 Farm-product Raw Materials, NEC *see* NAICS 42259: Other Farm Product Raw Material Wholesalers

5162 Plastics Materials & Basic Forms & Shapes *see* NAICS 42261: Plastics Materials & Basic Forms & Shapes Wholesalers

5169 Chemicals & Allied Products, NEC *see* NAICS 42269: Other Chemical & Allied Products Wholesalers

5171 Petroleum Bulk Stations & Terminals *see* NAICS 454311: Heating Oil Dealers; NAICS 454312: Liquefied Petroleum Gas Dealers; NAICS 42271: Petroleum Bulk Stations & Terminals

5172 Petroleum & Petroleum Products Wholesalers, Except Bulk Stations & Terminals *see* NAICS 42272: Petroleum & Petroleum Products Wholesalers

5181 Beer & Ale *see* NAICS 42281: Beer & Ale Wholesalers

5182 Wine & Distilled Alcoholic Beverages *see* NAICS 42282: Wine & Distilled Alcoholic Beverage Wholesalers

5191 Farm Supplies *see* NAICS 44422: Nursery & Garden Centers - Retail; NAICS 42291: Farm Supplies Wholesalers

5192 Books, Periodicals, & Newspapers *see* NAICS 42292: Book, Periodical & Newspaper Wholesalers

5193 Flowers, Nursery Stock, & Florists' Supplies *see* NAICS 42293: Flower, Nursery Stock & Florists' Supplies Wholesalers; NAICS 44422: Nursery & Garden Centers - Retail

5194 Tobacco & Tobacco Products *see* NAICS 42294: Tobacco & Tobacco Product Wholesalers

5198 Paint, Varnishes, & Supplies *see* NAICS 42295: Paint, Varnish & Supplies Wholesalers; NAICS 44412: Paint & Wallpaper Stores

5199 Nondurable Goods, NEC *see* NAICS 54189: Other Services Related to Advertising; NAICS 42299: Other Miscellaneous Nondurable Goods Wholesalers

RETAIL TRADE

5211 Lumber & Other Building Materials Dealers *see* NAICS 44411: Home Centers; NAICS 42131: Lumber, Plywood, Millwork & Wood Panel Wholesalers; NAICS 44419: Other Building Material Dealers

5231 Paint, Glass, & Wallpaper Stores *see* NAICS 42295: Paint, Varnish & Supplies Wholesalers; NAICS 44419: Other Building Material Dealers; NAICS 44412: Paint & Wallpaper Stores

5251 Hardware Stores *see* NAICS 44413: Hardware Stores

5261 Retail Nurseries, Lawn & Garden Supply Stores *see* NAICS 44422: Nursery & Garden Centers; NAICS 453998: All Other Miscellaneous Store Retailers; NAICS 44421: Outdoor Power Equipment Stores

5271 Mobile Home Dealers *see* NAICS 45393: Manufactured Home Dealers

5311 Department Stores *see* NAICS 45211: Department Stores

5331 Variety Stores *see* NAICS 45299: All Other General Merchandise Stores

5399 Miscellaneous General Merchandise Stores *see* NAICS 45291: Warehouse Clubs & Superstores; NAICS 45299: All Other General Merchandise Stores

5411 Grocery Stores *see* NAICS 44711: Gasoline Stations with Convenience Stores; NAICS 44511: Supermarkets & Other Grocery Stores; NAICS 45291: Warehouse Clubs & Superstores; NAICS 44512: Convenience Stores

5421 Meat & Fish Markets, Including Freezer Provisioners *see* NAICS 45439: Other Direct Selling Establishments; NAICS 44521: Meat Markets; NAICS 44522: Fish & Seafood Markets

5431 Fruit & Vegetable Markets *see* NAICS 44523: Fruit & Vegetable Markets

5441 Candy, Nut, & Confectionery Stores *see* NAICS 445292: Confectionary & Nut Stores

5451 Dairy Products Stores *see* NAICS 445299: All Other Specialty Food Stores

5461 Retail Bakeries *see* NAICS 722213: Snack & Nonalcoholic Beverage Bars; NAICS 311811: Retail Bakeries; NAICS 445291: Baked Goods Stores

5499 Miscellaneous Food Stores *see* NAICS 44521: Meat Markets; NAICS 722211: Limited-service Restaurants; NAICS 446191: Food Supplement Stores; NAICS 445299: All Other Specialty Food Stores

5511 Motor Vehicle Dealers *see* NAICS 44111: New Car Dealers

5521 Motor Vehicle Dealers *see* NAICS 44112: Used Car Dealers

5531 Auto & Home Supply Stores *see* NAICS 44132: Tire Dealers; NAICS 44131: Automotive Parts & Accessories Stores

5541 Gasoline Service Stations *see* NAICS 44711: Gasoline Stations with Convenience Store; NAICS 44719: Other Gasoline Stations

5551 Boat Dealers *see* NAICS 441222: Boat Dealers

5561 Recreational Vehicle Dealers *see* NAICS 44121: Recreational Vehicle Dealers

5571 Motorcycle Dealers *see* NAICS 441221: Motorcycle Dealers

5599 Automotive Dealers, NEC *see* NAICS 441229: All Other Motor Vehicle Dealers

5611 Men's & Boys' Clothing & Accessory Stores *see* NAICS 44811: Men's Clothing Stores; NAICS 44815: Clothing Accessories Stores

5621 Women's Clothing Stores *see* NAICS 44812: Women's Clothing Stores

5632 Women's Accessory & Specialty Stores *see* NAICS 44819: Other Clothing Stores; NAICS 44815: Clothing Accessories Stores

5641 Children's & Infants' Wear Stores *see* NAICS 44813: Children's & Infants' Clothing Stores

5651 Family Clothing Stores *see* NAICS 44814: Family Clothing Stores

5661 Shoe Stores *see* NAICS 44821: Shoe Stores

5699 Miscellaneous Apparel & Accessory Stores *see* NAICS 315: Included in Apparel Manufacturing Subsector Based on Type of Garment Produced; NAICS 44819: Other Clothing Stores; NAICS 44815: Clothing Accessories Stores

5712 Furniture Stores *see* NAICS 337122: Nonupholstered Wood Household Furniture Manufacturing; NAICS 33711: Wood Kitchen Cabinet & Counter Top Manufacturing; NAICS 337121: Upholstered Household Furniture Manufacturing; NAICS 44211: Furniture Stores

5713 Floor Covering Stores *see* NAICS 44221: Floor Covering Stores

5714 Drapery, Curtain, & Upholstery Stores *see* NAICS 442291: Window Treatment Stores; NAICS 45113: Sewing, Needlework & Piece Goods Stores; NAICS 314121: Curtain & Drapery Mills

5719 Miscellaneous Homefurnishings Stores *see* NAICS 442291: Window Treatment Stores; NAICS 442299: All Other Home Furnishings Stores

5722 Household Appliance Stores *see* NAICS 443111: Household Appliance Stores

5731 Radio, Television, & Consumer Electronics Stores *see* NAICS 443112: Radio, Television, & Other Electronics Stores; NAICS 44131: Automotive Parts & Accessories Stores

5734 Computer & Computer Software Stores *see* NAICS 44312: Computer & Software Stores

5735 Record & Prerecorded Tape Stores *see* NAICS 45122: Prerecorded Tape, Compact Disc & Record Stores

5736 Musical Instrument Stores *see* NAICS 45114: Musical Instrument & Supplies Stores

5812 Eating & Drinking Places *see* NAICS 72211: Full-service Restaurants; NAICS 722211: Limited-service Restaurants; NAICS 722212: Cafeterias; NAICS 722213: Snack & Nonalcoholic Beverage Bars; NAICS 72231: Foodservice Contractors; NAICS 72232: Caterers; NAICS 71111: Theater Companies & Dinner Theaters

5813 Drinking Places *see* NAICS 72241: Drinking Places

5912 Drug Stores & Proprietary Stores *see* NAICS 44611: Pharmacies & Drug Stores

5921 Liquor Stores *see* NAICS 44531: Beer, Wine & Liquor Stores

5932 Used Merchandise Stores *see* NAICS 522298: All Other Non-depository Credit Intermediation; NAICS 45331: Used Merchandise Stores

5941 Sporting Goods Stores & Bicycle Shops *see* NAICS 45111: Sporting Goods Stores

5942 Book Stores *see* NAICS 451211: Book Stores

5943 Stationery Stores *see* NAICS 45321: Office Supplies & Stationery Stores

5944 Jewelry Stores *see* NAICS 44831: Jewelry Stores

5945 Hobby, Toy, & Game Shops *see* NAICS 45112: Hobby, Toy & Game Stores

5946 Camera & Photographic Supply Stores *see* NAICS 44313: Camera & Photographic Supplies Stores

5947 Gift, Novelty, & Souvenir Shops *see* NAICS 45322: Gift, Novelty & Souvenir Stores

5948 Luggage & Leather Goods Stores *see* NAICS 44832: Luggage & Leather Goods Stores

5949 Sewing, Needlework, & Piece Goods Stores *see* NAICS 45113: Sewing, Needlework & Piece Goods Stores

5961 Catalog & Mail-order Houses *see* NAICS 45411: Electronic Shopping & Mail-order Houses

5962 Automatic Merchandising Machine Operator *see* NAICS 45421: Vending Machine Operators

5963 Direct Selling Establishments *see* NAICS 72233: Mobile Foodservices; NAICS 45439: Other Direct Selling Establishments

5983 Fuel Oil Dealers *see* NAICS 454311: Heating Oil Dealers

5984 Liquefied Petroleum Gas Dealers *see* NAICS 454312: Liquefied Petroleum Gas Dealers

5989 Fuel Dealers, NEC *see* NAICS 454319: Other Fuel Dealers

5992 Florists *see* NAICS 45311: Florists

5993 Tobacco Stores & Stands *see* NAICS 453991: Tobacco Stores

5994 News Dealers & Newsstands *see* NAICS 451212: News Dealers & Newsstands

5995 Optical Goods Stores *see* NAICS 339115: Ophthalmic Goods Manufacturing; NAICS 44613: Optical Goods Stores

5999 Miscellaneous Retail Stores, NEC *see* NAICS 44612: Cosmetics, Beauty Supplies & Perfume Stores; NAICS 446199: All Other Health & Personal Care Stores; NAICS 45391: Pet & Pet Supplies Stores; NAICS 45392: Art Dealers; NAICS 443111: Household Appliance Stores; NAICS 443112: Radio, Television & Other Electronics Stores; NAICS 44831: Jewelry Stores; NAICS 453998: All Other Miscellaneous Store Retailers

FINANCE, INSURANCE, & REAL ESTATE

6011 Federal Reserve Banks *see* NAICS 52111: Monetary Authorities-central Banks

6019 Central Reserve Depository Institutions, NEC *see* NAICS 52232: Financial Transactions Processing, Reserve, & Clearing House Activities

6021 National Commercial Banks *see* NAICS 52211: Commercial Banking; NAICS 52221: Credit Card Issuing; NAICS 523991: Trust, Fiduciary & Custody Activities

6022 State Commercial Banks *see* NAICS 52211: Commercial Banking; NAICS 52221: Credit Card Issuing; NAICS 52219: Other Depository Intermediation; NAICS 523991: Trust, Fiduciary & Custody Activities

6029 Commercial Banks, NEC *see* NAICS 52211: Commercial Banking

6035 Savings Institutions, Federally Chartered *see* NAICS 52212: Savings Institutions

6036 Savings Institutions, Not Federally Chartered *see* NAICS 52212: Savings Institutions

6061 Credit Unions, Federally Chartered *see* NAICS 52213: Credit Unions

6062 Credit Unions, Not Federally Chartered *see* NAICS 52213: Credit Unions

6081 Branches & Agencies of Foreign Banks *see* NAICS 522293: International Trade Financing; NAICS 52211: Commercial Banking; NAICS 522298: All Other Non-depository Credit Intermediation

6082 Foreign Trade & International Banking Institutions *see* NAICS 522293: International Trade Financing

6091 Nondeposit Trust Facilities *see* NAICS 523991: Trust, Fiduciary, & Custody Activities

6099 Functions Related to Deposit Banking, NEC *see* NAICS 52232: Financial Transactions Processing, Reserve, & Clearing House Activities; NAICS 52313: Commodity Contracts Dealing; NAICS 523991: Trust, Fiduciary, & Custody Activities; NAICS 523999: Miscellaneous Financial Investment Activities; NAICS 52239: Other Activities Related to Credit Intermediation

6111 Federal & Federally Sponsored Credit Agencies *see* NAICS 522293: International Trade Financing; NAICS 522294: Secondary Market Financing; NAICS 522298: All Other Non-depository Credit Intermediation

6141 Personal Credit Institutions *see* NAICS 52221: Credit Card Issuing; NAICS 52222: Sales Financing; NAICS 522291: Consumer Lending

6153   Short-term Business Credit Institutions, Except Agricultural *see* NAICS 52222: Sales Financing; NAICS 52232: Financial Transactions Processing, Reserve, & Clearing House Activities; NAICS 522298: All Other Non-depository Credit Intermediation

6159   Miscellaneous Business Credit Institutions *see* NAICS 52222: Sales Financing; NAICS 532: Included in Rental & Leasing Services Subsector by Type of Equipment & Method of Operation; NAICS 522293: International Trade Financing; NAICS 522298: All Other Non-depository Credit Intermediation

6162   Mortgage Bankers & Loan Correspondents *see* NAICS 522292: Real Estate Credit; NAICS 52239: Other Activities Related to Credit Intermediation

6163   Loan Brokers *see* NAICS 52231: Mortgage & Other Loan Brokers

6211   Security Brokers, Dealers, & Flotation Companies *see* NAICS 52311: Investment Banking & Securities Dealing; NAICS 52312: Securities Brokerage; NAICS 52391: Miscellaneous Intermediation; NAICS 523999: Miscellaneous Financial Investment Activities

6221   Commodity Contracts Brokers & Dealers *see* NAICS 52313: Commodity Contracts Dealing; NAICS 52314: Commodity Brokerage

6231   Security & Commodity Exchanges *see* NAICS 52321: Securities & Commodity Exchanges

6282   Investment Advice *see* NAICS 52392: Portfolio Management; NAICS 52393: Investment Advice

6289   Services Allied with the Exchange of Securities or Commodities, NEC *see* NAICS 523991: Trust, Fiduciary, & Custody Activities; NAICS 523999: Miscellaneous Financial Investment Activities

6311   Life Insurance *see* NAICS 524113: Direct Life Insurance Carriers; NAICS 52413: Reinsurance Carriers

6321   Accident & Health Insurance *see* NAICS 524114: Direct Health & Medical Insurance Carriers; NAICS 52519: Other Insurance Funds; NAICS 52413: Reinsurance Carriers

6324   Hospital & Medical Service Plans *see* NAICS 524114: Direct Health & Medical Insurance Carriers; NAICS 52519: Other Insurance Funds; NAICS 52413: Reinsurance Carriers

6331   Fire, Marine, & Casualty Insurance *see* NAICS 524126: Direct Property & Casualty Insurance Carriers; NAICS 52519: Other Insurance Funds; NAICS 52413: Reinsurance Carriers

6351   Surety Insurance *see* NAICS 524126: Direct Property & Casualty Insurance Carriers; NAICS 52413: Reinsurance Carriers

6361   Title Insurance *see* NAICS 524127: Direct Title Insurance Carriers; NAICS 52413: Reinsurance Carriers

6371   Pension, Health, & Welfare Funds *see* NAICS 52392: Portfolio Management; NAICS 524292: Third Party Administration for Insurance & Pension Funds; NAICS 52511: Pension Funds; NAICS 52512: Health & Welfare Funds

6399   Insurance Carriers, NEC *see* NAICS 524128: Other Direct Insurance Carriers

6411   Insurance Agents, Brokers, & Service *see* NAICS 52421: Insurance Agencies & Brokerages; NAICS 524291: Claims Adjusters; NAICS 524292: Third Party Administrators for Insurance & Pension Funds; NAICS 524298: All Other Insurance Related Activities

6512   Operators of Nonresidential Buildings *see* NAICS 71131: Promoters of Performing Arts, Sports & Similar Events with Facilities; NAICS 53112: Lessors of Nonresidential Buildings

6513   Operators of Apartment Buildings *see* NAICS 53111: Lessors of Residential Buildings & Dwellings

6514   Operators of Dwellings Other than Apartment Buildings *see* NAICS 53111: Lessors of Residential Buildings & Dwellings

6515   Operators of Residential Mobile Home Sites *see* NAICS 53119: Lessors of Other Real Estate Property

6517   Lessors of Railroad Property *see* NAICS 53119: Lessors of Other Real Estate Property

6519   Lessors of Real Property, NEC *see* NAICS 53119: Lessors of Other Real Estate Property

6531   Real Estate Agents & Managers *see* NAICS 53121: Offices of Real Estate Agents & Brokers; NAICS 81399: Other Similar Organizations; NAICS 531311: Residential Property Managers; NAICS 531312: Nonresidential Property Managers; NAICS 53132: Offices of Real Estate Appraisers; NAICS 81222: Cemeteries & Crematories; NAICS 53139: Other Activities Related to Real Estate

6541   Title Abstract Offices *see* NAICS 541191: Title Abstract & Settlement Offices

6552   Land Subdividers & Developers, Except Cemeteries *see* NAICS 23311: Land Subdivision & Land Development

6553   Cemetery Subdividers & Developers *see* NAICS 81222: Cemeteries & Crematories

6712   Offices of Bank Holding Companies *see* NAICS 551111: Offices of Bank Holding Companies

6719   Offices of Holding Companies, NEC *see* NAICS 551112: Offices of Other Holding Companies

6722   Management Investment Offices, Open-end *see* NAICS 52591: Open-end Investment Funds

6726   Unit Investment Trusts, Face-amount Certificate Offices, & Closed-end Management Investment Offices *see* NAICS 52599: Other Financial Vehicles

6732   Education, Religious, & Charitable Trusts *see* NAICS 813211: Grantmaking Foundations

6733   Trusts, Except Educational, Religious, & Charitable *see* NAICS 52392: Portfolio Management; NAICS 523991: Trust, Fiduciary, & Custody Services; NAICS 52519: Other Insurance Funds; NAICS 52592: Trusts, Estates, & Agency Accounts

6792   Oil Royalty Traders *see* NAICS 523999: Miscellaneous Financial Investment Activities; NAICS 53311: Owners & Lessors of Other Non-financial Assets

6794   Patent Owners & Lessors *see* NAICS 53311: Owners & Lessors of Other Non-financial Assets

6798   Real Estate Investment Trusts *see* NAICS 52593: Real Estate Investment Trusts

6799   Investors, NEC *see* NAICS 52391: Miscellaneous Intermediation; NAICS 52392: Portfolio Management; NAICS 52313: Commodity Contracts Dealing; NAICS 523999: Miscellaneous Financial Investment Activities

SERVICE INDUSTRIES

7011   Hotels & Motels *see* NAICS 72111: Hotels & Motels; NAICS 72112: Casino Hotels; NAICS 721191: Bed & Breakfast Inns; NAICS 721199: All Other Traveler Accommodation

7021   Rooming & Boarding Houses *see* NAICS 72131: Rooming & Boarding Houses

7032   Sporting & Recreational Camps *see* NAICS 721214: Recreational & Vacation Camps

7033   Recreational Vehicle Parks & Campsites *see* NAICS 721211: Rv & Campgrounds

7041   Organization Hotels & Lodging Houses, on Membership Basis *see* NAICS 72111: Hotels & Motels; NAICS 72131: Rooming & Boarding Houses

7211   Power Laundries, Family & Commercial *see* NAICS 812321: Laundries, Family & Commercial

7212   Garment Pressing, & Agents for Laundries *see* NAICS 812391: Garment Pressing & Agents for Laundries

7213   Linen Supply *see* NAICS 812331: Linen Supply

7215   Coin-operated Laundry & Drycleaning *see* NAICS 81231: Coin-operated Laundries & Drycleaners

7216   Drycleaning Plants, Except Rug Cleaning *see* NAICS 812322: Drycleaning Plants

7217   Carpet & Upholstery Cleaning *see* NAICS 56174: Carpet & Upholstery Cleaning Services

7218   Industrial Launderers *see* NAICS 812332: Industrial Launderers

7219   Laundry & Garment Services, NEC *see* NAICS 812331: Linen Supply; NAICS 81149: Other Personal & Household Goods Repair & Maintenance; NAICS 812399: All Other Laundry Services

7221   Photographic Studios, Portrait *see* NAICS 541921: Photographic Studios, Portrait

7231   Beauty Shops *see* NAICS 812112: Beauty Salons; NAICS 812113: Nail Salons; NAICS 611511: Cosmetology & Barber Schools

7241   Barber Shops *see* NAICS 812111: Barber Shops; NAICS 611511: Cosmetology & Barber Schools

7251   Shoe Repair Shops & Shoeshine Parlors *see* NAICS 81143: Footwear & Leather Goods Repair

7261   Funeral Services & Crematories *see* NAICS 81221: Funeral Homes; NAICS 81222: Cemeteries & Crematories

7291   Tax Return Preparation Services *see* NAICS 541213: Tax Preparation Services

7299   Miscellaneous Personal Services, NEC *see* NAICS 62441: Child Day Care Services; NAICS 812191: Diet & Weight Reducing Centers; NAICS 53222: Formal Wear & Costume Rental; NAICS 812199: Other Personal Care Services; NAICS 81299: All Other Personal Services

7311   Advertising Agencies *see* NAICS 54181: Advertising Agencies

7312   Outdoor Advertising Services *see* NAICS 54185: Display Advertising

7313   Radio, Television, & Publishers' Advertising Representatives *see* NAICS 54184: Media Representatives

7319   Advertising, NEC *see* NAICS 481219: Other Nonscheduled Air Transportation; NAICS 54183: Media Buying Agencies; NAICS 54185: Display Advertising; NAICS 54187: Advertising Material Distribution Services; NAICS 54189: Other Services Related to Advertising

7322   Adjustment & Collection Services *see* NAICS 56144: Collection Agencies; NAICS 561491: Repossession Services

7323   Credit Reporting Services *see* NAICS 56145: Credit Bureaus

7331   Direct Mail Advertising Services *see* NAICS 54186: Direct Mail Advertising

7334   Photocopying & Duplicating Services *see* NAICS 561439: Business Service Centers

7335   Commercial Photography *see* NAICS 481219: Other Nonscheduled Air Transportation; NAICS 541922: Commercial Photography

7336   Commercial Art & Graphic Design *see* NAICS 54143: Graphic Design Services

7338   Secretarial & Court Reporting Services *see* NAICS 56141: Document Preparation Services; NAICS 561492: Court Reporting & Stenotype Services

7342   Disinfecting & Pest Control Services *see* NAICS 56172: Janitorial Services; NAICS 56171: Exterminating & Pest Control Services

7349   Building Cleaning & Maintenance Services, NEC *see* NAICS 56172: Janitorial Services

7352   Medical Equipment Rental & Leasing *see* NAICS 532291: Home Health Equipment Rental; NAICS 53249: Other Commercial & Industrial Machinery & Equipment Rental & Leasing

7353   Heavy Construction Equipment Rental & Leasing *see* NAICS 23499: All Other Heavy Construction; NAICS 532412: Construction, Mining & Forestry Machinery & Equipment Rental & Leasing

7359   Equipment Rental & Leasing, NEC *see* NAICS 53221: Consumer Electronics & Appliances Rental; NAICS 53231: General Rental Centers; NAICS 532299: All Other Consumer Goods Rental; NAICS 532412: Construction, Mining & Forestry Machinery & Equipment Rental & Leasing; NAICS 532411: Commercial Air, Rail, & Water Transportation Equipment Rental & Leasing; NAICS 562991: Septic Tank & Related Services; NAICS 53242: Office Machinery & Equipment Rental & Leasing; NAICS 53249: Other Commercial & Industrial Machinery & Equipment Rental & Leasing

7361   Employment Agencies *see* NAICS 541612: Human Resources & Executive Search Consulting Services; NAICS 56131: Employment Placement Agencies

7363   Help Supply Services *see* NAICS 56132: Temporary Help Services; NAICS 56133: Employee Leasing Services

7371   Computer Programming Services *see* NAICS 541511: Custom Computer Programming Services

7372   Prepackaged Software *see* NAICS 51121: Software Publishers; NAICS 334611: Software Reproducing

7373   Computer Integrated Systems Design *see* NAICS 541512: Computer Systems Design Services

7374   Computer Processing & Data Preparation & Processing Services *see* NAICS 51421: Data Processing Services

7375   Information Retrieval Services *see* NAICS 514191: Online Information Services

7376   Computer Facilities Management Services *see* NAICS 541513: Computer Facilities Management Services

7377   Computer Rental & Leasing *see* NAICS 53242: Office Machinery & Equipment Rental & Leasing

7378   Computer Maintenance & Repair *see* NAICS 44312: Computer & Software Stores; NAICS 811212: Computer & Office Machine Repair & Maintenance

7379   Computer Related Services, NEC *see* NAICS 541512: Computer Systems Design Services; NAICS 541519: Other Computer Related Services

7381   Detective, Guard, & Armored Car Services *see* NAICS 561611: Investigation Services; NAICS 561612: Security Guards & Patrol Services; NAICS 561613: Armored Car Services

7382   Security Systems Services *see* NAICS 561621: Security Systems Services

7383   News Syndicates *see* NAICS 51411: New Syndicates

7384   Photofinishing Laboratories *see* NAICS 812921: Photo Finishing Laboratories; NAICS 812922: One-hour Photo Finishing

7389   Business Services, NEC *see* NAICS 51224: Sound Recording Studios; NAICS 51229: Other Sound Recording Industries; NAICS 541199: All Other Legal Services; NAICS 81299: All Other Personal Services; NAICS 54137: Surveying & Mapping Services; NAICS 54141: Interior Design Services; NAICS 54142: Industrial Design Services; NAICS 54134:

Drafting Services; NAICS 54149: Other Specialized Design Services; NAICS 54189: Other Services Related to Advertising; NAICS 54193: Translation & Interpretation Services; NAICS 54135: Building Inspection Services; NAICS 54199: All Other Professional, Scientific & Technical Services; NAICS 71141: Agents & Managers for Artists, Athletes, Entertainers & Other Public Figures; NAICS 561422: Telemarketing Bureaus; NAICS 561431: Private Mail Centers; NAICS 561439: Other Business Service Centers; NAICS 561491: Repossession Services; NAICS 56191: Packaging & Labeling Services; NAICS 56179: Other Services to Buildings & Dwellings; NAICS 561599: All Other Travel Arrangement & Reservation Services; NAICS 56192: Convention & Trade Show Organizers; NAICS 561591: Convention & Visitors Bureaus; NAICS 52232: Financial Transactions, Processing, Reserve & Clearing House Activities; NAICS 561499: All Other Business Support Services; NAICS 56199: All Other Support Services

7513   Truck Rental & Leasing, Without Drivers see NAICS 53212: Truck, Utility Trailer & Rv Rental & Leasing

7514   Passenger Car Rental see NAICS 532111: Passenger Cars Rental

7515   Passenger Car Leasing see NAICS 532112: Passenger Cars Leasing

7519   Utility Trailer & Recreational Vehicle Rental see NAICS 53212: Truck, Utility Trailer & Rv Rental & Leasing

7521   Automobile Parking see NAICS 81293: Parking Lots & Garages

7532   Top, Body, & Upholstery Repair Shops & Paint Shops see NAICS 811121: Automotive Body, Paint, & Interior Repair & Maintenance

7533   Automotive Exhaust System Repair Shops see NAICS 811112: Automotive Exhaust System Repair

7534   Tire Retreading & Repair Shops see NAICS 326212: Tire Retreading; NAICS 811198: All Other Automotive Repair & Maintenance

7536   Automotive Glass Replacement Shops see NAICS 811122: Automotive Glass Replacement Shops

7537   Automotive Transmission Repair Shops see NAICS 811113: Automotive Transmission Repair

7538   General Automotive Repair Shops see NAICS 811111: General Automotive Repair

7539   Automotive Repair Shops, NEC see NAICS 811118: Other Automotive Mechanical & Electrical Repair & Maintenance

7542   Carwashes see NAICS 811192: Car Washes

7549   Automotive Services, Except Repair & Carwashes see NAICS 811191: Automotive Oil Change & Lubrication Shops; NAICS 48841: Motor Vehicle Towing; NAICS 811198: All Other Automotive Repair & Maintenance

7622   Radio & Television Repair Shops see NAICS 811211: Consumer Electronics Repair & Maintenance; NAICS 443112: Radio, Television & Other Electronics Stores

7623   Refrigeration & Air-conditioning Services & Repair Shops see NAICS 443111: Household Appliance Stores; NAICS 81131: Commercial & Industrial Machinery & Equipment Repair & Maintenance; NAICS 811412: Appliance Repair & Maintenance

7629   Electrical & Electronic Repair Shops, NEC see NAICS 443111: Household Appliance Stores; NAICS 811212: Computer & Office Machine Repair & Maintenance; NAICS 811213: Communication Equipment Repair &

Maintenance; NAICS 811219: Other Electronic & Precision Equipment Repair & Maintenance; NAICS 811412: Appliance Repair & Maintenance; NAICS 811211: Consumer Electronics Repair & Maintenance

7631   Watch, Clock, & Jewelry Repair see NAICS 81149: Other Personal & Household Goods Repair & Maintenance

7641   Reupholster & Furniture Repair see NAICS 81142: Reupholstery & Furniture Repair

7692   Welding Repair see NAICS 81149: Other Personal & Household Goods Repair & Maintenance

7694   Armature Rewinding Shops see NAICS 81131: Commercial & Industrial Machinery & Equipment Repair & Maintenance; NAICS 335312: Motor & Generator Manufacturing

7699   Repair Shops & Related Services, NEC see NAICS 561622: Locksmiths; NAICS 562991: Septic Tank & Related Services; NAICS 56179: Other Services to Buildings & Dwellings; NAICS 48839: Other Supporting Activities for Water Transportation; NAICS 45111: Sporting Goods Stores; NAICS 81131: Commercial & Industrial Machinery & Equipment Repair & Maintenance; NAICS 11521: Support Activities for Animal Production; NAICS 811212: Computer & Office Machine Repair & Maintenance; NAICS 811219: Other Electronic & Precision Equipment Repair & Maintenance; NAICS 811411: Home & Garden Equipment Repair & Maintenance; NAICS 811412: Appliance Repair & Maintenance; NAICS 81143: Footwear & Leather Goods Repair; NAICS 81149: Other Personal & Household Goods Repair & Maintenance

7812   Motion Picture & Video Tape Production see NAICS 51211: Motion Picture & Video Production

7819   Services Allied to Motion Picture Production see NAICS 512191: Teleproduction & Other Post-production Services; NAICS 56131: Employment Placement Agencies; NAICS 53222: Formal Wear & Costumes Rental; NAICS 53249: Other Commercial & Industrial Machinery & Equipment Rental & Leasing; NAICS 541214: Payroll Services; NAICS 71151: Independent Artists, Writers, & Performers; NAICS 334612: Prerecorded Compact Disc , Tape, & Record Manufacturing; NAICS 512199: Other Motion Picture & Video Industries

7822   Motion Picture & Video Tape Distribution see NAICS 42199: Other Miscellaneous Durable Goods Wholesalers; NAICS 51212: Motion Picture & Video Distribution

7829   Services Allied to Motion Picture Distribution see NAICS 512199: Other Motion Picture & Video Industries; NAICS 51212: Motion Picture & Video Distribution

7832   Motion Picture Theaters, Except Drive-ins. see NAICS 512131: Motion Picture Theaters, Except Drive-in

7833   Drive-in Motion Picture Theaters see NAICS 512132: Drive-in Motion Picture Theaters

7841   Video Tape Rental see NAICS 53223: Video Tapes & Disc Rental

7911   Dance Studios, Schools, & Halls see NAICS 71399: All Other Amusement & Recreation Industries; NAICS 61161: Fine Arts Schools

7922   Theatrical Producers & Miscellaneous Theatrical Services see NAICS 56131: Employment Placement Agencies; NAICS 71111: Theater Companies & Dinner Theaters; NAICS 71141: Agents & Managers for Artists, Athletes, Entertainers & Other Public Figures;

NAICS 71112: Dance Companies; NAICS 71131: Promoters of Performing Arts, Sports, & Similar Events with Facilities; NAICS 71132: Promoters of Performing Arts, Sports, & Similar Events Without Facilities; NAICS 51229: Other Sound Recording Industries; NAICS 53249: Other Commercial & Industrial Machinery & Equipment Rental & Leasing

7929   Bands, Orchestras, Actors, & Other Entertainers & Entertainment Groups *see* NAICS 71113: Musical Groups & Artists; NAICS 71151: Independent Artists, Writers, & Performers; NAICS 71119: Other Performing Arts Companies

7933   Bowling Centers *see* NAICS 71395: Bowling Centers

7941   Professional Sports Clubs & Promoters *see* NAICS 711211: Sports Teams & Clubs; NAICS 71141: Agents & Managers for Artists, Athletes, Entertainers , & Other Public Figures; NAICS 71132: Promoters of Arts, Sports & Similar Events Without Facilities; NAICS 71131: Promoters of Arts, Sports, & Similar Events with Facilities; NAICS 711219: Other Spectator Sports

7948   Racing, Including Track Operations *see* NAICS 711212: Race Tracks; NAICS 711219: Other Spectator Sports

7991   Physical Fitness Facilities *see* NAICS 71394: Fitness & Recreational Sports Centers

7992   Public Golf Courses *see* NAICS 71391: Golf Courses & Country Clubs

7993   Coin Operated Amusement Devices *see* NAICS 71312: Amusement Arcades; NAICS 71329: Other Gambling Industries; NAICS 71399: All Other Amusement & Recreation Industries

7996   Amusement Parks *see* NAICS 71311: Amusement & Theme Parks

7997   Membership Sports & Recreation Clubs *see* NAICS 71391: Golf Courses & Country Clubs; NAICS 71394: Fitness & Recreational Sports Centers; NAICS 71399: All Other Amusement & Recreation Industries

7999   Amusement & Recreation Services, NEC *see* NAICS 561599: All Other Travel Arrangement & Reservation Services; NAICS 48799: Scenic & Sightseeing Transportation, Other; NAICS 71119: Other Performing Arts Companies; NAICS 711219: Other Spectator Sports; NAICS 71392: Skiing Facilities; NAICS 71394: Fitness & Recreational Sports Centers; NAICS 71321: Casinos; NAICS 71329: Other Gambling Industries; NAICS 71219: Nature Parks & Other Similar Institutions; NAICS 61162: Sports & Recreation Instruction; NAICS 532292: Recreational Goods Rental; NAICS 48711: Scenic & Sightseeing Transportation, Land; NAICS 48721: Scenic & Sightseeing Transportation, Water; NAICS 71399: All Other Amusement & Recreation Industries

8011   Offices & Clinics of Doctors of Medicine *see* NAICS 621493: Freestanding Ambulatory Surgical & Emergency Centers; NAICS 621491: Hmo Medical Centers; NAICS 621112: Offices of Physicians, Mental Health Specialists; NAICS 621111: Offices of Physicians

8021   Offices & Clinics of Dentists *see* NAICS 62121: Offices of Dentists

8031   Offices & Clinics of Doctors of Osteopathy *see* NAICS 621111: Offices of Physicians; NAICS 621112: Offices of Physicians, Mental Health Specialists

8041   Offices & Clinics of Chiropractors *see* NAICS 62131: Offices of Chiropractors

8042   Offices & Clinics of Optometrists *see* NAICS 62132: Offices of Optometrists

8043   Offices & Clinics of Podiatrists *see* NAICS 621391: Offices of Podiatrists

8049   Offices & Clinics of Health Practitioners, NEC *see* NAICS 62133: Offices of Mental Health Practitioners; NAICS 62134: Offices of Physical, Occupational, & Speech Therapists & Audiologists; NAICS 621399: Offices of All Other Miscellaneous Health Practitioners

8051   Skilled Nursing Care Facilities *see* NAICS 623311: Continuing Care Retirement Communities; NAICS 62311: Nursing Care Facilities

8052   Intermediate Care Facilities *see* NAICS 623311: Continuing Care Retirement Communities; NAICS 62321: Residential Mental Retardation Facilities; NAICS 62311: Nursing Care Facilities

8059   Nursing & Personal Care Facilities, NEC *see* NAICS 623311: Continuing Care Retirement Communities; NAICS 62311: Nursing Care Facilities

8062   General Medical & Surgical Hospitals *see* NAICS 62211: General Medical & Surgical Hospitals

8063   Psychiatric Hospitals *see* NAICS 62221: Psychiatric & Substance Abuse Hospitals

8069   Specialty Hospitals, Except Psychiatric *see* NAICS 62211: General Medical & Surgical Hospitals; NAICS 62221: Psychiatric & Substance Abuse Hospitals; NAICS 62231: Specialty Hospitals

8071   Medical Laboratories *see* NAICS 621512: Diagnostic Imaging Centers; NAICS 621511: Medical Laboratories

8072   Dental Laboratories *see* NAICS 339116: Dental Laboratories

8082   Home Health Care Services *see* NAICS 62161: Home Health Care Services

8092   Kidney Dialysis Centers *see* NAICS 621492: Kidney Dialysis Centers

8093   Specialty Outpatient Facilities, NEC *see* NAICS 62141: Family Planning Centers; NAICS 62142: Outpatient Mental Health & Substance Abuse Centers; NAICS 621498: All Other Outpatient Care Facilities

8099   Health & Allied Services, NEC *see* NAICS 621991: Blood & Organ Banks; NAICS 54143: Graphic Design Services; NAICS 541922: Commercial Photography; NAICS 62141: Family Planning Centers; NAICS 621999: All Other Miscellaneous Ambulatory Health Care Services

8111   Legal Services *see* NAICS 54111: Offices of Lawyers

8211   Elementary & Secondary Schools *see* NAICS 61111: Elementary & Secondary Schools

8221   Colleges, Universities, & Professional Schools *see* NAICS 61131: Colleges, Universities & Professional Schools

8222   Junior Colleges & Technical Institutes *see* NAICS 61121: Junior Colleges

8231   Libraries *see* NAICS 51412: Libraries & Archives

8243   Data Processing Schools *see* NAICS 611519: Other Technical & Trade Schools; NAICS 61142: Computer Training

8244   Business & Secretarial Schools *see* NAICS 61141: Business & Secretarial Schools

8249   Vocational Schools, NEC *see* NAICS 611513: Apprenticeship Training; NAICS 611512: Flight Training; NAICS 611519: Other Technical & Trade Schools

8299   Schools & Educational Services, NEC *see* NAICS 611512: Flight Training; NAICS 611692: Automobile Driving Schools; NAICS 61171: Educational Support Services; NAICS 611691: Exam Preparation & Tutoring; NAICS 61161: Fine Arts Schools; NAICS 61163: Language Schools; NAICS 61143: Professional & Management Development Training Schools; NAICS 611699: All Other Miscellaneous Schools & Instruction

8322 Individual & Family Social Services *see* NAICS 62411: Child & Youth Services; NAICS 62421: Community Food Services; NAICS 624229: Other Community Housing Services; NAICS 62423: Emergency & Other Relief Services; NAICS 62412: Services for the Elderly & Persons with Disabilities; NAICS 624221: Temporary Shelters; NAICS 92215: Parole Offices & Probation Offices; NAICS 62419: Other Individual & Family Services

8331 Job Training & Vocational Rehabilitation Services *see* NAICS 62431: Vocational Rehabilitation Services

8351 Child Day Care Services *see* NAICS 62441: Child Day Care Services

8361 Residential Care *see* NAICS 623312: Homes for the Elderly; NAICS 62322: Residential Mental Health & Substance Abuse Facilities; NAICS 62399: Other Residential Care Facilities

8399 Social Services, NEC *see* NAICS 813212: Voluntary Health Organizations; NAICS 813219: Other Grant-making & Giving Services; NAICS 813311: Human Rights Organizations; NAICS 813312: Environment, Conservation & Wildlife Organizations; NAICS 813319: Other Social Advocacy Organizations

8412 Museums & Art Galleries *see* NAICS 71211: Museums; NAICS 71212: Historical Sites

8422 Arboreta & Botanical or Zoological Gardens *see* NAICS 71213: Zoos & Botanical Gardens; NAICS 71219: Nature Parks & Other Similar Institutions

8611 Business Associations *see* NAICS 81391: Business Associations

8621 Professional Membership Organizations *see* NAICS 81392: Professional Organizations

8631 Labor Unions & Similar Labor Organizations *see* NAICS 81393: Labor Unions & Similar Labor Organizations

8641 Civic, Social, & Fraternal Associations *see* NAICS 81341: Civic & Social Organizations; NAICS 81399: Other Similar Organizations; NAICS 92115: American Indian & Alaska Native Tribal Governments; NAICS 62411: Child & Youth Services

8651 Political Organizations *see* NAICS 81394: Political Organizations

8661 Religious Organizations *see* NAICS 81311: Religious Organizations

8699 Membership Organizations, NEC *see* NAICS 81341: Civic & Social Organizations; NAICS 81391: Business Associations; NAICS 813312: Environment, Conservation, & Wildlife Organizations; NAICS 561599: All Other Travel Arrangement & Reservation Services; NAICS 81399: Other Similar Organizations

8711 Engineering Services *see* NAICS 54133: Engineering Services

8712 Architectural Services *see* NAICS 54131: Architectural Services

8713 Surveying Services *see* NAICS 54136: Geophysical Surveying & Mapping Services; NAICS 54137: Surveying & Mapping Services

8721 Accounting, Auditing, & Bookkeeping Services *see* NAICS 541211: Offices of Certified Public Accountants; NAICS 541214: Payroll Services; NAICS 541219: Other Accounting Services

8731 Commercial Physical & Biological Research *see* NAICS 54171: Research & Development in the Physical Sciences & Engineering Sciences; NAICS 54172: Research & Development in the Life Sciences

8732 Commercial Economic, Sociological, & Educational Research *see* NAICS 54173: Research & Development in the Social Sciences & Humanities; NAICS 54191: Marketing Research & Public Opinion Polling

8733 Noncommercial Research Organizations *see* NAICS 54171: Research & Development in the Physical Sciences & Engineering Sciences; NAICS 54172: Research & Development in the Life Sciences; NAICS 54173: Research & Development in the Social Sciences & Humanities

8734 Testing Laboratories *see* NAICS 54194: Veterinary Services; NAICS 54138: Testing Laboratories

8741 Management Services *see* NAICS 56111: Office Administrative Services; NAICS 23: Included in Construction Sector by Type of Construction

8742 Management Consulting Services *see* NAICS 541611: Administrative Management & General Management Consulting Services; NAICS 541612: Human Resources & Executive Search Services; NAICS 541613: Marketing Consulting Services; NAICS 541614: Process, Physical, Distribution & Logistics Consulting Services

8743 Public Relations Services *see* NAICS 54182: Public Relations Agencies

8744 Facilities Support Management Services *see* NAICS 56121: Facilities Support Services

8748 Business Consulting Services, NEC *see* NAICS 61171: Educational Support Services; NAICS 541618: Other Management Consulting Services; NAICS 54169: Other Scientific & Technical Consulting Services

8811 Private Households *see* NAICS 81411: Private Households

8999 Services, NEC *see* NAICS 71151: Independent Artists, Writers, & Performers; NAICS 51221: Record Production; NAICS 54169: Other Scientific & Technical Consulting Services; NAICS 51223: Music Publishers; NAICS 541612: Human Resources & Executive Search Consulting Services; NAICS 514199: All Other Information Services; NAICS 54162: Environmental Consulting Services

PUBLIC ADMINISTRATION

9111 Executive Offices *see* NAICS 92111: Executive Offices

9121 Legislative Bodies *see* NAICS 92112: Legislative Bodies

9131 Executive & Legislative Offices, Combined *see* NAICS 92114: Executive & Legislative Offices, Combined

9199 General Government, NEC *see* NAICS 92119: All Other General Government

9211 Courts *see* NAICS 92211: Courts

9221 Police Protection *see* NAICS 92212: Police Protection

9222 Legal Counsel & Prosecution *see* NAICS 92213: Legal Counsel & Prosecution

9223 Correctional Institutions *see* NAICS 92214: Correctional Institutions

9224 Fire Protection *see* NAICS 92216: Fire Protection

9229 Public Order & Safety, NEC *see* NAICS 92219: All Other Justice, Public Order, & Safety

9311 Public Finance, Taxation, & Monetary Policy *see* NAICS 92113: Public Finance

9411 Administration of Educational Programs *see* NAICS 92311: Administration of Education Programs

9431   Administration of Public Health Programs *see* NAICS
       92312: Administration of Public Health Programs

9441   Administration of Social, Human Resource & Income
       Maintenance Programs *see* NAICS 92313: Administra-
       tion of Social, Human Resource & Income Mainte-
       nance Programs

9451   Administration of Veteran's Affairs, Except Health In-
       surance *see* NAICS 92314: Administration of Vet-
       eran's Affairs

9511   Air & Water Resource & Solid Waste Management *see*
       NAICS 92411: Air & Water Resource & Solid Waste
       Management

9512   Land, Mineral, Wildlife, & Forest Conservation *see*
       NAICS 92412: Land, Mineral, Wildlife, & Forest
       Conservation

9531   Administration of Housing Programs *see* NAICS 92511:
       Administration of Housing Programs

9532   Administration of Urban Planning & Community & Rural
       Development *see* NAICS 92512: Administration of Ur-
       ban Planning & Community & Rural Development

9611   Administration of General Economic Programs *see*
       NAICS 92611: Administration of General Economic
       Programs

9621   Regulations & Administration of Transportation Pro-
       grams *see* NAICS 488111: Air Traffic Control;
       NAICS 92612: Regulation & Administration of Trans-
       portation Programs

9631   Regulation & Administration of Communications, Elec-
       tric, Gas, & Other Utilities *see* NAICS 92613: Regula-
       tion & Administration of Communications, Electric,
       Gas, & Other Utilities

9641   Regulation of Agricultural Marketing & Commodity *see*
       NAICS 92614: Regulation of Agricultural Marketing
       & Commodity

9651   Regulation, Licensing, & Inspection of Miscellaneous
       Commercial Sectors *see* NAICS 92615: Regulation,
       Licensing, & Inspection of Miscellaneous Commercial
       Sectors

9661   Space Research & Technology *see* NAICS 92711: Space
       Research & Technology

9711   National Security *see* NAICS 92811: National Security

9721   International Affairs *see* NAICS 92812: International
       Affairs

9999   Nonclassifiable Establishments *see* NAICS 99999: Un-
       classified Establishments

NAICS to SIC
Conversion Guide

The following listing cross-references five- and six-digit 1997 North American Industry Classification System (NAICS) codes with four-digit 1987 Standard Industrial Classification (SIC) codes. Because the systems differ in specificity, some NAICS categories correspond to more than one SIC category. Please refer to the introduction under "About Industry Classification" for more information.

AGRICULTURE, FORESTRY, FISHING, & HUNTING

11111   Soybean Farming *see* SIC 0116: Soybeans

11112   Oilseed Farming *see* SIC 0119: Cash Grains, NEC

11113   Dry Pea & Bean Farming *see* SIC 0119: Cash Grains, NEC

11114   Wheat Farming *see* SIC 0111: Wheat

11115   Corn Farming *see* SIC 0115: Corn; SIC 0119: Cash Grains, NEC

11116   Rice Farming *see* SIC 0112: Rice

111191   Oilseed & Grain Combination Farming *see* SIC 0119: Cash Grains, NEC

111199   All Other Grain Farming *see* SIC 0119: Cash Grains, NEC

111211   Potato Farming *see* SIC 0134: Irish Potatoes

111219   Other Vegetable & Melon Farming *see* SIC 0161: Vegetables & Melons; SIC 0139: Field Crops Except Cash Grains

11131   Orange Groves *see* SIC 0174: Citrus Fruits

11132   Citrus Groves *see* SIC 0174: Citrus Fruits

111331   Apple Orchards *see* SIC 0175: Deciduous Tree Fruits

111332   Grape Vineyards *see* SIC 0172: Grapes

111333   Strawberry Farming *see* SIC 0171: Berry Crops

111334   Berry Farming *see* SIC 0171: Berry Crops

111335   Tree Nut Farming *see* SIC 0173: Tree Nuts

111336   Fruit & Tree Nut Combination Farming *see* SIC 0179: Fruits & Tree Nuts, NEC

111339   Other Noncitrus Fruit Farming *see* SIC 0175: Deciduous Tree Fruits; SIC 0179: Fruit & Tree Nuts, NEC

111411   Mushroom Production *see* SIC 0182: Food Crops Grown Under Cover

111419   Other Food Crops Grown Under Cover *see* SIC 0182: Food Crops Grown Under Cover

111421   Nursery & Tree Production *see* SIC 0181: Ornamental Floriculture & Nursery Products; SIC 0811: Timber Tracts

111422   Floriculture Production *see* SIC 0181: Ornamental Floriculture & Nursery Products

11191   Tobacco Farming *see* SIC 0132: Tobacco

11192   Cotton Farming *see* SIC 0131: Cotton

11193   Sugarcane Farming *see* SIC 0133: Sugarcane & Sugar Beets

11194   Hay Farming *see* SIC 0139: Field Crops, Except Cash Grains, NEC

111991   Sugar Beet Farming *see* SIC 0133: Sugarcane & Sugar Beets

111992   Peanut Farming *see* SIC 0139: Field Crops, Except Cash Grains, NEC

111998   All Other Miscellaneous Crop Farming *see* SIC 0139: Field Crops, Except Cash Grains, NEC; SIC 0191: General Farms, Primarily Crop; SIC 0831: Forest Products; SIC 0919: Miscellaneous Marine Products; SIC 2099: Food Preparations, NEC

112111   Beef Cattle Ranching & Farming *see* SIC 0212: Beef Cattle, Except Feedlots; SIC 0241: Dairy Farms

112112   Cattle Feedlots *see* SIC 0211: Beef Cattle Feedlots

11212   Dairy Cattle & Milk Production *see* SIC 0241: Dairy Farms

11213   Dual Purpose Cattle Ranching & Farming No SIC equivalent

11221   Hog & Pig Farming *see* SIC 0213: Hogs

11231   Chicken Egg Production *see* SIC 0252: Chicken Eggs

11232   Broilers & Other Meat Type Chicken Production *see* SIC 0251: Broiler, Fryers, & Roaster Chickens

11233   Turkey Production *see* SIC 0253: Turkey & Turkey Eggs

11234   Poultry Hatcheries *see* SIC 0254: Poultry Hatcheries

11239   Other Poultry Production *see* SIC 0259: Poultry & Eggs, NEC

11241   Sheep Farming *see* SIC 0214: Sheep & Goats

11242   Goat Farming *see* SIC 0214: Sheep & Goats

112511   Finfish Farming & Fish Hatcheries *see* SIC 0273: Animal Aquaculture; SIC 0921: Fish Hatcheries & Preserves

112512   Shellfish Farming *see* SIC 0273: Animal Aquaculture; SIC 0921: Fish Hatcheries & Preserves

112519   Other Animal Aquaculture *see* SIC 0273: Animal Aquaculture

11291   Apiculture *see* SIC 0279: Animal Specialties, NEC

11292   Horse & Other Equine Production *see* SIC 0272: Horses & Other Equines

11293   Fur-Bearing Animal & Rabbit Production *see* SIC 0271: Fur-Bearing Animals & Rabbits

11299   All Other Animal Production *see* SIC 0219: General Livestock, Except Dairy & Poultry; SIC 0279: Animal Specialties, NEC; SIC 0291: General Farms, Primarily Livestock & Animal Specialties;

11311   Timber Tract Operations *see* SIC 0811: Timber Tracts

11321   Forest Nurseries & Gathering of Forest Products *see* SIC 0831: Forest Nurseries & Gathering of Forest Products

11331   Logging *see* SIC 2411: Logging

114111   Finfish Fishing *see* SIC 0912: Finfish

114112   Shellfish Fishing *see* SIC 0913: Shellfish

114119   Other Marine Fishing *see* SIC 0919: Miscellaneous Marine Products

11421   Hunting & Trapping *see* SIC 0971: Hunting & Trapping, & Game Propagation;

115111   Cotton Ginning *see* SIC 0724: Cotton Ginning

115112   Soil Preparation, Planting, & Cultivating *see* SIC 0711: Soil Preparation Services; SIC 0721: Crop Planting, Cultivating, & Protecting

115113   Crop Harvesting, Primarily by Machine *see* SIC 0722: Crop Harvesting, Primarily by Machine

115114   Other Postharvest Crop Activities *see* SIC 0723: Crop Preparation Services For Market, Except Cotton Ginning

115115   Farm Labor Contractors & Crew Leaders *see* SIC 0761: Farm Labor Contractors & Crew Leaders

115116   Farm Management Services *see* SIC 0762: Farm Management Services

11521   Support Activities for Animal Production *see* SIC 0751: Livestock Services, Except Veterinary; SIC 0752: Animal Specialty Services, Except Veterinary; SIC 7699: Repair Services, NEC

11531   Support Activities for Forestry *see* SIC 0851: Forestry Services

MINING

211111   Crude Petroleum & Natural Gas Extraction *see* SIC 1311: Crude Petroleum & Natural Gas

211112   Natural Gas Liquid Extraction *see* SIC 1321: Natural Gas Liquids

212111   Bituminous Coal & Lignite Surface Mining *see* SIC 1221: Bituminous Coal & Lignite Surface Mining

212112   Bituminous Coal Underground Mining *see* SIC 1222: Bituminous Coal Underground Mining

212113   Anthracite Mining *see* SIC 1231: Anthracite Mining

21221   Iron Ore Mining *see* SIC 1011: Iron Ores

212221   Gold Ore Mining *see* SIC 1041: Gold Ores

212222   Silver Ore Mining *see* SIC 1044: Silver Ores

212231   Lead Ore & Zinc Ore Mining *see* SIC 1031: Lead & Zinc Ores

212234   Copper Ore & Nickel Ore Mining *see* SIC 1021: Copper Ores

212291   Uranium-Radium-Vanadium Ore Mining *see* SIC 1094: Uranium-Radium-Vanadium Ores

212299   All Other Metal Ore Mining *see* SIC 1061: Ferroalloy Ores, Except Vanadium; SIC 1099: Miscellaneous Metal Ores, NEC

212311   Dimension Stone Mining & Quarrying *see* SIC 1411: Dimension Stone

212312   Crushed & Broken Limestone Mining & Quarrying *see* SIC 1422: Crushed & Broken Limestone

212313   Crushed & Broken Granite Mining & Quarrying *see* SIC 1423: Crushed & Broken Granite

212319   Other Crushed & Broken Stone Mining & Quarrying *see* SIC 1429: Crushed & Broken Stone, NEC; SIC 1499: Miscellaneous Nonmetallic Minerals, Except Fuels

212321   Construction Sand & Gravel Mining *see* SIC 1442: Construction Sand & Gravel

212322   Industrial Sand Mining *see* SIC 1446: Industrial Sand

212324   Kaolin & Ball Clay Mining *see* SIC 1455: Kaolin & Ball Clay

212325   Clay & Ceramic & Refractory Minerals Mining *see* SIC 1459: Clay, Ceramic, & Refractory Minerals, NEC

212391   Potash, Soda, & Borate Mineral Mining *see* SIC 1474: Potash, Soda, & Borate Minerals

212392   Phosphate Rock Mining *see* SIC 1475: Phosphate Rock

212393   Other Chemical & Fertilizer Mineral Mining *see* SIC 1479: Chemical & Fertilizer Mineral Mining, NEC

212399   All Other Nonmetallic Mineral Mining *see* SIC 1499: Miscellaneous Nonmetallic Minerals, Except Fuels

213111   Drilling Oil & Gas Wells *see* SIC 1381: Drilling Oil & Gas Wells

213112   Support Activities for Oil & Gas Operations *see* SIC 1382: Oil & Gas Field Exploration Services; SIC 1389: Oil & Gas Field Services, NEC

213113   Support Activities for Coal Mining *see* SIC 1241: Coal Mining Services

213114   Support Activities for Metal Mining *see* SIC 1081: Metal Mining Services

213115   Support Activities for Nonmetallic Minerals, Except Fuels *see* SIC 1481: Nonmetallic Minerals Services, Except Fuels

UTILITIES

221111   Hydroelectric Power Generation *see* SIC 4911: Electric Services; SIC 4931: Electric & Other Services Combined; SIC 4939: Combination Utilities, NEC

221112   Fossil Fuel Electric Power Generation *see* SIC 4911: Electric Services; SIC 4931: Electric & Other Services Combined; SIC 4939: Combination Utilities, NEC

221113   Nuclear Electric Power Generation *see* SIC 4911: Electric Services; SIC 4931: Electric & Other Services Combined; SIC 4939: Combination Utilities, NEC

221119   Other Electric Power Generation *see* SIC 4911: Electric Services; SIC 4931: Electric & Other Services Combined; SIC 4939: Combination Utilities, NEC

221121   Electric Bulk Power Transmission & Control *see* SIC 4911: Electric Services; SIC 4931: Electric & Other Services Combined; SIC 4939: Combination Utilities, NEC

221122   Electric Power Distribution *see* SIC 4911: Electric Services; SIC 4931: Electric & Other Services Combined; SIC 4939: Combination Utilities, NEC

22121   Natural Gas Distribution *see* SIC 4923: Natural Gas Transmission & Distribution; SIC 4924: Natural Gas Distribution; SIC 4925: Mixed, Manufactured, or Liquefied Petroleum Gas Production and/or Distribution; SIC 4931: Electronic & Other Services Combined; SIC 4932: Gas & Other Services Combined; SIC 4939: Combination Utilities, NEC

22131   Water Supply & Irrigation Systems *see* SIC 4941: Water Supply; SIC 4971: Irrigation Systems

22132   Sewage Treatment Facilities *see* SIC 4952: Sewerage Systems

22133   Steam & Air-Conditioning Supply *see* SIC 4961: Steam & Air-Conditioning Supply

CONSTRUCTION

23311   Land Subdivision & Land Development *see* SIC 6552: Land Subdividers & Developers, Except Cemeteries

23321   Single Family Housing Construction *see* SIC 1521: General contractors-Single-Family Houses; SIC 1531: Operative Builders

23322   Multifamily Housing Construction *see* SIC 1522: General Contractors-Residential Building, Other Than Single-Family; SIC 1531: Operative Builders

23331   Manufacturing & Industrial Building Construction *see* SIC 1531: Operative Builders; SIC 1541: General Contractors-Industrial Buildings & Warehouses

23332   Commercial & Institutional Building Construction *see* SIC 1522: General Contractors-Residential Building Other than Single-Family; SIC 1531: Operative Builders; SIC 1541: General Contractors-Industrial Buildings & Warehouses; SIC 1542: General Contractor-Nonresidential Buildings, Other than Industrial Buildings & Warehouses

23411   Highway & Street Construction *see* SIC 1611: Highway & Street Construction, Except Elevated Highways

23412   Bridge & Tunnel Construction *see* SIC 1622: Bridge, Tunnel, & Elevated Highway Construction

2349   Other Heavy Construction

23491   Water, Sewer, & Pipeline Construction *see* SIC 1623: Water, Sewer, Pipeline, & Communications & Power Line Construction

23492   Power & Communication Transmission Line Construction *see* SIC 1623: Water, Sewer, Pipelines, & Communications & Power Line Construction

23493   Industrial Nonbuilding Structure Construction *see* SIC 1629: Heavy Construction, NEC

23499   All Other Heavy Construction *see* SIC 1629: Heavy Construction, NEC; SIC 7353: Construction Equipment Rental & Leasing

23511   Plumbing, Heating & Air-Conditioning Contractors *see* SIC 1711: Plumbing, Heating & Air-Conditioning

23521   Painting & Wall Covering Contractors *see* SIC 1721: Painting & Paper Hanging; SIC 1799: Special Trade Contractors, NEC

23531   Electrical Contractors *see* SIC 1731: Electrical Work

23541   Masonry & Stone Contractors *see* SIC 1741: Masonry, Stone Setting & Other Stone Work

23542   Drywall, Plastering, Acoustical & Insulation Contractors *see* SIC 1742: Plastering, Drywall, Acoustical, & Insulation Work; SIC 1743: Terrazzo, Tile, Marble & Mosaic work; SIC 1771: Concrete Work

23543   Tile, Marble, Terrazzo & Mosaic Contractors *see* SIC 1743: Terrazzo, Tile, Marble, & Mosaic Work

23551   Carpentry Contractors *see* SIC 1751: Carpentry Work

23552   Floor Laying & Other Floor Contractors *see* SIC 1752: Floor Laying & Other Floor Work, NEC

23561   Roofing, Siding & Sheet Metal Contractors *see* SIC 1761: Roofing, Siding, & Sheet Metal Work

23571   Concrete Contractors *see* SIC 1771: Concrete Work

23581   Water Well Drilling Contractors *see* SIC 1781: Water Well Drilling

23591   Structural Steel Erection Contractors *see* SIC 1791: Structural Steel Erection

23592   Glass & Glazing Contractors *see* SIC 1793: Glass & Glazing Work; SIC 1799: Specialty Trade Contractors, NEC

23593   Excavation Contractors *see* SIC 1794: Excavation Work

23594   Wrecking & Demolition Contractors *see* SIC 1795: Wrecking & Demolition Work

23595   Building Equipment & Other Machinery Installation Contractors *see* SIC 1796: Installation of Erection of Building Equipment, NEC

23599   All Other Special Trade Contractors *see* SIC 1799: Special Trade Contractors, NEC

FOOD MANUFACTURING

311111   Dog & Cat Food Manufacturing *see* SIC 2047: Dog & Cat Food

311119   Other Animal Food Manufacturing *see* SIC 2048: Prepared Feeds & Feed Ingredients for Animals & Fowls, Except Dogs & Cats

311211   Flour Milling *see* SIC 2034: Dehydrated Fruits, Vegetables & Soup Mixes; SIC 2041: Flour & Other Grain Mill Products

311212   Rice Milling *see* SIC 2044: Rice Milling

311213   Malt Manufacturing *see* SIC 2083: Malt

311221   Wet Corn Milling *see* SIC 2046: Wet Corn Milling

311222   Soybean Processing *see* SIC 2075: Soybean Oil Mills; SIC 2079: Shortening, Table Oils, Margarine, & Other Edible Fats & Oils, NEC

311223   Other Oilseed Processing *see* SIC 2074: Cottonseed Oil Mills; SIC 2079: Shortening, Table Oils, Margarine & Other Edible Fats & Oils, NEC; SIC 2076: Vegetable Oil Mills, Except Corn, Cottonseed, & Soybean

311225   Fats & Oils Refining & Blending *see* SIC 2077: Animal & Marine Fats & Oil, NEC; SIC 2074: Cottonseed Oil Mills; SIC 2075: Soybean Oil Mills; SIC 2076: Vegetable Oil Mills, Except Corn, Cottonseed, & Soybean; SIC 2079: Shortening, Table Oils, Margarine, & Other Edible Fats & Oils, NEC

31123   Breakfast Cereal Manufacturing *see* SIC 2043: Cereal Breakfast Foods

311311   Sugarcane Mills *see* SIC 2061: Cane Sugar, Except Refining

311312   Cane Sugar Refining *see* SIC 2062: Cane Sugar Refining

311313   Beet Sugar Manufacturing *see* SIC 2063: Beet Sugar

31132   Chocolate & Confectionery Manufacturing from Cacao Beans *see* SIC 2066: Chocolate & Cocoa Products

31133   Confectionery Manufacturing from Purchased Chocolate *see* SIC 2064: Candy & Other Confectionery Products

31134   Non-Chocolate Confectionery Manufacturing *see* SIC 2064: Candy & Other Confectionery Products; SIC 2067: Chewing Gum; SIC 2099: Food Preparations, NEC

311411   Frozen Fruit, Juice & Vegetable Manufacturing *see* SIC 2037: Frozen Fruits, Fruit Juices, & Vegetables

311412   Frozen Specialty Food Manufacturing *see* SIC 2038: Frozen Specialties, NEC

311421   Fruit & Vegetable Canning *see* SIC 2033: Canned Fruits, Vegetables, Preserves, Jams, & Jellies; SIC 2035: Pickled Fruits & Vegetables, Vegetable Sauces, & Seasonings & Salad Dressings

311422   Specialty Canning *see* SIC 2032: Canned Specialties

311423   Dried & Dehydrated Food Manufacturing *see* SIC 2034: Dried & Dehydrated Fruits, Vegetables & Soup Mixes; SIC 2099: Food Preparation, NEC

311511   Fluid Milk Manufacturing *see* SIC 2026: Fluid Milk

311512   Creamery Butter Manufacturing *see* SIC 2021: Creamery Butter

311513   Cheese Manufacturing *see* SIC 2022: Natural, Processed, & Imitation Cheese

311514   Dry, Condensed, & Evaporated Dairy Product Manufacturing *see* SIC 2023: Dry, Condensed & Evaporated Dairy Products

31152   Ice Cream & Frozen Dessert Manufacturing *see* SIC 2024: Ice Cream & Frozen Desserts

311611   Animal Slaughtering *see* SIC 0751: Livestock Services, Except Veterinary; SIC 2011: Meat Packing Plants; SIC 2048: Prepared Feeds & Feed Ingredients for Animals & Fowls, Except Dogs & Cats

311612   Meat Processed from Carcasses *see* SIC 2013: Sausages & Other Prepared Meats; SIC 5147: Meat & Meat Products

311613   Rendering & Meat By-product Processing *see* SIC 2077: Animal & Marine Fats & Oils

311615   Poultry Processing *see* SIC 2015: Poultry Slaughtering & Processing

311711   Seafood Canning *see* SIC 2077: Animal & Marine Fats & Oils; SIC 2091: Canned & Cured Fish & Seafood

311712   Fresh & Frozen Seafood Processing *see* SIC 2077: Animal & Marine Fats & Oils; SIC 2092: Prepared Fresh or Frozen Fish & Seafood

311811   Retail Bakeries *see* SIC 5461: Retail Bakeries

311812   Commercial Bakeries *see* SIC 2051: Bread & Other Bakery Products, Except Cookies & Crackers; SIC 2052: Cookies & Crackers

311813   Frozen Bakery Product Manufacturing *see* SIC 2053: Frozen Bakery Products, Except Bread

311821   Cookie & Cracker Manufacturing *see* SIC 2052: Cookies & Crackers

311822   Flour Mixes & Dough Manufacturing from Purchased Flour *see* SIC 2045: Prepared Flour Mixes & Doughs

311823   Pasta Manufacturing *see* SIC 2098: Macaroni, Spaghetti, Vermicelli & Noodles

31183   Tortilla Manufacturing *see* SIC 2099: Food Preparations, NEC

311911   Roasted Nuts & Peanut Butter Manufacturing *see* SIC 2068: Salted & Roasted Nuts & Seeds; SIC 2099: Food Preparations, NEC

311919   Other Snack Food Manufacturing *see* SIC 2052: Cookies & Crackers; SIC 2096: Potato Chips, Corn Chips, & Similar Snacks

31192   Coffee & Tea Manufacturing *see* SIC 2043: Cereal Breakfast Foods; SIC 2095: Roasted Coffee; SIC 2099: Food Preparations, NEC

31193   Flavoring Syrup & Concentrate Manufacturing *see* SIC 2087: Flavoring Extracts & Flavoring Syrups

311941   Mayonnaise, Dressing & Other Prepared Sauce Manufacturing *see* SIC 2035: Pickled Fruits & Vegetables, Vegetable Seasonings, & Sauces & Salad Dressings; SIC 2099: Food Preparations, NEC

311942   Spice & Extract Manufacturing *see* SIC 2087: Flavoring Extracts & Flavoring Syrups; SIC 2095: Roasted Coffee; SIC 2099: Food Preparations, NEC; SIC 2899: Chemical Preparations, NEC

311991   Perishable Prepared Food Manufacturing *see* SIC 2099: Food Preparations, NEC

311999   All Other Miscellaneous Food Manufacturing *see* SIC 2015: Poultry Slaughtering & Processing; SIC 2032: Canned Specialties; SIC 2087: Flavoring Extracts & Flavoring Syrups; SIC 2099: Food Preparations, NEC

BEVERAGE & TOBACCO PRODUCT MANUFACTURING

312111   Soft Drink Manufacturing *see* SIC 2086: Bottled & Canned Soft Drinks & Carbonated Water

312112   Bottled Water Manufacturing *see* SIC 2086: Bottled & Canned Soft Drinks & Carbonated Water

312113   Ice Manufacturing *see* SIC 2097: Manufactured Ice

31212   Breweries *see* SIC 2082: Malt Beverages

31213   Wineries *see* SIC 2084: Wines, Brandy, & Brandy Spirits

31214   Distilleries *see* SIC 2085: Distilled & Blended Liquors;

31221   Tobacco Stemming & Redrying *see* SIC 2141: Tobacco Stemming & Redrying

312221   Cigarette Manufacturing *see* SIC 2111: Cigarettes

312229   Other Tobacco Product Manufacturing *see* SIC 2121: Cigars; SIC 2131: Chewing & Smoking Tobacco & Snuff; SIC 2141: Tobacco Stemming & Redrying

TEXTILE MILLS

313111   Yarn Spinning Mills *see* SIC 2281: Yarn Spinning Mills; SIC 2299: Textile Goods, NEC

313112   Yarn Texturing, Throwing & Twisting Mills *see* SIC 2282: Yarn Texturing, Throwing, Winding Mills

313113   Thread Mills *see* SIC 2284: Thread Mills; SIC 2299: Textile Goods, NEC

31321   Broadwoven Fabric Mills *see* SIC 2211: Broadwoven Fabric Mills, Cotton; SIC 2221: Broadwoven Fabric Mills, Manmade Fiber & Silk; SIC 2231: Broadwoven Fabric Mills, Wool; SIC 2299: Textile Goods, NEC

313221   Narrow Fabric Mills *see* SIC 2241: Narrow Fabric & Other Smallware Mills: Cotton, Wool, Silk & Manmade Fiber; SIC 2299: Textile Goods, NEC

313222   Schiffli Machine Embroidery *see* SIC 2397: Schiffli Machine Embroideries

31323   Nonwoven Fabric Mills *see* SIC 2297: Nonwoven Fabrics; SIC 2299: Textile Goods, NEC

313241   Weft Knit Fabric Mills *see* SIC 2257: Weft Knit Fabric Mills; SIC 2259: Knitting Mills NEC

313249   Other Knit Fabric & Lace Mills *see* SIC 2258: Lace & Warp Knit Fabric Mills; SIC 2259: Knitting Mills NEC

313311   Broadwoven Fabric Finishing Mills *see* SIC 2231: Broadwoven Fabric Mills, Wool; SIC 2261: Finishers of Broadwoven Fabrics of Cotton; SIC 2262: Finishers of Broadwoven Fabrics of Manmade Fiber & Silk; SIC 2269: Finishers of Textiles, NEC; SIC 5131: Piece Goods & Notions

313312   Textile & Fabric Finishing Mills *see* SIC 2231: Broadwoven Fabric Mills, Wool; SIC 2257: Weft Knit Fabric Mills; SIC 2258: Lace & Warp Knit Fabric Mills; SIC 2269: Finishers of Textiles, NEC; SIC 2282: Yarn Texturizing, Throwing, Twisting, & Winding Mills; SIC 2284: Thread Mills; SIC 2299: Textile Goods, NEC; SIC 5131: Piece Goods & Notions

31332   Fabric Coating Mills *see* SIC 2295: Coated Fabrics, Not Rubberized; SIC 3069: Fabricated Rubber Products, NEC

TEXTILE PRODUCT MILLS

31411   Carpet & Rug Mills *see* SIC 2273: Carpets & Rugs

314121   Curtain & Drapery Mills *see* SIC 2391: Curtains & Draperies; SIC 5714: Drapery, Curtain, & Upholstery Stores

314129   Other Household Textile Product Mills *see* SIC 2392: Housefurnishings, Except Curtains & Draperies

314911   Textile Bag Mills *see* SIC 2392: Housefurnishings, Except Curtains & Draperies; SIC 2393: Textile Bags

314912   Canvas & Related Product Mills *see* SIC 2394: Canvas & Related Products

314991   Rope, Cordage & Twine Mills *see* SIC 2298: Cordage & Twine

314992   Tire Cord & Tire Fabric Mills *see* SIC 2296: Tire Cord & Fabrics

314999   All Other Miscellaneous Textile Product Mills *see* SIC 2299: Textile Goods, NEC; SIC 2395: Pleating, Decorative & Novelty Stitching, & Tucking for the Trade; SIC 2396: Automotive Trimmings, Apparel Findings, & Related Products; SIC 2399: Fabricated Textile Products, NEC

APPAREL MANUFACTURING

315111   Sheer Hosiery Mills *see* SIC 2251: Women's Full-Length & Knee-Length Hosiery, Except socks; SIC 2252: Hosiery, NEC

315119   Other Hosiery & Sock Mills *see* SIC 2252: Hosiery, NEC

315191   Outerwear Knitting Mills *see* SIC 2253: Knit Outerwear Mills; SIC 2259: Knitting Mills, NEC

315192   Underwear & Nightwear Knitting Mills *see* SIC 2254: Knit Underwear & Nightwear Mills; SIC 2259: Knitting Mills, NEC

315211   Men's & Boys' Cut & Sew Apparel Contractors *see* SIC 2311: Men's & Boys' Suits, Coats, & Overcoats; SIC 2321: Men's & Boys' Shirts, Except Work Shirts; SIC 2322: Men's & Boys' Underwear & Nightwear; SIC 2325: Men's & Boys' Trousers & Slacks; SIC 2326: Men's & Boys' Work Clothing; SIC 2329: Men's & Boys' Clothing, NEC; SIC 2341: Women's, Misses', Children's, & Infants' Underwear & Nightwear; SIC 2361: Girls', Children's, & Infants' Dresses, Blouses & Shirts; SIC 2369: Girls', Children's, & Infants' Outerwear, NEC; SIC 2384: Robes & Dressing Gowns; SIC 2385: Waterproof Outerwear; SIC 2389: Apparel & Accessories, NEC; SIC 2395: Pleating, Decorative & Novelty Stitching, & Tucking for the Trade

315212   Women's & Girls' Cut & Sew Apparel Contractors *see* SIC 2331: Women's, Misses', & Juniors' Blouses & Shirts; SIC 2335: Women's, Misses' & Juniors' Dresses; SIC 2337: Women's, Misses', & Juniors' Suits, Skirts, & Coats; SIC 2339: Women's, Misses', & Juniors' Outerwear, NEC; SIC 2341: Women's, Misses', Children's, & Infants' Underwear & Nightwear; SIC 2342: Brassieres, Girdles, & Allied Garments; SIC 2361: Girls', Children's, & Infants' Dresses, Blouses, & Shirts; SIC 2369: Girls', Children's, & Infants' Outerwear, NEC; SIC 2384: Robes & Dressing Gowns; SIC 2385: Waterproof Outerwear; SIC 2389: Apparel & Accessories, NEC; SIC 2395: Pleating, Decorative & Novelty Stitching, & Tucking for the Trade

315221   Men's & Boys' Cut & Sew Underwear & Nightwear Manufacturing *see* SIC 2322: Men's & Boys' Underwear & Nightwear; SIC 2341: Women's, Misses', Children's, & Infants' Underwear & Nightwear; SIC 2369: Girls', Children's, & Infants' Outerwear, NEC; SIC 2384: Robes & Dressing Gowns

315222   Men's & Boys' Cut & Sew Suit, Coat & Overcoat Manufacturing *see* SIC 2311: Men's & Boys' Suits, Coats, & Overcoats; SIC 2369: Girls', Children's, & Infants' Outerwear, NEC; SIC 2385: Waterproof Outerwear

315223   Men's & Boys' Cut & Sew Shirt Manufacturing *see* SIC 2321: Men's & Boys' Shirts, Except Work Shirts; SIC 2361: Girls', Children's, & Infants' Dresses, Blouses, & Shirts

315224   Men's & Boys' Cut & Sew Trouser, Slack & Jean Manufacturing *see* SIC 2325: Men's & Boys' Trousers & Slacks; SIC 2369: Girls', Children's, & Infants' Outerwear, NEC

315225   Men's & Boys' Cut & Sew Work Clothing Manufacturing *see* SIC 2326: Men's & Boys' Work Clothing

315228   Men's & Boys' Cut & Sew Other Outerwear Manufacturing *see* SIC 2329: Men's & Boys' Clothing, NEC; SIC 2369: Girls', Children's, & Infants' Outerwear, NEC; SIC 2385: Waterproof Outerwear

315231   Women's & Girls' Cut & Sew Lingerie, Loungewear & Nightwear Manufacturing *see* SIC 2341: Women's, Misses', Children's, & Infants' Underwear & Nightwear; SIC 2342: Brassieres, Girdles, & Allied Garments; SIC 2369: Girls', Children's, & Infants' Outerwear, NEC; SIC 2384: Robes & Dressing Gowns; SIC 2389: Apparel & Accessories, NEC

315232   Women's & Girls' Cut & Sew Blouse & Shirt Manufacturing *see* SIC 2331: Women's, Misses', & Juniors' Blouses & Shirts; SIC 2361: Girls', Children's, & Infants' Dresses, Blouses & Shirts

315233   Women's & Girls' Cut & Sew Dress Manufacturing *see* SIC 2335: Women's, Misses', & Juniors' Dresses; SIC 2361: Girls', Children's, & Infants' Dresses, Blouses & Shirts

315234   Women's & Girls' Cut & Sew Suit, Coat, Tailored Jacket & Skirt Manufacturing *see* SIC 2337: Women's, Misses', & Juniors' Suits, Skirts, & Coats; SIC 2369: Girls', Children's, & Infants' Outerwear, NEC; SIC 2385: Waterproof Outerwear

315238   Women's & Girls' Cut & Sew Other Outerwear Manufacturing *see* SIC 2339: Women's, Misses', & Juniors' Outerwear, NEC; SIC 2369: Girls', Children's, & Infants' Outerwear, NEC; SIC 2385: Waterproof Outerwear

315291   Infants' Cut & Sew Apparel Manufacturing *see* SIC 2341: Women's, Misses', Children's, & Infants' Underwear & Nightwear; SIC 2361: Girls', Children's, & Infants' Dresses, Blouses, & Shirts; SIC 2369: Girls', Children's, & Infants' Outerwear, NEC; SIC 2385: Waterproof Outerwear

315292   Fur & Leather Apparel Manufacturing *see* SIC 2371: Fur Goods; SIC 2386: Leather & Sheep-lined Clothing

315299   All Other Cut & Sew Apparel Manufacturing *see* SIC 2329: Men's & Boys' Outerwear, NEC; SIC 2339: Women's, Misses', & Juniors' Outerwear, NEC; SIC 2389: Apparel & Accessories, NEC

315991   Hat, Cap & Millinery Manufacturing *see* SIC 2353: Hats, Caps, & Millinery

315992   Glove & Mitten Manufacturing *see* SIC 2381: Dress & Work Gloves, Except Knit & All-Leather; SIC 3151: Leather Gloves & Mittens

315993   Men's & Boys' Neckwear Manufacturing *see* SIC 2323: Men's & Boys' Neckwear

315999   Other Apparel Accessories & Other Apparel Manufacturing *see* SIC 2339: Women's, Misses', & Juniors' Outerwear, NEC; SIC 2385: Waterproof Outerwear; SIC 2387: Apparel Belts; SIC 2389: Apparel & Accessories, NEC; SIC 2396: Automotive Trimmings, Apparel Findings, & Related Products; SIC 2399: Fabricated Textile Products, NEC

LEATHER & ALLIED PRODUCT MANUFACTURING

31611   Leather & Hide Tanning & Finishing *see* SIC 3111: Leather Tanning & Finishing; SIC 3999: Manufacturing Industries, NEC

316211   Rubber & Plastics Footwear Manufacturing *see* SIC 3021: Rubber & Plastics Footwear

316212   House Slipper Manufacturing *see* SIC 3142: House Slippers

316213   Men's Footwear Manufacturing *see* SIC 3143: Men's Footwear, Except Athletic

316214   Women's Footwear Manufacturing *see* SIC 3144: Women's Footwear, Except Athletic

316219   Other Footwear Manufacturing *see* SIC 3149: Footwear Except Rubber, NEC

316991   Luggage Manufacturing *see* SIC 3161: Luggage

316992   Women's Handbag & Purse Manufacturing *see* SIC 3171: Women's Handbags & Purses

316993   Personal Leather Good Manufacturing *see* SIC 3172: Personal Leather Goods, Except Women's Handbags & Purses

316999   All Other Leather Good Manufacturing *see* SIC 3131: Boot & Shoe Cut Stock & Findings; SIC 3199: Leather Goods, NEC

Wood Product Manufacturing

321113   Sawmills *see* SIC 2421: Sawmills & Planing Mills, General; SIC 2429: Special Product Sawmills, NEC

321114   Wood Preservation *see* SIC 2491: Wood Preserving

321211   Hardwood Veneer & Plywood Manufacturing *see* SIC 2435: Hardwood Veneer & Plywood

321212   Softwood Veneer & Plywood Manufacturing *see* SIC 2436: Softwood Veneer & Plywood

321213   Engineered Wood Member Manufacturing *see* SIC 2439: Structural Wood Members, NEC

321214   Truss Manufacturing *see* SIC 2439: Structural Wood Members, NEC

321219   Reconstituted Wood Product Manufacturing *see* SIC 2493: Reconstituted Wood Products

321911   Wood Window & Door Manufacturing *see* SIC 2431: Millwork

321912   Cut Stock, Resawing Lumber, & Planing *see* SIC 2421: Sawmills & Planing Mills, General; SIC 2426: Hardwood Dimension & Flooring Mills; SIC 2429: Special Product Sawmills, NEC; SIC 2439: Structural Wood Members, NEC

321918   Other Millwork *see* SIC 2426: Hardwood Dimension & Flooring Mills; SIC 2421: Sawmills & Planing Mills, General; SIC 2431: Millwork

32192   Wood Container & Pallet Manufacturing *see* SIC 2441: Nailed & Lock Corner Wood Boxes & Shook; SIC 2448: Wood Pallets & Skids; SIC 2449: Wood Containers, NEC; SIC 2499: Wood Products, NEC

321991   Manufactured Home Manufacturing *see* SIC 2451: Mobile Homes

321992   Prefabricated Wood Building Manufacturing *see* SIC 2452: Prefabricated Wood Buildings & Components

321999   All Other Miscellaneous Wood Product Manufacturing *see* SIC 2426: Hardwood Dimension & Flooring Mills; SIC 2499: Wood Products, NEC; SIC 3131: Boot & Shoe Cut Stock & Findings; SIC 3999: Manufacturing Industries, NEC; SIC 2421: Sawmills & Planing Mills, General; SIC 2429: Special Product Sawmills, NEC

Paper Manufacturing

32211   Pulp Mills *see* SIC 2611: Pulp Mills

322121   Paper Mills *see* SIC 2611: Pulp Mills; SIC 2621: Paper Mills

322122   Newsprint Mills *see* SIC 2621: Paper Mills

32213   Paperboard Mills *see* SIC 2611: Pulp Mills; SIC 2631: Paperboard Mills

322211   Corrugated & Solid Fiber Box Manufacturing *see* SIC 2653: Corrugated & Solid Fiber Boxes

322212   Folding Paperboard Box Manufacturing *see* SIC 2657: Folding Paperboard Boxes, Including Sanitary

322213   Setup Paperboard Box Manufacturing *see* SIC 2652: Setup Paperboard Boxes

322214   Fiber Can, Tube, Drum, & Similar Products Manufacturing *see* SIC 2655: Fiber Cans, Tubes, Drums, & Similar Products

322215   Non-Folding Sanitary Food Container Manufacturing *see* SIC 2656: Sanitary Food Containers, Except Folding; SIC 2679: Converted Paper & Paperboard Products, NEC

322221   Coated & Laminated Packaging Paper & Plastics Film Manufacturing *see* SIC 2671: Packaging Paper & Plastics Film, Coated & Laminated

322222   Coated & Laminated Paper Manufacturing *see* SIC 2672: Coated & Laminated Paper, NEC; SIC 2679: Converted Paper & Paperboard Products, NEC

322223   Plastics, Foil, & Coated Paper Bag Manufacturing *see* SIC 2673: Plastics, Foil, & Coated Paper Bags

322224   Uncoated Paper & Multiwall Bag Manufacturing *see* SIC 2674: Uncoated Paper & Multiwall Bags

322225   Laminated Aluminum Foil Manufacturing for Flexible Packaging Uses *see* SIC 3497: Metal Foil & Leaf

322231   Die-Cut Paper & Paperboard Office Supplies Manufacturing *see* SIC 2675: Die-Cut Paper & Paperboard & Cardboard; SIC 2679: Converted Paper & Paperboard Products, NEC

322232   Envelope Manufacturing *see* SIC 2677: Envelopes

322233   Stationery, Tablet, & Related Product Manufacturing *see* SIC 2678: Stationery, Tablets, & Related Products

322291   Sanitary Paper Product Manufacturing *see* SIC 2676: Sanitary Paper Products

322292   Surface-Coated Paperboard Manufacturing *see* SIC 2675: Die-Cut Paper & Paperboard & Cardboard

322298   All Other Converted Paper Product Manufacturing *see* SIC 2675: Die-Cut Paper & Paperboard & Cardboard; SIC 2679: Converted Paper & Paperboard Products, NEC

Printing & Related Support Activities

323110   Commercial Lithographic Printing *see* SIC 2752: Commercial Printing, Lithographic; SIC 2771: Greeting Cards; SIC 2782: Blankbooks, Loose-leaf Binders & Devices; SIC 3999: Manufacturing Industries, NEC

323111   Commercial Gravure Printing *see* SIC 2754: Commercial Printing, Gravure; SIC 2771: Greeting Cards; SIC 2782: Blankbooks, Loose-leaf Binders & Devices; SIC 3999: Manufacturing Industries, NEC

323112   Commercial Flexographic Printing *see* SIC 2759: Commercial Printing, NEC; SIC 2771: Greeting Cards; SIC 2782: Blankbooks, Loose-leaf Binders & Devices; SIC 3999: Manufacturing Industries, NEC

323113   Commercial Screen Printing *see* SIC 2396: Automotive Trimmings, Apparel Findings, & Related Products; SIC 2759: Commercial Printing, NEC; SIC 2771: Greeting Cards; SIC 2782: Blankbooks, Loose-leaf Binders & Devices; SIC 3999: Manufacturing Industries, NEC

323114   Quick Printing *see* SIC 2752: Commercial Printing, Lithographic; SIC 2759: Commercial Printing, NEC

323115   Digital Printing *see* SIC 2759: Commercial Printing, NEC

323116   Manifold Business Form Printing *see* SIC 2761: Manifold Business Forms

323117   Book Printing *see* SIC 2732: Book Printing

323118   Blankbook, Loose-leaf Binder & Device Manufacturing *see* SIC 2782: Blankbooks, Loose-leaf Binders & Devices

323119   Other Commercial Printing *see* SIC 2759: Commercial Printing, NEC; SIC 2771: Greeting Cards; SIC 2782: Blankbooks, Loose-leaf Binders & Devices; SIC 3999: Manufacturing Industries, NEC

323121   Tradebinding & Related Work *see* SIC 2789: Bookbinding & Related Work

323122   Prepress Services *see* SIC 2791: Typesetting; SIC 2796: Platemaking & Related Services

PETROLEUM & COAL PRODUCTS MANUFACTURING

32411   Petroleum Refineries *see* SIC 2911: Petroleum Refining

324121   Asphalt Paving Mixture & Block Manufacturing *see* SIC 2951: Asphalt Paving Mixtures & Blocks

324122   Asphalt Shingle & Coating Materials Manufacturing *see* SIC 2952: Asphalt Felts & Coatings

324191   Petroleum Lubricating Oil & Grease Manufacturing *see* SIC 2992: Lubricating Oils & Greases

324199   All Other Petroleum & Coal Products Manufacturing *see* SIC 2999: Products of Petroleum & Coal, NEC; SIC 3312: Blast Furnaces & Steel Mills

CHEMICAL MANUFACTURING

32511   Petrochemical Manufacturing *see* SIC 2865: Cyclic Organic Crudes & Intermediates, & Organic Dyes & Pigments; SIC 2869: Industrial Organic Chemicals, NEC

32512   Industrial Gas Manufacturing *see* SIC 2813: Industrial Gases; SIC 2869: Industrial Organic Chemicals, NEC

325131   Inorganic Dye & Pigment Manufacturing *see* SIC 2816: Inorganic Pigments; SIC 2819: Industrial Inorganic Chemicals, NEC

325132   Organic Dye & Pigment Manufacturing *see* SIC 2865: Cyclic Organic Crudes & Intermediates, & Organic Dyes & Pigments

325181   Alkalies & Chlorine Manufacturing *see* SIC 2812: Alkalies & Chlorine

325182   Carbon Black Manufacturing *see* SIC 2816: Inorganic pigments; SIC 2895: Carbon Black

325188   All Other Basic Inorganic Chemical Manufacturing *see* SIC 2819: Industrial Inorganic Chemicals, NEC; SIC 2869: Industrial Organic Chemicals, NEC

325191   Gum & Wood Chemical Manufacturing *see* SIC 2861: Gum & Wood Chemicals

325192   Cyclic Crude & Intermediate Manufacturing *see* SIC 2865: Cyclic Organic Crudes & Intermediates & Organic Dyes & Pigments

325193   Ethyl Alcohol Manufacturing *see* SIC 2869: Industrial Organic Chemicals

325199   All Other Basic Organic Chemical Manufacturing *see* SIC 2869: Industrial Organic Chemicals, NEC; SIC 2899: Chemical & Chemical Preparations, NEC

325211   Plastics Material & Resin Manufacturing *see* SIC 2821: Plastics Materials, Synthetic & Resins, & Nonvulcanizable Elastomers

325212   Synthetic Rubber Manufacturing *see* SIC 2822: Synthetic Rubber

325221   Cellulosic Organic Fiber Manufacturing *see* SIC 2823: Cellulosic Manmade Fibers

325222   Noncellulosic Organic Fiber Manufacturing *see* SIC 2824: Manmade Organic Fibers, Except Cellulosic

325311   Nitrogenous Fertilizer Manufacturing *see* SIC 2873: Nitrogenous Fertilizers

325312   Phosphatic Fertilizer Manufacturing *see* SIC 2874: Phosphatic Fertilizers

325314   Fertilizer Manufacturing *see* SIC 2875: Fertilizers, Mixing Only

32532   Pesticide & Other Agricultural Chemical Manufacturing *see* SIC 2879: Pesticides & Agricultural Chemicals, NEC

325411   Medicinal & Botanical Manufacturing *see* SIC 2833: Medicinal Chemicals & Botanical Products

325412   Pharmaceutical Preparation Manufacturing *see* SIC 2834: Pharmaceutical Preparations; SIC 2835: In-Vitro & In-Vivo Diagnostic Substances

325413   In-Vitro Diagnostic Substance Manufacturing *see* SIC 2835: In-Vitro & In-Vivo Diagnostic Substances

325414   Biological Product Manufacturing *see* SIC 2836: Biological Products, Except Diagnostic Substance

32551   Paint & Coating Manufacturing *see* SIC 2851: Paints, Varnishes, Lacquers, Enamels & Allied Products; SIC 2899: Chemicals & Chemical Preparations, NEC

32552   Adhesive Manufacturing *see* SIC 2891: Adhesives & Sealants

325611   Soap & Other Detergent Manufacturing *see* SIC 2841: Soaps & Other Detergents, Except Specialty Cleaners; SIC 2844: Toilet Preparations

325612   Polish & Other Sanitation Good Manufacturing *see* SIC 2842: Specialty Cleaning, Polishing, & Sanitary Preparations

325613   Surface Active Agent Manufacturing *see* SIC 2843: Surface Active Agents, Finishing Agents, Sulfonated Oils, & Assistants

32562   Toilet Preparation Manufacturing *see* SIC 2844: Perfumes, Cosmetics, & Other Toilet Preparations

32591   Printing Ink Manufacturing *see* SIC 2893: Printing Ink

32592   Explosives Manufacturing *see* SIC 2892: Explosives

325991   Custom Compounding of Purchased Resin *see* SIC 3087: Custom Compounding of Purchased Plastics Resin

325992   Photographic Film, Paper, Plate & Chemical Manufacturing *see* SIC 3861: Photographic Equipment & Supplies

325998   All Other Miscellaneous Chemical Product Manufacturing *see* SIC 2819: Industrial Inorganic Chemicals, NEC; SIC 2899: Chemicals & Chemical Preparations, NEC; SIC 3952: Lead Pencils & Art Goods; SIC 3999: Manufacturing Industries, NEC

PLASTICS & RUBBER PRODUCTS MANUFACTURING

326111   Unsupported Plastics Bag Manufacturing *see* SIC 2673: Plastics, Foil, & Coated Paper Bags

326112   Unsupported Plastics Packaging Film & Sheet Manufacturing *see* SIC 2671: Packaging Paper & Plastics Film, Coated, & Laminated

326113   Unsupported Plastics Film & Sheet Manufacturing *see* SIC 3081: Unsupported Plastics Film & Sheets

326121   Unsupported Plastics Profile Shape Manufacturing *see* SIC 3082: Unsupported Plastics Profile Shapes; SIC 3089: Plastics Product, NEC

326122   Plastics Pipe & Pipe Fitting Manufacturing *see* SIC 3084: Plastics Pipe; SIC 3089: Plastics Products, NEC

32613   Laminated Plastics Plate, Sheet & Shape Manufacturing *see* SIC 3083: Laminated Plastics Plate, Sheet & Profile Shapes

32614   Polystyrene Foam Product Manufacturing *see* SIC 3086: Plastics Foam Products

32615   Urethane & Other Foam Product Manufacturing *see* SIC 3086: Plastics Foam Products

32616   Plastics Bottle Manufacturing *see* SIC 3085: Plastics Bottles

326191   Plastics Plumbing Fixture Manufacturing *see* SIC 3088: Plastics Plumbing Fixtures

326192   Resilient Floor Covering Manufacturing *see* SIC 3069: Fabricated Rubber Products, NEC; SIC 3996: Linoleum, Asphalted-Felt-Base, & Other Hard Surface Floor Coverings, NEC

326199   All Other Plastics Product Manufacturing *see* SIC 3089: Plastics Products, NEC; SIC 3999: Manufacturing Industries, NEC

326211   Tire Manufacturing *see* SIC 3011: Tires & Inner Tubes

326212   Tire Retreading *see* SIC 7534: Tire Retreading & Repair Shops

32622   Rubber & Plastics Hoses & Belting Manufacturing *see* SIC 3052: Rubber & Plastics Hose & Belting

326291   Rubber Product Manufacturing for Mechanical Use *see* SIC 3061: Molded, Extruded, & Lathe-Cut Mechanical Rubber Goods

326299   All Other Rubber Product Manufacturing *see* SIC 3069: Fabricated Rubber Products, NEC

NONMETALLIC MINERAL PRODUCT MANUFACTURING

327111   Vitreous China Plumbing Fixture & China & Earthenware Fittings & Bathroom Accessories Manufacturing *see* SIC 3261: Vitreous China Plumbing Fixtures & China & Earthenware Fittings & Bathroom Accessories

327112   Vitreous China, Fine Earthenware & Other Pottery Product Manufacturing *see* SIC 3262: Vitreous China Table & Kitchen Articles; SIC 3263: Fine Earthenware Table & Kitchen Articles; SIC 3269: Pottery Products, NEC

327113   Porcelain Electrical Supply Manufacturing *see* SIC 3264: Porcelain Electrical Supplies

327121   Brick & Structural Clay Tile Manufacturing *see* SIC 3251: Brick & Structural Clay Tile

327122   Ceramic Wall & Floor Tile Manufacturing *see* SIC 3253: Ceramic Wall & Floor Tile

327123   Other Structural Clay Product Manufacturing *see* SIC 3259: Structural Clay Products, NEC

327124   Clay Refractory Manufacturing *see* SIC 3255: Clay Refractories

327125   Nonclay Refractory Manufacturing *see* SIC 3297: Nonclay Refractories

327211   Flat Glass Manufacturing *see* SIC 3211: Flat Glass

327212   Other Pressed & Blown Glass & Glassware Manufacturing *see* SIC 3229: Pressed & Blown Glass & Glassware, NEC

327213   Glass Container Manufacturing *see* SIC 3221: Glass Containers

327215   Glass Product Manufacturing Made of Purchased Glass *see* SIC 3231: Glass Products Made of Purchased Glass

32731   Cement Manufacturing *see* SIC 3241: Cement, Hydraulic

32732   Ready-Mix Concrete Manufacturing *see* SIC 3273: Ready-Mixed Concrete

327331   Concrete Block & Brick Manufacturing *see* SIC 3271: Concrete Block & Brick

327332   Concrete Pipe Manufacturing *see* SIC 3272: Concrete Products, Except Block & Brick

32739   Other Concrete Product Manufacturing *see* SIC 3272: Concrete Products, Except Block & Brick

32741   Lime Manufacturing *see* SIC 3274: Lime

32742   Gypsum & Gypsum Product Manufacturing *see* SIC 3275: Gypsum Products; SIC 3299: Nonmetallic Mineral Products, NEC

32791   Abrasive Product Manufacturing *see* SIC 3291: Abrasive Products

327991   Cut Stone & Stone Product Manufacturing *see* SIC 3281: Cut Stone & Stone Products

327992   Ground or Treated Mineral & Earth Manufacturing *see* SIC 3295: Minerals & Earths, Ground or Otherwise Treated

327993   Mineral Wool Manufacturing *see* SIC 3296: Mineral Wool

327999   All Other Miscellaneous Nonmetallic Mineral Product Manufacturing *see* SIC 3272: Concrete Products, Except Block & Brick; SIC 3292: Asbestos Products; SIC 3299: Nonmetallic Mineral Products, NEC

PRIMARY METAL MANUFACTURING

331111   Iron & Steel Mills *see* SIC 3312: Steel Works, Blast Furnaces , & Rolling Mills; SIC 3399: Primary Metal Products, NEC

331112   Electrometallurgical Ferroalloy Product Manufacturing *see* SIC 3313: Electrometallurgical Products, Except Steel

33121   Iron & Steel Pipes & Tubes Manufacturing from Purchased Steel *see* SIC 3317: Steel Pipe & Tubes

331221   Cold-Rolled Steel Shape Manufacturing *see* SIC 3316: Cold-Rolled Steel Sheet, Strip & Bars

331222   Steel Wire Drawing *see* SIC 3315: Steel Wiredrawing & Steel Nails & Spikes

331311   Alumina Refining *see* SIC 2819: Industrial Inorganic Chemicals, NEC

331312   Primary Aluminum Production *see* SIC 3334: Primary Production of Aluminum

331314   Secondary Smelting & Alloying of Aluminum *see* SIC 3341: Secondary Smelting & Refining of Nonferrous Metals; SIC 3399: Primary Metal Products, NEC

331315   Aluminum Sheet, Plate & Foil Manufacturing *see* SIC 3353: Aluminum Sheet, Plate, & Foil

331316   Aluminum Extruded Product Manufacturing *see* SIC 3354: Aluminum Extruded Products

331319   Other Aluminum Rolling & Drawing *see* SIC 3355: Aluminum Rolling & Drawing, NEC; SIC 3357: Drawing & Insulating of Nonferrous Wire

331411   Primary Smelting & Refining of Copper *see* SIC 3331: Primary Smelting & Refining of Copper

331419   Primary Smelting & Refining of Nonferrous Metal *see* SIC 3339: Primary Smelting & Refining of Nonferrous Metals, Except Copper & Aluminum

331421   Copper Rolling, Drawing & Extruding *see* SIC 3351: Rolling, Drawing, & Extruding of Copper

331422   Copper Wire Drawing *see* SIC 3357: Drawing & Insulating of Nonferrous Wire

331423   Secondary Smelting, Refining, & Alloying of Copper *see* SIC 3341: Secondary Smelting & Refining of Nonferrous Metals; SIC 3399: Primary Metal Products, NEC

331491   Nonferrous Metal Rolling, Drawing & Extruding *see* SIC 3356: Rolling, Drawing & Extruding of Nonferrous Metals, Except Copper & Aluminum; SIC 3357: Drawing & Insulating of Nonferrous Wire

331492   Secondary Smelting, Refining, & Alloying of Nonferrous Metal *see* SIC 3313: Electrometallurgical Products, Except Steel; SIC 3341: Secondary Smelting & Reining of Nonferrous Metals; SIC 3399: Primary Metal Products, NEC

331511   Iron Foundries *see* SIC 3321: Gray & Ductile Iron Foundries; SIC 3322: Malleable Iron Foundries

331512   Steel Investment Foundries *see* SIC 3324: Steel Investment Foundries

331513   Steel Foundries, *see* SIC 3325: Steel Foundries, NEC

331521   Aluminum Die-Castings *see* SIC 3363: Aluminum Die-Castings

331522   Nonferrous Die-Castings *see* SIC 3364: Nonferrous Die-Castings, Except Aluminum

331524   Aluminum Foundries *see* SIC 3365: Aluminum Foundries

331525   Copper Foundries *see* SIC 3366: Copper Foundries

331528   Other Nonferrous Foundries *see* SIC 3369: Nonferrous Foundries, Except Aluminum & Copper

FABRICATED METAL PRODUCT MANUFACTURING

332111   Iron & Steel Forging *see* SIC 3462: Iron & Steel Forgings

332112   Nonferrous Forging *see* SIC 3463: Nonferrous Forgings

332114   Custom Roll Forming *see* SIC 3449: Miscellaneous Structural Metal Work

332115   Crown & Closure Manufacturing *see* SIC 3466: Crowns & Closures

332116   Metal Stamping *see* SIC 3469: Metal Stampings, NEC

332117   Powder Metallurgy Part Manufacturing *see* SIC 3499: Fabricated Metal Products, NEC

332211   Cutlery & Flatware Manufacturing *see* SIC 3421: Cutlery; SIC 3914: Silverware, Plated Ware, & Stainless Steel Ware

332212   Hand & Edge Tool Manufacturing *see* SIC 3423: Hand & Edge Tools, Except Machine Tools & Handsaws; SIC 3523: Farm Machinery & Equipment; SIC 3524: Lawn & Garden Tractors & Home Lawn & Garden Equipment; SIC 3545: Cutting Tools, Machine Tools Accessories, & Machinist Precision Measuring Devices; SIC 3799: Transportation Equipment, NEC; SIC 3999: Manufacturing Industries, NEC

332213   Saw Blade & Handsaw Manufacturing *see* SIC 3425: Saw Blades & Handsaws

332214   Kitchen Utensil, Pot & Pan Manufacturing *see* SIC 3469: Metal Stampings, NEC

332311   Prefabricated Metal Building & Component Manufacturing *see* SIC 3448: Prefabricated Metal Buildings & Components

332312   Fabricated Structural Metal Manufacturing *see* SIC 3441: Fabricated Structural Metal; SIC 3449: Miscellaneous Structural Metal Work

332313   Plate Work Manufacturing *see* SIC 3443: Fabricated Plate Work

332321   Metal Window & Door Manufacturing *see* SIC 3442: Metal Doors, Sash, Frames, Molding & Trim; SIC 3449: Miscellaneous Structural Metal Work

332322   Sheet Metal Work Manufacturing *see* SIC 3444: Sheet Metal Work

332323   Ornamental & Architectural Metal Work Manufacturing *see* SIC 3446: Architectural & Ornamental Metal Work; SIC 3449: Miscellaneous Structural Metal Work; SIC 3523: Farm Machinery & Equipment

33241   Power Boiler & Heat Exchanger Manufacturing *see* SIC 3443: Fabricated Plate Work

33242   Metal Tank Manufacturing *see* SIC 3443: Fabricated Plate Work

332431   Metal Can Manufacturing *see* SIC 3411: Metal Cans

332439   Other Metal Container Manufacturing *see* SIC 3412: Metal Shipping Barrels, Drums, Kegs, & Pails; SIC 3429: Hardware, NEC; SIC 3444: Sheet Metal Work; SIC 3499: Fabricated Metal Products, NEC; SIC 3537: Industrial Trucks, Tractors, Trailers, & Stackers

33251   Hardware Manufacturing *see* SIC 3429: Hardware, NEC; SIC 3499: Fabricated Metal Products, NEC

332611   Steel Spring Manufacturing *see* SIC 3493: Steel Springs, Except Wire

332612   Wire Spring Manufacturing *see* SIC 3495: Wire Springs

332618   Other Fabricated Wire Product Manufacturing *see* SIC 3315: Steel Wiredrawing & Steel Nails & Spikes; SIC 3399: Primary Metal Products, NEC; SIC 3496: Miscellaneous Fabricated Wire Products

33271   Machine Shops *see* SIC 3599: Industrial & Commercial Machinery & Equipment, NEC

332721   Precision Turned Product Manufacturing *see* SIC 3451: Screw Machine Products

332722   Bolt, Nut, Screw, Rivet & Washer Manufacturing *see* SIC 3452: Bolts, Nuts, Screws, Rivets, & Washers

332811   Metal Heat Treating *see* SIC 3398: Metal Heat Treating

332812   Metal Coating, Engraving , & Allied Services to Manufacturers *see* SIC 3479: Coating, Engraving, & Allied Services, NEC

332813   Electroplating, Plating, Polishing, Anodizing & Coloring *see* SIC 3399: Primary Metal Products, NEC; SIC 3471: Electroplating, Plating, Polishing, Anodizing, & Coloring

332911   Industrial Valve Manufacturing *see* SIC 3491: Industrial Valves

332912   Fluid Power Valve & Hose Fitting Manufacturing *see* SIC 3492: Fluid Power Valves & Hose Fittings; SIC 3728: Aircraft Parts & Auxiliary Equipment, NEC

332913   Plumbing Fixture Fitting & Trim Manufacturing *see* SIC 3432: Plumbing Fixture Fittings & Trim

332919   Other Metal Valve & Pipe Fitting Manufacturing *see* SIC 3429: Hardware, NEC; SIC 3494: Valves & Pipe Fittings, NEC; SIC 3499: Fabricated Metal Products, NEC

332991   Ball & Roller Bearing Manufacturing *see* SIC 3562: Ball & Roller Bearings

332992   Small Arms Ammunition Manufacturing *see* SIC 3482: Small Arms Ammunition

332993   Ammunition Manufacturing *see* SIC 3483: Ammunition, Except for Small Arms

332994   Small Arms Manufacturing *see* SIC 3484: Small Arms

332995   Other Ordnance & Accessories Manufacturing *see* SIC 3489: Ordnance & Accessories, NEC

332996   Fabricated Pipe & Pipe Fitting Manufacturing *see* SIC 3498: Fabricated Pipe & Pipe Fittings

332997   Industrial Pattern Manufacturing *see* SIC 3543: Industrial Patterns

332998   Enameled Iron & Metal Sanitary Ware Manufacturing *see* SIC 3431: Enameled Iron & Metal Sanitary Ware

332999   All Other Miscellaneous Fabricated Metal Product Manufacturing *see* SIC 3291: Abrasive Products; SIC 3432: Plumbing Fixture Fittings & Trim; SIC 3494: Valves & Pipe Fittings, NEC; SIC 3497: Metal Foil & Leaf; SIC 3499: Fabricated Metal Products, NEC; SIC 3537: Industrial Trucks, Tractors, Trailers, & Stackers; SIC 3599: Industrial & Commercial Machinery & Equipment, NEC; SIC 3999: Manufacturing Industries, NEC

MACHINERY MANUFACTURING

333111 Farm Machinery & Equipment Manufacturing *see* SIC 3523: Farm Machinery & Equipment

333112 Lawn & Garden Tractor & Home Lawn & Garden Equipment Manufacturing *see* SIC 3524: Lawn & Garden Tractors & Home Lawn & Garden Equipment

33312 Construction Machinery Manufacturing *see* SIC 3531: Construction Machinery & Equipment

333131 Mining Machinery & Equipment Manufacturing *see* SIC 3532: Mining Machinery & Equipment, Except Oil & Gas Field Machinery & Equipment

333132 Oil & Gas Field Machinery & Equipment Manufacturing *see* SIC 3533: Oil & Gas Field Machinery & Equipment

33321 Sawmill & Woodworking Machinery Manufacturing *see* SIC 3553: Woodworking Machinery

33322 Rubber & Plastics Industry Machinery Manufacturing *see* SIC 3559: Special Industry Machinery, NEC

333291 Paper Industry Machinery Manufacturing *see* SIC 3554: Paper Industries Machinery

333292 Textile Machinery Manufacturing *see* SIC 3552: Textile Machinery

333293 Printing Machinery & Equipment Manufacturing *see* SIC 3555: Printing Trades Machinery & Equipment

333294 Food Product Machinery Manufacturing *see* SIC 3556: Food Products Machinery

333295 Semiconductor Machinery Manufacturing *see* SIC 3559: Special Industry Machinery, NEC

333298 All Other Industrial Machinery Manufacturing *see* SIC 3559: Special Industry Machinery, NEC; SIC 3639: Household Appliances, NEC

333311 Automatic Vending Machine Manufacturing *see* SIC 3581: Automatic Vending Machines

333312 Commercial Laundry, Drycleaning & Pressing Machine Manufacturing *see* SIC 3582: Commercial Laundry, Drycleaning & Pressing Machines

333313 Office Machinery Manufacturing *see* SIC 3578: Calculating & Accounting Machinery, Except Electronic Computers; SIC 3579: Office Machines, NEC

333314 Optical Instrument & Lens Manufacturing *see* SIC 3827: Optical Instruments & Lenses

333315 Photographic & Photocopying Equipment Manufacturing *see* SIC 3861: Photographic Equipment & Supplies

333319 Other Commercial & Service Industry Machinery Manufacturing *see* SIC 3559: Special Industry Machinery, NEC; SIC 3589: Service Industry Machinery, NEC; SIC 3599: Industrial & Commercial Machinery & Equipment, NEC; SIC 3699: Electrical Machinery, Equipment & Supplies, NEC

333411 Air Purification Equipment Manufacturing *see* SIC 3564: Industrial & Commercial Fans & Blowers & Air Purification Equipment

333412 Industrial & Commercial Fan & Blower Manufacturing *see* SIC 3564: Industrial & Commercial Fans & Blowers & Air Purification Equipment

333414 Heating Equipment Manufacturing *see* SIC 3433: Heating Equipment, Except Electric & Warm Air Furnaces; SIC 3634: Electric Housewares & Fans

333415 Air-Conditioning & Warm Air Heating Equipment & Commercial & Industrial Refrigeration Equipment Manufacturing *see* SIC 3443: Fabricated Plate Work; SIC 3585: Air-Conditioning & Warm Air Heating Equipment & Commercial & Industrial Refrigeration Equipment

333511 Industrial Mold Manufacturing *see* SIC 3544: Special Dies & Tools, Die Sets, Jigs & Fixtures, & Industrial Molds

333512 Machine Tool Manufacturing *see* SIC 3541: Machine Tools, Metal Cutting Type

333513 Machine Tool Manufacturing *see* SIC 3542: Machine Tools, Metal Forming Type

333514 Special Die & Tool, Die Set, Jig & Fixture Manufacturing *see* SIC 3544: Special Dies & Tools, Die Sets, Jigs & Fixtures, & Industrial Molds

333515 Cutting Tool & Machine Tool Accessory Manufacturing *see* SIC 3545: Cutting Tools, Machine Tool Accessories, & Machinists' Precision Measuring Devices

333516 Rolling Mill Machinery & Equipment Manufacturing *see* SIC 3547: Rolling Mill Machinery & Equipment

333518 Other Metalworking Machinery Manufacturing *see* SIC 3549: Metalworking Machinery, NEC

333611 Turbine & Turbine Generator Set Unit Manufacturing *see* SIC 3511: Steam, Gas, & Hydraulic Turbines, & Turbine Generator Set Units

333612 Speed Changer, Industrial High-Speed Drive & Gear Manufacturing *see* SIC 3566: Speed Changers, Industrial High-Speed Drives, & Gears

333613 Mechanical Power Transmission Equipment Manufacturing *see* SIC 3568: Mechanical Power Transmission Equipment, NEC

333618 Other Engine Equipment Manufacturing *see* SIC 3519: Internal Combustion Engines, NEC; SIC 3699: Electrical Machinery, Equipment & Supplies, NEC

333911 Pump & Pumping Equipment Manufacturing *see* SIC 3561: Pumps & Pumping Equipment; SIC 3743: Railroad Equipment

333912 Air & Gas Compressor Manufacturing *see* SIC 3563: Air & Gas Compressors

333913 Measuring & Dispensing Pump Manufacturing *see* SIC 3586: Measuring & Dispensing Pumps

333921 Elevator & Moving Stairway Manufacturing *see* SIC 3534: Elevators & Moving Stairways

333922 Conveyor & Conveying Equipment Manufacturing *see* SIC 3523: Farm Machinery & Equipment; SIC 3535: Conveyors & Conveying Equipment

333923 Overhead Traveling Crane, Hoist & Monorail System Manufacturing *see* SIC 3536: Overhead Traveling Cranes, Hoists, & Monorail Systems; SIC 3531: Construction Machinery & Equipment

333924 Industrial Truck, Tractor, Trailer & Stacker Machinery Manufacturing *see* SIC 3537: Industrial Trucks, Tractors, Trailers, & Stackers

333991 Power-Driven Hand Tool Manufacturing *see* SIC 3546: Power-Driven Handtools

333992 Welding & Soldering Equipment Manufacturing *see* SIC 3548: Electric & Gas Welding & Soldering Equipment

333993 Packaging Machinery Manufacturing *see* SIC 3565: Packaging Machinery

333994 Industrial Process Furnace & Oven Manufacturing *see* SIC 3567: Industrial Process Furnaces & Ovens

333995 Fluid Power Cylinder & Actuator Manufacturing *see* SIC 3593: Fluid Power Cylinders & Actuators

333996 Fluid Power Pump & Motor Manufacturing *see* SIC 3594: Fluid Power Pumps & Motors

333997 Scale & Balance Manufacturing *see* SIC 3596: Scales & Balances, Except Laboratory

333999 All Other General Purpose Machinery Manufacturing *see* SIC 3599: Industrial & Commercial Machinery & Equipment, NEC; SIC 3569: General Industrial Machinery & Equipment, NEC

COMPUTER & ELECTRONIC PRODUCT MANUFACTURING

334111 Electronic Computer Manufacturing see SIC 3571: Electronic Computers

334112 Computer Storage Device Manufacturing see SIC 3572: Computer Storage Devices

334113 Computer Terminal Manufacturing see SIC 3575: Computer Terminals

334119 Other Computer Peripheral Equipment Manufacturing see SIC 3577: Computer Peripheral Equipment, NEC; SIC 3578: Calculating & Accounting Machines, Except Electronic Computers; SIC 3699: Electrical Machinery, Equipment & Supplies, NEC

33421   Telephone Apparatus Manufacturing see SIC 3661: Telephone & Telegraph Apparatus

33422   Radio & Television Broadcasting & Wireless Communications Equipment Manufacturing see SIC 3663: Radio & Television Broadcasting & Communication Equipment; SIC 3679: Electronic Components, NEC

33429   Other Communications Equipment Manufacturing see SIC 3669: Communications Equipment, NEC

33431   Audio & Video Equipment Manufacturing see SIC 3651: Household Audio & Video Equipment

334411 Electron Tube Manufacturing see SIC 3671: Electron Tubes

334412 Printed Circuit Board Manufacturing see SIC 3672: Printed Circuit Boards

334413 Semiconductor & Related Device Manufacturing see SIC 3674: Semiconductors & Related Devices

334414 Electronic Capacitor Manufacturing see SIC 3675: Electronic Capacitors

334415 Electronic Resistor Manufacturing see SIC 3676: Electronic Resistors

334416 Electronic Coil, Transformer, & Other Inductor Manufacturing see SIC 3661: Telephone & Telegraph Apparatus; SIC 3677: Electronic Coils, Transformers, & Other Inductors; SIC 3825: Instruments for Measuring & Testing of Electricity & Electrical Signals

334417 Electronic Connector Manufacturing see SIC 3678: Electronic Connectors

334418 Printed Circuit/Electronics Assembly Manufacturing see SIC 3679: Electronic Components, NEC; SIC 3661: Telephone & Telegraph Apparatus

334419 Other Electronic Component Manufacturing see SIC 3679: Electronic Components, NEC

334510 Electromedical & Electrotherapeutic Apparatus Manufacturing see SIC 3842: Orthopedic, Prosthetic & Surgical Appliances & Supplies; SIC 3845: Electromedical & Electrotherapeutic Apparatus

334511 Search, Detection, Navigation, Guidance, Aeronautical, & Nautical System & Instrument Manufacturing see SIC 3812: Search, Detection, Navigation, Guidance, Aeronautical, & Nautical Systems & Instruments

334512 Automatic Environmental Control Manufacturing for Residential, Commercial & Appliance Use see SIC 3822: Automatic Controls for Regulating Residential & Commercial Environments & Appliances

334513 Instruments & Related Products Manufacturing for Measuring, Displaying, & Controlling Industrial Process Variables see SIC 3823: Industrial Instruments for Measurement, Display, & Control of Process Variables; & Related Products

334514 Totalizing Fluid Meter & Counting Device Manufacturing see SIC 3824: Totalizing Fluid Meters & Counting Devices

334515 Instrument Manufacturing for Measuring & Testing Electricity & Electrical Signals see SIC 3825: Instruments for Measuring & Testing of Electricity & Electrical Signals

334516 Analytical Laboratory Instrument Manufacturing see SIC 3826: Laboratory Analytical Instruments

334517 Irradiation Apparatus Manufacturing see SIC 3844: X-Ray Apparatus & Tubes & Related Irradiation Apparatus; SIC 3845: Electromedical & Electrotherapeutic Apparatus

334518 Watch, Clock, & Part Manufacturing see SIC 3495: Wire Springs; SIC 3579: Office Machines, NEC; SIC 3873: Watches, Clocks, Clockwork Operated Devices, & Parts

334519 Other Measuring & Controlling Device Manufacturing see SIC 3829: Measuring & Controlling Devices, NEC

334611 Software Reproducing see SIC 7372: Prepackaged Software

334612 Prerecorded Compact Disc , Tape, & Record Reproducing see SIC 3652: Phonograph Records & Prerecorded Audio Tapes & Disks; SIC 7819: Services Allied to Motion Picture Production

334613 Magnetic & Optical Recording Media Manufacturing see SIC 3695: Magnetic & Optical Recording Media

ELECTRICAL EQUIPMENT, APPLIANCE, & COMPONENT MANUFACTURING

33511   Electric Lamp Bulb & Part Manufacturing see SIC 3641: Electric Lamp Bulbs & Tubes

335121 Residential Electric Lighting Fixture Manufacturing see SIC 3645: Residential Electric Lighting Fixtures; SIC 3999: Manufacturing Industries, NEC

335122 Commercial, Industrial & Institutional Electric Lighting Fixture Manufacturing see SIC 3646: Commercial, Industrial, & Institutional Electric Lighting Fixtures

335129 Other Lighting Equipment Manufacturing see SIC 3648: Lighting Equipment, NEC; SIC 3699: Electrical Machinery, Equipment, & Supplies, NEC

335211 Electric Housewares & Household Fan Manufacturing see SIC 3634: Electric Housewares & Fans

335212 Household Vacuum Cleaner Manufacturing see SIC 3635: Household Vacuum Cleaners; SIC 3639: Household Appliances, NEC

335221 Household Cooking Appliance Manufacturing see SIC 3631: Household Cooking Equipment

335222 Household Refrigerator & Home Freezer Manufacturing see SIC 3632: Household Refrigerators & Home & Farm Freezers

335224 Household Laundry Equipment Manufacturing see SIC 3633: Household Laundry Equipment

335228 Other Major Household Appliance Manufacturing see SIC 3639: Household Appliances, NEC

335311 Power, Distribution & Specialty Transformer Manufacturing see SIC 3548: Electric & Gas Welding & Soldering Equipment; SIC 3612: Power, Distribution, & Speciality Transformers

335312 Motor & Generator Manufacturing see SIC 3621: Motors & Generators; SIC 7694: Armature Rewinding Shops

335313 Switchgear & Switchboard Apparatus Manufacturing see SIC 3613: Switchgear & Switchboard Apparatus

335314 Relay & Industrial Control Manufacturing see SIC 3625: Relays & Industrial Controls

335911 Storage Battery Manufacturing see SIC 3691: Storage Batteries

335912 Dry & Wet Primary Battery Manufacturing *see* SIC
        3692: Primary Batteries, Dry & Wet

335921 Fiber-Optic Cable Manufacturing *see* SIC 3357: Draw-
        ing & Insulating of Nonferrous Wire

335929 Other Communication & Energy Wire Manufacturing *see*
        SIC 3357: Drawing & Insulating of Nonferrous Wire

335931 Current-Carrying Wiring Device Manufacturing *see* SIC
        3643: Current-Carrying Wiring Devices

335932 Noncurrent-Carrying Wiring Device Manufacturing *see*
        SIC 3644: Noncurrent-Carrying Wiring Devices

335991 Carbon & Graphite Product Manufacturing *see* SIC
        3624: Carbon & Graphite Products

335999 All Other Miscellaneous Electrical Equipment & Com-
        ponent Manufacturing *see* SIC 3629: Electrical Indus-
        trial Apparatus, NEC; SIC 3699: Electrical Machinery,
        Equipment, & Supplies, NEC

TRANSPORTATION EQUIPMENT MANUFACTURING

336111 Automobile Manufacturing *see* SIC 3711: Motor Vehi-
        cles & Passenger Car Bodies

336112 Light Truck & Utility Vehicle Manufacturing *see* SIC
        3711: Motor Vehicles & Passenger Car Bodies

33612   Heavy Duty Truck Manufacturing *see* SIC 3711: Motor
        Vehicles & Passenger Car Bodies

336211 Motor Vehicle Body Manufacturing *see* SIC 3711: Mo-
        tor Vehicles & Passenger Car Bodies; SIC 3713:
        Truck & Bus Bodies; SIC 3714: Motor Vehicle Parts
        & Accessories

336212 Truck Trailer Manufacturing *see* SIC 3715: Truck Trailers

336213 Motor Home Manufacturing *see* SIC 3716: Motor Homes

336214 Travel Trailer & Camper Manufacturing *see* SIC 3792:
        Travel Trailers & Campers; SIC 3799: Transportation
        Equipment, NEC

336311 Carburetor, Piston, Piston Ring & Valve Manufacturing
        see SIC 3592: Carburetors, Pistons, Piston Rings, &
        Valves

336312 Gasoline Engine & Engine Parts Manufacturing *see* SIC
        3714: Motor Vehicle Parts & Accessories

336321 Vehicular Lighting Equipment Manufacturing *see* SIC
        3647: Vehicular Lighting Equipment

336322 Other Motor Vehicle Electrical & Electronic Equipment
        Manufacturing *see* SIC 3679: Electronic Components,
        NEC; SIC 3694: Electrical Equipment for Internal
        Combustion Engines; SIC 3714: Motor Vehicle Parts
        & Accessories

33633   Motor Vehicle Steering & Suspension Components
        Manufacturing *see* SIC 3714: Motor Vehicle Parts &
        Accessories

33634   Motor Vehicle Brake System Manufacturing *see* SIC
        3292: Asbestos Products; SIC 3714: Motor Vehicle
        Parts & Accessories

33635   Motor Vehicle Transmission & Power Train Parts Man-
        ufacturing *see* SIC 3714: Motor Vehicle Parts & Ac-
        cessories

33636   Motor Vehicle Fabric Accessories & Seat Manufactur-
        ing *see* SIC 2396: Automotive Trimmings, Apparel
        Findings, & Related Products; SIC 2399: Fabricated
        Textile Products, NEC; SIC 2531: Public Building &
        Related Furniture

33637   Motor Vehicle Metal Stamping *see* SIC 3465: Automo-
        tive Stampings

336391 Motor Vehicle Air-Conditioning Manufacturing *see* SIC
        3585: Air-Conditioning & Warm Air Heating Equipment
        & Commercial & Industrial Refrigeration Equipment

336399 All Other Motor Vehicle Parts Manufacturing *see* SIC
        3519: Internal Combustion Engines, NEC; SIC 3599:
        Industrial & Commercial Machinery & Equipment,
        NEC; SIC 3714: Motor Vehicle Parts & Accessories

336411 Aircraft Manufacturing *see* SIC 3721: Aircraft

336412 Aircraft Engine & Engine Parts Manufacturing *see* SIC
        3724: Aircraft Engines & Engine Parts

336413 Other Aircraft Part & Auxiliary Equipment Manufactur-
        ing *see* SIC 3728: Aircraft Parts & Auxiliary Equip-
        ment, NEC

336414 Guided Missile & Space Vehicle Manufacturing *see* SIC
        3761: Guided Missiles & Space Vehicles

336415 Guided Missile & Space Vehicle Propulsion Unit &
        Propulsion Unit Parts Manufacturing *see* SIC 3764:
        Guided Missile & Space Vehicle Propulsion Units &
        Propulsion Unit Parts

336419 Other Guided Missile & Space Vehicle Parts & Auxil-
        iary Equipment Manufacturing *see* SIC 3769: Guided
        Missile & Space Vehicle Parts & Auxiliary Equipment

33651   Railroad Rolling Stock Manufacturing *see* SIC 3531:
        Construction Machinery & Equipment; SIC 3743:
        Railroad Equipment

336611 Ship Building & Repairing *see* SIC 3731: Ship Building
        & Repairing

336612 Boat Building *see* SIC 3732: Boat Building & Repairing

336991 Motorcycle, Bicycle, & Parts Manufacturing *see* SIC
        3944: Games, Toys, & Children's Vehicles, Except
        Dolls & Bicycles; SIC 3751: Motorcycles, Bicycles &
        Parts

336992 Military Armored Vehicle, Tank & Tank Component
        Manufacturing *see* SIC 3711: Motor Vehicles & Passen-
        ger Car Bodies; SIC 3795: Tanks & Tank Components

336999 All Other Transportation Equipment Manufacturing *see*
        SIC 3799: Transportation Equipment, NEC

FURNITURE & RELATED PRODUCT MANUFACTURING

33711   Wood Kitchen Cabinet & Counter Top Manufacturing
        see SIC 2434: Wood Kitchen Cabinets; SIC 2541:
        Wood Office & Store Fixtures, Partitions, Shelving, &
        Lockers; SIC 5712: Furniture Stores

337121 Upholstered Household Furniture Manufacturing *see*
        SIC 2512: Wood Household Furniture, Upholstered;
        SIC 2515: Mattress, Foundations, & Convertible Beds;
        SIC 5712: Furniture

337122 Nonupholstered Wood Household Furniture Manufactur-
        ing *see* SIC 2511: Wood Household Furniture, Except
        Upholstered; SIC 5712: Furniture Stores

337124 Metal Household Furniture Manufacturing *see* SIC
        2514: Metal Household Furniture

337125 Household Furniture Manufacturing *see* SIC 2519:
        Household Furniture, NEC

337127 Institutional Furniture Manufacturing *see* SIC 2531:
        Public Building & Related Furniture; SIC 2599: Furni-
        ture & Fixtures, NEC; SIC 3952: Lead Pencils,
        Crayons, & Artist's Materials; SIC 3999: Manufactur-
        ing Industries, NEC

337129 Wood Television, Radio, & Sewing Machine Cabinet
        Manufacturing *see* SIC 2517: Wood Television, Radio,
        Phonograph, & Sewing Machine Cabinets

337211 Wood Office Furniture Manufacturing *see* SIC 2521:
        Wood Office Furniture

337212 Custom Architectural Woodwork & Millwork Manufac-
        turing *see* SIC 2541: Wood Office & Store Fixtures,
        Partitions, Shelving, & Lockers

337214 Nonwood Office Furniture Manufacturing *see* SIC 2522: Office Furniture, Except Wood

337215 Showcase, Partition, Shelving, & Locker Manufacturing *see* SIC 2542: Office & Store Fixtures, Partitions, Shelving & Lockers, Except Wood; SIC 2541: Wood Office & Store Fixtures, Partitions, Shelving, & Lockers; SIC 2426: Hardwood Dimension & Flooring Mills; SIC 3499: Fabricated Metal Products, NEC

33791 Mattress Manufacturing *see* SIC 2515: Mattresses, Foundations & Convertible Beds

33792 Blind & Shade Manufacturing *see* SIC 2591: Drapery Hardware & Window Blinds & Shades

MISCELLANEOUS MANUFACTURING

339111 Laboratory Apparatus & Furniture Manufacturing *see* SIC 3829: Measuring & Controlling Devices, NEC

339112 Surgical & Medical Instrument Manufacturing *see* SIC 3841: Surgical & Medical Instruments & Apparatus; SIC 3829: Measuring & Controlling Devices, NEC

339113 Surgical Appliance & Supplies Manufacturing *see* SIC 2599: Furniture & Fixtures, NEC; SIC 3842: Orthopedic, Prosthetic, & Surgical Appliances & Supplies

339114 Dental Equipment & Supplies Manufacturing *see* SIC 3843: Dental Equipment & Supplies

339115 Ophthalmic Goods Manufacturing *see* SIC 3851: Opthalmic Goods; SIC 5995: Optical Goods Stores

339116 Dental Laboratories *see* SIC 8072: Dental Laboratories

339911 Jewelry Manufacturing *see* SIC 3469: Metal Stamping, NEC; SIC 3479: Coating, Engraving, & Allied Services, NEC; SIC 3911: Jewelry, Precious Metal

339912 Silverware & Plated Ware Manufacturing *see* SIC 3479: Coating, Engraving, & Allied Services, NEC; SIC 3914: Silverware, Plated Ware, & Stainless Steel Ware

339913 Jewelers' Material & Lapidary Work Manufacturing *see* SIC 3915: Jewelers' Findings & Materials, & Lapidary Work

339914 Costume Jewelry & Novelty Manufacturing *see* SIC 3479: Coating, Engraving, & Allied Services, NEC; SIC 3499: Fabricated Metal Products, NEC; SIC 3961: Costume Jewelry & Costume Novelties, Except Precious Metal

33992 Sporting & Athletic Goods Manufacturing *see* SIC 3949: Sporting & Athletic Goods, NEC

339931 Doll & Stuffed Toy Manufacturing *see* SIC 3942: Dolls & Stuffed Toys

339932 Game, Toy, & Children's Vehicle Manufacturing *see* SIC 3944: Games, Toys, & Children's Vehicles, Except Dolls & Bicycles

339941 Pen & Mechanical Pencil Manufacturing *see* SIC 3951: Pens, Mechanical Pencils, & Parts

339942 Lead Pencil & Art Good Manufacturing *see* SIC 2531: Public Buildings & Related Furniture; SIC 3579: Office Machines, NEC; SIC 3952: Lead Pencils, Crayons, & Artists' Materials

339943 Marking Device Manufacturing *see* SIC 3953: Marking Devices

339944 Carbon Paper & Inked Ribbon Manufacturing *see* SIC 3955: Carbon Paper & Inked Ribbons

33995 Sign Manufacturing *see* SIC 3993: Signs & Advertising Specialties

339991 Gasket, Packing, & Sealing Device Manufacturing *see* SIC 3053: Gaskets, Packing, & Sealing Devices

339992 Musical Instrument Manufacturing *see* SIC 3931: Musical Instruments

339993 Fastener, Button, Needle & Pin Manufacturing *see* SIC 3965: Fasteners, Buttons, Needles, & Pins; SIC 3131: Boat & Shoe Cut Stock & Findings

339994 Broom, Brush & Mop Manufacturing *see* SIC 3991: Brooms & Brushes; SIC 2392: Housefurnishings, Except Curtains & Draperies

339995 Burial Casket Manufacturing *see* SIC 3995: Burial Caskets

339999 All Other Miscellaneous Manufacturing *see* SIC 2499: Wood Products, NEC; SIC 3999: Manufacturing Industries, NEC

WHOLESALE TRADE

42111 Automobile & Other Motor Vehicle Wholesalers *see* SIC 5012: Automobiles & Other Motor Vehicles

42112 Motor Vehicle Supplies & New Part Wholesalers *see* SIC 5013: Motor Vehicle Supplies & New Parts

42113 Tire & Tube Wholesalers *see* SIC 5014: Tires & Tubes

42114 Motor Vehicle Part Wholesalers *see* SIC 5015: Motor Vehicle Parts, Used

42121 Furniture Wholesalers *see* SIC 5021: Furniture

42122 Home Furnishing Wholesalers *see* SIC 5023: Homefurnishings

42131 Lumber, Plywood, Millwork & Wood Panel Wholesalers *see* SIC 5031: Lumber, Plywood, Millwork, & Wood Panels; SIC 5211: Lumber & Other Building Materials Dealers - Retail

42132 Brick, Stone & Related Construction Material Wholesalers *see* SIC 5032: Brick, Stone, & Related Construction Materials

42133 Roofing, Siding & Insulation Material Wholesalers *see* SIC 5033: Roofing, Siding, & Insulation Materials

42139 Other Construction Material Wholesalers *see* SIC 5039: Construction Materials, NEC

42141 Photographic Equipment & Supplies Wholesalers *see* SIC 5043: Photographic Equipment & Supplies

42142 Office Equipment Wholesalers *see* SIC 5044: Office Equipment

42143 Computer & Computer Peripheral Equipment & Software Wholesalers *see* SIC 5045: Computers & Computer Peripherals Equipment & Software

42144 Other Commercial Equipment Wholesalers *see* SIC 5046: Commercial Equipment, NEC

42145 Medical, Dental & Hospital Equipment & Supplies Wholesalers *see* SIC 5047: Medical, Dental & Hospital Equipment & Supplies

42146 Ophthalmic Goods Wholesalers *see* SIC 5048: Ophthalmic Goods

42149 Other Professional Equipment & Supplies Wholesalers *see* SIC 5049: Professional Equipment & Supplies, NEC

42151 Metal Service Centers & Offices *see* SIC 5051: Metals Service Centers & Offices

42152 Coal & Other Mineral & Ore Wholesalers *see* SIC 5052: Coal & Other Mineral & Ores

42161 Electrical Apparatus & Equipment, Wiring Supplies & Construction Material Wholesalers *see* SIC 5063: Electrical Apparatus & Equipment, Wiring Supplies & Construction Materials

42162 Electrical Appliance, Television & Radio Set Wholesalers *see* SIC 5064: Electrical Appliances, Television & Radio Sets

42169 Other Electronic Parts & Equipment Wholesalers *see* SIC 5065: Electronic Parts & Equipment, NEC

42171 Hardware Wholesalers *see* SIC 5072: Hardware

42172 Plumbing & Heating Equipment & Supplies Wholesalers *see* SIC 5074: Plumbing & Heating Equipment & Supplies

42173   Warm Air Heating & Air-Conditioning Equipment & Supplies Wholesalers *see* SIC 5075: Warm Air Heating & Air-Conditioning Equipment & Supplies

42174   Refrigeration Equipment & Supplies Wholesalers *see* SIC 5078: Refrigeration Equipment & Supplies

42181   Construction & Mining Machinery & Equipment Wholesalers *see* SIC 5082: Construction & Mining Machinery & Equipment

42182   Farm & Garden Machinery & Equipment Wholesalers *see* SIC 5083: Farm & Garden Machinery & Equipment

42183   Industrial Machinery & Equipment Wholesalers *see* SIC 5084: Industrial Machinery & Equipment; SIC 5085: Industrial Supplies

42184   Industrial Supplies Wholesalers *see* SIC 5085: Industrial Supplies

42185   Service Establishment Equipment & Supplies Wholesalers *see* SIC 5087: Service Establishment Equipment & Supplies Wholesalers

42186   Transportation Equipment & Supplies Wholesale, *see* SIC: 5088: Tranportation Equipment & Supplies, Except Motor Vehicles

42191   Sporting & Recreational Goods & Supplies Wholesalers *see* SIC 5091: Sporting & Recreational Goods & Supplies

42192   Toy & Hobby Goods & Supplies Wholesalers *see* SIC 5092: Toys & Hobby Goods & Supplies

42193   Recyclable Material Wholesalers *see* SIC 5093: Scrap & Waste Materials

42194   Jewelry, Watch, Precious Stone & Precious Metal Wholesalers *see* SIC 5094: Jewelry, Watches, Precious Stones, & Precious Metals

42199   Other Miscellaneous Durable Goods Wholesalers *see* SIC 5099: Durable Goods, NEC; SIC 7822: Motion Picture & Video Tape Distribution

42211   Printing & Writing Paper Wholesalers *see* SIC 5111: Printing & Writing Paper

42212   Stationary & Office Supplies Wholesalers *see* SIC 5112: Stationery & Office Supplies

42213   Industrial & Personal Service Paper Wholesalers *see* SIC 5113: Industrial & Personal Service Paper

42221   Drug, Drug Proprietaries & Druggists' Sundries Wholesalers *see* SIC 5122: Drugs, Drug Proprietaries, & Druggists' Sundries

42231   Piece Goods, Notions & Other Dry Goods Wholesalers *see* SIC 5131: Piece Goods, Notions, & Other Dry Goods

42232   Men's & Boys' Clothing & Furnishings Wholesalers *see* SIC 5136: Men's & Boys' Clothing & Furnishings

42233   Women's, Children's & Infants' & Accessories Wholesalers *see* SIC 5137: Women's, Children's, & Infants' Clothing & Accessories

42234   Footwear Wholesalers *see* SIC 5139: Footwear

42241   General Line Grocery Wholesalers *see* SIC 5141: Groceries, General Line

42242   Packaged Frozen Food Wholesalers *see* SIC 5142: Packaged Frozen Foods

42243   Dairy Product Wholesalers *see* SIC 5143: Dairy Products, Except Dried or Canned

42244   Poultry & Poultry Product Wholesalers *see* SIC 5144: Poultry & Poultry Products

42245   Confectionery Wholesalers *see* SIC 5145: Confectionery

42246   Fish & Seafood Wholesalers *see* SIC 5146: Fish & Seafoods

42247   Meat & Meat Product Wholesalers *see* SIC 5147: Meats & Meat Products

42248   Fresh Fruit & Vegetable Wholesalers *see* SIC 5148: Fresh Fruits & Vegetables

42249   Other Grocery & Related Products Wholesalers *see* SIC 5149: Groceries & Related Products, NEC

42251   Grain & Field Bean Wholesalers *see* SIC 5153: Grain & Field Beans

42252   Livestock Wholesalers *see* SIC 5154: Livestock

42259   Other Farm Product Raw Material Wholesalers *see* SIC 5159: Farm-Product Raw Materials, NEC

42261   Plastics Materials & Basic Forms & Shapes Wholesalers *see* SIC 5162: Plastics Materials & Basic Forms & Shapes

42269   Other Chemical & Allied Products Wholesalers *see* SIC 5169: Chemicals & Allied Products, NEC

42271   Petroleum Bulk Stations & Terminals *see* SIC 5171: Petroleum Bulk Stations & Terminals

42272   Petroleum & Petroleum Products Wholesalers *see* SIC 5172: Petroleum & Petroleum Products Wholesalers, Except Bulk Stations & Terminals

42281   Beer & Ale Wholesalers *see* SIC 5181: Beer & Ale

42282   Wine & Distilled Alcoholic Beverage Wholesalers *see* SIC 5182: Wine & Distilled Alcoholic Beverages

42291   Farm Supplies Wholesalers *see* SIC 5191: Farm Supplies

42292   Book, Periodical & Newspaper Wholesalers *see* SIC 5192: Books, Periodicals, & Newspapers

42293   Flower, Nursery Stock & Florists' Supplies Wholesalers *see* SIC 5193: Flowers, Nursery Stock, & Florists' Supplies

42294   Tobacco & Tobacco Product Wholesalers *see* SIC 5194: Tobacco & Tobacco Products

42295   Paint, Varnish & Supplies Wholesalers *see* SIC 5198: Paints, Varnishes, & Supplies; SIC 5231: Paint, Glass & Wallpaper Stores

42299   Other Miscellaneous Nondurable Goods Wholesalers *see* SIC 5199: Nondurable Goods, NEC

RETAIL TRADE

44111   New Car Dealers *see* SIC 5511: Motor Vehicle Dealers, New and Used

44112   Used Car Dealers *see* SIC 5521: Motor Vehicle Dealers, Used Only

44121   Recreational Vehicle Dealers *see* SIC 5561: Recreational Vehicle Dealers

441221 Motorcycle Dealers *see* SIC 5571: Motorcycle Dealers

441222 Boat Dealers *see* SIC 5551: Boat Dealers

441229 All Other Motor Vehicle Dealers *see* SIC 5599: Automotive Dealers, NEC

44131   Automotive Parts & Accessories Stores *see* SIC 5013: Motor Vehicle Supplies & New Parts; SIC 5731: Radio, Television, & Consumer Electronics Stores; SIC 5531: Auto & Home Supply Stores

44132   Tire Dealers *see* SIC 5014: Tires & Tubes; SIC 5531: Auto & Home Supply Stores

44211   Furniture Stores *see* SIC 5021: Furniture; SIC 5712: Furniture Stores

44221   Floor Covering Stores *see* SIC 5023: Homefurnishings; SIC 5713: Floor Coverings Stores

442291 Window Treatment Stores *see* SIC 5714: Drapery, Curtain, & Upholstery Stores; SIC 5719: Miscellaneous Homefurnishings Stores

442299 All Other Home Furnishings Stores *see* SIC 5719: Miscellaneous Homefurnishings Stores

443111 Household Appliance Stores *see* SIC 5722: Household Appliance Stores; SIC 5999: Miscellaneous Retail Stores, NEC; SIC 7623: Refrigeration & Air-Conditioning Service & Repair Shops; SIC 7629: Electrical & Electronic Repair Shops, NEC

443112 Radio, Television & Other Electronics Stores *see* SIC 5731: Radio, Television, & Consumer Electronics Stores; SIC 5999: Miscellaneous Retail Stores, NEC; SIC 7622: Radio & Television Repair Shops

44312 Computer & Software Stores *see* SIC 5045: Computers & Computer Peripheral Equipment & Software; SIC 7378: Computer Maintenance & Repair `; SIC 5734: Computer & Computer Software Stores

44313 Camera & Photographic Supplies Stores *see* SIC 5946: Camera & Photographic Supply Stores

44411 Home Centers *see* SIC 5211: Lumber & Other Building Materials Dealers

44412 Paint & Wallpaper Stores *see* SIC 5198: Paints, Varnishes, & Supplies; SIC 5231: Paint, Glass, & Wallpaper Stores

44413 Hardware Stores *see* SIC 5251: Hardware Stores

44419 Other Building Material Dealers *see* SIC 5031: Lumber, Plywood, Millwork, & Wood Panels; SIC 5032: Brick, Stone, & Related Construction Materials; SIC 5039: Construction Materials, NEC; SIC 5063: Electrical Apparatus & Equipment, Wiring Supplies, & Construction Materials; SIC 5074: Plumbing & Heating Equipment & Supplies; SIC 5211: Lumber & Other Building Materials Dealers; SIC 5231: Paint, Glass, & Wallpaper Stores

44421 Outdoor Power Equipment Stores *see* SIC 5083: Farm & Garden Machinery & Equipment; SIC 5261: Retail Nurseries, Lawn & Garden Supply Stores

44422 Nursery & Garden Centers *see* SIC 5191: Farm Supplies; SIC 5193: Flowers, Nursery Stock, & Florists' Supplies; SIC 5261: Retail Nurseries, Lawn & Garden Supply Stores

44511 Supermarkets & Other Grocery Stores *see* SIC 5411: Grocery Stores

44512 Convenience Stores *see* SIC 5411: Grocery Stores

44521 Meat Markets *see* SIC 5421: Meat & Fish Markets, Including Freezer Provisioners; SIC 5499: Miscellaneous Food Stores

44522 Fish & Seafood Markets *see* SIC 5421: Meat & Fish Markets, Including Freezer Provisioners

44523 Fruit & Vegetable Markets *see* SIC 5431: Fruit & Vegetable Markets

445291 Baked Goods Stores *see* SIC 5461: Retail Bakeries

445292 Confectionery & Nut Stores *see* SIC 5441: Candy, Nut & Confectionery Stores

445299 All Other Specialty Food Stores *see* SIC 5499: Miscellaneous Food Stores; SIC 5451: Dairy Products Stores

44531 Beer, Wine & Liquor Stores *see* SIC 5921: Liquor Stores

44611 Pharmacies & Drug Stores *see* SIC 5912: Drug Stores & Proprietary Stores

44612 Cosmetics, Beauty Supplies & Perfume Stores *see* SIC 5087: Service Establishment Equipment & Supplies; SIC 5999: Miscellaneous Retail Stores, NEC

44613 Optical Goods Stores *see* SIC 5995: Optical Goods Stores

446191 Food Supplement Stores *see* SIC 5499: Miscellaneous Food Stores

446199 All Other Health & Personal Care Stores *see* SIC 5047: Medical, Dental, & Hospital Equipment & Supplies; SIC 5999: Miscellaneous Retail Stores, NEC

44711 Gasoline Stations with Convenience Stores *see* SIC 5541: Gasoline Service Station; SIC 5411: Grocery Stores

44719 Other Gasoline Stations *see* SIC 5541: Gasoline Service Station

44811 Men's Clothing Stores *see* SIC 5611: Men's & Boys' Clothing & Accessory Stores

44812 Women's Clothing Stores *see* SIC 5621: Women's Clothing Stores

44813 Children's & Infants' Clothing Stores *see* SIC 5641: Children's & Infants' Wear Stores

44814 Family Clothing Stores *see* SIC 5651: Family Clothing Stores

44815 Clothing Accessories Stores *see* SIC 5611: Men's & Boys' Clothing & Accessory Stores; SIC 5632: Women's Accessory & Specialty Stores; SIC 5699: Miscellaneous Apparel & Accessory Stores

44819 Other Clothing Stores *see* SIC 5699: Miscellaneous Apparel & Accessory Stores; SIC 5632: Women's Accessory & Specialty Stores

44821 Shoe Stores *see* SIC 5661: Shoe Stores

44831 Jewelry Stores *see* SIC 5999: Miscellaneous Retailer, NEC; SIC 5944: Jewelry Stores

44832 Luggage & Leather Goods Stores *see* SIC 5948: Luggage & Leather Goods Stores

45111 Sporting Goods Stores *see* SIC 7699: Repair Shops & Related Services, NEC; SIC 5941: Sporting Goods Stores & Bicycle Shops

45112 Hobby, Toy & Game Stores *see* SIC 5945: Hobby, Toy, & Game Stores

45113 Sewing, Needlework & Piece Goods Stores *see* SIC 5714: Drapery, Curtain, & Upholstery Stores; SIC 5949: Sewing, Needlework, & Piece Goods Stores

45114 Musical Instrument & Supplies Stores *see* SIC 5736: Musical Instruments Stores

451211 Book Stores *see* SIC 5942: Book Stores

451212 News Dealers & Newsstands *see* SIC 5994: News Dealers & Newsstands

45122 Prerecorded Tape, Compact Disc & Record Stores *see* SIC 5735: Record & Prerecorded Tape Stores

45211 Department Stores *see* SIC 5311: Department Stores

45291 Warehouse Clubs & Superstores *see* SIC 5399: Miscellaneous General Merchandise Stores; SIC 5411: Grocery Stores

45299 All Other General Merchandise Stores *see* SIC 5399: Miscellaneous General Merchandise Stores; SIC 5331: Variety Stores

45311 Florists *see* SIC 5992: Florists

45321 Office Supplies & Stationery Stores *see* SIC 5049: Professional Equipment & Supplies, NEC; SIC 5112: Stationery & Office Supplies; SIC 5943: Stationery Stores

45322 Gift, Novelty & Souvenir Stores *see* SIC 5947: Gift, Novelty, & Souvenir Shops

45331 Used Merchandise Stores *see* SIC 5932: Used Merchandise Stores

45391 Pet & Pet Supplies Stores *see* SIC 5999: Miscellaneous Retail Stores, NEC

45392 Art Dealers *see* SIC 5999: Miscellaneous Retail Stores, NEC

45393 Manufactured Home Dealers *see* SIC 5271: Mobile Home Dealers

453991 Tobacco Stores *see* SIC 5993: Tobacco Stores & Stands

453998 All Other Miscellaneous Store Retailers *see* SIC 5999: Miscellaneous Retail Stores, NEC; SIC 5261: Retail Nurseries, Lawn & Garden Supply Stores

45411 Electronic Shopping & Mail-Order Houses *see* SIC 5961: Catalog & Mail-Order Houses

45421 Vending Machine Operators *see* SIC 5962: Automatic Merchandise Machine Operators

454311 Heating Oil Dealers *see* SIC 5171: Petroleum Bulk Stations & Terminals; SIC 5983: Fuel Oil Dealers

454312 Liquefied Petroleum Gas Dealers *see* SIC 5171: Petroleum Bulk Stations & Terminals; SIC 5984: Liquefied Petroleum Gas Dealers

454319 Other Fuel Dealers *see* SIC 5989: Fuel Dealers, NEC

45439   Other Direct Selling Establishments *see* SIC 5421: Meat & Fish Markets, Including Freezer Provisioners; SIC 5963: Direct Selling Establishments

TRANSPORTATION & WAREHOUSING

481111   Scheduled Passenger Air Transportation *see* SIC 4512: Air Transportation, Scheduled

481112   Scheduled Freight Air Transportation *see* SIC 4512: Air Transportation, Scheduled

481211   Nonscheduled Chartered Passenger Air Transportation *see* SIC 4522: Air Transportation, Nonscheduled

481212   Nonscheduled Chartered Freight Air Transportation *see* SIC 4522: Air Transportation, Nonscheduled

481219   Other Nonscheduled Air Transportation *see* SIC 0721: Crop Planting, Cultivating, & Protecting; SIC 7319: Advertising, NEC; SIC 7335: Commercial Photography

482111   Line-Haul Railroads *see* SIC 4011: Railroads, Line-Haul Operating

482112   Short Line Railroads *see* SIC 4013: Railroad Switching & Terminal Establishments

483111   Deep Sea Freight Transportation *see* SIC 4412: Deep Sea Foreign Transportation of Freight

483112   Deep Sea Passenger Transportation *see* SIC 4481: Deep Sea Transportation of Passengers, Except by Ferry

483113   Coastal & Great Lakes Freight Transportation *see* SIC 4424: Deep Sea Domestic Transportation of Freight; SIC 4432: Freight Transportation on the Great Lakes - St. Lawrence Seaway; SIC 4492: Towing & Tugboat Services

483114   Coastal & Great Lakes Passenger Transportation *see* SIC 4481: Deep Sea Transportation of Passengers, Except by Ferry; SIC 4482: Ferries

483211   Inland Water Freight Transportation *see* SIC 4449: Water Transportation of Freight, NEC; SIC 4492: Towing & Tugboat Services

483212   Inland Water Passenger Transportation *see* SIC 4482: Ferries; SIC 4489: Water Transportation of Passengers, NEC

48411   General Freight Trucking, Local *see* SIC 4212: Local Trucking without Storage; SIC 4214: Local Trucking with Storage

484121   General Freight Trucking, Long-Distance, Truckload *see* SIC 4213: Trucking, Except Local

484122   General Freight Trucking, Long-Distance, Less Than Truckload *see* SIC 4213: Trucking, Except Local

48421   Used Household & Office Goods Moving *see* SIC 4212: Local Trucking Without Storage; SIC 4213: Trucking, Except Local; SIC 4214: Local Trucking With Storage

48422   Specialized Freight Trucking, Local *see* SIC 4212: Local Trucking without Storage; SIC 4214: Local Trucking with Storage

48423   Specialized Freight Trucking, Long-Distance *see* SIC 4213: Trucking, Except Local

485111   Mixed Mode Transit Systems *see* SIC 4111: Local & Suburban Transit

485112   Commuter Rail Systems *see* SIC 4111: Local & Suburban Transit

485113   Bus & Motor Vehicle Transit Systems *see* SIC 4111: Local & Suburban Transit

485119   Other Urban Transit Systems *see* SIC 4111: Local & Suburban Transit

48521   Interurban & Rural Bus Transportation *see* SIC 4131: Intercity & Rural Bus Transportation

48531   Taxi Service *see* SIC 4121: Taxicabs

48532   Limousine Service *see* SIC 4119: Local Passenger Transportation, NEC

48541   School & Employee Bus Transportation *see* SIC 4151: School Buses; SIC 4119: Local Passenger Transportation, NEC

48551   Charter Bus Industry *see* SIC 4141: Local Charter Bus Service; SIC 4142: Bus Charter Services, Except Local

485991   Special Needs Transportation *see* SIC 4119: Local Passenger Transportation, NEC

485999   All Other Transit & Ground Passenger Transportation *see* SIC 4111: Local & Suburban Transit; SIC 4119: Local Passenger Transportation, NEC

48611   Pipeline Transportation of Crude Oil *see* SIC 4612: Crude Petroleum Pipelines

48621   Pipeline Transportation of Natural Gas *see* SIC 4922: Natural Gas Transmission; SIC 4923: Natural Gas Transmission & Distribution

48691   Pipeline Transportation of Refined Petroleum Products *see* SIC 4613: Refined Petroleum Pipelines

48699   All Other Pipeline Transportation *see* SIC 4619: Pipelines, NEC

48711   Scenic & Sightseeing Transportation, Land *see* SIC 4119: Local Passenger Transportation, NEC; SIC 4789: Transportation Services, NEC; SIC 7999: Amusement & Recreation Services, NEC

48721   Scenic & Sightseeing Transportation, Water *see* SIC 4489: Water Transportation of Passengers, NEC; SIC 7999: Amusement & Recreation Services, NEC

48799   Scenic & Sightseeing Transportation, Other *see* SIC 4522: Air Transportation, Nonscheduled; SIC 7999: Amusement & Recreation Services, NEC

488111   Air Traffic Control *see* SIC 4581: Airports, Flying Fields, & Airport Terminal Services; SIC 9621: Regulation & Administration of Transportation Programs

488119   Other Airport Operations *see* SIC 4581: Airports, Flying Fields, & Airport Terminal Services; SIC 4959: Sanitary Services, NEC

48819   Other Support Activities for Air Transportation *see* SIC 4581: Airports, Flying Fields, & Airport Terminal Services

48821   Support Activities for Rail Transportation *see* SIC 4013: Railroad Switching & Terminal Establishments; SIC 4741: Rental of Railroad Cars; SIC 4789: Transportation Services, NEC

48831   Port & Harbor Operations *see* SIC 4491: Marine Cargo Handling; SIC 4499: Water Transportation Services, NEC

48832   Marine Cargo Handling *see* SIC 4491: Marine Cargo Handling

48833   Navigational Services to Shipping *see* SIC 4492: Towing & Tugboat Services; SIC 4499: Water Transportation Services, NEC

48839   Other Support Activities for Water Transportation *see* SIC 4499: Water Transportation Services, NEC; SIC 4785: Fixed Facilities & Inspection & Weighing Services for Motor Vehicle Transportation; SIC 7699: Repair Shops & Related Services, NEC

48841   Motor Vehicle Towing *see* SIC 7549: Automotive Services, Except Repair & Carwashes

48849   Other Support Activities for Road Transportation *see* SIC 4173: Terminal & Service Facilities for Motor Vehicle Passenger Transportation; SIC 4231: Terminal & Joint Terminal Maintenance Facilities for Motor Freight Transportation; SIC 4785: Fixed Facilities & Inspection & Weighing Services for Motor Vehicle Transportation

48851   Freight Transportation Arrangement *see* SIC 4731: Arrangement of Transportation of Freight & Cargo

488991   Packing & Crating *see* SIC 4783: Packing & Crating

488999   All Other Support Activities for Transportation *see* SIC 4729: Arrangement of Passenger Transportation, NEC; SIC 4789: Transportation Services, NEC

49111   Postal Service *see* SIC 4311: United States Postal Service

49211   Couriers *see* SIC 4215: Courier Services, Except by Air; SIC 4513: Air Courier Services

49221   Local Messengers & Local Delivery *see* SIC 4215: Courier Services, Except by Air

49311   General Warehousing & Storage Facilities *see* SIC 4225: General Warehousing & Storage; SIC 4226: Special Warehousing & Storage, NEC

49312   Refrigerated Warehousing & Storage Facilities *see* SIC 4222: Refrigerated Warehousing & Storage; SIC 4226: Special Warehousing & Storage, NEC

49313   Farm Product Warehousing & Storage Facilities *see* SIC 4221: Farm Product Warehousing & Storage

49319   Other Warehousing & Storage Facilities *see* SIC 4226: Special Warehousing & Storage, NEC

INFORMATION

51111   Newspaper Publishers *see* SIC 2711: Newspapers: Publishing or Publishing & Printing

51112   Periodical Publishers *see* SIC 2721: Periodicals: Publishing or Publishing & Printing

51113   Book Publishers *see* SIC 2731: Books: Publishing or Publishing & Printing

51114   Database & Directory Publishers *see* SIC 2741: Miscellaneous Publishing

511191   Greeting Card Publishers *see* SIC 2771: Greeting Cards

511199   All Other Publishers *see* SIC 2741: Miscellaneous Publishing

51121   Software Publishers *see* SIC 7372: Prepackaged Software

51211   Motion Picture & Video Production *see* SIC 7812: Motion Picture & Video Tape Production

51212   Motion Picture & Video Distribution *see* SIC 7822: Motion Picture & Video Tape Distribution; SIC 7829: Services Allied to Motion Picture Distribution

512131   Motion Picture Theaters, Except Drive-Ins. *see* SIC 7832: Motion Picture Theaters, Except Drive-In

512132   Drive-In Motion Picture Theaters *see* SIC 7833: Drive-In Motion Picture Theaters

512191   Teleproduction & Other Post-Production Services *see* SIC 7819: Services Allied to Motion Picture Production

512199   Other Motion Picture & Video Industries *see* SIC 7819: Services Allied to Motion Picture Production; SIC 7829: Services Allied to Motion Picture Distribution

51221   Record Production *see* SIC 8999: Services, NEC

51222   Integrated Record Production/Distribution *see* SIC 3652: Phonograph Records & Prerecorded Audio Tapes & Disks

51223   Music Publishers *see* SIC 2731: Books: Publishing or Publishing & Printing; SIC 2741: Miscellaneous Publishing; SIC 8999: Services, NEC

51224   Sound Recording Studios *see* SIC 7389: Business Services, NEC

51229   Other Sound Recording Industries *see* SIC 7389: Business Services, NEC; SIC 7922: Theatrical Producers & Miscellaneous Theatrical Services

513111   Radio Networks *see* SIC 4832: Radio Broadcasting Stations

513112   Radio Stations *see* SIC 4832: Radio Broadcasting Stations

51312   Television Broadcasting *see* SIC 4833: Television Broadcasting Stations

51321   Cable Networks *see* SIC 4841: Cable & Other Pay Television Services

51322   Cable & Other Program Distribution *see* SIC 4841: Cable & Other Pay Television Services

51331   Wired Telecommunications Carriers *see* SIC 4813: Telephone Communications, Except Radiotelephone; SIC 4822: Telegraph & Other Message Communications

513321   Paging *see* SIC 4812: Radiotelephone Communications

513322   Cellular & Other Wireless Telecommunications *see* SIC 4812: Radiotelephone Communications; SIC 4899: Communications Services, NEC

51333   Telecommunications Resellers *see* SIC 4812: Radio Communications; SIC 4813: Telephone Communications, Except Radiotelephone

51334   Satellite Telecommunications *see* SIC 4899: Communications Services, NEC

51339   Other Telecommunications *see* SIC 4899: Communications Services, NEC

51411   News Syndicates *see* SIC 7383: News Syndicates

51412   Libraries & Archives *see* SIC 8231: Libraries

514191   On-Line Information Services *see* SIC 7375: Information Retrieval Services

514199   All Other Information Services *see* SIC 8999: Services, NEC

51421   Data Processing Services *see* SIC 7374: Computer Processing & Data Preparation & Processing Services

FINANCE & INSURANCE

52111   Monetary Authorities - Central Bank *see* SIC 6011: Federal Reserve Banks

52211   Commercial Banking *see* SIC 6021: National Commercial Banks; SIC 6022: State Commercial Banks; SIC 6029: Commercial Banks, NEC; SIC 6081: Branches & Agencies of Foreign Banks

52212   Savings Institutions *see* SIC 6035: Savings Institutions, Federally Chartered; SIC 6036: Savings Institutions, Not Federally Chartered

52213   Credit Unions *see* SIC 6061: Credit Unions, Federally Chartered; SIC 6062: Credit Unions, Not Federally Chartered

52219   Other Depository Credit Intermediation *see* SIC 6022: State Commercial Banks

52221   Credit Card Issuing *see* SIC 6021: National Commercial Banks; SIC 6022: State Commercial Banks; SIC 6141: Personal Credit Institutions

52222   Sales Financing *see* SIC 6141: Personal Credit Institutions; SIC 6153: Short-Term Business Credit Institutions, Except Agricultural .; SIC 6159: Miscellaneous Business Credit Institutions

522291   Consumer Lending *see* SIC 6141: Personal Credit Institutions

522292   Real Estate Credit *see* SIC 6162: Mortgage Bankers & Loan Correspondents

522293   International Trade Financing *see* SIC 6081: Branches & Agencies of Foreign Banks; SIC 6082: Foreign Trade & International Banking Institutions; SIC 6111: Federal & Federally-Sponsored Credit Agencies; SIC 6159: Miscellaneous Business Credit Institutions

522294   Secondary Market Financing *see* SIC 6111: Federal & Federally Sponsored Credit Agencies

522298   All Other Nondepository Credit Intermediation *see* SIC 5932: Used Merchandise Stores; SIC 6081: Branches & Agencies of Foreign Banks; SIC 6111: Federal &

Federally-Sponsored Credit Agencies; SIC 6153: Short-Term Business Credit Institutions, Except Agricultural; SIC 6159: Miscellaneous Business Credit Institutions

52231   Mortgage & Other Loan Brokers *see* SIC 6163: Loan Brokers

52232   Financial Transactions Processing, Reserve, & Clearing House Activities *see* SIC 6019: Central Reserve Depository Institutions, NEC; SIC 6099: Functions Related to Depository Banking, NEC; SIC 6153: Short-Term Business Credit Institutions, Except Agricultural; SIC 7389: Business Services, NEC

52239   Other Activities Related to Credit Intermediation *see* SIC 6099: Functions Related to Depository Banking, NEC; SIC 6162: Mortgage Bankers & Loan Correspondents

52311   Investment Banking & Securities Dealing *see* SIC 6211: Security Brokers, Dealers, & Flotation Companies

52312   Securities Brokerage *see* SIC 6211: Security Brokers, Dealers, & Flotation Companies

52313   Commodity Contracts Dealing *see* SIC 6099: Functions Related to depository Banking, NEC; SIC 6799: Investors, NEC; SIC 6221: Commodity Contracts Brokers & Dealers

52314   Commodity Brokerage *see* SIC 6221: Commodity Contracts Brokers & Dealers

52321   Securities & Commodity Exchanges *see* SIC 6231: Security & Commodity Exchanges

52391   Miscellaneous Intermediation *see* SIC 6211: Securities Brokers, Dealers & Flotation Companies; SIC 6799: Investors, NEC

52392   Portfolio Management *see* SIC 6282: Investment Advice; SIC 6371: Pension, Health, & Welfare Funds; SIC 6733: Trust, Except Educational, Religious, & Charitable; SIC 6799: Investors, NEC

52393   Investment Advice *see* SIC 6282: Investment Advice

523991 Trust, Fiduciary & Custody Activities *see* SIC 6021: National Commercial Banks; SIC 6022: State Commercial Banks; SIC 6091: Nondepository Trust Facilities; SIC 6099: Functions Related to Depository Banking, NEC; SIC 6289: Services Allied With the Exchange of Securities or Commodities, NEC; SIC 6733: Trusts, Except Educational, Religious, & Charitable

523999 Miscellaneous Financial Investment Activities *see* SIC 6099: Functions Related to Depository Banking, NEC; SIC 6211: Security Brokers, Dealers, & Flotation Companies; SIC 6289: Services Allied With the Exchange of Securities or Commodities, NEC; SIC 6799: Investors, NEC; SIC 6792: Oil Royalty Traders

524113 Direct Life Insurance Carriers *see* SIC 6311: Life Insurance

524114 Direct Health & Medical Insurance Carriers *see* SIC 6324: Hospital & Medical Service Plans; SIC 6321: Accident & Health Insurance

524126 Direct Property & Casualty Insurance Carriers *see* SIC 6331: Fire, Marine, & Casualty Insurance; SIC 6351: Surety Insurance

524127 Direct Title Insurance Carriers *see* SIC 6361: Title Insurance

524128 Other Direct Insurance Carriers *see* SIC 6399: Insurance Carriers, NEC

52413   Reinsurance Carriers *see* SIC 6311: Life Insurance; SIC 6321: Accident & Health Insurance; SIC 6324: Hospital & Medical Service Plans; SIC 6331: Fire, Marine, & Casualty Insurance; SIC 6351: Surety Insurance; SIC 6361: Title Insurance

52421   Insurance Agencies & Brokerages *see* SIC 6411: Insurance Agents, Brokers & Service

524291 Claims Adjusters *see* SIC 6411: Insurance Agents, Brokers & Service

524292 Third Party Administration for Insurance & Pension Funds *see* SIC 6371: Pension, Health, & Welfare Funds; SIC 6411: Insurance Agents, Brokers & Service

524298 All Other Insurance Related Activities *see* SIC 6411: Insurance Agents, Brokers & Service

52511   Pension Funds *see* SIC 6371: Pension, Health, & Welfare Funds

52512   Health & Welfare Funds *see* SIC 6371: Pension, Health, & Welfare Funds

52519   Other Insurance Funds *see* SIC 6321: Accident & Health Insurance; SIC 6324: Hospital & Medical Service Plans; SIC 6331: Fire, Marine, & Casualty Insurance; SIC 6733: Trusts, Except Educational, Religious, & Charitable

52591   Open-End Investment Funds *see* SIC 6722: Management Investment Offices, Open-End

52592   Trusts, Estates, & Agency Accounts *see* SIC 6733: Trusts, Except Educational, Religious, & Charitable

52593   Real Estate Investment Trusts *see* SIC 6798: Real Estate Investment Trusts

52599   Other Financial Vehicles *see* SIC 6726: Unit Investment Trusts, Face-Amount Certificate Offices, & Closed-End Management Investment Offices

REAL ESTATE & RENTAL & LEASING

53111   Lessors of Residential Buildings & Dwellings *see* SIC 6513: Operators of Apartment Buildings; SIC 6514: Operators of Dwellings Other Than Apartment Buildings

53112   Lessors of Nonresidential Buildings *see* SIC 6512: Operators of Nonresidential Buildings

53113   Lessors of Miniwarehouses & Self Storage Units *see* SIC 4225: General Warehousing & Storage

53119   Lessors of Other Real Estate Property *see* SIC 6515: Operators of Residential Mobile Home Sites; SIC 6517: Lessors of Railroad Property; SIC 6519: Lessors of Real Property, NEC

53121   Offices of Real Estate Agents & Brokers *see* SIC 6531: Real Estate Agents Managers

531311 Residential Property Managers *see* SIC 6531: Real Estate Agents & Managers

531312 Nonresidential Property Managers *see* SIC 6531: Real Estate Agents & Managers

53132   Offices of Real Estate Appraisers *see* SIC 6531: Real Estate Agents & Managers

53139   Other Activities Related to Real Estate *see* SIC 6531: Real Estate Agents & Managers

532111 Passenger Car Rental *see* SIC 7514: Passenger Car Rental

532112 Passenger Car Leasing *see* SIC 7515: Passenger Car Leasing

53212   Truck, Utility Trailer, & RV Rental & Leasing *see* SIC 7513: Truck Rental & Leasing Without Drivers; SIC 7519: Utility Trailers & Recreational Vehicle Rental

53221   Consumer Electronics & Appliances Rental *see* SIC 7359: Equipment Rental & Leasing, NEC

53222   Formal Wear & Costume Rental *see* SIC 7299: Miscellaneous Personal Services, NEC; SIC 7819: Services Allied to Motion Picture Production

53223   Video Tape & Disc Rental *see* SIC 7841: Video Tape Rental

532291 Home Health Equipment Rental *see* SIC 7352: Medical Equipment Rental & Leasing

532292 Recreational Goods Rental *see* SIC 7999: Amusement & Recreation Services, NEC

532299 All Other Consumer Goods Rental *see* SIC 7359: Equipment Rental & Leasing, NEC

53231   General Rental Centers *see* SIC 7359: Equipment Rental & Leasing, NEC

532411 Commercial Air, Rail, & Water Transportation Equipment Rental & Leasing *see* SIC 4499: Water Transportation Services, NEC; SIC 4741: Rental of Railroad Cars; SIC 7359: Equipment Rental & Leasing, NEC

532412 Construction, Mining & Forestry Machinery & Equipment Rental & Leasing *see* SIC 7353: Heavy Construction Equipment Rental & Leasing; SIC 7359: Equipment Rental & Leasing, NEC

53242   Office Machinery & Equipment Rental & Leasing *see* SIC 7359: Equipment Rental & Leasing; SIC 7377: Computer Rental & Leasing

53249   Other Commercial & Industrial Machinery & Equipment Rental & Leasing *see* SIC 7352: Medical Equipment Rental & Leasing; SIC 7359: Equipment Rental & Leasing, NEC; SIC 7819: Services Allied to Motion Picture Production; SIC 7922: Theatrical Producers & Miscellaneous Theatrical Services

53311   Owners & Lessors of Other Nonfinancial Assets *see* SIC 6792: Oil Royalty Traders; SIC 6794: Patent Owners & Lessors

PROFESSIONAL, SCIENTIFIC, & TECHNICAL SERVICES

54111   Offices of Lawyers *see* SIC 8111: Legal Services

541191 Title Abstract & Settlement Offices *see* SIC 6541: Title Abstract Offices

541199 All Other Legal Services *see* SIC 7389: Business Services, NEC

541211 Offices of Certified Public Accountants *see* SIC 8721: Accounting, Auditing, & Bookkeeping Services

541213 Tax Preparation Services *see* SIC 7291: Tax Return Preparation Services

541214 Payroll Services *see* SIC 7819: Services Allied to Motion Picture Production; SIC 8721: Accounting, Auditing, & Bookkeeping Services

541219 Other Accounting Services *see* SIC 8721: Accounting, Auditing, & Bookkeeping Services

54131   Architectural Services *see* SIC 8712: Architectural Services

54132   Landscape Architectural Services *see* SIC 0781: Landscape Counseling & Planning

54133   Engineering Services *see* SIC 8711: Engineering Services

54134   Drafting Services *see* SIC 7389: Business Services, NEC

54135   Building Inspection Services *see* SIC 7389: Business Services, NEC

54136   Geophysical Surveying & Mapping Services *see* SIC 8713: Surveying Services; SIC 1081: Metal Mining Services; SIC 1382: Oil & Gas Field Exploration Services; SIC 1481: Nonmetallic Minerals Services, Except Fuels

54137   Surveying & Mapping Services *see* SIC 7389: Business Services, NEC; SIC 8713: Surveying Services

54138   Testing Laboratories *see* SIC 8734: Testing Laboratories

54141   Interior Design Services *see* SIC 7389: Business Services, NEC

54142   Industrial Design Services *see* SIC 7389: Business Services, NEC

54143   Graphic Design Services *see* SIC 7336: Commercial Art & Graphic Design; SIC 8099: Health & Allied Services, NEC

54149   Other Specialized Design Services *see* SIC 7389: Business Services, NEC

541511 Custom Computer Programming Services *see* SIC 7371: Computer Programming Services

541512 Computer Systems Design Services *see* SIC 7373: Computer Integrated Systems Design; SIC 7379: Computer Related Services, NEC

541513 Computer Facilities Management Services *see* SIC 7376: Computer Facilities Management Services

541519 Other Computer Related Services *see* SIC 7379: Computer Related Services, NEC

541611 Administrative Management & General Management Consulting Services *see* SIC 8742: Management Consulting Services

541612 Human Resources & Executive Search Consulting Services *see* SIC 8742: Management Consulting Services; SIC 7361: Employment Agencies; SIC 8999: Services, NEC

541613 Marketing Consulting Services *see* SIC 8742: Management Consulting Services

541614 Process, Physical, Distribution & Logistics Consulting Services *see* SIC 8742: Management Consulting Services

541618 Other Management Consulting Services *see* SIC 4731: Arrangement of Transportation of Freight & Cargo; SIC 8748: Business Consulting Services, NEC

54162   Environmental Consulting Services *see* SIC 8999: Services, NEC

54169   Other Scientific & Technical Consulting Services *see* SIC 0781: Landscape Counseling & Planning; SIC 8748: Business Consulting Services, NEC; SIC 8999: Services, NEC

54171   Research & Development in the Physical Sciences & Engineering Sciences *see* SIC 8731: Commercial Physical & Biological Research; SIC 8733: Noncommercial Research Organizations

54172   Research & Development in the Life Sciences *see* SIC 8731: Commercial Physical & Biological Research; SIC 8733: Noncommercial Research Organizations

54173   Research & Development in the Social Sciences & Humanities *see* SIC 8732: Commercial Economic, Sociological, & Educational Research; SIC 8733: Noncommercial Research Organizations

54181   Advertising Agencies *see* SIC 7311: Advertising Agencies

54182   Public Relations Agencies *see* SIC 8743: Public Relations Services

54183   Media Buying Agencies *see* SIC 7319: Advertising, NEC

54184   Media Representatives *see* SIC 7313: Radio, Television, & Publishers' Advertising Representatives

54185   Display Advertising *see* SIC 7312: Outdoor Advertising Services; SIC 7319: Advertising, NEC

54186   Direct Mail Advertising *see* SIC 7331: Direct Mail Advertising Services

54187   Advertising Material Distribution Services *see* SIC 7319: Advertising, NEC

54189   Other Services Related to Advertising *see* SIC 7319: Advertising, NEC; SIC 5199: Nondurable Goods, NEC; SIC 7389: Business Services, NEC

54191   Marketing Research & Public Opinion Polling *see* SIC 8732: Commercial Economic, Sociological, & Educational Research

541921 Photography Studios, Portrait *see* SIC 7221: Photographic Studios, Portrait

541922 Commercial Photography *see* SIC 7335: Commercial Photography; SIC 8099: Health & Allied Services, NEC

54193   Translation & Interpretation Services *see* SIC 7389: Business Services, NEC

54194   Veterinary Services *see* SIC 0741: Veterinary Services for Livestock; SIC 0742: Veterinary Services for Animal Specialties; SIC 8734: Testing Laboratories

54199   All Other Professional, Scientific & Technical Services *see* SIC 7389: Business Services

MANAGEMENT OF COMPANIES & ENTERPRISES

551111 Offices of Bank Holding Companies *see* SIC 6712: Offices of Bank Holding Companies

551112 Offices of Other Holding Companies *see* SIC 6719: Offices of Holding Companies, NEC

551114 Corporate, Subsidiary, & Regional Managing Offices (No SIC Equivalent)

ADMINISTRATIVE & SUPPORT, WASTE MANAGEMENT & REMEDIATION SERVICES

56111   Office Administrative Services *see* SIC 8741: Management Services

56121   Facilities Support Services *see* SIC 8744: Facilities Support Management Services

56131   Employment Placement Agencies *see* SIC 7361: Employment Agencies; SIC 7819: Services Allied to Motion Pictures Production; SIC 7922: Theatrical Producers & Miscellaneous Theatrical Services

56132   Temporary Help Services *see* SIC 7363: Help Supply Services

56133   Employee Leasing Services *see* SIC 7363: Help Supply Services

56141   Document Preparation Services *see* SIC 7338: Secretarial & Court Reporting

561421 Telephone Answering Services *see* SIC 7389: Business Services, NEC

561422 Telemarketing Bureaus *see* SIC 7389: Business Services, NEC

561431 Private Mail Centers *see* SIC 7389: Business Services, NEC

561439 Other Business Service Centers *see* SIC 7334: Photocopying & Duplicating Services; SIC 7389: Business Services, NEC

56144   Collection Agencies *see* SIC 7322: Adjustment & Collection Services

56145   Credit Bureaus *see* SIC 7323: Credit Reporting Services

561491 Repossession Services *see* SIC 7322: Adjustment & Collection; SIC 7389: Business Services, NEC

561492 Court Reporting & Stenotype Services *see* SIC 7338: Secretarial & Court Reporting

561499 All Other Business Support Services *see* SIC 7389: Business Services, NEC

56151   Travel Agencies *see* SIC 4724: Travel Agencies

56152   Tour Operators *see* SIC 4725: Tour Operators

561591 Convention & Visitors Bureaus *see* SIC 7389: Business Services, NEC

561599 All Other Travel Arrangement & Reservation Services *see* SIC 4729: Arrangement of Passenger Transportation, NEC; SIC 7389: Business Services, NEC; SIC 7999: Amusement & Recreation Services, NEC; SIC 8699: Membership Organizations, NEC

561611 Investigation Services *see* SIC 7381: Detective, Guard, & Armored Car Services

561612 Security Guards & Patrol Services *see* SIC 7381: Detective, Guard, & Armored Car Services

561613 Armored Car Services *see* SIC 7381: Detective, Guard, & Armored Car Services

561621 Security Systems Services *see* SIC 7382: Security Systems Services; SIC 1731: Electrical Work

561622 Locksmiths *see* SIC 7699: Repair Shops & Related Services, NEC

56171   Exterminating & Pest Control Services *see* SIC 4959: Sanitary Services, NEC; SIC 7342: Disinfecting & Pest Control Services

56172   Janitorial Services *see* SIC 7342: Disinfecting & Pest Control Services; SIC 7349: Building Cleaning & Maintenance Services, NEC; SIC 4581: Airports, Flying Fields, & Airport Terminal Services

56173   Landscaping Services *see* SIC 0782: Lawn & Garden Services; SIC 0783: Ornamental Shrub & Tree Services

56174   Carpet & Upholstery Cleaning Services *see* SIC 7217: Carpet & Upholstery Cleaning

56179   Other Services to Buildings & Dwellings *see* SIC 7389: Business Services, NEC; SIC 7699: Repair Shops & Related Services, NEC

56191   Packaging & Labeling Services *see* SIC 7389: Business Services, NEC

56192   Convention & Trade Show Organizers *see* SIC 7389: Business Services, NEC

56199   All Other Support Services *see* SIC 7389: Business Services, NEC

562111 Solid Waste Collection *see* SIC 4212: Local Trucking Without Storage; SIC 4953: Refuse Systems

562112 Hazardous Waste Collection *see* SIC 4212: Local Trucking Without Storage; SIC 4953: Refuse Systems

562119 Other Waste Collection *see* SIC 4212: Local Trucking Without Storage; SIC 4953: Refuse Systems

562211 Hazardous Waste Treatment & Disposal *see* SIC 4953: Refuse Systems

562212 Solid Waste Landfill *see* SIC 4953: Refuse Systems

562213 Solid Waste Combustors & Incinerators *see* SIC 4953: Refuse Systems

562219 Other Nonhazardous Waste Treatment & Disposal *see* SIC 4953: Refuse Systems

56291   Remediation Services *see* SIC 1799: Special Trade Contractors, NEC; SIC 4959: Sanitary Services, NEC

56292   Materials Recovery Facilities *see* SIC 4953: Refuse Systems

562991 Septic Tank & Related Services *see* SIC 7359: Equipment Rental & Leasing, NEC; SIC 7699: Repair Shops & Related Services, NEC

562998 All Other Miscellaneous Waste Management Services *see* SIC 4959: Sanitary Services, NEC

EDUCATIONAL SERVICES

61111   Elementary & Secondary Schools *see* SIC 8211: Elementary & Secondary Schools

61121   Junior Colleges *see* SIC 8222: Junior Colleges & Technical Institutes

61131   Colleges, Universities & Professional Schools *see* SIC 8221: Colleges, Universities, & Professional Schools

61141   Business & Secretarial Schools *see* SIC 8244: Business & Secretarial Schools

61142   Computer Training *see* SIC 8243: Data Processing Schools

61143   Professional & Management Development Training *see* SIC 8299: Schools & Educational Services, NEC

611511 Cosmetology & Barber Schools *see* SIC 7231: Beauty Shops; SIC 7241: Barber Shops

611512 Flight Training *see* SIC 8249: Vocational Schools, NEC; SIC 8299: Schools & Educational Services, NEC

611513 Apprenticeship Training *see* SIC 8249: Vocational Schools, NEC

611519 Other Technical & Trade Schools *see* SIC 8249: Vocational Schools, NEC; SIC 8243: Data Processing Schools

61161 Fine Arts Schools *see* SIC 8299: Schools & Educational Services, NEC; SIC 7911: Dance Studios, Schools, & Halls

61162 Sports & Recreation Instruction *see* SIC 7999: Amusement & Recreation Services, NEC

61163 Language Schools *see* SIC 8299: Schools & Educational Services, NEC

611691 Exam Preparation & Tutoring *see* SIC 8299: Schools & Educational Services, NEC

611692 Automobile Driving Schools *see* SIC 8299: Schools & Educational Services, NEC

611699 All Other Miscellaneous Schools & Instruction *see* SIC 8299: Schools & Educational Services, NEC

61171 Educational Support Services *see* SIC 8299: Schools & Educational Services NEC; SIC 8748: Business Consulting Services, NEC

HEALTH CARE & SOCIAL ASSISTANCE

621111 Offices of Physicians *see* SIC 8011: Offices & Clinics of Doctors of Medicine; SIC 8031: Offices & Clinics of Doctors of Osteopathy

621112 Offices of Physicians, Mental Health Specialists *see* SIC 8011: Offices & Clinics of Doctors of Medicine; SIC 8031: Offices & Clinics of Doctors of Osteopathy

62121 Offices of Dentists *see* SIC 8021: Offices & Clinics of Dentists

62131 Offices of Chiropractors *see* SIC 8041: Offices & Clinics of Chiropractors

62132 Offices of Optometrists *see* SIC 8042: Offices & Clinics of Optometrists

62133 Offices of Mental Health Practitioners *see* SIC 8049: Offices & Clinics of Health Practitioners, NEC

62134 Offices of Physical, Occupational & Speech Therapists & Audiologists *see* SIC 8049: Offices & Clinics of Health Practitioners, NEC

621391 Offices of Podiatrists *see* SIC 8043: Offices & Clinics of Podiatrists

621399 Offices of All Other Miscellaneous Health Practitioners *see* SIC 8049: Offices & Clinics of Health Practitioners, NEC

62141 Family Planning Centers *see* SIC 8093: Speciality Outpatient Facilities, NEC; SIC 8099: Health & Allied Services, NEC

62142 Outpatient Mental Health & Substance Abuse Centers *see* SIC 8093: Specialty Outpatient Facilities, NEC

621491 HMO Medical Centers *see* SIC 8011: Offices & Clinics of Doctors of Medicine

621492 Kidney Dialysis Centers *see* SIC 8092: Kidney Dialysis Centers

621493 Freestanding Ambulatory Surgical & Emergency Centers *see* SIC 8011: Offices & Clinics of Doctors of Medicine

621498 All Other Outpatient Care Centers *see* SIC 8093: Specialty Outpatient Facilities, NEC

621511 Medical Laboratories *see* SIC 8071: Medical Laboratories

621512 Diagnostic Imaging Centers *see* SIC 8071: Medical Laboratories

62161 Home Health Care Services *see* SIC 8082: Home Health Care Services

62191 Ambulance Services *see* SIC 4119: Local Passenger Transportation, NEC; SIC 4522: Air Transportation, Nonscheduled

621991 Blood & Organ Banks *see* SIC 8099: Health & Allied Services, NEC

621999 All Other Miscellaneous Ambulatory Health Care Services *see* SIC 8099: Health & Allied Services, NEC

62211 General Medical & Surgical Hospitals *see* SIC 8062: General Medical & Surgical Hospitals; SIC 8069: Specialty Hospitals, Except Psychiatric

62221 Psychiatric & Substance Abuse Hospitals *see* SIC 8063: Psychiatric Hospitals; SIC 8069: Specialty Hospitals, Except Psychiatric

62231 Specialty Hospitals *see* SIC 8069: Specialty Hospitals, Except Psychiatric

62311 Nursing Care Facilities *see* SIC 8051: Skilled Nursing Care Facilities; SIC 8052: Intermediate Care Facilities; SIC 8059: Nursing & Personal Care Facilities, NEC

62321 Residential Mental Retardation Facilities *see* SIC 8052: Intermediate Care Facilities

62322 Residential Mental Health & Substance Abuse Facilities *see* SIC 8361: Residential Care

623311 Continuing Care Retirement Communities *see* SIC 8051: Skilled Nursing Care Facilities; SIC 8052: Intermediate Care Facilities; SIC 8059: Nursing & Personal Care Facilities, NEC

623312 Homes for the Elderly *see* SIC 8361: Residential Care

62399 Other Residential Care Facilities *see* SIC 8361: Residential Care

62411 Child & Youth Services *see* SIC 8322: Individual & Family Social Services; SIC 8641: Civic, Social, & Fraternal Organizations

62412 Services for the Elderly & Persons with Disabilities *see* SIC 8322: Individual & Family Social Services

62419 Other Individual & Family Services *see* SIC 8322: Individual & Family Social Services

62421 Community Food Services *see* SIC 8322: Individual & Family Social Services

624221 Temporary Shelters *see* SIC 8322: Individual & Family Social Services

624229 Other Community Housing Services *see* SIC 8322: Individual & Family Social Services

62423 Emergency & Other Relief Services *see* SIC 8322: Individual & Family Social Services

62431 Vocational Rehabilitation Services *see* SIC 8331: Job Training & Vocational Rehabilitation Services

62441 Child Day Care Services *see* SIC 8351: Child Day Care Services; SIC 7299: Miscellaneous Personal Services, NEC

ARTS, ENTERTAINMENT, & RECREATION

71111 Theater Companies & Dinner Theaters *see* SIC 5812: Eating Places; SIC 7922: Theatrical Producers & Miscellaneous Theatrical Services

71112 Dance Companies *see* SIC 7922: Theatrical Producers & Miscellaneous Theatrical Services

71113 Musical Groups & Artists *see* SIC 7929: Bands, Orchestras, Actors, & Entertainment Groups

71119 Other Performing Arts Companies *see* SIC 7929: Bands, Orchestras, Actors, & Entertainment Groups,; SIC 7999: Amusement & Recreation Services, NEC

711211 Sports Teams & Clubs *see* SIC 7941: Professional Sports Clubs & Promoters

711212 Race Tracks *see* SIC 7948: Racing, Including Track Operations

711219 Other Spectator Sports *see* SIC 7941: Professional Sports Clubs & Promoters; SIC 7948: Racing, Includ-

ing Track Operations; SIC 7999: Amusement &
Recreation Services, NEC

71131   Promoters of Performing Arts, Sports & Similar Events
with Facilities *see* SIC 6512: Operators of Nonresidential Buildings; SIC 7922: Theatrical Procedures &
Miscellaneous Theatrical Services; SIC 7941: Professional Sports Clubs & Promoters

71132   Promoters of Performing Arts, Sports & Similar Events
without Facilities *see* SIC 7922: Theatrical Producers
& Miscellaneous Theatrical Services; SIC 7941: Professional Sports Clubs & Promoters

71141   Agents & Managers for Artists, Athletes, Entertainers &
Other Public Figures *see* SIC 7389: Business Services,
NEC; SIC 7922: Theatrical Producers & Miscella-
neous Theatrical Services; SIC 7941: Professional
Sports Clubs & Promoters

71151   Independent Artists, Writers, & Performers *see* SIC
7819: Services Allied to Motion Picture Production;
SIC 7929: Bands, Orchestras, Actors, & Other Entertainers & Entertainment Services; SIC 8999: Services,
NEC

71211   Museums *see* SIC 8412: Museums & Art Galleries

71212   Historical Sites *see* SIC 8412: Museums & Art Galleries

71213   Zoos & Botanical Gardens *see* SIC 8422: Arboreta &
Botanical & Zoological Gardens

71219   Nature Parks & Other Similar Institutions *see* SIC 7999:
Amusement & Recreation Services, NEC; SIC 8422:
Arboreta & Botanical & Zoological Gardens

71311   Amusement & Theme Parks *see* SIC 7996: Amusement
Parks

71312   Amusement Arcades *see* SIC 7993: Coin-Operated
Amusement Devices

71321   Casinos *see* SIC 7999: Amusement & Recreation Services, NEC

71329   Other Gambling Industries *see* SIC 7993: Coin-Operated
Amusement Devices; SIC 7999: Amusement & Recreation Services, NEC

71391   Golf Courses & Country Clubs *see* SIC 7992: Public
Golf Courses; SIC 7997: Membership Sports & Recreation Clubs

71392   Skiing Facilities *see* SIC 7999: Amusement & Recreation Services, NEC

71393   Marinas *see* SIC 4493: Marinas

71394   Fitness & Recreational Sports Centers *see* SIC 7991:
Physical Fitness Facilities; SIC 7997: Membership
Sports & Recreation Clubs; SIC 7999: Amusement &
Recreation Services, NEC

71395   Bowling Centers *see* SIC 7933: Bowling Centers

71399   All Other Amusement & Recreation Industries *see* SIC
7911: Dance Studios, Schools, & Halls; SIC 7993:
Amusement & Recreation Services, NEC; SIC 7997:
Membership Sports & Recreation Clubs; SIC 7999:
Amusement & Recreation Services, NEC

Accommodation & Foodservices

72111   Hotels & Motels *see* SIC 7011: Hotels & Motels; SIC
7041: Organization Hotels & Lodging Houses, on
Membership Basis

72112   Casino Hotels *see* SIC 7011: Hotels & Motels

721191 Bed & Breakfast Inns *see* SIC 7011: Hotels & Motels

721199 All Other Traveler Accommodation *see* SIC 7011: Hotels & Motels

721211 RV Parks & Campgrounds *see* SIC 7033: Recreational
Vehicle Parks & Campgrounds

721214 Recreational & Vacation Camps *see* SIC 7032: Sporting
& Recreational Camps

72131   Rooming & Boarding Houses *see* SIC 7021: Rooming
& Boarding Houses; SIC 7041: Organization Hotels &
Lodging Houses, on Membership Basis

72211   Full-Service Restaurants *see* SIC 5812: Eating Places

722211 Limited-Service Restaurants *see* SIC 5812: Eating
Places; SIC 5499: Miscellaneous Food Stores

722212 Cafeterias *see* SIC 5812: Eating Places

722213 Snack & Nonalcoholic Beverage Bars *see* SIC 5812:
Eating Places; SIC 5461: Retail Bakeries

72231   Foodservice Contractors *see* SIC 5812: Eating Places

72232   Caterers *see* SIC 5812: Eating Places

72233   Mobile Foodservices *see* SIC 5963: Direct Selling Establishments

72241   Drinking Places *see* SIC 5813: Drinking Places

Other Services

811111 General Automotive Repair *see* SIC 7538: General Automotive Repair Shops

811112 Automotive Exhaust System Repair *see* SIC 7533: Automotive Exhaust System Repair Shops

811113 Automotive Transmission Repair *see* SIC 7537: Automotive Transmission Repair Shops

811118 Other Automotive Mechanical & Electrical Repair &
Maintenance *see* SIC 7539: Automotive Repair Shops,
NEC

811121 Automotive Body, Paint & Interior Repair & Maintenance *see* SIC 7532: Top, Body, & Upholstery Repair
Shops & Paint Shops

811122 Automotive Glass Replacement Shops *see* SIC 7536:
Automotive Glass Replacement Shops

811191 Automotive Oil Change & Lubrication Shops *see* SIC
7549: Automotive Services, Except Repair & Carwashes

811192 Car Washes *see* SIC 7542: Carwashes

811198 All Other Automotive Repair & Maintenance *see* SIC
7534: Tire Retreading & Repair Shops; SIC 7549: Automotive Services, Except Repair & Carwashes

811211 Consumer Electronics Repair & Maintenance *see* SIC
7622: Radio & Television Repair Shops; SIC 7629:
Electrical & Electronic Repair Shops, NEC

811212 Computer & Office Machine Repair & Maintenance *see*
SIC 7378: Computer Maintenance & Repair; SIC
7629: Electrical & Electronic Repair Shops, NEC; SIC
7699: Repair Shops & Related Services, NEC

811213 Communication Equipment Repair & Maintenance *see*
SIC 7622: Radio & Television Repair Shops; SIC
7629: Electrical & Electronic Repair Shops, NEC

811219 Other Electronic & Precision Equipment Repair &
Maintenance *see* SIC 7629: Electrical & Electronic
Repair Shops, NEC; SIC 7699: Repair Shops & Re-
lated Services, NEC

81131   Commercial & Industrial Machinery & Equipment Repair & Maintenance *see* SIC 7699: Repair Shops &
Related Services, NEC; SIC 7623: Refrigerator & Air-
Conditioning Service & Repair Shops; SIC 7694: Armature Rewinding Shops

811411 Home & Garden Equipment Repair & Maintenance *see*
SIC 7699: Repair Shops & Related Services, NEC

811412 Appliance Repair & Maintenance *see* SIC 7623: Refrig-
eration & Air-Conditioning Service & Repair Shops;
SIC 7629: Electrical & Electronic Repair Shops, NEC;
SIC 7699: Repairs Shops & Related Services, NEC

81142   Reupholstery & Furniture Repair *see* SIC 7641: Re-
upholstery & Furniture Repair

81143   Footwear & Leather Goods Repair *see* SIC 7251: Shoe
Repair & Shoeshine Parlors; SIC 7699: Repair Shops
& Related Services

81149 Other Personal & Household Goods Repair & Maintenance *see* SIC 3732: Boat Building & Repairing; SIC 7219: Laundry & Garment Services, NEC; SIC 7631: Watch, Clock, & Jewelry Repair; SIC 7692: Welding Repair; SIC 7699: Repair Shops & Related Services, NEC

812111 Barber Shops *see* SIC 7241: Barber Shops

812112 Beauty Salons *see* SIC 7231: Beauty Shops

812113 Nail Salons *see* SIC 7231: Beauty Shops

812191 Diet & Weight Reducing Centers *see* SIC 7299: Miscellaneous Personal Services, NEC

812199 Other Personal Care Services *see* SIC 7299: Miscellaneous Personal Services, NEC,

81221 Funeral Homes *see* SIC 7261: Funeral Services & Crematories

81222 Cemeteries & Crematories *see* SIC 6531: Real Estate Agents & Managers; SIC 6553: Cemetery Subdividers & Developers; SIC 7261: Funeral Services & Crematories

81231 Coin-Operated Laundries & Drycleaners *see* SIC 7215: Coin-Operated Laundry & Drycleaning

812321 Laundries, Family & Commercial *see* SIC 7211: Power Laundries, Family & Commercial

812322 Drycleaning Plants *see* SIC 7216: Drycleaning Plants, Except Rug Cleaning

812331 Linen Supply *see* SIC 7213: Linen Supply; SIC 7219: Laundry & Garment Services, NEC,

812332 Industrial Launderers *see* SIC 7218: Industrial Launderers

812391 Garment Pressing, & Agents for Laundries *see* SIC 7212: Garment Pressing & Agents for Laundries

812399 All Other Laundry Services *see* SIC 7219: Laundry & Garment Services, NEC

81291 Pet Care Services *see* SIC 0752: Animal Speciality Services, Except Veterinary

812921 Photo Finishing Laboratories *see* SIC 7384: Photofinishing Laboratories

812922 One-Hour Photo Finishing *see* SIC 7384: Photofinishing Laboratories

81293 Parking Lots & Garages *see* SIC 7521: Automobile Parking

81299 All Other Personal Services *see* SIC 7299: Miscellaneous Personal Services, NEC; SIC 7389: Miscellaneous Business Services

81311 Religious Organizations *see* SIC 8661: Religious Organizations

813211 Grantmaking Foundations *see* SIC 6732: Educational, Religious, & Charitable Trust

813212 Voluntary Health Organizations *see* SIC 8399: Social Services, NEC

813219 Other Grantmaking & Giving Services *see* SIC 8399: Social Services, NEC

813311 Human Rights Organizations *see* SIC 8399: Social Services, NEC

813312 Environment, Conservation & Wildlife Organizations *see* SIC 8399: Social Services, NEC; SIC 8699: Membership Organizations, NEC

813319 Other Social Advocacy Organizations *see* SIC 8399: Social Services, NEC

81341 Civic & Social Organizations *see* SIC 8641: Civic, Social, & Fraternal Organizations; SIC 8699: Membership Organizations, NEC

81391 Business Associations *see* SIC 8611: Business Associations; SIC 8699: Membership Organizations, NEC

81392 Professional Organizations *see* SIC 8621: Professional Membership Organizations

81393 Labor Unions & Similar Labor Organizations *see* SIC 8631: Labor Unions & Similar Labor Organizations

81394 Political Organizations *see* SIC 8651: Political Organizations

81399 Other Similar Organizations *see* SIC 6531: Real Estate Agents & Managers; SIC 8641: Civic, Social, & Fraternal Organizations; SIC 8699: Membership Organizations, NEC

81411 Private Households *see* SIC 8811: Private Households

PUBLIC ADMINISTRATION

92111 Executive Offices *see* SIC 9111: Executive Offices

92112 Legislative Bodies *see* SIC 9121: Legislative Bodies

92113 Public Finance *see* SIC 9311: Public Finance, Taxation, & Monetary Policy

92114 Executive & Legislative Offices, Combined *see* SIC 9131: Executive & Legislative Offices, Combined

92115 American Indian & Alaska Native Tribal Governments *see* SIC 8641: Civic, Social, & Fraternal Organizations

92119 All Other General Government *see* SIC 9199: General Government, NEC

92211 Courts *see* SIC 9211: Courts

92212 Police Protection *see* SIC 9221: Police Protection

92213 Legal Counsel & Prosecution *see* SIC 9222: Legal Counsel & Prosecution

92214 Correctional Institutions *see* SIC 9223: Correctional Institutions

92215 Parole Offices & Probation Offices *see* SIC 8322: Individual & Family Social Services

92216 Fire Protection *see* SIC 9224: Fire Protection

92219 All Other Justice, Public Order, & Safety *see* SIC 9229: Public Order & Safety, NEC

92311 Administration of Education Programs *see* SIC 9411: Administration of Educational Programs

92312 Administration of Public Health Programs *see* SIC 9431: Administration of Public Health Programs

92313 Administration of Social, Human Resource & Income Maintenance Programs *see* SIC 9441: Administration of Social, Human Resource & Income Maintenance Programs

92314 Administration of Veteran's Affairs *see* SIC 9451: Administration of Veteran's Affairs, Except Health Insurance

92411 Air & Water Resource & Solid Waste Management *see* SIC 9511: Air & Water Resource & Solid Waste Management

92412 Land, Mineral, Wildlife, & Forest Conservation *see* SIC 9512: Land, Mineral, Wildlife, & Forest Conservation

92511 Administration of Housing Programs *see* SIC 9531: Administration of Housing Programs

92512 Administration of Urban Planning & Community & Rural Development *see* SIC 9532: Administration of Urban Planning & Community & Rural Development

92611 Administration of General Economic Programs *see* SIC 9611: Administration of General Economic Programs

92612 Regulation & Administration of Transportation Programs *see* SIC 9621: Regulations & Administration of Transportation Programs

92613 Regulation & Administration of Communications, Electric, Gas, & Other Utilities *see* SIC 9631: Regulation & Administration of Communications, Electric, Gas, & Other Utilities

92614 Regulation of Agricultural Marketing & Commodities *see* SIC 9641: Regulation of Agricultural Marketing & Commodities

92615   Regulation, Licensing, & Inspection of Miscellaneous Commercial Sectors *see* SIC 9651: Regulation, Licensing, & Inspection of Miscellaneous Commercial Sectors

92711   Space Research & Technology *see* SIC 9661: Space Research & Technology

92811   National Security *see* SIC 9711: National Security

92812   International Affairs *see* SIC 9721: International Affairs

99999   Unclassified Establishments *see* SIC 9999: Nonclassifiable Establishments

INDEX

This index contains references to topics, companies, associations, government agencies, and specific legislation cited in the Encyclopedia. Citations are followed by the volume number and page number(s) in which the company, association, agency, or legislative act is discussed. Topics of essays appear in boldface.

A

INDEX

INDEX

INDEX

INDEX

INDEX

INDEX

INDEX

CONTRIBUTOR NOTES

Aaron, Sunder. Freelance writer; MBA, University of Michigan, Ann Arbor.

Alberts, Daniel J. Technical writer based in Sterling Heights, Michigan; author of computer software and hardware operations manuals; a recognized member of the Society for Technical Communication.

Amerman, Don. Freelance writer and editor based in Saylorsburg, Pennsylvania; *writes regularly for* The Journal of Commerce.

Armstrong, Robin. Freelance writer; contributor to *Contemporary Musicians, Contemporary Black Biography,* and *International Dictionary of Opera.*

Azzata, Gerry. Freelance writer and researcher based in Medford, Massachusetts; former academic reference librarian with graduate degrees in law and library science; has written numerous materials in the areas of law, business, health, and online research.

Baker, Sandy. Freelance writer, researcher, and editor from Normal, Illinois; also has work experience in employee communications, university public relations, textbook publishing, and newspaper reporting.

Baker, Suzanne. Freelance writer; MBA, University of Michigan, Ann Arbor.

Balch, Trudy. Freelance writer.

Ballard, Andrew. Freelance writer

Barduson, Thomas. MBA and freelance writer and researcher.

Barnett, Kris. Adjunct English Instructor at the University of New Haven and freelance writer based in Portland, Connecticut.

Beard, James L. Freelance writer and essay author; CPA and MBA candidate, Oral Roberts University, Tulsa, Oklahoma.

Bellenir, Karen Freelance writer and editor.

Bennett, Bill. Business writer and researcher; MBA, University of Oregon, Eugene.

Berger, Percy Lee. J.D. and MBA candidate, University of Michigan, Ann Arbor; associate editor, *Michigan Journal of International Law;* freelance writer.

Berry, Pamela. Freelance writer and editor.

Bianco, David P. Freelance writer, editor, and publishing consultant; has contributed to the *Encyclopedia of Business,* the *International Directory of Company Histories,* and other reference publications, and edited several reference books on business topics.

Bilas, Wendy Johnson. Freelance writer; MBA in marketing, Wake Forest University; director of marketing for the Charlotte Symphony Orchestra.

Black, Virginia Mayo. Freelance reporter and editor based in Madison, Wisconsin; writer for newspapers and magazines covering business and general news topics.

Blumenfield, Steven. MBA candidate, University of Chicago; managing editor, *Chicago Business.*

Bodine, Paul S. Freelance writer and editor based in Milwaukee, Wisconsin; currently an independent contract editor for McGraw-Hill Professional Publishing, New York University Press, and the University of Michigan Press; his work has appeared in the *Milwaukee Journal* and the *Baltimore Sun.*

Boyer, Dean. Former newspaper reporter; freelance writer in Seattle area.

Brennan, Carol. Freelance writer and regular contributor to numerous Gale titles; her work also appears regularly in *Hour Detroit;* a graduate of Wayne State University, Detroit, Michigan, in 1988 with a B.A. in history.

Briggs, Karen. Freelance writer and editor based in Toronto, Ontario, Canada; has written for over 20 general-interest magazines in Canada, the United States, Great Britain, and Bermuda.

Brinker, Kaye. Freelance writer based in Brooklyn Heights, New York; former advertising copywriter; contributor to *Discount Merchandiser, Advertising Career Directory,* and *Bank Security Report.*

Brooke, Bob. Freelance writer and author of six books; writes weekly for the *Philadelphia Business Journal* and has also been published in *Business Traveler (US/UK), Mexico Business, The Rotarian, Delta Sky,* and the Rand McNally *Guide to World Business.*

Brooks, Jeanette. Technical writer and editor specializing in technical training and manufacturing.

Brown, Susan. Freelance writer.

Broyles, Michael J. Ph.D. ABD working on his thesis at the University of Western Ontario; has also written for the *Encyclopedia of Latin American History.*

Burke, Andrew. Freelance writer

Burnett-Balga, Beth. Freelance writer and full-time communications manager based in Atlanta, Georgia; has published articles in *Resource, American City and County,* and *World Wastes* magazines.

Burton-Faulkner, Kimberly. Freelance writer and editor based in Ann Arbor, Michigan; has written for the *Detroit Free Press Magazine;* master's candidate, University of Michigan, Ann Arbor.

Calhoun, Lisa. Freelance writer based in San Antonio, Texas; has written for a range of magazines on subjects from new media to Russian mafia; degree in professional writing from Baylor University, Waco, Texas.

Casey, Jim. Freelance technical writer based in Galveston, Texas; systems operator of CompuServe forums; former computer programmer and electrical engineer.

Cohen, Kerstan B. Freelance writer and French translator; editor for *Letter-Ex* poetry review.

Cohen, Paula Hartman. Freelance writer.

Cohn, Lynne M. Writer, poet, and editor; has written for *New York Newsday, Michigan Living,* and *Woman's own,* as well as her own published work of poetry.

Collins, Cheryl. Freelance writer and researcher.

Cook, Allan R. Freelance writer and journalist; graduate student in English, Oakland University, Rochester, Michigan.

Costilow, Donald R. Graphic artist/illustrator, Monongahela Power Company; instructor of business, Fairmont State College, Fairmont, West Virginia.

Covell, Jeffrey L. Freelance writer and corporate history contractor.

Creighton, Kevin. Freelance writer; MBA. University of Michigan, Ann Arbor.

Cuene, Jim. Freelance writer; graduate student in American Studies, Purdue University, West Lafayette, Indiana.

Daily, Kristine. Freelance writer; MBA candidate, Boston College.

Daniels, Garth K. Business consultant in corporate strategy and new venture development; adjunct faculty member, Westminster College, Salt Lake City, Utah.

Day, Holly L. Freelance writer and editor living in Minneapolis, Minnesota; her fiction and nonfiction writing has appeared in over 800 publications internationally.

Dee, James P. Freelance writer based in Pittsburgh, Pennsylvania; specialist in business and legal writing, editing, and project management.

Distelzweig, Howard. Freelance writer and editor based in Ann Arbor, Michigan; has written for *The Family: A Catholic Perspective, Credo,* and other periodicals.

Dorman, Evelyn. Freelance journalist, public relations, French teacher, tutor, and graduate student; Contributor to *Brides Today, Lerner-Pulitzer* newspapers, the *Chicago Sun Times,* and the *International Directory of Company Histories.*

Dougal, April S. Archivist and freelance writer specializing in business and social history in Cleveland, Ohio.

Eigo, Tim. Freelance business and law writer based in Phoenix, Arizona; received M.A. from the University of Notre Dame and J.D. from the University of California, Hastings College of Law.

Estioco, Rose M. Freelance writer and editor based in Detroit, Michigan, with writing experience on a variety of subjects including health care, science, aging, and business.

Evans, Ken. Doctoral candidate in Economics, University of Michigan, Ann Arbor.

Fagan, Dave. Business and technical writer and freelance journalist under the name Fagan Communications in Seattle, Washington; he writes regularly for *Downtown Source,* a weekly newspaper owned by *The Seattle Times;* his professional honors include writing awards from the Society of Professional Journalists in 1995 and 1996.

Fishel, Larry. Freelance writer and chemist based in East Lansing, Michigan.

Fisher, Rogene M. Freelance writer and editor.

Gallagher, Elizabeth A. Freelance writer.

Gallagher, John. Freelance writer.

Gallman, Jason. Freelance writer; graduate student in literature, Purdue University, West Lafayette, Indiana.

Gasbarre, April Dougal. Freelance writer specializing in business and social history in Cleveland, Ohio.

Genaway, David C. Library Director Emeritus, Youngstown State University, Ohio; president of Genaway & Associates, Inc. based in Canfield, Ohio; founded the national Conference on Integrated Online Library Systems, editor/compiler/publisher of the proceedings of seven national conferences; author of several books and 20 articles. Ph.D., University of Minnesota and M.A.L.S., University of Michigan.

Giglierano, Joan. Independent information professional and former business librarian based in Columbus, Ohio.

Glover, Beaird. Freelance writer.

Gluskin, Lisa. Writer and editor based in San Francisco; editor of *And . . .* arts and culture magazine.

Grant, Tina. Freelance writer and editor.

Grensing-Pophal, Lin. Business author and consultant in Chippewa Falls, Wisconsin; BA in psychology and M.A. in Organizational Management; author of four books on employee management and marketing issues; frequent contributor to business and trade publications.

Griffin, Attrices Dean. Freelance researcher and writer; former owner of research and technical writing firm.

Gundersen, Linda. Freelance editor and writer based in Doylestown, Pennsylvania; contributor to *The Strategic Healthcare Atlas,* freelancer for Aetna/U.S. Healthcare and Springhouse Corp., a publisher of nursing textbooks.

Gustafson, Randy. Freelance writer; MBA, University of Michigan, Ann Arbor.

Hammond, Nancy. Freelance writer and researcher working in the Detroit, Michigan.

Harris, Lisa. Graduate student in business, Chattanooga, Tennessee.

Harrison, Susan R. Writer and educator.

Hedden, Heather. Business periodical abstractor and indexer, Information Access Company, Foster City, California; senior staff writer, *Middle East Times,* Cairo Bureau, 1991-92.

Heil, Karl. Freelance writer; M.A. in linguistics, Eastern Michigan University, Ypsilanti, Michigan.

Henderson, Tona. Freelance consultant, Internet trainer, and business researcher; business librarian at The Pennsylvania State University, University Park, Pennsylvania.

Hernandez, Rolando. Computer systems analyst, project leader, and knowledge engineer.

Hillstrom, Laurie Collier. Freelance writer and editor; MBA, University of Michigan, Ann Arbor; former editor of *Authors and Artists for Young Adults,* and *Major Authors and Illustrators for Young Children and Young Adults.*

Hillyer, Richard. Freelance writer and editor, poet, and part-time English teacher; Ph.D. in English, University of Michigan, Ann Arbor.

Hornbeck, Diane M. Co-owner of Home Based Data Services, Inc., offering services to the publishing industry; graduate of Wayne State University, Detroit, Michigan, with a degree in mass communications.

Hoyt, Douglas. Freelance writer.

Huerster, Paricia G. Freelance writer and editor.

Hunt, Christopher. Freelance writer and editor; former advertising copyeditor in Japan; contributor to *Mainichi Daily News, The Japan Times, Canadian Biker, Exile,* and *Intertext.*

Ingram, Frederick. Freelance writer based in Sumter, South Carolina; contributor to *Encyclopedia of Business, Encyclopedia of Consumer Brands,* and *The Disaster Planning Handbook.*

Isaacs, McAllister III. Freelance writer and editor of *Textile World.*

Jacobson, Robert R. Freelance writer and musician.

Jeffrey, Tim. Playwright, short story writer, and freelance writer based in Detroit, Michigan.

Jochnowitz, Marinell. Writer and editor based in San Francisco, California.

Jones, J. Jacob. Graduate student in American History, Purdue University, West Lafayette, Indiana.

Joseph, Leslie. Freelance writer and editor based in Birmingham, Michigan; worked on *Lifetime Book of Mone Management, Chronology of 20th Century Eastern European History,* and *Contemporary Heroes and Heroines, Book II* as a editor for Gale Research.

Kalfatovic, Mary C. Freelance writer and librarian in the Washington, D.C. area; has written on film, theater, and entertainment for a variety of publications, and the author of *Montgomery Clift: A Bio-bibliography.*

Kaufman, Scott. Freelance writer.

King, Brett Allan. Freelance writer.

King, Daniel. Freelance writer; doctoral candidate in economics, New School for Social Research, New York, New York.

King, Susan Wood. Freelance writer and communications specialist based in Research Triangle Park, North Carolina.

Kirchner, Joseph. Freelance writer based in Alexandria, Virginia.

Kirn, Kathy. Freelance writer and owner of KMK Communications based in Baltimore, Maryland; experienced in corporate communications, public relations, and technical writing.

Kitsuse, Alicia. Freelance writer and editor based in Boulder, Colorado.

Kleiman, Robert T., Ph.D. Professor of Finance at Oakland University, Rochester, Michigan, and a nationally known consultant; frequently used as a source in such publications as *Money* magazine and the *Wall Street Journal.*

Kline, Trish. Freelance writer experienced in business script writing, public relations and advertising/marketing; the author of children's books, teacher's guides, and educational software.

Knes, Michael E. Freelance writer and librarian.

Knight, Judson. Freelance writer and editor; partner in the Knight Agency, specializing in literary representation.

Kody, John. Freelance writer.

Kolberg, Sharyn. Freelance writer and editor based in New York, New York; has written and ghostwritten dozens of non-fiction books, articles, and audio tapes.

Koserowski, Laurette. Freelance writer and assistant editor of *Traditional Quilter* magazine.

Kucera, David. Ph.D. candidate in Economics, New School for Social Research, New York, New York.

Kuhn, Karyn Bober. Freelance writer and editor.

Lawrie, Laura. Freelance writer, editor, and publishing consultant based in Arizona; has worked on *The Association of MBAs Guide to Business Schools, The New Grove Dictionary of Opera,* and *The Macmillian Dictionary of Art.* Currently the managing editor of *American Behavioral Scientist.*

Leahy, Norman W. Writer and researcher living in Richmond, Virginia; his work has appeared in such publications as the *Christian Science Monitor, USA Today, The San Diego Union-Tribune* and the *Washington Times;* M.A. in writing from Johns Hopkins University, Baltimore, Maryland.

Leotta, Joan. Freelance business and travel writer and storyteller in Burke, Virginia; published a book on writing techniques for hotel managers; writes poetry fiction, and nonfiction for children.

Levine, David. Regular contributor to Gale Research on numerous titles including *Exploring Law and Society* and *American Decades.*

Levine, Kathie. Attorney and freelance writer; contributing editor for *California Employer Advisor;* contributor to *San Francisco Business Times* and *Marin Independent Journal.*

Lewis, Scott M. Freelance writer and editor; contributing editor, *Option;* staff editor, *Security, Distributing and Marketing,* 1989-90.

MacFarlane, K. Thomas. Freelance writer.

Malkin, Shula. Freelance writer

Mandeville, Gertrude. Freelance writer.

Maschinot, Michael. Freelance writer.

Mason, Todd. Manager of Information Systems at Michigan Credit Union League and freelance writer/computer consultant.

Maxfield, Doris. Owner of Written Expressions, an editorial services business; contributor to numerous reference publications; former editor of *Online Database Search Services Directory* and *Charitable Organizations of the U.S.*

McDonald, Avril. Freelance writer.

McInerney, Merry. Freelance writer.

McKelvey, Paul S. Principal, McKelvey & Associates, Slidell, Louisiana; Extensive writing on international commerce, inland waterways and ports, and shipbuilding; member of New Orleans Press Club, International Association of Business Communicators, Public Relations Society of America, and Society for Technical Communication.

McNulty, Mary. Freelance writer and editor based in Chicago, Illinois; regular Gale contributor since 1988 whose work has also appeared in the *Chicago Tribune.*

Meyer, Bruce. Senior Editor for *Rubber & Plastics News,* Akron, Ohio.

Mogelonsky, Marcia. Freelance writer.

Mogul, Jonathan. Freelance writer based in Washington D.C.; Ph.D. in history from the University of Michigan, Ann Arbor.

Moncada, Patricia. Freelance editor based in Burke, Virginia; M.A. in English and American Literature from Southern Illinois University at Edwardsville.

Mote, Dave. Freelance writer and editor based in Indianapolis, Indiana; president of information retrieval company Performance Database.

Mote, Michelle. Freelance writer and professional educator.

Motta, Paolo. Freelance writer.

Nash, Margo. Freelance writer.

Neilson, Susan. Business reference librarian at the Charleston County Library, Charleston, South Carolina.

Nelson, Roxanne. Freelance writer based in San Francisco, California; regular contributor to *Living Healthy;* currently writing a book on sleep disorders.

Neubauer, Joan R. Owner, Word Wright International, Houston, Texas; public speaker, teacher, author of *Tell Them Like it Really Was: The Five Step Method to Writing Your Story,* and publisher of "The Last Word."

Norman, Bill. Former newspaper reporter and editor based in northern Illinois.

Oleck, Joan. Freelance writer in Brooklyn, New York; contributor to *New York Times, New Woman, Washington Journalism Review,* and other business publications.

Opdycke, Betty. Freelance writer.

Ossip, Kathleen. Freelance writer.

Paulson, Linda. Graduate of Columbia University Graduate School of Journalism, New York, New York; currently a contributor for numerous regional and national publications on a variety of topics.

Peck, Matthew C. M.A., Wayne State University, Detroit, Michigan; faculty member at the University of North Alabama, Florence.

Pederson, Jay P. Freelance writer and editor.

Pendergast, Sara. Freelance writer and copyeditor.

Pendergast, Tom. Freelance writer and editor; graduate student in American studies, Purdue University, West Lafayette, Indiana.

Pennie, Ariel. Freelance writer.

Pennington-Boyce, Amy. Consultant, researcher, and freelance business writer based in Ypsilanti, Michigan; provides services to profit and nonprofit organizations and to individuals regarding commercial and philanthropic development in the the former Soviet Union, international business, healthcare, and public relations.

Pitts, Lee. Executive editor, *Livestock Market Digest;* author of several books and a syndicated humor column.

Plamondon, Scott. Freelance writer.

Poss, Andrew. Freelance writer based in Buffalo, New York; Ph.D. in chemistry from the University of Rochester, New York.

Powell, Tami L. Freelance writer based in La Crescent, Minnesota; specializing in technical writing and editing, including computer software manuals.

Quagliana, Catherine A. Freelance writer and editor based in Austin, Texas.

Ratcliffe, Mary. Freelance writer and editor; author of brochures, newsletters, press releases, and advertising copy.

Rhodes, Scott. Freelance writer and funeral director based in Burlington, North Carolina.

Rooks, Alan. Freelance writer.

Ross-Flanigan, Nancy. Freelance writer based in Belleville, Michigan; has written for *Technology Review, The Dallas Morning News, The Harley-Davidson Enthusiast,* and other national publications; former science writer for the *Detroit Free Press.*

Rothman, Howard. Book author, magazine writer, and Web content provider based in Colorado; books include *RX Inc.: The Small Business Handbook for Building a Healthier Workforce, Companies with a Conscience: Intimate Portraits of Twelve Firms That Make a Difference,* and *All That Once Was Good: Inside America's National Pastime.*

Roy, Soumya. Freelance writer; MBA candidate, Temple University, Philadelphia, Pennsylvania.

Salamie, Dave. Co-owner of InfoWorks Development Group, a reference publication development and editorial services company; contributor to such reference works as *International Directory of Company Histories* and *International Dictionary of Films and Filmmakers.*

Sarich, John A. Freelance writer and editor; graduate student in economics, New School for Social Research, New York, New York.

Schneider, Bob. Freelance writer and Japanese translator; CPA, MBA, and New York Stock Exchange supervisory analyst.

Scott, Paula Pyzik. Freelance writer and video producer based in Ada, Ohio; contributed to numerous reference publications including *Contemporary Authors, Native American Tribes,* and *Newsmakers.*

Seablom, Kathy. Freelance writer.

Sharp, Arthur G. Business faculty member of Naugatuck Valley Community/Technical College, Waterbury Connecticut.

Sheil, Richard. Freelance writer, MBA candidate, University of Wisconsin;emMadison.

Sheldon, AnnaMarie. Freelance writer.

Shelton, Sonya. Freelance writer and editor based in Seattle, Washington; former editor of *RadioActive, Screamer,* and *Image* magazines; has written for various consumer and business magazines, corporate marketing, and reference books for over 12 years.

Shepherd, Kenneth R. Freelance writer based in Detroit, Michigan; history teacher at Henry Ford Community College, Dearborn.

Sherman, Fran Shonfeld. Freelance writer and editor; former contributor to *Compton's Encyclopedia* and *Britannica Book of the Year;* has worked on the online version of *Compton's Interactive Encyclopedia.*

Shugg, Elizabeth P. Freelance writer and editor specializing in corporate communications literature and feature writing for magazines and newspapers; she writes for regional newspapers in North Carolina as well as national magazines such as *Coastal Living* and *WebGuide.*

Spencer, Dorothy. Freelance writer and editor.

Sprinkle, David. Freelance writer and editor.

Stanley, Jill. Freelance writer.

Steward, Celeste. Adult reference librarian for Contra Costa County Library, Pinole, California; former news reporter and contributor to *What Do I Read Next* CD-ROM.

Stong, Jennifer. Freelance writer.

Straub, Deborah Gillan. Freelance writer and editor based near Grand Rapids, Michigan; has compiled several reference works published by Gale Research, including *Voices of Multicultural America* and *Contemporary Heroes and Heroines.*

Sturzenacker, Gloria. Freelance writer and editor based in New York, New York; former editor of the New York City Fire Department training magazine and local government reporter in public radio; editor of a variety of consumer and trade magazines.

Summers, Shannon. Freelance writer.

Swartz, Mark. Manuscript editor for the journals division of the University of Chicago Press.

Theodoroff, Mike. Freelance writer.

Thor, Angela. Information specialist based in Syracuse, New York; indexed *Higher & Higher* magazine and several historical books.

Thuermer, Karen. Editor and writer on international topics for 16 years; former editor of *Global Trade Magazine;* currently contributes to *International Business, Journal of Commerce,* and *World Trade* among others; masters degree in journalism form Penn State University, Hershey, Pennsylvania.

Tilak, Visi. Freelance writer based in Detroit, Michigan; regular contributor to national and international periodicals, she also writes corporate literature and is a freelance marketing communications consultant; M.A. in English and M.S. in journalism and mass communication.

Trimarco, Paola. Freelance business and health writer based in Washington, D.C.; Ph.D., University of Edinburgh, Scotland.

Urbiel, Martha. Librarian based in Hillsdale, New Jersey; regular contributor to Gale Research publications including *Children's Book Review Index.*

Vecchiolla, Richard R. Freelance writer and researcher focusing on shareholders rights and total quality management issues; J.D. candidate, Georgetown University, Washington, D.C.

Viswanathan, Shoba. Freelance writer and editor currently working as a senior editor in an electronic publishing company based in the San Francisco Bay area, California.

Von Heitman, Khatanga. Freelance writer.

Vyn, Kathleen. Freelance writer based in Chicago, Illinois; M.A. in creative writing from San Francisco State University, California; has written two nonfiction books, and her articles have been published in the *Chicago Tribune,* the *San Francisco Examiner, American Health, Omni,* and other publications.

Waters, John K. Freelance writer and editor based in California; author of *Silicon Valley: Inventing the future* and *The Bay Area: California Gateway to the Future;* contributor to *San Jose Magazine, South Bay Accent,* and *The Silicon Valley Insider.*

Wagner, Katherine. Freelance writer and editor based in Chicago, Illinois; correspondent for a variety of general-interest and business publications, and has edited catalogs, brochures, and travel guides.

Weaver, Danialle. Professional business and technology writer in Port Orange, Florida; has covered the energy and electricity industries since 1986 for publications such as *The Electric Daily, The Energy Daily,* and *Warfield's Business & Technology.*

Weber, Nathan. Freelance writer.

Weisman, Charlotte. Freelance writer and editor located in Wayne, Pennsylvania; has worked on various publications in Miami and Philadelphia recruiting and working with authors, editing their copy, and purchasing printing.

Westbrook, M. David. Freelance writer.

Wilson, Valerie. Freelance writer.

Wingett, Jeffery T. Freelance writer; MBA from California Polytechnic State University, San Luis Obispo.

Winters, Elaine. An award winning writer whose work has appeared in print and online; currently based in Berkeley, California; has also worked in Asia and the South Pacific.

Withem, Karen. Freelance writer.

Wolf, Gillian. Freelance writer based in Evanston, Illinois; ten years of experience, in history, corporate history, and biography.

Wolfe, Joanne. Freelance writer, editor and desktop publishing service provider based in Springfield, Oregon.

Woodward, Nancy Hatch. Freelance writer based in Chattanooga, Tennessee; contributes regularly to several business and health oriented publications.

Yocca, Beth. Freelance writer.

York, Leslee. Freelance writer.

Zrinsky, Christine M. Freelance writer and editor; director of individual gifts, Chicago Symphony Orchestra.